Seventh Edition
Blue Book
Tactical Firearms Values

by S.P. Fjestad

Edited by John B. Allen and David Kosowski

$34.95
Publisher's Softcover
Suggested List Price

TABLE OF CONTENTS

GENERAL INFORMATION

While many of you have probably dealt with our company for years, it may be helpful for you to know a little bit more about our operation, including information on how to contact us regarding our various titles and other informational services.

Blue Book Publications, Inc.
8009 34th Avenue South, Suite 250
Minneapolis, MN 55425 USA
GPS Coordinates: N44° 51 28.44, W93° 13.1709
Phone: 952-854-5229 • Customer Service (domestic and Canada): 800-877-4867
Fax: 952-853-1486 (available 24 hours a day)
Website: www.bluebookofgunvalues.com

General Email: support@bluebookinc.com - we check our email at 9am, 12pm, and 4pm M - F (excluding major U.S. holidays). Please refer to individual email addresses listed below with phone extension numbers.

To find out the latest information on our products, including availability and pricing, consumer related services, and up-to-date industry information (blogs, trade show recaps with photos/captions, upcoming events, feature articles, etc.), please check our website, as it is updated on a regular basis. Surf us - you'll have fun!

Since our phone system is equipped with voice mail, you may also wish to know extension numbers, which have been provided below:

Ext. 1000 - Beth Schreiber	(beths@bluebookinc.com)	Ext. 1600 - John B. Allen	(johna@bluebookinc.com)
Ext. 1200 – Karl Stoffels	(karls@bluebookinc.com)	Ext. 1800 - Tom Stock	(toms@bluebookinc.com)
Ext. 1300 - S.P. Fjestad	(stevef@bluebookinc.com)	Ext. 1900 – Sarah Peterson	(SarahS@bluebookinc.com)
Ext. 1400 - Kayla McCarthy	(KaylaM@bluebookinc.com)	Ext. 2000 - Adam Burt	(adamb@bluebookinc.com)
Ext. 1500 - Clint H. Schmidt	(clints@bluebookinc.com)	Ext. 2200 – Shauna Ritter	(shaunar@bluebookinc.com)

Office hours are: 8:30am - 5:00pm CST, Monday - Friday.

Additionally, an after-hours message service is available for ordering. All orders are processed within 24 hours of receiving them, assuming payment and order information is correct. Depending on the product, we typically ship UPS, Media Mail, or Priority Mail. Expedited shipping services are also available domestically for an additional charge. Please contact us directly for an expedited shipping quotation.

All correspondence regarding technical information/values on guns or guitars is answered in a FIFO (first in, first out) system. That means that letters, faxes, and email are answered in the order in which they are received, even though some people think that their emails take preference over everything else.

Online subscriptions and informational services are available for the *Blue Book of Gun Values, Blue Book of Tactical Firearms Values, Blue Book of Modern Black Powder Arms, Blue Book of Antique American Firearms & Values, American Gunsmiths, Blue Book of Airguns, Ammo Encyclopedia, Blue Book of Pool Cues, Blue Book of Electric Guitars, Blue Book of Acoustic Guitars,* and the *Blue Book of Guitar Amplifiers.*

As this edition goes to press, the following titles/products are currently available, unless otherwise specified:

37th Edition *Blue Book of Gun Values* by S.P. Fjestad

7th Edition *Blue Book of Tactical Firearms Values* by S.P. Fjestad

37th Edition *Blue Book of Gun Values* CD-ROM

Ammo Encyclopedia, 5th Edition by Michael Bussard

Seven Serpents – The History of Colt's Snake Guns by Gurney Brown

Blue Book Pocket Guide for Browning/FN/FN America LLC Firearms & Values 4th Edition by S.P. Fjestad

Blue Book Pocket Guide for Colt Dates of Manufacture, 2nd Edition by R.L. Wilson

Blue Book Pocket Guide for Colt Firearms & Values, 4th Edition by S.P. Fjestad

Blue Book Pocket Guide for Marlin Firearms & Values, 1st Edition by S.P. Fjestad

Blue Book Pocket Guide for Mossberg Firearms & Values, 1st Edition by S.P. Fjestad

Blue Book Pocket Guide for Remington Firearms & Values, 4th Edition by S.P. Fjestad

Blue Book Pocket Guide for Smith & Wesson Firearms & Values, 4th Edition by S.P. Fjestad

Blue Book Pocket Guide for Sturm Ruger Firearms & Values, 4th Edition by S.P. Fjestad

Blue Book Pocket Guide for Winchester Firearms & Values, 4th Edition by S.P. Fjestad

11th Edition *Blue Book of Airguns* by Dr. Robert D. Beeman & John B. Allen

3rd Edition *The Book of Colt Firearms* by R.L. Wilson

Book of Colt Paper 1834-2011 by John Ogle

The Book of Colt Memorabilia by John Ogle

The Book of Colt Memorabilia Pricing Guide by John Ogle

L.C. Smith Production Records by Jim Stubbendieck

American Engravers III - Masterpieces in Metal by America's Engraving Artisans by C. Roger Bleile

Mario Terzi – Master Engraver by Elena Micheli-Lamboy & Stephen Lamboy

American Gunsmiths, 2nd Edition by Frank Sellers

Parker Gun Identification & Serialization, compiled by Charlie Price and edited by S.P. Fjestad

If you would like to get more information about any of the above publications/products, simply check our websites: www.bluebookofgunvalues.com and www.bluebookofguitarvalues.com.

We would like to thank all of you for your business in the past – you are the reason we are successful. Our goal remains the same – to give you the best products, the most accurate and up-to-date information for the money, and the highest level of customer service available in today's marketplace. If something's right, tell the world over time. If something's wrong, please tell us immediately – we'll make it right.

FOREWORD
by S.P. Fjestad

Tac7's Manuscript Supervisor, Lisa Beuning and the Author/Publisher wrapping up yet another manuscript, the 8th one so far this year! Lisa has been analyzing and disseminating firearms catalogs/brochures and price sheets for decades giving her a unique perspective and constant exposure to new products and developing trends. This has lead to Lisa launching a new blog and it's for everyone. Be sure to follow each bi-weekly installment – visit www.bluebookofgunvalues.com

Welcome to the 7th Edition *Blue Book of Tactical Firearms Values*, now the largest and most up-to-date book and database ever created specifically for the ever-expanding field of tactical firearms. If you like this publication, you may also want to purchase an online subscription which contains thousands of images. It is also updated monthly – please visit **www.bluebookofgunvalues.com**.

A LITTLE HISTORY AND FIGHTING THE BELT

This title was initially released during 2009, and started out with 360 pages. Seven years later the page count is now close to 700, including 635 manufacturers/trademarks, over 6,500 individual gun model descriptions, and over 50,000 values! Fifteen years ago there were less than 25 AR-15 manufacturers/trademarks. This newest 7th Edition now contains over 250! Variations of semi-auto pistols have also skyrocketed, and this remains the only source book for complete information and up-to-date values on tactical handguns, shotguns, and rifles.

2008 will go down in tactical firearms history as the year this segment of the marketplace was turned upside down when the Obama administration took over the White House. Even though there was no federal anti-gun legislation enacted that year, tactical firearms and ammunition demand spiked after an unprecedented amount of fear, greed, and speculation amongst gun owners. This didn't stop until late 2013, and for a few years, this marketplace returned to more normal supply and demand economics. Currently, there are very few back-orders on most tactical firearms – supply has finally caught up with demand, and now many consumers can buy their tactical firearms for less than the manufacturer's MSRs.

ANOTHER BLACK STORM BREWING?

After watching both Donald Trump and Hillary Clinton give their victory speeches last night after winning the primary election in New York State by considerable margins, the Presidential election this fall will be the most important one since Abraham Lincoln was elected before the Civil War started. For the first time in American history, the Democratic Party is divided and the Republican Party is experiencing a hostile take over. While we're not exactly sure what will happen or what we're going to get if Trump is elected, all gun owners can be guaranteed what will happen if another Clinton takes office. She has already stated her anti-gun objectives, and they include aggressive anti-gun legislation, allowing states/individuals to sue firearms manufacturers for "wrongful deaths", and dismantling the Second Amendment. As the election gets closer and if Clinton gets the Democratic

presidential nomination, you might see another run on "black" tactical guns – no different than the last half of 2008. Regardless, this is one year where tactical firearms supply/demand economics could change significantly in a relatively short period of time. Also, we all remember what happened immediately after the Sandy Hook tragedy.

DATA ENTRY GONE GONZO

We used to think about the tactical firearms industry as almost a part-time job in terms of data entry. No longer! In recent years, the increased amount of tactical companies and their offerings have been staggering. This is easily evident when considering the book has doubled in size in seven years. Most AR-15 manufacturers now offer a wide variety of tactical enhancements as standard features, including quad rail assemblies, various sight combinations, new/improved finishes, and perhaps the most popular new accessory for 2016 – threaded barrels for suppressors. Still classified as an NFA item, many gun owners are hoping that suppressors will be reclassified by the BATFE. After all, as restrictive as England is with its anti-gun laws, citizens can easily buy suppressors with a minimum of paperwork. The reason? Even anti-gun politicians recognize that hearing loss is a legitimate health concern that can be helped with less noise – this includes silenced firearms.

MUCHO GRACCI

In wrapping up Tac7, I would like to thank our entire staff for its dedication, perseverance, and commitment to both quality products and services. Special thanks goes out to Lisa Beuning and John Allen for gathering much of the information used in this text, in addition to the countless hours spent on data entry. All of the contributing editors and firearms industry personnel also deserve kudos for the help and support they have provided over the years. Finally, no book or online database can be successful unless you embrace and support this product. For that, we all are very grateful and will continue to expand this publication to make sure it stays the best value for the money.

Sincerely,

signature

S.P. Fjestad
Author & Publisher
Blue Book of Tactical Firearms Values

ACKNOWLEDEMENTS

The publisher would like to express his thanks to the following people and companies for their contributions in this 7th Edition:

David Kosowski
John B. Allen
Lisa Beuning
JP Enterprises
STI International, Inc.
G. Brad Sullivan
William Peets
Robert "Doc" Adelman
Michael Kassnar – IWI US, Inc.
Randy Luth
Tom Spithaler – Olympic Arms
Linda Powell - Mossberg
Bud Fini – SIG Arms

Mark Eliason – Windham Weaponry
Mark Westrom – Armalite
Jeff Swisher & Angela Harrell – H&K USA
Dr. Leonardo M. Antaris
Michael Tenny – Cheaper Than Dirt
Stanley Ruselowski
Richard Fitzpatrick – Magpul Industries
Paul Pluff – Smith & Wesson
Richard Churchill – Colt
Chad Hiddleson
Chris Killoy - Sturm Ruger & Co.
Ginger Roberge - Knights's Armament

CREDITS

Cover Design and Art Director – Clint H. Schmidt
Manuscript Supervision – Lisa Beuning
Proofing – Lisa Beuning, Sarah Peterson, Kayla McCarthy, John B. Allen, and David Kosowski
Printing – Bang Printing, located in Brainerd, MN

ABOUT THE FRONT COVER

This edition's front cover features a JP Enterprises CTR-02 engraved limited edition rifle in .223 Rem. cal. This limited edition rifle has a Presentation Grade Finish and custom engraving executed by Brian Powley. Current MSR is $4,839. For more information, please visit www.jprifles.com.

Also pictured is the DVC 3-Gun semi-auto pistol from STI International in 9mm Para. cal. It features a special slide with six cut-outs reducing the overall weight, TiN coated barrel, skeletonized trigger, and hand stippled grips by Extreme Shooters of Arizona. Current MSR is $2,999. For more information, please visit www.stiguns.com.

ABOUT THE BACK COVER

The back cover features Standard Manufacturing Company's DP-12 Home Defense double barrel shotgun. Its unique bullpup action chambered for 12 ga. utilizes two separate threaded barrels (18 ½ in.) and magazines (14 shot capacity total) allowing the shooter to get two shots off for each "pump" of the pistol grip slide action. This new shotgun also features a receiver machined from aircraft grade aluminum, inline feeding, bottom loading and ejection, ambidextrous operation, 34-slot Picatinny rail, dual spring rubber recoil pad, and shell indicator windows. Current MSR is $1,395. For more information, please visit www.standardmfgllc.com.

MEET THE STAFF

Many of you may want to know what the person on the other end of the telephone/fax/email looks like, so here are the faces that go with the voices and emails.

S.P. Fjestad
Author/Publisher

John B. Allen
Author & Associate Editor Arms Division

David Kosowski
Copy Editor

Lisa Beuning
Modern Gun Manuscript Supervisor

Kayla McCarthy
Antique Manuscript Supervisor

Adam Burt
President

Tom Stock
CFO

Clint H. Schmidt
Art Director

Karl Stoffels
Lead Software Developer

Sarah Peterson
Web Media Manager/Proofreader

Beth Schreiber
Operations Manager

Shauna Ritter
Operations

DEFINITIONS OF TACTICAL FIREARMS
For Revolvers, Rifles, Semi-Auto Pistols, and Shotguns

Like beauty, the descriptive adjective "tactical" as applied to firearms lies in the eyes of the beholder. That said, determining if a specific firearm is a tactical weapon is more often than not a subjective and emotional process. But that process also depends upon several generally accepted criteria, i.e. the firearm's finish, design, specific components, and/or accessories. Whether a firearm is "tactical" may also depend upon the circumstances associated with how or when that firearm is utilized. The author and editors have devoted a considerable amount of effort in defining "tactical", and determining the criteria for a firearm's inclusion in this book. We could be neither all-inclusive, nor overly restrictive, as that would diminish this book's utility. But we believe those criteria have been fairly and equitably applied. We recognize that you may not find a specific firearm(s), which you consider to be tactical, within these pages. We also expect that you will question why some firearms were included. Your comments, critiques, and suggestions are always welcome, as this newest Seventh Edition of the *Blue Book of Tactical Firearms Values* remains a work-in-progress.

Author's Note: Original military contract firearms, including variations of rifles, shotguns, and pistols, are NOT included in this text (i.e., M1 Carbines, M1 Garands, Enfields, Trench Guns, etc.). Please refer to the *Blue Book of Gun Values* for current listings and values of these firearms (www.bluebookofgunvalues.com). Fully auto military contract firearms (and/or variations) that have been converted, modified, or redesigned by military arsenals and/or contracts for semi-auto operation only are included.

TACTICAL REVOLVERS
Tactical revolvers have at least three of the following factory/manufacturer standard features or options:
- Non-glare finish (generally but there may be exceptions)
- Mil-Std 1913 Picatinny or equivalent rail(s)
- Combat style grips (wood or synthetic)
- Fixed or adjustable low profile primary sights
- Auxiliary aiming/sighting/illumination equipment
- Compensators or barrel porting
- Combat triggers and hammers

Note: In addition to the above, open or iron sights for tactical revolvers may be Tritium illuminated "night sights", fiber optic, "three dot" (which are now essentially "factory standard" for most handguns), or other visually-enhanced types. The benefits of attaching a suppressor to a revolver's barrel are negated as it is impossible to suppress the noise and flash which emanates from the barrel/cylinder gap.

TACTICAL RIFLES/CARBINES
Tactical rifles and carbines (semi-auto, bolt action, or slide action) have at least two of the following factory/manufacturer standard features or options:
- Magazine capacity over ten rounds
- Non-glare finish (generally, but there may be exceptions)
- Mil-Std 1913 Picatinny or equivalent rail(s)
- Mostly synthetic stocks which may be fixed, folding, collapsible, adjustable, or with/without pistol grip
- Some "Assault Weapon" Ban characteristics, such as flash suppressors, detachable magazines, bayonet lugs, or threaded barrels

Note: In addition to the above, tactical rifles normally have attachments for single-, traditional two-, or three-point slings. Open or iron sights may be Tritium illuminated "night sights", fiber optic, or other visually-enhanced types. The capability to attach a suppressor is not by itself sufficient to include a firearm in this book.

For Revolvers, Rifles, Semi-Auto Pistols, and Shotguns

TACTICAL SEMI-AUTO PISTOLS

Tactical semi-auto pistols have at least three of the following factory/manufacturer standard features or options:

Magazine capacity over ten rounds if caliber is less than .45 ACP cal.

Non-glare finish (generally, but there may be exceptions)

Mil-Std 1913 Picatinny or equivalent rail(s)

Combat style grips (wood or synthetic)

Fixed or adjustable low profile primary sights, or high profile sights for use with a suppressor

Auxiliary aiming/sighting/illumination equipment

Compensators, barrel porting, or threaded muzzles

Note: In addition to the above, tactical semi-auto pistols may have a lanyard attachment device. Open or iron sights may be Tritium illuminated "night sights", fiber optic, "three dot" types (which are now essentially "factory standard" for most handguns) or other visually-enhanced types. The capability to attach a suppressor is not by itself sufficient to include a firearm in this book.

TACTICAL SHOTGUNS

Tactical shotguns (semi-auto or slide action) have at least two of the following factory/manufacturer standard features or options:

Higher capacity (than sporting/hunting shotguns) magazines, or magazine extensions

Non-glare finish (generally, but there may be exceptions)

Mil-Std 1913 Picatinny or equivalent rail(s)

Mostly synthetic stocks which may be fixed, folding, collapsible, adjustable, or with/without pistol grip

Some "Assault Weapon" Ban characteristics, such as bayonet lugs, or detachable "high capacity" magazines

Rifle or ghost ring sights (usually adjustable)

Short (18-20 inches) barrel with a fixed cylinder choke, or a breaching/stand-off device

Note: In addition to the above, tactical shotguns normally have attachments for single-, traditional two-, or three-point slings. Open or iron sights may be Tritium illuminated "night sights", fiber optic, "three dot", or other visually-enhanced types.

CZ-USA's new Scorpion EVO 3 S1 pistol in 9mm Para. cal.

HOW TO USE THIS BOOK

The values listed in this Seventh Edition of the *Blue Book of Tactical Firearms Values* are based on the national average retail prices gathered from gun shows, dealers, and auction sites. Do not expect to walk into a gun/pawn shop or trade/gun show and think that the proprietor/dealer will pay you the retail value listed within this text for your gun(s). Resale offers on most models could be anywhere from close to retail to up to 50% less than the values listed, depending on condition, availability and overall supply/demand economics. Prices paid by dealers will be dependent upon locality, desirability, dealer inventory, and potential profitability. In other words, if you want to receive 100% of the price (retail value), then you have to do 100% of the work (become the retailer, which also includes assuming 100% of the risk).

Percentages of original finish, (condition factors with corresponding prices/values, if applicable) are listed between 60% and 100%. Please consult the Photo Percentage Grading System (PPGS), available at no charge online at www.www.bluebookofgunvalues.com and also included in the *Blue Book of Gun Values*.

Included in this Seventh Edition is the most extensive Glossary ever compiled for tactical firearms, sights, and optics. Combined with the Anatomy illustrations, this will help you immensely in determining correct terminology on the wide variety of tactical firearms available in today's marketplace. Also see Abbreviations for more detailed information about both nomenclature and terminology abbreviations.

This book contains three unique Trademark Indexes – one for current tactical firearms manufacturers, importers, and distributors, one for accessories, and the third for ammunition. These Trademark Indexes are actually a source book unto themselves, and include the most recent emails, websites, and other pertinent contact information for these companies.

The Index might be the fastest way to find the make/model you are looking for. To find a model in this text, first look under the name of the manufacturer, trademark, brand name, and in some cases, the importer. Next, find the correct category name (if any), which are typically Pistols, Revolvers, Rifles and Shotguns. In some cases, models will appear with MSRs only after the heading/category description.

Once you find the correct model or sub-model, determine the specimen's percentage of original condition, and find the corresponding percentage column showing the value of a currently manufactured or discontinued model. **Editor/Publisher's note: Law enforcement and military models, full auto machine guns and other Class III variations, in addition to NFA items (with the exception of factory silencers on currently manufactured guns) are NOT included in this text/database.**

For the sake of simplicity, the following organizational framework has been adopted throughout this publication.

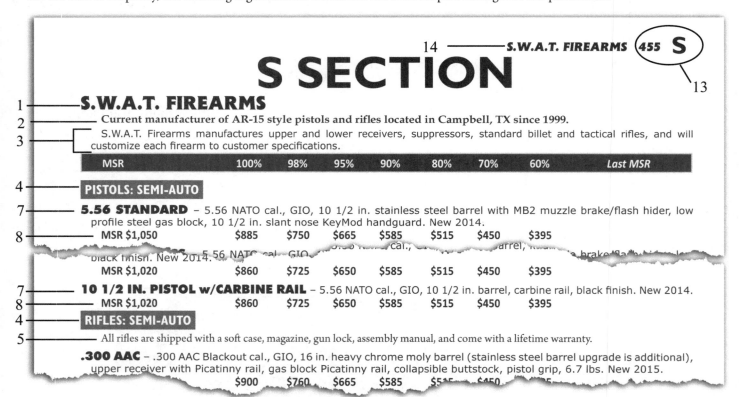

1. Manufacturer Name or Trademark – brand name, importer, trademark or manufacturer is listed alphabetically in uppercase bold face type.

2. Manufacturer Status – This information is listed directly beneath the manufacturer/trademark heading, providing current status and location along with importer information for foreign trademarks.

3. Manufacturer Description – These notes may appear next under individual heading descriptions and can be differentiated by the typeface. This will be specific information relating to the trademark or models.

4. Category Name – (normally, in alphabetical sequence) in upper case (inside a screened gray box), referring to various tactical configurations, including Pistols, Revolvers, Rifles, and Shotguns.

5. Category Note – May follow a category name to help explain the category, and/or provide limited information on models and current MSRs.

6. Value Additions/Subtractions – Value add ons or subtractions may be encountered directly under individual price lines or in some cases, category names, and are typically listed in either dollar amounts or percentages. These individual lines appear bolder than other descriptive typeface. On many guns less than 15 years old, these add/subtract adjustments will reflect the

	$975	$800	$665	$535	$465	$415	$365	$1,199

7 — **MODEL P224** – 9mm Para., 357 SIG, or .40 S&W cal., 3 1/2 in. barrel, DA/SA or DAK trigger, alloy frame with stainless steel slide, 10 or 12 (9mm Para. only) shot mag., satin nickel slide and controls (P224 Nickel), Siglite night sights, wood (disc.) or one-piece enhanced E2 (new 2013) grips, 25.4 oz. Mfg. 2012-2015.

8 — $925 $775 $650 $525 $450 $400 $350 $1,142 — 12

6 — **Add $57 for satin nickel slide and controls (Model P224 Nickel).**

10 — * *Model P224 SAS Gen. 2* – 9mm Para., .40 S&W, or .357 Sig cal., DA/SA or DAK (9mm only), similar to P224, except has Sig Anti-Snag (SAS) treatment on slide and frame, black Nitron finish, dehorned metal parts, SRT, Siglite night sights, and one-piece enhanced E2 grip, 29 oz. Mfg. 2012-2015.

8 — $950 $795 $665 $535 $465 $415 $365 $1,176 — 12

10 — * *Model P224 Extreme* – 9mm Para. or .40 S&W cal., DA/SA, 3 1/2 in. barrel, 10 or 12 shot mag., short reset trigger, Siglite night sights, Hogue Black and Grey Extreme G-10 grips, black Nitron finish, Nitron stainless steel slide, 29 oz. Mfg. 2012-2015.

8 — $975 $800 $665 $535 $465 $415 $365 $1,199 — 12

...x – .40 S&W cal. only, DA/SA, 3 1/2 in. barrel, 10...

	$1,195	$1,050	$900	$800	$700	$575	$475

7 — **SIG 516** – 5.56 NATO cal., short stroke GPO, 3 or 4 position gas valve, various configurations. New 2011.

10 — * *SIG 516 Basic Patrol* – 5.56 NATO cal., GPO, polymer handguard and 2 Picatinny rails - one on top of receiver and the other in front of handguard, 16 in. free floating barrel with muzzle brake, Magpul stock and pistol grip, 30 shot mag. Mfg. 2011 only.

8 — $1,095 $950 $800 $700 $600 $500 $425 $1,252 — 12

10 — * *SIG 516 Patrol* – 5.56 NATO or 7.62x39mm (mfg. 2012 only) cal., GPO, 16 in. free floating barrel with muzzle brake, Magpul MOE adj. stock and MOE grip, rear charging handle, free floating quad Picatinny rail, 3 position gas valve, 30 shot mag., ladder rail covers (new 2012), Pmag (new 2012), aluminum KeyMod handguard (new 2016), Black, Flat Dark Earth (new 2012) or OD Green (mfg. 2012-2015) finish. New 2011.

8 — MSR $1,794 $1,525 $1,350 $1,175 $1,000 $900 $775 $625

6 — **Add $54 for Flat Dark Earth finish (new 2012).**

10 — * *SIG 516 Carbon Fiber* – 5.56 NATO cal., GPO, 16 in. barrel, flip-up sights, carbon fiber forend and choice of carbon fiber SIG or Rifle stock, 30 shot Lancer mag. Mfg. 2014-2015.

8 — $1,700 $1,495 $1,275 $1,100 $950 $825 $650 $2,004 — 12

6 — **Add $192 for carbon fiber rifle stock and forend.**

10 — * *SIG 516 SRP (Sight Ready Platform)* – 5.56 NATO cal., GPO, 16 in. barrel, 30 shot mag., aluminum handguard, ...Green finish. Mfg. 2015 only.

$1,450 095

last factory MSRs (manufacturer's suggested retail price) for that option, and need to be either added or subtracted to ascertain the original MSR.

7. Model Name and Description – Model Name appears flush left, is bold faced in all upper-case letters, either in chronological order (normally) or alphabetical order (sometimes, the previous model name and/or close sub variation will appear at the end in parentheses). Model descriptions follow and usually start out with caliber/gauge, type of action, barrel length, important features, weight, and year(s) of manufacture/importation.

8. Value line – This pricing information will follow directly below the model name and description. The information appears in descending order from left to right with the values corresponding to a condition factor shown in the Grading Line near the top of the page. A pricing line with an MSR automatically indicates the gun is currently manufactured, and the MSR (Manufacturer's Suggested Retail) is shown left of the 100% column. 100% price on a currently manufactured gun also assumes not previously sold at retail. In some cases, N/As (Not Applicable) are listed and indicate that either there is no MSR on this particular model or the condition factor is not frequently encountered, and the value is not predictable. On a currently manufactured gun, the lower condition specimens will bottom out at a value, and a lesser condition gun value will approximate the lowest value listed. Recently manufactured 100% specimens without boxes, warranties, etc., that are currently manufactured must be discounted slightly (5%-20%, depending on the desirability of make and model).

9. Grading Line – The 100%-60% grading line will normally appear at or near the top of each page.

10. Sub-model Name and Description – Variations within a model appear as sub-models, and they are differentiated from model names because they are preceded by a bullet, indented, and are in upper and lower case type, and are usually followed by a short description.

11. Model Note (not shown) – Model notes and other pertinent information may follow price lines and value additions/subtractions. These appear in different type, and should be read since they contain both important and other critical, up-to-date information.

12. On many discontinued models and sub-models, an italicized value may appear at the end of the price line, indicating the last manufacturer's suggested retail price (LAST MSR).

13. Alphabetical Designator/Page Number – Capital letter indicating which alphabetical section you are in and the page number you are on.

14. Manufacturer Heading/Continued Heading – Continued Headings may appear at the top of the page, indicating a continuation of information for the manufacturer/trademarks from the previous page.

ANATOMY OF A TACTICAL SEMI-AUTO HANDGUN

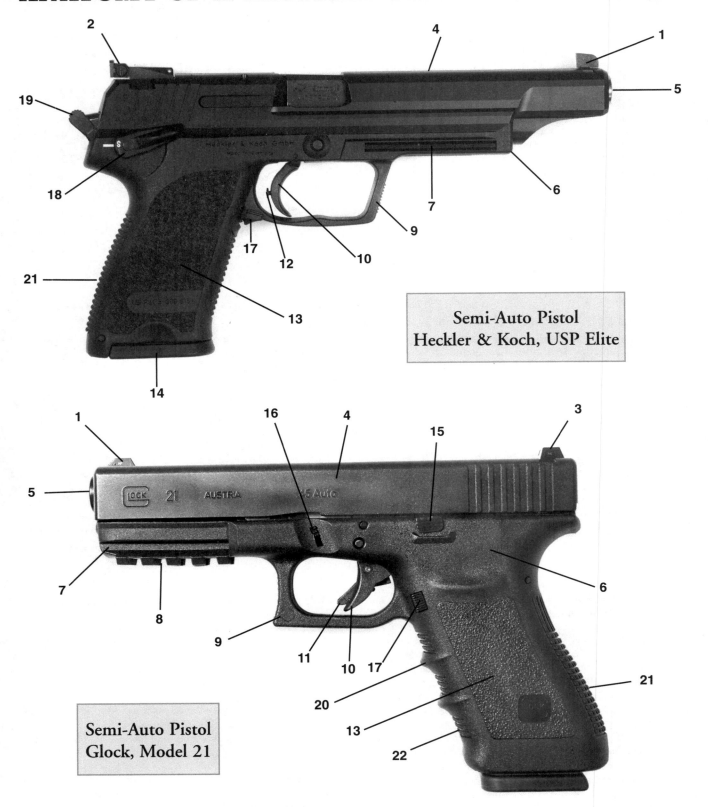

Semi-Auto Pistol
Heckler & Koch, USP Elite

Semi-Auto Pistol
Glock, Model 21

1.	Fixed blade front sight	9.	Trigger guard	17.	Magazine release
2.	Adj. rear sight	10.	Trigger	18.	Safety/decocking lever
3.	Fixed rear sight	11.	Trigger safety	19.	Hammer
4.	Slide	12.	Trigger overtravel stop	20.	Contoured finger grooves
5.	Barrel muzzle	13.	Grip frame	21.	Checkered rear grip frame
6.	Frame	14.	Magazine	22.	Checkered front grip frame
7.	Accessory/equipment rail	15.	Slide stop		
8.	Picatinny rail	16.	Takedown lever		

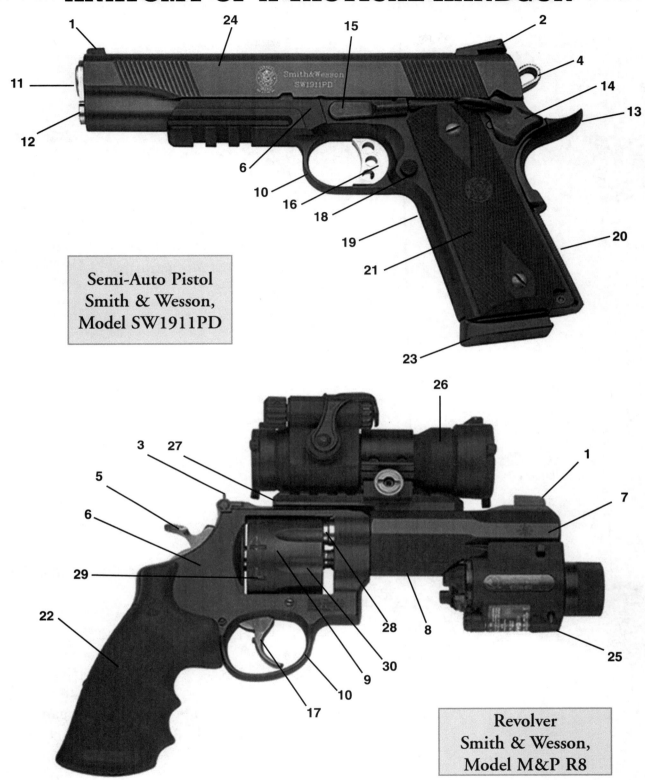

Semi-Auto Pistol
Smith & Wesson,
Model SW1911PD

Revolver
Smith & Wesson,
Model M&P R8

1.	Fixed blade front sight	11.	Barrel muzzle	21.	Grip
2.	Low profile combat rear sight	12.	Recoil spring guide rod	22.	Finger grooved grip
3.	Adj. blade rear sight	13.	Beavertail grip safety	23.	Magazine
4.	Skeletonized hammer	14.	Safety lever	24.	Slide with front and rear serrations
5.	Hammer with full spur	15.	Slide stop lever	25.	Flashlight (accessory)
6.	Frame	16.	Skeletonized trigger	26.	Reflex sight
7.	Barrel	17.	Trigger with over travel stop	27.	Picatinny rail
8.	Barrel lug	18.	Magazine release	28.	Breech end of barrel
9.	Cylinder	19.	Checkered front grip strap	29.	Cylinder stop notch
10.	Trigger guard	20.	Checkered rear grip strap	30.	Cylinder flute

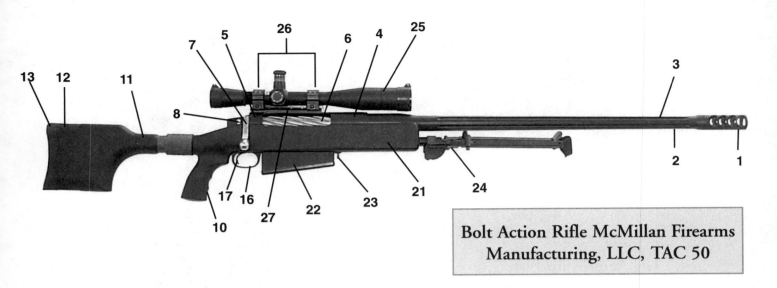

Bolt Action Rifle McMillan Firearms Manufacturing, LLC, TAC 50

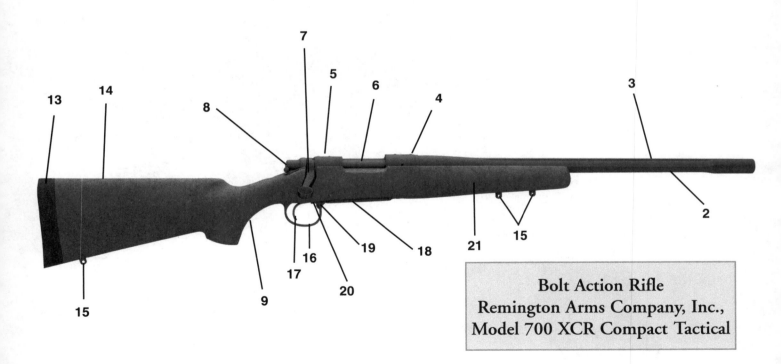

Bolt Action Rifle Remington Arms Company, Inc., Model 700 XCR Compact Tactical

1. Muzzle brake	10. Full pistol grip	19. Floor plate release
2. Barrel	11. Takedown buttstock	20. Bolt release lever
3. Barrel fluting	12. Buttstock spacers	21. Forend
4. Front receiver ring	13. Buttpad	22. Detachable box magazine
5. Rear receiver bridge	14. Buttstock	23. Magazine release
6. Bolt	15. Sling swivel stud	24. Detachable military style bipod
7. Bolt handle	16. Trigger guard	25. Variable power scope w/target turrets
8. Safety	17. Trigger	26. Scope rings
9. Semi-pistol grip	18. Hinged floor plate	27. Picatinny rail (scope base)

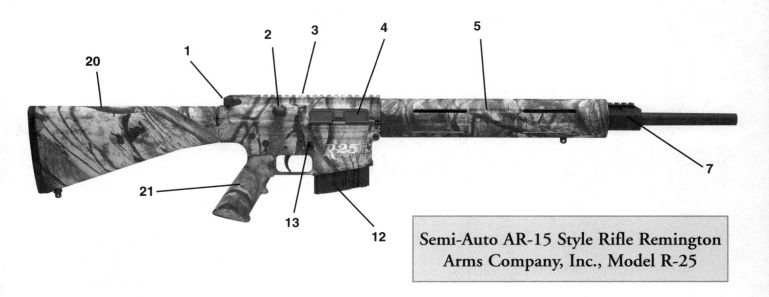

Semi-Auto AR-15 Style Rifle Remington Arms Company, Inc., Model R-25

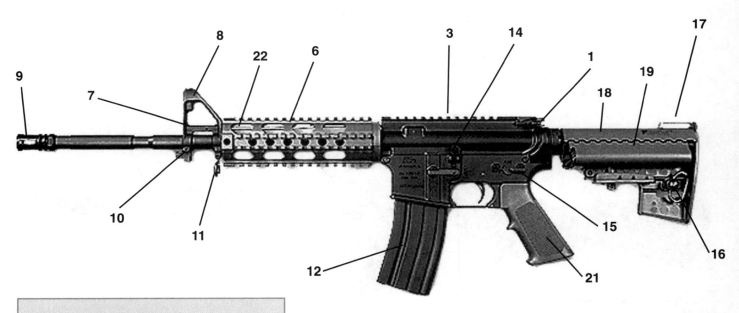

Semi-Auto AR-15/M4 Style Rifle DSA Inc., ZM-4 Carbine

1.	Charging handle	9.	Flash suppressor	17.	Single point sling attachment
2.	Forward bolt assist	10.	Bayonet mounting lug	18.	Collapsible stock
3.	Flat-top upper w/Picatinny rail	11.	Front sling swivel	19.	Cheekpiece
4.	Ejection port dust cover	12.	Detachable box magazine	20.	Fixed buttstock
5.	Free floating forearm	13.	Magazine release button	21.	Pistol grip
6.	Quad rail forearm	14.	Bolt release lever	22.	Gas tube
7.	Gas block w/Picatinny rail	15.	Safety lever		
8.	A2 style front sight	16.	Rear sling swivel		

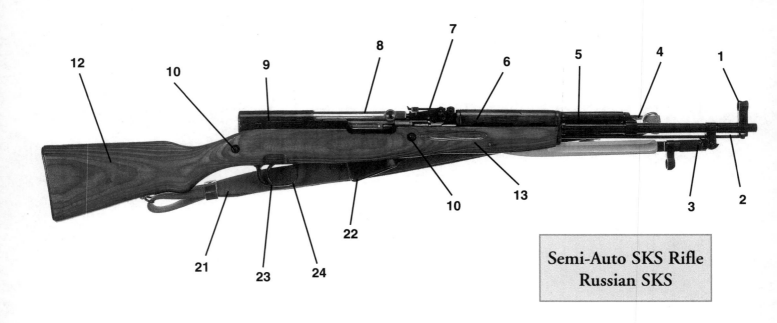

**Semi-Auto SKS Rifle
Russian SKS**

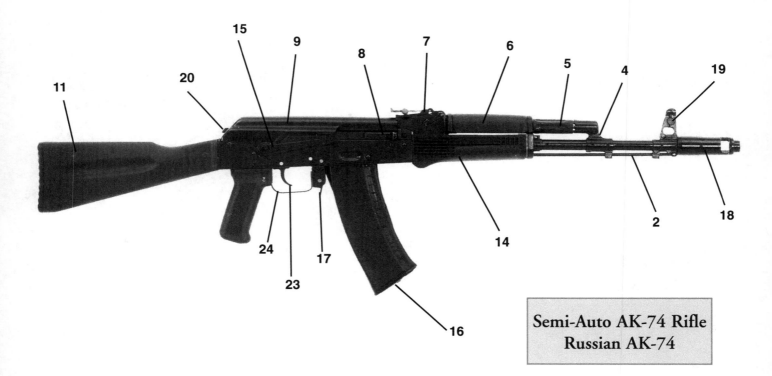

**Semi-Auto AK-74 Rifle
Russian AK-74**

1.	Hooded adjustable front sight	9.	Receiver cover	17.	Magazine release lever
2.	Cleaning rod	10.	Stock reinforcing cross bolts	18.	Flash suppressor
3.	Non-detachable folding bayonet	11.	Fixed buttstock	19.	Adjustable front sight
4.	Gas block	12.	Buttstock	20.	Takedown button
5.	Gas tube	13.	Forend	21.	Sling
6.	Handguard	14.	Forearm	22.	Non-detachable box magazine
7.	Rear tangent adjustable sight	15.	Safety lever	23.	Trigger
8.	Bolt	16.	Detachable box magazine	24.	Trigger guard

**Semi-Auto HK Style Rifle
PTR 91 Inc., Model PTR-91**

**Semi-Auto AR-15 Style Rifle
Olympic Arms Inc., OA-93 Carbine**

1.	Flash suppressor	7.	Free floating forearm	13.	Adjustable diopter rear sight
2.	Hooded front sight	8.	Shell deflector	14.	Stamped sheet metal receiver
3.	Charging handle	9.	Skeleton side folding stock	15.	Fire control group
4.	Bipod mounting adapter	10.	Adjustable cheekpiece	16.	Accessory and optics rail
5.	Bipod	11.	Sling attachment bar		
6.	Ventilated forearm	12.	Adjustable LOP (length of pull) buttpad		

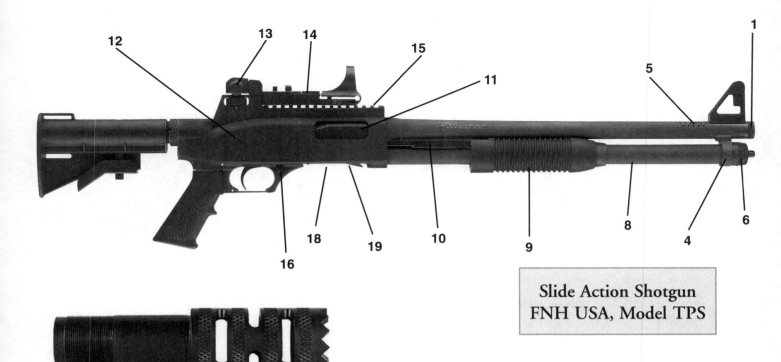

Slide Action Shotgun
FNH USA, Model TPS

Door Breaching
Attachment

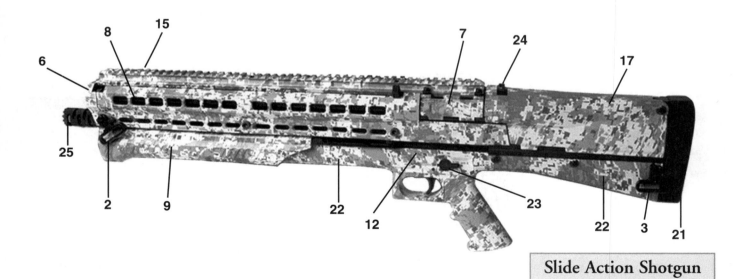

Slide Action Shotgun
Utas - USA
Model UTS-15

1.	Removable choke tube	10.	Action bar	19.	Carrier
2.	Front sling swivel	11.	Bolt	20.	Recoil absorbing pistol grip
3.	Rear sling swivel	12.	Receiver	21.	Recoil pad
4.	Forward magazine tube barrel band	13.	Back up iron sights	22.	Lower stock
5.	Barrel porting	14.	Reflex sight	23.	Safety lever
6.	Magazine end cap	15.	Picatinny rail	24.	Shell stop/mag. selector
7.	Left loading port door	16.	Safety button	25.	Tactical choke tube
8.	Magazine tube	17.	Upper stock		
9.	Forearm	18.	Loading port		

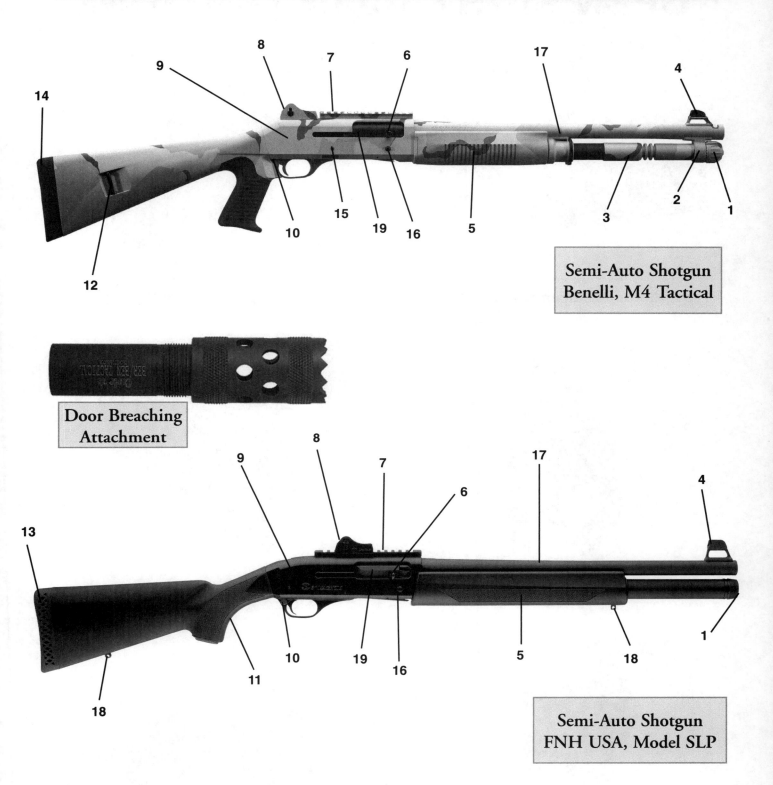

Semi-Auto Shotgun
Benelli, M4 Tactical

Door Breaching
Attachment

Semi-Auto Shotgun
FNH USA, Model SLP

1.	Magazine end cap	8.	Adjustable ghost-ring rear sight	15.	Takedown pin
2.	Forward magazine tube barrel band	9.	Receiver	16.	Action release button
3.	Magazine tube extension	10.	Safety	17.	Fixed choke barrel
4.	Elevated front sight	11.	Semi-pistol grip	18.	Sling swivel stud
5.	Forearm	12.	Side mount sling bar	19.	Ejection port w/charging handle slot
6.	Charging handle	13.	Ventilated recoil pad		
7.	Picatinny rail	14.	Solid recoil pad		

OPEN SIGHT ILLUSTRATIONS

Low Profile Handgun Combat Sights

Flip-Up Aperture Rear Sight

AR-15 Style Front Sight

AK Style Tangent Rear Sight

Adjustable Hooded Rifle Front Sight

Rifle or Shotgun Ghost Ring Rear Sight

OPEN SIGHT ILLUSTRATIONS

Elevated Rifle or Shotgun Front Sight

Tactical Shotgun Sight

Rail Mounted Laser Sight

Internal Guide Rod Laser Sight

Grip Mounted Laser Sight

OPTICAL SIGHT ILLUSTRATIONS

Compact Fixed Power Scope

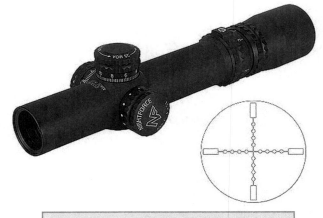

Compact Adjustable Power Scope with Mil-Dot Reticle

Full Size Fixed Power Scope with Mil-Dot Reticle and Target Turrets

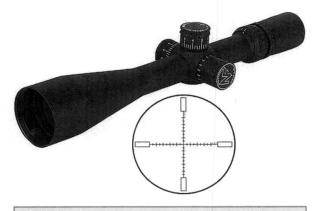

Full Size Adjustable Power Scope with Duplex Reticle and Target Turrets

Tube Style Reflex Dot Sight

Tubeless Style Reflex Dot Sight

Compact Reflex Dot Sight

GUN QUESTIONS/APPRAISALS POLICY

Whether we wanted it or not, Blue Book Publications, Inc. has ended up in the driver's seat as the clearing house for gun information. Because the volume of gun questions now requires almost full-time attention, we have developed a standardized policy that will enable us to provide you with the service you have come to expect from Blue Book Publications, Inc. To that end, we have extended all of these services to our website (www.bluebookofgunvalues.com).

To ensure that the research department can answer every gun question with an equal degree of thoroughness, an extensive firearms research center has been established. It includes a massive library with well over 1,500 reference books, thousands of both new and old factory catalogs/brochures, price sheets, most major auction catalogs, and dealer inventory listings. It's a huge job, and unlike Wikipedia, we answer every question like we could go to court on it.

ONLINE SELF SERVICE

Customers can answer most of their gun questions themselves. Simply visit www.bluebookofgunvalues.com and click on Appraisals and Evaluations under the Information & Services tab for more information and pricing on these service options. It certainly is a big help to know the manufacturer/trademark and the model to use this service. To further assist you, on our website every firearms manufacturer, category, and model is listed, and a model description is also provided free of charge. This will enable the consumer to ensure he/she selects the right make/model, or manufacturer/trademark before payment is made. There are two different levels of self service. Purchase information and current values on a single model or a one, two, or three-year online subscription for unlimited access to the *Blue Book of Tactical Firearms Values*. Color images are also available for many models and variations.

PHONE GUN QUESTIONS

The charge is $10 per gun value question, $15 per gun if the firearm's make and/or model needs to be identified first. Phone gun questions are payable with a major credit card. All phone gun questions are answered when time is permitting, on a first-come, first-serve basis. All value requests will be given within a range only, based on the accuracy of information the consumer provides – this is the most critical element of phone gun questions. Gun question telephone hours are 2:30 p.m. to 5:00 p.m., M-F, CST, no exceptions please. Phone gun questions are typically answered in 5 business days or less, unless the research staff has a production commitment or is away attending trade/gun shows.

APPRAISAL INFORMATION

Written appraisals will be performed only when time is permitting and if the following criteria are met. Research staff personnel must have good quality photos/images, a complete description(s), including manufacturer's name, model, gauge or caliber, barrel length, and other pertinent information. On some firearms, depending on the manufacturer/trademark and model, a factory letter may be necessary. Remember, since these written appraisals are done without physically inspecting the firearm(s), the appraised value(s) will only be as accurate as the information our research staff receives. High quality images are the single most important element on written appraisals. The charge for a written appraisal is 2% of the appraised value with a minimum of $30 per gun. For email appraisals, please refer to www.bluebookofgunvalues.com. Please allow 2-3 weeks response time per appraisal request.

FIREARMS RESEARCH

Firearms research services can be provided at $150 per hour, time permitting. Consumers need to email in their request(s) and exactly what they want done, and BBP will provide an estimate for its services before starting.

ADDITIONAL SERVICES

Individuals requesting a photocopy of a particular page or section from any edition for insurance or reference purposes will be billed at $5 per page, up to 5 pages, and $3.50 per page thereafter. Please direct all gun questions and appraisals to:

Blue Book Publications, Inc.
Attn: Research Dept.
8009 34th Ave. S., Suite 250
Minneapolis, MN 55425 USA
Phone: 952-854-5229, ext. 1600 • Fax: 952-853-1486 • www.bluebookofgunvalues.com
Email: guns@bluebookinc.com
Use "Firearm Inquiry" in the subject line or it may get deleted.

INTERESTED IN BUYING OR SELLING FIREARMS?

Over the course of many editions, we have received multiple requests for providing referrals for when buying, selling, or trading firearms. As Blue Book Publications, Inc. is a publisher, not a gun shop, this service is provided for the benefit of the buyer/seller to ensure they are treated fairly. There is no charge for this service, nor do we receive a commission (a thank you would be appreciated, however!). Our established international network of reliable dealers and collectors allows your particular buy or sell request to be referred to the most appropriate company/individual based on both your geographic location and area of collectibility. All replies are treated with strict confidentiality.

Please direct all inquiries to John Allen (see contact information above).

If this is an email request, please use "Referral" in the subject line or it may get deleted.

GRADING CRITERIA

The old, NRA method of firearms grading – relying upon adjectives such as "Excellent" or "Fair" – has served the firearms community for a many years. Today's dealers/collectors, especially those who deal in modern guns, have turned away from the older subjective system. There is too much variance within some of the older subjective grades, therefore making accurate grading difficult.

Most dealers and collectors are now utilizing what is essentially an objective method for deciding the condition of a gun: THE PERCENTAGE OF ORIGINAL FACTORY FINISH(ES) REMAINING ON THE GUN. After looking critically at a variety of firearms and carefully studying the Photo Percentage Grading System™ (available free of charge on our website: www.bluebookofgunvalues.com, it will soon become evident if a specific a gun has 98%, 90%, 70% or less finish remaining. Remember, sometimes an older gun described as NIB can actually be 98% or less condition, simply because of the wear accumulated by taking it in and out of the box and handling it too many times. Every gun's unique condition factor – and therefore the price – is best determined by the percentage of original finish(es) remaining, with the key consideration being the overall frame/receiver finish. The key word here is "original", for if anyone other than the factory has refinished the gun, its value as a collector's item has been diminished, with the exception of rare and historical pieces that have been properly restored. Every year, top quality restorations have become more accepted, and prices have gone up proportionately with the quality of the workmanship. Also popular now are antique finishes, and a new question has come up, "what is 100% antique finish on new reproductions?" Answer – a gun that started out as new, and then has been aged to a lower condition factor to duplicate natural wear and tear.

It is important to remember that most tactical firearms have either a parkerized, phosphated, matte black, or camouflaged finish which is very durable and resistant to wear and extreme weather conditions. Because of this, observing wear on the breech block, internal firing mechanism, and in the barrel may be the only way to accurately determine condition as these black/camo wonders get used, since most of them are all going to look 98% or better from the outside!

Every gun's unique condition factor – and therefore the price – is best determined by the percentage of original finish(es) remaining, with the key consideration being the overall frame/receiver finish. The key word here is "original", for if anyone other than the factory has refinished the gun, its value as a collector's item has been diminished, with the exception of rare and historical pieces that have been properly restored.

Note where the finishes of a firearm typically wear off first. These are usually places where the gun accumulates wear from holster/case rubbing, and contact with the hands or body over an extended period of time. A variety of firearms have been shown in four-color to guarantee that your "sampling size" for observing finishes with their correct colors is as diversified as possible.

It should be noted that the older a collectible firearm is, the smaller the percentage of original finish one can expect to find. Some very old and/or very rare firearms are sought by collectors in almost any condition!

For your convenience, NRA Condition Standards are listed on page 39. Converting from this grading system to percentages can now be done accurately. Remember the price is wrong if the condition factor isn't right!

GRADING SYSTEM CONVERSION GUIDELINES

New/Perfect 100% condition with or without box. 100% on currently manufactured firearms assumes NIB (New In Box) condition and not sold previously at retail.

Mint typically 98%-99% condition, depending on the age of the firearm. Probably sold previously at retail, and may have been shot occasionally.

Excellent 95%+ - 98% condition (typically).

Very Good 80% - 95% condition (all parts/finish should be original).

Good 60% - 80% condition (all parts/finish should be original).

Fair 20% - 60% condition (all parts/finish may or may not be original, but must function properly and shoot).

Poor under 20% condition (shooting not a factor).

NRA CONDITION STANDARDS

The NRA conditions listed below have been provided as guidelines to assist the reader in converting and comparing condition factors. In order to use this book correctly, the reader is urged to examine these images of NRA condition standards. Once the gun's condition has been accurately assessed, only then can values be accurately ascertained.

NRA MODERN CONDITION DESCRIPTIONS

New – not previously sold at retail, in same condition as current factory production.

Perfect – in new condition in every respect.

Excellent – new condition, used but little wear, no noticeable marring of wood or metal, bluing near perfect (except at muzzle or sharp edges).

Very Good – in perfect working condition, no appreciable wear on working surfaces, no corrosion or pitting, only minor surface dents or scratches.

Good – in safe working condition, minor wear on working surfaces, no broken parts, no corrosion or pitting that will interfere with proper functioning.

Fair – in safe working condition, but well worn, perhaps requiring replacement of minor parts or adjustments which should be indicated in advertisement, no rust, but may have corrosion pits which do not render article unsafe or inoperable.

NRA ANTIQUE CONDITION DESCRIPTIONS

Factory New – all original parts; 100% original finish; in perfect condition in every respect, inside and out.

Excellent – all original parts; over 80% original finish; sharp lettering, numerals and design on metal and wood; unmarred wood; fine bore.

Fine – all original parts; over 30% original finish; sharp lettering, numerals and design on metal and wood; minor marks in wood; good bore.

Very Good – all original parts; none to 30% original finish; original metal surfaces smooth with all edges sharp; clear lettering, numerals and design on metal; wood slightly scratched or bruised; bore disregarded for collectors firearms.

Good – less than 20% original finish, some minor replacement parts; metal smoothly rusted or lightly pitted in places, cleaned or reblued; principal lettering, numerals and design on metal legible; wood refinished, scratched, bruised or minor cracks repaired; in good working order.

Fair – less than 10% original finish, some major parts replaced; minor replacement parts may be required; metal rusted, may be lightly pitted all over, vigorously cleaned or reblued; rounded edges of metal and wood; principal lettering, numerals and design on metal partly obliterated; wood scratched, bruised, cracked or repaired where broken; in fair working order or can be easily repaired and placed in working order.

Poor – little or no original finish remaining, major and minor parts replaced; major replacement parts required and extensive restoration needed; metal deeply pitted; principal lettering, numerals and design obliterated, wood badly scratched, bruised, cracked or broken; mechanically inoperative, generally undesirable as a collector's firearm.

PPGS – FIREARMS GRADING MADE EASY

The Photo Percentage Grading System™ (PPGS) is available free of charge on our website at www.bluebookofgunvalues.com. If you carefully study all the images, and thoroughly read the accompanying captions, the color images will help you accurately determine condition better than anything that's ever been published or posted online. This revised Photo Percentage Grading System™ (PPGS) includes images of both NRA new and antique condition factors, in addition to all the 100%-10% percentage conditions for revolvers, pistols, rifles, and shotguns.

After more than 24 editions, the Photo Percentage Grading System™ has now become the industry standard for visibly ascertaining various condition factors based on a percentage system. The PPGS also retains the "PPGS-o-meters" whenever possible, so you can get a quick fix on condition factors.

Condition factors pictured (indicated by PPGS-o-meters), unless otherwise noted, refer to the percentage of a gun's remaining finish(es), including blue, case colors, nickel, or another type of original finish remaining on the frame/receiver. On older guns, describing the receiver/frame finish accurately is absolutely critical to ascertain an accurate grade, which will determine the correct value.

Additional percentages of condition may be used to describe other specific parts of a gun (i.e. barrel, wood finish, plating, magazine tube, etc.). Percentages of patina/brown or other finish discoloration factors must also be explained separately when necessary, and likewise be interpolated accurately. With antiques, the overall percentage within this text is NOT an average of the various condition factors, but again, refers to the overall original condition of the frame/receiver. Being able to spot original condition has never been more important, especially when the prices get into four, five, and six figures. Remember, the price is wrong if the condition factor isn't right!

Now, more than ever, it takes well-trained senses of sight, hearing, touch, and smell, with a direct connection to the most powerful computer ever built, a trained human brain, to accurately fingerprint a gun's correct condition factor. Regardless of how much knowledge you've accumulated from books, websites, auction catalogs, dealer listings, etc., you're still in potential danger as a buyer if you can't figure out a gun's condition factor(s) accurately. More than anything else, an older gun's overall condition must "add up" (i.e., an AR-15 with visible barrel wear should not have a bright blue magazine tube, and a Model 1911 Colt with 98% frame finish should not have an 80% slide).

While the Photo Percentage Grading System™ certainly isn't meant to be the Last Testament on firearms grading, it hopefully goes a lot further than anything else that's been published or posted on the web on the subject. Once you've accumulated the experience necessary to grade guns accurately, a ten-second "CAT scan" is usually all the time that is needed to zero in on each gun's unique condition factor.

In closing, the publisher wishes to express his thanks and gratitude to Pat Hogan, Judy Voss, and Matt Parise at Rock Island Auctions, and Dr. Leonardo Antaris, M.D. for authorizing the use of their digital images for the Photo Percentage Grading System™ (PPGS).

Sincerely,

S.P. Fjestad
Author & Publisher - *Blue Book of Tactical Firearms Values*

A SECTION

2 VETS ARMS CO., LLC

Current custom AR-15 style rifle manufacturer located in Eufaula, OK.

MSR	100%	98%	95%	90%	80%	70%	60%	Last MSR

RIFLES: SEMI-AUTO

2 Vets Arms Co., LLC is a female Service-connected Disabled Veteran Owned Business (SDVOB) that specializes in building high performance custom rifles for American patriots with an emphasis on serving the U.S. Military Veteran and those actively serving in the U.S. Armed Forces. A portion of the proceeds from each sale goes to support honored military veterans and veteran support organizations.

.300 BLACKOUT – .300 AAC Blackout cal., GIO, 16 in. free floating stainless steel barrel, low profile gas block, carbine length free float quad rail, optional lightweight free float tube, or PRI carbon fiber free float forend, side charging upper receiver, 2VA lower receiver and parts kit, Magpul MOE grip and trigger guard, and CTR Mil-Spec (standard or five optional style) buttstock.

	100%	98%	95%	90%	80%	70%	60%	Last MSR
	$1,400	$1,235	$1,100	$960	$815	$700	$575	*$1,675*

5.56mm RIFLE – 5.56 NATO cal., GIO, 16 in. free floating M4 profile stainless barrel, option of A2 front sight or low pro gas block, side charging upper receiver, 2 VA lower receiver and parts kit, Magpul MOE grip, trigger guard, and CTR Mil-Spec buttstock.

	100%	98%	95%	90%	80%	70%	60%	Last MSR
	$1,025	$925	$800	$685	$595	$515	$440	*$1,199*

6.8 SPC II – 6.8 SPC II cal., GIO, match grade 16, 18, or 20 in. free floating stainless steel barrel, low profile gas block, standard rifle length free float quad rail or optional lightweight quad rail, free float tube or PRI carbon fiber tube, side charging upper receiver, 2 Vets Arms lower receiver and parts kit, Magpul MOE grip and trigger guard, Magpul CTR Mil-Spec (standard or five optional) buttstock.

	100%	98%	95%	90%	80%	70%	60%	Last MSR
	$1,375	$1,215	$1,075	$950	$815	$700	$575	*$1,650*

2VA 5.56 ALPHA – 5.56 NATO cal., GIO, 16 in. stainless steel match barrel with full flutes, mid-length gas system, billet side charged upper receiver, forged lower receiver, B5 SOPMOD Alpha stock, BCM Gunfighter grip, KNS anti-rotation pins, Geissele SAA fire controls, Battle Arms Development ambi selector, Phase 5 enhanced side charged compatible BAD lever, 13 in. KeyMod compatible free float rail. New 2014.

	100%	98%	95%	90%	80%	70%	60%	
MSR $1,875	$1,575	$1,385	$1,200	$1,065	$900	$775	$625	

2VA 5.56 BRAVO – 5.56 NATO cal., GIO, 16 in. chrome moly barrel, A2 front sight base, billet side charged upper receiver, forged lower receiver, B5 Bravo stock and forend, Umbrella Corp. grip, G.I. fire controls, Phase 5 enhanced side charged compatible BAD lever. New 2014.

	100%	98%	95%	90%	80%	70%	60%	
MSR $1,300	$1,100	$995	$875	$735	$650	$550	$465	

2VA 6.8 DMR – 6.8 SPC cal., GIO, 20 in. stainless steel match barrel, billet side charged upper receiver, forged lower receiver, intermediate-length gas system, Battle Comp BABC compensator, B5 SOPMOD Alpha stock, BCM Gunfighter grip, 15 in. tactical Evo rail, adj. two-stage trigger. Mfg. 2014-2015.

	100%	98%	95%	90%	80%	70%	60%	Last MSR
	$1,560	$1,375	$1,190	$1,050	$900	$775	$625	*$1,849*

2VA LRRP – 5.56 NATO or .300 AAC Blackout cal., GIO, 16 in. stainless steel barrel with mid-length gas system, 10 in. tactical lightweight Evolution rail and Texas Custom Guns micro gas block, B5 Systems SOPMOD Alpha buttstock, Bravo Company Mfg. Gunfighter grip, LAR side charged upper receiver, 2VA forged lower receiver. Disc. 2015.

	100%	98%	95%	90%	80%	70%	60%	Last MSR
	$1,375	$1,215	$1,075	$950	$815	$700	$575	*$1,650*

Add $25 for .300 AAC Blackout cal.

2VA SOPMOD – 5.56 NATO or .300 AAC Blackout cal., GIO, 16 in. stainless steel barrel, mid-length gas system, 10 in. Spectre quad rail covering Texas Custom Guns micro gas block, B5 SOPMOD Alpha buttstock, Bravo Company Mfg. Gunfighter grip, LAR side charged upper receiver, 2VA lower receiver.

	100%	98%	95%	90%	80%	70%	60%	
MSR $1,499	$1,275	$1,125	$1,025	$875	$750	$625	$525	

2VA 308 SPECIAL PURPOSE RIFLE – .308 Win. cal., 18 in. fluted stainless steel match grade barrel with black Nitride finish, 15 in. lightweight free float tube, ambidextrous side charging system and safety selector, two-stage Geissele trigger, B5 Systems Bravo collapsible buttstock, 7 lbs. 13 oz. New 2015.

	100%	98%	95%	90%	80%	70%	60%	
MSR $1,875	$1,575	$1,385	$1,200	$1,065	$900	$775	$625	

2A ARMAMENT LLC

Current AR-15 style carbine/rifle manufacturer located in Boise, ID beginning 2015.

RIFLES: SEMI-AUTO

BLR-16 RIFLE – 5.56 NATO cal., mid-length gas system, 16 in. pencil profile stainless steel barrel, titanium T3 compensator, Magpul PMAG, ALG-ACT trigger group, Mission First Minimalist stock, Magpul MIAD grip, 15 in. extruded BL-RAIL, M-LOK, or KeyMod handguard, billet upper and lower receiver, Type III hardcoat anodized black finish, 5 lbs. New 2016.

	100%	98%	95%	90%	80%	70%	60%	
MSR $2,177	$1,835	$1,600	$1,350	$1,175	$1,000	$860	$715	

MSR	100%	98%	95%	90%	80%	70%	60%	*Last MSR*

BLR-CARBON RIFLE – 5.56 NATO cal., mid-length gas system, 16 in. Proof Research carbon fiber barrel, titanium T3 compensator, flared magwell, Magpul PMAG, CMC two-stage trigger, Magpul CTR stock, Magpul MIAD grip, 15 in. extruded BL-RAIL, M-LOK, or KeyMod handguard, billet upper and lower receivers, 2A-Gray Cerakote finish, 5 1/2 lbs. New 2016.

MSR	100%	98%	95%	90%	80%	70%	60%
MSR $3,689	$3,125	$2,725	$2,225	$1,915	$1,600	$1,340	$1,150

A.A. ARMS INC.

Previous manufacturer located in Monroe, NC until 1999.

CARBINES: SEMI-AUTO

AR9 CARBINE – 9mm Para. cal., similar action to AP9, except has carbine length barrel and side-folding metal stock. Banned 1994.

	100%	98%	95%	90%	80%	70%
	$750	$625	$550	$475	$425	$375	$325

PISTOLS: SEMI-AUTO

AP9 MINI-SERIES PISTOL – 9mm Para. cal., blowback design, phosphate/blue or nickel finish, 2 barrel lengths, 10 (C/B 1994) or 20* shot mag. Disc. 1999, parts cleanup during 2000.

100%	98%	95%	90%	80%	70%	60%	*Last MSR*
$425	$375	$325	$275	$225	$200	$175	*$245*

Add $20 for nickel finish.
Add $200 for AP9 long barrel Target Model (banned 1994).

A & B HIGH PERFORMANCE FIREARMS

Previous competition pistol manufacturer located in Arvin, CA.

PISTOLS: SEMI-AUTO

OPEN CLASS – 9mm Para. or .38 Super cal., SA, competition M1911-styled action, STI frame, Ultimatch or Hybrid compensated barrel, Caspian slide, C-More scope, blue or chrome finish.

100%	98%	95%	90%	80%	70%	60%	*Last MSR*
$2,800	$2,300	$1,875	$1,600	$1,375	$1,000	$750	*$2,800*

A.R. SALES

Previous manufacturer located in South El Monte, CA, circa 1968-1977.

RIFLES: SEMI-AUTO

MARK IV SPORTER – .308 Win. cal., M-14 style action, adj. sights. Approx. 200 mfg.

100%	98%	95%	90%	80%	70%	60%
$725	$650	$575	$500	$450	$400	$350

A06 ARMS

Current AR-15 style carbine/rifle manufacturer located in Fairplay, CO beginning 2013.

ADC (ARMI DALLERA CUSTOM)

Current pistol and tactical semi-auto rifle manufacturer and customizer located in Concesio, Italy. Previously located in Gardone, Italy. No current U.S. importer.

ADC manufactures high quality custom pistols, mainly of M1911 design, and a tactical black rifle based on the AR-15 style. Many options and configurations are available. ADC also provides a complete range of customizing and gunsmithing services. Please contact the company directly for more information, U.S. availability, and current pricing (see Trademark Index).

AK-47 DESIGN CARBINES, RIFLES, & PISTOLS

Select-fire military design rifle originally designed in Russia (initials refer to Avtomat Kalashnikova, 1947). The AK-47 was officially adopted by Russia in 1949. Russian-manufactured select fire AK-47s have not been manufactured since the mid-1950s. Semi-auto AK-47 and AKM clones are currently manufactured by several arsenals in China including Norinco and Poly Technologies, Inc. (currently illegal to import), in addition to being manufactured in other countries including the Czech Republic, Bulgaria, Russia, Egypt, and Hungary. On April 6th, 1998, recent "sporterized" variations (imported 1994-1998) with thumbhole stocks were banned by presidential order. Beginning in 2000, AK-47s were being assembled in the U.S., using both newly manufactured and older original military parts and components.

AK-47s and variations are not rare - approximately 75 million AK-47s and over 100 million AK-74 design carbine/rifles have been manufactured since 1947.

AK-47/AK-74/AKM HISTORY

Since the early 1950s, the AK-47/AK-74/AKM series of select fire rifles has been the standard issue military rifle of the former Soviet Union and its satellites. It continues to fulfill that role reliably today. The AK series of rifles, from the early variants of the AK-47 through the AKM and

AK-74, is undoubtedly the most widely used military small arms design in the world. Developed by Mikhail Kalashnikov (the AK stands for Avtomat Kalashnikova) in 1946, the AK went into full production in 1947 in Izhevsk, Russia. In 1953, the milled receiver was put into mass production. Since then, variants of the original AK-47 have been manufactured by almost every former Soviet bloc country and some free world nations, including Egypt. The AK action is the basis for numerous other weapons, including the RPK (Ruchnoy Pulemyot Kalashnikova).

The AK-47 was replaced in 1959 by the AKM, and retained the same basic design. The rifle was simply updated to incorporate easier and more efficient production methods, using a stamped, sheet metal receiver that was pinned and riveted in place, rather than a milled receiver. Other changes included a beavertail forearm, muzzle compensator, and an anti-bounce device intended to improve controllability and increase accuracy.

The AK was designed to be, and always has been, a "peasant-proof" military weapon. It is a robust firearm, both in design and function. Its record on the battlefields around the world is impressive, rivaled only by the great M1 Garand of the U.S. or bolt rifles such as the English Mark III Enfield. The original AK-47 prototypes are on display in the Red Army Museum in Moscow.

All of the current semi-auto AK "clones" are copies of the AKM's basic receiver design and internal components minus the full-auto parts. The Saiga rifle (see separate listing), manufactured by the Izhevsk Machining Plant, in Izhevsk, Russia, is the sole Russian entry into this market. It is available in the standard 7.62x39 mm, 5.45x39 mm (disc.) and 20 gauge or .410 bore. Molot (hammer) JSC also exports semi-automatic AKs to the U.S. under the trade name Vepr. (see separate listing). Saiga is imported by RWC (Russian Weapon Company), and the Vepr. is imported by Robinson Armaments. Molot was the home of the PPSh-41 sub-machine gun during WWII, and also manufactured the RPK and the RPK-74. Other AK European manufacturers include companies in the Czech Republic, Bulgaria, and the former Yugoslavia. The Egyptian-made Maahdi AK clones were also available in the U.S. market.

Interest in the Kalashnikov design is at an all-time high due to the availability of high quality military AK-74, AKS-74, AKS-74U, and RPK-74 parts kits. Some models, such as those produced by Marc Krebs, are of very high quality. Currently, it is hard to go to a gun show or page through a buy/sell firearms magazine and not see a variety of parts, accessories, and high capacity magazines available for many of the AK variants. For shooters, the value represented by these guns is undeniable for the price point.

Values for almost all of the imported AK clones are based solely on their use as sporting or target rifles. Fit and finish varies by country and importer. Most fall on the "low" side. Interest peaked prior to the passage of the 1994 Crime Bill and both AK clones and their "high capacity" magazines were bringing a premium for a short period of time in 1993 and 1994. However, interest waned during 1995-97, and the reduced demand lowered prices. In November of 1997, the Clinton Administration instituted an "administrative suspension" on all import licenses for these types of firearms in order to do a study on their use as "sporting firearms."

On April 6th, 1998, the Clinton Administration, in the political wake of the Jonesboro tragedy, banned the further import of 58 "assault-type" rifles, claiming that these semi-automatics could not be classified as sporting weapons - the AK-47 and most related configurations were included. During 1997, firearms importers obtained permits to import almost 600,000 reconfigured rifles - approximately only 20,000 had entered the country when this ban took effect. When the ban began, applications were pending to import an additional 1,000,000 guns. Previously, thumbhole-stocked AK Sporters were still legal for import, and recent exporters included the Czech Republic, Russia, and Egypt.

AK-47 DESIGN CARBINES, RIFLES, & PISTOLS: RECENT/CURRENT MFG. & IMPORTATION

The following is a listing of both current and recent manufacturers and importers that offer/have offered AK-47 design carbines, rifles, and pistols for sale domestically. Please look under each current company, importer, or brand name/trademark heading for up-to-date information and values on current makes and models that are offered.

These companies include: AKS (AK-47, AK-74, & AKM Copies), American Arms, Inc., American Tactical Imports, Armory USA LLC, Armscor, Arsenal JSCompany(Arsenal Bulgaria), Arsenal Inc., Arsenal USA LLC, B-West, Baikal, Bingham Ltd., Blackheart International LLC, Bushmaster Firearms International LLC, CZ (Ceska Zbrojovka), Century International Arms, Inc., Czechpoint Inc., E.D.M. Arms, E.M.F. Co. Inc., European American Armory Corp., Feather Industries, Inc., Federal Ordnance Inc., FEG, German Sport Guns GmbH, Hakim, Hesse Arms, I.O., Inc., Inter Ordnance of America, LP, Interarms Arsenal, Intrac Arms International Inc., K.B.I., K-VAR Corp., Liberty Arms International, LLC, M+M, Inc., Mitchell Arms, Inc., Molot JSCo, Navy Arms Company, Norinco, Ohio Ordnance Works Inc., Poly Technologies, Inc., Rasheed (Rashid), Robinson Armament Co., Russian American Armory Company, Russian Weapon Company, SAIGA, Samco Global Arms, Inc., Sarco, Inc., Sentinel Arms, TG International, Valmet Inc., Vector Arms Inc., Vepr, Vulcan Armament, and ZDF Import/Export.

CARBINES/RIFLES: SEMI-AUTO, AK-47, AK-74, & AKM MODELS

"AK-47" stands for Automatic Kalashnikov Rifle, 1947 Model, first developed in the former Soviet Union by Mikhail Kalashnikov, who passed away in 2013. This gas-operated military rifle was originally designed for select-fire operation, and quickly gained acceptance within the Soviet Union's military forces. While very early military production used stamped receivers, problems in the manufacturing process forced the adoption of milled receivers, which took more time, but solved all of the earlier production problems. The arsenals of Soviet satellite countries, as well as China also began producing AK-47s for military use, but later also began producing semi-auto variations for commercial sales. In 1959, the AKM (M designates modernized or upgraded) was developed with a stamped receiver and also featured a slanted muzzle brake - it was also approximately 33% lighter than the earlier milled AK-47s. There are far more AKMs available in the American marketplace for sale than semi-auto AK-47s. Chinese importation stopped during late 1990.

AK-47/AKM – 7.62x39mm (most common cal., former Russian M43 military), 5.45x39mm (Romanian mfg. or Saiga/MAK - recent mfg. only), or .223 Rem. cal., semi-auto Kalashnikov action, stamped (most common) or milled (pre-1959) receiver, typically 16 1/2 in. barrel, 5, 10, or 30* (C/B 1994) shot curved mag., wood or synthetic stock and forearm except on folding stock model, 1994-early 1998 importation typically had newer "sporterized" fixed stocks with thumbholes, may be supplied with bayonet, sling, cleaning kit, patterned after former military production rifle of China and Russia.

* AK-47/AKM Post-WWII-Pre-1994 Mfg./Importation – 7.62x39mm (most common cal., former Russian M43 military), 5.45x39mm (Romanian mfg. or Saiga/MAK - recent mfg. only), or .223 Rem. cal., semi-auto Kalashnikov

MSR	100%	98%	95%	90%	80%	70%	60%	Last MSR

action, stamped (most common) or milled receiver, typically 16 1/2 in. barrel, 5, 10, or 30* (C/B 1994) shot mag., wood or synthetic stock and forearm except on folding stock model, may be supplied with bayonet, sling, cleaning kit, patterned after former military production rifle of Russia and China. Check markings and/or proofs on gun for country of origin and possible importer.

	100%	98%	95%	90%	80%	70%	60%
Romanian mfg.	$1,650	$1,450	$1,250	$1,125	$900	$750	$575
Yugoslavian mfg.	$1,550	$1,350	$1,165	$1,050	$850	$700	$550
Hungarian mfg.	$1,750	$1,550	$1,325	$1,175	$950	$775	$625
Bulgarian mfg.	$1,450	$1,250	$1,075	$950	$800	$650	$500
Egyptian mfg.	$1,500	$1,300	$1,125	$1,000	$825	$675	$525

Add 20% for milled receiver.

Add 10% for chrome-lined barrel.

Add 10% for older folding stock variations.

Values are for original guns completely manufactured in the countries listed above and will have various import markings stamped on the receiver or barrel.

* *AK-47/AKM 1994-2004 Mfg.* – most feature "sporterized" fixed stocks with thumbholes to comply with the GCA of 1994.

	100%	98%	95%	90%	80%	70%	60%
	$950	$825	$725	$625	$525	$425	$325

* *AK-47/AKM Post 2004 Mfg./Importation* – most AK-47/AKMs manufactured/imported after 1998 utilize plastic/synthetic furniture, stamped receivers, and folding/telescoping stocks which have different components and construction from those rifles/carbines produced before 1998. Recent U.S. assembly refers to an original stamped European (mostly FEG) or milled receiver with U.S. assembly, using either new parts or matched, older unused original Eastern European-manufactured parts (BATFE 922.R compliant). This newest generation of AK-47/AKMs typically have features as described above, and cannot be sold in several states. Check city and state laws regarding high capacity magazine compliance.

	100%	98%	95%	90%	80%	70%	60%
	$650	$575	$495	$450	$350	$295	$225

The most desirable configuration of these recently assembled rifles/carbines has a folding/collapsible stock, high capacity mag., barrel compensator, and a bayonet lug.

These post-2004 AK-47/AKM variations typically do not have import markings, which indicates they have been made up as "parts guns" assembled from various manufacturers, and have usually been put together in the U.S. recently. Additional AK-47 listings can be found under current individual manufacturers and importers listed separately in this text (i.e., Arsenal Inc., Century International, Interarms, etc.).

AK-74/AKM – 5.45x39mm cal., semi-auto action based on the AKM, imported from Bulgaria and other previous Eastern bloc countries, in addition to recent assembly in the U.S., using FEG receivers, Bulgarian parts sets, and additional U.S.-made components.

	100%	98%	95%	90%	80%	70%	60%
Bulgarian mfg.	$1,450	$1,275	$1,075	$975	$800	$650	$500
Recent U.S. assembly	$650	$575	$500	$425	$350	$300	$275

Add 10%-15% for 5.45x39 mm cal. on Eastern European mfg. (non-recent import).

PISTOLS: SEMI-AUTO, AK-47 VARIATIONS

AK-47 PISTOLS – 7.62x39mm, or .223 Rem. cal., patterned after the AK-47 rifle/carbine, barrel length approx. 12 1/4 in., but can vary according to mfg., typically wood furniture, 5 to 30 shot mag. (depends on configuration), adj. rear sight, pistol grip, parkerized finish most common, recent Romanian mfg., approx. 5 lbs.

	100%	98%	95%	90%	80%	70%	60%
	$475	$425	$375	$325	$275	$250	$225

A M A C

See the "Iver Johnson" section in the I section. AMAC stands for American Military Arms Corporation. Manufactured in Jacksonville, AR. AMAC ceased operations in early 1993.

A.M.S.D. (ADVANCED MILITARY SYSTEM DESIGN)

Current manufacturer located in Geneva, Switzerland. No current U.S. importation. Previously distributed 2010-2012 by Loki Weapon Systems, located in Coalgate, OK.

RIFLES: BOLT ACTION

TACTEN RIFLE – .338 Lapua cal., tactical stock, bipod, two 10 shot mags., muzzle brake, two-stage trigger, includes cleaning kit and case. Disc. 2015.

Prices on this model were P.O.R.

OM 50 NEMESIS – various cals., 27 1/2 in. barrel, high performance muzzle brake, box mag., Picatinny top and side rails, adj. folding stock, adj. two-stage trigger, extended forend, adj. ground spike, scope rings, includes bipod, field cleaning kit, tool kit and fitted storage case. Disc. 2010.

MSR	100%	98%	95%	90%	80%	70%	60%	Last MSR

In 2010, AMSD sold the rights to the OM 50 Nemesis to the Swiss company San Swiss Arms AG (SAN). The model is now called the SAN 511. Rifles sold by AMSD before December 2010 are covered by AMSD's 25 year warranty. Please refer to the San Swiss listing in the S section for current listings.

AMP TECHNICAL SERVICE GmbH

Previous manufacturer located in Puchheim, Germany. Previously imported and distributed 2001-2004 by CQB Products, located in Tustin, CA.

RIFLES: BOLT ACTION

DSR-1 – .300 Win. Mag., .308 Win., or .338 Lapua cal., bullpup design with in-line stock, receiver is made from aluminum, titanium, and polymers, internal parts are stainless steel, two-stage adj. trigger, 4 or 5 shot mag., 25.6 in. Lothar Walther fluted barrel with muzzle brake and vent. shroud, includes bipod, ambidextrous 3-position safety, 13 lbs. Imported 2002-2004.

	100%	98%	95%	90%	80%	70%	60%	Last MSR
	$7,295	$6,300	$5,200	$4,100	$3,000	$2,500	$2,000	$7,795

Add $100 for .300 Win. Mag. or $300 for .338 Lapua cal.

AR 57 LLC (57CENTER LLC)

Current AR-15 style rifle manufacturer located in Woodinville, WA. Previously located in Bellevue and Redmond, WA.

CARBINES: SEMI-AUTO

AR57A1 - PDW – 5.7x28mm cal., 16 in. barrel, flash suppressor, black matte finish, ergonomic design custom grip with battery and accessory compartment, 50 shot box magazine runs horizontally over barrel and can be inserted from top or side of weapon, Mil-Spec fire control group, M-4 carbine 6-position stock with forged aluminum stock tube, front and rear upper Picatinny rails between mag., lower accessory rails, includes four 50 shot mags. Mfg. 2010-2013.

	100%	98%	95%	90%	80%	70%	60%	Last MSR
	$1,100	$975	$825	$750	$600	$500	$400	$1,099

AR57 GEN II/LEM – 5.7x28mm cal., 16 in. fluted barrel with flash hider, ambidextrous mag. release and charging handle, carbine buffer, semi-auto bolt, ergonomic design custom grip with battery and accessory compartment, extended rear quad rail, includes two 50 shot mags. New 2013.

MSR	100%	98%	95%	90%	80%	70%	60%	
$1,099	$975	$850	$725	$675	$550	$450	$350	

AR-7 INDUSTRIES, LLC

Previous manufacturer located in Geneseo, IL 1998-2004. Previously located in Meriden, CT, from 1998 to early 2004.

In February 2004, AR-7 Industries, LLC was purchased by ArmaLite, Inc., and recent manufacture was in Geneseo, IL.

RIFLES: BOLT ACTION

AR-7 TAKEDOWN – .22 LR cal., bolt action variation of the AR-7 Explorer rifle, similar takedown/storage configuration, 2 1/2 lbs. Advertised 2002 only.

While advertised during 2002, this model was never manufactured.

RIFLES: SEMI-AUTO

AR-7 EXPLORER RIFLE – .22 LR cal., takedown barrelled action stores in synthetic stock which floats, 8 shot mag., aperture rear sight, 16 in. barrel (synthetic sleeve with steel liner), black matte finish on AR-7, silvertone on AR-7S (disc. 2000), camouflage finish on AR-7C, two-tone (silver receiver with black stock and barrel) on AR-7T (disc. 2000), walnut finish on AR-W (mfg. 2001-2002), stowed length 16 1/2 in., 2 1/2 lbs. Mfg. late 1998-2004.

	100%	98%	95%	90%	80%	70%	60%	Last MSR
	$175	$150	$125	$110	$100	$90	$80	$200

Add $15 for camouflage or walnut finish.

This model was also previously manufactured by Survival Arms, Inc. and Charter Arms - see individual listings for information.

AR-7 SPORTER (AR-20) – .22 LR cal., 16 1/2 in. steel barrel with vent. aluminum shroud, metal skeleton fixed stock with pistol grip, 8 (new 2001) or 16 shot "flip clip" (optional) mag., 3.85 lbs. Mfg. late 1998-2004.

	100%	98%	95%	90%	80%	70%	60%	Last MSR
	$175	$150	$125	$110	$100	$90	$80	$200

Add $100 for sporter conversion kit (includes aluminum shrouded barrel, pistol grip stock, and 16 shot flip clip).

This model was also previously manufactured by Survival Arms, Inc. - see individual listing for information.

AR-7 TARGET – .22 LR cal., 16 in. bull barrel with 7/8 in. cantilever scope mount, tube stock with pistol grip, 8 shot mag., 3-9x40mm compact rubber armored scope was optional, 5.65 lbs. Mfg. 2002-2004.

	100%	98%	95%	90%	80%	70%	60%	Last MSR
	$195	$175	$150	$125	$105	$95	$80	$210

Add $60 for compact scope.

MSR		100%	98%	95%	90%	80%	70%	60%	*Last MSR*

AR-15 STYLE CARBINES, RIFLES, PISTOLS, & SHOTGUNS

AR-15 HISTORY

AR-15 refers to the model nomenclature originally given to the select-fire, gas-operated carbine/rifle featuring synthetic furniture and chambered in 5.56 NATO cal., and developed by Eugene Stoner in 1957. At the time, he was under contract by the Armalite division of the Fairchild Aircraft Corp. In 1958, this new AR-15 lost out in military competition to the select-fire M-14 manufactured by Springfield Armory. After losing this competition, Fairchild Aircraft Corp. thought their new carbine/rifle design would never prove to be successful or obtain a military contract. As a result, during 1959 it sold the design and all future manufacturing rights to Colt. In 1962, the U.S. Department of Defense Advanced Research Projects Agency (ARPA) purchased 1,000 AR-15 rifles from Colt which were immediately sent to South Vietnam for field trials. In 1963, Colt was awarded an 85,000 rifle contract for the U.S. Army (designated XM16E1), and another 19,000 for the U.S. Armed Forces (designated M-16). This new select-fire M-16 was a direct variation of Stoner's original AR-15 design, but had U.S. ordnance markings. In 1963, a presidential order given to the U.S. Army made the M-16 its official service rifle.

In 1966, because of the U.S. involvement in the escalating war in Vietnam, the U.S. government submitted an order for 840,000 M-16s to be delivered to the U.S. Armed Forces at a cost of $92 million. The rest like they say is history.

AR-15 INFORMATION AND RECENT/CURRENT MANUFACTURERS & IMPORTERS

Because of the consumer popularity and resulting proliferation of the semi-auto AR-15 style carbines/rifles over the past twenty years, there are many companies who now offer the AR-15 style platform for sale with their brand name or trademark stamped on the guns. However, there are only four primary domestic manufacturers which currently produce the majority of lower receivers for the AR marketplace. The following listing includes those manufacturers of AR-15 lower receivers, in addition to those brand names, trademarks, and private labels for other companies.

Lewis Machine & Tool = LMT, Lauer (disc.), DS Arms, PWA, Eagle, Knights Armament, Barrett, Bushmaster (possibly).

Continental Machine & Tool = Stag, RRA, High Standard, Noveske (disc.), Century, Global Tactical, CLE, S&W, MGI (1st variation), Wilson Tactical (not all models), Colt, Ratworx.

LAR = Grizzly, Bushmaster (L Prefix), Ameetech, DPMS (possibly), CMMG, Double Star, Fulton, Spike's Tactical, Noveske.

Mega Machine Shop = Mega, Gunsmoke, Dalphon, POF (forged), Alexander Arms, Singer, Spike's Tactical (disc.).

Additional smaller AR-15 lower receiver manufacturers include JV Precision (Double Star, LRB), Olympic (Olympic, SGW, Tromix, Palmetto, Dalphon, Frankford, Century (disc.), Superior (Superior Arms, Lauer), Grenadier Precision, and Sabre Defense (disc.).

Some companies also manufacture custom cut lower receivers out of solid billets, and they include MGI, Cobb, JP, Socom, Sun Devil, POF, and S&W (Performance Center).

In most cases, the markings on forged lower receivers that appear on the magazine well generally indicate the company or trademark that assembled the lower receiver while the markings that appear above the trigger guard indicate the manufacturer of the lower receiver.

The following is a listing of both current and recent manufacturers and importers that offer/have offered complete AR-15 style carbines, rifles, and pistols for sale domestically. Please look under each current company, importer, or brand name/trademark heading for up-to-date information and values on the makes and models that are offered.

These companies include: 2 Vets Arms Co. LLC, 2A Armament LLC, A06 Arms, Accurate Tool & Mfg. Co., Adams Arms, Adcor Defense, Adeq Firearms Co., Advanced Armament Corp., Aero Precision USA, Aklys Defense LLC, AKSA Arms (shotguns), Alan & William Arms, Inc., Alaska Magnum AR's, Alberta Tactical Rifle Supply, Alexander Arms LLC, Ambush Firearms, American Precision Arms, American Spirit Arms, American Spirit Arms Corp., American Tactical Imports, AM-TAC Precision, Anderson Manufacturing, Angstadt Arms, AR57 LLC (57Center LLC), Archer Manufacturing, Ares Defense Systems Inc., Armalite Inc., Arizona Armory, Arms LLC, Arms Room LLC, Arms Tech Ltd., Astra Arms S.A., Australian Automatic Arms Pty. Ltd., Aztek Arms, Barnes Precision Machine, Inc., Barrett Firearms Manufacturing, Inc., Battle Arms Development, Inc., Battle Rifle Company, Bazooka Brothers Mfg., Black Dawn Industries, Black Forge, Blackheart International LLC, Black Ops Technologies, Black Rain Ordnance, Black Rifle Company LLC, Black Weapons Armory, BlueGrass Armory, Bobcat Weapons Inc., Bold Ideas (Colt), Bohica, Bravo Company Mfg. Inc., Budischowsky, Bushmaster Firearms International LLC, C3 Defense, Inc., CMMG, Inc., Carbon 15, Cavalry Arms Corporation, Chattahoochee Gun Works, LLC, Christian Armory Works, Christensen Arms, Century International Arms, Inc., Cobb Manufacturing, Inc., Colt's Manufacturing Company, Inc., Controlled Chaos Arms, Coronado Arms, Core Rifle Systems, Crossfire LLC, Crusader Weaponry, DAR GmbH, DPMS Firearms, LLC, DRD Tactical, DSA Inc., Daewoo, Charles Daly (1976-2010), Dane Armory LLC, Daniel Defense, Dark Storm Industries, LLC (DSI), Del-Ton Incorporated, Desert Ordnance, Desert Tech, Devil Dog Arms, DEZ Tactical Arms, Dlask Arms Corp., Double D Armory, Ltd, Double Star Corp., Dreadnaught Industries LLC, E.M.F. Company, Inc., Eagle Arms, Inc., East Ridge Gun Co., Edward Arms Company, Entreprise Arms Inc., Evolution USA, Firebird Precision, Fulton Armory, GA Precision, G.A.R. Arms, Gilboa, Gun Room Co., LLC, Gunsmoke Enterprises, GWACS Armory, Hahn Tactical, Halo Arms, LLC, Hatcher Gun Company, Head Down Products LLC, Hera Arms, Hesse Arms, High Standard Manufacturing Co., HM Defense & Technology, Hodge Defense Systems, Hogan Manufacturing LLC, Houston Firearms, Houlding Precision Firearms, Huldra Arms, Husan Arms, Intacto Arms, Integrity Arms & Survival, Interarms Arsenal, Intercontinental Arms Inc., Invincible Arms, LLC, Iron Ridge Arms Co., Israel Military Industries (Galil), J.B. Custom Inc., JP Enterprises, Inc., JR Carbines LLC, Jard, Inc., Jesse James Firearms Unlimited, Juggernaut Tactical, K.B.I. Inc., King's Arsenal, Knight's Armament Company, L.A.R. Manufacturing, Inc., LRB Arms, LWRC International, Inc., Larue Tactical, Lauer Custom Weaponry, Legion Firearms LLC, Leitner-Wise Defense, Inc., Leitner-Wise Rifle Co. Inc., Les Baer Custom, Inc., Lewis Machine & Tool Company (LMT), Liberty Arms International LLC, Lithgow Arms, Loki Weapon Systems, Inc., Lone Star Armament, Inc., Lone Star Tactical Supply, Luvo Prague Ltd. (Luvo Arms), MBA Associates, MG Arms Incorporated, MGI, Maunz Match Rifles LLC (Karl Maunz), McDuffee Arms, Microtech Small Arms Research Inc. (MSAR), Miller Precision Arms, Miltac Industries, LLC, Mossberg, O.F. & Sons., Inc., Mohawk Armory, Nemesis Arms, New Evolution Military Ordnance (NEMO), Newtown Firearms, Next Generation

MSR	100%	98%	95%	90%	80%	70%	60%	Last MSR

Arms, North Eastern Arms, Northern Competition, Nosler, Inc., Noveske Rifleworks, LLC, Oberland Arms, Ohio Ordnance Works, Inc., Olympic Arms, Inc., Osprey Armament, Palmetto State Defense, Patriot Ordnance Factory (POF), Peace River Classics, Phase5 Tactical, Precision Firearms, Precision Reflex, Inc., Predator Custom Shop, Primary Weapons Systems (PWS), ProArms Armory s.r.o., Professional Ordnance, Inc., Proof Research, Quality Arms, Quality Parts Co., R Guns, R.I.P. Tactical, RND Manufacturing, Radical Firearms, LLC, Red X Arms, Remington Arms Company, Inc., Rhino Arms, Robinson Armament Co., Rock River Arms, Inc., Rocky Mountain Arms, Inc., Russian American Armory Company, SD Tactical Arms, SI Defense, St. George Arms, SMI Arms, SOG Armory, STI International, S.W.A.T. Firearms, Sabre, Sabre Defence Industries LLC, Scorpion Tactical, Seekins Precision, Sharps Milspec, Sharps Rifle Company, Sig Sauer, Sionics Weapon Systems, Smith & Wesson, Southern Gun Company, Specialized Dynamics, Specialized Tactical Systems, Spike's Tactical, LLC, Spirit Gun Manufacturing Company LLC, Stag Arms, Sterling Arsenal, Stoner Rifle, Sturm, Ruger & Co., Inc., Sun Devil Manufacturing LLC, Superior Arms, Tactical Arms Manufacturing, Tactical Armz, Tactical Rifles, Tactical Supply, Tactical Weapons Solutions, Templar Custom LLC, Templar Tactical Arms LLC, Templar Tactical Firearms, Texas Black Rifle Company, Texas Custom Guns, Thureon Defense, TNW Firearms, Inc., Tromix Corporation, Troy Defense, USA Tactical Firearms, Uselton Arms, VM Hy-Tech LLC, Valor Arms, Victor Arms Corporation, Vigilant Arms, Viking Armament Inc., Vltor Weapon Systems, Volquartsen Custom, Ltd., Vulcan Armament, Inc., WMD Guns, War Sport, Wilson Combat, Windham Weaponry, Wyoming Arms, LLC, Xtreme Machining, Yankee Hill Machine Co., Inc. (YHM), Z-M Weapons, Zenith Firearms, Zombie Defense.

ACCU-MATCH INTERNATIONAL INC.

Previous handgun and pistol parts manufacturer located in Mesa, AZ circa 1996.

PISTOLS: SEMI-AUTO

ACCU-MATCH PISTOL – .45 ACP cal., patterned after the Colt Govt. 1911, SA, competition pistol, stainless steel construction, 5 1/2 in. match grade barrel with 3 ports, recoil reduction system, 8 shot mag., 3-dot sight system. Approx. 160 mfg. 1996 only.

	100%	98%	95%	90%	80%	70%	60%	Last MSR
	$795	$700	$625	$550	$450	$375	$325	*$840*

ACCURACY INTERNATIONAL LTD.

Current rifle manufacturer located in Portsmouth, England, with offices in Fredericksburg, VA. Currently distributed by Mile High Shooting Accessories, located in Broomfield, CO, SRT Supply, located in St. Petersburg, FL, Tac Pro Shooting Center, located in Mingus, TX, and by Euro Optic Limited, located in Montoursville, PA. Previously imported by Accuracy International North America, located in Orchard Park, NY until circa 2005, and 1998-2005 in Oak Ridge, TN. Also previously imported until 1998 by Gunsite Training Center, located in Paulden, AZ.

RIFLES: BOLT ACTION

In addition to the models listed, Accuracy International also makes military and law enforcement rifles, including the SR98 Australian, G22 German, and the Dutch SLA. On Models AE, AW, AWP, and AWM listed in this section, many options and configurations are available which will add to the base prices listed.

Add $255 for Picatinny rail on all currently manufactured rifles (standard on Model AE and AW50).

AE MODEL – .243 Win., .260 Rem., .308 Win., or 6.5 Creedmoor cal., 5 shot mag., 20 or 24 in. stainless barrel, Harris bipod attachment point, four sling attachment points, Picatinny rail, black, green, or dark earth finish, approx. 8 1/2 lbs. Importation began 2002.

MSR $3,600	$3,325	$2,775	$2,400	$2,000	$1,700	$1,425	$1,200	

Add $307 for adj. cheekpiece (disc. 2012) or $422 for folding stock.
Add $213 for standard muzzle brake.
Add $357 for butt spike.
Add $454 for 26 in. barrel.

AT 308 – .308 Win. cal., 20, 24, or 26 in. stainless steel plain barrel, threaded for A1 muzzle brake, Quickloc quick release barrel system bolted and bonded to aluminum chassis, detachable 10 shot double stack mag., extractor, 3 pos. safety, two-stage adj. trigger, fixed stock with adj. cheekpiece and LOP, pistol grip, fixed buttpad with spacers, 1913 action rail, black, green, or pale brown stock, black metal finish, 13.9 lbs. New 2014.

MSR $3,550	$3,300	$2,750	$2,400	$2,000	$1,700	$1,425	$1,200	

AW MODEL – .243 Win. (new 2000), .260 Rem., .300 Win. Mag., .308 Win., .338 Lapua (disc. 2012), or 6.5 Creedmoor cal., precision bolt action featuring 20, 24, 26, or 27 (disc.) in. 1:12 twist stainless steel barrel with or w/o muzzle brake, 3-lug bolt, 10 shot detachable mag., green synthetic folding (military/LE only) thumbhole adj. stock, AI bipod, 14 lbs. Importation began 1995.

MSR $6,050	$5,500	$4,650	$4,000	$3,400	$2,850	$2,200	$1,800	

Add $203 for fluted barrel.
Add $257 for Picatinny rail or $422 for folding stock.
Add $342 for threaded barrel with muzzle brake.
Add $357 for butt spike.
Add $797 for .300 Win. Mag. cal. with 20 or 26 in. fluted and threaded barrel.
Add $376 for AW-F Model (disc. 2002).

MSR	100%	98%	95%	90%	80%	70%	60%	Last MSR

AWP MODEL – similar to AW Model, except has 20 or 24 in. barrel w/o muzzle brake, 15 lbs. Imported 1995-2007.

	$4,250	$3,650	$3,150	$2,650	$2,150	$1,800	$1,500	*$4,600*

Add $310 for AWP-F Model (disc. 2002).

AW50 – .50 BMG, advanced ergonomic design, features built-in anti-recoil system, 5 shot mag., adj. third supporting leg, folding stock, 27 in. fluted barrel with muzzle brake, Picatinny rail, approx. 30 lbs. Mfg. 1998-2012.

	$12,500	$10,500	$8,750	$7,500	$6,250	$4,950	$3,750	*$13,096*

AWM MODEL (SUPER MAGNUM) – .300 Win. Mag. or .338 Lapua cal., 6-lug bolt, 26 or 27 in. 1:9/1:10 twist stainless steel fluted barrel with muzzle brake, 5 shot mag., 15 1/2 lbs. Imported 1995-2009.

	$5,600	$5,100	$4,675	$3,800	$2,950	$2,500	$1,750	*$5,900*

Add $100 for .338 Lapua cal.
Add $324 for AWM-F Model (disc. 2002).

AX MODEL – .243 Win., .260 Rem., .308 Win., .338 Lapua, or 6.5 Creedmoor cal., 10 shot mag., 20, 24, 26, or 27 in. barrel with or w/o muzzle brake, Picatinny rail included, pistol grip with adj. cheekpiece, fixed butt pad with additional spacers, choice of green, black, or dark earth finished hardware, folding chassis.

MSR $6,500	$6,000	$5,200	$4,600	$4,000	$3,350	$2,750	$2,250	

Add $226 for muzzle brake.
Add $959 for .338 Lapua cal.

* AX50 – .50 BMG cal., 27 in. stainless match grade barrel with triple chamber muzzle brake, proofed steel action bolted to aluminum chassis, 5 shot detachable mag., Mil-Std 1913 action and forend rail, 6 lug 60 degree bolt with A1 leaf spring extractor, 2-pos. safety, two-stage trigger, integrated quick adjust butt spike, left folding stock, quick adjust butt and cheekpiece, choice of green, black, or dark earth finished hardware, 27 1/2 lbs.

MSR $10,610	$9,650	$8,750	$8,000	$7,250	$6,500	$5,750	$4,950	

AXMC (MULTI CALIBER) – .308 Win., .300 Win. Mag., or .338 Lapua Mag. cal., sniper configuration, solid steel, flat bottomed action bolts to combat tested AI chassis, 20, 24, 26, or 27 in. stainless steel plain barrel threaded for muzzle, 3-pos. safety, two-stage trigger, detachable 10 shot CIP length double stack mag., 6 lug, 60 degree bolt with leaf spring extractor, right side folding stock over bolt, adj. cheekpiece, adj. buttpad with spacers, pistol grip, Picatinny rail, 16 in. forend tube rail, accessory rails, black or green stock with black metalwork or pale brown stock and metalwork, 14.6 lbs. New 2014.

Please contact the importers or the factory directly for U.S. retail pricing and availability on this model.

AX308 – .308 Win. cal., 20, 24, or 26 in. stainless steel plain barrel, threaded for muzzle brake, detachable 10 shot double stack mag., 3-pos. safety, two-stage trigger, right side folding stock with adj. cheekpiece, adj. buttpad with spacers, pistol grip, Picatinny rail, 13 in. forend tube and accessory rails, 60 degree bolt with leaf spring extractor, available with black or green stock with black metal work or pale brown stock and metalwork, 13.9 lbs. New 2014.

Please contact the importers or the factory directly for U.S. retail pricing and availability on this model.

PALMAMASTER – .308 Win. cal., available with either NRA prone or UIT style stock, 30 in. stainless steel fluted barrel, designed for competition shooting, laminated stock. Disc. 2002.

	$2,600	$2,350	$2,100	$1,900	$1,700	$1,500	$1,250	*$2,850*

CISMMASTER – .22 BR, 6mm BR, .243 Win., .308 Win., 6.5x55mm, or 7.5x55mm cal., designed for slow and rapid fire international and military shooting competition, 10 shot mag., 2-stage trigger. Disc. 2002.

	$3,175	$2,850	$2,600	$2,350	$2,100	$1,900	$1,700	*$3,480*

VARMINT RIFLE – .22 Middlested, .22 BR, .22-250 Rem., .223 Rem., 6mm BR, .243 Win., .308 Win., or 7mm-08 Rem. cal., 26 in. fluted stainless steel barrel. Mfg. 1997-2002.

	$3,200	$2,725	$2,350	$1,950	$1,675	$1,475	$1,300	*$3,650*

ACCURACY X, INC.

Current rifle and semi-auto pistol manufacturer founded by competitive shooter Steve Huff, located in Virginia.

PISTOLS: SEMI-AUTO

PRO PLUS – .45 ACP cal., 1911 style, polished match barrel, 2 tuned mags., opened ejection port, tuned ejector and extractor, match hammer sear, match sights or scope/dot rail, high textured grips, high grip beavertail grip safety, forged slide and frame, checkering on front strap and mainspring, match grade slide stop, includes hard storage case, avail. in Wadgun and Metallic Sight configurations. New 2015.

MSR $3,495	$3,150	$2,755	$2,365	$2,140	$1,750	$1,425	$1,100	

PRO SERIES DEFENDER – .45 ACP cal., 1911-style, 5 in. barrel, 7 shot mag., adj. sights, beavertail safety, drop forged match fitted slide and frame.

MSR $2,995	$2,695	$2,360	$2,020	$1,835	$1,480	$1,215	$950	

MSR	100%	98%	95%	90%	80%	70%	60%	Last MSR

PRO SERIES GUARDIAN – .45 ACP cal., 4 in. barrel, 7 shot mag., beavertail safety, drop forged match fitted slide and frame, with or without bobtail.

MSR $3,028	$2,725	$2,385	$2,050	$1,855	$1,500	$1,225	$955	

Add $170 for bobtail.

PRO SERIES RECON – .45 ACP cal., 1911-style, 5 in. barrel, 7 shot mag., tactical sights, beavertail safety, drop forged match fitted slide and frame.

MSR $3,195	$2,875	$2,515	$2,155	$1,955	$1,580	$1,295	$1,000	

X SERIES 6 INCH LONGSIDE
Custom order, prices start at $3,499.

X SERIES ACTION PISTOL METALLIC/PPC – 1911-style.
Custom order, prices start at $3,499.

X SERIES BULLSEYE WADGUN – 1911-style.
Custom order, prices start at $3,499.

X SERIES COMMANDER/CARRY – 1911-style.
Custom order, prices start at $3,499.

X SERIES DEFENSE/TACTICAL – 1911-style.
Custom order, prices start at $3,499.

X SERIES IDPA/LIMITED 10 – 1911-style.
Custom order, prices start at $3,499.

X SERIES OPEN/COMPENSATED – 1911-style.
Custom order, prices start at $3,499.

X SERIES SERVICE PISTOL (HARDBALL) – 1911-style.
Custom order, prices start at $3,499.

RIFLES: BOLT ACTION

Accuracy X currently offers a sniper style bolt action tactical rifle. Since all guns are built per individual customer specifications, please contact the company directly for more information, including options, availability, and pricing (see Trademark Index).

ACCURATE TOOL & MFG. CO.

Current custom manufacturer located in Lexington, KY.

PISTOLS: SEMI-AUTO

Accurate Tool & Mfg. Co. also offers custom built 1911 pistols styled like Government, Commander, and Officer models. The following listings reflect base MSR only. Please contact the company directly for additional options, upgrades, availability, and pricing (see Trademark Index).

AR PISTOL – 5.56 NATO or .300 AAC Blackout cal., 7 1/2-8 1/2 in. cold hammer forged barrel, 20 shot mag., extended feed ramps, pistol-length gas system, flat-top upper receiver, forged lower receiver with extension, H buffer, and flip-up rear sight, Samson Evo handguard, Thordsen cheek riser, Mil-Spec phosphate finish.

MSR $1,345	$1,145	$1,015	$885	$740	$675	$575	$475	

RIFLES: SEMI-AUTO

The following models reflect base MSR only. Please contact the company directly for additional options, upgrades, availability, and pricing (see Trademark Index).

AR-10 – .308 Win. cal., match grade stainless steel barrel with Lantac flash suppressor or silencer mount of choice, 20 shot mag., extended feed ramp, mid-length gas system, forged flat-top upper and forged lower receiver with H buffer and flip-up rear sight, CMR rail system (one-piece free float handguard), in-house Cerakote finish of choice.

MSR $2,995	$2,550	$2,225	$1,825	$1,575	$1,300	$1,100	$950	

CLASSIC CARBINE – 5.56 NATO cal., 16 in. M4 profile barrel, M4 feed ramp barrel extension, enhanced flared magwell, M4 stock, carbine-length gas system, aluminum forged upper and lower receivers, Type III hardcoat anodized finish.

MSR $1,020	$865	$750	$650	$585	$515	$450	$395	

LE CARBINE – 5.56 NATO cal., 16 in. cold hammer forged barrel with A2 flash suppressor, one 30 shot mag. included, fixed front sight base, flip-up rear sight (on lower only), extended feed ramp, carbine-length gas system, flat-top upper and forged lower with Mil-Spec rec. extension and H buffer, standard M4 type handguard, Mil-Spec phosphate finish.

MSR $1,290	$1,095	$965	$825	$725	$625	$535	$450	

MSR	100%	98%	95%	90%	80%	70%	60%	Last MSR

LE MIDDY – 5.56 NATO cal., 16 in. cold hammer forged barrel with A2 flash suppressor, 30 shot mag., F marked front sight base, mid-length gas system, extended feed ramps, flat-top upper rec., forged lower receiver with extension, H buffer, and flip-up rear sight, Mil-Spec phosphate finish.

	100%	98%	95%	90%	80%	70%	60%	
MSR $1,290	$1,095	$965	$825	$725	$625	$535	$450	

ACTION ARMS LTD.

Previous firearms importer and distributor until 1994, located in Philadelphia, PA.

Only Action Arms Models AT-84S, AT-88S, and the Model B Sporter will be listed under this heading. Galil, Timberwolf, and Uzi trademarks can be located in their respective sections.

CARBINES: SEMI-AUTO

MODEL B SPORTER – 9mm Para. cal., patterned after the original Uzi Model B Sporter, 16.1 in. barrel, fires from closed bolt, thumbhole stock with recoil pad, 10 shot mag., adj. rear sight, 8.8 lbs. Limited importation from China 1994 only.

	100%	98%	95%	90%	80%	70%	60%	Last MSR
	$695	$625	$550	$475	$435	$385	$335	*$595*

ACTION LEGENDS MFG., INC.

Previous manufacturer, importer, and distributor until circa 2006 and located in Houston, TX.

RIFLES

MODEL 888 M1 CARBINE – .22 LR or .30 Carbine cal., 18 in. barrel, mfg. from new original M1 parts and stock and unused GI parts, 10, 15, or 30 shot mag., choice of birch or walnut stock, parkerized finish, metal or wood handguard, 5 1/2 lbs.

	100%	98%	95%	90%	80%	70%	60%	Last MSR
	$675	$625	$550	$495	$425	$375	$325	*$650*

Add $11 for .22 LR cal.
Add $31 for walnut/metal forearm or $47 for walnut/wood forearm.

ADAMS ARMS

Current rifle manufacturer established circa 2007, located in Palm Harbor, FL. Adams Arms also manufactures a complete line of accessories for the AR-15 platform, in addition to barrels, upper assemblies, and free floating rails.

PISTOLS: SEMI-AUTO

TACTICAL EVO BASE PISTOL – 5.56 NATO cal., GPO, 7 1/2 in. Government contour heavy barrel with A2 flash hider, 30 shot GI aluminum mag., Samson free-float lightweight modular rail system, no sights, adj. gas block, forged lower receiver with beveled magwell, forged A4 flat-top upper receiver with M4 feed ramps and Picatinny rail, pistol buffer tube, A2 grip, hardcoat black anodized finish. New 2015.

	100%	98%	95%	90%	80%	70%	60%	
MSR $1,098	$900	$790	$675	$610	$500	$400	$325	

TACTICAL EVO UPGRADED PISTOL – 5.56 NATO cal., GPO, 7 1/2 in. heavy contour pistol length or 11 1/2 in. carbine length VooDoo barrel with A2 flash hider, 30 shot GI aluminum mag., flat-top Picatinny rail, three adj. gas settings, extended Samson Evolution rail, pistol buffer tube, ambidextrous safety, beveled magwell, Samson fixed front and rear sights, upgraded JP fire control group, Ergo grip, hardcoat anodized black finish, approx. 6 lbs. New 2015.

	100%	98%	95%	90%	80%	70%	60%	
MSR $1,099	$900	$790	$675	$610	$500	$400	$325	

XLP EVO UPGRADED PISTOL – .300 AAC Blackout cal., GPO, 12 1/2 in. medium contour barrel with VDI .30 cal. Jet compensator and black Nitride finish, 30 shot GI aluminum mag., Samson free-float lightweight modular rail system, XLP low profile gas block, upgraded JP Fire Control group, Mil-Spec forged upper and lower receiver, M4 feed ramps, beveled magwell, flat-top Picatinny rail, pistol buffer tube, 12 in. Evolution handguard, no sights, Magpul MOE grip, JP trigger, 5.95 lbs. New 2015.

	100%	98%	95%	90%	80%	70%	60%	
MSR $1,605	$1,365	$1,195	$1,025	$930	$750	$625	$500	

RIFLES: SEMI-AUTO

Adams Arms manufactures a complete line of AR-15 platform rifles. For more information on options, availability, and delivery time, please contact the company directly (see Trademark Index).

Adams Arms manufactures the Huldra line of AR-15 style rifles/carbines exclusively for Fleet Farm and also manufactures the Korstog AR-15s. Please refer to the H and K section for a current listing.

MID BASE – 5.56 NATO cal., GPO, 16 in. Government contour Melonited barrel with A2 flash hider, Mil-Spec 6-position retractable stock, 30 shot GI aluminum magazine, Mil-Spec forged upper and lower receiver with Picatinny rail, black hardcoat anodized, Kryptek Highlander, Kryptek Nomad, or Kryptek Typhon camo (new 2015) finish, ribbed mid-length M4 style molded polymer handguards with lower heat shield, 6.4 lbs.

	100%	98%	95%	90%	80%	70%	60%	
MSR $1,016	$865	$755	$650	$590	$475	$400	$325	

Add $139 for Kryptek Highlander, Nomad, or Typhon finish (new 2015).

MSR	100%	98%	95%	90%	80%	70%	60%	Last MSR

CARBINE BASE – .223 Rem. cal., GPO, similar to Mid Base model, except has 16 in. M4 Profile 4150 CM Melonited barrel, and short forearm.

| MSR $994 | $850 | $745 | $640 | $580 | $475 | $400 | $325 | |

Add $515 for Carbine MOE model with Magpul handguards, stock, grip, and PMag.

MID TACTICAL EVO – 5.56 NATO cal., GPO, 16 in. Government contour 4150 CM Melonited barrel with A2 flash hider, 30 shot GI aluminum mag., Picatinny flat-top rail with dry lube internal finish and laser engraved, Samson free-float lightweight modular rail system, Mil-Spec forged upper and lower receiver, beveled magwell, M4 feed ramps, enhanced 6-pos. buttstock, hardcoat black anodized, Kryptek Highlander, Kryptek Nomad, or Kryptek Typhon camo (new 2015) finish, 7 lbs.

| MSR $1,349 | $1,150 | $1,000 | $865 | $780 | $635 | $525 | $425 | |

Add $139 for Kryptek Highlander, Nomad, or Typhon camo finish (new 2015).

* Mid Tactical Evo XLP – 5.56 NATO cal., 16 in. Government contour Melonited barrel with A2 flash hider, 30 shot GI aluminum mag., XLP multi-adj. low profile gas block, forged lower receiver with beveled magwell, forged M4 upper with M4 feed ramps and Picatinny rail, Samson free-float lightweight modular rail system, Vltor IMOD collapsible stock, hardcoat black anodized finish, 7 lbs. Disc. 2015.

| | $1,185 | $1,035 | $890 | $800 | $650 | $550 | $425 | *$1,389* |

CARBINE TACTICAL EVO – 5.56 NATO cal., GPO, 16 in. M4 profile Melonited barrel with A2 flash hider, 30 shot GI aluminum mag., Samson free-float lightweight modular rail system, no sights, forged lower with beveled magwell and A4 flat-top upper receiver with M4 feed ramps and Picatinny rail, Ergo grip, enhanced 6-position buttstock, hardcoat black anodized finish, 7 lbs.

| MSR $1,327 | $1,125 | $985 | $845 | $765 | $625 | $525 | $425 | |

MID TACTICAL ELITE – 5.56 NATO cal., GPO, 16 in. Government Contour Melonited barrel with A2 flash hider, VLTOR IMOD collapsible stock, Ergo grip, 30 shot GI aluminum magazine, Samson free float lightweight modular quad rail system, Mil-Spec forged upper and lower receiver, hardcoat anodized finish, Picatinny flat-top rail with dry lube internal finish and laser engraved. Disc. 2015.

| | $1,150 | $1,000 | $865 | $780 | $635 | $525 | $425 | *$1,349* |

CARBINE TACTICAL ELITE – 5.56 NATO cal., GPO, similar to Mid Tactical Elite, except has 16 in. M4 Contour Melonited barrel. Disc. 2015.

| | $1,125 | $985 | $845 | $765 | $625 | $525 | $425 | *$1,327* |

C.O.R. ULTRA LITE RIFLE – 5.56 NATO cal., 16 1/2 in. Ultra Lite contour Melonited barrel with VDI Jet Compensator, Hiperfire HiperTouch 24 Competition Fire Control, 30 shot GI aluminum mag., no sights, Samson free-float lightweight modular rail system, forged lower with beveled magwell, forged M4 upper with M4 feed ramps and flat-top Picatinny rail, Evolution Rail handguard, hand stop, 2 in. rails, QD mount, Magpul MOE stock, Magpul K2 grip, hardcoat black anodized finish. New 2015.

| MSR $1,800 | $1,525 | $1,335 | $1,145 | $1,035 | $850 | $700 | $550 | |

MID EVO ULTRA LITE – 5.56 NATO cal., GPO, 16 in. Ultra Lite barrel with Jet Compensator and black Nitride finish, 30 shot GI aluminum mag., Samson free-float lightweight modular rail system, forged A4 flat-top upper receiver with Picatinny rail, M4 feed ramps, forged lower with beveled magwell, Evolution Rail handguard, no sights, enhanced 6-pos. buttstock, Ergo grip, hardcoat black anodized finish, 6.7 lbs. New 2015.

| MSR $1,743 | $1,485 | $1,300 | $1,115 | $1,010 | $815 | $675 | $525 | |

SMALL FRAME .308 ALPHA-S RIFLE – .308 Win. cal., XLP low profile block, 18 in. barrel, VDI Jet compensator, 20 shot mag., AR gold trigger, Luth-AR adj. buttstock, Magpul K2 grip, Samson 15 in. evolution rail, hardcoat black anodized finish, 8.85 lbs. New 2015.

| MSR $2,266 | $1,925 | $1,685 | $1,425 | $1,250 | $1,050 | $900 | $750 | |

SMALL FRAME .308 PATROL BATTLE RIFLE – .308 Win. cal., 16 in. barrel, VDI Jet compensator, 20 shot mag., enhanced SOPMOD buttstock, Magpul K2 grip, Samson extended evolution rail, hardcoat black anodized finish, 8.15 lbs. New 2015.

| MSR $1,776 | $1,495 | $1,315 | $1,150 | $1,025 | $875 | $750 | $615 | |

SMALL FRAME .308 PATROL ENHANCED – .308 Win. cal., 16 in. barrel, 20 shot mag., enhanced SOPMOD buttstock, Magpul K2 grip, Magpul MOE handguard, hardcoat black anodized finish, 7.8 lbs. New 2015.

| MSR $1,489 | $1,260 | $1,120 | $985 | $835 | $725 | $615 | $515 | |

ULTRA LITE ADVANCED DISSIPATOR RIFLE – 5.56 NATO cal., GPO, 16 1/2 in. match grade Ultra Lite VooDoo barrel, 30 shot Magpul PMag., Diamondhead D45 Swing Sights, low mass bolt carrier, forged lower receiver with beveled magwell, forged M4 upper with M4 feed ramps and flat-top Picatinny rail, Magpul MOE handguard and trigger guard, Magpul MOE stock and grip, hardcoat black anodized finish. New 2015.

| MSR $1,326 | $1,125 | $985 | $845 | $765 | $625 | $525 | $425 | |

MSR	100%	98%	95%	90%	80%	70%	60%	Last MSR

ADCO ARMS INC. (ADCO SALES INC.)

Adco Sales Inc. was a previous importer of Diamond shotguns circa 2007-2012 manufactured by Vega in Istanbul, Turkey. Adco Arms Inc. currently imports accessories only and is located in Woburn, MA. During 2012, the name Adco Sales Inc. was changed to Adco Arms Inc.

SHOTGUNS: SLIDE ACTION

All Adco slide action shotguns were manufactured in Turkey.

MARINER MODEL – 12 ga., 3 in. chamber, choice of 18 1/2 plain or 22 in. VR barrel with chokes, 5 shot mag., black synthetic stock and forearm. Imported 2003-2006.

$250	$225	$200	$175	$150	$135	$110	*$319*

ADCOR DEFENSE

Current manufacturer located in Baltimore, MD.

Adcor Defense currently manufactures AR-15 style rifles/carbines.

RIFLES/CARBINES

A-556 ELITE – 5.56 NATO cal., GPO, 16, 18, or 20 in. chrome lined free floating barrel, forward placed reversible/ambidextrous charging handle, multi-purpose regulator, optics ready, ejection port dust wiper, two-piece keyed quad rail system, tool-less field strip design, custom rifle stock, custom ergonomic rifle grip with aggressive texturing. New 2013.

MSR $2,295	$1,950	$1,725	$1,450	$1,250	$1,050	$900	$750

A-556 ELITE GI – 5.56 NATO cal., GIO, 16, 18 (disc. 2015), or 20 (disc. 2015) in. chrome lined barrel with or without ambidextrous forward charging handle, multi-position gas regulator with removable gas tube, ejection port dust wiper, key-locked, highly rigid rail system mounts to upper receiver, upper and lower rails separate with push of a button, no tools needed, custom rifle stock, custom ergonomic rifle grip with aggressive texturing, 6.9 lbs. New 2013.

MSR $1,995	$1,700	$1,500	$1,250	$1,100	$950	$825	$675

B.E.A.R. – 5.56 NATO cal., GPO with multi-position regulator, 16 or 18 in. free floating chrome lined barrel, forward placed reversible/ambidextrous charging handle, ejection port dust wiper, two-piece keyed quad rail system, aluminum alloy receivers and rail systems, configured with sights or optics ready, 6.45-7.6 lbs. Disc. 2013.

$1,885	$1,650	$1,425	$1,275	$1,050	$850	$650	*$2,092*

* **B.E.A.R. Elite** – 5.56 NATO cal., GPO, similar to B.E.A.R., except has hammer forged chrome lined barrels, comes with sights or optics ready, also features Magpul MOE rifle stock, Magpul MOE ergonomic rifle grip with aggressive texturing, 6.45-7.6 lbs. Disc. 2015.
Retail pricing was never made available for this model.

B.E.A.R. GI – 5.56 NATO cal., GIO with multi-position gas regulator and removable gas tube, 16 or 18 in. chrome lined barrel, with or w/o ambidextrous forward placed charging handle, ejection port dust wiper, key-locked, highly rigid rail system mounts to upper receiver, upper and lower rails separate with the push of a button, no special tools needed, approx. 6.8 lbs. Disc. 2014.

$1,750	$1,525	$1,325	$1,195	$975	$795	$625	

* **B.E.A.R. GI Elite** – 5.56 NATO cal., GIO, similar to B.E.A.R. GI, except also features hammer forged chrome lined barrels, Magpul MOE rifle stock, Magpul MOE ergonomic rifle grip with aggressive texturing, approx. 6.8 lbs. Disc. 2015.
Retail pricing was never made available for this model.

B.E.A.R. LIMITED EDITION SIGNATURE SERIES – 5.56 NATO cal., 18 or 20 in. hammer forged, chrome lined barrel, full billet upper and lower receiver, Magpul pistol grip and buttstock, AMBI Products ambidextrous fire selector switch, matte black finish, hand built and signed by Michael Brown. Mfg. mid-2013.

$2,040	$1,785	$1,525	N/A	N/A	N/A	N/A	*$2,399*

ADEQ FIREARMS COMPANY

Previous manufacturer located in Tampa, FL 2010-2014.

Adeq Firearms Company manufactured custom and standard production AR-15 style firearms, sniper rifles, 1911 pistols, and firearm suppression systems. Alongside the civilian sales, the company handled custom built firearms for law enforcement and government agencies, as well as security contract operating companies. In addition, the company made a limited number of custom arsenal rebuilds of classic vintage military weapons based on parts availability.

PISTOLS: SEMI-AUTO

VIGILUM 1911 STYLE TACTICAL PISTOL – 9mm Para., .40 S&W, or .45 ACP cal., full sized 1911-style, GIO, match grade barrel, trigger, hammer, and sear, G10 grip, with or w/o rail, parkerized finish, 3-dot Novak low profile sights, 2.6 lbs. Mfg. 2011-2013.

$1,950	$1,700	$1,465	$1,325	$1,075	$880	$685	*$2,300*

MSR	100%	98%	95%	90%	80%	70%	60%	Last MSR

CK 6 – .45 ACP cal., limited production gun utilizing custom production frames and slides. Mfg. 2014 only.

| | $2,550 | $2,225 | $1,915 | $1,735 | $1,400 | $1,150 | $895 | $3,000 |

PALADIN DAGGER – .22 LR (special order by request) or 5.56 NATO cal., custom built with Paladin lower receiver. Mfg. 2012-2014.

| | $1,025 | $895 | $775 | $695 | $565 | $460 | $360 | $1,200 |

RIFLES: BOLT ACTION

INTERCEPTOR – .308 Win. or .300 Win. Mag. cal., Rem. 700 action, Lilja barrel, APO chassis, tactical and hunter variations. Mfg. 2014 only.

| | $2,725 | $2,385 | $2,050 | $1,850 | $1,500 | $1,225 | $950 | $3,200 |

Add $300 for tactical variation.

RIFLES: SEMI-AUTO

L-TAC (LIGHTWEIGHT TACTICAL RIFLE) – 5.56 NATO cal., GIO, available in three configurations: standard forged lower receiver with ultralight barrel and furniture (weighs 5.2 lbs.), the Gen 2 with ultralight lower receiver (weighs less than 5 lbs.), or the L-Tac SBR with 11 1/2 in. barrel and ultralight alloy lower receiver (approx. 5 lbs.), optional Gen 3 with both ultralight upper and lower receivers. Mfg. 2013 only.

| | $1,450 | $1,275 | $1,100 | $975 | $800 | $650 | $525 | $1,600 |

PALADIN PATROL CARBINE – 5.56 NATO, 6.8 SPC, 7.62x39mm (disc.) or .300 AAC Blackout cal., rotary bolt GIO, available in semi-auto, auto, or 3-round bursts (NFA rules apply), 16 or 18 in. chrome lined barrel, A2 front and quick detach A2 rear sights, Mil-Spec forged aluminum upper and lower receivers with anodized finish, Manganese phosphate barrel finish, standard A2 round mid-length handguards, GI pistol grip, Rogers 6-position adj. commercial tube buttstock, SST, includes cable lock, sling, and owner's manual, 5.8 lbs. Mfg. 2011-2014.

| | $925 | $810 | $695 | $625 | $525 | $450 | $395 | $1,082 |

Add $218 for Magpul MOE stock (Carbine 02).

Add $318 for Troy free float forearm, Magpul stock, and BUIS (Carbine 03).

PALADIN ULTRALIGHT – 5.56 NATO cal., Magtech magnesium infused lower receiver, 16 in. Voodoo Tactical barrel, Magpul stock, pistol grip. Mfg. 2013-2014.

| | $1,500 | $1,315 | $1,125 | $1,025 | $825 | $675 | $525 | $1,776 |

PRECISION LONG RANGE RIFLE – 7.62 NATO cal., GIO, 18 in. fluted bull barrel with GoGun flash hider, anodized receiver and Manganese phosphate barrel finish, PRi Gen3 carbon fiber forearm handguards, Magpul PRS buttstock, SST, includes Leupold Mark IV ER/T optics, pelican case, sniper data book, and cleaning kit, 11.6 lbs. Mfg. 2011-2013.

| | $1,950 | $1,700 | $1,465 | $1,325 | $1,075 | $880 | $685 | $2,300 |

RECON – 5.56 or 7.62 NATO cal., 16 (5.56 NATO cal.) in. Nitride or 18 (7.62 NATO cal.) in. SASS fluted barrel, LanTac flash hider, Dueck offset sights (18 in. barrel only), Magpul ACS stock, Troy MRF handguard, Ergo pistol grip. Mfg. 2014 only.

| | $1,875 | $1,640 | $1,400 | $1,275 | $1,025 | $850 | $650 | $2,200 |

Add $300 for 7.62 NATO cal.

VENATOR BATTLE RIFLE – 7.62 NATO cal., rotary bolt GIO, AR-15 style, 16, 18, or 20 in. chrome lined barrel with GoGun Talon muzzle brake, A2 front and quick detach A2 rear sights, Mil-Spec anodized receiver finish and Manganese phosphate barrel finish, free float aluminum handguard with Troy Alpha rail system, 6-position adj. commercial tube buttstock, SST, 20 shot detachable box mag., 8.1 lbs. Mfg. 2011-2014.

| | $1,625 | $1,425 | $1,225 | $1,100 | $900 | $725 | $575 | $1,800 |

ADVANCED ARMAMENT CORP.

Current manufacturer of AR-15 style rifles, barrels, upper receivers, silencers, muzzle brakes, flash hiders and accessories located in Lawrenceville, GA. Advanced Armament Corp. is part of the Freedom Group.

RIFLES: BOLT ACTION

MODEL 7 – .300 AAC Blackout cal., Rem. Model 7 bolt action, 16 in. threaded black nitride barrel, black glass filled polymer stock with adj. cheek riser, X-Mark Pro trigger, includes 20 MOA scope rail, 6 lbs. 8 oz.

| MSR $899 | $775 | $685 | $615 | $550 | $485 | $415 | $370 | |

RIFLES: SEMI-AUTO

MPW – 5.56 NATO or .300 AAC Blackout cal., GIO, 16 in. barrel with AAC 51T Blackout flash hider, nickel boron coated bolt carrier and cam pin, free floating quad rail sized to match length of barrel, 6-position Magpul CTR stock, Magpul MOE grip, Geissele two stage trigger.

| MSR $1,600 | $1,350 | $1,200 | $1,075 | $950 | $815 | $700 | $575 | |

MSR	100%	98%	95%	90%	80%	70%	60%	*Last MSR*

RIFLES: SINGLE SHOT

HANDI-RIFLE – .300 AAC Blackout cal., H&R Handi-Rifle break action, 16.2 in. threaded barrel, black glass filled polymer stock and furniture, H&R transfer bar trigger, 6.9 lbs. New 2012.

MSR $360	$325	$285	$250	$230	$215	$200	$190	

AERO PRECISION USA

Current semi-auto rifle manufacturer located in Tacoma, WA.

CARBINES/RIFLES: SEMI-AUTO

Aero Precision USA offers a complete line of AR-15 upper and lower receivers, as well as parts. Guns can be built per individual customer specifications. Please contact the company directly for more information including pricing and availability (see Trademark Index).

AC-15 COMPLETE RIFLE – 5.56 NATO cal., carbine-length gas system, 16 in. M4 profile barrel with A2 flash hider, Magpul 30 shot PMag., Magpul MBUS rear and A2 front sights, M4 collapsible stock, A2 pistol grip, M4 carbine handguard with double heat shield, hardcoat black anodized finish, 6.24 lbs. New 2016.

MSR $699	$615	$540	$470	$400	$350	$310	$295	

AC-15M MID-LENGTH COMPLETE RIFLE – 5.56 NATO cal., mid-length gas system, 16 in. barrel with A2 flash hider, 30 shot Magpul PMag., Magpul MBUS rear and A2 front sights, M4 collapsible stock, A2 pistol grip, M4 upper and Gen 2 lower receiver with flared magwell, M4 mid-length handguard with heat shield, hardcoat anodized black finish. New 2016.

MSR $740	$640	$550	$470	$400	$350	$310	$295	

AR15 BLACKHAWK COMPLETE – 5.56 NATO cal., 16 in. barrel with A2 flash hider, mid-length upper receiver with COP (Continuous Optics Platform), low profile gas block, standard charging handle, forged alum. upper and lower receiver, marked "Cal Multi", works with standard AR-15 components and magazines, threaded rear takedown pin detent hole, Magpul MOE pistol grip stock, Aero Precision billet trigger guard, configured rail system, matte black, FDE/Desert, OD/Olive, Titanium, Tungsten, or Burnt Bronze finish. Disc. 2015.

	$1,100	$995	$875	$735	$650	$550	$465	*$1,300*

Add $150 for FDE/Desert, OD/Olive, Titanium, Tungsten, or Burnt Bronze finish.

AR15 BLACKHAWK ELITE – 5.56 NATO cal., carbine length gas system, forged aluminum construction, 16 in. barrel with A2 flash hider, mid-length upper receiver with Continuous Optics Platform, M4 feed ramps, free float handguard rail system, fully enclosed dust cover pin, works with standard AR-15 components and magazines, threaded rear takedown pin detent hole, adj. tactical stock, hardcoat anodized matte black finish. Disc. 2015.

	$1,200	$1,075	$950	$800	$700	$600	$495	*$1,400*

AR15 M4E1 COMPLETE RIFLE – 5.56 NATO or .223 Wylde cal., 16 in. mid-length barrel with A2 flash hider, 15 in. KeyMod handguard, M4E1 upper, billet trigger guard, Magpul MOE grip, Magpul STR stock, black or FDE (disc. 2015) finish.

MSR $974	$825	$700	$630	$570	$500	$425	$380	

Add $25 for .223 Wylde cal.
Add $100 for FDE finish (disc. 2015).

C.O.P. (CONTINUOUS OPTICS PLATFORM) – 5.56 NATO cal., 16 in. M4 barrel, mid-length COP receiver, billet trigger guard, integrated upper receiver and handguard system, MOE grip, black or FDE finish. Disc. 2015.

	$1,100	$995	$875	$735	$650	$550	$465	*$1,299*

Add $150 for FDE finish.

C.O.P. M4 COMPLETE RIFLE – 5.56 NATO cal., carbine-length gas system, low profile gas block, 16 in. M4 profile barrel, M4 collapsible stock, A2 pistol grip, C.O.P. M4 upper receiver with rail panels, Gen 2 lower with flared magwell, black anodized finish. New 2016.

MSR $1,050	$885	$785	$685	$600	$535	$465	$415	

M5 .308 COMPLETE RIFLE 16 IN. (M5E1) – .308 Win. cal., 16 in. chrome moly barrel with A2 flash hider, low profile gas block, forged alum. construction, custom integrated upper receiver and free floated handguard system, standard charging handle, works with standard DPMS .308 components and magazines, threaded rear takedown pin detent hole, integrated trigger guard, standard Mil-Spec receiver extension, Magpul STR stock, Magpul MOE pistol grip, EK12 handguard, continuous top rail, matte black hardcoat anodized or FDE/Desert finish.

MSR $1,325	$1,115	$995	$875	$735	$650	$550	$465	

Add $75 for FDE/Desert finish.

MSR	100%	98%	95%	90%	80%	70%	60%	Last MSR

* **M5 .308 Complete Rifle 18 or 20 In. (M5E1)** – .308 Win. cal., 18 or 20 in. chrome moly barrel with A2 flash hider, low profile gas block, forged alum. construction, custom integrated upper receiver and free floated handguard system, standard charging handle, works with standard DPMS .308 components and magazines, threaded rear takedown pin detent hole, integrated trigger guard, standard Mil-Spec receiver extension, Magpul PRS stock, Magpul MOE pistol grip, EK12 handguard, continuous top rail, matte black hardcoat anodized or FDE/Desert finish.

| MSR $1,550 | $1,315 | $1,165 | $1,050 | $915 | $785 | $665 | $550 | |

Add $10 for 20 in. barrel.

Add $75 for FDE/Desert finish on 18 in. barrel, or $85 for FDE/Desert finish on 20 in. barrel.

M16A4 SPECIAL EDITION COMPLETE RIFLE – 5.56 NATO cal., rifle length gas system, 20 in. barrel with A2 flash hider, Magpul 30 shot PMag., A2 front sight block with bayonet lug, A2 stock and grip, M4 upper receiver, A2 detachable carry handle, rifle length A2 style handguard, Special Edition M16A4 lower receiver with custom engraving, M16A4 sling, Black anodized finish, 8 lbs. New 2016.

| MSR $1,050 | $885 | $785 | $685 | $600 | $535 | $465 | $415 | |

AKLYS DEFENSE LLC

Current rifle manufacturer founded in 2014, located in Baton Rouge, LA.

Aklys Defense also manufactures parts, accessories, and firearms-related gear. Please contact the company directly for more information on these products (see Trademark Index).

RIFLES: BOLT ACTION

HADES – .50 BMG cal., built on custom 22 in. match grade Safety Harbor AR-15 upper, Aklys forged lower receiver, 5 shot mag., choice of TI-7, PRS, or UBR stock, black, tan, or OD Green finish. New 2014.

| MSR $4,400 | $4,000 | $3,600 | $3,250 | $2,850 | $2,500 | $2,250 | $1,950 | |

JAVELIN – .308 Win. cal., rifle based on the Mossberg MVP Predator, AR style mags., adj. trigger, Mono-Core design suppressor, laminate sporter style wood stock, 10 lbs. New 2014.

| MSR $1,995 | $1,750 | $1,500 | $1,275 | $1,100 | $950 | $775 | $650 | |

RIFLES: SEMI-AUTO

FALCATA MOE – 5.56 NATO or .300 AAC Blackout cal., 16 in. M4 profile barrel with A2 flash hider, M4 feed ramps, forged aluminum upper and lower receivers with Type III hardcoat black anodized finish, Magpul MBUS rear sight, Magpul high temperature polymer forearm, 6-pos. collapsible Magpul stock, Magpul grip, black, Dark Desert Brown, OD Green, Pink, Tan, or custom Cerakote finish, 6.6 lbs. New 2014.

| MSR $895 | $795 | $695 | $625 | $550 | $475 | $395 | $350 | |

Add $10 for Dark Desert Brown or Pink finish.

Add $145 for custom Cerakote finish.

FALCATA ELITE – 5.56 NATO or .300 AAC Blackout cal., 16 or 18 in. melonited chrome moly barrel with competition muzzle brake, 12.3 (16 in. model) or 15 in. (18 in. model) Samson rail, TI-7 stock with battery compartments, black, Dark Brown, Flat Dark Earth, Olive Drab, or Pink finish. New 2014.

| MSR $1,285 | $1,150 | $1,000 | $875 | $775 | $650 | $550 | $450 | |

FALCATA HEAVY RIFLE – .308 Win. cal., 18 in. stainless carbon fiber barrel with MOJO magnum muzzle brake, 12 in. rail, collapsible or Magpul PRS stock, black, FDE, or OD Green finish. New 2014.

| MSR $1,750 | $1,550 | $1,350 | $1,075 | $925 | $800 | $700 | $600 | |

AKSA ARMS

Current trademark of AR-15 style shotguns, conversions, O/U shotguns, SXS shotguns, single shot shotguns, lever-action shotguns, semi-auto shotguns, and slide-action shotguns. Currently manufactured by Silah Insaat Metal SAN. Tic. LTD. STI, located in Konya, Turkey.

Please contact the manufacturer directly for domestic availability for AKSA Arms branded firearms (see Trademark Index).

ALAN & WILLIAM ARMS, INC.

Current semi-auto rifle manufacturer established in 2012, located in Cheyenne Wells, CO.

RIFLES: SEMI-AUTO

Many options and upgrades are available, and each rifle can be customized per individual specifications. Please contact the company directly for pricing and availability (see Trademark Index).

AR-15 – 5.56 NATO cal., chrome lined bore and chamber, CNC machined aircraft grade aluminum lower receiver, cold hammer forged barrel, M4 feed ramp barrel extension and flat-top receiver, Geissele super semi-automatic (SSA) two-stage trigger, BCM Gunfighter charging handle and bolt, Manganese phosphate barrel finish, hardcoat anodized matte black finish.

| MSR $2,100 | $1,795 | $1,575 | $1,325 | $1,150 | $995 | $850 | $700 | |

MSR		100%	98%	95%	90%	80%	70%	60%	*Last MSR*

ALASKA MAGNUM AR'S

Current manufacturer located in Fairbanks, AK.

Alaska Magnum AR's manufactures AR-15 style rifles designed as true big game rifles.

RIFLES: SEMI-AUTO

GRIZZLY – 6.9 AR Short or .460 GrizzinatAR cal., 18 in. match grade stainless steel barrel with muzzle brake, adj. rifle length gas system, flat-top upper with Picatinny rail handguard, alum. upper and lower receivers, synthetic stock, non-slip ergonomic ambidextrous grip, free float forend, nickel bolt carrier group, stainless steel firing pin, Cerakote finish.

| MSR $3,999 | | $3,595 | $3,150 | $2,695 | $2,450 | $1,975 | $1,625 | $1,250 | |

KODIAK – 6.9 AR Long, .300 RCM, .338 RCM, or .375 GrizzinatAR cal., 20 in. match grade stainless steel barrel with muzzle brake, adj. rifle length gas system, flat-top upper with Picatinny rail handguard, alum. upper and lower receivers, nickel bolt carrier group, synthetic buttstock, non-slip ergonomic ambidextrous grip, free float forend, Cerakote finish.

| MSR $3,999 | | $3,595 | $3,150 | $2,695 | $2,450 | $1,975 | $1,625 | $1,250 | |

WOLVERINE – .450 Bushmaster cal., 18 in. match grade stainless steel barrel with muzzle brake, adj. rifle length gas system, flat-top upper with Picatinny rail handguard, synthetic buttstock, free float forend, non-slip ergonomic ambidextrous grip, Cerakote finish.

| MSR $2,999 | | $2,695 | $2,350 | $2,025 | $1,850 | $1,475 | $1,225 | $950 | |

ALBERTA TACTICAL RIFLE SUPPLY

Current manufacturer located in Calgary, Alberta, Canada.

RIFLES

Alberta Tactical Rifle Supply builds custom made bolt action and AR-15 style carbines and rifles in a variety of configurations and calibers, including .50 BMG. Each gun is built per customer's specifications, and the possibilities are unlimited. Please contact the company directly for a listing of available options, delivery time, and an individualized price quotation (see Trademark Index).

ALCHEMY ARMS COMPANY

Previous manufacturer located in Auburn, WA, 1999-circa 2006.

PISTOLS: SEMI-AUTO

SPECTRE STANDARD ISSUE (SI) – 9mm Para., .40 S&W, or .45 ACP cal., SA, SFO, full size design, hammerless firing mechanism, linear action trigger, keyed internal locking device, aluminum receiver with 4 1/2 in. match grade stainless steel barrel and slide, tactical rail, various silver/black finishes, lowered ejection port, 10 shot double column mag, 32 oz. Mfg. 2000-2006.

| | | $675 | $585 | $525 | $465 | $415 | $350 | $300 | *$749* |

SPECTRE SERVICE GRADE (SG & SGC) – similar to Spectre Standard Issue, except does not have tactical rail and rounded trigger guard, SGC is Commander style with 4 in. barrel and weighs 27 oz. Mfg. 2000-2006, SGC mfg. 2001-2006.

| | | $675 | $585 | $525 | $465 | $415 | $350 | $300 | *$749* |

SPECTRE TITANIUM EDITION (TI/TIC) – similar to Spectre Series, except features a titanium slide with aluminum receiver, 22 (TIC is Commander style) or 24 oz. Mfg. 2000-2006.

| | | $895 | $775 | $675 | $575 | $500 | $450 | $395 | *$999* |

ALEXANDER ARMS LLC

Current manufacturer of AR-15 style rifles located in Radford, VA. Law enforcement, military, dealer, and consumer sales.

RIFLES: SEMI-AUTO

Add $130 for Shilen barrel.

.50 BEOWULF – .50 Beowulf cal., AR-15 style, GIO, shoots 300-400 grain bullet at approx. 1,800 feet per second, forged upper and lower receiver, 7 shot mag., rotary locking bolt and gas delay mechanism, various configurations include Entry, Over Match kit, Over Match Plus kit, Over Match Tactical kit, Precision Entry, Precision kit, AWS, and Law Enforcement (POR). New 2002.

* **Beowulf Overwatch .50** – similar to .50 Beowulf, GIO, except has 24 in. stainless steel barrel, extended range model, shoots 334 grain bullet at approx. 2,000 feet per second, 9 1/4 lbs. Mfg. 2004-2005.

| | | $1,550 | $1,355 | $1,160 | $1,055 | $850 | $695 | $540 | *$1,789* |

* **Beowulf Entry 16** – .50 Beowulf cal., GIO, 16 1/2 in. chrome moly barrel, mid-length A2 handguard, Picatinny rail, 7 shot mag., forged flat-top receiver, black or Coyote Brown (disc.) A2 stock.

| MSR $1,111 | | $925 | $850 | $725 | $625 | $550 | $475 | $425 | |

MSR	100%	98%	95%	90%	80%	70%	60%	Last MSR

* **Beowulf Hunter** – .50 Beowulf cal., 16 in. chrome moly barrel, forged flat-top receiver, G10 rifle handguard, tactical trigger, B5 Systems SOPMOD collapsible stock, Ergo grip, Kryptek Highlander camo finish. New 2015.

MSR $1,750	$1,485	$1,315	$1,150	$1,025	$875	$750	$615	

* **Beowulf Precision 16** – .50 Beowulf cal., GIO, 16 in. chrome moly barrel, composite free float G10 handguards, Picatinny rail, low profile gas block, 7 shot mag., forged flat-top receiver, black furniture standard or optional camo upgrades available.

MSR $1,356	$1,135	$1,015	$885	$740	$675	$575	$475	

* **Beowulf AWS 16 (Advanced Weapons System)** – .50 Beowulf cal., GIO, 16 1/2 in. chrome moly barrel, low profile gas block, forged flat-top receiver with Picatinny rail, free float Midwest Industries four rail handguard system, black A2 stock, 7 shot mag., includes soft carry bag.

MSR $1,506	$1,275	$1,125	$1,025	$875	$750	$625	$525	

* **Beowulf Overmatch Plus** – .50 Beowulf cal., GIO, 16 in. chrome moly barrel, forged flat-top receiver, detachable iron sights and rear carry handle, mid-length A2 handguard, Picatinny rail, 7 shot mag., black A2 stock.

MSR $1,211	$1,025	$925	$800	$685	$595	$515	$440	

* **Beowulf 24 Overwatch** – .50 Beowulf cal., GIO, 24 in. barrel, full length free float handguard, standard trigger and buttstock, Picatinny rail. Disc. 2009.

	$1,525	$1,350	$1,175	$1,050	$900	$775	$625	$1,789

* **Beowulf Piston Rifle** – .50 Beowulf cal., GPO, 10 shot mag., 16 1/2 in. threaded barrel with no standard muzzle device, Picatinny rail receiver, M4 stock, Samson EX handguard, includes soft carry bag. Mfg. 2012-2013.

	$1,700	$1,500	$1,250	$1,100	$950	$825	$675	$2,000

GENGHIS – 5.45x39mm cal., GIO, M4 styling with 16 in. stainless steel barrel, forged upper and lower receiver, 10 shot mag., various configurations included Entry ($1,066 last MSR), Over Match kit ($1,158 last MSR), Over Match Plus kit ($1,267 last MSR), and Over Match Tactical kit ($1,372 last MSR). Mfg. 2002-2005.

6.5 GRENDEL – 6.5 Grendel cal., GIO, M4 styling with 16, 18 1/2, 19, 20, or 24 in. stainless steel barrel, 10 shot mag. New 2004.

* **Grendel Overwatch 6.5** – 6.5 Grendel cal., GIO, 24 in. stainless steel barrel with match chamber, extremely accurate, forged and hard anodized upper and lower receiver. Mfg. 2004-disc.

	$1,275	$1,125	$1,025	$875	$750	$625	$525	$1,499

* **Grendel 20 (19.5) Entry** – 6.5 Grendel cal., GIO, 19 1/2 (disc.) or 20 in. stainless steel fully lapped threaded barrel with A2 flash hider, A2 buttstock, Ergo grip, G10 composite free float handguard, flat-top receiver with Picatinny rail, 10 shot mag., black A2 stock.

MSR $1,150	$975	$885	$765	$655	$575	$495	$435	

* **Grendel 24 Overwatch** – 6.5 Grendel cal., GIO, 24 in. stainless steel fully lapped threaded barrel with A2 flash hider, A2 buttstock, Ergo grip, composite free float G10 handguard, flat-top receiver with Picatinny rail, low profile gas block, black hardware.

MSR $1,250	$1,050	$950	$815	$715	$625	$535	$450	

* **Grendel AWS** – 6.5 Grendel cal., GIO, 20 or 24 in. stainless steel fully lapped threaded barrel with A2 flash hider, free float Midwest Industries railed handguard, Picatinny rail, 10 shot mag., A2 stock, black furniture.

MSR $1,230	$1,040	$925	$800	$685	$595	$515	$440	

Add $100 for 24 in. barrel.

* **Grendel Hunter** – 6.5 Grendel cal., GIO, 19 1/2 in. stainless steel fully lapped threaded barrel, flat-top receiver, full length military handguard, Picatinny rail, black or coyote brown stock, 10 shot mag., standard trigger. Disc. 2012.

	$1,150	$1,030	$900	$750	$650	$550	$465	$1,370

* **Grendel Hunter 18** – 6.5 Grendel cal., 18 in. fluted stainless steel barrel, 10 shot mag., G10 rifle handguard, tactical trigger, MK10 3 in. Picatinny rail installed on top of handguard, B5 Systems SOPMOD collapsible stock, Kryptek Highlander camo finish, ships in soft carry bag. New 2015.

MSR $1,750	$1,485	$1,315	$1,150	$1,025	$875	$750	$615	

* **Grendel SC Hunter** – 6.5 Grendel cal., 18 in. stainless steel fluted barrel, 10 shot mag., forged receiver, Titanium side charging handle, G10 rifle handguard, B5 Systems SOPMOD collapsible stock, tactical trigger, Kryptek Highlander camo dip finish. New 2015.

MSR $1,920	$1,635	$1,425	$1,200	$1,075	$925	$795	$650	

* **Grendel Incursion** – 6.5 Grendel cal., 16 in. lightweight Melonited button rifled barrel, flat-top receiver, MK10 free float handguard, M4 stock, military trigger, ships in soft cover bag. New 2015.

MSR $1,100	$925	$850	$725	$625	$550	$475	$425	

MSR	100%	98%	95%	90%	80%	70%	60%	Last MSR

* **Grendel Tactical 16** – 6.5 Grendel cal., GIO, 16 in. threaded barrel with or w/o flutes, A2 flash hider, M4 style or folding stock, with or w/o rail, mid-length handguard, 10 shot mag., fixed or folding sights, includes soft carry bag. Disc. 2015.

	100%	98%	95%	90%	80%	70%	60%	Last MSR
	$1,375	$1,215	$1,075	$950	$815	$700	$575	$1,650

* **Grendel Ultralight** – 6.5 Grendel cal., GIO, 16, 18, or 20 in. unthreaded free floating 5R cut rifled barrel with six straight flutes, integral three prong flash hider (16 or 18 in. barrel only), vented composite handguard, M4 collapsible stock, Enedine buffer. Disc. 2012.

	100%	98%	95%	90%	80%	70%	60%	Last MSR
	$1,795	$1,575	$1,325	$1,150	$995	$850	$700	$2,100

* **Grendel Sniper Rifle (GSR Series)** – 6.5 Grendel cal., GIO, 10 shot mag., 16 (disc. 2014), 20 (new 2015), 24 (new 2015), or 28 (disc.) in. fluted barrel, A2 flash hider, side charging handle, billet receiver, Magpul PRS stock, blade style single stage tactical trigger, MK10 vented composite handguard, LaRue SPR mount and Ergo Deluxe grip, black or FDE finish, includes soft carry bag. New 2012.

MSR $3,190	$2,725	$2,375	$1,925	$1,650	$1,375	$1,150	$995	

* **Grendel MK3 Gas Piston** – 6.5 Grendel cal., GPO, 16, 18, or 24 in. button rifled and fluted Lite series barrel with AAC flash hider, 10 shot mag., black or tactical dark earth furniture, includes soft carry bag. Mfg. 2012-2013.

	100%	98%	95%	90%	80%	70%	60%	Last MSR
	$1,825	$1,600	$1,340	$1,150	$995	$850	$700	$2,150

* **Lite 16/Lite 18 (Grendel Lightweight Rifle)** – 6.5 Grendel cal., GIO, lightweight 16, 18, 20 (disc. 2014), or 24 (mfg. 2014 only) in. button rifled fluted stainless steel barrel with A2 flash hider, 10 shot mag., M4 folding stock, composite free floating handguard, black furniture, includes soft carry bag. New 2012.

MSR $1,380	$1,150	$1,030	$900	$750	$685	$585	$485	

Add $100 for 18 in. barrel.
Add $88 for 24 in. barrel (mfg. 2014 only).

* **GDMR** – 6.5 Grendel cal., GIO, 16 (disc.), 20, or 24 in. stainless barrel with A2 flash hider, 10 shot mag., full tactical model, LaRue four rail handguard, sight base, bipod mount, Magpul rail covers, tactical single stage trigger, Troy fold up front and rear back up iron sights, Magpul PRS OD Green or black (disc.) stock, Ergo grip, removable top Picatinny rail. Disc. 2013, reintroduced 2015.

MSR $2,890	$2,460	$2,125	$1,750	$1,500	$1,225	$1,025	$900	

.17 HMR – .17 HMR cal., GIO, 18 in. stainless steel button rifled barrel with spiral flutes, 10 shot mag., flat-top receiver with Picatinny rail, six vent A1 flash hider, G10 composite handguard, non-vented mid-length free float tube, includes two mags., black, Kryptek Yeti camo, or Muddy Girl camo finish. New 2011.

MSR $995	$850	$725	$650	$585	$515	4450	$395	

5.56 NATO RIFLE – 5.56 NATO cal., GIO, two 30 shot mags., 16 or 20 (disc. 2014) in. fluted barrel with A2 flash hider, flat-top receiver with Picatinny rail, free-floated G10 (disc.) or MK10 composite handguard, M4 stock, A2 grip, black furniture, includes soft carry bag. New 2012.

MSR $1,100	$925	$850	$725	$625	$550	$475	$425	

Add $88 for 20 in. barrel (disc. 2014).

.300 AAC BLACKOUT RIFLE – .300 AAC Blackout cal., GIO, 16 in. fluted stainless steel barrel with AAC Blackout flash hider, 30 shot mag., G10 free floated composite handguard, M4 stock, A2 grip, black furniture, includes soft carry bag. New 2012.

MSR $1,100	$925	$850	$725	$625	$550	$475	$425	

ULFBERHT – .338 Lapua cal., based on the Russian DP 28 machine gun, adj. GPO, 27 1/2 in. chrome moly steel barrel with flash hider, includes four 10 shot mags., dual ejectors, plate extractor, flat-top continuous top rail, hard anodized handguard, Ergo Deluxe grip, folding modified Magpul PRS stock, Geissele SSA two-stage trigger, hard case, a wide variety of additional accessories such as slings and bipods are available on this model. New 2014.

MSR $5,800	$4,950	$4,350	$3,800	$3,100	$2,675	$2,450	$2,100	

The name Ulfberht comes from Norse legend - it was a unique type of sword made and carried by the Vikings over 1,000 years ago.

ALPINE INDUSTRIES

Previous manufacturer located in Los Angeles, CA.

Alpine Industries was a commercial M1 carbine manufacturer which produced approximately 17,000 guns between 1962-1965. Guns were made with newly manufactured cast receivers and military surplus parts, including some from England.

AMBUSH FIREARMS

Current AR-15 style semi-auto rifle manufacturer located in Black Creek, GA, with facilities in Ridgeland, SC.

CARBINES: SEMI-AUTO

All Ambush rifles come with a lifetime guarantee.

MSR	100%	98%	95%	90%	80%	70%	60%	Last MSR

AMBUSH A11 6.8/5.56 – 5.56 NATO (new 2012), or 6.8 SPC cal., AR-15 style, 18 in. barrel with Magpul MOE adj. stock, free floating full length Picatinny modular rail, with two smaller rails on bottom and front, black (standard), pink (mfg. 2013), Mossy Oak Break-Up Infinity (mfg. 2012-2013), Realtree AP (disc. 2015), Realtree Extra (new 2016), or Kryptek Highlander (new 2016) camo coverage, pistol grip, 5 shot mag., Geissele super semi-auto trigger, 6 lbs. New 2011.

| MSR $1,799 | $1,525 | $1,395 | $1,195 | $1,085 | $875 | $725 | $595 | |

AMBUSH 300 AAC BLACKOUT – .300 AAC Blackout (7.62x35mm) cal., 16 in. barrel, otherwise similar to Ambush 6.8/5.56, available in black, Realtree AP (disc. 2015), Realtree Extra (new 2016), or Mossy Oak Blaze Pink (disc.) finish, 6 1/2 lbs. New 2012.

| MSR $1,799 | $1,525 | $1,395 | $1,195 | $1,085 | $875 | $725 | $595 | |

Subtract $40 for Mossy Oak Blaze Pink finish (disc.).

DD5 AMBUSH – .308 Win. cal., black or Realtree Xtra camo finish. New 2016.

| MSR $2,899 | $2,475 | $2,150 | $1,775 | $1,525 | $1,250 | $1,050 | $925 | |

AMERICAN ARMS, INC.

Previous importer and manufacturer located in North Kansas City, MO, until 2000. American Arms imported various Spanish shotguns (Indesal, Lanber, Norica, and Zabala Hermanos), Italian shotguns including F. Stefano, several European pistols and rifles, and Sites handguns (1990-2000) mfg. in Torino, Italy. This company also manufactured several pistols in North Kansas City, MO. For more information and pricing on Norica airguns previously imported by American Arms, please refer to the *Blue Book of Airguns* by Dr. Robert Beeman & John Allen (also available online).

In late 2000, TriStar Sporting Arms, Ltd. acquired the parts inventory for some models previously imported by American Arms, Inc. Original warranties from American Arms do not apply to TriStar Sporting Arms, Ltd.

RIFLES: SEMI-AUTO

MODEL ZCY 308 – .308 Win. cal., GPO, AK-47 type action, Yugoslavian mfg. Imported 1988 only.

| | $775 | $650 | $550 | $450 | $400 | $375 | $350 | *$825* |

MODEL AKY 39 – 7.62x39mm cal., GPO, AK-47 type action, teakwood fixed stock and grip, flip up Tritium front and rear night sights, Yugoslavian mfg. Imported 1988-1989 only.

| | $650 | $550 | $495 | $440 | $395 | $350 | $300 | *$559* |

This model was supplied with sling and cleaning kit.

* **Model AKF 39 Folding Stock** – 7.62x39mm cal., folding stock variation of the Model AKY-39. Imported 1988-89 only.

| | $725 | $625 | $550 | $475 | $425 | $375 | $325 | *$589* |

EXP-64 SURVIVAL RIFLE – .22 LR cal., takedown rifle stores in oversize synthetic stock compartment, 21 in. barrel, 10 shot mag., open sights, receiver grooved for scope mounting, cross bolt safety, 40 in. overall length, 7 lbs. Imported 1989-90 only.

| | $150 | $135 | $125 | $115 | $105 | $95 | $85 | *$169* |

AMERICAN DEFENSE MANUFACTURING

Current AR-15 style rifle manufacturer located in New Berlin, WI.

RIFLES: SEMI-AUTO

All American Defense Manufacturing products are 100% designed by shooters and built in the USA. In addition to AR-15 rifles, American Defense Manufacturing also manufactures the patented Auto Lock System, as well as mounts, rings, bases, and other AR-15 accessories.

UIC (UNIVERSAL IMPROVED CARBINE) MOD 1 – 5.56 NATO or .300 AAC Blackout cal., 16 in. lightweight contour chrome lined barrel with Griffin Armament Tactical compensator, fully ambidextrous lower billet receiver, forged Mil-Spec upper receiver, ADM HD buffer, Mil-Spec bolt carrier group, Type III Teflon hardcoat black finish. New 2015.

| MSR $1,500 | $1,275 | $1,125 | $1,025 | $875 | $750 | $625 | $525 | |

UIC (UNIVERSAL IMPROVED CARBINE) MOD 2 – 5.56 NATO or .300 AAC Blackout cal., 16 in. lightweight contour chrome lined barrel with Griffin Armament Flash compensator, billet upper receiver, ADM heavy duty gas tube, two stage adj. trigger, fully ambidextrous lower billet receiver and charging handle, ADM buffer, choice of Low Light, KeyMod, or M-LOK rail system, steel end plate, Type III Teflon hardcoat Black, Flat Dark Earth, ADM Grey, ADM Bronze, or ADM Green finish. New 2015.

| MSR $1,750 | $1,485 | $1,315 | $1,150 | $1,025 | $875 | $750 | $615 | |

Add $150 for Flat Dark Earth, Grey, Bronze, or Green finish.

MSR	100%	98%	95%	90%	80%	70%	60%	Last MSR

UIC (UNIVERSAL IMPROVED CARBINE) MOD 3 – 5.56 NATO or .300 AAC Blackout cal., 16 in. lightweight contour chrome lined barrel with Griffin Armament Flash compensator, low profile adj. gas block (features 3 settings), billet upper receiver, ADM heavy duty gas tube, two stage adj. trigger, fully ambidextrous lower billet receiver and charging handle, ADM buffer, choice of Low Light, KeyMod, or M-LOK rail system, steel end plate, Type III Teflon hardcoat Black, Flat Dark Earth, ADM Grey, ADM Bronze, or ADM Green finish. New 2015.

MSR $2,050	$1,750	$1,525	$1,275	$1,100	$950	$825	$675	

Add $150 for Flat Dark Earth, ADM Grey, ADM Bronze, or ADM Green finish.

UIC 10A – .308 Win. cal., AR-15 style, available in four configurations: DMR, Battle Rifle, Heavy Recon, or CSASS, 16 or 18 in. stainless steel Nitride finished Hybrid profile barrel, ADM, SureFire, AAC, or Griffin suppressor, includes two 25 shot Magpul PMAGs, A2S or adj. two-stage trigger, Magpul MBUS Pro sights, Magpul MOE SL or Magpul ACS stock, Magpul MOE grip, ergonomic fully ambidextrous controls, BCM Gunfighter Mod 4 charging handle, steel end plate, 13 1/2 or 15 in. HDRI forearm rail systems in either Low Light, KeyMod, or M-LOK pattern, AR-10 length carbine receiver extensions, ADM adjustable two-stage fire control group, Type III hardcoat anodized black finish, 8 lbs. (Battle Rifle), 8 lbs. 4 oz. (Heavy Recon), or 9 lbs. 4 oz. (DMR and CSASS models). New 2016.

MSR $2,170	$1,840	$1,600	$1,375	$1,150	$995	$850	$700	

Add $54 for DMR or CSASS configurations.

AMERICAN INTERNATIONAL CORP.

Previous manufacturer and importer located in Salt Lake City, UT, circa 1972-1984. American International was a wholly owned subsidiary of ARDCO (American Research & Development). ARDCO's previous name was American Mining & Development. American International imported firearms from Voere, located in Kufstein, Austria. American Arms International (AAI) was another subsidiary of ARDCO.

In 1979, after American International Corp. had dissolved, AAI resumed production using mostly Voere parts. After running out of Voere parts, late production featured U.S. mfg. receivers (can be recognized by not having a pivoting barrel retainer slotted on the bottom of the receiver). American Arms International declared bankruptcy in 1984.

CARBINES: SEMI-AUTO

AMERICAN 180 AUTO CARBINE (M-1) – .22 LR cal., a specialized design for military use, 177 round drum mag., 16 1/2 in. barrel, aperture sight, high impact plastic stock and forearm, aluminum alloy receiver with black finish. Semi-auto variation mfg. 1979-c.1984. Total Voere production (denoted by A prefix serial number) between 1972 and 1979 was 2,300 carbines (includes both full and semi-auto versions). Later mfg. was marked either M-1 (semi-auto) or M-2 (fully auto). "B" serial number prefix was introduced in 1980, and barrel markings were changed to "Amer Arms Intl, SLC, UT."

	$725	$600	$475	$375	$350	$325	$295	

Add $550 for Laser Lok System - first commercially available laser sighting system.
Add approx. $300 for extra drum mag. and winder (fragile and subject to breakage).

AMERICAN PRECISION ARMS

Current manufacturer established in 2001, located in Jefferson, GA.

RIFLES: BOLT ACTION

All MSRs are considered base price. Many options and custom services are also available. Please contact the company directly for pricing and availability (see Trademark Index).

.308 RAVEN – .308 Win. cal., Rem. 700 action, 22 in. fluted barrel, Remington factory trigger, APA tactical bolt knob, oversized precision ground recoil lug, Guncote Black finish. Mfg. 2009-2011.

	$3,050	$2,675	$2,295	$2,075	$1,685	$1,375	$1,100	$3,395

CRITTER GET'R – .300 Win. Mag. cal., APA Genesis Hunting action, 24 in. stainless steel barrel, corrosion resistant finish, APA tactical bolt knob and bipod stud, Timney trigger, one piece fluted bolt, M16 style extractor, side bolt release, McMillan stock.

MSR $5,315	$4,525	$3,950	$3,350	$3,000	$2,425	$1,975	$1,550	

DO IT ALL APR – .308 Win. cal., APA Genesis action with pinned recoil lug, 22 in. contour barrel, McMillan HTG stock, spiral fluted bolt, mini-16 extractor, APA bolt knob, Timney trigger, Sage finish, includes one 10 shot mag. and royal gun case, 9 1/4 lbs. Disc. 2015.

	$4,350	$3,800	$3,250	$2,900	$2,500	$1,900	$1,475	$5,099

GENESIS HUNTER – various cals., customer supplied action, match grade barrel, reworked trigger, precision ground recoil lug, recessed target crown, dual dovetail rings and bases, metal finish, McMillan Hunting stock. Disc. 2010.

	$2,200	$1,925	$1,650	$1,495	$1,225	$1,000	$800	$2,450

MSR	100%	98%	95%	90%	80%	70%	60%	Last MSR

GENESIS TACTICAL – .223 Rem., .300 Win. Mag., or .308 Win. cal., customer supplied action, match grade Broughton stainless Sendero contour barrel, recessed target crown, free-floating bedding job with pillars, APA oversized precision ground recoil lug, McMillan HTG stock, KG baked on finish. Disc. 2010.

	$2,200	$1,925	$1,650	$1,495	$1,225	$1,000	$800	$2,450

MEAT STICK – .300 Win. Mag. cal., APA Genesis Hunting action, one-piece bolt body, 25 in. match grade stainless barrel, fluted bolt, pinned recoil lug, side bolt release, Williams steel trigger guard, McMillan HTG stock with adj. cheekpiece, APA tactical bipod stud, corrosion resistant finish, 20 in. MOA rail, M16 style extractor. New 2013.

MSR $5,784	$4,995	$4,400	$3,750	$3,325	$2,700	$2,175	$1,675	

PARAGON – .223 Rem. or .308 Win. cal., APA Genesis receiver includes side bolt release, M16 style extractor, one-piece bolt, 20 (.223 Rem.) or 22 (.308 Win.) in. stainless steel match grade barrel, uses A1 or AW mags., Manners TF1 folding stock, two side flush cups, APA tactical bipod stud, 13 1/2 in. LOP with Decelerator pad, Huber trigger, Cerakote coating, tan finish. New 2013.

MSR $6,840	$5,825	$5,050	$4,350	$3,900	$3,150	$2,550	$1,995	

REVELATION HUNTER – various cals., customer supplied action, match grade barrel, recessed target crown, hard chrome parts, Sako claw-style extractor, Jewel trigger, Sunny Hill trigger guard, customer choice of fiberglass stock, free-floating full length bedding with stainless or titanium pillars. Disc. 2010.

	$3,100	$2,725	$2,325	$2,110	$1,700	$1,400	$1,100	$3,450

REVELATION TACTICAL – various cals., customer supplied action, match grade Broughton barrel, recessed target crown, claw style Sako extractor, Jewell trigger, choice of McMillan, A3, A4, or A5 stock, free-floating bedding with stainless pillars, APA oversized tactical bolt handle, Badger rings, base, and trigger guard. Disc. 2011.

	$3,595	$3,150	$2,700	$2,450	$1,975	$1,625	$1,300	$3,995

RIFLES: SEMI-AUTO

All MSRs reflected base pricing. Many options and custom services were also available.

LYCAN – .223 Rem. cal., 16 or 18 in. Broughton threaded barrel, McCormick match trigger, dual spring extractor, Hogue grip, SOPMOD adj. stock, Larue or Knight (disc.) forend, black or nickel boron (disc.) finish. Disc. 2011.

	$3,100	$2,725	$2,325	$2,110	$1,700	$1,400	$1,100	$3,450

URBAN SNIPER .223 – .223 Rem. cal., 20 in. Broughton 5C stainless barrel, 20 shot mag., JP match grade trigger, standard carrier assembly, LMT SOPMOD adj. stock, Badger Ordnance forend, DPMS PSG-1 style grip. Disc. 2011.

	$2,200	$1,925	$1,650	$1,495	$1,225	$1,000	$800	$2,450

URBAN SNIPER .308 – .308 Win. cal., 20 in. Rock Creek 5R stainless barrel, 10 shot mag., DPMS upper and lower receiver, standard carrier assembly, JP match grade trigger, Magpul PRS adj. stock, Badger Ordnance forend. Disc. 2011.

	$2,785	$2,450	$2,100	$1,900	$1,550	$1,275	$1,000	$3,098

RIFLES: TARGET

American Precision Arms builds custom target rifles per customer's specifications. All models are POR, and a wide variety of options are available. Please contact the company directly for more information including pricing, options, and delivery time (see Trademark Index).

SHOTGUNS: SLIDE ACTION

In addition to rifles, American Precision Arms offered a shotgun modification service on customer supplied Remington 870s. Prices began at $1,395.

AMERICAN SPIRIT ARMS

Current manufacturer established circa 1995, located in Scottsdale, AZ. In April 2015, American Spirit Arms announced its sale to American Spirit Investments, LLC, and emphasized focus on their patented AR-15 side charger technology. They confirmed that the American Spirit Arms brand will be retained.

PISTOLS: SEMI-AUTO

American Spirit Arms previously offered a 5.56 NATO cal. AR-15 style pistol with A2 fixed carry handle (last MSR was $1,199, disc. 2012).

9MM PISTOL A2 – 9mm Para. cal., 7 1/2 in. chrome moly barrel, 25 shot mag., forged lower and forged A2 upper receiver with fixed carry handle, fixed front iron sight base, includes hard carry case.

MSR $1,300	$1,100	$995	$875	$735	$650	$550	$465	

A2 PISTOL – 5.56 NATO cal., 7 1/2 in. chrome moly barrel, forged lower receiver and forged A2 upper with fixed carry handle, 30 shot mag., includes hard case. Disc. 2014.

	$1,160	$1,030	$900	$750	$650	$550	$465	$1,390

MSR	100%	98%	95%	90%	80%	70%	60%	Last MSR

AR-15 PISTOL WITH HANDGUARD – 5.56 NATO cal., 7 1/2 in. chrome moly barrel, forged A3 flat-top upper receiver, Picatinny rail, carbine-length free float handguard, 30 shot mag., includes hard carry case. Disc. 2014.

	$1,135	$920	$890	$735	$650	$550	$465	*$1,350*

AR-15 PISTOL WITH QUAD RAIL – 5.56 NATO cal., 7 1/2 in. chrome moly barrel, forged A3 (disc. 2014) or side charging flat-top upper receiver, forged lower, Picatinny rail, quad rail with gas block, 30 shot mag., includes hard carry case.

MSR $1,400	$1,200	$1,075	$950	$800	$700	$600	$495	

SIDE CHARGING 9MM PISTOL (FLAT TOP 9MM PISTOL) – 9mm Para. cal., 7 1/2 in. chrome moly barrel, 25 shot mag., forged lower and forged A3 (disc. 2015) or side charging (new 2015) flat-top upper receiver, Picatinny rail, fixed front iron sight base, includes hard carry case.

MSR $1,400	$1,200	$1,075	$950	$800	$700	$600	$495	

RIFLES/CARBINES: SEMI-AUTO

American Spirit Arms manufactures a wide variety of AR-15 style semi-auto carbines and rifles based on the AR-15, M16, and the M4 in 5.56 NATO, .223 Rem., 9mm Para., and .308 Win. cal. A complete line of options, accessories, and parts are available. Base models are listed. Additionally, ASA has a Custom Shop for custom order rifles only built to customer specifications. Please contact the company directly regarding pricing for options and accessories (see Trademark Index).

ASA-A2 RIFLE – 5.56 NATO cal., GIO, 20 in. Govt. profile barrel, 30 shot mag., fixed carry handle, M4 feed ramps, fixed (A2) buttstock, includes hard carrying case. Disc. 2014.

	$1,100	$995	$875	$735	$650	$550	$465	*$1,296*

ASA-A320(G) SIDE CHARGING RIFLE – 5.56 NATO cal., GIO, 20 in. chrome moly barrel, 30 shot mag., choice of flat-top or fixed carry handle, side charging upper with Picatinny rail (became standard 2015), forged lower, gas block with Picatinny rail, rifle-length handguard, M4 feed ramps, A2 fixed stock, includes hard carrying case.

MSR $1,300	$1,100	$995	$875	$735	$650	$550	$465	

ASA-DISSIPATOR A2 CARBINE – 5.56 NATO cal., GIO, 16 in. M4 barrel, forged A2 upper receiver with fixed carry handle, 30 shot mag., adj. open rear sights, M4 feed ramps, A2 fixed buttstock, Dissipator CAR length gas system, front and rear sling swivels, includes hard carrying case. Disc. 2014.

	$1,150	$1,030	$900	$750	$650	$550	$465	*$1,386*

ASA-M4A2 CARBINE – 5.56 NATO cal., GIO, 16 in. barrel, 30 shot mag., fixed carry handle, 6-pos. M4 collapsible stock, includes hard carrying case. Disc. 2014.

	$1,100	$995	$875	$735	$650	$550	$465	*$1,296*

ASA-M4A3 SIDE CHARGING CARBINE – 5.56 NATO cal., GIO, 16 in. M4 barrel with Nitride finish, 30 shot PMAG, A2 fixed front sight or gas block, flat side charging upper with Picatinny rail (became standard 2015), M4 feed ramps, carbine-length gas system, 6-position collapsible stock, front and rear sling swivels, includes hard carrying case.

MSR $1,300	$1,100	$995	$875	$735	$650	$550	$465	

ASA-M4CS1 SIDE CHARGING CARBINE – 5.56 NATO cal., GIO, 16 in. M4 profile barrel with A2 flash hider, 30 shot PMAG, low profile gas block, M4 feed ramps, flat-top receiver (side charging upper became standard 2015) with Picatinny rail, carbine-length gas system, 10 in. Samson Evo quad rail, tactical trigger guard, Ergo grip, Magpul MOE collapsible buttstock, black or Flat Dark Earth finish, includes hard carrying case. New 2013.

MSR $1,476	$1,250	$1,110	$965	$800	$700	$600	$495	

ASA-M4CS2 SIDE CHARGING CARBINE – 5.56 NATO cal., GIO, 16 in. M4 profile barrel with A2 flash hider, 30 shot PMAG, flat-top upper receiver (side charging upper became standard 2015) with Picatinny rail, carbine-length gas system, M4 feed ramps, Midwest Industries Gen 2 drop-in quad rail, tactical trigger guard, A2 fixed front sight or gas block, Magpul MOE collapsible buttstock, Flat Dark Earth or OD Green furniture, includes hard carrying case. New 2013.

MSR $1,476	$1,250	$1,110	$965	$800	$700	$600	$495	

ASA-MID-LENGTH SIDE CHARGING RIFLE (A3 M16 RIFLE) – 5.56 NATO cal., 16 in. nitrided mid-length barrel, 30 shot mag., M4 feed ramps, forged lower and flat-top upper (side charging upper became standard 2015) receiver with Picatinny rail, CAR-length gas system, gas block with 1913 rail, front and rear sling swivels, 6-pos. buttstock, includes hard carrying case.

MSR $1,300	$1,100	$995	$875	$735	$650	$550	$465	

ASA-SIDE CHARGING DISSIPATOR (A3G CARBINE) – 5.56 NATO cal., GIO, 16 in. chrome moly barrel, 30 shot mag., M4 feed ramps, gas block with Picatinny rail, Magpul MOE rifle-length handguard with dissipator CAR-length gas system underneath, flat-top upper receiver (side charging upper became standard 2015) with Picatinny rail, forged lower, front and rear sling swivels, Magpul 6-pos. stock, includes hard carrying case.

MSR $1,400	$1,200	$1,075	$950	$800	$700	$600	$495	

MSR	100%	98%	95%	90%	80%	70%	60%	*Last MSR*

ASA-SPR SIDE CHARGING RIFLE (ASA-SPR) – 5.56 NATO (disc.) or .308 Win. (new 2015) cal., GIO, 18 in. stainless steel heavy profile barrel with A2 flash hider, mid-length gas system, 30 shot PMAG, flat-top upper (side charging upper became standard in 2015) receiver, low profile gas block, 12 in. Samson Evo quad rail, two stage trigger, M4 feed ramps, Ergo grip, MOE trigger guard, VLTOR Emod stock, includes hard carrying case. New 2013.

| MSR $2,800 | $2,375 | $2,075 | $1,725 | $1,475 | $1,200 | $1,025 | $895 | |

ASA-9mm AR-15 RIFLE M4/A2 CARBINE – 9mm Para. cal., GIO, 16 in. lightweight barrel, 25 shot mag., forged upper with fixed carrying handle, forged lower, fixed front sight base, adj. open rear sights, drop-in magwell adapter, 4-pos. collapsible CAR stock, front and rear sling swivels, includes hard carrying case.

| MSR $1,200 | $1,025 | $925 | $800 | $685 | $595 | $515 | $440 | |

ASA-9mm SIDE CHARGING RIFLE M4 CARBINE (A3G CARBINE) – 9mm Para. cal., GIO, 16 in. chrome moly barrel, 25 shot mag., flat-top receiver (side charging upper became standard 2015) with Picatinny rail, forged lower receiver, gas block with Picatinny rail, drop-in magwell adapter, front and rear sling swivels, 4-pos. collapsible CAR stock, includes hard carrying case.

| MSR $1,300 | $1,100 | $995 | $875 | $735 | $650 | $550 | $465 | |

ASA SIDE CHARGING BULL BARREL CARBINE (ASA-BULL A3 CARBINE) – 5.56 NATO cal., GIO, 16 in. stainless steel bull barrel, flat-top upper (side charging upper option became available 2015) with Picatinny rail, forged lower receiver, carbine-length gas system, M4 feed ramps, free float handguard with gas block, choice of 6-pos. collapsible or fixed A2 stock, includes 30 shot PMAG and hard carrying case.

| MSR $1,600 | $1,350 | $1,200 | $1,075 | $950 | $815 | $700 | $575 | |

ASA-BULL A3 RIFLE – 5.56 NATO cal., GIO, 24 in. bull barrel, fixed buttstock. Disc. 2012.

| | $1,300 | $1,150 | $1,000 | $875 | $750 | $625 | $500 | *$1,475* |

ASA-BULL BARREL FLAT TOP RIFLE – .223 Rem. cal., 24 in. stainless steel bull barrel, forged A3 flat-top upper receiver with Picatinny rail, free float handguard with gas block, 30 shot mag., M4 feed ramps, A2 buttstock, includes hard carrying case. Disc. 2014.

| | $1,525 | $1,350 | $1,175 | $1,050 | $900 | $775 | $625 | *$1,800* |

ASA-BULL SIDE CHARGER CARBINE – 5.56 NATO cal., 24 in. stainless steel bull barrel, 30 shot mag., aluminum flat-top side charge upper receiver, Picatinny rail, forged lower receiver, front and rear sling swivels, M4 feed ramps, standard A2 buttstock, includes hard carrying case. Disc. 2014.

| | $1,700 | $1,500 | $1,250 | $1,100 | $950 | $825 | $675 | *$2,000* |

ASA-BULL SIDE CHARGER CARBINE/RIFLE – .223 Rem. cal., GIO, 16 (carbine) or 24 (rifle) in. stainless steel bull barrel, features left side charger, Magpul PRS stock with circular free floating handguard and gas block. Disc. 2014.

| | $1,550 | $1,325 | $1,175 | $1,00 | $875 | $775 | $675 | *$1,725* |

ASA-308 SIDE CHARGER CARBINE/RIFLE – .308 Win. cal., GIO, 16 (standard-disc. 2012 or bull - new 2013), 20 (bull) or 24 (disc. 2011) in. bull barrel, flat-top receiver with Picatinny rail, full length quad rail became standard 2012, Hogue grip, two-stage trigger, Magpul CTR stock, includes two 20 shot AR-10 mags. Disc. 2014.

| | $2,200 | $1,925 | $1,600 | $1,375 | $1,125 | $975 | $850 | *$2,600* |

Add $450 for 20 in. bull barrel.

Subtract approx. $600 if without full length quad rail.

ASA 20 INCH 308 SIDE CHARGER RIFLE – .308 Win. cal., 20 in. stainless steel bull barrel, JP compensator, rifle length gas system, ASA aerospace aluminum lower and flat-top side charging upper receiver with Picatinny rail, low profile gas block, Nitrided carrier, Hogue grip, Harris bipod, Magpul PRS stock, includes 20 shot Armalite Gen2 mag. and hard carrying case. New 2015.

| MSR $3,050 | $2,575 | $2,240 | $1,825 | $1,575 | $1,300 | $1,100 | $950 | |

AMERICAN SPIRIT ARMS CORP.

Previous rifle and components manufacturer 1998-2005, located in Tempe, AZ. Previously located in Scottsdale, AZ.

RIFLES: SEMI-AUTO

The following listings are for AR-15 style rifles/carbines using GIO operation.

Add $25 for green furniture, $65 for black barrel finish, $75 for fluted barrel, $125 for porting, $119 for two-stage match trigger, and $55 for National Match sights on .223 cal. models listed below.

ASA 24 IN. BULL BARREL FLAT-TOP RIFLE – .223 Rem. cal., AR-15 style, GIO, forged steel lower receiver, forged aluminum flat-top upper receiver, 24 in. stainless steel bull barrel, free floating aluminum handguard, includes Harris bipod. Mfg. 1999-2005.

| | $850 | $700 | $625 | $550 | $500 | $450 | $400 | *$950* |

MSR	100%	98%	95%	90%	80%	70%	60%	Last MSR

ASA 24 IN. BULL BARREL A2 RIFLE – .223 Rem. cal., similar to ASA Bull Barrel Flat-top, except features A2 upper receiver with carrying handle and sights. Mfg. 1999-2005.

	$875	$725	$650	$565	$500	$450	$400	$980

OPEN MATCH RIFLE – .223 Rem. cal., GIO, 16 in. fluted and ported stainless steel match barrel with round shroud, flat-top without sights, forged upper and lower receiver, two-stage match trigger, upgraded pistol grip, individually tested, USPSA/IPSC open class legal. Mfg. 2001-2005.

	$1,350	$1,100	$950	$825	$725	$650	$525	$1,500

LIMITED MATCH RIFLE – .223 Rem. cal., GIO, 16 in. fluted stainless steel match barrel with round shroud with staggered hand grip, National Match front and rear sights, two-stage match trigger, upgraded pistol grip, individually tested, USPSA/IPSC open class legal. Mfg. 2001-2005.

	$1,175	$975	$825	$725	$650	$525	$475	$1,300

DCM SERVICE RIFLE – .223 Rem. cal., GIO, 20 in. stainless steel match barrel with ribbed free floating shroud, National Match front and rear sights, two-stage match trigger, pistol grip, individually tested. Mfg. 2001-2005.

	$1,175	$975	$825	$725	$650	$525	$475	$1,300

ASA 16 IN. M4 RIFLE – .223 Rem. cal., GIO, 16 in. barrel with muzzle brake, aluminum flat-top upper receiver, non-collapsible stock and M4 handguard. Mfg. 2002-2005.

	$795	$700	$625	$525	$450	$400	$350	$905

ASA 20 IN. A2 RIFLE – .223 Rem. cal., GIO, 20 in. National Match barrel, A2 receiver. Mfg. 1999-2005.

	$765	$640	$565	$500	$425	$350	$300	$820

ASA CARBINE WITH SIDE CHARGING RECEIVER – .223 Rem. cal., GIO, 16 in. National Match barrel with slotted muzzle brake, aluminum side charging flat-top upper receiver, M4 handguard. Mfg. 2002-2004.

	$865	$750	$650	$565	$500	$450	$400	$970

C.A.R. POST-BAN 16 IN. CARBINE – .223 Rem. cal., GIO, non-collapsible stock, Wilson 16 in. National Match barrel. Mfg. 1999-2005.

	$775	$650	$575	$500	$450	$400	$350	$830

ASA 16 IN. BULL BARREL A2 INVADER – .223 Rem. cal., GIO, 16 in. stainless steel barrel, forged steel lower receiver, forged aluminum A2 upper receiver, free floating aluminum handguard, carrying handle, includes Harris bipod. Mfg. 1999-2005.

	$860	$725	$630	$550	$500	$450	$400	$955

ASA 9MM A2 CAR CARBINE – 9mm Para. cal., GIO, forged upper and lower receiver, non-collapsible CAR stock, 16 in. Wilson heavy barrel w/o muzzle brake, with birdcage flash hider (pre-ban) or muzzle brake (post-ban), includes 9mm conversion block, 25 shot modified Uzi mag. Mfg. 2002-2005.

	$860	$725	$630	$550	$500	$450	$400	$950

Add $550 per extra 25 shot mag.

ASA 9MM FLAT-TOP CAR RIFLE – 9mm Para. cal., similar to A2 CAR Carbine, except has flat-top w/o sights. Mfg. 2002-2005.

	$860	$725	$630	$550	$500	$450	$400	$950

ASA 16 IN. TACTICAL RIFLE – .308 Win. cal., GIO, 16 in. stainless steel air gauged regular or match barrel, side charging handle, Hogue pistol grip, guaranteed 1/2 MOA accuracy, individually tested, 8 3/4 lbs. Mfg. 2002-2005.

	$1,475	$1,200	$995	$850	$750	$650	$525	$1,675

Add $515 for Match Rifle (includes fluted and ported barrel, two stage trigger, and hard chromed bolt and carrier).

ASA 24 IN. MATCH RIFLE – .308 Win. cal., GIO, 24 in. stainless steel air gauged match barrel with or w/o fluting/porting, side charging handle, Hogue pistol grip, guaranteed 1/2 MOA accuracy, individually tested, approx. 12 lbs. Mfg. 2002-2005.

	$1,475	$1,200	$995	$850	$750	$650	$525	$1,675

Add $515 for Match Rifle (includes fluted and ported barrel, two stage trigger, and hard chromed bolt and carrier).

AMERICAN TACTICAL IMPORTS (ATI)

Current importer located in Summmerville, SC, beginning late 2013. Previously located in Rochester, NY.

American Tactical Imports imports a wide variety of firearms and products, including pistols, AR-15 style and AK-47 design semi-auto rifles, and shotguns. Trademarks, imports, and private labels include Alpha shotguns, American Tactical Imports (ATI), Cavalry O/Us (new 2013), FMK (disc. 2013), Firepower Xtreme, German Sport Guns (GSG), Head Down Products (mfg. 2012-2013), ISSC (new 2015), Masterpiece Arms (MPA, disc. 2011), Omni, Ottoman Shotguns (disc. 2011), Tisas (imported 2008-2011), and Xtreme Rifles (disc. 2012). Please see individual listings for current model information and pricing. For current tactical model listings and MSRs/values, please refer to the most recent edition of the *Blue Book of Tactical Firearms Values* or visit www.bluebookofgunvalues.com.

MSR	100%	98%	95%	90%	80%	70%	60%	Last MSR

CARBINES/RIFLES: SEMI-AUTO

AT-15 – 5.56 NATO cal., AR-15 style, GIO, 16 in. barrel with muzzle brake, flat-top receiver with mid-length quad rail, post front sight, collapsible stock, 30 shot mag. Limited importation 2011 only.

	$650	$595	$525	$465	$435	$400	$375	*$719*

AT-47 – 5.56x45 cal., AK-47 design, GPO, 16 in. M4 barrel, blued finish, A3 flat-top, 10 shot mag., 6-position original underfolding stock, original wood furniture, includes hard case, unissued M70 Yugo parts kit. New 2014.

MSR $870	$735	$650	$580	$515	$450	$385	$340	

AT-47 MILLED – 7.62x39mm cal., AK-47 design, GPO, 16 1/2 in. match ER Shaw barrel, blue finish, mfg. from unissued Bulgarian parts kit, wood furniture, 30 shot mag., milled receiver, includes hard case. Disc. 2013.

	$725	$675	$600	$550	$450	$350	$275	*$790*

Add $120-$150 for Strikeforce Elite package with adj. polymer stock, pistol grip, recoil system, removable cheekpiece and three Picatinny rails (new 2012).

AT-47 STAMPED – 7.62x39mm cal., AK-47 design, GPO, similar to AT-47 Milled, except has stamped receiver. Mfg. in the U.S. 2011-2013.

	$525	$450	$410	$325	$275	$225	$200	*$600*

Add $120-$150 for Strikeforce Elite package with adj. polymer stock, pistol grip, recoil system, removable cheekpiece and three Picatinny rails (new 2012).

HDH16 CARBINE – 5.56 NATO cal., GIO, 10 or 30 shot mag., 16 in. heavy barrel, A3 flat-top receiver with Picatinny rail, 6-position stock, black hardware and finish, includes hard case. Mfg. 2012-2013.

	$650	$575	$525	$475	$425	$395	$325	*$750*

MILSPORT M4 CARBINE – 5.56 NATO cal., GIO, 30 shot PMAG, 16 in. barrel, A3 flat-top receiver with Picatinny rail, tubular ribbed handguard, forged aluminum upper and billet alum. lower, 7 in. drop-in quad rail, 6-position stock, black hardware and finish, includes hard case. New 2012.

MSR $770	$660	$575	$510	$440	$385	$340	$325	

MILSPORT M4 9MM – 9mm Para. cal., 16 in. barrel, A2 flash hider, 30 shot mag., 10 in. free float KeyMod rail, forged upper and billet lower receiver, 6-position Rogers Super-Stoc, black finish. New 2012.

MSR $900	$775	$685	$615	$550	$485	$415	$370	

V916/VX916 CARBINE – 5.56 NATO cal., GIO, 10 or 30 shot mag., 16 in. heavy barrel, flat-top receiver with Picatinny rail, 9 or 13 in. quad rail, 6-position stock, black hardware and finish, includes hard case. Mfg. 2012-2013.

	$775	$675	$575	$500	$450	$400	$350	*$889*

Add $20 for 13 in. quad rail (Model VX916).

.300 AAC CARBINE – .300 AAC blackout cal., GIO, 10 or 30 shot mag., 16 in. heavy barrel with muzzle brake, 6-position stock, flat-top receiver with Picatinny rail, 9 in. quad rail, black hardware and finish. Mfg. 2012-2013.

	$875	$750	$675	$575	$475	$400	$350	*$999*

OMNI 22 (VK22 STANDARD) – .22 LR cal., AR-15 style, GIO, 16 in. barrel, fixed or telestock, black finish, flat-top receiver with Picatinny rail, 10 or 28 shot mag. Disc. 2013.

	$425	$375	$325	$275	$250	$225	$200	*$470*

OMNI 22 OPS (VK22 TACTICAL) – .22 LR cal., AR-15 style, GIO, 16 in. barrel, fixed or telestock, black finish, flat-top receiver, 10 or 28 shot mag., quad rail, vertical foregrip, tactical rear sight. Disc. 2013.

	$465	$425	$385	$335	$295	$250	$225	*$520*

OMNI 556 – 5.56 NATO cal., GIO, 10 or 30 shot mag., 16 in. M4 style barrel, fixed or telescoping stock, 7 in. quad rail, flat-top receiver with Picatinny rail, Omni polymer lower receiver, black furniture. New 2013.

MSR $650	$575	$495	$425	$350	$295	$240	$200	

OMNI HYBRID M4 – 5.56 NATO cal., GPO, 16 in. barrel, 10 or 30 shot mag., flat-top polymer lower receiver, interlock hammer and trigger pin retainment system, enhanced trigger guard, beveled magwell, 6-position adj. stock, matte black finish, includes AR-15 parts kit, 7 lbs. New 2014.

MSR $620	$550	$485	$425	$375	$325	$275	$250	

OMNI HYBRID 22 COMBO – .22 LR cal. with complete 5.56 aluminum upper and Hybrid lower receiver, 16 in. barrel, 28 (.22 LR) or 30 (5.56) shot PMAG, 10 in. quad rail, 6-position stock, black finish. New 2015.

MSR $790	$675	$600	$525	$450	$400	$350	$295	

OMNI HYBRID 300 AAC BLACKOUT – .300 AAC Blackout cal., 16 in. barrel, 30 shot PMAG, complete Hybrid lower and aluminum upper receiver, 7 in. quad rail, 6-pos. stock, black finish, 6 1/2 lbs. New 2015.

MSR $650	$575	$500	$450	$395	$350	$325	$295	

MSR	100%	98%	95%	90%	80%	70%	60%	Last MSR

OMNI HYBRID MAXX – 5.56 NATO cal., 16 in. M4 black Nitride coated barrel, flat-top, optics ready, 10 or 30 shot PMAG, complete Omni Hybrid upper and lower polymer receiver, 6-pos. stock, black or FDE (new 2016) finish, 6 1/4 lbs. New 2015.

MSR $680	$590	$500	$435	$365	$325	$280	$265	

OMNI HYBRID 5.56 MAXX – 5.56 NATO cal., 16 in. barrel, 30 shot PMag, 7 in. quad rail, complete Omni Hybrid polymer upper and lower receiver, 6-pos. stock, black or FDE (new 2016) finish, 6 1/2 lbs. New 2015.

MSR $680	$590	$500	$435	$365	$325	$280	$265	

OMNI HYBRID MAXX 22 COMBO – .22 LR cal. with complete Omni Hybrid 5.56 upper and lower receiver, 16 in. barrel, 10 in. free float quad rail, 28 (.22 LR) or 30 (5.56) shot PMAG, black or FDE (new 2016) finish. New 2015.

MSR $770	$650	$575	$495	$450	$375	$315	$265	

OMNI HYBRID MAXX 300 – .300 AAC Blackout cal., 16 in. barrel, 30 shot PMAG, complete Omni Hybrid polymer upper and lower receiver, 7 in. quad rail, 6-pos. stock, black or FDE (new 2016) finish, 6 1/2 lbs. New 2015.

MSR $747	$650	$575	$510	$440	$385	$340	$325	

OMNI HYBRID TRANSLUCENT MAXX – 5.56 NATO cal., 16 in. black Nitride coated barrel, two 30 shot PMAGs, 10 in. free float quad rail, low profile gas block, metal reinforced polymer upper and lower receivers, 6-pos. Rogers Super-Stoc, black finish. New 2015.

MSR $700	$615	$540	$470	$400	$350	$310	$295	

PISTOLS: SEMI-AUTO

BB6 – 9mm Para. cal., polymer frame, 5 in. barrel, 15 or 18 shot mag., steel slide, integrated optics mount, quick view "gutter" sight, five different safeties, black finish. Mfg. by BB Techs of Austria. Importation began 2016.

MSR $730	$625	$520	$435	$375	$325	$280	$265	

FX 45K – .45 ACP cal., SA, 5 in. threaded barrel with muzzle cap, 8 shot mag., lower front Picatinny rail, bobbed hammer, beavertail safety, extended ambidextrous safety lever, skeletonized aluminum trigger, checkered mahogany grips, low profile rear sight, blued or Flat Dark Earth (new 2014) finish. Mfg. 2013-2014.

	$635	$550	$495	$450	$400	$350	$300	$740

Add $50 for Flat Dark Earth finish (new 2014).

FX FAT BOY – .45 ACP cal., 3.2 in. barrel, SA, blue finish, 10 or 12 shot double stack mag., all steel serrated grips, lightweight configuration became standard 2013. Mfg. by Shooters Arms Manufacturing in the Phillipines mid-2010-2014.

	$610	$525	$450	$400	$350	$300	$250	$720

FX G.I. – .45 ACP cal., SA, 1911 style frame, 4 1/4 in. barrel, blue finish, 8 shot mag., double diamond checkered wood grips, military style rear slide serrations, slide stop, safety lever, matte black trigger, round hammer, beavertail grip safety. Mfg. by Shooters Arms Manufacturing in the Phillipines beginning mid-2010.

MSR $490	$400	$325	$300	$265	$245	$225	$200	

* **FX G.I. Enhanced** – .45 ACP cal., similar to G.I. model, except has Novak sights. Mfg. mid-2010-2014.

	$475	$415	$350	$315	$260	$225	$195	$565

FX MILITARY – .45 ACP cal., 1911 style frame, 5 in. barrel, SA, blue finish, 8 shot mag., double diamond checkered wood grips, military style rear slide serrations, slide stop, safety lever and trigger. Mfg. by Shooters Arms Manufacturing in the Phillipines beginning mid-2010.

MSR $490	$400	$325	$300	$265	$245	$225	$200	

FX TITAN – .45 ACP cal., SA, 1911 style frame, 3 5/8 in. bull barrel, blue (Titan), NiBX (new 2013) finish or stainless steel (Titan SS, disc. 2012), 7 shot mag., double diamond checkered wood grips, low profile rear sights, stainless steel slide, rear slide serrations, military style slide stop, safety lever, skeletonized aluminum trigger. Mfg. by Shooters Arms Manufacturing in the Phillipines mid-2010-2014.

	$495	$435	$365	$315	$275	$235	$195	$590

Add $80 for NiBX finish (new 2013).
Add $100 for Titan SS (stainless steel), disc. 2012.

* **FX Titan Lightweight** – .45 ACP cal., similar to Titan, except has 3 1/8 in. bull barrel, NiBX finish only. Mfg. 2013-2014.

	$500	$440	$365	$315	$275	$235	$195	$610

FX THUNDERBOLT – .45 ACP cal., 1911 style frame, 5 in. non-ported or ported (new 2012) barrel, SA, blue finish or stainless steel (mfg. 2012 only), 8 shot mag., lower Picatinny rail standard, matte chrome round hammer and extended safety, beavertail with safety, dovetail front sight, Champion rear sight, aluminum trigger, double diamond checkered wood grips, wide front and rear slide serrations. Mfg. by Shooters Arms Manufacturing in the Phillipines mid-2010-2014.

	$740	$625	$550	$475	$400	$350	$295	$858

Add $42 for FX Thunderbolt E with ported slide (new 2012) or $40 for FX Thunderbolt SS with stainless construction (mfg. 2012 only).

MSR	100%	98%	95%	90%	80%	70%	60%	Last MSR

FXH-45 – .45 ACP cal., 5 in. steel match grade barrel, 8 shot mag., custom designed steel slide, polymer frame with built-in finger grooves, accepts Glock front and rear sights, black finish. New 2015.

MSR $700	$600	$515	$435	$375	$325	$280	$265	

FXH-45C – .45 ACP cal., 4 1/4 in. steel match grade barrel, 8 shot mag., custom designed steel slide, polymer frame with built-in finger grooves, accepts Glock front and rear sights, black finish. New 2015.

MSR $700	$600	$515	$435	$375	$325	$280	$265	

FXH-45D – .45 ACP cal., 3 1/4 in. steel match grade barrel, 7 shot mag., custom designed steel slide, polymer frame with built-in finger grooves, accepts Glock front and rear sights, black finish. New 2015.

MSR $700	$600	$515	$435	$375	$325	$280	$265	

AT CS9 SERIES – 9mm Para. cal., 4 in. barrel, DA/SA, Picatinny rail, ported slide, 18 shot mag., blue, chrome, or two tone finish. Mfg. in Turkey. Limited importation 2010-2011 only.

	$335	$295	$250	$230	$185	$150	$115	$380

Add $60 for chrome finish.

AT CS40 SERIES – .40 S&W cal., 4 in. barrel, DA/SA, Picatinny rail, 12 shot mag., blue, chrome, or two tone finish. Mfg. in Turkey. Limited importation 2010-2011 only.

	$360	$315	$270	$245	$200	$160	$125	$406

Add $15 for two tone or $40 for chrome finish.

AT C45 SERIES – .45 ACP cal., 4.6 in. barrel, DA/SA, Picatinny rail, ported slide, 9 shot mag., blue, chrome, or two tone finish. Mfg. in Turkey. Limited importation 2010-2011 only.

	$325	$285	$245	$220	$180	$145	$115	$370

Add $36 for chrome finish.

AT FS9 SERIES – 9mm Para. cal., 5 in. barrel, DA/SA, Picatinny rail, ported slide, 18 shot mag., blue, chrome, or two tone finish, mfg. in Turkey. Limited importation 2010-2011 only.

	$335	$295	$250	$230	$185	$150	$115	$380

Add $60 for chrome finish.

AT FS40 SERIES – .40 S&W cal., 5 in. barrel, DA/SA, Picatinny rail, 12 shot mag., blue, chrome, or two tone finish, mfg. in Turkey. Limited importation 2010-2011 only.

	$360	$315	$270	$245	$200	$160	$125	$406

Add $14 for two tone or $40 for chrome finish.

AT HP9 SERIES – 9mm Para. cal., 5 in. barrel, DA/SA, 18 shot mag., blue, chrome, or two tone finish, mfg. in Turkey. Limited importation 2010-2011 only.

	$335	$295	$250	$230	$185	$150	$115	$380

Add $31 for chrome finish.

AT MS380 SERIES – .380 ACP cal., 3.9 in. barrel, DA/SA, 12 shot mag., black, chrome, or two tone finish, mfg. in Turkey. Disc. 2011.

	$335	$295	$250	$230	$185	$150	$115	$380

Add $20 for chrome or black finish.

MILSPORT AR-15 PISTOL – 9mm Para. cal., 5 1/2 in. barrel, 2 in. flash can, 17 shot mag., billet lower, 7 in. KeyMod handguard, billet lower and forged upper receiver, black finish. New 2012.

MSR $870	$735	$650	$580	$515	$450	$385	$340	

OMNI HYBRID – 5.56 NATO cal., 7 1/2 in. barrel, 30 shot PMAG, Omni Hybrid lower and aluminum upper receiver, 7 in. free float quad rail, black finish, 4 3/4 lbs. New 2015.

MSR $600	$525	$450	$400	$350	$300	$275	$250	

OMNI HYBRID 300 – .300 AAC Blackout cal., 8 1/2 in. barrel, 30 shot PMAG, complete Omni Hybrid lower and aluminum upper receiver, 7 in. free float rail, black finish. New 2015.

MSR $670	$575	$500	$425	$395	$315	$260	$200	

OMNI HYBRID MAXX – 5.56 NATO cal., 7 1/2 in. barrel, 30 shot PMAG, 7 in. free float quad rail, complete OMNI Hybrid polymer upper and lower receiver, black finish, 4 3/4 lbs. New 2015.

MSR $670	$585	$500	$435	$365	$325	$280	$265	

OMNI HYBRID MAXX 300 – .300 AAC Blackout cal., 8 1/2 in. barrel, 30 shot PMAG, complete OMNI Hybrid polymer upper and lower receiver, 7 in. free float rail, optics ready, black finish, 4.95 lbs. New 2015.

MSR $680	$590	$500	$435	$365	$325	$280	$265	

MSR	100%	98%	95%	90%	80%	70%	60%	Last MSR

OMNI HYBRID AR-15 – 5.56 NATO or .300 AAC Blackout cal., 7 1/2 or 8 1/2 in. barrel, two 30 shot PMAGs, complete Omni Hybrid polymer lower receiver, 7 in. buffer tube, 7 in. free float quad rail, flip up iron or red-dot sights, black Nitride finish, 4 3/4-5.2 lbs. New 2015.

MSR $620	$565	$500	$4560	$400	$365	$335	$295	

Add $50 for flip-up iron sights or $60 for red dot sights.

SHOTGUNS: SEMI-AUTO

ALPHA FIELD – 12 ga., 3 in. chamber, inertia recoil system, 28 in. barrel, wide vent. rib, fiber optic front sight, checkered Turkish walnut stock and forearm, powder coat finish. New 2015.

MSR $550	$450	$365	$315	$275	$235	$200	$185	

ALPHA HD – 12 ga., 3 in. chamber, inertia recoil system, 18 1/2 in. barrel, 5 shot, blade sights, synthetic stock and forearm. New 2015.

MSR $470	$400	$350	$300	$270	$225	$185	$150	

ALPHA SPORT – 12 ga., 3 in. chamber, 26 in. barrel, inertia recoil system, synthetic stock and forearm. New 2015.

MSR $500	$425	$350	$315	$275	$235	$200	$185	

OMNI HYBRID MAXX – .410 bore, 2 1/2 in. chamber, GPO, 18 1/2 in. threaded barrel, Remington style chokes, 15 shot mag., 10 in. free floating quad rail, ambidextrous sling plate, Omni Hybrid lower receiver, 6-pos. adj. Super-Stoc, black finish, 6 1/2 lbs. New 2015.

MSR $930	$790	$685	$615	$550	$485	$415	$370	

TAC-SX2 (TAC-S) – 12 ga., 3 in. chamber, 18 1/2 in. barrel, blue finish, matte black synthetic pistol grip stock and forearm. Importation began 2014.

MSR $330	$280	$240	$215	$190	$170	$160	$150	

* **TAC-SX2 Combo (TAC-S Combo)** – 12 ga., similar to TACSX2, except is two barrel set, features 18 1/2 in. cyl. barrel and 28 in. vented ribbed barrel with 3 choke tubes. Importation began 2014.

MSR $420	$365	$325	$285	$260	$230	$200	$180	

SHOTGUNS: SLIDE ACTION

TAC-PX2 (TAC-P) – 12 ga., 3 in. chamber, 18 1/2 in. barrel, 5 shot, forearm with Picatinny rail, matte black finish, fixed synthetic stock with pistol grip, trigger guard mounted safety, ramped front sight, rubber buttpad, 5.95 lbs. New 2013.

MSR $280	$250	$200	$175	$155	$140	$125	$115	

* **TAC-PX2 Combo (TAC-P Combo)** – 12 ga., similar to TACPX2, except includes extra barrel and choke tubes. Mfg. 2014-2015.

	$335	$285	$245	$220	$180	$145	$115	*$350*

AM-TAC PRECISION

Previous manufacturer of AR-15 style carbines/rifles located in Garden City, ID from 2009-2015.

RIFLES: SEMI-AUTO

AM-TAC Precision produced firearms, components, and tactical products for the professional and recreational user.

LTC RIFLE – 5.56 NATO or .300 AAC Blackout cal., GIO, 16 in. stainless steel match grade barrel, "Jake Brake" muzzle device, KeyMod Rail System V2 handguard with Qik System, 30 shot mag., forged receivers, MBUS front and flip up rear sights, ALG Act combat trigger, BCM Mod 4 charging handle, QD endplate, enhanced trigger guard, Magpul MOE grip, MOE Mil-Spec 6-position stock, black finish, 6.28-6.6 lbs. Disc. 2015.

	$1,750	$1,525	$1,325	$1,200	$975	$795	$625	*$1,969*

Add $30 for .300 AAC Blackout cal.

PREDITOR ELITE RIFLE – 5.56 NATO or .300 AAC Blackout cal., GIO, 16 in. stainless steel match grade barrel, thread protector, 13 in. KeyMod rail system handguard, forged receivers, Magpul MOE grip, fixed A2 rifle stock, ALG Act combat trigger, BCM Mod 4 charging handle, QD endplate, enhanced trigger guard, 10 or 20 shot mag., two-color Cerakote camo finish. Disc. 2015.

	$1,825	$1,600	$1,375	$1,250	$1,000	$825	$700	*$2,049*

AMTEC 2000, INC.

Previous trademark incorporating Erma Werke (German) and H & R 1871 (U.S.) companies located in Gardner, MA until 1999. Amtec 2000, Inc. previously imported the Erma SR 100 rifle (see listing in Erma Suhl section).

MSR	100%	98%	95%	90%	80%	70%	60%	Last MSR

REVOLVERS

5 SHOT REVOLVER – .38 S&W cal., 5 shot double action, swing-out cylinder, 2 or 3 in. barrel, transfer bar safety, Pachmayr composition grips, high polish blue, matte electroless nickel, or stainless steel construction, fixed sights, approx. 25 oz., 200 mfg. 1996-99, all were distributed and sold in Europe only (no U.S. pricing).

ANDERSON MANUFACTURING

Current rifle manufacturer established during 2010, located in Hebron, KY. Distributor and dealer sales.

CARBINES/RIFLES: SEMI-AUTO

Anderson Manufacturing utilizes a proprietary metal treatment for all its rifles and carbines called RF-85. This metal treatment reduces friction on steel surfaces by 85, and RF-85 treated weapons do not require any wet lubricants, which also result in less dirt and carbon fouling in the action.

Add approx. $270 for RF85 No Lube treatment on all currently manufactured models.

3-GUN ELITE – .223 Wylde cal., 18 in. heavy barrel, Lantac Dragon .223/5.56 muzzle brake, 30 shot mag., forged receiver, steel adj. gas block, 15 in. EXT free float forearm, Magpul PRS buttstock, Magpul grip, 8 1/2 lbs.
Please contact the company directly for pricing and availability for this model.

AM10-BD – .308 Win. cal., GIO, 18 in. heavy barrel with flash hider, free float forearm, Magpul MOE buttstock and pistol grip, Picatinny rail and elevated modular rail, black furniture, 8.5 lbs. Disc. 2014.

MSR	100%	98%	95%	90%	80%	70%	60%	Last MSR
	$1,150	$925	$890	$735	$650	$550	$465	*$1,365*

.308 HUNTER (AM10-HUNTER) – .308 Win. cal., 18 in. chrome moly barrel with Anderson Knight Stalker flash hider, 20 shot mag., optic ready, forged receiver, stainless steel trigger and hammer, EXT free float forearm, low profile gas block, Magpul grip, Ti7 buttstock, black furniture, 8.9 lbs. New 2015.

MSR	100%	98%	95%	90%	80%	70%	60%	Last MSR
MSR $1,158	$985	$875	$750	$675	$550	$475	$425	

AM10-MSR – .308 Win. cal., GIO, 22 in. fluted barrel with crowned muzzle, low profile gas block, 14 1/4 in. free float forearm, A2 buttstock and pistol grip, black furniture, 9 lbs. Disc. 2014.

MSR	100%	98%	95%	90%	80%	70%	60%	Last MSR
	$1,100	$995	$875	$735	$650	$550	$465	*$1,319*

AM15-HBOR16/AM15-HBOR20 – .223 Rem. cal., GIO, 16 or 20 in. heavy barrel with target crown and flash suppressor, Wilson target trigger, Magpul PRS adj. stock, Magpul MIAD grip, front mounted low profile gas block, free floated handguard with upper and lower Picatinny rails, tactical charging handle, hard anodized finish, aluminum flat-top receiver, includes two-30 shot magazines and black hard case, 9.44 lbs. Disc. 2014.

MSR	100%	98%	95%	90%	80%	70%	60%	Last MSR
	$1,200	$1,075	$950	$800	$700	$600	$495	*$1,411*

Add $50 for 20 in. barrel.
Add $210 for AM-15HBOR16-Billet or AM-15HBOR20-Billet models (disc. 2012).

AM15-M416 (M4 CARBINE) – .223 Rem. or 6.8 SPC cal., GIO, 16 in. M4 heavy barrel with Phantom flash hider, front mounted low profile gas block, Magpul MOE 6-position adj. pistol grip stock, quad rail forend with upper and lower Picatinny rails, 8 in. free float modular forearm, hard anodized finish, aluminum flat-top receiver, includes two 30 shot Magpul magazines and black hard case, 6.3 lbs. Disc. 2014.

MSR	100%	98%	95%	90%	80%	70%	60%	Last MSR
	$875	$740	$650	$585	$515	$450	$395	*$1,038*

Add $50 for 6.8 SPC cal.
Add $210 for AM15M416-Billet model in .223 Rem. cal. (disc. 2012), or $337 for AM15M416-Billet model in 6.8 SPC cal. (disc. 2012).

* AM15-M416 Camo – .223 Rem. cal., similar to AM15-M416, except features 8 in. free float CAMO forearm, A2 pistol grip, tactical intent buttstock, and Digital Camo coverage. Mfg. 2013-2014.

MSR	100%	98%	95%	90%	80%	70%	60%	Last MSR
	$975	$875	$740	$625	$550	$475	$425	*$1,152*

* M4 LE (AM15-M416 LE) – 5.56 NATO/.223 Rem. cal., 16 in. M4 contour barrel with flash hider, A2 front sight, 30 shot mag., 6 in. free float modular forearm, A2 buttstock and grip, 6.4 lbs.

MSR	100%	98%	95%	90%	80%	70%	60%	Last MSR
MSR $918	$785	$685	$615	$550	$485	$415	$370	

* M4 Tiger (AM15-M416 Tiger) – 5.56 NATO cal., 16 in. chrome moly M4 contour barrel with Knight Stalker flash hider, 30 shot mag., low profile gas block, EXT free float forearm, Magpul buttstock and pistol grip, Tiger striped finish on upper and lower receivers, stainless steel trigger and hammer, ambi sling mount, 6.3 lbs. New 2013.

MSR	100%	98%	95%	90%	80%	70%	60%	Last MSR
MSR $1,127	$935	$850	$725	$625	$550	$475	$425	

* AM15-M416 ZE – .223 Rem. cal., similar to AM15-M416, except features 8 in. free float ZOMBIE forearm. Disc. 2014.

MSR	100%	98%	95%	90%	80%	70%	60%	Last MSR
	$915	$800	$665	$585	$515	$450	$395	*$1,078*

M4 (CURRENT MFG.) – 5.56 NATO cal., 16 in. M4 heavy barrel with Anderson Knight Stalker flash hider, 30 shot mag., low profile gas block, forged receiver, Picatinny rail, EXT free float forearm, Magpul buttstock and grip, black furniture, 6.3 lbs.

MSR	100%	98%	95%	90%	80%	70%	60%	Last MSR
MSR $987	$835	$730	$625	$570	$485	$415	$370	

MSR		100%	98%	95%	90%	80%	70%	60%	Last MSR

AM15-VS24 (HEAVY BARREL VARMINTER) – .223 Rem. cal., GIO, 24 in. stainless steel fluted bull barrel with target crown, flat-top receiver, 14 in. free float modular forearm tube, Magpul PRS buttstock, Ergo tactical deluxe palm shelf pistol grip, two 30 shot mags., low profile gas block, tactical charging handle, Timney trigger, black furniture, includes Harris bipod and black hard case, 9.44 lbs. Disc. 2014.

		$1,425	$1,245	$1,100	$970	$815	$700	$575	$1,681

Add $210 for AM-15VS24-Billet model (disc. 2012).

300 BLACKOUT (AM15-BLACKOUT) – .300 AAC Blackout cal., 16 in. barrel with Anderson Knight Stalker flash hider, low profile gas block, forged receiver, 30 shot mag., EXT free float forearm, stainless steel trigger and hammer, Magpul buttstock and grip, Picatinny rail, ambi sling mount, 6.2 lbs. New 2015.

MSR $1,078		$900	$760	$665	$585	$515	$450	$395	

OPTIC READY (AM15-AOR/HEAVY BARREL CARBINE) – 5.56 NATO cal., GIO, 16 in. M4 contour heavy barrel with A2 flash hider and Picatinny rail, 30 shot mag., front mounted low profile gas block, hard anodized finish with a forged aluminum flat-top receiver, ribbed oval M4 handguard, optic ready front sight, 6-position collapsible buttstock, A2 pistol grip, includes hard case, 6.4 lbs.

MSR $811		$695	$615	$550	$475	$420	$365	$335	

Add $210 for AM15-AOR16 Billet model (disc. 2012).

SNIPER (AM15-SNIPER) – 5.56 NATO cal., 24 in. stainless steel fluted barrel, 30 shot mag., EXT free float forearm, Magpul PRS buttstock, Ergo pistol grip, black furniture, 12 1/4 lbs. New 2015.

MSR $2,079		$1,775	$1,540	$1,275	$1,115	$950	$825	$675	

PISTOLS: SEMI-AUTO

AM15 7.5 PISTOL – 5.56 NATO cal., 7 1/2 in. barrel with Knight Stalker flash hider, low profile gas block, 30 shot mag., forged receiver, Anderson's EXT free float forearm, Magpul grip, black finish, 4.9 lbs. New 2015.

MSR $1,012		$925	$850	$725	$625	$550	$475	$425	

Add $270 for RF85 No Lube treatment.

ANGSTADT ARMS

Current manufacturer located in Charlotte, NC.

Angstadt Arms specializes in lightweight personal defense weapons for civilian and law enforcement use.

PISTOLS: SEMI-AUTO

UDP-9 – 9mm Para. cal., GIO, 6 in. chrome moly barrel with A2 flash suppressor, accepts Glock magazines, standard pistol buffer tube, alum. upper and lower receiver with matte black hardcoat anodized finish, flared magwell, integrated oversized trigger guard, Odin Works 5 1/2 in. free float KeyMod handguard with continuous top Picatinny rail, B5 Systems pistol grip, 5 lbs. New 2015.

MSR $1,249		$1,050	$950	$815	$715	$625	$535	$450	

UDP-9 PDW (PERSONAL DEFENSE WEAPON) – 9mm Para. cal., 16 in. chrome moly barrel, A2 style flash suppressor, flared magwell, integrated oversized trigger guard, Magpul MOE stock, K2 pistol grip, billet aluminum lower and slick side upper receiver, Odin Works 12 1/2 in. free float KeyMod handguard with continuous top Picatinny rail, matte black hardcoat anodized finish, 5 lbs.

MSR $1,599		$1,350	$1,200	$1,075	$950	$815	$700	$575	

RIFLES: SEMI-AUTO

UDP-9 RIFLE – 9mm Para. cal., GIO, AR-15 style, 16 in. chrome moly barrel with A2 flash suppressor and black phosphate finish, accepts Glock mags., billet aluminum lower with flared magwell, integrated oversized trigger guard, Odin Works 12 1/2 in. free-float KeyMod handguard with continuous top Picatinny rail, Magpul MOE stock, K2 pistol grip, matte black hardcoat anodized finish, 5 lbs. New 2015.

MSR $1,499		$1,275	$1,125	$1,025	$875	$750	$625	$525	

ANSCHÜTZ

Current manufacturer (J. G. Anschütz, GmbH & Co. KG) established in 1856 and currently located in Ulm, Germany. Both sporting rifles and target/competition rifles are currently imported begininng 2015 by Anschutz North America, located in Trussville, AL. Sporting rifles were previously imported by Steyr Arms, Inc. located in Bessemer, AL 2010-2015. Previously located in Trussville, AL until 2013. Merkel USA imported Anschutz from 2006-2010, until the company was purchased by Steyr Arms, Inc.

Target/competition rifles are also being imported currently by Champion's Choice, Inc. located in La Vergne, TN, Champion Shooters Supply located in New Albany, OH, and Altius Handcrafted Firearms located in West Yellowstone, MT.

MSR	100%	98%	95%	90%	80%	70%	60%	Last MSR

Sporting rifles were imported 1996-2003 by Tristar Sporting Arms. Ltd., located in N. Kansas City, MO. Previously distributed until 2000 by Go Sportsmens Supply, located in Billings, MT. Previously imported and distributed through 1995 in the U.S. by Precision Sales International Inc., located in Westfield, MA.

Anschütz was founded by Julius Gottfried Anschütz in 1856, and located in Zella-Mehlis, Germany until 1945. WWII nearly ended the company. Members of the Anschütz family were evacuated to West Germany after the war, while the company's possesions were expropriated and dismantled. Brothers Max & Rudolf Anschütz, grandsons of Julius, re-established the company in Ulm after WWII. In 1968, Max Anschütz turned over general management to his son Dieter (4th generation), who retired on March 31, 2008. The family business is now managed by Dieter's two sons, Jochen (President) and Uwe.

For more information and current pricing on both new and used Anschütz airguns, please refer to the *Blue Book of Airguns* by Dr. Robert Beeman & John Allen (now online also).

RIFLES: SEMI-AUTO

MSR RX 22 – .22 LR cal., blowback action, 16 1/2 in. plain barrel, full length Picatinny rail with integrated quad rail in forend, folding iron sights, forward cocking lever, folding adj. plastic stock, pistol grip, 2, 5, 10, 20 or 22 shot mag., choice of black (Black Hawk) or Desert tan finish, ambidextrous safety, adj. trigger, approx. 7 lbs. Mfg. by ISSC in Ried, Austria 2012-2015.

	$575	$500	$450	$400	$360	$330	$295	*$895*

MSR RX PRECISION – .22 LR cal., blowback action, 16 1/2 in. plain barrel, full length Picatinny rail with folding iron sights, forward cocking lever, 10 shot mag., choice of aluminum anodized or flat black receiver, ambidextrous safety, skeletonized non-folding wood buttstock painted gray, Competition Model has 11 mm prism rail and buttplate carrier with rubber buttplate, pistol grip, adj. trigger, approx. 7 lbs. Mfg. by ISSC in Ried, Austria 2012-2015.

	$650	$550	$475	$425	$375	$350	$325	*$995*

ANZIO IRONWORKS CORP.

Current manufacturer established during 2000, located in St. Petersburg, FL. Anzio Ironworks has been making gun parts and accessories since 1994. Dealer and consumer sales.

RIFLES: BOLT ACTION

.50 BMG SINGLE SHOT TAKEDOWN MODEL – .50 BMG cal., modified bullpup configuration, tube stock with 2 in. buttpad, 17 in. barrel with match or military chambering and muzzle brake, automatic ambidextrous safety and decocking mechanism, takedown action allowing disassembly in under 25 seconds, adj. target trigger, inclined sight mounting rail, cased, 25 lbs. Mfg. 2000-2002.

	$4,200	$4,000	$3,500	$2,350	$2,000	$1,800	$1,600	*$2,500*

Add $150 for 29 in. barrel or $1,050 for 29 in. barrel assembly.

.50 BMG SINGLE SHOT TITANIUM TAKEDOWN MODEL – .50 BMG cal., modified bullpup configuration, tube stock, 16 in. barrel with match or military chambering and muzzle brake, automatic ambidextrous safety and decocking mechanism, interrupted thread lockup, takedown action allowing disassembly in under 12 seconds, adj. target trigger, Picatinny rail mount, cased, 11 lbs. Limited mfg. 2002 only.

	$5,700	$5,000	$4,000	$3,500	$3,500	$3,000	$2,500	*$3,200*

Add $250 for 29 in. barrel, $350 for custom barrel length to 45 in., or $1,050 for 29 in. barrel assembly.

.50 BMG SINGLE SHOT MODEL LTD. – .50 BMG cal., laminated wood stock, butter knife bolt handle, bolt complete with ejector and extractor, parkerized finish, inclined sight mounting rail, 17 in. barrel with match or military chambering and muzzle brake, 21 lbs. Limited mfg. 2002 only.

	$2,500	$2,200	$1,950	$1,675	$1,400	$1,200	$1,000	*$2,750*

Add $150 for 29 in. barrel or $250 for custom barrel length to 45 in.

.50 BMG SINGLE SHOT MODEL – .50 BMG cal., 29 1/2 in. Lothar Walther match grade barrel, AR-15 trigger and safety, fixed metal buttstock with shrouded barrel and optional muzzle brake, 22 lbs. Mfg. 2003-2006.

	$1,800	$1,625	$1,400	$1,200	$1,000	$900	$800	*$1,995*

.50 BMG TAKEDOWN COMPETITION RIFLE – .50 BMG cal., 30 in. free floating match grade stainless steel takedown barrel with clamshell muzzle brake, 20 minute inclined sight mounting rail, all steel receiver, hand polished trigger, knurled steel handguard, titanium firing pin, .49 MOA guaranteed, black or green Duracoat finish, includes fitted pelican case. New 2005.

MSR $4,200	$3,675	$3,150	$2,750	$2,400	$2,100	$1,900	$1,700	

.338 LAPUA TAKEDOWN RIFLE – .338 Lapua cal., 26 or 29 in. Supermatch chrome moly free floated barrel or stainless heavy target free floated barrel, all steel receiver, hand polished trigger, titanium firing pin, solid or vented steel handguard, 5 shot detachable box mag., black or green Duracoat finish, includes fitted pelican case.

MSR $4,700	$4,225	$3,695	$3,175	$2,875	$2,325	$1,900	$1,475	

Please call the manufacturer directly for more info. on custom camo patterns and colors, as well as other options available on this model.

MSR		100%	98%	95%	90%	80%	70%	60%	Last MSR

.50 BMG SUPER LIGHTWEIGHT REPEATER MODEL – .50 BMG cal., lightweight model with 18 in. Lothar Walther fluted target barrel with 3 (standard) or 5 shot detachable mag., titanium muzzle brake, scope rail, bipod, and sling, includes fitted case, 13 1/2 lbs. New 2003.

	MSR $4,995	$4,500	$3,950	$3,300	$2,775	$2,350	$2,125	$1,850	

Add $250 for bipod.

Add $250 for 22 or 26 in. Lothar Walther fluted barrel.

.50 BMG TAKEDOWN LIGHTWEIGHT RIFLE – .50 BMG cal., lightweight model with 30 in. Supermatch chrome moly free floated takedown barrel with clamshell muzzle brake, 20 minute incline scope rail, all steel receiver, hand polished trigger, 3 (standard) or 5 (optional) shot round detachable box mag., knurled steel handguard, titanium firing pin, Cryo treated barrel, black or green Duracoat finish, fitted Pelican case.

	MSR $5,700	$5,125	$4,495	$3,850	$3,495	$2,825	$2,300	$1,800	

ANZIO .50 BMG STANDARD REPEATER – .50 BMG cal., 18 or 26 in. Lothar Walther free floated stainless match grade barrel, 3 shot mag., Pachmayr Magnum recoil pad, 3 lug steel bolt, all steel receiver, guaranteed 1 MOA, Black Duracoat, Tiger Stripe Desert, Winter camo, or Urban Digital camo finish, fitted Pelican case, 18-24 lbs. New 2004.

	MSR $3,995	$3,475	$2,850	$2,400	$2,000	$1,750	$1,500	$1,350	

Add $300 for left-hand action.

Add $350 for Tiger Stripe Desert or Winter camo finish.

Add $425 for Urban Digital camo finish.

ANZIO 20/50 RIFLE – 20mm or .50 BMG cal., single shot or mag. fed configuration, 36, 40 (standard), or 45 in. takedown barrel, black or camo patterned finish, includes fitted Pelican case. New 2013.

	MSR $7,500	$6,750	$5,900	$5,075	$4,595	$3,725	$3,050	$2,375	

Add $300 for 45 in. barrel.

Add $300 for camo pattern finish.

Add $1,000 for mag. fed configuration.

ANZIO SINGLE SHOT 50 – .50 BMG cal., 21 in. free floating target barrel, all steel and alloy receiver, Pachmayr white line recoil pad, Black, Tiger Stripe, Desert, Winter camo, or Urban Digital camo finish, 21 lbs. New 2012.

	MSR $2,500	$2,250	$1,975	$1,695	$1,525	$1,250	$1,025	$800	

Add $300 for left-hand action.

Add $350 for Tiger Stripe, Desert, or Winter camo finish.

Add $425 for Urban Digital camo finish.

MAG. FED RIFLE – 14.5x114mm, 20mm Vulcan (requires $200 transfer tax in states where legal), or Anzio .20-50 cal., single shot or repeater, 49 in. match grade fluted takedown barrel with heavy duty clamshell brake, detachable 3 shot box mag., fully adj. rear monopod, titanium firing pin, bipod, scope rail, customer choice of Duracoat color finish, oversized bolt handle. New 2008.

	MSR $11,900	$11,900	$9,950	$8,750	$8,000	$7,250	$6,500	$5,750	

Add $1,100 for handguard, free floating barrel, and adj. bipod.

Add $3,200 for suppressor.

Subtract $2,100 for single shot.

Subtract $4,400 for Anzio .20-50 cal. (single shot) or $3,400 for mag. fed .20-50 cal.

ARCHER MANUFACTURING

Current AR-15 style pistol and rifle manufacturer established during 2015, located in Hutto, TX.

PISTOLS: SEMI-AUTO

AM-15 PISTOL – 5.56 NATO or .300 AAC Blackout cal., Geissele low profile gas block, 7 or 9 in. Shilen match grade barrel, Geissele MK4 M-LOK handguard, Magpul Gen2 MBUS sights, Phase 5 Hex 2 pistol buffer assembly, Sig pistol stabilizing brace, Type III hardcoat anodized black finish. New 2015.

	MSR $1,595	$1,350	$1,200	$1,075	$950	$815	$700	$575	

RIFLES: SEMI-AUTO

AM-10 – .243 Win., 6.5mm Creedmoor, .260 Rem., 7mm-08, or .308 Win. cal., 16, 18, 21, or 23 in. Shilen match grade barrel, Magpul MBUS ProL sights, ALG Defense quality Mil-Spec trigger, Magpul CTR buttstock, billet DPMS compatible matched receiver set, Midwest Industries 308 SS M-LOK handguard, Geissele low profile gas block, BCM Gunfighter Mod 4 charging handle, Type III hardcoat anodized black finish. New 2015.

	MSR $2,095	$1,795	$1,575	$1,325	$1,150	$995	$850	$700	

AM-10 PREMIUM – .243 Win., 6.5mm Creedmoor, .260 Rem., 7mm-08, or .308 Win. cal., 16, 18, 21, or 23 in. Shilen match grade barrel, Magpul MBUS ProL sights, Geissele SSA trigger, Magpul UBR stock, MIAD grip, billet DPMS compatible matched receiver set, Midwest Industries 308 SS M-LOK handguard, Geissele low profile gas block, BCM

MSR	100%	98%	95%	90%	80%	70%	60%	Last MSR

Gunfighter Mod 4 charging handle, BattleComp BABC, H Series Cerakote finish in OD Green, FDE, Grey, or Two-Tone (OD Green or FDE w/black furniture). New 2015.

| MSR $2,495 | $2,125 | $1,875 | $1,550 | $1,325 | $1,100 | $950 | $825 | |

AM-15/AM-15F – 5.56 NATO or .300 AAC Blackout cal., Geissele low profile gas block, 16 in. Shilen match grade barrel, ALG Defense quality Mil-Spec trigger, Magpul Gen2 MBUS sights, Magpul CTR buttstock, BCM Gunfighter Mod 4 charging handle, ALG Defense 15 in. EMR V2 or V3 handguard, ALG Defense True Mil-Spec polished buffer tube and buffer system, forged receiver set with forward assist (AM-15F), or billet matched receiver set (AM-15), Armor Black, Magpul FDE, or Mil-Spec OD Green finish or Hill Country or Urban Jungle Cerakote camo finish. New 2015.

| MSR $1,595 | $1,350 | $1,200 | $1,075 | $950 | $815 | $700 | $575 | |

Add $100 for billet matched receiver set (AM-15).

Add $150 for Hill Country or Urban Jungle Cerakote camo finish.

ARCHER MOUNTAIN CARBINE – 5.56 NATO or .300 AAC Blackout cal., Geissele low profile gas block, 16 in. Shilen match grade barrel, ALG Defense quality Mil-Spec trigger, Magpul Gen2 MBUS sights, Magpul CTR buttstock, BCM Gunfighter Mod 4 charging handle, ALG Defense 15 in. EMR V2 or V3 handguard, ALG Defense True Mil-Spec polished buffer tube and buffer system, Robar PolymAR polymer receiver set, Armor Black, Magpul FDE, or Mil-Spec OD Green finish or Hill Country or Urban Jungle Cerakote camo finish. New 2015.

| MSR $1,695 | $1,450 | $1,275 | $1,125 | $1,000 | $850 | $735 | $595 | |

Add $150 for Hill Country or Urban Jungle Cerakote camo finish.

ARES DEFENSE SYSTEMS INC.

Current manufacturer established in 1997, located in Melbourne, FL.

RIFLES: SEMI-AUTO

Ares Defense Systems manufactures quality firearms and firearm accessories for military, law enforcement, and the sporting market. Current mission configurable weapons available for military and law enforcement only include: ARES-16 MCR, ARES-16 AMG-1, and the ARES-16 AMG-2.

ARES-15 MCR (MISSION CONFIGURABLE RIFLE) – 5.56 NATO cal., AR-15 style, GPO, 16 1/4 in. barrel, patented upper receiver system allows multiple configurations, including a 3-second barrel change, 6-pos. telescoping stock, Mil-Spec handguard with rail interface system, optional belt feed module, approx. 7 1/2 lbs. New 2014.

| MSR $2,566 | $2,185 | $1,910 | $1,640 | $1,485 | $1,200 | $985 | $825 | |

Add $1,984 for belt feed module.

ARES-15 MCR SUB CARBINE – 5.56 NATO cal., GPO, 16 1/4 in. quick change barrel, 30 shot mag., patented upper receiver system, left-side folding buttstock assembly, Mil-Spec co-planar handguard with rail interface system, includes SKB briefcase system, 7 1/2 lbs. New 2014.

| MSR $3,789 | $3,225 | $2,820 | $2,420 | $1,975 | $1,650 | $1,375 | $1,175 | |

ARES SCR (SPORT CONFIGURABLE RIFLE) – 5.56 NATO or 7.62x39mm cal., GIO, 16 1/4 or 18 in. light barrel, sporterized configuration with standard flat-top upper receiver or flat-top with dust cover, Magpul MOE handguard, modular design permits changing calibers, supplied with 5 shot mag., Sporter, Sporter Short, or Monte Carlo stock, 5.7 lbs. New 2014.

| MSR $865 | $735 | $650 | $580 | $515 | $450 | $385 | $340 | |

Add $30 for flat-top upper receiver with dust cover.

ARIZONA ARMORY

Current AR-15 style rifle manufacturer located in Phoenix, AZ since 2007.

RIFLES: SEMI-AUTO

All rifles can be customized per individual specifications with a wide variety of upgrades and options. Conversion kits, Magpul, Midwest Industries, and Yankee Hill upgrade packages also available.

AA-15 CARBINE – 5.56 NATO cal., GIO, 16 in. M4 chrome moly barrel, AZA billet lower, AZA billet A3 flat-top slick side upper, CAR 4-position stock, CAR handguard, 30 shot mag.

| MSR $775 | $665 | $590 | $515 | $440 | $385 | $340 | $325 | |

AA-15 M4A3 BASIC – 5.56 NATO cal., GIO, 16 in. M4 chrome moly barrel, AZA billet lower and A3 flat-top upper with forward assist, M4 handguards, M4 6-position stock, 30 shot mag.

| MSR $875 | $740 | $675 | $580 | $515 | $450 | $385 | $340 | |

AA-15 M4A3 OPERATOR – 5.56 NATO cal., GIO, 16 in. M4 chrome lined barrel with M4 feed ramp, A2 flash suppressor, M4 double heat shield handguards, AZA billet lower and A3 flat-top upper with forward assist, two stage National Match trigger, M4 6-position stock, 30 shot mag.

| MSR $985 | $840 | $725 | $650 | $565 | $495 | $420 | $375 | |

MSR	100%	98%	95%	90%	80%	70%	60%	Last MSR

AA-15 18 SPR – .223 Rem. cal., GIO, 18 in. stainless steel 1x8 SPR barrel, rifle length YHM lightweight railed free float handguards, low profile gas block, AZA billet lower and slick side A3 upper, two stage match trigger, A2 stock, YHM QDS folding back-up iron sights, 20 shot mag.

	100%	98%	95%	90%	80%	70%	60%
MSR $1,075	$900	$760	$665	$585	$515	$450	$395

AA-15 20V/T – .223 Rem./5.56 NATO (.223 Wylde chamber) cal., GIO, Walther 20 in. stainless steel target crown barrel, aluminum free float tube, AZA billet lower and A3 billet slick side upper, adj. JP trigger, A2 stock, single Picatinny rail gas block, optic ready no sights, 5 shot mag.

	100%	98%	95%	90%	80%	70%	60%
MSR $1,025	$860	$725	$650	$585	$515	$450	$395

AA-15 20M – 5.56 NATO cal., GIO, 20 in. stainless steel match barrel with A2 flash suppressor, AZA billet lower, A2 forged upper with National Match A2 rear sight assembly, National Match front sight, A2 free float handguards, adj. trigger, anti-rotation trigger/hammer pins, 30 shot mag. Disc. 2014.

This model was available as a special order and was POR.

AA-15 9MM – 9mm Para. cal., GIO, 16 in. chrome moly barrel with A2 flash suppressor, AZA billet lower, A3 billet smooth side upper with 9mm door kit, standard trigger group, CAR 4-position stock with 9mm buffer, CAR handguards, 9mm mag. block adapter with last round bolt hold open, 32 shot mag.

	100%	98%	95%	90%	80%	70%	60%
MSR $975	$840	$725	$650	$565	$495	$420	$375

ARLINGTON ORDNANCE

Previous importer located in Westport, CT until 1996. Formerly located in Weston, CT.

CARBINES/RIFLES: SEMI-AUTO

M1 GARAND RIFLE – .30-06 cal., imported from Korea in used condition, various manufacturers, with import stamp. Imported 1991-96.

	100%	98%	95%	90%	80%	70%	60%
	$825	$750	$675	$550	$500	$475	$450

Add $40 for stock upgrade (better wood).

* **Arsenal Restored M1 Garand Rifle** – .30-06 or .308 Win. cal., featured new barrel, rebuilt gas system, and reinspected components. Imported 1994-1996.

	100%	98%	95%	90%	80%	70%	60%
	$850	$700	$650	$600	$575	$550	$500

Add 5% for .308 Win. cal.

TROPHY GARAND – .308 Win. cal. only, action was original Mil-Spec, included new barrel and checkered walnut stock and forend, recoil pad. Imported 1994-1996.

	100%	98%	95%	90%	80%	70%	60%	Last MSR
	$925	$825	$725	$675	$575	$525	$475	$695

T26 TANKER – .30-06 or .308 Win. cal., included new barrel and other key components, updated stock finish. Imported 1994-1996.

	100%	98%	95%	90%	80%	70%	60%
	$850	$700	$650	$600	$575	$550	$500

.30 CAL. CARBINE – .30 Carbine cal., 18 in. barrel, imported from Korea in used condition, various manufacturers, with import stamp. Imported 1991-1996.

	100%	98%	95%	90%	80%	70%	60%
	$725	$650	$575	$525	$475	$425	$400

Add approximately $55 for stock upgrade (better wood).

MODEL FIVE CARBINE – while advertised, this model never went into production.

ARMALITE

Previous manufacturer located in Costa Mesa, CA, approx. 1959-1973.

RIFLES: SEMI-AUTO

AR-7 EXPLORER – .22 LR cal., 16 in. aluminum barrel with steel liner, aperture rear sight, takedown action and barrel store in hollow plastic stock in either brown (rare), black, or multi-color, gun will float, designed by Gene Stoner, mfg. 1959-73 by Armalite, 1973-90 by Charter Arms, 1990-97 by Survival Arms located in Cocoa, FL, and by AR-7 Industries, LLC, located in Meriden, CT, 1998-2004. Current mfg. beginning 1997 by Henry Repeating Arms Co. located in NJ.

	100%	98%	95%	90%	80%	70%	60%
Black/Multi-color stock	$400	$375	$325	$275	$250	$215	$190
Brown stock	$550	$500	$450	$375	$325	$260	$220

Some unusual early Costa Mesa AR-7 variations have been observed with ported barrels, extendable wire stock, hooded front sight, and hollow pistol grip containing a cleaning kit, perhaps indicating a special military contract survival weapon.

AR-7 CUSTOM – similar to AR-7 Explorer, only with custom walnut stock including cheekpiece, pistol grip. Mfg. 1964-70.

	100%	98%	95%	90%	80%	70%	60%
	$325	$300	$265	$235	$200	$190	$180

MSR	100%	98%	95%	90%	80%	70%	60%	Last MSR

AR-180 – .223 Rem. cal., GPO, 18 1/4 in. barrel, folding stock. Manufactured by Armalite in Costa Mesa, CA, 1969-1972, Howa Machinery Ltd., Nagoya, Japan, 1972 and 1973, and by Sterling Armament Co. Ltd., Dagenham, Essex, England.

	100%	98%	95%	90%	80%	70%	60%	Last MSR
Sterling Mfg.	$1,750	$1,600	$1,450	$1,300	$1,225	$1,125	$1,050	
Howa Mfg.	$2,100	$1,900	$1,800	$1,650	$1,500	$1,300	$1,150	
Costa Mesa Mfg.	$2,100	$1,900	$1,800	$1,650	$1,500	$1,300	$1,150	

ARMALITE, INC.

Current manufacturer located in Geneseo, IL. New manufacture began in 1995 after Eagle Arms, Inc. purchased the ArmaLite trademarks. The ArmaLite trademark was originally used by Armalite (no relation to ArmaLite, Inc.) during manufacture in Costa Mesa, CA, approx. 1959-1973 (see Armalite listing above). Dealer and distributor sales.

PISTOLS: SEMI-AUTO

AR-10 PISTOL – 7.62x51mm/.308 Win. cal., carbine length gas system, 13.9 in. black Cerakoted stainless steel barrel, threaded with flash suppressing compensator, 20 shot Magpul PMAG, folding receiver extension, arm brace, 12 in. aluminum tactical KeyMod handguard, Raptor ambidextrous charging handle, Mil-Std 1913 rail, two stage precision trigger, Magpul K2 pistol grip, 8.8 lbs. New 2015.

	100%	98%	95%	90%	80%	70%	60%	
MSR $2,699	$2,425	$2,125	$1,825	$1,650	$1,350	$1,100	$875	

AR-24 (ULTIMATE) – 9mm Para. cal., full size (AR-24-15 w/4.67 in. barrel) or compact (AR-24K-13 w/3.89 in. barrel) frame, DA/SA, blowback operation, 10, 13 (compact only), or 15 shot mag., 3-dot sights with fixed or adj. rear sight, black parkerized finish, checkered polymer grips, includes case and two magazines, 35 oz. Mfg. by Sarzsilmaz in Turkey. Imported 2007-2013.

	100%	98%	95%	90%	80%	70%	60%	Last MSR
	$475	$415	$355	$325	$260	$215	$165	*$550*

Add $81 for Model AR-24-10C/15C Combat/Tactical Custom pistol with C-suffix (full or compact size), adj. rear sight and checkered grip straps.

AR-24-15 – 9mm Para. cal., DA/SA, full size frame, 4.67 in. barrel, blowback operation, all steel construction, 15 shot mag., 3-dot sights with fixed or adj. rear sight, black parkerized finish, checkered polymer grips, serrated front and back strap, includes case and two magazines, 35 oz. Mfg. by Sarzsilmaz in Turkey. Imported 2007-2013.

	100%	98%	95%	90%	80%	70%	60%	Last MSR
	$475	$415	$355	$325	$260	$215	$165	*$550*

* **AR-24-15C Combat Custom** – 9mm Para. cal., similar to AR-24-15, except has fully adj. rear sight, checkered front and back strap. Mfg. by Sarzsilmaz in Turkey. Imported 2007-2013.

	100%	98%	95%	90%	80%	70%	60%	Last MSR
	$550	$480	$415	$375	$305	$250	$195	*$631*

AR-24K-13 COMPACT – 9mm Para. cal., similar to AR-24-15, except has 3.89 in. barrel and 13 shot mag., approx. 31 oz. Mfg. by Sarzsilmaz in Turkey. Imported 2007-2013.

	100%	98%	95%	90%	80%	70%	60%	Last MSR
	$475	$415	$355	$325	$260	$215	$165	*$550*

Add $81 for Model AR-24-10C/15C Combat/Tactical Custom pistol with C-suffix (full or compact size), adj. rear sight and checkered grip straps.

* **AR-24K-13C Combat Custom Compact** – 9mm Para. cal., similar to AR-24K-13, except has fully adj. rear sight, checkered front and back strap, 13 shot mag., 32 oz. Mfg. by Sarzsilmaz in Turkey. Imported 2007-2013.

	100%	98%	95%	90%	80%	70%	60%	Last MSR
	$550	$480	$415	$375	$305	$250	$195	*$631*

M-15 PISTOL – 5.56x45mm/.223 Rem. cal., 6 or 11 1/2 in. double lapped chrome lined barrel with flash suppressing compensator, 20 shot Magpul PMAG, folding receiver extension, arm brace, 5 in. light contour aluminum KeyMod handguard, Raptor ambidextrous charging handle, Mil-Std 1913 rail, two stage precision trigger, 6 lbs. New 2015.

	100%	98%	95%	90%	80%	70%	60%	
MSR $2,099	$1,875	$1,625	$1,375	$1,150	$975	$825	$675	

Add $150 for 11 1/2 in. barrel.

RIFLES: BOLT ACTION

AR-30(M) – .300 Win. Mag., .308 Win., or .338 Lapua cal., scaled down AR-50, repeater, Shilen modified single stage trigger, w/o muzzle brake, 5 shot detachable mag., 26 in. chrome moly barrel, 12 lbs. Mfg. 2003-2012.

	100%	98%	95%	90%	80%	70%	60%	Last MSR
	$1,850	$1,575	$1,350	$1,125	$1,000	$900	$800	*$2,021*

Add $140 for .338 Lapua cal.

AR-30A1 STANDARD – .300 Win. Mag. or .338 Lapua cal., 24 or 26 in. chrome moly barrel with muzzle brake, modified octagonal receiver, metal standard fixed stock, SST, 12.8-13.4 lbs. New 2013.

	100%	98%	95%	90%	80%	70%	60%	
MSR $3,264	$2,900	$2,550	$2,175	$1,975	$1,600	$1,300	$1,025	

Add $140 for .338 Lapua cal.

MSR	100%	98%	95%	90%	80%	70%	60%	Last MSR

* **AR-30A1 Target** – .300 Win. Mag. or .338 Lapua cal., Target configuration, 26 in. chrome moly barrel with muzzle brake, 5 shot mag., fixed buttstock with adj. cheekpiece, steel V-block bedding system, SST, 15.4 lbs. New 2013.

| MSR $3,460 | $3,125 | $2,735 | $2,350 | $2,125 | $1,725 | $1,400 | $1,095 | |

Add $139 for .338 Lapua cal.

AR-31 – .308 Win. cal., 18 or 24 in. double lapped chrome moly barrel with muzzle brake, 10 shot mag. (accepts AR-10B double stack mags.), SST, detachable sight rail and accessory rails, adj. pistol grip stock, matte black finish, 14 lbs. New 2014.

| MSR $3,460 | $3,125 | $2,735 | $2,350 | $2,125 | $1,725 | $1,400 | $1,095 | |

AR-50A1 (AR-50) – .50 BMG or .416 Barrett (mfg. 2013-2014, AR-50A1B-416) cal., single shot bolt action with octagonal receiver integrated into a skeletonized aluminum stock with adj. cheekpiece and recoil pad, 30 in. tapered barrel w/o sights and sophisticated muzzle brake (reduces felt recoil to approx. .243 Win. cal.), removable buttstock, right or left (disc. 2013) hand action, single stage trigger, approx. 34 lbs. New 1999.

| MSR $3,359 | $3,195 | $2,925 | $2,600 | $2,400 | $2,175 | $2,000 | $1,875 | |

Add $420 for left-hand action (disc. 2013).

During 2004, this model was produced with a special commemorative stamp notation on the left side of the receiver.

AR-50A1BNM (NATIONAL MATCH) – .50 BMG cal., similar to AR-50A1, except features 33 in. chrome moly fluted National Match barrel, right or left-hand action, also includes ArmaLite Skid System, 33.6 lbs. New 2013.

| MSR $4,230 | $3,800 | $3,325 | $2,850 | $2,575 | $2,100 | $1,725 | $1,325 | |

RIFLES: SEMI-AUTO

All ArmaLite AR-15 style semi-auto rifles have a limited lifetime warranty. Some previously manufactured models had stainless steel barrels and NM triggers at an additional charge. Descriptions and pricing are for currently manufactured models.

Beginning 2009, a forward bolt assist became standard on all AR-10A4 upper receivers.

Add $99-$228 for A4 carry handle assembly.

Add $150 for 100% Realtree Hardwoods or Advantage Classic camo finish (disc.).

AR-10 SERIES – various configurations, GIO, with or w/o sights and carry handle, choice of standard green, black (new 1999), or camo (disc.) finish, supplied with two 10 shot mags. (until 2004), current mfg. typically ships with one 10 round and one 20 round mag., during 2014, several variations of the AR-10 Series now accepts third party polymer mags., two-stage NM trigger became standard during 2008. New late 1995.

* **AR-10A2 Rifle (Infantry)** – .243 Win. (disc. 2003) or 7.62 NATO cal., GIO, 20 in. chrome-lined threaded barrel with flash suppressor, forged A2 upper with forward assist and A2 front sight, forged lower with tactical two-stage trigger, carry handle, Hi-Cap stock, Black or Green finish, includes one 10 shot mag., one 20 shot mag., sling, and hard case, 9.2 lbs. Disc. 2013.

| | $1,325 | $1,160 | $995 | $900 | $730 | $595 | $465 | $1,583 |

* **AR-10A2 Carbine** – 7.62 NATO cal., GIO, 16 in. threaded barrel with flash suppressor, forged A2 upper with forward assist and A2 front sight, forged lower receiver, tactical two-stage trigger, 6-pos. collapsible stock with extended tube, Black or Green finish, includes one 10 shot mag., one 20 shot mag., sling, and hard case, 9 lbs. Disc. 2013.

| | $1,325 | $1,160 | $995 | $900 | $730 | $595 | $465 | $1,583 |

Add $74 for 4-way quad rail on front of forearm (mfg. 2004-2008).

* **AR-10A4 Rifle SPR - Special Purpose Rifle** – .243 Win. (disc. 2003, reintroduced 2011-2013, black only) or 7.62 NATO cal., GIO, 20 in. chrome lined barrel with flash suppressor, forged flat-top upper receiver with Picatinny rail and gas block, forward assist, forged lower with tactical two-stage trigger, removable front sight, A2 stock, black (BF) or Green (F, disc. 2013) finish, w/o carry handle, includes one 10 shot mag., one 20 shot mag. (disc. 2014), sling, and hard case, 8.9 lbs.

| MSR $1,571 | $1,325 | $1,160 | $995 | $900 | $730 | $595 | $465 | |

Add $35 for permanently affixed muzzle brake (10A4BF-2, new 2013).

* **AR-10A4 Carbine** – 7.62 NATO cal., similar to AR-10A4 SPR Rifle, except has 16 in. barrel, mid-length handguard, and 6-position collapsible stock with G.I. Diameter extension tube, 7.8 lbs. Disc. 2014.

| | $1,325 | $1,160 | $995 | $900 | $730 | $595 | $465 | $1,571 |

Add $414 for SIR System (Selective Integrated Rail System, mfg. 2004-2006).

* **AR-10A4 Mod 1** – .308 Win. cal., GIO, 16 in. barrel with flash suppressor, forged one-piece upper receiver/rail system with detachable side and bottom rails, two-stage tactical trigger, collapsible tube stock with pistol grip, black finish and furniture.

While this model was advertised during 2012, it never went into production.

MSR	100%	98%	95%	90%	80%	70%	60%	Last MSR

* **AR-10A2 Carbine (AR-10A4 Tactical Carbine)** – 7.62 NATO/.308 Win. cal., GIO, 16 in. double lapped chrome lined chrome moly barrel with flash suppressor, two-stage tactical trigger, anodized aluminum receiver, forged aluminum A4 flat-top upper receiver with Picatinny rail and permanent carry handle, A2 front sight, 20 shot Magpul PMAG, aluminum handguard tube, 6-pos. collapsible stock, 9 lbs. New 2014.

MSR $1,571 $1,325 $1,160 $995 $900 $730 $595 $465

* **AR-10A4243BF** – .243 Win. cal., 20 in. match grade chrome moly barrel, two-stage tactical trigger, anodized aluminum lower receiver, forged flat-top upper receiver with Picatinny gas block, forward assist, fixed polymer stock, includes one 5 shot and one 10 shot mag., sling, 9 lbs. Disc. 2013.

    $1,325 $1,160 $995 $900 $730 $595 $465   *$1,571*

* **AR-10B Rifle** – .308 Win. cal., patterned after the early Armalite AR-10 rifle, GIO, featuring tapered M16 handguards, pistol grip, distinctive charging lever on top inside of carry handle (cannot be used to mount sighting devices), original brown color, 20 in. barrel, 9 1/2 lbs. Mfg. 1999-2008.

    $1,425 $1,245 $1,070 $970 $785 $640 $500   *$1,698*

* **AR-10A Carbine (A10A4CBF/CF)** – 7.62 NATO/.308 Win. cal., 16 in. double lapped chrome lined chrome moly threaded barrel with flash suppressor, two-stage tactical trigger, anodized aluminum lower receiver, forged flat-top upper receiver with Picatinny rail and forward assist, 6-pos. collapsible stock, 20 shot Magpul PMag., standard 8 in. handguard, Picatinny rail gas block, matte black (CBF) or green (CF, disc. 2014) finish, 7 3/4 lbs. New 2013.

MSR $1,571 $1,325 $1,160 $995 $900 $730 $595 $465

* **AR-10 National Match** – 7.62 NATO cal., GIO, 20 in. stainless steel match barrel with stainless A2 flash suppressor, forged flat-top receiver with Picatinny rail and forward assist, NM quad rail free float handguard, carry handle, forged lower with two-stage NM trigger, 10 shot mag., Mil-Std 1913 rail handguard, extended elevation NM sights, includes two 20 shot mags., USMC sling, black hard case, 11 1/2 lbs. Mfg. 2009-2013.

    $1,995 $1,745 $1,495 $1,355 $1,095 $900 $700   *$2,365*

AR-10SOF (SPECIAL OPERATION FORCES) CARBINE – .308 Win. cal., GIO, available in either A2 or A4 configurations, fixed tube stock, 16 in. barrel, black finish only. Mfg. 2003-2004.

    $1,250 $1,095 $940 $850 $690 $565 $440   *$1,503*

Add $52 for A2 configuration (includes Picatinny rail).

* **AR-10T Carbine (10TCBNF, Navy Model)** – 7.62 NATO cal., 16 in. triple lapped stainless barrel with A2 flash suppressor, forged flat-top upper with Picatinny rail and forward assist, Picatinny gas block, round mid-length free floating handguard, forged lower with two-stage NM trigger, Hi-Cap stock, Black finish, includes two 10 shot mags. and hard case, 8 1/2 lbs. Mfg. 2004-2012.

    $1,595 $1,395 $1,195 $1,085 $875 $720 $560   *$1,914*

* **AR-10T Rifle** – .243 Win. (mfg. 1995-2003, and 2009-2010), .260 Rem. (mfg. 2009-2013), .300 RSUM (mfg. 2004-2008, Ultra Mag. Model), 7mm-08 Rem. (mfg. 2009-2010), .338 Federal (mfg. 2009-2013), or 7.62 NATO cal., GIO, features 20 (7.62 NATO), 22 (.338 Federal or .260 Rem., disc. 2013), or 24 (disc. 2008) in. stainless steel heavy match barrel, two-stage NM trigger, black fiberglass (disc. 2008) or aluminum handguard tube, fixed A2 buttstock, flat-top receiver with Picatinny rail, w/o sights or carry handle, forward bolt assist became standard in 2009, Green (disc. 2013) or Black finish, includes one (new 2014) or two (disc. 2013) 10 shot mags. and hard case, 9 1/2 - 10 1/2 lbs.

MSR $1,899 $1,625 $1,425 $1,200 $1,075 $925 $795 $650

Add $80 for .338 Federal cal. (disc. 2013).
Add $214 for .300 RSUM cal. (disc. 2008).
Add $250 for Lothar Walther barrel (disc.).

* **AR10B Target (10TBNF/NF)** – .308 Win. cal., 20 in. triple lapped stainless steel match grade barrel, forged flat-top receiver, NM two-stage trigger, Picatinny gas block, fixed polymer stock, free float handguard, pistol grip, 10 shot mag., hard anodized matte black (BNF) or green (NF, disc. 2013) finish, 10.3 lbs. Disc. 2015.

    $1,595 $1,395 $1,195 $1,085 $875 $720 $560   *$1,914*

AR-10 SUPER SASS RIFLE (10SBF) – 7.62 NATO cal., GIO, mock AAC (disc.) or A2 flash suppressor, 20 in. triple lapped ceramic coated stainless steel threaded barrel with A2 flash suppressor, forged flat-top upper receiver with Picatinny rail, forward assist, adj. gas block, SuperSASS quad rail free floating handguard with rail covers, forged lower receiver, 20 shot mag., fully adj. Sniper stock, black finish, two-stage NM trigger, available with various accessories, includes one 10 shot mag., one 20 shot mag., USMC quick adjust sling, sling swivel mount, and hard case, 9.4-11.8 lbs.

MSR $3,100 $2,650 $2,2275 $1,850 $1,575 $1,300 $1,100 $895

* **AR-10A Super SASS Rifle (A10SBF)** – 7.62 NATO/.308 Win. cal., 20 in. Cerakote stainless steel match threaded barrel with flash suppressor, 20 shot Mapgul PMag., National Match two-stage trigger, Armalite floating rail systems handguard, Gas Buster charging handle, quad Mil-Std 1913 rail, Magpul PRS stock, 11.8 lbs. New 2012.

MSR $3,099 $2,650 $2,2275 $1,850 $1,575 $1,300 $1,100 $895

This model has magazine interchangeability with the AR-10B.

MSR	100%	98%	95%	90%	80%	70%	60%	Last MSR

»AR-10 CSASS (AR-10A Super SASS Carbine - A10SCBF) – 7.62 NATO/.308 Win. cal., 16 in. Cerakoted stainless steel match threaded barrel with flash suppressor, 20 shot Magpul PMag., Armalite floating rail systems handguard, Gas Buster charging handle, National Match two-stage trigger, quad Mil-Std 1913 rail, B5 buttstock, 9.1 lbs. New 2014.

| MSR $3,099 | $2,650 | $2,2275 | $1,850 | $1,575 | $1,300 | $1,100 | $895 | |

This model has magazine interchangeability with the AR-10B.

AR-10 DSR10 – 7.62x55mm/.308 Win. cal., 16 in. double lapped chrome lined barrel with flash suppressor, 20 shot Magpul PMAG, 8 in. handguard, Mil-Std 1913 rail gas block, single-stage trigger, 6-position collapsible buttstock, 7.9 lbs. New 2015.

| MSR $1,050 | $885 | $785 | $685 | $600 | $535 | $465 | $415 | |

AR-10 QUAD-RAIL (AR-10A4 LOW PROFILE CARBINE) – 7.62x51mm/.308 Win. cal., 16 in. double lapped chrome-lined chrome moly threaded barrel with flash suppressor, anodized aluminum receiver, forged aluminum upper receiver with free float quadrail handguards, low profile gas block, 20 shot Magpul PMAG, two-stage tactical trigger, B5 adjustable stock, 8.8 lbs. New 2014.

| MSR $1,850 | $1,600 | $1,400 | $1,175 | $1,050 | $900 | $775 | $625 | |

AR-10 TACTICAL – 7.62x51mm/.308 Win. cal., 16, 18, or 20 in. black Cerakoted stainless steel threaded barrel with flash hiding compensator, 25 shot Magpul PMag., 15 in. KeyMod handguard, full length Picatinny rail, Magpul MBUS flip-up sights, Raptor ambidextrous charging handle, two-stage precision trigger, MOE+ pistol grip, Magpul STR Multi-position collapsible (16 or 18 in.) or MBA-1 (20 in.) buttstock, 8.8 lbs. New 2015.

| MSR $1,999 | $1,700 | $1,500 | $1,250 | $1,100 | $950 | $825 | $675 | |

Add $100 for 18 or 20 in. barrel.

AR-10 VSR (VERSATILE SPORTING RIFLE) – 7.62x51mm/.308 Win. cal., 18 in. black Cerakoted stainless steel threaded barrel with knurled thread protector, 20 shot Magpul PMag., top Picatinny rail, 15 in. free-floating VSR handguard, Raptor ambidextrous charging handle, two-stage trigger, MBA-1 lightweight precision buttstock adjustable for LOP and comb height, 8.8 lbs. New 2015.

| MSR $1,899 | $1,625 | $1,425 | $1,200 | $1,075 | $925 | $795 | $650 | |

AR-10 3-GUN COMPETITION RIFLE – 7.62x51mm/.308 Win. cal., 18 in. stainless steel barrel, 25 shot Magpul PMag., 15 in. free floating 3-Gun handguard, ambidextrous safety and Raptor charging handle, two inch Mil-Std. rail section, Timney 3 lb. single stage trigger, Ergo wide grip, lightweight MBA-1 buttstock is adjustable for cheekpiece and LOP, 8.9 lbs. New 2015.

| MSR $2,199 | $1,875 | $1,650 | $1,400 | $1,200 | $1,025 | $875 | $725 | |

AR-180B – .223 Rem. cal., GPO, polymer lower receiver with formed sheet metal upper, standard AR-15 trigger group/magazine, incorporates the best features of the M15 (lower group with trigger and magwell) and early AR-180 (gas system, which keeps propellant gas outside of the receiver) rifles, 19.8 in. barrel with integral muzzle brake, 6 lbs. Mfg. 2003-2007.

| | $650 | $575 | $500 | $460 | $420 | $365 | $325 | *$750* |

For more information on the original ArmaLite AR-180 and variations, please refer to the previous ArmaLite listing.

M4A1C CARBINE – features GIO, 16 in. chrome-lined 1:9 twist heavy barrel with National Match sights and detachable carrying handle, grooved barrel shroud, 7 lbs. Disc. 1997.

| | $795 | $700 | $600 | $525 | $450 | $375 | $350 | *$935* |

M4C CARBINE – similar to M4A1C Carbine, except has non-removable carrying handle and fixed sights, 7 lbs. Disc. 1997.

| | $725 | $625 | $525 | $475 | $450 | $395 | $350 | *$870* |

M15 RIFLE/CARBINE VARIATIONS – .223 Rem. cal. standard unless otherwise noted, GIO, various configurations, barrel lengths, sights, and other features.

* **M15 22 LR Carbine** – .22 LR cal., GIO, 16 in. barrel with A2 flash suppressor, standard .223 lower with .22 LR upper receiver, forward assist, 6 in. handguard, Picatinny gas block. Mfg. 2011 only.

| | $575 | $500 | $430 | $390 | $350 | $295 | $250 | *$749* |

* **M15A4 SPR Mod 1 (15SPR1CB)** – 5.56 NATO, 6.8 SPC (mfg. 2012-2013, reintroduced 2016), or 7.62x39mm (mfg. 2012-2013) cal., GIO, 16 in. chrome-lined threaded barrel with flash hider, gas block with rail, forged flat-top receiver with Picatinny rail and laser engraved rail numbering, three extra detachable rails, collapsible stock, tactical two-stage trigger, aluminum lower receiver, ARMS polymer (disc. 2013) or flip up front and rear sights, black furniture, includes one 30 shot mag., sling, and hard case, 6 1/2 lbs. New mid-2010.

| MSR $1,589 | $1,350 | $1,175 | $1,000 | $900 | $730 | $600 | $475 | |

Add $35 for mid-length free floating quad rail (disc. 2013).

Add $160 for 7.62x39mm cal. (disc. 2013).

Add $155 for 6.8 SPC cal.

MSR	100%	98%	95%	90%	80%	70%	60%	Last MSR

* **M15A2/A4 National Match Rifle** – .223 Rem. cal., features GIO, 20 in. stainless steel NM sleeved 1:8 twist barrel with flash suppressor, forged A2 receiver with NM hooded rear sights and A2 NM clamp on front sight, forged lower with NM two-stage trigger, grooved barrel shroud, Black or Green furniture, with or w/o detachable carrying handle, includes one 30 shot mag., USMC quick adjust sling, and hard case, 9 lbs. Disc. 2013.

	$1,175	$1,030	$880	$800	$645	$530	$410	$1,422

* **M15A2 Golden Eagle** – .223 Rem. cal., similiar to M15A2 National Match Rifle, except has 20 in. heavy barrel, 9.4 lbs. Limited mfg. 1998 only.

	$1,100	$965	$825	$750	$600	$495	$385	$1,350

* **M15A2 Service Rifle** – 5.56 NATO cal., GIO, includes 20 in. chrome-lined 1:9 twist barrel, green or black furniture, forged A2 receiver, fixed stock, A2 front sight, tactical two-stage trigger, flash suppressor, carrying handle, includes one 30 shot mag., sling, and hard case, 8.2 lbs. Disc. 2013.

	$950	$830	$715	$645	$525	$430	$335	$1,174

* **M15A2 Carbine** – 5.56 NATO cal., similar to M15A2 Service Rifle, except has 16 in. barrel, 6-position collapsible stock with G.I. diameter extension tube, includes one 30 shot mag., sling, and hard case, 7 lbs. Disc. 2013.

	$950	$830	$715	$645	$525	$430	$335	$1,174

* **M15A4 National Match SPR** – .223 Rem. cal., similar to M15A2 National Match, except has forged flat-top receiver with Picatinny rail and NM detachable carry handle, includes one 30 shot mag., USMC quick adjust sling, and hard case, 9.8 lbs. Disc. 2013.

	$1,175	$1,030	$880	$800	$645	$530	$410	$1,435

* **M15A4 SPR (Special Purpose Rifle, 15A4/15A4B)** – 5.56 NATO cal., GIO, 20 in. chrome-lined H-Bar threaded barrel, gas block with rail, forged flat-top upper with Picatinny rail, forged lower with tactical two-stage trigger, Hi-Cap stock, Green (15A4) or Black (15A4B) finish, includes one 30 shot mag., sling, and hard case, 7.8 lbs. Disc. 2013.

	$875	$765	$655	$595	$480	$395	$300	$1,073

* **M15A4 SPR II National Match (Special Purpose Rifle)** – 5.56 NATO cal., similar to M15A4 SPR, except has triple lapped rifled barrel, strengthened free floating barrel sleeve and two-stage match trigger, green or black furniture. Mfg. 2003-2005.

	$1,195	$1,025	$880	$800	$645	$530	$410	$1,472

* **M15A4 Carbine** – 5.56 NATO, 6.8 SPC (mfg. 2009-2013, reintroduced 2016), or 7.62x39mm (mfg. 2009-2013) cal., 16 in. chrome moly threaded barrel, forged flat-top upper with Picatinny rail, gas block with rail, forged lower with tactical two-stage trigger, 6-pos. collapsible stock with G.I. diameter extension tube, green (15A4C) or black (15A4CB) furniture, includes one 30 shot mag., sling, and hard case, 6 1/2-7 lbs.

MSR $1,073	$875	$765	$655	$595	$480	$395	$300	

Add $42 for 6.8 SPC cal.

Add $42 for 7.62x39mm cal. (disc. 2013).

Subtract $60 for fixed front sight w/detachable carry handle (disc.).

* **M15A4 CBA2K** – 5.56 NATO cal., GIO, 16 in. double lapped chrome lined barrel, flash suppressor, two-stage tactical trigger, forged flat-top receiver with Picatinny rail, A2 front sight, 8 in. mid-length handguard, forged lower receiver, 6-position collapsible stock with G.I. diameter extension tube, includes one 30 shot mag., sling, and hard case, 6 1/2 lbs. Mfg. 2008-2013.

	$825	$700	$665	$595	$525	$450	$365	$1,031

* **M15ARTN** – .223 Rem. cal., GIO, 20 in. stainless steel barrel, National Match trigger, green or black finish. Mfg. 2004-2007.

	$1,075	$965	$825	$750	$600	$495	$385	$1,322

* **M-15T Target (15A4TBN Rifle Eagle Eye)** – .223 Rem. cal. w/Wylde chamber, GIO, 20 or 24 (disc. 2009) in. stainless steel heavy barrel, two-stage NM trigger, smooth green or black fiberglass (disc. 2008) or lightweight aluminum round floating handguard, Picatinny front sight rail but w/o sights and carrying handle, A2 stock, black or green furniture, includes one 10 shot mag. and hard case, 8.6 lbs. Disc. 2005, reintroduced 2007.

MSR $1,318	$1,100	$995	$875	$735	$650	$550	$465	

* **M-15 TARGET (15TBN)** – .223 Rem. cal., GIO, 18 in. triple lapped stainless steel match threaded barrel with flash suppressor, forged flat-top upper receiver with Picatinny rail, free float quad rail handguards, includes one 10 shot mag., collapsible stock, two-stage NM trigger, pistol grip, matte black finish, 7.9 lbs. New 2014.

MSR $1,449	$1,175	$1,030	$880	$800	$645	$530	$410	

* **M15A4T Carbine (Eagle Eye)** – features GIO, 16 in. stainless steel 1:9 twist heavy barrel, picatinny rail, smooth fiberglass handguard tube, two-stage trigger, 7.1 lbs. Mfg. 1997-2004.

	$1,125	$965	$825	$750	$600	$495	$385	$1,383

* **M15A4 Predator** – similar to M15A4T Eagle Eye, except has 1:12 twist barrel. Disc. 1996.

	$1,100	$965	$825	$750	$600	$495	$385	$1,350

MSR		100%	98%	95%	90%	80%	70%	60%	Last MSR

* **M15A4 Action Master** – GIO, includes 20 in. stainless steel 1:9 twist barrel, two-stage trigger, muzzle brake, Picatinny flat-top design w/o sights or carrying handle, 9 lbs. Disc. 1997.

| | | $950 | $830 | $715 | $645 | $525 | $430 | $335 | *$1,175* |

* **M15SOF (Special Operation Forces) Carbine** – .223 Rem. cal., GIO, available in either A2 or A4 configurations, fixed tube stock, 16 in. barrel, black finish only. Mfg. 2003-2004.

| | | $895 | $785 | $670 | $610 | $490 | $405 | $315 | *$1,084* |

Add $69 for A2 configuration (includes Picatinny rail).

M-15 DSR15/DSR15F – 5.56x45mm/.223 Wylde cal., 16 in. double lapped chrome lined barrel with flash suppressor, 30 shot Magpul PMAG, 8 in. handguard, Mil-Std 1913 rail gas block or A2 front sight base (DSR15F), single-stage trigger, 6-position collapsible buttstock, 6.1 lbs. New 2015.

| MSR $799 | | $685 | $615 | $550 | $475 | $420 | $365 | $335 | |

M15 LIGHT TACTICAL CARBINE – 5.56 NATO, 6.8 SPC, or 7.62x39mm cal., mid-length GIO, 16 in. chrome lined threaded barrel, flash suppressor, 30 shot mag., single stage trigger, forged aluminum receivers, top Picatinny rail, 10 in. aluminum tactical KeyMod handguard, anodized black finish, 6 lbs. New 2016.

| MSR $999 | | $850 | $725 | $650 | $585 | $515 | $450 | $395 | |

M-15 PISTON – 5.56 NATO cal., GPO, 16 in. chrome moly barrel, 30 shot Magpul PMag., 15 in. piston KeyMod handguard, Raptor ambidextrous charging handle, Mil-Std 1913 rail, two-stage precision trigger, Magpul STR buttstock adjustable for LOP and comb height, 7.3 lbs. New 2015.

| MSR $2,249 | | $1,915 | $1,685 | $1,425 | $1,225 | $1,035 | $885 | $735 | |

M-15 TACTICAL – 5.56x45mm/.223 Wylde cal., GIO, 16 or 18 in. black Cerakoted stainless steel threaded barrel with flash hiding compensator, 30 shot Magpul PMag., two-stage precision trigger, full length Picatinny rail, 15 in. aluminum tactical KeyMod handguard, Magpul STR multi-position collapsible stock, 7.2 lbs. New 2015.

| MSR $1,599 | | $1,350 | $1,200 | $1,075 | $950 | $815 | $700 | $575 | |

Add $100 for 18 in. barrel.

M-15 VSR (VERSATILE SPORTING RIFLE) – 5.56x45mm/.223 Wylde cal., GIO, 18 in. black Cerakoted stainless steel threaded barrel with knurled thread protector, 20 shot Magpul PMag., 15 in. free floating VSR handguard, Raptor ambidextrous charging handle, top Picatinny rail, two-stage precision trigger, MBA-1 lightweight buttstock adj. for LOP and comb height, 7 1/2 lbs. New 2015.

| MSR $1,349 | | $1,135 | $1,015 | $885 | $740 | $675 | $575 | $475 | |

M-15 3-GUN COMPETITION RIFLE – 5.56x45mm/.223 Wylde cal., GIO, 18 in. free floating stainless steel barrel, adj. gas block, 30 shot Magpul PMag., 12 in. free-floating 3-Gun handguard, two inch Mil-Std. rail section, Timney 3 lb. single stage trigger, MBA-1 lightweight precision buttstock adjustable for LOP and comb height, 6.6 lbs. New 2015.

| MSR $1,699 | | $1,450 | $1,275 | $1,125 | $1,000 | $850 | $735 | $595 | |

LEC15A4CBK (LAW ENFORCEMENT CARBINE) – 5.56 NATO cal., GIO, 16 in. double lapped chrome lined threaded barrel, forged flat-top receiver with Picatinny rail, flash suppressor, A2 front sight, 8 in. handguard, tactical two-stage trigger, 6-position collapsible stock with G.I. diameter extension tube, includes one 30 shot mag., sling, and hard case, 6 1/2 lbs. New 2009.

| MSR $989 | | $850 | $725 | $650 | $585 | $515 | $450 | $395 | |

ARMAMENT TECHNOLOGY

Previous firearms manufacturer located in Halifax, Nova Scotia, Canada 1988-2003.

Armament Technology discontinued making bolt action rifles in 2003. Currently, the company is distributing optical rifle sights only.

RIFLES: BOLT-ACTION

AT1-C24 TACTICAL RIFLE – .308 Win. or .300 Win. Mag. (disc. 2000) cal., similar to AT1-M24, except has detachable mag., adj. cheekpiece, and buttstock adj. for LOP, includes 3.5-10x30mm tactical scope and Mil-Spec shipping case, 1/2 in. MOA guaranteed, available in left-hand action, 14.9 lbs. Mfg. 1998-2003.

| | | $4,095 | $3,650 | $2,775 | $2,250 | $1,825 | $1,500 | $1,275 | *$4,195* |

AT1-C24B TACTICAL RIFLE – .308 Win. cal., similar to AT1-C24, except is not available in left-hand, 15.9 lbs. Mfg. 2001-2003.

| | | $4,250 | $3,750 | $2,850 | $2,300 | $1,850 | $1,525 | $1,300 | *$4,695* |

AT1-M24 TACTICAL RIFLE – .223 Rem. (new 1998), .308 Win., or .300 Win. Mag. (disc. 2000) cal., tactical rifle with competition tuned right-hand or left-hand Rem. 700 action, stainless steel barrel, Kevlar reinforced fiberglass stock, Harris bipod, matte black finish, competition trigger, 1/2 in. MOA guaranteed, 14.9 lbs. Disc. 2003.

| | | $4,350 | $3,850 | $2,850 | $2,350 | $1,900 | $1,600 | $1,350 | *$4,495* |

MSR	100%	98%	95%	90%	80%	70%	60%	Last MSR

ARMAMENT TECHNOLOGY CORP.

Previous manufacturer located in Las Vegas, NV between 1972 and 1978.

RIFLES: SEMI-AUTO

In addition to the models listed below, ATC also manufactured the "Firefly II", a select fire pistol.

M-2 FIREFLY – 9mm Para. cal., unique gas delayed blowback action, collapsible stock, very limited mfg., 4 3/4 lbs.

	100%	98%	95%	90%	80%	70%	60%
	$695	$625	$550	$475	$395	$350	$295

ARMITAGE INTERNATIONAL, LTD.

Previous manufacturer located in Seneca, SC until 1990.

PISTOLS: SEMI-AUTO

SCARAB SKORPION – 9mm Para. cal., design patterned after the Czech Model 61, blowback operation, SFO, 4.63 in. barrel, matte black finish, 12 shot (standard) or 32 shot (optional) mag., 3 1/2 lbs. Mfg. in U.S. 1989-1990 only.

	100%	98%	95%	90%	80%	70%	60%	Last MSR
	$695	$625	$550	$500	$425	$375	$325	$400

Add $45 for threaded flash hider or imitation suppressor.

Only 602 Scarab Skorpions were manufactured during 1989-1990.

ARMORY USA LLC

Previous manufacturer/importer until 2008, located in Houston, TX. Previous company name was Arsenal USA LLC.

RIFLES: SEMI-AUTO

Armory USA, LLC produced a variety of AK-47/AKM/AK-74 semi-auto rifles. Early rifles used Bulgarian milled receivers, later versions were built using sheet metal receivers made in Hungary by FEG.

During 2004, Armory USA began production of 1.6 mm thick U.S. made AK receivers, which were sold as both receivers and complete rifles. Production of 1 mm thick receivers began in Jan. 2005. Models not listed here may have been assembled by other manufacturers using these receivers. During 2004, Armory USA began assembling rifles at a new factory in Kazanlak, Bulgaria. Some components were made in the U.S., in compliance with the BATFE.

Please refer to the Arsenal USA listing for pre-2004 manufactured/imported rifles.

MODEL SSR-56-2 – 7.62x39mm cal., Armory USA made 1.6mm receiver wall thickness, Poly-Tec barrel assembly, Bulgarian internal parts. Approx. 400 mfg. during 2004.

	100%	98%	95%	90%	80%	70%	60%	Last MSR
	$750	$700	$675	$650	$600	$500	$475	$500

MODEL AMD-63-2 UP – 7.62x39mm cal., Armory USA made 1.6mm receiver wall thickness, Hungarian parts, underfolding buttstock. Approx. 125 mfg. 2004.

	100%	98%	95%	90%	80%	70%	60%	Last MSR
	$950	$900	$850	$800	$700	$650	$600	$600

Add $200 for milled receiver.

MODEL SSR-85C-2 – 7.62x39mm cal., assembled in Bulgaria, marked "ISD Ltd", blonde wood and black polymer furniture. Imported 2004-2006.

	100%	98%	95%	90%	80%	70%	60%	Last MSR
	$795	$750	$700	$650	$600	$525	$475	$550

Add $100 for side folding buttstock (Model SSR-85C-2 SF).

MODEL SSR-74-2 – 5.45x39mm cal., assembled in Bulgaria, marked "ISD Ltd", blonde wood and black polymer furniture. Imported 2005-2008.

	100%	98%	95%	90%	80%	70%	60%	Last MSR
	$775	$725	$695	$625	$600	$525	$475	$550

ARMS LLC

Current manufacturer located in Oregon since 2008.

PISTOLS: SEMI-AUTO

Arms LLC currently manufactures the ARMS-5 and ARMS-15 AR-15 style pistols. Each model is built to customer specifications. Please contact the company directly for more information including options, pricing, and availability (see Trademark Index).

RIFLES: SEMI-AUTO

Arms LLC currently manufactures the following AR-15 style models: ARMS-15 Classic, ARMS-15 Elite Custom, ARMS-15 Quadrail, ARMS-15 Long Range, ARMS-5 SBR, and the ARMS-5 rifle. Each model is built to customer specifications. Please contact the company directly for more information including options, pricing, and availability (see Trademark Index).

MSR	100%	98%	95%	90%	80%	70%	60%	*Last MSR*

ARMS RESEARCH ASSOCIATES

Previous manufacturer located in Stone Park, IL until 1991.

Arms Research Associates manufactured a KF-System Carbine that was select-fire NFA Class III only. Most NFA firearms are not included in this database.

CARBINES: SEMI-AUTO

KF SYSTEM – 9mm Para. cal., 18 1/2 in. barrel, vent. barrel shroud, 20 or 36 shot mag., matte black finish, 7 1/2 lbs., select-fire NFA class III transferable only.

	100%	98%	95%	90%	80%	70%	60%	Last MSR
	$395	$350	$300	$275	$250	$230	$210	*$379*

ARMS ROOM LLC

Current manufacturer of pistols and AR-15 style carbines/rifles located in Orlando, FL.

RIFLES: SEMI-AUTO

All rifles are 100% American made and include a custom presentation box, Mil-Spec cleaning kit, Magpul 30 shot mag., gun lock, operator's manual and a lifetime warranty.

MARK WALTERS SIGNATURE RIFLE – 5.56 NATO cal., mid-length gas system, 16 in. stainless steel barrel, GT Micro Predator flash hider, 30 shot PMAG, GT extended mag. release, stainless steel low profile gas block, integral trigger guard, MBUS Pro front and rear sights, Rogers Super-Stoc, MOE pistol grip, GT ambi selector, custom Mark Walters Edition laser engraving, GT Ultra slimline octagonal 5-sided KeyMod free floating handguard with monolithic top rail, Type III hardcoat anodized black finish.

	100%	98%	95%	90%	80%	70%	60%
MSR $1,495	$1,275	$1,125	$1,025	$875	$750	$625	$525

TAR-15 BOOT RIFLE PACKAGE – 5.56 NATO cal., carbine length GIO, 16 in. chrome moly barrel, M4 barrel profile, fixed front sight base, black anodized finish, A2 flash hider, double heat shield handguards, M16 bolt carrier group, flat-top upper with M4 cuts, Magpul Gen 2 rear flip up sight, Mil-Spec upper and lower parts, M4 stock and buffer tube.

	100%	98%	95%	90%	80%	70%	60%
MSR $895	$775	$685	$615	$550	$485	$415	$370

TAR-15 GRUNT RIFLE PACKAGE – 5.56 NATO cal., GIO, 16 in. chrome moly barrel, M4 barrel profile, fixed front sight base, black anodized finish, A2 flash hider, two-piece drop in quad rail, M16 bolt carrier group, flat-top upper with M4 cuts, Magpul Gen 2 rear flip up sight, Arms Room lower receiver, Mil-Spec upper and lower parts, Rogers Super-Stoc and buffer tube, Magpul MOE Plus grip.

	100%	98%	95%	90%	80%	70%	60%
MSR $1,035	$875	$740	$650	$585	$515	$450	$395

TAR-15 SAPPER RIFLE PACKAGE – 5.56 NATO cal., GIO, 16 in. chrome moly barrel, M4 barrel profile, Magpul MBUS folding front and rear sights, black anodized finish, Phantom flash hider, free float quad rail, M16 bolt carrier group, flat-top upper with M4 cuts, Arms Room lower receiver, Mil-Spec upper and lower parts, M4 stock and buffer tube, M4 grip, front sight adj. tool.

	100%	98%	95%	90%	80%	70%	60%
MSR $1,085	$900	$800	$685	$600	$535	$465	$415

TAR-15 SCOUT RIFLE PACKAGE – 5.56 NATO cal., GIO, 16 in. chrome moly barrel, M4 barrel profile, Magpul MBUS folding front and rear sights, black anodized finish, twisted Phantom flash hider, free float quad rail, M16 bolt carrier group, flat-top upper with M4 cuts, Arms Room lower receiver, Mil-Spec upper and lower parts, Rogers Super-Stoc and Mil-Spec buffer tube, Ergo or Magpul MOE grip, front sight adj. tool.

	100%	98%	95%	90%	80%	70%	60%
MSR $1,115	$925	$850	$725	$625	$550	$475	$425

ZMB-02 ZOMBIE KILLER CARBINE – 5.56 NATO cal., GIO, 16 in. chrome moly barrel, black and green two-tone finish, Phantom flash hider, OD or black quad rail, front and rear sights, pistol grip and magazine, M16 bolt carrier group, M4 cut, Mil-Spec upper and lower parts, Rogers Super-Stoc and Mil-Spec buffer tube, laser etched ejection port door, Zombie engraved logo with color fill, "LIVE - DEAD - UNDEAD" selector designations, includes soft case. Disc. 2014.

	100%	98%	95%	90%	80%	70%	60%	Last MSR
	$1,110	$995	$875	$735	$650	$550	$465	*$1,324*

PISTOLS: SEMI-AUTO

SPIKE'S TACTICAL PISTOL – .22 LR cal., GIO, SA, Mil-Spec parkerized finish, 16 in. barrel, chrome moly match grade air gauged Lothar Walther M4 upper, Arms Room or Spike's Tactical lower, receiver end cap, no rear sight or optional MBUS Magpul or Daniel Defense rear sight, heat treated bolt, M4 or Magpul AFG handguard w/Ergo bolt-on rail. Disc. 2014.

	100%	98%	95%	90%	80%	70%	60%	Last MSR
	$660	$580	$510	$440	$385	$340	$325	*$775*

Add $50 for MBUS Magpul or $60 for Daniel Defense rear sight.
Add $25 for Spike's Tactical lower.
Add $35 for Magpul AFG handguard.

TAR-15 ENTRY – 5.56 NATO cal., 7 1/2 in. threaded barrel, low profile gas block, solid tube handguard with textured grip knurling, three removable rails, M4 feed ramps, Type III hardcoat anodized black finish. New 2015.

	100%	98%	95%	90%	80%	70%	60%
MSR $699	$615	$540	$470	$400	$350	$310	$295

MSR	100%	98%	95%	90%	80%	70%	60%	Last MSR

TAR-15 STRYKER – 5.56 NATO cal., 7 1/2 in. threaded barrel, pistol length gas system, lightweight aluminum removable side and bottom rails, three section rails included, forged upper and lower receivers, M4 feed ramps, integrated enhanced trigger guard, milled mfg. engravings, Type III hardcoat anodized black finish. New 2015.

MSR $799	$685	$615	$550	$475	$420	$365	$335	

ARMS TECH LTD.

Previous manufacturer located in Phoenix, AZ, 1987-2012.

RIFLES: BOLT ACTION

SBA 2000 – 7.62x51 cal., Sako 75 action, 24 in. fixed barrel, suppressor ready, fully adj. stock, 12 lbs. Disc. 2012.
Retail pricing was not made available for this model.

SMIR (SUPER MATCH INTERDICTION RIFLE) – .300WM cal., 26 in. barrel, 13 3/4 lbs. Disc. 2012.
Last MSR in 2012 was $9,000.

TTR-50 (TACTICAL TAKEDOWN RIFLE) – .50 BMG cal., mission configurable heavy sniper rifle, comes standard with a MD50 B suppressor, OAL 59 3/8 in., 26 lbs. Disc. 2012.
Last MSR in 2012 was $9,000.

TTR-700 (TACTICAL TAKEDOWN RIFLE) – 7.62x51 cal., Rem. 700 bolt action, mission configurable sniper rifle, 17 or 24 in. barrel, includes soft "computer case" or optional Pelican hard case, 10.4 lbs. Disc. 2012.
Last MSR in 2012 was $4,500.

VOYAGER – takedown hunting rifle. Disc .2012.
Last MSR in 2012 was $3,000.

RIFLES: SEMI-AUTO

Previously, the company also offered the Urban Support Rifle for the civilian marketplace.

SUPER MATCH INTERDICTION POLICE MODEL – .243 Win., .300 Win. Mag., or .308 Win. (standard) cal., AR-15 style, GIO, features 22 in. free floating Schnieder or Douglas air gauged stainless steel barrel, McMillan stock, updated trigger group, detachable box mag., 13 1/4 lbs. Limited mfg. 1996-98.

	$3,950	$3,650	$3,300	$3,000	$2,750	$2,350	$2,000	$4,800

SHOTGUNS: SLIDE ACTION

ALPHA ENTRY – 12 ga., utilizes Rem. 870 action, 17 in. barrel, folding stock, 8 lbs. Disc. 2012.
Retail pricing was not made available for this model.

ARMSCOR

Current trademark of firearms manufactured by Arms Corporation of the Philippines (manufacturing began 1952) established in 1985 (Armscor Precision - API). The Armscor trademark is not being imported into the U.S. currently, but still exists in some foreign marketplaces. Previously imported and distributed 1999-2014 by Armscor Precision International (full line), located in Pahrump, NV. Previously imported 1995-1999 by K.B.I., Inc. located in Harrisburg, PA, by Ruko located in Buffalo, NY until 1995 and by Armscorp Precision Inc. located in San Mateo, CA until 1991.

In 1991, the importation of Arms Corporation of the Philippines firearms was changed to Ruko Products, Inc., located in Buffalo, NY. Barrel markings on firearms imported by Ruko Products, Inc. state "Ruko-Armscor" instead of the older "Armscorp Precision" barrel markings. All Armscorp Precision, Inc. models were discontinued in 1991.

The models listed also provide cross-referencing for older Armscorp Precision and Ruko imported models.

PISTOLS: SEMI-AUTO

All semi-auto pistols were discontinued during 2008, and currently Armscor manufactured pistols can be found under the Rock Island Armory trademark.

M-1911-A1 FS (FULL SIZE STANDARD) – .45 ACP cal., patterned after the Colt Govt. Model, SA, 7 shot mag. (2 provided), 5 in. barrel, parkerized (disc. 2001), blue (new 2002), two-tone (new 2002), or stainless steel (new 2002), skeletonized combat hammer and trigger, front and rear slide serrations, hard rubber grips, 38 oz. Imported 1996-97, reintroduced 2001-2008.

	$350	$300	$280	$260	$240	$220	$200	$399

Add $31 for two-tone finish.
Add $75 for stainless steel.

This model was also available in a high capacity configuration (Model 1911-A2 HC, 13 shot mag., $519 last MSR).

MSR	100%	98%	95%	90%	80%	70%	60%	Last MSR

M-1911-A1 MS (COMMANDER) – .45 ACP cal., SA, Commander configuration with 4 in. barrel, otherwise similar to M-1911 A1 Standard, rear slide serrations only. Imported 2001-2008.

| | $360 | $300 | $280 | $260 | $240 | $220 | $200 | $408 |

Add $37 for two-tone finish.
Add $90 for stainless steel.

M-1911-A1 CS (OFFICER) – .45 ACP cal., SA, officer's configuration with 3 1/2 in. barrel, checkered hardwood grips, 2.16 lbs. Imported 2002-2008.

| | $370 | $310 | $285 | $265 | $245 | $220 | $200 | $423 |

Add $52 for two-tone finish.
Add $105 for stainless steel.

M-1911-A1 MEDALLION SERIES – 9mm Para., .40 S&W, or .45 ACP cal., 5 in. barrel, SA, customized model including many shooting enhancements, match barrel, hand fitted slide and frame, choice of checkered wood or Pachmayr grips, available in either Standard or Tactical variation, blue, two-tone or chrome finish. Imported 2002-2008.

| | $445 | $350 | $310 | $285 | $260 | $240 | $220 | $539 |

Add $129 for Tactical Model, add $198 for Tactical Model two-tone, or $203 for Tactical Model chrome.

RIFLES: SEMI-AUTO

M-1600 – .22 LR cal., GIO, 10 or 15 (disc.) shot mag., 18 in. barrel, copy of the Armalite M16, ebony stock, 5 1/4 lbs. Importation disc. 2014.

| | $180 | $150 | $130 | $110 | $100 | $80 | $70 | |

* **M-1600R** – similar to M-1600, except has stainless steel retractable buttstock and vent. barrel hood, 7 1/4 lbs. Importation disc. 1995, reintroduced 2008-2011.

| | $155 | $135 | $115 | $105 | $85 | $70 | $55 | |

M-AK22(S) – .22 LR cal., copy of the famous Russian Kalashnikov AK-47 rifle, 18 1/2 in. barrel, 10 or 15 (disc.) shot mag., mahogany stock and forearm, 7 lbs. Importation disc. 2014.

| | $185 | $160 | $140 | $125 | $100 | $85 | $65 | |

* **M-AK22(F)** – similar to M-AK22, except has metal folding stock, and 30 shot mag. Disc. 1995.

| | $275 | $240 | $205 | $185 | $150 | $125 | $95 | $299 |

MIG 22 STANDARD – .22 LR cal., GIO, 18 in. barrel, blowback action, 15 shot detachable box mag., matte black finish, fixed synthetic stock, top Picatinny rail. Imported mid-2012-2014.
Retail pricing was never established for this model.

MIG 22 TARGET – .22 LR cal., GIO, 18 in. heavy barrel, blowback action, 15 shot detachable box mag., matte black finish, skeletonized aluminum stock, top Picatinny rail, 8 lbs. Imported mid-2012-2014.
Retail pricing was never established for this model.

SHOTGUNS: SLIDE ACTION

M-30 DG (DEER GUN) – 12 ga. only, law enforcement version of M-30, 20 in. plain barrel, iron sights, 7 shot mag., approx. 7 lbs. Importation disc. 1999, resumed during 2001.

| | $165 | $140 | $120 | $100 | $85 | $75 | $70 | $195 |

M-30SAS1 – 12 ga. only, riot configuration with 20 in. barrel and vent. barrel shroud, and Speedfeed 4 shot (disc.) or 6 shot mag., regular synthetic buttstock and forearm, matte finish, 8 lbs. Imported 1996-1999 and 2001-2008.

| | $180 | $155 | $130 | $110 | $95 | $85 | $75 | $211 |

Add $56 for Speedfeed stock (new 2002).

M-30 R6/R8 (RIOT) – 12 ga. only, similar to M-30DG, except has front bead sight only, 5 or 7 shot mag., cyl. bore. Importation disc. 1999, reintroduced 2001-2008.

| | $155 | $135 | $110 | $90 | $80 | $75 | $70 | $181 |

Add $7 for 7 shot mag.

M-30BG – 12 ga. only, 18 1/2 in. barrel, 5 shot mag., polymer pistol grip and forearm. New 2004.
This model is currently not being imported into the United States.

M-30F/FS – similar to M-30BG, except has additional folding metal stock unit. Disc. 2008.

| | $180 | $155 | $130 | $110 | $95 | $85 | $75 | $211 |

M30 C (COMBO) – 12 ga., 20 in. barrel, 5 shot mag., unique detachable black synthetic buttstock which allows pistol grip only operation. Disc. 1995.

| | $210 | $175 | $145 | $120 | $100 | $90 | $80 | $289 |

MSR	100%	98%	95%	90%	80%	70%	60%	Last MSR

M30 RP (COMBO) – 12 ga. only, same action as M-30 DG, interchangeable black pistol grip, 18 1/4 in. plain barrel w/front bead sight, 6 1/4 lbs. Disc. 1995.

	$210	$175	$145	$120	$100	$90	$80	$289

ARMSCORP USA, INC.

Previous manufacturer and importer located in Baltimore, MD. Currently Armscorp USA deals in parts only.

PISTOLS: SEMI-AUTO

HI POWER – 9mm Para. cal., patterned after Browning design, 4 2/3 in. barrel, DA/SA, military finish, 13 shot mag., synthetic checkered grips, spur hammer, 2 lbs. mfg. in Argentina, imported 1989-90 only.

	$395	$350	$295	$275	$250	$225	$200	$450

Add $15 for round hammer.
Add $50 for hard chrome finish w/combat grips (disc. 1989).

RIFLES: SEMI-AUTO

M-14 RIFLE (NORINCO PARTS) – .308 Win. cal., 20 shot mag., mfg. M-14 using Norinco parts, wood stock. Mfg. 1991-92 only.

	$1,225	$1,150	$1,050	$975	$875	$775	$675	$688

M-14R RIFLE (USGI PARTS) – .308 Win. cal., 10 (C/B 1994) or 20* shot mag., newly manufactured M-14 using original excellent condition forged G.I. parts including USGI fiberglass stock with rubber recoil pad. Mfg. 1986-2006.

	$1,925	$1,675	$1,400	$1,275	$1,125	$1,000	$850	$1,895

Add $80 for medium weight National Match walnut stock (M-14RNS).
Add $25 for G.I. buttplate (disc.).
Add $45 for USGI birch stock (M-14RNSB, disc.).

M-14 BEGINNING NATIONAL MATCH – .308 Win. cal., mfg. from hand selected older USGI parts, except for new receiver and new USGI air gauged premium barrel, guaranteed to shoot 1 1/4 in. group at 100 yards. Mfg. 1993-96.

	$2,050	$1,650	$1,350	$1,225	$1,125	$1,025	$925	$1,950

M-14 NMR (NATIONAL MATCH) – .308 Win. cal., built in accordance with USAMU Mil-Spec standards, 3 different barrel weights to choose from, NM rear sight system, calibrated mag., leather sling, guaranteed 1 MOA. Mfg. 1987-2006.

	$2,675	$2,125	$1,750	$1,400	$1,200	$1,075	$950	$2,850

M-21 MATCH RIFLE – .308 Win. cal., NM rear lugged receiver, choice of McMillan fiberglass or laminated wood stock, guaranteed 1 MOA accuracy.

	$3,475	$2,900	$2,325	$2,000	$1,650	$1,350	$1,175	$3,595

T-48 FAL ISRAELI PATTERN RIFLE – .308 Win. cal., mfg. in the U.S. to precise original metric dimensions (parts are interchangeable with original Belgium FAL), forged receiver, hammer forged chrome lined Mil-Spec. 21 in. barrel (standard or heavy) with flash suppressor, adj. front sight, aperture rear sight, 10 lbs. Imported 1990-92.

	$1,650	$1,475	$1,300	$1,150	$1,075	$975	$875	$1,244

This model was guaranteed to shoot within 2.5 MOA with match ammunition.

* **T-48 FAL L1A1 Pattern** – .308 Win. cal., fully enclosed forend with vents, 10 lbs. Imported 1992 only.

	$1,675	$1,500	$1,325	$1,175	$1,100	$1,000	$900	$1,181

Add $122 for wood handguard sporter model (limited supply).

* **T-48 Bush Model** – similar to T-48 FAL, except has 18 in. barrel, 9 3/4 lbs. Mfg. 1990 only.

	$1,625	$1,450	$1,325	$1,175	$1,025	$925	$850	$1,250

FRHB – .308 Win. cal., Israeli mfg. with heavy barrel and bipod. Imported 1990 only.

	$2,175	$1,900	$1,600	$1,425	$1,325	$1,225	$1,175	$1,895

FAL – .308 Win. cal., Armscorp forged receiver, 21 in. Argentinian rebuilt barrel, manufactured to military specs., supplied with one military 20 shot mag., aperture rear sight, 10 lbs. Mfg. 1987-89.

	$1,800	$1,575	$1,425	$1,250	$1,125	$1,025	$925	$875

Subtract $55 if without flash hider.
Add $75 for heavy barrel with bipod (14 lbs.).
Add $400 (last retail) for .22 LR conversion kit.

This model was guaranteed to shoot within 2.5 MOA with match ammunition.

* **FAL Bush Model** – similar to FAL, except has 18 in. barrel with flash suppressor, 9 3/4 lbs. Mfg. 1989 only.

	$2,200	$2,050	$1,925	$1,825	$1,750	$1,500	$1,250	$900

MSR	100%	98%	95%	90%	80%	70%	60%	Last MSR

* **FAL Para Model** – similar to FAL Bush Model, except has metal folding stock, leaf rear sight. Mfg. 1989 only.

| | $2,400 | $2,150 | $1,050 | $1,950 | $1,750 | $1,650 | $1,550 | $930 |

* **FAL Factory Rebuilt** – factory (Argentine) rebuilt FAL without flash suppressor in excellent condition with Armscorp forged receiver, 9 lbs. 10 oz. Disc. 1989.

| | $1,675 | $1,450 | $1,195 | $1,025 | $950 | $775 | $695 | $675 |

Add 20% for heavy barrel variation manufactured in Argentina under license from F.N.

M36 ISRAELI SNIPER RIFLE – .308 Win. cal., gas operated semi-auto, bullpup configuration, 22 in. free floating barrel, Armscorp M14 receiver, 20 shot mag., includes flash suppressor and bipod, 10 lbs. Civilian offering 1989 only.

| | $3,050 | $2,650 | $2,425 | $2,200 | $2,050 | $1,925 | $1,750 | $3,000 |

ARSENAL FIREARMS

Current pistol manufacturer located in Gardone, Italy. Currently imported beginning late 2013 by EAA Corp., located in Rockledge, FL. Previously distributed by Apex International, located in Middletown, CT.

PISTOLS: SEMI-AUTO

AF2011-DOUBLE BARREL PISTOL – .38 Super or .45 ACP cal., unique design allows side by side 4.92 in. barrels, double hammer with single spur, double independent or single trigger uses two single 8 shot magazines paired together with single floorplate, choice of blue steel with walnut grips and fixed sights, or stainless steel with rubber grips and adj. sights, approx. 51 oz. New 2012.

| MSR $4,400 | $3,995 | $3,550 | $3,100 | $2,750 | $2,300 | $2,100 | $1,950 | |

Add $700 for stainless steel construction with rubber grips and adj. sights.

STRIKE ONE – 9mm Para. or .40 S&W cal., 5 in. barrel, 17 shot mag., matte black finish, lower accessory rail, fully guided, non-tilting barrel locking system, beveled magwell, ambidextrous mag. release and safety, short travel trigger, polymer or aluminum frame, approx. 27 oz. New 2013.

| MSR $800 | $695 | $625 | $525 | $475 | $400 | $350 | $295 | |

Add $2,600 for aluminum frame.

ARSENAL INC.

Current importer of non-military Arsenal 2000 JSCo (Bulgarian Arsenal), established during 2001, located in Las Vegas, NV. Dealer and distributor sales.

PISTOLS: SEMI-AUTO

SAM7K – 7.62x39mm cal., GPO, 10 1/2 in. chrome lined cold hammer forged barrel, SA, milled receiver, short gas system, front sight block/gas block combination, 5 shot mag., black polymer furniture, original pistol grip with ambidextrous safety lever, aperture rear sight, AK scope rail, includes sling and cleaning kit. Importation beginning 2013.

| MSR $1,199 | $1,025 | $925 | $800 | $685 | $595 | $515 | $440 | |

Add $70 for quad Picatanny rail.
Add $300 for integrated tactical light.
Add $100 for Sig Sauer SB15 pistol stabilizing brace.

SLR-106U/UR – 5.56 NATO cal., GIO, 10 1/2 in. chrome lined hammer forged barrel, SA, front sight block, gas block combination, faux flash hider, 5 shot mag., stamped receiver, black polymer furniture, includes sling and cleaning kit, 5 1/2 lbs. Imported beginning 2013.

| MSR $1,025 | $860 | $725 | $650 | $585 | $515 | $450 | $395 | |

Add $44 for quad Picatanny rail.
Add $74 for Sig Sauer SB15 pistol stabilizing brace.

RIFLES: SEMI-AUTO

Arsenal Inc. is the exclusive licensed manufacturer of various Arsenal Bulgaria AK-47 design rifles which conform 100% to Arsenal Bulgaria specifications and manufacturing procedures. Models are built on forged and milled receivers with CNC technology, and feature solid, under-folding or side-folding stock.

Additionally, Arsenal Inc. has also imported AK-47 design configurations with a thumbhole stock design (pre-2004). Values for these earlier models will be slightly less than current models with fixed or collapsible stocks.

SAM-5 SERIES – .223 Rem. cal., patterned after the AK-47, 16.3 in. barrel, black (SA M-5) or green (SA M-5G, disc. 2005) synthetic furniture with pistol grip, approx. 8.1 lbs. Mfg. 2003-2009.

| | $710 | $620 | $530 | $480 | $390 | $320 | $250 | $800 |

Add $75 for SA M-5 R with scope rail (new 2007).
Add $10 for SA M-5G (disc. 2005).
Add $75 for SA M-5S with scope rail (limited edition, disc. 2005).
Add $80 for SA M-5SG (disc. 2005).

MSR	100%	98%	95%	90%	80%	70%	60%	Last MSR

SAM-7 S – 7.62x39mm cal., milled receiver, also available in carbine, otherwise similar to SA M-5, R Series with scope rail became standard 2009. Mfg. 2003-2011.

	$1,395	$1,295	$1,050	$850	$750	$650	$550	$1,550

Add $35 for SA M-7S with scope rail (disc.).
Add $5 for SA M-7G with OD green furniture (disc.)
Add $40 for SA M-7SG with scope rail (disc.)
Subtract approx. 15% if w/o scope rail (disc.)

SAM-7 CLASSIC – 7.62x39mm cal., features blonde wood stock, pistol grip and forearm, double stack magazine, heavy barrel and slanted gas block, Warsaw Pact buttstock, less than 200 mfg. 2001-circa 2008.

	$1,750	$1,500	$1,250	$1,125	$900	$775	$650	$1,995

SAM-7 A1/SAM-7 A1 R – 7.62x39mm cal., milled receiver, front sight gas block w/bayonet lug, 24mm flash hider, cleaning rod, accessory lug, black polymer furniture, NATO buttstock. Mfg. 2007-2009.

	$850	$745	$635	$580	$465	$380	$295	$960

Add $75 for SAM-7 A1 R w/scope rail.

SAM-7 R – 7.62x39mm cal., Bulgarian hammer forged receiver and 16.3 in. barrel with 14mm muzzle threads, U.S. made trigger group, cleaning rod, bayonet lug, black polymer furniture, AK scope rail. New 2012.

MSR $1,299	$1,100	$995	$875	$735	$650	$550	$465	

Add $50 for quad Picatinny rail.

SAM-7 R LAS VEGAS RIFLE – 7.62x39mm cal., 16.3 in. chrome lined hammer forged barrel, removable 4-port muzzle brake, 10 shot mag., cleaning rod, bayonet lug, milled and forged receiver, features Arsenal Las Vegas silver color medallion embedded in the stock, black polymer furniture, intermediate length trapdoor buttstock, AK scope rail.

MSR $1,349	$1,135	$1,015	$885	$740	$675	$575	$475	

$100 from sales of each unit of these rifles will be donated to the Las Vegas area council of Boy Scouts of America.

SAM-7 SF – 7.62x39mm cal., Bulgarian hammer forged receiver and 16.3 in. barrel, front sight gas block with bayonet lug, 24mm flash hider, cleaning rod, accessory lug, black polymer furniture, right hand side folding stock, ambidextrous safety, scope rail. Mfg. 2007-2009, reintroduced 2013.

MSR $1,449	$1,235	$1,100	$985	$835	$725	$615	$515	

Add $50 for quad rail.

SAM-7 SFC/SAM-7 SFK – 7.62x39mm cal., U.S. mfg., milled receiver, front sight/gas block combination with 24mm thread protector, cleaning rod, black polymer furniture, right hand side folding tubular buttstock, ambidextrous safety, scope rail, SAM-7 SFK model with short gas system and laminated wood Krinkov handguards became standard 2009. Mfg. 2007-2011, limited production SFK SBR model 2013-14.

	$2,725	$2,395	$2,050	$1,850	$1,500	$1,225	$950	$3,200

SAM-7 UF – 7.62x39mm cal., Bulgarian hammer forged receiver and 16.3 in. barrel with removable 14mm muzzle nut, milled receiver, front sight gas block with bayonet lug, cleaning rod, accessory lug, black polymer furniture, under-folding stock, ambidextrous safety. Importation beginning 2014.

MSR $1,299	$1,100	$995	$875	$735	$650	$550	$465	

SA RPK-3R – 5.45x39mm, milled receiver, RPK heavy barrel, removable flash hider, folding bipod, blonde wood furniture or black polymer, paddle style buttstock, scope rail, one 45 shot mag., sling, oil bottle, and cleaning kit. Mfg. 2011, reintroduced 2015.

MSR $2,750	$2,325	$2,225	$1,675	$1,450	$1,175	$1,015	$885	

SA RPK-5 (S) – .223 Rem. cal., features blonde wood stock, RPK heavy barrel, 14mm muzzle threads, pistol grip and forearm, 23 1/4 in. barrel with folding tripod, approx. 11 lbs. RPK-5 R Model has scope rail. Limited edition 2003-2014.

	$2,125	$1,875	$1,595	$1,450	$1,175	$950	$750	$2,500

SA RPK-7 – 7.62x39mm cal., paddle style buttstock, folding bipod, no scope rail, otherwise similar to SA RPK-5 (S). Limited edition 2003-2005, reintroduced 2007-2009.

	$995	$870	$745	$675	$545	$450	$350	$1,250

Add $75 for SA RPK-7 R with scope rail.

SA M-7 CLASSIC – 7.62x39mm cal., chrome lined hammer forged heavy barrel, muzzle nut, 30 shot mag., slanted gas block, milled receiver, cleaning rod, bayonet lug, blonde wood furniture, Warsaw Pact buttstock, U.S. mfg.

MSR $1,995	$1,700	$1,500	$1,250	$1,100	$950	$825	$675	

SAS M-7 – 7.62x39mm cal., U.S. mfg., authentic semi-auto version of Bulgarian model AR M1F with vertical gas block and BATFE-approved fixed metal underfolding-style stock. Mfg. 2004-2007.

	$1,075	$940	$800	$730	$590	$485	$375	$1,250

MSR	100%	98%	95%	90%	80%	70%	60%	Last MSR

SAS M-7 CLASSIC – 7.62x39mm cal., U.S. mfg., authentic semi-auto version of Russian 1953 Model AKS-47 with slant gas block and BATFE-approved fixed metal underfolding-style stock, blonde furniture, heavy barrel. Limited edition 2001-circa 2014.

	100%	98%	95%	90%	80%	70%	60%	Last MSR
	$1,750	$1,500	$1,250	$1,125	$900	$775	$650	*$1,995*

SLR 101 S – 7.62x39mm cal., similar to SA M-7, except has thumbhole synthetic stock, available in black (SLR 101SB1) or OD Green (SLR 101SG1). Mfg. 2003-2005.

	100%	98%	95%	90%	80%	70%	60%	Last MSR
	$595	$550	$500	$450	$400	$350	$325	*$410*

Add $100 for SLR 101SB1.
Add $110 for SLR 101SG1.

* **SLR-101S (Recent Importation)** – 7.62x39mm cal., 16 1/4 in. chrome lined hammer forged barrel, milled receiver, 14mm muzzle threads, muzzle brake, cleaning rod, black polymer furniture, intermediate length buttstock, scope rail, 10 shot mag., includes sling and cleaning kit. Imported 2013.

	100%	98%	95%	90%	80%	70%	60%	Last MSR
	$875	$775	$650	$595	$475	$395	$300	*$1,019*

SLR 101SB/SG – 7.62x39mm cal., double stack mag., side mount scope rail, 16 in. barrel, standard military stock configuration. Mfg. 2004-2005.

	100%	98%	95%	90%	80%	70%	60%	Last MSR
	$725	$650	$600	$550	$475	$425	$350	*$655*

Add $45 for SG Model with green polymer stock.

SLR-104 SERIES – 5.45x39mm cal., stamped receiver, 16 1/4 in. chrome lined hammer forged barrel with removable muzzle brake, bayonet lug, accessory lug, black left-side folding stock, stainless steel heat shield, scope rail, 30 shot mag., two-stage trigger. Importation began late 2013.

MSR	100%	98%	95%	90%	80%	70%	60%	Last MSR
$1,099	$925	$850	$725	$625	$550	$475	$425	

Add $80 for quad Picatinny rail.
Add $200 for SLR-104 UR model with front sight block and gas block combination.
Add $200 for short gas-block system and side scope rail (disc. 2015).
Add $320 for skeletonized folding buttstock with short gas-block system and side scope rail (disc. 2015).

SLR-105 SERIES – 5.45x39.5mm cal., stamped receiver, cleaning rod, black polymer furniture, NATO buttstock. Mfg. 2007-2009.

	100%	98%	95%	90%	80%	70%	60%	Last MSR
	$695	$650	$600	$550	$475	$425	$350	*$475*

Add $50 for SLR-105 R with scope rail.
Add $150 for SLR-105 A1 model with front sight gas block, bayonet lug, and 24mm muzzle brake.
Add $200 for SLR-105 A1 R model with scope rail.

SLR-106 SERIES – 5.56 NATO cal., Bulgarian stamped receiver, 16.3 in. barrel with 24mm muzzle brake, left-side wire (disc. 2011) or solid black polymer (new 2012) folding stock, gas block with bayonet lug, accessory lug (optional), stainless steel heat shield, two-stage trigger, Black or Desert Sand (disc.) furniture. Imported 2007-2015.

	100%	98%	95%	90%	80%	70%	60%	Last MSR
	$885	$785	$685	$600	$535	$465	$415	*$1,049*

Add $50 for side scope rail (current).
Add $30 for Desert Sand finish and side scope rail (disc.).
Add $50 for SLR-106 CR with front sight and gas block combined (new 2012).
Add $50 for SLR-106 FR with scope and forend rails.
Subtract approx. $250 if with wire folding stock (disc. 2011).
Add $205 for SLR-106 UR Model with scope rail.
Add $90 for SLR-106 U Model with combination short-stroke gas block and front sight system and black furniture (current).
Add $179 for SLR-106 Model with removable muzzle attachment (disc.).

The SLR-106 UR Model is also available as a short barreled rifle.

SLR-107 SERIES – 7.62x39mm cal., Bulgarian stamped receiver, 16.3 in. barrel with 24mm removable muzzle brake, left-side wire (disc. 2011) folding solid polymer (new 2012) stock, gas block with bayonet lug, accessory lug, side mounted accessory rail, stainless steel heat shield, two-stage trigger, black, plum (new 2014) or Desert Sand/Tan finish. New 2008.

MSR	100%	98%	95%	90%	80%	70%	60%	Last MSR
$999	$850	$725	$650	$585	$515	$450	$395	

Add $150 for quad rail.
Add $20 for plum or Desert Sand/Tan finish.
Subtract $149 for left-side folding stock (Model SLR-107F).
Subtract $149 for SLR-107 FR Model with scope rail (disc.).
Subtract $149 for SLR-107 UR Model with combination short-stroke gas block and front sight system and black furniture and scope rail.

The SLR-107 UR Model is also available as a short barreled rifle.

MSR	100%	98%	95%	90%	80%	70%	60%	Last MSR

ARSENAL JSCOMPANY (ARSENAL BULGARIA)

Current manufacturer located in Kazanlack, Bulgaria. Currently imported by Arsenal, Inc., located in Las Vegas, NV. Previously imported exclusively in 1994-1996 by Sentinel Arms located in Detroit, MI. For currently imported models, please refer to the Arsenal, Inc. listing.

The artillery arsenal in Rousse began operating in 1878, and was managed by Russian officers until 1884, when a Bulgarian was appointed the director. In 1891, the factory was transferred to Sofia, and was renamed the Sofia Artillery Arsenal until the entire facility was moved to Kazanlak in 1924. At that point, the name was changed to the State Military Factory. After WWII, the arsenal diversified into civilian production, and its Cold War security name was "Factory 10". In 1958, the first AK-47 design under Russian license came off the assembly line, and in 1982, the one millionth AK-47 had been manufactured.

PISTOLS: SEMI-AUTO

MAKAROV MODEL – 9mm Makarov cal., 3 2/3 in. barrel, 8 shot mag., black synthetic grips, blue finish. Disc. 1996.

	100%	98%	95%	90%	80%	70%	60%
	$185	$165	$125	$115	$105	$95	$85

RIFLES: SEMI-AUTO

BULGARIAN SA-93 – 7.62x39mm cal., Kalashnikov with hardwood thumbhole stock, 16.3 in. barrel, 5 shot detachable mag., 9 lbs. Disc. 1996.

	100%	98%	95%	90%	80%	70%	60%
	$800	$715	$625	$550	$600	$475	$450

* Bulgarian SA-93L – 7.62x39mm cal., similar to Bulgarian SA-93 except has 20 in. barrel, with or without optics, 9 lbs. Disc. 1996.

	100%	98%	95%	90%	80%	70%	60%
	$795	$725	$650	$595	$550	$495	$450

Add $145 with optics.

BULGARIAN SS-94 – 7.62x39mm cal., Kalashnikov action, thumbhole hardwood stock, 5 shot detachable mag., 9 lbs. Disc. 1996.

	100%	98%	95%	90%	80%	70%	60%
	$625	$550	$475	$425	$375	$350	$325

ARSENAL USA LLC

Previous manufacturer/importer from 1999-2004, located in Houston, TX. During September 2004, Arsenal USA LLC changed its name to Armory USA LLC. Please refer to the Armory USA LLC listing for recently manufactured rifles.

RIFLES: SEMI-AUTO

MODEL SSR-99 – 7.62x39mm cal., Bulgarian milled receiver and parts, black polymer furniture. Less than 300 mfg. 1999-2000.

	100%	98%	95%	90%	80%	70%	60%	Last MSR
	$825	$750	$700	$650	$600	$550	$500	*$600*

MODEL K-101 – .223 Rem. cal., Bulgarian milled receiver and parts, black polymer furniture. Less than 200 mfg. 1999-2000.

	100%	98%	95%	90%	80%	70%	60%	Last MSR
	$875	$775	$700	$650	$600	$550	$500	*$600*

MODEL SSR-99P – 7.62x39mm cal., Bulgarian milled receiver and parts, with rare Polish grenade launching variant parts, Polish wood furniture. Less than 500 mfg. 1999-2001.

	100%	98%	95%	90%	80%	70%	60%	Last MSR
	$875	$775	$700	$650	$600	$550	$500	*$600*

MODEL SSR-85B – 7.62x39mm cal., Hungarian FEG receiver and Polish AKM parts, blonde Hungarian wood furniture, small number produced using ITM U.S. made receiver. Approx. 1,200 mfg. 2000-2003.

	100%	98%	95%	90%	80%	70%	60%	Last MSR
	$875	$775	$700	$650	$600	$550	$625	*$450*

MODEL AMD-63 – 7.62x39mm cal., Hungarian FEG receiver and Polish AKM parts, unique metal lower handguard with pistol grip. 200 mfg. 2000-2003.

	100%	98%	95%	90%	80%	70%	60%	Last MSR
	$875	$775	$700	$650	$600	$550	$500	*$600*

MODEL SSR-56 – 7.62x39mm cal., Hungarian FEG receiver, Poly-Tec barrel assembly and Bulgarian internal parts. Approx. 500 mfg. 2002-2003.

	100%	98%	95%	90%	80%	70%	60%	Last MSR
	$775	$700	$650	$600	$550	$500	$450	*$450*

ASHBURY PRECISION ORDNANCE

Current manufacturer established in 1995, located in Charlottesville, VA. APO is a division of the Ashbury International Group, Inc. Consumer direct sales.

MSR	100%	98%	95%	90%	80%	70%	60%	Last MSR

RIFLES: BOLT ACTION

Ashbury Precision Ordnance (APO) makes a high quality line of precision tactical rifles called the Asymmetric Warrior Series (ASW) and a Tactical Competition Rifle Series (TCR). During 2014, APO also released a SuperSport precision rifle available in .338 Lapua Mag., .300 Win. Mag., or 6.5 Creedmoor cal. Prices on this model are POR. Specifications, features, and options vary from model to model, so please contact the manufacturer directly for more information and current availability (see Trademark Index).

ASW50 – .50 BMG cal., McMillan bolt action repeater, Pinnacle Series 27 (disc.) or 29 in. fluted contour barrel with muzzle brake, target crown, ambidextrous paddle lever magazine release, 5 shot detachable box mag., Huber Tactical two stage trigger, Quattro carbon fiber heat/Mirage Mitigating Ergonomic forend, continuous full-length Mil-Std 1913 rail, fully adj. PBA-H shoulder stock, Limbsaver recoil pad, Magpul M1AD grip set, Picatinny bottom accessory rail, black, Flat Dark Earth, OD Green, or Nordic Gray finish, 25 3/4 lbs.

	100%	98%	95%	90%	80%	70%	60%
MSR $12,575	$11,250	$10,000	$9,200	$8,000	$6,750	$5,500	$4,500

ASW338LM – .338 Lapua Mag. cal., Surgeon XL-II bolt action repeater, similar to ASW50 except has Pinnacle Series 20 or 27 in. fluted stainless steel barrel, target crown with AAC Blackout muzzle brake, and 10 shot double stack mag., 15-17 lbs.

	100%	98%	95%	90%	80%	70%	60%
MSR $8,550	$7,850	$7,100	$6,400	$5,500	$4,600	$3,700	$2,850

Add $200 for 10 shot mag.

ASW300 – .300 Win. Mag. cal., Surgeon XL-II bolt action receiver, Pinnacle Series 20 or 24 (disc.) in. fluted stainless steel barrel with AAC Blackout muzzle brake, target crown, ambidextrous paddle lever magazine release, 5 shot single stack mag., two-stage trigger, Quattro carbon fiber heat/Mirage Mitigating Ergonomic forend, continuous full-length Mil-Std 1913 rail, fully adj. PBA-H shoulder stock, Limbsaver recoil pad, Magpul M1AD grip, black, Flat Dark Earth, OD Green, or Nordic Gray finish, 13 lbs.

	100%	98%	95%	90%	80%	70%	60%
MSR $8,500	$7,825	$7,100	$6,400	$5,500	$4,600	$3,700	$2,850

ASW308 – .308 Win. Mag. cal., similar to ASW300, except has Surgeon 591-11 bolt action receiver, 20 in. fluted stainless steel barrel, 5 or 10 shot detachable box mag., and is available in A3 configuration, approx. 12 1/2 lbs.

	100%	98%	95%	90%	80%	70%	60%
MSR $7,700	$7,000	$6,200	$5,500	$4,700	$4,000	$3,250	$2,550

ASW 6.5 CM – 6.5 Creedmoor cal., otherwise similar to ASW308. Mfg. mid-2014-2015.

	100%	98%	95%	90%	80%	70%	60%	Last MSR
	$7,000	$6,200	$5,500	$4,700	$4,000	$3,250	$2,550	$7,700

ASW223 – .223 Rem. cal., 10 shot double stack mag., otherwise similar to ASW308. New 2012.

	100%	98%	95%	90%	80%	70%	60%
MSR $7,700	$7,000	$6,200	$5,500	$4,700	$4,000	$3,250	$2,550

MODULAR SPORT HUNTER (MSH) – .22-250 Rem., 6.5 Creedmoor, .308 Win., or .300 WSM cal., Saber SX, LX, or EX bolt action receiver, 16, 20, or 24 in. fluted stainless steel button rifled barrel, alloy construction, 5 shot mag., single stage trigger, fixed HTA ergonomically adj. shoulder stock, Sporter forend with dual sling studs, Ergo Slimline grip, Black Cerakote finish. New 2015.

Please contact the company directly for more information including price, options, and availability (see Trademark Index).

SABER PRECISION RIFLE (SPR) – .223 Rem., .308 Win., or .300 AAC Blackout cal., Saber SX bolt action receiver, Pinnacle Series 16 1/2 or 20 in. fluted stainless steel button rifled barrel, 5 shot mag., SABER-FORSST Modular Rifle Chassis System (MRCS), alloy construction, one-piece monolithic top rail, single stage trigger, Quattro Alloy Series V17 Mod-1 forend, 12 in. accessory rail mounts, tactical adj. shoulder stock, Ergo Slimline grip, choice of Cerakote color finish. New 2015.

Please contact the company directly for more information including price, options, and availability (see Trademark Index).

SUPERSPORT .375CT-XLR – .375 CheyTac cal., 28 in. match grade stainless steel barrel, 7 shot detachable box mag., Arclight muzzle brake, 40-MOA monolithic rail, two-stage trigger, Desert Tan finish, ergonomic adj. folding stock, pistol grip, oversized bolt handle, 22 lbs., 8 oz. New 2013.

	100%	98%	95%	90%	80%	70%	60%
MSR $7,425	$6,800	$5,850	$5,100	$4,300	$3,550	$2,900	$2,350

TCR338 – .338 Norma Mag. cal., Surgeon bolt action receiver, Pinnacle Series 27 in. fluted stainless steel barrel with FTE muzzle brake, ambidextrous paddle lever magazine release, 5 shot detachable box mag., two-stage trigger, integral scope rail, Quattro carbon fiber heat/Mirage Mitigating Ergonomic forend, hand tool adj. Saber (HTA) shoulder stock, Limbsaver recoil pad, Magpul M1AD grip, 4 in. Picatinny top and bottom accessory rail, Black, Flat Dark Earth, OD Green, or Nordic Gray finish, 14 lbs.

	100%	98%	95%	90%	80%	70%	60%
MSR $7,295	$6,650	$5,750	$5,000	$4,200	$3,500	$2,850	$2,300

TCR223 – .223 Rem. cal., Surgeon RSR bolt action receiver, Pinnacle Series 20 (disc.) or 22 in. fluted stainless steel barrel, target crown, available in A3 configuration with 5 or 10 shot mag., tactical two-stage trigger, MOD-O Quattro carbon fiber forend, Mil-Std 1913 accessory rail, fixed Saber HTA ergonomic shoulder stock, ambidextrous paddle lever magazine release, Magpul M1AD modular grip, Limbsaver recoil pad, black, Flat Dark Earth, OD Green, or Nordic Gray finish, 12 lbs. New 2012.

	100%	98%	95%	90%	80%	70%	60%
MSR $6,325	$5,650	$5,100	$4,500	$3,900	$3,300	$2,700	$2,100

MSR	100%	98%	95%	90%	80%	70%	60%	Last MSR

TCR260 – .260 Rem. cal., similar to TCR223, except has 24 in. barrel and 10 shot detachable box mag.

| MSR $6,325 | $5,650 | $5,100 | $4,500 | $3,900 | $3,300 | $2,700 | $2,100 | |

TCR300 – .300 Win. Mag. cal., similar to TCR338, except has a 24 in. barrel.

| MSR $7,295 | $6,650 | $5,750 | $5,000 | $4,200 | $3,500 | $2,850 | $2,300 | |

TCR308 – .308 Win. Mag. cal., similar to TCR223, except has 20 in. barrel.

| MSR $6,325 | $5,650 | $5,100 | $4,500 | $3,900 | $3,300 | $2,700 | $2,100 | |

TCR6.5 – 6.5 Creedmoor cal., similar to TCR223, except has 24 in. barrel. New 2012.

| MSR $6,325 | $5,650 | $5,100 | $4,500 | $3,900 | $3,300 | $2,700 | $2,100 | |

ASP

Previously manufactured customized variation of a S&W Model 39-2 semi-auto pistol (or related variations) manufactured by Armament Systems and Procedures located in Appleton, WI.

PISTOLS: SEMI-AUTO

ASP – 9mm Para. cal., compact, DA/SA, see-through grips with cut-away mag. making cartridges visible, Teflon coated, re-contoured lightened slide, combat trigger guard, spurless hammer, and mostly painted Guttersnipe rear sight (no front sight), supplied with 3 mags., 24 oz. loaded. Approx. 3,000 mfg. until 1981.

| | $3,500 | $1,500 | $1,275 | $1,050 | $875 | $775 | $695 | |

Add $200 for Tritium filled Guttersnipe sight.

This pistol is marked "ASP" on the magazine extension.

ASTRA ARMS S.A.

Current manufacturer established in 2008 and located in Sion, Switzerland. No current U.S. importation.

Astra Arms manufactures a line of AR-15 style tactical rifles called the Sturmgewher 4 Series. Current models include the Carbine and Commando. These models are not currently imported into the U.S. Please contact the company directly for more information, including availability and pricing (see Trademark Index).

AUSTRALIAN AUTOMATIC ARMS PTY. LTD.

Previous manufacturer located in Tasmania, Australia. Previously imported and distributed by California Armory, Inc. located in San Bruno, CA.

PISTOLS: SEMI-AUTO

SAP – .223 Rem. cal., GIO, 10 1/2 in. barrel, SA, 20 shot mag., fiberglass stock and forearm, 5.9 lbs. Imported 1986-1993.

| | $795 | $700 | $600 | $550 | $500 | $475 | $450 | *$799* |

RIFLES: SEMI-AUTO

SAR – .223 Rem. cal., GIO, AR-15 style, 16 1/4 or 20 in. (new 1989) barrel, 5 or 20 shot M16 style mag., fiberglass stock and forearm, 7 1/2 lbs. Imported 1986-89.

| | $1,250 | $1,000 | $900 | $800 | $775 | $750 | $700 | *$663* |

Add $25 for 20 in. barrel.

This model was also available in a fully automatic version (AR).

SP – .223 Rem. cal., GIO, AR-15 style, sporting configuration, 16 1/4 or 20 in. barrel, wood stock and forearm, 5 or 20 shot M16 style mag., 7 1/4 lbs. Imported late 1991-93.

| | $850 | $750 | $650 | $600 | $550 | $500 | $475 | *$879* |

Add $40 for wood stock.

AUSTRALIAN INTERNATIONAL ARMS

Previous manufacturer and exporter located in Brisbane, Australia until circa 2009. Previously, Australian International Arms worked in cooperation with ADI Limited Lithgow, formerly Small Arms Factory, known for its SMLE No. I MKIII and L1A1 rifles. AIA outsourced the manufacture of its designs and specifications. Previously imported in North America by Marstar Canada, located in Ontario, Canada, and imported and distributed until 2004 by Tristar Sporting Arms, Ltd., located in N. Kansas City, MO.

RIFLES: BOLT ACTION, ENFIELD SERIES

M10-A1 – 7.62x39mm cal., redesigned and improved No. 4 MK2 action, parkerized finish, all new components, teak furniture with No. 5 Jungle Carbine style stock with steel or brass buttplate, 20 in. chrome lined barrel with muzzle

MSR	100%	98%	95%	90%	80%	70%	60%	Last MSR

brake, adj. front sight, 10 shot mag., Picatinny rail, 8.3 lbs.
While advertised in 2007, this model never went into production.

* ***M10-A2*** – 7.62x39mm cal., similar to M10A2, except has No. 8 style forend, Monte Carlo stock, and 16.1 in. chrome lined barrel. Limited importation 2003-2004 by Tristar.

	$750	$700	$600	$525	$450	$375	$300	$659

M10-B1 – .308 Win. cal., redesigned and improved No. 4 MK2 action, matte blue finish, all new components, teak furniture with sporter carbine style stock and steel buttplate, 22 in. barrel, adj. front sight, 10 shot mag., Picatinny rail, 8.3 lbs. Imported 2006-disc.

	$575	$500	$425	$350	$300	$275	$250	$675

* ***M10-B2*** – .308 Win. cal., similar to M10-B1, except has brass buttplate, gloss blue finish, 25 in. chrome lined bull barrel, and bipod stud, 10 1/2 lbs. Imported 2006-disc.

	$650	$525	$425	$350	$300	$275	$225	$760

* ***M10-B3*** – .308 Win. cal., similar to M10-B1, except has chrome steel buttplate, gloss blue finish, and 22 in. lightweight barrel, 7 1/2 lbs. Limited importation 2006-disc.

	$900	$800	$700	$600	$500	$425	$350	$1,000

NO.4 MK IV – .308 Win. cal., parkerized finish, 25.2 in. chrome lined medium weight barrel, teak furniture with steel buttplate, 9.1 lbs. Prototype only imported by Tristar. Limited importation beginning 2006.

	$575	$500	$425	$350	$300	$275	$250	$675

Add $440 for walnut stock, glass bedding, target barrel, elevated Picatinny rail, and accessories (disc.).

M 42 – .308 Win. cal., 27.6 in. barrel with mahogany stock and extra cheekpiece, blue printed action, bright metal/barrel finish, includes Picatinny rail, 8.2 lbs. Imported 2003-2004.

	$1,125	$950	$800	$650	$550	$450	$350	$1,295

AUTO-ORDNANCE CORP.

Current manufacturer with facilities located in Worcester, MA, and corporate offices in Blauvelt, NY. Auto-Ordnance Corp. became a division of Kahr Arms in 1999. Auto-Ordnance Corp. was a division of Gun Parts Corp. until 1999. Previously located in West Hurley, NY. Consumer, dealer, and distributor sales.

CARBINES: SEMI-AUTO

For Thompson semi-auto carbine models, please refer to the Thompson listing.

AUTO-ORDNANCE M1-CARBINE (.30 CAL.) – .30 Carbine cal., 18 in. barrel, birch (disc.) or walnut (standard beginning 2008) stock, all new parts, parkerized receiver, metal handguard, aperture rear sight, and bayonet lug, 10 (new 2005) or 15 shot mag., 5.4 lbs. New 2004.

MSR $856	$725	$635	$550	$500	$400	$325	$275	

* ***Auto-Ordnance M1 Carbine Paratrooper (AOM150)*** – .30 Carbine cal., similar to .30 cal. M1 Carbine, except has folding stock, walnut handguard, parkerized finish, 15 shot mag. New 2008.

MSR $941	$795	$695	$595	$540	$435	$360	$295	

* ***Auto-Ordnance M1 Carbine Tactical*** – .30 Carbine cal., similar to .30 cal. M1 carbine, except has black polymer folding stock, metal handguard, 15 shot mag. Mfg. 2008-2012.

	$650	$575	$475	$375	$325	$300	$275	$792

AUTO-ORDNANCE 1927 A-1 STANDARD – .45 ACP cal., 16 in. plain barrel, solid steel construction, standard military sight, walnut stock and horizontal forearm. Disc. 1986.

	$570	$490	$430	$360	$315	$290	$270	$575

PISTOLS: SEMI-AUTO

During 1997, Auto Ordnance discontinued all calibers on the pistols listed below, except for .45 ACP or 9mm Para. cal. Slide kits were available for $179. Also, conversion units (converting .45 ACP to .38 Super or 9mm Para.) were available for $195.

All current Auto Ordnance 1911 Models include a spent cartridge case, plastic carrying case, and cable lock.

1911 COMPETITION – .38 Super (1996 only) or .45 ACP cal., SA, competition features included compensated barrel, commander hammer, flat mainspring housing, white 3-dot sighting system, beavertail grip safety, black textured wraparound grips. Mfg. 1993-1996.

	$530	$415	$375	$330	$300	$285	$270	$636

Add $10 for .38 Super cal.

MSR	100%	98%	95%	90%	80%	70%	60%	Last MSR

* 1911 A1 WWII Parkerized – .45 ACP cal., 5 in. barrel, no frills variation of the 1911 A1, military parkerizing, G.I. detailing with military style roll stamp, plastic or checkered walnut (disc. 2001, reintroduced 2007) grips, and lanyard loop. New 1992.

| MSR $688 | $585 | $510 | $440 | $400 | $325 | $275 | $225 | |

Add $17 for wood grips with U.S. logo (new 2007).

AXELSON TACTICAL

Current manufacturer and dealer located in Minden, NV.

PISTOLS: SEMI-AUTO

COMBAT 5.56 PISTOL – 5.56 NATO cal., 12 1/2 in. Faxon barrel, Talon muzzle brake, carbine length gas tube, BCM low profile gas block and buffer system, forged aluminum upper and lower receivers, 9 in. GunRec slim profile M-LOK rail system, ALG combat trigger, CMMG lower parts kit, BCM Gunfighter Mod 4 charging handle, B5 systems Bravo buttstock, BCM Gunfighter Mod 1 grip, Type III hardcoat anodized black finish. New 2016.

| MSR $1,629 | $1,350 | $1,200 | $1,075 | $950 | $815 | $700 | $575 | |

COMBAT 300 BLK PISTOL – .300 AAC Blackout cal., Type III hardcoat anodized finish. New 2016.

| MSR $1,729 | $1,465 | $1,275 | $1,125 | $1,000 | $850 | $735 | $595 | |

RIFLES: SEMI-AUTO

AXE AR15 – 5.56 NATO cal., 16 in. barrel, Talon muzzle brake, 12 in. slim profile M-LOK rail system, "Arch Angel" charging handle, M4 style billet aluminum lower receiver, ALG combat trigger group, B5 Systems enhanced SOPMOD buttstock, BCM Gunfighter Mod 0 pistol grip, FDE finish. New 2016.

| MSR $2,299 | $1,950 | $1,725 | $1,450 | $1,250 | $1,050 | $900 | $750 | |

Add $50 for Battle Axe, Desert Axe, Freedom Axe, Night Axe, Na Koa Ke Kai, Reaper, and Spartan models featuring different finishes.

AXE AR15 PRECISION ELITE – 5.56 NATO cal., 16 in. Proof Research barrel (chambered in .223 Wylde cal.), BattleComp muzzle brake, Seekins adj. gas block, 14 in. Centurion Arms rail system, AXTS ambidextrous Raptor charging handle, M4 style billet aluminum lower receiver, Geissele SSA-E trigger, B5 Systems enhanced SOPMOD buttstock, BCM pistol grip, FDE finish. New 2016.

| MSR $2,299 | $1,950 | $1,725 | $1,450 | $1,250 | $1,050 | $900 | $750 | |

Add $50 for Battle Axe, Desert Axe, Freedom Axe, Night Axe, Na Koa Ke Kai, Reaper, and Spartan models featuring different finishes.

"AXE" SPECIAL PURPOSE RIFLE – 5.56 NATO cal. chambered for .223 Wylde, GIO, stainless steel 18 in. barrel with muzzle brake, 15 shot mag., Magpul MBUS PRO sights, enhanced SOPMOD stock, 15 in. free floating rail system, 3 color camouflage finish with Cerakote. Limited mfg. 2015.

| | $3,695 | $3,235 | $2,770 | $2,515 | $2,030 | $1,665 | $1,295 | *$3,695* |

This model was designed to honor Matt Axelson as well as the other SEAL team members of Operation Red Wings who lost their lives in 2005 while fighting the Taliban in Afghanistan.

COMBAT 300BLK – .300 AAC Blackout cal., 16 in. Faxon chrome lined barrel, Talon muzzle brake, BCM carbine length gas tube, low profile gas block, and buffer system, forged aluminum upper and lower receivers, 14 in. slim profile lightweight M-LOK rail system, Geissele SSAE enhanced trigger, CMMG lower parts kit, BCM Gunfighter Mod 4 charging handle, B5 Systems Bravo buttstock, BCM Gunfighter Mod 1 grip, Type III hardcoat anodized black finish. New 2016.

| MSR $1,749 | $1,485 | $1,315 | $1,150 | $1,025 | $875 | $750 | $615 | |

COMBAT 308 – .308 Win. cal., 16 in. Faxon barrel, Battlecomp BABC muzzle brake, forged aluminum upper and lower receivers, BCM mid-length gas tube, low profile gas block, and buffer system, BCM Gunfighter 762 charging handle, Centurion Arms CMR rail system, Geissele SSAE trigger, CMMG lower parts kit, B5 Systems enhanced SOPMOD buttstock, BCM Gunfighter grip, Type III hardcoat anodized finish. New 2016.

| MSR $2,849 | $2,425 | $2,100 | $1,750 | $1,500 | $1,225 | $1,035 | $910 | |

COMBAT 5.56 SPR – 5.56 NATO cal., 18 in. Faxon chrome lined barrel, Talon muzzle brake, BCM carbine length gas tube, low profile gas block, and buffer system, forged aluminum upper and lower receivers, 14 in. slim profile lightweight M-LOK rail system, ALG combat trigger, Strike Industries charging handle with extended latch, B5 Systems Bravo buttstock, BCM Gunfighter Mod 1 grip, Type III hardcoat anodized black finish. New 2016.

| MSR $1,899 | $1,625 | $1,425 | $1,200 | $1,075 | $925 | $795 | $650 | |

COMBAT 5.56 – 5.56 NATO cal., 16 or 18 in. Faxon chrome lined barrel, Talon muzzle brake, BCM gas tube, low profile gas block, and buffer system, Strike Industries charging handle with extended latch, forged aluminum upper and lower receivers, 14 in. slim profile lightweight M-LOK rail, ALG combat trigger, B5 Systems Bravo buttstock, BCM Gunfighter Mod 1 grip, Type III hardcoat anodized black finish. New 2016.

| MSR $1,649 | $1,400 | $1,235 | $1,100 | $975 | $830 | $720 | $585 | |

MSR	100%	98%	95%	90%	80%	70%	60%	Last MSR

"DIETZ" SPECIAL PURPOSE RIFLE – 5.56 NATO cal., 16 in. Faxon chrome lined barrel, Talon muzzle brake, Bravo Company carbine length gas tube, gas block, and buffer system, BCM Gunfighter Mod 1 charging handle, Axelson Tactical forged aluminum upper and lower receivers with hardcoat anodized finish, 12 in. slim profile M-LOK rail system, ALG combat trigger, B5 Systems SOPMOD stock, BCM Gunfighter Mod 1 grip, serial numbers Dietz01-Dietz99. Only 99 rifles mfg. beginning 2016.

| MSR $3,595 | $3,050 | $2,675 | $2,175 | $1,875 | $1,550 | $1,300 | $1,125 | |

REAPER01 AR10 – .308 Win. cal., 16 in. Proof Research barrel, "Talon" muzzle brake, low profile gas block, Centurion Arms 14 in. slim profile rail system, AXTS ambidextrous Raptor charging handle, forged aluminum M4 lower receiver, Geissele SSA-E trigger, Battle Arms Development ambidextrous selector lever, Seekins Precision mag. release button, Magpul PRS buttstock, B5 Systems pistol grip. New 2016.

| MSR $3,849 | $3,275 | $2,875 | $2,365 | $2,000 | $1,675 | $1,425 | $1,200 | |

AZTEK ARMS

Previous rifle manufacturer located in Mapleton, UT until 2015.

RIFLES: BOLT ACTION

AVENGER BPR (BACKPACK RIFLE) – various cals., interchangeable calibers and shooting configurations, 10 or 20 shot mag., accepts all AR-15 mags., secondary safety that blocks the firing pin, billet upper and lower aluminum receivers, Samson Mfg. KeyMod 9 in. handguard, AR-15 trigger, 5-pos. adj. Magpul MOE folding stock and Magpul MOE grip, black finish, breaks down in under a minute for storage. Mfg. 2015 only.

| | $1,275 | $1,125 | $1,025 | $875 | $750 | $625 | $525 | $1,499 |

H 1200 LONG RANGE HUNTER – 7mm Rem. Mag., 7mm Ultra, .300 Win., .300 WSM, 300 Ultra, or .338 Ultra cal., 25 or 27 in. match grade Schneider fluted barrel with muzzle brake, Picatinny rail, Black CORAL stock, hinged trigger guard, extended box mag., Shilen match trigger, Cerakote coating on all metal surfaces, 6 3/4-7 1/2 lbs. Disc. 2015.

| | $3,650 | $3,175 | $2,625 | $2,185 | $1,800 | $1,500 | $1,300 | $4,295 |

H 1500 LONG RANGE HUNTER – 7mm Rem. Mag., 7mm Ultra, .300 Win. Mag., .300 Ultra, or .338 Edge cal., 26 (7mm Rem or .300 Win. only) or 28 in. fluted match grade Schneider LRC barrel with muzzle brake, Picatinny rail, Shilen match trigger, includes one 5 shot detachable mag., Cerakote coating, 9-10 1/2 lbs. Disc. 2015.

| | $3,750 | $3,300 | $2,725 | $2,275 | $1,900 | $1,625 | $1,400 | $4,395 |

H 2000 LONG RANGE HUNTER – 7mm Rem. Mag., 7mm Ultra, .300 Win. Mag., .300 Ultra, .338 Ultra, or .338 Edge cal., 28 or 30 in. match grade heavy contour fluted barrel with muzzle brake, black MOMBA stock with adj. LOP and cheekpiece, Picatinny rail, Shilen match trigger, detachable magazine trigger guard, includes one 5 shot mag., Cerakote coating, 11 1/2-12 lbs. Disc. 2015.

| | $4,100 | $3,600 | $3,100 | $2,525 | $2,100 | $1,800 | $1,575 | $4,795 |

T1200 TACTICAL URBAN – .243 Win., .260 Rem., .308 Win. Mag., and 6.5 Creedmoor cal., 20, 24, or 26 in. match grade heavy contour barrel, Tan ALPHA stock, Picatinny rail, one 5 shot mag., detachable magazine trigger guard, Shilen match trigger, Cerakote coating, 10 1/2-12 lbs. Disc. 2015.

| | $3,485 | $3,025 | $2,500 | $2,085 | $1,725 | $1,450 | $1,250 | $4,095 |

T 1500 TACTICAL RANGER – 7mm Rem. Mag. or .300 Win. Mag. cal., 26 in. match grade heavy contour barrel, Picatinny rail, McMillan adj. A5 stock in black, OD Green, or tan, one 5 shot mag., detachable magazine trigger, Shilen match trigger, Cerakote coating, 10 1/2-12 lbs. Disc. 2015.

| | $3,650 | $3,175 | $2,625 | $2,185 | $1,800 | $1,500 | $1,300 | $4,295 |

T 2000 TACTICAL MAXRANGE – .338 Norma or .338 Lapua cal., 27 in. match grade Schneider body guard contour barrel with muzzle brake, Picatinny rail, Shilen match trigger, one 5 shot mag., detachable magazine trigger, McMillan adj. A5 stock in black, OD Green, or tan, Cerakote coating, 10 1/2-12 lbs. Disc. 2015.

| | $4,100 | $3,600 | $3,100 | $2,525 | $2,100 | $1,800 | $1,575 | $4,795 |

RIFLES: SEMI-AUTO

Aztek Arms manufactured AR-15 style rifles in various configurations until 2015.

B SECTION

BCM EUROPEARMS

Current manufacturer located in Torino, Italy. No current U.S. importation.

BCM Europearms manufactures high quality bolt action competiton, hunting, and tactical/Law Enforcement rifles; the Storm semi-auto pistol (in 9x21mm and .40 S&W); and customized Remington 700 rifles. The "Barrel Block" competition rifle features a monolithic stock with integrally machined bedding (no separate bedding components) which allows both action and barrel to free float. The barrel and action are held in the stock by a "cap" which clamps over the barrel's chamber and is attached to the stock, not the action, by eight screws.

Currently these models are not being imported into the U.S. Please contact the company directly for more information, U.S. availability, and pricing (see Trademark Index).

BWE FIREARMS

Current rifle manufacturer and customizer with gunsmithing services established during 2002, and located in Longwood, FL.

BWE Firearms is a full service custom gunsmith shop specializing in NFA (Class III) firearms. It is also a Class II manufacturer. Please contact the company directly for more information on their models and services (see Trademark Index).

RIFLES: BOLT ACTION

BWE Firearms manufactured a bolt action rifle based on the Remington Model 700 long action. It was chambered for the .300 Blackout/Whisper, .338 Thumper, or .50 Thumper caliber, and features included blue printed actions, fully adjustable Bell and Carlson tactical stock, and Picatinny rail. Finishes included bead blast, polished blue, or parkerizing.

BAIKAL

Current trademark of products manufactured by the Russian Federal State Unitary Plant "Izhevsky Mechanichesky Zavod" (FSUP IMZ), located in Izhevsk, Russia. Currently imported by U.S. Sporting Goods, Inc. located in Rockledge, FL beginning 2011. Previously imported from late 1998 until 2004 by European American Armory Corp., located in Sharpes, FL, and from 1993-1996 by Big Bear, located in Dallas, TX.

Baikal SxS and O/U hunting guns (including air guns) were imported and distributed exclusively 2005-2009 by U.S. Sporting Goods (USSG), located in Rockledge, FL. Many Baikal shotguns and rifles were marketed domestically by Remington under the Spartan Gunworks trademark until 2008. See listings under Spartan Gunworks for more information.

Please contact the importer directly for more information and availability on Baikal firearms (see Trademark Index).

Baikal (the name of a lake in Siberia) was one of the key holding companies from the former Soviet Union, specializing in the production of firearms, and science intensive, complex electronic equipment.

The company was founded in 1942 as part of the Russian National Defense Industry. At that time, the plant produced world renowned Tokarev TT pistols. Upon conclusion of WWII, the company expanded its operation to include non-military firearms (O/U, SxS, and single barrel shotguns). FSUP IMZ is one of the world's largest manufacturers of military and non-military firearms. The total amount of guns produced by the FSUP IMZ is 680,000 units per year. The products range from various smoothbore guns, including slide action and self-loading models, rifled and combination guns, to a full array of sporting, civil, and combat pistols, including the internationally famous Makarov pistol. Since 2000, Baikal has produced a new pistol for the Russian Army which was developed by the enterprise designers and named after the group's leader - the Yarygin pistol.

FSUP IMZ features efficient manufacturing capacity and the unique intellectual potential of its qualified engineers-and-technicians staff. The FSUP IMZ is also undertaking the task of reintroducing the world to the "Russian Custom Gunsmith". There is a gunsmith school at the factory area for custom, one-of-a-kind hand engraved shotguns and rifles. The guns produced by the school feature high-quality assembly, attractive appearance, and high functional quality according to the best traditions of Russian gunmakers.

In the past, Baikal shotguns have had limited importation into the U.S. 1993 marked the first year that Baikals were officially (and legally) imported into the U.S. because of Russia's previous export restrictions. In prior years, however, a few O/Us have been seen for sale and have no doubt been imported into this country one at a time. Currently produced Baikals are noted for their good quality at low-level costs.

MSR	100%	98%	95%	90%	80%	70%	60%	Last MSR

RIFLES: SEMI-AUTO

MP161K – .17 HMR (disc. 2010), .22 LR, or .22 WMR (disc. 2010) cal., 19 1/2 in. accurized barrel, grey polymer thumbhole pistol grip stock with adj. LOP and cheekpiece height, 10 shot mag., integral Picatinny rail, adj. open sight, loaded chamber indicator, trigger guard mounted bottom safety, blue recoil pad and inserts in the forend. Importation began 2009.

MSR $437	$375	$325	$275	$250	$200	$175	$140

Add 20% for .17 HMR or .22 WMR cal. (disc. 2010).

MSR	100%	98%	95%	90%	80%	70%	60%	Last MSR

BARNES PRECISION MACHINE, INC.

Current semi-auto pistol and rifle manufacturer located in Apex, NC. Dealer and consumer direct sales.

PISTOLS: SEMI-AUTO

CQB PISTOL – 5.56 NATO or .300 AAC Blackout cal., 7 1/2 in. stainless steel barrel with A2 flash hider, breaching tip, BPM bolt carrier group with nickel boron coating, Magpul MBUS sights with front sight adjustment tool, Sig SB15 stabilizing brade, Magpul MOE grip, forged upper and lower receivers, PSFFRS Ultralite Extreme 7 in. handguard with quick detach sling swivel inserts, Black or Flat Dark Earth finish. New 2015.

| MSR $1,308 | $1,100 | $995 | $875 | $735 | $650 | $550 | $465 | |

Add $34 for Flat Dark Earth finish.

RIFLES: SEMI-AUTO

Barnes also manufactures AR-15 parts and accessories. Many options are available for each rifle. Please contact the company directly for a complete list and pricing (see Trademark Index). All rifles include a plastic hard case and one Magpul PMAG.

Add $272 for Basic Robar NP3 coating rifle upgrade.

Add $433 for Maritime Robar NP3 coating rifle upgrade.

BPM CQB .308 RIFLE – .308 Win. cal., 16 in. stainless steel match grade barrel, flash hider, 20 shot mag., Geissele G2S trigger or Hyperfire 24e, MBUS, Magpul MOE stock, Magpul grip, 14 in. ULE handguard, billet upper and lower receivers, includes standard enhanced battle rifle package (EBR), Black or FDE finish. New 2016.

Please contact the company directly for pricing on this model.

BPM LONG RANGE .308 RIFLE – .308 Win. cal., 20 in. stainless steel match grade barrel, flash hider, 20 shot mag., Geissele G2S trigger or Hyperfire 24e, MBUS, Magpul MOE rifle stock, Magpul grip, 14 in. ULE handguard, billet upper and lower receivers, includes standard enhanced battle rifle package (EBR), Black or FDE finish. New 2016.

Please contact the company directly for pricing on this model.

CQB PATROLMAN'S CARBINE – 5.56 NATO cal., .223 Wylde chambered, GPO, 16 or 18 (new 2014) in. BPM stainless steel match barrel, stainless steel low profile gas block, A2 style flash hider, 12 in. Ultralite XT modular free float rail system, optional sling swivels, Magpul MBUS Gen2 sights, 6-position MOE adj. stock, Picatinny rail, breaching tip, Black or FDE finish, includes hard plastic Patriot AR case. Disc. 2014.

| | $1,100 | $995 | $875 | $735 | $650 | $550 | $465 | *$1,308* |

Add $11 for 18 in. barrel (new 2014).

Add $28 for FDE finish.

* **CQB Patrolman's Carbine .300 Blackout** – .300 AAC Blackout cal., GIO, carbine length adj. gas system, 16 in. stainless steel barrel with BPMA2 style flash hider, breaching tip, Magpul MOE stock and pistol grip, Magpul MBUS sights, flat-top Picatinny rail receiver with 12 in. quad rail, includes plastic hard case, black finish. New 2013.

| MSR $1,636 | $1,375 | $1,215 | $1,075 | $950 | $815 | $700 | $575 | |

* **CQB Patrolman's Carbine MOE Package** – 5.56 NATO cal., .223 Wylde chambered, GPO, 16 or 18 (new 2014) in. BPM stainless steel match barrel, stainless steel low profile gas block, A2 style flash hider, 12 in. Ultralite Extreme handguard w/quick detach sling swivel inserts and removable bipod stud, Magpul MBUS Gen2 sights, 6-position Magpul MOE adj. stock, Magpul grip, Picatinny rail, breaching tip, black finish, includes hard plastic Patriot AR case.

| MSR $1,308 | $1,100 | $995 | $875 | $735 | $650 | $550 | $465 | |

Add $34 for 18 in. barrel.

MARITIME CQB PATROLMAN'S CARBINE – 5.56 NATO cal., .223 Wylde chambered, GPO, 16 in. stainless steel match barrel with A2 flash hider, 12 in. Ultralite Extreme handguard w/quick detach sling swivel inserts and removable bipod stud, Magpul MBUS sights with front sight adjustment tool, Magpul MOE stock and grip, Picatinny rail, breaching tip, Robar NP3 coating on upper, lower, and parts kit, includes hard plastic Patriot AR case. New 2015.

| MSR $1,824 | $1,550 | $1,355 | $1,175 | $1,050 | $900 | $775 | $625 | |

DESIGNATED MARKSMAN RIFLE – 5.56 NATO cal., GIO, 18 in. BPM stainless steel match barrel, 2 in. Ultralite XT modular free-float rail system, optional sling swivels, A2 fixed (disc. 2013), Magpul PRS or MOE stock, Picatinny rail, Miculek muzzle brake, Hiperfire match trigger, black finish.

| MSR $1,612 | $1,375 | $1,200 | $1,075 | $950 | $815 | $700 | $575 | |

THREE GUN MATCH CARBINE – 5.56 NATO cal., .223 Wylde chambered, GIO, 16 or 18 in. BPM stainless steel match barrel, adj. gas system, Robar NP3 electroless nickel or black finish, 12 in. Ultralite PSFFRS handguard with optional sling swivels, Magpul MOE or ACE SOCOM rifle length stock, Picatinny rail, Miculek muzzle compensator, Hiperfire match trigger.

| MSR $1,571 | $1,325 | $1,160 | $1,040 | $885 | $750 | $625 | $525 | |

Add $11 for 18 in. barrel.

MSR	100%	98%	95%	90%	80%	70%	60%	Last MSR

BARRETT FIREARMS MANUFACTURING, INC.

Current rifle manufacturer established in 1982, located in Murfreesboro, TN. Dealer direct sales.

RIFLES: BOLT ACTION

MODEL 90 – .50 BMG cal., 29 in. match grade barrel with muzzle brake, 5 shot detachable box mag., includes extendible bipod legs, scope optional, 22 lbs. Mfg. 1990-1995.

	100%	98%	95%	90%	80%	70%	60%	Last MSR
	$3,450	$2,950	$2,400	$2,150	$1,875	$1,600	$1,500	$3,650

Add $1,150 for Swarovski 10X scope and rings.

MODEL 95(M) – .50 BMG cal., 29 in. match grade fluted barrel with high efficiency muzzle brake, 5 shot detachable box mag., includes extendible bipod legs, full length M1913 receiver optics rail, scope optional, includes carrying case, 22 1/2 lbs. New 1995.

MSR $6,671	$6,250	$5,700	$5,050	$4,250	$3,500	$2,750	$2,200

Add $1,413 for Leupold scope and Barrett ultra high rings (new 2012).

Add $2,839 for rifle system including Leupold scope, BORS ultra high rings, 120 rounds of XM33 ammo, Pelican case, and bipod (new 2011).

Add $2,978 for QDL suppressor (new 2013).

MODEL 98B – .338 Lapua cal., 20 in. heavy unfluted, 26 (new 2013), or 27 (disc. 2012) in. fluted barrel, includes two 10 shot detachable mags. with muzzle brake, adj. stock, Harris bipod, monopod, full length M1913 optics receiver rail with 3 accessory rails on shroud, two sling loops, adj. trigger, ergonomic bolt handle, black finish, air/watertight case, 13 1/2 lbs. New 2009.

MSR $4,827	$4,400	$3,975	$3,600	$3,100	$2,800	$2,500	$2,150

Add $153 for 26 in. fluted barrel (new 2013).

Add $1,412 for Leupold scope and Barrett ultra high rings (new 2012).

Add $2,839 for Leupold scope, BORS, and Barrett ultra high rings.

Add $1,300 for Leupold scope and cleaning kit (disc. 2012).

MODEL 98B FIELDCRAFT – .260 Rem., .300 Win. Mag., .308 Win., .338 Lapua (new 2016), 6.5 Creedmoor, or 7mm Rem. Mag. cal., 18, 22, or 24 in. light barrel, 10 shot detachable box magazine, adj. cheekpiece, adj. match trigger, 8 in. scope rail, black anodized finish or Cerakote finishes in Tungsten Grey, Burnt Bronze, Multi-Role Brown, OD Green, or FDE. New 2015.

MSR $4,113	$3,750	$3,250	$2,775	$2,515	$2,050	$1,675	$1,300

Add $306 for .300 Win. Mag. or 7mm Rem. Mag. cal.

Add $386 for .338 Lapua cal. (new 2016).

MODEL 98B LEGACY – .338 Lapua cal., 26 in. fluted barrel, 10 shot detachable box magazine, adj. cheekpiece, adj. match grade trigger, quick detach sling loop sockets, 18 in. scope rail, black finish. Mfg. 2015 only.

	100%	98%	95%	90%	80%	70%	60%	Last MSR
	$3,195	$2,795	$2,395	$2,175	$1,750	$1,450	$1,125	$3,552

MODEL 98B TACTICAL – .300 Win. Mag., .308 Win., or .338 Lapua (new 2016) cal., 16, 22, or 24 in. heavy barrel with muzzle brake, 10 shot detachable box magazine, adj. cheekpiece, adj. match grade trigger, 17 in. scope rail, black anodized or Tungsten Grey Cerakote receiver finish. New 2015.

MSR $4,419	$3,995	$3,500	$3,000	$2,700	$2,185	$1,795	$1,395

Add $204 for .300 Win. Mag. or $280 for .338 Lapua (new 2016) cal.

MODEL 99 – .416 Barrett (32 in. barrel only) or .50 BMG cal., single shot, 25 (disc.) or 29 in. (.50 BMG cal. only) lightweight fluted, or 32 in. heavy barrel with muzzle brake, straight through design with pistol grip and bipod, full length M1913 receiver optics rail, Black, Brown (disc.), Silver (disc.), or Tan Cerakote (new 2012) finish, 23-25 lbs. New 1999.

MSR $3,967	$3,600	$3,250	$2,825	$2,475	$2,175	$1,775	$1,400

Add $102 for Tan Cerakote finish.

Add $153 for fluted barrel.

Add $1,412 for Leupold scope and Barrett Ultra high rings (new 2012).

Add $2,839 for Leupold scope, BORS, and Barrett Ultra high rings (new 2012).

Add $2,978 QDL suppressor (new 2013).

Add $251 for Bushnell Elite 10x scope (disc.).

MODEL MRAD – .260 Rem. (new 2016), .300 Win. Mag. (new 2014), .308 Win. (new 2014), .338 Lapua, 6.5 Creedmoor (new 2016), or 7mm Rem. Mag. (new 2016) cal., 17 (.308 Win. only, new 2014), 20 (new 2012), 22 (.308 Win. only, new 2014), 24 (new 2013), 24 1/2 (disc. 2013), 26 (new 2013) or 27 (mfg. 2012 only) in. fluted, heavy, or carbon fiber barrel with muzzle brake, features aluminum receiver with modular construction including user-changeable barrel system, match grade trigger, thumb operated safety, ambidextrous mag. release, 21 3/4 in. M1913 optics rail plus side rails on vent forend, folding stock with adj. cheekpiece, Multi-Role Brown, Black anodized (new 2013), Grey

MSR	100%	98%	95%	90%	80%	70%	60%	Last MSR

Cerakote (new 2014), OD Green Cerakote (new 2014), or Tan Cerakote (new 2014) finish, includes two 10 shot mags., two sling loops, three accessory rails, and Pelican case, 12-14.8 lbs. New mid-2011.

| MSR $6,000 | $5,700 | $5,350 | $4,800 | $4,300 | $3,750 | $3,150 | $2,600 | |

Add $154 for 20, 22, 24, or 26 in. fluted barrel.

Add $975 for carbon fiber barrel.

Add $1,565 (heavy or fluted) or $2,380 (carbon fiber) for barrel conversion kit (includes complete barrel assembly, bolt, case, and one 10 shot mag. - new 2014).

RIFLES: SEMI-AUTO

MODEL 82 RIFLE – .50 BMG cal., semi-auto recoil operation, 33-37 in. barrel, 11 shot mag., 2,850 FPS muzzle velocity, scope sight only, parkerized finish, 35 lbs. Mfg. 1982-1987.

| | $5,000 | $4,350 | $3,950 | $3,450 | $2,700 | $2,150 | $1,800 | |

Last MSR for consumers was $3,180 in 1985

This model underwent design changes after initial production. Only 115 were mfg. starting with ser. no. 100.

MODEL 82A1 – .416 Barrett (new 2010) or .50 BMG cal., short recoil operating system, variant of the original Model 82, back-up iron sights, fitted hard case, 20, 29 (new late 1989), or 33 (disc. 1989) in. fluted (current mfg.) or unfluted (disc.) barrel, current mfg. has muzzle brake, 10 shot detachable or fixed (.416 Barrett cal. only) mag., Black anodized or Tan Cerakote (new 2013) finish, 32 1/2 lbs. for 1989 and older mfg., approx. 30 lbs. for 1990 mfg. and newer. Current mfg. includes elevated M1913 optics rail, watertight case, and cleaning kit.

| MSR $9,119 | $9,120 | $8,000 | $7,000 | $6,150 | $5,575 | $4,525 | $3,700 | |

Add $204 for Tan Cerakote finish (new 2013).

Add $1,413 for Leupold scope, Barrett ultra high rings, and Monopod (new 2012).

Add $2,839 for Leupold scope, BORS, Barrett ultra high rings, and Monopod (new 2012).

Add $384 for pack-mat backpack case (new 1999).

Add $2,800 for rifle system including Leupold scope, ultra high rings, Pelican case, and detachable bipod (mfg. 2011-2014).

Add approx. $4,900 per upper conversion kit (disc. 2014).

Add $1,500 for Leupold Mark IV 4.5-14x50mm scope (disc. 2011).

Add $1,325 for Swarovski 10X scope and rings (disc.).

This model boasts official U.S. military rifle (M107) status following government procurement during Operation Desert Storm. In 1992, a new "arrowhead" shaped muzzle brake was introduced to reduce recoil.

MODEL 82A1 LEGACY – .50 BMG or .416 Barrett cal., recoil operated design, 24 in. non-fluted barrel with 2-port arrow head muzzle brake, 10 shot detachable box mag., 9 in. scope rail with 27 MOA taper, black finish, includes one 10 shot mag. and bipod. Mfg. 2015 only.

| | $7,775 | $7,000 | $6,125 | $5,250 | $4,760 | $3,850 | $3,150 | $7,777 |

Add approx. $5,000 for upper conversion kit.

MODEL 98 – .338 Lapua Mag. cal., 10 shot box mag., 24 in. match grade barrel with muzzle brake, bipod, 15 1/2 lbs. While advertised during mid-1999, this model was never produced.

MODEL 107A1 – .50 BMG cal., 20 (new 2012) or 29 in. fluted barrel with four port titanium muzzle brake, integrated M1913 full length receiver optics rail including flip up iron sights, features new bolt carrier group and aluminum recoil buffer system, Black (new 2013), Multi-Role Brown Cerakote (new 2014), Grey Cerakote (new 2014), OD Green Cerakote (new 2014), or Tan Cerakote finish, detachable adj. lightweight bipod, monopod on buttstock, 10 shot mag., 30.9 lbs. New mid-2011.

| MSR $12,281 | $12,280 | $11,000 | $9,700 | $8,300 | $7,500 | $6,300 | $4,995 | |

Add $1,413 for Leupold scope and Barrett ultra high rings (new 2012, Black Cerakote finish only).

Add $2,839 for Leupold scope, BORS, and Barrett ultra high rings (new 2012, Black Cerakote finish only).

Add $2,978 for QDL suppressor (new 2013).

MODEL M468 – 6.8 SPC cal., aluminum upper and lower receiver, 16 in. barrel with muzzle brake, 5, 10, or 30 shot mag., dual spring extractor system, folding front and rear sight, gas block, two-stage trigger, integrated rail system, choice of full or telescoping 4-position stock, 8 lbs. Mfg. 2005-2008.

| | $2,400 | $2,050 | $1,675 | $1,375 | $1,175 | $995 | $875 | $2,700 |

Add $1,590 for Model M468 upper conversion kit.

MODEL REC7 – 5.56 NATO or 6.8 SPC cal., AR-15 style, GPO, aluminum upper and lower receiver, 16 in. chrome lined barrel with A2 flash hider, 30 shot mag., folding front and ARMS rear sight, single stage trigger, ARMS selective integrated rail system (disc.) or Omega X rail (current mfg.), 6-position MOE stock, includes tactical soft case and two mags., 7.62 lbs. Mfg. 2008-2013.

| | $1,950 | $1,700 | $1,475 | $1,325 | $1,075 | $875 | $675 | $1,950 |

Add $1,650 per individual upper conversion kit.

Add $676 for Aimpoint Micro T-1 optics (mfg. 2011-2012).

MSR	100%	98%	95%	90%	80%	70%	60%	Last MSR

MODEL REC7 DI – 5.56 NATO, 6.8 SPC, or .300 AAC Blackout cal., GIO, 16 or 18 in. match grade stainless steel barrel, muzzle brake, 20 (18 in.) or 30 (16 in.) shot mag., ALG Defense ACT trigger, Barrett 15 in. KeyMod handguard, Bravo Company Gunfighter charging handle, Black, Tungsten Grey, OD Green, Flat Dark Earth, Multi-Role Brown, or Burnt Bronze receiver finish. New 2016.

| MSR $1,899 | $1,625 | $1,425 | $1,200 | $1,075 | $925 | $795 | $650 | |

MODEL REC7 GEN II – 5.56 NATO or 6.8 SPC cal., GPO, 16 in. barrel, Magpul MOE pistol grip stock, PWS Triad flash suppressor, PRI flip up iron sights, Geissele SSA trigger, BCM charging handle, beveled magwell, Barrett handguard with KeyMod, available in Black, Tungsten Grey, Flat Dark Earth, or OD Green finish, 30 shot mag., includes one KeyMod rail attachment and soft carrying case. New 2014.

| MSR $2,499 | $2,125 | $1,875 | $1,550 | $1,325 | $1,100 | $950 | $825 | |

* **Model REC7 Gen II DMR** – 5.56 NATO or 6.8 SPC cal., GPO, 18 in. barrel, Barrett muzzle brake, 20 shot mag., Magpul MBUS Pro sights, Magpul MOE pistol grip stock, Geissele trigger, Barrett handguard with KeyMod rail attachment, available in Black, Grey, Flat Dark Earth, or OD Green finish, includes soft carrying case. New 2016.

| MSR $2,799 | $2,375 | $2,075 | $1,725 | $1,475 | $1,200 | $1,025 | $895 | |

* **Model REC7 Gen II Flyweight** – 5.56 NATO cal., GPO, 16 in. lightweight barrel, thread protector, PWS Triad flash suppressor, 20 shot mag., Geissele trigger, Magpul MOE pistol grip stock, Barrett handguard with KeyMod rail attachment, Black, Grey, Flat Dark Earth or OD Green finish, includes soft carrying case. New 2016.

| MSR $2,199 | $1,875 | $1,650 | $1,400 | $1,200 | $1,025 | $875 | $725 | |

BATTLE ARMS DEVELOPMENT, INC. (B.A.D., INC.)

Current manufacturer located in Henderson, NV since 2009.

Battle Arms Development, Inc. (B.A.D. Inc.) is a design, research, and development firm focusing on small arms design including firearm components, tools, gauges, accessories, and complete weapon systems. All B.A.D. Inc. products are 100% made in the U.S.A.

RIFLES: SEMI-AUTO

BAD556-LW THE 300 SPARTAN RIFLE – 5.56 NATO cal., 16 in. Ultramatch Lightrigid stainless steel fluted barrel (.223 Wylde chamber), VG6 Epsilon compensator or BattleComp, Magpul Gen 2 PMAG with MAGPOD floorplate, low profile Grade 5 titanium gas block, stainless steel mid-length gas tube, lightweight billet aluminum upper and lower receivers, Fortis Shift short angled foregrip, BCM Gunfighter charging handle, 14 in. Fortis Switch 556 rail system, Mil-Spec ejection port cover, Ambi safety selector, CMC trigger, Mil-Spec carbine buffer tube, MFT Battlelink Minimalist stock, MFT G27 tactical pistol grip, 300 Spartan inspired custom theme Cerakote paint job, includes hard rifle case, 5.7 lbs.

| MSR $3,100 | $2,625 | $2,285 | $1,875 | $1,600 | $1,325 | $1,115 | $965 | |

BAD556-LW VADER RIFLE – 5.56 NATO cal., 16 in. Ultramatch Lightrigid stainless steel fluted barrel (.223 Wylde chamber), VG6 Epsilon compensator or BattleComp, Magpul Gen 2 PMAG with MAGPOD floorplate, low profile Grade 5 titanium gas block, stainless steel mid-length gas tube, lightweight billet aluminum upper and lower receivers, Fortis Shift short angled foregrip, BCM Gunfighter charging handle, 14 in. Fortis Switch 556 rail system, Mil-Spec ejection port cover, Ambi safety selector, CMC trigger, Sabertube buffer tube with lightweight stock, 3-position adj. tactical grip, Darth Vader inspired custom theme Cerakote paint job, includes hard rifle case, 5.4 lbs.

| MSR $3,150 | $2,675 | $2,335 | $1,900 | $1,625 | $1,350 | $1,130 | $980 | |

BATTLE RIFLE COMPANY

Current manufacturer of AR-15 style pistols and rifles located in Houston, TX. Previously located in Seabrook, TX.

PISTOLS: SEMI-AUTO

BR4 ATTACHE 5.56 – 5.56 NATO cal., 7 1/2, 10 1/2, or 11 1/2 in. barrel with A2 flash suppressor, black finish.

| MSR $1,195 | $1,025 | $925 | $800 | $685 | $595 | $515 | $440 | |

Add $100 for 10 1/2 or 11 1/2 in. barrel.
Add $100 for optional Sig Brace.

BR4 ATTACHE 9MM – 9mm Para. cal., blowback action, Colt SMG configuration with 32 shot straight mag., pistol buffer tube with Nomex cover, single point sling adapter, Ergo pistol grip, black finish. New 2015.

| MSR $1,395 | $1,195 | $1,075 | $950 | $800 | $700 | $600 | $495 | |

Add $100 for optional Sig Brace.

RIFLES: SEMI-AUTO

In addition to Cerakote and Duracoat fiinishes, Battle Rifle Company also added custom painting to their rifles beginning in 2016. Colors include: Afghanatan, Artic Jungle, Concrete Jungle, Deep Jungle, Desert Jungle, Norway, Scorched Earth, Sedona, Tundra, Pinko, Battle Royale, and NWU Type 3.

MSR	100%	98%	95%	90%	80%	70%	60%	Last MSR

BR308 (WARHAMMER) – .308 Win. cal., GIO, 16, 18, or 20 in. barrel with Disintegrator flash suppressor, Geissele SSA trigger system, enhanced combat stock system w/sling swivel attachment and easy grip adjustments, cheek weld designed finish w/Battle Rifle logo, Harris style bipod (18 or 20 in. only), forearm grip (16 in. only), 6-position buffer tube, ambi charging handle, Magpul front and rear MBUS sights, custom ambi pistol grip, heavy buffer, low profile gas block, additional rails for lights/optics, ambi fire control selector switch (option), includes one mag. and tactical bag.

MSR $2,695	$2,295	$2,010	$1,725	$1,575	$1,275	$1,050	$850	

Add $100 for 18 in. barrel or $200 for 20 in. barrel.

BR4 DMR – 5.56 NATO cal., flash suppressor, standard, ECS, or Magpul PRS stock, Ergo pistol grip, Black finish. New 2016.

MSR $1,795	$1,525	$1,335	$1,150	$1,050	$850	$685	$550	

BR4 LIT-CARBINE – 5.56 NATO or .300 AAC Blackout cal., 16 or 20 (new 2015) in. SOCOM profile barrel with flash suppressor, 12 or 15 in. free float Gen. 2 SS rail, SST, sling adaptor, enhanced combat stock with Battle Rifle logo, Black furniture, available with KeyMod rail. Disc. 2015.

	$1,450	$1,275	$1,125	$1,000	$850	$735	$595	*$1,695*

Add $100 for 20 in. barrel (new 2015).
Add $100 for KeyMod option with 12 in. rail. or $100 for 15 in. rail (disc. 2014).
Add $200 for .300 Blackout cal. or $200 for KeyMod option with 15 in. rail (disc. 2014).

BR4 ODIN – 5.56 NATO cal., 16 in. cryogenically treated barrel with Battle Rifle flash suppressor, mid-length gas port, 12 1/2 in. KeyMod rail, B.A.D. lever, custom ALG trigger, MFT Minimalist stock, Ergo pistol grip, black furniture, 6.1 lbs. New 2015.

MSR $1,795	$1,525	$1,335	$1,150	$1,050	$850	$685	$550	

BR4 SPARTAN – 5.56 NATO, 6.8 SPC (disc. 2015), 7.62x6mm (mfg. 2014-2015), or .300 AAC Blackout (disc. 2013) cal., GIO, choice of 16 in. Hbar profile or SOCOM profile barrel with flash suppressor, gas block with A2 front sight tower, collapsible stock, forged aluminum flat-top upper receiver with Picatinny rail and laser engraved, lower receiver with matching two-piece quad rail, polished trigger, black furniture, Ergo pistol grip, buttstock pad, includes one 30 shot mag. and black case, 6 1/2 lbs.

MSR $1,195	$1,025	$895	$775	$695	$575	$475	$375	

Add $100 for 6.8 SPC or 7.62x6mm (new 2014) cal.
Add $246 for .300 AAC Blackout cal. (disc. 2013).

BR4 SPECIAL PURPOSE RIFLE (SPR) – 5.56 NATO cal., 18 in. stainless steel barrel, muzzle brake, Geissele SSA trigger, Magpul flip up sights, Magpul ACS stock, Ergo pistol grip, nickel boron bolt carrier group, 15 in. Battle Rifle HEXRail, single point endplate. New 2016.

MSR $1,895	$1,625	$1,425	$1,200	$1,075	$925	$795	$650	

BR4 SPECTRE – 5.56 NATO, 6.8 SPC, or .300 AAC Blackout cal., 16 in. HBar or SOCOM profile barrel with BRC Disintegrator flash suppressor, custom ALG trigger, 12 in. free float quad rail, FAB Defense folding sights, Ergo pistol grip, buttstock pad, micro gas block under quad rail, SST, Hogue buttstock with QD points, Black or FDE (new 2015) furniture.

MSR $1,195	$1,025	$895	$775	$695	$575	$475	$375	

Add $100 for FDE finish (new 2015).

BR4 SPR – .223 Wylde cal., 18 in. stainless steel barrel, muzzle brake, Geissele SSA trigger, Magpul flip-up sights, Magpul ACS stock, Ergo pistol grip, nickel boron BCG, 15 in. battle rifle HexRail, single point end plate, Black finish. New 2016.

Please contact the company directly for pricing on this model (see Trademark Index).

BR4 STRYKER – 5.56 NATO cal., 16 in. M4 or SOCOM profile barrel with flash suppressor, flip-up front sight, quad rail with continuous top rail, Ergo pistol grip, buttstock pad, SST, single point sling adapter. Disc. 2014.

	$1,250	$1,095	$950	$850	$700	$600	$495	*$1,395*

BR4 TRIDENT – 5.56 NATO cal., 16 in. stainless steel barrel, muzzle brake, stainless steel springs, fire control group, pins, and lower parts, "F" type front sight base, Magpul flip up rear sight, specially designed for MARSEC (Maritime Security), bayonet lug, sling swivel, high temp Cerakote finished upper and lower receivers, buffer tube, 7 in. free float slim quad rail, M4 buttstock, M4 pistol grip. New 2016.

MSR $1,595	$1,350	$1,200	$1,075	$950	$815	$700	$575	

BR4 TROOPER – 5.56 NATO cal., 16 in. M4 profile barrel with A2 flash hider, 30 shot mag., carbine or mid-length, optional quad rail, carry handle with sights, collapsible or MOE stock, Black furniture.

MSR $995	$850	$725	$650	$585	$515	$450	$395	

Add $100 for mid-length, quad rail or MOE stock (disc. 2014).
Add $154 for mid-length MOE Trooper model (disc. 2014).

MSR	100%	98%	95%	90%	80%	70%	60%	Last MSR

BR4 WOLVERINE – 5.56 NATO or .300 AAC Blackout cal., 16 in. M4 profile barrel, 5 1/2 in. simulated suppressor, 15 1/2 in. KeyMod rail, front and rear flip-up sights, Ergo pistol grip, Mission First Tactical stock, single point sling adaptor, Black furniture. Mfg. 2014 only.

	$1,350	$1,200	$1,075	$950	$815	$700	$575	$1,595

Add $100 for .300 Blackout cal.

BR15 DMR – 5.56 NATO cal., 20 in. heavy barrel with flash suppressor, rifle length quad rail, Harris style bipod, SST or 2-stage trigger, Ergo pistol grip, standard, ECS, or Magpul PRS stock, Black furniture.

MSR $1,695	$1,450	$1,275	$1,125	$1,000	$850	$735	$595	

Add $200 for Magpul PRS stock (disc. 2014).

BR15 LIT-RIFLE – 5.56 NATO or .300 AAC Blackout cal., GIO, light infantry tactical rifle, 16 (disc. 2013) or 20 in. threaded, chrome lined barrel with flash suppressor, Magpul MBUS front and rear sights, M16 bolt carrier with nickel finish, forged flat-top upper receiver with Picatinny rail and laser and free float 12 (16 in. barrel, disc. 2013) or 15 (20 in. barrel) in. rail, forged aluminum lower receiver, polished trigger, ECS stock, single point sling endplate, includes one 30 shot mag. and black case, 6.7-7.9 lbs. Disc. 2014.

	$1,450	$1,275	$1,125	$1,000	$850	$735	$595	$1,695

Add $100 for 2-stage trigger option.

BR15 STANDARD – 5.56 NATO cal., 20 in. barrel with A2 flash suppressor, 30 shot mag., rifle length polymer handguards, carry handle rear sight, standard A2 fixed stock and pistol grip, SST, Black furniture. Disc. 2015.

	$1,100	$995	$875	$735	$650	$550	$465	$1,295

BR15 PATROLMAN – 5.56 NATO cal., similar to BR4, except features 16 in. steel straight profile barrel with flash suppressor, available with carbine or mid-length forearm, 7 1/2 lbs. Disc. 2013.

	$1,225	$1,080	$950	$800	$700	$600	$495	$1,449

BR15 VARMITEER – 5.56 NATO cal., 18 or 20 in. heavy barrel, low profile gas block, 10 shot mag., rifle length forend tube, optics ready, Ergo pistol grip, Magpul stock, available in Black, Desert Tan pattern, or Woodland pattern finish. Disc. 2014.

	$1,150	$1,000	$875	$735	$650	$550	$465	$1,295

BR15 6mmx45 – 6mmx45 cal., AR-15 style, 18 or 20 in. barrel, mid (18 in.) or rifle (20 in.) length gas sytem, KeyMod 15 1/2 in. rail, ECS stock, Black furniture, includes bipod. Disc. 2014.

	$1,350	$1,200	$1,075	$950	$815	$700	$575	$1,595

Add $100 for 20 in. barrel.

BR16 PRECISION TACTICAL RIFLE – 5.56 NATO cal., GIO, 20 in. heavy threaded barrel with flash suppressor, gas block with A2 front sight tower, forged aluminum flat-top upper with Picatinny rail and laser engraved, two-piece quad rail, forged alum. lower receiver, polished trigger, black furniture, fixed or adj. stock, includes one 30 shot mag., bipod match 600 meter sights, and black case. Disc. 2013.

	$1,450	$1,275	$1,125	$1,000	$850	$735	$595	$1,695

Add $100 for Magpul PRS or CAA Ansl adj. stock.

DEFENDER – 5.56 NATO cal., 16 in. barrel, A2 flash suppressor, M4 buttstock, Mil-Spec pistol grip, rail height front gas block, M4 handguards. New 2016.

MSR $798	$685	$615	$550	$475	$420	$365	$335	

BAZOOKA BROTHERS MFG.

Current manufacturer of AR-15 style carbines/rifles, pistols, and components established circa 2002, located in Russiaville, IN.

RIFLES/CARBINES: SEMI-AUTO

MODEL B-AR45 CARBINE – more research is pending for info on this model.

MSR $1,370	$1,150	$1,030	$900	$750	$685	$585	$485	

PISTOLS: SEMI-AUTO

MODEL B-AR45 PISTOL – 8 or 10 in. barrel, M4 or quad rail handguard, buffer tube, RMW extreme upper receiver, black finish.

Please contact the company directly for more information including price, options, and availability (see Trademark Index).

BENELLI

Current manufacturer established in 1967, located in Urbino, Italy. Benelli USA was formed during late 1997, and is currently importing all Benelli shotguns and rifles. Benelli pistols (and air pistols) are currently imported by Larry's Guns, located in Gray, ME beginning 2003. Company headquarters are located in Accokeek, MD. Shotguns

MSR	100%	98%	95%	90%	80%	70%	60%	Last MSR

were previously imported 1983-1997 by Heckler & Koch, Inc., located in Sterling, VA. Handguns were previously imported until 1997 by European American Armory, located in Sharpes, FL, in addition to Sile Distributors, Inc., until 1995, located in New York, NY, and Saco, located in Arlington, VA.

For more information on Benelli air pistols, please refer to the *Blue Book of Airguns* by Dr. Robert Beeman and John Allen (also available online).

RIFLES: SEMI-AUTO

MR1 CARBINE/RIFLE – 5.56 NATO cal., self-adjusting gas operation (similar to the Benelli M4 shotgun used by the Marines) with rotating bolt head featuring three lugs, accepts 5 shot AR-15 style mags., 16, or 20 (Europe only) in. barrel, regular or pistol grip, rifle sights, includes Picatinny rail with ghost ring sights, push button safety on trigger guard, black finish, approx. 8 lbs. Imported late 2009-2015.

	100%	98%	95%	90%	80%	70%	60%	Last MSR
	$1,175	$1,000	$875	$750	$650	$550	$450	$1,339

* **MR1 ComforTech Carbine** – 5.56 NATO, 16 in. barrel features black pistol grip ComforTech stock, otherwise similar to MR1 Carbine/Rifle. Imported 2011-2015.

	100%	98%	95%	90%	80%	70%	60%	Last MSR
	$1,275	$1,075	$925	$775	$675	$575	$475	$1,469

SHOTGUNS: SEMI-AUTO, 1985-OLDER

Benelli semi-auto 3rd generation (inertia recoil) shotguns were imported starting in the late 1960s. The receivers were mfg. of light aluminum alloy - the SL-80 Model 121 had a semi-gloss, anodized black finish, the Model 123 had an ornate photo-engraved receiver, the Model Special 80 had a brushed, white nickel-plated receiver, and the Model 121 M1 had a matte finish receiver, barrel, and stock. All 12 ga. SL-80 Series shotguns will accept 2 3/4 or 3 in. shells, and all SL-80 Series 12 ga. Models have interchangeable barrels (except the 121 M1) with 4 different model receivers (121, 121 M1, 123, and Special 80). All 4 models had fixed choke barrels.

The SL-80 Series shotguns were disc. during 1985, and neither H&K nor Benelli USA has parts for these guns. Some misc. parts still available for the 12 ga. from Gun Parts Corp. (see Trademark Index for more information).

Approx. 50,000 SL-80 series shotguns were mfg. before discontinuance - choke markings (located on the side or bottom of the barrel) are as follows: * full choke, ** imp. mod., *** mod., **** imp. cyl. SL-80 series guns used the same action (much different than current mfg.) and all had the split receiver design. Be aware of possible wood cracking where the barrel rests on the thin area of the forend and also on the underside of the buttstock behind trigger guard.

The marketplace for older Benelli semi-auto shotguns has changed recently, with more interest being shown on these older models as they represent a value compared to Benelli's new offerings. As a result of this additional interest and demand, values have gone up, after being dormant for many years.

100% values within this section assume NIB condition.

Subtract 5% for "SACO" importation (Saco was located in Arlington, VA).

SL-80 SERIES MODEL 121 M1 POLICE/MILITARY – 12 ga. only, similar in appearance to the Super 90 M1, hardwood stock, 7 shot mag., matte metal and wood finish, most stocks had adj. lateral sling attachment inside of buttstock, 18 3/4 in. barrel. Disc. 1985.

	100%	98%	95%	90%	80%	70%	60%
	$600	$525	$450	$400	$325	$250	$225

Since many of this model were sold to the police and military, used specimens should be checked carefully for excessive wear and/or possible damage. Since these guns usually saw extensive use, they are much less desirable than other SL-80 listed in this section, It is also difficult to find commonly needed parts for these guns. These models are not rare, but fewer have been traded, most likely due to poor sales history.

SHOTGUNS: SEMI-AUTO, 1986-NEWER

Unless indicated otherwise, all currently manufactured Benelli shotguns utilize a red fiber optic sight, and are equipped with a patented Benelli keyed chamber lock. As of 2011, Benelli had manufactured well over 2 million shotguns in many configurations.

M1 DEFENSE (SUPER 90) – similar to Super 90 Slug, except has pistol grip stock, 7.1 lbs. Disc. 1998.

	100%	98%	95%	90%	80%	70%	60%	Last MSR
	$700	$560	$425	$325	$300	$270	$250	$851

Add $41 for ghost-ring sighting system.

M1 PRACTICAL (SUPER 90) – 12 ga. only, 3 in. chamber, 26 in. plain barrel with muzzle brake, designed for IPSC events, extended 8 shot tube mag., oversized safety, speed loader, larger bolt handle, Mil-Spec adj. ghost ring sight and Picatinny rail, black regular synthetic stock and forearm, matte metal finish, includes 3 choke tubes, 7.6 lbs. Mfg. 1998-2004.

	100%	98%	95%	90%	80%	70%	60%	Last MSR
	$925	$785	$675	$575	$450	$350	$300	$1,285

M1 TACTICAL (SUPER 90) – 12 ga. only, 3 in. chamber, 18 1/2 in. barrel, fixed rifle or ghost ring sighting system, available with synthetic pistol grip or standard buttstock, includes 3 choke tubes, 5 shot mag., 6.7 - 7 lbs. Mfg. 1993-2004.

	100%	98%	95%	90%	80%	70%	60%	Last MSR
	$725	$600	$525	$425	$335	$275	$250	$975

Add $50 for ghost ring sighting system.

Add $50-$65 for pistol grip stock.

MSR	100%	98%	95%	90%	80%	70%	60%	Last MSR

* M1 Tactical M – similar to M1 Tactical, except has military ghost ring sights and standard synthetic stock, 7.1 lbs. Mfg. 1999-2000.

	100%	98%	95%	90%	80%	70%	60%	Last MSR
	$725	$600	$525	$425	$335	$275	$250	*$960*

Add $10 for pistol grip stock.

M1 ENTRY (SUPER 90) – 12 ga. only, 14 in. barrel, choice of synthetic pistol grip or standard stock, choice of rifle or ghost ring sights, 5 shot mag. (2 shot extension), approx. 6.7 lbs. Mfg. 1992-2006.

	100%	98%	95%	90%	80%	70%	60%	Last MSR
	$810	$675	$585	$450	$395	$340	$310	

Add $15 for synthetic pistol grip stock.
Add $65 for ghost ring sighting system.

This model required special licensing (special tax stamp) for civilians, and was normally available to law enforcement/military only.

M2 – 12 ga., 2 3/4 or 3 in. chamber, 18 1/2 in. barrel, open or ghost ring sights, matte black finish, pistol grip or straight grip stock, includes three choke tubes, 6.7 lbs. New 2013.

MSR $1,549	100%	98%	95%	90%	80%	70%	60%
	$1,300	$1,125	$975	$885	$715	$585	$450

M2 THREE GUN – 12 ga., 3 in. chamber, 21 in. VR barrel with Crio chokes, 3 shot mag., HiViz sights, black synthetic ComforTech stock, designed for 3 gun competition, 7.3 lbs. New 2012.

MSR $2,499	100%	98%	95%	90%	80%	70%	60%
	$2,225	$1,875	$1,600	$1,350	$1,150	$925	$750

M2 PRACTICAL – 12 ga. only, 3 in. chamber, 26 in. compensated barrel with ghost ring sights, designed for IPSC competition, 8 shot mag., Picatinny rail. Limited importation 2005.

	100%	98%	95%	90%	80%	70%	60%	Last MSR
	$1,135	$965	$825	$650	$550	$475	$425	*$1,335*

M2 TACTICAL – 12 ga. only, 3 in. chamber, Inertia Driven system, 18 1/2 in. barrel with choice of pistol grip, regular stock, or ComforTech stock configuration, matte finish, 5 shot mag., AirTouch checkering pattern on stock and forearm, open rifle or ghost ring sights, 6.7-7 lbs. New 2005.

MSR $1,359	100%	98%	95%	90%	80%	70%	60%
	$1,225	$1,050	$900	$775	$650	$500	$400

Add $110 for ghost ring sights w/ComforTech stock.
Subtract $110 for tactical open rifle sights.

M3 CONVERTIBLE AUTO/PUMP (SUPER 90) – 12 ga. only, 3 in. chamber, defense configuration incorporating convertible (fingertip activated) pump or semi-auto action, 19 3/4 in. cyl. bore barrel with ghost ring or rifle (disc. 2007) sights, 5 shot mag., choice of standard black polymer stock or integral pistol grip (disc. 1996, reintroduced 1999), approx. 7.3 lbs. Imported 1989-2015.

	100%	98%	95%	90%	80%	70%	60%	Last MSR
	$1,375	$1,175	$1,025	$900	$800	$700	$600	*$1,589*

Add $110 for folding stock (mfg. 1990-disc.) - only available as a complete gun.
Add $340 for Model 200 Laser Sight System with bracket (disc.).
Subtract approx. 10% for rifle sights (disc. 2007).

M4 TACTICAL – 12 ga. only, 3 in. chamber, consumer version of the U.S. Military M4, includes Auto Regulating Gas Operating (ARGO) system, dual stainless self cleaning pistons, 4 shot mag., matte black phosphated metal standard, H2O coating (mfg. 2012 and 2014), Cerakote AIDE (new 2016), or 100% Desert camo coverage (except for pistol grip, mfg. 2007-2012), 18 1/2 in. barrel with ghost ring sights, pistol grip, tactical (new 2012), telescoping (new 2012), or non-collapsible (disc. 2004) stock and forearm, Picatinny rail, approx. 7.8 lbs. Importation began late 2003.

MSR $1,999	100%	98%	95%	90%	80%	70%	60%
	$1,750	$1,500	$1,250	$1,050	$925	$850	$750

Add $300 for Cerakote AIDE finish (new 2016) with ghost ring sights and choice of pistol grip or tactical stock.
Add $300 for ATI Raven stock (mfg. 2013 only).
Add $100 for 100% Desert camo coverage (mfg. 2007-2012).
Add $500 for pistol grip or tactical stock with H20 coating (new 2014).
Add $370 for tactical stock with H2O coating (mfg. 2012 only) or $500 for telescoping stock with H2O coating (mfg. 2012 only).

M1014 LIMITED EDITION – similar to M4, except only available with non-collapsible stock, U.S. flag engraved on receiver, 8 lbs. Limited edition of 2,500 mfg. 2003-2004.

	100%	98%	95%	90%	80%	70%	60%	Last MSR
	$1,375	$1,100	$950	$825	$725	$650	$600	*$1,575*

* Super Black Eagle II Slug – 12 ga. only, 3 in. chamber, 24 in. barrel with rifled bore and adj. sights, includes Picatinny rail, choice of satin walnut (disc. 2012) stock and forearm or black synthetic stock, ComforTech became standard 2007, or 100% camo coverage of Timber HD (disc. 2008) or Realtree APG HD, approx. 7.4 lbs. New 2004.

MSR $1,899	100%	98%	95%	90%	80%	70%	60%
	$1,750	$1,475	$1,275	$1,050	$850	$625	$525

Add $100 for 100% camo treatment.
Subtract approx. $100 if with satin walnut stock and forearm.

SHOTGUNS: SLIDE-ACTION

All currently manufactured Benelli shotguns are equipped with a patented Benelli keyed chamber lock.

MSR	100%	98%	95%	90%	80%	70%	60%	Last MSR

* *Nova Tactical (Special Purpose Smooth Bore)* – 12 ga. only, 3 1/2 in. chamber, similar action to Nova, features 18 1/2 in. cyl. bore barrel with choice of rifle or ghost ring (new 2000) sights, black synthetic stock and forearm only, 7.2 lbs. New 1999.

| MSR $419 | $350 | $285 | $260 | $230 | $210 | $200 | $190 | |

Add $40 for ghost ring sights.

* *SuperNova Tactical* – 12 ga., 18 or 18 1/2 in. barrel with choice of ComforTech or pistol grip synthetic stock, matte finish or Desert camo (mfg. 2007-2012, pistol grip only), choice of rifle or ghost ring sights. New 2006.

| MSR $619 | $550 | $480 | $415 | $350 | $310 | $270 | $255 | |

Add $60 for ghost ring sights.

Add $170 for Desert camo w/pistol grip and ghost ring sights (mfg. 2007-2012).

* *SuperNova Slug* – 12 ga., 3 in. chamber, features 24 in. rifled bore drilled and tapped barrel with adj. rifle sights, black synthetic ComforTech or 100% coverage Realtree APG HD camo stock and forearm, 8.1 lbs. New 2007.

| MSR $829 | $700 | $575 | $450 | $375 | $325 | $275 | $250 | |

Add $100 for 100% camo coverage.

Add $10 for Field & Slug combo with extra 26 in. Field barrel (mfg. 2007 only).

BERETTA

Current manufacturer with headquarters located in Brescia, Italy since 1526. Current manufacturing locations include Brescia, Italy, Accokeek, MD, and Gallatin, TN (new 2014). The company name in Italy is Fabbrica d'Armi Pietro Beretta. Beretta U.S.A. Corp. was formed in 1977 and is located in Accokeek, MD. Beretta U.S.A. Corp. has been importing Beretta Firearms exclusively since 1980. 1970-1977 manufacture was imported exclusively by Garcia. Distributor and dealer direct sales.

Beretta is one of the world's oldest family owned industrial firms, having started business in 1526. In addition to Beretta owning Benelli, Stoeger, and Franchi, the company also purchased Sako and Tikka Companies in late 1999, Aldo Uberti & Co. in 2000, Burris Optics in 2002, and Steiner International Optics. Beretta continues to be a leader in firearms development and safety, and shooters attest to the reliability of their guns worldwide.

On January 29, 2014, Beretta announced that the company will expand its U.S. operations by building a new firearms manufacturing plant in Gallatin, Tennessee.

For more information and current pricing on both new and used Beretta precision airguns, please refer to the *Blue Book of Airguns* by Dr. Robert Beeman & John Allen (also available online).

PISTOLS: SEMI-AUTO, POST WWII MFG.

On Beretta's large frame pistols, alphabetical suffixes refer to the following: F Model - double/single action system with external safety decocking lever, G Model - double/single action system with external decocking only lever, D Model - double action only without safety lever, DS Model - double action only with external safety lever. Pistols have been manufactured in both Italy and America, and country of origin can be determined on the slide legend.

Information and values for state compliant variations are not listed.

The models in this section appear in numerical sequence.

MODEL PX4 STORM – 9mm Para, .40 S&W, or .45 ACP (new 2007) cal., single/double action, 3.2 (Compact model) or 4 in. barrel, polymer frame, locked breech with rotating barrel system, matte black finish with plastic grips, Pronox (disc.) or Super Luminova 3-dot night sights, 9 (.45 ACP only), 10, 14, or 17 shot mag. (varies due to caliber), accessory rail on lower frame, approx. 27 1/2 oz. New mid-2005.

| MSR $650 | $545 | $485 | $410 | $360 | $300 | $275 | $250 | |

Add $50 for .45 ACP cal. (new 2007).

The trigger mechanism of this gun can be customized to four different configurations: Type F (single/double action decocker and manual safety), Type D (DAO with spurless hammer, LE only), Type G (single/double action decocker with no manual safety, LE only), or Type C (constant action, spurless hammer). Values are for Type C and Type F variations.

* *Model PX4 Storm Inox* – 9mm Para. or .40 S&W cal., similar to Model PX4 Storm, except has stainless steel construction, and 10, 14, or 17 shot only. New 2012.

| MSR $700 | $575 | $500 | $425 | $360 | $300 | $275 | $250 | |

* *Model PX4 Storm Special Duty* – .45 ACP cal. only, DA/SA, 4.6 in. extended barrel, Type F action only, dark earth polymer frame and matte black slide, includes one 9 shot flush and two 10 shot extended mags., Commander style hammer, lower Picatinny rail, ambidextrous safety, two additional backstraps and waterproof case, 28.6 oz.

| MSR $1,150 | $975 | $825 | $700 | $600 | $500 | $425 | $350 | |

* *Model PX4 Storm Compact* – 9mm Para., .40 S&W (new 2012), or .45 ACP (new 2015) cal., similar to Model PX4 Storm, except has compact frame and 3.2 in. barrel, 8 (.45 ACP), 10, 12 (.40 S&W only, new 2012) or 15 (9mm Para. cal. only) shot mag., 27.3 oz. New late 2010.

| MSR $650 | $545 | $485 | $410 | $360 | $300 | $275 | $250 | |

Add $50 for .45 ACP cal. (new 2015).

MSR	100%	98%	95%	90%	80%	70%	60%	Last MSR

* Model PX4 Storm Sub-Compact – 9mm Para. or .40 S&W cal., similar to Model PX4 Storm, except has 10 or 13 (9mm Para. cal. only) shot mag., has sub-compact frame with 3 in. barrel, includes three backstraps, 26 oz. New 2007.

MSR $650	$545	$485	$410	$360	$300	$275	$250	

ARX 160 – .22 LR cal., 9 in. barrel with flash suppressor, 20 shot STANAG Type mag., matte black finish, Mil-Std. 1913 upper and lower rails, polymer flip-up sights, adj. folding stock, pistol grip, ambidextrous mag. release, 5.7 lbs. Mfg. 2013-2014.

	100%	98%	95%	90%	80%	70%	60%	Last MSR
	$475	$425	$375	$325	$275	$250	$225	*$545*

Pistols: Semi-Auto, Model 92 & Variations - 4.9 in. barrel

MODEL 90-TWO TYPE F – 9mm Para. or .40 S&W cal., 4.9 in. barrel, DA/SA, matte metal finish, removable single piece wraparound grip in two sizes, internal recoil buffer and captive recoil spring guide assembly, low profile fixed sights, 10, 12 (.40 S&W cal.), or 17 (9mm Para. cal.) shot mag., lower accessories rail with cover, 32 1/2 oz. Mfg. 2006-2009.

	100%	98%	95%	90%	80%	70%	60%	Last MSR
	$600	$525	$450	$375	$330	$300	$275	*$700*

MODEL 92FS VERTEC – 9mm Para. cal., DA/SA, straight backstrap grip, special short reach trigger, thin dual textured grip panels, and integral accessory rail on lower frame, removable front sight, beveled magwell, 10 shot mag., Bruniton finish, 32.2 oz. Mfg. 2002-2005.

	100%	98%	95%	90%	80%	70%	60%	Last MSR
	$635	$495	$440	$385	$340	$300	$275	*$760*

Add $25 for B-Lok safety system using key lock (mfg. 2003).

* Model 92FS Vertec Stainless (Inox) – stainless variation of the Model 92FS Vertec. Mfg. 2002-2005.

	100%	98%	95%	90%	80%	70%	60%	Last MSR
	$670	$525	$425	$360	$315	$260	$225	*$825*

Add $170 for laser grips (new 2004).
Add $25 for B-Lok safety system using key lock (mfg. 2003).

MODEL 92F WITH U.S. M9 MARKED SLIDE/FRAME – 9mm Para. cal., 100 mfg. with special serial no. range, "BER" prefix, government assembly numbers on frame, slide, hammer, mag. etc., includes plastic case and cleaning brush. Mfg. for the Armed Forces Reserve shooters, identical to military M9, except for serial number.

	100%	98%	95%	90%	80%	70%	60%	
	$1,750	$1,525	$1,350	$1,100	$950	$825	$700	

MODEL 92A1 – 9mm Para. cal., DA/SA, 4.9 in. barrel, three 10 or 17 shot mags., removable front sight, frame accessory rail, internal recoil buffer, rounded trigger guard, captive recoil spring assembly, black Bruniton finish, plastic grips, 34.4 oz, mfg. in Italy. New 2010.

MSR $775	$650	$550	$475	$425	$350	$285	$250	

M9A1 – 9mm Para. cal., DA/SA, features accessory rail on lower frame and checkered grip straps, 10 or 15 shot mag., 3-dot sights, beveled magwell, Black Bruniton finish, 35.3 oz. New 2006.

MSR $775	$650	$565	$485	$435	$365	$315	$265	

Pistols: Semi-Auto, Model 92 & Variations - 4.7 in. barrel

MODEL 92FS INOX TACTICAL – 9mm Para. cal., 4.7 in. barrel, DA/SA, features satin matte finished stainless steel slide and alloy frame, rubber grips, Tritium sights. Mfg. 1999-2000.

	100%	98%	95%	90%	80%	70%	60%	Last MSR
	$695	$560	$480	$425	$375	$325	$295	*$822*

MODEL 92G ELITE IA (BRIGADIER) – 9mm Para. cal., similar to Model 92FS Brigadier, DAO, except has 4.7 in. stainless barrel and many standard I.D.P.A. competition features including front and rear serrated slide, skeletonized hammer, and removable three-dot sighting system, plastic grips, includes Elite engraving on slide, 35.3 oz. Mfg. 1999-2005.

	100%	98%	95%	90%	80%	70%	60%	Last MSR
	$725	$585	$495	$425	$360	$300	$275	*$875*

* Model 92G Elite II (Brigadier) – similar to Model 92G Elite, except has stainless steel slide with black "Elite II" markings, target barrel crown, extended mag. release, optimized trigger mechanism, front and back strap checkering, low profile Novak rear sight, 35 oz. Mfg. mid-2000-2005.

	100%	98%	95%	90%	80%	70%	60%	Last MSR
	$815	$635	$530	$450	$385	$325	$295	*$985*

Pistols: Semi-Auto, Model 92 & Variations - 4.3 in. barrel

MODEL 92F/92FS COMPACT – similar to Model 92F, except has 4.3 in. barrel, DA/SA, 13 shot mag., plastic or wood grips, 31 1/2 oz. While temporarily suspended in 1986, production was resumed 1989-1993.

	100%	98%	95%	90%	80%	70%	60%	Last MSR
	$550	$450	$415	$375	$335	$300	$275	*$625*

Add $20 for checkered walnut grips (Model 92F Wood).
Add $65 for Trijicon sight system.

MODEL 92F & 92FS CENTURION – 9mm Para. cal., similar to Model 92F, except has compact barrel slide unit with full size frame, 4.3 in. barrel, choice of plastic or wood grips, 3 dot sight system, same length as Model 92F Compact, 10 (C/B 1994) or 15* shot mag., 33.2 oz. Mfg. 1992-98.

	100%	98%	95%	90%	80%	70%	60%	Last MSR
	$525	$435	$395	$365	$335	$300	$275	*$613*

MSR	100%	98%	95%	90%	80%	70%	60%	Last MSR

Add approx. $20 for checkered walnut grips (Model 92F Wood).
Add $90 for Tritium sight system (mfg. 1994-98).
Add 10% for Trijicon sights (disc).

MODEL 92FS COMPACT RAIL STAINLESS (INOX)
– 9mm Para. cal., 4 1/4 in. barrel, aluminum alloy frame, stainless steel slide, 10 (disc. 2014) or 13 shot mag., 1913 style lower accessory rail, combat trigger guard, ambidextrous safety, 32 oz. New 2013.

	100%	98%	95%	90%	80%	70%	60%	Last MSR
MSR $850	$695	$595	$500	$450	$375	$325	$285	

Pistols: Semi-Auto, Model 96 & Variations, Recent Mfg.

The models in this section appear in approximate chronological sequence.

MODEL 96A1
– .40 S&W, DA/SA, DA/SA, 4.9 in. barrel, three 10 or 11 shot mags., removable front sight, frame accessory rail, internal recoil buffer, rounded trigger guard, captive recoil spring assembly, ambidextrous safety, black Bruniton finish, plastic grips, 34.4 oz, mfg. in Italy. New 2010.

	100%	98%	95%	90%	80%	70%	60%	Last MSR
MSR $775	$650	$575	$495	$440	$360	$300	$285	

RIFLES: SEMI-AUTO, RECENT MFG.

BM-59 M-1 GARAND
– with original Beretta M1 receiver, M-14 style detachable mag., only 200 imported into the U.S.

	100%	98%	95%	90%	80%	70%	60%	Last MSR
	$3,200	$2,900	$2,400	$1,800	$1,500	$1,300	$1,175	*$2,080*

BM-62
– similar to BM-59, except has flash suppressor and is Italian marked.

	100%	98%	95%	90%	80%	70%	60%	Last MSR
	$3,200	$2,900	$2,400	$1,800	$1,500	$1,300	$1,175	

AR-70
– .222 Rem. or .223 Rem. cal., 5, 8, or 30 shot mag., diopter sights, epoxy finish, 17.72 in. barrel, 8.3 lbs.

	100%	98%	95%	90%	80%	70%	60%	Last MSR
	$1,925	$1,675	$1,375	$1,150	$1,025	$850	$750	*$1,065*

1989 Federal legislation banned the importation of this model into U.S.

ARX 100
– 5.56 NATO cal., lightweight techno-polymer receiver, no pins, matte black or FDE (new 2016) finish, 16 in. quick change cold hammer forged barrel with flash suppressor, can be removed and replaced with various lengths and calibers in a matter of seconds, 30 shot mag., ambidextrous magazine release, accepts AR magazines, case projection can be switched from right to left with a simple push of a button, telescoping folding stock, ambidextrous safety selector, all critical controls are ambidextrous, quad Picatinny rails with full-length upper. Mfg. in the U.S. New mid-2013.

	100%	98%	95%	90%	80%	70%	60%	Last MSR
MSR $1,950	$1,725	$1,525	$1,275	$1,125	$915	$750	$575	

ARX 160
– .22 LR cal., 18.1 in. barrel with flash suppressor, 10 (new 2014), 14 (mfg. 2013 only), or 20 (new 2014) shot STANAG-Type mag., matte black finish, quad Picatinny rails with full-length upper, polymer flip-up sights, adj. folding stock, pistol grip, ambidextrous safety lever and mag. release, 6 lbs. 6 oz. Imported 2013-2015.

	100%	98%	95%	90%	80%	70%	60%	Last MSR
	$515	$440	$375	$335	$315	$285	$250	*$575*

CX4 STORM CARBINE
– 9mm Para. (92 Carbine), .40 S&W (96 Carbine) or .45 ACP (8045 Carbine, disc. 2013.) cal., blowback single action, Giugiaro design featuring tactical styling with one-piece matte black synthetic stock with thumbhole, rubber recoil pad and stock cheekpiece, quad Picatinny rails, ghost ring sights, 16.6 in. hammer forged barrel, reversible crossbolt safety, mag. button, bolt handle, and ejection port, mag. capacities vary depending on caliber, current mfg. has 8 (.45 ACP cal.), 14 (.40 S&W cal., Px4 Storm mag.), 15 (9mm Para. with high cap Model 92 mag.), or 17 (high cap PX4 Storm mag.) shot mag., (this series also accepts Models 96, 8000, 8040, and 8045 pistol mags.), 29.7 in. overall length, 5 3/4 lbs. Mfg. mid-2003-2014.

	100%	98%	95%	90%	80%	70%	60%	Last MSR
	$795	$625	$550	$495	$450	$395	$350	*$915*

Add $95 for 92 Carbine package (includes scope, 9mm Para. (disc. 2005) or .40 S&W cal.). Disc.
Add $50 for top rail (only available in 9mm Para. or .40 S&W cal., mfg. 2006-2007).

This model has been available in many variations - 8045 (.45 ACP), 92 Carbine (8000, 9mm Para.), 92 Carbine package (w/scope), and 96 Carbine (8040, .40 S&W).

RX4 STORM CARBINE
– .223 Rem. cal., ARGO, gas operating system, available in collapsible five position telescoping stock or sporter style stock with optional pistol grip, black matte finish, ghost ring sights, includes 5 and 10 shot AR-15 style magazines. Limited importation 2007-2008.

	100%	98%	95%	90%	80%	70%	60%	Last MSR
	$1,100	$925	$800	$700	$600	$525	$450	*$1,100*

While advertised, only a few samples were brought into the U.S.

SHOTGUNS: SEMI-AUTO

It is possible on some of the following models to have production variances occur including different engraving motifs, stock configurations and specifications, finishes, etc. These have occurred when Beretta changed from production of one model to another. Also, some European and English distributors have sold their excess inventory through Beretta U.S.A., creating additional variations/configurations that are not normally imported domestically. While sometimes rare, these specimens typically do not command premiums over Beretta's domestic models.

MSR	100%	98%	95%	90%	80%	70%	60%	Last MSR

The following Beretta semi-auto models have been listed in numerical sequence, if possible, disregarding any alphabetical suffix or prefix.

Note: values are for unaltered guns.

Subtract 10% on the following factory multi-choke models if w/o newer Beretta Optima-chokes (12 ga. only, became standard 2003).

* ***Model 1200 Riot*** – 12 ga. only, 2 3/4 or 3 in. chamber, 20 in. cyl. bore barrel with iron sights, extended mag. Imported 1989-90 only.

	$400	$375	$350	$295	$250	$225	$200	$660

* ***Model 1201 FP (Riot)*** – 12 ga., riot configuration featuring 18 (new 1997) or 20 (disc. 1996) in. cylinder bore barrel, 5 shot mag, choice of adj. rifle sights (disc.), Tritium sights (disc. 1998) or ghost ring (new 1999, Tritium front sight insert) sights, matte wood (disc.) or black synthetic stock and forearm, matte metal finish (disc.), 6.3 lbs. Mfg. 1991-2004.

	$725	$595	$500	$400	$300	$250	$200	$890

Add $80 for Tritium sights (mfg. 1997-98).

Add $45 for pistol grip configuration (Model 1201 FPG3 - mfg. 1994 only).

TX4 STORM – 12 ga., 3 in. chamber, gas operated, dual lug action with rotating bolt, 18 in. OptimaBore barrel with OptimaChoke HP cylinder tube, optional TX4 Stand Off Device, 5 shot mag., matte black finish, alloy receiver with integral Picatinny rail, black synthetic stock, ghost ring rear sight, elevated post front sight, includes plastic case, approx. 6.4 lbs. Mfg. 2010-2011.

	$1,200	$995	$850	$725	$625	$525	$450	$1,450

BERGARA

Current rifle and barrel manufacturer located in Bergara, Spain. Barrels and Apex rifles imported by Connecticut Valley Arms, located in Duluth, GA, bolt action rifles are currently imported by Black Powder Products, located in Duluth, GA.

Bergara manufactures high quality rifle barrels, in addition to bolt action rifles and single shot Apex rifles imported by Connecticut Valley Arms. Please refer to the Connecticut Valley Arms section for current single shot rifle information and pricing.

RIFLES: BOLT ACTION

Add $200 for KDF muzzle brake.

BCR17 MEDIUM TACTICAL – .308 Win. cal., 22 in. nitride finished stainless steel contoured barrel, Timney or Shilen trigger, pillar bedded with Marine Tex steel filled epoxy, custom machined 20 MOA Picatinny rail, Badger M-4 bottom metal, McMillan A1-3 stock, olive finish with tan and black marbling, 9.9 lbs. Mfg. 2013-2015.

	$3,800	$3,400	$2,975	$2,550	$2,310	$1,870	$1,525	$4,000

MEDIUM TACTICAL CHASSIS STOCK – .308 Win. cal., 22 in. stainless steel barrel, Bergara custom action, 5 shot detachable mag., Timney trigger, Bergara custom Picatinny rail, screwed and pinned, APO Sporter Modular chassis stock, adj. comb height, 10 1/2 lbs. Mfg. 2014-2015.

	$4,200	$3,825	$3,350	$2,875	$2,600	$2,100	$1,725	$4,500

BCR19 HEAVY TACTICAL – .308 Win. or .300 Win. Mag. cal., 26 in. nitride finished stainless steel contoured barrel, 5 shot detachable mag., Timney or Shilen trigger, pillar bedded with Marine Tex steel filled epoxy, custom machined 20 MOA Picatinny rail, Badger M-5 bottom metal, six flush cups, bipod mounting stud, McMillan A-4 stock with adj. butt and comb., OD Green finish, 12 1/2 lbs. Mfg. 2013-2015.

	$4,200	$3,825	$3,350	$2,875	$2,600	$2,100	$1,725	$4,500

HEAVY TACTICAL – .308 Win. cal., Bergara custom action, 24 in. stainless steel barrel, nitride barrel finish, 10 shot detachable mag., Timney trigger, full length unitized Monolithic rail, tubular aluminum forend with accessory rails and flush cups, APO Mod-1 Chassis folding stock, adj. comb height, rear mono pod, 10 1/2 lbs. New 2014.

MSR $4,750	$4,150	$3,550	$3,250	$2,750	$2,150	$1,775	$1,525	

BERSA

Current manufacturer established circa 1958 and located in Ramos Mejia, Argentina. Currently distributed exclusively by Eagle Imports, Inc. located in Wanamassa, NJ. Previously imported and distributed before 1988 by Rock Island Armory located in Geneseo, IL, Outdoor Sports Headquarters, Inc. located in Dayton, OH, and R.S.A. Enterprises, Inc. located in Ocean, NJ. Distributor sales only.

PISTOLS: SEMI-AUTO

THUNDER PRO HC 9/40 – 9mm Para. or .40 S&W cal., DA/SA, 4 1/4 in. barrel with interchangeable Sig Sauer type 3 dot sights, alloy frame/steel slide, 17 (9mm Para. cal.), or 13 (.40 S&W cal.) shot mag., checkered black polymer

MSR	100%	98%	95%	90%	80%	70%	60%	Last MSR

grips, integral locking system, Picatinny lower rail, polygonal rifling, loaded chamber indicator, ambidextrous releases, matte black or duo-tone finish, 30.7 oz.

| MSR $505 | $430 | $375 | $325 | $290 | $235 | $195 | $150 | |

Add $6 for duo-tone finish.

BPCC (BP9/BP40CC) – 9mm Para., .380 ACP, or .40 S&W cal., 3.3 in. barrel, DAO, SFO, 7 (.40 S&W) or 8 shot mag., interchangeable Sig Sauer type front and Glock type rear sights, loaded chamber indicator, Black, Olive Drab (new 2014), Flat Dark Earth (new 2016), or Urban Grey (new 2016) high impact polymer frame with integral grips and front Picatinny rail, Matte Black or Duotone finish, ambidextrous mag. release, steel slide, 21.5 oz. New 2010.

| MSR $430 | $390 | $340 | $295 | $265 | $215 | $175 | $135 | |

Add $10 for Duotone finish.

BINGHAM, LTD.

Previous manufacturer located in Norcross, GA circa 1976-1985.

RIFLES: SEMI-AUTO

PPS 50 – .22 LR cal. only, blowback action, 50 round drum mag., standard model has beechwood stock. Disc. 1985.

| | $250 | $225 | $195 | $180 | $145 | $135 | $125 | *$230* |

Add 15% for deluxe model with walnut stock.

Add 20% for Duramil model with chrome finish and walnut stock.

This model was styled after the Soviet WWII Model PPSh Sub Machine Gun.

AK-22 – .22 LR cal. only, blowback action, styled after AK-47, 15 shot mag. standard, 29 shot mag. available. Standard model had beechwood stock. Disc. 1985.

| | $250 | $225 | $195 | $180 | $145 | $135 | $125 | *$230* |

Add $20 for Deluxe model with walnut stock.

GALIL-22 – .22 LR cal. only, patterned after Galil rifle. Disc.

| | $250 | $225 | $195 | $180 | $145 | $135 | $125 | |

FG-9 – 9mm Para. cal., blowback action, 20 1/2 in. barrel.

While advertised during 1984, this gun never went into production.

BLACK DAWN ARMORY (BLACK DAWN INDUSTRIES)

Current manufacturer of semi-auto pistols and rifles located in Sedalia, MO since 2010.

Black Dawn Armory currently manufactures a complete line of AR-15 style rifles as well as designing their own parts. Their Pro-Shop offers accessories geared toward the AR market, and they also have their own in-house Custom Shop that offers a wide range of services and finish options.

PISTOLS: SEMI-AUTO

BDP-556-10DMM – 5.56 NATO cal., 10 1/2 in. barrel, Magpul PMAG, enhanced trigger guard, ALG Defense QMS trigger, Ergo grip, T6 aluminum upper and lower receivers, laser engraved T-marks, M4 feed ramps, 9 in. MMR free float forend, Odin Works pistol buffer tube, ambi sling mount, Type III hardcoat anodized finish in Black, FDE, or OD Green. New 2016.

Please contact the manufacturer directly for pricing and availability for this model.

BDP-300-8SFC – .300 AAC Blackout cal., 8 1/2 in. barrel, Magpul PMAG, ALG Defense QMS trigger, enhanced trigger guard, Ergo grip, 7 in. MFRC free float forend, T6 aluminum upper and lower receivers, laser engraved T-marks, M4 feed ramps, Odin Works pistol buffer tube, ambi sling mount, Type III hardcoat anodized black finish. New 2016.

Please contact the manufacturer directly for pricing and availability for this model.

RIFLES: SEMI-AUTO

BDR-10 – .308 Win. cal., GIO, 16 or 20 in. M4 profile barrel, Magpul MOE collapsible stock, Magpul MOE grip, flared magwell, free floating handguard, Magpul 20 shot PMAG, black anodized finish, includes hard case. Mfg. 2012-2014.

Retail pricing was never made available for this model.

BDR-15A – 5.56 NATO/.223 Rem. cal., GIO, 16 in. M4 profile barrel with A2 flash hider, A2 front sight, MBUS rear sight, 30 shot mag., Magpul MOE collapsible stock, Magpul MOE grip, enhanced trigger guard, flared magwell, ambi. sling mount, M4 feed ramp, carbine length MFR rail, available in black, Flat Dark Earth, or OD Green finish, includes hard case and one 30 shot PMAG, 6 lbs. 10 oz. Mfg. 2012-2014.

| | $1,075 | $950 | $815 | $685 | $595 | $515 | $440 | *$1,249* |

MSR	100%	98%	95%	90%	80%	70%	60%	Last MSR

BDR-15B – 5.56 NATO/.223 Rem. cal., GIO, 16 in. M4 profile barrel with A2 flash hider, MBUS front and rear sights, 30 shot mag., Magpul MOE collapsible stock, Magpul MOE grip, enhanced trigger guard, flared magwell, ambi. sling mount, M4 feed ramp, mid-length MFR rail, available in black, Flat Dark Earth, or OD Green finish, includes hard case and one 30 shot PMAG, 6 lbs. 15 oz.

| MSR $1,279 | $1,085 | $950 | $825 | $685 | $595 | $515 | $440 | |

BDR-556-16APFC-BLK (BDR-15AP) – 5.56 NATO/.223 Rem. cal., GPO, 16 in. M4 profile barrel with A2 flash hider, A2 front sight, MBUS rear sight, 30 shot mag., Magpul MOE collapsible stock, Magpul MOE grip, enhanced trigger guard, flared magwell, ambi sling mount, M4 feed ramp, carbine length MFR rail, black, FDE (disc. 2014), or OD Green (disc. 2014) finish, includes hard case and one 30 shot PMAG, 6 lbs. 10 oz. New 2012.

| MSR $1,549 | $1,315 | $1,165 | $1,050 | $915 | $785 | $665 | $550 | |

BDR-556-16BPFM (BDR-15BP) – 5.56 NATO/.223 Rem. cal., GPO, 16 in. M4 profile barrel with A2 flash hider, MBUS front and rear sights, 30 shot mag., Magpul MOE collapsible stock, Magpul MOE grip, enhanced trigger guard, flared magwell, ambi. sling mount, M4 feed ramp, mid-length MFR rail, available in black, Flat Dark Earth (disc. 2014), or OD Green (disc. 2014) finish, includes hard case and one 30 shot PMAG, 6 lbs. 15 oz.

| MSR $1,549 | $1,315 | $1,165 | $1,050 | $915 | $785 | $665 | $550 | |

BDR-556-16M (BDR-15M) – 5.56 NATO/.223 Rem. cal., GIO, 16 in. M4 profile barrel with A2 flash hider, A2 front sight, MBUS rear sight, 30 shot mag., Magpul MOE collapsible stock, Magpul MOE grip, enhanced trigger guard, flared magwell, ambi. sling mount, M4 feed ramp, carbine length MFR rail, available in black, Flat Dark Earth (disc. 2015), or OD Green (disc. 2015) finish, includes hard case and one 30 shot PMAG, 7 lbs.

| MSR $1,549 | $1,315 | $1,165 | $1,050 | $915 | $785 | $665 | $550 | |

BDR-556-16MP (BDR-15MP) – 5.56 NATO/.223 Rem. cal., GPO, 16 in. M4 profile barrel with A2 flash hider, A2 front sight, MBUS rear sight, 30 shot mag., Magpul MOE collapsible stock, Magpul MOE grip, enhanced trigger guard, flared magwell, ambi. sling mount, M4 feed ramp, carbine length MFR rail, available in black, Flat Dark Earth (disc. 2015), or OD Green (disc. 2015) finish, includes hard case and one 30 shot PMAG, 7 lbs. New 2012.

| MSR $1,549 | $1,315 | $1,165 | $1,050 | $915 | $785 | $665 | $550 | |

BDR-556-20EML (BDR-15E) – 5.56 NATO/.223 Rem. cal., AR-15 style, GIO, 20 in. M4 profile heavy barrel, target crown, 30 shot mag., enhanced trigger guard, ALG Defense QMS trigger, no sights, Magpul MOE fixed A2 stock, Ergo grip, 15 in. free floating handguard, M4 feed ramps, black anodized finish, 8 lbs. 9 oz.

| MSR $1,299 | $1,100 | $995 | $875 | $735 | $650 | $550 | $465 | |

BDR-300-16FFM (BDR-15BLK) – .300 AAC Blackout cal., GIO, 16 in. M4 profile barrel with A2 flash hider, no sights, 30 shot mag., Magpul MOE collapsible stock, Magpul MOE grip, enhanced trigger guard, flared magwell, ambi. sling mount, M4 feed ramp, mid-length MFR rail, available in black, Flat Dark Earth, or OD Green finish, includes hard case and one 30 shot PMAG, 6 lbs. 11 oz. New 2012.

| MSR $1,299 | $1,100 | $995 | $875 | $735 | $650 | $550 | $465 | |

BDR-16A – 5.56 NATO/.223 Rem. cal., GIO, 16 in. barrel, A2 front sight, MBUS rear sight, Magpul MOE collapsible stock, Magpul MOE grip, available in black, Flat Dark Earth, or OD Green finish. New 2015.

| MSR $1,249 | $1,075 | $950 | $815 | $685 | $595 | $515 | $440 | |

* **BDR-16AP** – 5.56 NATO cal., similar to BDR-16A, except features GPO. New 2015.

| MSR $1,475 | $1,250 | $1,110 | $965 | $800 | $700 | $600 | $495 | |

BDR-16 BLK – .300 AAC Blackout cal., 16 in. barrel, free float MFR handguard, ION bonded heavy bolt carrier group, forged aluminum upper and lower receivers, Magpul pistol grip, MOE collapsible stock, black, FDE, or OD Green finish, 6 lbs. 7 oz. New 2015.

| MSR $1,250 | $1,075 | $950 | $815 | $685 | $595 | $515 | $440 | |

BDR-16M – 5.56 NATO cal., GIO, 16 in. barrel, A2 front sight, MBUS rear sight, Magpul MOE handguard, ION bonded heavy bolt carrier group, forged aluminum upper and lower receivers, Magpul pistol grip, MOE collapsible stock, black, Flat Dark Earth, or OD Green finish, 7 lbs. New 2015.

| MSR $1,199 | $1,025 | $925 | $800 | $685 | $595 | $515 | $440 | |

* **BDR-16MP** – 5.56 NATO cal., similar to BDR-16M, except features GPO. New 2015.

| MSR $1,399 | $1,200 | $1,075 | $950 | $800 | $700 | $600 | $495 | |

ALPHA – 5.56 NATO cal., GIO, custom built model featuring 16 in. M4 profile barrel with A2 muzzle brake and M4 extensions, fixed A2 front sight, forged aluminum upper and lower receivers, flat-top upper receiver w/M4 feed ramp, enhanced flared magwell, standard A2 grip, 6-position collapsible stock, black anodized finish, accessories include Black Dawn rear flip sight, two 30 shot mags., and a case, 9 lbs. Disc. 2014.

Retail pricing was never made available for this model.

MSR	100%	98%	95%	90%	80%	70%	60%	Last MSR

BRAVO – 5.56 NATO cal., GIO, custom built model similar to Alpha, except accessories include extended Black Dawn MFR free float rail enclosing a low profile gas block, Black Dawn front and rear flip up sights, two 30 shot mags., and hard case. Disc. 2014.
    Retail pricing was never made available for this model.

CHARLIE EDITION – 5.56 NATO cal., custom built model similar to Alpha, except features GPO, accessories include a Black Dawn rear flip up sight, two 30 shot mags., hard case. Disc. 2014.
    Retail pricing was never made available for this model.

DELTA EDITION – 5.56 NATO cal., custom built model featuring GPO, 16 in. M4 profile barrel and M4 extensions, forged aluminum upper and lower receivers, flat-top upper receiver w/M4 feed ramps, enhanced flared magwell, standard A2 grip, 6-position collapsible stock, black anodized finish, accessories include Black Dawn MFR free float rail enclosing a Black Dawn low profile gas block, front and rear flip up sights, two 30 shot mags., and hard case, 9 lbs. Disc. 2014.
    Retail pricing was never made available for this model.

ECHO EDITION – 5.56 NATO cal., GIO, custom built model featuring 20 in. H-Bar profile barrel, M4 extensions, 11 in. target crown, fluted and vented free float tube forend with sling swivel stud, 4 rail Picatinny gas block, flat-top upper receiver with M4 feed ramp, enhanced flared magwell, A2 fixed stock, Hogue overmolded pistol grip, black anodized finish, accessories include two 20 shot mags. and hard case. Disc. 2014.
    Retail pricing was never made available for this model.

MOE EDITION – 5.56 NATO cal., GIO, custom built model featuring 16 in. M4 profile barrel with A2 muzzle brake and M4 extensions, fixed A2 front and Magpul MBUS rear sights, forged aluminum lower and flat-top upper receiver w/M4 feed ramps, enhanced flared magwell, Magpul MOE carbine length handguard, Magpul MOE pistol grip and Magpul MOE 6-position collapsible stock, black anodized finish, includes one 30 shot mag. and hard case, 9 lbs. Disc. 2014.
    Retail pricing was never made available for this model.

ZOMBIE SLAYER – 5.56 NATO cal., GIO, custom built model similar to Alpha, except accessories included are one 30 shot Zombie magazine and hard case. Disc. 2014.
    Retail pricing was never made available on this model.

BLACK FORGE LLC

The assets of Black Forge were acquired by Invincible Arms, LLC located in Willoughby, OH, beginning 2015. Invincible Arms operates that brand exclusively as the parts and components arm of the company. Black Forge previously manufactured semi-auto pistols and rifles until 2014, and was located in Orlando, FL.

PISTOLS: SEMI-AUTO

TIER 1 PISTOL – 5.56 NATO cal., AR-15 style, GIO, aluminum flat-top A3 upper receiver, aluminum forged lower receiver, 10 1/2 in. carbine length barrel with Carlson Comps TAC brake, 10 1/2 in. modular rail system with full-length top Picatinny rail, two 3 in. and one 5 in. rail sections, M4 feed ramps, 30 shot detachable mag., Black Forge winter trigger guard, single stage trigger, Magpul industries or U.S. Palm Battle grip, investment cast fire controls, Carpenter M16 LEO bolt carrier group with Black Forge NiPhos coating, hardcoat anodized matte black finish. Mfg. 2014-2015.

	100%	98%	95%	90%	80%	70%	60%	Last MSR
	$1,125	$995	$850	$775	$625	$500	$425	*$1,250*

* **Tier 1 Pistol SIG PSB** – 5.56 NATO cal., similar to Tier 1 pistol, except has fully adj. SIG PSB tactical style stock. Mfg. 2014-2015.

	100%	98%	95%	90%	80%	70%	60%	Last MSR
	$1,250	$1,095	$950	$850	$695	$575	$450	*$1,385*

RIFLES: SEMI-AUTO

All Black Forge rifles and carbines came with a limited lifetime warranty.

A3 FLAT-TOP CARBINE – 5.45x39mm (disc. 2014) or 5.56 NATO cal., GIO, 16 1/2 in. chrome moly steel barrel with A2 birdcage flash hider, A3 flat-top removable carry handle, A2 front sight post gas block, adj. rear sights, 6-position collapsible stock and poly grip with Mil-Spec size buffer tube, double shield M4 handguard, black furniture. Disc. 2015.

	100%	98%	95%	90%	80%	70%	60%	Last MSR
	$800	$700	$625	$550	$485	$415	$370	*$949*

    Add $100 for 5.45x39mm cal. (disc. 2014).

BADGER – .223 Rem., 5.45x39mm, or 7.62x39mm cal., AK-47 design, GIO, 16 1/2 in. hammer forged heavy chrome lined barrel with Phantom muzzle brake and internal recoil reducer, factory integrated adj. sights, M4 Magpul MOE collapsible stock and ACE sidefolder, 4-way adj. milled Red Star Arms trigger system, high grade polymer Scorpion grip, 4-rail Picatinny adapter system, black finish. Disc. 2013.

	100%	98%	95%	90%	80%	70%	60%	Last MSR
	$1,395	$1,225	$1,050	$950	$775	$625	$525	*$1,550*

BF15 M4 TIER 1 – 5.56 NATO cal., AR-15 style, GIO, 16 1/2 in. M4 barrel with A2 birdcage flash suppressor, F-Marked A2 front sight post gas block, 30 shot mag., aluminum flat-top A3 upper receiver w/Picatinny rail, Magpul MBUS Gen2 or A.R.M.S. rear flip up sight, double shield M4 handguard, Magpul (disc. 2013) or Black Forge winter (new 2014) trigger guard, alum. forged lower receiver w/Black Forge logo, SST, Rogers Super-Stoc with Cam-Lock System, 6-position

MSR	100%	98%	95%	90%	80%	70%	60%	Last MSR

collapsible stock w/buffer tube, Magpul MOE or U.S. Palm Battle (new 2014) grip, black furniture, Black Forge Niphos coating (new 2014). Disc. 2015.

	$935	$850	$725	$625	$550	$475	$425	$1,099

BF15 M4 TIER 2 – 5.56 NATO or 5.45x39mm (disc. 2014) cal., GIO, 16 1/2 in. M4 barrel with A2 birdcage flash hider, F-Marked A2 front sight post gas block, alum. flat-top A3 upper receiver with Mil-Spec 1913 Picatinny rail system featuring M4 feed ramps, alum. forged lower receiver with Black Forge logo, SST, Magpul Industries MBUS Gen 2 or A.R.M.S. rear flip up sight, double shield M4 handguard, 6-pos. collapsible stock with Mil-Spec size buffer tube, standard M4 furniture and manganese phosphate BCG finish, black, Kryptek Typhon or Urban Red camo (new 2014) finish. Disc. 2015.

	$900	$795	$675	$610	$515	$440	$395	$999

Add $100 for 5.45x39mm cal. (disc. 2014).

Add $100 for Urban Red camo (new 2014) or Kryptek Typhon finish.

BF15 M4 TIER 3 – 5.56 NATO cal., GIO, 16 1/2 in. M4 barrel with A2 birdcage flash hider, F-Marked A2 front sight post gas block, alum. flat-top A3 upper receiver with Mil-Spec Picatinny rail system featuring M4 feed ramps, double shield M4 handguard, forged alum. lower, SST, 6-pos. collapsible stock with Mil-Spec size buffer tube, black furniture. Mfg. 2014-2015.

	$775	$685	$615	$550	$485	$415	$370	$899

BF15 TIER 1R – .300 AAC Blackout cal., 16 1/2 in. M4 barrel with Carlson Impact muzzle brake, low profile gas block, 13 1/2 in. modular rail system full length top Picatinny rail, two 3 in. and one 5 in. rail sections, aluminum flat-top A3 upper receiver, M4 feed ramps, alum. forged lower with Black Forge logo and safety designations, Black Forge winter trigger guard, Rogers Super-Stoc with innovative cam-lock system, stainless springs, Magpul Industries or U.S. Palm Battle grip, Black Forge Ni-Phos BCG coating, 6-pos. collapsible stock with Mil-Spec size buffer tube. Disc. 2015.

	$1,225	$1,075	$950	$800	$700	$600	$495	$1,425

BF15 TIER 2R – 5.56 NATO cal., 16 1/2 in. M4 barrel with A2 bird cage flash hider, low profile gas block, 13 1/2 in. modular rail system with full length top Picatinny rail, two 3 inch and one 5 in. rail sections, alum. flat-top A3 upper receiver with 1913 Picatinny rail system featuring M4 feed ramps, alum. forged lower receiver with Black Forge logo and safety designations, stainless springs, 6-pos. collapsible stock with Mil-Spec size buffer tube, black furniture. Disc. 2015.

	$975	$875	$740	$625	$550	$475	$425	$1,150

BF15 YOUTH M4 – 5.56 NATO cal., GIO, 16 1/2 in. threaded barrel with F-marked A2 front sight post gas block, aluminum flat-top A3 upper with Mil-Spec Picatinny rail system featuring M4 feed ramps, SST, forged lower receiver, 6-pos. Roger's Super Stock with buffer tube, slim carbine handguards, M4 accessories, black furniture, anodized type 2 color DiamondDyze finish in orange, violet, green, blue, or red. Disc. 2015.

	$835	$725	$625	$575	$485	$415	$370	$979

MID-PISTON DRIVEN CARBINE – 5.56 NATO cal., Adams Arms mid-length piston driven operating system, aluminum flat-top A3 upper receiver with Mil-Spec 1913 Picatinny rail system and M4 feed ramps, aluminum forged lower receiver, 16 1/2 in. Voodoo Innovations Government Contour barrel with VG6 Epsilon muzzle brake, 30 shot detachable mag., Black Forge winter trigger guard, B5 SOPMOD stock with Damage Industries QD stock endplate, Damage Industries vertical grip, Magpul MOE grip, sling swivels, billet charging handle with V3 extended latch, Odin Works 9 in. KeyMod rail, custom Cerakote finish in Blue Titanium, Foliage Green, and Flat Dark Earth. Mfg. 2014-2015.

	$1,350	$1,200	$1,075	$950	$815	$700	$575	$1,599

Add $50 for Blue Titanium finish.

CAR PISTON DRIVEN CARBINE – 5.56 NATO cal., similar to Mid-Piston Driven Carbine, except has Roger's Superstoc and PWS enhanced buffer tube, available in sniper green, sniper gray, and burnt bronze finish. Mfg. 2014-2015.

	$1,320	$1,150	$1,040	$875	$750	$625	$525	$1,549

Subtract $150 for Burnt Bronze finish.

KALASHNIKOV – 7.62x54R cal., AK-47 design, GIO, 23 in. hammer forged heavy chrome lined barrel, Mojo MicroClick rear peep sight and factory front sight, RPK front trunnion, quick detach Advanced Armament Corps. Blackout muzzle brake with suppressor, spring-loaded UTG bipod in the front, and a monopod grip attached to the Magpul PRS adj. stock via a Picatinny rail underneath, Surefire SGM handguard, 4-way adj. milled Red Star Arms trigger guard, Magpul MOE pistol gip, black finish. Disc. 2013.

	$1,775	$1,550	$1,325	$1,200	$975	$800	$675	$1,975

OPERATOR – .308 Win. cal., GIO, 16 1/2 in. barrel, Tromix charging handle and shark muzzle brake, 6-position Magpul MOE stock and ACE Pig Nose adapter, one-piece milled Texas Weapons Systems dog leg rail w/Picatinny rail, flip up Magpul MBUS sights, Magpul MOE grip, 4-rail Midwest Rail adapter system, black furniture. Disc. 2013.

	$1,465	$1,275	$1,125	$1,000	$850	$735	$595	$1,725

OPERATOR GEN 2 – 5.45x39mm cal., GIO, 16 1/2 in. barrel, built on Russian Vepr receiver, includes one 30 shot mag. Disc. 2013.

	$1,275	$1,125	$1,025	$875	$750	$625	$525	$1,495

MSR	100%	98%	95%	90%	80%	70%	60%	Last MSR

RPK – 5.45x39mm cal., GIO, AK-47 design, 23 in. hammer forged heavy chrome lined barrel, built on Russian Vepr 5.45 receiver, Russian red birch laminate original club foot style stock, pistol grip, and handguard, AK Cage Brake, UTG Dragon Claw clamp-on bipod, adj. sights, black finish. Disc. 2013.

	100%	98%	95%	90%	80%	70%	60%	Last MSR
	$1,375	$1,215	$1,075	$950	$815	$700	$575	$1,650

STINGER – 5.45x39mm cal., GIO, 16 in. barrel, 30 shot mag., Vepr RBK receiver, black furniture. Disc. 2013.

	100%	98%	95%	90%	80%	70%	60%	Last MSR
	$1,365	$1,200	$1,075	$950	$815	$700	$575	$1,625

TACTICAL BLACK POLY – .223 Rem., 5.45x39mm, or 7.62x39mm cal., AK-47 design, GIO, 16 1/2 in. hammer forged heavy chrome lined barrel with Afghan era AK-74 style muzzle brake, black polymer stock, adj. sights, 4-way adj. milled Red Star Arms trigger system, integrated bullet guide, internal recoil reducer, adapter block, black finish. Disc. 2013.

	100%	98%	95%	90%	80%	70%	60%	Last MSR
	$1,135	$920	$890	$735	$650	$550	$465	$1,350

Add $75 for .223 Rem. cal.

* ***Tactical Plum Poly*** – .223 Rem., 5.45x39mm, or 7.62x39mm cal., GIO, similar to Tactical Black Poly, except features an ACE 8 1/2 in. skeleton stock with a sidefolder adapter, and comes with a Phantom muzzle brake, factory plum colored pistol grip and two-piece handguard. Disc. 2013.

	100%	98%	95%	90%	80%	70%	60%	Last MSR
	$1,250	$1,110	$965	$800	$700	$600	$495	$1,475

Add $75 for .223 Rem. cal.

VEPR TACTICAL 308 – .308 Win. cal., GIO, 16 1/2 in. barrel with Razr muzzle brake and internal recoil reducer, 10 or 20 shot mag., 4-way adj. milled trigger intrafuse handguard, ACE skeleton stock, Vepr adapter block, Hogue polymer grip, HK front and rear sights, black furniture. Disc. 2013.

	100%	98%	95%	90%	80%	70%	60%	Last MSR
	$1,375	$1,215	$1,075	$950	$815	$700	$575	$1,650

WA-SPr 74 – 5.45x39mm cal., AK-47 design, GIO, 16 1/2 in. hammer forged heavy chrome lined barrel, ACE lightweight stock braided in paracord for comfort and design matched with an Ace sidefolder adapter, 30 shot mag., 4-way adj. milled Red Star Arms trigger system and one-piece recoil reducer, Cerakote firearm coatings in Burnt Bronze with Cerakote Ceramic Micro Clear finish, includes matching Para Patriot Single Point Sling set. Disc. 2013.

	100%	98%	95%	90%	80%	70%	60%	Last MSR
	$2,125	$1,875	$1,550	$1,325	$1,100	$950	$825	$2,375

WOLVERINE – .223 Rem., 5.45x39mm, or 7.62x39mm cal., AK-47 design, GIO, 16 1/2 in. hammer forged heavy chrome lined barrel, factory integrated adj. sights, Russian red birch laminate stock, two-piece handguard and slant muzzle brake with crush washer, bullet guide, 4-way adj. milled Red Star Arms trigger system, black finish. Disc. 2013.

	100%	98%	95%	90%	80%	70%	60%	Last MSR
	$1,135	$920	$890	$735	$650	$550	$465	$1,350

Add $75 for .223 Rem. cal.

SHOTGUNS: SEMI-AUTO

Modified Izhmash, Saiga, and Vepr shotguns were also available in various configurations - prices ranged from $699-$1,295.

SAIGA 12 CHAOS – 12 ga., 18.1 in. smooth bore barrel with Tromix Mini-Monster muzzle brake, 12 shot mag., Chaos Titan quad rail system, monolithic Picatinny rail, iron sights, Ergo F93 AR-15 side folding stock, Red Star Arms 4-way adj. milled fire control group, TAC-47 gas plug, black finish.

	100%	98%	95%	90%	80%	70%	60%	Last MSR
	$1,525	$1,350	$1,150	$1,050	$850	$675	$550	$1,695

VEPR 12 TROMIX SF – 12 ga., threaded, chrome lined barrel, Tromix side-folding stock, Demon brake and Red Star Arms adj. milled trigger, hinged dust cover w/Picatinny rail, Molot polymer pistol grip, upper and lower handguard, Tromix charging handle, 5 shot mag., adj. rear sight, black furniture.

	100%	98%	95%	90%	80%	70%	60%	Last MSR
	$1,725	$1,525	$1,300	$1,175	$950	$775	$600	$1,899

BLACKHEART INTERNATIONAL LLC

Current manufacturer located in Clarksburg, WV. Previously located in Fairmont and Philippi, WV. The company also manufactures separate components for AR-15 style carbines/rifles, in addition to custom bolt actions and barreled actions.

PISTOLS: SEMI-AUTO

BHI-15 S2 AR57 PISTOL – 5.7x28mm cal.,12 in. free float barrel, aluminum upper and lower receiver, Geissele Super Dynamic Combat trigger, Wolff trigger springs, Stark SE-1 pistol grip, black anodized finish. Disc 2014.

	100%	98%	95%	90%	80%	70%	60%	Last MSR
	$1,100	$995	$875	$735	$650	$550	$465	$1,304

RIFLES: BOLT ACTION

BHI manufactures custom bolt action guns for competition, sporting, and military/LE applications. They are built on the BBG bolt action and are available in .300 Win. Mag., .300 AAC Blackout, .308 Win., and .300 Lapua calibers. Each rifle is custom built by their master gunsmith. Please contact the company directly for more information, including pricing and available options (see Trademark Index).

BHI also offered a line of tactical and sport bolt action models. They included the BBG Light Sniper - last MSR was $4,054, BBG Hunter - last MSR was $3,321, BBG F-Class - last MSR was $3,324, and the BBG Tactical - last MSR was $4,579.

MSR	100%	98%	95%	90%	80%	70%	60%	Last MSR

RIFLES: SEMI-AUTO

Blackheart International also makes a variety of NFA carbines for military and law enforcement.

3g PRO – 5.56 NATO cal., AR-15 style, 16 in. Wilson Combat match grade stainless steel barrel with Rolling Thunder compensator, mid-length gas system, 30 shot mag., BHI aluminum free-float modular handguard with full-length top rail, Geissele Super Dynamic Combat two-stage trigger group, Mil-Spec A3 flat-top aluminum upper and BHI-15 Multi caliber aluminum lower receiver, MBUS Pro Offset sights, BHI-Stark pistol grip, Magpul CTR collapsible stock, hardcoat black anodized finish. New 2015.

MSR $2,395	$2,050	$1,800	$1,500	$1,300	$1,075	$935	$795

B10.762RA – 7.62x39mm cal., AK-47 design, 16 1/2 in. barrel, threaded muzzle, 30 shot mag., bayonet lug, G2 single-hook trigger group, CAA or Hogue quad rail forend, adj. sights, BHI-Stark pistol grip, Phoenix KickLite (recoil reduction) stock, black finish. New 2015.

MSR $925	$785	$685	$615	$550	$485	$415	$370

B10.762RB – 7.62x39mm cal., AK-47 design, 16 1/2 in. barrel, threaded muzzle, 30 shot mag., bayonet lug, G2 single-hook trigger group, CAA or Hogue quad rail forend, adj. sights, BHI-Stark pistol grip, Phoenix Technologies AK buttstock with internal storage compartment, soft buttpad, black finish. New 2015.

MSR $845	$725	$650	$580	$515	$450	$385	$340

B10.762RC – 7.62x39mm cal., AK-47 design, 16 1/2 in. barrel, threaded muzzle, 30 shot mag., bayonet lug, G2 single-hook trigger group, CAA front rail system, adj. sights, BHI-Stark pistol grip, Phoenix Technologies Field buttstock featuring a soft recoil pad and 6-position LOP, black finish. New 2015.

MSR $865	$735	$650	$580	$515	$450	$385	$340

BHI-15 (A) – 5.56 NATO cal., AR-15 style, GIO, 16 in. chrome lined barrel, 30 shot mag., manganese phosphate barrel finish, A2 flash hider, standard collapsible stock, polycarbonate handguard, A3 flat-top upper and aluminum lower, hardcoat black anodized finish, standard charging handle, front post sight, rear aperture sight, Mil-Spec trigger group, Wolff springs, detachable carry handle. Disc. 2014.

	$1,050	$950	$815	$685	$595	$515	$440	*$1,245*

BHI-15 MIL-SPEC2 AR57 RIFLE – 5.7x28mm cal., 16 in. free float fluted barrel and Gen 2 receiver, alum. upper and lower receivers, Mil-Spec trigger group, A2 pistol grip, black hardcoat anodized finish, 5.91 lbs. Disc. 2014.

	$1,200	$1,075	$950	$800	$700	$600	$495	*$1,411*

BHI-15 S2 – 5.56 NATO cal., AR-15 style, GIO, 16 in. chrome lined barrel with Surefire flash hider/suppressor adapator, flat-top receiver with Picatinny rail, 30 shot mag., manganese phosphate barrel finish, Magpul CTR collapsible stock, aluminum free-float tube, mid-length handguard, hardcoat black anodized finish, PRI Gasbuster charging handle, Geissele SSA 2-stage trigger, Wolff springs, Stark SE-1 pistol grip, titanium firing pin. Disc. 2014.

	$1,795	$1,575	$1,325	$1,150	$995	$850	$700	*$2,095*

Add $1,800 for BHI-15 S Executive Package - a complete tactical support system for your rifle including Harris bipod and adapter, Magpul flip up front and rear sights, Aimpoint Micro-H1 with QD mount and lens covers, Insight M3X tactical illuminator light, J. Dewey field cleaning kit, hard travel case with padded nylon case, and more.

BHI-15 S2 AR57 RIFLE – 5.7x28mm cal., 16 in. free float fluted barrel, milled aluminum lightweight AR57 upper receiver, and BHI-15 S2 lower receiver, Geissele Super Dynamic Combat trigger, Wolff trigger springs, Stark SE-1 pistol grip, hardcoat black anodized finish, 6.15 lbs. Disc. 2014.

	$1,465	$1,275	$1,125	$1,000	$850	$735	$595	*$1,721*

BHI-15 SPR2 (SPECIAL PURPOSE RIFLE) – 5.56 NATO cal., AR-15 style, GIO, 20 in. chrome lined barrel with Surefire flash hider/suppressor adaptor, manganese phosphate barrel finish, 20 shot mag., flat-top receiver with Picatinny rail, aluminum free float tube, rifle length handguard, PRI Gasbuster charging handle, Geissele SSA two-stage trigger, Mil-Spec A3 flat-top upper, aluminum lower, hard chromed titanium firing pin, Magpul PRS adj. stock, adj. DPMS Panther Tactical grip, oversized magwell, hardcoat anodized black finish. Disc. 2014.

	$2,100	$1,850	$1,575	$1,425	$1,150	$950	$750	*$2,475*

Add $1,600 for BHI-15 SPR Executive Package - a complete tactical support system for your rifle including Leupold Mark-AR 3x9 scope, Harris bipod and adapter, Magpul flip up front and rear sights, Freedom Reaper Scope mount, J. Dewey field cleaning kit, hard travel case with padded nylon case, and more.

SAAK.545R – 5.45x39mm cal., AK-47design, 16 1/2 in. barrel, threaded muzzle, bayonet lug, 30 shot mag., adj. sights, G2 single-hook trigger group, side folding stock, black finish. New 2015.

MSR $1,195	$1,025	$925	$800	$685	$595	$515	$440

SAAK.762R – 7.62x39mm cal., AK-47 design, 16 1/2 in. barrel with threaded muzzle, 30 shot mag., adj. sights, bayonet lug, G2 single-hook trigger group, original wood on grip and forend, underfolding stock, black phosphate receiver and barrel finish. New 2015.

MSR $845	$725	$650	$580	$515	$450	$385	$340

MSR	100%	98%	95%	90%	80%	70%	60%	Last MSR

SAAK.762R GRUNT – 7.62x39mm cal., AK-47 design, 16 1/2 in. barrel with slant-style flash hider/compensator, forward Picatinny rail, 30 shot mag., G2 single-hook trigger group, bayonet lug, Krebs Custom Enhanced safety selector, Hogue overmolded rubber handguard with attachable rails, Stark-BHI pistol grip, ACE Skeleton side folding stock, black phosphate barrel and receiver finish, includes BHI AK-47 tactical sling. New 2015.

	100%	98%	95%	90%	80%	70%	60%
MSR $1,045	$885	$785	$685	$600	$535	$465	$415

* **SAAK.762R Grunt TC** – 7.62x39mm cal., similar to Grunt, except has Stark-BHI or Hogue pistol grip, and Woodland/Urban Tactical Camo furniture. New 2015.

MSR $1,169	$995	$885	$765	$655	$575	$495	$435

SAAK.762R GRUNT PRO – 7.62x39mm cal., AK-47 design, 16 in. barrel with slant style flash hider/compensator, 30 shot mag., G2 single hook trigger group, bayonet lug, Hogue overmolded rubber handguard with attachable rails, Stark-BHI pistol grip, Krebs safety selector, optic rail/receiver cover, ACE Skeleton side folding stock with cushioned rubber buttplate, black phosphate finish, includes BHI AK-47 tactical sling. New 2015.

MSR $1,245	$1,050	$950	$850	$715	$625	$535	$450

* **SAAK.762R Grunt Pro TC** – 7.62x39mm cal., similar to Grunt Pro, except has 16 1/2 in. barrel, 10 shot mag., Stark-BHI or Hogue pistol grip, and Woodland/Urban Tactical Camo finish. New 2015.

MSR $1,435	$1,220	$1,085	$965	$815	$715	$600	$500

SAAK.762R SOPMOD (BHI SOPMOD AK) – 7.62x39mm cal., AK-47 design, 16 in. hammer forged chrome-lined barrel, AK-74 style flash hider, 30 shot polymer mag., Magpul CTR collapsible and folding stock, Stark-BHI pistol grip, widened mag. release lever, CCA aluminum quad rail forend, Tritium front and rear sights, offset vertical grip, quick attach scope mount, enhanced selector lever, includes AKARS sight mounting system, black phosphate finish, 8.7 lbs.

MSR $1,565	$1,325	$1,165	$1,050	$915	$785	$665	$550

SAAR.308R AR-10 CARBINE – .308 Win. cal., 16 in. stainless steel barrel with Surefire SOCOM muzzle brake adapter, 20 shot mag., BHI free-float modular handguard with full-length top rail, Geissele Super Dynamic Combat trigger, BHI .308/7.62 flat-top aluminum upper and lower receivers, BHI-Stark pistol grip, Magpul CTR collapsible stock, hardcoat black anodized finish. New 2015.

MSR $3,100	$2,635	$2,300	$1,900	$1,600	$1,450	$1,185	$950

SAAR.308R AR-10 SPECIAL PURPOSE RIFLE – .308 Win. cal., 20 in. stainless steel barrel with black phosphate finish and Surefire muzzle brake/suppressor adapter or A2 compensator, 20 shot mag., BHI rifle-length modular handguard with top rail, BHI .308/7.62 flat-top aluminum upper and lower receivers, Geissele Super Dynamic Combat trigger, DMPS grip, Magpul PRS stock, hardcoat black anodized finish. New 2015.

MSR $3,500	$2,975	$2,600	$2,230	$2,025	$1,650	$1,350	$1,050

SAAR.556BLK – .300 AAC Blackout cal., AR-15 style, 16 in. barrel with black phosphate finish and A2 muzzle, 30 shot mag., BHI free-float modular handguard with full-length top rail, Geissele Super Dynamic Combat trigger, Mil-Spec A3 flat-top aluminum upper and BHI-15 multi caliber aluminum lower receivers, BHI-Stark pistol grip, Magpul CTR collapsible stock, hardcoat black anodized finish. New 2015.

MSR $2,049	$1,750	$1,530	$1,315	$1,190	$965	$825	$675

SAAR.556R – 5.56 NATO cal., AR-15 style, 16 in. barrel with black Nitride finish and A2 compensator, 30 shot mag., BHI free-float modular handguard, Mil-Spec A3 flat-top aluminum upper and BHI-15 multi-caliber lower receivers, Mil-Spec trigger, BHI-Stark pistol grip, six-pos. collapsible stock, hardcoat black anodized finish. New 2015.

MSR $1,149	$975	$885	$765	$655	$575	$495	$435

SAAR.556RE – 5.56 NATO cal., 16 in. stainless steel barrel with A2 compensator, carbine-length gas system, 30 shot mag., BHI free-float modular handguard, ALG Defense Advanced Combat trigger, Mil-Spec A3 flat-top aluminum and BHI-15 multi-caliber lower receivers, BHI-Stark pistol grip, Magpul CTR collapsible stock, hardcoat black anodized finish. New 2015.

MSR $1,295	$1,100	$995	$875	$735	$650	$550	$465

SAAR.556RSE – 5.56 NATO cal., AR-15 style, 16 in. barrel with black Nitride finish and Surefire muzzle brake/suppressor adapter, carbine length gas system, 30 shot mag., PRI Gasbuster charging handle, BHI free-float modular handguard with full-length top rail, Geissele Super Dynamic Combat two-stage trigger, BHI-Stark pistol grip, Mil-Spec A3 flat-top aluminum upper and BHI-15 multi caliber aluminum lower receiver, Magpul CTR collapsible stock, hardcoat black anodized finish. New 2015.

MSR $1,995	$1,700	$1,500	$1,250	$1,100	$950	$825	$675

SAAR.556SPR – 5.56 NATO cal., AR-15 style, 20 in. barrel with black Nitride finish and Surefire suppressor adapter or A2 muzzle brake, rifle length gas system, 20 shot mag., PRI Gasbuster charging handle, BHI free float modular handguard with full-length top rail, Geissele Super Dynamic Combat trigger, Mil-Spec A3 flat-top upper and BHI-15 multi caliber lower receiver, Magpul PRS stock, hardcoat black anodized finish. New 2015.

MSR $2,495	$2,125	$1,875	$1,550	$1,325	$1,100	$950	$825

MSR	100%	98%	95%	90%	80%	70%	60%	Last MSR

SHOTGUNS: SLIDE ACTION

BH-870-4 – 12 ga., 2 3/4 or 3 in. chamber, Rem. 870 action, 18 1/2 in. barrel, matte black finish, 7 shot, collapsible adj. pistol grip tactical stock, Picatinny rails on the magazine clamp and saddle rail. New 2013.
Please contact the company directly for pricing and availability for this model (see Trademark Index).

BLACKOPS TECHNOLOGIES
Previous manufacturer located in Columbia Falls, MT until 2014.

PISTOLS: SEMI-AUTO

CLASSIC 1911 – 9mm Para., 10mm, .40 S&W, or .45 ACP cal., Government or Commander frame, 5 in. KART National Match barrel, SA, precision tuned trigger, custom made VZ grips, fixed sights with Tritium inserts optional. Mfg. 2013-2014.

| | $2,725 | $2,385 | $2,050 | $1,850 | $1,500 | $1,225 | $1,000 | *$3,195* |

RECON 1911 – 9mm Para., 10mm, .40 S&W, or .45 ACP cal., Government or Commander frame, 4 1/4 in. KART National Match barrel, SA, precision tuned trigger, custom made VZ grips, full perimeter precision TiG magwell, max bevel MSH, fixed sights with Tritium inserts optional. Mfg. 2013-2014.

| | $2,800 | $2,450 | $2,100 | $1,900 | $1,550 | $1,275 | $1,000 | *$3,295* |

RIFLES: BOLT ACTION

INFIDEL – .223 Rem., .260 Rem., .300 Win., .308 Win., or .338 Lapua Mag. cal., Rem. 700 action, 22 in. stainless steel contour barrel, BlackOps recoil lug, Picatinny rail, X-Mark Pro trigger, AICS or AX variant stock, Cerakote finish. Disc. 2014.

| | $3,175 | $2,775 | $2,375 | $2,175 | $1,750 | $1,425 | $1,110 | *$3,725* |

JAEGER – .300 Win. Mag. or .338 LM cal., Model 911 action, 20 or 22 in. barrel with Surefire muzzle brake/suppressor adapter, pinned recoil lug, Manners MCS-T4A or T6 A stock, Timney trigger, embedded front rail night vision mount, Picatinny rail, Cerakote finish, shipped in fitted Pelican case. Disc. 2014.

| | $5,100 | $4,475 | $3,825 | $3,475 | $2,800 | $2,300 | $1,775 | *$5,995* |

KUKRI – .260 Rem. or .308 Win. cal., Model 911 action, 18 in. Bartlein Kukri contour barrel, Manners MCS-T or T3 stock, Timney trigger, black finish, shipped in fitted Pelican case. Disc. 2014.

| | $4,025 | $3,525 | $3,025 | $2,750 | $2,225 | $1,825 | $1,425 | *$4,725* |

PERSEUS – .308 Win. cal., Model 911 action, 19 in. RECON contour barrel, Timney trigger, Manners MCS-T4A or T6A stock, embedded front rail night vision mount, shipped in fitted Pelican case. Disc. 2014.

| | $4,875 | $4,275 | $3,650 | $3,325 | $2,675 | $2,195 | $1,725 | *$5,725* |

RANCH RIFLE – .223 Rem. or .308 Win. cal., Model 911 action, 16 1/2 in. Bartlein Specter contour stainless steel barrel, BlackOps Precision Ranch rifle stock, Timney trigger, Picatinny rail, M16 style extractor and plunger ejector, black finish. Disc. 2014.

| | $4,025 | $3,525 | $3,025 | $2,750 | $2,225 | $1,825 | $1,425 | *$4,725* |

RAVAGE – .17 HMR, .17 M2, .22 LR, or .22 WMR cal., Model 605 action, 18 in. Kreiger Specter contour barrel, Blackops Precision Ranch rifle stock, Specter night vision mount (optional), Timney trigger, includes Pelican case. Disc. 2014.

| | $4,250 | $3,725 | $3,200 | $2,900 | $2,350 | $1,925 | $1,500 | *$4,725* |

RECON – .308 Win. cal., Model 911 action, 18 in. Bartlein Kukri contour stainless steel barrel with Surefire muzzle brake and suppressor adapter, Manners MCS-T6 or T6-A stock, EFR night vision mount, Timney trigger, Nitride or Cerakote finish, precision Pillar system, enhanced heavy duty DBM, ground recoil lug, shipped in custom fitted Pelican case. Disc. 2014.

| | $4,700 | $4,125 | $3,525 | $3,200 | $2,585 | $2,125 | $1,675 | *$5,525* |

SPECTER-BABR – .308 Win. cal., Model 911 action, 18 in. Bartlein Specter contour barrel, Manners MCS Series of stocks, integral back-up iron sight system, EFR or Specter night vision mount, Timney trigger, black finish, shipped in custom fitted Pelican case. Disc. 2014.

| | $5,625 | $4,925 | $4,225 | $3,825 | $3,095 | $2,550 | $2,000 | *$6,625* |

BLACK RAIN ORDNANCE, INC.
Current rifle and pistol manufacturer established in 2008, located in Neosho, MO. Dealer and distributor sales.

PISTOLS: SEMI-AUTO

BRO SPEC16 PISTOL – 5.56 NATO or .300 AAC Blackout cal., low profile gas block, 10 1/2 in. chrome moly barrel with A2 flash hider, Mil-Spec GI trigger, MOE grip, black Nitride bolt and carrier groups, forged upper/lower receivers, forged charging handle, 10 in. M-LOK handguard, black finish. New 2016.

| MSR $899 | $775 | $685 | $615 | $550 | $485 | $415 | $370 | |

MSR	100%	98%	95%	90%	80%	70%	60%	Last MSR

PG5 – .223 Rem. cal., GPO, 7 1/5 in. stainless fluted black barrel with HCC flash hider, 30 shot PMag., 7 in. quad rail, adj. low profile gas block, milled billet aluminum receiver, black MOE grip, black anodized finish, 5 lbs. 4 oz. Mfg. 2015 only.

	$1,600	$1,400	$1,200	$1,095	$900	$775	$625	*$1,889*

PG9 – .223 Rem. cal., GPO, 7 1/2 in. stainless steel fluted barrel, 30 shot PMag., black 7 in. quad rail, milled billet aluminum receiver, adj. low profile gas block, black MOE grip, Norguard finish, 5 lbs. 4 oz. Mfg. 2015 only.

	$1,600	$1,400	$1,200	$1,095	$900	$775	$625	*$1,889*

RIFLES: SEMI-AUTO

COMPETITION SERIES - BRO COMP3G – 5.56 NATO or .308 Win. cal., rifle length gas system, adj. gas block, 16 or 18 in. fluted stainless steel barrel, Competition compensator, BRO-DIT trigger with KNS, Luth AR MBA-1 stock, MOE grip, billet receivers, 17 3/4 in. SLM M-LOK handguard, Black, Blue Titanium, or Smith's Grey finish. New 2016.

MSR $2,299	$1,950	$1,725	$1,450	$1,250	$1,050	$900	$750	

Add $600 for .308 Win. cal.

HUNTING SERIES - BRO PREDATOR .308 – .308 Win. cal., rifle length gas system, adj. gas block, 18, 20, or 24 in. fluted stainless steel barrel, Competition compensator, BRO-DIT trigger with KNS, Magpul PRS stock, MIAD grip, billet receivers, 15 in. M-LOK handguard, Black, FDE, or OD Green finish. New 2016.

MSR $2,449	$2,075	$1,815	$1,500	$1,300	$1,075	$935	$795	

HUNTING SERIES - BRO PREDATOR 5.56 – 5.56 NATO cal., adj. gas block, rifle length gas system, 18, 20, or 24 in. fluted stainless steel barrel, BRO-DIT trigger with KNS, Magpul PRS stock, MOE grip, billet receivers, 15 in. M-LOK handguard, Black, FDE, or OD Green finish. New 2016.

MSR $1,849	$1,575	$1,385	$1,185	$1,065	$915	$785	$635	

RECON SERIES - BRO FORCE – 5.56 NATO, .300 AAC Blackout, or .308 Win. cal., adj. gas block, 16 in. Divot mid-length gas stainless barrel, milled flash suppressor, nickel boron bolt carrier, aluminum billet receivers, BRO-DIT trigger with KNS, UBR stock, MOE grip, 15 in. M-LOK handguard, Skulls or Digi-Tan finish. New 2016.

MSR $1,949	$1,650	$1,440	$1,200	$1,075	$925	$795	$650	

Add $600 for .308 Win. cal.

RECON SERIES - BRO SCOUT – 5.56 NATO, .300 AAC Blackout, or .308 Win. cal., mid-length gas system, adj. gas block, 16 in. lightweight profile barrel, slim milled flash suppressor, BRO-DIT trigger with KNS, MFT Minimalist stock, MOE grip, billet receivers, 15 in. SLM M-LOK handguard, Smith's Grey, FDE, or OD Green Cerakote finish. New 2016.

MSR $1,799	$1,525	$1,350	$1,175	$1,050	$900	$775	$625	

Add $600 for .308 Win. cal.

RECON SERIES - BRO URBAN – 5.56 NATO, .300 AAC Blackout, or .308 Win. cal., adj. gas block, 16 in. double flute stainless barrel, milled flash suppressor, mid-length gas system, aluminum billet receivers, BRO-DIT trigger with KNS, MOE SL stock, MOE grip, 12 in. M-LOK handguard, Black or Norguard finish. New 2016.

MSR $1,699	$1,450	$1,275	$1,125	$1,000	$850	$735	$595	

Add $600 for .308 Win. cal.

SPEC SERIES - BRO SPEC15 CARBINE – 5.56 NATO or .300 AAC Blackout cal., low profile gas block, 10 1/2 in. chrome moly barrel with A2 flash hider, Mil-Spec GI trigger, MOE grip, forged upper/lower receivers, forged charging handle, 10 in. M-LOK handguard, black finish. New 2016.

MSR $899	$775	$685	$615	$550	$485	$415	$370	

LIMITED EDITION NRA RIFLE – .223 Rem. cal., GPO, 16 in. custom stainless two-tone barrel with straight flute and round competition compensator, 30 shot PMag., adj. low profile gas block, milled billet aluminum receiver, MOE stock and grip, black anodized finish, officially licensed by the NRA, 6 lbs. 7 oz. Limited mfg. 2015 only.

	$1,875	$1,650	$1,425	$1,300	$1,050	$875	$725	*$2,209*

PG1 – .223 Rem. cal., GPO or GIO, 20 shot mag., 16 in. slim blast stainless steel barrel with flash suppressor, detachable folding sights, flat-top Picatinny rail with 7 in. black barrel quad rail, black pistol grip and collapsible MOE stock, Pink Splash receiver finish. Disc. 2015.

	$1,725	$1,525	$1,300	$1,175	$950	$825	$675	*$2,039*

Add $350 for PG1 with gas piston operation.

PG2 – .223 Rem. cal., GIO or GPO, 20 shot mag., 16 in. partially fluted black barrel with flash suppressor, flat-top Picatinny rail with 7 in. FDE quad rail, FDE UBR stock, Digital Tan receiver finish, detachable folding sights. Disc. 2015.

	$2,050	$1,800	$1,550	$1,400	$1,125	$925	$795	*$2,439*

Add $360 for PG2 with gas piston operation.

MSR	100%	98%	95%	90%	80%	70%	60%	Last MSR

PG3 – .223 Rem. cal., GIO or GPO, 20 shot mag., 16 in. black/white finished partially spiral fluted barrel with flash suppressor, flat-top Picatinny rail with 7 in. black quad rail, black UBR stock, Silver Skulls receiver finish, detachable folding sights, 7 lbs. 4 oz. Disc. 2015.

| | $1,995 | $1,750 | $1,500 | $1,350 | $1,100 | $900 | $750 | $2,379 |

Add $400 for PG3 with gas piston operation.

PG4 – .223 Rem. cal., GIO, 20 shot mag., 24 in. partially fluted black bull barrel, flat-top Picatinny rail with 12 in. black or FDE (disc. 2012, reintroduced 2015) quad rail, black PRS stock, black or FDE (disc. 2012, reintroduced 2015) finish. Disc. 2015.

| | $1,895 | $1,650 | $1,425 | $1,300 | $1,050 | $875 | $725 | $2,239 |

Add $30 for FDE finish (disc. 2012, reintroduced 2015).

PG5 – .223 Rem. cal., GIO or GPO, 20 shot mag., 16 in. partially fluted stainless black barrel with flash suppressor, flat-top Picatinny rail with 7 in. black quad rail, black MOE stock, black finish, detachable folding sights, 6 lbs. 7 oz. Disc. 2015.

| | $1,795 | $1,575 | $1,325 | $1,150 | $995 | $850 | $700 | $2,109 |

Add $330 for PG5 with gas piston operation.

PG6 – .223 Rem. cal., GIO or GPO, adjustable low profile gas block, 16 in. partially fluted black barrel with flash suppressor, milled billet aluminum receiver, flat-top Picatinny rail with 9 in. FDE quad rail, FDE MOE stock, detachable folding sights, 30 shot PMAG, black anodized receiver finish, 6 lbs., 7 oz. Disc. 2015.

| | $1,795 | $1,575 | $1,325 | $1,150 | $995 | $850 | $700 | $2,109 |

Add $360 for PG6 with gas piston operation.

PG7 – Disc. 2011.

| | $1,675 | $1,465 | $1,250 | $1,150 | $950 | $825 | $675 | $1,989 |

PG8 – Disc. 2011.

| | $1,675 | $1,465 | $1,250 | $1,150 | $950 | $825 | $675 | $1,989 |

PG9 – .223 Rem. cal., GIO or GPO, 20 shot mag., 16 in. M4 partially fluted MACH barrel with flash suppressor, flat-top Norguard finished receiver with 7 in. black quad rail, black pistol grip and MOE stock, detachable folding sights, 6 lbs. 7 oz. Disc. 2015.

| | $1,795 | $1,575 | $1,325 | $1,150 | $995 | $850 | $700 | $2,109 |

Add $350 for PG9 with gas piston operation.

PG11 – .223 Rem. cal., GIO, 20 shot mag., 18 or 20 (disc. 2014) in. partially fluted black barrel with compensator, no sights, flat-top Picatinny rail with 12 in. black or Flat Dark Earth modular rail, black or FDE UBR stock, black, Digital Tan, Flat Dark Earth, Norguard, Pink Splash, or Silver Skulls receiver finish, 7 lbs. 10 oz. Disc. 2015.

| | $2,275 | $1,925 | $1,625 | $1,390 | $1,125 | $975 | $850 | $2,689 |

Add $40 for Digital Tan, Flat Dark Earth, Norguard, Pink Splash, or Silver Skulls finish.

PG12 – .308 Win. cal., GIO, 20 shot mag., 18 (disc. 2014) or 20 in. partially fluted black or stainless finished barrel with compensator, flat-top Picatinny rail with 12 in. black or FDE modular rail, black or FDE PRS stock, black, Digital Tan, FDE, Norguard, Pink Splash, or Silver Skulls finish, 9 lbs. 8 oz. Disc. 2015.

| | $2,695 | $2,350 | $2,025 | $1,850 | $1,475 | $1,225 | $995 | $3,189 |

Add $40 for Digital Tan, FDE, Norguard, Pink Splash, or Silver Skulls finish.

PG13 – .308 Win. cal., GIO, 20 shot mag., 18 in. partially spiral fluted black/white finished barrel with flash suppressor, no sights, Silver Skull finished receiver with flat-top Picatinny rail and 9 in. black modular rail, black pistol grip and UBR stock, 9 lbs. 8 oz. Disc. 2015.

| | $2,575 | $2,250 | $1,925 | $1,750 | $1,425 | $1,150 | $950 | $3,049 |

PG14 – .308 Win. cal., GIO, 20 shot mag., 18 in. partially fluted stainless barrel with flash suppressor, Norguard finished receiver with Picatinny rail and 9 in. Black modular rail, Black pistol grip and MOE stock, no sights, 8 lbs. 13 oz. Disc. 2015.

| | $2,285 | $1,925 | $1,625 | $1,390 | $1,125 | $975 | $850 | $2,699 |

PG15 – .308 Win. cal., GIO, 18 or 20 in. partially fluted black barrel with compensator, milled billet aluminum receiver, adj. low profile gas block, flat-top Picatinny rail with 12 in. black modular rail, 20 shot mag., black MOE stock, MIAD grip, black or FDE receiver finish, 8 lbs. 1 oz. Mfg. 2013-2015.

| | $2,375 | $2,075 | $1,725 | $1,475 | $1,200 | $1,025 | $895 | $2,809 |

Add $50 for FDE (Flat Dark Earth) finish.

PG16 – .308 Win. cal., GIO, 20 shot mag., 24 in. partially fluted black bull barrel, flat-top Picatinny rail with 12 in. black or FDE modular rail, black or FDE pistol grip and PRS stock, black or FDE finish, no sights, 11 lbs. Disc. 2015.

| | $2,425 | $2,100 | $1,740 | $1,475 | $1,200 | $1,025 | $895 | $2,869 |

Add $30 for FDE (Flat Dark Earth) finish.

MSR		100%	98%	95%	90%	80%	70%	60%	Last MSR

PG17 – .223 Rem. cal., GIO, 20 shot mag., 18 or 24 in. partially fluted black bull barrel, no sights, flat-top Picatinny rail with 9 or 12 in. black or FDE modular rail, black or FDE pistol grip and UBR stock, black or FDE finish. Disc. 2013.

		$2,150	$1,875	$1,625	$1,450	$1,185	$975	$750	$2,359

Add $30 for FDE (flat dark earth) finish.

BLACK RIFLE COMPANY LLC

Previous rifle and accessories manufacturer located in Clackamas, OR until 2014.

CARBINES/RIFLES: SEMI-AUTO

BRC FORGED RECEIVER MOE CARBINE – AR-15 style, GIO, stainless steel low profile gas block, 16 in. M4 Isonite barrel with Victory compensator/flash hider, Magpul MOE stock and grip, tactical trigger, forged upper and lower receiver, CNC machined quad rail, hardcoat anodized Cerakote ceramic coating, black or Flat Dark Earth finish. Disc. 2014.

		$1,675	$1,475	$1,250	$1,150	$925	$775	$625	$1,849

BRC FORGED RECEIVER MID-LENGTH CARBINE – AR-15 style, GIO, similar to BRC Forged Receiver MOE Carbine, except has 16 in. mid-length gas medium contour isonite barrel, Black, Dark Earth, Olive Drab, Sniper Gray, or White finish. Disc. 2014.

		$1,675	$1,475	$1,250	$1,150	$925	$775	$625	$1,849

BRC BILLET MID-LENGTH CARBINE – AR-15 style, GIO, similar to BRC Forged MOE Carbine, except has 16 in. gas medium contour barrel, billet mid-length receiver, Magpul MOE stock and grip standard, other stock options are available, choice of Black, Dark Earth, Olive Drab, Sniper Gray, or White finish. Disc. 2014.

		$1,675	$1,475	$1,250	$1,150	$925	$775	$625	$1,849

Add $50 for 14 1/2 in. pinned compensator.

BRC SASS RIFLE – 6.8 SPC cal., AR-15 style, GIO, billet receivers, 18 in. match grade barrel with Victory compensator, 13 in. MQR rail, Magpul PRS stock, Ergo grip, tactical latch, stainless steel polished carrier with MP tested bolt. Disc. 2014.

		$1,875	$1,650	$1,400	$1,200	$1,025	$875	$725	$2,200

BLACK WEAPONS ARMORY

Previous custom manufacturer located in Tucson, AZ until 2014.

RIFLES: SEMI-AUTO

Black Weapons Armory manufactured custom AR-15 rifles built to customer specifications and gunsmithing as well as AR-15 parts and accessories. Previous models included the PUG (Practical Ugly Gun) - last MSR in 2014 was $2,050.

BLASER

Currently manufactured by Blaser Jagdwaffen GmbH in Isny im Allgäu, Germany. Currently imported and distributed beginning late 2006 by Blaser USA, located in San Antonio, TX. Previously located in Stevensville, MD. Previously imported and distributed 2002-2006 by SIG Arms located in Exeter, NH, and circa 1988-2002 by Autumn Sales Inc. located in Fort Worth, TX. Dealer sales.

The Blaser Company was founded in 1963 by Horst Blaser. In 1986, the company was taken over by Gerhard Blenk. During 1997, the company was sold to SIG. In late 2000, SIG Arms AG, the firearms portion of SIG, was purchased by two Germans, Michael Lüke and Thomas Ortmeier, who have a background in textiles. Today the Lüke & Ortmeier group (L&O Group) includes independently operational companies such as Blaser Jadgwaffen GmbH, Mauser Jagdwaffen GmbH, J.P. Sauer & Sohn GmbH, SIG-Sauer Inc., SIG-Sauer GmbH and SAN Swiss Arms AG.

Blaser currently makes approximately 20,000 rifles and shotguns annually, with most being sold in Europe.

RIFLES: BOLT ACTION

The R-93 rifle system's biggest advantage is its component interchangeability. Both barrels and bolt heads/assemblies can be quickly changed making the R-93 a very versatile rifle platform. Many special orders and features are available; please contact Blaser USA directly for additional information, including pricing and availability (see Trademark Index).

Add $415 for saddle scope mount on all current Blaser rifles.

Add $355 for left-hand stock available on currently manufactured R-8 and R-93 models.

Add $242 for Kickstop recoil pad on currently manufactured Blaser rifles.

Beginning late 2006, Blaser began offering graded wood between grades 3-11 on most models. Please refer to these listings under each current model.

R-93 TACTICAL 2 – please refer to listing in the Sig Sauer section under the Rifles: Bolt Action category.

This model is distributed by Sig Sauer Inc., located in Exeter, NH.

MSR	100%	98%	95%	90%	80%	70%	60%	Last MSR

BLUEGRASS ARMORY

Current rifle manufacturer located in Ocala, FL. Previously located in Richmond, KY. Consumer direct sales. During 2010, Bluegrass Armory was purchased by Good Times Outdoors.

RIFLES: BOLT ACTION

VIPER XL 50 – .50 BMG or .510 DTC Europ cal., single shot action with 3-lug bolt, 29 in. chrome moly steel barrel with muzzle brake, one-piece frame with aluminum stock (choice of gray, OD green, or black), incorporates Picatinny rail, includes detachable bipod, right or left hand, approx. 24 lbs. New 2003.

| MSR $3,499 | $3,250 | $2,950 | $2,700 | $2,500 | $2,300 | $2,100 | $1,950 | |

Add $100 for OD Green or Grey finish.

MOONSHINER – .308 Win., .300 Win. Mag., or .338 Lapua cal., Bullpup configuration with twin lugs, 21, 24, or 26 in. barrel with muzzle brake, 8 in. Picatinny rail on top of receiver plus 3 on forearm, detachable mag., soft contoured recoil pad with storage compartment in stock, available in Coytoe Tan, OD Green, or Tactical Black finish, 11 lbs. New 2011.

| MSR $2,995 | $2,750 | $2,400 | $2,100 | $1,750 | $1,475 | $1,125 | $975 | |

BOBCAT WEAPONS INC.

Previous manufacturer from April, 2003-circa 2006 and located in Mesa, AZ. During late 2006, the company name was changed to Red Rock Arms.

Please refer to Red Rock Arms in the R section for current information and pricing.

RIFLES: SEMI-AUTO

BW-5 MODEL – 9mm Para. cal., stamped steel or polymer (Model BW-5 FS) lower receiver, roller lock delayed blowback operating system, 16 1/2 in. stainless steel barrel, choice of black, desert tan, OD green, or camo stock, pistol grip, and forearm, Model BW-5 FS has fake suppressor, paddle mag. release and 8 7/8 in. barrel, 10 shot mag., approx. 6.4 lbs. Mfg. 2003-2006.

| | $1,175 | $995 | $875 | $800 | $725 | $650 | $575 | *$1,350* |

Add $275 for Model BW-5 FS.

BOHICA

Previous manufacturer and customizer located in Sedalia, CO, circa 1993-1994.

RIFLES: SEMI-AUTO

M16-SA – .223 Rem., .50 AE, or various custom cals., AR-15 style, GIO, 16 or 20 in. barrel, A2 sights, standard handguard, approx. 950 were mfg. through September 1994.

| | $1,375 | $1,225 | $1,000 | $850 | $725 | $600 | $525 | |

Add $100 for flat-top receiver with scope rail.
Add $65 for two-piece, free floating handguard.

In addition to the rifles listed, Bohica also manufactured a M16-SA Match variation (retail was $2,295, approx. 10 mfg.), a pistol version of the M16-SA in both 7 and 10 in. barrel (retail was $1,995, approx. 50 mfg.), and a limited run of M16-SA in .50 AE cal. (retail was $1,695, approx. 25 mfg.).

BRAVO COMPANY MFG. INC.

Current rifle manufacturer located in Hartland, WI.

CARBINES/RIFLES: SEMI-AUTO

Bravo Company Mfg., Inc. manufactures a line of AR-15 style rifles with many available options and accessories. The company is also a dealer/distributor for other companies that specialize in tactical gear.

A4 RIFLE – 5.56 NATO cal., GIO, polymer handguards, detachable carry handle with windage and elevation adj. 600m rear sight, black hardcoat anodized finish, fixed buttstock, Mil-Spec F-marked forged front sights, M4 flat-top receiver, Mod 4 charging handle, chrome lined bore and chamber, MOE enhanced trigger guard, M4 feed ramp barrel extension. Disc. 2014.

| | $1,035 | $925 | $800 | $685 | $595 | $515 | $440 | *$1,219* |

BCM PRECISION 18 RIFLE – 5.56 NATO cal., 18 in. steel barrel, M4 feed ramp barrel extension, forged aluminum lower and flat-top upper receivers, BCM Mod 4 charging handle, tactical handguard, mid-length GIO, Magpul MOE enhanced trigger guard, M4 stock, hardcoat anodized finish, 6 lbs. 10 oz. Mfg. 2015 only.

Retail pricing was not made available for this model.

MSR	100%	98%	95%	90%	80%	70%	60%	Last MSR

BCM SAM-RIFLE – 5.56 NATO cal., 20 in. heavy profile stainless steel barrel, M4 feed ramp barrel extension, forged aluminum lower and flat-top upper receivers, rifle length GIO, BCM Mod 4 charging handle, Magpul MOE enhanced trigger guard, KAC free-float handguard, taper pinned KAC folding front sight, A2 fixed stock, hardcoat anodized finish. Mfg. 2015 only.

	$925	$850	$725	$625	$550	$475	$425	*$1,099*

EAG TACTICAL CARBINE – 5.56 NATO cal., 14 1/2 in. Government profile barrel with permanently attached A2X flash hider for a civilian legal 16 in. barrel, M4 feed ramp barrel extension, mid-length GIO, F-marked forged front sight and pinned front sight base, BCM Mod 3 charging handle, forged aluminum lower and flat-top upper receivers, LaRue Tactical 9 in. Stealth free float handguard, Troy Industries/BCM folding battle sight, three TangoDown SCAR rail covers, TangoDown QD vertical Grip-K, Battle Grip, and PR#4 sling mount, Magpul MOE enhanced trigger guard, Magpul MOE stock, also includes SureFire G2 LED illuminator and VTAC light mount, black or FDE finish. New 2015.

MSR $2,263	$1,925	$1,685	$1,425	$1,225	$1,035	$885	$735	

CAR-16LW MOD 0 CARBINE – 5.56 NATO cal., GIO, 16 in. lightweight barrel, basic rifle with double heat shield handguards, no rear sight, black hardcoat anodized finish, adj. Magpul stock, Mil-Spec F-marked forged front sight, M4 flat-top receiver, upper Picatinny rail, Mod 4 charging handle, chrome lined bore and chamber. Disc. 2014.

	$925	$850	$725	$625	$550	$475	$425	*$1,099*

CAR-16LW MOD 1 CARBINE – 5.56 NATO cal., similar to CAR-16LW, except has detachable carry handle with windage and elevation adj. 600m rear sight. Disc. 2014.

	$1,035	$925	$800	$685	$595	$515	$440	*$1,219*

HALEY STRATEGIC JACK CARBINE – 5.56 NATO cal., 14 1/2 in. Govt. profile barrel with permanently attached BCM Gunfighter compensator for a civilian legal 16 in. barrel, M4 feed ramp barrel extension, forged aluminum lower and flat-top upper receivers, mid-length GIO, Geissele super modular rail, BCM Mod 4 charging handle, ALG Defense ACT trigger, enhanced trigger guard, diopter front folding battle sight and rear battle sight, B5 Systems SOPMOD Bravo stock, Haley Strategic Thorntail offset light mount, hardcoat anodized finish, 6 lbs. 11 oz. New 2015.

MSR $2,263	$1,925	$1,685	$1,425	$1,225	$1,035	$885	$735	

M4 MOD 0 CARBINE – 5.56 NATO cal., GIO, 16 in. barrel, basic rifle with double heat shield handguards, no rear sight, black hardcoat anodized finish, adj. Magpul stock, Mil-Spec F-marked forged front sight, M4 flat-top receiver, upper Picatinny rail, Mod 4 charging handle, chrome lined bore and chamber, MOE enhanced trigger guard, M4 feed ramp barrel extension.

MSR $1,202	$1,025	$925	$800	$685	$595	$515	$440	

M4 MOD 1 CARBINE – 5.56 NATO cal., GIO, 16 in. barrel, double heat shield handguards, detachable carry handle with windage and elevation adj. 600m rear sight, black hardcoat anodized finish, adj. Magpul stock, Mil-Spec F-marked forged front sight, M4 flat-top receiver, Mod 4 charging handle, chrome lined bore and chamber, MOE enhanced trigger guard, M4 feed ramp barrel extension, 6.9 lbs.

MSR $1,334	$1,120	$995	$875	$735	$650	$550	$465	

M4 MOD 2 CARBINE – 5.56 NATO cal., GIO, 16 in. barrel, drop in tactical handguard, folding rear battle sight, black hardcoat anodized finish, adj. Magpul stock, Mil-Spec F-marked forged front sight, M4 flat-top receiver, quad rail, Mod 4 charging handle, chrome lined bore and chamber, MOE enhanced trigger guard, M4 feed ramp barrel extension.

MSR $1,509	$1,275	$1,125	$1,025	$875	$750	$625	$525	

M4 MOD 3 CARBINE – 5.56 NATO cal., GIO, 16 in. M4 barrel, F-marked forged front sight, pinned front sight base, folding rear iron sight, M4 feed ramp barrel extension, BCM Mod 4 charging handle, forged aluminum upper and lower receivers, tactical handguard with double heat shield, carbine length GIO, Magpul MOE enhanced trigger guard, M4 stock, hardcoat anodized finish, 6 lbs. 8 oz. Disc. 2015.

Retail pricing was not available for this model.

MID-16 MOD 0 CARBINE – 5.56 NATO cal., GIO, 16 in. barrel, basic rifle with Magpul MOE handguards, no rear sight, black hardcoat anodized finish, adj. Magpul stock, Mil-Spec F-marked forged front sight, M4 flat-top receiver, upper Picatinny rail, Mod 4 charging handle, chrome lined bore and chamber, M4 feed ramp barrel extension.

MSR $1,218	$1,035	$925	$800	$685	$595	$515	$440	

MID-16 MOD 2 CARBINE – 5.56 NATO cal., GIO, 16 in. barrel, drop in tactical handguard, folding rear battle sight, black hardcoat anodized finish, adj. Magpul stock, Mil-Spec F-marked forged front sight, M4 flat-top receiver, quad rail, Mod 4 charging handle, chrome lined bore and chamber, MOE enhanced trigger guard, M4 feed ramp barrel extension.

MSR $1,534	$1,290	$1,125	$1,025	$875	$750	$625	$525	

MID-16 MOD 3 CARBINE – 5.56 NATO cal., 16 in. Government profile steel barrel, M4 feed ramp, F-marked forged front sight, pinned front sight base, folding rear iron sight, mid-length GIO, BCM Mod 4 charging handle, forged aluminum upper and lower receivers, modular tactical handguard, Magpul MOE enhanced trigger guard, M4 stock, hardcoat anodized finish, 6 lbs. 11 oz. Mfg. 2015 only.

Retail pricing was not available for this model.

MSR	100%	98%	95%	90%	80%	70%	60%	Last MSR

MID-16LW MOD 0 CARBINE – 5.56 NATO cal., GIO, 16 in. lightweight barrel, M4 flat-top receiver, black hardcoat anodized finish, adj. Magpul stock, Mil-Spec F-marked forged front sights, Mod 4 charging handle, chrome lined bore and chamber, Magpul MOE enhanced trigger guard. Mfg. 2011-2015.

	$935	$850	$725	$625	$550	$475	$425	*$1,119*

MK12 MOD 0 – 5.56 NATO cal., GIO, 18 in. MK12 profile stainless steel barrel with flash hider or compensator, PRI Gen III 12 in. carbon fiber handguard, optics ready railed upper receiver, forged aluminum lower, BCM Mod 4 charging handle, PRI folding front sight base, Magpul MOE enhanced trigger guard, A2 fixed stock, hardcoat anodized finish in black or FDE. New 2015.

MSR $2,550	$2,150	$1,890	$1,550	$1,325	$1,100	$950	$825	

Add $150 for FDE (Flat Dark Earth) finish.

RECCE-16 CARBINE – 5.56 NATO cal., GIO, 16 in. Government profile steel barrel, A2 flash hider, Magpul MOE handguards, adj. Magpul stock, M4 flat-top receiver, full length quad rail, Mod 4 charging handle, chrome lined bore and chamber, M4 feed ramp barrel extension, MOE enhanced trigger guard, black hardcoat anodized finish, 6 lbs. 10 oz.

MSR $1,400	$1,200	$1,075	$950	$800	$700	$600	$495	

RECCE-16 PRECISION CARBINE – 5.56 NATO cal., GIO, 16 in. medium profile stainless steel barrel, A2 flash hider, free float rail system, mid-length GIO, tactical handguard, M4 feed ramp barrel extension, BCM Mod 4 charging handle, forged aluminum flat-top upper and lower receivers, Magpul MOE enhanced trigger guard, M4 stock, black hardcoat anodized finish. Disc. 2015.

	$1,175	$1,050	$925	$750	$665	$565	$475	*$1,399*

RECCE-16 KMR-A – 5.56 NATO cal., mid-length GIO, 16 in. Govt. profile barrel, Mod 0 compensator, Mod 0 buttstock, Mod 3 pistol grip, KMR Alpha-15 handguard, Mod 4 charging handle, QD endplate, M4 feed ramp flat-top with laser T markings, aluminum forged upper and lower receivers, black or Dark Bronze finish, 6 lbs. New 2016.

MSR $1,400	$1,200	$1,075	$950	$800	$700	$600	$495	

Add $100 for Dark Bronze finish.

RECCE-16 KMR-A .300 BLACKOUT – .300 AAC Blackout cal., carbine-length GIO, 16 in. BCM enhanced profile barrel, Mod 1 compensator, Mod 0 buttstock, Mod 3 pistol grip, KMR Alpha-13 handguard, Mod 4 charging handle, QD endplate, M4 feed ramp flat-top with laser T markings, aluminum forged upper and lower receivers, black finish, 6 lbs. New 2016.

MSR $1,500	$1,275	$1,125	$1,025	$875	$750	$625	$525	

RECCE-16 KMR-LIGHTWEIGHT – 5.56 NATO cal., mid-length GIO, 16 in. standard enhanced lightweight profile barrel, Mod 0 compensator, Mod 0 buttstock, Mod 3 pistol grip, KMR Alpha-15 handguard, Mod 4 charging handle, QD endplate, M4 feed ramp flat-top with laser T markings, aluminum forged upper and lower receivers, black finish, 6 lbs. New 2016.

MSR $1,490	$1,260	$1,120	$985	$835	$725	$615	$515	

RECCE-16 KMR-A PRECISION – 5.56 NATO cal., mid-length GIO, 16 in. Govt. profile stainless steel barrel, Mod 0 compensator, Mod 0 buttstock, Mod 3 pistol grip, aluminum forged flat-top upper and lower receivers, KMR Alpha-15 handguard, Mod 4 charging handle, M4 feed ramp extension, black finish, 6 1/2 lbs. New 2016.

MSR $1,630	$1,365	$1,200	$1,075	$950	$815	$700	$575	

RECCE-18 KMR-A PRECISION – 5.56 NATO cal., rifle length GIO, 18 in. Govt. profile stainless steel barrel, Mod 0 compensator, Mod 0 buttstock, Mod 3 pistol grip, aluminum forged flat-top upper and lower receivers, KMR Alpha-15 handguard, Mod 4 charging handle, M4 feed ramp extension, black finish, 6 1/2 lbs. New 2016.

MSR $1,650	$1,400	$1,235	$1,100	$975	$830	$720	$585	

PISTOLS: SEMI-AUTO

RECCE-9 KMR-A PISTOL – .300 AAC Blackout cal., pistol length GIO, 9 in. BCM enhanced profile barrel, Mod 1 7.62 compensator, Mod 3 pistol grip, KMR Alpha 8 handguard, Mod 4 charging handle, forged aluminum flat-top upper and lower receivers, M4 feed ramp extension, Type III hardcoat anodized black finish, 4.9 lbs. New 2016.

MSR $1,500	$1,275	$1,125	$1,025	$875	$750	$625	$525	

RECCE-11 KMR-A PISTOL – 5.56 NATO cal., carbine length GIO, 11 1/2 in. Govt. profile or enhanced lightweight barrel, Mod 0 compensator, Mod 3 pistol grip, KMR Alpha-10 handguard, Mod 4 charging handle, forged aluminum flat-top upper and lower receivers, black finish, 5.1 lbs. New 2016.

MSR $1,400	$1,200	$1,075	$950	$800	$700	$600	$495	

RECCE-12 KMR-A PISTOL – .300 AAC Blackout cal., pistol length GIO, 12 1/2 in. BCM enhanced profile barrel, Mod 1 7.62 compensator, Mod 3 pistol grip, KMR-10 handguard, Mod 4 charging handle, forged aluminum flat-top upper and lower receivers, M4 feed ramp extension, Type III hardcoat anodized black finish, 5.2 lbs. New 2016.

MSR $1,500	$1,275	$1,125	$1,025	$875	$750	$625	$525	

MSR		100%	98%	95%	90%	80%	70%	60%	Last MSR

BREN 10 (PREVIOUS MFG.)

Previous trademark manufactured 1983-1986 by Dornaus & Dixon Ent., Inc., located in Huntington Beach, CA.

Bren 10 magazines played an important part in the failure of these pistols to be accepted by consumers. Originally, Bren magazines were not shipped in some cases until a year after the customer received his gun. The complications arising around manufacturing a reliable dual caliber magazine domestically led to the downfall of this company. For this reason, original Bren 10 magazines are currently selling for $150-$175 if new (watch for fakes). Standard Black Hogue grips selling for $75-$100.

PISTOLS: SEMI-AUTO

Note: the Bren 10 shoots a Norma factory loaded 10mm auto. cartridge. Ballistically, it is very close to a .41 Mag. Bren pistols also have unique power seal rifling, with five lands and grooves. While in production, Bren pistols underwent four engineering changes, the most important probably being re-designing the floorplate of the magazine to prevent the magazine from dislocating as the pistol recoiled.

100% values in this section assume NIB condition. Add 5% for extra original factory mag. Subtract 10% without box/manual.

BREN 10 MILITARY/POLICE MODEL – 10mm cal. only, DA/SA, identical to standard model, except has all black finish, 5 in. barrel, "83MP" ser. no. prefix. Mfg. 1984-1986.

		100%	98%	95%	90%	80%	70%	60%	Last MSR
		$2,650	$2,300	$2,100	$1,850	$1,250	$900	$700	*$550*

BREN 10 SPECIAL FORCES MODEL – 10mm cal. only, DA/SA, 4 in. barrel, commercial version of the military pistol submitted to the U.S. gov't. Model D has dark finish. Model L has light finish, "SFD" ser. no. prefix on Model D, "SFL" ser. no. prefix on Model L. Disc. 1986.

		100%	98%	95%	90%	80%	70%	60%	Last MSR
Dark finish - Model D		$2,675	$2,250	$2,100	$1,850	$1,450	$975	$600	
Light finish - Model L		$3,675	$2,975	$2,750	$2,100	$1,650	$1,050	$675	*$600*

BREN 10 (RECENT MFG.)

Previous trademark manufactured in limited quantities from 2010-2011 by Vltor Mfg., located in Tucson, AZ. Vltor Mfg. was acquired by Abrams Airborne Manufacturing, Inc. in 2004. Previously distributed exclusively until early 2011 by Sporting Products, LLC, located in W. Palm Beach, FL.

PISTOLS: SEMI-AUTO

Very few of the following pistols were actually mass produced.

SM SERIES – 10mm or .45 ACP cal., 5 in. barrel, DA/SA, stainless steel frame with blue slide, 10 (SM45) or 15 (SM10) shot mag., two-tone finish, synthetic grips, approx. 500 (SM10) or 300 (SM45) were scheduled to be mfg., but very few were produced mid-2010-2011.

		100%	98%	95%	90%	80%	70%	60%	Last MSR
		$1,095	$995	$875	$750	$650	$550	$450	*$1,200*

SMV SERIES – 10mm or .45 ACP cal., 5 in. barrel, DA/SA, stainless steel frame, hard chrome slide, 10 (SMV10) or 15 (SMV15) shot mag., black synthetic grips, approx. 500 (SMV10) or 300 (SMV45) were scheduled to be produced, but very few were mfg. mid-2010-2011.

		100%	98%	95%	90%	80%	70%	60%	Last MSR
		$1,175	$1,050	$925	$800	$700	$600	$495	*$1,299*

SFD45 – .45 ACP cal., 4 in. barrel, DA/SA, matte black finished frame and slide, synthetic grips, 10 shot mag., approx. 500 were scheduled to be produced, but very few were mfg. mid-2010-2011.

		100%	98%	95%	90%	80%	70%	60%	Last MSR
		$995	$895	$800	$700	$600	$500	$425	*$1,100*

SFL45 – .45 ACP cal., 4 in. barrel, DA/SA, matte finished stainless steel frame, hard chrome slide, 10 shot mag., synthetic grips, two-tone finish, approx. 200 were scheduled to be produced, but very few were mfg. mid-2010-2011.

		100%	98%	95%	90%	80%	70%	60%	Last MSR
		$1,095	$995	$875	$750	$650	$550	$450	*$1,200*

BRILEY

Current trademark of pistols and rimfire semi-auto rifles with choke tubes currently manufactured in Houston, TX. Current pistol and rifle manufacture is sub-contracted to other manufacturers using the Briley trademark. Briley has previously produced both pistols and rifles, including those listed, in addition to manufacturing a complete line of top quality shotgun barrel tubes and chokes since 1976. Additionally, beginning late March, 2006-2007 Briley Manufacturing imported and distributed Mauser Models 98 and 03 bolt action rifles from Germany.

PISTOLS: SEMI-AUTO

Briley still has some new old stock pistols remaining. Please check their website for availability and pricing (see Trademark Index).

Add $30 for ambidextrous safety. Add $225 for custom mag well. Add $175 for hard chrome finish. Add $157 for Tritium night sights.

MSR	100%	98%	95%	90%	80%	70%	60%	Last MSR

PLATE MASTER – 9mm Para. or .38 Super cal., SA, features 1911 Govt. length frame, Briley TCII titanium barrel compensator, Briley scope mount, and other competition features, hot blue finish. Mfg. 1998-2004.

| | $1,675 | $1,325 | $1,075 | $895 | $775 | $625 | $575 | *$1,895* |

Add $175 for hard chrome finish.

EL PRESIDENTE – 9mm Para. or .38 Super cal., SA, top-of-the-line competition model with Briley quad compensator with side ports, checkered synthetic grips and front grip strap, squared off trigger guard. Mfg. 1998-2004.

| | $2,250 | $1,925 | $1,625 | $1,325 | $1,075 | $875 | $750 | *$2,550* |

Add $175 for hard chrome finish.

BROLIN ARMS, INC.

Previous importer of handguns (FEG mfg.), rifles (older Mauser military, see Mauser listing), shotguns (Chinese mfg.), and airguns from 1995 to 1999. Previously located in Pomona, CA, until 1999, and in La Verne, CA until 1997.

PISTOLS: SEMI-AUTO, SINGLE ACTION

PATRIOT SERIES MODEL P45 COMP – .45 ACP cal., similar to Legend Series Model L45, except has one-piece match 4 in. barrel with integral dual port compensator, 7 shot mag., Millett or Novak combat sights (new 1997), test target provided, choice of blue or satin (frame only) finish, 38 oz. Mfg. 1996-97 only.

| | $585 | $475 | $415 | $365 | $325 | $285 | $250 | *$649* |

Add $70 for Novak combat sights (new 1997).
Add $20 for T-tone finish (frame only).

* ***Patriot Series Model P45C (Compact)*** – .45 ACP cal., similar to Model P45 Comp, except has 3 1/4 in. barrel with integral conical lock-up system, 34 1/2 oz. Mfg. 1996-97.

| | $610 | $495 | $425 | $375 | $325 | $285 | $250 | *$689* |

Add $70 for Novak combat sights.
Add $20 for T-tone finish (frame only).

* ***Patriot Series Model P45T*** – features standard frame with compact slide, 3 1/4 in. barrel, 35 1/2 oz. Mfg. 1997 only.

| | $620 | $500 | $425 | $375 | $325 | $285 | $250 | *$699* |

Add $60 for Novak combat sights (new 1997).
Add $10 for T-tone finish (frame only).

TAC 11 – .45 ACP cal., 5 in. conical barrel w/o bushing, beavertail grip safety, 8 shot mag., T-tone or blue finish, Novak low profile combat or Tritium sights, black rubber contour grips, 37 oz. Mfg. 1997-98.

| | $595 | $485 | $425 | $365 | $325 | $285 | $250 | *$670* |

Add $90 for Tritium sights (disc. 1997).

* ***Tac 11 Compact*** – similar to Tac 11, except has shorter barrel. Mfg. 1998 only.

| | $610 | $495 | $435 | $365 | $325 | $285 | $250 | *$690* |

Add $60 for hard chrome finish.

PISTOLS: SEMI-AUTO, DOUBLE ACTION

The following models had limited manufacture 1998 only.

TAC SERIES SERVICE MODEL – .45 ACP cal., full sized service pistol, DA/SA, 8 shot single column mag., front and rear slide serrations, combat style trigger guard, royal or satin blue finish, low profile 3-dot sights. Mfg. 1998 only.

| | $360 | $315 | $285 | $260 | $240 | $220 | $200 | *$400* |

Add $20 for royal blue finish.

TAC SERIES FULL SIZE MODEL – 9mm Para., .40 S&W, or .45 ACP cal., DA/SA, similar to Tac Series Service Model, except longer barrel, checkered walnut or plastic grips, 8 (.45 ACP only) or 10 shot mag. Mfg. 1998 only.

| | $360 | $315 | $285 | $260 | $240 | $220 | $200 | *$400* |

Add $20 for royal blue finish.

TAC SERIES COMPACT MODEL – 9mm Para. or .40 S&W cal., DA/SA, shortened barrel/slide with full size frame, 10 shot mag. Mfg. 1998 only.

| | $360 | $315 | $285 | $260 | $240 | $220 | $200 | *$400* |

Add $20 for royal blue finish.

TAC SERIES BANTAM MODEL – 9mm Para. or .40 S&W cal., super compact size, DA/SA, with concealed hammer, all steel construction, 3-dot sights. Mfg. 1998 only.

| | $360 | $315 | $285 | $260 | $240 | $220 | $200 | *$399* |

MSR	100%	98%	95%	90%	80%	70%	60%	Last MSR

BANTAM MODEL – 9mm Para. or .40 S&W cal., DA/SA, super compact size, concealed hammer, all steel construction, 3-dot sights, royal blue or matte finish. Limited mfg. by FEG 1999 only.

| | $360 | $315 | $285 | $260 | $240 | $220 | $200 | $399 |

SHOTGUNS: SEMI-AUTO

MODEL SAS-12 – 12 ga. only, 2 3/4 in. chamber, 24 in. barrel with IC choke tube, 3 (standard) or 5 shot (disc. late 1998) detachable box mag., synthetic stock and forearm, gas operated. Mfg. 1998-99.

| | $445 | $385 | $335 | $300 | $280 | $260 | $240 | $499 |

Add $39 for extra 3 or 5 (disc.) shot mag.

SHOTGUNS: SLIDE ACTION

Brolin shotguns were manufactured in China by Hawk Industries, and were unauthorized copies of the Remington Model 870. Most of these slide action models were distributed by Interstate Arms, and it is thought that Norinco or China North Industries were connected to the manufacturer during the importation of these shotguns.

LAWMAN MODEL – 12 ga. only, 3 in. chamber, action patterned after the Rem. Model 870 (disc. 1998) or the Ithaca Model 37 (new 1999) 18 1/2 in. barrel, choice of bead, rifle (disc. 1998), or ghost ring (disc. 1998) sights, matte (disc. 1998), nickel (disc. 1997), royal blue (new 1998), satin blue (new 1998) or hard chrome finish, black synthetic or hardwood stock and forearm, 7 lbs. Mfg. in China 1997-99.

| | $165 | $155 | $145 | $135 | $125 | $115 | $105 | $189 |

Add $20 for nickel finish (disc. 1997).
Add $20 for hard chrome finish.
Add $20 for ghost ring sights.

BROWN PRECISION, INC.

Current manufacturer established in 1968, located in Los Molinos, CA. Previously manufactured in San Jose, CA. Consumer direct sales.

Brown Precision Inc. manufactures rifles primarily using Remington or Winchester actions and restocks them using a combination of Kevlar, fiberglass, and graphite (wrinkle finish) to save weight. Stock colors are green, brown, grey, black, camo brown, camo green, or camo grey. Chet Brown pioneered the concept of the fiberglass rifle stock in 1965. He started blueprinting actions and using stainless steel match grade barrels on hunting rifles in 1968, and became the first custom gunmaker to use high tech weather-proof metal finishes on hunting rifles during 1977.

RIFLES: BOLT ACTION

Brown Precision will also stock a rifle from a customer supplied action. This process includes a Brown Precision stock, custom glass bedding, recoil pad, stock finish, etc. Prices begin at $995.

LAW ENFORCEMENT SELECTIVE TARGET – .308 Win. cal., Model 700 Varmint action with 20, 22, or 24 in. factory barrel, O.D. green camouflage treatment. Disc. 1992.

| | $995 | $870 | $745 | $675 | $545 | $450 | $350 | $1,086 |

This model could have been special ordered with similar options from the Custom High Country Model, with the exception of left-hand action.

TACTICAL ELITE – various cals. and custom features, includes fully blueprinted Rem. 700 action, Shilen select match grade stainless steel barrel, custom chamber, recessed target crown, glass bedded Brown Precision Tactical Elite style stock, Teflon metal finish (choice of color), customized per individual order. New 1997.

| MSR $6,195 | $5,675 | $5,100 | $4,275 | $3,650 | $3,200 | $2,700 | $2,050 | |

Subtract $1,600 if action is supplied by customer.
Add $675 for 3 way adj. buttplate (disc.).

THE UNIT – .270 Win., .300 Win. Mag., .300 Wby. Mag., .338 Win. Mag., 7mm-08 Rem., 7mm Rem. Mag., or 7mm STW cal., Rem. 700 BDL or Win. Mod. 70 controlled feed action, various lengths match grade stainless steel barrel with cryogenic treatment, Teflon or electroless nickel finish, Brown Precision Kevlar or graphite reinforced fiberglass stock, includes 60 rounds of custom ammo. Limited mfg. 2001 only.

| | $3,225 | $2,820 | $2,420 | $2,195 | $1,775 | $1,450 | $1,130 | $3,795 |

Add $500 for Win. Model 70 Super Grade action with controlled round feeding.
Add $200 for left-hand action.
Subtract $600 if action was supplied by customer.

BROWNING

Current manufacturer with U.S. headquarters located in Morgan, UT. Browning guns originally were manufactured in Ogden, UT, circa 1880. Browning firearms are manufactured by Fabrique Nationale in Herstal and Liège, Belgium. Beginning 1976, Browning also contracted with Miroku of Japan and A.T.I. in Salt Lake City, UT to manufacture both

MSR	100%	98%	95%	90%	80%	70%	60%	Last MSR

long arms and handguns. In 1992, Browning (including F.N.) was acquired by GIAT of France. During late 1997, the French government received $82 million for the sale of F.N. Herstal from the Walloon business region surrounding Fabrique Nationale in Belgium.

The category names within the Browning section have been arranged in an alphabetical format: - PISTOLS (& variations), RIFLES (& variations), SHOTGUNS (& variations), SPECIAL EDITIONS, COMMEMORATIVES & LIMITED MFG., and SHOT SHOW SPECIALS.

The author would like to express his sincere thanks to the Browning Collector's Association, including members Rodney Herrmann, Richard Spurzem, Jim King, Bert O'Neill, Jr., Anthony Vanderlinden, Richard Desira, Gary Chatham, Bruce Hart, and Glen Nilson for continuing to make their important contributions to the Browning section.

In addition to the models listed within this section, Browning also offered various models/variations that were available only at the annual SHOT SHOW beginning 2004. More research is underway to identify these models, in addition to their original MSRs (if listed).

PISTOLS: SEMI-AUTO, CENTERFIRE, F.N. PRODUCTION UNLESS OTHERWISE NOTED

HI-POWER: POST-1954 MFG. – 9mm Para. or .40 S&W (mfg. 1995-2010) cal.,SA, similar to FN Model 1935, has BAC slide marking, 10 (C/B 1994) or 13* shot mag., 4 5/8 in. barrel, polished blue finish, checkered walnut grips, fixed sights, molded grips were introduced in 1986 (disc. in 2000), ambidextrous safety was added to all models in 1989, approx. 32 (9mm Para.) or 35 (.40 S&W) oz., mfg. by FN in Belgium, imported 1954-2000, reintroduced 2002.

* ***Hi-Power Standard - Polished Blue Finish (Imported 1954-2000)*** – 9mm Para. or .40 S&W (new 1995-) cal., includes fixed front and lateral adj. rear sight, 32 or 35 oz.

	100%	98%	95%	90%	80%	70%	60%
	$875	$700	$550	$475	$425	$350	$325

Add 50% for ring hammer and internal extractor.
Add 20% for ring hammer and external extractor (post 1962 mfg.).
Add 30% for thumb print feature.
Add 15% for T-prefix serial number.
Older specimens in original dark green, maroon, or red/black plastic boxes were mfg. 1954-1965 and are scarce - add $100+ in value. Black pouches (circa 1965-1968, especially with gold metal zipper) will also command a $25-$50 premium, depending on condition.

Major identifying factors of the Hi-Power are as follows: the "Thumb-Print" feature was mfg. from the beginning through 1958. Old style internal extractor was mfg. from the beginning through 1962, the "T" SN prefix (T-Series start visible extractor) was mfg. 1963-mid-1970s for all U.S. imports by BAC, 69C through 77C S/N prefixes were mfg. 1969-1977. Rounded type Ring Hammers with new external extractor were mfg. from 1962-1972 (for U.S. imports by BAC, much later on FN marked pistols). Spur Hammers have been mfg. 1972-present, and the "245" S/N prefix has been mfg. 1977-present. During 2010, all Hi-Powers featured a 75th Anniversary logo etched onto the top of the slide.

* ***Hi-Power Standard with Adj. Rear Sight*** – 9mm Para. or .40 S&W cal. (disc. 2010), similar to Hi-Power Standard blue, except has adj. rear sight.

MSR $1,200	100%	98%	95%	90%	80%	70%	60%
	$925	$735	$595	$495	$435	$395	$360

* ***Hi-Power Mark III*** – 9mm Para. or .40 S&W (mfg. 1994-2000, reintroduced 2003-2010) cal., 4 5/8 in. barrel, non-glare matte blue (disc. 2005) or black epoxy (new 2006) finish, 10 or 13 shot mag., ambidextrous safety, tapered dovetail rear fixed sight, single action trigger, two-piece molded grips, Mark III designation became standard in 1994, approx. 35 oz. Imported 1985-2000, reintroduced 2002.

MSR $1,110	100%	98%	95%	90%	80%	70%	60%
	$875	$600	$500	$435	$375	$335	$315

Add 50% for black epoxy military FN model marked "Made in Belgium." (without Assembled in Portugal) with box and accessories.

* ***Hi-Power Practical Model*** – 9mm Para. or .40 S&W (new 1995) cal., features blue (disc. 2005) or black epoxy slide, silver-chromed frame finish, wraparound Pachmayr rubber grips, round style serrated hammer, and choice of adj. sights (mfg. 1993-2000) or removable front sight, 36 (9mm Para.) or 39 (.40 S&W) oz. Imported 1990-2000, reintroduced 2002-2006.

	100%	98%	95%	90%	80%	70%	60%	Last MSR
	$725	$600	$525	$450	$425	$400	$375	*$863*

Add $58 for adj. sights (disc. 2000).

* ***Hi-Power GP Competition*** – 9mm Para. cal., competition model with 6 in. barrel, detent adj. rear sight, rubber wraparound grips, front counterweight, improved barrel bushing, decreased trigger pull, approx. 36 1/2 oz.

	100%	98%	95%	90%	80%	70%	60%
	$995	$895	$725	$600	$550	$500	$450

The original GP Competition came in a black plastic case w/accessories and is more desirable than later imported specimens which were computer serial numbered and came in a styrofoam box. Above prices are for older models - subtract 10% if newer model (computer serial numbered). This model was never cataloged for sale by BAC in the U.S., and it is not serviced by Browning.

* ***Hi-Power Tangent Rear Sight & Slotted*** – 9mm Para. cal., variation with grip strap slotted to accommodate shoulder stock. Early pistols had "T" prefixes. Later pistols had spur hammers and are in the serial range 73CXXXX-74CXXXX.

	100%	98%	95%	90%	80%	70%	60%
	$1,550	$1,300	$1,100	$900	$775	$650	$525

MSR	100%	98%	95%	90%	80%	70%	60%	Last MSR

Add $200 if with "T" prefix.

Add $50 for original pouch and instruction booklet.

This variation will command a premium; beware of fakes, however (carefully examine slot milling and look for ser. no. in 3 places).

Vektor Arms in N. Salt Lake, UT, imported this model again in limited quantities circa 2004 with both the "245" and seldom seen "511" (includes wide trigger, loaded chamber indicator and external extractor) ser. no. prefixes. These guns are not arsenal refinished or refurbished, and were sold in NIB condition, with two 13 shot mags. Original pricing was $895 for the "245" prefix, and $995 for the "511" prefix.

PRO-9/PRO-40 – 9mm Para. or .40 S&W cal., DA/SA, 4 in. barrel, 10, 14 (.40 S&W cal. only), or 16 (9mm Para. cal. only) shot mag., ambidextrous decocking and safety, black polymer frame with satin stainless steel slide, under barrel accessory rail, interchangeable backstrap inserts, fixed sights only, 30 (9mm Para.) or 33 oz. Mfg. in the U.S. by FNH USA 2003-2006.

	100%	98%	95%	90%	80%	70%	60%	Last MSR
	$525	$430	$370	$350	$315	$295	$260	*$641*

Please refer to FNH USA handgun listing for current manufacture.

SHOTGUNS: SEMI-AUTO, AUTO-5 1903-1998, 2012-CURRENT MFG.

BROWNING CHOKES AND THEIR CODES (ON REAR LEFT-SIDE OF BARREL)

* designates full choke (F).

*- designates improved modified choke (IM).

** designates modified choke (M).

**- designates improved cylinder choke (IC).

**$ designates skeet (SK).

*** designates cylinder bore (CYL).

INV. designates barrel is threaded for Browning Invector choke tube system.

INV. PLUS designates back-bored barrels.

Miroku manufactured A-5s can be determined by year of manufacture in the following manner: RV suffix - 1975, RT - 1976, RR - 1977, RP - 1978, RN - 1979, PM - 1980, PZ - 1981, PY - 1982, PX - 1983, PW - 1984, PV - 1985, PT - 1986, PR - 1987, PP - 1988, PN - 1989, NM - 1990, NZ - 1991, NY - 1992, NX - 1993, NW - 1994, NV - 1995, NT - 1996, NR - 1997, NP - 1998, ZY - 2012, ZX - 2013, ZW - 2014, ZV - 2015, ZT - 2016.

Browning resumed importation from F.N. in 1946. On November 26, 1997, Browning announced that the venerable Auto-5 would finally be discontinued. Final shipments were made in February, 1998. Over 3 million A-5s were manufactured by Fabrique Nationale in all configurations between 1903-1976. 1976-1998 manufacture was by Miroku in Japan. The A-5 was reintroduced in 2012 with a Kinematic Drive System, aluminum receiver, and a fixed barrel.

NOTE: Barrels are interchangeable between older Belgian A-5 models and recent Japanese A-5s manufactured by Miroku, if the gauge and chamber length are the same. A different barrel ring design and thicker barrel wall design might necessitate some minor sanding of the inner forearm on the older model, but otherwise, these barrels are fully interchangeable.

NOTE: The use of steel shot is recommended ONLY in those recent models manufactured in Japan - NOT in the older Belgian variations.

The "humpback" design on the Auto-5 (both Belgian and Japanese mfg.) features recoil operation with a scroll engraved steel receiver. During 1909, Browning introduced the magazine cutoff, and moved the safety from inside to the front of the triggerguard. 1946-1951 mfg. has a safety in front of triggerguard. 1951-1976 mfg. has crossbolt safety behind the trigger. Post-war 16 ga. imports by Browning are chambered for 2 3/4 in., and have either a horn (disc. 1964) or plastic (1962-1976) buttplate, high luster wood finish (disc. 1962) or glossy lacquer (1962-1976) finish. Walnut buttstock has either round knob pistol grip (disc. 1967) or flat knob (new 1967). In today's Auto-5 marketplace, all gauges of the A-5 have become extremely collectible. Obviously, the Belgian A-5s are the most desirable. However, the pre-1998 Miroku guns are gaining in collectible popularity. It also has become very apparent that the demand for the FN lightweight 20 ga. has superceded the Sweet 16 due to availablilty. Both the lightweight 20 ga. and the Sweet 16 are the most desirable and have seen a dramatic increase in collectibility. Rarity of configurations such as choke designations, and barrel lengths are very important factors in determining value. Older rare barrels such as the solid rib and the 16 and 20 ga. guns with shorter barrels and open chokes are more desirable than a 30 in. 12 ga. gun with full choke barrel.

The publisher would like to thank Mr. Richard "Doc" Desira for his recent contributions to the Auto-5/A-5 section.

Add 15% for NIB condition on Belgian mfg. Auto-5 models only, depending on desirability. Beware of reproduced boxes and labels, especially on the more desirable configurations.

Add 15% for the round knob (rounded pistol grip knob on stock, pre-1967 mfg.) variation on FN models only, depending on desirability.

Add $250-$500 per additional barrel, depending on the gauge, barrel length, choke, condition, and rarity (smaller gauge open chokes are the most desirable).

Add 20% for reddish stock and forearm configurations (Belgian mfg. - pre 1962).

Add 15% on FN models with blonde stock and forearm - mfg. mid-1960s.

MSR	100%	98%	95%	90%	80%	70%	60%	Last MSR

AUTO-5 POLICE CONTRACT – 12 ga. only, 5 or 8 (factory extended) shot mag., black enamel finish on receiver and barrel, can be recognized by the European "POL" police markings below serial number, 24 in. barrel. Imported in limited quantities during 1999.

	MSR	100%	98%	95%	90%	80%	70%	Last MSR
5 shot mag.	N/A	$700	$650	$625	$575	$525	$500	
8 shot mag.	N/A	$1,300	$1,095	$995	$895	$850	$750	

BRÜGGER & THOMET

Current manufacturer located in Thun, Switzerland. Currently imported by D.S.A., located in Barrington, IL.

Brügger and Thomet also manufactures a wide variety of high quality tactical style and select-fire rifles and pistols. During 2004, the company purchased all rights to the TMP pistol, and SMG from Steyr Arms in Austria. After many design improvements the TP-9 pistol platform was released.

PISTOLS: SEMI-AUTO

TP-9 – 9mm Para. or .45 ACP (new late 2011) cal., 5.1 in. barrel, SA, short recoil delayed blowback, features ambidextrous and trigger safeties, polymer frame construction in choice of Black, OD Green, or Desert Tan finish, full length upper integrated Picatinny rail with partial lower rail in front of trigger guard, 10 or 30 shot mag., adj. rear sight with post front sight, includes hard case, 44 oz. Importation disc. 2011.

	100%	98%	95%	90%	80%	70%	60%	Last MSR
	$1,650	$1,475	$1,300	$1,125	$900	$800	$700	*$1,795*

This model is also available in a select-fire variation available to law enforcement and government agencies.

BUDISCHOWSKY

Previous trade name of firearms designed by Edgar Budischowsky, initially manufactured in Ulm, Germany by Korriphila GmbH, and subsequently by Norton Armament Corporation (NORARMCO) in Mt. Clemens, MI.

PISTOLS: SEMI-AUTO

SEMI-AUTO PISTOL – .223 Rem. cal., 11 5/8 in. barrel, 20 or 30 shot mag., fixed sights, a novel tactical designed type pistol.

	100%	98%	95%	90%	80%	70%	60%
	$470	$415	$385	$360	$305	$250	$220

RIFLES: SEMI-AUTO

TACTICAL DESIGN RIFLE – .223 Rem. cal., 18 in. barrel, wood tactical stock.

	100%	98%	95%	90%	80%	70%	60%
	$500	$440	$415	$385	$330	$275	$250

TACTICAL DESIGN RIFLE W/FOLDING STOCK – .223 Rem. cal., 18 in. barrel, folding stock.

	100%	98%	95%	90%	80%	70%	60%
	$575	$500	$450	$425	$395	$360	$330

BULLSEYE GUN WORKS

Previous manufacturer located in Miami, FL circa 1954-1959.

CARBINES: SEMI-AUTO

Bullseye Gun Works initially started as a gun shop circa 1954, and several years later, they started manufacturing M1 carbines using their own receivers and barrels. Approx. 2,000 - 2,500 were manufactured with their name on the receiver side until the company was reorganized as Universal Firearms Corporation circa late 1950s. Values are typically in the $200 - $350 range, depending on originality and condition.

BUL LTD. (TRANSMARK)

Current pistol manufacturer located in Tel Aviv, Israel since 1990. Bul M1911 parts are currently being imported by All America Sales, Inc. located in Piggot, AR. Previously imported 2003-early 2010 by K.B.I., located in Harrisburg, PA. Previously imported and distributed in North America during 2009 by Legacy Sports International, located in Reno, NV, and during 2002 by EAA Corp., located in Sharpes, FL. Previously imported and distributed 1997-2001 by International Security Academy (ISA) located in Los Angeles, CA, and from 1996-1997 by All America Sales, Inc. located in Memphis, TN. Dealer sales only.

PISTOLS: SEMI-AUTO

Please refer to the Charles Daly section in this text for most recent information and prices on Charles Daly imported Bul Transmark pistols (domestic imports were marked Charles Daly 2004-early 2010). Non-domestic Bul Pistols are typically marked Bul M-5 on left side of slide except for the Cherokee and Storm models. M-5 frame kits were previously available at $399 retail.

BUL CHEROKEE – 9mm Para. cal., DA/SA, full size black polymer frame with finger groove grips, integral Picatinny rail, DA, exposed hammer, double stack 17 shot mag., squared off trigger guard, includes hard case, cleaning kit and two mags. Imported 2009.

	100%	98%	95%	90%	80%	70%	60%	Last MSR
	$495	$435	$370	$335	$270	$225	$175	*$575*

MSR	100%	98%	95%	90%	80%	70%	60%	Last MSR

* **Bul Cherokee Compact** – 9mm Para. cal., similar to the Cherokee, except has compact polymer frame. Imported 2009.

	$495	$435	$370	$335	$270	$225	$175	$575

BUSHMASTER FIREARMS INTERNATIONAL

Current trademark of carbines, rifles, and pistols established in 1978, and currently manufactured in Huntsville, AL beginning late 2011 and company headquarters located in Madison, NC. Previously located in Windham, ME until 2011. On March 31, 2011, Freedom Group Inc. announced that Bushmaster's manufacturing facility in Windham, ME would be closing, and new Bushmaster products would be produced in other Freedom Group facilities. The previous company name was Bushmaster Firearms, and the name changed after the company was sold on April 13, 2006 to Cerberus, and became part of the Freedom Group Inc. Older mfg. was by Gwinn Arms Co. located in Winston-Salem, NC 1972-1974. The Quality Parts Co. gained control in 1986. Distributor, dealer, or consumer direct sales.

During 2003, Bushmaster purchased Professional Ordnance, previous maker of the Carbon 15 Series of semi-auto pistols and rifles/carbines. Carbon 15s are still made in Lake Havasu City, AZ, but are now marked with the Bushmaster logo. For pre-2003 Carbon 15 mfg., please refer to the Professional Ordnance section in this text.

Bushmaster formed a custom shop during 2009, and many configurations are now available by special order only. Please contact Bushmaster directly for more information and availability on these special order guns.

PISTOLS: SEMI-AUTO

BUSHMASTER PISTOL – .223 Rem. cal., AK-47 design, top (older models with aluminum receivers) or side mounted charging handle (most recent mfg.), steel frame on later mfg., 11 1/2 in. barrel, parkerized finish, adj. sights, 5 1/4 lbs.

	$625	$550	$450	$400	$375	$350	$300	$375

Add $40 for electroless nickel finish (disc. 1988).
Add $200 for matte nickel finish (mfg. circa 1986-1988).

This model uses a 30 shot M-16 mag. and the AK-47 gas piston operating system.

During 1985-1986, a procurement officer for the U.S. Air Force ordered 2,100 of this model for pilot use with a matte nickel finish. Eventually, this officer was retired or transferred, and the replacement officer turned down the first batch, saying they were "too reflective". Bushmaster then sold these models commercially circa 1986-1988.

CARBON-15 TYPE P21S/TYPE 21 – 5.56 NATO cal., GIO, ultra lightweight carbon fiber upper and lower receivers, 7 1/4 in. "Profile" stainless steel barrel, quick detachable muzzle compensator, ghost ring sights, 10 or 30 (new late 2004) shot mag., A2 pistol grip, also accepts AR-15 type mags., Stoner type operating sytem, tool steel bolt, extractor and carrier, 40 oz. Mfg. 2003-2012 (Bushmaster mfg.).

	$725	$625	$550	$475	$400	$325	$295	$871

Subtract approx. $200 if without full-length barrel shroud and Picatinny rail (Type 21, disc. 2005).

CARBON-15 TYPE 97/TYPE P97S – GIO, similar to Professional Ordnance Carbon 15 Type 20, except has fluted barrel, Hogue overmolded pistol grip and chrome plated bolt carrier, Type 97S has full length barrel shroud, upper and lower Picatinny rail, 46 oz. Mfg. 2003-2012 (Bushmaster mfg.).

	$695	$600	$525	$450	$375	$300	$285	$825

Add $78 for Model P97S with full length barrel shroud and lower Picatinny rail.
Subtract approx. $100 if w/o full length barrel shroud and lower Picatinny rail (disc.)

CARBON-15 9MM – 9mm Para. cal., blowback operation, carbon fiber composite receivers, 7 1/2 in. steel barrel with A1 birdcage flash hider, A2 front sight, full-length Picatinny optics rail, Neoprene foam sleeve over buffer tube, 10 or 30 shot mag., 4.6 lbs. Mfg. 2006-2012.

	$785	$710	$625	$550	$475	$400	$325	$871

PIT VIPER AP-21 – 5.56 NATO cal., GIO, 7 1/4 in. barrel with birdcage flash suppressor, visible upper gas transfer tube, receiver Picatinny rail, approx. 3 1/2 lbs. Limited mfg. 2011 only.

	$725	$625	$550	$475	$400	$325	$295	$873

XM-15 PATROLMAN'S AR PISTOL – 5.56 NATO cal., GIO, 7 or 10 1/2 in. stainless steel barrel with A2 flash hider, knurled free float tubular handguard, flat-top receiver with Picatinny rail, Phase 5 ambi single point sling attachment, A2 pistol grip and standard trigger guard, aluminum pistol buffer tube with foam featuring laser engraved Bushmaster logo, 30 shot mag., approx. 5 1/2 lbs. Mfg. 2013-2015.

	$825	$700	$600	$525	$450	$375	$325	$973

XM-15 ENHANCED PATROLMAN'S AR PISTOL – 5.56 NATO cal., GIO, 7 or 10 1/2 in. stainless steel barrel with AAC 3 prong flash hider, free float lightweight quad rail handguard, Phase 5 ambi single point sling attachment, Magpul MOE pistol grip and trigger guard, aluminum pistol buffer tube with foam featuring laser engraved Bushmaster logo, 30 shot mag. Mfg. 2013-2015.

	$995	$875	$750	$675	$550	$450	$350	$1,229

MSR	100%	98%	95%	90%	80%	70%	60%	Last MSR

RIFLES: BOLT ACTION

BA50 CARBINE/RIFLE – .50 BMG cal., 22 (carbine, disc. 2011) or 30 (rifle) in. Lothar Walther free floating barrel with vent. forend, AAC Cyclops muzzle brake/silencer adapter (new 2014), 10 shot mag., left side bolt handle, full length receiver Picatinny rail, Magpul PRS adj. buttstock with LimbSavr recoil pad, high efficiency recoil reducing muzzle brake, steel bipod with folding legs, ErgoGrip deluxe tactical pistol grip, aluminum lower receiver, manganese phosphate finish on steel parts, hard anodized black finish on aluminum parts, includes Storm hardcase and two mags., 20 or 27 lbs. New 2009.

| MSR $5,657 | $4,995 | $4,500 | $4,000 | $3,500 | $3,000 | $2,650 | $2,300 | |

Last MSR on the carbine was $5,261.

RIFLES: SEMI-AUTO

All current AR-15 style Bushmaster rifles are shipped with a hard plastic lockable case. Most Bushmaster barrels are marked "5.56 NATO", and can be used safely with either 5.56 NATO (higher velocity/pressure) or .223 Rem. cal. ammo.

Information and values for state compliant variations are not listed.

During 2006, Bushmaster began offering a complete gas piston upper receiver/barrel assembly. Last MSRs ranged from $580-$990, depending on caliber and configuration.

The XM-10 typically refers to 7.62 NATO cal., and XM-15 refers to 5.56 NATO cal. on the current models listed.

.300 AAC BLACKOUT – .300 AAC Blackout cal., GIO, 16 in. M4 contour barrel with AAC Blackout muzzle brake, Magpul ACS stock and MOE grip, free floating quad rail, 30 shot mag. (AR compatible), flat-top receiver with Picatinny rail, 6 1/2 lbs. Mfg. 2012-2015.

| | $1,275 | $1,125 | $1,025 | $875 | $750 | $625 | $525 | *$1,508* |

.450 CARBINE/RIFLE – .450 Bushmaster cal., GIO, 16 (carbine) or 20 in. chrome moly steel barrel, 5 shot mag., forged aluminum receiver, A2 pistol grip, solid A2 buttstock with trapdoor, A3 flat-top upper receivers with Picatinny rail, free floating vented aluminum forend, 8 1/2 lbs. New 2008.

| MSR $1,299 | $1,100 | $995 | $875 | $735 | $650 | $550 | $465 | |

6.8mm SPC/7.62x39mm CARBINE – 6.8mm SPC or 7.62x39mm (new 2010) cal., GIO, 16 in. M4 profile barrel with Izzy muzzle brake, 6-position telescoping stock, available in A2 (disc. 2012) or A3 configuration, 26 shot mag., includes black web sling, extra mag. and lockable carrying case, approx. 7 lbs. Mfg. late 2006-late 2013.

| | $1,200 | $1,075 | $950 | $800 | $700 | $600 | $495 | *$1,402* |

Add $100 for A3 configuration (disc. 2010).

BUSHMASTER RIFLE – 5.56 NATO cal., GPO, top (older models with aluminum receivers) or side mounted charging handle (recent mfg.), steel receiver (current mfg.), 18 1/2 in. barrel, parkerized finish, adj. sights, wood stock, 6 1/4 lbs., base values are for folding stock model.

| | $625 | $550 | $500 | $475 | $425 | $400 | $350 | *$350* |

Add $40 for electroless nickel finish (disc. 1988).

Add $65 for fixed rock maple wood stock.

This model uses a 30 shot M-16 mag. and the AK-47 gas piston system.

* ***Bushmaster Rifle Combination System*** – GPO, includes rifle with both metal folding stock and wood stock with pistol grip.

| | $750 | $675 | $625 | $575 | $525 | $475 | $450 | *$450* |

TARGET/COMPETITION A-2/A-3 RIFLE (XM15-E2S) – 5.56 NATO cal., GIO, patterned after the Colt AR-15, 20, 24 (disc. 2012), or 26 (disc. 2002) in. Govt. spec. match grade chrome lined or stainless steel (new 2002) barrel with A2 flash hider, 10 or 30 shot mag., manganese phosphate or Realtree Camo (20 in. barrel only, mfg. 2004 - late 2006) finish, rear sight adj. for windage and elevation, cage flash suppressor (disc. 1994), approx. 8.3 lbs. Mfg. began 1989 in U.S.

| MSR $969 | $825 | $700 | $630 | $570 | $500 | $425 | $380 | |

Add $30 for A3 configuration with removable carry handle.

Add $88 for stainless steel barrel with A3 removable carry handle (disc. 2015).

Add $194 for heavy 1 in. diameter competition barrel (disc. 2011).

Add $50 for fluted barrel or $40 for stainless steel barrel (mfg. 2002-2009).

Add $10 for 24 in. (disc. 2012) or $25 for 26 in. (disc. 2002) barrel.

Add $60 for Realtree Camo finish (disc.).

HEAVY BARREL CARBINE A-2/A-3 (XM15-E2S, SHORTY CARBINE) – 5.56 NATO cal., GIO, 11 1/2 (LE only, disc. 1995), 14 (LE only, disc. 1994), or 16 in. heavy barrel with birdcage flash suppressor, 30 shot mag., choice of A2 or A3 configuration, fixed (disc.) or telescoping buttstock, approx. 7.4 lbs. Mfg. began 1989.

| MSR $895 | $775 | $685 | $615 | $550 | $485 | $415 | $370 | |

Add $525 for A3 configuration with removable carry handle.

This model does not have the target rear sight system of the XM15-E2S rifle.

MSR	100%	98%	95%	90%	80%	70%	60%	Last MSR

* **M4 Post-Ban Carbine (XM15-E2S)** – 5.56 NATO cal., GIO, 16 in. barrel, fixed or telestock (new late 2004) tubular stock, pistol grip, black, Flat Dark Earth, OD Green, phosphate (disc.), A-TACS camo, or Desert Camo (stock, pistol grip, and forearm only, disc. 2005) finish, M4 carbine configuration with permanently attached Izzy muzzle brake, 30 shot mag. became standard in late 2004. Mfg. 2003-2015.

| | $1,125 | $1,000 | $875 | $735 | $650 | $550 | $465 | *$1,331* |

Add $107 for A-TACS camo.
Add $35 for desert camo finish (disc. 2005).
Add $85 for A3 removable carrying handle (disc. 2012).

* **XM-15 Limited Edition 20th Anniversary Rifle** – GIO, 20 in. barrel, features 20th Anniversary engraving on upper and lower receiver, special medallion in buttstock, includes hardwood presentation case. Limited mfg. 1998-99.

| | $1,275 | $1,095 | $985 | $800 | $650 | $525 | $450 | |

* **XM-15 Limited Edition 25th Anniversary Carbine** – GIO, skeletonized tubular stock, pistol grip, A-3 type flat-top with flip-up sights, laser engraved 25th anniversary crest on lower magwell, nickel plated ejection port cover. Limited mfg. of 1,500 during 2003.

| | $1,275 | $1,095 | $985 | $800 | $650 | $525 | $450 | *$1,695* |

* **E2 Carbine** – 5.56 NATO cal., GIO, 16 in. match chrome lined barrel with new M16A2 handguard and short suppressor, choice of A1 or E2 sights. Mfg. 1994-95.

| | $775 | $675 | $575 | $475 | $425 | $400 | $350 | |

Add approx. $50 for E2 sighting system.

AK CARBINE – 5.56 NATO cal., 17 in. barrel featuring AK-47 style muzzle brake, telestock standard, choice of A2 or A3 configuration, ribbed oval forearm, approx. 7 1/2 lbs. Mfg. 2008-2010.

| | $875 | $750 | $675 | $550 | $450 | $400 | $350 | *$1,215* |

Add $85 for A3 removable carry handle.

DISSIPATOR CARBINE – 5.56 NATO cal., GIO, 16 in. heavy barrel with full length forearm and special gas block placement (gas block system is located behind the front sight base and under the rifle length handguard), A2 or A3 style with choice of solid buttstock or 6-position telestock, 30 shot mag., lockable carrying case. Mfg. 2004-2010.

| | $875 | $750 | $675 | $550 | $450 | $395 | $350 | *$1,246* |

Add $25 for telestock.
Add $50 for fluted barrel (disc. 2005).
Add $115 for A3 removable carrying handle.

MOE DISSIPATOR CARBINE – 5.56 NATO cal., GIO, 16 in. barrel with chrome-lined bore and chamber, mid-length gas system, flat-top with Picatinny rail, features Magpul Original Equipment (MOE) accessories such as 30 shot PMag., rifle-length handguard, MBUS rear flip sight, Magpul MOE adj. stock with rubber buttpad, MOE grip, Black finish, 6.42 lbs. New 2011.

| MSR $1,099 | | | $925 | $850 | $725 | $625 | $550 | $475 | $425 |

MOE .223 MID-LENGTH – 5.56 NATO cal., GIO, 16 in. barrel with chrome-lined bore and chamber, Magpul MOE stock, mid-length handguard, pistol grip, and MBUS rear flip sight, Magpul 30 shot PMag., Black or Flat Dark Earth (disc. 2014) finish, 6 1/2 lbs. New 2011.

| MSR $1,099 | | | $925 | $850 | $725 | $625 | $550 | $475 | $425 |

MOE .308 MID-LENGTH – .308 Win. cal., GIO, otherwise similar to MOE .223 Mid-length, except has 20 shot mag., Black, OD Green, or FDE finish, 6.1 lbs. Mfg. 2011-2015.

| | $1,315 | $1,165 | $1,050 | $915 | $785 | $665 | $550 | *$1,546* |

MOE M4-TYPE CARBINE/A-TACS CARBINE – 5.56 NATO cal., GIO, 16 in. heavy profile M4 barrel, 30 shot PMag., Magpul adj. A-frame buttstock, Magpul MOE handguard, grip, enhanced trigger guard, and Magpul MBUS rear flip sight, Black, OD Green (disc. 2014), FDE (disc. 2014), or A-TACS camo (disc. 2014) finish, 6.42 lbs. New 2011.

| MSR $1,099 | | | $925 | $850 | $725 | $625 | $550 | $475 | $425 |

Add $106 for A-TACS camo (disc. 2014).

M4 A.R.M.S. CARBINE – 5.56 NATO cal., GIO, 16 in. chrome moly vanadium steel barrel with chrome lined bore and chamber, 30 shot mag., A3 removable carry handle, black, Foliage Green (new 2010), or Flat Dark Earth (new 2010) anodized finish, Magpul adj. buttstock with optional MOE (new 2010), Hogue pistol grip, optional Troy four rail handguard and front sights or A.R.M.S. 41-B front and rear flip-up sights (new 2010, became standard 2011), 6.2 lbs. Mfg. 2009-2011.

| | $875 | $750 | $675 | $550 | $450 | $400 | $350 | *$1,247* |

Subtract approx. 10% if without A.R.M.S. front and rear flip up sights.

MSR	100%	98%	95%	90%	80%	70%	60%	Last MSR

PATROLMAN'S CARBINE – 5.56 NATO, 6.8 SPC, or 7.62x39mm NATO cal., GIO, 16 in. standard barrel, choice of A2 (bullet button) or A3 configuration, two piece tubular handguard, 6-position adj. stock, black finish only, approx. 6 1/2 lbs. Disc. 2013.

	$950	$800	$725	$600	$485	$400	$350	$1,275

Add 10% for 6.8 Rem. SPC or 7.62x39 NATO cal. (A3 configuration only).

M4 PATROLMAN'S CARBINE – 5.56 NATO cal., GIO, choice of A2 or A3 configuration, 16 in. chrome-lined M4 barrel with A2 flash hider, 30 shot mag., 6-position telestock, detachable carry handle (A3 only), black anodized finish, approx. 6 1/2 lbs. New 2009.

MSR $895	$775	$685	$615	$550	$485	$415	$370	

Add $52 for A3 detachable carry handle.

M4 A3 PATROLMAN'S CARBINE CERAKOTE – 5.56 NATO cal., GIO, 16 in. M4 barrel with A2 flash hider, A3 upper with removable carry handle, A2 carbine two-piece handguard, 6-position M4 stock, 30 shot mag., choice of OD Green or FDE Cerakote finished receiver, 6.7 lbs. Mfg. 2013-2014.

	$1,125	$995	$875	$735	$650	$550	$465	$1,321

M4 A3 PATROLMAN'S CARBINE W/QUAD RAIL – 5.56 NATO cal., 16 in. M4 chrome lined barrel with A2 flash hider, 30 shot mag., aluminum free float quad rail handguard, forged A3 flat-top upper with detachable carry handle, forged lower with 6-position lightweight M4 stock. New 2011.

MSR $1,099	$925	$850	$725	$625	$550	$475	$425	

M17S BULLPUP – 5.56 NATO cal., GIO, semi-auto bullpup configuration featuring gas operated rotating bolt, 10 (C/B 1994) or 30* shot mag., 21 1/2 plain or 22 (disc.) in. barrel with flash suppressor (disc.), glass composites and aluminum construction, phosphate coating, 8 1/4 lbs. Mfg. 1992-2005.

	$750	$650	$525	$475	$425	$400	$385	$765

MODULAR CARBINE – 5.56 NATO cal., GIO, 16 in. barrel with flash suppressor, includes many Bushmaster modular accessories, such as skeleton telestock and four-rail free floating tubular forearm, detachable folding front and rear sights, 10 or 30 (new late 2004) shot mag., 6.3 lbs. Mfg. 2004-2014.

	$1,495	$1,325	$1,150	$1,025	$875	$750	$615	$1,793

SUPERLIGHT CARBINE – 5.56 NATO cal., GIO, 16 in. lightweight barrel, choice of fixed (disc.), 6-position telestock, or stub (disc.) stock with finger groove pistol grip, A2 or A3 type configuration, 30 shot mag., black finish, 5.8 - 6 1/4 lbs. Mfg. 2004-2013.

	$1,050	$925	$825	$750	$600	$500	$400	$1,291

Subtract 5% if without telestock.

Subtract approx. $75 if without A-3 removable carry handle.

ACR BASIC A-TACS CARBINE – 5.56 NATO cal., GPO, 16 1/2 in. barrel with A2 flash hider, 30 shot PMag, fixed A-frame composite stock with rubber butt pad and sling mounts, Black (disc. 2013), Coyote Brown (disc. 2010), or A-TACS camo finish, 8.2 lbs. Disc. 2014.

	$2,200	$1,925	$1,600	$1,375	$1,125	$975	$850	$2,604

ACR BASIC FOLDER – .223 Rem. or 6.8 SPC (mfg. 2013-2015) cal., GPO, 16 1/2 in. barrel with A2 flash hider, 30 shot PMAG, Magpul MBUS front/rear flip up sights, composite handguard with heat shield, folding and 6-position polymer stock with rubber butt pad and sling mount, Black or Coyote Brown finish, 8.2 lbs. New mid-2011.

MSR $2,149	$1,825	$1,595	$1,375	$1,150	$995	$850	$700	

ACR BASIC ORC CARBINE – 5.56 NATO cal., GPO, 16 1/2 in. barrel with muzzle brake, full-length top Picatinny rail w/o sights and fixed stock, 30 shot mag., Black or Coyote Brown finish, 8.2 lbs. Mfg. 2011-2013.

	$1,725	$1,475	$1,350	$1,085	$895	$695	$525	$2,343

ACR DMR – 5.56 NATO cal., 18 1/2 in. stainless steel Melonite-treated melonite barrel, AAC 51T Blackout flash hider, Geissele trigger, ACR railed handguard, Magpul PRS style stock, 8 3/4 lbs. Mfg. 2014-2015.

	$2,375	$2,075	$1,775	$1,625	$1,300	$1,075	$925	$2,799

ACR ENHANCED – 5.56 NATO or 6.8 SPC (while advertised in 2010, this caliber hasn't been mfg. to date) cal., Bushmaster proprietary GPO, modular design allows caliber interchangeability by changing the barrel, magazine, and bolt head, 16 1/2 in. chrome moly steel barrel with Melonite coating, AAC Blackout NSM flash hider, ambidextrous controls, adj. two-position gas piston, 30 shot mag., folding or 6-position telestock, black or Coyote Brown finish, three sided aluminum handguard, Magpul MBUS front/rear flip up sights, upper and lower accessory rails, includes sling, hardcase and extra mag., 8.2 lbs. New 2010.

MSR $2,249	$1,915	$1,685	$1,425	$1,225	$1,035	$885	$735	

ACR ORC BULLET BUTTON – .223 Rem. cal., 16 in. M4 contour barrel with A2 flash hider, 10 shot mag., Bullet Button lower receiver. New 2015.

MSR $2,249	$1,915	$1,685	$1,425	$1,225	$1,035	$885	$735	

MSR	100%	98%	95%	90%	80%	70%	60%	Last MSR

ACR PATROL CARBINE – 5.56 NATO or 6.8 SPC cal., GPO, 16 1/2 in. chrome moly steel barrel with Melonite coating, AAC Blackout flash hider, ratchet-style suppressor mounting, 30 shot mag., fixed stock, adj. cheekpiece, Picatinny rail, includes sling and three mags, 8.2 lbs. Mfg. 2010-2014.

| | $2,100 | $1,850 | $1,575 | $1,425 | $1,150 | $950 | $825 | $2,552 |

ACR SPECIAL PURPOSE CARBINE – 5.56 NATO cal., GPO, 16 1/2 in. cold hammer forged barrel, folding and 6-position telescoping polymer stock with rubber buttpad and sling mounts, quad Picatinny rails, and includes three 30 shot PMAG magazines and soft nylon case, Black finish only, 8.3 lbs. Mfg. 2011-2014.

| | $2,375 | $2,075 | $1,775 | $1,625 | $1,300 | $1,075 | $925 | $2,799 |

ORC (OPTICS READY CARBINE) ACR – 5.56 NATO or .308 Win. (mfg. 2010-2012) cal., GPO, 16 in. barrel with A2 birdcage flash suppressor, receiver length Picatinny rail with risers ready for optical sights, 6-position telestock, 30 shot mag., oval M4 type forearm, 6 lbs. Mfg. 2008-2013.

| | $925 | $850 | $725 | $625 | $550 | $475 | $425 | $1,112 |

Add $239 for .308 Win. cal. (mfg. 2010-2012).

ORC BASIC FOLDER CARBINE – 5.56 NATO cal., GPO, 16 1/2 in. barrel with muzzle brake, similar to ACR Enhanced Carbine, except does not have 3-sided aluminum handguard with Picatinny rails, Black or Coyote Brown finish, 8.2 lbs. Mfg. 2011 only.

| | $1,995 | $1,775 | $1,575 | $1,395 | $1,150 | $950 | $725 | $2,490 |

ORC 5.56 – 5.56 NATO cal., GPO, 16 or 18 (disc.) in. heavy profile barrel with flash suppressor, full-length receiver Picatinny rail, heavy oval handguard, 6-position telescoping stock, 10 or 30 shot mag., Black finish, 7 3/4 lbs. Mfg. 2011-2014.

| | $900 | $785 | $685 | $600 | $535 | $465 | $415 | $1,083 |

ORC .308 – 7.62 NATO cal., GPO, 16 or 18 (disc.) in. heavy profile barrel with A2 flash suppressor, full-length receiver Picatinny rail, heavy oval handguard, 6-position telescoping stock, 20 shot mag., Black finish, 7 3/4 lbs. Mfg. 2011-2015.

| | $1,225 | $1,085 | $965 | $815 | $715 | $600 | $500 | $1,438 |

MOE/ORC GAS PISTON CARBINE – 5.56 NATO cal., GPO, 16 in. barrel, MOE carbine features many Magpul accessories, is available in Black, OD Green, or Flat Dark Earth finish, ORC model does not have MOE features, but 6-position tactical stock and receiver length Picatinny rail with risers for optics, approx. 6.3 lbs. Mfg. 2011-2012.

| | $995 | $875 | $750 | $650 | $550 | $475 | $400 | $1,247 |

Add $89 for ORC model.

Add $100-$149 for extra Magpul features on MOE model.

GAS PISTON CARBINE – 5.56 NATO cal., GPO, similar to AK-47s and FALs, 16 in. M4 profile barrel with flash suppressor, telestock, ribbed oval forearm with flip-up sight. Mfg. 2008-2010.

| | $1,325 | $1,125 | $1,025 | $825 | $675 | $525 | $450 | $1,850 |

HUNTER – .308 Win. cal., GIO, 20 in. fluted barrel, vented free floating aluminum forearm tube, 10 shot mag., Hogue rubberized pistol grip (Hunter) or A2 grip (Vista, disc. late 2011), Grey/Green or camo finish, 8.2 lbs. Mfg. 2011-2013.

| | $1,225 | $1,050 | $950 | $775 | $650 | $550 | $450 | $1,685 |

Add $100 for Vista Hunter model (disc. late 2011).

PREDATOR – 5.56 NATO cal., GIO, includes DCM (disc.) 20 in. extra fluted, or stainless steel (disc. 2006) varmint barrel, two-stage competition trigger, rubberized pistol grip, flat-top receiver with mini-risers (adds 1/2 in. height for scope mounting), free floating vented tube forearm, 10 shot mag., controlled ejection path, choice of black or A-TACS Digital Camo (new 2011, compliant configuration only) finish, 8 lbs. Mfg. 2006-2013.

| | $1,075 | $950 | $825 | $700 | $575 | $500 | $450 | $1,415 |

Add $104 for A-TACS Digital Camo finish (compliant configuration only).

The stainless variation included an adj. ergonomic pistol grip.

DCM COMPETITION RIFLE – 5.56 NATO cal., GIO, includes DCM competition features such as modified A2 rear sight, 20 in. extra heavy 1 in. diameter competition barrel, custom trigger job, and free-floating handguard. Mfg. 1998-2005.

| | $1,250 | $1,095 | $950 | $850 | $700 | $575 | $450 | $1,495 |

DCM-XR COMPETITION RIFLE – 5.56 NATO cal., GIO, 20 in. extra heavy competition barrel, dual aperture rear sight and competition ground for clarity front sight, free-floating ribbed forearm, competition trigger, choice of A2 solid or A3 removable carry handle, 13 1/2 lbs. Mfg. 2008-2010.

| | $850 | $725 | $675 | $550 | $450 | $400 | $350 | $1,150 |

Add $100 for A3 removable carry handle.

MSR	100%	98%	95%	90%	80%	70%	60%	Last MSR

CARBINE-15 COMPETITION – 5.56 NATO cal., GIO, various configurations, choice of extra heavy or heavy barrel in 20 or 24 in. with or w/o muzzle brake, A2 or A3 configuration, various type of sights, 8.5-13.85 lbs. Mfg. 2011 only.

| | $825 | $700 | $650 | $525 | $425 | $375 | $325 | $1,112 |

Add approx. $75 for A3 removable carry handle.
Add $194 for heavy 1 in. diameter competition barrel.

CARBON-15 R21 – 5.56 NATO cal., GIO, ultra lightweight carbon fiber upper and lower receivers, 16 in. "Profile" stainless steel barrel, quick detachable muzzle compensator, Stoner type operating system, tool steel bolt, extractor and carrier, optics mounting base, fixed tube stock, 10 or 30 (new late 2004) shot mag., also accepts AR-15 type mags., 3.9 lbs. Mfg. 2003-2009 (Bushmaster mfg.).

| | $825 | $725 | $625 | $550 | $450 | $375 | $300 | $990 |

* **Carbon-15 Lady** – 5.56 NATO cal., GIO, 16 in. barrel, includes overall tan finish (except for barrel) and webbed tube stock with recoil pad, chrome/nickel plating on small parts, supplied with soft case, 4 lbs. Mfg. 2004-2006.

| | $825 | $725 | $625 | $550 | $450 | $375 | $300 | $989 |

CARBON-15 (R97/97S) – 5.56 NATO cal., AR-15 style, GIO, ultra lightweight carbon fiber upper and lower receivers, hard chromed tool steel bolt, extractor and carrier, 16 in. fluted stainless steel barrel, quick detachable muzzle compensator, optics mounting base, 10 or 30 (new late 2004) shot mag., quick detachable stock, also accepts AR-15 type mags., 3.9 or 4.3 (Model 97S) lbs. Mfg. 2003-2010.

| | $995 | $895 | $800 | $725 | $600 | $475 | $400 | $1,300 |

Subtract approx. $175 without Picatinny rail and "Scout" extension, double walled heat shield foregrip, ambidextrous safety, and multi-carry silent sling (Model Type 97, disc. 2005).

CARBON-15 .22 LR – .22 LR cal., GIO, similar to Carbon-15 R21, 16 in. barrel, Picatinny rail, 10 shot mag., fixed stock, approx. 4.4 lbs. Disc. 2009.

| | $575 | $500 | $450 | $375 | $300 | $250 | $225 | $790 |

Bushmaster also made a Carbon-15 .22 rimfire upper receiver/barrel assembly, which is exclusively designed for Bushmaster lower receivers - last MSR was $387 (new 2005).

CARBON-15 9MM – 9mm Para. cal., blowback operation, carbon fiber composite receiver, 16 in. steel barrel with A1 birdcage flash suppressor, A2 front sight and dual aperture rear sight, Picatinny optics rail, collapsible stock, 10 or 30 shot mag., 5.7 lbs. Mfg. 2006-2012.

| | $775 | $675 | $575 | $525 | $425 | $350 | $275 | $933 |

CARBON-15 TOP LOADING RIFLE – 5.56 NATO cal., GIO, carbon fiber composite receiver, 16 in. M4 profile barrel with Izzy suppressor, A2 front sight and dual aperture rear sight, Picatinny optics rail, collapsible stock, 10 shot top-loading internal mag., 5.8 lbs. Mfg. 2006-2010.

| | $775 | $675 | $600 | $500 | $400 | $325 | $250 | $1,100 |

CARBON-15 MODEL 4 CARBINE – 5.56 NATO cal., GIO, carbon composite receiver, collapsible tube stock, 14 1/2 (LE only), or 16 (disc. 2012) in. barrel with compensator, 30 shot mag., semi-auto design styled after the military M4, 5 1/2 lbs. Mfg. 2005-2013.

| | $725 | $650 | $575 | $500 | $450 | $375 | $300 | $956 |

CARBON-15 FLAT-TOP CARBINE – 5.56 NATO cal., GIO, 16 in. M4 barrel, muzzle fitted with "IZZY" flash hider, 30 shot mag., receiver length Picatinny rail with dual aperture flip-up rear sight, 6-position stock, Black finish, 5 1/2 lbs. Mfg. 2006-2015.

| | $815 | $700 | $630 | $570 | $500 | $425 | $380 | $956 |

CARBON-15 SUPERLIGHT ORC W/RED DOT – 5.56 NATO cal., GIO, 16 in. super light contour barrel with A2 flash hider, 10 (disc. 2013) or 30 shot mag., red dot optical sight with rings and riser blocks, 6-position stock, black finish. Mfg. 2012-2015.

| | $725 | $650 | $580 | $515 | $450 | $385 | $340 | $866 |

CARBON-15 M4 QUAD RAIL – 5.56 NATO cal., GIO, 16 in. M4 barrel with A2 flash hider, 30 shot mag., fixed front sight base and bayonet lug, Mission First Tactical polymer quad rail with rail covers, 6-position stock, black finish, 6 1/4 lbs. Mfg. 2014-2015.

| | $725 | $650 | $580 | $515 | $450 | $385 | $340 | $866 |

CARBON-15 C22 COMBO – .22 LR and 5.56 NATO cals., GIO, includes two barrels chambered for .22 LR and 5.56 NATO cals., flat-top receiver with Picatinny rail, 16 in. M4 style barrels with A2 flash hiders, fixed front sight base, Mission First Tactical polymer quad rail with rail covers, 6-position stock, supplied with 25 shot (.22 LR cal.) and 30 shot (5.56 NATO) magazines. Mfg. 2013-2015.

| | $1,035 | $925 | $800 | $685 | $595 | $515 | $440 | $1,222 |

MSR	100%	98%	95%	90%	80%	70%	60%	Last MSR

CARBON 22 – .22 LR cal., 16 in. M4 contour barrel with A2 flash hider, 25 shot mag., 6 position stock assembly, Mission First Tactical polymer quad rail with rail covers. Mfg. 2014-2015.

	$450	$395	$350	$300	$275	$250	$225	$499

V-MATCH COMPETITION RIFLE – 5.56 NATO cal., GIO, top-of-the line match/competition rifle, flat-top receiver with extended aluminum barrel shroud, choice of 20, 24, or 26 (disc. 2002) in. barrel, 8.3 lbs. Mfg. 1994-2010.

	$925	$825	$700	$650	$525	$425	$325	$1,115

Add $50 for fluted barrel.
Add $10 for 24 in. or $25 for 26 (disc. 2002) in. barrel.
Add $117 for A-3 removable carry handle.

    * **V-Match Commando Carbine** – 5.56 NATO cal., GIO, 16 in. barrel. Mfg. 1997-2010.

	$925	$825	$700	$650	$525	$425	$325	$1,105

Add $50 for fluted barrel.
Add $117 for A-3 removable carry handle.

VARMINTER – 5.56 NATO cal., GIO, includes DCM 24 in. extra heavy fluted or stainless steel varmint barrel, competition trigger, rubberized pistol grip, flat-top receiver with mini-risers (adds 1/2 in. height for scope mounting), free floating vented tube forearm, 5 shot mag., controlled ejection path, choice of Black or A-TACS Digital camo (new 2011, compliant configuration only) finish. Mfg. 2002-2013.

	$1,150	$995	$900	$825	$650	$550	$425	$1,430

Add $71 for stainless steel barrel (compliant variation only).
Add $105 for A-TACS Digital camo coverage (compliant configuration only).
    The stainless variation includes an adj., ergonomic pistol grip.

VARMINTER W/2020 OPTICS – 5.56 NATO cal., GIO, 24 in. fluted barrel, features Remington's new 2020 Digital Optic System, Magpul stock, includes wheeled hard case with custom fitted foam insert. Mfg. 2014 only.

	$4,500	$4,000	$3,650	$3,350	$3,000	$2,750	$2,500	$5,000

BUSHMASTER .308 SERIES – .308 Win. cal., GIO, 16 or 20 in. phosphate coated heavy alloy steel barrel with Izzy compensator, 20 shot mag., solid buttstock or skeletonized stock, available in A2 or A3 style with a variety of configurations, including muzzle brakes, flash suppressors, and sighting options. Mfg. late 2004-2005.

	$1,375	$1,200	$1,050	$975	$785	$650	$500	$1,750

Add $25 for A3 removable carry handle.
Add $10 for 20 in. barrel.
Add $50 (16 in. barrel) or $60 (20 in. barrel) for skeletonized stock.
Add approx. $100 for free-floating foream.

XM-10 .308 ENHANCED ORC – .308 Win. cal., GIO, 16 in. chrome lined barrel, Troy modular free-floating handguard, Magpul PRS stock and MIAD grip, two-stage trigger, 9 lbs. New 2014.

MSR $1,599	$1,350	$1,200	$1,075	$950	$815	$700	$575	

XM-10 DMR – 7.62 NATO cal., 18 1/2 in. stainless Cerakote bull barrel, Troy free-floating handguard, Magpul PRS stock, MIAD grip and trigger guard, AAC 51T Blackout muzzle brake, Gieselle trigger, 10 1/2 lbs. Mfg. 2014 only.

	$1,700	$1,500	$1,250	$1,100	$950	$825	$675	$1,999

XM-15 TACTICAL ORC (BASIC TACTICAL CARBINE) – 5.56 NATO cal., GIO, 16 in. mid-length stainless steel barrel with AAC 51T Blackout flash hider, 15 in. Barnes Precision modular free-float handguard, Magpul MOE grip, Magpul MOE stock, two-stage match trigger, enhanced trigger guard, 7 3/4 lbs. Mfg. 2014-2015.

	$1,135	$1,015	$885	$740	$675	$575	$475	$1,350

XM-15 QRC (QUICK RESPONSE CARBINE) – 5.56 NATO cal., GIO, 16 in. superlight contour chrome moly barrel with A2 birdcage-type flash hider, 10 shot mag., quick detach Mini red dot sight, forged lower and A3 flat-top upper receiver, 6-position collapsible M4 stock, Melonite coated barrel. New 2016.

MSR $769	$660	$575	$510	$440	$385	$340	$325	

XM-15 3-GUN ENHANCED CARBINE – 5.56 NATO cal., GIO, 16 in. mid-length stainless steel barrel, Rolling Thunder compensator, 15 in. AP Custom carbon fiber handguard, Timney trigger, Magpul MIAD grip, Magpul MOE stock, PVD bolt carrier group, crimson anodized receiver, Bravo Company charging handle, ambi selector switch, Arrendondo mag. release, Black finish, 7 3/4 lbs. Mfg. 2014-2015.

	$1,485	$1,315	$1,150	$1,025	$875	$750	$615	$1,750

C SECTION

C3 DEFENSE, INC.

Previous manufacturer of AR-15 style rifles, upper/lower receivers, and related components located in Hiram, GA until 2013.

MSR	100%	98%	95%	90%	80%	70%	60%	Last MSR

RIFLES: SEMI-AUTO

C3 Defense discontinued all manufacture of complete firearms in 2013. C3 Defense also offered the short barrel C315 Clandestine Series for military/law enforcement.

C315 RANGER – .223 Rem. cal., GIO, 16 in. barrel, matte black finish, forged upper and lower, flared magwell, M4 feed ramps, Mil-Spec trigger group, A2 front post sight, 30 shot mag., 6-position retractable stock, A2 grip, M16 bolt carrier group, Magpul rear MBUS.

	100%	98%	95%	90%	80%	70%	60%	Last MSR
	$850	$725	$650	$585	$515	$450	$395	*$995*

C315 RECON – .223 Rem. cal., GIO, 16 in. barrel, matte black finish, forged upper and lower, flared magwell, M4 feed ramps, Mil-Spec trigger group, A2 front sight, 30 shot mag., Magpul MOE stock and grip, M16 bolt carrier group, Magpul MBUS and polymer extended trigger guard.

	100%	98%	95%	90%	80%	70%	60%	Last MSR
	$925	$850	$725	$625	$550	$475	$425	*$1,112*

C315 SFR (STANDARD FULL RIFLE) – .223 Rem. cal., GIO, 16 in. barrel, matte black finish, billet upper and lower, flared magwell, tension screw, front textured grip, M4 feed ramps, Mil-Spec trigger group, A2 front sight, 30 shot mag., Magpul MOE stock, A2 grip, Magpul extended trigger guard, carbine length handguard with rail.

	100%	98%	95%	90%	80%	70%	60%	Last MSR
	$1,195	$1,000	$875	$775	$675	$575	$475	*$1,349*

C315 EFR (ENHANCED FULL RIFLE) – .223 Rem. or .300 AAC Blackout cal., GIO, 16 in. barrel, matte black finish, enhanced billet upper and lower, flared magwell, tension screw, front textured grip, M4 feed ramps, Mil-Spec trigger group, 13 in. free float handguard with rail, 30 shot mag., Magpul MOE stock and grip, Magpul front and rear MBUS, Triad flash suppressor, M16 bolt carrier group.

	100%	98%	95%	90%	80%	70%	60%	Last MSR
	$1,325	$1,160	$1,040	$885	$750	$625	$525	*$1,579*

C315 EFR OW (OVERWATCH) – .223 Rem. or 6.8 SPC cal., GIO, 18 in. stainless steel barrel with fitted bolt, matte black finish, enhanced billet upper and lower, flared magwell, tension screw, front textured grip, M4 feed ramps, two-stage match trigger, 13 in. free float handguard with rail, chromed NM bolt carrier, 20 shot mag., Magpul UBR stock and MIAD grip, Magpul front and rear MBUS, Triad flash suppressor.

	100%	98%	95%	90%	80%	70%	60%	Last MSR
	$2,175	$1,995	$1,775	$1,525	$1,300	$1,150	$875	*$2,539*

CETME

Previous manufacturer located in Madrid, Spain. CETME is an abbreviation for Centro Estudios Technicos de Materiales Especiales.

RIFLES: SEMI-AUTO

AUTOLOADING RIFLE – 7.62x51mm NATO cal., 17 3/4 in. barrel, roller lock delayed blowback action, similar to HK-91 in appearance, wood military style stock, aperture rear sight.

	100%	98%	95%	90%	80%	70%	60%	Last MSR
	$2,950	$2,650	$2,350	$2,000	$1,725	$1,500	$1,350	

The H&K G3 is the next generation of this rifle, and many parts are interchangeable between the CETME and the G3.

CMMG, INC.

Current manufacturer of AR-15 style carbines/rifles and related components and accessories established in 2002, located in Fayette, MO.

PISTOLS: SEMI-AUTO

MK3 K – .308 Win. cal., 12 1/2 in. barrel with A2 muzzle compensator, billet receivers, single stage trigger, Magpul MOE pistol grip, RKM11 KeyMod free-floating handguard, 7 1/2 lbs. New 2015.

MSR	100%	98%	95%	90%	80%	70%	60%	
$1,550	$1,320	$1,155	$1,040	$875	$750	$625	$525	

MK4 K – 5.56 NATO cal., 12 1/2 in. barrel with A2 muzzle compensator, RKM11 KeyMod free-floating handguard, Magpul MOE pistol grip and trigger guard, single stage trigger, 6 lbs. New 2015.

MSR	100%	98%	95%	90%	80%	70%	60%	
$1,000	$850	$725	$650	$585	$515	$450	$395	

MK4 PDW – .300 AAC Blackout cal., 8 in. medium taper barrel with A2 muzzle compensator, 30 shot Magpul PMAG, single stage trigger, free-floating KeyMod handguard, Magpul MOE pistol grip, ambidextrous rear sling mount, 5.3 lbs. New mid-2014.

MSR	100%	98%	95%	90%	80%	70%	60%	
$1,000	$850	$725	$650	$585	$515	$450	$395	

MSR	100%	98%	95%	90%	80%	70%	60%	Last MSR

MK9 PDW – 9mm Para. cal., 8 1/2 in. barrel with A2 muzzle compensator, 32 shot mag., free-floating KeyMod handguard, Magpul MOE pistol grip and MOE trigger guard, single stage trigger, ambidextrous rear sling mount, 5.3 lbs. New mid-2014.

| MSR $1,100 | $925 | $850 | $725 | $625 | $550 | $475 | $425 | |

MK47 MUTANT AKS8 – 7.62x39mm cal., 8 in. medium taper barrel, KRINK muzzle device, 30 shot Magpul AK/AKM MOE mag., SST, Magpul MOE pistol grip, billet receivers, RKM9 KeyMod handguard, Black finish. New 2016.

| MSR $1,550 | $1,315 | $1,165 | $1,050 | $915 | $785 | $665 | $550 | |

MK47 MUTANT K – 7.62x39mm cal., 10 in. medium taper barrel, muzzle brake, accepts all standard AK mags., Magpul MOE pistol grip, billet aluminum receivers, RKM9 KeyMod handguard, Black finish. New 2016.

| MSR $1,500 | $1,275 | $1,125 | $1,025 | $875 | $750 | $625 | $525 | |

RIFLES: SEMI-AUTO

.22 LR SERIES

* **M4 Profile Model 22A7C3D** – .22 LR cal., AR-15 style, GIO, 16 in. WASP treated chrome moly steel M4 barrel, phosphated bolt group, 6-position stock, 25 shot grey mag., optics ready with railed gas block or low profile railed gas block, Black finish. Disc. 2013.

| | $650 | $575 | $510 | $440 | $385 | $340 | $325 | $750 |

* **Lightweight Model 22A1CF6** – .22 LR cal., AR-15 style, GIO, 16 in. WASP treated chrome moly steel M4 lightweight barrel, stainless steel bolt group with BHOA and forward assist adapter, M4 handguard, 6-position stock, 25 shot Evolution mag., "F" marked front sight base and Magpul MBUS rear sight, Black finish. Disc. 2013.

| | $725 | $650 | $580 | $515 | $450 | $385 | $340 | $830 |

.300 AAC BLACKOUT SERIES

* **Model 30AF8A6** – .300 AAC Blackout cal., GIO, 16 in. M300 profile WASP treated chrome moly steel barrel, optics ready with low profile gas block, K9 quad rail, mid-length free float tube, 6-position stock, 30 shot Magpul Pmag., Black finish. Disc. 2013.

| | $850 | $725 | $650 | $585 | $515 | $450 | $395 | $1,000 |

* **Model 30A77E1 Stainless** – .300 AAC Blackout cal., GIO, 16 in. M300 profile stainless steel barrel, mid-length handguard, carbine low pro gas block, 6-position stock, 30 shot Magpul Pmag., "F" marked front sight base and Magpul MBUS rear sight, Black finish. Disc. 2013.

| | $885 | $750 | $665 | $585 | $515 | $450 | $395 | $1,050 |

* **Model 30AF8DF** – .300 AAC Blackout cal., GIO, 16 in. M300 profile WASP treated chrome moly barrel, Revolution handguard with 5 slot rails and Revolution modular handguard panels, "F" marked front sight base and Magpul MBUS rear sight, 6-position stock, 30 shot Pmag., Black finish. Disc. 2013.

| | $885 | $750 | $665 | $585 | $515 | $450 | $395 | $1,050 |

.308 MK3 SERIES

– .308 Win./7.62 NATO cal., GIO, standard barrel options include 16 or 18 in. stainless steel medium contour or a hammer forged chrome lined barrel, aluminum upper and lower receivers, uses SR25 or LR308 mags., and can be configured with Magpul MOE stocks, MOE pistol grips, and CMMG two-stage triggers. Disc. 2013.

* **Model 38A20FB** – .308 Win. cal., GIO, 18 in. medium contour stainless steel threaded barrel, low profile gas block, 10 in. modular free float tube, 4-slot rail, Mil-Spec 6-position stock, standard trigger, 20 shot Pmag., black finish. Disc. 2013.

| | $1,225 | $1,090 | $950 | $800 | $700 | $600 | $495 | $1,450 |

* **Model 38AB136** – .308 Win. cal., GIO, 16 in. medium contour cold hammer forged stainless steel barrel, low profile gas block, 10 in. mod. free float tube, three 4-slot rails, Mil-Spec 6-position Magpul MOE stock and grip, 2-stage trigger, 20 shot Pmag., black finish. Disc. 2013.

| | $1,350 | $1,200 | $1,075 | $950 | $815 | $700 | $575 | $1,600 |

* **Model 38A6DFO** – .308 Win. cal., GIO, 16 in. hammer forged barrel, low profile gas block, mod. free float tube, 4-slot rail, Magpul MOE stock and grip, 2-stage trigger, 20 shot Pmag., Black finish. Disc. 2013.

| | $1,560 | $1,375 | $1,190 | $1,050 | $900 | $775 | $625 | $1,850 |

* **Model 38AF432** – .308 Win. cal., GIO, 18 in. threaded hammer forged barrel, low profile gas block, 10 in. modular free float tube, 4-slot rail, 6-position stock, 20 shot Pmag., Black finish. Disc. 2013.

| | $1,450 | $1,275 | $1,125 | $1,000 | $850 | $735 | $595 | $1,700 |

5.56 HAMMER FORGED SERIES

– 5.56 NATO cal., GIO, 16 in. hammer forged chrome-lined M4, M10, or Government profile barrel, 30 shot Magpul Pmag., "F" marked front sight base, with or w/o Magpul MBUS rear sight, Black or FDE finish, other options available. Disc. 2013.

MSR	100%	98%	95%	90%	80%	70%	60%	Last MSR

* **Model 55AD33B** – 5.56 NATO cal., GIO, 16 in. hammer forged chrome-lined barrel, mid-length low profile gas block, "F" marked front sight base and Magpul MBUS rear sight, Magpul MOE rifle length handguard, Mil-Spec 6-position Magpul MOE stock and grip, 30 shot Magpul Pmag., Black finish. Disc. 2013.

	$1,050	$950	$815	$685	$595	$515	$440	$1,250

* **Model 55AD3A1** – 5.56 NATO cal., GIO, 16 in. M10 profile cold hammer forged chrome-lined barrel, mid-length handguard, "F" marked front sight base and Magpul MBUS rear sight, 6-position stock, 30 shot Pmag., Black finish. Disc. 2013.

	$975	$885	$750	$625	$550	$475	$425	$1,180

* **Model 55AD37C** – 5.56 NATO cal., GIO, 16 in. M10 profile hammer forged chrome-lined barrel, "F" marked front sight base and Magpul MBUS rear sight, mid-length low pro gas block, Magpul MOE rifle length handguard in Flat Dark Earth, Mil-Spec 6-position Magpul MOE stock and grip in Flat Dark Earth, 30 shot Magpul Pmag. in FDE finish. Disc. 2013.

	$1,050	$950	$815	$685	$595	$515	$440	$1,250

* **Model 55AD3B2** – 5.56 NATO cal., GIO, 16 in. M10 profile hammer forged chrome-lined barrel, "F" marked front sight base and rear sight, mid-length low pro gas block, Mil-Spec 6-position stock, 30 shot Magpul Pmag., Black finish. Disc. 2013.

	$1,025	$925	$800	$685	$595	$515	$440	$1,200

* **Model 55A8433** – 5.56 NATO cal., GIO, 16 in. M4 profile hammer forged chrome-lined barrel, "F" marked front sight base and rear sight, Mil-Spec 6-position stock, 30 shot Magpul Pmag., Black finish. Disc. 2013.

	$975	$875	$740	$625	$550	$475	$425	$1,150

* **Model 55A5252** – 5.56 NATO cal., GIO, 16 in. Government profile hammer forged chrome-lined barrel, "F" marked front sight base and Magpul MBUS rear sight, Magpul MOE mid-length handguard, Mil-Spec 6-position Magpul MOE stock and grip, 30 shot Magpul Pmag., Black finish. Disc. 2013.

	$1,050	$950	$815	$685	$595	$515	$440	$1,250

* **Model 55A5244** – 5.56 NATO cal., GIO, 16 in. Government profile hammer forged chrome-lined barrel, "F" marked front sight base and Magpul MBUS rear sight, Magpul MOE mid-length handguard, Mil-Spec 6-position Magpul MOE stock and grip, 30 shot Magpul Pmag., Flat Dark Earth furniture. Disc. 2013.

	$1,050	$950	$815	$685	$595	$515	$440	$1,250

* **Model 55A526D** – 5.56 NATO cal., GIO, 16 in. Government profile hammer forged chrome-lined barrel, "F" marked front sight base and rear sight, Mil-Spec 6-position stock, 30 shot Magpul Pmag., Black finish. Disc. 2013.

	$1,025	$925	$800	$685	$595	$515	$440	$1,200

5.56 LE SERIES – 5.56 NATO cal., GIO or GPO, WASP (Weapon Armament Surface Protection) finish, the nitriding conversion is applied to the barrel inside and out, along with the front sight base and uppers, 16 in. chrome moly M4 or bull barrel, 30 shot Magpul PMAG., LE rifles use "T" marked upper receivers with M4 feed ramps and forged lower receivers with Mil-Spec components, Black or FDE finish. Disc. 2013.

* **Model 55AE1AD** – 5.56 NATO cal., GIO or GPO, 16 in. WASP treated M4 profile chrome moly steel barrel, "T" marked front sight base, rear sight, M4 handguard, Mil-Spec 6-position stock, A2 pistol grip, 30 shot Magpul Pmag., Flat Dark Earth furniture. Disc. 2013.

	$800	$700	$615	$550	$485	$415	$370	$950

* **Model 55AE1BB** – 5.56 NATO cal., GPO or GIO, 16 in. WASP treated M4 profile chrome moly steel barrel, optics ready with piston system, Mil-Spec 6-position stock, 30 shot Magpul Pmag., black finish. Disc. 2013.

	$885	$750	$665	$585	$515	$450	$395	$1,050

* **Model 55AED49** – 5.56 NATO cal., GIO or GPO, 16 in. WASP treated chrome moly steel bull barrel, optics ready with low profile gas block, carbine length round free float tube, Mil-Spec 6-position stock, 30 shot Magpul Pmag., black finish. Disc. 2013.

	$725	$650	$580	$515	$450	$385	$340	$850

* **Model 55AEDA5** – 5.56 NATO cal., GIO or GPO, 16 in. WASP treated chrome moly steel bull barrel, optics ready with piston system, Revolution handguard with 5 slot rails, Mil-Spec 6-position stock, 30 shot Magpul Pmag., black finish. Disc. 2013.

	$1,025	$925	$800	$685	$595	$515	$440	$1,200

5.56 STAINLESS STEEL SERIES – 5.56 NATO cal., GIO, 16, 18, 22, or 24 in. stainless steel M4 profile or Bull barrel, with or w/o fluting, low profile gas block, A1 or 6-position stock, 30 shot Magpul Pmag., free float tube, Black finish. Disc. 2013.

* **Model 55ABB89** – 5.56 NATO cal., GIO, 16 in. stainless steel bull barrel, carbine length round free float handguard tube, low profile gas block, 6-position stock, 30 shot Magpul Pmag., Black finish. Disc. 2013.

	$775	$685	$615	$550	$485	$415	$370	$900

MSR	100%	98%	95%	90%	80%	70%	60%	Last MSR

* **Model 55A3C9E** – 5.56 NATO cal., GIO, 18 in. stainless steel Bull barrel, optics ready with low profile gas block, mid-length round free float tube, Mil-Spec 6-position stock, 30 shot Magpul Pmag., Black finish. Disc. 2013.

	$790	$685	$615	$550	$485	$415	$370	*$930*

* **Model 55A8EDC** – 5.56 NATO cal., GIO, 22 in. stainless steel Bull barrel, optics ready low profile gas block, rifle length round free float tube, A1 stock, 30 shot Magpul Pmag., Black finish. Disc .2013.

	$815	$700	$615	$550	$485	$415	$370	*$980*

* **Model 55AE392** – 5.56 NATO cal., GIO, 25 in. stainless steel fluted barrel, optics ready with low profile gas block, rifle length round free float tube, A1 stock, 30 shot Magpul Pmag., Black finish. Disc. 2013.

	$925	$850	$725	$625	$550	$475	$425	*$1,100*

* **Model 55A3866** – 5.56 NATO cal., GIO, 16 in. stainless steel M4 profile barrel, optics ready with railed gas block, Mil-Spec 6-position stock, 30 shot Magpul Pmag., Black finish. Disc. 2013.

	$800	$700	$615	$550	$485	$415	$370	*$950*

MK3 – .308 Win. cal., 18 in. stainless steel heavy taper barrel with A2 compensator, RKM15 KeyMod free float handguard, billet aluminum receiver, SST, A2 pistol grip, A1 buttstock, 20 shot PMag., 9.3 lbs. New 2014.

MSR $1,600	$1,375	$1,200	$1,075	$950	$815	$700	$575	

MK3 3GR – .308 Win. cal., 18 in. stainless steel heavy taper barrel with CMMG SV muzzle brake, RKM15 KeyMod free float handguard, Billet aluminum receiver, Geissele automatics SSA trigger, Magpul MOE pistol grip, trigger guard, buttstock, 9.4 lbs. New 2014.

MSR $1,850	$1,575	$1,375	$1,190	$1,050	$900	$775	$625	

MK3 CBR (CARBINE BATTLE RIFLE) – .308 Win. cal., GIO, 16 in. nitrided stainless steel match barrel, Surefire SOCOM suppressor adapter muzzle brake, full length free float Revo KeyMod handguard and KeyMod accessory attachment system, one 5-slot rail, Magpul MOE pistol grip and ACS-L buttstock, Geissele Super semi-auto 2-stage trigger, two-position selector safety, 5, 10 or 20 shot Pmag., Black or Flat Dark Earth (new 2016) finish, 8.7 lbs.

MSR $2,000	$1,700	$1,500	$1,250	$1,100	$950	$825	$675	

Add $150 for Flat Dark Earth finish (new 2016).

MK3 D – .308 Win. cal., GIO, 16 in. chrome-lined hammer forged barrel with A2 compensator, RKM15 KeyMod free float handguard, Billet alum. receiver, SST, 20 shot PMag., Magpul MOE pistol grip and stock, Black furniture, 8.2 lbs. Mfg. 2014 only.

	$1,700	$1,500	$1,250	$1,100	$950	$825	$675	*$2,000*

MK3 T – .308 Win. cal., 16.1 in. medium taper profile barrel with A2 compensator, RKM15 KeyMod free float handguard, Billet alum. receiver, SST, A2 pistol grip, M4 buttstock, Black furniture, 8.1 lbs. New 2014.

MSR $1,650	$1,400	$1,225	$1,100	$950	$815	$700	$575	

MK4 – 5.56 NATO cal., 14 1/2 in. chrome lined barrel with permanently attached A2 compensator (to meet minimum requirements), 30 shot PMAG, single stage trigger, MBUS rear sight, M4 buttstock, A2 pistol grip, forged aluminum receivers, M4 two-piece handguard, Black finish, 6 1/2 lbs.

MSR $1,150	$960	$875	$740	$625	$550	$475	$425	

MK4 3GR – 5.56 NATO cal., 18 in. stainless steel medium taper profile barrel with CMMG SV muzzle brake, RKM14 KeyMod free float handguard, Geissele SSA two-stage trigger, Magpul MOE pistol grip, trigger guard, rifle buttstock, Black furniture, 7 lbs. New 2014.

MSR $1,400	$1,200	$1,075	$950	$800	$700	$600	$495	

MK4 A4 (GOVERNMENT PROFILE MODEL 22A6A1F) – .22 LR or 5.56 NATO (new 2014) cal., AR-15 style, GIO, 20 in. WASP treated chrome moly steel Government profile barrel with A2 compensator, stainless steel bolt group with BHOA and forward assist adapter, "F" marked front sight base and Magpul MBUS rear sight, A2 two-piece handguard, A1 (disc.) or M4 buttstock with A2 pistol grip, 25 shot Evolution mag., black finish, 6 1/2 lbs.

MSR $925	$785	$685	$615	$550	$485	$415	$370	

Add $225 for 5.56 NATO cal.

MK4 D – 5.56 NATO cal., 16.1 in. medium taper hammer forged barrel with A2 compensator, RKM14 KeyMod free float handguard, forged aluminum receiver, SST, Magpul MOE pistol grip, trigger guard, and buttstock, 6.4 lbs.

MSR $1,400	$1,200	$1,075	$950	$800	$700	$600	$495	

MK4 HT – .22 LR, 5.56 NATO, or .300 AAC Blackout cal., GIO or GPO (5.56 NATO cal. only), 16.1 in. heavy taper chrome moly or stainless steel barrel with castellated thread protector, RKM KeyMod free float handguard, forged aluminum receiver, ST, A2 pistol grip and M4 buttstock, black furniture, 7 lbs. New 2014.

MSR $925	$785	$685	$615	$550	$485	$415	$370	

Add $125 for stainless steel barrel.
Add $175 for 5.56 NATO or .300 AAC Blackout cal.
Add $425 for GPO (gas piston operation).

MSR	100%	98%	95%	90%	80%	70%	60%	Last MSR

MK4LE – 9mm Para. (disc. 2014), .22 LR, 5.56 NATO, or .300 AAC Blackout cal., AR-15-style, GIO, 16 in. WASP treated chrome moly steel M4 profile barrel or M300 multi-role profile barrel (.300 AAC Blackout cal. only) with A2 compensator, M4 two-piece handguard, M4 buttstock with A2 pistol grip, 30 shot, forged aluminum receiver, SST, black furniture, "F" marked front sight base and MBUS rear sight, 6.2 lbs.

   MSR $850 $725 $650 $580 $515 $450 $385 $340

   Add $100 for 5.56 NATO cal., $150 for .300 AAC Blackout, or $250 for 9mm Para. cal. (disc. 2014).

   * **MK4LE Optics Ready** – 9mm Para. (disc. 2014), .22 LR, 5.56 NATO, or .300 AAC Blackout cal., similar to MK4LE, except has railed gas block and no sights.

   MSR $825 $700 $615 $550 $475 $420 $365 $335

   Add $100 for 5.56 NATO cal., $125 for .300 Blackout cal., or $250 for 9mm Para. cal. (disc. 2014).

MK4LEM – 5.56 NATO cal., GIO, 16 in. chrome moly steel medium taper profile barrel with A2 compensator, mid-length two-piece handguard, forged aluminum receiver, SST, M4 buttstock with A2 pistol grip, black furniture, 6 1/2 lbs. New 2014.

   MSR $950 $800 $700 $615 $550 $485 $415 $370

MK4 RCE – 5.56 NATO or .300 AAC Blackout cal., gas operated, 16 in. stainless steel medium taper profile barrel with CMMG SV brake, M4 flat-top upper receiver, aluminum lower, RKM14 KeyMod free-float handguard, Geissele two-stage trigger, 30 shot mag., Magpul MOE pistol grip, MOE trigger guard, CTR buttstock, black with Nitrided or stainless barrel or Flat Dark Earth (new 2015) finish, 6.7 lbs. New 2014.

   MSR $1,400 $1,200 $1,075 $950 $800 $700 $600 $495

   Add $100 for Flat Dark Earth finish (new 2015).

   Subtract $50 for black with stainless barrel.

MK4 S – 5.56 NATO cal., 18 in. stainless steel medium taper barrel with A2 compensator, RKM14 KeyMod free float handguard, forged aluminum receiver, SST, A2 pistol grip, M4 buttstock, Black furniture, 6.7 lbs.

   MSR $1,100 $925 $850 $725 $625 $550 $475 $425

MK4 T – 9mm Para. (disc. 2014), .22 LR, .300 AAC Blackout, or 5.56 NATO cal., 16.1 in. medium taper chrome moly or stainless steel barrel with A2 compensator, RKM11 KeyMod free float handguard, forged aluminum receiver, SST, A2 pistol grip, M4 buttstock, 6.3 lbs. New 2014.

   MSR $900 $775 $685 $615 $550 $485 $415 $370

   Add $100 for stainless steel barrel.

   Add $150 for 5.56 NATO or .300 AAC Blackout cal. or $250 for 9mm Para. cal. (disc. 2014).

MK4 V – 5.56 NATO cal., 24 in. fluted medium contour stainless steel barrel with target crown, RKM14 KeyMod free float handguard, forged alum. receiver, SST, A2 pistol grip, A1 fixed buttstock, 7 1/2 lbs. New 2014.

   MSR $1,250 $1,050 $950 $815 $685 $595 $515 $440

MK4 V2 – 5.56 NATO cal., 24 in. fluted barrel, target crown, 30 shot PMag., Geissele SSA trigger, RKM14 KeyMod handguard, Magpul MOE pistol grip, stock, and trigger guard, 7 1/2 lbs. New 2015.

   MSR $1,500 $1,275 $1,125 $1,025 $875 $750 $625 $525

MK9LE – 9mm Para. cal., 16.1 in. barrel with A2 compensator, utilizing Colt pattern magazines, 32 shot mag., "F" marked front sight base and MBUS rear sight, M4 type 2-piece handguard, forged receivers, single stage trigger, A2 pistol grip, M4 buttstock with 6-position receiver extension, Black finish, 6.2 lbs. New 2015.

   MSR $1,100 $925 $850 $725 $625 $550 $475 $425

   * **MK9LE OR** – 9mm Para. cal., similar to MK9LE, except has no sights, comes ready to accept your favorite optic or iron sights, 7.2 lbs. New 2015.

   MSR $1,075 $900 $760 $665 $585 $515 $450 $395

MK9 T – 9mm Para. cal., 16.1 in. M4 barrel with A2 compensator, 32 shot mag., free floating RKM11 handguard, forged receivers, A2 pistol grip, M4 buttstock with 6-pos. receiver extension, single stage trigger, 6.3 lbs. New 2015.

   MSR $1,150 $960 $875 $740 $625 $550 $475 $425

MK47 MUTANT SERIES – 7.62 NATO cal., GIO, 16.1 in. free floated barrel, fully modular, interchangable trigger assembly, rail, grip, buffer tube assembly, buttstock, muzzle brake, and gas system, uniquely engineered upper and lower receivers using billet aluminum, the lower receiver is designed to accept standard AK magazines, full length Picatinny rail, optics ready, only 7.2 lbs. New 2015.

   * **MK47 MUTANT AKM** – 7.62 NATO cal., 16.1 in. barrel with SV muzzle brake, 30 shot AKM PMag., RKM15 handguard, mid-sized billet receivers, single stage trigger, MOE pistol grip, CTR buttstock, 7.2 lbs. New 2015.

   MSR $1,650 $1,375 $1,215 $1,075 $950 $815 $700 $575

   * **MK47 MUTANT AKM2** – 7.62 NATO cal., 16.1 in. barrel with SV muzzle brake, 30 shot AKM PMag., RKM15 handguard, mid-sized billet aluminum receiver based on MK3 platform, Geissele SSA trigger, Magpul MOE pistol grip, CTR buttstock, top of the line Mutant rifle offering the most features, 7.2 lbs. New 2015.

   MSR $1,850 $1,575 $1,375 $1,190 $1,050 $900 $775 $625

MSR	100%	98%	95%	90%	80%	70%	60%	Last MSR

* **MK47 MUTANT AKS13** – 7.62x39mm cal., pinned gas block, 13 in. medium taper barrel with KRINK muzzle device pinned and welded to meet the 16 in. legal requirement, 30 shot AK PMAG (accepts standard AK mags.), single stage Mil-Spec trigger, Magpul CTR stock, MOE pistol grip, billet aluminum receivers, RKM15 KeyMod handguard, Black furniture, 7.4 lbs. New 2016.

MSR $1,750	$1,485	$1,315	$1,150	$1,025	$875	$750	$615	

* **MK47 MUTANT T** – 7.62 NATO cal., GIO, 16.1 in. barrel with A2 compensator, 30 shot AKM PMag., RKM15 handguard, billet receivers, single stage trigger, A2 pistol grip stock, this is the entry-level Mutant designed to give the user the opportunity to upgrade as they see fit, 7.2 lbs. New 2015.

MSR $1,500	$1,275	$1,125	$1,025	$875	$750	$625	$525	

C Z (CESKÁ ZBROJOVKA)

Current manufacturer located in Uhersky Brod, Czech Republic since 1936. Previous manufacture was in Strakonice, Czechoslovakia circa 1923-late 1950s. Newly manufactured CZ firearms are currently imported exclusively by CZ USA located in Kansas City, KS. Previously imported by Magnum Research, Inc. located in Minneapolis, MN until mid-1994. Previously imported before 1994 by Action Arms Ltd. located in Philadelphia, PA. Dealer and distributor sales.

For CZ manufactured airguns, please refer to the *Blue Book of Airguns* by Dr. Robert Beeman and John Allen (now online also).

CZ USA currently has four product lines, which include CZ (pistols, rifles, and shotguns), Safari Classics (best quality bolt action rifles), Dan Wesson (semi-auto pistols), and Brno (combination guns and rifles). Please refer to the individual listings for more information and current values.

PISTOLS: SEMI-AUTO, RECENT MFG.

CZ-75 P-01 – 9mm Para. cal., based on CZ-75 design but with metallurgical improvements, DA/SA, aluminum alloy frame, hammer forged 3.7 in. barrel, 10 or 14 (new 2005) shot mag., fixed sights, swappable safety (new 2016)/decocker, includes M3 rail on bottom of frame, checkered rubber grips, matte black polycoat finish, 27.2 oz. Importation began 2003.

MSR $627	$545	$480	$420	$365	$315	$275	$250	

Add $99 for tactical block with bayonet (mfg. 2006-2012).
Add $67 for Crimson Trace laser grips (mfg. 2007-2010).

CZ-75 P-06 – .40 S&W cal., 3.7 in. hammer forged barrel, 10 shot mag., light aluminum alloy frame, M3 rail, dual slide serrations, squared trigger guard, checkered black rubber grips, fixed night sights, decocker, black polycoat finish, 1.82 lbs. Mfg. 2008-2009, reintroduced 2011.

MSR $680	$575	$500	$450	$395	$335	$295	$265	

Add $99 for tactical block with bayonet (disc. 2012).

CZ P-07 DUTY – 9mm Para. or .40 S&W cal., DA/SA, 3.8 in. standard or threaded (new 2012) barrel, black polycoat or OD Green (new 2012) polymer frame with black slide, squared off trigger guard, 10 (9mm only), 12 (.40 S&W only) or 16 shot mag., fixed sights, decocking lever, Omega trigger system, 27 oz. Mfg. 2009-2013.

	$435	$370	$325	$280	$260	$240	$220	*$483*

Add $13 for .40 S&W cal.
Add $6 for OD Green frame in 9mm Para. cal. with 16 shot mag. (new 2012).
Add $45 for threaded barrel (9mm Para. cal. only) with black finish (new 2012).

CZ P-09 (P-09 DUTY) – 9mm Para. or .40 S&W cal., full size variation of the P-07 Duty, 4 1/2 in. barrel, 15 (.40 S&W) or 19 (9mm Para.) shot staggered mag., includes lower Picatinny rail and low profile sights, Omega SA/DA trigger, black polymer frame and black steel slide, polymer grips, approx. 30 oz. New 2013.

MSR $530	$475	$400	$350	$315	$285	$250	$225	

Add $14 for .40 S&W cal.
Add $47 for suppressor ready (9mm Para. only), 19 shot mag. New 2014.

CZ-40B/CZ-40P – .40 S&W cal. only, CZ-75B operating mechanism in alloy (CZ-40B) or polymer (CZ-40P) M1911 style frame, DA/SA, black polycoat finish, 10 shot double column mag., fixed sights, firing pin block safety. Limited importation 2002 only, reintroduced 2007 only.

	$425	$365	$325	$290	$275	$250	$225	*$499*

* **CZ-40 P Compact** – .40 S&W cal., 1,500 imported 2004, reimported 2006.

	$325	$285	$265	$245	$225	$200	$175	*$370*

CZ-75 SERIES – 9mm Para. or .40 S&W (disc. 1997, reintroduced 1999) cal., Poldi steel, selective double action, double action only, or single action only, frame safety, 4 3/4 in. barrel, 10 (C/B 1994, standard for .40 S&W cal.), 15* (disc.), or 16 (9mm Para. cal. only) shot mag., currently available in black polycoat/polymer (standard, DA and SA only), matte blue (disc. 1994), high polish (disc. 1994), glossy blue (mfg. 1999-2010), dual tone (mfg. 1998-2012), satin nickel (mfg. 1994-2012), high polished stainless steel, or matte stainless steel (new 2006) finish, black plastic grips, non-suffix early guns did not have a firing pin block safety, reversible mag. release, or ambidextrous safety, and

MSR	100%	98%	95%	90%	80%	70%	60%	Last MSR

were usually shipped with two mags., B suffix model nomenclature was added 1998, and designated some internal mechanism changes, BD suffix indicates decocker mechanism, 34.3 oz. New 1975.

Add 10% with lanyard loop.

These early pistols sell for $1,200 if NIB condition, chrome engraved $1,650 (NIB), factory competition $1,500 (NIB).

"First Model" variations, mostly imported by Pragotrade of Canada, are identifiable by short slide rails, no half-cock feature, and were mostly available in high polish blue only. Current values range from $275-$595, depending on original condition.

* **CZ-75 Semi-Compact** – 9mm Para. cal. only, 13 shot mag., choice of black polymer, matte, or high polish blue finish. Imported 1994 only.

| | $350 | $300 | $275 | $250 | $230 | $250 | $200 | *$519* |

Add $20 for matte blue finish.
Add $40 for high polish blue finish.

* **CZ-75 B Military** – 9mm Para. cal. Imported 2000-2002.

| | $365 | $315 | $270 | $250 | $225 | $210 | $195 | *$429* |

* **CZ-75 B Tactical** – similar to CZ-75 B, except has OD green frame and matte black slide, includes CZ knife. Limited importation during 2003:

| | $425 | $355 | $305 | $270 | $225 | $210 | $195 | *$499* |

CZ-75 COMPACT – 9mm Para. or .40 S&W (mfg. 2005-2010) cal. only, 3.7 in. barrel, steel frame, 10 (C/B 1994), 13* (disc.), or 14 shot mag., fixed sights, checkered walnut (disc.) or plastic grips, manual safety, black, glossy blue (disc. 2006), dual tone (disc. 2012), or satin nickel (disc. 2012) finish, 33 oz. New 1993.

| MSR $581 | $495 | $435 | $375 | $325 | $275 | $250 | $225 | |

Add $41 for glossy blue (disc. 2006), dual tone (disc. 2012), or satin nickel (disc. 2012) finish.
Add $41 for .40 S&W cal. (disc. 2010).
Add $99 for tactical block with bayonet (.40 S&W cal. only) mfg. 2006-2012.
Add $431 for CZ Kadet .22 LR adapter I or II (includes .22 LR upper slide assembly and mag., mfg. 1998-disc.).

* **CZ-75 D PCR Compact** – 9mm Para. cal., 3.7 in. barrel, black polymer alloy frame, decocker, PCR stands for Police of Czech Republic, 10 or 14 shot mag., black rubber grip, fixed snag free sights, loaded chamber indicator, 1.7 lbs. Importation began 2000.

| MSR $599 | $515 | $465 | $400 | $350 | $300 | $265 | $235 | |

* **CZ-75 Compact SDP** – 9mm Para. cal., DA/SA, 3.7 in. barrel, black alloy frame with black aluminum grips, lower Picatinny rail, low profile Tritium two-dot night sights, 14 shot mag., front and rear slide serrations, bobbed hammer, 28 1/2 oz. New 2013.

| MSR $1,453 | $1,265 | $1,075 | $925 | $800 | $700 | $600 | $500 | |

CZ-75 KADET – .22 LR cal., black polymer finish, 10 shot mag, 4.7 in. barrel, 37.9 oz. Mfg. 1999-2004, reintroduced 2006-2012.

| | $560 | $500 | $450 | $400 | $350 | $300 | $275 | *$690* |

CZ-75 SHADOW – 9mm Para. cal., DA/SA or SAO (new 2013), black or dual-tone finish, competition hammer/trigger with beavertail frame, stainless steel guide rod, ambidextrous extended manual safety, new style 85 combat trigger, includes two 16 (SAO, new 2013), or 18 shot mags. and test target, fiber optic front sight and shadow rear sight, checkered black plastic grips, 39 oz. Mfg. in Czech Republic, assembled in USA. Mfg. 2011-2013.

| | $915 | $800 | $725 | $650 | $575 | $500 | $425 | *$1,053* |

Subtract $74 for SAO (new 2013, includes two 16 shot mags.).

* **CZ-75 Shadow T** – 9mm Para. cal., similar to CZ-75 Shadow, except is DA/SA, and has black rubber grips and full adj. rear sight. Mfg. 2011-2013.

| | $1,075 | $940 | $815 | $725 | $650 | $575 | $500 | *$1,180* |

CZ-75 SHADOW CTS LS-P – 9mm Para. cal., DA/SA, black polycoat frame/grips, satin nickel long slide, adj. sights. Mfg. by Custom Shop 2012-2013.

| | $1,300 | $1,150 | $1,025 | $875 | $775 | $675 | $550 | *$1,521* |

CZ-75 TS CZECHMATE – 9mm Para. cal., includes two 5.4 in. barrels and all accessories necessary to shoot in IPSC open or limited division, aluminum grips, competition hammer, undercut trigger guard, three 20 shot mags. and one 26 shot mag., black polycoat finish. Custom Shop mfg. New 2011.

| MSR $3,317 | $2,850 | $2,475 | $2,150 | $1,825 | $1,500 | $1,250 | $1,000 | |

CZ-75 SP-01 – 9mm Para. cal., 4 3/4 in. barrel, includes lower Picatinny rail, ambidextrous thumb safety, adj. Tritium sights, matte black polycoat finish, decocker, checkered black rubber grips, two 10 or 18 shot mags, 38 oz. New 2006.

| MSR $680 | $575 | $485 | $410 | $350 | $300 | $275 | $250 | |

MSR	100%	98%	95%	90%	80%	70%	60%	Last MSR

* **CZ-75 SP-01 Phantom** – 9mm Para. cal., SA/DA, polymer frame with accessory rail, steel slide, fixed sights, two interchangable grip inserts, decocking lever, 19 shot mag. (also fits standard CZ-75 models), black polycoat finish, squared off trigger guard, 28.2 oz. Mfg. 2009-2013.

	$520	$440	$375	$325	$275	$250	$225	$595

* **CZ-75 SP-01 Accu-Shadow** – 9mm Para. cal., 4.6 in. barrel, features Accu-Bushing system enabling precise barrel placement and better accuracy, competition hammer, lighter springs, short reset disconnector, fiber optic front and Hajo serrated target rear sight, lower Picatinny rail, black finish, 38 1/2 oz. Mfg. 2013-2014.

	$1,475	$1,295	$1,075	$925	$800	$700	$600	$1,715

* **CZ-75 SP-01 Shadow Custom** – 9mm Para. cal., adj. competition rear and fiber optic front sight, 19 shot mag., custom tuned action and trigger, competition hammer, reduced power springs, stainless guide rod, thin black aluminum grips, dual tone finish, Custom Shop mfg. 2011 only.

	$1,050	$900	$750	$600	$500	$400	$325	$1,199

* **CZ-75 SP-01 Shadow Target** – 9mm Para. cal., similar to SP-01 Series, except has custom shop target features, including Champion style hammer, fiber optic front sight and competition rear sight, extended mag. release, fully beveled magwell, 19 shot mag., rubber grips, 2.6 lbs. Custom Shop mfg. 2010-2014.

	$1,175	$995	$825	$700	$600	$500	$425	$1,361

CZ-75 SP-01 TACTICAL – 9mm Para. or .40 S&W cal., 4.6 in. barrel, 12 or 18 shot mag., lower Picatinny rail, decocker, Tritium sights, black rubber grips, black polycoat finish.

MSR $680	$575	$485	$440	$395	$340	$315	$285	

Add $79 for .40 S&W cal.

Add $99 for tactical block with bayonet (disc. 2012).

CZ-83 – .32 ACP (disc. 1994, reintroduced 1999-2002 and 2006), .380 ACP (new 1986), or 9mm Makarov (mfg. 1999-2001) cal., modern design, 3-dot sights, 3.8 in. barrel, DA/SA, choice of carry models, blue (disc. 1994), glossy blue (new 1998), satin nickel (new 1999, not available in .32 ACP), or black polymer (disc. 1997) finish, black synthetic grips, 10 (C/B 1994), 12* (.380 ACP) or 15* (.32 ACP) shot mag., 26.2 oz. Mfg. began 1985, but U.S. importation started in 1992. Importation disc. 2012.

	$375	$315	$265	$235	$200	$175	$160	$452

Add $36 for satin nickel.

CZ-85, CZ-85 B – 9mm Para. or 9x21mm (imported 1993-94 only) cal., DA/SA, variation of the CZ-75 with ambidextrous controls, 4.6 in. barrel, new plastic grip design, sight rib, available in black polycoat, matte blue (disc. 1994), glossy blue (mfg. 2001 only), or high-gloss blue (9mm Para. only, disc. 1994) finish, includes firing pin block and finger rest trigger, plastic grips, 10, 15 (disc.), or 16 shot mag. New 2005, B suffix model nomenclature was added during 1998, approx. 2.2 lbs.

MSR $628	$525	$465	$410	$375	$330	$295	$275	

Add $431 for CZ Kadet .22 LR adapter (includes .22 LR upper slide assembly and mag., mfg. 1998 only).

* **CZ-85 Combat** – 9mm Para. cal., similar to CZ-85B, except has fully adj. rear sight, available in black polymer, matte blue (disc. 1994), glossy blue (mfg. 2001-2010), dual-tone (disc. 2012), satin nickel (disc. 2012), or high-gloss blue (disc. 2010) finish, walnut (disc. 1994) or black plastic (new 1994) grips, extended mag. release, drop free 15 (mfg. 1995-2011) or 16 shot mag. Importation began 1992.

MSR $664	$550	$465	$425	$375	$350	$325	$295	

Add $26 for glossy blue (disc. 2010), satin nickel (disc. 2012), or dual-tone (disc. 2012) finish.

Add $291 for CZ Kadet .22 LR adapter (includes .22 LR upper slide assembly and mag., mfg. 1998 only).

CZ-2075 RAMI – 9mm Para. or .40 S&W cal., DA/SA, 3 in. barrel, double stack 7 (.40 S&W cal. new 2012), 8 (.40 S&W cal.), 10 (9mm Para. cal., flush fit) or 14 (9mm Para. cal., disc. 2013) shot mag. with finger extension, snag free (disc.) or fixed sights, black polycoat finish with black rubber checkered grips, alloy or polymer (mfg. 2006-2011) frame, 25 oz. New 2005.

MSR $614	$510	$445	$375	$325	$300	$250	$225	

Add $19 for .40 S&W cal. with 7 shot mag. (new 2012).

Subtract approx. $100 for polymer frame with black polycoat finish (disc. 2011).

* **CZ-2075 RAMI BD** – 9mm Para. cal., DA/SA, 3 in. barrel, 10 or 14 shot mag., similar to CZ-2075 RAMI, except has decocking lever, weight reduction scallop on slide, Tritium 3-dot night sights, 23 1/2 oz. New 2009.

MSR $680	$590	$480	$425	$385	$350	$325	$295	

CZ VZ 61 SKORPION – imported by CZ 2009-2010. Please refer to this model listing in the Skorpion section.

RIFLES: BOLT ACTION, CENTERFIRE, COMMERCIAL MFG.

Ceská Zbrojovka began manufacturing rifles circa 1936. Long gun production was discontinued between 1948-1964, with the exception of the massive military contracts during that time period.

MSR	100%	98%	95%	90%	80%	70%	60%	Last MSR

* CZ 527 M1 American – .223 Rem. cal., styling similar to U.S. military M1 carbine featuring 3 shot flush detachable mag., no sights, redesigned trigger guard (new 2015), walnut (disc. 2013) or black synthetic stock, approx. 6 lbs. New 2008.

| MSR $665 | $555 | $475 | $420 | $365 | $335 | $295 | $250 | |

Add $66 for walnut stock (disc. 2013).

CZ 550 MAGNUM H.E.T. (HIGH ENERGY TACTICAL) – .300 Win. Mag., .300 Rem. Ultra Mag., or .338 Lapua cal., 28 in. barrel, flat black finish, Kevlar tactical stock, 4 to 6 shot fixed mag., SST, muzzle brake, oversized bolt handle, 13 lbs. Mfg. 2009-2013.

| | $3,500 | $3,125 | $2,625 | $2,250 | $1,950 | $1,575 | $1,325 | *$3,929* |

CZ 550 URBAN COUNTER SNIPER – .308 Win. cal., 16 in. barrel with SureFire muzzle brake, OD Green Kevlar stock, 10 shot mag. Mfg. 2010-2013.

| | $2,275 | $2,000 | $1,750 | $1,500 | $1,250 | $1,000 | $825 | *$2,530* |

CZ 700 SNIPER – .308 Win. cal., sniper design features forged billet receiver with permanently attached Weaver rail, 25.6 in. heavy barrel w/o sights, 10 shot detachable mag., black synthetic thumbhole stock with adj. cheekpiece and buttplate, large bolt handle, fully adj. trigger, 11.9 lbs. Limited importation 2001 only.

| | $1,875 | $1,575 | $1,250 | $1,025 | $895 | $775 | $650 | *$2,097* |

CZ 700M1 SNIPER – .308 Win. cal., similar to CZ 700 Sniper, except has laminated stock, limited importation 2001 only.

| | $1,875 | $1,575 | $1,250 | $1,025 | $895 | $775 | $650 | |

CZ 750 SNIPER – .308 Win. cal., sniper design, 26 in. barrel w/muzzle brake, includes two 10 shot mags., thread protector, and mirage shield, black synthetic thumbhole stock w/adj. comb, scope mounting via detachable Weaver rail or integral CZ 19mm dovetail, 11.9 lbs. Limited mfg. 2006-2015.

| | $1,775 | $1,550 | $1,250 | $1,050 | $925 | $775 | $675 | *$1,999* |

RIFLES: SEMI-AUTO

CZ-M52 (1952) – 7.62x45mm Czech cal., 20 2/3 in. barrel, 10 shot detachable mag., tangent rear sight, this model was also imported briefly by Samco Global Arms, Inc. located in Miami, FL.

| | $550 | $450 | $350 | $300 | $250 | $200 | $150 | |

CZ-M52/57 (1957) – 7.62x39mm cal., later variation of the CZ-M52.

| | $425 | $375 | $325 | $300 | $250 | $200 | $150 | |

CZ 512 TACTICAL – .22 LR or .22 WMR cal., 16 1/2 in. threaded Sporter barrel, 10 or 25 shot detachable single stack mag., top Picatinny rail, Crossbolt safety, 6-position stock with adj. comb, black finish, 6.1 lbs. New 2016.

| MSR $493 | $420 | $350 | $300 | $275 | $250 | $225 | $195 | |

Add $31 for .22 WMR cal.

CZ 805 BREN S1 CARBINE – 5.56 NATO cal., AR-15 style, aluminum frame, 16.2 in. cold hammer forged threaded barrel with two port muzzle brake, 30 shot STANAG mag., flip-up adj. iron sights, folding adj. stock, polymer grips, ambi thumb safety, top and bottom Picatinny rails, black or FDE finish, 8.02 lbs. New 2016.

| MSR $1,999 | $1,700 | $1,500 | $1,250 | $1,100 | $950 | $825 | $675 | |

CZ SCORPION EVO 3 S1 CARBINE – 9mm Para. cal., fiber reinforced polymer frame, 16 1/2 in. barrel with either a two-port compensator or faux suppressor, 20 shot double stack polymer mag., low-profile aluminum adj. sights, folding adj. stock, black polymer grips, ambi thumb safety, non-reciprocating charging handle, forend with M-LOK attachment points, top Picatinny rail, black finish, 6.1 lbs. New 2016.

| MSR $1,049 | $885 | $785 | $685 | $600 | $535 | $465 | $415 | |

VZ 58 MILITARY/TACTICAL SPORTER – 7.62x39mm cal., short stroke GPO, milled receiver, 16.14 in. barrel, tilting breech block, choice of Zytel skeletonized (Tactical) or plastic impregnated wood (Military) stock, alloy 30 shot mag., 7.32 lbs. Mfg. 2008-2011.

| | $925 | $850 | $750 | $650 | $550 | $450 | $350 | *$999* |

Add $30 for Tactical Sporter model (available with synthetic or folding (new 2010) stock).

SHOTGUNS: SEMI-AUTO

CZ 712 PRACTICAL G2 (CZ 712 PRACTICAL) – 12 ga., 3 in. chamber, 22 in. barrel with 5 choke tubes, 9 shot extended mag., 6-position M4 style adj. stock, matte black finish, 8.1 lbs. Mfg. 2014-2015.

| | $595 | $550 | $495 | $450 | $415 | $385 | $335 | *$699* |

In 2015 this model was updated and nomenclature changed to CZ 712 Practical G2.

MSR	100%	98%	95%	90%	80%	70%	60%	*Last MSR*

SHOTGUNS: SLIDE ACTION

CZ 612 HC-P – 12 ga., 20 in. barrel with cyl. choke tube, tactical configuration features black polymer pistol grip stock and grooved forearm, ghost ring sights with fiber optic dots, matte black metal finish, 6 1/2 lbs. Mfg. 2013-2015.

	$310	$285	$250	$225	$200	$185	$170	*$369*

CZ 612 HOME DEFENSE – 12 ga., 18 1/2 in. barrel with fixed cyl. choke and front bead sight, black synthetic stock and forearm, matte black metal finish, 6 lbs. Mfg. 2013-2015.

	$265	$235	$210	$190	$170	$150	$135	*$304*

Add $105 for Home Defense Combo two barrel set with extra 26 in. barrel (new 2014).

CZ (STRAKONICE)

Current manufacturer established in 1919 and located in Strakonice, Czech Republic. No current U.S. importation. Previously imported by Adco Sales, Inc., located in Woburn, MA.

PISTOLS: SEMI-AUTO

Older Strakonice manufacture can be found in the CZ (Ceska Zbrojovka) section.

CZ-TT – 9mm Para., .40 S&W, or .45 ACP cal., DA/SA, polymer frame, 3.77 in. ported or unported barrel, matte finish, 10 shot mag., 26.1 oz. Imported 2004-2006.

	$450	$415	$375	$325	$295	$275	$250	*$479*

Add $30 for ported barrel (disc.).
Add $40 for ported barrel and slide serrations (disc.).
Add $399 for conversion kit with one mag.

CZ-T POLYMER COMPACT – similar to CZ-TT, except has shorter barrel. Limited importation 2004 only.

	$475	$425	$375	$325	$295	$275	$225	*$559*

CZ ST9 – 9mm Para. cal., 5 in. barrel, 16 shot mag., DA/SA, manual safety lever, matte blue finish, checkered wood grips.

This model has not been imported into the U.S.

CADEX DEFENCE

Current bolt action rifle and accessories manufacturer with U.S.A. office located in Valdosta, GA.

RIFLES: BOLT ACTION

CDX30 GUARDIAN LITE RIFLE – .308 Win. cal., 20 or 24 in. fluted match grade barrel with threaded muzzle, M16-style extractor, oversized trigger guard and mag. release, reverse folding buttstock, rubberized Ergo grip with finger grooves, detachable base, full length lite top rail, tool-free adj. butt pad, adj. LOP and cheek rest, Black, Tan, Hybrid Tan/Black, OD Green, or Hybrid Green/Black finish, 14.2 lbs. New 2015.

MSR $6,000	$5,100	$4,475	$3,825	$3,475	$2,800	$2,350	$2,000	

CDX30 GUARDIAN TAC RIFLE – .308 Win. cal., 20 or 24 in. fluted match grade barrel with threaded muzzle, multiple magazine sleeves, oversized trigger guard and mag. release, fully adj. stock with integrated monopod attachment, rubberized Ergo grip with finger grooves, detachable base, full length lite top rail, Black, Tan, or Hybrid Tan/Black finish, 14.6 lbs. New 2015.

MSR $5,200	$4,425	$3,875	$3,325	$3,025	$2,500	$2,100	$1,625	

CDX33 PATRIOT LITE RIFLE – .338 Lapua cal., 27 in. fluted match grade barrel with threaded muzzle, M16-style extractor, oversized trigger guard and mag. release, reverse folding buttstock, rubberized Ergo grip with finger grooves, detachable base, full length lite top rail, tool-free adj. butt pad, adj. LOP and cheek rest, Black, Tan, Hybrid Tan/Black, OD Green, or Hybrid Green/Black finish, 14.2 lbs. New 2015.

MSR $6,000	$5,100	$4,475	$3,825	$3,475	$2,800	$2,350	$2,000	

CDX33 PATRIOT TAC RIFLE – .338 Lapua cal., 27 in. fluted match grade barrel with threaded muzzle, multiple magazine sleeves, oversized trigger guard and mag. release, fully adj. stock with integrated monopod attachment, rubberized Ergo grip with finger grooves, detachable base, full length lite top rail, Black, Tan, or Hybrid Tan/Black finish, 14.6 lbs. New 2015.

MSR $5,200	$4,425	$3,875	$3,325	$3,025	$2,500	$2,100	$1,625	

CDX-40 SHADOW – .408 CheyTac cal., 29 or 32 in. fluted Bartlein stainless steel barrel, single or double stage trigger, oversized trigger guard and mag. release, folding buttstock, adj. buttpad, LOP, and cheek rest, Ergo finger grooved grips, detachable base, full length light top rail, Cerakote finish in Black, Tan, OD Green, Hybrid Black/Tan, or Hybrid Black/Green, 8 1/2 lbs. New 2016.

Please contact the company directly for pricing and availability for this model.

MSR	100%	98%	95%	90%	80%	70%	60%	Last MSR

CDX-50 TREMOR – .50 BMG cal., 29 in. fluted match grade heavy stainless steel barrel, barrel band and threaded muzzle, 5 shot, stainless action and bolt, single or double stage trigger, oversized trigger guard and mag. release, folding buttstock, tool-free adj. cheek rest and LOP, detachable base, dual top rail, Cerakote finish in Black, Tan, OD Green, Hybrid Black/Tan, or Hybrid Black/Green, 23.8 lbs. New 2016.

MSR $8,500 $7,250 $6,500 $5,750 $5,250 $4,500 $3,750 $3,000

CDX300 FREEDOM LITE RIFLE – .300 Win. Mag. cal., 24 or 26 in. fluted match grade barrel with threaded muzzle, M16-style extractor, oversized trigger guard and mag. release, reverse folding buttstock, rubberized Ergo grip with finger grooves, detachable base, full length lite top rail, tool-free adj. buttpad, adj. LOP and cheek rest, Black, Tan, Hybrid Tan/Black, OD Green, or Hybrid Green/Black finish, 14.2 lbs. New 2015.

MSR $6,000 $5,100 $4,475 $3,825 $3,475 $2,800 $2,350 $2,000

CDX300 FREEDOM TAC RIFLE – .300 Win. Mag. cal., 24 or 26 in. fluted match grade barrel with threaded muzzle, multiple magazine sleeves, oversized trigger guard and mag. release, fully adj. stock with integrated monopod attachment, rubberized Ergo grip with finger grooves, detachable base, full length lite top rail, Black, Tan, or Hybrid Tan/Black finish, 14.6 lbs. New 2015.

MSR $5,200 $4,425 $3,875 $3,325 $3,025 $2,500 $2,100 $1,625

CALICO LIGHT WEAPONS SYSTEMS

Current manufacturer established during 1986, and located in Cornelius, OR, previously located in Hillsboro, OR from 2002-2010, located in Sparks, NV 1998-2001, and in Bakersfield, CA.

CARBINES: SEMI-AUTO

Extra magazines are currently priced as follows: $141 for 100 shot 9mm Para. cal., $118 for 50 shot 9mm Para. cal., or $125 for 100 shot .22 LR cal.

LIBERTY I/II & LIBERTY 50-100 – 9mm Para. cal., 16.1 in. barrel, downward ejection, retarded blowback CETME type action, aluminum alloy receiver, synthetic stock with pistol grip (some early post-ban specimens had full wood stocks with thumbhole cutouts), 50 or 100 shot helical feed mag., ambidextrous safety, 7 lbs. Mfg. 1995-2001, reintroduced late 2007.

MSR $710 $625 $550 $500 $450 $400 $350 $300

Add $70 for Liberty 50 Tactical with quad rails (new 2010).
Add $189 for Liberty I Tactical with quad rails (new 2010), or $197 for Liberty II Tactical with quad rails (new 2010).
Add $119 for Liberty I with skeletal adj. stock, or $137 for Liberty II with fixed stock.
Add $46 for Liberty 100 (100 shot mag.), or $116 for Liberty 100 Tactical with quad rails (new 2010).
Current MSR is for the Liberty 50 Model.

M-100 – .22 LR cal., blowback action, folding buttstock, 100 shot helical feed mag., alloy frame, aluminum receiver, ambidextrous safety, 16.1 in. shrouded barrel with flash suppressor/muzzle brake, adj. sights, 4.2 lbs. empty. Mfg. 1986-1994, reintroduced late 2007.

MSR $573 $515 $450 $400 $350 $300 $275 $250

* **M-100 Tactical** – similar to M-100, except has quad Picatinny rails. New 2010.

MSR $643 $550 $475 $425 $375 $325 $300 $275

* **M-100 FS** – similar to M-100, except has solid stock and barrel does not have flash suppressor. Mfg. 1996-2001, reintroduced late 2007.

MSR $573 $515 $450 $400 $350 $300 $275 $250

* **M-100 FS Tactical** – similar to M-100 FS, except has quad Picatinny rail. New 2010.

MSR $643 $550 $475 $425 $375 $325 $300 $275

M-101 – while advertised, this model never went into production.

M-105 SPORTER – similar to M-100, except has walnut distinctively styled buttstock and forend, 4 3/4 lbs. empty. Mfg. 1989-1994.

   $650 $550 $495 $450 $350 $295 $250   *$335*

M-106 – while advertised, this model never went into production.

M-900 – 9mm Para. cal., retarded blowback action, wood (disc.) or collapsible buttstock (current mfg.), cast aluminum receiver with stainless steel bolt, static cocking handle, 16 in. barrel, fixed rear sight with adj. post front, 50 (standard) or 100 shot helical feed mag., ambidextrous safety, black polymer pistol grip and forend, approx. 3.7 lbs. Mfg. 1989-1990, reintroduced 1992-1993, again during 2007-2010.

   $775 $700 $650 $600 $500 $450 $400   *$875*

Add $157 for 100 shot mag.

MSR	100%	98%	95%	90%	80%	70%	60%	Last MSR

* **M-900S** – similar to M-900, except has non-collapsible shoulder stock. Disc. 1993.

| | $650 | $550 | $475 | $400 | $350 | $300 | $275 | $632 |

* **M-901 Canada Carbine** – 9mm Para. cal., similar to M-900, except has 18 1/2 in. barrel and sliding stock. Disc. 1992.

| | $675 | $595 | $550 | $475 | $350 | $300 | $285 | $643 |

This model was also available with solid fixed stock (Model 901S).

M-951 TACTICAL CARBINE – 9mm Para. cal., 16.1 in. barrel, similar appearance to M-900 Carbine, except has muzzle brake and extra pistol grip on front of forearm, 4 3/4 lbs. Mfg. 1990-94.

| | $750 | $700 | $675 | $650 | $600 | $475 | $450 | $556 |

* **M-951S** – similar to M-951, except has synthetic buttstock. Mfg. 1991-94.

| | $650 | $595 | $525 | $450 | $400 | $350 | $300 | $567 |

PISTOLS: SEMI-AUTO

LIBERTY III – 9mm Para. cal., 6 in. ported barrel, choice of 50 or 100 shot mag., ribbed forend, 2 1/4 lbs. w/o mag. New 2010.

| MSR $783 | $700 | $625 | $550 | $500 | $450 | $400 | $350 | |

Add $70 for Liberty III Tactical with quad rails (new 2011).

M-110 – .22 LR cal., blowback action, 6 in. barrel with muzzle brake, 100 round helical feed mag., includes notched rear sight and adj. windage front sight, 10 1/2 in. sight radius, ambidextrous safety, pistol grip storage compartment, 2.21 lbs. empty. Mfg. 1989-2001, reintroduced 2007.

| MSR $619 | $550 | $475 | $375 | $325 | $275 | $225 | $200 | |

M-950 – 9mm Para. cal., same operating mechanism as the M-900 Carbine, 6 in. barrel, 50 (standard) or 100 shot helical feed mag., 2 1/4 lbs. empty. Mfg. 1989-1994, mfg. late 2007-2010.

| | $775 | $700 | $650 | $600 | $500 | $450 | $400 | $872 |

CANIK55

Current trademark of pistols manufactured by Samsun Domestic Defence and Industry Corporation (a subsidiary of Aral Industry Corporation), established in 1997 and located in Samsun, Turkey. Currently imported beginning 2013 by Tristar, located in N. Kansas City, MO, and beginning 2014 by Century International Arms, Inc., located in Delray Beach, FL. Previously imported circa mid-2010-2011 by Canik-USA, located in Pueblo West, CO.

PISTOLS: SEMI-AUTO

Canik55 is a line of good quality semi-auto 1911-style pistols, including the Shark Series, Stingray Series, TP-9 Series (new 2012, SFO), Piranha Series, LSC Series, S-FC 100 Series, MKEK Series, and Dolphin Series. Currently, only some of these models are being imported into the U.S. Please contact the importers directly for more information, including pricing and U.S. availability (see Trademark Index).

CARACAL

Current manufacturer of semi-auto pistols established in 2006, and located in the Abu Dhabi, United Arab Emirates. Currently imported beginning 2011 by Caracal USA, located in Newinton, NH. Previously located in Trussville, AL and Knoxville, TN. Currently distributed in Italy exclusively by Fratelli Tanfoglio Snc, located in Brescia, Italy.

In 2016, Caracal joined forces with Wilcox Industries Corp. located in Newington, NH.

PISTOLS: SEMI-AUTO

MODEL C – 9mm Para., 9x21mm, .357 SIG, or .40 S&W cal., modified Browning-type blowback design, DAO, SFO, 3.66 in. barrel, 14 shot mag., ribbed black polymer frame with colored inserts and Picatinny rail in front of trigger guard, matte black slide with rear slide serrations and integral sights (fiber optic front sight), Glock style trigger safety, cocking indicator, approx. 25 oz. Disc.

| | $550 | $450 | $415 | $375 | $335 | $300 | $275 | $625 |

Caracal has issued a recall on all of its Model C pistols following an incident where one gun suffered a catastrophic slide failure. The company advises owners not to load or use any Model C pistol and to contact Caracal immediately at 205-655-7050. Caracal is offering a full refund of the purchase price on all C Model pistols.

MODEL F – similar to Model C, except has 4.1 in. barrel and 18 shot mag., 26 1/2 oz.

| | $550 | $450 | $415 | $375 | $335 | $300 | $275 | $625 |

MODEL SC – 9mm Para. or 9x21mm cal., similar to Model C, except is compact variation with 3.38 in. barrel and 13 shot mag., approx. 23 oz. Limited mfg. 2009-2011.

| | $550 | $450 | $415 | $375 | $335 | $300 | $275 | $625 |

MSR	100%	98%	95%	90%	80%	70%	60%	Last MSR

MODEL CAL .40 – .40 S&W cal., 4.1 in. barrel, 14 shot mag., SFO, lightweight polymer frame, lower accessory rail, corrosion resistant matte black finish, low profile slide, short trigger pull, ambidextrous mag. release, approx. 27 oz. New 2013.

Please contact Caracal USA directly for current pricing on this model.

MODEL CP660 – 9mm Para., modified Browning-type blowback design, double action, SFO, 4.1 in. barrel, 18 shot mag., ribbed black polymer frame with colored inserts and Picatinny rail in front of trigger guard, dovetail widened rear sight notch, deeper slide serrations, altered firing pin unit in the slide, and drop safety. New mid-2014.

Please contact Caracal USA directly for current pricing on this model.

RIFLES: BOLT ACTION

MODEL CSR – .308 Win. cal., 20 or 32 in. hammer forged threaded barrel, folding adj. skeletonized stock, pistol grip, quad rail, 10 shot mag., adj. match grade trigger, black finish, approx. 11 lbs. New 2012.

Please contact Caracal USA directly for current pricing on this model.

RIFLES: SEMI-AUTO

MODEL CC10 – 9mm Para. cal., modern bullpup design with skeletonized stock with grip safety, full length Picatinny rail, sights integrated into the frame, 18 shot detachable mag., right hand ejection with bolt lever on left side, black finish, choice of 9.3 (CC10-SB, LE only) or 16.1 (CC10 LB) in. barrel. New 2012.

Please contact Caracal USA directly for current pricing on this model.

CARBON 15

Please refer to the Professional Ordnance (discontinued mfg.) and Bushmaster (current mfg.) listings for more information on this trademark.

CAVALRY ARMS CORPORATION

Previous manufacturer located in Gilbert, AZ until 2010 and previously located in Mesa, AZ.

CARBINES/RIFLES: SEMI-AUTO

Cavalry Arms Corporation manufactured the CAV-15 Series, patterned after the AR-15 style carbine/rifle. Cavalry Arms also made conversions for select slide action shotguns.

CAV-15 SCOUT CARBINE – .223 Rem. cal., GIO, 16 in. chrome lined barrel, A2 flash hider, A3 flat-top upper receiver, longer sight radius, stand alone rear sight, Black, Green, or Coyote Brown finish, C6 handguards. Disc. 2010.

MSR	100%	98%	95%	90%	80%	70%	60%	Last MSR
	$765	$675	$580	$515	$450	$385	$340	$850

Add $199 for drop in rail system.
Add $259 for free float system.
Add $92 for YHM flip up front or rear sight.

CAV-15 RIFLEMAN – .223 Rem. cal., GIO, 20 in. chrome lined Govt. profile barrel, A2 flash hider, A3 flat-top upper receiver, stand alone rear sight, Black, Green, or Coyote Brown finish, A2 handguard. Disc. 2010.

MSR	100%	98%	95%	90%	80%	70%	60%	Last MSR
	$765	$675	$580	$515	$450	$385	$340	$850

Add $279 mid-length free float system.
Add $310 for rifle length free float system.
Add $92 for YHM flip up front or rear sight.

CENTURION ORDNANCE, INC.

Previous importer located in Helotes, TX. Centurion Ordnance also imported Aguila ammunition.

SHOTGUNS: SLIDE ACTION

POSEIDON – 12 ga., 1 3/4 in. chamber (shoots "mini-shells" and slugs), 18 1/4 in. smoothbore barrel, 13 in. LOP, black synthetic stock and forearm, 6 shot mag., adj. rear sight, 5 lbs., 5 oz. Limited importation 2001.

MSR	100%	98%	95%	90%	80%	70%	60%	Last MSR
	$285	$250	$225	$200	$185	$170	$155	

While prototypes of this model were imported briefly during 2001, this gun never made it into the consumer marketplace.

Mini-shells retailed for $12.60 for a box of 20 (shot sizes include 7, #4 & #1 buckshot).

CENTURY ARMS (CENTURY INTERNATIONAL ARMS, INC.)

Current importer and distributor founded in 1961 with current corporate offices located in Delray Beach, FL. Century International Arms, Inc. was previously headquartered in St. Albans, VT until 1997, and Boca Raton, FL from 1997-2004. The company rebranded in late 2014 and is now known as Century Arms.

Century Arms imports a large variety of used military rifles, shotguns, and pistols. Because inventory changes daily, especially on tactical style rifles, carbines and pistols, please contact the company directly for the most recent offerings

MSR	100%	98%	95%	90%	80%	70%	60%	Last MSR

and pricing (see Trademark Index).

Additionally, Century Arms imports a wide range of accessories, including bayonets, holsters, stocks, magazines, grips, mounts, scopes, misc. parts, new and surplus ammunition, etc., and should be contacted directly (see Trademark Index) for a copy of their most recent catalog, or check their web site for current offerings.

PISTOLS: SEMI-AUTO

Century International Arms Inc. also imports Arcus pistols from Bulgaria and Daewoo pistols from South Korea. Please refer to the individual sections for more information.

M-1911 STYLE PISTOLS – .45 ACP cal., SA, patterned after the Colt Govt. Model 1911, choice of 4 1/4 (Blue Thunder Commodore, Commodore 1911, or GI-Officer's Model) or 5 (SAM Elite/SAM Standard, Military, or SAM Chief/Falcon or Scout) ported (disc. 2002) or unported barrel, 7 or 8 shot mag., various configurations and finishes, target features are available on select models, approx. 41 oz. Imported from the Phillipines beginning 2001, current mfg. is from Shooter's Arms.

| No MSR | $500 | $450 | $375 | $350 | $275 | $225 | $175 | |

Add $35 for Commodore Blue Thunder Model with squared off trigger guard (disc. 2013).

C93 PISTOL – 5.56 NATO or 7.62x39mm (new 2013) cal., patterned after the H&K MP-5 using a roller lock delayed blowback system and fluted chamber, 8 1/2 in. barrel with flash suppressor, adj. rear sight, includes two 40 shot mags., 6.4 lbs. Imported 2012-2014.

| | $900 | $795 | $675 | $625 | $495 | $400 | $315 | |

CENTURION 39 AK PISTOL – 7.62x39mm cal., AK-47 design, features 11 3/8 in. barrel with M16 style birdcage muzzle brake, machined receiver, quad Picatinny rails, Tapco G2 trigger, ergonomic pistol grip, black polymer furniture, optional Shark Fin front sight, 5.4 lbs. Mfg. in the U.S. beginning 2011.

| MSR $735 | $650 | $575 | $510 | $440 | $385 | $340 | $325 | |

COLEFIRE MAGNUM – 7.62 Tokarev cal., styled after the Sterling Mk7 pistol, manganese phosphate finish coated with black wrinkle paint, enlarged and knurled charging handle, 4 1/2 in. barrel, SA, optional accessory rail. Imported 2013.

| | $250 | $225 | $195 | $175 | $140 | $115 | $90 | |

This model did not include a magazine (sold separately).

CZ 999/CZ 999 COMPACT – 9mm Para. cal., 3 1/2 (Compact) or 4 1/4 in. barrel, DA/SA, 15 shot double column mag., ambidextrous controls, white dot sights, inertial firing pin, loaded chamber indicator, decocking lever, mfg. by Zastava. Imported 2013-2014.

| | $470 | $410 | $350 | $325 | $260 | $210 | $175 | |

DRACO – 7.62x39mm cal., blonde wood forend, 12 1/4 in. barrel, 30 shot mag., approx. 5 1/2 lbs. Imported 2010-2012.

| | $395 | $350 | $300 | $265 | $235 | $200 | $185 | *$450* |

PAP M92 PV – 7.62x39mm cal., GPO, AK-47 design, 10 in. cold hammer forged barrel, 30 shot mag., dual aperture Krinkov style rear sight, bolt hold-open notch on selector, steel alloy bolt and barrel, stamped receiver, hinged top cover, 6.6 lbs., mfg. by Zastava. Importation began 2013.

| MSR $535 | $475 | $400 | $340 | $285 | $250 | $230 | $220 | |

Add $30 for Krinkov muzzle brake.

PAP M85 PV – .223 Rem. cal., GPO, AK-47 design, 10 in. cold hammer forged barrel, 30 shot mag., dual aperture Krinkov style rear sight, bolt hold-open notch on selector, steel alloy bolt and barrel, stamped receiver, hinged top cover, 6.4 lbs., mfg. by Zastava. Importation began 2013.

| MSR $535 | $475 | $400 | $340 | $285 | $250 | $230 | $220 | |

Add $30 for Krinkov muzzle brake.

P1 Mk 7 – 9mm Para. cal., 3.7 in. stainless steel barrel, polymer frame, integral Picatinny rail, fully ambidextrous, four interchangeable grip backstraps, matte black finish, includes two 15 shot mags., 24 oz. Mfg. by Grand Power, importation began mid-2013.

| No MSR | $500 | $440 | $375 | $340 | $275 | $225 | $175 | |

RIFLES/CARBINES: SEMI-AUTO

AES10-B RPK STYLE – 7.62x39mm cal., 23 1/8 in. heavy barrel with folding bipod, laminated stock and forend, includes two AK style 40 shot mags., 10.9 lbs. Imported 2012.

| | $575 | $500 | $450 | $400 | $375 | $350 | $325 | *$675* |

AK-74 BULLPUP – 5.45x39mm cal., AK-47 design, 16 1/4 in. barrel with muzzle brake, vent. handguard, top Picatinny rail, two 30 shot mags., 7.35 lbs. Limited importation 2010-2011.

| | $575 | $500 | $425 | $365 | $335 | $295 | $275 | *$650* |

MSR	100%	98%	95%	90%	80%	70%	60%	Last MSR

AK-74 SPORTER – 5.45x39mm cal., AK-47 design, 16 1/4 in. barrel with muzzle brake, side mount rail, bayonet lug, fixed wood stock, includes two 30 shot mags., sling, mag. pouch, cleaning rod and oil bottle, 7.6 lbs. Importation began 2014.

| No MSR | $790 | $695 | $595 | $535 | $435 | $350 | $275 | |

AKMS – 7.62x39mm cal., AK-47 design, 16 1/4 in. barrel with muzzle brake, features laminate wood handguards, pistol grip, and steel folding buttstock with skeleton buttplate, includes two 30 shot mags., 7.8 lbs. Imported 2011-2013.

| | $625 | $550 | $500 | $425 | $350 | $275 | $225 | *$700* |

C15A1 SPORTER – 5.56 NATO cal., AR-15 style, based on M16A1, GIO, triangular "Vietnam era" style handguard, 16 in. barrel with muzzle brake, fixed stock, includes two original Colt 30 shot mags. (disc. 2011) or fixed 10 shot mag. (current mfg.), choice of green polymer or walnut wood furniture, A3 carry handle and sights. Importation began mid-2010.

   This model is POR.

   Add 15% for High Cap Mag. model

C15 M4 – 5.56 NATO cal., AR-15 style, 16 in. barrel with birdcage muzzle brake, flat-top receiver with detachable carry handle, adj. T6 stock, one 30 shot mag. Importation began 2014.

| No MSR | $700 | $615 | $525 | $475 | $385 | $315 | $250 | |

CENTURION 39 – 7.62x39mm cal., 16 1/2 in. barrel, V-shape Chevron compensator, available in Tactical (fixed black synthetic stock) or Sporter (black synthetic stock) configurations, black finish, fixed buttstock with pistol grip, four Picatinny rails, includes two 30 shot mags., 8.2 lbs. All parts mfg. in U.S. beginning mid-2010.

| No MSR | $800 | $700 | $600 | $550 | $450 | $360 | $295 | |

   * Centurion 39 Classic – 7.62x39mm cal., similar to Centurion 39, except has laminated wood stock in Black (new 2014), Brown (new 2014), and Blonde (new 2014), adj. rear sight. All parts mfg. in U.S. beginning mid-2010.

| No MSR | $800 | $700 | $600 | $550 | $450 | $360 | $295 | |

CENTURION UC-9 CARBINE – 9mm Para. cal., patterned after the Israeli sub-machine gun, straight blowback closed bolt action, 16 in. barrel, blue finish, folding steel stock, includes two 32 shot all steel double column mags., approx. 9 lbs. Importation began mid-2012.

| No MSR | $900 | $795 | $675 | $610 | $495 | $400 | $315 | |

CETME SPORTER – .308 Win. cal., new mfg. Cetme action, 19 1/2 in. barrel, 20 shot mag., choice of blue or Mossy Oak Break-Up camo (disc.) metal finish, wood (disc.) or synthetic stock, pistol grip, and vent. forearm, refinished condition only, 9.7 lbs. Imported 2002-2011.

| | $550 | $475 | $400 | $350 | $300 | $275 | $250 | *$635* |

DEGTYAREV MODEL – top mounted magazine, semi-auto version of the Soviet model, available in three variations.

   * DP 28 – 7.62x54R cal., 23.8 in. barrel, gas operated, 47 shot drum mag., full shoulder stock.

| | $3,500 | $3,060 | $2,625 | $2,380 | $1,925 | $1,575 | $1,225 | |

   * DPM 28 – 7.62x54R cal., 23.8 in. barrel, gas operated, 47 shot drum mag., pistol grip stock.

| | $3,500 | $3,060 | $2,625 | $2,380 | $1,925 | $1,575 | $1,225 | |

   * DTX Tank Model – 7.62x54R cal., 23.8 in. barrel, 50 shot drum mag., collapsible stock, approx. 10 lbs.

| | $3,500 | $3,060 | $2,625 | $2,380 | $1,925 | $1,575 | $1,225 | |

DPM – 7.62x54R cal., semi-auto closed bolt copy of the WWII Soviet machine gun, 23.8 in. barrel, 47 shot pan magazine mounted on top of receiver, adj. sights, wood furniture, blued metal, includes bipod, 18 1/2 lbs. w/out mag. Imported 2011-2012.

| | $1,775 | $1,575 | $1,350 | $1,150 | $950 | $750 | $675 | *$2,000* |

DRAGUNOV – 7.62x54R cal., new CNC milled receiver, Dragunov configuration, thumbhole stock, 26 1/2 in. barrel, supplied with scope and cleaning kit. Mfg. in Romania. Disc. 2010.

| | $975 | $855 | $730 | $665 | $535 | $440 | $340 | |

FAL SPORTER – .308 Win. cal., U.S. mfg., new barrel and receiver, synthetic furniture, 20 shot mag. Imported 2004-2006.

| | $850 | $745 | $635 | $580 | $465 | $380 | $295 | |

G-3 SPORTER – .308 Win. cal., mfg. from genuine G3 parts, and American made receiver with integrated scope rail, includes 20 shot mag., 19 in. barrel, pistol grip stock, matte black finish, refinished condition only, 9.3 lbs. Imported 1999-2006.

| | $785 | $685 | $590 | $535 | $430 | $355 | $275 | |

GOLANI SPORTER – .223 Rem. cal., 21 in. barrel, 35 shot mag., folding stock, optional bayonet lug, approx. 8 lbs., mfg. in Israel.

| | $625 | $550 | $500 | $425 | $350 | $275 | $225 | *$700* |

   Add $30 for bayonet lug (disc.).

MSR	100%	98%	95%	90%	80%	70%	60%	Last MSR

GORIUNOV SG43 – 7.62x54R cal., copy of Soviet model, gas operated, 28.3 in. barrel, 250 shot belt fed, charging handle, spade grips, includes wooden crate, folding carriage, 3 ammo belts, 96 lbs. Importation disc. 2011.

| | $4,750 | $4,200 | $3,750 | $3,250 | $2,650 | $2,100 | $1,850 | *$5,325* |

GP 1975 – 7.62x39mm cal., AK-47 design, 16 1/4 in. barrel, black synthetic furniture, new U.S. receiver and barrel, includes two 30 shot mags., approx. 7.4 lbs. Importation disc. 2011.

| | $595 | $425 | $375 | $325 | $275 | $250 | $225 | *$675* |

Add approx. $140 for collapsible stock and Picatinny rail forearm.

GP WASR-10 HIGH-CAP SERIES – 7.62x39mm cal., AK-47 design, 16 1/4 in. barrel, various configurations, includes two 30 shot double stack mags., 7 1/2 lbs. Mfg. by Romarm of Romania.

| MSR $670 | $585 | $510 | $435 | $365 | $325 | $280 | $265 | |

Add $10 for bayonet.
Add $133 for 100 shot drum mag.
Add $250 for factory installed slide fire stock (new 2014).
Add $67 for recoilless buttstock (new 2012).
Add $60 for 50th Anniversary model with Century Arms logo on back right of receiver (only 50 mfg. during 2012).

GP WASR-10 LO-CAP – 7.62x39mm cal., AK-47 design, 16 1/4 in. barrel, wood stock and forearm, includes one 5 and one 10 shot single stack mags., 7 1/2 lbs. Mfg. by Romarm of Romania. Importation disc. 2011.

| | $400 | $350 | $315 | $275 | $250 | $225 | $200 | *$450* |

L1A1/R1A1 SPORTER – .308 Win. cal., current mfg. receiver patterned after the British L1A1, includes carrying handle, synthetic furniture, 20 shot mag., 22 1/2 in. barrel, fold over aperture rear sight, 9 1/2 lbs. Mfg. in U.S., disc. 2010.

| | $975 | $850 | $750 | $650 | $575 | $500 | $450 | |

Subtract approx. $200 for L1A1 Sporter.

M70 SERIES – 7.62x39mm cal., based on Yugoslavian Paratrooper model, 16 1/4 in. barrel, includes two 30 shot double stack mags., classic wood furniture (disc.) or black polymer upper and lower handguards, black under folding stock (AB2) or fixed synthetic stock (B1), slant muzzle brake, bayonet lug, approx. 7 1/2 lbs. Limited importation beginning 2013.

| No MSR | $660 | $575 | $495 | $450 | $365 | $295 | $230 | |

Add $40 for AB2 Model.

M-76 SNIPER/SPORTER MODEL – 8mm Mauser cal., semi-auto version of the Yugoslav M76, new U.S. receiver and 21 1/2 in. barrel, includes original scope, mount, and 10 shot mag., 11.3 lbs. Importation disc. 2011.

| | $1,495 | $1,200 | $1,000 | $875 | $750 | $650 | $550 | *$1,725* |

MEXSAR – .22 LR cal., 21 1/4 in. barrel, 16 shot mag., fiber optic front sight, uncheckered pistol grip hardwood stock, dovetailed for scope mounts, blue finish, 6.2 lbs. Importation began 2014.

| No MSR | $230 | $200 | $175 | $150 | $125 | $100 | $80 | |

PAP M77 PS – .308 Win. cal., 16 1/4 in. cold hammer forged barrel, 30 shot mag., black polymer thumbhole stock with upper and lower handguard, Picatinny rail, dust cover, mfg. by Zastava. Importation began 2013.

| No MSR | $650 | $575 | $495 | $440 | $360 | $295 | $250 | |

PAP SERIES – 7.62x39 or 7.62x51mm cal., 16 1/4 in. cold hammer forged barrel, choice of classic wood stock with pistol grip, black thumbhole stock with polymer handguard, or T6 collapsible stock with plastic handguard, 10 or 30 shot mag., accessory rail, 7.7-8 lbs. Mfg. by Zastava. Importation began 2013.

| No MSR | $580 | $510 | $435 | $395 | $325 | $260 | $200 | |

Add $80 for Hi-Cap Model with fixed wood buttstock, handguard, and two 30 shot mags (new 2014).
Add $120 for DF Model with T6 collapsible stock.

RAS47 – 7.62x39mm cal., AK-47 design, 16 1/2 in. barrel, slant muzzle brake, stamped receiver, two 30 shot Magpul mags., T-shaped magazine catch, side scope rail, bolt hold open safety, AK sights, compatibility with AKM furniture, AK stock, pistol grip, and handguard, includes enhanced dust cover, 7.8 lbs. New 2015.

| MSR $799 | $685 | $615 | $550 | $475 | $420 | $365 | $335 | |

* ***RAS47 Black*** – 7.62x39mm cal., similar to RAS47, except has RAK-1 enhanced trigger group, Magpul MOE AK furniture, black nitrite finish, 7.37 lbs. New mid-2015.

| MSR $799 | $685 | $615 | $550 | $475 | $420 | $365 | $335 | |

S.A.R. 1 – 7.62x39mm cal., AK-47 design, 16 1/2 in. barrel, wood stock and forearm, scope rail mounted on receiver, includes one 10 and two 30 shot double stack mags., 7.08 lbs. Mfg. by Romarm of Romania. Importation disc. 2003.

| | $750 | $655 | $560 | $510 | $410 | $335 | $260 | |

S.A.R. 2 – 5.45x39mm cal., AK-47 design, 16 in. barrel, wood stock and forearm, includes one 10 and one 30 shot double stack mags., 8 lbs. Mfg. by Romarm of Romania. Importation disc. 2003.

| | $750 | $655 | $560 | $510 | $410 | $335 | $260 | |

MSR	100%	98%	95%	90%	80%	70%	60%	Last MSR

S.A.R. 3 – .223 Rem. cal., AK-47 design, 16 in. barrel, wood stock and forearm, includes one 10 and one 30 shot double stack mag., 8 lbs. Mfg. by Romarm of Romania. Importation disc. 2003.

| | $750 | $655 | $560 | $510 | $410 | $335 | $260 | |

SAIGA SERIES – 5.45x39mm or 7.62x39mm cal., 16 1/4 (Hi-Cap) or 16 1/2 in. chrome lined barrel, 10 or 30 (Hi-Cap) shot mag., iron sights, fixed plastic straight grip stock with pistol grip or checkered synthetic pistol grip stock, side mount rail, matte black finish, approx. 8 lbs. Importation began 2014.

| No MSR | $650 | $575 | $495 | $450 | $375 | $295 | $250 | |

Add $310 for Hi-Cap Model.

STERLING SA – 9mm Para. cal., blowback action, semi-auto version of the Sterling submachine gun, 16 1/4 in. barrel, American made receiver and barrel, original style crinkle painted finish, folding stock, includes two 34 shot mags., available in Type I (disc.) or Type II, L sight with 100 and 200 yard apertures, front post sight, full length heat shield, unique port feed angle, 9.2 lbs.

| No MSR | $550 | $475 | $415 | $375 | $300 | $250 | $195 | |

TANTAL SPORTER – 5.45x39mm cal., 18 in. barrel, parkerized finish, side folding wire stock, flash hider, includes extra mag., 8 lbs.

| | $475 | $400 | $350 | $300 | $275 | $250 | $225 | *$550* |

VZ2008 SPORTER – 7.62x39mm cal., copy of the Czech VZ58, 16 1/4 in. barrel, steel receiver, dull matte finish, bead blasted metal parts, wood or plastic (disc. 2011) buttstock, CA compliant, 7 lbs. Importation disc. 2011, resumed 2014.

| No MSR | $600 | $525 | $450 | $410 | $325 | $275 | $210 | |

RIFLES: SLIDE ACTION

PAR 1 OR 3 – 7.62x39mm (PAR 1) or .223 Rem. (PAR 3) cal., AK-47 receiver design, 10 shot mag., accepts double stack AK magazines, wood stock, pistol grip, and forearm, 20.9 in. barrel, 7.6 lbs. Mfg. by PAR, and imported 2002-2009.

| | $360 | $300 | $275 | $250 | $225 | $200 | $175 | |

SHOTGUNS

SAS-12 SEMI-AUTO – 12 ga. only, 2 3/4 in. chamber, detachable 3 (Type II) or 5 shot mag., black synthetic stock and forearm, 22 or 23 1/2 in. barrel. Mfg. by PRC in China.

| | $225 | $195 | $170 | $155 | $125 | $100 | $80 | |

Add approx. $25 for ghost ring rear with blade front or bead sight.

CATAMOUNT FURY I SEMI-AUTO – 12 ga., 2 3/4 or 3 in. chamber, adj. gas system, 20.1 in. barrel, includes 3 choke tubes, full, modified, and cylinder bore, Picatinny rail mounted to hinged dust cover, fixed combat sights, AK-style safety lever, 5 shot AK style detachable box mag., fixed black synthetic stock with pistol grip, matte black finish, 8.7 lbs. New 2013.

| MSR $670 | $585 | $515 | $435 | $365 | $325 | $280 | $265 | |

MODEL IJ2 SLIDE ACTION – 12 ga. only, 2 3/4 or 3 in. chamber, 19 in. barrel with ghost ring sights or fiber optic front sights, fixed choke only, 7.2 lbs. Mfg. in China.

| | $200 | $175 | $150 | $135 | $110 | $90 | $70 | |

ULTRA 87 SLIDE ACTION – 12 ga., 3 in. chamber, 19 in. barrel with iron sights, optional pistol grip, metal heatshield (disc.), fixed black synthetic (current mfg.) or side folding (disc.) stock, 8.2 lbs.

| | $185 | $160 | $145 | $130 | $115 | $100 | $90 | *$200* |

Add $65 for extra 28 in. barrel.

MKA 1919 – 12 ga., AR-15 style, gas operation, aluminum alloy upper, one piece polymer lower receiver, pistol grip fixed stock, matte black or 100% camo finish, right side magwell mag. release, bolt stop, 5 shot detachable mag., A2 removable carry handle and front sight, three internal chokes, integral Picatinny rail, approx. 6 1/2 lbs. Imported from Turkey beginning mid-2012.

| No MSR | $850 | $750 | $640 | $575 | $475 | $385 | $300 | |

CHARLES DALY: 1976-2010

Previous manufactured trademark imported late 1996-early 2010 by KBI, Inc. located in Harrisburg, PA. Previously imported by Outdoor Sports Headquarters, Inc. located in Dayton, OH until 1995.

In 1976, Sloan's Sporting Goods sold the Daly division to Outdoor Sports Headquarters, Inc., a sporting goods wholesaler located in Dayton, OH. OSHI continued the importation of high-grade Daly shotguns, primarily from Italy and Spain. By the mid-1980s, the Charles Daly brand was transformed into a broad consumer line of excellent firearms and hunting accessories.

In 1996, OSHI was sold to Jerry's Sports Center, Inc. of Forest City, PA, a major wholesaler of firearms and hunting supplies. Within a few months of Jerry's acquisition of OSHI, K.B.I., Inc. of Harrisburg, PA, purchased the Charles Daly trademark from JSC. As it turned out, Michael Kassnar, president of K.B.I., Inc., had produced almost all of the Charles Daly

MSR	100%	98%	95%	90%	80%	70%	60%	Last MSR

products for OSHI from 1976-1985 in his capacity of president of Kassnar Imports, Inc. K.B.I., Inc. resurrected the complete line of O/U and SxS shotguns in early 1997.

In 1998, the line expanded to include rimfire rifles and the first pistol produced under the Daly name, a Model 1911-A1 in .45 ACP cal. In 1999, semi-auto and slide action shotguns were also reintroduced. In 2000, the additions included 3 1/2 in. slide actions and semi-autos, Country Squire .410 bore shotguns, bolt action centerfire rifles, and the DDA 10-45, the first double action pistol produced under the Charles Daly name.

During 2004, Charles Daly began importing Bul Transmark pistols from Israel. In 2007, the Little Sharps single shot rifles were introduced.

In 2008, a Charles Daly Defense line was established, which includes AR-15 style semi-auto rifles.

On Jan. 29, 2010, K.B.I. announced it was shutting its doors and discontinued importation of all models.

PISTOLS: SEMI-AUTO

During 2001, the nomenclature on these 1911 models was changed to include a new "E" prefix. The "E" stands for enhanced, and features included extended high-rise beavertail grip safety, combat trigger, combat hammer, beveled magwell, flared and lowered ejection port, dovetailed front and low profile rear sights, and hand checkered double diamond grips. The Enhanced pistols were manufactured by Armscor of the Philipines. M-5 pistols are manufactured by Bul Transmark in Israel.

GOVERNMENT 1911-A2 FIELD EFS HC – .40 S&W or .45 ACP cal., 5 in. barrel, SA, similar to Government 1911 A-1 Field EFS, 13 (.45 ACP cal.), or 15 (.40 S&W cal.) shot mag., blue finish only. Imported 2005-2007.

	100%	98%	95%	90%	80%	70%	60%	Last MSR
	$595	$520	$445	$405	$325	$270	$210	$725

Add $124 for Target Model (.45 ACP cal. only, new 2005).

MODEL DDA 10-45 FS (DOUBLE ACTION) – .40 S&W (disc. 2001) or .45 ACP cal., DA/SA, 4 3/8 in. barrel, polymer frame with checkering, double stack 10 shot mag. with interchangeable base plate (allowing for extra grip length), matte black or two-tone (new 2001) finish, 28 1/2 oz. Imported 2000-2002.

	100%	98%	95%	90%	80%	70%	60%	Last MSR
	$450	$395	$340	$305	$250	$205	$160	$519

Add $40 for two-tone finish.

* **Model DDA 10-45 CS** – similar to Model DDA 10-45 FS, except has 3 5/8 in. barrel, 26 oz. Imported 2000-2002.

	100%	98%	95%	90%	80%	70%	60%	Last MSR
	$450	$395	$340	$305	$250	$205	$160	$519

Add approx. $10 for colored frame (yellow, OD green, or fuschia, new 2001) and compensated barrel.

FIELD HP HI-POWER – 9mm Para. cal., SA, 4 3/4 in. barrel, patterned after the Browning Hi-Power, blue or hard chrome (mfg. 2005) finish, 10 or 13 shot mag., XS Express sight system, mfg. in U.S. Mfg. late 2003-2006.

	100%	98%	95%	90%	80%	70%	60%	Last MSR
	$385	$335	$290	$260	$210	$175	$135	$458

Add $120 for hard chrome finish (mfg. 2005).

This model has been produced both by Dan Wesson (2003-2004) and Magnum Research (2005-2006).

CD9 – 9mm Para. cal., 4.46 in. barrel, SA, SFO, black polymer frame and finish, striker fired, adj. sights, trigger safety, forward/lower accessory rail, 10 or 15 shot mag., three grip inserts. Imported 2009 only.

	100%	98%	95%	90%	80%	70%	60%	Last MSR
	$375	$330	$280	$255	$205	$170	$130	$437

G4 1911 SERIES – .45 ACP cal., SA, 5 in. barrel, 7 shot, black finish carbon or stainless steel construction, beveled magwell, flared and lowered ejection port, beavertail grip safety, internal extractor, Novak sights, three slot aluminum trigger, available in Standard, Target, and Tactical configurations, mfg. in Israel. Imported 2009 only.

	100%	98%	95%	90%	80%	70%	60%	Last MSR
	$750	$655	$565	$510	$415	$340	$265	$867

Add $96 for either Tactical or Target model.
Add $96 for stainless steel.
Add $354 for .22 LR conversion kit.

M-5 FS STANDARD (BUL 1911 GOVERNMENT) – 9mm Para. (new 2010), .40 S&W or .45 ACP cal., 5 in. barrel, polymer double column frame, SA, steel slide, aluminum speed trigger, checkered front and rear grip straps, blue or chrome finished slide, 10, 14, or 17 (9mm Para. cal.) shot staggered mag., 31-33 oz. Mfg. by Bul Transmark in Israel. Imported 2004-2009.

	100%	98%	95%	90%	80%	70%	60%	Last MSR
	$665	$580	$500	$450	$365	$300	$235	$803

* **M-5 MS Standard Commander** – .40 S&W or .45 ACP cal., similar to M-5 FS Standard, except has 4 1/3 in. barrel, 29-30 oz. Imported 2004-2009.

	100%	98%	95%	90%	80%	70%	60%	Last MSR
	$665	$580	$500	$450	$365	$300	$235	$803

* **M-5 Ultra-X** – 9mm Para. or .45 ACP cal., 10 or 12 (9mm Para. cal. only) shot mag., compact variation with 3.15 in. barrel. Imported 2005-2009.

	100%	98%	95%	90%	80%	70%	60%	Last MSR
	$665	$580	$500	$450	$365	$300	$235	$803

MSR	100%	98%	95%	90%	80%	70%	60%	Last MSR

JERICHO SERIES – 9mm Para., .40 S&W, or .45 ACP cal., 3 1/2 (Compact), 3.82 (Mid-Size), or 4.41 (Full Size) in. barrel, DA/SA, 10, 12, 13, or 15 shot mag., polymer or steel frame with black or chrome (Mid-size .45 ACP cal. only) finish, combat style trigger guard, slide mounted thumb decocker, two slot accessory rail (except Compact), ergonomic grips, mfg. by IWI, Ltd. (formerly IMI) in Israel. Limited importation 2009.

	$595	$520	$445	$405	$325	$270	$210	$699

Add $198 for steel frame and chrome finish (Full or Mid-size only).

ZDA MODEL – 9mm Para. or .40 S&W cal., DA/SA, 4 1/8 in. barrel, 12 (.40 S&W cal.) or 15 (9mm Para. cal.) shot mag., mfg. by Zastava. Limited importation 2005 only.

	$490	$430	$370	$335	$270	$220	$170	$589

RIFLES/CARBINES: SEMI-AUTO

All recently manufactured semi-auto rifles have forged aluminum alloy receivers that are hard coat milspec anodized and Teflon coated, manganese phosphate barrel (except stainless), radiused aluminum magazine release button, aluminum trigger guard, safety selector position on right side of receiver, dust cover, brass deflector, forward assist, and include one magazine and hard plastic carrying case. All recently manufactured rifles were covered by a lifetime repair policy.

D-M4/D-M4P CARBINE – 5.56 NATO cal., GIO, 16 in. chrome moly match barrel with M-203 mounting groove, 10, 20, or 30 shot mag., forged "F" front sight base with bayonet lug and rubber coated sling swivel, A3 detachable carry handle, T-Marked flat-top upper, 6-position telestock, A2 birdcage flash hider, oval double heat shield M4 forend. Mfg. 2008-2009.

	$925	$810	$695	$630	$510	$415	$325	$1,143

Add $90 for M4 feed ramps (Model DM-4).

D-M4LE CARBINE – 5.56 NATO cal., GIO, similar to D-M4 carbine, except has Mil-Spec diameter receiver extension with "H" buffer. Mfg. 2008-2009.

	$1,275	$1,115	$955	$865	$700	$575	$445	$1,373

D-M4S CARBINE – GIO, similar to D-M4 carbine, except has two Picatinny riser blocks, oval double heat shield M4 forend with QD sling swivel and swivel/bipod stud installed, Magpul enhanced trigger guard. Mfg. 2008-2009.

	$1,025	$895	$770	$695	$565	$460	$360	$1,189

D-M4LX CARBINE – 5.56 NATO cal., GIO, 16 in. chrome moly H-bar fluted match barrel, M4 feed ramps, T-Marked flat-top upper, flip up rear sight, folding front gas block with bayonet lug, aluminum free floating quad rail forend with swiveling sling stud, nine 5-slot low profile ladder style quad rail covers, Ace M4 SOCOM standard length telestock with half buttpad, Phantom flash suppressor, Ergo Ambi AR grip. Mfg. 2008-2009.

	$1,650	$1,445	$1,240	$1,120	$910	$745	$580	$1,783

D-M4LT CARBINE – 5.56 NATO cal., GIO, Mil-Spec diameter receiver extension with "H" buffer, chrome lined lightweight A1 barrel, permanently attached Phantom suppressor, slim carbine type forend, 30 shot Magpul PMAG black mag. Limited mfg. 2009.

	$1,275	$1,115	$955	$865	$700	$575	$445	$1,373

Add $890 for permanently attached Smith Vortex flash suppressor, Magpul CTR stock with buttpad, and Daniel Defense light rail (Model D-M4LTD, mfg. 2009 only).

Add $1,050 for Vltor Modstock, mid-length gas system, Smith Vortex suppressor, Daniel Defense light rail, and Magpul grip (Model D-M4MG, mfg. 2009 only).

Add $150 for A2 birdcage flash hider, full length handguard, Troy flip-up BUIS (Model D-M4MLL, mfg. 2009 only).

D-MCA4 RIFLE – .223 Rem. cal., 20 in. chrome-lined Govt. profile barrel with A2 birdcage flash hider, 30 shot Mil-Spec mag., A3 detachable carry handle, forged front sight base, A2 handguard, A2 buttstock. Limited mfg. 2009.

	$1,175	$1,030	$880	$800	$645	$530	$410	$1,317

Add $622 for KAC M5 quad rail with KAC panels (Model D-MCA4-M5).

D-M4LED CARBINE – 5.56 NATO cal., GIO, 16 in. chrome lined Govt. profile barrel, Flat Dark Earth finish, Magpul CTR Mil-Spec buttstock, A2 birdcage flash hider, M4 feed ramps, Daniel Defense light rail, Magpul MIAD grip, Troy rear BUIS. Limited mfg. 2009.

	$1,925	$1,675	$1,500	$1,250	$1,050	$875	$725	$2,209

D-MR20 RIFLE – 5.56 NATO cal., GIO, 20 in. Wilson Arms stainless steel fluted bull barrel, Magpul PRS II stock, three slot riser blocks, Daniel Defense light rail forearm with Picatinny rail gas block, two-stage match trigger, Phantom suppressor, 20 shot mag. Mfg. 2009.

	$1,825	$1,595	$1,370	$1,240	$1,005	$820	$640	$1,979

DR-15 TARGET – 5.56 NATO cal., GIO, 20 in. chrome moly match H-bar barrel, A2 upper with carry handle, fixed A2 buttstock, A2 birdcage flash hider, forged front sight tower with bayonet lug and rubber coated sling swivel. Limited mfg. 2008.

	$895	$785	$670	$610	$490	$405	$315	$1,089

MSR	100%	98%	95%	90%	80%	70%	60%	Last MSR

DV-24 MATCH TARGET/VARMINT – 5.56 NATO cal., GIO, 24 in. free float match stainless steel bull barrel, T-Marked flat-top upper, two Picatinny riser blocks, ported aluminum tube forend with swivel/bipod stud installed, Ace skeletonized buttstock, Picatinny rail milled gas block, two-stage match trigger. Mfg. 2008-2009.

| | $1,250 | $1,095 | $940 | $850 | $690 | $565 | $440 | *$1,389* |

JR CARBINE – 9mm Para. (JR9), .40 S&W (JR40), or .45 ACP (JR45) cal., GIO, 16 1/4 in. triangular contoured barrel, 13 (.45 ACP), 15 (.40 S&W), or 17 (9mm) shot mag., features unique magwell interchangability, allowing the owner to use handgun magazine of choice, matte black synthetic 6-position telescoping AR stock, anodized aluminum receiver, Picatinny rail, free float quad rail forearm, ergonomic AR grip, includes two mags., approx. 6 1/2 lbs. Disc. 2009.

| | $875 | $775 | $700 | $625 | $550 | $475 | $400 | *$987* |

SHOTGUNS: SEMI-AUTO

The Charles Daly "Novamatic" shotguns were produced in 1968 by Breda in Italy. The Novamatic series was not imported by Outdoor Sport Headquarters, Inc.

TACTICAL – 12 ga., 18 1/2 in. barrel, matte black synthetic pistol grip stock, Picatinny rail, ghost ring sights, extended tactical choke tube. Limited mfg. 2009.

| | $495 | $435 | $370 | $335 | $270 | $225 | $175 | *$587* |

Add $80 for 100% A-Tacs camo finish (new 2010).

SHOTGUNS: SLIDE ACTION

TACTICAL – 12 or 20 (new 2009) ga., 3 in. chamber, 18 1/2 in. cyl. bore barrel with front sight, black synthetic stock and forearm or 100% camo coverage (new 2009), matte blue metal or chrome finish, 6 lbs. Imported 2000-2009.

| | $250 | $220 | $190 | $170 | $140 | $115 | $90 | *$289* |

Add $24 for Field Tactical AW with chrome finish and adj. sights.
Add $74 for pistol grip stock, ghost ring sights, and MC1 multichoke.
Add $134 for pistol grip stock, ghost ring sights, Picatinny rail, and extended choke tube.
Add $124 for camo with ghost ring and fiber optic sights (new 2009).

CHARLES DALY: 2011-PRESENT

Current registered trademark of shotguns imported by Samco Global Arms located in Miami, FL.

During Sept. 2012, Samco Global Arms, Inc. purchased the Charles Daly trademarks from the Kassnar family. On Akkar and Charles Daly shotguns imported by Samco during 2011-2012, service can be provided directly by Samco. Samco can also supply service parts and accessories for Charles Daly semi-auto, pump, and O/U shoguns imported by K.B.I., Inc. and made by the Akkar factory in Turkey, from 1999 through 2010. These models are identifiable by the serial number. Samco cannot provide direct service and/or parts for any other firearms imported by K.B.I. Inc. or others, that were sold under the Charles Daly name. Parts for other Charles Daly firearms imported by K.B.I., Inc., such as 1911 pistols made in the Phillipines - contact Armscor. Shotguns made in Italy, contact Sabatti, or Fausti. For Miroku shotguns made in Japan, contact Browning, etc.

SHOTGUNS: SEMI-AUTO

MODEL 600 HD (HOME DEFENSE) – 12 ga., 3 in. chamber, 18 1/2 in. chrome moly steel barrel, cyl. choke, bead sight, Black synthetic stock, blue finish. New 2012.

| MSR $509 | $450 | $395 | $340 | $300 | $250 | $200 | $150 | |

* ***Model 600 HD-LH (Left Hand)*** – 12 ga., similar to Model 600 HD, except features camo stock and left-hand action. New 2013.

| MSR $541 | $485 | $425 | $375 | $325 | $275 | $225 | $175 | |

MODEL 600 THD (TACTICAL) – 12 ga., 3 in. chamber, 18 1/2 in. chrome moly steel barrel, MC chokes, ghost ring sights, Picatinny rail, Black synthetic pistol grip stock with blue finish or full digital camo. New 2012.

| MSR $613 | $540 | $475 | $400 | $375 | $300 | $250 | $200 | |

Add $94 for full digital camo stock and finish.

CHARTER ARMS

Previously manufactured by Charco, Inc. located in Ansonia, CT 1992-1996. Previously manufactured by Charter Arms located in Stratford, CT 1964-1991.

The company's first model was the Undercover.

PISTOLS: SEMI-AUTO

EXPLORER II & S II PISTOL – .22 LR cal., SA survival pistol, barrel unscrews, 8 shot mag., black, gold (disc.), silvertone, or camouflage finish, 6, 8, or 10 in. barrels, simulated walnut grips. Disc. 1986.

| | $90 | $80 | $70 | $60 | $55 | $50 | $45 | *$109* |

This model uses a modified AR-7 action.
Manufacture of this model was by Survival Arms located in Cocoa, FL.

MSR	100%	98%	95%	90%	80%	70%	60%	Last MSR

RIFLES: SEMI-AUTO

AR-7 EXPLORER RIFLE – .22 LR cal., SA, takedown, barreled action stores in Cycolac synthetic stock, 8 shot mag., adj. sights, 16 in. barrel, black finish on AR-7, silvertone on AR-7S. Camouflage finish new 1986 (AR-7C). Mfg. until 1990.

	$125	$100	$85	$75	$65	$55	$50	*$146*

In 1990, the manufacturing of this model was taken over by Survival Arms located in Cocoa, FL. Current mfg. AR-7 rifles will be found under the Henry Repeating Arms Company.

CHATTAHOOCHEE GUN WORKS, LLC

Current custom manufacturer located in Phenix City, AL.

PISTOLS: SEMI-AUTO

Chattahoochee Gun Works previously manufactured the CGW-15 AR-15 style pistol in 5.56 NATO cal. (last MSR was $1,500).

RIFLES: SEMI-AUTO

CGW-15 B 16 M1 – 5.56 NATO cal., 16 in. chrome moly barrel (.223 Wylde chambered), mid-length GIO, low profile gas block, solid billet lower receiver and forged T-marked upper, Midwest Industries free float rail system, Gunfighter charging handle, Magpul CTR stock, A2 grip, black finish.

MSR $1,550		$1,315	$1,165	$1,050	$915	$785	$665	$550

CGW-15 B 16-R1V – 5.56 NATO cal., 16 in. stainless steel barrel, A2 flash hider, A4 barrel extension, extended feed ramps, mid-length GIO, low profile gas block, solid billet upper and lower receiver, CGW Gunfighter charging handle, H-buffer, 13 1/2 or 15 in. KeyMod free float handguard, Magpul MOE pistol grip carbine stock, Magpul MOE or Ergo grip, hardcoat anodized finish, Ni-Teflon, Magpul Gray, FDE, or OD Green finish upgrades also available.

MSR $1,999		$1,875	$1,650	$1,400	$1,200	$1,025	$875	$725

CGW-15 R16B-KAC-1 – 5.56 NATO cal., 16 in. stainless steel barrel (.223 Wylde chambered), A2 flash hider, A4 barrel extension, mid-length GIO, low profile gas block, H-buffer, extended feed ramps, billet lower, forged T-marked upper, Knights Armament with front sight 12 1/2 in. free float handguard w/1913 rails, CGW Gunfighter charging handle, Magpul CTR stock, Magpul MOE+ grip, hardcoat anodized finish.

MSR $1,700		$1,450	$1,275	$1,125	$1,000	$850	$735	$595

CGW-15 SM-16 – 5.56 NATO cal., 16 in. cold hammer forged lightweight profile barrel, A2 flash suppressor, 30 shot mag., mid-length GIO, F-marked fixed front sight base, Magpul MBUS rear sight, flat-top upper and forged Mil-Spec lower receiver, Magpul MOE mid-length handguards, forged charging handle, Magpul MOE carbine stock, Mil-Spec trigger group, Mil-Spec heavy phosphate finish.

MSR $1,225		$1,025	$925	$800	$685	$595	$515	$440

CGW-15 16 IN. NICKEL TEFLON – 5.56 NATO or .300 AAC Blackout cal., 16 in. stainless steel barrel, A2 or Blackout 51 T flash suppressor, 30 shot mag., mid-length GIO, CGW low profile gas block, solid billet upper and lower receivers with Nickel Teflon finish, Mil-Spec receiver extension, CGW KeyMod rail, free float handguard w/Picatinny rail, Magpul MOE+ grip, staked endplate, H-Buffer, CGW Gunfighter charging handle, engraved Chattahoochee Gun Works logo, Magpul CTR stock.

MSR $1,950		$1,650	$1,450	$1,225	$1,085	$935	$800	$660

CGW 7.62 – 7.62 NATO cal., 20 in. Kreiger barrel, SureFire muzzle brake or AAC BrakeOut adaptor muzzle device, rifle length GIO, 20 shot PMAG, solid billet upper and lower receiver, Superior Weapons Systems E1 free float tube, Geissele SSA trigger, Magpul CTR stock, Magpul + grip.

MSR $2,499		$2,125	$1,875	$1,550	$1,325	$1,100	$950	$825

CGW 7.62 16 IN. – 7.62 NATO cal., 16 or 18 in. match grade stainless steel barrel, black or bead blasted finish, A2 muzzle brake, 20 shot PMAG, mid-length GIO, solid billet upper and lower receiver, Superior Weapons Systems E1 free float tube or 15 in. KeyMod rail, VLTOR IMOD or Magpul CTR stock, Magpul + or Ergo grip.

MSR $2,100		$1,795	$1,575	$1,325	$1,150	$995	$850	$700

CHEYTAC USA, LLC

Current manufacturer located in Nashville, GA. Previously located in Arco, ID. Previously distributed by SPA Defense, located in Ft. Lauderdale, FL, and by Knesek Guns, Inc., located in Van Buren, AR. Dealer sales.

RIFLES: BOLT ACTION

Cheytac previously manufactured the following models: M300 A5 McMillan, M300 Precision Engagement Rifle, Perses Tactical Engagement Rifle, Vidar, and Safeside.

M200 INTERVENTION – .375 CheyTac or .408 CheyTac cal., 29 in. takedown/interchangeable barrel, removable muzzle brake, 7 shot detachable box mag., adj. match trigger, CNC machined receiver, integral bipod and monopod,

MSR	100%	98%	95%	90%	80%	70%	60%	Last MSR

5-position fully adj. stock, Cerakote ArmorBlack (standard), FDE, OD Green, Nordic Gray, Tungsten, or Kryptek camo finish, includes custom case, 6 1/2 lbs.

Current MSR is $11,500-$11,960, depending on finish.

M300 INTERVENTION CARBON FIBER – .375 CheyTac or .408 CheyTac cal., 29 in. fluted barrel, detachable muzzle brake, 7 shot detachable box mag., adj. match trigger, integral trigger guard and magwell, ambi paddle lever mag. release, carbon fiber ergonomic enclosed forend with free floating barrel channel, full length Picatinny rails, flush cup swing swivel attachment points, fully adj. folding buttstock, Ergo tactical handle grip, Push Button Adjustable Hybrid (PBA-H) shoulder stock, adj. cheekpiece, premium Limbsaver custom recoil pad, Cerakote ArmorBlack (standard), FDE, OD Green, Nordic Gray, Tungsten, or Kryptek camo finish, includes CheyTac USA logo and laser engraving and custom case, 21 lbs.

Current MSR is $10,500-$10,960, depending on finish.

M300 INTERVENTION COMPOSITE – .375 CheyTac or .408 CheyTac cal., 29 in. fluted barrel, removable muzzle brake, 7 shot detachable box mag., Picatinny rail mount, adj. match trigger, V-Block stock with adj. cheekpiece, flush cups for sling mounts, OD Green or Kryptek camo finish, includes custom case, 19 lbs.

Current MSR is $8,500-$8,960, depending on finish.

XTREME LONG DISTANCE RIFLE – .300 Win. Mag., .308 Win., .375 Cheytac, .338 Lapua, .or .408 CheyTac cal., 29 in. fluted barrel, muzzle brake, 7 shot box mag., lightweight aluminum chassis with built in V block design, 40 MOA optic rail, adj. target trigger, fully adj. stock, ergonomic pistol grip, sling mounting flush cups, Cerakote ArmorBlack (standard), FDE, OD Green, Nordic Gray, Tungsten, or Kryptek camo finish, includes custom case, 19 lbs.

Current MSR is $8,500-$8,960, depending on finish.

CHIAPPA FIREARMS LTD.

Current manufacturer established during 2008 and located in Dayton, OH. Previously marketed until 2014 by MKS Supply, located in Dayton, OH with sales through various domestic distributors. Chiappa Firearms Ltd. is one division of the Chiappa Group, which includes Armi Sport (replica firearms manufacturer established in 1958), Chiappa Firearms Ltd. (firearms manufacturer), Kimar Srl (firearms manufacturer), Costa Srl (metal surface finish treatment), ACP (laser training system), and AIM (video/target simulations).

Chiappa Firearms Ltd. manufactures a wide variety of firearms including reproductions and replicas. The models listed in this section were marketed exclusively by MKS Supply, Inc. until 2014, and are marked Chiappa Firearms on the guns. Chiappa also manufactures private label guns for Cimarron Firearms, Legacy Sports, and Taylor's and Company. Please refer to these sections for more information on those Chiappa mfg. models.

PISTOLS: SEMI AUTO

M FOUR-22 – .22 LR cal., blowback action, replica of the M4 carbine, 6 in. steel barrel, blue finish, fire control group, finger groove pistol grip, dust cover, adj. sights, 10 or 28 shot mag., faux flash hider, machined quad rail forearm, includes two mags. New 2011.

MSR $489	$400	$350	$300	$265	$235	$220	$210	

RIFLES: SEMI-AUTO

M-22 SERIES – While a Carbine, National Match, and Precision Match were advertised during 2011, this series never went into production and was not imported.

M FOUR-22 – .22 LR cal., blowback action, 5, 10 or 28 shot, 16 in. barrel with flash hider, forward assist and bolt release, black or tan finish, fixed tube stock, ribbed tube-type forearm, A-4 adj. sights, Picatinny flat-top, detachable carry handle, accepts Mil-Spec handguards, 5 1/2 lbs. Disc. 2012.

	$360	$325	$300	$265	$230	$200	$180	*$419*

Add $30 for red dot scope.

M1 CARBINE – please refer to listing under Citadel.

M1-9 CARBINE – 9mm Para. cal., 19 in. matte blue barrel and receiver, two 10 shot mags., polymer or wood stock, dovetail rail for scope mounts.

MSR $599	$510	$450	$385	$350	$285	$235	$185	

Add $80 for wood stock.

M FOUR-22 GEN II PRO CARBINE/RIFLE – .22 LR cal., blowback action, 16 in. heavy match threaded barrel, 10 or 28 shot mag., 7.8 (Carbine) or 11.8 (Rifle) in. free floating aluminum quad rail with 8-position Picatinny rail, pistol grip, 6-position collapsible stock, parkerized or Muddy Girl finish. New 2013.

MSR $538	$450	$400	$360	$325	$285	$260	$240	

Add $30 for rifle configuration with 11.8 in. quad rail.
Add $60 for Muddy Girl finish.

Chiappa also offers an M Four-22 conversion unit (upper only) - current MSR is $329-$379, depending on forend length (new 2012).

MSR	100%	98%	95%	90%	80%	70%	60%	Last MSR

M FOUR-22 GEN II RIFLE – .22 LR cal., blowback action, Black or Tan (new 2015) polymer frame, 16 in. heavy match threaded barrel, 10 or 28 shot mag., fixed stock, matte black barrel and receiver. New 2014.

MSR $499	$450	$385	$330	$285	$250	$230	$220	

Add $10 for Black polymer frame.

AK-22 RIFLE – .22 LR cal., blued steel receiver, 17 1/4 in. blue barrel, synthetic or wood stock, includes two 10 shot mags., 6-6.7 lbs. New 2014.

MSR $429	$365	$325	$275	$250	$200	$165	$130	

Add $35 for wood stock.

RAK-22 RIFLE – .22 LR cal., blowback action, 17 1/4 in. blued barrel, two 10 shot mags., wood stock with synthetic pistol grip, 6.6 lbs. New 2016.

MSR $529	$465	$385	$330	$285	$250	$230	$220	

SHOTGUNS: SLIDE ACTION

C6 SERIES – 12 ga., 3 in. chamber, 18 1/2 in. barrel with fixed front sight and one Rem. choke, 5 shot mag., choice of black synthetic stock with pistol grip or pistol grip only, or four-position adj. stock (black finish only), matte black or satin nickel finish. New 2013.

MSR $389	$325	$275	$250	$225	$200	$175	$150	

Add $10 for field stock with pistol grip.
Add $40 for satin nickel finish.
Add $50 for 20 ga. Youth model with Next G1 camo stock and forend.

C6 FIELD PUMP SHOTGUN – 12 or 20 ga., 3 in. chamber, 26 in. barrel, interchangeable choke tubes, 5 shot, synthetic stock, black or RealTree Xtra Green camo (20 ga. only) finish, 5.4-6.4 lbs. New 2016.

MSR $409	$350	$300	$275	$250	$200	$165	$135	

C6 MAG PUMP SHOTGUN – 12 ga., 3 1/2 in. chamber, 24 or 28 in. barrel, interchangeable choke tubes, 5 shot, fiber optic front sight, Realtree Max-5 or Realtree Xtra Green camo finish, 6.7 lbs. New 2016.

MSR $519	$450	$395	$340	$300	$250	$200	$175	

Add $30 for Realtree Xtra Green camo finish.

C9 SERIES – 12 ga. only, 3 in. chamber, 22 in. barrel, black synthetic stock with pistol grip, 8 shot mag., fixed or fiber optic front, ghost ring Picatinny rear sight, matte black or satin nickel finish. New 2013.

MSR $349	$300	$265	$225	$200	$175	$150	$125	

Add $28 for satin nickel finish.
Add $35 for full length pistol grip stock, ghost ring sights and rail, and breecher tube.

CHRISTENSEN ARMS

Current rifle manufacturer established in 1995, and currently located in Gunnison, UT. Previously located in Fayette, UT during 2000-2010, and in St. George, UT during 1995-99. Direct sales only.

PISTOLS: SEMI-AUTO

* ***Tactical Government (Tactical Lite)*** – .45 ACP cal., similar to Government model, except has Picatinny rail, and flared magwell. Mfg. 2011-2015.

	$2,825	$2,350	$2,050	$1,775	$1,500	$1,250	$1,050	*$3,250*

Add $1,000 for titanium frame.

RIFLES: BOLT ACTION

In addition to the models listed below, Christensen Arms also offers the Carbon One Custom barrel installed on a customer action (any caliber) for $1,100 ($875 if short chambered by competent gunsmith), as well as providing a Carbon Wrap conversion to an existing steel barrel ($675). Additionally, a Custom Long Range Package is available for $6,695, as well as an Extreme Long Range Package for $4,650.

Add $1,200 for titanium action, $195 for titanium muzzle brake, $275 for Jewell trigger, $150 for Teflon coated action, $150 for Realtree (disc. 2013), Mossy Oak (disc. 2013), King's Desert (mfg. 2011-2013), King's Snow (mfg. 2011-2013) or Natural Gear (disc. 2010) camo stock. Add $200 for Camo stock dip (new 2014), $250 for lightened action (disc. 2013), $150 for Black Nitride action, $200 for natural graphite stock finish, $945 for Tier 1 Sporting stock, $1,000 for Tier 1 thumbhole stock on the models listed below.

BA TACTICAL – .223 Rem.-.338 Lapua Mag. cal., 20-27 in. carbon fiber wrapped barrel with target contour and stainless steel side-port muzzle brake, 5 shot detachable mag., 3-way adj. single stage trigger, hand-laid fiberglass stock, adj. cheekpiece via inserts, adj. LOP via 1/4 in. spacers, front stud with five flush cups, integral full-length 1913 Mil-Std rails, painted black/gray webbing, approx. 7.7-8.1 lbs. New 2016.

MSR $2,799	$2,525	$2,210	$1,895	$1,715	$1,395	$1,150	$885	

Add $200 for .338 Lapua Mag. cal.

MSR	100%	98%	95%	90%	80%	70%	60%	Last MSR

* BA Tactical VTAC – .223 Rem., 6.5 Creedmoor, .308 Win., or .300 AAC Blackout cal., similar to BA Tactical, except has 16 in. barrel, 7.1-7 1/2 lbs. New 2016.

| | MSR $2,799 | $2,525 | $2,210 | $1,895 | $1,715 | $1,395 | $1,150 | $885 | |

CARBON ONE EXTREME – various cals., 18-26 in. carbon wrap free floating barrel, choice of carbon classic or thumbhole Christensen Arms stock, Teflon coated and lightened action, 3 lb. trigger pull, 5 1/2-7 lbs. Mfg. 2007-2012.

| | $2,875 | $2,400 | $1,900 | $1,500 | $1,200 | $975 | $800 | *$3,295* |

CARBON ONE RANGER (CONQUEST) – .50 BMG cal., single shot (disc. 2010) or repeater (5 shot), McMillan stainless steel bolt action, max barrel length is 32 in. with muzzle brake, Christensen composite stock with bipod, approx. 16 (single shot) - 24 lbs. Mfg. 2001-2014.

| | $8,200 | $6,700 | $5,450 | $4,500 | $3,750 | $2,850 | $2,500 | *$8,995* |

Add $300 for Tac-50 stock.
Add $240 for Atlas Bipod BT10.
Add $200 for camo stock dip.
Subtract 20% for a single shot action (disc. 2010).

CARBON ONE TACTICAL – various cals., grey synthetic stock, various barrel lengths, stainless steel free floating Shilen barrel with muzzle brake, glass bedded barrel assembly, precision trigger, many options available per customer request, 5.5-7 lbs. Mfg. 2010-2012.

| | $4,150 | $3,650 | $3,250 | $1,825 | $2,300 | $1,950 | $1,700 | *$4,595* |

CARBON RANGER – .50 BMG cal., large diameter graphite barrel casing (up to 36 in. long), no stock or forearm, twin rails extending from frame sides are attached to recoil pad, Omni Wind Runner action, bipod and choice of scope are included, 25-32 lbs. Limited mfg. 1998-2000 only.

| | $9,950 | $8,900 | $8,000 | $7,100 | $6,200 | $5,300 | $4,400 | *$10,625* |

TACTICAL FORCE MULTIPLIER (TFM) CARBON – .223 Rem. (disc. 2015), 6.5 Creedmoor, .300 Win. Mag., .308 Win., or .338 Lapua cal., carbon fiber barrel with titanium muzzle brake, glass bedded, adj. Timney trigger, drop-box magazine, tactical bolt knob, adj. tactical stock in hand-laid Tier 1 carbon, integral Picatinny rail, black nitride coating, 7.1 lbs. New 2014.

| | MSR $4,899 | $4,400 | $3,850 | $3,300 | $2,995 | $2,425 | $1,985 | $1,550 | |

Add $200 for .338 Lapua Mag. cal.

* Tactical Force Multiplier (TFM) Steel – similar to TFM Carbon model, except features steel barrel. Disc. 2015.

| | $4,350 | $3,800 | $3,275 | $2,950 | $2,395 | $1,950 | $1,525 | *$4,845* |

* Tactical Force Multiplier (TFM) VTAC – 6.5 Creedmoor, .300 AAC Blackout, or .308 Win. Mag. cal., 16 in. carbon fiber wrapped barrel with target contour and muzzle brake, 5 shot detachable mag., 3-way adj. single stage trigger, Aerograde carbon fiber TFM stock, front stud with five flush cups, Natural carbon fiber finish, 7.1-7 1/2 lbs. New 2016.

| | MSR $4,899 | $4,400 | $3,850 | $3,300 | $2,995 | $2,425 | $1,985 | $1,550 | |

RIFLES: SEMI-AUTO

Christensen Arms also offered a Carbon One Challenge drop-in barrel (16 oz.) for the Ruger Model 10/22. Last MSR was $499 (disc. 2010).

CARBON ONE CHALLENGE (CUSTOM) – .17 HMR, .22 LR, or .22 WMR cal., features Ruger 10/22 Model 1103 action with modified bolt release, synthetic bull barrel with precision stainless steel liner, 2 lb. Volquartsen trigger, Fajen brown laminated wood (disc.) or black synthetic stock with thumbhole, approx. 3.5-4 lbs. Mfg. 1996-2010.

| | $1,500 | $1,250 | $1,050 | $875 | $750 | $600 | $500 | *$1,750* |

Add $350 for .17 HMR or .22 WMR cal.

The 100% price represents the base model, with no options.

CARBON CHALLENGE II – similar to Carbon Challenge I, except has AMT stainless receiver and trigger, black synthetic stock, approx. 4 1/2 lbs. Limited mfg. 1997-1998 only.

| | $1,150 | $975 | $875 | $800 | $725 | $650 | $525 | *$1,299* |

CA-10 RECON – .243 Win., 6.8 Creedmoor, .308 Win., or .338 Federal cal., GIO, features 16-24 in. carbon fiber match grade barrel, various stock configurations, flat-top receiver with Picatinny rail, adj. Timney trigger, carbon handguard, 20 shot mag., black carbon fiber or camo forearm finish, 6-8 lbs. Mfg. 2011-2013.

| | $2,995 | $2,650 | $2,250 | $2,035 | $1,650 | $1,350 | $1,050 | *$3,575* |

Subtract $200 for steel barrel.

CARBON ONE CA-15 SERIES (AR-15) – .223 Rem. cal., GIO, forged aluminum upper and lower receiver, choice of round shroud with quad rails or integrated forearm with full Picatinny rail on top, adj. stock, carbon fiber wrapped stainless steel barrel, ambidextrous charging handle, Timney adj. drop-in trigger, 30 shot detachable AR-15 style mag., 5.5 - 7 lbs. Mfg. 2009-2010.

| | $2,500 | $2,195 | $1,875 | $1,700 | $1,375 | $1,125 | $875 | *$2,950* |

MSR	100%	98%	95%	90%	80%	70%	60%	Last MSR

CA-15 PREDATOR – .223 Rem., .204 Ruger, 6.8 SPC, or 6.5 Grendel, GIO, 20 or 24 in. carbon fiber match grade barrel, collapsible stock, flat-top receiver with Picatinny rail, ambidextrous controls, adj. Timney trigger, 20 shot mag., Hogue pistol grip, black, King's Desert Shadow, or King's Snow Shadow finish, 5.5-7 lbs. Mfg. 2011-2012.

| | $2,550 | $2,225 | $1,925 | $1,750 | $1,400 | $1,150 | $900 | *$2,995* |

CA-15 RECON – .204 Ruger, .223 Rem./5.56 NATO (.223 Wylde chamber), 6.5 Grendel, 6.8 SPC or .300 AAC cal., GPO, 16 or 20 in. match grade carbon fiber barrel, carbon fiber handguard with built-in Picatinny rails, choice of adj. stock, adj. Timney trigger, titanium birdcage flash suppressor, 30 shot mag., Hogue pistol grip, factory black synthetic, Digital Desert Brown, King's Desert Shadow, or King's Snow Shadow finish, 5.5-7 lbs. Mfg. 2011-2015.

| | $3,000 | $2,625 | $2,250 | $2,040 | $1,650 | $1,350 | $1,050 | *$3,395* |

CA-15 VTAC – .223 Wylde or .300 AAC Blackout cal., GIO, 16 in. straight fluted stainless steel black nitride finished barrel or carbon fiber wrapped barrel, flash hider, flared magwell, VTAC self-contained trigger, BCM Gunfighter stock, Magpul MOE pistol grip, 15 in. free-float KeyMod handguard with integral rails, machined billet upper and lower receivers, Picatinny rail, Type III hardcoat black anodized finish. New mid-2015.

| MSR $2,699 | | $2,425 | $2,125 | $1,825 | $1,650 | $1,350 | $1,100 | $875 | |

Add $200 for carbon fiber wrapped barrel and titanium flash hider.

CA-10 DMR – .243 Win. (new 2016), .260 Rem. (new 2016), 6.5 Creedmoor (new 2016), or .308 Win. cal., GIO, 18-24 in. match grade carbon wrapped stainless steel barrel, threaded with titanium side baffle brake, Christensen LTM trigger, carbon fiber handguard with integrated carbon Picatinny rails, nitride bolt carrier finish, ambidextrous mag. release, extended charging handle, oversized bolt release, Hogue overmolded grip, Magpul adj. STR buttstock, Type III hard black anodized or Cerakote finish in Burnt Bronze or Tungsten, 7.1 lbs. New 2014.

| MSR $3,799 | | $3,225 | $2,825 | $2,325 | $1,975 | $1,650 | $1,375 | $1,175 | |

CD-15 RECON – .223 Wylde or 5.56 NATO cal., GIO, 16-24 in. match grade carbon wrapped barrel, OSS suppressor, Christensen LTM trigger, aluminum receiver, carbon fiber handguard with integrated carbon Picatinny rails, nickel boron coated bolt carrier, ambidextrous magazine release, oversized bolt release, extended charging handle, Hogue overmolded grip, hard black anodized Type III or Cerakote receiver colors, numerous finish options available, 7.3 lbs. Mfg. 2014-2015.

| | $4,400 | $3,850 | $3,300 | $2,990 | $2,420 | $1,975 | $1,550 | *$4,890* |

CHRISTIAN ARMORY WORKS

Current custom rifle manufacturer located in Rock Spring, GA.

RIFLES: SEMI-AUTO

Christian Armory Works currently manufactures rifles in several calibers and configurations. Current models include: Standard NP3 Tactical rifles starting at $1,897 and CAW-10 .308 models starting at $1,499. Please contact the company directly for more information on options, pricing, and availability (see Trademark Index).

CIMARRON F.A. CO.

Current importer, distributor, and retailer located in Fredricksburg, TX. Cimarron is currently importing A. Uberti, D. Pedersoli, Chiappa Firearms, Pietta, and Armi-Sport firearms and black powder reproductions and replicas. Previous company name was Old-West Co. of Texas. Dealer sales only.

Please refer to the *Blue Book of Modern Black Powder Arms* by John Allen (also online) for more information and prices on Cimarron's lineup of modern black powder models.

PISTOLS: SEMI-AUTO

M4-22 – .22 LR cal., AR-15 style, blowback action, 6 in. barrel with muzzle brake, quad rail, includes A2 carry handle, black finish, 5, 10, or 28 shot Atchison style conversion mag., cased with cleaning kit, 3.9 lbs. Mfg. by Armi Chiappa in Italy. Imported 2011-2012.

| | $450 | $375 | $325 | $275 | $250 | $225 | $195 | *$587* |

CITADEL

Current trademark imported beginning 2009 by Legacy Sports International, located in Reno, NV.

CARBINES: SEMI-AUTO

M1 CARBINE – .22 LR cal., M1 design, 18 in. threaded (new 2013) barrel with fixed front sight and adj. rear sight, black synthetic, Harvest Moon camo (mfg. 2013-2015), Muddy Girl camo (new 2013), Outshine camo (mfg. 201302915), or wood (new 2012) stock, 10 shot mag., blued finish, 4.8 lbs. Mfg. by Chiappa in Italy, importation began 2011.

| MSR $309 | | $265 | $235 | $200 | $185 | $170 | $160 | $150 | |

Add $70 for Muddy Girl, Harvest Moon (disc. 2015), or Outshine camo (mfg. 2013-2015) stock.
Add $100 for wood stock (new 2012).

MSR	100%	98%	95%	90%	80%	70%	60%	Last MSR

PISTOLS: SEMI-AUTO

M-1911 – .45 ACP cal., full size 1911 style frame, 5 in. barrel, SA, matte black, brushed nickel (mfg. 2010-2014), or polished nickel (mfg. 2010-2014), steel slide, 8 shot, skeletonized hammer and trigger, Novak sights, lowered and flared ejection port, extended ambidextrous safety, checkered wood or Hogue wraparound (available in black, green, or Sand, new 2010) grips, includes two magazines and lockable plastic case, 2.3 lbs. Imported 2009-2014, reintroduced 2016.

    MSR $592 $495 $425 $395 $365 $325 $275 $250

    Add $39 for Hogue wraparound grips in black, green, or Sand.

    Add $89 for brushed nickel (disc. 2014) or $108 for polished nickel (disc. 2014).

    Add $250 for Wounded Warrior Project configuration with matte black finish (disc.).

    * **M-1911 Compact** – .45 ACP cal., 3 1/2 in. barrel, 6 shot, similar to Citadel M-1911 FS, except has compact frame, not available in polished nickel, 2.1 lbs. Imported 2009-2014, reintroduced 2016.

    MSR $592 $495 $425 $395 $365 $325 $275 $250

    Add $39 for Hogue grips in Black, OD Green, or Sand. Add $89 for brushed nickel (disc. 2014).

SHOTGUNS: SLIDE ACTION

CITADEL LE TACTICAL – 12 ga., 20 (disc. 2011) or 22 (new 2012) in. barrel, 7 shot mag., matte black finish, available in Standard, Spec-Ops (features Blackhawk Spec-Ops stock with recoil reduction), Talon (features thumbhole stock with Blackhawk recoil reduction), or Pistol grip w/heat shield (features interchangeable stock and removable pistol grip) configuration, approx. 5.8-7 lbs. Mfg. in the U.S. 2010-2012.

               $385 $335 $285 $240 $210 $180 $150   *$466*

    Add $41 for Pistol grip w/heat shield or $166 for either Spec-Ops or Talon configuration.

CIVILIAN FORCE ARMS

    Current 1911 style pistol and AR-15 style pistol, rifle, and parts and accessories manufacturer located in Yorkville, IL beginning late 2014.

    Civilian Force Arms was founded by former Army soldier and Purple Heart recipient Yonas Hagos. Yonas prides himself on producing weapons that are American Made, Built To Survive™.

PISTOLS: 1911 STYLE

    All CFA firearms carry a lifetime warranty for any mechanical or manufacturer defects. Each model comes with a hard case, two magazines, gun lock, and manual.

ASSASSIN 1911 .45 ACP – . 45 ACP cal., full size carbon steel frame, stainless steel Operator lower frame, 4 1/4 (Commander) or 5 (Government) in. carbon steel slide, 5 in. stainless bull barrel, 8 shot mag., adj. rear and ramp front sights, high cut checkered front strap, Wilson Combat beavertail grip and thumb safety, contoured magwell, CFA custom VZ double diamond grips, 2.6 lbs. New late 2014.

    MSR $1,499 $1,350 $1,185 $1,025 $925 $750 $625 $525

    * **Assassin 1911 Gunner's Edition** – .45 ACP cal., full size carbon steel frame, stainless steel Operator lower frame, 5 in. carbon steel slide, 5 in. stainless bull barrel, 8 shot mag., high cut checkered front strap, Lo-Mount adj. rear sight with improved ramp front sight, Wilson Combat beavertail grip and thumb safety, Wilson Combat contoured magwell, CFA custom VZ double diamond grips, 2.6 lbs. New 2016.

    MSR $1,499 $1,350 $1,185 $1,025 $925 $750 $625 $525

BLACK WIDOW 1911 – . 45 ACP cal., full size carbon steel frame, stainless steel Operator lower frame, 4 1/4 (Commander) or 5 (Government) in. carbon steel slide, 5 in. stainless bull barrel, black receiver, 8 shot mag., adj. rear and ramp front sights, high cut checkered front strap, Wilson Combat beavertail grip and thumb safety, contoured magwell, CFA custom VZ double diamond grips, 2.6 lbs. New 2015.

    MSR $1,499 $1,350 $1,185 $1,025 $925 $750 $625 $525

BLUE VIPER 1911 – .45 ACP cal., full size stainless steel frame and receiver, 5 in. stainless bull barrel, 5 in. carbon steel slide, one 8 shot mag., contoured magwell, low mount adj. rear and improved ramp front sights, high cut checkered front strap, Wilson Combat beavertail grip and thumb safety, CFA custom VZ grips, 2.6 lbs. New 2015.

    MSR $1,499 $1,350 $1,185 $1,025 $925 $750 $625 $525

CAPONE – .45 ACP cal., full size stainless steel frame, 5 in. carbon steel slide, 5 in. stainless steel bull barrel, 8 shot mag., Lo-Mount adj. rear sight with improved ramp front sight, black receiver, high cut checkered front strap, Wilson Combat beavertail grip and thumb safety, contoured magwell, CFA custom VZ grips, 2.6 lbs.

    MSR $1,499 $1,350 $1,185 $1,025 $925 $750 $625 $525

RENEGADE – .45 ACP cal., full size carbon steel frame, 5 in. carbon steel slide, 5 in. stainless steel bull barrel, 8 shot mag., black receiver, high cut checkered front strap, Wilson Combat beavertail grip and thumb safety, contoured magwell, CFA custom VZ grips, Lo-Mount adj. rear sight with improved ramp front sight, 2.6 lbs.

    MSR $1,299 $1,150 $1,000 $875 $785 $625 $525 $425

MSR	100%	98%	95%	90%	80%	70%	60%	Last MSR

SCORPION 1911 – .45 ACP cal., full size FDE frame, FDE receiver, 5 in. stainless bull barrel, 5 in. carbon steel slide, one 8 shot mag., contoured magwell, low mount adj. rear and improved ramp front sights, high cut checkered front strap, Wilson Combat beavertail grip and thumb safety, CFA custom VZ grips, 2.6 lbs. New 2015.

MSR $1,599	$1,450	$1,275	$1,095	$985	$800	$675	$550	

PISTOLS: SEMI-AUTO

All CFA firearms carry a lifetime warranty for any mechanical or manufacturer defects. Each model comes with a hard case, two magazines, gun lock, and manual.

SWEEPER-15 – .223 Rem./5.56 NATO cal., GIO, 7 1/2 in. M4 profile chrome moly barrel, Phantom muzzle brake, 30 shot mag., aluminum trigger guard, A.R.M.S. flip up front and rear sights, Sig brace, MFT Engage black pistol grip, manual safety, low profile gas block, forged aluminum M4A4 flat-top upper w/Picatinny rail, 9 in. Midwest Industries G2 T-Series rail, BCM Mod 4 charging handle, hardcoat anodized black finish, 6.2 lbs.

MSR $1,699	$1,450	$1,275	$1,125	$1,000	$850	$735	$595	

SWEEPER-15 GEN2 – .223 Rem./5.56 NATO cal., GPO, 10 1/2 in. M4 profile chrome moly threaded barrel, Phantom muzzle brake, 30 shot mag., aluminum trigger guard, A.R.M.S. flip-up front and rear sights, Sig Brace Gen2, MFT black pistol grip, manual safety, M4 feed ramps, forged aluminum M4A4 flat-top upper w/Picatinny rail, Adam Arms .740 piston, 9.2 in. black Fortis Rev carbine cutout rail, BCM Mod 4 charging handle, hardcoat black anodized finish, 6.4 lbs.

MSR $1,849	$1,575	$1,385	$1,185	$1,065	$915	$785	$635	

XENA-15 GEN3 – .223 Rem./5.56 NATO cal., GIO, 10 1/2 in. M4 profile chrome moly barrel, A2 flash hider, aluminum trigger guard, MFT black pistol grip, manual safety, M4 feed ramps, forged aluminum M4A4 flat-top upper w/Picatinny rail, carbine plastic handguard, AR15 pistol buffer tube kit, standard Mil-Spec charging handle, hardcoat anodized black finish, 6.2 lbs.

MSR $829	$700	$615	$550	$475	$420	$365	$335	

XENA-15 GEN4 – .223 Rem./5.56 NATO cal., GIO, 10 1/2 in. M4 profile chrome moly barrel, A2 flash hider, 30 shot mag., aluminum trigger guard, A.R.M.S. flip-up front and rear sights, Magpul MOE black plastic grip, manual safety, M4 feed ramps, Mil-Spec charging handle, carbine quad rail, AR15 pistol buffer tube kit, forged aluminum M4A4 flat-top upper w/Picatinny rail.

MSR $849	$725	$650	$580	$515	$450	$385	$340	

RIFLES: SEMI-AUTO

All CFA firearms carry a lifetime warranty for any mechanical or manufacturer defects. Each model comes with a hard case, two magazines, gun lock, and manual, unless otherwise noted.

BLACK RUSSIAN AK47 CLASSIC – 7.62x39mm cal., 16 1/4 in. Green Mountain threaded barrel, two 30 shot Magpul MOE AK PMAGs, stamped CFA receiver with scope rail, classic wood stock, AK47 grip, Fenocite KG/KG GunKote (black) finish.

MSR $1,199	$1,025	$925	$800	$685	$595	$515	$440	

BLACK RUSSIAN AK47 MOE1 – 7.62x39mm cal., AK-47 design, 16 1/4 in. Green Mountain threaded barrel, 30 shot Magpul MOE AK PMAG, stamped CFA receiver with scope rail, Magpul Zhukov AK side folding stock, M-LOK compatible forearm, Magpul MOE AK47 grip, KG Gunkote (black) finish.

MSR $1,299	$1,100	$995	$875	$735	$650	$550	$465	

BLACK RUSSIAN AK47 MOE2 – 7.62x39mm cal., AK-47 design, 16 1/4 in. Green Mountain threaded barrel, 30 shot Magpul MOE AK PMAG, stamped CFA receiver w/scope rail, Magpul MOE AK47 grip, Magpul Zhukov AK side folding stock, M-LOK compatible forearm, KG Gunkote (black) finish.

MSR $1,299	$1,100	$995	$875	$735	$650	$550	$465	

DAKOTA-15 – .223 Rem./5.56 NATO cal., GIO, 18 in. straight flute heavy chrome moly barrel, Phantom 3102 flash hider, 30 shot mag., low profile gas block, manual safety, M4A4 forged aluminum flat-top upper w/Picatinny rail, Nickel Boron bolt carrier group, M4 feed ramps, 6-position Mil-Spec Mission First Tactical BMS-Battlelink stock, MFT Engage black pistol grip, aluminum trigger guard, 15 in. Fortis Rev2 rail, BCM Mod 4 charging handle, CAA bipod, hardcoat black anodized finish, 8.2 lbs.

MSR $1,899	$1,625	$1,425	$1,200	$1,075	$925	$795	$650	

DAKOTA-15 HUNTER EDITION – .223 Rem./5.56 NATO cal., GIO, 18 in. straight flute heavy chrome moly barrel, Phantom 3102 flash hider, 30 shot mag., low profile gas block, manual safety, M4A4 forged aluminum flat-top upper rec. w/Picatinny rail, M4 feed ramps, 6-position Mil-Spec Mission First Tactical BMS-Battlelink stock, MFT Engage black pistol grip, aluminum trigger guard, 15 in. Fortis Rev2 rail with Multi-Cam finish, BCM Mod 4 charging handle, CAA bipod, 8.2 lbs.

MSR $2,099	$1,795	$1,575	$1,325	$1,150	$995	$850	$700	

MSR	100%	98%	95%	90%	80%	70%	60%	Last MSR

HAGOS-15 – .223 Rem./5.56 NATO or .300 AAC Blackout cal., GIO, 16 in. M4 profile chrome moly barrel, Phantom muzzle brake, low profile gas block, 30 shot mag., manual safety, A.R.M.S. flip-up front and rear sights, M4 feed ramps, 15 in. Midwest Industries SS Series Gen2 rail, forged aluminum M4A4 flat-top upper w/Picatinny rail, BCM Mod 4 charging handle, 6-position Mil-Spec Mission First Tactical BMS-Battlelink Minimalist stock, MFT Engage black pistol grip, hardcoat black anodized finish, 6 1/2 lbs.

| MSR $1,499 | $1,275 | $1,125 | $1,025 | $875 | $750 | $625 | $525 | |

Add $100 for .300 AAC Blackout cal.

KATY-15 – .223 Rem./5.56 NATO or .300 AAC Blackout cal., GIO, 16 in. M4 profile chrome moly barrel, Phantom muzzle brake, low profile gas block, 30 shot mag., manual safety, A.R.M.S. flip-up front and rear sights, M4 feed ramps, 12 in. Midwest Industries T-Series rail, forged aluminum M4A4 flat-top upper w/Picatinny rail, BCM Mod 4 charging handle, 6-position Mil-Spec Mission First Tactical BMS-Battlelink Minimalist stock, MFT Engage black pistol grip, hardcoat black anodized finish, 7 lbs.

| MSR $1,099 | $925 | $850 | $725 | $625 | $550 | $475 | $425 | |

Add $100 for .300 AAC Blackout cal.

NATALIA-15 – .223 Rem./5.56 NATO cal., GPO, 16 in. M4 profile chrome lined barrel (.223 Wylde chamber), Lantac Dragon threaded muzzle brake, low profile gas block, 30 shot mag., A.R.M.S. flip up front and rear sight, manual safety, forged aluminum M4A4 flat-top upper w/Picatinny rail, M4 feed ramps, machined aluminum trigger guard, 9 in. Fortis Rev carbine cutout rail, BCM Mod 4 charging handle, 6-position Mi-Spec Mission First Tactical BMS (Battlelink Minimalist Stock), MFT Engage black pistol grip, hardcoat anodized black finish, 6.8 lbs

| MSR $2,199 | $1,875 | $1,650 | $1,400 | $1,200 | $1,025 | $875 | $725 | |

NATASHA – .223 Rem./5.56 NATO or .300 AAC Blackout cal., GIO, 16 in. M4 profile chrome moly barrel (.223 Wylde chamber), threaded Phantom muzzle brake, 30 shot mag., manual safety, A.R.M.S. flip up front and rear sights, forged aluminum M4A4 flat-top upper w/Picatinny rail, M4 feed ramps, BCM Mod 4 charging handle, 15 in. Midwest Industries T-Series Gen2 rail, 6-position Mil-Spec MFT Battlelink Minimalist stock, MFT Engage black pistol grip, machined aluminum trigger guard, hardcoat anodized black finish, 7.1 lbs.

| MSR $1,599 | $1,350 | $1,200 | $1,075 | $950 | $815 | $700 | $575 | |

Add $100 for .300 AAC Blackout cal.

OPERATOR-15 – .223 Rem./5.56 NATO cal., GIO, 16 in. M4 profile chrome moly barrel (.223 Wylde chamber), threaded Phantom muzzle brake, 30 shot mag., low profile gas block, manual safety, forged aluminum M4A4 flat-top upper w/Picatinny rail, M4 feed ramps, 15 in. CFA free float quad rail, machined aluminum enhanced trigger guard, A.R.M.S. front and rear flip up sights, BCM Mod 4 charging handle, 6-position Mil-Spec MFT Battlelink Minimalist stock, MFT Engage black pistol grip, hardcoat anodized black finish, 7 1/2 lbs.

| MSR $1,599 | $1,350 | $1,200 | $1,075 | $950 | $815 | $700 | $575 | |

PATRIOT-15 – .223 Rem./5.56 NATO cal., GIO, 16 in. M4 profile chrome moly barrel, threaded Lantac Dragon muzzle brake, low profile gas block, 30 shot mag., A.R.M.S. front and rear flip up sights, forged aluminum M4A4 flat-top upper w/Picatinny rail, M4 feed ramps, BCM Mod 4 charging handle, manual ambidextrous safety, 14.8 in. Fortis Rev rail, drop-in trigger, 6-position Mil-Spec MFT Battlelink Minimalist stock, MFT EPGI16 Engage pistol grip, hardcoat anodized black finish, 7.2 lbs.

| MSR $2,299 | $1,950 | $1,725 | $1,450 | $1,250 | $1,050 | $900 | $750 | |

PHANTOM-15 – 223 Rem./5.56 NATO cal., GIO, 16 in. M4 profile chrome moly barrel, CFA muzzle brake, low profile gas block, 30 shot mag., manual safety, A.R.M.S. flip-up front and rear sights, M4 feed ramps, CFA 12 in. Phantom rail, forged aluminum M4A4 flat-top upper w/Picatinny rail, BCM Mod 4 charging handle, 6-position Mil-Spec Mission First Tactical BMS-Battlelink Minimalist stock, MFT Engage black pistol grip, hardcoat black anodized finish, 7 lbs.

| MSR $1,299 | $1,100 | $995 | $875 | $735 | $650 | $550 | $465 | |

REACHER-308 – .308 Win./7.62 NATO cal., GIO, 18 in. stainless steel barrel, threaded low profile CFA muzzle brake, 20 shot mag., manual ambidextrous safety, billet aluminum AR10 type flat-top upper w/Picatinny rail, VLTOR BCM Mod 4 charging handle, 12 in. CFA 308 rail, 6-position Mil-Spec MFT Battlelink Minimalist stock, MFT Engage black pistol grip, hardcoat anodized black finish, 9 1/2 lbs.

| MSR $2,299 | $1,950 | $1,725 | $1,450 | $1,250 | $1,050 | $900 | $750 | |

REACHER-308 GEN2 – .308 Win./7.62 NATO cal., GIO, 20 in. stainless steel barrel, threaded low profile Fortis muzzle brake, 20 shot mag., manual ambidextrous safety, machined aluminum trigger guard, billet aluminum AR10 type flat-top upper w/Picatinny rail, VLTOR BCM Mod 4 charging handle, 15 in. Fortis Switch 308 rail, Mako SSR25 Sniper buttstock w/adj. cheek well, MFT Engage pistol grip, CAA bipod, hardcoat anodized black finish, 12 lbs.

| MSR $2,699 | $2,295 | $2,010 | $1,725 | $1,450 | $1,275 | $1,050 | $875 | |

REACHER EVO-308 – .308 Win./7.62 NATO cal., GIO, 18 in. stainless steel barrel, 20 shot mag., manual ambidextrous safety, billet aluminum AR10 type flat-top upper w/Picatinny rail, 9 in. UTG two-piece rail, machined aluminum trigger guard, 6-position Mil-Spec MFT Battlelink Minimalist stock, MFT Engage black pistol grip, hardcoat anodized black or FDE finish, 9 1/2 lbs.

| MSR $1,799 | $1,525 | $1,350 | $1,175 | $1,050 | $900 | $775 | $625 | |

MSR	100%	98%	95%	90%	80%	70%	60%	Last MSR

REACHER EVO-308 SCORPION – .308 Win./7.62 NATO cal., GIO, 18 in. stainless steel barrel, threaded low profile CFA Shark muzzle brake, 20 shot mag., manual ambidextrous safety, billet aluminum AR10 type flat-top upper w/Picatinny rail, 13 in. UTG Super Slip LR308 rail, VLTOR BCM Mod 4 charging handle, machined aluminum trigger guard, 6-position Mil-Spec MFT Battlelink Minimalist stock, MFT Engage black pistol grip, hardcoat anodized black finish, 9 1/2 lbs.

| MSR $1,899 | $1,625 | $1,425 | $1,200 | $1,075 | $925 | $795 | $650 | |

REACHER-308 SNIPER EDITION – .308 Win./7.62 NATO cal., GIO, 18 in. stainless steel barrel, threaded low profile muzzle brake, 20 shot mag., manual ambidextrous safety, VLTOR BCM Mod 4 charging handle, billet aluminum AR10 type flat-top upper w/Picatinny rail, 12 in. Phantom 308 rail, Mako SSR25 Sniper buttstock w/adj. cheek well, MFT Engage pistol grip, hardcoat anodized black finish, CAA bipod, 11 lbs.

| MSR $2,599 | $2,200 | $1,925 | $1,600 | $1,375 | $1,125 | $975 | $850 | |

SALLY-15 – .223 Rem./5.56 NATO or .300 AAC Blackout cal., GIO, 16 in. M4 profile chrome moly barrel, Phantom muzzle brake, low profile gas block, 30 shot mag., manual safety, A.R.M.S. flip-up front and rear sights, M4 feed ramps, 12 in. Midwest Industries S-Series rail, forged aluminum M4A4 flat-top upper w/Picatinny rail, BCM Mod 4 charging handle, 6-position Mil-Spec Mission First Tactical BMS-Battlelink Minimalist stock, MFT Engage black pistol grip, hardcoat black anodized finish, 6.8 lbs.

| MSR $1,099 | $925 | $850 | $725 | $625 | $550 | $475 | $425 | |

Add $100 for .300 AAC Blackout cal.

SCORPION-15 – .223 Rem./5.56 NATO cal., GIO, 16 in. M4 profile chrome moly barrel (.223 Wylde chamber), Shark threaded muzzle brake, low profile gas block, 30 shot mag., manual safety, A.R.M.S. front and rear flip up sights, BCM Mod 4 charging handle, forged aluminum M4A4 flat-top upper w/Picatinny rail, M4 feed ramps, 15 in. Leaper Slim rail, machined aluminum enhanced trigger guard, 6-position Mil-Spec MFT Battlelink Minimalist stock, MFT Engage black pistol grip, hardcoat anodized black finish, 6 1/2 lbs.

| MSR $1,199 | $1,025 | $925 | $800 | $685 | $595 | $515 | $440 | |

XENA-15 – .223 Rem./5.56 NATO cal., GIO, 16 in. M4 profile chrome moly barrel, A2 flash hider, 30 shot mag., manual safety, M4 feed ramps, forged aluminum M4A4 flat-top upper receiver with Picatinny rail, aluminum trigger guard, buffer tube, carbine handguard, front sight post and rear MFT back-up sight, standard charging handle, 6-position Mil-Spec MFT stock, MFT Engage black pistol grip, hardcoat black anodized finish, 6.3 lbs.

| MSR $799 | $685 | $615 | $550 | $475 | $420 | $365 | $335 | |

XENA-15 A2 – .223 Rem./5.56 NATO cal., GIO, 20 in. M4 profile chrome moly barrel, A2 flash hider, 30 shot mag., manual safety, front iron sight post, rear carry handle fixed sight, standard charging handle, M4A4 forged aluminum flat-top upper with Picatinny rail, M4 feed ramps, rifle length handguard, fixed A2 buttstock, A2 pistol grip, hardcoat black anodized finish, 8 1/2 lbs.

| MSR $1,099 | $925 | $850 | $725 | $625 | $550 | $475 | $425 | |

XENA-15 GEN2 MOE – .223 Rem./5.56 NATO cal., GIO, 16 in. M4 profile chrome moly barrel (.223 Wylde chamber), threaded A2 flash hider, 30 shot mag., manual safety, front iron sight post, A.R.M.S. flip up or Magpul rear sight, CFA True Mil-Spec Gen3 charging handle, forged aluminum M4A4 flat-top upper w/Picatinny rail, M4 feed ramps, Magpul carbine plastic handguard, 6-position Mil-Spec Magpul MOE stock, Magpul MOE black pistol grip, hardcoat anodized black finish, 6 1/2 lbs.

| MSR $829 | $700 | $615 | $550 | $475 | $420 | $365 | $335 | |

XENA-15 GEN3 – .223 Rem./5.56 NATO cal., GIO, 16 in. M4 profile chrome moly barrel, A2 flash hider, 30 shot mag., manual safety, A.R.M.S. flip-up front and rear sights, Mil-Spec standard charging handle, M4 feed ramps, M4A4 forged aluminum flat-top upper w/Picatinny rail, carbine plastic handguard, 6-position Mil-Spec MFT stock, MFT Engage black pistol grip, hardcoat black anodized finish, 6 1/2 lbs.

| MSR $829 | $700 | $615 | $550 | $475 | $420 | $365 | $335 | |

* XENA-16 GEN3 Sport – .223 Rem./5.56 NATO cal., GIO, 16 in. M4 profile chrome moly barrel, A2 flash hider, 30 shot mag., manual safety, M4 feed ramps, M4A4 forged aluminum flat-top upper w/Picatinny rail, Mil-Spec charging handle, carbine plastic handguard, 6-position Mil-Spec MFT stock, MFT Engage black pistol grip, hardcoat anodized black finish, 6.4 lbs.

| MSR $789 | $675 | $590 | $510 | $440 | $385 | $340 | $325 | |

XENA-15 GEN4 – .223 Rem./5.56 NATO cal., GIO, 16 in. M4 profile chrome moly barrel, A2 flash hider, 30 shot mag., manual safety, A.R.M.S. flip-up front and rear sights, M4 feed ramps, carbine UTG aluminum handguard, M4A4 forged aluminum flat-top upper w/Picatinny rail, CFA Mil-Spec Gen3 charging handle, 6-position Mil-Spec MFT stock, MFT Engage black pistol grip, hardcoat black anodized finish, 6.7 lbs.

| MSR $849 | $725 | $650 | $580 | $515 | $450 | $385 | $340 | |

* XENA-15 GEN4 Sport – .223 Rem./5.56 NATO cal., GIO, 16 in. M4 profile chrome moly barrel, A2 flash hider, 30 shot mag., manual safety, M4 feed ramps, carbine UTG handguard, M4A4 forged aluminum flat-top upper w/ Picatinny rail, 6-position Mil-Spec MFT stock, MFT Engage black pistol grip, hardcoat black anodized finish, 6.4 lbs.

| MSR $809 | $685 | $615 | $550 | $475 | $420 | $365 | $335 | |

MSR	100%	98%	95%	90%	80%	70%	60%	Last MSR

XENA-15 GEN4.1 – .223 Rem./5.56 NATO cal., GIO, 16 in. M4 profile chrome moly barrel, A2 flash hider, 30 shot mag., manual safety, A.R.M.S. flip-up front and rear sights, Mil-Spec charging handle, M4 feed ramps, M4A4 forged aluminum flat-top upper w/Picatinny rail, carbine UTG aluminum slim handguard, 6-position Mil-Spec MFT stock, MFT Engage black pistol grip, hardcoat black anodized finish, 6.6 lbs.

| MSR $869 | $735 | $650 | $580 | $515 | $450 | $385 | $340 | |

XENA-15 GEN4 HUNTER EDITION – .223 Rem./5.56 NATO cal., GIO, 18 in. M4 profile fluted chrome moly barrel, A2 flash hider, 30 shot mag., manual safety, front iron sight post, flip-up rear sight, aluminum trigger guard, Mil-Spec charging handle, M4 feed ramps, carbine UTG aluminum handguard, M4A4 forged aluminum flat-top upper receiver w/Picatinny rail, 6-position Mil-Spec MFT stock, MFT Engage black pistol grip, Multi-Cam finish, 9 lbs.

| MSR $1,149 | $975 | $885 | $765 | $655 | $575 | $495 | $435 | |

XENA-15 2.0 – .223 Rem./5.56 NATO cal., GIO, 16 in. M4 profile chrome moly barrel, A2 flash hider, 30 shot mag., manual safety, M4 feed ramps, forged aluminum M4A4 flat-top upper receiver w/Picatinny rail, aluminum trigger guard, buffer tube, carbine two-piece quad rail, front sight post and rear MFT back-up sight, standard Mil-Spec charging handle, 6-position Mil-Spec MFT stock, MFT Engage black pistol grip, hardcoat black anodized finish, 6.5 lbs.

| MSR $849 | $725 | $650 | $580 | $515 | $450 | $385 | $340 | |

CLARIDGE HI-TEC INC.

Previous manufacturer located in Northridge, CA 1990-1993. In 1990, Claridge Hi-Tec, Inc. was created and took over Goncz Armament, Inc.

All Claridge Hi-Tec firearms utilized match barrels mfg. in-house, which were button-rifled. The Claridge action is an original design and does not copy other actions. Claridge Hi-Tec models can be altered (Law Enforcement Companion Series) to accept Beretta 92F or Sig Model 226 magazines.

PISTOLS: SEMI-AUTO

Add $40 for polished stainless steel frame construction.

L-9 PISTOL – 9mm Para., .40 S&W, or .45 ACP cal., blowback telescoping bolt operation, SA, 7 1/2 (new 1992) or 9 1/2 (disc. 1991) in. shrouded barrel, aluminum receiver, choice of black matte, matte silver, or polished silver finish, one-piece grip, safety locks firing pin in place, 10 (disc.), 17 or 30 shot double row mag., adj. sights, 3 3/4 lbs. Mfg. 1991-1993.

| | $595 | $525 | $375 | $300 | $265 | $225 | $200 | *$598* |

Add $395 for a trigger activated laser sight available in Models M, L, C, and T new mfg.

S-9 PISTOL – similar to L-9, except has 5 in. non-shrouded threaded barrel, 3 lbs. 9 oz. Disc. 1993.

| | $695 | $625 | $550 | $475 | $350 | $280 | $250 | *$535* |

T-9 PISTOL – similar to L-9, except has 9 1/2 in. barrel. Mfg. 1992-93.

| | $550 | $495 | $375 | $300 | $265 | $225 | $200 | *$598* |

M PISTOL – similar to L Model, except has 7 1/2 in. barrel, 3 lbs. Disc. 1991.

| | $575 | $515 | $375 | $300 | $265 | $225 | $200 | *$720* |

CARBINES: SEMI-AUTO

C-9 CARBINE – same cals. as L and S Model pistols, 16.1 in. shrouded barrel, choice of black graphite composite or uncheckered walnut stock and forearm, 5 lbs. 12 oz. Mfg. 1991-1993.

| | $650 | $595 | $525 | $450 | $395 | $350 | $300 | *$675* |

Add $74 for black graphite composite stock.
Add $474 for integral laser model (with graphite stock).

This model was available with either gloss walnut, dull walnut, or black graphite composite stock.

LAW ENFORCEMENT COMPANION (LEC) – 9mm Para., .40 S&W, or .45 ACP cal., 16 1/4 in. button rifled barrel, black graphite composition buttstock and foregrip, buttstock also provides space for an extra mag., available in either aluminum or stainless steel frame, matte black finish, available with full integral laser sighting system. Limited mfg. 1992-93.

| | $750 | $650 | $575 | $495 | $425 | $375 | $325 | *$749* |

Add $400 for integral laser sighting system.

CLARK CUSTOM GUNS, INC.

Current custom gun maker and gunsmith located in Princeton, LA. Clark Custom Guns, Inc. has been customizing various configurations of handguns, rifles, and shotguns since 1950. It would be impossible to list within the confines of this text the many conversions this company has performed. Please contact the company directly (see Trademark Index) for an up-to-date price sheet and catalog on their extensive line-up of high quality competition pistols and

MSR	100%	98%	95%	90%	80%	70%	60%	Last MSR

related components. Custom revolvers, rifles, and shotguns are also available in addition to various handgun competition parts, related gunsmithing services, and a firearms training facility called The Shootout.

The legendary James E. Clark, Sr. passed away during 2000. In 1958, he became the first and only full-time civilian to win the National Pistol Championships.

PISTOLS: SEMI-AUTO

Clark Custom Guns manufactures a wide variety of M1911 style handguns, including the Premium Bullseye Pistols (MSR $2,445-$4,625), Custom Combat Hardball (MSR $2,225-$2,950), Custom Combat SWAR/SWCAT (MSR $1,065-$1,255), Game Master (MSR $1,995), SSR (MSR $1,444-$1,744), 1911 Race Gun (MSR $3,295-$3,695), Meltdown (MSR $2,395), and the Lightweight revolver (MSR $1,495). Previously manufactured models include: Bullseye Pistol (last MSR in 2013 was $1,695-$3,100), Millennium Meltdown (damascus slide, only 50 mfg. during 2000 - MSR was $3,795), .460 Rowland Hunter LS (last MSR $2,640), and the Unlimited (last MSR $3,395-$3,790). Clark will also build the above configurations on a customer supplied gun - prices are less. Please contact the company directly regarding more information on its wide variety of pistols, including availability and pricing (see Trademark Index).

CLIFTON ARMS

Previous manufacturer of custom rifles from 1992-1997 located in Medina, TX. Clifton Arms specialized in composite stocks (with or without integral, retractable bipod).

Clifton Arms manufactured composite, hand laminated stocks, which were patterned after the Dakota 76 stock configuration.

RIFLES: BOLT ACTION

CLIFTON SCOUT RIFLE – .243 Win. (disc. 1993), .30-06, .308 Win., .350 Rem. Mag., .35 Whelen, 7mm-08 Rem. (disc. 1993), or .416 Rem. Mag. cal., choice of Dakota 76, pre-64 Winchester Model 70, or Ruger 77 MK II (standard) stainless action with bolt face altered to controlled round feeding, Shilen stainless premium match grade barrel, Clifton synthetic stock with bipod, many other special orders were available. Mfg. 1992-97.

	100%	98%	95%	90%	80%	70%	60%
	$3,000	$2,350	$1,650	$$1,455	$1,195	$1,010	$835

This model was available as a Standard Scout (.308 Win. cal. with 19 in. barrel), Pseudo Scout (.30-06 cal. with 19 1/2 in. barrel), Super Scout (.35 Whelen or .350 Rem. Mag. with 20 in. barrel), or African Scout (.416 Rem. Mag. with 22 in. barrel).

COBB MANUFACTURING, INC.

Previous rifle manufacturer located in Dallas, GA until 2007.

On Aug. 20, 2007, Cobb Manufacturing was purchased by Bushmaster, and manufacture was moved to Bushmaster's Maine facility. Please refer to the Bushmaster section for current information.

RIFLES: BOLT ACTION

MODEL FA50 (T) – .50 BMG cal., straight pull bolt action, lightweight tactical rifle, standard A2 style stock, ergonomic pistol grip, parkerized finish, Lothar Walther 22 or 30 in. barrel, recoil reducing Armalite muzzle brake, padded Mil-spec sling, includes two 10 shot mags., detachable M60 bipod, watertight case, 29 lbs. Disc. 2007.

	100%	98%	95%	90%	80%	70%	60%	Last MSR
	$6,275	$5,300	$4,500	$3,900	$2,700	$2,300	$2,100	$6,995

Add $300 for 22 in. barrel.
Add $1,000 for Ultra Light model with lightweight 22 or 30 in. barrel.
Add $89 for additional 10 shot mag.

RIFLES: SEMI-AUTO

MCR (MULTI-CALIBER RIFLE) SERIES – available in a variety of calibers from 9mm Para. to .338 Lapua, offered in MCR 100, MCR 200, MCR 300, and MCR 400 configurations, variety of stock, barrel and finish options. Mfg. 2005-2007.
Prices on this series started at $3,000, and went up according to options chosen by customer.

COBRAY INDUSTRIES

Please refer to S.W.D. Inc. in the S section.

COLT'S MANUFACTURING COMPANY, LLC

Current manufacturer with headquarters located in West Hartford, CT.

Manufactured from 1836-1842 in Paterson, NJ; 1847-1848 in Whitneyville, CT; 1854-1864 in London, England; and from 1848-date in Hartford, CT. Colt Firearms became a division of Colt Industries in 1964. In March 1990, the Colt Firearms Division was sold to C.F. Holding Corp. located in Hartford, CT, and the new company was called Colt's Manufacturing Company, Inc. The original Hartford plant was closed during 1994, the same year the company was sold again to a new investor group headed by Zilkha Co., located in New York, NY. During 1999, Colt Archive Properties LLC, the historical research division, became its own entity.

MSR	100%	98%	95%	90%	80%	70%	60%	Last MSR

In late 1999, Colt discontinued many of their consumer revolvers, but reintroduced both the Anaconda and Python Elite through the Custom Shop. Production on both models is now suspended. The semi-auto pistols remaining in production are now referred to as Model "O" Series.

In November 2003, Colt was divided into two separate companies, Colt Defense LLC (military/law enforcement) and Colt's Manufacturing Company LLC (handguns and match target rifles). The largest portion of Colt Defense's business is now in sporting rifles, a line of business the company got back into during 2011. Military orders have been on the decline since 2009.

During 2013, Colt Defense LLC acquired Colt's Manufacturing LLC for $60.5 million and reunited Colt's military and civilian handgun businesses. By combining the two companies after a decade long split, Colt Defense has eliminated the risk that its contract with Colt's Manufacturing to sell commercial firearms to civilian sportsmen and hunters under its namesake brand wouldn't be extended beyond March 2014. The company plans to remain in West Hartford.

For more information and current pricing on both new and used Colt airguns, please refer to the *Blue Book of Airguns* by Dr. Robert Beeman & John Allen (also available online). For more information and current pricing on both new and used Colt black powder reproductions and replicas, please refer to the *Blue Book of Modern Black Powder Arms* by John Allen (also available online).

PISTOLS: SEMI-AUTO, SINGLE ACTION, RECENT/CURRENT MFG.

Factory Colt abbreviations used on its price sheets are as follows: B - blue, BPF - black powder frame, BRS - Bomar rear sights, BSTS - bright polished stainless steel, CARS - Colt adjustable rear sight, CC/B - colored case/blue, CCBS - Colt Champion Bomar style sight, CCES - Colt Champion Elliason style sights, CER - Cerakote, FDE - Flat Dark Earth, F-H - Front Heinie sight, FOA - Fiber optic front, adj. rear, FXS - fixed sights, GE - gold enhancement, HBAR - heavy barrel, HC - hard chrome, IBFDE - Ion Bond FDE finish, L/W - lightweight, M - matte black, MP - Magpul accessories, NBRFFO - Novak Black Rear Front Fiber Optic, NM - National Match, NNS - Novak Night Sights, R - accessory rail, SE - semi-automatic enhanced, STS - stainless steel, TT - Two Tone, WDS - white dot sights, WDC - white dot carry, and WDCN - white dot carry Novak sights.

Some Series 80 pistols, including Gold Cups and Defenders with slanted slide serrations, polished ejection port, and beavertail safety are more desirable than standard models without these features. See individual models for pricing.

SPECIAL COMBAT GOVERNMENT CARRY MODEL O (SERIES 80) – .45 ACP cal., 5 in. throated barrel, flared ejection port, skeletonized trigger, custom tuning, blue or royal blue (disc.), hard chrome (disc.), or two-tone (disc.) finish, bar-dot-bar (disc. 2000) or Novak (new 2009) night sights, and ambidextrous safety. Mfg. 1992-2000, reintroduced 2009.

MSR $2,099	$1,775	$1,450	$1,125	$950	$775	$675	$575	

SPECIAL COMBAT GOVERNMENT CMC MARINE MODEL O – .45 ACP cal., full size with 5 in. National Match stainless steel barrel, front and rear slide serrations, features Desert Tan cerakote finish, stainless steel frame and slide, Novak night sights with Trijicon inserts, serrated grip straps with lanyard loop, aluminum trigger, unique patterned grips, G10 composite grips, lower Picatinny rail, includes Pelican case with two 7 shot mags, cleaning kit, and test target. Mfg. for United States Marine Corps by the Custom Shop, limited civilian availability. Mfg. 2013-2015.

	$2,600	$2,100	$1,750	$1,200	$775	$675	$575	*$2,149*

DEFENDER SERIES MODEL O – 9mm Para., .40 S&W (mfg. 1999 only) or .45 ACP cal., 3 in. barrel with 3-dot (disc.) or white dot carry Novak sights, 7 shot mag., rubber wrap-around grips with finger grooves, lightweight perforated trigger, stainless steel slide and frame - frame finished in matte stainless, firing pin safety, 22 1/2 oz. New 1998.

MSR $899	$775	$650	$550	$475	$425	$375	$325	

Note: Colt has issued a factory recall on the safety for this model sold after March 2007 in the following ser. no. range: DR33036 - DR35948 X. Colt will send you a new recoil spring assembly kit that includes the Guide Pad to replace in your pistol.

* ***Defender Plus*** – .45 ACP cal., similar to Defender Model O, except has aluminum frame and 8 shot mag. Mfg. 2002-2003.

	$875	$775	$700	$625	$575	$550	$475	*$876*

RAIL GUN SERIES MODEL O – .45 ACP cal., 5 in. barrel, 8 shot mag., stainless, two-tone (disc.), or Cerakote (new 2011) finish, white dot carry Novak sights, similar to Government Stainless model, except has Picatinny rail underneath frame in front of trigger guard. New 2009.

MSR $1,199	$1,025	$895	$725	$625	$525	$450	$395	

Add $50 for Cerakote finish (new 2011).

NEW AGENT SA MODEL O – 9mm Para. (disc. 2012) or .45 ACP cal., 3 in. barrel, Series 80 firing pin safety system, hammerless, 7 shot mag., double diamond slim fit or Crimson Trace (new 2012) grips, black anodized aluminum frame, blue finish, beveled magwell, skeletonized trigger, snag free trench style sights, front strap serrations, captive recoil spring system. Mfg. 2008-mid-2015.

	$925	$795	$650	$550	$450	$400	$350	*$1,078*

MSR	100%	98%	95%	90%	80%	70%	60%	Last MSR

Add $288 for Crimson Trace laser grips (new 2012).

Add 10% for 9mm Para. cal. (disc. 2012).

Note: Colt has issued a factory recall on the safety for this model sold after March 2007 in the following ser. no. range: GT01001-GT04505 XX. These pistols must be returned to Colt's factory for part(s) replacement.

GOVERNMENT MODEL 1911A1 .22 CAL. RAIL GUN – .22 LR cal., similar to Government Model 1911 .22 cal., except has lower Picatinny rail on frame, double slide serrations, skeleton trigger, low mount 3-dot combat style sights, beavertail grip safety and Commander style hammer, black or FDE (new 2013) finish, 36 oz. Mfg. by Umarex in Germany beginning 2011 and imported/distributed by Walther Arms.

MSR $449	$385	$325	$285	$240	$215	$195	$185

Add $50 for FDE finish (new 2013).

This model is also available in a Gold Cup variation - please refer to the listing in the Pistols: Semi-Auto, National Match Models - WWII & Post-WWII category.

RIFLES: BOLT ACTION, CENTERFIRE

COLT PRECISION RIFLE (M2012SA308) – .308 Win. cal., tactical configuration featuring 22 in. heavy match grade spiral fluted stainless steel barrel with muzzle brake, skeletonized adj. forged aluminum stock, pistol grip, vent. aluminum handguard with 2/3 length Picatinny rail, 5 or 10 shot mag., black finish, Timney single stage adj. trigger, 13.2 lbs. Mfg. by Cooper Firearms of Montana 2013-2015.

	$3,300	$2,950	$2,600	$2,300	$2,000	$1,850	$1,625	$3,799

RIFLES: SEMI-AUTO, CENTERFIRE, AR-15 & VARIATIONS

The AR-15 rifle and variations are the civilian versions of the U.S. armed forces M-16 model, which was initially ordered by the U.S. Army in 1963. Colt's obtained the exclusive manufacturing and marketing rights to the AR-15 from the Armalite division of the Fairchild Engine and Airplane Corporation in 1961.

Factory Colt AR-15 receivers are stamped with the model names only (Sporter II, Government Model, Colt Carbine, Sporter Match H-Bar, Match Target), but are not stamped with the model numbers (R6500, R6550, R6521, MT6430, CR6724). Because of this, if an AR-15 rifle/carbine does not have its original box, the only way to determine whether the gun is pre-ban or not is to look at the serial number and see if the configuration matches the features listed below within the two pre-ban subcategories.

AR-15 production included transition models, which were made up of obsolete and old stock parts. These transition models include: blue label box models having large front takedown pins, no internal sear block, 20 in. barrel models having bayonet lugs, misstamped nomenclature on receivers, or green label bolt assemblies.

Rifling twists on the Colt AR-15 have changed throughout the years, and barrel twists are stamped at the end of the barrel on top. They started with a 1:12 in. twist, changed to a 1:7 in. twist (to match with the new, longer .223 Rem./5.56mm SS109-type bullet), and finally changed to a 1:9 in. twist in combination with 1:7 in. twist models as a compromise for bullets in the 50-68 grain range. Current mfg. AR-15s/Match Targets have rifling twists/turns incorporated into the model descriptions.

Colt's never sold pre-ban lower receivers individually. It only sold completely assembled rifles.

A Colt letter of provenance for the following AR-15 models is $100 per gun.

AR-15, Pre-Ban, 1963-1989 Mfg. w/Green Label Box

Common features of 1963-1989 mfg. AR-15s are bayonet lug, flash hider, large front takedown pin, no internal sear block, and w/o reinforcement around the magazine release button.

AR-15 boxes during this period of mfg. had a green label with serial number affixed on a white sticker. Box is taped in two places with brown masking tape. NIB consists of the rifle with barrel stick down the barrel, plastic muzzle cap on flash hider, factory tag hanging from front sight post, rifle in plastic bag with ser. no. on white sticker attached to bag, cardboard insert, accessory bag with two 20 round mags., manual, sling, and cleaning brushes. Cleaning rods are in separate bag.

Pre-ban parts rifles are rifles, which are not assembled in their proper factory configuration. Counterfeit pre-ban rifles are rifles using post-ban receivers and assembled into a pre-ban configuration (it is a felony to assemble or alter a post-ban rifle into a pre-ban configuration).

Add $100 for NIB condition.

Add $300 for early green label box models with reinforced lower receiver.

SP-1 (R6000) – .223 Rem. cal., GIO, original Colt tactical configuration without forward bolt assist, 20 in. barrel with 1:12 in. twist, identifiable by the triangular shaped handguards/forearm, no case deflector, A1 sights, finishes included parkerizing and electroless nickel, approx. 6 3/4 lbs. Ser. no. range SP00001-SP5301 (1976). Mfg. 1963-1984.

	$2,100	$1,975	$1,850	$1,725	$1,600	$1,500	$1,200

Add 40%-60% for mint original models with early two and three digit serial numbers.

Pre-ban serialization is ser. no. SP360,200 and lower.

Early SP-1s were packaged differently than later standard green box label guns.

MSR	100%	98%	95%	90%	80%	70%	60%	Last MSR

* SP-1 Carbine (R6001) – .223 Rem. cal., similar to SP-1, except has 16 in. barrel, ribbed handguards, collapsible buttstock, high gloss finish.

| | $2,900 | $2,700 | $2,425 | $2,225 | $2,075 | $1,900 | $1,650 | |

Mint original condition models with early two and three digit serial numbers are selling in the $3,250 - $3,500 range.

Pre-ban serialization is ser. no. SP360200 and lower.

Early SP-1s were packaged differently than later standard green box label guns.

SPORTER II (R6500) – .223 Rem. cal., GIO, various configurations, receiver stamped "Sporter II", 20 in. barrel, 1:7 twist, A1 sights and forward assist, disc.

| | $1,875 | $1,650 | $1,475 | $1,300 | $1,175 | $1,075 | $995 | |

Serial numbers SP360200 and below are pre-ban.

* Sporter II Carbine (R6420) – .223 Rem. cal., similar to Sporter II, except has 16 in. barrel, A1 sights and collapsible buttstock.

| | $2,225 | $2,000 | $1,850 | $1,675 | $1,525 | $1,425 | $1,275 | |

Serial numbers SP360200 and below are pre-ban.

GOVERNMENT MODEL (R6550) – .223 Rem. cal., GIO, receiver is stamped Government Model, 20 in. barrel with 1:7 in. twist and bayonet lug, A2 sights, forward assist and brass deflector, very desirable because this model has the closest configurations to what the U.S. military is currently using.

| | $2,250 | $2,100 | $1,950 | $1,800 | $1,650 | $1,400 | $1,200 | |

In 1987, Colt replaced the AR-15A2 Sporter II Rifle with the AR-15A2 Govt. Model. This new model has the 800 meter rear sighting system housed in the receiver's carrying handle (similar to the M-16 A2).

Serial numbers GS008000 and below with GS prefix are pre-ban.

* Government Model (6550K) – .223 Rem. cal., similar to R6550, except does not have bayonet lug, originally supplied with .22 L.R. cal. conversion kit.

| | $2,050 | $1,900 | $1,750 | $1,600 | $1,450 | $1,250 | $1,100 | |

Subtract $300 w/o conversion kit.

Serial numbers GS008000 and below with GS prefix are pre-ban.

* Government Model (R6550CC) – .223 Rem. cal., similar to R6550, except has Z-Cote tiger striped camo finish, very scarce (watch for cheap imitation paint jobs).

| | $3,500 | $3,350 | $3,100 | $2,800 | $2,600 | $2,400 | $2,000 | |

Serial numbers GS008000 and below with GS prefix are pre-ban.

H-BAR MODEL (R6600) – GIO, H-Bar model with 20 in heavy barrel, 1:7 twist, forward assist, A2 sights, brass deflector, 8 lbs. New 1986.

| | $2,050 | $1,900 | $1,750 | $1,600 | $1,400 | $1,200 | $1,000 | |

Serial numbers SP360200 and below are pre-ban.

* H-Bar (R6600K) – similar to R6600, except has no bayonet lug, supplied with .22 LR cal. conversion kit.

| | $1,975 | $1,825 | $1,675 | $1,525 | $1,375 | $1,225 | $1,100 | |

Subtract $300 if w/o conversion kit.

Serial numbers SP360200 and below are pre-ban.

* Delta H-Bar (R6600DH) – similar to R6600, except has 3-9x rubber armored scope, removable cheekpiece, adj. scope mount, and black leather sling, test range selected for its accuracy, aluminum transport case. Mfg. 1987-1991.

| | $2,300 | $2,150 | $1,925 | $1,775 | $1,575 | $1,375 | $1,125 | *$1,460* |

Serial numbers SP360200 and below are pre-ban.

AR-15, Pre-Ban, 1989-Sept. 11, 1994 Mfg. w/Blue Label Box

Common features of 1989-1994 AR-15 production include a small front takedown pin, internal sear block, reinforcement around the mag. release button, flash hider, no bayonet lug on 20 in. models, A2 sights, brass deflector, and forward bolt assist. Models R6430 and 6450 do not have A2 sights, brass deflector, or forward bolt assist.

Blue label boxed AR-15s were mfg. between 1989-Sept. 11, 1994. Please refer to box description under Pre-1989 AR-15 mfg.

Pre-ban parts rifles are rifles which are not assembled in their proper factory configuration. Counterfeit pre-ban rifles are rifles using post-ban receivers and assembled into a pre-ban configuration.

Add $100 for NIB condition.

MSR	100%	98%	95%	90%	80%	70%	60%	Last MSR

AR-15A3 TACTICAL CARBINE (R-6721) – .223 Rem. cal., GIO, M4 flat-top with 16 in. heavy barrel, 1:9 twist, A2 sights, pre-ban configuration with flash hider, bayonet lug, and 4-position, collapsible stock, removable carry handle, 134 were sold commercially in the U.S., most collectible AR-15. Mfg. 1994 only.

	100%	98%	95%	90%	80%	70%	60%
S/N 134 and lower	$2,975	$2,500	$2,275	$2,050	$1,900	$1,775	$1,600
S/N 135 and higher	$1,250	$1,075	$950	$850	$750	$650	$550

On the R-6721, serial numbers BD000134 and below are pre-ban.

Please note the serial number cutoff on this model, as Colt shipped out a lot of unstamped post-ban law enforcement only "LEO" rifles before finally stamping them as a restricted rifle.

GOVERNMENT CARBINE (R6520) – .223 Rem cal., GIO, receiver is stamped Government Carbine, two-position collapsible buttstock, 800 meter adj. rear sight, 16 in. barrel bayonet lug, 1:7 twist, shortened forearm, 5 lbs. 13 oz. Mfg. 1988-94.

	100%	98%	95%	90%	80%	70%	60%	Last MSR
	$2,275	$2,125	$2,025	$1,875	$1,750	$1,625	$1,425	*$880*

Add $200 for green label box.

On the R6520, serial numbers GC018500 and below are pre-ban.

Please note the serial number cutoff on this model, as Colt shipped out a lot of unstamped post-ban law enforcement only "LEO" rifles before finally stamping them as a restricted rifle.

This model was manufactured in both green and blue label configurations.

COLT CARBINE (R6521) – receiver is stamped Colt Carbine, similar to R6520, except has no bayonet lug, 16 in. barrel, 1:7 twist. Disc. 1988.

	100%	98%	95%	90%	80%	70%	60%	Last MSR
	$2,150	$2,000	$1,850	$1,700	$1,625	$1,475	$1,300	*$770*

Serial numbers CC001616 and below are pre-ban.

SPORTER LIGHTWEIGHT (R6530) – .223 Rem. cal., GIO, receiver is stamped Sporter Lightweight, 16 in. barrel, 1:7 twist, similar to R6520, except does not have bayonet lug or collapsible stock.

	100%	98%	95%	90%	80%	70%	60%	Last MSR
	$1,650	$1,500	$1,350	$1,100	$1,000	$900	$800	*$740*

Serial numbers SI027246 and below are pre-ban.

9mm CARBINE (R6430) – 9mm Para. cal., similar to R6450 Carbine, except does not have bayonet lug or collapsible stock. Mfg. 1992-1994.

	100%	98%	95%	90%	80%	70%	60%
	$1,950	$1,800	$1,650	$1,500	$1,375	$1,275	$1,175

Serial numbers NL004800 are pre-ban.

9mm CARBINE (R6450) – 9mm Para. cal., GIO, carbine model with 16 in. barrel, 1:10 twist, bayonet lug, w/o forward bolt assist or brass deflector, two-position collapsible stock, 20 shot mag., 6 lbs. 5 oz.

	100%	98%	95%	90%	80%	70%	60%	Last MSR
	$2,250	$2,100	$1,950	$1,800	$1,725	$1,575	$1,400	*$696*

On the R6450, serial numbers TA010100 are pre-ban.

Please note the serial number cutoff on this model, as Colt shipped out a lot of unstamped post-ban law enforcement only "LEO" rifles before finally stamping them as a restricted rifle.

This model was manufactured with either a green or blue label.

7.62x39mm CARBINE (R6830) – 7.62x39mm cal., GIO, 16 in. barrel w/o bayonet lug, 1:12 twist, fixed buttstock. Mfg. 1992-1994.

	100%	98%	95%	90%	80%	70%	60%
	$1,850	$1,700	$1,550	$1,400	$1,275	$1,175	$1,075

Serial numbers LH011326 are pre-ban.

TARGET COMPETITION H-BAR RIFLE (R6700) – .223 Rem. cal., GIO, flat-top upper receiver for scope mounting, 20 in. H-Bar barrel (1:9 in. twist), quick detachable carry handle with a 600-meter rear sighting system, dovetailed upper receiver grooved to accept Weaver style scope rings, 8 1/2 lbs.

	100%	98%	95%	90%	80%	70%	60%
	$1,850	$1,700	$1,550	$1,400	$1,200	$1,025	$875

Serial numbers CH019500 and below are pre-ban.

COMPETITION H-BAR CUSTOM SHOP (R6701) – .223 Rem. cal., similar to the R6700, but with detachable scope mount, custom shop enhancements added to trigger and barrel, 2,000 mfg. from Colt Custom Shop.

	100%	98%	95%	90%	80%	70%	60%
	$1,950	$1,800	$1,650	$1,500	$1,350	$1,200	$1,050

MATCH H-BAR (R6601) – GIO, heavy 20 in. H-Bar barrel with 1:7 twist, fixed buttstock. 8 lbs.

	100%	98%	95%	90%	80%	70%	60%
	$1,750	$1,600	$1,450	$1,300	$1,150	$1,025	$950

MSR	100%	98%	95%	90%	80%	70%	60%	Last MSR

* Delta H-Bar (R6601DH) – similar to R6601, except has 3-9x rubber armored variable scope, removable cheekpiece, adj. scope mount, black leather sling, test range selected for its accuracy, aluminum transport case. Mfg. 1987-91.

| | $2,450 | $2,300 | $2,150 | $2,000 | $1,850 | $1,700 | $1,550 | *$1,460* |

Serial numbers MH086020 and below are pre-ban.

SPORTER TARGET (R6551) – similar to R6601, except had 20 in. barrel with reduced diameter underneath handguard, 7 1/2 lbs.

| | $1,750 | $1,600 | $1,450 | $1,300 | $1,150 | $1,050 | $950 | |

On the R6551, serial numbers ST038100 and below are pre-ban.

AR-15, Post-Ban, Mfg. Sept. 12, 1994-Present

During 2007, Colt released the M-5 Military Carbine and the LE 10-20, with 11 1/2, 14 1/2, or 16 in. barrel. These guns were only available for military and law enforcement.

During 2013, Colt released a line of competition rifles, manufactured under license by Bold Ideas of Texas, located in Breckenridge, TX. Every rifle/carbine comes with a 100 yard target.

State compliant variations are not listed in this text. Values are typically similar to the models from which they were derived.

Add $368 for Colt Scout C-More Sight (disc.).
Add $444 for Colt Tactical C-More Sight (disc.).

COMPETITION CRP-18 WITH GUNGODDESS TOUCH – .223 Rem. cal., GIO, 18 in. match grade stainless steel fluted barrel with triple port muzzle brake, 30 shot round Magpul mag., enlarged trigger guard, Geissele two-stage match trigger, Magpul CTR 6-pos. adj. stock with locking adjustments, Magpul MOE grip, matched bolt and carrier with H-buffer, GunGoddess 15 in. free-float handguard, one 2 in. accessory rail, Colt Competition charging handle with extended tactical latch, black finish, 7.22 lbs. New 2015.

| MSR $1,995 | $1,725 | $1,500 | $1,295 | $1,150 | $925 | $750 | $625 | |

Add $130 for Robin Egg Blue, Pink, Bright Purple, Snow White, Crimson, Zombie Green, Brushed Nickel, or Crushed Silver furniture.

COMPETITION PRO – .223 Rem. Wylde cal., GIO, 18 in. match grade stainless steel fluted barrel, fully adj. gas block, triple chamber or Sure-Fire muzzle brake, forged upper and lower receiver, flat-top with Picatinny rail, 30 shot mag., matte black finish, Geissele two-stage match trigger, Magpul adj. stock, grip, and forend, approx. 7 lbs. Mfg. 2013.

| | $1,825 | $1,525 | $1,295 | $1,175 | $950 | $775 | $600 | *$2,029* |

PRO CRB-16 – .300 AAC Blackout or .300 Whisper (new 2014) cal., GIO, patented low profile adj. gas block, forged and precision fitted upper and lower receivers, matte black finish, 16 in. match grade air gauged stainless steel barrel with Colt competition triple port muzzle brake, 10 or 30 shot aluminum mag., Geissele two-stage match trigger, Magpul enlarged trigger guard, Magpul STR six position adj. stock with locking adjustments, Magpul MOE grip with extended backstrap, Hogue 12 in. multi-piece slotted float tube handguard, Competition charging handle with extended tactical latch, matched bolt and bolt carrier with H-buffer, 13 slot Picatinny rail on flat-top upper receiver, 6.7 lbs. Mfg. 2013-2015.

| | $1,525 | $1,275 | $1,075 | $950 | $775 | $650 | $550 | *$1,799* |

PRO CRC-22 – 6.5 Creedmoor cal., adj. gas system, 22 in. stainless HBAR+ heavy barrel, PRS adj. stock, ProBrake, 3 rails, 20 shot mag. Mfg. 2014-2015.

| | $2,550 | $2,150 | $1,800 | $1,500 | $1,250 | $1,125 | $925 | *$2,979* |

PRO CRG-20 – 6.5mm Grendel cal., GIO, patented low profile adj. gas block, forged and precision fitted upper and lower receivers, matte black finish, 20 in. match grade air gauged chrome moly steel custom barrel with black nitrided finish, 10 or 25 shot aluminum mag., Colt competition match target trigger, nickel Teflon coated, 15 in. vented modular float tube handguard, 10 in. top mounted Picatinny handguard rail with 23 slots and 2-3 accessory rails, oversized trigger guard, Magpul CTR 6-position adj.buttstock with locking adjustments, Magpul MOE pistol grip with extended backstrap, competition charging handle with extended tactical latch, matched bolt and bold carrier with H-buffer, 13 slot Picatinny rail on flat-top upper receiver. Limited mfg. 2013 only.

| | $1,400 | $1,225 | $1,050 | $950 | $775 | $625 | $495 | *$1,649* |

PRO CRL-16 – .308 Win. cal., GIO, low profile adj. gas block, CNC machined and precision fitted upper and lower receivers, matte black finish, 16 in. tapered midweight match grade air gauged polished stainless steel custom barrel with triple port muzzle brake, 10 or 20 shot Magpul mag., integral enlarged trigger guard, Geissele two-stage SSA-E match trigger, Magpul CTR six position adj. stock with locking adjustments, Magpul MOE pistol grip with extended backstrap, 12 1/2 in. float tube handguard, top mounted Picatinny handguard rail, two 3 in. accessory rails, competition charging handle with extended tactical latch, matched bolt and bolt carrier, 18 slot Picatinny rail on flat-top upper receiver. New 2013.

| MSR $2,339 | $1,995 | $1,750 | $1,495 | $1,350 | $1,095 | $900 | $700 | |

PRO CRL-20 – .308 Win. cal., similar to Pro CRL-16, except has 20 in. tapered heavy barrel with six flutes. New 2013.

| MSR $2,979 | $2,550 | $2,225 | $1,925 | $1,735 | $1,400 | $1,150 | $895 | |

MSR	100%	98%	95%	90%	80%	70%	60%	Last MSR

PRO CRP-16 – 5.56 NATO cal., GIO, low profile adj. gas block, forged and precision fitted upper and lower receivers, matte black finish, 16 in. two-diameter heavy weight match grade air gauged polished stainless steel barrel, triple port muzzle brake, 10 or 30 shot Magpul mag., Geissele two-stage match trigger, Magpul enlarged trigger guard, Magpul CTR six position adj. stock with locking adjustments, Magpul MOE grip with extended backstrap, competition 12 in. vented modular float tube handguard, 5 1/2 in. top mounted Picatinny handguard rail with 11 slots, two 3 in. accessory rails, competition charging handle with extended tactical latch matched bolt and bolt carrier with H-buffer, 13 slot Picatinny rail on flat-top upper receiver. New 2013.

| MSR $1,899 | | $1,625 | $1,425 | $1,225 | $1,100 | $895 | $725 | $575 | |

PRO CRP-18 THREE-GUN MATCH RIFLE – 5.56 NATO cal., similar to CRP-16, except has 18 in. custom fluted mid-weight barrel, 15 in. vented modular float tube handguard, and full length Picatinny top handguard rail with one 2 in. accessory rail. New 2013.

| MSR $2,019 | | $1,725 | $1,500 | $1,295 | $1,150 | $925 | $750 | $625 | |

PRO CRP-20 LONG RANGE VARMINT/RIFLE – 5.56 NATO cal., similar to Pro CRP-18, except has 20 in. heavy barrel and 10 in. top mounted Picatinny handguard rail with 23 slots, and two 3 in. accessory rails. Mfg. 2013-2015.

| | | $1,625 | $1,425 | $1,225 | $1,100 | $895 | $725 | $575 | $1,899 |

Add $100 for PRS adj. stock with 3 rails or quad rails.

EXPERT CRE-16 – 5.56 NATO cal., similar to Expert CRE-18, except has 16 in. barrel. Mfg. 2014-2015.

| | | $1,375 | $1,200 | $1,050 | $935 | $750 | $625 | $495 | $1,599 |

EXPERT CRE-18/CRE-18 RR – 5.56 NATO cal., GIO, low profile gas block, forged and precision fitted upper and lower receivers, matte black finish, 18 in. midweight match grade air gauged polish stainless steel barrel, 10 or 30 shot Magpul mag., competition nickel Teflon coated match target trigger, enlarged Magpul trigger guard, Magpul MOE four position adj. stock or CTR adj. stock (Model CRE-18 RR, new 2014), Expert Brake (CRE-18) or ProBrake (CRE-18 RR, mfg. 2014-2015), 15 in. vented modular float tube handguard, 5 1/2 in. top mounted Picatinny handguard rail with 11 slots, two 3 in. accessory rails with five slots each or quad rails (CRE-18 RR, disc. 2015), Hogue rubber finger groove grip, competition charging handle with extended tactical latch, matched bolt and bolt carrier with H-buffer, 13 slot Picatinny rail on flat-top upper receiver. New 2013.

| MSR $1,599 | | $1,375 | $1,200 | $1,050 | $935 | $750 | $625 | $495 | |

Add $100 for CRE-18 RR model with quad rails and ProBrake (mfg. 2014-2015).

SPORTING RIFLE CSR-1516/CSR-1518 – .223 Rem. or 5.56 NATO cal., GIO, solid steel machined low profile gas block, forged alloy upper and lower receivers, matte black finish, 16 (CSR-1516) or 18 (CSR-18) in. midweight match grade chrome moly black manganese phosphate threaded steel barrel with standard flash suppressor, 10 or 30 shot mag., nickel Teflon coated match target trigger, adj. six position carbine (CSR-16) or rifle stock with wide cheekpiece (CSR-18), rubber over-molded finger groove grip with integral beavertail, 12 in. float tube handguard, standard charging handle, bolt, and bolt carrier, top mounted seven slot accessory rail. Mfg. 2013-2015.

| | | $850 | $750 | $650 | $575 | $475 | $385 | $300 | $990 |

Add $59 for CSR-18.

MARKSMAN CRX-16/CRX-16E – .223 Rem. cal., GIO, low profile gas block, forged and precision fitted upper and lower receivers, matte black finish, 16 in. midweight match grade manganese phosphated chrome moly steel barrel, Expert Brake, 10 or 30 shot Magpul mag., competition match target nickel Teflon coated trigger, enlarged Magpul trigger guard, carbine style four position adj. buttstock or Magpul MOE fixed rifle stock (CRX-16E), checkered A2 style finger groove grip, 12 in. vented modular float tube handguard, 5 1/2 in. top mounted Picatinny handguard rail with 11 slots, two 3 in. accessory rails with five slots each, matched bolt and bolt carrier with H-buffer, 13 slot Picatinny rail on flat-top upper receiver. New 2013.

| MSR $1,399 | | $1,200 | $1,075 | $950 | $815 | $715 | $605 | $505 | |

TACTICAL PATROL CARBINE CRX-16 RR – 5.56 NATO cal., low pro gas system, 16 in. chrome moly M4 contour barrel, ProBrake, quad rails, CTR stock, 6 lb. trigger, 30 shot mag. Mfg. 2014-2015.

| | | $1,175 | $1,050 | $895 | $800 | $675 | $575 | $450 | $1,379 |

COLT ACCURIZED RIFLE (CR6720/CR6724) – .223 Rem. cal., GIO, 20 (CR6720) or 24 (CR6724, disc. 2012, reintroduced 2014) in. stainless match barrel, matte finish, accurized AR-15, 8 (disc. 1998) or 9 (new 1999) shot mag., 9.41 lbs. New 1997.

| MSR $1,374 | | $1,095 | $950 | $825 | $750 | $600 | $500 | $400 | |

MATCH TARGET COMPETITION H-BAR RIFLE (MT6700/MT6700C) – .223 Rem. cal., GIO, features flat-top upper receiver for scope mounting, 20 in. barrel (1:9 in. twist), quick detachable carry handle which incorporates a 600-meter rear sighting system, counterbored muzzle, dovetailed upper receiver is grooved to accept Weaver style scope rings, supplied with two 5 (disc.), 8 (disc.), or 9 (new 1999) shot mags., cleaning kit, and sling, matte black finish, 8 1/2 lbs. Mfg. 1992-2013.

| | | $975 | $850 | $725 | $675 | $535 | $450 | $395 | $1,230 |

Add $57 for compensator (MT6700C, mfg. 1999-disc).

MSR	100%	98%	95%	90%	80%	70%	60%	Last MSR

MATCH TARGET COMPETITION H-BAR II (MT6731) – .223 Rem. cal., GIO, flat-top, 16.1 in. barrel (1:9 in.), 9 shot mag., matte finish, 7.1 lbs. Mfg. 1995-2012.

	$950	$825	$700	$650	$525	$425	$395	$1,173

MATCH TARGET LIGHTWEIGHT (MT6430, MT6530, or MT6830) – .223 Rem. (MT6530, 1:7 in. twist), 7.62x39mm (MT6830, disc. 1996, 1:12 in. twist), or 9mm Para. (MT6430, disc. 1996, 1:10 in. twist) cal., GIO, features 16 in. barrel (non-threaded per C/B 1994), initially shorter stock and handguard, rear sight adjustable for windage and elevation, includes two detachable 5, 8, or 9 (new 1999) shot mags., approx. 7 lbs. Mfg. 1991-2002.

	$895	$795	$675	$625	$525	$425	$395	$1,111

Add $200 for .22 LR conversion kit (disc. 1994).

MATCH TARGET M4 CARBINE (MT6400/MT6400R) – .223 Rem. cal., GIO, similar to current U.S. armed forces M4 model, except semi-auto, 9 or 10 shot mag., 16.1 in. barrel, 1:7 in. twist, matte black finish, fixed tube buttstock, A3 detachable carrying handle, 7.3 lbs. Mfg. 2002-2013.

	$950	$850	$750	$650	$450	$425	$395	$1,211

Add $341 for quad accessory rail (MT6400R).

MATCH TARGET 6400001 – 5.56 NATO cal., GIO, 16.1 in. M4 barrel with flash suppressor, flat-top receiver, fixed tube stock, 10 shot mag., Magpul Gen. II rear back up sight, two-piece ribbed handguard with post front sight, black finish, 7 lbs. Mfg. 2013 only.

	$1,300	$1,100	$975	$825	$725	$575	$500	$1,461

MATCH TARGET 6400R001 – 5.56 NATO cal., 16.1 in. M4 barrel with flash suppressor, 10 shot mag., flat-top receiver with Picatinny rail integrated with quad rail handguard, Magpul Gen. II rear sight and flip up adj. post front sight, black finish, 7.2 lbs. Mfg. 2013 only.

	$1,595	$1,375	$1,250	$1,000	$825	$650	$550	$1,825

MATCH TARGET H-BAR RIFLE (MT6601/MT6601C) – .223 Rem. cal., GI, heavy 20 in. H-Bar barrel, 1:7 in. twist, A2 sights, 8 lbs. Mfg. 1986-2010.

	$1,125	$975	$875	$775	$675	$600	$550	$1,218

Add $200 for .22 LR conversion kit (mfg. 1990-94).
Add $1 for compensator (MT6601C, new 1999).

TACTICAL ELITE MODEL (TE6700) – .223 Rem. cal., GIO, 20 in. heavy barrel, 1:8 in. twist, Hogue finger groove pistol grip, Choate buttstock, fine tuned for accuracy, scope and mount included, approx. 1,000 rifles made by the Custom Shop circa 1996-97.

	$1,650	$1,450	$1,250	$1,075	$900	$725	$575	

TARGET GOVT. MODEL RIFLE (MT6551) – .223 Rem. cal., GIO, semi-auto version of the M16 rifle with forward bolt assist, 20 in. barrel (1:7 in.), straight line black nylon stock, aperture rear and post front sight, 5, 8, or 9 (new 1999) shot mags., 7 1/2 lbs. Disc. 2002.

	$925	$810	$700	$650	$550	$450	$400	$1,144

Add $200 for .22 LR conversion kit (mfg. 1990-94).

SPORTER CARBINE (SP6920) – .223 Rem. cal., GIO, has M-4 features including flat-top receiver with A3 removeable carry handle, 16.1 in. barrel with flash hider, 4-position collapsible buttstock, ribbed oval handguard, matte black finish, 5.95 lbs. Mfg. 2011 only.

	$995	$875	$775	$675	$600	$500	$400	$1,155

Add 15% for the legal LE6920 variation that were sold to civilians.

The last 100 carbines of the Model LE6920 marked "Law Enforcement Carbine" and "Restricted" were sold as commercial guns to FFL dealers. Each of these has a factory letter stating as such.

COLT SPORTER (SP6940) – .223 Rem. cal., GIO, flat-top receiver with full-length quad Picatinny rails, 16.1 in. fully floated barrel, flip up adj. sights, 4-position collapsible stock, 1-piece monolithic upper receiver, 20 shot mag., matte black metal finish, 6.1 lbs. Mfg. 2011 only.

	$1,275	$1,000	$900	$800	$700	$625	$550	$1,500

Add 15% for the legal LE6940 variation that were sold to civilians.

The last 100 carbines of the Model LE6940 marked "Law Enforcement Carbine" and "Restricted" were sold as commercial guns to FFL dealers. Each of these has a factory letter stating as such.

SP901 RIFLE – .308 Win. cal., GIO, 16 in. full floated heavy chrome lined barrel, direct gas system, locking bolt, matte black finish, one piece monolithic upper receiver with rail, upper receiver can be swapped out for .223, ambidextrous operating controls, flip up post sights, bayonet lug and flash hider. Mfg. mid-2011.

While advertised in 2011, this model never went into production (see LE901-16S).

MSR	100%	98%	95%	90%	80%	70%	60%	Last MSR

COLT CARBINE AR6450 – 9mm Para. cal., GIO, 16.1 in. barrel with flash suppressor, A3 detachable carrying handle, 32 shot mag., grooved aluminum handguard, A2 post front sight, adj. Rogers Super-Stoc, matte finish, 6.35 lbs. Mfg. 2012 only.

| | $1,050 | $925 | $850 | $725 | $600 | $550 | $425 | $1,176 |

COLT CARBINE AR6520TRI – 5.56 NATO cal., GIO, 16.1 in. barrel, matte black finish, 30 shot mag., adj. sights. Mfg. 2013 only.

| | $1,050 | $925 | $850 | $725 | $600 | $550 | $425 | $1,223 |

LIGHTWEIGHT CARBINE (AR6720) – 5.56 NATO cal., GIO, 16.1 in. light barrel with flash hider and A2 front sight, 30 shot round PMAG, ribbed aluminum forearm, A3 detachable carrying handle, MBUS Gen 2 rear sight, matte black finish, adj. stock, 6.2 lbs. New 2012.

| MSR $929 | $795 | $695 | $625 | $550 | $485 | $415 | $370 | |

COLT CARBINE AR6720LECAR – 5.56 NATO cal., GIO, 16.1 in. barrel, Magpul Gen. II rear sight with adj. post front sight, 30 shot mag., matte black finish, 6 lbs. Mfg. 2013 only.

| | $1,250 | $1,075 | $925 | $825 | $675 | $550 | $425 | $1,468 |

TACTICAL CARBINE (AR6721) – 5.56 NATO cal., GIO, 16.1 in. heavy barrel with flash hider and A2 front sight, 30 shot PMAG, MBUS Gen 2 rear sight, ribbed aluminum forearm, A3 detachable carrying handle, matte black finish, adj. stock, 7.3 lbs. New 2012.

| MSR $929 | $795 | $695 | $625 | $550 | $485 | $415 | $370 | |

9MM CARBINE (AR6951) – 9mm Para. cal., GIO, 16.1 in. barrel with flash suppressor, 32 shot mag., folding rear sight, adj. Rogers Super-Stoc, flat-top receiver, A3 detachable carrying handle, grooved aluminum handguard, choice of matte black or Muddy Girl (AR6951MPMG, limited mfg. 2015 only) finish, 6.4 lbs. New 2012.

| MSR $1,099 | $1,050 | $950 | $850 | $725 | $600 | $550 | $425 | |

Last MSR for Muddy Girl finish was $1,567 in 2015.

Add $319 for Muddy Girl camo finish (limited mfg. 2015 only).

AR15 A4 RIFLE – 5.56 NATO cal., GIO, 20 in. barrel with flash suppressor, 30 shot mag., flat-top receiver with removable carry handle, A2 style buttstock and front sight, ribbed handguard, black finish, 7.7 lbs. New 2013.

| MSR $999 | $850 | $725 | $650 | $585 | $515 | $450 | $395 | |

AR15 A4MP-FDE – 5.56 NATO cal., GIO, 20 in. barrel with flash suppressor, Flat Dark Earth (FDE) furniture, 30 shot mag., 2/3 quad rail with cover, A2 front sight with Magpul Gen. II rear sight, fixed stock, matte black barrel, matte black or FDE (new 2014) receiver finish, 7 1/2 lbs. Mfg. 2013-2014.

| | $1,095 | $975 | $850 | $725 | $600 | $550 | $425 | $1,304 |

Add $35 for FDE receiver finish.

COLT CARBINE AR-6821/AR-6821MP-R – .300 AAC Blackout cal., AR-6821 is similar to AR-6720, AR-6821MP-R has Magpul furniture and accessory rail. Mfg. 2015 only.

| | $965 | $825 | $725 | $650 | $550 | $450 | $400 | $1,155 |

Add $113 for Magpul furniture and accessory rail.

COLT CARBINE CR6724001 – 5.56 NATO cal., GIO, 24 in. stainless barrel without sights, one-piece flat-top upper receiver with integrated 2/3 length quad Picatinny rail, fixed non-adj. stock, 10 shot mag., black finish, 8.8 lbs. Mfg. 2013-2015.

| | $1,425 | $1,250 | $1,075 | $975 | $825 | $725 | $575 | $1,653 |

AR-15 SCOPE (3X/4X) AND MOUNT – initially offered with 3x magnification scope, then switched to 4x. Disc.

| | $395 | $300 | $240 | $185 | $160 | $130 | $115 | $344 |

LE901-16S (SP901) – .308 Win. cal., GIO, 16.1 in. heavy full floated barrel with bayonet lug and flash hider, flat-top with Picatinny rail, one-piece upper receiver with BUIS, ambidextrous controls, flip up adj. front sight post, flip-up adj. rear sight, 20 shot mag., fixed stock, matte black finish, 9.4 lbs. Mfg. 2012-2015.

| | $2,275 | $1,995 | $1,700 | $1,550 | $1,250 | $1,025 | $795 | $2,544 |

M.A.R.C.901 MONOLITHIC – .308 Win. cal., GIO, 16.1 or 18 (LE901-18SE, mfg. 2015 only) in. heavy full floated barrel with bayonet lug and flash hider, 20 shot mag., one-piece monolithic flat-top upper receiver with Picatinny rail, BUIS, ambidextrous controls, adj. VLTOR buttstock, matte black or FDE (LE901FDE-16SE) finish, 9.4 lbs. New 2015.

| MSR $1,999 | $1,725 | $1,500 | $1,295 | $1,150 | $925 | $750 | $625 | |

Add $100 for FDE finish (model LE901FDE-16SE), disc. 2015.

M.A.R.C.901 CARBINE (AR901-16S) – .308 Win. cal., 16.1 in. heavy free-floating barrel with muzzle brake, 20 shot mag., retractable B5 Bravo buttstock, flat-top receiver with full length Picatinny rail, vent tubular handguard with 3 Picatinny rails. New 2015.

| MSR $1,399 | $1,200 | $1,075 | $950 | $800 | $700 | $600 | $495 | |

MSR	100%	98%	95%	90%	80%	70%	60%	Last MSR

LE6900 – 5.56 NATO cal., GIO, 16.1 in. barrel, no sights, 30 shot mag., matte black finish, 6 lbs. Mfg. 2012-mid 2013.

	$800	$725	$625	$550	$475	$425	$395	*$899*

LE6920 M4 CARBINE – 5.56 NATO cal., GIO, 16.1 in. barrel with bayonet lug and flash hider, adj. front sight post, ribbed handguard, Magpul Gen2 back-up rear sight, flat-top receiver with Picatinny rail, collapsible stock, 30 shot mag., matte black finish, 6.9 lbs. New 2012.

MSR $999	$850	$725	$650	$585	$515	$450	$395	

LE6920AE – 5.56 NATO cal., 16.1 in. barrel, ambidextrous mag. release, bolt catch and fire selector, 30 shot PMag., MBUS rear Gen. 2 sights, collapsible stock, matte black finish, 6.38 lbs. New 2014.

MSR $1,374	$1,225	$1,075	$925	$825	$675	$550	$425	

LE6920-OEM1/OEM2 M4 – 5.56 NATO cal., 16.1 in. barrel with muzzle brake, includes pistol grip and rear buffer tube, flat-top receiver with Picatinny rail, no furniture, OEM1 includes A2 style front sight. New 2015.

MSR $799	$685	$615	$550	$475	$425	$375	$340	

LE6920 SOCOM – 5.56 NATO cal., GIO, 16.1 in. barrel with bayonet lug and flash hider, flat-top receiver with BUIS, Knights Armament rail system, 30 shot mag., adj. front sight post, flip up adj. rear sight, non-adj. tube stock, matte black finish, 7.2 lbs. Mfg. 2012-2014.

	$1,395	$1,220	$1,050	$950	$775	$625	$495	*$1,602*

LE6920MP-R – 5.56 NATO cal., 16.1 in. barrel, 30 shot PMag., MBUS rear Gen. 2 sight, Troy rail, Magpul MOE furniture, Black furniture, 7.11 lbs. Mfg. 2014-2015.

	$1,125	$985	$850	$775	$625	$500	$400	*$1,268*

LE6920MP & VARIATIONS – 5.56 NATO cal., GIO, 16.1 in. barrel with bayonet lug and flash hider, 30 shot PMAG, adj. front sight post, MBUS Gen2 back up rear sight, Magpul MOE carbine collapsible stock with MOE handguard and pistol grip, flat-top receiver with Picatinny rail, MOE trigger guard, Magpul MOE furniture in black (LE6920MP-B), A-TACS Foliage/Green (LE6920MPFG, new 2013), Olive Drab (LE6920MP-OD), USA One Nation Hydro-dipped (LE6920MP-USA, new 2014), ATAC camo hydro-dipped (LE6920MPATAC, new 2014), or Steel Gray (LE6920MP-STG, new 2015) 6.9 lbs. Mfg. 2012-mid-2015.

	$1,095	$950	$825	$750	$600	$500	$400	*$1,229*

Add $87 for USA One Nation Hydro-Dipped Magpul furniture (LE6920-USA, new 2014).

Add $166 for ATACS Foliage/Green finish (LE6920MPFG).

Add $247 for ATAC camo Hydro-Dipped Magpul furniture (LE6920MPATAC, new 2014).

* *LE6920MPG* – 5.56 NATO cal., similar to LE6920MP, except features Olive Drab Green upper and lower receivers, OD Green Magpul furniture (LE6920MPG-OD) or Black Magpul furniture (LE6920MPG-B, new 2014), vertical grip. Mfg. 2012-mid-2015.

	$1,195	$1,050	$895	$825	$650	$550	$425	*$1,361*

* *LE6920MPFDE* – 5.56 NATO cal., similar to LE6920MP, except features Flat Dark Earth Magpul MOE furniture with vertical grip, Flat Dark Earth finish. Mfg. 2012-mid-2015.

	$1,195	$1,050	$895	$825	$650	$550	$425	*$1,361*

* *LE6920MPFDE-R* – 5.56 NATO cal., similar to LE6920MP, except features Flat Dark Earth coated upper and lower receivers, FDE Troy Rail, FDE Magpul furniture. Mfg. 2014-mid-2015.

	$1,350	$1,175	$1,025	$925	$750	$625	$475	*$1,572*

LE6920MPS-B/FDE – 5.56 NATO cal., 16.1 in. barrel, 30 shot round PMAG mag., MBUS Gen 2 rear sight, Magpul MOE SL carbine vertical pistol grip stock, Magpul MOE SL handguard, Flat Dark Earth furniture.

MSR $1,049	$885	$785	$685	$600	$535	$465	$415	

LE6940 M4 MONOLITHIC – 5.56 NATO cal., GIO, 16.1 in. full floated barrel with bayonet lug and flash hider, 1-piece upper receiver, 30 shot mag., flip-up adj. front sight post, Magpul Gen2 back-up rear sight, collapsible stock, matte black finish, 6.9 lbs. New 2012.

MSR $1,399	$1,200	$1,075	$950	$800	$700	$600	$495	

LE6940P – 5.56 NATO cal., GPO, 16.1 in. full floated barrel with bayonet lug and flash hider, 1-piece upper receiver, 30 shot mag., flip-up adj. front sight post, Magpul Gen2 back-up rear sight, collapsible stock, matte black finish, 6.9 lbs. Mfg. 2012-mid-2015.

	$1,750	$1,525	$1,325	$1,195	$975	$795	$625	*$2,105*

* *LE6940MPFG* – 5.56 NATO cal., similar to LE6940P, except features A-TACS Forest Green Camo. Mfg. 2012-2013.

	$1,195	$1,050	$895	$825	$650	$550	$425	*$1,395*

LE6940AE-3G – 5.56 NATO cal., 16.1 in. barrel, Colt articulating piston system, lower receiver features ambidextrous operating controls and 3 operating controls on both sides, monolithic upper is fully modular with smooth handguard allowing for different rail locations, A2 grip, M4 buttstock, 30 shot Pmag., MBUS rear Gen. 2 sight, Black furniture, 7.2 lbs. Mfg. 2014-2015.

	$1,650	$1,450	$1,250	$1,125	$925	$750	$575	*$1,945*

MSR	100%	98%	95%	90%	80%	70%	60%	Last MSR

LT6720-R – 5.56 NATO cal., 16.1 in. barrel, 30 shot PMag., MBUS front and rear Gen. 2 sights, Troy rail, Magpul ACS telescoping stock, Black Magpul furniture, matte black finish, 6.48 lbs. New 2014.

MSR $1,321	$1,125	$985	$850	$775	$625	$500	$400	

   * LT6720MPMG – 5.56 NATO cal., 16.1 in. light contour barrel wih bird cage flash hider, 30 shot mag., Magpul MBUS sights, Magpul ACS Muddy Girl camo telescoping stock, Magpul stock, trigger guard, and pistol grip, Muddy Girl camo finish, 6.2 lbs. Mfg. 2014-mid-2015.

	$1,250	$1,075	$900	$800	$700	$600	$500	$1,448

EXPANSE M4 – 5.56 NATO cal., GIO, 16.1 in. barrel, 30 shot round aluminum mag., adj. front sight post, flat-top Picatinny rail, matte black finish, 6.44 lbs. New 2016.

MSR $699	$615	$540	$470	$400	$350	$310	$295	

RIFLES: SEMI-AUTO, RIMFIRE, AR-15 & VARIATIONS

The following models are manufactured by Carl Walther, located in Ulm, Germany, under license from New Colt Holding Corp., and imported/distributed by Walther Arms.

M4 CARBINE – .22 LR cal., GIO, 16.2 in. shrouded barrel, flat-top receiver, 10 or 30 shot mag., detachable carry handle, single left-side safety lever, four position retractable stock, ribbed aluminum handguard, black finish, approx. 6 lbs. Mfg. by Umarex under license from Colt and imported by Walther Arms. New 2009.

MSR $569	$475	$400	$350	$315	$285	$250	$225	

   * M4 Ops – .22 LR cal., GIO, 16.2 in. barrel, 10 or 30 shot mag., aluminum upper and lower receiver, black finish, quad tactical rail interface system with elongated Picatinny rail on top of barrel and frame, inline barrel/stock design, cartridge case deflector, muzzle compensator, detachable rear sight, four position collapsible stock, ejection port cover, approx. 6 1/2 lbs. Mfg. by Umarex under license from Colt and imported by Walther Arms. New 2009.

MSR $599	$515	$435	$375	$340	$310	$285	$250	

M16 – .22 LR cal., GIO, 21.2 in. barrel, 10 or 30 shot mag., flat-top receiver with detachable carry handle, fixed stock, elongated ribbed aluminum handguard, removable rear sight, ejection port cover, single left-side safety lever, black finish, approx. 6 1/4 lbs. Mfg. 2009-2010.

	$575	$525	$475	$425	$395	$375	$350	$599

   * M16 SPR (Special Purpose Rifle) – .22 LR cal., GIO, 21.2 in. barrel, 30 shot mag., black finish, fixed stock, aluminum upper and lower receiver, quad tactical rail interface system with Picatinny rail, flip up front and rear sights, inline barrel/stock design, cartridge case deflector, muzzle compensator. Mfg. 2009-2010.

	$625	$575	$525	$475	$450	$415	$395	$670

COMMANDO ARMS

Previous manufacturer located in Knoxville, TN.

Commando Arms became the new name for Volunteer Enterprises in the late 1970s.

CARBINES: SEMI-AUTO

MARK 45 – .45 ACP cal., carbine styled after the Thompson sub-machine gun, 16 1/2 in. barrel.

	$495	$425	$350	$315	$280	$225	$195	

COMMANDO ARMS (NEW MFG.)

Current trademark of shotguns manufactured in Konya, Turkey. Currently imported under private label by Webley & Scott, SKB, and Dickinson.

SHOTGUNS

Current SxS models include the Estate, Prestige, Plantation, and the Classic (disc.). Current O/U models include the Classic (disc.), Elite, Estate (disc.), Gold, Hunter, Royal, Osso, Trap and Skeet, and the Ultra (disc.). Current semi-auto models include the Gold and Classic Series. Current single barrel models include the Century III and Star Series (disc.). Slide action defense guns include the Pump Series. Please contact the company directly for more information, including U.S. availability and pricing on non-Webley & Scott, SKB, and/or Dickinson labeled models (see Trademark Index).

COMPETITIVE EDGE GUNWORKS LLC

Previous rifle manufacturer located in Bogard, MO until 2013.

RIFLES: BOLT ACTION

Competitive Edge Gunworks LLC built custom order bolt action rifles based on its patented action. Tactical, Hunting, Varmint, and Competition configurations were available.

MSR	100%	98%	95%	90%	80%	70%	60%	Last MSR

CONTROLLED CHAOS ARMS

Current custom AR-15 style manufacturer located in Baxter, IA.

Controlled Chaos Arms builds and manufactures AR rifles and carbines, and offers other firearm industry products such as suppressors, gunsmithing services, provides finishes and weapon maintenance, as well as gun and rifle training. Please contact the company directly for more information on all their products and services including current models, options, pricing, and availability (see Trademark Index).

RIFLES: SEMI-AUTO

AR-15 CARBINE PACKAGE – 5.56 NATO cal., GIO, 16 in. M4 profile barrel with A2 birdcage flash hider, tactical charging handle assembly, removable rear sight, Gen2 six-position stock, standard trigger, Ergo pistol grip, M4 polished feed ramp, includes soft case, takedown tool, and two Extreme Duty 30 shot mags.

MSR $1,300	$1,100	$995	$875	$735	$650	$550	$465	

CORE RIFLE SYSTEMS

Current trademark of carbines, rifles, and pistols manufactured by Good Time Outdoors, Inc. (GTO), located in Ocala, FL.

PISTOLS: SEMI-AUTO

CORE15 ROSCOE R1 PISTOL – 5.56 NATO cal., 10 1/2 in. carbine length gas system barrel with Midwest Industries flash hider and black Nitride finish, Magpul 30 shot mag., Core15 KeyMod 9 1/2 in. rail, KAK Industries pistol buffer tube, forged M4 upper and T6 lower receivers, beveled magwell, M4 feed ramps, Picatinny flat-top rail, stainless steel gas tube, Hardcore V.2 charging handle, oversized trigger guard, Ergo Swift grip, 5.6 lbs. New 2015.

MSR $880	$765	$675	$595	$525	$460	$390	$340	

* **CORE15 Roscoe RB1 Pistol** – 5.56 NATO cal., similar to Roscoe R1, except also features Sig Sauer SB15 pistol stabilizing brace, 6.7 lbs. New 2015.

MSR $990	$850	$725	$650	$585	$515	$450	$395	

CORE15 300BO ROSCOE R2 PISTOL – .300 AAC Blackout cal., 9 1/2 in. pistol length gas system barrel with Midwest Industries flash hider and black Nitride finish, Magpul 30 shot mag., Core15 KeyMod 9 1/2 in. rail, KAK Industries pistol buffer tube, forged M4 upper and T6 lower receivers, beveled magwell, M4 feed ramps, Picatinny flat-top rail, stainless steel gas tube, Hardcore V.2 charging handle, oversized trigger guard, Ergo Swift grip, 5.6 lbs. New 2015.

MSR $880	$765	$675	$595	$525	$460	$390	$340	

* **CORE15 300BO Roscoe RB2 Pistol** – .300 AAC Blackout cal., similar to 300 BO Roscoe R2, except includes Sig Sauer SB15 pistol stabilizing brace, 6.7 lbs. New 2015.

MSR $990	$850	$725	$650	$585	$515	$450	$395	

RIFLES: SEMI-AUTO

GTO Guns manufactures a complete line of AR-15 style carbines and rifles, in addition to uppers in various cals., lower receivers, and related accessories.

CORE15 HOGUE KeyMod RIFLE – 5.56 NATO or .300 AAC Blackout cal., mid-length GIO, 16 in. Govt. profile barrel with black Nitride or black phosphate finish, 30 shot PMAG, oversized trigger guard, Hogue 6-position retractable stock, Hogue pistol grip, KeyMod 12 1/2 in. rail, Hardcore V.2 billet charging handle, stainless steel gas tube, Mil-Spec buffer tube, forged upper and lower receivers, beveled magwell, M4 feed ramps, flat-top Picatinny rail, Type III hardcoat anodized finish, 6 1/2 lbs. New 2016.

MSR $1,000	$850	$725	$650	$585	$515	$450	$395	

Add $100 for .300 AAC Blackout cal.

CORE15 KeyMod LW – 5.56 NATO cal., low pro gas block, 14 1/2 in. pencil profile barrel with pinned and welded Yankee Hill Phantom flash hider, black Nitride finish, Mission First Tactical 30 shot mag., oversized trigger guard, Mission First Tactical Minimalist stock, Ergo black Suregrip, CORE15 KeyMod 12 1/2 in. rail, Mil-Spec buffer tube, Hardcore V.2 billet charging handle, Mil-Spec forged upper and lower receivers, flat-top Picatinny rail, Type III hardcoat anodized finish, 5 lbs. 14 oz.

MSR $1,000	$850	$725	$650	$585	$515	$450	$395	

CORE15 M4 PISTON RIFLE – 5.56 NATO cal., AR-15 style, utilizes Core15/Adams Arms GPO, 16 in. M4 chrome-lined barrel with A2 flash hider, M1913 Picatinny optics rails, Magpul 20 shot PMAG, Tapco 6-position adj. stock, M4 style thermoset molded polymer handguards with dual heat shields, A2 pistol grip, flat-top receiver, matte black finish or custom colors also available, marked GTO near gas block, 6.2 lbs. New 2011.

MSR $1,290	$1,100	$940	$840	$675	$550	$475	$375	

CORE15 M4 RIFLE – 5.56 NATO cal., utilizes standard GIO, A2 elevated front sight, with one Picatinny rail, otherwise similar to Core15 M4 Piston Rifle, 5.9 lbs. New 2011.

MSR $930	$815	$675	$625	$550	$475	$400	$350	

MSR		100%	98%	95%	90%	80%	70%	60%	Last MSR

CORE15 M4 SCOUT RIFLE – 5.56 NATO cal., GIO, 16 in. M4 profile barrel with A2 flash hider, Mil-Spec forged upper and lower receiver, stainless steel gas tube, chrome lined stainless steel bolt carrier, 30 shot mag., 6-position retractable stock, M4 style thermoset molded polymer handguards, A2 pistol grip, Hardcore billet charging handle, Type III Class II hardcoat anodized finish in black, OD Green, or FDE, 6 lbs. New 2014.

| MSR $825 | | $735 | $625 | $550 | $495 | $425 | $375 | $325 | |

* CORE15 KeyMod Scout – 5.56 NATO or .300 AAC Blackout (new 2016) cal., carbine length gas system, 16 in. mid-length profile barrel, low profile gas block, forged lower and upper with flat-top Picatinny rail, 12 1/2 in. Core15 KeyMod rail system, 6-pos. retractable stock, black Nitride finish, 6 1/2 lbs. New 2015.

| MSR $900 | | $785 | $665 | $575 | $500 | $425 | $375 | $325 | |

Add $250 for .300 AAC Blackout cal. (new 2016).

CORE15 MFT KeyMod RIFLE – 5.56 NATO or .300 AAC Blackout cal., carbine length GIO, 16 in. Govt. profile barrel with black Nitride or black phosphate finish, MFT 30 shot mag., oversized trigger guard, Mission First Tactical Minimalist stock, MFT G27 grip, low profile gas block, KeyMod 12 1/2 in. rail, Hardcore V.2 billet charging handle, stainless steel gas tube, Mil-Spec buffer tube, forged upper and lower receivers, beveled magwell, flat-top Picatinny rail, Type III hardcoat anodized finish, 6 1/2 lbs. New 2016.

| MSR $980 | | $825 | $700 | $630 | $570 | $500 | $425 | $380 | |

Add $80 for .300 AAC Blackout cal.

CORE15 MOE .300 BLACKOUT RIFLE – .300 AAC Blackout cal., GIO, 16 in. stainless steel barrel with SureFire 3 prong flash hider, forged T6 M4 flat-top upper with internal dry lube and Laser-T markings, V.2 charging handle, forged lower receiver with hardcoat anodized finish, M4 feed ramps, and beveled magwell, Magpul MOE 6-position stock and pistol grip, Magpul MOE handguard, Magpul 30 shot PMAG, black furniture, 5.8 lbs. New 2013.

| MSR $1,280 | | $1,100 | $940 | $840 | $675 | $550 | $475 | $375 | |

CORE15 MOE M4 RIFLE – 5.56 NATO cal., 16 in. M4 profile barrel with A2 flash hider, choice of GIO or GPO, 30 shot Magpul mag., forged upper and lower receivers, M4 feed ramps, Magpul MOE handguard, MBUS rear sight, Magpul MOE 6-position stock and pistol grip, oversized trigger guard, black furniture, low profile or Picatinny gas block, 5.9-6.2 lbs. New 2012.

| MSR $1,140 | | $1,000 | $840 | $750 | $600 | $500 | $450 | $350 | |

Add $450 for Core15 MOE M4 Piston rifle with gas piston assembly.

CORE15 MOE MID-LENGTH RIFLE – 5.56 NATO cal., GIO, 18 in. heavy stainless steel barrel with polygonal rifling and A2 flash hider, Magpul MOE 6-position pistol grip stock, Magpul 30 shot PMAG, oversized trigger guard, forged upper receiver with flat-top Picatinny rail, forged lower with M4 feed ramps and beveled magwell, enclosed vent. forearm, black furniture, 6.2 lbs. Mfg. 2012-2014.

| | | $1,250 | $1,075 | $975 | $795 | $650 | $495 | $400 | *$1,420* |

* Core15 MOE Mid-Length Piston Rifle – 5.56 NATO cal., similar to Core15 MOE Mid-Length rifle, except has GPO, Magpul MOE handguard, MOE Black or Desert Tan (mfg. 2012 only) hardware, 6.9 lbs. Mfg. 2012-2014.

| | | $1,525 | $1,295 | $1,175 | $950 | $775 | $600 | $500 | *$1,730* |

CORE15 MOE M-LOK RIFLE – 5.56 NATO or .300 AAC Blackout cal., carbine length GIO, 16 in. Govt. profile barrel with black Nitride or black phosphate finish, A2 flash hider, 30 shot PMAG, oversized trigger guard, CORE15 A Frame front sight, Magpul MOE 6-position retractable stock, Magpul MOE M-LOK carbine length forearm, Magpul MOE grip, Hardcore V.2 charging handle, stainless steel gas tube, Mil-Spec buffer tube, forged T6 lower with beveled magwell, forged T6 M4 upper receiver with M4 feed ramps, flat-top Picatinny rail, laser engraved T-markings, Type III hardcoat anodized finish, 6 lbs. New 2016.

| MSR $1,140 | | $975 | $885 | $765 | $655 | $575 | $495 | $435 | |

Add $140 for .300 AAC Blackout cal.

* CORE15 MOE M-LOK Piston Rifle – 5.56 NATO cal., GPO, 16 in. Govt. profile barrel with black Nitride finish, 30 shot PMAG, oversized trigger guard, Magpul MOE 6-position retractable stock, Magpul MOE M-LOK carbine length forearm, Magpul MOE grip, Hardcore V.2 charging handle, stainless steel gas tube, Mil-Spec buffer tube, forged T6 lower with beveled magwell, forged T6 M4 upper receiver with M4 feed ramps, flat-top Picatinny rail, laser engraved T-markings, Type III hardcoat anodized finish, 6 lbs. New 2016.

| MSR $1,590 | | $1,340 | $1,180 | $1,050 | $915 | $785 | $665 | $550 | |

CORE15 SCOUT UL II RIFLE – 5.56 NATO or .300 AAC Blackout cal., carbine length gas system, 16 in. Govt. profile barrel with A2 flash hider and black Nitride or black phosphate finish, Hexmag 30 shot mag., oversized trigger guard, A frame front sight base, CORE15 6-position retractable stock, A2 pistol grip, beveled magwell, Midwest Industries SS Series drop-in modular rail, Mil-Spec forged T6 lower and M4 upper receiver with M4 feed ramps, flat-top Picatinny rail, Mil-Spec buffer tube, Hardcore V.2 billet charging handle, Type III hardcoat anodized finish, 6 lbs. 5 oz.

| MSR $950 | | $815 | $700 | $630 | $570 | $500 | $425 | $380 | |

Add $140 for .300 AAC Blackout cal.

MSR	100%	98%	95%	90%	80%	70%	60%	Last MSR

CORE15 TAC M4 RIFLE – 5.56 NATO cal., GIO, 16 in. M4 profile barrel with A2 flash hider, 30 shot Magpul mag., forged T6 lower receiver with beveled magwell, forged M4 upper receiver with flat-top Picatinny rail, Hardcore V.2 charging handle, free floating quad rail, oversized trigger guard, forged "F" marked A frame front sight base and Magpul MBUS rear sight, Magpul MOE 6-position pistol grip stock, 5.9 lbs. New 2012.

| MSR $1,280 | $1,100 | $940 | $840 | $675 | $550 | $475 | $375 | |

* **CORE15 Tac M4 Piston Rifle** – 5.56 NATO cal., GPO, similar to Core15 Tac M4 Rifle, except has Monolithic Melonite coated bolt carrier group, Picatinny flat-top gas bloc, and Magpul MOE MBUS front and rear sights, 6.2 lbs. New 2012.

| MSR $1,730 | $1,525 | $1,295 | $1,175 | $950 | $775 | $600 | $500 | |

CORE15 TAC M4 UL RIFLE – 5.56 NATO cal., GIO, 16 in. chrome moly M4 profile barrel with A2 flash hider, stainless steel gas tube, A frame front sight base (forged), optional low profile or Picatinny gas block, Magpul MBUS rear sight, 6-position retractable stock with A2 pistol grip, Magpul 30 shot PMAG, forged upper receiver with flat-top Picatinny rail and M4 feed ramps, forged lower with beveled magwell, black furniture, 5.2 lbs. New 2013.

| MSR $1,170 | $1,025 | $865 | $775 | $650 | $550 | $450 | $375 | |

CORE15 TAC M4 V.2 RIFLE – 5.56 NATO cal., 16 in. M4 profile barrel with A2 flash hider, choice of GIO or GPO, flat-top model with full length Picatinny rail on top of receiver and quad rail, Magpul ACS 6-position pistol grip stock, 30 shot Magpul mag., approx. 6 lbs. Mfg. 2012-2013.

| | $1,150 | $975 | $885 | $725 | $585 | $475 | $400 | *$1,299* |

CORE15 TAC 6.5 GRENDEL RIFLE – 6.5mm Grendel cal., rifle length GIO, 18 or 20 in. fluted barrel with black Nitride finish or stainless steel, Lantac Dragon muzzle brake, ASC 25 shot stainless steel mag., oversized trigger guard, Hogue 6-position retractable stock, Hogue pistol grip, KeyMod 15 in. rail, Hardcore V.2 billet charging handle, stainless steel gas tube, low profile gas block, forged upper and lower receivers, M4 feed ramps, flat-top Picatinny rail, beveled magwell, 6 1/2 lbs. New 2016.

| MSR $1,490 | $1,260 | $1,100 | $985 | $835 | $725 | $615 | $515 | |

Add $50 for stainless steel barrel.

CORE15 TAC II .300 BLACKOUT RIFLE – .300 AAC Blackout cal., carbine length GIO, 16 in. stainless steel barrel, forged T6 M4 flat-top upper with internal dry lube and Laser-T markings, V.2 charging handle, Gen 2 free float mid-length quad rail, forged lower receiver with anodized finish, M4 feed ramps, beveled magwell, Magpul ACS 6-position stock, Magpul MOE pistol grip, Magpul 30 shot PMAG, low profile gas block, black furniture, 5.9 lbs. Mfg. 2013-2015.

| | $1,200 | $1,040 | $925 | $750 | $615 | $475 | $400 | *$1,390* |

CORE15 TAC II M4 RIFLE – 5.56 NATO cal., GIO, 16 in. M4 profile barrel with A2 flash hider, forged lower receiver with M4 feed ramps and beveled magwell, forged upper receiver with full length flat-top Picatinny rail, Gen 2 mid-length two-piece quad rail, Magpul ACS 6-position pistol grip stock, 30 shot Magpul mag., V.2 charging handle, oversized trigger, 5.9 lbs. Mfg. 2012-2014.

| | $1,150 | $1,000 | $900 | $750 | $600 | $475 | $400 | *$1,300* |

CORE15 TAC III RIFLE – 5.56 NATO cal., GIO, 16 in. chrome moly barrel with A2 flash hider, low profile gas block, forged lower receiver with beveled magwell, forged upper with M4 feed ramps, flat-top Picatinny rail, Gen 2 SS Series free float forearm, stainless steel gas tube, V.2 charging handle, Magpul MOE MBUS front and rear sights, Magpul MOE 6-position pistol grip stock, Magpul 30 shot PMAG, oversized trigger guard, black, Burnt Bronze (new 2016), or Sniper Gray (new 2016) finish, 5.9 lbs. New 2013.

| MSR $1,390 | $1,200 | $1,040 | $925 | $750 | $615 | $475 | $400 | |

Add $110 for Burnt Bronze or Sniper Grey finish (new 2016).

CORE15 TAC MID-LENGTH RIFLE – 5.56 NATO cal., GIO, 18 in. heavy stainless steel match grade barrel with polygonal rifling and A2 flash hider, forged upper and lower receivers, flat-top receiver with Gen 2 mid-length two-piece quad rail system, V.2 charging handle, Magpul UBR buttstock, Magpul MIAD grip, Magpul 30 shot PMAG, black finish, 8 lbs. Mfg. 2012-2014.

| | $1,425 | $1,225 | $1,100 | $895 | $725 | $575 | $475 | *$1,630* |

* **Core15 TAC Mid-Length Piston Rifle** – 5.56 NATO cal., GPO, similar to Core15 TAC Mid-Length rifle, except has mid-length GPO, adjustable gas settings, Picatinny flat-top gas block, 8.5 lbs. Mfg. 2012-2014.

| | $1,625 | $1,395 | $1,250 | $1,025 | $835 | $650 | $525 | *$1,850* |

CORE15 HARDCORE SYSTEM X RIFLES – 5.56 NATO cal., GIO, 16 or 18 in. barrel, Magpul Gen3 20 or 30 shot mag., 15 in. aluminum KeyMod rail, H2 buffer, angled groove low pro gas block, Magpul MBUS Pro front and rear sights, integral oversized trigger guard, ambidextrous safety, Core15 Hardcore billet solid aluminum alloy upper and lower receivers, Nickel Boron bolt carrier group, stainless steel gas tube, Hardcore scalloped billet charging handle. New 2015.

All X System rifles also include a Boyt HM 44 hardshell case, Magpul 20 and 30 shot magazines, range log, Otis Technologies MSR/AR cleaning system and a Frog Lube Tube.

MSR	100%	98%	95%	90%	80%	70%	60%	Last MSR

CORE15 HARDCORE SYSTEM X1 – 5.56 NATO or 6.5mm Grendel (new 2016) cal., GIO, 16 or 18 (new 2016) in. mid-length fluted barrel with LanTac Dragon muzzle brake, black Nitride finish or stainless steel (new 2016, 18 in. barrel only), Magpul Gen3 20 or 30 shot mag., Magpul MBUS Pro front and rear sights, Magpul ACS stock, black Hogue rubber grip, in-house Sniper Grey Cerakote finish. New 2015.

	100%	98%	95%	90%	80%	70%	60%	
MSR $2,500	$2,125	$1,860	$1,600	$1,450	$1,175	$975	$775	

CORE15 HARDCORE SYSTEM X2 – 5.56 NATO or 6.5mm Grendel (new 2016) cal., GIO, 16 or 18 (new 2016) in. mid-length fluted barrel with LanTac Dragon muzzle brake and black Nitride or stainless steel (new 2016, 18 in. barrel only) finish, Magpul Gen3 20 or 30 shot mag., Magpul MBUS Pro front and rear sights, Magpul UBR collapsible stock, black Hogue rubber grip, in-house Sniper Grey Cerakote finish, includes Leupold MK6 1x16x20 scope with mount and adj. Atlas BT10 Bipod 1913 Picatinny rail mount. New 2015.

	100%	98%	95%	90%	80%	70%	60%	
MSR $5,500	$4,675	$4,095	$3,500	$3,185	$2,575	$2,100	$1,650	

CORE15 HARDCORE SYSTEM X3 – 5.56 NATO or 6.5mm Grendel (new 2016) cal., GIO, 18 or 20 (new 2016) in. fluted rifle length barrel with black Nitride or stainless steel (new 2016, 20 in. barrel only) finish, Magpul Gen3 20 or 30 shot mag., Magpul MBUS Pro front and rear sights, Magpul ACS stock, black Hogue rubber grip, in-house Sniper Grey Cerakote finish. New 2015.

	100%	98%	95%	90%	80%	70%	60%	
MSR $2,600	$2,225	$1,950	$1,675	$1,525	$1,225	$1,000	$800	

CORE15 HARDCORE SYSTEM X4 – 5.56 NATO or 6.5mm Grendel (new 2016) cal., GIO, 18 or 20 (new 2016) in. fluted rifle length barrel with black Nitride or stainless steel (new 2016, 20 in. barrel only) finish, Magpul Gen3 20 or 30 shot mag., Magpul MBUS Pro front and rear sights, Magpul UBR collapsible stock, black Hogue rubber grip, includes Leupold MK6 3x18x44 scope with mount, adj. Atlas BT10 bipod 1913 Picatinny rail mount. New 2015.

	100%	98%	95%	90%	80%	70%	60%	
MSR $5,600	$4,775	$4,185	$3,585	$3,250	$2,625	$2,150	$1,700	

CORE30 MOE RIFLE – .308 Win. cal., GIO, 16 in. CMV mid-length barrel with SureFire SOCOM 3 Prong flash hider, low profile gas block, Magpul MOE 6-position stock and grip, Magpul 20 shot PMAG, Magpul MOE mid-length forearm, aluminum alloy lower and upper with Picatinny rail and Laser engraved T-markings, integral oversized trigger guard, V3 billet charging handle, hardcoat anodized finish, 8 lbs. New 2013.

	100%	98%	95%	90%	80%	70%	60%	
MSR $1,950	$1,700	$1,440	$1,300	$1,050	$875	$750	$650	

CORE30 MOE LR RIFLE – .308 Win. cal., GIO, 18 in. CMV mid-length barrel with SureFire SOCOM muzzle brake, low profile gas block, aluminum alloy upper receiver with Picatinny rail, Geissele SSA-E two-stage match trigger, integral oversized trigger guard, MOE mid-length forearm, Magpul MOE 6-position stock and grip, V3 billet charging handle, anodized finish, Magpul 20 LR PMAG, 8 1/2 lbs. New 2013.

	100%	98%	95%	90%	80%	70%	60%	
MSR $2,350	$2,050	$1,750	$1,550	$1,250	$1,025	$900	$750	

CORE30 MOE M-LOK – 6.5mm Creedmoor cal., low profile gas block, 20 or 22 in. barrel with black Nitride finish, SureFire SOCOM 3 Prong flash hider, Magpul 20 shot PMAG, integral oversized trigger guard, Magpul MOE 6-position stock, Magpul MOE mid-length forearm, Magpul MOE griip, V.3 billet charging handle, Mil-Spec buffer tube, aluminum alloy upper with Picatinny rail and laser engraved T-markings, Type III hardcoat anodized finish, 8 lbs. New 2016.

	100%	98%	95%	90%	80%	70%	60%	
MSR $2,000	$1,700	$1,500	$1,250	$1,100	$950	$825	$675	

* **CORE30 MOE M-LOK Stainless** – 6.5mm Creedmoor cal., similar to CORE30 MOE M-LOK, except has 20 or 22 in. fluted stainless steel barrel with bead blasted finish. New 2016.

	100%	98%	95%	90%	80%	70%	60%	
MSR $2,400	$2,050	$1,800	$1,500	$1,300	$1,075	$935	$795	

CORE30 TAC RIFLE – .308 Win. cal., GIO, 16 in. CMV mid-length barrel with SureFire SOCOM muzzle brake, low profile gas block, Magpul 20 shot LR PMAG, Magpul ACS 6-position stock, Magpul MOE grip, Samson STAR 13.2 in. quad rail, V3 billet charging handle, integral oversized trigger guard, hardcoat anodized finish, Geissele SSA-E two stage match trigger, aluminum alloy lower and upper receiver with Picatinny rail and laser engraved T-markings, black furniture, 9 lbs. Mfg. 2013-2014, reintroduced 2016.

	100%	98%	95%	90%	80%	70%	60%	
MSR $2,470	$2,100	$1,840	$1,575	$1,350	$1,125	$950	$800	

CORE30 TAC LR RIFLE – .308 Win. cal., GIO, 18 in. stainless steel match grade mid-length barrel with SureFire SOCOM muzzle brake, low profile gas block, Magpul 20 LR PMAG, aluminum alloy upper receiver with Picatinny rail, Geissele SSA-E two-stage match trigger, integral oversized trigger guard, Magpul UBR stock, Magpul MIAD grip, APEX Gator grip, 15 in. free float modular forearm, V3 billet charging handle, anodized finish, 9 1/2 lbs. New 2013.

	100%	98%	95%	90%	80%	70%	60%	
MSR $2,880	$2,500	$2,125	$1,900	$1,675	$1,350	$1,000	$895	

CORE30 TAC II RIFLE – .308 Win. or 6.5mm Creedmoor cal., GIO, 16, 18, 20, or 22 in. fluted (6.5mm Creedmoor only) or non-fluted barrel with black Nitride finish or stainless steel, SureFire SOCOM muzzle brake, 20 shot Magpul PMAG, single stage trigger, integral oversized trigger guard, Magpul ACS 6-position stock, Magpul MOE grip, 15 in. KeyMod rail, V.3 billet charging handle, low profile gas block, Mil-Spec buffer tube, aluminum alloy upper and lower receivers, Picatinny rail, Type III hardcoat anodized finish, 9 lbs. New 2016.

	100%	98%	95%	90%	80%	70%	60%	
MSR $2,400	$2,050	$1,800	$1,500	$1,300	$1,075	$935	$795	

Add $70 for 6.5mm Creedmoor cal.

MSR	100%	98%	95%	90%	80%	70%	60%	Last MSR

CORONADO ARMS

Current rifle manufacturer located in Dixon, CA.

CARBINES/RIFLES: SEMI-AUTO

CA-15 CARBINE – 5.56 NATO or 6.8 SPC cal., AR-15 style, GIO, Lothar Walther button rifled barrel, 10 shot mag., Geissele trigger, extended upper and lower receivers, flared and broached magwell, Magpul MOE grip, Magpul STR stock, black hardcoat anodized finish, 7 1/4 lbs.

MSR $1,650	$1,400	$1,235	$1,100	$975	$830	$720	$585

CA-15 COMPETITION CARBINE – .223 Wylde chamber, GIO, 16 in. stainless steel barrel with Crosshill Technologies X-Comp Compensator or muzzle brake, 10 shot mag., Gunfighter Industries Mod 4 charging handle, Geissele 3-gun trigger, KeyMod rifle length handguard, extended upper receiver, adj. gas block, Magpul STR stock, Magpul MOE grip, approx. 8 lbs. New 2015.

MSR $1,995	$1,700	$1,500	$1,250	$1,100	$950	$825	$675

CA-15 RIFLE – 5.56 NATO or 6.8 SPC cal., AR-15 style, GIO, Lothar Walther button rifled and fluted bull barrel, 10 shot mag., mid-length gas system, Geissele two-stage trigger, extended upper and lower receivers, flared and broached magwell, Magpul MOE grip, Magpul PRS stock, black hardcoat anodized finish. New 2014.

MSR $2,450	$2,095	$1,825	$1,525	$1,315	$1,085	$940	$815

CA-15 COMPETITION RIFLE – 5.56 NATO cal., GIO, 18 in. button rifled barrel, .223 Wylde chamber, Competition muzzle brake, rifle length gas system, adj. gas block, 10 shot mag., Gunfighter Industries Mod 4 charging handle, Geissele two-stage trigger, KeyMod rifle length handguard, Magpul MOE+ grip, Magpul PRS stock, 9 1/2 lbs. New 2016.

MSR $2,550	$2,165	$1,900	$1,550	$1,350	$1,115	$965	$835

CROSS CANYON ARMS

Current bolt action rifle manufacturer located in Ogden, UT. Previously located in West Haven, UT.

RIFLES: BOLT ACTION

Cross Canyon Arms manufactures high quality custom bolt action hunting and tactical style rifles chambered for its proprietary Tejas cartridge, as well as short and long actions calibers. **Current models include:** the GC-1000 Hunter ($4,999 MSR or $5,738 for Highcomb stock), GC 1300-XLR ($5,499 for Highcomb or Sporter stock), GC 1000-CORPS ($6,133 for McMillan or $5,922 for Bell & Carlson stock), GC 750-MAX ($5,000 for Sporter stock), XC-500 ($4,000), Big Cottonwood ($2,750 for Sporter or $3,000 for Highcomb stock), Big Cottonwood Varmint ($2,750 for laminate, $3,000 for McMillan, $2,876 for H&S Precision, or $2,836 for Bell & Carlson stock), Big Cottonwood Tactical ($3,395 for McMillan, $3,195 for H&S Precision, or $2,985 for Bell & Carlson stock), Big Cottonwood Teton ($2,750 for Sporter stock). **Previous models included:** Grand Canyon Hunter Extreme Range (last MSR was $5,488 for Sporter stock or $5,738 for Highcomb stock), Grand Canyon Varmint (last MSR was $5,613 for H&S Precision or $5,837 for McMillan stock), Grand Canyon Tactical (last MSR was $5,922, $5,723 for Bell & Carlson, or $6,133 for McMillan stock), Grand Canyon Teton (last MSR was $5,938, $5,488 for Sporter or $5,738 for Highcomb stock), Grand Canyon Dangerous Game (last MSR was $5,688 or $5,488 for Sporter stock), 1/2 Canyon (last MSR was $4,450), Africa Game (dangerous game cals., last MSR was $5,213 for short action or $5,288 for long action), Grand Teton (last MSR was $5,213 for short action or $5,288 for long action), Death Valley (last MSR was $5,213 for short action or $5,288 for long action), and the King's Canyon (last MSR was $2,395). A multitude of options and finishes are available. Please contact the company for more information, including options, delivery time, and pricing (see Trademark Index).

CROSSFIRE LLC

Previous manufacturer located in La Grange, GA 1998-2001.

COMBINATION GUNS

CROSSFIRE MK-I – 12 ga. (3 in. chamber) over .223 Rem. cal., unique slide action O/U design allows stacked shotgun/rifle configuration, 18 3/4 in. shotgun barrel with invector chokes over 16 1/4 in. rifle barrel, detachable 4 (shotgun) and 5 (rifle) shot mags., open sights, Picatinny rail, synthetic stock and forearm, choice of black (MK-I) or RealTree 100% camo (MK-1RT) finish, single trigger with ambidextrous fire control lever, 8.6 lbs. Limited mfg. mid-1998-2001.

	$1,295	$1,150	$995	$895	$795	$695	$595	$1,895

Add $100 for camo finish.

CRUSADER WEAPONRY

Previous manufacturer located in Murray, UT until 2015.

PISTOLS: SEMI-AUTO

G20 WRATH – 10mm cal., SA, SFO, Generation 3 Glock frame, tungsten guide rod, factory weight recoil spring, ghost ring tactical 5 lb. connector (hand fit), extended slide stop, PSI Tac-Rac plug/tool, Trijicon night sights, Slipstream Permanent Pistol Treatment. Disc. 2014.

	$675	$600	$500	$475	$375	$300	$250	$769

MSR	100%	98%	95%	90%	80%	70%	60%	Last MSR

GLOCK PHANTOM (G21 Phantom) – 9mm Para., .40 S&W, .45 ACP, or 10mm cal., SFO, large frame, Tungsten guide rod, extended slide stop, grip plug, ST-2 Permanent Slipstream Treatment. Disc. 2015.

	$660	$575	$510	$440	$385	$340	$325	$769

* ***Glock Reaper (G23 Reaper)*** – 9mm Para. or .40 S&W cal., SFO, mid-compact frame, otherwise similar to Glock Phantom. Disc. 2015.

	$625	$540	$510	$440	$385	$340	$325	$725

* ***Glock Specter (G26 Specter)*** – 9mm Para. or .40 S&W cal., SFO, sub-compact frame, otherwise similar to Glock Phantom. Disc. 2015.

	$625	$540	$510	$440	$385	$340	$325	$725

RIFLES: SEMI-AUTO

BROADSWORD – 7.62 NATO cal., AR-10 patterned rifle, 16, 18, 20, or 24 in. polygonal rifled barrel with BattleComp compensator, billet receiver, Apex free floating handguard, accepts Magpul PMAGs, treated with Slipstream weapon lubricant, includes Plano tactical hard case. Disc. 2015.

	$2,515	$2,185	$1,800	$1,550	$1,275	$1,075	$935	$2,950

GUARDIAN – 5.56 NATO or 6.8 SPC cal., mid-length gas system, 16 in. polygonal rifled barrel with Vortex flash hider, free float handguard, Magpul CTR buttstock, Magpul MIAD grip, Magpul MBUS back-up sights, ambi single point sling attachment, quad rail forend with end cap, Slipstream basic rifle treatment, includes Bulldog hard sided rifle case. Disc. 2015.

	$1,700	$1,500	$1,250	$1,100	$950	$825	$675	$2,000

LONGBOW – 7.62 NATO cal., 24 in. polygonal rifled barrel with BattleComp muzzle brake, Magpul PRS stock, DPMS Panther target grip, JP adj. trigger, Apex handguard, Slipstream basic rifle treatment (Cerakote finishes and airburshed camo are optional), rifle gas system with low profile gas block. Disc. 2015.

	$2,815	$2,465	$1,995	$1,700	$1,400	$1,200	$1,035	$3,297

PALADIN – 5.56 NATO cal., 20 or 24 in. match grade polygonal rifled heavy barrel with target crown, rifle length gas system, low profile gas block, APEX free float tube forearm, target grip, JP trigger, Magpul PRS stock, Slipstream treatment, includes hard case. Disc. 2015.

	$1,795	$1,575	$1,325	$1,150	$995	$850	$700	$2,100

TEMPLAR – 5.56 NATO cal., AR-15 style, mid-length gas system, 18 in. polygonal rifled barrel with BattleComp compensator, Magpul UBR buttstock, Magpul MIAD grip, Magpul MBUS sights, Apex handguard with top rail, Slipstream basic rifle treatment, Plano tactical hard rifle case. Disc. 2015.

	$1,875	$1,650	$1,400	$1,200	$1,025	$875	$725	$2,200

SHOTGUNS: SLIDE ACTION

WRAITH – 12 or 20 ga., adj. rifle sights, extended 6 shot mag., stainless steel magazine follower, Mesa Tactical SureShell shotshell carrier, oversized safety button, Speedfeed stock set, action job, trigger job, Slipstream treatment, Dark Grey Cerakote finish (other colors and camo available upon request). Disc. 2015.

	$850	$725	$650	$585	$515	$450	$395	$999

CZECHPOINT INC.

Current distributor located in Knoxville, TN.

Czechpoint Inc. distributes tactical style semi-auto rifles, including a line of AK-47 design carbines/rifles with milled receivers in various configurations, Skorpion pistols (see model listing under Skorpion heading), and revolvers manufactured in the Czech Republic by D-Technik, Alfa Proj., and others. Please contact the company directly regarding current model availability and pricing (see Trademark Index).

NRA
STAND AND FIGHT

As a member, you will receive these benefits:

- ★ 24/7 defense of your firearm freedoms
- ★ Choice of an award-winning magazine
- ★ $2,500 in ArmsCare® firearms insurance
- ★ $5,000 Life & Accidental Insurance ($10,000 for Life Members)
- ★ Access to NRA's hunting, shooting, and safety programs

JOIN NRA TODAY!

NRA membership is regularly $40 per year. But if you act today, we'll sign you up for a full year of NRA membership for just $25!

Name: _____ XR029490
     First   Last   M.I.

Address: _____

City: _____ State: _____ Zip: _____ D.O.B. ____/____/____

Phone: _____ E-mail: _____

Magazine choice: ☐ *American Rifleman* ☐ *American Hunter* ☐ *America's 1ST Freedom*

Please enclose $25 for your One-Year Membership

☐ Check or money order enclosed, payable to: "NRA"   ☐ Please charge my: ☐ VISA ☐ MasterCard ☐ AMEX ☐ DISCOVER

[Card Number]   Exp. Date: [MO] [YR]

Signature: _____

NRA

To join instantly call 1-800-672-0004

Mail application with payment to:
National Rifle Association of America
c/o Recruiting Programs Department
11250 Waples Mill Road
Fairfax, VA 22030

Contributions, gifts or membership dues made or paid to the National Rifle Association of America are not refundable or transferable and are not deductible as charitable contributions for Federal income tax purposes. International memberships: add $5 for Canadian and $10 for all other countries. Please allow 4 - 6 weeks for membership processing. This membership offer can not be combined with any other discounts or offers. Membership starts the day of processing of dues payments by NRA. Three dollars and seventy-five cents of the annual membership fee is designated for magazine subscription. Insurance benefits are subject to the conditions contained in the Master Policy on file at NRA headquarters at the time a claim arises. There are special exclusions and limitations to such policy. Furthermore, NRA and the Insurers specifically reserve the right to alter or change any conditions in the Master Policy, including, but not limited to, reductions in the amount of coverage, and the cancellation or non-renewal of such policy. Annual Junior members are not eligible for insurance benefits. Affinity card available for applicants who meet all the credit criteria. The moving discount is off the Interstate Commerce Commission approved tariff rate. For specific state by state disclosures, please visit http://www.nra.org/NRA-UniformDisclosureStatement.pdf

D SECTION

D&L SPORTS, INC.

Current manufacturer located in Chino Valley, AZ.

Gunsmith Dave Lauck manufactures a complete line of 1911 style custom pistols, AR-15 style semi-auto carbines, and precision bolt action rifles. A wide variety of options and accessories are available. Additionally, D&L offers custom gunsmithing services. Please contact the company directly for more information, including pricing, options, and delivery time (see Trademark Index).

D.A.R. GmbH (DYNAMICS ARMS RESEARCH)

Current AR-15 style rifle and carbine manufacturer located in Fraureuth, Germany (previously located in Lichentanne, Germany). No current U.S. importation.

RIFLES: SEMI-AUTO

D.A.R. currently manufactures a variety of good quality AR-15 style carbines and rifles in various configurations. Additionally, the company also manufactures a variety of AR-15 style components and mounts. Please contact the company directly for U.S. availability and pricing (see Trademark Index).

DPMS FIREARMS (LLC)

Current trademark manufactured in St. Cloud, MN and by Remington Arms Co. in Huntsville, AL beginning late 2014. Previous manufacturer established in 1986 and located in St. Cloud and Becker, MN. Previous company name was DPMS, Inc. (Defense Procurement Manufacturing Services, Inc.) DPMS Firearms assembles high quality AR-15 style rifles, in addition to related parts and components. Distributor and dealer sales.

In December 2007, Cerberus Capital Management acquired the assets of DPMS. The new company name became DPMS Firearms, LLC, and currently is DPMS Firearms.

MSR	100%	98%	95%	90%	80%	70%	60%	Last MSR

PISTOLS: SEMI-AUTO

PANTHER .22 LR PISTOL – .22 LR cal., GIO, blowback action, 8 1/2 in. heavy chrome moly steel barrel, 10 shot mag., black aircraft aluminum flat-top upper receiver, black forged aircraft aluminum lower receiver, phosphate and hard chrome finished bolt and carrier, aluminum trigger guard, ribbed aluminum tubular handguard, no sights, 4 1/4 lbs. Limited mfg. 2006-2007.

	100%	98%	95%	90%	80%	70%	60%	Last MSR
	$700	$625	$550	$475	$425	$375	$325	$850

PISTOLS: SLIDE ACTION

PANTHER PUMP PISTOL – .223 Rem. cal., GIO, 10 1/2 in. threaded heavy barrel, aluminum handguard incorporates slide action mechanism, pistol grip only (no stock), carrying handle with sights, 5 lbs. Disc. 2007.

	100%	98%	95%	90%	80%	70%	60%	Last MSR
	$1,200	$1,025	$925	$825	$700	$575	$495	$1,600

RIFLES: SEMI-AUTO

Each new DPMS rifle/carbine comes equipped with two mags. (high cap where legal), a nylon web sling, and a cleaning kit. Post-crime bill manufactured DPMS rifles may have pre-ban features, including collapsible stocks, high capacity mags, and a flash hider/compensator. Models with these features are not available in certain states.

The Panther AR-15 Series was introduced in 1993 in various configurations, including semi-auto GIO and slide action, and feature a tactical design in various barrel lengths and configurations, with a 10 or 30 shot mag.

300 AAC BLACKOUT – .300 AAC Blackout cal., 16 in. heavy chrome lined barrel, equipped with Blackout suppressor adapter or an inert slipover mock suppressor (disc. 2014), AP4 stock, choice of carbine or mid-length handguard, 7-7 1/2 lbs. New 2012.

MSR $1,149	100%	98%	95%	90%	80%	70%	60%	Last MSR
	$975	$885	$765	$655	$575	$495	$435	

COMPACT HUNTER – .308 Win. cal., 16 in. Teflon coated stainless steel barrel, B5 System SOPMOD stock, two-stage match trigger, carbon fiber free float handguard, Hogue rubber pistol grip, 7 3/4 lbs. Mfg. 2012-2014.

	100%	98%	95%	90%	80%	70%	60%	Last MSR
	$1,275	$995	$850	$725	$600	$525	$450	$1,499

LITE HUNTER (PANTHER LITE 308/338) – .243 Win., .260 Rem., .308 Win. or .338 Federal cal., 18 (disc. 2012) or 20 (new 2012) in. free-floating barrel, no sights, carbon fiber free-floating handguard, bipod stud, A3 style flat-top, Picatinny rail, A2 stock (new 2012), Hogue rubber grips, various accessories and options available. Mfg. 2009-2014.

	100%	98%	95%	90%	80%	70%	60%	Last MSR
	$1,275	$995	$850	$725	$600	$525	$450	$1,499

LONG RANGE LITE – .308 Win. cal., 24 in. stainless steel barrel, A2 fixed stock, two-stage match trigger, carbon fiber free float handguard, Hogue rubber pistol grip, 10 1/4 lbs. Mfg. 2012-2014.

	100%	98%	95%	90%	80%	70%	60%	Last MSR
	$1,275	$995	$850	$725	$600	$525	$450	$1,499

MSR	100%	98%	95%	90%	80%	70%	60%	Last MSR

MOE WARRIOR – 5.56 NATO cal., 16 in. heavy barrel, Magpul MOE stock, handguard, and pistol grip, back-up sights, sling adapter, enhanced trigger guard, suppressor adapter, black or Dark Earth Magpul MOE furniture, 7.3 lbs. Mfg. 2012-2014.

	100%	98%	95%	90%	80%	70%	60%	Last MSR
	$975	$850	$725	$625	$525	$475	$425	$1,159

TAC2 – 5.56 NATO cal., 16 in. barrel with Panther flash hider, Magpul ACS stock, MOE pistol grip, new M111 modular handguard system, utilizes a full rifle length gas system, A2 front and Magpul rear sights, 8 1/2 lbs. New 2012.

MSR $1,249	$1,050	$950	$815	$715	$625	$535	$450	

TAC20 – .308 Win. cal., 20 in. heavy chrome moly barrel, A2 fixed stock, detachable carry handle, Panther flash hider, 11 1/2 lbs. Mfg. 2012-2015.

	$1,050	$900	$775	$675	$575	$500	$450	$1,299

TPR (TACTICAL PRECISION RIFLE) – 5.56 NATO cal., 20 in. heavy stainless steel barrel with AAC flash hider, M1911 modular handguard, Magpul MOE pistol grip and B5 Systems SOPMOD stock, two stage trigger, 7 3/4 lbs. New 2012.

MSR $1,249	$1,050	$950	$815	$715	$625	$535	$450	

PANTHER A2/A3 CLASSIC – 5.56 NATO cal., 16 (disc.) or 20 in. heavy barrel, ribbed barrel shroud, A3 stock with detachable carrying handle with sights, or A2 fixed stock, 9 lbs. Disc. 2015.

	$825	$700	$600	$500	$450	$395	$350	$980

Add $76 for left-hand variation (Southpaw Panther, disc.)

* **Panther Classic Bulldog** – 20 in. stainless fluted bull barrel, flat-top, adj. buttstock, vented free float handguard, 11 lbs. Disc. 1999.

	$995	$850	$725	$625	$550	$475	$425	$1,219

PANTHER CARBINE 16 – 5.56 NATO cal., 16 in. heavy barrel with A2 birdcage flash hider, A3 flat-top upper, Pardus 6-position collapsible stock, GlacierGuard handguard, A2 pistol grip, 7.1 lbs. Disc. 2015.

	$825	$700	$600	$500	$450	$395	$350	$979

PANTHER 7.62x39mm CARBINE/RIFLE – 7.62x39mm Russian cal., 16 or 20 in. heavy barrel, black Zytel buttstock with trap door assembly, A2 flash hider, A2 pistol grip, 7-9 lbs. Mfg. 2000-2011.

	$695	$600	$525	$450	$400	$375	$335	$850

Add $10 for 20 in. barrel.

PANTHER DCM – .223 Rem. cal., 20 in. stainless steel heavy barrel, National Match sights, two-stage trigger, black Zytel composition buttstock, 9 lbs. Mfg. 1998-2003, reintroduced 2006-2012.

	$925	$800	$675	$595	$525	$450	$400	$1,129

PANTHER CLASSIC SIXTEEN – 5.56 NATO cal., 16 in. lightweight chrome moly (new 2012) or heavy (disc. 2011) barrel with A2 birdcage flash hider, adj. sights, black Zytel composition buttstock (disc.) or A2 fixed pistol grip stock, 7.1 lbs. Mfg. 1998-2014.

	$695	$625	$550	$500	$450	$400	$350	$859

Add $55 for Panther Free Float Sixteen with free floating barrel and vent. handguard (disc. 2008).

A1 LITE 20 (PANTHER LITE A1/A3) – 5.56 NATO cal., 16 (disc.) or 20 (new 2007) in. post-ban chrome moly barrel with A2 birdcage flash hider (new 2007), 1:9 in. twist, non-collapsible fiberite CAR (disc.) or A2 fixed pistol grip stock, choice of forged A1 upper with forward bolt assist or A3 (disc.) carry handle, black Teflon finish, 6-7.3 lbs. Mfg. 2002-2014.

	$695	$625	$550	$450	$400	$360	$325	$829

LITE 16 A3 – 5.56 NATO cal., 16 in. lightweight barrel with A2 birdcage flash hider, forged upper and lower receivers, GlacierGuard handguard, Pardus stock, A2 sights, 6 lbs.

MSR $829	$700	$615	$550	$475	$420	$365	$335	

PANTHER LO-PRO CLASSIC – 5.56 NATO cal., 16 in. bull barrel, A2 fixed stock, flat-top low profile upper receiver with push pin, 7 3/4 lbs. Mfg. 2002-2012.

	$625	$575	$525	$475	$425	$395	$350	$769

PANTHER TUBER – 5.56 NATO cal., 16 in. post-ban heavy free float barrel with full length 2 in. diameter aluminum free float handguard, adj. A2 rear sights. Mfg. 2002-2008.

	$625	$550	$500	$465	$435	$400	$375	$754

PANTHER A2 TACTICAL – 5.56 NATO cal., 16 in. heavy manganese phosphated barrel, standard A2 handguard, 9 3/4 lbs. Mfg. 2004-2013.

	$695	$625	$550	$475	$425	$395	$350	$859

MSR	100%	98%	95%	90%	80%	70%	60%	Last MSR

PANTHER AP4 CARBINE – 5.56 NATO cal., 16 in. M4 contour barrel with A2 flash hider, with or w/o attached Miculek compensator, fixed fiberglass reinforced polymer M4 stock, 7 1/4 lbs. Mfg. 2004-2012.

	$775	$700	$625	$550	$475	$425	$375	$959

Add $54 for Miculek compensator.

* ***Panther AP4 Carbine (Disc.)*** – 6.8x43mm SPC or 5.56x45mm cal., 16 in. barrel, collapsible stock, includes carrying handle, 6 1/2 lbs. Disc.

	$750	$675	$600	$525	$450	$400	$360	$904

PANTHER AP4 A2 CARBINE – 5.56 NATO cal., 16 in. chrome moly steel heavy barrel with A2 flash hider, standard A2 front sight assembly, A2 fixed carry handle and adj. rear sight, forged aircraft aluminum upper and lower receiver, hardcoat anodized Teflon coated black finish, AP4 6-position telescoping fiber reinforced polymer stock, GlacierGuard handguard, 7.1 lbs. New 2006.

MSR $945	$815	$700	$630	$570	$500	$425	$380	

PANTHER A2 CARBINE "THE AGENCY" – 5.56 NATO cal., 16 in. chrome moly steel barrel with A2 flash hider, A3 flat-top forged receiver, two-stage trigger, tactical charging handle, package includes Surefire quad rail and flashlight, EoTech and "Mangonel" rear sights, Ergo Suregrip forearm and collapsible stock, supplied with two 30 shot mags., 7 lbs. Mfg. 2007-2012.

	$1,625	$1,400	$1,175	$995	$850	$725	$600	$2,069

LR-6.5 (PANTHER 6.5) – 6.5mm Creedmoor cal., 24 in. stainless steel free float bull barrel, single rail gas block, no sights, ribbed aluminum free float tube handguard, bipod stud, A3 style flat-top, black Teflon coated, standard A2 black Zytel Mil-Spec stock, A2 pistol grip, 11.3 lbs. Mfg. 2009-2014.

	$995	$875	$750	$650	$575	$500	$450	$1,239

PANTHER 6.8mm CARBINE/RIFLE – 6.8x43mm Rem. SPC cal., 16 (new 2007) or 20 in. chrome moly manganese phosphated steel barrel with A2 flash hider, standard A2 front sight assembly, A3 flat-top upper receiver with detachable carry handle and adj. rear sight, aluminum aircraft alloy lower receiver, black standard A2 Zytel Mil-Spec stock with trap door assembly, A2 handguard, includes two 25 shot mags., approx. 9 lbs. Mfg. 2006-2011.

	$825	$725	$650	$575	$500	$450	$395	$1,019

Add $10 for 20 in. barrel.

PANTHER 6.8 SPCII HUNTER – 6.8x43mm Rem. SPC cal., 18 in. steel barrel with Miculek compensator, aluminum A3 flat-top with forward assist, black Zytel skeletonized A2 stock, mid-length carbine fiber free-floating forearm tube, 7.65 lbs. Mfg. 2011-2012.

	$995	$875	$750	$625	$550	$475	$395	$1,269

PANTHER RECON MID-LENGTH CARBINE – 5.56 NATO or 7.62 NATO (mfg. 2012-2014) cal., 16 in. stainless steel heavy barrel with AAC blackout flash hider, flat-top aluminum upper receiver with Magpul BUIS front and rear sights, mid-length quad rail free floating forearm tube, Magpul MOE stock and pistol grip, 7.7 lbs. New 2011.

MSR $1,197	$975	$825	$700	$600	$525	$475	$400	

Add $430 for .308 Recon (mfg. 2012-2014).

PANTHER LBR CARBINE – 5.56 NATO cal., 16 in. lightweight stainless barrel with A2 flash hider, muzzle brake, flat-top receiver with integral Picatinny rail, Magpul MOE stock with A2 pistol grip, vent free floating handguard with front upper Picatinny rail, 7 1/4 lbs. New 2011.

MSR $979	$830	$700	$630	$570	$500	$425	$380	

* ***Panther LBR DIVA Edition*** – 5.56 NATO cal., similar to Panther LBR, except has 16 in. chrome moly barrel and Leopard print especially for women. Mfg. 2012-2014.

	$825	$725	$625	$495	$450	$395	$350	$979

PRAIRIE PANTHER – 20 in. heavy fluted free float barrel, flat-top, vented handguard, 8 3/4 lbs. Disc. 1999.

	$795	$725	$625	$550	$475	$425	$375	$959

PRAIRIE PANTHER (CURRENT MFG.) – .223 Rem. or 6.8 SPC (black finish only, disc. 2014) cal., 20 in. stainless steel fluted heavy barrel, target crown, carbon fiber free float tube, no sights, hard anodized finish, choice of black with carbon fiber handguard (mfg. 2011-2015), King's Desert Shadow (Desert), King's Snow Shadow (mfg. 2011-2015) or Mossy Oak Brush (Brush) camo coverage, A3 Picatinny rail flat-top, tactical charging handle assembly, Magpul winter trigger guard, skeletonized black Zytel Mil-Spec stock with trap door assembly, A2 pistol grip stock, two-stage trigger, approx. 7.1 lbs. New 2010.

MSR $1,249	$1,050	$950	$815	$715	$625	$535	$450	

Subtract approx. $60 for black finish (disc. 2015).
Add $30 for 6.8 SPC cal. (black finish only, disc. 2014).

MSR	100%	98%	95%	90%	80%	70%	60%	Last MSR

ARCTIC PANTHER – .223 Rem. cal., 20 in. barrel, similar to Prairie Panther, except has white powder coat finish on receiver and aluminum handguard, railed gas block, 9 lbs. Mfg. 1997-2015.

	$975	$825	$700	$600	$525	$460	$415	$1,197

PANTHER BULL/SWEET 16 – .223 Rem. cal., features 16 (Sweet 16), 20, or 24 in. stainless free float bull barrel, flat-top, aluminum forearm, A2 fixed stock, aluminum pistol grip, A2 handguard, railed gas block/optics ready, 7 3/4-9 1/2 lbs.

MSR $979	$830	$700	$630	$570	$500	$425	$380	

Add $10 for 20 in. barrel (Panther Bull 20).

Add $20 for 24 in. barrel (Panther Bull 24).

* ***Panther Bull Classic*** – .223 Rem. cal., 20 in. long one in. bull barrel, adj. sights, 10 lbs. Mfg. 1998-2008.

	$750	$650	$575	$525	$450	$400	$360	$910

Add $200 for SST lower.

* ***Panther Bull Twenty-Four Special*** – 5.56 NATO cal., 24 in. stainless fluted barrel, adj. A2 buttstock with sniper pistol grip, JP trigger, 10 1/4 lbs. Mfg. 1998-2015.

	$1,095	$875	$750	$625	$525	$460	$415	$1,348

* ***Panther Super Bull*** – .223 Rem. cal., 16, 20, or 24 in. extra heavy free float bull barrel, flat-top receiver, handguard, approx. 11 lbs. Mfg. 1997-98, 24 in. model reintroduced during late 2004, disc. 2006.

	$975	$850	$725	$625	$525	$450	$400	$1,199

* ***Panther Super Bull 24*** – 24 in. extra heavy stainless steel bull barrel (1 1/8 in. diameter barrel), flat-top, hi-rider upper receiver, skeletonized A2 buttstock, 11 3/4 lbs. Mfg. 1999-2004.

	$975	$850	$725	$625	$525	$450	$400	$1,199

PANTHER PARDUS – .223 Rem. cal., 16 in. stainless steel free float bull barrel, integrated compensator, titanium nitride plated steel bolt and carrier, three rail extruded upper receiver, aluminum alloy upper and lower receiver, Teflon coated tan or black 6-position telescoping fiber reinforced polymer stock, curved and serrated buttplate, four-rail aluminum handguard, no sights, includes two 30 shot mags., 8.1 lbs. Mfg. 2006-2008.

	$1,295	$1,150	$950	$800	$675	$575	$525	$1,600

PANTHER MK-12 5.56 NATO – 5.56 NATO cal., 18 in. stainless heavy free float barrel with flash hider, one-piece four rail tube and six long rail covers, A3 flat-top receiver, 5-position SOPMOD collapsible stock with tactical pistol grip, two-stage trigger, two 30 round mags., Midwest Industry flip-up sights, 8 3/4 lbs. Mfg. 2007-2014.

	$1,350	$1,150	$950	$800	$700	$600	$500	$1,649

PANTHER MK-12 7.62 NATO – 7.62 NATO cal., 18 in. stainless steel heavy barrel, flash hider, Midwest Industries flip up rear sight, gas block with flip up front sight, A3 Picatinny rail flat-top, aluminum lower receiver, integral trigger guard, Magpul CTR adj. stock, Hogue rubber grip with finger grooves, two-stage match trigger, hardcoat anodized black finish, four rail free float tube, six rail covers, approx. 9.6 lbs. Mfg. 2010-2014.

	$1,450	$1,225	$975	$850	$725	$625	$525	$1,799

PANTHER SDM-R – .223 Rem. cal., 20 in. heavy stainless free float barrel with A2 flash hider, four rail aluminum tube, pistol grip stock, National Match front sight, Harris bipod with rail adapter, two 30 shot mags., 8.85 lbs. Mfg. 2007-2008.

	$1,150	$1,025	$925	$800	$675	$575	$475	$1,404

PANTHER 20TH ANNIVERSARY – .223 Rem. cal., 20 in. stainless steel fluted bull barrel, phosphated steel bolt and carrier, hi-rider forged high polished chrome upper and lower receiver with commemorative engraving, chrome plated charging handle, semi-auto trigger group, aluminum trigger guard and mag. release button, A2 black Zytel Mil-Spec stock with trap door assembly and engraved DPMS logo, no sights, vented aluminum handguard, includes two 30 shot mags., approx. 9 1/2 lbs. Limited mfg. of 100 rifles in 2006.

	$1,795	$1,575	$1,350	$1,225	$985	$825	$625	$1,995

PANTHER RACE GUN – .223 Rem. cal., 24 in. stainless steel barrel with Hot Rod handguard, IronStone steel and aluminum stock with rubber buttplate and brass weights, 16 lbs. Mfg. 2001-2008.

	$1,425	$1,250	$1,050	$950	$850	$725	$600	$1,724

PANTHER SINGLE SHOT – 5.56 NATO cal., 20 in. barrel, A2 black Zytel stock and handguard, single shot only w/o magazine, 9 lbs. Disc. 2008.

	$650	$575	$500	$450	$400	$350	$300	$819

AP4 .22 CAL. CARBINE – .22 LR cal., GIO, 16 in. barrel, GlacierGuard M4 handguard, A2 pistol grip and flash hider, AP4 stock with detachable carry handle, 6 1/2 lbs. Disc. 2014.

	$725	$625	$525	$450	$395	$350	$295	$935

MSR	100%	98%	95%	90%	80%	70%	60%	Last MSR

.22 CAL. BULL CARBINE – .22 LR cal., GIO, 16 in. bull barrel, aluminum handguard, A2 pistol grip and flash hider, fixed A2 stock, no sights, 7.3 lbs. Disc. 2015.

	$750	$675	$600	$525	$450	$395	$325	$935

PANTHER .22 RIFLE – .22 LR cal., AR-15 style receiver, GIO, 16 in. bull barrel, black Teflon metal finish, Picatinny rail, black Zytel A2 buttstock, 7.8 lbs. Mfg. 2003-2008.

	$650	$550	$500	$450	$400	$375	$350	$804

PANTHER DCM .22 LR RIFLE – .22 LR cal., GIO, 20 in. fluted stainless steel H-Bar barrel with 1:16 in. twist, A2 upper receiver with National Match sights, black Teflon finish, A2 stock and handguards, also available with optional DCM handguard system. Mfg. 2004-2008.

	$795	$675	$600	$525	$450	$395	$350	$994

PANTHER AP4 .22 LR RIFLE – .22 LR cal., GIO, 16 in. M4 contoured barrel, M4 handguards and pinned carstock, A3 flat-top upper receiver, detachable carry handle with A2 sights and black Teflon finish, 6 1/2 lbs. Mfg. 2004-2008.

	$695	$625	$550	$475	$400	$350	$300	$894

PANTHER LR-.308 – .308 Win. cal., 24 in. free float bull barrel with 1:10 in. twist, ribbed aluminum forearm tube, aircraft alloy upper/lower, A2 fixed pistol grip stock, black Teflon finish, 11 1/4 lbs. Mfg. mid-2003-2014.

	$975	$875	$750	$650	$575	$500	$450	$1,199

* *Panther LR-.308B* – .308 Win. cal., similar to Long Range Rifle, except has 18 in. chrome moly bull barrel and carbine length aluminum handguard. Mfg. late 2003-2012.

	$975	$875	$750	$650	$575	$500	$450	$1,189

* *Panther LR-.308T* – 7.62 NATO cal., similar to .308B, except has 16 in. H-Bar barrel. Mfg. 2004-2012.

	$975	$875	$750	$650	$575	$500	$450	$1,189

* *Panther LR-.308 AP4* – 7.62 NATO cal., similar to Panther .308 Long Range, except has AP4 six position telescoping fiber reinforced polymer stock. Disc. 2012.

	$1,050	$975	$775	$675	$575	$500	$450	$1,299

* *Panther LR-.308 Classic* – 7.62 NATO cal., similar to Panther LR-308, except has 20 in. barrel, A3 style flat-top receiver and removeable carry handle. Mfg. mid-2008-2014.

	$975	$875	$750	$650	$575	$500	$450	$1,199

PANTHER LR-308C – .308 Win. cal., 20 in. heavy steel free float barrel, features A3 flat-top receiver with detachable carrying handle, standard A2 front sight assembly, four rail standard length tube, two 19 shot mags., 11.1 lbs. Mfg. 2007-2008.

	$995	$875	$775	$675	$575	$500	$425	$1,254

PANTHER LRT-SASS – 7.62 NATO cal., 18 in. stainless steel contoured barrel with Panther flash hider, A3 style flat-top upper receiver solid alumnium lower receiver, AR-15 trigger group, ambi-selector, JP adj. trigger, black waterproof Vltor Clubfoot carbine 5 position (disc.) or Magpul stock, vented handguard and Panther tactical pistol grip, Magpul sights, approx. 11 1/2 lbs. Mfg. 2006-2014.

	$1,725	$1,500	$1,250	$1,025	$875	$750	$625	$2,179

PANTHER MINI-SASS – 5.56 NATO cal., 18 in. stainless steel fluted barrel with Panther flash hider, forged A3 flat-top upper receiver, aircraft aluminum alloy lower receiver, aluminum trigger guard, Magpul PRS stock, tactical pistol grip, Magpul sights, includes Harris bipod, 10 1/4 lbs. New 2008.

MSR $1,599	$1,350	$1,200	$1,075	$950	$815	$700	$575	

PANTHER LR-30S – .300 RSUM cal., 20 in. stainless steel free float fluted bull barrel, aluminum upper and lower receiver, hardcoat anodized Teflon coated black skeletonized synthetic stock, integral trigger guard, ribbed aluminum tube handguard, includes two 4 shot mags., nylon web sling and cleaning kit. Mfg. 2004-2008.

	$995	$875	$750	$650	$550	$500	$425	$1,255

PANTHER LR-204 – .204 Ruger cal., 24 in. fluted stainless steel bull barrel, no sights, A3 flat-top forged upper and lower receiver, semi-auto trigger group, standard A2 black Zytel Mil-Spec stock with trap door assembly, includes two 30 shot mags., 9 3/4 lbs. Mfg. 2006-2015.

	$995	$875	$750	$650	$550	$500	$425	$1,213

PANTHER LR-243 – .243 Win. cal., 20 in. chrome moly steel heavy (disc. 2012) or lightweight (Lite Hunter) free float barrel, no sights, raised Picatinny rail, aluminum upper and lower receiver, standard AR-15 trigger group, skeletonized black Zytel Mil-Spec stock with trap door assembly, ribbed aluminum free float handguard, includes two 19 shot mags., 10 3/4 lbs. Mfg. 2006-2013.

	$1,195	$975	$850	$725	$600	$525	$450	$1,499

MSR	100%	98%	95%	90%	80%	70%	60%	Last MSR

PANTHER LR-260 SERIES – .260 Rem. cal., 18 (mfg. 2007-2012, LR-260L), 20 (LR-260H, Lite Hunter) or 24 (LR-260) in. stainless steel fluted bull barrel, no sights, raised Picatinny rail, thick walled aluminum upper receiver, solid lower receiver, standard AR-15 trigger group, integral trigger guard, A2 black Zytel stock with trap door assembly, includes two 19 shot mags., 11.3 lbs. Mfg. 2006-2014.

	$995	$875	$750	$650	$550	$500	$425	$1,239

Add $260 for 18 in. barrel (LR-260L) with skeletonized stock, Miculek compensator and JRD trigger (disc. 2012).

PANTHER ORACLE – 5.56 NATO or 7.62 NATO (disc. 2015) cal., 16 in. chrome moly heavy barrel, A2 flash hider, gas block with single rail, no sights, GlacierGuards oval carbine length handguard, A3 Picatinny flat-top, hard anodized black finish, integral trigger guard, Pardus 6-position telescoping stock with cheekpiece, A2 pistol grip, curved and serrated buttplate, multiple sling slots, approx. 8.3 lbs. New 2010.

* **Panther Oracle 5.56 NATO cal.**

MSR $655	$575	$500	$435	$365	$325	$280	$265	

Add $30 for stainless steel barrel (disc. 2014).
Add $80 for quad rail handguard (disc. 2014).
Add $110 for ATACS Oracle Carbine (includes ATACS camo coverage), mfg. 2011-2014.

* **Panther Oracle 7.62 NATO cal.** – Disc. 2015.

	$895	$800	$700	$625	$550	$500	$450	$1,099

Add $90 for ATACS Oracle Carbine (includes ATACS camo coverage), new 2011.

PANTHER SPORTICAL – 5.56 NATO or 7.62 NATO cal., 16 in. chrome moly heavy or lite contour barrel, single rail gas block, A2 flash hider, various rails and accessories. Mfg. mid-2008-2015.

	$625	$575	$500	$450	$400	$350	$295	$746

Add $367 for 7.62 NATO cal.

PANTHER REPR – 7.62 NATO cal., 18 in. chrome moly (disc.) or 20 in. fluted stainless steel free float barrel, Gem Tech flash hider/suppressor, micro gas block, A3 style flat-top upper receiver, milled aluminum lower receiver, hardcoat anodized coyote brown finish, removable hinged trigger guard, Picatinny rail, four rail tube handguard, Magpul PRS stock, Hogue rubber grip with finger grooves, 9 1/2 lbs. Mfg. 2009-2014.

	$2,000	$1,725	$1,400	$1,200	$975	$850	$725	$2,589

PANTHER RAPTR CARBINE – 5.56 NATO cal., 16 in. chrome moly steel contoured barrel, 30 shot mag., flash hider, A2 front sight, Mangonel flip up rear sight, Ergo Z-Rail two-piece four rail handguard, Crimson Trace vertical grip with integrated light and laser combination, A3 Picatinny rail flat-top, hardcoat anodized black finish, dust cover, aluminum trigger guard, AP4 6-position telescoping polymer stock, Ergo Ambi SureGrip, 8.2 lbs. Mfg. 2010-2011.

	$1,350	$1,150	$950	$825	$725	$600	$500	$1,649

PANTHER CSAT TACTICAL – 5.56 NATO cal., 16 in. chrome moly steel contoured barrel, 30 shot mag., A2 front sight assembly with A2 front sight post, detachable rear sight, four rail free float tube, A3 Picatinny rail flat-top, aluminum lower receiver, Magpul CTR adj. stock, Magpul MIAD pistol grip, 7.8 lbs. Mfg. 2010-2012.

	$1,450	$1,250	$1,025	$850	$725	$625	$550	$1,799

PANTHER CSAT PERIMETER – 5.56 NATO cal., similar to Tactical, except has 16 in. heavy barrel, approx. 8 lbs. Mfg. 2010-2011.

	$1,450	$1,250	$1,025	$850	$725	$625	$550	$1,799

PANTHER 3G1 – 5.56 NATO or 7.62 NATO (mfg. 2012-2014) cal., 18 in. stainless standard or heavy barrel, 30 shot mag., Miculek compensator, no sights, VTAC modular handguard, bipod stud, A3 Picatinny rail flat-top, black anodized finish, aluminum trigger guard, JP adj. trigger group, Magpul CTR adj. stock, Hogue rubber pistol grip, 7 3/4 lbs. New 2010.

MSR $1,399	$1,200	$1,075	$950	$800	$700	$600	$495	

Add $400 for 7.62 NATO cal. (mfg. 2012-2014).

PANTHER 3G2 – 5.56 NATO cal., 16 in. stainless lightweight barrel with Miculek compensator, Magpul STR buttstock, M111 modular handguard, Ergo rubber pistol grip, and Magpul Gen. 2 BUIS sights, enhanced charging handle, two stage trigger, 7 lbs., 2 oz. Mfg. 2013-2015.

	$1,175	$950	$825	$700	$600	$525	$450	$1,420

GII AP4 – .308 Win. cal., 16 in. lightweight chrome lined barrel with Cancellation Brake flash hider, forged anodized Teflon coated upper and lower receiver, F marked front sight base, Magpul BUIS rear sight, 6-position M4 collapsible stock, carbine length Glacier Guard handguard, A2 pistol grip, matte black finish, 7 1/4 lbs. New 2014.

MSR $1,399	$1,200	$1,075	$950	$800	$700	$600	$495	

GII BULL 24 – .308 Win. cal., 24 in. stainless steel bull barrel, A2 stock, aluminum free float handguard, and no flash hider, 10 lbs. New 2014.

MSR $1,299	$1,100	$995	$875	$735	$650	$550	$465	

MSR	100%	98%	95%	90%	80%	70%	60%	Last MSR

GII HUNTER – .243 Rem. (mfg. 2015 only), .260 Rem. (mfg. 2015 only), .308 Win., or .338 Federal (mfg. 2015 only) cal., 20 in. stainless steel barrel with target crown, no sights, Hogue pistol grip, carbon fiber free float tube handguard, Magpul MOE stock. New 2014.

| MSR $1,599 | $1,350 | $1,200 | $1,075 | $950 | $815 | $700 | $575 | |

GII COMPACT HUNTER – .243 Win., .260 Rem., .308 Win., or .338 Federal cal., 18 in. stainless Teflon coated barrel, carbon fiber free float tube handguard, Magpul MOE stock, Hogue pistol grip, black finish. New 2015.

| MSR $1,599 | $1,350 | $1,200 | $1,075 | $950 | $815 | $700 | $575 | |

GII MOE – .308 Win. cal., 16 in. lightweight chrome-lined barrel, Magpul BUIS sights, MOE carbine stock, Magpul MOE pistol grip, and carbine length MOE handguard. New 2014.

| MSR $1,499 | $1,275 | $1,125 | $1,025 | $875 | $750 | $625 | $525 | |

GII RECON – .308 Win. cal., 16 in. stainless steel bead blasted mid-length barrel with Advanced Armament Blackout silencer adapter, mid-length gas system, forged anodized Teflon coated A3 type upper and lower receiver, Magpul front and rear BUIS sight, Magpul MOE 6-position collapsible stock, Magpul MOE pistol grip, four rail free float tube handguard, matte black finish, 8 1/2 lbs. New 2014.

| MSR $1,659 | $1,400 | $1,235 | $1,100 | $975 | $830 | $720 | $585 | |

GII SASS – .308 Win. cal., mid-length gas system, 18 in. Teflon coated stainless steel fluted bull barrel with Panther flash hider, forged anodized Teflon coated A3 type upper and lower receiver, Magpul front sight and rear BUIS sight, Magpul PRS rifle stock, Harris bipod and adapter, Panther tactical grip, four rail free float tube handguard, matte black finish, 10 1/2 lbs. New 2014.

| MSR $2,279 | $1,940 | $1,685 | $1,425 | $1,225 | $1,030 | $885 | $735 | |

GEN I ORACLE – 7.62 NATO cal., compact, 16 in. heavy barrel, optics ready, GlacierGuard handguard, black finish. New 2016.

| MSR $954 | $815 | $700 | $630 | $570 | $500 | $425 | $380 | |

RIFLES: SLIDE ACTION

PANTHER PUMP RIFLE – .223 Rem. cal., GIO, 20 in. threaded heavy barrel with flash hider, aluminum handguard incorporates slide action mechanism, carrying handle with sights, bayonet lug, designed by Les Branson, 8 1/2 lbs. Disc. 2009.

| | $1,350 | $1,125 | $995 | $875 | $725 | $575 | $495 | *$1,700* |

DRD TACTICAL

Current semi-auto pistol and rifle manufacturer. Dealer and distributor sales.

CARBINES/RIFLES: SEMI-AUTO

CDR-15 – 5.56 NATO or .300 AAC Blackout cal., GIO, hammer forged 16 in. chrome lined or Melonite coated (.300 AAC Blackout only) barrel, carbine or mid-length gas block, 30 shot mag., billet receiver, Magpul CTR stock, MOE grip, 13 in. QD tactical rail, parkerized or matte black finish, custom cut foam hard case, 6.9 lbs.

| MSR $2,091 | $1,785 | $1,565 | $1,325 | $1,150 | $995 | $850 | $700 | |

Add $109 for .300 AAC Blackout cal.

G762 – 7.62x51mm NATO cal., GIO, hammer forged chrome lined 16 or 18 in. barrel, 20 shot mag., accepts standard G3/HK 91 magazines, billet upper and lower receiver, 1913 mounting rail accepts Magpul L4 panels at 3, 6, and 9 o'clock positions, tactical buttstock, black hardcoat anodized finish, includes hard case, 8.7 lbs. Disc. 2015.

| | $2,775 | $2,430 | $2,080 | $1,885 | $1,525 | $1,250 | $1,000 | *$3,250* |

KIVAARI 338 – .338 Lapua Mag. cal., GIO, 24 in. quick takedown barrel with Silencer Co. QD muzzle brake, billet aluminum receiver, ambidextrous safety, bolt catch, and mag. release, non-reciprocating left side charging handle, two 10 shot mags., 17 in. Magpul M-LOK rail, Magpul PRS fully adj. stock, includes Atlas adj. bipod and choice of Tactical Tailor Trekker backpack or hard case, 14.6 lbs. New mid-2015.

| MSR $6,900 | $5,875 | $5,140 | $4,400 | $3,995 | $3,230 | $2,650 | $2,075 | |

M762 – 7.62x51mm NATO cal., GIO, hammer forged chrome lined 16 or 18 in. barrel with flash suppressor, two 20 shot round PMAGs, billet upper and lower receiver, Magpul MOE stock/grip, quick takedown 13 in. rail, includes hard case with pistol tray, black hardcoat anodized finish, 8.7 lbs.

| MSR $3,250 | $2,775 | $2,430 | $2,080 | $1,885 | $1,525 | $1,250 | $1,000 | |

PARATUS P762 GEN 2 – 7.62x51mm NATO cal., GIO, designed for quick takedown, hammer forged chrome lined 16 or 18 in. barrel, 20 shot mag., billet upper and lower receiver, 1913 mounting rail, Magpul adj. folding stock and grips, Geissele two-stage trigger, black hardcoat anodized or nickel boron finish, includes small hard case, backpack, or diplomatic attaché case, 9.2 lbs.

| MSR $6,000 | $5,100 | $4,465 | $3,825 | $3,475 | $2,800 | $2,300 | $1,800 | |

MSR	100%	98%	95%	90%	80%	70%	60%	Last MSR

PISTOLS: SEMI-AUTO

CDR15 10.5 – .223 Rem./5.56 NATO cal., GIO, 10 1/2 in. melanite coated steel barrel with flash hider, 30 shot Magpul PMag., billet aluminum receivers, DRD QD 7 in. 1913 rail with Magpul L-4 rail panels, hardcoat black anodized finish, 5.2 lbs. Mfg. 2015 only.

	$850	$725	$650	$585	$515	$450	$395	$995

CDR15 11.5 – 5.56 NATO cal., GIO, 11 1/2 in. hammer forged barrel, 30 shot Magpul PMag., DRD quick takedown 7 in. rail with Magpul L-4 rail panels, billet aluminum receivers, hardcoat black anodized finish, 5.4 lbs. Mfg. 2015 only.

	$960	$875	$740	$625	$550	$475	$425	$1,150

M762 – 7.62x51mm NATO/.308 cal., GIO, 12 in. Lothar-Walther stainless steel barrel with Noveske KX3 flash suppressor, 20 shot mag., AR15-type safety selector, Magpul MOE grips, Sig SB15 pistol stabilizing brace, DRD QD 13 in. 1913 rail with Magpul L-4 rail panels, hardcoat black anodized finish, includes custom cut foam hard case with pistol tray, 8.8 lbs. Mfg. 2015 only.

	$2,550	$2,225	$1,825	$1,575	$1,300	$1,100	$950	$2,995

M762 12 IN. – 7.62 NATO cal., GIO, 12 in. stainless steel barrel, two 20 shot Magpul PMags., billet aluminum receivers, DRD quick takedown 9 in. rail with Magpul L4 rail panels, hardcoat black anodized finish, 8 1/2 lbs. Mfg. 2015 only.

	$1,575	$1,380	$1,190	$1,050	$900	$775	$625	$1,850

DSA INC.

Current manufacturer, importer, and distributor of semi-auto rifles and related components located in Barrington, IL. Previously located in Round Lake and Grayslake, IL.

DSA Inc. is a manufacturer of FAL design and SA58 style rifles for both civilian and law enforcement purposes (L.E. certificates must be filled out for L.E. purchases). Until recently, DSA, Inc. also imported a sporterized Sig 550 rifle.

PISTOLS: SEMI-AUTO

SA58 TACTICAL PISTOL – 7.62 NATO cal., 8 in. barrel with A2 flash hider, based on SA58 FAL design, detachable 10 or 20 shot mag., Type 1 or 2 receiver, black glass filled nylon furniture, Para. extended scope mount, lightweight alloy lower receiver, SAW pistol grip, folding cocking handle, includes sling and hard case, 9 1/2 lbs. New 2013.

MSR $1,695	$1,475	$1,275	$1,150	$950	$775	$625	$550	

RIFLES: BOLT ACTION

DS-MP1 – .308 Win. cal., 22 in. match grade barrel, Rem. 700 action with Badger Ordnance precision ground heavy recoil lug, trued bolt face and lugs, hand lapped stainless steel barrel with recessed target crown, black McMillan A5 pillar bedded stock, Picatinny rail, includes test target guaranteeing 1/2 MOA at 100 yards, black or camo Duracoat finish, 11 1/2 lbs. Mfg. 2004-2009.

	$2,500	$2,150	$1,800	$1,550	$1,250	$1,000	$850	$2,800

RIFLES: SEMI-AUTO

The SA-58 and ZM-4 rifles listed are available in a standard DuraCoat solid or camo pattern finishes. Patterns include: ACU, Advanced Tiger Stripe, Afghan, AmStripe, Belgian, Belgian Digital, Belgian Advanced Tiger Stripe, Black Forest MirageFlage, Desert MirageFlage, MultiColor, OD MirageFlage, Mossy Oak Breakup (disc.), Rhodesian, Thailand Marine, Tiger Stripe (disc.), Underbrush (disc.), Urban MirageFlage, Urban Tiger Stripe, Vietnam Tiger stripe (disc.), Wilderness MirageFlage, Winter Twig (disc.), or Woodland Prestige. DSA Inc. makes three types of forged steel receivers, and they are distinguished by the machining cuts on Types I and II, and no cuts on Type III.

Add $50 for MK16 fluted M4 barrel.
Add $65 for stainless steel M4 barrel.
Add $90 for Magpul MOE furniture.

DS-AR SERIES – .223 Rem cal., GIO, available in a variety of configurations including carbine and rifle, standard or bull barrels, various options, stock colors and features. Mfg. 2006-2008.

	$875	$775	$675	$575	$495	$450	$395	$1,000

Add $243 for SOPMOD Carbine. Add $30 for 1R Carbine. Add $150 for 1V Carbine. Add $130 for S1 Bull rifle. Add $500 for DCM rifle. Add $30 for XM Carbine.
Add $1,395 - $1,515 for monolithic rail platform. Add $675 for Z4 GTC Carbine with corrosion resistant operating system.

DS-CV1 CARBINE – 5.56 NATO cal., GIO, 16 in. chrome moly D4 barrel with press on mock flash hider, fixed Shorty buttstock, D4 handguard and heatshield, forged front sight base, forged lower receiver, forged flat-top upper receiver, variety of Duracoat solid or camo finishes available, 6 1/4 lbs. Mfg. 2004-2005.

	$775	$700	$625	$550	$500	$450	$400	$850

MSR	100%	98%	95%	90%	80%	70%	60%	Last MSR

DS-LE4 CARBINE – 5.56 NATO cal., GIO, 16 in. chrome moly D4 barrel with threaded A2 flash hider, collapsible CAR buttstock, D4 handguard with heatshield, forged lower receiver, forged front sight base with bayonet lug, forged flat-top upper receiver, Duracoat solid or camo finish, 6.15 or 6 1/4 lbs. Mfg. 2004-2012.

  Retail pricing was not available for this model.

DS-S1 – .223 Win. cal., GIO, 16, 20, or 24 in. match chamber stainless steel free float bull barrel, A2 buttstock, aluminum handguard, Picatinny gas block sight base, forged lower receiver, NM two-stage trigger, forged flat-top upper receiver, optional fluted barrel, variety of Duracoat solid or camo finishes available, 8-10 lbs. Mfg. 2004-2005.

	$825	$750	$625	$525	$425	$375	$325	$950

IMBEL 58 – .308 Win. cal., Imbel FAL standard rifle with 21 in. original Imbel barrel, DSA Type 1 carry handle cut receiver, original flash hider, U.S. humpback stock and handguard. Mfg. 2011-2012.

	$875	$775	$650	$525	$450	$375	$325	$995

RPD CARBINE – 7.62x39 cal., 17 1/2 in. fluted barrel, billet machined receiver, belt fed, quad rail handguard, SAW style pistol grip, fully adj. AR15 style stock, lightweight alloy lower trigger frame, includes two 100 shot belt and drum sets, carry bag, sling, hard case, approx. 14 lbs. New 2013.

MSR $2,850	$2,425	$2,100	$1,750	$1,500	$1,225	$1,035	$910	

RPD TRADITIONAL RIFLE – 7.62x39 cal., 20 1/2 in. barrel, billet machined receiver, belt fed, wood stock, includes two 100 shot belt and drum sets, carry bag, sling, hard case, approx. 17 lbs. New 2013.

MSR $2,200	$1,875	$1,650	$1,400	$1,200	$1,025	$875	$725	

SA58 STANDARD RIFLE/CARBINE – .308 Win/7.62x51mm cal., FAL design using high precision CNC machinery, 16 (carbine, disc.), 18 (carbine, disc.), 19 (disc. 2012), 21 (rifle), or 24 (bull only, disc. 2009) in. steel or stainless steel (disc.) barrel, Belgian flash hider, black synthetic (disc.), X-Series, or Humpback stock, pistol grip (standard 2001) attached to frame, 10 or 20 shot mag., lightweight alloy lower receiver, Type 1 or 2 receiver, includes sling and hard case, 8.7-11 lbs.

MSR $1,700	$1,450	$1,275	$1,125	$1,000	$850	$735	$595	

Add $150 for bull barrel (disc. 2009).
Add $250 for stainless steel barrel (disc.).

* **SA58 Standard Rifle Predator** – .243 Win., .260 Rem., or .308 Win. cal., Type 1 or Type 3 receiver, 16 or 19 in. barrel with target crown, green fiberglass furniture, Picatinny rail, 5 or 10 shot mag., approx. 9 lbs. Mfg. 2003-2012.

	$1,525	$1,275	$1,050	$875	$775	$675	$575	$1,750

* **SA58 Standard Rifle Gray Wolf** – .300 WSM (disc. 2005) or .308 Win. cal., Type 1 or Type 3 receiver, 21 in. bull barrel with target crown, gray aluminum handguard, synthetic stock and adj. pistol grip, Picatinny rail, 5 or 10 shot mag., approx. 13 lbs. Mfg. 2003-2010.

	$1,950	$1,750	$1,450	$1,250	$1,050	$875	$775	$2,295

* **SA58 Standard Rifle Collectors Series** – .308 Win. cal., configurations included the Congo ($1,970 - last MSR), Para Congo ($2,220 - last MSR), and the G1 ($2,000 - last MSR). Mfg. 2003-2010.
  Add $230 for Duracoat finish.

* **SA58 Standard Rifle T48 Replica** – .308 Win. cal., 10 or 20 shot fixed mag., stripper clip top cover, cryogenically treated barrel, wood furniture, replica Browning flash hider. Imported 2002-2008.

	$1,500	$1,275	$1,050	$850	$725	$625	$525	$1,795

* **SA58 Tactical Carbine** – similar to SA58 Standard Rifle, except has 16 1/4 in. barrel, 8 1/4 lbs. Mfg. 1999-2012.

	$1,495	$1,250	$1,050	$875	$775	$675	$575	$1,700

Add $275 for Para folding stock.
Add $200 for SA58 Lightweight Carbine with aluminum receiver components (disc. 2004).
Add $250 for SA58 Stainless Steel Carbine (included scope mount through 2000).
Subtract 5% if w/o fluted barrel (became standard 2009).

SA58 CARBINE – 7.62x51mm cal., 16 1/4 or 18 in. threaded barrel with Belgian flash hider, 20 shot mag., Type I or II receiver, glass filled nylon furniture, lightweight alloy lower receiver, X-Series or Humpback stock, includes sling and hard case. New 2011.

MSR $1,700	$1,450	$1,275	$1,125	$1,000	$850	$735	$595	

SA58 CTC (COMPACT TACTICAL CARBINE) – .308 Win./7.62 NATO cal., 16 1/2 in. fluted medium contour barrel with A2 flash hider, detachable 10 or 20 shot mag., SA58 Type I or II receiver, lightweight aluminum lower, short military grade handguard, folding Para stock, synthetic pistol grip, front sight post, rear peep sight, includes adj. sling and hard gun case, 8.25 lbs.

MSR $1,975	$1,660	$1,465	$1,225	$1,085	$935	$800	$660	

Subtract $275 for X-Series or Humpback stock.

MSR	100%	98%	95%	90%	80%	70%	60%	Last MSR

SA58 DMR (DESIGNATED MARKSMAN RIFLE) – .308 Win./7.62 NATO cal., 16 1/2 in. fluted barrel, Type 1 receiver, detachable 10 or 20 shot mag., lightweight aluminum A2 Hampton lower, Vltor CAS-V short rail handguard/ bipod, front sight post, M16A2 adj. rear sight, Magpul PRS fixed buttstock, Saw pistol grip, SA58 extended Extreme Duty scope mount, 12 .4 lbs. New 2015.

Please contact the manufacturer directly for pricing on this model.

SA58 MEDIUM CONTOUR – .223 Rem. (disc.) or .308 Win./7.62 NATO cal., standard configuration, 21 in. medium contour barrel with Belgian short flash hider, detachable 10 or 20 shot mag., Type I or II receiver, lightweight alloy (disc.) or aluminum lower, injection molded fiberglass reinforced handguard, front sight post and rear peep sight, standard synthetic or X-Series buttstock, synthetic pistol grip. New 2011.

MSR $1,700	$1,495	$1,250	$1,050	$875	$775	$675	$575	

Add $150 for .223 Rem. cal. (disc.).

SA58 PLUMP CONTOUR – .223 Rem. (disc.) or .308 Win./7.62 NATO cal., standard configuration, 21 in. plump contour barrel with Belgian waffle short flash hider, detachable 10 or 20 shot mag., Type I or II receiver, lightweight alloy (disc.) or aluminum lower, injection molded fiberglass reinforced handguard, front sight post and rear peep sight, standard synthetic or X-Series buttstock, synthetic pistol grip. New 2011.

MSR $1,700	$1,495	$1,250	$1,050	$875	$775	$675	$575	

Add $150 for .223 Rem. cal. (disc.).

SA58 PARA CARBINE/RIFLE – 7.62x51mm cal., 16, 18, or 21 in. threaded barrel with Belgian flash hider, Type I or II receiver, lightweight alloy Para lower receiver, 20 shot mag., glass filled nylon furniture, Para. folding stock, includes sling and hard case. New 2011.

MSR $1,975	$1,675	$1,460	$1,225	$1,085	$935	$800	$660	

SA58 PREDATOR – .308 Win./7.62 NATO cal., standard configuration, 16 or 19 in. medium contour barrel with target crown, detachable 5 or 10 shot mag., SA58 Type 1 receiver, lightweight aluminum lower, injection molded fiberglass reinforced handguard with OD Green finish, adj. front sight post and rear peep sights, standard synthetic or X-Series buttstock and synthetic pistol grip in OD Green finish, SA58 Extreme Duty scope mount, also includes adj. sling and hard gun case. New 2015.

Please contact the company directly for pricing, options, and availability for this model (see Trademark Index).

SA58 SPARTAN – .308 Win. cal., 16 or 18 in. barrel with Steyr short flash hider (disc.) or YHM Phantom flash hider, Type 1 non-carry handle cut receiver with Spartan Series logo, aluminum lower receiver, DSA custom shop speed trigger, tactical para. rear sight, post front sight, standard synthetic buttstock, SAW pistol grip, military grade handguard, Black DuraCoat finish or Black with OD Green finish, three detachable 20 shot mags., adj. sling and case. Mfg. 2009-2015.

	$2,200	$1,925	$1,600	$1,375	$1,125	$975	$850	*$2,595*

* **SA58 Spartan Tactical** – 7.62 NATO cal., 16 in. fluted medium contour barrel with Trident flash hider, Type 1 Spartan marked receiver, short gas system handguards, DSA speed trigger, three 20 shot mags., SOCOM Para folding stock, SAW pistol grip, all black or black/green DuraCoat finish. Disc. 2015.

	$2,375	$2,075	$1,725	$1,475	$1,200	$1,025	$895	*$2,795*

SA58 SPR (SPECIAL PURPOSE RIFLE) – .308 Win./7.62 NATO cal., 19 in. fully fluted premium barrel, Trident (disc.) or SilencerCo trifecta (new 2015) flash hider, Type I forged receiver, detachable 10 or 20 shot mag., match grade speed trigger, long rail interface handguard, extended Extreme Duty scope mount, SPR side folding adj. stock, SAW pistol grip, Magpul Pro front and rear steel sights, ambidextrous safety, BT Industries vertical front grip and adj. monopod (new 2015), rail mounted bipod, DuraCoat finish, includes adj. sling, hard case, and Leupold 3.5x10x40 MK4 optic (new 2015), 13.8 lbs. New 2009.

MSR $5,795	$4,950	$4,350	$3,800	$3,100	$2,675	$2,450	$2,100	

SA58 TARGET – .308 Win./7.62 NATO cal., 21 in. premium medium contour barrel with target crown, Type 1 receiver, lightweight aluminum lower, alloy free-float tube with textured finish, elevated front sight post and rear peep sight, detachable 10 or 20 shot mag., standard synthetic or X-Series buttstock, synthetic pistol grip, includes hard gun case, 11.1 lbs. New 2015.

Please contact the company directly for pricing, options, and availability for this model.

SA58 VOYAGER – .308 Win./7.62 NATO cal., 21 in. premium threaded barrel with Belgian short flash hider, detachable 10 or 20 shot mag., Type 1 None carry handle cut cast receiver, lightweight aluminum lower, injection molded fiberglass reinforced military grade handguard, Holland style rear sight, adj. post front sight, standard synthetic buttstock and pistol grip, includes adj. sling and hard gun case, 9.75 lbs. New 2014.

MSR $1,200	$1,025	$925	$800	$685	$595	$515	$440	

MSR	100%	98%	95%	90%	80%	70%	60%	*Last MSR*

STG58 AUSTRIAN FAL – .308 Win. cal., features choice of DSA Type I or Type II upper receiver, carry handle, steel lower receiver, rifle has long flash hider, carbine has Steyr short flash hider, steel handguard with bipod cut, metric FAL buttstock and pistol grip, adj. front and rear sight, 10 or 20 shot detachable mag., 10-10.4 lbs. Imported 2006-2008, reimported 2011-2012.

	$995	$895	$800	$700	$600	$500	$400	*$1,150*

Add $50 for carbine.
Add $290 for rifle with folding stock (disc. 2008).
Add $340 for carbine with folding stock (disc. 2008).

ZM-4 SERIES – .223 Rem./5.56 NATO or .300 AAC Blackout (disc. 2015) cal., GIO, 16 or 20 in. barrel, forged upper and lower receiver, various configurations, black finish, detachable magazine, hard case. New 2004.

* **ZM-4 .300 Blackout** – .300 AAC Blackout cal., GIO, 16 in. blue or stainless steel barrel with Trident flash hider, A3 flat-top alloy receiver, forged front sight base with bayonet lug, M4 handguard with heat shield, Hogue pistol grip, 6-position collapsible M4 stock, matte black finish. Mfg. 2013-2015.

	$725	$650	$580	$515	$450	$385	$340	*$853*

Add $20 for stainless steel barrel.

* **ZM-4 A2 Carbine** – 5.56 NATO cal., 16 in. M4 barrel with A2 flash hider, alloy upper and lower receiver, A2 carry handle receiver, forged front sight base with bayonet lug, M4 handguard with heat shield, 6-position collapsible M4 stock. Disc. 2015.

	$695	$615	$550	$475	$420	$365	$335	*$831*

* **ZM-4 A2 Rifle** – 5.56 NATO cal., 20 in. M4 barrel with A2 flash hider, alloy upper and lower receiver, A2 carry handle receiver, forged front sight base with bayonet lug, rifle length handguard with heat shield, fixed A2 stock, Hogue pistol grip. Disc. 2015.

	$710	$630	$550	$475	$420	$365	$335	*$844*

* **ZM-4 Flat-Top Carbine With Rail** – 5.56 NATO cal., 16 in. M4 barrel with A2 flash hider, alloy lower and A3 flat-top upper receiver, forged front sight base with bayonet lug, folding detachable rear sight, carbine length quad rail handguard, 6-pos. collapsible M4 stock, Hogue pistol grip. Mfg. 2015 only.

	$885	$785	$685	$600	$535	$465	$415	*$1,050*

* **ZM-4 Gas Piston CQB** – .223 Rem. cal., GPO, 16 in. chrome lined free floating barrel, Mil-Spec forged lower receiver, CQB forged upper receiver, one piece bolt carrier, quick change barrel system, collapsible CAR stock, detachable 30 shot mag., A2 flash hider. Disc. 2010.

	$2,425	$2,150	$1,625	$1,475	$1,300	$1,125	$950	*$2,870*

* **ZM-4 MIDFAL** – 5.56 NATO cal., 16 in. chrome moly barrel with FAL Belgian style flash hider, detachable mag., forged alloy lower and flat-top upper receiver, forged front sight base with bayonet lug, enhanced steel charging handle and Delta ring, ambi selector switch, folding rear iron sight, Magpul enhanced trigger guard, Magpul MOE mid-length handguard, Magpul MOE pistol grip, Magpul or ACE fixed skeleton stock, includes hard gun case. Mfg. 2013-2015.

	$800	$700	$615	$550	$485	$415	$370	*$936*

* **ZM-4 Mid-Length Carbine** – 5.56 NATO cal., 16 in. fluted or non-fluted mid-length barrel with A2 flash hider, M4 A3 flat-top receiver, forged front sight base with bayonet lug, mid-length handguards with heat shield, alloy upper and lower receiver, 6-pos. collapsible M4 stock, Hogue pistol grip.

MSR $834	$710	$625	$550	$475	$420	$365	$335	

Add $13 for fluted barrel.

* **ZM-4 MK16 (Enhanced Carbine)** – 5.56 NATO cal., GIO, 16 in. enhanced MK16 fluted M4 barrel with YHM muzzle brake, alloy lower and A3 flat-top upper receiver, forged front sight base with bayonet lug, ambidextrous selector switch, enhanced Delta ring, Magpul MOE handguard, six position MOE stock, Magpul MOE pistol grip, matte black finish. Mfg. 2013-2015.

	$790	$685	$615	$550	$485	$415	$370	*$929*

* **ZM-4 M.R.C. (MULTI-ROLE CARBINE)** – 5.56 NATO cal., GIO, 16 in. chrome lined heavy barrel, 3 prong Trident flash hider, steel low profile gas block, Magpul PMAG, Magpul MBUS front and rear sights, 13 1/2 in. Diamondhead USA VRS-T handguard, BCM Ambi Gunfighter charging handle, Mil-Spec 6-position buffer tube, B5 Systems SOPMOD stock, Hogue pistol grip. New 2016.

MSR $1,275	$1,060	$950	$815	$715	$625	$535	$450	

* **ZM-4 Spartan** – .223 Rem. cal., GIO, 16 in. fluted chrome moly barrel, Yankee Hill Machine Phantom flash hider, Mil-Spec forged lower and flat-top upper receiver, forged front sight base with lug, Magpul trigger guard, Robar NP3 bolt, carrier, and charging handle, Hogue pistol grip, SOPMOD collapsible stock, and two-piece rail system became standard 2013, 6.65 lbs. Disc. 2014.

	$1,225	$1,075	$925	$825	$700	$575	$450	*$1,455*

MSR	100%	98%	95%	90%	80%	70%	60%	Last MSR

»**ZM-4 Spartan Leo** – 5.56 NATO cal., 16 in. fluted chrome moly barrel with Yankee Hill Machine Phantom flash hider, detachable mag., forged lower with Spartan Series logo, forged flat-top upper with mid-length gas system and forged front sight base, Rock River Arms competition trigger, Magpul trigger guard, Yankee Hill Machine two-piece rail system and plastic handguard, LMT SOPMOD collapsible stock, Hogue pistol grip, includes hard gun case, 7 lbs. Disc. 2015.

	100%	98%	95%	90%	80%	70%	60%	Last MSR
	$1,235	$1,100	$985	$835	$725	$615	$515	$1,455

* **ZM-4 Standard Flat-Top Carbine** – .223 Rem./5.56 NATO cal., GIO, 16 in. chrome moly M4 barrel with A2 flash hider, detachable mag., Mil-Spec forged lower and A3 flat-top upper receiver, forged front sight base with bayonet lug, M4 handguard with heat shield, 6-pos. collapsible M4 stock, Hogue pistol grip, includes hard gun case, 6 1/4 lbs.

MSR $850								
	$725	$650	$580	$515	$450	$385	$340	

Subtract $62 if without chrome lined barrel.

* **ZM-4 Standard Flat-Top Rifle** – 5.56 NATO cal., 20 in. M4 barrel with A2 flash hider, alloy lower and A3 flat-top upper receiver, forged front sight base with bayonet lug, rifle length handguard with heat shield, fixed A2 stock, Hogue pistol grip.

MSR $820								
	$695	$615	$550	$475	$420	$365	$335	

* **ZM-4 Standard MRP** – .223 Rem. cal., GIO, 16 or 18 in. chrome lined (16 in.) or stainless steel free float barrel, Mil-Spec forged lower receiver, LMT MRP forged upper receiver with 20 1/2 in. full length quad rail, LMT enhanced bolt, dual extractor springs, collapsible CAR stock, detachable 30 shot mag., A2 flash hider. Disc. 2010.

	100%	98%	95%	90%	80%	70%	60%	Last MSR
	$2,275	$1,995	$1,750	$1,550	$1,325	$1,125	$950	$2,695

Add $100 for stainless steel barrel.

* **ZM-4 War Z M4 Rifle** – 5.56 NATO cal., GIO, 16 in. lightweight stainless steel barrel, SureFire Pro Comp muzzle device, Magpul PMAG, steel micro gas block, A.R.M.S. front and rear sights, 15 in. Midwest Industries Gen III stainless steel handguard, forged lightweight enhanced upper receiver, BCM Ambi Gunfighter charging handle, Mil-Spec 6-position buffer tube, enhanced trigger guard, B5 Systems SOPMOD stock, Magpul MIAD pistol grip, Seekins Precision ambi selector switch. New 2016.

MSR $1,495								
	$1,275	$1,125	$1,025	$875	$750	$625	$525	

* **ZM-4 WerkerZ V1 Rifle** – 5.56 NATO cal., GIO, 16 in. fluted steel barrel, 3 prong Trident flash hider, Magpul PMAG, Magpul MOE M-LOK handguard, enhanced contour delta ring, Picatinny gas block, forged lightweight enhanced upper receiver, Mil-Spec forged alloy charging handle, enhanced trigger guard, B5 Systems SOPMOD stock, Magpul MOE pistol grip. New 2016.

MSR $965								
	$820	$700	$630	$570	$500	$425	$380	

* **ZM-4 WerkerZ V2 Rifle** – 5.56 NATO cal., GIO, 16 in. fluted heavy chrome lined barrel, 3 prong Trident flash hider, Magpul PMAG, Magpul SL Series M-LOK handguard, enhanced contour delta ring, Picatinny gas block, forged lightweight enhanced upper receiver, forged steel charging handle, Mil-Spec 6-position buffer tube, enhanced trigger guard, B5 Systems SOPMOD stock, Magpul MOE pistol grip. New 2016.

MSR $1,065								
	$890	$785	$685	$600	$535	$465	$415	

Z-IAR RIFLE – 5.56 NATO cal., GIO, 16 in. chrome moly fluted barrel with A2 flash hider, detachable mag., forged lower with ambi safety switch, forged flat-top upper with steel charging handle, Vltor rail interface handguard system with customizable rails, Vltor collapsible stock, incorporates new features such as Bufferloc and Keyloc technologies, includes hard gun case, 8.4 lbs. Mfg. 2015 only.

Retail pricing wasn't made available for this model.

DAEWOO

Previous commercial firearms manufacturer located in Korea. Previous limited importation by Century International Arms, located in Delray Beach, FL. Previous importation included Kimber of America, Inc. until 1997, Daewoo Precision Industries, Ltd., until mid-1996, located in Southampton, PA, and previously distributed by Nationwide Sports Distributors 1993-96. Previously imported by KBI, Inc. and Firstshot, Inc., both located in Harrisburg, PA, and B-West located in Tucson, AZ.

Daewoo made a variety of firearms available for commercial use, and most of these were never imported into the U.S.

PISTOLS: SEMI-AUTO

DH380 – .380 ACP cal., DA/SA, styled after the Walther PPK. Imported 1995-96.

	100%	98%	95%	90%	80%	70%	60%	Last MSR
	$330	$285	$260	$235	$210	$185	$165	$375

DH40 – .40 S&W cal., otherwise similar to DP51, 32 oz. Imported 1995-disc.

	100%	98%	95%	90%	80%	70%	60%	
	$325	$270	$245	$225	$200	$185	$170	

MSR	100%	98%	95%	90%	80%	70%	60%	Last MSR

DP51 STANDARD/COMPACT – 9mm Para. cal., "fast action" allows lowering hammer w/o depressing trigger, 3 1/2 (DP51 C or S, disc.) or 4.1 (DP51) in. barrel, 10 (C/B 1994), 12* (.40 S&W), or 13* (9mm Para.) shot mag., 3-dot sights, tri-action mechanism (SA, DA, or fast action), ambidextrous manual safety, alloy receiver, polished or sandblasted black finish, 28 or 32 oz., includes lockable carrying case with accessories. Imported in various configurations circa 1991-2009.

| | $315 | $265 | $240 | $220 | $200 | $185 | $170 | |

Add 10% for DP51 Compact (disc.).

DP52 – .22 LR cal., DA/SA, similar to DH380, 3.8 in. barrel, alloy receiver, 10 shot mag., blue finish, 23 oz. Imported 1994-96.

| | $320 | $275 | $225 | $200 | $180 | $165 | $150 | *$380* |

RIFLES: SEMI-AUTO

MAX II (K2) – .223 Rem. cal., 18 in. barrel, gas operated rotating bolt, folding fiberglass stock, interchangeable mags. with the Colt M16, 7 lbs. Importation disc. 1986.

| | $950 | $875 | $800 | $725 | $625 | $550 | $475 | *$609* |

MAX I (K1A1) – similar to Max II (K2), except has retractable stock. Importation disc. 1986.

| | $1,050 | $925 | $850 | $750 | $650 | $575 | $500 | *$592* |

DR200 – .223 Rem. cal., sporterized stock, 10 shot mag. Imported 1995-96.

| | $650 | $550 | $475 | $425 | $395 | $375 | $350 | *$535* |

DR300 – 7.62x39mm cal., with or w/o thumbhole stock. Importation disc.

| | $650 | $550 | $475 | $425 | $395 | $375 | $350 | |

DAKOTA ARMS, INC.

Current manufacturer and previous importer established in 1986, located in Sturgis, SD. Dealer and direct sales through manufacturer only. This company is not affiliated with Dakota Single Action Revolvers.

On June 5, 2009, Remington Arms Company purchased Dakota Arms, Inc.

Dakota Arms Inc. also owned the rights to Miller Arms and Nesika actions. Please refer to these individual sections for more information.

Dakota Arms models listed below were also available with many custom options. Left-hand actions were available on all bolt action rifles at no extra charge. Actions (barreled or unbarreled) may have been purchased separately.

RIFLES: BOLT ACTION

DAKOTA LONGBOW T-76 TACTICAL – .300 Dakota Mag., .300 Win. Mag. (new 2006), .330 Dakota Mag., .308 Win. (new 2006), .338 Lapua Mag., or .338 Dakota Mag. cal., 28 in. stainless barrel, long range tactical design, black synthetic stock with adj. comb, includes Picatinny optical rail, Model 70 style trigger, matte finish metal, controlled round feeding, and deployment kit, 13.7 lbs. Mfg. 1997-2009.

| | $4,300 | $3,760 | $3,225 | $2,925 | $2,365 | $1,935 | $1,505 | *$4,795* |

DAKOTA SCIMITAR TACTICAL – .308 Win. or .338 Lapua cal., 24 or 27 in. match grade chrome moly barrel, 2nd generation Longbow with solid top receiver, long and short action, one-piece bolt handle, oversized claw extraction system, true controlled round feed, three postition safety, non-glare matte black finish, synthetic stock, optical rail. Mfg. 2008-2009.

| | $5,850 | $5,120 | $4,385 | $3,980 | $3,215 | $2,630 | $2,045 | *$6,295* |

DAN WESSON

Current trademark manufactured by Dan Wesson Firearms beginning 2005, located in Norwich, NY. Distributed beginning 2005 by CZ-USA, located in Kansas City, KS. Previously manufactured by New York International Corp. (NYI) located in Norwich, NY 1997-2005. Distributor and dealer sales.

PISTOLS: SEMI-AUTO

Until 2005, Dan Wesson manufactured a complete line of .45 ACP 1911 style semi-auto pistols. Previously manufactured models include: Seven (last MSR was $999), Seven Stainless (last MSR was $1,099), Guardian (last MSR was $799), the Guardian Deuce (last MSR was $799), the Dave Pruit Signature Series (last MSR was $899), and the Hi-Cap (last MSR was $689).

DISCRETION – 9mm Para. or .45 ACP cal., 5 3/4 in. extended match grade stainless steel threaded barrel, suppressor ready, 8 or 10 shot mag., light rails, competition-inspired hammer, serrated trigger, adj. night sights, G10 grips, manual thumb and grip safety, Black Duty finish. New 2016.

| MSR $2,142 | | $1,885 | $1,650 | $1,415 | $1,280 | $1,050 | $875 | $700 | |

MSR	100%	98%	95%	90%	80%	70%	60%	Last MSR

ELITE SERIES HAVOC – .38 Super or 9mm Para. cal., 4 1/4 (disc.) or 5 in. barrel with compensator, SA, all steel construction, designed for Open IPSC/USPSA Division, C-More red dot sights, 21 shot mag., matte black finish, 38 oz. New 2011.

| MSR $4,299 | $3,700 | $3,225 | $2,800 | $2,400 | $2,000 | $1,650 | $1,400 | |

ELITE SERIES MAYHEM – .40 S&W cal., SA, Limited IPSC/USPSA, stainless steel frame, 6 in. bull barrel with tactical rail, 18 shot mag., adj. fiber optic sights, G10 grips, ambi thumb/grip safety, matte black finish, 38 3/4 oz. New 2011.

| MSR $3,899 | $3,400 | $2,950 | $2,550 | $2,100 | $1,800 | $1,500 | $1,325 | |

ELITE SERIES TITAN – 10mm cal., 4 3/4 in. bull barrel, SA, 13 shot mag., all steel construction, lower frame tactical rail, matte black finish, Tritium sights, G10 grips, snake scale serrations on the slide, 26 oz. New 2011.

| MSR $3,829 | $3,350 | $2,925 | $2,550 | $2,100 | $1,800 | $1,500 | $1,325 | |

GUARDIAN – 9mm Para., .38 Super (new 2014), or .45 ACP (new 2011) cal., 8 or 9 shot mag., 4 1/4 in. barrel, SA, Commander-length slide and black light alloy Commander frame, Bobtail mainspring housing, Tritium sight, checkered Cocobolo grips, Black Duty finish, 28.8 oz. New 2010.

| MSR $1,558 | $1,350 | $1,150 | $950 | $825 | $725 | $625 | $525 | |

Add $61 for .45 ACP cal. (new 2011).

RZ-45 HERITAGE – .45 ACP cal. only, 8 shot mag., 5 in. barrel, stainless steel frame, SA, fixed night sights, manual thumb safety, rubber grips, 38 1/2 oz. New 2009.

| MSR $1,298 | $1,075 | $900 | $800 | $700 | $600 | $500 | $400 | |

SPECIALIST – 9mm Para. (new 2016) or .45 ACP cal., SA, 5 in. barrel, forged stainless steel slide, 8 or 9 (new 2016) shot mag., extended magazine release, undercut trigger guard, Tritium night sights, G10 VZ Operator II grips, ambidextrous thumb safety, serrated rib, frame has lower Picatinny rail, recessed slide stop, matte stainless or Black Duty finish. New 2012.

| MSR $1,701 | $1,450 | $1,275 | $1,125 | $1,000 | $850 | $735 | $595 | |

Add $311 for Black Duty finish.

VALOR – 9mm Para. (new 2016) or .45 ACP cal., SA, 5 in. barrel, 8 or 9 (9mm, new 2016) shot mag., adj. (disc.) or Heinie Ledge Straight 8 (new 2010) Tritium night sights, VZ slimline G10 grips, manual thumb and grip safety, choice of black ceramic coated (disc.), Black Duty finish, or matte stainless steel (new 2010), 38 oz. New 2008.

| MSR $1,701 | $1,450 | $1,275 | $1,125 | $1,000 | $850 | $735 | $595 | |

Add $311 for Black Duty finish.

VALOR COMMANDER – 9mm Para. or .45 ACP cal., SA, 4 1/4 in. barrel, 8 or 9 shot mag., stainless steel, fixed Tritium night sights, G10 grips, manual thumb and grip safety, bead blasted or Black Duty finish, 2.2 lbs. New 2016.

| MSR $1,701 | $1,450 | $1,275 | $1,125 | $1,000 | $850 | $735 | $595 | |

Add $311 for Black Duty finish.

* **V-Bob Black/V-Bob Stainless (Valor Bobtail Commander)** – 9mm Para. (new 2016) or .45 ACP cal., 4 1/4 in. barrel, 8 or 9 (new 2016) shot mag., fixed Tritium night sights, double diamond Black/Gray G10 grips and Black Duty finish or Black G10 grips with matte stainless finish, manual thumb and grip safety, Ed Brown bobtail commander style features, 35.2 oz. New 2010.

| MSR $1,766 | $1,485 | $1,315 | $1,150 | $1,025 | $875 | $750 | $615 | |

Add $311 for Black Duty finish.

REVOLVERS: DOUBLE ACTION

Dan Wesson has also manufactured a variety of revolver packages that were available by special order only.

MODEL 715 SMALL FRAME SERIES – .357 Mag. cal., 6 shot, stainless steel, 2 1/2, 4, 6, 8, or 10 in. heavy barrel with VR and full ejector shroud, rubber wraparound finger groove grips, interchangeable barrels. Mfg. 2002-2004.

| | $625 | $550 | $475 | $425 | $375 | $325 | $275 | $709 |

Add $50 for 4 in., $90 for 6 in., $150 for 8 in., or $190 for 10 in. barrel.

This model was also available as a pistol pack with four barrels and case. MSR was $1,699.

DANE ARMORY LLC

Previous AR-15 style rifle manufacturer located in Mesa, AZ until 2013.

RIFLES: SEMI-AUTO

All rifles included a case and manual.

DCM SERVICE AR-15 – .223 Rem. cal., National Match barrel and chromed bolt carrier, free float forend tube, F-marked front sight base, fixed synthetic stock, matte black finish, A4 configuration with carry handle, pistol grip. Disc. 2013.

| | $1,575 | $1,375 | $1,175 | $1,075 | $865 | $710 | $550 | $1,850 |

MSR	100%	98%	95%	90%	80%	70%	60%	Last MSR

HIGH POWER MATCH AR – .223 Rem. or .308 Win. cal., heavy barrel, Dane Armory exclusive free float handguard, Sinclair or Centra sight options, wide variety of stocks, handguard, and accessories. Disc. 2013.
  Base price on this model was $1,950.

PISTOL CALIBER AR – .223 Rem. or .308 Win. cal., heavy barrel, Dane Armory exclusive free float handguard, Sinclair or Centra sight options, wide variety of stocks, handguard, and accessories. Disc. 2013.
  Base price on this model was $2,150.

DANIEL DEFENSE

Current AR-15 style rifle and related components manufacturer located in Savannah, GA, with facilities also located in Ridgeland, SC.

CARBINES: SEMI-AUTO

In addition to the models listed below, Daniel Defense can build a custom rifle based on customer specifications. Please contact the company directly for this service (see Trademark Index). Daniel Defense also offers a complete line of tactical accessories and parts. All carbines and rifles come with a limited lifetime warranty.

DDM4 CARBINE SERIES – 5.56 NATO cal., GIO, 16 in. chrome lined barrel, A2 birdcage flash hider, 10, 20, or 30 shot mag., Mil-Spec enhanced magwell, A4 feed ramp, A1.5 BUIS sight, pinned "F" marked front sight base, Omega X rails, Magpul 5-position collapsible buttstock, A2 vertical grip, includes plastic case.

* **DDM4V1** – 5.56 NATO cal., GIO, 16 in. chrome lined M4 barrel, standard or lightweight (new 2012) barrel, curved and serrated front sight, DDM4 rail, QD swivel attachment points, original Daniel Defense rifle, black finish, 6.7 lbs.

MSR	100%	98%	95%	90%	80%	70%	60%	Last MSR
MSR $1,799	$1,620	$1,420	$1,215	$1,100	$890	$750	$650	

* **DDM4V2** – 5.56 NATO cal., GIO, 16 in. chrome lined barrel, similar to DDM4V1, except lightweight configuration with Omega X 7.0 rail system, also available with lightweight carbine barrel (DDM4V2LW). Mfg. 2011-2013.

MSR	100%	98%	95%	90%	80%	70%	60%	Last MSR
	$1,575	$1,375	$1,125	$925	$800	$700	$600	$1,759

* **DDM4V3** – 5.56 NATO or 6.8 SPC (mfg. 2012-2015) cal., mid-length GIO, 16 in. chrome lined Government profile barrel or lightweight carbine barrel (DDM4V3LW, disc. 2015) with flash suppressor, curved and serrated front sight, 9 in. free float Omega quad rail, black finish, 6 1/2 lbs.

MSR	100%	98%	95%	90%	80%	70%	60%	Last MSR
MSR $1,799	$1,620	$1,420	$1,215	$1,100	$890	$750	$650	

* **DDM4V4** – 5.56 NATO cal., GIO, 16 in. hammer forged carbine barrel, pinned low profile gas block, Omega X 9.0 rail system, available in lightweight profile (disc. 2011), no sights, fixed sights, or flip up sights. Disc. 2013.

MSR	100%	98%	95%	90%	80%	70%	60%	Last MSR
	$1,475	$1,275	$1,050	$900	$775	$650	$550	$1,639

Add $120 for fixed sights. Add $299 for flip up sights (disc. 2011).

* **DDM4V5** – 5.56 NATO or .300 AAC Blackout (mfg. mid-2012-2014) cal., GIO, 16 in. hammer forged Govt. or lightweight barrel, DD improved flash suppressor, 30 shot mag., pinned low profile gas block, Omega X 12.0 rail system, no sights, fixed sights, or flip up sights, Type III hardcoat anodized black, Daniel Defense Tornado or Mil-Spec+ Cerakote finish, 6.4 lbs.

MSR	100%	98%	95%	90%	80%	70%	60%	Last MSR
MSR $1,689	$1,440	$1,250	$1,115	$985	$840	$725	$590	

Add $235 for Daniel Defense Tornado or Mil-Spec+ Cerakote finish.
Add $299 for flip up sights (disc. 2011).

» **DDM4V5S** – 5.56 NATO cal., AR-15 style, mid-length GIO, 14 1/2 in. (16.1 w/muzzle) Govt. profile chrome moly barrel with extended DD improved flash suppressor (pinned and welded to reach the NFA required barrel length), Daniel Defense buttstock, vertical grip and pistol grip, DDM4 Rail 12.0 with Mil-Std Picatinny rail with QD swivel attachment points, Type III hardcoat anodized black or Mil-Spec+ Cerakote finish, 6.23 lbs. New 2016.

MSR	100%	98%	95%	90%	80%	70%	60%	Last MSR
MSR $1,769	$1,495	$1,320	$1,150	$1,025	$875	$750	$615	

Add $155 for Mil-Spec+ Cerakote finish.

* **DDM4V7** – 5.56 NATO or 6.8 SPC (disc. 2014) cal., GIO, 16 (5.56 NATO) or 18 (6.8 SPC, disc. 2014) in. standard or lightweight barrel with flash hider, with or w/o sights, flat-top receiver, full length top Picatinny rail, forearm features three modular Picatinny rails that are moveable, 30 shot mag., Type III hardcoat anodized black or Mil-Spec+ Cerakote finish, 6 1/2 lbs. New 2012.

MSR	100%	98%	95%	90%	80%	70%	60%	Last MSR
MSR $1,599	$1,350	$1,200	$1,075	$950	$815	$700	$575	

Add $110 for fixed sights.
Add $150 for Mil-Spec+ Cerakote finish.

* **DDM4V9** – 5.56 NATO cal., low profile gas block, mid-length gas system, GIO, 16 in. Govt. profile chrome moly barrel, Daniel Defense flash suppressor, CNC machined aluminum upper and lower receiver, glass filled polymer adj. buttstock with soft touch overmolding, flared magwell, vertical grip and pistol grip, 15 in. quad rail aluminum handguard, 3 low profile rail ladders, 6-position receiver extension, 30 shot PMAG, no sights, M16 chrome lined bolt carrier group, H buffer, hardcoat anodized finish, 6.6 lbs. New 2014.

MSR	100%	98%	95%	90%	80%	70%	60%	Last MSR
MSR $1,689	$1,440	$1,250	$1,115	$985	$840	$725	$590	

MSR	100%	98%	95%	90%	80%	70%	60%	Last MSR

»**DDM4V9 S2W (Strength to Weight)** – 5.56 NATO cal., similar to DDM4V9, except has 18 in. S2W cold hammer forged profile barrel, black finish, 7 1/2 lbs. Mfg. 2014-2015.

	$1,440	$1,250	$1,115	$985	$840	$725	$590	*$1,689*

»**DDM4V9 Lightweight** – 5.56 NATO cal., similar to DDM4V9, except has 16 in. lightweight profile barrel and Daniel Defense Tornado Cerakote finish, 6.34 lbs. New 2014.

MSR $1,840	$1,550	$1,365	$1,175	$1,050	$900	$775	$625	

* **DDM4V11** – 5.56 NATO cal., 16 in. cold hammer forged Govt. or lightweight barrel with mid-length GIO, DD improved flash suppressor, 15 in. SLiM rail with KeyMod attachments, top Picatinny rail, iron sights, Type III hardcoat anodized black, Cerakote finish in Mil-Spec+ or Tornado, or Kryptek Typhon (new 2016) finish, 6.28 lbs. New 2015.

MSR $1,599	$1,350	$1,200	$1,075	$950	$815	$700	$575	

Add $50 for Kryptek Typhon finish (new 2016).
Add $160 for Mil-Spec+ or Tornado Cerakote finish.

* **DDM4V11 Pro** – 5.56 NATO cal., 18 in. cold hammer forged S2W barrel with DD Muzzle Climb Mitigator Gen II muzzle, rifle length GIO, 30 shot Magpul PMAG, Geissele Super Dynamic 3-Gun trigger, machined alum. upper and lower receivers with M4 feed ramps and enhanced flared magwell, 15 in. SLiM rail, Vltor BCM Gunfighter Mod 4 charging handle, top Picatinny rail with KeyMod attachment, 6-pos. aluminum receiver extension, polymer pistol grip buttstock with Soft Touch overmolding, black hardcoat anodized finish, 7 1/2 lbs. New 2015.

MSR $1,849	$1,575	$1,385	$1,185	$1,065	$915	$785	$635	

* **DDM4V11 SLW** – 5.56 NATO cal., AR-15 style, mid-length gas system, 14 1/2 in. (16 in. w/muzzle) cold hammer forged lightweight profile barrel, pinned and welded extended flash suppressor (to reach NFA requirements), polymer pistol grip buttstock with Soft Touch overmolding, free floating Slim Rail 12.0 handguard, KeyMod attachments, full-length top Picatinny rail, Type III hardcoat anodized black or Cerakote finishes in Mil-Spec+ or Daniel Defense Tornado, 6.09 lbs. New 2016.

MSR $1,669	$1,410	$1,235	$1,100	$975	$830	$720	$585	

Add $190 for Mil-Spec+ or Daniel Defense Tornado Cerakote finish.

DDM4 ISR (INTEGRALLY SUPPRESSED RIFLE) – .300 AAC Blackout cal., GIO, 16.1 in. S2W barrel (10.3 in. barrel with permanently attached suppressor), integral suppressor, 30 shot Magpul PMAG, pistol length gas system, 12 in. modular float rail with three modular Picatinny rail sections, 6-pos. aluminum receiver extension, enhanced flared magwell, rear receiver QD swivel, M4 feed ramps, polymer pistol grip buttstock with Soft Touch overmolding, black finish, 7 1/2 lbs. Mfg. 2015 only.

	$2,600	$2,275	$1,950	$1,770	$1,430	$1,175	$925	*$2,899*

DD5V1 – .308 Win. cal., AR-15 style, mid-length GIO, 16 in. cold hammer forged chrome moly barrel, extended DD Superior suppression device, flared magwell, integral oversized trigger guard, Geissele SSA-two-stage trigger, ambidextrous safety selector, 15 in. Picatinny top rail, KeyMod handguard, configurable modular charging handle, Type III hardcoat anodized black, Mil-Spec+ Cerakote, or Kryptek Typhon finish, 8.3 lbs. New 2016.

MSR $2,899	$2,475	$2,150	$1,775	$1,525	$1,250	$1,050	$925	

Add $150 for Mil-Spec+ Cerakote or Kryptek Typhon finish.

DD CARBINE SERIES – 5.56 NATO or 6.8 SPC cal., GIO, 16 in. chrome lined barrel, similar to DDM4 Series, except Mil-Spec buttstock. New 2010.

* **DDXV/XV EZ** – GIO, 16 in. cold hammer forged barrel, "F" marked fixed front sight base, flared magwell on lower receiver, Magpul enhanced trigger guard, M16 bolt carrier group, rear receiver QD sling swivel attachment, with (XV EZ) or w/o (XV, disc. 2011) EZ CAR 7.0 rail system and A1 fixed rear sight. Disc. 2013.

	$1,275	$1,100	$950	$825	$700	$600	$500	*$1,419*

Add $68 for EZ CAR 7.0 rail system.
Add $129 for XVM model with mid-length barrel.

* **DDV6.8** – 6.8 SPC cal., GIO, 16 in. cold hammer forged mid-length barrel, Omega X 9.0 VFG and A1.5 fixed rear sight. Disc. 2011.

	$1,375	$1,100	$975	$850	$725	$625	$525	*$1,537*

M4A1 – 5.56 NATO cal., AR-15 style, carbine length GIO with pinned low profile gas block, 14 1/2 in. (16 in. w/ muzzle) cold hammer forged M4 profile barrel with pinned and welded (to reach NFA requirements) DD improved flash suppressor, M4A1 RIS II rail system, Type III hardcoat anodized black or Mil-Spec+ Cerakote finish, 6 3/4 lbs. New 2016.

MSR $1,819	$1,525	$1,350	$1,175	$1,050	$900	$775	$625	

Add $160 for Mil-Spec+ Cerakote finish.

MSR	100%	98%	95%	90%	80%	70%	60%	Last MSR

MK12 – 5.56 NATO cal., GIO, 18 in. cold hammer forged stainless steel MK12 barrel, DD improved flash suppressor, rifle length gas system, 20 shot Magpul PMAG, upper receiver with 12 in. M4 free floating rail, Geissele SSA two-stage trigger, 6-pos. aluminum receiver extension, Vltor Mod 4 charging handle, polymer pistol grip buttstock with Soft Touch overmolding, Type III hardcoat anodized black, DD Tornado Cerakote, or Kryptek Typhon (new 2016) finish, 7.41 lbs. New mid-2014.

| MSR $1,999 | $1,700 | $1,500 | $1,250 | $1,100 | $950 | $825 | $675 | |

Add $50 for Kryptek Typhon finish (new 2016).
Add $160 for Daniel Defense Tornado Cerakote finish.

PISTOLS: SEMI-AUTO

DDMK18 – 5.56 NATO cal., GIO, 10.3 in. cold hammer forged Govt. profile barrel with DD improved flash suppressor, carbine length gas system, pistol receiver extension, MK18 RIS II rail system, black or FDE hardcoat anodized finish, 5.4 lbs. New 2015.

| MSR $1,699 | $1,450 | $1,275 | $1,125 | $1,000 | $850 | $735 | $595 | |

Add $250 for Law Tactical Gen III adaptor (new 2016).

DDM4300 – .300 AAC Blackout cal., GIO, 10.3 in. cold hammer forged S2W barrel with DD improved flash suppressor, pistol length gas system, pinned low-profile gas block, 30 shot Magpul PMAG, pistol receiver extension, 9 in. M4 rail, polymer pistol grip with Soft Touch overmolding, black finish, 5.3 lbs. New 2015.

| MSR $1,699 | $1,450 | $1,275 | $1,125 | $1,000 | $850 | $735 | $595 | |

DARK STORM INDUSTRIES, LLC (DSI)

Current AR-15 style rifle manufacturer as well as AR-15 parts and accessories manufacturer/distributor, located in Oakdale, NY since 2013.

PISTOLS: SEMI-AUTO

DS-9 HAILSTORM – 9mm Para. cal., black or FDE finish.

| MSR $1,095 | $925 | $850 | $725 | $625 | $550 | $475 | $425 | |

Add $100 for FDE finish.

RIFLES: SEMI-AUTO

DS-9 LIGHTNING – 9mm Para. cal., GIO, 16 in. SOCOM profile threaded stainless steel barrel with Competition compensator, Glock 17 shot mag., billet aluminum lower and forged upper receiver with forward assist and ejection port cover, 9mm nickel boron coated bolt carrier group, ambidextrous safety selector, 11 in. forearm Troy Battle Alpha rail, trigger lock, Magpul CTR adj. stock, Hogue pistol grip, black or FDE finish.

| MSR $1,295 | $1,100 | $995 | $875 | $735 | $650 | $550 | $465 | |

* **DS-9 Lightning Featureless** – 9mm Para. cal., GIO, 16 in. SOCOM profile stainless steel barrel, Glock 10 shot mag., Billet aluminum lower and forged upper receiver with forward assist and ejection port cover, nickel boron coated 9mm bolt carrier group, Spec Ops Gen 2 charging handle, DSI billet ambidextrous safety selector, 11 in. forearm Troy Battle Alpha rail, Thordsen FRS-15 Gen. 2 rifle stock with rubber buttpad, Thordsen enhanced buffer tube cover with QD sling sockets, ambidextrous sling plate, black or FDE finish.

| MSR $1,295 | $1,100 | $995 | $875 | $735 | $650 | $550 | $465 | |

Add $100 for FDE finish.

DS-9 MOE – 9mm Para. cal., GIO, 16 in. M4 profile threaded Nitrite barrel with A2 style Birdcage flash hider, Glock 17 shot mag., Billet aluminum lower and forged upper receiver with forward assist and ejection port cover, trigger lock, 7 in. Magpul MOE drop-in forearm, rail front sight block, Magpul MOE adj. stock and pistol girp, black, pink, grey, FDE, or OD Green finish.

| MSR $995 | $850 | $725 | $650 | $585 | $515 | $450 | $395 | |

* **DS-9 MOE Featureless** – 9mm Para. cal., GIO, 16 in. M4 profile barrel, Glock 10 shot mag., Billet aluminum lower and forged upper receiver with forward assist and ejection port cover, Magpul MOE 7 in. drop-in forearm, rail front sight block, Thordsen FRS-15 rifle stock, Thordsen standard buffer tube cover, trigger lock, black, pink, grey, FDE, or OD Green finish.

| MSR $995 | $850 | $725 | $650 | $585 | $515 | $450 | $395 | |

Add $100 for FDE or OD Green finish.

DS-9 TYPHOON – 9mm Para. cal., GIO, 16 in. M4 profile threaded Nitrite barrel with CQB compensator, Glock 17 shot mag., trigger lock, billet aluminum lower, forged upper rec. with forward assist and ejection port cover, ambidextrous safety selector, DSI Ultralight narrow profile KeyMod 12 in. forearm, Magpul CTR adj. stock, Hogue pistol grip, ambidextrous sling plate, black, FDE, or OD Green finish, 6 lbs. 4 oz.

| MSR $1,195 | $1,025 | $925 | $800 | $685 | $595 | $515 | $440 | |

Add $100 for FDE or OD Green finish.

MSR	100%	98%	95%	90%	80%	70%	60%	Last MSR

* DS-9 Typhoon Featureless – 9mm Para. cal., GIO, 16 in. M4 profile Nitride barrel, Glock 10 shot mag., billet aluminum lower and forged upper rec. with forward assist and ejection port cover, Spec Ops Gen 2 charging handle, ambidextrous safety selector, DSI Ultralight narrow profile KeyMod 12 in. forearm, trigger lock, Thordsen FRS-15 Gen 2 rifle stock with rubber buttpad, Thordsen enhanced buffer tube cover with QD sling sockets, ambidextrous sling plate, black, FDE, or OD Green finish.

MSR $1,195	$1,025	$925	$800	$685	$595	$515	$440

Add $100 for FDE or OD Green finish.

DS-15 LIGHTNING – 5.56 NATO, .300 AAC Blackout, or .458 SOCOM cal., micro gas block and carbine GIO, 16 in. stainless steel threaded barrel with Competition compensator, fixed or detachable 10 shot Magpul PMAG, no sights, trigger lock, FX billet lower receiver, forged upper w/forward assist and ejection port cover, 11 in. Troy Battle rail Alpha forearm, Magpul CTR adj. stock, Hogue pistol grip, black or FDE finish.

MSR $1,195	$1,025	$925	$800	$685	$595	$515	$440

Add $100 for .458 SOCOM cal.

* DS-15 Lightning Featureless – 5.56 NATO, .300 AAC Blackout, or .458 SOCOM cal., micro gas block and carbine GIO, 16 in. stainless steel barrel, 10 shot Magpul PMAG, no sights, trigger lock, billet lower receiver, forged upper w/ forward assist and ejection port cover, NiB M16 bolt carrier group, Spec Ops Gen 2 charging handle, ambidextrous safety selector, 11 in. Troy Battle Alpha rail forearm, Thordsen FRS-15 Gen 2 rifle stock with rubber buttpad, Thordsen enhanced buffer tube w/QD sling sockets, black or FDE finish.

MSR $1,195	$1,025	$925	$800	$685	$595	$515	$440

Add $100 for .458 SOCOM cal.

DS-15 MOE – 5.56 NATO or .300 AAC Blackout cal., rail gas block and carbine GIO, 16 in. M4 profile threaded barrel with A2 style Birdcage flash hider, 20 shot fixed or detachable Magpul PMAG, trigger lock, no sights, Magpul MOE 7 in. drop-in forearm, Magpul MOE adj. pistol grip stock, billet lower receiver and forged upper with forward assist and ejection port cover, black, grey, pink, FDE, or OD Green finish.

MSR $895	$775	$685	$615	$550	$485	$415	$370

Add $50 for .300 AAC Blackout cal.

* DS-15 MOE Featureless – 5.56 NATO or .300 AAC Blackout cal., rail gas block and carbine GIO, 16 in. SOCOM profile blued barrel, 10 shot Magpul PMAG, no sights, trigger lock, billet lower receiver and forged upper with forward assist and ejection port cover, M16 bolt carrier group, Magpul MOE 7 in. drop-in forearm, Thordsen FRS-15 rifle stock, Thordsen standard buffer tube cover, black, grey, pink, FDE, or OD Green finish.

MSR $895	$775	$685	$615	$550	$485	$415	$370

Add $50 for .300 AAC Blackout cal.

DS-15 SPORT – 5.56 NATO cal., rail gas block and carbine GIO, 16 in. SOCOM profile barrel, 30 shot fixed or detachable Magpul PMAG, billet lower and forged sport upper receiver, trigger lock, M16 bolt carrier group, DSI 7 in. drop-in quad rail forearm, M4 style adj. pistol grip stock, black finish.

MSR $795	$685	$615	$550	$475	$420	$365	$335

* DS-15 Sport Featureless – 5.56 NATO cal., rail gas block and carbine GIO, 16 in. SOCOM profile barrel, 10 shot Magpul PMAG, trigger lock, no sights, FX billet lower receiver and forged Sport side upper, M16 bolt carrier group, DSI 7 in. quad rail forearm, M4 style pinned stock, Spur Gen 2 grip, black finish.

MSR $795	$685	$615	$550	$475	$420	$365	$335

DS-15 THUNDER – 5.56 NATO or .300 AAC Blackout cal., micro gas block and carbine GIO, 16 in. threaded barrel with Competition compensator, fixed or detachable 10 shot Magpul PMAG, no sights, trigger lock, FX billet lower receiver, forged upper w/forward assist and ejection port cover, 10 1/4 in. Diamondhead VRS-T forearm, Magpul STR adj. stock, Hogue pistol grip, black finish.

MSR $1,395	$1,200	$1,075	$950	$800	$700	$600	$495

* DS-15 Thunder Featureless – 5.56 NATO or .300 AAC Blackout cal., micro gas block and carbine GIO, 16 in. barrel, 10 shot detachable Magpul PMAG, no sights, trigger lock, Thordsen FRS-15 rifle stock with rubber buttpad, black finish.

MSR $1,395	$1,200	$1,075	$950	$800	$700	$600	$495

DS-15 TYPHOON – 5.56 NATO or .300 AAC Blackout cal., micro gas block and carbine GIO, 16 in. M4 profile threaded barrel with CQB compensator, fixed or detachable 10 shot PMAG, trigger lock, no sights, FX billet lower receiver, forged upper with forward assist and ejection port cover, M16 bolt carrier group, ambidextrous safety selector, DSI Ultralight narrow profile KeyMod 12 in. forearm, Magpul CTR adj. stock, Hogue pistol grip, ambidextrous sling plate, black, FDE, or OD Green finish, 6 lbs. 15 oz.

MSR $1,095	$925	$850	$725	$625	$550	$475	$425

Add $100 for FDE or OD Green finish.

MSR	100%	98%	95%	90%	80%	70%	60%	*Last MSR*

* **DS-15 Typhoon Featureless** – 5.56 NATO or .300 AAC Blackout cal., micro gas block and carbine GIO, 16 in. SOCOM profile barrel, 10 shot Magpul PMAG, trigger lock, no sights, billet lower receiver, forged upper w/forward assist and ejection port cover, Spec Ops Gen 2 charging handle, ambidextrous safety selector, DSI Ultralight narrow profile KeyMod 12 in. forearm, Thordsen FRS-15 Gen 2 rifle stock with rubber buttpad, Thordsen enhanced buffer tube cover w/QD sling sockets, ambidextrous sling plate, black, FDE, or OD Green finish, 6 lbs. 12 oz.

| MSR $1,095 | $925 | $850 | $725 | $625 | $550 | $475 | $425 | |

Add $100 for FDE or OD Green finish.

DAUDSONS ARMOURY

Current manufacturer located in Peshawar, Pakistan. No current U.S. importation.

Daudsons Armoury's origins stretch back over two centuries dealing in the sporting arms and defense firearms trade. The company provides firearms for the armed forces of Pakistan as well as the Defense Ministry.

Daudsons Armoury manufactures the DSA line of 12 ga. shotguns. Basic models include: DSA Royal, DSA Regal, DSA Super Deluxe, DSA Shooter, DSA Commando, DSA Sure Shot, and the DSA Security. All are manufactured from high grade alloy steel, with black synthetic stocks and forearms, and all parts are completely interchangeable. Daudsons also manufactures double barrel rifles and a semi-auto .22 cal. rifle. For more information on these guns, including pricing and U.S. availability, please contact the company directly (see Trademark Index).

DEL-TON INCORPORATED

Current rifle and pistol manufacturer located in Elizabethtown, NC. Dealer sales. Previously distributed until 2011 by American Tactical Imports, located in Rochester, NY.

CARBINES/RIFLES: SEMI-AUTO

Del-Ton manufactures a wide variety of AR-15 style carbines/rifles, as well as a full line of rifle kits. Many options, accessories, and parts are also available. Please contact the company for more information, including current availability and options (see Trademark Index). All rifles include a hard case, two mags., and buttstock cleaning kit.

A2 CARBINE – .223 Rem. cal., GIO, 16 in. heavy chrome moly barrel, fixed A2 stock, CAR handguard with single heat shield, A2 flash hider, black furniture, carry handle, includes sling. Disc. 2012.

| | $650 | $575 | $510 | $440 | $385 | $340 | $325 | *$750* |

A2 DT-4 CARBINE – .223 Rem. cal., GIO, 16 in. chrome moly barrel, 6-position M4 stock, 30 shot mag., CAR handguard with single heat shield, A2 flash hider, black furniture, includes sling. Disc. 2012.

| | $650 | $575 | $510 | $440 | $385 | $340 | $325 | *$750* |

ALPHA 220H – 5.56 NATO cal., GIO, 20 in. chrome moly heavy profile barrel with threaded muzzle and A2 flash hider, forged aluminum T6 upper and lower receiver, 30 shot mag., A2 configuration with rear sight, rifle length handguard with single heat shield, standard A2 Black Zytel buttstock with trap door assembly, A2 grip, Black furniture, 8.2 lbs.

| MSR $918 | $780 | $685 | $615 | $550 | $485 | $415 | $370 | |

ALPHA 320H – 5.56 NATO cal., GIO, similar to Alpha 220H, except features M4 feed ramps, no sights, and A3 flat-top receiver, 8 lbs.

| MSR $822 | $700 | $615 | $550 | $475 | $420 | $365 | $335 | |

ALPHA 320G (STANDARD GOVERNMENT PROFILE RIFLE) – 5.56 NATO cal., GIO, 20 in. chrome moly standard or heavy profile barrel with threaded muzzle and A2 flash hider, Government profile, M4 feed ramps, A2 reinforced Zytel buttstock, A2 grip, 30 shot mag., standard length handguard with single heat shield, black furniture, forged aluminum upper and lower receivers, A3 flat-top or A2 upper with carry handle, includes sling, 7.4 lbs.

| MSR $822 | $700 | $615 | $550 | $475 | $420 | $365 | $335 | |

ALPHA 320P – 5.56 NATO cal., GIO, post ban rifle, 20 in. heavy chrome moly barrel with crowned muzzle, M4 feed ramps, 10 shot mag., fixed A2 reinforced Zytel buttstock with trap door assembly, A2 grip, black furniture, rifle length handguard with single heat shield, flat-top A3 or A2 upper with carry handle, includes sling, 7.8 lbs. Disc. 2013.

| | $685 | $615 | $550 | $475 | $420 | $365 | $335 | *$780* |

DTI-4 CARBINE – .223 Rem. cal., GIO, 16 in. chrome moly M4 profile barrel, six position M4 stock, 30 shot mag., CAR handguard with single heat shield, A2 flash hider, black furniture, A3 flat-top or A2 upper with carry handle, includes sling. Disc. 2012.

| | $650 | $575 | $510 | $440 | $385 | $340 | $325 | *$750* |

DTI-15 CARBINE – .223 Rem. cal., GIO, 16.1 in. barrel, 30 shot mag., hard anodized black oxide finish, adj. 6-position collapsible stock with M249-style pistol grip, fixed front sights, approx. 7 3/4 lbs. Mfg. mid-2011-2012.

| | $725 | $650 | $580 | $515 | $450 | $385 | $340 | *$859* |

MSR	100%	98%	95%	90%	80%	70%	60%	Last MSR

DTI ECHO 7.62x39 – 7.62x39mm cal., carbine length GIO, 16 in. heavy profile barrel, threaded muzzle, A2 flash hider, aluminum trigger guard and mag. catch button, front sight base, M4 buttstock, A2 grip, forged aluminum lower and A3 flat-top upper with Picatinny rail, M4 feed ramps, right hand ejection, aluminum Delta ring carbine length handguard with single heat shield, H buffer, 6.6 lbs. New 2016.

	100%	98%	95%	90%	80%	70%	60%	
MSR $753	$650	$575	$510	$440	$385	$340	$325	

DTI EVOLUTION – 5.56 NATO cal., GIO, lightweight profile 16 in. chrome-lined barrel with threaded muzzle and A2 flash hider, low profile gas block, M4 feed ramps, Samson Evolution free float forend with accessory rails, Samson quick flip dual aperture rear sight, Samson folding front sight, forged aluminum upper and lower receiver, A3 flat-top with white T marks, hardcoat anodized metal finish, two-stage trigger, Magpul CTR stock, buffer tube, Magpul MOE + grip, black or Dark Earth furniture, 6 1/2 lbs. New 2013.

	100%	98%	95%	90%	80%	70%	60%	
MSR $1,319	$1,100	$995	$875	$735	$650	$550	$465	

DTI EXTREME DUTY – 5.56 NATO cal., GIO, 16 in. hammer forged chrome lined barrel with threaded muzzle/A2 flash hider, Black finish, T6 aluminum upper and lower receiver, M4 carbine handguard with double heat shield, M4 5-position reinforced fiber buttstock with Mil-Spec buffer tube, A2 grip, Samson quick flip dual aperture rear sight, 6.4 lbs. New 2012.

	100%	98%	95%	90%	80%	70%	60%	
MSR $1,119	$935	$850	$725	$625	$550	$475	$425	

DTI TRX MID-LENGTH RIFLE/CARBINE – 5.56 NATO cal., GIO, 16 in. barrel, A2 flash hider, threaded muzzle, Troy TRX battlerail handguard, 30 shot mag., and BattleAx CQB adj. stock, Black or Tan finish, 7.2 lbs. Mfg. 2012 only.

	100%	98%	95%	90%	80%	70%	60%	Last MSR
	$1,050	$950	$815	$685	$595	$515	$440	*$1,250*

DT SPORT CARBINE – 5.56 NATO cal., GIO, lightweight profile 16 in. barrel with threaded muzzle/A2 flash hider, forged aluminum A3 flat-top upper receiver with forward assist, forged alum. lower with A2 grip, M4 6-position buttstock with commercial buffer tube, oval ribbed handguard with A2 front sight and single heat shield, 10 or 30 shot mag., manganese phosphated under front sight base, 5.8 lbs. Mfg. 2011-2015.

	100%	98%	95%	90%	80%	70%	60%	Last MSR
	$615	$540	$470	$400	$350	$310	$295	*$697*

* **DT Sport Lite** – 5.56 NATO cal., carbine length GIO, 16 in. lightweight profile barrel, threaded muzzle, A2 flash hider, aluminum trigger guard, M4 6-pos. buttstock, A2 grip, forged aluminum A3 flat-top upper and lower receivers, H buffer, aluminum Delta ring carbine length handguard with single heat shield, black finish, 5.8 lbs. New 2016.

	100%	98%	95%	90%	80%	70%	60%	
MSR $649	$575	$500	$435	$365	$325	$280	$265	

* **DT Sport OR** – 5.56 NATO cal., GIO, similar to DT Sport Carbine, except is Optics Ready, so does not include the A2 front sight tower, manganese phosphated under low profile gas block, 5.6 lbs. New 2013.

	100%	98%	95%	90%	80%	70%	60%	
MSR $705	$615	$540	$470	$400	$350	$310	$295	

ECHO 216 (A2 LIGHTWEIGHT) – 5.56 NATO cal., GIO, 16 in. chrome moly M4 barrel with threaded muzzle and A2 flash hider, forged T6 aluminum upper and lower receiver, carry handle, 30 shot mag., carbine length handguard with single heat shield, A2 configuration with rear sight, M4 5-position stock with buffer tube, A2 grip, Black furniture, 6.6 lbs. New 2012.

	100%	98%	95%	90%	80%	70%	60%	
MSR $891	$750	$665	$580	$515	$450	$385	$340	

* **Echo 216F** – 5.56 NATO cal., GIO, similar to Echo 216, except features A2 reinforced Zytel buttstock with trap door assembly, 6.8 lbs. Mfg. 2012-2013.

	100%	98%	95%	90%	80%	70%	60%	Last MSR
	$685	$615	$550	$475	$420	$365	$335	*$788*

* **Echo 216H** – 5.56 NATO cal., GIO, similar to Echo 216, except features 16 in. chrome moly heavy barrel, A2 reinforced Zytel buttstock and A2 grip, trap door assembly, 7 lbs. Disc. 2014.

	100%	98%	95%	90%	80%	70%	60%	Last MSR
	$685	$615	$550	$475	$420	$365	$335	*$793*

ECHO 300 BLK – .300 AAC Blackout cal., GIO, 16 in. heavy profile barrel with A2 flash hider, M4 Mil-Spec buttstock, forged aluminum upper with Picatinny rail, M4 feed ramps, carbine length aluminum Delta ring single heat shield handguard, Black finish.

	100%	98%	95%	90%	80%	70%	60%	
MSR $891	$750	$665	$580	$515	$450	$385	$340	

ECHO 308 – .308 Win. cal., GIO, 16 in. heavy profile barrel with A2 style flash hider, Magpul 20 shot PMAG, integral trigger guard, knurled aluminum forend, M4 buttstock, M4 feed ramps, forged aluminum receiver, carbine length knurled free-float handguard tube, Black finish.

	100%	98%	95%	90%	80%	70%	60%	
MSR $948	$815	$700	$630	$570	$500	$425	$380	

ECHO 316 – 5.56 NATO cal., GIO, 16 in. barrel with threaded muzzle and Manganese phosphated finish, A2 flash hider, forged aluminum upper and lower receiver, hardcoat anodized Mil-Spec matte black finish, aluminum trigger guard, M4 front sight base, M4 five position reinforced fiber buttstock with Mil-Spec buffer tube, carbine length aluminum delta ring single heat shield handguards, A2 grip, A3 flat-top. New 2014.

	100%	98%	95%	90%	80%	70%	60%	
MSR $753	$650	$575	$510	$440	$385	$340	$325	

MSR	100%	98%	95%	90%	80%	70%	60%	Last MSR

ECHO 316L KeyMod – 5.56 NATO cal., GIO, 16 in. lightweight profile barrel, threaded muzzle, A2 flash hider, aluminum trigger guard and mag. catch button, front sight base, M4 5-pos. buttstock, A2 grip, M4 feed ramps, forged aluminum lower and A3 upper with Picatinny rail, round forward assist, right-hand ejection, H buffer, Samson Evolution KeyMod carbine length handguard, 7.2 in. free-float rail, hardcoat anodized Black finish, 5.8 lbs. New 2016.

	100%	98%	95%	90%	80%	70%	60%	Last MSR
MSR $921	$785	$685	$615	$550	$485	$415	$370	

ECHO 316L LIGHTWEIGHT CARBINE – 5.56 NATO cal., GIO, 16 in. chrome moly barrel with A2 flash hider and threaded muzzle, forged T6 aluminum upper and lower receiver, carbine length handguard with single heat shield, 6-position M4 reinforced carbon fiber buttstock, 5.8 lbs. Mfg. 2012 only.

	100%	98%	95%	90%	80%	70%	60%	Last MSR
	$650	$575	$510	$440	$385	$340	$325	*$750*

ECHO 316H – 5.56 NATO cal., GIO, 16 in. chrome moly heavy barrel with threaded muzzle and A2 flash hider, M4 feed ramps, carbine length handguard with single heat shield, front sight base, T6 aluminum upper and lower, A3 flat-top with white T marks, M4 5-position reinforced carbon buttstock with buffer tube, A2 grip, black furniture, 6.6 lbs. New 2012.

	100%	98%	95%	90%	80%	70%	60%	Last MSR
MSR $753	$650	$575	$510	$440	$385	$340	$325	

* ***Echo 316H OR*** – 5.56 NATO cal., GIO, similar to Echo 316H, except has single rail gas block and is optics ready, 6.4 lbs. Mfg. 2013-2015.

	100%	98%	95%	90%	80%	70%	60%	Last MSR
	$695	$615	$550	$475	$420	$365	$335	*$816*

ECHO 316M – 5.56 NATO cal., GIO, 16 in. barrel with threaded muzzle and A2 flash hider, 30 shot mag., aluminum trigger guard, F-marked front sight base, M4 5-position buttstock, M4 feed ramps, carbine length aluminum Delta ring single heat shield handguard, forged lower and flat-top upper receivers, hardcoat anodized black finish, 6.6 lbs. New 2016.

	100%	98%	95%	90%	80%	70%	60%	Last MSR
MSR $822	$700	$620	$550	$475	$420	$365	$335	

ECHO 316 MOE – 5.56 NATO cal., GIO, 16 in. chrome moly heavy profile barrel, threaded muzzle, A2 flash hider, A3 flat-top, Magpul MOE polymer stock with buffer tube and Magpul MOE grip, 30 shot PMag, forged T6 aluminum upper and lower receiver, Magpul MOE carbine length handguard with heat resistant construction, OD Green, Black or Tan finish, 6.8 lbs. Mfg. 2012-2015.

	100%	98%	95%	90%	80%	70%	60%	Last MSR
	$735	$650	$580	$515	$450	$385	$340	*$877*

ECHO 316 MLOK – 5.56 NATO cal., carbine length GIO, 16 in. heavy profile barrel, threaded muzzle, A2 flash hider, front sight base, Magpul MOE 5-pos. stock, forged aluminum lower and A3 flat-top upper with Picatinny rail, M4 feed ramps, Magpul MOE H buffer, Magpul MLOK carbine length aluminum delta ring handguard, Black or FDE finish, 6.8 lbs. New 2016.

	100%	98%	95%	90%	80%	70%	60%	Last MSR
MSR $863	$735	$650	$580	$515	$450	$385	$340	

ECHO 316 OR – 5.56 NATO cal.

	100%	98%	95%	90%	80%	70%	60%	Last MSR
MSR $816	$700	$620	$550	$475	$420	$365	$335	

ECHO 316P – 5.56 NATO cal., GIO, M4 Post Ban rifle, 16 in. chrome moly barrel with pinned YHM muzzle brake, 10 shot mag., M4 feed ramps, forged aluminum T6 upper and lower receivers, A3 flat-top upper, pinned M4 reinforced carbon fiber buttstock with commercial buffer tube, black furniture, carbine length handguard with single heat shield, 6.9 lbs.

	100%	98%	95%	90%	80%	70%	60%	Last MSR
MSR $822	$700	$620	$550	$475	$420	$365	$335	

ECHO 316PF (POST-BAN CARBINE) – 5.56 NATO cal., GIO, A3 Post Ban rifle, 16 in. heavy profile chrome moly barrel with target crowned muzzle, no flash hider, 10 shot mag., M4 feed ramps, fixed A2 reinforced Zytel buttstock with trap door assembly, A2 grip, black furniture, carbine length handguard with single heat shield, forged aluminum T6 upper and lower receivers, A3 upper, 6.9 lbs. Disc. 2013.

	100%	98%	95%	90%	80%	70%	60%	Last MSR
	$685	$615	$550	$475	$420	$365	$335	*$780*

M4 CARBINE – .223 Rem. cal., GIO, 16 in. chrome moly barrel, 30 shot mag., black furniture, six position M4 stock, CAR handguard with single heat shield, A2 flash hider, includes sling. Disc. 2012.

	100%	98%	95%	90%	80%	70%	60%	Last MSR
	$650	$575	$510	$440	$385	$340	$325	*$750*

Add $9 for Tapco Model with Tapco buttstock, SAW grip, polymer mags., and short vertical grip (new 2012).

SIERRA 3G – .223 Wylde cal., mid-length GIO, 16 in. lightweight profile barrel, DTI brake, Magpul 30 shot PMAG, Magpul CTR stock, Magpul Ergo grip, Samson Evolution KeyMod free-float forend, Black finish. New late 2015.

	100%	98%	95%	90%	80%	70%	60%	Last MSR
MSR $1,319	$1,110	$995	$875	$735	$650	$550	$465	

SIERRA 216H (A2 MID-LENGTH CARBINE) – 5.56 NATO cal., GIO, 16 in. chrome moly barrel with threaded muzzle and A2 flash hider, heavy profile, forged aluminum T6 upper and lower receiver, carry handle, 30 shot mag., A2 configuration with rear sight, A2 reinforced Zytel buttstock with trap door assembly, A2 grip, mid-length handguard with single heat shield, Black furniture, 7.4 lbs. Disc. 2014.

	100%	98%	95%	90%	80%	70%	60%	Last MSR
	$685	$615	$550	$475	$420	$365	$335	*$793*

MSR	100%	98%	95%	90%	80%	70%	60%	Last MSR

SIERRA 316H (MID-LENGTH CARBINE) – 5.56 NATO cal., GIO, 16 in. mid-length chrome moly barrel with A2 flash hider, heavy profile, 30 shot mag., black furniture, M4 5-position buttstock, A2 grip, Mil-Spec buffer tube, forged aluminum T6 upper and lower receiver, A3 flat-top, mid-length handguard with single heat shield, M4 feed ramps, 7 lbs.

MSR $753	$650	$575	$510	$440	$385	$340	$325	

SIERRA 316 MLOK – 5.56 NATO cal., mid-length GIO, 16 in. heavy profile barrel, threaded muzzle/A2 flash hider, 30 shot mag., Magpul MOE trigger guard, front sight base, Magpul MOE grip, M4 feed ramps, forged aluminum lower and A3 flat-top upper with Picatinny rail, round forward assist, H buffer, Magpul MOE mid-length aluminum Delta ring handguard, black, Dark Earth, or OD Green finish, 7 lbs. New 2016.

MSR $858	$725	$650	$580	$515	$450	$385	$340	

SIERRA 316 MOE – 5.56 NATO cal., GIO, 16 in. chrome moly barrel, threaded muzzle, A2 flash hider, A3 flat-top, Magpul MOE polymer stock and Magpul MOE grip and trigger guard, 30 shot PMag, forged T6 aluminum upper and lower receiver, Magpul MOE mid-length handguard with heat resistant polymer construction, OD Green (disc. 2015), Black or Dark Earth (disc. 2015) finish, 7.1 lbs. Mfg. 2012-2015.

	$735	$650	$580	$515	$450	$385	$340	$877

SIERRA 316P – 5.56 NATO cal., GIO, A3 mid-length post ban rifle, 16 in. chrome moly barrel with pinned YHM muzzle brake, 10 shot mag., M4 feed ramps, pinned M4 reinforced carbon fiber buttstock with commercial buffer tube, black furniture, mid-length handguard with single heat shield, A3 flat-top, forged aluminum T6 upper and lower receivers, 6.9 lbs. Disc. 2013.

	$685	$615	$550	$475	$420	$365	$335	$806

PISTOLS: SEMI-AUTO

LIMA KeyMod PISTOL – 5.56 NATO cal., AR-15 style, 7 1/2 in. barrel with A2 flash hider, 30 shot mag., aluminum trigger guard, M4 feed ramps, pistol length handguard, Samson Evolution KeyMod 6 1/2 in. free float rail, forged aluminum lower and flat-top upper receivers, pistol buffer tube, hardcoat anodized black finish, 4.8 lbs. New 2016.

MSR $877	$750	$655	$580	$515	$450	$385	$340	

DEMRO

Previous manufacturer located in Manchester, CT.

RIFLES: SEMI-AUTO

T.A.C. MODEL 1 RIFLE – .45 ACP or 9mm Luger cal., blowback operation, 16 7/8 in. barrel, open bolt firing system, lock-in receiver must be set to fire, also available in carbine model.

	$650	$595	$525	$475	$425	$395	$360	

XF-7 WASP CARBINE – .45 ACP or 9mm Luger cal., blowback operation, 16 7/8 in. barrel.

	$650	$595	$525	$475	$425	$395	$360	

Add $45 for case.

DERYA INTERNATIONAL ARMS COMPANY (DERYA HUNTING ARMS)

Current manufacturer established in 2000, and located in Konya, Turkey. Distributed in the U.S. since 2012 by Advanced Tactical Imports, located in Huntsville, AL.

Derya International Arms Company currently manufactures semi-auto, slide action, O/U, and single shot shotguns in various configurations, in addition to air rifles and tactical accessories. Please contact the importer directly for more information, values, and availability (see Trademark Index).

DESERT ORDNANCE

Current rifle manufacturer located in McCarren, NV. Current distributor for U.S. Ordnance.

RIFLES: BOLT ACTION

Desert Ordnance offers several bolt action models, including the Desert Dog Custom, Coyote, and the Prong Horn, in various calibers, colors, and stock options. Please contact the company directly for more information, including pricing and availability (see Trademark Index).

RIFLES: SEMI-AUTO

Desert Ordnance offers a complete line of AR-15 style tactical and hunting rifles, mostly in 5.56 NATO cal. Many options and configurations are available, as well as a wide variety of parts and accessories. Please contact the company directly for more information, including pricing and availability (see Trademark Index).

MSR	100%	98%	95%	90%	80%	70%	60%	Last MSR

DESERT TECH (DESERT TACTICAL ARMS)

Current rifle manufacturer located in West Valley City, UT beginning 2014. Previously named Desert Tactical Arms located in Salt Lake City, UT from 2007-2013.

RIFLES: BOLT ACTION

SRS-A1 (STEALTH RECON SCOUT) – .260 Rem. (new 2014), .300 Win. Mag., .308 Win., .338 Lapua Mag. (new 2014), 6.5 Creedmoor (new 2014), 6.5x47 Lapua (new 2014), or 7mm WSM (new 2014) cal., GIO, 5 or 6 shot detachable box mag., bullpup design with 22 or 26 in. free floating threaded chrome moly match grade barrel, right or left (new 2015) hand action, fully adj. match trigger, quad rail, monolithic upper aluminum receiver, black, OD Green (disc. 2014), or FDE finish, adj. buttstock and cheekpiece, DT Monopod included (beginning 2015), 11 lbs., 8 oz. New 2013.

MSR $4,995	$4,250	$3,750	$3,250	$2,625	$2,200	$1,875	$1,625

Add $200 for .300 Win. Mag. cal.

Add $200 for OD Green (disc. 2014) or FDE finish.

Add $350 for .338 Lapua Mag. and DT brake.

Add $1,645-$2,095 for conversion kit, depending on caliber.

Please contact the company directly for more information on the wide variety of options and accessories available for this model.

SRS-A1 COVERT (STEALTH RECON SCOUT) – .243 Win. (disc. 2013), .300 Win. Mag., .308 Win. or .338 Lapua cal., GIO, 16 or 18 in. match grade free floating barrel, 5 or 6 shot mag., bullpup designed to be eleven inches shorter than conventional M16A2 rifles, tactical stock with adj. LOP, pistol grip, Black, Coyote Brown (disc. 2013), Flat Dark Earth, or Olive Drab (disc. 2014) finish, full length rail, ambidextrous mag release, DT Monopod included (beginning 2015), right or left (new 2015) hand action, 9.4-15.1 lbs.

MSR $4,995	$4,250	$3,750	$3,250	$2,625	$2,200	$1,875	$1,625

Add $200 for .300 Win. Mag.

Add $200 for OD Green (disc. 2014) or Flat Dark Earth finish.

Add $350 for .338 Lapua cal. with DT brake.

Add $1,645-$2,095 for conversion kit, depending on caliber.

RIFLES: SEMI-AUTO

Desert Tech currently manufacutures accessories, ammunition, silencers, and conversion kits. Please contact the company directly for more information on these products (see Trademark Index).

HTI SNIPER – .50 BMG, .375 CheyTac, .408 CheyTac (new 2014), or .416 Barrett (new 2014) cal., GIO, 29 in. match grade, free floating, fluted barrel, 5 shot mag., ergonomic stock, designed to be lighter and more portable, compact bullpup design, black, OD Green (disc. 2014), or FDE finish, DT Monopod included (beginning 2015), 19.4 lbs. New 2012.

MSR $7,495	$6,375	$5,580	$4,780	$4,335	$3,500	$2,875	$2,250

Add $100 for .50 BMG cal.

Add $200 for FDE or OD Green (disc. 2014) finish.

MDR RIFLE – .223 Rem., .308 Win., or 7.62x39mm cal., bullpup design, 16 in. barrel, 20 or 30 shot mag., fully ambidextrous, lightweight, ergonomic, Black/Tan finish, 7 1/2 lbs. New 2015.

MSR $1,999	$1,700	$1,500	$1,250	$1,100	$950	$825	$675

Add $250 for 7.62x51mm cal.

DESERT TOYS

Previous rifle manufacturer located in Mesa, AZ.

RIFLES: BOLT ACTION

REBEL – .50 BMG cal., single shot, 18 or 26 in. barrel, black finish. Disc.

Base price for this model was $2,950.

DETONICS DEFENSE TECHNOLOGIES, LLC

Current semi-auto pistol manufacturer located in Millstadt, IL since 2007.

During 2013, Detonics changed its name to Detonics Defense Technologies, LLC.

MSR	100%	98%	95%	90%	80%	70%	60%	Last MSR

PISTOLS: SEMI-AUTO

COMBAT MASTER HT – .40 S&W cal., 3 1/2 in. barrel, SAO, 7 shot mag., two-tone Cerakote finish, stainless steel frame, low profile sights, aluminum/dymondwood grips, 30 oz. New 2010.

| MSR $1,849 | $1,575 | $1,380 | $1,180 | $1,075 | $875 | $725 | $550 | |

DTX – 9mm Para. or .40 S&W cal., DAO, 4 1/4 in. barrel, two-tone Cerakote finish, aluminum/polymer frame, 14 (.40 S&W) or 16 (9mm Para.) shot, low profile sights, aluminum/polymer grips, 25 1/2 oz. Mfg. mid-2011-2014.

| | $995 | $850 | $725 | $625 | $500 | $400 | $300 | *$1,099* |

NEMESIS HT – .40 S&W cal., similar to Combat Master HT, except has 5 in. barrel, 9 shot, 38 oz. Mfg. 2011-2014.

| | $1,915 | $1,675 | $1,435 | $1,300 | $1,050 | $860 | $675 | *$2,249* |

MTX – .45 ACP cal., DAO, 4 1/4 in. match barrel, black finish, 10 shot mag., aluminum frame with steel receiver, fixed combat sights, 27 oz. New 2014.

| MSR $1,500 | $1,350 | $1,125 | $925 | $800 | $675 | $575 | $500 | |

DETONICS FIREARMS INDUSTRIES

Previous manufacturer located in Bellevue, WA 1976-1988. Detonics was sold in early 1988 to the New Detonics Manufacturing Corporation, a wholly owned subsidiary of "1045 Investors Group Limited."

Please refer to the New Detonics Manufacturing Corporation listing in the N section for complete model listings of both companies.

DETONICS USA

Previous manufacturer located in Pendergrass, GA circa 2004-mid-2007.

PISTOLS: SEMI-AUTO

SCOREMASTER – .45 ACP cal., stainless steel construction, 5 in. barrel, SAO, 7 shot, MMC adj. rear sight, logo engraved checkered rosewood grips, available in Tactical (adj. sights and rail) or Target (Bo-Mar adj. sights, ext. slide stop, mag. release, and ambidextrous safety) configuration, 43 oz.

| | $1,475 | $1,250 | $1,050 | $925 | $800 | $775 | $625 | *$1,650* |

MILITARY TACTICAL – .45 ACP cal., SAO, black bonded finish, adj. sights, includes rail, forward serrations, checkered front strap, and lanyard ring.

| | $1,750 | $1,525 | $1,350 | $1,125 | $950 | $800 | $675 | *$1,975* |

DEVIL DOG ARMS

Current handgun and AR-15 style rifle, parts, and accessories manufacturer located in Lake Zurich, IL.

HANDGUNS: SEMI-AUTO

DDA-1911 CLASSIC HANDGUN – .45 ACP cal., 5 in. match grade stainless barrel, 7 shot mag., heat treated steel frame with front strap and undercut trigger guard, heat treated steel Classic flat-top slide with front and rear grid cocking serrations, 3-hole skeletonized trigger with set screw, high ride beavertail grip safety and single sided thumb safety, XS-Sight Novak front and rear sights, G10 grip panels, black Nitride, FDE Cerakote, and NiB-X finish, 37.2 oz. New 2015.

| MSR $1,299 | $1,100 | $950 | $850 | $750 | $650 | $550 | $450 | |

DDA-1911-TACTICAL HANDGUN – .45 ACP cal., 5 in. match grade stainless barrel, 7 shot mag., heat treated steel frame with integral tactical rail, DDA style front strap and undercut trigger guard, heat treated steel Classic flat-top slide with front and rear grid cocking serrations, 3-hole skeletonized trigger with set screw, G10 grip panels, XS-Sight Novak Tritium front and rear sights, high ride beavertail grip safety and single sided thumb safety, black Nitride, FDE Cerakote, and NiB-X finish, 37.2 oz. New 2015.

| MSR $1,449 | $1,250 | $1,075 | $975 | $875 | $775 | $675 | $550 | |

DDA-15B-EPP – 5.56 NATO cal., GIO, 10 1/2 in. M4 profile barrel with DDA Tri-Comp tactical muzzle brake, 3D billet machined lower and A4 flat-top upper receiver, M4 feed ramp, DDA billet charging handle, Geissele ALG Defense trigger, DDA 9 in. aluminum free float octagon KeyMod handguard, Magpul MBUS polymer flip up sights, Magpul MOE rubberized pistol grip, hardcoat anodized finish in black or FDE, 7 lbs.

| MSR $1,549 | $1,325 | $1,150 | $1,025 | $950 | $825 | $725 | $625 | |

DDA-15B-MPP – 5.56 NATO cal., semi-auto, GIO, 7 1/2 in. M4 profile barrel with DDA tactical muzzle brake and Nitride finish, 3D billet machined lower and A4 flat-top upper receiver, M4 feed ramp, DDA billet charging handle, Geissele ALG Defense trigger, DDA 6 1/2 in. aluminum free float octagon KeyMod handguard, Magpul MBUS polymer flip up sights, Magpul MOE rubberized pistol grip, hardcoat anodized finish in black or FDE, 6 lbs. 3 oz.

| MSR $1,399 | $1,175 | $1,050 | $950 | $850 | $750 | $650 | $525 | |

MSR	100%	98%	95%	90%	80%	70%	60%	Last MSR

DDA-WATCHDOG DEFENDER HANDGUN – .45 Colt/.410 shotgun cal., 3 1/2 in. stainless steel interchangeable barrel, 2 shot mag., rebounding hammer, retracting firing pins, automatic extractor, spring-loaded cammed locking lever, stainless steel frame with integrated trigger guard, DDA Black Ash grip panels, Crossbolt safety, blade front and fixed rear sights, satin polish finish, 22 oz. New 2015.

MSR $599	$525	$475	$425	$375	$300	$250	$200	

RIFLES: SEMI-AUTO

DDA-10B-CERBERUS – 7.62 NATO cal., GIO, 18 in. match grade competition profile stainless steel barrel with DDA Tri-Comp Precision muzzle brake, 3D billet machined lower and flat-top upper receiver, DDA tactical mag. release, ambi selector and billet ambi-charging handle, Dueck Defense Rapid Transition Offset sights, CMC single stage competition trigger, 15 in. aluminum free float octagon Hex or KeyMod handguard, Magpul PRS Sniper adj. buttstock, Accu-Grip Adj. Competition pistol grip, NiB-X coated, 10 lbs. New 2015.

MSR $3,299	$2,825	$2,475	$2,025	$1,750	$1,475	$1,250	$1,075	

DDA-10B-MRP – 7.62 NATO cal., GIO, 18 in. LM profile stainless steel barrel with DDA Tri-Comp precision muzzle brake, 3D billet machined lower and flat-top upper receiver, DDA tactical mag. release, ambi-selector, and billet charging handle, Geissele ALG Defense Combat trigger, DDA 15 in. aluminum free float octagon HEX or KeyMod handguard, Magpul MBUS polymer flip up sights, Magpul MOE rifle buttstock, Magpul MOE rubberized pistol grip, hardcoat anodized finish in black or FDE, 9 lbs. 4 oz.

MSR $1,999	$1,700	$1,500	$1,250	$1,100	$950	$825	$675	

DDA-10B-PRP – 7.62 NATO cal., GIO, 20 in. match grade precision bull stainless steel barrel with DDA Tri-Comp Precision muzzle brake, 3D billet machined lower and flat-top upper receiver, DDA tactical mag. release, ambi selector and billet charging handle, HiperFire 24C trigger, no sights, 15 in. aluminum free float octagon Hex or KeyMod handguard, Ergo Tactical Palm Suregrip pistol grip, Magpul PRS Sniper adj. buttstock, hardcoat anodized finish in black or FDE, 11 lbs. 9 oz. New 2015.

MSR $2,799	$2,375	$2,075	$1,725	$1,475	$1,200	$1,025	$895	

DDA-10B-TRP – 7.62 NATO cal., GIO, 16 in. tactical grade stainless steel barrel with DDA tactical flash suppressor, 3D billet machined lower and flat-top upper receiver, DDA tactical mag. release, ambi selector, and billet ambi-charging handle, HiperFire 24 trigger, 15 in. aluminum free float octagon Hex or KeyMod handguard, Magpul MBUS polymer flip up sights, Magpul MIAD adj. pistol grip, Falcon F93 8-pos. tactical entry buttstock, hardcoat anodized finish in black or FDE, 9 lbs. 8 oz. New 2015.

MSR $2,499	$2,125	$1,875	$1,550	$1,325	$1,100	$950	$825	

DDA-15B-BRP – .300 AAC Blackout cal., GIO, 16 in. LM profile stainless steel barrel with DDA Tri-Comp Precision muzzle brake, 3D billet machined lower and A4 flat-top upper receiver, M4 feed ramp, tactical mag. release, ambi selector, and billet charging handle, Magpul MBUS polymer flip up sights, DDA 15 in. aluminum free-float octagon HEX or KeyMod handguard, HiperFire 24 trigger, Magpul CTR 6-pos. buttstock, Magpul MOE rubberized pistol grip, hardcoat anodized finish in black or FDE, 7 lbs. 3 oz.

MSR $1,899	$1,625	$1,425	$1,200	$1,075	$925	$795	$650	

DDA-15B-CRP – 5.56 NATO cal., GIO, 18 in. match grade competition profile stainless steel barrel with DDA 3Gun Competition muzzle brake, 3D billet machined lower and A4 flat-top upper receiver, M4 feed ramp, DDA tactical mag. release, ambi selector, and billet ambi charging handle, DDA 15 in. aluminum free float octagon HEX or KeyMod handguard, HiperFire 24 3G or 24C trigger, Magpul STR 6-pos. buttstock, Magpul MIAD adj. pistol grip, hardcoat anodized finish in black or FDE, 8 lbs.

MSR $1,999	$1,700	$1,500	$1,250	$1,100	$950	$825	$675	

DDA-15B-DMRP – 5.56 NATO cal., GIO, 18 in. match grade competition profile stainless steel barrel with DDA 3Gun Competition muzzle brake, 3D billet machined lower and A4 flat-top upper receiver, M4 feed ramp, DDA tactical mag. release, ambi selector, and billet charging handle, HiperFire 24E trigger, DDA aluminum free float 15 in. octagon HEX or KeyMod handguard, Magpul MIAD adj. pistol grip, Magpul PRS Sniper adj. buttstock, hardcoat anodized finish in black or FDE, 8 lbs.

MSR $2,099	$1,795	$1,575	$1,325	$1,150	$995	$850	$700	

DDA-15B-ERP – 5.56 NATO cal., GIO, 16 in. HP profile barrel with black Nitride finish and DDA Tri-Comp tactical muzzle brake, 3D billet lower and A4 flat-top upper receiver, M4 feed ramp, Geissele ALG defense trigger, DDA 13 in. aluminum free float octagon HEX or KeyMod handguard, Magpul MBUS polymer flip up sights, Magpul CTR 6-pos. buttstock, Magpul MOE rubberized pistol grip, hardcoat anodized finish in black or FDE, 7 lbs. 9 oz.

MSR $1,549	$1,325	$1,150	$1,050	$925	$795	$675	$550	

DDA-15B-MRP – 5.56 NATO cal., GIO, 16 in. M4 profile barrel with black Nitride finish and DDA tactical muzzle brake, Geissele ALG defense trigger, Magpul MOE polymer ergonomic handguard, Magpul MBUS polymer flip up sights, 3D billet lower and A4 flat-top upper receiver, M4 feed ramp, Magpul MOE rubberized pistol grip, Magpul MOE 6-pos. buttstock, hardcoat anodized finish in black or FDE, 6 lbs. 13 oz.

MSR $1,399	$1,200	$1,075	$950	$800	$700	$600	$500	

MSR	100%	98%	95%	90%	80%	70%	60%	Last MSR

DDA-15B-ORTHROS – 5.56 NATO cal., GIO, 18 in. match grade competition profile stainless steel barrel with DDA 3Gun Competition muzzle brake, 3D billet machined lower and A4 flat-top upper receiver, M4 feed ramp, DDA tactical mag. release, ambi selector and billet ambi charging handle, Dueck Defense Rapid Transition Offset sights, CMC single stage competition trigger, 15 in. aluminum free float octagon Hex or KeyMod handguard, Falcon F93 8-pos. Tactical Entry buttstock, Accu-Grip Adj. Competition pistol grip, NiB-X coated, 7 lbs. 8 oz. New 2015.

| MSR $2,799 | $2,375 | $2,075 | $1,725 | $1,475 | $1,200 | $1,025 | $895 | |

DDA-15B-TRP – 5.56 NATO cal., GIO, 16 in. M4 profile barrel with black Nitride finish and DDA tactical flash suppressor, 3D billet machined lower and A4 flat-top upper receiver, M4 feed ramp, DDA 15 in. aluminum free float octagon HEX or KeyMod handguard, Magpul MBUS polymer flip up sights, tactical mag. release, ambi selector, and billet charging handle, Magpul ACS 6-pos. buttstock, Magpul MIAD adj. pistol grip, HiperFire 24 trigger, hardcoat anodized finish in black or FDE, 7 lbs. 9 oz.

| MSR $1,899 | $1,625 | $1,425 | $1,200 | $1,075 | $925 | $795 | $650 | |

GG2G (GIRL'S GUIDE TO GUNS) SERIES – This series was done in collaboration with Natalie Foster, creator of Girl's Guide to Guns to bring color and design to her Devil Dog Arms custom rifles to suit the style and wardrobe of the most discerning female shooters. DuraCoat Signature colors available are Fast as Lightning, Audrey's Arsenal, Gunning For You, Blushing Bullet, UnderCover, Bullet Breeze, Silver Bullet, Kiss My AK, and Champagne & Lead. New 2015.

* **GG2G-15 Classic** – 5.56 NATO cal., GIO, 16 in. M4 profile chrome moly barrel with DDA Tri-Comp tactical muzzle brake and Nitride finish, 3D billet lower and A4 flat-top upper receiver, M4 feed ramp, Geissele/ALG Mil-Spec Combat trigger, 13 in. aluminum free float octagon Hex handguard, Magpul MBUS polymer flip up sights, Magpul MOE 6-pos. buttstock, Magpul MOE+ rubberized pistol grip, DuraCoat Signature color finish, 6 lbs. 8 oz. New 2015.

| MSR $1,499 | $1,275 | $1,125 | $1,025 | $875 | $750 | $625 | $525 | |

* **GG2G-15 Natalie Signature** – 5.56 NATO cal., GIO, 18 in. match grade competition stainless steel barrel with 3Gun Competition muzzle brake, 3D billet lower and A4 flat-top upper receiver, M4 feed ramp, HiperFire 24 trigger, Magpul MBUS polymer flip up sights, 15 in. aluminum free float octagon Hex handguard, Magpul STR 6-pos. buttstock, Magpul MOE+ rubberized pistol grip, NiB-X coating on metal parts, DuraCoat Signature color finish, 7 lbs. New 2015.

| MSR $1,799 | $1,525 | $1,350 | $1,175 | $1,050 | $900 | $775 | $625 | |

DEZ TACTICAL ARMS, INC.

Current AR-15 style rifle manufacturer located in south central WI since 2012.

CARBINES/RIFLES: SEMI-AUTO

BR4-15 CARBINE MIL-SPEC – 5.56 NATO cal., GIO, 16 in. CMV steel barrel with black Nitride finish, 30 shot mag., A2 front sight base with carbine length gas tube, forged receivers, M4 feed ramps, charging handle, M4 military style forearm, stainless steel trigger, tactical 6-position buttstock, Mil-Spec grip, includes Plano hard plastic case, 6 lbs. 10 oz. New 2015.

| MSR $899 | $775 | $685 | $615 | $550 | $485 | $415 | $370 | |

COMPETITION RIFLE – 5.56 NATO cal., GIO, 18 in. fluted heavy contour stainless steel barrel, 3 port compensator or YHM Phantom muzzle brake, 30 shot E-Lander mag., adj. low profile gas system, forged aluminum A4 upper and lower receiver, M4 feed ramps, charging handle, nickel boron bolt carrier group, DEZ Arms 15 in. Compeition KeyMod free float handguard, Magpul extended trigger guard, Hiperfire Hipertouch trigger, Mil-Spec carbine assembly with FAB Defense 6-position buttstock, adj. cheek riser, ambi Ergo grip, includes Plano hard plastic case, 8 lbs. New 2015.

| MSR $1,849 | $1,575 | $1,375 | $1,190 | $1,050 | $900 | $775 | $625 | |

COVERT OPS CARBINE V2 – .223 Rem. cal., GIO, 16 in. HBar chrome moly button rifled barrel, 30 shot Magpul PMAG with transparent round count window, forged upper receiver with M4 grooved feed ramps, charging handle with extended tactical latch, forged aluminum lower receiver, Mil-Spec bolt carrier group, carbine length gas tube, YHM smooth profile mid-length free floating forearm with end cap, stainless steel military grade trigger, YHM Phantom muzzle brake, FAB Defense 6-position adj. stock with adj. cheekpiece, ambi Ergo grip (v2) or UTG combat sniper grip with FAB Defense magwell grip, 7.1 lbs.

| MSR $1,399 | $1,200 | $1,075 | $950 | $800 | $700 | $600 | $495 | |

COVERT OPS CARBINE V3 – 5.56 NATO cal., 16 in. match grade rifle. New 2015.

| MSR $1,399 | $1,200 | $1,075 | $950 | $800 | $700 | $600 | $495 | |

DTA-4 CARBINE – .223 Rem. cal., GIO, 16 in. chrome moly button rifled barrel, 30 shot aluminum mag., forged upper receiver with M4 grooved feed ramps and charging handle, A2 front sight base with carbine length gas tube, military handguard, M4 military style carbine length forearm, forged aluminum lower receiver, A2 flash hider, stainless steel military grade trigger, tactical 6-position collapsible adj. stock, military style grip, approx. 6 1/2 lbs.

| MSR $1,099 | $925 | $850 | $725 | $625 | $550 | $475 | $425 | |

* **DTA-4 Carbine Optic Ready** – .223 Rem. cal., GIO, similar to DTA-4, except has top rail gas block instead of A2 front sight base. New 2015.

| MSR $1,099 | $925 | $850 | $725 | $625 | $550 | $475 | $425 | |

MSR	100%	98%	95%	90%	80%	70%	60%	Last MSR

DTA-4 ENHANCED CARBINE – .223 Rem. or .300 AAC Blackout cal., GIO, 16 in. chrome moly button rifled barrel, 30 shot Magpul PMAG, forged upper receiver with M4 grooved feed ramps, A2 front sight base with carbine length gas tube, Magpul MOE handguard, carbine length forearm, forged aluminum lower receiver, A2 flash hider, stainless steel military grade trigger, Magpul MOE 6-position adj. stock, Israeli grip, approx. 6 lbs. 13 oz.

| MSR $1,219 | $1,035 | $925 | $800 | $685 | $595 | $515 | $440 | |

Add $15 for .300 AAC Blackout cal.

DARK ASSAULT CARBINE – 7.62 NATO cal., GIO, 16 in. HBAR match grade barrel with flash suppressor, 30 shot mag., low profile gas block with carbine length gas tube, YHM Diamond profile free floating mid-length handguard with end cap, forged receivers, ALG Defense trigger, M4 feed ramps, charging handle, 6-pos. shock absorbing buttstock with adj. cheek riser, Ambi Ergo grip and FAB Defense magwell grip, black finish, includes Plano hard plastic case, 8 lbs. 6 oz. New 2015.

| MSR $1,499 | $1,275 | $1,125 | $1,025 | $875 | $750 | $625 | $525 | |

FLAWLESS RIFLE – .223 Rem. cal., GIO, 20 or 24 in. chrome moly HBar button rifled diamond fluted barrel, 30 shot Magpul PMAG with transparent round count window, forged upper receiver with M4 grooved feed ramps and charging handle with extended tactical latch, forged aluminum lower receiver, Mil-Spec bolt carrier group, quad rail with rifle length gas tube, YHM diamond profle free floating rifle length forearm with end cap, stainless steel military grade trigger, .50 cal. style flash enhancer, FAB Defense 6-position adj. stock with adj. cheekpiece, Ergo SureGrip, 9 lbs. Disc. 2014.

| | $1,350 | $1,200 | $1,075 | $950 | $815 | $700 | $575 | *$1,600* |

Add $10 for 24 in. barrel.

TRU-FLIGHT CARBINE – .223 Rem. cal., GIO, 16 in. chrome moly button rifled barrel, 30 shot Magpul PMAG with transparent round count window, forged upper receiver with M4 grooved feed ramps and extended charging handle, forged aluminum lower receiver, Mil-Spec bolt carrier group, single rail Picatinny gas block with carbine length gas tube, YHM carbine length free floating forearm, stainless steel military grade trigger, three port compensator, FAB Defense 6-position adj. stock with adj. cheekpiece, Israeli grip with FAB Defense magwell grip, 6.8 lbs. Disc. 2014.

| | $1,150 | $1,030 | $900 | $750 | $650 | $550 | $465 | *$1,370* |

TWISTED ELITE CARBINE – .223 Rem. cal., GIO, 16 in. chrome moly HBar button rifled twist fluted barrel, 30 shot Magpul PMAG with transparent round count window, forged upper receiver with M4 grooved feed ramps and extended charging handle, forged aluminum lower receiver, Mil-Spec bolt carrier group, low profile gas block with carbine length gas tube, YHM carbine length free floating "Todd Jarrett Competition" forearm, stainless steel military grade trigger, YHM Phantom muzzle brake, FAB Defense 6-position adj. stock with adj. cheekpiece, Ergo SureGrip with FAB Defense magwell grip, black or FDE (new 2015) finish, 7.2 lbs.

| MSR $1,419 | $1,200 | $1,075 | $950 | $800 | $700 | $600 | $495 | |

Add $150 for FDE finish (new 2015).

ULTRA LIGHT RIFLE – 5.56 NATO cal., GIO, 16 in. match grade chrome moly barrel, YHM Phantom Comp/flash hider, 30 shot Magpul PMAG, low profile gas block with carbine length gas tube, Mil-Spec A4 forged aluminum upper and lower receiver, M4 feed ramps, charging handle, Nitride coated bolt carrier group, DEZ Arms KeyMod carbine length free float handguard, ALG Defense Q.M.S. trigger, Mil-Spec carbine assembly with 6-position stock, A2 pistol grip, 6.2 lbs. New 2015.

| MSR $1,299 | $1,100 | $995 | $875 | $735 | $650 | $550 | $465 | |

HUNTER RIFLE – 6.8 SPC cal., GIO, match grade 16 in. heavy contour barrel, enhanced flash hider, 25 shot mag., adj. low profile carbine length gas tube, YHM TJ Competition mid-length free float handguard, continuous top Picatinny rail, nickel Teflon coated ALG ACT trigger system, nickel boron bolt carrier group, Mil-Spec A4 forged aluminum upper and lower receiver, Magpul extended trigger guard, M4 grooved feed ramps, extended charging handle, Magpul MOE fixed rifle stock, ambi Ergo grip, includes hard plastic Plano case, 7 lbs. 15 oz. New 2016.

| MSR $1,459 | $1,235 | $1,100 | $985 | $835 | $725 | $615 | $515 | |

DIAMOND

Trade name on shotguns manufactured by Matsan A.S. located in Istanbul, Turkey since 1962. Currently imported by Adco Arms Co., Inc., located in Woburn, MA.

Matsan A.S. manufactures high quality, reliable semi-auto, slide action, O/U, and SxS shotguns in various gauges and configurations. Please contact the company directly for more information on current models, pricing, and availability (see Trademark Index).

DIAMONDBACK FIREARMS

Current pistol and AR-15 style rifle manufacturer located in Cocoa, FL. Distributor and dealer sales.

During late 2012, Taurus Holdings purchased an exclusive global distribution agreement with Diamondback Firearms, LLC. Taurus will assume all sales and marketing efforts of the Diamondback branded products from its Miami office.

MSR	100%	98%	95%	90%	80%	70%	60%	Last MSR

PISTOLS: SEMI-AUTO

DB15 – 5.56 NATO or .300 AAC Blackout cal., GIO, 7 1/2 or 10 1/2 in. chrome moly barrel, forged aluminum lower and A3 flat-top forged aluminum upper receiver, SST, no sights, Diamondback aluminum modified four rail handguard, A2 style pistol grip, black, Flat Dark Earth, or OD Green finish. New 2014.

MSR $899	$800	$700	$600	$550	$450	$350	$275	

Add $15 for Flat Dark Earth or OD Green finish.

RIFLES: SEMI-AUTO

DB10 – .308 Win. cal., GIO, 18 in. HBAR barrel with A2 flash hider and black nitride finish, 20 shot mag., low profile gas block, no sights, CNC machined billet aluminum lower with custom trigger guard and T Marked upper receiver, Odin KeyMod rail, Magpul ACS stock, Magpul MOE Plus pistol grip, black anodized or Flat Dark Earth finish, 8.5 lbs. New 2015.

MSR $2,049	$1,750	$1,550	$1,295	$1,150	$985	$865	$725	

Add $33 for Flat Dark Earth finish.

DB10 ELITE – .308 Win. cal., 18 in. heavy barrel with JP compensator, 20 shot Magpul mag., CNC machined billet lower with custom trigger guard and T marked upper receiver, CMC trigger, 15 in. LW KeyMod rail, no sights, Magpul PRS stock, Ergo SureGrip grip, black anodized or Flat Dark Earth finish, 10 1/2 lbs. New 2015.

MSR $2,619	$2,215	$1,935	$1,600	$1,375	$1,125	$975	$850	

Add $34 for Flat Dark Earth finish.

DB15 5.56 NATO – 5.56 NATO cal., GIO, 16 in. chrome moly M4 contour free floating barrel with A2 flash hider, A3 flat-top upper receiver, Diamondback aluminum modified four rail or standard 2-piece handguard, 4-position M4 stock, black or Flat Dark Earth finish, available with no sights, A2 front sights, or Magpul sights, 6.65 lbs. New 2013.

MSR $756	$650	$575	$510	$440	$385	$340	$325	

Add $141 for Magpul sights.
Add $143 for A2 front sights.
Add $263 for four rail handguard or $296 for four rail handguard and Magpul sights.
Add $285 for Flat Dark Earth finish and four rail handguard.

* **DB15 Camo** – 5.56 NATO cal., 16 in. chrome moly M4 contour free-floating barrel with A2 flash hider, M4 stock, A2 style pistol grip, forged lower and A3 flat-top upper receiver, Diamondback aluminum modified four rail handguard, no sights or Magpul sights, Digital Green Camo or Digital Tan Camo finish, 6.65 lbs. New 2013.

MSR $1,221	$1,035	$935	$805	$675	$585	$500	$425	

Add $33 for Magpul sights.

* **DB15 Fluted** – 5.56 NATO cal., GIO, 16 or 18 in. fluted barrel, 13 1/2 in. fluted Underside KeyMod rail or 15 in. Elite KeyMod rail, forged upper and lower receivers, A2 style pistol grip, ATI Strikeforce stock with aluminum civilian buffer tube assembly, no sights, black anodized or Stone Grey finish, 6.65 lbs. New 2015.

MSR $1,589	$1,350	$1,200	1,075	$950	$815	$700	$575	

Add $360 for 15 in. Elite KeyMod rail and Stone Grey finish.

* **DB15 Nickel** – 5.56 NATO cal., GIO, 30 shot mag., 16 in. M4 contour free floating barrel with A2 flash hider, A3 flat-top upper receiver, aluminum four rail handguard, nickel boron coating, 6-position Magpul CTR stock, Magpul MIAD grip, no sights, 6.65 lbs. New 2013.

MSR $1,199	$1,025	$925	$795	$665	$575	$510	$435	

Add $28 for MagPul sights.

DB15 .300 BLACKOUT – .300 AAC Blackout cal., GIO, 16 in. chrome moly M4 contour free float barrel with A2 flash hider, forged lower and A3 flat-top upper receiver, no sights, A2 front sights, or Magpul sights, Diamondback aluminum modified four rail or standard 2-piece handguard, A2 style pistol grip, ATI Strikeforce stock with aluminum civilian buffer tube assembly, black or Flat Dark Earth finish, 6.65 lbs.

MSR $1,010	$850	$725	$650	$585	$515	$450	$395	

Add $10 for A2 front sight only.
Add $130 for four rail handguard, no sights.
Add $160 for Flat Dark Earth finish or $198 for FDE finish with Magpul sights.
Add $231 for four rail handguard with MagPul sights.

* **DB15 .300 Blackout Camo** – .300 AAC Blackout cal., 16 in. chrome moly M4 contour free floating barrel with A2 flash hider, M4 stock, A2 style pistol grip, forged lower and A3 flat-top upper receiver, Diamondback aluminum modified four rail handguard, no sights or Magpul sights, Digital Green Camo or ATAC Camo finish, 6.65 lbs.

MSR $1,264	$1,050	$950	$815	$685	$595	$515	$440	

Add $104 for Magpul sights.
Add $104 for ATAC camo finish with Magpul sights.

MSR	100%	98%	95%	90%	80%	70%	60%	Last MSR

* **DB15 .300 Blackout Nickel** – .300 AAC Blackout cal., GIO, 16 in. M4 contour free floating barrel with A2 flash hider, forged lower and A3 flat-top upper receiver, aluminum four rail handguard, nickel boron coating, 6-position Magpul CTR stock, Magpul MIAD grip, no sights or Magpul sights, 6.65 lbs. New 2013

MSR $1,244	$1,040	$940	$810	$670	$585	$525	$435	

Add $99 for Magpul sights.

DLASK ARMS CORP.

Current manufacturer and distributor located in British Columbia, Canada. Direct sales.

PISTOLS: SEMI-AUTO

Dlask Arms Corp. manufactures custom M-1911 style custom guns for all levels of competition. Previous models included the TC Tactical Carry ($1,250 last MSR), Gold Team ($2,000 last MSR), Silver Team L/S ($1,700 last MSR), and the Master Class ($3,500 last MSR). Dlask also imported a DAC 394 during 1997-1998, it's a 9mm Para. copy of the Sig 225. Values ranged from $225-$400, depending on condition. In addition, Dlask also manufactures a wide variety of custom parts for the M-1911. For more information, please contact the company directly (see Trademark Index).

DLASK 1911 – .45 ACP cal., available in all calibers, Suregrip safety by Ed Brown, slide fit to frame, Novak fixed sight, full length guide rod, black checkered grips.

MSR $1,250	$1,125	$975	$850	$775	$625	$500	$400	

DLASK 1911 PRO – .45 ACP cal., avail. in all calibers, adj. rear sight and dovetail front sight, Suregrip safety by Ed Brown, slide is fit to frame, checkered brown grips, includes full length guide rod. New 2008.

MSR $1,560	$1,400	$1,225	$1,050	$950	$775	$625	$500	

DLASK 1911 PRO PLUS – .45 ACP cal., other cals. available, hand fit, will accept all standard parts, adj. rear sight and dovetail front, ambidextrous safety, Suregrip safety by Ed Brown, includes full length guide rod. New 2008.

MSR $2,500	$2,250	$1,975	$1,695	$1,525	$1,250	$1,015	$800	

DLASK 1911 SLICK – .45 ACP cal., tactical 1911 style, heavy flanged, tapered cone match grade barrel, Tactical Novak sights, extreme dehorn. Mfg. mid-2011-2014.

	$1,250	$1,095	$950	$850	$700	$575	$450	*$1,400*

RIFLES: SEMI-AUTO

BASIC DAR 22 – .22 LR cal., GIO, 16 1/2 in. barrel, Dlask DAR 22 receiver with integral Picatinny rail, Black, OD Green, or Tan Brown Hogue overmolded stock, anodized black finish. New 2012.

MSR $700	$615	$540	$470	$400	$350	$310	$295	

DAR-701 TARGET – AR-15 style, GIO, 22, 24, or 26 in. stainless steel or blue barrel, aluminum alloy construction, two front sling swivels on the tube. Disc. 2013.

	$1,975	$1,725	$1,475	$1,350	$1,075	$900	$700	*$2,200*

DOLPHIN GUN COMPANY

Current rifle manufacturer located in Lincolnshire, United Kingdom. No current U.S. importation.

Dolphin Gun Company was founded circa 2006 by competitive shooters Mik Maksimovic and Pete Hobson. The company builds custom competition "F Class" and tactical style rifles, utilizing Accuracy International or tactical style stocks. Many calibers and options are available. Please contact the company directly for more information, including pricing, delivery time, availability, gun services, etc. (see Trademark Index).

DOMINION ARMS

Previous trademark of slide action shotguns manufactured by Rauch Tactical, located in Blaine, WA.

Rauch manufactured 12 ga. tactical style slide action shotguns until circa 2010.

DOUBLE D ARMORY, LTD

Current AR-15 style rifle manufacturer located in Greenwood Village, CO since 2012. Dealer and distributor sales.

RIFLES: SEMI-AUTO

Double D Armory also manufactures AR-15 parts as well as their own hardcoat anodized proprietary camo patterns called COVERCEAL™.

MODEL SST 5.56 NATO – 5.56 NATO cal., GIO, 16 in. Lothar Walther match grade stainless steel barrel with polygonal rifling and black Nitride finish, A2 flash suppressor, 30 shot mag., mid-length gas system, nickel boron bolt carrier group, aluminum billet upper and lower receiver, M4 feed ramps, Bravo Co. Gunfighter Mod 4 charging handle, 15 in. enhanced free floating handguard, ALG Defense combat trigger, oversized trigger guard, flared magwell, B5 Systems 6-pos. collapsible stock, Magpul MOE+ or B5 Systems grip, full-length top Picatinny rail, choice of hardcoat anodized proprietary camo pattern finish, 6.2 lbs. New 2015.

MSR $1,949	$1,650	$1,450	$1,225	$1,085	$935	$800	$660	

MSR	100%	98%	95%	90%	80%	70%	60%	Last MSR

MODEL SST .300 BLACKOUT – .300 AAC Blackout cal., 16 in. standard Lothar Walther barrel, carbine length gas system, otherwise similar to Model SST 5.56, 6.2 lbs. New 2015.

	100%	98%	95%	90%	80%	70%	60%
MSR $1,949	$1,650	$1,450	$1,225	$1,085	$935	$800	$660

DOUBLESTAR CORP.

Current manufacturer located in Winchester, KY. Distributed by J&T Distributing. Dealer sales only.

Doublestar Corp. currently also manufactures AR-15 accessories and uppers.

PISTOLS: SEMI-AUTO

1911 COMBAT PISTOL – .45 ACP cal., SA, forged steel frame, stainless steel slide, optional 1913 Picatinny rail, Novak white dot front and LoMount rear sights, memory groove beavertail grip safety, 8 shot mag., 25 LPI checkering, black Nitride or nickel finish, 39 oz. Mfg. 2010-2014.

	100%	98%	95%	90%	80%	70%	60%	Last MSR
	$1,800	$1,575	$1,350	$1,225	$995	$825	$625	$2,000

Add $150 for nickel finish.

C2 – .45 ACP cal., 4 1/4 in. barrel, 8 shot mag., forged steel frame and slide, funneled magwell, 25 LPI checkering, Novak sights, Greider hand-tuned trigger, Wilson "Bulletproof" internals, rounded butt or Bobtail, DLC Black or Smoke Grey Ion Bond finish, 34.6 oz. New 2015.

	100%	98%	95%	90%	80%	70%	60%
MSR $1,999	$1,700	$1,500	$1,250	$1,100	$950	$825	$675

Add $57 for Smoke Grey Ion Bond finish w/out bobtail or $225 with bobtail.

Add $167 if without bobtail (Black Ion Bond finish).

C2G – .45 ACP cal., 5 in. barrel, Novak 8 shot mag., Novak sights, with or without Picatinny rail, funneled magwell, 25 LPI checkering, DLC Black or Smoke Grey Ion Bond finish, 39 oz. New 2015.

	100%	98%	95%	90%	80%	70%	60%
MSR $1,929	$1,640	$1,425	$1,200	$1,075	$925	$795	$650

Add $75 for Smoke Grey Ion Bond finish (railed model).

Add $45 if without Picatinny rail or $58 for Smoke Grey Ion Bond finish and no Picatinny rail.

C2G 10MM X PISTOL – 10mm cal., forged frame and slide, 5 in. Clark match ramped barrel and match barrel bushing, Greider trigger. New 2016.

	100%	98%	95%	90%	80%	70%	60%
MSR $2,178	$1,835	$1,600	$1,350	$1,175	$1,000	$860	$715

C2S – .45 ACP cal., 3 1/2 in. Storm Lake stainless barrel, full melt barrel bushing, 8 shot mag., Novak sights, round butt or bobtail, funneled magwell, 25 LPI checkering, DLC Black or Smoke Grey Ion Bond finish, 33 oz. New 2015.

	100%	98%	95%	90%	80%	70%	60%
MSR $2,074	$1,785	$1,525	$1,275	$1,125	$975	$850	$685

Add $168 for bobtail model.

PHD 1911 – .45 ACP cal., 5 in. barrel, XS express sights with a Tritium front sight, round butt, Wilson Combat high-ride beavertail grip safety, rear cocking serrations, flat-top serrated slide, black finish, 34.9 oz. New 2016.

	100%	98%	95%	90%	80%	70%	60%
MSR $1,364	$1,140	$1,015	$885	$740	$675	$575	$475

DSC .300 BLACKOUT AR PISTOL – .300 AAC Blackout cal., 7 1/2 or 9 in. rifled barrel, pistol length free float aluminum handguard, pistol tube, 4 3/4 lbs. New 2014.

	100%	98%	95%	90%	80%	70%	60%
MSR $1,407	$1,250	$1,075	$950	$800	$700	$600	$495

MINI DRAGON DSC 7.5 AR PISTOL – 5.56 NATO, .300 AAC Blackout, or 9mm Para. cal., AR-15 style, GIO, 7 1/2 in. chrome moly steel heavy barrel, 30 shot mag., pistol length free-float aluminum handguard, Picatinny rail gas block, forged lower and A3 flat-top upper receiver with M4 feed ramps, forward assist, dust cover, DSC pistol tube, A2 grip, hardcoat anodized finish, 4.7 lbs.

	100%	98%	95%	90%	80%	70%	60%
MSR $838	$700	$620	$550	$475	$420	$365	$335

MINI DRAGON DSC 10.5 AR PISTOL – 5.56 NATO or 9mm Para. cal., AR-15 style, GIO, 10 1/2 in. chrome moly steel heavy barrel with A2 muzzle, single heat shield CAR handguard, A2 upper receiver, front sight tower, DSC pistol tube, A2 pistol grip, 5 1/2 lbs.

	100%	98%	95%	90%	80%	70%	60%
MSR $1,284	$1,075	$965	$820	$715	$625	$535	$450

Add $220 for 9mm Para. cal.

MINI DRAGON DSC 11.5 AR PISTOL – 5.56 NATO or 9mm Para. (disc.) cal., AR-15 style, GIO, 11 1/2 in. chrome moly steel heavy barrel with A2 muzzle, 30 shot mag., front sight tower, CAR length polymer handguard, T6 aluminum A3 flat-top upper receiver with M4 feed ramps, forward assist, dust cover, A2 pistol grip, hardcoat anodized finish, 5.7 lbs.

	100%	98%	95%	90%	80%	70%	60%
MSR $1,284	$1,075	$965	$820	$715	$625	$535	$450

Add $220 for 9mm Para. cal. (disc.).

DSC STAR-15 PISTOL – .223 Rem. cal., AR-15 style, GIO, 7 1/2, 10 1/5, or 11 1/2 in. chrome moly match barrel, A2 flash hider, front sight assembly or rail gas block. Disc. 2010.

	100%	98%	95%	90%	80%	70%	60%	Last MSR
	$875	$750	$675	$600	$525	$450	$395	$950

MSR	100%	98%	95%	90%	80%	70%	60%	Last MSR

RIFLES/CARBINES: SEMI-AUTO

Double Star Corp. makes a complete line of AR-15 style carbines/rifles, as well as a line of SBRs (Short Barreled Rifles) for military/law enforcement.

ARC (ALWAYS READY CARBINE) – 5.56 NATO cal., GIO, low profile gas block, 16 in. lightweight barrel, A2 flash hider, 30 shot mag., Samson folding front and rear sights, Ace SOCOM stock, Ergo Sure grip, 15 in. Samson Evolution free floating handguard, aluminum Mil-Spec flat-top upper, M4 feed ramps, forward assist, dust cover, DSC TAC latch charging handle, hardcoat anodized black finish, 6.8 lbs. New 2016.

| MSR $1,371 | $1,150 | $1,030 | $900 | $750 | $685 | $585 | $485 | |

BUMP DRAGON – New 2016.

| MSR $1,284 | $1,075 | $965 | $815 | $715 | $625 | $535 | $450 | |

MDM (MODERN DESIGNATED MARKSMAN) – 5.56 NATO cal., GIO, 16 in. stainless steel Wilson air gauged barrel, A2 flash hider, 30 shot mag., no sights, Magpul ACS buttstock, Hogue pistol grip, low profile gas block, 15 in. Samson Evolution free floating handguard, aluminum Mil-Spec flat-top upper receiver, M4 feed ramps, forward assist, dust cover, standard charging handle, 8.35 lbs. New 2016.

| MSR $1,570 | $1,325 | $1,170 | $1,050 | $915 | $785 | $665 | $550 | |

DSC .204 RUGER – .204 Ruger cal., GIO, 20 or 24 in. stainless steel fluted or non-fluted bull barrel, Picatinny rail gas block, Mil-Spec flat-top, free float aluminum tube handguard, A2 pistol grip and buttstock. Mfg. 2013 only.

| | $995 | $900 | $800 | $700 | $600 | $500 | $425 | $1,125 |

DSC .300 BLACKOUT – .300 AAC Blackout cal., GIO, 16 in. HBAR barrel, black nitride coating, Picatinny rail gas block, CAR handguard, Mil-Spec flat-top with M4 feed ramp, A2 pistol grip, 6-position commercial spec DS-4 stock, 6.7 lbs. New 2013.

| MSR $954 | $815 | $700 | $630 | $570 | $500 | $425 | $380 | |

DSC 3 GUN RIFLE – 5.56 NATO cal., AR-15 style, GIO, 30 shot, 18 in. fluted stainless heavy barrel with Carlson Comp muzzle brake, DSC enhanced trigger guard, Timney trigger, Samson 15 in. Evolution handguard, Ace ARFX buttstock, Hogue or Ergo ambi SureGrip, 7 1/2 lbs. New 2012.

| MSR $1,543 | $1,310 | $1,145 | $1,035 | $880 | $760 | $635 | $535 | |

DSC COMMANDO – 5.56 NATO cal., GIO, 16 in. chrome moly HBAR lightweight barrel, permanently attached flash hider, Picatinny rail gas block or "F" marked FSB, two-piece CAR length polymer handguard, Mil-Spec flat-top or A2 upper receiver, A2 pistol grip, 6-position DS-4 buttstock, front sight base, 6.45 lbs. New 2013.

| MSR $1,400 | $1,200 | $1,075 | $950 | $800 | $700 | $600 | $495 | |

DSC C3 CONSTANT CARRY CARBINE – 5.56 NATO cal., GIO, 16 in. lightweight A-1 profile barrel, steel low profile gas block, Samson Evolution 9 in. handguard, Mil-Spec flat-top with M4 feed ramp, A2 pistol grip, Ace Ltd. AR-UL-E buttstock, Magpul MBUS front and rear sights, 5 1/2 lbs. New 2013.

| MSR $1,197 | $1,025 | $925 | $800 | $685 | $595 | $515 | $440 | |

DSC CRITTERSLAYER – .223 Rem. cal., AR-15 style, GIO, 24 in. fluted Shaw barrel, full length Picatinny rail on receiver and Badger handguard, two-stage match trigger, palmrest, ergonomic pistol grip with finger grooves, includes Harris LMS swivel bipod, flat-top or high rise upper receiver, 11 1/2 lbs. Disc. 2010.

| | $1,300 | $1,150 | $925 | $850 | $750 | $650 | $550 | $1,430 |

Add $40 for ported barrel.

* **DSC CritterSlayer Jr.** – .223 Rem. cal., GIO, similar to CritterSlayer, except has 16 in. barrel and fully adj. A2 style buttstock, DSC flat-top or high rise upper receiver. Disc. 2010.

| | $1,050 | $875 | $775 | $675 | $575 | $475 | $400 | $1,150 |

Add $65 for detachable carrying handle or $35 for removable front sight.
Add $200 for Enhanced CritterSlayer Jr. with 16 in. Expedition barrel, CAR handguard, and adj. buttstock.

DSC DEER RIFLE – 6.8 SPC cal., AR-15 style, GIO, 20 in. chrome moly heavy barrel with A2 phantom flash hider, 5 shot mag., Ace ARFX skeleton stock, Next Camo water transfer finish, winter trigger guard, 7 3/4 lbs. Mfg. 2012-2014.

| | $1,295 | $1,125 | $875 | $800 | $700 | $600 | $500 | $1,450 |

DSC DS-4 – 5.56 NATO, 6.5 Grendel, 6.8 SPC, or 7.62x39mm (disc.) cal., GIO, AR-15 style, patterned after the Military M-4, GIO, 16 in. chrome moly barrel with Phantom A2 flash hider, 30 shot mag., double heat shield handguard, A2 or flat-top upper receiver with M4 feed ramps, forward assist, dust cover, A2 pistol grip, 6-position buttstock, matte black, tactical pink (disc.), or OD Green (disc.) finish, 6.3 lbs.

| MSR $931 | $800 | $695 | $620 | $550 | $485 | $415 | $370 | |

DSC DS-4 FDE – 5.56 NATO cal., GIO, 16 in. chrome moly M4 barrel, Flat Dark Earth Teflon coated finish, Picatinny rail gas block or "F" marked FSB, double heat shield two-piece polymer handguard, flat-top upper receiver, A2 pistol grip, 6-position buttstock, Magpul Rear BUIS, FDE finish. New mid-2012.

| MSR $1,390 | $1,160 | $1,035 | $900 | $750 | $685 | $585 | $485 | |

MSR	100%	98%	95%	90%	80%	70%	60%	Last MSR

* DSC DS-4 OD – 5.56 NATO cal., similar to DS-4 FDE, except features OD Green finish. New mid-2012.

MSR $1,390	$1,160	$1,035	$900	$750	$685	$585	$485

DSC DS-4 MOE – 5.56 NATO cal., AR-15 style, GIO, 16 in. chrome moly barrel, Magpul MOE features include handguard, upper receiver, pistol grip, enhanced trigger guard, rear BUIS, 6-position commercial spec Magpul MOE stock, 30 shot mag., FDE finish, 6.3 lbs.

MSR $1,476	$1,245	$1,100	$985	$835	$725	$615	$515

DSC EXPEDITION CARBINE/RIFLE – 5.56 NATO cal., AR-15 style, GIO, 16 or 20 (disc.) in. lightweight contour barrel with integrated muzzle brake, single heat shield CAR handguard, A2 or flat-top upper receiver, A2 pistol grip, A2 or 6-position commercial spec stock, 6.35 lbs. Disc. 2014.

	100%	98%	95%	90%	80%	70%	Last MSR
	$925	$825	$675	$550	$450	$395	$350	*$1,030*

Add $65 for detachable carry handle (disc.).

DSC LIGHTWEIGHT TACTICAL – 5.56 NATO cal., GIO, fluted 16 in. chrome moly HBAR barrel, Picatinny rail gas block or "F" marked FSB, single heat shield two-piece CAR length polymer handguard, Mil-Spec flat-top or A2 upper receiver, D-4 six position buttstock, 6.9 lbs. New mid-2012.

MSR $1,400	$1,200	$1,075	$950	$800	$700	$600	$495

DSC MARKSMAN RIFLE – 5.56 NATO cal., AR-15 style, GIO, 20 in. Wilson Arms stainless steel barrel, Daniel Defense free float handguard, Picatinny rail gas block, A2 Phantom flash hider, Magpul PRS buttstock, adj. LOP, Magpul MIAD pistol grip, two-stage trigger, front and rear flip sight, approx. 9 lbs.

MSR $1,804	$1,525	$1,350	$1,175	$1,050	$900	$775	$625

Add $185 for bipod.

DSC MIDLENGTH CARBINE – 5.56 NATO cal., 16 in. heavy barrel with A2 flash hider, 30 shot alum. mag., front sight tower, mid-length polymer handguard, DS-4 stock, A2 pistol grip, 6.7 lbs. New 2014.

MSR $1,350	$1,135	$1,015	$885	$740	$675	$575	$475

DSC MIDNIGHT DRAGON – 5.56 NATO cal., AR-15 style, GIO, 24 in. stainless steel bull barrel with spiral fluting and black nitride coating, aluminum free float handguard with bipod stud, A3 flat-top upper receiver, Ace ARFX buttstock, Ergo tactical pistol grip, DSC two-stage trigger, Badger TAC latch, DSC enhanced trigger guard, 9 1/4 lbs. New 2012.

MSR $1,115	$930	$850	$725	$625	$550	$475	$425

DSC MSD MIL-SPEC DRAGON – 5.56 NATO cal., 16 in. barrel, "F" marked front sight tower, DS-4 Mil-Spec stock, 6.1 lbs. New 2014.

MSR $1,088	$900	$785	$685	$600	$535	$465	$415

DSC PATROL RIFLE – 5.56 NATO cal., AR-15 style, GIO, 16 in. chrome moly lightweight barrel with A2 phantom flash hider, Slimline quad rail handguard with three low profile rail covers, flip up rear sight, six position DS-4 buttstock, Hogue overmolded pistol grip, 6 1/2 lbs.

MSR $1,089	$900	$785	$685	$600	$535	$465	$415

DSC STAR-CAR CARBINE – 5.56 NATO, 6.5 Grendel, 6.8 SPC, or 9mm Para. cal., AR-15 style, GIO, 16 in. chrome moly steel heavy barrel with Phantom A2 flash hider, 30 shot mag., single heat shield CAR handguard, A2 or flat-top upper receiver, standard A2 pistol grip, fixed post-ban CAR type stock, 6.7 lbs.

MSR $890	$750	$665	$580	$515	$450	$385	$340

Add $75 for 6.8 SPC, $125 for 6.5 Grendel, or $220 for 9mm Para. cal.

DSC STAR M4 CARBINE – .223 Rem. cal., AR-15 M4 carbine design, GIO, fixed M4 style post-ban buttstock, 16 in. barrel, M4 handguard, 6.76 lbs. Disc. 2012.

	100%	98%	95%	90%	80%	70%	Last MSR
	$825	$725	$650	$565	$500	$465	$430	*$910*

Add $85 for detachable carrying handle.

DSC STAR DISSIPATOR – 5.56 NATO cal., AR-15 style, GIO, 16 in. dissipator chrome moly steel barrel with full length handguard, A2 or 6 position CAR buttstock, A2 or flat-top upper receiver, 6.9 lbs. Disc. 2014.

	100%	98%	95%	90%	80%	70%	Last MSR
	$925	$825	$700	$625	$525	$425	$350	*$1,030*

DSC STAR 10-B RIFLE – .308 Win. cal., 18 in. stainless steel button rifled and threaded barrel with Bullseye muzzle brake, AR stock with laser etched position marks and 7-position tube, Ergo tactical pistol grip with textured finger grooves, Samson Evo handguard, billet upper and lower receivers, Gunfighter charging handle, Type III hardcoat anodized black finish, approx. 10 lbs. New 2015.

MSR $2,567	$2,175	$1,900	$1,550	$1,350	$1,115	$965	$835

DSC STAR-15 LIGHTWEIGHT TACTICAL – .223 Rem. cal., AR-15 style, GIO, 16 in. fluted H-Bar barrel with attached muzzle brake, shorty A2 buttstock, A2 or flat-top upper receiver, 6 1/4 lbs. Disc. 2004, reintroduced 2009-2010.

	100%	98%	95%	90%	80%	70%	Last MSR
	$825	$725	$650	$565	$500	$465	$430	*$930*

Add $65 for detachable carrying handle.

MSR	100%	98%	95%	90%	80%	70%	60%	Last MSR

DSC STAR-15 RIFLE/CARBINE – 5.56 NATO, 6.5 Grendel, 6.8 SPC, or 7.62x39mm (disc. 2013) cal., AR-15 style, GIO, 16 (disc.) or 20 in. match barrel with A2 flash hider, ribbed forearm, two-piece rifle handguard, standard A2 buttstock and pistol grip, A2 or flat-top upper receiver, 8 lbs.

MSR	100%	98%	95%	90%	80%	70%	60%	Last MSR
MSR $1,326	$1,115	$995	$875	$735	$650	$550	$465	

Add $65 for flat-top with detachable carrying handle.
Add $75 for 6.8 SPC,or 7.62x39mm (disc. 2013) cal. or $125 for 6.5 Grendel cal.

DSC STAR-15 9MM CARBINE – 9mm Para. cal., AR-15 style, GIO, 16 in. barrel, ribbed forearm, A2 or flat-top upper receiver, 7 1/2 lbs. Mfg. 2004, reintroduced 2009-2010.

	100%	98%	95%	90%	80%	70%	60%	Last MSR
	$950	$825	$725	$650	$575	$500	$450	$1,080

Add $65 for detachable carry handle.

DSC STAR-15 6.8 SPC RIFLE/CARBINE – 6.8 SPC cal., GIO, 16 or 20 in. chrome moly barrel, A2 upper or flat-top, A2 (rifle) or 6-position DS-4 buttstock, 7-8 lbs. Disc. 2010.

	100%	98%	95%	90%	80%	70%	60%	Last MSR
	$825	$725	$650	$565	$500	$465	$430	$935

Add $65 for detachable carry handle.

DSC STAR-15 6.8 SPC SUPER MATCH RIFLE – 6.8 SPC cal., GIO, 20, 22, or 24 in. free float super match stainless steel bull barrel, Picatinny rail gas block, two-piece NM free floating handguard. Disc. 2010.

	100%	98%	95%	90%	80%	70%	60%	Last MSR
	$950	$825	$725	$650	$575	$500	$450	$1,075

DSC STAR-15 .204 RUGER RIFLE – .204 Ruger cal., GIO, 24 in. chrome moly barrel, A2 buttstock, A2 flash hider. Disc. 2010.

	100%	98%	95%	90%	80%	70%	60%	Last MSR
	$925	$850	$750	$650	$575	$500	$450	$1,050

DSC STAR-15 6.5 GRENDEL CARBINE/RIFLE – 6.5 Grendel cal., GIO, 16 or 20 in. chrome moly barrel, A2 or 6-position (Carbine) buttstock. Disc. 2010.

	100%	98%	95%	90%	80%	70%	60%	Last MSR
	$875	$775	$675	$600	$525	$450	$395	$985

Add $65 for detachable carry handle.

DSC STAR-15 6.5 GRENDEL SUPER MATCH RIFLE – 6.5 Grendel cal., GIO, 20, 22, or 24 in. free-floating match bull barrel, A2 buttstock, Picatinny rail gas block, two-piece NM free floating handguard. Disc. 2010.

	100%	98%	95%	90%	80%	70%	60%	Last MSR
	$995	$875	$775	$675	$575	$475	$400	$1,125

DSC STAR-15 DCM SERVICE RIFLE – 5.56 NATO cal., AR-15 style, GIO, 20 in. free-float match barrel, National Match front and rear sights, two-stage match trigger, DCM handguard, 8 lbs. Disc.

	100%	98%	95%	90%	80%	70%	60%	Last MSR
	$900	$825	$725	$650	$550	$485	$440	$1,000

DSC SUPERMATCH RIFLE – 5.56 NATO, 6.5 Grendel, or 6.8 SPC cal., AR-15 style, GIO, 16, 20, 22 (disc. 2013), or 24 in. free-float stainless steel Super Match barrel, 10 shot alum. mag., flat-top or high rise upper receiver, includes Picatinny rail and one-piece National Match handguard, A2 stock, 7.8 - 9 3/4 lbs.

MSR	100%	98%	95%	90%	80%	70%	60%	Last MSR
MSR $1,020	$860	$725	$650	$585	$515	$450	$395	

Add $65 for 6.8 SPC or $115 for 6.5 Grendel cal.

DSC TARGET CARBINE – .223 Rem. cal., AR-15 style, GIO, 16 in. dissipator barrel with full length round one-piece National Match handguard, flip up sights, Picatinny rail, flat-top upper receiver. Disc.

	100%	98%	95%	90%	80%	70%	60%	Last MSR
	$1,050	$875	$775	$695	$625	$550	$485	$1,175

DSC ZOMBIE SLAYER – 5.56 NATO cal., AR-15 style, GIO, 14 1/2 in. DS4 barrel (16 in. with permanently attached A2 phantom flash hider), flat-top upper receiver with detachable GI carry handle, two 30 shot magazines, 6-position D4 stock, double heat shield handguards, USMC multi-purpose bayonet, "Zombie Slayer" lasered lower, 6.1 lbs. Mfg. 2012-2014.

	100%	98%	95%	90%	80%	70%	60%	Last MSR
	$1,100	$975	$875	$775	$675	$575	$475	$1,245

DORKAS FOREIGN TRADE

Current exporter of Turkish-made shotguns located in Konya, Turkey. No current U.S. importer.

Dorkas currently distributes and exports hunting and tactical shotguns manufactured in Turkey by Özkanlar (Akrep, Kobra, Bavyer and Lupus trademarks), Turkuaz, and Mertmak. Please contact the company directly for current information, including U.S. availability and pricing (see Trademark Index).

DRAKE ASSOCIATES

Current rifle manufacturer located in Shelter Island, NY. Dealer, law enforcement/military, and civilian sales.

RIFLES: BOLT ACTION

TIER 1 HUNTER STALKER – .223 Rem., .30-06, 7mm Rem. Mag., .308 Win. or .300 Win. Mag. cal., super match chamber, right or left hand Rem. 700 action, 16 1/2 or 20 in. single point cut competition barrel with target crown,

MSR	100%	98%	95%	90%	80%	70%	60%	Last MSR

AAC Blackout 51T muzzle brake or DRAKE 3 port removable muzzle brake with Hex, Remington X-Mark Pro adj. trigger, Hunter Stalker LWSS Universal Chassis in black, Flat Dark Earth, or OD Green, bipod attachment point, FAB Defense GL SHOCK CP with cheek riser kit, Hogue pistol grip, 20 MOA long rail, three 9 o'clock Picatinny rails with QD Swivel hard point, Mil-Spec tube, Cerakote barrel and action finish, includes case.

| MSR $3,336 | $2,850 | $2,500 | $2,150 | $1,950 | $1,575 | $1,285 | $1,000 | |

TIER 1 STALKER M24E – .30-06, 7mm Rem. Mag., .308 Win. or .300 Win. Mag. cal., super match chamber, right hand only Rem. 700 short or long action, 26 in. single point cut competition barrel with target crown, AAC Blackout 51T muzzle brake or DRAKE 3 port removable muzzle brake with Hex, Remington X-Mark Pro adj. trigger, 20 MOA long rail, three 9 o'clock Picatinny rails with QD Swivel hard point, Mil-Spec tube, choice of Strike Dual 30 or Strike Dual 33 Chassis in black, Flat Dark Earth or Pink Warrior finish, Cerakote barrel and action finish, includes case.

| MSR $4,999 | $4,250 | $3,725 | $3,195 | $2,895 | $2,350 | $1,925 | $1,495 | |

TIER 2 STALKER – .223 Rem., .30-06, 7mm Rem. Mag., .308 Win. or .300 Win. Mag. cal., right hand only Rem. 700 action, 16 1/2, 20, or 26 in. SPS or varmint barrel, Remington X-Mark Pro adj. trigger, 20 MOA long rail, three 9 o'clock Picatinny rails with QD Swivel hard point, Hogue pistol grip, Mil-Spec tube, choice of Cadex Field Strike, Strike Dual 30 or Strike Dual 33 Chassis in Black, Flat Dark Earth, OD Green, or Pink Warrior finish, bipod attachment point, Cerakote barrel and action finish, includes case.

| MSR $2,995 | $2,550 | $2,225 | $1,925 | $1,750 | $1,400 | $1,150 | $895 | |

Add $1,000 for Strike Dual 30 or 33 Chassis.

This model comes with an SPS barrel in 16 1/2 or 20 inches only with flash hider, and the varmint barrel is only available in .300 Win Mag., .30-06, or 7mm Rem. Mag.

TIER 3 HUNTER STALKER – .223 Rem., .30-06, 7mm Rem. Mag., .308 Win., .300 AAC Blackout, or .300 Win. Mag. cal., right or left hand action, 16 1/2, 20, or 26 in. SPS or varmint barrel, Remington X-Mark Pro adj. trigger, Hunter Stalker LWSS Universal Chassis in black, Flat Dark Earth, or OD Green finish, bipod attachment point, FAB Defense GL SHOCK CP with cheek riser kit, Hogue pistol grip, 20 MOA long rail, three 9 o'clock Picatinny rails with QD Swivel hard point, Mil-Spec tube, includes case.

| MSR $2,295 | $1,950 | $1,700 | $1,465 | $1,325 | $1,075 | $880 | $685 | |

TIER 4 SPECIAL APPLICATION STALKER – .300 Win. Mag., .338 Lapua, .416 Rem. Mag., or .50 BMG cal., super match chamber, right hand McMillan G30 or TAC50 action, 26 in. M24 profile single cut competition fluted or non-fluted barrel with target crown, AAC Blackout or Drake 3 port removable muzzle brake with Hex (MK13 only) or Rangemaster Precision Arms removable muzzle brake (MK15 only), Timney (MK13), Huber (MK15), or X-Treme (MK15) adj. trigger, Strike Dual 33 or Dual 50 Chassis in black, Flat Dark Earth, OD Green or Pink Warrior finish, 20 (MK13) or 40 (MK15) MOA long rail, 2 and 4 in. 3/6/9 o'clock Picatinny rail kits, QD Swivel hard point, Cerakote action and barrel finish.

| MSR $6,495 | $5,525 | $4,850 | $4,150 | $3,750 | $3,050 | $2,485 | $2,000 | |

Add $2,200 for Tac 50 MK15 configuration in .416 Rem. Mag. or .50 BMG cal.

E SECTION

E.D.M. ARMS

Current manufacturer established in 1997, located in Hurricane, UT since 2008. Previously located in Redlands, CA 1997-2008. Dealer and consumer direct sales.

MSR	100%	98%	95%	90%	80%	70%	60%	Last MSR

RIFLES: BOLT ACTION

WINDRUNNER MODEL 96 (XM107) – .338 Lapua (mfg. 2002-2010) or .50 BMG cal., takedown repeater action, EDM machined receiver, fully adj. stock, match grade 28 in. detachable barrel that removes within seconds, allowing exact head space every time the barrel is reinstalled, includes two 5 (.50 BMG cal.) or 8 (.338 Lapua) shot mags., Picatinny rail, and bipod, 24 (Lightweight Tactical Takedown) or 36 lbs.

| MSR $7,500 | $6,900 | $6,375 | $5,575 | $4,775 | $4,325 | $3,500 | $2,875 | |

Add $1,000 for left hand action.

   * ***Windrunner Model 96 SS99*** – similar to Windrunner, except is single shot, w/o mag., includes bipod and sling, 32 lbs. New 2002.

| MSR $5,250 | $4,850 | $4,475 | $4,150 | $3,450 | $2,850 | $2,250 | $1,850 | |

MODEL 06 MINI-WINDRUNNER – .308 Win. cal., 20 in. barrel, 10 shot mag., Picatinny rail, lightweight, tactical, takedown version of the Windrunner Model 96, 11.2 lbs. Mfg. 2007-2010.

| | $3,750 | $3,300 | $2,900 | $2,550 | $2,175 | $1,800 | $1,500 | *$4,250* |

MODEL XM04 CHEYENNE TACTICAL – .408 CheyTac cal., takedown repeater, tactical bolt action configuration, 5 shot mag., 30 in. fluted barrel with suppressor, desert camo finish, retractable stock, effective range is 2,500+ yards, 27 lbs. New 2002.

| MSR $6,750 | $6,400 | $5,500 | $5,000 | $4,500 | $4,000 | $3,500 | $3,000 | |

Subtract $1,400 for single shot action (disc.).

MODEL 12 – .223 Rem. or 7.62 NATO cal., fluted barrel with muzzle brake, 4 shot detachable mag., Savage AccuTrigger standard, includes twin rail adj. stock with heavy recoil pad, receiver with Picatinny rail, pistol grip, guaranteed one MOA at 100 yards. New 2012.

| MSR $2,975 | $2,675 | $2,250 | $1,875 | $1,600 | $1,400 | $1,200 | $1,000 | |

MODEL 50 – .50 BMG cal., single shot, twin rail adj. skeletonized stock, Picatinny rail and bipod. Mfg. 2003.

| | $3,750 | $3,250 | $2,850 | $2,450 | $2,050 | $1,650 | $1,275 | *$4,250* |

MODEL 98 – .338 Lapua cal., takedown repeating bolt action, single rail adj. stock, pistol grip, 22 lbs. New 2003.

| MSR $6,750 | $6,325 | $5,500 | $5,000 | $4,500 | $4,000 | $3,500 | $2,750 | |

510 DTC EUROP – .50 DTC Europ cal. (1 in. shorter than .50 BMG), designed for CA shooters and legal in CA. Mfg. 2007-2008.

| | $7,000 | $6,200 | $5,500 | $5,000 | $4,500 | $4,000 | $3,500 | *$7,500* |

RIFLES: SEMI-AUTO

WINDRUNNER .50 CAL. – .50 BMG cal., 28 in. Lilja match grade chrome moly barrel, integrated Picatinny rail, removable black stock with cheekrest and adj. buttpad. Mfg. 2006-2013.

| | $8,650 | $7,875 | $6,890 | $5,900 | $5,355 | $4,350 | $3,550 | *$9,250* |

E.M.F. CO., INC.

Current importer and distributor established 1956, located in Santa Ana, CA. Distributor and dealer sales. E.M.F. stands for Early & Modern Firearms Inc.

For information on Great Western Arms Co., Dakota Single Action and Hartford revolvers, rifles, and carbines imported by E.M.F., please refer to the Great Western Arms Co., Dakota Single Action Revolvers and Hartford sections. Please refer to the *Blue Book of Modern Black Powder Arms* by John Allen (also online) for more information and prices on E.M.F.'s lineup of modern black powder models.

PISTOLS: SEMI-AUTO

All current semi-auto pistols are manufactured in the U.S.

HARTFORD 1911-A1 – .45 ACP cal., 5 in. barrel, SA, 7 shot mag., patterned after original 1911, parkerized finish, fixed sights, flat or arched mainspring housing, black Ergo, brown plastic military, ultra stag, or checkered hardwood grips, includes two mags. Mfg. 2009-2013.

| | $515 | $465 | $400 | $360 | $330 | $300 | $275 | *$585* |

MSR	100%	98%	95%	90%	80%	70%	60%	Last MSR

HARTFORD 1911 COMBAT MODEL – .45 ACP cal., 7 shot mag., similar to 1911-A1 model, except has choice of fixed Tritium low profile or adj. sights with Tritium inserts, parkerized, blue, Duracoat, or nickel finish, black Ergo or checkered hardwood grips, includes two mags, lock, and hard case. Mfg. 2009-2013.

| | $595 | $525 | $450 | $395 | $360 | $330 | $300 | *$685* |

HARTFORD 1911 CCC MODEL – .45 ACP cal., 4 1/4 in. barrel, SA, 8 shot mag., choice of fixed low profile, Novak style fixed night, or Bo-Mar adj. sights, parkerized, blue, stainless, Duracoat, or nickel finishes, includes two mags., lock, and hard case. Mfg. 2009-2013.

| | $950 | $825 | $700 | $575 | $475 | $425 | $375 | *$1,075* |

Add $710 for night sights and skip checkered grips.

FMK MODEL 9C1 – 9mm Para. cal., 4 in. barrel, SA, SFO, lightweight polymer frame, 10 or 14 shot mag., blue steel slide with engraved Bill of Rights, five interchangable front sights, eighteen interchangable rear sights, "Mag Out" safety, striker indicator, loaded chamber indicator, black or desert tan finish, includes two mags., lock, and case, 23 1/2 oz. Mfg. by FMK Firearms beginning 2009.

| MSR $400 | | $360 | $325 | $285 | $260 | $235 | $215 | $200 | |

RIFLES: SEMI-AUTO

J R CARBINE – 9mm Para., .40 S&W, or .45 ACP cal., GIO, blowback operation, utilizes standard M4/AR-15 furniture and trigger components, right or left-hand action, Glock magazine, can be converted to other popular pistol mags., flat-top receiver, quad rail forend, black adj. stock, extended pistol grip, tri-flatted barrel design, patented ejection and extraction features, compatible with AR-15 accessories. Mfg. in U.S.A. by J R Carbines, LLC mid-2010-2013.

| | $675 | $600 | $525 | $475 | $425 | $400 | $350 | *$750* |

Please refer to Just Right Carbines listing for current manufacture.

RIFLES: SEMI-AUTO, REPRODUCTIONS

These models are authentic shooting reproductions previously manufactured in Italy.

AP 74 – .22 LR or .32 ACP cal., GIO, copy of the Colt AR-15, 15 shot mag., 20 in. barrel, 6 3/4 lbs. Importation disc. 1989.

| | $350 | $295 | $250 | $200 | $175 | $155 | $145 | *$295* |

Add $25 for .32 ACP cal.

* **AP74 Sporter Carbine** – .22 LR cal. only, GIO, wood sporter stock. Importation disc. 1989.

| | $375 | $325 | $275 | $225 | $195 | $175 | $160 | *$320* |

* **AP74 Paramilitary Paratrooper Carbine** – .22 LR cal. only, GIO, folding wire, black nylon, or wood folding stock. Importation disc. 1987.

| | $395 | $350 | $300 | $260 | $215 | $175 | $165 | *$325* |

Add $10 for wood folding stock.

* **AP74 "Dressed" Military Model** – GIO, with Cyclops scope, Colt bayonet, sling, and bipod. Disc. 1986.

| | $395 | $350 | $300 | $265 | $240 | $220 | $200 | *$450* |

GALIL – .22 LR cal. only, reproduction of the Israeli Galil. Importation disc. 1989.

| | $350 | $295 | $250 | $200 | $175 | $155 | $145 | *$295* |

KALASHNIKOV AK-47 – .22 LR cal. only, reproduction of the Russian AK-47, semi-auto. Importation disc. 1989.

| | $350 | $295 | $250 | $200 | $175 | $155 | $145 | *$295* |

FRENCH M.A.S. – .22 LR cal. only, reproduction of the French bullpup combat rifle, with carrying handle, 29 shot mag. Importation disc. 1989.

| | $375 | $325 | $265 | $240 | $220 | $200 | $185 | *$320* |

M1 CARBINE – .30 cal. only, copy of the U.S. Military M1 Carbine. Disc. 1985.

| | $295 | $250 | $225 | $200 | $175 | $150 | $125 | *$205* |

Add 50% for Paratrooper variation.

EAGLE ARMS, INC.

Previous manufacturer located in Geneseo, IL. Previous division of ArmaLite, Inc. 1995-2002, located in Geneseo, IL. Manufacture of pre-1995 Eagle Arms rifles was in Coal Valley, IL.

During 1995, Eagle Arms, Inc. reintroduced the ArmaLite trademark. The new company was organized under the ArmaLite name. In 2003, Eagle Arms became a separate company, and no longer a division of ArmaLite.

Eagle Arms also made lower receivers only.

MSR	100%	98%	95%	90%	80%	70%	60%	Last MSR

RIFLES: SEMI-AUTO, RECENT MFG.

On the following M-15 models manufactured 1995 and earlier, A2 accessories included a collapsible carbine type buttstock (disc. per 1994 C/B) and forward bolt assist mechanism. Accessories are similar, with the addition of National Match sights. The A2 suffix indicates the rifle is supplied with carrying handle, A4 designates a flat-top receiver, some are equipped with a detachable carrying handle.

AR-10 MATCH RIFLE – .308 Win. cal., GIO, very similar to the Armalite AR-10 A4 rifle, 20 or 24 (Match rifle) in. chrome moly barrel, A2 (Service rifle) or A4 style flat-top upper receiver (no sights), black stock with pistol grip and forearm, 10 shot mag., 9.6 lbs. Mfg. 2001-2005.

	$925	$850	$750	$650	$550	$450	$395	$1,000

Add $65 for Service rifle with A2 front/rear sights.

Add $480 for 24 in. barrel and aluminum free floating handguard.

MODEL M15 A2/A4 RIFLE (EA-15 E-1) – .223 Rem. or .308 Win. cal., patterned after the Colt AR-15A2, GIO, 20 in. barrel, A2 sights or A4 flat-top, with (pre 1993) or w/o forward bolt assist, 7 lbs. Mfg. 1990-1993, reintroduced 2002-2005.

	$750	$675	$600	$550	$500	$450	$395	$795

Add $40 for .223 cal. flat-top (Model E15A4B).

Add $205 for .308 Win. cal. flat-top.

Add 10% for .308 Win. cal.

* **Model M15 A2/A4 Rifle Carbine (EA9025C/EA9027C)** – GIO, features collapsible (disc. per C/B 1994) or fixed (new 1994) buttstock and 16 in. barrel, 5 lbs. 14 oz. Mfg. 1990-95, reintroduced 2002-2005.

	$750	$675	$600	$550	$500	$450	$395	$795

Add $40 for flat-top (Model E15A4CB).

1997 retail for the pre-ban models was $1,100 (EA9396).

Beginning 1993, the A2 accessory kit became standard on this model.

* **Model M15 A2 H-BAR Rifle (EA9040C)** – GIO, features heavy Target barrel, 8 lbs. 14 oz., includes E-2 accessories. Mfg. 1990-95.

	$850	$750	$675	$575	$525	$450	$395	$895

1997 retail for this pre-ban model was $1,100 (EA9200).

* **Model M15 A4 Rifle Eagle Spirit (EA9055S)** – GIO, includes 16 in. premium air gauged National Match barrel, fixed stock, full length tubular aluminum handguard, designed for IPSC shooting, includes match grade accessories, 8 lbs. 6 oz. Mfg. 1993-95, reintroduced 2002 only.

	$800	$700	$625	$550	$500	$450	$395	$850

The 1995 pre-ban variation of this model retailed at $1,475 (EA9603).

* **Model M15 A2 Rifle Golden Eagle (EA9049S)** – similar to M15 A2 H-BAR, except has National Match accessories and two-stage trigger, 20 in. extra heavy barrel, 12 lbs. 12 oz. Mfg. 1991-1995, reintroduced 2002 only.

	$1,000	$875	$775	$675	$575	$475	$425	$1,125

The 1997 pre-ban variation of this model retailed at $1,300 (EA9500).

* **Model M15 A4 Rifle Eagle Eye (EA9901)** – GIO, includes 24 in. free floating 1 in. dia. barrel with tubular aluminum handguard, weighted buttstock, designed for silhouette matches, 14 lbs. Mfg. 1993-95.

	$1,350	$1,175	$995	$850	$725	$625	$525	$1,495

* **Model M15 Rifle Action Master (EA9052S)** – GIO, match rifle, flat-top, solid aluminum handguard tube, for free floating 20 in. barrel with compensator, N.M. accessories, fixed stock, 8 lbs. 5 oz. Mfg. 1992-95, reintroduced 2002 only.

	$750	$675	$600	$550	$500	$450	$395	$850

The 1995 pre-ban variation of this model retailed at $1,475 (EA5600).

* **Model M15 A4 Rifle Special Purpose (EA9042C)** – GIO, 20 in. barrel, flat-top (A4) or detachable handle receiver. Disc. 1995.

	$895	$825	$725	$625	$525	$450	$395	$955

The 1995 pre-ban variation of this model retailed at $1,165 (EA9204).

* **Model M15 A4 Rifle Predator (EA9902)** – GIO, post-ban only, 18 in. barrel, National Match trigger, flat-top (A4) or detachable handle receiver. Mfg. 1995 only.

	$1,225	$1,050	$925	$825	$700	$600	$495	$1,350

EAST RIDGE/STATE ARMS GUN COMPANY, INC.

Current rifle manufacturer located in Bancroft, WI.

The East Ridge Gun Company, Inc. manufactures the State Arms Gun Co. .50 BMG cal. bolt action rifles. East Ridge purchased the State Arms Gun Company in 2001, and combined the company names.

MSR	100%	98%	95%	90%	80%	70%	60%	Last MSR

RIFLES: BOLT ACTION, SINGLE SHOT

BIG BERTHA – .50 BMG cal., 36 in. Lothar Walther premium target bull barrel, muzzle brake, all steel bipod, special tactical or custom laminated wood stock, scope rail, approx. 40 lbs.

MSR $2,750	$2,475	$2,165	$1,850	$1,685	$1,365	$1,115	$865	

COMPETITOR 2000 – .50 BMG cal., 30 or 36 in. Lothar Walther fluted bull barrel, extra large muzzle brake, all steel bipod, adj. aluminum stock with military hardcoat finish, scope mount, Jewell trigger, pistol grip with palm swell, accuracy guaranteed to be less than 1 minute of angle with custom ammo.

MSR $3,400	$3,075	$2,695	$2,300	$2,095	$1,695	$1,385	$1,075	

LIGHT WEIGHT COMPETITOR – .50 BMG cal., 30 in. Lothar Walther fluted bull stainless or chrome moly barrel, reduced weight muzzle brake, adj. skeletonized aluminum stock with black hardcoat finish, scope mounting rail, Jewell trigger, sniper type pistol grip with palm swell, optional carrying handle, 28 lbs. Disc. 2010.

	$3,075	$2,695	$2,300	$2,095	$1,695	$1,385	$1,075	*$3,400*

Add $200 for stainless steel barrel.

REBEL – .50 BMG cal., 36 in. Lothar Walther bull barrel, muzzle brake, all steel bipod, adj. aluminum tactical stock with removable carrying handle, or custom laminated wood stock, scope rail, AR-15 grip, approx. 38 lbs.

MSR $2,650	$2,375	$2,050	$1,750	$1,550	$1,250	$1,025	$800	

Add $200 for custom laminated wood stock.

SHORTY – .50 BMG cal., 30 in. Lothar Walther tapered barrel, muzzle brake, all steel bipod, adj. aluminum tactical stock with removable carry handle, or custom laminated wood stock, scope rail, approx. 31 lbs.

MSR $2,450	$2,150	$1,895	$1,625	$1,450	$1,150	$925	$715	

Add $200 for custom laminated wood stock.

TITAN BENCH – .50 BMG cal., 30 in. Lothar Walther stainless steel fluted barrel, muzzle brake, adj. trigger, bench rest style laminated stock in choice of colors, precision ground tapered or flat steel scope base, 26 lbs. 6 oz.

MSR $2,550	$2,295	$2,015	$1,725	$1,560	$1,260	$1,035	$800	

ED BROWN CUSTOM, INC.

Previous rifle manufacturer circa 2000-2014, located in Perry, MO. During 2009, the rifle division was transferred to Ed Brown Products, Inc.

Please refer to Ed Brown Products, Inc. for currently manufactured rifles.

RIFLES: BOLT ACTION

702 LIGHT TARGET (TACTICAL) – .223 Rem. or .308 Win. cal., features Ed Brown short repeater action, aluminum trigger guard and floorplate, 21 in. match grade barrel, includes Talley scope mounts, approx. 8 3/4 lbs. Disc. 2005.

	$2,495	$2,185	$1,870	$1,695	$1,370	$1,125	$875	*$2,495*

A3 TACTICAL – various cals., top-of-the-line sniper weapon, 26 in. heavyweight match grade hand lapped barrel, Shilen trigger, McMillan fiberglass A-3 tactical stock, 11 1/4 lbs. Disc. 2008.

	$2,995	$2,620	$2,245	$2,035	$1,645	$1,350	$1,050	*$2,995*

ED BROWN PRODUCTS, INC.

Current manufacturer established during 1988 located in Perry, MO. Consumer direct sales.

PISTOLS: SEMI-AUTO

All the models in this category except the Classic Custom are available with Gen. III black coating at no extra charge.

The following MSRs represent each model's base price, with many options available at additional charge.

Add $75 for ambidextrous safety on certain models.

COMMANDER BOBTAIL – various cals., M1911 style, SA, carry configuration, features round butt variation of the Class A Limited frame, incorporating frame and grip modifications, including a special housing w/o checkering, 4 1/4 in. barrel, Hogue exotic wood grips, 34 oz. Disc. 2003.

	$2,350	$2,055	$1,760	$1,600	$1,290	$1,055	$820	*$2,350*

EXECUTIVE ELITE – .45 ACP cal., M1911 style, 5 in. barrel, SA, choice of all blue/blue, stainless blue (disc.), stainless/stainless, or stainless/stainless with Black Gen4 slide/barrel, features Hardcore components, flared and lowered ejection port, Commander style hammer, 25 LPI checkering on front and rear grip strap, beveled magwell, fixed 3-dot night sights, checkered Cocobolo wood grips, 34 oz. New 2004.

MSR $2,895	$2,675	$2,300	$1,925	$1,675	$1,325	$1,075	$850	

EXECUTIVE CARRY – .45 ACP cal., similar to Executive Elite, except has 4 1/4 in. barrel and Bobtail grip, 34 oz. New 2004.

MSR $3,145	$2,825	$2,500	$2,050	$1,825	$1,425	$1,175	$925	

MSR	100%	98%	95%	90%	80%	70%	60%	Last MSR

EXECUTIVE TARGET – .45 ACP cal., similar to Executive Elite, except modified for target and range shooting, adj. Ed Brown rear sight, 5 in. barrel, single stack mag., matte stainless or matte black Gen. III stainless finish, Cocobolo diamond checkered grips, approx. 38 oz. Mfg. 2006-disc.

| | $2,675 | $2,400 | $2,000 | $1,800 | $1,425 | $1,175 | $925 | *$2,945* |

Add $75 for California Executive Target Model with matte blue frame/slide finish and black Gen II coating.

KOBRA – .45 ACP cal., 1911 style, 7 shot, 5 in. barrel, SA, features "snakeskin" metal treatment on frame, mainspring housing and slide, 3-dot night sights, exotic wood grips, matte stainless or matte black Gen. III stainless finish, 39 oz. New 2002.

| MSR $2,695 | $2,475 | $2,125 | $1,825 | $1,575 | $1,250 | $995 | $775 | |

KOBRA CARRY – .45 ACP cal., 1911 style, 4 1/4 in. barrel, SA, features Bobtail and "snakeskin" metal treatment on frame, mainspring housing and slide, 3-dot night sights, matte stainless or matte black Gen. III stainless finish, 34 oz. New 2002.

| MSR $2,945 | $2,725 | $2,350 | $2,000 | $1,750 | $1,425 | $1,100 | $875 | |

* ***Kobra Carry Lightweight*** – .45 ACP cal., 7075 aluminum single stack Commander frame and Bobtail housing, 4 1/4 in. barrel, 10-8 black sight, front night sight, slim Cocobolo wood grips, black Gen. III coating, 27 oz. New 2010.

| MSR $3,320 | $3,075 | $2,725 | $2,300 | $1,900 | $1,550 | $1,200 | $975 | |

SPECIAL FORCES – .45 ACP cal., 1911 style, 7 shot mag., 5 in. barrel, SA, Commander style hammer, special Chainlink treatment on front and rear grip straps, checkered diamond pattern Cocobolo grips, 3-dot night sights, Generation III black coating applied to all metal surfaces, 38 oz. New 2006.

| MSR $2,695 | $2,475 | $2,100 | $1,800 | $1,550 | $1,225 | $995 | $775 | |

Add $100 for stealth gray Gen. III (disc.) or Gen4 finish and carbon fiber grips (new 2011).
Add $75 for California Special Forces Model with matte blue frame/slide finish and black G3 (disc.) or Gen4 coating.

SPECIAL FORCES LIGHT RAIL – .45 ACP cal., 5 in. barrel, SA, forged Government style frame with integral light rail, Chainlink treatment on forestrap and mainspring housing, fixed 3-dot night sights, traditional square cut cocking serrations, diamond cut wood grips, approx. 40 oz. Mfg. 2009-2012.

| | $2,275 | $1,975 | $1,725 | $1,550 | $1,275 | $1,050 | $825 | *$2,395* |

SPECIAL FORCES CARRY/CARRY II – .45 ACP cal., 4 1/2 in. Commander style barrel, SA, single stack bobtail frame, 8 shot, Chainlink treatment on forestrap and mainspring housing, stainless or optional Gen. III finish, low profile combat rear sights, fixed dovetail 3-dot night front sights, diamond cut wood grips, approx. 35 oz. New 2009.

| MSR $2,945 | $2,600 | $2,250 | $1,900 | $1,700 | $1,350 | $1,100 | $855 | |

JIM WILSON SPECIAL LIMITED EDITION – .45 ACP cal., SA, features black frame with Jim Wilson signature on slide, smooth Tru-Ivory grips, 7 shot mag., 38 oz. Limited mfg. 2007.

| | $2,295 | $2,010 | $1,720 | $1,560 | $1,260 | $1,035 | $800 | *$2,295* |

JEFF COOPER COMMEMORATIVE LIMITED EDITION – .45 ACP cal., 5 in. barrel, SA, Govt. style, forged frame and slide, matte finish, square cut serrations on rear of slide, Jeff Cooper signature on slide, fixed Novak Lo-mount dovetail rear sight, dovetail front sight, 7 shot mag., exhibition grade Cocobolo grips with Jeff Cooper pen and sword logo, includes limited edition leather bound copy of *Principles of Self Defense*, 38 oz. Limited mfg. 2008.

| | $2,295 | $2,010 | $1,720 | $1,560 | $1,260 | $1,035 | $800 | *$2,295* |

MASSAD AYOOB SIGNATURE EDITION – .45 ACP cal., 4 1/4 in. barrel, Commander bobtail stainless steel frame, SA, 25 LPI checkering on frame and mainspring housing, Massad Ayoob signature on right side of slide, ambidextrous safety, fixed 3-dot sights, black G10 checkered grips, 4 1/2 lb. trigger pull, includes a copy of *Gun Digest Book of Concealed Carry* by Massad Ayoob. Limited mfg. 2009-2010.

| | $2,700 | $2,365 | $2,025 | $1,835 | $1,485 | $1,215 | $945 | *$2,700* |

CHAMPION MOLON LABE 1911 – .45 ACP cal., 5 in. barrel, designed by certified law enforcement instructor Dave Champion, hand fitted and assembled, "Molon Labe" in Greek letters is laser engraved on the left side of the frame, "Champion" is laser engraved on the right side of the slide, custom G10 grips with engraved Spartan battle helmet, custom Snakeskin metal treatment on front and back grip straps, wide notch rear sight with Tritium front night sight, solid aluminum trigger, black Gen. III coating. Limited mfg. 2011 only.

| | $2,595 | $2,150 | $1,850 | $1,625 | $1,450 | $1,275 | $1,050 | *$2,595* |

RIFLES: BOLT ACTION

In August of 2010, Ed Brown Products announced that all bolt action rifle production had been put on hold indefinitely. The following last MSRs represent each model's base price, and many options were available at additional cost. Beginning 2006, all M-702 actions were disc. in favor of Ed Brown's new Model 704 controlled feed action with spring-loaded extractor integral with the bolt. All recently manufactured rifles have stainless steel barrels and the entire rifle is coated with Generation III black coating (new 2007).

MSR	100%	98%	95%	90%	80%	70%	60%	Last MSR

A5 TACTICAL – .300 Win. Mag. or .308 Win. cal., features adj. McMillan A-5 tactical stock, 5 shot detachable mag., black finish, Shilen trigger, 12 1/2 lbs. Mfg. 2008-2010.

| | $4,495 | $3,935 | $3,370 | $3,055 | $2,470 | $2,025 | $1,575 | $4,495 |

M40A2 MARINE SNIPER – .30-06 or .308 Win. cal., 24 in. match grade barrel, special McMillan GP fiberglass tactical stock with recoil pad, Woodlands camo is molded into stock, this model is a duplicate of the original McMillan Marine Sniper rifle used in Vietnam, except for the Ed Brown action, 9 1/4 lbs. Mfg. 2002-2010.

| | $3,695 | $3,235 | $2,770 | $2,515 | $2,030 | $1,665 | $1,295 | $3,695 |

EDWARD ARMS COMPANY

Current manufacturer located in Phoenix, AZ.

Edward Arms Company manufactures precision weapon systems from the AR-15 platform to custom 1911 handguns.

RIFLES: SEMI-AUTO

MSRs reflect base pricing only. Please contact the company directly for more information including options, availability, and delivery time (see Trademark Index).

15V2L RIFLE – 5.56 NATO cal., AR-15 style, 16 in. chrome lined barrel, YHM lightweight rifle length quad rail, 6-position Mil-Spec tube, Tungsten buffer, Magpul CTR buttstock, Ergo grip, black receivers and rail, four grip/stock colors available.

| MSR $1,860 | $1,575 | $1,385 | $1,185 | $1,065 | $915 | $785 | $635 | |

B.A.R. RIFLE – 5.56 NATO cal., AR-15 style, 16 in. chrome lined barrel, 12 1/2 or 15 in. Samson Evolution rifle length rail, 6-pos. Mil-Spec tube, Tungsten buffer, Magpul CTR buttstock, Ergo grip, black receiver and rail, four grip/stock colors available.

| MSR $1,750 | $1,485 | $1,315 | $1,150 | $1,025 | $875 | $750 | $615 | |

EA10 L.R.T. (LONG RANGE TACTICAL) – .308 Win. cal., AR-15 style, 18 in. stainless steel threaded barrel, mid-length gas system, 13.8 in. Troy Battle rail, Timney trigger, integral trigger guard, Battle Arms Development ambi-lever, AR10 billet charging handle, billet machined lower and flat-top upper receiver with laser T-marks, Magpul PRS AR10 stock, Ergo grip, Type III hardcoat anodized finish (optional colors available), includes U.S. Peace Keeper case.

| MSR $3,000 | $2,550 | $2,225 | $1,825 | $1,575 | $1,300 | $1,100 | $950 | |

SLR COMBAT RIFLE – 5.56 NATO cal., AR-15 style, 16 in. chrome lined barrel, YHM SLR rifle length forearm, 6-pos. Mil-Spec tube, Tungsten buffer, Magpul CTR buttstock, Ergo grip, black receivers and rail, four grip/stock colors available.

| MSR $2,000 | $1,700 | $1,500 | $1,250 | $1,100 | $950 | $825 | $675 | |

EMTAN KARMIEL LTD.

Current rifle manufacturer and parts supplier located in Karmiel, Israel. No current U.S. importation.

RIFLES: SEMI-AUTO

Emtan Karmiel Ltd. currently manufactures the MZ-15B, MZ-15F, and MZ-4B in various AR-15 style configurations. Please contact the manufacturer directly for more information including pricing, options, and U.S. availability (see Trademark Index).

ENFIELD AMERICA, INC.

Previous manufacturer located in Atlanta, GA.

PISTOLS: SEMI-AUTO

MP-9 – 9mm Para. cal., design similar to MP-45. Mfg. 1985.

| | $550 | $475 | $425 | $350 | $295 | $260 | $240 | |

Add $150 for carbine kit.

MP-45 – .45 ACP cal., 4 1/2, 6, 8, 10, or 18 1/2 in. shrouded barrel, parkerized finish, 10, 30, 40, or 50 shot mag., 6 lbs. Mfg. 1985 only.

| | $550 | $475 | $425 | $350 | $295 | $260 | $240 | $350 |

ENFIELDS

Originally manufactured by the Royal Small Arms Factory at Enfield situated on the northern outskirts of London, in Middlesex, England. Various Enfield rifles, carbines and revolvers were produced and/or converted by other British factories (B.S.A., L.S.A., S.S.A., N.R.F., P. Webley & Son, Webley & Scott Ltd., Albion Motors, W.W. Greener, Westley Richards, Vickers (VSM), ROF Fazakerley, ROF Maltby, BSA Shirley (M47C), as well as Australia at Lithgow (from 1913), in Canada at Long Branch (from 1941), the United States by Stevens-Savage (also from 1941), RFI Ishapore, India (from 1905), Nakhu, Pyuthan and Sundrijal in Nepal (from 1911), and at Wah Cantt in Pakistan (from the late 1950s).

The publisher would like to thank Mr. Bob Maze and Mr. Ian Skennerton for making the following information available.

MSR	100%	98%	95%	90%	80%	70%	60%	Last MSR

RIFLES & CARBINES

.303 RIFLE No. 1 Mk III* H.T. SNIPER – factory fitted telescopic sight and heavy barrel, converted at Lithgow, Australia at the end of WWII, special bedding of furniture, some were also fitted with a cheekpiece, British and Lithgow actions.

| | $7,000 | $6,000 | $5,500 | $5,000 | $4,250 | $3,750 | $3,250 | |

Buyer beware - check for authentic serial numbers, as there have been some fakes on this model.

.303 No. 3 Mk I* (T) (PATTERN 1914 SNIPER) – converted in England by Periscope Prism Co. (1918) & B.S.A. (1938) from Winchester rifles, the Pattern 1918 telescope on crawfoot mounts was fitted.

| | $8,500 | $7,500 | $6,000 | $5,250 | $4,750 | $4,000 | $3,750 | |

.303 No. 3 Mk I* (T) A SNIPER – converted in England by Alex Martin in WWII from Winchester MK I* (F) rifles, Great War Aldis and P.P. Co. telescopes (ex-SMLE snipers) were fitted, original SMLE rifle engraved number is usually visible, usually scope is offset (left) of the bore line. 421 mfg. beginning of WWII.

| | $7,500 | $6,750 | $6,000 | $5,250 | $4,750 | $4,000 | $3,500 | |

.303 No. 5 MK. I JUNGLE CARBINE – 20 1/2 in. barrel with flash hider, lightened action body and shortened furniture. From 1944, for service in the Far East.

| | $850 | $750 | $650 | $575 | $475 | $385 | $300 | |

Add 50% for BSA Shirley (M47C) rifle grenade trials rifles with serial numbers beginning with "BB" and a hung trigger.
Add approx. $2,500 for the .22 No. 5 Mk I rifle produced during 1945 in limited quantities for trials.
Subtract 20% for Indian service issues that have a transverse wood screw in the forend which is less desirable.

Beware of recently imported (circa 1990s) No. 4 rifles converted to appear as Jungle Carbines. These models do not have the lightning cuts on the receiver, barrel, and trigger guard.

7.62mm L42A1 SNIPER – Enfield conversion and extensive rebuild of the No. 4 Mk I(T) sniper rifle, fitted with an upgraded No. 32 telescopic sight to L1A1, half-stocked furniture, 7.62mm magazine with integral ejector, with heavy target barrel.

| | $8,500 | $7,750 | $7,250 | $6,750 | $5,750 | $5,250 | $4,500 | |

Add 30% for Iraq war issue with 6x Schmidt & Bender scope (beware of non-originals!)

ENTRÉPRISE ARMS INC.

Previous manufacturer located in Irwindale, CA, circa 1996-2009.

PISTOLS: SEMI-AUTO

The models listed are patterned after the Colt M1911, but have "Widebody" frames.

ELITE SERIES – .45 ACP cal., 3 1/4 in. barrel, features steel 1911 Widebody frame, flat mainspring housing, flared ejection port, 10 shot mag., bead blasted black oxide finish, tactical sights, 36 oz. Mfg. 1997-2009.

* **Elite Series P325**

| | $625 | $565 | $500 | $450 | $400 | $360 | $330 | *$700* |

* **Elite Series P425** – similar to Elite P325, except has 4 1/4 in. barrel, 38 oz. Mfg. 1997-2009.

| | $625 | $565 | $500 | $450 | $400 | $360 | $330 | *$700* |

* **Elite Series P500** – similar to Elite P325, except has 5 in. barrel, 40 oz. Mfg. 1997-2009.

| | $625 | $565 | $500 | $450 | $400 | $360 | $330 | *$700* |

TACTICAL SERIES – .45 ACP cal., 3 1/4 in. barrel, SA, features Tactical Widebody with "De-horned" slide and frame allowing snag-free carry, narrow ambidextrous thumb safety, 10 shot mag., low profile Novak or ghost ring sights, squared trigger guard, flat mainspring housing, matte black oxide finish, 36 oz. New 1997.

* **Tactical Series P325**

| | $875 | $750 | $650 | $575 | $500 | $450 | $395 | *$979* |

* **Tactical Series P325 Plus** – similar to P325, except has short Officer's length slide/barrel fitted onto a full Government frame, designed as concealed carry pistol. Mfg. 1998-2009.

| | $875 | $750 | $650 | $575 | $500 | $450 | $395 | *$979* |

* **Tactical Series P425** – similar to Tactical P325, except has 4 1/4 in. barrel, 38 oz. Mfg. 1997-2009.

| | $875 | $750 | $650 | $575 | $500 | $450 | $395 | *$979* |

* **Tactical Series P500** – similar to Tactical P325, except has 5 in. barrel, 40 oz. Mfg. 1997-2009.

| | $875 | $750 | $650 | $575 | $500 | $450 | $395 | *$979* |

MSR	100%	98%	95%	90%	80%	70%	60%	Last MSR

CARBINES: SEMI-AUTO

STG58C CARBINE/SCOUT – .308 Win. cal., tactical design, 16 1/2 in. barrel with muzzle brake, synthetic pistol grip stock, last shot bolt hold open, adj. gas system, Mil-Spec black oxide finish, 20 shot mag., 200-600 meter aperture sights, supplied with black nylon sling, various configurations, approx. 9 lbs. Mfg. 2000-2009.

* **STG58C Carbine Scout** – Entreprise Type 03 receiver, integral bipod, includes carry handle.

MSR	100%	98%	95%	90%	80%	70%	60%	Last MSR
	$1,075	$875	$750	$625	$575	$500	$450	$1,199

* **STG58C Carbine** – Entreprise Type 01 receiver, machined aluminum free floating handguards, carry handle.

MSR	100%	98%	95%	90%	80%	70%	60%	Last MSR
	$1,200	$995	$850	$750	$625	$550	$500	$1,399

FAL CARBINE MODEL – .308 Win. cal., 18 in. barrel, detachable 10 or 20 shot mag., parkerized finish, Entreprise Type 03 steel receiver, injection molded handguard and standard buttstock with pistol grip, zero climb muzzle brake, adj. gas system, carry handle, adj. front sight, adj. rear aperture sight, 9.3 lbs. Mfg. 2009 only.

MSR	100%	98%	95%	90%	80%	70%	60%	Last MSR
	$875	$775	$650	$550	$500	$450	$400	$979

FAL PARA CARBINE MODEL – .308 Win. cal., 18 in. barrel, detachable 10 or 20 shot mag., parkerized finish, Entreprise Type 03 steel receiver, paratrooper folding stock with pistol grip, zero climb muzzle brake, adj. gas system, carry handle, adj. front sight, adj. rear aperture sight, 9.8 lbs. Mfg. 2009 only.

MSR	100%	98%	95%	90%	80%	70%	60%	Last MSR
	$1,125	$900	$775	$650	$600	$500	$450	$1,249

RIFLES: SEMI-AUTO

STG58C RIFLE – .308 Win. cal., choice of 16 1/2, 21, or 24 in. barrel with muzzle brake, synthetic pistol grip stock, last shot bolt hold open, adj. gas system, Mil-Spec black oxide finish, 20 shot mag., 200-600 meter aperture sights, supplied with black nylon sling, various configurations, 8 1/2-13 lbs. Mfg. 2000-2009.

* **STG58C Rifle Lightweight Model** – 16 1/2 in. barrel, Entreprise Type 03 receiver, 8 1/2 lbs.

MSR	100%	98%	95%	90%	80%	70%	60%	Last MSR
	$1,050	$900	$800	$725	$650	$600	$550	$1,199

* **STG58C Rifle Standard Model** – 21 in. barrel, Entreprise Type 03 receiver, integral bipod, 9.8 lbs.

MSR	100%	98%	95%	90%	80%	70%	60%	Last MSR
	$795	$700	$625	$525	$475	$425	$375	$899

Add $100 for CA configuration.

* **STG58C Rifle Government Model** – 21 in. barrel, Entreprise Type 01 receiver, integral bipod, 9 1/2 lbs.

MSR	100%	98%	95%	90%	80%	70%	60%	Last MSR
	$1,050	$900	$800	$725	$650	$600	$550	$1,199

* **STG58C Rifle Target Model** – 21 in. free float barrel, Entreprise Type 01 receiver, with aluminum handguard, 11 1/2 lbs.

MSR	100%	98%	95%	90%	80%	70%	60%	Last MSR
	$1,200	$995	$850	$750	$625	$550	$500	$1,399

* **STG58C Rifle Match Target Model** – 24 in. free-float match heavy barrel, Entreprise Type 01 receiver, with aluminum handguard, 13 lbs.

MSR	100%	98%	95%	90%	80%	70%	60%	Last MSR
	$1,825	$1,650	$1,475	$1,200	$1,000	$850	$750	$1,999

FAL TARGET MODEL – .308 Win. cal., 21 in. barrel, detachable 10 or 20 shot mag., Entreprise Type 03 receiver, parkerized finish, injection molded free floating aluminum handguard, match grade trigger, lapped fitted bolt and carrier, iron sights, zero climb muzzle brake, injection molded standard buttstock with pistol grip, adj. front sight, adj. rear aperture sight, 9.9 lbs. Mfg. 2009 only.

MSR	100%	98%	95%	90%	80%	70%	60%	Last MSR
	$1,050	$900	$800	$725	$650	$600	$550	$1,199

FAL GOVERNMENT MODEL – .308 Win. cal., 21 in. barrel, detachable 10 or 20 shot mag., adj. gas system, carry handle, Entreprise Arm steel receiver, parkerized finish, steel handguard, zero climb muzzle brake, injection molded standard buttstock with pistol grip, adj. front sight, adj. rear aperture sight, 9.9 lbs. Mfg. 2009 only.

MSR	100%	98%	95%	90%	80%	70%	60%	Last MSR
	$1,000	$875	$775	$700	$600	$500	$450	$1,149

FAL STANDARD MODEL – .308 Win. cal., 21 in. barrel, detachable 10 or 20 shot mag., adj. gas system, carry handle, Entreprise Type 03 receiver, parkerized finish, injection molded handguard, zero climb muzzle brake, injection molded standard buttstock with pistol grip, adj. front sight, adj. rear aperture sight, 9 1/2 lbs. Mfg. 2009 only.

MSR	100%	98%	95%	90%	80%	70%	60%	Last MSR
	$850	$750	$650	$550	$500	$450	$400	$959

ERMA SUHL, GmbH

Previous manufacturer located in Suhl, Germany January 1998 - circa 2004. Erma Suhl purchased the remaining assets of Erma-Werke.

RIFLES: BOLT ACTION

SR100 SNIPER RIFLE – .300 Win. Mag., .308 Win., or .338 Lapua Mag. cal., tactical rifle featuring brown laminated wood stock with thumbhole, adj. buttplate/cheekpiece, and vent. forend, forged aluminum receiver, 25 1/2 or 29 1/2

MSR	100%	98%	95%	90%	80%	70%	60%	Last MSR

in. barrel, muzzle brake, adj. match trigger, approx. 15 lbs. Limited importation 1997-98 only.

| | $6,500 | $5,750 | $5,000 | $4,350 | $3,750 | $3,000 | $2,350 | $8,600 |

This model was imported exclusively by Amtec 2000, Inc., located in Gardner, MA.

Most recent importation was in .300 Win. Mag., and included a Steyr scope mount.

ERMA-WERKE

Previous manufacturer located in Dachau, Germany (Erma-Werke production) until bankruptcy occurred in October of 1997. Pistols were previously imported and distributed by Precision Sales International, Inc. located in Westfield, MA, Nygord Precision Products located in Prescott, AZ, and Mandall's Shooting Supplies, Inc. located in Scottsdale, AZ. Previously distributed by Excam located in Hialeah, FL.

Erma-Werke also manufactured private label handguns for American Arms Inc. (refer to their section for listings).

RIFLES

Models listed were available from Mandall Shooting Supplies, unless otherwise noted.

EM-1 .22 CARBINE – .22 LR cal., M1 copy, 10 or 15 shot mag., 18 in. barrel, rear adj. aperture sight, 5.6 lbs. Mfg. 1966-97.

| | $365 | $295 | $250 | $215 | $190 | $175 | $160 | $400 |

EGM-1 – similar to EM-1 except for unslotted buttstock, 5 shot mag.

| | $260 | $230 | $195 | $175 | $150 | $125 | $100 | $295 |

ESCORT

Current trademark of shotguns manufactured by Hatsan Arms Co., located in Izmir, Turkey and imported beginning 2002 by Legacy Sports International, located in Reno, NV. Previously located in Alexandria, VA.

SHOTGUNS: O/U

* **Escort Shorty Home Defense** – 12 ga. only, 3 in. chambers, 18 in. VR barrels with choke tubes, fiber optic front sight, accessory rail on lower barrel, nickel plated receiver, black synthetic stock with adj. comb and vent recoil pad, 7 lbs. New 2011.

| MSR $663 | $575 | $500 | $450 | $365 | $325 | $285 | $265 |

SHOTGUNS: SEMI-AUTO

Beginning 2004, all models have a round back receiver with 3/8 in. dovetail milled along top for mounting sights. Beginning in 2009, all Escort semi-auto shotguns use a bottom feed system similar to a Remington 11-87.

ESCORT SERIES - 3 IN. – 12 or 20 (new 2005) ga., 3 in. chamber, gas operated action with 2 position adj. screw (disc. 2003), 20 (disc. 2008), 22 (AS Youth and PS Slug, new 2005), 24 (disc. 2008), 26 (new 2005), or 28 in. VR barrel with 3 multi-chokes, blue finish, vent recoil pad, gold trigger, checkered walnut (Model AS) or polymer (Model PS) black or 100% camo coverage Mossy Oak Break-Up (disc. 2004), Mossy Oak Obsession (mfg. 2005-2008), Shadowgrass (disc. 2008), King's Woodland (mfg. 2009-2010), King's Desert (mfg. 2009-2010), King's Snow (mfg. 2009-2010), or Muddy Girl (new 2013) camo stock and forearm, 6.4-7 lbs. Importation began 2002.

| MSR $489 | $395 | $350 | $325 | $285 | $250 | $225 | $195 |

Add $169 for AS Supreme model with gloss finished walnut stock and forearm (disc.). Add $99 for Model PS Slug with rifled slug barrel and cantilever mount (disc. 2011).

Add $182 for AS Select Model with select walnut (mfg. 2007-2008). Add $100 for 100% camo coverage (disc. 2010). Add $74 for HiViz Spark front sight and King's Field metal finish (mfg. 2009). Add $175 for Model PS Slug Combo (mfg. 2006-2008). Add $81 for 24 in. barrel with Model PS TriViz sights and Mossy Oak Break Up camo coverage (disc. 2004).

* **Escort Series - 3 in. - Aimguard** – similar to Escort model, except has black chrome finish, black polymer stock, 18 (new 2006) or 20 (disc. 2005) in. barrel, cylinder bore. Imported 2004-2007.

| | $340 | $295 | $275 | $250 | $230 | $215 | $195 | $392 |

* **Escort Series 3 In. Home Defense** – 12 ga., 18 in. barrel with cyl. bore choke, muzzle brake, receiver features upper Picatinny rail, adj. ghost ring rear sight and adj. fiber optic front sight, black MP-SA TacStock2 with cushioned pistol grip, forearm has Picatinny rail on bottom, recoil pad, built-in holder for 2 extra shells, 6.9 lbs. New 2011.

| MSR $531 | $475 | $415 | $350 | $325 | $275 | $215 | $175 |

GLADIUS HOME DEFENSE – 12 or 20 ga., 18 in. cyl. bore barrel with muzzle brake, alum. alloy receiver, adj. ghost ring rear and fiber optic front sights, upper Picatinny rail, extended length forend with Picatinny rail, black or Marine (disc.) finish, forend pistol grip, black synthetic stock with cushioned pistol grip, recoil pad, adj. cheek pad, built-in holder for 2 extra shells, sling swivel studs, 6.8 lbs. New 2014.

| MSR $580 | $525 | $475 | $400 | $350 | $300 | $250 | $185 |

Add $27 for Marine finish (disc.).

MSR	100%	98%	95%	90%	80%	70%	60%	Last MSR

TURKEY/COYOTE TACTICAL – 12 ga., FAST loading system, 24 in. chrome moly barrel, extended full choke Turkey tube, fiber optic ghost ring sights, 100% Realtree AP camo stock with cushioned pistol grip, built-in shell storage in the stock, upper and lower Picatinny rails, mag. cut off, sling swivel studs included, 7.4 lbs. New 2013.

| MSR $659 | $595 | $525 | $450 | $400 | $325 | $275 | $215 | |

SHOTGUNS: SLIDE ACTION

ESCORT SERIES – 12 or 20 (new 2005) ga., 3 in. chamber, matte blue finish, black synthetic or 100% camo (disc.) stock and forearm, 18 (Aimguard or MarineGuard Model), 22 (Field Slug, mfg. 2005-2011), 24 (Turkey, includes extra turkey choke tube and FH TriViz sight combo with Mossy Oak Break Up [disc. 2004] or Obsession camo coverage, disc. 2008), 26 (new 2005, Field Hunter), or 28 (Field Hunter) in. barrel, alloy receiver with 3/8 in. milled dovetail for sight mounting, trigger guard safety, 4 or 5 shot mag. with cut off button, two stock adj. shims, 6.4-7 lbs. Importation began 2003.

* **Escort Series Aimguard** – 12 ga., 3 in. chamber, 18 in. barrel, fixed cyl. bore choke, 5 shot mag., matte black synthetic stock, includes sling swivel studs, large slide release button, 6.4 lbs.

| MSR $312 | $260 | $225 | $195 | $175 | $150 | $135 | $120 | |

* **Escort Series Marine Guard** – 12 ga., 18 in. barrel with black synthetic stock, nickel receiver, 5 shot mag., fixed cyl. bore choke, 6.4 lbs.

| MSR $380 | $325 | $285 | $250 | $225 | $200 | $185 | $150 | |

* **Escort Series Home Defense (Tactical Entry/Special Ops)** – 12 ga. only, 3 in. chamber, 18 in. barrel, synthetic stock, cushioned vertical pistol grip, available in a variety of configurations, forearm features upper and lower Picatinny rail, current mfg. features the MP-P/A TacStock2 with pistol grip and built in holder for two extra shells, fiber optic front sight, fully adj. ghost ring rear, 6.85 lbs. New 2009.

| MSR $393 | $350 | $295 | $260 | $225 | $200 | $180 | $160 | |

Subtract approx. 15% if w/o TacStock2 (new 2010).

GLADIUS HOME DEFENSE – 20 ga., 2 3/4 or 3 in. chamber, 18 in. cyl. bore barrel with muzzle brake, alum. alloy receiver, adj. ghost ring rear and fiber optic front sights, upper Picatinny rail, extended length forend with Picatinny rail, forend pistol grip, black synthetic stock with cushioned pistol grip, recoil pad, adj. cheek pad, built-in holder for 2 extra shells, sling swivel studs, 6.8 lbs. New 2014.

| MSR $485 | $425 | $375 | $325 | $300 | $250 | $200 | $150 | |

EUROPEAN AMERICAN ARMORY CORP.

Current importer and distributor established in late 1990, located in Rockledge, FL. Previously located in Sharpes, FL 1990-2006. Distributor and dealer sales.

EAA currently imports the Tanfoglio Witness series of semi-auto pistols, located in Italy, H. Weihrauch revolvers, located in Germany, and select Zastava firearms, located in Serbia. All guns are covered by EAA's lifetime limited warranty. EAA has also imported various trademarks of long guns, including Saiga, and Izhmash. Please refer to those individual sections.

Baikal shotguns, Zastava Z98 and Z5 bolt actions, Sarpa slide action shotguns manufactured by Sarzilmaz, and Sabatti double rifles are currently imported by U.S. Sporting Goods Inc. Please refer to individual listings for more information and current pricing.

PISTOLS: SEMI-AUTO

EAA has issued a safety upgrade notice regarding any Witness style semi-auto pistol bearing a serial number between AE00000 - AE700000. Owners are requested to field strip the pistol and send the slide assembly directly to EAA. EAA will replace the firing pin and return it to you. See Trademark Index for contact information.

The following Witness pistols also have a .22 LR conversion kit available for $234.

WITNESS EA 9 SERIES – 9mm Para. cal., action patterned after the CZ-75, DA/SA, 4 1/2 in. unported or ported (polymer, New Frame only, new 2002) barrel, steel or polymer frame/steel slide (new 1997), 10 (C/B 1994), 16*, or 18 (new late 2004) shot mag., choice of Wonder (new 1997), stainless steel (disc. 1996), blue, blue/chrome (disc. 1993), or brushed chrome (disc. 1996) finish, combat sights, black neoprene grips, 33 oz. Importation began late 1990.

| MSR $607 | $495 | $430 | $375 | $320 | $285 | $230 | $185 | |

Add $145 for 9mm Para/.22 LR combo.
Subtract $36 for polymer New Frame.

* **Model EA 9 (L) Compact** – similar to EA 9, except has 3 5/8 in. unported or ported (polymer frame only, mfg. 2002-2006) barrel and 10 (C/ B 1994), 12 (new late 2004), or 13* shot mag., 27 oz.

| MSR $607 | $495 | $430 | $375 | $320 | $285 | $230 | $185 | |

Subtract $36 for polymer frame.
Add $10-$20 for ported barrel (polymer frame only, disc. 2006).

MSR	100%	98%	95%	90%	80%	70%	60%	Last MSR

WITNESS EA 10 SUPER SERIES
– 10mm cal., action patterned after the CZ-75, DA/SA, 4 1/2 in. barrel, polymer or steel frame, 10, 12*, or 15 (new late 2004) shot mag., choice of stainless steel (disc.), blue, chrome (disc.), or Wonder (new 1999) finish, combat sights, black neoprene grips, 33 oz. Imported 1994 only, and again begining 1999.

MSR $607	$495	$430	$375	$320	$285	$230	$185	

Add $30 for chrome finish (disc.).
Add $65 for stainless steel (disc.).
Subtract $36 for polymer frame.

* **Model EA 10 Carry Comp** – similar to EA 10, except has 4 1/2 in. compensated barrel, blue or Wonder (new 2005) finish. Mfg. 1999-2005.

	$415	$365	$310	$280	$230	$185	$145	$489

Subtract $20 for blue finish.

* **Model EA 10 Compact** – similar to EA 10, except has 3 5/8 in. barrel, 8 or 12 (new late 2004) shot mag., 27 oz.

MSR $607	$495	$430	$375	$320	$285	$230	$185	

Subtract $36 for polymer frame.

WITNESS EA 38 SUPER SERIES
– .38 Super cal., action patterned after the CZ-75, DA/SA, 4 1/2 in. barrel, steel or polymer frame/steel slide (mfg. 1997-2004), 10 (C/B 1994), 18 (new late 2004) or 19* shot mag., choice of Wonder (heat treated grey satin finish, new 1997), stainless steel (disc. 1996), blue (disc.), blue/chrome (disc. 1994), or brushed chrome (disc. 1996) finish, combat sights, black neoprene grips, 33 oz. Importation began 1994.

MSR $607	$495	$430	$375	$320	$285	$230	$185	

Subtract $31 for polymer frame (disc. 2004).

* **Model EA 38 Compact** – similar to EA 38 Super Series, except has 3 5/8 in. unported or ported barrel, choice of matte blue or Wonder finish, 30 oz. Mfg. 1999-2004.

	$370	$325	$275	$250	$205	$165	$130	$449

Subtract $20 for polymer frame.
Add $20 for Wonder finish or ported barrel (polymer frame only).

WITNESS EA 40 SERIES
– .40 S&W cal., action patterned after the CZ-75, DA/SA, 4 1/2 in. barrel, steel or polymer frame/steel slide (new 1997), 10 (C/B 1994), 12*, or 15 (new late 2004) shot mag., choice of Wonder (new 1997), stainless steel (disc. 1996), blue, blue/chrome (disc.), or brushed chrome (disc. 1996) finish, combat sights, black neoprene grips, 33 oz. Importation began late 1990.

MSR $607	$495	$430	$375	$320	$285	$230	$185	

Subtract $36 for polymer New Frame.

* **Model EA 40 (L) Compact** – similar to EA 40, except has 3 5/8 in. unported or ported barrel, 9 or 12 (new late 2004) shot mag.

MSR $607	$495	$430	$375	$320	$285	$230	$185	$557

Subtract $36 for polymer frame.
Add $10-$20 for ported barrel (polymer frame only, disc. 2005).

WITNESS EA 41 SERIES
– .41 Action Express cal., action patterned after the CZ-75, DA/SA, 4 1/2 in. barrel, steel frame, 11 shot mag., blue, blue/chrome, or brushed chrome finish, combat sights, black neoprene grips, 33 oz. Importation disc. 1993.

	$450	$395	$335	$305	$245	$200	$155	$595

Add $40 for blue/chrome or brushed chrome finish.

* **Model EA 41 Compact** – similar to EA 41, except has 3 1/2 in. barrel and 8 shot mag.

	$495	$435	$370	$335	$270	$225	$175	$625

Add $40 for blue/chrome or brushed chrome finish.

WITNESS EA 45 SERIES
– .45 ACP cal., action patterned after the CZ-75, DA/SA, 4 1/2 in. standard or compensated (mfg. 1998-2005) barrel, steel frame, polymer full size frame (new 2004), or polymer frame/steel slide (new 1997), 10 (C/ B 1994) or 11* shot mag., choice of Wonder (new 1997), stainless steel (disc. 1996), blue, blue/chrome (disc. 1993), or brushed chrome (disc. 1996) finish, combat sights, walnut grips, 35 oz. Importation began late 1990.

MSR $607	$495	$430	$375	$320	$285	$230	$185	

Add $145 for .45 ACP/.22 LR combo.
Add $40 for ported barrel (steel only, with Wonder finish, disc. 2004).
Subtract $36 for polymer frame or blue finish.

* **Model EA 45 (L) Compact** – similar to EA 45, except has 3 5/8 in. unported or ported barrel and 8 shot mag., 26 oz.

MSR $607	$495	$430	$375	$320	$285	$230	$185	

Add $30 for ported barrel (polymer frame only, disc. 2004).
Add $50 for single port barrel compensator or carry configuration with compensator (disc.).
Subtract $36 for polymer frame.

MSR	100%	98%	95%	90%	80%	70%	60%	Last MSR

WITNESS P CARRY – 9mm Para., 10mm, .40 S&W, or .45 ACP cal., SA/DA, 3.6 in. barrel, 10 (.45 ACP), 15 (10mm or .40 S&W), or 17 (9mm Para.) shot mag., full size polymer frame, compact slide, Commander style, integral M-1913 rail, two-tone finish with Wonder finished slide, 29 oz. New 2006.

| MSR $691 | $560 | $465 | $410 | $360 | $325 | $265 | $225 | |

WITNESS CARRY COMP GUN – .38 Super (disc. 1997), 9mm Para. (disc. 1997), .40 S&W cal. (disc. 1997), 10mm (disc. 1994, reintroduced 1999), or .45 ACP cal., DA/SA, full size frame with compact slide and 1 in. compensator, 10 (C/B 1994), 12* (.40 S&W), or 16* (9mm Para.) shot mag., Wonder (new 1997), blue, Duo-Tone (disc. 1994) finish. Imported 1992-2004.

| | $425 | $370 | $320 | $290 | $235 | $190 | $150 | $479 |

Add $10 for Wonder finish.

WITNESS ELITE MATCH – 9mm Para., 10mm, .38 Super, .40 S&W, or .45 ACP cal., SA, 4 3/4 in. barrel, two-tone finish, checkered black polymer grips, extended mag. release, 10 (.45 ACP), 15 (.40 S&W or 10mm), or 17 (9mm Para. or .38 Super) shot mag., approx. 44 oz. New mid-2013.

| | $625 | $525 | $450 | $385 | $340 | $315 | $275 | $778 |

WITNESS GOLD TEAM XTREME – 9mm Para. or .38 Super cal., SA/DA, 5 1/4 in. barrel with polygonal rifling, 17 shot extended mag., specially tuned by the Tanfoglio custom shop, white checkered aluminum grips, features many Xtreme components such as hammer, trigger, guide rod, and firing pin, ported barrel and slide, two-tone ceramic coating with matte silver frame, slide, and matte black frame, includes some shooting accessories, approx. 48 oz. New 2015.

| MSR $5,884 | $4,995 | $4,400 | $3,800 | $3,150 | $2,500 | $2,000 | $1,750 | |

WITNESS LIMITED CUSTOM XTREME – 9mm Para. or .40 S&W cal., SA/DA, 4 3/4 in. barrel with polygonal rifling, 14 (.40 S&W) or 17 (9mm Para.) shot extended mag., white checkered grips, features many Xtreme components such as aluminum grips, hammer, trigger, guide rod, firing pin, and fiber optic front sight, black ceramic coated, includes some shooting accessories, approx. 45 oz. New 2015.

| MSR $1,961 | $1,695 | $1,450 | $1,200 | $1,000 | $850 | $725 | $625 | |

WITNESS MATCH XTREME – 9mm Para., .40 S&W, 10mm, or .45 ACP cal., SA/DA, 6 in. barrel with polygonal rifling, 10 (.45 ACP), 14 (.40 S&W), or 17 (9mm Para.) shot extended mag., black aluminum checkered grips, features many Xtreme components such as hammer, trigger, guide rod, firing pin, and fiber optic front sight, two-tone ceramic coated finish, includes some shooting accessories, approx. 47 oz. New 2015.

| MSR $1,879 | $1,600 | $1,400 | $1,150 | $950 | $825 | $725 | $625 | |

WITNESS STOCK II XTREME – 9mm Para. or .40 S&W cal., SA/DA, 4 1/2 in. barrel with polygonal rifling, 14 (.40 S&W) or 17 (9mm Para.) shot extended mag., white checkered grips, features many Xtreme components such as aluminum grips, hammer, trigger, guide rod, firing pin, and fiber optic front sight, two-tone ceramic finish with bronze colored slide and matte black frame, includes some shooting accessories, approx. 44 oz. New 2015.

| MSR $1,961 | $1,695 | $1,450 | $1,200 | $1,000 | $850 | $725 | $625 | |

WITNESS STOCK III XTREME – 9mm Para. or .40 S&W cal., SA/DA, 4 1/2 in. barrel with polygonal rifling, 14 (.40 S&W) or 17 (9mm Para.) shot extended mag., black checkered aluminum grips, features many Xtreme components such as hammer, trigger, guide rod, firing pin, and fiber optic front sight, two-tone ceramic finish with bronze colored frame and matte black slide, includes some shooting accessories, approx. 45 oz. New 2015.

| MSR $1,404 | $1,200 | $1,000 | $875 | $750 | $650 | $550 | $475 | |

SAR K2 – 9mm Para., .40 S&W (disc. 2013), 10mm (disc. 2013) or .45 ACP cal., 4 1/2 in. barrel, DA/SA, 14 (.45 ACP), 17 (.40 S&W and 10mm), or 18 (9mm Para.) shot mag., all steel frame, steel or stainless steel slide, ergonomic grip, accessory rail, extended beavertail, elongated squared trigger guard with serrations, removable dovetail front sight, fully adj. rear sight assembly, blue finish, mfg. by Sarsilmaz for Turkish military, 40 oz. Importation began mid-2011.

| MSR $459 | $390 | $335 | $285 | $250 | $225 | $200 | $185 | |

Add $104 for stainless steel.
Add $277 for .45 ACP cal.
Add $354 for Sport Configuration in .45 ACP cal.
Add $521 for stainless steel in .45 ACP cal.

SAR K2P – 9mm Para. cal., 3.8 in. barrel, blue or stainless, lower accessory rail, 16 shot mag., ambidextrous safety, full size grip, compact slide, polymer frame, 24 oz. Mfg. 2013 only.

| | $365 | $325 | $275 | $250 | $200 | $165 | $125 | $433 |

Add $98 for stainless.

SAR ST10 – 9mm Para. cal., 4.4 in. barrel, blue or two-tone finish, ergonomic polymer grips, steel frame and slide, adj. rear sights, lower accessory rail, 16 shot mag., removable dovetail front sight, includes carry case, holster, two-pocket mag. pouch, two mags., lock and cleaning tools, 34 oz. New mid-2013.

| | $650 | $575 | $495 | $450 | $400 | $365 | $335 | $754 |

Add $69 for stainless steel.

MSR	100%	98%	95%	90%	80%	70%	60%	*Last MSR*

SARGUN – 9mm Para., .40 S&W, or .45 ACP cal., 4 1/2 in. barrel, polymer frame, blue or stainless steel slide, 15 or 17 shot mag., matte black finish, ambidextrous controls, loaded chamber indicator, adj. front and rear sights, integral accessory rail, includes case, holster, and other shooting accessories, 20 oz. New mid-2013.

	$540	$475	$425	$360	$325	$295	$250	*$613*

Add $26 for 9mm Para. or $64 for .40 S&W cal.

Add $101 for stainless.

ZASTAVA EZ – 9mm Para., .40 S&W, or .45 ACP (disc. 2010) cal., DA/SA, ambidextrous controls, 10 (.45 ACP), 11 (.40 S&W), or 15 (9mm Para.) shot mag., 4 in. barrel, aluminum frame, accessory rail, spur hammer, blue or chrome finish, 33 oz. Imported 2007-2011.

	$495	$435	$375	$335	$285	$250	$215	*$573*

Add $47 for chrome finish (disc. 2010).

* **Zastava EZ Compact** – similar to Zastava EZ Model, except has compact frame, 7 (.45 ACP), 8 (.40 S&W), or 12 shot mag., 3 1/2 in. barrel. Imported 2007-2010.

	$495	$435	$375	$335	$285	$250	$215	*$573*

Add $47 for chrome finish (disc. 2010).

Subtract 10% if without ported barrel (disc. 2010).

ZASTAVA EZ CARRY – 9mm Para. or .40 S&W cal., full size frame, 3 1/2 in. ported barrel, DA/SA, 10 or 14 shot mag. Imported 2010-2011.

	$550	$495	$450	$395	$350	$300	$250	*$619*

RIFLES

Some EAA rifles were manufactured by Sabatti in Italy (est. 1674), Lu-Mar in Italy, and H. Weihrauch in Germany (see separate listing in the H. Weihrauch section). Imported 1992-96.

ZASTAVA PAP 762 SEMI-AUTO – 7.62x39mm cal., patterned after the AK-47, blonde hardwood thumbhole stock and furniture, 10 shot mag., 16 3/4 in. barrel, removable accessory rail, 10 lbs. Imported 2008-2013.

	$435	$375	$335	$295	$265	$240	$220	*$488*

TANFOGLIO WITNESS APPEAL SEMI-AUTO – .22 LR or .22 WMR cal., bullpup design, 16 in. barrel with muzzle brake, elevated Picatinny rail, adj. front and rear sights, ambidextrous controls, black polymer thumbhole stock with pistol grip has adj. LOP, 10 shot mag., front and rear sling mounts, black finish, 4.8 lbs. Importation began 2012.

MSR $450	$385	$335	$295	$260	$240	$220	$195	

Add $17 for .22 WMR cal.

M-93 BLACK ARROW BOLT ACTION – .50 BMG cal., Mauser action, 36 in. fluted heavy barrel with muzzle brake, adj. folding bipod, iron sights, detachable 5 shot mag., carry handle, detachable scope mount, wood case, 35 lbs. Mfg. by Zastava, imported 2007-2011.

	$6,400	$5,800	$5,000	$4,250	$3,500	$2,900	$2,300	*$6,986*

SHOTGUNS: SLIDE ACTION

MODEL PM2 – 12 ga. only, unique 7 shot detachable mag., 20 in. barrel, black wood stock and composite forearm, dual action bars, cross-bolt safety on trigger guard, available in matte blue or chrome finish, 6.81 lbs. Imported 1992 only.

	$550	$480	$410	$375	$300	$245	$190	*$695*

Add $200 for night sights.

Add $75 for matte chrome finish.

EVANS ARMS

Current pistol manufacturer located in Clairton, PA. Previously named Night Owl Firearms until 2015.

PISTOLS: SEMI-AUTO

NO9 – 9mm Para. cal., SFO, 4.17 in. barrel, polymer frame with steel slide, 10, 15, 17, 18, or 20 shot mag., 3-dot fixed sights, single action trigger, right or left-hand action, lower Picatinny rail, black or FDE frame finish, 31 oz.

MSR $650	$575	$500	$435	$365	$325	$280	$265	

EVOLUTION USA

Current rifle manufacturer located in White Bird, ID since 1984. Distributor and dealer sales.

RIFLES: BOLT ACTION

Evolution USA uses four different types of actions for its rifles. They include the MSR-10 that is a faceted and highly customized Remington M700 receiver, the MSX-10 that uses a Post-64 Classic Win. Model 70 with claw extractor, the Pre-64 Win. Model 70 action, and the Mauser Express 98 action manufactured by CZ USA. Most models can be ordered by selecting one of the previous receivers.

MSR	100%	98%	95%	90%	80%	70%	60%	Last MSR

BOLT ACTION SNIPER/VARMINT SERIES – various cals., 3 different configurations include Sniper, Informal Target Varmint, and Field Grade Varmint, features match barrel, action, and tuned trigger. Disc. 2000.

Prices for the Sniper rifle started at approx. $3,000 while the Varmint guns started at approx. $2,000.

RIFLES: SEMI-AUTO

GRENADA – .223 Rem. cal., GIO, design based on the AR-15 with flat upper receiver, 17 in. stainless steel match barrel with integral muzzle brake, NM trigger. Disc. 2000.

	$985	$825	$675	$600	$525	$465	$400	$1,195

DESERT STORM – similar to Grenada, except has 21 in. match barrel. Disc. 2003.

	$975	$825	$665	$560	$500	$450	$400	$1,189

IWO JIMA – GIO, carrying handle incorporating iron sights, 20 in. stainless steel match barrel, A2 HBAR action, tubular handguard. Limited mfg.

	$1,000	$875	$775	$700	$600	$475	$425	

RIFLES : SINGLE SHOT

PHANTOM III SINGLE SHOT – .50 BMG or .700 NE cal., Evolution M-2000 stainless single shot action, 28 in. Lilja match barrel with flutes and muzzle brake, approx. 30 lbs. Mfg. 2000-2011.

	$4,700	$4,300	$3,850	$3,500	$2,950	$2,400	$2,250	$4,700

Add $1,700 for Delta Model (50-80 lbs.) or .700 NE cal. (24-30 lbs.), disc.

EXCAM

Previous importer and distributor located in Hialeah, FL, which went out of business late 1990. Excam distributed Dart, Erma, Tanarmi, Targa, and Warrior exclusively in the U.S. These trademarks will appear under Excam. All importation of Excam firearms ceased in 1990.

All Targa and Tanarmi pistols were manufactured in Gardone V.T., Italy. All Erma and Warrior pistols and rifles were manufactured in W. Germany. Senator O/U shotguns were manufactured by A. Zoli located in Brescia, Italy.

HANDGUNS: TANARMI MFG.

TA 41 SERIES SEMI-AUTO – .41 Action Express cal., action similar to TA 90 Series, 11 shot mag., matte blue (Model TA 41B) or matte chrome (Model TA 41C) finish, combat sights, black neoprene grips, 38 oz. Imported 1989-90.

	$450	$390	$360	$330	$295	$265	$240	$490

Add $70 for adj. target sights (Model TA 41BT).

TA 90 SERIES SEMI-AUTO – 9mm Para. cal., double action, copy of the CZ-75, 4 3/4 in. barrel, steel frame, 15 shot mag., matte blue (Model TA 90B) or matte chrome finish (Model TA 90C), combat sights, wood (disc. 1985) or neoprene grips, 38 oz. New 1985.

	$365	$300	$260	$225	$205	$190	$180	$415

Add $85 for adj. target sights (TA 90BT).

Earlier models featured a polished blue finish and nickel steel alloy frame (35 oz.).

RIFLES: ERMA MFG.

EM 1 CARBINE – .22 LR or .22 WMR cal., semi-auto, copy of the original M1 carbine, 19 1/2 in. barrel, 15 shot, iron sights, blue only. ESG 22 is .22 WMR (12 shot). Disc. 1985.

	$175	$155	$140	$125	$115	$100	$90	$195

Add $100 for ESG 22, .22 WMR cal.

EXCEL ARMS

Current trademark of pistols and rifles manufactured by Excel Industries, Inc., located in Ontario, CA. Previously located in Chino, CA.

PISTOLS: SEMI-AUTO

ACCELERATOR MP – .17 HMR (MP-17), .17 Mach 2 (new 2007, SP-17), .22 LR (new 2007, SP-22), or .22 WMR (MP-22) cal., 6 1/2 (new 2007) or 8 1/2 in. barrel, SA, polymer frame with stainless steel slide, adj. sights, 9 shot mag., 45 or 54 oz. Mfg. 2005-2009.

	$385	$325	$285	$260	$240	$220	$195	$433

Add $63 for red/green dot optic sight or $87 for 4x32mm scope with illuminated crosshairs.
Add $87 for choice of Realtree Hardwoods HD Green or Digital Desert camo coverage (new 2008).

MP-17 – .17 HMR cal., 8 1/2 in. barrel, SA, 9 shot, stainless steel, polymer grip, adj. sights, available with red dot optic or scope and rings, matte black, Digital Desert or Realtree Hardwoods HD camo. Mfg. late 2008-2010.

	$375	$325	$285	$260	$240	$220	$195	$433

Add $63 for red dot optic front sight. Add $87 for scope and rings. Add $87 for camo.

MSR	100%	98%	95%	90%	80%	70%	60%	Last MSR

MP-22 – .22 WMR cal., 6 1/2 or 8 1/2 in. stainless steel bull barrel, SA, 9 shot, polymer grip, adj. sights, integral Weaver base, available with red dot optic or scope and rings, stainless steel, Black Cerakote, Digital Desert (disc. 2010) or Realtree Hardwoods HD camo (disc. 2010), 3 3/8 lbs. New late 2008.

	100%	98%	95%	90%	80%	70%	60%	Last MSR
MSR $477	$415	$345	$300	$260	$240	$220	$195	

Add $71 for red dot optic front sight. Add $97 for scope and rings. Add $87 for camo (disc. 2010).

MP-5.7 – 5.7x28mm cal., stainless steel construction, 8 1/2 in. bull barrel with integral top Picatinny rail, SA, fully adj. target sights, available with red dot optic or scope and rings, polymer grip, 9 shot mag., blow-back action, last round hole open, stainless steel or black Cerakote finish, 3 3/8 lbs. New 2011.

	100%	98%	95%	90%	80%	70%	60%	Last MSR
MSR $615	$550	$475	$425	$375	$300	$250	$200	

Add $70 for red dot optic sights. Add $96 for scope and rings.

X-5.7P – 5.7x28mm cal., 8 1/2 in. barrel, SA, 10 or 25 shot mag., no sights or adj. iron sights (25 shot mag. only), Black finish. New 2011.

	100%	98%	95%	90%	80%	70%	60%	Last MSR
MSR $715	$650	$575	$500	$450	$400	$350	$295	

Add $121 for adj. iron sights (25 shot mag. only).

X-9P – 9mm Para. cal., 8 1/2 in. barrel, 10 or 17 shot mag., with or w/o adj. sights, black finish, 4 1/2 lbs. New 2016.

	100%	98%	95%	90%	80%	70%	60%	Last MSR
MSR $715	$650	$575	$500	$450	$400	$350	$295	

Add $121 for adj. iron sights.
Add $280 for adj. iron sights, pistol brace, and one 30 shot Glock compatible mag. (X-9P B).

X-22P – .22 LR cal., 4 1/2 in. barrel, SA, black synthetic stock, 10 or 25 shot mag., adj. sights, Picatinny rail. New 2009.

	100%	98%	95%	90%	80%	70%	60%	Last MSR
MSR $455	$400	$335	$290	$250	$225	$200	$185	

X-30P – .30 Carbine cal., features aluminum frame with integral Picatinny rail, 8 1/2 in. partially shrouded barrel, delayed blowback action, tilted black synthetic pistol grip with finger grooves, 10 or 20 shot mag., no sights or adj. iron sights (20 shot mag. only), black finish, 4 1/2 lbs. New 2011.

	100%	98%	95%	90%	80%	70%	60%	Last MSR
MSR $715	$650	$575	$500	$450	$400	$350	$295	

Add $121 for adj. iron sights (20 shot mag. only).

SP-17 – .17 Mach 2 cal., 6 1/2 or 8 1/2 in. barrel, SA, 10 shot, stainless steel, polymer grip, adj. sights, available with red dot optic or scope and rings, matte black, Digital Desert or Realtree Hardwoods HD camo. Mfg. late 2008-2010.

	100%	98%	95%	90%	80%	70%	60%	Last MSR
	$375	$325	$285	$260	$240	$220	$195	*$433*

Add $63 for red dot optic front sight. Add $87 for scope and rings. Add $87 for camo.

SP-22 – .22 LR cal., 6 1/2 or 8 1/2 in. barrel, SA, 10 shot, stainless steel, polymer grip, adj. sights, available with red dot optic or scope and rings, matte black, Digital Desert or Realtree Hardwoods HD camo. Mfg. late 2008-2010.

	100%	98%	95%	90%	80%	70%	60%	Last MSR
	$375	$325	$285	$260	$240	$220	$195	*$433*

Add $63 for red dot optic front sight. Add $87 for scope and rings. Add $87 for camo.

RIFLES: SEMI-AUTO

CR-9 – 9mm Para. cal., stainless steel construction, 18 in. stainless bull barrel, full length Weaver rail and two side rails, adj. and detachable sights, 10 shot mag., nylon sling and detachable swivels. Mfg. 2008.

	100%	98%	95%	90%	80%	70%	60%	Last MSR
	$550	$480	$415	$375	$305	$250	$195	*$635*

MR/SR SERIES – .17 HMR (MR17), .17 Mach 2 (SR17, new 2007), .22 LR (SR22, new 2007), or .22 WMR (MR22) cal., black composite stock with large thumbhole, fluted 18 in. stainless steel barrel and receiver with shroud, black, silver, or camo finish, fully adj. sights, 9 shot mag., standard package is supplied with red dot optic and hard sided case, 8 lbs. Mfg. 2004-2009.

	100%	98%	95%	90%	80%	70%	60%	Last MSR
	$435	$380	$325	$295	$240	$195	$150	*$488*

Add $195 for choice of Realtree Hardwoods HD Green or Digital Desert camo coverage (new 2008).
Add $35 for red dot optical sight.
Add $147 for iron sights or 3-9x40mm scope.
Add $231 for iron sights and 6x9 in. bipod.

MR-17 – .17 HMR cal., 18 in. bull barrel, 9 shot mag., silver or black shroud, available options include no sights, red dot optic, iron sights, scope and rings, sling, bipod, side rails, and flashlight, black, Digital Desert or Realtree Hardwoods HD Green camo. Mfg. late 2008-2010.

	100%	98%	95%	90%	80%	70%	60%	Last MSR
	$425	$370	$320	$290	$235	$190	$150	*$488*

Add $35 for red dot optic sights. Add $147 for iron sights or 3-9x40mm scope. Add $84 for bipod (iron sights or scope only). Add $257 for side rails and flashlight. Add $195 for camo.

The no sight model is only available with one magazine - all other variations include two.

MSR	100%	98%	95%	90%	80%	70%	60%	Last MSR

MR-22 – .22 WMR cal., 18 in. bull barrel, 9 shot mag., silver or black shroud, full length top Picatinny rail, available options include no sights, red dot optic, iron sights, scope and rings, sling, bipod, side rails, and flashlight, blowback action, black, Digital Desert (disc. 2010) or Realtree Hardwoods HD Green camo (disc. 2010) finish, 8 lbs. New late 2008.

| MSR $538 | $450 | $385 | $335 | $300 | $250 | $195 | $150 | |

Add $39 for red dot optic sights. Add $162 for iron sights or 3-9x40mm scope. Add $255 for bipod (iron sights or scope only). Add $446 for side rails and flashlight. Add $195 for camo (disc. 2010).

The no sight model is only available with one magazine - all other variations include two.

* **MR-22 Camo** – .22 WMR cal., similar to MR-22, except features Desert Digital or Timbers Edge camo stock and shroud, no sights. Mfg. 2014 only.

| | $510 | $450 | $385 | $350 | $275 | $225 | $185 | $600 |

MR-22 TIM WELLS SIGNATURE RIFLE – .22 LR or .22 WMR cal., 18 in. stainless steel fluted bull barrel, 9 shot mag., full length Weaver rail integrated into the aluminum shroud, polymer composite pistol grip stock, Kryptek Highlander camo finish, includes 3-9x40 scope and sling studs, Relentless Pursuit TV logo on buttstock, 8 lbs. New 2015.

| MSR $732 | $625 | $545 | $470 | $425 | $350 | $285 | $225 | |

MR-5.7 – 5.7x28mm cal., 18 in. fluted bull barrel, 9 shot mag., black or silver shroud, full length upper Picatinny rail, no sights, black synthetic pistol grip stock with thumbhole, last round hole open, 8 lbs. New 2011.

| MSR $672 | $595 | $515 | $460 | $400 | $350 | $300 | $275 | |

Add $163 for 3.9x40mm scope.

SR-17 – .17 Mach 2 cal., 18 in. bull barrel, 10 shot mag., silver or black shroud, available options include no sights, red dot optic, iron sights, scope and rings, sling, bipod, side rails, and flashlight, black, Digital Desert or Realtree Hardwoods HD Green camo. Mfg. 2008-2010.

| | $425 | $370 | $320 | $290 | $235 | $190 | $150 | $488 |

Add $35 for red dot optic sights. Add $147 for iron sights or 3-9x40mm scope. Add $84 for bipod (iron sights or scope only). Add $257 for side rails and flashlight. Add $195 for camo.

The no sight model is only available with one magazine - all other variations include two.

SR-22 – .22 LR cal., 18 in. bull barrel, 10 shot mag., silver or black shroud, available options include no sights, red dot optic, iron sights, scope and rings, sling, bipod, side rails, and flashlight, black, Digital Desert or Realtree Hardwoods HD Green camo. Mfg. late 2008-2010.

| | $425 | $370 | $320 | $290 | $235 | $190 | $150 | $488 |

Add $35 for red dot optic sights. Add $147 for iron sights or 3-9x40mm scope. Add $84 for bipod (iron sights or scope only). Add $257 for side rails and flashlight. Add $195 for camo.

The no sight model was only available with one magazine - all other variations included two.

X-9R – 9mm Para. cal., 16 in. barrel, 10 or 17 shot mag., compatible with Glock magazines, with or w/o adj. sights, collapsible stock, top Picatinny rail, manual bolt hold open feature, black finish, 6 1/4 lbs. New 2016.

| MSR $795 | $725 | $650 | $575 | $500 | $450 | $400 | $350 | |

Add $121 for adj. iron sights (17 shot mag. only).

X-22R – .22 LR cal., 18 in. barrel, fixed (mfg. 2011-2015) or collapsible black synthetic stock, blowback action, no sights, 10 or 25 shot mag., drilled and tapped, accepts Ruger 10/22 mags., 4 3/4 lbs. New 2009.

| MSR $504 | $450 | $400 | $350 | $300 | $250 | $200 | $175 | |

Add $90 for 3-9x40 scope.
Add $15 for fixed stock (mfg. 2011-2015).

X-30R – .30 Carbine cal., 18 in. partially shrouded barrel, aluminum receiver with integral Picatinny top rail, blow-back action, fixed or collapsible stock, no sights or adj. iron sights (20 shot mag. only), 10 or 20 shot mag., approx. 6 1/4 lbs. New 2011.

| MSR $795 | $725 | $650 | $575 | $500 | $450 | $400 | $350 | |

Add $15 for fixed stock (10 shot mag. only).
Add $121 for adj. iron sights (20 shot mag. only).

X-5.7R – 5.7x28mm cal., otherwise similar to the X-30R, 10 or 25 shot mag. New 2011.

| MSR $795 | $725 | $650 | $575 | $500 | $450 | $400 | $350 | |

Add $15 for fixed stock (10 shot mag. only).
Add $121 for adj. iron sights (25 shot mag. only).

F SECTION

F&D DEFENSE
Current manufacturer located in New Braunfels, TX.

MSR	100%	98%	95%	90%	80%	70%	60%	Last MSR

RIFLES: SEMI-AUTO

FD308 – .308 Win. cal., FAL type action with GPO, 16, 17 (disc. 2013), 18 (new 2014), 21 (disc. 2013), or 22 (new 2014) in. stainless barrel with two chamber muzzle brake, full length Picatinny rail with folding battle Tritium sights, side charging system with integrated forward asssist, removeable guide rails, Geissele trigger group, tan Magpul UBR stock and pistol grip, storage compartment in the buttstock, 8.7 lbs. New 2012.

MSR $3,395 $2,895 $2,525 $2,050 $1,750 $1,450 $1,225 $1,050

Add $100 for 22 in. barrel.

FD338 – .338 Lapua Mag. cal., GPO, 22 or 25 in. stainless steel barrel, 10 or 15 shot double stack mags., non-reciprocating side charging handle, matched lower, upper, rail, bolt, and extension, Geissele trigger group, full length Picatinny rail, Magpul PRS stock and pistol grip. New 2013.

MSR $5,450 $4,625 $4,050 $3,475 $2,950 $2,500 $2,050 $1,700

FD260 – .260 Rem. cal., similar to FD338, except has 22 in. stainless Bartlein barrel, Magpul 20 shot PMAG.

MSR $3,595 $3,050 $2,675 $2,175 $1,875 $1,550 $1,300 $1,125

FD65C – 6.5mm Creedmoor cal., similar to FD338, except has 22 in. barrel.

MSR $3,595 $3,050 $2,675 $2,175 $1,875 $1,550 $1,300 $1,125

FD458 – .458 FND chambered, GIO, 18 in. stainless steel barrel, built on the FD338 chassis and action, 10 or 15 shot double stack mag., non-reciprocating side charging handle, matched lower, upper, rail, bolt, and extension, Geissele trigger, full length Picatinny rail, Magpul UBR stock and pistol grip.

MSR $5,950 $5,050 $4,420 $3,790 $3,435 $2,780 $2,275 $1,775

FEG
Current manufacturer located in Hungary (FÉG stands for Fegyver és Gépgyár) since 1891. Previously imported 2007-2010 by SSME Deutsche Waffen, Inc., located in Plant City, FL. A few models were imported by Century International Arms located in Delray Beach, FL (see additional information under the Century International Arms in this text). Previously imported and distributed by K.B.I., Inc. located in Harrisburg, PA, and distributed until 1998 by Interarms located in Alexandria, VA.

RIFLES: SEMI-AUTO

MODEL SA-85M – 7.62x39mm cal., sporter rifle utilizing AKM action, 16.3 in. barrel, 6 shot detachable mag., thumbhole stock, 7 lbs. 10 oz. Imported 1991, banned 1998.

$550 $480 $410 $375 $300 $245 $190   *$429*

SA-85 S (SA-2000M) – .223 Rem. (disc. 2000) or 7.62x39mm cal., sporter rifle with skeletonized Choate synthetic stock, 16.3 (new 2007) or 17 3/4 (disc. 2000) in. barrel with muzzle brake, 6, 10, or 30 shot detachable mag. Imported 1999-2000, reimported 2007-2011.

$950 $830 $710 $645 $520 $425 $330   *$1,075*

F.I.E.
Previous importer (F.I.E. is the acronym for Firearms Import & Export) located in Hialeah, FL until 1990.

F.I.E. filed bankruptcy in November of 1990 and all models were discontinued. Some parts or service for these older firearms may be obtained through Numrich Gun Parts Corp. (see Trademark Index), even though all warranties on F.I.E. guns are void.

PISTOLS: SEMI-AUTO, TITAN SERIES

SPECTRE PISTOL – 9mm Para. or .45 ACP cal., double action, unique triple action blowback system with two piece bolt, 6 in. barrel, military style configuration, adj. sights, 30 or 50 (optional with unique 4 column configuation) shot mag., 4.8 lbs. Mfg. 1989-90 only.

$675 $600 $525 $480 $440 $400 $360   *$718*

Add $14 for mag. loading tool.

KG-99 – 9mm Para. cal., 36 shot mag. Mini-99 also available with 20 shot mag. and 3 in. barrel. Disc. 1984.

$550 $475 $440 $400 $365 $330 $300

This model was not manufactured but sold by F.I.E.

MSR	100%	98%	95%	90%	80%	70%	60%	Last MSR

RIFLES: SEMI-AUTO

PARA RIFLE – .22 LR cal., tactical designed rifle with tube stock (is also magazine), includes green cloth case with white stenciled letters, takedown, 11 shot mag., matte black receiver finish, approx. 4 lbs. Mfg. by L. Franchi between 1979-84. Imported into the U.S. from 1985-1988.

	100%	98%	95%	90%	80%	70%	60%	Last MSR
	$325	$275	$225	$195	$155	$130	$110	*$225*

8,000 of this model were manufactured by L. Franchi. 5,000 went to the Italian Government and were used as training rifles (with German scopes). The remainder were imported by F.I.E. (without scopes).

SPECTRE CARBINE – 9mm Para. cal., same action as Spectre pistol, collapsible metal buttstock, 30 or 50 (opt.) shot mag., adj. rear sight, with pistol and forearm grip. Mfg. 1989-disc.

	100%	98%	95%	90%	80%	70%	60%	Last MSR
	$550	$450	$375	$300	$275	$250	$225	*$700*

FMK FIREARMS

Current pistol manufacturer located in Placentia, CA. Dealer direct sales beginning 2014. Previously distributed by American Tactical Imports, located in Rochester, NY until 2013.

PISTOLS: SEMI-AUTO

FMK 9C1/9C1G2 – 9mm Para. cal., SFO, SA, 4 in. stainless steel barrel, features FAT trigger mechanism for quick and short trigger pull, polymer frame with steel slide, 10, 14, or 17 shot mag., Glock compatible sight system, loaded chamber indicator, shock absorbing backstrap, with or w/o Bill of Rights engraving, black or satin nickel plated slide or black with silver slide (new 2016), black, Dark Earth, OD Green, Urban Grey, pink, Crimson Red (new 2016), or Tiffany Blue (new 2016) frame finish, Picatinny rail, trigger safety, includes two mags., 23 1/2 oz. New 2010.

MSR $410	100%	98%	95%	90%	80%	70%	60%
	$350	$300	$265	$240	$220	$200	$180

Add $5 for Bill of Rights engraving.
Add $10 for black with silver slide (new 2016).

Approximately 1,000 9C1 models were manufactured before the 9C1G2 became available. The 9C1G2 comes with either a Fast Action Trigger (Glock style) or double action only.

FMR

Current rifle manufacturer located in Pantin, France. No current U.S. importation.

RIFLES: BOLT ACTION

FMR owns the rights to the French trademark Unique, and manufactures a line of bolt action rifles based on the original Unique design. All rifles have an aluminum ERGAL or stainless steel action, interchangeable barrels and fully adjustable stocks. The RS1 Sniper is available as a single shot or a repeater, and has an MSR of €1,930. The RS1 Commando has a heavy barrel and muzzle brake and has an MSR of €1,570. Various options are also available, including an unmodified adjustable stock for the CZ22. Please contact the company directly for more information, including options, pricing, and U.S. availability (see Trademark Index).

FN AMERICA LLC (FNH USA)

Current manufacturer and importer established in 1998, located in McLean, VA. Dealer and distributor sales.

In the U.S., FN (Fabrique Nationale) is represented by two entities - FNH USA, which is responsible for sales, marketing, and business development, and FNM, which stands for FN Manufacturing, which handles manufacturing. FNH USA has two separate divisions - commercial/law enforcement, and military operations. FN Manufacturing is located in Columbia, SC. Design, research and development are conducted under the authority of FN Herstal S.A. In mid-2014, it was announced that the consolidation of FN Manufacturing LLC and FNH USA LLC would be called FN America LLC, and headquarters will remain in McLean.

Some of the firearms that FNM currently produces for the U.S. government are M16 rifles, M249 light machine guns, and M240 medium machine guns. FNM also produces the FNP line of handguns for the commercial, military, and law enforcement marketplaces. FNM is one of only three small arms manufacturers designated by the U.S. government as an industry base for small arms production. In November 2004, the FN model was chosen by the U.S. Special Operations Command (USSOCOM) for the new SCAR military rifle.

CARBINES/RIFLES: SEMI-AUTO

FN15 1776 – 5.56x45mm cal., 16 in. alloy steel button-broached barrel, A2 style compensator, 30 shot Magpul PMAG Gen 3, optics ready Mil-Std 1913 flat-top rail, 6-pos. collapsible stock, two-piece single heat shield, oval handguard, sling attachments, matte black finish, 6.6 lbs. New 2015.

MSR $899	100%	98%	95%	90%	80%	70%	60%
	$775	$685	$615	$550	$485	$415	$370

FN15 CARBINE – 5.56x45mm cal., 16 in. barrel with A2 style compensator, 30 shot alum. mag., A2 style front sights, removable M4 style rear carrying handle, flat-top upper receiver with rail, two-piece oval handguard, 6-pos. collapsible stock, matte black finish, 6.94 lbs. New 2014.

MSR $1,149	100%	98%	95%	90%	80%	70%	60%
	$975	$885	$765	$655	$575	$495	$435

MSR	100%	98%	95%	90%	80%	70%	60%	Last MSR

FN15 COMPETITION – 5.56x45mm cal., 18 in. cold hammer forged barrel, SureFire ProComp 556 muzzle brake, steel low profile gas block, 30 shot mag., Timney trigger, Magpul MOE-SL collapsible buttstock, Magpul MOE black pistol grip, rifle length gas system, H2 buffer, nickel boron bolt carrier group, extended rifle length M-LOK 16 in. handguard, ambidextrous bolt release, billet aluminum upper and lower receiver with anodized blue finish, 8.1 lbs. New 2016.
   Please contact the manufacturer directly for pricing and availability for this model.

FN15 DMR – 5.56x45mm cal., 18 in. chrome-lined free-floating barrel with Surefire Pro Comp 556 muzzle brake, 30 shot Magpul PMag., Magpul MBUS Pro sights, Timney competition trigger, Midwest Industries SSM M-LOK 15 in. handguard, flat-top receiver with rail, Magpul STR buttstock, Magpul MOE grip, matte black finish, 7.2 lbs. New 2015.

MSR $1,899	$1,625	$1,425	$1,200	$1,075	$925	$795	$650	

FN15 MILITARY COLLECTOR M4 – 5.56x45mm cal., 16 in. button-broached barrel, 30 shot AR style mag., A2 style front and adj. rear sights, 6-pos. stock with sling mount, M4 pistol grip, ambi safety lever, Knights Armament M4 RAS adapter rail with rail covers, hard anodized aluminum flat-top receiver with Picatinny rail, matte black finish, 6.6 lbs. New 2015.

MSR $1,749	$1,485	$1,315	$1,150	$1,025	$875	$750	$615	

FN15 MILITARY COLLECTOR M16 – 5.56x45mm cal., 20 in. button-broached barrel, A2 compensator, 30 shot aluminum AR style mag., A2 style front and adj. rear sights, fixed A2 buttstock, M16 pistol grip, ambi selector, Knights Armament M5 RAS adaptor rail with rail covers, hard anodized aluminum flat-top receiver with Picatinny rail, matte black finish, 8.2 lbs. New 2015.

MSR $1,749	$1,485	$1,315	$1,150	$1,025	$875	$750	$615	

FN M249S MILITARY COLLECTOR – 5.56x45mm cal., GPO, closed bolt operation, formed steel frame, 20 1/2 in. cold hammer forged steel barrel, quick change barrel capability, 30 shot mag., ergonomic polymer buttstock, crossbolt safety, removable heat shield, folding steel bipod, folding carry handle, flip up feed tray cover and feed mechanism, top cover integrated Mil-Std 1913 rail system, non-reciprocating charging handle, 17 lbs. New 2016.
   Please contact the manufacturer directly for pricing and availability for this model.

FN15 MOE SLG – 5.56x45mm cal., 16 in. alloy steel button-broached barrel, A2 compensator, 30 shot Magpul PMAG, Magpul MBUS rear and A2 style front sights, Magpul MOE SL gray buttstock and grip, hard anodized aluminum receiver, Magpul MOE SL gray M-LOK carbine handguard, forward assist, matte black/gray finish, 6.8 lbs. New 2015.

MSR $1,199	$1,025	$925	$800	$685	$595	$515	$440	

FN15 PATROL CARBINE – 5.56x45mm cal., 16 in. alloy steel button-broached, chrome lined barrel, 30 shot mag., Samson flip up rear sights, pistol grip, Midwest Industries drop-in 7 in. quad rail/forearm, black finish, 6 lbs. New 2016.
   Please contact the manufacturer directly for pricing and availability for this model.

FN15 RIFLE – 5.56x45mm cal., 20 in. barrel with A2 compensator, 30 shot mag., flat-top receiver with rail, A2-style front sights, removable carrying handle, two-piece ribbed round handguard with heat shields, fixed stock with sling mount and storage compartment, matte black finish, 7.97 lbs. New 2014.

MSR $1,149	$975	$885	$765	$655	$575	$495	$425	

FN15 SPORTING – .223 Rem. cal., 18 in. match grade cold hammer forged free-floating barrel with Surefire Procomp 556 muzzle brake, 30 shot mag., Timney competition trigger, flat-top receiver with rail, Samson Evolution 15 in. handguard, Magpul CTR buttstock, Magpul MOE grip, matte black finish, 7.7 lbs. New 2015.

MSR $1,749	$1,485	$1,315	$1,150	$1,025	$875	$750	$615	

FN15 TACTICAL – 5.56x45mm cal., 16 in. match grade free floating barrel with FNH USA 3-prong flash hider, 30 shot Magpul PMAG, alum. flat-top receiver with rail, Magpul MBUS sights, Midwest Industries LWM 12 in. handguard with M-LOK accessory mounting system, Magpul MOE grip, enhanced combat trigger, Magpul MOE SL buttstock, matte black finish, 6.6 lbs. New 2015.

MSR $1,479	$1,250	$1,100	$985	$835	$725	$615	$515	

FN15 TACTICAL .300 BLK – .300 AAC Blackout cal., 16 in. match grade hammer forged, free floating barrel, SureFire ProComp 762 muzzle brake, low profile gas block, 30 shot mag., Magpul front and rear sight assembly, Magpul MOE-SL buttstock and MOE pistol grip, carbine length gas system, H buffer, lightweight 12 in. M-LOK rail, 6 3/4 lbs. New 2016.

MSR $1,479	$1,250	$1,100	$985	$835	$725	$615	$515	

FNAR STANDARD – .308 Win. cal., 16 (new 2010) or 20 in. light or heavy fluted contoured barrel, 10 or 20 shot detachable box mag., one-piece M-1913 optical rail, three accessory rails attached to forearm, matte black synthetic pistol grip stock with soft cheekpiece, adj. comb, ambidextrous mag. release, 8.8-9 lbs. Mfg. 2009-2013.

	$1,550	$1,325	$1,100	$975	$850	$725	$650	*$1,699*

FNAR COMPETITION – 7.62x51mm cal., gas operated, 20 in. fluted barrel, target crowned, front barrel mounted sight rail for aftermarket sights, 20 shot detachable box mag., alum. alloy receiver with one-piece Mil-Std 1913 optics rail, hard anodized blue receiver finish with Team FNH USA markings, blue/grey laminated stock assembly with checkered gripping surfaces, adj. for cheekpiece, non-slip recoil pad, crossbolt safety, 8.9 lbs. New 2013.

MSR $1,767	$1,500	$1,315	$1,150	$1,025	$875	$750	$615	

MSR	100%	98%	95%	90%	80%	70%	60%	Last MSR

PS90 – 5.7x28mm cal., blowback operation, bullpup configuration, 16 in. barrel, 10 or 30 shot box mag. runs horizontally along the top, empty cases are ejected downward, integrated muzzle brake, Olive Drab or black finish, configurations include PS90 RD with reflex sight module (mfg. 2009), PS90 USG with non-magnifying black reticle optical sight, and the PS90 TR with three M-1913 rails for optional optics, 6.3 lbs. Disc. 2011.

	100%	98%	95%	90%	80%	70%	60%	Last MSR
	$1,925	$1,675	$1,450	$1,295	$1,075	$925	$800	$2,199

Add $391 for red-dot sights.

FS2000 STANDARD/TACTICAL – .223 Rem. cal., bullpup configuration, 17.4 in. barrel, gas operated with rotating bolt, 10 or 30 shot AR-15 style mag., empty cases are ejected through a forward port, includes 1.6x optical sighting package on Standard Model (disc. 2010), Tactical Model features emergency back up folding sights, CQB model features lower accessory rail, ambidextrous polymer stock, top mounted M-1913 rail, Olive Drab Green or black finish, 7.6 lbs. Disc. 2013.

	100%	98%	95%	90%	80%	70%	60%	Last MSR
	$2,425	$2,100	$1,825	$1,675	$1,450	$1,250	$995	$2,779

* PS90 Standard – 5.7x28mm cal., blowback operation, 16 in. hammer forged barrel with ported muzzle brake, 10 (new 2012) or 30 shot mag., alloy upper receiver, bottom ejection port, forward handstop, 1913 accessory rail and back-up iron sight, molded-in rear sling attachment point, ambidextrous charging handles, synthetic thumbhole bullpup design, sliding trigger, enlarged trigger guard, black or Olive Drab Green finish, 6.28 lbs. New 2010.

MSR $1,449	100%	98%	95%	90%	80%	70%	60%	
	$1,235	$1,100	$985	$835	$725	$615	$515	

SCAR 16S – .223 Rem. cal., semi-auto only version of U.S. SOCOM's newest service rifle, gas operated short stroke piston system, free floating 16 1/4 in. barrel with hard chrome bore, 10 or 30 shot detachable box mag., folding open sights, fully ambidextrous operating controls, three optical rails, side folding polymer stock, A2 pistol grip, fully adj. comb and LOP, black or Flat Dark Earth finish on receiver and stock, 7 1/4 lbs. New 2009.

MSR $2,995	100%	98%	95%	90%	80%	70%	60%	
	$2,695	$2,375	$2,050	$1,850	$1,575	$1,275	$1,050	

SCAR 17S – .308 Win. cal., 10 or 20 shot mag., otherwise similar to SCAR 16S, 8 lbs. New 2009.

MSR $3,349	100%	98%	95%	90%	80%	70%	60%	
	$2,925	$2,550	$2,175	$1,900	$1,575	$1,275	$1,050	

SCAR 20S – 7.62x51mm cal., GPO, 20 in. cold hammer forged free floating barrel, 10 shot mag., enlarged trigger guard, adj. folding front and rear sights, adj. non-folding polymer stock, adj. cheekpiece, A2 black pistol grip, ambidextrous safety lever and mag. release, Monolithic receiver, top Picatinny rail, Flat Dark Earth finish, 42 1/2 in. OAL. New 2016.
Please contact the manufacturer directly for pricing and availability for this model.

PISTOLS: SEMI-AUTO

In addition to the models listed, FNH USA also imported the HP-SA ($800 last MSR), and the HP-SFS until 2006.

All FNP guns come standard with three magazines and a lockable hard case.

FNP-9 – 9mm Para. cal., 4 in. barrel, 10 or 16 (disc. 2010) shot mag., polymer frame, matte black or matte stainless steel slide, DA/SA, matte black or Flat Dark Earth (mfg. 2010 only) finish, ambidextrous frame mounted decocker, underframe rail, interchangeable backstrap inserts, 25.2 oz. Disc. 2011.

	100%	98%	95%	90%	80%	70%	60%	Last MSR
	$575	$495	$435	$380	$340	$300	$275	$649

Add $125 for night sights (disc. 2009).
Add $50 for USG operation (DA/SA, ambidextrous frame mounted decocker/manual safety), disc. 2010.

FNP-9M – 9mm Para. cal., 3.8 in. barrel, DA/SA, 10 or 15 shot mag., polymer frame, similar to the FNP-9, except is smaller frame, 24.8 oz. Disc. 2008.

	100%	98%	95%	90%	80%	70%	60%	Last MSR
	$525	$450	$400	$365	$335	$300	$275	$593

Add $118 for night sights.

FNP-357 – .357 SIG cal., similar to FNP-9, black finish only, 14 shot mag., 27.2 oz. Mfg. 2009.

	100%	98%	95%	90%	80%	70%	60%	Last MSR
	$565	$475	$425	$375	$335	$300	$275	$629

Add $65 for USG operation (features ambidextrous frame mounted decocker/manual safety levers).

FNP-40 – .40 S&W cal., 4 in. barrel, 10 or 14 (disc. 2010) shot mag., DA/SA, black or Flat Dark Earth (mfg. 2010 only) polymer frame, optional stainless steel slide, underframe rail, interchangeable backstrap, external hammer, 25.2 or 26.7 oz. Disc. 2011.

	100%	98%	95%	90%	80%	70%	60%	Last MSR
	$575	$495	$435	$380	$340	$300	$275	$649

Add $125 for night sights (disc. 2009).
Add $50 for USG operation (features ambidextrous frame mounted decocker/manual safety levers), disc. 2010.

FNP-45 – .45 ACP cal., 4 1/2 in. barrel, DA/SA, 10 (disc. 2011), 14, or 15 (new 2011) shot mag., polymer frame, matte black finish with optional stainless steel slide, or Flat Dark Earth (new 2010) finish, external extractor, underframe rail, interchangeable backstraps, 33.2 oz. Disc. 2013.

	100%	98%	95%	90%	80%	70%	60%	Last MSR
	$725	$625	$575	$525	$450	$400	$350	$795

Add $125 for night sights (disc.).
Subtract approx. 5% if without USG operation (features ambidextrous frame mounted decocker/manual safety levers).

MSR	100%	98%	95%	90%	80%	70%	60%	Last MSR

Add approx. $186 for pistol package, which includes three mags., molded polymer holster, double mag. pouch, and training barrel (mfg. 2009 only).

* **FNP-45 Competition** – .45 ACP cal., DA/SA, matte black finish, 15 shot mag., lower accessory rail, interchangeable arched and flat backstrap inserts with lanyard holes, 33.2 oz. Mfg. 2011-2012.

	$1,075	$925	$825	$725	$625	$550	$475	*$1,239*

* **FNP-45 Tactical** – .45 ACP cal., 5.3 in. threaded barrel, 15 shot mag., DA/SA, polymer frame with Mil-Std 1913 mounting rail and interchangeable backstraps with lanyard eyelets, serrated trigger guard, ambidextrous mag. release, manual safety and slide stop, fixed combat sights, black or Flat Dark Earth finish, stainless steel slide, includes fitted soft case. Mfg. 2010-2012.

	$1,200	$1,025	$875	$775	$675	$575	$495	*$1,395*

FNS-9 – 9mm Para. cal., DAO, SFO, 4 in. cold hammer forged stainless steel barrel, 10 or 17 shot mag., matte black or matte silver slide finish, fixed 3-dot sights or night sights, external extractor with loaded chamber indicator, front and rear cocking serrations, black or FDE (disc.) finished polymer frame, lower accessory rail, two interchangeable backstraps with lanyard eyelets, serrated trigger guard, fully ambidextrous slide stop lever and mag. release, 25.2 oz. New 2012.

MSR $599		$525	$465	$400	$340	$300	$265	$250

Add $50 for night sights or for left-hand action.
Add $66 for 10 shot mag. with left-hand action.

* **FNS-9 Compact** – 9mm Para. cal., similar to FNS-9, except has 3.6 in. barrel, 12 or 17 shot mag., matte black or matte silver slide, matte black finished frame, 23.4 oz. New 2015.

MSR $599		$525	$465	$400	$340	$300	$265	$250

Add $50 for night sights.

FNS-9 LONGSLIDE (COMPETITION) – 9mm Para. cal., striker fired, DAO, SFO, 5 in. hammer forged stainless steel barrel, stainless steel slide, fixed 3 dot sights, loaded chamber indicator, front and rear cocking serrations, 17 shot mag., Mil-Std 1913 accessory mounting rail, serrated trigger guard, black frame finish, 27.2 oz. New 2013.

MSR $649		$575	$500	$435	$365	$325	$280	$265

FNS-40 – .40 S&W cal., DAO, SFO, 4 in. cold hammer forged stainless steel barrel, 14 shot mag., matte black or matte silver slide finish, black or Flat Dark Earth (disc.) finished polymer frame, fixed 3-dot sights or night sights, external extractor with loaded chamber indicator, front and rear cocking serrations, lower accessory rail, two interchangeable backstraps with lanyard eyelets, serrated trigger guard, fully ambidextrous slide stop lever and mag. release, 27.5 oz. New 2012.

MSR $599		$525	$465	$400	$340	$300	$265	$250

Add $50 for night sights or for left-hand action.
Add $66 for 10 shot mag. with left-hand action.

* **FNS-40 Compact** – .40 S&W cal., similar to FNS-40, except has 3.6 in. barrel, 10 or 14 shot mag., matte black or matte silver slide, matte black polymer frame, 25.8 oz. New 2015.

MSR $599		$525	$465	$400	$340	$300	$265	$250

Add $50 for night sights.

FNS-40 LONGSLIDE – .40 S&W cal., striker fired, DAO, SFO, 5 in. hammer forged stainless steel barrel, stainless steel slide, fixed 3 dot sights, loaded chamber indicator, front and rear cocking serrations, 14 shot mag., Mil-Std 1913 accessory mounting rail, serrated trigger guard, black frame finish, 29.5 oz. New 2013.

MSR $649		$575	$500	$435	$365	$325	$280	$265

FNX-9 – 9mm Para. cal., DA/SA, semi-auto pistol, 4 in. barrel, 10 (new 2012) or 17 shot mag., serrated trigger guard, deep V fixed combat sights, four interchangeable backstrap inserts, ambidextrous mag. release and manual safety, front and rear cocking serrations, Mil-Std mounting rail, matte black or matte black with stainless steel slide, 21.9 oz. New 2010.

MSR $699		$615	$540	$470	$400	$350	$310	$295

Add $50 for night sights (disc. 2013).

* **FNX-9 Compact** – 9mm Para. cal., DA/SA, semi-auto pistol, 3 in. barrel, 17 shot mag., serrated trigger guard, deep V fixed combat sights, ambidextrous mag. release and manual safety, front and rear cocking serrations, Mil-Std mounting rail, matte black, 17.9 oz. New 2014.

MSR $699		$615	$540	$470	$400	$350	$310	$295

Add $50 for night sights.

FNX-40 – .40 S&W cal., DA/SA, semi-auto pistol, 4 in. barrel, 10 (new 2012) or 14 shot mag., serrated trigger guard, deep V fixed combat sights, four interchangeable backstrap inserts, ambidextrous mag. release and manual safety, front and rear cocking serrations, Mil-Std mounting rail,, matte black or matte black with stainless steel slide, 24.4 oz. New 2010.

MSR $699		$615	$540	$470	$400	$350	$310	$295

Add $50 for night sights (disc. 2013).

MSR		100%	98%	95%	90%	80%	70%	60%	Last MSR

FNX-45 – .45 ACP cal., DA/SA, 4 1/2 in. stainless steel barrel, 10, 12 (disc. 2013), or 15 shot mag., matte black or stainless steel slide, low profile fixed 3-dot sights, external extractor with loaded chamber indicator, matte black polymer frame, front and rear cocking serrations, two interchangeable backstrap inserts, lower accessory rail, ambidextrous decocking levers, ring style external hammers, black or Flat Dark Earth finish, 33.2 oz. New 2012.

| | MSR $824 | $695 | $615 | $550 | $475 | $420 | $365 | $335 | |

* ***FNX-45 Tactical*** – .45 ACP cal., similar to FNX-45, except has threaded barrel, 15 shot mag., high profile night sights, includes fitted Cordura nylon soft case, 33.6 oz. New 2012.

| | MSR $1,349 | $1,135 | $1,015 | $885 | $740 | $675 | $575 | $475 | |

FIVE-SEVEN – 5.7x28mm cal., SA, SFO, 4 3/4 in. cold hammer forged stainless steel barrel with hard chrome chamber and bore, polymer encased steel slide, USG (disc. 2012) or MK2 variation, 10 or 20 shot mag., reversible mag. release, textured grip, black, OD Green (disc. 2011) or Flat Dark Earth finish, polymer frame, Mil-Std mounting, ambidextrous manual safety, magazine disconnect safety, choice of fixed 3-dot (standard mfg.), adj. (USG model), C-More fixed (disc.), or C-More fixed night sights (disc.), underframe rail, includes three mags., hard case and cleaning kit, 20.8 oz.

| | MSR $1,349 | $1,135 | $1,015 | $885 | $740 | $675 | $575 | $475 | |

Add 10% for early mfg. that incorporated a larger trigger guard than current mfg.

RIFLES: BOLT ACTION

FNH USA imports a wide range of tactical rifle systems for military and law enforcement only. FNH USA also imported a line of modular system rifles, including the Ultima Ratio Intervention, the Ultima Ratio Commando II, and the .338 Lapua Model. Please contact the company directly for more information, including availability and pricing (see Trademark Index).

BALLISTA – .308 Win. (mfg. 2013 only), .300 Win. Mag. (mfg. 2013 only), or .338 Lapua cal., 26 in. fluted barrel, ambidextrous fully adj. folding stock, 5 or 8 shot detachable box mag., aluminum alloy receiver with top mounted mil-std 1913 rail plus multiple rail segments for other accessories, fully adj. single or two-stage trigger, Flat Dark Earth or Desert Tan finish, 14 1/2 lbs. Mfg. by Unique Alpine AG. New 2013.

| | MSR $7,499 | $6,950 | $6,400 | $5,800 | $5,200 | $4,500 | $3,650 | $2,875 | |

PBR (PATROL BOLT RIFLE) – .300 WSM (XP Model) or .308 Win. cal., 22 in. heavy free floating barrel standard, stippled black Hogue overmolded stock, Picatinny rail, four shot fixed or removable box mag., some models may be marked "FN Herstal", later production marked "FNH", approx. 9 1/2 lbs.

| | | $1,075 | $925 | $825 | $750 | $625 | $500 | $425 | *$1,075* |

Add $170 for XP Model in .300 WSM cal.

SPR A1/A1a – .308 Win. cal., 20 in. fluted (A1a) or 24 (A1) in. non-fluted cold hammer forged free-floating barrel, recessed target crown, 4 shot detachable box mag., pre-'64 Model 70 action, external claw extractor, matte black McMillan fiberglass stock with adj. comb and LOP, textured gripping surfaces, premium recoil pad, multiple steel sling swivel studs, knurled bolt handle, 3-pos. safety, blade ejector, 1-piece steel 1913 optics rail, matte black finish, 11.8-12.4 lbs.

| | MSR $2,245 | $2,000 | $1,775 | $1,575 | $1,375 | $1,175 | $975 | $750 | |

Subtract $246 for A1 model with non-fluted barrel.

SPR A2 – .308 Win. cal., similar to A1, 20 in. fluted or 24 in. non-fluted barrel, 11.6 or 12.2 lbs. Disc. 2009.

| | | $2,500 | $2,185 | $1,875 | $1,700 | $1,375 | $1,125 | $875 | *$2,745* |

SPR A3 G (SPECIAL POLICE RIFLE) – .308 Win. cal., 24 in. fluted barrel with hard chromed bore, hinged floorplate, one-piece steel Mil-Std 1913 optical rail, A3 fiberglass tactical stock with adj. comb and LOP, steel sling studs, designed to achieve 1/2 MOA accuracy standard, 14.3 lbs.

| | MSR $3,495 | $3,175 | $2,750 | $2,350 | $2,125 | $1,700 | $1,395 | $1,075 | |

SPR A5M – .308 Win. or .300 WSM cal., steel construction, 20 or 24 in. non-fluted free-floating barrel, target crown, 4 or 5 shot mag., controlled round feed with external claw extractor, blade ejector, one-piece steel Mil-Std 1913 optics rail, 2-lever adj. trigger, 3-position safety, McMillan fiberglass stock with adj. LOP and cheekpiece, textured gripping surfaces, multiple sling/bipod studs, matte black finish, 11.3-11.8 lbs.

| | MSR $2,899 | $2,625 | $2,325 | $1,975 | $1,750 | $1,475 | $1,250 | $950 | |

Add $100 for traditional hinged floorplate in .300 WSM cal. or $200 for hinged floorplate in .308 Win. cal. (both disc. 2013).

SPR A5M XP – .308 Win. cal., steel construction, 20 or 24 in. chrome lined free floating heavy fluted barrel, threaded muzzle, recessed target crown, 5 shot box mag., controlled round feed with external claw extractor, blade ejector, one piece 20 MOA optics rail, McMillan fiberglass stock with adj. LOP and cheekpiece, textured gripping surfaces, multiple sling/bipod studs, 6 integral quick detach sling mounts, premium recoil pad, 2-lever adj. trigger, 3-pos. safety, oversized bolt handle, ambidextrous mag. release, matte black finish, 11 1/2-11 3/4 lbs. New 2013.

| | MSR $2,899 | $2,625 | $2,325 | $1,975 | $1,750 | $1,475 | $1,250 | $950 | |

Add $200 for TBM (tactical box mag.) with 20 or 24 in. fluted barrel (mfg. 2011-2013).

MSR	100%	98%	95%	90%	80%	70%	60%	Last MSR

PSR I – .308 Win. cal., 20 in. fluted or 24 in. non-fluted barrel, 3, 4, or 5 shot internal mag., FN tactical sport trigger system, hinged floorplate, matte black McMillan sporter style fiberglass stock, raised comb, recoil pad, steel sling studs, 7.7 or 8.7 lbs. Disc. 2009.

	$2,000	$1,750	$1,500	$1,360	$1,100	$900	$700	*$2,253*

PSR II/III – .308 Win. or .300 WSM (PSR II) cal., 22 in. fluted or 24 in. non-fluted barrel, 3, 4 (PSR III), or 5 shot internal or detachable box mag., FN tactical sport trigger system, matte olive drab McMillan sporter style fiberglass stock, raised comb, recoil pad, steel sling studs, 8.7 - 9.8 lbs. Disc. 2009.

	$2,000	$1,750	$1,500	$1,360	$1,100	$900	$700	*$2,253*

TSR XP/XP USA (TACTICAL SPORT RIFLES) – .223 Rem. (XP USA), 7.62x39mm (XP USA, disc. 2009), .300 WSM (disc. 2013), or .308 Win. (disc. 2013) cal., Model 70 short (XP) or ultra short (XP USA) action, 20 in. fluted (disc. 2010), 20 or 24 (disc. 2013) in. non-fluted barrel, 3, 4 (detachable box mag., XP Model only), 5, or 6 shot mag., one-piece steel Mil-Std 1913 optical rail, full aluminum bedding block molded into FN/Hogue synthetic stock, Olive Drab overmolded surface, recoil pad, steel sling studs, 8.7-10.1 lbs. Disc. 2015.

	$1,050	$925	$800	$700	$600	$500	$400	*$1,199*

Add $100 for .300 WSM cal. with floorplate (disc. 2013).

SHOTGUNS

FNH USA manufactured tactical style shotguns, including the FN Police Shotgun ($500 last MSR) and the FN Tactical Police Shotgun (with or w/o fixed stock, $923 last MSR).

FN SLP STANDARD (MODEL SLP - SELF LOADING POLICE) – 12 ga., 3 in. chamber, semi-auto, gas system, 18 in. barrel with standard invector chokes, 6 shot extended tube mag., high profile adj. rear sights, two-piece bolt, alum. alloy receiver, top mounted one-piece 1913 rail, two steel sling swivel studs, crossbolt safety, matte black synthetic stock with checkered gripping panels on forearm and grip, non-slip recoil pad, matte black finish, 7.7 lbs. New 2008.

MSR $1,379	$1,150	$1,030	$900	$750	$685	$585	$485	

FN SLP COMPETITION – 12 ga., 3 in. chamber, semi-auto, gas operated with one interchangeable gas piston, 22 (disc. 2014) or 24 (new 2015) in. VR barrel with IC Invector Plus extended choke tubes, crossbolt safety, flip-up rear and fiber optic front sights, 8 shot extended tube mag. with blue aluminum tube cover, aluminum alloy receiver with enlarged loading port and blue hard anodized finish, matte black synthetic stock with checkered gripping panels on forearm and grip, non-slip recoil pad, sling swivel studs, 7 1/2 lbs. New 2013.

MSR $1,449	$1,235	$1,100	$985	$835	$725	$615	$515	

FN SLP TACTICAL – 12 ga., 3 in. chamber, semi-auto, gas operated, 18 in. barrel with standard invector choke tubes, 6 shot extended tube mag., high profile adj. ghost ring rear and wing protected front sights, alum. alloy receiver, top mounted rail, crossbolt safety, two steel sling swivel studs, forward mounted 1913 tri-rail mount, matte black synthetic pistol grip stock with 3 interchangeable cheekpieces and 3 interchangeable recoil pads, checkered gripping surfaces on forearm and grip, matte black finish, 7.4 lbs.

MSR $1,479	$1,250	$1,100	$985	$835	$725	$615	$515	

FN SLP MK1 – 12 ga., 3 in. chamber, semi-auto, active valve gas system, 22 in. barrel with standard invector chokes, 8 shot extended mag. tube with aluminum tube cover, low profile adj. rear and red fiber optic front sights, two-piece bolt, alum. alloy receiver, top mounted Cantilever Weaver-pattern accessory rail, two steel sling swivels, matte black synthetic stock with checkered gripping surfaces on forearm and grip, non-slip recoil pad, crossbolt safety, matte black finish, 8.2 lbs.

MSR $1,324	$1,125	$1,000	$875	$735	$650	$550	$465	

FN SLP MK1 TACTICAL – 12 ga., 3 in. chamber, semi-auto, active valve gas system, 18 in. barrel with standard invector interchangeable choke tubes, 6 shot extended tube mag. with aluminum mag. tube cover, forward mounted 1913 tri-rail mount, low profile adj. folding rear and red fiber optic front sights, two-piece bolt, matte black synthetic pistol grip stock with interchangeable comb inserts and recoil pads, crossbolt safety, matte black finish, 7.9 lbs.

MSR $1,429	$1,225	$1,100	$950	$800	$700	$600	$495	

MODEL SC1 O/U – 12 ga., 2 3/4 in. chambers, 28 (disc. 2013) or 30 in. VR barrel with invector plus choking, silver receiver, blue/gray, black, or green adj. comb laminate stock with recoil pad. New 2011.

MSR $2,449	$2,150	$1,850	$1,625	$1,400	$1,175	$940	$815	

P-12 SLIDE ACTION – 12 ga., 2 3/4 or 3 in. chrome lined chamber, 18 in. cantilever barrel, matte black finish, aluminum alloy receiver, checkered synthetic stock, recoil pad, Invector cylinder choke Weaver rail pattern, sling swivels, 7 lbs., 7 oz. New 2013.

MSR $669	$595	$525	$450	$395	$360	$330	$295	

MSR	100%	98%	95%	90%	80%	70%	60%	Last MSR

FABARM, S.p.A.

Current manufacturer established in 1900 and located in Brescia, Italy. Currently imported by Fabarm USA beginning 2012, and located in Cambridge, MD. Previously imported by Tristar, located in Kansas City, MO circa 2007-2009. Select models previously retailed until 2012 by Bill Hanus Birdguns, LLC, located in Newport, OR. Previously imported by SIG Arms during 2005, located in Exeter, NH, and by Heckler & Koch, Inc. 1998-2004. Certain models had limited importation by Ithaca Acquisition Corp. located in King Ferry, NY during 1993-1995. Previously imported and distributed (1988-1990) by St. Lawrence Sales, Inc. located in Lake Orion, MI. Previously imported until 1986 by Beeman Precision Arms, Inc. located in Santa Rosa, CA.

Fabarm currently manufactures approx. 35,000 long guns annually.

Fabarm manufactures a wide variety of shotguns, rifles, and double rifles in assorted configurations, with many options available. Most models, however, are not currently being imported into the U.S. at this time. Please contact the importer directly for more information, including current model availability and pricing (see Trademark Index).

SHOTGUNS: SEMI-AUTO

The following previously manufactured models are gas operated, self compensating, have 4 shot mags., aluminum receivers, twin action bars, blue receiver with photo etched game scene engraving, and checkered walnut stock and forearm.

Add $25 for De Luxe engraving or camouflage wood finish.

TACTICAL SEMI-AUTO – 12 ga. only, 3 in. chamber, 20 in. barrel with TriBore choke system with cylinder choke, tactical configuration with large cocking handle, oversized safety, black polymer stock and forearm, pistol grip stock design new 2003, choice of Picatinny rail with either integral rear or fixed front and ghost ring (new 2003) sight, 5 shot mag., 6.6 lbs. Imported 2001-2004.

	$875	$775	$650	$575	$515	$450	$400	$1,025

SHOTGUNS: SLIDE ACTION

The following models are variations of the same action based on a twin bar slide system, alloy receiver with anti-glare finish (including barrel), rear trigger guard safety, and 2 3/4 or 3 in. shell interchangeability.

Add $25 for camouflage wood finish on the following models.

MODEL S.D.A.S.S. – 12 ga. only, 3 in. chamber, originally designed for police and self defense use, 8 shot tube mag., 20 or 24 1/2 in. barrel threaded for external choke tubes, approx. 6 lbs. 6 oz. Imported 1989-90.

	$325	$285	$260	$230	$195	$160	$140	$415

This model with 24 1/2 in. barrel is threaded for external multi-chokes which can add up to 6 in. to the barrel length - available for a $17 extra charge.

* **Model S.D.A.S.S. Special Police** – 12 ga., similar to Model S.D.A.S.S. except has special heavy 20 in. cylinder bored barrel, VR, cooling jacket, 6 shot mag., rubber recoil pad. Imported 1989-90.

	$340	$295	$265	$230	$195	$160	$140	$440

* **Model S.D.A.S.S. Martial** – 12 ga. only, 18, 20, 28, 30, or 35 1/2 (disc. 1989) in. barrel, fixed sights and choke, approx. 6 1/4 lbs. Imported 1989-90.

	$330	$290	$260	$225	$190	$160	$140	$424

Add $41 for VR barrel.
Add $20 for 35 1/2 (disc. 1989) in. barrel.
Add $33 for multi-choke (plain rib with 1 choke and wrench).
Add $65 for innerchoke (includes 1 choke and wrench - VR barrel only).

FP6 – 12 ga. only, 3 in. chamber, 20 or 28 (new 2001) in. shrouded barrel (non-ported TriBore system became standard 2000) with vent. heat shield, with or w/o Picatinny rail, with (new 2003) or w/o ghost ring rear sight, camo (new 2001), matte, or carbon fiber (new 2000) finished metal, 100% Mossy Oak camo (mfg. 2001-2003) or black synthetic stock and forearm, pistol grip stock design new 2003, various security configurations, includes locking plastic case, 6 1/2-7 lbs. Imported 1998-2005.

	$460	$400	$365	$325	$295	$265	$240	

Subtract $30 for 100% Mossy Oak Break-up camo coverage (disc. 2003).

FABRIQUE NATIONALE

Current manufacturer located in Herstal, near Liege, Belgium. The current company name is "Group Herstal." However, the company is better known as "Fabrique Nationale" or "Fabrique Nationale d'Armes de Guerre". FN entered into their first contract with John M. Browning in 1897 for the manufacture of their first pistol, the FN 1899 Model. Additional contracts were signed and the relationship further blossomed with the manufacture of the A-5 shotgun. FN was acquired by GIAT of France in 1992. In late 1997, the company was purchased by the Walloon government of Belgium. Additional production facilities are located in Portugal, Japan, and the U.S.

MSR	100%	98%	95%	90%	80%	70%	60%	Last MSR

Also see: Browning Arms under Rifles, Shotguns, and Pistols, and FN AMERICA LLC (FNH USA) for current offerings in the U.S.

The author would like to express his sincere thanks to Anthony Vanderlinden for making FN contributions to this edition.

RIFLES: BOLT ACTION

FN SNIPER RIFLE (MODEL 30) – .308 Win. cal., this model was a Mauser actioned Sniper Rifle equipped with 20 in. extra heavy barrel, flash hider, separate removable diopter sights, Hensoldt 4x scope, hardcase, bipod, and sling. 51 complete factory sets were imported into the U.S., with additional surplus rifles that were privately imported.

| | $4,750 | $4,250 | $4,000 | $3,500 | $3,000 | $2,750 | $2,500 | |

Subtract 15% if removable diopter sights or bipod is missing.

Subtract 10% if scope is not marked with F.N. logo.

Values assume complete factory outfit with all accessories.

RIFLES: SEMI-AUTO

MODEL 1949 – 7x57mm Mauser, 7.65mm Mauser, 7.92mm Mauser, or .30-06 cal., (.308 Win. cal. for Argentine conversion rifles), gas operated, 10 shot box mag. (20 round detachable mag. for Argentine conversions), 23 in. barrel, military rifle, tangent rear sight.

	100%	98%	95%	90%	80%	70%	60%
Columbia	$1,700	$1,400	$1,150	$1,000	$900	$750	$700
Luxembourg	$1,500	$1,250	$1,000	$900	$800	$650	$600
Venezuela	$1,350	$1,100	$900	$850	$700	$600	$550
Argentina	N/A	$1,250	$1,100	$950	$850	$750	$650
Egyptian	$1,600	$1,350	$1,100	$995	$895	$725	$675

Add $100 for detachable grenade launcher.

Subtract 30% for U.S. rebuilt, non-matching rifles with reproduction stocks.

Original FN-49 sniper rifles are extremely rare and may add $2,500+.

Beware of U.S. assembled "sniper" configurations, and Belgian military "ABL" scopes mounted on other contract rifles and sold as original sniper configurations.

FN-49 contract rifles not listed above are very rare in the U.S. and will demand a premium.

Carefully inspect black paint finish for factory originality, as all FN-49s were factory painted.

RIFLES: SEMI-AUTO, FAL/LAR/CAL/FNC SERIES

After tremendous price increases between 1985-88, Fabrique Nationale decided in 1988 to discontinue this series completely. Not only are these rifles not exported to the U.S. any longer, but all production has ceased in Belgium as well. The only way FN will produce these models again is if they are given a large military contract - in which case a "side order" of commercial guns may be built. 1989 Federal legislation regarding this type of tactical design also helped push up prices to their current level. FAL rifles were also mfg. in Israel by I.M.I.

F.N. FAL – semi-auto, French designation for the F.N. L.A.R. (light automatic rifle), otherwise similar to the L.A.R.

| | $4,175 | $3,950 | $3,750 | $3,475 | $3,150 | $3,100 | $2,750 |

* F.N. FAL G

	100%	98%	95%	90%	80%	70%	60%
Standard	$4,800	$4,000	$3,500	$2,950	$2,450	$2,150	$2,000
Paratrooper	$5,200	$4,400	$3,900	$3,350	$2,850	$2,550	$2,400
Heavy Barrel	$6,800	$6,250	$4,950	$4,400	$3,750	$3,250	$2,750
Lightweight	$5,200	$4,250	$3,750	$3,100	$2,600	$2,350	$2,100

Values listed assume inclusion of factory bipod.

The Standard G Series was supplied with a wooden stock and wood or nylon forearm. The Heavy Barrel variant had all wood furniture and was supplied with a bipod. The Lightweight Model had an aluminum lower receiver, piston tube and magazine.

G Series FALs were imported between 1959-1962 by Browning Arms Co. This rifle was declared illegal by the GCA of 1968, and was exempted 5 years later. Total numbers exempted are: Standard - 1,822, Heavy Barrel - 21, and Paratrooper - 5.

F.N. L.A.R. COMPETITION (50.00, LIGHT AUTOMATIC RIFLE) – .308 Win. (7.62x51mm) cal., semi-auto, competition rifle with match flash hider, 21 in. barrel, adj. 4 position fire selector on automatic models, wood stock, aperture rear sight adj. from 100-600 meters, 9.4 lbs. Mfg. 1981-83.

| | $4,250 | $4,025 | $3,850 | $3,625 | $3,450 | $3,175 | $2,950 |

This model was designated by the factory as the 50.00 Model.

Mid-1987 retail on this model was $1,258. The last MSR was $3,179 (this price reflected the last exchange rate and special order status of this model).

MSR	100%	98%	95%	90%	80%	70%	60%	Last MSR

* **FN L.A.R. Competition Heavy barrel rifle (50.41 & 50.42)** – barrel is twice as heavy as standard L.A.R., includes wood or synthetic stock, short wood forearm, and bipod, 12.2 lbs. Importation disc. 1988.

| | $4,495 | $4,275 | $4,150 | $4,000 | $3,675 | $3,500 | $3,250 | |

Add $500 for walnut stock.

Add $350 for match sights.

There were 2 variations of this model. The Model 50.41 had a synthetic buttstock while the Model 50.42 had a wood buttstock with steel buttplate incorporating a top extension used for either shoulder resting or inverted grenade launching.

Mid-1987 retail on this model was $1,497 (Model 50.41) or $1,654 (Model 50.42). The last MSR was $3,776 (this price reflected the last exchange rate and special order status of this model).

* **FN L.A.R. Competition Paratrooper rifle (50.63 & 50.64)** – similar to L.A.R. model, except has folding stock, 8.3 lbs. Mfg. 1950-88.

| | $4,275 | $3,700 | $3,300 | $3,000 | $2,550 | $2,300 | $2,150 | |

There were 2 variations of the Paratrooper L.A.R. Model. The Model 50.63 had a stationary aperture rear sight and 18 in. barrel. The Model 50.64 was supplied with a 21 in. barrel and had a rear sight calibrated for either 150 or 200 meters. Both models retailed for the same price.

Mid-1987 retail on this model was $1,310 (both the Model 50.63 and 50.64). The last MSR was $3,239 (this price reflected the last exchange rate and special order status of this model).

CAL – originally imported in 1980, FN's .223 CAL military rifle succeeded the .308 FAL and preceeded the .223 FNC, at first declared illegal but later given amnesty, only 20 imported by Browning.

| | $7,800 | $7,000 | $6,250 | $5,500 | $4,750 | $4,100 | $3,600 | |

FNC MODEL – .223 Rem. (5.56mm) cal., lightweight combat carbine, 16 or 18 1/2 in. barrel, NATO approved, 30 shot mag., 8.4 lbs. Disc. 1987.

| | $2,950 | $2,700 | $2,550 | $2,100 | $1,900 | $1,650 | $1,500 | |

Add $350 for Paratrooper model (16 or 18 1/2 in. barrel).

While rarer, the 16 in. barrel model incorporated a flash hider that did not perform as well as the flash hider used on the standard 18 1/2 in. barrel.

Mid-1987 retail on this model was $749 (Standard Model) and $782 (Paratrooper Model). The last MSR was $2,204 (Standard Model) and $2,322 (Paratrooper Model) - these prices reflected the last exchange rate and special order status of these models.

FAXON FIREARMS

Current rifle manufacturer located in Cincinnati, OH.

RIFLES: SEMI-AUTO

ARAK-21 XRS RIFLE – 5.56 NATO, 7.62 NATO (new 2015), or .300 AAC Blackout cal., utilizes both AR-15 and AK-47 design elements, gas piston actuated (four position), 16 or 20 in. barrel with A2 flash supressor, MAG tactical lower, upper receiver with charging block and standard charging handle, aluminum full length upper Picatinny rails and partial lower and side rails, three insulating shims, bolt carrier assembly, lower recoil lug with spring guide rod, dual recoil spring system, 30 shot mag., matte black, blue, silver, green or red finish, includes plastic hard case.

| MSR $1,899 | $1,775 | $1,540 | $1,350 | $1,075 | $950 | $825 | $695 | |

Add $265 for extra BAU (barrel assembly unit).

This model is also available in single barrel or multiple barrel steel or stainless steel packages. Please contact the company directly for pricing and availability (see Trademark Index).

ARAK-31 XRS RIFLE – .308 Win., .300 AAC Blackout, 5.56 NATO, or 6.5mm Creedmoor cal., GPO, LR-308 barrel with custom Trunion, billet upper and lower receivers, forward reversible charging handles, ambi safety, magazine catch, and bolt release, compatible with LR-308 DPMS lower receivers, integrated Magpul M-LOK System, removal-protected gas adjuster, Battle Arms Development BAD-ASS selector, HiperFire trigger, B5 Bravo stock, black anodized, OD Green, or FDE Cerakote finish, 9 lbs. Mfg. 2015 only.

| | $2,125 | $1,875 | $1,550 | $1,325 | $1,100 | $950 | $825 | *$2,499* |

FEATHER INDUSTRIES, INC.

Previous manufacturer located in Boulder, CO until 1995.

RIFLES: SEMI-AUTO

AT-22 – .22 LR cal., semi-auto blowback action, 17 in. detachable shrouded barrel, collapsible metal stock, adj. rear sight, with sling and swivels, 20 shot mag., 3 1/4 lbs. Mfg. 1986-95.

| | $325 | $275 | $250 | $240 | $230 | $220 | $215 | *$250* |

MSR	100%	98%	95%	90%	80%	70%	60%	Last MSR

F2 – similar to AT-22, except is equipped with a fixed polymer buttstock. Mfg. 1992-95.

| | $295 | $240 | $215 | $200 | $185 | $175 | $160 | *$280* |

AT-9 – 9mm Para. cal., semi-auto blowback action, 16 in. barrel, available with 10 (C/B 1994), 25*, 32 (disc.), or 100 (disc. 1989) shot mag., 5 lbs. Mfg. 1988-95.

| | $850 | $775 | $700 | $650 | $600 | $550 | $500 | *$500* |

Add $250 for 100 shot drum mag.

F9 – similar to AT-9, except is equipped with a fixed polymer buttstock. Mfg. 1992-95.

| | $725 | $675 | $600 | $550 | $485 | $450 | $375 | *$535* |

SATURN 30 – 7.62x39mm Kalashnikov cal., semi-auto, gas operated, 19 1/2 in. barrel, composite stock with large thumbhole pistol grip, 5 shot detachable mag., drilled and tapped for scope mounts, adj. rear sight, 8 1/2 lbs. Mfg. 1990 only.

| | $800 | $700 | $625 | $575 | $525 | $450 | $425 | *$695* |

KG-9 – 9mm Para. cal., semi-auto blowback action, 25 or 50 shot mag., tactical configuration. Mfg. 1989 only.

| | $850 | $775 | $700 | $650 | $600 | $550 | $500 | *$560* |

Add $100 for 50 shot mag.

SAR-180 – .22 LR cal., semi-auto blowback action, 17 1/2 in. barrel, 165 shot drum mag., fully adj. rear sight, walnut stock with combat style pistol grip and forend, 6 1/4 lbs. Mfg. 1989 only.

| | $695 | $625 | $575 | $525 | $475 | $440 | $400 | *$500* |

Add $250 for 165 shot drum mag.
Add $200 for retractable stock.
Add $395 for laser sight.

This variation was also manufactured for a limited time by ILARCO (Illinois Arms Company), previously located in Itasca, IL.

KG-22 – .22 LR cal., similar to KG-9, 20 shot mag. Mfg. 1989 only.

| | $395 | $350 | $300 | $275 | $255 | $245 | $235 | *$300* |

FEATHER USA/AWI LLC

Previous firearms and current parts manufacturer established 1996, located in Eaton, CO.

PISTOLS: SEMI-AUTO

TACTICAL PISTOL SERIES – 9mm Para., .357 Sig., .40 S&W, .45 ACP, 10mm, or .460 Rowland cal., blowback action, steel construction, 9.2 in. barrel, SA, front and rear sights, scope rail, super rails, pre-drilled for sling, accepts high cap Glock magazines, Black matte finish, no tools needed for takedown or cleaning, includes Backpack carry case, 4 1/2 lbs.

| | $550 | $475 | $425 | $375 | $300 | $250 | $200 | *$619* |

Add $150 for high accuracy bull barrel on any caliber.

RIFLES: SEMI-AUTO

BACKPACKER SERIES – 9mm Para., .22 LR, .357 Sig., .40 S&W, .45 ACP, 10mm, or .460 Rowland cal., takedown action, modular design, 17.2 in. barrel, 2-position steel stock, 8 shot mag., pre-drilled for scope rail, super rails, and sling, Black matte finish, includes case that is waterproof and floatable, 2 1/2 lbs. (.22 LR).

| | $350 | $300 | $275 | $250 | $200 | $150 | $125 | *$399* |

Add $250 for 9mm Para., .357 Sig., .40 S&W, .45 ACP, 10mm, or .460 Rowland cal.

DELUXE SERIES – 9mm Para., .22 LR, .357 Sig., .40 S&W, .45 ACP, 10mm, or .460 Rowland cal., takedown action, modular design, 17.2 in. barrel, front and rear sight, 2-position steel stock, scope rail, super rails and pre-drilled for sling, 10 or 20 shot mag., Black matte finish, includes case (holds rifle and optional 4 mags., barrel, barrel shroud, bipod, front grip, car stock), 2 1/2-5 lbs.

| | $450 | $400 | $350 | $300 | $250 | $200 | $150 | *$499* |

Add $100 for high accuracy fluted barrel (.22 LR).
Add $250 for 9mm Para., .357 Sig., .40 S&W, .45 ACP, 10mm, or .460 Rowland cal.
Add $350 for high accuracy tapered bull barrel for all calibers except .22 LR.

TACTICAL RIGID STOCK SERIES – 9mm Para., .357 Sig., .40 S&W, .45 ACP, 10mm, or .460 Rowland cal., blowback action, modular design, 17.2 in. barrel, front and rear sights, drilled and tapped for sling and comes standard with scope rail and super rail system, includes full tactical carry case, 6 1/2 lbs.

| | $750 | $650 | $575 | $525 | $425 | $350 | $275 | *$849* |

Add $150 for high accuracy bull barrel on any caliber.

MSR	100%	98%	95%	90%	80%	70%	60%	Last MSR

FEDERAL ENGINEERING CORPORATION

Previous manufacturer located in Chicago, IL.

RIFLES: SEMI-AUTO

XC-220 – .22 LR cal., 16 5/16 in. barrel, 28 shot mag., machined steel action, 7 1/2 lbs. Mfg. 1984-89.

	$495	$450	$400	$350	$320	$295	$275	

XC-450 – .45 ACP cal. only, 16 1/2 in. barrel length, 30 shot mag., fires from closed bolt, machined steel receiver, 8 1/2 lbs. Mfg. 1984-89.

	$950	$825	$750	$675	$600	$550	$500	

XC-900 – 9mm Para. cal., 16 1/2 in. barrel length, 32 shot mag., fires from closed bolt, machined receiver action, 8 lbs. Mfg. 1984-89.

	$950	$825	$750	$675	$600	$550	$500	

FEDERAL ORDNANCE, INC.

Previous manufacturer, importer, and distributor located in South El Monte, CA from 1966-1992. Briklee Trading Co. bought the remaining assets of Federal Ordnance, Inc. in late 1992, and continued to import various firearms until circa 1998.

Federal Ordnance imported and distributed both foreign and domestic military handguns and rifles until 1992. In addition, they also fabricated firearms using mostly newer parts.

RIFLES/CARBINES

M-14 SEMI-AUTO – .308 Win. cal., legal for private ownership (no selector), 20 shot mag., refinished original M-14 parts, available in either filled fiberglass, G.I. fiberglass, refinished wood, or new walnut stock. Mfg. 1986-91.

	$1,275	$1,075	$995	$940	$865	$800	$750	*$700*

Add $50 for filled fiberglass stock.
Add $110 for refinished wood stock.
Add $190 for new walnut stock with handguard.

During the end of production, Chinese parts were used on this model. Values are the same.

TANKER GARAND SEMI-AUTO – .30-06 or .308 Win. cal., original U.S. GI parts, 18 in. barrel, new hardwood stock, parkerized finish. Mfg. began late 1991.

	$975	$900	$850	$800	$750	$700	$625	

CHINESE RPK 86S-7 SEMI-AUTO – 7.62x39mm cal., semi-auto version of the Peoples Republic of China RPK light machine gun, 75 shot drum mag., 23 3/4 in. barrel, with bipod. Imported 1989 only.

	$1,450	$1,275	$1,075	$1,000	$825	$775	$650	*$500*

Add $100 for 75 shot drum mag.

FIERCE FIREARMS, LLC

Current custom manufacturer located in Gunnison, UT.

Fierce Firearms manufactures custom bolt action rifles in various calibers to customer specifications with many options to choose from including stainless steel or titanium action, stainless steel or carbon barrels, stock dipping, paint jobs, and various finishes.

RIFLES: BOLT ACTION

TACTICAL EDGE – .300 Win., .308 Win., or .338 Lapua cal., stainless steel match grade barrel with 5 flutes, target crown, 3-position True Lock safety, tactical style receiver with built-in Picatinny rail, speed detachable box mag., Triad bolt, Last Guard coating on barrel and action, carbon fiber stock available in Black & Gray, Camo, or True Timber finish. New 2014.

MSR $3,295	$2,975	$2,600	$2,225	$2,025	$1,635	$1,350	$1,050	

Add $125 for Camo or True Timber finish.

57 CENTER LLC

Please refer to AR57 LLC listing in the A section.

FIREARMS INTERNATIONAL, INC.

Current manufacturer established in 1998, located in Houston, TX. Dealer sales.

In September, 2004, a new company called Crusader Group Gun Company, Inc. was formed, and is the corporate parent of Firearms International, Inc., High Standard Manufacturing Co., AMT-Auto Mag, and Arsenal Line Products.

While IAI (Israel Arms International) was originally established to market firearms manufactured by Israel Arms, Ltd. through Firearms International, Inc., IAI defaulted on this agreement without any sales being made.

MSR	100%	98%	95%	90%	80%	70%	60%	Last MSR

RIFLES/CARBINES: SEMI-AUTO

M1 CARBINE – .30 Carbine cal., 18 in. barrel, parkerized finish, wood stock, adj. rear sight, 10 shot mag., mfg. in the U.S., and patterned after the WWII design, 5 1/2 lbs. Limited mfg. 2001-2003.

	$500	$425	$375	$335	$300	$275	$250	$575

P50 RIFLE/CARBINE – .50 BMG cal., designed by Robert Pauza, gas operation, 24 or 29 in. barrel, MOA accuracy at 1,000 yards, includes two 5 shot mags. and hard case, 25 (carbine) or 30 lbs. Limited mfg. 2001-2003.

	$7,500	$6,750	$5,750	$5,000	$4,500	$4,000	$3,500	$7,950

FIREBIRD PRECISION

Current manufacturer located in Mountainair, NM.

Firebird Precision builds custom made AR-15 style rifles and shotguns in a variety of configurations and calibers. Each gun is built to individual customer specifications, and a wide variety of options and features are available. Please contact the company directly for available options, delivery time, and an individualized price quotation (see Trademark Index).

FIRESTORM

Previous trademark of pistols and revolvers manufactured by Industria Argentina, Fabrinor, S.A.L., and Armscor. Distributed (master distributor) and imported from late 2000-2011 by SGS Imports, International Inc., located in Wanamassa, NJ.

PISTOLS: SEMI-AUTO

Beginning 2004, all Firestorm pistols were available with an integral locking system (ILS).

FIRESTORM SERIES – .22 LR, .32 ACP (disc. 2007), or .380 ACP cal., DA/SA, 3 1/2 or 6 (.22 LR cal. only, Sport Model) in. barrel, matte or duo-tone finish, 7 (.380 ACP) or 10 (.22 LR or .32 ACP) shot mag., 3 dot combat sights, anatomic rubber grips with finger grooves, 23 oz. Imported 2001-2011.

	$280	$235	$185	$155	$145	$135	$125	$329

Add $6 for duo-tone finish.

MINI-FIRESTORM – 9mm Para., .40 S&W, or .45 ACP (new 2002) cal., DA/SA, 3 1/2 in. barrel, nickel, matte or duo-tone finish, 7 (.45 ACP cal.), 10, or 13 (9mm Para. only) shot mag., 3 dot sights, polymer grips, safeties include manual, firing pin, and decocking, 24 1/2 - 27 oz. Imported 2001-2009.

	$365	$315	$275	$230	$195	$180	$165	$425

Add $10 for duo-tone finish.
Add $20 for nickel finish.

FIRESTORM 45 GOVERNMENT – .45 ACP cal., SA, 5 1/8 in. barrel, matte or duo-tone finish, 7 shot mag., anatomic rubber grips with finger grooves, 36 oz. Imported 2001-2005.

	$260	$230	$200	$180	$165	$150	$135	$309

Add $8 for duo-tone finish.

FIRESTORM 45 GOVT. 1911 – .45 ACP cal., SA, patterned after the M1911, choice of matte or deluxe blue finish, 7 shot mag., current mfg. has skeletonized hammer, forward slide serrations, Novak style sights, diamond checkered walnut grips, and flared ejection port, 36 oz. Imported 2006-2007, reintroduced 2009.

	$395	$360	$330	$295	$275	$250	$200	$460

Add $39 for deluxe blue finish.

FORT SOE SIA

Current trademark manufactured by the Science Industrial Association Fort of the Ministry of Internal Affairs of Ukraine, located in Vinnitsa, Ukraine. No current U.S. importation.

The Ministry manufactures a line of good quality semi-auto pistols and semi-auto rifles in various tactical configurations with a wide variety of options. Currently, these guns are not imported into the U.S. Please contact the company directly for more information, including pricing and availability (see Trademark Index).

FORT WORTH FIREARMS

Previous manufacturer located in Fort Worth, TX 1995-2000.

SHOTGUNS: SLIDE ACTION

GL 18 – 12 ga. only, security configuration with 18 in. barrel with perforated shroud, thumb operated laser/xenon light built into end of 7 shot mag. tube, ammo storage. Mfg. 1995-96.

	$295	$265	$240	$210	$190	$170	$160	$347

MSR	100%	98%	95%	90%	80%	70%	60%	*Last MSR*

FOSTECH MFG.

Current semi-auto shotgun and accessories manufacturer located in Seymour, IN.

SHOTGUNS: SEMI-AUTO

ORIGIN 12 TACTICAL SHOTGUN – 12 ga., GIO, 18 1/2 in. quick change barrel, 8 shot standard detachable box mag., 20 or 30 shot drum mags. are optional, 3 point operational trigger, last shot bolt hold-open, choice of hard black, hard nickel, or hard black with nickel internals, includes all-weather tactical hard case, 9 lbs. 3 oz. New 2015.

	100%	98%	95%	90%	80%	70%	60%
MSR $2,600	$2,400	$2,250	$2,000	$1,750	$1,500	$1,300	$1,100

Add $100 for hard black finish with nickel internals or $200 for hard nickel finish.

FOX CARBINE

Previous rifle trademark manufactured by FoxCo Products Inc., located in Manchester, CT, and by Tri-C Corporation, located in Meridan, CT circa 1974-1976.

CARBINES: SEMI-AUTO

FOX CARBINE – 9mm Para. (mfg. by FoxCo Products) or .45 ACP (mfg. by Tri-C Corp.) cal., patterned after the Tommy Gun, 16 in. barrel with muzzle brake, grip safety, open bolt with fixed firing pin, removable wood rear stock and grooved forearm, uses M-3 30 shot mags., three safeties including a three-digit combination lock on left side of frame, loaded chamber indicator, adj. rear sight, matte metal finish, approx. 8 lbs.

100%	98%	95%	90%	80%	70%	60%
$995	$875	$750	$625	$550	$500	$450

In 1977, the rights to manufacture the FoxCo carbine were sold to Demro Products Inc., which continued to manufacture this configuration until the mid-1980s.

FRANCHI, LUIGI

Current manufacturer established during 1868, located in Brescia, Italy. In 1987, Franchi was sold to Socimi, then to Beretta, and most recently to Benelli. This trademark has been imported for approximately the past 50 years. Currently imported exclusively by Benelli USA, located in Accokeek, MD, since 1998. Previously imported and distributed by American Arms, Inc. located in North Kansas City, MO. Some models were previously imported by FIE firearms located in Hialeah, FL.

Also see Sauer/Franchi heading in the S section.

SHOTGUNS: SEMI-AUTO & SLIDE ACTION

MODEL 612 DEFENSE – 12 ga. only, 18 1/2 in. barrel with cyl. bore, matte finish metal with black synthetic stock and forearm, 6 1/2 lbs. Imported 2000-2002.

100%	98%	95%	90%	80%	70%	60%	*Last MSR*
$525	$450	$375	$325	$285	$265	$245	*$635*

This model was previously designated the Variopress 612 Defense.

SAS-12 – 12 ga. only, 3 in. chamber, slide action only, synthetic stock with built-in pistol grip, 8 shot tube mag., 21 1/2 in. barrel, 6.8 lbs. Imported 1988-90 only.

100%	98%	95%	90%	80%	70%	60%	*Last MSR*
$600	$525	$450	$395	$350	$295	$250	*$473*

This model was imported exclusively by FIE Firearms located in Hialeah, FL.

SPAS-12 – 12 ga., 2 3/4 in. chamber, tactical shotgun, slide action or semi-auto operation, 5 (new 1991) or 8 (disc.) shot tube mag., alloy receiver, synthetic stock with built-in pistol grip (limited quantities were also mfg. with a folding stock or metal fixed stock), one-button switch to change operating mode, 21 1/2 in. barrel, 8 3/4 lbs. Importation disc. 1994.

100%	98%	95%	90%	80%	70%	60%	*Last MSR*
$1,500	$1,300	$1,175	$1,000	$900	$800	$700	*$769*

This model was imported exclusively by FIE Firearms located in Hialeah, FL until 1990.

SPAS-15 – 12 ga. only, 2 3/4 in. chamber, tactical shotgun, slide action or semi-auto operation, 6 shot detachable box mag., 21 1/2 in. barrel, lateral folding skeleton stock, carrying handle, one button switch to change operating mode, 10 lbs. Limited importation 1989 only.

Even though the retail was in the $700 range, demand and rarity have pushed prices up dramatically, with NIB examples in the $5,000 - $7,500 range.

This model had very limited importation (less than 200) as the BATFE disallowed further importation almost immediately.

LAW-12 – 12 ga. only, 2 3/4 in. chamber, gas operated semi-auto, synthetic stock with built-in pistol grip, 5 (new 1991) or 8 (disc.) shot tube mag., 21 1/2 in. barrel, 6 3/4 lbs. Imported 1988-94.

100%	98%	95%	90%	80%	70%	60%	*Last MSR*
$570	$485	$400	$360	$320	$300	$280	*$719*

MSR	100%	98%	95%	90%	80%	70%	60%	Last MSR

FRANKLIN ARMORY

Current manufacturer of semi-auto pistols and rifles/carbines located in Morgan Hill, CA and Minden, NV.

Franklin Armory specializes in producing legal firearms for restrictive jurisdictions such as California (O7/FFL and Class II SOT manufacturer), as well as for the non-restrictive states.

PISTOLS: SEMI-AUTO

SALUS PISTOL – 5.56 NATO, 7.62x39mm (disc. 2015) or .450 BM (new 2015) cal., GIO, 7 1/2 in. barrel with threaded barrel, crowned muzzle and Triad flash hider, 30 shot mag., knurled free float handguard tube, aluminum upper and lower receiver with full Picatinny rail, forward assist, flared magwell, padded receiver extension/buffer tube, Ergo Ambi SureGrip, black finish, includes tactical soft side case.

MSR $1,495		$1,275	$1,125	$1,025	$875	$750	$625	$525

Add $145 for .450 BM (new 2015).
Add $155 for 7.62x39mm cal. (disc. 2015).

SE-SSP 7 1/2 IN. PISTOL – 5.56 NATO, 7.62x39mm (disc. 2015), or .450 BM (new 2015) cal., GIO, 7 1/2 in. barrel with A2 flash hider (compensator on .450 BM), single rail Picatinny gas block, optional forged front sight gas block with integral bayonet lug and front sling swivel, knurled free float handguard tube, forged aluminum lower and A4 upper receiver with full Picatinny rail, forward assist, ambi sling mount, padded receiver extension/buffer tube, A2 pistol grip, 30 shot mag., black finish, includes tactical soft side case.

MSR $1,040		$870	$740	$650	$585	$515	$450	$395

Add $15 for forged front sight gas block.
Add $135 for 7.62x39mm cal. (disc. 2015).
Add $315 for .450 BM cal. (new 2015).

SE-SSP 11 1/2 IN. PISTOL – 5.56 NATO, 6.8 SPC, 7.62x39mm, .300 AAC Blackout (disc. 2015) or .450 Bushmaster cal., GIO, 11 1/2 in. threaded barrel, crowned muzzle, hider or compensator (on .450 Bushmaster only), CAR handguards with alum. liners, A4 forged aluminum flat-top upper receiver, otherwise similar to SE-SSP 7 1/2 in. pistol.

MSR $1,020		$860	$725	$650	$585	$515	$450	$395

Add $20 for forged front sight gas block.
Add $50 for .300 AAC Blackout cal. (disc. 2015).
Add $155 for 7.62x39mm cal.
Add $180 for .450 Bushmaster cal.
Add $215 for 6.8 SPC cal.

XO-26S SALUS PISTOL – 5.56 NATO, 6.8 SPC, 7.62x39mm, .300 AAC Blackout, or .450 Bushmaster cal., GIO, 11 1/2 in. threaded barrel, crowned muzzle, Phantom toothed flash hider, 9 (450 Bushmaster), 25 (6.8 SPC), or 30 shot mag., low profile gas block, carbine length gas system, full Picatinny rail, forward assist, 9 in. KeyMod rail handguard, pop up front and rear MBUS sights, billet aluminum upper and lower receivers, flared magwell, integral cold weather trigger guard, EPG16 grip, Black, Desert Smoke, or Olive Drab Green finish.

MSR $1,875		$1,575	$1,385	$1,200	$1,065	$900	$775	$625

Add $25 for .300 AAC Blackout cal.
Add $125 for .450 BM cal.
Add $140 for 7.62x39mm cal., or $225 for 6.8 SPC cal.

XO-26 R2 (XO-26) – 5.56 NATO, 6.8 SPC, .300 AAC Blackout, 7.62x39mm (disc. 2015), or .450 Bushmaster cal., GIO, 11 1/2 in. barrel with Phantom toothed flash hider or Ross Schuler Compensator (on .450 Bushmaster only), Specter length free float forearm quad rail, low profile gas block, forged aluminum lower and A4 flat-top upper with full Picatinny rail, pop-up front and rear sights, forward assist, ambi sling mount, custom tuned trigger, padded receiver extension/buffer tube, Magpul MIAD grip, 9 (.450 Bushmaster), 25 (6.8 SPC), or 30 shot mag., black finish, includes tactical soft side case.

MSR $1,470		$1,245	$1,100	$985	$835	$725	$615	$515

Add $20 for .300 AAC Blackout cal.
Add $130 for .450 Bushmaster or $160 for 6.8 SPC cal.
Add $140 for 7.62x39mm cal. (disc. 2015).

* **XO-26b** – 5.56 NATO, 6.8 SPC, .300 AAC Blackout (disc. 2015), or 7.62x39mm (disc. 2015) cal., 11 1/2 in. barrel with A2 or Toothed flash hider, carbine length gas system, forged aluminum A4 flat-top upper with full Picatinny rail, 25 (6.8 SPC) or 30 shot mag., Magpul MOE handguard, forward assist, forged aluminum lower with ambi sling mount, padded receiver/extension buffer tube, Magpul MIAD grip, hardcoat anodized black finish.

MSR $1,130		$940	$850	$725	$625	$550	$475	$425

Add $225 for 6.8 SPC cal.
Add $45 for .300 AAC Blackout (disc. 2015) or $170 for 7.62x39mm cal. (disc.2015).

MSR	100%	98%	95%	90%	80%	70%	60%	Last MSR

XOW – 5.56 NATO, 7.62x39mm, or .450 Bushmaster (new 2015) cal., GIO, 7 1/2 in. barrel with PWS CQB flash hider, A4 forged aluminum flat-top upper receiver with carbine length forearm quad rail, rail covers, Magpul RVG forward vertical grip, Magpul MBUS pop-up front and rear sights, forward assist, full Picatinny rail, forged alum. lower receiver with ambi sling mount, padded receiver extension/buffer tube, Magpul MIAD grip, Magpul enhanced trigger guard, PWS enhanced padded buffer tube, 30 shot mag., Black, FDE, or Olive Drab Green furniture, includes tactical soft side case. Disc. 2015.

MSR $1,850 $1,560 $1,375 $1,190 $1,050 $900 $775 $625

Add $100 for 7.62x39mm or $200 for .450 Bushmaster (new 2015) cal.

RIFLES: SEMI-AUTO

3GR – 5.56 NATO cal., GIO, 18 in. barrel with threaded muzzle crown, EGW compensator, A4 forged aluminum upper receiver with Desert Smoke finish, full Picatinny rail, ambi tac latch, forward assist, forged aluminum lower receiver with black finish, Ergo Ambi SureGrip and Magpul MOE trigger guard, 10 or 20 shot mag., Ace ARFX stock with bottom Picatinny rail, adj. comb and LOP, sling mountable. Disc. 2013.

     $1,475 $1,300 $1,100 $1,000 $825 $675 $525   *$1,650*

* **3GR-L** – 5.56 NATO cal., GIO, 18 in. fluted barrel with threaded muzzle crown and compensator, low profile adj. gas block, mid-length gas system, FSR 13 in. rail system, 10 or 20 shot mag., integral cold weather trigger guard, Magpul PRS stock with bottom Picatinny rail, Ergo Ambi SureGrip, flared magwell, push button QD sling mounts, ambi tac latch, forward assist, forged aluminum lower receiver with black finish, adj. comb and LOP, aluminum upper and lower receivers with Desert Smoke finish.

MSR $2,310 $1,950 $1,725 $1,450 $1,250 $1,050 $900 $750

Add $390 for the Franklin Armory Binary Firing System (3-position selectable trigger system), new 2016.

10-8 R2 (10-8 CARBINE) – 5.56 NATO, 6.8 SPC, 7.62x39mm (disc. 2015), or .300 AAC Blackout (new 2016) cal., GIO, 16 in. medium contour barrel with Triad flash suppressor, forged front sight, free float forearm quad rail, A4 forged aluminum upper receiver with full Picatinny rail, Magpul MBUS rear sight, forward assist, forged aluminum lower receiver with custom tuned trigger, Ergo Gapper, Ergo Ambi SureGrip, M4 6-position adj. stock with rear sling mount positions, 10, 20, 25 (6.8 SPC only), or 30 shot mag., black furniture.

MSR $1,335 $1,115 $1,000 $875 $735 $650 $550 $465

Add $20 for .300 AAC Blackout cal. (new 2016).

Add $150 for 6.8 SPC cal.

Add $155 for 7.62x39mm cal. (disc. 2015).

F17-L – .17 WSM cal., GPO, 20 in. stainless steel bull barrel, target crown, free float fluted and vented handguard, forward assist, alum. upper and lower receivers, anodized Olive Drab Green finish, flared magwell, integral cold weather trigger guard, 10 shot mag., Magpul MOE rifle stock, Magpul MIAD adj. grip, ambidextrous push button QD sling mounts. New mid-2014.

MSR $2,000 $1,700 $1,500 $1,250 $1,100 $950 $825 $675

F17-M4 – .17 WSM cal., GPO, 16 in. medium contour barrel, threaded muzzle crown, A2 flash hider, 10 shot mag., M4 6-position stock, A2 grip, forged aluminum upper and lower, TML-7 free float and knurled handguard, M-LOK compatible forward slots, forward assist, Type III hardcoat anodized black finish.

MSR $1,500 $1,275 $1,125 $1,025 $875 $750 $625 $525

F17-SPR – .17 WSM cal., GPO, 18 in. chrome moly barrel, 10 shot mag., MFT Battlelink Minimalist stock, rubber buttpad, Mission First Tactical EPG16 grip, forged aluminum upper and lower receivers, free float knurled handguard, M-LOK compatible forward slots, forward assist, Type III hardcoat anodized black finish. New 2016.

MSR $1,800 $1,525 $1,350 $1,175 $1,050 $900 $775 $625

F17-V4 – .17 WSM Rimfire cal., GPO, 20 in. bull barrel, target crown with recessed muzzle crown, 10 shot mag., forged aluminum upper and lower receivers, TML-12 free-float knurled handguard, integral tripod adapter, forward assist, A2 grip, A2 stock with storage compartment, black finish. New 2015.

MSR $1,500 $1,275 $1,125 $1,025 $875 $750 $625 $525

FEATURELESS RIFLE – 5.56 NATO cal., GIO, 16 in. HBAR contour barrel with threaded muzzle crown and Phantom brake, Magpul MOE handguard, A4 forged aluminum upper receiver with full Picatinny rail and forward assist, forged alum. lower receiver with Hammerhead grip, 10 or 20 shot mag., ACE ARUL stock with rubber buttpad, alum. receiver extension, Black, Flat Dark Earth (FDE), FOL, or Olive Drab Green furniture. Disc. 2013.

     $1,025 $925 $800 $685 $595 $515 $440   *$1,200*

HBAR 16 IN. – 5.56 NATO, 6.8 SPC, or 7.62x39mm cal., GIO, 16 in. HBAR contour barrel, threaded muzzle crown with A2 flash hider, CAR handguards, Picatinny rail gas block with carbine length gas system, or optional forged front sight gas block with integral bayonet lug and front sling swivel, A4 forged aluminum upper receiver with full Picatinny rail and forward assist, forged alum. lower receiver with A2 pistol grip, 10, 20, 25 (6.8 SPC only), or 30 shot mag., M4 6-position collapsible stock with rear sling mounts and alum. receiver extension, black furniture.

MSR $1,080 $910 $775 $675 $595 $515 $450 $395

MSR	100%	98%	95%	90%	80%	70%	60%	Last MSR

Add $20 for forged front sight gas block.
Add $95 for 6.8 SPC cal.
Add $140 for 7.62x39mm cal.

* **HBAR 20 IN.** – 5.56 NATO, 6.8 SPC, 7.62x39mm, or .450 Bushmaster cal., GIO, similar to HBAR 16 in., except has 20 in. HBAR contour barrel, threaded muzzle crown with flash hider or compensator (.450 Bushmaster only), A2 handguard, forged front sight gas block with integral bayonet lug and front sling swivel, or optional Picatinny rail gas block with carbine length gas system, A2 stock with storage compartment.

| MSR $1,095 | $925 | $850 | $725 | $625 | $550 | $475 | $425 | |

Add $20 for forged front sight gas block.
Add $90 for 6.8 SPC cal.
Add $130 for 7.62x39mm cal.
Add $165 for .450 Bushmaster cal.

LTW – 5.56 NATO cal., GIO, 16 in. lightweight contour barrel with A2 flash hider, Picatinny rail gas block with carbine length gas system, optional forged front sight gas block with integral bayonet lug and front sling swivel, CAR handguard, A4 forged aluminum upper receiver with full Picatinny rail and forward assist, forged alum. lower receiver with A2 pistol grip, 30 shot mag., M4 6-position collapsible stock with rear sling mounts and alum. receiver extension, black furniture. Disc. 2015.

| | $925 | $850 | $725 | $625 | $550 | $475 | $425 | $1,100 |

Add $25 for forged front sight gas block.

M4 – 5.56 NATO or .300 AAC Blackout cal., GIO, 16 in. M4 contour barrel with threaded muzzle crown A2 flash hider, M4 double heat shield handguard with aluminum liners, forged front sight gas block with integral bayonet lug and front sling swivel or optional Picatinny rail gas block, A4 forged aluminum upper receiver with full Picatinny rail and forward assist, forged alum. lower receiver, 10, 20, or 30 shot mag., M4 6-position collapsible stock with aluminum CAR receiver extension, A2 pistol grip, black furniture.

| MSR $1,100 | $925 | $850 | $725 | $625 | $550 | $475 | $425 | |

Add $25 for forged front sight gas block.
Add $45 for .300 AAC Blackout cal.
Add $425 for the Franklin Armory Binary Firing System (3-position selectable trigger system), new 2016.

M4-HTF – 5.56 NATO cal., GIO, 16 in. M4 contour fluted barrel, steel construction, low-pro gas block, EGW compensator, forged aluminum A4 upper receiver with Specter length free float forearm quad rail, pop up front and rear sights, forward assist, forged aluminum lower receiver with Ergo Gapper, Ergo Ambi SureGrip, ACE ARFX stock with rubber buttpad and foam padded receiver extension, 10, 20, or 30 shot mag., black furniture. Disc. 2015.

| | $1,475 | $1,290 | $1,125 | $1,000 | $850 | $735 | $595 | $1,735 |

M4-L – 5.56 NATO or .300 AAC Blackout cal., GIO, 16 in. M4 contour barrel, threaded muzzle crown with A2 flash hider, forged front sight with carbine length gas system, Magpul MOE carbine length handguard, 10 or 20 shot mag., Magpul ACS stock with integral storage compartment, aluminum upper and lower receivers, Black, Desert Smoke, or Olive Drab Green finish, full Picatinny rail with MBUS rear sight, Magpul MIAD adj. grip.

| MSR $1,770 | $1,500 | $1,310 | $1,140 | $1,000 | $850 | $735 | $595 | |

Add $65 for .300 AAC Blackout cal.

* **M4-OPL** – 5.56 NATO or .300 AAC Blackout cal., GPO, similar to M4-L, except utilizes the Osprey Defense Piston System.

| MSR $2,200 | $1,875 | $1,650 | $1,400 | $1,200 | $1,025 | $875 | $725 | |

Add $70 for .300 AAC Blackout cal.

M4-MOE – 5.56 NATO or .300 AAC Blackout cal., GIO, 16 in. M4 contour barrel with threaded muzzle crown A2 flash hider, Magpul MOE handguard, forged front sight gas block with integral bayonet lug and front sling swivel or optional Picatinny rail gas block, A4 forged aluminum upper receiver with full Picatinny rail and forward assist, forged alum. lower receiver with Magpul MOE grip and trigger guard, 10 or 20 shot mag., Magpul MOE 6-position collapsible stock with rubber buttpad, aluminum carbine length receiver extension, black furniture.

| MSR $1,200 | $1,025 | $925 | $800 | $685 | $595 | $515 | $440 | |

Add $25 for forged front sight gas block.
Add $60 for .300 AAC Blackout cal.

PRAEFECTOR – 5.56 NATO, 6.8 SPC, or .450 BM cal., 20 in. medium contour barrel with Revere compensator, 9, 25, or 30 shot mag., low profile gas block, forged aluminum lower and A4 upper receivers, full Picatinny rail, forward assist, FSR 15 in. handguard, Ergo Ambi Sure grip, Magpul MOE rifle stock, black finish. New 2015.

| MSR $1,420 | $1,210 | $1,075 | $950 | $800 | $700 | $600 | $495 | |

Add $135 for 6.8 SPC or $150 for .450 BM cal.

MSR	100%	98%	95%	90%	80%	70%	60%	Last MSR

SLT-M MILITIA MODEL – 7.62 NATO cal., 20 in. barrel, rifle length gas system, 10 or 20 shot mag., Libertas billet machined upper receiver with Smoke Composites 15 in. carbon fiber handguard, forward assist, Osprey Defense gas piston, Diamond Head front and rear sights, alum. lower with ambidextrous controls, flared magwell, integral Cold Weather trigger guard, Ergo Ambi Sure grip, Smoke Composites A2 carbon fiber stock, Black, Desert Smoke, or Olive Drab Green finish. New 2015.

  Please contact the company directly for pricing and availability on this model.

TMR-L – 5.56 NATO or 6.8 SPC cal., GIO, 20 in. full heavy contour barrel with recessed muzzle crown, low profile gas block with rifle length gas system, aluminum upper and lower receiver with Black, Desert Smoke, or Olive Drab Green finish, full Picatinny rail, Gen. 1 tac latch, flared magwell, 10 or 20 shot mag., Magpul PRS stock with bottom Picatinny rail, adj. comb and LOP, Ergo Ambi SureGrip.

| MSR $2,035 | $1,715 | $1,500 | $1,250 | $1,100 | $950 | $825 | $675 | |

  Add $45 for 6.8 SPC cal.

V1 – 5.56 NATO cal., GIO, 24 in. full heavy contour stainless steel fluted barrel with recessed muzzle crown, single rail Picatinny rail gas block, free float fluted and vented handguard with bipod stud, A4 forged aluminum upper receiver with full picatinny rail, Gen 1 tac latch, forward assist, forged aluminum lower receiver with Magpul MIAD adj. grip, Magpul MOE trigger guard, 10 shot mag., Magpul PRS stock, adj. comb and LOP, bottom Picatinny rail, black furniture.

| MSR $1,700 | $1,450 | $1,275 | $1,125 | $1,000 | $850 | $735 | $595 | |

  * V2 – 5.56 NATO or 6.5mm Grendel (disc. 2015) cal., similar to V1, except does not have fluted barrel.

| MSR $1,560 | $1,310 | $1,150 | $1,040 | $875 | $750 | $625 | $525 | |

  Add $100 for 6.5mm Grendel cal. (disc. 2015).

V3 – 5.56 NATO or 6.5mm Grendel cal., GIO, 24 in. full heavy contour stainless steel barrel with recessed muzzle crown, single rail Picatinny rail gas block with rifle length gas system, free float fluted and vented handguard, A4 forged aluminum upper receiver with full Picatinny rail, forward assist, forged aluminum lower receiver with A2 grip, 10 shot mag, A2 stock with storage compartment and rear sling mount, black furniture. Disc. 2015.

| | $935 | $850 | $725 | $625 | $550 | $475 | $425 | *$1,125* |

  Add $85 for 6.5mm Grendel cal.

  * V4 – 5.56 NATO or 6.8 SPC cal., 20 in. full heavy contour barrel, recessed muzzle crown, rifle length gas system, 10 shot mag., single rail Picatinny gas block, forged aluminum upper and lower receivers, full Picatinny rail, forward assist, TML-12 free float handguard with M-LOK slots and integral tripod adapter, A2 stock with storage compartment for cleaning kit, A2 grip, Type III hardcoat anodized black finish.

| MSR $1,135 | $950 | $850 | $725 | $625 | $550 | $475 | $425 | |

  Add $50 for 6.8 SPC cal.

V1-L – 5.56 NATO cal., GIO, 24 in. full heavy contour stainless steel fluted barrel with recessed muzzle crown, Picatinny rail gas block with rifle length gas system, fluted and vented free float rail with sling/bipod stud, aluminum upper receiver with free float fluted and vented handguard, Gen 1 tac latch, forward assist, alum. lower receiver with flared magwell, push button QD sling mounts, Magpul MIAD adj. grip, 10 or 20 shot mag., Magpul PRS stock, adj. comb and LOP, bottom Picatinny rail, black furniture.

| MSR $2,090 | $1,795 | $1,575 | $1,325 | $1,150 | $995 | $850 | $700 | |

  * V2-L – 5.56 NATO or 6.5 Grendel (disc. 2015) cal., similar to V1-L, except does not have fluted barrel.

| MSR $2,000 | $1,700 | $1,500 | $1,250 | $1,100 | $950 | $825 | $675 | |

  Add $115 for 6.5 Grendel cal. (disc. 2015).

FULTON ARMORY

Current rifle manufacturer and parts supplier located in Savage, MD. Dealer sales.

CARBINES/RIFLES: SEMI-AUTO

Fulton Armory makes a comprehensive array of the four U.S. Gas Operated Service Rifles: M1 Garand, M1 Carbine, M14 and AR-15-style, including corresponding commercial versions and upper receiver assemblies and related parts and components. All current models are described below. For a listing of previously manufactured models, please refer to our online version at www.bluebookofgunvalues.com.

FAR-15 A2 SERVICE RIFLE – .223 Rem./5.56 NATO cal., 20 in. HBAR profile chrome-lined barrel with A2 flash suppressor, A2 upper receiver, FA lower with Accu-Wedge, single stage trigger, M16 bolt carrier group, 12 in. round A2 handguard with heat shields, GI front sight with bayonet lug, fixed A2 buttstock with A2 buttplate and aluminum door assembly, carry handle, A2 pistol grip, includes 10 shot mag. and black nylon "Silent" sling, 8.05 lbs.

| MSR $1,210 | $1,025 | $925 | $800 | $685 | $595 | $515 | $440 | |

MSR	100%	98%	95%	90%	80%	70%	60%	Last MSR

FAR-15 A4 SERVICE RIFLE – .223 Rem./5.56 NATO cal., 20 in. HBAR profile chrome-lined barrel with A2 flash suppressor, A3/A4 numbered upper receiver, FA lower with Accu-Wedge, GI front sight with bayonet lug, fixed A2 buttstock with buttplate and aluminum door assembly, A2 pistol grip, 12 in. round A2 handguard with heat shields, single stage trigger, includes one 10 shot mag. and black nylon "Silent" sling.

| MSR $1,130 | $940 | $850 | $725 | $625 | $550 | $475 | $425 | |

FAR-15 GUARDIAN – .223 Rem./5.56 NATO cal., 20 in. HBAR (Guardian-H) or "Pencil" (Guardian-L) profile chrome-lined barrel with A2 flash suppressor, A3/A4 flat-top numbered upper receiver and FA lower with Accu-Wedge, 13 1/2 in. Diamondhead VRS-X handguard float tube, modular rail system, low profile steel gas block, 2-stage non-adj. trigger, fixed A2 buttstock with A2 buttplate and aluminum door assembly, right-handed Ergo SureGrip, includes one 10 shot mag. and black nylon "Silent" sling, 6.85-7.95 lbs.

| MSR $1,450 | $1,225 | $1,090 | $950 | $800 | $700 | $600 | $495 | |

FAR-15 LEGACY RIFLE – .223 Rem./5.56 NATO cal., 20 in. "Pencil" profile chrome-lined barrel with M16 3-prong muzzle brake, M16 Slick Side upper receiver with A1 rear sight, Slick-Side chrome bolt carrier with forward assist notches, USGI M16 triangular handguard, GI gas block with bayonet lug, A1 round front sight post, FA lower receiver with Accu-Wedge, USGI M16 grip, single stage trigger, A1 fixed buttstock, includes one 10 shot mag. and black nylon "Silent" sling, 6 3/4 lbs.

| MSR $1,270 | $1,060 | $950 | $815 | $685 | $595 | $515 | $440 | |

FAR-15 LIBERATOR – .223 Rem./5.56 NATO cal., 20 in. HBAR (Liberator-H) or "Pencil" (Liberator-L) profile chrome-lined barrel with A2 flash suppressor, A3/A4 flat-top numbered upper and FA lower receiver with Accu-Wedge, 12 in. Daniel Defense Lite rail with rail covers, low profile steel gas block, 2-stage non-adj. trigger, fixed A2 buttstock with A2 buttplate and aluminum door assembly, right-handed Ergo SureGrip, includes one 10 shot mag. and black nylon "Silent" sling, 7-8.1 lbs.

| MSR $1,700 | $1,450 | $1,275 | $1,125 | $1,000 | $850 | $735 | $595 | |

FAR-15 PEERLESS NM A2 SERVICE RIFLE – .223 Rem./5.56 NATO cal., 20 in. HBAR profile stainless steel barrel with A2 flash suppressor, National Match 2-stage trigger, 12 in. round floated and modified A2 handguard, steel float tube, Northern Competition NM rear sight with hooded aperture, custom pillared rear sight base and power wedge front sight base with NM front sight post, A2 upper with fixed carry handle, FA lower with Accu-Wedge, A2 buttstock with A2 buttplate, A2 pistol grip, includes one 10 shot mag. and black nylon "Silent" sling, 9.85 lbs.

| MSR $1,600 | $1,350 | $1,200 | $1,075 | $950 | $815 | $700 | $575 | |

FAR-15 PEERLESS NM A4 SERVICE RIFLE – .223 Rem./5.56 NATO cal., 20 in. HBAR profile stainless steel barrel with A2 flash suppressor, A3/A4 flat-top numbered upper receiver with detachable carry handle and rear sight base, FA lower with Accu-Wedge and marked "US Rifle", Northern Competition National Match hooded aperture rear sight, NM front sight post and drilled and tapped front sight base, 12 in. round A2 handguard modified for steel float tube, GI gas block with bayonet lug, A2 buttstock with A2 buttplate, A2 pistol grip, non-adj. 2-stage NM trigger, includes one 10 shot mag. and black nylon "Silent" sling, 11 1/4 lbs.

| MSR $1,750 | $1,475 | $1,290 | $1,125 | $1,000 | $850 | $735 | $595 | |

FAR-15 PHANTOM – .223 Rem./5.56 NATO cal., 20 in. HBAR (Phantom-H) or "Pencil" (Phantom-L) profile chrome-lined barrel with A2 flash suppressor, A3/A4 flat-top numbered upper, FA lower with Accu-Wedge, 13 1/2 in. Diamondhead VRS-T handguard float tube, modular rail system, low profile steel gas block, 2-stage non-adj. trigger, fixed A2 buttstock with A2 buttplate and aluminum door assembly, right-handed Ergo SureGrip, includes one 10 shot mag. and black nylon "Silent" sling, 7-8.10 lbs.

| MSR $1,450 | $1,225 | $1,090 | $950 | $800 | $700 | $600 | $495 | |

FAR-15 PREDATOR VARMINT RIFLE – .223 Rem./5.56 NATO cal., GIO, 24 in. stainless steel bull barrel with plain muzzle, compression fit gas block, flat-top upper, bolt carrier drilled and tapped for side cocking handle, forged lower receiver with Accu-Wedge, fixed A2 buttstock with A2 buttplate and aluminum door assembly, Ergo SureGrip, single stage trigger, includes one 10 shot mag. and Nylon "Silent" sling.

| MSR $1,250 | $1,050 | $950 | $815 | $685 | $595 | $515 | $440 | |

* **FAR-15 Predator Varmint Lite** – .223 Rem./5.56 NATO cal., 20 in. HBAR profile stainless steel barrel with threaded muzzle and A2 flash suppressor, A3/A4 flat-top numbered upper and FA lower receiver with Accu-Wedge, 2-stage non-adj. match trigger, 12 in. PVR round knurled handguard float tube with bipod stud, compression fit gas block, fixed A2 buttstock with A2 buttplate and aluminum door assembly, right-handed Ergo SureGrip, includes one 10 shot mag., nylon "Silent" sling, 8.05 lbs.

| MSR $1,200 | $1,025 | $925 | $800 | $685 | $595 | $515 | $440 | |

FAR-15 STOWAWAY – .223 Rem./5.56 NATO cal., 16 in. "Pencil" profile chrome-lined barrel with A2 flash suppressor, GI M16 bolt carrier, barrel extension, and extractor, A1 C7 forged upper receiver, 7 in. triangular handguard with heat shields, front sight gas block with bayonet lug, FA lower receiver with Accu-Wedge, Shorty fixed buttstock, A2 pistol grip, single stage trigger, includes one 10 shot mag., black nylon "Silent" sling, 5 3/4 lbs.

| MSR $800 | $685 | $615 | $550 | $475 | $420 | $365 | $335 | |

MSR	100%	98%	95%	90%	80%	70%	60%	Last MSR

FAR-308 LIBERATOR – .308 Win./7.62 NATO cal., 18 1/2 in. lightweight chrome moly (Liberator-L) or medium weight stainless steel (Liberator-H) barrel with A2 flash suppressor, compression fit gas block, A3/A4 flat-top upper and FA lower with modified Accu-Wedge, DPMS pattern parts, nickel boron bolt carrier group, 12 in. Liberator .308 handguard float tube, lightweight 4-rail with rail covers, 2-stage non-adj. trigger, fixed A1 buttstock with A2 buttplate and aluminum door assembly, right-handed Ergo SureGrip, includes one 10 shot mag. and black nylon "Silent" sling, 9 1/4-9 3/4 lbs.

| MSR $1,800 | $1,525 | $1,350 | $1,175 | $1,050 | $900 | $775 | $625 | |

FAR-308 M110 SERVICE RIFLE – .308 Win./7.62 NATO cal., 20 in. M110 stainless steel barrel with A2 flash suppressor, compression fit gas block with top rail, A3/A4 flat-top upper and FA lower with modified Accu-Wedge, DPMS Pattern parts, nickel boron bolt carrier group with staked key, extended bolt stop, 12 in. Liberator handguard float tube, lightweight 4-rail with rail covers, 2-stage non-adj. trigger, fixed A1 buttstock with A2 buttplate and aluminum door assembly, A2 pistol grip, includes one 10 shot mag. and black nylon "Silent" sling, 10.85 lbs.

| MSR $1,800 | $1,525 | $1,350 | $1,175 | $1,050 | $900 | $775 | $625 | |

FAR-308 PVR-H – .308 Win./7.62 NATO cal., 24 in. match quality stainless steel heavy bull barrel with A2 flash suppressor, compression fit gas block, high rise side-cocking upper receiver with nickel boron bolt carrier group, FA lower with modified Accu-Wedge, DPMS pattern parts, 2-stage match trigger, 12 in. round knurled PVR handguard float tube, fixed A1 buttstock with A2 buttplate and aluminum door assembly, right-handed Ergo SureGrip, includes one 10 shot mag. and black nylon "Silent" sling, 10.6 lbs.

| MSR $1,600 | $1,350 | $1,200 | $1,075 | $950 | $815 | $700 | $575 | |

FAR-308 PVR-L – .308 Win./7.62 NATO cal., 20 in. M110 match grade stainless steel barrel with A2 flash suppressor, compression fit gas block, A3/A4 flat-top upper receiver and FA lower with modified Accu-Wedge, DPMS pattern parts, nickel boron bolt carrier group, 12 in. round knurled handguard float tube, 2-stage non-adj. trigger, fixed A1 buttstock with A2 buttplate and aluminum door assembly, right-handed Ergo SureGrip, includes one 10 shot mag. and black nylon "Silent" sling, 9.8 lbs.

| MSR $1,600 | $1,350 | $1,200 | $1,075 | $950 | $815 | $700 | $575 | |

FAR-6.5 PVR – 6.5 Creedmoor cal., 24 in. match quality stainless steel heavy bull barrel with A2 flash suppressor, compression fit gas block, high rise side-cocking upper receiver with nickel boron bolt carrier group, FA lower with modified Accu-Wedge, DPMS pattern parts, 2-stage match trigger, 12 in. round knurled PVR handguard float tube, fixed A1 buttstock with A2 buttplate and aluminum door assembly, right-handed Ergo SureGrip, includes one 10 shot mag. and black nylon "Silent" sling, 10.85 lbs.

| MSR $1,600 | $1,350 | $1,200 | $1,075 | $950 | $815 | $700 | $575 | |

M1 GARAND SERVICE RIFLE – .30-06 cal., GIO, 24 in. GI contour barrel, USGI receiver, walnut stock and handguard with linseed oil finish, includes 8 shot clip and canvas sling.

| MSR $1,900 | $1,625 | $1,425 | $1,200 | $1,075 | $925 | $795 | $650 | |

* ***M1 Garand Enhanced Service Rifle*** – .30-06 cal., GIO, similar to M1 Garand Service Rifle, except comes standard with several National Match upgrades including remove spacer, Loctite and epoxy front handguard hardware, knurl and Loctite lower band to barrel, and modified trigger.

| MSR $2,000 | $1,700 | $1,500 | $1,250 | $1,100 | $950 | $825 | $675 | |

M1 PEERLESS SERVICE RIFLE – .30-06 cal., GIO, 24 in. GI contour barrel, milled trigger guard, USGI receiver, rear sight, National Match upgrades, glass bedded action, walnut stock with linseed oil finish, includes 8 shot mag. and canvas sling.

| MSR $2,750 | $2,340 | $2,050 | $1,750 | $1,590 | $1,285 | $1,050 | $850 | |

M1 SERVICE CARBINE – .30 Carb. cal., GIO, 18 in. barrel, barrel band with bayonet lug, Fulton Armory's M1 carbine receiver, walnut stock with Linseed oil finish, includes one 10 shot mag., oiler, and canvas sling.

| MSR $1,500 | $1,275 | $1,125 | $1,025 | $875 | $750 | $625 | $525 | |

* ***M1A1 Paratrooper Carbine*** – .30 Carb. cal., GIO, similar to M1 Service Carbine, except features a high quality reproduction of the folding wood "Paratrooper" stock with matching wood handguard.

| MSR $1,500 | $1,275 | $1,125 | $1,025 | $875 | $750 | $625 | $525 | |

M1A1 SCOUT CARBINE – .30 Carb. cal., National Match barrel, Type 3 barrel band with bayonet lug, FA M1 carbine receiver, Picatinny mounting system, aluminum Scout rail, folding polymer Choate stock, includes one 10 shot mag. and canvas sling.

| MSR $1,500 | $1,275 | $1,125 | $1,025 | $875 | $750 | $625 | $525 | |

* ***M3 Scout Carbine*** – .30 Carb. cal., GIO, similar to M1 Service Carbine, except features a Picatinny handguard rail for mounting a wide variety of optics.

| MSR $1,600 | $1,350 | $1,200 | $1,075 | $950 | $815 | $700 | $575 | |

MSR	100%	98%	95%	90%	80%	70%	60%	Last MSR

M1C ENHANCED SNIPER RIFLE – .30-06 cal., GIO, 24 in. GI contour barrel with T-37 pronged flash suppressor, USGI receiver (drilled, tapped, and fitted to the scope mount by Griffin & Howe, Inc.), Griffin & Howe scope mount, National Match upgrades, walnut stock with linseed oil finish, includes 8 shot mag., tan leather sling, tan leather lace-up cheekpiece, and professionally fitted. Disc. 2014.

	$2,350	$2,050	$1,775	$1,600	$1,300	$1,075	$825	*$2,600*

M1C PEERLESS SNIPER RIFLE – .30-06 cal., GIO, 24 in. GI contour barrel with T-37 pronged flash suppressor, USGI receiver (drilled, tapped, and fitted to the scope mount by Griffin & Howe, Inc.), milled trigger guard, National Match upgrades, glass bedded action, walnut stock and handguard with linseed oil finish, includes 8 shot mag., tan leather lace-up cheekpiece, tan leather M1907 sling. Disc. 2014.

	$2,875	$2,525	$2,150	$1,950	$1,575	$1,300	$1,000	*$3,200*

M1E SCOUT RIFLE – .30-06 cal., GIO, 24 in. GI contour barrel, walnut stock with linseed oil finish, USGI receiver, Super Scout rear handguard with 3-way Picatinny rail, iron sights, includes 8 shot mag. and canvas sling.

MSR $2,050		$1,740	$1,525	$1,300	$1,185	$950	$825	$675	

M14 EBR-RI (ENHANCED BATTLE RIFLE - ROCK ISLAND) – .308 Win./7.62 NATO cal., 22 in. GI contour chrome moly barrel, NM flash suppressor with bayonet lug, Sage EBR tactical chassis system, FA heat treated receiver, Mil-Spec parts throughout, Picatinny rails with detachable forearm, Sage telescoping buttstock with adj. cheek rest and buttpad (integrated with stock), includes one 10 shot mag. and black nylon "Silent" sling, 11.15 lbs.

MSR $3,500		$2,975	$2,575	$2,075	$1,765	$1,450	$1,225	$1,050	

M14 MOD 1 SOCOM – .308 Win./7.62 NATO cal., 16 in. SOCOM GI contour barrel with A2 flash suppressor, Sage EBR Op rod guide block, SEI gas cylinder lock with dovetail, Picatinny rails, Sage tactical aluminum chassis, Magpul CTR buttstock, includes one 10 shot mag. and black nylon "Silent" sling.

MSR $3,875		$3,275	$2,850	$2,340	$1,975	$1,650	$1,375	$1,175	

M14 SCOUT – .308 Win./7.62 NATO cal., 18 1/2 in. GI contour barrel with NM flash suppressor and bayonet lug, 10 shot mag., FA Gen III Scout rail, 3-way Picatinny rail, oil-finished walnut stock, rubber recoil pad, includes one mag. and canvas sling.

MSR $2,900		$2,475	$2,150	$1,775	$1,525	$1,250	$1,050	$925	

M14 SCOUT 16 – .308 Win./7.62 NATO cal., 16 in. SOCOM 1x10 GI contour barrel with A2 flash suppressor, 10 shot mag., Super Scout handguard, 3-way Picatinny rail, oil-finished walnut stock, rubber recoil pad, front sight base, canvas sling.

MSR $2,900		$2,475	$2,150	$1,775	$1,525	$1,250	$1,050	$925	

M14 SERVICE RIFLE – .308 Win./7.62 NATO cal., GIO, 22 in. 1x12 GI contour barrel with National Match flash suppressor and bayonet lug, brown reinforced fiberglass handguard, 10 shot mag., walnut stock with linseed oil finish, includes canvas sling.

MSR $2,700		$2,275	$1,925	$1,625	$1,390	$1,125	$975	$850	

M14 ENHANCED SERVICE RIFLE – .308 Win./7.62 NATO cal., GPO, 22 in. GI Contour chrome moly barrel with National Match flash suppressor with bayonet lug, Fulton Armory's M14 semi-auto receiver, National Match upgrades include gas cylinder with welded front band, Sadlak NM Op rod spring guide, modified trigger, and modified handguard, fiberglass reinforced brown handguard, GI Contour walnut stock with linseed oil finish, includes one 10 shot mag. and canvas sling.

MSR $2,900		$2,475	$2,150	$1,775	$1,525	$1,250	$1,050	$925	

M14 PEERLESS NM SERVICE RIFLE – .308 Win./7.62 NATO cal., GPO, 22 in. medium contour stainless steel barrel, National Match flash suppressor with bayonet lug, hand milled trigger guard latch, aperture sights, fiberglass reinforced brown handguard, threaded M14 rear lug receiver glass bedded to heavy contour walnut stock with linseed oil finish or McMillan fiberglass stock, glass bedded action, includes National Match upgrades (including Sadlak tin gas piston, ferrule with modified front end, front sling swivel and front sight, modified trigger and handguard), one 10 shot mag., and canvas sling.

MSR $3,600		$3,050	$2,675	$2,275	$2,075	$1,680	$1,375	$1,125	

M21 ENHANCED SNIPER RIFLE – .308 Win./7.62 NATO cal., GIO, 22 in. GI contour chrome moly barrel, National Match flash suppressor with bayonet lug, Fulton Armory marked "M21" receiver with scope mount and Picatinny rail, fiberglass reinforced brown handguard, GI contour walnut stock with linseed oil finish, adj. cheekpiece, and front stock swivel with Picatinny rail, includes National Match upgrades, one 10 shot mag. and canvas sling.

MSR $3,200		$2,725	$2,385	$2,050	$1,850	$1,500	$1,225	$995	

M25 PEERLESS SNIPER RIFLE – .308 Win./7.62 NATO cal., GPO, 22 in. medium contour stainless steel barrel, NM flash suppressor with bayonet lug, 10 shot mag., FA receiver marked "M21", FA scope mount, front stock swivel with Picatinny rail, hand-milled trigger guard latch, National Match upgrades include modified trigger, black reinforced fiberglass handguard, McMillan M2A stock with adj. cheekpiece, includes one mag. and canvas sling.

MSR $4,450		$3,775	$3,315	$2,725	$2,275	$1,900	$1,625	$1,400	

MSR		100%	98%	95%	90%	80%	70%	60%	Last MSR

M39 EMR (ENHANCED MARKSMAN RIFLE) – .308 Win./7.62 NATO cal., 22 in. GI contour chrome moly barrel, NM flash suppressor with bayonet lug, Picatinny rails with detachable forearm, FA scope mount installed in the Sage EBR tactical chassis system, Sage telescoping buttstock with adj. cheek rest and butt pad (integrated with stock), includes one 10 shot mag. and black nylon "Silent" sling, 11.9 lbs.

MSR $3,725		$3,135	$2,725	$2,200	$1,885	$1,550	$1,300	$1,125	

MK14 MOD 0 EBR – .308 Win./7.62 NATO cal., 18 1/2 in. GI contour chrome moly barrel with direct connect SEI Vortex flash suppressor, FA heat treated receiver, front sight relocated to the gas cylinder lock with dovetail, installed in the Sage EBR tactical chassis system, Picatinny rails, detachable forearm (integrated with stock), Sage telescoping buttstock with adj. cheek rest and butt pad, includes one 10 shot mag. and black nylon "Silent" sling, 11 lbs.

MSR $3,700		$3,125	$2,725	$2,200	$1,885	$1,550	$1,300	$1,125	

* **MK14 MOD 1 EBR** – .308 Win./7.62 NATO cal., similar to MK14 Mod 0 EBR, except has CQB aluminum Sage tactical chassis system and Magpul CTR buttstock, 9.85 lbs.

MSR $3,775		$3,175	$2,765	$2,215	$1,885	$1,550	$1,300	$1,125	

* **MK14 MOD 2 EBR** – .308 Win./7.62 NATO cal., similar to MK14 Mod 0 EBR, except has 22 in. barrel, Sage PMRI (Precision Marksman Rock Island) tactical chassis sytem which includes an integrated Magpul PRS2 buttstock, 12 lbs.

MSR $4,000		$3,400	$2,975	$2,475	$2,075	$1,725	$1,450	$1,250	

T26 GARAND TANKER – .30-06 cal., GIO, 18 1/4 in. Tanker contour barrel and shortened "Tanker Variant" front handguard, USGI receiver, walnut stock with linseed oil finish, includes 8 shot mag. and canvas sling, 8 1/2 lbs.

MSR $2,100		$1,795	$1,575	$1,325	$1,150	$995	$850	$700	

* **T26S Garand Tanker Scout** – .30-06 cal., GIO, similar to T26 Garand Tanker, except comes standard with Super Scout rear handguard with 3-way Picatinny rail.

MSR $2,350		$1,975	$1,740	$1,450	$1,250	$1,050	$900	$750	

FUSION FIREARMS

Current 1911-style semi-auto pistol manufacturer established in 2005, located in Venice, FL.

PISTOLS: SEMI-AUTO

There are literally dozens of available options for each pistol. Matched pairs and multi-caliber options are also available - prices range from $1,795-$3,295, depending on options. Please contact the company directly for more information regarding pricing and available options (see Trademark Index).

All pistols come with a lifetime limited warranty.

Values listed are for base model only without options.

T-COMM TACTICAL COMMANDER – .357 SIG., .38 Super, .40 S&W, 9x23mm, 9mm Para., 10mm, .400 Corbon, or .45 ACP cal., similar to Pro Series Commander, except has lower tactical rail.

MSR $1,995		$1,695	$1,485	$1,275	$1,150	$925	$765	$595	

G SECTION

GA PRECISION

Current manufacturer established in 1999, located in N. Kansas City, MO.

MSR	100%	98%	95%	90%	80%	70%	60%	Last MSR

RIFLES: BOLT ACTION

BASE CUSTOM – customer choice of caliber, Rem. 700 short or long action, GIO, 20-26 in. stainless steel barrel with 5R rifling, McMillan M40A-1 HTG stock with Pachmayr Decelerator recoil pad, three sling studs, Rem. X-Mark trigger, custom steel trigger guard, matte Cerakote finish in OD Green, Mil-Spec OD, Black, or Coyote Tan finish.

| MSR $3,200 | $2,725 | $2,375 | $1,925 | $1,650 | $1,375 | $1,150 | $995 | |

CRUSADER – .308 Win. cal., Templar short action, GIO, 23 in. stainless steel barrel, M16 extractor, left side bolt release, McMillan A5 stock in GAP camo pattern, 5 and 10 shot detachable mag., matte Cerakote OD Green finish, T.A.B. Gear sling in OD Green also included.

| MSR $3,990 | $3,400 | $2,975 | $2,475 | $2,075 | $1,725 | $1,450 | $1,250 | |

FBI HRT – .308 Win. cal., Templar short action, GIO, 22 in. stainless steel barrel with Surefire suppressor/muzzle brake, 5 and 10 shot detachable mag., McMillan A3-5 adj. stock in OD Green, adj. cheekpiece, spacer system butt pad, left side bolt release, EFR rail installed, OD Green matte Cerakote finish, T.A.B. Gear sling in OD Green also included.

| MSR $4,600 | $3,900 | $3,450 | $2,875 | $2,375 | $2,000 | $1,725 | $1,500 | |

GAP-10 – .260 Rem. or .308 Win. cal., GIO, 16-22 in. stainless steel barrel, 20 shot mag., GAP-10 upper and lower receiver with Sniper/Tac handguard, rifle length or mid-length handguard, A2 stock standard (Magpul PRS optional), SST, ambidextrous bolt release, Badger Ordnance Universal safety, includes one-piece scope mount, matte black hardcoat anodized finish. New 2012.

| MSR $2,750 | $2,300 | $1,940 | $1,625 | $1,390 | $1,125 | $975 | $850 | |

GLADIUS – .308 Win. cal., Rem. 700 action, GIO, 18 in. stainless steel special Gladius contour barrel with Surefire brake/adaptor, Manners T-2A stock in Multicam camo pattern, adj. KMW Loggerhead cheek, 5 and 10 shot detachable mag. system, matte black Cerakote finish, includes T.A.B. Gear sling in OD Green.

| MSR $4,100 | $3,485 | $3,025 | $2,500 | $2,090 | $1,735 | $1,450 | $1,250 | |

HOSPITALLER – .308 Win. cal., Surgeon Mod. 591 integral short action, GIO, 24 in. stainless steel fluted barrel, Manners T4 adj. stock, KMW cheekpiece, Pachmayr Decelerator pad, 5 shot detachable box mag., matte Cerakote OD Green, Tan, or Black finish.

| MSR $4,500 | $3,825 | $3,350 | $2,750 | $2,290 | $1,900 | $1,625 | $1,400 | |

NON-TYPICAL – .243 Win., .260 Rem., .270 WSM, .300 WSM, .308 Win., .325 WSM, 7mm-08, 7mm WSM, all Remington RSAUMs, custom .338 WSM and .358 WSM cal., custom GAP Templar Hunter short action, GIO, 25 in. stainless steel contour barrel, B&C GAP Hunter integral aluminum stock in OD Green with black/tan webbing, Pachmayr Decelerator pad, Rem. X-Mark Pro trigger, custom steel trigger guard, M16 extractor, 1913 rail, matte Cerakote finish in OD Green, Tan, or Black, leather Montana rifle sling included, 7 lbs. 3 oz.

| MSR $2,995 | $2,550 | $2,225 | $1,825 | $1,575 | $1,300 | $1,100 | $950 | |

ROCK – customer choice of caliber, Rem. 700 short or long action, GIO, 22 in. stainless steel fluted barrel, McMillan M40A1 HTG stock with choice of camo, Pachmayer Decelerator pad installed, matte Cerakote finish in OD Green, Coyote Tan, or Black.

| MSR $3,495 | $2,975 | $2,575 | $2,075 | $1,765 | $1,450 | $1,225 | $1,050 | |

THUNDER RANCH – .308 Win. cal., Templar short action, GIO, 22 in. stainless steel barrel, Manners MCS-T molded-in Field Grade GAP camo stock, 5 and 10 shot mag., OD Cerakote finish, M16 extractor, left-side bolt release, marked with TR logo and comes with a special certificate from Thunder Ranch, T.A.B. Gear sling in OD Green also included.

| MSR $3,870 | $3,275 | $2,850 | $2,340 | $1,975 | $1,650 | $1,375 | $1,175 | |

XTREME HUNTER – 6.5 SAUM 4S cal., Templar short action Hunter, 24 in. fluted #3 contour stainless steel barrel, Vais micro muzzle brake, detachable box mag., X-Mark Pro trigger, M16 extractor, oversized tactical bolt knob, Manners super light carbon fiber stock, matte Cerakote finish in customer's choice of color, leather Montana gun sling, 7 1/2 lbs. New 2014.

| MSR $4,370 | $3,725 | $3,285 | $2,700 | $2,275 | $1,850 | $1,600 | $1,350 | |

USMC M40A1 – 7.62 NATO cal., Rem. 700 short action, 25 in. USMC contour stainless steel barrel, matte black finish, steel trigger guard, McMillan M40A1-HTG stock in Forest Camo, red 1/2 in. Pachmayr recoil pad, custom made trigger guard and floorplate.

| MSR $3,700 | $3,125 | $2,725 | $2,200 | $1,890 | $1,560 | $1,300 | $1,125 | |

MSR	100%	98%	95%	90%	80%	70%	60%	Last MSR

USMC M40A3 – 7.62 NATO cal., Rem. 700 short action, 25 in. USMC contour stainless steel barrel, matte black finish, Badger Ordnance M5 trigger guard, McMillan A4 stock with OD Green molded-in color, adj. saddle cheekpiece, spacer system buttpad.

| MSR $3,970 | $3,375 | $2,950 | $2,475 | $2,075 | $1,725 | $1,450 | $1,250 | |

USMC M40A5 – 7.62 NATO cal., Rem. 700 short action, 25 in. USMC contour stainless steel barrel, Surefire comp/suppressor, matte black finish, Badger M5 DBM trigger guard, one 5 shot mag., adj. McMillan A4 stock in OD Green, PGW PVS-22 night vision mount mounted in stock, spacer system LOP adjustment.

| MSR $4,490 | $3,825 | $3,350 | $2,750 | $2,290 | $1,900 | $1,625 | $1,400 | |

US ARMY M-24 – .308 Win. or .300 Win. Mag. cal., Rem. 700 Long action, 24 in. stainless steel barrel, matte black finish, steel M-24 trigger guard, drilled and tapped, one-piece M24 steel scope base, black HS Precision M-24 stock, adj. LOP, matte black Cerakote finish.

| MSR $3,670 | $3,100 | $2,700 | $2,195 | $1,885 | $1,560 | $1,300 | $1,125 | |

G.A.C. RIFLES Srl

Current rifle manufacturer established in 1993, and currently located in Corner Spa, Brescia, Italy. No current U.S. importation.

RIFLES: BOLT ACTION

G.A.C. Rifles manufactures top quality target rifles for a variety of shooting disciplines. Guns are individually ordered. Please contact the company directly for potential U.S. importation/availability, pricing, and length of delivery time (see Trademark Index).

G.A.R. ARMS

Current AR-15 style manufacturer located in Fairacres, NM.

CARBINES/RIFLES: SEMI-AUTO

GR-15 MTCSS – .223 Wylde cal., GIO, 16 in. LW50 stainless steel barrel, Phantom flash hider, YHM quad rail gas block, Daniel Defense 9 in. modular free float rail, Magpul bolt catch B.A.D. lever (battery assist device), two-stage match trigger, Hogue grip, Magpul PRS black sniper stock, charging handle with tactical latch, A3 flat-top upper, Magpul alum. trigger guard, two 30 shot mags., includes hard rifle case.

| MSR $1,800 | $1,525 | $1,350 | $1,175 | $1,050 | $900 | $775 | $625 | |

GR-15 ORHS (OPTICS READY HUNTER STANDARD) – 5.56 NATO cal., GIO, 16 or 20 in. E.R. Shaw chrome moly heavy weight barrel, M4 feed ramps, charging handle, free float aluminum forend, Mil-Spec trigger, 5 (20 in.) or 10 (16 in.) shot mag., A3 flat-top upper, high riser block for optics, A2 fixed stock, hard rifle case.

| MSR $1,270 | $1,080 | $950 | $815 | $685 | $595 | $515 | $440 | |

Add $10 for 20 in. barrel.

GR-15 STAINLESS 16 IN. – .223 Rem. cal., GIO, 16 in. stainless steel bison barrel, carbine length free floating handguard, charging handle, forged alum. lower and A3 flat-top upper receiver, right hand ejection, two 20 shot mags., A2 buttstock.

| MSR $1,205 | $1,025 | $925 | $800 | $685 | $595 | $515 | $440 | |

  * GR-15 Stainless 20 In. – .223 Wylde cal., similar to A3 Stainless 16 in., except features 20 in. stainless steel barrel and rifle length handguard.

| MSR $1,217 | $1,025 | $925 | $800 | $685 | $595 | $515 | $440 | |

GR-15 STANDARD CARBINE – 5.56 NATO cal., GIO, 16 in. Government contour M4 barrel with A2 flash hider, threaded muzzle, M4 feed ramps, parkerized finish, charging handle, carbine length handguard with single heat shield, forged aluminum lower and A3 flat-top upper receiver, right hand ejection, 6-position collapsible buttstock, single rail gas block, 30 shot mag., standard sling, includes hard rifle case.

| MSR $910 | $775 | $685 | $615 | $550 | $485 | $415 | $370 | |

  * GR-15 Standard Rifle – 5.56 NATO cal., similar to GR-15 A3 Standard Carbine, except features 20 in. barrel, rifle length handguard, and A2 fixed buttstock.

| MSR $950 | $800 | $700 | $615 | $550 | $485 | $415 | $370 | |

GR-15 TAC DEFENDER – 5.56 NATO cal., GIO, 16 in. Government contour barrel with A2 flash hider, Troy Industries 7, 10, or 13.8 in. free float quad rails, M4 feed ramps, charging handle, forged alum. lower receiver and A3 flat-top upper, ejection port cover and round forward assist, right hand ejection, 6-position collapsible buttstock, carbine length handguard and single heat shield (13.8 in. model only), black or FDE parkerized finish.

| MSR $1,060 | $900 | $750 | $665 | $585 | $515 | $450 | $395 | |

Add $100 for 7 in. Troy Industries free float quad rail.

Add $131 for 13.8 in. Troy Industries free float quad rail.

MSR		100%	98%	95%	90%	80%	70%	60%	Last MSR

GR-15 TACDE7 – 5.56 NATO cal., GIO, elite version of Tac Defender model, 16 in. M4 barrel, parkerized finish, M4 feed ramps, Troy 7 in. free float quad rail in FDE, Troy rail covers in FDE, single rail gas block, YHM (disc.) or Troy gas block mounted flip up front sight, YHM (disc.) or Troy flip up rear sight, Vortex (disc.) or Troy Medieval flash suppressor, Magpul trigger guard in FDE, Troy Battle Axe pistol grip FDE, Troy Battle Axe CQB lightweight stock in FDE, Troy 30 shot Battlemag, Troy rifle sling, charging handle with tactical latch, two-stage match trigger.

| MSR $1,884 | | $1,600 | $1,400 | $1,200 | $1,075 | $900 | $775 | $625 | |

* **GR-15 TACDE10** – 5.56 NATO cal., similar to GR-15 TACDE7, except features Troy 10 in. free float quad rail, black finish.

| MSR $1,917 | | $1,635 | $1,425 | $1,200 | $1,075 | $925 | $795 | $650 | |

GR-15 TAC EVO (EVOLUTION) – 5.56 NATO cal., GIO, 16 in. Government contour barrel with A2 flash hider, threaded muzzle, parkerized finish, M4 feed ramps, charging handle, Samson 7 in. free float with add-on rails, forged alum. lower receiver and forged A3 flat-top upper, M4 collapsible buttstock, two 30 shot mags., right hand ejection, includes hard rifle case.

| MSR $1,158 | | $985 | $875 | $740 | $625 | $550 | $475 | $425 | |

GR-15 TACE CARBINE – 5.56 NATO cal., GIO, 16 in. fluted barrel, parkerized finish, M4 feed ramps, two-stage match trigger, A3 flat-top upper, Midwest Industries flash hider/impact device, Midwest Industries free float quad rail, gas block with flip up front and rear sights, Magpul ACS stock, Magpul OD Green 30 shot mag., Magpul enhanced aluminum trigger guard, Hogue OD Green pistol grip.

| MSR $1,760 | | $1,495 | $1,300 | $1,125 | $1,000 | $850 | $735 | $595 | |

GR-15 TACPB CARBINE – 5.56 NATO cal., GIO, 16 in. barrel, parkerized finish, M4 feed ramps, Mil-Spec trigger, Troy Industries free float 7.2 in. Alpha BattleRail, YHM single rail gas block, Troy Industries rear flip up Tritium Battlesight, Troy Industries front gas block mounted flip up Battlesight, Magpul MOE fixed stock, standard A2 pistol grip, charging handle with tactical latch, 30 shot mag., includes hard rifle case.

| MSR $1,600 | | $1,350 | $1,200 | $1,075 | $950 | $815 | $700 | $575 | |

GR-15 TACTC – 5.56 NATO cal., GIO, 16 in. M4 barrel with A2 flash hider, charging handle, Tapco M4 6-position commercial stock, Tapco saw cut pistol grip, Tapco vertical foregrip and Tapco Intrafuse handguard with quad rails for mounting lights/lasers, Tapco bipod, two Tapco 30 shot mags., Tapco sling system, includes hard rifle case.

| MSR $1,223 | | $1,040 | $925 | $800 | $685 | $595 | $515 | $440 | |

GR-15 TACTICAL CARBINE – 5.56 NATO cal., GIO, 16 in. Govt. contour M4 barrel with A2 flash hider, parkerized finish, M4 feed ramps, charging handle, carbine length handguard, single heat shield, drop-in quad rails, A3 flat-top forged alum. upper and lower receiver, right-hand ejection, M4 6-position collapsible buttstock, two 30 shot mags., includes hard rifle case.

| MSR $1,000 | | $850 | $725 | $650 | $585 | $515 | $450 | $395 | |

GR-15 VTAC DEFENDER – 5.56 NATO cal., GIO, 16 in. Govt. contour barrel with A2 flash hider, Troy Industries 9 in. VTAC free float rails, charging handle, forged alum. A3 flat-top upper receiver, forged lower, right hand ejection, two 30 shot mags., M4 collapsible buttstock, parkerized finish, includes hard rifle case.

| MSR $1,090 | | $925 | $850 | $725 | $625 | $550 | $475 | $425 | |

GR-15 ZTAC ZOMBIE TACTICAL CARBINE – 5.56 NATO cal., GIO, 16 in. M4 Govt. contour barrel with A2 flash hider, parkerized finish, M4 feed ramps, Ergo Z free float rail, Ergo vertical forward grip, Ergo ambidextrous pistol grip in Zombie Green, Ergo Zombie Green magwell cover, Ergo Zombie Green rail covers and ladder rail covers, Zombie Hunter dust cover, Zombie Hunter magazine catch, Zombie Hunter charging handle, front and rear flip up sights, Ergo F93 eight position stock, BullDog Zombie coffin soft rifle case.

| MSR $1,620 | | $1,375 | $1,200 | $1,075 | $950 | $815 | $700 | $575 | |

GWACS ARMORY

Current manufacturer of AR-15 style carbines/rifles, receivers, and accessories, located in Tulsa, OK.

RIFLES: SEMI-AUTO

CAV-15 – 5.56 NATO cal., gas operated, 16 in. chrome moly Nitride M4 Wilson barrel contour with A2 flash suppressor, flat-top receiver with tactical A4 quad rail, Magpul MOE stock, Magpul MOE handguard, Magpul Gen2 backup rear sight, standard charging handle, Mil-Spec trigger assembly, M16 bolt carrier group, optics ready, black, Coyote Tan, Flat Dark Earth, OD Green, or Zombie Green, approx. 6 lbs.

| MSR $839 | | $715 | $625 | $550 | $475 | $420 | $365 | $335 | |

CAV-15 MKII LWT – 5.56 NATO cal., AR-15 style, 16 in. chrome moly matte light contour "pencil" barrel with A2 flash hider, heat resistant GlacierGuard polymer handguard, single rail gas block, ejection port door, forward assist, charging handle, bolt and carrier assembly, black finish, 5 lbs. 12 oz.

| MSR $600 | | $525 | $465 | $400 | $340 | $300 | $265 | $250 | |

MSR	100%	98%	95%	90%	80%	70%	60%	Last MSR

CAV-15 TACTICAL A4 MOE – 5.56 NATO cal., 16 in. chrome moly Nitride M4 Wilson barrel with A2 flash hider, MKII lower with carbine buffer and Mil-Spec trigger assembly, alum. flat-top upper with charging handle, MOE handguard, gas block, black finish, 6 lbs. 2 oz.

MSR $691	$595	$525	$450	$400	$325	$280	$265	

GALIL

Current trademark manufactured by Israel Weapon Industries Ltd. (IWI), formerly Israel Military Industries (IMI). Currently imported by IWI US, Inc. located in Harrisburg, PA beginning late 2014. Galil semi-auto sporterized rifles and variations with thumbhole stocks were banned in April, 1998. Beginning late 1996, Galil rifles and pistols were available in selective fire mode only (law enforcement, military only) and are currently imported by IWI US, Inc., previously imported by UZI America, Inc., a subsidiary of O.F. Mossberg & Sons, Inc. Previously imported by Action Arms, Ltd. located in Philadelphia, PA until 1994, by Springfield Armory located in Geneseo, IL, and Magnum Research, Inc., located in Minneapolis, MN.

Magnum Research importation can be denoted by a serial number prefix "MR", while Action Arms imported rifles have either "AA" or "AAL" prefixes.

PISTOLS: SEMI-AUTO

GALIL ACE PISTOL (GAP39) – 7.62x39mm cal., closed rotating bolt, long stroke GPO, milled steel receiver, 8.3 in. barrel, 2-piece Picatinny Tri-Rail forearm system w/removable covers and protected pressure switch area, 30 shot standard AK-style mag., adj. rear and Tritium post front sights, OAL 18 in., parkerized finish, 6 lbs. Imported late 2014-2015.

	$1,500	$1,300	$1,100	$1,000	$800	$700	$500	$1,749

On December 28, 2015 IWI US, Inc. conducted a recall of all Galil ACE (GAP39) pistols that have a receiver with a 3-pin (3-hole) fire control group construction. There are no safety issues involved with this recall. FFL Dealers and Consumers should contact IWI US, Inc. at (717) 695-2081, email recall@iwi.

GALIL ACE PISTOL (GAP39-II) – 7.62x39mm cal., closed rotating bolt, long stroke GPO, milled steel receiver, 8.3 in. barrel, 2-piece Picatinny top rail, Tri-Rail forearm system w/removable covers and protected pressure switch area, 30 shot standard AK-style mag., fully adj. sights with Tritium front post, 18 in. OAL, parkerized finish, 6 lbs. w/o mag. New 2016.

MSR $1,749	$1,500	$1,300	$1,100	$1,000	$800	$700	$500	

GALIL ACE PISTOL (GAP39SB) – 7.62x39mm cal., closed rotating bolt, long stroke GPO, milled steel receiver, 8.3 in. barrel, 2-piece Picatinny top rail, Tri-Rail forearm system w/removable covers and protected pressure switch area, 30 shot standard AK-style mag., fully adj. sights with Tritium front post, side folding stabilizing brace, 26 3/4 in. OAL, parkerized finish, 6 1/2 lbs. w/o mag. New 2016.

MSR $1,849	$1,600	$1,400	$1,175	$1,050	$850	$750	$550	

RIFLES: SEMI-AUTO

Models 329, 330 (Hadar II), 331, 332, 339 (sniper system with 6x40 mounted Nimrod scope), 361, 372, 386, and 392 all refer to various configurations of the Galil rifle.

MODEL AR – .223 Rem. or .308 Win. cal., gas operated, rotating bolt, 16.1 (.223 Rem. cal. only) or 19 (.308 Win. cal. only) in. barrel, parkerized, folding stock, flip up Tritium night sights, 8.6 lbs.

	$3,150	$2,650	$2,475	$2,150	$1,925	$1,750	$1,625	$950

Add $500 for .308 Win. cal.

MODEL ARM – .223 Rem. or .308 Win. cal., similar to Model AR, except includes folding bipod, vented hardwood handguard, and carrying handle.

	$3,450	$3,100	$2,850	$2,600	$2,300	$2,100	$1,900	$1,050

Add $500 for .308 Win. cal.

GALIL SPORTER – .223 Rem. or .308 Win. cal., gas operated, rotating bolt, 16.1 or 19 in. barrel, parkerized, one-piece thumbhole stock, 4 (.308 Win.) or 5 (.223 Rem.) shot mag., choice of wood (disc.) or polymer handguard, 8 1/2 lbs. Imported 1991-93.

	$1,650	$1,525	$1,375	$1,200	$1,100	$1,000	$950	$950

Add $400 for .308 Win. cal.

HADAR II – .308 cal., gas operated, tactical type configuration, 18 1/2 in. barrel, 4 shot (standard) or 25 shot mag., adj. rear sight, one-piece walnut thumbhole stock with pistol grip and forearm, recoil pad, 10.3 lbs. Imported 1989 only.

	$1,575	$1,375	$1,275	$1,050	$950	$825	$750	$998

SNIPER OUTFIT – .308 Win. cal., limited production, sniper model built to exact I.D.F. specifications for improved accuracy, 20 in. heavy barrel, hardwood folding stock (adj. recoil pad and adj. cheekpiece) and forearm, includes

MSR	100%	98%	95%	90%	80%	70%	60%	Last MSR

Tritium night sights, bipod, detachable 6x40mm Nimrod scope, two 25 shot mags., carrying/storage case, 14.1 lbs. Imported 1989 only.

	100%	98%	95%	90%	80%	70%	60%	Last MSR
	$6,500	$5,750	$5,000	$4,350	$3,750	$3,250	$2,850	$3,995

GALIL ACE RIFLE (GAR1639) – 7.62x39mm cal., closed rotating bolt, long stroke GPO, milled steel receiver, 16 in. barrel, 2-piece Picatinny top rail, Tri-Rail forearm system w/removable covers and protected pressure switch area, 30 shot standard AK-style mag., fully adj. sights with Tritium front post, side folding adj. telescoping buttstock w/two position removable comb, 34 1/2 in. OAL, parkerized finish, 7 1/2 lbs. w/o mag. New 2016.

MSR $1,899	$1,650	$1,450	$1,250	$1,100	$900	$800	$600	

GAMBA, RENATO

Current trademark established in 1748, and located in Gardone V.T., Italy. Gamba firearms are currently manufactured by Bre-Mec srl beginning 2007, and are not currently being imported into the U.S. Previously imported in limited quantities circa 2005-2010 by Renato Gamba U.S.A., located in Walnut, CA. The U.S. service center is located in Bernardsville, NJ. Gamba of America, a subsidiary of Firing Line, located in Aurora, CO, was the exclusive importer and distributor for Renato Gamba long guns from 1996-2000. Pistols were previously imported and distributed (until 1990) by Armscorp of America, Inc. located in Baltimore, MD. Shotguns were previously (until 1992) imported by Heckler & Koch, Inc. located in Sterling, VA.

Filli Gamba (Gamba Brothers) was founded in 1946. G. Gamba sold his tooling to his brother, Renato, in 1967 when Renato Gamba left his brothers and S.A.B. was formed. Filli Gamba closed in 1989 and the Zanotti firm was also purchased the same year.

Renato Gamba firearms have had limited importation since 1986. In 1989, several smaller European firearms companies were purchased by R. Gamba and are now part of the Renato Gamba Group - they include Gambarmi and Stefano Zanotti. The importation of R. Gamba guns changed in 1990 to reflect their long term interest in exporting firearms to America. Earlier imported models may be rare but have not enjoyed much collectibility to date.

SHOTGUNS: SLIDE ACTION

MODEL 2100 – 12 ga., 3 in. chamber, 19 1/2 in. barrel, 7 shot mag., law enforcement configuration with matte black metal and wood, 6.62 lbs. Limited importation.

	$325	$250	$225	$200	$180	$160	$145	$715

GERMAN SPORT GUNS GmbH

Current firearms and air soft manufacturer and distributor located in Ense-Höingen, Germany. Currently imported by American Tactical Imports, located in Rochester, NY.

In May 2013, the L&O Group (owners of Blaser, Mauser, J.P. Sauer & Sohn, John Rigby, and Sig Sauer) purchased a majority stake in German Sport Guns. The L&O Group is owned by Michael Lüke and Thomas Ortmeier.

CARBINES: SEMI-AUTO

GSG-522 LW CARBINE (GSG-522) – .22 LR cal., semi-auto design patterned after the H&K MP-5 with forearm cocking handle, 16 1/2 in. barrel with choice of flash hider or faux elongated suppressor, open sights, 10 or 22 shot detachable mag., aluminum (disc. 2014) or lightweight polymer upper and lower receiver, Picatinny rail, ambidextrous safety, black, camo (disc. 2011), or nickel (disc. 2011) finish, synthetic, lightweight synthetic (became standard 2015), or wood fixed (disc.) stock with pistol grip, optional textured pistol grip, Weaver rail, and gold accents (disc. 2012), 6.2-6.6 lbs. New 2002, importation began 2008.

MSR $300	$265	$235	$210	$190	$170	$160	$150	

Add $47 for 110 round drum mag. (new 2013).

Add approx. $75 if without lightweight stock.

Add $28 for nickel (disc. 2011) or $51 for camo finish (special order only, disc. 2011).

Add $47 for wood (disc. 2011).

Add $115 for gold accents (disc. 2012).

* **GSG-522 LW/GSG-522 Retractable Stock** – .22 LR cal., 16 1/4 in. barrel with choice of flash hider or faux elongated suppressor, open sights, 22 shot detachable mag., rail system, black finish, lightweight synthetic retractable stock, optional textured pistol grip and integrated Weaver rail. New 2013.

MSR $320	$280	$245	$220	$200	$175	$165	$155	

GSG-522 SD LW (GSG-522 SD) – .22 LR cal., similar to GSG-522, except has textured pistol grip and integrated Weaver rail as standard, ribbed handguard and barrel shroud, black finish only, lightweight stock became standard 2015.

MSR $320	$280	$245	$220	$200	$175	$165	$155	

Add $40 for 110 round drum mag. (new 2013).

Add $25 for retractable stock (new 2013).

Add approx. $100 if without lightweight stock.

MSR	100%	98%	95%	90%	80%	70%	60%	*Last MSR*

GSG MP-40 – .22 LR cal., 17.2 in. barrel, blued finish, 10 or 28 shot mag., black Bakelite furniture, all metal construction, iron sights, shipped in WWII period-style wooden crate, approx. 9 lbs. New 2014.

MSR $540	$485	$425	$375	$325	$275	$240	$210	

GSG STG-44 – .22 LR cal., 17.2 in. barrel, 10 or 25 shot detachable mag., adj. trigger (new 2013), patterned after the Nazi Sturmgewehr 44, wood furniture with metal or black stained wood furniture (new 2015), blue finish, optional WWII period style wooden crate made in U.S., 9.4 lbs. New 2012.

MSR $430	$375	$325	$295	$275	$250	$225	$195	

Subtract $40 for black stained wood furniture (GSG STG-44 Black, new 2015).

Add $25 for wooden crate (disc.).

GSG AK-47 (KALASHNIKOV) – .22 LR cal., patterned after the AK-47 design action, blowback operated, 10, 15 (disc.), 22 (disc.), or 24 (new 2011) shot mag., 16 1/2 in. barrel with protected front sight, available with black synthetic or hardwood pistol grip (mfg. 2012 only) stock. New 2009.

MSR $416	$360	$315	$285	$265	$240	$215	$190	

Add $174 for hardwood stock and gold receiver (mfg. 2012 only).

Add $120-$150 for Strikeforce Elite package with adj. polymer stock, pistol grip, recoil system, removable cheekpiece and three Picatinny rails (mfg. 2012-2014).

* ***Kalashnikov Rebel*** – .22 LR cal., 16 1/2 in. barrel, wood furniture, features strapping tape wrapped around front of upper handguard and magazine, red bandana added to buttstock, 10 or 24 shot mag., 7 lbs. Mfg. 2013-2015.

	$425	$375	$325	$285	$260	$230	$200	*$483*

Add $120-$150 for Strikeforce Elite package with adj. polymer stock, pistol grip, recoil system, removable cheekpiece and three Picatinny rails (disc. 2014).

PISTOLS: SEMI-AUTO

GSG-522 LW (GSG-522 P) – .22 LR cal., 9 in. barrel with flash suppressor, 10 or 22 shot mag., choice of standard or lightweight (new 2013) configuration, black finish, patterned after the MP-5 pistol, adj. diopter rear sight with optional Picatinny rail, top lever charging, integrated Weaver rail (new 2011), textured pistol grip, integrated sling bracket, 5.89 lbs. New 2009.

MSR $300	$260	$240	$220	$200	$185	$175	$165	

GSG-522 PK – .22 LR cal., 10 or 22 shot mag., 4 5/8 in. barrel flush with top of frame, forward mounted charging lever, blued finish, operating mechanism similar to GSG-522 P, integrated Weaver rail and textured pistol grip (new 2011), 5.2 lbs. New 2009.

MSR $421	$365	$335	$315	$285	$265	$245	$225	

GSG-922 – .22 LR cal., 3.4 in. threaded barrel, SA, with or w/o faux suppressor, beavertail grip safety, 3-hole skeleton trigger, lower Picatinny rail, checkered black plastic or walnut (new 2015) grips, compatible with 1911 parts, black finish. New mid-2012.

MSR $380	$340	$300	$275	$250	$225	$200	$185	

Add $30 for faux suppressor (disc. 2014).

GSG 1911 SERIES – .22 LR cal., patterned after the M1911, 5 in. barrel, SA, front and rear slide serrations, checkered diamond walnut (GSG 1911) or plastic grips in Tan (GSG Tan), Green (GSG Green), or Black (GSG Black, disc. 2014) grips, skeletonized trigger and hammer, beavertail grip safety, 10 shot mag. New 2009.

MSR $300	$275	$250	$225	$210	$195	$185	$175	

Subtract $10 for GSG Black Model (disc. 2014).

Add $180 for .22 LR conversion kit (new 2013).

* ***GSG 1911 Series Target Model*** – .22 LR cal., similar to 1911 Series, except has threaded barrel and target style checkered molded grips, adj. rear sights, Picatinny under rail. New late 2013.

MSR $340	$300	$275	$250	$225	$210	$195	$185	

GSG 1911 AD OPS – .22 LR cal., similar to GSG 1911, except has black plastic grips, lower Picatinny rail, and threaded barrel with 4 in. faux suppressor.

MSR $310	$280	$255	$230	$215	$200	$190	$180	

MP-40 – .22 LR cal., 10 in. barrel, 10 or 28 shot mag., black finish. New 2015.

MSR $540	$475	$425	$375	$325	$275	$250	$225	

GIBBS GUNS, INC.

Previously manufactured by Volunteer Enterprises in Knoxville, TN and previously distributed by Gibbs Guns, Inc. located in Greenback, TN.

MSR	100%	98%	95%	90%	80%	70%	60%	Last MSR

CARBINES

MARK 45 CARBINE – .45 ACP cal. only, based on M6 Thompson machine gun, 16 1/2 in. barrel, 5, 15, 30, or 90 shot mag. U.S. mfg. Disc. 1988.

	100%	98%	95%	90%	80%	70%	60%	Last MSR
	$750	$625	$525	$450	$375	$330	$300	*$279*

Add $200 for 90 shot mag.
Add 10% for nickel plating.

GIBBS RIFLE COMPANY, INC.

Current manufacturer, importer, and distributor located in Martinsburg, WV. Gibbs manufactured rifles with the Gibbs trademark in Martinsburg, WV 1991-1994, in addition to importing Mauser-Werke firearms until 1995. Dealer and distributor sales.

In the past, Gibbs Rifle Company, Inc. imported a variety of older firearms, including British military rifles and handguns (both original and refurbished condition), a good selection of used military contract pistols and rifles, in addition to other shooting products and accessories, including a bipod patterned after the Parker-Hale M-85.

Gibbs Rifle Company, Inc. has imported and manufactured military collectibles, historical remakes, and special sporting rifles. All rifles are carefully inspected, commercially cleaned and boxed to ensure their quality, and all have a limited lifetime warranty. Gibbs Rifle Company, Inc. also offered membership in the Gibbs Military Collectors Club, an organization dedicated to military firearms collectors.

RIFLES: BOLT ACTION

ENFIELD NO. 5 JUNGLE CARBINE – .303 British cal., older No. 4 Enfield barreled action with newly manufactured stock, bayonet lug and flash hider have been added, 20 in. barrel, 7 3/4 lbs. Imported 1999-2004, reintroduced 2010 with camo synthetic stock.

	100%	98%	95%	90%	80%	70%	60%	Last MSR
	$400	$350	$300	$265	$235	$200	$175	

A bayonet and scabbard were also available for this model.

ENFIELD NO. 7 JUNGLE CARBINE – .308 Win. cal., older 2A action with reconfigured original wood, flash hider and bayonet lug have been added, 20 in. barrel, 8 lbs. Imported 1999-2004.

	100%	98%	95%	90%	80%	70%	60%	Last MSR
	$375	$325	$285	$265	$250	$225	$200	*$200*

QUEST EXTREME CARBINE – .303 British cal., updated No. 5 Enfield action, 20 in. barrel with compensator/flash hider, electroless nickel metal finish, new buttstock with survival kit packaged in butt trap, 7 3/4 lbs. Imported 2000-2004.

	100%	98%	95%	90%	80%	70%	60%	Last MSR
	$375	$325	$285	$265	$250	$225	$200	*$250*

QUEST II – .308 Win. cal., modern 2A Enfield barreled action, mfg. from chrome vanadium steel, 20 in. barrel with compensator/flash hider and adj. rear sight, front sight protector, pre-fitted see-through scope mount accepts all Weaver based optics and accessories, electroless nickel finish, hardwood stock with survival kit included, 12 shot mag., 8 lbs. Imported 2001-2004.

	100%	98%	95%	90%	80%	70%	60%	Last MSR
	$375	$325	$265	$235	$200	$185	$170	*$280*

QUEST III – .308 Win. cal., similar to Quest II, except has black synthetic stock, w/o survival kit. Imported 2002-2004.

	100%	98%	95%	90%	80%	70%	60%	Last MSR
	$395	$345	$280	$240	$200	$185	$170	*$300*

MODEL 85 SNIPER RIFLE – .308 Win. cal., 24 in. heavy barrel, 10 shot mag., camo green synthetic McMillan stock with stippling, built in adj. bipod and recoil pad, enlarged contoured bolt, adj. sights, 12 lbs. 6 oz.

	100%	98%	95%	90%	80%	70%	60%	Last MSR
	$3,950	$3,650	$3,250	$2,850	$2,400	$2,000	$1,650	*$2,050*

M1903-A4 SPRINGFIELD SNIPER MODEL – .30-06 cal., replica of original M1903-A3 Springfield, drilled and tapped, Redfield replica rings and mounts, new C stock, barrel marked with modern dates of mfg., includes U.S. issue leather sling and OD Green canvas carrying case. M73G2 scope became standard during 2012. New 2009.

MSR	100%	98%	95%	90%	80%	70%	60%	Last MSR
$1,250	$1,100	$975	$875	$775	$675	$575	$475	

M1903-A4-82 SPRINGFIELD SNIPER MODEL – .30-06 cal., similar to M1903, except has improved M82 rifle scope and 7/8 in. rings. Mfg. 2010-2012.

	100%	98%	95%	90%	80%	70%	60%	Last MSR
	$1,075	$950	$825	$700	$600	$500	$400	*$1,200*

M1903-A4-84 SPRINGFIELD SNIPER MODEL – .30-06 cal., similar to M1903A4-82, except has improved M84 rifle scope and 7/8 in. rings. Mfg. 2010-2012.

	100%	98%	95%	90%	80%	70%	60%	Last MSR
	$1,100	$950	$825	$700	$600	$500	$400	*$1,250*

GILA RIVER GUN WORKS

Current custom rifle manufacturer located in Pocatello, ID. Previously located in Yuma, AZ.

RIFLES: CUSTOM

Michael Scherz specializes in high-quality, bolt action rifles in .550 Magnum caliber. During late 2011 Gila River Tactical was formed and is a division of Gila River Gun Works. This tactical division offers a wide variety of long range precision tactical rifles. Please contact the company directly for more information, including pricing and availability (see Trademark Index).

GILBOA

Current trademark manufactured by Silver Shadow Advanced Security Systems Ltd., located in Kiryat Ono, Israel. Currently imported and distributed by LDB Supply, located in Dayton, OH.

CARBINES/PISTOLS: SEMI-AUTO

Silver Shadow manufactures the Gilboa line of AR-15 semi-auto carbines and pistols in 5.56x45mm, .223 Rem., 7.62x39mm, 7.62x51mm, .308 Win., and 9mm Para. cals. in various tactical configurations. All models are also available in full auto for military/law enforcement. Please contact the distributor directly for more information regarding pricing, availability, and the wide variety of options (see Trademark Index).

RIFLES: BOLT ACTION

SAVANNAH – .223 Rem. cal., GPO, fully machined solid aluminum aircraft alloy billet upper and lower receivers, 18 in. free floating bull chrome lined barrel, 10, 20, or 30 shot mag., also accepts any standard AR-15 style magazine, folding stock, flat-top with Picatinny top rail.
   Please contact the distributor directly for pricing and availability on this model (see Trademark Index).

GIRSAN MACHINE & LIGHT WEAPON INDUSTRY COMPANY

Current handgun and shotgun manufacturer established in 1994, located in Giresun, Turkey. Currently imported by Zenith Firearms, located in Afton, VA.

PISTOLS: SEMI-AUTO

Girsan manufactures a complete line of good quality semi-auto pistols in a variety of configurations, calibers, frame sizes, and finishes. Many options are available. Current models include: MC13, MC14, Compact M.C., Regard M.C., Tugra, Zirve (disc.), Bora, Bora Light, MC 21, MC23, MC 25, MC27, MC27E, MC T40, MC R40, MC C40, MC 21.40, MC 21.45, MC 23.40, MC 23.45, MC 1911, MC 1911S. Please contact the importer directly for more information, including U.S. availability and pricing (see Trademark Index).

SHOTGUNS: SEMI-AUTO

During 2012, the company also expanded its line into the 312 series of semi-auto hunting and tactical shotguns. Please contact the company directly for more information including current models, pricing, and U.S. availability (see Trademark Index).

GLOCK

Currently manufactured by Glock GmbH in Austria beginning 1983. Sales in the U.S. began in 1986. Glock also opened a production facility for manufacturing its polymer frames and assembling complete pistols in Smyrna, GA during late 2005. Exclusively imported and distributed by Glock, Inc. USA, located in Smyrna, GA. Distributor and dealer sales.

All Glock pistols have a "safe action" constant operating system (double action mode) which includes trigger safety, firing pin safety, and drop safety. Glock pistols have only 35 parts for reliability and simplicity of operation. With approximately 170 or more variations, over 10 million Glock semi-auto pistols have been manufactured since 1983.

In 1995 the Glock Collector's Association was formed. To date Glock has manufactured commemoratives (see Pistols: Semi-Auto, Commemoratives in this section), specially marked, and engraved models, plus the agency and police marked variations. By joining the Glock Collector's Association, members can find out the history of the most desirable G17-G43 civilian models. Please refer to Firearms/Shooting Organizations for more information on the Glock Collector's Association, including how to join.

PISTOLS: SEMI-AUTO

To date, there have been four generations of Glock pistols. Generation 1 (Gen 1), circa 1986-1988 features a pebbled finish frame without horizontal grooves on the front or back strap. Generation 2 (Gen 2), circa 1988-1997 can be identified by a checkered grenade finish with horizontal grooves on both the front and rear grip straps. Generation 3 (Gen 3), circa 1995-current started out with transition finger grooves and no front rail with thumb rests, then transitioned into finger grooves and a rail with thumb rests, checkered finished frame. This was followed by Variant 2 which is identified by an (extreme polymid traction) Rough Textured Frame (RTF-2), finger grooves rail, with recessed thumb rests. During 2010, Glock introduced Generation 4 (Gen 4, RTF-4) Rough Textured Frame, this enables standard frame Glock pistols to adopt the new short frame technology, which can be almost instantly fitted to any hand size, and features the (less polymid traction) Rough Textured Frame with recessed thumb rests, finger grooves, rail, and interchangeable frame back straps. It also includes a reversible enlarged magazine catch, dual recoil spring assembly, and a new trigger system, and in 2014, the first model Generation 4 (Gen4) features slim frame (less than 1 inch width), sub-compact "Less Aggressive" "Rough Textured Frame" (RTF) with thumb rest, reversible enlarged magazine catch, dual recoil spring assembly and new trigger system with no finger grooves and rail, single stack magazine. Glock has been transitioning all its pistols to Gen 4 since 2010.
   Add $18 for adj. rear sight, $22 for Glock steel sights (new 2004), or $47 for Glock night sights (new 2004).
   Add $80 for fixed Meprolight sight or $105 for fixed Trijicon sight (disc. 2003-2004, depending on model.)

MSR	100%	98%	95%	90%	80%	70%	60%	Last MSR

Add $25 for internal locking system (ILS) on most currently manufactured models listed below (new 2004).

Add $95 for tactical light or $284 for tactical light with laser for most currently manufactured pistols listed below.

MODEL 17/17C GEN 1, GEN 2, GEN 3 (SPORT/SERVICE)
– 9mm Para. cal., striker fired constant double action mode, polymer frame, mag., trigger and other pistol parts, 4.48 in. hexagonal rifled barrel, Gen1 (new 1986), Gen2 (new 1989), Gen3 (new 1998) or Gen4 (new 2010), with (Model 17C, Gen2 checkered grip, new 1997) (Model 17, 17C Gen3 ported non-ported (new 1997-98), steel slide and springs, 5 1/2 lb. trigger pull, 10 (C/B 1994), 17* (reintroduced late 2004), or 19* (reintroduced late 2004) shot mag., adj. (Sport Model) or fixed (Service Model) rear sight, standard black or optional OD/Olive Drab (Green) (Gen3 only 2005-current, limited mfg.), or FDE/Flat Dark Earth (Light Brown) (Gen3 2012-current limited mfg.) finish, includes a lockable pistol box, cable lock, cleaning rod, and other accessories, extra mag. and a spare rear sight, 24 3/4 oz. Importation began late 1985.

MSR $599	$475	$425	$395	$365	$335	$295	$250

Add $22 for Model 17C with fixed rear sight (new 1997).

Add $119 for competition model w/adj. sights (Model 17CC, mfg. 2000-2003).

This model is still available with the RTF-2 finish (extreme polymid traction) Rough Textured Frame (Model 17 RTF-2 mfg. 2009).

During 2011 Glock released its 25th Silver Anniversary Limited Edition of the Model 17 Gen4. It featured a 25 year marking on the top of the slide in addition to special 25th year silver medallion inletted in polymer frame - only 2,500 were produced.

All Gen3-4 models have recessed thumb rests and finger grooved mounting accessories rail, except Gen3 standard, compact, sub-compact Transition models (mfg. 1995-1998) have finger grooves, but no mounting accessories rail. Gen4 sub-compact slim frame (less than 1 in. width) "Less Aggressive" Rough Textured Frame (RTF) with thumb rests, reversible enlarged magazine catch, dual recoil spring assembly and new trigger system with no finger grooves and accessories rail. New 2014.

* **Model 17L Gen 1, Gen 2, Gen 3 (Sport/Service Competition)** – 9mm Para. cal., 6.02 in. ported/non-ported barrel, slotted relieved slide, recalibrated trigger pull (4 1/2 lb. pull), adj. rear sight, 26.3 oz. mfg. Gen1 pebbled grip (new 1988), Gen2 non-ported checkered grip, has no mounting accessories rail (new 1990), Gen3 non-ported has thumb rests, finger grooves, mounting accessories rail (new 1998).

MSR $750	$625	$550	$475	$425	$350	$325	$275

Add $28 for adj. sight.

Early Gen1 production with barrel ports, will command a high premium (new 1988).

This model is a long barreled competition version of the Model 17 "pebbled frame".

* **Model 17 TB Gen 3 (Sport/Service)** – 9mm Para. cal., similar to Model 17, except features the new TB "Threaded Barrel" for a suppressor-ready design, roughly .5 in. longer than the 4.48 in. barrel, finger grooves, mounting accessories rail and elevated sights. New 2014.

MSR $649	$525	$450	$400	$365	$335	$295	$250

MODEL 17 GEN 4 25TH SILVER ANNIVERSARY LIMITED EDITION
– 9mm Para. cal., Glock steel sights only, features 25th year silver medallion inletted in polymer frame and special inscription in back of slide on top, includes silver case. 2,500 to be mfg. during 2011.

MSR $850	$700	$600	$500	$450	$375	$350	$295

MODEL 17 GEN 4
– 9mm Para. cal., similar to Model 17 Gen 3, except features (less polymid traction) Rough Textured Frame (RTF-4) with recessed thumb rests, finger grooves rail, and interchangeable frame back straps, includes a reversible enlarged magazine catch, dual recoil spring assembly, and a new trigger system, fixed rear, adj. rear Glock steel, or Glock night sights, standard black or optional FDE/Flat Dark Earth (light brown) (2012-current, limited mfg.) or gray (2015-current, limited mfg.) finish. All Gen4 models shipped with 3 magazines, except Sub-Compact Models have 2 mags. New 2010.

MSR $649	$540	$440	$400	$375	$335	$295	$250

* **Model 17 MOS Gen 4 Competition (Sport/Service)** – 9mm Para. cal., adj. rear sight, similar to Model 17 Gen 4, except has Glock MOS, and lower rail for mounting accessories. New 2015.

MSR $726	$625	$550	$495	$440	$375	$325	$250

MODEL 18/18C GEN1, GEN2, GEN3 SELECTIVE FIRE CONTROL
– 9mm Para. cal., similar to Model 17, except has Selective Fire Control with non interchangeable parts, with hexagonal rifled barrels. Gen1 pebbled finish frame has ported/non-ported barrel. New 1988. Gen2 checkered grip has ported/non-ported barrel. New 1996. Model 18C Gen3 finger grooves, mounting accessories rail has ported/non-ported barrel, 19 shot mag., optional 33 shot mag., 24oz. New 1997.

Available for law enforcement and military units only (USA).

MODEL 19/19C COMPACT GEN 1, GEN 2, GEN 3 (SPORT/SERVICE)
– 9mm Para. cal., 4.01 in. barrel with hexagonal rifling ported (Model 19C, Gen2 checkered grip, new 1997), or unported barrel and checkered grip Gen2 has no accessories rail, (new 1988). 10 (C/B 1994), 15* (reintroduced late 2004), or 17* (reintroduced late 2004) shot mag., fixed (Service Model) or adj. (Sport Model) rear sight, 23 1/2 oz., Gen1 cut-down pebbled grip, has no mounting

MSR	100%	98%	95%	90%	80%	70%	60%	Last MSR

accessories rail (new 1988), Gen3 early transition model has finger grooves, thumb rests, no mounting accessories rail, (new 1997), standard black or optional OD/Olive Drab (green) (Gen3 only 2005-current, limited mfg.) or FDE/Flat Dark Earth (light brown) (Gen3 2012-current, limited mfg.) finish. Later Gen3 models ported/non-ported barrel have thumb rests, finger grooves, mounting accessories rail, (new 1997-98).

MSR $599	$475	$425	$395	$365	$335	$295	$250	

Add $22 for Model 19C with fixed sight only (new 1997).

Add $119 for competition model w/adj. sights (Model 19CC, mfg. 2000-2003).

This model is still available with RTF-2 finish (extreme polymid traction, Rough Textured Frame, Model 19 RTF-2, mfg. 2009).

This model is similar to Model 17, except has scaled down dimensions.

During 1996, AcuSport Corp. commissioned Glock to make a special production run of matching 9mm Para. cal. sets. Each set consists of a Model 19 and 26 with serialization as follows: Model 19 (ser. prefix AAA0000-AAA0499) and Model 26 (ser. prefix AAB0000-AAB0499).

* **Model 19 TB Compact Gen 3 (Sport/Service)** – 9mm Para. cal., compact size to the Model 17, except features the new TB "Threaded Barrel" for a suppressor-ready design, roughly .5 in. longer than the 4.01 in. barrel, finger grooves, mounting accessories rail and elevated sights. New 2014.

MSR $649	$525	$450	$400	$365	$335	$295	$250	

MODEL 19 GEN 4 – 9mm Para. cal., similar to Model 19, except features (less polymid traction) Rough Textured Frame (RTF-4) with recessed thumb rests, finger grooves, rail, and interchangeable frame back straps, includes a reversible enlarged magazine catch, dual recoil spring assembly, and a new trigger system, fixed rear, adj. rear Glock steel, or Glock night sights, standard black or optional FDE/Flat Dark Earth (light brown) (2012-current, limited mfg.) or gray (2015-current, limited mfg.) finish. New 2010.

MSR $649	$500	$440	$400	$375	$335	$295	$250	

* **Model 19 MOS Gen 4 Competition (Sport/Service)** – 9mm Para. cal., adj. rear sight, similar to Model 17 Gen 4, except has Glock MOS, and lower rail for mounting accessories. New 2015.

MSR $726	$625	$550	$495	$440	$375	$325	$250	

MODEL 20/20C GEN 2, GEN 3 (SPORT/SERVICE) – 10mm Norma cal., similar to Model 17 features except has 4.61 in. barrel ported/non-ported Model 20-20C, Gen3 with hexagonal rifling, optional 6 in. "Hunting Barrel" factory available. Early transition model has recessed thumb rests, finger grooves, no mounting accessories rail (new 1997), 10 (C/B 1994) or 15* (reintroduced late 2004) shot mag., larger slide and receiver, fixed (Service Model) or adj. (Sport Model) rear sight, Gen3 ported/non-ported barrel have recessed thumb rests, finger grooves, mounting accessories rail, (new 1997-98), Gen2 non-ported barrel, checkered grip, has no mounting accessories rail, standard black or optional OD/Olive Drab (green) (Gen3 only 2005-current, limited mfg.) or FDE/Flat Dark Earth (light brown) (Gen3 2012-current, limited mfg.) finish, 30 oz. New 1990.

MSR $637	$500	$440	$410	$375	$350	$325	$295	

Add $39 for compensated barrel (Model 20C, fixed sight only, new 1997).

Add $145 for competition model w/adj. sights (Model 20CC, mfg. 2000-2003).

* **Model 20SF Gen 3** – 10mm Norma cal., similar to Model 20, except has Gen3 (short frame), have recessed thumb rests, finger grooves, mounting accessories rail, 4.61 in. barrel with hexagonal rifling, 15 shot mag., all Glock sight options available, new trigger position, 30.7 oz. New 2009.

MSR $637	$500	$440	$410	$375	$350	$325	$295	

MODEL 20 GEN 4 – 10mm Norma cal., similar to Model 20 except features (less polymid traction) Rough Textured Frame (RTF-4) with recessed thumb rests, finger grooves, rail and interchangeable frame back straps, includes a reversible enlarged magazine catch, dual recoil assembly and new trigger system, fixed rear, adj. rear Glock steel or Glock night sights, standard black or optional FDE/Flat Dark Earth (light brown) (2013-current, limited mfg.) or gray (2015-current, limited mfg.) finish. New 2012.

MSR $687	$535	$460	$425	$395	$365	$335	$300	

MODEL 21/21C GEN 2, GEN 3 (SPORT/SERVICE) – .45 ACP cal., similar to Model 17, except has 4.61 in. barrel with octagonal rifling ported/non-ported Model 21-21C, Gen3 early transition model has recessed thumb rests, finger grooves, no mounting accessories rail (new 1997), 10 (C/B 1994) or 13* (reintroduced late 2004) shot mag., Gen3 ported/non-ported barrel, have recessed thumb rests, finger grooves, mounting accessories rail (new 1997-98), Gen2 non-ported barrel, checkered grip, has no mounting accessories rail, standard black or optional OD/Olive Drab (green) (Gen3 only 2005-current, limited mfg.) finish, FDE/Flat Dark Earth (Gen3 2012-current, limited mfg.) finish, 29 oz. New 1990.

MSR $637	$500	$440	$410	$375	$350	$325	$295	

Add $39 for compensated barrel (Model 21C, fixed rear sight only, new 1997).

Add $145 for competition model w/adj. sights (Model 21CC, mfg. 2000-2003).

MSR	100%	98%	95%	90%	80%	70%	60%	Last MSR

* Model 21SF Gen 3 – .45 ACP cal., similar to Model 21, except has Gen3 (short frame), new trigger position, recessed thumb rests, finger grooves, mounting accessories rail, 4.61 in. barrel with octagonal rifling, 13 shot mag., 29 oz. (new 2007). Gen3 RTF-2 (extreme polymid traction) Rough Textured Frame (new 2009).

MSR $637	$500	$440	$410	$375	$350	$325	$295	

* Model 21SF TB Gen 3 (Sport/Service) – .45 ACP cal., similar to Model 21, except has Gen 3 (short frame), new trigger position, recessed thumb rests, finger grooves, mounting accessories rail, elevated sights, features the new TB "Threaded Barrel" for a suppressor-ready design, roughly .5 in. longer than the 4.61 in. barrel. New 2014.

MSR $649	$525	$450	$400	$365	$335	$295	$250	

MODEL 21 GEN 4
– .45 ACP cal., similar to Model 21, except features (less polymid traction) Rough Textured Frame (RTF-4) with recessed thumb rests, finger grooves rail and interchangeable frame back straps, includes a reversible enlarged magazine catch, dual recoil spring assembly, and a new trigger system, fixed rear, adj. rear Glock steel, or Glock night sights, standard black or optional FDE/Flat Dark Earth (light brown) (2012-current, limited mfg.) or gray (2015-current, limited mfg.) finish. New 2011.

MSR $687	$535	$460	$430	$395	$365	$335	$300	

MODEL 22/22C GEN 2, GEN 3 (SPORT/SERVICE)
– .40 S&W cal., similar to Model 17, except has 4.48 in. barrel with hexagonal barrel ported Model 22C Gen2 checkered grip (new 1997), 10 (C/B 1994), 15* (reintroduced late 2004), 17, or 22 shot mag., all Glock sight variations available, Gen3 has ported/non-ported barrel, have recessed thumb rests, finger grooves mounting accessories rail (new 1997-98), Gen2 has non-ported barrel, checkered grip has no mounting accessories rail, standard black or optional OD/Olive Drab (green) (Gen3 only 2005-current, limited mfg.) or FDE/Flat Dark Earth (light brown) (Gen3 2012-current, limited mfg.) finish, 25 1/2 oz. New 1990.

MSR $599	$475	$425	$395	$365	$335	$295	$250	

Add $22 for Model 22C with compensated barrel (fixed rear sight only, new 1997).

Add $119 for competition model with adj. sights (Model 22CC, mfg. 2000-2003).

This model is still available with RTF-2 finish (extreme polymid traction, Rough Textured Frame, Model 22 RTF-2, mfg. 2009).

MODEL 22 GEN 4
– .40 S&W cal., similar to Model 22, except features (less polymid traction) Rough Textured Frame (RTF-4) with recessed thumb rests, finger grooves rail and interchangeable frame back straps, includes a reversible enlarged magazine catch, dual recoil spring assembly, and a new trigger system, fixed rear, adj. rear Glock steel, or Glock night sights, standard Black or optional FDE/Flat Dark Earth (Light Brown) (2012-current, limited mfg.) or Gray (2015-current, limited mfg.) finish. New 2010.

MSR $649	$500	$440	$400	$375	$350	$325	$295	

MODEL 23/23C GEN 2, GEN 3 COMPACT (SPORT/SERVICE)
– .40 S&W cal., compact variation of the Model 22, 4.01 in. barrel with hexagonal rifling ported (Model 23C), Gen2 checkered grip (new 1997), 10 (C/B 1994), 13* (reintroduced 2004), or 15 shot mag., available in all Glock sight variations, Gen3 ported/non-ported barrel have recessed thumb rests, finger grooves, mounting accessories rail (new 1997-98), Gen2 non-ported barrel, checkered grip has no mounting accessories rail, standard black or optional OD/Olive Drab (green) (Gen3 only 2005-current, limited mfg.) or FDE/Flat Dark Earth (light brown) (Gen3 2012-current, limited mfg.) finish, 23 1/2 oz. New 1990.

MSR $599	$475	$425	$395	$365	$335	$295	$250	

Add $22 for compensated barrel Model 23C (fixed rear sight only, new 1997).

Add $145 for competition model w/adj. sights (Model 23CC, mfg. 2000-2003).

This model is still available with RTF-2 finish (extreme polymid traction) Rough Textured Frame (Model 22 RTF-2 mfg. 2009).

During 1996, AcuSport Corp. commissioned Glock to make a special production run of matching .40 S&W cal. sets. Each set consists of a Model 23 and 27 with serialization as follows: Model 23 (ser. prefix AAC0000-AAC1499) and Model 27 (ser. prefix AAD0000-AAD1499).

* Model 23 TB Gen 3 Compact (Sport/Service) – .40 S&W cal., similar to Model 22, except compact size, features the new TB "Threaded Barrel" for a suppressor-ready design, roughly .5 in. longer than the 4.01 in. barrel, finger grooves, mounting accessories rail, and elevated sights. New 2014.

MSR $649	$525	$450	$400	$365	$335	$295	$250	

MODEL 23 GEN 4
– .40 S&W cal., similar to Model 23 Compact, except features (less polymid traction) Rough Textured Frame (RTF-4) with recessed thumb rests, finger grooves, rail, and interchangeable frame back straps, includes a reversible enlarged magazine catch, dual recoil spring assembly, and a new trigger system, fixed rear, adj. rear Glock steel, or Glock night sights, standard black or optional FDE/Flat Dark Earth (light brown) (2012-current, limited mfg.) or gray (2015-current, limited mfg.) finish. New 2010.

MSR $649	$500	$440	$400	$375	$335	$295	$250	

MSR	100%	98%	95%	90%	80%	70%	60%	Last MSR

MODEL 24/24C GEN 2, GEN 3 COMPETITION (SPORT/SERVICE) – .40 S&W cal., Gen3, similar to Model 22, except has 6.02 in. barrel with hexagonal rifling, internally compensated, recessed thumb rest, finger grooves, accessory rail ported (Model 24C, new 1999), adj. rear sight, 10, 15, 17, or 22 shot mag., recalibrated trigger pull (4 1/2 lb. pull), Gen2 checkered grip has no rail, "P" ported/non-ported series, 29 1/2 oz. New 1994.

MSR $750	$625	$550	$475	$425	$350	$325	$275

Add $40 for compensated barrel (Model 24C).

MODEL 25 COMPACT GEN 3 (SPORT/SERVICE) – .380 ACP cal., similar to Model 19 Compact, except has 4.02 in. barrel, 15 or 17 shot mag., recessed thumb rest, finger grooves, accessory rail, 22.5 oz. New 2008.

This model is available for law enforcement only (USA).

MODEL 26 GEN 3 SUB-COMPACT – 9mm Para. cal., sub-compact variation of the Model 19 Compact, except has shortened grip, 3.42 in. barrel with hexagonal rifling, 10 or 12 shot mag., available with all Glock sight variations, thumb rest, finger grooves, no mounting rail, first Gen3 production run Transition model, standard black or optional OD/Olive Drab (green) (Gen3 only 2005-current, limited mfg.) or FDE/Flat Dark Earth (light brown) (Gen3 2012-current, limited mfg.) finish, 21 3/4 oz. New 1995.

MSR $599		$475	$425	$395	$365	$335	$295	$250

MODEL 26 GEN 4 – 9mm Para. cal., similar to Model 26 Sub-Compact, except features (less polymid traction) Rough Textured Frame (RTF-4) with recessed thumb rests, finger grooves, and interchangeable frame back straps, includes a reversible enlarged magazine catch, dual recoil spring assembly, and a new trigger system, fixed rear, adj. rear Glock steel, or Glock night sights, standard black or optional FDE/Flat Dark Earth (light brown) (2012-current, limited mfg.) or gray (2015-current, limited mfg.) finish. New 2010.

MSR $649		$500	$440	$400	$375	$335	$295	$250

MODEL 27 GEN 3 SUB-COMPACT – .40 S&W cal., sub-compact variation of the Model 23 Compact, except has shortened grip, 3.42 in. barrel with hexagonal rifling, 9 or 10 shot mag., all Glock sight variations available, thumb rest, finger grooves, no mounting rail, standard black or optional OD/Olive Drab (green) (Gen3 only, 2005-current, limited mfg.) or FDE/Flat Dark Earth (light brown) (Gen3 2012-current, limited mfg.) finish, 21 3/4 oz. New 1995.

MSR $599		$475	$425	$395	$365	$335	$295	$250

MODEL 27 GEN 4 – .40 S&W cal., similar to Model 27 Sub-Compact, except features (less polymid traction) Rough Textured Frame (RTF-4) with recessed thumb rests, finger grooves, and interchangeable frame back straps, includes a reversible enlarged magazine catch, dual recoil spring assembly, and a new trigger system, fixed rear, adj. rear Glock steel, or Glock night sights, standard black or optional FDE/Flat Dark Earth (light brown) (2012-current, limited mfg.) or gray (2015-current, limited mfg.) finish. New 2010.

MSR $649		$500	$440	$400	$375	$335	$295	$250

MODEL 28 GEN 3 SUB-COMPACT – .380 ACP cal., similar to Model 26/27/33/39 Sub-Compact, except has scaled down dimensions with 3.42 in. barrel, thumb rest, finger grooves, no mounting rail, approx. 20 oz. New 1998.

This model is available for law enforcement only (USA).

MODEL 29 GEN 3 SUB-COMPACT – 10mm Norma cal., sub-compact variation of the Model 20, featuring 3.77 in. barrel with hexagonal rifling, 10 shot mag., all Glock sight variations are available, thumb rest, finger grooves, with or w/o (early mfg.) rail, standard black or optional OD/Olive Drab (green) (Gen3 only 2005-current, limited mfg.) finish, 27 oz. New 1996.

MSR $637		$500	$440	$410	$375	$350	$325	$295

* **Model 29SF Gen 3** – 10mm Norma cal., 3.77 in. barrel, Gen3, short frame, all Glock sight options available, new trigger position, thumb rest, finger grooves, mounting accessories rail, otherwise similar to Model 29. New 2009.

MSR $637		$500	$440	$410	$375	$350	$325	$295

MODEL 29 GEN 4 – 10mm Norma cal., similar to Model 29 Sub-compact except features (less polymid traction) Rough Textured Frame (RTF-4) with recessed thumb rest, finger grooves, rail and interchangeable frame back straps, reversible enlarged magazine catch, dual recoil spring assembly, and new trigger system, fixed rear, adj. rear Glock steel, or Glock night sights. New 2012.

MSR $637		$500	$440	$410	$375	$350	$325	$295

MODEL 30 GEN 3 SUB-COMPACT – .45 ACP cal., sub-compact variation of the Model 21 featuring 3.77 in barrel with octagonal rifling, mag. extension, 10 shot mag., all Glock sight options available, thumb rest, finger grooves, with or w/o (early mfg.) rail, standard black or optional OD/Olive Drab Green (Gen3 only 2005-current, limited mfg.) finish, 26 1/2 oz. New 1996.

		$500	$440	$410	$375	$350	$325	$295

* **Model 30SF Gen 3** – .45 ACP cal., 3.77 in. barrel, Gen3 short frame, all Glock sight options available, new trigger position, thumb rest, finger grooves, mounting accessory rail, otherwise similar to Model 30. New 2008.

MSR $637		$500	$440	$410	$375	$350	$325	$295

MSR	100%	98%	95%	90%	80%	70%	60%	Last MSR

* Model 30S Gen 3 – .45 ACP cal., 3.78 in. barrel, Gen3 short frame, all Glock sight options available, new trigger position, recessed thumb rest, finger grooves, accessory rail, otherwise similar to Model 30SF. Model 36 slim style slide. New 2012.

| MSR $637 | $500 | $440 | $410 | $375 | $350 | $325 | $295 | |

MODEL 30 GEN 4 – .45 ACP cal, similar to Model 30 Sub-compact except features (less polymid traction) Rough Textured Frame (RTF-4) with recessed thumb rest, finger grooves, rail and interchangeable frame back straps, reversible enlarged magazine catch, dual recoil spring assembly, and new trigger system, fixed rear, adj. rear Glock steel, or Glock night sights. New 2012.

| MSR $637 | $500 | $440 | $410 | $375 | $350 | $325 | $295 | |

MODEL 31/31C GEN 2, GEN 3 (SPORT/SERVICE) – .357 SIG cal., similar to Model 22, 4.48 in. barrel with hexagonal rifling, ported/non-ported (Model 31-31C Gen3) thumb rests, finger grooves, mounting accessories rail (new 1997-98), all Glock sight options available, 10, 15, or 16 shot mag., Model 31 Gen2 non-ported barrel, checkered grip has no mounting accessories rail, standard black or optional OD/Olive Drab (green) (Gen3 only 2005-current, limited mfg.) finish, 26 oz. New 1997.

| MSR $599 | $475 | $425 | $395 | $365 | $335 | $295 | $250 | |

Add $22 for compensated barrel (Model 31C, fixed rear sight only, new 1998).

Add $119 for competition model w/adj. sights (Model 31CC, mfg. 2000-2004).

MODEL 31 GEN 4 – .357 SIG cal., similar to Model 31, except features (less polymid traction) Rough Textured Frame (RTF-4) with recessed thumb rests, finger grooves rail, and interchangeable frame back straps, includes a reversible enlarged magazine catch, dual recoil spring assembly, and a new trigger system, fixed rear, adj. rear Glock steel, or Glock night sights. New 2010.

| MSR $649 | $500 | $440 | $400 | $375 | $335 | $295 | $250 | |

MODEL 32/32C COMPACT GEN 2, GEN 3 (SPORT/SERVICE) – .357 SIG cal., similar to Model 23, 4.01 in. barrel with hexagonal rifling ported/non-ported (Model 32-32C Gen3), thumb rests, finger grooves, mounting accessories rail (new 1997-98), Model 32 Gen2 non-ported barrel checkered grip, has no mounting accessories rail, all Glock sight options are available, 10, 13, or 14 shot mag., standard black or optional OD/Olive Drab (green) (Gen3 only 2005-current, limited mfg.) finish, 24 oz. New 1997.

| MSR $599 | $475 | $425 | $395 | $365 | $335 | $295 | $250 | |

Add $22 for compensated barrel (Model 32C, fixed rear sight only, new 1998).

Add $119 for competition model w/adj. sights (Model 32CC, mfg. 2002-2004).

MODEL 32 GEN 4 – .357 SIG cal., similar to Model 32 Compact, except features (less polymid traction) Rough Textured Frame (RTF-4) with recessed thumb rests, finger grooves, rail, and interchangeable frame back straps, includes a reversible enlarged magazine catch, dual recoil spring assembly, and a new trigger system, fixed rear, adj. rear Glock steel, or Glock night sights. New 2012.

| MSR $649 | $500 | $440 | $400 | $375 | $335 | $295 | $250 | |

MODEL 33 GEN 3 SUB-COMPACT – .357 SIG cal., sub-compact variation of the Model 32 Compact, shortened grip, 3.42 in. barrel with hexagonal rifling, 9 or 10 shot mag., thumb rest, finger grooves, no mounting rail, standard black or optional OD/Olive Drab (green) (Gen 3 only 2005-current, limited mfg.) finish, 22 oz. New 1997.

| MSR $599 | $475 | $425 | $395 | $365 | $335 | $295 | $250 | |

MODEL 33 GEN 4 – .357 SIG cal., similar to Model 33 Sub-compact, except features (less polymid traction) Rough Textured Frame (RTF-4) with recessed thumb rests, finger grooves, and interchangeable back straps, includes a reversible enlarged magazine catch, dual recoil spring assembly, and a new trigger system, fixed rear, adj. rear Glock steel, or Glock night sights. New 2012.

| MSR $614 | $535 | $450 | $375 | $325 | $295 | $260 | $225 | |

MODEL 34 GEN 3 COMPETITION (SPORT/SERVICE) – 9mm Para. cal., similar features as the Model 17, except has 5.31 in. barrel, recalibrated trigger pull (4 1/2 pull), relieved slide, with hexagonal rifling, extended slide stop lever and magazine catch, adj. rear sights, target grips have recessed thumb rests, mounting accessories rail, 10, 17, or 19 shot mag., standard black or optional OD/Olive Drab (green) (Gen3 only 2005-current, limited mfg.) or FDE/Flat Dark Earth (light brown) (Gen3 2012-current, limited mfg.) finish, 25.75 oz. New 1998.

| MSR $679 | $595 | $525 | $465 | $415 | $360 | $315 | $285 | |

MODEL 34 GEN 4 – 9mm Para. cal., similar to Model 34, except features (less polymid traction) Rough Textured Frame (RTF-4) with recessed thumb rests, finger grooves, rail, and interchangeable frame back straps, includes a reversible enlarged magazine catch, dual recoil spring assembly, and a new trigger system, adj. rear sight only, standard black or optional FDE/Flat Dark Earth (light brown) (2012-current, limited mfg.) or gray (2015-current, limited mfg.) finish. New 2011.

| MSR $729 | $625 | $550 | $495 | $440 | $375 | $325 | $300 | |

MSR	100%	98%	95%	90%	80%	70%	60%	Last MSR

* Model 34 MOS Gen 4 Competition (Sport/Service) – 9mm Para. cal., similar to Model 34, except has Glock MOS, adjustable rear sights, finger grooves, mounting accessories rail. New 2015.

| MSR $840 | $725 | $600 | $500 | $435 | $375 | $325 | $295 | |

MODEL 35 GEN 3 COMPETITION (SPORT/SERVICE) – .40 S&W cal., 10, 15, 16, or 22 shot mag., recessed thumb rest, finger grooves, accessory rail, otherwise similar to Model 34, standard black or optional OD/Olive Drab (green) (Gen3 only 2005-current, limited mfg.) or FDE/Flat Dark Earth (light brown) (Gen3 2012-current, limited mfg.) finish, 27.5 oz. New 1998.

| MSR $679 | $595 | $525 | $465 | $415 | $360 | $315 | $285 | |

MODEL 35 GEN 4 – .40 S&W cal., similar to Model 35, except features (less polymid traction) Rough Textured Frame (RTF-4) with recessed thumb rests, finger grooves, rail, and interchangeable frame back straps, includes a reversible enlarged magazine catch, dual recoil spring assembly, and a new trigger system, adj. rear sight only, standard black or optional FDE/Flat Dark Earth (light brown) (2012-current, limited mfg.) or gray (2015-current, limited mfg.) finish. New 2010.

| MSR $729 | $625 | $550 | $495 | $440 | $375 | $325 | $300 | |

* Model 35 MOS Gen 4 Competition (Sport/Service) – .40 S&W cal., similar to Model 35, except has Glock MOS, adjustable rear sight, finger grooves, mounting accessories rail. New 2015.

| MSR $840 | $725 | $600 | $500 | $435 | $375 | $325 | $295 | |

MODEL 36 GEN 3 SUB-COMPACT – .45 ACP cal., similar to Model 30 Sub-compact, except has single column 6 shot mag., 3.77 in. barrel with octagonal rifling, recessed thumb rest, finger grooves, no rail, all Glock sight options are available, slimmest Glock .45 ACP cal. for concealment, standard black or optional OD/Olive Drab (green) (Gen3 only 2005-current, limited mfg.) finish, 22 1/2 oz. New 1999.

| MSR $637 | $500 | $440 | $410 | $375 | $350 | $325 | $295 | |

MODEL 37 GEN 3 (SPORT/SERVICE) – .45 G.A.P. (Glock Automatic Pistol) cal., 4.48 in. barrel with octagonal rifling, all Glock sight options are available, similar to Model 17, except has extended slide stop lever, wider and heavier slide, improved locking block and ejector, 10 shot semi-staggered column mag., recessed thumb rest, finger grooves, accessory rail, standard black or optional OD/Olive Drab (green) (Gen3 only 2005-current, limited mfg.) finish, 28 3/4 oz. New 2003.

| MSR $614 | $535 | $450 | $375 | $325 | $295 | $260 | $225 | |

MODEL 37 GEN 4 – .45 G.A.P. (Glock Automatic Pistol) cal. similar to Model 37, except features (less polymid traction) Rough Textured Frame (RTF-4) with recessed thumb rests, finger grooves, rail, and interchangeable frame back straps, includes a reversible enlarged magazine catch, dual recoil spring assembly, and a new trigger system, fixed rear, adj. rear Glock steel, or Glock night sights. New 2010.

| MSR $664 | $575 | $495 | $425 | $375 | $325 | $300 | $275 | |

MODEL 38 GEN 3 COMPACT (SPORT/SERVICE) – .45 G.A.P. cal., similar to Model 37, except has 4.01 in. barrel with octagonal rifling, 8 shot semi-staggered column mag., thumb rest, finger grooves, accessory rail, all Glock sight options are available, standard black or optional OD/Olive Drab Green (Gen3 only 2005-current, mfg. limited) finish, 26 oz. New 2005.

| MSR $614 | $535 | $450 | $375 | $325 | $295 | $260 | $225 | |

MODEL 39 GEN 3 SUB-COMPACT – .45 G.A.P. cal., sub-compact variation of the Model 38 Compact, except has shortened grip, 6 shot semi-staggered column mag., 3.42 in. barrel with octagonal rifling, all Glock sight options are available, recessed thumb rest, finger grooves, no rail, standard black or optional OD/Olive Drab Green (Gen3 only 2005-current, limited mfg.) finish, 22 oz. New 2005.

| MSR $614 | $535 | $450 | $375 | $325 | $295 | $260 | $225 | |

MODEL 40 MOS GEN 4 COMPETITION (SPORT/SERVICE) – 10mm Norma cal., similar to the Model 41, except has 6.01 in. hexagonal rifled barrel recalibrated trigger pull (4 1/2 lb. pull) with Glock MOS (Modular Optic System) adjustable rear sight, 10 or 15 shot mag., 31.32 oz. New 2015.

| MSR $840 | $725 | $600 | $500 | $435 | $375 | $325 | $295 | |

MODEL 41 GEN 4 COMPETITION (SPORT/SERVICE) – .45 ACP cal., Gen4 similar to Model 21, except has 5.31 in. barrel, recalibrated 4 1/2 lb. trigger pull, (less polymid traction) Rough Textured Frame (RTF-4), recessed thumb rest, finger grooves, rail, interchangeable frame backstrap, reversible enlarged magazine catch, dual recoil spring assembly, new trigger system, octagonal rifling, adj. rear Glock sights, 10 or 13 shot mag., standard black or optional gray (2015-current, limited mfg.) finish, 27 oz. New 2013.

| MSR $749 | $675 | $575 | $495 | $425 | $375 | $325 | $295 | |

* Model 41 MOS Gen 4 Competition (Sport/Service) – .45 ACP cal., similar to Model 41, except has Glock MOS, adjustable rear sight. New 2015.

| MSR $840 | $725 | $600 | $500 | $435 | $375 | $325 | $295 | |

MSR	100%	98%	95%	90%	80%	70%	60%	Last MSR

MODEL 42 GEN 4 SUB-COMPACT – .380 ACP cal., (Gen4) features "Less Aggressive" Polymid Traction Rough Textured Frame (RTF) single column, fires from standard Glock locked breech, 3.25 in. barrel with hexagonal rifling, 6 shot mag., measures less than 1 inch width, slimmest Glock frame for concealment, reversible enlarged magazine catch, dual recoil spring assembly, new trigger system, thumb rest, no finger grooves and rail, 5 1/2 lb. trigger pull, adj. rear Glock sights, standard black or optional FDE/Flat Dark Earth (light brown) (2015-current, limited mfg.) finish, 13 3/4 oz. New 2013.

| MSR $499 | $475 | $425 | $365 | $335 | $300 | $275 | $250 | |

This model is manufactured in the U.S.

Blue Book Publications selected this model as one of its Top 10 Industry Awards from all the new firearms at the 2014 SHOT Show.

MODEL 43 GEN 4 SUB-COMPACT – 9mm Para. cal., (Gen4) features "Less Aggressive" Polymid Traction Rough Textured Frame (RTF) single column, fires from standard Glock locked breech, 3.39 in. barrel with hexagonal rifling, 6 shot mag., measures less than 1 inch width, slimmest Glock 9mm frame for concealment, reversible enlarged magazine catch, dual recoil spring assembly, new trigger system, thumb rests, no finger grooves and rail, 5 1/2 lb. trigger pull, adj. rear Glock sights, 17.95 oz. Mfg. in Austria. New 2015.

| MSR $599 | $540 | $475 | $430 | $380 | $350 | $325 | $295 | |

GONCZ ARMAMENT, INC.

Previous manufacturer located in North Hollywood, CA circa 1984-1990.

While advertised, BATF records indicate very few Goncz pistols or carbines were actually produced. All of these guns were prototypes or individually hand-built and none were ever mass produced through normal fabrication techniques.

In 1990, Claridge Hi-Tec, Inc. purchased Goncz Armament, Inc.

GRAND POWER s.r.o.

Current manufacturer established in 2002, located in the Slovakia. Currently imported beginning 2014 by Eagle Imports, located in Wanamassa, NJ, and by Century International Arms beginning in 2013, located in Delray Beach, FL. Previously imported until 2007 by STI International, located in Georgetown, TX.

PISTOLS: SEMI-AUTO

K100 – 9mm Para. cal., 4 1/4 in. barrel, 15 shot mag., plastic front and drift adj. steel rear sights, includes four removable polymer hand grips, deep front and rear slide serrations, Picatinny rail on frame, Black finish, 1.81 lbs.

| MSR $629 | $535 | $475 | $400 | $365 | $295 | $240 | $185 | |

K100 X-TRIM – 9mm Para. cal., SA/DA, 4 1/4 in. barrel, 15 shot mag., side adj. steel Dynamic rear sight and fiber optic front sight, blue finish, 1.74 lbs.

| MSR $865 | $735 | $650 | $550 | $500 | $400 | $330 | $250 | |

P1 – 9mm Para. cal., SA/DA, compact version of the K100 model, features 3.66 in. barrel, 15 shot mag., side adj. steel rear sight and plastic front sight, blue finish, 1.7 lbs.

| MSR $629 | $535 | $475 | $400 | $365 | $295 | $240 | $185 | |

P1 ULTRA – 9mm Para. cal., SA/DA, 3.66 in. barrel, 15 shot mag., side adj. Dynamic rear sight and fiber optic front sight, blue finish, 1.61 lbs.

| MSR $789 | $675 | $595 | $500 | $460 | $375 | $300 | $235 | |

P11 – 9mm Para. cal., SA/DA, sub-compact model featuring 3.35 in. barrel, 12 shot mag., blue finish, 1.62 lbs.

| MSR $615 | $525 | $460 | $400 | $350 | $295 | $235 | $185 | |

P40 – .40 S&W cal., SA/DA, 4 1/4 in. barrel with unique rotating barrel mechanism, 14 shot mag., steel dismantling catch, rounded slide, blue finish, 1.94 lbs.

| MSR $819 | $700 | $615 | $525 | $475 | $385 | $315 | $250 | |

P45 – .45 ACP cal., SA/DA, 4 1/4 in. barrel, 10 shot mag., steel dismantling catch, blue finish, 1.87 lbs.

| MSR $819 | $700 | $615 | $525 | $475 | $385 | $315 | $250 | |

CP380D – .380 ACP cal., includes decocker, blue finish. New 2016.

| MSR $528 | $450 | $400 | $365 | $335 | $300 | $275 | $250 | |

P4010M – 10mm cal., blue finish. New 2016.

| MSR $819 | $700 | $615 | $525 | $475 | $385 | $315 | $250 | |

X-CALIBUR – 9mm Para. cal., SA/DA, 4.99 in. barrel, 15 shot mag., side adj. steel Elliason rear sight and fiber optic front sight, extended slide, blue finish, 1.95 lbs.

| MSR $999 | $850 | $750 | $650 | $575 | $475 | $385 | $300 | |

MSR	100%	98%	95%	90%	80%	70%	60%	Last MSR

GRENDEL, INC.

Previous manufacturer located in Rockledge, FL, circa 1990-1995.

PISTOLS: SEMI-AUTO

MODEL P-30 – .22 WMR cal., blowback action, 5 in. barrel, hammerless, matte black finish, 10 (C/B 1994) or 30* shot mag., 21 oz. Mfg. 1990-95.

	$350	$300	$250	$225	$200	$185	$175	$225

Add $25 for electroless nickel finish (disc. 1991).

Add $35 for scope mount (Weaver base).

* **Model P-30M** – similar to Model P-30, except has 5.6 in. barrel with removable muzzle brake. Mfg. 1990-95.

	$350	$300	$250	$225	$200	$185	$175	$235

Add $25 for electroless nickel finish (disc. 1991).

MODEL P-30L – similar to Model P-30, except has 8 in. barrel with removable muzzle brake, 22 oz. Mfg. 1991-92.

	$395	$350	$325	$285	$250	$230	$220	$280

Add $15 for Model P-30LM that allows for fitting various accessories.

MODEL P-31 – .22 WMR cal., same action as P-30, except has 11 in. barrel, enclosed synthetic barrel shroud and flash hider, 48 oz. Mfg. 1990-95.

	$450	$400	$365	$325	$290	$265	$235	$345

RIFLES & CARBINES

MODEL R-31 – .22 WMR cal., similar design to Model P-31 pistol, except has 16 in. barrel and telescoping stock, 64 oz. Mfg. 1991-1995.

	$495	$450	$425	$375	$335	$310	$285	$385

SRT-20F COMPACT – .243 Win. or .308 Win. cal., bolt action based on the Sako A2 action, 20 in. match grade finned barrel with muzzle brake, folding synthetic stock, integrated bipod rest, no sights, 9 shot mag., 6.7 lbs. Disc. 1989.

	$775	$725	$675	$595	$565	$540	$520	$525

Grendel previously manufactured the SRT-16F, SRT-20L, and SRT-24 - all were disc. 1988. Values are approx. the same as the SRT-20F.

GUNCRAFTER INDUSTRIES

Current pistol manufacturer located in Huntsville, AR.

PISTOLS: SEMI-AUTO

MODEL NO. 1 – .45 ACP or .50 GI cal., 1911 style, SA, 7 shot mag., 5 in. heavy match grade barrel, parkerized or hard chrome finish, front strap checkering, Heinie Slant Pro Tritium sights, Aluma checkered grips, includes two mags. and cordura case, 41.3 oz.

MSR $3,185	$2,925	$2,400	$2,050	$1,775	$1,575	$1,350	$1,075	

MODEL NO. 2 – .45 ACP (disc. 2015) or .50 GI cal., 1911 style, 7 shot mag., 5 in. heavy match grade barrel, full profile slide with dust cover frame, integral light rail, parkerized or hard chrome finish, front strap checkering, Heinie Slant Pro Tritium sights, Aluma checkered grips, includes two mags. and cordura case, 45.9 oz.

MSR $3,185	$2,925	$2,400	$2,050	$1,775	$1,575	$1,350	$1,075	

MODEL NO. 3 – .50 GI cal., similar to Model No. 1, except has Commander style frame. New 2010.

MSR $3,185	$2,925	$2,400	$2,050	$1,775	$1,575	$1,350	$1,075	

PISTOL WITH NO NAME – 9mm Para., 10mm, .38 Super, or .45 ACP cal., available with 4 1/2 (either Commander size, or with Officer size frame, Commander size slide/barrel), or 5 in. Match Grade barrel and Government full size frame, single side thumb safety, beveled magwell, solid match trigger, shredder grips, slide top serrations, G.I. Tritium sights, fully dehorned, black melonite finish, includes two mags. and GI logo cordura case, 38 oz. New 2010.

MSR $2,695	$2,400	$2,050	$1,750	$1,550	$1,250	$1,000	$800	

Add $250 for 9mm Para. or .38 Super cal. or $300 for 10mm cal.

Add $335 for No Name Longslide in .45 ACP or $635 for No Name Longslide in 10mm cal.

GUN ROOM CO., LLC

Please refer to the Noreen Firearms LLC listing in the N section.

H SECTION

HM DEFENSE & TECHNOLOGY

Current AR-15 style rifle manufacturer, located in Mount Orab, OH.

MSR	100%	98%	95%	90%	80%	70%	60%	Last MSR

PISTOLS: SEMI-AUTO

HMP15F-556 – 5.56 NATO/.223 Rem. cal., 9 1/2 in. straight fluted stainless steel barrel with flash hider, Magpul PMAG, MOE Magpul black grip, steel gas block, 9 1/4 in. free-floated Picatinny rail, buffer tube with foam pad, full forged receiver, Type III hardcoat black anodized finish.

MSR $845	$725	$650	$580	$515	$450	$385	$340	

HMP15F-300 – .300 AAC Blackout cal., 10 1/2 in. straight fluted stainless steel barrel with flash hider, Magpul PMAG, MOE Magpul black grip, 9 1/4 in. free-floated Picatinny rail, full forged receiver, steel gas block, buffer tube with foam pad, Type III hardcoat black anodized finish.

MSR $845	$725	$650	$580	$515	$450	$385	$340	

RIFLES: SEMI-AUTO

HM15F-300 – .300 AAC Blackout cal., 16 in. spiral fluted stainless barrel, HM black flash hider, Magpul PMAG, MOE Magpul black stock, MOE Magpul black grip, 12 in. Picatinny rail, QD end plate, hard anodized black finish.

MSR $895	$775	$685	$615	$550	$485	$415	$370	

HM15-SPFSS-300 – .300 AAC Blackout cal., 16 in. spiral fluted stainless barrel, Mil-Spec black flash hider, Magpul PMAG, full billet upper and lower receiver, MOE Magpul black stock, MOE Magpul black grip, carbine length or 14 in. Picatinny rail, hardcoat anodized black finish.

MSR $1,495	$1,275	$1,125	$1,025	$875	$750	$625	$525	

Add $50 for 14 in. Picatinny rail (HM15-SPFSS-300-LR).

HM15F-556 – 5.56 NATO/.223 Rem. cal., 16 in. spiral fluted CrMo black barrel, VI-556 black flash hider, Magpul PMAG, Magpul MOE Black grip, 12 in. Picatinny rail, carbine gas system, steel gas block, QD endplate, full forged receiver, Type III black anodized hardcoat finish.

MSR $945	$815	$700	$630	$570	$500	$425	$380	

HM15-MB-556 – 5.56 NATO cal., 16 in. HM Monobloc barrel, V1-556 black flash hider, 30 shot mag., mid-length gas system, integral gas block, billet lower, 12 in. Picatinny HM Defense rail (accepts Magpul MOE 1913 style rail sections), Magpul MOE black buttstock, Magpul MOE black grip, QD endplate, Type III hardcoat anodized black finish, includes special serial number. New 2016.

MSR $1,495	$1,275	$1,125	$1,025	$875	$750	$625	$525	

HM15-SPFCR-556 – 5.56 NATO/.223 Rem. cal., 16 in. spiral fluted CrMo black barrel, VI-556 black flash hider, 30 shot mag., MOE Magpul black stock, MOE Magpul black grip, full billet upper and lower receiver, 12 (HM15-SPFCR-556-F) or 14 in. Picatinny rail, QD endplate, steel gas block, carbine gas system, Type III hardcoat adonized finish.

MSR $1,195	$1,025	$925	$800	$685	$595	$515	$440	

Add $50 for 14 in. Picatinny rail (HM15-SPFCR-556-LR).

HM15-SPFCR-556-FDE – 5.56 NATO/.223 Rem. cal., 16 in. spiral fluted CrMo black barrel, V1-556 black flash hider, 30 shot mag., carbine gas system, steel gas block, 12 in. Picatinny rail, billet lower receiver with FDE Cerakote finish, Magpul MOE black stock, Magpul MOE black grip, QD endplate. New 2016.

MSR $1,295	$1,100	$995	$875	$735	$650	$550	$465	

HM15F-556-S – 5.56 NATO/.223 Rem. cal., 16 in. CrMo black barrel, V1-556 flash hider, 30 shot mag., steel gas block, carbine gas system, 9 in. Picatinny rail (accepts Magpul MOE 1913 style rail sections), Mil-Spec adj. stock, Type III hardcoat anodized black finish. New 2016.

MSR $745	$650	$575	$510	$440	$385	$340	$325	

H-S PRECISION, INC.

Current custom pistol and rifle manufacturer located in Rapid City, SD since 1990. H-S Precision, Inc. also manufactures synthetic stocks and custom machine barrels as well. Dealer and consumer direct sales.

H-S Precision introduced the aluminum bedding block for rifle stocks in 1981, and has been making advanced composite synthetic stocks and custom ballistic test barrels for more than two decades.

In addition to the following models, H-S Precision, Inc. also built rifles using a customer's action (mostly Remington 700 or Winchester Post-'64 Model 70). 2004 MSRs ranged from $1,520-$1,830.

MSR	100%	98%	95%	90%	80%	70%	60%	Last MSR

RIFLES: BOLT ACTION, PRO-SERIES 2000

All H-S Precision rifles feature Kevlar/graphite laminate stocks, cut rifle barrels, and other high tech innovations including a molded aluminum bedding block system. Beginning in 1999, H-S Precision began utilizing their H-S 2000 action, and model nomenclature was changed to begin with Pro-Series 2000.

Add $200 for left-hand action on select models.

PRO-SERIES 2000 HEAVY TACTICAL HTR (HEAVY TACTICAL MARKSMAN) – various cals., 20-26 in. stainless fluted barrel standard, Remington BDL (disc. 1999) or Pro-Series 2000 (new 2000) action. New 1990.

| MSR $3,795 | $3,400 | $3,050 | $2,675 | $2,295 | $2,075 | $1,675 | $1,375 | |

Add $100 for extended barrel port (Model HTR EP, disc.).

PRO SERIES 2000 RAPID DEPLOYMENT RIFLE (RDR) – .308 Win. cal., Pro-Series 2000 stainless steel short action only, 20 in. fluted barrel, black synthetic stock with or w/o thumbhole, black Teflon metal finish, approx. 7 1/2 lbs. New 2000.

| MSR $3,495 | | $3,125 | $2,800 | $1,375 | $2,100 | $1,700 | $1,375 | $1,075 |

Add $400 for thumbhole stock (RDT model, new 2006).

Add $125 for PST60A Long Range stock (disc.).

PRO-SERIES 2000 SHORT TACTICAL (STR) – .204 Ruger-.325 WSM cal., matte Teflon finished action and barrel, 20 in. fluted barrel with standard porting, Pro Series Tactical stock. New 2004.

| MSR $3,795 | | $3,400 | $3,050 | $2,675 | $2,295 | $2,075 | $1,675 | $1,375 |

PRO-SERIES 2000 TAKEDOWN TACTICAL LONG RANGE (TTD) – various short and long action cals., 20-22 in. stainless steel barrel, Remington BDL takedown action, matte blue finish. Mfg. 1990-2005, reintroduced 2008.

| MSR $5,995 | | $5,450 | $4,995 | $4,500 | $4,100 | $3,700 | $3,200 | $2,750 |

Add $100 for extended barrel port (Model TTD EP, disc.).

Add $2,995 - $3,595 for extra takedown barrel, depending on cartridge case head size.

TAKEDOWN LONG RANGE (TACTICAL MARKSMAN) – .223 Rem., .243 Win., .30-06, .308 Win., 7mm Rem. Mag., .300 Win. Mag., or .338 Win. Mag. cal., includes "kwik klip" and stainless fluted barrel. Mfg. 1990-97.

| | $2,495 | $2,050 | $1,675 | $1,350 | $995 | $850 | $750 | *$2,895* |

A complete rifle package consisting of two calibers (.308 Win. and .300 Win. Mag.), scope and fitted case was available for $5,200 retail.

HAGELBERG ARMS DESIGN

Current manufacturer located in Denmark. No current U.S. importation.

RIFLES: BOLT ACTION, SINGLE SHOT

FH-50 – .50 BMG cal., loaded from the buttstock (buttstock is bolt), 23.6 (Variant K) or 35.8 (Variant L) in. barrel, pistol grip, approx. 27 lbs.

Please contact the company directly for pricing and U.S. availability on this model.

HAHN TACTICAL

Current AR-15 style rifle and parts manufacturer, located in Winchester, VA, since 2015.

PISTOLS: SEMI-AUTO

REAPER PISTOL – 5.56 NATO, .223 Wylde, or .300 AAC Blackout cal., 10 in. black Nitrided barrel, Black Rain Ordnance flash hider, Spikes JACK billet lower with a Hahn Tactical upper, 9 in. custom skeleton-themed handguard, Sig stabilizing brace, Magpul MOE backup sights, Mil-Spec trigger with Hahn Tactical adjuster, Magpul MOE grip, custom Cerakote finish. New 2015.

| MSR $1,700 | | $1,450 | $1,275 | $1,125 | $1,000 | $850 | $735 | $595 |

RIFLES: SEMI-AUTO

FREEDOM-15 TACTICAL RIFLE – 5.56 NATO, .223 Wylde, or .300 AAC Blackout cal., 16 in. lightweight fluted black Nitride barrel, Yankee Hill Machine Phantom flash hider/compensator, Hahn Tactical forged aluminum upper and lower with flared magwell, 13 in. handguard, Mil-Spec trigger with Hahn Tactical adjuster, Magpul MOE back up sights, Magpul MOE grip, Magpul CTR stock. New 2015.

| MSR $1,500 | | $1,275 | $1,125 | $1,025 | $875 | $750 | $625 | $525 |

PRECISION 15 – 5.56 NATO, .223 Wylde, or .300 AAC Blackout cal., 16 in. lightweight fluted black Nitride barrel, Yankee Hill Machine Phantom flash hider/compensator, 15 in. handguard, Mil-Spec trigger with Hahn Tactical adjustor, T6 aluminum billet upper and lower, Magpul MOE back up sights, Magpul CTR stock, Magpul MOE grip. New 2015.

| MSR $2,000 | | $1,700 | $1,500 | $1,250 | $1,100 | $950 | $825 | $675 |

MSR	100%	98%	95%	90%	80%	70%	60%	Last MSR

HAKIM

Previous trademark of rifle adopted by the Egyptian army during the early 1950s.

RIFLES: SEMI-AUTO

HAKIM – 7.92x57mm or 8x57mm cal., gas operated, 25.1 in. barrel with muzzle brake, cocking the bolt is done by sliding the top cover forward, then pulling it back, manual safety is located in rear of receiver, 10 shot detachable box mag., can also be reloaded using stripper clips, adj. rear sight, hardwood stock, 9.7 lbs. Approx. 70,000 mfg. circa 1950s-1960s, with Swedish machinery.

	100%	98%	95%	90%	80%	70%	60%
	$495	$450	$400	$360	$320	$285	$245

HALO ARMS, LLC

Previous rifle manufacturer located in Phoenixville, PA from 2003-2013.

Halo Arms also manufactured custom alloy stocks.

RIFLES

Halo Arms, LLC manufactured good quality AR-15 style rifles in commercial, military, and law enforcement configurations.

HA 50 FTR SINGLE SHOT – .50 BMG cal., GIO, 22 in. chrome moly barrel, special order only, matte black finish or optional colors, muzzle brake, vertical aluminum front grip, bipod, Picatinny rail, flip up front sights, rear iron sights, standard AR trigger, unique bottom load/eject operation.

	100%	98%	95%	90%	80%	70%	60%	Last MSR
	$4,100	$3,850	$3,500	$3,150	$2,700	$2,400	$2,000	*$4,350*

Add $300 for deployment package, which includes Storm hard case, cleaning rods, and ammo pouch.

HA 50 LRR SINGLE SHOT – .50 BMG cal., GIO, long range rifle. Disc. 2008.

	100%	98%	95%	90%	80%	70%	60%	Last MSR
	$4,200	$3,900	$3,500	$3,150	$2,700	$2,400	$2,000	*$4,500*

HA 308 FTR BOLT ACTION – .308 Win. cal., field tactical rifle, GIO, 24 in. heavy contour chrome moly barrel, 5 shot internal mag. with screw removable floorplate, three position safety, matte black finish or optional colors, Picatinny rail, right hand bolt and ejection port, full length vented free float tube with rail attachment points, hand tuned trigger, 11 1/2 lbs. Disc. 2009.

	100%	98%	95%	90%	80%	70%	60%	Last MSR
	$1,295	$1,100	$925	$800	$675	$575	$475	*$1,375*

F-BAR BOLT ACTION – .204 Ruger, .22-250 Rem., .223 Rem., .243 Win., or .308 Win. cal., GIO, matte black finish standard, custom colors available, 24 in. heavy contour chrome moly barrel, 5 shot, full length vented free float tube, Picatinny rail, hand tuned trigger, 11 1/2 lbs.

	100%	98%	95%	90%	80%	70%	60%	Last MSR
	$1,375	$1,200	$1,025	$900	$775	$650	$525	*$1,455*

Add $18 for tube Picatinny rail.
Add $25 for vertical grip or bipod mount.
Add $45 for monopod.

MAXIMUS BOLT ACTION – .416 Barrett or .50 BMG cal., GIO, 22 or 30 in. sporter contour chrome moly target barrel, matte black finish standard, custom colors available, benchrest single shot, integral flat bottom, full length forearm, Picatinny rail, dual stock struts, muzzle brake, Jewell trigger, two-position safety, 25 lbs.

	100%	98%	95%	90%	80%	70%	60%	Last MSR
	$4,750	$4,250	$3,600	$3,000	$2,500	$2,000	$1,625	*$5,185*

Add $18 for Picatinny rail forearm.
Add $25 for vertical grip.
Add $30 for bipod mount.
Add $55 for monopod.

M-BAR MONOLITH BOLT ACTION – .204 Ruger, .22-250 Rem., .223 Rem., .243 Win., or .308 Win. cal., GIO, matte black finish standard, custom colors available, 24 in. heavy contour chrome moly barrel, 5 shot, Picatinny rail, hand tuned trigger, three position safety, 11 1/2 lbs.

	100%	98%	95%	90%	80%	70%	60%	Last MSR
	$1,325	$1,175	$1,000	$875	$750	$650	$525	*$1,395*

Add $18 for tube Picatinny rail.
Add $25 for vertical grip or bipod mount.
Add $45 for monopod.

HARRINGTON & RICHARDSON, INC.

Previous manufacturer located in Gardner, MA - formerly from Worcester, MA. Successors to Wesson & Harrington, manufactured from 1871 until January 24, 1986. H & R 1871, LLC was formed during 1991 (an entirely different company). H & R 1871, LLC is not responsible for the warranties or safety of older pre-1986 H & R firearms.

A manufacturer of utilitarian firearms for over 115 years, H & R ceased operation on January 24, 1986. Even though new manufacture (under H & R 1871, LLC) is utilizing the H & R trademark, the discontinuance of older models in either NIB or

MSR	100%	98%	95%	90%	80%	70%	60%	Last MSR

mint condition may command slight asking premiums, but probably will not affect values on those handguns only recently discontinued. Most H & R firearms are still purchased for their shooting value rather than collecting potential. In recent years, pre-1950s examples have become increasingly more collectible.

Further recent research indicates that many H&R frames were manufactured and stamped with serial numbers in the mid-1930s, but not assembled as complete guns until the WWII era. Therefore, H&R serial numbers alone will not always indicate the variation number.

Please refer to H & R listing in the Serialization section online at www.bluebookofgunvalues.com for alphabetical suffix information on how to determine year of manufacture for most H & R firearms between 1940-1982.

The author would like to thank the late Mr. Jim Hauff and the late Mr. W.E. "Bill" Goforth for providing pricing and information on many of the H&R models.

RIFLES

MODEL 60 REISING SEMI-AUTO – .45 ACP cal., delayed blowback action, 18 1/4 in. barrel, parkerized finish, 10 or 20 shot detachable box mag., front post and adj. rear sight, pistol grip walnut stock, sling swivels, semi-auto version of the Model 50. Mfg. 1944-1946.

	100%	98%	95%	90%	80%	70%	60%
	$2,800	$2,400	$1,925	$1,575	$1,275	$1,050	$900

MODEL M-4 SURVIVAL – .22 Hornet cal., 5 shot mag., 14 or 16 in. barrel, wire collapsible stock. Mfg. for U.S. military during the 1950s.

	100%	98%	95%	90%	80%	70%	60%
	$2,000	$1,650	$1,425	$1,125	$965	$855	$750

Add $400 for barrels less than 16 in. (sales restricted).

This model was packaged in survival kits for U.S. pilots, and is usually encountered with a replacement barrel of 16 inches or more.

MODEL M-1 GARAND – refer to U.S. Military Long Arms in the U section.

MODEL T-48 FAL/T223 (H&R MFG. FAL) – .308 Win. cal., 20 shot mag., selective fire. Approx. 200 mfg. for U.S. military during the 1960s.

Recent values are approx. $10,000 for 98% condition.

Since sales of this rifle are restricted, it is not often encountered in the used marketplace.

M-14 RIFLE/GUERILLA GUN – .308 Win. cal., selective fire, 20 shot mag., Guerilla gun mfg. in prototype only. Mfg. for the U.S. military during the 1960s.

Recent values are approx. $20,000 for 98% condition.

Since sales of this rifle are restricted, it is not often encountered in the used marketplace.

M-16 AUTOMATIC BATTLE RIFLE – 5.56 NATO cal., selective fire, 20 or 30 shot mag. Mfg. for the U.S. military during the 1960s-1970s.

Recent values are approx. $15,000 for 98% condition.

Since sales of this rifle are restricted, it is not often encountered in the used marketplace.

T-223 (H&R MFG. H&K 93) – .223 Rem. or .308 Win. cal., selective fire, 20 shot mag. Approx. 200 mfg. for the U.S. military during the 1960s.

Recent values are approx. $15,000 for 98% condition.

Since sales of this rifle are restricted, it is not often encountered in the used marketplace.

HARRIS GUNWORKS

Previous firearms manufacturer located in Phoenix, AZ 1995-March 31, 2000. Previously named Harris-McMillan Gunworks and G. McMillan and Co., Inc.

RIFLES: BOLT ACTION

M-40 SNIPER RIFLE – .308 Win. cal., Remington action with McMillan match grade heavy contour barrel, fiberglass stock with recoil pad, 4 shot mag., 9 lbs. Mfg. 1990-2000.

	100%	98%	95%	90%	80%	70%	60%	Last MSR
	$1,825	$1,450	$1,125	$925	$800	$700	$600	$2,000

M-86 SNIPER RIFLE – .300 Phoenix (disc. 1996), .30-06 (new 1989), .300 Win. Mag., or .308 Win. cal., fiberglass stock, variety of optical sights. Mfg. 1988-2000.

	100%	98%	95%	90%	80%	70%	60%	Last MSR
	$2,450	$2,000	$1,675	$1,325	$1,000	$895	$800	$2,700

Add $300 for .300 Phoenix cal. with Harris action (disc. 1996).
Add $200 for takedown feature (mfg. 1993-96).

M-87 LONG RANGE SNIPER RIFLE – .50 BMG cal., stainless steel bolt action, 29 in. barrel with muzzle brake, single shot, camo synthetic stock, accurate to 1,500 meters, 21 lbs. Mfg. 1988-2000.

	100%	98%	95%	90%	80%	70%	60%	Last MSR
	$3,450	$2,800	$2,375	$2,000	$1,850	$1,700	$1,575	$3,885

MSR	100%	98%	95%	90%	80%	70%	60%	Last MSR

* M-87R Long Range Sniper Rifle – similiar specs. as Model 87, except has 5 shot fixed box mag. Mfg. 1990-2000.

	100%	98%	95%	90%	80%	70%	60%	Last MSR
	$3,725	$2,950	$2,550	$2,200	$2,000	$1,850	$1,700	$4,000

M-88 U.S. NAVY – .50 BMG cal., reintroduced U.S. Navy Seal Team shell holder single shot action with thumbhole stock (one-piece or breakdown two-piece), 24 lbs. Mfg. 1997-2000.

	100%	98%	95%	90%	80%	70%	60%	Last MSR
	$3,250	$2,600	$2,200	$1,625	$1,250	$1,125	$900	$3,600

Add $300 for two-piece breakdown stock.

M-89 SNIPER RIFLE – .308 Win. cal., 28 in. barrel with suppressor (also available without), fiberglass stock adj. for length and recoil pad, 15 1/4 lbs. Mfg. 1990-2000.

	100%	98%	95%	90%	80%	70%	60%	Last MSR
	$2,875	$2,525	$2,250	$1,875	$1,650	$1,325	$1,100	$3,200

Add $425 for muzzle suppressor (disc. 1996).

M-92 BULL PUP – .50 BMG cal., bullpup configuration with shorter barrel. Mfg. 1993-2000.

	100%	98%	95%	90%	80%	70%	60%	Last MSR
	$4,300	$3,250	$2,750	$2,300	$2,050	$1,850	$1,700	$4,770

M-93 – .50 BMG cal., similar to M-87, except has folding stock and detachable 5 or 10 shot box mag. Mfg. 1993-2000.

	100%	98%	95%	90%	80%	70%	60%	Last MSR
	$3,800	$3,250	$2,750	$2,300	$2,000	$1,850	$1,700	$4,150

Add $300 for two-piece folding stock or dovetail combo quick disassembly fixture.

M-95 TITANIUM/GRAPHITE – .50 BMG cal., features titanium alloy M-87 receiver with graphite barrel and steel liner, single shot or repeater, approx. 18 lbs. Mfg. 1997-2000.

	100%	98%	95%	90%	80%	70%	60%	Last MSR
	$4,650	$4,175	$3,475	$2,875	$2,300	$2,050	$1,850	$5,085

Add $165 for fixed mag.
Add $315 for detachable mag.

RIFLES: SEMI-AUTO

M-96 – .50 BMG cal., gas-operated with 5 shot detachable mag., carry handle scope mount, steel receiver, 30 lbs. Mfg. 1997-2000.

	100%	98%	95%	90%	80%	70%	60%	Last MSR
	$6,200	$5,625	$5,075	$4,650	$4,175	$3,475	$2,875	$6,800

HATCHER GUN COMPANY

Current custom pistol, rifle, and shotgun manufacturer located in Elsie, NE and established in 1983.

Hatcher Gun Company manufactures custom pistols, rifles, and shotguns for both the civilian and law enforcement marketplaces. Rifles include a series of AR-15 models in various barrel lengths and configurations, pistols include a bolt action model based on the Remington XP-100, and shotguns include modified Saiga semi-autos, NFA items include short barreled Saiga's and SxS shotguns. Please contact the company directly for more information, availability, and pricing (see Trademark Index).

HEAD DOWN PRODUCTS, LLC

Current AR-15 style semi-auto rifle manufacturer located in Dallas, GA. Previously distributed until 2013 by American Tactical Imports, located in Rochester, NY.

CARBINES/RIFLES: SEMI-AUTO

All Head Down rifles are available in a short barreled configuration for military/law enforcement, include a hard case and limited lifetime warranty.

ARCADIUS-DMR .308 BILLET RIFLE – .308 Win. cal., 22 in. stainless steel HDP profile barrel with PVX muzzle device, rifle-length gas system, 20 shot PMAG 15 in. HD Gen II Mod II rail, single stage drop-in trigger, ambi Raptor charging handle with Head Down skull engraved, billet upper and lower receivers, integral trigger guard, flared magwell, Magpul PRS stock, Ergo ambi pistol grip, Type III hardcoat anodized finish. New 2015.

MSR $2,199							
	$1,875	$1,650	$1,400	$1,200	$1,025	$875	$725

ARCADIUS-MR .308 BILLET RIFLE – .308 Win. cal., 18 in. stainless steel HDP profile barrel with PVX muzzle device, 20 shot PMAG, mid-length gas system, 15 in. HD Gen II MOD II rail, single stage drop-in trigger, ambi Raptor charging handle with Head Down skull engraved, billet upper and lower receivers, integral trigger guard, flared magwell, Magpul PRS stock, Ergo ambi pistol grip, Type III hardcoat anodized finish. New 2015.

MSR $2,099							
	$1,795	$1,575	$1,325	$1,150	$995	$850	$700

ARCADIUS-PR .308 BILLET RIFLE – .308 Win. cal., 16 in. stainless steel HDP profile barrel with PVX muzzle device, 20 shot PMAG, mid-length gas system, 13 in. HD Gen II Mod II rail, single stage drop-in trigger, ambi Raptor charging handle with Head Down skull engraved, billet upper and lower receivers, integral trigger guard, flared magwell, HDF stock, Ergo ambi grip, Type III hardcoat anodized finish. New 2015.

MSR $1,899							
	$1,625	$1,425	$1,200	$1,075	$925	$795	$650

MSR	100%	98%	95%	90%	80%	70%	60%	Last MSR

ARCADIUS-S .308 BILLET RIFLE – .308 Win. cal., 16 in. stainless steel HDP profile barrel with A2 flash hider, 20 shot PMAG, carbine length gas system, 10 in. HD Gen II MOD II rail, billet upper and lower receivers, integral trigger guard, flared magwell, 6-pos. stock, Mil-Spec plastic pistol grip, Type III hardcoat anodized finish. New 2015.

| MSR $1,659 | $1,375 | $1,215 | $1,075 | $950 | $815 | $700 | $575 | |

HDX TAC7 – 5.56 NATO cal., GIO, 16 in. profile Melonite coated barrel, 7 in. free floating rail system handguard, matte black hardcoat anodized finish, 6-position collapsible stock with standard pistol grip, two 30 shot mags., A2 flash hider, forged upper and lower receiver, flared magwell, vertical bipod grip, two rail covers. Disc. 2013.

| | $925 | $850 | $725 | $625 | $550 | $475 | $425 | *$1,099* |

MK12 BILLET RIFLE – 5.56 NATO cal., GIO, 18 in. HDP profile barrel with A2 flash hider, 20 shot Lancer mag., 15 in. Provectus rail system, single stage drop-in trigger, ambi Raptor charging handle with Head Down skull engraved, milled billet upper and lower receivers, integral trigger guard, flared magwell, HDF stock, Ergo rubber ambi pistol grip, hardcoat anodized finish, includes hard rifle case. Mfg. 2013-2015.

| | $1,625 | $1,425 | $1,200 | $1,075 | $925 | $795 | $650 | *$1,899* |

PREDATOR PACKAGE + NIGHTVISION KIT – 5.56 NATO cal., 16 in. HDP profile barrel with A2 flash hider, two 20 shot Lancer mags., mid-length gas system, HD Provectus 13 in. rail system, single stage drop-in trigger, Luna Gen 2+ Nightvision scope, Luna extended range laser IR, Magpul rail mounted sling adapter, ambi Raptor charging handle with Head Down skull engraved, billet upper and lower receivers, integral trigger guard, flared magwell, HDF stock, Ergo rubber ambi pistol grip, hardcoat anodized finish, includes custom foam hard case. New 2015.

| MSR $4,500 | $3,825 | $3,345 | $2,870 | $2,600 | $2,100 | $1,725 | $1,400 | |

PROVECTUS PV9 GEN I BILLET RIFLE – .300 AAC Blackout or 5.56 NATO cal., GIO, 16 in. HDP profile barrel with PVX muzzle device, flat-top Picatinny receiver with integrated 9, 13, or 15 in. Provectus quad rail, billet upper/lower receiver, HDF 6-position buttstock, Ergo rubber ambi pistol grip, 30 shot Lancer mag., integral trigger guard, flared magwell, Type III hardcoat anodized finish. New 2013.

| MSR $1,650 | $1,375 | $1,215 | $1,075 | $950 | $815 | $700 | $575 | |

Add $85 for 13 in. or $350 for 15 in. Provectus quad rail.

Add $100 for .300 AAC Blackout cal.

PROVECTUS PV10 GEN II BILLET RIFLE – 5.56 NATO cal., 16 in. HDP profile barrel with PVX muzzle device, 30 shot Lancer mag., mid-length gas system, HD Gen II 10 in. rail system, single stage drop-in trigger, ambi Raptor charging handle with Head Down skull engraved, HDF Stock, Ergo rubber ambi grip, milled billet upper and lower receivers, integral trigger guard, flared magwell, Type III hardcoat anodized finish. New 2015.

| MSR $1,650 | $1,375 | $1,215 | $1,075 | $950 | $815 | $700 | $575 | |

PROVECTUS PV13 BILLET RIFLE – 5.56 NATO or .300 AAC Blackout cal., GIO, 16 in. HDP profile barrel, PVX muzzle device, matte black hardcoat anodized finish, HD Gen II 13 in. Provectus rail system handguard, HDF adj. stock with Ergo rubber ambi pistol grip, 30 shot Lancer mag., nickel boron carrier group, precision milled upper and lower receiver, integral trigger guard, flared magwell, Type III hardcoat anodized finish.

| MSR $1,650 | $1,375 | $1,215 | $1,075 | $950 | $815 | $700 | $575 | |

Add $125 for .300 AAC Blackout cal.

PROVECTUS PV15 GEN II BILLET RIFLE – 5.56 NATO or .300 AAC Blackout cal., GIO, 16 in. profile Melonite coated barrel, matte black hardcoat anodized finish, 15 in. Provectus rail system handguard, HDF adj. stock with Ergo rubber ambi pistol grip, 30 shot Lancer mag., A2 flash hider, Geissle two-stage trigger, nickel boron carrier group, precision milled upper and lower receiver, integral trigger guard, flared magwell.

| MSR $1,650 | $1,375 | $1,215 | $1,075 | $950 | $815 | $700 | $575 | |

Add $115 for .300 AAC Blackout cal.

TRITON M4 BILLET RIFLE (HDX M4) – 5.56 NATO cal., GIO, 16 in. profile Melonite coated barrel, matte black hardcoat anodized finish, Mil-Spec handguard, 6-position collapsible stock with standard pistol grip, 30 shot mag., A2 flash hider, forged upper and lower receiver, flared magwell.

| MSR $849 | $725 | $650 | $580 | $515 | $450 | $385 | $340 | |

TRITON 7 BILLET RIFLE – 5.56 NATO cal., 15 in. HDP profile barrel with A2 flash hider, 30 shot Lancer mag., carbine length gas system, 7 in. two-piece carbine length quad rail, milled billet upper and lower receivers, flared magwell, integral trigger guard, A2 adj. stock, plastic grip, Type III hardcoat anodized finish. New 2015.

| MSR $899 | $775 | $685 | $615 | $550 | $485 | $415 | $370 | |

TRITON 10 GEN II BILLET RIFLE (HDX TAC10) – 5.56 NATO cal., GIO, 16 in. profile Melonite coated steel barrel, 10 in. free floating rail system handguard, matte black hardcoat anodized finish, 6-position collapsible stock with standard pistol grip, 30 shot Lancer mag., A2 flash hider, forged upper and lower receiver, flared magwell, vertical bipod grip, two rail covers, Mil-Spec bolt carrier group.

| MSR $999 | $850 | $725 | $650 | $585 | $515 | $450 | $395 | |

MSR	100%	98%	95%	90%	80%	70%	60%	Last MSR

TRITON 12 BILLET RIFLE (HDX TAC12) – 5.56 NATO cal., GIO, 16 in. profile Melonite coated steel barrel, 12 in. free floating rail system handguard, matte black hardcoat anodized finish, 6-position collapsible stock with standard pistol grip, two 30 shot mags., A2 flash hider, forged upper and lower receiver, flared magwell, vertical bipod grip, two rail covers, Mil-Spec bolt carrier group.

MSR $1,099	$925	$850	$725	$625	$550	$475	$425	

TRITON 15 GEN II BILLET RIFLE – 5.56 NATO cal., GIO, 16 in. HDP profile barrel with A2 flash hider, 30 shot Lancer mag., billet upper and lower receivers, 15 in. free floating quad rail, MFT stock, plastic Mil-Spec grip, Type III hardcoat anodized finish. New 2015.

MSR $1,149	$960	$875	$740	$625	$550	$475	$425	

PISTOLS: SEMI-AUTO

PROVECTUS PV9 BILLET PISTOL – 5.56 NATO cal., 7 1/2 in. HDP profile barrel with A2 flash hider, 30 shot Lancer mag., HD Provectus 9 in. rail system, single stage drop-in trigger, integral trigger guard, ambi Raptor charging handle with Head Down skull engraved, milled billet upper and lower receivers, flared magwell, SIG brace, Ergo rubber ambi grip, hardcoat anodized finish, includes hard rifle case. New 2015.

MSR $1,650	$1,375	$1,215	$1,075	$950	$815	$700	$575	

TRITON BILLET PISTOL – 5.56 NATO cal., 7 1/2 in. HDP profile barrel with A2 flash hider, 30 shot Lancer mag., 7 in. CAR length quad rail, integral trigger guard, flared magwell, SIG stock, plastic grip, Type III hardcoat anodized finish. New 2015.

MSR $1,199	$1,025	$925	$800	$685	$595	$515	$440	

HECKLER & KOCH

Current manufacturer established in 1949, and located in Oberndorf/Neckar, Germany. Currently imported and distributed beginning mid-2008 by H & K USA, located in Columbus, GA. .22 LR cal. pistols and rifles are currently imported by Walther Arms, located in Fort Smith, AR. Previously imported by Merkel USA, located in Trussville, AL, by Heckler & Koch, Inc. located in Sterling, VA (previously located in Chantilly, VA). During 2004, H & K built a new plant in Columbus, GA, primarily to manufacture guns for American military and law enforcement.

In early 1991, H & K was absorbed by Royal Ordnance, a division of British Aerospace (BAE Systems) located in England. During December 2002, BAE Systems sold Heckler & Koch to a group of European investors. Heckler & Koch, Inc. and HKJS GmbH are wholly owned subsidiaries of Suhler Jag und Sportwaffen Holding GmbH and the sole licensees of Heckler & Koch commercial firearms technology.

PISTOLS: SEMI-AUTO, RECENT MFG.

USP and USP Compact (with bobbed hammer) Models are divided into 10 variants. They include: USP Variant 1 (DA/SA with control safety decocking lever on left), USP Variant 2 (DA/SA with control safety decocking lever on right), USP Variant 3 (DA/SA with control safety decocking lever on left), USP Variant 4 (DA/SA with control safety decocking lever on right), USP Variant 5 (DAO with control safety decocking lever on left), USP Variant 6 (DAO with control safety decocking lever on right), USP Variant 7 (DAO with no control lever), USP Variant 9 (DA/SA with safety control lever on left), and USP Variant 10 (DA/SA with safety control lever on right). Please contact your H&K dealer for pricing on these variants.

LEM refers to Law Enforcement Modification (enhanced DAO and conventional SA/DA with serrated decocking button on rear of frame).

All currently manufactured H&K pistols feature a patented lock-out safety device which blocks the hammer strut and slide.
Add $65 for variant change or night sights prior to shipping on currently manufactured USP and USP Compact models.
Add $387 for laser sighting device BA-6 (mfg. 2002-2005).

HK-4 – First and Second Variations. Mfg. 1968-1973.

* **HK-4 First Variation** – .22 LR, .25 ACP, .32 ACP, or .380 ACP, DA, blowback action; 8 (.380 ACP), 9 (.32 ACP), or 10 (.22 LR or .25 ACP) shot mag., high polished blue finish on slide, matte black finish, brown checkered plastic grips with HK logo, fixed front sight, adj. rear sight, firing pin block safety mounted on the left side of the slide, 18 oz. Mfg. 1967-1970.

	$485	$435	$360	$300	$265	$220	$195	

An early four barrel set in all calibers with recoil springs, 4 mags., .22 cal. ejector, bolt tool and four plastic fitted cases is currently priced in the $2,000 range.
A late four barrel set in all calibers with recoil springs, 4 mags., .22 cal. ejector, bolt tool and two cardboard fitted cases is currently priced in the $1,500 range.

* **HK-4 Second Variation** – .380 ACP cal., 8 shot mag., DA, blue finish, blowback action, adj. rear sight, 22 LR cal. conversion kit with 10 round magazine offered as an option, fixed front sight, adj. rear sight, firing pin block safety mounted on the left side of the slide, 18 oz. Mfg. 1971-1973.

	$475	$425	$355	$300	$260	$220	$195	

Add approx. 10%-15% for .22 LR cal. conversion kit.

MSR	100%	98%	95%	90%	80%	70%	60%	Last MSR

HK-4 COMMEMORATIVE COMBO – includes one .22 LR cal. and one .380 ACP cal. barrel, in wooden presentation with gold plating for H&R. Mfg. 1971.

	100%	98%	95%	90%	80%	70%	60%	Last MSR
	$950	$850	$750	$650	$550	$450	$400	

P9S – .45 ACP or 9mm Para. cal., DA/SA combat model, 4 in. barrel, roller lock delayed blowback action, blue (early mfg.) or phosphate finish, sculptured plastic grips, fixed sights. Although production ceased in 1984, limited quantities were available until 1989.

	100%	98%	95%	90%	80%	70%	60%	Last MSR
	$950	$875	$775	$650	$525	$450	$375	$1,299

Add 20% for .45 ACP.

Add 50% for pistols marked "P9".

P9S TARGET – .45 ACP or 9mm Para. cal., 4 in. barrel, DA/SA, phosphate finish, adj. sights and trigger. Although production ceased in 1984, limited quantities were available until 1989.

	100%	98%	95%	90%	80%	70%	60%	Last MSR
	$1,500	$1,275	$1,050	$925	$800	$700	$600	$1,382

Add 20% for .45 ACP cal.

P9S COMPETITION KIT SPORT MODEL – 9mm Para. or .45 ACP (rare) cal., similar to P9S Target, except extra 5 1/2 in. barrel and weight, competition walnut grip, 2 slides, with factory case. Disc. 1984.

	100%	98%	95%	90%	80%	70%	60%	Last MSR
Sport 1	$3,000	$2,650	$2,300	$2,050	$1,800	$1,600	$1,400	
Sport 2	$4,000	$3,500	$3,000	$2,500	$2,000	$1,600	$1,400	
Sport 3	$5,000	$4,500	$4,000	$3,500	$3,000	$2,500	$2,000	$2,250

P7 PSP – 9mm Para. cal., SFO, older variation of the P7 M8, without extended trigger guard, ambidextrous mag. release (European style), or heat shield. Standard production ceased 1986. A reissue of this model was mfg. in 1990, with approx. 150 produced. Limited quantities remained through 1999.

	100%	98%	95%	90%	80%	70%	60%	Last MSR
	$1,200	$1,075	$900	$800	$700	$600	$500	
European Model	$2,000	$1,800	$1,500	$1,300	$1,000	$800	$700	$1,111

The PSP is serial numbered 001-239. The PSP/P7 is serial numbered 240-251, and the P7 serialization starts at 252.

P7 M8 – 9mm Para. cal., unique squeeze cocking single action, SFO, extended square combat type trigger guard with heat shield, 4.13 in. fixed barrel with polygonal rifling, 8 shot mag., ambidextrous mag. release, fixed 3-dot sighting system, stippled black plastic grips, black phosphate or nickel (mfg. 1992-2000) finish, includes 2 mags., 28 oz. Disc. 2005.

	100%	98%	95%	90%	80%	70%	60%	Last MSR
	$2,250	$2,000	$1,750	$1,500	$1,175	$800	$650	$1,515

Add 30% for nickel/hard chrome finish.

Add $100 for Tritium sights (various colors, new 1993).

Add $1,200 for .22 LR conversion kit (barrel, slide, and two mags., disc. 1999).

P7 M13 – similar to P7 M8, only with staggered 13 shot mag., SFO, 30 oz. Disc. 1994.

	100%	98%	95%	90%	80%	70%	60%	Last MSR
	$3,200	$2,825	$2,500	$2,250	$1,875	$1,475	$1,250	$1,330

Add 20% for nickel/hard chrome finish.

Add $85 for Tritium sights (various colors, new 1993).

Add $150 for factory wood grips.

P7 M10 – .40 S&W cal., similar specifications as P7 M13, except has 10 shot mag., SFO, 39 oz. Mfg. 1991-1994.

	100%	98%	95%	90%	80%	70%	60%	Last MSR
	$3,200	$2,825	$2,500	$2,250	$1,875	$1,475	$1,250	$1,315

Add 20% for nickel/hard chrome finish.

Add $85 for Tritium sights (various colors, new 1993).

P7 K3 – .22 LR or .380 ACP cal., uses unique oil-filled buffer to decrease recoil, 3.8 in. barrel, matte black or nickel (less common) finish, 8 shot mag. (includes 2), 26 1/2 oz. Mfg. 1988-94.

	100%	98%	95%	90%	80%	70%	60%	Last MSR
	$2,200	$1,950	$1,750	$1,475	$1,250	$1,050	$875	$1,100

Add $1,500 for .22 LR conversion kit.

Add $1,000 for .32 ACP conversion kit.

Add $85 for Tritium sights (various colors, new 1993).

HK45 – .45 ACP cal., DA/SA and variants (10), 10 shot mag., 4.53 in. O-ring barrel with polygonal rifling, features black, OD Green (new 2015), or tan (new 2015) Cerakote slide and polymer frame with finger groove grips, integrated Picatinny rail, low profile 3-dot sights, interchangable grip panels, twin slide serrations, internal mechanical recoil reduction system reduces recoil 30%, ambidextrous controls, includes one additional backstrap and two 10 shot mags., 27.7 oz. New 2008.

MSR	100%	98%	95%	90%	80%	70%	60%	Last MSR
$1,199	$1,025	$900	$800	$675	$550	$500	$450	

Add $100 for LEM trigger DAO.

Add $100 for three 10 shot mags. and night sights.

MSR	100%	98%	95%	90%	80%	70%	60%	Last MSR

* **HK45 Tactical** – .45 ACP cal., choice of DA/SA with safety decocking lever on left or LEM trigger, or DAO with no safety/decocking lever, with threaded barrel, high profile Tritium three-dot sights (new 2015), choice of black, tan, or green frame, includes one additional backstrap. New 2013.

| MSR $1,399 | $1,225 | $1,050 | $925 | $800 | $675 | $550 | $475 | |

Add $100 for LEM trigger DAO, or for three 10 shot mags.

HK45 COMPACT – .45 ACP cal., 3.9 in. barrel, 8 or 10 shot mag. with ginger grip floorplate, small grip frame, ambidextrous slide release levers, bobbed hammer, 3-dot sights, adj. backstrap, black, OD Green (new 2015), or tan (new 2015) Cerakoted slide and matching polymer frame, includes 2 magazines and one additional backstrap, 28.5 oz. New 2008.

| MSR $1,199 | $1,025 | $900 | $800 | $675 | $550 | $500 | $450 | |

Add $100 for LEM trigger DAO or three 8 shot mags. with night sights.

* **HK45 Compact Tactical** – .45 ACP cal., similar to HK45 Compact, except has 4.57 in. threaded barrel, safety/decocking lever on left side, spur hammer, high profile Tritium three-dot sights (new 2015), includes 2 magazines, and one additional backstrap, 29 oz. New 2011.

| MSR $1,399 | $1,225 | $1,050 | $925 | $800 | $675 | $550 | $475 | |

Add $100 for decocking lever on left side, LEM trigger, or for two 10 shot mags. and one 8 shot mag.

HK-416 – .22 LR cal., 10 or 20 shot mag., pistol variation of the Model 416 rifle, blowback action, 9 in. barrel, SA, steel receiver, fixed front sight, external safety, quad Picatinny rail with open sights, including diopter adj. rear sight, black finish, approx. 5 lbs, mfg. by Carl Walther in Ulm, Germany, and imported by Walther Arms. New mid-2009.

| MSR $499 | $450 | $395 | $360 | $330 | $300 | $265 | $235 | |

P30 – 9mm Para. or .40 S&W (new 2011) cal., 3.86 in. barrel with polygonal rifling, 10 (CA only), 13 (.40 S&W cal.) or 15 (9mm Para. cal. only) shot mag., 3-dot sights, lower Picatinny rail, self decocking DA spur hammer, multiple trigger variants including DA/SA, or standard (disc. 2012) or lightened LEM DAO (new 2012) trigger, firing pin block safety, loaded chamber indicator, ergonomic grips with interchangeable side panels and backstraps, double slide serrations, internal recoil reduction system, approx. 23 oz. Importation began mid-2007.

| MSR $1,099 | $950 | $795 | $675 | $550 | $450 | $400 | $375 | |

Add $100 for three extra magazines and night sights (new 2014).

* **P30L** – similar to P30, except has 4 1/2 in. barrel and 1/2 in. longer slide, 27.5 oz. New 2009.

| MSR $1,149 | $975 | $825 | $695 | $575 | $475 | $425 | $395 | |

Add $100 for three 15 shot magazines and night sights (new 2014).

* **P30LS** – DA/SA, similar to P30L, except has ambidextrous safety lever/rear decocking button, and includes two 15 shot magazines.

| MSR $1,149 | $975 | $825 | $695 | $575 | $475 | $425 | $395 | |

Add $100 for three 15 shot magazines and night sights (new 2014).

* **P30S** – 9mm Para. or .40 S&W cal., DA/SA, 3.85 in. barrel with polygonal rifling and lower Picatinny rail, two 13 or 15 (9mm Para. cal. only) shot mags., spur hammer with decocking lever on back of frame, 3-dot sights, ergonomic grips with interchangeable side panels and backstraps, firing pin block safety and ambidextrous safety lever, double slide serrations, internal recoil reduction system, loaded chamber indicator.

| MSR $1,099 | $950 | $795 | $675 | $550 | $450 | $400 | $375 | |

Add $100 for three 15 shot magazines and night sights (new 2014).

* **P30SK Sub Compact** – 9mm Para cal., ergonomic polymer frame with lower Picatinny rail, with or w/o ambidextrous dual magazine release and manual safety levers, 3.27 in. barrel with polygonal rifling, 10 shot mag., trigger variants include conventional DA/SA with spur hammer and serrated decocking button on rear of frame or LEM enhanced DAO with "light strike V1" trigger setup and bobbed hammer, 3-dot sights, grips with interchangeable side panels and backstraps, firing pin block safety, loaded chamber indicator, double slide serrations, HK Lock-Out safety device, approx. 24 oz. Importation began 2016.

| MSR $719 | $650 | $575 | $500 | $450 | $400 | $350 | $300 | |

Add $100 for three 10 shot magazines and night sights.

P2000 – 9mm Para., .357 SIG (mfg. 2005-2012), or .40 S&W cal., DA/SA or LEM (Law Enforcement Modification) DAO (w/o control lever), compact design, patterned after USP Compact Model, features pre-cocked hammer system with very short trigger reset distance, lockout safety device, 3-dot sights, 3.66 in. barrel with polygonal rifling, 10 or 12 shot mag. with finger extension, or optional 13 shot mag. (new late 2004), with or w/o decocker, interchangeable rear grip panels, black finish, approx. 25 oz.

| MSR $799 | $695 | $625 | $550 | $475 | $400 | $350 | $300 | |

Add $100 for three 13 shot magazines and night sights (new 2014).
Add $100 for three 12 shot mags. (.40 S&W) and night sights or three 10 shot mags. (.40 S&W only).
Subtract approx. $50 for .357 SIG cal. (mfg. 2005-2012).

MSR	100%	98%	95%	90%	80%	70%	60%	Last MSR

* **P2000 SK Sub Compact** – 9mm Para. or .40 S&W cal., similar to P2000, choice of LEM (Law Enforcement Modification) or regular DA/SA trigger system, 3.26 in. barrel, 9 (.357 SIG (disc. 2012) or .40 S&W cal.) or 10 (9mm Para.) shot mag., approx. 24 oz. Importation began 2005.

| MSR $799 | $695 | $625 | $550 | $475 | $400 | $350 | $300 | |

Add $100 for three 9 or 10 shot magazines and night sights (new 2014).
Subtract approx. $50 for .357 SIG cal. (mfg. 2005-2012).

USP CUSTOM COMBAT – 9mm Para. or .40 S&W cal., DA/SA, Variant 1, Novak combat sight system, includes jet funnel kit and two 16 (.40 S&W cal.) or 18 (9mm Para. cal.) shot mags. Mfg. 2009.

| | $1,150 | $975 | $875 | $775 | $675 | $550 | $450 | *$1,295* |

USP COMBAT COMPETITION – 9mm Para. or .40 S&W cal., 4 1/4 in. barrel, includes jet funnel kit with two 16 (.40 S&W) or 18 (9mm Para.) mags., Novak combat sight system, DA/SA or LEM trigger (became standard mid-2008), lower accessory rail on frame, 26 1/2 oz. Imported 2007-2010.

| | $1,250 | $1,025 | $925 | $825 | $700 | $600 | $500 | *$1,450* |

Subtract approx. $100 if w/o LEM trigger.

USP COMPETITION – similar to USP Combat Competition, except features LEM match trigger system. Imported 2007-2008.

| | $1,125 | $975 | $850 | $750 | $625 | $500 | $450 | *$1,279* |

USP 9 – 9mm Para. cal., available in 9 variants of DA/SA/DAO, 4 1/4 in. barrel with polygonal rifling, Browning-type action with H & K recoil reduction system, polymer frame, all metal surfaces specially treated, can be carried cocked and locked, stippled synthetic grips, bobbed hammer, 3-dot sighting system, multiple safeties, 10 (C/B 1994), 15 (new late 2004), or 16* shot polymer mag., 26.5 oz. New 1993.

| MSR $979 | $835 | $725 | $600 | $500 | $450 | $400 | $350 | |

Add $70 for LEM trigger, DAO and two 10 or 15 shot mags.
Add $100 for three 15 shot magazines and night sights (new 2014).
Add $170 for LEM trigger, DAO, three 15 shot mags. and night sights.
Add $107 for Tritium sights (various colors, mfg. 1993-2010).

* **USP 9 SD** – similar to USP 9, except has adj. target sights and 4.7 in. threaded barrel, approx. 27 oz. Imported 2004-2006, reintroduced 2011.

| MSR $1,399 | $1,225 | $1,050 | $925 | $800 | $675 | $550 | $475 | |

* **USP 9 Stainless** – similar to USP 9, except has satin finished stainless steel slide. Mfg. 1996-2001.

| | $700 | $565 | $475 | $415 | $360 | $300 | $255 | *$817* |

USP 9 COMPACT – 9mm Para. cal., compact variation of the USP 9 featuring 3.58 in. barrel, 10 or 13 (new late 2004) shot mag., LEM trigger became available 2003, 25.5 oz. New 1997.

| MSR $999 | $850 | $750 | $650 | $525 | $450 | $400 | $375 | |

Add $100 for LEM trigger, DAO and two 10 or 13 shot mags.
Add $100 for three 13 shot magazines with night sights (new 2014).
Add $200 for LEM trigger, DAO, three 13 shot mags., and night sights.

* **USP 9 Compact Stainless** – similar to USP 9 Compact, except has satin finished stainless steel slide. Mfg. 1997-2004.

| | $735 | $595 | $500 | $430 | $375 | $315 | $270 | *$849* |

* **USP 9 Compact LEM** – 9mm Para. cal., DAO, blue finish only, LEM trigger mechanism decreases trigger pull to 7 1/2 - 8 1/2 lbs., 24 1/2 oz. Imported 2003-2004.

| | $695 | $575 | $495 | $450 | $400 | $350 | $315 | *$799* |

USP 9 TACTICAL – 9mm Para. cal., DA/SA, 4.86 in. threaded O-ring barrel, match grade trigger, adj. target sights, fixed grips, safety/decocking lever on left, two 10 or 15 shot mags., black finish, 28 oz. New 2015.

| MSR $1,349 | $1,195 | $1,000 | $900 | $800 | $675 | $550 | $475 | |

Add $100 for three 15 shot mags. and adj. night sights.

USP 9x19 TACTICAL – 9mm Para. cal. enhanced variation of the USP 9, 4.92 in. threaded barrel with rubber o-ring, 10 or 15 shot mag., adj. target type sights and trigger, approx. 28 1/2 oz. Mfg. 2007-2010.

| | $975 | $850 | $750 | $625 | $525 | $450 | $400 | *$1,112* |

USP 357 – .357 SIG cal., available in 4.25 (Standard, disc. 2004) or 3.58 (Compact) in. barrel, 10 or 12 (optional beginning 2004) shot mag., black finish, approx. 24.5 oz. Imported 2001-2005.

| | $695 | $560 | $500 | $450 | $395 | $350 | $300 | *$799* |

Subtract $30 for Standard Model (disc. 2004).

MSR	100%	98%	95%	90%	80%	70%	60%	Last MSR

USP 40 – .40 S&W cal., similar to USP 9, 9 variants of DA/SA/DAO, 10 (C/B1994), 13* (reintroduced late 2004), or 16 (optional, new 2005, needs jet funnel modification) shot mag., LEM trigger (new 2013), 27.75 oz. New 1993.

MSR $979 $835 $725 $600 $500 $450 $400 $350

Add $70 for LEM trigger (new 2013), DAO and two 10 or 13 shot mags.

Add $107 for Tritium sights (various colors, mfg. 1993-disc.).

A Desert Tan finish became available during 2005 at no extra charge (includes matching nylon carrying case). Limited mfg. 2005-2006.

* ***USP 40 Stainless*** – similar to USP 40, except has satin finished stainless steel slide. Mfg. 1996-2003.

     $700 $565 $470 $415 $360 $300 $255   *$817*

USP 40 COMPACT – .40 S&W cal., compact variation of the USP 40 featuring 3.58 in. barrel, 10 or 12 (new late 2004) shot mag., LEM trigger became available 2002, 27 oz. New 1997.

MSR $999 $850 $750 $650 $525 $450 $400 $375

Add $100 for LEM trigger, DAO, and two 10 or 12 shot mags.

Add $100 for three 12 shot magazines with night sights (new 2014).

A Desert Tan finish became available during 2005-2006 at no extra charge (includes matching nylon carrying case). Grey was also available in limited quantities during 2005 only.

* ***USP 40 Compact Stainless*** – similar to USP 40 Compact, except has satin finished stainless steel slide. Mfg. 1997-2004.

     $735 $595 $500 $430 $375 $315 $270   *$849*

* ***USP 40 Compact LEM*** – .40 S&W cal., DAO, blue finish only, LEM trigger mechanism decreases trigger pull to 7 1/2 - 8 1/2 lbs., 24 1/2 oz. Imported 2002-2005.

     $695 $575 $495 $450 $400 $350 $315

USP 40 TACTICAL – .40 S&W cal., enhanced variation of the USP 40, 4.92 in. threaded barrel with rubber o-ring, 10 (standard) or 13 shot mag., adj. target type sights and match trigger, 30 1/2 oz. New 2005.

MSR $1,349 $1,150 $995 $850 $750 $625 $550 $495

Add $100 for three 13 shot mags and adj. night sights (new 2014).

USP 45 – .45 ACP cal., similar to USP 9, 9 variants of DA/SA/DAO, 10 (C/B 1994), 12 (new late 2004) or 13* shot mag., 27 3/4 oz. New 1995.

MSR $999 $850 $750 $650 $525 $450 $400 $375

Add $100 for LEM trigger, DAO (new 2011), or $200 for three magazines and night sights.

Add $107 for Tritium sights (various colors, mfg. 1993-2010).

A desert tan or green finish became available during 2005-2006 at no extra charge (includes matching nylon carrying case). Grey was also available in limited quantities during 2005 only.

* ***USP 45 Stainless*** – similar to USP 45, except has satin finished stainless steel slide. Mfg. 1996-2003.

     $760 $600 $500 $430 $375 $315 $270   *$888*

* ***USP 45 Match Pistol*** – .45 ACP cal., features 6.02 in. barrel with polygonal rifling, micrometer adj. high relief and raised rear sight, raised target front sight, 10 shot mag., barrel weight, fluted, and ambidextrous safety, choice of matte black or stainless steel slide, supplied with additional o-rings and setup tools, 38 oz. Mfg. 1997-98.

     $2,150 $1,850 $1,575 $1,300 $1,050 $900 $800   *$1,369*

Add $72 for stainless steel slide model.

USP 45 COMPACT – .45 ACP cal., compact variation of the USP 45, featuring 3.8 in. barrel, 8 shot mag., 28 oz. New 1998.

MSR $1,049 $895 $775 $650 $550 $475 $425 $375

Add $100 for LEM trigger, DAO (new 2011).

Add $200 for three magazines and night sights.

* ***USP 45 Compact Stainless*** – similar to USP 45 Compact, except has satin finished stainless steel slide. Mfg. 1998-2004.

     $775 $615 $510 $440 $385 $325 $275   *$894*

* ***USP 45 Compact 50th Anniversary*** – commemorates the 50th year of H & K (1950-2000), 1 of 1,000 special edition featuring high polish blue slide with 50th Anniversary logo engraved in gold and silver, supplied with presentation wood case and commemorative coin. Limited mfg. 2000 only.

     $1,150 $895 $795   N/A   N/A   N/A   N/A   *$999*

USP 45 TACTICAL PISTOL – .45 ACP cal., enhanced variation of the USP 45, 5.09 in. threaded barrel with rubber o-ring, 10 or 12 (new late 2004) shot mag., adj. 3-dot target type sights and match trigger, limited availability, 36 oz. New 1998.

MSR $1,349 $1,195 $1,000 $900 $800 $675 $550 $475

Add $100 for three 12 shot magazines and adj. night sights.

A Desert Tan finish became available during 2005-2006 at no extra charge (includes matching nylon carrying case).

MSR	100%	98%	95%	90%	80%	70%	60%	Last MSR

* USP 45 Tactical Pistol Compact – .45 ACP cal., compact variation of the USP 45 Tactical, 3.78 in. barrel, 8 shot mag., 28 oz. Imported 2006-2012.

	$1,100	$950	$850	$750	$650	$550	$450	$1,242

USP EXPERT – 9mm Para. (mfg. 2003-2005, reintroduced 2013), .40 S&W (mfg. 2002-2009), or .45 ACP (disc. 2009) cal., features new slide design with 5.2 in. barrel, 10 (standard), 12 (.45 ACP, disc. 2009), 13 (.40 S&W, disc. 2009), 15 (9mm Para.) or 18 (new 2013) shot mag., match grade SA or DA trigger pull, recoil reduction system, reinforced polymer frame, adj. rear sight, approx. 30 oz. Imported 1999-2009, reintroduced 2013.

MSR $1,399	$1,225	$1,050	$925	$800	$675	$550	$475	

Add $100 for jet funnel frame and two 18 shot mags. (new 2013).

USP ELITE – 9mm Para. (disc. 2005) or .45 ACP cal., long slide variation of the USP Expert, 6.2 in. barrel, match trigger parts, target sights, ambidextrous control levers, blue finish, includes two 10 shot mags. or 12 (.45 ACP) or 15 (9mm Para.) shot mag. Imported 2003-2009.

	$1,375	$1,150	$1,000	$900	$800	$700	$600	$1,406

MARK 23 SPECIAL OPERATIONS PISTOL – .45 ACP cal., 5.87 in. threaded barrel with O-ring and polygonal rifling, DA/SA, polymer frame with ribbed integral grips, 3-dot sights, 10 or 12 (optional beginning late 2004) shot mag., squared off trigger guard, lower frame is grooved for mounting accessories, mechanical recoil reduction system, 39 oz. Limited availability. New 1996.

MSR $2,299	$2,050	$1,775	$1,525	$1,250	$1,000	$875	$775	

The "MK23" is the official military design that is not available to civilians.

A Desert Tan finish became available during 2005-2006 at no extra charge (includes matching nylon carrying case).

SP 89 – 9mm Para. cal., roller lock delayed blowback, 4 1/2 in. barrel, 15 shot mag., adj. aperture rear sight (accepts HK claw-lock scope mounts), 4.4 lbs. Mfg. 1990-1993.

	$4,950	$4,500	$4,150	$4,000	$3,750	$3,625	$3,500	$1,325

VP 70Z – 9mm Para. cal., 18 shot, DAO, SFO, 4 1/2 in. barrel, parkerized finish, plastic receiver/grip assembly. Disc. 1984.

	$750	$675	$600	$550	$500	$450	$400	

Add 125% if frame cut for shoulder stock (Model VP 70M, NFA Class III).

The majority of pistols that were cut for shoulder stock are the Model VP 70M, and are subject to NFA Class III regulation. A complete M stock with sear is also considered NFA.

VP9 – 9mm Para. cal., 4.09 in. barrel, 15 shot mag., fixed three dot steel luminous sights, polymer frame, lower Picatinny rail, front and rear slide serrations, cock firing pin indicator, trigger has safety latch, removable side panels and backstrap, black finish, 25 1/2 oz. New mid-2014.

MSR $719	$650	$575	$500	$450	$400	$350	$300	

Add $100 for three 10 or 15 shot mags. and night sights.

VP40 – .40 S&W cal., polymer frame w/lower Picatinny rail, 4.09 in. barrel, 13 shot mag., trigger safety latch, fixed three dot luminous sights, grips have removable side panels and backstrap, cocked firing pin indicator, front and rear slide serrations, black finish, 1.8 lbs. New 2016.

MSR $719	$650	$575	$500	$450	$400	$350	$300	

Add $100 for three 10 or 13 shot mags. and night sights.

RIFLES: BOLT ACTION

BASR – .22 LR, .22-250 Rem., 6mm PPC, .300 Win. Mag., .30-06, or .308 Win. cal., Kevlar stock, stainless steel barrel, limited production. Special order only. Mfg. 1986 only.

	$5,750	$5,000	$4,500	$4,000	$3,650	$3,300	$2,600	$2,199

Less than 135 of this variation were manufactured and they are extremely rare. Contractual disputes with the U.S. supplier stopped H & K from receiving any BASR models.

RIFLES: SEMI-AUTO

Most of the models listed, being of a tactical design, were disc. in 1989 due to Federal legislation. Sporterized variations mfg. after 1994 with thumbhole stocks were banned in April, 1998.

In 1991, the HK-91, HK-93, and HK-94 were discontinued. Last published retail prices (1991) were $999 for fixed stock models and $1,199 for retractable stock models.

In the early '70s, S.A.C.O. importers located in Virginia sold the Models 41 and 43 which were the predecessors to the Model 91 and 93, respectively. Values for these earlier variations will be higher than values listed.

MSR	100%	98%	95%	90%	80%	70%	60%	Last MSR

G3 SEMI-AUTO – .308 Win. cal., patterned after the H&K G3 select-fire military rifle, two variations were imported by Golden State Arms circa 1962.

	100%	98%	95%	90%	80%	70%	60%	Last MSR
	$8,500	$7,500	$6,500	$5,500	$4,750	$4,000	$3,250	

SR-9 – .308 Win. cal., semi-auto sporting rifle, 19.7 in. barrel, Kevlar reinforced fiberglass thumbhole stock and forearm, 5 shot mag., diopter adj. rear sight, accepts H & K claw-lock scope mounts. Mfg. 1990-93.

| | $2,075 | $1,725 | $1,400 | $1,225 | $1,075 | $950 | $850 | *$1,199* |

While advertised again during 1998, this model was finally banned in April, 1998.

SR-9T – .308 Win. cal., precision target rifle with adj. MSG 90 buttstock and PSG-1 trigger group, 5 shot mag. Mfg. 1992-93.

| | $2,795 | $2,375 | $2,050 | $1,775 | $1,375 | $1,295 | $1,050 | *$1,725* |

While advertised again during 1998, this model was finally banned in April, 1998.

SR-9TC – .308 Win. cal., similar to SR-9T except has PSG-1 adj. buttstock. Mfg. 1993 only.

| | $3,350 | $2,925 | $2,600 | $2,275 | $1,925 | $1,475 | $1,250 | *$1,995* |

While advertised again during 1998, this model was finally banned in April, 1998.

PSG-1 – .308 Win. cal. only, high precision marksman's rifle, 5 shot mag., adj. buttstock, includes accessories (Hensholdt illuminated 6x42mm scope) and case, 17.8 lbs. Importation disc. 1998.

| | $13,950 | $12,500 | $10,950 | $9,500 | $8,500 | $7,500 | $7,000 | *$10,811* |

MODEL 41 A-2 – .308 Win. cal., predecessor to the Model 91 A-2, originally imported by Golden State Arms.

| | $4,500 | $4,000 | $3,750 | $3,500 | $3,350 | $3,200 | $3,000 | |

MODEL 43 A-2 – predecesor to the Model 93 A-2. Disc.

| | $4,500 | $4,000 | $3,750 | $3,500 | $3,350 | $3,200 | $3,000 | |

MODEL 91 A-2 – .308 Win. cal., roller lock delayed blowback action, attenuated recoil, black cycolac stock, 17.7 in. barrel, 20 shot mag., 9.7 lbs. Importation disc. 1989.

* **Model 91 A-2 Fixed stock model**

| | $2,350 | $2,000 | $1,800 | $1,600 | $1,400 | $1,250 | $1,000 | *$999* |

Add $200 for Desert camo finish.
Add $275 for NATO black finish.

* **Model 91 A-2 SBF (Semi-Beltfed)** – supplied with bipod and M60 link (200 shot with starter tab) and MG42 modified belt (49 shot with fixed starter tab), limited mfg. Disc.

| | $10,500 | $9,500 | $8,500 | N/A | N/A | N/A | N/A | |

* **Model 91 A-3** – with retractable metal stock.

| | $3,100 | $2,900 | $2,700 | $2,500 | $2,150 | $2,000 | $1,895 | *$1,114* |

Add $775 for .22 LR conversion kit.

* **Model 91 A-2 Package** – includes A.R.M.S. mount, B-Square rings, Leupold 3-9x compact scope with matte finish. Importation disc. 1988.

| | $3,150 | $2,750 | $2,400 | $2,150 | $1,900 | $1,700 | $1,475 | *$1,285* |

Add 30% for retractable stock.

MODEL 93 A-2 – .223 Rem. cal., smaller version of the H & K 91, 25 shot mag., 16.14 in. barrel, 8 lbs.

* **Model 93 A-2 Fixed stock model**

| | $2,500 | $2,250 | $2,000 | $1,750 | $1,500 | $1,250 | $1,000 | *$946* |

Add 10% for desert camo finish.
Add 15% for NATO black finish.

* **Model 93 A-3** – with retractable metal stock.

| | $3,400 | $3,250 | $3,000 | $2,800 | $2,650 | $2,500 | $2,250 | *$1,114* |

* **Model 93 A-2 Package** – includes A.R.M.S. mount, B-Square rings, Leupold 3-9x compact scope with matte finish. Importation disc. 1988.

| | $3,500 | $3,100 | $2,850 | $2,550 | $2,400 | $2,100 | $1,895 | *$1,285* |

Add 10% for retractable stock.

MODEL 94 CARBINE A-2 – 9mm Para. cal., semi-auto carbine, 16.54 in. barrel, aperture rear sight, 15 shot mag. New 1983.

* **Model 94 Carbine A-2 Fixed stock model**

| | $3,950 | $3,750 | $3,500 | $3,400 | $3,000 | $2,600 | $2,500 | *$946* |

MSR	100%	98%	95%	90%	80%	70%	60%	Last MSR

* Model 94 Carbine A-3 – retractable metal stock.

	100%	98%	95%	90%	80%	70%	60%	Last MSR
	$4,150	$3,900	$3,700	$3,550	$3,200	$2,800	$2,700	$1,114

* Model 94 Carbine A-2 Package – includes A.R.M.S. mount, B-Square rings, Leupold 3-9x compact scope with matte finish. Importation disc. 1988.

	100%	98%	95%	90%	80%	70%	60%	Last MSR
	$4,300	$3,875	$3,650	$3,300	$3,000	$2,800	$2,500	$1,285

Add 10% for retractable stock.

* Model 94 Carbine A-2 SGI – 9mm Para. cal., target rifle, aluminum alloy bipod, Leupold 6X scope, 15 or 30 shot mag. Imported 1986 only.

	100%	98%	95%	90%	80%	70%	60%	Last MSR
	$3,950	$3,750	$3,500	$3,000	$2,750	$2,500	$2,150	$1,340

MODEL HK 416 – .22 LR cal., GIO, 10 or 20 shot mag., blowback action with last shot bolt hold open, 16.1 in. barrel with muzzle brake, H&K style diopter sight, black ergonomic pistol grip with storage compartment, manual safety, steel flat-top receiver with quad Picatinny rail, H&K style 5 position buttstock with storage compartment and recoil pad, black finish, 6.8 lbs, mfg. by Carl Walther in Ulm, Germany. Mfg. mid-2010-2011.

	100%	98%	95%	90%	80%	70%	60%	Last MSR
	$500	$450	$400	$375	$350	$325	$295	$569

MODEL 416 D145RS – .22 LR cal., GIO, blowback action, 16.1 in. barrel, fixed front sight, adj. rear sight, external safety, 10 or 20 shot mag., metal receiver, black finish, upper and lower rail interface system, pistol grip with compartment, adj. buttstock, functional dust cover, 6.8 lbs., mfg. by Carl Walther in Ulm, Germany, and imported by Umarex USA. New late 2009.

MSR	100%	98%	95%	90%	80%	70%	60%	
$599	$550	$495	$450	$395	$350	$300	$275	

MODELS SL6 & SL7 CARBINE – .223 Rem. (HK-SL6) or .308 Win. (HK-SL7) cal., roller lock delayed blowback action, 17.71 in. barrel, reduced recoil, vent. wood handguard, 3 or 4 shot mag., matte black metal finish, 8.36 lbs. Importation disc. 1986.

	100%	98%	95%	90%	80%	70%	60%	
	$1,650	$1,450	$1,250	$1,050	$925	$800	$650	

Add $250-$300 for factory H & K scope mount system.
Add $200 for .308 Win. cal.

These models were the last sporter variations H & K imported into the U.S. - no U.S. importation since 1986.

MODEL SL8-1 – .223 Rem. cal., short stroke piston actuated gas operating system, advanced grey carbon fiber polymer construction based on the German Army G36 rifle, thumbhole stock with adj. cheekpiece and buttstock, 10 shot mag., modular and removable Picatinny rail, removable sights, 20.8 in. cold hammer forged heavy barrel, adj. sights, 8.6 lbs. Imported 2000-2003, reimported 2007-2010.

	100%	98%	95%	90%	80%	70%	60%	Last MSR
	$1,950	$1,650	$1,500	$1,350	$1,200	$1,000	$900	$2,449

Add $338 for carrying handle with 1.5X-3x optical sights (disc. 2009).
Add $624 for carrying handle with 1.5X-3x optical sights and red dot reflex sight (disc. 2009).

MODEL SL8-6 – .223 Rem. cal., similar to SL8-1, except has elevated Picatinny rail that doubles as carrying handle. Mfg. 2010-2011.

	100%	98%	95%	90%	80%	70%	60%	Last MSR
	$1,950	$1,650	$1,500	$1,350	$1,200	$1,000	$900	$2,388

MODEL USC .45 ACP CARBINE – .45 ACP cal., similar design/construction as the Model SL8-1, except is blowback action, and has 16 in. barrel and grey skeletonized buttstock, 10 shot mag., 6 lbs. Imported 2000-2003, reimported beginning 2007-2011.

	100%	98%	95%	90%	80%	70%	60%	Last MSR
	$1,500	$1,275	$1,050	$925	$825	$725	$625	$1,788

MR556A1 CARBINE – 5.56 NATO cal., GPO, 10 or 30 shot steel mag., 16 1/2 in. heavy barrel with muzzle brake, free floating rail system handguard with four Mil-Std 1913 Picatinny rails, Picatinny rail machined into top of upper receiver, two-stage trigger, diopter sights, black anodized finish, adj. buttstock with (disc. 2013) or w/o (new 2014) storage compartment, HK pistol grip with optional configurations, 7.6 lbs. Mfg. in the U.S. using American and German made components. New 2009.

MSR	100%	98%	95%	90%	80%	70%	60%	
$3,399	$3,050	$2,625	$2,300	$2,000	$1,700	$1,500	$1,250	

MR762A1 CARBINE – 7.62x51mm cal., GPO, 16 1/2 in. barrel, free floating rail system, flip up front and diopter rear sights, black anodized finish, 10 or 20 shot polymer mag., upper and lower accessory rails, adj. buttstock with storage compartment, pistol grip with optional configurations, 9.84-10.4 lbs. Limited mfg. in the U.S. New late 2009.

MSR	100%	98%	95%	90%	80%	70%	60%	
$3,999	$3,600	$3,150	$2,700	$2,350	$1,950	$1,725	$1,400	

MODEL MP5 A5 – .22 LR cal., blowback action, 10 or 25 shot mag., 16.1 in. barrel with compensator, black finish, metal receiver, Navy pistol grip, H&K adj. front and rear sights, 3 lug, standard forearm, retractable stock, external safety, 5.9 lbs., mfg. by Carl Walther in Ulm, Germany, imported by Umarex USA. New late 2009.

MSR	100%	98%	95%	90%	80%	70%	60%	
$499	$450	$395	$360	$330	$300	$275	$250	

MSR	100%	98%	95%	90%	80%	70%	60%	Last MSR

MODEL MP5 SD – .22 LR cal., blowback action, 10 or 25 shot mag., 16.1 in. barrel with compensator, black finish, metal receiver, adj. rear sights, interchangeable front post sight, 3 lug imitation, SD type ribbed forearm, Navy pistol grip, retractable stock, external safety, 5.9 lbs. Mfg. by Carl Walther in Ulm, Germany, imported by Umarex USA. New late 2009.

| MSR $599 | $525 | $475 | $425 | $395 | $360 | $330 | $300 | |

SHOTGUNS: SEMI-AUTO

Benelli shotguns previously imported by H&K can be found under Benelli.

MODEL 512 – 12 ga. only, mfg. by Franchi for German military contract, rifle sights, matte finished metal, walnut stock, fixed choke pattern diverter giving rectangular shot pattern. Importation disc. 1991.

| | $1,500 | $1,300 | $1,100 | $925 | $800 | $700 | $600 | |

Last Mfg.'s Wholesale was $1,895.

HEINIE SPECIALTY PRODUCTS

Previous pistol manufacturer established in 1973, located in Quincy, IL. Heinie currently manufactures sights only.

Heinie manufactured both scratch built personal defense and tactical/carry 1911 packages in a wide variety of chamberings.

HENRY REPEATING ARMS COMPANY

Current rifle manufacturer established during 1997, located in Bayonne, NJ beginning 2008, with manufacturing facilities in Rice Lake, WI beginning in 2014. Previously located in Brooklyn, NY. Distributor and dealer sales.

RIFLES: SEMI-AUTO

U.S. SURVIVAL AR-7 – .22 LR cal., patterned after the Armalite AR-7 with improvements, takedown design enables receiver, two 8 shot mags., and barrel to stow in ABS plastic stock, 100% Mossy Oak Break-Up camo (new 2000) or weather resistant silver (disc.) or black (new 1999) stock/metal finish, adj. rear and blade front sights, 16 1/2 in. long when disassembled and stowed in stock, includes plastic carrying case, 3 1/2 lbs. New 1997.

| MSR $290 | $250 | $215 | $190 | $175 | $165 | $155 | $145 | |

Add $60 for 100% camo finish (new 2000).

HERA ARMS

Current firearms manufacturer located in Triefenstein, Germany. No current U.S. importation.

Hera Arms manufactures a complete line of AR-15 style semi-auto rifles in .223 Rem cal., as well as several styles of conversions for SIG, Glock, Walther, CZ, and H&K pistols. Hera Arms also manufactures a variety of tactical accessories geared towards military, law enforcement, and sport shooters. Please contact the company directly for more information, including options, U.S. availability, and pricing (see Trademark Index).

HESSE ARMS

Previous manufacturer located in Inver Grove Heights, MN.

Hesse Arms manufactured very limited quantities of semi-auto pistols, bolt action rifles, and semi-auto rifles.

PISTOLS: SEMI-AUTO

HAR-15 – .223 Rem. cal., features carbon/Aramid fiber flat-top upper receiver, 7 1/2 in. barrel, 100% parts interchangeability with AR-15 type firearms. Mfg. 2002 only.

| | $995 | $870 | $745 | $675 | $545 | $450 | $350 | *$850* |

RIFLES: BOLT ACTION

M98 V5 – .220 Swift, .22-250 Rem., or .308 Win. cal., Mauser M98 action, 26 in. barrel with recessed crown and fully stressed relieved, competition stock with vent forearm, fully adj. trigger. Mfg. 1999-2002.

| | $650 | $570 | $490 | $440 | $360 | $295 | $230 | *$640* |

HBR 50 – .50 BMG cal., single shot action, 34 in. match barrel with muzzle brake, adj. buttstock and trigger. Mfg. 2001-2002.

| | $2,250 | $1,970 | $1,690 | $1,530 | $1,240 | $1,015 | $790 | *$1,650* |

RIFLES: SEMI-AUTO, CENTERFIRE

HAR-15A2 SERIES – .223 Rem. cal., AR-15 type action, various configurations, barrel lengths and options. Mfg. 1997-2002.

* ***Standard Rifle/Carbine*** – features Mil-Spec parts, 16 (carbine) or 20 (rifle) in. heavy match grade barrel.

| | $850 | $745 | $640 | $580 | $470 | $385 | $300 | *$779* |

MSR	100%	98%	95%	90%	80%	70%	60%	Last MSR

* Bull Gun – features 16 in. stainless steel barrel with special front sight base.

| | $900 | $790 | $675 | $610 | $495 | $405 | $315 | $825 |

* Dispatcher – features 16 in. barrel with full length handguards, 7.9 lbs. Mfg. 1999-2002.

| | $875 | $765 | $655 | $595 | $480 | $395 | $305 | $799 |

* .50 Action Express – .50 AE cal., 16 or 20 in. barrel, fixed tube stock, 10 shot mag., 6.9-7.3 lbs. Mfg. 1999-2002.

| | $1,150 | $1,005 | $865 | $780 | $635 | $520 | $405 | $1,100 |

* X-Match – 20 in. heavy barrel with A3 flat-top receiver, free floating aluminum forearm tube, 8.7-9.6 lbs. Mfg. 1999-2002.

| | $800 | $700 | $600 | $545 | $440 | $360 | $280 | |

* National Match – features 1/2 minute match sights, CMP legal free-floating handguards, match bolt carrier, adj. trigger, individually tested.

| | $1,150 | $1,005 | $865 | $780 | $635 | $520 | $405 | $1,100 |

* Omega Match – top-of-the-line features, including 16 in. stainless steel barrel, hooked style stock with pistol grip, flat-top receiver, capable of 1/4 in. groups.

| | $1,250 | $1,095 | $940 | $850 | $690 | $565 | $440 | $1,100 |

* High Grade – custom built per individual order.

| | $1,550 | $1,355 | $1,165 | $1,055 | $855 | $700 | $545 | $1,399 |

ULTRA RACE – 24 in. stainless barrel, vented free-floating handguard, flat-top upper receiver, Palma style rear sight, globe front sight, fully adj. skeleton stock. Mfg. 2001-2002.

| | $2,100 | $1,840 | $1,575 | $1,430 | $1,155 | $945 | $735 | $1,999 |

FAL/FALO SERIES – .308 Win. cal., action patterned after the F.N. FAL, various barrel lengths and configurations. Mfg. 1997-2002.

* FAL-H Standard Rifle – features 24 in. barrel, synthetic stock.

| | $1,150 | $1,005 | $865 | $780 | $635 | $520 | $405 | $1,100 |

* FAL-H/FALO Congo Carbine – features 16 in. barrel.

| | $1,300 | $1,140 | $975 | $885 | $715 | $585 | $455 | $1,150 |

* FALO Tactical – features free floating handguard assembly, flat-top receiver.

| | $1,550 | $1,355 | $1,165 | $1,055 | $855 | $700 | $545 | $1,400 |

* FAL-H/FALO High Grade – custom built per individual order.

| | $1,550 | $1,355 | $1,165 | $1,055 | $855 | $700 | $545 | $1,400 |

H91 RIFLE SERIES – .308 Win. cal., 18 1/4 in. barrel, action patterned after the H&K 91, approx. 9 lbs. Mfg. 2000-2002.

| | $1,450 | $1,270 | $1,090 | $985 | $800 | $655 | $510 | $1,250 |

Add $600 for Marksman Rifle variation (special receiver with strengthening rails).

* H91 Precision – 26 in. barrel, tuned "set" trigger, free floating polymer forearm, receiver has specially designed inserts for strength and stability, 12.4 lbs. Mfg. 2000-2002.

| | $3,300 | $2,890 | $2,475 | $2,245 | $1,815 | $1,485 | $1,155 | $3,250 |

H94 CARBINE – .9mm Para. cal., copy of H&K MP5, stamped steel receiver, integral scope mount, 9 in. (A2 or pinned telescoping stock), or 5.5 in. barrel (fixed folding stock). Mfg. 2002 only.

| | $1,950 | $1,705 | $1,465 | $1,325 | $1,075 | $880 | $685 | $1,850 |

M14H STANDARD RIFLE – .308 Win. cal., semi-auto version of the M14 rifle, choice of walnut or wrinkle coat synthetic stock, supplied with extra 10 shot mag. and original M14 stock. Mfg. 1997-1999.

| | $1,050 | $920 | $790 | $715 | $580 | $475 | $370 | $999 |

Add $110 for M14HE2 variation.

* M14H Brush Rifle – features black synthetic stock with 18 in. barrel. Mfg. 1997-1999.

| | $1,100 | $965 | $825 | $750 | $605 | $495 | $385 | $1,059 |

MODEL 47 RIFLE – 7.62x39mm or .308 Win. (new 2000) cal., Kalashnikov type action in various configurations, including RPK and STG 940, black synthetic stock, 16 1/4, 20 (disc. 1999), or 22 (.308 Win.) in. barrel. Mfg. 1997-2002.

| | $675 | $590 | $505 | $460 | $370 | $305 | $235 | $570 |

Add $270 for RPK or STG 940 configuration.
Add $329 for .308 Win. cal.

MSR	100%	98%	95%	90%	80%	70%	60%	Last MSR

RIFLES: SEMI-AUTO, RIMFIRE

H22 SERIES – .22 LR cal., stainless steel Ruger 10/22 action, various configurations and features. Models included the Standard (last MSR $460), Wildcat (last MSR $559), Competition (last MSR $560), and Tiger Shark (last MSR $830). Very limited mfg. 1997-2000.

Limited availability precludes accurate pricing on this model.

HI-POINT FIREARMS

Current trademark marketed by MKS Supply, Inc. located in Dayton, Ohio. Hi-Point firearms have been manufactured by Beemiller Inc. located in Mansfield, OH since 1988. Dealer and distributor sales.

Prior to 1993, trademarks sold by MKS Supply, Inc. (including Beemiller, Haskell Manufacturing, Inc., Iberia Firearms, Inc., and Stallard Arms, Inc.) had their own separate manufacturers' markings. Beginning in 1993, Hi-Point Firearms eliminated these individualized markings and chose instead to have currently manufactured guns labeled "Hi-Point Firearms". All injection molding for Hi-Point Firearms is done in Mansfield, OH.

CARBINES: SEMI-AUTO

MODEL 995TS – 9mm Para. cal., 16 1/2 in. barrel, 10 shot mag., Weaver style rails, internal recoil buffer in stock, last round lock open, apperture rear (disc.) or fully adj. sights, one-piece camo (disc.) or black polymer skeletonized stock features pistol grip (target stock became standard 2013), parkerized or chrome (disc. 2007) finish, sling, swivels, and scope base, 6 1/4 lbs. New 1996.

MSR $297	$275	$250	$225	$210	$200	$190	$180	

Add $30 for forward grip (995TS FG) or $50 for forward grip and flashlight (995TS FGFL).
Add $38 for 4x32 scope (995TS 4x32) or for red dot scope (995TS RD).
Add $57 for Pro Pack Kit with target stock (new 2011, 995TS PRO).
Add $110 for laser sight (995TS LAZ).
Add $152 for forward grip, flashlight, and laser sight (new 2011, 995TS FGFL-LAZ).
Add $143 for 4x RGB scope (995TS 4xRGB).
Add $10 for chrome finish (disc. 2007).
Add $15 for camo stock (mfg. 2002-disc.).
Add $85 for detachable compensator, laser, and mount (mfg. 1999-2010).

This model is manufactured by Beemiller, located in Mansfield, OH.

* ***Model 995TS Camo*** – 9mm Para. cal., 16 1/2 in. barrel, 10 shot mag., Weaver style rails, internal recoil buffer in stock, last round lock open, fully adj. sights, sling, swivels, and scope base, all-weather polymer skeletonized stock, Hydro dipped Desert Digital Camo (995TS DD), Pink Camo (995TS PI), or Woodland Style Camo (995TS WC) finish, 6 1/4 lbs. New 2015.

MSR $359	$310	$270	$235	$210	$175	$150	$125	

MODEL 4095TS – .40 S&W cal., 17 1/2 in. barrel, 10 shot mag., Weaver style rails, aperture rear (disc.) or fully adj. sights (Ghost ring rear peep and post front), one-piece camo (disc.) or black polymer skeletonized stock features pistol grip (target stock became standard 2013), parkerized or chrome (disc. 2007) finish, sling, swivels, and scope base, 7 lbs. Mfg. 2003-2008, reintroduced 2011.

MSR $315	$285	$260	$235	$220	$210	$200	$190	

Add $24 for forward grip (4095TS FG) or $44 for forward grip and flashlight (4095TS FGFL).
Add $104 for laser (4095TS-LAZ).
Add $146 for forward grip, flashlight, and laser (new 2011, 4095TS FGFL-LAZ).
Add $32 for 4x32 scope or red dot scope.
Add $137 for 4x RGB scope (4095TS 4xRGB, new 2013).
Add $51 for Pro Pack Kit with target stock (new 2011).
Add $85 for detachable compensator, laser, and mount (mfg. 1999-2010).

* ***Model 4095TS Camo*** – .40 S&W cal., 16 1/2 in. barrel, 10 shot mag., Weaver style rails, sling, swivels, and scope base, fully adj. sights, all-weather polymer skeletonized stock, Hydro dipped Desert Digital Camo (4095TS DD), Pink Camo (4095TS PI), or Woodland Style Camo (4095TS WC) finish, 6 1/4 lbs. New 2015.

MSR $371	$315	$275	$235	$215	$175	$150	$125	

MODEL 4595TS – .45 ACP cal., 17 1/2 in. barrel, 9 shot mag., adj. peep sight, black polymer stock (target stock became standard 2013), Weaver style rails, sling, swivels, and scope base, black finish, 7 lbs. New 2011.

MSR $330	$295	$270	$245	$230	$220	$210	$200	

Add $30 for forward grip (4595TS FG) or $50 for forward grip and flashlight (4595TS FGFL).
Add $38 for 4x32 scope (4595TS 4x32) or red dot scope (4595TS RD). Add $109 for laser sight (4595TS-LAZ).
Add $57 for Pro Pack Kit with target stock (new 2011).
Add $142 for 4x RGB scope (new 2013).
Add $152 for forward grip, flashlight, and laser sight (new 2011, 4595TS FGFL-LAZ).

MSR	100%	98%	95%	90%	80%	70%	60%	Last MSR

* **Model 4595TS Camo** – .45 ACP cal., 16 1/2 in. barrel, 9 shot mag., fully adj. sights, Weaver style rails, sling, swivels, and scope base, all-weather polymer skeletonized stock, Hydro dipped Desert Digital Camo (4595TS DD), Pink Camo (4595TS PI), or Woodland Style Camo (4595TS WC) finish, 6 1/4 lbs. New 2015.

MSR $392	$335	$295	$250	$230	$185	$150	$125	

HIGH STANDARD

Previous manufacturer located in New Haven, Hamden, and East Hartford, CT. High Standard Mfg. Co. was founded in 1926. They entered the firearms business when they purchased Hartford Arms and Equipment Co. in 1932. The original plant was located in New Haven, CT. During WWII High Standard operated plants in New Haven and Hamden. After the war, the operations were consolidated in Hamden. In the late 1940's and early 1950's the pistol plant was located in East Haven but the guns continued to be marked New Haven. In 1968, the company was sold to the Leisure Group, Inc. A final move was made to East Hartford, CT in 1977 where they remained until the doors were closed in late 1984. In early 1978, the Leisure Group sold the company to the management and the company became High Standard, Inc.

Many collectors have realized the rarity and quality factors this trademark has earned. 13 different variations (Models C, A, D, E, H-D, H-E, H-A, H-B First Model, G-380, GD, GE, and Olympic, commonly called the GO) had a total production of less than 28,000 pistols. For these reasons, top condition High Standard pistols are getting more difficult to find each year.

As a final note on High Standard pistols, they are listed under the following category names: Letter Series, Letter Series w/Hammer, Lever Letter Series, Lever Name Series, 100 Series, 101 Series, 102 Series, 103 Series, 104 Series, 105 Series, 106 Series - Military Models, 107 Series, Conversion Kits, and SH Series.

Note: catalog numbers were not always consistent with design series, and in 1966-1967 changed with accessories offered, but not design series.

The approx. ser. number cut-off for New Haven, CT marked guns is 442,XXX.

The approx. ser. number range for Hamden, CT marked guns is 431,XXX-2,500,811, G 1,001-G 13,757 (Shipped) or G15,650 (Packed) or ML 1,001-ML 23,065. One exception is a 9211 Victor serial number 3,000,000 shipped 1 March, 1974.

The first gun shipped 16 June, 1977 from E. Hartford was a Victor 9217 serial number EH0001.

The approx. ser. number ranges for E. Hartford, CT manufacture is ML 25,000-ML 86,641 and SH 10,001-SH 34,034. One exception is a single gun numbered ML90,000.

All "V" marked guns were shipped during June 1984 or later independent of serial number.

Original factory boxes have become very desirable. Prices can range from $50-$100 for a good condition Model 106 or 107 factory box to over $150 for an older box of a desirable model.

SHOTGUNS: DEFENSE & LAW ENFORCEMENT

SEMI AUTOMATIC MODEL – 12 ga., 20 in. cylinder bore barrel, 4 shot mag., recoil pad walnut stock and forearm.

	$325	$300	$275	$250	$225	$200	$150	

MODELS 10A/10B SEMI-AUTO – 12 ga., combat model, 18 in. barrel, semi-auto, unique bullpup design incorporates raked pistol grip in front of receiver and metal shoulder pad attached directly to rear of receiver, black Cycolac plastic shroud and pistol grip, very compact size (28 in. overall). Disc.

* **Model 10-A Semi-Auto** – 4 shot mag., fixed carrying handle and integral flashlight. Between 1,700 and 1,800 were produced beginning 1967.

	$875	$795	$725	$650	$575	$500	$425	

* **Model 10-B Semi-Auto** – 12 ga., folding carrying handle, provisions made for attaching a Kel-lite flashlight to receiver top, extended blade front sight, 4 shot mag., carrying case.

	$850	$775	$715	$650	$575	$515	$450	

Add 15% for flashlight.

SLIDE ACTION RIOT SHOTGUN – 12 ga. only on the Flite King Action, 18 or 20 in. barrel, police riot gun, available with or w/o rifle sights, plain pistol grip oiled walnut stock & forearm, changed to walnut stained and lacquered birch in the mid-1970s.

	$325	$275	$250	$200	$175	$125	$115	

HIGH STANDARD MANUFACTURING CO.

High Standard is a current trademark of firearms manufactured by Firearms International Inc., established in 1993 and located in Houston, TX.

This company was formed during 1993, utilizing many of the same employees and original material vendors which the original High Standard company used during their period of manufacture (1926-1984). During 2004, Crusader Group Gun Company, Inc. was formed, and this new company includes the assets of High Standard Manufacturing Co, Firearms International Inc., AMT-Auto Mag, Interarms, and Arsenal Line Products.

MSR	100%	98%	95%	90%	80%	70%	60%	Last MSR

RIFLES/CARBINES: SEMI-AUTO

HSA-15 – 5.56 NATO or 6x45mm (new 2012) cal., AR-15 style, A2 configuration, 16 (carbine), or 20 (rifle) in. barrel with muzzle brake, fixed (rifle) or collapsible (carbine) stock, 30 shot mag., with or w/o adj. sights.

MSR $925	$850	$750	$650	$575	$525	$475	$425	

Add $40 for adj. sights.

Subtract $72 for 6x45mm cal. (new 2012).

HSA-15 CRUSADER – 5.56 NATO cal., 16 in. M4 barrel with A2 flash hider, alum. forged upper and lower receivers, 30 shot mag., quad rail in choice of carbine, mid, or rifle length, low profile gas block or Picatinny gas block, M4 style 6-position adj. stock, ambidextrous safety, Ergo pistol grip, ambidextrous single point sling adaptor, black or tan finish. New 2014.

MSR $1,200	$1,075	$950	$800	$725	$600	$485	$375	

HSA-15 ENFORCER – 5.56 NATO or .300 AAC Blackout cal., 16 in. M4 style barrel with A2 flash hider, 30 shot mag., alum. forged upper and lower receivers with hardcoat anodized finish, quad rail in choice of carbine, mid, or rifle length, low profile gas block or Picatinny rail, M4 6-position adj. stock, Ergo pistol grip, front and rear flip up rail mounted sights, ambidextrous single point sling adaptor, black or tan finish. New 2014.

MSR $1,100	$975	$850	$725	$675	$550	$450	$350	

Add $50 for .300 AAC Blackout cal.

HSA-15 NATIONAL MATCH – 5.56 NATO cal., AR-15 style, available with either 20 in. (National Match) or 24 in. (Long Range Rifle) fluted barrel, includes Knight's military two-stage trigger. Mfg. 2006-2012.

	$1,125	$950	$850	$750	$650	$550	$495	*$1,238*

Add $12 for Long Range Rifle.

M-4 CARBINE – 5.56 NATO or 9mm Para. cal., 16 in. barrel, fixed A2 (.223 Rem. cal. only, new 2010) or six position adj. stock, fixed or adj. sights. New 2009.

MSR $880	$825	$725	$625	$550	$475	$400	$350	

Add $30 for 9mm Para. cal. (adj. stock only).

Add $35 for adj. sight (disc.).

Add $65 for quad rail with Picatinny gas block.

Add $450 for chrome lined barrel, free floating quad rails, flip up sights, flash hider and two-stage match trigger (.223 Rem. cal. only, disc. 2009).

M-4 ENFORCER CARBINE – 5.56 NATO cal., 16 in. barrel with A2 flash hider, Socom style 6-position collapsible stock, flip up battle sights, full length flat-top receiver, YHM quad rail with smooth sides, Ergo grip, 30 shot mag. New 2012.

MSR $2,275	$1,950	$1,700	$1,475	$1,250	$1,050	$875	$725	

HOGAN MANUFACTURING LLC

Current AR-15 style carbine/rifle manufacturer located in Glendale, AZ.

RIFLES: SEMI-AUTO

H-223 STANDARD CARBINE – .223 Rem. cal., AR-15 style, GPO, 16 in. button rifled barrel with 5 prong muzzle brake, aluminum alloy free floating monolithic Tactical or Hunter handguards, aluminum forged lower and A3 flat-top upper receiver, Hogan "Gold Standard" trigger system, VLTOR 6-position retractable buttstock with Mil-Spec tube, rubber buttpad, Ergo pistol grip, black or OD Green anodized, Dark Earth or OD Green Cerakote, or NP3 finish, includes hard case with foam liner, one Magpul PMAG, Ergo LowPro rail covers.

MSR $2,099	$1,795	$1,575	$1,325	$1,150	$995	$850	$700	

Add $200 for Dark Earth or OD Green Cerakote finish.

* ***H-223 Designated Marksman*** – .223 Rem. cal., GPO, similar to H-223 Standard carbine, except features 18 in. barrel, 7 lbs. 3 oz. (with Hunter X-Rail) or 8 lbs. 3 oz. (with Tactical X-rail).

MSR $2,099	$1,795	$1,575	$1,325	$1,150	$995	$850	$700	

Add $200 for Dark Earth or OD Green Cerakote finish.

* ***H-223 Sniper Elite*** – .223 Rem. cal., GPO, similar to H-223 Standard Carbine, except features 20 in. barrel, 8 lbs. 5 oz.

MSR $2,274	$1,925	$1,690	$1,425	$1,225	$1,035	$885	$735	

Add $200 for Dark Earth or OD Green Cerakote finish.

H-223 HERO MODEL – .223 Rem. cal., AR-15 style, GPO, 16 in. barrel with A2 flash hider, Magpul MOE mid-length plastic handguard, forged alum. A3 flat-top upper, alum. alloy lower receiver, M4 retractable buttstock with Mil-spec tube, A2 pistol grip, black anodized finish.

MSR $1,399	$1,200	$1,075	$950	$800	$700	$600	$495	

MSR	100%	98%	95%	90%	80%	70%	60%	Last MSR

H-308 STANDARD CARBINE – .308 Win. cal., AR-15 style, GPO, 16 in. button rifled barrel with 5 prong muzzle brake, aluminum alloy free floating monolithic Tactical or Hunter handguards, aluminum forged lower and A3 flat-top upper receiver, Hogan "Gold Standard" trigger system, VLTOR 6-position retractable buttstock with Mil-Spec tube, rubber buttpad, Ergo pistol grip, black or OD Green anodized, Dark Earth or OD Green Cerakote, or NP3 finish, includes hard case with foam liner, one Magpul PMAG, Ergo LowPro rail covers.

| MSR $2,290 | $1,950 | $1,725 | $1,450 | $1,250 | $1,050 | $900 | $750 | |

Add $200 for Dark Earth or OD Green Cerakote finish.

* **H-308 Designated Marksman** – .308 Win. cal., GPO, similar to H-308 Standard carbine, except features 18 in. barrel.

| MSR $2,290 | $1,950 | $1,725 | $1,450 | $1,250 | $1,050 | $900 | $750 | |

Add $200 for Dark Earth or OD Green Cerakote finish.

* **H-308 Sniper Elite** – .308 Rem. cal., GPO, similar to H-308 Standard Carbine, except features 20 in. barrel.

| MSR $2,290 | $1,950 | $1,725 | $1,450 | $1,250 | $1,050 | $900 | $750 | |

Add $200 for Dark Earth or OD Green Cerakote finish.

HOLLOWAY ARMS CO.

Previous manufacturer located in Fort Worth, TX.

Holloway made very few rifles or carbines before operations ceased and existing specimens are scarce.

RIFLES: SEMI-AUTO

HAC MODEL 7 RIFLE – .308 Win. cal., gas operated, 20 in. barrel, adj. front and rear sights, 20 shot mag., side folding stock, right or left-hand action. Mfg. 1984-1985 only.

| | $3,750 | $3,350 | $3,100 | $2,800 | $2,650 | $2,350 | $2,000 | $675 |

* **HAC Model 7C Rifle Carbine** – 16 in. carbine, same general specifications as Model 7. Disc. 1985.

| | $3,750 | $3,350 | $3,100 | $2,800 | $2,650 | $2,350 | $2,000 | $675 |

Also available from the manufacturer were the Models 7S and 7M (Sniper and Match models).

HOLMES FIREARMS

Previous manufacturer located in Wheeler, AR. Previously distributed by D.B. Distributing, Fayetteville, AR.

PISTOLS: SEMI-AUTO

These pistols were manufactured in very limited numbers, most were in prototype configuration and exhibit changes from gun to gun. These models were open bolt and subject to 1988 federal legislation regulations.

MP-83 – 9mm Para. or .45 ACP cal., 6 in. barrel, walnut stock and forearm, blue finish, 3 1/2 lbs.

| | $700 | $600 | $500 | $450 | $400 | $375 | $350 | $450 |

Add 10% for deluxe package.
Add 40% for conversion kit (mfg. 1985 only).

MP-22 – .22 LR cal., steel and aluminum construction, 6 in. barrel, similar appearance to MP-83, 2 1/2 lbs. Mfg. 1985 only.

| | $395 | $360 | $320 | $285 | $250 | $230 | $210 | $400 |

SHOTGUNS

COMBAT 12 – 12 ga., riot configuration, cylinder bore barrel. Disc. 1983.

| | $795 | $720 | $650 | $595 | $550 | $500 | $450 | $750 |

HOULDING PRECISION FIREARMS

Current AR-15 style manufacturer located in Cincinnati, OH beginning mid-2015. Previously located in Madera, CA.

RIFLES: SEMI-AUTO

HPF-15 MOE – 5.56 NATO cal., GIO, 16 in. M4 barrel with HPF Irish Curse muzzle brake, BTE SST, Magpul MBUS sights, MOE handguard, Magpul MOE 6-position stock, Magpul MOE grip, Cerakote finish, 8.4 lbs.

| MSR $1,599 | $1,350 | $1,180 | $1,015 | $925 | $750 | $625 | $500 | |

HPF-15 MOE-C – 5.56 NATO cal., GIO, 16 in. M4 profile barrel with Troy Medieval muzzle brake, modular two-piece handguard, pistol grip, integrated oversized trigger guard, flared magwell, receiver height gas block, all Magpul MOE furniture including MOE carbine length handguard, grip, stock, and Magpul MBUS sights, Cerakote ceramic finish, 7 lbs. Disc. 2014.

| | $1,525 | $1,350 | $1,150 | $1,050 | $850 | $700 | $575 | $1,799 |

MSR	100%	98%	95%	90%	80%	70%	60%	Last MSR

HPF-15 MOE-M – 5.56 NATO cal., GIO, 16 in. mid-length barrel with Troy muzzle brake, integrated oversized trigger guard, flared magwell, BTE receiver height gas block, all Magpul MOE furniture including MOE mid-length handguard, grip, 6-position stock, and Magpul MBUS sights, Cerakote ceramic finish, 7 lbs. Disc. 2014.

| | $1,525 | $1,350 | $1,150 | $1,050 | $850 | $700 | $575 | *$1,799* |

HPF-15 MOE-R – 5.56 NATO cal., GIO, 18 in. rifle length barrel with Troy muzzle brake, integrated oversized trigger guard and flared magwell, BTE receiver height gas block, all Magpul MOE furniture including MOE rifle-length handguard, grip, 6-position stock, and Magpul MBUS sights, Cerakote ceramic finish, 7 lbs. Disc. 2014.

| | $1,525 | $1,350 | $1,150 | $1,050 | $850 | $700 | $575 | *$1,799* |

HPF-15 UBR – 5.56 NATO cal., GIO, 16 or 18 in. mid-length match grade barrel with custom muzzle brake, diamond head gas block, interchangeable Picatinny rail segments, two-stage Geissele trigger, aluminum upper and lower receivers, polished M4 feed ramps, Troy or JP Enterprise modular handguard, integrated oversized trigger guard and flared magwell, Ergo grip or Magpul Plus grip, Magpul ACS or Vltor collapsible buttstock, Magpul MBUS sights or optic ready, Cerakote finish, 6.14 lbs.

| MSR $2,350 | $2,125 | $1,850 | $1,595 | $1,450 | $1,175 | $950 | $750 | |

HPF-3 TGR – 5.56 NATO cal., GIO, 16 or 18 in. barrel by Daniel Defense, JP Enterprise tactical compensator or Talon brake, Geissele Super 3-gun SST, HPF upper and lower receiver, large latch BCM Gunfighter charging handle, Magpul plus grip, Magpul ACS stock. Mfg. 2013 only.

| | $2,150 | $1,875 | $1,625 | $1,450 | $1,175 | $975 | $750 | *$2,403* |

HPF-15 TGR – 5.56 NATO cal., GIO, 16 or 18 in. mid-length barrel with custom muzzle brake, Vltor low profile gas block, large or medium latch BCM Gunfighter charging handle, polished M4 feed ramps, 15 in. Troy modular handguard, Magpul BUIS sights or optic ready, billet aluminum upper and lower receiver, integrated oversized trigger guard and flared magwell, Geissele SSA two-stage or duty trigger, Ergo grip or Magpul Plus grip, Magpul ACS or Vltor collapsible stock, 6.14 lbs.

| MSR $2,499 | $2,250 | $1,975 | $1,700 | $1,525 | $1,250 | $1,025 | $800 | |

HOUSTON ARMORY

Previous rifle manufacturer located in Stafford, TX until 2015.

RIFLES

Houston Armory manufactured a line of AR-15 style semi-auto rifles, including the .440 Hash (last MSR was $3,485), .50 Beowulf (last MSR ws $3,485), H300IC (last MSR was $3,085), H16IC (last MSR ws $3,085), H308IC (last MSR was $4,085), and HASPR16 (last MSR was $2,890). Houston Armory also offered a bolt action rifle (last MSR range was $1,900-$2,900), as well as a complete line of suppressors.

HOWA

Current manufacturer established in 1967, located in Tokyo, Japan. Howa sporting rifles are currently imported beginning Oct. 1999 by Legacy Sports International, LLC, located in Reno, NV. Previously located in Alexandria, VA. Previously imported until 1999 by Interarms/Howa, located in Alexandria, VA, Weatherby (Vanguard Series only), Smith & Wesson (pre-1985), and Mossberg (1986-1987).

RIFLES: BOLT ACTION

Howa also manufactures barreled actions in various configurations. MSRs range from $476-$596. During mid-2011, detachable magazines became available for all Model 1500s.

MODEL 1500 PCS – .308 Win. cal., police counter sniper rifle featuring 24 in. barrel, choice of blue metal or stainless steel, black synthetic or checkered walnut stock, no sights, approx. 9.3 lbs. Imported 1999-2000.

| | $385 | $335 | $290 | $260 | $210 | $175 | $135 | *$465* |

Add $20 for wood stock.
Add $60 for stainless steel.

HULDRA ARMS

Current trademark of AR-15 style semi-auto rifles manufactured by Adams Arms and sold exclusively by Fleet Farm.

RIFLES: SEMI-AUTO

All rifles include magazine and soft sided tactical case.

MARK IV CARBINE – 5.45x39mm or 5.56 NATO cal., AR-15 style, GPO, 16 in. M4 contour barrel with A2 flash hider, SST, 6-position tactical buttstock with A2 pistol grip, M4 handguards, forged aluminum upper and lower receivers, 6.2 lbs.

| MSR $950 | $815 | $700 | $630 | $570 | $500 | $425 | $380 | |

Add $65 for 5.45x39mm cal.

MSR	100%	98%	95%	90%	80%	70%	60%	Last MSR

MARK IV TACTICAL ELITE – 5.56 NATO cal., AR-15 style, GPO, 16 in. Government contour barrel with A2 flash hider, SST, Vltor IMOD Mil-Spec stock with non-slip removable buttpad, Ergo ambi pistol grip, free floating extended quad rail forearm with Picatinny rail, forged aluminum upper and lower receivers, includes magazine and soft sided tactical case, 7.2 lbs.

MSR $1,450	$1,235	$1,100	$985	$835	$725	$615	$515	

MARK IV TACTICAL EVO – 5.56 NATO cal., 14 1/2 in. Government contour barrel with permanently affixed elongated flash hider, M4 feed ramps, mid-length gas system, SST, Samson Evolution Series aluminum forearm, Mil-Spec hardcoat anodized finish, 6.8 lbs. Disc. 2014.

	$1,200	$1,075	$950	$800	$700	$600	$495	*$1,400*

X-PRE 1 – 5.56 NATO cal., GPO, 16 in. medium contour fluted stainless steel barrel with Adams Arms compensator, SST, Vltor IMOD Mil-Spec stock with non-slip removable buttpad, Ergo ambi grip, monolithic fluted forearm, forged aluminum upper and lower receivers, 7.2 lbs. Disc. 2013.

	$1,800	$1,575	$1,350	$1,225	$990	$825	$675	*$2,000*

X-PRE 2 – 5.56 NATO cal., GPO, 18 in. Ultra lite match grade barrel with Adams Arms Jet compensator, Mega Arms MKM upper receiver and free float KeyMod, Hipertouch 24 3G trigger, Luth MBA-1 stock, Magpul MOE K-2 grip, approx. 7 1/2 lbs. New 2015.

MSR $2,000	$1,700	$1,500	$1,250	$1,100	$950	$825	$675	

HUSAN ARMS

Current manufacturer of semi-auto rifles and shotguns located in Konya, Turkey. Shotguns currently imported by Century Arms (Century International Arms, Inc.), located in Delray Beach, FL, and by RAAC, located in Scottsburg, IN.

Husan Arms manufactures a complete line of AR-15 style semi-auto rifles with various stock options and receiver finishes. Currently, these models are not imported into the U.S. Husan also manufactures the MKA 1919 12 ga. AR-15 style shotgun. Please refer to the importer's listings for more information.

I SECTION

IAI INC. - AMERICAN LEGENDS

Previous manufacturer, importer, and distributor located in Houston, TX. Firearms were manufactured by Israel Arms International, Inc., located in Houston, TX. IAI designates Israel Arms International, and should not be confused with Irwindale Arms, Inc. (also IAI).

The models listed were part of an American Legend Series that are patterned after famous American and Belgian military carbines/rifles and semi-auto pistols.

MSR	100%	98%	95%	90%	80%	70%	60%	Last MSR

CARBINES/RIFLES: SEMI-AUTO

MODEL 888 M1 CARBINE – .22 LR or .30 Carbine cal., 18 in. barrel, mfg. from new original M1 parts and stock by IAI (barrel bolt and receiver) and unused GI parts, 10 shot mag., choice of birch or walnut stock, parkerized finish, metal or wood handguard, 5 1/2 lbs. Mfg. by IAI in Houston, TX 1998-2004.

	$675	$595	$565	$435	$395	$315	$295	*$556*

Add $11 for .22 LR cal. Add $31 for walnut/metal forearm or $47 for walnut/wood forearm.

MODEL 333 M1 GARAND – .30-06 cal., patterned after the WWII M1 Garand, 24 in. barrel, internal magazine, 8 shot en-bloc clip, parkerized finish, 9 1/2 lbs. Mfg. 2003-2004.

	$950	$875	$775	$625	$525	$400	$350	*$972*

PISTOLS: SEMI-AUTO

MODEL 2000 – .45 ACP cal., patterned after the Colt Govt. 1911, 5 or 4 1/4 (Commander configuration, Model 2000-C) in. barrel, SA, parkerized finish, plastic or rubber finger groove grips, 36-38 oz. Mfg. in South Africa 2002-2004.

	$415	$365	$325	$295	$275	$250	$225	*$465*

I.O., INC.

Current manufacturer/importer (I.O., Inc. stands for Inter Ordnance) established in 2008, located in Palm Bay, FL. Previously located in Monroe, NC until mid-2013.

PISTOLS: SEMI-AUTO

HELLCAT .380 II – .380 ACP cal., 2 3/4 in. steel alloy barrel with 6 grooves, DAO, SFO, 6 shot stainless steel mag., fixed sights, available in three finishes, includes custom pocket pouch, 9.4 oz. Disc. 2013.

	$200	$175	$150	$135	$110	$90	$75	*$250*

HELLPUP – 7.62x39mm cal., AK-47 design, 9 1/4 in. barrel, Krinkov style flash hider, 30 shot metal mag., adj. front and rear sights, black polymer furniture, tactical pistol grip, Mil-Spec receiver, parkerized finish, 5 lbs. Mfg. by Radom, importation disc. 2013.

	$775	$700	$625	$550	$475	$400	$325	*$864*

M214 NANO – 7.62x39mm cal., AK-47 design, 7 in. barrel, 30 shot mag., parkerized finish, 5 1/2 lbs. New 2016.

MSR $675	$585	$500	$435	$365	$325	$280	$265	

M215 MICRO FL-7 – 5.56x45mm or .300 AAC Blackout cal., 7 in. barrel, 30 shot mag., forged T6 upper and lower receivers, free float handguard, hardcoat anodized finish, 4.3 lbs. New 2015.

MSR $750	$675	$600	$525	$450	$375	$325	$275	

M215 MICRO QR-7 – 5.56x45mm or .300 AAC Blackout cal., 7 in. barrel, 30 shot mag., forged T6 upper and lower receivers, 4 in. (Micro QR-7/4) or full-length free float quad rail, hard anodized finish, 4.3 lbs. New 2015.

MSR $750	$675	$550	$475	$425	$375	$325	$275	

M215 MICRO QR-10 – 5.56x45mm or .300 AAC Blackout cal., 10 in. barrel, 30 shot mag., T6 upper and lower receivers, full-length quad rail, hard anodized finish, 4.3 lbs. New 2015.

MSR $750	$675	$550	$475	$425	$375	$325	$275	

POLISH PPS-43C – 9x19mm (new 2014) or 7.62x25mm TT cal., SA, stamped steel barrel and receiver, L-shaped flip up rear sight, fixed blade front sight, muzzle brake, stock has no function and is permanently fixed in its folded position, safety located at front of trigger guard, includes 2 (9x19mm cal.) or 4 curved box magazines (each holds 35 rounds) and cleaning kit. Mfg. at Radom Plant in Poland.

MSR $600	$535	$475	$400	$350	$295	$235	$185	

RADOM 47P (POLISH AK PISTOL) – 7.62x39mm cal., AK-47 design, 9 1/4 or 11 1/2 (disc.) in. barrel with Krinkov style flash hider, two 30 shot waffle pattern polymer mags., Mil-Spec receiver, wood (disc.) or tactical pistol grip, black polymer furniture, parkerized finish, 5 lbs. Mfg. by Radom. Importation began 2014.

MSR $700	$595	$525	$450	$400	$350	$300	$250	

MSR	100%	98%	95%	90%	80%	70%	60%	*Last MSR*

VENOM .45 1911 – .45 ACP cal., 4 in. stainless steel barrel with chamber indicator, full size grip and frame, Commander size slide, 8 shot mag., tapered magwell, lightweight adj. trigger, ambi safety, low profile sights, built-in Picatinny rail, serrated forward slide, diamond checkered Hogue grips, includes foam lined carry case, parkerized (disc. 2015) or Cerakote finish, 2 lbs. New 2014.

	100%	98%	95%	90%	80%	70%	60%	
MSR $600	$535	$475	$400	$350	$295	$235	$185	

Subtract approx. $65 for parkerized finish.

RIFLES: SEMI-AUTO

AK22 – Disc. 2010.

Last MSR in 2010 was $500.

AK47-C – AK-47 style, fixed, folding, collapsible or polymer stock (Galil-type forearm), synthetic or wood stock. Disc. 2010.

Last MSR in 2010 was $500-$670, depending on stock.

AKM247 – 7.62x39mm cal., AK-47 design, 16 1/4 in. barrel, 30 shot mag., Mil-Spec receiver, bayonet lug, bolt hold open, recoil buffer, accepts all standard AK and RPK mags., adj. front and rear sights, tactical pistol grip and sling swivel, black polymer furniture, fixed or underfolding (new 2016, AKM247 UF) stock, parkerized finish, 8 lbs. New 2015.

	100%	98%	95%	90%	80%	70%	60%	
MSR $600	$525	$465	$400	$340	$300	$265	$250	

Add $100 for underfolding stock (new 2016, AKM247 UF).

AKM247C – 7.62x39mm cal., 16 1/2 in. barrel, 30 shot mag., bayonet lug, adj. sights, tactical pistol grip and sling swivels, precision machined scope mount rail on left side of receiver, laminated wood furniture, parkerized finish, 8 lbs. New 2015.

	100%	98%	95%	90%	80%	70%	60%	
MSR $675	$585	$500	$435	$365	$325	$280	$265	

Add $25 for underfolding stock (AKM247C UF).

AKM247E – 7.62x39mm cal., GPO, 16 1/4 in. barrel, Mil-Spec receiver, adj. sights, handguard with built-in accessory rail, tactical pistol grip and sling swivel, bayonet lug, black polymer furniture, parkerized finish, 7 lbs. New 2015.

Please contact the company directly for pricing and availability for this model.

AKM247H – 7.62x39mm cal., AK-47 design, 16 in. barrel, 30 shot mag., Mil-Spec receiver, bayonet lug, bolt hold open, recoil buffer, lower handguard, adj. front and rear sights, Hogue pistol grip, black polymer furniture, parkerized finish, 7 lbs. Mfg. 2015 only.

	100%	98%	95%	90%	80%	70%	60%	
	$545	$485	$415	$350	$310	$275	$260	*$620*

AKM247SB SF/UF – 7.62x39mm cal., AK-47 design, 16 in. barrel, permanently attached barrel extension, 30 shot mag., side folding or underfolding stock, parkerized finish, 8 lbs. New 2016.

	100%	98%	95%	90%	80%	70%	60%	
MSR $950	$815	$700	$630	$570	$500	$425	$380	

Add $68 for underfolding stock (AKM247SB UF).

AKM247T – 7.62x39mm cal., AK-47 design, 16 in. barrel with Phantom flash hider, 30 shot mag., CNC machined scope mount rail, tactical quad rail, parkerized finish, 8 lbs. New 2015.

	100%	98%	95%	90%	80%	70%	60%	
MSR $647	$575	$500	$435	$365	$325	$280	$265	

AR-15A1 – .223 Rem. cal., 16.1 in. barrel, two 30 shot mags., I.O. made lower receiver machined solid aircraft aluminum billets, fixed black polymer stock and forend, pistol grip, carry handle, original Colt Vietnam style upper receiver and bolt assembly. New 2014.

	100%	98%	95%	90%	80%	70%	60%	
MSR $900	$775	$685	$615	$550	$485	$415	$370	

BSR-74 – 5.45x39mm cal., AK-47 style, 16.1 in. chrome lined barrel with bayonet lug, removable compensator, 30 shot detachable mag., matte black finish, wood or polymer furniture, wood stock with sling swivel or wire folding stock, pistol grip. Mfg. in Bulgaria, assembled in the U.S. Imported 2014 only.

	100%	98%	95%	90%	80%	70%	60%	
	$625	$540	$470	$400	$350	$310	$295	*$730*

Add $100 for wire folding stock.

CAR-15 – .223 Rem. cal., 16.1 in. barrel with flash hider, two 30 shot mags., I.O. made lower receiver machined out of solid aircraft aluminum billets, matte black finish, adj. 6-position stock, pistol grip, carry handle, original Colt Vietnam style upper receiver and bolt assembly. Mfg. 2014 only.

	100%	98%	95%	90%	80%	70%	60%	
	$685	$615	$550	$475	$420	$365	$335	*$790*

CASAR AK – Disc. 2011.

Last MSR in 2011 was $648.

HELLHOUND TACTICAL – 7.62x39mm cal., AK-47 design, aluminum quad rail tactical handguard, 30 shot mag., CNC machined scope mount rail, parkerized finish, fixed polymer or wire folding stock. Mfg. 2011-2014.

	100%	98%	95%	90%	80%	70%	60%	
	$685	$615	$550	$475	$420	$365	$335	*$800*

MSR	100%	98%	95%	90%	80%	70%	60%	Last MSR

M214 – 7.62x39mm cal., AK-47 design, 16 in. barrel with Phantom flash hider, two 30 shot mags. (one clear, one black), fully heat treated receiver, extra long mag. release, full length quad rail, bolt hold open, recoil buffer, scope mount rail on left side of receiver, gas block/front sight combo, new trigger group, black polymer furniture, choice of tactical club foot or lateral folding stock, includes foam-lined hardshell case, 9 lbs. New 2015.

	100%	98%	95%	90%	80%	70%	60%	
MSR $740	$640	$555	$470	$400	$350	$310	$295	

Add $10 for side folding stock.

M214 SNIPER – 7.62x39mm cal., 21.4 in. heavy fluted barrel with compensator, 30, 40, or 75 shot mag., quad rail, adj. bipod, recoil buffer, bolt hold open, fully adj. stock, neoprene pistol grip, scope mount, parkerized finish, 10 1/2 lbs. New 2015.

	100%	98%	95%	90%	80%	70%	60%	
MSR $905	$775	$685	$615	$550	$485	$415	$370	

Add $121 for 1.5-4x40BE illuminated scope.
Add $100 for Russian 6x41 scope (mfg. 2015 only).

M215 A FRAME – 5.56x45mm cal., 16 in. barrel, 30 shot mag., flat-top receiver, Picatinny rail, front sight, round polymer forend, hard anodized finish, 6 lbs. New 2015.

	100%	98%	95%	90%	80%	70%	60%	
MSR $590	$525	$465	$400	$340	$300	$265	$250	

M215 LOW PROFILE – 5.56x45mm cal., 16 in. barrel, 30 shot mag., flat-top receiver, Picatinny rail, two-piece quad rail, low profile gas block, hard anodized finish, 6 lbs. New 2015.

	100%	98%	95%	90%	80%	70%	60%	
MSR $620	$650	$575	$510	$440	$385	$340	$325	

POLISH BERYL "ARCHER" – 7.62x39mm cal., AK-47 design, 16 1/4 in. hammer forged barrel with flash hider, 30 shot mag., Mil-Spec receiver, tactical pistol grip, black polymer furniture, collapsible stock, features a bolt hold open integrated into the safety lever on right side of receiver, and FB (Fabryka Broni) trademark on left side of receiver, adj. front and rear sights, tactical swivel sling, 7 lbs. Mfg. in Radom, Poland.

	100%	98%	95%	90%	80%	70%	60%	
MSR $1,380	$1,150	$1,030	$900	$750	$650	$550	$465	

RADOM 47 – 7.62x39mm cal., AK-47 design, 16 1/4 in. hammer forged chrome lined barrel, Mil-Spec receiver, adj. front and rear sights, black tactical pistol grip and sling swivel, parkerized finish, 7 lbs. Mfg. at Radom Plant in Poland. Importation began 2015.

	100%	98%	95%	90%	80%	70%	60%	
MSR $570	$515	$450	$375	$325	$285	$260	$240	

Add $30 for folding stock (Radom 47FS).

RADOM W – 7.62x39mm cal., AK-47 design, 16 1/4 in. barrel, Mil-Spec receiver, adj. front and rear sights, wood furniture, black tactical pistol grip and sling swivel, 7 lbs. Mfg. at Radom Plant in Poland. Importation began 2015.

	100%	98%	95%	90%	80%	70%	60%	
MSR $600	$525	$465	$400	$340	$300	$265	$250	

SPORTER – 7.62x39mm cal., AK-47 design, 16 1/4 in. barrel, 30 shot, Mil-Spec receiver, Picatinny rail forearm, black polymer fixed or Tantal folding stock, tactical pistol grip, tactical sling swivel, CNC machined scope mount rail, adj. front and rear sights, available in parkerized, dark earth, or pink finish/furniture, 7 lbs. Mfg. 2011-2014.

	100%	98%	95%	90%	80%	70%	60%	Last MSR
	$675	$615	$550	$475	$420	$365	$335	*$790*

Add $10 for Tantal folding stock.

* ***Laminate Sporter*** – 7.62x39mm cal., similar to Sporter model, except features laminate wood stock, parkerized finish only. Imported 2011-2014.

	100%	98%	95%	90%	80%	70%	60%	Last MSR
	$650	$575	$510	$440	$385	$340	$325	*$750*

* ***Polish Sporter*** – 7.62x39mm cal., similar to Laminate Sporter model, except does not have scope mount rail. Imported 2014 only.

	100%	98%	95%	90%	80%	70%	60%	Last MSR
	$625	$540	$470	$400	$350	$310	$295	*$720*

SPORTER ECON – 7.62x39mm cal., AK-47 design, 16 1/4 in. barrel, Mil-Spec receiver, 30 shot mag., Picatinny rail forearm, black polymer stock, tactical pistol grip, tactical sling swivel, adj. front and rear sights, parkerized finish, 7 lbs. Disc. 2013.

	100%	98%	95%	90%	80%	70%	60%	Last MSR
	$590	$500	$435	$365	$325	$280	$265	*$677*

STG-22 – Disc. 2010.

Last MSR in 2010 was $500.

STG2000-C – 7.62x39mm cal., AK-47 design, 16 1/4 in. barrel, 30 shot mag., Mil-Spec receiver, Picatinny rail, tactical pistol grip, tactical sling swivel, CNC machined scope mount rail, front sight/gas block, black polymer stock, parkerized, dark earth, or pink furniture. Disc. 2014.

	100%	98%	95%	90%	80%	70%	60%	Last MSR
	$685	$615	$550	$475	$420	$365	$335	*$800*

VEPR IV – please refer to Vepr. section for this model.

SHOTGUNS: SEMI-AUTO

Please refer to Vepr. section.

MSR	100%	98%	95%	90%	80%	70%	60%	Last MSR

ISSC HANDELSGESELLSCHAFT

Current manufacturer of semi-auto firearms located in Ried, Austria. Currently imported by American Tactical Imports located in Summerville, SC beginning 2015. Previously imported by Legacy Sports International located in Reno, NV late 2011-2014, and by Austrian Sporting Arms, located in Ware, MA until 2011.

PISTOLS: SEMI-AUTO

M22 – .22 LR cal., patterned after the Glock semi-auto, 4, 4 3/4 (new 2012), or 5 1/2 (new 2012) in. threaded (new 2012), standard, or target (new 2012) barrel, SA, 10 shot mag., white dot front and adj. rear sights, lower accessory rail, loaded chamber indicator, safety decocker, magazine disconnect, black polymer frame with contoured grip, adj. rear sight, black, two-tone Desert Tan, OD Green, pink, Harvest Moon camo (new 2013), Outshine camo (new 2013), or Muddy Girl camo (new 2013) finish, with or w/o brushed chrome (new 2012) slide, 21 oz. Imported 2009-2014.

	$365	$325	$285	$265	$245	$225	$200	$429

Add $72 for Harvest Moon camo, Outshine camo, or Muddy Girl camo (new 2013) stock.
Add $110 for 4 3/4 in. threaded barrel.
Add $38 for 5 1/2 in. target barrel.

M22 GEN2 – .22 LR cal., 4 in. barrel, two 10 shot mags., five safeties. New 2015.

MSR $220	$195	$175	$150	$135	$100	$90	$75	

RIFLES: SEMI-AUTO

MK22 – .22 LR cal., 10 or 22 shot mag., 16.6 in. Lothar Walther match barrel with muzzle brake, multiple charge bar locations on right and left side of receiver, ambidextrous safety and mag. release, black or Desert Tan (new 2012) finish, variable and folding adj. open sight, Picatinny quad rail, fixed, folding or collapsible stock with adj. cheekpiece, features UCAS (Universal Cocking Adaptation System), 6 1/2 lbs. Imported 2011-2014.

	$575	$500	$450	$400	$365	$335	$300	$665

Add $37 for Desert Tan finish.

INGRAM

Previously manufactured until late 1982 by Military Armament Corp. (MAC) located in Atlanta, GA.

PISTOLS: SEMI-AUTO

MAC 10 – .45 ACP or 9mm Para. cal., open bolt, semi-auto version of the sub-machine gun, 10 (.45 ACP cal.), 16 (9mm Para. cal.), 30 (.45 ACP cal.), or 32 (9mm Para. cal.) shot mag., compact all metal welded construction, rear aperture and front blade sight. Disc. 1982.

	$950	$875	$800	$700	$650	$575	$525	

Add approx. $160 for accessories (barrel extension, case, and extra mag.).

MAC 10A1 – similar to MAC 10 except fires from a closed bolt.

	$395	$375	$350	$280	$265	$225	$210	

MAC 11 – similar to MAC 10 except in .380 ACP cal.

	$750	$695	$650	$575	$550	$535	$485	

INTACTO ARMS

Current manufacturer established in 2008, located in Boise, ID.

CARBINES/RIFLES: SEMI-AUTO

Intacto Arms manufactures a complete line of semi-auto rifles and carbines based on the AR-15 and the AR-10 platforms. A wide variety of options and accessories are available. Please contact the company directly for more information (see Trademark Index). All rifles and carbines come with a lifetime guarantee.

BATTLE TAC – .204 Ruger, .22 LR, .223 Rem., .243 Win., .300 AAC Blackout, .300 WSM, 7.62x39mm, or 6.8 SPC cal., 16 in. stainless steel match grade barrel with A2 Predator flash hider, 30 shot PMAG, mid-length low profile gas block, solid billet machined upper and lower, nickel boron bolt carrier group (new 2016), 9 1/2, 12 1/2, or 15 1/2 in. extruded or round free floating handguard, 4 QD sling mount positions and continuous top Picatinny rail, ALG-QMS trigger (new 2016), Magpul CTR adj. stock, Magpul MOE+ grip, matte black or Flat Dark Earth finish, includes tactical soft carrying case.

MSR $2,000	$1,700	$1,500	$1,250	$1,100	$950	$825	$675	

Add $800 for UBL configuration (Under Barrel Launcher).
Add $100 for any caliber other than .223 Rem.
This model is available with a 9 1/2, 12 1/2, or 15 1/2 in. round or forged handguard at no additional charge.

MSR		100%	98%	95%	90%	80%	70%	60%	Last MSR

BATTLE TAC SPECIAL CALIBER – .204 Ruger, .22 LR, .243 Win., .300 AAC Blackout, .300 WSM, 7.62 NATO, or 6.8 SPC cal., customer's choice of caliber, barrel length, and gas system, stainless steel match barrel, Phantom Persuasion flash hider, Magpul 30 shot mag., solid billet upper and lower receiver, nickel boron bolt carrier group, mid-length gas block, ALG QMS trigger, 9 1/2, 12 1/2, or 15 1/2 in. extruded or round free float handguard, Picatinny top rail, Magpul CTR stock, MOE grip, black, FDE, or custom Cerakote finish, includes 34 in. Bulldog 5-pocket tactical soft carrying case. New 2015.

| | MSR $2,000 | $1,700 | $1,500 | $1,250 | $1,100 | $950 | $825 | $675 | |

Add $299 for custom Cerakote finish.

CARBON TAC – .308 Win. cal., AR-10 style, 18 1/2 in. National Match chrome moly stainless steel barrel, Doublestar 308 Carlson flash hider, 20 shot PMAG, solid billet CNC machined upper and lower, chrome bolt carrier group, knurled exterior, crenelated muzzle end, Magpul CTR collapsible stock, Precision Reflex 12 1/2 in. carbon fiber triangular free float handguard with rails, matte black finish, includes soft carrying case.

| | MSR $3,500 | $2,975 | $2,575 | $2,075 | $1,765 | $1,450 | $1,225 | $1,050 | |

This model can be completely customized per individual customer specifications.

FULL BATTLE RIFLE – .223 Rem. cal., 16.1 in. stainless steel match grade barrel with Phantom Persuasion flash hider, mid-length gas system, 30 shot Magpul PMAG, Magpul MBUS sights, solid billet machined upper and lower receiver, 9 1/2, 12 1/2, or 15 1/2 in. extruded or round free floating handguard, 4 QD sling mount positions and continuous Picatinny top rail, Magpul ACS adj. stock, Magpul ASAP sling mount, Magpul AFG2 forward grip, Magpul MOE+ grip, Geissele two-stage trigger, nickel boron bolt carrier group, BCM Gunfighter charging handle, JP silent buffer system, JP original complete adjustable fire control system (new 2016), matte black, FDE, or custom Cerakote finish, includes tactical soft carrying case.

| | MSR $2,500 | $2,125 | $1,875 | $1,550 | $1,325 | $1,100 | $950 | $825 | |

Add $299 for custom Cerakote finish.

This model can be completely customized per individual customer specifications.

ICARUS 7 – .223 Rem. cal., 16 in. chrome moly barrel, mid-length F-Mark front sight gas system, solid billet machined lower, forged flat-top upper, G.I. issue standard dual heat shield handguard, matte black finish, includes soft carrying case.

| | MSR $900 | $775 | $685 | $615 | $550 | $485 | $415 | $370 | |

MANTIS RIFLE – .223 Rem. cal., 18 (new 2016) or 20 in. stainless steel match grade barrel with Phantom Persuasion Tip flash hider, 10 and 30 shot PMAG, mid-length low profile gas block, solid billet machined upper and lower receiver, JP original complete adjustable fire control system (new 2016), nickel boron bolt carrier group (new 2016), 4 QD sling mount positions and continuous top Picatinny rail, 15 1/2 in. extruded or round free floating handguard, BCM Gunfighter large latch charging handle, JP silent buffer system, Magpul PRS or UBR (new 2016) stock, Magpul MOE+ grip, bipod, matte black, FDE, or custom Cerakote finish, includes tactical soft carrying case.

| | MSR $2,600 | $2,200 | $1,925 | $1,600 | $1,375 | $1,125 | $975 | $850 | |

Add $299 for custom Cerakote finish.

This model can be completely customized per individual customer specifications.

MID TAC – .223 Rem. or .300 AAC Blackout (stainless only) cal., 16 in. black phosphate or stainless steel barrel, 30 shot PMAG, mid-length low profile gas block, ALG-QMS trigger (new 2016), solid billet machined lower, forged flat-top upper, 4 QD sling mount positions and Picatinny top rail, 9 1/2, 12 1/2, or 15 1/2 in. extruded or round free floating handguard, adj. tactical (disc. 2015) or Magpul MOE (new 2016) stock, Magpul MOE grip (new 2016), matte black finish, includes soft carrying case.

| | MSR $1,400 | $1,200 | $1,075 | $950 | $800 | $700 | $600 | $495 | |

Add $100 for stainless steel.
Add $100 for .300 AAC Blackout cal.

M.O.E. – .223 Rem. cal., 16 in. chrome moly or stainless steel barrel, mid-length F-Mark front sight gas system, solid billet machined lower, forged flat-top upper, Magpul MOE handguard, Magpul MOE+ grip, Magpul MOE stock, 30 shot Magpul PMAG, matte black finish, includes soft carrying case.

| | MSR $1,100 | $925 | $850 | $725 | $625 | $550 | $475 | $425 | |

Add $100 for stainless steel.

PISTOLS: SEMI-AUTO

All 1911 style pistols can be customized per individual customer specifications, and Cerakoted in any color of the customer's choosing.

BATTLE TAC PISTOL – .223 Rem. cal., AR-15 style, solid billet CNC machined upper and lower, 7 or 10 1/2 in. stainless steel match barrel, Magpul flip up front and rear sight with single or double rail gas block, nickel boron bolt carrier group (new 2016), 6 1/2 or 9 1/2 in. forged or free float handguard, ALG-QMS trigger (new 2016), matte black finish, includes soft carrying case.

| | MSR $1,700 | $1,450 | $1,275 | $1,125 | $1,000 | $850 | $735 | $595 | |

MSR	100%	98%	95%	90%	80%	70%	60%	Last MSR

1911 GOVERNMENT – .45 ACP cal., full size Government style frame, 5 in. barrel, rear slide serrations, ambidextrous thumb safety, skeletonized trigger, high grip beavertail, checkered polymer grips, stippled front and rear backstrap.

MSR $2,899	$2,475	$2,150	$1,775	$1,525	$1,250	$1,050	$925

* 1911 Government Tactical – .45 ACP cal., similar to Government model, except has flared magwell and accessory rail.

MSR $2,899	$2,475	$2,150	$1,775	$1,525	$1,250	$1,050	$925

1911 COMMANDER – .45 ACP cal., similar to 1911 Government model, except has full size Commander style frame, 4 1/4 in. barrel, and double diamond checkered wood grips.

MSR $2,899	$2,475	$2,150	$1,775	$1,525	$1,250	$1,050	$925

1911 OFFICER – .45 ACP cal., similar to 1911 Government model, except has compact frame and 3 1/2 in. barrel.

MSR $2,899	$2,475	$2,150	$1,775	$1,525	$1,250	$1,050	$925

INTEGRITY ARMS & SURVIVAL

Current custom AR-15 style manufacturer located in Jefferson, GA. Previously located in Watkinsville, GA.

PISTOLS: SEMI-AUTO

.300 BLK PISTOL – .300 AAC Blackout cal., 12 1/2 in. Melonite treated barrel, Noveske KX5 muzzle device, pistol lengh gas system, Mil-Spec single stage trigger, forged matched set upper and lower receivers, 13 in. slim free float handguard, ambidextrous safety, Ergo grip, SIG arm brace on rear, hardcoat anodized finish.

MSR $1,250	$1,050	$950	$815	$715	$625	$535	$450

SIDE CHARGING AR PISTOL – 5.56 NATO cal., 10 1/2 in. barrel, Troy Industries Claymore muzzle brake, billet machined lower and non-reciprocating side charging upper receiver, M4 feed ramps, deluxe pistol buffer tube with Tungsten filled heavy buffer, quick detach endplate, ALG Defense QMS trigger group, Dark Earth Hogue rubber grip with beavertail, Troy Industries 11 in. Bravo handguard.

MSR $1,300	$1,100	$995	$875	$735	$650	$550	$465

CARBINES/RIFLES: SEMI-AUTO

Integrity Arms & Survival manufactures custom AR-15 style rifles in 5.56 NATO, 6.8 SPC, .223 Wylde, or .300 AAC Blackout caliber per customer specifications. **Previously manufactured models include:** Burnt Bronze Battle Rifle (last MSR was $1,350), Civilian Service Carbine (last MSR was $1,300), Premium Lightweight Wylde Chambered Carbine (last MSR was $1,050), Side Charging Burnt Bronze Carbine (last MSR was $1,500), Special Purpose Rifle (last MSR was $1,590), Foliage Green Premium Carbine (last MSR in 2014 was $1,300), Tungsten Grey Carbine (last MSR in 2014 was $1,350) and Muddy Girl Carbine (last MSR in 2014 was $900).

BATTLE WORN SIDE CHARGING CARBINE – 5.56 NATO cal., Melonite treated barrel, mid-length gas sytem, billet lower and non-reciprocating side charging upper receiver, 12 in. free floating slim KeyMod handguard, Mil-Spec single stage trigger, VLTOR IMOD Clubfoot stock, Ergo ambi Suregrip, Battle Worn Cerakote finish.

MSR $1,400	$1,200	$1,075	$950	$800	$700	$600	$495

BASIC M4 CARBINE – 5.56 NATO/.223 Rem. cal., 16 in. barrel (.223 Wylde chambered), M16 type bolt carrier group, forged upper and lower receiver, MIl-Spec single stage trigger, Magpul MOE handguard and stock, hardcoat anodized finish.

MSR $850	$725	$650	$580	$515	$450	$385	$340

ULTRALIGHT FIGHTING CARBINE (UFC) – 5.56 NATO/.223 Rem. cal., 16 in. Melonite treated barrel, mid-length gas system, forged upper and lower receiver, M4 feed ramps, Magpul Gen2 MBUS front and rear sights, rifle length carbon fiber free float handguard, Magpul MOE 6-position collapsible stock, Hogue beavertail soft rubber grip with finger grooves, 5.95 lbs.

MSR $1,250	$1,050	$950	$815	$715	$625	$535	$450

INTERARMS ARSENAL

Current trademark of firearms imported and distributed by High Standard Manufacturing Company, located in Houston, TX.

RIFLES: SEMI-AUTO

POLISH MODEL WZ.88 TANTAL – 5.45x39mm cal., choice of side folding stock with wood forend furniture or fixed stock, chrome lined barrel. Mfg. in U.S.

MSR $619	$525	$465	$415	$365	$335	$300	$275

Add $10 for side folding stock.

POLISH UNDERFOLDER – 7.62x39mm cal., underfolding stock.

MSR $975	$825	$675	$575	$475	$400	$350	$300

MSR	100%	98%	95%	90%	80%	70%	60%	Last MSR

HUNGARIAN ADM 65 STYLE AKM – 7.62x39mm cal., side folding stock.

MSR $837	$750	$650	$525	$475	$425	$375	$350

Add $28 for wood stock.
Add $38 for Tactical model.

HUNGARIAN UNDERFOLDER – 7.62x39mm cal., underfolding stock.

MSR $875	$735	$650	$580	$515	$450	$385	$340

AKM SERIES – 7.62x38mm cal., black polymer stock, Russian, Egyptian or Polish configurations.

MSR $619	$525	$465	$415	$365	$335	$300	$275

Add $40 for Polish import with under folding stock (AKMS Model).

AK-74 – 5.45x39mm cal., Bulgarian style mfg., choice of wood or polymer furniture.

MSR $679	$575	$500	$450	$400	$350	$300	$275

AK-47 – 7.62x39mm cal., AK-47 design with milled receiver, choice of Yugoslavian Zastava or other Eastern Bloc mfg.

MSR $1,195	$1,050	$925	$800	$675	$550	$475	$400

AR-15 A2 RIFLE – 5.56 NATO cal., AR-15 style, GIO, choice of flat-top (no sights), or A2 configuration, 20 in. barrel with flash hider, choice of black synthetic fixed or collapsible stock, 30 shot mag.

MSR $925	$825	$750	$675	$600	$525	$450	$400

Add $40 for A2 adj. sights.

M4 CARBINE – 5.56 NATO cal., GIO, 16 in. barrel with muzzle brake, choice of flat-top or A2 configuration, M4 6-position collapsible stock.

MSR $880	$740	$650	$580	$515	$450	$385	$340

Add $35 for A2 configuration.

INTERCONTINENTAL ARMS INC.

Previous importer located in Los Angeles, CA circa 1970s.

Intercontinental Arms Inc. imported a variety of SA revolvers, an AR-15 type semi-auto rifle, a derringer, a rolling block single shot rifle, and a line of black powder pistol reproductions and replicas. While these firearms were good, utilitarian shooters, they have limited desirability in today's marketplace. The single action revolvers manufactured by Hämmerli are typically priced in the $200-$395 range, the derringer is priced in the $115-$175 range, the AR-15 copy is priced in the $425-$675 range, and the single shot rolling block rifle is priced in the $150-$200 range, depending on original condition.

INTERDYNAMIC OF AMERICA, INC.

Previous distributor located in Miami, FL 1981-84.

PISTOLS: SEMI-AUTO

KG-9 – 9mm Para. cal., 3 in. barrel, SA, open bolt, tactical design pistol. Disc. approx. 1982.

	$850	$800	$700	$675	$650	$600	$575

KG-99 – 9mm Para. cal., 3 in. barrel, SA, tactical design pistol, closed bolt, 36 shot mag., 5 in. vent. shroud barrel, blue only, a stainless steel version of the KG-9. Mfg. by Interdynamic 1984 only.

	$425	$375	$325	$275	$250	$225	$195

*** KG-99M Mini Pistol**

	$495	$450	$400	$325	$275	$250	$225

INTERSTATE ARMS CORP.

Current importer located in Billerica, MA.

Interstate Arms Corp. has imported a variety of Chinese made cowboy action shotguns and reproductions, as well as pistols from Turkey.

SHOTGUNS: SLIDE ACTION

MODEL 97T WWI TRENCH GUN – 12 ga. only, authentic reproduction of the original Winchester WWI Trench Gun, complete with shrouded barrel, proper markings, finish, and wood. Imported mid-2002-2006, reintroduced 2010. Mfg. by Sun City Machinery Ltd.

MSR $465	$395	$350	$295	$275	$215	$180	$160

MODEL 372 – 12 ga., 3 in. chamber, 18 1/2 in. barrel with heat shield and ghost ring sights, bottom ejection port, cylinder choke, black synthetic stock and forearm. Limited importation 2007-2009.

	$200	$175	$150	$135	$110	$90	$70	*$250*

MSR	100%	98%	95%	90%	80%	70%	60%	Last MSR

HAWK 982 – 12 ga. only, 3 in. chamber, defense configuration with 18 1/2 in. cylinder bore barrel with fixed choke, black synthetic stock and forearm, matte black metal finish, current mfg. uses ghost ring sights. Importation began 2001.

	100%	98%	95%	90%	80%	70%	60%	
MSR $293	$260	$230	$200	$185	$170	$160	$150	

INTRAC ARMS INTERNATIONAL INC.

Previous importer located in Knoxville, TN. Intrac imported trademarks manufactured by Arsenal Bulgaria, and by IM Metal Production facility in Croatia late 2000-2004. Previously imported by HS America, located in Knoxville, TN.

RIFLES: SEMI-AUTO

ROMAK 1 & 2 – 7.62x39mm (Romak 1) or 5.45x39mm (Romak 2) cal., AK-47 copy with 16 1/2 in. barrel and scope mount on left side of receiver, wood thumbhole stock, includes 5 and 10 shot mags., and accessories. Imported 2002-2004.

	$595	$550	$525	$475	$450	$400	$350	$329

SLR-101 – similar to Romak, except has 17 1/4 in. cold hammer forged barrel and black polymer stock and forearm, includes 2 mags. and accessories. Imported 2002-2004.

	$650	$575	$500	$450	$425	$350	$325	$359

ROMAK 3 – 7.62x54R cal., based on current issue PSL/FPK sniper configuration, 5 or 10 shot mag., last shot bolt hold open, 26 1/2 in. barrel with muzzle brake, Mil-Spec scope with range finder, bullet drop compensator and illuminated recticle. Imported 2002-2004.

	$900	$825	$750	$650	$575	$525	$475	$899

INTRATEC

Previous manufacturer located in Miami, FL circa 1985-2000.

PISTOLS: SEMI-AUTO

TEC-DC9 – 9mm Para. cal., 5 in. shrouded barrel, SA, matte black finish, 10 (C/B 1994) or 32* shot mag. Mfg. 1985-1994.

	$475	$425	$375	$300	$275	$225	$200	$269

* **TEC-9DCK** – similar to TEC-9, except has new durable Tec-Kote finish with better protection than hard chrome. Mfg. 1991-94.

	$495	$465	$425	$375	$325	$295	$260	$297

* **TEC-DC9S** – matte stainless version of the TEC-9. Disc. 1994.

	$550	$500	$450	$400	$350	$300	$250	$362

Add $203 for TEC-9 with accessory package (deluxe case, 3-32 shot mags., tactical design grip, and recoil compensator).

TEC-DC9M – mini version of the Model TEC-9, including 3 in. barrel and 20 shot mag. Disc. 1994.

	$495	$465	$425	$375	$325	$295	$260	$245

* **TEC-DC9MK** – similar to TEC-9M, except has Tec-Kote rust resistant finish. Mfg. 1991-94.

	$525	$450	$400	$350	$300	$250	$200	$277

* **TEC-DC9MS** – matte stainless version of the TEC-9M. Disc. 1994.

	$575	$500	$450	$400	$350	$300	$275	$339

TEC-22 "SCORPION" – .22 LR cal., 4 in. barrel, SA, ambidextrous safety, military matte finish, or electroless nickel, 30 shot mag., adj. sights, 30 oz. Mfg. 1988-1994.

	$375	$325	$275	$225	$200	$175	$160	$202

Add $20 for Tec-Kote finish.

* **TEC-22N** – similar to TEC-22, except has nickel finish. Mfg. 1990 only.

	$395	$345	$300	$275	$250	$230	$220	$226

Add $16 for threaded barrel (Model TEC-22TN).

TEC-22T – threaded barrel variation of the TEC-22 "Scorpion." Mfg. 1991-94.

	$395	$350	$300	$250	$225	$195	$175	$161

Add $23 for Tec-Kote finish.

AB-10 – 9mm Para. cal., design similar to Luger, 2 3/4 in. non-threaded barrel, SA, choice of 32* (limited supply) or 10 shot mag., black synthetic frame, firing pin safety block, black or stainless steel finish, 45 oz. Mfg. 1997-2000.

	$325	$275	$235	$200	$180	$160	$150	$225

Add $20 for stainless steel (new 2000).
Add $100 for 32 shot mag.

MSR	100%	98%	95%	90%	80%	70%	60%	Last MSR

INTRATEC U.S.A., INC.

Previous manufacturer located in Miami, FL.

CARBINES

TEC-9C – 9mm Para. cal., carbine variation with 16 1/2 in. barrel, 36 shot mag.

Only 1 gun mfg. 1987 - extreme rarity precludes pricing.

PISTOLS: SEMI-AUTO

TEC-9 – 9mm Para. cal., 5 in. shrouded barrel, SA, 32 shot mag. Disc.

	100%	98%	95%	90%	80%	70%	60%
	$550	$495	$450	$395	$350	$295	$250

INVINCIBLE ARMS LLC

Current AR-15 style rifle, parts, and accessories manufacturer located in Willoughby, OH beginning 2015.

PISTOLS: SEMI-AUTO

BLACK FORGE TIER 1 PISTOL – 5.56 NATO cal., AR-15 style, GIO, aluminum flat-top A3 upper receiver, aluminum forged lower receiver, 10 1/2 in. carbine length barrel with Carlson Comps TAC brake, 10 1/2 in. modular rail system with full-length top Picatinny rail, two 3 in. and one 5 in. rail sections, M4 feed ramps, 30 shot detachable mag., Black Forge winter trigger guard, single stage trigger, Magpul Industries or U.S. Palm Battle grip, investment cast fire controls, Carpenter M16 LEO bolt carrier group with Black Forge NiPhos coating, hardcoat anodized matte black finish.

Please contact the company directly for pricing, options, and availability for this model.

* ***Black Forge Tier 1 SIG PSB*** – 5.56 NATO cal., similar to Tier 1 pistol, except has fully adj. SIG PSB tactical style stock.

Please contact the company directly for pricing, options, and availability for this model.

CARBINES/RIFLES: SEMI-AUTO

.300 BLACKOUT – .300 AAC Blackout cal., GIO, 16 1/2 in. M4 barrel, Lancer Systems Viper muzzle brake and 30 shot mag., KeyMod rail systems w/Picatinny rail sections, front and rear back up iron sights, Fortis REV free float rail system handguard, aluminum flat-top upper receiver with Mil-Spec Picatinny rail, M4 feed ramp, forged aluminum lower w/Invincible Arms logo, low profile gas block, stainless steel gas tube, Mil-Spec buffer tube, Invincible Arms laser engraved charging handle, oversized trigger guard, Hiperfire Hipertouch single stage trigger, Rogers Super-Stoc 6-position telescoping stock, A2 pistol grip, 6.8 lbs.

MSR $1,525	100%	98%	95%	90%	80%	70%	60%
	$1,295	$1,140	$1,035	$880	$760	$635	$535

.458 SOCUM – .458 SOCOM cal., GIO, 16 1/2 in. heavy barrel, muzzle brake with crush washer, Lancer Systems 30 shot mag., combination KeyMod rail systems w/Picatinny rail sections, front and rear back up iron sights, free floating railed handguard, aluminum flat-top upper receiver with Mil-Spec Picatinny rail, M4 feed ramp, forged aluminum lower w/Invincible Arms logo, low profile gas block, stainless steel gas tube, Mil-Spec buffer tube, Invincible Arms laser engraved charging handle, oversized trigger guard, Hiperfire Hipertouch single stage trigger, Rogers Super-Stoc 6-position telescoping stock, Magpul Gen1 MOE pistol grip, 7.8 lbs.

MSR $1,525	100%	98%	95%	90%	80%	70%	60%
	$1,295	$1,140	$1,035	$880	$760	$635	$535

5.56 OPTICS READY CARBINE – 5.56 NATO cal., GIO, 16 1/2 in. M4 barrel, A2 flash hider w/crush washer, 30 shot mag., no sights, M4 style dual heat shield handguard, aluminum flat-top upper w/Mil-Spec 1913 Picatinny rail system, M4 feed ramps, low profile gas block, stainless steel gas tube, Mil-Spec buffer tube, Invincible Arms laser engraved charging handle, forged aluminum lower w/Invincible Arms logo, oversized trigger guard, single stage trigger, Invincible Arms 6-position telescoping stock, A2 pistol grip, 6 1/2 lbs.

MSR $821	100%	98%	95%	90%	80%	70%	60%
	$685	$615	$550	$475	$420	$365	$335

5.56 PREDATOR RIFLE – 5.56 NATO cal., GIO, 18 in. heavy barrel, Lancer Systems muzzle brake w/crush washer, Lancer Systems 20 shot mag., no sights, Lancer Systems carbon fiber free floating handguard, aluminum flat-top upper w/Mil-Spec 1913 Picatinny rail system, M4 feed ramps, low profile gas block, stainless steel gas tube, Mil-Spec buffer tube, Invincible Arms laser engraved charging handle w/extended latch, aluminum forged lower with IA logo, oversized trigger guard, Hiperfire Hipertouch single stage trigger, Magpul UBR 6-position telescoping stock, Magpul MOE Gen 1 pistol grip, 7.1 lbs.

MSR $2,898	100%	98%	95%	90%	80%	70%	60%
	$2,475	$2,150	$1,775	$1,525	$1,250	$1,050	$925

5.56 VARMITER RIFLE – 5.56 NATO cal., GIO, 18 in. heavy barrel, Lancer Systems Viper muzzle brake w/crush washer, Lancer Systems 20 shot mag., no sights, low profile gas block, aluminum flat-top upper with Mil-Spec 1913 Picatinny rail system, M4 feed ramps, Lancer Systems carbon fiber free float handguard, Mil-Spec buffer tube, stainless steel gas tube, IA laser engraved charging handle with extended latch, forged aluminum lower with IA logo, oversized trigger guard, Hiperfire Hipertouch single stage trigger, Magpul UBR 6-position telescoping stock, Magpul MOE Gen 1 pistol grip, 6.9 lbs.

MSR $2,898	100%	98%	95%	90%	80%	70%	60%
	$2,475	$2,150	$1,775	$1,525	$1,250	$1,050	$925

MSR	100%	98%	95%	90%	80%	70%	60%	*Last MSR*

5.56 TACTICAL CARBINE – 5.56 NATO cal., GIO, 16 in. M4 barrel, Lancer Systems Viper muzzle brake w/crush washer, Lancer Systems 30 shot mag., combination KeyMod rail system with 1913 Picatinny rail sections, front and rear back up iron sights, Fortis REV free float handguard, aluminum flat-top upper with Mil-Spec Picatinny rail, M4 feed ramps, low profile gas block, stainless steel gas tube, Mil-Spec buffer tube, IA laser engraved charging handle, forged aluminum lower with IA logo, oversized trigger guard, Hiperfire Hipertouch single stage trigger, Rogers Super-Stoc 6-position telescoping stock, Magpul MOE Gen 1 pistol g rip, 7.4 lbs.

MSR $1,525	$1,295	$1,140	$1,035	$880	$760	$635	$535	

IRON BRIGADE ARMORY

Current rifle manufacturer located in Jacksonville, NC established 1979. Consumer direct sales through FFL.

RIFLES: BOLT ACTION

Iron Brigade Armory currently manufactures the following bolt action rifles: XM-3 Rifle - MSR $8,295, Chandler M40 Long Range Precision Rifle - MSR $5,995, M40 USM Chandler Urban Model - MSR $6,900, TAC-100 Tactical Standard Grade (rifle only) - MSR $2,295, TAC-200 Tactical Standard Grade (with optics) - MSR $3,195, TAC-300 Tactical Standard Grade (complete) - MSR $3,595, TAC-400 Tactical Super Grade (rifle only) - MSR $2,850, TAC-500 Tactical Super Grade (with optics) - MSR $3,750, and TAC-600 Tactical Super Grade (complete) - MSR $4,150. Several options and upgrades are available on each model. Please contact the company directly for more information, availability, and current prices (see Trademark Index).

IRON RIDGE ARMS CO.

Current AR-15 style rifle manufacturer located in Longmount, CO.

Iron Ridge Arms Co. manufactures the AR-15 style IRA-X Rifle platform available in three different configurations. Current lead time for individual rifles is approximately six months. Please contact the company directly for more information including customizing, options, pricing, and availability (see Trademark Index).

ISRAEL ARMS INTERNATIONAL, INC.

Previous importer and manufacturer located in Houston, TX, 1997-2004. Please refer to IAI Inc. - American Legend listing in this section.

ISRAEL ARMS LTD.

Previous manufacturer located in Kfar Saba, Israel. Imported and distributed exclusively by Israel Arms International, Inc. located in Houston, TX 1997-2001.

RIFLES: SEMI-AUTO

MODEL 333 M1 GARAND – .30-06 cal., 24 in. barrel, parts remanufactured to meet GI and Mil-Specs, parkerized finish, 8 shot en bloc clip, 9 1/2 lbs. Mfg. 2000-2001.

	$895	$850	$800	$700	$600	$500	$400	*$852*

MODEL 444 FAL – .308 Win. cal., patterned after the FN FAL model. Mfg. by Imbel, located in Brazil, 2000-2001.

	$925	$850	$795	$725	$675	$595	$550	*$897*

ISRAEL MILITARY INDUSTRIES (IMI)

Previous manufacturer established 1933-circa 2009, and located in Israel.

IMI manufactured guns (both new and disc. models) include Galil, Jericho, Magnum Research, Timberwolf, Uzi, and others, and can be located in their respective sections.

ITHACA GUN COMPANY (NEW MFG.)

Current manufacturer established in 2006, located in Upper Sandusky, OH, with facilities in Aynor, SC, beginning 2014.

During December of 2007, Ithaca Gun Company bought out the remaining assets and equipment of Ithaca Gun Company LLC and moved production to Upper Sandusky, OH.

SHOTGUNS: SLIDE ACTION

MODEL 37 DEERSLAYER II – 12 or 20 ga., 3 in. chamber, 24 in. fixed barrel, 5 shot, bottom ejection, gold plated trigger, fiber optic rifle sight, drilled and tapped for scope mounts, fancy AAA walnut stock, with or without thumbhole, Pachmayr recoil pad, sling swivel studs, Weaver scope base, matte blue finish, 6.8-7 1/2 lbs.

MSR $1,029	$950	$825	$700	$575	$475	$375	$325	

MSR	100%	98%	95%	90%	80%	70%	60%	Last MSR

MODEL 37 DEERSLAYER III – 12 or 20 ga., 3 in. chamber, 26 in. fluted fixed barrel, 5 shot, bottom ejection, gold plated trigger, fancy AAA walnut stock, with or without thumbhole, Pachmayr recoil pad, sling swivel studs, Weaver scope base, matte blue finish, 8.1-9 1/2 lbs.

MSR $1,350	$1,175	$1,000	$875	$775	$675	$575	$475	

MODEL 37 DEFENSE – 12 or 20 ga., 3 in. chamber, 18 1/2 or 20 in. fixed barrel with standard cylinder bore, 5 or 8 shot, brass bead front sight, matte blued finish, walnut or synthetic buttstock and forend, black Pachmayr Decelerator pad, 6.8-7.1 lbs.

MSR $799	$695	$625	$525	$425	$350	$300	$250	

Add $86 for synthetic stock.

MODEL 37 HOG SLAYER – 12 ga., 20 in. rifled barrel, 5 shot, rifled sights, synthetic stock, matte blue or camo finish, 7 lbs.

MSR $895	$775	$650	$550	$475	$400	$350	$295	

Add $55 for camo finish.

MODEL 37 TACTICAL – 12 ga., 18 1/2 or 20 in. barrel, 5 or 8 shot, synthetic Mark 5, pistol grip adj., or side folding stock, 6-7.7 lbs.

MSR $799	$695	$625	$525	$425	$350	$300	$250	

MODEL 37 TURKEY SLAYER – 12 or 20 ga., 3 in. chamber, 23 in. free-floating fixed barrel, extended extra-full turkey choke, 5 shot, bottom ejection, fiber optic sights, camo, synthetic or thumbhole stock, sling swivel studs, drilled and tapped for scope mounts, weather-resistant matte finish, 7.6-8.2 lbs.

MSR $940	$750	$650	$550	$450	$375	$325	$275	

MODEL 37 WATERFOWL – 12 or 20 ga., 3 in. chamber, 28 or 30 in. VR barrel, three choke tubes, 5 shot, bottom ejection, synthetic stock, steel shot compatible, PermaGuard matte black or 100% camo finish, 7.2 lbs.

MSR $895	$775	$650	$550	$475	$400	$350	$295	

ITHACA GUN COMPANY LLC (OLDER MFG.)

Previous manufacturer located in Ithaca, NY from 1883-1986, King Ferry, NY circa 1989-2005, and Auburn, NY right before it closed in June, 2005.

Ithaca Gun Company, LLC had resumed production on the Model 37 slide action shotgun and variations during 1989, and then relocated to King Ferry, NY shortly thereafter. In the past, Ithaca also absorbed companies including Syracuse Arms Co., Lefever Arms Co., Union Fire Arms Co., Wilkes-Barre Gun Co., as well as others.

SHOTGUNS: SLIDE ACTION

In 1987, Ithaca Acquisition Corp. reintroduced the Model 37 as the Model 87. Recently manufactured Model 87s are listed in addition to both new and older Model 37s (produced pre-1986). During late 1996, Ithaca Gun Co., LLC resumed manufacture of the Model 37, while discontinuing the Model 87.

Over 2 million Model 37s have been produced.

Model 37s with ser. nos. above 855,000 will accept both 2 3/4 and 3 in. chambered barrels interchangeably. Earlier guns have incompatible threading for the magnum barrels.

MODEL 37 DS POLICE SPECIAL – 12 ga. only, 18 1/2 in. barrel with rifle sights, Parkerized finish on metal, oil finished stock, typically subcontracted by police departments or law enforcement agencies, with or without unit code markings.

	$325	$275	$235	$200	$185	$170	$160	

MODEL 37 PROTECTION SERIES – 12 ga. only, 18 1/2 or 20 in. smoothbore barrel w/o chokes, 5 or 8 shot tube mag., approx. 6 3/4 lbs. Limited mfg. 2005.

	$425	$375	$325	$275	$250	$225	$195	*$482*

Add $27 for 20 in. barrel.

MODEL 87 MILITARY & POLICE – 12 (3 in.) or 20 (new 1989) ga., short barrel Model 37 w/normal stock or pistol grip only, 18 1/2, 20, or 24 3/4 (scarce) in. barrel, choice of front bead or rifle sights, front blade was usually a fluorescent orange plastic, 5, 8, or 10 shot. Originally disc. 1983, reintroduced 1989-95.

	$265	$230	$200	$180	$170	$160	$150	*$323*

Add $104 for nickel finish (mfg. 1991-92 only).

IVER JOHNSON ARMS, INC. (NEW MFG.)

Current manufacturer established during 2004, located in Rockledge, FL. Dealer and distributor sales.

During 2013, Iver Johnson Arms produced a 1911A1 Carbine/Rifle with Mech-Tech Systems upper and Iver Johnson lower (last MSR $775).

MSR	100%	98%	95%	90%	80%	70%	60%	Last MSR

PISTOLS: 1911 STYLE

Iver Johnson Arms, Inc. previously manufactured the Raven Series in both .22 LR and .45 ACP cals. until 2009, and the last MSR was $532. Also discontinued during 2009 was the Frontier Four Derringer and the Model PM 30G M1 Carbine. The Trojan was discontinued in 2012 (last MSR was $574). The 1911 A1 Thrasher was disc. in 2013, last MSR was $608-$817.

1911A1 – 9mm Para. or .45 ACP cal., GI style parts, Government size frame, 5 in. barrel, forged slide, 8 shot mag., GI rear sight with fixed blade front sight, vertical rear serrations, finger relief cut near trigger, flat, serrated metal mainspring housing, walnut logo engraved or Black Dymondwood dual texture (new 2014, Digital finish models only) grips, matte blue, Pink Duracoat, Muddy Girl (new 2015), Kryptek Gray and Black hydrographic (new 2016), OD Green Cerakote, Coyote Tan Cerakote, Digital Navy (new 2014) or Digital Snow (new 2014) finish, 2.4 lbs.

| MSR $532 | $460 | $395 | $350 | $295 | $265 | $235 | $200 | |

Add $157 for OD Green or Coyote Tan Cerakote finish.
Add $170 for Pink Duracoat finish.
Add $204 for Muddy Girl (new 2015) or Kryptek Grey and Black hydrographic finish (new 2016).
Add $238 for Digital Navy or Digital Snow finish (new 2014).

* **1911A1 Boa** – .45 ACP cal., similar to 1911A1, except features Boa snakeskin hydrographic finish and black Dymondwood snakeskin grips. New 2014.

| MSR $770 | $650 | $575 | $495 | $440 | $375 | $325 | $275 | |

* **1911A1 Copperhead** – .45 ACP cal., similar to 1911A1, except features high grade epoxy base coat with hydrographic snakeskin printing in tan, black Dymondwood grips with snakeskin texture and logo. New 2014.

| MSR $770 | $650 | $575 | $495 | $440 | $375 | $325 | $275 | |

* **1911A1 Water Moccasin** – .45 ACP cal., similar to 1911A1, except features high grade epoxy base coat with hydrographic snakeskin printing in dark green, synthetic white pearlized grips with black engraved owl logo. New 2014.

| MSR $770 | $650 | $575 | $495 | $440 | $375 | $325 | $275 | |

* **1911A1 Zombie** – .45 ACP cal., similar to 1911A1, except features fixed sights, Zombie green slide with hydrographic zombie print, black frame and parts, and Zombie engraved pearlized green Hogue grips. New 2014.

| MSR $743 | $635 | $550 | $475 | $425 | $350 | $300 | $250 | |

EAGLE – 9mm Para. or .45 ACP cal., Commander size frame, 5 in. barrel, forged slide, Millet white outline fully adj. rear sight with dovetail front sight, beveled magwell, skeleton hammer and 3-hole trigger, lowered and flared ejection port, beavertail grip safety with memory cut, extended slide stop and thumb safety, angled front and rear serrations, walnut large diamond wood or rosewood double border/diamond with engraved logo (polished models only) grips, high luster polished blue (.45 ACP), all matte blue (9mm Para.), OD Green Cerakote, or Coyote Tan Cerakote finish, 2.4 lbs.

| MSR $713 | $625 | $550 | $475 | $395 | $325 | $295 | $250 | |

Add $57 for high luster polished blue finish.
Add $77 for ported slide.
Add $81 for OD Green or Coyote Tan Cerakote finish.

EAGLE LR – .45 ACP cal., deluxe 1911 style, Government size frame, 5 in. barrel, forged slide, 3 notch Picatinny rail system, beveled magwell, lowered and flared ejection port, Millett white outline fully adj. rear sight with dovetail front sight, angled rear and front serrations, skeleton hammer and 3-hole trigger, beavertail grip safety w/memory cut, extended slide stop and thumb safety, black Dymondwood grips with dual texture, matte blue finish, 2 1/2 lbs.

| MSR $959 | $825 | $725 | $625 | $550 | $475 | $375 | $295 | |

* **Eagle LR Zombie** – .45 ACP cal., similar to Eagle LR, except features Zombie engraved pearlized green Hogue grips, Zombie green slide with hydrographic zombie print, Black frame and parts, 2 1/2 lbs. New 2014.

| MSR $1,079 | $925 | $825 | $695 | $625 | $525 | $425 | $325 | |

EAGLE XL – .45 ACP or 10mm (new 2016) cal., 6 in. barrel, with or without ported slide, lowered and flared ejection port, skeleton hammer, 3-hole trigger, fully adj. rear sight with dovetail front sight, walnut or Dymondwood (10mm only, new 2016) grips, beavertail grip safety with memory cut, extended slide stop and thumb safety, matte blue finish, 2 lbs. 10 oz. New 2015.

| MSR $845 | $725 | $640 | $540 | $495 | $425 | $350 | $300 | |

Add $20 for 10mm cal.
Add $75 for magna ported barrel and slide.

FALCON – .45 ACP cal., Series 70 1911, Commander size frame, 4 1/4 in. barrel, combat style round hammer, GI rear sight w/fixed blade front sight, vertical rear serrations, walnut logo engraved grips, matte blue finish, 2.2 lbs.

| MSR $538 | $460 | $395 | $350 | $295 | $265 | $235 | $200 | |

MSR	100%	98%	95%	90%	80%	70%	60%	*Last MSR*

HAWK – 9mm Para. or .45 ACP cal., Commander size frame, 4 1/4 in. barrel, forged slide, Novak style LoMount fixed rear sight with dovetail front sight, beveled magwell, skeleton hammer and 3-hole trigger, lowered and flared ejection port, beavertail grip safety with memory cut, extended slide stop and thumb safety, angled front and rear serrations, walnut large diamond wood or rosewood double border/diamond with engraved logo (polished models only) grips, high luster polished blue (.45 ACP), all matte blue (9mm Para.), OD Green Cerakote, or Coyote Tan Cerakote finish, 2.2 lbs.

| MSR $698 | $615 | $540 | $460 | $385 | $315 | $285 | $240 | |

Add $51 for high luster polished blue finish.
Add $81 for OD Green or Coyote Tan Cerakote finish.
Add $105 for LoMount Trijicon night sights.

* ***Hawk Digital Navy/Digital Snow*** – .45 ACP cal., similar to Hawk, except features Digital Navy or Digital Snow hydrographic finish and black Dymondwood dual texture grips. New 2014.

| MSR $860 | $735 | $650 | $550 | $500 | $425 | $350 | $300 | |

Add $106 for LoMount Trijicon night sights.

THRASHER – 9mm Para. or .45 ACP cal., Officer size 1911, 3.12 in. bull barrel, two stage recoil spring system, fixed GI style sights, lowered and flared ejection port, GI style trigger, thumb safety, and slide stop, round combat style hammer, beavertail grip safety, walnut, large diamond checkered grips with engraved owl logo, matte blue finish, includes one magazine, 1.9 lbs.

| MSR $636 | $550 | $480 | $415 | $375 | $300 | $275 | $240 | |

* ***Thrasher Polished*** – 9mm Para., .40 S&W, or .45 ACP cal., Officer size 1911, 3.12 in. barrel, two stage recoil spring system, LoMount Novak style rear and Dovetail front sight, lowered and flared ejection port, front and rear serrations, 3-hole trigger and extended thumb safety, round, combat style hammer, beavertail grip safety, rosewood double border, large diamond checkered grips with engraved logo, polished matte blue or polished stainless finish, includes one magazine, 1.9 lbs.

| MSR $749 | $635 | $550 | $475 | $425 | $350 | $300 | $250 | |

Add $102 for polished stainless finish.
Add $105 for Trijicon night sights.

SHOTGUNS: O/U

IJ600 – 12, 20 ga., or .410 bore, 28 in. VR barrel with internal chokes, bead front sight, walnut stock and forend with checkering, selector switch on safety, engraved receiver in black or silver, 7 lbs. 5 oz. New 2015.

| MSR $540 | $475 | $415 | $385 | $350 | $315 | $285 | $235 | |

SHOTGUNS: SEMI-AUTO

HP18 – 12 or 20 ga., 18 in. barrel with muzzle brake, Picatinny rail with adj. rear sight, fiber optic front sight, two-piece pistol grip full stock (removable leaving pistol grip), rubber buttpad, matte black finish, 6 lbs. 6 oz. New 2015.

| MSR $420 | $375 | $335 | $300 | $275 | $250 | $225 | $195 | |

IJ500 – 12 or 20 ga., 2 3/4 or 3 in. chamber, 28 in. VR barrel with bead sight and internal chokes, walnut stock and forend with checkering, black receiver and barrel, 7 lbs. 2 oz. New 2015.

| MSR $420 | $375 | $335 | $300 | $275 | $250 | $225 | $195 | |

15 SA – 12 ga., 2 3/4 or 3 in. chamber, AR-15 style, 20 in. barrel, three removable chokes, 5 shot mag., fully adj. rear sight, synthetic stock with rubber butt pad, top and bottom rail, detachable carry handle, black finish, 7 lbs. 12 oz. New 2016.

| MSR $445 | $395 | $350 | $310 | $285 | $255 | $225 | $195 | |

SHOTGUNS: SLIDE ACTION

PAS12 – 12 ga., 2 3/4 or 3 in. chamber, 18 in. smooth bore barrel, 4 shot mag., alum. lightweight receiver with machined top rails for ring mounts, polymer stock in black, Cerakote OD Green, Cerakote Coyote Tan, Duracoat Pink, Boa, Copperhead, Water Moccasin, Digital Navy, Digital Snow, or Muddy Girl finish, black polymer medium length forend with deep ribbing, sling swivels, extended bolt release latch, cross trigger block safety, blade front sight, avail. with or w/o muzzle brake, includes gun lock and manual, 6 lbs. Mfg. by Armed in Turkey.

| MSR $294 | $250 | $225 | $190 | $170 | $140 | $115 | $90 | |

Add $11 for muzzle break.
Add $81 for Cerakote OD Green, Cerakote Coyote Tan, or Duracoat Pink finish.
Add $135 for Digital Navy, Digital Snow, or Muddy Girl finish.
Add $162 for Boa, Copperhead, or Water Moccasin Hydrographic snake print finish.

* ***PAS12 Adj. Sight*** – 12 ga., similar to PAS12, except has white dot fully adj. rear sight with fiber optic front sight, available with muzzle brake, 6 lbs. Mfg. by Armed in Turkey.

| MSR $312 | $265 | $230 | $200 | $180 | $145 | $120 | $95 | |

Add $11 for muzzle brake.

MSR	100%	98%	95%	90%	80%	70%	60%	Last MSR

* **PAS12 Combo** – 12 ga., similar to PAS12, except has either 28 or 30 in. VR barrel with bead sight, includes 3 internal chokes for long barrel, black finish. Mfg. by Armed in Turkey.

| MSR $397 | $340 | $300 | $250 | $230 | $185 | $155 | $120 | |

* **PAS12 PG** – 12 ga., similar to PAS12, except features 2-piece pistol grip stock, no muzzle brake available, 6 lbs. Mfg. by Armed in Turkey.

| MSR $327 | $280 | $245 | $210 | $190 | $155 | $125 | $100 | |

* **PAS12 PG-R/C** – 12 ga., 2 3/4 or 3 in. chamber, 18 in. smooth bore barrel with muzzle brake, 4 shot mag., Picatinny rail on alum. lightweight receiver, 2-piece pistol grip stock with rubber pad, black, Digital Navy (new 2014) or Digital Snow (new 2014) finish, black polymer medium length forend with deep ribbing, sling swivels, extended bolt release latch, cross trigger block safety, fiber optic sight, includes gun lock and manual, 6 lbs. Mfg. by Armed in Turkey.

| MSR $346 | $300 | $265 | $225 | $200 | $165 | $135 | $100 | |

Add $134 for Digital Navy or Digital Snow finish (new 2014).

* **PAS12 Rail** – 12 ga., similar to PAS12, except features Picatinny rail on top of receiver with fiber optic front sight, 6 lbs. Mfg. by Armed in Turkey.

| MSR $310 | $265 | $230 | $200 | $180 | $145 | $120 | $95 | |

Add $11 for muzzle brake.

* **PAS12 Satin** – 12 ga., similar to PAS12, except features all satin finish and no muzzle brake, 6 lbs. Mfg. by Armed in Turkey.

| MSR $365 | $310 | $270 | $235 | $210 | $170 | $140 | $110 | |

PAS20 – 20 ga., 18 in. barrel, straight stock, black finish. New 2015.

| MSR $294 | $250 | $225 | $190 | $170 | $140 | $115 | $90 | |

* **PAS 20 PG-R/C** – 20 ga., 18 in. barrel with muzzle brake, fiber optic front sight, two-piece pistol grip stock, Picatinny rail, black finish. New 2015.

| MSR $346 | $300 | $265 | $225 | $200 | $165 | $135 | $100 | |

IVER JOHNSON ARMS & CYCLE WORKS

Previously located in Worchester, MA, 1883-1890, Fitchburg, MA, 1890-1975, Middlesex, NJ 1975-1983 (name changed to Iver Johnson Arms Inc.) and Jacksonville, AR 1984-1993. Formerly Johnson Bye & Co. 1871-1883. Renamed Iver Johnson's Arms & Cycle Works mid-year 1894-1975 (incorporated as Iver Johnson's Arms & Cycle Works Inc. in 1915). Renamed Iver Johnson's Arms & Cycle Works in 1891 with manufacturing moving to Fitchburg, MA. In 1975 the name changed to Iver Johnson's Arms, Inc., and two years later, company facilities were moved to Middlesex, NJ. In 1982, production was moved to Jacksonville, AR under the trade name Iver Johnson Arms, Inc. In 1983, Universal Firearms, Inc. was acquired by Iver Johnson Arms, Inc.

The author and publisher would like to thank the late Mr. Bill Goforth for providing much of the information on Iver Johnson Arms & Cycle Works.

PISTOLS: SEMI-AUTO

I.J. SUPER ENFORCER (M1 CARBINE) – .30 Carbine cal., gas operated pistol version of the M1 Carbine, 5, 10, or 15 shot mag., walnut stock, fires from closed bolt, 9 1/2 in. barrel, 4 lbs. Mfg. 1978-1993.

| | $850 | $745 | $640 | $580 | $470 | $385 | $300 | |

UNIVERSAL ENFORCER (M1 CARBINE) – .30 Carbine cal., gas operated, blue finish, single action, pistol version of the M1 carbine, 5, 10, or 15 shot mag., 9 1/2 in. barrel, hardwood stock, fires from close bolt, trigger block safety, 4 lbs. Mfg. 1986.

| | $850 | $745 | $640 | $580 | $470 | $385 | $300 | |

RIFLES

Iver Johnson's first rifle was manufactured in 1928 and remained the only rifle manufactured entirely within the Iver Johnson factory in Fitchburg. The later .22 cal. rifles were all imported from either Canada or Germany, except the Lil Champ Model, which was manufactured in Jacksonville, AR. The M1 Carbine models were manufactured in either Middlesex, NJ or Jacksonville, AR.

I.J. SEMI-AUTO CARBINE – .22 LR cal., 15 shot mag., recoil operated, blue finish, copy of the M1 carbine, 18 1/2 in. barrel, military type front sight protected by wings, rear aperture adj. sight, walnut finished hardwood stock and handguard, sling swivels, imported from Germany, 5 3/4 lbs. Mfg. 1985-1990.

| | $425 | $365 | $315 | $275 | $235 | $195 | $175 | |

I.J. MAGNUM SEMI-AUTO CARBINE – .22 WMR cal., gas operated, otherwise similar to Semi-Auto Carbine, imported from Germany. Mfg. 1985-1990.

| | $525 | $465 | $395 | $340 | $295 | $250 | $220 | |

MSR	100%	98%	95%	90%	80%	70%	60%	Last MSR

I.J. PLAINSFIELD SEMI-AUTO CARBINE – .30 Carbine, 9mm Para. (new 1986), or 5.7mm (disc. 1986) cal., gas operated, copy of WWII U.S. Military Carbine, 5, 10, 15, or 30 shot detachable mag., stainless steel or blue finish, 18 in. barrel, American walnut or hardwood stock, model names and numbers changed several times, M2 full auto model available during the 1980s, 6 1/2 lbs. Mfg. 1978-1993.

| | $450 | $395 | $335 | $285 | $245 | $210 | $180 | |

Add 10% for walnut stock.
Add 20% for stainless steel.
Add 35% for 5.7mm cal. (Spitfire Model) or 9mm Para. cal.

I.J. PARATROOPER SEMI-AUTO CARBINE – .30 Carbine cal., gas operated, copy of WWII U.S. Military Carbine, 5, 10, 15, or 30 shot detachable mag., stainless steel or blue finish, 18 in. barrel, American walnut or hardwood stock, with collapsible stock extension, model names and numbers changed several times, M2 full auto model available with 12 in. barrel, 4 1/2 lbs. Mfg. 1978-1989.

| | $595 | $550 | $500 | $460 | $430 | $395 | $360 | |

Add 10% for walnut stock.
Add 20% for stainless steel.

I.J. SURVIVAL CARBINE SEMI-AUTO – .30 Carbine or 5.7mm cal., gas operated, copy of WWII military carbine, 5, 10, 15, or 30 shot detachable mag., stainless steel or blue finish, Zytel black plastic pistol grip stock, 6 1/2 lbs.

| | $450 | $395 | $335 | $285 | $245 | $210 | $180 | |

Add 20% for stainless steel.
Add 35% for 5.7mm cal. (Spitfire Model).

* **I.J. Survival Carbine Semi-Auto w/Folding Stock** – .30 Carbine or 5.7mm cal., similar to Survival Carbine, except has folding stock. Mfg. 1983-1989.

| | $585 | $500 | $425 | $375 | $325 | $275 | $235 | |

Add 20% for stainless steel.
Add 35% for 5.7mm cal. (Spitfire Model).

I.J. UNIVERSAL CARBINE SEMI-AUTO – .30 Carbine or .256 Win. Mag. cal., gas operated, GI military type carbine, 5 or 10 shot detachable mag., 18 in. barrel, stainless steel or blue finish, walnut stained hardwood, sling swivel, drilled and tapped, known as Model 1003 (.30 Carbine) or Model 1256 (.256 Win. Mag., 5 shot only). Mfg. 1986.

| | $450 | $395 | $335 | $285 | $245 | $210 | $180 | |

Iver Johnson marked models are rare.

I.J. UNIVERSAL PARATROOPER SEMI-AUTO CARBINE – .30 Carbine cal., similar to Universal Carbine model, except has Schmeisser-type hardwood folding stock, 5 or 10 shot detachable mag., drilled and tapped. Mfg. 1986.

| | $550 | $475 | $415 | $360 | $315 | $265 | $230 | |

Iver Johnson marked models are rare.

MODEL 5100 BOLT ACTION SNIPER – .338 Win., .416 Win., or .50 BMG cal., single shot, free floating 29 in. barrel, no sights, drilled and tapped, marketed with Leupold Ultra M1 20X scope, adj. composite stock, adj. trigger, two different model numbers, 36 lbs. Limited mfg. 1985-1993.

| | $4,550 | $3,775 | $3,375 | $3,000 | $2,600 | $2,300 | $2,000 | |

NOTES

J SECTION

J.B. CUSTOM INC.

Current manufacturer and restorer located in Huntertown, IN. Previously located in Fort Wayne, IN. Consumer direct sales.

J.B. Custom also offers service parts and restoration services for Winchester commemorative lever action rifles and carbines.

PISTOLS: SEMI-AUTO

J.B. Custom builds custom semi-auto pistols based on the 1911 design, including the Diamond Match (MSR $2,595), the Tactical Masterpiece (MSR $2,595), the Diamond Jim Gambler (MSR $2,895), the Elite Officer (MSR $1,995), and the Elite Command (MSR $1,995).

RIFLES: SEMI-AUTO

J.B. Custom builds two types of AR-15 style rifles in .223 Rem. cal. - the Target Sniper (MSR$1,195) and the M-4 (MSR $995). Please contact the manufacturer directly for more information including options and availalility (see Trademark Index).

J.L.D. ENTERPRISES, INC.

Previous rifle manufacturer located in Farmington, CT. In 2006, the company name was changed to PTR 91, Inc. The company was re-organized circa 2010 and is now known as PTR Industries, Inc.

Please refer to PTR Industries, Inc. listing for current information.

JMC FABRICATION & MACHINE, INC.

MSR	100%	98%	95%	90%	80%	70%	60%	Last MSR

Previous manufacturer located in Rockledge, FL 1997-99.

RIFLES: BOLT ACTION

MODEL 2000 M/P – .50 BMG cal., rapid takedown, 30 in. barrel, matte black finish, cast aluminum stock with Pachmayr pad, fully adj. bipod, 10 shot staggered mag., two-stage trigger, includes 24X U.S. Optics scope, prices assume all options included, 29 1/2 lbs. Limited mfg. 1998-99.

	100%	98%	95%	90%	80%	70%	60%	Last MSR
	$7,950	$7,400	$6,800	$6,150	$5,500	$4,900	$4,200	$8,500

Subtract $2,800 if w/o options.

JP ENTERPRISES, INC.

Current manufacturer and customizer established in 1978, located in Hugo, MN beginning 2010, previously located in White Bear Lake, MN 2000-2009, Vadnais Heights, MN 1998-2000, and in Shoreview, MN 1995-98. Distributor, dealer, and consumer sales.

JP Enterprises is a distributor for Infinity pistols, and also customizes Remington shotgun Models 11-87, 1100, and 870, the Remington bolt action Model 700 series, Glock pistols, and the Armalite AR-10 series.

JP Enterprises also manufactures a complete line of high quality parts and accessories for AR-15 style rifles, including upper and lower assemblies, sights and optics, machined receivers, barrels/barrel kits, fire control kits, handguards, etc. and gunsmithing services. Please contact the company directly for more information and pricing regarding these parts, accesssories, and services (see Trademark Index).

PISTOLS: SEMI-AUTO

Level I & Level II custom pistols were manufactured 1995-97 using Springfield Armory slides and frames. Only a few were made, and retail prices were $599 (Level I) and $950 (Level II).

GMR-13 – 9mm Para. cal., blowback action, 10 1/2 in. JP Supermatch button rifled barrel with standard profile compensator, JP modular handguard, Phase 5 buffer tube, matte black receiver finish. New 2015.

MSR	100%	98%	95%	90%	80%	70%	60%
MSR $1,499	$1,425	$1,250	$1,075	$975	$785	$650	$500

JP-15 PISTOL – .223 Rem. cal., Low Mass Operating System (LMOS), 10 1/2 in. JP Supermatch barrel with black Teflon finish, JP Tactical Recoil Eliminator muzzle, JP small frame receiver with matte black finish, Phase 5 Buffer tube, Hogue pistol grip. New 2015.

MSR	100%	98%	95%	90%	80%	70%	60%
MSR $1,699	$1,615	$1,415	$1,210	$1,100	$890	$725	$575

RIFLES: BOLT ACTION

MOR-07 – .260 Rem., 7mm WSM (new 2009), or .308 Win. cal., 24 in. stainless steel cryo-treated bull barrel, benchrest quality bolt action, Picatinny rail, JP Tactical Chassis system, Timney trigger, benchrest or tactical style forend, Precision grip system, matte black hardcoat anodized finish, 10 shot detachable mag., includes hard case. Disc. 2010.

	100%	98%	95%	90%	80%	70%	60%	Last MSR
	$4,250	$3,850	$3,350	$2,925	$2,500	$2,000	$1,600	$4,499

MSR	100%	98%	95%	90%	80%	70%	60%	Last MSR

MR-10 – .260 Rem. (new 2012), 7mm WSM (new 2012), .308 Win., .300 WSM, or 6.5 Creedmoor cal., 3 lug short through bolt action with upper Picatinny rail, spiral cut bolt, 24 in. JP Supermatch fluted stainless steel barrel with large profile JP compensator, folding Magpul stock with tactical grip including palmrest, benchrest style forend or JP modular handguard system. New 2011.

	100%	98%	95%	90%	80%	70%	60%	
MSR $3,999	$3,850	$3,500	$3,150	$2,700	$2,300	$1,900	$1,650	

RIFLES: SEMI-AUTO

The rifles in this section utilize a modified AR-15 style operating system.

BARRACUDA 10/22 – .22 LR cal., features customized Ruger 10/22 action with reworked fire control system, choice of stainless bull or carbon fiber superlight barrel, 3 lb. trigger pull, color laminated "Barracuda" skeletonized stock. Mfg. 1997-2003.

	100%	98%	95%	90%	80%	70%	60%	Last MSR
	$1,075	$950	$775	$650	$575	$475	$400	$1,195

A-2 MATCH – .223 Rem. cal., GIO, JP-15 lower receiver with JP fire control system, 20 in. JP Supermatch cryo-treated stainless barrel, standard A2 stock and pistol grip, DCM type free float forend, Mil-Spec A2 upper assembly with Smith National Match rear sight. Mfg. 1995-2003.

	100%	98%	95%	90%	80%	70%	60%	Last MSR
	$1,525	$1,300	$1,100	$925	$825	$700	$600	$1,695

AR-10T – .243 Win. or .308 Win. cal., GIO, features Armalite receiver system with JP fire control, flat-top receiver, vent. free floating tubular handguard, 24 in. cryo treated stainless barrel, black finish. Mfg. 1998-2004.

	100%	98%	95%	90%	80%	70%	60%	Last MSR
	$2,175	$1,825	$1,600	$1,450	$1,150	$875	$750	$2,399

Add $150 for anodized upper assembly in custom color.
Add $350 for laminated wood thumbhole stock.

* **AR-10LW** – GIO, lightweight variation of the Model AR-10T, includes 16-20 in. cryo treated stainless barrel, composite fiber tubular handguard, black finish only, 7-8 lbs. Mfg. 1998-2004.

	100%	98%	95%	90%	80%	70%	60%	Last MSR
	$2,175	$1,825	$1,600	$1,450	$1,150	$875	$750	$2,399

Add $200 for detachable sights.

CTR-02 COMPETITION TACTICAL RIFLE – .204 Ruger (mfg. 2012-2015), .22 LR (new 2016), .300 AAC Blackout (new 2016), .223 Rem., or 6.5 Grendel (new 2012) cal., GIO, state-of-the-art advanced AR design with many improvements, integral ACOG interface, beveled magwell, 10 shot mag., JP recoil eliminator and fire control system, 1/4 MOA possible, JP Supermatch polished stainless steel barrel, rifle or mid-length JP modular handguard system, Hogue pistol grip, JP low mass or full mass operating system, black synthetic A2 or ACE ARFX buttstock, black Teflon over hardcoat anodized finish. New 2002.

	100%	98%	95%	90%	80%	70%	60%	
MSR $2,499	$2,375	$2,080	$1,780	$1,615	$1,300	$1,075	$850	

Add $599 for presentation grade finish (disc. 2011).

CTR-02 ENGRAVED EDITION RIFLE – .223 Rem. cal., 20 in. JP Supermatch medium contour barrel with polished stainless finish, JP large profile compensator, T6 billet upper and lower receivers with black hardcoat anodizing on aluminum components and Presentation Grade finish with hand engraving, JP MK III 2XL Signature handguard system, JP adj. minimized gas block, Ace ARFX buttstock, Hogue pistol grip, includes polished JP scope mount and accessory pack. New 2015.

	100%	98%	95%	90%	80%	70%	60%	
MSR $4,839	$4,595	$4,025	$3,450	$3,125	$2,525	$2,075	$1,625	

GRADE II – .223 Rem. cal., GIO, features Mil-Spec JP lower receiver with upper assembly finished in a special two-tone color anodizing process, JP fire control, 18-24 in. cryo treated stainless barrel, composite skeletonized stock, Harris bipod, choice of multi-color or black receiver and forend, includes hard case. Mfg. 1998-2002.

	100%	98%	95%	90%	80%	70%	60%	Last MSR
	$1,750	$1,500	$1,275	$1,025	$825	$700	$600	$1,895

Add $200 for laminated wood thumbhole stock.

GRADE III (THE EDGE) – .223 Rem. cal., GIO, RND machined match upper/lower receiver system, 2-piece free floating forend, standard or laminated thumbhole wood stock, 18 to 24 in. barrel (cryo treated beginning 1998) with recoil eliminator, includes Harris bipod, top-of-the-line model, includes hard case. Mfg. 1996-2002.

	100%	98%	95%	90%	80%	70%	60%	Last MSR
	$2,550	$2,125	$1,750	$1,450	$1,150	$875	$750	$2,795

Add $250 for laminated thumbhole stock.

JP-15 & VARIATIONS (GRADE I A-3 FLAT TOP) – .204 Ruger (mfg. 2012-2015), .223 Rem., .22 LR, .300 AAC Blackout, or 6.5 Grendel (new 2012) cal., GIO, features Eagle Arms (disc. 1999), DPMS (disc. 1999) or JP15 lower assembly with JP fire control system, Mil-Spec A-3 type upper receiver with 18 or 24 in. JP Supermatch cryo-treated stainless barrel, JP Compensator, 10 shot mag., synthetic modified thumbhole (disc. 2011), synthetic A2 or ACE ARFX buttstock (new 2012), Magpul MOE, or laminated wood thumbhole (disc. 2002) stock, JP vent. two-piece free float forend, recoil eliminator, black Teflon hardcoat anodized finish, JP Compensator muzzle treatment, Hogue pistol grip. New 1995.

	100%	98%	95%	90%	80%	70%	60%	
MSR $1,999	$1,900	$1,660	$1,425	$1,290	$1,050	$855	$665	

Add $400 for NRA Hi-Power version with 24 in. bull barrel and sight package (disc. 2002).
Add $200 for laminated wood thumbhole stock (disc. 2002).
Subtract $300 for Duty Defense rifle (JP-15D), disc.

MSR		100%	98%	95%	90%	80%	70%	60%	Last MSR

* JP-15 Gladiator – .223 Rem. cal., 16 in. Supermatch barrel with black Teflon finish, Tactical compensator with crush washer, Mil-Spec forged upper and lower receivers, 2 and 4 in. full length top rail, extra long JP Rapid Configuration handguard, Magpul BUIS sights, Magpul CTR stock, Magpul MIAD grips, VTAC sling, matte black hardcoat anodized finish, includes accessory pack. New 2015.

MSR $2,049 $1,950 $1,700 $1,465 $1,325 $1,075 $880 $685

* JP-15 Grade I IPSC Limited Class – similar to Grade I, except has quick detachable match grade iron sights, Versa-pod bipod. Mfg. 1999-2004.

    $1,650 $1,400 $1,150 $995 $775 $625 $550   *$1,795*

* JP-15 Grade I Tactical/SOF – similar to Grade I, all matte black non-glare finish, 18, 20, or 24 in. Supermatch barrel. Mfg. 1999-2003.

    $1,425 $1,225 $1,050 $925 $800 $700 $600   *$1,595*

Add $798 for Trijicon ACOG sight with A-3 adapter.

* JP-15 ORRC – .223 Rem. cal., 16 or 18 in. JP Supermatch barrel with black Teflon finish, tactical profile JP compensator, extra long JP Rapid Configuration handguard, forged upper and lower receivers, MOE trigger guard, TI-7 (disc.) or A2 fixed stock, Hogue pistol grip, matte black hardcoat anodized finish, includes accessory pack, 6.8-7 lbs. New 2013.

MSR $1,699 $1,615 $1,415 $1,210 $1,100 $890 $725 $565

* JP-15 Patrol Rifle – .223 Rem. cal., FMOS (Full Mass Operating System), 16 in. JP Supermatch light contour barrel, JP tactical compensator, black Teflon barrel finish, Mil-Spec forged upper and lower receiver set, rifle length rapid configuration handguard, Magpul MOE trigger guard, TI-7 buttstock, A2 grip, matte black finish, 6.7 lbs. New 2016.

MSR $1,509 $1,275 $1,125 $1,025 $875 $750 $625 $525

* JP-15/VTAC Kyle Lamb Signature Rifle – .223 Rem. cal., GIO, JP FMOS (Full Mass Operating System), 16 in. JP Supermatch barrel, tactical compensator with crush washer, rifle-length JP rapid configuration handguard, Mil-Spec forged upper/lower receiver, Magpul CTR buttstock, Hogue pistol grip, black Teflon finish, accessory pack included, 6.4 lbs.

MSR $1,899 $1,800 $1,575 $1,350 $1,225 $990 $810 $630

JP-22R – .22 LR cal., 18 in. Supermatch light contour stainless steel barrel, A2 or ACE ARFX buttstock, Hogue pistol grip, extra long JP rapid configuration handguard system, matte black finish. New mid-2014.

MSR $1,349 $1,275 $1,115 $955 $865 $700 $575 $450

Add $150 for polished compensator (Model JP-15/22LR-C).

LRP-07 – .260 Rem., .308 Win., 6.5 Creedmoor (new 2012), 6mm Creedmoor, or .338 Federal (mfg. 2012-2015) cal., GIO, 18 (LRP-07H, Hunter's package) or 22 in. stainless steel cryo-treated barrel, left side charging system (new 2009), tactical compensator, matte black hardcoat anodizing, aluminum components, 10 or 19 shot mag., A2 or ACE ARFX, Tactical TI-7, or Magpul MOE stock, JP modular handguard, JP low mass operating system, Hogue pistol grip, upper accessory rail.

MSR $3,299 $3,135 $2,745 $2,350 $2,130 $1,725 $1,410 $1,100

Add $100 for Hunter's package.

Add $295 for Bench Rest variation with 22 in. barrel.

* SASS LRP-07 – .308 Win. cal., similar to LRP-07, except has SASS (Semi-Auto Sniper System) package that includes 20 in. Supermatch barrel, Magpul PRS buttstock, Magpul MIAD grip, scope mount, three 20 shot mags., and soft backpack case. Mfg. 2013-2014.

    $4,375 $3,830 $3,280 $2,975 $2,400 $1,975 $1,550   *$4,600*

Add $500 for suppressor.

Add $1,375 for Leupold Mark 4 scope.

Add $1,599 for Bushnell Elite Tactical scope.

Add $2,500 for U.S. Optics SN-3-T-PAL scope.

LRP-07 BILLET BEAUTY SPECIAL EDITION RIFLE – .308 Win. cal., 20 in. JP Supermatch medium contour barrel with custom Cerakote finish, JP large profile compensator, T6 billet upper and lower receivers, JP extra long rapid configuration handguard system, JP adj. minimized gas block, Magpul MOE fixed stock, Magpul MIAD grip, the paint scheme of the Bomber is captured by a special two-tone Cerakote treatment coupled with OD Green Magpul furniture and black accents in the trigger, safety, charging handle slider and mag. release, the stock features a printed homage to the B-17 tail markings, the sides of the magwell have been fitted with plates displaying both the period Army Air Force logo and specially commissioned nose art of the Billet Beauty. Limited mfg. of 25 pieces beginning 2015.

The current MSR for this model is $4,649.

This model pays special tribute to the B-17 bomber, and is in commemoration of American airmen who took to the skies in defense of liberty. It is styled after the iconic aircraft that carried America to victory in WWII.

NC-22 – .22 LR cal., precision machined Nordic Component upper receiver, 18 in. lightweight stainless steel barrel with JP Compensator, extra long JP modular handguard system, matte black anodized hardcoat finish. Mfg. 2013-2014.

    $1,425 $1,250 $1,075 $975 $785 $650 $500   *$1,499*

MSR	100%	98%	95%	90%	80%	70%	60%	Last MSR

PSC-11 – .204 Ruger (mfg. 2012-2015), .223 Rem., .22 LR (new 2016), .300 AAC Blackout (new 2016), or 6.5 Grendel (new 2012) cal., GIO, JP adjustable gas system, JP Supermatch polished stainless barrel, JP Compensator, billet upper with left side charging system, MK III handguard system, A2 or ACE ARFX buttstock, Hogue pistol grip, small frame with upper accessory rail, matte black hardcoat anodized finish on aluminum components. New 2011.

MSR $2,599	$2,475	$2,165	$1,855	$1,685	$1,360	$1,125	$875	

PSC-12 – .260 Win. (disc.), .308 Win., 6.5 Creedmoor (disc.), or 6.5 Grendel (disc.) cal., GIO, large frame, JP Supermatch button rifled barrel with polished stainless finish, JP Compensator, JP adjustable gas system, dual charging upper assembly compatible with DPMS lower receivers, MK III handguard system, A2 or ACE ARFX buttstock, Hogue pistol grip, JP fire control trigger. New 2012.

MSR $3,499	$3,325	$2,910	$2,495	$2,260	$1,830	$1,500	$1,175	

SCR-11 – .22 LR (new mid-2014), .204 Ruger (disc. 2015), .300 AAC Blackout (new 2016), .223 Rem., or 6.5 Grendel cal., competition side-charging rifle with left side charge system, features JP Supermatch polished stainless barrel with JP compensator, flat-top receiver with Picatinny rail, vent. modular handguard, choice of A2 or ACE ARFX buttstock, Hogue pistol grip, matte black hardcoat anodized finish on aluminum components. New 2011.

MSR $2,699	$2,565	$2,245	$1,925	$1,745	$1,410	$1,155	$900	

5.11 ALWAYS BE READY EDITION RIFLES – JP Enterprises has joined forces with 5.11 Tactical to create a series of precision rifles in 5.11 Storm Grey. Three configurations are available and each rifle includes a Cerakote finish upgrade in 5.11 Storm Grey, custom laser markings, and a full tactical rail package. New 2015.

* ***JP-15ABR*** – .223 Rem. cal., 16 in. medium contour JP Supermatch barrel with black Teflon finish, tactical compensator with crush washer, Mil-Spec forged upper and lower receivers, extra long JP Rapid Configuration handguard, TI-7 buttstock, MOE trigger guard, Hogue pistol grip, 5.11 Storm Grey Cerakote finish, 7.2 lbs. New 2015.

MSR $2,499	$2,375	$2,080	$1,780	$1,615	$1,300	$1,070	$830	

* ***LRP-07 ABR*** – .308 Win. cal., 20 in. medium contour barrel with large profile compensator and black Teflon finish, billet aluminum upper and lower receiver with left-side charging system, minimized black JP adj. gas block, extra long JP modular handguard, black Magpul PRS stock, Magpul MIAD black grip, accessories include extra long 14 1/2 in. top rail, 2 and 4 in. modular rails, and JP swivel mount adaptor, 5.11 Storm Grey Cerakote over hardcoat anodized finish with 5.11 logo. New 2015.

MSR $4,539	$4,310	$3,775	$3,235	$2,930	$2,370	$1,940	$1,510	

* ***SCR-11 ABR*** – .223 Rem. cal., 18 in. JP Supermatch medium contour barrel with small profile compensator and black Teflon finish, T6 upper and lower receivers with left-side charging system on upper receiver, extra long JP modular handguard, flip-up iron sights, 2 in. front sight rail, 2 and 4 in. modular rail piece, Magpul UBR stock, Hogue pistol grip, Storm Grey Cerakote finish. New 2015.

MSR $3,899	$3,700	$3,240	$2,775	$2,515	$2,035	$1,665	$1,300	

JACKSON RIFLES

Previous rifle manufacturer located in Castle Douglas, Scotland. Currently, the company manufactures and distributes parts for custom rifles.

Jackson Rifles manufactured high quality long-range competition rifles, including the J5-P (single shot) and the J5-T (bolt action repeater), available in both right and left-hand actions.

JAMES RIVER ARMORY

Current manufacturer and restoration company specializing in military firearms from WWI and WWII, located in Burgaw, NC. Previously located in Baltimore, MD.

RIFLES/CARBINES: SEMI AUTO

James River Armory currently restores selected military WWI and WWII rifles, and puts on new Criterion barrels and in some cases, new stocks. When completed, all rifles are test fired for safety. Please contact the company directly for current model availability and pricing on its restored military firearms (see Trademark Index).

Current offerings include the M1 Garand (MSR $1,495), AK-47 (MSR $849), Rockola M14F (MSR $2,395), Rockola M1 Carbine (MSR $1,295), and the Rockola T3 Carbine (MSR $1,695).

JARD, INC.

Current pistol and AR-15 style rifle manufacturer located in Sheldon, IA.

PISTOLS: SEMI-AUTO

J21 – .22 LR cal., blowback operation, 7 in. free-floating barrel, upper Picatinny rail, side charging handle, free-floating handguard, with or w/o rails and muzzle brake. New 2014.

MSR $715	$625	$540	$470	$400	$350	$310	$295	

Add $47 for rails and muzzle brake.

MSR	100%	98%	95%	90%	80%	70%	60%	Last MSR

J23 – .223 Wylde cal., free-floating barrel and handguard, standard AR lower, Picatinny rail upper, side charging handle, includes rails and muzzle brake. New 2014.

| MSR $1,009 | $850 | $725 | $650 | $585 | $515 | $450 | $395 | |

RIFLES: BOLT ACTION

MODEL J70 – free float barrel, modular design, multiple handle options, single stack magazine, black finish. New mid-2013. While advertised during 2013, as of May, 2015 the Model H70 has yet to go into production.

RIFLES: SEMI-AUTO

MODEL J16 – .223/5.56 NATO cal., GIO, 16 in. barrel, 20 shot mag., folding/telescoping stock, free floating barrel and handguard, Picatinny rail upper, JARD sight compensation system, optional quad rail or muzzle brake, Black finish.

| MSR $1,015 | $860 | $725 | $650 | $585 | $515 | $450 | $395 | |

Add $100 for quad rail kit. Add $75 for muzzle brake.

MODEL J17 – .17 HMR or .22 WMR cal., blowback operation, adj. stock, pistol grip, Picatinny rail receiver, detachable magazine, side charging handle, ergonomic safety and magazine release operation, Black finish.

| MSR $1,000 | $850 | $725 | $650 | $585 | $515 | $450 | $395 | |

MODEL J18 – .243 WSSM, .25 WSSM, or 7mm WSSM cal., GIO, 22 in. barrel, enlarged bolt design, side charging handle, flat-top Picatinny rail, free floating barrel and handguard, QD sling stud standard, 3 shot mag.

| MSR $1,181 | $975 | $885 | $750 | $635 | $550 | $475 | $425 | |

MODEL J19 – .223/5.56 NATO cal., GIO, standard AR lower, left non-reciprocating charging handle, right fold adj. length stock with adj. cheek pad, Picatinny rail upper, free float barrel and forearm, JARD sight compensation system, brass deflector.

| MSR $1,446 | $1,225 | $1,090 | $950 | $800 | $700 | $600 | $495 | |

MODEL J22 – .22 LR cal., blowback operation, 16.2 in. barrel, 26 shot mag., side charging handle, upper Picatinny rail, free floating barrel and handguard, pistol grip, quad rail/muzzle brake is optional, Black finish.

| MSR $735 | $640 | $550 | $475 | $400 | $350 | $310 | $295 | |

Add $99 for quad rail/muzzle brake.

MODEL J48 – .223 Wylde cal., GIO, 18 5/8 in. barrel, AR mag., right ejection, right side charging, rotating bolt, AR trigger, stock, and grip. New 2014.

| MSR $1,125 | $935 | $850 | $725 | $625 | $550 | $475 | $425 | |

MODEL J50 – .50 BMG cal., GIO, rotating bolt, 30 in. fixed barrel, free floating handguard, detachable 5 shot mag., adj. trigger, Black finish, 24 lbs. Disc. 2014.

| | $7,600 | $6,650 | $5,700 | $5,175 | $4,175 | $3,425 | $2,675 | *$8,450* |

MODEL J67 – 9mm Para. cal., bullpup configuration, blowback design, 16 3/4 in. barrel, uses standard Glock magazines, QD sling mounts, M-LOK compatible slots, ambidextrous charging handle.

| MSR $900 | $775 | $685 | $615 | $550 | $485 | $415 | $370 | |

MODEL J71 – .17 HMR or .17 WSM cal., blowback action, 20 in. button rifled barrel, detachable mag., adj. stock, side charging handle, Picatinny rail receiver.

| MSR $1,192 | $1,025 | $925 | $800 | $685 | $595 | $515 | $440 | |

MODEL J1022 – .22 LR cal., blowback operation, accepts Ruger 10/22 magazines/barrels/stocks, Sporter or heavy barrel (multiple barrel configurations available), Picatinny rail standard, side charging handle, Jard Sporter trigger standard, Hogue or wood laminate thumbhole stock.

| MSR $549 | $495 | $435 | $365 | $315 | $275 | $250 | $230 | |

Add $15 for sporter barrel with Hogue stock. Add $75 for heavy barrel with wood laminate thumbhole stock.

JARRETT RIFLES, INC.

Current manufacturer established in 1979, located in Jackson, SC. Direct custom order sales only.

RIFLES: BOLT ACTION

Jarrett Rifles, Inc. is justifiably famous for its well-known Beanfield rifles (refers to shooting over a beanfield at long range targets). A Jarrett innovation is the Tri-Lock receiver, which has 3 locking lugs, and a semi-integral recoil lug. Jarrett blueprints every action for proper dimensioning and rigid tolerances, and this explains why their rifles have set rigid accuracy standards.

A wide variety of options are available for Jarrett custom rifles (holders of 16 world records in rifle accuracy). Jarrett also manufactures its own precision ammunition for discriminating shooters/hunters. The manufacturer should be contacted directly for pricing and availability regarding these special order options, and custom gunsmithing services (see Trademark Index).

Current pricing does not include 11% excise tax or scope.

MSR	100%	98%	95%	90%	80%	70%	60%	Last MSR

BENCHREST/YOUTH/TACTICAL – various cals., various configurations depending on application. Mfg. 1999-disc.

| | $4,625 | $4,150 | $3,650 | $3,150 | $2,750 | $2,150 | $1,750 | *$4,625* |

ORIGINAL BEANFIELD RIFLE – built on customer supplied action, choice of caliber, stock style, color, barrel length and finish, with or w/o muzzle brake, supplied with 20 rounds of ammo and test target. New 2005.

| MSR $6,050 | $5,500 | $4,995 | $4,500 | $3,925 | $3,400 | $3,000 | $2,600 | |

.50 CAL. – .50 BMG cal., McMillan custom receiver, choice of repeater or single shot, 30 or 34 in. barrel with muzzle brake, 28-45 lbs. Mfg. 1999-2003.

| | $8,050 | $6,500 | $5,300 | $4,350 | $3,650 | $3,000 | $2,500 | *$8,050* |

Add $300 for repeater action.

JERICHO (CURRENT MFG.)

Current trademark of pistols manufactured by IWI Ltd., and currently imported by IWI USA, Inc., located in Harrisburg, PA. Dealer and distributor sales.

PISTOLS: SEMI AUTO

On the following models, add approx. $124 for pistol kit (includes hardshell case, Mepro Tritium sights, J-Gear Kit w/UpLula).

PL POLYMER FRAME 910/4010 SERIES – 9mm Para. or .40 S&W cal., SA/DA, blowback action, polymer frame, 4.4 in. barrel, 10 shot mag., adj. sights, black finger groove grips, features lower Picatinny rail in front of squared off trigger guard, matte black finish, includes carrying case, 28 oz. New 2016.

| MSR $559 | $475 | $425 | $375 | $325 | $295 | $275 | $250 | |

* **PSL-910/PSL-4010** – 9mm Para. or .40 S&W cal., SA/DA, blowback action, medium frame, 3.8 in. barrel, 10 shot mag., adj. sights, black finger groove grips, features lower Picatinny rail in front of squared off trigger guard, matte black finish, includes carrying case, 28 oz. New 2016.

| MSR $559 | $475 | $425 | $375 | $325 | $295 | $275 | $250 | |

* **FS-910/FS-4010** – 9mm Para., .40 S&W cal., SA/DA, blowback action, steel frame, 4.4 in. barrel, 10 shot mag., adj. sights, features lower Picatinny rail in front of squared off trigger guard, matte black finish, includes carrying case, approx. 36 oz. New 2016.

| MSR $655 | $575 | $495 | $450 | $375 | $325 | $295 | $275 | |

PL POLYMER FRAME 941 SERIES

* **PL-9/PL-40** – 9mm Para. or .40 S&W cal., SA/DA, blowback action, polymer frame, 4.4 in. barrel, 12 or 16 shot mag., adj. sights, black finger groove grips, features lower Picatinny rail in front of squared off trigger guard, matte black finish, includes carrying case, 28 oz. New 2015.

| MSR $559 | $475 | $425 | $375 | $325 | $295 | $275 | $250 | |

* **PSL-9/PSL-40** – 9mm Para. or .40 S&W cal., SA/DA, blowback action, polymer frame, 3.8 in. barrel, 12 or 16 shot mag., adj. sights, black finger groove grips, features lower Picatinny rail in front of squared off trigger guard, matte black finish, includes carrying case, 25.5 oz. New 2015.

| MSR $559 | $475 | $425 | $375 | $325 | $295 | $275 | $250 | |

F STEEL FRAME 941 SERIES

* **F-9/F-40** – 9mm Para. or .40 S&W cal., SA/DA, blowback action, steel frame, 4.4 in. barrel, 12 (.40 S&W cal.) or 16 shot mag., adj. sights, features lower Picatinny rail in front of squared off trigger guard, matte black finish, includes carrying case, 36.8 oz. New 2015.

| MSR $655 | $575 | $495 | $450 | $375 | $325 | $295 | $275 | |

* **FS-9/FS-40/FS-45** – 9mm Para., .40 S&W, or .45 ACP cal., SA/DA, blowback action, steel frame, 3.8 in. barrel, 10 (.45 ACP), 12 (.40 S&W) or 16 (9mm Para) shot mag., adj. sights, features lower Picatinny rail in front of squared off trigger guard, matte black finish, includes carrying case, approx. 36 oz. New 2015.

| MSR $655 | $575 | $495 | $450 | $375 | $325 | $295 | $275 | |

* **F-910/F-4010** – 9mm Para. or .40 S&W cal., SA/DA, blowback action, steel frame, 4.4 in. barrel, 10 shot mag., adj. sights, features lower Picatinny rail in front of squared off trigger guard, matte black finish, includes carrying case, 36.8 oz. New 2016.

| MSR $655 | $575 | $495 | $450 | $375 | $325 | $295 | $275 | |

JERICHO (PREVIOUS MFG.)

Previous trademark of Israel Military Industries (I.M.I.). Previously imported by K.B.I., Inc. located in Harrisburg, PA.

PISTOLS: SEMI-AUTO

JERICHO 941 – 9mm Para. cal. or .41 Action Express (by conversion only) cal., DA/SA, 4.72 in. barrel with polygonal

MSR	100%	98%	95%	90%	80%	70%	60%	Last MSR

rifling, all steel fabrication, 3 dot Tritium sights, 11 or 16 (9mm Para.) shot mag., ambidextrous safety, polymer grips, decocking lever, 38 1/2 oz. Imported 1990-1992.

	100%	98%	95%	90%	80%	70%	60%	Last MSR
	$625	$550	$475	$425	$375	$325	$295	*$649*

Add $299 for .41 AE conversion kit.

Industrial hard chrome or nickel finishes were also available for all Jericho pistols.

* ***Jericho 941 Pistol Package*** – includes 9mm Para. and .41 AE conversion kit, cased with accessories. Mfg. 1990-91 only.

	100%	98%	95%	90%	80%	70%	60%	Last MSR
	$850	$775	$700	$625	$575	$495	$450	*$775*

JESSE JAMES FIREARMS UNLIMITED

Current pistol, rifle, and silencer manufacturer located in Dripping Springs, TX.

RIFLES: SEMI-AUTO

NOMAD AR 10 – .308 Win. cal., GIO, Proof Research carbon fiber barrel, JJFU needle bearing trigger, milled billet upper and lower, M-LOK system option at the end of handguard.

MSR $5,000	$4,250	$3,750	$3,250	$2,625	$2,200	$1,875	$1,625	

NOMAD AR-15 – .223 Rem. or .300 AAC Blackout cal., GIO, AR-15 style, 16 or 22 in. chrome-lined match grade barrel w/muzzle brake, two-stage trigger, ACS or Magpul UBR stock, JJFU Skelly grip, billet aluminum upper and lower receivers, Tungsten or Sandman finish.

MSR $3,499	$2,975	$2,600	$2,100	$1,800	$1,500	$1,250	$1,075	

JOHNSON AUTOMATICS, INC.

Previous manufacturer located in Providence, RI. Johnson Automatics, Inc. moved many times during its history, often with slight name changes. M.M. Johnson, Jr. died in 1965, and the company continued production at 104 Audubon Street in New Haven, CT as Johnson Arms, Inc., mostly specializing in sporter semi-auto rifles with Monte Carlo stocks in .270 Win. or .30-06 cal.

RIFLES: SEMI-AUTO

MODEL 1941 – .30-06 or 7x57mm cal., 22 in. removable air cooled barrel, recoil operated, perforated metal handguard, aperture sight, military stock. Most were made for Dutch military, some used by U.S. Marine Paratroopers, during WWII all .30-06 and 7x57mm were ordered by South American governments.

	$7,350	$6,750	$6,000	$5,250	$4,500	$3,950	$3,250	

MilTech offers a restored version of this model. Inspect this model carefully for originality before considering a possible purchase. Values are somewhat lower for restored guns.

JUGGERNAUT TACTICAL

Current AR-15 style gun and accessories manufacturer located in Orange, CA. Dealer and consumer direct sales through FFL.

RIFLES: SEMI-AUTO

JT-10 – .308 Win. cal., GIO, 18 in. stainless steel fluted barrel with JT compensator, 10 or 30 shot mag., extended M4 feed ramps, mid-length gas system, billet lower and flat-top upper receivers, 12, 15, or 16 1/2 in. free float KeyMod rail, extended latch charging handle, ALG QMS trigger, 6-pos. receiver extension, carbine buffer, MFT Battlelink Minimalist stock, Hogue pistol grip, includes two rifle carry bag, Mil-Spec phosphate finish in various colors, 6 lbs. New 2015.

MSR $1,699	$1,450	$1,275	$1,125	$1,000	$850	$735	$595	

JT-15 – 5.56 NATO cal., AR-15 style, GIO, 16 or 18 in. stainless steel fluted barrel with JT compensator, 10 or 30 shot mag., extended M4 feed ramps, mid-length gas system, billet lower and flat-top upper receiver, 9, 12, or 15 in. free-float KeyMod rail, extended latch charging handle, ALG QMS trigger, no sights, 6-pos. receiver extension, carbine buffer, MFT Battlelink Minimalist stock with JT Hogue pistol grip, Mil-Spec phosphate finish in various colors, approx. 6 lbs. New 2015.

MSR $1,495	$1,275	$1,125	$1,025	$875	$750	$625	$525	

JUST RIGHT CARBINES

Current trademark of carbines established in 2011, and manufactured in Canandaigua, NY. Dealer and distributor sales. Previously distributed by LDB Supply LLC located in Dayton, OH, by American Tactical Imports (ATI), located in Rochester, NY, and by E.M.F., located in Santa Ana, CA.

MSR	100%	98%	95%	90%	80%	70%	60%	Last MSR

CARBINES: SEMI-AUTO

JUST RIGHT CARBINE STANDARD – 9mm Para., .40 S&W, or .45 ACP (new mid-2011) cal., blowback action, 16 1/4 (disc.) or 17 in. barrel, features ambidextrous bolt handle and ejection, flat-top receiver with Picatinny rail, half length barrel quad rail or takedown tube, uses Glock or M1911 (.45 ACP only) magazines, collapsible 6-position stock, matte black, Desert Camo (new 2013), Muddy Girl (new 2013), ReaperZ Green (new 2013), A-TACS Foliage Green (new 2014), or Snow Ghost (new 2014) finish, approx. 6 1/2 lbs. New 2011.

| MSR $774 | $695 | $610 | $525 | $475 | $400 | $350 | $300 | |

Add $25 for .40 S&W cal.

Add $50 for .45 ACP cal.

Add $75 for Desert Camo, Muddy Girl camo, ATACS Foliage Green, or Snow Ghost finish.

Add $95 for Reaper Z Green and 33 shot mag. (new 2013).

Add $100 for tactical package (includes red dot scope, forward folding grip, Tuff1 grip cover and two magazines).

MARINE – 9mm Para., .40 S&W, or .45 ACP cal., straight blowback operation, 17 in. stainless barrel with Birdcage muzzle brake, takedown tube, Glock style mags., top Picatinny rail, 6-pos. collapsible M4 buttstock, Electroless nickel plated finish, 6 1/2 lbs. New 2015.

| MSR $874 | $725 | $650 | $580 | $515 | $450 | $385 | $340 | |

M&P TACTICAL – 9mm Para. or .40 S&W cal., straight blowback operation, 17 in. threaded or unthreaded barrel, 15 or 17 shot M&P mag., free-floating quad rail or takedown tube, collapsible or fixed stock, pistol grip, black finish. New 2015.

| MSR $824 | $695 | $620 | $550 | $475 | $420 | $365 | $335 | |

NOTES

K SECTION

K.B.I., INC.

Previous importer and distributor located in Harrisburg, PA until Jan. 29, 2010. Distributor sales.

K.B.I., Inc. imported Charles Daly semi-auto pistols, Bul Transmark semi-auto pistols, SA revolvers, AR-15 style rifles, and shotguns in many configurations, including O/U, SxS, semi-auto, lever action, and slide action. K.B.I. also imported Armscor (Arms Corp. of the Philippines), FEG pistols, and Liberty revolvers and SxS coach shotguns. These models may be found within their respective alphabetical sections. K.B.I. previously imported the Jericho pistol manufactured by I.M.I. from Israel. Older imported Jericho pistols may be found under its own heading in this text, and more recently imported pistols are listed under the Charles Daly listing.

MSR	100%	98%	95%	90%	80%	70%	60%	Last MSR

RIFLES: BOLT ACTION

KASSNAR GRADE I – available in 9 cals., GIO, thumb safety that locks trigger, with or w/o deluxe sights, 22 in. barrel, 3 or 4 shot mag., includes swivel posts and oil finished standard grade European walnut with recoil pad, 7 1/2 lbs. Imported 1989-93.

	100%	98%	95%	90%	80%	70%	60%	Last MSR
	$445	$385	$325	$275	$225	$195	$175	$499

NYLON 66 – .22 LR cal., GIO, patterned after the Remington Nylon 66. Imported until 1990 from C.B.C. in Brazil, South America.

	100%	98%	95%	90%	80%	70%	60%	Last MSR
	$125	$110	$95	$85	$75	$70	$65	$134

MODEL 122 – .22 LR cal., GIO, bolt action design with mag. Imported from South America until 1990.

	100%	98%	95%	90%	80%	70%	60%	Last MSR
	$125	$110	$95	$85	$75	$70	$65	$136

MODEL 522 – .22 LR cal., GIO, bolt action design with tube mag. Imported from South America until 1990.

	100%	98%	95%	90%	80%	70%	60%	Last MSR
	$130	$115	$100	$85	$75	$70	$65	$142

BANTAM SINGLE SHOT – .22 LR cal., GIO, youth dimensions. Imported 1989-90 only.

	100%	98%	95%	90%	80%	70%	60%	Last MSR
	$110	$90	$85	$75	$70	$65	$60	$120

KDF, INC.

Previous rifle manufacturer until circa 2007 and current custom riflesmith specializing in restocking and installing muzzle brakes, in addition to supplying specialized rifle parts. Located in Seguin, TX. KDF utilized Mauser K-15 actions imported from Oberndorf, Germany for many rifle models. Previously, KDF rifles were manufactured by Voere (until 1987) in Vöhrenbach, W. Germany.

Older KDF rifles were private labeled by Voere and marked KDF. Since Voere was absorbed by Mauser-Werke in 1987, model designations changed. Mauser-Werke does not private label (i.e. newer guns are marked Mauser-Werke), and these rifles can be found under the Mauser-Werke heading in this text.

RIFLES: OLDER VOERE MFG. (PRE-1988)

* **K-15 Swat Rifle** – .308 Win. cal. standard, 24 or 26 in. barrel, parkerized metal, oil finished target walnut stock, 3 or 4 shot detachable mag., 10 lbs. Importation disc. 1988.

	100%	98%	95%	90%	80%	70%	60%	Last MSR
	$1,475	$1,250	$1,000	$850	$725	$650	$575	$1,725

KSN INDUSTRIES LTD.

Previous distributor (1952-1996) located in Houston, TX. Previously imported until 1996 exclusively by J.O. Arms, Inc. located in Houston, TX. Currently manufactured Israel Arms, Ltd. pistols may be found under their individual listing.

PISTOLS: SEMI-AUTO

The pistols listed were mfg. by Israel Arms, Ltd.

KAREEN MK II – 9mm Para. or .40 S&W (new late 1994) cal., SA, 4.64 in. barrel, two-tone finish, rubberized grips, regular or Meprolite sights, 10 (C/B 1994), 13*, or 15* shot mag., 33 oz. Imported 1993-1996.

	100%	98%	95%	90%	80%	70%	60%	Last MSR
	$360	$305	$255	$225	$200	$185	$170	$411

Add approx. $160 for two-tone finish with Meprolite sights.

* **Kareen Mk II Compact** – compact variation with 3.85 in. barrel. Imported 1993-96.

	100%	98%	95%	90%	80%	70%	60%	Last MSR
	$415	$360	$315	$255	$225	$200	$185	$497

K-VAR CORP.

Current importer located in Las Vegas, NV. MSR Distribution is the distributor for K-Var Corp.

K-VAR Corp. currently distributes Saiga rifles and shotguns, in addition to importing select Zastava bolt action rifles and pistols,

MSR	100%	98%	95%	90%	80%	70%	60%	*Last MSR*

Vepr rifles mfg. by Molot, Arsenal Inc. SLR series, AK-47 design rifles and an RPK milled rifle. Additionally, K-Var Corp. manufactures a Model SA M-7 SFK AK-47 design rifle in the U.S. See separate listings for Saiga rifles/shotguns, Zastava bolt action rifles, Vepr rifles, Arsenal, and the RPK model. Please contact the company directly for availability and pricing (see Trademark Index).

KAHR ARMS

Current manufacturer established in 1993, with headquarters located in Blauvelt, NY, and manufacturing in Worchester, MA. Construction is underway in Lord's Valley, PA to build a new manufacturing facility which should be operational sometime during 2015. Distributor and dealer sales.

Kahr order number nomenclature is as follows:

M= Steel frame, 3-3.1 in. barrel, PM= Polymer frame, 3.1-3.24 in. barrel, KP= Polymer frame, 3.54-3.6, 2.53 in. barrel, K= Steel frame, 3.465-3.5 in. barrel, TP=Polymer frame, 3.965-4.04 in. barrel, KT= Steel frame, 3.965-4 in. barrel, CM= Polymer frame, 3-3.14 in. barrel, CW= Polymer frame, 3.65-3.64 in. barrel, CT= Polymer frame, 4-4.04 in. barrel.

First three numbers - 383= .380 ACP, 909= 9mm, 919= 9mm with External Safety, 404= .40 S&W, 414= .40 S&W with External Safety, 454= .45 ACP.

4th number - 0= Carbon steel, black oxide (disc.), 1= Carbon steel, nickel finish (disc.), 2= Carbon steel, black T finish (disc.), 3= Matte stainless steel, 4= Blackened stainless steel, 6= Polished stainless steel, Elite98 (disc.), 8= Polished stainless steel, Elite.

Letters at end - A= Required for certain older inventory items, N= Tritium night sights, NOVAK= Novak low profile Tritium night sights

PISTOLS: SEMI-AUTO

All premim Kahr pistols are supplied with three magazines, hard polymer case, trigger lock, and five-year warranty. The premium pistols feature Lothar Walther polygonal rifled match grade barrels.

All value series Kahr pistols (CM, CW, CT) are supplied with one magazine, trigger lock, are shipped in a cardboard box, and have a five-year warranty.

CW9 – 9mm Para. cal., DAO, 3.6 in. barrel, black polymer frame, matte stainless steel slide, 7 shot mag., textured polymer grips, adj. rear sight, pinned in polymer front sight, white dot combat sights or rear day and front night sights (new 2016), 15.8 oz. New 2005.

MSR $449	$385	$335	$295	$260	$210	$175	$135

Add $46 for rear day and front night sights (new 2016).

CW40 – .40 S&W cal., DAO, 3.6 in. barrel, black polymer frame, matte stainless steel slide, 6 shot mag., textured polymer grips, adj. rear sight, pinned in polymer front sight, white dot combat sights, 16.8 oz. New 2008.

MSR $449	$385	$335	$295	$260	$210	$175	$135

CW45 – .45 ACP cal., DAO, 3.64 in. barrel, 6 shot mag., black polymer frame, matte stainless steel slide, adj. rear sight, pinned in polymer front sight, white dot combat sights, textured polymer grips, 19.7 oz. New 2008.

MSR $449	$385	$335	$295	$260	$210	$175	$135

K9 COMPACT – 9mm Para. cal., trigger cocking, DAO with passive striker block, locked breech with Browning type recoil lug, steel construction, 3 1/2 in. barrel with polygonal rifling, 7 shot mag., wraparound black polymer grips, matte black, black titanium (Black-T, mfg. 1997-98), or electroless nickel (mfg. 1996-99) finish, 25 oz. Mfg. 1993-2003.

	$560	$485	$435	$385	$340	$315	$285	*$648*

Add $74 for electroless nickel finish (disc.).
Add $126 for black titanium finish (Black-T, disc.).
Add $103 for Tritium night sights (new 1996).

* ***K9 Compact Stainless*** – 9mm Para. cal., 3 1/2 in. barrel, similar to K9 Compact, except is matte finished stainless steel, NYCPD specs became standard 2006 (trigger LOP is 1/2 in. compared to 3/8 in.). New 1998.

MSR $880	$750	$650	$565	$510	$415	$340	$275

Add $135 for Tritium night sights.
Add $38 for matte blackened stainless steel finish (new 2004).

KP9 GEN2 – 9mm Para. cal., black polymer frame, 3 1/2 in. barrel, 7 shot, matte stainless slide, short trigger with trigger safety, Truglo TFX Tritium/fiber optic day/night sights, accessory rail, ships with three magazines and high impact polymer case. New 2015.

MSR $976	$825	$700	$625	$550	$485	$415	$370

P9 POLYMER COMPACT – 9mm Para. cal., DAO, 3.6 in. barrel, lightweight black polymer frame, 7 shot mag., matte stainless slide, "Browning-type" recoil lug, passive striker block, no magazine disconnect, black textured polymer grips, drift adj. white bar-dot combat sights, 17.9 oz. New 1999.

MSR $762	$650	$575	$500	$450	$360	$295	$230

Add $121 for Tritium night sights (new 2000).
Add $48 for matte black stainless slide (new 2004).
Add $114 for external safety and loaded chamber indicator with new enhanced trigger (new 2012).

MSR	100%	98%	95%	90%	80%	70%	60%	Last MSR

MK9 MICRO SERIES – 9mm Para. cal., micro compact variation of the K9 Compact featuring 3 in. barrel, double action only with passive striker block, overall size is 4 in. H x 5 1/2 in. L, duo-tone finish with stainless frame and black titanium slide, includes two 6 shot flush floorplate mags. Mfg. 1998-99.

	100%	98%	95%	90%	80%	70%	60%	Last MSR
	$650	$575	$515	$465	$425	$395	$375	$749

Add $85 for Tritium night sights.

* MK9 Micro Series Elite 2000 Stainless – similar to MK9 Elite 98 Stainless, except features black stainless frame and slide, black Roguard finish. Mfg. 2001-2002.

	100%	98%	95%	90%	80%	70%	60%	Last MSR
	$575	$485	$425	$360	$315	$260	$225	$694

PM9 MICRO POLYMER COMPACT – 9mm Para. cal., 3 in. barrel with polygonal rifling, black polymer frame, trigger cocking DAO, matte stainless steel slide, 6 or 7 (with mag. grip extension, disc.) shot mag., 16 oz. New 2003.

MSR $810	$685	$600	$515	$465	$375	$310	$240	

Add $125 for Tritium night sights.
Add $53 for matte blackened stainless slide (new 2004).
Add $18 for external safety, loaded chamber indicator (new 2010), and enhanced trigger (new 2012).
Add $263 for custom engraved slide (Custom Shop only, mfg. 2012-2015)
Add $168 for stainless slide with Crimson Trace trigger guard laser (mfg. 2010-2014).

TP9 – 9mm Para. cal., 4 in. barrel, 8 shot mag., black polymer frame, matte stainless slide, Elite 98 trigger, white bar dot sights (new 2006), textured black polymer grips, 20 oz. Mfg. 2004-2014.

	100%	98%	95%	90%	80%	70%	60%	Last MSR
	$600	$500	$425	$360	$315	$260	$225	$697

Add $141 for Novak night sights.

TP9 GEN2 4 IN. – 9mm Para. cal., black polymer frame, 4 in. barrel, 8 shot, matte stainless slide, short trigger with trigger safety, Truglo TFX Tritium/fiber optic day/night sights, accessory rail, ships with three magazines and high impact polymer case. New 2015.

MSR $976	$825	$700	$625	$550	$485	$415	$370	

TP9 GEN2 5 IN. – 9mm Para. cal., black polymer frame, 5 in. barrel, 8 shot, matte satinless slide with front slide serrations, short trigger with trigger safety, co-witness white three dot sights, mount for reflex sights, accessory rail, ships with three mags. in a high impact polymer case. New 2015.

MSR $1,015	$860	$725	$650	$585	$515	$450	$395	

TP9 GEN2 6 IN. – 9mm Para. cal., black polymer frame, 6 in. compensated barrel, 8 shot, short trigger with trigger safety, co-witness white three dot sights, Leupold Delta Point Reflex Sight, matte stainless slide with front slide serrations, accessory rail, matte finish. New 2015.

MSR $1,566	$1,315	$1,155	$1,040	$875	$750	$625	$525	

K40 COMPACT – .40 S&W cal., DAO, 3 1/2 in. barrel, 6 shot mag., locked breech with Browning type recoil lug, wraparound black polymer grips, matte black or electroless nickel finish (disc. 1999), 26 oz. Mfg. 1997-2003.

	100%	98%	95%	90%	80%	70%	60%	Last MSR
	$560	$485	$435	$385	$340	$315	$285	$648

Add $103 for Tritium night sights (new 1997).
Add $74 for electroless nickel finish (disc. 1999).
Add $126 for black titanium finish (Black-T, disc. 1998).

* K40 Compact Stainless – .40 S&W cal., DAO, 3 1/2 in. barrel, 6 shot mag., matte stainless steel, wraparound textured soft polymer black grips, drift adj. white bar-dot combat sights, Browning type recoil lug, passive striker block, no magazine disconnect, 24.1 oz. New 1997.

MSR $880	$750	$650	$565	$510	$415	$340	$275	

Add $135 for Tritium night sights.
Add $38 for matte black stainless steel (new 2004).

P40 COMPACT POLYMER – .40 S&W cal., DAO, 3.6 in. barrel w/polygonal rifling, black polymer frame, matte stainless steel slide, 6 shot mag., Browning type recoil lug, passive striker block, drift adj. white bar-dot combat sights, textured polymer black grips, 18.9 oz. New 2001.

MSR $762	$650	$575	$500	$450	$360	$295	$230	

Add $121 for Tritium night sights.
Add $48 for matte black stainless slide (new 2004).
Add $114 for external safety and loaded chamber indicator, and enhanced trigger (new 2015).

MK40 MICRO – .40 S&W cal., micro compact variation of the Compact K40, featuring 3 in. barrel, matte stainless frame and slide, supplied with one 5 shot and one 6 shot (with grip extension) mag., wraparound textured hard nylon black grips, 25 oz. New 1999.

MSR $880	$750	$650	$565	$510	$415	$340	$275	

Add $107 for Tritium night sights.

MSR	100%	98%	95%	90%	80%	70%	60%	Last MSR

PM40 COMPACT POLYMER – .40 S&W cal., black polymer frame, 3 in. barrel, supplied with one 5 shot and one 6 shot (with grip extension) mag., matte finished stainless slide, drift adj. white bar-dot combat sights, textured polymer black grips, 17 oz. New 2004.

| MSR $810 | $685 | $600 | $515 | $465 | $375 | $310 | $240 | |

Add $125 for Tritium night sights.
Add $53 for matte black stainless slide (new 2005).
Add $18 for external safety and loaded chamber indicator with enhanced trigger (new 2012).
Add $168 for stainless slide and Crimson Trace trigger guard laser (mfg. 2010-2014).

TP40 – .40 S&W cal., DAO, "Browning - type" recoil lug, passive striker block, black polymer frame, 4 in. barrel with polygonal rifling, 7 shot mag., no magazine disconnect, matte stainless slide, white bar-dot sights, textured black polymer grips. Mfg. 2006-2014.

| | $600 | $500 | $425 | $370 | $325 | $285 | $250 | *$697* |

Add $141 for Novak night sights (TP40 Tactical).

KP45 GEN2 – .45 ACP cal., 3 1/2 in. barrel, black polymer frame, 6 shot, matte stainless slide, accessory rail, short trigger with trigger safety, Truglo TFX Tritium/fiber optic day/night sights. New 2015.

| MSR $976 | $825 | $700 | $625 | $550 | $485 | $415 | $370 | |

P45 POLYMER – .45 ACP cal., DAO, black polymer frame with matte or black stainless steel slide, 3.54 in. barrel, 6 shot mag., ribbed grip straps, low profile white dot combat sights, textured black polymer grips, 18 1/2 oz. New 2005.

| MSR $829 | $700 | $615 | $525 | $475 | $385 | $315 | $250 | |

Add $120 for Novak night sights.
Add $51 for black stainless slide (new 2006).

PM45 POLYMER – .45 ACP cal., black polymer frame, 3.24 in. barrel, 5 shot mag., matte stainless or blackened stainless slide, white bar dot combat or Novak night sights, textured black polymer grips, Crimson Trace trigger guard laser (mfg. 2011-2014), approx. 19 oz. New 2007.

| MSR $880 | $750 | $650 | $565 | $510 | $415 | $340 | $275 | |

Add $119 for Novak night sights.
Add $51 for black stainless steel slide (new late 2008).
Add $89 for Crimson Trace trigger guard laser (mfg. 2011-2014).

TP45 POLYMER – .45 ACP cal., DAO, black polymer frame, 4.04 in. barrel, 7 shot mag., matte stainless steel slide, white bar dot combat sights, textured black polymer grips, approx. 23 oz. Mfg. 2007-2014.

| | $600 | $500 | $425 | $370 | $325 | $285 | $250 | *$697* |

Add $142 for Novak sights.

TP45 GEN2 – .45 ACP cal., 4 in. barrel, black polymer frame, 7 shot, matte stainless slide, accessory rail, short trigger with trigger safety, Truglo TFX Tritium/fiber optic day/night sights. New 2015.

| MSR $976 | $825 | $700 | $625 | $550 | $485 | $415 | $370 | |

TP45 GEN2 5 IN. – .45 ACP cal., black polymer frame, 5 in. barrel, 8 shot, matte stainless slide with front slide serrations, short trigger with trigger safety, co-witness white three dot sights, short trigger with trigger safety, accessory rail, mount for reflex sights. New 2015.

| MSR $1,015 | $860 | $725 | $650 | $585 | $515 | $450 | $395 | |

TP45 GEN2 6 IN. – .45 ACP cal., 6 in. compensated barrel, 8 shot, short trigger with trigger safety, co-witness white three dot sights, Leupold Delta Point Reflex Sight, matte stainless slide with front slide serrations, accessory rail, matte finish. New 2015.

| MSR $1,566 | $1,315 | $1,155 | $1,040 | $875 | $750 | $625 | $525 | |

KALASHNIKOV USA

Current importer of AK-47 design rifles and shotguns located in Tullytown, PA.

RIFLES: SEMI-AUTO

Current rifles being imported by Kalashnikov USA include: US132, US132L, US132S, US132SS, US132W, US132Z, US132F1, and US109T. For values and more information, please contact the importer directly (see Trademark Index).

SHOTGUNS: SEMI-AUTO

Current shotguns being imported by Kalashnikov USA include: US109T and US109L. For values and more information, please contact the importer directly (see Trademark Index).

MSR		100%	98%	95%	90%	80%	70%	60%		Last MSR

KEL-TEC CNC INDUSTRIES, INC.

Current manufacturer established in 1991, located in Cocoa, FL. Dealer sales.

CARBINES/RIFLES: SEMI-AUTO

All Kel-Tec firearms are available in OD Green, Desert Tan, and Black Cerakote finishes. Other colors are available by special order.

CMR30 – .22 Win. Mag. cal., 16.1 in. threaded barrel, 30 shot mag., single action trigger, ambidextrous safety, Magpul flip-up sights, upper and lower Picatinny rail, collapsible stock with nylon buttplate, Zytel grips, 3.8 lbs. New 2015.

MSR $630		$550	$475	$425	$365	$295	$250	$200	

M43 BULLPUP – .223 Rem. cal., short stroke piston system, 17.4 in. barrel, downward brass ejection system, pistol grip, ambidextrous bolt release, manually locked back charging handle, heat shield over piston, accepts standard AR-15 magazines, integral folding sights, wood furniture, parkerized finish, approx. 7 lbs. Mfg. late 2014-2015.

		$1,600	$1,395	$1,195	$1,075	$875	$725	$625		*$1,900*

SUB-9/SUB-40 CARBINE – 9mm Para. or .40 S&W cal., unique pivoting 16.1 in. barrel rotates upwards and back, allowing overall size reduction and portability (16 in. x 7 in.), interchangeable grip assembly will accept most popular double column high capacity handgun mags., including Glock, S&W, Beretta, SIG, or Kel-Tec, tube stock with polymer buttplate, matte black finish, 4.6 lbs. Mfg. 1997-2000.

		$350	$300	$265	$240	$220	$200	$180	

Last MSR on the SUB-9 carbine was $700.

Last MSR on the SUB-40 carbine was $725.

Add $25 for .40 S&W cal.

SUB-2000 CARBINE – 9mm Para. or .40 S&W (new 2004) cal., similar to Sub-9/Sub-40, but features a completely new design, 16.1 in. barrel, aperture rear and adj. front sights, internal keyed deployment lock, push bolt safety, choice of blued, parkerized, or hard chrome finish with black, OD Green, or tan grips, 4 lbs. Mfg. 2001-2015.

		$350	$300	$265	$240	$220	$200	$180		*$409*

Add $32 for parkerized finish.
Add $42 for hard chrome finish.
Add $9 for OD Green or tan grips with parkerized finish. Add $12 for OD Green or tan grips with blued or hard chrome finish.

This model accepts magazines from the Glock 17, 19, 22, or 23, Beretta 92 or 96, S&W Model 59, or Sig 226.

SUB-2000 GEN 2 – 9mm Para. or .40 S&W cal., updated version of the Sub-2000, blowback action, 16 in. threaded barrel, will accept most double column handgun mags. such as Beretta, Glock, or S&W, larger ejection port, front sight is now constructed of aluminum, sight can be removed to add a flash hider, stock is now adj. to three different positions, top and bottom integral Picatinny rails are standard, includes 5 Magpul M-Lok slots per side, grip updated with ergonomic groove, "Gator Grip" texturing was added to grip, stock, and forend for better control, includes single point sling attachment and webbing sling loop, folding buttstock, 4 1/4 lbs. New 2016.

MSR $500		$450	$395	$340	$300	$250	$200	$160	

SU-16 SERIES CARBINE/RIFLE – 5.56 NATO cal., unique downward folding stock, forearm folds down to become a bipod, 16 (new 2005) or 18 1/2 in. barrel, Picatinny receiver rail, M16 breech locking and feeding system, choice of black, OD Green (new 2012), or tan (new 2012) synthetic stock (stores extra mags.) and forearm, approx. 4.7 lbs. New 2003.

* **SU-16A** – 5.56 NATO cal., 18 1/2 in. barrel, 10 shot AR-15 compatible mag., right hand reciprocating bolt handle and mag. catch, buttstock can store two 10 shot mags., black, OD Green, or tan finish, 5 lbs.

MSR $676		$575	$500	$450	$400	$350	$300	$275	

Add $140 for OD Green or tan finish.

* **SU-16B** – 5.56 NATO cal., similar to SU-16, except has lightened 16 in. barrel, 4 1/2 lbs.

MSR $718		$615	$550	$475	$425	$375	$325	$295	

* **SU-16C** – .300 AAC Blackout (new 2013) or 5.56 NATO cal., similar to SU-16A, except has 16 in. barrel, front sight is integrated into the gas block, integrated bipod, Picatinny rail, and also has a true folding stock, parkerized finish with black polymer components, 4.7 lbs.

MSR $794		$675	$575	$495	$450	$385	$335	$315	

* **SU-16CA** – 5.56 NATO cal., hybrid of the SU-16C and SU-16A models, 16 in. barrel with chrome-lined bore and chamber and threads, front sight is integrated into the gas block, buttstock can store two 10 shot mags., parkerized finish with black polymer components, folding buttstock. New 2016.

MSR $795		$675	$575	$495	$450	$385	$335	$315	

* **SU-16E** – .223 Rem. or .300 AAC Blackout cal., 16 in. barrel, flat-top Picatinny receiver, collapsible buttstock, pistol grip, small quad rail, accepts AR-15 compatible magazines, black, OD Green, or tan finish, 4.7 lbs. New 2012.

MSR $901		$825	$725	$625	$525	$450	$395	$350	

Add $138 for OD Green or Tan finish.

MSR	100%	98%	95%	90%	80%	70%	60%	Last MSR

* SU-16F – 5.56 NATO cal., similar to SU-16A, except has Canadian black or choice of OD Green or tan finish. Mfg. 2012-2014.

	$585	$515	$465	$415	$360	$310	$285	*$682*

Add $140 for OD Green or tan finish.

SU-22 RIFLE SERIES – .22 LR cal., blowback action, 16 in. barrel, 26 shot mag., adj. sights, ejectors, Picatinny rail on top of receiver and bottom of aluminum quad forearm, crossbolt safety, black synthetic stock, parkerized finish, 4 lbs. New 2008.

MSR $547	$475	$415	$355	$325	$260	$215	$180

Add $10 for under folding stock with 15 shot mag. (SU-22C).
Add $41 for pistol grip style AR stock (SU-22E).
Add $126 for OD Green or Tan finish.

RMR-30 CARBINE – .22 WMR cal., 16.1 in. threaded barrel, rifle version of the PMR-30 featuring a skeletonized collapsible stock, upper and lower Picatinny rails, flat-top design, ambidextrous operating handles, aluminum construction, 30 shot mag., 3.8 lbs. Mfg. 2011-2014.

	$500	$400	$350	$300	$275	$225	$200	*$588*

RFB CARBINE – .308 Win. cal., GPO, bullpup configuration with pistol grip and rear detachable mag., 18 (Carbine), or 32 (Target, disc. 2012) in. barrel with A2 style flash hider, Picatinny rail, front ejection from tube located above barrel, 10 or 20 shot mag., accepts FAL type mags., tilting breech block design, ambidextrous controls, black synthetic lower, adj. trigger, choice of black, OD Green, or tan finish, 8.1-11.3 lbs. New 2009.

MSR $1,930	$1,625	$1,400	$1,200	$1,075	$875	$725	$625

Add $158 for OD Green or tan finish.

* RFB Hunter – .308 Win. cal., similar to RFB Carbine, except has 24 in. heavy profile threaded barrel, includes hard case, thread protector, and one 20 shot mag., 9.7 lbs. New 2009.

MSR $2,204	$1,875	$1,525	$1,300	$1,125	$1,000	$900	$775

Add $75 for OD Green or Tan finish.

RDB – .223 Rem. or .300 AAC Blackout (new 2016) cal., adj. short stroke GPO, bullpup design, 17.3, 20, or 24 (new 2016) in. barrel with A2 flash hider, downward brass ejection system, pistol grip, ambidextrous bolt release, manually locked back charging handle, polymer Picatinny top and bottom rail, accepts standard AR-15 magazines, polymer furniture, matte black finish, approx. 7 lbs. New late 2014.

MSR $1,545	$1,325	$1,160	$995	$900	$725	$600	$485

RDB-C – .223 Rem. or 6.5 Grendel cal., downward ejecting bullpup design, 20 in. barrel, 10 shot mag., push buttun mag. release, polymer furniture, hunter-style fixed stock, grip, and forend, push button safety, FDE or OD Green finish, 7 lbs. New 2016.

Please contact the company directly for pricing and availability on this model.

PISTOLS: SEMI-AUTO

PLR-16 – 5.56 NATO cal., GPO, 9.2 in. threaded barrel, upper frame has integrated Picatinny rail, 10 shot detachable mag., adj. sights, black composite frame, 3.2 lbs. New 2006.

MSR $676	$585	$525	$450	$395	$350	$295	$250

Add $119 for OD Green or tan finish.

PLR-22 – .22 LR cal., blowback action, 10.1 in. barrel, 26 shot mag., ejector, adj. sights, integrated Picatinny rail, black, tan, or OD Green composite frame, 2.8 lbs. New 2008.

MSR $398	$330	$295	$250	$235	$210	$190	$170

Add $193 for OD Green or tan finish.

PF-9 – 9mm Para. cal., similar operating system as P-11, DAO, 3.1 in. barrel, single stack 7 shot mag., includes lower accessory rail, adj. sights, black, grey, or Olive Drab grips, blued, parkerized, or hard chrome finish, 12.7 oz. Limited mfg. 2006, reintroduced 2008.

MSR $356	$285	$230	$195	$175	$155	$135	$125

Add $45 for parkerized finish.
Add $60 for hard chrome finish.

PMR-30 – .22 WMR cal., blowback action, 4.3 in. barrel, 30 shot mag., aluminum frame, manual safety, fiber optic sights, steel slide and barrel, Zytel grips, black, OD green, tan, or titanium finish, lower Picatinny rail, 13.6 oz. New 2010.

MSR $455	$500	$440	$365	$335	$315	$295	$275

Add $27 for OD green or tan finish.
Add approx. $125 for titanium barrel finish.

MSR	100%	98%	95%	90%	80%	70%	60%	Last MSR

SHOTGUNS: SLIDE ACTION

KSG – 12 ga., 2 3/4 in. chamber, unique bullpup configuration, utilizing an 18 1/2 in. cyl. bore barrel, twin mag. tubes under the barrel allow 14 shot capacity, downward ejection, steel and polymer construction, upper and lower Picatinny rails w/o sights, pistol grip, 26.1 in. overall length, 6.9 lbs. New 2011.

	MSR $990	$875	$775	$675	$575	$500	$425	$350

Add $50 for OD Green or Tan finish.

KEPPELER - TECHNISCHE ENTWICKLUNGEN GmbH

Current rifle manufacturer located in Fichtenberg, Germany. No current U.S. importation.

Keppeler manufactures a wide variety of top quality rifles, in many target configurations (including UIT-CISM, Prone, Free, and Sniper Bullpup). Both metric and domestic calibers are available as well as a variety of special order options. Keppeler also manufactures precision caliber conversion tubes for the shotgun barrel(s) on combination guns and drillings. Please contact the factory directly for more information and current pricing (see Trademark Index).

KIMBER

Current trademark manufactured by Kimber Mfg., Inc., established during 1997, with company headquarters and manufacturing located in Elmsford, NY. Previously located in Yonkers, NY until 2011. Previous rifle manufacture was by Kimber of America, Inc., located in Clackamas, OR circa 1993-1997. Dealer sales.

PISTOLS: SEMI-AUTO

Kimber pistols, including the very early models marked "Clackamas, Oregon", have all been manufactured in the Yonkers, NY plant. Prior to the 1998 production year, the "Classic" model pistols were alternately roll-scrolled "Classic", "Classic Custom" or "Custom Classic". During 1997-98, the "Classic" moniker was dropped from Kimber pistol nomenclature as a specific model.

All Kimber 1911 pistols are shipped with a lockable high impact synthetic case with cable lock and one magazine, beginning 1999.

Beginning in 2001, the "Series II" pistol, incorporating the Kimber Firing Pin Safety System, was again phased into some centerfire models. All pistols incorporating the firing pin block have the Roman Numeral "II" following the name of the pistol presented on the slide directly under the ejection port. This conversion was completed by February 2002, and about 50% of subsequent Kimber 1911 pistol production have been Series II. There was no "Series I" pistol per se, but pre-series II models are often referred to in that manner.

During 2003, external extractors were phased out of many .45 ACP models. Due to consumer demand, production was phased back to traditional (internal) extractors during 2006.

All three changes (disuse of the term "Classic" for pistols, Series II safety system, and external extractor) were "phased in" throughout normal production cycles. Therefore, no distinctive cut-off dates or serial numbering series were established to identify specific product runs or identify when these features were incorporated.

Almost all Kimber pistols (exceptions are Royal II, Classic Carry Pro, rimfires and some pistols sold in California) have stainless steel match grade barrels beginning 2013.

Add $339 for .22 LR cal. or $344-$379 for .17 Mach 2 cal. (mfg. 2005-2006) conversion kit for all Mil-spec 1911 pistols (includes complete upper assembly, lightweight aluminum slide, premium bull barrel, and 10 shot mag.). Available in satin black and satin silver. Kimber began manufacture of these kits in early 2003. Prior to that, they were manufactured by a vendor.

AEGIS II SERIES – 9mm Para. cal., SA, 3 (Ultra), 4 (Pro), or 5 (Custom) in. stainless steel barrel, 8 or 9 shot mag., aluminum frame w/satin silver premium KimPro II finish, matte black slide, thin rosewood grips, 30 LPI front strap checkering, high relief cut under trigger guard, Tactical Wedge 3-dot (green) night sights, bumped and grooved grip safety, hammer, thumb safety and mag. release button are bobbed, Carry Melt treatment on both frame and slide, 25 oz. New 2006.

	MSR $1,331	$1,125	$975	$850	$725	$625	$525	$450

COVERT II SERIES – .45 ACP cal., SA, 3 (Ultra Covert II), 4 (Pro Covert II), or 5 (Custom Covert II) in. bushingless barrel, aluminum frame, lanyard ring and magazine with extended bumper (Pro Covert or Custom Covert only), Carry Melt treatment, 30 LPI front strap checkering, bumped and grooved beavertail grip safety, Tactical Wedge 3-dot (green) night sights, digital camo Crimson Trace Lasergrips, Desert Tan finish, matte black oxide slide, approx. 25-30 oz. New 2007.

	MSR $1,657	$1,495	$1,300	$1,100	$1,025	$900	$775	$650

CUSTOM II – .45 ACP or 9mm Para. (new 2016) cal., patterned after the Colt Government Model 1911, 5 in. barrel, SA, matte black or two-tone (new 2016) slide and frame finish, 7 shot mag., steel frame, match grade barrel, bushing and trigger group, lowered and flared ejection ports, three-hole trigger, dovetail mounted sights, frame machined from solid steel, high ride beavertail grip safety, choice of rubber, laminated wood (disc.), walnut (disc.), or rosewood grips, 38 oz. New 1995.

	MSR $837	$775	$675	$575	$500	$400	$325	$275

Add $34 for walnut (disc.) or rosewood grips.

Add $117 for night sights.

Add $185 for Royal II finish (polished blue and checkered rosewood grips, disc. 2010 and replaced by new Custom Shop version with same name)

This series' nomenclature added the Roman numeral "II" during 2001.

MSR	100%	98%	95%	90%	80%	70%	60%	Last MSR

* **Custom Target II** – .45 ACP cal., similar to Custom II, except features Kimber adj. rear sight. New 1998.

    MSR $974 $860 $725 $675 $595 $425 $400 $365

CUSTOM STAINLESS II – .38 Super (advertised in 1999, mfg. late 2005-2008), 9mm Para. (advertised in 1999, new 2008), .40 S&W (mfg. 1999-2007), or .45 ACP cal., similar to Custom II, except has stainless steel slide and frame.

    MSR $998 $850 $750 $650 $550 $450 $360 $280

    Add $18 for 9mm Para. or $11 for .40 S&W (disc. 2007) cal.

    Add $130 for night sights (.45 ACP cal. only).

    Add $143 for high polish stainless in .38 Super cal. only (mfg. late 2005-2008).

    Subtract $27 for Stainless Limited Edition marked "Stainless LE" (disc. 1998).

* **Custom Stainless Target II** – similar to Custom Stainless II, except is available in .38 Super (new 2002), 9mm Para., 10mm (new 2003), or .45 ACP cal., features Kimber adj. rear sight. New 1998.

    MSR $1,108 $975 $850 $725 $625 $500 $425 $350

    Add $84 for .38 Super, 10mm, or 9mm Para. cal.

    Add $100 for .40 S&W cal. (disc. 2002).

    Add $130 for high polish stainless in .38 Super cal. only (mfg. late 2005-2008).

ECLIPSE II SERIES – 10mm (Eclipse Custom II, new 2004) or .45 ACP cal., SA, stainless steel slide and frame, black matte finish with brush polished flat surfaces for elegant two-tone finish, Tritium night sights, target models have adj. bar/dot sights, silver/grey laminated double diamond grips or Crimson Trace Lasergrips (new 2015), black small parts, 30 LPI front strap checkering, include Eclipse Ultra II (3 in. barrel, short grip), Eclipse Pro II and Eclipse Pro-Target II (4 in. barrel, standard grip, disc. 2012), Eclipse Custom II, and Eclipse Target II (full size). New 2002.

    MSR $1,351 $1,165 $975 $825 $750 $650 $550 $450

    Add $42 for Eclipse Target II in .45 ACP cal. or Eclipse Pro-Target II (disc. 2012).

    Add $238 for Crimson Trace Lasergrips (new 2015).

    The initial Custom Shop version of these pistols was mfg. during late 2001, featuring an ambidextrous thumb safety, and "Custom Shop" markings on left side of slide, 7,931 were mfg.

GOLD MATCH II – .45 ACP cal., SA, 5 in. stainless steel match barrel and bushing, premium aluminum match grade trigger, ambidextrous thumb safety became standard in 1998, 8 shot mag., Kimber adj. sight, fancy checkered rosewood grips in double diamond pattern, high polish blue, hand fitted barrel by Kimber Custom Shop, 38 oz.

    MSR $1,393 $1,250 $1,125 $950 $850 $700 $575 $450

    This series' nomenclature added the Roman numeral "II" during 2001.

* **Gold Match Stainless II** – .38 Super (advertised in 1999, never mfg.), 9mm Para. (advertised in 1999, mfg. 2008-2014), .40 S&W (mfg. 1999-2007), or .45 ACP cal., similar to Gold Match, except is stainless steel, 38 oz.

    MSR $1,574 $1,375 $1,175 $1,025 $900 $750 $625 $550

    Add $75 for 9mm Para. (disc. 2014), or $100 for .40 S&W (disc. 2007) cal.

TEAM MATCH II – 9mm Para. (new 2009), .45 ACP, or .38 Super (limited mfg. 2003-2004, reintroduced 2006-2010) cal., same pistol developed for USA Shooting Team (2004 Olympics Rapid Fire Pistol Team) competition, satin finish stainless steel frame and slide, 5 in. match grade barrel, SA, 30 LPI front strap checkering, match grade trigger, Tactical Extractor system (disc.) or internal extractor, extended magwell, 8 shot mag., laminated red/white/blue grips, 38 oz. Total production just over 10,000 units. Later mfg. had a gold logo on slide, red/blue grips and black DLC coating on slide. Mfg. 2003-2012.

                    $1,315 $1,150 $975 $775 $725 $575 $450   *$1,563*

    Add $13 for 9mm Para. cal.

    Add $48 for .38 Super cal. (disc. 2010).

    A $100 donation was made to the U.S.A. Shooting Team for every Team Match II sold.

* **Team Match II (Current Mfg.)** – 9mm Para. or .45 ACP cal., SA, same pistol developed for USA Shooting Team (2004 Olympics Rapid Fire Pistol Team) competition, 5 in. match grade barrel and bushing, front serrations, satin finish stainless steel frame, stainless steel slide with black diamond-like coating finish and 24Kt. gold USA shooting team logo, 30 LPI front strap checkering, full-length guide rod, ambidextrous thumb safety, match grade trigger, extended magwell, 8 shot mag., laminated red and blue G10 grips, 38 oz. New 2014.

    MSR $1,868 $1,595 $1,395 $1,195 $1,085 $875 $725 $560

    Add $14 for 9mm Para. cal.

    A $100 donation is made to the U.S.A. Shooting Team for every Team Match II sold.

SUPER MATCH II – .45 ACP cal. only, 5 in. barrel, SA, top-of-the-line model, two-tone stainless steel construction, KimPro finish on slide, match grade trigger, Custom Shop markings, accuracy guarantee, 38 oz. New 1999.

    MSR $2,313 $2,075 $1,800 $1,575 $1,350 $1,100 $900 $750

    This series' nomenclature added the Roman numeral "II" during 2001.

MSR	100%	98%	95%	90%	80%	70%	60%	Last MSR

LTP II – .45 ACP cal., designed for Limited Ten competition, Tactical Extractor, steel frame and slide, KimPro finish, 20 LPI front strap checkering, 30 LPI checkering under trigger guard, tungsten guide rod, flat-top serrated slide, beveled magwell, ambidextrous thumb safety, adj. rear sight. Mfg. by Custom Shop 2002-2006.

	$1,850	$1,620	$1,385	$1,260	$1,015	$830	$645	*$2,106*

RIMFIRE TARGET – .17 Mach 2 (mfg. 2004-2005) or .22 LR cal., 5 in. barrel, SA, 10 shot mag., aluminum frame with satin silver or matte black finish (black anodized finish was disc. in 2006), black oxide steel or satin stainless slide (.17 Mach 2 cal. only), black synthetic double diamond grips, Kimber adj. rear sight, 28 oz. New 2003.

MSR $871	$775	$675	$575	$500	$400	$325	$275	

Add $339 for black or silver conversion kit.

Add $75 for .17 Mach 2 cal. (disc. 2005).

RIMFIRE SUPER – .22 LR cal., 5 in. barrel, 10 shot mag., aluminum frame with satin silver KimPro II finish, front strap checkering, aluminum flat-top slide with matte black KimPro II finish and aggressive fluting on upper sides, full length guide rod, premium aluminum trigger, ambidextrous safety, rosewood grips with logo inserts, 23 oz. Mfg. by Kimber Custom Shop beginning 2004.

MSR $1,220	$1,075	$925	$800	$700	$600	$500	$425	

POLYMER – .45 ACP cal., SA, widened black polymer frame offering larger mag. capacity, choice of fixed (Polymer) or adj. Kimber target (Polymer Target, disc. 1999) rear sight, matte black slide, 10 shot mag., 34 oz. Mfg. 1997-2001.

	$675	$595	$500	$450	$375	$300	$225	*$795*

Add $88 for Polymer Target.

All Polymer models were disc. in 2002 in favor of the new "Ten" Series with improved Kimber made frame. Magazines are interchangeable.

* **Polymer Stainless** – .38 Super (advertised in 1999, never mfg.), 9mm Para. (advertised in 1999, never mfg.), .40 S&W (mfg. 1999 only), or .45 ACP cal., similar to Polymer, except has satin finish stainless steel slide. Mfg. 1998-2001.

	$745	$650	$550	$500	$410	$335	$250	*$856*

Add $88 for Polymer Stainless Target (disc. 1999).

* **Polymer Gold Match** – .45 ACP cal. only, similar to Gold Match, except has polymer frame, supplied with 10 shot double stack mag., 34 oz. Mfg. 1999-2001.

	$925	$810	$695	$630	$510	$415	$325	*$1,041*

»**Polymer Gold Match Stainless** – similar to Gold Match, except has polymer frame and stainless steel slide, 34 oz. Mfg. 1999-2001.

	$1,025	$895	$770	$695	$565	$460	$360	*$1,177*

* **Polymer Pro Carry** – .45 ACP cal. only, 4 in. bushingless bull barrel, steel slide, 32 oz. Mfg. 1999-2001.

	$725	$635	$545	$495	$400	$325	$255	*$814*

»**Polymer Pro Carry Stainless** – similar to Polymer Pro Carry, except has stainless steel slide. Mfg. 1999-2001.

	$755	$660	$565	$515	$415	$340	$265	*$874*

* **Polymer Ultra Ten II** – .45 ACP cal., black polymer frame with aluminum frame insert, stainless slide, 3 in. barrel, 10 shot staggered mag., low profile sights, lighter version of the Polymer Series frame, Kimber Firing Pin Safety, 24 oz.

While advertised during 2001 with an MSR of $896, this model was manufactured in prototypes only.

COMPACT II – .45 ACP cal., SA, 4 in. barrel, .4 in. shorter aluminum or steel frame, 7 shot mag., Commander style hammer, single recoil spring, low profile combat sights, checkered black synthetic grips, 28 (aluminum) or 34 (steel) oz. Mfg. 1998-2001.

	$635	$555	$475	$430	$350	$285	$220	*$764*

* **Compact Stainless II** – .40 S&W (mfg. 1999-2001) or .45 ACP cal., stainless steel slide, 4 in. bull barrel, 4 in. shorter aluminum (disc., reintroduced 2009) or stainless (mfg. 2002-2008) frame, 7 shot mag., Commander style hammer, single recoil spring, low profile combat sights, black synthetic grips, 34 oz. Mfg. 1998-2013.

	$925	$825	$725	$625	$525	$450	$350	*$1,052*

Add $32 for .40 S&W cal. (disc. 2001).

This model's nomenclature added the Roman numeral "II" during 2001.

COMBAT CARRY – .40 S&W or .45 ACP cal., 4 in. barrel, SA, carry model featuring aluminum frame and trigger, stainless steel slide, Tritium night sights, and ambidextrous thumb safety, 28 oz. Limited mfg. 1999 only.

	$940	$825	$700	$650	$515	$425	$325	*$1,044*

Add $30 for .40 S&W cal.

MSR	100%	98%	95%	90%	80%	70%	60%	Last MSR

MASTER CARRY SERIES – .45 ACP cal., SA, 3 (Ultra), 4 (Pro), or 5 (Custom) in. stainless steel barrel, aluminum frame on Carry Pro and Carry Ultra models, stainless steel frame on Carry Custom, black KimPro II finish on slide and satin finish frame, skeletonized trigger, includes Crimson Trace master series laser grips with red beam, round heel frame, tactical wedge night sights, 25-30 oz. New 2013.

MSR $1,568	$1,325	$1,175	$1,025	$900	$775	$650	$550	

PRO CARRY II – 9mm Para. (new mid-2005), .40 S&W (disc. 2001) or .45 ACP cal., SA, 4 in. barrel, 7 or 8 shot mag., full length guide rod, aluminum frame, steel slide, aluminum match grade trigger, fixed low profile sights, full length black synthetic double diamond grips, matte black or two-tone (new 2016) finish, 28 oz. New 1999.

MSR $919	$800	$725	$650	$575	$500	$425	$350	

Add $50 for 9mm Para. cal.

Add $35 for .40 S&W cal. (disc.).

Add $120 for night sights (.45 ACP cal. only).

This series' nomenclature added the Roman numeral "II" during 2001.

* **Stainless Pro Carry II** – .40 S&W (disc. 2007), .45 ACP, or 9mm Para. cal., similar to Pro Carry, except has stainless steel slide, 28 oz. New 1999.

MSR $1,016	$900	$800	$700	$600	$500	$400	$300	

Add $50 for 9mm Para. cal.

Add $112 for night sights (.45 ACP cal. only).

Add $38 for .40 S&W (disc. 2007) cal.

Add $295 for Crimson Trace grips (.45 ACP cal. only, disc. 2009).

* **Pro Carry HD II** – .38 Super (new 2002) or .45 ACP cal., similar to Pro Carry Stainless, except has heavier stainless steel frame, 35 oz. New 2001.

MSR $1,046	$925	$825	$700	$600	$500	$425	$350	

Add $48 for .38 Super cal.

ULTRA CARRY II – .40 S&W (disc. 2001) or .45 ACP cal., SA, 3 in. barrel, aluminum frame with matte black finish, 7 shot mag., full length guide rod, steel slide, fixed low profile sights, black synthetic double diamond grips, black or two-tone (new 2016) finish, 25 oz. New 1999.

MSR $919	$800	$725	$650	$575	$500	$425	$350	

Add $120 for night sights.

Add $39 for .40 S&W cal. (disc. 2001).

Add $375 for Crimson Trace grips (disc. 2009).

This series' nomenclature added the Roman numeral "II" during 2001.

* **Stainless Ultra Carry II** – 9mm Para. (new 2008), .40 S&W (disc. 2007), or .45 ACP cal., similar to Ultra Carry II, except has stainless steel slide. New 1999.

MSR $1,016	$900	$800	$700	$600	$500	$400	$300	

Add $50 for 9mm Para. (new 2008) or $45 for .40 S&W cal. (disc. 2007).

Add $109 for night sights (.45 ACP cal. only, disc. 2009).

CRIMSON CARRY II – .45 ACP cal., SA, satin silver aluminum frame, 3 (Ultra), 4 (Pro), or 5 (Custom) in. stainless steel barrel, matte black slide with black sights, shortened slide stop pin, beveled frame, extended thumb safety, rosewood Crimson Trace laser grips with double diamond checkering and Kimber logo. New mid-2008.

MSR $1,206	$1,050	$900	$800	$700	$600	$500	$400	

Add $87 for Crimson Trace laser grips with green beam (new 2013).

SUPER CARRY SERIES – .45 ACP cal., SA, 3 (Ultra), 4 (Pro), or 5 (Custom) in. barrel, stainless steel slide, aluminum frame, KimPro II finish, night sights, rounded edges, checkered double Dymondwood or Micarta (Ultra+, new 2011) grips, recessed slide stop pin with surrounding bevel, rear slide serrations. New 2010.

MSR $1,596	$1,350	$1,150	$975	$875	$775	$650	$525	

* **Super Carry HD Series** – .45 ACP cal., 3 (Ultra), 4 (Pro), or 5 (Custom) in. barrel, similar to Super Carry, except has matte black finish and G10 checkered blue/black Micarta grips, 32 oz. New 2011.

MSR $1,699	$1,525	$1,315	$1,100	$1,025	$900	$775	$650	

SOLO CARRY – 9mm Para. cal., DA, SFO, micro-compact aluminum frame, 2.7 in. stainless steel barrel, 6 or 8 (extended mag.) shot, matte black (Solo Carry) or satin silver (Solo Carry Stainless) KimPro II finish, stainless steel slide, amidextrous thumb safety, black synthetic removable grips, rosewood grips with special logo (new 2015), or Crimson Trace Lasergrips (new 2015), ambidextrous mag. release, 3-dot sights, 17 oz. New 2011.

MSR $815	$725	$625	$525	$450	$395	$340	$315	

Add $34 for rosewood grips with special logo (new 2015).

Add $258 for Crimson Trace Lasergrips (new 2015).

MSR	100%	98%	95%	90%	80%	70%	60%	Last MSR

* Solo CDP (LG) – 9mm Para. cal., SFO, 2.7 in. barrel, matte black aluminum frame with satin stainless steel slide, 6 or 8 shot mag., checkered front and back strap, fixed 3 dot Tritium night sights and rosewood Crimson Trace laser grips, 17 oz. New late 2011.

| MSR $1,223 | $1,050 | $875 | $750 | $675 | $550 | $450 | $350 | |

* Solo Carry DC – 9mm Para. cal., SA, SFO, 2.7 in. barrel, black DLC finished slide and barrel, night sights, Carry Melt treatment, 6 shot mag., 17 oz. New 2012.

| MSR $904 | $795 | $725 | $650 | $575 | $500 | $425 | $350 | |

Add $300 for Crimson Trace laser grips (Solo Carry DC-LG).

* Solo Sapphire – 9mm Para. cal., DA, SFO, 2.7 in. stainless steel barrel, ambidextrous thumb safety, bright polished blue PVD accents and engraved stainless steel slide, night sights, Micarta grips, 17 oz. New 2015.

| MSR $1,291 | $1,150 | $1,000 | $875 | $775 | $625 | $500 | $395 | |

MICRO 9 CRIMSON CARRY – 9mm Para. cal., satin aluminum frame, 3.15 in. stainless steel barrel, 6 shot, steel slide with matte black finish, rosewood with Crimson Trace laser grips, full length guide rod, 15.6 oz. New 2016.

| MSR $894 | $785 | $675 | $575 | $500 | $400 | $325 | $275 | |

MICRO 9 STAINLESS – 9mm Para. cal., satin aluminum frame with silver finish, 3.15 in. stainless steel barrel, stainless steel slide, rosewood grips, 15.6 oz. New 2016.

| MSR $654 | $575 | $500 | $450 | $400 | $350 | $300 | $250 | |

MICRO 9 TWO-TONE – 9mm Para. cal., 3.15 in. stainless steel ramped barrel, 6 shot, stainless steel slide with matte black finish, solid aluminum match grade trigger, rosewood grips, full length guide rod, two-tone slide and frame finish, 15.6 oz. New 2016.

| MSR $654 | $575 | $500 | $450 | $400 | $350 | $300 | $250 | |

MICRO ADVOCATE – .380 ACP cal., 2 3/4 in. barrel, 7 shot, fixed night sights, purple/black or brown/black G10 grips, includes extended magazine, matte black slide finish, 13.4 oz. New mid-2015.

| MSR $714 | $615 | $525 | $475 | $425 | $375 | $325 | $275 | |

MICRO CDP – .380 ACP cal., SA, 2 3/4 in. barrel, 6 shot mag., stainless steel slide and barrel, aluminum frame, 30 LPI front strap checkering, steel dovetail mounted 3-dot night sights, ambidextrous thumb safety, high cut under the trigger guard, double diamond checkered rosewood grips, matte black finish, checkered mainspring housing, 13.4 oz. Built in Kimber Custom Shop. New late 2012.

| MSR $951 | $850 | $725 | $675 | $595 | $425 | $400 | $365 | |

Add $259 for Crimson Trace laser grips (LG Model).

MICRO CARRY – .380 ACP cal., SA, 2 3/4 in. stainless steel barrel, aluminum frame, stainless steel slide, all satin or black frame finish, 6 shot mag., steel sights, black synthetic double diamond grips or Crimson Trace Lasergrips (new 2015), 15.4 oz. New 2013.

| MSR $651 | $575 | $500 | $450 | $415 | $385 | $350 | $295 | |

Add $28 for all satin finish (Micro Carry Stainless).
Add $145 for Micro Carry Advocate model with purple/black grips (new 2015).
Add $260 for Crimson Trace Lasergrips (Micro Crimson Carry, new 2015).

* Micro Bel Air – .380 ACP cal., 2 3/4 in. barrel, 6 or 7 shot, fixed low profile sights, ivory Micarta grips, two-position safety, mirror polish stainless steel frame, Bel Air Blu KimPro II finish, 13.04 oz. New 2016.

| MSR $802 | $695 | $600 | $550 | $500 | $450 | $395 | $350 | |

* Micro Sapphire – .380 ACP cal., DA, SFO, 2 3/4 in. stainless steel barrel, ambidextrous thumb safety, bright polished blue PVD accents and engraved stainless steel slide, night sights, Micarta grips, 13.4 oz. New 2015.

| MSR $1,014 | $900 | $800 | $700 | $600 | $500 | $400 | $300 | |

MICRO RAPTOR – .380 ACP cal., 2 3/4 in. stainless steel barrel, aluminum or steel frame, stainless steel slide, 6 shot mag., full length guide rod, high cut under trigger guard, solid aluminum match grade trigger, side and top slide scaling, front strap scale serrations, Carry Melt treatment, Tritium 3-dot night sights, Zebra wood grips with scale pattern and Kimber logo, Black or Satin Silver finish, 13.4 oz. New 2015.

| MSR $951 | $850 | $725 | $675 | $595 | $425 | $400 | $365 | |

Add $21 for stainless steel slide, frame, and Satin Silver finish (Micro Raptor Stainless).

CUSTOM TLE II – 10mm (new 2012) or .45 ACP cal., 5 in. barrel, SA, tactical law enforcement pistol (TLE) with exactly the same features as the Kimber pistols carried by LAPD SWAT, black oxide coated frame and slide, same features as Custom II, except has 30 LPI front strap checkering and night sights, integrated mainspring lanyard slot (new 2016), flat-top slide (new 2016), aggressive G10 grips (new 2016), approx. 38 oz. New 2003.

MSR	100%	98%	95%	90%	80%	70%	60%	Last MSR

* **Custom TLE II** – 9mm Para. (new 2014, TFS model only), 10mm (new 2013) or .45 ACP cal., 5 in. stainless steel barrel, 7 shot mag., full length guide rod, steel frame and slide with matte black finish, front strap checkering, front serrations, Tritium 3-dot night sights, double diamond black synthetic grips, 38 oz.

| MSR $1,080 | $950 | $825 | $700 | $625 | $525 | $425 | $350 | |

Add $61 for 10mm cal.
Add $73 for TFS Model with threaded barrel (new 2014).
Add $134 for 9mm Para. cal. with threaded barrel (TFS model).
Add $274 for Crimson Trace laser grips (disc. 2010).

* **Stainless TLE II** – .45 ACP cal., similar to TLE II, except has stainless steel slide and frame. New 2004.

| MSR $1,211 | $1,050 | $925 | $800 | $725 | $600 | $500 | $425 | |

* **Custom TLE/RL II** – 9mm Para. (new 2014), 10mm (new 2013) or .45 ACP cal., similar to Custom TLE II, except has Picatinny rail machined into the frame to accept optics and other tactical accessories. New 2003.

| MSR $1,178 | $1,050 | $925 | $800 | $725 | $600 | $500 | $425 | |

Add $74 for 10mm cal.
Add $73 for TFS Model with threaded barrel (new 2014).
Add $148 for 9mm Para. (TFS model only, new 2014).

* **Stainless TLE/RL II** – .45 ACP cal., similar to Custom TLE/RL II, except is stainless. New 2004.

| MSR $1,323 | $1,150 | $975 | $825 | $750 | $650 | $550 | $450 | |

* **Pro TLE/RL II** – .45 ACP cal., similar to Custom TLE/RL II, except has 4 in. bushingless bull barrel. New 2004.

| MSR $1,248 | $1,075 | $950 | $825 | $725 | $625 | $525 | $425 | |

* **Stainless Pro TLE/RL II** – .45 ACP cal., similar to Stainless TLE/RL II, except has 4 in. bushingless bull barrel. New 2004.

| MSR $1,379 | $1,225 | $1,050 | $900 | $800 | $700 | $600 | $475 | |

* **Pro TLE II (LG)** – .45 ACP cal., similar to Custom TLE/RL II, except has 4 in. bushingless bull barrel and Crimson Trace laser grips (disc. 2008 only). Mfg. 2006-2008, reintroduced 2010.

| MSR $1,150 | $995 | $850 | $725 | $650 | $575 | $500 | $425 | |

Add $74 for threaded barrel (TFS model, new 2015).
Subtract $240 if w/o Crimson Trace laser grips (mfg. 2008 only).

* **Stainless Pro TLE II** – .45 ACP cal., similar to Pro TLE II, except is stainless steel, and Crimson Trace laser grips optional.

| MSR $1,253 | $1,075 | $950 | $825 | $725 | $625 | $525 | $425 | |

Add $265 for Crimson Trace laser grips.

ULTRA TLE II – .45 ACP cal., 3 in. bull barrel, SA, 7 shot mag., dovetail mounted night sights, matte black finish, aluminum frame. New 2010.

| MSR $1,007 | $900 | $800 | $700 | $600 | $500 | $400 | $300 | |

Add $243 for Crimson Trace laser grips.

* **Stainless Ultra TLE II** – .45 ACP cal., similar to Ultra TLE II, except is stainless steel. New 2010.

| MSR $1,136 | $995 | $850 | $725 | $625 | $500 | $425 | $350 | |

Add $265 for Crimson Trace laser grips.

TACTICAL II SERIES – 9mm Para. (Tactical Pro II, new 2004) or .45 ACP cal., SA, lightweight tactical pistol, gray anodized (disc. 2008) or gray KimPro II finished frame with black steel slide, fixed Tritium 3-dot night sights, extended magwell, 30 LPI front strap checkering, black/gray laminated logo grips, 7 shot mag. with bumper pad, available in Tactical Ultra II (3 in. barrel, short grip, 25 oz.), Tactical Pro II (4 in. barrel, standard grip, 28 oz.), Tactical Custom II (5 in. barrel, standard grip, 31 oz.). Tactical Custom HD II (.45 ACP only, new 2009), or Tactical Entry II (.45 ACP only, includes integral rail and night sights). New 2003.

| MSR $1,317 | $1,125 | $975 | $850 | $725 | $600 | $525 | $400 | |

Add $34 for Tactical Pro II in 9mm Para. cal.
Add $70 for Tactical Custom HD II.
Add $173 for Tactical Entry II.

A Custom Shop version of the Pro Tactical II was manufactured in 2002, but without checkering and night sights.

STAINLESS TEN II – .45 ACP cal., SA, high capacity polymer frame, stainless steel slide with satin finish, impressed front grip strap checkering and serrations under trigger guard, textured finish, polymer grip safety and mainspring housing, 10 or 13 (new 2005) round double stack mag., includes Ultra Ten II (3 in. barrel, short grip, disc. 2003), Pro Carry Ten II (4 in. barrel, standard grip), Stainless Ten II (full size), and Gold Match Ten II (stainless steel barrel, polished stainless steel slide flats, hand fitted barrel/bushing to slide, adj. sight), 14 (pre-ban) round mags. also available, accepts magazines from older Kimber mfg. polymer pistols. Mfg. 2002-2007.

| | $715 | $625 | $535 | $485 | $395 | $320 | $250 | $812 |

Add $9 for Pro-Carry Ten II, $35 for Ultra Ten II (disc. 2003), or $294 for Gold Match Ten II.

MSR	100%	98%	95%	90%	80%	70%	60%	Last MSR

* **BP Ten II** – similar to Stainless Ten II, except has black oxide carbon steel slide, and aluminum frame for lighter weight. Mfg. 2003-2007.

| | $570 | $500 | $425 | $385 | $315 | $255 | $200 | *$652* |

* **Pro BP Ten II** – similar to Pro Carry Ten II, except has black oxide carbon steel slide, and aluminum frame for lighter weight. Mfg. 2003-2007.

| | $570 | $500 | $425 | $385 | $315 | $255 | $200 | *$666* |

CDP II (CUSTOM DEFENSE PACKAGE) SERIES

– 9mm Para. (new 2008), .40 S&W (disc. 2007), or .45 ACP cal., Custom Shop pistol featuring Tritium night sights, stainless steel slide with black anodized aluminum frame, 3 in. (Ultra CDP II, 25 oz.), Ultra+ (3-inch barrel with full length grip, new 2011), 4 in. (Pro CDP II and Compact CDP II, 28 oz.), or 5 in. (Custom CDP II, 31 oz.) barrel, SA, Carry Melt treatment, ambidextrous thumb safety, double diamond pattern checkered rosewood grips, 30 LPI checkered front strap and under trigger guard (new 2003), two-tone finish. New 2000.

| MSR $1,331 | $1,150 | $1,000 | $875 | $775 | $625 | $525 | $400 | |

Add $28 for 9mm Para cal. (new 2008).

Add $300 for Crimson Trace laser grips (new 2010).

Add $40 for .40 S&W cal., available in either Ultra CDP II or Pro CDP II configuration (disc. 2007).

The Pro CDP II has a full length grip frame.

This series' nomenclature added the Roman numeral "II" during 2001.

ULTRA TEN CDP II

– .45 ACP cal., SA, 3 in. barrel, stainless steel slide with black polymer frame, Tritium night sights, carry bevel treatment, standard manual safety, 10 shot mag., 24 oz. Mfg. 2003 only.

| | $825 | $720 | $620 | $560 | $455 | $370 | $290 | *$926* |

RAPTOR II

– .45 ACP cal., SA, 5 in. stainless barrel with engraved "Raptor II" and "Custom Shop", full size carbon steel or stainless steel (new 2008) frame with "scales" on front strap, continuing on slide in lieu of standard serrations, flats on frame and slide polished, black oxide finish, back cut flat-top, black anodized trigger, ambidextrous safety, scaled Zebra wood grip panels with Kimber logo, fixed slant night sights, 38 oz. New mid-2004.

| MSR $1,434 | $1,250 | $1,075 | $925 | $800 | $700 | $600 | $475 | |

Add $134 for stainless steel frame (new 2008).

PRO RAPTOR II

– .45 ACP cal., SA, 4 in. stainless barrel with engraved "Pro Raptor II" and "Custom Shop", full size stainless steel frame with "scales" on front strap, continuing on carbon steel slide in lieu of standard serrations, flats on frame and slide polished, black oxide finish, back cut flat-top, black anodized trigger, ambidextrous safety, scaled Zebra wood grip panels with Kimber logo, fixed slant night sights, 38 oz. New mid-2004.

| MSR $1,295 | $1,100 | $975 | $850 | $725 | $600 | $525 | $450 | |

Add $120 for Stainless Pro Rapter II (new 2009).

ULTRA RAPTOR II

– .45 ACP cal., SA, 3 in. ramped bushingless barrel, lightweight aluminum frame, scale serrations on flat-top slide and front strap, feathered logo wood grips, flats on frame and slide polished, night sights, all-matte black finish. Mfg. by Custom Shop. New 2006.

| MSR $1,295 | $1,100 | $975 | $850 | $725 | $600 | $525 | $450 | |

Add $120 for Stainless Ultra Raptor II.

GRAND RAPTOR II

– .45 ACP cal., SA, 5 in. barrel, full-size stainless steel frame, blued slide, flats on frame and slide polished, two-tone finish, scale rosewood grips with Kimber logo, extended ambidextrous thumb safety, bumped beavertail grip safety, night sights, mfg. by Custom Shop. New 2006.

| MSR $1,657 | $1,495 | $1,300 | $1,100 | $1,025 | $900 | $775 | $650 | |

WARRIOR

– .45 ACP cal., SA, production began following adoption of this pistol by the Marine Expeditionary Unit (MEU) Special Operations Capable (SOC), Detachment 1 (Det. 1), civilian version with 5 in. barrel, Series I (no firing pin block), carbon steel slide and frame, integral Picatinny light rail, internal extractor, lanyard loop, bumped grip safety, G-10 material grip (coyote brown), wedge night sights, ambidextrous safety, GI length (standard) guide rod finished in black KimPro II, 38 oz. New mid-2004.

| MSR $1,512 | $1,325 | $1,150 | $975 | $850 | $725 | $600 | $550 | |

* **Warrior SOC** – .45 ACP cal., 5 in. barrel, tan/green KimPro II finish, lower front rail with removable Desert Tan Crimson Trace Rail Master laser sight, ambidextrous thumb safety, lanyard ring, textured G10 grips, 40 oz. New 2013.

| MSR $1,665 | $1,495 | $1,300 | $1,100 | $1,025 | $900 | $775 | $650 | |

» **Warrior SOC TFS** – .45 ACP cal., similar to the Warrior SOC, except has 5 1/2 in. barrel threaded for suspension (TFS) and a thread protector cap, 40 oz. New 2015.

| MSR $1,738 | $1,545 | $1,325 | $1,100 | $1,025 | $900 | $775 | $650 | |

MSR	100%	98%	95%	90%	80%	70%	60%	*Last MSR*

DESERT WARRIOR – .45 ACP cal., 5 in. stainless steel barrel, 7 shot mag., steel frame and slide, Tactical Wedge Tritium night sights, Kimber tactical rail, ambidextrous thumb safety, steel mainspring housing with lanyard ring, Dark Earth KimPro II metal finish and light tan G-10 grips. New mid-2005.

	100%	98%	95%	90%	80%	70%	60%	
MSR $1,512	$1,325	$1,150	$975	$850	$725	$600	$550	

* ***Desert Warrior TFS*** – .45 ACP cal., similar to Desert Warrior, except has 5 1/2 in. stainless steel barrel threaded for suspension (TFS), and thread protector cap, 40 oz. New 2015.

	100%	98%	95%	90%	80%	70%	60%	
MSR $1,586	$1,375	$1,175	$1,025	$900	$750	$625	$550	

KPD – while advertised during 2006-2007, this model never went into production.

SIS SERIES – .45 ACP cal., SA, stainless steel slide, frame, and serrated mainspring housing, 7 or 8 shot mag., 3 (Ultra), 4 (Pro), or 5 (Custom or Custom RL) in. barrel, SIS night sights, cocking shoulder for one-hand cocking, lightweight hammer, solid trigger, slide serrations, gray KimPro II finish, beavertail grip safety, stippled black laminate logo grips, ambidextrous thumb safety, choice of rounded frame and mainspring housing (SIS Ultra), Picatinny rail (SIS Pro & Custom RL), standard length guide rod (Custom & Custom RL), 31-39 oz. Mfg. 2008-2009.

	100%	98%	95%	90%	80%	70%	60%	*Last MSR*
	$1,250	$1,095	$935	$850	$685	$560	$435	*$1,427*

Add $95 for SIS Custom RL model with standard length guide rod and Picatinny rail.

Pistols: Kimber Non-Cataloged Models

Over the years, Kimber has manufactured a number of models that did not appear in their catalog. To help identify non-cataloged models, pistols are listed in two categories: Custom Shop/Special Edition Pistols and Limited Edition Pistols.

Pistols: Kimber Custom Shop/Special Editions, Single Action

Beginning in 1998, the Kimber Custom Shop began producing special edition pistols. Special edition models have been issued in either fixed numbers, or time limited. Where available, time limited models show the actual number produced. All models are .45 ACP caliber unless otherwise specified.

CLASSIC CARRY ELITE – .45 ACP cal., round heel steel frame with highly polished flats, 5 in. barrel, fine line engraving on stainless slide, 24 LPI front strap checkering, bi-tone gunmetal/rose gold PVD finish, 38 oz. New 2015.

	100%	98%	95%	90%	80%	70%	60%	
MSR $2,495	$2,175	$1,850	$1,600	$1,390	$1,125	$925	$800	

CLASSIC CARRY PRO – .45 ACP cal., steel frame and slide, 4 in. bushingless match grade bull barrel, round heel frame, charcoal blue metal finish, G10 ivory grips, night sights, front strap checkering, 35 oz. New 2012.

	100%	98%	95%	90%	80%	70%	60%	
MSR $1,785	$1,575	$1,340	$1,100	$1,025	$900	$775	$650	

ELITE CARRY – black anodized compact aluminum frame, stainless slide, 4 in. barrel, meltdown treatment on slide and frame, Tritium night sights, 20 LPI checkered front strap, ambidextrous safety, aluminum match trigger, hand checkered rosewood grips, 28 oz. 1,200 mfg. 1998.

Last MSR was $1,019.

ROYAL CARRY – compact aluminum frame, 4 in. bushingless barrel, highly polished blue, night sights, ambidextrous safety, hand checkered rosewood grips, 28 oz. 600 mfg. 1998.

Last MSR was $903.

GOLD GUARDIAN – highly polished stainless steel slide and frame, hand fitted 5 in. match barrel and bushing, Tritium night sights, ambidextrous safety, extended magwell, skeletonized match trigger, hand checkered rosewood grips, 38 oz. 300 mfg. 1998.

Last MSR was $1,350.

STAINLESS COVERT – meltdown stainless slide and frame finished in silver KimPro, 4 in. barrel, 30 LPI front strap checkering, 3-dot Tritium night sights, hand checkered rosewood grips, 34 oz. 1,000 mfg. 1999.

Last MSR was $1,135.

PRO ELITE – aluminum frame with silver KimPro finish, stainless slide with black KimPro finish, full meltdown treatment on slide and frame, 4 in. barrel, 30 LPI front strap checkering, 3-dot Tritium night sights, hand checkered rosewood grips, 28 oz. 2,500 mfg. 1999.

Last MSR was $1,140.

ULTRA ELITE – aluminum frame with black KimPro finish, satin stainless slide, full meltdown treatment on slide and frame, 3 in. barrel, 30 LPI front strap checkering, 3-dot Tritium night sights, hand checkered rosewood grips, 25 oz. 2,750 mfg. 1999.

Last MSR was $1,085.

HERITAGE EDITION – black oxide steel frame and slide, 30 LPI front strap checkering, ambidextrous safety, premium aluminum trigger, NSSF Heritage medallion and special markings on slide, ser. no. begins with KHE, 38 oz. 1,041 mfg. 2000.

Last MSR was $1,065.

MSR	100%	98%	95%	90%	80%	70%	60%	Last MSR

STAINLESS GOLD MATCH SE II – .38 Super or .45 ACP cal., stainless steel frame and slide, 5 in. barrel, serrated flat-top slide, 30 LPI front strap checkering, hand checkered rosewood grips, ambidextrous safety, polished flats, ser. no. begins with KSO, 38 oz. 260 (.38 Super) and 294 (.45 ACP) mfg. 2001.

Last MSR was $1,487.

Add $88 for .38 Super cal.

ULTRA SHADOW II – black steel slide and anodized aluminum frame, 3 in. barrel, fixed Tritium night sights, 30 LPI front strap checkering, grey laminate grips, silver grip and thumb safeties and mainspring housing, ser. no. begins with KUSLE, 25 oz.

Last MSR was $949.

PRO SHADOW II – black steel slide and anodized aluminum frame, 4 in. barrel, fixed Tritium night sights, 30 LPI front strap checkering, grey laminate grips, silver grip and thumb safeties and mainspring housing, ser. no. begins with KPSLE, 28 oz.

Last MSR was $949.

ULTRA CDP ELITE II – .45 ACP cal., first Kimber .45 pistols with ramped match grade barrels, black anodized aluminum frame, black oxide carbon steel slide, 3 in. barrel, Carry Melt treatment for rounded and blended edges, Meprolight 3-dot Tritium night sights, 30 LPI checkering on front strap and under trigger guard, ambidextrous thumb safety and charcoal/ruby laminated logo grips, 25 oz. Mfg. 2002-Jan. 2003.

Last MSR was $1,216.

ULTRA CDP ELITE STS II – .45 ACP cal., first Kimber .45 pistols with ramped match grade barrels, silver anodized aluminum frame, satin stainless steel slide, 3 in. barrel, Carry Melt treatment for rounded and blended edges, Meprolight 3-dot Tritium night sights, 30 LPI checkering on front strap and under trigger guard, ambidextrous thumb safety and charcoal/ruby laminated logo grips, 25 oz. Mfg. 2002-Jan. 2003.

Last MSR was $1,155.

ULTRA RCP II – .45 ACP cal., SA, (Refined Carry Pistol), 3 in. stainless steel barrel, 7 shot mag., black anodized frame (disc.) or aluminum frame with Matte Gray KimPro II finish, Carry Melt treatment, steel slide with Matte Black KimPro II finish, no sights, bobbed mag. release, hammer, beavertail grip safety and thumb safety, round mainspring housing and rear of frame, thin black Micarta grip panels (disc. 2014), Rosewood double diamond Crimson Trace lasergrips with Kimber logo became standard 2015, older mfg. had distinctive "hook" on hammer, new mfg. has straight hammer, 25 oz. Mfg. 2003-2005 by Custom Shop, reintroduced 2007.

MSR $1,651	$1,495	$1,300	$1,100	$1,025	$900	$775	$650

Subtract approx. $300 if without Crimson Trace Lasergrips.

ULTRA SP II – special anodized frame colors (black/blue, black/red, and black/silver) with black oxide slide, 7 shot mag., 3 in. bushingless barrel, 3-dot sights, Carry Melt treatment, ball milled Micarta grips, standard fixed sights, 25 oz. Mfg. 2003-2005.

	$1,025	$900	$800	$725	$625	$575	$495	*$1,175*

25th ANNIVERSARY CUSTOM LIMITED EDITION – .45 ACP cal., black oxide frame and slide, 5 in. barrel, premium aluminum trigger, fancy walnut anniversary logo grips, "1979-2004" engraving on slide, Series I safeties and traditional extractor, ser. no. range is KAPC0001-KAPC1911. Limited production of 1,911 during 2004-2005.

	$825	$725	$650	$575	$500	$425	$350	*$923*

* **25th Anniversary Custom Limited Edition Gold Match** – blued frame and slide, deep polish on flats, 5 in. stainless barrel, premium aluminum trigger, ambidextrous safety, adj. sights, fancy walnut anniversary logo grips, "1979-2004" engraving in slide, Series I safeties and traditional extractor, ser. no. range KAPG0001-KAPG0500, 38 oz. Limited production of 500 during 2004-2005.

	$1,175	$995	$875	$775	$700	$625	$550	*$1,357*

* **25th Anniversary Custom Limited Edition Pistol Set** – includes one Custom (ser. no. range KMSC0001-KMSC250) and one Gold Match (ser. no. range KMSG0001 - KMSG250), matched ser. nos., wood presentation case. Limited production of 250 during 2004-2005.

	$2,250	$2,000	$1,775	$1,525	$1,300	$1,100	$900	*$2,620*

CENTENNIAL EDITION – .45 ACP cal., steel frame with finish by Turnbull Restoration, ivory grips, adj. target sights, light scroll engraving, aluminum trigger, includes presentation case, Limited mfg. of 250 during 2010.

	$3,995	$3,650	$3,275	N/A	N/A	N/A	N/A	*$4,352*

AMETHYST ULTRA II – 9mm Para. or .45 ACP cal., round heel frame, 3 in. barrel, Tactical Wedge night sights, G10 grips, ambidextrous safety, highly polished stainless steel slide with amethyst purple PVD coating and cut scroll engraving and border, amethyst purple PVD-coated small parts, 25 oz. Special Edition mfg. by the Custom Shop beginning 2016.

MSR $1,652	$1,495	$1,300	$1,100	$1,025	$900	$775	$650

MSR	100%	98%	95%	90%	80%	70%	60%	Last MSR

DIAMOND ULTRA II – 9mm Para. or .45 ACP cal., aluminum round heel frame, 3 in. barrel, mirror-polished stainless steel slide and small parts, cut scroll engraving and border, Tactical Wedge night sights, G10 grips, ambidextrous safety, satin silver finish, 25 oz. New mid-2015.

| MSR $1,652 | $1,495 | $1,300 | $1,100 | $1,025 | $900 | $775 | $650 | |

ONYX ULTRA II – 9mm Para. or .45 ACP cal., 3 in. stainless steel barrel, 7 or 8 shot mag., ambidextrous thumb safety, full length guide rod, aluminum frame with satin silver finish, PVD coating on small parts, stainless steel slide with high polish deep black PVD coating and cut scroll engraving and border, Tactical Wedge night sights, solid aluminum match grade trigger, black Micarta thin grips, 25 oz. New 2015.

| MSR $1,652 | $1,495 | $1,300 | $1,100 | $1,025 | $900 | $775 | $650 | |

SAPPHIRE ULTRA II – 9mm Para. cal., 3 in. barrel, G10 grips, polished stainless steel slide and small parts feature a bright blue PVD finish with fine engraved border accents, rounded heel, ambidextrous thumb safety, Tactical Wedge nightsights. New 2012.

| MSR $1,652 | $1,495 | $1,300 | $1,100 | $1,025 | $900 | $775 | $650 | |

SAPPHIRE PRO II – 9mm Para. cal., 4 in. stainless steel barrel, 9 shot mag., aluminum frame with Satin Silver KimPro II finish, polished blue PVD finish on slide and small parts, stainless steel slide with engraving, full length guide rod, ambidextrous safety, Tactical Wedge 3-dot green Tritium night sights, blue/black G10 thin grips, 28 oz. New 2015.

| MSR $1,652 | $1,495 | $1,300 | $1,100 | $1,025 | $900 | $775 | $650 | |

STAINLESS II (CLASSIC ENGRAVED EDITION) – .45 ACP cal., 5 in. stainless steel barrel, stainless steel frame and slide, high grade walnut grips with ivory Micarta checkered inlay, accent-engraved mainspring housing, full coverage vine and leaf tool engraving with stipple relief on frame and slide, satin silver finish, 38 oz. New mid-2015.

Please contact the manufacturer directly for pricing and availability on this model.

ROYAL II – .45 ACP cal., 5 in. barrel, steel frame and slide, fixed low profile sights, aluminum match grade trigger, charcoal blue finish, solid bone grips, 38 oz. Mfg. by the Custom Shop beginning 2010.

| MSR $2,020 | $1,850 | $1,575 | $1,325 | $1,100 | $950 | $825 | $700 | |

GOLD COMBAT II – .45 ACP cal. only, 5 in. barrel (bushingless bull became standard 2008), SA, full size carry pistol based on the Gold Match, steel frame and slide, stainless steel match grade barrel and bushing, matte black KimPro II finish, serrated flat-top and scalloped French shoulders also became standard 2008, Tritium night sights, checkered walnut (disc. 2008) or 24 LPI herringbone pattern Micarta grips, ambidextrous thumb safety, extended and beveled magwell, full length guide rod, 38 oz, mfg. by Custom Shop. Mfg. 1994-2008, reintroduced 2011.

| MSR $2,307 | $2,075 | $1,800 | $1,575 | $1,375 | $1,100 | $900 | $750 | |

This series' nomenclature added the Roman numeral "II" during 2001.

* **Gold Combat Stainless II** – similar to Gold Combat, except is all stainless steel. Mfg. 1994-2008, reintroduced 2011.

| MSR $2,251 | $2,000 | $1,775 | $1,550 | $1,375 | $1,100 | $900 | $700 | |

* **Gold Combat RL II** – .45 ACP cal., similar to Gold Combat, except has Picatinny rail machined into the lower forward frame to accept optics and other tactical accessories. Mfg. 1994-2008, reintroduced 2011.

| MSR $2,405 | $2,100 | $1,800 | $1,575 | $1,375 | $1,125 | $925 | $800 | |

Pistols: Kimber Limited Editions, Single Action

Kimber has produced limited runs of pistols for dealer groups, NRA, sporting goods stores, law enforcement agencies, special requests, etc. Limited run pistols can be as small as 25 mfg.

PRO CARRY SLE – all stainless steel slide and frame, 4 in. barrel, identical to Stainless Pro Carry Model, except has stainless frame, mfg. for Kimber Master Dealers, cataloged in 2001, later production known as Pro Carry HD II, 1,329 mfg. during 2000.

Last MSR was $815.

PRO COMBAT – black oxide stainless steel frame and slide, 4 in. barrel, ambidextrous safety, Tritium 3-dot night sights, match grade aluminum trigger, 30 LPI front strap checkering, hand checkered rosewood grips, 35 oz. Marketed by RGuns. 52 mfg. 2000.

Last MSR was $860.

TARGET ELITE II – two-tone stainless frame and slide, black oxide coating on frame, slide natural stainless, adj. rear sight, rosewood double diamond grips, sold through stores affiliated with Sports Inc. buying group, 38 oz. 220 mfg. 2001.

Last MSR was $950.

CUSTOM DEFENDER II – two-tone stainless frame and slide, black oxide coating on frame, slide natural stainless, fixed low profile rear sight, double diamond rosewood grips, sold only through stores affiliated with National Buying Service, 38 oz. 290 mfg. 2001.

Last MSR was $839.

MSR	100%	98%	95%	90%	80%	70%	60%	*Last MSR*

CUSTOM ECLIPSE II – stainless slide and frame, 5 in. barrel, black oxide finish brush polished on the flats, 30 LPI front strap checkering, adj. night sights, laminated grey grips, ser. no. begins with KEL, 38 oz. 4,522 mfg. 2001.

Last MSR was $1,121.

PRO ECLIPSE II – stainless steel frame and slide, 4 in. barrel, black oxide finish brush polished on the flats, 30 LPI front strap checkering, fixed 3-dot night sights, laminated grey grips, ambidextrous safety, ser. no. begins with KRE, 35 oz. 2,207 mfg. 2001.

Last MSR was $1,065.

ULTRA ECLIPSE II – stainless steel frame and slide, 3 in. barrel, black oxide finish brush polished on the flats, 30 LPI front strap checkering, fixed 3-dot night sights, laminated grey grips, ambidextrous safety, 34 oz. 1,202 mfg. 2001.

Last MSR was $1,054.

STRYKER TEN II – Ultra Ten II with black polymer frame and frame insert and small parts, natural stainless slide, 25 oz. 200 mfg. 2002.

Last MSR was $850.

LAPD SWAT – black oxide coated stainless frame and slide, 5 in. barrel, low profile Meprolight 3-dot night sights, 30 LPI front strap checkering, black rubber double diamond grips, 38 oz. 300 mfg. 2002.

Following extensive testing to select a duty pistol, LAPD SWAT chose a Kimber Stainless Custom II and had it enhanced to their specifications. This model was made strictly for law enforcement and not sold to the public. A civilian version called the Tactical law Enforcement (TLE) Series went into production in 2003. Pistols marked "LAPD SWAT" were not sold to the public.

NRA EPOCH II – stainless slide and frame, 5 in. barrel, black oxide finish brush polished on flats, 30 LPI front strap checkering, standard safety, fixed Tritium night sights, laminated grey grips, ser. no. begins with KNRAE, Friends of NRA pistol available only at NRA banquets, 38 oz. 58 mfg. 2002.

This model had no established MSR.

THE BOSS II – limited edition to commemorate Blythe Sports 50th anniversary, stainless steel slide and frame, Carry Melt treatment, fixed white dot sights, premium aluminum 2 hole trigger, 5 in. barrel, engraved "The BOSS II" on ejection port side, and "SPECIAL EDITION", black and sliver laminate grips with Blythe 50th anniversary logo in center on white insert, ser. no. KBSS000-KBSS024, 25 mfg.

This model had no established MSR.

ECLIPSE CLE II – 5 in. barrel, Eclipse Custom II finish on slide with black over stainless frame (no front strap checkering), charcoal/ruby Kimber logo grips, sold only through stores affiliated with National Buying Service, 38 oz. 271 mfg. 2003.

Last MSR was $917.

* ***Eclipse PLE II*** – similar to Eclipse CLE II, except has 4 in. bushingless barrel, sold only through stores affiliated with Sports Inc. buying group, 35 oz. 232 mfg. 2003.

Last MSR was $877.

* ***Eclipse ULE II*** – Eclipse Ultra II finish on slide with black over stainless frame (no front strap checkering), 3 in. bushingless barrel, charcoal/ruby Kimber logo grips, sold only through stores affiliated with National Buying Service, 34 oz. 227 mfg. 2003.

Last MSR was $890.

TEAM MATCH II 38 SUPER – .38 Super cal., identical to original Team Match II, with .38 Super ramped barrel, match grade chamber, bushing and trigger group, special Team Match features including 30 LPI checkered front strap, adj. sight, extended magwell, premium aluminum trigger and red, white, and blue USA Shooting Team logo grips, 38 oz. Mfg. 2003-2004.

MSR	100%	98%	95%	90%	80%	70%	60%	*Last MSR*
	$1,150	$995	$875	$775	$675	$575	$475	*$1,352*

MCSOCOM ICQB (2004) – .45 ACP cal., at the request of the Marine Corps Special Operations Command (MCSOCOM) Detachment 1 (Det. 1), Kimber produced Interim Close Quarters Battle (ICQB) 1911 patterned pistols in accordance with very high specific requirements: steel frame and slide finished in matte black, internal extractor, GI length guide rod and plug, light rail, bumped grip safety and ambidextrous manual safety, lanyard loop, Simonich G-10 "Gunner" grips, and Novak Lo-Mount night sights.

There was no MSR on this model, as it was not available for sale to the general public.

The civilian version of this pistol is called the Warrior.

TARGET MATCH – .45 ACP cal., oversized 5 in. stainless steel barrel, matte black frame and slide with brush polished flats, high relief cut under trigger guard, wide cocking serrations, solid match trigger, engraved bullseye inlaid burl walnut logo grips, 30 LPI checkering on front strap and under trigger guard, special ser. no. starting with "KTM", 38 oz. 1,000 mfg. 2006-2009.

MSR	100%	98%	95%	90%	80%	70%	60%	*Last MSR*
	$1,215	$1,025	$875	$775	$700	$600	$500	*$1,427*

MSR	100%	98%	95%	90%	80%	70%	60%	Last MSR

CLASSIC TARGET II – .45 ACP cal., two-tone stainless steel frame, matte black oxide slide, no cocking serrations, adj. sights, premium match grade trigger, smooth/stippled logo grips, match grade chamber, barrel, and barrel bushing, 38 oz. Sold exclusively through Gander Mountain. Mfg. 2006-2008.

	$825	$675	$555	$460	$395	$350	$300	$999

FRANKLIN CUSTOM II – similar to Custom II, silver finished slide stop, bushing, mag. release, grip safety and mainspring housing, red, white and blue laminate grips with Franklin's Gun Shop logo, commemorates 44th anniversary of Franklin's Gun Shop, ser. no. KFGS01 - KFGS50, 50 mfg. 2006.
This model had no established MSR.

RIFLES: BOLT ACTION

The models listed feature a Mauser style action with controlled round feeding and extraction.

MODEL 84M LPT (LIGHT POLICE TACTICAL) – .223 Rem. or .308 Win. cal., 24 in. matte blue heavy sporter contour fluted barrel, 5 shot mag., Picatinny rail, oversize bolt handle, sling swivels, recoil pad, full length Mauser claw extractor, 3-position Model 70 style safety, adj. trigger, black laminate stock with panel stippling, 8 lbs., 7 oz. New 2008.

MSR $1,495	$1,295	$1,075	$925	$825	$725	$625	$500	

MODEL 8400 ADVANCED TACTICAL II – .308 Win., .300 Win. Mag., or 6.5 Creedmoor (new 2015) cal., 24 or 26 in. match grade stainless steel threaded barrel with SureFire muzzle brake, full-length Mauser claw extractor, controlled round feeding, Manners MCS-TF4 folding stock with adj. comb, oversized bolt knob and extended bolt handle, upper and lower Picatinny rails, 5 or 10 shot detachable box mag., KimPro II Desert Tan finish. New 2014.

MSR $4,351	$3,695	$3,235	$2,775	$2,515	$2,025	$1,675	$1,295	

* **Model 8400 Advanced Tactical SOC** – .308 Win., .300 Win. Mag., or 6.5 Creedmoor (new 2015) cal., 24 or 26 in. stainless steel threaded barrel with SureFire muzzle brake and matte KimPro II finish, 5 shot detachable box mag., Kimber modular chassis system, side folding stock with adj. comb, integral rear monopod, two Mil-Spec rails on forearm, Cerakote Flat Dark Earth finish, 11 lbs. 6 oz. New 2014.

MSR $4,419	$3,750	$3,275	$2,825	$2,550	$2,075	$1,695	$1,325	

MODEL 8400 PATROL/POLICE TACTICAL – .300 Win. Mag. or .308 Win. (new 2010) cal., 20 (Patrol), 24, or 26 in. match grade barrel, chamber, and trigger, trued bolt face, custom McMillan glass bedded stock, fixed Picatinny rail, enlarged bolt handle and knob, 8 3/4 lbs. Mfg. 2009-2013.

	$1,325	$1,160	$995	$900	$725	$595	$475	$1,495

MODEL 8400 PATROL TACTICAL – .308 Win. or .300 Win. Mag. cal., 24 or 26 in. match grade stainless steel fluted barrel, full-length Mauser claw extractor, controlled round feeding, Manners MCS-T6 reinforced carbon fiber black synthetic stock with squared forend and grooved forearm, vertical pistol grip, ambidextrous palm swell, oversized bolt knob and extended bolt handle, top rail, 5 or 10 shot detachable box mag., 8 lbs. 12 oz. New 2014.

MSR $2,447	$2,075	$1,825	$1,550	$1,400	$1,150	$935	$725	

MODEL 8400 TACTICAL SERIES – .300 Win. Mag. or .308 Win. cal., matte blue (Tactical) or KimPro II Dark Earth (Advanced Tactical) finish, grey (Tactical) or Desert Camo (Advanced Tactical) McMillan synthetic stock, 24 in. fluted bull barrel, 5 shot mag., 9 lbs., 4 oz. Mfg. 2007-2013.

	$1,675	$1,450	$1,250	$1,125	$900	$750	$575	$1,971

Add $680 for Advanced Tactical with Desert Tan or black Pelican case.

KIMEL INDUSTRIES, INC.

Previously manufactured until late 1994 by A.A. Arms located in Monroe, NC. Previously distributed by Kimel Industries, Inc. located in Matthews, NC.

CARBINES: SEMI-AUTO

AR-9 CARBINE – 9mm Para. cal., carbine variation of the AP-9 with 16 1/2 in. barrel, 20 shot mag., and steel rod folding stock. Mfg. 1991-94.

	$625	$550	$475	$425	$365	$315	$275	$384

PISTOLS: SEMI-AUTO

AP-9 PISTOL – 9mm Para. cal., SA, blowback operation, bolt knob on left side of receiver, 5 in. barrel with vent. shroud, front mounted 10 (C/B 1994) or 20* shot detachable mag., black matte finish, adj. front sight, 3 lbs. 7 oz. Mfg. 1989-1994.

	$475	$425	$375	$325	$300	$275	$250	$279

* **AP-9 Pistol Mini** – compact variation of the AP-9 Model with 3 in. barrel, blue or nickel finish. Mfg. 1991-94.

	$550	$500	$425	$375	$325	$300	$275	$273

MSR	100%	98%	95%	90%	80%	70%	60%	*Last MSR*

* **AP-9 Pistol Target** – target variation of the AP-9 with 12 in. match barrel with shroud, blue finish only. Mfg. 1991-94.

	$600	$550	$475	$425	$375	$350	$325	*$294*

* **P-95 Pistol** – similar to AP-9, except without barrel shroud and is supplied with 5 shot mag., parts are interchangeable with AP-9. Mfg. 1990-91 only.

	$395	$350	$300	$250	$200	$175	$150	*$250*

KING'S ARSENAL

Current manufacturer established in 2011, located in Abilene, TX.

PISTOLS: SEMI-AUTO

King's Arsenal offers the Kustom 1911 in Officer, Commander, or full size Government configurations, with carbon steel, stainless, or titanium frames. A wide variety of options and accessories are available. Prices range from $1,200-$3,500, depending on the configuration. Please contact the company directly for a price quote and available options (see Trademark Index).

RIFLES: BOLT ACTION

King's Arsenal also offers the Royalty line of custom made bolt action rifles. Please contact the company directly for pricing and available options (see Trademark Index).

XKALIBER – .50 BMG cal., 28 in. light contour Lija barrel, repeater, McMillan muzzle brake, Shilen trigger, lightweight chassis, 25 lbs.

Please contact the manufacturer directly for pricing and options.

RIFLES: SEMI-AUTO

Add $110 for Samson Quad Rail.
Add $99 for custom barrel fluting.
Add $75 for bull barrel.
Add $75 for 6.8 SPC or 6.5 Grendel cal.
Add $49 for nickel boron bolt carrier group coating.

KROWN 15 BASE MODEL – 5.56 NATO, 6.8 SPC, or 6.5 Grendel cal., GIO, 16, 18, or 20 in. barrel, lightweight or midweight, King's Arsenal upper and lower, M4 collapsible stock with A2 grip, A2 flash hider, 15 in. Samson Evo handguard or 12.4 in. quad rail.

MSR $1,785	$1,525	$1,335	$1,150	$1,035	$840	$685	$535	

Add $109 for Magpul CTR stock.

KROWN 15 KUSTOM MODEL – 5.56 NATO, 6.8 SPC, 6.5 Grendel, or .300 AAC Blackout cal., GIO, 16, 18, or 20 in. Noveske stainless steel barrel, lightweight or midweight, King's Arsenal upper and lower, Geissele SSA trigger, Magpul CTR stock, King's Arsenal grip, A2 flash hider, 15 in. Samson Evo handguard or 12.4 in. quad rail.

MSR $2,285	$1,995	$1,750	$1,475	$1,325	$1,075	$880	$685	

Add $75 for Noveske Switchblock.
Add $75 for .300 Blackout cal.
Add $165 for Geissele SD3G trigger.

KINTREK, INC.

Previous rifle manufacturer located in Owensboro, KY.

RIFLES: SEMI-AUTO

BULLPUP MODEL – .22 LR cal., bullpup configuration, hinged dust cover, clear Ram-Line type coil spring mag., black synthetic thumbhole stock, A2 style front/rear sight. Disc.

	$350	$300	$250	$225	$200	$175	$150	

KNIGHT'S ARMAMENT COMPANY

Current manufacturer established in 1983, located in Titusville, FL. Previously located in Vero Beach, FL. Dealer and consumer direct sales.

RIFLES: SEMI-AUTO

Some of the models listed were also available in pre-ban configurations. SR-25 Enhanced Match model has 10 or 20 shot mag. Some of the following models, while discontinued for civilian use, may still be available for military/law enforcement.

STONER SR-15 M-5 RIFLE – .223 Rem. cal., GIO, 20 in. standard weight barrel, flip-up low profile rear sight, two-stage target trigger, 7.6 lbs. Mfg. 1997-2008.

	$1,775	$1,550	$1,300	$1,100	$900	$825	$725	*$1,837*

MSR	100%	98%	95%	90%	80%	70%	60%	Last MSR

* ***Stoner SR-15 M-4 Carbine*** – .223 Rem. cal., similar to SR-15 rifle, except has 16 in. barrel, choice of fixed synthetic or non-collapsible buttstock. Mfg. 1997-2005.

	100%	98%	95%	90%	80%	70%	60%	Last MSR
	$1,495	$1,250	$1,050	$925	$825	$725	$625	$1,575

Add $100 for non-collapsible buttstock (SR-15 M-4 K-Carbine, disc. 2001).

* ***SR-15 E3 Mod 2 URX 4 KeyMod (Stoner SR-15 URX E3 Carbine)*** – 5.56 NATO cal., GIO, features 16 in. free floating barrel with URX forearm, E3 type rounded lug improved bolt. New 2004.

MSR $2,312	$2,150	$1,900	$1,600	$1,450	$1,200	$950	$750	

* ***SR-15 E3 Mod 2 URX 4 M-Lok*** – 5.56 NATO. cal., E3 type rounded lug improved bolt, AR-15 style, gas impingement operation, 16 in. free floating barrel, URX4 M-Lok handguard. New 2016.

MSR $2,450	$2,200	$1,900	$1,650	$1,500	$1,200	$1,000	$750	

SR-15E IWS LIGHT PRECISION RIFLE – 5.56 NATO cal., 18 in. match stainless steel barrel with custom match chamber, URX (upper receiver extending) free floated barrel system, IWS lower, 2-stage match trigger, ambidextrous controls, black furniture, 7.38 lbs.

	$2,450	$2,150	$1,850	$1,650	$1,350	$1,100	$850	

SR-15 E3 LPR MOD 2 M-LOK – 5.56 NATO cal., 18 in. match stainless steel barrel with custom match chamber, free floated barrel system, 2-stage match trigger, URX4 M-LOK handguard, IWS lower, ambidextrous controls, black furniture, 7.38 lbs. New 2016.

MSR $2,700	$2,450	$2,150	$1,850	$1,650	$1,350	$1,100	$850	

STONER SR-15 MATCH RIFLE – .223 Rem. cal., GIO, flat-top upper receiver with 20 in. match grade stainless steel free floating barrel with RAS forend, two-stage match trigger, 7.9 lbs. Mfg. 1997-2008.

	$1,850	$1,625	$1,375	$1,150	$950	$850	$750	$1,972

SR-15 MOD 2 – 5.56 NATO cal., 16 in. hammer forged chrome-lined barrel, mid-length gas system, ambi bolt release, selector, and mag. release, drop-in two-stage trigger, black finish, 6 3/4 lbs. New 2015.

Please contact the company directly for pricing, options, and availability.

SR-15 E3 LPR MOD 2 KeyMod (LIGHT PRECISION RIFLE) – 5.56 NATO cal., Mod 2 Gas System, 18 in. match grade stainless steel barrel with a custom match chamber and QDC flash eliminator, adj. micro sights, two-stage match trigger, multi-lug improved E3 bolt, 6-pos. SOPMOD stock, URX 4 handguard with KeyMod mounting points, standard ambidextrous lower receiver, black finish, 7 1/2 lbs. New 2015.

MSR $2,700	$2,450	$2,150	$1,850	$1,650	$1,350	$1,100	$850	

STONER SR-25 SPORTER – .308 Win. cal., GIO, 20 in. lightweight barrel, AR-15 configuration with carrying handle, 5, 10, or 20 (disc. per C/B 1994) shot detachable mag., less than 2 MOA guaranteed, non-glare finish, 8.8 lbs. Mfg. 1993-97.

	$2,650	$2,250	$1,900	$1,600	$1,300	$1,000	$850	$2,995

* ***Stoner RAS Sporter Carbine (SR-25 Carbine)*** – .223 Rem. cal., GIO, 16 in. free floating barrel, grooved non-slip handguard, removable carrying handle, 7 3/4 lbs. Mfg. 1995-2005.

	$3,100	$2,650	$2,200	$1,800	$1,500	$1,250	$1,000	$3,495

Subtract 15% if w/o RAS.

In 2003, the Rail Adapter System (RAS) became standard on this model.

SR-25 STANDARD MATCH – .308 Win. cal., GIO, free-floating 24 in. match barrel, fiberglass stock, includes commercial gun case and 10 shot mag. Disc. 2008.

	$3,600	$3,300	$2,950	$2,600	$2,300	$2,000	$1,600	$3,918

SR-25 RAS MATCH – .308 Win. cal., similar to SR-25 Standard, except has 24 in. free floating match barrel and flat-top receiver, less than 1 MOA guaranteed, RAS became standard 2004, 10 3/4 lbs. Mfg. 1993-2008.

	$3,350	$2,800	$2,300	$1,800	$1,500	$1,250	$1,000	$3,789

Subtract approx. 15% if w/o Rail Adapter System (RAS).

Over 3,000 SR-25s were mfg.

* ***SR-25 RAS Match Lightweight*** – .308 Win. cal., GIO, 20 in. medium contour free floating barrel, 9 1/2 lbs. Mfg. 1995-2004.

	$2,950	$2,550	$2,175	$1,700	$1,400	$1,200	$995	$3,244

Add approx. 15% for Rail Adapter System.

SR-25 E2 ACC KeyMod (ADVANCED COMBAT CARBINE) – 7.62 NATO cal., 16 in. rifled chrome-lined barrel with 5-slot flash hider, ambi controls, carbon cutter bolt carrier, multi-lug improved E2 bolt, drop-in two-stage trigger, URX handguard, two-stage match trigger, black finish, 8.4 lbs. New 2015.

MSR $4,861	$4,500	$3,950	$3,400	$3,050	$2,500	$2,000	$1,600	

MSR	100%	98%	95%	90%	80%	70%	60%	Last MSR

SR-25 E2 ACC URX4 M-LOK – 7.62 NATO cal., 16 in. rifled chrome-lined barrel with 5-slot flash hider, ambi controls, carbon cutter bolt carrier, multi-lug improved E2 bolt, drop-in two-stage trigger, URX handguard, two-stage match trigger, black finish, 8.4 lbs. New 2016.

| MSR $4,861 | $4,500 | $3,950 | $3,400 | $3,050 | $2,500 | $2,000 | $1,600 | |

SR-25 E2 APC (ADVANCED PRECISION CARBINE) KeyMod – 7.62 NATO cal., 16 in. barrel with QDC flash suppressor, URX 4 free floating barrel system, drop-in two stage trigger, ambi bolt release, selector, and mag. release, black furniture, 9.12 lbs. New mid-2014.

| MSR $4,861 | $4,550 | $4,000 | $3,400 | $3,100 | $2,500 | $2,050 | $1,600 | |

SR-25 E2 APC M-LOK – 7.62 NATO cal., 16 in. barrel with QDC flash suppressor, URX 4 free floating barrel system, drop-in two stage trigger, ambi bolt release, selector, and mag. release, black furniture, 9.12 lbs. New 2016.

| MSR $4,861 | $4,550 | $4,000 | $3,400 | $3,100 | $2,500 | $2,050 | $1,600 | |

SR-25 E2 APR (ADVANCED PRECISION RIFLE) KeyMod – 7.62 NATO cal., 20 in. match barrel with QDC flash suppressor, ambi controls, drop-in two-stage trigger, E2 bolt and gas system, URX 4 handguard, black finish, 10 1/2 lbs. New 2015.

| MSR $4,861 | $4,550 | $4,000 | $3,400 | $3,100 | $2,500 | $2,050 | $1,600 | |

SR-25 E2 APR M-LOK – 7.62 NATO cal., 20 in. match barrel with QDC flash suppressor, ambi controls, drop-in two-stage trigger, E2 bolt and gas system, URX 4 handguard, black finish, 10 1/2 lbs. New 2016.

| MSR $4,861 | $4,550 | $4,000 | $3,400 | $3,100 | $2,500 | $2,050 | $1,600 | |

SR-25 ENHANCED MATCH RIFLE/CARBINE – .308 Win. cal., GIO, 16 or 20 in. barrel, 10 or 20 shot mag., URX rail system, two-stage trigger, ambidextrous mag. release, integrated adj. folding front sight, micro adj. folding rear sight, EM gas block, combat trigger guard, chrome plated multi-lug bolt and bolt carrier, fixed or nine position adj. stock, black anodized finish, flash hider (carbine only), approx. 8 1/2 lbs. Disc. 2013.

| | $4,750 | $4,375 | $3,750 | $3,400 | $2,750 | $2,250 | $1,750 | $4,994 |

Add $625 for 16 in. carbine.

SR-25 MK11 MOD O CIVILIAN DELUXE SYSTEM PACKAGE – .308 Win. cal., GIO, consumer variation of the Navy Model Mark Eleven, Mod O, w/o sound suppressor, includes Leupold 3.5-10X scope, 20 in. military grade match barrel, backup sights, cell-foam case and other accessories. Mfg. 2003-2008.

| | $7,950 | $7,250 | $6,350 | $5,850 | $5,100 | $4,500 | $4,000 | $8,534 |

SR-25 MK11 MATCH RIFLE – .308 Win. cal., GIO, includes MK11 Mod O features and 20 in. heavy barrel. Mfg. 2004-2008.

| | $5,675 | $5,200 | $4,775 | $4,400 | $3,750 | $3,150 | $2,700 | $6,325 |

SR-25 MK11 CARBINE – .308 Win. cal., GIO, includes MK11 Mod O features and 16 in. match grade stainless steel barrel with muzzle brake, URX 4x4 rail forend, 4-position buttstock. Mfg. 2005-2013.

| | $6,350 | $5,800 | $5,200 | $4,700 | $3,950 | $3,400 | $2,850 | $6,636 |

SR-25 BR CARBINE – .308 Win. cal., similar to SR-25 MK11 Carbine, except has chrome lined steel barrel. Mfg. 2005-2008.

| | $5,675 | $5,200 | $4,775 | $4,400 | $3,750 | $3,150 | $2,700 | $6,307 |

SR-30 – .300 AAC Blackout cal., 16 in. stainless steel barrel with QDC flash suppressor, URX 3.1 free floating rail system, micro front and rear iron sights, E3 bolt, ambi controls, 2-stage trigger, fully adj. SOPMOD stock, black furniture, 6 1/2 lbs. Mfg. mid-2014-2015.

| | $2,300 | $2,050 | $1,750 | $1,600 | $1,300 | $1,050 | $800 | $2,632 |

The SR-30 and SR-30 E3 Mod 2 M-LOK are available in SBR configuration for the Military and Law Enforcement with a 9.5 in. barrel.

SR-M110 SASS – 7.62x51mm cal., GIO, 20 in. military match grade barrel, full RAS treatment on barrel, civilian variation of the Army's semi-auto sniper rifle system, includes Leupold long-range tactical scope, 600 meter back up iron sights, system case and other accessories. Mfg. 2006-2009.

| | $13,000 | $11,000 | $9,500 | $8,000 | $7,000 | $6,000 | $5,000 | $14,436 |

"DAVID TUBB" COMPETITION MATCH RIFLE – .260 Rem. or .308 Win. cal., GIO, incorporates refinements by David Tubb, top-of-the-line competition match rifle, including adj. and rotating buttstock pad. Mfg. 1998 only.

| | $5,200 | $4,000 | $3,600 | $3,150 | $2,700 | $2,300 | $1,995 | $5,995 |

STONER SR-50 – .50 BMG cal., GIO, features high strength materials and lightweight design, fully locked breech and two lug rotary breech bolt, horizontal 5 shot box mag., tubular receiver supports a removable barrel, approx. 31 lbs. Limited mfg. 2000, non-commercial sales only.

Last MSR was $6,995.

Extreme rarity factor precludes accurate pricing on this model.

MSR	100%	98%	95%	90%	80%	70%	60%	Last MSR

KORRIPHILA

Previous trademark manufactured until 2004 by Intertex, located in Eislingen, Germany. Previously imported 1999-2004 by Korriphila, Inc., located in Pineville, NC., and by Osborne's located in Cheboygan, MI until 1988.

PISTOLS: SEMI-AUTO

Less than 30 Korriphila pistols were made annually.

HSP 701 – 7.65 Luger, .38 Super, 9mm Para., 9mm Police, 9mm Steyr, .45 ACP, or 10mm Norma cal., DA/SA, Budischowsky delayed roller lock system assists in recoil reduction, 40% stainless steel parts, 4 or 5 in. barrel, blue or satin finish, walnut grips, 7 or 9 shot mag., based on earlier HSP 70, approx. 2.6 lbs, very limited production.

	$6,500	$5,500	$3,750	$2,950	$2,150	$1,850	$1,675

KORSTOG

Current trademark of AR-15 style rifles manufactured by Adams Arms, and retailed exclusively by Fleet Farm.

Korstog is an ancient Norwegian word meaning "crusade."

CARBINES/RIFLES: SEMI-AUTO

All rifles include a soft sided tactical case.

BRANN – 5.56 NATO cal., carbine length GIO, 16 in. Melonite coated chrome moly valadium steel barrel with M4 contour, high quality aluminum forged upper and lower receivers, aluminum precision machined receiver extension/buffer tube, hardcoat anodized finish, SST, F-marked front sight base and A2 front sight post, 6-position tactical buttstock with carbine USGI forearm, A2 grip, upper receiver adaptable for rear sight or optics, A4 flat-top receiver with M4 feed ramps. New 2013.

MSR $900		$750	$650	$550	$485	$425	$350	$300

JAGER – 5.56 NATO cal., rifle length GIO, 20 in. heavy precision fluted stainless steel barrel with Adams Arms Jet compensator, low profile gas block, high quality aluminum upper and lower receivers, hardcoat anodized finish, JP-EZ single stage trigger, no sights, Magpul PRS precision adjustable stock with 15 in. Samson Evolution Series T6 aluminum Mil-zdpec forearm, Ergo Ambi grip, A4 flat-top receiver with M4 feed ramps, steel bolt carrier group, heat-treated gas key, 9.1 lbs. New 2013.

MSR $1,950		$1,650	$1,450	$1,375	$1,095	$875	$725	$625

VAR – 5.56 NATO cal., mid-length GIO, 16 in. Melonite coated chrome moly valadium steel barrel with permanently attached flash hider, low profile gas block, high quality aluminum forged upper and lower receivers, machined aluminum Mil-Spec receiver extension/buffer tube, hardcoat anodized finish, JP-EZ single stage trigger, no sights, 6-position Vltor IMOD collapsible stock with Sampson Evolution Series T6 aluminum forearm, Ergo Ambi grip, A4 flat-top receiver with M4 feed ramps, steel bolt carrier group, heat-treated gas key. New 2013.

MSR $1,450		$1,225	$1,050	$950	$800	$700	$600	$500

VOLI – 5.56 NATO cal., mid-length GIO, 16 in. Melonite coated chrome moly valadium steel barrel, high quality aluminum upper and lower receivers, hardcoat anodized finish, SST, F-marked front sight base and A2 Magpul front sight post, Magpul MBUS Gen 2 rear sight, 6-position Magpul MOE adjustable collapsible stock, pistol grip, A4 flat-top receiver with M4 feed ramps, steel bolt carrier group, heat treated gas key. New 2013.

MSR $1,150		$950	$850	$715	$685	$495	$415	$350

KRICO

Current trademark manufactured by Kriegeskorte Handels GmbH, located in Pyrbaum, Germany. No current U.S. importation. Previously imported exclusively mid-2005-2010 by Northeast Arms LLC, located in Fort Fairfield, ME. Previously distributed by Precision Sales, Int'l, located in Westfield, MA 1999-2002. Previously manufactured in Vohburg-Irsching, Germany 1996-1999, and in Fürth-Stadeln, Germany by Sportwaffenfabrik Kriegeskorte GmbH pre-1996.

During 2000, Krico was purchased by Marocchi. Krico has been imported/distributed by over ten U.S. companies/individuals. Krico manufactures high quality rifles, and to date, has mostly sold their guns in Europe. Many of the discontinued models listed may still be current within the European marketplace. Please contact the company directly for more information, including U.S. availability and pricing (see Trademark Index). The Krico name is an abridgement of the family name Kriegeskorte.

RIFLES: BOLT ACTION

MODEL 640 DELUXE/SUPER SNIPER – .223 Rem. or .308 Win. cal., 23 in. barrel, select walnut stock has stippled hand grip, adj. cheekpiece and vent. forearm, engine turned bolt assembly, 3 shot mag., match trigger, 10 lbs. Importation disc. 1988.

	$1,795	$1,650	$1,475	$1,325	$1,200	$1,100	$995	*$1,725*

This model was known as the 650 Sniper/Match until 1986.

MSR	100%	98%	95%	90%	80%	70%	60%	*Last MSR*

KRISS ARMS GROUP (KRISS SYSTEMS SA)

Current manufacturer of civilian and law enforcement firearms established in 2008 with factories located in Etoy, Switzerland, and Chesapeake, VA. Previously located in Nyon, Switzerland and Virginia Beach, VA. Distributor and dealer sales.

KRISS USA, Inc. is the North American extension of the Switzerland based KRISS Group, the pioneers of recoil mitigation technology and the world leaders in firearms innovation. KRISS USA manufactures, imports, and distributes KRISS Group firearms and accessories under KRISS, the brand dedicated recoil mitigation and firearms technology; SPHINX, the brand dedicated to precision manufacturing and performance pistols; KRYTAC, the brand dedicated to training and firearms safety; and DEFIANCE, the brand dedicated to firearms enhancements designed to aid the shooter in overcoming asymmetric warfare conditions. The company's previous name was Transformational Defense Industries, Inc. In late 2010, the company acquired Swiss pistol maker Sphinx Sytems Ltd.

PISTOLS: SEMI-AUTO

KRISS VECTOR SDP – 9mm Para. or .45 ACP cal., pistol variation of the KRISS Vector carbine, patented KRISS Super V Recoil Mitigation System, 5 1/2 or 6 1/2 (disc.) in. barrel with 1/2x28RH thread pitch, full length Mil-Std 1913 Picatinny top receiver rail and Picatinny bottom accessory rail, compatible with Glock pistol magazines, flip sights, short throw safety lever, combat pivoting trigger, quick detach sling mount, 5.4 lbs. New 2011.

MSR $1,349	$1,225	$1,075	$925	$850	$675	$550	$450

Add $100 for .45 ACP cal.

RIFLES: SEMI-AUTO

KRISS USA, Inc. also manufactures a select fire Vector submachine gun, chambered in .45 ACP and 9mm Para. cal. for military and law enforcement only, and the KRISS Vector SBR, a short barreled rifle variation of the KRISS Vector chambered in .45 ACP and 9mm Para. cal. Please contact the company directly for more information on these models (see Trademark Index).

KRISS VECTOR CRB – 9mm Para. or .45 ACP cal., carbine variation of the KRISS Vector, patented KRISS Super V Recoil Mitigation System, 16 in. barrel and barrel shroud, compatibe with Glock pistol magazines, flip up front and rear sights, full length Mil-Std 1913 Picatinny top receiver rail and Picatinny bottom accessory rail, short throw safety lever, combat pivoting trigger, adj. M4 stock, 5.8 lbs. New 2011.

MSR $1,499	$1,350	$1,180	$1,015	$925	$750	$625	$500

Add $20 for .45 ACP cal.

Add $884 for TacPac option (includes tactical sling, bipod grip pod system, Surefire tactical light, and L-3 Eotech holographic sight system), mfg. 2012-disc.

KRISS VECTOR CRB ENHANCED – 9mm Para. or .45 ACP cal., carbine enhanced variation of the KRISS Vector, patented KRISS Super V Recoil Mitigation System, 16 in. barrel and enhanced barrel shroud, compatible with Glock pistol magazines, combat pivoting trigger, flip sights, adj. M4 stock, Magpul RVG vertical grip, short throw safety lever, KRISS hand stop, full length Mil-Std 1913 Picatinny top receiver rail and Picatinny bottom accessory rail, Combat Grey Cerakote finish. New 2015.

MSR $1,699	$1,525	$1,350	$1,150	$1,050	$850	$700	$550

Add $20 for .45 ACP cal.

NOTES

L SECTION

L.A.R. MANUFACTURING, INC.

Previous rifle manufacturer established in 1968, located in West Jordan, UT until 2012. L.A.R. was acquired by the Freedom Group in late 2012 and closed its doors during 2013.

In addition to its .50 cal. bolt action rifles, L.A.R. also made upper receiver assemblies, and associated parts/accessories for AR-15 style carbines/rifles.

MSR	100%	98%	95%	90%	80%	70%	60%	Last MSR

PISTOLS: SEMI-AUTO

GRIZZLY WIN. MAG. MARK I – .357 Mag., .357/.45 Grizzly Win. Mag. (new 1990), .45 ACP, 10mm, or .45 Win. Mag. cal., single action, based on the Colt 1911 design, 5.4 in. (new 1986), 6 1/2 in., 8 in. (new 1987), or 10 in. (new 1987) barrel, parkerized finish, 7 shot mag., ambidextrous safeties, checkered rubber grips, adj. sights, 48 oz. empty. Also can be converted to .45 ACP, 10mm (new 1988), .357 Mag., or .30 Mauser (disc.). Mfg. 1984-1999.

* *Grizzly Win. Mag. Mark I Short Barrel Lengths* – 5.4 or 6 1/2 in. barrel.

	$875	$675	$625	$525	$495	$475	$450	$1,000

Add $14 for .357 Mag. cal.
Add $150 for hard chrome or nickel frame.
Add $260 for full hard chrome or nickel frame.
Add $233-$248 for cal. conversion units.

Conversion units include .357 Mag., 10mm, .40 S&W (1991-1993 only), and .45 ACP cals.

* *Grizzly Win. Mag. Mark I Long Barrel Lengths* – .357 Mag., .45 Win. Mag., or .357/.45 Grizzly Win. Mag. (new 1990) cal., 8 or 10 in. barrel, extended slides. Disc. 1995.

	$1,195	$975	$895	$800	$725	$650	$575	$1,313

Add $62 for 10 in. barrel.
Add $24 for .357 Mag.
Add $143 for scope mounts (disc.).
Add $110 for muzzle compensator.

* *Grizzly Win. Mag. Mark I State Special Edition* – .45 Grizzly Win. Mag., 50 mfg. beginning 1998 to commemorate each state (ser. numbers match the order each state was admitted to the union), features gold etchings on frame, gold small parts, faux mother-of-pearl grips, cased. Limited mfg. 1998-99.
Regional demand/interest preclude accurate pricing on this model.

GRIZZLY .44 MAG. MARK 4 – .44 Mag. cal., choice of lusterless blue, parkerized, chrome, or nickel finish, 5.4 or 6 1/2 in. barrel, adj. sights. Mfg. 1991-99.

	$875	$715	$635	$550	$495	$475	$450	$1,014

GRIZZLY .50 MARK 5 – .50 Action Express cal., single action semi-auto, 5.4 or 6 1/2 in. barrel, 6 shot mag., checkered walnut grips, 56 oz. Mfg. 1993-99.

	$1,475	$1,275	$1,050	$895	$775	$700	$625	$1,152

Add $178-$189 per coversion unit (new 1996).

GRIZZLY WIN. MAG. MARK II – similar to Mark I, except has fixed sights, standard safeties, and different metal finish. Mfg. 1986 only.

	$625	$550	$525	$495	$475	$450	$425	$550

Add $25 for .357 Mag.

RIFLES: BOLT ACTION

GRIZZLY BIG BOAR COMPETITOR RIFLE – .50 BMG cal., single shot, bolt action design in bullpup configuration, alloy steel receiver and bolt, 36 in. heavy barrel with compensator, thumb safety, match or field grade, includes bipod, scope mount, leather cheek pad and hard carry case, 30.4 lbs. Mfg. 1994-2011.

	$2,150	$1,725	$1,575	$1,375	$1,175	$1,050	$950	$2,350

Add $100 for parkerizing.
Add $250 for nickel trigger housing finish.
Add $350 for full nickel frame (disc. 2010).
Add $250 for stainless steel Lothar Walther barrel (disc. 2010).
Add $522 for redesigned (2002) tripod and pintle mount.
Last MSR was $4,841 for the Big Bore Hunter Rifle Package in 2011. This included: Nightforce scope and rings, cleaning kit, tripod with pintle mount, drag bag, and hard carry case.

MSR	100%	98%	95%	90%	80%	70%	60%	Last MSR

GRIZZLY T-50 – .50 BMG cal., single shot, 32-36 in. barrel with muzzle brake, extended barrel shroud with top and bottom Picatinny rails, black parkerized finish, cheek saddle on frame, carry handle in front of trigger guard, extended bolt handle, 30 1/2 - 32 lbs. Mfg. 2009-2012.

	100%	98%	95%	90%	80%	70%	60%	Last MSR
	$3,000	$2,800	$2,600	$2,400	$2,200	$2,000	$1,800	*$3,200*

MSR on the A T-50 Tactical Package was $5,618. This package included: Nightforce scope and rings, cleaning kit, heavy duty bipod, carry handle, Accu-Shot monopod, drag bag, and hard carry case.

RIFLES: SEMI-AUTO

GRIZZLY 15 – .223 Rem. cal., GIO, patterned after the AR-15, available in either A2 or A3 configuration, limited mfg. 2004-2005.

	100%	98%	95%	90%	80%	70%	60%	Last MSR
	$825	$725	$650	$575	$525	$475	$425	*$795*

Add $85 for detachable carry handle.

GRIZZLY A2 SPEC CARBINE – 5.56 NATO cal., AR-15 style, GIO, 16 in. M4 chrome moly threaded barrel with A2 birdcage flash suppressor, 5 position collapsible carbine stock, Grizzly A2 aluminum upper receiver, Mil-Spec forged aluminum LAR Grizzly lower receiver, Mil-Spec or LAR split carbine quad rail handguard, A2 front sight, standard trigger group, A2 Mil-Spec pistol grip. Mfg. 2011-2012.

	100%	98%	95%	90%	80%	70%	60%	Last MSR
	$895	$775	$675	$575	$525	$475	$425	*$999*

GRIZZLY A3 SPEC CARBINE – 5.56 NATO cal., GIO, similar to Grizzly A2 Spec Carbine, except has Grizzly A3 aluminum flat-top upper receiver. Mfg. 2011-2012.

	100%	98%	95%	90%	80%	70%	60%	Last MSR
	$880	$765	$675	$575	$525	$475	$425	*$979*

OPS-4 GRIZZLY H-TACTICAL – 5.56 NATO cal., AR-15 style, GPO, 16 in. M4 chrome moly threaded barrel with A2 birdcage flash suppressor, 5 position collapsible carbine stock, LAR side charged forged aluminum flat-top upper receiver, Mil-Spec forged aluminum LAR Grizzly lower receiver, Mil-Spec or LAR split carbine quad rail handguard, hard anodized aluminum charging handle. Mfg. 2011-2012.

	100%	98%	95%	90%	80%	70%	60%	Last MSR
	$975	$850	$725	$625	$550	$500	$450	*$1,111*

OPS-4 GRIZZLY HUNTER – .223 Rem./5.56 NATO (.223 Wylde chamber) cal., AR-15 style, GIO, 18, 20, or 24 in. bull chrome moly (20 or 24 in.) or stainless steel (18 or 20 in.) barrel, standard A2 black stock, standard trigger or two stage match trigger group, OPS-4 side charged forged aluminum flat-top upper receiver, Mil-Spec forged aluminum LAR Grizzly lower receiver, LAR free float tube rifle length handguard, LAR aluminum gas block, hard anodized aluminum charging handle. Mfg. 2011-2012.

	100%	98%	95%	90%	80%	70%	60%	Last MSR
	$885	$765	$675	$575	$525	$475	$425	*$989*

OPS-4 GRIZZLY OPERATOR – 5.56 NATO cal., AR-15 style, GIO, 16 in. chrome moly heavy threaded barrel with 5 port muzzle brake and compensator, Magpul CTR collapsible stock, Hogue rubber grip with finger grooves or Magpul MIAD pistol grip, standard trigger group, OPS-4 side charged forged aluminum flat-top upper receiver, Mil-Spec forged aluminum LAR Grizzly lower receiver, LAR mid-length quad rail handguard, LAR aluminum gas block with rail, hard anodized aluminum charging handle. Mfg. 2011-2012.

	100%	98%	95%	90%	80%	70%	60%	Last MSR
	$975	$825	$725	$625	$550	$500	$450	*$1,099*

OPS-4 GRIZZLY PRECISION OPERATOR – .223 Rem./5.56 NATO (.223 Wylde chamber) cal., AR-15 style, GIO, 18 or 20 in. bull stainless steel barrel, Magpul PRS stock, Magpul pistol grip and trigger guard or Magpul MIAD, standard trigger or 2 stage match trigger group, LAR rifle length free floating quad rail handguard, LAR aluminum low profile gas block, otherwise similar to OPS-4 Grizzly Operator. Mfg. 2011-2012.

	100%	98%	95%	90%	80%	70%	60%	Last MSR
	$1,125	$950	$825	$725	$625	$550	$475	*$1,299*

OPS-4 GRIZZLY SPEC CARBINE – 5.56 NATO cal., AR-15 style, GIO, 16 in. M4 chrome moly threaded barrel with A2 Birdcage flash suppressor, standard trigger group, 5 position collapsible carbine stock, OPS-4 side charged forged aluminum flat-top upper receiver, Mil-Spec forged aluminum LAR Grizzly lower receiver, A2 front sight, Mil-Spec or LAR split carbine quad rail handguard, hard anodized aluminum charging handle. Mfg. 2011-2012.

	100%	98%	95%	90%	80%	70%	60%	Last MSR
	$865	$750	$675	$575	$525	$475	$425	*$959*

OPS-4 GRIZZLY SPEC RIFLE – 5.56 NATO cal., AR-15 style, GIO, 20 in. chrome moly heavy threaded barrel with A2 birdcage flash suppressor, standard trigger or 2 stage match trigger group, standard A2 black stock, otherwise similar to OPS-4 Grizzly Spec Carbine. Mfg. 2011-2012.

	100%	98%	95%	90%	80%	70%	60%	Last MSR
	$895	$775	$675	$575	$525	$475	$425	*$999*

OPS-4 GRIZZLY STANDARD CARBINE – 5.56 NATO cal., AR-15 style, GIO, 16 in. M4 chrome moly threaded barrel with A2 birdcage flash suppressor, standard trigger group, 5 position collapsible carbine stock, LAR side charged forged aluminum flat-top upper receiver, Mil-Spec forged aluminum LAR Grizzly lower receiver, LAR aluminum gas block with rail, full chrome bolt carrier and gas key, hard anodized aluminum charging handle. Mfg. 2011-2012.

	100%	98%	95%	90%	80%	70%	60%	Last MSR
	$895	$775	$675	$575	$525	$475	$425	*$999*

MSR	100%	98%	95%	90%	80%	70%	60%	Last MSR

OPS-4 GRIZZLY STANDARD RIFLE – 5.56 NATO cal., AR-15 style, GIO, 20 in. chrome moly heavy threaded barrel with A2 birdcage flash suppressor, standard trigger or 2 stage match trigger group, standard A2 black stock, otherwise similar to OPS-4 Grizzly Standard Carbine. Mfg. 2011-2012.

	$975	$850	$725	$625	$550	$500	$450	*$1,099*

OPS-22 TERMINATOR – .22 LR cal., GIO, 16 in. carbon steel barrel, free float tube, 30 shot mag., collapsible buttstock. Mfg. 2011-2012.

	$575	$500	$425	$375	$325	$295	$275	*$649*

L E S INCORPORATED

Previous manufacturer located in Morton Grove, IL.

PISTOLS: SEMI-AUTO

P-18 ROGAK – 7.65mm Para. (limited mfg.) or 9mm Para. cal., DA/SA gas delayed blowback, 18 shot, 5 1/2 in. barrel, stainless steel, black plastic grips with partial thumb rest. Disc.

	$450	$395	$350	$325	$295	$275	$250	
High Polish Finish	$525	$450	$395	$375	$325	$295	$275	

Add 25% for 7.65mm Para. cal.

This pistol was patterned after the Steyr Model GB. Approx. 2,300 P-18s were mfg. before being disc.

LRB ARMS

Current manufacturer located in Floral Park, NY. Currently distributed by LRB of Long Island, NY.

RIFLES: SEMI-AUTO

M14SA BASE – .308 Win./7.62 NATO cal., GIO, 22 in. barrel with NM modified flash suppressor, 10 shot mag., hammer forged receiver, forged LRB bolt, reconditioned brown fiberglass or New Boyds walnut stock, sling.

MSR $2,541	$2,150	$1,890	$1,550	$1,325	$1,100	$950	$825	

Add $133 for Boyds walnut stock.

M14SA CLASSIC – .308 Win./7.62 NATO cal., GIO, authentic Vietnam era "As Issue" rifle, Criterion 22 in. chrome-lined barrel with USGI flash suppressor, 10 shot mag., M14SA receiver, LRB bolt, USGI reconditiond brown fiberglass or USGI reconditioned walnut stock, sling.

MSR $2,641	$2,225	$1,940	$1,600	$1,375	$1,125	$975	$850	

Add $83 for walnut stock.

M14SA TANKER – .308 Win./7.62 NATO cal., GIO, Criterion 18 1/2 in. chrome-lined barrel with LRB muzzle brake, 10 shot mag., M14SA receiver, LRB bolt, USGI reconditioned brown fiberglass or New Boyds walnut stock, sling.

MSR $2,663	$2,240	$1,960	$1,600	$1,375	$1,125	$975	$850	

Add $83 for walnut stock.

M14SA MEDIUM MATCH – .308 Win./7.62 NATO cal., GIO, choice of 22 in. stainless steel or chrome moly barrel with NM modified flash suppressor, NM front and rear sight, NM spring guide, Boyds walnut stock, 10 shot mag., sling.

MSR $3,005	$2,550	$2,225	$1,825	$1,575	$1,300	$1,100	$950	

M25 MEDIUM MATCH – .308 Win./7.62 NATO cal., choice of 22 in. stainless steel or chrome moly barrel with NM modified flash suppressor, M25 receiver, LRB bolt, NM front and rear sight, NM spring guide, unitized gas cylinder, Boyds walnut stock, 10 shot mag., sling.

MSR $3,090	$2,625	$2,275	$1,850	$1,590	$1,310	$1,100	$950	

M25 TANKER – .308 Win./7.62 NATO cal., GIO, Criterion 18 1/2 in. chrome-lined barrel with LRB muzzle brake, 10 shot mag., M25 receiver, USGI reconditioned brown fiberglass or New Boyds walnut stock, sling.

MSR $2,748	$2,275	$1,925	$1,625	$1,390	$1,125	$975	$850	

Add $134 for walnut stock.

10TH ANNIVERSARY SPECIAL – .308 Win./7.62 NATO cal., GIO, choice of 22 in. stainless steel or chrome moly barrel with USGI flash suppressor, NM front sight, NM OP rod spring guide, Boyds M1A style walnut stock, laser engraved number on left side of receiver, buttstock displays a 10th Anniversary coin mounted on right side. Limited mfg. of 200 beginning 2012. Disc. 2013.

	$2,325	$2,025	$1,750	$1,575	$1,275	$1,050	$825	*$2,592*

LWRC INTERNATIONAL, INC.

Current manufacturer of pistols, rifles, and related AR-15 accessories. Established during 2006, located in Cambridge, MD. Dealer and distributor sales.

MSR	100%	98%	95%	90%	80%	70%	60%	Last MSR

PISTOLS: SEMI-AUTO

M6A2-PSD (PERSONAL SECURITY DETAIL) – 5.56 NATO cal., GPO, 8 in. ultra compact hammer forged steel barrel, A2 flash hider, 30 shot Magpul PMAG, MIAD pistol grip, shortened recoil system, Troy front sight, folding BUIS rear sight, NiCorr surface treatment, black, FDE, Patriot Brown, or OD Green finish, 5 1/2 lbs.

| MSR $2,139 | $1,900 | $1,665 | $1,425 | $1,275 | $1,050 | $850 | $675 | |

Add $153 for FDE, OD Green, or Patriot Brown finish.

M6IC-PSD (PERSONAL SECURITY DETAIL) – 5.56 NATO cal., GPO, 8 1/2 in. cold hammer forged barrel with high efficiency flash hider, Monoforge upper receiver with modular 7 in. rail system, fully ambidextrous lower receiver with dual controls, enhanced fire control group, ambidextrous charging handle, Skirmish flip-up sights, PSD pistol buffer tube recoil system, Magpul MOE grip, black anodized or Cerakote finish in Patriot Brown, OD Green, or Flat Dark Earth, 5.9 lbs. New 2015.

| MSR $2,274 | $2,025 | $1,765 | $1,500 | $1,360 | $1,100 | $900 | $700 | |

Add $153 for Patriot Brown, OD Green, or Flat Dark Earth Cerakote finish.

SIX8-PSD – 6.8 SPC cal., GPO, 8 1/2 in. cold hammer forged barrel with high efficiency flash hider, 30 shot Magpul mag., enlarged ejection port, fully ambidextrous lower receiver, full Picatinny quad rail, LWRCI pistol buffer tube, enhanced fire control group, ambidextrous charging handle, rail skins, Skirmish back-up iron sights, Magpul MOE grip, black anodized or Cerakote finishes in Patriot Brown, OD Green, or Flat Dark Earth, 6 1/4 lbs. New 2015.

| MSR $2,192 | $1,960 | $1,710 | $1,450 | $1,315 | $1,065 | $875 | $700 | |

Add $153 for Patriot Brown, OD Green, or Flat Dark Earth Cerakote finish.

RIFLES: SEMI-AUTO

LWRC manufactures a complete line of short-stroke, gas-piston operated AR-15 style, M-16, and M4 semi-auto rifles. These models have a wide variety of sights, accessories, and related hardware available. Please contact the company directly for more information on the available options (see Trademark Index).

M6-A3 – 5.56 NATO or 6.8 SPC cal., GPO, 16.1 or 18 in. barrel, A2 flash hider, 30 shot mag., Vltor EMod adj. stock, Magpul MIAD pistol grip, integrated flip down sight, ARM-R free float rail system, front sight is folding and incorporated in gas block, Olive Drab or black finish, 7.3 lbs.

| | $2,075 | $1,775 | $1,575 | $1,400 | $1,125 | $975 | $800 | *$2,317* |

M6-A4 – 5.56 NATO or 6.8 SPC cal., GPO, 16 1/2 in. hammer forged steel barrel, 30 shot mag., Vltor EMod adj. stock, Magpul MIAD pistol grip, folding rear BUIS sight, folding front sight incorporated in gas block, front handle, quad rail, black finish, 7.4 lbs.

While advertised during 2011, this model has yet to be manufactured.

M6-G – 5.56 NATO or 6.8 SPC cal., GPO, 16.1 in. hammer forged steel barrel, 30 shot mag., Magpul MOE pistol grip stock, folding BUIS front and rear sights, enhanced fire control group, black finish, approx. 7 lbs.

While advertised during 2011, this model has yet to be manufactured.

M6-IC BASIC – 5.56 NATO cal., GPO, 16 in. fluted (first 500) or non-fluted barrel with A2 Birdcage flash hider, Monoforge upper receiver, 9 in. M6 modular rail, FDE (initial run of 500 only) or Black finish, Magpul MOE pistol grip stock, 7.3 lbs. Mfg. 2013-2014.

| | $2,115 | $1,850 | $1,585 | $1,450 | $1,175 | $950 | $750 | *$2,349* |

Add $100 for fluted barrel.

M6-IC-A2 – 5.56 NATO cal., GPO, 16.1 in. cold hammer forged match grade barrel, Birdcage flash hider, 6-position Vltor EMod or Magpul MOE stock, Magpul MIAD pistol grip, 30 shot mag., folding BUIS front and rear sights, mid-length free float rail system, black, FDE, OD Green, or Patriot Brown finish, 7.3 lbs.

| MSR $2,249 | $2,050 | $1,790 | $1,525 | $1,375 | $1,125 | $925 | $725 | |

Add $153 for FDE, OD Green, or Patriot Brown finish.

M6-IC-A5 – 5.56 NATO cal., GPO, 16.1 in. spiral fluted cold hammer forged barrel, full length top Picatinny rail, ambidextrous charging handle, LWRCI enhanced fire control group, fully ambidextrous lower receiver, dual controls, 12 in. user configurable rail system, LWRCI adj. compact stock with integrated sling mounting points, Magpul MOE grip, black anodized or Cerakote finish in Patriot Brown, OD Green, or FDE, 7 lbs. New 2015.

| MSR $2,599 | $2,340 | $2,050 | $1,755 | $1,590 | $1,285 | $1,075 | $850 | |

Add $153 for Patriot Brown, OD Green, or FDE Cerakote finish.

M6-IC ENHANCED – 5.56 NATO cal., GPO, 16.1 in. helical fluted barrel with A2 Birdcage flash hider, 30 shot PMAG, ambidextrous charging handle, 12 in. IC modular rail, Magpul MIAD pistol grip stock, LWRCI folding BUIS front and rear sights, black, OD Green, FDE, or Patriot Brown Cerakote finish, 7.1 lbs. New 2014.

| MSR $2,549 | $2,275 | $1,990 | $1,700 | $1,525 | $1,250 | $1,025 | $800 | |

Add $153 for FDE, OD Green, or Patriot Brown finish.

MSR	100%	98%	95%	90%	80%	70%	60%	Last MSR

M6-IC-SPR – 5.56 NATO cal., GPO, 16.1 in. spiral fluted barrel with A2 Birdcage flash hider, 30 shot PMAG, ambidextrous charging handle, 12 in. IC modular rail, Magpul MIAD pistol grip stock, LWRCI folding BUIS front and rear sights, black, OD Green, FDE, or Patriot Brown finish, 7.1 lbs. New 2014.

| MSR $2,396 | $2,140 | $1,865 | $1,585 | $1,450 | $1,175 | $950 | $750 | |

Add $153 for FDE, OD Green, or Patriot Brown finish.

M6-SL (STRETCH LIGHTWEIGHT) – 5.56 NATO cal., GPO, 16 in. light contour cold hammer forged barrel, A2 flash hider, 30 shot mag., MOE mid-length handguard and pistol grip, EXO (nickel boron) plated advanced combat bolt, one-piece coated carrier, and enhanced fire control group, Daniel Defense fixed rear sight, fixed A2 front sight, 6-position Magpul CTR stock, black, FDE, Patriot Brown, or OD Green finish, 6.6 lbs.

| MSR $1,709 | $1,515 | $1,300 | $1,100 | $900 | $775 | $650 | $575 | |

Add $102 for FDE, Patriot Brown, or OD Green finish.

M6-SPR (SPECIAL PURPOSE RIFLE) – 5.56 NATO or 6.8 SPC cal., GPO, 16.1 in. cold hammer forged fluted barrel, A2 flash hider, 30 shot mag., Magpul ACS stock, Magpul MIAD pistol grip, folding BUIS front and rear sights, black, OD Green, FDE or Patriot Brown finish, SPR-MOD rail, Bravo Company Mod4 Gunfighter charging handle, nickel coated bolt carrier and fire control group, Skirmish sights, 7.3 lbs. Disc. 2014.

| | $2,225 | $1,950 | $1,675 | $1,525 | $1,225 | $1,000 | $800 | *$2,479* |

R.E.P.R. (RAPID ENGAGEMENT PRECISION RIFLE) STRAIGHT – 7.62 NATO cal., GPO, 16, 18 (disc.), or 20 in. cold hammer forged heavy straight arrel, A2 Birdcage flash hider, Geissele two-stage trigger, 6-position Vltor Emod (disc.), Magpul UBR (disc.), B5 SOPMOD (16 in. model) or Magpul PRS (20 in. model) stock, 5, 10, or 20 shot mag., Magpul MIAD pistol (disc.) or Magpul MOE Plus grip, folding BUIS (disc.) or Skirmish back-up iron sights, sculpted ARM-R top rail, adj. two position gas block, ambidextrous bolt release, left side mounted non-reciprocating charging handle, 12 1/2 in. modular rail system, black anodized or Cerakote finishes in Patriot Brown, OD Green, or FDE, 9.3-11 1/4 lbs.

| MSR $3,672 | $3,290 | $2,885 | $2,465 | $2,200 | $1,775 | $1,450 | $1,150 | |

Add $153 for Patriot Brown, OD Green, or FDE Cerakote finish.
Add $204 for 20 in. barrel.

R.E.P.R. SPIRAL – 7.62mm NATO cal., GPO, 16 or 20 in. spiral fluted cold hammer forged barrel, A2 Birdcage flash hider, two position adj. gas block, side mounted non-reciprocating charging handle, Skirmish back-up iron sights, Geissele two-stage trigger, 12 1/2 in. modular rail system, B5 SOPMOD adj. stock (16 in. model) or Magpul PRS adj. stock (20 in. model), Magpul MOE Plus grip, black anodized or Cerakote finishes in FDE, Patriot Brown, or OD Green, 9-11 1/4 lbs. New 2012.

| MSR $3,825 | $3,435 | $3,000 | $2,575 | $2,325 | $1,885 | $1,550 | $1,200 | |

Add $153 for Patriot Brown, OD Green, or FDE Cerakote finish.
Add $204 for 20 in. barrel.

SIX8-A2 – 6.8 SPC cal., GPO, 16.1 in. cold hammer forged barrel with LWRCI flash hider, 30 shot PMAG, nickel boron coated bolt carrier group, enlarged ejection port, enhanced fire control group, claw extractor, LWRC compact stock and Magpul MOE plus grip, 9 in. Picatinny quad rail, Mil-Spec trigger, Skirmish back-up iron sights, two-position safety, fully ambidextrous, black anodized, FDE, Patriot Brown, or OD Green Cerakote finish, 7.3 lbs. New 2013.

| MSR $2,294 | $2,050 | $1,790 | $1,525 | $1,375 | $1,125 | $925 | $725 | |

Add $153 for FDE, Patriot Brown, or OD Green Cerakote finish.

SIX8-A5 – 6.8 SPC cal., GPO, 16.1 in. cold hammer forged barrel with high efficiency flash hider, 30 shot Magpul mag., enlarged ejection port, 12 in. user configurable rail, Skirmish back-up iron sights, LWRCI enhanced fire control group, ambidextrous charging handle, compact stock with integral sling attachment point, Magpul MOE grip, black anodized or Cerakote finishes in Patriot Brown, OD Green, or FDE, 7.3 lbs. New 2014.

| MSR $2,651 | $2,225 | $1,940 | $1,600 | $1,375 | $1,125 | $975 | $850 | |

Add $153 for Cerakote finish in Patriot Brown, OD Green, or FDE.

SIX8-SPR – 6.8 SPC cal., GPO, 16.1 in. cold hammer forged heavy barrel with LWRCI flash hider, Magpul 30 shot mag., dual extractor springs, claw extractor, enlarged ejection port, LWRCI Skirmish sights, LWRCI adj. compact stock with integrated quick-detach points, nickel boron coated bolt carrier group, enhanced fire control group, full length Picatinny top rail, 12 in. user configurable rail system, ambidextrous charging handle, dual control fully ambidextrous lower receiver, black anodized or Cerakote finishes in FDE, OD Green, or Patriot Brown, 7 1/4 lbs. New 2013.

| MSR $2,549 | $2,275 | $1,990 | $1,700 | $1,525 | $1,250 | $1,025 | $800 | |

Add $153 for FDE, Patriot Brown, or OD Green finish.

IC-DI – 5.56 NATO cal., GIO, 16.1 in. cold hammer forged spiral fluted heavy barrel, A2 flash hider, LWRCI advanced trigger guard, LWRCI compact stock w/QD sling, angled ergonomic foregrip, Magpul MOE+ grip, modular one-piece free float rail, ambidextrous charging handle, Mil-Spec 6-position buffer tube, Monoforge one-piece upper, fully ambidextrous lower receiver, Type III hardcoat anodized black finish, 6.7 lbs. New late 2015.

| MSR $1,599 | $1,350 | $1,200 | $1,075 | $950 | $815 | $700 | $575 | |

MSR	100%	98%	95%	90%	80%	70%	60%	*Last MSR*

C.S.A.S.S. – 7.62 NATO cal., GPO, 16.1 or 20 in. cold hammer forged spiral fluted heavy barrel, Geissele SSA two-stage precision trigger, LWRCI Skirmish BUIS, B5 SOPMOD (16.1 in. model) or Magpul PRS (Precision Rifle/Sniper, 20 in. model) stock, Magpul MOE Plus grip, 12 1/2 in. modular rail system, top side ambidextrous charging handle, nickel Teflon coated bolt carrier group, billet aluminum C.S.A.S.S. upper and lower receivers, black anodized or Cerakote finishes in FDE, Olive Drab, or Patriot Brown, 8 3/4-10 3/4 lbs. New 2016.

Please contact the manufacturer directly for pricing and availability on this model.

LABANU INCORPORATED

Labanu, Inc. SKSs were manufactured by Norinco in China, and imported exclusively until 1998 by Labanu, Inc., located in Ronkonkoma, NY.

RIFLES: SEMI-AUTO

MAK 90 SKS SPORTER RIFLE – 7.62x39mm cal., sporterized variation of the SKS with thumbhole stock, 16 1/2 in. barrel, includes accessories, 5 lbs. Importation began 1995, banned 1998.

	100%	98%	95%	90%	80%	70%	60%	*Last MSR*
	$625	$550	$475	$425	$375	$325	$295	*$189*

LAKESIDE MACHINE LLC

Previous manufacturer located in Horseshoe Bend, AR until late 2013. Previously located in Pound, WI.

RIFLES: SEMI-AUTO

Lakeside manufactured half-scale, semi-auto, belt fed replicas of many of America's famous machine guns, including the 1919 A4 ($3,995 last MSR), 1919 M37 ($3,895 last MSR, only 2 mfg.), 1917 A1 ($4,495 last MSR), M2 HB ($4,995 last MSR), M2 WC ($5,495 last MSR), and a dual mount M2 HB (was POR). Calibers included: .22 LR, .17 Mach 2 (optional), and .22 WMR. Additionally, Lakeside also manufactured a semi-auto, closed bolt, belt fed .22 LR cal. Model Vindicator BF1 with 16 1/4 in. shrouded barrel ($2,695 last MSR).

LANCER SYSTEMS

Current AR-15 style rifle and accessories manufacturer located in Allentown, PA.

RIFLES: SEMI-AUTO

All L15 models ship with three 30 shot mags. and two 20 shot mags.

All L30 models ship with one 20 shot mag. and one 10 shot mag.

Add approx. $40 for Raddlock Device.

L15 COMPETITION – 5.56 NATO cal., .223 Wylde chamber, GIO, 18 in. stainless steel White Oak barrel, Wheaton Arms (disc.) or Lancer Nitrous compensator, extra long free floating handguard, LCS-A1-R Lancer fixed stock, Ergo grip, CMC trigger, 7.7 lbs. New 2013.

MSR $2,225	100%	98%	95%	90%	80%	70%	60%
	$1,975	$1,750	$1,475	$1,225	$1,000	$850	$750

L15 DMR – 5.56 NATO cal., .223 Wylde chamber, 18 in. White Oak barrel with thread protector, Geissele Hi-Speed National Match two-stage trigger, B5 SOPMOD Bravo stock, Ergo grip, rifle length gas system, 15 in. Lancer LCH5 handguard, 7.3 lbs.

Please contact the company directly for pricing, options, and availability on this model.

L15 OUTLAW – 5.56 NATO cal., .223 Wylde chamber, 17 in. mid-weight profile Bartlein stainless steel barrel, Lancer Nitrous compensator, Geissele Super Dynamic 3-Gun trigger, LCS-A1-R fixed stock, Ergo grip, rifle length adj. gas block, Raptor charging handle, 15 in. Lancer LCR5 round handguard, 6 3/4 lbs.

MSR $2,725	100%	98%	95%	90%	80%	70%	60%
	$2,295	$1,995	$1,650	$1,425	$1,160	$1,000	$875

L15 PATROL – 5.56 NATO cal., 16 in. mid-weight CHF chrome lined barrel, Battle Comp compensator, Mil-Spec trigger, B5 Bravo stock, BCM Gunfighter grip, mid-length gas system, Lancer LCH5 12 in. handguard with 2 in. sight rail, single point sling mount, 6 1/2 lbs.

MSR $1,950	100%	98%	95%	90%	80%	70%	60%
	$1,650	$1,450	$1,225	$1,085	$935	$800	$660

L15 SUPER COMPETITION – 5.56 NATO cal., .223 Wylde chamber, GIO, upgraded version of the L15 Competition featuring 17 in. stainless steel Krieger barrel, Wheaton Arms SS (disc.) or Lancer Nitrous compensator, rifle length gas system, 15 in. Lancer LCH5 octagon handguard, EFX-A2 (disc.) or Lancer LCS-A1-R fixed stock, Ergo grip, CMC trigger, 7 1/2 lbs. New 2013.

MSR $2,525	100%	98%	95%	90%	80%	70%	60%
	$2,300	$1,925	$1,600	$1,275	$1,075	$875	$775

L15 SHARP SHOOTER – 5.56 NATO cal., GIO, 20 in. heavy profile Krieger barrel, Lancer extra long free-float handguard, tactical Magwell lower receiver, EFX-A2 fixed stock, Ergo grip, CMC trigger, 8.9 lbs. Mfg. 2013-2015.

	100%	98%	95%	90%	80%	70%	60%	*Last MSR*
	$1,925	$1,675	$1,400	$1,150	$975	$775	$700	*$2,180*

MSR	100%	98%	95%	90%	80%	70%	60%	Last MSR

L15 SPORTER – 5.56 NATO cal., GIO, 16 in. lightweight CHF chrome lined barrel with A2 flash hider, mid-length gas system, Lancer handguard with 2 in. sight rail, tactical magwell lower receiver, F93 Pro stock, Ergo grip, Mil-Spec trigger, 7.4 lbs. New 2013.

MSR $1,750	$1,575	$1,375	$1,125	$900	$775	$675	$575	

L30 HEAVY METAL – 7.62 NATO cal., .308 Obermeyer chamber, 18 in. stainless steel White Oak barrel, Lancer Nitrous compensator, Geissele SD3G trigger, Lancer LCS stock, Ergo Tactical Deluxe grip, rifle length adj. gas block, Lancer carbon fiber handguard, 9 1/2 lbs.

MSR $3,345	$2,840	$2,480	$2,000	$1,700	$1,400	$1,200	$1,035	

L30 LTR – 7.62 NATO or 6.5 Creedmoor cal., 24 in. stainless steel Bartlein barrel, Lancer Viper muzzle brake, rifle length adj. gas block, billet aluminum upper with integral carbon fiber handguard and Picatinny rail, oversized mag. release button, ambidextrous bolt release, mission configurable lower receiver, Geissele Hi-Speed National Match trigger, KFS TacMod stock, Ergo Tactical Deluxe grip, 12 1/2 lbs.

MSR $4,200	$3,575	$3,125	$2,600	$2,175	$1,800	$1,500	$1,300	

L30 MBR (MODERN BATTLE RIFLE) – 7.62 NATO cal., 16 in. black nitride barrel, Lancer Nitrous compensator, Mil-Spec trigger, B5 SOPMOD stock, Ergo grip, rifle length gas system, Lancer carbon fiber handguard, 9 lbs.

MSR $2,560	$2,170	$1,900	$1,550	$1,350	$1,115	$965	$835	

LARUE TACTICAL

Current manufacturer located in Leander, TX.

RIFLES: SEMI-AUTO

OBR (OPTIMIZED BATTLE RIFLE) – 5.56 NATO (new 2011) or .308 Win./7.62 NATO cal., AR-15 style, GIO, 16.1, 18, or 20 in. stainless steel barrel, adj. gas block, 20 shot box mag., flared magwell, A2 fixed stock, black anodized finish, Mil-Std 1913 one-piece upper rail, Troy front and optional BUIS rear sight, A2 flash hider, detachable side rails, approx. 10 lbs.

5.56 MSR $2,245	$2,500	$2,150	$1,875	$1,700	$1,375	$1,125	$875	
7.62 MSR $3,370	$3,750	$3,150	$2,850	$2,350	$1,900	$1,450	$1,150	

A variety of accessories are available on this model for additional cost.

PREDATOBR – 5.56 NATO or 7.62 NATO cal., GIO, 16.1 or 18 in. threaded barrel, 30 shot, Picatinny rail, 6-position Retract Action Trigger (R.A.T.) stock. New 2014.

5.56 MSR $2,245	$2,150	$2,000	$1,800	$1,600	$1,400	$1,200	$1,000	
7.62 MSR $3,370	$3,250	$2,850	$2,400	$2,150	$1,750	$1,450	$1,150	

A variety of accessories are available on this model for additional cost.

PREDATAR – 5.56 NATO or .308 Win. /7.62 NATO (new 2013) cal., GIO, 16.1 or 18 in. contoured stainless steel barrel, skeletonized handguard, A2 flash hider, quad rail forend, black phosphate finish, 6-position Magpul stock, 30 shot mag., charging lever, forward assist, Geissele two-stage trigger, approx. 6 1/2 lbs. New mid-2011.

5.56 MSR $1,807	$1,995	$1,750	$1,495	$1,350	$1,050	$900	$700	
7.62 MSR $2,932	$3,000	$2,650	$2,250	$2,050	$1,650	$1,350	$1,050	

A variety of accessories are available on this model for additional cost.

COSTA SIGNATURE EDITION – 5.56 NATO cal., GIO, 16.1 in. barrel, SureFire muzzle brake, FDE KG GunKote finish, "COSTA LUDUS" logo engraved on left side of receiver, black parts and rail covers, first 500 units are match numbered on the upper and lower. Mfg. 2013-2015.

	N/A	$4,500	$4,000	$3,500	$3,000	$2,500	$2,000	*$2,895*

FDE LIMITED EDITION PREDATAR – 7.62 NATO cal., AR-15 style, GIO w/PST (port selector technology), 16 in. heavy barrel, LaRue M308 TranQuilo muzzle brake, 1/10 twist, 3-20 round mags., FDE Cerakote finish w/select black parts and GAP rail covers. Approx. 125 mfg. Disc.

Rarity precludes accurate pricing on this model.

UDE LIMITED EDITION PREDATOBR – 5.56 NATO cal., AR-15 style, GIO w/PST (port selector technology), 16 in. barrel, LaRue M556 TranQuilo muzzle brake, 1/8 twist, 2-30 round mags., black LaRue MBT trigger, UDE LaRue RAT stock and A-PEG pistol grip, UDE GAP rail covers and index clips, UDE finish w/select black part. Approx. 125 mfg. numbered 001-125. Disc.

	$3,000	$2,625	$2,250	$2,050	$1,650	$1,350	$1,050	

MSR		100%	98%	95%	90%	80%	70%	60%	*Last MSR*

LASERAIM ARMS, INC.

Previous distributor located in Little Rock, AR. Previously manufactured until 1999 in Thermopolis, WY. Laseraim Arms, Inc. was a division of Emerging Technologies, Inc.

PISTOLS: SEMI-AUTO

SERIES I – .40 S&W, .400 Cor-Bon (new 1998), .45 ACP, or 10mm cal., SA, 3 3/8 (Compact Model), 5, or 6 in. barrel with compensator, ambidextrous safety, all stainless steel metal parts are Teflon coated, beveled magwell, integral accessory mounts, 7 (.45 ACP) or 8 (10mm or .40 S&W) shot mag., 46 or 52 oz. Mfg. 1993-99.

		$325	$295	$265	$215	$185	$150	$125	*$349*

Add $120 for wireless laser combo (new 1997).

* ***Series I Compact*** – .40 S&W or .45 ACP cal., 3 3/8 in. non-ported slide and fixed sights. Mfg. 1993-99.

		$325	$295	$265	$215	$185	$150	$125	*$349*

Series I Illusion and Dream Team variations were made during 1993-94. Retail prices respectively were $650 and $695.

SERIES II – .40 S&W (disc. 1994), .45 ACP, or 10mm cal., SA, similar technical specs. as the Series I, except has non-reflective stainless steel finish, fixed or adj. sights, and 3 3/8 (Compact Model, .45 ACP only), 5, or 7 (.45 ACP only) in. non-compensated barrel, 37 or 43 oz. Mfg. 1993-1996.

		$485	$385	$300	$240	$210	$180	$155	*$550*

Series II Illusion and Dream Team variations were made during 1993-94. Retail prices respectively were $500 and $545.

SERIES III – .45 ACP cal., 5 in. ported barrel, SA, serrated slide, Hogue grips. Mfg. 1994-disc.

		$595	$465	$415	$375	$345	$310	$275	*$675*

SERIES IV – .45 ACP cal., 3 3/8 (Compact Model) or 5 in. ported barrel, SA, serrated slide, diamond checkered wood grips. Mfg. 1994-disc.

		$550	$450	$400	$360	$330	$300	$265	*$625*

LAUER CUSTOM WEAPONRY

Current manufacturer of AR-15 style carbines/rifles located in Chippewa Falls, WI.

RIFLES: SEMI-AUTO

Please contact the manufacturer directly for current pricing and availability on these models (see Trademark Index).

LCW15 BATTLE RIFLE – 5.56 NATO cal., AR-15 style, GIO (available with LCW's MaxGas proprietry high performance gas system), 16 in. barrel, A3 flat-top or A2 carry handle on upper receiver, shorty carbine handguard, A2 buttstock, one 30 shot GI mag., black or Afghan camo finish.

LCW15 TARGET RIFLE – 5.56 NATO cal., GIO (MaxGas proprietary gas system), 24 in. stainless steel bull barrel, matching serial number on upper and lower receiver, A3 flat-top upper receiver, match target trigger, free float aluminum handguard, A2 buttstock, one 20 shot mag., includes hard case and ear plugs.

LCW15 URBAN RESPONDER – 5.56 NATO cal., AR-15 style, GIO, CQB precision carbine, M4 barrel with A2 flash hider, TriPower illuminated sight, M6 tactical laser illuminator with remote switch, lightweight 4-rail tactical free float handguard, forward grip, compact skeleton stock, tactical grip with storage compartment, DPMS quick response rear flip up sight, A.R.M.S. 17 mount, LCW 3-point tactical sling, 30 shot mag., Urban MirageFlage finish, 7 1/2 lbs.

VINDICATOR – .22 LR cal., GIO, belt fed model. Disc. 2014.

LAW ENFORCEMENT ORDNANCE CORPORATION

Previous manufacturer located in Ridgway, PA until 1990.

SHOTGUNS: SEMI-AUTO

STRIKER-12 – 12 ga., 12 shot rotary mag., 18 1/4 in. alloy shrouded barrel with PG extension, folding or fixed tactical design stock, 9.2 lbs., limited mfg. 1986-1990.

		$1,000	$875	$750	$675	$600	$550	$500	*$725*

Add $200 for folding stock.
Add $100 for Marine variation ("Metal Life" finish).

Earlier variations were imported and available to law enforcement agencies only. In 1987, manufacture was started in PA and these firearms could be sold to individuals (18 in. barrel only). This design was originally developed in South Rhodesia.

LAZZERONI ARMS COMPANY

Current manufacturer located in Tucson, AZ since 1995. Direct/dealer sales.

MSR	100%	98%	95%	90%	80%	70%	60%	Last MSR

RIFLES: BOLT ACTION

Lazzeroni ammunition is precision loaded in Lazzeroni's Tucson facility under rigid tolerances. All ammunition is sealed for absolute weatherproofing. Lazzeroni proprietary calibers are already established as being extremely effective at long distances.

MODEL L2012/L2005 GLOBAL HUNTER SERIES – available in various Lazzeroni proprietary cals., various configurations including Short Magnum Lite, Long Magnum Lite, Long Magnum Thumbhole, Long Magnum Special Long Range (disc. 2010), Short Magnum Dangerous Game (disc. 2010) and Long Magnum Dangerous Game, features stainless steel receiver, match grade fluted or unfluted barrel with muzzle brake, Jewell competition trigger, diamond fluted or helical cut bolt shaft, titanium firing pin, Limbsavr recoil pad, slim line graphite composite stock, approx. 6.1-8.7 lbs. Mfg. 2005-disc.

	100%	98%	95%	90%	80%	70%	60%	Last MSR
	$4,650	$4,250	$3,600	$3,100	$2,650	$2,150	$1,675	*$5,000*

Add $1,000 for heavy barrel Long Magnum (disc. 2010).

Add $3,000 for Dangerous Game (Model L2012-LD) or Long Magnum Tactical Model (Model L2012-TAC, mfg. 2011-2013).

LEGACY SPORTS INTERNATIONAL

Current importer located in Reno, NV. Previously located in Alexandria, VA.

Legacy Sports International imports a wide variety of firearms trademarks in various configurations, including pistols, rifles, and shotguns. Trademarks include: Citadel, Escort, Howa, ISSC (disc. 2014), Pointer, Puma (disc. 2015), and Verona (disc.). Please refer to these individual listings.

LEGION FIREARMS LLC

Current firearms and accessories manufacturer located in Temple, TX.

CARBINES: SEMI-AUTO

LF-10D CARBINE – .308 Win. or 7.62x51 NATO cal., GIO, 16 in. stainless steel barrel, three land polygonal rifling, M4 feed ramps, hex milled fluting, SureFire muzzle brake, micro MOA adj. gas block, aluminum aircraft grade nickel boron coated upper and lower receiver, 12 in. Legion quad-channel concept handguard, ceramic wear resistant coating, Raptor .308 charging handle, ambidextrous bolt release, Phase 5 tactical REVO sling attachment system, BAD lever 90 degree ambi safety selector, Magpul MOE pistol grip, B5 Systems enhanced SOPMOD stock, H3 heavy buffer, steel bolt carrier, single stage trigger, available in Alpha Grey, Burnt Bronze, Flat Dark Earth, OD Green, Sniper Grey, or Black finish. New 2011.

MSR $3,390	$3,100	$2,875	$2,515	$2,150	$1,950	$1,575	$1,295

LF-15D CARBINE – 5.56 NATO cal., GIO, 16 in. stainless steel barrel, three land polygonal rifling, M4 feed ramps, hex milled fluting, aluminum aircraft grade nickel boron coated upper and lower receiver, Wilson Combat handguard, ceramic wear resistant coating, drilled and tapped, ambidextrous bolt release, available in Alpha Grey, Burnt Bronze, Flat Dark Earth, OD Green, Sniper Grey, or Black finish, Noveske QD endplate, single stage trigger, adj. tactical stock, H2 heavy buffer, lightweight billet modular design. New 2011.

MSR $2,390	$2,175	$1,995	$1,775	$1,525	$1,375	$1,115	$910

PISTOLS: SEMI-AUTO

LF-P – 9mm Para., .40 S&W, or .45 ACP cal., 5 in. stainless steel threaded or non-threaded barrel, SA, 1911 style chrome moly frame and slide, 13 (.45 ACP), 18 (.40 S&W), or 20 (9mm Para.) shot mag., omni-directional serrations, EGW melt barrel bushing, Legion hex hammer, Ameri Glow rear sights, STI machined front sights, Springco cryotreated recoil and mainspring, custom trigger assembly, available in Flat Dark Earth, Naked Nickel Boron, Burnt Bronze, OD Green, or black finish, includes three magazines.

MSR $2,595	$2,350	$2,200	$1,925	$1,650	$1,495	$1,210	$995

LEITNER-WISE DEFENSE, INC.

Current AR-15 style parts/accessories manufacturer located in Alexandria, VA. The company discontinued its semi-auto line of rifles circa 2010.

RIFLES: SEMI-AUTO

M.U.L.E. MOD. 1 (MODULAR URBAN LIGHT ENGAGEMENT CARBINE) – 5.56 NATO cal., GPO, 16 in. steel barrel standard, other lengths optional, op-rod operating system, single stage trigger, Magpul ACS buttstock, MOE pistol grip, black finish, upper and lower rails, 30 shot mag., flared magwell, E sights, includes one mag., manual, and cleaning kit, 7.9 lbs. Disc. circa 2010.

	$1,550	$1,375	$1,175	$1,000	$850	$700	$575	*$1,680*

Add $100 for precision trigger.

M.U.L.E. MOD. 2 (MODULAR URBAN LIGHT ENGAGEMENT CARBINE) – .308 Win. cal., GPO, 16 or 20 in. steel barrel, similar to Mod. 1, except has heavier barrel, 8 1/2 lbs. Disc. circa 2010.

	$1,895	$1,700	$1,500	$1,300	$1,100	$900	$700	*$2,100*

Add $100 for 20 in. barrel.

MSR	100%	98%	95%	90%	80%	70%	60%	Last MSR

LEITNER-WISE RIFLE CO. INC.

Previous manufacturer located in Springfield, VA circa 2006. Previously located in Alexandria, VA 1999-2005.

RIFLES: SEMI-AUTO

LW 15.22 – .22 LR or .22 WMR cal., GIO, patterned after the AR-15, 16 1/2 or 20 in. barrel, forged upper and lower receivers, choice of carry handle or flat-top upper receiver, forward bolt assist, last shot hold open, 10 or 25 shot mag. Mfg. 2000-2005.

	$775	$675	$600	$550	$500	$450	$425	*$850*

Add $50 for A2 carrying handle.

LW 15.499 – .499 (12.5x40mm) cal., receiver and action patterned after the AR-15, Mil-Spec standards, 16 1/2 in. steel or stainless steel barrel, flat-top receiver, 5 (disc.), 10, or 14 (new 2006) shot mag., approx. 6 1/2 lbs. Mfg. 2000-2005.

	$1,350	$1,150	$995	$875	$750	$675	$600

Add $92 for stainless steel barrel.

LW 6.8/5.56 S.R.T. – 5.56x45mm NATO or 6.8x43mm SPC cal., 16.1 in. barrel, hard chrome lined bore, gas operated, locking bolt, Troy front and rear sights, forged T7075 aluminum flat-top upper receiver, 6-position collapsible stock, Picatinny rail, removable carry handle, A2 flash hider, LW forged lower receiver, 28 or 30 shot mag., 5.38 lbs. Ltd. mfg. 2006.

	$2,050	$1,800	$1,600	$1,400	$1,200	$1,000	$850

Add $100 for 6.8x43mm SPC cal.

LES BAER CUSTOM, INC.

Current manufacturer and customizer established in 1993, located in LeClaire, IA since 2008. Previously located in Hillsdale, IL until 2008. Dealer sales only.

PISTOLS: SEMI-AUTO, 1911 SERIES, SINGLE ACTION

The following current models are available with the following features unless otherwise noted: lowered and flared ejection port, tuned and polished extractor, Baer extended ejector, and beveled magwell.

Add $70 for Tactical Package (rounds the edges of the pistol).

ULTIMATE MASTER COMBAT SERIES – .38 Super, .400 Cor-Bon, or .45 ACP cal., steel frame and slide with blued finish, compensated, 5 or 6 in. barrel, two 8 shot mags., checkered Cocobolo grips, low mount LBC adj. sight with hidden rear leaf, dovetailed front sight, double serrated slide, deluxe Commander hammer and sear, full length recoil rod, extended ambi safety, speed trigger.

* Compensated Model – .38 Super or .45 ACP cal., compensated barrel.

MSR $3,240	$2,700	$2,400	$2,075	$1,775	$1,575	$1,350	$995

Add $150 for .38 Super cal.

* 5 Inch Model – .38 Super, .400 Cor-Bon, or .45 ACP cal., 5 in. barrel.

MSR $3,040	$2,550	$2,250	$1,975	$1,700	$1,525	$1,275	$925

Add $50 for .400 Cor-Bon cal. Add $100 for .38 Super cal.

* 6 Inch Model – .38 Super, .400 Cor-Bon, or .45 ACP cal., 6 in. barrel.

MSR $3,140	$2,625	$2,350	$2,050	$1,775	$1,575	$1,350	$995

Add $70 for .400 Cor-Bon cal. Add $80 for .38 Super cal.

NATIONAL MATCH HARDBALL PISTOL – .45 ACP cal., NM steel frame, slide, and 5 in. barrel with stainless bushing, 7 shot mag., blued finish, checkered front strap, checkered Cocobolo grips, low mount LBC adj. sight with hidden rear leaf, dovetailed front sight, rear serrated slide, match trigger.

MSR $2,310	$2,050	$1,800	$1,500	$1,225	$1,025	$875	$775

BULLSEYE WADCUTTER PISTOL – .45 ACP cal., NM frame, slide, and barrel with stainless bushing, 7 shot mag., blued finish, checkered Cocobolo grips, double serrated slide, high checkered front strap, Baer deluxe hammer and sear, beavertail grip safety with pad, Baer speed trigger, optical scope mount.

MSR $2,390	$2,100	$1,825	$1,525	$1,250	$1,050	$895	$795

Add $60 for 6 in. slide with Lo-Mount LBC adj. sights and Baer optical mount.

PPC DISTINGUISHED MATCH PISTOL – 9mm Para. or .45 ACP cal., NM steel frame, slide, and barrel with stainless bushing, 8 shot mag., 5 in. barrel, blued finish, checkered Cocobolo grips, PPC sight, Baer dovetail front sight, double serrated slide, Baer deluxe Commander hammer and sear, beavertail grip safety with pad, Baer speed trigger, extended ambi safety.

MSR $2,980	$2,600	$2,300	$2,000	$1,775	$1,525	$1,275	$1,050

Subtract $490 for .45 ACP cal.

PPC OPEN CLASS – 9mm Para. or .45 ACP cal., similar to PPC Distinguished Match, except features 6 in. barrel.

MSR $2,695	$2,400	$2,100	$1,850	$1,600	$1,325	$1,100	$900

Add $400 for 9mm Para. cal. with supported chamber.

MSR	100%	98%	95%	90%	80%	70%	60%	Last MSR

PREMIER II 5 INCH MODEL – .38 Super, .400 Cor-Bon, or .45 ACP cal., NM steel frame, slide, and barrel with stainless bushing, 5 in. barrel, low mount LBC adj. sight with hidden rear leaf, dovetail front sight, two 8 shot mags., blued finish or stainless steel (disc. 2015), checkered Cocobolo grips, beavertail grip safety with pad, speed trigger, extended ambi safety.

	100%	98%	95%	90%	80%	70%	60%	
MSR $2,180	$1,875	$1,575	$1,275	$1,075	$950	$800	$725	

Add $80 for stainless steel (disc. 2015).
Add $200 for .400 COR-BON cal. Add $440 for .38 Super cal.
Add $580 for .45 ACP/.400 COR-BON dual cylinder combo.

PREMIER II 6 INCH MODEL – .38 Super or .45 ACP cal., similar to Premier II 5 Inch Model, except features 6 in. barrel, blued finish only.

	100%	98%	95%	90%	80%	70%	60%	
MSR $2,390	$2,100	$1,825	$1,525	$1,250	$1,050	$895	$795	

Add $100 for .400 COR-BON cal. Add $450 for .38 Super cal.

PREMIER II SUPER-TAC – 38 Super, .400 Cor-Bon, .45 ACP, or .45 ACP/.400 Cor-Bon combo cal., NM steel frame, barrel with stainless bushing, two 8 shot mags., NM steel frame, slide, and barrel with stainless bushing, Baer speed trigger, low mount LBC adj. rear sight and Baer dovetail front sight, both fitted with Tritium night sights, checkered Cocobolo grips, extended ambi safety, beavertail grip safety with pad, deburred for tactical carry, DuPont S coating, 45 ACP/.400 Cor-Bon dual cylinder combo.

	100%	98%	95%	90%	80%	70%	60%	
MSR $2,650	$2,350	$2,075	$1,825	$1,575	$1,325	$1,100	$900	

Add $60 for .400 Cor-Bon cal.
Add $280 for .38 Super cal.
Add $540 for .45 ACP/.400 Cor-Bon dual cylinder combo.

PROWLER III – .45 ACP cal., NM steel frame, slide, and 5 in. barrel with tapered cone stub weight, Bear reverse plug, slide fitted to frame, double serrated slide, low mount BoMar sight with hidden leaf rear, dovetail front sight, checkered slide stop, Baer speed trigger, deluxe Commander hammer, beavertail grip safety with pad, extended ambi safety, blued finish, two 8 shot mags., checkered Cocobolo grips. Disc. 2014.

	100%	98%	95%	90%	80%	70%	60%	Last MSR
	$2,400	$2,125	$1,800	$1,575	$1,300	$1,100	$925	*$2,710*

CUSTOM CARRY – .38 Super (4 1/4 in. only), or .45 ACP cal., NM steel frame, slide, and barrel with stainless bushing, 4 1/4 (Comanche length) or 5 in. throated barrel, blued or stainless steel finish, deluxe fixed combat sight, dovetail front sight, improved ramp style night sights, double serrated slide, checkered slide stop, Baer speed trigger, extended ambi safety, two 8 shot mags., checkered Cocobolo grips.

	100%	98%	95%	90%	80%	70%	60%	
MSR $2,190	$1,875	$1,575	$1,275	$1,075	$950	$800	$725	

Add $100 for stainless steel finish.
Add $360 for .38 Super cal. with 4 1/4 in. barrel and stainless steel finish.

SUPER COMANCHE – .38 Super cal., steel construction only, 4 1/4 in. throated barrel, NM slide with rear serrations only, stainless steel bushing, deluxe fixed combat rear sight with night sight, dovetail front sight ramp style with night sight, blue finish or optional chrome or DuPont S finish, checkered slide stop, speed trigger, extended ambi safety, checkered Cocobolo grips, high checkered front strap, two 9 shot mags. with base pads. Mfg. 2013-2015.

	100%	98%	95%	90%	80%	70%	60%	Last MSR
	$2,275	$2,025	$1,775	$1,525	$1,275	$1,075	$875	*$2,550*

ULTIMATE RECON PISTOL – .45 ACP cal., full size Caspian frame with integral Picatinny rail system for frame mounted light, comes standard with a Streamlight TLR-1, NM slide and 5 in. barrel with stainless bushing, deluxe fixed combat rear sight with night sights, dovetail front sight, double serrated slide, bead blast blue finish or optional bead blast chrome finish, deluxe hammer and sear, checkered slide stop, speed trigger, tactical style extended combat safety, checkered Cocobolo grips, high checkered front strap, two 8 shot mags.

	100%	98%	95%	90%	80%	70%	60%	
MSR $2,650	$2,350	$2,075	$1,825	$1,575	$1,325	$1,100	$900	

Add $260 for bead blast chrome finish.

ULTIMATE TACTICAL CARRY – .45 ACP cal., 5 in. barrel with stainless match bushing, three stainless steel 8 shot mags., steel NM frame and slide, lowered and flared ejection port, tuned extractor, deluxe hammer and sear, aluminum match trigger, LBC deluxe fixed combat rear sight with Tritium inserts, dovetail front sight with Tritium insert, deluxe special slim line grips, combat extended safety, checkered slide stop, blued finish, deluxe special slim line grips.

	100%	98%	95%	90%	80%	70%	60%	
MSR $2,215	$1,895	$1,595	$1,275	$1,075	$950	$800	$725	

THUNDER RANCH SPECIAL – .45 ACP cal., 5 in. stainless barrel, steel slide with front and rear serrations, beavertail grip safety with pad, high checkered front strap, LBC deluxe fixed combat rear and dovetail front sights with Tritium inserts, lowered and flared ejection port, extended ejector, combat extended safety, aluminum match trigger, deluxe Commander hammer and sear, beveled magwell, deluxe special slim line grips with Thunder Ranch logo, three stainless steel 7 shot mags., special Thunder Ranch logo engraved on slide, special serial numbers with "TR" prefix, blued finish.

	100%	98%	95%	90%	80%	70%	60%	
MSR $2,290	$1,950	$1,625	$1,300	$1,075	$950	$800	$725	

MSR	100%	98%	95%	90%	80%	70%	60%	Last MSR

SHOOTING USA CUSTOM PISTOL – .45 ACP cal., similar to Premier II 5 in. model, except also features tactical extended safety, a special serial number prefix with "S USA" and the number, the famous Shooting USA logo engraved on the right side of the slide, blued finish, two 8 shot stainless steel mags., and a special DVD produced by Shooting USA.

| MSR $2,180 | $1,875 | $1,575 | $1,275 | $1,075 | $950 | $800 | $725 | |

CUSTOM CENTENNIAL MODEL 1911 PISTOL – .45 ACP cal., made to commemorate the 100th anniversary year of "Old Ironsides", similar to Premier II 5 in. model, except features rear serrated slide with the model name engraved on the slide, ivory grips, deluxe charcoal blue finish, extended tactical safety, three 8 shot mags., special presentation box. Disc. 2015.

| | $3,875 | $3,450 | $2,975 | $2,450 | $2,000 | $1,675 | $1,425 | *$4,350* |

1911 S.R.P. (SWIFT RESPONSE PISTOL) – .45 ACP cal., NM steel frame and slide with front and rear serrations, 4 1/4 (Comanche Model) or 5 in. barrel with stainless match bushing, deluxe fixed combat sight, dovetail front sight, checkered slide stop, speed trigger, deluxe Commander hammer, beavertail grip safety with pad, tactical style ambi safety, Tritium night sights installed front and rear, Deburred for tactical carry, DuPont S coating on complete pistol, three 8 shot mags., checkered Cocobolo grips, special wooden presentation box with glass lid.

| MSR $2,840 | $2,500 | $2,175 | $1,900 | $1,625 | $1,350 | $1,100 | $900 | |

MONOLITH – .38 Super or .45 ACP cal., NM steel Monolith frame, Monolith flat bottom double serrated slide, 5 in. barrel with stainless match bushing, low mount LBC adj. sight with hidden rear leaf, Baer dovetail front sight, checkered slide stop, speed trigger, deluxe Commander hammer, beavertail grip safety with pad, extended ambi safety, two 8 shot mags., checkered Cocobolo grips, blued finish, extra long dust cover.

| MSR $2,320 | $2,050 | $1,800 | $1,500 | $1,225 | $1,025 | $875 | $775 | |

Add $420 for supported chamber .38 Super.

* ***Monolith Heavyweight*** – .38 Super or .45 ACP cal., similar to Monolith, except has a heavier frame.

| MSR $2,370 | $2,075 | $1,825 | $1,500 | $1,250 | $1,050 | $895 | $795 | |

Add $310 for supported chamber .38 Super.

MONOLITH COMANCHE – .45 ACP cal., NM steel Monolith frame, Monolith flat bottom double serrated slide, 4 1/4 in. barrel with stainless match bushing, Tritium night sights front and rear and deluxe fixed rear sight, checkered slide stop, speed trigger, deluxe Commander hammer, beavertail grip safety with pad, extended ambi safety, two 8 shot mags., checkered Cocobolo grips, blued finish, extra long dust cover, also includes front and rear Tritium night sights and deluxe fixed rear sight, edges are rounded for tactical carry.

| MSR $2,380 | $2,100 | $1,825 | $1,525 | $1,250 | $1,050 | $895 | $795 | |

* ***Monolith Comanche Heavyweight*** – .45 ACP cal., similar to Monolith Comanche, except dust cover is slightly thicker to add weight and is flat on the bottom.

| MSR $2,415 | $2,125 | $1,850 | $1,525 | $1,250 | $1,050 | $895 | $795 | |

STINGER MODEL – .45 ACP cal., NM Stinger frame, NM Commanche length slide with rear serrations, slide fitted to frame, 4 1/4 in. barrel with stainless bushing, low mount combat fixed rear sight, dovetail front sight, checkered slide stop, speed trigger, deluxe Commander hammer, beavertail grip safety with pad, extended ambi safety, two 7 shot mags., checkered Cocobolo grips, blued finish.

| MSR $2,240 | $1,925 | $1,600 | $1,275 | $1,075 | $950 | $800 | $725 | |

* ***Stinger Model Stainless*** – .45 ACP cal., similar to Stinger Model, except features stainless steel frame and slide.

| MSR $2,310 | $2,050 | $1,800 | $1,500 | $1,225 | $1,025 | $875 | $775 | |

.38 SUPER STINGER – .38 Super cal., NM Stinger frame, NM Commanche length slide with rear serrations only, 4 1/4 in. barrel with supported chamber and stainless steel bushing, deluxe fixed combat rear sight with night sight, dovetail ramp type with night sight, checkered slide stop, speed trigger, deluxe Commander hammer, beavertail grip safety with pad, tactical ambi safety, three 8 shot mags. with pads, checkered Cocobolo grips, blue finish or optional chrome or DuPont S finish. New 2013.

| MSR $2,840 | $2,500 | $2,175 | $1,900 | $1,625 | $1,350 | $1,100 | $900 | |

GT MONOLITH STINGER – .45 ACP or .38 Super cal., Officer size frame, 4 1/4 in. slide (Comanche length), extra long dust cover matches length of slide, Rolo night sights, includes three mags., checkered Cocobolo grips, blue (standard) or chrome (optional) finish. New 2015.

| MSR $2,915 | $2,550 | $2,275 | $1,975 | $1,750 | $1,500 | $1,250 | $1,000 | |

Add $175 for .38 Super cal. Add $300 for chrome finish.

* ***GT Monolith Stinger Heavyweight*** – .45 ACP or .38 Super cal., similar to GT Monolith Stinger, except has extra heavy dust cover with a flat bottom. New 2015.

| MSR $3,015 | $2,625 | $2,325 | $2,000 | $1,775 | $1,525 | $1,250 | $1,000 | |

Add $175 for .38 Super cal.

BOSS – .45 ACP cal., similar to the Premier II series, except features blued slide, extended combat safety, rear cocking serrations on the slide, fiber optic front sight, chromed complete lower, special tactical package.

| MSR $2,560 | $2,275 | $2,025 | $1,775 | $1,525 | $1,275 | $1,075 | $875 | |

MSR	100%	98%	95%	90%	80%	70%	60%	Last MSR

HEMI 572 – .45 ACP cal., inspired by Chrysler's fast and fearsome 1970 Hemi Cuda, double serrated slide, fiber optic front sight with green insert, Hex head grip screws, special tactical package with ambi safety, VZ black recon grips, complete hard chrome finish on all major components, DuPont S coating on slide stop, mag. catch and mag. catch lock, two 8 shot mags. New 2013.

MSR $2,690	$2,400	$2,100	$1,850	$1,600	$1,325	$1,100	$900

BLACK BAER – 9mm Para. cal., SA, steel NM frame and slide, NM supported barrel with stainless bushing, two 9 shot mags., tuned extractor, extended ejector, deluxe hammer and sear, Baer deluxe fixed rear combat night sight, dovetail front sights, black recon grips, tactical extended combat safety, rear serrated slide, checkered slide stop, DuPont S coating on entire pistol. New 2016.

MSR $3,159	$2,725	$2,400	$2,050	$1,800	$1,525	$1,250	$1,000

CONCEPT I/CONCEPT II – .45 ACP cal., NM steel frame and slide, 5 in. barrel with stainless bushing, slide fitted to frame, double serrated slide, LBC adj. deluxe low mount rear sight with hidden leaf, dovetail front sight, or deluxe fixed combat sight (Concept II), checkered slide stop, fitted speed trigger with action job, deluxe Commander hammer, beavertail grip safety with pad, extended ambi safety, two 8 shot mags., checkered Cocobolo grips, blued finish.

MSR $2,020	$1,775	$1,595	$1,350	$1,150	$975	$825	$700

* **Concept III/Concept IV** – .45 ACP cal., similar to Concept I/Concept II, except has stainless steel frame and blued steel slide, and checkered front strap.

MSR $2,260	$1,925	$1,600	$1,300	$1,075	$950	$800	$725

* **Concept V** – .45 ACP cal., similar to Concept I, except both frame and slide are stainless steel, available with 5 or 6 in. barrel, LBC adj. rear sight, checkered front strap.

MSR $2,240	$1,900	$1,595	$1,300	$1,075	$950	$800	$725

Add $105 for 6 in. barrel.

* **Concept VI** – .45 ACP cal., similar to Concept V, except has 5 in. barrel, Baer deluxe fixed combat rear sight.

MSR $2,290	$1,950	$1,625	$1,300	$1,075	$950	$800	$725

* **Concept VII** – .45 ACP cal., similar to Concept I, except has Commanche size 4 1/4 in. barrel, all blued steel, Baer deluxe fixed combat rear sight, and checkered front strap.

MSR $2,230	$1,895	$1,595	$1,275	$1,075	$950	$800	$725

* **Concept VIII** – .45 ACP cal., similar to Concept I, except has Commanche size 4 1/4 in. barrel, all stainless steel, Baer deluxe fixed combat rear sight, and checkered front strap.

MSR $2,280	$1,950	$1,625	$1,300	$1,075	$950	$800	$725

LIMITED EDITION LES BAER PRESENTATION GRADE 1911 – .45 ACP cal., similar to Premier II, except also features detailed hand chiseled engraving, special charcoal blueing on all polished surfaces, rich nitre blue is used on pins, thumb safety, slide stop, grip screws, mag catch lock and hammer, real ivory grips, "LBC" engraving on top of the slide is inlaid with gold, optional to add name of the recipient engraved on the slide with the legend "To (name) by Les Baer", includes special presentation box.

MSR $7,140	$6,600	$5,950	$5,500	$4,750	$4,000	$3,250	$2,500

Add $220 for name engraving on slide.

CUSTOM 25TH ANNIVERSARY SPECIAL COLLECTORS MODEL – .45 ACP cal., similar to Premier II, except also includes hand engraving on both sides of the slide and frame, Les Baer's actual signature and the legend "25th Anniversary" have been engraved, then inlaid with white gold on the top of the slide, rich charcoal blue finish, real ivory grips, also includes a special presentation box. Limited mfg. disc. 2015.

	$7,250	$6,400	$5,800	$5,000	$4,250	$3,500	$2,700	$7,940

RIFLES: BOLT ACTION

CUSTOM TACTICAL VARMINT CLASSIC – .243 Win., .260 Rem., .300 Win. Mag. (new 2011) or .308 Win. cal., 24 in. match grade barrel, Still Tac 30 action and thick lug, Timney match trigger, front and back of action are glass bedded and lug is bedded into Bell & Carlson precision varmint stock, fitted Wyatts precision floorplate with box mag., Picatinny one piece rail, DuPont S coated finish. Mfg. 2010-2011.

	$3,250	$2,850	$2,450	$2,000	$1,650	$1,375	$1,125	$3,410

Add $150 for .300 Win. Mag. cal. with Harris bipod and muzzle brake.

CUSTOM TACTICAL/TACTICAL RECON – .243 Win., .260 Rem., .308 Win., .338 Lapua, 6.5x284 Norma, or .300 Win. Mag. cal., 24, 26, or 27 in. match grade barrel with or w/o muzzle brake, Still Tac 30 action and thick lug, Timney match trigger, front and back of action are glass bedded and lug is bedded into Bell & Carlson adj. stock, fitted Wyatts precision floorplate with box mag., Picatinny one piece rail, DuPont S coated finish, Harris bipod. Limited mfg. 2011 only.

	$3,300	$2,950	$2,500	$2,075	$1,695	$1,375	$1,125	$3,560

Add $200 for .300 Win. Mag. with enforcer muzzle brake or $330 for .338 Lapua with enforcer muzzle brake.

MSR	100%	98%	95%	90%	80%	70%	60%	Last MSR

RIFLES: SEMI-AUTO

CUSTOM ULTIMATE AR MODEL – .204 Ruger (new 2004), .223 Rem., or 6.5 Grendel (mfg. 2007-2009) cal., 18-24 in. stainless steel barrel, Picatinny flat-top rail, individual rifles are custom built with no expense spared, everything made in-house ensuring top quality and tolerances, all models are guaranteed to shoot 1/2-3/4 MOA groups, various configurations include Varmint Model (disc.), Super Varmint Model, Super Match Model (new 2002), M4 Flat-Top Model, Thunder Ranch (disc. 2010), CMP Competion, and IPSC Action Model. New 2001.

MSR $2,590	$2,375	$2,050	$1,800	$1,575	$1,350	$1,125	$900	

Add $50 for Super Varmint model in .223 Rem. or $280 in .204 Ruger cal. Add $950 with scope package.
Add $150 for Super Match model in .223 Rem. or $370 in .204 Ruger cal. Add $1,359 with scope package.
Add $300 for IPSC action model or $1,350 with scope package.
Add $349 for Thunder Ranch rifle (disc. 2010). Add $849 for CMP competition rifle (disc.).
Add $245 for Super Varmint model (.204 Ruger cal., disc.) or $210 for 6.5 Grendel cal. with M4 style barrel (disc.).

CUSTOM NRA MATCH RIFLE – .223 Rem. cal., 30 in. bench rest stainless steel barrel, 30 shot mag., forged upper and lower receivers, Picatinny flat-top rail, LBC chromed bolt, extracter, and National Match carrier, Geissele two-stage trigger, free float handguard with locking ring, custom grip with extra material under the trigger guard, Dupont S coating on upper, lower, and small parts, available with or without sights package.

MSR $2,950	$2,675	$2,300	$1,995	$1,750	$1,500	$1,250	$1,000	

Add $1,040 for sights package.

CUSTOM SPECIAL TACTICAL RIFLE – .223 Rem., 16 in. stainless steel fluted bench rest barrel, two 20 shot mags., Geissele non-adj. two-stage trigger, free float handguard with mounted sling stud, forged upper and lower receivers, Picatinny style flat-top rail, extractor, unique sighting system, includes nylon weather proof sling and lockable front sling swivel, detachable carry handle, Dupont S coating, 7 lbs. 6 oz. New 2011.

MSR $2,720	$2,475	$2,100	$1,875	$1,625	$1,425	$1,150	$925	

.264 LBC-AR M4 FLATTOP – .264 LBC-AR cal., 16 in. medium weight barrel, two 14 shot mags., 9 in. four-way handguard with locking ring and integral Picatinny rail system, VersaPod installed, free float handguard, fixed stock, Dupont S coating, black finish, includes soft rifle case. New 2010.

MSR $2,790	$2,525	$2,125	$1,895	$1,625	$1,425	$1,150	$925	

.264 LBC-AR SUPER MATCH – .264 LBC-AR cal., stainless steel barrel, fixed stock, black finish, 14 shot mag., features similar to Super Match Model in .223 cal. New 2010.

MSR $2,840	$2,575	$2,150	$1,900	$1,625	$1,425	$1,150	$925	

.264 LBC-AR SUPER VARMINT – .264 LBC-AR cal., stainless steel bench rest barrel, two 14 shot mags., fixed stock, black finish, features similar to Super Varmint model in .223 cal. New 2010.

MSR $2,640	$2,425	$2,075	$1,850	$1,600	$1,400	$1,125	$895	

6x45 ULTIMATE AR – 6x45mm cal., 18-24 in. stainless steel barrel, available in Super Varmint, Super Match, and M4 Flat-top configurations, black finish, fixed stock, similar to Ultimate AR in .223 configuration. New 2010.

MSR $2,640	$2,425	$2,075	$1,850	$1,600	$1,400	$1,125	$895	

Add $100 for Super Match model.

POLICE SPECIAL – .223 Rem., .264 LBC-AR (disc.), or 6x45mm (disc.) cal., 16 in. precision button rifled steel barrel, 14 or 30 shot mag., removable carry handle with rear sight, Picatinny flat-top upper rail, National Match chromed carrier, flip up front sight, six position ATI collapsible stock with adj. cheekpiece and grip, Picatinny four-way handguard, A2 flash hider, Timney match trigger group, lockable sling swivel mounted on stud on four-way handguard, includes two mags. Mfg. 2010-2014.

	$1,625	$1,425	$1,150	$1,000	$875	$750	$625	*$1,790*

.308 LBC ULTIMATE MATCH/SNIPER – .308 Win. cal., 18 or 20 in. stainless steel barrel with precision cut rifling, matte black finish, 20 shot mag., machined upper and lower, no forward assist, Picatinny flat-top rail, steel gas block, free float handguard with lock ring, two-stage trigger group, Dupont S coating on barrel, Harris bipod, fixed or adj. Magpul stock, with or w/o enforcer muzzle brake, available in Match or Sniper configuration. New 2011.

MSR $3,640	$3,275	$2,825	$2,500	$2,200	$1,950	$1,725	$1,500	

Add $30 for Match model with PRS Magpul stock or $300 for Sniper model with adj. stock and enforcer muzzle brake.

.308 ULTIMATE MONOLITH SWAT MODEL – .308 Win. cal., 18 or 24 in. stainless steel barrel with precision cut rifling, matte black finish, 20 shot mag., similar to .308 Ultimate Match/Sniper, except has integrated Mil-Std 1913 Picatinny rail system, Magpul PRS adj. stock, Versa pod and adapter, integral trigger guard is bowed on bottom so shooter can wear gloves. New 2011.

MSR $4,390	$3,950	$3,600	$3,100	$2,775	$2,475	$2,250	$1,825	

MSR	100%	98%	95%	90%	80%	70%	60%	*Last MSR*

LEWIS MACHINE & TOOL COMPANY (LMT)

Current tactical rifle and accessories manufacturer established in 1980, and located in Milan, IL.

CARBINES/RIFLES: SEMI-AUTO

LMT manufactures AR-15 style rifles and carbines.

CQB MRP DEFENDER MODEL 16 (CQB16) – 5.56 NATO cal., GIO, low profile gas block, 16 in. chrome lined barrel with A2 birdcage compensator, 30 shot mag., standard trigger, Defender lower with SOPMOD stock, tactical charging handle assembly, includes sling, heavy duty push button swivels, manual, tactical adj. front and rear sights, torque wrench/driver, and three rail panels, 6.8 lbs.

| MSR $2,100 | $1,875 | $1,550 | $1,350 | $1,225 | $975 | $800 | $625 | |

CQB MRP DEFENDER 6.8 (CQB16 6.8) – 6.8 SPC cal., similar to CQB MRP Defender Model 16, except has 25 shot mag. New 2010.

| MSR $2,198 | $1,975 | $1,725 | $1,475 | $1,350 | $1,085 | $895 | $695 | |

CQB MRP DEFENDER PISTON 16 (CQBPS16) – 5.56 NATO cal., GPO, 16 in. barrel, tactical charging handle assembly, Defender lower with SOPMOD buttstock, 30 shot mag., standard trigger group, includes sling, tactical front and rear sights, torque wrench/driver, and three rail panels. New 2010.

| MSR $2,351 | $2,100 | $1,750 | $1,500 | $1,375 | $1,100 | $900 | $700 | |

CQB MRP DEFENDER PISTON 16 (CQBPS68) – 6.8 SPC cal., GPO, similar to CQBPS16, except has piston 25 shot mag. New 2014.

| MSR $2,508 | $2,250 | $1,975 | $1,695 | $1,550 | $1,250 | $1,025 | $795 | |

CQB MRP MODEL 16 (CQB16300) – .300 Whisper cal., GIO, 16 in. chrome lined barrel, tactical charging handle, Defender lower with SOPMOD buttstock and standard trigger group, adj. rear sight, tactical front sight, 30 shot mag., includes torque wrench, 3 rail panels, and sling.

| MSR $2,100 | $1,875 | $1,550 | $1,350 | $1,225 | $975 | $800 | $625 | |

CQBODGB – 5.56 NATO cal., GIO, 16 in. heavy barrel with A2 birdcage compensator, 30 shot mag., low profile gas block, CQB MRP upper, tactical charging handle, tactical sights, three rail panels, Defender lower with SOPMOD buttstock, Olive Drab Green finish, includes sling, 6.8 lbs.

| MSR $2,100 | $1,875 | $1,550 | $1,350 | $1,225 | $975 | $800 | $625 | |

CQBPU16 – 5.56 NATO cal., GPO, 16 in. chrome lined barrel, charging handle, H2 buffer, includes torque wrench and 3 rail panels. Disc. 2013.

| | $1,395 | $1,225 | $1,050 | $950 | $775 | $625 | $500 | *$1,558* |

CMP556 – 5.56 NATO cal., GIO, 20 in. ultra cut rifled stainless steel barrel, 30 shot mag., standard flat-top upper receiver, charging handle, Defender lower with fixed rifle length buttstock and standard trigger group, includes sling.

| MSR $2,100 | $1,875 | $1,550 | $1,350 | $1,225 | $975 | $800 | $625 | |

COMPLIANT CQB MRP DEFENDER MODEL 16 (CompCQB16) – 5.56 NATO cal., GIO, 16 in. chrome lined target style barrel, tactical charging handle, Defender lower receiver with fixed SOPMOD buttstock and standard trigger group, tactical sights, 10 shot mag., has three rail panels, push button swivel, and includes sling.

| MSR $2,100 | $1,875 | $1,550 | $1,350 | $1,225 | $975 | $800 | $625 | |

COMPLIANT DEFENDER STANDARD MODEL 16 (COMP16) – 5.56 NATO cal., GIO, 16 in. chrome lined target style barrel, standard flat-top upper receiver, 10 shot mag., tactical charging handle assembly, Defender lower with fixed SOPMOD buttstock, standard trigger group, includes sling, tactical adj. rear sight, and heavy duty push button swivel.

| MSR $1,685 | $1,500 | $1,250 | $1,075 | $975 | $825 | $675 | $550 | |

DEFENDER STANDARD MODEL 16 (STD16) – 5.56 NATO cal., GIO, 16 in. chrome lined barrel, flat-top upper receiver, tactical charging handle assembly, standard trigger and bolt, Defender lower with SOPMOD buttstock, tactical adj. rear sight, 5.9 - 6.2 lbs.

| MSR $1,594 | $1,425 | $1,225 | $1,075 | $950 | $775 | $650 | $500 | |

DEFENDER STANDARD PATROL MODEL 16 (SPM16) – 5.56 NATO cal., GIO, similar to Defender Standard Model 16, except has Generation 2 collapsing buttstock. New 2010.

| MSR $1,371 | $1,225 | $1,075 | $900 | $800 | $675 | $550 | $495 | |

LM8MRP/LM8MRPSS – 5.56 NATO cal., GIO, 16 in. chrome lined or stainless steel barrel, 30 shot mag., tactical charging handle, Defender lower receiver with SOPMOD buttstock and standard trigger group, tactical sights, four rail segments, rubberized grip panels, includes sling. New 2012.

| MSR $2,254 | $2,025 | $1,750 | $1,450 | $1,300 | $1,050 | $875 | $725 | |

Add $133 for 16 in. stainless steel barrel (LM8MRPSS).

MSR	100%	98%	95%	90%	80%	70%	60%	Last MSR

LM8MRPSC (SLK8) – 5.56 NATO cal., GIO, 16 or 20 in. ultra match stainless steel barrel, 30 shot mag., two stage trigger, no sights, four rail segments, six rubberized grip panels, heavy duty push-button swivels, Long Slick upper receiver with SOPMOD 6-position adj. stock, tactical charging handle with Ergo Battle Grip, two position selector safety, Type III hardcoat anodized finish, 7 lbs. 2 oz. New 2014.

MSR $2,405	$2,050	$1,800	$1,500	$1,300	$1,075	$935	$795

LM8MWSLTFDE – .308 Win. cal., GIO, 16 in. chrome lined barrel with A2 birdcage compensator, 20 shot mag., low profile gas block, tactical charging handle, two-stage trigger, tactical sights, ambi selector and mag release, four rail segments, Slick upper receiver, Defender lower with SOPMOD buttstock, Flat Dark Earth finish, 5 QD sling swivel attachment points, includes sling, 9.3 lbs. New 2015.

MSR $3,349	$3,015	$2,650	$2,200	$1,875	$1,550	$1.300	$1,125

LM8MWS SLICK RECEIVER RIFLE – .308 Win. cal., GIO, 16 in. chrome lined barrel or 16 in. stainless steel barrel with matte blackened finish, 20 shot mag., monolithic rail platform, Defender lower with SOPMOD stock, rubberized grip panels, two stage trigger, includes sling, manual, tactical front and rear sights, torque wrench/driver, and four rail panels. New 2010.

MSR $3,149	$2,825	$2,475	$2,125	$1,850	$1,525	$1,250	$975

Add $563 for matte black stainless steel barrel (LM8MWSF).

LM308 COMP16 – .308 Win. cal., GIO, 16 in. crowned target barrel, 10 shot mag., tactical charging handle, two stage match trigger, ambi selector, tactical sights, SOPMOD buttstock, includes 3 rail panels. New 2012.

MSR $3,003	$2,700	$2,350	$2,000	$1,750	$1,450	$1,175	$975

LM8308SS SHARPSHOOTER WEAPON SYSTEM – .308 Win. cal., GIO, 16 in. stainless steel matte black barrel, tactical charging handle, SOPMOD buttstock, flip up sights, includes eight 20 shot magazines, cleaning kit, Harris bipod and pelican case, Flat Dark Earth furniture. New 2012.

MSR $5,198	$4,675	$4,200	$3,600	$3,250	2,800	$2,400	$2,000

LM308MWSE MODULAR WEAPON SYSTEM – .308 Win. cal., GIO, 16 in. chrome lined barrel, two stage match trigger, SOPMOD buttstock, tactical sights, 20 shot mag., tactical charging handle, includes 3 rail panels, sling. New 2012.

MSR $3,003	$2,700	$2,350	$2,000	$1,750	$1,450	$1,175	$975

* **LM308MWSF/MWSK Modular Weapon System Stainless** – .308 Win. cal., similar to Modular Weapon System (LM308MWSE), except features 16 or 20 in. stainless steel barrel with tactically flat matte blackened finish. New 2012.

MSR $3,566	$3,200	$2,800	$2,400	$2,175	$1,750	$1,450	$1,125

LIBERTY ARMS INTERNATIONAL LLC

Previous importer and manufacturer located in Victoria, TX until circa 2015. Previously located in Albion, NY until 2010.

RIFLES: SEMI-AUTO

Liberty Arms assembled an AK-47 design carbine manufactured from U.S. milled or stamped receivers, U.S. chrome lined barrels, and Bulgarian manufactured part kits. MSRs were $900 for the milled receiver, and $750 for the stamped receiver. Additionally, the company imported a variety of European firearms and ammunition.

LIBERTY ARMS WORKS, INC.

Previous manufacturer located in West Chester, PA circa 1991-1996.

PISTOLS: SEMI-AUTO

L.A.W. ENFORCER – .22 LR, 9mm Para., 10mm, .40 S&W (new 1994), or .45 ACP cal., patterned after the Ingram MAC 10, SA, 6 1/4 in. threaded barrel, closed bolt operation, manual safety, 10 (C/B 1994) or 30* shot mag., 5 lbs. 1 oz. Mfg. 1991-96.

	$575	$500	$450	$415	$385	$335	$295	$545

LITHGOW ARMS

Current civilian and military rifle manufacturer located in Lithgow, Australia. No U.S. importation.

RIFLES: SEMI-AUTO

LA 101 CROSSOVER – .17 HMR, .22 LR, or .22 WMR cal., cold hammer forged barrel, 5 or 10 shot removable single stack mag., integrated trigger guard, single stage trigger, matte Armor Black or Titanium Cerakote finished polymer or timber stock, walnut brown laminate, or Turkish walnut stock, rubber recoil pad, adj. LOP, two segments of Weaver accessory rails, right or left-hand action.

Please contact the manufacturer directly for pricing and availability for this model.

MSR		100%	98%	95%	90%	80%	70%	60%	Last MSR

LA 102 CROSSOVER – .223 Rem., .243 Win., or .308 Win. cal., cold hammer forged threaded barrel, 3 or 4 shot removable single stack box mag., single stage trigger, reinforced polymer, walnut brown laminate, or Turkish walnut stock, rubber recoil pad, adj. LOP, three position bolt shroud mounted safety with indicator, three sling studs, steel receiver with Picatinny rail, Cerakote Titanium H series treated barrel and receiver.

Please contact the company directly for pricing and availability for this model.

LJUNGMAN

Previously manufactured by Carl Gustaf, located in Eskilstuna, Sweden.

RIFLES: SEMI-AUTO

AG 42 – 6.5x55mm Swedish cal., 10 shot mag., wood stock, tangent rear and hooded front, bayonet lug, designed in 1941.

		$850	$700	$600	$495	$450	$400	$365	

This was the first mass produced, direct gas operated rifle. This weapon was also used by the Egyptian armed forces and was known as the Hakim, and chambered in 8x57mm Mauser.

LOKI WEAPON SYSTEMS, INC.

Previous manufacturer and distributor circa 2009-2012 and located in Coalgate, OK.

Loki Weapon Systems manufactured AR-15 style tactical rifles and 1911 style pistols. Loki was also the U.S. distributor until 2012 for A.M.S.D., located in Geneva, Switzerland.

CARBINES/RIFLES: SEMI-AUTO

Other calibers were available by request. Loki offered a limited lifetime warranty on all rifles and carbines.

FENRIR – 5.56 NATO, .300 Whisper, .458 SOCOM, 6.5mm Grendel, 6.8 SPC, or 6.8 Grendel cal., 16 in. barrel, 40 shot mag., mid length gas operating system, M4 ramps and extension, machined upper and lower, Fail Zero coated bolt carrier group, 12 in. eight sided forend with full length Picatinny rail, YHM Phantom flash hider, Ergo F93 eight position stock, hard case, approx. 8 lbs. Mfg. 2009-2011.

		$1,450	$1,295	$1,125	$900	$800	$700	$600	$1,575

Subtract $125 for ambidextrous safety selector and 15 in. eight sided forend.

HUNTING RIFLE – .223 Rem./5.56 NATO (.223 Wylde chamber) cal., 20 in. varmint barrel, eight sided forend with three Picatinny rails, single stage trigger, 10 shot mag., fixed stock with Ergo grip, includes hard case. Mfg. mid-2010-2011.

		$1,475	$1,295	$1,125	$900	$800	$700	$600	$1,625

PRECISION SNIPER TACTICAL RIFLE – .223 Rem./5.56 NATO (.223 Wylde chamber) cal., M4 upper and lower, 18 in. fluted stainless steel barrel, three port compensator, eight sided forend with full length Picatinny rail, ambidextrous safety, two-stage trigger, 30 shot mag., F93 Ergo stock and grip, includes hard case. Disc. 2011.

		$1,625	$1,475	$1,295	$1,125	$900	$800	$700	$1,795

LWSF 3G COMPETITION – 5.56 NATO cal., 18 in. double fluted stainless steel barrel, 15 in. vented carbon fiber forend, Vltor A2 fixed stock, adj. gas block, lightened buffer system and carrier, standard Mil-Spec charging handle, hardcoat anodized Teflon coated black finish, two-stage trigger, integrated CQB Magwell grip with XL magwell and Ergo pistol grip, Nordic Corvette compensator, approx. 6 1/2 lbs. Mfg. 2012.

		$1,675	$1,450	$1,225	$1,050	$900	$750	$675	$1,850

LWSF DMR (DESIGNATED MARKSMAN) – .223 Rem./5.56 NATO (.223 Wylde chamber) cal., 20 in. fluted stainless steel SDMR contoured barrel with Rolling Thunder compensator, standard Mil-Spec charging handle, A2 stock with Magpul MOE grip, hardcoat anodized Teflon coated black finish, multiple picatinny rails, LOKI 14.5 handguard, pinned Lo Pro gas block, M4 feed ramps, 7.8 lbs. Mfg. 2012.

		$1,495	$1,300	$1,100	$900	$700	$600	$550	$1,645

LWSF MAGPUL MOE – .264 LBC, .300 Blackout, or 5.56 NATO cal., 16.1 in. chrome moly vanadium alloy barrel, A2 birdcage flash hider, Magpul MOE stock with pistol grip, mid-length forend and low profile gas block or YHM flip sight tower gas block, integrated Picatinny rail, oversized trigger guard, hardcoat anodized Teflon coated finish, forward assist and dust cover, polished M4 feed ramps, fail zero full-auto bolt carrier, nickel-boron coated charging handle and fire control group, approx. 6 1/2 lbs. Mfg. 2012 only.

		$1,195	$1,000	$850	$725	$600	$500	$450	$1,349

LWSF PATROL – .264 LBC, .300 AAC Blackout, or 5.56 NATO cal., 16 (.300 BLK cal.), 18 (.264 LBC) or 18 in. double fluted stainless steel barrel, mid-length gas block, phantom flash hider, Vltor EMOD retractable stock with Magpul MOE grip, full length Picatinny rail, free floating forend, integrated winter trigger guard, creep-adj. polished trigger, M4 feed ramps, forward assist and dust cover, black hardcoat anodized finish, also available with optional tactical comp or Battlecomp, 7 1/2 lbs. Mfg. 2012.

		$1,275	$1,075	$975	$775	$625	$525	$475	$1,479

MSR	100%	98%	95%	90%	80%	70%	60%	Last MSR

LWSF STD – .300 AAC Blackout, 6.5mm Grendel, or 5.56 NATO cal., 16.1 in. chrome moly vanadium alloy barrel, A2 birdcage flash hider, Magpul MOE stock, low profile gas block with rail, black hardcoat anodized finish, mid-length free floating forend, standard M4 pistol grip, oversized trigger guard, integrated CQB Magwell grip with XL magwell, fail zero full-auto rated bolt carrier, polished M4 feed ramps, forward assist and dust cover, optional YHM flip sight tower gas block, Vltor EMOD or Ergo F93 stock, 6.7 lbs. Mfg. 2012 only.

	$1,195	$1,000	$850	$725	$600	$500	$450	$1,349

LWSF TACTICAL – .300 AAC Blackout or 5.56 NATO cal., 16 in. Nitride treated M4 barrel, 14 1/2 in. modular forend, A2 birdcage flash hider, Vltor EMOD 6-position retractable stock with Magpul MOE grip, black hardcoat anodized Teflon coated finish, NiB-X coated full-auto rated bolt carrier, integrated winter trigger guard, CQB Magwell grip with XL magwell, creep-adj. polished trigger, optional 9 in. top rail and three 3 in. rails or Troy TRX Extreme handguard, standard Mil-Spec charging handle, forward assist and M4 feed ramps. Mfg. 2012 only.

	$1,300	$1,100	$1,000	$800	$650	$550	$500	$1,525

LWS M4 MOE – 5.56 NATO cal., 16 in. nitride treated barrel, M4 extension, A2 birdcage flash hider, 6-position Magpul MOE stock with pistol grip and trigger guard, standard A2 sight post low profile gas block with integrated rail or YHM gas block with integrated flip up front sight, Mil-Spec BCG nickel boron bolt carrier, mid-length handguard, black hardcoat anodized Teflon coated finish, forward assist and dust cover, creep-adj. hand stoned trigger, standard Mil-Spec charging handle. Mfg. 2012 only.

	$895	$825	$750	$650	$550	$450	$350	$999

LWS M4 PATROL – .300 BLK or 5.56 NATO cal., 16 in. nitride treated barrel, M4 extension, A2 birdcage flash hider, choice of 6-position Magpul MOE stock with pistol grip and trigger guard, EMOD or F93 collapsible stock and Ergo pistol grip, Mil-Spec BCG nickel boron bolt carrier, Loki 12 in. rifle length handguard, black hardcoat anodized Teflon coated finish, forward assist and dust cover, creep-adj. hand stoned trigger, standard Mil-Spec charging handle, optional 12 in. top Picatinny rail and three 3 in. side and bottom rails. Mfg. 2012 only.

	$1,050	$925	$825	$700	$600	$500	$400	$1,199

LWS M4 STD – .300 BLK or 5.56 NATO cal., 16 in. nitride treated barrel, M4 extension, 6-position Magpul MOE stock with M4 pistol grip and trigger guard, black, Flat Dark Earth, or OD Green hardcoat anodized Teflon coated finish, M4 flat-top upper, 30 shot PMAG, creep-adj. hand stoned single stage trigger, standard Mil-Spec charging handle, low profile gas block with integrated rail, mid-length handguard, includes case. Mfg. 2012 only.

	$925	$850	$775	$675	$575	$475	$375	$1,049

LWS M4 TACTICAL – .300 BLK or 5.56 NATO cal., 16 in. Nitride treated M4 barrel, 14 1/2 in. free floating forend, A2 birdcage flash hider, choice of 6-position Magpul MOE, EMOD, or F93 stock with Ergo pistol grip, black hardcoat anodized Teflon coated finish, standard Mil-Spec charging handle, forward assist and dust cover, mid-length gas system, optional 9 in. Picatinny rail, three 3 in. side and bottom rails, hand stoned trigger, XL modular handguard. Mfg. 2012 only.

	$1,075	$925	$825	$700	$600	$500	$400	$1,225

PISTOLS: SEMI-AUTO

Loki manufactured custom built 1911 style pistols in .45 ACP cal. Base price began at $1,800 and went up according to options and accessories.

LONE STAR ARMAMENT, INC.

Previous pistol manufacturer located in Stephenville, TX circa 1970-2004. During 2003, Lone Star Armament was absorbed by STI, located in Georgetown, TX.

PISTOLS: SEMI-AUTO

Lone Star Armament manufactured a lineup of M1911 style pistols. Models included: Ranger Match ($1,595 last MSR), Lawman Match ($1,595 last MSR), Lawman Series ($1,475 last MSR), Ranger Series ($1,475 last MSR), and the Guardian Series ($895 last MSR).

LONE STAR TACTICAL SUPPLY

Previous firearms and current accessories manufacturer located in Tomball, TX.

In addition to manufacturing semi-auto pistols, rifles, and shotguns, Lone Star is also a dealer for Saiga rifles, and offers many shooting accessories.

PISTOLS: SEMI-AUTO

COMPETITION 9 – 9mm Para. cal., SFO, SA, TimberWolf frame, choice of 2 quick change grips, rounded trigger guard, extended beaver tail, round mag. catch, improved checkering, extended slide lock and slide stop, two Glock 17 shot mags., forged stainless steel slides, front and rear cocking serrations, bull nose, beveled rails, lowered ejection port, adj. rear sights. Mfg. disc.

	$650	$575	$510	$440	$385	$340	$325	$750

MSR	100%	98%	95%	90%	80%	70%	60%	Last MSR

COMPETITION 40 – .40 S&W cal., SFO, SA, similar to Competition 9, except features two Glock 17 shot mags. Mfg. disc.

	100%	98%	95%	90%	80%	70%	60%	Last MSR
	$650	$575	$510	$440	$385	$340	$325	*$750*

DUTY 9 – 9mm Para. cal., SFO, SA, TimberWolf frame, choice of 2 quick change grips, rounded trigger guard, extended beaver tail, round mag. catch, improved checkering, extended slide lock and slide stop, two Glock 17 shot mags., forged stainless steel slides, front and rear cocking serrations, bull nose, beveled rails, lowered ejection port, standard sights. Disc.

	100%	98%	95%	90%	80%	70%	60%	Last MSR
	$650	$575	$510	$440	$385	$340	$325	*$750*

DUTY 40 – .40 S&W cal., SFO, SA, similar to Duty 9, except features two Glock 15 shot mags. Disc.

	100%	98%	95%	90%	80%	70%	60%	Last MSR
	$650	$575	$510	$440	$385	$340	$325	*$750*

Add $120 for diamond speed sights with Tritium inserts.

RIFLES: SEMI-AUTO

BORDER PATROL – .223 Rem./5.56 NATO (.223 Wylde chamber) cal., AR-15 style, GIO, 16 in. chrome moly barrel with A2 flash hider, extended M4 feed ramps, "F" marked A2 front sight base, forged charging handle, laser engraved "T" markings, dry film lube inside upper receiver, ST-T2 Tungsten buffer, Lone Star Tactical logo, bullet pictogram selector markings, 6-position stock, 6-position buffer tube, castle nut, staked latch plate, standard pistol grip, Black finish. Mfg. for Lone Star Tactical by Spike's Tactical. Mfg. disc.

	100%	98%	95%	90%	80%	70%	60%	Last MSR
	$925	$810	$700	$625	$525	$450	$395	*$1,025*

SHOTGUNS

870 TACTICAL – 12 ga.,18 1/2 in. tactical barrel, 2 shot magazine extension, XS front sight blade, XS ghost ring sight rail, Blackhawk recoil reducing stock with powerpack, forward handguard, 870 Picatinny rail forward handguard, receiver drilled and tapped for scope mounts, sidesaddle ammunition carrier, Blackhawk recoil reducing stock with powerpack, forward handguard, black finish.

	100%	98%	95%	90%	80%	70%	60%	Last MSR
	$775	$675	$575	$525	$425	$350	$275	*$850*

SAIGA 12 – 12 ga., Kalashnikov style, Blackhawk SpecOps recoil reducing stock, Lone Star stock adapter with single point sling capability, custom trigger, TAC-47 custom 3-position gas plug, Tromix Shark Break door breacher muzzle brake, SGM forward handguard, SGM tactical 10 shot mag., custom textured pistol grip and forward handguard. Mfg. disc.

	100%	98%	95%	90%	80%	70%	60%	Last MSR
	$1,350	$1,175	$1,025	$925	$750	$625	$475	*$1,500*

LOSOK CUSTOM ARMS

Current semi-auto rifle manufacturer located in Delaware, OH.

RIFLES: SEMI-AUTO

VALKYR – various cals. between .30-06-.458 Win. Mag., various barrel configurations 18 in. to 28 in. sporter through heavy, choice of M1 Garand or M14 operating system, milled receiver, modified M1918 Browning BAR magazine, McMillan stock, Picatinny top rail, 16 1/2 lbs. New 2012.

Please contact the company directly for pricing and availability for this model.

LUSA USA

Previous manufacturer located in Hooksett, NH until circa 2008.

CARBINES: SEMI-AUTO

Lusa USA manufactured a 9mm Para. cal. carbine with a 16 in. barrel in three configurations - the 94 LE (last MSR $1,295), 94 SP89 Pistol (last MSR $999), 94 SA (A2 Standard, last MSR $999), the 94 PDW (side folding stock, last MSR $1,099), and the 94 AWB (fixed stock, last MSR $999-$1,099).

LUVO PRAGUE LTD.

Current pistol and rifle manufacturer located in Praha 2-Vinohrady, Czech Republic. No current U.S. importation.

PISTOLS: SEMI-AUTO

Luvo Prague Ltd. currently manufactures the following pistols: CZ TT9, CZ TT40, CZ TT45, and CZ ST9 in various calibers and finishes. Please contact the manufacturer directly for more information including pricing, options, and U.S. availability (see Trademark Index).

RIFLES: SEMI-AUTO

Luvo Prague Ltd. currently manufactures the following AR-15 style rifles: LA-10, LA-11, LA-15, LA-16, LA-110 SASS, CZ Reliable V22, VZ-58V, and VZ-58P. Please contact the manufacturer directly for more information including price, options, and U.S. availability (see Trademark Index).

NOTES

M SECTION

M+M INDUSTRIES (M+M, INC.)

Current importer and distributor located in Northglenn, CO. Previously located in Eastlake, CO.

MSR	100%	98%	95%	90%	80%	70%	60%	Last MSR

PISTOLS: SEMI-AUTO

SAN SG553 – 5.56 NATO cal., upper receiver has Picatinny rail with integrated synthetic handguard, pistol grip, muzzle brake, 30 shot mag. Mfg. in Switzerland. Importation began 2013.

MSR $3,500	$2,975	$2,600	$2,230	$2,025	$1,635	$1,350	$1,050	

RIFLES: BOLT ACTION

SAN 511 PRECISION .50 BMG – .50 BMG cal., 17 1/2, 22, 27 1/2, 32, or 36 in. free floated barrel with muzzle brake, 5 shot detachable box mag., aluminum alloy receiver, adj. rear support leg, folding adj. bipod, telescope or night sights, integral Picatinny rail, side folding shoulder stock, approx. 32 lbs.

MSR $18,505	$16,650	$13,950	$11,795	$10,250	$9,000	$7,850	$6,600	

RIFLES: SEMI-AUTO

M10-762 RIFLE – 7.62x39mm cal., AK-47 design, 16 1/4 in. cold hammer forged chrome lined barrel with muzzle brake, 30 shot double stack polymer mag., combination gas block and front sight, RPK graduated rear sight, steel quick detachable scope mounting rail, removable fire control retaining plate, Hogue rubber overmolded forend with customizable Picatinny rails, choice of fixed Phoenix Technologies survival adj. 6-position Kicklite or Field stock, Hogue pistol grip, single hook trigger group, matte black finish, approx. 7 lbs. Imported from Romania with six U.S. made parts and assembled in America.

MSR $750	$625	$550	$495	$450	$400	$375	$350	

MG ARMS INCORPORATED

Current manufacturer established in 1980, located in Spring, TX. MG Arms Incorporated was previously named Match Grade Arms & Ammunition. Consumer direct sales.

PISTOLS: SEMI-AUTO

WRAITHE – 9mm Para. (new 2014) or .45 ACP cal., M1911 design, 4 1/4 in. match grade barrel, SA, aluminum alloy frame, choice of fixed or night sights, 3 1/2 lb. trigger, custom grip panels, high ride beavertail safety, choice of black, Olive Drab, Desert Tan, or titanium finish. New 2013.

MSR $3,195	$2,800	$2,400	$2,125	$1,800	$1,400	$1,150	$925	

RIFLES: BOLT ACTION

BANSHEE – various cals., blueprinted Rem. action, cryogenically treated stainless steel National Match medium (Banshee Lite) or heavy taper fluted barrel, 5 or 10 shot detachable mag., tactical bolt handle, custom bedded full length aluminum pillar block, 2 1/2 lb. custom trigger, Varmint weight fully adj. or lightweight non-adj. (Banshee Lite) fiberglass stock, includes Picatinny scope base. New 2012.

MSR $3,395	$2,885	$2,525	$2,165	$1,960	$1,585	$1,300	$1,075	

Add $150 for left-hand action.

Subtract $200 for Banshee Lite.

MGA SILVER EDITION – various cals., Model 7015 action, match grade #3 taper barrel, tuned trigger, 20 oz. fiberglass stock, PTFE metal finish. Mfg. 2009-2010.

	$2,450	$2,200	$1,925	$1,700	$1,500	$1,300	$1,050	*$2,635*

SIGNATURE CLASSIC – various cals., Nesika Hunter action (disc.) or Stiller action, PacNor or Hart stainless steel barrel with Super Eliminator muzzle brake, Jewell trigger, choice of Cascade fiberglass (disc.) or AAA fancy wood stock, matte stainless steel, black, or Cerakote finish. Limited mfg. (approx. 10 guns per year) beginning 2000.

MSR $9,495	$9,495	$8,250	$7,000	$5,750	$4,500	$3,500	$3,000	

Subtract approx. 35% if with Cascade fiberlass stock (disc).

ULTRA-LIGHT MODEL – various cals., lightened and skeletonized Wby. Vanguard (disc. 2004), Rem. 700 (new 2005), or Win. Model 70 action, stainless steel National Match barrel, Super Eliminator muzzle brake, bolt fluted and skeletonized, Sako style extractor, Jewell trigger, Teflon metal finish, textured epoxy stock with Pachmayr Decelerator pad, variety of camo finishes on stock, 5 1/2 lbs.

MSR $3,895	$3,350	$3,150	$2,900	$2,450	$2,075	$1,750	$1,425	

Add $500 for Win. Model 70 action.

MSR	100%	98%	95%	90%	80%	70%	60%	Last MSR

VARMINTER – various cals., squared and lapped Rem. M700 action, stainless steel National Match barrel with Super Eliminator muzzle brake, black Teflon metal finish, camo epoxy stock.

	$2,625	$2,300	$2,000	$1,650	$1,325	$1,050	$925	*$2,895*

RIFLES: SEMI-AUTO

BEHEMOTH – .50 BMG cal., 24, 29, or 31 in. stainless steel match grade skip line fluted barrel with Super Eliminator muzzle brake, 5 shot detachable mag., Picatinny style handrail with KeyMods, fully machined stainless steel lower receiver, choice of fully adjustable or skeletonized custom buttstock, PTFE or ceramic metal finish. New 2015.

MSR $12,200	$11,000	$9,000	$7,250	$6,500	$5,500	$5,000	$4,500	

CK-4 – .223 Rem. or .300 Fireball cal., AR-15 style, GIO, 16 or 20 in. barrel with flash hider (16 in. only), 20 or 30 shot mag., MGA 3-piece lower receiver, A3 flat-top receiver, 6-position collapsible stock, free floating quad rail handguard, choice of PTFE resin finish, basic, or camo coverage. Mfg. 2011-2015.

	$1,695	$1,475	$1,275	$1,150	$925	$775	$595	*$$1,995*

K-YOTE VARMINT SYSTEM – various cals. from .17 Rem.-.458 Lott, AR-15 style, GIO, choice of round fluted or 10 sided match grade fully free-floating barrel in 20, 24, or 26 in. lengths, custom target trigger, standard or camo finish four rail aluminum handguard, adj. stock, A3 flat-top upper receiver, machined lower receiver, scope rail. New 2009.

MSR $3,695	$3,450	$3,100	$2,850	$2,550	$2,300	$2,250	$1,995	

TARANIS – 5.56 NATO or .300 AAC Blackout cal., AR-15 style, GIO, 16 in. lightweight match grade tapered barrel with titanium flash hider, 20 or 30 shot mag., upper receiver with flat-top Picatinny rail, carbon fiber handguard, CTR 6-position collapsible stock, PTFE resin, basic, or zebra camo finish. New 2013.

MSR $2,195	$1,975	$1,750	$1,425	$1,150	$995	$850	$675	

MGI

Current rifle manufacturer located in Old Town, ME. Previously located in Bangor, ME until late 2010.

PISTOLS: SEMI-AUTO

HYDRA VIPERA 5.56 MODULAR PISTOL – 5.56 NATO/.223 Rem. cal., 7 in. barrel, aluminum construction, Mil-Spec internal parts, QCB upper receiver and modular lower, AR-15 mags., black finish. New 2015.

MSR $1,289	$1,075	$965	$825	$685	$595	$515	$440	

HYDRA VIPERA 7.62x39 MODULAR PISTOL – 7.62x39 cal., 7 in. barrel, aluminum construction, Mil-Spec internal parts, QCB upper receiver and modular lower, AK-47 mags., black finish. New 2015.

MSR $1,289	$1,075	$965	$825	$685	$595	$515	$440	

This model is designed to use standard Warsaw Pact metal magazines and Thermold polymer magazines.

HYDRA VIPERA 9mm SMG-9C MODULAR PISTOL – 9mm SMG-9C cal., 7 1/2 in. barrel, fires 9mm ammo from standard Colt style magazines, aluminum construction, Mil-Spec internal parts, QCB upper receiver and modular lower, black finish. New 2015.

MSR $1,289	$1,075	$965	$825	$685	$595	$515	$440	

HYDRA VIPERA .300 BLACKOUT MODULAR PISTOL – .300 AAC Blackout cal., 7 in. barrel, AR-15 mags., aluminum construction, Mil-Spec internal parts, QCB upper receiver and modular lower, black finish. New 2015.

MSR $1,289	$1,075	$965	$825	$685	$595	$515	$440	

RIFLES: SEMI-AUTO

MARCK 15-001/003 (HYDRA) – .223 Rem./5.56 NATO cal., AR-15 style, GIO, complete weapon system, A2 front sight base (Marck-15-001) or low profile gas block (Marck-15-003), 16 in. barrel, modular lower receiver with a 5.56mm magwell, QCB-D upper receiver, change barrels in seconds with no tools required, and utilize the correct magazine for the caliber you desire, black or Muddy Girl finish. A wide variety of configurations are available.

MSR $1,299	$1,100	$995	$875	$735	$650	$550	$465	

* **Marck 15 Piston** – 5.56 NATO cal., similar to Marck-15 Base System, except features GPO.

MSR $1,599	$1,425	$1,245	$1,075	$975	$775	$650	$500	

* **Marck 15-AK47-001** – 7.62x39mm cal., similar to Marck-15 Base System, except offered in AK configuration utilizing standard AK-47 magazines and includes A2 front sight base.

MSR $1,374	$1,150	$1,030	$900	$750	$685	$585	$485	

* **Marck 15-AK47-003** – 7.62x39mm cal., similar to Marck-15 Base System, except offered in AK configuration utilizing standard AK-47 magazines and includes enhanced reliability firing pin and bolt and low profile gas block.

MSR $1,299	$1,100	$995	$875	$735	$650	$550	$465	

MSR	100%	98%	95%	90%	80%	70%	60%	Last MSR

* **Marck 15-6.5-003** – 6.5mm Grendel cal., 16 in. barrel, low profile gas block, MGI modified bolt carrier, MGI modular lower receiver with AR magwell, QCB-D upper receiver, top Picatinny rail, black finish, includes foam padded case. New 2015.

| MSR $1,400 | $1,200 | $1,075 | $950 | $800 | $700 | $600 | $495 | |

* **Marck 15-6.8-003** – 6.5mm Grendel cal., 16 in. barrel, low profile gas block, MGI modified bolt carrier, MGI modular lower receiver with AR magwell, QCB-D upper receiver, top Picatinny rail, black finish, includes foam padded case. New 2015.

| MSR $1,299 | $1,100 | $995 | $875 | $735 | $650 | $550 | $465 | |

* **Marck 15-450T-003** – .450 Thumper cal., 16 in. barrel, modified bolt carrier, MGI modular lower receiver with 5.56 AR magwell, MGI QCB-D upper receiver, top Picatinny rail, black finish, includes foam padded case. New 2015.

| MSR $1,495 | $1,275 | $1,120 | $975 | $800 | $700 | $600 | $495 | |

* **Marck 15-50BW** – .50 Beowulf cal., MGI rate and recoil reducing buffer, top Picatinny rail, black finish, includes foam padded case. New 2015.

| MSR $1,499 | $1,275 | $1,125 | $1,025 | $875 | $750 | $625 | $525 | |

* **Marck 15-300BO-003** – .300 AAC Blackout cal., otherwise similar to Marck15-003 with low profile gas block, black finish.

| MSR $1,299 | $1,100 | $995 | $875 | $735 | $650 | $550 | $465 | |

* **Marck 15-308 Configuration (.308 Hydra)** – .308 Win. cal., similar to Marck-15-001/003, except offered in .308 configuration, takes a modified M14 magazine, includes a rate recoil reducing buffer and 18 in. barrel. Disc. 2014.

| | $1,575 | $1,375 | $1,175 | $1,075 | $875 | $725 | $550 | $1,750 |

* **Marck 15-SMG-9C** – 9mm Para. cal.,16 in. blowback barrel and 9mm blowback bolt, utilzes Colt style 9mm SMG mags., modular lower receiver with a 9mm SMG magwell, QCB-D upper receiver, black finish. New 2015.

| MSR $1,299 | $1,100 | $995 | $875 | $735 | $650 | $550 | $465 | |

* **Marck 15-2545-003** – .25-45 Sharps cal., 16 in. SRC barrel, low profile gas block, MGI modular lower receiver, AR magwell, MGI QCB-D (Quick Change Barrel Upper Receiver), MGI D-Fender D-Ring, M4 profile 6-position Mil-Spec stock, includes hard case. New 2016.

| MSR $1,399 | $1,200 | $1,075 | $950 | $800 | $700 | $600 | $495 | |

M-K SPECIALTIES INC.

Previous rifle manufacturer circa 2000-2002 located in Grafton, WV.

RIFLES: SEMI-AUTO

M-14 A1 – .308 Win. cal., forged M-14 steel receiver using CNC machinery to original government specifications, available as Rack Grade, Premier Match, or Tanker Model, variety of National Match upgrades were available at extra cost, base price is for Rack Grade. Mfg. 2000-2002.

| | $1,475 | $1,275 | $995 | $875 | $750 | $625 | $500 | $1,595 |

National Match upgrades ranged from $345-$955.

MK ARMS INC.

Previous manufacturer located in Irvine, CA circa 1992.

CARBINES: SEMI-AUTO

MK 760 – 9mm Para. cal., steel frame, 16 in. shrouded barrel, fires from closed bolt, 14, 24, or 36 shot mag., parkerized finish, folding metal stock, fixed sights. Mfg. 1983-approx. 1992.

| | $725 | $650 | $575 | $525 | $475 | $415 | $375 | $575 |

MKA ARMS

Current manufacturer located in Konya, Turkey with headquarters in Istanbul. No current U.S. importation.

MKA Arms manufactures an AR-15 style gas operated semi-automatic shotgun in 12 ga. Various configurations are available. Please contact the manufacturer directly for more information and possible U.S. availability (see Trademark Index).

MKE

Current manufacturer located in Ankara, Turkey. MKE guns and ammunition are currently imported by Zenith Firearms, located in Afton, VA. Previously imported beginning 2011 by American Tactical Imports, located in Rochester, NY. Previously distributed by Mandall Shooting Supplies, Inc., located in Scottsdale, AZ.

MKE manufactures a wide variety of military and law enforcement models, in addition to a line of consumer semi-auto hunting rifles and a semi-auto pistol. Please contact the importer directly for more information, including pricing and availability (see Trademark Index).

MSR	100%	98%	95%	90%	80%	70%	60%	Last MSR

PISTOLS: SEMI-AUTO

AT-94P – 9mm Para. cal., MP5 style, 16.4 in. barrel, matte black finish, roll locked delayed blowback system, 30 shot mag. Imported 2011-2012.

| | $1,395 | $1,200 | $1,000 | $850 | $700 | $600 | $525 | $1,596 |

AT-94K – 9mm Para. cal., MP5 style, roll locked delayed blowback system, 4 1/2 in. barrel, matte black finish, 30 shot mag., open sights. Imported 2011-2012.

| | $1,395 | $1,200 | $1,000 | $850 | $700 | $600 | $525 | $1,596 |

RIFLES/CARBINES: SEMI-AUTO

AT-94R2 CARBINE – 9mm Para. cal., 16.4 in. barrel, patterned after H&K Model 94, roll delayed blowback action, A2 style MP5 stock, steel receiver, matte black finish, 10 shot detachable box mag. Imported 2011-2012.

| | $1,350 | $1,125 | $900 | $800 | $700 | $600 | $500 | $1,550 |

AT-43 RIFLE – .223 Rem. cal., 17 in. barrel, patterned after H&K Model 93, roll delayed blowback action, A2 style fixed stock, steel receiver, matte black finish, 30 shot detachable box mag. Imported 2011-2012.

| | $1,300 | $1,075 | $875 | $775 | $675 | $575 | $475 | $1,495 |

MKS SUPPLY, INC.

Marketing company representing various companies including Hi-Point Firearms and Inland Mfg. Previously represented Chiappa Firearms Ltd. MKS firearms were manufactured by Chiappa Firearms Ltd. located in Dayton, OH until 2014. Please refer to Hi-Point Firearms and Inland Mfg. sections for individual model listings.

SHOTGUNS

MKS Supply, Inc. offered the following shotguns until 2014: Aimpro Tactical 590 A1 with choice of 18 1/2 or 20 in. barrel with Hogue standard stock, and TacStar side saddle - MSRs were $897 and $945, Aimpro Tactical 590 A1 Breacher - last MSR was $868, and the Aimpro Tactical 590 A1 Elite with holographic sight and other accessories - last MSR was $1,495.

MMC ARMORY

Current AR-15 style manufacturer established in 2008, located in Mark, IL.

PISTOLS: SEMI-AUTO

MA15 CQP (CLOSE QUARTER PISTOL) – 5.56 NATO or .300 AAC Blackout cal., black furniture. Disc. 2014.

| | $1,750 | $1,525 | $1,325 | $1,200 | $975 | $795 | $700 | $1,950 |

RIFLES: SEMI-AUTO

MA15 3GCR (3 GUN COMPETITION READY) – 5.56 NATO cal., GIO, 17 in. barrel with compensator, 15 in. Troy Alpha handguard, single stage drop in velocity trigger, nickel coated bolt carrier group, low profile gas block, ambidextrous charging handle, 30 shot mag., flat trigger guard, Rogers Super-Stoc and 6-position polished buffer tube, polymer A2 style grip, black furniture, 6.2 lbs. New 2014.

| MSR $1,709 | $1,525 | $1,325 | $1,150 | $1,050 | $850 | $695 | $550 | |

MA15 PATROL ELITE – 5.56 NATO or .300 AAC Blackout cal., GIO, 16 in. chrome moly M4 profile nitride hardened barrel, nickel boron coated carrier group, polished buffer tube, single stage trigger, matte black or Muddy Girl (new 2014) finish, two-piece mid-length handguard with double heat shield, 6-position collapsible polymer stock, A2 style pistol grip, Picatinny gas block, 30 shot mag., A2 dimension compensator, flat Mil-Spec trigger guard, 6.1 lbs.

| MSR $1,339 | $1,125 | $975 | $890 | $735 | $650 | $550 | $465 | |

Add $214 for Muddy Girl furniture (new 2014).

MA15 PREDATOR XV – 5.56 NATO or .300 AAC Blackout (new 2015) cal., GIO, 17.1 in. threaded barrel with M4 extension and thread protector, 30 shot mag., enhanced SST, hardcoat anodized receivers with M4 feed ramps and flared magwell, 13 in. Troy Alpha rail, low profile gas block, ambidextrous charging handle, Troy 13 in. Bravo handguard, Rogers Super-Stoc and 6-position polished buffer tube, A2 style pistol grip, black furniture, 6.2 lbs. Mfg. 2014 only.

| | $1,350 | $1,180 | $1,050 | $885 | $750 | $625 | $525 | $1,599 |

MA15 RECON – 5.56 NATO or .300 AAC Blackout cal., GIO, 16 in. chrome moly M4 profile nitride hardened barrel, available with flash hider or compensator, nickel boron coated carrier group, polished buffer tube, single stage drop in velocity trigger, matte black finish, 13 in. Troy Bravo quad rail handguard, 6-position Rogers Super-Stoc collapsible polymer stock, A2 style grip, 30 shot mag., A2 dimension compensator, winter trigger guard, low profile gas block, ambidextrous charging handle, 6.8 lbs.

| MSR $1,599 | $1,350 | $1,180 | $1,050 | $885 | $750 | $625 | $525 | |

Add $60 for compensator.

MSR	100%	98%	95%	90%	80%	70%	60%	Last MSR

MA15 TACTICAL – 5.56 NATO or .300 AAC Blackout cal., GIO, 16 in. chrome moly Nitride hardened barrel with M4 extension, available with flash hider or compensator, nickel boron coated carrier group, polished buffer tube, SST, matte black finish, 13 in. Troy Alpha modular handguard with movable Picatinny rail, 6-position Rogers Super-Stoc collapsible polymer stock, A2 style grip, 30 shot mag., A2 dimension compensator, flat trigger guard, low profile gas block, ambidextrous charging handle, 6.1 lbs.

	MSR $1,579	$1,335	$1,175	$1,050	$885	$750	$625	$525	

Add $60 for compensator.

MAADI-GRIFFIN CO.

Previous rifle manufacturer located in Mesa, AZ until 2003. Consumer direct sales.

RIFLES: SEMI-AUTO

MODEL MG-6 – .50 BMG cal., gas operated, bullpup configuration, one piece cast lower receiver, 5, 10, or 15 shot side mounted mag., 26-30 in. barrel, includes bipod, hard carrying case, and 3 mags., 23 lbs. Mfg. 2000-2003.

		$5,500	$4,750	$3,850	$3,250	$2,600	$2,200	$1,800	*$5,950*

Add $450 for MK-IV tripod.

RIFLES: SINGLE SHOT

MODEL 89 – .50 BMG cal., one piece cast lower receiver, 36 in. barrel, felt recoil is less than 12 ga., tig-welded interlocking assembly, no screws, tripod optional, 22 lbs. Mfg. 1990-2003.

		$3,100	$2,750	$2,400	$2,050	$1,775	$1,500	$1,250	*$3,150*

Add $600 for stainless steel.

MODEL 92 CARBINE – .50 BMG cal., 20 in. barrel, 5 lb. trigger pull, 18 1/2 lbs. Mfg. 1990-2003.

		$2,950	$2,550	$2,225	$1,875	$1,650	$1,400	$1,200	*$2,990*

Add $650 for stainless steel.

MODEL 99 – .50 BMG cal., similar to Model 89, except has 44 in. barrel, 28 lbs. Mfg. 1999-2003.

		$3,150	$2,725	$2,450	$2,050	$1,775	$1,500	$1,250	*$3,350*

Add $650 for stainless steel.

MAGNUM RESEARCH, INC.

Current trademark of pistols and rifles with company headquarters located in Blauvelt, NY beginning 2010, with manufacturing facilities located in Pillager, MN, and by I.W.I. (Baby and Desert Eagle Series), located in Israel. During June of 2010, Kahr Arms purchased the assets of Magnum Research, Inc. Desert Eagle Series was manufactured 1998-2008 by IMI, located in Israel. Previously manufactured by Saco Defense located in Saco, ME during 1995-1998, and by TAAS/IMI (Israeli Military Industries) 1986-1995. .22 Rimfire semi-auto pistols (Mountain Eagle) were previously manufactured by Ram-Line. Single shot pistols (Lone Eagle) were manufactured by Magnum Research sub-contractors. Distributed by Magnum Research, Inc., in Minneapolis, MN. Dealer and distributor sales.

PISTOLS: SEMI-AUTO, RIMFIRE

THE MOUNTAIN EAGLE – .22 LR cal., SA, 6 (new 1995) or 6 1/2 (disc. 1994) in. polymer and steel barrel, features alloy receiver and polymer technology, matte black finish, adj. rear sight, 15 or 20 shot mag. 21 oz. Mfg. 1992-96.

		$185	$155	$135	$115	$100	$85	$75	*$239*

*   ***The Mountain Eagle Compact Edition*** – similar to Mountain Eagle, except has 4 1/2 in. barrel with shortened grips, adj. rear sight, 10 or 15 shot mag., plastic case, 19.3 oz. Mfg. 1996 only.

		$165	$135	$120	$105	$95	$80	$70	*$199*

*   ***The Mountain Eagle Target Edition*** – .22 LR cal., Target variation of the Mountain Eagle, featuring 8 in. accurized barrel, 2-stage target trigger, jeweled bolt, adj. sights with interchangeable blades, 23 oz. Mfg. 1994-96.

		$235	$185	$150	$135	$120	$105	$95	*$279*

PICUDA MLP-1722 – .17 Mach 2 or .22 LR cal., 10 in. graphite barrel, no sights, features MLR-22 frame, choice of laminated nutmeg, forest camo, or pepper colored Barracuda stock, integral scope base, target trigger, 10 shot mag., approx. 3 lbs. Mfg. 2007-2009.

		$595	$525	$450	$400	$350	$300	$250	*$699*

PISTOLS: SEMI-AUTO, CENTERFIRE

IMI SP-21 – 9mm Para., .40 S&W, or .45 ACP cal., DA/SA, traditional Browning operating system, SFO, polymer frame with ergonomic design, 3.9 in. barrel with polygonal rifling, 10 shot mag., finger groove grips, 3 dot adj. sights, reversible mag. release, multiple safeties, matte black finish, decocking feature, approx. 29 oz. Limited importation from IMI late 2002-2005.

		$550	$395	$335	$300	$280	$260	$240	*$499*

The IMI SP-21 uses the same magazines as the Baby Eagle pistols. This model is referred to the Barak SP-21 in Israel.

MSR	100%	98%	95%	90%	80%	70%	60%	Last MSR

PISTOLS: SEMI-AUTO, CENTERFIRE - EAGLE SERIES

Magnum Research also offers a Collector's Edition Presentation Series. Special models include a Gold Edition (serial numbered 1-100), a Silver Edition (serial numbered 101-500), and a Bronze Edition (serial numbered 501-1,000). Each pistol from this series is supplied with a walnut presentation case, 2 sided medallion, and certificate of authenticity. Prices are available upon request by contacting Magnum Research directly.

Alloy frames on the Desert Eagle Series of pistols were discontinued in 1992. However, if sufficient demand warrants, these models will once again be available to consumers at the same price as the steel frames.

Beginning late 1995, the Desert Eagle frame assembly for the .357 Mag., .44 Mag., and .50 AE cals. is based on the .50 caliber frame. Externally, all three pistols are now identical in size. This new platform, called the Desert Eagle Pistol Mark XIX Component System, enables .44 Mag. and .50 AE conversions to consist of simply a barrel and a magazine - conversions to or from the .357 Mag. also include a bolt.

The slide assembly on the Mark I and Mark VII is physically smaller than the one on a Mark XIX. Also, the barrel dovetail on top is 3/8 in. on a Mark I or Mark VII, while on a Mark XIX, it is 7/8 in., and includes cross slots for scopes.

Individual Desert Eagle Mark XIX 6 in. barrels are $408-$601, depending on finish, and 10 in. barrels are $509, depending on finish. Add $129 for Trijicon night sights (new 2006). Add $92 for Hogue Pau Ferro wooden grips (new 2007), $50 for Hogue soft rubber grips with finger grooves, or $130 for Hogue anodized black aluminum "Reaper" engraved or "The Bone Yard" engraved grips. During 2015, Magnum Research introduced 6 in. barrels in a variety of finishes that include the Clam Pack - a case, and two extra magazines. MSRs range from $476-$656, depending on metal finish.

MR9/MR40 EAGLE – 9mm Para. or .40 S&W cal., SA, SFO, fully adj. rear sight, 4 (9mm Para. cal., disc. 2013), 4.15 (.40 S&W cal., disc. 2013), or 4 1/2 (new 2014) in. barrel, interchangeable palm swells, 10, 11 (.40 S&W cal.), or 15 (9mm Para. cal.) shot mag., lower Picatinny rail, internal safeties, square trigger guard, cooperative manufacturing effort with Carl Walther supplying the black polymer frame with integral steel rails, while the stainless steel slide and barrel are manufactured and assembled in Pillager, MN, approx. 25 oz. New 2011.

| MSR $559 | $475 | $425 | $375 | $325 | $295 | $275 | $250 | |

* The Baby Eagle II Semi-Compact – 9mm Para., .40 S&W (polymer frame only), or .45 ACP cal., similar to Baby Eagle II Full Size, except has 3.7 (disc.), or 3.93 (new 2011) in. barrel. Imported 2008-2014 by I.W.I.

| | $560 | $475 | $425 | $375 | $325 | $275 | $225 | $656 |

Subtract $27 for polymer frame.
Add $235 for brushed or polished chrome (disc. 2009).

MARK I DESERT EAGLE .357 MAG – .357 Mag. cal., SA, similar to Mark VII, except has standard trigger and safety lever is teardrop shaped, and slide catch release has single serration. Disc.

| | $925 | $825 | $725 | $625 | $525 | $450 | $400 | |

MARK XIX .357 MAG. DESERT EAGLE – .357 Mag. cal., features .50 cal. frame and slide, SA, 6 or 10 (disc. 2011) in. barrel, full Picatinny top rail with fixed sights became standard late 2009 (U.S. mfg.), standard Black, Brushed Chrome, Matte Chrome, Polished Chrome, Bright Nickel, Satin Nickel, 24K Gold, Titanium Gold, or Titanium Gold w/ Tiger Stripes finish, 4 lbs., 6 oz. Mfg. by Saco 1995-98, by IMI 1998-2009, and domestically beginning 2010.

| MSR $1,572 | $1,350 | $1,180 | $1,015 | $925 | $750 | $625 | $500 | |

Add $138 for integral muzzle brake (new 2015).
Add $276 for Brushed Chrome, Matte Chrome, Polished Chrome, Bright Nickel or Satin Nickel finish.
Add $510 for 24K Gold or Titanium Gold finish.
Add $623 for Titanium Gold w/Tiger Stripe finish.
Add $87 for 10 in. barrel (disc. 2011).

MARK VII .357 MAG. DESERT EAGLE – .357 Mag. cal., SA, gas operated, 6 (standard barrel length), 10, or 14 in. barrel length with 3/8 in. dovetail rib, steel (58.3 oz.) or alloy (47.8 oz.) frame, adj. trigger, safety lever is hook shaped, slide catch/release lever has three steps, adaptable to .44 Mag. with optional kit, 9 shot mag. (8 for .44 Mag.). Mfg. 1983-95, limited quantities were made available again during 1998 and 2001.

| | $1,100 | $1,000 | $875 | $750 | $650 | $550 | $475 | $929 |

Add approx. $150 for 10 or 14 in. barrel (disc. 1995).
Add $495 for .357 Mag. to .41 Mag./.44 Mag. conversion kit (6 in. barrel). Disc. 1995.
Add approx. $685 for .357 Mag. to .44 Mag. conversion kit (10 or 14 in. barrel). Disc. 1995.

* Mark VII .357 Mag. Desert Eagle Stainless Steel – similar to .357 Mag. Desert Eagle, except has stainless steel frame, 58.3 oz. Mfg. 1987-95.

| | $1,100 | $1,000 | $875 | $750 | $650 | $550 | $475 | $839 |

Add approx. $150 for 10 or 14 in. barrel.

MARK VII .41 MAG. DESERT EAGLE – .41 Mag. cal., SA, similar to .357 Mag. Desert Eagle, except has 6 in. barrel only, 8 shot mag., steel (62.8 oz.) or alloy (52.3 oz.) frame. Mfg. 1988-1995, limited quantities available during 2001.

| | $1,050 | $975 | $850 | $725 | $625 | $525 | $475 | $899 |

Add $395 for .41 Mag. to .44 Mag. conversion kit (6 in. barrel only).

MSR	100%	98%	95%	90%	80%	70%	60%	Last MSR

* Mark VII .41 Mag. Desert Eagle Stainless Steel – similar to .41 Mag. Desert Eagle, except has stainless steel frame, 58.3 oz. Mfg. 1988-95.

| | $1,100 | $1,000 | $875 | $750 | $650 | $550 | $475 | *$949* |

MARK I DESERT EAGLE .44 MAG.
– .44 Mag. cal., SA, similar to Mark VII, except has standard trigger and safety lever is teardrop shaped, and slide catch release has single serration. Disc.

| | $1,200 | $1,075 | $925 | $775 | $675 | $575 | $495 | |

MARK XIX .44 MAG. DESERT EAGLE
– .44 Mag. cal., features .50 cal. frame and slide, SA, 6 or 10 in. barrel, full Picatinny top rail with fixed sights became standard late 2009 (U.S. mfg.), standard Black, brushed chrome, polished chrome, matte chrome, satin nickel, bright nickel, 24K Gold, Titanium Gold, Titanium Gold w/Tiger Stripes, Kryptek Highlander (new 2015), or Burnt Bronze Cerakote (new 2015) finish, 4 lbs., 6 oz. Mfg. by Saco 1995-98, by IMI 1998-2009, domestically by CCI beginning 2009, and by I.W.I. beginning 2012.

| MSR $1,572 | $1,350 | $1,180 | $1,015 | $925 | $750 | $625 | $500 | |

Subtract $42 for Israel mfg.

Add $88 for 10 in. barrel or $138 for integral muzzle brake (new 2015).

Add $140 for Burnt Bronze Cerakote finish (new 2015).

Add $140 for Tungsten Cerakote (Dark Graphite Gray) with Black appointments (new 2016).

Add $221 for Kryptek Highlander pattern finish (new 2015).

Add $314 for Brushed chrome, matte chrome, polished chrome, satin nickel, or bright nickel finish.

Add $552 for 24K Gold or Titanium Gold finish. Add $664 for Titanium Gold w/Tiger Stripes finish.

Add $199 for black muzzle brake (limited mfg. 2010 only).

Add $238 for 6 in. barrel with muzzle brake, black finish (mfg. 2013-2014), or $615 for muzzle brake with brushed or polished chrome (mfg. 2013-2014).

MARK VII .44 MAG. DESERT EAGLE
– .44 Mag. cal., SA, similar to .357 Desert Eagle, 8 shot mag., steel (62.8 oz.) or alloy (52.3 oz.) frame. Originally mfg. 1986-1995, re-released 1998-2000.

| | $1,100 | $1,000 | $875 | $750 | $650 | $550 | $475 | *$1,049* |

Add $100 for 10 (current) or 14 (disc. 1995) in. barrel.

Add $475 for .44 Mag. to .357 Mag. conversion kit (6 in. barrel). Disc. 1995.

Add $675 for .44 Mag. to .357 Mag. conversion kit (10 or 14 in. barrel). Disc. 1995.

Add $395 for .44 Mag. to .41 Mag. conversion kit (6 in. barrel). Disc. 1995.

* Mark VII .44 Mag. Desert Eagle Stainless Steel – similar to .44 Mag. Desert Eagle, except has stainless steel frame, 58.3 oz. Mfg. 1987-95.

| | $1,175 | $1,050 | $900 | $775 | $675 | $575 | $475 | *$949* |

Add approx. $210 for 10 or 14 in. barrel.

MARK VII .50 AE DESERT EAGLE
– .50 AE cal., SA, 6 in. barrel with 7/8 in. rib with cross slots for Weaver style rings, steel only, black standard finish, frame slightly taller than the Mark VII .357 Mag./.44 Mag., 7 shot mag., 72.4 oz. Mfg. 1991-1995 by IMI, limited quantities were made available again during 1998 only.

| | $1,175 | $950 | $825 | $700 | $575 | $500 | $450 | *$1,099* |

This cartridge utilized the same rim dimensions as the .44 Mag. and was available with a 300 grain bullet. The .50 Action Express cal. has 20%-25% more stopping power than the .44 Mag., with a minimal increase in felt recoil.

MARK XIX CUSTOM 440
– .440 Cor-Bon cal., SA, similar to Mark XIX .44 Mag. Desert Eagle, 6 or 10 in. barrel, standard black finish, rechambered by MRI Custom Shop, limited mfg. 1999-2001.

| | $1,175 | $995 | $850 | $725 | $575 | $500 | $450 | *$1,389* |

Add $40 for 10 in. barrel.

MARK XIX .50 AE DESERT EAGLE
– .50 AE cal., SA, larger frame, 6 or 10 in. barrel, full Picatinny top rail with fixed sights became standard late 2009 (U.S. mfg.), standard black finish, 4 lbs., 6 oz. Mfg. by Saco 1995-1998, by IMI (1998-2008 disc.), I.W.I. (new 2009), and CCI in the U.S. beginning 2010.

| MSR $1,572 | $1,350 | $1,180 | $1,015 | $925 | $750 | $625 | $500 | |

Add $32 for domestic mfg.

Add $121 for 10 in. barrel.

Add $140 for Burnt Bronze Cerakote finish (new 2015).

Add $140 for Tungsten Cerakote (Dark Graphite Gray) with Black appointments (new 2016).

Add $170 for integral muzzle brake (new 2015).

Add $350 for brushed chrome, matte chrome, polished chrome, bright nickel or satin nickel finish.

Add $595 for 24K Gold or Titanium Gold finish. Add $706 for Titanium Gold w/Tiger Stripes finish.

Add $209 for muzzle brake (black finish, 6 in. barrel only, disc. 2014) or $592 for muzzle brake with brushed chrome (mfg. 2011-2014) or polished chrome (mfg. 2013-2014).

MSR	100%	98%	95%	90%	80%	70%	60%	Last MSR

MARK XIX 3 CAL. COMPONENT SYSTEM – includes Mark XIX .44 Mag. Desert Eagle and 5 barrels including .357 Mag. (6 and 10 in.), .44 Mag., and .50 AE (6 and 10 in.) cals., .357 bolt assembly and ICC aluminum carrying case. Also available in custom finishes at extra charge. Mfg. 1998-2011.

	$3,900	$3,450	$2,800	$2,400	$2,000	$1,750	$1,500	$4,402

* ***Mark XIX 3 Cal. Component System (6 or 10 in. Barrel)*** – includes component Mark XIX system in 6 or 10 in. barrel only. Mfg. 1998-2011.

	$2,550	$2,225	$1,775	$1,500	$1,250	$1,000	$850	$2,910

Add $262 for 10 in. barrel (disc. 2011).

RIFLES: BOLT-ACTION

Magnum Research still offers Mountain Eagle centerfire rifles that can be custom ordered directly from the factory. Current MSRs range from $2,307-$3,400. Please contact Magnum Research directly for information on pricing and available configurations (see Trademark Index). Values listed below represent the last retail pricing available.

MOUNTAIN EAGLE TACTICAL RIFLE – .223 Rem. (new 2002), .22-250 Rem. (new 2002), .308 Win., .300 Win. Mag., or .300 WSM (new 2002) cal., accurized Rem. M-700 action, 26 in. Magnum Lite barrel, H-S Precision tactical stock, adj. stock and trigger, 9 lbs., 4 oz. Mfg. 2001-standard production stopped 2011, currently special order.

	$2,150	$1,825	$1,475	$1,150	$850	$700	$575	$2,475

Add $96 for any cal. other than .300 WSM (disc. 2011).

MAJESTIC ARMS, LTD.

Previous firearms manufacturer established during 2000, and located on Staten Island, NY. The company now produces firearms components, conversion kits, and accessories.

CARBINES: SEMI-AUTO

MA 2000 – .22 LR cal., Henry Repeating Arms Co. AR-7 takedown action, fiber optic sights, American walnut forearm, pistol grip, and buttplate, fixed tubular stock with butt bag, 16 1/4 in. Lothar Walther barrel with crown, black Teflon or silver bead blast finish, 4 lbs. Mfg. 2000-2008.

	$350	$295	$250	$225	$195	$175	$150	$389

MA 4 – .17 HMR, .17 Mach 2 (new 2005), .22 LR (new 2005), or .22 WMR cal., takedown action, traditional or wire frame stock, interchangeable barrel/bolt assembly.

While intially advertised during 2004 with an MSR of $399, this model did not go into production past the prototype stage.

SHOTGUNS: SLIDE ACTION

BASE-TAC – 12 or 20 ga., 3 in. chamber, based on M870 Remington action, approx. 18 in. barrel with ghost ring sights, black synthetic (12 ga.) or hardwood stock and forearm, extended 6 shot tube mag., 6-7 lbs. Mfg. 2004-2010.

	$675	$575	$500	$450	$400	$350	$300	$759

Add $30 for 20 ga.

MARLIN FIREARMS COMPANY

Current trademark with headquarters located in Madison, NC beginning 2010. Currently manufactured by Remington in Ilion, NY beginning early 2011. Previous manufacturer located in North Haven, CT (1969-2010), and in New Haven, CT (1870-1969). The Marlin company manufactured firearms between 1870-2010. Distributor sales only.

On Nov. 10th, 2000, Marlin Firearms Company purchased H&R 1871, Inc. This includes the brand names Harrington & Richardson, New England Firearms, and Wesson & Harrington (please refer to individual sections in this text).

During 2005, Marlin Firearms Company once again started manufacturing an L.C. Smith line of both SxS and O/U shotguns.

Remington Arms Company, Inc. and The Freedom Group acquired Marlin Firearms Company, H&R 1871, LLC., New England Firearms (NEF), and L.C. Smith brand in January of 2008. The Freedom Group, Inc. announced the closure of its Marlin manufacturing facility, located in North Haven, Connecticut. During 2011, production was moved to Ilion, NY. Marlin Firearms Company had been a family-owned and operated business from 1921-2007.

SHOTGUNS: BOLT ACTION

* ***Model 512DL Slugmaster*** – similar to Model 512 Slugmaster, except has black Rynite stock, Fire Sights (with red fiber optic inserts) became standard 1998. Disc. 1998.

	$310	$230	$200	$180	$160	$145	$130	$372

* ***Model 512P Slugmaster*** – 12 ga., 3 in. chamber, features 21 in. ported fully rifled barrel with front and rear Fire Sights (high visibility red and green fiber optic inserts), 2 shot detachable box mag., black fiberglass synthetic stock with molded-in checkering, receiver is drilled and tapped, 8 lbs. Mfg. 1999-2001.

	$315	$235	$200	$180	$165	$155	$145	$388

MSR		100%	98%	95%	90%	80%	70%	60%	Last MSR

MASTERPIECE ARMS

Current pistol and rifle manufacturer located in Comer, GA. Previously located in Carrollton, GA until 2013, also previously located in Braselton, GA. Dealer sales only.

CARBINES: SEMI-AUTO

MPA manufactures a line of semi-auto carbines patterned after the MAC Series with 30 or 35 shot mags. (interchangable with its pistols).

MPA20DMG CARBINE – 9mm Para. cal., side cocker, 16.2 in. threaded barrel, barrel extension, low profile mag. release, hammer with disconnect, adj. front and rear sights, side folder stock, "Decal Grip" grip panels, machined aluminum lower receiver, free floating aluminum extrusion handguard, scope mount, MPA polymer case, Cerakote Burnt Bronze (standard), Black, Gunmetal, Tungsten, Sniper Green, or FDE finish. New 2015.

| MSR $899 | | $775 | $685 | $615 | $550 | $485 | $415 | $370 | |

MPA20SST CARBINE – 9mm Para. cal., side cocker, 16 in. threaded barrel with muzzle brake, 30 shot polymer mag., adj. front sight, MPA low profile buttstock, AR-15 handguard, scope mount, MPA aluminum quad rail, includes mag. loader and gun case. New 2016.

| MSR $816 | | $695 | $615 | $550 | $475 | $420 | $365 | $335 | |

MPA460 CARBINE – .460 Rowland cal., 16 in. threaded barrel, 30 shot mag., side cocking, muzzle brake, black finish, with or w/o .45 ACP upper. Mfg. 2010 only.

| | | $725 | $650 | $575 | $500 | $425 | $375 | $325 | *$800* |

Add $54 for scope mount, handguard, and Mark III tactical scope.

MPAR556/MPAR300 – 5.56 NATO or .300 AAC Blackout (new 2014) cal., 16.26 in. barrel with combat muzzle brake, short stroke piston, ATACS Hydrographic (new 2014), phosphate or hardcoat anodized finish, two-piece free floating aluminum handguard with front cover and Picatinny rails, MBA buttsock, side folding design, locked bolt action, side charging handle, forward assist, angled foregrip, full length top rail, dust cover on side charger, full length scope mount, accepts M16 magazines, 7.8 lbs. New 2013.

| MSR $951 | | $815 | $700 | $630 | $570 | $500 | $425 | $380 | |

Add $108 for ATACS Hydrographic finish (new 2014), 5.56 NATO cal. only.

MPAR556 GEN II RIFLE – 5.56 NATO cal., GPO, 16 in. barrel with black Nitride finish, adj. gas block with four settings, last round bolt hold open, full length top rail, non-reciprocating side charger with forward assist and dust cover, aluminum handguard with front cover, side rails, QD mount on handguard and buttstock, angled foregrip, side folding collapsible stock, black, Cerakote, or ATAC finish, 7.8 lbs. New 2015.

| MSR $1,020 | | $865 | $755 | $650 | $590 | $515 | $450 | $395 | |

Add $113 for Cerakote or ATAC finish.

MPAR 6.8 CAMO – 6.8 SPC cal., short stroke piston operating system, 16 in. threaded barrel with 3-baffle muzzle brake, locked bolt, steel receiver, 25 shot mag., modular free-floating MPA aluminum handguard with fixed top and bottom Picatinny rails, side charging handle doubles as forward assist, bufferless recoil system, full length scope mount, adj. telescopic, folding MPA buttstock, side folding design, quick detach sling points, black (mfg. 2014 only) or MultiCam Hydrographic finish. New 2014.

| MSR $1,089 | | $925 | $810 | $695 | $625 | $535 | $465 | $415 | |

Subtract approx. $60 for black finish.

MPA5700DMG – 5.7x28mm cal., side cocker, fully machined frame, 16 in. threaded barrel with muzzle brake, 20 shot polymer mag., adj. front sight, MPA low profile buttstock, fully machined grips, MPA aluminum extruded quad rail, scope mount, black Cerakote finish (other colors available upon request). New 2016.

| MSR $899 | | $775 | $685 | $615 | $550 | $485 | $415 | $370 | |

MPA9300DMG CARBINE – 9mm Para. cal., side cocker, 16.2 in. threaded barrel, barrel extension, low profile mag. release, accepts standard Glock style mags., hammer with disconnect plus original hammer, adj. front and rear sights, side folding stock, "Decal Grip" grip panels, machined aluminum lower receiver, free floating aluminum extrusion handguard, scope mount, Cerakote Burnt Bronze (standard), Black, Sniper Green, Gunmetal, Tungsten, or FDE finish, includes MPA polymer case, 5 lbs. New 2015.

| MSR $966 | | $820 | $700 | $630 | $570 | $500 | $425 | $380 | |

MPA9300SST CARBINE – 9mm Para. cal., side cocker, 16 in. threaded barrel with muzzle brake, 30 shot polymer mag., hammer with disconnect, adj. front and rear sight, MPA low profile buttstock, scope mount, molded pistol grip cover, MPA aluminum quad rail, includes mag. loader and gun case. New 2016.

| MSR $816 | | $695 | $615 | $550 | $475 | $420 | $365 | $335 | |

MSR	100%	98%	95%	90%	80%	70%	60%	Last MSR

MPA MINI TACTICAL CARBINE – 9mm Para. cal., side cocker, 16 in. threaded barrel with birdcage muzzle brake, 30 shot mag., mag. loader, adj. front and rear sights, tactical pistol grip, aluminum quad rail, multi-reticle hollow sight, MPA low profile aluminum or side folding (new 2014) stock. Mfg. 2011-2014.

| | $725 | $625 | $525 | $450 | $425 | $400 | $375 | $816 |

Add $53 for side folding stock.

Models MPA9300SST and MPA9300SST-SF

MPA TACTICAL CARBINE – 9mm Para. or .45 ACP cal., side charger, 16 in. threaded barrel, scope mount, 30 (.45 ACP cal.) or 35 (9mm Para. cal.) shot mag., Intrafuse handguard and vertical grip, Defender stock, multi-reticle hollow sight. Mfg. 2011-2012.

| | $850 | $750 | $650 | $575 | $500 | $425 | $375 | $956 |

Add $16 for .45 ACP cal.

.45 ACP SIDE COCKING CARBINE (SIDE COCKING MODEL) – 9mm Para. (MPA20SST, disc. 2014), .45 ACP (MPA1SST), or 5.7x28mm (MPA5700SST, disc. 2014) cal., side cocker, 16 in. threaded barrel with muzzle brake, 20 (5.7x28mm only, disc.) or 30 shot mag., scope mount, mag. loader, MPA low profile aluminum or side folding (mfg. 2014 only) stock, MPA aluminum handguard, adj. front and rear sights, quick mag. release, tactical pistol grip (9mm Para. only, disc. 2014).

| MSR $816 | $695 | $615 | $550 | $475 | $420 | $365 | $335 | |

Add $53 for side folding stock (disc. 2014).

TOP COCKING MODEL – 9mm Para. (MPA20T-A) or .45 ACP (MPA1T-A) cal., top cocking, 16 in. threaded barrel, black skeletonized stock, 30 shot mag. Disc. 2010.

| | $480 | $425 | $360 | $325 | $265 | $215 | $170 | $530 |

Add $30 for .45 ACP cal.

PISTOLS: SEMI-AUTO

MPA manufactures a line of tactical style pistols patterned after the original MAC Series from Ingram.

MPA10T – .45 ACP cal., top cocking, 6 or 10 (disc.) in. threaded barrel, 30 shot mag., short Picatinny rail mounted to lower receiver for attachment of flashlight, barrel extension, magazine loader, quick magazine release, adj. front and rear sights.

| MSR $499 | $450 | $385 | $330 | $285 | $250 | $230 | $220 | |

Add $80 for 10 in. barrel and AR-15 handguard (disc.).

* **MPA10SST** – .45 ACP cal., similar to MPA10T, except is side cocking, available with optional muzzle brake.

| MSR $574 | $510 | $435 | $365 | $315 | $275 | $250 | $230 | |

MPA30DMG – 9mm Para. cal., 5 1/2 in. threaded barrel, side cocker, multi-caliber pistol (utilizing a change of the bolt and barrel it can be modified to fire .40 S&W or .357 Sig cal.), adj. front and rear sights, L-Bracket with QD sling plate, fully machined aluminum pistol grip that accepts Glock Magazines, lower Picatinny rail, hammer with disconnect, low profile mag. release and "Decal Grip" grip panels, scope mount, Cerakote finish in Flat Dark Earth, Tungsten, Burnt Bronze, or Black, includes MPA polymer case. New 2015.

| MSR $679 | $585 | $500 | $435 | $365 | $325 | $280 | $265 | |

MPA30T – 9mm Para. cal., top cocking, 6 in. threaded barrel, 30 shot mag., barrel extension, mag. loader, adj. front and rear sights, quick mag. release, flashlight lower Picatinny rail, hammer with disconnect.

| MSR $499 | $425 | $370 | $320 | $290 | $235 | $190 | $150 | |

* **MPA30SST** – 9mm Para. cal., similar to MPA30T, except is side cocking.

| MSR $574 | $495 | $425 | $375 | $325 | $275 | $225 | $195 | |

MPA57DMG – 5.7x28mm cal., side cocker, 5 in. threaded barrel with muzzle brake, 20 shot polymer mag., fully machined grips, fully machined aluminum receiver, scope mount, black Cerakote finish. New 2016.

| MSR $680 | $590 | $500 | $435 | $365 | $325 | $280 | $265 | |

MPA57SST – 5.7x28mm cal., side cocker, 5 in. threaded barrel, 20 shot mag., scope mount, muzzle brake, adj. front and rear sights, quick mag. release, flashlight lower Picatinny rail, hammer with disconnect, black, ATACS (disc. 2014), or Grim Reaper finish.

| MSR $605 | $515 | $450 | $385 | $350 | $285 | $240 | $185 | |

Add $60 for ATACS (MPA57SSA-ATACS, disc. 2014) or Grim Reaper (MPA57SST-GR) finish.

MPA570SST – 5.7x28mm cal., side cocker, 8 in. threaded barrel, muzzle brake, 20 shot mag., scope mount, short aluminum handguard, angled foregrip, adj. front and rear sights, quick mag. release, flashlight lower Picatinny rail, hammer with disconnect, Black finish.

| MSR $756 | $645 | $565 | $485 | $440 | $355 | $300 | $235 | |

MSR	100%	98%	95%	90%	80%	70%	60%	Last MSR

MPA930DMG – 9mm Para. cal., side cocker, 3 1/2 in. threaded barrel with thread protector, accepts standard Glock mags., adj. front and rear sights, QD flush cup for single point sling system, aluminum pistol grip with "Decal Grip" grip panels, fully machined aluminum lower receiver, scope mount, hammer with disconnect, Cerakote finish in black, Flat Dark Earth, Burnt Bronze, or Tungsten, includes MPA polymer case. New 2015.

	100%	98%	95%	90%	80%	70%	60%	Last MSR
MSR $679	$575	$500	$430	$390	$315	$275	$225	

MPA930 MINI PISTOL – 9mm Para. cal., 3 1/2 in. threaded barrel, SA, 35 shot mag., optional scope mount, black finish. Disc. 2013.

	100%	98%	95%	90%	80%	70%	60%	Last MSR
	$375	$325	$275	$225	$200	$175	$150	*$489*

Add $81 for side cocker with scope mount.

MPA930T MINI PISTOL – 9mm Para. cal., top cocking, 4 1/2 in. threaded barrel, 30 shot mag., mag. loader, barrel extension, adj. front and rear sights, quick mag. release, hammer with disconnect, black, vamo (Model MPA930T-AC), or Grim Reaper (MPA930T-GR) finish.

	100%	98%	95%	90%	80%	70%	60%	Last MSR
MSR $499	$425	$370	$320	$290	$235	$190	$150	

Add $45 for camo (MPA930T-AC) or Grim Reaper (MPA930T-GR) finish.

* ***MPA930SST Mini Pistol*** – 9mm Para. cal., similar to MPA930T, except is side cocking and features tactical pistol grip, flashlight lower Picatinny rail.

	100%	98%	95%	90%	80%	70%	60%	Last MSR
MSR $574	$495	$425	$375	$325	$275	$225	$195	

* ***MPA930SST Limited Edition*** – 9mm Para. cal., side cocker, 3 1/2 in. threaded barrel with combat/high precision muzzle brake, 35 shot mag., mag. loader, Cerakote barrel extension, scope mount, multi-reticle holosight 40 Lumens flashlight, lower rail, L-Bracket mounted QD sling system with special MPA engraving, E-Clip removal tool, includes Certificate of Authenticity, engraved with "X of 100" (depending on which number you receive), two-tone Cerakote finish (upper and lower receiver are FDE, grip inlay, sight blocks, and other hardware is black Cerakote). Limited mfg. of 100 models. New 2015.

MSR is $600

MPA930SST-X – 9mm Para. cal., 3 1/2 in. threaded barrel, 35 shot polymer mag., safety barrel extension, scope mount, lower rail, 40 Lumen flashlight, multi reticle holosight.

	100%	98%	95%	90%	80%	70%	60%	Last MSR
MSR $657	$575	$500	$435	$365	$325	$280	$265	

MPA935SST – 9mm Para. cal., side cocker, 8 in. threaded barrel, 30 shot mag., short handguard, angled foregrip, quick release mag. catch, adj. front and rear sight, hammer with disconnect, includes barrel extension, pistol grip cover, and scope mount. New 2015.

	100%	98%	95%	90%	80%	70%	60%	Last MSR
MSR $678	$575	$500	$430	$390	$315	$275	$225	

MPA22T MINI PISTOL – .22 LR cal., 5 in. threaded barrel, SA, 30 shot mag., top cocker or side cocker with scope mount, black finish. Mfg. 2010-2012.

	100%	98%	95%	90%	80%	70%	60%	Last MSR
	$385	$350	$315	$275	$250	$225	$195	*$440*

Add $85 for side cocker with scope mount.

MPA460 PISTOL – .460 Rowland cal., 6 or 10 in. threaded barrel, SA, 30 shot mag., side cocker, scope mount, muzzle brake, black finish. Mfg. 2009-2010.

	100%	98%	95%	90%	80%	70%	60%	Last MSR
	$495	$450	$395	$365	$335	$300	$275	*$580*

Add $90 for .45 ASP upper.
Add $96 for 10 in. barrel.

MPA TACTICAL PISTOL – 9mm Para. or .45 ACP cal., side cocker, 6 in. threaded barrel, SA, 30 (.45 ACP) or 35 (9mm) shot mag., multi-reticle hollow sight, includes Picatinny rail, flashlight and pressure switch, adj. front and rear sights, quick magazine release, safety barrel extension, tactical pistol grip. New 2011.

	100%	98%	95%	90%	80%	70%	60%	Last MSR
MSR $657	$575	$525	$450	$400	$350	$300	$275	

Model MPA10SST-X and MPA30SST-X

MPA MINI TACTICAL PISTOL – .22 LR (disc. 2012) or 9mm Para. cal., side cocker, 3 1/2 (9mm Para. cal.) or 5 (.22 LR cal., disc. 2012) in. threaded barrel, SA, 30 (.22 LR cal.) or 35 (9mm Para. cal.) shot mag., multi-reticle red-dot sight, adj. front and rear sights, tactical pistol grip, includes flashlight, ring rail, and safety extension. New 2011.

	100%	98%	95%	90%	80%	70%	60%	Last MSR
MSR $657	$575	$525	$450	$400	$350	$300	$275	

Model MPA930SST-X

MPA SUB-COMPACT – .32 ACP or .380 ACP cal., DAO, 2 1/4 in. barrel, sub-compact design, 6 shot mag., solid steel construction, black or two-tone finish, black synthetic grips, 11.8 oz. Mfg. 2011-2012.

	100%	98%	95%	90%	80%	70%	60%	Last MSR
	$275	$250	$225	$195	$175	$150	$135	*$323*

Add $23 for two-tone finish.

MSR	100%	98%	95%	90%	80%	70%	60%	Last MSR

MPAM11-9SA – 9mm Para. cal., M11 frame, 5 1/2 in. threaded barrel with thread protector, 30 shot MPA polymer mag., adj. front and fixed rear sights, quick release mag. catch, black finish. New 2015.

MSR $393	$350	$315	$275	$245	$215	$195	$175	

MPAR556-P GEN II – 5.56x45mm cal., GPO, side cocker, 11 in. threaded barrel, 30 shot mag., non-reciprocating charging handle with forward assist, locked triangular bolt design, extruded aluminum handguard, angled foregrip, side rail and QD mount, no sights, black, Burnt Bronze, Flat Dark Earth, or Tungsten finish. New 2015.

MSR $945	$800	$700	$600	$545	$450	$375	$300	

Add $54 for Burnt Bronze, Flat Dark Earth, or Tungsten finish.

RIFLES: BOLT ACTION

MPA BA LITE RIFLE – 6mm, .243, 6.5mm Creedmoor, 7mm, .280 Win., .308 Win., .300 Win. Mag., .300 Ultra, .338 Win., or .338 Lapua Mag. cal., Kelblys Atlas Tactical action, 20-27 in. Spencer/MPA stainless steel barrel with Alamo Four Start Cowl Induction brake, 5 shot mag., Rifle Basix LV1 trigger, MPA buttstock with adj. LOP and cheek riser, MPA lightweight chassis, lower Picatinny rail, spigot mount ready, Cerakote finish in Black, FDE, Gunmetal, Tungsten, or Burnt Bronze, includes Plano basic rifle case. New 2016.

MSR $2,999	$2,550	$2,225	$1,825	$1,575	$1,300	$1,100	$950	

MPA BOLT ACTION RIFLE – .300 Win. Mag., .308 Win., .338 Lapua, 6mm, 6.5mm, or 6.5 Creedmoor cal., 24 in. Sendero Profile or 26 in. heavy varmint (.300 Win Mag. only) hand lapped stainless steel threaded barrel with muzzle brake, Timney trigger, aluminum V-bedded chassis, Rem. 700 type action, stainless one-piece fluted bolt, ground recoil lugs, AICS or AW 5 or 10 shot mag., upper and lower Picatinny rail, MPA buttstock with adj. cheek riser and adj. LOP, night vision bridge, black, FDE, or Cerakote (multiple colors) finish, includes monopod, 12 1/2-13 lbs. New 2014.

MSR $3,000	$2,595	$2,275	$1,950	$1,750	$1,425	$1,175	$950	

Add $150 for 6mm, 6.5mm, or 6.5 Creedmoor cal.

Add $250 for .300 Win. Mag. or .338 Lapua cal.

MPA 5.56x45mm BOLT ACTION SPORTING RIFLE – 5.56x45mm cal., match grade barrel, 10 shot mag., full feature handguard, side charging handle with forward assist, Mil-Spec fire control group, side folding stock, black finish. New 2015.

MSR $750	$635	$575	$475	$425	$375	$325	$275	

The MSR listed reflects the base model. Many other upgrades and features are available including 6.8 SPC or .300 AAC Blackout cal. and Cerakote finishes. Please contact the company directly for more information on these upgrades including price and availability (see Trademark Index).

MPA6547 BA RIFLE – 6.5x47 Lapua cal., Stillers Precision TAC Series action, Spencer/MPA stainless steel 24 in. Sendero profile barrel, Alamo Four Start Cowl induction brake, 10 shot Accurate/AICS mag., Rifle Basix LV1 trigger, night vision bridge, MPA buttstock with adj. cheekpiece, LOP, and monopod, MPA tactical aluminum or Competition chassis, lower mounted Picatinny rail, Cerakote finish (multiple colors available), includes Plano basic rifle case. New 2016.

MSR $3,250	$2,775	$2,425	$1,965	$1,685	$1,385	$1,175	$1,025	

MPA 6.5BA CREEDMORE RIFLE – 6.5mm Creedmoor cal., Stillers Precision TAC Series action, 24 in. Spencer/MPA stainless steel threaded Sendero profile barrel with muzzle brake, 10 shot AICS mag., Timney trigger, night vision bridge, removable front bridge, MPA buttstock with adj. cheek riser, LOP, and monopod, MPA tactical aluminum chassis, lower mounted Picatinny rail, barrier stop, Cerakote finish (multiple colors available), includes Plano basic rifle case, 12 1/2 lbs., New 2016.

MSR $3,150	$2,675	$2,335	$1,900	$1,625	$1,350	$1,130	$980	

MAUNZ MATCH RIFLES LLC (MAUNZ, KARL)

Current manufacturer located in Grand Rapids, OH. Previously located in Toledo and Maumee, OH circa 1960s-1987.

RIFLES: SEMI-AUTO

Maunz Rifles were manufactured in Toledo and Maumee Ohio from 1960's until 1987 by Karl Maunz for high-end military, law enforcement and competition. Models included the Model 87 Maunz Match Rifle, Model 77 Service Match Rifle, Model 67 Match Grade for practice, Model 67 Sniper Rifle, Model 57 and the Model 47 rifle. All models made on or prior to 2011 are custom order only.

MODEL 57 M1A – various cals. including .30-06, .308 Win., .276 Maunz or .45 Maunz (rare), other custom calibers were available, utilizes M1 Garand receiver with M14 parts, National Match barrel, custom-built glass bedded stock.

	$1,800	$1,600	$1,350	$1,125	$900	$775	$625	

MODEL 66 MATCH SERVICE RIFLE – .308 Win. cal., 22 in. barrel, M1A configuration with M1 and M14 G.I. parts, fiberglass stock, NM sights, M1 trigger assembly, 10 lbs., approx. 200 mfg.

	$2,500	$2,250	$2,000	$1,800	$1,500	$1,250	$1,050	

MODEL 67 MATCH GRADE PRACTICE RIFLE – 7.62 NATO/.308 Win. (.308x224, .308x244, .308x264), 6.30 Maunz, .338 Maunz (ltd. mfg.), or .45 Maunz (ltd. mfg.) cal., other custom calibers were available, M1A configuration with combination of M1 Garand and M14 parts, not allowed for service rifle competition.

	$2,000	$1,775	$1,525	$1,250	$1,000	$875	$700	

MSR	100%	98%	95%	90%	80%	70%	60%	Last MSR

MODEL 67 ASSAULT SNIPER RIFLE – 7.62 NATO/.308 Win. (.308x224, .308x244, .308x264), or 6.30 Maunz cal., 22 in. barrel standard, medium and heavy barrels were also available, M14 sights standard, 5, 10, 20, or 30 shot mag.

| | $2,000 | $1,775 | $1,525 | $1,250 | $1,000 | $875 | $700 | |

MODEL 77 – .308 Win. cal., utilized M1A Springfield receiver initially, followed by Valley Ordnance mfg., receiver has removable lug under the barrel, red, white and blue laminated stock, ser. no. 000011-005040.

| | $2,100 | $1,800 | $1,500 | $1,250 | $1,050 | $925 | $800 | |

MODEL 77 SERVICE MATCH RIFLE – 7.62 NATO/.308 Win. cal., custom calibers were also available, 22 in. barrel standard, medium and heavy barrels were also available, 5, 10, or 20 shot mag., NM/2A sights, special removable front globe sight, charcoal grey parkerized finish, heavyweight Kevlar or graphite/fiberglass stock with black gel coat, red/white/blue stocks also available.

| | $2,850 | $2,650 | $2,400 | $2,000 | $1,900 | $1,700 | $1,300 | |

MODEL 87 – various cals., 26 in. medium weight barrel, synthetic stock, G.I. parts with TRW bolts, satin black finish, open sights, ser. nos. 00001-03030, 11 lbs. Mfg. 1985-89.

| | $2,300 | $2,200 | $2,100 | $2,000 | $1,900 | $1,700 | $1,500 | |

MODEL 87 MATCH RIFLE – 7.62 NATO/.308 Win. (.308x224, .308x244, .308x264), 6.30 Maunz, .338 Maunz (ltd. mfg.), or .45 Maunz (ltd. mfg.) cal., other custom calibers were available, charcoal grey parkerized finish, heavyweight Kevlar or graphite/fiberglass stock with black gel coat, red/white/blue stocks also available.

| | $2,500 | $2,300 | $2,150 | $2,000 | $1,900 | $1,700 | $1,500 | |

MODEL 007 – .30 Custom, 6.30 Maunz, or .45 Maunz cal., accuracy metal full lined bedded with long action to accept the M1 Garand bolt, modified M14 type gas system, stainless steel or metal receiver, scope mount, classic wood, heavyweight Kevlar, or graphite/fiberglass stock covered in black gel coat, accepts many different type of magazines, custom weight barrels available.

| MSR $1,650 | $1,650 | $1,550 | $1,500 | $1,450 | $1,350 | $1,200 | $1,000 | |

MODEL 007 NRA MATCH RIFLE – chambered in 6.30 Maunz caliber with die sets for 6mm, 6.5mm, 7mm, 7.62x51mm, and .30-06 cal., 50 mfg. - one for each state, custom fit to the shooter and using his chosen serial number.

| | $1,650 | $1,550 | $1,500 | $1,450 | $1,350 | $1,200 | $1,000 | |

MODEL 97 MATCH/HUNTING RIFLE – chambered for 17 to 45Maunz calibers, modeled after the AR-10 and AR-15, GIO, custom weight barrels, fiberglass stock, custom color stock or classic wood stock with patent pending.

| MSR $1,850 | $1,700 | $1,575 | $1,350 | $1,100 | $900 | $850 | $750 | |

MODEL 97 SERVICE RIFLE – 5.56 NATO or .223 Rem. cal., modeled after the US M16/AR-15, GIO, black gel coated GI fiberglass stock.

| MSR $1,250 | $1,175 | $1,075 | $950 | $850 | $750 | $700 | $650 | |

MODEL 97 TARGET RIFLE – .243 Win. or .308 Win. cal., modeled after the AR-10 and AR-15, custom weight barrels, custom classic wood stock with patent pending. New 2016.

| MSR $2,400 | $2,175 | $1,900 | $1,625 | $1,475 | $1,195 | $980 | $800 | |

MODEL M14SA – service Standard grade rifle modeled after the M14.

Previous MSR on this model was $1,400.

MODEL M16SA – Service Standard grade rifle modeled after the M16.

Previous MSR on this model was $650.

MAUSER JAGDWAFFEN GmbH

Current trademark established during 1871, and currently owned by SIG Arms AG beginning late 2000. Mauser Model 98 Magnum bolt action rifles are currently manufactured by Mauser Jagdwaffen GmbH, located in Isny, Germany. Currently imported by Blaser USA, beginning circa 2012. Previously imported by Mauser USA, located in San Antonio, TX, 2009-2012.

In late 2000, SIG Arms AG, the firearms portion of SIG, was purchased by two Germans named Michael Lüke and Thomas Ortmeier, who have a background in textiles. Today the Lüke & Ortmeier group (L&O Group) includes independently operational companies such as Blaser Jadgwaffen GmbH, Mauser Jagdwaffen GmbH, J.P. Sauer & Sohn GmbH, SIG-Sauer Inc., SIG-Sauer GmbH and SAN Swiss Arms AG.

From late March, 2006-2009, Models 98 and 03 were distributed exclusively by Briley Manufacturing, located in Houston, TX. The former transition name was Mauser Jagd-und Sportwaffen GmbH. On January 1, 1999, Mauser transferred all production and distribution rights of both hunting and sporting weapons to SIG-Blaser. Mauser-Werke Oberndorf Waffensysteme GmbH continues to manufacture military defense contracts (including making small bore barrel liners for tanks), in addition to other industrial machinery.

MSR		100%	98%	95%	90%	80%	70%	60%	Last MSR

Previously imported exclusively by Brolin Arms, located in Pomona, CA during 1997-98 only. During 1998, the company name was changed from Mauser-Werke Oberndorf Waffensysteme GmbH. During 1994, the name was changed from Mauser-Werke to Mauser-Werke Oberndorf Waffensysteme GmbH. Previously imported by GSI located in Trussville, AL, until 1997, Gibb's Rifle Co., Inc. until 1995, Precision Imports, Inc. located in San Antonio, TX until 1993, and KDF located in Seguin, TX (1987-89).

PISTOLS: SEMI-AUTO, RECENT IMPORTATION

M-2 – .357 SIG (disc. 2001), .40 S&W, or .45 ACP cal., short recoil operation, SFO, rotating 3.54 in. barrel lockup, manual safety, 8 (.45 ACP) or 10 shot, DAO, hammerless, aluminum alloy frame with nickel chromium steel slide, black finish, includes case and trigger lock, approx. 29 or 32 1/2 oz. Mfg. by SIG in Europe, limited importation 2000-04.

| | | $450 | $400 | $350 | $300 | $275 | $250 | $225 | |

RIFLES: BOLT ACTION, RECENT PRODUCTION

Values on currently manufactured models include single rifle case, scope mount, and matching sling.

Add $520 for left-hand action. Add $1,287 per interchangeable standard cal. barrel. Add $988 per bolt assembly, and/or $390 per bolt head. Add $996 for barrel fluting (standard cals. only). Beginning late 2006, Mauser began grading wood between grades 2-11. Grade 2 is standard wood, and the following additional charges apply to the additional wood upgrades (2016 MSRs): Grade 3 - $335, N/A domestically, Grade 4 - $555, Grade 5 - $1,120, Grade 6 - $2,235, Grade 7 - $3,353, Grade 8 - $4,688, Grade 9 - $6,030, Grade 10 - $7,815, Grade 11 - from $10,045.

MODEL SR 93 – .300 Win. Mag. cal., precision rifle employing skeletonized cast magnesium/aluminum stock, combination right-hand/left-hand bolt, adj. ergonomics, 27 in. fluted barrel with muzzle brake, integrated bipod, 4 or 5 shot mag., approx. 13 lbs. without accessories. Disc. 1996.

| | | $20,000 | $17,250 | $14,750 | $11,950 | $8,700 | $6,500 | $5,000 | $21,995 |

* **Model 2000 Classic Sniper** – .300 Win. Mag. or .308 Win. cal., features heavy fluted barrel, special set trigger system, bipod rail, and other special shooting performance features, satin blue metal finish, custom built with individual certificate. Limited importation 1998 only.

| | | $1,900 | $1,550 | $1,350 | $1,100 | $900 | $775 | $650 | $2,200 |

LIGHTNING SNIPER MODEL – .300 Win. Mag. or .308 Win. cal., slide-bolt action, features free floating heavy fluted barrel w/o sights, special wood or synthetic stock with built-in bipod rail, detachable mag., satin blue metal finish. Limited importation 1998 only.

| | | $895 | $775 | $675 | $600 | $525 | $475 | $425 | $1,000 |

* **Lightning Sniper Model Stainless** – similar to Lightning Sniper Model, except is satin stainless steel. Limited importation 1998 only.

| | | $895 | $775 | $675 | $600 | $525 | $475 | $425 | $1,000 |

MAVERICK ARMS, INC.

Currently manufacturer located in Eagle Pass, TX, who completed a major expansion during 2014. Administrative offices are at O.F. Mossberg & Sons, located in North Haven, CT. Distributor sales only.

SHOTGUNS

Beginning 1992, all Maverick slide action shotguns incorporate twin slide rails in the operating mechanism.

* **Model 88 Field Slide Action Security** – 12 ga., 3 in. chamber, 18 1/2 (6 shot) or 20 (8 shot) in. barrel with cyl. bore fixed choke, bead sights, regular or pistol grip (disc. 1997) synthetic stock, 6 or 8 shot, plain synthetic forearm, matte blue metal finish, 6 1/4-6 1/2 lbs. New 1993.

| MSR $293 | | $250 | $220 | $190 | $170 | $140 | $115 | $90 | |

Add $7 for 8 shot model with 20 in. barrel (disc. 2009).
Add $98 for bullpup configuration (6 or 9 shot, disc. 1994).
Add $47-$65 for combo package (disc.).

* **Model 88 Field Slide Action Combat** – 12 ga. only, combat design featuring pistol grip stock and forearm, black synthetic stock is extension of receiver, 18 1/2 in. cyl. bore barrel with vented shroud with built-in carrying handle, open sights. Mfg. 1990-92.

| | | $375 | $330 | $280 | $255 | $205 | $170 | $130 | $282 |

MODEL HS-12 TACTICAL O/U – 12 ga., 2 3/4 or 3 in. chambers, 18 1/2 in. barrels, cylinder bore or Imp. Mod chokes, matte black finish, synthetic stock, rear slot sight with fiber optic front sight, no under barrel mounted Picatinny rail beginning 2012. Mfg. 2011-2015.

| | | $475 | $415 | $355 | $325 | $260 | $215 | $165 | $564 |

Add $18 for choke tubes.

MSR		100%	98%	95%	90%	80%	70%	60%	Last MSR

MODEL HS-12 THUNDER RANCH – 12 ga., 3 in. chamber, 2 shot, 18 1/2 in. barrel, matte black finish, side mounted Picatinny rails, tang mounted safety and barrel selector, checkered black synthetic pistol grip stock and forearm with nylon shell holder, fiber optic front sight, engraved Thunder Ranch logo, 6 1/4 lbs. New 2013.

	MSR $594		$485	$425	$365	$335	$300	$275	$250

MAWHINNEY, CHUCK

Current trademark of sniper rifles manufactured by Rifle Craft, Ltd. located in the United Kingdom. Imported by Chuck Mawhinney, located in Baker City, OR.

RIFLES: BOLT ACTION

M40 SNIPER – .308 Win. cal., based on the M700 Remington action, 24 in. matte black pillar bedded free floating barrel, walnut stock, engraved aluminum floorplate with Chuck Mawhinney's signature (former sniper for the Marines), includes 3-9x40mm Leupold scope. Serial numbered 1-103. New 2012.

	MSR $5,000		$5,000	$4,400	$3,750	$3,150	$2,500	$2,000	$1,650

MAXIMUS ARMS, LLC

Current pistol manufacturer, gunsmith, and customizer established in 1991 and located in Gallatin, TN. Consumer and dealer sales.

While Maximus Arms LLC has been in gunsmithing business for more than 20 years, the company started manufacturing its own guns during 2010. The company has its own foundry, and uses 17-4PH stainless steel for all its custom guns.

PISTOLS: SEMI-AUTO

CENTURION – .45 ACP cal., full-size semi-auto, match grade barrel, high rise beavertail safety, flared magwell, front and rear slide serrations, adj. trigger, polished feed ramp, lowered and flared ejection ports, checkered grips, steel or Damascus slide, two magazines and an airline approved gun case.

	MSR $1,776		$1,625	$1,425	$1,225	$1,100	$900	$725	$575

Add $1,124 for Centurion model with Damascus slide.

GLADIATOR – .45 ACP cal., full-size semi-auto, 5 in. throated match barrel, 8 shot mag., checkered wood grips, high rise beavertail safety, Commander style hammer, Sprinco recoil reduction system, flared magwell, front and rear slide serrations, match trigger, polished feed ramp, lowered and flared ejection ports, extended thumb safety, extended mag. release, ghost ring fully adj. rear sight and fiber optic front sight, integral Picatinny tactical rail, loaded chamber indicator, exotic wood grips, 36.6 oz.

	MSR $1,776		$1,625	$1,425	$1,225	$1,100	$900	$725	$575

McCANN INDUSTRIES

Previous rifle and current accessories manufacturer located in Spanaway, WA.

McCann Industries manufactured new Garand semi-auto rifles with design improvements that utilize a .338 or .458 Mag cal. cartridge (not Win. Mag.), in addition to a .300 Win. Mag. bolt action pistol. For more information, including pricing and availability, contact the company directly (see Trademark Index).

MCDUFFEE ARMS

Current AR-15 rifle manufacturer established in 2010, located in Westminster, CO.

McDuffee Arms is a family owned and operated business specializing in AR-15 rifles and receivers. They offer a lifetime warranty on all their products.

RIFLES: SEMI-AUTO

BANSHEE 3G – 3-gun competition rifle, 18 in. stainless steel barrel with stainless steel muzzle brake, iron sights, ultra slim-line free float handguard, aluminum lower, A3 flat-top upper, power extractor spring, 6-pos. adj. stock, Type III hardcoat anodized finish, 7.2 lbs. New 2014.

	MSR $990		$850	$725	$650	$585	$515	$450	$395

Add $10 for NorGuard coating or $15 for nickel boron bolt carrier group.

BANSHEE AR-15 CARBINE – 5.56 NATO, .300 AAC Blackout (disc. 2015), or 7.62x39mm cal., 16 in. M4 contour chrome moly barrel, railed gas block, free float quad rail handguards, A3 flat-top upper receiver, billet aluminum lower, 6-position adj. stock, power extractor spring, Type III hardcoat anodized black finish, 6.6 lbs.

	MSR $800		$685	$615	$550	$475	$420	$365	$335

Add $15 for 9 in., $20 for 13 in., or $30 for 15 in. handguard.
Add $15 for NorGuard coating or $30 for nickel boron bolt carrier group.
Add $25 for 7.62x39mm cal. or $50 for .300 AAC Blackout cal (disc. 2015).

MSR	100%	98%	95%	90%	80%	70%	60%	Last MSR

* **Banshee AR-15 Carbine SS** – 5.56 NATO, .300 AAC Blackout, 6.8 SPC (disc. 2015), or 7.62x39mm (disc. 2015) cal., similar to Banshee AR-15 Carbine, except features 16 in. M4 contour stainless steel barrel and steel flash suppressor, 6.6 lbs.

| MSR $850 | $725 | $650 | $580 | $515 | $450 | $385 | $340 | |

Add $10 for 9 in., $40 for 13 in., or $45 for 15 in. handguard.

Add $15 for NorGuard coating or $30 for nickel boron bolt carrier group.

Add $40 for .300 AAC Blackout, $35 for 7.62x39mm (disc. 2015), or $120 for 6.8 SPC (disc. 2015) cal.

BANSHEE AR-15 RIFLE – .223 Wylde cal., 20 in. stainless steel barrel and stainless steel custom flash suppressor, billet aluminum lower, railed gas block, A3 flat-top upper, full length free float quad rail handguard, 6-pos. adj. stock, black Type III hardcoat anodized finish.

| MSR $1,010 | $850 | $725 | $650 | $585 | $515 | $450 | $395 | |

Add $10 for 15 in. handguard.

Add $15 for NorGuard coating or $30 for nickel boron bolt carrier group.

MLR-308 BROADSWORD – .308 Win. cal., 20 in. heavy stainless steel barrel with stainless steel muzzle brake, 10 shot Magpul PMAG, billet aluminum lower, integral Winter trigger guard, nickel boron bolt carrier group, H3 heavy buffer, free-float super slim handguard, A3 flat-top upper, railed gas block, Magpul CTR adj. stock, Ergo grip, Type III hardcoat anodized finish. New 2014.

| MSR $1,400 | $1,200 | $1,075 | $950 | $800 | $700 | $600 | $495 | |

Add $25 for nickel boron bolt carrier group or $40 for NorGuard coating.

McMILLAN BROS. RIFLE CO.

Previous division of McMillan Group International, located in Phoenix, AZ. Dealer and consumer direct sales. During 1998, the company name changed from McBros Rifles to McMillan Bros. Rifle Co. The company name changed again during 2007 to McMillan Firearms Manufacturing. Please refer to McMillan Firearms Manufacturing, LLC listing for recent models.

RIFLES: BOLT ACTION

MCR TACTICAL – .308 Win. or .300 Win. Mag. cal. Mfg. 1993-2007.

| | $2,950 | $2,400 | $1,900 | $1,500 | $1,250 | $1,050 | $925 | $3,300 |

This model was formerly designated the MCR Sniper Model.

* **MCRT Tactical** – .300 Win. Mag. or .338 Lapua (new 1998), similar to MCR Tactical. Mfg. 1993-2007.

| | $3,050 | $2,550 | $2,100 | $1,825 | $1,550 | $1,375 | $1,100 | $3,500 |

Add $500 for .338 Lapua Mag (muzzle brake is standard).

This model was formerly designated the MCRT Sniper Model.

BIG MAC/BOOMER – .50 BMG cal., available as either single shot sporter, repeater sporter, light benchrest, or heavy benchrest variation. Mfg. 1993-2007.

| | $4,450 | $3,850 | $3,250 | $2,700 | $2,225 | $1,825 | $1,525 | $4,900 |

Add $300 for repeating action.

Add $500 for Tactical 50 variation.

Add $100 for Tactical single shot.

Add $100 for heavy benchrest variation.

McMILLAN FIREARMS MANUFACTURING, LLC

Current manufacturer located in Phoenix, AZ beginning 2007.

McMillan Group International is a group of McMillan family companies: McMillan Fiberglass Stocks, McMillan Firearms Manufacturing, and McMillan Machine Company. In 2014, the company was acquired by Strategic Armory Corps. This company also owns ArmaLite, Surgeon Rifles, AWC Silencers, and AWC Ammo.

RIFLES: BOLT ACTION, TACTICAL SERIES

TAC-300 – .300 Win. Mag. cal., 26 in. medium heavy free floating contoured threaded stainless steel barrel, detachable 5 shot box mag. or hinged floorplate, drilled and tapped, McMillan G30 long action, A-5 fiberglass buttstock with adj. cheekpiece and LOP, black, OD, gray (disc.), or tan Cerakote finish, two sling swivels, 11 lbs.

| MSR $6,750 | $5,725 | $5,000 | $4,295 | $3,895 | $3,150 | $2,575 | $2,000 | |

TAC-308 – .308 Win. cal., 20 (disc.) or 24 in. match grade stainless steel medium heavy contoured threaded barrel with cap, detachable 5 shot box mag., drilled and tapped, McMillan G31 short action, A-3 fiberglass buttstock with adj. cheekpiece and LOP spacer system, black, OD, gray (disc.), dark earth (disc.), or tan Cerakote finish, two sling swivels.

| MSR $6,495 | $5,525 | $4,825 | $4,150 | $3,750 | $3,050 | $2,475 | $1,925 | |

MSR	100%	98%	95%	90%	80%	70%	60%	Last MSR

TAC-338 – .338 Lapua cal., 26 1/2 in. match grade stainless steel medium heavy contoured threaded barrel with muzzle brake, detachable 5 shot box mag. or hinged floorplate, drilled and tapped, McMillan G30 short action, A-5 fiberglass buttstock with adj. cheekpiece and LOP spacer system, Cerakote finish in Black, OD, Gray (disc.), Dark Earth (disc.), or Tan, 6 flushmount cups with sling loops, 13 lbs.

MSR $6,895	$5,850	$5,125	$4,395	$3,975	$3,225	$2,625	$2,050	

TAC-416 R/SS – .416 Barrett cal., single shot action, 29 in. match grade Navy contour or 30 in. light contour fluted threaded barrel with muzzle brake, drilled and tapped, McMillan synthetic stock with butthook and adj. saddle style cheekpiece, six flushmount cups with sling loops, bipod, Decelerator pad, spacer system, adj. trigger, black, olive, gray, tan, or dark earth finish. New 2013.

MSR $9,990	$8,495	$7,425	$6,375	$5,775	$4,675	$3,825	$2,975	

TAC-50 A1 – .50 BMG cal., 29 in. match grade Navy contour fluted threaded barrel with muzzle brake, drilled and tapped, 5 shot detachable box mag., Jewell bottom safety trigger, McMillan synthetic stock with butthook and adj. saddle style cheekpiece, A1 bipod, Decelerator pad, black, OD, gray (disc.), tan, or dark earth (disc.) Cerakote finish, 26 lbs.

MSR $9,990	$8,495	$7,425	$6,375	$5,775	$4,675	$3,825	$2,975	

TAC-50 A1-R2 – .50 BMG cal., similar to Tac-50 A1, except has McMillan Tac-50 A1-R2 stock and R2 recoil mitigation system. New 2013.

MSR $11,990	$10,195	$8,925	$7,650	$6,925	$5,600	$4,595	$3,575	

TAC-50C – .50 BMG cal., folding Cadex Dual Strike chassis system, 29 in. match grade Navy contour fluted and threaded barrel with muzzle brake, 5 shot detachable box mag., Cadex Dual Strike with adj. cheekpiece with option for vertical adjustment, adj. LOP, and Decelerator pad, Jewell bottom safety trigger, tan, OD, or black Cerakote finish, 24 lbs. New 2016.

Please contact the manufacturer directly for pricing and availability on this model.

ALIAS STAR – 6.5x47 Lapua, 6.5mm Creedmoor, or .308 Win. cal., 18 to 24 in. stainless steel match grade barrel, threaded muzzle with thread cap, detachable 10 or 20 shot mag., tactical pistol grip, matte black finish, tube or quad rail forend, Anschutz trigger, includes case, 11.6 lbs. Mfg. 2013-2015.

	$7,350	$6,825	$6,000	$5,150	$4,675	$3,775	$3,000	*$8,300*

ALIAS TARGET – .260 Rem., 6.5x47 Lapua, 6.5mm Creedmoor, .308 Win., .308 Palma, or 6XC cal., 24 to 30 in. barrel, includes two detachable 10 shot mags. and one single shot loading block, competition pistol grip, matte black finish, competition buttstock and forend, Anschutz trigger, 12 lbs. Mfg. 2013-2015.

	$7,350	$6,825	$6,000	$5,150	$4,675	$3,775	$3,000	*$8,300*

CS5 STANDARD – .308 Win cal., matte black finish, 18 1/2 in. stainless steel match grade barrel with threaded muzzle and thread cap., 10 or 20 shot detachable box magazine, Anschutz trigger, adj. buttstock, pistol grip, tactile safety button, upper Picatinny rail, optional suppressor and bipod, includes full-size gun case. Mfg. 2012-2015.

Retail priciing was never made available for this model.

RIFLES: SEMI-AUTO

M1A – .308 Win. cal., 18 or 20 in. barrel, 10 shot mag., McMillan MFS-14 modular tactical system, SOCOM five position adj. buttstock, pistol grip with finger groove, M3A fiberglass stock with saddle type cheekpiece, Picatinny style side and bottom rails, four flushmount cups with sling swivels, two-stage military trigger, many other options available.

	$2,995	$2,750	$2,450	$2,125	$1,800	$1,525	$1,300	*$3,399*

Add $200 for compact model with 18 in. barrel.

M3A – .308 Win. cal., features McMillan M3A fiberglass stock with adj. cheekpiece, standard or full length upper handguard tactical rail. Mfg. 2011-2012.

Retail pricing was not obtainable for this model.

McMILLAN, G. & CO., INC.

Previous trademark established circa 1988, located in Phoenix, AZ.

G. McMillan & Co., Inc. had various barrel markings from 1988-1995 including G. McMillan, Harris - McMillan, and Harris Gunworks.

RIFLES: BOLT ACTION

The models listed were also available with custom wood stocks at varying prices. McMillan also manufactured a custom rifle from a supplied action. Features included new barreling, a fiberglass stock, matte black finish, and range testing to guarantee 3/4 M.O.A. Prices started at $1,400.

Add $150 for stainless steel receiver on most models.

M-40 SNIPER RIFLE – .308 Win. cal., Remington action with McMillan match grade heavy contour barrel, fiberglass stock with recoil pad, 4 shot mag., 9 lbs. Mfg. 1990-95.

	$1,775	$1,475	$1,150	$925	$825	$725	$625	*$1,800*

MSR	100%	98%	95%	90%	80%	70%	60%	Last MSR

M-86 SNIPER RIFLE – .300 Phoenix, .30-06 (new 1989), .300 Win. Mag. or .308 Win. cal., fiberglass stock, variety of optical sights. Mfg. 1988-95.

| | $1,825 | $1,500 | $1,150 | $975 | $85 | $775 | $675 | $1,900 |

Add $550 for .300 Phoenix cal.
Add $200 for takedown feature (new 1993).

* **M-86 Sniper Rifle System** – includes Model 86 Sniper Rifle, bipod, Ultra scope, rings, and bases. Cased. Mfg. 1988-92.

| | $2,460 | $2,050 | $1,825 | $1,600 | $1,350 | $1,100 | $950 | $2,665 |

M-87 LONG RANGE SNIPER RIFLE – .50 BMG cal., stainless steel bolt action, 29 in. barrel with muzzle brake, single shot, camo synthetic stock, accurate to 1,500 meters, 21 lbs. Mfg. 1988-95.

| | $3,650 | $2,950 | $2,500 | $2,150 | $1,900 | $1,700 | $1,575 | $3,735 |

* **M-87 Long Range Sniper Rifle System** – includes Model 87 Sniper Rifle, bipod, 20X Ultra scope, rings, and bases. Cased. Mfg. 1988-92.

| | $4,200 | $3,400 | $2,875 | $2,550 | $2,250 | $2,100 | $1,800 | $4,200 |

* **M-87R Long Range Sniper Rifle** – same specs. as Model 87, except has 5 shot fixed box mag. Mfg. 1990-95.

| | $3,995 | $3,300 | $2,700 | $2,300 | $2,000 | $1,850 | $1,700 | $4,000 |

Add $300 for Combo option.

M-89 SNIPER RIFLE – .308 Win. cal., 28 in. barrel with suppressor (also available without), fiberglass stock adj. for length and recoil pad, 15 1/4 lbs. Mfg. 1990-95.

| | $2,200 | $1,825 | $1,575 | $1,250 | $1,050 | $875 | $750 | $2,300 |

Add $425 for muzzle suppressor.

M-92 BULLPUP – .50 BMG cal., bullpup configuration with shorter barrel. Mfg. 1993-95.

| | $3,750 | $2,950 | $2,550 | $2,200 | $2,000 | $1,850 | $1,700 | $4,000 |

M-93SN – .50 BMG cal., similar to M-87, except has folding stock and detachable 5 or 10 shot box mag. Mfg. 1993-95.

| | $3,950 | $3,250 | $2,750 | $2,300 | $2,000 | $1,850 | $1,700 | $4,300 |

.300 PHOENIX LONG RANGE RIFLE – .300 Phoenix cal., special fiberglass stock featuring adj. cheekpieces to accommodate night vision optics, adj. buttplate, 29 in. barrel, conventional box mag., 12 1/2 lbs. Mfg. 1992 only.

| | $2,700 | $2,195 | $1,850 | $1,450 | $1,100 | $925 | $825 | $3,000 |

.300 Phoenix was a cartridge developed to function at ranges in excess of 800 yards. It produced muzzle velocities of 3,100 ft. per second with a 250 grain bullet.

MCREES PRECISION

Previous firearms and current accessories manufacturer located in Lesterville, MO. McRees Precision is a division of McRees Multi Services. Consumer sales through FFL dealers.

RIFLES: BOLT ACTION

McRees Precision manufactured a bolt action rifle in various calibers with a 22 in. barrel. All rifles were guaranteed at least 1/2 MOA at 100 yards.

METROARMS CORPORATION

Current manufacturer of American Classic trademarked 1911 style semi-auto pistols imported and distributed by Eagle Imports, located in Wanamassa, NJ.

MetroArms Corporation was established in late 2011 under the expertise of former competitive shooter Hector Rodriquez.

PISTOLS: SEMI-AUTO: AMERICAN CLASSIC SERIES

AMERICAN CLASSIC COMMANDER MODEL – 9mm Para. (new 2013) or .45 ACP cal., SA, 4 1/4 in. barrel, 8 (.45 ACP) or 9 (9mm) shot mag., Blue, Hard Chrome (disc. 2015), or Duotone (new 2012) finish, steel frame and slide, Novak rear sight, dovetail front sight, flared and lowered ejection port, extended slide stop, beavertail grip safety, combat hammer, combat trigger, rear slide serrations, diamond cut checkered mahogany grips, approx. 36 oz. New 2010.

| MSR $624 | $520 | $450 | $375 | $325 | $295 | $275 | $250 | |

Add $75 for duo-tone finish (new 2012).
Add $95 for hard chrome finish (disc. 2015).

AMERICAN CLASSIC AMIGO MODEL – .45 ACP cal., SA, Officer's Model configuration, 3 1/2 in. barrel, 7 shot mag., steel frame and slide, Dovetail front and Novak-style rear sights, diamond cut checkered mahogany grips, Beavertail grip/extended thumb safety, Deep Blue, Hard Chrome, or Duotone (new 2012) finish, approx. 32 1/2 oz. New 2011.

| MSR $714 | $610 | $515 | $425 | $365 | $325 | $285 | $250 | |

Add $90 for hard chrome finish.
Add $60 for duo-tone finish (new 2012).

MSR	100%	98%	95%	90%	80%	70%	60%	Last MSR

AMERICAN CLASSIC TROPHY MODEL – .45 ACP cal., 5 in. barrel, 8 shot mag., steel frame and slide, SA, dovetail fiber optic front sight, adj. Novak rear sight, flared and lowered ejection port, ambidextrous thumb safety, reverse plug recoil system with full length guide rod, beveled magwell, combat hammer and trigger, front and rear slide serrations, diamond cut checkered mahogany grips, checkered mainspring housing, hard chrome finish, approx. 38 oz. New 2010.

MSR $819	$715	$625	$575	$495	$450	$425	$375	

PISTOLS: SEMI-AUTO, MAC SERIES

MAC 1911 BOBCUT – .45 ACP cal., SA, 4 1/4 in. barrel, steel frame, blue, hard chrome, or black chrome (new 2014) finish, 8 shot mag., hammer forged steel slide, fully adj. Novak style rear sight, dovetail fiber optic front sight, custom hardwood grips with MAC logo, approx. 35 oz. New 2013.

MSR $902	$765	$675	$575	$525	$425	$350	$275	

Add $76 for hard chrome finish.
Add $143 for black chrome finish (new 2014).

MAC 1911 BULLSEYE – .45 ACP cal., SA, 6 in. ramped match bull barrel, 8 shot mag., dovetail front and fully adj. Bomar-type rear sights, custom hardwood grips with MAC logo, ambidextrous thumb safety, flared and lowered ejection port, skeletal combat hammer and trigger, wide front and rear slide serrations, Blue, hard chrome, or black chrome (mfg. 2014 only) finish, approx. 47 oz. New 2013.

MSR $1,219	$1,040	$910	$780	$700	$575	$475	$365	

Add $75 for hard chrome finish.

MAC 1911 CLASSIC – .45 ACP cal., SA, 5 in. ramped match bull barrel, 8 shot mag., steel frame, hammer forged steel slide, fully adj. Bomar style rear sight, dovetail fiber optic front sight, flared and lowered ejection port, standard slide stop, enhanced beavertail grip safety, skeletal hammer, combat trigger, wide front and rear slide serrations, ambidextrous thumb safety, custom hardwood grips with MAC logo, wide magwell, blue, hard chrome, or black chrome (new 2015) finish, approx. 41 oz. New 2013.

MSR $1,045	$895	$795	$650	$595	$475	$395	$300	

Add $75 for hard chrome finish.
Add $159 for black chrome finish (new 2015).

MAC 3011 SSD – .45 ACP or .40 S&W (new 2014) cal., SA, steel frame, 5 in. ramped match grade bull barrel, 14 (.45 ACP) or 15 (.40 S&W) shot mag., hammer forged steel slide, fully adj. Bomar style rear sight, dovetail fiber optic front sight, flared and lowered ejection port, standard slide stop, enhanced beavertail grip safety, skeletal hammer, combat trigger, wide front and rear slide serrations, ambidextrous thumb safety, aluminum grips with MAC logo, wide magwell, blue or hard chrome finish, approx. 46 oz. New 2013.

MSR $1,136	$975	$865	$735	$650	$525	$425	$325	

Add $76 for hard chrome finish.

PISTOLS: SEMI-AUTO, SPS SERIES

SPS Series pistols are manufactured by S.P.S. in Spain, then assembled in the U.S.

SPS PANTERA – 9mm Para. (new 2016), .45 ACP, or .40 S&W (new 2014) cal., SA, 5 in. ramped match bull barrel, 12 (.45 ACP) or 16 (.40 S&W, new 2014) shot mag., steel frame, hammer forged steel slide, fully adj. Bomar style rear sight, dovetail fiber optic front sight, flared and lowered ejection port, standard slide stop, enhanced beavertail grip safety, skeletal hammer, lightweight polymer trigger, wide front and rear slide serrations, ambidextrous thumb safety, glass filled nylon polymer grips with S.P.S. logo, wide magwell, black chrome finish, approx. 37 oz. New 2013.

MSR $1,895	$1,600	$1,400	$1,200	$1,095	$875	$725	$550	

SPS VISTA – 9mm Para. (Vista Short) or .38 Super (Vista Long) cal., SA, 5 1/2 in. ramped match threaded barrel, steel frame, 21 shot mag., hammer forged steel slide, scope mount, flared and lowered ejection port, standard slide stop, enhanced beavertail grip safety, skeletal hammer, lightweight polymer trigger, wide front and rear slide serrations, ambidextrous thumb safety, glass filled nylon polymer grips with S.P.S. logo, wide magwell, black chrome finish, approx. 42-43 oz. New 2013.

MSR $2,450	$2,175	$1,900	$1,625	$1,475	$1,195	$975	$750	

MICOR DEFENSE, INC.

Current manufacturer established in 1999, located in Decatur, AL.

Micor manufactures a line of defense products available to the general public, as well as custom weapons and products for the defense and other related industries. Micor consists of two companies - Micor Industries, Inc. and Micor Defense, Inc.

RIFLES: SEMI-AUTO

Micor manufactures the Leader 416 semi-auto bullpup rifle, Leader T2 semi-auto rifle, and the Leader 338 Bullpup rifle. Additionally, Micor offers the Gatekeeper 50 (Leader 50), a lightweight .50 BMG cal. rifle (MSR $9,995). All models were designed by Charles St. George, original designer of the Bushmaster M17 bullpup rifle. Please contact the company directly for pricing, availability, and options (see Trademark Index).

MSR	100%	98%	95%	90%	80%	70%	60%	Last MSR

MICROTECH SMALL ARMS RESEARCH, INC. (MSAR)

Current rifle manufacturer located in Bradford, PA.

CARBINES/RIFLES: SEMI-AUTO

MSAR manufactures American-made semi-auto bullpup carbines and rifles, patterned after the Steyr AUG.

STG-556 – .223 Rem. cal., 16 or 20 in. chrome lined barrel, gas operated rotating bolt, short piston drive, 10, 20, 30, or 42 shot mag., black, tan, or OD Green finish, with or w/o 9 in. Picatinny rail, right or left-hand ejection, synthetic stock, 7.2 lbs.

MSR $1,839	$1,675	$1,400	$1,200	$995	$800	$700	$625

Add $156 for 1.5x Optic.

* **STG-556 Gebirgsjager Limited Edition** – similar to STG-556, engraved Edelweiss flower insignia, except includes all OD Green finish, 1.5x CQB optical sight, 6 in. Picatinny side rail, three 30 shot mags., OD Green Currahee knife with nylon sheath, Giles sling with Uncle Mike's sling swivels, custom Pelican 1700 green case, and certificate of authenticity.

	$3,495	$3,100	$2,750	$2,525	$2,300	$2,100	$1,875

STG-680 – 6.8 Rem. cal., 16 or 20 in. chrome lined barrel, 10, 20, 30, or 42 shot mag., black, tan, or OD Green synthetic stock, with or w/o 9 in. Picatinny rail, right or left-hand action, 7.2 lbs.

	$1,725	$1,575	$1,395	$1,275	$1,150	$995	$825

Add $156 for 1.5x Optic.

STG-E4 – 5.56 NATO or .300 AAC Blackout cal., semi-auto rifle, bull pup design, gas operated rotating bolt short piston drive, 16 1/2 or 18 1/2 in. chrome moly barrel with dedicated sound flash suppressor, 9 in. Picatinny rail, re-engineered bolt carrier, black composite stock with quick detach shell deflector, improved trigger modual, 2-position safety, 30 shot mag., 7.2 lbs. New 2013.

MSR $2,200	$1,975	$1,675	$1,450	$1,200	$1,000	$800	$700

MILLER PRECISION ARMS

Current AR-15 manufacturer located in Columbia Falls, MT.

RIFLES: SEMI-AUTO

MPA300 GUARDIAN – .300 Win. Mag. cal., 20 in. stainless steel ultra match SPR barrel, Precision Reflex forearm, Magpul PRS stock, Dark Earth Cerakote finish.

MSR $5,399	$4,850	$4,250	$3,650	$3,300	$2,675	$2,195	$1,700

MPAR 10 – .308 Win. cal., 16-24 in. stainless steel SPR contour barrel, free float aluminum forearm, LMT SOPMOD stock, bead blasted stainless steel finish.

MSR $2,199	$1,975	$1,725	$1,475	$1,350	$1,075	$900	$700

MPAR 15 – 5.56 NATO cal., 16 in. M4 button rifled chrome moly barrel, Troy Industries forearm, Magpul MOE stock, Black anodized finish.

MSR $1,599	$1,425	$1,250	$1,075	$975	$775	$650	$500

MPA 556 – .223 Wylde cal., 18 in. stainless steel ultra match SPR barrel, Hammerhead muzzle brake, precision machined billet upper and lower receiver, forward assist, Picatinny flat-top rail, extractor, Geissele two-stage trigger, Precision Reflex free float carbon fiber handguard, integral trigger, LMT SOPMOD stock, Armour Black Cerakote finish.

MSR $3,600	$3,250	$2,850	$2,450	$2,225	$1,800	$1,475	$1,150

MPA 762 – .308 Win. cal., 18 in. stainless steel ultra match SPR contour barrel, Precision Reflex Delta forearm, LMT SOPMOD stock, anodized finish.

MSR $3,750	$3,375	$2,950	$2,525	$2,300	$1,850	$1,525	$1,175

MILTAC INDUSTRIES, LLC

Current AR-15 manufacturer located in Boise, ID.

PISTOLS: SEMI-AUTO

AR-15 PISTOL – 5.56 NATO/.223 Rem. or .300 AAC Blackout cal., GIO, 7 1/2 or 10 1/2 in. stainless steel barrel with KAK Industry "flash can", Sig Sauer SB15 arm brace, Magpul MOE grip, Troy Alpha (disc.) or MT Sierra Tango (new 2015) rail, 30 shot Magpul PMAG, Cerakote finish in Black, Burnt Bronze, Flat Dark Earth, OD Green, or Tactical Grey. New mid-2014.

MSR $1,099	$925	$850	$725	$625	$550	$475	$425

RIFLES: SEMI-AUTO

ALPHA SERIES – 5.56 NATO cal., GIO, 16 in. M4 chrome lined barrel with Smith Enterprises Vortex flash hider, two Magpul 30 shot PMAGs, 13 in. modular free float Alpha rail, Geissele Super two-stage trigger, flared magwell, oversized

MSR	100%	98%	95%	90%	80%	70%	60%	Last MSR

trigger guard, 3D engraving on lower receiver, Troy Industries M4 flip up iron battle sights, hardcoat anodized and Cerakote finish in black, FDE, or two-tone, Magpul 6-position collapsible or extended stock, Magpul MIAD grip, includes Crossfire tactical carry case, 6 lbs. 12 oz.

MSR $2,389	$2,015	$1,765	$1,475	$1,265	$1,050	$950	$750	

BRAVO SERIES – .300 AAC Blackout cal., GIO, 16 in. stainless barrel with SP ATC muzzle brake, two Magpul 30 shot PMAGs, 13 in. modular free float Alpha rail, Geissele Super two-stage trigger, flared magwell, oversized trigger guard, 3D engraving on lower receiver, Troy Industries M4 flip up iron battle sights, hardcoat anodized and Cerakote finish in black, FDE, or two-tone, Magpul 6-position collapsible or extended stock, Magpul MIAD grip, includes Crossfire tactical carry case, 7 lbs. 4 oz.

MSR $2,389	$2,015	$1,765	$1,475	$1,265	$1,050	$950	$750	

COMBAT SERIES – 5.56 NATO/.223 Rem. cal., GIO, 16 in. steel barrel with A4 flash hider, 30 shot Magpul PMAG, M4 double heat shield, 6-pos. stock, A2 black plastic grip, hardcoat anodized finish in Black, Flat Dark Earth, or Two-Tone, 6 1/4 lbs. New mid-2014.

MSR $1,199	$1,025	$925	$800	$685	$595	$515	$440	

COMPETITION SERIES – 5.56 NATO/.223 Rem. cal., GIO, 18 in. stainless steel Match Grade 3-gun threaded barrel, Geissele Match 3-Gun trigger, nickel boron bolt, oversized trigger guard, Cerakote finish. New mid-2014.

MSR $2,789	$2,335	$1,965	$1,650	$1,400	$1,125	$975	$850	

ECHO SERIES – 5.56 NATO cal., GIO, 16 in. M4 chrome lined barrel with Smith Enterprises Vortex or YHM (new 2014) flash hider, 13 in. modular free float Alpha or Sierra Tango (new 2014) rail, nickel boron bolt carrier group, flared magwell, oversized trigger guard, 3D engraving on lower receiver, no sights, hardcoat anodized and Cerakote finish in black, FDE, or two-tone, Magpul MOE carbine Mil-Spec stock, Magpul MOE grip, 6 lbs. 4 oz.

MSR $1,789	$1,510	$1,310	$1,150	$1,015	$860	$735	$595	

SIX SERIES – 6.8 SPC or 6.5mm Grendel cal., 16 or 20 in. stainless steel threaded barrel, Geissele two-stage trigger, nickel boron bolt, Cerakote finish. New mid-2014.

MSR $2,639	$2,225	$1,940	$1,600	$1,375	$1,125	$975	$850	

MITCHELL ARMS, INC.

Previous manufacturer, importer, and distributor located in Fountain Valley, CA.

Mitchell Centerfire Pistols

1911 GOLD/SIGNATURE SERIES (WIDE BODY) – .45 ACP cal., features new tapered barrel slide lock-up, SA, full length guide rod recoil buffer assembly, beveled magwell, blue (disc. 1995) or stainless steel, 10 (C/B 1994) or 13* shot mag., walnut checkered grips, fixed or adj. sights. Mfg. 1994-1997.

> *** 1911 Gold/Signature Series (Wide Body) Tactical Model** – stainless steel, features elongated grip safety and serrated front slide, adj. rear sight. Mfg. 1996-97.

	$795	$675	$575	$480	$410	$350	$295	*$895*

RIFLES: DISC.

LW22 SEMI-AUTO – .22 LR cal., 10 shot mag., composite or skeleton stock, patterned after Feather Industries semi-auto. Limited mfg. 1996-97.

	$300	$265	$240	$220	$195	$175	$160	*$275*

Add $30 for composite stock.

LW9 SEMI-AUTO – 9mm Para. cal., semi-auto, blowback action, composite or skeleton stock, patterned after Feather Industries 9mm Para. semi-auto. Limited mfg. 1996-97.

	$550	$495	$450	$395	$365	$335	$295	*$500*

Add $35 for composite stock.

M-16A3 – .22 LR, .22 WMR (disc. 1987), or .32 ACP cal., patterned after Colt's AR-15, GIO. Mfg. 1987-94.

	$450	$395	$350	$300	$275	$250	$225	*$266*

Add 20% for .22 WMR cal. or .32 ACP (disc. 1988).

CAR-15/22 – .22 LR cal., GIO, carbine variation of M16 with shorter barrel and collapsible stock. Mfg. 1990-94.

	$495	$450	$395	$350	$300	$275	$250	*$266*

GALIL – .22 LR or .22 WMR cal., patterned after Galil rifle, choice of wood stock or folding stock (new 1992). Mfg. 1987-1993.

	$395	$350	$295	$265	$230	$200	$185	*$359*

MAS – .22 LR or .22 WMR cal., patterned after French MAS rifle. Mfg. 1987-93.

	$395	$350	$295	$265	$230	$200	$185	*$359*

Add $75 for .22 WMR cal. (disc. 1988).

MSR	100%	98%	95%	90%	80%	70%	60%	Last MSR

PPS-30/50 – .22 LR cal., patterned after the Russian WWII PPS military rifle, full length barrel shroud, 20 shot banana mag., adj. rear sight, walnut stock. Mfg. 1989-94.

| | $325 | $275 | $250 | $225 | $200 | $185 | $170 | *$266* |

Add $150 for 50 shot drum magazine.

AK-22 – .22 LR or .22 WMR (new 1988) cal., copy of the famous Russian AK-47, fully adj. sights, built-in cleaning rod, high quality European walnut or folding stock, 20 shot mag. Mfg. 1985-94.

| | $325 | $275 | $250 | $225 | $200 | $185 | $170 | *$266* |

Add $40 for folding stock.

AK-47 – 7.62x39mm cal., copy of the original Kalashnikov AK-47, semi-auto, teak stock and forend, 30 shot steel mag., last shot hold open. Mfg. in Yugoslavia. Imported 1986-89.

| | $1,895 | $1,700 | $1,550 | $1,400 | $1,300 | $1,200 | $1,100 | *$675* |

Add $100 for steel folding buttstock.
Add $200 for 75 shot steel drum mag.

.308 WIN. NATO AK-47 (M77B1) – .308 Win. cal., milled receiver, adj. gas port, otherwise similar to AK-47 except has scope rail, day/night Tritium sights, and 20 shot mag. Imported 1989 only.

| | $1,895 | $1,700 | $1,550 | $1,400 | $1,300 | $1,200 | $1,100 | *$775* |

Add $600 for military issue sniper scope and rings.

M76 – 7.92mm cal., similar to AK-47, except has longer barrel and frame set up for scope mount, counter sniper design, 10 shot mag., mfg. to Mil-Spec. Imported 1986-1989.

| | $2,000 | $1,875 | $1,650 | $1,475 | $1,200 | $950 | $850 | *$1,995* |

SKS-M59 – 7.62x39mm cal., copy of the SKS-M59 standard rifle, full walnut stock, fully adj. sights, gas operated. Mfg. in Yugoslavia. Imported 1986-1989.

| | $775 | $675 | $550 | $450 | $400 | $350 | $300 | *$699* |

R.P.K. – 7.62x39mm or .308 Win. cal., forged heavy barrel with cooling fins, teak stock, detachable bipod. Importation disc. 1992.

| | $1,300 | $1,100 | $975 | $850 | $750 | $650 | $550 | *$1,150* |

Add $845 for .308 Win. cal.

MODEL M-90 – 7.62x39mm or .308 Win. cal., AK-47 type action, in various configurations (heavy barrel, folding or fixed stock, finned barrel, etc.), plastic thumbhole stock, 5 shot mag., limited importation from Yugoslavia 1991-92.

| | $1,100 | $900 | $800 | $700 | $650 | $600 | $550 | *$829* |

Add 20% for folding stock.
Add 10% for .308 Win. cal. (wood stock only).
This model was subjected to modification due to ATF regulations after arrival in the U.S.

SHOTGUNS: SLIDE ACTION

MODEL 9108/9109 – 12 ga. only, all-purpose self-defense model featuring 20 in. barrel with 7 shot mag., choice of military green (special order), brown walnut, or black regular or pistol grip stock and forearm. Mfg. 1994-96.

| | $240 | $195 | $175 | $160 | $145 | $130 | $120 | *$279* |

Add $20 for adj. rear rifle sight (Model 9109).
Add $20 for interchangeable choke tube (Model 9108 only).

MODEL 9111/9113 – 12 ga. only, 18 1/2 in. barrel with bead sights, 6 shot mag., choice of brown or green synthetic (special order), brown walnut or black regular or pistol grip stock and forearm. Mfg. 1994-96.

| | $240 | $195 | $175 | $160 | $145 | $130 | $120 | *$279* |

Add $20 for adj. rear rifle sight (Model 9113).
Add $20 for interchangeable choke tube (Model 9111 only).

MODEL 9114 – 12 ga. only, designed for police and riot control, choice of synthetic pistol grip or top folding (disc. 1994) buttstock, 20 in. barrel with iron sights, 6 shot mag. Mfg. 1994-96.

| | $295 | $255 | $210 | $180 | $160 | $145 | $130 | *$349* |

MODEL 9115 – 12 ga. only, design based on Special Air Services riot gun, 18 1/2 in. barrel with vent. heat shield, parkerized finish, 6 shot mag., stealth grey stock featuring 4 shell storage. Mfg. 1994-96.

| | $295 | $255 | $210 | $180 | $160 | $145 | $130 | *$349* |

Add $20 for interchangeable choke tube.

MITCHELL'S MAUSERS

Current importer located in Fountain Valley, CA.

Please refer to the Escalade and Sabre sections for previously imported semi-auto and slide action shotguns.

MSR	100%	98%	95%	90%	80%	70%	60%	Last MSR

PISTOLS: SEMI-AUTO

Mitchell's Mausers previously imported older Luger pistols in many variations. Last MSRs circa 2010 on the following models were: P08 WWI 4 in. $4,995, P08 WWII 4 in. $4,495, Navy Model 6 in. $6,495, Artillery Model 8 in. $7,995, P08 Treaty of Versailles $5,995, and $9,995 for Carbine w/stock. All were restored and were cased with accessories. Additionally, the company also imported a restored WWII P.38, cased with accessories - last MSR was $1,295.

FALCON SERIES – 9mm Para., .40 S&W, or .45 ACP cal., DA/SA operation, Browning locking system operation, 3.9 (semi-compact) or 4 1/4 (compact) in. barrel, low profile sights, aluminum frame with steel frame and barrel, 12, 16, or 20 shot mag., loaded chamber indicator, approx. 32 oz. Mfg. in Serbia. Importation began late 2011.

MSR $795	$725	$650	$575	$495	$425	$350	$295	

RIFLES: BOLT ACTION

Beginning 1999, Mitchell's Mausers imported a sizeable quantity of WWII Mauser 98Ks manufactured in Yugoslavia during/after WWII. These guns are basically in new condition, having been only test fired over the past 50 years. They are supplied with bayonet and scabbard, military leather sling, original field cleaning kit, and leather ammo pouch. Caliber is 8mm Mauser (7.9x57mm), and all parts numbers match on these rifles.

MODEL M48 – 8mm Mauser cal., original Mauser 98K rifle manufactured with German technology in Serbia, various grades, matching serial numbers on all parts. Importation began 2006.

MSR $349	$325	$295	$275	$250	$240	$230	$220	

The above price is for the Service grade rifle without accessories. Add $100 for Collector Grade, $150 for Custom Select Grade, $200 for BO (Stealth), $200 for Premium Grade, $250 for Premium Select Grade, and $300 for Premium Grade BO (Stealth).
A special Museum Grade with bayonet, scabbard, belt hanger, and other accessories was also available for $1,000.

TANKER MAUSER M63 (MODEL M48) – .243 Win., .270 Win., .30-06, 8mm Mauser, or .308 Win. cal., similar to Model 48, except the barrel length is 17.4 in., 5 shot internal mag., 1400m adj. rear sight, hardwood stock with semi-gloss finish, 7.4 lbs. Imported 2006-approx. 2010.

	$450	$395	$375	$345	$295	$265	$235	*$495*

NEW K98 – 8mm Mauser cal., original WWII Mauser mfg., all matching parts, various configurations available, including Souvenir, Collector, and Premium Grades.

MSR $789	$725	$625	$525	$450	$395	$350	$295	

BLACK ARROW – .50 BMG cal., Mauser action, 5 shot detachable box mag., fluted and compensated barrel, includes bipod and quick detachable scope mount, shock absorbing buttstock. Imported 2003-2006.

	$5,750	$4,950	$4,275	$3,600	$3,000	$2,400	$2,150	*$6,500*

SOVIET MOSIN-NAGANT – various cals., original gun dated 1942 to commemorate the battle of Stalingrad. Limited importation 2009.

U.S. pricing was not available on this model.

RIFLES: SEMI-AUTO

BLACK LIGHTNING – .17 Mach 2 (disc.), .17 HMR (disc.), .22 LR (disc.), or .22 WMR cal., black polymer oversized thumbhole stock with full length aluminum shroud and Picatinny rail, 18 in. stainless steel fluted heavy barrel, stainless steel action, 9 shot mag., detachable carry handle, detachable front sight, sling swivels. New 2006.

MSR $595	$500	$450	$375	$350	$300	$250	$200	

PPSH 41/22/PPS50/22 – .22 LR cal., patterned after the Russian PPSh-41, 16.1 in. barrel, features stained hardwood stock, full length perforated barrel heat shield, fixed sights, 10, 30, or 50 shot detachable drum magazine, 4.4 lbs. Importation began 2012.

MSR $495	$450	$400	$350	$300	$275	$250	$225	

Add $150 for 50 shot detachable drum mag.
Add $39 for reflex rear sight (new 2014).

MOHAWK ARMORY

Current AR-15 style manufacturer located in Midway, TN.

Mohawk Armory offers a line of AR-15 style semi-auto rifles and pistols. The company is also a Class III dealer and offers many products for law enforcement/military. Please contact the company directly for more information, including pricing and available options (see Trademark Index).

MOLOT

Current manufacturer established during 1941, and located in Vyatskie Polyany, Kirov region, Russia.

Currently manufactured trademarks include: Vepr. rifles and shotguns, a SKS semi-auto rifle line, several models of bolt action rifles, including target models, in addition to Becas slide action and semi-auto shotguns. Please refer to these sections for more information.

MSR	100%	98%	95%	90%	80%	70%	60%	Last MSR

MOSSBERG, O.F. & SONS, INC.
Current manufacturer located in North Haven, CT, 1962-present and New Haven, CT, 1919-1962.

Oscar Mossberg developed an early reputation as a designer and inventor for the Iver Johnson, Marlin-Rockwell, Stevens, and Shattuck Arms companies. In 1915, he began producing a 4-shot, .22 LR cal. palm pistol known as the "Novelty," with revolving firing pin. After producing approx. 600 of these pistols, he sold the patent to C.S. Shattuck, which continued to manufacture guns under the name "Unique." The first 600 had no markings except serial numbers, and were destined for export to South America. Very few of these original "Novelty" pistols survived in this country, and they are extremely rare specimens.

Mossberg acquired Advanced Ordnance Corp. during 1996, a high quality manufacturer utilizing state-of-the-art CNC machinery.

RIFLES: BOLT ACTION, CURRENT PRODUCTION

MODEL 802 PLINKSTER – .22 LR cal., 18 or 21 (disc. 2014) in. barrel with adj. iron sights, aluminum alloy receiver, blue or brushed chrome (21 in. barrel only, mfg. 2007-2014) finish, wood (new 2009), black synthetic, black pink (new 2009), or pink marble (new 2009) synthetic stock with (disc. 2012) or w/o thumbhole, Sport Grip skeletonized stock became optional mid-2012, 10 shot mag., approx. 4 lbs. New 2006.

MSR $190	$170	$150	$130	$115	$95	$75	$60

Add $12 for 4x scope (802 Plinkster Scoped Combo).
Add $20 for brushed chrome finish (mfg. 2007-2014).
Add $44 for Classic wood, or synthetic sport grip stock in Pink or Pink Marble finish.

MODEL 817 – .17 HMR cal., 21 in. barrel, 5 shot detachable mag., Weaver style scope bases, alum. alloy receiver, blue or brushed chrome finish, black synthetic, wood, thumbhole (tip-down forend became standard with thumbhole during 2009, disc. 2012) or Sports Grip skeletonized (new mid-2012) stock, approx. 4 1/2 - 4 3/4 lbs. New 2007.

MSR $223	$185	$160	$140	$125	$100	$85	$65

Add $16 for brushed chrome finish.
Add $43 for wood or thumbhole (disc. 2009) stock.
Add $82 for Roadblocker muzzle brake (mfg. 2010-2012).
Add $14 for 3-9x40mm scope or $55 for 3-16x50mm scope with bipod (with Roadblocker muzzle brake only, mfg. 2010-2012).

MVP FLEX – 5.56mm or 7.62 NATO cal., 18 1/2 or 20 in. threaded or non-threaded sporter or medium bull barrel, matte blue finish, spiral fluted bolt, optional A2 flash suppressor, 10 shot mag., LBA trigger, Picatinny top rail, FLEX TLS-compatible six position adj. stock in black or tan (new 2014), 6 1/2-7 lbs. New 2013.

MSR $727	$625	$545	$470	$425	$345	$285	$260

Add $15 for threaded barrel with A2 flash suppressor.

MVP PATROL – 5.56mm, 7.62 NATO, or .300 ACC Blackout (mfg. 2014 only) cal., 16 1/4 in. medium bull threaded or non-threaded barrel, spiral fluted bolt, LBA adj. trigger, matte blue finish, textured stock in black or Tan (new 2014) with checkered grip and forend, 10 shot mag., no sights or rifle sights, Picatinny rail, 6 3/4 - 7 1/2 lbs. New 2013.

MSR $694	$585	$500	$425	$375	$300	$250	$200

Add $16 for threaded barrel and A2 flash suppressor.

RIFLES: LEVER ACTION

MODEL 464 SPX – .22 LR (disc. 2013, reintroduced 2015) or .30-30 Win. cal., 16 1/4, 18 (.22 LR, new 2015), or 18 1/2 (disc. 2013) in. barrel with A2 style flash suppressor or muzzle brake, 7 (.30-30 Win. cal.) or 14 (disc. 2013) shot mag., matte black finish, 6-position adj. tactical stock with elevated comb, tri-rail forearm with ladder rail covers, adj. fiber optic sights or dovetail receiver, drilled and tapped, 6 (.22 LR cal.) or 7 (.30-30 Win. cal.) lbs. New 2012.

MSR $540	$485	$415	$350	$325	$260	$225	$175

Subtract $30 for .22 LR cal.

MODEL 464 ZMB – .30-30 Win. cal., 6 (disc. 2013) or 7 (new 2014) shot mag., compact 16 1/4 in. barrel with removable A2 flash suppressor, matte blue finish, six position adj. tactical stock, tri-rail forend with rail covers, 3-dot adj. fiber optic or rifle sights, drilled and tapped, sling swivel studs, ZMB receiver engraving, 7 lbs. Mfg. 2012-2014.

	$480	$410	$350	$300	$250	$210	$175	*$581*

RIFLES: SEMI-AUTO

At the SHOT Show during 2014, Mossberg unveiled its new Duck Commander Series. Please refer to individual listings.

* *Model 702 Bantam Plinkster* – .22 LR cal., 18 in. barrel, blue finish, 10 shot mag., 12 1/4 in. LOP, adj. rifle sights, Black or Pink synthetic stock, 4 lbs. New 2006.

MSR $190	$170	$150	$130	$115	$95	$75	$60

Add $12 for scoped combo with 4x scope.
Add $44 for Pink synthetic stock.

MSR	100%	98%	95%	90%	80%	70%	60%	Last MSR

MODEL 715T TACTICAL CARRY (TACTICAL 22)

MODEL 715T TACTICAL CARRY (TACTICAL 22) – .22 LR cal., AR-15 style, GIO, 18 in. barrel, matte black finish, 10 or 25 shot mag., synthetic fixed or 6-position adj. stock, front post sight, adj. rifle sights, Picatinny quad rail forend, handle mounted top rail, mag. loading assist tool, integrated A2 style carry handle, 5 1/4 lbs. Mfg. 2011-2015.

| | $255 | $215 | $175 | $150 | $125 | $100 | $95 | $308 |

MODEL 715T FLAT-TOP

MODEL 715T FLAT-TOP – .22 LR cal., GIO, 16 1/4 in. barrel with A2 style muzzle brake, blue barrel finish, 10 or 25 shot mag., flat-top with full length top rail, removeable/adj. sights or 30mm red dot sights, fixed or adj. synthetic stock, Black, Mossy Oak Brush (disc. 2015), or Muddy Girl (new 2014) camo finish, 5 1/2 - 5 3/4 lbs. New 2012.

| MSR $372 | $320 | $280 | $240 | $220 | $175 | $150 | $125 | |

Add $10 for removable A2 style Picatinny mounted front and rear sights.
Add $66 for Muddy Girl camo finish (new 2014).
Add $69 for Mossy Oak Brush camo finish (disc. 2015).

MMR HUNTER

MMR HUNTER – 5.56 NATO cal., GIO, 20 in. carbon steel barrel with black phosphate metal finish, 5 shot mag., SST, anodized aluminum receiver, Picatinny top rail, A2 black synthetic stock, SE-1 pistol grip with battery compartment, checkered aluminum tubular forend, Mossy Oak Treestand or Mossy Oak Brush camo finish, no sights, 7 1/2 lbs. Mfg. mid-2011-2015.

| | $895 | $775 | $675 | $625 | $550 | $475 | $400 | $1,028 |

Add $99 for camo finish.

MMR TACTICAL

MMR TACTICAL – 5.56 NATO cal., GIO, 16 1/4 in. carbon steel barrel with black phosphate metal finish, 10 or 30 shot mag., SST, anodized aluminum receiver, black synthetic fixed or 6-position collapsible stock, A2 style muzzle brake, no sights or removable Picatinny rail, Stark SE-1 deluxe pistol grip, quad rail forend, approx. 7 - 7 1/2 lbs. Mfg. mid-2011-2015.

| | $875 | $775 | $650 | $550 | $450 | $395 | $350 | $987 |

Add $41 for Picatinny rail.

SHOTGUNS: SEMI-AUTO, RECENT PRODUCTION

In 1985, Mossberg purchased the parts inventory and manufacturing rights for the shotguns that Smith & Wesson discontinued in 1984. These 1000 Series models (manufactured in Japan) are identical to those models which S&W discontinued. Parts and warranties are not interchangeable.

Beginning 1989, all Mossbergs sold in the U.S. and Canada have been provided with a Cablelock which goes through the ejection port, making the gun's action inoperable.

To celebrate its 75th anniversary, Mossberg released a new Crown Grade variation within most models during 1994, including the slide action 500 and 835 Series. These can be differentiated from previous manufacture by cut checkering, redesigned walnut or American hardwood stocks and forearms, screw-in choke tubes, and 4 different camo patterns. The Crown Grade was discontinued in 2000.

At the SHOT Show during 2014, Mossberg unveiled its new Duck Commander Series. Please refer to individual listings.

* Model 930 Special Purpose Home Security – 12 ga., 3 in. chamber, 5 shot, 18 1/2 in. cylinder bore barrel, bead sights, blue finish, black synthetic stock, 7 1/4 lbs. New 2007.

| MSR $662 | $550 | $475 | $400 | $375 | $300 | $250 | $200 | |

* Model 930 Special Purpose Roadblocker – 12 ga., 3 in. chamber, 18 1/2 in. barrel with large muzzle brake, 5 shot, matte blue finish, black synthetic stock, 7 3/4 lbs. Mfg. 2009-2011.

| | $575 | $495 | $415 | $375 | $300 | $245 | $190 | $670 |

* Model 930 Special Purpose SPX – 12 ga., 3 in. chamber, 8 shot mag., 18 1/2 in. cylinder bore barrel, Picatinny top rail, LPA ghost ring rear or XS ghost ring (mfg. 2015 only) sights, and winged fiber optic front sight, Black synthetic stock with (new 2009) or w/o pistol grip, Matte Blue or Coyote Tan (new 2013) finish, 7 3/4 lbs. New 2008.

| MSR $851 | $710 | $610 | $525 | $475 | $385 | $315 | $250 | |

Add $104 for full length pistol grip stock (new 2009).
Add $164 for pistol grip stock with Coyote Tan finish (new 2013).
Add $47 for XS sights w/pistol grip (mfg. 2015 only).

* Model 930 Special Purpose SPX Blackwater Series – 12 ga., 3 in. chamber, 8 shot, 18 1/2 in. cylinder bore barrel, receiver mounted sliding safety, matte black finish with Blackwater logo on right side of receiver, black composite pistol grip stock, Picatinny rail, XS sights: Ghost ring rear/AR-style Tritium stripe front, oversized cocking handle and bolt release, 7 3/4 lbs. Mfg. 2011-2014.

| | $750 | $650 | $575 | $510 | $415 | $350 | $275 | $891 |

* Model 930 Tactical – 12 ga., 3 in. chamber, 5 shot, 18 1/2 in. Standoff cylinder bore barrel, white dot sights, with or w/o heat shield, matte blue finish, black synthetic stock, 7 1/4 lbs. New mid-2008.

| MSR $714 | $585 | $500 | $425 | $395 | $315 | $275 | $225 | |

Add $25 for heat shield (new 2011).

MSR	100%	98%	95%	90%	80%	70%	60%	Last MSR

MODEL 930 JM PRO SERIES – 12 ga., 3 in. chamber, 22 or 24 in. VR barrel, 9 or 10 shot, matte black or Kryptek Typhon camo (new 2014, 24 in. bbl. only) synthetic stock, fiber optic front sight, engraved receiver, beveled loading gate, shorter forend, extended magazine tube, adj. overtravel, built to Jerry Miculek's specifications. New 2012.

| MSR $790 | $675 | $590 | $500 | $460 | $375 | $300 | $250 | |

Add $29 for Kryptek Typhon camo finish (new 2014).

* ***Model 9200 Crown Semi-Auto Jungle Gun*** – 12 ga. only, 18 1/2 in. plain barrel with cyl. bore, parkerized metal, synthetic stock. Mfg. 1998-2001.

| | $610 | $535 | $455 | $415 | $335 | $275 | $215 | *$704* |

SHOTGUNS: SLIDE ACTION, RECENT PRODUCTION

In 1985, Mossberg purchased the parts inventory and manufacturing rights for the shotguns that Smith & Wesson discontinued in 1984. These 3000 Series models (manufactured in Japan) are identical to those models which S&W discontinued. Parts and warranties are not interchangeable.

Beginning 1989, all Mossbergs sold in the U.S. and Canada have been provided with a Cablelock which goes through the ejection port, making the gun's action inoperable.

To celebrate its 75th anniversary, Mossberg released a new Crown Grade variation within most models during 1994, including the slide action 500 and 835 Series. These can be differentiated from previous manufacture by cut checkering, redesigned walnut or American hardwood stocks and forearms, screw-in choke tubes, and 4 different camo patterns. The Crown Grade was discontinued in 2000.

On April 30, 2013, Mossberg announced the manufacture of its 10 millionth Mossberg 500 model.

At the SHOT Show during 2014, Mossberg unveiled its new Duck Commander Series. Please refer to individual listings.

MODEL 500 BULLPUP – 12 ga., 18 1/2 (6 shot) or 20 (9 shot) in. barrel, bullpup configuration, 6 or 9 shot mag., includes shrouded barrel, carrying handle, ejection port in stock, employs high impact materials. Mfg. 1986-90.

| | $650 | $525 | $450 | $415 | $325 | $275 | $215 | *$425* |

Add $15 for 8 shot mag. (disc.).

MODEL 500 CAMPER – 12, 20 ga., or .410 bore only, 18 1/2 in. barrel, synthetic pistol grip (no stock), camo carrying case optional, blued finish. Mfg. 1986-90 only.

| | $250 | $220 | $185 | $170 | $135 | $110 | $85 | *$276* |

Add $25 for .410 bore.
Add $30 for camo case.

* ***Model 500 Turkey Synthetic Thumbhole*** – 12 ga., 3 in. chamber, 6 shot, 20 in. VR barrel, X-Factor ported tube, adj. fiber optic sights, Black synthetic thumbhole stock with matte blue finish or synthetic thumbhole stock with 100% Mossy Oak New Break-Up (disc. 2011), Mossy Oak Break-Up Infinity (mfg. 2012-2013), Realtree Hardwoods HD Green (disc. 2012), or Realtree Extra Green (new 2013) camo coverage, 7 lbs. Mfg. 2007-2014.

| | $415 | $365 | $310 | $275 | $225 | $185 | $150 | *$484* |

Add $59 for Realtree Extra Green camo coverage (new 2013).

MODEL 500 CHAINSAW – 12 ga., 3 in. chamber, 18 1/2 in. stand-off barrel with cyl. bore choke, 6 shot mag., pistol grip synthetic stock, matte black finish, easily removable unique "chainsaw" forend grip provides muzzle control and stability, drilled and tapped, tri-rail forend, white dot sights, 6 lbs. New 2011.

| MSR $531 | $450 | $395 | $340 | $300 | $250 | $200 | $160 | |

MODEL 500 CHAINSAW ZMB – 12 ga., 3 in. chamber, 18 1/2 in. stand-off barrel with cyl. bore choke, 6 shot mag., matte black finish, easily removable unique "chainsaw" forend grip provides muzzle control and stability, drilled and tapped, tri-rail forend, white dot sights, includes light and laser combo, ZMB engraved logo on receiver, pistol grip black synthetic stock, 6 lbs. Mfg. 2012-2014.

| | $550 | $475 | $425 | $375 | $300 | $250 | $200 | *$650* |

MODEL 500 CRUISER – 12, 20, or .410 (new 1993) ga., 3 in. chamber, 14 (12 ga. only, Law Enforcement Model, disc. 1995), 18 1/2, 20, or 21 (20 ga. only - mfg. 1995-2002) in. cylinder bore barrel, shroud is available in 12 ga. only, 6 or 8 (12 ga. only) shot mag., bead sights, Black synthetic pistol grip or Black synthetic stock with pistol grip conversion kit, right or left (new 2015) hand configuration, 5 1/2 - 6 1/2 lbs. New 1989.

| MSR $452 | $385 | $335 | $290 | $260 | $210 | $175 | $135 | |

Add $17 for heat shield around barrel (12 ga. only).
Add $17 for 20 ga. with pistol grip conversion kit.
Add $17 for 8 shot (20 in. barrel, 12 ga. only).
Add $31 for left-hand configuration (new 2015).
Add $96 for 14 in. barrel (disc.).
Add approx. $34 for camper case (1993-1996).

MSR	100%	98%	95%	90%	80%	70%	60%	Last MSR

* **Model 500 Crusier Blackwater Series** – 12 ga., 3 in. chamber, 18 1/2 in. cylinder bore barrel, synthetic pistol grip, matte black finish, white dot front sight, ported stand off door breacher at muzzle, 6 shot, half-round ribbed forearm with nylon web strap, Blackwater logo on right side of receiver, approx. 6 lbs. Mfg. 2011-2014.

| | $425 | $375 | $325 | $295 | $250 | $200 | $150 | *$493* |

* **Model 500 Cruiser Mil-Spec** – 12 ga. only, 20 in. cylinder bored barrel with bead sights, built to Mil-Specs., parkerized finish. Mfg. 1997 only.

| | $395 | $345 | $295 | $270 | $215 | $180 | $140 | *$478* |

* **Model 500 Cruiser Road Blocker** – 12 ga. only, 3 in. chamber, 6 shot, 18 1/2 in. heavy walled barrel with heat shield and large muzzle brake, bead sights, matte blue metal finish, Black synthetic pistol grip (no stock), 5 3/4 lbs. Mfg. 2009-2014.

| | $475 | $415 | $350 | $325 | $250 | $200 | $160 | *$562* |

* **Model 500 Cruiser Tactical Light Forend** – 12 ga., 3 in. chamber, 6 shot, 18 1/2 in. cylinder bore barrel, white dot sights, matte blue metal finish, integrated Insight tactical light forend with 3-function ambidextrous touchpad, Black synthetic pistol grip, 5 3/4 lbs. Mfg. 2008-2015.

| | $560 | $475 | $415 | $375 | $300 | $250 | $200 | *$670* |

* **Model 500 Cruiser Tactical Tri-Rail w/Center Mass Laser** – 12 ga., 3 in. chamber, 6 shot, 18 1/2 in. cylinder bore barrel, bead sight, LaserLyte Center Mass laser with three modes (constant on, pulse, and auto off) mounted on tactical tri-rail forend, full length bottom Picatinny rail, Black synthetic pistol grip, matte blue metal finish, 5 3/4 lbs. Mfg. 2014.-2015

| | $585 | $500 | $425 | $395 | $315 | $260 | $200 | *$695* |

MODEL 500 GHOST RING SIGHT – 12 ga. only, 3 in. chamber, 18 1/2 or 20 in. cyl. bore or Accu-choke (20 in. only - new 1995) barrel, 6 or 9 shot tube mag., blue or parkerized finish, synthetic field stock, includes ghost ring sighting device. Mfg. 1990-97.

| | $270 | $235 | $200 | $185 | $150 | $120 | $95 | *$332* |

Add $53 for parkerized finish.
Add $49 for 9 shot mag. (20 in. barrel only).
Add $123 for Accu-choke barrel (parkerized finish only).
Add $134 for Speedfeed stock (new 1994 - 9 shot, 20 in. barrel only).

MODEL 500 HOME SECURITY HS410 – 20 (1996 only) ga. or .410 bore, 3 in. chamber, 18 1/2 in. barrel with spreader choke, Model 500 slide-action, 6 shot mag., blue metal finish, Black or Muddy Girl (new 2014) synthetic field stock with pistol grip forearm, 5 1/2 lbs. New 1990.

| MSR $463 | $395 | $350 | $300 | $275 | $215 | $175 | $150 | |

Add $28 for Muddy Girl camo stock and forend (new 2014).

* **Model 500 Home Security Laser .410** – includes laser sighting device in right front of forearm. Mfg. 1990-93.

| | $400 | $350 | $300 | $270 | $220 | $180 | $140 | *$451* |

MODEL 500 J.I.C. (JUST IN CASE) – 12 ga., 3 in. chamber, 18 1/2 or 20 (new 2013) in. cyl. bore barrel, 6 or 8 (new 2013) shot, comes with pistol grip, impact resistant tube and strap, available in four configurations: 5.11 Pack (w/takedown 500 and tools), Cruiser (survival kit in a can, blue metal, OD Green tube), Mariner (multi-tool and knife, Orange tube, Marinecote finish), Sandstorm (Desert camo tube and finish, disc. 2014), or Black (8 shot only, new 2013), 5 1/2 lbs. New 2007.

| MSR $484 | $410 | $360 | $310 | $280 | $225 | $185 | $150 | |

Add $62 for Sandstorm model (disc. 2014) or $143 for Mariner model.

MODEL 500 MARINER – 12 ga. only, 3 in. chamber, 18 1/2 or 20 (disc.) in. cyl. bore barrel, 6 or 9 (disc. 2008) shot, bead, fixed (disc.), or ghost ring (mfg. 1995-99) sights, Marinecote finish on all metal parts (more rust-resistant than stainless steel), full-length black synthetic stock with pistol grip conversion kit, 5 3/4- 6 3/4 lbs.

| MSR $616 | $525 | $460 | $395 | $355 | $290 | $235 | $185 | |

Add $51 for 9 shot model with 20 in. barrel (disc. 2008).
Add $68 for ghost ring rear sight (disc. 1999).
Add $23 for Speedfeed stock (mini-combo only - disc.).

MODEL 500 PERSUADER – 12 or 20 (new 1995) ga., 6 or 8 shot, 18 1/2 in. plain or Standoff barrel, cyl. bore or Accu-chokes (mfg. 1995-disc.), optional rifle (12 ga./20 in. cyl. bore barrel only), bead, white dot, or ghost ring (new 1999-2004, reintroduced 2013 only) sights, blue, matte (new 2006, 12 ga. only), or parkerized (12 ga. with ghost ring sights only, disc. 2004) finish, Speedfeed stock was disc. 1990, optional bayonet lug, plain pistol grip wood (disc. 2004), Black synthetic stock with or w/o pistol grip, right or left (20 ga. only, new 2015) hand configuration, 5 1/2-7 1/2 lbs.

| MSR $452 | $385 | $335 | $290 | $260 | $210 | $175 | $135 | |

Add $17 for pistol grip.
Add $46 for 20 ga. with Standoff barrel (new 2009).

MSR	100%	98%	95%	90%	80%	70%	60%	Last MSR

Add $14 for left-hand configuration (20 ga. only, new 2015).
Add $18 for tri-rail Picatinny forend (mfg. 2011-2013).
Add $159 for ghost ring sights (mfg. 1999-2004, 2013 only).
Add $127 for parkerized finish and ghost ring sights (disc. 2004).
Add $40 for combo with pistol grip (disc.).
Add $23 for rifle sights (disc., 12 ga. only).

* **Model 500 Persuader Night Special Edition** – 12 ga. only, includes synthetic stock and factory installed Mepro-Light night sight bead sight, only 300 mfg. for Lew Horton Distributing in 1990 only.

	100%	98%	95%	90%	80%	70%	60%	Last MSR
	$350	$260	$225	$200	$160	$135	$115	*$296*

MODEL 500 TACTICAL
– 12 ga. only, 3 in. chamber, 18 1/2 in. cylinder bore barrel, 6 shot, 6-position adj. tactical black synthetic stock, choice of matte blue or Marinecoate (disc. 2015) finish, right or left (new 2015) hand configuration, 6 3/4 lbs. New 2006.

MSR $584	$500	$440	$375	$340	$275	$225	$175	

Add $14 for left-hand configuration (new 2015).
Add $156 for Marinecote finish (disc. 2015).

* **Model 500 Tactical Tri-Rail w/Center Mass Laser** – 12 ga., 3 in. chamber, 8 shot, 20 in. cylinder bore barrel, matte blue metal finish, bead sights, Laserlyte Center Mass laser with three modes (constant on, pulse, and auto off) mounted on tactical tri-rail forend, Black synthetic stock, 7 lbs. New 2014.

MSR $695	$595	$525	$450	$400	$325	$275	$210	

MODEL 500 SPX SPECIAL PURPOSE
– 12 ga. only, 3 in. chamber, 18 1/2 in. cylinder bore barrel with M16 style front sight, LPA ghost ring rear sight, Picatinny rail, matte blue metal finish, 6-pos. adj. tactical black synthetic stock with pistol grip, 6 3/4 lbs. New 2009.

MSR $710	$605	$530	$455	$410	$335	$275	$215	

MODEL 500 SPECIAL PURPOSE
– 12 ga. only, 18 in. cylinder bored barrel, choice of blue or parkerized finish, synthetic stock with or without Speedfeed. Disc. 1996.

	100%	98%	95%	90%	80%	70%	60%	Last MSR
	$350	$295	$250	$225	$200	$175	$160	*$378*

Add $21 for Speedfeed stock.
Add $76 for ghost ring sight (parkerized finish only).

MODEL 500 SPECIAL PURPOSE (RECENT MFG.)
– 12 ga., 2 3/4 or 3 in. chamber, 18 1/2 in. cylinder bore barrel, 6 shot, matte blue finish, synthetic stock, plain bead sight, recoil reduction system. Mfg. 2013-2014.

	$425	$375	$325	$295	$235	$195	$150	*$493*

MODEL 500 THUNDER RANCH
– 12 ga., 3 in. chamber, 18 1/2 in. cylinder bore barrel, 5 shot mag., matte black synthetic stock with 12 3/4 in. LOP, white dot sights, tri-rail Picatinny forend, non-glare matte blue metal finish, sling swivel studs, Thunder Ranch logo engraved on receiver, includes black padded sling. New mid-2011.

MSR $498	$425	$375	$325	$295	$250	$200	$160	

* **Model 500 Flex Hunting 20 Ga.** – 20 ga., 3 in. chamber, 24 (X Factor ported chokes) or 26 in. VR barrel, choice of matte blue (26 in.) or OD Green (24 in.) metal finish, 6 shot, TLS Tool-less Locking System, choice of Black synthetic or 100% Mossy Oak Break Up Infinity camo stock and Field forend, twin bead or adj. fiber optic sights, 7 lbs. New 2014.

MSR $473	$395	$350	$300	$275	$215	$175	$150	

Add $107 for Mossy Oak Break Up Infinity camo stock and OD Green metal finish.

MODEL 500 FLEX TACTICAL
– 12 or 20 (new 2014) ga., 3 in. chamber, 6 shot, 20 in. cylinder bore barrel, matte blue, OD Green (disc. 2015), or Tan barrel finish, XS ghost ring or plain bead sight, Picatinny top rail, tactical railed forend, standard or six position adj. Black synthetic stock, TLS Tool-less locking system, 6 1/4-6 3/4 lbs. New mid-2012.

MSR $630	$535	$470	$400	$365	$295	$240	$185	

Add $29 for Tan barrel finish.
Add $8 for XS ghost ring sight with OD Green barrel finish (disc. 2015).

* **Model 535 ATS Thumbhole Turkey** – 12 ga., 3 1/2 in. chamber, 20 in. VR barrel with X-factor ported choke tube, 6 shot, adj. fiber optic sights, synthetic thumbhole stock, Matte Blue (Black stock) or 100% Mossy Oak New Break-Up (disc. 2011), Mossy Oak Break-Up Infinity (new 2012), Realtree Hardwoods HD Green (disc. 2012), or Realtree Extra Green (new 2013) camo coverage, 7 lbs. Mfg. 2007-2014.

	$425	$375	$325	$295	$250	$200	$150	*$503*

Add $74 for 100% camo coverage.

MODEL 500/590 INTIMIDATOR LASER
– 12 ga. only, 3 in. chamber, 18 1/2 (Model 500) or 20 (Model 590) in. cyl. bore barrel, 6 (Model 500) or 9 (Model 590) shot tube mag., blue or parkerized finish, synthetic field stock, includes laser sighting device. Mfg. 1990-93.

MSR	100%	98%	95%	90%	80%	70%	60%	Last MSR

* Model 500 Intimidator

	$500	$385	$340	$300	$265	$230	$195	$505

Add $22 for parkerized finish.

* Model 590 Intimidator

	$550	$495	$440	$375	$340	$295	$260	$556

Add $45 for parkerized finish.

MODEL 590 SPECIAL PURPOSE SLIDE ACTION
– 12 ga., 3 in. chamber, 9 shot mag., 20 in. cyl. bore barrel with or w/o (disc. 2015) heat shield and bayonet lug, bead or ghost ring sights, blue, matte blue (new 2016), or parkerized (disc. 2015) finish, Black synthetic stock with or w/o (disc. 2015) Speedfeed, right or left (new 2015) hand configuration, with (new 2016) or w/o tri-rail forend, 7 1/4 lbs. New 1987.

MSR $542	$460	$400	$345	$315	$255	$200	$160	

Add $84 for ghost ring sights.
Add $53 for ghost ring sights, matte blue finish, and tri-rail forend (new 2016).
Add $14 for left-hand configuration (new 2015).
Add $41 for parkerized finish (disc. 2015).
Add $33 for Speedfeed (blue, disc. 1999) or $96 for Speedfeed (parkerized, disc. 2015) stock.
Add $75 for heavy barrel with ghost ring sights, metal trigger guard and safety (disc. 2011).

* Model 590 Special Purpose Bullpup – similar to Model 500 Bullpup except is 9 shot and has 20 in. barrel. Mfg. 1989-90 only.

	$650	$525	$450	$410	$325	$275	$210	$497

* Model 590 Special Purpose Double Action – 12 ga. only, 3 in. chamber, world's first double action shotgun (long trigger pull), 18 1/2 or 20 in. barrel, 6 or 9 shot, bead or ghost ring sights, black synthetic stock and forearm, top tang safety, parkerized metal finish, 7-7 1/4 lbs. Mfg. 2000-2003.

	$450	$395	$335	$305	$245	$200	$155	$510

Add $31 for 9 shot capacity.
Add $48 for ghost ring sights.
Add $124 for Speedfeed stock (20 in. barrel with ghost ring sights only).

* Model 590 Special Purpose Line Launcher – special purpose Marine and rescue shotgun with blaze orange synthetic stock, line dispensing canister, floating and distance heads, nylon and spectra line refills, includes case and two boxes of launching loads.

	$850	$745	$635	$580	$465	$380	$295	$927

* Model 590 Special Purpose Mariner – 12 ga., 3 in. chamber, 9 shot, 20 in. cylinder bore barrel, bead sights, Marinecote finish, full-length Black synthetic stock and pistol grip conversion kit, 6-7 lbs. Mfg. 1989-1993, reintroduced 2009.

MSR $678	$575	$500	$430	$390	$315	$255	$200	

Add 5% for Speedfeed stock (disc. 1990).
Subtract 10% if w/o pistol grip adapter (disc.)

* Model 590 Tactical Light Forend – 12 ga., 3 in. chamber, 9 shot, 20 in. cylinder bore barrel with heat shield, bead sight, matte blue metal finish, integrated Insight tactical light forend with 3-function ambidextrous touchpad, Black synthetic stock, 7 1/4 lbs. Disc. 2015.

	$595	$525	$450	$400	$325	$275	$225	$720

* Model 590 Tactical Tri-Rail 9 Shot – 12 ga., 3 in. chamber, 9 shot, 20 in. cylinder bore barrel, Parkerized finish, heat shield, bead sight, tactical tri-rail forend, Black synthetic stock with shell storage (Speedfeed), 7 1/4 lbs. Mfg. 2011-2015.

	$575	$500	$425	$385	$310	$250	$200	$681

MODEL 590 FLEX TACTICAL
– 12 ga., 3 in. chamber, 9 shot, 20 in. cylinder bore barrel, matte blue finish, bead sight, six position adj. black synthetic stock with rail, 7 lbs. New mid-2012.

MSR $652	$550	$480	$415	$375	$300	$250	$200	

MODEL 590A1 SLIDE ACTION
– 12 ga., 3 in. chamber, 6 (disc. 2015), 7 (new 2016) or 9 shot mag., 18 1/2 or 20 (new 2010) in. cylinder bore heavy barrel, parkerized finish, choice of 3-dot (disc. 2015), bead, or ghost ring sight, metal trigger guard and top safety, synthetic or Speedfeed (disc. 2015) stock, with (new 2016) or w/o tri-rail forend, Black finish, 7- 7 1/2 lbs. New 2009.

MSR $587	$500	$440	$375	$340	$275	$225	$175	

Add $43 for ghost ring sights.
Add $56 for Speedfeed stock (disc. 2015).
Add $70 for 9 shot/bead sights or $106 for 9 shot/ghost ring sights.
Add $159 for synthetic stock with 4-shell storage.
Add $94 for choice of 3-dot or ghost rings sights with Speedfeed stock (disc. 2015).

MSR	100%	98%	95%	90%	80%	70%	60%	Last MSR

* **Model 590A1 Adj. Stock** – 12 ga. only, 3 in. chamber, 20 in. heavy walled cylinder bore barrel, 6 or 9 shot, 3-dot (6 shot) or ghost ring (9 shot) sights, six position adj. aluminum stock with pistol grip, Black finish, 6 3/4-7 lbs. Mfg. 2009-2015.

| | $700 | $610 | $525 | $475 | $375 | $315 | $250 | $839 |

Add $53 for 6 shot with 3-dot sights.

* **Model 590A1 With LPA Adj. Trigger** – 12 ga., 3 in. chamber, 6 shot, 18 1/2 in. fluted cylinder bore barrel, Parkerized finish, 3-dot sights, LPA adj. trigger, Black synthetic stock, 6 3/4 lbs. Mfg. 2011-2014.

| | $550 | $475 | $415 | $375 | $300 | $250 | $200 | $640 |

* **Model 590A1 Compact/Bantam** – 12 ga., 3 in. chamber, 6 shot, 18 1/2 in. heavy walled cylinder bore barrel, Parkerized finish, 13 in. LOP, ghost ring sights, Black synthetic stock, 7 lbs. Mfg. 2009-2015.

| | $595 | $510 | $450 | $400 | $325 | $275 | $225 | $712 |

* **Model 590A1 Mariner** – 12 ga. only, 3 in. chamber, 6 (disc. 2015) or 7 (new 2015) shot, 18 1/2 in. heavy walled cyl. bore barrel with bead sights, Marinecote finish, black synthetic stock, with (new 2016) or w/o tri-rail forend, 6 3/4 lbs. New 2009.

| MSR $734 | $625 | $550 | $475 | $425 | $350 | $285 | $225 | |

* **Model 590A1 Special Purpose (Disc.)** – 12 ga., marked 590A1 on receiver, parkerized, ghost ring rear sight, synthetic stock and forend, ramp front sight. Disc. 1997.

| | $550 | $480 | $410 | $375 | $300 | $245 | $190 | |

* **Model 590A1 Special Purpose Blackwater Series** – 12 ga., 3 in. chamber, 20 in. heavy wall cylinder bore barrel, 9 shot extended mag., military trigger guard, bayonet lug, parkerized metal finish, matte black furniture, Blackwater logo on right side of receiver, top Picatinny rail, integral adj. ghost ring rear sight, white post front sight, half-round ribbed forearm with three Picatinny rails, Speedfeed buttstock with two spare shell holders on each side, rubber buttpad, 7 1/4 lbs. Mfg. 2011-2014.

| | $650 | $575 | $500 | $450 | $375 | $300 | $250 | $754 |

* **Model 590A1 SPX** – 12 ga. only, 3 in. chamber, 9 shot, 20 in. heavy walled cyl. bore barrel, ghost ring rear and winged fiber optic front sights, parkerized finish, black synthetic stock and forearm, includes M9 bayonet and scabbard, receiver Picatinny rail, 7 lbs. New 2009.

| MSR $875 | $750 | $655 | $575 | $525 | $475 | $425 | $395 | |

* **Model 590A1 Tactical Light Forend 6 Shot** – 12 ga., 3 in. chamber, 6 shot, 18 1/2 in. heavy walled cylinder bore barrel, Parkerized metal finish, metal trigger guard and safety, clean out tube, bead sight, features Insight tactical light forend, Black synthetic stock, 6 3/4 lbs. Disc. 2015.

| | $635 | $550 | $475 | $425 | $350 | $275 | $225 | $764 |

* **Model 590A1 Tactical Tri-Rail Adjustable 9 Shot** – 12 ga., 3 in. chamber, 20 in. Parkerized heavy walled barrel, 9 shot extended tube mag., ghost ring sights, tri-rail forend, 6-position adj. aluminum pistol grip stock, matte black finish, 7 3/4 lbs. New 2013.

| MSR $853 | $725 | $650 | $580 | $515 | $450 | $385 | $340 | |

MODEL 835 ULTI-MAG WATERFOWL – 12 ga., 3 1/2 in. chamber, 6 shot, 26 (mfg. 2004-2008) or 28 in. VR ported/overbored barrel, Modified tube or Accu-Mag Set chokes, Dual Bead or fiber optic front sights, Blue finish with wood stock (disc. 2015), Matte Blue finish with Black synthetic stock, or synthetic stock with 100% Mossy Oak Shadow Grass (mfg. 2000-2007), Mossy Oak New Break-Up (disc. 2011), Mossy Oak Duck Blind (mfg. 2007-2012), Mossy Oak Shadowgrass Blades (new 2013), or Advantage Max-4 (mfg. 2004-2015) camo coverage, 7 3/4 lbs.

| MSR $503 | $425 | $370 | $320 | $290 | $235 | $190 | $150 | |

Add $82 for Mossy Oak Shadowgrass Blades (new 2013) or Advantage Max-4 (disc. 2015) camo coverage.

* **Model 3000 Law Enforcement** – 12 or 20 ga. only, 18 1/2 or 20 in. cylinder bore only, rifle or bead sights. Mfg. 1986-87 only.

| | $325 | $285 | $245 | $220 | $180 | $145 | $115 | $362 |

Add $25 for rifle sights.
Add $33 for black Speedfeed stock.

N SECTION

NAVY ARMS COMPANY

Current importer established during 1956, and located in Martinsburg, WV beginning 2014. Previously located in Ridgefield, NJ, 1962-2002. Navy Arms imports were fabricated by various manufacturers including the Italian companies Davide Pedersoli & Co., Pietta & Co., and A. Uberti & C. Navy Arms also owns Old Western Scrounger ammo, which markets obsolete and hard-to-find ammo. Distributor and dealer sales.

Navy Arms has also sold a wide variety of original military firearms classified as curios and relics. Handguns included the Mauser Broomhandle, Japanese Nambu, Colt 1911 Government Model, Tokarev, Browning Hi-Power, S&W Model 1917, and others. Rifles included Mauser contract models, Japanese Type 38s, Enfields, FNs, Nagants, M1 Carbines, M1 Garands, Chinese SKSs, Egyptian Rashids, French MAS Model 1936s, among others. Most of these firearms are priced in the $75-$500 price range depending on desirability of model and condition.

In 2014, Navy Arms made an agreement with Browning Arms Company, licensees of the Winchester brand name for firearms, to have Winchester-branded 1873 replica rifles made for Navy Arms with features and upgrades unique to Navy Arms guns. These improvements include a factory installed short-stroke kit, squared off shotgun style buttstock, and deluxe grade American walnut stocks fully checkered with an oil finish and full octagonal barrels. Navy Arms receives these guns from Winchester without finish on the metal. The receiver and all furniture are then bone color case-hardened and the barrels blued. These guns will be produced annually on a limited basis and are only available from Navy Arms. For information and up-to-date pricing regarding recent Navy Arms black powder models, please refer to the *Blue Book of Modern Black Powder Arms* by John Allen (also online).

MSR	100%	98%	95%	90%	80%	70%	60%	Last MSR

RIFLES: MODERN PRODUCTION

In addition to the models listed, Navy Arms in late 1990 purchased the manufacturing rights of the English firm Parker-Hale. In 1991, Navy Arms built a manufacturing facility, Gibbs Rifle Co., located in Martinsburg, WV and produced these rifles domestically 1991-1994 (see Gibbs Rifle Co. listing for more info on models the company currently imports).

RPKS-74 – .223 Rem. or 7.62x39mm (new 1989) cal., semi-auto version of the Chinese RPK Squad Automatic Weapon, Kalashnikov action, 19 in. barrel, integral folding bipod, 9 1/2 lbs. Imported 1988-89 only.

	$525	$445	$350	$250	$195	$175	$150	$649

MODEL 1 CARBINE/RIFLE – .45-70 Govt. cal., action is sporterized No. 1 MKIII Enfield, choice of 18 (carbine) or 22 (rifle) in. barrel with iron sights, black Zytel Monte Carlo (rifle) or straight grip walnut (carbine) stock, 7 (carbine) or 8 1/2 (rifle) lbs. Limited importation 1999 only.

	$325	$255	$200	$175	$160	$145	$130	$375

MODEL 4 CARBINE/RIFLE – .45-70 Govt. cal., action is sporterized No. 4 MKI Enfield, choice of 18 (carbine) or 22 (rifle) in. barrel, blue metal, choice of checkered walnut Monte Carlo (rifle) or uncheckered straight grip (carbine, disc. 1999) stock, 7 or 8 lbs. Mfg. 1999-2001.

	$325	$255	$200	$175	$160	$145	$130	$375

NEMESIS ARMS

Current rifle manufacturer located in Park City, KY since 2015. Previously located in Calimesa, CA.

RIFLES: BOLT ACTION

VALKYRIE – choice of caliber, ambidextrous takedown rifle system, 16 or 20 in. barrel, 10 shot mag., steel alloy upper and billet lower receiver, collapsible stock, includes Versapod and both left and right-hand bolts. New 2015.

MSR $5,350	$4,550	$4,050	$3,500	$2,850	$2,450	$2,075	$1,825	

VANQUISH (WINDRUNNER) – .243 Win., .260 Rem., 6.5mm Creedmoor (new 2011), .300 Win. (new 2013), .308 Win., or .338 Federal cal., take down action, 16 or 20 in. chrome moly steel heavy fluted barrel, steel alloy upper, steel lower, adj. stock, 10 shot detachable mag., Weaver rail, Versapod bipod, collapsible stock, 12 lbs.

MSR $4,500	$3,850	$3,250	$2,850	$2,450	$2,150	$1,750	$1,450	

During 2010, this model's nomenclature changed from Windrunner to the Vanquish.

NEMO (NEW EVOLUTION MILITARY ORDNANCE)

Current centerfire rifle manufacturer located in Kalispell, MT. Dealer sales.

RIFLES: SEMI-AUTO

NEMO manufactures many variations of rifles built on the AR-15 style platform. It currently sells weapon systems to the military, law enforcement, special operations, and the civilian marketplace. NEMO also makes tactical bolt action rifles per individual specifications.

MSR		100%	98%	95%	90%	80%	70%	60%	Last MSR

OMEN MATCH – 7mm Rem. Mag. or .338 Win. Mag. cal., 24 in. stainless steel fluted barrel with B1 Tri Lug suppressor ready muzzle brake, adj. gas block, two 14 shot polymer mags., billet aluminum receivers with Custom Tiger Stripe anodized finish, two detachable accessory rails, nickel boron bolt carrier group, steel side charging handle, Geissele two-stage trigger, NEMO integrated free floated customizable handguard, Magpul PRS Sniper stock, Hogue overmolded pistol grip, Black finish, includes custom drag bag, 12.6 lbs. New 2014.

| MSR $6,075 | | $5,150 | $4,550 | $3,950 | $3,600 | $2,950 | $2,450 | $2,000 | |

OMEN/OMEN MATCH 2.0 – .300 Win. Mag. cal., GIO, 22 in. match grade (disc. 2013) or fluted stainless steel (new 2014) barrel with NEMO PC Tornado flash hider (disc. 2013) or NEMO A-10 muzzle brake (new 2014), nickel boron barrel extension and feed ramp, two NEMO 14 shot mags., Geissele two-stage trigger, two detachable handguard accessory rails with built-in QD mounts, NEMO integrated free floated customizable handguard with hard black anodized finish, low profile (disc. 2013) or adj. (new 2014) gas block, NEMO steel side charging handle, Mako adj. SSR-25 sniper stock and Hogue overmolded pistol grip with Black finish, Tru-Spec Drag Bag, Billet upper and lower receivers with SF Tiger Stripe finish, 10 1/2 lbs. New 2012.

| MSR $5,699 | | $4,850 | $4,250 | $3,640 | $3,300 | $2,675 | $2,185 | $1,700 | |

  Add $151 for Magpul PRS stock (new 2015).

  The Omen model was upgraded in 2014 and renamed the Omen Match 2.0.

OMEN PRATKA – .300 Win. Mag. cal., GIO, 20 in. ultra-lightweight fluted stainless steel barrel with NEMO A-10 muzzle brake, two NEMO 14 shot polymer mags., nickel boron barrel extension and feed ramp, steel side charging handle, Geissele two-stage trigger, NEMO integrated free floated customizable handguard with Black anodized finish, two detachable handguard accessory rails with built-in QD mounts, Mission First Tactical Battlelink ultra lightweight minimalist stock with sling mounts and Hogue overmolded pistol grip with Black finish, includes carry case, 9 1/2 lbs. New 2014.

| MSR $3,999 | | $3,400 | $2,975 | $2,550 | $2,325 | $1,875 | $1,550 | $1,300 | |

OMEN RECON – .300 Win. Mag. cal., 18 in. fluted stainless steel barrel with B1 Tri Lug suppressor ready muzzle brake, adj. gas block, nickel boron barrel extension, feed ramp, bolt release, and bolt carrier with recoil reduction system, Geissele two-stage trigger, two 14 shot polymer mags., billet aluminum receivers with Custom Tiger Stripe finish, NEMO integrated free float customizable handguard with Black finish, two detachable handguard accessory rails with built-in QD mounts, steel side charging handle, Mission First Tactical Battlelink collapsible carbine stock with adj. cheekpiece, Hogue overmolded pistol grip, Black finish, includes custom drag bag, 10 lbs. New 2014.

| MSR $5,699 | | $4,850 | $4,250 | $3,640 | $3,300 | $2,675 | $2,185 | $1,700 | |

OMEN WATCHMAN 2.0 – .300 Win. Mag. cal., adj. gas block, 24 in. carbon fiber barrel with B1 Tri Lug suppressor ready muzzle brake, Picatinny rail on top of aluminum free-float integrated customizable handguard and billet aluminum receiver, both with Custom Tiger Stripe anodized finish, Geissele SSA-E two-stage trigger, nickel boron bolt carrier group, steel side charging handle, two 14 shot polymer mags., ambidextrous safety, two detachable accessory rails, Magpul PRS Sniper stock, Hogue overmolded pistol grip, Black finish, includes custom drag bag, 12.6 lbs. New 2014.

| MSR $7,475 | | $6,350 | $5,575 | $4,775 | $4,350 | $3,500 | $2,875 | $2,450 | |

TANGO2 – 5.56 NATO/.223 Rem. cal., GIO, 16 in. NEMO stainless steel barrel with PC Tornado flash hider, Billet upper and lower receivers with SF Tiger Stripe finish, Geissele two-stage trigger, rifle length free float KeyMod handguard with removable rail system in Black, low profile gas block, charging handle with tactical latch, Troy micro sights, Mission First Tactical Battlelink collapsible stock with optional cheek riser, Hogue overmolded pistol grip, ambi safety, one PMag., Timney trigger, Black finish, foam lined case, 7 lbs.

| MSR $2,975 | | $2,525 | $2,225 | $1,900 | $1,725 | $1,400 | $1,150 | $975 | |

* **TANGO6** – .300 AAC Blackout cal., GIO, 16 in. NEMO stainless steel barrel with NEMO flash hider, low profile gas block, billet aluminum receivers with Custom Tiger Stripe finish, Troy micro sights, two KeyMod Picatinny accessory rails, charging handle with tactical latch, nickel boron bolt carrier assembly, Geissele two-stage trigger, rifle length free float KeyMod handguard, Mission First Tactical Battlelink collapsible stock with optional cheek riser, Hogue overmolded pistol grip, Black finish, includes foam lined case, 7 lbs.

| MSR $2,975 | | $2,525 | $2,225 | $1,900 | $1,725 | $1,400 | $1,150 | $975 | |

TANGO8 – .308 Win. cal., 16 in. stainless steel barrel with NEMO flash hider and black nitride finish, low profile gas block, Geissele SSA-E two-stage trigger, NEMO integrated free floated customizable handguard, two detachable handguard accessory rails with built-in QD mounts, Troy micro sights, charging handle with tactical latch, billet aluminum receiver with Custom Tiger Stripe finish, NEMO adj. buttstock assembly with battery storage, Hogue overmolded pistol grip, Black finish, includes one Magpul PMag. and foam lined case.

| MSR $4,200 | | $3,575 | $3,125 | $2,675 | $2,425 | $1,975 | $1,625 | $1,250 | |

* **Tango8 MSP** – .308 Win. cal., 16 in. stainless barrel with NEMO muzzle brake, Troy Micro back up iron sights, nickel boron bolt carrier group, low profile gas block, Battle Arms ambi safety selector, BCM Gunfighter charging handle with tactical latch, two detachable handguard accessory rails with built in QD mounts, rifle length free floated handguard, Geissele two-stage trigger, Magpul PRS buttstock, Hogue overmolded pistol grip, black finish, includes one Magpul PMAG and foam lined case, 8.7 lbs.

| MSR $4,825 | | $4,100 | $3,600 | $3,100 | $2,525 | $2,100 | $1,800 | $1,575 | |

MSR	100%	98%	95%	90%	80%	70%	60%	*Last MSR*

* *Tango 8 SASS* – .308 Win. cal., same as Tango 8, except features 20 in. SASS Profile stainless steel barrel, NEMO rifle-length integrated free floated customizable handguard, Magpul PRS buttstock, black finish, 10.8 lbs.

MSR $4,675	$3,975	$3,475	$3,000	$2,700	$2,185	$1,800	$1,475	

Ti ONE TITANIUM RIFLE – .308 Win. cal., AR-15 style, GIO, 16 in. stainless steel H-Bar profile barrel, titanium matched receiver set, customizable tube handguard, Troy Tritium micro set back up iron sights, titanium Picatinny handguard rails, low profile gas block, charging handle with tactical latch, 6-pos. buttstock, Hogue grip with battery management system, titanium DRK compensator, Timney trigger, titanium buffer tube, black Nitride finish, 8.65 lbs. Serial No. 1.

Current MSR on this rifle is $95,000.

NESIKA

Current trademark of actions and rifles (new 2014) manufactured by Nesika Bay Precision, Inc., located in Sturgis, SD. Actions are currently distributed by Dakota Arms. Nesika also manufactured rifles circa 2004-2005. Previously located in Poulsbo, WA until 2003. Dealer and consumer sales.

On June 5, 2009, Remington Arms Company purchased Dakota Arms, Inc., including the rights to Nesika.

RIFLES: BOLT ACTION

In 2014, Nesika once again began offering its proprietary actions. Current models include the Tactical Model (MSR $1,400-$1,700), Classic Model (MSR $1,275-$1,475), Hunter Model (MSR $1,050-$1,450), and Round Model (MSR $1,000-$1,350).

Nesika also sold its proprietary rifle actions until 2009 in Classic ($1,275 - $1,475 MSR), Round ($1,000 - $1,350 MSR), Hunter ($1,050 - $1,450 MSR), and Tactical ($1,400 - $1,700 MSR) configurations and in a variety of cals. A Model NXP bolt action single shot pistol model was also available. Last MSR was $1,100 circa 2008.

URBAN TACTICAL – various tactical cals., heavy duty receiver with Picatinny rail and fluted 24 or 28 in. barrel, detachable box mag., black synthetic stock with adj. recoil pad. Mfg. 2004-2005.

	$4,500	$4,000	$3,500	$3,000	$2,500	$2,000	$1,650	*$5,040*

Add $160 for heavy .308 Win. cal. or $520 for Lapua or Lazzeroni Warbird or Patriot cals.

NEW DETONICS MANUFACTURING CORPORATION

Previous manufacturer located in Phoenix, AZ 1989-1992. Formerly named Detonics Firearms Industries (previous manufacturer located in Bellevue, WA 1976-1988). Detonics was sold in early 1988 to the New Detonics Manufacturing Corporation, a wholly owned subsidiary of "1045 Investors Group Limited."

PISTOLS: SEMI-AUTO, STAINLESS

MARK I – .45 ACP cal., matte blue. Disc. 1981.

	$550	$450	$395	$335	$290	$245	$215	

COMBATMASTER MC1 (FORMERLY MARK I) – .45 ACP, 9mm Para., or .38 Super cal., 3 1/2 in. barrel, two-tone (slide is non-glare blue and frame is matte stainless) finish, 6 shot mag., fixed sights, 28 oz. Disc. 1992.

	$775	$575	$450	$385	$335	$280	$235	*$920*

Add $15 for OM-3 model (polished slide - disc. 1983).
Add $100 for 9mm Para. or .38 Super cal. (disc. 1990).

This model was originally the MC1, then changed to the Mark I, then changed back to the MC1.

COMBATMASTER MARK V – .45 ACP, 9mm Para., or .38 Super cal., 3 1/2 in. barrel, matte stainless finish, fixed sights, 6 (.45 ACP) or 7 (9mm Para. and .38 Super) shot mag., 29 oz. empty. Disc. 1985.

	$620	$550	$495	$430	$375	$315	$270	*$689*

Add $100 for 9mm Para. or .38 Super cal.

MILITARY COMBAT MC2 – .45 ACP, 9mm Para., or .38 Super cal., dull, non-glare combat finish, fixed sights. Comes with camouflaged pile-lined wallet, and Pachmayr grips. Disc. 1984.

	$621	$560	$500	$430	$375	$315	$270	

Add $55 for 9mm Para. or .38 Super.

SERVICEMASTER – .45 ACP cal. only, shortened version of the Scoremaster, non-glare combat finish, 4 1/4 in. barrel, coned barrel system, 8 shot mag., interchangeable front and adj. rear sights, 39 oz. Disc. 1986.

	$825	$675	$575	$480	$410	$350	$295	*$686*

NEW ENGLAND FIREARMS

Current trademark established during 1987, located and previously manufactured in Gardner, MA until Nov. 1, 2007. Beginning Nov. 1, 2007, the NEF trademark applies to imported guns only. Distributor sales.

During late Jan. of 2008, Remington acquired the Marlin Firearms Company, which had purchased the H&R, New England Firearms (NEF), and L.C. Smith brands during 2000. On May 31st, 2007, Remington Arms Co. was acquired by Cerberus Capital.

MSR	100%	98%	95%	90%	80%	70%	60%	*Last MSR*

During 2000, Marlin Firearms Co. purchased the assets of H&R 1871, Inc., and the name was changed to H&R 1871, LLC. Brand names include Harrington & Richardson, New England Firearms, and Wesson & Harrington.

All NEF firearms utilize a transfer bar safety system and have a $10 service plan which guarantees lifetime warranty. New England Firearms should not be confused with New England Arms Corp.

RIFLES: SINGLE SHOT

Beginning Nov. 1, 2007, H&R 1871 decided that all products built in the USA will carry the H&R brand name, and all imported products will be sold under the NEF brand name. The Handi-Rifle, Super Light Handi-Rifle, Sportster, and Survivor are now under the H&R brand name.

SURVIVOR – .223 Rem., .308 Win. (new 1999), .357 Mag. (disc. 1998) or .410/45 LC (new 2007) cal., similar in design to the Survivor Series shotgun, removable forearm with ammo storage, thumbhole stock with storage compartment, no iron sights, 20 (.410/45 LC cal. only) or 22 in. barrel, blue or nickel finish, .357 Mag. cal. has open sights, .223 Rem. and .308 Win. cal. have heavy barrels and scope mount rail, 6 lbs. Mfg. 1996-2008.

	$230	$180	$145	$110	$80	$70	$60	*$281*

Add approx. $15 for nickel finish (disc. 1998, reintroduced 2007 for .410/45 LC cal. only).
Subtract $76 for .410/45 LC cal. (new 2007).

SHOTGUNS: SINGLE SHOT

Beginning Nov. 1, 2007, H&R 1871 decided that all products built in the U.S.A. will carry the H&R brand name, and all imported products will be sold under the NEF brand name. The Pardner Series and Tracker Slug are now under the H&R brand name.

SURVIVOR SERIES – 12 (disc. 2003), 20 (disc. 2003) ga. or .410/.45 LC (new 1995) bore, 3 in. chamber, 20 (.410/.45 LC) or 22 in. barrel with Mod. choke, blue or electroless nickel finish, synthetic thumbhole designed hollow stock with pistol grip, removable forend holds additional ammo, sling swivels, and black nylon sling, 13 1/4 in. LOP, 6 lbs. Mfg. 1992-93, reintroduced 1995-2006.

	$175	$150	$120	$100	$85	$75	$65	*$219*

Add $18 for electroless nickel finish.
Subtract 20% for 12 or 20 ga.

SHOTGUNS: SLIDE ACTION

Beginning Nov. 1, 2007, H&R 1871 decided that all products built in the U.S.A. will carry the H&R brand name, and all imported products will be sold under the NEF brand name. The Pardner Series is now under the H&R brand name.

* ***Pardner Pump Protector*** – .12 ga., black synthetic stock, 18 1/2 in. barrel, bead front sight, matte finished metal, swivel studs, vent. recoil pad, 5 shot tube mag., crossbolt safety. Mfg. 2006-2007.

	$155	$135	$115	$100	$85	$75	$65	*$186*

* ***Pardner Pump Slug*** – 12 or 20 ga., takedown action, 21 (20 ga.) or 22 (12 ga.) in. rifled barrel, matte metal finish, black synthetic (12 ga.) or walnut (20 ga.) pistol grip stock with fluted comb, swivel studs, vent. recoil pad, ramp front sight, adj. rear sight, drilled and tapped, 5 shot mag., crossbolt safety, approx. 6 1/2 lbs. Mfg. 2006-2008.

	$250	$215	$190	$160	$140	$115	$100	*$298*

Add $33 for full cantilever scope mount (new 2009). Add $44 for walnut stock and forearm.

NEWTOWN FIREARMS

Current manufacturer located in Hangtown, CA.

CARBINES: SEMI-AUTO

NF-15/GEN 2 TACTICAL – 5.56 NATO cal., AR-15 style, choice of GIO or GPO, 16 in. match grade Vanadium steel fluted barrel with flash hider, quad Picatinny rail, black furniture, collapsible stock, sub MOA accuracy guaranteed, 10 or 20 shot mag., 8 lbs. Disc. 2013.

	$2,775	$2,300	$1,950	$1,575	$1,250	$1,000	$875	*$2,950*

NF-15 GEN 3 MATCH – .223 Wylde cal., GPO, 16 in. McGowen H-Bar match stainless steel barrel with black nitride coating, Gen-3 Mil-Spec T6 heavy mass billet upper and lower receiver set, Timney match trigger, modular free float quad rail, Adams Arms 4-pos. carbine length piston system with Adams Arms piston carrier, Battle Arms ambi safety, billet tactical charging handle, Magpul ACS Mil-Spec stock, Ergo Suregrip pistol grip. New 2014.

MSR $2,800	$2,375	$2,075	$1,775	$1,625	$1,300	$1,075	$925	

GEN-4 NF-15 – .223 Wylde cal., GPO, 16 in. McGowen H-Bar match stainless steel barrel with black Nitride coating and Barnes Precision A2 enhanced flash hider, billet tactical latch charging handle, Battle Arms ambidextrous safety selector, Gen-4 Mil-Spec T6 forged or Gen-4 Mil-Spec T6 billet lower receiver, forged upper receiver, modular free float quad rail, handguard with low heat-sync barrel nut, Barnes Precision gas block or Troy low pro gas block, 6-pos. carbine buffer tube, Magpul CTR stock, Ergo Sure pistol grip. New 2014.

MSR $1,499	$1,275	$1,125	$950	$875	$700	$575	$475	

Add $200 for Gen. 4 Mil-Spec T6 billet lower receiver.

MSR	100%	98%	95%	90%	80%	70%	60%	Last MSR

GEN-4 NF-15 PISTON – .223 Wylde cal., S.M.A.A.R.T. infinitely adj. GPO system, 16 in. McGowen H-Bar match stainless steel barrel with black Nitride coating and Barnes Precision A2 enhanced flash hider, Gen-4 Mil-Spec T6 forged or Gen-4 Mil-Spec billet lower receiver, forged upper receiver, ACT combat trigger, modular free float quad rail, handguard with low heat-sync barrel nut, 6-pos. carbine buffer tube, billet tactical latch charging handle, Battle Arms ambidextrous safety selector, Magpul CTR stock, Ergo Sure pistol grip. New 2014.

| MSR $2,099 | $1,785 | $1,575 | $1,350 | $1,225 | $975 | $800 | $675 | |

Add $300 for Gen-4 Mil-Spec T6 billet lower receiver.

NEXT GENERATION ARMS

Previous rifle manufacturer located in Hayden, ID until circa 2012.

RIFLES: SEMI-AUTO

Next Generation Arms manufactured AR-15 style rifles with an emphasis on being lighter, shorter, more reliable and easier to clean. There were many configurations possible, but most used a Noveske 14 1/2 in. barrel and a Geissele trigger. These are combined with advanced design and manufacturing as well as ceramic coatings.

NIGHTHAWK CUSTOM

Current manufacturer located in Berryville, AR, since 2004. Consumer custom order sales.

PISTOLS: SEMI-AUTO, SINGLE ACTION

Nighthawk Custom offers a complete line of high quality 1911 style semi-auto pistols. Please contact the company directly for more information on custom pistols, a wide variety of options, gunsmithing services and availability (see Trademark Index).

Add $199-$295 for Crimson Trace laser grips on any applicable model (not bobtail). Add $150 for Ed Brown bobtail. Add $120 for ambidextrous safety. Add $425 for Complete Hard Chrome Finish.

10-8 – .45 ACP cal., 5 in. barrel, SA, green or black linen Micarta grips, black Perma Kote finish, 8 shot, Hilton Yam/10-8 performance designed U-notched rear and serrated front sights with Tritium inserts, low profile Dawson Light Speed Rail, front/rear cocking serrations, long solid trigger with hidden fixed over travel stop, strong side only safety, 42 oz. Mfg. 2009-2010.

| | $2,350 | $2,025 | $1,650 | $1,325 | $1,175 | $900 | $775 | $2,595 |

AAC (ADVANCED ARMAMENT CORPORATION) – 9mm Para. or .45 ACP cal., 5 in. threaded barrel, SA, stainless steel thread protector, done in collaboration with Advanced Armament Corporation, lightening cuts on the top and sides of the slide, mainspring housing and front strap that match the Advanced Armament M4-2000 suppressor, tall Heinie Slant Pro Straight Eight front sights designed for use with suppressor, black Perma Kote finish in black, ultra thin Nighthawk Custom Alumagrips, solid, black aluminum trigger, 39 oz. New 2010.

| MSR $3,495 | $3,150 | $2,700 | $2,375 | $1,850 | $1,525 | $1,300 | $1,075 | |

Add $100 for AAC Recon Model with integrated lower rail.

BOB MARVEL CUSTOM 1911 – 9mm Para. (new 2015) or .45 ACP cal., 4 1/4 in. barrel, proprietary bull barrel system, hand stippling on top of slide, bull nose front taper, fully adjustable sights, one-piece mainspring housing and magwell, high cut front strap, lightweight aluminum medium solid match trigger, Nighthawk Custom/Marvel EVERLAST recoil system, black Melonite finish, 2 lbs. 6 oz. New 2012.

| MSR $3,995 | $3,575 | $3,100 | $2,650 | $2,050 | $1,700 | $1,475 | $1,300 | |

Add $200 for 9mm Para. cal. (new 2015).

BROWNING HI POWER – 9mm Para. cal., hand textured (stippled) frame and trigger guard, crowned barrel, two 13 shot mags., competition steel hammer, Heinie Slant Pro black rear and Nighthawk (14K) gold bead front sights, custom select Cocobolo checkered grips with NH logo, custom extended beavertail, contoured magwell, French border, Cerakote satin rust resistant finish. New 2016.

| MSR $2,895 | $2,600 | $2,275 | $1,950 | $1,775 | $1,425 | $1,175 | $925 | |

CHRIS COSTA RECON – 9mm Para. (2012 only) or .45 ACP cal., 5 in. crowned barrel and beveled flush with the bushing, 8 (.45 ACP) or 10 (9mm Para.) shot mag., fully machined slide and one piece mainspring housing, top serrations, red fiber optic or Tritium dot front sights, EVERLAST recoil system, magwell with rounded butt, Jardine Tactical Hook rear sights, extreme high cut checkered front strap, integrated recon light rail, multi-faceted slide top, lightweight aluminum medium solid match trigger, 10-8 Performance Hyena Brown grips, black Melonite finish, COSTA logo engraved in silver, 2 lbs. 6 oz. Mfg. 2012-2015.

| | $3,325 | $2,875 | $2,500 | $1,950 | $1,600 | $1,375 | $1,150 | $3,695 |

* **Chris Costa Compact** – .45 ACP cal. only, similar to Chris Costa Recon, except has smaller, officer-style frame, 4 1/4 in. barrel, black 10-8 Performance 5 LPI grips, 2 lbs. 4 oz. Mfg. 2012-2015.

| | $3,325 | $2,875 | $2,500 | $1,950 | $1,600 | $1,375 | $1,150 | $3,695 |

MSR	100%	98%	95%	90%	80%	70%	60%	Last MSR

DOMINATOR – .45 ACP cal., 5 in. crowned match grade barrel, stainless steel frame with black Perma Kote slide, Nighthawk Custom fully adjustable rear sights, 8 shot, hand serrated rear og slide with serrated top slide, front and rear slide serrations, 25 LPI checkering on front strap, Cocobolo double diamond grips with laser engraved Nighthawk Custom logo, 40 oz.

| MSR $3,450 | $3,100 | $2,650 | $2,325 | $1,800 | $1,475 | $1,250 | $1,025 | |

Add $100 for Recon Model with integrated lower rail (disc. 2014).
Add $350 for the FLX high capacity double stack frame (disc. 2011).

ENFORCER – .45 ACP cal., SA only, 5 in. barrel, Novak low mount Tritium or Heinie Slant Pro night sights, extended tactical mag. catch, aggressive no slip G10 Golf Ball grips or Mil-Tac G-10 spiral logo grips in either black/gray or black/green (new 2012), unique frame with integrated plunger tube and magwell, hand serrations on rear of slide with serrated top slide, front and rear slide cocking serrations, lanyard loop mainspring housing, completely dehorned and ready for carry, Perma Kote finish in black, green, sniper gray, coyote tan, or titanium blue, 39 oz.

| MSR $3,395 | $3,050 | $2,600 | $2,275 | $1,750 | $1,425 | $1,200 | $975 | |

Add $100 for Recon Model with integrated lower rail (disc. 2014).

FALCON – 9mm Para., 10mm, or .45 ACP cal., 5 in. match grade stainless steel or carbon steel crowned barrel with chamfered bushing, one-piece fully machined mainspring/magwell combination, rear cocking serrations, golf ball dimple-pattern G10 grips in Coyote Tan, Black, or OD Green finish with or without the Nighthawk logo, Heinie ledge rear sight, 39 oz. New 2011.

| MSR $3,395 | $3,050 | $2,600 | $2,275 | $1,750 | $1,425 | $1,200 | $975 | |

* ***Falcon Commander*** – .45 ACP cal., similar to Falcon, except in Commander size. New 2013.

| MSR $3,395 | $3,050 | $2,600 | $2,275 | $1,750 | $1,425 | $1,200 | $975 | |

GA PRECISION MODEL – Nighthawk's Ever-last recoil system, Heinie Ledge night sights, thick tactical bushing and smooth recoil spring plug, serrated rear of slide, bevel and recess slide stop, custom one-piece MSH and magwell, Nitride Black out finish. New 2016.

| MSR $3,695 | $3,325 | $2,910 | $2,495 | $2,260 | $1,830 | $1,500 | $1,175 | |

GRP (GLOBAL RESPONSE PISTOL) – 9mm Para. (new 2012), 10mm (new 2012), or .45 ACP cal., SA only, 5 in. match grade barrel, 8 shot mag., match grade trigger, front and rear cocking serrations, Heinie or Novak Extreme Duty adj. night sights, Gator Back (disc.) or Golf Ball grips, Perma Kote ceramic based finish in Black, Sniper Gray, Green, Coyote Tan, or Titanium Blue, tactical single side or Ambi safety, 2 lb. 7 oz.

| MSR $2,995 | $2,550 | $2,225 | $1,825 | $1,575 | $1,300 | $1,100 | $950 | |

Add $100 for GRP II with 4 1/4 in. barrel (disc. 2011).
Add $200 Crimson Trace laser grips (disc. 2014).
Add $350 for the FLX high capacity double stack frame (disc. 2011).

* ***GRP Recon*** – 9mm Para., 10mm, or .45 ACP cal., similar to GRP, except includes frame with integrated lower rail for Surefire X300 weapon light, 2 lb. 9 oz.

| MSR $3,195 | $2,875 | $2,525 | $2,175 | $1,675 | $1,325 | $1,150 | $995 | |

Add $200 Crimson Trace laser grips (disc. 2014).

GRIFFON – 9mm Para. cal., Griffon Industries designed 1911, Government frame, 5 in. fitted threaded barrel, three Chip McCormick mags. laser engraved with the Griffon logo, 10-8 Performance flat trigger, VZ Super Scoop grips with magazine button relief scallop, recon rail, wide rear cocking serrations, Griffon Industries logo, with or w/o Trijicon RMR cut slide, includes Griffon Industries pistol pouch, carbon fiber holster and double mag. carrier, limited edition custom Griffon Industries morale patch. New 2016.

| MSR $5,995 | $5,395 | $4,725 | $4,050 | $3,675 | $2,975 | $2,450 | $1,900 | |

HEINE LADY HAWK – 9mm Para. or .45 ACP cal., 4 1/4 in. crowned match grade barrel, ultra thin aluminum grips, Heinie Slant Pro Straight Eight sights, modified ultra thin chain link front strap and mainspring housing for reduced grip circumference, titanium blue Perma Kote finish with hard chromed controls, 36 oz.

| MSR $3,495 | $3,150 | $2,700 | $2,375 | $1,850 | $1,525 | $1,300 | $1,075 | |

Add $200 for anodized aluminum lightweight frame.
Add $200 for complete stainless steel model.
Add $100 for Recon Model with integrated lower rail (disc. 2014).

HEINIE LONG SLIDE – 10mm or .45 ACP cal., 6 in. match grade barrel, black Perma Kote ceramic based finish, Cocobolo wood grips with Heinie logo, Nighthawk Custom fully adjustable rear or fixed sights, 25 LPI checkering on front strap, contoured for carry, 44 oz.

| MSR $3,795 | $3,400 | $2,950 | $2,600 | $2,000 | $1,650 | $1,450 | $1,200 | |

Add $100 for Recon Model with integrated lower rail.
Add $150 for extended magazine well.
Add $350 for unique Nighthawk Custom camouflage finish; available in Digital, Woodland or Desert Camo (disc. 2011).

MSR	100%	98%	95%	90%	80%	70%	60%	Last MSR

HEINIE PDP – .45 ACP cal., 4 1/4 (Commander size) or 5 (Government size) in. Heinie match grade barrel, Cocobolo wood grips with Heinie logo, fixed sights, scalloped front strap and mainspring housing, extended combat safety, contoured for carry magwell, Heinie match hammer, sear, and disconnector, serrated rear of slide & slide top, Heinie aluminum trigger, tactical mag release, 38 oz.

MSR $3,395	$3,050	$2,600	$2,275	$1,750	$1,425	$1,200	$975

HEINIE SIGNATURE SERIES – 9mm Para. cal., available in Competition, Government Recon, and Officer Compact configurations, features silver Heinie Signature Series engraved logo on right of slide, features same thin frame as Lady Hawk model.

* ***Heinie Signature Series Compact*** – 9mm Para. cal., similar to the RECON and the Competition model, except has smaller officer-style frame designed for concealed carry, 4 1/2 in. barrel, and G10 grips. New 2012.

MSR $3,495	$3,150	$2,700	$2,375	$1,850	$1,525	$1,300	$1,075

* ***Heinie Signature Series Competition*** – 9mm Para. cal., 5 in. barrel, hand signed thin grip panels, fully machined one piece mainspring housing and magwell combination that has been thinned and scalloped, red fiber optic front sights, black Heinie Slant Pro rear sights, hand serrated rear of slide, slide top serrations, crowned and recessed match grade barrel, tool steel hammer and hammer strut, lightweight aluminum match grade trigger, recessed slide stop, chamfered frame, 40 oz. New 2012.

MSR $3,495	$3,150	$2,700	$2,375	$1,850	$1,525	$1,300	$1,075

* ***Heinie Signature Series RECON*** – 9mm Para. cal., 5 in. match grade barrel, similar features as the Competition, except has integrated recon light rail X300 tactical light, and Heine Slant Pro Night Sights. New 2012.

MSR $3,595	$3,200	$2,750	$2,425	$1,900	$1,575	$1,350	$1,125

HEINIE TACTICAL CARRY – .45 ACP cal., 5 in. Heinie match grade barrel, black Perma Kote ceramic based finish, double diamond Cocobolo or aluminum grips with Heinie logo, Heinie Straight Eight Slant Pro night sights, Heinie trigger, complete carry dehorned, Heinie signature magwell, flat slide top with 40 LPI serrations, done in collaboration with renowned gunsmith Richard Heinie, 40 oz. Disc. 2013.

	$3,600	$3,250	$2,850	$2,450	$2,000	$1,600	$1,200	*$3,895*

KESTREL – .45 ACP cal., forged frame, 4 1/4 in. Commander length slide, match grade crowned and recessed barrel, beveled magwell, tactical checkered extended mag. release, Heinie Slant Pro Straight Eight night sights, Nighthawk Custom ultra-thin alumagrips, hand serrated rear of slide, Heinie Signature scalloped front strap and contoured mainspring housing, black Nitride finish with stainless controls. New 2016.

MSR $3,495	$3,150	$2,700	$2,375	$1,850	$1,525	$1,300	$1,075

PREDATOR – 9mm Para., 10mm, or .45 ACP cal., SA only, 5 in. stainless steel barrel, black Perma Kote ceramic based finish with black slide, double diamond Cocobolo, walnut, or black cristobal checkered grips, Heinie Slant Pro Straight Eight or Novak Lo-Mount night sights, hand checkering on rear of slide with serrated top slide, front and rear slide serrations, 25 LPI checkering on front strap, unique one piece precision fit barrel designed to reduce muzzle flip and felt recoil, one inch at 25 yards guaranteed accuracy, top-of-the-line model, available in Black, Sniper Gray, Coyote Tan, Titanium Blue, Hard Chrome, or Stainless steel, 32-34 oz.

MSR $3,595	$3,200	$2,750	$2,425	$1,900	$1,575	$1,350	$1,125

Add $100 for Recon Model with integrated lower rail.

Add $350 for the FLX high capacity double stack frame. (9mm & 10mm Government size only, disc. 2011)

* ***Predator II*** – 9mm Para., 10mm, or .45 ACP cal., similar to Predator, except has 4 1/4 in. barrel, checkered rear of slide, top serrations, 2 lbs. 4 oz.

MSR $3,595	$3,200	$2,750	$2,425	$1,900	$1,575	$1,350	$1,125

* ***Predator III*** – 9mm Para., 10mm, or .45 ACP cal., similar to Predator, except features Officer frame and 4 1/4 in. barrel, 2 lbs. 6 oz.

MSR $3,595	$3,200	$2,750	$2,425	$1,900	$1,575	$1,350	$1,125

* ***Predator T5*** – 9mm Para. cal., 5 in. stainless steel bull barrel, stainless steel frame, Nighthawk two-piece magwell, single side safety, Heinie Ledge Straight Eight front and rear Tritium night sights, thinned Cocobolo grips with diamond checkering, black Nitride finish, 40.3 oz. New 2015.

MSR $3,795	$3,400	$2,950	$2,600	$2,000	$1,650	$1,450	$1,200

SHADOW HAWK COMMANDER – 9mm Para. cal., 4 1/4 in. custom match carbon steel barrel, stainless steel frame, one-piece magwell, Heinie Ledge Straight Eight front and rear Tritium night sights, black and gray spiral cut custom grips, black Nitride finish, 36.7 oz. New 2015.

MSR $3,795	$3,400	$2,950	$2,600	$2,000	$1,650	$1,450	$1,200

SHADOW HAWK GOVERNMENT – 9mm Para. cal., 5 in. barrel, stainless steel frame, single side safety, Heinie Ledge Straight Eight front and rear Tritium night sights, aggressive cocking serrations, one-piece steel magwell/ mainspring housing, black flat-faced trigger, front strap checkering, high beavertail, recessed and beveled slide stop, black and gray spiral cut G10 grips, black Nitride finish, 39 oz. New 2015.

MSR $3,795	$3,400	$2,950	$2,600	$2,000	$1,650	$1,450	$1,200

MSR	100%	98%	95%	90%	80%	70%	60%	Last MSR

* ***Shadow Hawk Government With Trijicon RMR*** – 9mm Para. cal., similar to Shadow Hawk Government, except features a mounted Trijicon RMR (Ruggedized Miniature Reflex) sight, front and rear Trijicon Tall Tritium night sights, 37.4 oz. New 2015.

| MSR $4,895 | $4,500 | $3,975 | $3,625 | $3,025 | $2,675 | $2,475 | $2,225 | |

SILENT HAWK – .45 ACP cal., Commander recon frame and Commander slide, threaded barrel with protector, two Nighthawk Custom 8 shot stainless mags., G10 black and gray spiral cut grips with mag. release cutout and Nighthawk logo, custom checkering on front strap of frame, one-piece mainspring housing and magwell, custom NH/SilencerCo brand logos on slide and behind rear cocking serrations, hand serrated rear of slide, tri-cut top slide and custom cocking serrations to match Osprey silencer, Nitride Black Out finish, built for SilencerCo. New 2016.

| MSR $4,295 | $3,850 | $3,375 | $2,895 | $2,625 | $2,125 | $1,750 | $1,375 | |

T3 – 9mm Para., .40 S&W (disc. 2011) or .45 ACP cal., 4 1/4 in. match grade stainless steel fully crowned barrel, Officer size frame, extended magwell, flush forged slide stop with chamfered frame, tactical mag. release, unique Nighthawk T3 magwell, horizontally serrated no-snag mainspring housing and rear of slide, skeletonized aluminum match trigger, Heinie straight 8 slant pro sights, Perma Kote finish, in black, gun metal grey, green, coyote tan, titanium blue, or hard chrome, 38 oz.

| MSR $3,350 | $3,000 | $2,550 | $2,250 | $1,700 | $1,375 | $1,175 | $950 | |

Add $200 for anodized aluminum lightweight frame.

Add $495 for T3 Comp model (.45 ACP cal. only), with Schuemann AET hybrid comp. ported barrel (mfg. 2010-disc.).

* ***T3 Stainless*** – 9mm Para, .40 S&W (disc. 2011) or .45 ACP cal., similar to T3, except stainless steel.

| MSR $3,550 | $3,175 | $2,725 | $2,400 | $1,875 | $1,550 | $1,325 | $1,100 | |

* ***T3 Thin*** – similar to the T3, except is smaller design for concealed carry. New 2012.

| MSR $3,550 | $3,175 | $2,725 | $2,400 | $1,875 | $1,550 | $1,325 | $1,100 | |

T4 – 9mm Para. cal., 3.8 in. crowned barrel, Bob Marvel Everlast recoil system, steel, aluminum, or stainless steel (new 2015) proprietary thin frame, ultra-thin G10 grips. New 2013.

| MSR $3,395 | $3,050 | $2,600 | $2,275 | $1,750 | $1,425 | $1,200 | $975 | |

Add $200 for aluminum or stainless steel (new 2015) frame.

TALON – 9mm Para., .40 S&W (disc. 2011), 10mm, or .45 ACP cal., 5 in. match grade barrel, lightweight aluminum match trigger, hand checkering on rear of slide with serrated top slide, front and rear slide serrations, 25 LPI checkering on front strap, Novak night sights, Cocobolo, walnut, or black cristobal grips, tactical mag. release, Perma Kote ceramic based finish in black, Sniper Gray, Coyote Tan, Titanium Blue, hard chrome, or Diamond Black option available, 36-41 oz.

| MSR $3,195 | $2,875 | $2,525 | $2,175 | $1,675 | $1,325 | $1,150 | $875 | |

Add $199 for Crimson Trace Lasergrips with Nighthawk logo.

Add $100 for Recon Model with integrated lower rail.

Add $200 for anodized aluminum lightweight frame.

Add $350 for the FLX high capacity double stack frame (disc. 2011).

* ***Talon II*** – 9mm Para., .40 S&W (disc. 2011), 10mm, or .45 ACP cal., similar to Talon, except features Commander size frame, 4 1/4 in. barrel, 2 lbs. 4 oz.

| MSR $3,195 | $2,875 | $2,525 | $2,175 | $1,675 | $1,325 | $1,150 | $875 | |

» **Talon II Bobtail** – 9mm Para., .40 S&W (disc. 2011), 10mm, or .45 ACP cal., similar to Talon II, except features Ed Brown Bobtail.

| MSR $3,345 | $3,000 | $2,550 | $2,250 | $1,700 | $1,375 | $1,175 | $950 | |

* ***Talon IV*** – similar to Talon, except compact model with 3.6 in. barrel, gray frame and black slide, rear slide serrations, and black grips. Disc. 2010.

| | $2,225 | $1,950 | $1,600 | $1,300 | $1,050 | $875 | $750 | *$2,425* |

VIP (VERY IMPRESSIVE PISTOL) – crowned barrel, 14K gold-plated front bead sight, Heinie Black rear sight, giraffe bone grips, deep hand engraving featured throughout, custom vertical front strap and mainspring serrations, hand serrated rear of slide and ejector, classic antique nickel finish, includes custom Cocobolo hardwood presentation case. New 2016.

| MSR $7,995 | $7,195 | $6,295 | $5,395 | $4,895 | $3,950 | $3,250 | $2,525 | |

WAR HAWK COMPACT – .45 ACP cal., 4 1/4 in. barrel, stainless steel Officer size frame, one-piece mainspring housing/magwell, Heinie Slant Pro night rear and Tritium front sights, Everlast Recoil System, solid aluminum match grade trigger, tri-cut slide with bold angles, heavy bevel on bottom of slide, thin G10 grips in Hyena brown, War Hawk logo engraved on slide, black Nitride finish, 34.7 oz. New 2015.

| MSR $3,895 | $3,500 | $2,975 | $2,625 | $2,025 | $1,675 | $1,475 | $1,225 | |

MSR	100%	98%	95%	90%	80%	70%	60%	Last MSR

WAR HAWK GOVERNMENT – .45 ACP cal., full size Government frame, 5 in. barrel, one-piece mainspring housing/magwell, solid aluminum match grade trigger, Everlast Recoil System, multi-faceted slide, serrated arrow style slide top, heavy bevel on bottom of slide, War Hawk logo engraved on slide, aggressive G10 grips in Hyena Brown, tactical magazine catch, Jardine Hook rear sight and red fiber optic front sights, black Nitride finish, 39.6 oz. New 2015.

| MSR $3,895 | $3,500 | $2,975 | $2,625 | $2,025 | $1,675 | $1,475 | $1,225 | |

WAR HAWK RECON – .45 ACP cal., 5 in. barrel, one-piece mainspring housing/magwell, solid aluminum match grade trigger, multi-faceted slide, serrated arrow style slide top, War Hawk logo engraved on slide, Everlast Recoil System, aggressive G10 grips in Hyena Brown, Jardine black rear sight and red fiber optic front, integrated recon accessory rail, extended tactical mag catch, black Nitride finish, 39.6 oz. New 2015.

| MSR $3,995 | $3,575 | $3,100 | $2,650 | $2,050 | $1,700 | $1,475 | $1,300 | |

RIFLES: BOLT ACTION

HUNTING RIFLE – various cals., bolt action, available in Hunting, Varmint, and Bench Rest configurations, Broughton barrel, synthetic stock. Disc. 2011.

| | $3,500 | $3,100 | $2,650 | $2,250 | $1,800 | $1,375 | $1,125 | *$3,895* |

TACTICAL RIFLE – .308 Win., 7mm Rem. Mag., .300 Rem. Mag., or .338 Lapua cal., with or w/o Surgeon action, with or w/o bolt on Picatinny rail with choice of 0 or 20 MOA integral elevation, Jewell trigger, Perma Kote finish in choice of Desert Sand, OD Green, Sniper Gray, Desert camo, Woodland camo, or Urban camo finish, tactical synthetic stock with adj. comb. Mfg. 2009-2011.

| | $3,800 | $3,350 | $2,900 | $2,500 | $2,000 | $1,500 | $1,225 | *$4,250* |

Add $550 for short Surgeon action.

Add $595 for 100% coverage Custom woodland or digital camouflage finish.

Add $625 for Magnum Surgeon action.

Add $650 for long Surgeon action.

Add $875 for XL action in .338 Lapua cal.

SHOTGUNS

OVERSEER MODEL 1 – 12 ga., hand honed action and rails, 6 shot mag., two shot extension tube, Nighthawk's black custom tactical ghost ring rear sight and front red fiber optic sight, Hogue overmolded stock, receiver mounted Picatinny rail, 6 round side shell carrier, black Cerakote finish. New 2016.

| MSR $1,525 | $1,285 | $1,125 | $1,025 | $875 | $750 | $625 | $525 | |

* ***Overseer Model 2*** – 12 ga., similar to Overseer Model 1, except has SGA Magpul stock and forend upgrade with black finish and adaptor plates. New 2016.

| MSR $1,690 | $1,435 | $1,250 | $1,115 | $985 | $840 | $725 | $590 | |

* ***Overseer Model 3*** – 12 ga., similar to Overseer Model 1, except has SGA Magpul stock and forend upgrade with adaptor plates, custom Shadow Tan camo stock finish. New 2016.

| MSR $2,040 | $1,725 | $1,510 | $1,250 | $1,100 | $950 | $825 | $675 | |

* ***Overseer Model 4*** – 12 ga., similar to Overseer Model 1, except has SGA Magpul stock and forend upgrade with adaptor plates, Surefire Z2X combat light (320 Lumens, LED), barrel clamp with swivel and Picatinny rail, and custom Shadow Urban camo stock finish. New 2016.

| MSR $2,270 | $1,925 | $1,685 | $1,425 | $1,225 | $1,035 | $885 | $735 | |

* ***Overseer Model 5*** – 12 ga., similar to Overseer Model 1, except has SGA Magpul stock and forend upgrade with adaptor plates, custom Battle Worn Silver Patriot Complete finish. New 2016.

| MSR $2,115 | $1,800 | $1,575 | $1,325 | $1,150 | $995 | $850 | $700 | |

* ***Overseer Model 6*** – 12 ga., similar to Overseer Model 1, except has collapsible stock upgrade with Hogue pistol grip, Surefire forend (DSF870) light and forend for 870, includes ambidextrous momentary/constant on switches, isolated selector switch for high (600 lumens) and low (200 lumens) output modes, breeching device with 3-shot extension. New 2016.

| MSR $2,190 | $1,875 | $1,650 | $1,400 | $1,200 | $1,025 | $875 | $725 | |

TACTICAL SLIDE ACTION – 12 ga., reworked 3 in. chambered action for faster, smoother cycling, Hogue overmolded style stock with 12 or 14 in. LOP, Big Dome large safety, 2-shot extension, fully adjustable and protected ghost ring rear sight with red fiber optic front, 4 or 6 round shell carrier, Rust-Proof ceramic finish in a variety of colors including camo, (Hillbilly223 camo finish became standard in 2014). Disc. 2015.

| | $1,250 | $1,095 | $925 | $800 | $600 | $550 | $475 | *$1,450* |

Add $35 for Tritium front sight upgrade.

Add $75 for Picatinny rail on top of receiver.

Add $85 for magazine clamp with rail & swing swivel.

Add $125 for breaching tool.

Add $125 for Surefire Tactical light with ring mount.

Add $165 for 5-position stock.

MSR	100%	98%	95%	90%	80%	70%	60%	Last MSR

TACTICAL SEMI-AUTO – 12 ga., 2 3/4 in. chamber, 18 in. barrel, pistol grip synthetic stock, Surefire forend weapon light, hand tuned action, rust-proof ceramic finish in a variety of colors including camouflage patterns, tactical charging handle on the bolt, fully adjustable and protected ghost ring rear sight, red fiber optic front sight, 2-shot extension, 4 or 6 round shell carrier. Disc. 2011.

	100%	98%	95%	90%	80%	70%	60%	Last MSR
	$1,800	$1,550	$1,250	$1,125	$800	$675	$550	$2,060

Add $35 for Tritium front sight blade.
Add $75 for Picatinny rail on top of receiver.
Add $299 for Surefire forend tactical weapon light.

NOREEN FIREARMS LLC

Current manufacturer located in Belgrade, MT.

RIFLES: BOLT ACTION

ULR (ULTRA LONG RANGE) – .338 Lapua, .408 CheyTac, .416 Barrett, or .50 BMG cal., single shot, 32 (disc.) or 34 in. button rifled chrome moly barrel, Noreen muzzle brake, tactical black or desert camo finish, shell holder bolt, Timney adj. trigger, Picatinny top rail, folding rotating bipod, collapsible shoulder stock, A2 grip, 32 lbs.

MSR $2,000	$1,700	$1,500	$1,250	$1,100	$950	$825	$675	

ULR EXTREME – .50 BMG, .50 DTC, .416 Barrett, .408 CheyTac, or .338 Lapua cal., single shot, 34 in. barrel with muzzle brake, barrel shroud, Timney adj. trigger, fully adj. XLR folding stock, cheek rest, and recoil pad, Ergo grip, XLR chassis system, top Picatinny rail, black finish, 32 lbs.

MSR $3,600	$3,050	$2,675	$2,175	$1,875	$1,550	$1,300	$1,125	

RIFLES: SEMI-AUTO

BAD NEWS GEN II (BAD NEWS ULTRA LONG RANGE -ULR) – .300 Win. Mag. (disc.), .338 Norma (mfg. 2014-2015), or .338 Lapua cal., GPO, 26 in. barrel, custom muzzle brake, aluminum receiver, Mil-Spec (disc.) or match (new 2016) trigger, 5 or 10 shot detachable box mag., one piece bolt carrier, Picatinny quad rail on handguard, Magpul PRS adj. stock, matte black finish, 13 lbs.

MSR $5,996	$5,450	$4,475	$3,825	$3,475	$2,800	$2,295	$1,775	

In 2016, this model's nomenclature changed to Bad News Gen. II because it received upgraded receivers, handguard, billet magazines, and a new adj. gas block.

BBN223 – 5.56x45mm cal., GIO, 16 in. barrel with Noreen flash hider, Mil-Spec trigger, Magpul MBUS flip up sights, 6-position collabsible stock, A2 pistol grip, sling mounts, 6 lbs. New 2016.

MSR $1,300	$1,100	$995	$875	$735	$650	$550	$465	

BN36 CARBINE ASSASSIN – .30-06 cal., GIO, 16 in. barrel with flash hider, 20 shot mag., Mil-Spec trigger, enlarged trigger guard, collapsible stock, A2 pistol grip, black finish, 7 lbs. New 2016.

MSR $1,700	$1,450	$1,275	$1,125	$1,000	$850	$735	$595	

BN36 CARBINE ASSASSIN-X – .30-06 cal., GIO, 16 in. barrel with flash hider, 20 shot mag., Mil-Spec trigger, Luth AR stock, Tactical Dynamics pistol grip, black finish, 7 lbs. New 2016.

MSR $2,000	$1,700	$1,500	$1,250	$1,100	$950	$825	$675	

Blue Book Publications selected this model as one of its Top 10 Industry Awards from all the new firearms at the 2016 SHOT Show.

BN36 LONG RANGE ASSASSIN (BN36 SEMI-AUTO) – .25-06 Rem., .270 Win., .30-06, .300 Win. Mag., or 7mm rem. Mag. (new 2016) cal., GIO, 22 in. chrome moly barrel, Noreen design muzzle brake, side charging, matte black finish, fixed A2 (disc.) or Luth AR stock with pistol grip, 5, 10, or 20 shot box mag., Mil-Spec or optional match trigger, 9 lbs. New 2013.

MSR $2,000	$1,700	$1,500	$1,250	$1,100	$950	$825	$675	

BN308 – .308 Win. cal., GIO, 16 in. barrel with flash hider, 20 shot mag., Mil-Spec trigger, Luth AR stock, Tactical Dynamics pistol grip, updated forearm (new 2016) with Picatinny rail, Type III hardcoat anodized black finish, 8 lbs. New 2015.

MSR $2,000	$1,700	$1,500	$1,250	$1,100	$950	$825	$675	

BN408 - "THE BEAST" – .408 CheyTac cal., piston driven, side charging semi-auto, 28 in. barrel with black Nitride finish, Noreen muzzle brake, 10 shot double stack billet mag., match trigger, adj. AR-15 collapsible stock, A2 pistol grip, monolithic upper receiver, continuous Picatinny rail, ambidextrous controls, includes rear monopod and bipod, black oxide finish, 23 lbs. New 2016.

Current MSR for this model is $12,990.

MSR		100%	98%	95%	90%	80%	70%	60%	Last MSR

NORINCO

Current division of China North Industries Corp. established in 1981, and located in Beijing, China. Norinco currently manufactures small arms and large military weapons for commercial, law enforcement, and military applications. No current U.S. importation. Distributed exclusiely throughout Europe by Norconia GmbH established during 1988, and located in Rottendorf, Germany. Previously imported and distributed exclusively by Interstate Arms Corp., located in Billerica, MA. Previous importers have included: Norinco Sports U.S.A., located in Diamond Bar, CA, Century International Arms, Inc. located in St. Albans, VT; China Sports, Inc. located in Ontario, CA; Interarms located in Alexandria, VA; KBI, Inc. located in Harrisburg, PA; and others.

Norinco pistols, rifles, and shotguns are manufactured in the People's Republic of China by China North Industries Corp. (Norinco has over 100 factories). Currently, due to government legislation, Norinco cannot legally sell weapons in the U.S.

RIFLES: SEMI-AUTO

TYPE 84S AKS RIFLE – .223 Rem. cal., semi-auto Kalashnikov action, 16.34 in. barrel, hardwood stock and pistol grip, 30 shot mag., 1,000 meter adj. rear sight, includes bayonet and sheath, 8.87 lbs. Imported 1988-89 only.

		$1,450	$1,250	$1,150	$1,000	$925	$875	$795	$350

* ***Type 84S-1 AKS Rifle*** – similar to Type 84S AKS except has under-folding metal stock. Imported 1989 only.

		$1,600	$1,500	$1,400	$1,250	$1,100	$1,000	$900	$350

* ***Type 84S-3 AKS Rifle*** – similar to Type 84S AKS except has composite fiber stock (1 1/2 in. longer than wood stock). Imported 1989 only.

		$1,295	$1,100	$1,000	$950	$900	$800	$750	$365

* ***Type 84S-5 AKS Rifle*** – similar to Type 84S AKS except has side-folding metal stock. Imported 1989 only.

		$1,600	$1,500	$1,450	$1,350	$1,200	$1,100	$1,000	$350

NHM-90/91 (AK-47 THUMBHOLE) – .223 Rem. or 7.62x39mm cal., features new thumbhole stock for legalized import, 5 shot mag. Imported 1991-1993, configuration was restyled and renamed NHM-90/91 in 1994.

		$750	$675	$575	$500	$450	$350	$300	$375

NHM-90/91 SPORT – 7.62x39mm cal., choice of 16.34 (NHM-90) or 23.27 (NHM-91) in. barrel, hardwood thumbhole stock, NHM-91 has bipod, 5 shot mag., 9-11 lbs. Imported 1994-95.

		$550	$500	$450	$425	$385	$350	$325	

The .223 Rem. cal. was also available for the Model NHM-90. Each Model NHM-90/91 was supplied with three 5 shot mags., sling, and cleaning kit.

MODEL B THUMBHOLE – 9mm Para. cal., patterned after the Uzi, features sporterized thumbhole wood stock, 10 shot mag. Importation 1995 only.

		$795	$695	$600	$550	$500	$450	$400	$625

R.P.K. RIFLE – 7.62x39mm cal., includes bipod. Importation disc. 1993.

		$1,200	$1,000	$900	$800	$725	$650	$600	$600

TYPE SKS – .223 Rem. or 7.62x39mm cal., SKS action, 20.47 in. barrel, 10 (C/B 1994) or 30* shot mag., 1,000 meter adj. rear sight, hardwood stock, new design accepts standard AK mag., with or w/o folding bayonet, 8.8 lbs. Imported 1988-1989, reintroduced 1992-95 with Sporter configuration stock.

		$475	$400	$350	$325	$300	$250	$225	$150

Add $100 for synthetic stock and bayonet.
Subtract 15% if refinished.

TYPE 81S AKS RIFLE – 7.62x39mm cal., semi-auto Kalashnikov action, 17 1/2 in. barrel, 5, 30, or 40 shot mag., 500 meter adj. rear sight, fixed wood stock, hold open device after last shot, 8 lbs. Imported 1988-1989.

		$1,200	$1,000	$900	$800	$725	$650	$600	$385

* ***Type 81S-1 AKS Rifle*** – similar to Type 81S AKS except has under-folding metal stock. Imported 1988-89.

		$1,300	$1,075	$950	$850	$750	$625	$575	$385

TYPE 56S-2 – 7.62x39mm cal., older Kalashnikov design with side-folding metal stock. Importation disc. 1989.

		$1,500	$1,350	$1,200	$1,100	$1,000	$900	$800	$350

TYPE 86S-7 RPK RIFLE – 7.62x39mm cal., AK action, 23.27 in. heavy barrel with built-in bipod, in-line buttstock, 11.02 lbs. Imported 1988-1989.

		$1,500	$1,275	$1,075	$950	$850	$750	$650	$425

MSR	100%	98%	95%	90%	80%	70%	60%	Last MSR

TYPE 86S BULLPUP RIFLE – 7.62x39mm cal., bullpup configuration with AK action, under-folding metal stock, 17 1/4 in. barrel, ambidextrous cocking design, folding front handle, 7 lbs. Imported 1989 only.

	100%	98%	95%	90%	80%	70%	60%	Last MSR
	$1,850	$1,650	$1,500	$1,250	$1,100	$1,000	$900	$400

DRAGUNOV (MODEL 350 NDM-86) – 7.62x54mm Russian, sniper variation of the AK-47, features 24 in. barrel with muzzle brake, special laminated skeletonized wood stock with vent. forearm, detachable 10 shot mag., 8 lbs. 9 oz. Importation disc. 1995.

	100%	98%	95%	90%	80%	70%	60%	Last MSR
	$2,950	$2,650	$2,400	$2,250	$2,000	$1,850	$1,650	$3,080

This model was also imported by Gibbs Rifle Co. located in Martinsburg, WV.

* ***Dragunov Carbine*** – similar to Dragunov rifle, except shorter barrel, various accessories including a lighted scope were also offered, plastic furniture.

	100%	98%	95%	90%	80%	70%	60%
	$1,200	$1,000	$875	$775	$675	$600	$550

OFFICERS NINE – 9mm Para. cal., 16.1 in. barrel, action patterned after the IMI Uzi, 32 shot mag., black military finish, 8.4 lbs. Limited 1988-89.

	100%	98%	95%	90%	80%	70%	60%	Last MSR
	$1,100	$995	$850	$725	$650	$575	$500	$450

SHOTGUNS: SEMI-AUTO

* ***Model 2000 Field Defense*** – 12 ga. only, 2 3/4 in. chamber, 18 1/2 in. barrel with cyl. choke tube and choice of bead, rifle, or ghost ring sights, matte black metal finish, black synthetic stock and forearm with recoil pad. Limited importation 1999 only.

	100%	98%	95%	90%	80%	70%	60%	Last MSR
	$245	$225	$190	$175	$160	$155	$145	$282

Add $5 for rifle sights.
Add $17 for ghost ring sights.

SHOTGUNS: SLIDE ACTION

* ***Model 98 Field Defense*** – 12 ga. only, 3 in. chamber, 18 1/2 in. barrel with cyl. choke tube and choice of bead, rifle, or ghost ring sights, matte black metal finish, black synthetic stock and forearm with recoil pad. Limited importation 1999 only.

	100%	98%	95%	90%	80%	70%	60%	Last MSR
	$170	$150	$130	$115	$100	$90	$80	$190

Add $15 for ghost ring sights.

NORTHERN COMPETITION

Current rifle manufacturer located in Racine, WI. Consumer direct sales through FFL.

RIFLES: SEMI-AUTO

Northern Competition manufactures a line of AR-15 style rifles in various calibers and configurations. Current/recent models are described within this section. Previous models included the Predator and Ranch models.

CHEETAH – .22-250, .243 Win., or .308 Win. cal., AR-15 style, GIO, 24 or 26 in. chrome moly barrel, quad rail Picatinny handguard, Magpul PRS stock, NM 2-stage trigger, one 19 shot Magpul mag., Black finish, 12 1/2 lbs. Disc. 2013.

	100%	98%	95%	90%	80%	70%	60%	Last MSR
	$1,725	$1,500	$1,250	$1,100	$950	$825	$675	$2,019

COUGAR – .22-250, .243 Win., or .308 Win. cal., AR-15 style, GIO, 24 or 26 in. chrome moly barrel, single stage trigger, A2 style buttstock, pistol grip, Black finish, 12 lbs. Disc. 2013.

	100%	98%	95%	90%	80%	70%	60%	Last MSR
	$1,460	$1,275	$1,125	$1,000	$850	$735	$595	$1,719

COMPLETE SERVICE RIFLE (NCSR15) – .22-250, .243 Win., or .308 Win. cal., AR-15 style Classic A2 design, pre or post-ban configuration, GIO, 20 in. heavy barrel, A2 style buttstock, two-stage trigger, charging handle, NM float tube assembly, NM front sight housing, NM double pinned minute sights, Black finish.

MSR	100%	98%	95%	90%	80%	70%	60%
$1,495	$1,275	$1,125	$1,025	$875	$750	$625	$525

Add $200 for Geissele trigger.

NOSLER, INC.

Current rifle, ammunition, and bullet manufacturer located in Bend, OR.

Founded in 1948, Nosler, Incorporated is a family owned company. Nosler is most known for revolutionizing the hunting bullet industry with bullets such as the Partition®, Ballistic Tip®, AccuBond®, E-Tip®, and most recently the AccuBond® LR. With the company motto of "Quality First", Nosler manufactures premium component bullets, reloading brass, ammunition, and semi-custom rifles for domestic and international customers making Nosler a comprehensive shooting products company.

MSR	100%	98%	95%	90%	80%	70%	60%	Last MSR

RIFLES: BOLT ACTION

MODEL 48 SERIES – various cals., features NoslerCustom push feed action, 3 or 4 shot mag., 24-26 in. barrel w/o sights, standard, 2, or 3 position safety, Rifle Basix or Timney trigger, various synthetic or wood stocks, Cerakote and Microslick metal coating. Guaranteed accuracy at 100 yards, available in production and Custom configurations, approx. 6 1/4 - 8 3/4 lbs. New 2005.

* **Model 48 Custom** – various cals., features Kevlar/carbon fiber stock in various colors or fancy walnut stock, Cerakote finish, various barrel lengths between 20-26 in., available in Long Range, Expedition, High Country, and Brush Country packages, 6 1/2-7 1/2 lbs.

| MSR $3,795 | $3,350 | $2,750 | $2,375 | $2,025 | $1,825 | $1,475 | $1,200 | |

Add $200 for factory installed muzzle brake.
Add $100 for detachable magazine.
Add $100 for 3-position safety.
Add $250 for factory installed open sights.
Add $100 for extra fancy walnut with blackwood endcap and gripcaps.

* **Model 48 Custom Varmint** – .204 Ruger, .223 Rem., or .22-250 Rem. cal., features Coyote tan Kevlar/carbon fiber stock, Graphite Black or Coyote Tan Cerakote, 7 1/4 lbs. Disc. 2011.

| | $2,650 | $2,200 | $1,800 | $1,450 | $1,150 | $1,000 | $900 | *$2,995* |

* **Model 48 Heritage** – various cals., Nosler 48 action, stainless match grade barrel, glass bedding, hinged floorplate, 2-position Rocker safety, fancy walnut stock with 20 LPI checkering, Cerakote All-Weather finish. New 2014.

| MSR $1,895 | $1,625 | $1,425 | $1,225 | $1,100 | $900 | $725 | $575 | |

* **Model 48 Legacy** – various cals., features deluxe checkered walnut stock, special engraved floorplate bearing the signature of John A. Nosler, no sights, Midnight Blue Cerakote finish, 7 1/2 - 8 lbs. Disc. 2013.

| | $2,295 | $2,000 | $1,725 | $1,550 | $1,250 | $1,025 | $800 | *$2,695* |

* **Model 48 Patriot** – various cals., Nosler Model 48 action, stainless match grade barrel, lightweight Aramid fiber reinforced composite stock, 2-position Rocker safety, glass and aluminum pillar bedding, hinged floorplate, Cerakote All-Weather finish. New 2014.

| MSR $1,795 | $1,525 | $1,325 | $1,125 | $995 | $800 | $650 | $525 | |

* **Model 48 Professional** – various cals., features black Bell & Carlson composite stock, matte black Cerakote finish, no sights, 6 1/2 -7 1/2 lbs. Mfg. 2012-2013.

| | $2,295 | $2,000 | $1,725 | $1,550 | $1,250 | $1,025 | $800 | *$2,695* |

Add $100 for detachable magazine.
Add $200 for factory installed muzzle brake.

* **Model 48 Trophy** – various cals., features black and spiderweb gray Bell & Carlson composite stock, magnesium color Cerakote finish, blind bottom magazine, no sights, 6 1/2-7 lbs. Disc. 2013.

| | $1,800 | $1,575 | $1,300 | $1,050 | $875 | $750 | $625 | *$1,995* |

Add $200 for factory installed muzzle brake.

* **Model 48 Outfitter** – various cals., Nosler Model 48 action, 22 in. stainless match grade barrel, adj. open sights, glass and aluminum pillar bedding, blind-bottom internal magazine, 2-position Rocker safety, black and spiderweb gray Bell & Carlson lightweight Aramid fiber reinforced composite stock, magnesium color Cerakote finish. New 2013.

| MSR $1,895 | $1,625 | $1,425 | $1,225 | $1,100 | $900 | $725 | $575 | |

* **Model 48 Custom Long Range Package** – various cals., NoslerCustom push feed action, 26 in. Magnum contoured barrel with removable muzzle brake, 3 or 4 shot mag., Kevlar/carbon fiber stock, includes Pelican hard case, Woodland color with C2 finish, includes Nightforce scope and rings, supplied with Picatinny scope base. New 2015.

| MSR $5,830 | $5,400 | $4,750 | $4,200 | $3,550 | $3,000 | $2,675 | $2,275 | |

* **Model 48 Custom Expedition Package** – various cals., NoslerCustom push feed action, 26 in. Magnum contoured barrel with removable muzzle brake, 3 or 4 shot mag., Kevlar/carbon fiber stock, includes Pelican hard case, Obsidian color with C2 finish, includes Swarovski scope and Talley rings. New 2015.

| MSR $6,245 | $5,700 | $4,995 | $4,300 | $3,600 | $3,050 | $2,700 | $2,300 | |

* **Model 48 Custom High Country Package** – various cals., NoslerCustom push feed action, 24 or 26 in. Magnum contoured barrel with removable muzzle brake, 3 or 4 shot mag., Kevlar/carbon fiber stock, includes Pelican hard case, Onyx color with C2 finish, includes Zeiss Conquest scope and Talley rings. New 2015.

| MSR $5,775 | $5,350 | $4,700 | $4,150 | $3,500 | $3,000 | $2,675 | $2,275 | |

* **Model 48 Custom Brush Country Package** – various Mag. cals., NoslerCustom push feed action, 26 in. Magnum contoured barrel with removable muzzle brake, 3 or 4 shot mag., open sights, Kevlar/carbon fiber stock, includes Pelican hard case, Onyx color with C2 finish, includes Leupold scope and rings. New 2015.

| MSR $5,840 | $5,400 | $4,750 | $4,200 | $3,550 | $3,000 | $2,675 | $2,275 | |

MSR	100%	98%	95%	90%	80%	70%	60%	Last MSR

CUSTOM LIMITED EDITION SERIES – .280 Ackley Improved (Series 2), .300 WSM (Series 1, limited quantities), or .338 Win. Mag. (Series 3) cal., features NoslerCustom barreled action with 3-position safety, integral Leupold QD scope mounts, 24 in. barrel w/o sights, fancy checkered walnut stock with forend and pistol grip caps, Pachmayr Decelerator recoil pad, only 500 of each series mfg. (ser. no. range 001-500), shipped in Kalispel Aluminum case or Pelican Polymer hard case with leather sling, 9 lbs. New 2005.

| MSR $4,495 | $4,200 | $3,800 | $3,350 | $2,875 | $2,475 | $2,150 | $1,750 | |

Add $200 for Series 1 in .300 WSM cal. (limited quantities).

The Series 1 rifle comes with a Leupold VXIII 2.5-8x36 scope calibrated for the Nosler ammunition sold with the rifle.

The Series 2 rifles comes with a Leupold VXIII 2.5-8x36, VXIII 3.5-10x40, or VXIII 4.5-14x40 scope, calibrated for the Nosler ammunition sold with the rifle.

The Series 3 rifle comes with Leupold VXIII 2.5-8x36mm, VXIII 3.5-10x40, or VXIII 4.5-14x40 scope, calibrated for the Nosler ammunition sold with the rifle.

SANCTUARY EDITION SERIES – .270 WSM cal. only, 24 in. barrel w/o sights, matte black Cerakote finish, fancy grade checkered bubinga wood stock with forend and pistol grip caps, Pachmayr Decelerator recoil pad, integral Leupold QD scope mounts, only 25 mfg. (ser. no. range 001-025 w/SE prefix), shipped in Americase hard case with Leupold LPS or VX7 scope. Disc. 2014.

| | $5,100 | $4,500 | $4,000 | $3,450 | $2,950 | $2,650 | $2,250 | *$5,495* |

RIFLES: SEMI-AUTO

VARMAGEDDON 5.56 NATO – 5.56 NATO cal., AR-15 style, GIO, 18 in. stainless steel barrel, Noveske Gen. III upper and lower receiver with Picatinny rail and integrated 13 1/2 in. NSR handguard with KeyMod system, extended feed ramp, Magpul PRS stock, MOE grip, Geissele SD-E trigger. New 2013.

| MSR $2,995 | $2,725 | $2,400 | $2,075 | $1,775 | $1,575 | $1,350 | $1,100 | |

Add $900 for package with Leupold Varmageddon scope and CDS turret.

NOVESKE RIFLEWORKS LLC

Current manufacturer located in Grants Pass, OR. Dealer and distributor sales.

CARBINES/RIFLES: SEMI-AUTO

.300 BLK CARBINE LO-PRO/NSR – .300 AAC Blackout cal., GIO, 16 in. stainless steel barrel, low-profile gas block pinned to barrel, forged Gen. II lower, forged Vltor MUR upper with anti-rotation interfaced with handguard, Gun Fighter charging handle, 11 in. free float handguard with 1913 rails or 13 1/2 in. NSR free floating handguard with 1913 top rail, Blackout 51T flash suppressor, Mil-Spec receiver extension, black finish, extended feed ramp, H2 buffer, Vltor IMOD carbine stock, flip up front and rear sights, approx. 6 lbs. Disc. 2013.

| | $1,975 | $1,735 | $1,450 | $1,250 | $1,050 | $900 | $750 | *$2,335* |

Add $160 for Lo-Pro Model.

BASIC LIGHT RECCE CARBINE – 5.56 NATO cal., GIO, 16 in. cold hammer forged chrome lined barrel, forged lower, flat-top upper, Gun Fighter charging handle, mid-length A2 handguards, Blackout flash suppressor, Mil-Spec receiver extension, black phosphate finish, approx. 6 lbs.

| MSR $1,730 | $1,465 | $1,275 | $1,125 | $1,000 | $850 | $735 | $595 | |

GEN III RIFLE – 5.56 NATO or .300 AAC Blackout cal., 16 or 18 in. barrel, 30 shot mag., carbine or mid-length gas system, Gen. III upper receiver with extended feed ramps and anti-rotation interface with handguard, Raptor ambidextrous charging handle, Gen. III lower receiver with 6-pos. receiver extension, ALG Defense ACT trigger, Noveske 13 1/2 in. quad rail with 1913 rails, NSR 13 1/2 in. free floating handguard with top Picatinny rail, Noveske Signature back up iron sights by Troy Ind., Magpul STR carbine stock, MIAD pistol grip, Black Cerakote finish. New mid-2014.

| MSR $2,575 | $2,175 | $1,900 | $1,560 | $1,325 | $1,100 | $950 | $825 | |

Add $20 for 18 in. barrel.

GEN III SWITCHBLOCK RIFLE – 5.56 NATO cal., 16 in. barrel, mid-length gas system, Gen. III upper receiver with extended feed ramps, Raptor ambidextrous charging handle, Gen. III lower receiver with 6-pos. receiver extension, staked Noveske QD end plate, ALG Defense ACT trigger, 11 1/2 in. Noveske split rail w/1913 rails, Noveske Signature back up iron sights by Troy Ind., 30 shot mag., Magpul STR Carbine stock, MIAD pistol grip, Black Cerakote finish. New mid-2014.

| MSR $2,930 | $2,495 | $2,175 | $1,800 | $1,525 | $1,250 | $1,050 | $925 | |

INFANTRY RIFLE – 5.56 NATO or .300 AAC Blackout cal., 16 in. barrel, 30 shot mag., Lo-Pro gas block, carbine or mid-length gas system, Gen. I flat-top upper receiver with extended feed ramps, MOD 4 Gun Fighter charging handle, Gen. I forged lower receiver with 6-pos. receiver extension, ALG Defense ACT trigger, Noveske Signature back-up iron sights by Troy Ind., Noveske 11 in. quad rail w/1913 rails, Magpul CTR stock, Magpul MOE grip.

| MSR $2,365 | $1,975 | $1,740 | $1,450 | $1,250 | $1,050 | $900 | $750 | |

MSR	100%	98%	95%	90%	80%	70%	60%	Last MSR

LIGHT RECCE CARBINE – 5.56 NATO or .300 AAC Blackout cal., GIO, 16 in. cold hammer forged chrome lined barrel, low-profile gas block or Switchblock pinned to barrel, forged Gen. II lower, forged Vltor upper with anti-rotation interfaced with handguard, Gun Fighter charging handle, NSR 13 1/2 in. free float handguard with 1913 top rail or 11 1/2 in. free float handguard with 1913 rails (Switchblock only), Blackout 51T flash suppressor, ALG combat trigger, Mil-Spec receiver extension, black phosphate finish, approx. 6 lbs. Disc. 2013.

	$1,885	$1,650	$1,400	$1,200	$1,025	$875	$725	*$2,215*

Add $320 for Switchblock.
Subtract $35 for 5.56 NATO cal.

LIGHT RECCE LO-PRO CARBINE – 5.56 NATO cal., GIO, 16 in. cold hammer forged chrome lined barrel, Lo-Pro gas block pinned to barrel, forged Gen. II lower, forged Vltor MUR upper with anti-rotation interfaced with handguard, Gun Fighter charging handle, 11 in. free float handguard with 1913 top rail, Blackout flash suppressor, Mil-Spec receiver extension, black phosphate finish, extended feed ramp, approx. 6 lbs. Disc. 2013.

	$1,975	$1,740	$1,450	$1,250	$1,050	$900	$750	*$2,340*

RECON CARBINE – 5.56 NATO cal., GIO, 16 in. stainless steel barrel, low-profile gas block, forged Gen. II lower, forged Vltor upper receiver featuring an anti-rotation interface with handguard, Gun Fighter charging handle, 11 in. free float handguard with 1913 rails or NSR 13 1/2 in. free float handguard with 1913 top rail, Blackout flash suppressor, ALG combat trigger, Mil-Spec receiver extension, black finish, Vltor IMOD carbine stock, H buffer, flip up front and rear sights, extended feed ramps, optional Switchblock pinned to barrel, approx. 6 lbs. Disc. 2013.

	$2,125	$1,850	$1,525	$1,310	$1,075	$935	$795	*$2,485*

Add $195 for Switchblock.
Subtract $160 for NSR handguard.

ROGUE HUNTER – 5.56 NATO cal., GIO, 16 or 18 in. lightweight stainless steel barrel, low-profile gas block pinned to barrel, forged lower, M4 upper, Gun Fighter charging handle, 13 1/2 in. free float handguard with 1913 top rail, A2 flash suppressor, ALG combat trigger, Mil-Spec receiver extension, black finish, Vltor IMOD carbine stock, H buffer, Tango Down pistol grip, 30 shot mag., extended feed ramp, approx. 6 lbs., 4 oz.

MSR $1,825	$1,535	$1,350	$1,175	$1,050	$900	$775	$625	

Add $20 for 18 in. barrel.

SHOOTING TEAM RIFLE – 5.56 NATO cal., 18 in. stainless steel barrel, 30 shot mag., Gen. III upper receiver with extended feed ramps and anti-rotation interface with handguard, Gen. III lower receiver, Geissele DMR trigger, STS ambidextrous selector, Raptor ambidextrous charging handle, 16.7 in. free floating handguard with Picatinny top rail, Magpul PRS stock, MIAD pistol grip, Cerakote (Tungsten) finish. New mid-2014.

MSR $3,010	$2,560	$2,225	$1,825	$1,575	$1,300	$1,100	$950	

SPR – 5.56 NATO cal., GIO, 18 in. stainless steel barrel, low-profile gas block pinned to barrel, forged Gen II lower, forged Vltor MUR upper featuring an anti-rotation interface with handguard, Gun Fighter charging handle, NSR 13 1/2 in. free float handguard with 1913 top rail, Blackout flash suppressor, ALG combat trigger, Mil-Spec receiver extension, black finish, Vltor IMOD carbine stock, H buffer, flip up front and rear sights, extended feed ramp, approx. 6 lbs. Disc. 2013.

	$1,975	$1,740	$1,450	$1,250	$1,050	$900	$750	*$2,350*

NOWLIN MFG., INC.

Previous custom handgun manufacturer. Nowlin Guns continues to manufacture a wide variety of pistol components. The company was established in 1982, and is currently located in Claremore, OK.

PISTOLS: SEMI-AUTO

Nowlin discontinued all its pistols in late 2010. The following is a listing of its products with last MSRs. Nowlin Mfg., Inc. manufactured a complete line of high quality M1911 A1 styled competition and defense pistols, available in 9mm Para., 9x23mm, .38 Super, .40 S&W, or .45 ACP cal. Various frame types are available, including a variety of Nowlin choices. Recent models (available in blue or nickel finish) included the NRA Bianchi Cup (approx. 1997 retail was $2,750 - disc.), 007 Compact ($1,395 - disc.), Compact X2 ($1,436 - disc.), Match Classic ($1,695 - disc. 2010), Crusader ($1,999 - disc. 2010), Avenger w/STI frame ($2,279 - disc. 2010), Challenger ($2,049 - disc. 2010), World Cup PPC ($2,219 - disc. 2010), STI High Cap. Frame ($1,595 - disc. 1999), Mickey Fowler Signature Series ($2,187 - disc. 2010), Compact Carry ($1,695 - disc. 1999), Compact 4 1/4 in. ($1,750, .45 ACP, disc. 2002), Gladiator ($1,447 in .45 ACP cal., disc. 2002), Match Master ($2,795 - disc. 2010), Bianchi Cup Master Grade ($5,019, .38 Super cal., disc. 2010) and the Custom Shop Excaliber Series ($3,029 - disc. 2010).

NOTES

O SECTION

OBERLAND ARMS

Current manufacturer located in Huglfing, Germany. Previously located in Habach, Germany. No current U.S. importation.

Oberland Arms manufactures a wide variety of high quality rifles, including an OA-15 series based on the AR-15 style carbine/rifle. Oberland Arms also used to manufacture pistols. Many rifle options and configurations are available. Please contact the company directly for more information, including pricing, options, and U.S. availability (see Trademark Index).

OHIO ORDNANCE WORKS, INC.

Current rifle and related components manufacturer established in 1981, and located in Chardon, OH.

Ohio Ordnance Works also manufactures machine guns, components, and accessories.

MSR	100%	98%	95%	90%	80%	70%	60%	Last MSR

RIFLES: SEMI-AUTO

MODEL BAR 1918A3 – .30-06 cal., patterned after the original Browning BAR (M1918A2) used during WWI, all steel construction utilizing original parts except for lower receiver, 24 in. barrel, original folding type rear sight, matte metal and wood finish, Bakelite or American walnut stock and forearm, 20 lbs.

| MSR $4,300 | $3,650 | $3,195 | $2,750 | $2,475 | $2,000 | $1,650 | $1,275 | |

Add $598 for 1918A3 SLR Bundle - includes two 20 shot mags., two 30 shot mags., carrying handle, web sling, bipod, flash hider, bolt open hold device, cleaning kit, and custom cut pelican case.

COLT 1918 SLR (MODEL BAR A1918 SLR) – .30-06 cal., similar to Model BAR 1918A3, except does not have A3 carry handle. Mfg. 2005-2007, reintroduced 2015.

| MSR $8,799 | $7,895 | $6,900 | $5,925 | $5,375 | $4,350 | $3,550 | $2,795 | |

MODEL 1928 BROWNING – .30-06, 7.65mm, .308 Win., or 8mm (disc.) cal., semi-auto action patterned after the 1928 Browning watercooled machine gun, blue (disc.) or parkerized finish, includes tripod, water hose, ammo can, 3 belts, and belt loader. Limited production late 2001-2007.

| | $3,750 | $3,400 | $3,000 | $2,650 | $2,300 | $2,100 | $1,900 | *$4,000* |

Add $200 for .308 Win. or 8mm (disc.) cal. Add approx. $2,000 for blue finish (limited mfg.).

MODEL M-240 SLR – 7.62 NATO cal., belt fed, gas operated, 20 in. barrel, adj. sights, air cooled, fires from closed bolt, sling, cleaning kit, ruptured case extractor, gas regulator cleaning tool, disassembly tools, 2500 M-13 links, custom fit hard case, 24.2 lbs. New 2007.

| MSR $13,918 | $11,850 | $10,375 | $8,895 | $8,000 | $6,800 | $5,600 | $4,500 | |

MODEL VZ2000/VZ2000 SBR – 7.62x39mm cal., Czech VZ 58 copy, new milled receiver, original barrels, heat cured paint finish (matches original Czech finish), choice of bakelite furniture with folding stock or pistol grip with quad Picatinny rail and vertical grip (VZ2000 Tactical), includes four 30 shot mags., pouch, sling, cleaning kit, original bayonet, 6 lbs. Disc. 2014.

| | $875 | $765 | $650 | $595 | $475 | $395 | $300 | *$1,026* |

MODEL 1917A1 WATERCOOLED – .30-06 or .308 Win. cal., semi-auto copy of the military 1917A1 machine gun, various packages are available. Mfg. 2011-2012.

| | $6,500 | $5,750 | $5,000 | $4,650 | $4,250 | $3,850 | $3,450 | *$5,000* |

Add $1,005 for deluxe package including 1917A1 tripod.
Add $1,500 for "The Works" package including 1917A1 tripod, water hose and can, wooden box, and linker.

MODEL 1919A4 SEMI-AUTO BELTFED – .308 Win. cal., copy of military 1919A4 machine gun, various packages available. Mfg. 2011-2012.

| | $3,250 | $2,650 | $2,200 | $1,800 | $1,650 | $1,500 | $1,375 | *$2,000* |

Add $550 for Deluxe Package including M2 tripod and pintle.
Add $945 for "The Whole Enchilada" package including M2 tripod with pintle, trunnion shield, 1919A4 linker, and .30-06 barrel.

H.C.A.R. (HEAVY COUNTER ASSAULT RIFLE) – .30-06 cal., fires from closed bolt, 16 in. threaded barrel with Surefire muzzle brake, 30 shot mag., Troy Industries front and rear flip-up sights, newly designed handguard with four integrated Picatinny rails, ambidextrous bolt release, hydraulic buffer system, newly designed trigger, ergonomic pistol grip, Magpul CTR buttstock, custom hard case. New 2015.

| MSR $4,700 | $4,350 | $3,850 | $3,330 | $2,950 | $2,500 | $2,150 | $1,825 | |

OLYMPIC ARMS, INC.

Current manufacturer established during 1976, located in Olympia, WA. Sales through Olympic dealers only.

Olympic Arms, Inc. was founded by Robert C. Schuetz, and began as Schuetzen Gun Works (SGW) in 1956, manufacturing barrels in Colorado Springs, Colorado. Prior to that Mr. Schuetz had been partnered in business with well known gunsmith P.O. Ackley. In 1975 the company moved to Olympia, Washington, and while its business in rifle barrels and barrel blanks thrived, it also began manufacturing complete custom bolt action rifles. In 1982, Schuetzen Gun Works began to

MSR	100%	98%	95%	90%	80%	70%	60%	Last MSR

manufacture AR-15/M16 rifles and components under the trade name of Olympic Arms, Inc., while custom bolt action rifles continued to be produced under the SGW brand. In late 1987, Olympic Arms, Inc. acquired Safari Arms of Phoenix, AZ. As of Jan. 2004, the Safari Arms product name was discontinued, and all 1911 style products are now being manufactured in the Olympic Arms facility in Olympia, WA. Schuetzen Pistol Works is the in-house custom shop of Olympic Arms. Olympic Arms is one of the few AR-15 manufacturers to make every major component part in-house.

PISTOLS: SEMI-AUTO

Please refer to the Safari Arms section for previously manufactured pistols made under the Safari Arms trademark.

On July 10, 2014, Olympic Arms announced the cancellation of all 1911 pistols, as well as 1911 frames and slides.

BIG DEUCE – .45 ACP cal., 6 in. longslide version of the MatchMaster, SA, matte black slide with satin stainless steel frame, smooth walnut (disc.) or Cocobolo grips with double diamond checkering, double slide serrations, 44 oz. Mfg. 1995-2004, reintroduced 2006-2014.

	100%	98%	95%	90%	80%	70%	60%	Last MSR
	$1,025	$900	$725	$600	$500	$400	$350	*$1,164*

BLAK-TAC MATCHMASTER – .45 ACP cal., 5 in. National Match barrel, SA, 7 shot mag., widened and lowered ejection port, Blak-Tac treated frame and slide, low profile combat sights, adj. trigger, approx. 40 oz. Mfg. 2003-2008.

	100%	98%	95%	90%	80%	70%	60%	Last MSR
	$875	$775	$675	$575	$500	$450	$400	*$995*

COHORT – .45 ACP cal., Enforcer slide and MatchMaster frame, 4 in. stainless steel barrel, SA, beavertail grip safety, extended thumb safety and slide release, commander style hammer, smooth walnut grips with laser etched Black Widow logo (disc.) or checkered walnut grips, finger grooved front grip strap, fully adj. rear sight, 37 oz. Mfg. 1995-2014.

	100%	98%	95%	90%	80%	70%	60%	Last MSR
	$850	$750	$650	$550	$450	$400	$350	*$974*

ENFORCER – .45 ACP cal., 3.8 (disc.) or 4 in. bushingless stainless bull barrel, SA, 6 shot mag., shortened grip, available with max hard finish aluminum frame, parkerized, electroless nickel, or lightweight (disc.) anodized finishes, Triplex counterwound self-contained spring recoil system, flat or arched mainspring housing, adj. sights, ambidextrous safety, neoprene or checkered walnut grips, finger grooved front grip strap, 27 (lightweight model) or 35 oz. Disc. mid-2014.

	100%	98%	95%	90%	80%	70%	60%	Last MSR
	$870	$740	$650	$585	$515	$450	$395	*$1,034*

This model was originally called the Black Widow. After Safari Arms became Schuetzen Pistol Works, this model was changed extensively to include stainless construction, beavertail grip safety, and combat style hammer.

MATCHMASTER – .45 ACP cal., similar to the Enforcer, except has 5 or 6 in. barrel and 7 shot mag. rounded (R/S) or squared off trigger guard, finger grooved front grip strap, single or double (6 in. barrel) slide serrations, approx. 40 oz. Disc. mid-2014.

	100%	98%	95%	90%	80%	70%	60%	Last MSR
	$870	$740	$650	$585	$515	$450	$395	*$1,034*

Add $70 for 6 in. barrel.

K22 – .22 LR cal., GIO, SA, 6 1/2 in. button rifled stainless steel barrel, forged flat-top with Picatinny rails, gas block, free floating aluminum tube handguard with knurling, non-chromed bore, A2 flash suppressor, 4.3 lbs. Mfg. 2011-mid-2014.

	100%	98%	95%	90%	80%	70%	60%	Last MSR
	$775	$675	$575	$475	$425	$395	$375	*$896*

K23P SERIES – 5.56 NATO cal., GIO, SA, 6 1/2 in. chrome moly steel button rifled barrel with A2 flash suppressor, forged A2 upper with fully adj. rear sight, post front sight, no bayonet lug, free floating aluminum tube handguard with knurling, carbon recoil buffer in back of frame, with (K23P-FT) or w/o (K23P) flat-top receiver, 5.12 lbs. New 2007.

MSR $876	100%	98%	95%	90%	80%	70%	60%	
	$735	$650	$580	$515	$450	$385	$340	

Add $91 for optics ready flat-top receiver and gas block (K23P-OR, new 2016).

Add $95 for A3 upper receiver (disc. 2011) or $91 for A3 upper w/Picatinny rail and Firsh handguard (K23P-A3TC, disc. 2011, reintroduced 2016).

K24P – 5.56 NATO, .300 AAC Blackout, or 7.62x39mm cal., GIO, 11 1/2 in. button rifled barrel, choice of A2 fixed sights with carry handle or flat-top (K24P-FT), pistol grip with Fiberite ribbed handguard, extended recoil buffer in back of pistol grip, matte black finish, 6.77 lbs. New 2015.

MSR $896	100%	98%	95%	90%	80%	70%	
	$775	$685	$615	$550	$485	$415	$370

K24P-OR – 5.56 NATO, .300 AAC Blackout, or 7.62x39mm cal., GIO, 11 1/2 in. button rifled barrel, no sights, pistol grip with Fiberite ribbed handguard, Picatinny flat-top with forward top rail on barrel, extended recoil buffer in back of pistol grip, matte black finish, 6.77 lbs. New 2015.

MSR $935	100%	98%	95%	90%	80%	70%	
	$790	$685	$615	$550	$485	$415	$370

K24P-9 – 9mm Para., 10mm, .40 S&W, or .45 ACP cal., GIO, 11 1/2 in. button rifled barrel, A2 sights, pistol grip with Fiberite ribbed handguard, extended recoil buffer in back of pistol grip, matte black finish, 6.77 lbs. New 2015.

MSR $928	100%	98%	95%	90%	80%	70%	
	$790	$685	$615	$550	$485	$415	$370

K24P-9-OR – 9mm Para., 10mm, .40 S&W, or .45 ACP cal., GIO, 11 1/2 in. button rifled barrel, A2 sights, pistol grip with Fiberite ribbed handguard, Picatinny flat-top w/forward top rail on barrel, extended recoil buffer in back of pistol grip, matte black finish, 6.77 lbs. New 2015.

MSR $974	100%	98%	95%	90%	80%	70%	
	$825	$700	$630	$570	$500	$425	$380

MSR	100%	98%	95%	90%	80%	70%	60%	Last MSR

OA-93 PISTOL – .223 Rem. (older mfg.), 5.56 NATO, or 7.62x39mm (very limited mfg., disc.) cal., GIO, 6 (most common, disc.), 6 1/2 (new 2005), 9 (disc.), or 14 (disc.) in. button rifled stainless steel threaded barrel with Phantom flash suppressor, forged flat-top upper receiver utilizes integral scope mount base, 30 shot mag., free-floating aluminum handguard tube with knurling, without buffer tube stock or charging handle, 4 lbs. 3 oz., approx. 500 mfg. 1993-94 before Crime Bill discontinued production, reintroduced late 2004.

| MSR $1,268 | $1,050 | $900 | $825 | $750 | $700 | $650 | $550 | |

Last MSR in 1994 was $2,700

Add 100% for 7.62x39mm cal.

OA-96 AR PISTOL – .223 Rem. cal., GIO, 6 in. barrel only, similar to OA-93 Pistol, except has pinned (fixed) 30 shot mag. and rear takedown button for rapid reloading, 5 lbs. Mfg. 1996-2000.

| | $775 | $650 | $575 | $495 | $450 | $395 | $350 | *$860* |

OA-98 PISTOL – .223 Rem. cal., GIO, skeletonized, lightweight version of the OA-93/OA-96, 6 1/2 in. non-threaded barrel, 10 shot fixed (disc.) or detachable (new 2006) mag., denoted by perforated appearance, 3 lbs. Mfg. 1998-2003, reintroduced 2005-2007.

| | $875 | $775 | $675 | $575 | $475 | $425 | $375 | *$1,080* |

RIFLES: BOLT ACTION

In 1993, Olympic Arms purchased the rights, jigs, fixtures, and machining templates for the Bauska Big Bore Magnum Mauser action. Please contact Olympic Arms (see Trademark Index) for more information regarding Bauska actions both with or without fluted barrels.

ULTRA CSR TACTICAL RIFLE – .308 Win. cal., Sako action, 26 in. broach cut heavy barrel, Bell & Carlson black or synthetic stock with aluminum bedding, Harris bipod, carrying case. Mfg. 1996-2000.

| | $1,450 | $1,250 | $1,100 | $1,000 | $800 | $700 | $600 | *$1,140* |

COUNTER SNIPER RIFLE – .308 Win. cal., bolt action utilizing M-14 mags., 26 in. heavy barrel, camo-fiberglass stock, 10 1/2 lbs. Disc. 1987.

| | $1,300 | $1,100 | $975 | $895 | $750 | $650 | $600 | *$1,225* |

SURVIVOR I CONVERSION UNIT – .223 Rem. or .45 ACP cal., converts M1911 variations into carbine, bolt action, collapsible stock, 16 1/4 in. barrel, 5 lbs.

| | $275 | $225 | $195 | $150 | $125 | $110 | $95 | |

This kit was also available for S&W and Browning Hi-Power models.

RIFLES: SEMI-AUTO

Olympic Arms is currently shipping high capacity mags. with its rifles/carbines to those states where legal.

The PCR (Politically Correct Rifle) variations listed refer to those guns manufactured after the Crime Bill was implemented in September 1994 through 2004. PCR rifles have smooth barrels (no flash suppressor), a 10 shot mag., and fixed stocks. Named models refer to the original, pre-ban model nomenclature.

Olympic Arms has also made some models exclusively for distributors. They include the K30R-16-SST (Sports South, LLC), K16-SST (Sports South, LLC), and the PP FT M4 SS (Lew Horton). Please contact these distributors for more information, availability, and pricing.

COMPETITOR RIFLE – .22 LR cal., GIO, Ruger 10/22 action with 20 in. barrel featuring button cut rifling, Bell & Carlson thumbhole fiberglass stock, black finish and matte stainless fluted barrel, includes bipod, 6.9 lbs. Mfg. 1996-99.

| | $500 | $450 | $400 | $360 | $330 | $300 | $275 | *$575* |

ULTRAMATCH/PCR-1 – .223 Rem. cal., GIO, AR-15 action with modifications, 20 or 24 in. match stainless steel barrel, Picatinny flat-top upper receiver, Williams set trigger optional, scope mounts, 10 lbs. 3 oz. Mfg. 1985-disc.

* **Ultramatch PCR-1** – disc. 2004.

| | $850 | $750 | $675 | $625 | $575 | $525 | $475 | *$1,074* |

* **Ultramatch PCR-1P** – .223 Rem. cal., GIO, premium grade ultramatch rifle with many shooting enhancements, including Maxhard treated upper and lower receiver, 20 or 24 in. broach cut Ultramatch bull barrel, 1x10 in. or 1x8 in. rate of twist. Mfg. 2001-2004.

| | $1,050 | $925 | $825 | $725 | $625 | $550 | $495 | *$1,299* |

* **Ultramatch UM-1** – .223 Rem. cal., GIO, 20 in. stainless Ultramatch barrel with non-chromed bore, gas block, free floating aluminum tube with knurling, approx. 8 1/2 lbs. Disc. 1994, reintroduced late 2004-2012.

| | $1,075 | $950 | $850 | $750 | $650 | $550 | $495 | |

Last MSR in 1994 was $1,515, Last MSR in 2012 was $1,329

* **Ultramatch UM-1P** – .223 Rem. cal., similar to UM-1 Ultramatch, except has 20 (disc. 2006) or 24 in. Ultramatch bull stainless barrel, premium grade ultramatch rifle with many shooting enhancements, 9 1/2 lbs. New 2005.

| MSR $1,624 | $1,375 | $1,200 | $1,075 | $950 | $815 | $700 | $575 | |

INTERCONTINENTAL – .223 Rem. cal., GIO, synthetic wood-grained thumbhole buttstock and aluminum handguard, 20 in. Ultramatch barrel (free floating). Mfg. 1992-1993.

| | $1,350 | $1,050 | $875 | $750 | $600 | $550 | $495 | *$1,371* |

MSR	100%	98%	95%	90%	80%	70%	60%	Last MSR

INTERNATIONAL MATCH – .223 Rem. cal., similar to Ultramatch, except has custom aperture sights. Mfg. 1991-93.

	$1,150	$975	$875	$750	$650	$575	$525	$1,240

SERVICE MATCH/PCR SERVICE MATCH – .223 Rem. cal., AR-15 action with modifications, GIO, 20 in. SS Ultramatch barrel, carrying handle, standard trigger, choice of A1 or A2 flash suppressor (Service Match only), 8 3/4 lbs.

* ***Service Match SM-1*** – GIO, 9.7 lbs., disc. 1994, reintroduced late 2004-2012.

	$995	$875	$775	$675	$575	$500	$450	

Last MSR in 1994 was $1,200, Last MSR in 2012 was $1,273

* ***Service Match SM-1P Premium Grade*** – .223 Rem. cal., GIO, Maxhard upper and lower receiver, 20 in. broach cut Ultramatch super heavy threaded barrel (1 turn in 8 in. is standard), flash suppressor, 2-stage CMP trigger, Blak-Tak Armour bolt carrier assembly, Bob Jones NM interchangeable rear sight system, AC4 pneumatic recoil buffer, Turner Saddlery competition sling, GI style pistol grip. Mfg. 2005-2012.

	$1,350	$1,050	$875	$750	$600	$550	$495	$1,728

* ***Service Match PCR*** – disc. late 2004.

	$750	$675	$625	$550	$500	$450	$400	$1,062

* ***Service Match PCR-SMP Premium Grade*** – .223 Rem. cal., Maxhard upper and lower receiver, 20 in. broach cut Ultramatch super heavy barrel (1 turn in 8 in. is standard), 2-stage CMP trigger, Blak-Tak Armour bolt carrier assembly, Bob Jones NM interchangeable rear sight system, AC4 pneumatic recoil buffer, Turner Saddlery competition sling, GI style pistol grip. Mfg. 2004 only.

	$950	$800	$700	$600	$525	$475	$425	$1,613

MULTIMATCH ML-1/PCR-2 – .223 Rem. cal., tactical short range rifle, 16 in. Ultramatch barrel with A2 upper receiver, aluminum collapsible (Multimatch ML-1) or fixed (PCR-2) stock, carrying handle, A2 flash suppressor (Multimatch ML-1 only). Mfg. 1991-2012.

* ***Multimatch ML-1*** – 7.35 lbs. Disc. 2012.

	$950	$800	$700	$600	$525	$475	$425	

Last MSR in 1994 was $1,200, Last MSR in 2012 was $1,188

* ***Multimatch PCR-2*** – disc. late 2004.

	$750	$675	$625	$550	$500	$450	$400	$958

MULTIMATCH ML-2/PCR-3 – .223 Rem. cal., GIO, Picatinny flat-top upper receiver with stainless steel 16 in. Ultramatch bull (new 2005) barrel, carrying handle (disc.), approx. 7 1/2 lbs. Mfg. 1991-2015.

* ***Multimatch ML-2*** – .223 Rem. cal., 16 in. Ultramatch stainless steel bull barrel, crowned muzzle, forged flat-top with Picatinny rails, gas block with Picatinny rails, free floating tubular aluminum handguard with knurling, A2 stock with trapdoor, 7 1/2 lbs. Disc. 1994, reintroduced late 2004.

	$1,050	$925	$825	$725	$625	$550	$495	

Last MSR in 1994 was $1,200, Last MSR in 2015 was $1,253

* ***Multimatch PCR-3*** – disc. late 2004.

	$850	$750	$675	$625	$575	$525	$475	$958

AR-15 MATCH/PCR-4 – .223 Rem. cal., GIO, patterned after the AR-15 with 20 in. barrel and solid synthetic stock, 8 lbs. 5 oz. Mfg. 1975-2004.

* ***PCR-4***

	$850	$750	$675	$625	$575	$525	$475	$803

* ***AR-15 Match***

	$1,075	$935	$825	$725	$625	$550	$495	$1,075

CAR-15/PCR-5 – GIO, modified AR-15 with choice of 11 1/2 (disc. 1993) or 16 in. barrel, stow-away pistol grip and collapsible stock (CAR-15 only), 7 lbs. Mfg. 1975-1998, PCR-5 reintroduced 2000-2004.

* ***PCR-5*** – .223 Rem., 9mm Para. (new 1996), .40 S&W (new 1996), or .45 ACP (new 1996) cal., GIO. Disc. 1998, reintroduced 2000-2004.

	$950	$800	$700	$600	$525	$475	$425	$755

Add $45 for 9mm Para., .40 S&W, or .45 ACP cal.

* ***CAR-15*** – .223 Rem., 9mm Para., .40 S&W, .45 ACP, or 7.62x39mm cal.

	$1,050	$925	$825	$725	$625	$550	$495	$1,030

Add $170 for pistol cals.

CAR-97 – .223 Rem., 9mm Para., 10mm, .40 S&W, or .45 ACP cal., similar to PCR-5, except has 16 in. button rifled barrel, A2 sights, fixed CAR stock, post-ban muzzle brake, approx. 7 lbs. Mfg. 1997-2004.

	$795	$700	$635	$550	$500	$450	$400	$780

Add approx. $65 for 9mm Para., .40 S&W, or .45 ACP cal.

MSR	100%	98%	95%	90%	80%	70%	60%	Last MSR

* CAR-97 M4 – .223 Rem. cal., M4 configuration with contoured barrel, GIO, fixed carbine tube stock, factory installed muzzle brake, oversized shortened handguard. Mfg. 2003-2004.

	$750	$675	$625	$550	$500	$450	$400	$839

Add $95 for detachable carrying handle (new 2004).

PCR-6 – 7.62x39mm cal., 16 in. barrel, post-ban only, GIO, A2 stowaway stock, carrying handle, 7 lbs. Mfg. 1995-2002.

	$795	$700	$635	$550	$500	$450	$400	$870

PCR-7 ELIMINATOR – .223 Rem. cal., similar to PCR-4, except has 16 in. barrel, 7 lbs. 10 oz. Mfg. 1999-2004.

	$750	$675	$625	$550	$500	$450	$400	$844

PCR-8 – .223 Rem. cal., same configuration as the PCR-1, except has standard 20 in. stainless steel heavy bull barrel with button rifling. Mfg. 2001-2004.

	$725	$650	$595	$550	$500	$450	$400	$834

* PCR-8 Mag. – .223 WSSM or .243 WSSM cal., otherwise similar to PCR-8. Mfg. 2004.

	$825	$725	$650	$575	$525	$450	$400	$1,074

This model was also scheduled to be available in .308 Olympic Mag. and 7mm Olympic Mag. cals.

PCR-9/10/40/45 – 9mm Para., 10mm, .40 S&W, or .45 ACP cal., similar to PCR-5 Carbine except for pistol cal., GIO, A2 upper standard, 16 in. barrel, A2 buttstock, Mil-Spec lower receiver. Mfg. 2001-2004.

	$775	$695	$625	$550	$500	$450	$400	$835

PCR-16 – .223 Rem. cal., GIO, 16 in. match grade bull barrel, two-piece aluminum free-floating handguard, Picatinny receiver rail, 7 1/2 lbs. Mfg. 2003-2004.

	$750	$675	$625	$550	$500	$450	$400	$714

PCR-30 – .30 Carbine cal., GIO, forged aluminum receiver with matte black anodizing, parkerized steel parts, A2 adj. rear sight, accepts standard GI M1 .30 Carbine mags., 16 in. barrel with 1 turn in 12 in. twist, 7.15 lbs. Mfg. 2004.

	$825	$725	$650	$575	$525	$450	$400	$899

PLINKER – .223 Rem. cal., similar to PCR-5, except has 16 in. button rifled barrel standard, A1 sights, cast upper/lower receiver, 100% standard Mil-Spec parts, 7 lbs. Mfg. 2001-2004.

	$595	$525	$450	$400	$365	$335	$300	$598

PLINKER PLUS – 5.56 NATO cal., similar to Plinker, except has 16 (disc. 2009, reintroduced 2011) in. button rifled threaded chrome moly steel barrel with A2 flash suppressor, standard A1 upper, cast upper/lower receiver, 100% standard Mil-Spec parts, A2 stock with trapdoor, 7-8.4 lbs. Mfg. 2005-2015.

	$635	$560	$485	$415	$365	$325	$300	$727

* Plinker Plus Compact – 5.56 NATO cal., 16 in. button rifled chrome moly steel barrel with A2 flash suppressor, forged A1 upper with windage only adjustment, elevation adj. front sight post with bayonet lug, Fiberite carbine length handguard, A2 stock with trapdoor, Pink handguard and stock, 7.37 lbs. New 2015.

MSR $688	$590	$500	$435	$365	$325	$280	$265	

* Plinker Plus Flat Top – 5.56 NATO cal., similar to Plinker Plus, except has flat-top with Picatinny rails, M4 six point collapsible stock. New 2012.

MSR $714	$615	$540	$470	$400	$350	$310	$295	

* Plinker Plus 20 – 5.56 NATO cal., 20 in. button rifled threaded chrome moly steel barrel with A2 flash suppressor, choice of forged A1 upper or flat-top upper with Picatinny rails, adj. post front sight with bayonet lug, 100% standard Mil-Spec parts, A2 stock with trapdoor, 7-8.4 lbs. New 2012.

MSR $740	$650	$575	$510	$440	$385	$340	$325	

FAR-15 – .223 Rem. cal., GIO, featherweight model with A1 contour lightweight button rifled 16 in. barrel, fixed collapsible stock, 9.92 lbs. Mfg. 2001-2004.

	$700	$635	$585	$535	$485	$435	$385	$822

GI-16 – 5.56 NATO cal., GIO, forged aluminum receiver with black matte finish, A1 type upper receiver, parkerized steel parts, A1 adj. rear sights, 16 in. button rifled match grade barrel, M4 collapsible stock, 6.6 lbs. Mfg. 2004, reintroduced 2006-2012.

	$750	$675	$625	$550	$500	$450	$400	$857

GI-20 – .223 Rem. cal., similar to GI-16, except has 20 in. heavy barrel and A2 lower receiver, 8.4 lbs. Mfg. 2004.

	$650	$565	$475	$425	$375	$350	$315	$749

OA-93 CARBINE – .223 Rem. cal., GIO, 16 in. threaded barrel, design based on OA-93 pistol, aluminum side folding stock, flat-top receiver, round aluminum handguard, Vortex flash suppressor, 7 1/2 lbs. Mfg. 1995, civilian sales disc. 1998, reintroduced 2004-2007.

	$1,050	$925	$825	$725	$625	$550	$495	

Last MSR in 1998 was $1,550. Last MSR in 2007 was $1,074.

MSR	100%	98%	95%	90%	80%	70%	60%	Last MSR

* **OA-93PT Carbine** – .223 Rem. cal., GIO, aluminum forged receiver, black matte hard anodized finish, no sights, integral flat-top upper receiver rail system, match grade 16 in. chrome moly steel barrel with removable muzzle brake, push button removable stock, vertical pistol grip, 7.6 lbs. Mfg. 2004 only, reintroduced 2006-2007.

	$875	$765	$685	$625	$575	$525	$475	$1,074

LTF/LT-MIL4 LIGHTWEIGHT TACTICAL RIFLE – 5.56 NATO cal., GIO, available in LTF (fluted), LT-M4 (new 2011), or LT-MIL4 (disc. 2009) configuration, black matte anodized receiver, Firsh type forearms with Picatinny rails, parkerized steel parts, adj. flip-up sight system, 16 in. non-chromed fluted, M4 stainless steel (new 2011), or MIL4 threaded barrel with flash suppressor, tube style Ace FX buttstock, 6.4 lbs. Mfg. 2005-2015.

	$1,025	$925	$825	$725	$625	$550	$495	$1,240

Subtract $97 for M4 style stainless steel barrel (new 2011).
Subtract approx. 10% if w/o fluted barrel.

LTF PREDATOR – .204 Ruger (new 2012), 5.56 NATO, 7.62 NATO (disc. 2015), or 6.8 SPC (new 2012) cal., 16 in. button rifled chrome moly barrel with A2 flash suppressor, forged flat-top with Picatinny rails, gas block with Picatinny rail, free floating aluminum tube handguard, Ergo grip, Ace FX skeleton stock, black or 100% camo coverage, 6.44 lbs. New 2011.

MSR $1,026	$860	$725	$650	$585	$515	$450	$395	

Add $115 for 100% camo coverage.

MPR .308-15 – 7.62 NATO cal., GIO, 16, 18, or 24 in. stainless steel ultra match button rifled barrel w/o sights, 10 shot mag., billet aluminum upper and lower, rifle length Predator aluminum free float handguard (16 in. barrel with knurling), designed to accept all standard AR-15 upper receivers as well as Olympic Arms .308 style lowers, two-position front pivot pin, forward Picatinny rails, A2 buttstock, 9 lbs. New 2015.

MSR $975	$825	$700	$630	$570	$500	$425	$380	

Add $224 for 18 in. barrel or $324 for 24 in. barrel.

K3B CARBINE – 5.56 NATO, 6.8 SPC (new 2016), or .300 AAC Blackout (new 2016) cal., GIO, 16 in. match grade chrome moly steel threaded heavy barrel with A2 flash suppressor, adj. A2 rear sight, Fiberite carbine length handguard, A2 (disc.) or M4 collapsible (new 2012) buttstock, adj. front post sight, A3 flat-top receiver became standard 2011, 6 3/4 lbs.

MSR $811	$685	$615	$550	$475	$420	$365	$335	

Add $20 for 6.8 SPC cal. (new 2016).

* **K3B-FAR Carbine** – 5.56 NATO cal., 16 in. FAR button rifled stainless steel barrel with A2 flash suppressor, forged A2 upper with fully adj. rear sight or flat-top upper, post front sight with bayonet lug, Fiberite carbine length handguard, M4 6-pos. collapsible stock, 6 lbs. New 2005.

MSR $844	$725	$650	$580	$515	$450	$385	$340	

* **K3B-M4 Carbine** – 5.56 NATO cal., 16 in. M4 button rifled stainless steel barrel with A2 flash suppressor, forged A2 upper with fully adj. rear sight or flat-top upper, post front sight with bayonet lug, Fiberite carbine length M4 handguard with heat shield, M4 6-pos. collapsible stock, 6.3 lbs. New 2005.

MSR $844	$725	$650	$580	$515	$450	$385	$340	

Add $65 for detachable carry handle (K3BM4A3).

* **K3B-M4-A3-TC Carbine** – 5.56 NATO cal., similar to K3B-M4, except is tactical carbine version with Firsh handguard, flat-top upper receiver with Picatinny rail, and detachable carry handle, 6.7 lbs. New 2005.

MSR $993	$850	$725	$650	$585	$515	$450	$395	

K4B/K4B68 – 5.56 NATO or 6.8 SPC (new 2010) cal., GIO, 20 in. match grade chrome moly steel button rifled threaded barrel with flash suppressor, adj. A2 rear sight, A2 buttstock, adj. front post sight, A2 upper receiver and handguard, 8 1/2 lbs.

MSR $844	$725	$650	$580	$515	$450	$385	$340	

Subtract $26 for flat-top upper with Picatinny rail (K4B-FT).

K4B-A4 – .223 Rem. cal., GIO, 20 in. barrel with A2 flash suppressor, elevation adj. post front sight, bayonet lug, Firsh rifle length handguard with Picatinny rails, flat-top receiver, 9 lbs. Mfg. 2006-2008.

	$750	$675	$625	$550	$500	$450	$400	$941

K7 ELIMINATOR – 5.56 NATO cal., GIO, 16 in. stainless steel threaded barrel with flash suppressor, adj. A2 rear sight, A2 buttstock, adj. front post sight, 6.8 lbs. New 2005.

MSR $909	$775	$685	$615	$550	$485	$415	$370	

Add $104 for K7-ORT (Optic Ready Tactical).

K8 – .204 Ruger (new 2012), 6.8 SPC (new 2012) or 5.56 NATO cal., GIO, 20 in stainless steel button rifled bull barrel, A2 buttstock, Picatinny flat-top upper receiver, gas block, free floating aluminum knurled tube, satin bead blast finish on barrel, 8 1/2 lbs. New 2005.

MSR $909	$775	$685	$615	$550	$485	$415	$370	

This model is marked "Target Match" on mag. well.

MSR	100%	98%	95%	90%	80%	70%	60%	Last MSR

* K8-MAG – similar to K8, except available in .223 WSSM, .243 WSSM, .25 WSSM, or .300 OSSM (new 2006) cals., and has 24 in. barrel, 5 shot mag., 9.4 lbs. New 2005.

| MSR $1,364 | $1,150 | $1,015 | $885 | $740 | $675 | $575 | $475 | |

K9/K10/K40/K45 – 9mm Para. (K9), 10mm Norma (K10), .40 S&W (K40), or .45 ACP (K45) cal., GIO, 16 in. threaded stainless steel barrel with flash suppressor, adj. A2 rear sight, 10 shot converted Uzi (10mm, .40 S&W or .45 ACP cal.) or 32 (9mm Para.) shot converted Sten detachable mag., Fiberite carbine length handguard, M4 6-pos. collapsible buttstock, bayonet lug, 6.7 lbs. New 2005.

| MSR $1,006 | $850 | $750 | $650 | $585 | $515 | $450 | $395 | |

* K9GL/K40GL – 9mm Para. or .40 S&W cal., 16 in. button rifled stainless steel barrel with flash suppressor, forged A2 upper with fully adj. rear sight, adj. post front sight with bayonet lug, lower receiver designed to accept Glock magazines, Fiberite carbine length handguard, M4 6-pos. collapsible stock, does not include magazine, 6.86 lbs. New 2005.

| MSR $1,157 | $975 | $885 | $765 | $655 | $575 | $495 | $435 | |

K16 – 5.56 NATO, 6.8 SPC (new 2012), 7.62x39mm (new 2012), or .300 AAC Blackout (new 2012) cal., GIO, 16 in. button rifled chrome moly bull barrel with crown muzzle, free floating aluminum tube handguard with knurling, forged flat-top upper receiver with Picatinny rails, gas block with Picatinny rails, A2 buttstock with trapdoor, 7 1/2 lbs. New 2005.

| MSR $831 | $700 | $625 | $550 | $475 | $420 | $365 | $335 | |

Add $52 for 7.62x39mm, 6.8 SPC, or .300 AAC Blackout cal.

K22 M4 – .22 LR cal., GIO, 16 in. stainless steel barrel, M4 six-point collapsible stock, forged A2 upper, adj. rear sight, adj. post front sight with bayonet lug, A1 flash suppressor, Fiberite carbine length handguard with heat shield, 6.6 lbs. Mfg. 2011-2012.

| | $850 | $750 | $675 | $625 | $575 | $525 | $475 | *$1,039* |

K22 RIMFIRE TARGET MATCH – .22 LR cal., GIO, 16 in. stainless steel bull barrel, A2 fixed trapdoor stock, flat-top with Picatinny rails, no sights, free floating aluminum handguard tube with knurling, muzzle crown, 8.6 lbs. Mfg. 2011-2015.

| | $700 | $635 | $585 | $535 | $485 | $435 | $385 | *$831* |

K22 SURVIVAL LIGHT – .22 LR cal., GIO, 16 in. stainless steel featherweight barrel, side folding stock, flat-top with Picatinny rails, gas block, free floating slotted aluminum handguard, A1 flash suppressor, 6 lbs. Mfg. 2011-2012.

| | $750 | $675 | $625 | $550 | $500 | $450 | $400 | *$883* |

K30 – .30 Carbine cal., similar to K16, except has A2 upper receiver, collapsible stock, and threaded barrel with flash suppressor, 6.6 lbs. Mfg. 2005-2006.

| | $700 | $635 | $585 | $535 | $485 | $435 | $385 | *$905* |

Add $95 for A3 upper receiver.

K30R – 7.62x39mm cal., GIO, 16 or 20 (new 2016) in. stainless steel barrel, 6-point M4 collapsible stock, A2 flash suppressor, pistol grip, matte black anodized receiver, parkerized steel parts, A2 upper with adj. rear sight, 6 3/4 lbs. New 2007.

| MSR $844 | $725 | $650 | $580 | $515 | $450 | $385 | $340 | |

Add $39 for 20 in. barrel or 16 in. bull barrel with flat-top (K30R16, new 2016).

K68 – 6.8 SPC cal., GIO, 16 or 20 (optional) in. M4 button rifled stainless steel barrel with A2 flash suppressor, A2 upper with adj. rear sight, post front sight with bayonet lug, Fiberite M4 carbine length handguard, 6-position M4 collapsible stock, matte black anodized receiver, parkerized steel parts, pistol grip, 6.62 lbs. New 2007.

| MSR $857 | $725 | $650 | $580 | $515 | $450 | $385 | $340 | |

K74 – 5.45x39mm cal., GIO, 16 in. button rifled stainless steel barrel with A2 flash suppressor, forged A2 upper with adj. rear sight and post front sight with bayonet lug, 6-position M4 collapsible stock, 6 3/4 lbs. New 2009.

| MSR $844 | $725 | $650 | $580 | $515 | $450 | $385 | $340 | |

UMAR (ULTIMATE MAGNUM AR) – .22-250 Rem., .223 WSSM (disc.), .243 WSSM (disc.), .25 WSSM (disc.), or .300 WSSM (disc.) cal., GIO, 24 in. heavy match grade stainless steel bull barrel, black matte anodized aluminum forged receiver, parkerized steel parts, flat-top/gas block with Picatinny rails, sling swivel mount, A2 stock w/trapdoor, Ergo tactical deluxe pistol grip, Predator Firsh free floating handguard, 9.4 lbs. New 2012.

| MSR $1,559 | $1,315 | $1,165 | $1,050 | $915 | $785 | $665 | $550 | |

Add $97 for fluted bull barrel (new 2016).

The upper receiver of this model will not work on standard AR-15 lowers.

GAMESTALKER CAMO – .204 Ruger (mfg. 2011 only), .243 WSSM, .25 WSSM, or .300 OSSM cal., GIO, 22 in. stainless steel barrel, flat-top upper receiver with Picatinny rail, ACE skeleton stock with Ergo SureGrip, 100% camo coverage, approx. 7 1/2 lbs. New 2010.

| MSR $1,364 | $1,150 | $975 | $885 | $740 | $675 | $575 | $475 | |

MSR	100%	98%	95%	90%	80%	70%	60%	Last MSR

GSG2 (GAMESTOCKER GEN 2) – 5.56 NATO, 6.8 SPC, or 7.62x39mm cal., GIO, 20 in. stainless steel barrel, flat-top upper receiver with Picatinny rail, free floating aluminum handguard, ACE FX skeleton stock with Ergo SureGrip, 100% camo coverage, approx. 7 1/2 lbs. New 2011.

	100%	98%	95%	90%	80%	70%	60%	Last MSR
MSR $1,234	$1,040	$925	$825	$725	$625	$525	$450	

MPR GAMESTOCKER – .243 Win., .308 Win., .260 Rem., .300 WSM, or 7mm-08 cal., matte black finish. New 2016.

	100%	98%	95%	90%	80%	70%	60%	Last MSR
MSR $1,689	$1,425	$1,250	$1,115	$985	$840	$725	$590	

OMEGA WEAPONS SYSTEMS INC.

Previous shotgun manufacturer established circa 1998, and located in Tucson, AZ. Previously distributed by Defense Technology, Inc., located in Lake Forest, CA.

SHOTGUNS: SEMI-AUTO

OMEGA SPS-12 – 12 ga. only, 2 3/4 in. chamber, gas operation, 5 shot detachable mag., 20 in. barrel, protected ghost ring rear and front sight, synthetic stock (with or w/o pistol grip) and forearm, 9 lbs. Mfg. 1998-2005.

	100%	98%	95%	90%	80%	70%	60%	Last MSR
	$195	$180	$165	$150	$135	$125	$115	$225

OMNI

Previous manufacturer located in Riverside, CA 1992-1998. During 1998, Omni changed its name to E.D.M. Arms. Previously distributed by First Defense International located in CA.

RIFLES: BOLT ACTION

LONG ACTION SINGLE SHOT – .50 BMG cal., competition single shot, chrome moly black finished receiver, 32-34 in. steel or stainless steel barrel with round muzzle brake, benchrest fiberglass stock, designed for FCSA competition shooting, 32 lbs. Mfg. 1996-98.

	100%	98%	95%	90%	80%	70%	60%	Last MSR
	$3,600	$3,200	$2,800	$2,500	$2,150	$1,800	$1,500	$3,500

Add $400 for painted stock (disc. 1996).

SHELL HOLDER SINGLE SHOT – similar to Long Action Single Shot, except has fiberglass field stock with bipod, 28 lbs. Mfg. 1997-98.

	100%	98%	95%	90%	80%	70%	60%	Last MSR
	$2,975	$2,750	$2,525	$2,150	$1,800	$1,500	$1,250	$2,750

MODEL WINDRUNNER – .50 BMG cal., long action, single shot or 3 shot mag., 1-piece I-beam, chrome moly black finished receiver, 36 in. barrel with round muzzle brake, fiberglass tactical stock, 35 lbs. Mfg. 1997-1998.

	100%	98%	95%	90%	80%	70%	60%	Last MSR
	$6,950	$6,425	$5,875	$5,325	$4,750	$4,175	$3,500	$7,500

Add $750 for 3 shot repeater.

MODEL WARLOCK – .50 BMG or 20mm cal., single, 3 (20mm), or 5 (.50 BMG) shot fixed mag., fiberglass field stock, massive design chrome moly black finished receiver, muzzle brake, 50 lbs. Mfg. 1997-1998.

	100%	98%	95%	90%	80%	70%	60%	Last MSR
	$10,750	$8,950	$7,750	$6,750	$5,500	$4,750	$3,950	$12,000

E.D.M. ARMS MODEL 97 – available in most cals. up to .308 Win., single shot or repeater (cals. .17 Rem. through .223 Rem. only), wire-cut one-piece receiver, black tactical stock with pillar-bedded chrome moly barrel, black finished receiver, unique trigger with safety, 9 lbs. Mfg. 1997-1998.

	100%	98%	95%	90%	80%	70%	60%	Last MSR
	$2,525	$2,150	$1,800	$1,500	$1,250	$1,100	$925	$2,750

E.D.M. ARMS WINDRUNNER WR50 – .50 BMG cal., sniper rifle, 5 shot mag., removable tactical adj. stock, takedown action with removable barrel, wire-cut one-piece receiver, titanium muzzle brake, blackened chrome moly barrel, approx. 29 lbs. Mfg. 1998 only.

	100%	98%	95%	90%	80%	70%	60%	Last MSR
	$11,750	$10,250	$9,500	$8,250	$7,000	$5,750	$4,500	$12,900

ORSIS

Current tactical rifle manufacturer located in Moscow, Russia. No current U.S. importation.

RIFLES

Orsis currently manufactures the following bolt action models: F-Class, SE T-5000 M, SE Hunter M, SE Alpine M, and Varmint M. Semi-auto models include: AR-10 National Match and the M-15 Carbine. Previous models included the T-500. Please contact the company directly for more information including pricing and U.S. availability (see Trademark Index).

OSPREY ARMAMENT

Current AR-15 style manufacturer located in Wilmington, NC.

RIFLES: SEMI-AUTO

Osprey Armament currently manufactures AR-15 style carbines/rifles, including the most recent X-Series models: Osprey CSASS Rifle (MSR $1,895) and the Osprey MK-12 Rifle (MSR $2,395). Please contact the company directly for more information including descriptions, options, and availability (see Trademark Index).

P/Q SECTIONS

P.A.W.S., INC.

Previous manufacturer located in Salem, OR. Distributor and dealer sales. Previously distributed by Sile Distributors, Inc. located in New York, NY.

MSR	100%	98%	95%	90%	80%	70%	60%	Last MSR

CARBINES: SEMI-AUTO

ZX6/ZX8 CARBINE – 9mm Para. or .45 ACP cal., semi-auto, 16 in. barrel, 10 or 32* shot mag., folding metal stock, matte black finish, aperture rear sight, partial barrel shroud, 7 1/2 lbs. Mfg. 1989-2004.

	$715	$635	$550	$475	$375	$300	$250	

The ZX6 is chambered for 9mm Para., while the ZX8 is chambered for .45 ACP.

PGW DEFENCE TECHNOLOGIES, INC.

Current manufacturer established in 1992, and located in Winnipeg, Manitoba, Canada. Previous company name was Prairie Gun Works until 2003. Currently imported by Trigger Time Gun Club, located in Longmont, CO. Previously imported by Leroy's Big Valley Gun Works, located in Glasgow, MT.

RIFLES: BOLT ACTION

PGW manufactures approx. 50-60 guns annually. They also sell their actions separately for $400-$2,300, depending on caliber and configuration.

LRT-3 (PGW/GIBBS) – .50 BMG cal., single shot action, Big Mac stock. Mfg. 1999-2009.

	$4,150	$3,700	$3,400	$3,100	$2,800	$2,500	$2,250	

PTR INDUSTRIES, INC.

Current pistol and rifle manufacturer located in Aynor, SC beginning in 2014. Previously located in Bristol, CT and Farmington, CT. Represented by Vincent A. Pestilli & Associates, located in Brownfield, ME. Previous company names were PTR 91, Inc. and J.L.D. Enterprises.

PISTOLS: SEMI-AUTO

The following models utilize a delayed blowback roller-lock system action.

PTR PDW – .308 Win. cal., 8 1/2 in. barrel with flash hider, tactical handguard, black aluminum butt cap, H&K type polymer trigger group, includes one 20 shot mag., approx. 7 1/2 lbs. New 2012.

MSR $1,029		$865	$725	$650	$585	$515	$450	$395

PTR PDW R – .308 Win. cal., 8 1/2 in. match grade bull barrel, removable flash hider, 20 shot mag., paddle mag. release, tactical aluminum handguard, sling mount end cap, welded scope mount, machined butt cap, black finish, 7.8 lbs. New 2015.

MSR $1,149		$975	$885	$765	$655	$575	$495	$435

PTR-32 PDW – 7.62x39mm cal., otherwise similar to PTR-91 PDW, except has one banana shaped 30 shot mag. Limited mfg. 2012 only.

	$1,050	$950	$800	$700	$600	$500	$450	*$1,199*

This model was also available with a Picatinny rail (Model PTW-32 PDW-R), limited mfg. 2012 only.

PTR 32K PDW R GEN 2 – 7.62x39mm cal., 12.7 in. match grade bull barrel, flash hider, 30 shot Magpul PMAG, H&K Navy type polymer trigger group, wide polymer handguard, machined butt cap, welded scope rail, sling swivel, drilled and tapped for AR-15 pig snout tube adapter, 8 lbs. Atlantic Firearms exclusive model.

MSR $1,149		$975	$885	$765	$655	$575	$495	$435

PTR 51P PDW R – .308 Win. or 7.62 NATO cal., 8 1/8 in. match grade bull barrel, flash hider, 20 shot mag., machined butt cap, drilled and tapped for AR15 tube adapter, H&K Navy type polymer trigger group, MP5 wide polymer handguard, welded scope rail, sling swivel, 7.8 lbs. Atlantic Firearms exclusive model.

MSR $1,125		$935	$850	$725	$625	$550	$475	$425

PTR K3P PDW R – .308 Win. or 7.62 NATO cal., 12.7 in. match grade bull barrel, flash hider, 20 shot mag., H&K Navy type polymer trigger group, HK 93 wide polymer handguard, machined butt cap, welded scope rail, sling swivel, drilled and tapped for AR15 pig snout tube adapter, 8 lbs. Atlantic Firearms exclusive model.

MSR $1,149		$975	$885	$765	$655	$575	$495	$435

PTR 32P PDW R GEN 2 – 7.62 NATO cal., 8 1/8 in. match grade bull barrel, flash hider, 30 shot Magpul PMAG, H&K Navy type polymer trigger group, MP5 wide polymer handguard, machined butt cap, welded scope rail, sling swivel, drilled and tapped for AR15 pig snout tube adapter, 7.8 lbs. Atlantic Firearms exclusive model.

MSR $1,075		$895	$785	$685	$600	$535	$465	$415

MSR	100%	98%	95%	90%	80%	70%	60%	*Last MSR*

RIFLES: SEMI-AUTO

The following rifles utilize an H&K style roller lock delayed blowback action. PTR-91 also manufactures the SBR (Short Barrel Rifle) for military/law enforcement.

PTR-91 AI – .308 Win. cal., match grade rifle with polymer trigger group, match grade barrel, H&K style hooded front blade and four position diopter rear sight, 20 shot mag., steel bipod, steel handguard with bipod recesses, pre-ban H&K flash hider, with (PTR-91 AI C) or w/o (PTR-91 AI F) muzzle brake with match grade barrel. Mfg. 2005-2008.

	100%	98%	95%	90%	80%	70%	60%	Last MSR
	$1,150	$925	$825	$725	$600	$500	$425	*$1,295*

PTR-91 CLASSIC – .308 Win. cal., 18 in. H&K type profile barrel with flash hider, 20 shot mag., black (Classic Black) or wood (Classic Wood) furniture with slimline handguard, black powdercoated finish, H&K navy type polymer trigger group. Limited mfg. 2012 only.

	100%	98%	95%	90%	80%	70%	60%	Last MSR
	$875	$750	$625	$550	$500	$450	$395	*$969*

Add $30 for Classic Wood.

PTR-91F – .308 Win. cal., 18 in. barrel with pre-ban H&K flash hider, 20 shot mag., CNC machined scope mounts, H&K style hooded front blade and four position diopter rear sight, H&K Navy type polymer trigger group, one-piece forged cocking handle, parkerized finish, black tactical handguard, black polymer fixed stock, black powdercoat finish, 9 1/2 lbs. Disc. 2015.

	100%	98%	95%	90%	80%	70%	60%	Last MSR
	$925	$850	$725	$625	$550	$475	$425	*$1,100*

Add $200 for tactical handguard, side folding stock, and pre-ban flash hider (PTR-91R, disc. 2008).
Add $200 for tactical handguard, side folding stock, and muzzle brake (PTR-91 RC, disc. 2008).

PTR-91FR – .308 Win. cal., 18 in. match grade bull barrel, flash hider, 20 shot mag., black tactical aluminum handguard with 6 in. rail, welded scope mount, H&K Navy type polymer trigger group housing, black polymer stock, black powdercoat finish, 9 3/4 lbs. New 2015.

	100%	98%	95%	90%	80%	70%	60%	
MSR $1,245	$1,050	$940	$800	$685	$595	$515	$440	

PTR-91 G.I. – .308 Win. cal., 18 in. H&K type profile tapered match grade barrel, flash hider, 20 shot mag., paddle magazine release (new 2016), H&K OD Green polymer fixed stock and slimline handguard, matte parkerized finish, 9 1/2 lbs. New 2012.

	100%	98%	95%	90%	80%	70%	60%	
MSR $955	$815	$700	$630	$570	$500	$425	$380	

* **PTR-G.I. R** – .308 Win. cal., 18 in. H&K profile match grade tapered barrel, flash hider, 20 shot mag., paddle magazine release (new 2016), OD Green polymer stock and slimline handguard, welded scope mount, classic fixed stock, matte parkerized finish, 9 3/4 lbs. New 2015.

	100%	98%	95%	90%	80%	70%	60%	
MSR $1,025	$860	$725	$650	$585	$515	$450	$395	

* **PTR-91 G.I. K** – .308 Win. cal., similar to PTR-91 G.I., except has 16 in. barrel. Mfg. 2014 only.

	100%	98%	95%	90%	80%	70%	60%	Last MSR
	$950	$850	$725	$625	$500	$450	$425	*$1,049*

PTR-91 KC – .308 Win. cal., "Kurz" law enforcement carbine with 16 in. barrel, H&K style hooded front blade and four position diopter rear sight, 10 (compliant) or 20 (disc.) shot mag., tropical green (disc.) or black furniture, wide handguard with bipod recesses, pre-ban H&K flash hider or welded muzzle compensator (PTR-91KC). Mfg. 2005-2014.

	100%	98%	95%	90%	80%	70%	60%	Last MSR
	$1,150	$1,025	$900	$800	$700	$600	$550	*$1,245*

Add $100 for PTR-91 KFO with side folding stock and pre-ban flash hider (disc. 2006).

PTR-91 KF – .308 Win. cal., 16 in. match grade bull barrel, 20 shot mag., black furniture with tactical handguard, pre-ban H&K flash hider, standard fixed stock, H&K Navy polymer trigger group, black powdercoat finish, 9 lbs. Disc. 2015.

	100%	98%	95%	90%	80%	70%	60%	Last MSR
	$925	$850	$725	$625	$550	$475	$425	*$1,100*

PTR-91 KFM4 – .308 Win. cal., "Kurz" paratrooper carbine, 16 in. barrel, H&K style hooded front blade and four position diopter rear sight, 20 shot mag., tropical green (disc.) or black furniture, wide handguard with bipod recesses and three complete rails, H&K Navy type polymer trigger group, M4 type 6-position telescoping stock and flash hider, 10 lbs. Mfg. 2005-2014.

	100%	98%	95%	90%	80%	70%	60%	Last MSR
	$1,295	$1,100	$975	$850	$725	$625	$575	*$1,450*

* **PTR-91 KFM4R** – .308 Win. cal., 16 in. match grade bull barrel with flash hider, H&K style hooded front blade and four position diopter rear sight, 20 shot mag., black polymer handguard, three complete rails, H&K Navy type polymer trigger group, M4 type 6-position telescoping stock, black powdercoat finish, welded scope mount, 11 lbs. New 2011.

	100%	98%	95%	90%	80%	70%	60%	
MSR $1,359	$1,135	$1,015	$885	$740	$675	$575	$475	

PTR-91 KPF GERMAN PARATROOPER – .308 Win. cal., 16 in. barrel, 20 shot mag., black furniture, three rails, pre-ban H&K flash hider, H&K Navy polymer trigger group, original German telescoping stock. Disc. 2014.

	100%	98%	95%	90%	80%	70%	60%	Last MSR
	$1,775	$1,575	$1,375	$1,150	$925	$800	$675	*$1,915*

Add $100 for welded scope mount (Model PTR-91 KPFR, mfg. 2011-2014).

MSR	100%	98%	95%	90%	80%	70%	60%	Last MSR

PTR-MSG 91 SNIPER – .308 Win. cal., 18 in. fluted target barrel, paddle magazine release (new 2016), black furniture, tactical aluminum handguard, welded Picatinny accessory rail, Harris bipod, adj. Magpul stock with cheekpiece, pre-ban H&K flash hider, with (Model PTR-MSG 91 C) or w/o (PTR-MSG 91) welded muzzle compensator.

| MSR $1,749 | $1,485 | $1,315 | $1,150 | $1,025 | $875 | $750 | $615 | |

PTR-MSG 91 SS SUPER SNIPER – .308 Win. cal., 20 in. fluted free floating match grade barrel, 10 shot mag., paddle magazine release (new 2016), free-floated black tactical super sniper handguard, welded Picatinny accessory rail, Harris bipod and adapter, no sights, welded scope mount, Magpul PRS2 stock, adj. cheekpiece and LOP, black powdercoat finish, 13 lbs.

| MSR $2,699 | $2,295 | $1,975 | $1,675 | $1,400 | $1,150 | $1,000 | $875 | |

PTR-91 MSR – .308 Win. cal., 18 in. crown tapered target barrel, 5 shot mag., H&K Navy type polymer trigger group, sling swivel, earth tone furniture with free floating handguard, 8 in. welded scope mount, black synthetic stock with adj. cheekpiece. Mfg. 2012-2015.

| | $925 | $850 | $725 | $625 | $550 | $475 | $425 | *$1,099* |

PTR-91 SC SQUAD CARBINE – .308 Win. cal., 16 in. fluted bull barrel, flash hider, 20 shot mag., H&K style hooded front blade and four position diopter rear sight, tactical aluminum handguard with three rails, welded Picatinny accessory rail, standard fixed polymer stock, with or w/o welded compensator (compliant model), black powdercoat finish, 9 1/2 lbs.

| MSR $1,299 | $1,100 | $995 | $875 | $735 | $650 | $550 | $465 | |

PTR-91T – .308 Win. cal., similar to Model PTR-91, except has green furniture and original H&K flash hider. Limited mfg. 2005.

| | $895 | $800 | $700 | $600 | $500 | $450 | $400 | *$995* |

PTR-32 KF – 7.62x39mm cal., 16 in. barrel, H&K style hooded front blade and four position diopter rear sight, 30 shot mag., black furniture, tactical aluminum handguard, pre-ban H&K flash hider, H&K Navy type polymer trigger group, standard stock. Disc. 2013.

| | $1,050 | $925 | $825 | $725 | $600 | $500 | $450 | *$1,175* |

Add $50 for welded scope mount (Model PTR-32KFR, new 2011).

PTR-32 KFR GEN 2 – 7.62x39mm cal., 16 in. match grade tapered barrel, flash hider, 30 shot mag., H&K Navy type polymer trigger group housing, black polymer handguard, welded scope mount, paddle magazine release, black polymer fixed stock, black powdercoat finish, 9 1/2 lbs.

| MSR $999 | $850 | $725 | $650 | $585 | $515 | $450 | $395 | |

PTR-32 KC – 7.62x39mm cal., 16 in. barrel, H&K style hooded front blade and four position diopter rear sight, 10 shot mag., black furniture, tactical aluminum handguard, H&K Navy type polymer trigger group, welded muzzle compensator. Disc. 2013.

| | $1,050 | $925 | $825 | $725 | $600 | $500 | $450 | *$1,175* |

Add $50 for welded scope mount (Model PTR-32 KCR, new 2011).

PTR-32 KFM4 – 7.62x39mm cal., 16 in. barrel, H&K style hooded front blade and four position diopter rear sight, 30 shot mag., black furniture, tactical aluminum handguard with three rails, pre-ban H&K flash hider, H&K Navy type polymer trigger group, M4 6-position telescoping stock. Disc. 2013.

| | $1,325 | $1,100 | $975 | $850 | $725 | $600 | $500 | *$1,485* |

Add $100 for welded scope mount (model PTR-32 KFM4R, new 2011).

PTR-32 KFM4R GEN 2 – 7.62x39mm cal., 16 in. match grade tapered barrel, flash hider, 30 shot mag., H&K Navy type polymer trigger group housing, black polymer M4 6-position collapsible stock, black tactical HK 91 length handguard with 6 in. rail, welded scope mount, paddle magazine release, black powdercoat finish, 11 lbs.

| MSR $1,359 | $1,135 | $1,015 | $885 | $740 | $675 | $575 | $475 | |

PTR-32 KCM4 – 7.62x39mm cal., 16 in. barrel, H&K style hooded front blade and four position diopter rear sight, 10 shot mag., black furniture, tactical aluminum handguard with three rails, H&K Navy type polymer trigger group, M4 style fixed stock, welded compensator. Disc. 2013.

| | $1,325 | $1,100 | $975 | $850 | $725 | $600 | $500 | *$1,485* |

Add $100 for welded scope mount (Model PTR-32 KCM4R, new 2011).

PTR-32 KPF – 7.62x39mm cal., 16 in. barrel, 30 shot mag., black furniture, three rails, original German telescoping stock. Mfg. 2011-2013.

| | $1,825 | $1,600 | $1,400 | $1,150 | $925 | $800 | $675 | *$1,980* |

Add $100 for welded scope mount (Model PTR-32 KPF4).

MSR	100%	98%	95%	90%	80%	70%	60%	Last MSR

PTR-32 SCCR – 7.62x39 cal., 16 in. match grade tapered barrel with flash hider, H&K Navy type polymer trigger group housing, 30 shot mag., paddle magazine release, welded scope mount, black polymer fixed stock with HK 93 length black tactical handguard, custom engraving with gold inlay showing "We the People" and "Shall not be infringed...", custom receiver engraving showing Palmetto Tree and Crescent Moon, black powdercoat finish, 9 1/2 lbs. Limited mfg. for Ellet Bros. distribution.

| MSR $1,099 | $925 | $850 | $725 | $625 | $550 | $475 | $425 | |

PTR SCCR – .308 Win. cal., 18 in. match grade bull barrel with flash hider, H&K navy type polymer trigger group housing, supplied with three 20 shot mags., welded scope mount, black polymer fixed stock with slimline polymer handguard, custom barrel engraving showing "We the People" and "Shall not be infringed...", custom receiver engraving showing Palmetto Tree and Crescent Moon, nickel color powdercoat finish, 9 1/2 lbs. New mid-2014.

| MSR $1,200 | $1,025 | $925 | $800 | $685 | $595 | $515 | $440 | |

PTR SFR – .308 Win. cal., 18 in. match grade H&K profile tapered barrel, flash hider, 20 shot mag., H&K Navy type polymer trigger group housing, black Choate side folding stock with black polymer slimline handguard, black powdercoated finish, welded scope mount, 9 lbs. Disc. 2015.

| | $1,100 | $995 | $875 | $735 | $650 | $550 | $465 | *$1,300* |

PTR TXR – .308 Win. cal., 16 in. match grade bull barrel, flash hider, 20 shot mag., polymer trigger group housing, black tactical handguard with 6 in. rail, welded scope mount, custom barrel engraving showing "Protect Our Border" and "Come And Take It", custom receiver engraving showing the outline of the state of Texas and star, black 6-position collapsible M4 stock, Flat Dark Earth Cerakote finish, 11 lbs. Limited mfg.

| MSR $1,300 | $1,100 | $995 | $875 | $735 | $650 | $550 | $465 | |

PTR A3R – .308 Win. cal., 18 in. match grade H&K profile tapered barrel, flash hider, 20 shot mag., paddle magazine release (new 2016), H&K Navy type polymer trigger group housing, black polymer fixed stock, black polymer H&K wide handguard, black powdercoated finish, welded scope mount, 10 lbs. Atlantic Firearms exclusive model.

| MSR $1,045 | $885 | $785 | $685 | $600 | $535 | $465 | $415 | |

PTR A3S – .308 Win. cal., 18 in. match grade H&K profile tapered barrel, flash hider, 20 shot mag., paddle magazine release (new 2016), H&K Navy type polymer trigger group housing, black polymer slimline handguard, fixed stock, black powdercoated finish, welded scope mount, 10 lbs. Atlantic Firearms exclusive model.

| MSR $999 | $850 | $725 | $650 | $585 | $515 | $450 | $395 | |

PALMETTO STATE ARMORY

Current pistol, rifle, and related parts manufacturer with corporate offices located in Columbia, SC.

PISTOLS: SEMI-AUTO

PSA 1911 STAINLESS – .45 ACP cal., 1911 style, 5 in. stainless steel barrel, 7 shot mag., stainless steel frame, combat hammer, tactical trigger with adj. stop, diamond checkered grip with extended beavertail and extended safety lever, blue or chrome slide with polished sides, 37 oz. New 2016.

Please contact the company directly for pricing and availability for this model.

CLASSIC FREEDOM KeyMod PISTOL – 5.56 NATO cal., 7 in. Melonite treated chrome moly barrel, A2 flash hider, M4 barrel extension, pistol length gas system, A2 grip, 6 in. lightweight KeyMod rail, low profile gas block, forged A3 upper receiver, forward assist, dust cover, aluminum lower with fluted T6 pistol buffer tube, hardcoat anodized black finish. New 2016.

Please contact the company directly for pricing and availability for this model.

RIFLES: SEMI-AUTO

PSA 9mm CLASSIC RIFLE – 9mm Para. cal., 16 in. chrome moly barrel, A2 flash hider, standard AR-15 magwell contains aluminum 9mm magazine adapter that accepts Colt style AR 9mm mags., single stage trigger, F-marked gas sight base, M4 carbine stock, A2 grip, mid-length handguard, forged aluminum upper and lower receiver, hardcoat anodized black finish. New 2016.

Please contact the company directly for pricing and availability for this model.

PSA CLASSIC FREEDOM RIFLE – 5.56 NATO cal., AR-15 style, 16 in. M4 barrel with A2 style muzzle, carbine length gas system, forged M4 receivers with heat shield, A2 style grip, carbine length buffer tube, M4 stock, black finish, 6.8 lbs.

| MSR $620 | $550 | $480 | $415 | $350 | $310 | $270 | $255 | |

PSA KS47 CLASSIC KeyMod RIFLE – 7.62x39 cal., mid-length gas system, 16 in. chrome moly medium profile barrel, A2 flash hider, low profile gas block, accepts standard AK-47 mags., extended AK-style mag. release outside of trigger guard, M4 carbine stock, 13 in. KeyMod free float handguard, forged upper and billet aluminum lower receiver, forward assist, dust cover, T6 buffer tube, hardcoat anodized black finish. New 2016.

Please contact the company directly for pricing and availability for this model.

MSR	100%	98%	95%	90%	80%	70%	60%	Last MSR

PSA MID-LENGTH MOE FREEDOM CARBINE – 5.56 NATO cal., GIO, AR-15 style, 16 in. stainless steel barrel with A2 flash hider, M4 barrel extension, 30 shot mag., mid-length gas system, F-marked gas sight base, forged upper and lower receivers, MOE furniture, hardcoat anodized black finish.

MSR $700	$615	$540	$470	$400	$350	$310	$295	

PSA MID STAINLESS FREEDOM RIFLE – 5.56 NATO cal., GIO, AR-15 style, 16 in. stainless steel barrel with A2 flash hider, M4 barrel extension, mid-length gas system, F-marked gas sight base, standard handguard, forged upper and lower receivers, buffer tube, 6-pos. M4 carbine stock, A2 style grip, hardcoat anodized black finish.

MSR $530	$465	$385	$330	$285	$250	$230	$220	

PSA MOE FREEDOM KeyMod RIFLE – 9mm Para. cal., GIO, AR-15 style, blowback action, 16 in. A2 style barrel, 32 shot round steel mag., forged aluminum upper and lower receivers, M4 flat-top slick side upper with feed ramp, PSA lightweight KeyMod w/QD points free-float handguard, T6 aluminum buffer tube, 6-pos. Magpul stock, hardcoat anodized black finish, 6 3/4 lbs.

MSR $950	$815	$700	$630	$570	$500	$425	$380	

PSA M4 MOE RIFLE WITH VORTEX OPTIC – 5.56 NATO cal., GIO, 16 in. chrome moly barrel, A2 flash hider, M4 barrel extension, carbine gas system, pinned F-marked front sight post, MOE carbine handguard, forged upper rec., 6-pos. buffer tube, MOE stock, Magpul MOE grip and trigger guard, hardcoat anodized black finish.

MSR $700	$615	$540	$470	$400	$350	$310	$295	

PSA PA10 .308 RIFLE – .308 Win. cal., GIO, AR-15 style, 16 in. stainless steel barrel with A2 flash hider, mid-length gas system, F-marked gas sight base, forged aluminum upper and lower receivers, forward assist and dust cover, buffer tube, 6-pos. M4 stock, single stage trigger, hardcoat anodized finish.

MSR $900	$775	$685	$615	$550	$485	$415	$370	

PSA PA10 MIAD RIFLE – .308 Win. cal., GIO, AR-15 style, 18 in. stainless steel A2-style barrel, M4 style extension, 20 shot mag., mid-length gas system, low profile gas block, forged aluminum flat-top upper with feed ramps, forward assist, dust cover, Midwest Industries SSK 15 in. free float handguard, T6 alum. extended buffer tube, 6-pos. Magpul MOE stock, hardcoat anodized black finish.

MSR $1,200	$1,025	$925	$800	$685	$595	$515	$440	

PSA PA10 MID-LENGTH MOE/BLACKHAWK RIFLE – .308 Win. cal., GIO, 18 in. stainless steel barrel with A2 flash hider, mid-length gas system, 20 shot Magpul mag., F-marked front sight base, Magpul MOE handguard, forged upper and lower receivers, Magpul MOE carbine stock, Blackhawk ergonomic grip, hardcoat anodized black finish.

MSR $900	$775	$685	$615	$550	$485	$415	$370	

PSA 308 STAINLESS KeyMod CLASSIC RIFLE – .308 Win. cal., mid-length GIO, 18 or 20 in. stainless steel barrel, A2 flash hider, single stage trigger, M4 carbine stock, A2 pistol grip, 13 or 15 in. PSA SR KeyMod rail, low profile gas block, forged aluminum upper and lower receiver, forward assist, dust cover, T6 buffer tube, hardcoat anodized black finish. New 2016.

Please contact the company directly for pricing and availability for this model.

PSAK-47 CLASSIC POLY – 7.62x39mm cal., AK-47 design, Melonite treated barrel and bolt, slanted muzzle brake, single stage trigger, 800 meter rear sight leaf, traditional polymer stock or hard wood furniture in blonde or red finish, stamped steel receiver. New 2016.

Please contact the manufacturer directly for pricing and availability for this model.

PSAK-47 MOE RIFLE – 7.62x39 cal., AK-47 design, Melonite treated barrel and bolt, slanted muzzle brake, steel receiver, single stage trigger, 800 meter rear sight leaf, Magpul MOE furniture, black oxide finish. New 2016.

Please contact the company directly for pricing and availability for this model.

PSAK-47 ZHUKOFF RIFLE – 7.62x39 cal., AK-47 design, Melonite treatet barrel and bolt, slanted muzzle brake, steel receiver, single stage trigger, 800 meter rear sight leaf, Zhukov folding stock and extended handguard, Magpul MOE grip. New 2016.

Please contact the company directly for pricing and availability for this model.

PALMETTO STATE DEFENSE, LLC

Current manufacturer located in Greer, SC.

RIFLES: SEMI-AUTO

Palmetto State Defense manufactures custom AR-15 style rifles in several calibers and configurations. Current models include: MOE 16 in. Carbine - MSR $1,149, M4 Carbine - MSR $1,049, A2.5 20 in. Rifle - MSR $1,299, Tactical Match - MSR $1,899, .300 BLK - MSR $1,199, and SRC (Suppressor Ready Carbine) - MSR $1,599. Previously manufactured models include: Limited Edition Blue, and Straightjacket. Please contact the company directly for more information including options, pricing, and availability (see Trademark Index).

MSR		100%	98%	95%	90%	80%	70%	60%		*Last MSR*

PARA USA, LLC

Previous manufacturer and trademark established in 1985 and discontinued in February of 2015. Previously located in Pineville, NC. Previous company names were Para-Ordnance Mfg. Inc. and Para USA Inc. Para-Ordnance Mfg. Inc was located in Scarborough, Ontario, Canada until June 2009. Previously located in Ft. Lauderdale, FL. Dealer and distributor sales.

Para-Ordnance Mfg. was founded by Ted Szabo and Thanos Polyzos. Szabo was born in Hungary and his family fled the country when the Russians invaded during the Hungarian Revolution of 1956. Polyzos was born in Greece and later emigrated to Canada.

On Jan. 30, 2012, Freedom Group, Inc. purchased the assets of Para USA, Inc. Manufacturing continued in Pineville, NC until the trademark was retired in February 2015.

PISTOLS: SEMI-AUTO

From 1985-2009, pistols were marked "Made in Canada" with a Canadian maple leaf on the slide.

In 1999, Para-Ordnance introduced their LDA trigger system, originally standing for Lightning Double Action. During 2002, all alloy frame pistols were discontinued, and the abbreviation LDA became Light Double Action. Beginning 2003, all Para-Ordnance models were shipped with two magazines. Beginning Jan. 1, 2004, all Para-Ordnance models were replaced for the general market (except California) with the introduction of the new Power Extractor (PXT) models. The Griptor system, featuring front grip strap grasping grooves, became available during 2005, and the accessory mounting rail option became available during 2006.

Previous Para-Ordnance model nomenclature typically listed the alphabetical letter of the series, followed by a one or two digit number indicating magazine capacity, followed by the number(s) of the caliber. Hence, a Model P14.45 is a P Series model with a 14 shot mag. in .45 ACP cal., and a 7.45LDA indicates a .45 ACP cal. in Light Double Action with a 7 shot mag.

Previous Para nomenclature typically features the configuration type on the left side of the slide. The model designation is located on the right side of the slide and underneath it on the frame the product code (new 2006)/order number (changed to product code during 2006), which is alpha-numeric, may also appear.

Para offered the following finishes on its pistols: Regal (black slide, black frame w/stainless fire controls), Midnight Blue (blue slide, blue frame w/blue fire controls), Coyote Brown, Covert Black (black slide, black frame, and black fire controls), Black Watch (black slide, green frame, green (double stack) or black (single stack) fire controls), Spec Ops (green slide, green frame w/black fire controls), or Sterling (all stainless, black slide w/polished sides), in addition to stainless steel construction.

6.45 LDA/LLDA – Models 6.45 LDA (changed to Para-Companion, marked Para-Companion on left side of slide and C7.45LDA on right side of slide) and 6.45 LLDA were advertised in the 2001 Para-Ordnance catalog (became the Para-Carry, marked Para-Carry on left side of slide and 6.45 LLDA on right side of frame), the 6.45 LLDA was never mfg., prototype only. Mfg. 2001-2003.

C SERIES MODELS – .45 ACP cal., DAO, 3 (Carry), 3 1/2 (Companion or Companion Carry), 4 1/2 (CCW or Tac-Four), or 5 in. barrel, stainless steel only, single or double (Tac-Four only) stack mag., 6 (Carry), 7, or 10 (Tac-Four only) shot mag., approx. 30-34 oz. Mfg. 2003.

		100%	98%	95%	90%	80%	70%	60%		Last MSR
		$775	$680	$580	$525	$425	$350	$270		*$939*

Add $70 for Companion Carry Model.

D SERIES MODELS – 9mm Para., .40 S&W, or .45 ACP cal., DAO, 3 1/2 or 5 in. barrel, 7 or 10 shot single stack mag., steel receiver, matte black finish or stainless steel. Mfg. 2003.

		100%	98%	95%	90%	80%	70%	60%		Last MSR
		$715	$625	$535	$485	$395	$320	$250		*$859*

Add $80 for stainless steel.

P SERIES MODELS – 9mm Para., .40 S&W, or .45 ACP cal., SA, 3 1/2, 4 1/4, or 5 in. barrel, 10 shot mag., matte black (5 in. barrel only) or stainless steel finish.

* ***P Series Model P12*** – .40 S&W (disc. 2002) or .45 ACP cal., compact variation of the P14 featuring 10 (C/B 1994) or 11* shot mag. and 3 1/2 in. barrel, 33 oz. with steel frame (disc. 2002) or 24 oz. with alloy frame (disc. 2002) or stainless steel (standard beginning 2003, duo-tone stainless was disc. 2000). Mfg. 1990-2003.

		100%	98%	95%	90%	80%	70%	60%		Last MSR
		$750	$655	$560	$510	$410	$335	$260		*$899*

Subtract 10% for steel frame (disc. 2002).

* ***P Series Model P13*** – .40 S&W (disc. 2000) or .45 ACP cal., similar to P14, except has 10 (C/B 1994) or 12* shot mag., 4 1/4 in. barrel, 35 oz. with steel frame (disc. 2002) or 25 oz. with alloy frame (disc. 2002), stainless steel became standard 2003 (duo-tone stainless was disc. 2000). Mfg. 1993-2003.

		100%	98%	95%	90%	80%	70%	60%		Last MSR
		$750	$655	$560	$510	$410	$335	$260		*$899*

* ***P Series Model P14*** – .40 S&W (mfg. 1996-2000) or .45 ACP cal., patterned after the Colt Model 1911A1 except has choice of alloy (matte black, disc. 2002), steel (matte black), or stainless steel (stainless or duo-tone finish) frame that has been widened slightly for extra shot capacity (13* shot), 10 shot (C/B 1994) mag., single action, 3-dot sight system, rounded combat hammer, 5 in. ramped barrel, 38 oz. with steel frame or 28 oz. with alloy frame (disc. 2002), duo-tone stainless steel was disc. 2000. Mfg. 1990-2003.

		100%	98%	95%	90%	80%	70%	60%		Last MSR
		$685	$600	$515	$465	$375	$310	$240		*$829*

Add $70 for stainless steel.

MSR	100%	98%	95%	90%	80%	70%	60%	Last MSR

* **P Series Model P16** – .40 S&W cal., otherwise similar to P14, steel or stainless steel (new 1997) frame only. New 1995-2002.

| | $640 | $560 | $480 | $435 | $350 | $290 | $225 | $750 |

Add $49 for stainless steel.
Add $35 for duo-tone stainless steel (disc. 2000).

* **P Series Model P18** – 9mm Para. cal., 5 in. ramped barrel, stainless steel, solid barrel bushing, flared ejection port, quadruple safety, adj. rear sight, 40 oz. Mfg. 1998-2003.

| | $800 | $700 | $600 | $545 | $440 | $360 | $280 | $960 |

PXT 1911 SINGLE STACK SERIES

PXT 1911 SINGLE STACK SERIES – .38 Super or .45 ACP cal., SA, features new power extractor design with larger claw (PXT), left slide is marked "Para 1911", right side marked with individual model names, various configurations, barrel lengths, and finishes, single stack mag., spurred or spurless (light rail models only) hammer. New 2004.

* **Slim Hawg** – .45 ACP cal. only, 3 in. barrel, 6 shot mag., 3-dot sights, choice of stainless steel (disc. 2009) or Covert Black (new 2006) finish, 24 or 30 (stainless) oz. Disc. 2012.

| | $850 | $750 | $650 | $595 | $475 | $395 | $325 | $949 |

Add $140 for stainless steel (disc. 2009).

* **Super Hawg Single Stack** – .45 ACP cal., similar to S14.45 Ltd., except has 6 in. barrel and stainless finish, 8 shot mag. Mfg. 2008-2010.

| | $1,250 | $1,095 | $935 | $850 | $685 | $560 | $435 | $1,369 |

* **GI Expert** – .45 ACP cal., 5 in. barrel, 8 shot mag., 3 dot sights, steel frame, black finish. Mfg. 2009-2012.

| | $575 | $495 | $425 | $375 | $300 | $245 | $200 | $649 |

»**GI Expert Stainless** – .45 ACP cal., 5 in. barrel, 8 shot mag., similar to GI Expert, except is weather resistant stainless steel. Mfg. 2010-2012.

| | $615 | $550 | $475 | $400 | $350 | $300 | $250 | $699 |

»**GI Expert ESP** – .45 ACP cal., 5 in. barrel, 8 shot mag., similar to GI Expert, except has beavertail grip safety with speed bump, lightweight match trigger with adj. overtravel, fiber optic front sight. Mfg. 2010.

| | $625 | $525 | $450 | $400 | $350 | $300 | $250 | $699 |

»**GI Expert LTC** – .45 ACP cal., 4 1/4 in. barrel, 8 shot mag., similar to GI Expert, except has compact frame, beavertail grip safety, competition trigger, fiber optic front sight, double diamond checkered wood grips, alloy receiver, black slide, black frame. Mfg. 2011-2012.

| | $700 | $625 | $525 | $425 | $375 | $325 | $295 | $799 |

* **1911 OPS** – .45 ACP cal. only, 3 1/2 in. barrel, 7 shot mag., 3-dot sights, stainless steel construction, 32 oz. Disc. 2008.

| | $975 | $855 | $730 | $665 | $535 | $440 | $340 | $1,099 |

* **1911 LTC** – 9mm Para. (mfg. 2008-2010) or .45 ACP cal., 4 1/4 in. barrel, 8 or 9 (9mm Para) shot mag., 3-dot sights, steel (disc.), alloy or stainless steel (disc. 2009) construction, Covert Black (9mm Para.) or Regal finish, 28 (alloy) or 35 oz. Disc. 2012.

| | $775 | $675 | $550 | $425 | $375 | $325 | $295 | $899 |

Add $20 for steel (disc.), or $150 for stainless steel (disc. 2009).

* **1911 SSP Series** – .38 Super (disc. 2008) or .45 ACP cal., 5 in. barrel, SA, 8 or 9 (.38 Super cal. only) shot mag., fiber optic (new 2011) 3-dot or Novak adj. (Tactical Duty Model only, disc.) sights, carbon or stainless steel (mfg. 2006-2008) construction, Black Covert (new 2008) or Regal (disc.) finish, steel frame (new 2011), stainless (disc. 2008), or bright stainless (.38 Super cal. only), premium Cocobolo (new 2011), checkered wood (disc.) or pearl (.38 Super cal.) grips, 39 oz. Disc. 2008, reintroduced 2011-2012.

| | $775 | $675 | $550 | $425 | $375 | $325 | $295 | $899 |

Add $230 for stainless steel.
Add $250 for .38 Super cal., or $280 for .38 Super with pearl grips.
Add $250 for Tactical Duty SSP with Novak adj. sights (disc. 2008).

* **1911 SSP Gun Rights** – .45 ACP cal., 14 shot, 5 in. barrel, stainless steel construction, 40 oz. Mfg. mid-2009-2011.

| | $1,025 | $895 | $775 | $695 | $565 | $475 | $375 | $1,149 |

Para USA made a donation to the NRA-ILA fund for every pistol sold.

* **1911 Black Ops** – .45 ACP cal., 5 in. stainless steel match grade ramped barrel, two 8 shot mags., stainless steel frame and slide, beavertail grip safety, adj. skeletonized trigger, G10 grips, Tritium front and rear night sights, oversized and flared ejection port, EGW HD extractor, full length one-piece guide rod, Ionbond finish, 40 oz. Mfg. 2012-2015.

| | $1,075 | $950 | $825 | $725 | $625 | $525 | $400 | $1,276 |

* **Black Ops 10.45** – .45 ACP cal., 5 in. stainless steel barrel, two double stack 10 shot mags., stainless steel slide and frame, adj. skeletonized trigger, beavertail grip safety, G10 grips, IonBond finish, Tritium front and rear night sights, oversized and flared ejection port, EGW HD extractor, checkered front strap, 41 oz. Mfg. 2013-2015.

| | $1,100 | $975 | $825 | $725 | $625 | $525 | $400 | $1,319 |

MSR		100%	98%	95%	90%	80%	70%	60%	Last MSR

* **Black Ops 14.45** – .45 ACP cal., similar to Black Ops 10.45, except has two 14 shot double stack mags., 41 oz. Mfg. mid-2012-2015.

		$1,100	$975	$825	$725	$625	$525	$400	$1,319

* **Black Ops Combat** – .45 ACP cal., 5 1/2 in. stainless steel match grade threaded barrel, two double stack 14 shot mags., stainless steel slide and frame, beavertail grip safety, adj. skeletonized trigger, checkered front strap, G10 grips, EGW HD extractor, IonBond finish, high profile night sights, 41 oz. Mfg. 2013-2015.

		$1,125	$975	$825	$725	$625	$525	$425	$1,345

* **Black Ops Recon** – 9mm Para. (new 2014) or .45 ACP cal., 4 1/4 in. stainless steel barrel, two double stack 14 or 18 (9mm) shot mags., stainless steel slide and frame, beavertail grip safety, adj. skeletonized trigger, G10 grips, IonBond finish, Tritium front and rear night sights, checkered front strap, EGW HD extractor, 41 oz. Mfg. 2013-2015.

		$1,100	$975	$825	$725	$625	$525	$400	$1,319

* **1911 Nite-Tac** – .45 ACP cal. only, 5 in. barrel, 8 shot mag., 3-dot sights, stainless steel construction, Covert Black finish or stainless, features light rail on frame, flush spurless hammer, 40 oz. Disc. 2008.

		$1,025	$875	$750	$650	$550	$450	$375	$1,149

* **Todd Jarrett USPSA Limited Edition** – .45 ACP cal., 5 in. barrel, 8 shot mag., features Novak adj. sights, steel construction, Covert Black/Sterling finish, 39 oz.

		$1,550	$1,355	$1,160	$1,055	$850	$695	$540	$1,729

PXT HIGH CAPACITY SERIES – 9mm Para., 40 S&W, or .45 ACP cal., SA, 10 shot or higher capacity mag., various barrel lengths, construction, and finishes.

* **Hawg 9** – 9mm Para. cal., compact frame, 12 shot mag., 3 in. ramped barrel with guide rod, dovetailed low mount 3-dot fixed sights, alloy receiver, steel slide, spurred competition hammer, match grade trigger, black polymer grips, Regal black finish, three safeties, 24 oz. Mfg. 2005-2010.

		$875	$765	$655	$595	$480	$395	$300	$959

* **Lite Hawg 9** – similar to Hawg 9, except is steel and has light rail, flush spurless hammer, Covert Black finish. Disc. 2008.

		$990	$865	$740	$675	$545	$445	$345	$1,099

* **Lite Hawg .45** – .45 ACP cal., similar to Lite Hawg 9, except has 10 shot mag., flush spurless hammer, Covert Black finish. Disc. 2008.

		$990	$865	$740	$675	$545	$445	$345	$1,099

* **Warthog** – .45 ACP cal., lightweight, compact design, 3 in. ramped stainless steel match grade barrel, steel or stainless steel frame, two double stack 10 shot mags., Tritium night (disc.) or 3-dot (upgraded fiber optic became standard during 2011) sights, spur competition hammer, match grade trigger, extended slide lock, beavertail grip and firing pin safeties, EGW HD extractor, black polymer grips, satin stainless steel or black Nitride (new 2011), Covert Black (Para-Kote, disc.), or Regal (disc.) finish, 24 or 31 oz. Mfg. 2004-2015.

		$750	$650	$565	$510	$415	$340	$265	$898

Add $35 for stainless steel.

* **Nite Hawg** – .45 ACP cal., 3 in. barrel, 10 shot mag., Tritium night sights, compact alloy frame, Covert Black finish, black plastic grips, 24 oz.

		$995	$870	$745	$675	$545	$450	$350	$1,099

* **Big Hawg** – .45 ACP cal., 5 in. barrel, 14 shot mag., 3-dot sights, alloy frame, Regal finish with chrome accents, black plastic grips, 28 oz.

		$875	$765	$655	$595	$480	$395	$300	$959

* **Super Hawg High Capacity** – .45 ACP cal., similar to S14.45 Ltd., except has 6 in. barrel and stainless finish. Mfg. 2008-2010.

		$1,250	$1,095	$935	$850	$685	$560	$435	$1,369

* **P14.45** – .45 ACP cal., 5 in. barrel, 14 shot mag., 3-dot (fiber optic became standard 2011) sights, Covert Black finish steel (new 2008) or stainless steel (disc.) construction, black synthetic grips, brushed stainless steel, 40 oz.

		$795	$725	$625	$575	$475	$375	$295	$879

Add $230 for stainless steel (disc.2009).

* **P14.45 Stainless** – .45 ACP cal., 5 in. barrel, 14 shot mag., similar to P14.45, except is all stainless steel, 40 oz. Mfg. 2012.

		$750	$650	$525	$425	$375	$325	$295	$899

Add $30 for light rail.

* **P14.45 Gun Rights** – .38 Super or .45 ACP cal., 8 or 9 shot, 5 in. barrel, steel or stainless steel construction, Covert Black or bright stainless, 39 oz. Mfg. mid-2009-2011.

		$1,025	$895	$775	$695	$565	$475	$375	$1,159

Para USA made a donation to the NRA-ILA fund for every pistol sold.

MSR		100%	98%	95%	90%	80%	70%	60%	Last MSR

* **P18.9** – 9mm Para. cal., 5 in. barrel, 18 shot mag., adj. sights, stainless steel construction, black synthetic grips, brushed stainless steel, 40 oz.

		$1,025	$895	$770	$695	$565	$460	$360	$1,139

* **S14.45 Limited (PXT High Capacity Limited)** – .45 ACP cal., single action, 10 (disc.) or 14 shot mag., adj. sights, 3 1/2 (stainless steel, disc. 2005), 4 1/4 (stainless steel, disc. 2005), or 5 (steel, disc. 2005, or stainless steel) in. barrel, Covert (disc. 2005) or Sterling finish, black synthetic grips, 40 oz.

		$1,150	$995	$850	$775	$625	$500	$395	$1,289

Add $110 for Long Slide Limited Model (mfg. 2011).

Add $75 for 3 1/2 or 4 1/4 in. barrel or stainless steel (disc. 2006).

* **S16.40 Limited (PXT High Capacity Limited)** – .40 S&W cal., single action, 10 (disc.) or 16 shot mag., adj. sights, 3 1/2 (stainless steel, disc. 2005), 4 1/4 (stainless steel, disc. 2005), or 5 (steel, disc. 2005, or stainless steel) in. barrel, Covert (disc. 2005) or Sterling finish, black synthetic grips, 40 oz.

		$1,150	$995	$850	$775	$625	$500	$395	$1,289

Add $75 for 3 1/2 or 4 1/4 in. barrel or stainless steel (disc. 2006).

* **S12-45 Limited** – .45 ACP cal., 3 1/2 in. ramped barrel, 10 or 12 shot mag., stainless steel frame with black slide, Novak adj. rear sight, spur competition hammer, checkered Cocobolo grips with gold medallions, 34 oz. Mfg. 2005-2006.

		$995	$870	$745	$675	$545	$450	$350	$1,105

* **18.9 Limited** – 9mm Para. cal., 5 in. barrel, stainless steel frame, black Sterling finish, stainless slide, 10 or 18 shot mag., fiber optic front sights, adj. rear sights, includes two mags. Mfg. 2011-2012.

		$1,150	$995	$850	$775	$625	$500	$395	$1,289

* **Todd Jarrett USPSA .40 Limited Edition** – .40 S&W cal., SA, 16 shot mag., 5 in. barrel, Novak adj. sights, steel construction, Covert Black/Sterling finish, flared magwell, black synthetic grips, 40 oz. Disc. 2008.

		$1,495	$1,310	$1,120	$1,015	$820	$675	$525	$1,729

14.45 TACTICAL – .45 ACP cal., 4 1/4 (disc.) or 5 in. match grade barrel, SA, 8 shot mag., stainless steel frame, black finish, checkered front grip strap, Ed Brown National Match bushing and slide stop, Tactical II hammer, power extractor, flat checkered mainspring housing, alloy base pads, fiber optic sights. Mfg. 2011-2012.

		$1,375	$1,200	$1,025	$925	$750	$625	$475	$1,599

16.40 TT – .40 S&W cal., SA, 16 shot mag., 5 in. barrel, stainless steel frame, duo-tone finish, adj. sights, 42 oz. Mfg. 2012.

		$1,695	$1,450	$1,250	$1,050	$875	$750	$650	$1,899

PXT LDA SINGLE STACK (CARRY OPTION SERIES) – 9mm Para. (new mid-2006), .45 GAP (new mid-2006) or .45 ACP cal., DAO, single stack mag., various barrel lengths and finishes, features Griptor grips (grooved front grip strap), spurless flush hammer and rounded grip safety.

* **Carry Gap** – .45 GAP cal., 3 in. barrel, 6 shot mag., 3-dot sights, steel frame, Covert Black finish, 30 oz. Disc. 2008.

		$975	$855	$730	$665	$535	$440	$340	$1,079

* **CCO Gap** – similar to Carry Gap, except has 7 shot mag. and 3 1/2 in. barrel, 31 oz. Mfg. 2006-2008.

		$975	$855	$730	$665	$535	$440	$340	$1,079

* **Covert Black Carry** – .45 ACP cal., 6 shot mag., 3 in. barrel, Novak adj. sights, stainless steel construction, Covert Black finish, 30 oz.

		$1,025	$895	$770	$695	$565	$460	$360	$1,149

* **Carry** – similar to Covert Black Carry, except has 3-dot sights and is brushed stainless steel.

		$1,025	$895	$770	$695	$565	$460	$360	$1,149

* **Carry 9** – 9mm Para. cal., 8 shot mag., 3 in. barrel, 3-dot sights, alloy frame, Covert Black finish, 24 oz. Mfg. mid-2006-2011.

		$900	$785	$675	$610	$495	$405	$315	$999

* **Stealth** – .45 ACP cal., 3 in. barrel, alloy frame, black anodized finish, night sights, 24 oz. Mfg. 2012-2013.

		$1,175	$1,025	$875	$800	$650	$525	$450	$1,339

* **PDA** – 9mm Para cal., 3 in. barrel with fiber optic front and two-dot rear sights, alloy frame with Sterling/Covert Black finish. Mfg. 2008-2011.

		$1,125	$975	$825	$750	$605	$495	$385	$1,249

* **PDA .45** – .45 ACP cal., 3 in. barrel with three dot sights, 6 shot mag., alloy frame with stainless/Covert Black finish. Mfg. 2008-2011.

		$1,150	$995	$850	$775	$625	$500	$395	$1,299

MSR	100%	98%	95%	90%	80%	70%	60%	Last MSR

* **CCO** – .45 ACP cal., 7 shot mag., 3 1/2 in. barrel, 3-dot sights, stainless steel construction, brushed stainless finish, 32 oz. Disc. 2008.

	100%	98%	95%	90%	80%	70%	60%	Last MSR
	$1,000	$875	$750	$680	$550	$450	$350	*$1,129*

* **CCW** – similar to CCO model, except has 4 1/4 in. barrel, 34 oz. Disc. 2008.

	$1,000	$875	$750	$680	$550	$450	$350	*$1,129*

* **Companion** – .45 ACP cal., 3 1/2 in. barrel, 7 shot mag., stainless steel frame, LDA trigger system, black finish, fiber optic front sight, 2-dot rear sight. Mfg. 2011-2012.

	$895	$775	$650	$595	$475	$395	$300	*$999*

* **Companion II** – .45 ACP cal., 4 1/4 in. barrel, 8 shot mag., stainless steel frame, black finish, fiber optic sight, single stack, DA trigger system, gold trigger, checkered wood grips with gold Para logo, includes two mags. Mfg. 2011.

	$750	$650	$525	$425	$375	$325	$295	*$899*

PXT LDA SINGLE STACK – .45 ACP cal., DAO, non-carry option models, spurless flush hammer, various configurations and barrel lengths.

* **CCO Companion Black Watch** – .45 ACP cal., 7 shot mag., 3 1/2 in. barrel, 3-dot sights, stainless steel construction, Black Watch finish, 32 oz.

	$975	$855	$730	$665	$535	$440	$340	*$1,099*

* **Covert Black Nite-Tac SS** – .45 ACP cal., 8 shot mag., 5 in. barrel, 3-dot sights, stainless steel construction, Covert Black finish, includes light rail, checkered wood grips, 40 oz. Mfg. 2006-2007.

	$1,000	$875	$750	$650	$550	$450	$375	*$1,125*

* **Nite-Tac SS** – .45 ACP cal., 8 shot mag., 5 in. barrel, 3-dot sights, stainless steel construction, brushed stainless finish, includes light rail, checkered wood grips, 40 oz. Mfg. 2006-2007.

	$1,000	$875	$750	$650	$550	$450	$375	*$1,125*

* **Tac-S** – .45 ACP cal., 8 shot mag., 4 1/4 in. barrel, 3-dot sights, steel frame, Spec Ops finish, 35 oz.

	$865	$755	$650	$590	$475	$390	$305	*$999*

PXT LDA HIGH CAPACITY (CARRY OPTION SERIES) – 9mm Para., .40 S&W, or .45 ACP cal., DAO, spurless flush hammer, rounded grip safety, various options, barrel lengths and magazine capacity.

* **Carry 12** – .45 ACP cal., 12 shot mag., 3 1/2 in. barrel, low mount 3-dot Tritium night sights, stainless steel construction, black synthetic grips, brushed stainless finish, 34 oz.

	$1,050	$920	$785	$715	$575	$470	$365	*$1,199*

* **Tac-Four** – .45 ACP cal., 13 shot mag., 4 1/4 in. barrel, 3-dot sights, stainless steel construction, black synthetic grips, brushed stainless finish, 36 oz.

	$960	$840	$735	$625	$525	$425	$350	*$1,099*

* **Tac-Forty** – .40 S&W cal., 15 shot mag., 4 1/4 in. barrel, 3-dot sights, stainless steel construction, black synthetic grips, brushed stainless finish, 36 oz. Mfg. 2007.

	$925	$825	$725	$625	$525	$425	$350	*$1,049*

* **Tac-Five** – 9mm Para cal., 18 shot mag., 5 in. barrel, Novak adj. sights, stainless steel construction, black synthetic grips, Covert Black finish, 37 1/2 oz. Mfg. 2007.

	$1,050	$920	$785	$715	$575	$470	$365	*$1,185*

This model was also available in a limited edition "Canadian Forces" model with a maple leaf on the slide.

PXT LDA HIGH CAPACITY SERIES – .45 ACP cal., DAO, 14 shot mag., 5 in. barrel, 3-dot sights, steel or stainless steel construction, spurless flush hammer, Covert Black finish or stainless steel.

* **Colonel** – .45 ACP cal., 4 1/4 in. ramped barrel, low mount white 3-dot fixed sights, steel frame, 10 or 14 shot mag., spur competition hammer, LDA trigger, black polymer grips with medallions, green spec. ops. finish, 37 oz. Mfg. 2005-2006.

	$795	$695	$595	$540	$435	$360	$280	*$899*

* **Covert Black Hi-Cap .45** – steel frame, Covert Black finish. Disc. 2008.

	$950	$830	$710	$645	$520	$425	$330	*$1,099*

* **Covert Black Nite-Tac .45** – steel frame, Covert Black finish, includes light rail. Mfg. 2006-2008.

	$955	$840	$730	$625	$525	$425	$350	*$1,099*

* **Coyote Brown Nite-Tac .45** – .45 ACP cal., similar to Covert Black Nite-Tac, except has adj. fiber optic sights and Coyote Brown finish.

	$1,175	$1,030	$880	$800	$645	$530	$410	*$1,349*

MSR	100%	98%	95%	90%	80%	70%	60%	Last MSR

* Hi-Cap .45 – stainless steel construction, brushed stainless finish. Disc. 2008.

	$955	$840	$730	$625	$525	$425	$350	$1,099

* Nite-Tac .45 – stainless steel construction, brushed stainless finish, includes light rail. Mfg. 2006-2008.

	$1,025	$900	$775	$650	$550	$450	$350	$1,199

PXT LDA HIGH CAPACITY LIMITED – 9mm Para., .40 S&W, or .45 ACP cal., DAO, 10, 14, 16, or 18 shot mag., steel or stainless steel, 5 in. barrel. Disc. 2006.

	$935	$800	$700	$600	$500	$400	$350	$1,035

Add $75 for stainless steel.

PXT LTC HIGH CAPACITY – .45 ACP cal., 4 1/4 in. barrel, DAO, 10 or 14 shot mag., 3-dot fixed sights, stainless steel frame, match grade trigger, black polymer grips with medallions, green spec. ops. finish, three safeties, 37 oz. Mfg. 2005-2006.

	$750	$655	$560	$510	$410	$335	$260	$855

S SERIES MODELS – .40 S&W or .45 ACP cal., SA, 3 1/2, 4 1/4, or 5 in. barrel, 10 shot mag., matte black (5 in. barrel only) or stainless steel finish.

* S Series Model S10 Limited – similar to P10, except has competition shooting features, including beavertail grip safety, competition hammer, tuned trigger, match grade barrel, front slide serrations, choice of steel or alloy frame with matte black finish or stainless steel, 40 oz. Mfg. 1999-2002.

	$765	$670	$575	$520	$420	$345	$270	$865

Add $10 for steel receiver.
Add $24 for stainless steel.

* S Series Model S12 Limited – .40 S&W (disc. 2002) or .45 ACP cal., similar to P12, except has competition shooting features, including beavertail grip safety, competition hammer, tuned trigger, match grade barrel, front slide serrations, choice of steel or alloy (disc. 2002) frame, matte black (disc. 2002) or stainless steel finish, 40 oz. Mfg. 1999-2003.

	$895	$785	$670	$610	$490	$405	$315	$1,049

Subtract 10% for steel frame (disc. 2002).

* S Series Model S13 Limited – .40 S&W (disc. 2002) or .45 ACP cal., similar to P13, except has competition shooting features, including beavertail grip safety, competition hammer, tuned trigger, match grade barrel, front slide serrations, choice of steel or alloy (disc. 2002) frame, matte black (disc. 2002) or stainless steel finish, 40 oz. Mfg. 1999-2003.

	$895	$785	$670	$610	$490	$405	$315	$1,049

* S Series Model S14 Limited – .40 S&W (disc. 2002) or .45 ACP cal., similar to P14, except has competition shooting features, including beavertail grip safety, competition hammer, tuned trigger, match grade barrel, front slide serrations, matte black or stainless steel, 40 oz. Mfg. 1998-2003.

	$850	$745	$635	$580	$465	$380	$295	$989

Add $60 for stainless steel.

* S Series Model S16 Limited – .40 S&W cal., similar to P16, except has 5 in. barrel and competition shooting features, including beavertail grip safety, competition hammer, tuned trigger, match grade barrel, front slide serrations, matte black steel or stainless steel, 40 oz. Mfg. 1998-2003.

	$850	$745	$635	$580	$465	$380	$295	$989

Add $60 for stainless steel.

T SERIES MODELS – 9mm Para., .40 S&W (stainless steel only), or .45 ACP cal., DAO, 5 in. barrel, 7 (.45 ACP cal. only, single stack mag.) or 10 shot mag., steel or stainless steel, matte black finish or stainless steel. Mfg. 2003.

	$825	$720	$620	$560	$455	$370	$290	$1,009

Add $80 for stainless steel.

RIFLES: SEMI-AUTO

TTR SERIES – .223 Rem. cal., tactical design, GIO, 16 1/2 in. chrome lined barrel, DIGS (delayed impingement gas system) operation, 30 shot mag., flip up front sight and adj. flip up rear sight, flat-top receiver with full length Picatinny rail, black finish, single stage trigger, available in Short Rail with fixed stock (TTR-XASF, mfg. 2009), or 5 position folding stock with Short Rail (TTR-XAS), Long Rail (TTR-XA), and Nylatron (TTR-XN, mfg. 2009) forearm configurations. Mfg. 2009-late 2011.

	$2,050	$1,800	$1,575	$1,350	$1,150	$975	$825	$2,397

Add $100 for Nylatron forearm (mfg. 2009).

MSR	100%	98%	95%	90%	80%	70%	60%	Last MSR

PARDINI, ARMI S.r.l.

Current manufacturer located in Lido di Camaiore, Italy. Currently imported by Pardini USA, LLC beginning 2012 located in Tampa, FL. Previously imported until 2012 by Larry's Guns, located in Gray, ME. Previously imported until 2004 by Nygord Precision Products located in Prescott, AZ, and distributed until 1996 by Mo's Competitor Supplies & Range, Inc. located in Brookfield, CT, and until 1990 by Fiocchi of America, Inc., located in Ozark, MO.

For more information and current pricing on both new and used Pardini airguns, please refer to the *Blue Book of Airguns* by Dr. Robert Beeman & John Allen (also online).

PISTOLS: SEMI-AUTO

PC45 – .40 S&W, .45 ACP, or 9x21mm cal., single action mechanism designed for stock competition category, adj. trigger pull. Limited importation by Nygord 2000-2004.

	$1,295	$1,050	$840	$715	$575	$500	$440

Add $75 for 6 in. barrel and slide.

* ***PC45S*** – .40 S&W, .45 ACP, or 9x21mm cal., similar to PC, except has compensator and scope mount with optical sight.

	$1,500	$1,250	$1,100	$950	$850	$725	$600

* ***PCS-Open*** – similar to PCS, except w/o scope and frame mount, top-of-the-line semi-auto.

	$1,650	$1,400	$1,250	$1,100	$950	$850	$725

GT9/PC40/GT45 DEFENSE/SPORT – 9mm Para., 9x21mm (disc. 2011), .40 S&W, or .45 ACP cal., 5 or 6 in. barrel, SA, diamond wood grips, matte silver, 13 or 17 (9x21mm) shot mag., black, silver, bronze, or two-tone finish. Importation began late 2004.

MSR $2,299	$2,075	$1,775	$1,450	$1,225	$995	$850	$750

Add $150 for 6 in. barrel.
Add $100 for silver or bronze (disc. 2013) finish.
Add $50 for .45 ACP cal.
Add $95 for 6 in. barrel and slide (disc.).
Add $700 for titanium finish in 9mm Para. cal. with 6 in. barrel only.
Add $999 for 9mm Para. or .40 S&W cal. conversion kit for GT45 Model (disc. 2013).
Add $230 for GT45S Model with compensator in silver finish (disc. 2011).

* ***GT9/GT40 Defense Sport Inox*** – 9mm Para. or .40 S&W (IPSC) cal., features 5 or 6 in. stainless steel barrel, black or Regal finish.

MSR $2,899	$2,500	$2,150	$1,850	$1,550	$1,275	$1,050	$875

Add $100 for Regal finish.
Add $800 for 5 in. barrel and 9mm Para. cal. or $1,100 for 9mm Para. cal. with 6 in. barrel (all disc. 2013).

PARKER-HALE LIMITED

Previous gun manufacturer located in Birmingham, England. Rifles were manufactured in England until 1991 when Navy Arms purchased the manufacturing rights and built a plant in West Virginia for fabrication. This new company was called Gibbs Rifle Company, Inc. and they manufactured models very similar to older Parker-Hale rifles during 1992-94. Shotguns were manufactured in Spain and imported by Precision Sports, a division of Cortland Line Company, Inc. located in Cortland, NY until 1993.

Parker was the previous trade name of the A.G. Parker Company, located in Birmingham, England, which was formed from a gun making business founded in 1890 by Alfred Gray Parker. The company became the Parker-Hale company in 1936. The company was purchased by John Rothery Wholesale circa 2000.

Parker-Hale Ltd. continues to make a wide variety of high quality firearms cleaning accessories for both rifles and shotguns, including their famous bipod.

RIFLES: BOLT ACTION

All Parker-Hale rifle importation was discontinued in 1991. Parker-Hale bolt action rifles utilize the Mauser M98 action and were offered in a variety of configurations. A single set trigger option was introduced in 1984 on most models, which allows either "hair trigger" or conventional single stage operation - add $85. Parker-Hale also used the Brno Model ZG-47 action. Please see the Brno section for this model.

MODEL 85 SNIPER RIFLE – .308 Win. cal., bolt action, extended heavy barrel, 10 shot mag., camo green synthetic stock with stippling, built in adj. bipod, enlarged contoured bolt, adj. recoil pad. Importation began 1989.

	$2,650	$2,250	$1,700	$1,475	$1,250	$1,050	$875	*$1,975*

PATRIOT ORDNANCE FACTORY (POF)

Current rifle manufacturer located in Glendale, AZ.

MSR	100%	98%	95%	90%	80%	70%	60%	Last MSR

CARBINES/RIFLES: SEMI-AUTO

Patriot Ordnance Factory manufactures AR-15 style rifles and carbines chambered in 5.56/.223 and 7.62/.308, as well as upper and lower receivers and various parts. The semi-auto carbines and rifles use a unique gas piston operating system that requires no lubrication. A wide variety of options are available for each model. Please contact the company directly for more information, including options and pricing (see Trademark Index).

P308 (P308 MID-LENGTH RIFLE) – .308 Win. cal., GPO, 16 1/2 or 20 in. heavy contour fluted barrel, 3-position gas regulation for normal, suppressed and single action modes, FMP-A3 muzzle device, corrosion resistant operating system, chrome plated Mil-Spec bolt, optional fixed hooded front sight, optional Troy or Diamondhead flip up sights, hunter/sniper or tactical aircraft aluminum alloy modular railed receiver, nickel, black, Olive Drab (new 2013), and Cerakote Burnt Bronze (new 2013) hardcoat anodized Teflon finish, oversized trigger guard, Magpul MOE pistol grip, Magpul CTR 6-position collapsible stock, Ergo ladder rail covers, sling, bipod mount, Magpul 20 shot PMAG, approx. 9 lbs. Disc. 2014.

	$2,675	$2,150	$1,825	$1,600	$1,350	$1,175	$1,000	$3,220

Add $100 for Olive Drab (new 2013) or Cerakote Burnt Bronze (new 2013) finish.
Add $25 for NP3 nickel/alloy plating.

P308 HUNTING RIFLE – .243 Win or .308 Win. cal., GPO, 20 in. heavy contour fluted barrel, 3-position gas regulation for normal, suppressed and single action modes, FMP-A3 muzzle device, corrosion resistant operating system, chrome plated Mil-Spec bolt, optional fixed hooded front sight, optional Troy or Diamondhead flip up sights, hunter/sniper aircraft aluminum alloy modular railed receiver, Olive Drab Cerakote finish, oversized trigger guard, Magpul MOE pistol grip, fixed polymer buttstock, Ergo ladder rail covers, sling, bipod mount, 5 shot stainless steel mag., approx. 9 lbs. Disc. 2013.

	$2,675	$2,150	$1,825	$1,600	$1,350	$1,175	$1,000	$3,220

P415 CARBINE – .223 Rem. cal., GPO, 16 in. heavy contour chrome lined fluted barrel, A3 muzzle device, corrosion resistant operating system, nickel plated A3 flat-top upper receiver and charging handle, M4 feed ramp, nickel and black hardcoat anodized Teflon finish, fixed removable hooded front sight, optional Troy flip up sight, single stage trigger, oversized trigger guard, Magpul CTR retractable 6-position buttstock, M4 plastic handguard or Predator P-9 tactical rail system, sling/bipod mount, approx. 7-7.4 lbs. Disc. 2011.

	$1,825	$1,650	$1,425	$1,295	$1,050	$875	$675	$1,999

Add $300 for Predator P-9 tactical rail system.

P415 MID-LENGTH RIFLE – 5.56 NATO cal., GPO, 16 1/2 or 18 in. chrome moly vanadium alloy, heavy contour, hand lapped button rifled fluted barrel, 3-position gas regulation for normal, suppressed and single action modes, FMP-A3 muzzle device, corrosion resistant operating system, chrome plated Mil-Spec bolt, optional fixed hooded front sight, optional Troy or Diamondhead flip up sights, hunter/sniper or tactical aircraft aluminum alloy modular railed receiver, nickel and black hardcoat anodized Teflon finish, oversized trigger guard, Magpul MOE pistol grip, Magpul CTR 6-position collapsible stock, Ergo ladder rail covers, sling, bipod mount, Magpul 30 shot PMAG, approx. 8 lbs. Mfg. 2012-2014.

	$2,100	$1,800	$1,750	$1,500	$1,050	$875	$725	$2,320

Add $30 for NP3 nickel/alloy plating (new 2014).

P415 HUNTING RIFLE – 5.56 NATO cal., GPO, 18 in. heavy contour fluted barrel, 3-position gas regulation for normal, suppressed and single action modes, FMP-A3 muzzle device, corrosion resistant operating system, chrome plated Mil-Spec bolt, optional fixed hooded front sight, optional Troy or Diamondhead flip up sights, hunter/sniper aircraft aluminum alloy modular railed receiver, Olive Drab Cerakote finish, oversized trigger guard, Magpul MOE pistol grip, fixed polymer buttstock, Ergo ladder rail covers, sling, bipod mount, 5 shot stainless steel mag., approx. 8 lbs. Disc. 2013.

	$1,825	$1,650	$1,425	$1,295	$1,050	$875	$675	$2,320

P415 RECON CARBINE – .223 Rem. cal., GPO, 16 in. heavy contour chrome lined fluted barrel, A3 muzzle device, corrosion resistant operating system, nickel plated A3 flat-top upper receiver and charging handle, M4 feed ramp, nickel and black hardcoat anodized Teflon finish, fixed removable hooded front sight, optional Troy flip up sight, single stage trigger, oversized trigger guard, Magpul PRS or 6-position adj. buttstock, tactical rail handguard, approx. 8 lbs. Disc. 2011.

	$1,825	$1,650	$1,425	$1,295	$1,050	$875	$675	$1,999

P415 SPECIAL PURPOSE RIFLE – .223 Rem. cal., GPO, 18 in. heavy contour chrome lined fluted barrel, A3 muzzle device, corrosion resistant operating system, nickel plated A3 flat-top upper receiver and charging handle, M4 feed ramp, nickel and black hardcoat anodized Teflon finish, fixed removable hooded front sight, optional Troy flip up sight, single stage trigger, Magpul PRS or 6-position adj. buttstock, tactical rail handguard, approx. 9 lbs. Disc. 2011.

	$1,825	$1,650	$1,425	$1,295	$1,050	$875	$675	$1,999

P15 PURITAN – 5.56 NATO or 7.62 NATO (new 2015) cal., GPO, 16 1/2 in. Nitride heat treated contour barrel with A2 flash hider, receiver height Picatinny flat-top gas block, ambidextrous safety selector, E2 extraction system, Magpul MOE buttstock, Magpul MOE pistol grip with mid-length polymer handguard, 30 shot PMAG, bayonet mount, QD sling mount, nickel boron coated bolt carrier, hardcoat black anodized finish, 6.7 lbs. New 2014.

MSR $1,470			$1,250	$1,110	$965	$800	$700	$600	$495

MSR	100%	98%	95%	90%	80%	70%	60%	Last MSR

GEN 4 P300 – .300 Win. Mag. cal., GPO, 18 or 24 in. barrel, 14 1/2 in. modular rail, NP3 coating, 9.2-9.8 lbs. New 2016.

| | MSR $3,500 | $2,975 | $2,575 | $2,075 | $1,750 | $1,450 | $1,225 | $1,050 |

GEN 4 P308 – .308 Win. cal., GPO, 16 1/2 or 20 in. heavy contour deep fluted barrel, triple port muzzle brake, 20 or 30 shot PMAG, no sights, 3-pos. adj. gas block, E2 extraction technology, ambidextrous fire controls, anti-tilt buffer tube, 11 1/2 or 14 1/2 in. modular free-floating rail, drop-in trigger system, Magpul CTR stock with buttpad, nickel boron bolt carrier group, black anodized, NP3 nickel alloy plating, or Cerakote Olive Drab, Burnt Bronze, or Tungsten finish, 8 lbs. 8 oz. New 2014.

| | MSR $2,730 | $2,325 | $2,000 | $1,640 | $1,400 | $1,125 | $975 | $850 |

Add $30 for NP3 nickel alloy plating.
Add $70 for 14 1/2 in. modular rail.
Add $120 for Cerakote finish in Olive Drab, Tungsten, or Burnt Bronze.

GEN 4 P415 – .223 Rem. cal., GPO, 16 1/2 or 18 in. deep fluted barrel with triple port muzzle brake, 30 shot PMAG, no sights, 3-pos. adj. gas block, E2 extraction technology, ambidextrous fire controls, anti-tilt buffer, 11 1/2 or 14 1/2 in. modular free-floating rail, drop-in trigger system, Magpul CTR stock with buttpad, nickel boron bolt carrier group, aluminum billet upper and lower receivers, black anodized, NP3 nickel alloy plating, Olive Drab, or Cerakote finish in Burnt Bronze or Tungsten, 7 lbs. New 2014.

| | MSR $2,025 | $1,725 | $1,510 | $1,250 | $1,100 | $950 | $825 | $675 |

Add $75 for NP3 nickel alloy plating or Olive Drab finish.
Add $125 for Burnt Bronze or Tungsten Cerakote finish.
Add $105 for 14 1/2 in. modular rail.

RENEGADE – 5.56 NATO cal., GIO, 16 1/2 in. Nitride heat treated Puritan barrel, A2 flash hider, Dictator 9-position adj. gas block with straight gas tube, Mil-Spec trigger, E2 Extraction Technology, Mission First Tactical magazine, grip, and stock, Mil-Spec upper and lower receiver, 14 1/2 in. M-LOK compatible Renegade rail, 4 integrated QD sling mounts, Type III hardcoat anodized black finish, 6.3 lbs. New 2016.

| | MSR $1,500 | $1,275 | $1,125 | $1,025 | $875 | $750 | $625 | $525 |

GEN 4 RENEGADE+ – 5.56 NATO cal., GIO, 16 1/2 in. Nitride heat treated Puritan barrel with Triple Port muzzle brake, mid-length Dictator 9-position adj. gas block with straight gas tube, E2 Extraction Technology, 3 1/2 lb. drop-in flat trigger, Mission First Tactical magazine, grip, and stock, Mil-Spec upper, 14 1/2 in. M-LOK compatible Renegade rail with 4 integrated QD sling mounts, ambidextrous QD endplate, Gen4 POF-USA billet lower receiver, completely ambidextrous, Ultimate bolt carrier group, Type 3 hardcoat anodized black finish, 6.4 lbs. New 2016.

| | MSR $1,900 | $1,625 | $1,425 | $1,200 | $1,075 | $925 | $795 | $650 |

GEN 4 SKIRMISH HEAVY – .308 Win. cal., GPO, 16 1/2 in. heavy barrel, 14 1/2 in. modular rail, extended handguard, ambidextrous controls, E2 extraction technology, fixed Magpul MOE stock, black anodized or NP3 finish, 8.4 lbs. New 2015.

| | MSR $2,820 | $2,395 | $2,085 | $1,725 | $1,475 | $1,200 | $1,025 | $895 |

Add $40 for NP3 coating.

GEN 4 SKIRMISH LIGHT – 5.56 NATO cal., GPO, 16 1/2 in. barrel, 14 1/2 in. modular rail, extended handguard, ambidextrous controls, E2 extraction technology, fixed Magpul MOE stock, black anodized or NP3 finish, 7.4 lbs. New 2015.

| | MSR $2,270 | $1,925 | $1,685 | $1,425 | $1,225 | $1,035 | $885 | $735 |

Add $20 for NP3 coating.

OLDE SCHOOL – .223 Rem./5.56 NATO or .308 Win./7.62 NATO cal., GIO, 16 1/2 in. barrel, E2 extraction technology, ambidextrous controls, straight Inconel gas tube, adj. gas system, 11 1/2 in. M-LOK handguard, black anodized or NP3 finish, 8.2 lbs. New 2015.

| | MSR $2,650 | $2,225 | $1,940 | $1,600 | $1,375 | $1,125 | $975 | $850 |

Add $40 for NP3 coating.

GEN 4 WAR HOG HEAVY – 7.62 NATO/.308 Win. cal., GPO, 16 1/2 in. match grade deep fluted heavy barrel with triple port muzzle brake, 20 shot PMAG, Gen 4 receivers, E2 extraction technology, 3-pos. adj. gas block, 14 1/2 in. free-floating monolithic M rail, no sights, ambidextrous controls, adj. Luth-AR MBA stock, Burnt Bronze Cerakote finish, 8.8 lbs. New 2015.

| | MSR $3,040 | $2,685 | $2,240 | $1,825 | $1,575 | $1,300 | $1,100 | $950 |

GEN 4 WAR HOG LIGHT – 5.56 NATO cal., GPO, 16 1/2 in. match grade deep fluted barrel with triple port muzzle brake, 30 shot PMAG, Gen 4 receivers, E2 extraction technology, EFP match trigger, 3-pos. adj. gas block, 14 1/2 in. free-floating monolithic M rail, no sights, ambidextrous controls, adj. Luth-AR MBA MOE stock, Burnt Bronze Cerakote finish, 7.7 lbs. New 2015.

| | MSR $2,350 | $1,975 | $1,740 | $1,450 | $1,250 | $1,050 | $900 | $750 |

MSR	100%	98%	95%	90%	80%	70%	60%	Last MSR

PISTOLS: SEMI-AUTO

P308 PISTOL – .308 Win. cal., GPO, 12 1/2 in. heavy contour fluted barrel, 3-position gas regulation for normal, suppressed and single action modes, FMP-A3 muzzle device, corrosion resistant operating system, chrome plated Mil-Spec bolt, optional fixed hooded front sight, optional Troy or Diamondhead flip up sights, hunter/sniper or tactical aircraft aluminum alloy modular railed receiver, nickel and black hardcoat anodized Teflon finish, oversized trigger guard, Magpul MOE pistol grip, PWS enhanced pistol buffer tube, Ergo ladder rail covers, sling, bipod mount, Magpul 20 shot PMAG, approx. 7 1/2 lbs. Disc. 2014.

	100%	98%	95%	90%	80%	70%	60%	Last MSR
	$2,850	$2,250	$1,900	$1,650	$1,350	$1,175	$1,000	*$3,220*

P415 PISTOL – 5.56 NATO cal., GPO, 7 1/4 or 10 1/2 in. heavy contour fluted barrel, 3-position gas regulation for normal, suppressed and single action modes, FMP-A3 muzzle device, chrome plated Mil-Spec bolt, optional fixed hooded front sight, optional Troy or Diamondhead flip up sights, hunter/sniper or tactical aircraft aluminum alloy modular railed receiver, nickel and black hardcoat anodized Teflon finish, oversized trigger guard, Magpul MOE pistol grip, PWS enhanced pistol buffer tube, Ergo ladder rail covers, sling, bipod mount, Magpul 30 shot PMAG, approx. 6 1/2 lbs. Disc. 2013.

	100%	98%	95%	90%	80%	70%	60%	Last MSR
	$2,075	$1,800	$1,525	$1,375	$1,100	$900	$725	*$2,320*

GEN 4 AR PISTOL 415 – .223 Rem./5.56 NATO cal., GPO, 7 1/4 or 10 1/2 in. deep fluted barrel, 6 or 9 in. modular rail, black anodized finish or NP3 coating, 5.7 lbs. New 2014.

MSR $2,130	100%	98%	95%	90%	80%	70%	60%	
	$1,810	$1,590	$1,325	$1,150	$995	$850	$700	

Add $30 for NP3 coating.

GEN 4 AR PISTOL 308 – .308 Win./7.62 NATO cal., GPO, 12 1/2 in. deep fluted barrel, 11 1/2 in. modular rail, black anodized finish or NP3 coating, 7.6 lbs. New 2014.

MSR $2,600	100%	98%	95%	90%	80%	70%	60%	
	$2,200	$1,925	$1,600	$1,375	$1,125	$975	$850	

Add $30 for NP3 coating.

RIFLES: BOLT ACTION

GEN 4 REVOLT – 5.56 NATO (light) or 7.62 NATO (heavy) cal., AR-15 style, straight pull action with feed assist, 18 1/2 in. lightweight or heavy fluted barrel, 14 1/2 in. M-LOK handguard, Gen 4 ambidextrous controls, E2 extraction technology, Luth-AR buttstock, Gen 4 ambidextrous controls, NP3 coating, includes permanent capture pin, 8.2-9.2 lbs. New 2015.

MSR $2,030	100%	98%	95%	90%	80%	70%	60%	
	$1,725	$1,500	$1,250	$1,100	$950	$825	$675	

Add $650 for .308 Win. cal. and heavy barrel.

PAUZA SPECIALTIES

Previous manufacturer located in Baytown, TX circa 1991-96. Previously distributed by U.S. General Technologies, Inc., located in South San Francisco, CA.

Pauza previously manufactured the P50 semi-auto rifle for Firearms International, Inc. - please refer to that section for current information.

RIFLES: SEMI-AUTO

P50 SEMI-AUTO – .50 BMG cal., semi-auto, 24 (carbine) or 29 (rifle) in. match grade barrel, 5 shot detachable mag., one-piece receiver, 3-stage gas system, takedown action, all exterior parts Teflon coated, with aluminum bipod, 25 or 30 lbs. Mfg. 1992-96.

	100%	98%	95%	90%	80%	70%	60%	Last MSR
	$5,950	$5,250	$4,600	$4,100	$3,650	$3,200	$2,800	*$6,495*

PEACE RIVER CLASSICS

Previous manufacturer located in Bartow, FL until 2001. Peace River Classics was a division of Tim's Guns.

RIFLES: SEMI-AUTO

PEACE RIVER CLASSICS SEMI-AUTO – .223 Rem. or .308 Win. (new 1998, possible prototypes only) cal., available in 3 configurations including the Shadowood, the Glenwood, and the Royale, GIO, hand-built utilizing Armalite action, patterned after the AR-15, match grade parts throughout, special serialization, laminate thumbhole stock. Very limited mfg. 1997-2001.

Last MSR on the .223 Rem. cal. in 2001 was $2,695, or $2,995 for .308 Win. cal

Due to this model's rarity factor, accurate values are hard to ascertain.

PETERS STAHL GmbH

Previous pistol manufacturer located in Paderborn, Germany until 2010. Previously imported until 2009 by Euro-Imports, located in Yoakum, TX. Previously distributed by Swiss Trading GmbH, located in Bozeman, MT. Previously imported 1998-1999 by Peters Stahl, U.S.A. located in Delta, UT, and by Franzen International Inc. located in Oakland, NJ until 1998.

MSR	100%	98%	95%	90%	80%	70%	60%	Last MSR

PISTOLS: SEMI-AUTO

Peters Stahl manufactured high quality semi-auto pistols based on the Model 1911 design, but had limited U.S. importation. Models included the Multicaliber, 92-Sport, O7-Sport, HC-Champion and variations, 1911-Tactical/Classic, PLS, and a .22 LR. Peters Stahl also manufactures multicaliber conversion kits of the highest quality. Recent models previously imported (until 2000) included the Model Millennium (MSR was $2,195), Match 22 LR (MSR was $1,995), Trophy Master (MSR was $1,995), Omega Match (MSR was $1,995), High Capacity Trophy Master (MSR was $1,695), O7 Multicaliber (MSR was $1,995), and the 92 Multicaliber (MSR was $2,610-$2,720). In the past, Peters Stahl has manufactured guns for Federal Ordnance, Omega, Schuetzen Pistol Works, and Springfield Armory.

PHASE5 TACTICAL

Current AR-15 pistol and rifle manufacturer, located in Roseville, CA.

PISTOL: SEMI-AUTO

AR-15 ATLAS ONE PISTOL - BILLET – 5.56 NATO cal., GIO, electroless nickel M4 barrel extension, CMC 3 1/2 lb. curved trigger group, Single Point Bungee Sling and ARMS 71L front and rear flip-up sights, matched Billet lower and upper receiver set, EN bolt carrier, EBRv2, REVO, ABL/CHA, 5 lbs. 4 oz. New 2016.

MSR $1,850	$1,575	$1,385	$1,185	$1,065	$915	$785	$635

AR-15 CQC PISTOL - FORGED – 5.56 NATO cal., GIO, compact frame, forged aluminum receivers. New 2016.

MSR $1,250	$1,050	$950	$815	$715	$625	$535	$450

RIFLES: SEMI-AUTO

AR-15 P5T15 – 5.56 NATO cal., mid-length GIO, 16 in. chrome lined, button rifled barrel, Winter Trigger guard, ARMS 71L flip up sights, Mission First Tactical Battlelink 6-pos. utility stock, Mission First Tactical Engaged pistol grip, Phase5 enhanced buffer spring, forged aluminum lower and upper receivers, Lo-Pro Nose Quad Rail, M4 extension/M4 feed ramps, ambidextrious Battle Latch charging handle, 7 lbs. 3 oz. New late 2015.

MSR $1,776	$1,495	$1,315	$1,150	$1,025	$875	$750	$615

PISTOL DYNAMICS

Current semi-auto pistol manufacturer located in Palm Bay, FL.

PISTOLS: SEMI-AUTO

Pistol Dynamics manufactures high quality 1911-style semi-auto pistols. Current models include the Signature (base price $3,800 MSR), Combat Special Evolution (base price $3,600 MSR), Scout (base price $2,900 MSR), Super Scout (base price $3,695), 1911 Anniversary, STI/SVI Limited, and the X-O (base price $2,400 MSR). Previous models include: Combat Special Classic (last MSR for base price was $4,600). Options and delivery times vary for each model. Please contact the company directly for availability and pricing (see Trademark Index).

POLY TECHNOLOGIES, INC.

Previously distributed by PTK International, Inc. located in Atlanta, GA. Previously imported by Keng's Firearms Specialty, Inc., located in Riverdale, GA. Manufactured in China by Poly Technologies, Inc.

Poly Technologies commercial firearms are made to Chinese military specifications and have excellent quality control. These models were banned from domestic importation due to 1989 Federal legislation.

RIFLES: SEMI-AUTO

Add 10% for NIB.

AKS-762 – 7.62x39mm or .223 Rem. cal., 16 1/4 in. barrel, semi-auto version of the Chinese AKM (Type 56) rifle, 8.4 lbs., wood stock. Imported 1988-1989.

	$1,495	$1,325	$1,100	$975	$875	$795	$750	*$400*

Add $100 for side-fold plastic stock.

This model was also available with a downward folding stock at no extra charge.

SKS – 7.62x39mm cal., 20 9/20 in. barrel, full wood stock, machined steel parts to Chinese military specifications, 7.9 lbs. Imported 1988-89.

	$550	$475	$400	$350	$300	$275	$250	*$200*

AK-47/S (LEGEND) – 7.62x39mm cal., 16 3/8 in. barrel, semi-auto configuration of the original AK-47, fixed, side-folding, or under-folding stock, with or w/o spike bayonet, 8.2 lbs. Imported 1988-89.

	$2,000	$1,800	$1,600	$1,350	$1,200	$1,000	$925	*$550*

Add 10% for folding stock.

The "S" suffix in this variation designates third model specifications.

* AK-47/S National Match Legend – utilizes match parts in fabrication.

	$1,950	$1,750	$1,550	$1,275	$1,050	$975	$900	

MSR		100%	98%	95%	90%	80%	70%	60%	Last MSR

RPK – 7.62x39mm cal. Disc.

		$1,475	$1,300	$1,150	$1,025	$925	$850	$775	

M-14/S – .308 Win. cal., 22 in. barrel, forged receiver, patterned after the famous M-14, 9.2 lbs. Imported 1988-89.

		$1,100	$950	$850	$775	$725	$650	$575	*$700*

PRECISION FIREARMS LLC

Current rifle manufacturer located in Martinsburg, WV beginning in late 2013. Previously located in Hagerstown, MD. Dealer and consumer sales through FFL.

RIFLES: BOLT ACTION

Precision Firearms offers a line of custom-made bolt action rifles built per individual customer specifications using Stiller Precision or Badger Ordnance actions and Bartlein or Lilja rifled barrels. Each rifle includes a hard case and one magazine. Delivery time is anywhere from 6 to 18 weeks. Please contact the company for more information, including available options and pricing (see Trademark Index).

CARBINES/RIFLES: SEMI-AUTO

AMAZON LIGHT WEIGHT RIFLE – various cals., mid-length GIO, lightweight cold hammer forged barrel with muzzle brake, aluminum billet lower and upper receiver, with or w/o sights, carbon figer handguard, BCM Gunfighter Mod 4 or Rainier XCT (disc.) ambi charging handle, Geissele or Timney trigger, Magpul ACS-L stock, PF, Hogue, Magpul, or Ergo grip, matte black finish, 6 1/2 lbs.

MSR $1,700		$1,450	$1,275	$1,125	$1,000	$850	$735	$595	

Add $195 for sights.

ARIES T1-B (ARIES T-1) – 5.56 NATO cal., Adams Arms GPO system, 16 in. mid-length German-made barrel with Battle Comp compensator, two Magpul mags., aluminum billet upper and lower receiver, M4 feed ramps, Troy folding sights, BAD-ASS ambi safety, Troy ambi bolt release, BCM Mod 4 charging handle, Magpul UBR stock, Hogue pistol grip, Geissele SSA-E trigger, matte black Nitride finish, includes tactical case.

MSR $2,300		$1,950	$1,725	$1,450	$1,250	$1,050	$900	$750	

ARION TYPE I – 6.5mm Grendel cal., 16 in. fluted barrel with PF LMD muzzle brake, Rainier Compensator, NOX, or AAC flash hider, aluminum billet upper and lower receiver, BAD-ASS ambi-safety, BCM Gunfighter charging handle, Geissele two-stage trigger, PF (disc. 2014) or integral (new 2015) trigger guard, nickel boron carrier group, 15 in. Geissele MK 3 (disc. 2014) or Geissele MK8 MLOK 13 in. handguard with three modular rails, rubberized grip, Magpul UBR stock with battery storage, matte black finish, includes sling and soft tactical case, optional Troy ambi bolt and mag. release,

MSR $2,200		$1,875	$1,650	$1,400	$1,200	$1,025	$875	$725	

Add $200 for sights.

EXCALIBUR 3 GUN RIFLE – 5.56 NATO cal., 18 or 20 in. German-made or Lilja match barrel, two Magpul mags., precision machined aluminum billet upper and lower receiver, Magpul ACS- L stock, Magpul MOE or Hogue grip, Lancer 15 in. competition handguard, aluminum trigger guard, Geissele Super 3 Gun trigger, Mil-Spec tube and buffer, sling with QD attachment, BCM Mod 4 charging handle, matte black finish, nickel boron coating, includes tactical case.

MSR $2,200		$1,875	$1,650	$1,400	$1,200	$1,025	$875	$725	

HAVOC SERIES – various cals., German-made barrel with black Nitride coating, precision machined aluminum billet upper and lower receiver, optional Magpul or Troy folding sights, Geissele 13 in. MK3 rail (disc. 2014) or Geissele 13 in. MK8 rail with MLOK (new 2015), BCM Mod 4 charging handle, Mil-Spec tube and buffer, two Magpul mags., Magpul MOE or PF Hogue grips, Geissele two-stage trigger, aluminum trigger guard, Magpul STR stock, sling and QD attachment, matte black finish, includes case.

MSR $1,800		$1,525	$1,350	$1,175	$1,050	$900	$775	$625	

Add $75 for Magpul or $200 for Troy folding sights.

THE KATANA 3G – .223 Rem./5/56 NATO cal. (.223 Wylde chamber), designed for 3 Gun Competition, stainless steel Lothar Walther barrel, precision machined aluminum billet upper and lower receiver, Samson, VTac, or ALG handguard, each rifle can be custom crafted per individual needs, includes tactical nylon carry case and 2 magazines. Disc. 2014.

		$1,450	$1,275	$1,125	$1,000	$850	$735	$595	*$1,700*

Add $200 for sights.

THE KATANA II – .223 Wylde cal., 16 in. free-floated stainless steel Lothar Walther barrel with PF NOX flash hider, two 30 shot Troy or Magpul mags., Troy 13 in. Vtac Alpha handguard, Geissele two-stage trigger, mid-length gas system, billet upper and lower receivers, M4 feed ramps, BCM Gunfighter Mod 4 charging handle, Magpul enhanced aluminum trigger guard, Magpul MOE rubberized grip, Magpul ACS-L stock with 6 positions and storage area in the stock, single point mount QD sling, includes soft tactical case.

MSR $1,700		$1,450	$1,275	$1,125	$1,000	$850	$735	$595	

Add $200 for sights.

MSR			100%	98%	95%	90%	80%	70%	60%	*Last MSR*

PRECISION SIDEWINDER AR-X08 RIFLE (PF-X08 LARGE FRAME AR) – .243 Win., .260 Rem., .308 Win., 6.5 Creedmoor, 6.5x47 Lapua, or 7mm-08 Rem. cal., Bartlein or Lilja barrel, PF muzzle device, Geissele SSA-E trigger, T6 aluminum billet lower and DPMS pattern upper receiver, integral Winter trigger guard, forward assist, port cover, shell deflector, Hogue grip, matte black finish, made to customer specifications.

    Base MSRs start at $3,200.

THE STIR (SOFT TARGET INTERDICTION RIFLE) – .204 Ruger, .223 Wylde, or 6.5 Grendel cal., 24 in. Bartlein, Lilja, or Lothar Walther barrel, precision machined aluminum billet upper and lower, upper receiver is heavily walled and matched for fit and finish, lower receiver has tension screw, aluminum or carbon fiber handguard, PF, Hogue, Magpul or Ergo grip, super match carrier, BCM Gunfighter Mod 3, Rainier XCT (disc.), or Armageddon ambi charging handle, Geissele or Timney trigger, Magpul PRS stock, matte black finish, optional barrel fluting, bipod, monopods, Vortex scope, muzzle brakes.

| MSR $2,300 | | | $1,950 | $1,725 | $1,450 | $1,250 | $1,050 | $900 | $750 | |

    Add $300 for fully equipped optional model without optics.

THE NIGHTSHADOW – 5.56 NATO cal., lightweight chrome-lined hammer forged barrel with BCM muzzle brake, precision machined upper and lower receivers, BCM KMR 13 in. handguard, BCM Gunfighter Mod 4 charging handle, Geissele two-stage trigger, PF Black Phalanx carrier group, with or w/o sights, Magpul CTR stock, PF rubberized grip, 6 lbs. New 2015.

| MSR $1,600 | | | $1,350 | $1,200 | $1,075 | $950 | $815 | $700 | $575 | |

    Add $195 for sights.

PRECISION REFLEX, INC.

Current AR-15 manufacturer located in New Bremen, OH.

RIFLES: SEMI-AUTO

Precision Reflex, Inc. manufactures AR-15 style rifles and shooting accessories for commercial, law enforcement, and military use. For more information on the many products they have available, please contact the company directly (see Trademark Index).

3 GUN SHOOTER RIFLE – 5.56 NATO or 6.8 SPC cal., 18 in. stainless steel barrel with threaded muzzle, M4 feed ramps, low profile steel gas block, forged upper and lower receivers, 15 in. black forearm, AR trigger, 6-position carbine stock with recoil pad, A2 pistol grip, flip-up rear sights, Gas Buster charging handle with military latch, 7 1/2 lbs. New 2014.

| MSR $1,320 | | | $1,175 | $1,025 | $875 | $800 | $650 | $525 | $425 | |

DELUXE RIFLE – 5.56 NATO or 6.8 SPC cal., 16 in. Douglas stainless steel or 17 in. Bergara chrome moly barrel, threaded muzzle, M4 feed ramps, flip-up front and rear sights, AR trigger, intermediate round forearm with natural finish, intermediate length top rail, 6-position carbine stock with recoil pad, A2 pistol grip, Gas Buster charging handle w/military latch, Black finish, 7.9 lbs. New 2014.

| MSR $1,325 | | | $1,175 | $1,025 | $875 | $800 | $650 | $525 | $425 | |

    Add $215 for Douglas stainless steel barrel.

ENTRY LEVEL RIFLE – 5.56 NATO cal., 17 in. Bergara chrome moly barrel, threaded muzzle, M4 feed ramps, forged upper and lower receivers, rifle length round forearm in Natural, Black, or Flat Dark Earth, AR trigger, 6-position carbine stock with recoil pad, A2 pistol grip, Gas Buster charging handle w/military latch, approx 8 lbs. New 2014.

| MSR $1,190 | | | $1,050 | $925 | $800 | $725 | $575 | $475 | $375 | |

    Add $30 for forearm with Black or Flat Dark Earth finish.

    * *Entry Level Rifle Stainless* – 5.56 NATO or 6.8 SPC cal., similar to Entry Level rifle, except features 16 in. stainless steel barrel, rifle length round forearm in Natural, Black, or Flat Dark Earth finish. New 2014.

| MSR $1,322 | | | $1,175 | $1,025 | $875 | $800 | $650 | $525 | $425 | |

    Add $11 for forearm with Black or Flat Dark Earth finish.

ENTRY LEVEL DELTA RIFLE – 5.56 NATO cal., 17 in. Bergara chrome moly barrel, threaded muzzle, M4 feed ramps, forged upper and lower receivers, rifle length Delta forearm in Black or Flat Dark Earth finish, AR trigger, 6-position carbine stock with recoil pad, A2 pistol grip, Gas Buster charging handle w/military latch, approx 8 lbs. New 2014.

| MSR $1,205 | | | $1,075 | $950 | $800 | $725 | $575 | $475 | $375 | |

    * *Entry Level Delta Rifle Stainless* – 5.56 NATO or 6.8 SPC cal., similar to Entry Level Delta rifle, except features 16 in. stainless steel barrel, rifle length Delta forearm in Black or Flat Dark Earth finish, approx 8 lbs. New 2014.

| MSR $1,339 | | | $1,200 | $1,050 | $900 | $800 | $650 | $525 | $425 | |

MARK 12 MOD O SPR RIFLE – 5.56 NATO or 6.8 SPC cal., 18 in. stainless steel barrel, threaded muzzle, forged upper and lower receivers, flip-up front and rear sights, AR trigger, Black rifle length forearm, full length SPR top rail, 6-position carbine stock with recoil pad, A2 pistol grip, Gas Buster charging handle w/military latch, 8.68 lbs. New 2014.

| MSR $1,790 | | | $1,625 | $1,425 | $1,225 | $1,100 | $900 | $725 | $575 | |

MSR	100%	98%	95%	90%	80%	70%	60%	Last MSR

* Mark 12 Mod Delta Rifle – 5.56 NATO or 6.8 SPC cal., similar to Mark 12 Mod O SPR rifle, except features a full length SPR Delta top rail, 7.9 lbs. New 2014.

| MSR $1,790 | $1,625 | $1,425 | $1,225 | $1,100 | $900 | $725 | $575 | |

MARK 12 MOD O SPR VARIANT RIFLE – 5.56 NATO or 6.8 SPC cal., 16 in. stainless steel or 17 in. Bergara chrome moly barrel, threaded muzzle, M4 feed ramps, forged upper and lower receivers, AR trigger, 6-position carbine stock with recoil pad, A2 pistol grip, Black finish, intermediate length top rail, flip-up front and rear sights, 7.9 lbs. New 2014.

| MSR $1,494 | $1,350 | $1,175 | $1,025 | $925 | $750 | $625 | $500 | |

Add $134 for stainless steel barrel in 5.56 NATO or $181 if in 6.8 SPC cal.

TACTICAL OPERATOR RIFLE – 5.56 NATO or 6.8 SPC cal., 16 in. Douglas stainless steel barrel or 17 in. Bergara (5.56 NATO only) chrome moly barrel, threaded muzzle, M4 feed ramps, forged upper and lower receivers, AR trigger, rifle length round forearm with Flat Dark Earth finish, flip-up front and rear sights, 6-position carbine stock with recoil pad, A2 pistol grip, top rail, Gas Buster charging handle w/military latch, 7.9 lbs. New 2014.

| MSR $1,504 | $1,350 | $1,175 | $1,025 | $925 | $750 | $625 | $500 | |

Add $134 for Douglas stainless steel barrel in 5.56 NATO or $171 if with 6.8 SPC cal.

PREDATOR CUSTOM SHOP

Current custom manufacturer located in Knoxville, TN.

RIFLES: BOLT ACTION

Predator Custom Shop manufactures custom bolt action rifles built to customer specifications. Base rifles start at $2,050. Please contact the company directly for more information including options, pricing, availability, and delivery time (see Trademark Index).

RIFLES: SEMI-AUTO

Predator Custom Shop manufactures custom AR-15 rifles built to customer specifications. Current models include the 5.56 Carnivore, and the 5.56 DMR. Please contact the company directly for more information including options, pricing, availability, and delivery time (see Trademark Index).

PREDATOR TACTICAL LLC

Current manufacturer located in Tempe, AZ since 2010.

Predator Tactical LLC was founded by champion competition shooter Matt Burkett. In early 2016, Industry Armament acquired Predator Tactical and plans to expand their current production and distribution operations.

PISTOLS: SEMI-AUTO

For the following models personalization is available on any part of the build and finishing. You can have your name on the magazines, side of the gun, etc. Each pistol also includes one hour of private training in Arizona by the Predator Team, one complete refinishing, and a range bag.

1911 SHRIKE – 9mm Para., 10mm, .38 Super, or .45 ACP cal., Caspian Arms frame, Briley custom match barrel with spherical bushing, 8 shot mag., stainless steel, high polished silver sides with engraved lettering and logos, checkering on front strap, Extreme Engineering hammer, sear, and disconnector.
Current MSR on this model is $3,575.

1911 TOTAL CUSTOM – .45 ACP cal., carbon frame and slide, 5 in. barrel with bushing, tactical guide rod, rosewood, walnut, or VZ OP2 black grips, blued finish.
Current MSR on this model is $3,250-$5,850, depending on customer specifications.

BANSHEE OPEN GUN – 9mm Para., .38 Super, .38 Super Comp., .40 S&W, or .45 ACP cal., STI tactical or standard frame, Shuemann Hybrid 3 port barrel, PT exclusive compensator, C-More scope, PT sideways mount or Allchin scope mount, Extreme Engineering hammer, sear, and disconnector, Aftec extractor, Dawson magwell, ambi safety, Ed Brown beavertail, blued, hard chrome, or PVD coated finish.
Current MSR on this model is $4,450-$5,575, depending on customer specifications.

IRON SHRIKE – .45 ACP cal., heat treated carbon steel Caspian Arms frame, checkering on front strap, tactical guide rod, G10 grips, adj. rear sight, front night sight, front and rear serrations, high grip beavertail safety, blued finish.
Current MSR on this model is $3,450.

NIGHT SHRIKE – .45 ACP cal., 4 in. ultra match barrel, stainless steel slide on top of aluminum short rail frame, high polished silver sides with engraved lettering and logos, stainless steel, checkering on front strap, tactical rail, tactical guide rod, adj. or fixed rear sights, front night sight, front and rear serrations, high grip beavertail, 8 shot mag.
Current MSR on this model is 3,950.

SCARAB – 9mm Para., 10mm, .38 Super, .38 Super Comp., .40 S&W, or .45 ACP cal., STI frame, Briley or Schuemann match barrel, Extreme Engineering hammer, sear, and disconnector, front and rear serrations, Ed Brown beavertail grip safety.
Current MSR on this model is $3,625-$5,175, depending on customer specifications.

MSR	100%	98%	95%	90%	80%	70%	60%	Last MSR

3 GUN NATION CUSTOM SCARAB – 9x19mm, .38 Super, .38 Super Comp., .40 S&W, or .45 ACP cal., STI frame, bull barrel, stainless billet machined slide, stainless small parts, Extreme Engineering fire control group, Burkett grip, two-tone finish.

Current MSR on this model is $3,495-$4,130, depending on customer specifications.

WRAITH OPEN GUN – 9mm Para., .38 Super, or .38 Super Comp. cal., STI frame, PT exclusive compensator, C-More scope, PT tactical side or PT Allchin scope mount, Extreme Engineering hammer, sear, and disconnector, Aftec extractor, ambi safety, Ed Brown beavertail, blued, hard chrome, or black Nitride finish.

Current MSR on this model is $4,750-$5,875, depending on customer specifications.

RIFLES: SEMI-AUTO

Predator Tactical offers customized rifles - base price for the PT-10 Model is $3,175 Please contact the company for more information, including pricing and availability (see Trademark Index).

PRIMARY WEAPONS SYSTEMS (PWS)

Current manufacturer located in Boise, ID.

Primary Weapons Systems manufactures a series of AR-15 style semi-auto pistols, rifles, and bolt action rifles, as well as SBR models for law enforcement and military.

PISTOLS: SEMI-AUTO

MK107 SERIES – .223 Rem./5.56 NATO (.223 Wylde chamber), 7.62x39mm (disc. 2012) cal., AR-15 style, GPO, 30 shot mag., 7 1/2 in. Isonite QPQ treated, 1:8 twist button rifled barrel. Mil-Spec upper and lower receiver, ALG Defense QMS trigger, enhanced bolt carrier group, PWS KeyMod rail system, BCM Gunfighter charging handle, Magpul MOE furniture and sights.

MSR $1,950	$1,700	$1,500	$1,275	$1,150	$950	$775	$600	

MK109 SERIES – .300 BLK cal., GPO, 9 3/4 in. stainless steel, 30 shot polymer mag., Isonite QPD treated, button rifled barrel, Mil-Spec upper and lower receiver, quad rail, available in matte black or Flat Dark Earth finish, enhanced charging handle and bolt carrier group, Micro-slicked Internals, Magpul XT rail panels, Magpul MOE grip, MBUS sights, approx. 5 1/5 lbs. Disc. 2012.

	$1,525	$1,300	$1,100	$925	$750	$675	$575	$1,700

Add $200 for Flat Dark Earth finish.

MK110 SERIES – .223 Rem. cal. (.223 Wylde chamber), GPO, similar to MK107 Series, except has 10 3/4 in. barrel. New 2014.

MSR $1,950	$1,700	$1,500	$1,275	$1,150	$950	$775	$600	

DI-10P MODERN MUSKET – .223 Rem./5/56 NATO (.223 Wylde chamber) cal., AR-15 style, 10 3/4 in. barrel with Sig Sauer SB15 stabilizing brace, matte black hardcoat anodized finish, 6 lbs. New mid-2014.

MSR $1,500	$1,275	$1,125	$950	$875	$700	$575	$450	

RIFLES: BOLT ACTION

MK3 SERIES – .308 Win. (new 2014), .300 Win. Mag., or .338 Lapua (new 2014) cal., 20 (.308 Win. cal. only) or 21 3/4 in. stainless steel barrel, 5 shot mag., Isonite QPQ treated barrel and receiver, Jewell trigger, PRC muzzle device, KRG Whisky-3 folding chassis, AI mag. compatibility, 11 1/2 lbs. New 2012.

MSR $7,000	$6,250	$5,475	$4,700	$4,250	$3,450	$2,825	$2,200	

T3 RIMFIRE SERIES – .22 LR cal., 21 1/2 in. barrel, choice of stock, Summit 10/22 action, 30 shot mag., approx. 4 lbs.

MSR $800	$675	$595	$500	$450	$375	$300	$235	

RIFLES: SEMI-AUTO

DI-16 MODERN MUSKET – .223 Rem./5.56 NATO (.223 Wylde chamber) cal., 16 in. barrel with removable flash suppressor, adj. tactical stock, pistol grip, quad rail, matte black hardcoat anodized finish, 6 lbs. 12 oz. New mid-2014.

MSR $1,500	$1,275	$1,125	$950	$875	$700	$575	$450	

MK1 SERIES – .223 Rem./5.56 NATO (.223 Wylde chamber), or .300 BLK cal., GPO, 16 or 18 (new 2014) in. stainless steel, Isonite QPD treated, button rifled barrel, 30 shot polymer mag., Mil-Spec upper and lower receiver, quad rail, available in matte black, flat dark earth, or Kryptek camo (new 2014) finish, enhanced bolt carrier group, Micro-slicked Internals, Magpul XT rail panels, Magpul MOE grip, MBUS sights, Triad 30 flash suppressor, ALG Defense QMS trigger, PWS KeyMod rail system, BCM GUNFIGHTER charging handle, approx. 7 lbs.

MSR $1,950	$1,695	$1,485	$1,275	$1,150	$925	$775	$600	

Add $50 for Kryptek camo finish.

Add $250 for Ranger proof logo.

MSR	100%	98%	95%	90%	80%	70%	60%	Last MSR

MK2 SERIES – .308 Win. cal., SR-25 platform, GPO, 16.1 or 20 in. Isonite QPD treated button rifled barrel, 30 shot polymer mag., Mil-Spec upper and lower receiver, quad rail, available in matte black or Flat Dark Earth finish, enhanced bolt carrier group, Micro-slicked Internals, Magpul XT rail panels, Magpul MOE grip, MBUS sights, ALG Defense QMS trigger, PWS KeyMod rail system, BCM Gunfighter charging handle, 8 lbs. 12 oz.

| MSR $2,600 | $2,250 | $1,925 | $1,750 | $1,425 | $1,150 | $900 | $850 | |

WOODLAND SPORTING RIFLE – .223 Rem./5.56 NATO (.223 Wylde chamber), or .300 BLK cal., GIO, 16.1 or 18 in. free floating stainless steel, Isonite QPQ treated, button rifled barrel, enhanced charging handle, PWS Mil-Spec upper and lower receiver, enhanced DI carrier, black olive (disc.) or walnut stock, 30 shot polymer mag. approx. 7 1/2 - 8 lbs. Mfg. 2012-2014.

| | | $1,325 | $1,160 | $1,000 | $900 | $725 | $600 | $500 | *$1,500* |

WRAITH 3GUN COMPETITION RIFLE – .223 Rem./5.56 NATO (.223 Wylde chamber) cal., GIO, 18 in. free floating stainless steel, Isonite QPQ treated, button rifled barrel, enhanced BCM Gunfighter charging handle, PWS Mil-Spec upper and lower receiver, enhanced DI carrier, black, olive or walnut stock, 30 shot polymer mag., Daniel Defense free float handguard, JP Tactical EZ trigger, 7 lbs., 5 oz. Mfg. 2012, reintroduced 2014.

| MSR $2,900 | $2,475 | $2,175 | $1,850 | $1,685 | $1,350 | $1,125 | $875 | |

This model is also available in an AR-10 platform chambered in .308 Win cal. with a 20 in. barrel. Please contact the custom shop for more information and pricing.

PROARMS ARMORY s.r.o.

Current manufacturer located in Czech Republic. No U.S. importation.

RIFLES: SEMI-AUTO

PAR MK3 – 5.56 NATO cal., GPO, 5, 10, 20, or 30 shot mag., 16 3/4 or 18 in. Lothar Walther barrel, four-position adj. gas block, aluminum alloy frame and upper receiver made on CNC, ergonomic beaver tail pistol grip, free float handguard with four fixed rails or KeyMod system in four different lengths, telescopic 6-position collapsible stock, folding MBUS sights.

Current retail price is €1,599, including VAT.

PAR MK3 SPARTAN – .223 Rem. or 7.62x39mm cal., GPO, AR-15 style, 16 3/4 in. barrel, A2 muzzle brake, 30 shot mag., folding MBUS, M4 collapsible stock, A2 grip, 4 rail or KeyMod handguard with hex wrench, black finish. New 2016.
Please contact the manufacturer directly for pricing on this model.

PROFESSIONAL ORDNANCE, INC.

Previous manufacturer located in Lake Havasu City, AZ 1998-2003. Previously manufactured in Ontario, CA circa 1996-1997. Distributor sales only.

During 2003, Bushmaster bought Professional Ordnance and the Carbon 15 trademark. Please refer to the Bushmaster section for currently manufactured Carbon 15 rifles and pistols (still manufactured in Lake Havasu City).

PISTOLS: SEMI-AUTO

CARBON-15 TYPE 20 – .223 Rem. cal., GIO, Stoner type operating system with recoil reducing buffer assembly, carbon fiber upper and lower receiver, hard chromed bolt carrier, 7 1/4 in. unfluted stainless steel barrel with ghost ring sights, 30 shot mag. (supplies were limited), also accepts AR-15 type mags., 40 oz. Mfg. 1999-2000.

| | $950 | $800 | $725 | $650 | $575 | $525 | $475 | *$1,500* |

CARBON-15 TYPE 21 – .223 Rem cal., GIO, ultra lightweight carbon fiber upper and lower receivers, 7 1/4 in. "Profile" stainless steel barrel, quick detachable muzzle compensator, ghost ring sights, 10 shot mag., also accepts AR-15 type mags., Stoner type operating system, tool steel bolt, extractor and carrier, 40 oz. Mfg. 2001-2003.

| | $850 | $750 | $675 | $600 | $550 | $500 | $450 | *$899* |

CARBON-15 TYPE 97 – .223 Rem. cal., similar to Carbon 15 Type 20, except has fluted barrel and quick detachable compensator, 46 oz. Mfg. 1996-2003.

| | $925 | $800 | $725 | $625 | $575 | $525 | $475 | *$964* |

RIFLES: SEMI-AUTO

CARBON-15 TYPE 20 – .223 Rem. cal., GIO, same operating system as the Carbon-15 pistol, 16 in. unfluted stainless steel barrel, carbon fiber buttstock and forearm, includes Mil-Spec optics mounting base, 3.9 lbs. Mfg. 1998-2000.

| | $975 | $850 | $795 | $725 | $650 | $550 | $475 | *$1,550* |

CARBON-15 TYPE 21 – .223 Rem. cal., GIO, ultra lightweight carbon fiber upper and lower receivers, 16 in. "Profile" stainless steel barrel, quick detachable muzzle compensator, Stoner type operating system, tool steel bolt, extractor and carrier, optics mounting base, quick detachable stock, 10 shot mag., also accepts AR-15 type mags., 3.9 lbs. Mfg. 2001-2003.

| | $975 | $850 | $795 | $725 | $650 | $550 | $475 | *$988* |

MSR	100%	98%	95%	90%	80%	70%	60%	Last MSR

CARBON-15 TYPE 97/97S – .223 Rem. cal., GIO, ultra lighweight carbon fiber upper and lower receivers, Stoner type operating system, hard chromed tool steel bolt, extractor and carrier, 16 in. fluted stainless steel barrel, quick detachable muzzle compensator, optics mounting base, quick detachable stock, 30 shot mag., also accepts AR-15 type mags., 3.9 lbs. Mfg. 2001-2003.

	$1,075	$900	$825	$750	$675	$600	$550	$1,120

Add $165 for Model 97S (includes Picatinny rail and "Scout" extension, double walled heat shield forearm, ambidextrous safety, and multi-point silent carry).

PROOF RESEARCH

Current rifle manufacturer located in Columbia Falls, MT. Consumer sales through FFL dealers.

RIFLES: BOLT ACTION

TERMINUS (MONTE CARLO) – various cals., Hunter action with 20 MOA integral rail, 16 1/2-30 in. carbon fiber wrapped Sendero or Sendero Light barrel, BDL hinged floorplate, Jewell or Timney trigger, optics are optional and customer defined, Kevlar Monte Carlo lightweight ergonomic stock with raised cheekpiece, Pachmayr recoil pad, Cerakote finish in Black, FDE, OD Green, Tungsten, or Sniper Gray, 6 lbs. 13 oz.

MSR $5,990	$5,390	$4,715	$4,050	$3,675	$2,975	$2,450	$1,900	

Add $300-$600 depending on caliber, action, and mag.

SUMMIT – .33 WSM BDL XM, 7mm WSM BDL XM, or .270 WSM BDL XM cal., Proof H6 bolt action, 22 or 24 (Sendero Light) in. Proof Research carbon fiber wrapped barrel, BDL (hinged floorplate), Jewell and Timney trigger, custom finished carbon fiber/Kevlar Summit stock, Pachmayr recoil pad, Black, Flat Dark Earth, Olive Drab, Sniper Gray, or Tungsten Cerakote finish, 6 lbs. 9 oz.-7 lbs. 3.8 oz.

MSR $5,840	$5,250	$4,595	$3,950	$3,575	$2,890	$2,375	$1,850	

Add $150 depending on caliber, action, and mag.

* **Summit YL** – .204 Ruger-.338 Win. Mag. cal., similar to Summit model, except developed for the female or youth shooter, features 16-26 in. barrel, Summit CFB lightweight stock with slim profile, and Leupold 4.5-14x40 CDX optics. Disc. 2014.

	$5,125	$4,485	$3,850	$3,485	$2,825	$2,300	$1,800	$5,700

TAC II – .243 Rem.-.338 Win. cals., AR-15 style, GIO, lightweight, long range rifle, Proof T6 action, 16 1/2-30 in. Proof Research carbon fiber wrapped Sendero barrel, Kevlar Tac II stock with adj. cheekpiece, Pachmayr recoil pad, vertical grip, and lower profile forearm, Jewell or Timney trigger, optics are optional and customer defined, Cerakote finish is standard, Flat Dark Earth, OD Green, camo, and other finishes available, 8.81 lbs.

MSR $6,690	$6,025	$5,275	$4,525	$4,100	$3,325	$2,725	$2,125	

Pricing is for base rifle only w/o options.
Add $100-$800 depending on caliber, action, and mag.

RIFLES: SEMI-AUTO

MONOLITHIC AR10 – .243 Rem.-.338 RCM cals., GIO, 20 in. carbon fiber wrapped barrel, carbine, mid-rifle, or rifle length available, Mega Machine Monolithic upper receiver, Mega Machine lower receiver, Magpul PRS stock is standard, Geissele trigger, Premier 3-15x50LT optics, LaRue Tactical LT 104 mount, anodized Type III black, Cerakote, and custom option finishes available. Disc. 2014.

	$3,075	$2,700	$2,300	$2,100	$1,700	$1,400	$1,075	$3,417

MONOLITHIC AR15 – .204 Ruger-6.8 SPC cal., GIO, 16 in. carbon fiber wrapped barrel, available in carbine, mid-length, and rifle length, Mega Machine Monolithic upper and matched lower receiver, Magpul ACS stock standard, Geissele trigger, optics are optional and customer defined, LaRue Tactical LT 104 mount, anodized Type II Black, OD Green, and other Cerakote custom finishes available. Disc. 2014.

	$2,800	$2,450	$2,100	$1,900	$1,550	$1,275	$975	$3,113

SOCOM I – 243 Rem.-.338 Win. cals., AR-15 style, GIO, "tactical hunter" rifle, Proof T6 action, 16-28 in. Proof Research carbon fiber wrapped barrel, Proof Socom I composite stock with adj. cheekpiece and straight grip, Jewell or Timney trigger, optics are optional and customer defined, Cerakote finish is standard, Flat Dark Earth, OD Green, camo, and other finishes available. Disc. 2014.

	$6,150	$5,375	$4,625	$4,175	$3,375	$2,775	$2,150	$6,850

TUBE GUN SYSTEM – .204 Ruger-.338 Win. cals., Proof C6 action, GIO, 16-28 in. Proof Research carbon fiber wrapped bull barrel, Eliseo tube chasis RTS stock, optics are optional and customer defined, Cerakote finish is standard, matte black and other custom colors are available. Disc. 2014.

	$4,250	$3,725	$3,200	$2,900	$2,350	$1,925	$1,500	$4,695

MSR	100%	98%	95%	90%	80%	70%	60%	Last MSR

PUMA

Previous trademark of firearms imported by Legacy Sports International LLC until 2014, located in Reno, NV. Previously located in Alexandria, VA.

RIFLES: SEMI-AUTO

PPS/22 – .22 LR cal., 16 in. shrouded barrel with open sights, choice of uncheckered wood or black, green, or sand colored synthetic or Wildcat tactical adj. stock, 10 (clip), 30 (clip or drum) or 50 shot drum mag., Wildcat stock includes optional Picatinny rail, pistol grip, and vertical forend grip, mfg. by Pietta. Mfg. 2009-2010.

	100%	98%	95%	90%	80%	70%	60%	Last MSR
	$475	$425	$375	$325	$295	$275	$250	$519

Add $40 for 50 shot drum mag or wood stock.

Add $50 for black, green, or sand colored, or Wildcat synthetic stock.

QUALITY ARMS

Current rifle manufacturer located in Rigby, ID.

RIFLES: BOLT ACTION

THE TAC 21 – .308 Win., 6.5x47 Lapua, or .338 Lapua cal., GIO, built on Rem. receiver, full length accessories mounting rail, Magpul PRS stock, Magpul pistol grip, heavy duty bipod, 5 or 10 shot AICS mag., American Defense 35mm quick detach scope mount and 6-25x56 LRS-1 Millett Tactical rifle scope, includes Condor drag bag.

MSR $2,195	$1,975	$1,730	$1,480	$1,345	$1,085	$890	$690	

RIFLES: SEMI-AUTO

6.5 GRENDEL – 6.5 Grendel cal., GIO, this rifle will be custom built, but basics specs are as follows: 18, 20, or 24 in. match grade free floated stainless barrel, tactical free float rail, front and rear Magpul or ARMS flip-up sights, SST, Magpul ACS 6-position collapsible stock, nickel plated 4 1/2 lb. single stage trigger, hammer, bolt, and carrier, 10 and 26 shot mag., includes black soft tactical case.

MSR $1,595	$1,350	$1,200	$1,075	$950	$815	$700	$575	

AMBI GEN 2 SIDE CHARGING – 5.56 NATO cal., 16 in. match grade free-floating medium contour stainless barrel, 30 shot Magpul mag., forged Mil-Spec lower and custom billet aluminum ambidextrous upper receiver, ambidextrous side charging handles, safety, and mag. release, nickel plated trigger, hammer, bolt, and carrier, Midwest Industries Gen 2 forend, Arms flip-up front and rear sights, Magpul ACS 6-pos. collapsible stock, includes black soft tactical case. New 2015.

MSR $1,495		$1,275	$1,125	$1,025	$875	$750	$625	$525

BATTLESTORM – 5.56 NATO cal., GIO, 16 in. free floated M4 profile barrel, free float lightweight Spectre length quad rail handguard with ladder rail covers and end cap, low profile gas block, front and rear RTS sights, Primary Arms 1-4x24 optical red dot scope, ergonomic pistol grip, Battle Blades knife and scabbard, winter trigger guard, nickel plated single stage trigger, hammer, bolt and carrier, Battlelink 6-position collapsible stock with storage, 30 shot Magpul mag., includes cleaning kit and black soft tactical case.

MSR $1,895		$1,625	$1,425	$1,200	$1,075	$925	$795	$650

BIG BORE 50 – .50 cal., 16 or 18 in. barrel, nickel plated trigger, hammer, bolt, and carrier, Midwest Industries Gen 2 free float forend, Arms flip-up front and rear sights, side charging billet upper and Mil-Spec lower receivers, Ace skeleton stock, Stark pistol grip with integrated Winter trigger guard, includes black soft tactical case. New 2015.

MSR $1,895		$1,625	$1,425	$1,200	$1,075	$925	$795	$650

DEVASTATOR – 5.56 NATO cal., GIO, 16 in. M4 profile barrel, free float carbine length quad rail handguard with ladder rail covers and end cap, YHM flip-up front sight gas block, rear flip-up sights, single stage trigger, 6-position collapsible stock, 30 shot Mapgul mag., forged upper and lower receivers, includes cleaning kit and black soft tactical case. Disc. 2014.

	$825	$725	$625	$565	$475	$400	$300	$975

DOMINATOR – 5.56 NATO cal., GIO, 18 in. free floated medium profile stainless barrel, low profile gas block, tactical free float rail or YHM custom rail, forged lower receiver, standard M3/M4 forged upper receiver, ergonomic grip, Magpul ACS 6-position collapsible stock, front and rear Magpul or ARMS polymer sights, Primary Arms M3 style red dot scope with cantilever mount, single point sling egg plate, single stage nickel plated trigger, hammer, and bolt carrier, 30 shot Magpul mag., includes black soft tactical case. Disc. 2014.

	$1,185	$1,035	$890	$800	$650	$550	$425	$1,395

HUNTER – 6.5 Grendel cal., 18 or 20 in. match grade free-floating medium contour stainless barrel, 10 or 26 shot mag., billet side charging upper receiver, Midwest Industries Gen 2 free float rail, nickel plated trigger, hammer, bolt, and carrier, Ace skeleton stock, Cerakote coating in 3-color camo, includes black soft tactical case. New 2015.

MSR $1,895		$1,625	$1,425	$1,200	$1,075	$925	$795	$650

MSR	100%	98%	95%	90%	80%	70%	60%	Last MSR

LIBERATOR – 5.56 NATO cal., GIO, 16 in. free floated M4 profile barrel, free float lightweight Spectre length quad rail handguard with ladder rail covers and end cap, low profile gas block, front and rear Magpul or ARMS flip-up polymer sights, forged Mil-Spec upper and lower receivers, Primary Arms red dot with cantilever mount, ergonomic pistol grip, upgraded 6-position collapsible stock, 30 shot Magpul mag., nickel plated single stage trigger, hammer, bolt, and carrier, includes black soft tactical case. Disc. 2014.

MSR	100%	98%	95%	90%	80%	70%	60%	Last MSR
	$1,100	$965	$825	$750	$600	$500	$400	$1,295

LRAR DOMINATOR – 5.56 NATO cal., GIO, 18 in. match grade free floated stainless barrel, tactical free float rail, front and rear Magpul or ARMS flip-up sight, Primary Arms M3 red dot with cantilever mount, Magpul ACS 6-position collapsible stock, nickel plated single stage trigger, hammer, bolt, and carrier, 30 shot Magpul mag., ambidextrous upper receiver with fully automatic upward opening ejection port doors, includes black soft tactical case. Disc. 2014.

MSR	100%	98%	95%	90%	80%	70%	60%	Last MSR
	$1,275	$1,115	$955	$865	$700	$600	$475	$1,495

M4 CARBINE – 5.56 NATO cal., GIO, 16 in. M4 barrel, forged lower receiver, A3/A4 forged flat-top upper, rear flip-up sight, forged front sight, A2 grip, M4 6-position collapsible stock, SST, 30 shot Magpul mag.

MSR $775	100%	98%	95%	90%	80%	70%	60%
	$650	$575	$510	$440	$385	$340	$325

ODIN – 5.56 NATO cal., 16 in. M4 profile barrel, 30 shot Magpul mag., Odin free-float forend, Primary Arms red dot with cantilever mount, Arms front and rear flip-up sights, Magpul MOE 6-position collapsible stock, Magpul K-Grip, forged upper and lower receivers, includes black soft tactical case. New 2015.

MSR $1,495	100%	98%	95%	90%	80%	70%	60%
	$1,275	$1,125	$1,025	$875	$750	$625	$525

THOR – 5.56 NATO cal., 16 in. free-floating M4 profile barrel, 30 shot Magpul mag., forged Mil-Spec upper and lower receivers, Arms front and rear flip-up sights, Troy Alpha rail, nickel plated trigger, hammer, bolt, and carrier, Magpul STR stock, Magpul K-Grip, includes black soft tactical case. New 2015.

MSR $1,235	100%	98%	95%	90%	80%	70%	60%
	$1,050	$950	$815	$685	$595	$515	$440

QUALITY PARTS CO./BUSHMASTER

Quality Parts Co. was a division of Bushmaster Firearms, Inc. located in Windham, ME that manufactured AR-15 type rifles and various components and accessories for Bushmaster. Please refer to the Bushmaster Firearms International listing in the B section for current model listings and values.

R SECTION

R GUNS

Current manufacturer, importer, and dealer located in Carpentersville, IL.

R Guns offers a line of AR-15 style rifles and carbines in various configurations, upper and lower receivers, accessories, and related components. Please contact the company directly for more information on its various models, availability, and pricing (see Trademark Index).

RAAC

Current importer located in Scottsburg, IN.

MSR	100%	98%	95%	90%	80%	70%	60%	Last MSR

RIFLES AND SHOTGUNS

Russian American Armory Company is an import company for Molot, located in Russia. Current product/model lines include Vepr. rifles, in addition to a line of bolt action rifles, including the LOS/BAR Series, CM-2 Target rifle, Korshun, and Sobol hunting model. Please check individual heading listings for current information, including U.S. availability and pricing. Please contact the company directly for current offerings (see Trademark Index).

MKA 1919 – 12 ga., 3 in. chamber, AR-15 style, self-adjusting GIO, 18 1/2 in. barrel with three choke tubes, 5 shot box mag., A2 configuration with carry handle and front sight, Picatinny rail, bolt hold open after last round, fixed or adj. synthetic stock, sling swivels, choice of matte black or 100% camo coverage. Mfg. in Turkey.

MSR $700		$650	$575	$525	$475	$435	$400	$375

Add $100 for 100% camo coverage.

Add $500 for flat top receiver and adj. stock.

R.I.P. TACTICAL

Current AR-15 manufacturer located in Utah.

RIFLES: SEMI-AUTO

R.I.P. Tactical builds custom AR-15 rifles to individual customer specifications. Current models include: RIP-BM (base model), RIP-NT (nickel Teflon coated), RIP-DC (camo), RIP-BA (black anodized), RIP-OD (ceramic coated dark green), and the RIP-SBR (short barreled rifle). Base MSR starts at $1,495. Several options are available for each model. Please contact the company directly for options, delivery time, and an individualized price quotation (see Trademark Index).

RND MANUFACTURING

Current manufacturer established in 1978, and located in Longmont, CO. Previously distributed by Mesa Sportsmen's Association, LLC located in Delta, CO. Dealer or consumer direct sales.

PISTOLS: SEMI-AUTO

RND PISTOL – 5.56 NATO cal., AR-15 style, GIO, round shrouded handguard, 7 1/2 in. barrel with muzzle brake, pistol grip, full length vent. Picatinny rail, titanium firing pin, 9 1/2 lbs. New 2010.

MSR $2,000		$1,800	$1,600	$1,350	$1,100	$900	$750	$650

RIFLES: SEMI-AUTO

RND EDGE SERIES – .223 Rem. (RND 400), .300 WSM (RND 1000, new 2003), .300 Ultra (RND 2100, new 2003), .308 Win. (RND 800, new 2010), .338 Lapua Mag. (RND 2000, new 1999), .375 Super Mag. (RND 2600), .408 CheyTac (RND 2500) or 7.62x39mm (disc.) cal., patterned after the AR-15 style, gas impingement operation, 18, 20, 24, or 26 in. barrel,, choice of synthetic (Grade I), built to individual custom order, handmade laminated thumbhole (Grade II, disc. 1998), or custom laminated thumbhole stock with fluted barrel (Grade III, disc. 1998), CNC machined, vented aluminum shroud, many options and accessories available, custom order only, approx. 11 1/2-16 lbs. New 1996.

Add $355 for Grade II (disc. 1998) or $605 for Grade III (disc.).

* **RND 400** – .223 Rem. cal., GIO, AR-15 style, 18-26 in. barrel, CNC machined upper and lower receivers, integral picatinny rail, titanium firing pin, free floating handguard, synthetic A2 style stock, hard black anodized with grey or black finish, 9.5 lbs.

MSR $2,295		$2,000	$1,750	$1,300	$1,050	$850	$750	$650

* **RND 800** – .308 Win./7.62 NATO cal., GPO, AR-15 style, 20-26 in. super match free floating barrel, CNC machined matched upper and lower receivers, left side non-reciprocating charging handle, hard black anodized with black or gray gun coat, integral Picatinny rail, titanium firing pin, modular handguard, adj. stock, 11 lbs. New 2010.

MSR $3,795		$3,400	$2,975	$2,550	$2,310	$1,875	$1,525	$1,200

MSR	100%	98%	95%	90%	80%	70%	60%	Last MSR

* **RND 1000** – .300 Win. Mag. cal., GPO, 20-26 in. Super match free floating barrel, CNC machined matched upper and lower receivers, left sided non-reciprocating charging handle, integral Picatinny rail, RND integrated buffer system, modular handguard, fully adj. stock, single feed double stack mag., hard black anodized with black or gray gun coat finish, 11 lbs. New 2003.

| MSR $2,295 | $2,000 | $1,750 | $1,300 | $1,050 | $850 | $750 | $650 | |

* **RND 2000** – .338 Lapua Mag. cal., GPO, AR-15 style, 20-26 in. Super match free floating barrel, CNC machined matched upper and lower receivers, left sided non-reciprocating charging handle, integral Picatinny rail, single feed double stack mag., RND integrated buffer system, modular handguard, fully adj. stock, hard black anodized with black or gray gun coat finish, 14 lbs. New 1999.

| MSR $4,795 | $4,325 | $3,785 | $3,250 | $2,950 | $2,375 | $1,950 | $1,525 | |

»**RND 2100** – .300 Rem. Ultra Mag. cal., otherwise similar to RND 2000. New 2003.

| MSR $4,795 | $4,325 | $3,785 | $3,250 | $2,950 | $2,375 | $1,950 | $1,525 | |

»**RND 2500** – .408 CheyTac cal., GPO, similar to RND 2000, except features 26 in. Super match free floating barrel, 18 lbs. New 2004.

| MSR $10,500 | $9,450 | $8,275 | $7,100 | $6,425 | $5,200 | $4,250 | $3,325 | |

»**RND 2600** – .375 CheyTac cal., GPO, 20-26 in. Super match free floating barrel, CNC machined matched upper and lower receivers, left sided non-reciprocating charging handle, integral Picatinny rail, single feed double stack mag., RND integrated buffer system, modular handguard, fully adj. stock, hard black anodized with black or gray gun coat finish, 18 lbs.

| MSR $10,500 | $9,450 | $8,275 | $7,100 | $6,425 | $5,200 | $4,250 | $3,325 | |

* **RND 3000** – .50 BMG cal., GPO, 26 in. Super match barrel with muzzle brake, full length integrated Picatinny rail, fully adj. stock, double stack mag., includes optics and scope, black or various camo colors, includes bipod, 28 lbs.

| MSR $11,500 | $10,350 | $9,250 | $8,250 | $7,500 | $6,750 | $6,000 | $5,250 | |

»**RND 3100** – .416 Rem. Mag. cal., otherwise similar to RND 3000. Mfg. 2012 only.

| | $10,350 | $9,250 | $8,250 | $7,500 | $6,750 | $6,000 | $5,250 | $11,500 |

RPB INDUSTRIES

Previous company located in Avondale, GA. RPB Industries' guns were made by Masterpiece Arms.

CARBINES: SEMI-AUTO

RPB CARBINE – .45 ACP cal., closed bolt blowback action, 16 1/4 in. barrel, fixed skeletonized stock and forearm pistol grip, accepts M-3 military submachine gun mags., black finish, 9 1/2 lbs. Mfg. 2000-2004.

| | $450 | $375 | $325 | $285 | $260 | $235 | $210 | |

Add $75 for Deluxe Model with EZ cocker and installed scope mount.

RADICAL FIREARMS, LLC

Current manufacturer and retail operation located in Stafford, TX.

Radical Firearms manufactures custom built AR-15s, AR-10s, bolt guns, and silencers in their fully tooled and operational gunsmithing facility.

RIFLES: SEMI-AUTO

RF-10 BILLET RIFLE (HUNTER LINE) – .308 Win. or 6.5 Creedmoor cal., 18 or 24 in. barrel, stainless steel Melonite custom brake, right or left-hand action, Mil-Spec trigger and mag. release, MBA-2 "Skullaton" stock, Ergo Suregrip, billet upper and lower matching set, Mil-Spec bolt catch, continuous top Picatinny rail, free floating rail system with KeyMod slots, 9 lbs. 3 oz.

| MSR $1,300 | $1,100 | $995 | $875 | $735 | $650 | $550 | $465 | |

RF .300 BLACKOUT COMPLETE RIFLE – .300 AAC Blackout cal., GIO, 16 in. HBAR Melonite barrel, A2 flash hider, M4 collapsible stock, A2 grip, low profile micro gas block, stainless pistol length gas tube, 10 in. free float FGS (Forward Guard Shield) rail or 12 in. free float FQR (First-Gen Quad) rail, Picatinny top or quad rails, forged upper and lower receivers.

| MSR $560 | $495 | $435 | $365 | $315 | $275 | $250 | $230 | |

Add $90 for 12 in. free float FQR rail.

RF 6.8 SPC COMPLETE RIFLE – 6.8 SPC II cal., 15 in. FHR rail. New 2016.

| MSR $800 | $685 | $615 | $550 | $475 | $420 | $365 | $335 | |

RF 5.56 SOCOM COMPLETE RIFLE – 5.56 NATO cal., GIO, 16 in. SOCOM barrel, A2 flash hider, M4 feed ramps, M4 collapsible stock, Ergo Suregrip, stainless carbine length gas system, low profile micro gas block, forged upper and lower receivers, Picatinny top rail, 12 in. free float FGS round rail.

| MSR $560 | $495 | $435 | $365 | $315 | $275 | $250 | $230 | |

MSR	100%	98%	95%	90%	80%	70%	60%	Last MSR

RF 7.62x39 COMPLETE RIFLE – 7.62x39 cal., GIO, 16 in. HBAR Melonite barrel, A2 flash hider, M4 or A2 collapsible stock, A2 grip, low profile micro gas block, stainless carbine length gas system, forged upper and lower receiver, Picatinny top rail, 12 in. free float FGS or FQR rail.

MSR $560 $495 $435 $365 $315 $275 $250 $230

Add $90 for A2 collapsible stock and 12 in. FQR rail.

RF 5.56 M4 COMPLETE RIFLE – 5.56 NATO cal., GIO, 16 in. M4 Melonite barrel, A2 flash hider, M4 feed ramps, M4 collapsible stock, Ergo Suregrip or A2 grip, stainless carbine length gas system, low profile micro gas block, forged upper and lower receivers, Picatinny top rail, 12 in. free float FGS round rail or FQR (First-Gen Quad) rail.

MSR $560 $495 $435 $365 $315 $275 $250 $230

Add $90 for 12 in. FQR rail and A2 grip.

RF COMPLETE RIFLE WITH 15 IN. FHR – 5.56 NATO or .300 AAC Blackout cal., 15 in. FHR rail. New 2016.

MSR $650 $575 $500 $435 $365 $325 $280 $265

RF 458 SOCOM COMPLETE RIFLE – .458 SOCOM cal., GIO, 16 in. HBAR Melonite barrel, Panzer brake, Luth-AR MBA-2 "Skullaton" stock, Ergo Suregrip, low profile micro gas block, stainless carbine length gas system, 12 in. free float FHR (First-Gen Hybrid Rail), quad Picatinny rails, forged upper and lower receiver.

MSR $1,000 $850 $725 $650 $585 $515 $450 $395

RF 6.5 GRENDEL COMPLETE RIFLE – 6.5 Grendel cal., 20 or 24 in. stainless steel match grade barrel, custom stainless Pepper Pot brake, Luth-AR modular MBA-1 stock, Mil-Spec grip, low profile gas block, 15 in. free float hybrid rail, M4 forged upper and lower receiver, standard charging handle.

MSR $1,030 $865 $725 $650 $585 $515 $450 $395

PISTOLS: SEMI-AUTO

RF COMPLETE AR PISTOL – 5.56 NATO or .300 AAC Blackout cal., 10 1/2 in. Melonite treated chrome moly barrel, extractor booster pre-installed, carbine length gas system, forged Mil-Spec upper receiver, M4 feed ramps, 10 in. FQR (First-Gen Quad Rail), pistol buffer assembly.

MSR $580 $520 $440 $365 $315 $275 $250 $230

RF COMPLETE AR PISTOL WITH SIG BRACE – 5.56 NATO or .300 AAC Blackout cal., 10 1/2 in. Melonite treated chrome moly barrel, pistol length gas system, extractor booster pre-installed, forged upper and lower receivers with M4 feed ramps, 10 in. FGS (Forward Guard Shield) round rail, pistol buffer assembly, Sig Tac arm brace.

MSR $650 $575 $500 $435 $365 $325 $280 $265

RF ROUND RAIL AR PISTOL – 5.56 NATO or 7.62x39 cal., 10 1/2 in. Melonite treated chrome moly barrel, full-length free float handguard, 10 in. FGS round rail.

MSR $550 $495 $435 $365 $315 $275 $250 $230

RF AR PISTOL WITH QUAD RAIL – .300 AAC Blackout cal., 10 1/2 in. Melonite treated chrome moly barrel, full-length free float handguard, 10 in. FGS round rail, Sig Tac arm brace.

MSR $680 $590 $500 $435 $365 $325 $280 $265

RADOM

Current trademark manufactured by Fabryka Broni, Lucznik - Radom Sp. z o.o., located in Radom, Poland. Currently imported on a limited basis by I.O., Inc., located in Monroe, NC. Previously manufactured 1925-1945 by the Polish Arsenal located in Radom, Poland & Steyr, Austria. Post WWII also manufactured by Z.M. Lucznik (Radom Factory) in Radom, Poland. Recent importation was by Dalvar of U.S.A., located in Seligman, AZ. Previously located in Richardson, TX and Henderson, NV.

RIFLES: SEMI-AUTO

Fabryka Broni Lucznik currently manufactures a variety of semi-auto rifles and carbines designed after the Model 96 Beryl rifle. Please contact the importer directly for U.S. availability and pricing (see Trademark Index).

RAMO DEFENSE SYSTEMS

Previous rifle manufacturer 1999-2003 and located in Nashville, TN.

RIFLES: BOLT ACTION

TACTICAL .308 – .308 Win. cal., Rem. M-700 long action, match grade stainless steel barrel, skeletonized black synthetic stock with cheekpad, matte black metal finish, 4 shot mag., 16 lbs. Mfg. 1999-2003.

$2,495 $2,100 $1,850 $1,600 $1,400 $1,200 $995   *$2,495*

MSR	100%	98%	95%	90%	80%	70%	60%	Last MSR

M91/M91A2 – .308 Win. or .300 Win. Mag. cal., Rem. M-700 long action, black Kevlar and fiberglass stock, matte black metal finish, 4 shot mag., 14 lbs. Mfg. 1999-2003.

	$2,695	$2,250	$1,950	$1,675	$1,475	$1,250	$995	$2,695

Add $200 for .300 Win. Mag. cal.

M600 SINGLE SHOT – .50 BMG cal., single shot, twin tube skeletonized stock with pistol grip and cheekpiece, 32 in. barrel with fins at breech and muzzle brake, 23 lbs. Mfg. 1999-2003.

	$4,195	$3,700	$3,200	$2,750	$2,250	$1,950	$1,675	$4,195

M650 REPEATER – .50 BMG cal., repeater action with 6 shot detachable rotary mag., stock and barrel (30 in.) similar to M600, approx. 30 lbs. Mfg. 1999-2003.

	$6,395	$5,750	$5,150	$4,500	$3,750	$3,000	$2,250	$6,395

RANGEMASTER PRECISION ARMS (RPA INTERNATIONAL LTD.)

Current rifle manufacturer located in Kent, England. Currently imported since 2014 by Accurate-Mag, located in Monroe, CT.

Company name changed in mid-2013 from RPA International Ltd. to Rangemaster Precision Arms.

RIFLES: BOLT ACTION LISTINGS

Rangemaster Precision Arms manufactures high quality bolt action rifles, including a tactical long range sniper model, the Rangemaster RM 7.62 Stubby (£4,175 MSR), Rangemaster RM 7.62 (£4,175 MSR), Rangemaster 338 (£4,430 MSR), and the Rangemaster 50 (£5,306 MSR). The Rangemaster Series includes a folding stock, stainless steel barrel and muzzle brake, Picatinny rails and tactical bipod. The Interceptor is available in a single shot (£2,533 MSR) and a Repeater (£2,813 MSR) version. The Hunter rifle comes with or w/o a thumbhole stock (£2,723 base MSR), Highland Stalker (£2,758 MSR), Woodland Stalker (£2,723 MSR). The Target Rifle Series includes the Elite Single Shot (£2,550 MSR), and the Ranger (£2,398 MSR). In mid-2015, RPA plans to introduce the Ultra tactical rifle (POR). All pricing does not include VAT. Additionally, the company makes custom rifles and actions. Please contact the company directly for complete pricing, U.S. availability and options (see Trademark Index).

RASHEED (RASHID)

Previous Egyptian military rifle mfg. circa mid-1960s.

RIFLES: SEMI-AUTO

RASHEED – 7.62x39mm cal., gas operated mechanism with tilting bolt, 20 1/2 in. barrel with folding bayonet, bolt cocking is by separate bolt handle installed on right side of receiver, detachable 10 shot mag., open type sights, hardwood stock with vent. forend, approx. 8,000 mfg. circa mid-1960s.

	$795	$700	$600	$500	$400	$300	$250	

RED ROCK ARMS

Current manufacturer established April 2003 and located in Mesa, AZ. During late 2006, the company name was changed from Bobcat Weapons, Inc. to Red Rock Arms.

PISTOLS: SEMI-AUTO

BWA5 FSA – 9mm Para. cal., H&K tactical design, roller lock delayed blowback action, 8.9 in. stainless steel barrel, black Duracoat finished stock, pistol grip, and forearm, 10, 30, or 40 shot mag., approx. 5.3 lbs. Mfg. 2007-2008.

	$1,525	$1,350	$1,125	$900	$775	$650	$550	$1,700

RIFLES: SEMI-AUTO

ATR-1 CARBINE – .223 Rem. cal., H&K tactical design, 16 1/4 in. barrel, adj. front and rear sight, black furniture, 30 shot AR-15 style mag., available with or w/o flash suppressor, 8 lbs. New 2007.

MSR $1,400	$1,250	$1,075	$925	$825	$750	$650	$575	

BW5 FSA – 9mm Para. cal., H&K tactical design, stamped steel lower receiver, roller lock delayed blowback action, 16 1/2 in. stainless steel barrel (3-lug barrel and 9 in. fake suppressor), black Duracoat finished stock, pistol grip, and forearm, 10, 30, or 40 shot mag., approx. 6.7 lbs. Mfg. 2006-2008.

	$1,525	$1,350	$1,125	$900	$775	$650	$550	$1,700

RED X ARMS

Current semi-auto rifle manufacturer located in central MN.

PISTOLS: SEMI-AUTO

RXA15 MOE PISTOL – 5.56 NATO cal., 7 1/2 in. stainless steel barrel with A2 compensator, 30 shot PMag., forged aluminum lower receiver and flat-top upper with M4 feed ramps, hardcoat black anodized finish, free-floating carbine length aluminum RSA quad rail handguard, low profile gas block, alum. charging handle, KAK Industries pistol tube

MSR	100%	98%	95%	90%	80%	70%	60%	Last MSR

with Sig brace, Magpul MOE grip and trigger guard, Black or FDE finish, includes two ladder rail covers and soft tactical case with mag. pouches.

| MSR $999 | $850 | $725 | $650 | $585 | $515 | $450 | $395 | |

RIFLES: SEMI-AUTO

RXA15 3G RIFLE – 5.56 NATO cal., 18 in. stainless steel heavy barrel with RXA SS tactical Gill muzzle brake, mid-length gas system with low profile gas block, T6 aluminum lower and upper receiver, 15 in. Samson Evolution rail system, BCM Mod 4 charging handle, Rock River 2-stage National Match trigger, Mil-Spec lower parts kit with enhanced trigger guard and MFT G2 grip, Magpul UBR buttstock, hardcoat anodized Class III black finish, includes one 30 shot round window PMag. and 42 in. soft tactical case.

| MSR $1,200 | $1,025 | $925 | $800 | $685 | $595 | $515 | $440 | |

RXA 300 BLACKOUT HBAR RIFLE – .300 AAC Blackout cal., 16 in. HBAR button rifled barrel with A2 compensator and Nitride coating, 30 shot PMag., T6 forged aluminum lower and flat-top upper receiver, M4 feed ramps, free-floating carbine length RXA modular alum. handguard, top rail gas block, M16 bolt carrier group, Mil-Spec alum. charging handle, 6-pos. adj. stock, hardcoat black anodized finish, includes 38 in. soft tactical case with mag. pouches.

| MSR $999 | $850 | $725 | $650 | $585 | $515 | $450 | $395 | |

RXA15 STAINLESS HBAR MOD RIFLE – 5.56 NATO cal., 16 in. stainless steel HBAR barrel with A2 compensator, carbine gas system, T6 forged aluminum lower and upper receiver with M4 feed ramps, carbine length RXA modular handguard, top rail gas block, M16 bolt carrier group, Mil-Spec charging handle, 6-pos. collapsible stock, hardcoat anodized black finish, includes one 30 shot round Pmag. and 38 in. soft tactical case.

| MSR $849 | $725 | $650 | $580 | $515 | $450 | $385 | $340 | |

RXA15 STAINLESS M4 MOE RIFLE – 5.56 NATO cal., 16 in. stainless steel M4 barrel with stainless steel A2 compensator, carbine gas system, T6 forged aluminum lower and upper receiver, M4 feed ramps, free-floating carbine length RXA alum. quad rail handguard, top rail gas block, M16 bolt carrier group, Mil-Spec alum. charging handle, Magpul MOE grip and trigger guard, Magpul MOE 6-pos. collapsible stock, Black, FDE, or OD Green finish, includes one 30 shot PMag., two ladder rail covers, and 38 in. soft tactical case with mag. pouches.

| MSR $1,049 | $885 | $750 | $665 | $585 | $515 | $450 | $395 | |

X-TREME 16 TACTICAL SS – 5.56 NATO cal., GIO, 16 in. button rifled stainless steel heavy H-Bar contour barrel, A2 birdcage muzzle brake, A3 aluminum flat-top upper and lower receiver, forward assist, dust cover, black hardcoat anodized finish, six position adj. M4 stock with sling hook, chrome lined bolt carrier and staked gas key, chrome plated firing pin, aluminum charging handle, 30 shot Magpul mag., two-piece quad rail aluminum handguard, carbine length gas tube, optional sights and bipod. Disc. 2014.

| | $650 | $575 | $525 | $475 | $450 | $425 | $395 | $725 |

GARY REEDER CUSTOM GUNS

Current custom manufacturer located in Flagstaff, AZ. Consumer direct sales.

HANDGUNS

For over 35 years, Gary Reeder has specialized in customizing revolvers from various manufacturers, and is now building several series of custom revolvers on his own frames, in addition to customizing customer supplied handguns. Gary also manufactures several series of Model 1911 style pistols built to customers specifications in .45 ACP and 10mm. Reeder currently produces well over 60 different series of custom hunting handguns, cowboy guns, custom 1911s, and large caliber hunting rifles. For more information on his extensive range of custom guns, please contact the factory directly (see Trademark Index).

REGENT

Current trademark of semi-auto pistols manufactured by Trabzon Gun Industry Corp., located in Turkey, imported by Umarex USA, Inc.

PISTOLS: SEMI-AUTO

R350CR – .45 ACP cal., 4 in. barrel, 7 shot mag., lower Picatinny rail, bobbed hammer and skeletonized trigger, checkered front grip strap, double diamond checkered Hogue synthetic grips, 35 oz. New 2012.

| MSR $499 | $425 | $375 | $350 | $325 | $300 | $275 | $250 | |

REMINGTON ARMS COMPANY, INC.

Current manufacturer and trademark established in 1816, with factories currently located in Ilion, NY, Lonoke, AR, Mayfield, KY, and Huntsville, AL.

Founded by Eliphalet Remington II and originally located in Litchfield, Herkimer County, NY circa 1816-1828. Remington established a factory in Ilion, NY next to the Erie Canal in 1828, and together with his sons Philo, Samuel, and Eliphalet III pioneered many improvements in firearms manufacture. Corporate offices were moved to Madison, NC in 1996. DuPont

MSR	100%	98%	95%	90%	80%	70%	60%	Last MSR

owned a controlling interest in Remington from 1933-1993, when the company was sold to Clayton, Dubilier & Rice, a New York City based finance company. The Mayfield, KY plant opened in 1997. On May 31st, 2007, a controlling interest in the company was sold to Cerberus Capital. Currently, Remington employs 2,500 workers in the U.S., including 1,000 in its Ilion, NY plant alone. Recently, Remington has acquired Harrington & Richardson Firearms (H & R), and Marlin Firearms. The company has moved manufacturing to their Remington plant in Ilion, New York. Remington management has every intention of keeping all three product identities separate.

During 2013, Remington made significant improvements, including the expansion of its ammunition facility, growth of its firearms manufacturing capacity, secured some competitive military and law enforcement contracts, and introduced a series of new products including the Ultimate Defense Handgun Ammunition and Model 783 bolt action rifle.

In February of 2014, Remington announced a major expansion with new manufacturing to occur at the old Chrylser building in Huntsville, AL. The company has indicated that more than 2,000 new jobs will be created in the next 10 years.

For recent information on long guns imported by Spartan Gun Works, a Remington subsidiary, please refer to the Spartan Gun Works listing in the S section.

PISTOLS: SEMI-AUTO, POST-WWII PRODUCTION

MODEL 1911 R1 CARRY – .45 ACP cal., 5 in. stainless steel match grade barrel and bushing, one 7 shot and one 8 shot mag., steel construction, bobbed hammer, skeletonized aluminum trigger, Novak low profile sights with Tritium front sight, partially checkered Cocobolo grips, ambidextrous safety, beavertail grip safety, satin black oxide finish, 38 1/2 oz. New 2013.

MSR $1,067	$925	$800	$700	$600	$550	$495	$450	

MODEL 1911 R1 ENHANCED – 9mm Para. (new 2014) or .45 ACP cal., SA, steel construction with blued finish, 5 in. barrel, 8 or 9 (9mm Para.) shot mag., front and rear slide serrations, skeletonized trigger, bobbed hammer, checkered black laminate grips, low profile rear sight and fiber optic front sight, 40 oz. New 2013.

MSR $903	$795	$700	$600	$550	$500	$450	$400	

Add $226 for Crimson Trace laser sight (.45 ACP cal. only), new 2014.

* **Model 1911 R1 Enhanced Stainless** – .45 ACP cal., 5 in. barrel, all stainless steel construction, features front and rear slide serrations, skeletonized trigger, bobbed hammer, checkered black laminate grips, 8 shot mag., low profile rear sight and fiber optic front sight, 40 oz. New 2013.

MSR $990	$850	$750	$650	$595	$475	$400	$325	

* **Model 1911 R1 Enhanced Threaded Barrel** – .45 ACP cal., features 5 3/4 in. threaded stainless steel barrel, all steel construction with blue finish, 8 shot mag., twin slide serrations, checkered black laminate grips, skeletonized trigger, bobbed hammer, 40 oz. New 2013.

MSR $959	$825	$725	$625	$550	$450	$375	$300	

RIFLES: SEMI-AUTO - CENTERFIRE

The models have been listed in numerical sequence for quick reference.

Remington also manufactures models R4, R5, R10, R11, and ACR for military and law enforcement only. These models are not covered in this text.

* **Model 7400 SP (Special Purpose)** – .270 Win. or .30-06 cal., similar to Model 7400, except has non-reflective matte finish on both wood and metalwork. Mfg. 1993-94.

	$435	$370	$300	$255	$230	$210	$185	$524

* **Model 7400 Weathermaster** – .270 Win. or .30-06 cal., features matte nickel plated receiver, barrel, and magazine, black synthetic stock and forearm, 22 in. barrel with open sights, 7 1/2 lbs. Mfg. 2003-2004.

	$495	$400	$315	$255	$230	$210	$185	$624

* **Model 7400 Synthetic** – same cals. as Model 7400, features black fiberglass reinforced synthetic stock and forend, matte black metal finish, 22 in. barrel only. Mfg. 1998-2006.

	$465	$385	$330	$285	$265	$240	$220	$589

» **Model 7400 Synthetic Carbine** – .30-06 cal., similar to Model 7400 Synthetic, except has 18 1/2 in. barrel. 7 1/4 lbs. Mfg. 1998-2006.

	$465	$385	$330	$285	$265	$240	$220	$589

MODEL R-15 – .450 Bushmaster cal., GIO, 18 in. fluted barrel, 4 shot detachable mag., receiver length Picatinny rail, ergonimic pistol grip, fixed stock, Mossy Oak Break-up camo coverage, approx. 7 3/4 lbs. Mfg. 2010-2015.

	$1,375	$1,200	$1,075	$925	$825	$725	$600	$1,499

MODEL R-15 HUNTER – .30 Rem. AR cal., GIO, 22 in. fluted barrel, receiver length Picatinny rail, ergonomic pistol grip, 4 shot detachable mag., 100% Realtree AP HD camo coverage, approx. 7 3/4 lbs. Mfg. 2009-2015.

	$1,150	$1,000	$900	$775	$700	$575	$450	$1,229

MSR	100%	98%	95%	90%	80%	70%	60%	Last MSR

MODEL R-15 VTR (VARMINT TARGET RIFLE) PREDATOR

MODEL R-15 VTR (VARMINT TARGET RIFLE) PREDATOR – .204 Ruger (disc. 2009) or .223 Rem. cal., GIO, 18 (carbine, .204 Ruger disc. 2009) or 22 in. free floating chrome moly fluted barrel, fixed or telestock (Carbine CS) with pistol grip, 5 shot fixed (new 2012, .223 Rem. cal. only) or detachable mag. (compatible with AR-15 style mags.), R-15 marked on magwell, single stage trigger, flat-top receiver with Picatinny rail, no sights, round vent. forearm, 100% Advantage Max-1 HD camo coverage except for barrel, includes lockable hard case, mfg. by Bushmaster in Windham, ME 2008-2011, and in Ilion, NY beginning 2011, 6 3/4 - 7 3/4 lbs. Mfg. 2008-2013.

	100%	98%	95%	90%	80%	70%	60%	Last MSR
	$1,150	$1,000	$900	$775	$700	$625	$550	*$1,327*

* **Model R-15 VTR Stainless** – .223 Rem. cal., 24 in. stainless triangular VTR barrel, OD Green upper and lower receiver, Advantage Max-1 HD camo finish on fixed stock, pistol grip, and tubed forearm, 7 3/4 lbs. New 2009.

MSR $1,299	$1,200	$1,050	$950	$800	$725	$600	$475	

* **Model R-15 VTR Thumbhole** – .223 Rem. cal., similar to VTR Stainless, except has 24 in. fluted barrel, OD Green camo thumbhole stock. Mfg. 2009-2010.

	$1,275	$1,125	$1,000	$900	$800	$700	$625	*$1,470*

* **Model R-15 VTR Byron South Signature Edition** – .223 Rem. cal., GIO, 18 in. barrel, Advantage Max-1 HD camo pistol grip stock. Mfg. mid-2008-2011.

	$1,625	$1,400	$1,225	$1,050	$900	$800	$700	*$1,845*

* **Model R-15 VTR Predator Carbine** – .223 Rem. cal., GIO, 18 (disc. 2013) or 22 in. free floating button rifled fluted barrel with recessed hunting crown, 5 shot mag., single stage trigger, receiver length Picatinny rail, ergonomic pistol grip, fixed or collapsible (CS, disc. 2013) synthetic stock, Advantage Max-1 HD camo coverage on stock, receiver, and forearm furniture, 6 3/4-7 3/4 lbs.

MSR $1,199	$1,150	$1,000	$900	$775	$700	$625	$550	

* **Model R-15 VTR Predator Magpul MOE** – .223 Rem. cal., GIO, 16, 18 (disc. 2015), or 22 in. fluted barrel with AAC Brakeout muzzle brake, wrap around rubber overmolding on Magpul grip, Magpul trigger guard, Magpul MOE fixed or adj. stock, 5 shot mag., two-stage match trigger, Mossy Oak Brush camo coverage on stock, receiver, and forearm furniture, 6 3/4-7 3/4 lbs.

MSR $1,199	$1,125	$995	$900	$775	$700	$625	$550	

MODEL R-25

MODEL R-25 – .243 Win., 7mm-08 Rem., or .308 Win. cal., GIO, 20 in. free floating fluted chrome moly barrel, single-stage trigger, ergonomic pistol grip fixed stock with 100% Mossy Oak Treestand camo coverage, front and rear sling swivels, 4 shot fixed (.308 Win. cal. only, new 2012) or detachable mag., R-25 marked on magwell, includes hard case, 7 3/4 lbs. Mfg. 2009-2014.

	$1,495	$1,225	$1,075	$950	$850	$750	$650	*$1,697*

MODEL R-25 GII

MODEL R-25 GII – .243 Win. (disc. 2015), .260 Rem. (disc. 2015), .308 Win./7.62 NATO, or 7mm-08 Rem. (disc. 2015) cal., AR-15 style, 20 in. fluted stainless barrel, 4 shot mag., vented carbon fiber free-float tube, forged anodized upper and lower receivers, improved extractor, steel feed ramp, dual ejectors, new Remington Hunter stock with SuperCell recoil pad, Hogue rubber pistol grip, single stage trigger, receiver length Picatinny rail, Mossy Oak Infinity Camo finish, 7 5/8 lbs. New 2015.

MSR $1,697	$1,495	$1,225	$1,075	$950	$850	$750	$650	

RIFLES: SLIDE ACTION, CENTERFIRE

* **Model 7600P Patrol Rifle** – .308 Win. cal., 16 1/2 in. barrel, synthetic stock, parkerized finish, Wilson Combat ghost ring sights, designed for police/law enforcement only.

Remington does not publish consumer retail pricing for this police/law enforcement model. Secondary prices for this model will be slightly higher than for current pricing on the Model 7600 Synthetic.

* **Model 7600 Synthetic** – .243 Win., .270 Win., .280 Rem. (mfg. 1998-2000), .30-06, or .308 Win. cal., 22 in. barrel only, features black fiberglass reinforced synthetic stock and forend, matte black metal finish, SuperCell recoil pad became standard 2011, 7 1/2 lbs. New 1998.

MSR $771	$610	$475	$385	$315	$265	$240	$225	

During 2007, Grice offered 500 Model 7600 QWAC (Quick Woods Action Carbine) in .308 Win. cal. with 18 1/2 in. barrels, Realtree AP camo synthetic stocks and fiber optic front and rear sights.

» **Model 7600 Synthetic Carbine** – .30-06 cal., similar to Model 7600 Synthetic, except has 18 1/2 in. barrel, SuperCell recoil pad became standard in 2011, 7 1/4 lbs. New 1998.

MSR $771	$610	$475	$385	$315	$265	$240	$225	

MODEL 7615

MODEL 7615 – .223 Rem., 10 shot AR-15 compatible detachable box mag., accepts AR-15 and M16 style magazines, 16 1/2 (tactical model with pistol grip and non-collapsible tube stock and Knoxx Special Ops NRS recoil suppressor), 18 1/2 (ranch rifle, walnut stock and forearm), or 22 (camo hunter, 100% Mossy Oak Brush camo coverage) in. barrel w/o sights, synthetic or walnut (ranch carbine) stock and forearm, drilled and tapped, approx. 7 lbs. Mfg. 2007-2008, mfg. in Ilion, NY.

	$790	$685	$575	$500	$450	$400	$350	*$955*

Add $54 for Camo Hunter with 100% camo coverage.

MSR	100%	98%	95%	90%	80%	70%	60%	Last MSR

MODEL 7615P PATROL RIFLE – .223 Rem. cal., 16 1/2 in. barrel, 10 shot or extended mag., synthetic stock, parkerized finish, accepts AR-15 and M16 style magazines, Wilson Combat ghost ring sights, designed for police/law enforcement, 7 lbs.

Remington does not publish consumer retail pricing for this police/law enforcement model. Secondary prices for this model will be slightly higher than for current pricing on the Model 7600 Carbine.

MODEL 7615 SPS – .223 Rem. cal., 16 1/2 in. blue barrel, Picatinny rail, action, slide release and safety based on the Model 870, 10 shot mag, accepts AR-15 and M16 style mags., black pistol grip synthetic stock. Mfg. 2008.

	100%	98%	95%	90%	80%	70%	60%	Last MSR
	$695	$625	$550	$500	$450	$400	$350	*$805*

This model was available through Remington Premier dealers only.

RIFLES: RIMFIRE, SEMI-AUTO

Please note: Model 597 rifles in .17 HMR caliber have been recalled by Remington - please visit Remington's website for more information: www.remington.com, or call 1-800-243-9700, #3.

* ***Model 597 Heavy Barrel*** – .22 LR cal., 16 1/2 in. heavy barrel w/o sights, scope rail installed, OD Green or A-TACS digital camo (disc. 2015) synthetic stock, 5 3/4 lbs. New 2012.

MSR $254	100%	98%	95%	90%	80%	70%	60%	
	$200	$160	$130	$110	$100	$85	$75	

Add $102 for A-TACS Digital camo stock and threaded barrel (disc. 2015).

* ***Model 597 AAC-SD*** – .22 LR cal., 16 1/2 in. threaded barrel with thread protector, accepts AAC and other flash hiders, muzzle brakes, or suppressors, black synthetic stock, includes scope rail, 10 shot mag., no sights, 5 1/2 lbs. Mfg. 2011-2014.

	100%	98%	95%	90%	80%	70%	60%	Last MSR
	$200	$160	$130	$110	$100	$85	$75	*$257*

MODEL 597 VTR (VARMINT TARGET RIFLE) – .22 LR or .22 WMR cal., 16 in. heavy barrel, 10 or 30 shot mag., Picatinny top rail, fixed A2 or Pardus collapsible stock with pistol grip, with (collapsible stock only) or w/o free floating quad rail, choice of matte black or A-TACS digital camo finish, nickel Teflon plating, 5 1/2 lbs. Mfg. 2010-2011.

	100%	98%	95%	90%	80%	70%	60%	Last MSR
	$415	$375	$330	$300	$275	$250	$225	*$465*

Add $26 for .22 WMR cal. (fixed A2 stock only).
Add $153 for A-TACS overmolded stock or free-floating quad rail system.

RIFLES: BOLT ACTION, MODEL 700 & VARIATIONS

Remington also currently manufactures Models M24, M24A2, M24A3, R700, XM2010, and MSR for military and law enforcement only. These models are not covered in this text.

Remington has issued a recall on Model 700s with the X-Mark Pro trigger manufactured between May 1, 2006-April 9, 2014. Please call 1-800-243-9700 to learn more about this recall.

Model 700s manufactured up until the early 1980s featured a riveted extractor, scrolled bolt, and typically nicer wood. These Model 700s if above 95% original condition will command a small premium - the better the condition, the larger the premium (i.e., NIB specimens typically have up to a 10% premium, depending on the caliber and features).

MODEL 700P & VARIATIONS – various cals., long or short action, various barrel lengths, designed for police/law enforcement and military, current configurations include: 700P, 700P TWS (Tactical Weapons System, includes scope, bipod and case), 700P LTR (Light Tactical Rifle), 700P LTR TWS (Light Tactical Rifle/Tactical Weapons System, includes scope, bipod, and case), 700P USR (Urban Sniper Rifle), Model M24/M24A2/M24A3 Sniper Weapon System (combination of Model 700 and Model 40-XB design, with scope, case, and bipod), and from the Remington Custom Shop Model 40-XS Tactical Rifle System, Model 40-XB Tactical, and the Model 40-XS 338 Tactical.

Remington does not publish consumer retail pricing for these police/law enforcement models. Secondary prices for base models w/o scopes and other options will be slightly higher than for current pricing on the Model 700BDL Custom Deluxe. Prices for rifles with scopes and other features will be determined by how much the individual options and accessories add to the base value.

MODEL 700 SPS (SPECIAL PURPOSE SYNTHETIC) – various cals., 24 or 26 in. barrel, black synthetic stock with SuperCell (became standard 2010) or R3 (disc. 2009) recoil pad, X-Mark Pro adj. trigger standard, approx. 7 3/8 lbs. Mfg. in Ilion, NY beginning 2005.

MSR $731	100%	98%	95%	90%	80%	70%	60%	
	$595	$500	$445	$375	$325	$275	$225	

This model is also available in left-hand action at no extra charge - calibers are .270 Win., .30-06, .300 Win. Mag., or 7mm Rem. Mag. (new 2009).

MODEL 700 SPS TACTICAL – .223 Rem. or .308 Win. cal., 20 in. heavy contour barrel, black oxide finish, black synthetic overmolded Hogue stock, X-Mark Pro adj. trigger, matte black finish, 7 1/2 lbs. Mfg. 2008, reintroduced 2010.

MSR $788	100%	98%	95%	90%	80%	70%	60%	
	$650	$550	$495	$425	$375	$325	$275	

This model was available through Remington Premier dealers only in 2008.

MSR	100%	98%	95%	90%	80%	70%	60%	Last MSR

* **Model 700 SPS Tactical AAC-SD** – .223 Rem., .300 AAC Blackout (new 2013) or .308 Win. cal., 16 1/2 (new 2013) or 20 (.308 only) in. heavy barrel with threaded muzzle, Hogue overmold Ghillie Green Pillar bedded stock, X-Mark Pro adj. trigger. New 2011.

| MSR $842 | $695 | $595 | $545 | $475 | $415 | $375 | $315 | |

* **Model 700 SPS Tactical Blackhawk** – .223 Rem. or .308 Win. cal., 20 in. triangular contoured barrel, Bell & Carlson Medalist adj. stock, pistol grip cap, steel floor plate and trigger guard, X-Mark Pro trigger, synthetic stock, tactical bolt handle, 8 1/2 lbs. Mfg. 2012 only.

| | $695 | $595 | $545 | $475 | $415 | $375 | $315 | $850 |

* **Model 700 SPS Tactical Laser Engraved** – .223 Rem. or .308 Win. cal., 16 1/2 in. barrel with threaded muzzle, laser engraved "Tactical" on barrel, carbon receiver and barrel with matte finish, Hogue Ghillie Green synthetic stock, X-Mark Pro externally adj. trigger, 7 1/2 lbs. Mfg. 2013-2014.

| | $675 | $575 | $525 | $450 | $395 | $350 | $295 | $842 |

MODEL 700 TACTICAL – 6.8 SPC cal., 20 in. parkerized barrel, synthetic stock, approx. 9 lbs. Limited availability 2005-2006.

| | $800 | $725 | $650 | $585 | $485 | $400 | $335 | $990 |

MODEL 700 TACTICAL CHASSIS – .300 Win. Mag., .308 Win. Mag., or .338 Lapua Mag. cal., 24 or 26 in. free floating barrel, AAC51-T muzzle brake (.338 Lapua only), Magpul MAG307 PRS fully adj. stock and pistol grip, target tactical bolt handle, ratchet mount muzzle brake, X-Mark Pro externally adj. trigger, ships in hard case. New 2014.

| MSR $2,900 | $2,425 | $2,095 | $1,875 | $1,675 | $1,475 | $1,250 | $1,025 | |

Add $200 for .308 Win. or $600 for .338 Lapua Mag. cal.

MODEL 700 TACTICAL TARGET – .308 Win. cal., 26 in. triangular contour barrel with 5-R tactical rifling, 4 shot mag., steel trigger guard and floor plate, X-Mark Pro adj. trigger, Bell & Carlson Medalist adj. stock, tactical bolt handle, OD Green finish, 11 3/4 lbs. Mfg. 2009-2014.

| | $1,875 | $1,600 | $1,375 | $1,150 | $1,025 | $900 | $700 | $2,138 |

MODEL 700 XCR TACTICAL – .223 Rem. (disc. 2015), .308 Win. or .300 Win. Mag. cal., 3-5 shot mag., 26 in. fluted stainless steel receiver/barrel with black TriNyte PVD coating, tactical Bell & Carlson OD Green with Black web stock with full length aluminum bedding, X-Mark Pro adj. trigger, 9 1/8 lbs. New 2007.

| MSR $1,525 | $1,250 | $1,065 | $935 | $835 | $725 | $585 | $450 | |

* **Model 700 XCR Tactical .338 Lapua** – .338 Lapua cal., 26 in. stainless steel receiver/barrel with black TriNyte PVD coating and AAC muzzle brake, 5 round detachable mag. box, steel trigger guard, steel trigger guard, X-Mark Pro adj. trigger, tactical Bell & Carlson OD Green stock with full length aluminum bedding. New 2011.

| MSR $2,493 | $2,095 | $1,800 | $1,575 | $1,325 | $1,175 | $1,000 | $775 | |

* **Model 700 XCR Tactical Compact** – .223 Rem. (disc. 2015) or .308 Win. cal., compact frame, 20 in. fluted varmint contour barrel, 3-5 shot mag., X-Mark Pro adj. trigger, tactical Bell & Carlson OD Green stock with full length aluminum bedding, 7 1/2 lbs. New 2008.

| MSR $1,525 | $1,250 | $1,065 | $935 | $835 | $725 | $585 | $450 | |

MODEL 2020 SPS TACTICAL – .308 Win. cal., Model 700 action, 26 in. (long range variation, .30-06 cal.) or 20 in. threaded (tactical variation, .308 Win.) barrel, Hogue overmolded green pillar bedded stock, 4 shot internal box magazine, features a TrackingPoint 3x-21x zoom scope with laser range finder, gyroscopes, and camera, programmable optics software adjusts for different ammunition, 10.3 lbs. Mfg. 2014-2015.

| | $4,950 | $4,250 | $3,800 | $3,400 | $3,000 | $2,600 | $2,200 | $5,575 |

Remington claims its 2020 system can make consistent accurate shots out to 500 yards.

RIFLES: BOLT ACTION, MODEL 40X & VARIATIONS

MODEL 40-XB TACTICAL – .308 Win. cal., 27 1/4 in. button rifled fluted stainless barrel, repeater action with adj. 40-X trigger, aluminum bedding block, Teflon coated metal, matte black H-S Precision synthetic tactical stock with vertical pistol grip, 10 1/4 lbs. New 2004.

| MSR $2,992 | $2,550 | $2,200 | $1,800 | $1,450 | $1,200 | $925 | $800 | |

MODEL 40-XB TDR/TIR (TARGET DEPLOYMENT/INTERDICTION RIFLE) – .308 Win. cal., super match stainless steel hand lapped barrel, BCS 1000 (TDR) or H-S PST25 tactical/vertical pistol grip stock (TIR), custom tuned match trigger, one-piece heavy duty steel trigger guard, heavy stainless recoil lug, integral mounting system with #8 screws, Picatinny rail, double pinned bolt handle, muzzle brake, MOA accuracy guaranteed to 600 yards, includes hard carrying case, mfg. by Custom Shop.

These models are POR.

MSR	100%	98%	95%	90%	80%	70%	60%	Last MSR

MODEL 40-XS TACTICAL – .308 Win. or .338 Lapua cal., stainless steel action and barrel, 24 or 26 in. heavy barrel, adj. trigger, non-reflective black polymer coating, titanium bedded McMillan A5 adj. stock, AR type extractor, detachable mag., muzzle brake (.338 Lapua cal.), steel trigger guard and floorplate, Mfg. by Custom Shop.

| MSR $4,400 | $3,675 | $3,050 | $2,500 | $2,000 | $1,650 | $1,350 | $1,175 | |

Add $550 for .338 Lapua cal.

Add $2,731 for Model 40-XS Tactical Weapons System with Harris bipod, Picatinny rail, Leupold Mark IV 3.5-10x40mm long range M1 scope, Turner AWS tactical sling, and military grade hard case.

MODEL 40-X TACTICAL MOD – .308 Win. cal., 20 in. barrel, barreled action colors include flat dark earth (FDE), OD Green, or black. Limited mfg. 2011 only.

| | $4,300 | $3,600 | $3,000 | $2,300 | $1,875 | $1,500 | $1,325 | $4,850 |

MODEL 40-X TDR – .308 Win. cal., repeater action, 20 in. barrel, features various stock/receiver colors, including black, OD Green, tan and Flat Dark Earth. Limited mfg. 2011 only.

| | $2,775 | $2,275 | $1,995 | $1,675 | $1,295 | $1,150 | $935 | $3,170 |

MODEL 40-X TIR – .308 Win. cal., repeater action, 20 in. barrel, stock/slash receiver colors include black/black, black/OD Green, or black/tan. Limited mfg. 2011 only.

| | $3,600 | $3,100 | $2,400 | $1,925 | $1,500 | $1,250 | $1,000 | $4,087 |

MODEL XM3 TACTICAL – .308 Win. cal., choice of steel or titanium action, match grade 18 1/2 in. stainless threaded barrel, Model 40-X action, custom bedded McMillan stock with adjustable LOP, Harris bipod, steel trigger guard, Nightfore NXS 3.5-15x50mm mil-dot scope, guaranteed MOA accuracy to 1,000 yards, Hardigg Storm case with all tools and maintenance equipment, mfg. by Custom Shop. Mfg. 2009-2011.

| | $9,250 | $8,000 | $7,000 | $6,000 | $5,000 | $4,000 | $3,500 | $10,281 |

Add $2,128 for steel action.

SHOTGUNS: SEMI-AUTO, DISC.

MODEL 48A RIOT GUN – 12 ga. only, 20 in. plain barrel.

| | $275 | $220 | $195 | $165 | $150 | $140 | $110 | |

Shotguns: Semi-Auto, Model 1100 & Variations

3 in. shells (12 or 20 ga.) may be shot in Magnum receivers only, regardless of what the barrel markings may indicate (the ejection port is larger in these Magnum models with "M" suffix serialization).

Model 1100 serial numbers on the receiver started with the number 1001. All but the early guns also have a prefix letter. All Model 1100 Remington shotguns were serial numbered in blocks of numbers. Each serial number has a suffix and the following indicates the meaning: V = 12 ga. standard, M = 12 ga. Mag., W = 16 ga., X = 20 ga., N = 20 ga. Mag., K = 20 ga. lightweight, U = 20 ga. lightweight Mag., J = 28 ga., H = .410 bore.

Remington MSRs on extra barrels (3 in. chamber standard) for the following currently manufactured models range from $258-$358 per barrel, depending on configuration.

Add $877 for custom shop Etchen stock and forearm installed on new Model 1100s (mfg. 2000-circa 2010).

MODEL 1100 TACTICAL – 12 ga. only, 3 in. chamber, choice of Speedfeed IV pistol grip or black synthetic stock and forearm, 6 (Speedfeed IV) or 8 (22 in. barrel only) shot mag., 18 (Speedfeed IV with fixed IC choke) or 22 (synthetic with Rem Chokes and HiViz sights) in. VR barrel, OD Green metal finish, R3 recoil pad, approx. 7 1/2 lbs. Disc. 2006.

| | $640 | $575 | $515 | $450 | $400 | $350 | $295 | $759 |

Add $40 for 22 in. barrel.

MODEL 1100 TAC-2/TAC-4 – 12 ga., 2 3/4 in. chamber, 18 (bead sight) or 22 in. VR barrel, Hi-Viz sights, bead blasted black oxide metal finish, black synthetic stock with (Tac-2 with SFIV stock) or w/o (Tac-4) pistol grip, fixed (18 in.) or Rem Chokes, 6 or 8 shot mag., sling swivels, R3 recoil pad, 7 1/2 - 7 3/4 lbs. Mfg. 2007-2015.

| | $795 | $675 | $575 | $500 | $450 | $400 | $350 | $943 |

Add $72 for Tac-4 with 4 shot mag. and 22 in. VR barrel.

Shotguns: Semi-Auto, Model 11-87 & Variations

Model 11-87 barrels will not fit the Model 1100 or Model 11-87 Super Magnum models.

Remington MSRs on extra barrels (3 in. chamber standard) for the following currently manufactured models range from $280-$358 per barrel, depending on configuration.

Many options are available from the Custom Shop, and are POR.

MODEL 11-87 P (POLICE) – 12 ga. only, 18 in. barrel, improved cylinder choke, synthetic stock, parkerized finish, choice of bead or rifle sights, 7 shot extended mag., designed for police/law enforcement.

Remington does not publish consumer retail pricing for this police/law enforcement model. Secondary prices for this model will be slightly higher than for current pricing on the Model 11-87 SPS.

MODEL 11-87 SPS (SPECIAL PURPOSE SYNTHETIC) – see individual sub-models listed below.

MSR		100%	98%	95%	90%	80%	70%	60%	Last MSR

* **Model 11-87 SPS 3 in. Magnum** – similar to Model 11-87 SP 3 in. Mag., except is supplied with black synthetic stock and forearm. Disc. 2004.

		$610	$475	$400	$360	$315	$275	$250	$791

* **Model 11-87 SPS-BG Camo (Special Purpose Synthetic Big Game)** – 12 ga. only, 21 in. plain barrel with rifle sights and Rem Choke. Mfg. 1994 only.

		$555	$425	$350	$290	$250	$225	$200	$692

* **Model 11-87 SP/SPS (Special Purpose Deer Gun)** – 12 ga. only, 3 in. chamber, 21 in. IC or Rem Choke (Model SP, mfg. 1989-2003) or fully rifled (new 1993, became standard 2004) barrel with rifle sights, parkerized metal with matte finished wood or black synthetic (Model SPS, new 1993) stock and forearm, vent. recoil pad, includes camouflaged nylon sling, 7 1/4 lbs. Mfg. 1987-2005.

		$695	$525	$450	$395	$350	$300	$250	$908

Subtract 10% for fixed choke barrel or if w/o cantilever (became standard 2005) scope mount.

Rem Chokes were standard on this model between 1989-1992.

SHOTGUNS: SLIDE ACTION, DISC.

MODEL 17R – 20 ga. only, security configuration, 20 in. cylinder bore barrel, 4 shot mag. Mfg. circa 1920s.

		$325	$265	$235	$200	$150	$120	$100	

MODEL 29R – 12 ga. only, security configuration, 20 in. cylinder bore barrel, 5 shot mag. Mfg. circa 1920s.

		$375	$325	$265	$235	$200	$150	$120	

MODEL 31R "RIOT" GRADE – features shortened barrel.

		$425	$365	$325	$295	$270	$230	$190	

SHOTGUNS: SLIDE ACTION, MODEL 870 & RECENT VARIATIONS

3 in. shells (12 or 20 ga.) may be shot in Magnum receivers only regardless of what the barrel markings may indicate (the ejection port is larger in these Magnum models with M suffix serialization).

Remington has manufactured many limited production runs for various distributors and wholesalers over the years. These shotguns are usually built to a specific configuration (gauge, stock, barrel length, finish, etc.), and are usually available until supplies run out. While these models are not included in this section, pricing in most cases will be similar to the base models from which they were derived.

In April 2009, Remington made its 10 millionth Model 870 slide action shotgun, making it the most manufactured shotgun in firearms history.

Remington also manufactures the Models R870 and MCS for military and law enforcement only. These models are not covered in this text.

Many custom shop options are available, all are POR.

Add 25%-35% for 16 ga. on older mfg., if original condition is 95%+.

Remington MSRs on extra barrels (3 in. chamber is standard, except for Skeet barrel) for the following currently manufactured models range from $140-$300 per barrel, depending on configuration.

MODEL 870 EXPRESS SYNTHETIC TACTICAL (HD, HOME DEFENSE) – 12 or 20 (new 2007, 7 shot mag. only) ga., 18 1/2 in. with fixed cyl. choked barrel with bead front sight, black synthetic stock and forend, black oxide metal finish, 7 1/2 lbs. New 1991.

MSR $420		$350	$295	$250	$225	$200	$185	$170	

Add $23 for 12 ga. 6 shot tube mag.

Add $39 for 20 ga. 7 shot tube mag. (disc. 2015).

Add $180 for ghost ring sights with Rem chokes.

* **Model 870 Express Tactical Knoxx 20 Ga.** – 20 ga., 18 1/2 in. barrel with fixed cyl. choke, 7 shot mag., Knoxx Spec-Ops stock, matte black finish, drilled and tapped, 6 lbs. Mfg. 2009-2015.

		$450	$375	$320	$280	$240	$210	$180	$555

* **Model 870 Express Tactical Camo** – 12 ga., 18 1/2 in. barrel with Rem choke, 6 shot mag. with 2 shot mag. extension, XS Ghost Ring Sight Rail and XSR Ghost Ring sights, Speedfeed IV pistol grip synthetic stock with A-TACS camo coverage, SuperCell recoil pad, 7 1/2 lbs. Mfg. 2010-2015.

		$585	$485	$435	$380	$325	$275	$225	$720

* **Model 870 Express Specialty** – 12 or 20 ga., 18 in. cylinder bore or Rem Choke barrel, folding or Knoxx Spec-Ops pistol grip stock, 2 or 7 shot mag extension. Mfg. 2008.

		$365	$315	$270	$235	$200	$180	$160	$452

Add $27 for 2 shot mag. extension with Knoxx Spec-Ops stock.

Add $53 for synthetic folding stock with 7 shot mag extension.

This model was available through Remington Premier dealers only.

MSR		100%	98%	95%	90%	80%	70%	60%	*Last MSR*

MODEL 870 SPECIAL PURPOSE MARINE MAGNUM – 12 ga. only, 3 in. chamber, 18 in. plain barrel bored cyl., electroless nickel plated metal finish, 6 or 7 (disc.) shot mag., R3 recoil pad became standard during 2004, sling swivels and Cordura sling, 7 1/2 lbs.

| MSR $841 | | $665 | $560 | $460 | $400 | $350 | $300 | $250 | |

Add $117 for XCS Marine Model with black TriNyte metal coating (mfg. 2007-2008).

MODEL 870 POLICE – 12 ga. only, 18 or 20 in. plain barrel, choice of blue or parkerized finish, bead or rifle (disc. 1995, 20 in. barrel only) sights, Police cylinder (disc.) or IC choke. Mfg. 1994-2006 (last year of civilian sales).

| | | $385 | $315 | $250 | $200 | $175 | $160 | $145 | *$492* |

Add $13 for parkerized finish.
Add $44 for rifle sights (disc. 1995).

Remington also offers a Model 870P, 870P MAX, 870MCS, and 870P Synthetic for police/law enforcement, featuring extended capacity magazines, improved cylinder chokes, collapsible stocks, with some models having shorter than 18 in. barrels. While Remington does not publish consumer retail pricing for these police/law enforcement models, secondary prices for these guns will be slightly higher than for current pricing on the Model 870 Police.

MODEL 870 TACTICAL – 12 ga. only, 3 in. chamber, 18 or 20 in. fixed IC choke barrel, 6 or 7 (20 in. barrel only) shot mag., OD Green metal finish, black synthetic tactical or Knoxx Spec-Ops adj. recoil absorbing stock with pistol grip, open sights, approx. 7 1/2 lbs. Mfg. 2006.

| | | $515 | $465 | $425 | $385 | $350 | $320 | $290 | *$599* |

Add $26 for Spec-Ops adj. stock.

MODEL 870 TAC-2/TAC-3 – 12 ga., 3 in. chamber, 18 or 20 (disc) in. cyl. bore barrel, black oxide metal finish, black synthetic stock and forearm, pistol grip with choice of Knoxx Spec-Ops folding stock (Tac-2 FS), Knoxx Spec-Ops tube stock or regular synthetic (disc. 2008) stock, 6 (Tac-2 w/18 in. barrel) or 8 (Tac-3 w/20 in. barrel, disc. 2008) shot mag., bead sights, R3 recoil pad on fixed stock, approx. 7 lbs. New 2007.

| MSR $750 | | $615 | $535 | $470 | $415 | $380 | $340 | $300 | |

MODEL 870 TACTICAL DESERT RECON – 12 ga., 18 or 20 in. barrel, Digital Tiger TSP Desert Camo stock and forend, special ported tactical extended Rem Choke tube, Speedfeed stock with 2 or 3 shot carrier. Mfg. 2008-2009.

| | | $575 | $500 | $450 | $400 | $365 | $335 | $295 | *$692* |

Add $67 for 20 in. barrel.

MODEL 870 RIOT – 12 ga. only, 18 or 20 in. barrel, choice of blue or parkerized metal finish. Disc. 1991.

| | | $295 | $265 | $225 | $200 | $170 | $150 | $130 | *$355* |

Add $40 for police rifle sights (20 in. barrel only).

MODEL 887 NITRO MAG TACTICAL – 12 ga., 3 in. chamber, 18 1/2 in. threaded barrel with Rem Choke and Hi-Viz front sight, black synthetic stock and forearm, 4 shot mag. and 2 shot extension with mag. tube hanger bracket, Picatinny rail, SuperCell recoil pad, ArmorLokt coated metal finish, 6 7/8 lbs. Mfg. 2010-2015.

| | | $425 | $380 | $335 | $295 | $260 | $230 | $195 | *$534* |

REPUBLIC ARMS, INC.

Previous manufacturer 1997-2001, and located in Chino, CA.

PISTOLS: SEMI-AUTO

THE PATRIOT – .45 ACP cal., DAO, ultra compact with 3 in. barrel, 6 shot mag., ultra compact black polymer frame and stainless steel slide (either brushed or with black Melonite coating, new 2000), locked breech action, checkered grips, 20 oz. Mfg. 1997-2001.

| | | $265 | $230 | $210 | $185 | $175 | $165 | $155 | *$299* |

REPUBLIC ARMS OF SOUTH AFRICA

Previous manufacturer located in Jeppestown, Union of South Africa. Previously imported until 2002 by TSF Ltd., located in Fairfax, VA.

PISTOLS: SEMI-AUTO

RAP 401 – 9mm Para. cal., 8 shot mag., otherwise similar to Rap-440. Importation 1999-circa 2002.

| | | $495 | $425 | $375 | $350 | $325 | $300 | $275 | |

RAP-440 – .40 S&W cal., compact DA/SA, 3 1/2 in. barrel with high contrast 3-dot sights, last shot hold open, hammer drop safety/decocking lever, firing pin block safety, 7 shot mag., all steel construction, 31 1/2 oz., includes case, spare magazine, and lock. Imported 1998-circa 2002.

| | | $545 | $475 | $425 | $395 | $375 | $330 | $300 | |

Add $50 for Trilux Tritium night sights.

MSR	100%	98%	95%	90%	80%	70%	60%	Last MSR

SHOTGUNS: SLIDE ACTION

MUSLER MODEL – 12 ga., lightweight shotgun, polymer reinforced stock and forearm, action opening release lever, action locks open after the last round. Imported 1998-circa 2002.

	$549	$475	$425	$395	$375	$330	$300	

REX FIREARMS

Current trademark of pistols imported by the Firearms Imports Manufacturers Exporters (FIME) Group, established in 2015 and located in Las Vegas, NV.

PISTOLS: SEMI-AUTO

REX 01 Zero1 – 9mm Para. cal., DA, 4.3 in. barrel, 17 shot mag., steel construction, 3 dot sights, black synthetic grips, ambidextrous safety, lower Picatinny rail, dual slide serrations, matte black finish, 29 oz. Mfg. by Arex in Slovenia. Importation began 2016.

MSR $599	$525	$450	$400	$365	$335	$300	$275	

RHINO ARMS

Current rifle manufacturer located in St. Louis, MO. Previously located in Washington, MO.

PISTOLS: SEMI-AUTO

MM-47 – 7.62x39mm cal., GPO, 7 1/2 in. medium contour barrel with Rhino Flash Tamer muzzle, Rhino buffer tube, 7 in. Rhino Ultra Light Series carbon fiber handguard, ambi safety, curved trigger, Suregrip grip. New 2015.

MSR $2,200	$1,875	$1,650	$1,400	$1,200	$1,025	$875	$725	

RA-4R V2P – 5.56 NATO or .300 AAC Blackout cal., 7 (Ultra Light) or 9 in. light contour barrel with Rhino Flash Tamer muzzle, adj. gas block, 9 or 12 in. M-LOK handguard, beveled magwell, ambi safety, Sig Sauer SB15 pistol stabilizing brace, standard charging handle, Rhino curved trigger, Suregrip grip, black finish. New 2015.

MSR $1,900	$1,625	$1,425	$1,200	$1,075	$925	$795	$650	

Add $50 for .300 AAC Blackout cal.

RA-15 – 5.56 NATO or .300 AAC Blackout cal., 10 1/2 in. light contour barrel with Rhino Flash Tamer muzzle, 9 in. Rhino Ultra Light Series Carbon fiber handguard, Rhino buffer tube, curved trigger, Suregrip grip, black finish. New 2015.

MSR $1,700	$1,450	$1,275	$1,125	$1,000	$850	$735	$595	

RIFLES: SEMI-AUTO

Rhino Arms manufactures a complete line of AR-15 style carbines/rifles.

DOUBLE V SERIES II 5.56/.300 BLACKOUT – 5.56 NATO or .300 AAC Blackout (new 2014) cal., GIO, 16 (5.56 NATO cal. only) or 18 (.300 AAC Blackout cal. only) in. chrome moly fluted bull with muzzle brake or non-fluted barrel, machined aluminum receiver, gas block with integrated Picatinny rail, free floating carbon fiber handguard, Ergo grip, 10 or 30 shot Rhino Skin coated mag., Magpul CTR stock standard, nickel boron coated precision bolt carrier group, 7.8 (5.56 NATO) or 8.1 lbs.

MSR $2,405	$2,050	$1,800	$1,500	$1,300	$1,075	$935	$795	

Add $270 for .300 AAC Blackout cal.
Add $45 for Magpul ACS stock, $155 for Magpul PRS stock, or $165 for Magpul UBR stock.

DOUBLE V SERIES II 308 (RA-5D) – .308 Win. cal., GIO, 18 in. chrome moly heavy fluted bull with muzzle brake or non-fluted barrel, aluminum upper and lower receiver, rail gas block, 10 or 20 shot mag., Rhino flash hider, free float tube, Magpul UBR or CTR stock, Ergo grip, anti-walk receiver retaining pins, 8.8 lbs.

MSR $3,015	$2,700	$2,365	$2,025	$1,835	$1,485	$1,215	$950	

Add $45 for Magpul ACS stock, $155 for Magpul PRS stock, or $165 for Magpul UBR stock.

MM-47 MSR – 7.62x39mm cal., GPO, 16 in. medium contour barrel with Rhino Flash Tamer muzzle, carbine length gas block, takes Magpul and surplus AK mags., 15 1/2 in. Rhino Ultra-Light handguard, enhanced bolt catch, ambi safety, Mapgul CTR stock, Suregrip grip, Rhino curved trigger. New 2015.

MSR $2,200	$1,875	$1,650	$1,400	$1,200	$1,025	$875	$725	

RA-4B SERIES – .223 Rem. cal., GIO, 16 or 20 (RA-4BV only) in. chrome moly heavy barrel, aluminum lower receiver, flat-top upper, A2 flash hider, choice of A2 buttstock (RA-4B or RA-4BV) or M4 buttstock (RA-4BG or RA-4BT), 10 or 30 shot mag., anti-walk receiver retaining pins. Disc. 2010.

	$895	$825	$750	$675	$595	$550	$495	$978

Add $44 for RA-4BG model with rail gas block and M4 buttstock.
Add $248 for RA-BT model with four rail handguard and M4 buttstock.
Add $119 for RA-4BV model with 20 in. barrel, free float tube and A2 buttstock.

MSR	100%	98%	95%	90%	80%	70%	60%	Last MSR

RA-4P SERIES – .223 Rem. cal., GIO, 16 or 20 (RA-4PV) in. chrome moly steel barrel, flat-top upper, aluminum lower, A2 or Rhino flash hider, 10 or 30 shot mag., Ergo grip, Magpul CTR or PRS buttstock, anti-walk receiver retaining pins. Disc. 2010.

	$1,150	$1,000	$875	$750	$625	$550	$500	$1,243

Add $35 for RA-4PG model with four rail gas block, CAR handguard, and CTR buttstock.
Add $185 for RA-4PT model with four rail gas block, four rail handguard, and CTR buttstock.
Add $247 for RA-PV model with four rail gas block, free float tube, and PRS buttstock.

RA-4R 3GR – 5.56 NATO cal., 16 or 18 in. light contour barrel with 1 in. Rhino muzzle brake, adj. gas block, Raptor extended ambi charging handle, 15 in. M-LOK handguard, low mass bolt carrier with titanium firing pin, extended bolt catch release, beveled magwell, ambi safety, Rhino straight trigger, ARFX stock with carbon fiber sleeve, Suregrip grip, black finish. New 2015.

MSR $2,400	$2,050	$1,800	$1,500	$1,300	$1,075	$935	$795	

RA-4R 50SCR (50 STATE COMPLIANT RIFLE) – 5.56 NATO or .300 AAC Blackout cal., 16 in. heavy barrel, target crown, 10 shot mag., adj. gas block, 13 1/2 in. T.R.I.M. handguard, standard charging handle, full mass bolt carrier, enhanced bolt catch, ambi safety, beveled magwell, Rhino curved trigger, New York stock, Suregrip grip, black finish. New 2015.

MSR $2,200	$1,875	$1,650	$1,400	$1,200	$1,025	$875	$725	

Add $50 for .300 AAC Blackout cal.

RA-4R ISR (INTEGRALLY SUPPRESSED RIFLE) – .300 AAC Blackout cal., 16.1 in. light contour barrel (7 1/2 in. barrel with titanium mono-core permanently attached brings overall length to 16.1 in.), integral suppressor, adj. gas block, 12 in. M-LOK handguard, low mass bolt carrier with titanium firing pin, extended bolt catch release, beveled magwell, ambi safety, extended ambi charging handle, Magpul UBR stock, Rhino curved trigger, Suregrip grip, black finish. New 2015.

MSR $3,400	$2,895	$2,535	$2,050	$1,750	$1,450	$1,225	$1,050	

RA-4R PDW (PERSONAL DEFENSE WEAPON) – 5.56 NATO or .300 AAC Blackout cal., compact non-NFA variation rifle, 14 1/2 in. light contour barrel with Rhino Flash Tamer muzzle, adj. gas block, 9 or 12 in. M-LOK handguard, extended charging handle, enhanced bolt catch, ambi safety, beveled magwell, Rhino curved trigger, quick extend PDW stock, Suregrip grip, black finish. New 2015.

MSR $2,300	$1,950	$1,725	$1,450	$1,250	$1,050	$900	$750	

Add $50 for .300 AAC Blackout cal.

RA-4R V2 – 5.56 NATO or .300 AAC Blackout cal., 16 in. heavy fluted barrel with Rhino muzzle brake, adj. gas block, 13 1/2 in. T.R.I.M. aluminum handguard with modular attachment points, standard charging handle, Rhino curved trigger, Magpul CTR stock, Suregrip grip, ambi safety, beveled magwell. New 2015.

MSR $2,200	$1,875	$1,650	$1,400	$1,200	$1,025	$875	$725	

Add $50 for .300 AAC Blackout cal.

RA-5R DMR – .260 Rem., .308 Win., 6mm Creedmoor, or 6.5mm Creedmoor cal., 22 in. heavy fluted barrel with Rhino muzzle brake, rifle length gas block, 17 in. M-LOK handguard, Raptor charging handle, low mass bolt carrier with titanium firing pin, enhanced bolt catch, ambi safety, two-stage trigger, Magpul PRS stock, Suregrip grip. New 2015.

MSR $3,550	$3,020	$2,645	$2,270	$2,055	$1,665	$1,375	$1,075	

RA-5R HMR (HEAVY METAL RIFLE) – .308 Win. cal., 16 in. light contour barrel with 1 in. muzzle brake, adj. gas block, 15 in. M-LOK handguard, Raptor charging handle, low mass bolt carrier with titanium firing pin, extended bolt catch, ambi safety, ARFX stock with carbon fiber sleeve, Rhino straight trigger, Suregrip grip. New 2015.

MSR $3,100	$2,635	$2,300	$1,975	$1,790	$1,450	$1,185	$1,000	

RA-5R HTR (HEAVY TACTICAL RIFLE) – .308 Win. cal., 16 in. pinned medium contour barrel with 1 in. Rhino muzzle brake, mid-length gas block, 12 1/2 in. KeyMod handguard, Raptor charging handle, full mass bolt carrier, enhanced bolt catch, ambi safety, Ace Socom stock, Suregrip grip, Rhino curved trigger. New 2015.

MSR $3,100	$2,635	$2,300	$1,975	$1,790	$1,450	$1,185	$1,000	

RA-5R V2 – .308 Win. cal., 18 in. heavy fluted barrel with Rhino muzzle brake, mid-length gas block, 13 1/2 in. RS KeyMod handguard, standard charging handle, full mass bolt carrier, enhanced bolt catch, ambi safety, beveled magwell, Rhino curved trigger, Magpul ACS stock, Suregrip grip, black finish. New 2015.

MSR $2,950	$2,500	$2,175	$1,775	$1,525	$1,250	$1,050	$925	

RA-15 MSR – 5.56 NATO cal., 16 in. light contour barrel with Rhino Flash Tamer muzzle, carbine length adj. gas block, 13 1/2 in. Rhino Ultra-Light handguard, standard charging handle, Magpul CTR stock, Rhino curved trigger, Suregrip grip. New 2015.

MSR $1,700	$1,450	$1,275	$1,125	$1,000	$850	$735	$595	

MSR	100%	98%	95%	90%	80%	70%	60%	Last MSR

RIFLES: BOLT ACTION

RA-PBA .338 – .338 Lapua Mag. cal., 26 in. brushed stainless steel barrel with compensator, AI bottom metal, extra deep fluted bolt pattern, custom trigger, Manners T2A stock. New 2015.

| MSR $5,000 | $4,250 | $3,720 | $3,190 | $2,890 | $2,350 | $1,925 | $1,500 | |

RA-PBA LONG ACTION – .300 Win. Mag. or 7mm Mag. cal., 26 in. Sendero brushed stainless steel barrel with Rhino compensator, extra deep fluted bolt pattern, A1 bottom metal, custom trigger, Manners T2A stock, OD Green finish. New 2015.

| MSR $4,500 | $3,825 | $3,350 | $2,875 | $2,600 | $2,100 | $1,725 | $1,350 | |

RA-PBA SHORT ACTION – .260 Rem., .308 Win., 6 Creedmoor, or 6.5 Creedmoor cal., 26 in. Sendero barrel with Black Nitride finish, Rhino compensator, extra deep fluted bolt pattern, A1 bottom metal, custom trigger, Manners T2A stock, Flat Dark Earth finish. New 2015.

| MSR $4,500 | $3,825 | $3,350 | $2,875 | $2,600 | $2,100 | $1,725 | $1,350 | |

RIB MOUNTAIN ARMS, INC.

Previous rifle manufacturer circa 1992-2000, and located in Beresford and Sturgis, SD.

RIFLES: BOLT ACTION

MODEL 92 – .50 BMG cal., match grade barrel with muzzle brake, long action, walnut thumbhole stock, Timney trigger, approx. 28 lbs. Mfg. 1997-2000.

| | $3,175 | $2,725 | $2,275 | $2,000 | $1,750 | $1,575 | $1,300 | $3,475 |

MODEL 93 – similar to Model 92, except has short action with removable shell holder bolt, approx. 25 lbs. Mfg. 1997-2000.

| | $3,175 | $2,725 | $2,275 | $2,000 | $1,750 | $1,575 | $1,300 | $3,475 |

RIFLES, INC.

Current custom rifle manufacturer located in Pleasanton, TX. Previously located in Cedar City, UT. Dealer or direct consumer sales.

Riflemaker and custom gunsmith Lex Webernick has been manufacturing lightweight sporting rifles for more than 20 years.

RIFLES: BOLT ACTION

On the following models, the customer must provide a Remington or Winchester action.

Add $175 for muzzlebrake (stainless quiet Slimbrake II) on Classic and Master Series.

CANYON – various cals., designed for long range shooting, synthetic stock with adj. cheekpiece available in 6 colors, stainless steel action/barrel with muzzle brake, 10 lbs. New 2011.

| MSR $3,500 | $3,150 | $2,650 | $2,100 | $1,775 | $1,500 | $1,215 | $1,000 | |

RITTER & STARK

Current manufacturer located in Ferlach, Austria beginning 2015. No current U.S. importation.

RIFLES: SEMI-AUTO

SX-1 MODULAR TACTICAL RIFLE – .308 Win., .300 Win. Mag., or .338 Lapua cal., AR-15 style, free floating match grade barrel, R&S muzzle brake, detachable box mag., interchangeable magwell, interchangeable trigger, adj. folding stock, adj. cheekpiece, pistol grip, 3-position safety, Mil-Std Picatinny rail mounted on barrel, quad rail forend, black finish. New 2016.

Please contact the company directly for more information including price, options, and U.S. availabilty.

RIVERMAN GUN WORKS

Current rifle manufacturer located in Coeur d'Alene, ID.

PISTOLS: SEMI-AUTO

RM9 – 9mm Para. cal., MP5 platform, 9 1/2 in. 3-lug barrel, choice of A2 or pistol cap, SEF trigger group, can be configured as a pistol, SBR, or fixed with faux suppressor to comply with rifle regulations, Gun Kote finish. Disc. 2015.

| | $2,250 | $1,975 | $1,700 | $1,525 | $1,250 | $1,025 | $800 | $2,500 |

RIFLES: BOLT ACTION

Each rifle is custom built to your specifications. Riverman Gun Works has many options and accessories available. For more information on these upgrades, please contact the manufacturer directly (see Trademark Index).

MSR	100%	98%	95%	90%	80%	70%	60%	Last MSR

MBR-10 (MODULAR BREAKDOWN RIFLE) – .243 Win., .260 Rem., .308 Win., .338 Federal, 7mm-08 Rem., or 6.5 Creedmoor cal., spring assisted bolt, 16 in. stainless barrel with RGW Serpent Series compensator, available in Tactical or Hunter configurations, standard AR mag., billet cut upper and lower receiver, A2 fixed or Minimalist stock, Hogue grip, 13 in. RGW Serpent Series KeyMod or M-LOK rail, Gun Kote (Tactical) or Camo Hydrographic dip (Hunter) finish, designed for quick and easy breakdown for changing barrels and/or calibers, includes case.

MSR $2,600	$,200	$1,925	$1,600	$1,375	$1,125	$975	$850	

MBR-15 – .204 Ruger, .223 Rem., .300 AAC Blackout, 6.5 Grendel, or 6.8 SPC cal., otherwise similar to MBR-10.

MSR $2,100	$1,875	$1,625	$1,400	$1,225	$925	$800	$700	

RIFLES: SEMI-AUTO

RM-15 – 7.62 NATO cal., 16 in. stainless barrel, billet cut upper and lower receiver, Winter trigger guard, Serpent Series KeyMod rail system, recessed mag. release, hard anodized, Gun Kote, Hydrographic Dip, or Cerakote finish, 6.6 lbs.

MSR $1,600	$1,350	$1,200	$1,075	$950	$815	$700	$575	

RM-308 – 7.62 NATO cal., 18 in. stainless barrel, billet cut upper and lower receiver, Winter trigger guard, Serpent Series KeyMod or M-LOK rail system, recessed mag. release, Minimalist stock, Hogue grip, hard anodized, Gun Kote, Hydrographic Dip, or Cerakote finish, 8 lbs.

MSR $2,150	$1,925	$1,685	$1,450	$1,310	$1,050	$875	$675	

THE ROBAR COMPANIES, INC.

Current manufacturer and customizer established during 1986, and located in Phoenix, AZ.

Robar is a leader in custom metal finishing, including combination finishes. These include the Roguard black finish, NP3 and NP3 Plus surface treatment, and additional finishes including bluing, electroless nickel, and PolyT2 metal finish. Please contact Robar directly (see Trademark Index) for more information, including current prices on their lineup of firearms, custom metal and wood finishes, and customizing services, including shotguns.

RIFLES

Robar manufactures the SR21 precision rifle based on the Remington 700 action (MSR $3,995), the SR60 Precision Rifle (MSR $3,495), SR90 Precision Rifle (MSR $4,295), QR2 Compact rifle (MSR $3,595), Thunder Ranch Rifle (MSR $4,950), and the RC50 .50 BMG rifle (MSR $7,995). A wide variety of options are available. Please contact Robar directly for more information, including availability and delivery time (see Trademark Index).

ROBERT HISSERICH COMPANY

Previous gunsmith and previous custom rifle manufacturer located in Mesa, AZ. Previous company name was Stockworks.

RIFLES: BOLT ACTION

ROBERT HISSERICH BOLT GUN – various cals., features Weatherby Vanguard action, Pac-Nor stainless steel barrel, Pachmayr Decelerator pad, hinged floorplate, black synthetic stock. Mfg. 2003-disc.

	$1,795	$1,500	$1,250	$1,050	$875	$750	$625	

LIGHTWEIGHT RIFLES SLR – various cals., Rem. long or short action, Kevlar/fiberglass MPI stock, match grade Pac-Nor barrel, straight flutes in bolt body, Timney trigger, straight line muzzle brake, pillar bedded action, free floating barrel, "window" cuts in action for lightening, black oxide finish on carbon or stainless steel, English or Claro walnut deluxe checkered stock, custom order only. Approx. 4 3/4-5 lbs.

	$2,600	$2,300	$2,000	$1,800	$1,600	$1,400	$1,200	

Add $200 for stainless steel.

SHARPSHOOTER – various cals., Win. Model 70 action with controlled feeding, precision long range hunting rifle with Schnieder stainless steel fluted barrel, laminated stock with ebony forend tip, titanium firing pin, pillar glass bedded with free floating barrel, includes Leupold 6.5-20x40mm scope, custom order only.

	$5,950	$5,100	$4,500	$3,900	$3,400	$2,850	$2,150	

ROBINSON ARMAMENT CO.

Current pistol and rifle manufacturer located in Salt Lake City, UT. Previously distributed by ZDF Import/Export, Inc., located in Salt Lake City, UT. Dealer and consumer direct sales.

PISTOLS: SEMI-AUTO

XCR-L MICRO PISTOL – 5.56 NATO, 6.8 SPC, .300 AAC Blackout (new 2015), 5.45x39mm, or 7.62x39mm cal., GPO, 7 (disc.) or 7 1/2 in. chrome lined barrel, upper, side, and lower rails, two stage trigger, accepts M16 magazines, left side charging handle, various sight options, Black, Flat Dark Earth, or Olive Drab finish, approx. 5 lbs. New 2010.

MSR $1,795	$1,525	$1,350	$1,175	$1,050	$900	$775	$625	

MSR	100%	98%	95%	90%	80%	70%	60%	Last MSR

XCR-M – .243 Win., .260 Rem., or 7.62 NATO cal., GPO, 9 1/2 in. barrel, 15 in. full top rail, 5 1/2 in. side and bottom rail, various options available, matte black, flat dark earth, or olive drab finish, 6.2 lbs. New 2012.

MSR $2,300	$1,950	$1,725	$1,450	$1,250	$1,050	$900	$750	

RIFLES: SEMI-AUTO

M96 EXPEDITIONARY RIFLE/CARBINE – .223 Rem. cal., GPO, tactical modular design, unique action allows accessory kit (new 2000) to convert loading from bottom to top of receiver, 16.2 (Recon Model, new 2001), 17 1/4 (carbine, new 2000) or 20 1/4 in. barrel with muzzle brake, stainless steel receiver and barrel, matte black finish metal, black synthetic stock and forearm, adj. sights, gas operated with adjustment knob, last shot hold open, rotating bolt assembly, 8 1/2 lbs. Mfg. 1999-2006.

	$1,495	$1,300	$1,100	$925	$850	$775	$700	

Add $750 for rifle/carbine with top feed.

XCR-L MODEL – .223 Rem., 6.8 SPC, 7.62x39mm, 5.45x39mm, .300 AAC Blackout (new 2015), or .308 Win. (mfg. 2008-2013) cal., GPO, tactical design, 16 or 18.6 in. full floating barrel, handguard with 8 in. side and bottom Picatinny rails, open sights, quick change barrel system, bolt hold open, side folding stock standard until 2008, stock configuration optional beginning 2009, two-stage trigger, uses M16 mags., black, Flat Dark Earth, or Olive Drab finish, 7 1/2 lbs. New 2006.

MSR $1,995	$1,700	$1,500	$1,250	$1,100	$950	$825	$675	

Add $560 for conversion kit (includes barrel, bolt, and 25 shot mag.).
Add $150-$250 for stock option, depending on configuration.
Add $50 for 18.6 in. barrel.
Add $32 for rail covers.
Add $200 for Flat Dark Earth or Olive Drab or $300 for white or tiger stripe.

The model nomenclature was changed from XCR to XCR-L (lightweight) during 2008.

XCR-M – .260 Rem., .243 Win., or 7.62 NATO cal., GPO, 16, 17, 18.6, or 20 in. light or heavy stainless steel barrel, 20 in. full top rail, 9 1/2 in. side and bottom rail, matte black, flat dark earth, olive drab, white, or tiger stripe finish, approx. 8 lbs. New 2012.

MSR $2,495	$2,125	$1,875	$1,550	$1,325	$1,100	$950	$825	

Add $200 for flat dark earth, olive drab, $300 white or tiger stripe finish.
Add $32 for rail covers.

ROCK ISLAND ARMORY (CURRENT MFG.)

Current trademark manufactured by Arms Corp. of the Philippines. Currently imported by Armscor Precision International, located in Pahrump, NV.

PISTOLS: SEMI-AUTO

M1911-A1 FSP – 9mm Para. (new 2011), .38 Super or .45 ACP cal., patterned after the Colt Govt. Model, SA, 7 shot mag. (2 provided), 5 in. barrel, parkerized (disc. 2001), nickel, blue (new 2002), two-tone (new 2002), or stainless steel (new 2002), skeletonized combat hammer and trigger, front and rear slide serrations, hard rubber grips, 38 oz. Imported 1996-97, reintroduced 2001.

No MSR	$395	$360	$320	$295	$280	$260	$240	

Add $10 for MSP Model or for .38 Super cal.
Add $18 for Duracoat finish.
Add $34 for two-tone finish.
Add $100 for stainless steel (disc. 2011)
Add $60 for a high capacity configuration (Model 1911-A2 HC, 13 shot mag., disc. 2009).
Add $60 for Model 1911-A1 FS RIA Tactical (.45 ACP cal. only) or $84 for FS RIA Tactical with Duracoat (new 2012).
Add $205 for Model 1911-A2 FS RIA Match Model (.45 ACP cal. only).
Add $55 for nickel finish (Model 1911-A1 FSNP).
Add $100 for night sights (new 2012).

PRO MATCH TAC ULTRA – .45 ACP cal., 6 in. barrel, 8 shot mag., Picatinny rail, skeletonized trigger, extended beavertail, adj. rear and fiber optic front sights, parkerized finish, 2 1/2 lbs. New 2015.

MSR $1,145	$995	$900	$775	$650	$575	$485	$435	

PRO MATCH ULTRA 6 IN./HC "BIG ROCK" – 10mm cal., 6 in. barrel, 8 or 16 (HC "Big Rock") shot mag., upper and lower Picatinny rails, extended beavertail, skeletonized trigger. New 2015.

MSR $1,187	$1,025	$925	$800	$675	$600	$500	$450	

Add $157 for 16 shot mag. (high capacity "Big Rock" model).

MSR	100%	98%	95%	90%	80%	70%	60%	Last MSR

TAC STANDARD FS (M1911-A1 FS TACTICAL) – .45 ACP cal., SA, skeletonized trigger, rear slide serrations, bobbed hammer, lower Picatinny rail, diamond checkered walnut grips, parkerized finish, 8 shot mag., standard or night sights, full dust cover rail, single stack. New 2011.

| MSR $696 | $525 | $450 | $400 | $365 | $335 | $300 | $275 | |

Add $121 for night sights.

TAC ULTRA CS – 9mm Para. or .45 ACP cal., compact model, combat hammer, skeletonized trigger, extended beavertail, G10 grip, tactical rail, ambidextrous safety and slide, full dust cover rail, 2-dot tactical adj. rear and fiber optic front sights, front and back wide-angled slide serrations. New 2014.

| MSR $799 | $715 | $635 | $565 | $525 | $485 | $435 | $385 | |

TAC ULTRA FS – .45 ACP, 10mm, .or 40 S&W (new 2015) cal., 8 shot, full dust cover rail, combat trigger, extended beavertail, 2-dot tactical adj. rear and orange fiber optic front sights, front and back wide-angled slide serrations, ambidextrous safety, tactical rail, single stack (.40 S&W only), G10 or VZ grip, 2 1/2 lbs.

| MSR $788 | $700 | $625 | $550 | $515 | $475 | $425 | $375 | |

Add $24 for 10mm cal.

* Tac Ultra FS HC (High Capacity) – 9mm Para., .45 ACP, or .40 S&W (new 2015) cal., similar to Tac Ultra FS, except has 14 (.45 ACP), 16 (.40 S&W), or 17 (9mm) shot, 3 lbs.

| MSR $859 | $750 | $650 | $575 | $540 | $495 | $445 | $395 | |

TAC ULTRA MS – 9mm Para., 10mm, .40 S&W, or .45 ACP cal., mid-size model, 8 or 9 (9mm only) shot, combat hammer, skeletonized trigger, extended beavertail, tactical rail, ambidextrous safety and slide, full dust cover rail, 2-dot tactical adj. rear and fiber optic front sights, front and back wide-angled slide serrations, G10 grip. New 2015.

| MSR $799 | $715 | $635 | $565 | $525 | $485 | $435 | $385 | |

Add $24 for 10mm cal.

TAC FS TITANIUM – .45 ACP cal., full size, 8 shot, titanium construction. New late 2015.

| MSR $1,156 | $1,000 | $900 | $775 | $650 | $575 | $485 | $435 | |

TCM TAC ULTRA FS – 9mm Para./.22 TCM cal., full size, 10 shot mag., combat trigger, 2-dot adj. rear LPA and TruGlo high visibility front sights, front and back wide angled slide serrations, full dust cover rail, ambidextrous safety, tactical rail, extended beavertail, G10 grips, Parkerized finish, includes 9mm conversion barrel, 3 lbs. New 2015.

| MSR $867 | $780 | $685 | $615 | $550 | $485 | $415 | $370 | |

* TCM Tac Ultra MS – 9mm Para./.22 TCM cal., similar to TCM Tac Ultra FS, except has mid-size frame. New 2015.

| MSR $882 | $790 | $685 | $615 | $550 | $485 | $415 | $370 | |

TCM TAC ULTRA FS HIGH CAP – 9mm Para./.22 TCM cal., full size, 17 shot mag., outfitted with an original Armscor cartridge, combat trigger, fiber optic front and adj. rear sights, tactical rail, extended beavertail, G10 grips, Parkerized finish, 3 lbs. New 2015.

| MSR $914 | $825 | $725 | $650 | $585 | $515 | $450 | $395 | |

* TCM Tac Ultra MS High Cap – 9mm Para./.22 TCM cal., similar to TCM Tac Ultra FS, except has mid-size frame, 2 1/2 lbs. New 2015.

| MSR $914 | $825 | $725 | $650 | $585 | $515 | $450 | $395 | |

XT 22 STANDARD – .22 LR cal., delayed blowback action, steel construction, 5 in. modular barrel, 10 or 15 shot mag., skeletonized trigger, bobbed hammer, integral rail mount, checkered synthetic grips, parkerized finish, 38 oz. New 2011.

| MSR $602 | $540 | $475 | $425 | $365 | $325 | $285 | $250 | |

* XT 22 Standard Combo – .22 LR/.45 ACP cal., steel construction, 5 in. modular barrel, 8 or 10 shot mag., delayed blowback action with integral rail mount, low profile snag free sights, checkered synthetic grips, parkerized finish, 2.22 lbs.

| MSR $900 | $800 | $675 | $600 | $560 | $515 | $460 | $415 | |

* XT 22 Magnum – .22 Mag. cal., steel construction, modular barrel, 15 shot mag., delayed blowback action with integral rail mount, low profile snag free sights, checkered synthetic grips, parkerized finish, 2.22 lbs. New late 2014.

| MSR $609 | $540 | $475 | $425 | $365 | $325 | $285 | $250 | |

* XT 22 TAC – .22 LR cal., steel construction, modular barrel, 10 shot mag., top Picatinny rail, skeletonized trigger, bobbed hammer, checkered synthetic grips, parkerized finish, 2.22 lbs. New late 2014.

| MSR $712 | $535 | $450 | $400 | $365 | $335 | $300 | $275 | |

MSR	100%	98%	95%	90%	80%	70%	60%	*Last MSR*

ROCK RIVER ARMS, INC.

Current handgun and rifle manufacturer established in 1996 and located in Colona, IL beginning 2004. Previously located in Cleveland, IL until 2003. Dealer and consumer direct sales.

CARBINES/RIFLES: SEMI-AUTO

Rock River Arms makes a variety of AR-15 style rifles/carbines in .223 Rem. cal. Previous models included the CAR UTE (disc. 2004, last MSR was $850), Tactical Carbine A2, M4 Entry (disc. 2003, last MSR was $875), and NM A2-DCM Legal (disc. 2005, last MSR was $1,265).

Beginning 2006, Rock River Arms released a series of rifles in 9mm Para. cal. Also during 2006, the company released a series of rifles in .308 Win. cal. A wide variety of options are available for each rifle. Base model assumes black furniture.

LAR-15 9.11 COMMEMORATIVE – .5.56 NATO or .223 Rem. cal., GIO, 16 in. lightweight chrome moly barrel, forged A4 upper receiver, low profile gas block, chromed bolt carrier group, RRA tactical muzzle brake, two-stage chrome trigger group, winter trigger guard, star safety, overmolded pistol grip, Hogue free float tube handguard, non-collapsible or 6-position tactical CAR stock, flat black finish with American flag, and "9*11 Tenth Year Commemoration" engraved on receiver. Limited mfg. mid-2011.

	100%	98%	95%	90%	80%	70%	60%	Last MSR
	$995	$850	$725	N/A	N/A	N/A	N/A	*$1,011*

Add $25 for non-collapsible stock, pinned/welded tactical muzzle brake, and 10 shot mag.

LAR-15 ATH (ADVANCED TACTICAL HUNTER) CARBINE – .223 Rem. cal., GIO, 18 in. heavy match cryo treated stainless steel barrel, muzzle brake, forged A4 upper and LAR-15 lower receiver, matte black finish, low profile gas block, two-stage trigger, Winter trigger guard, Star safety, Ergo SureGrip pistol grip, RRA Advanced half quad free float handguard with three rail covers, Operator CAR stock, 7.7 lbs. New 2011.

MSR $1,370	$1,165	$1,025	$900	$750	$650	$550	$465

LAR-15 CAR A2 – .223 Rem. cal., GIO, forged A2 upper receiver, 16 in. Wilson chrome moly barrel, A2 flash hider, two-stage match trigger, CAR length handguard, A2 pistol grip, fixed or tactical CAR stock, 7 1/2 lbs. Disc. 2012.

	$820	$700	$625	$550	$485	$415	$370	*$960*

Add $15 for six-position tactical stock.
Add $175 for tactical carry handle.
Add $145 for quad rail and tactical CAR stock.

LAR-15 CAR A4 – 5.56 NATO chambered for 5.56mm and .223 Rem. cal., GIO, 16 in. chrome moly barrel with A2 flash hider, two-stage trigger, gas block sight base or A2 front sight base, forged LAR-15 lower and forged A4 upper receiver, CAR length handguard, 6-pos. tactical CAR stock, overmolded A2 pistol grips, 7.1 lbs.

MSR $1,035	$865	$725	$650	$585	$515	$440	$395

Add $145 for left-hand (LAR-15LH Lef-T CAR A4, new 2013).

LAR-15 COYOTE CARBINE/RIFLE – .223 Rem. cal., GIO, forged A4 upper receiver, 16 (carbine) or 20 (rifle) in. Wilson chrome moly HBar barrel, Smith Vortex flash hider, Weaver style light varmint gas block with sight rail (disc. 2013) or low profile gas block (new 2014), two-stage match trigger, Winter trigger guard, Hogue rubber pistol grip, Hogue overmolded free float tube handguard (disc. 2013) or RRA deluxe extended free float rail (new 2014), ACE ARFX skeleton (disc. 2013) or RRA Operator A2 (new 2014) or Operator CAR (new 2014) stock, 8.4 lbs.

MSR $1,300	$1,100	$965	$875	$735	$650	$550	$465

Add $45 for 20 in. barrel (Coyote Rifle).
Add $145 for left-hand (LAR-15LH, Lef-T, new 2013).

LAR-15 DELTA CAR – .223 Rem. cal., GIO, forged upper and lower, 16 in. chrome moly HBAR barrel, A2 flash hider, low profile gas block, two-stage trigger, Winter trigger guard, Delta CAR stock, Ergo Suregrip, Delta quad rail CAR two-piece drop-in handguard, 7 lbs. New 2013.

MSR $1,085	$910	$765	$665	$585	$515	$450	$395

LAR-15 DELTA CAR MID-LENGTH – .223 Rem. cal., GIO, similar to Delta CAR, except has mid-length handguard, 7.3 lbs. New 2013.

MSR $1,100	$925	$850	$725	$625	$550	$475	$425

LAR-15 ELITE CAR A4 – 5.56 NATO chambered for 5.56mm and .223 cal., GIO, 16 in. chrome moly barrel with A2 flash hider, two stage trigger, Star safety, forged receivers, mid-length handguard, 6-pos. tactical CAR stock, Hogue rubber pistol grip, slide mount sling swivel, 7.7 lbs.

MSR $1,065	$900	$750	$665	$585	$515	$450	$395

Add $40 for chrome lined barrel.

LAR-15 ELITE CAR UTE2 – .223 Rem. cal., GIO, 16 in. Wilson chrome moly barrel, A2 flash hider, two-stage match trigger, mid-length handguard, forged Universal Tactical Entry 2 upper receiver, 6-pos. tactical CAR stock, Hogue rubber pistol grip, 7.7 lbs. Disc. 2012.

	$900	$750	$665	$585	$515	$450	$395	*$1,060*

MSR	100%	98%	95%	90%	80%	70%	60%	Last MSR

LAR-15 ELITE COMP – 5.56 NATO chambered for 5.56mm and .223 Rem. cal., GIO, 16 in. chrome lined barrel with tactical muzzle brake, forged receivers, flip front sight gas block assembly, two stage trigger, Winter trigger guard, Star safety, A.R.M.S. low profile flip-up rear sight, MagPul CTR (disc.) or Operator CAR stock, Ergo Suregrip pistol grip, features free floating half-round, half-quad handguard, 8.4 lbs. New 2008.

MSR $1,515	$1,285	$1,125	$1,025	$875	$750	$625	$525	

LAR-15 ENTRY TACTICAL – .223 Rem. cal., GIO, 16 in. chrome moly R-4 heavy barrel with A2 flash hider, two-stage trigger, forged lower and A4 upper receiver, Star safety, Hogue rubber pistol grip, R-4 handguard with double heat shields, 6-position tactical CAR stock, 7 1/2 lbs.

MSR $1,065	$900	$750	$665	$585	$515	$450	$395	

Add $40 for chrome lined barrel.

LAR-15 FRED EICHLER SERIES PREDATOR – .223 Wylde chamber for 5.56mm and .223 Rem. cal., GIO, 16 in. bead blasted stainless steel cryogenically treated barrel, low profile hidden gas block, chrome RRA National Match two-stage trigger with parkerized finish on trigger shoe, RRA winter trigger guard, RRA Fred Eichler Series free-floating handguard with full length Picatinny top rail and 2 1/2 in. rails, tan Hogue rubber grips, Operator A2 or CAR stock, 20 shot mag., forged A4 upper flat-top, custom muzzle brake, two-tone black/tan finish, includes hard case. New 2012.

MSR $1,510	$1,285	$1,125	$1,025	$875	$750	$625	$525	

LAR-15 FRED EICHLER SERIES PREDATOR 2 – .223 Wylde chamber for 5.56mm and .223 Rem. cal., GIO, 16 in. fluted stainless steel barrel with directionally tuned and ported muzzle brake, forged A4 upper, low profile gas block, two-stage chrome trigger, Winter trigger guard, Star safety, Fred Eichler Series free float extended length handguard with two rail covers and full top Picatinny rail, Operator A2 or CAR buttstock, Hogue rubber pistol grip, receivers and handguard finished in Cerakote Tan or Gunmetal Gray, 7.6 lbs. New 2015.

MSR $1,750	$1,475	$1,295	$1,125	$1,000	$850	$735	$595	

LAR-15 HUNTER – .223 Rem. cal., GIO, 16 in. chrome moly barrel with RRA tactical muzzle brake, forged A4 upper receiver, low profile gas block, two-stage trigger, Winter trigger guard, half-quad free float mid-length handguard with three rail covers, Operator CAR stock, Hogue rubber pistol grip, WYL-Ehide or PRK-Ehide (disc.) anodized camo finish, 7.6 lbs. New 2012.

MSR $1,550	$1,315	$1,150	$1,040	$875	$750	$625	$525	

LAR-15 IRS – 5.56 NATO chambered for 5.56mm and .223 cal., GIO, 16 or 18 (XL model only) in. fluted chrome moly barrel with RRA Helical brake, low profile gas block, forged upper and lower receivers, two stage trigger, Winter trigger guard, IRS CAR, MID, STD, or XL length handguard with integral folding sights, Operator CAR stock, Hogue pistol grip, 7.8-8 lbs. New 2015.

MSR $1,540	$1,310	$1,150	$1,040	$875	$750	$625	$525	

Add $25 for Mid-length handguard (LAR-15 MID).
Add $50 for STD length handguard (LAR-15 STD).
Add $80 for XL length handguard (LAR-15 XL).

LAR-15 LIGHTWEIGHT – 5.56 NATO chambered for 5.56mm and .223 cal., GIO, 16 in. chrome moly lightweight barrel with A2 flash hider, low profile gas block, two-stage trigger, Winter trigger guard, forged upper and lower receivers, carbon fiber free float extended handguard in CAR, MID, STD, or XL lengths, 6-pos. tactical CAR stock, Hogue rubber pistol grips, 5.6-6.1 lbs. New 2015.

MSR $1,325	$1,125	$995	$875	$735	$650	$550	$465	

Add $25 for mid-length handguard (Lightweight Mid model).
Add $50 for STD length handguard (Lightweight STD model).
Add $75 for XL length handguard (Lightweight XL model).

LAR-15 MID-LENGTH A2 – .223 Rem. cal., GIO, forged A2 upper receiver, 16 in. Wilson chrome moly barrel, two-stage match trigger, mid-length handguard, A2 pistol grips and buttstock, 7 1/2 lbs. Disc. 2012.

	$820	$700	$625	$550	$485	$415	$370	*$960*

Add $15 for six-position tactical stock.

LAR-15 MID-LENGTH A4 – 5.56 NATO chambered for 5.56mm and .223 Rem. cal., GIO, 16 in. chrome moly barrel with A2 flash hider, two-stage trigger, forged LAR-15 lower and forged A4 upper receiver, available with gas block sight base or A2 front sight base, mid-length handguard, 6-pos. tactical CAR stock, overmolded A2 pistol grip, 7.1 lbs.

MSR $1,035	$865	$725	$650	$585	$515	$440	$395	

Add $15 for six-position tactical stock.
Add $170 for quad rail and tactical stock.
Add $175 for tactical carry handle.

MSR	100%	98%	95%	90%	80%	70%	60%	Last MSR

LAR-15 LIGHTWEIGHT MOUNTAIN RIFLE – 5.56 NATO chambered for 5.56mm and .223 Rem. cal., GIO, 16 in. chrome moly lightweight barrel with A2 flash hider, lightweight low profile gas block, Star safety, two-stage trigger, Winter trigger guard, RRA lightweight aluminum Mountain Rifle handguard, 6-pos. tactical CAR stock, Hogue rubber pistol grip, 6.2 lbs. New 2015.

| MSR $1,150 | $975 | $875 | $740 | $625 | $550 | $475 | $425 | |

LAR-15 NATIONAL MATCH A2 – 5.56mm Wylde chambered for 5.56mm and .223 Rem. cal., GIO, 20 in. Wilson heavy match stainless steel barrel with A2 flash hider, 20 shot mag., two-stage match chrome trigger group, forged A2 upper receiver, A2 pistol grip and buttstock, free floating Thermo Mold handguard, match front and rear sights, 9.7 lbs.

| MSR $1,335 | $1,135 | $995 | $875 | $735 | $650 | $550 | $465 | |

LAR-15 NATIONAL MATCH A4 – .223 Rem. cal., GIO, similar to National Match A2 model, except has forged A4 upper receiver with NM carry handle, 9.7 lbs.

| MSR $1,415 | $1,210 | $1,075 | $950 | $800 | $700 | $600 | $495 | |

LAR-15 NSP CAR – 5.56 NATO chambered for 5.56mm and .223 cal., GIO, 16 in. fluted R4 profile chrome moly barrel with RRA Operator brake, forged upper and lower receivers, gas block with front sight base, RRA NSP flip front and rear sights, NSP two-piece drop-in CAR length rail, two-stage trigger, NSP CAR stock, NSP overmolded pistol grips, Black or Pink NSP handguard, stock, grip, sights, and magazine, 7 lbs. New 2015.

| MSR $1,120 | $935 | $850 | $725 | $625 | $550 | $475 | $425 | |

LAR-15 OPERATOR SERIES – .223 Rem. cal., GIO, 16 in. chrome moly barrel, tactical muzzle brake, forged LAR-15 lower, forged A4 upper receiver, upper Picatinny rail, Operator CAR stock, matte black finish, two-stage trigger, winter trigger guard, Ergo SureGrip, configurations include the Entry (R-4 handguard and barrel profile), the Tactical (R-4 handguard), and the Elite (half-quad free float handguard with mid-length gas system), designed for left-handed shooters, 7.2-8 lbs. New 2011.

| MSR $1,360 | $1,135 | $1,015 | $890 | $735 | $650 | $550 | $465 | |

Beginning 2013, this model became available in left-hand only (LAR-15LH, Lef-T).

LAR-15 OPERATOR III – 5.56 NATO cal., GIO, similar to Operator Series, except has low profile mid-length gas system, Operator muzzle brake, TRO free float mid-length handguard, Mil-Spec top rail, includes two 30 shot mags. and case, Hogue grip, 8 lbs. New 2014.

| MSR $1,065 | $900 | $750 | $665 | $585 | $515 | $450 | $395 | |

LAR-15 PREDATOR PURSUIT RIFLE/MID-LENGTH – .223 Wylde chamber for 5.56mm and .223 Rem. cal., GIO, 16 (Mid-length model only) or 20 (rifle length model only) in. air gauged heavy match stainless steel barrel, forged A4 upper, low profile gas block, two-stage match trigger, Winter trigger guard, Deluxe entended free float rail with rifle or mid-length handguard, A2 buttstock, Hogue rubber pistol grip, 7-7.9 lbs.

| MSR $1,305 | $1,100 | $995 | $875 | $735 | $650 | $550 | $465 | |

Add $35 for rifle length handguard (Predator Pursuit Rifle).

Add $145 for left-hand (LAR-15LH, Lef-T Predator Pursuit, new 2013).

LAR-15 PRO-SERIES ELITE – .223 Rem. cal., GIO, forged A4 upper receiver, chrome lined 16 in. Wilson chrome moly barrel, RRA tactical muzzle brake, flip front sight and gas block assembly, two-stage match trigger, Winter trigger guard, Badger tactical charging handle latch, A.R.M.S. #40L low profile flip up rear sight, Ergo sure-grip pistol grip, 6-position tactical CAR stock, MWI front sling adapter, MWI CAR stock end plate adapter loop rear sling mount, Daniel Defense 12.0 FSPM quad rail handguard, SureFire M910A-WH vertical foregrip weaponlight, Aimpoint Comp M2 red dot optical sight and QRP mount with spacer, 9 1/2 lbs. Disc. 2012.

| | $2,500 | $2,175 | $1,975 | $1,595 | $1,300 | $1,025 | $975 | *$2,750* |

LAR-15 PRO-SERIES GOVERNMENT – .223 Rem. cal., GIO, forged A4 upper receiver, 16 in. chrome lined Wilson chrome moly barrel, A2 flash hider, two-stage match trigger, flip up rear sight, Hogue rubber pistol grip, 6-position tactical CAR stock, Surefire M73 quad rail handguard, Surefire M951 WeaponLight light system, EOTech 552 Holosight red-dot optical sight, side mount sling swivel, 8.2 lbs. Disc. 2012.

| | $2,150 | $1,850 | $1,575 | $1,425 | $1,150 | $950 | $750 | *$2,375* |

LAR-15 R3 COMPETITION – .223 Wylde chambered for 5.56mm and .223 cal., GIO, 18 in. fluted stainless steel barrel with directionally-tuned and ported muzzle brake, 30 shot mag., low profile gas block, forged LAR-15 lower and forged A4 upper receiver, two-stage match trigger, Winter trigger guard, Star safety, RRA TRO-XL free float handguard, RRA adj. Operator A2 or CAR stock, Hogue rubber pistol grips, matte black finish, 7.6 lbs. New 2013.

| MSR $1,355 | $1,135 | $1,000 | $890 | $735 | $650 | $550 | $465 | |

LAR-15 STANDARD A2 – .223 Rem. cal., GIO, forged A2 upper receiver, 20 in. Wilson chrome moly barrel, A2 flash hider, two-stage match trigger, A2 pistol grip, handguard, and buttstock, 8.6 lbs. Disc. 2012.

| | $900 | $775 | $650 | $595 | $485 | $415 | $370 | *$980* |

MSR	100%	98%	95%	90%	80%	70%	60%	Last MSR

LAR-15 STANDARD A4 – .223 Wylde chamber for 5.56mm and .223 cal., GIO, 20 in. chrome moly HBAR barrel with A2 flash hider, A2 front sight base, forged LAR-15 lower and A4 upper receivers, two-stage trigger, A2 handguard, A2 buttstock, overmolded A2 pistol grip, 8.2 lbs.

	MSR $1,010	$860	$725	$650	$585	$515	$450	$395

Add $145 for left-hand (LAR-15LH, Lef-T, new 2013).

LAR-15 TACTICAL CAR UTE2 – .223 Rem. cal., GIO, forged Universal Tactical Entry 2 upper receiver, 16 in. Wilson chrome moly barrel, A2 flash hider, two-stage match trigger, Hogue rubber pistol grip, R-4 handguard, 6-position tactical CAR stock, 7 1/2 lbs. Disc. 2012.

	$965	$825	$700	$625	$515	$450	$395	*$1,060*

LAR-15 TACTICAL CAR A4 – .223 Rem. cal., GIO, 16 in. chrome moly barrel, A2 flash hider, forged A4 upper receiver, two-stage trigger, Hogue rubber pistol grip, R-4 handguard, 6-position tactical CAR stock, 7 1/2 lbs.

	MSR $1,065	$900	$750	$665	$585	$515	$450	$395

Add $40 for chrome lined barrel.

Add $115 for left-hand (LAR-15LH, Lef-T, mfg. 2013-2014).

LAR-15 TEXAS RIFLE – .223 Wylde chambered for 5.56mm or .223 cal., GIO, 16 in. fluted stainless steel barrel with Black Cerakote finish, tuned and ported muzzle brake, low profile gas block, two-stage chrome trigger, Winter trigger guard, forged A4 upper, Star safety, RRA Texas XL free float handguard with two rail covers, A2 or CAR buttstock, Hogue rubber pistol grip, BCM Gunfighter charging handle, receivers and handguard finished in Cerakote Magpul Flat Dark Earth, Burnt Bronze, or Barret Bronze, 7.6 lbs. New 2015.

	MSR $1,700	$1,450	$1,275	$1,125	$1,000	$850	$735	$595

LAR-15 VARMINT A4 – .223 Rem. or .308 Win. (mfg. 2010-2011) cal., GIO, 16, 18, 20, or 24 in. air gauged stainless steel bull barrel, forged A4 upper receiver, low profile gas block, two-stage trigger, Winter trigger guard, RRA TRO free float top rail handguard, Hogue rubber pistol grip, A2 buttstock, 8-10.2 lbs.

	MSR $1,255	$1,065	$950	$815	$685	$595	$515	$440

Add $15 for 18 in., $30 for 20 in., or $40 for 24 in. barrel.

Add $145 for left-hand (LAR-15LH, Lef-T Varmint A4, new 2013).

Add $395 for .308 Win. cal. (mfg. 2010-2011).

LAR-15 VARMINT EOP (ELEVATED OPTICAL PLATFORM) – .223 Wylde chambered for 5.56mm or .223 Rem. cal., GIO, 16, 18, 20, or 24 in. Wilson air gauged stainless steel bull barrel, forged EOP upper receiver, low profile gas block, Weaver style light varmint gas block with sight rail, two-stage match trigger, Winter trigger guard, knurled and fluted free floating aluminum tube (disc.) or TRO free float handguard, Hogue rubber pistol grip, A2 buttstock, 8.2-10 lbs.

	MSR $1,290	$1,095	$995	$875	$735	$650	$550	$465

Add $15 for 18, $30 for 20, or $40 for 24 in. barrel.

LAR-15 X-1 RIFLE – .223 Wylde chambered for 5.56 NATO or .223 cal., GIO, 18 in. fluted stainless steel barrel, RRA Beast or Hunter muzzle brake, forged upper and lower receivers, low profile gas block, two-stage trigger, Winter trigger guard, RRA TRO-XL extended length free float rail, Operator A2 or Operator CAR stock, Hogue rubber pistol grip, Black or Tan finish, includes 9 in. XL accessory rail and two 2 in. short accessory rails, 7.7 lbs. New 2014.

	MSR $1,495	$1,285	$1,120	$975	$800	$700	$600	$495

Add $50 for RRA Hunter muzzle brake and tan finish.

LAR-PDS CARBINE (PISTON DRIVEN SYSTEM) – .223 Rem. cal., GPO, 16 in. chrome moly barrel, A2 flash hider, black finish, full length upper and partial lower Picatinny rails, Hogue rubber pistol grip, ribbed forend, two-stage trigger, injection molded ribbed or tri-rail handguard, folding ambidextrous non-reciprocating charging handles, two-position regulator, side folding 6-position tactical stock with receiver extension storage compartment, approx. 7.4 lbs. New 2011.

	MSR $1,595	$1,350	$1,200	$1,075	$950	$815	$700	$575

Add $155 for tri-rail handguard.

LAR-6.8 CAR A2/A4 – 6.8 SPC cal., GIO, forged A2 (disc. 2012) or A4 upper receiver, 16 in. Wilson chrome moly barrel, A2 flash hider, two-stage match trigger, A2 pistol grip, 6-pos. tactical CAR stock, choice of CAR length or mid-length handguard, 7 1/2 lbs.

	MSR $1,055	$885	$750	$665	$585	$515	$450	$395

Add $50 for Operator stock.

LAR-6.8 COYOTE CARBINE – 6.8 SPC cal., GIO, forged A4 upper receiver, 16 in. Wilson chrome moly HBar barrel, Smith Vortex flash hider, Weaver style light varmint gas block with sight rail, two-stage match trigger, winter trigger guard, Hogue rubber pistol grip, Hogue overmolded free float tube handguard, A2 stock, 7 lbs.

	MSR $1,310	$1,100	$995	$875	$735	$650	$550	$465

MSR	100%	98%	95%	90%	80%	70%	60%	Last MSR

LAR-6.8 X-1 RIFLE – 6.8 SPC II cal., GIO, 18 in. fluted stainless steel HBAR barrel, RRA Beast or Hunter muzzle brake, low profile gas block, forged lower and A4 upper receiver, two-stage trigger, Winter trigger guard, RRA TRO-XL extended length free float rail, RRA Operator A2 or Operator CAR stock, Hogue rubber pistol grip, Black or Tan finish, includes one 9 in. XL accessory rail and two 2 in. short accessory rails for handguard, 7.9 lbs. New 2014.

	100%	98%	95%	90%	80%	70%	60%	
MSR $1,595	$1,350	$1,200	$1,075	$950	$815	$700	$575	

Add $50 for RRA Hunter muzzle brake and tan finish.

LAR-300 COYOTE CARBINE – .300 ACC Blackout cal., 16 in. chrome moly HBAR barrel with Smith Vortex flash hider, forged A4 upper, low profile gas block, two-stage trigger, Winter trigger guard, Deluxe extended free float CAR length handguard, Operator CAR stock, Hogue rubber pistol grip, 7.2 lbs. New 2015.

	100%	98%	95%	90%	80%	70%	60%	
MSR $1,295	$1,095	$995	$875	$735	$650	$550	$465	

LAR-300 CAR A4 – .300 ACC Blackout cal., GIO, 16 in. chrome moly HBAR barrel with A2 flash hider, forged A4 upper, two-stage trigger, CAR length handguard, 6-pos. tactical CAR stock, overmolded A2 grip, 7.1 lbs. New 2015.

	100%	98%	95%	90%	80%	70%	60%	
MSR $1,070	$900	$750	$665	$585	$515	$450	$395	

LAR-300 DELTA CAR – .300 ACC Blackout cal., GIO, 16 in. chrome moly barrel with A2 flash hider, low profile gas block, two-stage trigger, Winter trigger guard, Delta CAR stock, Ergo Suregrip pistol grip, Delta quad rail CAR length two-piece drop-in handguard, 7 lbs. New 2015.

	100%	98%	95%	90%	80%	70%	60%	
MSR $1,120	$935	$850	$725	$625	$550	$475	$425	

LAR-300 TACTICAL CAR A4 – .300 ACC Blackout cal., GIO, 16 in. chrome moly HBAR barrel with A2 flash hider, A2 front sight base with side mount sling swivel, two-stage trigger, R-4 handguard, 6-pos. tactical CAR stock, Hogue rubber grip, 7 1/2 lbs. New 2015.

	100%	98%	95%	90%	80%	70%	60%	
MSR $1,100	$925	$850	$725	$625	$550	$475	$425	

LAR-300 X-1 RIFLE – .300 ACC Blackout cal., GIO, 18 in. fluted stainless steel HBAR barrel, RRA Beast or Hunter muzzle brake, forged upper and lower receivers, low profile gas block, two-stage trigger, Winter trigger guard, RRA TRO-XL extended length free float rail, Operator A2 or Operator CAR stock, Hogue rubber pistol grip, black or tan finish, includes 9 in. XL accessory rail and two 2 in. short accessory rails, 7.9 lbs. New 2015.

	100%	98%	95%	90%	80%	70%	60%	
MSR $1,585	$1,350	$1,165	$1,050	$885	$750	$625	$525	

Add $50 for RRA Hunter muzzle brake and tan finish.

LAR-458 CAR A4 – .458 SOCOM cal., GIO, forged A4 upper receiver, 16 in. Wilson chrome moly bull barrel, A2 flash hider, Weaver style varmint gas block with sight rail, two-stage match trigger, knurled and fluted free floating aluminum tube handguard, A2 buttstock and pistol grip, 7.6 lbs.

	100%	98%	95%	90%	80%	70%	60%	
MSR $1,220	$1,035	$925	$800	$685	$595	$515	$440	

LAR-458 MID-LENGTH A4 – .458 SOCOM cal., GIO, forged A4 upper receiver, 16 in. chrome moly bull barrel, A2 flash hider, gas block with sight rail, two-stage match trigger, knurled and fluted free floating aluminum tube handguard, A2 buttstock and pistol grip, 7.8 lbs. New 2010.

	100%	98%	95%	90%	80%	70%	60%	
MSR $1,220	$1,035	$925	$800	$685	$595	$515	$440	

Add $290 for Operator model with half quad free float with full length top rail, Vortex flash hider and CAR stock (new 2010).

LAR-458 TACTICAL CARBINE – .458 SOCOM cal., GIO, 16 in. chrome moly bull barrel with Operator muzzle brake, forged A4 upper, low profile gas block, two-stage trigger, Winter trigger guard, RRA Deluxe extended free float rifle length handguard, NSP 6-pos. CAR stock, Hogue rubber pistol grip, 7.8 lbs. New 2015.

	100%	98%	95%	90%	80%	70%	60%	
MSR $1,415	$1,210	$1,075	$950	$800	$700	$600	$495	

LAR-458 X-1 RIFLE – .458 Socom cal., GIO, 18 in. fluted stainless steel bull barrel, RRA Beast or Hunter muzzle brake, low profile gas block, forged RRA LAR-458 lower and A4 upper receiver, two-stage trigger, Winter trigger guard, RRA TRO-XL extended length free float rail, RRA Operator A2 or Operator CAR stock, Hogue rubber pistol grip, black or tan finish, includes one 9 in. XL accessory rail and two 2 in. short accessory rails for handguard, 8.7 lbs. New 2014.

	100%	98%	95%	90%	80%	70%	60%	
MSR $1,595	$1,350	$1,200	$1,075	$950	$815	$700	$575	

Add $50 for RRA Hunter muzzle brake and tan finish.

LAR-8 MID LENGTH A2/A4 – .308 Win. cal., GIO, 16 in. barrel with A2 flash hider, CAR buttstock, gas block sight base, Hogue rubber grip, two stage trigger, forged A2 (disc. 2012) or A4 upper receiver, mid-length handguard, approx. 8 lbs. New 2010.

	100%	98%	95%	90%	80%	70%	60%	
MSR $1,335	$1,135	$995	$875	$735	$650	$550	$465	

LAR-8 ELITE OPERATOR – .308 Win. cal., GIO, 16 in. barrel, similar to Mid-length A4, except has advanced half quad rail, flip front sight, gas block sight base, Operator stock and Smith Vortex flash hider. New 2010.

	100%	98%	95%	90%	80%	70%	60%	
MSR $1,740	$1,475	$1,290	$1,125	$1,000	$850	$735	$595	

MSR	100%	98%	95%	90%	80%	70%	60%	Last MSR

LAR-8 STANDARD A2/A4 – .308 Win. cal., GIO, forged lower and A2 (disc. 2012) or A4 upper receiver, 20 in. chrome moly barrel, A2 flash hider, gas block sight base, two stage trigger, A2 buttstock, A2 handguard, Hogue rubber pistol grip, approx. 9 lbs. New 2010.

| MSR $1,370 | $1,165 | $1,025 | $900 | $750 | $650 | $550 | $465 | |

LAR-8 STANDARD OPERATOR – .308 Win. cal., GIO, 16 in. barrel, similar to LAR-8 Standard A4, except has advanced half quad rail, flip front sight, gas block sight base, Operator stock and Smith Vortex flash hider. New 2010.

| MSR $1,790 | $1,525 | $1,335 | $1,150 | $1,015 | $860 | $735 | $595 | |

LAR-8 PREDATOR HP – .308 Win. cal., GIO, forged lower and upper receiver, 20 in. bead blasted lightweight stainless steel barrel, gas block sight base, two stage trigger, A2 buttstock, free float tube handguard, Hogue rubber pistol grip, approx. 8.6 lbs. New 2010.

| MSR $1,690 | $1,435 | $1,255 | $1,100 | $960 | $815 | $700 | $575 | |

Add $50 for Operator A2 stock.

LAR-8 VARMINT A4 – .308 Win. cal., GIO, forged LAR-8 lower, forged A4 upper receiver with forward assist and port door, 20 or 26 in. cryo treated stainless steel bull barrel, varmint gas block with sight rail, two-stage trigger, winter trigger guard, Hogue rubber pistol grip, A2 buttstock, aluminum free float tube handguard, 10.4-11.6 lbs. New 2011.

| MSR $1,655 | $1,400 | $1,225 | $1,075 | $950 | $815 | $700 | $575 | |

Add $5 for 26 in. barrel.

LAR-8 X-1 RIFLE – 7.62 NATO cal., GIO, 18 in. fluted stainless steel HBAR barrel, RRA Beast or Hunter muzzle brake, RRA custom low profile gas block, forged lower and A4 upper with forward assist and port door, two-stage trigger, Winter trigger guard, RRA TRO-STD rifle length free float rail, RRA Operator A2 or Operator CAR stock, Hogue rubber pistol grip, Black or Tan finish, includes one 81/2 in. accessory rail and two 2 in. accessory rails for handguard, 9 1/2 lbs. New 2014.

| MSR $1,845 | $1,575 | $1,365 | $1,175 | $1,050 | $900 | $775 | $625 | |

Add $50 for RRA Hunter muzzle brake and tan finish.

LAR-9 CAR A2/A4 – 9mm Para. cal., GIO, forged A2 (disc. 2012) or A4 upper receiver, 16 in. Wilson chrome moly barrel, A1 flash hider, standard single stage trigger, CAR length handguard, A2 pistol grip, 6-position tactical CAR stock, approx. 7 lbs.

| MSR $1,180 | $975 | $885 | $750 | $635 | $550 | $475 | $425 | |

Add $50 for Operator stock.

LAR-9 MID-LENGTH A4 – 9mm Para. cal., GIO, forged A4 upper receiver, forged lower with integral magwell, 16 in. Wilson chrome moly barrel with gas block sight base, A2 flash hider, standard single stage trigger, mid-length handguard, Hogue pistol grip, 6-position tactical CAR stock, approx. 7 lbs.

| MSR $1,180 | $975 | $885 | $750 | $635 | $550 | $475 | $425 | |

Add $50 for Operator stock.

LAR-10 VARMINT A4 – .308 Win. cal., GIO, forged A4 upper reciever with forward assist and port door, 26 in. Wilson stainless steel bull barrel, Weaver type sight base gas block, two-stage match trigger, knurled and fluted free floating aluminum tube handguard, Hogue pistol grip, A2 buttstock, 11.6 lbs. Disc. 2010.

| | $1,150 | $920 | $890 | $735 | $650 | $550 | $465 | $1,350 |

LAR-10 MID-LENGTH A2/A4 – .308 Win. cal., GIO, forged A2 or A4 upper receiver with forward assist and ejection port door, 16 in. Wilson chrome moly barrel, A2 flash hider, A2 front sight or A4 gas block with sight base, two-stage match trigger, mid-length handguard, Hogue rubber pistol grip, 6-position tactical CAR stock, approx. 8 lbs. Disc. 2009.

| | $925 | $850 | $725 | $625 | $550 | $475 | $425 | $1,100 |

Add $50 for A2 sights.

LAR-10 STANDARD A2/A4 – .308 Win. cal., GIO, forged A2 or A4 upper receiver, with forward assist and ejection port door, 20 in. Wilson chrome moly barrel, A2 flash hider, A2 front sight or A4 gas block sight base, two-stage match trigger, A2 handguard, Hogue rubber pistol grip, A2 buttstock, 9.3 lbs. Disc. 2009.

| | $925 | $850 | $725 | $625 | $550 | $475 | $425 | $1,100 |

Add $45 for A2 sights.

LAR-40 MID-LENGTH A2/A4 – .40 S&W cal., GIO, forged A2 (disc. 2011) or A4 (new 2013) upper, 16 in. chrome moly barrel, A2 flash hider, two-stage match trigger, mid-length handguard, Hogue rubber pistol grip, 6-position tactical CAR stock, approx. 7 lbs. Mfg. 2010-2011, reintroduced 2013.

| MSR $1,260 | $1,065 | $950 | $815 | $685 | $595 | $515 | $440 | |

LAR-40 CAR A2/A4 – .40 S&W cal., GIO, forged A2 (disc. 2011) or A4 upper receiver, 16 in. chrome moly barrel, A2 flash hider, single stage trigger, R-4 handguard, 6-position tactical CAR stock with Hogue pistol grip, approx. 7 lbs. Disc. 2011, reintroduced 2013.

| MSR $1,260 | $1,065 | $950 | $815 | $685 | $595 | $515 | $440 | |

Add $145 for quad rail.
Add $50 for Operator stock.

MSR	100%	98%	95%	90%	80%	70%	60%	Last MSR

LAR-47 CAR A4 – 7.62x39mm cal., GIO, 16 in. chrome lined HBar barrel with A2 flash hider, gas block front sight base, forged lower and A4 upper, two-stage trigger, CAR handguard, 6-pos. CAR tactical stock, A2 pistol grip, ambidextrous mag. release, 6.4 lbs. New 2013.

MSR $1,270	$1,075	$955	$815	$685	$595	$515	$440	

LAR-47 COYOTE CARBINE – 7.62x39mm cal., GIO, 16 in. chrome lined HBAR barrel with Smith Vortex flash hider, low profile gas block, forged upper and lower receivers, two-stage trigger, ambidextrous mag. release, Deluxe extended free float rifle length handguard, 6-pos. CAR stock, Hogue rubber pistol grip, 7.8 lbs. New 2015.

MSR $1,740	$1,475	$1,285	$1,125	$1,000	$850	$735	$595	

LAR-47 DELTA CARBINE – 7.62x39mm cal., GIO, forged lower and A4 upper, 16 in. chrome lined HBar barrel with A2 flash hider, low profile gas block, two-stage trigger, two-piece Delta quad rail handguard, 6-pos. Delta CAR stock, Ergo Suregrip, ambidextrous mag. release, 7 3/4 lbs. New 2013.

MSR $1,545	$1,315	$1,155	$1,040	$875	$750	$625	$525	

LAR-47 TACTICAL COMP – 7.62x39mm cal., GIO, 16 in. chrome lined HBAR barrel with Operator brake, flip front sight gas block assembly, forged upper and lower receivers, two-stage trigger, ambidextrous mag. release, CAR length free float quad rail, Operator CAR stock, overmolded pistol grips, 7.8 lbs. New 2015.

MSR $1,500	$1,275	$1,125	$1,025	$875	$750	$625	$525	

LAR-47 X-1 RIFLE – 7.62x39mm cal., GIO, 18 in. fluted stainless steel bull barrel, RRA Beast or Hunter muzzle brake, forged upper and lower receivers, low profile gas block, two-stage trigger, RRA TRO-XL extended length free float rail, Operator A2 or Operator CAR stock, Hogue rubber pistol grip, Black or Tan finish, includes 9 in. XL accessory rail and two 2 in. short accessory rails for handguard, 8.2 lbs. New 2015.

MSR $1,600	$1,350	$1,200	$1,075	$950	$815	$700	$575	

Add $50 for RRA Hunter muzzle brake and tan finish.

TASC RIFLE – .223 Rem. cal., GIO, 16 in. Wilson chrome moly barrel, A2 flash hider, forged A2 upper receiver with lockable windage and elevation adj. rear sight, two-stage match trigger, Hogue rubber pistol grip, A2 buttstock or 6-position CAR tactical buttstock, choice of R-4 or mid-length handguard, approx. 7 1/2 lbs. Disc. 2009.

	$875	$765	$655	$595	$515	$450	$395	*$950*

Add $15 for six-position collapsible stock.

PRO-SERIES TASC – .223 Rem. cal., GIO, forged A2 upper receiver, chrome lined 16 in. Wilson chrome moly barrel, Smith Vortex flash hider, two-stage match trigger, oversize Winter trigger guard, A2 rear sight with lockable windage and elevation, Hogue rubber pistol grip, 6-position tactical CAR stock, Surefire M85 mid-length quad rail, graphite fore grip, EOTech 511 Holosight, Midwest Industries A2 adj. cantilever sight mount, 8.7 lbs. Disc. 2009.

	$1,700	$1,500	$1,250	$1,100	$950	$825	$675	*$2,000*

PISTOLS: SEMI-AUTO

Rock River Arms made a variety of high quality M-1911 based semi-autos through 2011. They specialized in manufacturing their own National Match frames and slides. Previous models included: the Standard Match (disc. 2003, last MSR was $1,150), Ultimate Match Achiever (disc. 2003, last MSR was $2,255), Matchmaster Steel (disc. 2001, last MSR was $2,355), Elite Commando (disc. 2005, last MSR was $1,725), Hi-Cap Basic Limited (disc. 2003, last MSR was $1,895), and the Doug Koenig Signature Series (disc. 2003, last MSR was $5,000, .38 Super cal.). Rock River Arms still offers parts, and reintroduced a 1911 model in 2013. In 2015, Rock River Arms reintroduced several of their renowned steel frame 1911-A1 models.

Add $200 for 1911-A1 Cerakote finish options in Barrett Bronze, Graphite Black, Gunmetal Gray, SOCOM Blue, Magpul Flat Dark Earth, Burnt Bronze, or Tan (new 2015).

1911 POLY – .45 ACP cal., SA, 1911 style polymer frame, 5 in. chrome moly barrel, steel slide, 7 shot mag., overmolded pistol grips, beavertail grip safety, Commander hammer, parkerized finish, aluminum speed trigger, dovetail front and rear sight, includes two mags., polymer holster, mag loader, lock and fitted case, 36 oz. Advertised 2013. Became available 2015.

MSR $925	$830	$725	$625	$565	$455	$375	$300	

1911-A1 BASIC LIMITED (BASIC LIMITED MATCH) – 9mm Para. (disc. 2010), .38 Super (disc. 2010), .40 S&W (disc. 2010), or .45 ACP cal., SA, 4 1/4 (disc. 2010), 5, or 6 (disc. 2010) in. slide with double serrations, National Match frame with beveled magwell, low mount Bo-Mar hidden leaf rear and RRA dovetail front sights, Match Commander hammer and match sear, extractor and extended ejector, lowered and flared ejection port, beavertail grip safety, aluminum speed trigger, two piece recoil guide rod and polished feed ramp, serrated slide stop and ambidextrous safety, deluxe checkered Rosewood grips, blue, hard chrome (disc. 2010), black "T" (disc. 2010), or black/green "T" duotone (disc. 2010) finish. Disc. 2010, reintroduced 2015.

MSR $1,950	$1,750	$1,530	$1,315	$1,190	$965	$800	$625	

Last MSR in 2010 was $1,840.

MSR	100%	98%	95%	90%	80%	70%	60%	Last MSR

1911-A1 BULLSEYE WADCUTTER

9mm Para. (disc. 2011), .38 Super (disc. 2011), .40 S&W (disc. 2011), or .45 ACP cal., SA, 4 1/4 (disc. 2011), 5, or 6 (disc. 2011) in. barrel, throated NM KART barrel w/NM bushing (new 2015), 7 shot mag., forged National Match frame with choice of RRA Slide mount, Bo-Mar rib (disc. 2011), Bullseye rib (new 2015), Caspian frame mount sights (disc. 2011), or Weigand 3rd Gen. frame mount, double slide serrations, beavertail grip safety with raised pad, serrated slide stop and two-piece recoil guide rod, lowered and flared ejection port, Commander hammer and match sear, aluminum speed trigger, checkered rosewood grips, blue, hard chrome (disc. 2011), black "T" (disc. 2011), or black/green "T" duotone (disc. 2011) finish. Disc. 2011, reintroduced 2015.

| MSR $2,500 | $2,250 | $1,970 | $1,690 | $1,530 | $1,250 | $1,025 | $800 | |

Last MSR in 2011 was $1,715

Add $100 for Bullseye rib (new 2015) or Weigand frame mount.
Add $35 for Caspian frame mount or Bo-Mar rib (disc. 2011).

1911-A1 CARRY PISTOL (BASIC CARRY)

.45 ACP cal., SA, 5 in. National Match barrel with double slide serrations, parkerized finish, checkered rosewood grips, RRA forged National Match frame, lowered and flared ejection port, RRA dovetail front sight with Tritium inserts, Heinie or Novak (new 2015) rear sight, Match Commander hammer and match sear, aluminum speed trigger, beavertail grip safety, standard (disc.) or tactical (new 2015) mag. catch, safety, and standard recoil system. Disc. 2010, reintroduced 2015.

| MSR $1,650 | $1,485 | $1,300 | $1,115 | $1,010 | $815 | $675 | $525 | |

1911-A1 LIMITED MATCH

9mm Para. (disc. 2010), .38 Super (disc. 2010), .40 S&W (disc. 2010), or .45 ACP cal., SA, 4 1/4 (disc. 2010), 5, or 6 (disc. 2010) in. barrel with double slide serrations and RRA borders, National Match frame with beveled magwell, checkered front and rear strap, low mount hidden leaf rear sight, RRA dovetail front sight, Match Commander hammer, aluminum speed trigger, beavertail grip safety with raised pad, deluxe checkered (disc. 2010) or G10 black laminate (new 2015) grips, two-piece recoil guide rod, blue (disc. 2010), brushed hard chrome, black "T" (disc. 2010), or black/green duotone (disc. 2010) finish, includes one magazine. Disc. 2010, reintroduced 2015.

| MSR $3,600 | $3,240 | $2,835 | $2,430 | $2,200 | $1,780 | $1,475 | $1,150 | |

Last MSR in 2010 was $2,185

1911-A1 NM HARDBALL (NATIONAL MATCH HARDBALL)

9mm Para. (disc. 2011), .38 Super (disc. 2011), .40 S&W (disc. 2011), or .45 ACP cal., SA, 4 1/4 (disc. 2011), 5, or 6 (disc. 2011) in. barrel, forged NM frame with beveled magwell, choice of rear or double (disc. 2011) slide serrations, aluminum speed trigger, checkered front strap, hidden leaf rear and dovetail front sights, lowered and flared ejection port, tuned and polished extractor and extended ejector, checkered rosewood (disc. 2011) or deluxe walnut grips, blue, hard chrome (disc. 2011), black "T" (disc. 2011), or black/green "T" duotone (disc. 2011) finish, includes one mag. Disc. 2011, reintroduced 2015.

| MSR $2,550 | $2,295 | $2,010 | $1,720 | $1,560 | $1,260 | $1,050 | $825 | |

Last MSR in 2010 was $1,550

1911-A1 TACTICAL PISTOL

9mm Para. (disc. 2011), .38 Super (disc. 2011), .40 S&W (disc. 2011), or .45 ACP cal., SA, 5 in. barrel with double slide serrations, checkered front strap, RRA bar stock frame with integral light rail, lowered and flared ejection port, RRA dovetail front sight with Tritium inserts, Heinie or Novak (new 2015) rear sight with Tritium inserts, alum. speed trigger, tuned and polished extractor, extended ejector, beavertail grip safety with raised pad, tactical mag. catch and safety, standard recoil system, completely dehorned for carry, checkered rosewood grips, blue, hard chrome (disc. 2011), black "T" (disc. 2011), or black/green "T" duotone (disc. 2011) finish. Disc. 2011, reintroduced 2015.

| MSR $2,200 | $1,980 | $1,735 | $1,485 | $1,350 | $1,095 | $895 | $720 | |

RRA PRO CARRY

9mm Para., .38 Super, .40 S&W, or .45 ACP cal., SA, 4 1/4, 5, or 6 in. barrel with slide serrations, RRA National Match frame, checkered front strap, lowered and flared ejection port, RRA dovetail front sight with Tritium inserts, Match Commander hammer, alum. speed trigger, tuned and polished extractor, extended ejector, deluxe rosewood grips, choice of Heinie or Novak rear sight with Tritium inserts, beavertail grip safety. Disc. 2010.

| | $1,675 | $1,465 | $1,255 | $1,140 | $920 | $755 | $585 | *$1,920* |

RRA SERVICE AUTO

9mm Para. cal., similar to RRA Pro Carry, except with 5 in. barrel and double slide serrations. Mfg. 2009-2010.

| | $1,575 | $1,380 | $1,180 | $1,070 | $865 | $710 | $550 | *$1,790* |

LIMITED POLICE COMPETITION

9mm Para. cal., 5 in. National Match barrel, SA, blue, hard chrome, black "T", or black/green "T" duotone finish, RRA forged National Match frame with beveled magwell with choice of 20, 25, or 30 LPI checkered front strap, double slide serrations, 3-position rear sight, choice of wide or narrow blade, RRA dovetail front sight, tall, thinned, and relieved for PPC, Smith & Alexander flared magwell, lowered and flared ejection port, Match Commander hammer and match sear, tuned and polished extractor and extended ejector, beavertail grip safety and flat checkered mainspring housing, deluxe checkered grips, ambidextrous safety, tuned and polished feed ramp, two-piece recoil spring guide rod. Disc. 2010.

| | $2,095 | $1,825 | $1,600 | $1,375 | $1,250 | $1,000 | $775 | *$2,375* |

MSR	100%	98%	95%	90%	80%	70%	60%	Last MSR

UNLIMITED POLICE COMPETITION – 9mm Para. cal., forged 6 in. National Match barrel, SA, RRA forged National Match frame with beveled magwell, choice of 20, 25, or 30 LPI checkered front strap, double slide serrations, similar configuration as Limited Police Competition. Disc. 2010.

	$2,095	$1,825	$1,600	$1,375	$1,250	$1,000	$775	$2,375

LAR-15 A4 – .223 Rem. cal., GPO, 7 or 10 1/2 in. chrome moly barrel with A2 flash hider, single stage trigger, Forged LAR-15 lower and A4 upper receivers, Hogue rubber pistol grip, pistol length handguard and TRO free float rail (7 in. barrel only) or R-4 handguard (10 1/2 in. barrel only), matte black finish, 5.2 lbs.

MSR $1,055	$895	$785	$670	$610	$490	$400	$325	

Add $120 for 7 in. barrel or for gas block sight base.

LAR-9 A4 – 9mm Para. cal., 7 or 10 1/2 (chrome lined) in. chrome moly barrel with A2 flash hider, single stage trigger, TRO free float rail and pistol length handguard (7 in. barrel) or R4 handguard (10 1/2 in. barrel), gas block sight base (10 1/2 in. only), RRA LAR-9 lower with integral magwell and forged A4 upper, Hogue rubber grip, includes one mag., 4.8 lbs.

MSR $1,205	$1,025	$895	$770	$695	$565	$475	$375	

Add $115 for 7 in. barrel.

LAR-40 – .40 S&W cal., GPO, 7 or 10 1/2 in. barrel, forged lower receiver with integral magwell, A2 or A4 upper, single stage trigger, Hogue rubber pistol grip, approx. 5 lbs. Mfg. 2010-2011.

	$1,050	$900	$800	$700	$600	$500	$400	$1,120

Add $45 for 7 in. barrel and free float tube handguard.
Add $10-$15 for gas block sight base.

PDS PISTOL (PISTON DRIVEN SYSTEM) – .223 Rem. or .300 AAC Blackout (new 2015) cal., GPO, 8 or 9 (new 2013) in. chrome moly barrel, features A2 flash hider, full length upper and partial lower Picatinny rails, Hogue rubber pistol grip, ribbed forend, single (disc. 2012) or two-stage (new 2013) stage trigger, injection molded ribbed handguard, folding ambidextrous non-reciprocating charging handles, two-position regulator, approx. 5 lbs. New 2010.

MSR $1,245	$1,050	$925	$795	$715	$580	$475	$400	

Add $65 for .300 AAC Blackout cal.
Add $150 for aluminum tri-rail handguard.

ROCKY MOUNTAIN ARMS, INC.

Current firearms manufacturer located in Longmont, CO since 1991.

Rocky Mountain Arms is a quality specialty manufacturer of rifles and pistols. All firearms are finished in a Dupont Teflon-S industrial coating called "Bear Coat".

PISTOLS: SEMI-AUTO

BAP (BOLT ACTION PISTOL) – .308 Win., 7.62x39mm, or 10mm Rocky Mountain Thunderer (10x51mm) cal., 14 in. heavy fluted Douglas Match barrel, Kevlar/graphite pistol grip stock, supplied with Harris bipod and black nylon case. Mfg. 1993 only.

	$1,425	$1,275	$1,100	$950	$825	$700	$575	$1,595

22K PISTOLS – .22 LR cal., AR style pistols featuring GIO, 7 in. barrel, choice of matte black or NATO Green Teflon-S finish, will use Colt conversion kit, choice of carrying handle or flat-top upper receiver, 10 or 30 shot mag., includes black nylon case. Mfg. 1993 only.

	$475	$425	$375	$350	$325	$295	$275	$525

Add $50 for flat-top receiver with Weaver style bases.

PATRIOT PISTOL – .223 Rem. cal., AR-15 style, GIO, 7 in. match barrel with integral Max Dynamic muzzle brake, available with either carrying handle upper receiver and fixed sights or flat-top receiver with Weaver style bases, fluted upper receiver became an option in 1994, accepts standard AR-15 mags, 21 in. OAL, 5 lbs. Mfg. 1993-94 (per C/B), reintroduced 2005.

MSR $3,000	$2,850	$2,500	$2,250	$2,000	$1,750	$1,500	$1,250	

KOMRADE – 7.62x39mm cal., floating 7 in. barrel, 5 shot mag., includes carrying handle upper receiver with fixed sights, red finish only, 5 lbs. Very limited mfg. was pre-ban 1994 only.

Last MSR was $1,995

Rarity precludes accurate pricing on this model. Recent sales with case in the $3,500 range.

RIFLES: BOLT ACTION

PROFESSIONAL SERIES – .223 Rem., .30-06, .308 Win., or .300 Win. Mag. cal., bolt action rifle utilizing modified Mauser action, fluted 26 in. Douglas premium heavy match barrel with integral muzzle brake, custom Kevlar-Graphite stock with off-set thumbhole, test target. Mfg. 1991-95.

	$2,050	$1,650	$1,275	$995	$850	$725	$600	$2,200

Add $100 for .300 Win. Mag. cal.
Add $300 for left-hand action.

MSR		100%	98%	95%	90%	80%	70%	60%	Last MSR

PRAIRIE STALKER – .223 Rem., .22-250 Rem., .30-06, .308 Win., or .300 Win. Mag. cal., choice of Remington, Savage, or Winchester barreled action, includes Choate ultimate sniper stock, lapped bolt and match crown, "Bear Coat" all-weather finish, includes factory test target. Limited mfg. 1998 only.

		$1,595	$1,350	$1,150	$950	$875	$775	$675	$1,795

* ***Prairie Stalker Ultimate*** – similar to Prairie Stalker, except custom barrel and caliber specifications are customer's choice. Limited mfg. 1998 only.

		$2,200	$1,875	$1,625	$1,400	$1,200	$1,000	$895	$2,495

PRO-VARMINT – .22-250 Rem., or .223 Rem. cal., RMA action, 22 in. heavy match barrel with recessed crown, "Bear Coat" metal finish, Choate stock with aluminum bedding. Mfg. 1999-2002.

		$995	$875	$800	$725	$650	$575	$450	$1,095

POLICE MARKSMAN – .308 Win. or .300 Win. Mag. cal., similar to Professional Series, except has 40X-C stock featuring adj. cheekpiece and buttplate, target rail, Buehler micro-dial scope mounting system. Mfg. 1991-95.

		$2,325	$1,995	$1,650	$1,325	$1,100	$900	$700	$2,500

Add $100 for .300 Win. Mag. cal.
Add $400 for left-hand action.
Add $400 for illuminated dot scope (4-12x56mm).

* ***Police Marksman II*** – .308 Win. cal., RMA action, 22 in. heavy match barrel with recessed crown, "Bear Coat" metal finish, Choate stock with aluminum bedding. Mfg. 1999-2002.

		$995	$875	$800	$725	$650	$575	$450	$1,095

PRO-GUIDE – .280 Rem., .35 Whelen, .308 Win., 7x57mm Mauser, or 7mm-08 Rem. cal., Scout Rifle design with 17 in. Shilen barrel, "Bear Coat" finish, approx. 7 lbs. Mfg. 1999-2002.

		$2,025	$1,800	$1,600	$1,425	$1,200	$1,000	$825	$2,295

NINJA SCOUT RIFLE – .22 WMR cal., takedown rifle based on Marlin action, black stock, 16 1/2 in. match grade crowned barrel, forward mounted Weaver style scope base, adj. rear sight, 7 shot mag. Mfg. 1991-95.

		$640	$575	$525	$460	$430	$390	$360	$695

Add $200 for illuminated dot scope (1.5-4X) w/extended eye relief.

SCOUT SEMI-AUTO – .22 WMR cal., patterned after Marlin action. Mfg. 1993-95.

		$650	$575	$495	$395	$350	$295	$260	$725

Add $200 for illuminated dot scope (1.5-4X) w/extended eye relief.

RIFLES: SEMI-AUTO

M-SHORTEEN – .308 Win. cal., compact highly modified M1-A featuring 17" match crowned barrel, custom front sight, mod. gas system, hand honed action and trigger, custom muzzle brake. Mfg. 1991-94.

		$1,650	$1,425	$1,175	$995	$850	$725	$600	$1,895

Add $200 for Woodland/Desert camo.

VARMINTER – .223 Rem. cal. only, AR-15 style, GIO, 20 in. fluted heavy match barrel, flat-top receiver with Weaver style bases, round metal National Match handguard, free float barrel, choice of NATO green or matte black Teflon-S finish, supplied with case and factory test target (sub-MOA accuracy). Mfg. 1993-94.

		$2,195	$1,800	$1,600	$1,400	$1,200	$1,000	$875	$2,495

PATRIOT MATCH RIFLE – .223 Rem. cal., AR-15 style, GIO, 20 in. Bull Match barrel, regular or milled upper and lower receivers, two-piece machined aluminum handguard, choice of DuPont Teflon finish in black or NATO green, 1/2 MOA accuracy, hard case. Mfg. 1995-97, reintroduced 2005.

MSR $2,500		$2,350	$2,050	$1,700	$1,425	$1,200	$1,000	$895	

SHOTGUNS: SLIDE ACTION

870 COMPETITOR – 12 ga., 3 in. chamber, security configuration with synthetic stock, hand-honed action, ghost ring adj. sights, "Bear Coat" finish, high visibility follower. Mfg. 1996-97.

		$695	$625	$550	$500	$450	$400	$360	$795

ROHRBAUGH FIREARMS CORP.

Current manufacturer located in Bayport, NY, previously located in Deer Park, NY.

PISTOLS: SEMI-AUTO

R-9 – 9mm Para. or .380 ACP (new 2007) cal., DAO, 2.9 in. barrel, free bored to reduce felt recoil, frame is 7075-T651 aluminum, stainless steel or black Stealth slide, 6 shot mag., parts cut from solid billets, all internal parts are stainless, short recoil locked breech with cam operated tilting barrel locking system, recessed hammer, carbon fiber (disc.) or G10

	MSR	100%	98%	95%	90%	80%	70%	60%	*Last MSR*

grips, no sights, 12.8 (carbon fiber grips) or 13 1/2 (G10 grips) oz. New 2003.

    MSR $1,150 $1,000 $875 $750 $680 $550 $450 $350

Add $45 for black Stealth slide.

* ***R9S Model*** – similar to Model R-9, except has fixed open sights, 9mm Para. cal. variations include Tribute (silver gun with black/blue CF grips, new 2012), Coyote (Coyote Tan metal finish, new 2012), and Covert (black with sights, new 2012). New 2004.

    MSR $1,150 $1,000 $875 $750 $680 $550 $450 $350

Add $45 for black Stealth slide.

Add $200 R9S Tribute (new 2012). Add $600 for R9S Coyote or Covert (new 2012).

Add $45 for Elite Custom Model (Model R9SE, disc.).

ROHRBAUGH ROBAR R9 SERIES – similar to original R9, except frame, barrel, slide and trigger are treated with Robar Industries NP3 coating (corrosion resistant and self lubricating), polished stainless steel, limited lifetime warranty. Mfg. 2010 only.

                   $1,500 $1,315 $1,125 $1,020 $825 $675 $525   *$1,795*

RUSSIAN AMERICAN ARMORY COMPANY

Please refer to the RAAC listing in this section.

RUSSIAN SERVICE PISTOLS AND RIFLES

Previously manufactured at various Russian military arsenals (including Tula).

RIFLES

Original Soviet Mosin-Nagant bolt action rifles/carbines include: M1891 rifle, M1891 Dragoon, M1891/30 Rifle, M1891/30 Sniper Model, M1910 Carbine, M1938 Carbine, and the M1944 Carbine. Values for these older original military configurations will approximate values listed for the original mfg. Mosin-Nagant.

TOKAREV M1938 & M1940 (SVT) SEMI-AUTO – 7.62x54R cal., SVT M40 is the more common variation, while the SVT M38 sniper is very rare, 10 shot mag., first Russian military semi-auto, large quantities manufactured beginning 1938, but original surviving specimens in excellent condition are now very scarce.

    SVT M38 $4,500 $4,000 $3,500 $3,000 $2,500 $2,000 $1,500

    SVT M40 $1,800 $1,500 $1,200 $1,000 $800 $700 $600

RPD SEMI-AUTO – 7.62x39mm cal., converted from belt fed to semi-auto only, fired from closed bolt, milled receiver, includes 50 shot mag., recent importation.

                   $3,795 $3,495 $2,950 $2,600 $2,300 $2,000 $1,750

NOTES

S SECTION

S.W.A.T. FIREARMS

Current manufacturer of AR-15 style pistols and rifles located in Campbell, TX since 1999.

S.W.A.T. Firearms manufactures upper and lower receivers, suppressors, standard billet and tactical rifles, and will customize each firearm to customer specifications.

MSR	100%	98%	95%	90%	80%	70%	60%	Last MSR

PISTOLS: SEMI-AUTO

5.56 STANDARD – 5.56 NATO cal., GIO, 10 1/2 in. stainless steel barrel with MB2 muzzle brake/flash hider, low profile steel gas block, 10 1/2 in. slant nose KeyMod handguard. New 2014.

MSR $1,050	$885	$750	$665	$585	$515	$450	$395	

5.56 STAINLESS – 5.56 NATO cal., GIO, 10 1/2 in. stainless steel barrel with MB2 muzzle brake/flash hider, low profile steel gas block, 10 in. slant nose KeyMod handguard. New 2014.

MSR $1,130	$935	$850	$725	$625	$550	$475	$425	

.300 BLACKOUT – .300 AAC Blackout cal., GIO, 10 1/2 in. black phosphate barrel with MB2 muzzle brake/flash hider, low profile steel gas block, 10 in. slant nose KeyMod handguard. New 2014.

MSR $1,130	$935	$850	$725	$625	$550	$475	$425	

7 1/2 IN. PISTOL W/KNURLED TUBE – 5.56 NATO cal., GIO, 7 1/2 in. barrel, knurled tube, top Picatinny rail, black finish. New 2014.

MSR $1,020	$860	$725	$650	$585	$515	$450	$395	

10 1/2 IN. PISTOL w/CARBINE RAIL – 5.56 NATO cal., GIO, 10 1/2 in. barrel, carbine rail, black finish. New 2014.

MSR $1,020	$860	$725	$650	$585	$515	$450	$395	

RIFLES: SEMI-AUTO

All rifles are shipped with a soft case, magazine, gun lock, assembly manual, and come with a lifetime warranty.

.300 AAC – .300 AAC Blackout cal., GIO, 16 in. heavy chrome moly barrel (stainless steel barrel upgrade is additional), upper receiver with Picatinny rail, gas block Picatinny rail, collapsible buttstock, pistol grip, 6.7 lbs. New 2015.

MSR $1,070	$900	$760	$665	$585	$515	$450	$395	

BASE HEAVY (BASE MODERN SPORTING RIFLE) – 5.56 NATO or 7.62 NATO (disc.) cal., GIO, 16 in. heavy chrome moly barrel, free float round knurled handguard or quad rail, flat-top upper with Picatinny rail, gas block Picatinny rail, collapsible buttstock, pistol grip, black finish, 7 lbs.

MSR $880	$740	$650	$580	$515	$450	$385	$340	

Add $210 for 7.62 NATO cal. (disc.).

* ***Base Heavy 2*** – 5.56 NATO cal., GIO, 16 in. heavy chrome moly barrel, billet upper and lower receiver, mid-length free floating rail, Ergo textured grip, 39 1/2 in. OAL

MSR $938	$800	$700	$615	$550	$485	$415	$370	

* ***Base Heavy 3*** – 5.56 NATO cal., GIO, 16 in. heavy chrome moly barrel, steel low profile gas block, rifle length free floating rail, billet upper and lower receivers, collapsible buttstock, Ergo tactical (palm swell) grip, 39 1/2 in. OAL.

MSR $1,150	$975	$885	$765	$655	$575	$495	$435	

BASE 20 – 5.56 NATO cal., GIO, 20 in. heavy chrome moly barrel, upper receiver with Picatinny rail, handguard tube, gas block Picatinny rail, fixed stock, pistol grip, black finish, 8.3 lbs. New 2015.

Please contact the company directly for pricing, options, and availability for this model (see Trademark Index).

COMPETITOR – 5.56 NATO cal., GIO, 16 in. heavy chrome moly barrel, MB-3 muzzle brake, low profile gas block, flip up iron sights, extended charging handle, billet upper and lower receiver, Magpul AVG stock, Ergo textured grip, 8.3 lbs.

MSR $1,260	$1,050	$950	$815	$715	$625	$535	$450	

DESERT STORM – 5.56 NATO cal., GIO, 16 in. lightweight chrome moly barrel with FH-1 flash hider, rifle length free float quad rail, Magpul MOE stock, Magpul AFG forward grip, Cerakote Magpul FDE finish, 6.97 lbs.

MSR $1,229	$1,035	$925	$800	$685	$595	$515	$440	

DRAGON SLAYER – 5.56 NATO cal., GIO, 16 in. barrel with MB-2 muzzle brake, mid-length free floating quad rail, low profile gas block, billet upper and lower receivers, Crimson Cerakote finish, 6.2 lbs.

MSR $1,160	$975	$885	$765	$655	$575	$495	$435	

M4 – 5.56 NATO cal., GIO, 16 in. M4 contour barrel with FH-1 flash hider, Ergo grip, carbine length free float quad rail, 7 lbs. Disc. 2015.

	$860	$725	$650	$585	$515	$450	$395	$1,014

MSR	100%	98%	95%	90%	80%	70%	60%	Last MSR

PRISON PINK CONVICTION – 5.56 NATO cal., GIO, 16 in. lightweight chrome moly barrel, 2-piece quad rail, Prison Pink Cerakote finish, 6.6 lbs. Disc. 2014.

	100%	98%	95%	90%	80%	70%	60%	Last MSR
	$1,225	$1,090	$950	$800	$700	$600	$495	*$1,458*

TASTANIUM DEVIL – 5.56 NATO cal., GIO, 20 in. heavy barrel with MB-3 muzzle brake, carbine length free float quad rail, Titanium Cerakote finish, 8.3 lbs. New 2014.

MSR $1,179	$990	$885	$765	$655	$575	$495	$435	

TOP GUN – 5.56 NATO cal., GIO, 16 in. heavy chrome moly barrel with MB-1 muzzle brake (disc.) or FH-1 flash hider, low profile gas block, two-stage trigger, billet upper and lower receivers, YHM quad rail, extended charging handle, Ergo (disc.) or Magpul AFG pistol grip, Magpul CTR stock, ambi-sling mount, 8.3 lbs.

MSR $1,187	$1,000	$900	$765	$655	$575	$495	$435	

S.W.D., INC.

Previous manufacturer located in Atlanta, GA.

Similar models have previously been manufactured by R.P.B. Industries, Inc. (1979-82), and met with BATF disapproval because of convertibility into fully automatic operation. "Cobray" is a trademark for the M11/9 semiautomatic pistol.

CARBINES

SEMI-AUTO CARBINE – 9mm Para. cal., same mechanism as M11, 16 1/4 in. shrouded barrel, telescoping stock.

	$550	$495	$450	$400	$325	$275	$235	

PISTOLS: SEMI-AUTO

COBRAY M-11/NINE mm – 9mm Para. cal., fires from closed bolt, SA, 3rd generation design, stamped steel frame, 32 shot mag., parkerized finish, similar in appearance to Ingram Mac 10.

	$475	$395	$350	$300	$295	$275	$250	

This model was also available in a fully-auto variation, Class III transferable only.

REVOLVERS

LADIES HOME COMPANION – .45-70 Govt. cal., double action design utilizing spring wound 12 shot rotary mag., 12 in. barrel, steel barrel and frame, 9 lbs. 6 oz. Mfg. 1990-94.

	$650	$525	$400	$360	$335	$310	$290	

SHOTGUNS: SINGLE SHOT

TERMINATOR – 12 or 20 ga., tactical design shotgun with 18 in. cylinder bore barrel, parkerized finish, ejector. Mfg. 1986-88 only.

	$150	$125	$95	$80	$70	$60	$55	*$110*

SD TACTICAL ARMS

Current rifle manufacturer located in Menomonie, WI.

CARBINES/RIFLES: SEMI-AUTO

SD Tactical Arms manufactures a line of AR style semi-auto carbines and rifles built per individual customer specifications. The company also offers a complete line of tactical gear and accessories, including rails and magazines. Since each rifle is built per custom order, please contact the company directly for pricing, available options, and delivery time (see Trademark Index).

SI DEFENSE, INC.

Current AR-15 style carbine/rifle manufacturer located in Kalispell, MT.

CARBINES/RIFLES: SEMI-AUTO

MID-LENGTH CUSTOM – .223 Rem./5.56x45mm cal., internal GIO system, 18 in. stainless steel fluted barrel with SI DRK muzzle brake, flip-up front and rear sights, billet upper and lower receivers, black mid-length handguard, Ace stock, black finish. Disc. 2013.

Retail pricing was not available on this model.

SI-C .223 STANDARD CARBINE – .223 Rem./5.56x45mm cal., internal gas block system, 16 in. parkerized barrel with SI DRK muzzle brake, A2 style fixed front sight, flip-up rear sight, billet upper and lower receivers, custom carbine length handguard, available in Black, Flat Dark Earth, or OD Green finish. Disc. 2014.

	$950	$865	$725	$625	$550	$475	$425	

SI-C ATC – 5.56 NATO cal., 16 in. M4 contour, nitride coated barrel with muzzle brake, 30 shot Magpul mag., 6-position adj. stock, 15 in. floating handguard, Hogue grip, fixed front and adj. rear sight, standard Black or Flat Dark Earth finish, 6 1/2 lbs. New 2014.

MSR $1,650	$1,375	$1,215	$1,075	$950	$815	$700	$575	

MSR	100%	98%	95%	90%	80%	70%	60%	Last MSR

SI-C M4 CARBINE – 5.56 NATO cal., nickel boron coated bolt carrier group, 16 in. M4 contour, nitride coated barrel with muzzle brake, 30 shot Magpul mag., Magpul MBUS flip-up rear sight, YHM flip-up front sight, 6-position adj. stock, Magpul MOE handguard, standard Black or Flat Dark Earth finish, 7 lbs. Mfg. 2014 only.

| | $1,025 | $925 | $800 | $85 | $595 | $515 | $440 | |

SI-C M406 – 5.56 NATO cal., AR-15 style, 16 in. barrel, carbine length gas system, black Nitride bolt carrier group, folding front and flip rear sights, Magpul CTR stock, 6.4 lbs. New 2015.

| MSR $1,250 | $1,050 | $950 | $815 | $685 | $595 | $515 | $440 | |

SI-D .308 AMBI CF BATTLE RIFLE – .308 Win. cal., 18 in. Proof Research match grade carbon fiber barrel, Fortis Red muzzle brake, 20 shot mag., hard black anodized billet upper and lower receiver, ambidextrous controls, quick snap dust cover, forward assist, flared magwell, integrated trigger guard, 15 1/2 in. lightweight free-floating KeyMod handguard, CMC trigger, ambi charging handle, Battle Arms Development selector, Mission First tactical stock, 8 1/2 lbs. New 2015.

| MSR $3,499 | $2,975 | $2,575 | $2,075 | $1,765 | $1,450 | $1,225 | $1,050 | |

SI-D .308 AMBI SS BATTLE RIFLE – .308 Win. cal., 16 in. stainless steel black Nitride barrel and DRK-SI-D muzzle brake, 20 shot mag., ambi billet upper and lower receivers, ambidextrous mirrored controls, quick snap dust cover, forward assist, flared magwell, integrated trigger guard, 15 1/2 in. lightweight free-floating KeyMod handguard, STD trigger, ambi charging handle, Battle Arms development selector, Mission First Tactical stock, 8 1/2 lbs. New 2015.

| MSR $2,850 | $2,400 | $2,090 | $1,725 | $1,475 | $1,200 | $1,025 | $895 | |

SI-D .308 BATTLE RIFLE – .308 Win./7.62 NATO cal., 16 1/2 in. parkerized barrel with SI DRK muzzle brake, A2 style fixed front sight, carbine length gas system, billet upper and lower receivers, SI Defense carbine handguard, 6-position adj. buttstock, black finish. Disc. 2014.

| | $1,575 | $1,385 | $1,200 | $1,065 | $900 | $775 | $625 | |

SI-D .308 CARBINE (HUNTING/SPORTSMAN) – .308 Win. cal., 16 in. M4 contour barrel with SI Defense DRK compensator, Weaver extra tall scope rings and Nikon 3x9 power scope with BDC reticle, free floating carbine length tube handguard, SI Defense adj. quad rail gas block, adj. 6-position Choate stock, 20 shot Magpul mag., Flat Dark Earth finish, 9.1 lbs. Disc. 2014.

| | $2,100 | $1,850 | $1,575 | $1,425 | $1,150 | $950 | $795 | |

SI-D .308 RIFLE – .308 Win. cal., 16 in. stainless steel barrel with Black Nitride finish, 20 shot mag., billet upper and lower receivers, flared magwell, forward assist, integrated trigger guard, single stage trigger, rifle length gas system, Magpul MBUS sights, Midwest Industries handguard, Magpul CTR stock, Hogue grip, 8 1/2 lbs. New 2015.

| MSR $1,800 | $1,525 | $1,350 | $1,175 | $1,050 | $900 | $775 | $625 | |

SI-D .300WM AMBI PETRA RIFLE – .300 WM cal. New 2015.

Please contact the company directly for more information including features, options, pricing, and availability (see Trademark Index).

TREAD – 5.56x45mm cal., 18 in. parkerized barrel with SI Defense DRK muzzle brake, flip-up front and rear sights, billet upper and lower receivers, custom handguard, Ace buttstock, "Don't Tread On Me" engraving, custom Timney skeletonized trigger group, extended charging handle latch, red and white colored lettering. Disc. 2013.

Retail pricing was not available on this model.

ST. GEORGE ARMS

Current trademark of semi-auto rifles manufactured by K&M Arms with company headquarters located in Murfreesboro, TN.

RIFLES: SEMI-AUTO

LEADER 50 A1 – .50 BMG cal., bullpup configuration, GIO, 24 in. barrel with large muzzle brake, 10 shot detachable box mag. (M82A1 type), AR-15 style pistol grip and safety lever, top Picatinny rail, includes front bipod and rear monopod, matte black finish, 20 lbs. New 2016.

| MSR $8,200 | $7,500 | $6,500 | $5,500 | $4,750 | $4,000 | $3,250 | $2,650 | |

Blue Book Publications selected this model as one of its Top 10 Industry Awards from all the new firearms at the 2016 SHOT Show.

SKS

SKS designates a semi-auto rifle design originally developed by the Russian military, and manufactured in Russia by both Tula Arsenal (1949-1956) and by Izhevsk Arsenal from 1953-1954. Currently manufactured in Russia, China, and many other countries. Previously manufactured in Russia, China (largest quantity), N. Korea, East Germany, Romania, Albania, Yugoslavia, and North Vietnam.

MSR	100%	98%	95%	90%	80%	70%	60%	*Last MSR*

SKS DEVELOPMENT & HISTORY

SKS (Samozaryadnyi Karabin Simonova) - developed by Sergei Gavrilovich Simonov in the late 1940s to use the 7.62 cartridge of 1943 (7.62x39mm). The SKS is actually based on an earlier design developed by Simonov in 1936 as a prototype self-loading military rifle. The SKS was adopted by the Soviet military in 1949, two years after the AK-47, and was originally intended as a complement to the AK-47s select-fire capability. It served in this role until the mid-to-late 1950s, when it was withdrawn from active issue and sent to reserve units and Soviet Youth "Pioneer" programs. It was also released for use in military assistance programs to Soviet Bloc countries and other "friendly" governments. Much of the original SKS manufacturing equipment was shipped to Communist China prior to 1960. Since then, most of the SKS carbines produced, including those used by the Viet Cong in Vietnam, have come from China.

Like the AK-47, the Simonov carbine is a robust military rifle. It, too, was designed to be used by troops with very little formal education or training. It will operate reliably in the harshest climatic conditions, from the Russian arctic to the steamy jungles of Southeast Asia. Its chrome-lined bore is impervious to the corrosive effects of fulminate of mercury primers and the action is easily disassembled for cleaning and maintenance.

The SKS and a modified sporter called the OP-SKS (OP stands for Okhotnichnyi Patron) are the standard hunting rifles for a majority of Russian hunters. It is routinely used to take everything from the Russian saiga antelope up to and including moose, boar, and brown bear. The main difference between the regular SKS and the OP variant is in the chamber dimensions and the rate of rifling. The OP starts as a regular SKS, then has the barrel removed and replaced with one designed to specifically handle a slightly longer and heavier bullet.

Prior to the "assault weapons" ban, hundreds of thousands of SKS carbines were imported into the U.S. The SKS was rapidly becoming one of the favorites of American hunters and shooters. Its low cost and durability made it a popular "truck gun" for those shooters who spend a lot of time in the woods, whether they are ranchers, farmers, or plinkers. While the Russian made SKS is a bonafide curio and relic firearm and legal for importation, the Clinton administration suspended all import permits for firearms having a rifled bore and ammunition from the former Soviet Union in early 1994. In order to get the ban lifted, the Russian government signed a trade agreement, wherein they agreed to deny export licenses to any American company seeking SKS rifles and a variety of other firearms and ammunition deemed politically incorrect by Clinton & Gore. The BATF then used this agreement as a reason to deny import licenses for any SKS from any country.

Most of the SKS carbines imported into the U.S. came from the Peoples Republic of China. They were a mix of refurbished military issue, straight military surplus, and even some new manufacture. Quality was rather poor. Compared to the SKS Chinese carbines, only a few Russian made SKSs ever made it into the U.S. All are from military stockpiles and were refurbished at the Tula Arms Works, probably the oldest continuously operating armory in the world. Recently, more SKS carbines have been imported from the former Yugoslavia by Century International Arms. These carbines carry the former Soviet Bloc designation of "Type 58" and feature milled receivers. Quality is generally good, and values are comparable to other Russian/European SKS imports. Values for unmodified Russian and Eastern European made SKS carbines (those with the original magazines and stock) are higher than the Chinese copies.

The most collectible SKS is East German mfg., and SKS rifles mfg. in N. Korea and N. Vietnam are also quite rare in the U.S.

Over 600 million SKS carbines have been manufactured in China alone, by over 45 different manufacturers, in addition to the millions manufactured in other former Soviet Bloc countries. The Simonov carbine was the best selling semi-auto rifle in America (and other countries) during 1993-94, and remains a popular choice for plinking, hunting, and protection in the new millennium.

RIFLES: SEMI-AUTO

SKS – 7.62x39mm Russian cal., Soviet designed, original Soviet mfg. as well as copies mfg. in China, Russia, Yugoslavia, and many other countries, gas operated weapon, 10 shot fixed mag., wood stock (thumbhole design on newer mfg.), with or w/o (newer mfg.) permanently attached folding bayonet, tangent rear and hooded front sight, no current importation from China, Russia, or the former Yugoslavia.

Please refer to individual importers for other SKS listings, including Norinco, Poly-Technologies, and Mitchell Arms.

* *SKS Mfg. in Russia, Yugoslavia, Romania*

	100%	98%	95%	90%	80%	70%	60%
	$495	$450	$375	$325	$275	$235	$195

* *SKS Chinese Recent Mfg. w/Thumbhole Stock*

	100%	98%	95%	90%	80%	70%	60%
	$375	$325	$275	$250	$225	$200	$175

SMI ARMS

Currrent pistol and rifle manufacturer located in Merriam, KS.

SMI Arms is a division of Signature Manufacturing. In addition to complete firearms built to order, SMI Arms/Signature Manufacturing also manufactures individual component parts and accessories for the AR-15/AK-47 platform.

PISTOLS: SEMI-AUTO

SMI ENFORCER AR15 PISTOL MOD 1 – 5.56 NATO or .300 AAC Blackout cal., pistol length gas system, 7 1/2 in. match grade M4 carbine barrel, target crown, birdcage flash hider, 30 shot mag., no sights, 7 in. free float ultralight slim KeyMod rail system, billet aluminum upper and lower receiver, flared magwell, pistol buffer tube only, standard Mil-Spec A2 pistol grip in black or FDE, standard Mil-Spec hardcoat anodized trigger guard, 6 lbs.

MSR $799	100%	98%	95%	90%	80%	70%	60%
	$685	$615	$550	$475	$420	$365	$335

MSR	100%	98%	95%	90%	80%	70%	60%	Last MSR

SMI ENFORCER AR15 PISTOL MOD 2 – 5.56 NATO or .300 AAC Blackout cal., pistol length gas system, 7 1/2 in. match grade M4 carbine barrel, target crown, birdcage flash hider, 30 shot Magpul mag., Magpul MBUS 2 front and rear sights, billet aluminum upper and lower receivers, 7 in. free float ultralight slim KeyMod rail system, SMI BETR tactical charging handle, single stage trigger, and Winter trigger guard, flared magwell, KAK Industries Shockwave blade pistol stabilizer, Magpul MOE grip, Magpul angled forearm grip, hardcoat anodized black or FDE finish, 6 lbs.

	100%	98%	95%	90%	80%	70%	60%	
MSR $1,299	$1,100	$995	$875	$735	$650	$550	$465	

RIFLES: SEMI-AUTO

AK STORM TACTICAL – 7.62x39 cal., 16 in. chrome lined black Nitride barrel, U.S. made slant brake and parkerized bent receiver, 30 shot mag., standard front and rear sights, Red Star Arms adj. trigger and FCG plate, Magpul MOE AK grip, Zhukov stock and furniture, built on Polish parts kit, ceramic single color finish, 7 lbs.

MSR $1,399	$1,200	$1,075	$950	$800	$700	$600	$495	

AK STORM TACTICAL SHOT 2016 EDITION – 7.62x39 cal., AK-47 design, 16 in. chrome lined black Nitride barrel, PWS FSC 47 flash suppressor, 30 shot mag., standard front and rear sights, Krebs enhanced safety, Manticore Arms alpha rail, Magpul MOE AK grip, MFT Minimalist stock, VLTOR stock adapter, Ultimak optics mount, Red Star Arms adj. trigger and FCG plate, ceramic single color finish, 7 1/2 lbs. Limited mfg. beginning 2016.

MSR $1,799	$1,525	$1,350	$1,175	$1,050	$900	$775	$625	

AK WOLVERINE – 7.62x39 cal., 16 in. chrome lined black Nitride barrel, U.S. made slant brake and parkerized bent receiver, standard front and rear sights, Tapco G2 trigger, Red Star Arms FCG plate, original wood furniture, built from Polish parts kit, 7 lbs.

MSR $999	$850	$725	$650	$585	$515	$450	$395	

BCR MOD 1 (BAD COMPANY RIFLE) – 5.56 NATO, .300 AAC Blackout, 7.62x30, 6.5 Grendel, or 6.8 SPC II cal., carbine length gas system, 16 in. match grade M4 carbine barrel, target crown, birdcage flash hider, 30 shot mag., billet aluminum upper and lower receiver, flared magwell, no sights, 13 in. free float ultralight slim KeyMod rail system, standard Mil-Spec charging handle and trigger guard, 6-position Mil-Spec buffer tube, Magpul MOE collapsible pistol grip stock, hardcoat anodized finish in black or FDE, 6.7 lbs.

MSR $1,099	$925	$850	$725	$625	$550	$475	$425	

BCR MOD 2 (BAD COMPANY RIFLE) – 5.56 NATO or .300 AAC Blackout cal., carbine length gas system, 16 in. match grade M4 carbine barrel, target crown, birdcage flash hider, includes two Mil-Spec aluminum 30 shot mags., billet aluminum upper and lower, Magpul MBUS 2 front and rear sights, 15 in. free float ultralight slim KeyMod rail system, 6-position Mil-Spec buffer tube, standard Mil-Spec charging handle, tuned trigger, and trigger guard, Magpul MOE collapsible pistol grip stock, hardcoat anodized finish in black or FDE, 6 1/2 lbs.

MSR $1,199	$1,025	$925	$800	$685	$595	$515	$440	

BCR MOD 3 (BAD COMPANY RIFLE) – 5.56 NATO, .300 AAC Blackout, 7.62x30, 6.5 Grendel, or 6.8 SPC II cal., 16 in. match grade M4 carbine barrel, target crown, birdcage flash hider, carbine length gas system, 30 shot mag., Magpul MBUS 2 front and rear sights, 15 in. free float ultralight slim KeyMod rail system, billet aluminum upper and lower receiver, flared magwell, SMI BETR tactical charging handle, 6-position Mil-Spec buffer tube, Magpul MOE collapsible pistol grip stock, BETR tactical Winter trigger guard, hardcoat anodized finish in black or FDE, 6 1/2 lbs.

MSR $1,249	$1,050	$950	$815	$715	$625	$535	$450	

BCR MOD 4 (BAD COMPANY RIFLE) – 5.56 NATO or .300 AAC Blackout cal., carbine length gas system, 16 in. match grade M4 carbine barrel, target crown, birdcage flash hider, includes two 30 shot Magpul mags., billet aluminum upper and lower receiver, flared magwell, Magpul MBUS 2 front and rear sights, 15 in. free float ultralight slim KeyMod rail system, SMI BETR tactical charging handle, single stage trigger, and Winter trigger guard, 6-position Mil-Spec buffer tube, Magpul MOE collapsible pistol grip stock, hardcoat anodized finish in black or FDE, 6 1/2 lbs.

MSR $1,399	$1,200	$1,075	$950	$800	$700	$600	$495	

STR MOD 1 (SPORTING TACTICAL RIFLE) – 5.56 NATO, 7.62x30, 6.5 Grendel, or 6.8 SPC II cal., carbine length gas system, 18 in. match grade barrel, target crown, birdcage flash hider, includes two Magpul 30 shot mags., Magpul MBUS 2 front and rear sights, 13 in. free float P-Mod KeyMod rail system, billet aluminum upper and lower receivers, flared magwell, nickel boron EXO finished bolt carrier group, SMI BETR tactical charging handle, single stage trigger, and Winter trigger guard, 6-position Mil-Spec buffer tube, MFT Minimalist collapsible pistol grp stock, hardcoat anodized finish in black or FDE, 6 1/2 lbs.

MSR $1,599	$1,350	$1,200	$1,075	$950	$815	$700	$575	

STR MOD 2 (SPORTING TACTICAL RIFLE) – 5.56 NATO, 7.62x30, 6.5 Grendel, or 6.8 SPC II cal., carbine length gas system, 18 in. match grade barrel, target crown, birdcage flash hider, Magpul MBUS 2 front and rear sights, 15 in. free float P-Mod KeyMod rail system, includes two Magpul 30 shot mags., billet aluminum upper and lower, flared magwell, nickel boron EXO finished bolt carrier group, SMI BETR tactical charging handle, single stage trigger, and Winter trigger guard, 6-position Mil-Spec buffer tube, MFT Minimalist collapsible pistol grip stock, hardcoat anodized finish in black or FDE, 6 1/2 lbs.

MSR $1,649	$1,400	$1,235	$1,100	$975	$830	$720	$585	

MSR	100%	98%	95%	90%	80%	70%	60%	Last MSR

STR MOD 3 (SPORTING TACTICAL RIFLE) – 5.56 NATO, 7.62x30, 6.5 Grendel, or 6.8 SPC II cal., carbine length gas system, 18 in. match grade barrel, target crown, birdcage flash hider, billet aluminum upper and lower receiver, flared magwell, 6-position Mil-Spec buffer tube, nickel boron EXO bolt carrier group, Magpul MBUS 2 front and rear sights, 17 in. free float P-Mod KeyMod rail system, SMI BETR tactical charging handle, single stage trigger, and Winter trigger guard, MFT Minimalist collapsible pistol grip stock, hardcoat anodized finish in black or FDE, includes two Magpul 30 shot mags., 6 1/2 lbs.

	100%	98%	95%	90%	80%	70%	60%	Last MSR
MSR $1,699	$1,450	$1,275	$1,125	$1,000	$850	$735	$595	

SRM ARMS

Current shotgun manufacturer located in Meridan, ID. Exclusively distributed by GSA Direct LLC located in Boise, ID. Dealer sales.

SHOTGUNS: SEMI-AUTO

MODEL 1216 – 12 ga., 3 in. chamber, 18 1/2 in. barrel with fixed choke, bullpup with pistol grip configuration, semi-auto roller-locked delayed blowback system, features a rotating detachable 16 shot mag with four separate tubes, ambidextrous receiver with tip up action, full length top Picatinny rail and three handguard rails, ghost rear and post front sights, matte black, FDE, or OD Green finish, 32 1/2 in. OAL, 7 1/4 lbs. New late 2011.

	100%	98%	95%	90%	80%	70%	60%	Last MSR
MSR $2,399	$2,050	$1,800	$1,500	$1,300	$1,075	$935	$795	

The concept of the SRM shotgun began in the early 2000s when special forces personnel described their dream shotgun to the SRM developers. The first model was previewed in 2008, with final versions arriving late 2011.

STI INTERNATIONAL

Current manufacturer established during 1993, and located in Georgetown, TX. Distributor and dealer sales.

In addition to manufacturing the pistols listed, STI International also makes frame kits in steel, stainless steel, aluminum, or titanium - please contact the company directly for pricing and availability (see Trademark Index).

PISTOLS: SEMI-AUTO, SINGLE ACTION

The beginning numerals on all STI pistols designate the barrel length, and most of the following models are listed in numerical sequence.

2.5 NEMESIS – 7mm Penna/7x23mm cal., 2 1/2 in. barrel. Mfg. 2010-2011.

	100%	98%	95%	90%	80%	70%	60%	Last MSR
	$840	$725	$625	$525	$450	$400	$350	$870

3.0 ELEKTRA – 9mm Para., .40 S&W (disc. 2012), or .45 ACP cal., forged aluminum frame, 3.24 in. bull barrel, stainless steel slide with Cerakote finish, black anodized or silver frame with Crimson Trace Laser (new 2015, black anodized only) or blue (disc. 2014), purple (disc. 2014), red (disc. 2014), or pink pearl (9mm only) grips, rear cocking serrations, beavertail grip safety, 6 or 8 shot mag., fixed Tritium 2 dot sights. New 2010.

	100%	98%	95%	90%	80%	70%	60%	Last MSR
MSR $1,399	$1,250	$1,095	$950	$850	$700	$600	$495	

Add $300 for Crimson Trace Laser grips (new 2015).

3.0 ESCORT – 9mm Para., .40 S&W (mfg. 2013-2014) or .45 ACP cal., 3.24 in. bull barrel, forged aluminum Officer length frame with silver Cerakote finish, STI Recoil Master, undercut trigger guard, bobbed grip safety, checkered Cocobolo grips, round top slide with rear cocking serrations and blued finish, adj. 3-dot sights, 6 or 8 shot mag., stippled front strap, 22.8 oz. New 2009.

	100%	98%	95%	90%	80%	70%	60%	Last MSR
MSR $1,299	$1,100	$995	$875	$735	$650	$550	$465	

3.0 OFF DUTY – 9mm Para. or .45 ACP cal., compact frame, blued or hard chrome matte finish, 3 in. barrel with blue slide, checkered Cocobolo grips, stippled front strap, competition front sight, tactical rear sight, 31.3 oz. Mfg. 2009-2013.

	100%	98%	95%	90%	80%	70%	60%	Last MSR
	$1,075	$950	$800	$725	$595	$485	$375	$1,265

3.0 ROGUE – 9mm Para. cal., 3 in. bull barrel, forged aluminum compact frame, STI stippled front strap, undercut trigger guard, blued slide with Duracoated frame, integral sights, 21 oz. Mfg. 2009.

	100%	98%	95%	90%	80%	70%	60%	Last MSR
	$925	$825	$725	$650	$575	$500	$425	$1,024

3.0 SHADOW – 9mm Para., .40 S&W, or .45 ACP cal., 3 in. bull barrel, matte black KG coated finish, forged aluminum frame, undercut trigger guard, stippled front strap, ultra thin G10 grips with STI logo, rear cocking serrations, curved trigger, beavertail grip safety, fixed Tritium 2 dot sights, 6 or 8 shot mag., 23.4 oz. Mfg. 2010-2014.

	100%	98%	95%	90%	80%	70%	60%	Last MSR
	$1,250	$1,095	$950	$850	$695	$565	$440	$1,472

3.0 SPARTAN III – 9mm Para. or .45 ACP cal., 1911 Commander steel frame, parkerized finish, bald front strap, hand checkered double diamond mahogany grips, rear slide serrations, STI long curved trigger, 3.24 in. chrome non-ramped bull bushing barrel, STI high ride beavertail grip safety, competition front sights, fixed rear sights, 6 or 8 shot mag., 32.7 oz. Mfg. 2012-2014.

	100%	98%	95%	90%	80%	70%	60%	Last MSR
	$650	$575	$495	$440	$360	$295	$225	$754

MSR	100%	98%	95%	90%	80%	70%	60%	Last MSR

3.0 TACTICAL – .38 Super, 9mm Para., .40 S&W, or .45 ACP cal., matte blue or hard chrome finish, 3 in. bull or threaded barrel, modular steel frame with integral tactical rail, flat-top slide with rear cocking serrations, black glass filled nylon polymer grips, long curved trigger, high ride beavertail grip safety, fixed rear sight, ramped front sight, 10, 12, 14, or 17 shot mag., 34 oz. Mfg. 2014-2015.

	$1,825	$1,595	$1,375	$1,240	$1,000	$825	$640	$2,144

Add $102 for Tritium sights, or $167 for threaded barrel with Tritium sights.
Add $340 for hard chrome finish.

* **3.0 Tactical Lite** – .38 Super, 9mm Para, .40 S&W, or .45 ACP cal., 3 in. bull or threaded barrel, 10, 12, 14, or 17 shot mag., with or w/o Tritium sights, blue finish. Mfg. 2014 only.

	$1,825	$1,595	$1,375	$1,240	$1,000	$825	$640	$2,144

Add $62 for Tritium sights or $167 for threaded barrel and Tritium sights.

3.0 TOTAL ECLIPSE – 9mm Para., .40 S&W, or .45 ACP cal., 3 in. barrel, skeletonized trigger, aluminum frame, polymer grips, beavertail safety, fixed 2-dot Tritium sights, blue finish, 23.1 oz. Mfg. 2011-2013.

	$1,575	$1,375	$1,175	$1,075	$865	$710	$550	$1,870

3.25 GP5 – 9mm Para. cal., 3 1/4 in. barrel, DAO, blue finish, chrome moly steel frame with integral tactical rail, textured polymer grips, double slide serrations, ambidextrous safety, internal extractor, adj. sights, 24.2 oz. Mfg. by Grand Power, Ltd. 2010-2011.

	$595	$550	$500	$450	$400	$375	$350	$663

3.4 BLS9/BLS40 – 9mm Para. or .40 S&W cal., blue finish, Govt. length grips, Heinie low mount sights, single stack mag., 30 oz. Mfg. 1999-2005.

	$765	$650	$565	$460	$400	$375	$350	$889

3.4 LS9/LS40 – 9mm Para. or .40 S&W (disc. 2008) cal., blue finish, Commander length grips, single stack mag., Heinie low mount rear sight, slide integral front sight, 28 oz. Mfg. 1999-2013.

	$925	$825	$725	$650	$575	$500	$425	$1,002

3.4 ESCORT – 9mm Para. or .45 ACP cal., 1911 forged aluminum Commander style frame, 3.4 in. ramped bull barrel, slide with rear cocking serrations, Duracoat finish with blue slide, undercut trigger guard, stippled front strap, rosewood grips, STI high ride beavertail grip safety, fixed Novak style 3-dot sights, 22.8 oz. Mfg. 2007-2008.

	$925	$825	$725	$650	$575	$500	$425	$1,024

3.9 FALCON – .38 Super, .40 S&W, or .45 ACP cal., STI standard frame, 3.9 in. barrel, size is comparable to Officers Model, adj. rear sight. Limited mfg. 1993-98.

	$1,875	$1,375	$1,175	$925	$850	$775	$675	$2,136

3.9 GUARDIAN – 9mm Para. (new 2009), .40 S&W (mfg. 2014 only), or .45 ACP cal., 1911 Commander style aluminum blue frame, 3.9 in. ramped bull barrel, stainless steel slide with polished sides, stippled front strap, undercut trigger guard, rosewood (disc.) or Cocobolo wood grips, fixed 3-dot sights, 6 or 8 shot mag., stainless/blue or hard chrome (disc. 2014) finish, 32.4 oz. New 2007.

MSR $1,299	$1,100	$995	$875	$735	$650	$550	$465	

Add $340 for hard chrome finish (disc. 2014).

3.9 STINGER – 9mm Para. or .38 Super cal., black frame, designed for IPSC and USPSA competition, 38 oz. Mfg. 2005-2008.

	$2,500	$2,225	$1,975	$1,750	$1,575	$1,375	$1,150	$2,773

3.9 TACTICAL – 9mm Para., .40 S&W, or .45 ACP cal., matte blue finish, 3.9 in. bull barrel, modular steel frame with integral tactical rail, flat-top slide with rear cocking serrations, black glass filled nylon polymer grips, long curved trigger, high ride beavertail grip safety, fixed rear sight, ramped front sight, 34 oz. Mfg. 2012-2013.

	$1,775	$1,500	$1,250	$1,000	$875	$800	$675	$2,109

3.9 V.I.P. – 9mm Para. (new 2009), .40 S&W (new 2009), or .45 ACP cal. only, aluminum frame, STI modular polymer frame, stainless steel slide, 3.9 in. bull barrel with STI Recoilmaster muzzle brake, 10, 13, or 16 shot double stack mag., STI fixed sights, blue or hard chrome finish or stainless steel, 25 oz. Mfg. 2001-2006, reintroduced 2009-2014.

	$1,500	$1,325	$1,125	$1,025	$825	$675	$525	$1,775

Add $340 for hard chrome finish.

4.0 SPARTAN IV – 9mm Para. or .45 ACP cal., 1911 Commander steel frame, parkerized finish, bald front strap, hand checkered double diamond mahogany grips, rear slide serrations, STI long curved trigger, 4.26 in. chrome non-ramped bull bushing barrel, STI high ride beavertail grip safety, competition front sights, fixed rear sights, 8 or 9 shot mag., 34.3 oz. Mfg. 2012-2014.

	$650	$575	$495	$440	$360	$295	$225	$754

MSR	100%	98%	95%	90%	80%	70%	60%	Last MSR

4.0 TACTICAL – 9mm Para., .40 S&W, or .45 ACP cal., matte blue or hard chrome finish, 3 in. bull or threaded barrel, modular steel frame with integral tactical rail, flat-top slide with rear cocking serrations, black glass filled nylon polymer grips, long curved trigger, high ride beavertail grip safety, fixed rear sight, ramped front sight, 10, 12, 14, or 17 shot mag., 34 oz. Mfg. 2014-2015.

| | $1,825 | $1,595 | $1,375 | $1,240 | $1,000 | $825 | $640 | $2,144 |

Add $102 for Tritium sights, or $167 for threaded barrel with Tritium sights.
Add $340 for hard chrome finish.

* 4.0 Tactical Lite – 9mm Para. or .45 ACP cal., 2011 platform, 4 in. bull or threaded barrel, 10, 12, or 17 shot mag., aluminum frame, full length tactical rail, fixed rear and ramped front sight, ambidextrous safety, tactical magwell, Black Cerakote finish, 32 oz. New 2014.

| MSR $2,199 | $1,825 | $1,595 | $1,375 | $1,240 | $1,000 | $825 | $640 | |

Add $100 for threaded barrel.

4.15 TACTICAL – 9mm Para., .40 S&W, or .45 ACP cal., blue steel, fixed sights, short trigger, ambidextrous safety, 34 1/2 oz. Mfg. 2004-2013.

| | $1,725 | $1,500 | $1,295 | $1,175 | $950 | $775 | $600 | $2,045 |

4.15 RANGER II (3.9 RANGER) – 9mm Para. (new 2009), .40 S&W (new 2009), or .45 ACP cal. only, Officer's Model with 3.9 (Ranger, disc. 2004) or 4.15 (Ranger II, new 2005) in. bull barrel and 1/2 in. shortened grip frame, blue or hard chrome (new 2014) steel frame with stainless steel slide, low mount STI/Heinie sights, 8 or 9 shot mag., 29 oz. Mfg. 2001-2014.

| | $1,000 | $875 | $750 | $675 | $550 | $450 | $350 | $1,181 |

Add $340 for hard chrome finish.
Add $192 for Ranger III configuration (mfg. 2010-2013).

4.15 DUTY CT – 9mm Para., .40 S&W or .45 ACP cal., 5 in. bull barrel, matte blue finish, integral tactical rail, flat-top slide with rear cocking serrations, ramped front sight, fixed rear sight, 36.6 oz. Mfg. 2006-2008.

| | $1,100 | $950 | $825 | $700 | $600 | $525 | $450 | $1,286 |

4.25 GP6 – 9mm Para. cal., 4 1/4 in. barrel, DA/SA, blue finish, chrome moly steel frame with integral tactical rail, textured polymer grips, double slide serrations, ambidextrous safety, internal extractor, adj. sights, 26.1 oz. Mfg. by Grand Power, Ltd. Mfg. 2009-2012.

| | $595 | $550 | $500 | $450 | $400 | $375 | $350 | $663 |

Add $34 for GP6-C model with fiber optic front sight and adj. rear sight (mfg. 2010-2011).

4.25 EL COMMANDANTE – 9mm Para. cal., blue matte finish, Government steel frame, 4.25 in. non-ramped bushing barrel, beavertail grip safety, steel trigger, single sided thumb safety, one-piece original GI style guide rod, GI steel sights, smooth wood grips, rear slide cocking serrations, 34 1/2 oz. Mfg. 2011 only.

| | $895 | $725 | $625 | $525 | $450 | $400 | $350 | $942 |

4.3 HAWK – various cals., 4.3 in. barrel, STI standard frame (choice of steel or aluminum), 27 or 31 oz. Mfg. 1993-1999.

| | $1,725 | $1,275 | $1,075 | $875 | $800 | $700 | $600 | $1,975 |

4.3 NIGHT HAWK – .45 ACP cal., 4.3 in. barrel, STI wide extended frame, blue finish, 33 oz. Limited mfg. 1997-99.

| | $1,875 | $1,375 | $1,175 | $925 | $850 | $775 | $675 | $2,136 |

5.0 APEIRO – .38 Super (mfg. 2014 only), 9mm Para., .40 S&W, or .45 ACP cal., 2011 platform, 5 in. Schuemann Island style bull barrel, 10, 12, 14, or 17 shot mag., oversized magwell, long wide steel frame, stainless steel slide with sabertooth serrations, blue finish, black glass filled nylon polymer grips, stainless flared and blended magwell, Dawson fiber optic front and adj. rear sights, ambidextrous safety, 38 oz. New 2010.

| MSR $2,699 | $2,285 | $1,995 | $1,650 | $1,425 | $1,160 | $1,000 | $875 | |

5.0 EAGLE – 9mm Para., .357 SIG, .38 Super (disc. 2011) .40 S&W, or .45 ACP cal., 5 in. barrel, STI standard full size wide body govt. model frame (choice of steel or aluminum), 10, 12, 14, or 17 shot double stack mag., fixed (new 2016) or adj. rear sight, fiber optic front sight, polished blue (disc. 2015), matte blue (new 2016), or hard chrome (mfg. 2014 only) finish, high ride beavertail grip safety, black glass filled nylon polymer grips, 31 or 35 oz.

| MSR $1,999 | $1,700 | $1,500 | $1,250 | $1,100 | $950 | $825 | $675 | |

Add $340 for hard chrome finish (disc. 2014).
Add $266 for .38 Super with .45 ACP conversion kit (disc. 2011).

5.0 EDGE – .38 Super (new 2014), 9mm Para., 10mm Norma (disc. 2008), .40 S&W, or .45 ACP cal., 5 in. bull barrel, designed for limited/standard IPSC competition, STI extended wide body frame, 10, 12, 14, or 17 shot double stack mag., full length dust cover and guide rod, fiber optic front sight, fully adj. rear sight, oversized magwell, stainless steel ambidextrous safety, blue or hard chrome (disc. 2014) finish, 39 oz. New 1998.

| MSR $2,199 | $1,860 | $1,625 | $1,395 | $1,260 | $1,025 | $835 | $650 | |

Add $340 for hard chrome finish (disc. 2014).

MSR		100%	98%	95%	90%	80%	70%	60%	Last MSR

5.0 EXECUTIVE – 9mm Para., .40 S&W, or .45 ACP cal., 2011 platform, STI long/wide frame, 5 in. bull barrel, 10, 12, 14, or 17 shot double stack mag., extended magazine release, oversized magwell, ambidextrous safety, stainless construction, grey nylon polymer grips and square trigger guard, hard chrome finish with black inlays, fiber optic front and STI adj. rear sights, Dawson Tool Less guide rod, approved for IPSC standard and USPSA limited edition, 38 oz. New 2001.

| MSR $2,699 | | $2,285 | $1,995 | $1,650 | $1,425 | $1,160 | $1,000 | $875 | |

* **5.0 Executive Special Edition** – 9mm Para., .40 S&W, or .45 ACP cal., ramped bull barrel, 24Kt. gold on all steel surfaces, checkered black grips, "Special Edition" engraved on slide, 39 oz. Mfg. 2005-2006.

| | | $2,625 | $2,325 | $2,000 | N/A | N/A | N/A | N/A | $2,930 |

* **5.0 Executive IPSC 30th Commemorative** – 9mm Para., .40 S&W, or .45 ACP cal., ramped bull barrel, two-tone hard chrome finish, special engraved slide with "IPSC 30th Anniversary" on side, 39 oz. Mfg. 2005-2006.

| | | $2,500 | $2,225 | $1,975 | N/A | N/A | N/A | N/A | $2,775 |

5.0 FB7 – 7mm or 9mm Para. cal., 5 in. barrel. Mfg. 2010-2011.

| | | $1,750 | $1,500 | $1,250 | $1,000 | $875 | $800 | $675 | $1,940 |

5.0 G.I. – .45 ACP cal., 5 in. non-ramped bushing barrel, matte blue finish, steel frame and trigger, beavertail grip safety, matte blue slide with rear cocking serrations, smooth wood grips, GI steel sights, 8 shot mag., 35.3 oz. Mfg. 2010-2014.

| | | $750 | $650 | $565 | $510 | $415 | $340 | $265 | $874 |

5.0 GM – 9mm Para .or .38 Super cal., race gun, modular steel frame, 5 in. one piece, rifle grade, stainless steel TruBor compensated barrel, drilled and tapped mag release, long curved trigger, C-More scope, stainless steel magwell, 2011 glass filled black polymer modular grips, high ride beavertail grip safety, ambidextrous thumb safety, hard chrome finish with blue color inlay, classic flat-top with slide lightening, sabertooth cocking serrations, recoil master guide rod, 17 or 20 shot mag., 44.6 oz. Mfg. 2014-2015.

| | | $3,125 | $2,735 | $2,350 | $2,125 | $1,725 | $1,400 | $1,095 | $3,682 |

5.0 LEGEND – .38 Super, 9mm Para., .40 S&W, or .45 ACP cal., 5 in. bull barrel, STI modular steel long wide frame, Tri-top forged slide with sabertooth cocking serrations and hard chrome with black inlay and polished sides, blue frame, black glass filled nylon polymer grips with hard chrome magwell, Dawson fiber optic front sights, adj. rear sight, 10, 12, 14, or 17 shot mag., 38 oz. Mfg. 2007-2015.

| | | $2,450 | $2,150 | $1,840 | $1,665 | $1,350 | $1,100 | $860 | $2,886 |

5.0 MARAUDER – 9mm Para. cal., 2011 platform, 5 in. barrel with bushing, 10 or 17 shot mag., fiber optic front and adj. TAS rear sights, short dust cover with tactical rail for light/laser mounting, tactical magwell with cutouts, Cerakote finish. New 2014.

| MSR $2,399 | | $2,050 | $1,800 | $1,500 | $1,300 | $1,075 | $935 | $795 | |

5.0 NITRO 10 – 10mm cal., 1911 style forged steel Government frame, 5 in. ramped bull barrel, 8 shot mag., one piece steel guide rod, long curved trigger, undercut trigger guard, competition front sight, fixed "Ledge" style rear sight, "Nitro" Cocobolo (disc. 2015) or VZ Operator II Marsoc G10 (new 2016) grips, polished blued slide, matte blued frame, high ride beavertail grip safety, single-sided thumb safety, classic slide with front and rear cocking serrations, 38.9 oz. New 2014.

| MSR $1,599 | | $1,350 | $1,200 | $1,075 | $950 | $815 | $700 | $575 | |

5.0 RANGEMASTER – .38 Super (mfg. 2014 only), 9mm Para. or .45 ACP cal., Master Series forged black frame, 5 in. ramped bull barrel, 8 or 9 shot mag., fully adj. rear sight, extended magwell, ambidextrous stainless steel safety, 30 LPI checkering, STI Recoilmaster guide rod, 2011 style trigger guard, Cocobolo wood grips, blue or hard chrome (disc. 2014) finish, 38 oz. New 2005.

| MSR $1,599 | | $1,350 | $1,200 | $1,075 | $950 | $815 | $700 | $575 | |

Add $340 for hard chrome finish (disc. 2014).

5.0 RANGEMASTER II – similar to Rangemaster, except does not have extended frame dust cover. Mfg. 2006.

| | | $1,175 | $965 | $850 | $725 | $625 | $525 | $475 | $1,344 |

5.0 SENTINEL – 9mm Para., .40 S&W, or .45 ACP cal., 1911 Govt. forged frame, 5 in. barrel, flat-top slide with rear cocking serrations, matte blue finish, front strap 30 LPI checkering, checkered steel D&T mainspring housing and flared magwell, STI competition front sights, adj. rear sight, thick rosewood grips, 38.3 oz. Mfg. 2007-2008.

| | | $1,395 | $1,200 | $1,025 | $875 | $750 | $625 | $550 | $1,598 |

5.0 SENTINEL PREMIER – 9mm Para. or .45 ACP cal., 1911 Govt. forged frame, 5 in. bull barrel with bushing, target crown, 6 shot mag., polished slide with rear cocking serrations, hard chrome finish, front strap 30 LPI checkering, checkered steel D&T mainspring housing and flared magwell, adj. Tritium sights, single-sided safety, black (disc. 2015) or VZ ETC Zebra G10 (new 2016) grips, 36.7 oz. New 2009.

| MSR $2,099 | | $1,795 | $1,575 | $1,325 | $1,150 | $995 | $850 | $700 | |

MSR	100%	98%	95%	90%	80%	70%	60%	Last MSR

5.0 SENTRY – 9mm Para., .40 S&W, or .45 ACP cal., 5 in. ramped barrel with bushing, classic polished flat-top slide with front and rear cocking serrations, checkered Cocobolo grips, blue or hard chrome finish, competition front and adj. rear sights, 6 or 9 shot mag., 35.3 oz. Mfg. 2009-2014.

	$1,495	$1,300	$1,125	$1,000	$825	$675	$525	$1,753

Add $315 for hard chrome finish.

5.0 SPARROW – .22 LR cal. only, unlocked blowback action, STI standard extended frame, 5.1 in. ramped bull barrel, fixed sights, blue finish, 30 oz. Limited mfg. 1998-1999 only.

	$1,025	$900	$800	$700	$600	$500	$400	$1,090

5.0 SPARTAN V – 9mm Para. (new 2013), or .45 ACP cal., 1911 Govt. steel frame, parkerized finish, bald front strap, hand checkered double diamond wood grips, front and rear slide serrations, STI long curved trigger, 5 in. chrome ramped bushing barrel, STI high ride beavertail grip safety, fiber optic front sights, adj. rear sights, 9 shot mag., 35.3 oz. Mfg. 2007-2015.

	$650	$575	$495	$440	$360	$295	$225	$754

5.0 STI 20TH ANNIVERSARY – 9mm Para., .40 S&W, or .45 ACP cal., 5 in. bull barrel, steel frame, PVD and TIN (titanium nitride) finish, black glass filled nylon polymer filled grips, TIN coated magwell, beavertail grip safety, Dawson fiber optic front and STI adj. rear sight, 38 oz. Limited edition of 200 during 2010.

	$3,300	$2,950	$2,600	N/A	N/A	N/A	N/A	$3,623

5.0 100TH ANNIVERSARY SPECIAL EDITION – .45 ACP cal., consists of 2 pistols - one is traditional GI style 1911, and the other gun is built on STI's patented high capacity modular frame, boxed with 2011 STI "challenge" coin, 500 sets mfg. 2011-2012.

	$3,875	$3,400	$2,900	$2,400	$2,100	$1,950	$1,700	$4,154

5.0 TACTICAL – 9mm Para., .40 S&W, or .45 ACP cal., 5 in. bull or threaded barrel, short trigger, ambidextrous safety, 10, 12, 14, or 17 shot mag., blue steel or hard chrome finish, fixed sights, 39 oz. Mfg. 2004-2015.

	$1,825	$1,595	$1,375	$1,240	$1,000	$825	$640	$2,144

Add $340 for hard chrome finish.

Add $102 for Tritium sights or $167 for Tritium sights and threaded barrel.

* **5.0 Tactical Lite** – similar to 5.0 Tactical, except stainless slide, alloy frame, fixed sights, 34 1/2 oz. Mfg. 2004-2005.

	$1,800	$1,525	$1,300	$1,050	$900	$825	$700	$2,002

5.0 TROJAN/TROJAN LITE – 9mm Para., .40 S&W, .38 Super, or .45 ACP, 5 in. barrel with bushing, cast steel or aluminum (Trojan Lite) frame, fiber optic front and fully adj. rear sight, Cocobolo wood grips, single stack mag., stainless steel available 2006-2011, stippled front strap and mainspring housing, matte blue, blue/anodized (Trojan Lite), or hard chrome (disc. 2014) finish, 8 or 9 shot mag., 34-42 oz. New 1999.

MSR $1,299	$1,100	$995	$875	$735	$650	$550	$465	

Add $100 for aluminum frame (Trojan Lite).

Add $340 for hard chrome finish (disc. 2014).

Add $288 for .38 Super with .45 ACP conversion kit (disc. 2011).

Add $412 for stainless steel (disc. 2011).

5.0 TRUBOR (COMPETITOR) – 9mm Para. or .38 Super cal. only, standard frame, classic slide with front and rear serrations, square hammer, compensator, double stack mag., match sear, STI "Alchin" style blast deflector mount, TruBor compensator became standard 2005, C-More rail scope, wide ambidextrous and grip safeties, 41.3 oz. Mfg. 1999-2011.

	$2,475	$2,050	$1,750	$1,450	$1,200	$995	$875	$2,864

5.0 TRUBOR GM – 9mm Para. or .38 Super cal., 5 in. TruBor bull barrel, hard chrome finish with blue color inlays, classic flat-top slide, sabertooth cocking serrations, blue glass filled nylon polymer grips with stainless steel magwell, drilled and tapped, C-More gray scope, 44.6 oz. Mfg. 2009-2011.

	$3,350	$3,000	$2,700	$2,250	$1,800	$1,400	$1,175	$3,655

5.0/5.5 TRUBOR – 9mm Para. or .38 Super cal., 2011 platform, modular steel frame, 5 or 5.5 (disc. 2013) in. TruBor barrel with 5-port competition proven compensator, 10 or 20 shot mag., full length guide rod, stainless steel spur hammer, black glass filled nylon polymer grips with aluminum magwell, lightened slide with front and rear cocking serrations, C-More railway red dot sight with blast deflector mount, ambidextrous thumb safety, polished blue or hard chrome (disc. 2014) finish, 41 oz. New 2012.

MSR $2,899	$2,475	$2,150	$1,775	$1,525	$1,250	$1,050	$925	

Add $347 for hard chrome finish (disc. 2014).

5.0 TRUSIGHT – 9mm Para., .40 S&W, or .45 ACP (disc. 2008) cal., 5 in. ramped bull barrel with expansion chamber, black glass filled nylon polymer grip with aluminum magwell, Dawson fiber optic front sight, adj. rear sight, blue finish with polished slide, 39 oz. Mfg. 2006-2009.

	$1,795	$1,525	$1,275	$1,050	$900	$825	$700	$1,985

MSR	100%	98%	95%	90%	80%	70%	60%	*Last MSR*

5.0 USPSA SINGLE STACK – 9mm Para., .38 Super (new 2013), .40 S&W, or .45 ACP cal., 5 in. stainless steel barrel with bushing, tri-top two-tone slide with sabertooth cocking serrations, blue frame, 30 LPI front strap checkering, checkered steel D&T mainspring housing and magwell, competition front and adj. rear sight, 8 or 9 shot mag., 38.3 oz. New 2009.

| MSR $1,976 | $1,675 | $1,475 | $1,250 | $1,140 | $925 | $750 | $585 | |

5.0 USPSA DOUBLE STACK – 9mm Para., .40 S&W, or .45 ACP cal., 5 in. stainless steel barrel, tri-top two-tone slide with sabertooth cocking serrations, blue frame, 30 LPI front strap checkering, checkered steel D&T mainspring housing and magwell, competition front and adj. rear sight, 38.3 oz. Mfg. 2009-2012.

| | $2,425 | $2,000 | $1,750 | $1,450 | $1,200 | $1,000 | $900 | *$2,818* |

5.0 IPSC DOUBLE STACK – 9mm Para., .40 S&W, or .45 ACP cal., 5 in. bull barrel, blue frame, two-tone hard chrome slide with sabertooth cocking serrations, Dawson fiber optic front and adj. rear sights, black glass filled nylon polymer grips with stainless steel magwell, 38 oz. Mfg. 2009-2012.

| | $2,425 | $2,000 | $1,750 | $1,450 | $1,200 | $1,000 | $900 | *$2,818* |

LEGACY MODEL – .45 ACP cal., 5 in. ramped STI bushing barrel, PVD finish, polished flat-top black slide, rear cocking serrations, front strap checkering, custom Cocobolo grips, ambidextrous thumb safety, ramped front sight, 36 oz. Mfg. 2006-2008.

| | $1,750 | $1,500 | $1,250 | $1,000 | $900 | $825 | $700 | *$1,929* |

5.1 LIMITED – while advertised during 1998 with an MSR of $1,699, this model never went into production.

5.5 EAGLE – various cals., features STI standard frame, 5 1/2 in. compensated barrel, 44 oz. Limited mfg. 1994-98.

| | $2,100 | $1,750 | $1,475 | $1,200 | $995 | $895 | $775 | *$2,399* |

5.5 GRANDMASTER – .38 Super cal. standard, custom order gun with any variety of options available, double stack mag., 42 oz. Mfg. 2001-2008.

| | $3,075 | $2,650 | $2,275 | $1,900 | $1,650 | $1,425 | $1,200 | *$3,371* |

5.5 STI GM – 9mm Para. or .38 Super cal., modular steel frame, 5.5 TruBor bull barrel with two inch integral compensator, hard chrome finish with blue, red, or black inlay, C-More red dot sight, blue glass filled polymer grips with stainless flared magwell and drilled and tapped mag. release, lightened slide with sabertooth cocking serrations, high ride beavertail grip safety, ambidextrous thumb safety, 10 or 20 shot mag., 44.6 oz. New 2012.

| MSR $3,682 | $3,125 | $2,735 | $2,350 | $2,125 | $1,725 | $1,400 | $1,095 | |

6.0 EAGLE – .38 Super (disc.), 9mm Para., .40 S&W, or .45 ACP cal., features STI super extended heavy steel frame, 6 in. barrel with bushing, blue or hard chrome (disc. 2014) finish, wide body with 10, 12, 14, or 17 shot double stack mag.,fiber optic front and fully adj. target style rear sights, ambidextrous safety, 42 oz. New 1998.

| MSR $2,199 | $1,900 | $1,665 | $1,425 | $1,295 | $1,050 | $850 | $665 | |

Add $340 for hard chrome finish (disc. 2014).
Add $267 for .38 Super with .45 ACP conversion kit (disc. 2008).

6.0 TROJAN – 9mm Para. or .45 ACP cal., similar to Trojan 5.0, except has 6 in. barrel and single stack mag., 36 oz. New 2000.

| MSR $1,555 | $1,325 | $1,160 | $995 | $900 | $725 | $595 | $465 | |

Add $143 for .38 Super with .45 ACP conversion kit (disc. 2008).

6.0 HUNTER – 10mm cal. only, 6 in. barrel, STI super extended heavy frame with single stack mag., blue finish, 51 oz. Only 2 mfg. 1998, disc. 2000.

| | $2,250 | $1,875 | $1,650 | $1,425 | $1,200 | $995 | $895 | *$2,485* |

Add $350 for Leupold 2X scope with terminator mount.

6.0 PERFECT 10 – 10mm Norma cal., 2011 platform, 6 in. bull barrel, blue or hard chrome (disc. 2014) finish with polished classic flat-top slide, front and rear cocking serrations, ramped front and Heinie fixed rear sights, 6 inch integral tactical rail, 10 or 14 shot mag., black glass filled nylon polymer grips with aluminum flared magwell, ambidextrous safety, 37 1/2 oz. New 2009.

| MSR $2,699 | $2,285 | $1,995 | $1,650 | $1,425 | $1,160 | $1,000 | $875 | |

Add $340 for hard chrome finish (disc. 2014).

6.0 TARGETMASTER – 9mm Para. or .45 ACP cal., Master Series forged black frame, 6 in. ramped bull barrel, two piece steel guide rod, 8 or 9 shot mag., undercut trigger guard, 30 LPI checkering, Aristocrat three position rear sight, extended magwell, ambidextrous stainless steel safety, Cocobolo wood grips, matte blued finish, 40 oz. New 2005.

| MSR $1,799 | $1,525 | $1,350 | $1,175 | $1,050 | $900 | $775 | $625 | |

Add $315 for hard chrome finish in 9mm Para. cal. (disc. 2014), or $340 for hard chrome finish in .45 ACP cal. (disc. 2014).

MSR	100%	98%	95%	90%	80%	70%	60%	Last MSR

6.0 .450 XCALIBER – .450 cal., single stack mag., V-10 barrel and slide porting, stainless grip and thumb safeties, adj. rear sight. Limited mfg. 2000-2002.

	$1,000	$850	$750	$650	$525	$450	$395	$1,122

6.0 .450+ XCALIBER – .450+ cal., otherwise similar to Xcaliber 6.0 .450, except has 6 in. frame with patented polymer grip and double stack mag. Limited mfg. 2000-2002.

	$1,775	$1,575	$1,350	$1,175	$995	$875	$775	$1,998

COSTA 5.0 – 9mm Para. or .45 ACP cal., 5 in. bull barrel, 10, 12, or 17 shot mag., black Diamond Like Carbon (DLC) finish. New 2016.

MSR $2,599 | $2,200 | $1,925 | $1,600 | $1,375 | $1,125 | $975 | $850

COSTA CARRY COMP – 9mm Para. or .45 ACP cal., 4 in. carry comp barrel, 10, 12, or 17 shot mag., Diamond Like Carbon (DLC) finish. New 2016.

MSR $3,299 | $2,815 | $2,465 | $1,995 | $1,700 | $1,400 | $1,200 | $1,035

COSTA VIP – 9mm Para. or .45 ACP cal., 4 in. bull barrel, 10 or 15 shot mag., black Diamond Like Carbon (DLC) finish. New 2016.

MSR $2,599 | $2,200 | $1,925 | $1,600 | $1,375 | $1,125 | $975 | $850

DUTY ONE – 9mm Para., .40 S&W (disc. 2014), or .45 ACP cal., 3 (ramped bull), 4.4 (bull disc. 2013, bushing new 2014), or in. ramped bull barrel, 6, 8, or 9 shot mag., forged steel frame with integral tactical rail, undercut trigger guard, front and rear slide serrations, fixed front and rear sights, G10 grip panels, Recoil Master (3 or 4 in. barrel) or full length guide rod (5 in. barrel), high ride beavertail grip safety, matte blue or hard chrome (mfg. 2014 only) finish, 36.3 oz. New 2013.

MSR $1,499 | $1,275 | $1,125 | $1,025 | $875 | $750 | $625 | $525

Add $79 for Tritium sights (4 in. barrel, disc.).
Add $363 for hard chrome finish (disc. 2014).

* **Duty One Lite** – 9mm Para. or .45 ACP cal., 3 (bull) or 4 (bushing) in. barrel, 6, 8, 9, or 10 shot mag., aluminum frame, fixed front and rear sights, unique cocking serrations on slide and frame, tactical accessory rail, blued/anodized finish. New 2014.

MSR $1,599 | $1,350 | $1,200 | $1,075 | $950 | $815 | $700 | $575

5.0 DUTY ONE – 9mm Para., .40 S&W (disc. 2014) or .45 ACP cal., 5.1 in. barrel with bushing, forged steel frame with integral tactical rail (new 2013), undercut trigger guard, front and rear slide serrations, checkered wood (disc. 2012) or G10 grip panels (new 2013), matte blue or hard chrome (mfg. 2014 only) finish, high ride beavertail grip safety, 8 or 9 shot mag., 37.2 oz. New 2005.

MSR $1,499 | $1,175 | $1,025 | $875 | $800 | $650 | $525 | $400

Add $363 for hard chrome finish (disc. 2014).
Add $79 for Tritium sights (disc.).

* **5.0 Duty One Lite** – 9mm Para. or .45 ACP cal., 5 in. barrel with bushing, 8 or 10 shot mag., aluminum frame, fixed front and rear sights, 1911 slide serrations, full length guide rod, tactical accessory rail, blued/anodized finish. New 2014.

MSR $1,599 | $1,350 | $1,200 | $1,075 | $950 | $815 | $700 | $575

DVC 3-GUN – 9mm Para. cal., 5.4 in. TiN coated barrel w/bushing, 10 or 20 shot mag., STI tactical aluminum magwell, STI adj. rear and fiber optic front sights, black DVC 2011 grip, ambi safety lever, accessory rail for light/laser sight, black Diamond Like Carbon (DLC) finish. New 2016.

MSR $2,999 | $2,550 | $2,225 | $1,825 | $1,575 | $1,300 | $1,100 | $950

DVC CLASSIC – 9mm Para., .40 S&W, or .45 ACP cal., forged Master Series frame, 5.4 in. bushing barrel, 8, 9, or 10 shot mag., extended base pads, Dawson Precision D&T mag. release, ICE magwell, fully adj. rear sight and fiber optic front, black VZ II Operator grips, tool-less guide rod, hard chrome finish. New 2016.

MSR $2,799 | $2,375 | $2,075 | $1,725 | $1,475 | $1,200 | $1,025 | $895

DVC LIMITED – 9mm Para. or .40 S&W cal., 2011 platform, 5 in. bull barrel with Titanium Nitrate finish, 10 or 20 shot mag., improved sear and hammer, new 2 lb. trigger, fiber optic front and adj. rear sights, Dawson Precision Tool Less guide rod, slide porting on top and sides, textured grips, hard chrome finish. New 2015.

MSR $2,999 | $2,550 | $2,225 | $1,825 | $1,575 | $1,300 | $1,100 | $950

DVC OPEN – 9mm Para. or .38 Super cal., entirely new design based off the 2011, 5 in. precision fit bull barrel with TruBor style integrated compensator and Titanium Nitride finish, 10 or 20 shot mag., Dawson Precision guide rod, reversible dual detent slide racker, mounted C-More 6MOA dot sight, hand textured grips, oversized competition magwell, hard chrome finish on all steel parts, 48 oz. New 2015.

MSR $3,999 | $3,400 | $2,975 | $2,475 | $2,075 | $1,725 | $1,450 | $1,250

MSR	100%	98%	95%	90%	80%	70%	60%	Last MSR

GUARDIAN 2011 – 9mm Para. cal., 2011 platform, lightweight aluminum narrow frame, 3.9 in. bull barrel, 10 or 15 shot double stack mag., stainless steel slide, TAS rear w/white dot front sights, black 2011 VIP grips, single side safety lever, black Cerakote frame finish. New 2016.

| MSR $1,899 | $1,625 | $1,425 | $1,200 | $1,075 | $925 | $795 | $650 | |

HEXTACTICAL DS – 9mm Para. or .45 ACP cal., 2011 platform, lightweight Tri-Topped slide, 4 or 5 in. bushing barrel, 10, 14, or 20 shot mag., extended base, flared magwell, rear ledge and fiber optic front sights, black double diamond grips, accessory rail, black Cerakote finish. New 2016.

| MSR $2,599 | $2,200 | $1,925 | $1,600 | $1,375 | $1,125 | $975 | $850 | |

HEXTACTICAL SS – 9mm Para. or .45 ACP cal., 1911 platform, lightweight Tri-Topped slide, 4 in. bull or 5 in. bushing barrel, 8 or 9 shot mag., flared magwell, fixed rear ledge and front fiber optic sights, VZ Alien grips, accessory rail, black Cerakote finish. New 2016.

| MSR $2,099 | $1,795 | $1,575 | $1,325 | $1,150 | $995 | $850 | $700 | |

LAWMAN – .38 Super (3 in. barrel, mfg. 2014 only), 9mm Para. or .45 ACP cal., 3 or 4.15 in. STI ramped bull barrel, polished blue finish, carbon steel slide, 8 or 9 shot mag., forged steel frame with 30 LPI front strap checkering, undercut trigger guard, G10 (disc. 2015) or VZ Double Diamond black and gray G10 grips (new 2016), front and rear slide cocking serrations, long curved aluminum trigger, high ride beavertail safety, recoil master guide rod, ramped front sight, tactical adj. rear sight, optional Tritium sights, 6 or 8 shot mag., single sided thumb safety, blue (disc.), black/green (disc.), brown/tan (disc.), or black Cerakote (new 2015) finish, 24.8 oz. New 2012.

| MSR $1,499 | $1,275 | $1,125 | $1,025 | $875 | $750 | $625 | $525 | |

Add $79 for Tritium sights (disc. 2014).

5.0 LAWMAN (LSA) – 9mm Para. (new 2013) or .45 ACP cal., 1911 Govt. style, 5 in. bushing barrel, hammer forged carbon steel frame, designed for duty, self-defense, IPSC, USPSA, and IDPA competition, fixed front sight with TAS rear sight, 8 or 9 shot mag., unique grip pattern (disc. 2015), VZ Double Diamond black and gray G10 grips (new 2016), 1911 slide serrations, blue (disc.), black/green (disc.), brown/tan (disc.) or black Cerakote (new 2015) finish, 36 oz. New 2005.

| MSR $1,499 | $1,275 | $1,125 | $1,025 | $875 | $750 | $625 | $525 | |

MATCH MASTER (4.15 MATCH MASTER) – .38 Super or 9mm Para. (new 2014) cal., 2011 platform, 4.26 in. TruBor barrel with T2 compensator, 10 or 20 shot mag., sabertooth front and rear cocking serrations, stainless steel spur hammer, black glass filled nylon polymer grips with aluminum magwell, drilled and tapped, C-More red dot scope with blast shield and thumb rest, ambidextrous safety, blue or hard chrome (mfg. 2014 only) finish with polished classic slide, 38.9 oz. New 2009.

| MSR $2,999 | $2,550 | $2,225 | $1,825 | $1,575 | $1,300 | $1,100 | $950 | |

Add $395 for hard chrome finish (mfg. 2014 only).

STEEL MASTER (4.15 STEEL MASTER) – 9mm Para. cal., 2011 platform, 4.26 in. Trubor barrel, T1 compensator, 10 or 20 shot mag., blue or hard chrome (mfg. 2014 only) finish with polished classic slide, sabertooth cocking serrations, stainless steel spur hammer, ambidextrous safety, C-More red dot scope with blast shield and thumbrest, black glass filled nylon polymer grips with aluminum magwell, 38.9 oz. New 2009.

| MSR $2,799 | $2,395 | $2,075 | $1,750 | $1,565 | $1,225 | $975 | $810 | |

Add $395 for hard chrome finish (mfg. 2014 only).

TACTICAL DS – 9mm Para., .40 S&W, or .45 ACP cal., 2011 platfom, steel frame, 4 or 5 in. threaded or non-threaded bull barrel, 10, 12, 14, or 17 shot mag., tactical magwell, fixed rear and ramped front sight, ambidextrous safety, full length tactical accessory rail, black Cerakote finish. New 2015.

| MSR $2,099 | $1,795 | $1,575 | $1,325 | $1,150 | $995 | $850 | $700 | |

Add $100 for threaded barrel.

TACTICAL SS – .38 Super (3 in. only, mfg. 2014), 9mm Para., .40 S&W (disc. 2014), or .45 ACP cal., 3, 4, or 5 in. ramped bull or threaded (new 2014) barrel, forged steel frame with integral tactical rail, 30 LPI front strap checkering, undercut trigger guard, VZ Aliens black and gray (new 2016) G10 grip panels, long curved trigger, high ride beavertail grip safety, ambidextrous thumb safeties, ramped front sight and fixed ledge rear sights or tall suppressor sights (threaded barrel models only, new 2016), 6, 8, or 9 shot mag., full length guide rod (5 in. only), matte blue (disc. 2014), hard chrome (mfg. 2014 only), or black Cerakote finish, 34-41 oz. New 2013.

| MSR $1,899 | $1,625 | $1,425 | $1,200 | $1,075 | $925 | $795 | $650 | |

Add $100 for threaded barrel and Tritium sights.
Add $340 for hard chrome finish (mfg. 2014 only).

RIFLES/CARBINES: SEMI-AUTO

STI SPORTING/TACTICAL CARBINE – .223 Rem. or 5.56 NATO cal., GIO, 16 in. stainless steel barrel, JP trigger group, STI Valkyrie handguard and gas block, Nordic tactical compensator, black Teflon coating, fixed A2 or collapsible buttstock, optional rails, approx. 7 lbs. Mfg. 2010-2014.

| | $1,225 | $1,075 | $925 | $835 | $675 | $550 | $425 | $1,455 |

MSR		100%	98%	95%	90%	80%	70%	60%	*Last MSR*

SWS 2000

Previous rifle manufacturer located in Krefeld, Germany until 2010. Previously imported until 2009 by Euro-Imports, located in Yoakum, TX.

RIFLES

SWS 2000 manufactured a variety of sporting and tactical style rifles in a variety of configurations.
Prices ranged from €2,600-€3,759 for sporting and hunting models, and €6,162-€7,910 for tactical rifles.

SABRE

Previous trademark of shotguns previously imported by Mitchell's Mausers, located in Fountain Valley, CA.

SHOTGUNS: SEMI-AUTO

SABRE – 12 ga. only, gas operated, 18 1/2 (w/o VR), 22, or 28 in. VR barrel with choke tubes, choice of black fiberglass or checkered walnut stock and forearm, configurations include Hunting, Turkey, Deer Hunter, and Police, mfg. in Turkey. Importation disc. 2007.

		100%	98%	95%	90%	80%	70%	60%	Last MSR
		$435	$375	$325	$275	$235	$210	$190	*$495*

Add $50 for Police model.

SABRE DEFENCE INDUSTRIES LLC

Previous manufacturer from 2002-2010, with production headquarters located in Nashville, TN, and sales offices located in Middlesex, U.K. This company was previously known as Ramo Mfg., Inc., which was founded in 1977. Sabre Defence was also the U.S. distributor for Sphinx pistols until 2009.

CARBINES/RIFLES: SEMI-AUTO

Sabre Defence Industries manufactured many variations of the XR15 line of tactical design carbines and rifles for civilians, law enforcement, and military.

XR15A3 COMPETITION EXTREME – .223 Rem. cal., GIO, 16, 18, or 20 in. stainless steel fluted barrel, 30 shot mag., A3 upper and matched lower, black anodized finish, CTR six position retractable stock, free float handguard, Ergo grip, match trigger, flip up sights, mid-length barrel assembly, M4 feed ramp, includes two mags., cleaning kit, and tactical case. Disc. 2010.

		100%	98%	95%	90%	80%	70%	60%	Last MSR
		$1,950	$1,700	$1,450	$1,275	$1,025	$850	$750	*$2,189*

XR15A3 COMPETITION SPECIAL – .223 Rem. or 6.5 Grendel cal., 16 (.223 Rem. cal. only), GIO, 18, or 20 in. stainless steel fluted barrel, 30 shot mag., A3 upper and matched lower, black anodized finish, A2 fixed stock, tubular free float handguard, Ergo grip, match trigger, mid-length barrel assembly, M4 feed ramp, includes two mags., cleaning kit, and tactical case. Disc. 2010.

		100%	98%	95%	90%	80%	70%	60%	Last MSR
		$1,700	$1,475	$1,250	$1,125	$895	$725	$575	*$1,899*

Add $200 for 6.5 Grendel cal.

XR15A3 COMPETITION DELUXE – .223 Rem. or 6.5 Grendel cal., GIO, 16, 18, or 20 in. stainless or vanadium steel fluted barrel, 25 (6.5 Grendel cal.) or 30 shot mag., A3 upper and matched lower, black anodized finish, five position retractable stock, tactical handguard, Ergo grip, match trigger, flip up sights, competition Gill-brake, fluted mid-length barrel assembly, M4 feed ramp, includes two mags., cleaning kit, and tactical case. Disc. 2010.

		100%	98%	95%	90%	80%	70%	60%	Last MSR
		$2,075	$1,815	$1,555	$1,415	$1,150	$950	$725	*$2,299*

Add $200 for 6.5 Grendel cal.
Add $300 for piston system upgrade (Competition Deluxe Piston, new 2010).

XR15A3 SPR – .223 Rem. or 6.5 Grendel cal., GIO, 16, 18, or 20 in. stainless or vanadium steel fluted barrel, 25 (6.5 Grendel cal.) or 30 shot mag., A3 upper and matched lower, black anodized finish, five position retractable stock, tactical handguard, Ergo grip, match trigger, flip up sights, bipod, fluted mid-length barrel assembly, M4 feed ramp, includes two mags., cleaning kit, and tactical case, 8.7 lbs. Disc. 2010.

		100%	98%	95%	90%	80%	70%	60%	Last MSR
		$2,250	$1,975	$1,695	$1,525	$1,225	$1,015	$785	*$2,499*

Add $200 for 6.5 Grendel cal.

XR15A3 M4 FLAT TOP – .223 Rem., 6.5 Grendel, or 7.62x39mm (disc. 2009) cal., GIO, 16 in. vanadium contoured barrel, 25 (6.5 Grendel cal. only) or 30 shot mag., A3 upper and matched lower, M4 oval handguard, flip up sights, black anodized finish, A2 grip, single stage trigger, six position collapsible stock, M4 feed ramp, A2 flash hider, includes two mags., cleaning kit, and tactical case, 6.4 lbs. Disc. 2010.

		100%	98%	95%	90%	80%	70%	60%	Last MSR
		$1,350	$1,150	$995	$875	$750	$650	$525	*$1,507*

Add $70 for 7.62x39mm cal. (disc. 2009).
Add $34 for chrome lined barrel.
Add $193 for 6.5 Grendel cal.

MSR	100%	98%	95%	90%	80%	70%	60%	Last MSR

XR15A3 M5 FLAT TOP – .223 Rem. or 6.5 Grendel cal., GIO, 16 in. vanadium contoured mid-length barrel, 25 (6.5 Grendel cal. only) or 30 shot mag., black anodized finish, A3 upper and matched lower, flip up sights, single stage trigger, six position collapsible stock, M4 feed ramp, A2 flash hider, mid-length handguard, Ergo grip, includes two mags., cleaning kit, and tactical case, 6 1/2 lbs. Disc. 2010.

	$1,350	$1,150	$995	$875	$750	$650	$525	$1,504

Add $195 for 6.5 Grendel cal.
Add $33 for chrome lined barrel.

XR15A3 M4 CARBINE – .223 Rem., 6.5 Grendel, or 7.62x39mm (disc. 2009) cal., GIO, 16 in. vanadium contoured alloy barrel, 25 (6.5 Grendel cal. only) or 30 shot mag., black anodized finish, A3 upper and matched lower, M4 oval handguard, forged front sight, no rear sight, A2 grip, single stage trigger, six position collapsible stock, M4 feed ramp, A2 flash hider, includes two mags., cleaning kit, and tactical case, 6.3 lbs. Disc. 2010.

	$1,195	$1,050	$875	$775	$650	$550	$450	$1,344

Add $100 for 7.62x39mm cal. (disc. 2009).
Add $33 for chrome lined barrel.
Add $205 for 6.5 Grendel cal.

XR15A3 PRECISION MARKSMAN RIFLE – .223 Rem. or 6.5 Grendel cal., GIO, 20 or 24 in. stainless steel barrel, 25 (6.5 Grendel cal.) or 30 shot mag., A3 upper and match lower, rail handguards, Ergo tactical deluxe grip with palm rest, match trigger, fluted mid-length barrel assembly, black anodized finish, M4 feed ramp, Magpul PRS adj. stock, includes Leupold 6.5-20x50 Mark IV scope (standard through 2009), two mags., cleaning kit and tactical case, approx. 10 lbs. Disc. 2010.

	$2,200	$1,950	$1,700	$1,475	$1,225	$1,000	$800	$2,415

Add $126 for 6.5 Grendel cal.
Add $1,185 for Leupold scope.

XR15A3 M4 TACTICAL – .223 Rem., 6.5 Grendel, or 7.62x39mm (disc. 2009) cal., GIO, 16 in. vanadium chrome lined contoured barrel, 25 (6.5 Grendel cal. only) or 30 shot mag., A3 upper and matched lower, multi-rail handguards, flip up sights, black anodized finish, Ergo grip, single stage trigger, six position collapsible stock, M4 feed ramp, A2 flash hider, tactical Gill-brake, includes two mags., cleaning kit, and tactical case, approx. 7 lbs. Disc. 2010.

	$1,825	$1,625	$1,400	$1,225	$975	$800	$650	$1,993

Add $40 for 7.62x39mm cal. (disc. 2009).
Add $176 for 6.5 Grendel cal.

* **M4 Tactical Piston Carbine** – .223 Rem. cal., 16 in. chrome moly steel barrel, 30 shot mag., similar to M4 Tactical, except has mid-length GPO, 7 lbs. Mfg. 2010 only.

	$2,250	$1,975	$1,695	$1,525	$1,225	$1,015	$785	$2,499

XR15A3 M5 CARBINE – .223 Rem., 6.5 Grendel, or 7.62x39mm (disc. 2009) cal., GIO, 16 in. vanadium contoured barrel, 25 (6.5 Grendel cal. only) or 30 shot mag., A3 upper and matched lower, mid-length handguards, black anodized finish, forged front sight, Ergo grip, single stage trigger, six position collapsible stock, M4 feed ramp, A2 flash hider, includes two mags., cleaning kit, and tactical case, 6.4 lbs. Disc. 2010.

	$1,195	$1,050	$875	$775	$650	$550	$450	$1,341

Add $30 for 7.62x39mm cal. (disc. 2009).
Add $33 for chrome lined barrel.
Add $208 for 6.5 Grendel cal.

M5 TACTICAL CARBINE – .223 Rem. or 6.5 Grendel cal., GIO, 16 in. chrome moly chrome lined barrel, 25 or 30 shot mag., free float quadrail handguards, flip up front and rear sights, collapsible buttstock, single stage Mil-Spec trigger, ergonomic pistol grip, trigger lock, sling, cleaning kit, and case, approx. 7 lbs. Mfg. 2009-2010.

	$1,925	$1,700	$1,475	$1,250	$1,025	$875	$725	$2,117

Add $235 for 6.5 Grendel cal.

* **M5 Tactical Piston Carbine** – .223 Rem. cal., 16 in. chrome moly steel barrel, 30 shot mag., similar to M5 Tactical, except has mid-length GPO, 7.3 lbs. Mfg. 2010.

	$2,250	$1,975	$1,695	$1,525	$1,225	$1,015	$785	$2,499

XR15A3 A4 RIFLE – .223 Rem. cal., GIO, 20 in. vanadium govt. contour barrel, 30 shot mag., black anodized finish, A3 upper and matched lower, A2 round handguard, forged front sight, A2 grip, single stage trigger, fixed A2 stock, M4 feed ramp, A2 flash hider, includes two mags., approx. 7.2 lbs. Disc. 2010.

	$1,215	$1,075	$895	$775	$650	$550	$450	$1,384

Add $34 for chrome lined barrel.

XR15A3 A2 NATIONAL MATCH – .223 Rem. cal., GIO, 20 in. stainless steel matte finished H-Bar barrel, 30 shot mag., black anodized finish, A3 upper and matched lower, NM handguards, forged front sights, NM rear sight, A2 grip, two-stage trigger, fixed A2 stock, M4 feed ramp, A2 flash hider, includes two mags. Disc. 2009.

	$1,525	$1,335	$1,150	$1,050	$850	$695	$550	$1,699

MSR	100%	98%	95%	90%	80%	70%	60%	*Last MSR*

XR15A3 FLAT TOP CARBINE – .223 Rem. cal., GIO, 16 in. vanadium barrel, 30 shot mag., A3 upper and matched lower, black anodized finish, CAR round handguards, flip up sights, Ergo grip, single stage trigger, six position collapsible stock, M4 feed ramp, A2 flash hider, includes two mags. Disc. 2009.

	$1,200	$1,050	$895	$825	$675	$550	$425	*$1,319*

Add $40 for chrome lined barrel.

XR15A3 HEAVY BENCH TARGET – .204 Ruger, .223 Rem., or 6.5 Grendel cal., GIO, 24 in. fluted match grade stainless steel heavy barrel, 4 (6.5 Grendel, disc. 2009), 10, or 25 (6.5 Grendel) shot mag., black anodized finish, A3 upper and matched lower, tubular free float handguards, flip up sights, Ergo grip, single stage adj. trigger, fixed A2 stock, sling swivel stud and bipod, includes two mags., cleaning kit, and tactical case, 9.3 lbs. Disc. 2010.

	$1,700	$1,475	$1,275	$1,125	$900	$750	$600	*$1,889*

Add $200 for 6.5 Grendel cal.

XR15A3 VARMINT – .223 Rem. cal., GIO, 20 in. fluted match grade stainless steel heavy barrel, 10 shot mag., A3 upper and matched lower, black anodized finish, tubular free float handguards, Ergo grip, match trigger, fixed A2 stock, sling swivel stud, includes two mags., cleaning kit, and tactical case. Disc. 2009.

	$1,550	$1,350	$1,175	$1,050	$850	$695	$550	*$1,709*

LIGHT SABRE – .223 Rem. cal., GIO, 16 in. chrome moly barrel, 30 shot mag., M5 carbine upper, forged front sight, one piece polymer lower assembly, single stage Mil-Spec trigger, 5.9 lbs. Mfg. 2009-2010.

	$1,100	$1,075	$925	$800	$675	$550	$425	*$1,229*

SACO DEFENSE INC.

Previous firearms manufacturer located in Saco, ME. Saco Defense was purchased by General Dynamics in July of 2000, and continues to produce guns for military defense contracts. This company was previously owned by Colt's Manufacturing Company, Inc. during late 1998-2000.

In the past, Saco Defense utilized their high-tech manufacturing facility to produce guns for Magnum Research, Weatherby (contract ended Sept., 2001), and others.

SAFARI ARMS

Previous trademark manufactured in Olympia, WA. M-S Safari Arms, located in Phoenix, AZ, was started in 1978 as a division of M-S Safari Outfitters. In 1987, Safari Arms was absorbed by Olympic Arms. Safari Arms manufactured 1911 style pistols since the acquisition of M-S Safari Arms in 1987. In Jan. 2004, the Safari Arms name was discontinued and all 1911 style pistols are now being manufactured by Olympic Arms. Please refer to the Olympic Arms section for currently manufactured models.

Safari Arms previously made the Phoenix, Special Forces, Camp Perry, and Royal Order of Jesters commemoratives in various configurations and quantities. Prices average in the $1,500 range except for the Royal Order of Jesters ($2,000).

SCHUETZEN PISTOL WORKS

Schuetzen Pistol Works is the current custom shop of Olympic Arms. Some of the pistols made by Safari Arms had the "Schuetzen Pistol Works" name on them (c. 1994-96). Until Jan. 2004, all pistols were are marked with the Safari Arms slide marking. All pistols, however, have been marked "Safari Arms" on the frame. The pistols formerly in this section have been moved to the PISTOLS: SEMI-AUTO category.

PISTOLS: SEMI-AUTO, SINGLE ACTION

Safari Arms manufactured mostly single action, semi-auto pistols derived from the Browning M1911 design with modifications. Please refer to Olympic Arms listing for currently manufactured pistols.

GI SAFARI – .45 ACP cal., patterned after the Colt Model 1911, Safari frame, beavertail grip safety and commander hammer, parkerized matte black finish, 39.9 oz. Mfg. 1991-2000.

	$500	$455	$395	$350	$295	$275	$250	*$550*

CARRYCOMP – .45 ACP cal., 5 in. barrel, utilizes W. Schuemann designed hybrid compensator system, 7 shot mag., rounded or squared off trigger guard, single slide serrations, finger grooved front grip strap, available in stainless steel or steel, 38 oz. Mfg. 1993-99.

	$1,030	$875	$750	$600	$500	$425	$375	*$1,160*

* **CarryComp Enforcer** – similar to Safari Arms Enforcer, except utilizes W. Schuemann designed hybrid compensator system, available in stainless steel or steel, 36 oz. Mfg. 1993-96.

	$1,175	$1,025	$875	$750	$600	$500	$425	*$1,300*

CARRIER – .45 ACP cal. only, reproduction of the original Detonics ScoreMaster, except has upgraded sights, custom made by Richard Niemer from the Custom Shop. New 1999-2001.

	$750	$625	$575	$500	$450	$400	$350	*$750*

MSR	100%	98%	95%	90%	80%	70%	60%	Last MSR

RENEGADE – .45 ACP cal., left-hand action (port on left side), 4 1/2 (4-star, disc. 1996) or 5 (new 1994) in. barrel, 6 shot mag., adj. sights, stainless steel construction, 36-39 oz. Mfg. 1993-98.

	$955	$800	$700	$600	$525	$450	$395	$1,085

Add $50 for 4-star (4 1/2 in. barrel, disc.).

RELIABLE – similar to Renegade, except has right-hand action. Mfg. 1993-98.

	$730	$620	$525	$450	$425	$400	$375	$825

Add $60 for 4-star (4 1/2 in. barrel, disc.).

GRIFFON PISTOL – .45 ACP cal., 5 in. stainless steel barrel, 10 shot mag., standard govt. size with beavertail grip safety, full-length recoil spring guide, commander style hammer, smooth walnut grips, 40 1/2 oz. Disc. 1998.

	$855	$725	$650	$575	$500	$450	$395	$920

SAFETY HARBOR FIREARMS, INC.

Current manufacturer located in Safety Harbor, FL.

Safety Harbor Firearms also manufactures a line of KEG (Kompact Entry Gun) slide action shotguns (12 and 20 ga.), in short barrel lengths that are classified as NFA weapons. Please contact the manufacturer directly for more information, availability and pricing for these models (see Trademark Index).

RIFLES: BOLT ACTION

SHF R50 – .50 BMG cal., 18, 22, or 29 in. barrel, side mounted 3 (disc. 2009) or 5 shot mag., black reinforced fixed tube stock with vent. recoil pad, partially shrouded barrel with muzzle brake, Picatinny rails, 16 1/2-20 lbs.

MSR $2,250	$1,915	$1,685	$1,425	$1,225	$1,035	$885	$735	

Add $150 for 29 in. barrel.

SHF S50 – .50 BMG cal., single shot, 18, 22, or 29 in. barrel, similar stock and handguard as the SHF R50, but in lightweight configuration. New mid-2009.

MSR $1,850	$1,575	$1,385	$1,185	$1,065	$915	$785	$635	

Add $100 for 29 in. barrel.

SHF R/S ZOMBIE – .50 BMG cal., choice of repeater or single shot action, 18 or 22 in. barrel. Mfg. 2014-2015.

	$1,995	$1,750	$1,500	$1,350	$1,095	$900	$800	$2,199

Add $500 for Mag. fed repeater action.

SAIGA

Current trademark manufactured by Izhmash, located in Izhevsk, Russia since 1807. Currently imported exclusively beginning 2012 by RWC Group LLC, located in Tullytown, PA. Previously imported by US Sporting Goods, Inc., located in Rockledge, FL, RAAC (Russian American Armory Company), located in Scottsburg, IN, Arsenal Inc., located in Las Vegas, NV, K-VAR Corp., located in Las Vegas, NV, and European American Armory Corp., located in Sharpes, FL.

On July 16, 2014, economic sanctions were placed against Russian firearms imports, and they are currently no longer allowed to be imported into the U.S. As a result, quantities of Saiga firearms may be in short supply.

CARBINES/RIFLES: SEMI-AUTO

SAIGA RIFLE – .223 Rem. (Model IZ-114), 5.45x39mm (Model IZ-240), or .308 Win. (Model IZ-139) cal., Kalashnikov type action, black synthetic or hardwood (new 2003, only available in .308 Win. cal.) stock and forearm, 16, 20, or 21 (.308 Win. cal. only) in. barrel length, matte black metal, 7-8 1/2 lbs. Imported 2002-2004, reintroduced 2006.

MSR $649	$600	$525	$450	$375	$300	$260	$230	

Add $200 for .308 Win. cal.

SAIGA 100 – .223 Rem., .30-06, .308 Win., or 7.62x39mm cal., hunting configuration with black synthetic stock, 3 or 10 shot mag., 22 in. barrel with open sights, 7.7 lbs. Imported 2006-disc.

	$650	$595	$550	$495	$450	$400	$350	

Add 15% for .308 Win. cal.

SAIGA CARBINE CONVERSION – 7.62x39mm cal., AK-style carbine, polymer furniture. New 2012.

MSR $900	$775	$675	$575	$525	$425	$350	$275	

Add $20 for Tuning B Model (CBS collapsible stock, RS47SET polymer forward handguard, four rails and G47 pistol grip).
Add $525 for Tuning C Model (ARSNL fully adj. stock, XRS47 aluminum 5 rails handguard, UPG47 pistol grip w/interchangeable finger grooves and backstraps).

MSR	100%	98%	95%	90%	80%	70%	60%	Last MSR

SGL21/26 SERIES – 7.62x39mm cal., Russian made, stamped receiver, original Russian chrome lined hammer forged barrel, front sight block with bayonet lug, gas block with accessory lug, US made double stage trigger group, 5 shot mag., 4000 meter rear sight leaf, scope rail, original Warsaw, NATO or black polymer side folding buttstock with trapdoor for cleaning kit, Black, OD Green, Plum, Desert Sand (new 2012) finish. Mfg. by Izhmash, imported by Arsenal, Inc. New 2011.

| MSR $959 | $825 | $725 | $625 | $575 | $450 | $375 | $295 | |

Add $10 for NATO buttstock.

Add $10 for 40 shot mag.

Add $105 for forend rails (new 2012).

Add $422 for black polymer side folding buttstock.

SGL31 – 5.45x39mm cal., Russian made, stamped receiver, 10 shot mag., 16.3 in. original Russian chrome lined hammer forged barrel, front sight block with bayonet lug, gas block with accessory lug, US made double stage trigger group, 1000 meter rear sight leaf, scope rail, original Warsaw or black polymer side folding buttstock with trapdoor for cleaning kit, Black, OD Green, Plum or Desert Sand (new 2012) finish. Mfg. by Izhmash, imported by Arsenal Inc. New 2011.

| MSR $1,499 | $1,275 | $1,125 | $995 | $875 | $750 | $625 | $495 | |

Add $10 for 30 shot mag.

Add $50 for Plum, Green, or Desert Sand (new 2012) finish.

Add $105 for forend rails (new 2012).

Add $150 for black polymer side folding buttstock.

RIFLES: BOLT ACTION

BI-7-2KO – .22 LR cal., straight pull action, 5 shot mag., screw adjustable for pull, travel, and release, oversized trigger guard, iron sights, birch stock with contoured pistol grip and cutout for 4 extra mags., integral rail on barrel, 7.7 lbs.

| MSR $1,299 | $1,050 | $900 | $800 | $700 | $600 | $500 | $425 | |

SHOTGUNS: SEMI-AUTO

SAIGA-12 – 12 or 20 ga., 3 in. chamber, 5 shot detachable box mag., Kalashnikov type action, black synthetic stock and forearm, 19-22 in. barrel length, matte black metal, with or w/o side rail, optional adj. leaf sight or notch rear sight, 6.7-10 lbs. Imported 2002-2004, reintroduced 2006.

| MSR $900 | $825 | $700 | $600 | $500 | $400 | $350 | $295 | |

Add $25 for adj. leaf sight or $13 for notch rear sights.

Add $50 for 20 ga.

Add $40 for RPK handguard (disc.).

Add 10% for choke tubes (12 ga. only, disc.).

* **Saiga .410 Bore** – .410 bore, 19 or 21 in barrel, 4 or 10 (disc.) shot detachable box mag., NATO or Warsaw Pact buttstock, with or w/o side scope rail, otherwise similar to Saiga Shotgun, approx. 6.6 lbs. Imported 2002-2004, reintroduced 2006.

| MSR $800 | $725 | $625 | $525 | $450 | $400 | $350 | $295 | |

* **Saiga Skeletonized Stock** – 12 ga. only, 19 in. barrel, plastic or laminated skeletonized stock, Picatinny rail, with or w/o magwell, 4 or 5 shot mag., AK sights. Imported 2012-2014.

| | $850 | $750 | $650 | $575 | $475 | $375 | $300 | $994 |

Add $81 for laminated stock.

* **Saiga Hunting Model** – 12 ga. only, 19 in. barrel, wooden or plastic Monte Carlo or hunting style stock, with or w/o magwell, Picatinny rail, optional leaf or AK sights, 4 or 5 shot mag. Imported 2012-2014.

| | $750 | $650 | $575 | $500 | $415 | $350 | $275 | $885 |

Add $45 for wooden stock.

Add $144 for optional leaf sight.

Add $80 for hunting stock.

SAKO, LTD.

Current rifle manufacturer established circa 1921 and located in Riihimäki, Finland. Current models are presently being imported by Beretta USA, located in Accokeek, MD. Previously imported by Stoeger Industries, Inc. located in Wayne, NJ, Garcia, and Rymac.

During 2000, Sako, Ltd. was purchased by Beretta Holding of Italy. All currently produced Sakos are imported by Beretta USA Corp. located in Accokeek, MD.

Beginning 2000, most Sako rifles (except the Action I in .223 Rem. cal.) are shipped with a Key Concept locking device. This patented system uses a separate key to activate an almost invisible lock which totally blocks the firing pin and prevents bolt movement.

MSR	100%	98%	95%	90%	80%	70%	60%	Last MSR

RIFLES: BOLT ACTION, RECENT PRODUCTION

Beginning late 2001, Sako established a custom shop, which allows the consumer to select from a wide variety of finishes, options, and special orders, including individual stock dimensions. Please contact Beretta USA for more information regarding the Sako custom shop.

All Sako left-handed models are available in medium or long action only.

Some older model TRG rifles (Models TRG-S, TRG-22, and TRG-42) have experienced firing pin breakage. Ser. no. ranges on these U.S. distributed rifles are 202238 - 275255 and 973815 - 998594. Please contact Beretta USA directly (str@berettausa.com or 800-803-8869) for a replacement firing pin assembly if you have a rifle within these serial number ranges.

MODEL TRG-21 – .308 Win. cal., bolt action, 25 3/4 in. stainless steel barrel, new design features modular synthetic stock construction with adj. cheekpiece and buttplate, cold hammer forged receiver, and resistance free bolt, 10 shot detachable mag., 10 1/2 lbs. Imported 1993-99.

	$2,300	$2,000	$1,800	$1,600	$1,400	$1,200	$975	$2,699

MODEL TRG-22 – .308 Win. cal., bolt action, 20 or 26 in. stainless steel barrel, updated TRG-21 design featuring adj. modular synthetic stock in Green, Desert Tan (disc.), or all black construction with adj. cheekpiece and buttplate, competition trigger, Picatinny rail became standard circa 2011, choice of blue (disc. 2002) or phosphate (new 2002) metal finish, cold hammer forged receiver, and resistance free bolt, 10 shot detachable mag., approx. 10 1/4 lbs. Importation began 2000.

MSR $3,500	$2,975	$2,465	$1,975	$1,750	$1,500	$1,250	$1,000	

Add $2,575 for folding stock in green finish.
Subtract approx. 10% if without Picatinny rail.

MODEL TRG-41 – .338 Lapua Mag. cal., similar to Model TRG-21, except has long action and 27 1/8 in. barrel, 7 3/4 lbs. Imported 1994-99.

	$2,700	$2,425	$2,150	$1,850	$1,625	$1,400	$1,200	$3,099

MODEL TRG-42 – .300 Win. Mag. (disc. 2012) or .338 Lapua Mag. cal., updated TRG-41 design featuring long action and 27 1/8 in. barrel, Picatinny rail became standard during 2011, choice of black composite/blue finish, desert tan (disc. 2013), or green composite/phosphate (new 2002) finish, 5 shot mag., 11 1/4 lbs. Importation began 2000.

MSR $4,550	$4,095	$3,595	$3,075	$2,795	$2,325	$1,925	$1,750	

Add $2,550 for folding stock with Picatinny rail (green finish only).
Subtract approx. $775 if without Picatinny rail (desert tan stock only).

MODEL TRG-S – available in medium action (disc. 1993) in .243 Win. or 7mm-08 cal., or long action in .25-06 Rem. (Mfg. 1994-98), .270 Win. (disc. 2000), 6.5x55mm Swedish (disc. 1998), .30-06 (disc.), .308 Win. (disc. 1995), .270 Wby. Mag. (disc. 1998), 7mm Wby. Mag. (Mfg. 1998), 7mm Rem. Mag. (disc.), .300 Win. Mag. (disc.), .300 Wby. Mag. (mfg. 1994-99), .30-378 Wby. Mag. (new 1998, 26 in. barrel only), .338 Win. Mag. (disc. 1999), .338 Lapua Mag. (new 1994), .340 Wby. Mag. (disc. 1998), 7mm STW (26 in. barrel only, disc. 1999), .375 H&H (disc. 1998), or .416 Rem. Mag. (disc. 1998) cal., black synthetic stock, Sporter variation derived from the Model TRG-21, 22 (disc.), 24 (Mag. cals. only, disc.), or 26 in. barrel, 3 or 5 shot detachable mag., fully adj. trigger, 60 degree bolt lift, matte finish, 8 1/8 lbs. Imported 1993-2004.

	$775	$650	$525	$475	$440	$415	$380	$896

SAMCO GLOBAL ARMS, INC.

Current importer and distributor located in Miami, FL. Dealer sales.

Samco Global Arms purchased the Charles Daly trademark in late 2012, and is currently importing a variety of Charles Daly shotgun configurations (see Charles Daly in the C section). Samco also imports Akkar shotguns from Turkey, as well as a variety of foreign and domestic surplus military rifles, including various contract Mausers, Loewe, Steyr, Czech, Lee Enfield, Mosin-Nagant, etc. Samco also imports European surplus pistols. Most of these guns offer excellent values to both shooters and collectors. Please contact the company directly for current availability and pricing, as its inventory changes weekly (see Trademark Index).

SAN SWISS ARMS AG

Current company established during late 2000, with headquarters located in Neuhausen, Switzerland.

In late 2000, SIG Arms AG, the firearms portion of SIG, was purchased by two Germans named Michael Lüke and Thomas Ortmeier, who have a background in textiles. Today the Lüke & Ortmeier group (L&O Group) includes independently operational companies such as Blaser Jadgwaffen GmbH, Mauser Jagdwaffen GmbH, John Rigby, J.P. Sauer & Sohn GmbH, SIG-Sauer Inc., SIG-Sauer GmbH and SAN Swiss Arms AG. Please refer to individual listings.

RIFLES

In 2010, San Swiss Arms purchased the rights to the A.M.S.D. Model OM 50 Nemesis. Model nomenclature has been changed to the San 511. Please contact the company directly for more information on this model including options, pricing, and U.S. availability (see Trademark Index).

MSR	100%	98%	95%	90%	80%	70%	60%	Last MSR

SARCO, INC.

Current importer and wholesaler located in Stirling, NJ.

Sarco Inc. imports a wide variety of foreign and domestic surplus military style rifles and shotguns that offer excellent values for the shooter. Please contact the company directly, as inventory changes constantly (see Trademark Index).

SARSILMAZ (SAR ARMS)

Current manufacturer established during 1880, and located in Istanbul, Turkey. Currently distributed by Davidson's, located in Prescott, AZ. Currently imported under private label by European American Armory, located in Rockledge, FL. Recently imported by Armalite, Inc., located in Geneseo, IL (refer to listings in Armalite section). Select slide action shotguns are imported by US Sporting Goods Inc. located in Rockledge, FL. Previously distributed 2000-2003 by PMC, located in Boulder City, NV. Previously imported and distributed until 2000 by Armsport, Inc. located in Miami, FL.

PISTOLS: SEMI-AUTO

Sarsilmaz manufactures a wide variety of semi-auto pistols in many configurations. Current models include the B6 Series, CM9, KILINC 2000 Mega and Light, P8 Series, and K2 Series. Please contact Sarsilmaz directly for more information, including pricing on its line of non-imported semi-auto pistols (see Trademark Index).

REVOLVERS

Sarsilmaz manufactures a line of double action revolvers in .38 Special and .357 Magnum caliber. Currently, these models are imported into the U.S. Please contact the manufacturer directly for more information (see Trademark Index).

RIFLES: SEMI-AUTO

Beginning in 2014, Sarsilmaz introduced the SAR 223 semi-auto rifle, based on the AR-15 design, and the 109T submachine gun. All rifles are gas piston operated, have adjustable telescoping tactical style stocks, matte black finish, and come with a 30 shot aluminum, steel, or polymer magazine.

SHOTGUNS

Sarsilmaz manufactures a variety of shotguns in O/U, semi-auto, and slide action configurations. Recent importation was by US Sporting Goods Inc. (see listings here).

SAR SEMI-AUTO SHOTGUN/SARSA – 12, 20, or 28 (disc.) ga., 2 or 3 (disc.) in. chamber, inertia/recoil operation, dual action bars, 22, 26, or 28 in. VR barrel with Benelli style choke tubes, aluminum receiver, steel bolt, polymer stock and forearm, choice of matte black or 100% camo finish, recoil pad, various configurations, 5.5-6.1 lbs. Importation began 2011.

| MSR $545 | $465 | $400 | $350 | $325 | $250 | $210 | $190 | |

Add $70 for 100% camo coverage (not available in 28 ga.).

SARSASP SEMI-AUTO – 12 ga., 3 in. chamber, 18 1/2 in. barrel, 5 shot mag, black polymer stock with pistol grip, top Picatinny rail, raised fiber optic front sight, adj. ghost ring rear sight, breach-style choke tube, 5 3/4 lbs. New mid-2013.

| MSR $659 | $560 | $495 | $425 | $380 | $310 | $250 | $195 | |

SAR SLIDE ACTION – 12, 20, or 28 (disc. late 2011) ga., 2 3/4, 3 or 3 1/2 in. (12 ga. only) chamber, dual action bars, 22, 26, or 28 in. VR barrel with Benelli style choke tube, aluminum receiver, polymer stock and forearm, choice of matte black or 100% camo coverage, various configurations, 5.7-6.2 lbs. Importation began 2011.

| MSR $381 | $325 | $285 | $250 | $230 | $210 | $190 | $175 | |

Add $67 for 100% camo coverage.

Add $81 for combo package with extra barrel (3 1/2 in. chamber only).

SAR SLIDE ACTION SPECIAL PURPOSE – 12 ga., 3 in. chamber, tactical configuration with black polymer pistol grip stock and extended grooved forearm, dual action bars, 18 1/2 in. fixed or screw in choke barrel with muzzle brake, aluminum receiver, optional Picatinny rail with ghost ring sight, 5 3/4 lbs. Importation began 2011.

| MSR $368 | $315 | $275 | $250 | $230 | $210 | $190 | $175 | |

Add $23 for Picatinny rail.

Subtract $67 for bead sights.

SARPASP SLIDE ACTION – 12 ga., 3 in. chamber, 18 1/2 in. barrel, 5 shot mag, black polymer stock with pistol grip, top Picatinny rail, raised fiber optic front sight, adj. ghost ring rear sight, breach-style choke tube, 5 3/4 lbs. New mid-2013.

| MSR $485 | $415 | $375 | $310 | $280 | $230 | $185 | $150 | |

MSR	100%	98%	95%	90%	80%	70%	60%	Last MSR

SAUER, J.P., & SOHN

Current manufacturer located in Eckernförde, Germany since 1751 (originally Prussia). Currently imported by Sauer USA, located in San Antonio, TX. Previously manufactured in Suhl pre-WWII. Previously imported and warehoused 1995-2007 by SIG Arms, located in Exeter, NH. Rifles were previously imported until 1995 by the Paul Company Inc. located in Wellsville, KS and until 1994 by G.U., Inc. located in Omaha, NE.

In 1972, J.P. Sauer & Sohn entered into a cooperative agreement with SIG. During 2000, SAN Swiss Arms AG purchased SIG Arms AG, including the J.P. Sauer & Sohn trademark. The L&O Group, an international industrial holding company, currently has controlling interest of J.P. Sauer and Sohns. Production remains in Eckernförde, Germany.

RIFLES: BOLT ACTION

Add $1,081-$2,156 per interchangeable barrel depending on rifle configuration on the following models where applicable.

Add $631-$677 per spare bolt, depending on rifle configuration.

Add $683 for left-hand.

Add $1,763 for Model 202 conversion kit or $1,917-$2,776 for Model 202 takedown conversion kit, depending on caliber.

SSE 3000 PRECISION RIFLE – .308 Win. cal., very accurate, law enforcement counter Sniper Rifle, built to customer specifications.

	100%	98%	95%	90%	80%	70%	60%
	$4,845	$3,655	$3,200	$2,850	$2,500	$2,275	$2,000

SSG 2000 – available in .223 Rem., 7.5mm Swiss, .300 Wby. Mag., or .308 Win. (standard) cal., bolt action, 4 shot mag., no sights, deluxe sniper rifle featuring thumbhole style walnut stock with stippling and thumbwheel adj. cheekpiece, 13 lbs. Importation disc. 1986.

	100%	98%	95%	90%	80%	70%	60%	Last MSR
	$2,480	$2,260	$1,950	$1,700	$1,500	$1,300	$1,100	$2,850

This model was available in .223 Rem., .300 Wby. Mag., or 7.5mm cal. by special order only.

SSG 3000 – .223 Rem., 22 1/2 in. barrel, Parker-Hale bipod, 2-stage match trigger, includes 2 1/2-10x52mm Zeiss scope, 200 mfg. for Swiss police.

	100%	98%	95%	90%	80%	70%	60%
	$12,000	$10,000	$8,500	$7,000	$6,750	$5,500	$4,250

SSG 3000 (CURRENT MFG.) – See listing under Sig-Sauer.

SAVAGE ARMS, INC.

Current manufacturer located in Westfield, MA since 1959, with sales offices located in Suffield, CT. Previously manufactured in Utica, NY - later manufacture was in Chicopee Falls, MA. Dealer and distributor sales.

This company originally started in Utica, NY in 1894. The Model 1895 was initially manufactured by Marlin between 1895-1899. After WWI, the name was again changed to the Savage Arms Corporation. Savage moved to Chicopee Falls, MA circa 1946 (to its Stevens Arms Co. plants). In the mid-1960s the company became The Savage Arms Division of American Hardware Corp., which later became The Emhart Corporation. This division was sold in September 1981, and became Savage Industries, Inc. located in Westfield, MA (since the move in 1960). On November 1, 1989, Savage Arms Inc. acquired the majority of assets of Savage Industries, Inc. On June 24, 2013, ATK acquired Caliber Company, the parent company of Savage Sports Corporation.

Savage Arms, Inc. will offer service and parts on their current line of firearms only (those manufactured after Nov. 1, 1995). These models include the 24, 99, and 110 plus the imported Model 312. Warranty and repair claims for products not acquired by Savage Arms, Inc. will remain the responsibility of Savage Industries, Inc. For information regarding the repair and/or parts of Savage Industries, Inc. firearms, please refer to the Trademark Index in the back of this text. Parts for pre-1989 Savage Industries, Inc. firearms may be obtained by contacting the Numrich Gun Parts Corporation located in West Hurley, NY (listed in Trademark Index).

For Savage Arms, Inc. pre-December 1968, serial number records can be researched from the original company ledgers for rifles, pistols, and shotguns that were serialized. The information will be furnished for Model 1895, 1899, and Model 99 rifles, semi-automatic pistols, and other pre-December 1968 serialized guns at a charge of $35 per gun. Information on other Savage non-serialized firearms, or post-December 1968 guns will be furnished at $25 per gun. A factory letter authenticating the configuration of a particular specimen may be obtained by contacting Mr. John Callahan (see Trademark Index for listings and address). Please allow 8 weeks for an adequate response.

For more Savage model information, please refer to the Serialization section in the back of this text.

Please refer to the *Blue Book of Modern Black Powder Arms* by John Allen (also online) for more information and prices on Savage's lineup of modern black powder models. For more information and current pricing on both new and used Savage airguns, please refer to the *Blue Book of Airguns* by Dr. Robert Beeman & John Allen (also online).

Black Powder Long Arms and Pistols - Reproductions & Replicas by Dennis Adler is also an invaluable source for most black powder reproductions and replicas, and includes hundreds of color images on most popular makes/models, provides manufacturer/trademark histories, and up-to-date information on related items/accessories for black powder shooting - www.bluebookofgunvalues.com

MSR	100%	98%	95%	90%	80%	70%	60%	*Last MSR*

RIFLES: CENTERFIRE, CURRENT/RECENT PRODUCTION

The 110 Series was first produced in 1958. Beginning in 1992, Savage Arms, Inc. began supplying this model with a master trigger lock, earmuffs, shooting glasses (disc. 1992), and test target.

Beginning 1994, all Savage rifles employ a laser etched bolt featuring the Savage logo. During 1996, Savage began using pillar bedded stocks for many of their rifles.

Recent Savage nomenclature usually involves alphabetical suffixes which mean the following: B - laminated wood stock, BT - laminated thumbhole stock, C - detachable box mag., EV - Evolution stock, F - composite/synthetic stock, G - hardwood stock, H - hinged floorplate, K - AccuStock or standard muzzle brake, AK - adj. muzzle brake with fluted barrel, L - left-hand, LE - Law Enforcement, NS - no sights, P - police (tactical) rifle, SB - smooth bore, SE - safari express, SR - suppressor ready, SS - stainless steel, SS-S - stainless steel single shot, T - Target (aperture rear sight), TR - tactical style rimfire, TRR - tactical style rimfire w/rail, U - high luster blue, blue metal finish and/or stock finish, V - Long Range (Varmint w/heavy barrel), XP - package gun (scope, sling, and rings/base), Y - Youth/Ladies Model. A 2 digit model number (10) designates new short action. A 3 digit model number (110) indicates long action.

Hence, the Model 111FCNS designates a 111 Series firearm with synthetic stock, detachable magazine, and no sights. Likewise, a Model 11FYCXP3 indicates a Model 11 Series with synthetic stock, youth dimensions, detachable magazine, is a packaged gun which includes scope. The Model 116FHSAK indicates a long action rifle with hinged floorplate, synthetic stock, stainless steel action/barrel with adj. muzzlebrake.

During 2003, Savage released its new patented AccuTrigger, which allows the consumer to adjust the trigger pull from the outside of the rifle from 1 1/2 lbs. - 6 lbs. using a proprietary tool. The AccuTrigger also has almost no trigger creep and is infinitely adjustable. Initially, it was released in all Varmint, LE, and heavy barrel long range rifles, and during 2004, the AccuTrigger became standard on nearly all Savage centerfire rifles, except the Model 11 and 11FCXP3 and 10/110G Package guns. During 2007, Savage began offering target actions with AccuTrigger, right bolt, and choice of left or right port ejection with .223 Rem. bolt head - MSR is $560-$595.

During 2008, Savage Arms introduced a new personal anti-recoil device (P.A.D.), which is installed in many Savage bolt action centerfire rifles. The P.A.D. reduces recoil by 45% from OEM solid and vented pads.

In 2009, Savage Arms introduced its Accustock, which incorporates a rigid aluminum rail and 3D bedding cradle that is firmly imbedded in the stock throughout the length of the rifles forend. Many Savage Centerfire rifles now incorporate the Accustock bedding system.

Also during 2009/2010, Savage introduced varmint short actions, along with both long and short sporter actions. Sporter actions had an MSR of $481, while the varmint short actions' MSR was $505. A dual port receiver, allowing left loading and right ejection was also released in 2009 - MSR was $595.

During 2010, Target actions became available in stainless steel only (in either single or dual port configuration) - MSR on the single port is $613, and $651 for the dual port.

During 2012, Savage introduced its new AXIS Series.

Whenever possible, the models within this category have been listed in numerical sequence.

Subtract approx. 10% on models listed below w/o AccuTrigger (became standard on all centerfire rifles in 2004).

MODEL 10BA/BAS-K – .308 Win. cal., 24 in. fluted heavy barrel with muzzle brake, short action, 10 shot detachable box mag., all aluminum AccuStock, AccuTrigger, Magpul PRS-G3 buttstock, Picatinny rail, no sights, matte blued finish, oversized bolt handle, 13.4 lbs. New 2009.

MSR	100%	98%	95%	90%	80%	70%	60%	Last MSR
MSR $2,446	$2,000	$1,750	$1,500	$1,360	$1,100	$900	$700	

* ***Model 10BAT/S-K*** – .308 Win. cal., 24 in. barrel with muzzle brake, short action, 10 shot detachable box mag., similar to Model 10BAS-K, except has tactical stock with adj. buttpad. Mfg. 2009-2010.

	$1,750	$1,450	$1,125	$925	$800	$700	$600	*$2,071*

MODEL 10 LAW ENFORCEMENT SERIES – .223 Rem., .260 Rem. (mfg. 1999-2001), .308 Win., or 7mm-08 (mfg. 1999-2001) cal., short action, tactical/law enforcement model, checkered black synthetic stock, features 20 (new 2006) or 24 in. heavy barrel w/o sights, AccuTrigger became standard 2003, 8 lbs. Mfg. 1998-2007.

	$505	$440	$380	$345	$280	$225	$175	*$621*

* ***Model 10FP/10FLP*** – .223 Rem. or .308 Win. cal., short action, 20 or 24 in. heavy free floating and button rifled barrel, 4 shot box mag., black McMillan synthetic sporter style stock, drilled and tapped, swivel stud, oversized bolt handle, 6 1/4 lbs. Mfg. 1998-2010.

	$625	$500	$425	$365	$335	$295	$275	*$775*

This model was also available in left-hand action (Model 10FLP, 24 in. barrel only, disc. 2009).

* ***Model 10FP Duty*** – similar to Model 10FP, except has open iron sights. Mfg. 2002 only.

	$435	$355	$290	$250	$215	$180	$165	*$525*

* ***Model 10FP 20 In. (LE1/LE1A)*** – .223 Rem. (LE1A only, disc. 2007) or .308 Win. cal., similar to Model 10FP, except has 20 in. heavy barrel with no sights, choice of standard (LE1, disc. 2005) or Choate (LE1A) stock (folding only, new 2006). Mfg. 2002-2010.

	$865	$695	$565	$475	$425	$350	$300	*$1,034*

Subtract 20% for standard stock (LE1).

MSR	100%	98%	95%	90%	80%	70%	60%	Last MSR

* **Model 10FP 26 In. (LE2/LE2A)** – .223 Rem. (LE2A only) or .308 Win. cal., similar to Model 10FP-LE1/LE1A, except has 26 in. heavy barrel and choice of standard (LE2, disc. 2005) or Choate stock (LE2A). Mfg. 2002-2006.

| | $625 | $500 | $400 | $360 | $330 | $300 | $275 | *$754* |

Subtract 20% for standard stock.

* **Model 10FP McMillan (LE2B)** – .308 Win. cal., short action, features McMillan tactical fiberglass stock with stippled grip areas, 4 shot mag., 26 in. heavy barrel. Mfg. 2003-2006.

| | $860 | $725 | $625 | $525 | $425 | $325 | $265 | *$1,033* |

* **Model 10FP H-S Precision** – .308 Win. cal., 24 in. barrel, features H-S Precision stock. Mfg. 2006 only.

| | $720 | $585 | $475 | $425 | $350 | $300 | $275 | *$864* |

* **Model 10FPCPXP/10FPXP (LE/LEA)** – .308 Win. cal. only, short action, features skeletonized synthetic stock, 24 (new 2006) or 26 (disc. 2005) in. barrel w/o sights, H-S Precision stock became standard 2006, LEA has Choate stock, LE has standard stock (disc. 2005), includes Burris (disc.) or Leupold (new 2004) 3.5-10x50mm scope with flip covers and sling, 4 shot internal (FPXP, disc. 2006) or detachable (FPCPXP, new 2007) mag., Harris bipod, aluminum case, 10 1/2 lbs. Mfg. 2002-2009.

| | $2,275 | $1,850 | $1,550 | $1,300 | $1,100 | $900 | $750 | *$2,715* |

Subtract 20% for LE standard stock or 10% for Choate stock (Model 10FPXP-LEA package).

* **Model 10FCP HS Precision** – .308 Win. cal., 24 in. barrel, features H-S Precision stock, 4 shot detachable box mag., matte blued finish, oversized bolt handle, no sights, 9.6 lbs. New 2007.

| MSR $1,315 | $1,100 | $925 | $750 | $650 | $550 | $475 | $400 | |

» **Model 10FCPXP H-S Precision Package** – .308 Win. cal., 24 in. barrel, includes top Picatinny rail, 3-9x40mm scope, and bipod, 9.6 lbs. Mfg. 2010-2011.

| | $2,550 | $2,250 | $1,900 | $1,625 | $1,275 | $1,000 | $875 | *$2,908* |

* **Model 10FCP Choate** – .308 Win. cal., 24 in. barrel, features Choate stock, detachable box mag. Mfg. 2007 only.

| | $700 | $575 | $475 | $425 | $350 | $300 | $275 | *$833* |

* **Model 10FCP McMillan** – .308 Win. cal., 24 in. heavy barrel, 4 shot detachable box mag., no sights, matte blued finish, oversized bolt handle, AccuTrigger, McMillan fiberglass stock, 10 lbs. New 2007.

| MSR $1,591 | $1,325 | $1,025 | $895 | $750 | $650 | $550 | $475 | |

* **Model 10 FCP-K/ Model 10 FLCP-K** – .223 Rem. or .308 Win. cal., short action, 24 in. heavy blue barrel with muzzle brake, 4 shot detachable box mag., drilled and tapped, black synthetic AccuStock with aluminum spine and 3-D bedding cradle, swivel stud for bipod, oversized bolt handle, 8.9 lbs. Mfg. 2009-2013.

| | $850 | $725 | $595 | $475 | $425 | $350 | $300 | *$975* |

This model was also available in left-hand action at no extra charge (Model 10 FLCP-K).

MODEL 10 PRECISION CARBINE – .223 Rem., .308 Win., or .300 AAC Blackout (mfg. 2012 only) cal., 20 in. matte blue free floating button rifled threaded (new 2012) or un-threaded (disc. 2011) barrel, 4 shot detachable box mag., swivel stud, oversized bolt handle, green camo AccuStock with aluminum spine and 3-D bedding cradle, 7 lbs. Mfg. 2009-2014.

| | $810 | $675 | $550 | $425 | $375 | $350 | $300 | *$952* |

MODEL 12 LONG RANGE PRECISION – .243 Win., .260 Rem., or 6.5 Creedmoor cal., short action, 26 in. fluted full profile barrel, Target AccuTrigger, H-S Precision fiberglass stock, 4 shot detachable box mag., no sights, oversized bolt handle, matte blued finish, 11 lbs. New 2011.

| MSR $1,288 | $1,050 | $910 | $750 | $650 | $550 | $475 | $400 | |

MODEL 12 LONG RANGE PRECISION VARMINTER REPEATER – .204 Ruger, .22-250 Rem., .223 Rem., or 6mm Norma BR cal., 26 in. barrel, short action, detachable box mag., target AccuTrigger. Mfg. 2008-2010.

| | $1,085 | $925 | $825 | $725 | $625 | $525 | $450 | *$1,319* |

MODEL 110-FP LAW ENFORCEMENT (TACTICAL POLICE) – .223 Rem. (disc. 1998), .25-06 Rem. (new 1995), .300 Win. Mag. (new 1995), .30-06 (mfg. 1996-2006), .308 Win. (disc. 1998), or 7mm Rem. Mag. (mfg. 1995-2007) cal., long action, 24 in. heavy barrel pillar bedded tactical rifle, all metal parts are non-reflective, 4 shot internal mag., black DuPont Rynite stock, right or left-hand (mfg. 1996-2001) action, drilled and tapped for scope mounts, AccuTrigger became standard 2003, 8 1/2 lbs. Mfg. 1990-2001, reintroduced 2003-2008.

| | $575 | $465 | $360 | $310 | $265 | $240 | $210 | *$678* |

Was also available in left-hand action at no additional charge (mfg. 1996-2001, Model 110-FLP).

* **Model 110FCP** – .25-06 Rem. or .300 Win. Mag. cal., 24 in. heavy barrel with Savage muzzle brake, 4 shot detachable box mag., black synthetic AccuStock with aluminum spine and 3-D bedding cradle, drilled and tapped, swivel stud for bipod, oversized bolt handle, 9 lbs. Mfg. 2009.

| | $725 | $600 | $500 | $425 | $375 | $350 | $300 | *$866* |

MSR	100%	98%	95%	90%	80%	70%	60%	Last MSR

MODEL 110BA/BAS – .300 Win. Mag. or .338 Lapua cal., right or left (110BA LH, new 2013) hand action, 26 in. fluted carbon steel barrel with muzzle brake, 5 or 6 shot detachable box mag., drilled and tapped, open sights, includes Picatinny top rail, matte black aluminum tactical AccuStock with handguard, AccuTrigger, 15 3/4 lbs. New 2010.

| MSR $2,638 | $2,175 | $1,900 | $1,625 | $1,450 | $1,150 | $925 | $775 | |

MODEL 110FCP HS PRECISION – .300 Win. Mag. or .338 Lapua cal., long action, 24 or 26 in. carbon steel heavy barrel, matte black metal finish, 4 shot detachable box mag., black HS Precision fiberglass stock with V-Block, drilled and tapped, AccuTrigger, oversized bolt handle, 9 lbs. New 2012.

| MSR $1,315 | $1,100 | $925 | $750 | $650 | $550 | $475 | $400 | |

Add $411 for .338 Lapua cal.

MODEL 111 HOG HUNTER – .338 Win. Mag. cal., long action, 4 shot internal box mag., 20 in. threaded barrel with iron sights, matte black metal finish, AccuTrigger, OD Green synthetic stock, 8 lbs. New 2012.

| MSR $560 | $475 | $425 | $365 | $335 | $295 | $265 | $235 | |

MODEL 111 LONG RANGE HUNTER – .25-06 Rem. (disc. 2014), 6.5x284 Norma, 7mm Rem. Mag., .300 Win. Mag., or .338 Lapua (new 2012) cal., 3 or 5 (.338 Lapua cal. only) shot mag., 26 in. fluted carbon steel barrel with adj. muzzle brake, drilled and tapped, AccuTrigger, Karsten adj. and detachable cheekpiece, matte black synthetic AccuStock and forearm, no sights, hinged floorplate, 8.65 lbs. New 2010.

| MSR $1,171 | $975 | $765 | $625 | $525 | $425 | $365 | $325 | |

Add $250 for .338 Lapua cal. (new 2012).

SCATTERGUN TECHNOLOGIES INC. (S.G.T.)

Current manufacturer located in Berryville, AR since 1999. Previously located in Nashville, TN 1991-1999. Distributor, dealer, and consumer sales.

During 1999, Wilson Combat purchased Scattergun Technologies. S.G.T. manufactures practical defense, tactical, and hunting shotguns in 12 ga. only, utilizing Remington Models 870 and 11-87 (disc.) actions in various configurations as listed. All shotguns feature 3 in. chamber capacity and parkerized finish.

SHOTGUNS: SEMI-AUTO

Add $15 for short stock on models listed.

Add $125 for Armor-Tuff finish on models listed.

K-9 MODEL – 12 ga., 18 in. barrel, adj. ghost ring sight, 7 shot mag., side saddle, synthetic buttstock and forearm. Disc. 2003.

| | $1,100 | $875 | $775 | $665 | $560 | $465 | $410 | *$1,325* |

URBAN SNIPER MODEL – 12 ga., 18 in. rifled barrel, scout optics, 7 shot mag., side saddle, synthetic buttstock, forearm and bipod. Disc. 1999.

| | $1,225 | $1,075 | $950 | $835 | $685 | $585 | $485 | *$1,390* |

SHOTGUNS: SLIDE ACTION

On the following models, Armor-Tuff finish became standard during 2003.

Add $15 for short stock on models listed.

Subtract approx. $100 if w/o Armor-Tuff finish.

STANDARD MODEL – 12 or 20 (disc. 2011) ga., 18 1/2 in. barrel, adj. ghost ring sight, 7 shot mag., side saddle, synthetic buttstock and forearm with 11,000 CP flashlight, Black, Green, Gray, Federal Brown, Flat Dark Earth, or Green Base Camo finish.

| MSR $1,540 | $1,315 | $1,165 | $1,050 | $915 | $785 | $665 | $550 | |

Add $400 for Green Base Camo.

EXPERT MODEL – 12 ga., 18 in. barrel with mod. choke, nickel/Teflon finished receiver, adj. ghost ring sight, forearm incorporates 11,000 CP flashlight. Mfg. 1997-2000.

| | $1,200 | $995 | $775 | $665 | $560 | $465 | $410 | *$1,350* |

PRACTICAL TURKEY MODEL – 20 in. barrel with extra full choke, adj. ghost ring sight, 5 shot mag. for 3 in. shells, synthetic buttstock and forearm. Mfg. 1995-99.

| | $545 | $500 | $465 | $405 | $350 | $290 | $250 | *$595* |

LOUIS AWERBUCK SIGNATURE MODEL – 18 in. barrel with fixed choke, adj. ghost ring sight, 5 shot mag., side saddle, wood buttstock with recoil reducer and forearm. Mfg. 1994-99.

| | $625 | $490 | $385 | $325 | $275 | $230 | $200 | *$705* |

F.B.I. MODEL – similar to Standard Model, except has 5 shot mag. Disc. 1999.

| | $715 | $625 | $490 | $420 | $370 | $305 | $265 | *$770* |

MSR	100%	98%	95%	90%	80%	70%	60%	Last MSR

MILITARY MODEL – 18 in. barrel with vent. handguard and M-9 bayonet lug, adj. ghost ring rear sight, 7 shot mag., synthetic stock and grooved corncob forearm. Mfg. 1997-98.

	100%	98%	95%	90%	80%	70%	60%	Last MSR
	$625	$490	$385	$325	$275	$230	$200	$690

PATROL MODEL – 18 in. barrel, adj. ghost ring sight, 5 shot mag., synthetic buttstock and forearm. Disc. 1999.

	100%	98%	95%	90%	80%	70%	60%	Last MSR
	$545	$500	$465	$405	$350	$290	$250	$595

BORDER PATROL (MODEL 20) – 12 or 20 (disc. 2011) ga., 18 1/2 or 20 (disc. 2011) in. barrel, similar to Patrol Model, except has 7 shot mag., synthetic stock and forearm, Black, FDE, OD Green, Green Base Camo, Gray Base Camo, or FDE Base Camo finish.

MSR	100%	98%	95%	90%	80%	70%	60%	Last MSR
MSR $1,135	$975	$885	$765	$655	$575	$495	$435	

Add $400 for Green, Gray, or FDE Base Camo.
Add $35 for 20 ga. (disc. 2011).

SCHMEISSER GmbH

Current manufacturer located in Krefeld, Germany. Some models are distributed by American Tactical Imports, located in Rochester, NY.

RIFLES: SEMI-AUTO

Schmeisser GmbH currently manufactures AR-15 style rifles in several calibers and configurations. Current models include AR15 M4, AR15 M5, AR15 A4 (16 and 20 in.), AR15 Ultramatch, AR15 Ultramatch STS, AR15 M4-Solid, and AR15 M5-Solid. Please contact the company directly for more information including options, pricing, and availability (see Trademark Index).

SCHUETZEN PISTOL WORKS

Schuetzen Pistol Works is the in-house custom shop of Olympic Arms. Schuetzen Pistol Works has been customizing Safari Arms and Olympic Arms 1911 style pistols since 1997. For currently manufactured pistols, please refer to the Olympic Arms listing. For discontinued models, please refer to the Safari Arms listing.

SCHWABEN ARMS GMBH

Current manufacturer located in Rottweil, Germany. No current U.S. importation.

Schwaben Arms GmbH manufactures 600-800 guns annually. Production includes an extensive lineup of quality tactical rifles and carbines, primarily patterned after H&K models and other historically significant military rifles/carbines, including a .308 Win. cal. semi-auto MP5. Both commercial and military/law enforcement models are available. Please contact the factory directly for U.S. availability and pricing (see Trademark Index).

SCORPION TACTICAL

Previous AR-15 rifle manufacturer and current AR-15 parts and accesories manufacturer, located in Leander, TX.

RIFLES: SEMI-AUTO

ATS-15 L1 – 5.56 NATO cal., GIO, 16 in. heavy barrel with A2 flash hider, 30 shot mag., fixed front and flip-up adj. rear sights, forged aluminum upper and lower receivers, standard AR charging handle, SST, standard plastic mid-length handguard with heat shield, 6-pos. sliding stock, plastic pistol grip, Black finish. Disc. 2014.

	100%	98%	95%	90%	80%	70%	60%	Last MSR
	$900	$800	$675	$625	$500	$400	$325	$999

ATS-15 L2 – 5.56 NATO cal., GIO, 16 in. heavy barrel with A2 flash hider, 30 shot Pmag., fixed front and Magpul MBUS rear sights, forged aluminum upper and lower receivers, standard AR charging handle, SST, mid-length drop-in quad rail, 6-pos. sliding stock, Ergo grip, Black finish. Disc. 2014.

	100%	98%	95%	90%	80%	70%	60%	Last MSR
	$1,150	$1,000	$875	$775	$650	$525	$400	$1,229

ATS-15 L3 – 5.56 NATO cal., GIO, 16 in. M4 profile barrel with A2 flash hider, 30 shot Pmag., Troy micro flip up Battlesight sights, forged aluminum upper and lower receivers, standard AR charging handle, SST, Magpul enhanced aluminum trigger guard, carbine-length free floating quad rail, Magpul 6-pos. CTR stock, Ergo grip, Black finish, 6.9 lbs. Disc. 2014.

	100%	98%	95%	90%	80%	70%	60%	Last MSR
	$1,300	$1,150	$975	$875	$725	$585	$475	$1,449

ATS-15 L5 – 5.56 NATO cal., GIO, 16 in. M4 profile barrel with A2 flash hider, 30 shot Pmag., Magpul Gen2 MBUS front and rear back up sights, forged aluminum upper and lower receivers, standard AR charging handle, SST, Magpul enhanced aluminum trigger guard, 13.8 in. Troy Alpha rail, Magpul ACS/Adaptable Carbine Storage stock, Ergo grip, FDE finish, 6.9 lbs. Disc. 2014.

	100%	98%	95%	90%	80%	70%	60%	Last MSR
	$1,975	$1,725	$1,475	$1,350	$1,085	$900	$725	$2,200

MSR	100%	98%	95%	90%	80%	70%	60%	Last MSR

SEEKINS PRECISION

Current manufacturer located in Lewiston, ID.

Seekins Precision currently manufactures complete AR-15 style rifles as well as AR-15 parts and accessories.

RIFLES: SEMI-AUTO

SP3G – .223 Rem./5.56 NATO (.223 Wylde chamber) cal., GIO, 18 in. 3G contoured super match barrel, 15 in. SP3R rail system, Melonite coated gas tube, bolt carrier, and adj. gas block, Magpul UBR stock, Ergo deluxe tactical pistol grip, Geissele Super 3-Gun trigger, BCM Mod 3 charging handle, SP billet lower Gen 2, Billet iMRT-3 upper, H buffer, M4 feed ramp, and SP Advanced Tactical Compensator. Disc. 2014.

	$2,525	$2,225	$1,900	$1,725	$1,400	$1,150	$900	*$2,800*

SP10 .308 – .308 Win. cal., 18 in. stainless steel match grade barrel, ATC brake, billet aluminum construction, adj. gas block, single stage trigger, 15 in. SP3R handguard, ambidextrous controls, top Picatinny rail, BCM Mod 3 charging handle, CMC trigger, Magpul STR stock, hardcoat anodized matte black finish, 8.9 lbs. New 2015.

MSR $2,489	$2,125	$1,875	$1,550	$1,325	$1,100	$950	$825	

SPBRV2 (BATTLEFIELD RIFLE) – .223 Wylde or .300 AAC Blackout cal., 16 in. stainless steel match grade barrel with flash hider, 12 in. SAR quad rail handguard, forged upper and lower, QMS trigger, BCM Mod 3 charging handle, Magpul MOE stock, Ergo grip, Melonite-coated gas components, 7.2 lbs. New 2015.

MSR $1,425	$1,215	$1,085	$965	$815	$715	$605	$505	

SPCBRV1 (COMBAT BILLET RIFLE) – .223 Rem./5.56 NATO (.223 Wylde chamber), or .300 AAC Blackout cal., GIO, 16 in. stainless steel barrel with flash hider, Melonite coated gas tube, bolt carrier and adj. gas block, Magpul MOE stock, Ergo pistol grip, ALG-ACT trigger, BCM Mod 3 charging handle, B.A.D. ambi selector, SP Gen2 billet lower, upper, and 12 in. BAR rail, H buffer, M4 feed ramp.

MSR $1,850	$1,575	$1,385	$1,185	$1,065	$915	$785	$635	

SPRO3G (PRO SERIES) – .223 Wylde or .300 AAC Blackout cal., 18 in. stainless ultra-match barrel, ATC muzzle brake, CNC machined billet upper and lower receivers, competition style free-float handguard, Melonite-coated gas tube, bolt carrier group, and adj. gas block, ambidextrous controls, CMC trigger, BCM Mod 3 charging handle, Magpul UBR stock, Ergo Deluxe grip, 8 1/2 lbs. New 2015.

MSR $2,250	$1,915	$1,685	$1,425	$1,225	$1,035	$885	$735	

SPROV3 (PRO SERIES) – .223 Wylde or .300 AAC Blackout cal., 16 in. stainless steel match grade barrel, flash hider, ambidextrous controls, CNC machined billet upper and lower receivers, Melonite-coated gas components, 15 in. MCSR handguard, ACT trigger, Magpul STR stock, Ergo Deluxe grip, 7 1/2 lbs. New 2015.

MSR $1,995	$1,700	$1,500	$1,250	$1,100	$950	$825	$675	

SENNI ARMS CO.

Current manufacturer located in Queensland, Australia. No current U.S. importation.

Senni Arms manufactures a complete line of 1911-style semi-auto pistols, including the Stinger, 2010, Black Snake, Lawson, Silhouette, Razorback, and the Trooper. Senni Arms also manufactures the Siege semi-auto tactical shotgun and the Elysium M4 semi-auto tactical carbine. Please contact the company directly for more information, including pricing and domestic availability (see Trademark Index).

SERBU FIREARMS, INC.

Current manufacturer located in Tampa, FL.

Serbu Firearms also manufactures a Super-Shorty short barreled slide action shotgun based on the Remington 870 or Mossberg 500. These shotguns are classified NFA only.

RIFLES: BOLT ACTION

BFG-50 RIFLE/CARBINE – .50 BMG cal., single shot bolt action, 22 (carbine), 29 1/2 (rifle), or 36 (alloy or stainless, new 2011) in. match grade barrel with muzzle brake, AR-15 style trigger and safety, Picatinny rail, parkerized finish, 17-22 lbs. New 1999.

MSR $2,395	$2,395	$2,150	$1,875	$1,625	$1,450	$1,185	$975	

Add $175 for bi-pod.

Add $400 for 36 in. barrel (alloy or stainless), new 2011.

BFG-50A – .50 BMG cal., gas operated, 26 in. barrel with 8 port Shark Brake muzzle brake, 10 shot mag., 3-lug bolt, sliding plate extrator, dual plunger ejectors, removable barrel extension and handguard, 23 lbs. New 2008.

MSR $7,200	$6,650	$5,750	$5,000	$4,100	$3,700	$3,400	$3,100	

MSR	100%	98%	95%	90%	80%	70%	60%	Last MSR

SERO LTD.

Current rifle manufacturer located in Budapest, Hungary. No U.S. importation.

RIFLES: SEMI-AUTO

GEPARD GM6 LYNX – 14.5x114mm Soviet or .50 BMG cal., bullpup configuration, 28 3/4 in. barrel with muzzle brake, 100% desert camo coverage, 5 shot mag. is located in back of the pistol grip, full Picatinny rail, 25.3 lbs. New 2012.

Please contact the company directly for U.S. availability and pricing.

SHARPS MILSPEC

Previous trademark and division of Sharps Rifle Company, located in Chamberlain, SD 2011 only.

RIFLES: SEMI-AUTO

SHARPS 2010 CARBINE – 5.56 NATO cal., AR-15 style, GPO, 16 in. 5 groove rifling barrel with muzzle brake, redesigned charging handle, aluminum free floating handguard with quad Picatinny rails, Magpul ACS buttstock and MIAD pistol grip, supplied with two 30 shot mags. Limited mfg. 2011 only.

	100%	98%	95%	90%	80%	70%	60%	Last MSR
	$2,425	$2,100	$1,800	$1,500	$1,250	$1,000	$850	$2,695

SHOOTERS ARMS MANUFACTURING INCORPORATED

Current manufacturer established in 1992, and located in Cebu, the Philippines. Currently imported by Century International Arms, located in Delray Beach, FL. Previously imported by Pacific Arms Corp. in Modesto, CA.

Shooter Arms Manufacturing Inc. makes semi-auto pistols, including the Elite, Commodore, Military, GI, Desert Storm, Seahawk, 1911A1, Eagle, Hawk, and the Trojan. Previous models have included the React, React-2, Military Enhanced, GI Enhanced, Elite Sport, Chief, Scout, Falcon, Raven, Omega, and Alpha. Shooters Arms Manufacuring Inc. also manufactures a revolver, the Protector, and a 12 ga. shotgun called the SAS 12. Please contact the importer directly for more information, including pricing and U.S. availability (see Trademark Index).

SIDEWINDER

Previous trademark manufactured by D-Max, Inc. located in Bagley, MN circa 1993-96. Dealer or consumer sales.

REVOLVERS

SIDEWINDER – .45 LC or 2 1/2/3 in. .410 bore shotshells/slugs, 6 shot, stainless steel construction, 6 1/2 or 7 1/2 in. bull barrel (muzzle end bored for removable choke), Pachmayr grips, transfer bar safety, adj. rear sight, unique design permits one cylinder to shoot above listed loads, cased with choke tube, 3.8 lbs. Mfg. 1993-1996.

	100%	98%	95%	90%	80%	70%	60%	Last MSR
	$695	$575	$475	$415	$360	$300	$255	$775

SIG ARMS AG

Current Swiss company (SIG) established during 1860 in Neuhausen, Switzerland. P 210 pistols are currently imported and distributed by Sig Sauer (formerly SIG Arms, Inc.), established in 1985, located in Exeter, NH. Previously located in Herndon, VA and Tysons Corner, VA.

In late 2000, SIG Arms AG, the firearms portion of SIG, was purchased by two Germans named Michael Lüke and Thomas Ortmeier, who have a background in textiles. Today the Lüke & Ortmeier group includes independently operational companies such as Blaser Jadgwaffen GmbH, Mauser Jagdwaffen GmbH, J.P. Sauer & Sohn GmbH, SIG-Sauer Inc., SIG-Sauer GmbH and SAN Swiss Arms AG. Please refer to individual listings.

PISTOLS: SEMI-AUTO

SIG Custom Shop variations of the P 210 were also available in three configurations - United We Stand ($8,990 last MSR) and two variations of the 50 Year Jubilee ($4,995 or $5,999 last MSR).

Add $1,473 for .22 LR conversion kit on the following models (not available on the P 210-8).

P 210 & VARIATIONS – 9mm Para. or 7.65mm Para. (disc.) cal., single action, 4 3/4 in. barrel, 8 shot mag., standard weapon of the Swiss Army, 2 lbs.

Originally mfg. in 1947, this pistol was first designated the SP 47/8 and became the standard military pistol of the Swiss Army in 1949. Later designated the P 210, this handgun has been mfg. continuously for over 55 years.

* **P 210 Danish Army M49** – Danish Army version of the Model P 210, approx. 25,000 mfg.

	100%	98%	95%	90%	80%	70%	60%	Last MSR
	$3,000	$2,500	$2,000	$1,750	$1,500	$1,250	$1,000	

* **P 210-1** – polished finish, walnut grips, special hammer, fixed sights. Importation disc. 1986.

	100%	98%	95%	90%	80%	70%	60%	Last MSR
	$2,500	$2,000	$1,500	$1,250	$1,000	$900	$750	$1,861

MSR	100%	98%	95%	90%	80%	70%	60%	Last MSR

* **P 210-2** – matte finish, field or combat (recent mfg.) sights, plastic (disc.) or wood grips. Limited importation 1987-2002.

	$1,800	$1,500	$1,200	$900	$750	$625	$550	$1,680

Add 50% for high polish Swiss Army pistols with "A" prefix.

Add 50% for West German Police Contract models with unique loaded chamber indicator on slide. Approx. 5,000 mfg. in "D" prefix serial range.

* **P 210-5** – matte finish, heavy frame, micrometer target sights, 150mm or 180mm (disc.) extended barrel, hard rubber (disc.) or wood (current mfg.) grips, bottom (EU) or push-button side mounted (U.S.) mag. release, very limited mfg. Limited importation 1997-2007.

	$2,250	$2,150	$1,675	$1,350	$1,125	$1,000	$895	

Add 15% for side mounted mag. release.

Add 50% for early mfg. guns.

* **P 210-6** – matte blue finish, fixed (recent importation) or micrometer sights, 120mm barrel, checkered walnut grips, bottom (EU) or push-button side mounted (U.S.) mag. release.

	$1,850	$1,700	$1,500	$1,300	$1,125	$1,000	$895	

* **P 210-7** – .22 LR or 9mm Para. cal., regular or target long barrel, limited importation. Disc.

	$3,500	$3,000	$2,700	$2,350	$2,000	$1,750	$1,500	

* **P 210-8** – features heavy frame, target sights, and wood grips. Special order only. Limited importation 2001-2003.

	$3,750	$3,250	$2,650	$2,300	$1,950	$1,600	$1,275	$4,289

* **P 210 Legend** – please refer to listing in the Sig Sauer section, new mfg.

RIFLES: BOLT ACTION

SHR 970 – .25-06 Rem., .270 Win., .280 Rem., .30-06, .308 Win., .300 Win. Mag., or 7mm Rem. Mag. cal., steel receiver, standard model featuring easy takedown (requires single tool) and quick change 22 or 24 (Mag. cals. only) in. barrel, detachable 3 or 4 shot mag., 65 degree short throw bolt, 3 position safety, standard medium gloss walnut stock with checkering, ultra-fast lock time, Nitrided bore, no sights, includes hard carry case, approx. 7.3 lbs. Mfg. 1998-2002.

	$475	$395	$350	$325	$295	$275	$250	$550

Add $395 for extra barrel.

* **SHR 970 Synthetic** – similar to SHR 970, except has checkered black synthetic stock with stippled grip. Mfg. 1999-2002.

	$445	$375	$325	$295	$275	$250	$230	$499

STR 970 LONG RANGE – .308 Win. or .300 Win. Mag. cal., inlcudes stippled black McMillan composite stock with precision bedding blocks, 24 in. fluted heavy barrel with integral muzzle brake and non-reflective Ilaflon metal coating, cased, 11.6 lbs. Mfg. 2000-2002.

	$875	$795	$675	$575	$525	$475	$425	$899

RIFLES: SEMI-AUTO

MODEL 1908 MONDRAGON – 7.5mm cal. and others, serial number is stamped externally in four locations, unique operating mechanism, first semi-auto military contract rifle, approx. 500 rifles Mexican contract.

	$30,000	$25,000	$20,000	$16,000	$13,000	$10,000	$7,000	

PE-57 – 7.5 Swiss cal. only, semi-auto version of the Swiss military rifle, 24 in. barrel, includes 24 shot mag., leather sling, bipod and maintenance kit. Importation disc. 1988.

	$8,000	$7,000	$6,000	$5,000	$4,000	$3,000	$2,500	$1,745

The PE-57 was previously distributed in limited quantities by Osborne's located in Cheboygan, MI.

SIG-AMT RIFLE – .308 Win. cal., semi-auto version of SG510-4 auto rifle, roller delayed blowback action, 5, 10, or 20 shot mag., 18 3/4 in. barrel, wood stock, folding bipod. Mfg. 1960-1988.

	$5,500	$4,500	$3,750	$3,250	$2,750	$2,250	$1,750	$1,795

SG 550/551 – .223 Rem. cal. with heavier bullet, Swiss Army's semi-auto version of a tactical design rifle (SIG 90), 20.8 (SG 550) or 16 in. (SG 551 Carbine) barrel, some synthetics used to save weight, 20 shot mag., diopter night sights, built-in folding bipod, 7.7 or 9 lbs.

	100%	98%	95%	90%	80%	70%	60%	Last MSR
SG 550 (Rifle)	$8,500	$7,750	$7,000	$6,250	$5,500	$4,950	$4,500	
SG 551 (Carbine)	$9,500	$9,000	$8,500	$8,000	$7,250	$6,500	$5,600	$1,950

This model had very limited domestic importation before 1989 Federal legislation banned its configuration.

SIG 556 – Please refer to the Sig Sauer section.

MSR	100%	98%	95%	90%	80%	70%	60%	Last MSR

SIG SAUER

Current firearms trademark manufactured by SIG Arms AG (Schweizerische Industrie-Gesellschaft) located in Neuhausen, Switzerland. Most models are currently manufactured in the U.S., and some models continue to be imported from Switzerland. Sig Sauer, Inc. was established in 2007, and is located in Exeter, NH. Previously imported and distributed from 1985-2006 by Sigarms, Inc. located in Exeter, NH. Previously located in Herndon, VA and Tysons Corner, VA.

In late 2000, SIG Arms AG, the firearms portion of SIG, was purchased by two Germans named Michael Lüke and Thomas Ortmeier (L&O Group), who have a background in textiles. Headquarters for L&O are in Emsdetten, Switzerland. Today the Lüke & Ortmeier group includes independently operational companies such as Blaser Jagdwaffen GmbH, Mauser Jagdwaffen GmbH, John Rigby, J.P. Sauer & Sohn GmbH, SIG-Sauer Inc., SIG-Sauer GmbH and SAN Swiss Arms AG. Please refer to individual listings.

On Oct. 1, 2007, SIG Arms changed its corporate name to Sig Sauer.

PISTOLS: SEMI-AUTO

Beginning 2001, SIG started manufacturing variations which are compliant by state. They include CA (10 shot mag. max only), MA (requires a loaded chamber indicator), and NY (must include empty shell casing) are priced slightly higher than the standard models available for the rest of the states.

The Sigarms Custom Shop, located in Exeter, NH, has recently been established, and offers a wide variety of custom shop services, including action enhancement, full servicing, DA/SA conversions, trigger and hammer modifications, barrel replacement, and many refinishing options. Please contact Sigarms Custom Shop directly for more information and current pricing on these services.

During 2005, the Sigarms Custom Shop produced 12 limited editions, including the P229 Rail (January), P245 w/nickel accents and Meprolight night sights (February), P220 .45 ACP Rail (March), P239 Satin Nickel w/Hogue rubber grips (April), GSR 1911 Reverse Two-Tone (May), P229 Satin Nickel Reverse Two-Tone (June), P232 Rainbow Titanium (July), P226 Rail (August), P220 Sport Stock (September), P239 w/extra .357 SIG cal. barrel (October), P228 Two-Tone (November), and the P226 package w/Oakley glasses (December).

Early SIG Sauer pistols can be marked either with the Herndon or Tysons Corner, VA barrel address, and can also be marked "W. Germany" or "Germany". Earlier mfg. had three proofmarks on the bottom front of the slide, with a fourth on the frame in front of the serial number. Early guns with these barrel markings will command a slight premium over prices listed below, if condition is 98%+. Current mfg. has Exeter, NH barrel address.

Add $379 for caliber X-Change kit on current models.

MODEL MCX 9 IN. – 5.56 NATO (mfg. 2015 only), 7.62x39mm (mfg. 2015 only), or .300 ACC Blackout cal., GPO, 9 in. barrel, 30 shot mag., aluminum handguard, folding sights, Black or FDE (new 2016) finish, includes SBX stabilizing devise and polymer hard case, with or without 5.56 NATO conversion kit. New 2015.

MSR $1,972	$1,675	$1,500	$1,325	$1,175	$975	$750	$625

Add $475 for 5.56 NATO conversion kit.

MODEL MCX 11 1/2 IN. – 5.56 NATO cal., 11 1/2 in. barrel, 30 shot aluminum mag., folding sights, aluminum KeyMod handguard, pistol stabilizing brace, Black or FDE finish. New 2016.

MSR $1,972	$1,675	$1,500	$1,325	$1,175	$975	$750	$625

MODEL MPX-P – 9mm Para. cal., AR-15 style pistol, GPO, 8 in. barrel, aluminum handguard, reflex sights, 30 shot mag., with or without pistol stablizing brace. Mfg. 2014-2015.

	$1,380	$1,100	$900	$700	$600	$550	$495	*$1,576*

Add $309 for pistol stabilizing brace (PSB).

MODEL MPX-P-9-KM – 9mm Para. cal., 8 in. barrel, 30 shot mag., folding sights, no stock, aluminum KeyMod handguard, handstop, black finish. New 2016.

MSR $1,500	$1,325	$1,175	$1,000	$900	$775	$650	$525

MODEL MPX-P-9-KM-PSB – 9mm Para. cal., 8 in. barrel, 30 shot mag., folding sights, aluminum KeyMod handguard, pistol stabilizing brace, black finish. New 2016.

MSR $1,794	$1,525	$1,350	$1,175	$1,050	$875	$725	$575

MOSQUITO – .22 LR cal., compact design similar to P226, 3.98 in. barrel, polymer frame, 10 shot mag., DA/SA, decocker, ambidextrous manual safety, Picatinny rail on bottom of frame, internal locking device, adj. rear sight, molded composite grips, black, nickel (mfg. 2007-2008), blue (disc. 2012), two-tone, Desert Digital camo (mfg. 2009-2012), pink (new 2009), reverse two-tone (new 2007), carbon fiber (mfg. 2012 only), Flat Dark Earth (FDE) frame (new 2012), multi-cam (mfg. 2012 only), OD frame (new 2012), or deep purple (new 2012) frame finish, 24.6 oz. Mfg. 2005-2014.

	$350	$300	$260	$230	$210	$190	$170	*$408*

Add $18 for hot pink frame, flat dark earth frame (new 2012), OD frame finish, or deep purple frame finish.
Add $34 for threaded barrel.
Add $15 for nickel (disc. 2008) finish. Add $79 for carbon fiber or multi-cam (mfg. 2012 only).
Add $112 for Desert Digital camo frame with threaded barrel, disc. 2012.
Add $142 for camo finish, threaded barrel, and tactical trainer package (disc. 2009).
Add $75 for long slide with barrel weight (black finish only, new 2007, Sporter model). Disc. 2012.

MSR	100%	98%	95%	90%	80%	70%	60%	Last MSR

MODEL P 210 LEGEND – 9mm Para. cal., SAO, 4 3/4 in. barrel with fixed 2-dot or adj. target sights, black Nitron finish, side release 8 shot mag., checkered wood grips, improved and extended beavertail, grooved grip straps, nickel plated safety, hammer, trigger, and slide release. Imported 2011-2014.

| | $2,175 | $1,925 | $1,700 | $1,475 | $1,250 | $1,050 | $875 | $2,428 |

Add $214 for adj. target sights.

For pre-2011 manufacture, please refer to listings in the Sig Arms AG section.

MODEL P 210 SUPER TARGET – 9mm Para. cal., SAO, 6 in. barrel, Nitron stainless steel slide and frame, 8 shot, redesigned 1911-style safety lever and extended slide catch lever, adj. target sights, enhanced controls, beavertail, stippled ergonomic wood grips with integral magwell, Black Nitron finish. Mfg. 2014 only.

| | $3,500 | $3,150 | $2,750 | $2,500 | $2,250 | $2,000 | $1,750 | $3,993 |

MODEL P220 – .22 LR (disc.), .38 Super (disc.), 7.65mm (disc.), 9mm Para. (disc 1991), or .45 ACP cal., 4.4 in. barrel, 7 (.45 ACP, disc.) or 8 shot mag., full size, DA/SA, SAO, or DAO (.45 ACP cal. only), decocking lever, choice of matte blue (disc. 2006), black nitron (new 2007), stainless steel (mfg. 2001-2007), K-Kote (disc. 1999), electroless nickel (disc. 1991), two-tone with nickel finished slide (disc. 2011), or Ilaflon (mfg. 2000 only) finish, lightweight alloy frame, black plastic grips, optional DAK trigger system (DAO with 6 1/2 lb. trigger pull) available during 2005 only, tactical rail became standard 2004 at no extra charge (blue or stainless only), contrast (disc. 2015) or Siglite night sights became standard 2016, approx. 30.4 or 41.8 (stainless steel) oz. New 1976.

| MSR $1,087 | | $950 | $735 | $625 | $525 | $450 | $400 | $350 |

Add $349 for .22 LR conversion kit (current mfg.) or $680 for older mfg. .22 LR conversion kit.

Subtract $114 for contrast sights (disc. 2015).

Add $149 for black stainless with Hogue rubber grips and Siglite night sights (mfg. 2012-2013).

Add $40 for DAK trigger system (limited mfg. 2005).

Add $103 for two-tone (nickel slide) finish (disc. 2011).

Add $100 for P220 SAO Model (single action only, disc. 2009).

Add $306 for Crimson Trace laser grips w/night sights (disc. 2009).

Add $95 for stainless steel frame & slide (mfg. 2001-2007).

Add $40 for Ilaflon finish (disc. 2000).

Add $45 for factory K-Kote finish (disc. 1999).

Add $70 for electroless nickel finish (disc. 1991).

Subtract 10% for "European" Model (bottom mag. release - includes 9mm Para. and .38 Super cals.).

Values are for .45 ACP cal. and assume American side mag. release (standard 1986).

This model was also available as a Custom Shop Limited Edition during July, 2004 (MSR was $800 and November, 2004 (MSR was $861).

* **Model P220 Combat** – .45 ACP cal., 4.4 in. non-threaded barrel, Flat Dark Earth finish, alloy frame, Nitron stainless slide, corrosion resistant parts, 8 shot mag., M1913 Picatinny rail, Siglite night sights, 30.4 oz. Mfg. 2007-2012, reintroduced 2014-2015.

| | $1,125 | $950 | $825 | $725 | $625 | $525 | $425 | $1,290 |

» **Model P220 Combat Threaded** – .45 ACP cal., DA/SA, 4.4 in. threaded barrel, Flat Dark Earth anodized alloy frame, Nitron stainless slide, corrosion resistant parts, 8 or 10 shot steel mag., M1913 Picatinny rail, Siglite night sights, polymer grip, 30.4 oz. Mfg. 2007-2012, reintroduced 2014.

| MSR $1,282 | | $1,075 | $915 | $800 | $725 | $625 | $525 | $425 |

* **Model P220 Elite/Dark Elite** – .45 ACP cal., similar to P220, except has short reset trigger, DA/SA or SAO, two-tone (limited mfg.), or black Nitron finish, 8 shot mag., ergonomic beavertail, Picatinny rail, front cocking serrations, custom shop wood or black aluminum (Dark Elite) grips. Mfg. 2007-2014.

| | $1,095 | $950 | $850 | $725 | $625 | $525 | $425 | $1,253 |

Add $61 for Elite Dark with threaded barrel (disc. 2012).

* **Model P220 Elite Stainless** – .45 ACP cal., DA/SA, 4.4. in. barrel, stainless steel frame and slide, 8 shot, Picatinny rail, short reset trigger, ergonomic beavertail grip, Siglite night sights, custom rosewood grips or checkered aluminum (Platinum Elite, disc. 2011) grips, 39.1 oz. New 2007.

| MSR $1,359 | | $1,215 | $1,015 | $900 | $800 | $700 | $600 | $500 |

Add $72 for platinum Elite with aluminum grips (stainless only), disc. 2011.

* **Model P220 Equinox** – .45 ACP cal., DA/SA, 4.4 in. barrel, lightweight hard anodized alloy frame, two-tone accented slide with Nitron finish, 8 shot, Picatinny rail, TruGlo TFO front sight, Siglite rear sight, black or gray laminated wood grips w/custom shop logo, 30.4 oz. Mfg. 2007-2015.

| | $1,125 | $950 | $850 | $725 | $625 | $525 | $425 | $1,290 |

* **Model P220 Extreme** – .45 ACP cal., DA/SA, 4 in. barrel, 8 shot mag., forward slide serrations, SRT trigger system, Siglite night sights, Hogue black and gray G-10 Extreme grips, black Nitron finish, approx. 30 oz. Mfg. 2012-2015.

| | $1,095 | $935 | $825 | $700 | $600 | $500 | $400 | $1,256 |

MSR		100%	98%	95%	90%	80%	70%	60%	Last MSR

* Model P220 Match – .45 ACP cal., similar to P220, except has 5 in. cold hammer forged barrel, DA/SA or SAO, ambidextrous safety, two-tone or stainless (Match Elite) finish, adj. sights, black polymer or custom shop wood (Super Match) grips, Elite Match became standard during 2010. Mfg. 2007-2012.

		$1,175	$975	$850	$725	$625	$550	$450	$1,368

Add $7 for Super Match model.

Subtract approx. $200 for Match (disc. 2009, last MSR was $1,170).

* Model P220 Match Elite (Recent Mfg.) – .45 ACP cal., DA/SA, full size frame, 5 in. barrel, 8 shot mag., beavertail frame, front strap checkering, SRT, Siglite night sights, adj. target sights, Picatinny rail, black anodize aluminum grips, stainless finish, 39.1 oz. Disc. 2015.

		$1,450	$1,275	$1,100	$985	$800	$650	$525	$1,713

* Model P220 Super Match (Current Mfg.) – .45 ACP cal., SAO, 5 in. barrel, 8 shot mag., lightweight alloy beavertail frame with hardcoat anodized finish, front strap checkering, front cocking serrations, adj. target sights, Picatinny rail, rosewood grips, Sig Sauer Custom Shop logo engraved on slide, natural stainless slide finish, 33.6 oz. Limited production Custom Shop model.

MSR $1,467		$1,275	$1,150	$1,000	$900	$750	$600	$475	

* Model P220 NRALE – .45 ACP cal., features NRA Law Enforcement logo and the words "NRA Law Enforcement" engraved in 24Kt. gold, Cocobolo grips with NRA medallions, gold trigger and appointments. Limited production of 1,000, including P226 NRALE 2002-2003.

		$850	$650	$495	N/A	N/A	N/A	N/A	$911

* Model P220 Scorpion Elite – .45 ACP cal., 4.4 in. threaded or non-threaded barrel, 8 shot mag., front cocking serrations, short reset trigger, Flat Dark Earth (FDE) metal finish, beavertail, Siglite night sights and Hogue G-10 Parana grips, 30.4 oz. Mfg. 2012-2015.

		$1,195	$1,025	$875	$750	$650	$550	$450	$1,348

Add $57 for threaded barrel.

* Model P220 Sport – .45 ACP cal., features 4.8 in. heavy compensated barrel, stainless steel frame and slide, 10 shot mag., target sights, improved trigger pull, single or double action, 46.1 oz. Imported 1999-2000, reintroduced 2003-2005.

		$1,375	$975	$800	$695	$585	$485	$415	$1,600

* Model P220 Stainless Nitron – .45 ACP cal., DA/SA, 4.4 in. barrel, 8 shot mag., Siglite night sights, Hogue rubber grips, all stainless Nitron finish, 39.1 oz. Disc. 2015.

		$975	$800	$665	$535	$465	$415	$365	$1,199

* Model P220 Stainless Reverse Two-Tone – .45 ACP cal., DA/SA, 4.4 in. barrel, 8 shot mag., Siglite night sights, Hogue rubber grips, all stainless reverse two-tone finish, Nitron coated slide, 39.1 oz. Disc. 2015.

		$975	$800	$665	$535	$465	$415	$365	$1,199

* Model P220R – .22 LR cal., 4.4 in. barrel, 10 shot mag., DA/SA, matte black anodized finish, adj. sights, otherwise similar to standard P220. Mfg. 2009-2012.

		$565	$500	$450	$395	$350	$300	$275	$642

* Model P220 TacPac – .45 ACP cal., features black Nitron finish, Siglite sights, one-piece enhanced E2 grip, STL 900L, includes holster. Mfg. 2013-2014.

		$1,075	$925	$825	$725	$625	$525	$425	$1,238

MODEL P220 .22 LR – .22 LR cal., full size, 4.4 in. barrel, DA/SA trigger, black anodized alloy slide, 10 shot mag., adj. sights, black anodized finish. Mfg. 2014-2015.

		$585	$495	$450	$400	$365	$335	$295	$685

MODEL P220 CARRY – .45 ACP cal., compact model w/full size frame, 3.9 in. barrel, 8 shot single stack mag., DA/SA, DAK, or SAO, black Nitron finish, Picatinny rail, black polymer factory grips, contrast (disc. 2015) or Siglite night sights. New 2007.

MSR $1,087		$885	$750	$635	$525	$450	$400	$350	

Subtract $114 for contrast sights (disc. 2015).

Add $100 for SAO trigger (disc. 2008).

* Model P220 Carry Elite – .45 ACP cal., DA/SA, 3.9 in. barrel, front cocking serrations, ergonomic beavertail grip, Picatinny rail, stainless or black Nitron (mfg. 2009-2012) finish, Siglite adj. combat night sights, wood (disc.) or Hogue aluminum grips, 30.4 oz. Mfg. 2007-2014.

		$1,250	$1,025	$895	$750	$650	$550	$450	$1,396

Subtract $140 for black nitron finish (disc. 2012).

MSR	100%	98%	95%	90%	80%	70%	60%	Last MSR

* **Model P220 Carry Stainless Elite** – .45 ACP cal., DA/SA, 3.9 in. barrel, 8 shot mag., front cocking serrations, SRT, Siglite night sights, natural stainless steel slide, Elite stainless steel beavertail frame, Hogue rubber (mfg. 2012-2013) or custom rosewood grips (new 2013), 39.1 oz. New 2012.

| MSR $1,359 | $1,215 | $1,000 | $900 | $800 | $700 | $600 | $500 | |

* **Model P220 Carry Equinox** – .45 ACP cal., DA/SA, 3.9 in. barrel, accessory rail, two-tone accented Nitron stainless steel slide with lightweight black hard-anodized frame, TruGlo TFO front sight, Siglite rear sight, black or grey laminated wood grips w/custom shop logo, 30.4 oz. Mfg. 2007-2015.

| | $1,095 | $935 | $825 | $700 | $600 | $500 | $400 | $1,256 |

* **Model P220 Carry SAS** – .45 ACP cal., DA/SA or SAO (disc. 2014), 3.9 in. barrel, SRT, Nitron or two-tone finish with black frame and stainless steel slide, Dehorning, SIG Anti-Snag treatment on slide/frame, custom shop brown wood grips (disc.) or one-piece black polymer grips, contrast (disc. 2013) or Siglite night sights (became standard 2014), Gen. 2 features became standard 2008, 30.4 oz. New 2010.

| MSR $1,119 | $915 | $775 | $650 | $525 | $465 | $415 | $365 | |

MODEL P220 COMPACT – .45 ACP cal., DA/SA or SAO (disc.), 3.9 in. barrel, compact beavertail frame, 6 shot mag., black Nitron or two-tone (disc. 2010) finish, contrast (disc.) or Siglite night sights, lower Picatinny rail, black polymer grips. Mfg. 2007-2013, reintroduced 2015 only.

| | $925 | $775 | $650 | $525 | $450 | $400 | $350 | $1,142 |

Add $75 for two-tone finish (disc. 2010).

* **Model P220 Compact SAS** – .45 ACP cal., DA/SA or SAO (disc.), 3.9 in. barrel, 6 shot mag., SRT, contrast (disc.) or Siglite night sights (became standard 2014), dehorned, black polymer or custom shop wood (disc.) grips, Gen. 2 features became standard 2012, Nitron stainless steel slide, SIG Anti-Snag treatment on slide/frame, 29.6 oz. Mfg. 2007-2015.

| | $975 | $800 | $665 | $535 | $465 | $415 | $365 | $1,199 |

MODEL P224 – 9mm Para., 357 SIG, or .40 S&W cal., 3 1/2 in. barrel, DA/SA or DAK trigger, alloy frame with stainless steel slide, 10 or 12 (9mm Para. only) shot mag., satin nickel slide and controls (P224 Nickel), Siglite night sights, wood (disc.) or one-piece enhanced E2 (new 2013) grips, 25.4 oz. Mfg. 2012-2015.

| | $925 | $775 | $650 | $525 | $450 | $400 | $350 | $1,142 |

Add $57 for satin nickel slide and controls (Model P224 Nickel).

* **Model P224 SAS Gen. 2** – 9mm Para., .40 S&W, or .357 Sig cal., DA/SA or DAK (9mm only), similar to P224, except has Sig Anti-Snag (SAS) treatment on slide and frame, black Nitron finish, dehorned metal parts, SRT, Siglite night sights, and one-piece enhanced E2 grip, 29 oz. Mfg. 2012-2015.

| | $950 | $795 | $665 | $535 | $465 | $415 | $365 | $1,176 |

* **Model P224 Extreme** – 9mm Para. or .40 S&W cal., DA/SA, 3 1/2 in. barrel, 10 or 12 shot mag., short reset trigger, Siglite night sights, Hogue Black and Grey Extreme G-10 grips, black Nitron finish, Nitron stainless steel slide, 29 oz. Mfg. 2012-2015.

| | $975 | $800 | $665 | $535 | $465 | $415 | $365 | $1,199 |

* **Model P224 Equinox** – .40 S&W cal. only, DA/SA, 3 1/2 in. barrel, 10 shot mag., two-tone polished Nitron slide finish, black hard anodized frame finish, TruGlo TFO front sight with Siglite rear night sight, Hogue black G-10 grips, 29 oz. Mfg. 2012-2015.

| | $1,095 | $935 | $825 | $700 | $600 | $500 | $400 | $1,256 |

MODEL P225 – 9mm Para. cal., DA/SA or DAO, similar to P220, shorter dimensions, 3.85 in. barrel, 8 shot single stack mag., thumb actuated mag. release, fully adj. sights, 28.8 oz. Disc. 1998.

| | $595 | $525 | $450 | $425 | $395 | $350 | $310 | $725 |

Add $45 for factory K-Kote finish.
Add $105 for Siglite night sights.
Add $45 for nickel finished slide (new 1992).
Add $70 for electroless nickel finish (disc. 1991).

This model was also available as a Custom Shop Limited Edition during March, 2004. MSR was $803.

MODEL P225 CLASSIC – 9mm Para. cal., DA/SA, 3.6 in. barrel, 8 shot steel mag., short reset trigger, Siglite night sights, black G10 grips, black finish. New 2016.

| MSR $1,175 | $950 | $785 | $650 | $535 | $465 | $415 | $365 | |

MODEL P225 HUNTER – 9mm Para. cal., SAO, 5 in. barrel, 8 shot steel mag., adj. sights, black G10 grips, camo frame finish. New 2016.

| MSR $1,467 | $1,275 | $1,150 | $1,000 | $900 | $750 | $600 | $475 | |

MODEL P226 – .357 SIG (new 1995), 9mm Para. (disc. 1997, reintroduced 1999), or .40 S&W (new 1998) cal., full size, choice of DA/SA or DAO (new 1992) operation, 10 (C/B 1994), 12 (new mid-2005, .357 SIG or .40 S&W cal.)

MSR	100%	98%	95%	90%	80%	70%	60%	Last MSR

or 15* (9mm Para. cal. only) shot mag., 4.4 in. barrel, alloy frame, currently available in blackened stainless steel (Nitron finish became standard 2000), two-tone (disc. 2011), reverse two-tone (.40 S&W cal. only - mfg. 2012 only), or nickel (disc. 2002) finish (stainless slide only), tactical rail became standard 2004, choice of traditional DA or DAK (disc.) trigger system (DAO with 6 1/2 lb. trigger pull, not available in all stainless) available beginning 2005, E2 grips became standard 2011, high contrast sights (9mm & .40 S&W, disc. 2015) or Siglite night sights became standard 2016, automatic firing pin block safety, 31.7 or 34 oz. New 1983.

| MSR $1,087 | $925 | $765 | $650 | $535 | $450 | $400 | $350 | |

Subtract $114 if with contrast sights (disc. 2015).
Add $339 for .22 LR cal. conversion kit.
Add $149 for reverse two-tone finish - all stainless with Siglite night sights and Hogue rubber grips (mfg. 2012 only).
Add $306 for Crimson Trace laser grips w/Siglite night sights (mfg. 2007).
Add $95 for stainless steel frame and slide (mfg. 2004-2005).
Add $103 for two-tone finish (nickel finished stainless steel slide) w/night sights, (disc. 2011).
Add $45 for K-Kote (Polymer) finish (mfg. 1992-97, 9mm Para. only).
Add $70 for electroless nickel finish (disc. 1991).

This model is also available in double action only (all finishes) at no extra charge.

This model was also available as a Custom Shop Limited Edition during Feb., 2004 (MSR was $1,085). A limited edition P226 America with blue titanium and gold finishes was also available from SIG's Custom Shop (MSR was $7,995).

This model is also available as the P226R Tactical, sold exclusively by Ellett Bros. distributors - no pricing information is available.

* ***Model P226 Combat*** – 9mm Para. cal., DA/SA, 4.4 in. threaded or non-threaded barrel, 10 or 15 shot mag., Siglite night sights, Flat Dark Earth frame and grips, black Nitron slide, Picatinny rail, 34 oz. Mfg. 2008-2012, reintroduced 2015 only.

| | $1,095 | $935 | $825 | $700 | $600 | $500 | $400 | *$1,256* |

»***Model P226 Combat Threaded Barrel*** – 9mm Para. cal., DA/SA, 4.4 in. threaded barrel, 10 or 15 shot mag., Siglite night sights, Flat Dark Earth frame and grips, black Nitron slide, Picatinny rail, 34 oz. Mfg. 2008-2012, reintroduced 2015.

| MSR $1,282 | $1,075 | $915 | $800 | $725 | $625 | $525 | $425 | |

* ***Model P226 Elite*** – 9mm Para., .357 SIG, or .40 S&W, or .45 ACP cal., DA/SA (disc.), 4.4 in. barrel, Beavertail Elite frame, 15 shot mag., forward cocking serrations, Siglite night sights, two-tone (disc.), or black Nitron finish, black polymer grips, 34.4 oz. Mfg. 2007-2015.

| | $1,095 | $935 | $825 | $700 | $600 | $500 | $400 | *$1,256* |

Add $72 for platinum Elite with aluminum grips (disc. 2011).
Add $71 for TB Model with threaded barrel (9mm Para. only), disc. 2012.

* ***Model P226 Dark Elite*** – 9mm Para., .357 SIG, or .40 S&W (new 2011), DA/SA, similar to P226, except has Black Nitron finish, 12 or 15 shot mag., aluminum checkered grips. Mfg. 2007-2014.

| | $1,050 | $925 | $825 | $725 | $625 | $525 | $425 | *$1,243* |

* ***Model P226 Elite Stainless*** – 9mm Para., .357 SIG (disc. 2012), .40 S&W (new 2011), or .45 ACP (disc. 2011) cal., DA/SA, 4.4 in. barrel, 10, 12, or 15 shot mag., SRT, ergonomic beavertail grip, front cocking serrations, front strap checkering, lower Picatinny rail, stainless steel, custom shop wood grips (disc.) or checkered Rosewood grips, Siglite night sights, 42.2 oz. New 2007.

| MSR $1,359 | $1,215 | $1,000 | $900 | $800 | $700 | $600 | $500 | |

* ***Model P226 Enhanced Elite*** – 9mm Para., .357 SIG (disc. 2015), or .40 S&W (disc. 2015) cal., DA/SA, 4.4 in. barrel, 12 (.357 Sig) or 15 shot mag., includes lower Picatinny rail in front of trigger guard, SRT, beavertail, Siglite night sights, E2 polymer grips, black Nitron finish, 34.4 oz. Mfg. 2011-2012, reintroduced 2015.

| MSR $1,174 | $950 | $785 | $650 | $535 | $465 | $415 | $365 | |

Add $34 for .40 S&W or $35 for 9mm Para. cal. (disc. 2015).

* ***Model P226 Engraved*** – 9mm Para. cal., DA/SA, full size frame, 4.4 in. barrel, 15 shot mag., polished Nitron stainless steel slide with custom engraving, black hardcoat anodized (mfg. 2015 only) or stainless steel frame and slide, Siglite night sights, custom wood grips with SIG medallion, 34 oz. New 2015.

| MSR $1,631 | $1,350 | $1,075 | $895 | $750 | $625 | $525 | $425 | |

Subtract $365 for black hardcoat anodized frame and slide (mfg. 2015 only).

* ***Model P226 Equinox*** – 9mm Para. (new 2015) or .40 S&W cal., DA/SA, 4.4 in. barrel, two-tone Nitron stainless steel slide, lightweight black anodized alloy frame, nickel accents, 12 shot mag., TruGlo TFO front sight, rear Siglite night sight, Picatinny rail, grey laminated wood grips, 34 oz., mfg. by the Custom Shop. Mfg. 2006-2012, reintroduced 2015 only.

| | $1,095 | $935 | $825 | $700 | $600 | $500 | $400 | *$1,256* |

MSR	100%	98%	95%	90%	80%	70%	60%	Last MSR

* **Model P226 Extreme** – 9mm Para. or .40 S&W cal., DA/SA, 4.4 in. barrel, 12 or 15 shot mag., SRT, front cocking serrations, Siglite night sights, lower Picatinny rail, Hogue Black and Grey Extreme Series G10 grips, black Nitron finish, 34 oz. Mfg. 2011-2015.

| | $1,095 | $935 | $825 | $700 | $600 | $500 | $400 | $1,256 |

* **Model P226 E2** – 9mm Para. cal., 15 shot mag., black Nitron finish, ergonomic slim profile one piece grips, Siglite night sights, short reset trigger, integral accessory rail, includes three mags. New 2010 only.

| | $1,000 | $895 | $775 | $675 | $575 | $525 | $450 | $1,149 |

* **Model P226 Jubilee** – 9mm Para. cal., limited edition commemorating SIG's 125th anniversary, features gold-plated small parts, carved select walnut grips, special slide markings, cased. Mfg. 1985 only.

| | $1,495 | $1,175 | $950 | $835 | $685 | $585 | $485 | $2,000 |

* **Model P226 MK25 Navy Version** – 9mm Para. cal., DA/SA, 4.4 in. barrel, three 15 shot mags., black Nitron or Flat Dark Earth (FDE, new 2014) finish with phosphated small components, features anchor engraving, Picatinny rail, UID label on right side of slide, Siglite night sights, black polymer grips, 34.4 oz. New 2012.

| MSR $1,141 | $935 | $775 | $650 | $535 | $465 | $415 | $365 | |

Add $54 for Flat Dark Earth finish (new 2014), or $54 for threaded barrel.

* **Model P226 NRALE** – .40 S&W cal., features NRA Law Enforcement logo and the words "NRA Law Enforcement" engraved in 24Kt. gold, Cocobolo grips with NRA medallions, gold trigger and appointments. Limited production of 1,000, including P220 NRALE, 2002-2003.

| | $850 | $650 | $495 | N/A | N/A | N/A | N/A | $911 |

* **Model P226R** – .22 LR cal., Nitron finish, adj. sights, DA/SA or SAO, 10 shot mag., with or w/o beavertail grips and stainless reverse two-tone. Mfg. 2009-2012.

| | $585 | $515 | $465 | $400 | $350 | $300 | $275 | $656 |

Add $33 for beavertail and stainless reverse two-tone.

* **Model P226 Scorpion Elite** – 9mm Para. cal. only, DA/SA, 4.4 in. threaded or non-threaded barrel, 10 or 15 shot mag., SRT, beavertail, Siglite night sights, Picatinny rail, Flat Dark Earth (FDE) finish, Hogue Extreme G-10 grips, 34 oz. Mfg. 2012 only, reintroduced 2015 only.

| | $1,125 | $950 | $825 | $725 | $625 | $525 | $425 | $1,348 |

Add $57 for threaded barrel.

* **Model P226 Special Editions** – 9mm Para. or .40 S&W (Cops Commemorative only, disc. 2008) cal., engraved, variations include Navy (black Nitron finish, phosphate components and anchor engraving), Cops Commemorative (Siglite night sights and wood grips, disc. 2008). Series disc. 2011.

| | $895 | $775 | $675 | $575 | $475 | $400 | $350 | $1,020 |

* **Model P226 Sport** – 9mm Para. cal., DA/SA or DAO, features 5.6 in. match or heavy compensated barrel, stainless steel frame and slide, 10 shot mag., target sights, improved trigger pull, rubber grips, 48.8 oz. Mfg. 2003-2005.

| | $1,375 | $975 | $800 | $695 | $585 | $485 | $415 | $1,600 |

* **Model P226 ST** – 9mm Para., .40 S&W, or .357 Mag. cal., 4.4 in. barrel, white stainless slide and frame, blue barrel, Picatinny rail, 10 shot mag., 38.8 oz.

While advertised during 2006, this model never went into production - prototypes only.

* **Model P226 Super Cap Tactical** – .40 S&W cal., similar to P226 Tactical, black Nitron finish, TruGlo front sight, Siglite rear sight, includes four 15 shot mags. Mfg. 2009-2010.

| | $1,025 | $925 | $825 | $725 | $625 | $525 | $425 | $1,156 |

* **Model P226 TACOPS** – 9mm Para., .357 SIG, or .40 S&W cal., DA/SA, 4.4 in. threaded (9mm only) or non-threaded barrel, 15 or 20 shot mag., Picatinny rail, SRT, TruGlo TFO front sight and Siglite rear night sight, Elite beavertail frame, front cocking serrations, polymer Magwell grips, black Nitron or Flat Dark Earth coated (FDE, mfg. 2015 only) finish, 34 oz. New 2011.

| MSR $1,282 | $1,075 | $925 | $825 | $725 | $625 | $525 | $425 | |

Add $22 for .357 Sig or 9mm Para. cal.
Add $77 for threaded barrel
Add $80 for FDE finish (mfg. 2015 only).

* **Model P226 TacPac** – 9mm Para. or .40 S&W cal., features black Nitron finish, Siglite sights, one-piece enhanced E2 grip, STL 900L, includes holster. Mfg. 2013-2014.

| | $1,075 | $950 | $825 | $725 | $625 | $525 | $425 | $1,238 |

* **Model P226 Tactical/Blackwater Tactical** – similar to P226, black Nitron finish, Picatinny rail, threaded barrel, post and dot contrast Siglite night sights, available in standard (disc. 2009) and Blackwater configuration (black Nitron finish, Siglite night sights, and wood grips). Mfg. 2007-2010.

| | $1,150 | $975 | $850 | $750 | $650 | $550 | $450 | $1,300 |

MSR	100%	98%	95%	90%	80%	70%	60%	Last MSR

Subtract approx. $50 for standard tactical - (disc. 2009, last MSR was $1,245).

* **Model P226 Tribal Nitron** – 9mm Para. cal., black hardcoat frame, polished tribal pattern Nitron slide, custom engraved tribal aluminum grips. Mfg. 2015 only.

| | $1,125 | $950 | $825 | $725 | $625 | $525 | $425 | $1,348 |

* **Model P226 Tribal Two-Tone** – 9mm Para. cal., black hardcoat frame, polished tribal pattern stainless steel slide, custom tribal engraved aluminum grips. Mfg. 2015 only.

| | $950 | $795 | $665 | $535 | $465 | $415 | $365 | $1,176 |

* **Model P226 USPSA** – 9mm Para. cal., short reset trigger, 4.4 in. barrel, 15 shot mag., Dawson fiber optic front sight, Warren rear sight, polymer grips, aluminum frame with stainless steel slide, black Nitron finish, USPSA engraving, includes three mags. Mfg. 2009-2010.

| | $1,095 | $950 | $825 | $725 | $625 | $525 | $400 | $1,246 |

MODEL P226 .22 LR – .22 LR cal., 4.4 in. barrel, DA/SA trigger, black anodized alloy slide, 10 shot mag., adj. sights, one-piece enhanced E2 grip, black anodized finish. Mfg. 2014 only.

| | $565 | $495 | $450 | $400 | $365 | $335 | $295 | $662 |

Add $23 for beavertail and short reset trigger (SRT).

MODEL P226 LEGION – 9mm Para., .40 S&W, or .357 Mag. cal., DA/SA, or SAO, 4.4 in. barrel, X-Ray3 day/night sights, 12 (.40 S&W or .357) or 15 shot mag., short reset trigger, black G10 grips, X-RAY, Gray finish. New 2016.

| MSR $1,359 | $1,275 | $1,050 | $925 | $800 | $700 | $600 | $500 | |

MODEL P226 X-FIVE – 9mm Para. or .40 S&W cal., SAO, adj. trigger, 5 in. stainless steel barrel and slide, ambidextrous thumb safety, all stainless construction with magwell, low profile adj. sights, 14 (.40 S&W) or 19 (9mm Para.) shot mag., available in blue, two-tone, stainless or black Nitron finish, checkered walnut grips, includes 25 meter test target, checkered front grip strap, 47.2 oz. Mfg. mid-2005-2012.

| | $2,400 | $2,050 | $1,700 | $1,400 | $1,225 | $1,000 | $850 | $2,747 |

* **Model P226 X-Five Competition** – 9mm Para. or .40 S&W cal., similar to X-Five, except has black polymer grips. Mfg. 2007-2012.

| | $1,725 | $1,475 | $1,250 | $1,050 | $875 | $700 | $650 | $1,976 |

* **Model P226 X-Five All Around** – 9mm Para. or .40 S&W cal., adj. sights, ergonomic beavertail grip, DA/SA, stainless slide and frame, black polymer grips. Mfg. 2007-2012.

| | $1,425 | $1,200 | $975 | $850 | $750 | $650 | $550 | $1,696 |

* **Model P226 X-Five Tactical** – 9mm Para. cal., SAO, black Nitron finish, contrast sights, lightweight alloy frame, Picatinny rail, ergonomic beavertail grips. Mfg. 2007-2012.

| | $1,425 | $1,200 | $975 | $850 | $750 | $650 | $550 | $1,696 |

MODEL P226 X SERIES – 9mm Para. or .40 S&W cal., individual models are marked on left side of slide between slide serrations. New series mfg. 2014 only.

* **Model P226 X All Around** – 9mm Para. or .40 S&W cal., DA/SA, natural stainless steel slide and frame extended for 5 in. barrel, adj. rear sight, front cocking serrations, integral Picatinny accessory rail, standard magazine and mag. catch, black laminated grips. Mfg. 2014 only.

| | $1,900 | $1,750 | $1,525 | $1,325 | $1,125 | $950 | $750 | $2,245 |

* **Model P226 X Classic** – 9mm Para. or .40 S&W cal., SAO, 5 in. barrel, natural stainless steel slide and frame, user adj. SAO trigger, fully adj. target sights, M1913 Picatinny accessory rail, custom walnut grips. Mfg. 2014 only.

| | $2,275 | $2,000 | $1,750 | $1,500 | $1,300 | $1,100 | $900 | $2,679 |

* **Model P226 X Entry** – 9mm Para. or .40 S&W cal., SAO, 5 in. barrel, natural stainless steel slide and frame, fixed rear sight, M1913 Picatinny accessory rail, standard magazine catch, black polymer grips. Mfg. 2014 only.

| | $1,495 | $1,300 | $1,125 | $995 | $850 | $700 | $575 | $1,763 |

* **Model P226 X Match** – 9mm Para. or .40 S&W cal., SAO, natural stainless steel slide and frame extended for a 5 in. barrel, front cocking serrations, skeletonized hammer, fully adj. target sights, M1913 Picatinny accessory rail, extended magazine catch, black laminate grips. Mfg. 2014 only.

| | $1,450 | $1,250 | $1,075 | $950 | $800 | $650 | $550 | $1,728 |

Add $1,192 for .40 S&W cal.
Add $1,078 for shorter barrel (XFive Match Short model).

* **Model P226 X Open** – 9mm Para. cal., SAO, natural stainless steel slide and frame, 5 in. barrel with compensator, user adj. SAO straight match trigger, Sport takedown lever, M1913 Picatinny accessory rail, black G10 grips, bridge mount, ambidextrous slide racker, extended magazine catch. Mfg. 2014 only.

| | $4,200 | $3,800 | $3,350 | $2,800 | $2,300 | $1,900 | $1,625 | $4,852 |

MSR		100%	98%	95%	90%	80%	70%	60%	Last MSR

* ***Model P226 X Super Match*** – 9mm Para. or .40 S&W cal., 5 or 6 (XSix Super Match) in. barrel, sport takedown lever, natural stainless steel slide and frame, fully adj. target sights, M1913 Picatinny accessory rail, extended magazine catch, black G10 grips, straight trigger. Mfg. 2014 only.

| | | $2,600 | $2,300 | $2,000 | $1,750 | $1,500 | $1,250 | $1,000 | *$3,042* |

Add $241 for 6 in. barrel (XSix Super Match model).

* ***Model P226 X Tactical*** – 9mm Para. or .40 S&W cal., SAO, Nitron slide, black alloy frame, black polymer grips. Mfg. 2014 only.

| | | $1,450 | $1,250 | $1,050 | $875 | $750 | $625 | $550 | *$1,678* |

MODEL P227 – .45 ACP cal., DA/SA, 4.4 in. stainless steel barrel, 10 shot mag., contrast sights (disc. 2015) or Siglite night sights, lower Picatinny rail, one-piece enhanced E2 grip, black Nitron or Flat Dark Earth (new 2015) finish, 32 oz. New 2013.

| MSR $1,087 | | $925 | $750 | $635 | $525 | $450 | $400 | $350 | |

Add $54 for Flat Dark Earth slide and frame finish (new 2015) with Siglite night sights.
Subtract $114 for contrast sights (disc. 2015).

* ***Model P227 Carry*** – .45 ACP cal., DA/SA, 3.9 in. stainless steel barrel, 10 shot mag., Siglite night sights, lower Picatinny rail, one-piece polymer grips, black Nitron finish, 30 1/2 oz. New 2013.

| MSR $1,087 | | $885 | $750 | $650 | $525 | $450 | $400 | $350 | |

* ***Model P227 Carry SAS*** – .45 ACP cal., Gen. 2, 3.9 in. stainless steel barrel, black Nitron finish, dehorning, SRT, contrast (disc.) or Siglite night sights, Sig anti-snag treatment on slide and frame with no rail, one piece ergonomic grips, 30 1/2 oz. New 2013.

| MSR $1,119 | | $915 | $765 | $650 | $535 | $465 | $415 | $365 | |

* ***Model P227 Enhanced Elite*** – .45 ACP cal., DA/SA, 4.4 in. barrel, 10 shot mag., beavertail, SRT, Siglite night sights, one-piece enhanced E2 grip, black Nitron finish. New 2015.

| MSR $1,174 | | $950 | $795 | $650 | $545 | $475 | $420 | $365 | |

* ***Model P227 Equinox*** – .45 ACP cal., DA/SA, 10 shot mag., two-tone polished Nitron finish, TruGlo TFO front sight, Siglite night sights, wood grips. New 2014.

| MSR $1,228 | | $1,050 | $915 | $815 | $725 | $625 | $525 | $425 | |

* ***Model P227R*** – .45 ACP cal., DA/SA, threaded barrel, 45 Nitron, Siglite sights, SRT, 10 or 14 shot mag., black Nitron finish. New 2014.

| MSR $1,290 | | $1,050 | $915 | $800 | $725 | $625 | $525 | $425 | |

* ***Model P227 TACOPS*** – .45 ACP cal., DA/SA, 4.4 in. barrel, four 14 shot mags., beavertail, SRT, TFO/Siglite night sight combo, G-10 Magwell grips, black Nitron finish, 35 oz. New 2015.

| MSR $1,359 | | $1,225 | $1,015 | $900 | $800 | $700 | $600 | $500 | |

* ***Model P227R TacPac*** – .45 ACP cal., DA/SA, 45 Nitron, Siglite sights, STL-900L, 10 shot mag., includes holster. Mfg. 2014 only.

| | | $1,050 | $950 | $825 | $725 | $625 | $525 | $425 | *$1,238* |

MODEL P228 (OLD MFG.) – 9mm Para., DA/SA or SAO (new 1992) operation, compact design, 3.86 in. (compact) barrel, 10 (C/B 1994) or 13* (reintroduced 2004) shot mag., automatic firing pin block safety, high contrast sights, alloy frame, choice of blue, Nitron (new 2004), nickel (mfg. 1991-97), or stainless steel (new 2004) slide, or K-Kote (disc. 1997) finish, 29.3 oz. Mfg. 1990-97, reintroduced 2004-2006.

| | | $700 | $600 | $500 | $450 | $400 | $350 | $310 | *$840* |

Add $50 for Siglite night sights.
Add $376 for .22 LR cal. conversion kit.
Add $45 for K-Kote (Polymer) finish (disc. 1997).
Add $45 for nickel finished slide (1991-97).
Add $70 for electroless nickel finish (disc. 1991).

This model was also available in double action only (all finishes) at no extra charge.

This model was also available as a Custom Shop Limited Edition during April, 2004 (MSR was $800).

MODEL P229 – .357 SIG (new 1995), 9mm Para. (mfg. 1994-96, reintroduced 1999), or .40 S&W cal., compact size, 3.9 in. barrel, choice of DA/SA or DAK trigger system (DAO with 6 1/2 lb. trigger pull) available beginning 2005, blackened Nitron or satin nickel (disc.) finished stainless steel slide with aluminum alloy frame, 10 (C/B 1994), 12* (.357 SIG or .40 S&W cal. only), or 13 (9mm Para. cal. only, new 2005) shot mag., E2 (enhanced ergonomics) grips became standard 2011, tactical rail became standard in 2004 (Nitron finish only), contrast (9mm or .40 S&W only, disc. 2015) or Siglite night sights became standard in 2016, includes lockable carrying case, 31.1 or 32.4 oz. New 1991.

| MSR $1,087 | | $925 | $765 | $650 | $525 | $450 | $400 | $350 | |

MSR	100%	98%	95%	90%	80%	70%	60%	Last MSR

Subtract $114 for contrast sights (disc. 2015).

Add $306 for Crimson Trace laser grips w/Siglite night sights (mfg. 2007-2008).

Add $180 for black Nitron finish with TruGlo TFO front and Siglite rear sights with four hi-cap mags. (Super Cap Tactical model, not available in .357 SIG cal.), disc. 2010.

Add $103 for two-tone finish (nickel finished stainless steel slide) with night sights (disc. 2011).

Add $349 for .22 LR cal. conversion kit.

This model was also available in double action only at no extra charge.

This model was also available as a Custom Shop Limited Edition during June, 2004 (MSR was $873), during August, 2004 (MSR was $916) and during Dec. 2004 (MSR was $844).

* **Model P229 Combat** – 9mm Para. cal., DA/SA, 3.9 in. barrel, 15 shot mag., Siglite night sights, FDE finished alloy frame, stainless steel slide with Nitron finish, Picatinny rail, vertical front strap serrations, FDE polymer grips, 32 oz. New 2015.

MSR $1,195	$1,035	$895	$800	$700	$600	$500	$400	

* **Model P229 Elite** – 9mm Para., .40 S&W, or .357 SIG cal., DA/SA or SAO, 3.9 in. barrel, 10, 12, or 13 shot mag., SRT, two-tone (disc.), or black Nitron finish, ergonomic beavertail, Picatinny rail, front cocking serrations, Siglite night sights, custom rosewood or aluminum grips (Platinum Elite, disc. 2011), 33.5 oz. Mfg. 2007-2012.

	$1,050	$925	$825	$725	$625	$525	$425	*$1,218*

Add $71 for TB model with threaded barrel.

Add $72 for platinum Elite with aluminum grips (disc. 2011).

* **Model P229 Elite Stainless** – 9mm Para. or .40 S&W cal., DA/SA, 3.9 in. barrel, stainless steel slide and frame, 10, 12 (.40 S&W only), or 15 (9mm Para.) shot mag., SRT, ergonomic beavertail, Picatinny rail, front cocking serrations, Siglite night sights, custom shop rosewood grips, natural stainless finish, 40.2 oz. New 2007.

MSR $1,359	$1,225	$1,015	$900	$800	$700	$600	$500	

* **Model P229 Elite Dark** – 9mm Para., .357 SIG (disc. 2012), or .40 S&W cal., DA/SA, 3.9 in. barrel, SRT (short reset trigger), Black Nitron finish, 12 or 15 shot mag., ergonomic beavertail, Picatinny rail, front cocking serrations, front strap checkering, Siglite night sights, custom aluminum grips. Mfg. 2009-2014.

	$1,050	$925	$825	$725	$625	$525	$425	*$1,243*

Add $71 for TB model with threaded barrel (disc. 2013).

* **Model P229 Enhanced Elite** – 9mm Para., .40 S&W (disc. 2015), or .357 SIG (disc. 2015) cal., DA/SA, 3.9 in. barrel, 10 (disc. 2015), 12 (disc. 2015), or 15 shot mag., beavertail frame with front strap checkering and accessory rail, SRT, E2 polymer grips, Siglite night sights, black Nitron finish, 32 oz. Mfg. 2011-2013, reintroduced 2015.

MSR $1,174	$950	$795	$650	$545	$475	$420	$365	

* **Model P229 Scorpion Elite** – 9mm Para. or .40 S&W cal., 3.9 in. threaded (9mm only) or non-threaded barrel, beavertail, SRT, Siglite night sights, Hogue Extreme G-10 grips, Flat Dark Earth (FDE) finish. Mfg. 2012-2015.

	$1,125	$950	$825	$725	$625	$525	$425	*$1,348*

Add $57 for threaded barrel (9mm Para. only).

* **Model P229 Equinox** – .40 S&W cal., 3.9 or 4.4 (disc.) in. barrel, two-tone Nitron stainless steel slide, lightweight black anodized alloy frame, nickel accents, 10 or 12 shot mag., TruGlo TFO front sight, rear Siglite night sight, Picatinny rail, grey laminated wood grips, 34 oz. Mfg. by the Custom Shop 2007-2012, reintroduced 2015.

MSR $1,195	$1,050	$900	$800	$700	$600	$500	$400	

* **Model P229 Extreme** – 9mm Para. cal., DA/SA, 3.9 in. barrel, 10 or 15 shot mag., front slide serrations, SRT, Siglite night sights, Picatinny rail, Hogue Extreme Series G10 grips, black Nitron finish, 32 oz. Mfg. 2012-2013, reintroduced 2015 only.

	$1,095	$935	$825	$700	$600	$500	$400	*$1,256*

* **Model P229 E2** – 9mm Para. cal., 15 shot mag., black Nitron finish, ergonomic slim profile one piece grips, Siglite night sights, short reset trigger, integral accessory rail, includes three mags. Mfg. 2010 only.

	$1,000	$895	$775	$675	$575	$525	$450	*$1,149*

* **Model P229 SAS** – 9mm Para., .357 SIG, or .40 S&W cal., DA/SA, 3.9 in. barrel, 12 or 13 shot mag., DAK (disc.) or SRT, smooth dehorned stainless steel slide with engraved custom shop logo, contrast (disc.) or Siglite night sights, lightweight black hard anodized frame, rounded trigger guard, checkered wood (disc.) or one-piece E2 grips, designed for snag-free profile for concealed carry, Generation II features became standard 2009, two-tone (disc.) or black Nitron (new 2009) finish, 32 oz. Mfg. by Custom Shop. Mfg. 2005-2012, reintroduced 2015 only.

	$950	$795	$665	$535	$465	$415	$365	*$1,176*

Add $30 for two-tone finish (disc. 2010).

MSR	100%	98%	95%	90%	80%	70%	60%	Last MSR

* **Model P229 M11-A1** – 9mm Para. cal., DA/SA, 3.9 in. threaded or non-threaded barrel, includes three 15 shot double stack mags., SRT, Siglite night sights, black polymer factory grips, black hard anodized frame finish with one piece stainless steel slide, corrosion protection on internal components, controls, and barrel, black nitron or Flat Dark Earth (new 2014) finish, 32 oz. New 2013.

| MSR $1,119 | $915 | $775 | $650 | $535 | $465 | $415 | $365 | |

Add $55 for Flat Dark Earth finish (new 2014) or threaded barrel (new 2014).

This model was previously incorrectly identified as a Model P228 M11-A1 (new mfg.).

* **Model P229 Sport** – .357 SIG or .40 S&W (new 2003) cal., DA/SA or SAO, 4.8 in. match or heavy (disc. 2000) compensated barrel, stainless steel frame and slide, target sights, improved trigger pull, 43.6 oz. Mfg. 1998-2000, reintroduced 2003-2005.

| | $1,375 | $975 | $800 | $695 | $585 | $485 | $415 | $1,600 |

* **Model P229 TacPac** – 9mm Para. or .40 S&W cal., features black nitron finish, Siglite sights, one-piece enhanced E2 grip, STL 900L, includes holster. Mfg. 2013-2014.

| | $1,075 | $950 | $825 | $725 | $625 | $525 | $425 | $1,238 |

* **Model P229 HF (Heritage Fund)** – .40 S&W cal., 10 shot, 3.9 in. barrel, slide marked "10th Anniversary P229", frame marked "1992-2002", gold engraving and accents, brushed stainless steel, gold trigger, Cocobolo Hogue grips with NSSF Heritage Fund medallion, includes wood display case. Limited mfg. late 2001-2004.

| | $1,195 | $750 | $600 | N/A | N/A | N/A | N/A | $1,299 |

* **Model P229R .22 LR** – .22 LR cal., DA/SA, 4.4 in. barrel, 10 shot mag., matte black anodized finish, adj. sights, E2 polymer grip, otherwise similar to standard P229. Mfg. 2009-2012, reintroduced 2015 only.

| | $725 | $625 | $550 | $475 | $400 | $350 | $275 | $858 |

MODEL P229 LEGION – 9mm Para., .40 S&W, or .357 Mag. cal., DA/SA, 3.9 in. barrel, 12 (.40 S&W or .357) or 15 shot mag., short reset trigger, black G10 grips, X-RAY, Gray frame finish. New 2016.

| MSR $1,359 | $1,275 | $1,050 | $925 | $800 | $700 | $600 | $500 | |

MODEL P230 – .22 LR (disc.).32 ACP, .380 ACP, or 9mm Ultra (disc.) cal., DA/SA or DAO, 7, 8, or 10 shot, 3.6 in. barrel, blue, composite grips, 17.6 oz. Mfg. 1976-1996.

| | $425 | $375 | $300 | $270 | $240 | $215 | $190 | $510 |

Add $35 for stainless slide (.380 ACP only).

* **Model P230 SL Stainless** – similar to Model P230, except stainless steel construction, 22.4 oz. Disc. 1996.

| | $480 | $400 | $375 | $315 | $270 | $230 | $200 | $595 |

MODEL P232 – .380 ACP cal., DA/SA or DAO, 3.6 in. barrel, 7 shot mag., aluminum alloy frame, compact personal size, blue (disc.), black nitron or two-tone stainless (disc. 2012) slide, automatic firing pin block safety, composite (disc.) or Hogue rubber grips, Siglite night sights (became standard 2010), 17.6 oz. Mfg. 1997-2014.

| | $725 | $650 | $550 | $475 | $425 | $350 | $295 | $809 |

Add $29 for two-tone finish (mfg. 2007-2012).
Subtract $71 if w/o Siglite night sights (became standard 2010).

* **Model P232 Stainless** – .380 ACP cal., similar to Model P232, except stainless steel construction, natural finish, 22.4 oz. Mfg. 1997-2014.

| | $795 | $650 | $525 | $450 | $375 | $325 | $295 | $889 |

Subtract approx. $75 if w/o Siglite night sights and Hogue grips (standard beginning 2007).

MODEL P238 – 9mm Para. (mfg. 2012 only), or .380 ACP cal., lightweight aluminum frame, 2.7 in. barrel, 6 shot mag., stainless steel slide, SAO trigger, thumb safety, black Nitron or two-tone finish, fixed or Siglite night sights, fluted grips (new 2012), 15.2 oz. Mfg. 2009-2013.

| | $550 | $475 | $450 | $375 | $340 | $300 | $275 | $679 |

Add $14 for two-tone finish.
Subtract $40 if w/o Siglite night sights (standard beginning 2010).

This model with specific features was disc. in 2013, and replacement model is the P238 Two-Tone Tribal (features black tribal engraving pattern on slide).

* **Model P238 Blackwood** – .380 ACP cal., SAO, 2.7 in. barrel, 6 shot, Siglite night sights, anodized alloy beavertail style frame, stainless steel slide, two-tone finish, blackwood grips, 15.2 oz. New 2010.

| MSR $706 | $615 | $565 | $475 | $425 | $385 | $325 | $285 | |

Add $28 for ambi safety (mfg. 2012 only).

* **Model P238 Desert** – .380 ACP cal., SAO, 2.7 in. barrel, X-Grip 7 shot mag., Siglite night sights, Hogue one-piece FDE rubber grips, ambi safety (mfg. 2012), Desert tan (two-tone FDE) finish. New 2012.

| MSR $738 | $615 | $565 | $485 | $435 | $395 | $335 | $295 | |

Add $28 ambi safety (mfg. 2012 only).

MSR	100%	98%	95%	90%	80%	70%	60%	Last MSR

* Model P238 Diamond Plate – .380 ACP cal., similar to Model P238, except has two-tone finish or black Nitron (mfg. 2012 only), "Diamond Plate" engraving, and black G10 grips. Mfg. 2011-2013.

	100%	98%	95%	90%	80%	70%	60%	Last MSR
	$650	$575	$475	$425	$375	$325	$275	*$752*

Add $28 for ambi safety (mfg. 2012 only).

* Model P238 Edge – .380 ACP cal., SAO, alloy beavertail style frame, 2.7 in. barrel, 6 shot steel mag., stainless steel slide with serrations, Siglite night sights, checkered black G10 grips, custom Edge PVD coated slide and controls, 20.1 oz. New 2015.

MSR $738	$665	$595	$495	$435	$395	$335	$295	

* Model P238 Engraved – .380 ACP cal., SAO, 2.7 in. barrel, 6 shot steel mag., polished Nitron engraved slide, Siglite night sights, rosewood grips with SIG medallion, black hardcoat anodized frame, 15.2 oz. New 2015.

MSR $760	$680	$615	$515	$450	$400	$340	$300	

* Model P238 Equinox – .380 ACP cal., SAO, beavertail style frame, 2.7 in. barrel, 6 shot mag., Siglite rear sight, TruGlo TFO front sight, custom black wood grips, ambi safety, two-tone Nitron finish, approx. 16 oz. New 2010.

MSR $738	$635	$575	$485	$435	$395	$335	$295	

Add $28 for ambi safety (mfg. 2012 only).

* Model P238 Extreme – .380 ACP cal., SAO, 2.7 in. barrel, X-Grip 7 shot mag., Siglite night sights, Black/Gray Hogue Extreme G10 grips, black nitron finish. New 2012.

MSR $738	$645	$585	$495	$435	$395	$335	$295	

* Model P238 HD – .380 ACP cal., SAO, 2.7 in. barrel, 6 shot mag., stainless beavertail style frame with black accents, stainless steel slide with slide serrations, Siglite night sights, black G10 polymer grips, includes lockable hard case, 20.1 oz. Mfg. 2015 only.

	$680	$615	$515	$450	$400	$340	$300	*$799*

* Model P238 HDW – .380 ACP cal., SAO, 2.7 in. barrel, 6 shot mag., stainless steel frame and slide, Siglite night sights, locked breech mechanism, frame mounted thumb safety, rosewood grips, natural stainless finish, 20.1 oz. Mfg. 2015 only.

	$680	$615	$515	$450	$400	$340	$300	*$799*

* Model P238 HD Nickel – .380 ACP cal., SAO, beavertail style stainless steel frame with nickel coating, 2.7 in. barrel, 6 shot mag., stainless steel slide with serrations, Siglite night sights, custom Blackwood grips with SIG medallion, 20.1 oz. New 2015.

MSR $793	$710	$625	$535	$485	$415	$350	$300	

* Model P238 Lady – .380 ACP cal., similar to Model P238, except built on red Cerakote alloy frame with "rose and scroll" 24K gold engraving, and rosewood grips. Mfg. 2011-2013.

	$650	$575	$475	$425	$375	$325	$275	*$752*

* Model P238 Nightmare – .380 ACP cal., SAO, anodized alloy beavertail style frame, 2.7 in. barrel, 6 shot mag., stainless steel slide with serrations, Siglite night sights, Hogue Black G10 grips, black Nitron finished frame and slide. New 2015.

MSR $738	$615	$565	$485	$435	$395	$335	$295	

* Model P238 Nitron – .380 ACP cal., SAO, 2.7 in. barrel, 6 shot mag., beavertail style frame, Siglite night sights, fluted polymer grips, black Nitron finish, 15.2 oz.

MSR $706	$615	$565	$475	$425	$385	$325	$285	

* Model P238 Polished – .380 ACP cal., SAO, 2.7 in. barrel, 6 shot, features polished frame and engraved stainless steel slide, Siglite night sights, choice of Hogue Pink Rubber (disc.), Pink Pearlite, Black Pearlite, or White Pearlite grips, 15.2 oz. New 2014.

MSR $799	$650	$595	$500	$450	$400	$340	$300	

* Model P238 Rainbow – .380 ACP cal., SAO, beavertail frame, 2.7 in. barrel, 6 shot mag., Siglite night sights, rosewood grips, Rainbow titanium slide and accents, 15.2 oz. New 2010.

MSR $738	$635	$575	$485	$435	$395	$335	$295	

* Model P238 Rosewood – .380 ACP cal., 2.7 in. barrel, 6 shot mag., beavertail style frame, Siglite night sights, rosewood grips, black Nitron finish, 15.2 oz. New 2010.

MSR $706	$615	$565	$475	$425	$385	$325	$285	

Add $29 for ambi safety (mfg. 2012 only).

* Model P238 SAS – .380 ACP cal., SAO, 2.7 in. barrel, 6 shot mag., dehorned frame and slide, Siglite night sights, Custom Shop (disc.) or brown Goncalo checkered wood grips, ambi safety (mfg. 2012 only), logo engraved on slide, two-tone finish. New 2011.

MSR $738	$635	$575	$485	$435	$395	$335	$295	

Add $29 for ambi safety (mfg. 2012 only).

MSR	100%	98%	95%	90%	80%	70%	60%	Last MSR

* **Model P238 Scorpion** – .380 ACP cal., 2.7 in. barrel, 7 shot mag., Siglite night sights, Black/Green Hogue G-10 grips, Ambi safety, Flat Dark Earth (FDE) finish. New 2012.

| MSR $760 | $650 | $595 | $500 | $450 | $400 | $340 | $300 | |

* **Model P238 Spartan** – .380 ACP cal., SAO, 2.7 in. barrel, stainless steel frame and slide, X-Grip 7 shot mag., slide is engraved with the Greek phrase "MOLON LABE", custom grips feature the inlaid Spartan helmet, Siglite night sights, oil-rubbed bronze PVD finish, 20.1 oz. New 2015.

| MSR $834 | $710 | $625 | $535 | $485 | $415 | $350 | $300 | |

* **Model P238 Stainless** – .380 ACP cal., similar to P238, except has stainless steel frame and slide, Siglite night sights, G10 or rosewood (disc. 2012) grips, approx. 20 oz. Mfg. 2010-2013.

| | $680 | $615 | $515 | $450 | $400 | $340 | $300 | $786 |

* **Model P238 Tactical Laser** – similar to Model P238, except has two-tone finish, black checkered aluminum grips, ambi safety (new 2012), ambi laser module. Mfg. 2010-2012.

| | $725 | $625 | $525 | $475 | $425 | $375 | $325 | $829 |

* **Model P238 Trigger Guard Laser** – .380 ACP cal., 6 shot mag., contrast sights, removable trigger guard laser, polymer grips, black Nitron finish. Mfg. 2015 only.

| | $680 | $615 | $515 | $450 | $400 | $340 | $300 | $799 |

* **Model P238 Two-Tone Tribal** – .380 ACP cal., SAO, 2.7 in. barrel, 6 shot, two-tone finish with Nitron tribal pattern engraving on slide, Siglite night sights, custom tribal engraved aluminum grips, 15.2 oz. Mfg. 2014-2015.

| | $665 | $595 | $495 | $435 | $395 | $335 | $295 | $776 |

* **Model P238 Rosewood Tribal** – .380 ACP cal., SAO, 2.7 in. barrel, 6 shot, two-tone nickel plated stainless slide with Rainbow titanium tribal pattern engraving, Siglite night sights, custom rosewood grips, 15.2 oz. Mfg. 2014-2015.

| | $665 | $595 | $495 | $435 | $395 | $335 | $295 | $776 |

MODEL P239 – .357 SIG, 9mm Para., or .40 S&W (new 1998) cal., compact personal size, DA/SA or DAO, 3.6 in. barrel, stainless steel slide and aluminum alloy frame, DAK trigger, firing pin block safety, 7 or 8 (9mm Para. only) shot mag., contrast or Siglite night sights, black polymer or one-piece enhanced E2 grip, black Nitron or two-tone (disc. 2009) finish, approx. 29 oz. Mfg. 1996-2015.

| | $925 | $775 | $650 | $525 | $450 | $400 | $350 | $1,142 |

Subtract $114 if without Siglite night sights.
Add $305 for Crimson Trace laser grips and night sights (mfg. 2007).
Add $135 for two-tone stainless slide with night sights (disc. 2009).

This model was also available as a Custom Shop Limited Edition during May, 2004 (MSR was $673).

* **Model P239 Rainbow** – .40 S&W cal., otherwise similar to Model P239, Rainbow titanium finish, Siglite night sights. Mfg. 2012 only.

| | $925 | $825 | $725 | $625 | $525 | $450 | $350 | $1,000 |

* **Model P239 SAS** – 9mm Para. (new 2008), .357 SIG (disc. 2012, reintroduced 2015), or .40 S&W cal., 3.6 in. barrel, 7 or 8 shot mag., DAK (disc.) or short reset trigger, smooth dehorned stainless steel slide, contrast (disc.) or Siglite night sights, lightweight black hard anodized frame, black Nitron or two-tone (disc. 2013) finish, rounded trigger guard, checkered/carved wood grips, designed for snag-free profile for concealed carry, Generation II features became standard 2009, 29 1/2 oz. Mfg. by Custom Shop beginning June, 2005.

| MSR $979 | $800 | $700 | $615 | $515 | $450 | $400 | $350 | |

Add $14 for two-tone finish (disc. 2013).

* **Model P239 Scorpion Elite** – 9mm Para., .357 Sig., or .40 S&W cal., DA/SA, 3.6 in. barrel, 7 or 8 shot mag., SRT, Siglite night sights, Flat Dark Earth finish, Hogue G10 Piranha grips, 29.5 oz. Mfg. 2014-2015.

| | $1,095 | $935 | $825 | $700 | $600 | $500 | $400 | $1,256 |

* **Model P239 Tactical** – 9mm Para. cal., DA/SA, 4 in. threaded barrel, 8 shot mag., front cocking serrations, SRT, Siglite night sights, black polymer grips, black Nitron finish, 29.5 oz. Mfg. 2010-2012, reintroduced 2015 only.

| | $1,095 | $935 | $825 | $700 | $600 | $500 | $400 | $1,256 |

MODEL P245 – .45 ACP cal., DA/SA, compact model featuring 3.9 in. barrel, includes 6 and 8 shot mag., blue, two-tone (disc. 2005), Ilaflon (mfg. 2000 only), or K-Kote (disc. 1999) finish, approx. 30 oz. Mfg. 1999-2006.

| | $695 | $585 | $495 | $440 | $400 | $350 | $310 | $840 |

Add $75 for Siglite night sights.
Add $56 for two-tone or K-Kote finish (disc.).
Add $50 for Ilaflon finish (mfg. 2000 only).

MSR	100%	98%	95%	90%	80%	70%	60%	Last MSR

MODEL P250 FULL SIZE – 9mm Para., .357 SIG (disc. 2010, reintroduced 2015 only), .40 S&W, or .45 ACP cal., DAO, full size frame, 4.7 in. barrel, steel frame with black polymer grip shell, features modular synthetic frame with removable fire control assembly, 10 (.45 ACP), 14 (.40 S&W and .357 SIG), or 17 (9mm Para.) shot mag., ambidextrous slide release lever, black Nitron or two-tone (disc. 2010) finish, contrast or Siglite night (disc. 2015) sights, integrated Picatinny rail, converts into various calibers by changing slides, grip modules, and magazine, 27.6 oz. Mfg. mid-2008-2013, reintroduced 2015.

MSR $480	$415	$395	$365	$325	$285	$260	$230	

Add $58 for Siglite night sights (disc. 2015).
Add $15 for two-tone finish (not available in .45 ACP cal.), disc. 2010.
Add $243 for 2 SUM package, includes sub-compact caliber exchange kit (not available in .357 SIG or .45 ACP cal.), disc.

* **Model P250 Compact** – 9mm Para., .357 SIG (disc. 2015), .380 ACP (new 2015), .40 S&W or .45 ACP cal., 3.9 in. threaded (9mm, 2015 only) or non-threaded barrel, 9 (.45 ACP), 10 (.22 LR), 13 (.357 SIG or .40 S&W) or 15 (9mm or .380 ACP) shot mag., contrast or Siglite night (disc. 2015) sights, interchangeable polymer grips, Picatinny rail, black Nitron ot two-tone (disc. 2010) finish, 24.6 oz. New mid-2008.

MSR $480	$425	$395	$365	$325	$285	$260	$230	

Add $58 for Siglite night sights (disc. 2015).
Add $195 for threaded barrel (9mm Para. cal. with Siglite night sights), (mfg. 2015 only).
Add $94 for ambidextrous manual safety (9mm Para. cal. only), mfg. 2012 only.
Add $141 for threaded barrel and Siglite night sights (9mm Para. cal. only), mfg. 2012 only.
Add $15 for two-tone finish (disc. 2010).
Add $215 for desert digital camo finish (9mm Para. cal. only), includes Siglite night sights, medium grips, and DAO (mfg. 2009-2010).

* **Model P250 Compact .22 LR** – .22 LR cal., DAO, 3.9 in. barrel, two 10 shot mags., adj. contrast sights, modular black polymer grips, M1913 accessory rail, black hardcoat anodized slide, 21.2 oz. New 2015.

MSR $434	$385	$350	$325	$285	$250	$225	$200	

* **Model P250 Compact Diamond** – similar to P250 Compact, except has black nitron or two-tone finish with "Diamond Plate" engraving, Siglite night sights. Mfg. 2012 only.

	$495	$425	$375	$325	$275	$250	$225	*$582*

Add $15 for two-tone finish (disc. 2010).
Add $215 for desert digital camo finish (9mm Para. cal. only), includes Siglite night sights, medium grips, and DAO (mfg. 2009-2010).

* **Model P250 Subcompact** – 9mm Para., .357 SIG (disc. 2015), .380 ACP (mfg. 2012-2015), .40 S&W, or .45 ACP cal., DAO, 3.6 in. barrel, 6 (.45 ACP), 10 (.357 SIG or .40 S&W), or 12 (9mm Para. or .380 ACP) shot mag., contrast or Siglite night (disc. 2015) sights, interchangeable polymer grips, black Nitron finish, 24.9 oz. New mid-2008.

MSR $480	$425	$395	$365	$325	$285	$260	$230	

Add $58 for Siglite night sights (disc. 2015).
Add $80 for integrated accessory rail (disc. 2015).
Add $172 for .380 ACP or .45 ACP with Siglite night sights (disc. 2015).
Add $15 for two-tone finish (9mm Para. or .40 S&W cal.), disc. 2010.
Add $375 for Desert Digital camo finish (9mm Para. cal. only), includes Siglite night sights, medium grips, and DAO (mfg. 2009-2010).

* **Model P250 TacPac** – 9mm Para. or .40 S&W cal., full size frame, Siglite sights, 14 or 17 shot mag., black Nitron finish, Picatinny rail, includes STL-900 compatible holster. Mfg. 2014-2015.

	$575	$525	$450	$395	$350	$300	$265	*$662*

MODEL P290RS (P290) – 9mm Para. or .380 ACP (new 2015) cal., DAO, sub-compact design utilizing light polymer black or pink (mfg. 2015 only) frame, 2.9 in. barrel, 6 or 8 (new 2012) shot mag., Re-strike firing pin (became standard in 2012), black polymer grips, contrast (new 2015) or Siglite night sights, options include integrated laser module and personalized grip inserts, black Nitron finish, 20 oz. New 2011.

MSR $488	$425	$385	$365	$325	$285	$260	$230	

Add $92 for integrated laser module (disc. 2015).
Subtract $57 if without Siglite night sights.

In 2014, the model nomenclature changed to P290RS.

* **Model P290RS Black Diamond Plate** – 9mm Para. cal., similar to Model P290RS, except has 6 shot mag., Nitron slide with diamond plate engraving, black polymer grips. Mfg. 2012 only.

	$510	$450	$385	$350	$285	$230	$185	*$595*

* **Model P290RS Enhanced** – 9mm Para. (disc. 2015) or .380 ACP (new 2015) cal., DAO, Re-strike firing pin, black polymer frame, 2.9 in. barrel, 6 or 8 (.380 ACP only) shot mag., Siglite night sights, Black and Green (disc. 2015) or Black and Pink (new 2015) Enhanced G10 grips, black Nitron/natural stainless steel slide, 20.5 oz. New 2014.

MSR $543	$465	$415	$375	$340	$300	$280	$250	

Subtract approx. $35 for 9mm Para. cal. (disc. 2015).

MSR	100%	98%	95%	90%	80%	70%	60%	Last MSR

* **Model P290RS ORB** – 9mm Para. cal., DAO, sub-compact, 2.9 in. barrel, 6 or 8 shot mag., Siglite night sights, removable enhanced G10 grip plates, oil rubbed bronze nitron coated slide, black polymer frame, 20.5 oz. New 2014.

| MSR $543 | $465 | $415 | $375 | $340 | $300 | $280 | $250 | |

* **Model P290RS Rainbow** – 9mm Para. cal., sub-compact frame, 2.9 in. barrel, 6 shot mag., Siglite night sights, black polymer grips, Rainbow Titanium finish, 20.5 oz. Mfg. 2015 only.

| | $485 | $425 | $375 | $340 | $300 | $280 | $250 | $570 |

* **Model P290RS Two-Tone** – 9mm Para. or .380 ACP (new 2015) cal., similar to P290RS, except has stainless steel slide, black polymer frame and grips, and optional integrated laser module (new 2014), 20.5 oz.

| MSR $488 | $425 | $375 | $325 | $300 | $250 | $200 | $150 | |

Add $92 for integrated laser module (mfg. 2014-2015).

Add $149 for .380 ACP cal. with integrated laser module (mfg. 2015 only).

MODEL P320 NITRON – 9mm Para., .357 SIG (new 2015), .40 S&W, or .45 ACP (new 2015) cal., SFO, DAO, full size frame, 4.7 in. barrel, 10 (.45 ACP), 14 (.357 SIG or .40 S&W) or 17 (9mm Para.) shot mag., contrast or Siglite night sights, interchangeable fire control assembly and grip panels, reversible mag. release, lower Picatinny rail, front and rear slide serrations, black Nitron finish, 29.4 oz. New 2014.

| MSR $679 | $595 | $525 | $485 | $450 | $395 | $325 | $295 | |

Subtract $82 if without Siglite night sights.

* **Model P320 Carry Nitron** – 9mm Para., .357 Sig., .40 S&W, or .45 ACP (new 2016) cal., 3.9 in. threaded (new 2015, 9mm only) or non-threaded barrel, 10 (.45 ACP), 14 (.357 SIG or .40 S&W) or 17 (9mm Para.) shot mag., contrast or Siglite night sights, interchangeable grip panels, lower Picatinny rail, front and rear slide serrations, black Nitron finish, 26 oz. New 2014.

| MSR $679 | $595 | $535 | $485 | $450 | $395 | $325 | $295 | |

Add $68 for threaded barrel (9mm Para. only, new 2015).

Subtract $82 if without Siglite night sights.

* **Model P320 Compact** – 9mm Para., .357 SIG, .40 S&W, or .45 ACP cal., SFO, DAO, compact frame, 3.9 in. barrel, 9 (.45 ACP), 13 (.40 S&W or .357 SIG), or 15 (9mm) shot mag., Picatinny rail, contrast or Siglite night sights, modular polymer or small (.45 ACP, FDE, new 2016) grips, Black Nitron or Flat Dark Earth Nitron finish. New 2015.

| MSR $679 | $595 | $535 | $495 | $450 | $395 | $325 | $295 | |

Add $68 for threaded barrel (9mm Para. cal. only).

Subtract $82 if without Siglite night sights.

* **Model P320 Subcompact** – 9mm Para. or .40 S&W (new 2016) cal., DAO, 3.6 in. barrel, 12 shot mag., contrast or Siglite night sights, modular polymer or medium (.40 S&W only, new 2016) grips, with or without accessory rail, Black Nitron finish. New 2015.

| MSR $679 | $595 | $535 | $485 | $450 | $395 | $325 | $295 | |

Subtract $82 if without Siglite night sights.

MODEL PM400 – 5.56 NATO cal., pistol equivalent of the M400 carbine/rifle, GIO, 11 1/2 in. barrel, flip-up rear sights, 30 shot, Picatinny flat-top upper, integral ambi QD sling, B5 Systems pistol grip, KeyMod handguard, FDE finish, with or w/o pistol stabilizing brace, 7 lbs. Mfg. 2014-2015.

| | $1,295 | $1,150 | $995 | $900 | $750 | $600 | $475 | $1,519 |

Subtract approx. $125 if without pistol stabilizing brace.

* **Model PM400 SWAT PSB** – 5.56 NATO cal., GIO, 11 1/2 in. barrel, 10 shot mag., aluminum handguard, pistol stabilizing brace, flip-up rear sight, integral ambi QD sling mounts, black finish, 6 lbs. New 2015.

| MSR $1,467 | $1,275 | $1,150 | $1,000 | $900 | $750 | $600 | $475 | |

* **Model PM400 Elite** – 5.56 NATO (new 2016) or .300 AAC Blackout cal., GIO, 9 in. barrel, 30 shot mag., flip-up front and rear sights, rotating locking bolt, integral ambi QD sling mounts, aluminum KeyMod handguard, pistol stabilizing brace, black finish, 6 lbs. New 2015.

| MSR $1,202 | $1,075 | $975 | $850 | $750 | $650 | $550 | $425 | |

Add $374 for .300 AAC Blackout cal.

MODEL P516 – 5.56 NATO cal., short stroke pushrod GPO with adj. gas valve, 7 or 10 (new 2012) in. barrel with muzzle brake, Magpul MOE grip, flip up adj. iron sights, 10 or 30 (disc.) shot mag., aluminum quad rail, black finish, with (new 2014) or without pistol stabilizing brace (PSB, became standard 2015). Mfg. 2011-2012, reintroduced 2014-2015.

| | $975 | $800 | $665 | $535 | $465 | $415 | $365 | $1,199 |

Subtract approx. $175 if without pistol stabilizing brace (PSB).

MSR	100%	98%	95%	90%	80%	70%	60%	Last MSR

MODEL P522

.22 LR cal., blowback action, 10.6 in. barrel, aluminum flat-top upper receiver, choice of polymer or quad rail (P522 SWAT) forend, flash suppressor, 10 or 25 shot polymer mag., ambidextrous safety selector, sling attachments, with (new 2014) or without pistol stabilizing brace (PSB, became standard 2015), approx. 6 1/2 lbs. Mfg. 2010 only, reintroduced 2014-2015.

	100%	98%	95%	90%	80%	70%	60%	Last MSR
	$525	$450	$400	$360	$315	$290	$260	*$628*

Subtract approx. $125 if without pistol stabilizing brace (PSB).

Add $71 for P522 SWAT model with quad rail forend (mfg. 2010 only).

Last MSR for P522 SWAT model (disc. 2010) was $643.

MODEL P556

5.56 NATO cal., GPO similar to SIG 556 carbine, 10 in. cold hammer forged barrel with A2 type flash suppressor, Picatinny top rail, pistol grip only, ribbed and vented black polymer forearm, black Nitron finish, mini red dot front sight, aluminum alloy two-stage trigger, ambidextrous safety, 30 shot mag (accepts standard AR-15 style mags.), 6.3 lbs. Mfg. 2009-2010.

	100%	98%	95%	90%	80%	70%	60%	Last MSR
	$1,825	$1,650	$1,450	$1,300	$1,200	$1,100	$1,000	*$1,876*

Add $147 for P556 SWAT model with quad rail forend.

* **Model P556 Lightweight** – similar to Model P556, except has lightweight polymer lower unit and forend. Mfg. 2010-2013.

	100%	98%	95%	90%	80%	70%	60%	Last MSR
	$1,075	$950	$825	$725	$625	$525	$425	*$1,207*

Add $133 for quad rail forend (SWAT Model).

MODEL P556xi

5.56 NATO (AR-15 style) or 7.62x39mm (AK-47 design) cal., GPO, 10 in. barrel, polymer handguard, flip up sights, 30 shot mag., with (became standard 2015) or without pistol stabilizing brace. New 2014.

MSR	100%	98%	95%	90%	80%	70%	60%	Last MSR
$1,663	$1,415	$1,250	$1,075	$965	$835	$695	$550	

Add $131 for 7.62x39mm cal. with AK-47 design.

Subtract approx. $120 if without pistol stabilizing brace (became standard 2015).

MODEL P556xi SWAT

5.56 NATO (AR-15 style) or 7.62x39mm (AK-47 design) cal., GPO, 10 in. barrel, aluminum handguard, flip up sights, 30 shot mag., pistol stabilizing brace. New 2015.

MSR	100%	98%	95%	90%	80%	70%	60%	Last MSR
$1,794	$1,525	$1,350	$1,175	$1,050	$875	$725	$575	

Add $141 for 7.62x39mm cal. with AK-47 design.

MODEL P716

7.62 NATO cal., short stroke GPO with 4-position gas valve, 12 in. barrel, 20 shot mag., locking flip-up front and rear sights, integral ambi QD sling mounts, includes pistol stabilizing brace (PSB), 8.6 lbs. Mfg. 2015 only.

	100%	98%	95%	90%	80%	70%	60%	Last MSR
	$2,085	$1,800	$1,575	$1,350	$1,100	$950	$825	*$2,456*

MODEL P938

9mm Para. cal., SAO, 3 in. barrel, lightweight aluminum frame, stainless steel slide, thumb safety, 6 shot, Siglite night sights, ambi safety, polymer grips, black Nitron finish, 16 oz. New 2012.

MSR	100%	98%	95%	90%	80%	70%	60%	Last MSR
$760	$650	$595	$500	$450	$400	$340	$300	

* **Model P938 Aluminum** – 9mm Para. cal., 3 in. barrel, 6 shot mag., Siglite night sights, ambi safety, black aluminum grips, black Nitron finish. Mfg. 2013-2015.

	100%	98%	95%	90%	80%	70%	60%	Last MSR
	$725	$575	$475	$425	$395	$350	$295	*$856*

* **Model P938 Black Rubber** – 9mm Para. cal., 3 in. barrel, 6 shot mag., black Nitron finish, Siglite night sights, ambi safety, black rubber grips. New 2013.

MSR	100%	98%	95%	90%	80%	70%	60%	Last MSR
$815	$695	$550	$465	$425	$395	$350	$295	

* **Model P938 Blackwood** – 9mm Para. cal., 3 in. barrel, 6 shot mag., black Nitron finish, Siglite night sights, ambi safety, Hogue blackwood grips, two-tone black Nitron frame/stainless slide finish. New 2012.

MSR	100%	98%	95%	90%	80%	70%	60%	Last MSR
$793	$685	$615	$535	$485	$415	$350	$300	

* **Model P938 Edge** – 9mm Para. cal., SAO, 3 in. barrel, 6 shot, stainless steel slide with serrations and Edge finish (custom PVD coating), Siglite night sights, thumb safety, checkered black G10 grips, shipped in lockable hard case with one 6 shot mag., 16 oz. New mid-2015.

MSR	100%	98%	95%	90%	80%	70%	60%	Last MSR
$815	$695	$550	$465	$425	$395	$350	$295	

* **Model P938 Equinox** – 9mm Para. cal., 3 in. barrel, features two-tone polished Nitron finish, TruGlo front and Siglite rear sights, ambi safety, Hogue black diamondwood grips. New 2012.

MSR	100%	98%	95%	90%	80%	70%	60%	Last MSR
$815	$695	$550	$465	$425	$395	$350	$295	

* **Model P938 Extreme** – 9mm Para. cal., SAO, black anodized beavertail style frame, 3 in. barrel, X-Grip 7 shot mag., Nitron-coated stainless slide, Siglite night sights, Hogue G10 Piranha grips in black and gray, ambi safety, black Nitron finish, 16 oz. New 2012.

MSR	100%	98%	95%	90%	80%	70%	60%	Last MSR
$815	$695	$550	$465	$425	$395	$350	$295	

MSR	100%	98%	95%	90%	80%	70%	60%	Last MSR

* **Model P938 Nightmare** – 9mm Para. cal., 3 in. barrel, 7 shot mag., black Nitron finish, Siglite night sights, ambi safety, Hogue Black G10 grips. New 2013.

| MSR $815 | $685 | $550 | $465 | $425 | $395 | $350 | $295 | |

* **Model P938 Polished** – 9mm Para. cal., 3 in. barrel, engraved slide, Siglite night sights, 6 shot mag., Rosewood medallion grips, ambi safety, polished Nitron coated finish. New 2015.

| MSR $815 | $695 | $550 | $465 | $425 | $395 | $350 | $295 | |

* **Model P938 Rosewood** – 9mm Para. cal., 3 in. barrel, 6 shot mag., black Nitron finish, Siglite night sights, ambi safety, rosewood grips. New 2012.

| MSR $793 | $685 | $615 | $535 | $485 | $415 | $350 | $300 | |

* **Model P938 Rosewood .22 LR** – .22 LR cal., SAO, lightweight microcompact frame, 3.3 in. barrel, 10 shot mag., adj. contrast or Siglite night sights, rosewood or black rubber grips, ambi safety, black hard anodized finish, 16 oz. Mfg. 2015 only.

| | $565 | $475 | $425 | $375 | $325 | $290 | $260 | $685 |

Add $34 for threaded barrel.

* **Model P938 Rosewood .22 LR Target** – .22 LR cal., SAO, 4.1 in. barrel, 10 shot mag., adj. contrast sights, rosewood grips, ambi safety, black finish. New 2015.

| MSR $651 | $575 | $525 | $485 | $450 | $395 | $325 | $295 | |

* **Model P938 SAS** – 9mm Para. cal., SAO, 3 in. barrel, Siglite night sights, Brown Goncalo checkered wood grips, ambi safety, dehorning, two-tone finish. Mfg. 2012-2013, reintroduced 2015.

| MSR $815 | $695 | $550 | $465 | $425 | $395 | $350 | $295 | |

* **Model P938 Scorpion** – 9mm Para. cal., SAO, 3 in. threaded (new 2015) or non-threaded barrel, 6 shot mag., Siglite night sights, ambi safety, Hogue G10 grips, Flat Dark Earth finish, 16 oz. Mfg. 2014-2015.

| | $775 | $600 | $500 | $450 | $425 | $365 | $315 | $913 |

Add $115 for threaded barrel (new 2015).

MODEL 1911 FULL SIZE (GSR REVOLUTION)

– .40 S&W (new 2014) or .45 ACP cal., SA, 5 in. match grade barrel, choice of white (disc.), standard blue (disc.), two-tone, reverse two-tone (mfg. 2007-2010), or black Nitron finish, includes two 8 shot mags., with or w/o under frame Picatinny rail, firing pin safety, front and rear strap checkering, Novak (disc.) or low profile sights, checkered wood (all stainless), rosewood, aluminum, or synthetic (blued stainless) grips, approx. 41 oz. Mfg. in Exeter, NH. Mfg. 2004-2015.

| | $925 | $775 | $650 | $525 | $450 | $400 | $350 | $1,142 |

Add $34 for M-1913 Picatinny rail.
Add $57 for Fastback rounded frame (with black Nitron finish and rosewood grips), new 2015.
Add $100 for platinum Elite with two-tone finish, adj. combat night sights and aluminum grips (mfg. 2008-2011).
Add $120 for Blackwater model (mfg. 2009-2010).
Subtract $40 for reverse two-tone finish (disc. 2010).

The abbreviation GSR on this model stands for Granite Series Revolution.

* **Model 1911 Desert** – .45 ACP cal., Desert Tan finish, contrast sights, Ergo XT OD Green grips, otherwise similar to the 1911. Mfg. 2012 only.

| | $950 | $825 | $725 | $625 | $525 | $450 | $375 | $1,070 |

* **Model 1911 Engraved Texas** – .45 ACP cal., SAO, 5 in. barrel, 8 shot mag., Siglite night sights, custom Texas grips, polished slide with gold or silver engraving. New 2015.

| MSR $1,522 | $1,325 | $1,175 | $1,000 | $900 | $775 | $650 | $525 | |

Add $141 for gold engraving.

* **Model 1911 Extreme** – .45 ACP cal., SAO, full size frame, 5 in. barrel, Magwell housing, two 8 shot mags., flat trigger, Siglite night sights, black/hray Hogue Extreme G-10 grips, ambi safety, integral accessory rail, black Nitron finish. Mfg. 2012 only, reintroduced 2015.

| MSR $1,174 | $950 | $800 | $700 | $575 | $475 | $415 | $375 | |

* **Model 1911 Fastback** – .45 ACP cal., Fastback rounded frame, two 8 shot mags., black Nitron finish, low profile night sights, rosewood grips, otherwise similar to the 1911. Mfg. 2012 only.

| | $1,025 | $875 | $750 | $625 | $525 | $450 | $375 | $1,170 |

* **Model 1911 Max** – .40 S&W (new 2014) or .45 ACP cal., Custom Competition, 5 in. barrel, 8 shot mag., forward cocking serrations, external extractor, flat trigger, Koenig speed hammer, fiber optic front and adj. rear sights, ICE Magwell, Wilson Mag., custom Hogue chainlink G-10 grips, Max logo, reverse two-tone finish, 41.6 oz. New 2012.

| MSR $1,663 | $1,425 | $1,275 | $1,100 | $965 | $835 | $695 | $550 | |

MSR	100%	98%	95%	90%	80%	70%	60%	Last MSR

* **Model 1911 Nickel Rail** – .45 ACP cal., SAO, full size stainless steel side and frame, 5 in. barrel, 8 shot mag., low profile night sights, integral 1913 accessory rail, custom Brown Vector grips, stainless steel magwell, nickel PVD finish, 41.6 oz. New 2015.

| MSR $1,141 | $925 | $775 | $650 | $535 | $465 | $415 | $365 | |

* **Model 1911 Nightmare** – .45 ACP or .357 SIG (new 2016) cal., SAO, Fastback rounded frame, 5 in. barrel, two 8 shot mags., stainless controls, Siglite night sights, black G-10 grips, black Nitron finish. New 2012.

| MSR $1,195 | $1,025 | $935 | $825 | $750 | $650 | $550 | $425 | |

* **Model 1911 POW-MIA** – .45 ACP cal., SAO, 5 in. barrel, two 8 shot steel mags., Siglite night sights, custom Hogue grips with POW-MIA seal, slide is engraved with barbed wire and there are dog tags and an American flag engraved with an inscription on the top of the slide, black Nitron finish. Mfg. 2012 only, reintroduced 2015.

| MSR $1,304 | $1,175 | $1,025 | $875 | $750 | $650 | $550 | $450 | |

Add $143 for custom engraved stainless, engraved KaBar knife, and Pelican case (mfg. 2012 only).

* **Model 1911 Scorpion** – .45 ACP cal., SAO, 5 in. barrel, 8 shot mag., front cocking serrations, low profile night sights, ambi safety, magwell housing, Hogue Extreme Series G10 grips, Flat Dark Earth (FDE) finish, 41.6 oz. Mfg. 2011-2015.

| | $1,000 | $825 | $700 | $575 | $475 | $415 | $375 | $1,233 |

Add $80 for threaded barrel.

* **Model 1911 Emperor Scorpion** – .45 ACP cal., SAO, full size frame, 5 in. barrel, two 8 shot mags., skeletonized combat hammer and trigger, Siglite night sights, Piranha Textured G-10 Magwell grips, ambi safety, mainspring housing, front cocking serrations, M1913 rail, Flat Dark Earth PVD finish. New 2015.

| MSR $1,174 | $1,000 | $825 | $700 | $575 | $475 | $415 | $375 | |

* **Model 1911 Emperor Scorpion** – .45 ACP cal., SAO, 5 in. barrel, 8 shot mag., low profile night sights, mainspring housing, skeletonized combat hammer and trigger, front cocking serrations, M1913 accessory rail, Piranha textured G10 magwell grips, Flat Dark Earth (FDE) finish, 41.6 oz. New 2015.

| MSR $1,213 | $990 | $820 | $695 | $575 | $475 | $415 | $375 | |

* **Model 1911 Spartan (Molon Labe)** – .45 ACP cal., SA, 5 in. barrel, features custom oil rubbed bronze Nitron finish with 24Kt. gold inlay Molon Labe engraving on slide (Ancient Greek meaning "Come and Take Them"), Hogue grips with Spartan helmet, and low profile sights, otherwise similar to the 1911. New late 2012.

| MSR $1,304 | $1,175 | $1,025 | $875 | $750 | $650 | $550 | $450 | |

* **Model 1911 Stainless** – .45 ACP cal., features stainless finish and blackwood grips, otherwise similar to the 1911. Disc. 2013.

| | $995 | $875 | $750 | $650 | $550 | $450 | $425 | $1,156 |

Subtract $43 if without M-1913 Picatinny rail (disc. 2012).

* **Model 1911 STX** – .45 ACP cal., SAO, full size frame, 5 in. barrel, 8 shot mag., adj. combat night sights, burled maple grips, ambi safety, beavertail grip safety, flat-top, reverse two-tone finish, 41.6 oz.

| MSR $1,174 | $950 | $795 | $675 | $575 | $475 | $415 | $375 | |

* **Model 1911 Super Target** – .45 ACP cal., SAO, full size frame, 5 in. barrel, 8 shot mag., adj. target rear and fiber optic front sights, beavertail grip safety, black Nitron or stainless steel finish, custom walnut or birch (stainless model) grips with SIG medallion, 41.6 oz. New 2015.

| MSR $1,609 | $1,425 | $1,250 | $1,075 | $950 | $825 | $675 | $550 | |

* **Model 1911 TTT** – .45 ACP cal., features two-tone finish, black controls, adj. combat night sights and wood grips, otherwise similar to the 1911. Disc. 2012.

| | $1,025 | $875 | $750 | $650 | $550 | $450 | $375 | $1,170 |

* **Model 1911 Tacops** – .45 ACP or .357 SIG (new 2016) cal., SAO, 5 in. threaded or non-threaded barrel, four 8 shot mags., Siglite night sights, Magwell Ergo XT grips, ambi thumb safety, integral accessory rail, black Nitron finish. New 2011.

| MSR $1,174 | $950 | $800 | $700 | $575 | $475 | $415 | $375 | |

Add $76 for threaded barrel.

* **Model 1911 Tacpac** – .45 ACP cal., features 1911 XO, holster with attached mag. pouch, magazine loader, and 3 magazines, otherwise similar to the 1911. Mfg. 2012-2013.

| | $950 | $825 | $725 | $625 | $525 | $450 | $375 | $1,070 |

* **Model 1911 Railed Tacpac** – .45 ACP cal., features 1911 XO with lower Picatinny rail, includes holster with attached mag. pouch and two magazines, laser module. Mfg. 2013-2015.

| | $925 | $775 | $650 | $525 | $450 | $400 | $350 | $1,142 |

MSR		100%	98%	95%	90%	80%	70%	60%	Last MSR

* **Model 1911 Target** – .45 ACP cal., features black Nitron or stainless finish, adj. target sights, and rosewood or blackwood grips. Mfg. 2011-2012.

		$975	$850	$725	$625	$525	4450	$400	$1,113

Add $29 for stainless finish with blackwood grips.

* **Model 1911 XO** – .45 ACP or .357 SIG (new 2016) cal., SAO, 5 in. match grade barrel, stainless steel slide and frame, beavertail grip safety, 8 shot mag., low profile contrast sights, Ergo XT grips, black Nitron or stainless (disc. 2012) finish, with (new 2016, .357 SIG only) or without accessory rail, 41.6 oz. New 2007.

MSR $1,010		$865	$725	$635	$535	$450	$400	$350	

Add $56 for .357 SIG cal. and accessory rail (new 2016).
Add $28 for stainless finish (disc. 2012).

MODEL 1911 TRADITIONAL FULL SIZE
– .45 ACP cal., 5 in. barrel, rounded top slide, front cocking serrations, stainless frame with matte black Nitron slide and small parts, 3 hole speed trigger, Hogue custom black wood grips, low profile Siglite night sights, two 8 shot mags., reverse two-tone finish, approx. 41 oz. Mfg. 2011-2012, reintroduced 2015 only.

		$950	$795	$665	$535	$465	$415	$365	$1,176

* **Model 1911 Traditional Compact** – .45 ACP or .357 SIG (new 2015) cal., compact slide with 3.9 in. barrel, rounded top slide, stainless frame, 3 hole speed trigger, Hogue custom black wood grips, low profile Siglite night sights, two 7 shot mags., stainless finish, approx. 35 oz. Mfg. 2011-2012, reintroduced 2015 only.

		$950	$795	$665	$535	$465	$415	$365	$1,176

* **Model 1911 Traditional Tacops** – .45 ACP or .357 SIG (mfg. 2015 only) cal., stainless frame, 5 in. barrel, 8 shot mag., low profile Siglite night sights, black Ergo XT grips, stainless magwell, ambi safety, M1913 rail, black Nitron finish, 41.6 oz. New 2012.

MSR $1,174		$950	$795	$650	$545	$475	$420	$365	

MODEL 1911 MATCH ELITE
– 9mm Para., .40 S&W, or .45 ACP cal., round top, 5 in. barrel, double slide serrations on frame, adj. target sights, 3 hole trigger, Hogue custom wood grips, choice of stainless or two-tone (.45 ACP cal. only) finish. Mfg. 2011-2012.

		$925	$875	$750	$650	$550	$450	$400	$1,170

MODEL 1911 TRADITIONAL STAINLESS STEEL
– 9mm Para., .38 Super (disc. 2015), .40 S&W, or .45 ACP cal., stainless steel. New 2014.

* **Model 1911 Traditional Stainless Match Elite** – 9mm Para., .38 Super (disc. 2015), .40 S&W, or .45 ACP (mfg. 2015 only) cal., SAO, stainless frame, 5 in. barrel, 8 or 9 shot mag., adj. sights, blackwood grips. New 2014.

MSR $1,141		$950	$775	$650	$535	$465	$415	$365	

* **Model 1911 Traditional Stainless Nightmare** – .45 ACP cal., Fastback frame, Siglite sights, Nitron finish. Mfg. 2014-2015.

		$1,095	$935	$825	$700	$600	$500	$400	$1,256

* **Model 1911 Traditional Stainless Scorpion** – .45 ACP cal., stainless steel frame, Siglite sights, Flat Dark Earth finish. Mfg. 2014-2015.

		$995	$825	$675	$545	$475	$420	$365	$1,233

* **Model 1911 Traditional Stainless Emperor Scorpion** – .45 ACP cal., SAO, Fastback frame, 4.2 in. barrel, two 8 shot mags., Siglite night sights, black G10 grips, ambi safety, Flat Dark Earth coated finish. New 2015.

MSR $1,174		$950	$800	$675	$545	$475	$420	$365	

MODEL 1911 CARRY (REVOLUTION)
– .45 ACP cal., carry configuration with short stainless slide, 4 in. barrel, stainless steel frame (disc. 2012) or black Nitron finish, Novak (disc. 2010) or low profile night sights, 8 shot mag., rosewood grips became standard with black Nitron finish during 2011, black wood grips became standard on stainless finish during 2011. Mfg. 2007-2012, reintroduced 2015 only.

		$925	$775	$650	$525	$450	$400	$350	$1,142

* **Model 1911 Carry Fastback** – .45 ACP cal., Fastback rounded frame, black Nitron finish, low profile night sights, two 8 shot mags., and rosewood grips, otherwise similar to the 1911 Carry. Mfg. 2012 only, reintroduced 2015 only.

		$975	$800	$665	$535	$465	$415	$365	$1,199

* **Model 1911 Carry Nightmare** – .45 ACP or .357 SIG (mfg. 2015 only) cal., SAO, Fastback rounded frame, 4.2 in. barrel, two 8 shot mags., stainless controls, Siglite night sights, black G-10 grips, black nitron finish. New 2012.

MSR $1,195		$1,050	$925	$825	$700	$600	$500	$400	

MSR	100%	98%	95%	90%	80%	70%	60%	Last MSR

* Model 1911 Carry Scorpion – .45 ACP cal., features Flat Dark Earth finish, low profile night sights, ambi safety, magwell housing, and Hogue Extreme Series G-10 grips, otherwise similar to 1911 Carry. Mfg. 2012-2015.

	$995	$825	$675	$545	$475	$420	$365	*$1,233*

Add $80 for threaded barrel.

* Model 1911 Carry Spartan – .45 ACP cal., SAO, 4.2 in. barrel, 8 shot mag., Siglite sights, Molon Labe engraved slide, oil-rubbed bronze Nitron finish with 24Kt. gold inlay engraving, Hogue custom Spartan grips, 38.8 oz. New 2014.

MSR $1,304	$1,195	$1,025	$875	$750	$650	$550	$450	

* Model 1911 Carry Tacops – .45 ACP cal., SAO, 4.2 or 4.9 in. threaded or non-threaded barrel, four 8 shot mags., Siglite night sights, Magwell Ergo XT grips, ambi thumb safety, M1913 rail, black Nitron finish. Mfg. 2012 only, reintroduced 2015.

MSR $1,174	$950	$800	$675	$545	$475	$420	$365	

Add $76 for threaded barrel.

MODEL 1911 COMPACT (REVOLUTION) – .45 ACP cal., SA, short slide and compact frame, 6 shot, stainless or black Nitron finish, 4 in. barrel, night sights. Mfg. 2007-2009.

	$975	$850	$725	$625	$525	$450	$400	*$1,170*

* Model 1911 Compact C3 – .45 ACP cal., SAO, 4.2 in. barrel, 7 shot mag., black hardcoat anodized alloy frame, stainless slide, low profile contrast sights, slim profile rosewood grips, two-tone finish. New 2011.

MSR $1,010	$865	$725	$640	$535	$450	$400	$350	

Add $214 for magwell and black CTC laser grips (mfg. 2012 only) or add $243 for magwell and wood grain CTC laser grips (mfg. 2012 only).

* Model 1911 Compact RCS – .45 ACP cal., dehorning and anti-snag treatment, black Nitron or two-tone finish, 7 shot, low profile night sights, custom wood grips, otherwise similar to 1911 Compact. Disc. 2012.

	$975	$850	$725	$625	$525	$450	$400	*$1,170*

Add $15 for two-tone finish.

* Model 1911 Compact Nickel – .45 ACP cal., SAO, 4.2 in. barrel, 7 shot mag., low profile night sights, custom Vector grips, Magwell, checkered front strap, nickel Nitron coated finish, 38.8 oz. New 2015.

MSR $1,141	$925	$775	$650	$535	$465	$415	$365	

MODEL 1911 ULTRA COMPACT – 9mm Para. (new 2015) or .45 ACP cal., 3.3 in. barrel, 3 hole trigger, aluminum frame, slim profile custom wood rosewood or blackwood grips, low profile night sights, two 7 or 8 (new 2016, 9mm only) shot mags., Nitron or two-tone finish, 28 oz. New 2011.

MSR $1,119	$900	$775	$650	$535	$465	$415	$365	

MODEL 1911-22 – .22 LR cal., black frame and slide finish, 5 in. barrel, low profile 3-dot contrast sights, 3 hole trigger, bobbed hammer, beavertail, Hogue custom rosewood grips, one 10 shot mag., black, camo (new 2013), Flat Dark Earth (new 2012), or OD Green (new 2012) finish, 34 oz. Mfg. 2011-2014.

	$395	$350	$315	$275	$260	$240	$200	*$460*

Add $58 for Flat Dark Earth, OD Green (new 2012), or camo (new 2013) finish.

MODEL SIG PRO SP2009 – 9mm Para. cal., otherwise identical to SP2340, 28 oz. Mfg. 1999-2005.

	$510	$450	$355	$290	$260	$220	$195	*$640*

Add $60 for Siglite night sights.
Add $31 for two-tone finish.

MODEL SIG PRO SP2022 – 9mm Para., .357 SIG, or .40 S&W cal., 10, 12 or 15 (9mm Para. cal. only) shot mag., 3.85 in. barrel, DA/SA, polymer frame, Picatinny rail, Nitron, blue, or two-tone (disc. 2005) stainless steel slide, black Nitron finish, convertible to DAO, optional interchangeable grips, 26.8 (9mm Para.) or 30 oz. Mfg. 2004-2007.

	$495	$440	$355	$290	$260	$220	$195	*$613*

Subtract 10% if w/o Siglite night sights (became standard 2007).

MODEL SIG PRO SP2340 – .357 SIG, or .40 S&W cal., features polymer frame and one-piece Nitron finished stainless steel or two-tone (new 2001) finished slide, 3.86 in. barrel, DA/SA, includes two interchangeable grips, 10 shot mag., approx. 30.2 oz. Mfg. 1999-2005.

	$510	$450	$355	$290	$260	$220	$195	*$640*

Add $60 for Siglite night sights.
Add $31 for two-tone finish.

MODEL SP2022 – 9mm Para., .357 SIG (mfg. 2015 only), or .40 S&W cal., DA/SA, 3.9 in. barrel, polymer frame with integrated lower Picatinny rail, choice of black Nitron or natural stainless slide, modular fire control unit, interchangeable grip assemblies, 10 (disc.) 12, or 15 (9mm Para. only) shot mag., contrast or Siglite night (disc. 2015) sights, two-tone, black Nitron, or FDE (new 2014) finish, 29 oz. New 2011.

MSR $543	$465	$415	$375	$340	$300	$280	$250	

MSR	100%	98%	95%	90%	80%	70%	60%	Last MSR

Add $68 for FDE or two-tone finish.
Add $141 for threaded barrel (9mm Para. only).
Add $35 for Siglite night sights (disc. 2015).
Add $92 for .357 SIG cal. with Siglite Night sights (mfg. 2015 only).

* ***Model SP2022 Diamond*** – 9mm Para. cal., similar to Model SP2022, except has two-tone or black Nitron finish with "Diamond Plate" engraving, and Siglite night sights. Mfg. 2012 only.

	$550	$475	$400	$350	$300	$250	$225	$626

* ***Model SP2022 TacPac*** – 9mm Para. or .40 S&W cal., 12 or 15 shot mag., Siglite sights, one-piece enhanced E2 grip, black Nitron finish, STL 900L, includes holster. Mfg. 2013-2015.

	$615	$550	$495	$450	$395	$325	$295	$719

RIFLES: BOLT ACTION

TACTICAL 2 – .223 Rem. (mfg. 2010-2012), .308 Win., .300 Win. Mag. (disc. 2013), or .338 Lapua cal., left or right-hand straight pull action, 24.7 (.308 Win. cal. only), 25.6 (.300 Win. cal. only, disc. 2013), or 27 (.338 Lapua cal. only) in. fluted barrel with muzzle brake, aluminum receiver, black hardcoat anodized finish, adj. single stage trigger, 4 or 5 shot polymer box mag., ambidextrous Blaser adj. composite pistol grip stock with adj. buttplate and cheekpiece, Picatinny rail, optional Harris bipod, 12 - 12 1/2 lbs. Mfg. 2007-2014.

	$3,700	$3,300	$2,900	$2,400	$1,900	$1,750	$1,500	$4,171

Add $303 for .338 Lapua cal.
Add $299-$565 per individual bolt head depending on caliber.
Add $1,689 per interchangeable barrel.

SIG 50 – .50 BMG cal., 29 in. fluted barrel with muzzle brake, 5 shot detachable mag., helical bolt, Desert Tan finish, detachable buttstock or McMillan tactical stock, includes bipod, 23.4 lbs. Mfg. 2011-2012, reintroduced 2014-2015.

	$9,100	$7,750	$6,350	$5,100	$4,850	$3,900	$3,200	$9,825

SSG 3000 PRECISION TACTICAL RIFLE – .308 Win. cal., modular design, ambidextrous McMillan tactical stock with adj. comb, 23.4 in. barrel with muzzle brake, folding aluminum chassis (new 2012), 5 shot detachable mag., supplied in 3 different levels, Level I does not have bipod or scope, cased, 12 lbs. Mfg. 2000-2012.

	$2,400	$2,100	$1,700	$1,500	$1,250	$1,000	$875	$2,799

Add $933 for folding aluminum chassis (new 2012).
Add $1,500 for Level II (includes Leupold Vari-X III 3.5-10x40mm duplex reticle scope and Harris bipod, disc.).
Add $2,300 for Level III (includes Leupold Mark 4 M1 10x40mm Mil-Dot reticle scope and Harris bipod, disc.).
Add $1,500 for .22 LR cal. conversion kit (disc.).

* ***SSG 3000 Patrol*** – .308 Win. cal., 18 or 23 1/2 in. barrel with (new 2014) or w/o threading, black or FDE (new 2014) finish, Patrol stock with integral aluminum bedding. Mfg. 2012-2015.

	$1,295	$1,100	$950	$825	$700	$575	$495	$1,499

RIFLES: SEMI-AUTO

State compliant rifles on some of the currently manufactured models listed within this section include CA, CO, HA, IL, MA, MD, NJ, and NY. Compliance features will vary from state to state, and typically, these compliant state MSRs are slightly higher than the standard models available from the rest of the states.

SIG M400 – 5.56 NATO cal., GIO, 16 in. barrel, A2 grip, M4 buttstock, 600 meter adj. and removable rear sight, 30 shot mag., includes hard case. Mfg. 2012-2015.

	$1,050	$925	$795	$700	$600	$500	$400	$1,233

Add $93 for aluminum quad rails (disc. 2014).
Add $40 for lightweight steady ready platform (mfg. 2012 only).

* ***SIG M400 B5 Series*** – 5.56 NATO cal., GIO, 16 in. barrel, 30 shot mag., rear flip up sights, B5 Systems SOPMOD 6-pos. telescoping stock, pistol grip, KeyMod carbine handguards, Picatinny rail, Gray or Foliage finish, 6.7 lbs. Mfg. 2015 only.

	$1,150	$1,000	$875	$775	$650	$550	$450	$1,348

* ***SIG M400 Carbon Fiber*** – 5.56 NATO cal., GIO, 16 in. barrel, carbon fiber forend or choice of SIG or carbon fiber rifle stock, 30 shot Lancer mag. Mfg. 2014-2015.

	$1,850	$1,625	$1,395	$1,275	$1,025	$850	$695	$2,170

Add $172 for carbon fiber forend and carbon fiber rifle stock.

* ***SIG M400 Classic*** – 5.56 NATO cal., GIO, M4 style polymer handguard, SIG grips, fixed front and rear flip-up sights, 30 shot mag., telestock, black finish. New 2014.

MSR $1,250	$1,065	$945	$815	$750	$650	$525	$425	

MSR	100%	98%	95%	90%	80%	70%	60%	Last MSR

* **SIG M400 Enhanced Carbine** – 5.56 NATO cal., GIO, features 16 in. barrel, MOE handguards, MOE grip, MOE stock, and flip up rear sights, available in black, OD Green, or Flat Dark Earth finish, otherwise similar to SIG M400. Mfg. 2012-2014.

	100%	98%	95%	90%	80%	70%	60%	Last MSR
	$1,200	$1,075	$925	$850	$700	$575	$450	$1,234

Add $66 for Flat Dark Earth finish.

* **SIG M400 Enhanced Patrol** – 5.56 NATO or .300 AAC Blackout cal., GIO, 16 in. barrel, flip up sights, 30 shot mag., polymer handguard, Black, Flat Dark Earth, OD Green (new 2015), or Muddy Girl (disc. 2015) finish. New 2014.

MSR $1,413	100%	98%	95%	90%	80%	70%	60%	
	$1,200	$1,075	$950	$825	$725	$595	$500	

Add $34 for Muddy Girl finish (disc. 2015).

* **SIG M400 Hunting** – 5.56 NATO cal., GIO, features 20 in. barrel, 1:8 twist, MOE handguard, MOE grip, optic ready, black or Mix Pine2 finish, otherwise similar to SIG M400. Mfg. 2012 only.

	100%	98%	95%	90%	80%	70%	60%	Last MSR
	$975	$875	$775	$675	$600	$550	$495	$1,099

Add $90 for Mix Pine2 finish.

* **SIG M400 Magpul** – 5.56 NATO cal., GIO, 20 in. barrel, black finish, Magpul rifle stock, MOE grip and forend. Mfg. 2014-2015.

	100%	98%	95%	90%	80%	70%	60%	Last MSR
	$1,095	$975	$850	$725	$625	$525	$425	$1,287

* **SIG M400 Predator** – 5.56 NATO or .300 AAC Blackout (new 2016) cal., GIO, 18 in. heavy match grade threaded and capped stainless steel barrel, 5 shot mag., Geissele two-stage match trigger, Hogue synthetic rubber grip stock with free float forend, flat-top upper, extended charging handle, no sights, aluminum handguard, Black finish, 7.6 lbs. New 2013.

MSR $1,446	100%	98%	95%	90%	80%	70%	60%	
	$1,225	$1,095	$950	$850	$750	$625	$525	

* **SIG M400 SWAT** – 5.56 NATO cal., GIO, 16 in. barrel, quad rail, SIG grip, M4 style buttstock, rear flip sight, 20 shot mag., black finish. Mfg. 2012 only, reintroduced 2014.

MSR $1,337	100%	98%	95%	90%	80%	70%	60%	
	$1,150	$1,015	$875	$800	$700	$575	$475	

* **SIG M400 Varmint** – 5.56 NATO cal., GIO, 22 in. heavy stainless steel barrel, 5 shot mag., match trigger. Mfg. 2014 only.

	100%	98%	95%	90%	80%	70%	60%	Last MSR
	$1,195	$1,050	$900	$800	$700	$575	$475	$1,395

* **SIG M400 Varminter** – 5.56 NATO cal., GIO, 22 in. heavy match grade stainless steel threaded and capped barrel, 5 shot mag., Geissele two-stage match trigger, Hogue rubber grip synthetic stock with free float forend, flat-top upper, extended charging handle, 8.1 lbs. Mfg. 2013-2014.

	100%	98%	95%	90%	80%	70%	60%	Last MSR
	$1,195	$1,050	$900	$800	$700	$575	$475	$1,395

SIG 516 – 5.56 NATO cal., short stroke GPO, 3 or 4 position gas valve, various configurations. New 2011.

* **SIG 516 Basic Patrol** – 5.56 NATO cal., GPO, polymer handguard and 2 Picatinny rails - one on top of receiver and the other in front of handguard, 16 in. free floating barrel with muzzle brake, Magpul stock and pistol grip, 30 shot mag. Mfg. 2011 only.

	100%	98%	95%	90%	80%	70%	60%	Last MSR
	$1,095	$950	$800	$700	$600	$500	$425	$1,252

* **SIG 516 Patrol** – 5.56 NATO or 7.62x39mm (mfg. 2012 only) cal., GPO, 16 in. free floating barrel with muzzle brake, Magpul MOE adj. stock and MOE grip, rear charging handle, free floating quad Picatinny rail, 3 position gas valve, 30 shot mag., ladder rail covers (new 2012), Pmag (new 2012), aluminum KeyMod handguard (new 2016), Black, Flat Dark Earth (new 2012) or OD Green (mfg. 2012-2015) finish. New 2011.

MSR $1,794	100%	98%	95%	90%	80%	70%	60%	
	$1,525	$1,350	$1,175	$1,000	$900	$775	$625	

Add $54 for Flat Dark Earth finish (new 2012).

* **SIG 516 Carbon Fiber** – 5.56 NATO cal., GPO, 16 in. barrel, flip-up sights, carbon fiber forend and choice of carbon fiber SIG or Rifle stock, 30 shot Lancer mag. Mfg. 2014-2015.

	100%	98%	95%	90%	80%	70%	60%	Last MSR
	$1,700	$1,495	$1,275	$1,100	$950	$825	$650	$2,004

Add $192 for carbon fiber rifle stock and forend.

* **SIG 516 SRP (Sight Ready Platform)** – 5.56 NATO cal., GPO, 16 in. barrel, 30 shot mag., aluminum handguard, Black or OD Green finish. Mfg. 2015 only.

	100%	98%	95%	90%	80%	70%	60%	Last MSR
	$1,450	$1,275	$1,095	$900	$800	$700	$600	$1,713

* **SIG 516 Sport Configuration Model (SCM)** – GPO, features fixed stock, A2 pistol grip, 10 shot mag. Mfg. 2011-2012.

	100%	98%	95%	90%	80%	70%	60%	Last MSR
	$1,375	$1,150	$1,000	$875	$750	$625	$525	$1,599

* **SIG 516 Precision Marksman** – GPO, features 18 in. free floating match barrel w/o muzzle brake, free floating quad Picatinny rail, 2 stage trigger, Magpul PRS stock, MIAD grip, 30 shot mag. Mfg. 2011-2013.

	100%	98%	95%	90%	80%	70%	60%	Last MSR
	$2,400	$2,100	$1,800	$1,625	$1,325	$1,075	$850	$2,399

MSR	100%	98%	95%	90%	80%	70%	60%	Last MSR

SIG 522 – .22 LR cal., 16 in. barrel, blowback action, 10 or 25 shot mag., black polymer lower receiver, folding/telescopic or non-folding Swiss style (disc.) stock, polymer (w/rail kit) or aluminum forend, flash suppressor, approx. 6 1/2 lbs. Mfg. 2009-2015.

Add $199 for mini red dot sight (disc. 2012).
Add $53 for non-folding stock (disc.).
Add $222 for rotary rear sight (disc. 2009).
Add $210 for Harris bipod (disc. 2010).
Add $66 (Variable Power) or $106 (Prismatic Scope) with polymer handguards and telescopic stock (mfg. 2011 only).

* **SIG 522 Classic** – .22 LR cal., 16 in. barrel, features folding/telescopic stock, polymer handguards, rail kit, 10 or 25 shot mag. Disc. 2015.

	100%	98%	95%	90%	80%	70%	60%	Last MSR
	$485	$425	$365	$330	$275	$225	$200	$570

* **SIG 522 Classic SWAT** – .22 LR cal., 16.6 in. barrel, features folding/telescopic stock, aluminum quad rail, 10 or 25 shot mag. Disc. 2015.

	100%	98%	95%	90%	80%	70%	60%	Last MSR
	$665	$585	$500	$450	$375	$300	$250	$776

* **SIG 522 Commando** – .22 LR cal., 16 in. barrel, polymer handguard, folding/telescopic stock, tactical training suppressor, rail kit. Mfg. 2011-2015.

	100%	98%	95%	90%	80%	70%	60%	Last MSR
	$565	$495	$425	$385	$310	$250	$225	$662

* **SIG 522 Commando SWAT** – .22 LR cal., quad rail handguard, folding/telescopic stock, tactical training suppressor. Mfg. 2012 only.

	100%	98%	95%	90%	80%	70%	60%	Last MSR
	$625	$550	$475	$400	$350	$300	$275	$707

* **SIG 522 Field** – .22 LR cal., 20 in. barrel, folding/telescopic stock, polymer handguard, rail kit, 10 shot mag. Mfg. 2012-2014.

	100%	98%	95%	90%	80%	70%	60%	Last MSR
	$465	$415	$365	$335	$300	$275	$250	$534

* **SIG 522 Target** – .22 LR cal., 20 in. barrel, Hogue free floating forend, folding/telescopic stock, variable power scope, 10 shot mag. Mfg. 2012-2015.

	100%	98%	95%	90%	80%	70%	60%	Last MSR
	$725	$635	$550	$475	$400	$325	$300	$856

SIG 551A1 – 5.56 NATO cal., GPO, 16 in. barrel, rotary bolt, utilizes original Swiss 550-style 20 or 30 shot translucent mags., black polymer folding skeletonized stock and forearm that surrounds barrel, gray finish, post front sights, adj. rotary diopter drum rear sight, two-stage trigger, top accessory rail, 7 lbs. Mfg. 2012-2014.

	100%	98%	95%	90%	80%	70%	60%	Last MSR
	$1,450	$1,300	$1,100	$925	$800	$675	$550	$1,599

SIG 556 CLASSIC – 5.56 NATO cal., GPO, rotary bolt, 16 in. barrel with muzzle brake, alloy trigger housing, polymer forearm or choice of SIG quad-rail (SWAT Model) or tri-rail, integrated Picatinny rails, two-stage trigger, collapsible or collapsible/folding tube stock, Magpul CTR Carbine stock type (SWAT) or M4 style stock (556ER or 556 Holo), 30 shot AR-15 type mag., 7.8-8.7 lbs. Mfg. 2007-2013.

	100%	98%	95%	90%	80%	70%	60%	Last MSR
	$1,265	$1,110	$950	$850	$700	$575	$450	$1,266

Add $133 for quad-rail system (Classic SWAT Model).
Add $45 for Holo model with holographic sight (disc. 2009).
Add $150 for collapsible stock with GLR and Stoplite (disc. 2009).
Add $306 for Classic 16 with adj. folding stock and red dot sight (disc. 2009).
Add $456 for Classic 17 with adj. folding stock and rotary sight (disc. 2009).
Add $300 for 16 in. barrel with GLR and Stoplite (disc. 2009).
Subtract $200 if w/o iron sights (became standard 2008).

* **SIG 556R** – 7.62x39mm cal., GPO, 16 in. barrel, polymer handguards or aluminum quad rail (mfg. 2012 only) forend, folding/telescopic (mfg. 2011 only), or Swiss style (new 2012) stock, mini red dot sight, 5 (Hunting Model, mfg. 2012 only) or 30 shot AK type mag. Mfg. 2011-2013.

	100%	98%	95%	90%	80%	70%	60%	Last MSR
	$1,330	$1,175	$1,000	$900	$750	$600	$475	$1,332

Add $34 for Hunting Model (mfg. 2012 only).
Add $133 for aluminum quad rail (mfg. 2012 only).

* **SIG 556 DMR** – 5.56 NATO cal., GPO, similar to Model 556, except has 18 in. heavy barrel w/o sights, adj. Magpul PRS stock, vented synthetic forearm, Picatinny rail on bottom of forearm and top of receiver, includes tactical bipod, 12 lbs. Mfg. 2008-2013.

	100%	98%	95%	90%	80%	70%	60%	Last MSR
	$1,730	$1,525	$1,300	$1,175	$950	$775	$600	$1,732

* **SIG 556 Patrol** – 5.56 NATO cal., GPO, similar to SIG 556, 16 in. barrel, 30 shot mag., steel upper receiver, choice of polymer (Patrol) or alloy quad rail (Patrol SWAT) forend, black anodized finish, A2 flash suppressor, folding collapsible Swiss style stock, rotary diopter sight, 7 1/2 lbs. Mfg. 2010-2013.

	100%	98%	95%	90%	80%	70%	60%	Last MSR
	$1,265	$1,110	$950	$850	$700	$575	$450	$1,266

Add $133 for SWAT model with quad rail forend.

MSR	100%	98%	95%	90%	80%	70%	60%	Last MSR

* SIG 556 xi Patrol Swat – 5.56mm NATO cal., GPO, 16 in. barrel, steel receiver with M1913 rail, flip-up front and rear sights, M1913 quad rail forend, removable barrel, ambi safety, ambi mag. release, Swiss style stock. Mfg. 2012 only.

	$1,295	$1,125	$1,000	$875	$750	$625	$475	*$1,424*

SIG 556xi – 5.56 NATO (AR-15 style), 7.62x39mm (AK-47 design), or .300 AAC Blackout (AR-15 style, mfg. 2014 only) cal., GPO, 16 in. barrel, flip-up sights, 30 shot mag., polymer handguard, folding stock, black finish. New 2014.

MSR $1,522	$1,295	$1,165	$1,015	$900	$800	$675	$525	

Add $141 for 7.62x39mm cal.

Add $133 for .300 AAC Blackout cal. (mfg. 2014 only).

SIG 556xi SWAT – 5.56 NATO (AR-15 style) or 7.62x39mm (AK-47 design) cal., GPO, 16 in. barrel, 30 shot mag., lock sights, folding stock, aluminum handguard, black finish. New 2015.

MSR $1,663	$1,415	$1,250	$1,075	$965	$835	$695	$550	

Add $131 for 7.62x39mm cal.

SIG 556/P226 MATCHED PAIR – 5.56 NATO/9mm Para. cals., GPO, includes matched set of Desert Digital Special Editions of SIG 556 ER folding stock and P226 pistol. Both rifle and pistol have unique matching serial numbers, includes Pelican hard carry case in Flat Dark Earth, certificate of authenticity. Limited production run of 1,500 sets. Mfg. 2012.

Retail pricing was not established on this set.

SIG 716 DMR (DESIGNATED MARKSMAN) – 7.62 NATO cal., short stroke pushrod operating system with 4 position gas valve, 16 in. free floating barrel, 2-stage match trigger, Magpul PMag., aluminum forend, Magpul UBR stock and MIAD grip, Picatinny rail, Black (mfg. 2015 only) or Flat Dark Earth (new 2016) furniture, 12.3 lbs. New 2015.

MSR $2,963	$2,600	$2,225	$1,925	$1,775	$1,450	$1,225	$1,000	

SIG 716 PATROL – 7.62 NATO cal., GPO, 16 in. barrel, 20 shot mag., MagPul ACS stock and MIAD grip, quad rail, Black, Flat Dark Earth, or OD Green (disc. 2015) finish. New 2011.

MSR $2,283	$1,965	$1,745	$1,525	$1,350	$1,150	$925	$750	

Add $55 for Flat Dark Earth finish (new 2012).

SIG 716 PRECISION MARKSMAN – 7.62 NATO cal., 18 in. barrel, short stroke GPO, four position gas valve, threaded muzzle, upper and lower rails, two-stage Geissele match trigger, MIAD grip, Magpul UBR stock, matte black finish, 20 shot PMag., bipod, folding back up iron sights, 11 lbs. Mfg. 2013 only.

	$2,250	$1,975	$1,695	$1,525	$1,240	$1,015	$795	*$2,666*

SIG SCM – 5.56 NATO cal., GIO, 16 in. barrel, 10 shot mag., steel upper receiver, polymer forend with lower accessory rail, Holo sight, aluminum lower, target crowned muzzle, A2 fixed stock, Picatinny top rail, approx. 8 lbs. Mfg. 2010-2011.

	$1,075	$950	$825	$725	$625	$525	$425	*$1,191*

SIG SCM 22 – .22 LR cal., 18 in. barrel, choice of polymer handguard, or aluminum quad rail, blow-back operating system, adj. iron sights, fixed stock, 10 shot mag. Mfg. 2011 only.

	$525	$450	$395	$350	$300	$275	$250	*$587*

Add $103 for aluminum quad rail.

SIG MCX – 5.56 NATO or .300 AAC Blackout cal., 16 in. barrel, 30 shot mag., KeyMod aluminum handguard, folding iron sights, thin folding stock, black anodized or Flat Dark Earth (new 2016) finish, 5.6 lbs. New 2015.

MSR $1,903	$1,610	$1,400	$1,200	$1,000	$900	$775	$625	

Add $272 for conversion kit.

SIG MPX – 9mm Para. cal., converts to .357 SIG or .40 S&W cal., closed, fully locked short stroke pushrod gas system, 16 in. free-float barrel with permanently attached muzzle brake, 30 shot mag., ambidextrous magazine release, MPX Reflex sight, telescoping or folding stock, pistol grip, ambidextrous safety selector, extended carbon fiber rail adaptable handguard (disc. 2015) or aluminum KeyMod handguard (new 2016), monolithic upper receiver with integral M1913 rail, AR-style controls, rear charging handle, matte black finish. New mid-2013.

MSR $1,957	$1,650	$1,450	$1,250	$1,050	$925	$750	$650	

SINO DEFENSE MANUFACTURING (SDM)

Current manufacturer of carbines/rifles and distributed exclusively by Prima Armi located in Pinerolo, Italy. No current U.S. importation.

SDM manufactures AR-15 style and AK-47 design rifles and carbines. Additionally, the company also makes a Dragunov and Mauser 98 style carbine, including a sniper variation. Please contact the company directly for more information, including U.S. availability and pricing (see Trademark Index).

MSR	100%	98%	95%	90%	80%	70%	60%	Last MSR

SIONICS WEAPON SYSTEMS

Current rifle manufacturer located in Tucson, AZ.

CARBINES/RIFLES: SEMI-AUTO, AR-15 STYLE

Sionics Weapon Systems also manufactures NFA items. Current models include Patrol SBR II, and Patrol SBR III. Please contact the company directly for more information and pricing (see Trademark Index).

PATROL LW-ENHANCED – 5.56 NATO cal., GIO, 16 in. lightweight Melonite barrel with A2 flash suppressor, M4 upper and forged aluminum lower receiver, mid-length gas system, Vltor Gun Fighter charging handle, ALG Defense QMS trigger, Vltor 5-pos. receiver extension, "H" buffer, Midwest Industries SSK 12 in. KeyMod handguard, B5 Systems Bravo stock, Ergo grip, 5 lbs. 9 oz. Disc. 2015.
   Retail pricing was not made available for this model.

PATROL RIFLE 0 – 5.56 NATO cal., 16 in. medium contour barrel with A2 flash suppressor, forged M4 upper and aluminum lower receiver, mid-length gas system, F-marked front sight base, Magpul MBUS rear sight, Vltor Gun Fighter charging handle, ALG Defense QMS trigger, Vltor 5-pos. receiver extension, carbine H buffer, Magpul MOE handguard, Ergo grip, Vltor IMOD stock, 6 lbs. 13 oz. New 2015.

MSR	100%	98%	95%	90%	80%	70%	60%
MSR $1,200	$1,025	$925	$800	$685	$595	$515	$440

PATROL RIFLE I – 5.56 NATO cal., GIO, 16 in. medium weight chrome lined barrel, A2 flash suppressor, 9 in. free-floating quad rail handguard, forged aluminum lower and upper receivers, M4 feed ramps, mid-length gas system, F-marked front sight base, Vltor Gun Fighter charging handle, ALG Defense QMS trigger, Carbine H buffer, Vltor 5-pos. receiver extension, Ergo grip, Vltor IMOD stock, 7 lbs.

MSR	100%	98%	95%	90%	80%	70%	60%
MSR $1,480	$1,250	$1,100	$985	$835	$725	$615	$515

PATROL RIFLE II – 5.56 NATO cal., GIO, 16 in. medium weight chrome lined barrel, A2 flash suppressor, 30 shot Magpul PMag., M4 upper receiver, mid-length gas system, Vltor Gun Fighter charging handle, forged aluminum lower, ALG Defense QMS trigger, Vltor 5-pos. receiver extension, Carbine H buffer, 12 in. free-floating quad rail handguard, Ergo grip, Vltor IMOD stock, 7 lbs.

MSR	100%	98%	95%	90%	80%	70%	60%
MSR $1,560	$1,325	$1,165	$1,050	$915	$785	$665	$550

PATROL RIFLE II PRO – 5.56 NATO cal., similar to Patrol Rifle II, except has 12 in. free float quad rail handguard and low profile gas block. Disc. 2013.

100%	98%	95%	90%	80%	70%	60%	Last MSR
$1,425	$1,250	$1,115	$985	$840	$725	$590	*$1,669*

PATROL RIFLE III – 5.56 NATO cal., GIO, 16 in. medium weight chrome lined barrel with A2 flash suppressor, 30 shot Magpul mag., mid-length gas system, M4 upper receiver, forged aluminum lower, single stage LE (disc.) or ALG Defense QMS trigger, "H" buffer, nickel treated M16 bolt carrier, 12.37 in. free floating "slick side" Samson EVO rail handguard, low profile gas block, Vltor Gun Fighter charging handle, Magpul MOE or Vltor IMOD stock, Magpul MOE or Ergo grip, 6 lbs. 6 oz.

MSR	100%	98%	95%	90%	80%	70%	60%
MSR $1,430	$1,215	$1,085	$965	$815	$715	$600	$500

   * *Patrol Rifle III XL* – 5.56 NATO cal., similar to Patrol Rifle III, except has 15 in. free floating Samson EVO rail handguard, 6 lbs. 8 oz.

MSR	100%	98%	95%	90%	80%	70%	60%
MSR $1,460	$1,240	$1,100	$985	$835	$725	$615	$515

PATROL RIFLE MK2 – 5.56 NATO cal., GIO, 16 in. medium contour barrel with A2 flash suppressor, mid-length gas system, forged M4 upper, forged aluminum lower, nickel plated bolt carrier group, Vltor Gun Fighter charging handle, ALG Defense QMS trigger, Vltor 5-pos. receiver extension, "H" buffer, 13 in. Geissele SMR MK2 rail handguard, Vltor IMOD stock, Ergo grip, 6 lbs. 13 oz. Disc. 2015.

100%	98%	95%	90%	80%	70%	60%	Last MSR
$975	$885	$765	$655	$575	$495	$435	*$1,150*

PATROL SSK-12/SSK-15 – 5.56 NATO cal., GIO, 16 in. barrel with A2 flash suppressor, M4 upper and forged aluminum lower receiver, 30 shot Magpul mag., low profile gas block, ALG Defense QMS trigger, "H" buffer, 12 (SSK-12) or 15 (SSK-15) in. SSK-KeyMod free-float handguard rail, Magpul MOE stock, Ergo grip. Disc. 2015.

100%	98%	95%	90%	80%	70%	60%	Last MSR
$895	$785	$685	$600	$535	$465	$415	*$1,070*

   Add $20 for 15 in. KeyMod rail.

PERIMETER MARKSMAN RIFLE – 5.56 NATO cal., GIO, 18 1/2 in. stainless steel chrome lined barrel, M4 upper receiver, Magpul MBUS front and rear sight, Sionics muzzle brake, nickel plated bolt carrier and key, heavy extractor spring, forged aluminum lower receiver, single stage LE trigger, 30 shot Magpul mag., standard rifle buffer, ACE skeleton stock, Magpul MOE grip, free floating 15 inch rail EVO handguard, low profile gas block, includes soft case. Disc. 2014.

100%	98%	95%	90%	80%	70%	60%	Last MSR
$1,450	$1,275	$1,125	$1,000	$850	$735	$595	*$1,709*

MSR	100%	98%	95%	90%	80%	70%	60%	Last MSR

SHADES OF GRAY PATROL LIGHTWEIGHT – 5.56 NATO cal., GIO, 16 in. lightweight barrel with A2 flash suppressor, M4 upper, forged aluminum lower, ALG Defense QMS trigger, 6-pos. Mil-Spec receiver extension, "H" buffer, 30 shot Magpul mag., 15 in. SSK-KeyMod free-float handguard, low profile gas block, mid-length gas system, Magpul MOE K2 grip in Stealth Gray, Magpul MOE SL stock in Stealth Gray. Mfg. 2015 only.

	$1,100	$995	$875	$735	$650	$550	$465	$1,320

SIRKIS INDUSTRIES, LTD.

Previous manufacturer located in Ramat-Gan, Israel. Previously imported and distributed by Armscorp of America, Inc. located in Baltimore, MD.

RIFLES

MODEL 36 SNIPER RIFLE – .308 Win. cal. only, gas operated action, carbon fiber stock, 22 in. barrel, flash suppressor, free range sights. Disc. 1985.

	$670	$580	$520	$475	$430	$390	$350	$760

SISK RIFLES LLC

Current rifle manufacturer located in Dayton, TX.

RIFLES: BOLT ACTION

Charlie Sisk builds high quality bolt action rifles per individual customer specifications. The STAR (Sisk Tactical Adaptive Rifle) has a base price of $6,495. Hunting models start at $5,600. A wide variety of options and accessories are available. Please contact the company directly for more information, including availability, delivery time, pricing and options (see Trademark Index).

SKORPION

Current semi-auto or select-fire pistol model manufactured in the Czech Republic. Currently imported by Czechpoint, Inc. located in Knoxville, TN beginning 2010. CZ USA purchased the VZ 61 Skorpions from Czechpoint between 2009-2010.

PISTOLS: SEMI-AUTO

SA VZ. 61 SCORPION (SKORPION) – .32 ACP, .380 ACP, or 9mm Makarov cal., semi-auto copy of VZ 61 Skorpion submachine gun, blue or nickel finish, SA, forward charging knob, steel frame, 4.52 in. barrel, 20 shot mag., hardwood grips, flip up rear sight, lanyard rings, wood or polymer grips, 41 oz.

MSR $595		$500	$440	$375	$340	$275	$225	$175

Add $20 for .380 ACP or 9mm Makarov cal.

SMITH & WESSON

Current manufacturer located in Springfield, MA, 1857 to date. Partnership with Horace Smith & Daniel B. Wesson 1856-1874. Family owned by Wesson 1874-1965. S&W became a subsidiary of Bangor-Punta from 1965-1983. Between 1983-1987, Smith & Wesson was owned by the Lear Siegler Co. On May 22, 1987, Smith & Wesson was sold to R.L. Tomkins, an English holding company. During 2001, Tomkins sold Smith & Wesson to Saf-T-Hammer, an Arizona-based safety and security company. Smith & Wesson was the primary distributor for most Walther firearms and accessories in the United States from 2002-2012. During 2012, Carl Walther GmbH Sportwaffen and Umarex announced the formation of Walther Arms, Inc. to import, sell, and market all Walther products in the U.S. beginning Jan. 1, 2013.

Smith & Wessons have been classified under the following category names - PISTOLS: LEVER ACTION, ANTIQUE, TIP-UPS, TOP-BREAKS, SINGLE SHOTS, EARLY HAND EJECTORS (Named Models), NUMBERED MODEL REVOLVERS (Modern Hand Ejectors), SEMI-AUTOS, RIFLES, and SHOTGUNS.

Each category is fairly self-explanatory. Among the early revolvers, Tip-ups have barrels that tip up so the cylinder can be removed for loading or unloading, whereas Top-breaks have barrels & cylinders that tip down with automatic ejection.

Hand Ejectors are the modern type revolvers with swing out cylinders. In 1957, S&W began a system of numbering all models they made. Accordingly, the Hand Ejectors have been divided into two sections - the Early Hand Ejectors include the named models introduced prior to 1958. The Numbered Model Revolvers are the models introduced or continued after that date, and are easily identified by the model number stamped on the side of the frame, visible when the cylinder is open. The author wishes to express his thanks to Mr. Sal Raimondi, Jim Supica, Rick Nahas, and Roy Jinks, the S&W Historian, for their updates and valuable contributions.

Factory special orders, such as ivory or pearl grips, special finishes, engraving, and other production rarities will add premiums to the values listed. After 1893, all ivory and pearl grips had the metal S&W logo medallions inserted on top.

FACTORY LETTER OF AUTHENTICITY - S&W charges $50 for a formal letter of authenticity. A form is available for downloading on their website: www.smith-wesson.com for this service. Turnaround time is usually 8-12 weeks.

For more information and current pricing on both new and used Smith & Wesson airguns, please refer to the *Blue Book of Airguns* by Dr. Robert Beeman & John Allen (also online).

MSR	100%	98%	95%	90%	80%	70%	60%	Last MSR

REVOLVERS: NUMBERED MODEL/RECENT MFG. (MODERN HAND EJECTORS)

Smith & Wesson handguns manufactured after 1957 are stamped with a model number on the frame under the cylinder yoke. The number is visible when the cylinder is open. All revolvers manufactured by S&W from 1946-1956 were produced without model numbers.

To locate a particular revolver in the following section, simply swing the cylinder out to the loading position and read the model number inside the yoke. The designation Mod. and a two- or three-digit number followed by a dash and another number designates which engineering change was underway when the gun was manufactured. Hence, a Mod. 15-7 is a Model 15 in its 7th engineering change (and should be indicated as such when ordering parts). Usually, earlier variations are the most desirable to collectors unless a particular improvement is rare.

Some models might have a few engineering changes listed, and that's because their values are different. However, if engineering changes are not listed individually, it means that the values are the same as for those without. Hence a Model 19-6 (.357 Combat Magnum) that's not listed simply means that its value is the same as an earlier variation, in this case, the Model 19-3.

Beginning 1994, S&W started providing synthetic grips and a drilled/tapped receiver for scope mounting on certain models.

S&W revolvers are generally categorized by frame size. Frame sizes are as follows: J-frame (small), K-frame (medium), L-frame (medium), N-frame (large), and X-frame (extra large). All currently manufactured S&W revolvers chambered for .38 S&W Spl. cal. will also accept +P rated ammunition.

Current S&W abbreviations for revolver feature codes used on its price sheets and literature are as follows: Grips: CTG - Crimson Trace laser grips, RG - rubber grips, WG - wood grips. Sights: ADJ - adjustable, ADJV - adjustable V-notch, BB - black blade, DWD - dovetail white dot, INTCH - interchangeable front, FIX - fixed, FO - fiber optic, GB - gold bead front, INTEG - integral front, PAT - Patridge front, NS - night sight, RR - red ramp front, SN - square notch, WB - white bead, and WO - white outline. Frame Material: AL - alloy, SS - stainless, CS - carbon steel. Frame Sizes: SM - Small/Compact, MD - Medium, LG - Large, XL - Extra Large. Older finish abbreviations include: ZB - Blue/Black, ZC - Clear Cote, ZG - Grey, ZM - Matte, ZS - Satin. Cylinder: CA - alloy, CC - carbon, CS - stainless, CT - titanium. Barrel: BF - full lug, BO - one piece, BP - PowerPort, BT - traditional, B2 - two piece. Action: DAO - double action only, SA/DA - single action/double action. Older finish abbreviations include: ZB - Blue/Black, ZC - Clear Cote, ZG - Grey, ZM - Matte, ZS - Satin. Cylinder: CA - alloy, CC - carbon, CS - stainless, CT - titanium.

Pre-2010 S&W abbreviations for revolver feature codes used on its price sheets and literature are as follows: Grips: GC - Crimson Trace laser grips, GR - rubber grips, GW - wood grips, GF - finger groove grips. Sights: SA - adj., SB - black blade front, SC - interchangeable front, SF - fixed, SG - gold bead front, SH - Hi-Viz, SI - integral front, SP - Patridge front, SN - front night, SR - red ramp front, SW - white outline adj. rear. Frame Material: FA - alloy, FS - stainless, FC - carbon.

During 2009, S&W started manufacture of the Classic Firearms series of revolvers. These guns incorporate many features of S&W's older and most famous/collectible revolvers, but have also been enhanced with modern engineering changes. This series is referred to as Classic or Classics in the model nomenclature, as opposed to Classic which indicates standard production S&W models and nomenclature.

Add 15%-20% for those models listed that are pinned and recessed (pre-1981 mfg.), if in 90% or better condition, or 10%-15% if condition is 60%-80%.

Earlier mfg. on the following models with lower engineering change numbered suffixes are more desirable than later mfg. (i.e., a Model 10-1 is more desirable than a Model 10-14).

Factory error stamped revolvers generally bring a small premium (5%-10%, if in 95%+ original condition) over a non-error gun, if the right collector is found.

N/As listed instead of values in this section indicate the value in that condition factor is not available. Since asking prices do fluctuate greatly in these higher condition factors, it is impossible to accurately ascertain a single value.

BODYGUARD 38 – .38 Spl. + P cal., 5 shot, DAO, 1.9 in barrel, small J-frame, internal hammer, aluminum alloy upper frame, steel reinforced polymer lower frame, stainless steel cylinder, ambidextrous cylinder release, fixed sights with Crimson Trace laser module next to cylinder latch behind the recoil shield, and activated with thumb, round butt with integrated black polymer grips, matte black finish, 14.3 oz. New late 2010.

MSR $539	$445	$395	$360	$320	$285	$260	$240	

GOVERNOR – .45 LC/.410 shotshell or .45 ACP/.410 shotshell, 2 1/2 in. shotshell, new Z-frame, 2 3/4 in. barrel, 6 shot, SA/DA, Tritium night front sight, fixed rear sight, Scandium alloy frame with stainless steel cylinder, matte black finish, black synthetic finger groove or Crimson Trace Laser grips, 29.6 oz. New 2011.

MSR $869	$695	$595	$475	$400	$350	$300	$275	

Add $310 for Crimson Trace laser grips.

MODEL 310 NIGHTGUARD – 10mm or .40 S&W cal., 2 1/2 in. barrel, matte black finish, Scandium alloy N-frame with stainless steel cylinder, 6 shot, SA/DA, XS 24/7 standard dot Tritium night front sight, fixed rear sight, Pachmayr grips, 28 oz. Mfg. 2009-2010.

	$895	$685	$530	$425	$350	$300	$275	*$1,185*

MODEL 315 NIGHTGUARD – .38 Spl. + P cal., 2 1/2 in. barrel, K-frame, blue/black finish, 6 shot, rubber grips, front night sight, fixed rear sight, alloy frame with stainless cylinder. Mfg. 2009 only. Scarce.

	$1,150	$1,000	$865	$775	$635	$525	$400	*$995*

MSR	100%	98%	95%	90%	80%	70%	60%	Last MSR

MODEL 325 PD-AIRLITE Sc – .45 ACP cal., 2 1/2 (disc. 2006) or 4 in. barrel, otherwise similar to Model 329 PD, approx. 21 1/2 - 25 oz. Mfg. 2004-2007.

| | $800 | $625 | $485 | $400 | $335 | $300 | $275 | *$1,067* |

MODEL 325 NIGHTGUARD – .45 ACP cal., two-piece 2 1/2 in. barrel, alloy frame with stainless steel cylinder, black alloy finish, 6 shot, N-frame, SA/DA, rubber grips, fixed rear sight with front night sight, 28 oz. Mfg. 2008-2012.

| | $825 | $650 | $525 | $425 | $350 | $300 | $275 | *$1,049* |

MODEL 327 PD-AIRLITE Sc – .357 Mag. cal., 8 shot, N-frame, 4 in. two-piece barrel, wood grips, Scandium frame with titanium cylinder, matte black finish, 26 1/2 oz. Mfg. 2008-2009.

| | $950 | $725 | $550 | $450 | $350 | $315 | $285 | *$1,264* |

MODEL 327 NIGHTGUARD – .357 Mag. cal., two-piece 2 1/2 in. barrel, alloy frame with stainless steel cylinder, black alloy finish, 8 shot, N-frame, SA/DA, rubber grips, fixed rear sight with front night sight, 27.6 oz. Mfg. 2008-2012.

| | $825 | $650 | $525 | $425 | $350 | $300 | $275 | *$1,049* |

MODEL 329 PD-AIRLITE Sc – .44 Mag. cal., 4 in. barrel, N-frame, 6 shot, Scandium frame and titanium cylinder with matte black metal finish, wood Ahrends grips with finger grooves, and Hogue rubber monogrip, Hi-Viz front sight, approx. 26 oz. New 2003.

| MSR $1,159 | $915 | $715 | $550 | $450 | $375 | $325 | $300 | |

MODEL 329 NIGHTGUARD – .44 Mag. cal., two-piece 2 1/2 in. barrel, alloy frame with stainless steel cylinder, black alloy finish, 6 shot, N-frame, SA/DA, rubber grips, fixed rear sight with front night sight, 29.3 oz. Mfg. 2008-2012.

| | $825 | $650 | $525 | $425 | $350 | $300 | $275 | *$1,049* |

MODEL 337 AIRLITE Ti CHIEFS SPECIAL – .38 S&W Spl.+P cal., J-frame, 5 shot, 1 7/8 in. barrel, similar design as the Model 331, 11.9 oz. Mfg. 1999-2003.

| | $675 | $595 | $500 | $460 | $370 | $300 | $235 | *$716* |

Add $24 for Dymondwood Boot grips (mfg. 1999 only).

MODEL 340 AIRLITE Sc CENTENNIAL – .357 Mag. cal., J-frame, 5 shot, 1 7/8 in. barrel only, Scandium alloy frame, barrel shroud, and yoke, titanium cylinder, two-tone matte stainless/grey finish, hammerless, Hogue Bantam grips, 12 oz. Mfg. 2001-2008.

| | $775 | $575 | $475 | $400 | $340 | $295 | $250 | *$1,019* |

MODEL 340 PD AIRLITE Sc (CENTENNIAL) – similar to Model 340 Airlite Sc, except has black/grey finish, Hi-Viz sight became standard 2009, also available with no internal lock (new 2011), "PD" marked, 12 oz. New 2000.

| MSR $1,019 | $795 | $625 | $500 | $400 | $340 | $295 | $250 | |

MODEL 340 M & P (CENTENNIAL) – .357 Mag. cal., 5 shot, J-frame, DAO, concealed hammer, 1 7/8 in. barrel, includes XS sights (24/7 Tritium night and integral U-notch), Scandium alloy frame with stainless steel cylinder, also available with no internal lock (new 2011), matte black finish, synthetic or Crimson Trace laser grips, "M&P" marked, 13.3 oz. New 2007.

| MSR $869 | $695 | $595 | $475 | $400 | $350 | $300 | $275 | |

Add $260 for Crimson Trace laser grips.

MODEL 342 AIRLITE Ti CENTENNIAL – .38 S&W Spl.+P cal., similar to Model 337, except is hammerless and double action only, matte stainless/grey finish, Uncle Mike's Boot grips, 12 oz. Mfg. 1999-2003.

| | $575 | $445 | $390 | $345 | $310 | $280 | $250 | *$734* |

Add $24 for Dymondwood Boot grips (mfg. 1999 only).

MODEL 342 PD AIRLITE Ti CENTENNIAL – .38 S&W Spl.+P cal., J-frame, 5 shot, double action only, aluminum alloy frame with titanium cylinder and stainless steel 1 7/8 in. barrel, hammerless, black/grey finish, "PD" marked, Hogue Bantam grips, 10.8 oz. Mfg. 2000-2003.

| | $595 | $460 | $390 | $340 | $310 | $280 | $250 | *$758* |

MODEL 351 PD AIRLITE Sc (CHIEFS SPECIAL) – .22 MRF (.22 WMR) cal., J-frame, 1 7/8 in. two-piece barrel, 7 shot, black finish, aluminum alloy frame and cylinder, wood grips, 10.6 oz. New 2004.

| MSR $759 | $575 | $495 | $400 | $350 | $300 | $275 | $225 | |

MODEL 357 PD – .41 Rem. Mag. cal., 6 shot, 4 in. two piece barrel, N frame, Scandium alloy frame with titanium cylinder, matte black finish, Ahrends wood grips with finger grooves, Hi-Viz front sight, adj. V-notch rear sight, 27 1/2 oz. Mfg. mid-2005-2007.

| | $815 | $575 | $475 | $400 | $340 | $300 | $275 | *$1,067* |

MSR	100%	98%	95%	90%	80%	70%	60%	*Last MSR*

MODEL 357 NIGHTGUARD – .41 Mag. cal., 2 1/2 in. barrel, N-frame, matte black metal finish, 6 shot, black synthetic grips, alloy frame with stainless steel cylinder, fixed rear sight, front night sight, 29.7 oz. Mfg. 2010 only.

| | $895 | $685 | $530 | $425 | $350 | $300 | $275 | *$1,185* |

MODEL 360 AIRLITE Sc CHIEFS SPECIAL – .357 Mag. cal., J-frame, 5 shot, 1 7/8 in. two piece barrel, Scandium alloy frame with titanium cylinder, matte stainless/grey finish, Hogue Bantam grips, fixed sights, 12 oz. Mfg. 2001-2007.

| | $775 | $575 | $475 | $400 | $340 | $295 | $250 | *$1,019* |

MODEL 360 PD AIRLITE Sc (CHIEFS SPECIAL) – .357 Mag. or .38 Spl. + P cal., J-frame, similar to Model 360 Airlite Sc Chiefs Special, except has matte stainless/grey finish, "PD" marked, Hi-Viz sight became standard 2009, 12 oz. New 2002.

| MSR $1,019 | $850 | $675 | $525 | $400 | $340 | $295 | $250 | |

MODEL 360 M & P (CHIEFS SPECIAL) – .357 Mag. cal., 5 shot, J-frame, SA/DA, 1 7/8 in. barrel, includes XS sights (24/7 Tritium night and integral U-notch), Scandium alloy frame with stainless steel cylinder, matte black finish, synthetic grips, M&P marked, 13.3 oz. Mfg. 2007-2012.

| | $725 | $600 | $475 | $350 | $300 | $250 | $225 | *$869* |

MODEL 386 AIRLITE Sc MOUNTAIN LITE – .357 Mag. cal., L-frame, 7 shot, 2 1/2 (new 2007) or 3 1/8 (disc. 2006) in. two piece stainless steel barrel with adj. rear and Hi-Viz front sight, Scandium alloy frame with titanium cylinder, two-tone matte stainless/grey finish, Hogue Bantam grips, 18 1/2 oz. Mfg. 2001-2007.

| | $650 | $510 | $420 | $365 | $325 | $295 | $265 | *$869* |

MODEL 386 PD AIRLITE Sc – .357 Mag. cal., L-frame, 7 shot, 2 1/2 in. stainless barrel with adj. black rear sight, Scandium alloy frame with titanium cylinder, black/grey finish, Hogue Bantam grips, 17 1/2 oz. Mfg. 2001-2005.

| | $665 | $500 | $415 | $355 | $315 | $285 | $250 | *$872* |

Add $22 for Hi-Viz front sight (disc. 2005).

MODEL 386 Sc/S – .357 Mag. cal., L-frame, 7 shot, 2 1/2 in. barrel, synthetic finger groove grips, matte black finish, Scandium alloy frame with stainless steel cylinder, red ramp front sight, adj. rear sight, 21.2 oz. Mfg. mid-2007-2008.

| | $775 | $600 | $475 | $385 | $335 | $295 | $265 | *$948* |

MODEL 386 NIGHTGUARD – .357 Mag. cal., two-piece 2 1/2 in. barrel, alloy frame with stainless cylinder, black alloy finish, 7 shot, L-frame, SA/DA, rubber grips, fixed rear sight with front night sight, 24 1/2 oz. Mfg. 2008-2012.

| | $750 | $595 | $500 | $450 | $400 | $350 | $325 | *$979* |

MODEL 396 AIRLITE Ti MOUNTAIN LITE – .44 S&W Spl. cal., L-frame, 5 shot, 3 1/8 in. two piece barrel, adj. rear and Hi-Viz front sight, aluminum alloy frame with titanium cylinder, matte stainless/grey finish, Hogue Bantam grips, 18 oz. Mfg. 2001-2004.

| | $625 | $475 | $400 | $355 | $315 | $285 | $250 | *$812* |

There has been one engineering change to this model.

MODEL 396 NIGHTGUARD – .44 Spl. cal., two-piece 2 1/2 in. barrel, alloy frame with stainless steel cylinder, black alloy finish, 5 shot, L-frame, SA/DA, rubber grips, fixed rear sight with front night sight, 24.2 oz. Mfg. 2008-2009.

| | $825 | $650 | $550 | $475 | $425 | $375 | $335 | *$1,074* |

MODEL 637 AIRWEIGHT (CHIEFS SPECIAL) – .38 S&W Spl.+P cal., J-frame, 5 shot, matte finish, alloy frame with 1 7/8 (current mfg.), 2 1/8 (PowerPort only, disc.), or 2 1/2 full lug (mfg. 2010 only) in. satin stainless steel barrel and cylinder, current production uses Uncle Mike's Boot, Crimson Trace Laser (new 2005), or pink (new 2012) grips, 15 oz., 560 mfg. during 1991, reintroduced 1996.

| MSR $469 | $355 | $315 | $275 | $225 | $190 | $170 | $150 | |

Add $20 for pink grips (new 2012).
Add $16 for Carry Combo configuration (mfg. 2004-2008).
Add $230 for Crimson Trace laser grips (new 2005).
Add $70 for Red LaserMax (new 2016).
Add $50 for 2 1/2 in. full lug barrel (mfg. 2010 only).
Add $142 for 2 1/8 in. barrel with PowerPort (Pro Series, mfg. 2009-2010).

MODEL 638 AIRWEIGHT (BODYGUARD) – .38 S&W Spl.+P cal., J-frame, 5 shot, alloy frame, 1 7/8 or 2 1/2 full lug (mfg. 2010 only) in. stainless steel barrel and cylinder, shrouded hammer, round butt, Uncle Mike's Boot, Crimson Trace Laser, or pink (new 2012) grips, 15 oz. 1,200 mfg. during 1990 only, reintroduced 1998.

| MSR $469 | $355 | $315 | $275 | $225 | $190 | $170 | $150 | |

Add $20 for pink grips (new 2012).
Add $24 for 2 1/2 in. full lug barrel (disc. 2010).
Add $230 for Crimson Trace laser grips (new 2010).
Add $70 for Red LaserMax (new 2016).

MSR		100%	98%	95%	90%	80%	70%	60%	Last MSR

MODEL 681 DISTINGUISHED SERVICE MAGNUM – .357 Mag. cal., stainless steel, 4 in. barrel, fixed sights, L-Frame. Mfg. 1980-1992.

		100%	98%	95%	90%	80%	70%	60%	Last MSR
		$425	$350	$275	$225	$175	$140	$125	*$412*

1991 mfg. includes square butt. There were 5 engineering changes to this model.

MODEL 686 DISTINGUISHED COMBAT MAGNUM – .357 Mag./.38 Spl.+ P cal., L-Frame, 6 shot, similar to Model 586, except has 2 1/2 (new 1990), 4, 6 (with (disc.) or w/o PowerPort), or 8 3/8 (disc. 2002) in. barrel, fixed (disc.) or adj. sights, blue, stainless, Midnight Black (ltd. ed. 1989 only, 2,876 mfg. in 6 in. barrel, and 1,559 mfg. in 4 in. barrel) finish, current production uses Hogue rubber grips, 35-51 oz. New 1980.

MSR $829		$600	$475	$350	$300	$250	$225	$200	

* **Model 686 Distinguished Combat Magnum Plus** – .357 Mag./.38 Spl.+ P cal., L-frame, 7 shot, 2 1/2, 3 (new 2007), 4, or 6 in. barrel, synthetic or Hogue rubber grips, stainless steel, round (2 1/2 in. barrel only) or square butt, white outline rear sight on 4 or 6 in. barrel, 34 1/2 - 43 oz. New 1996.

MSR $849		$615	$485	$350	$300	$250	$225	$200	

MODEL 686/686SSR PRO SERIES – .357 Mag./.38 Spl. + P cal., 6 shot, L-frame, 4 (Model 686SSR) or 5 (Model 686 with full moon clips, new 2010) in. barrel, SA/DA, interchangeable front sight, adj. rear sight, satin stainless (Model 686SSR) or bead (Model 686) finish, checkered wood grips, stainless steel frame and cylinder, forged hammer and trigger, custom barrel with recessed Precision crown, Bossed mainspring, and tuned action, 38.3 oz. New 2007.

MSR $999		$750	$615	$515	$400	$350	$325	$275	

Subtract $10 for full moon clips (Model 686, new 2010).

PISTOLS: SEMI-AUTO, CENTERFIRE

Listed in order of model number (except .32 and .35 Automatic Pistols). Alphabetical models will appear at the end of this section.

To understand S&W 3rd generation model nomenclature, the following rules apply. The first two digits (of the four digit model number) specify caliber. Numbers 39, 59, and 69 refer to 9mm Para. cal. The third digit refers to the model type. 0 means standard model, 1 is for compact, 2 is for standard model with decocking lever, 3 is for compact variation with decocking lever, 4 is for standard with double action only, 5 designates a compact model in double action only, 6 indicates a non-standard barrel length, 7 is a non-standard barrel length with decocking lever, and 8 refers to non-standard barrel length in double action only. The fourth digit refers to the material(s) used in the fabrication of the pistol. 3 refers to an aluminum alloy frame with stainless steel slide, 4 designates an aluminum alloy frame with carbon steel slide, 5 is for carbon steel frame and slide, 6 is a stainless steel frame and slide, and 7 refers to a stainless steel frame and carbon steel slide. Hence, a Model 4053 refers to a pistol in .40 S&W cal. configured in compact version with double action only and fabricated with an aluminum alloy frame and stainless steel slide.

A few semi-auto models have had engineering changes during their manufacture. These will be denoted by a dash followed by another number after the main model number. Unless there is an additional price line, models with engineering changes will have the same value as those without. This model nomenclature does not apply to 2 or 3 digit model numbers (i.e., Rimfire Models and the Model 52).

Current S&W abbreviations for pistol feature codes used on its price sheets and literature are as follows: Grips: CTG - Crimson Trace laser grips, PG - plastic grips, RG - rubber grips, WG - wood grips. Sights: ADJ - adjustable, ADJFO - adj. fiber optic, FIXEDB - fixed black, LMC - low mount carry, BB - black blade, BP - black post, FO - fiber optic, GB - gold bead - INTCH - interchangeable, NS - night sights, PAT - Patridge, RR - red ramp, WB - white bead, WD - white dot. Frames: AL - alloy, SS - stainless steel, CS - carbon steel, MCR - maximum corrosion resistant, (SM - stainless melonite), POLY - polymer. Safeties: AMBI - ambidextrous, MS - magazine safety, NMS - no magazine safety, IL - internal lock, TS - thumb safety, TLCI - tacticle loaded chamber indicator. Action: DA - double action only, SA - single action only, SA/DA - single action/double action, SF - striker fire.

Pre-2010 S&W abbreviations are as follows: Grips: GC - Crimson Trace laser grips, GR - rubber grips, GW - wood grips, GF - finger groove grips, GP - plastic grips. Sights: SA - adj., SB - black blade front, SC - interchangeable front, SD - dot front, SF - fixed, SG - gold bead front, SH - Hi-Viz, SL - Lo Mount Carry, SP - Patridge front, SR - red ramp front, SV - black post, S1 - front night. Frame Material: FA - alloy, FS - stainless, CF - carbon, FM - stainless Melonite, FP - polymer. Frame Sizes: SM - Small/Compact, MD - Medium, LG - Large, XL - Extra Large. Finishes: ZB - Blue/Black, ZC - Clear Cote, ZG - Grey, ZL - Melonite, ZM - Matte, ZS - Satin Stainless, ZT - Two-Tone, ZW - Camo. Barrel: BC - carbon, BL - light, BO - one piece, BS - stainless, BT - traditional, BX - heavy, B2 - two piece. Action: AD - double action only, AF - striker fire, AS - single action only, AT - traditional double action. Slide: DS - stainless steel, DC- carbon, DM - stainless Melonite.

When applicable, early variations of some of the older semi-auto models listed in this category will be more desirable than later mfg.

BODYGUARD 380 – .380 ACP cal., DAO (hammer fired), sub-compact, 2 3/4 in. barrel, 6 shot mag., black polymer frame, adj. sight, black polymer frame with integral laser and finger groove grips, with or w/o (new 2016) thumb safety, stainless steel slide with black Melonite finish, 11.85 oz. New mid-2010.

MSR $449		$385	$335	$290	$265	$245	$225	$200	

Add $70 for Crimson Trace Green Laserguard (new 2016).

MSR	100%	98%	95%	90%	80%	70%	60%	*Last MSR*

MODEL 59 – 9mm Para. cal., similar to Model 39, except has 14 shot mag., black nylon grips, DA/SA, total production approx. 231,841. Mfg. 1972-1981.

| | $550 | $400 | $350 | $275 | $250 | $225 | $215 | |

Add $50 for nickel finish.
Add $150 for smooth front (ungrooved) grip frame.
Add 200% for smooth front and rear grip straps (20 mfg.).

MODEL 410 – .40 S&W cal., Value Series, DA/SA, steel slide with alloy frame, blue finish, 4 in. barrel, 10 or 11 shot mag., single side safety, 3-dot sights, straight backstrap with synthetic grips, 28 1/2 oz. Mfg. 1996-2007.

| | $525 | $375 | $275 | $225 | $195 | $175 | $165 | *$687* |

Add $25 for Hi-Viz front sight (mfg. 2002-2003).

* Model 410S – .40 S&W cal., Value Series, similar to Model 410, except has stainless steel slide with alloy frame, 28 1/2 oz. Mfg. 2005-2006.

| | $545 | $375 | $275 | $245 | $205 | $175 | $165 | *$711* |

Add $100 for Crimson Trace laser grips.

MODEL 411 – .40 S&W cal., Value Series, 4 in. barrel, DA/SA, 11 shot mag., fixed sights, blue finish, aluminum alloy frame, manual safety. Mfg. 1992-1996.

| | $475 | $400 | $350 | $325 | $295 | $280 | $265 | *$525* |

MODEL 439 – 9mm Para. cal., DA/SA, 4 in. barrel, blue or nickel finish, alloy frame, 8 shot mag., checkered walnut grips, 30 oz. Mfg. 1981-1988.

| | $500 | $415 | $350 | $325 | $260 | $215 | $165 | *$472* |

Add $50 for nickel finish (disc. 1986). Add $26 for adj. sights.

Production began on February 26, 1981 with serial number A669101. The first few thousand were supplied with a short wide extractor before reverting back to the Model 39-2 style extractor. The gun was discontinued in the fall of 1988 and replaced by the third-generation Model 3904.

MODEL 457 COMPACT – .45 ACP cal., Value Series, DA/SA, alloy frame and steel slide, 3 3/4 in. barrel, single side safety, 3-dot sights, 7 shot mag., straight backstrap, blue finish only, black synthetic grips, 29 oz. Mfg. 1996-2006.

| | $525 | $365 | $270 | $225 | $195 | $175 | $165 | *$681* |

MODEL 459 – 9mm Para. cal., 14 shot version of Model 439, checkered nylon stocks, limited mfg. with squared-off trigger guard with serrations. Mfg. 1981-1988.

| | $450 | $400 | $350 | $300 | $275 | $255 | $240 | *$501* |

Add $25 for adj. sights.
Add $50 for nickel finish (disc. 1986).
Add 30% for Model 4590 (Transitional 5903).

Production started in 1981, at approximately serial number A668439, and was discontinued in 1988. It is estimated that the first 10,000 guns were produced with the short wide extractor.

MODEL 469 "MINI" – 9mm Para. cal., DA/SA, alloy frame, 12 shot finger extension mag., short frame, bobbed hammer, 3 1/2 in. barrel, sandblast blue or satin nickel finish, ambidextrous safety standard (1986), molded Delrin black grips, 26 oz. Mfg. 1983-1988.

| | $475 | $435 | $325 | $275 | $240 | $225 | $210 | *$478* |

The first eleven guns were completed in 1982 (serial numbers starting at A796437) and were used for test and evaluation samples. Full production began in August of 1983 with serial number A840000. 25 of the first 100 guns were nickel finish, class "A" engraved and shipped with a presentation case, marked "First 100". However while they were marked "First 100" they were not necessarily the first hundred serial numbers.

MODEL 559 – The Model 559 is the carbon steel version of the 14 round, double stack magazine second-generation pistol, DA/SA. The gun was introduced in 1980 with shipments starting in 1981, at approximately serial number A672725. The majority of the guns were produced with the short wide extractor. Only 200 to 250 were supplied with the Model 39-2 type extractor. After production of 10,609 units, 8,973 in blue finish and 1,636 in nickel, the gun was discontinued October 1982.

| | $600 | $525 | $450 | $375 | $275 | $250 | $225 | |

Add $50 for nickel finish. Add $30 for fixed rear sight.

MODEL 639 STAINLESS – 9mm Para. cal., DA/SA, similar to Model 439, only stainless steel, 8 shot mag., ambidextrous safety became standard 1986, 36 oz. Mfg. 1982-1988.

| | $475 | $400 | $350 | $300 | $250 | $200 | $165 | *$523* |

Add $27 for adj. sights.

The pistol was introduced on May 24, 1982, with serial number A769806. The gun was first available with the short wide extractor but that was changed to the Model 39-2 type on September 15, 1982 after approximately 600 had been produced.

MSR	100%	98%	95%	90%	80%	70%	60%	Last MSR

MODEL 645 STAINLESS – .45 ACP cal. only, 5 in. barrel, SA, 8 shot mag., squared-off trigger guard, black molded nylon grips, ambidextrous safety, fixed sights, 37 1/2 oz. Mfg. 1985-1988.

	$550	$475	$400	$350	$300	$250	$200	$622

Add approx. 25% for the approx. 479 Model 6450 "Interim" pistols were mfg. in 1988 only.

Add $27 for adj. sight.

The first 28 prototype pistols were produced in October 1984 and were serial numbered from A883222 to A883249. Production started in November 1985 with shipments starting in December of 1985 at serial number TAK0001.

MODEL 659 STAINLESS – 9mm Para. cal., DA/SA, similar to Model 459, only stainless steel, 14 shot mag., ambidextrous safety became standard 1986, 39 1/2 oz. Disc. 1988.

	$475	$400	$350	$300	$250	$215	$180	$553

Add approx. 30% for the approx. 150 Model 6590 "Interim" or "transitional" pistols were mfg. in 1988 only.

Add $27 for adj. sights.

The gun was introduced in 1982 beginning with serial number A782700 and was discontinued in 1988. It was replaced by the Model 5906. A limited number of this model were supplied with the short wide extractor and are considered scarce.

MODEL 669 STAINLESS – 9mm Para. cal., smaller version of Model 659 with 12 shot finger extension mag., 3 1/2 in. barrel, fixed sights, molded Delrin grips, ambidextrous safety standard, 26 oz. Mfg. 1986-88 only.

	$475	$375	$300	$250	$195	$165	$140	$522

Add approx. 30% for the approx. 150 Model 6690 "Interim" or "transitional" pistols were mfg. in 1988 only.

The Model 669 was introduced in 1985 beginning with serial number TAE 0001. The gun had a stainless steel slide and barrel with aluminum alloy frame. The first 100 guns were set aside for special orders; 25 of these were class "A" engraved by an outside contractor and marked "1 of 25." It took ten years for all of these engraved guns to be sold. In 1988 the Model 669 was discontinued and replaced by the Model 6906. Total production of the Model 669 was 54,074 pistols.

MODEL 908 COMPACT – 9mm Para. cal., Value Series, compact variation of the Model 909/910, DA/SA, 3 1/2 in. barrel, 3-dot sights, 8 shot mag., straight backstrap, 24 oz. Mfg. 1996-2007.

	$495	$355	$275	$230	$195	$175	$165	$648

* **Model 908S Compact** – Value Series, similar to Model 908, except has stainless steel slide with alloy frame, 24 oz. Mfg. 2003-2007.

	$495	$355	$275	$230	$195	$175	$165	$648

Add $24 for carry combo variation (includes Kydex carry holster, new 2004).

MODEL 910 FULL SIZE – Value Series, similar to Model 909, except has 10 or 15 shot mag., 28 oz. Mfg. 1994-2007.

	$450	$375	$300	$250	$210	$190	$175	$616

Add $22 for Hi-Viz front sight (disc. 2003).

MODEL 915 – 9mm Para. cal., Value Series, 4 in. barrel, fixed sights, 10 (C/B 1994) or 15* shot mag., manual safety, aluminum alloy frame, blue finish. Mfg. 1993-1994.

	$425	$350	$275	$225	$200	$190	$175	$467

MODEL 1006 STAINLESS – 10mm cal., stainless steel construction, 5 in. barrel, DA/SA, exposed hammer, 9 shot mag., fixed or adj. sights, ambidextrous safety, 26,979 units produced 1990-1993.

	$750	$650	$425	$350	$300	$245	$215	$769

Add $27 for adj. rear sight.

Product Codes: 104800, 105004, 108234, 108237.

MODEL 1026 STAINLESS – 10mm cal., 5 in. barrel, DA/SA, features frame mounted decocking lever, 9 shot mag., straight backstrap, 3,135 units produced 1990-1991 only.

	$850	$675	$550	$425	$325	$245	$215	$755

Product Codes: 105006, 105021, 108239.

MODEL 1046 STAINLESS – 10mm cal., 5 in. barrel, DAO, fixed sights, 9 shot mag., straight backstrap, 151 units produced 1991 only.

	$1,500	$1,200	$875	$550	$400	$300	$250	$747

Product Codes: 104602, 108233.

MODEL 1066 STAINLESS – 10mm cal., 4 1/4 in. barrel, DA/SA, 9 shot mag., straight backstrap, ambidextrous safety, traditional double action, fixed sights, 5,067 units produced 1990-1992.

	$750	$625	$500	$400	$325	$250	$225	$730

Add $75 for Tritium night sights - disc. 1991 (Model 1066-NS).

Product Codes: 105500, 108270.

Only 1,000 Model 1066-NSs were manufactured.

MSR	100%	98%	95%	90%	80%	70%	60%	Last MSR

MODEL 1076 STAINLESS – similar to Model 1026 Stainless, except has 4 1/4 in. barrel, 13,805 units produced 1990-93.

	100%	98%	95%	90%	80%	70%	60%	Last MSR
	$700	$625	$550	$450	$350	$300	$245	$778

Product Codes: 10506, 105021, 108239.

MODEL 1086 STAINLESS – similar to Model 1066 Stainless, except is double action only, 1,660 units produced 1990-1992.

	100%	98%	95%	90%	80%	70%	60%	Last MSR
	$900	$700	$525	$400	$325	$250	$210	$730

Product Codes: 106004, 108251.

MODEL SW1911 – .45 ACP cal., patterned after the Colt M1911, large frame, SA, 5 in. barrel, 8 shot single stack mag., alloy (disc. 2006), steel or stainless steel frame, steel slide, matte, blue/black (new 2005) or Clear Coat finish, patented S&W firing pin safety release activated by the grip safety, pinned-in external extractor, Wolff springs throughout, Texas Armament match trigger, Hogue rubber (standard) or wood (new 2004) grips, McCormick hammer and thumb safety, Briley barrel bushing, two Wilson magazines, full-length heavy guide rod, high profile Wilson beavertail safety, adj. rear black blade, or Novak Lo-Mount Carry sights, 39 oz. Mfg. 2003-2011.

	100%	98%	95%	90%	80%	70%	60%	Last MSR
	$875	$675	$525	$425	$375	$335	$300	$1,039

Add $60 for rear adj. sight.
Add $270 or Doug Koenig Model w/two-tone finish and adj. rear sight.

* **Model SW1911 Stainless** – features stainless steel frame and slide, checkered wood or black synthetic grips, 39.4 oz.

MSR $1,079	100%	98%	95%	90%	80%	70%	60%	
	$925	$725	$550	$425	$395	$350	$325	

Add $120 for wood grips and adj. rear sight.
Add $93 for matte finish with black blade front sight (disc. 2006).
Add $72 for tactical lower frame rail w/wood grips (mfg. 2006-2010).
Add $301 for Crimson Trace laser grips (mfg. 2005-2010).

* **Model SW1911 w/no firing pin block** – similar to SW1911, except does not have firing pin block, Melonite finish. Mfg. 2009-2011.

	100%	98%	95%	90%	80%	70%	60%	Last MSR
	$925	$750	$525	$450	$400	$375	$350	$1,099

MODEL SW1911 PD (Sc) – similar to Model SW1911, except has 4 1/4 or 5 (new 2007) in. barrel with small Scandium alloy frame, 8 shot, black finish, and wood grips. Mfg. 2004-2011.

	100%	98%	95%	90%	80%	70%	60%	Last MSR
	$950	$725	$550	$475	$425	$375	$325	$1,109

Add $240 for Crimson Trace laser grips.
Add $120 for Gunsite model with gold bead front sight.
Add $30 for tactical lower rail.

MODEL SW1911 E SERIES – .45 ACP cal., 4 1/4 (disc. 2012) or 5 (new 2011) in. barrel, SA, features front and rear scalloped slide serrations, 7 or 8 shot, white dot sights, alloy or stainless steel (new 2011) frame, blue/black (alloy frame), GI Bead (stainless) or Melonite (stainless) finish, wood or Crimson Trace Laser grips, approx. 40 oz. New 2009.

MSR $979	100%	98%	95%	90%	80%	70%	60%	
	$815	$665	$535	$450	$400	$350	$300	

Add $170 for Crimson Trace Laser grips.
Add $220 for 4 1/4 in. barrel with alloy frame (disc. 2012).
Add $420 for tactical rail (5 in. barrel only, stainless steel, new 2011).

SW1911 PRO SERIES – .45 ACP or 9mm Para. (new 2009) cal., SA, 5 in. barrel, 8 (.45 ACP) or 10 (9mm Para.) shot mag., 3-dot (9mm Para. cal. only), Novak fiber optic front and rear or Black Dovetail rear adj. sights, checkered wood grips, stainless steel frame and slide, satin stainless finish, Pro Series features include 300 LPI front strap checkering, hand polished barrel feed ramp, crisp 4 1/2 lb. trigger pull, full length guide rod, oversized external extractor, ambidextrous frame safety, precision crowned muzzle, 41 oz. New mid-2007.

MSR $1,459	100%	98%	95%	90%	80%	70%	60%	
	$1,150	$925	$775	$675	$575	$475	$425	

Add $120 for 9mm Para. cal. (new 2009).
Add $150 for adj. Black Dovetail rear sight (new late 2011).

* **SW1911 Pro Series Subcompact** – similar to SW1911 Pro Series, except has 3 in. barrel, 7 shot mag., and subcompact frame, 26 1/2 oz. New 2009.

MSR $1,229	100%	98%	95%	90%	80%	70%	60%	
	$950	$795	$675	$550	$450	$400	$350	

MODEL 3904 – 9mm Para. cal., DA/SA, aluminum alloy frame, 4 in. barrel with fixed bushing, 8 shot mag., Delrin one piece wraparound grips, exposed hammer, ambidextrous safety, beveled magwell, extended squared-off trigger guard, adj. or fixed rear sight, 3-dot sighting system, 28 oz. Mfg. 1989-1991.

	100%	98%	95%	90%	80%	70%	60%	Last MSR
	$475	$385	$350	$325	$300	$280	$265	$541

Add $25 for adj. rear sight.

MSR	100%	98%	95%	90%	80%	70%	60%	Last MSR

MODEL 3906 STAINLESS – stainless steel variation of the Model 3904, 35 1/2 oz. Mfg. 1989-91.

| | $510 | $435 | $375 | $315 | $270 | $230 | $200 | $604 |

Add $28 for adj. rear sight.

MODEL 3913 COMPACT STAINLESS – stainless steel variation of the Model 3914, 25 oz. Mfg. 1990-99.

| | $535 | $440 | $365 | $305 | $260 | $220 | $190 | $662 |

* *Model 3913NL Compact Stainless* – similar to Model 3913 Ladysmith, except does not have Ladysmith on the slide. Disc. 1994.

| | $550 | $475 | $395 | $350 | $295 | $250 | $220 | $622 |

* *Model 3913 LS Compact Stainless (Ladysmith)* – similar to Model 3913 Stainless, except is matte stainless with white Delrin grips and mag. does not have finger extension, includes case, 25 oz. Mfg. 1990-2006.

| | $710 | $525 | $400 | $335 | $290 | $245 | $215 | $901 |

MODEL 3913TSW TACTICAL – 9mm Para. cal., DA/SA, compact frame, 3 1/2 in. barrel, 8 shot mag., Novak Lo-Mount 2-dot sights, stainless steel slide, aluminum alloy frame, matte stainless finish, straight black backstrap synthetic grips, 24.8 oz. Mfg. 1998-2006.

| | $690 | $520 | $400 | $335 | $290 | $245 | $215 | $876 |

MODEL 3914 COMPACT – 9mm Para. cal., DA/SA, aluminum alloy frame, 3 1/2 in. barrel, hammerless, 8 shot finger extension mag., fixed sights only, ambidextrous safety, blue finish, straight backstrap grip, 25 oz. Mfg. 1990-1995.

| | $495 | $425 | $350 | $325 | $295 | $280 | $265 | $562 |

This model was also available with a single side manual safety at no extra charge - disc. 1991 (Model 3914NL).

* *Model 3914 Compact LadySmith* – similar to Model 3914, except has Delrin grips, 25 oz. Mfg. 1990-91 only.

| | $485 | $415 | $365 | $305 | $260 | $220 | $190 | $568 |

* *Model 3914 TSW* – similar to Model 3914, except slide is marked "9 Tactical", blue finish, 8 shot mag. 1,060 mfg. 1990 only.

| | $800 | $650 | $475 | $395 | $345 | $280 | $235 | |

MODEL 3953 COMPACT STAINLESS – 9mm Para. cal., DAO, aluminum alloy frame with stainless steel slide, compact model with 3 1/2 in. barrel, 8 shot mag. Mfg. 1990-1999.

| | $535 | $440 | $365 | $305 | $260 | $220 | $190 | $662 |

MODEL 3953TSW – similar to Model 3913TSW, except is DAO, 24.8 oz. Mfg. 1998-2002.

| | $615 | $475 | $380 | $320 | $275 | $230 | $200 | $760 |

MODEL 3954 – similar to Model 3953, except has blue steel slide. Mfg. 1990-92.

| | $475 | $395 | $350 | $325 | $295 | $280 | $265 | $528 |

MODEL 4003 STAINLESS – .40 S&W cal., DA/SA, 4 in. barrel, 11 shot mag., white dot fixed sights, ambidextrous safety, aluminum alloy frame with stainless steel slide, one piece Xenoy wraparound grips, straight gripstrap, 28 oz. Mfg. 1991-1993.

| | $575 | $495 | $395 | $330 | $285 | $240 | $215 | $698 |

* *Model 4003TSW Stainless* – similar to Model 4003 Stainless, but has aluminum alloy frame, 10 shot mag., stainless steel slide, S&W tactical features, including equipment rail and Novak Lo-Mount Carry sights, traditional double action only, satin stainless finish, 28 1/2 oz. Mfg. 2000-2004.

| | $700 | $600 | $500 | $450 | $400 | $360 | $330 | $940 |

MODEL 4004 – .40 S&W cal., similar to Model 4003, except has aluminum alloy frame with blue carbon steel slide. Mfg. 1991-92.

| | $540 | $460 | $375 | $325 | $295 | $280 | $265 | $643 |

MODEL 4006 STAINLESS – .40 S&W cal., 3 1/2 (Shorty Forty) or 4 in. barrel, DA/SA, 10 (C/B 1994) or 11* shot mag., satin stainless finish, exposed hammer, Delrin one piece wraparound grips, 3-dot sights, 38 1/2 oz. Mfg. 1990-1999.

| | $655 | $545 | $400 | $335 | $290 | $245 | $215 | $791 |

Add $31 for adj. rear sight.
Add $115 for fixed Tritium night sights (new 1992).

The bobbed hammer option on this model was disc. in 1991.

* *Model 4006TSW Stainless* – similar to Model 4006 Stainless, except has stainless steel frame and slide, S&W tactical features, including equipment rail, traditional double action only, 37.8 oz. Mfg. 2000-2004.

| | $700 | $600 | $500 | $450 | $400 | $360 | $330 | $963 |

Add $38 if w/o Novak Lo-Mount Carry (NLC) sights.
Add $133 for night sights (disc.).

MSR		100%	98%	95%	90%	80%	70%	60%	Last MSR

MODEL 4013 COMPACT STAINLESS – .40 S&W cal., DA/SA, 3 1/2 in. barrel, 8 shot mag., fixed sights, ambidextrous safety, alloy frame. Mfg. 1991-1996.

		$595	$485	$385	$330	$295	$280	$265	$722

MODEL 4013TSW TACTICAL – .40 S&W cal., DA/SA, 3 1/2 in. barrel, 9 shot mag. with reversible mag. catch, aluminum alloy frame with stainless steel slide, satin stainless finish, black synthetic grips, fixed 3-dot Novak Lo-Mount Carry sights, ambidextrous safety, 26.8 oz. Mfg. 1997-2006.

		$825	$630	$450	$385	$335	$280	$235	$1,021

MODEL 4014 COMPACT – similar to Model 4013, except is steel with blue finish. Mfg. 1991-93.

		$550	$475	$425	$375	$330	$300	$275	$635

MODEL 4026 STAINLESS – .40 S&W cal., traditional double action with frame mounted decocking lever, 10 (C/B 1994) or 11* shot mag., fixed sights, curved backstrap, 36 oz. Mfg. 1991-93.

		$625	$525	$400	$335	$290	$245	$215	$731

MODEL 4040 PD – .40 S&W cal., compact frame using Scandium, 3 1/2 in. barrel, DA/SA, Hogue rubber grips, Novak Lo-Mount Carry 3-dot sights, matte black finish, 25.6 oz. Mfg. 2003-2005.

		$625	$525	$400	$335	$290	$245	$215	$840

MODEL 4043 STAINLESS – .40 S&W cal., DAO, aluminum alloy frame with stainless steel slide, 4 in. barrel, 10 (C/B 1994) or 11* shot mag., one piece Xenoy wraparound grips, straight backstrap, white-dot fixed sights, 30 oz. Mfg. 1991-1999.

		$635	$510	$390	$325	$280	$240	$210	$772

*   ***Model 4043TSW Stainless*** – .40 S&W cal., DAO, similar to Model 4043 Stainless, but has S&W tactical features, including equipment rail, 28 1/2 oz. Mfg. 2000-2002.

		$650	$550	$425	$350	$290	$245	$215	$886

MODEL 4044 – .40 S&W cal., similar to Model 4043, except has carbon steel slide. Mfg. 1991-92.

		$540	$460	$375	$325	$295	$280	$265	$643

MODEL 4046 STAINLESS – similar to Model 4006 Stainless, except is DAO, 4 in. barrel only. Mfg. 1991-1999.

		$655	$540	$400	$335	$290	$245	$215	$791

Add $115 for Tritium night sights (new 1992).

*   ***Model 4046TSW Stainless*** – DAO, similar to Model 4046 Stainless, but has S&W tactical features, including equipment rail, 37.8 oz. Mfg. 2000-2002.

		$700	$625	$500	$455	$400	$360	$330	$907

Add $133 for night sights.

MODEL 4053 COMPACT STAINLESS – .40 S&W cal., DAO variation of the Model 4013. Mfg. 1991-1997.

		$625	$525	$400	$335	$290	$245	$215	$734

MODEL 4053TSW (TACTICAL) – .40 S&W cal., DAO, 3 1/2 in. barrel, 9 shot mag. with reversible mag. catch, alloy frame with stainless steel slide, satin stainless finish, black synthetic grips, fixed sights, ambidextrous safety, 26.8 oz. Mfg. 1997-2002.

		$730	$580	$425	$360	$315	$260	$225	$886

MODEL 4054 – .40 S&W cal., DAO variation of the Model 4014. Mfg. 1991-1992.

		$650	$550	$425	$350	$290	$245	$215	$629

MODEL 4056TSW (TACTICAL) – .40 S&W cal., DAO, 3 1/2 in. barrel, 9 shot mag. with reversible mag. catch, stainless steel frame and slide, satin stainless finish, black synthetic grips, fixed sights, ambidextrous safety, 37 1/2 oz. Mfg. 1997 only.

		$675	$575	$450	$350	$290	$245	$215	$844

MODEL 4505 – .45 ACP cal., carbon steel variation of the Model 4506, fixed or adj. rear sight. 1,200 mfg. 1991 only.

		$650	$550	$425	$350	$290	$245	$215	$660

Add $27 for adj. rear sight.

MODEL 4506 STAINLESS – .45 ACP cal., 5 in. barrel, DA/SA, 8 shot mag., combat trigger guard, exposed hammer, fixed or adj. rear sight, straight backstrap (curved is optional), Delrin one-piece grips, 40 1/2 oz. Mfg. 1990-1999.

		$680	$550	$410	$345	$300	$250	$220	$822

Add $33 for adj. rear sight.

Approx. 100 Model 4506s left the factory mismarked Model 645 on the frame. In NIB condition they are worth $700.

MODEL 4513TSW – .45 ACP cal., DAO, compact frame, 3 3/4 in. barrel, 7 shot mag., 3-dot Novak Lo-Mount Carry sights, stainless steel slide, aluminum alloy frame, satin stainless finish, 28.6 oz. Mfg. 1998-2004.

		$725	$625	$475	$395	$340	$285	$240	$980

MSR	100%	98%	95%	90%	80%	70%	60%	Last MSR

MODEL 4516 COMPACT STAINLESS – .45 ACP cal., bobbed hammer, compact variation of the Model 4506, 3 3/4 in. barrel, DA/SA, 7 shot mag., ambidextrous safety, fixed rear sight only, 34 oz. Mfg. 1990-1997.

| | $650 | $525 | $400 | $335 | $290 | $245 | $215 | $787 |

Original model is marked 4516 while later mfg. changed slide legend to read 4516-1. Original mfg. is more collectible and slight premiums are being asked.

MODEL 4526 STAINLESS – similar to Model 4506 Stainless, except has frame mounted decocking lever. Mfg. 1990-91 only.

| | $675 | $550 | $425 | $350 | $290 | $245 | $215 | $762 |

MODEL 4536 STAINLESS – .45 ACP cal., similar to Model 4516 Compact, except has frame mounted decocking lever only. Mfg. 1990-91 only.

| | $675 | $550 | $425 | $350 | $290 | $245 | $215 | $762 |

MODEL 4546 STAINLESS – .45 ACP cal., similar to Model 4506 Stainless, except is double action only. Mfg. 1990-91 only.

| | $675 | $550 | $425 | $350 | $290 | $245 | $215 | $735 |

MODEL 4553TSW – .45 ACP cal., similar to Model 4513TSW, except is double action only. Mfg. 1998-2002.

| | $755 | $595 | $450 | $385 | $335 | $280 | $235 | $924 |

MODEL 4556 STAINLESS – .45 ACP cal., DAO, 3 3/4 in. barrel, 7 shot mag., fixed sights. Mfg. 1991 only.

| | $675 | $550 | $425 | $350 | $290 | $245 | $215 | $735 |

MODEL 4563TSW – .45 ACP cal., DA/SA, 4 1/4 in. barrel, 8 shot mag., aluminum alloy frame with stainless steel slide, satin stainless finish, includes S&W tactical features, including equipment rail and Novak 3-dot sights, synthetic black straight backstrap grips, 30.6 oz. Mfg. 2000-2004.

| | $750 | $625 | $450 | $390 | $340 | $280 | $235 | $977 |

MODEL 4566 STAINLESS – .45 ACP cal., DA/SA, ambidextrous safety, 4 1/4 in. barrel, 8 shot mag. Mfg. 1990-1999.

| | $650 | $550 | $410 | $345 | $300 | $250 | $220 | $822 |

* Model 4566TSW Stainless – similar to Model 4566, except has ambidextrous safety, 39.1 oz. Disc. 2004.

| | $725 | $600 | $450 | $390 | $340 | $280 | $235 | $1,000 |

MODEL 4567-NS STAINLESS – similar to Model 4566 Stainless, except has Tritium night sights, stainless steel frame and carbon steel slide. 2,500 mfg. in 1991 only.

| | $650 | $550 | $425 | $350 | $290 | $245 | $215 | $735 |

MODEL 4576 STAINLESS – .45 ACP cal., features 4 1/4 in. barrel, DA/SA, frame mounted decocking lever, fixed sights. Mfg. 1990-1992.

| | $635 | $535 | $410 | $345 | $300 | $250 | $220 | $762 |

MODEL 4583TSW – similar to Model 4563TSW, except is DAO, 30.6 oz. Mfg. 2000-2002.

| | $700 | $575 | $450 | $380 | $330 | $275 | $230 | $921 |

MODEL 4586 STAINLESS – .45 ACP cal., full size 4 1/4 in. barrel, DAO, 8 shot mag. Mfg. 1990-1999.

| | $695 | $575 | $425 | $345 | $300 | $250 | $220 | $822 |

* Model 4586TSW Stainless – similar to Model 4566TSW, except is DAO, 39.1 oz. Mfg. 2000-2002.

| | $700 | $600 | $445 | $380 | $330 | $275 | $230 | $942 |

MODEL 5903 – 9mm Para. cal., DA/SA, 4 in. barrel, stainless steel slide and alloy frame, exposed hammer, 10 (C/B 1994) or 15* shot mag., adj. (disc. 1993) or fixed rear sight, ambidextrous safety. Mfg. 1990-1997.

| | $650 | $575 | $475 | $395 | $365 | $325 | $300 | $701 |

Add $30 for adj. rear sight (disc).
Add 20% for Model 5903 SSV, only 1,500 mfg.

* Model 5903TSW – 9mm Para. cal., DA/SA, aluminum alloy frame with stainless slide, satin stainless finish, includes S&W tactical features, such as equipment rail and Novak Lo-Mount Carry sights, black synthetic grips with curved backstrap, 28.9 oz. Mfg. 2000-2004.

| | $725 | $580 | $430 | $385 | $330 | $275 | $250 | $892 |

MODEL 5904 – 9mm Para. cal., similar to Model 5903, except has blue steel slide and blue alloy frame, 26 1/2 oz. Mfg. 1989-1998.

| | $535 | $445 | $360 | $330 | $300 | $280 | $265 | $663 |

Add $30 for adj. rear sight (disc. 1993).

MSR	100%	98%	95%	90%	80%	70%	60%	Last MSR

MODEL 5905 – 9mm Para. cal., similar to Model 5904, except has blue carbon steel frame and slide. Approx. 5,000 mfg. 1990-1991 only.

| | $650 | $575 | $500 | $440 | $375 | $335 | $300 | |

MODEL 5906 STAINLESS – 9mm Para. cal., stainless steel variation of the Model 5904, 37 1/2 oz. Mfg. 1989-1999.

| | $615 | $500 | $400 | $335 | $290 | $245 | $215 | $751 |

Add $37 for adj. rear sight.
Add $115 for Tritium night sights.
Add 100% for Model 5906M (South American military model with Melonite finish).

* ***Model 5906TSW Stainless*** – 9mm Para. cal., DA/SA, similar to Model 5906 Stainless, but has S&W tactical features, including equipment rail, 38.3 oz. Mfg. 2000-2004.

| | $650 | $575 | $475 | $350 | $300 | $265 | $235 | $915 |

Add $44 if w/o Novak Lo Mount Carry sight.
Add $132 for night sights (disc.).

MODEL 5924 – 9mm Para. cal., blue steel version of the 5903, 4 in. barrel, features frame mounted decocking lever, 15 shot mag., 37 1/2 oz. Mfg. 1990-91 only.

| | $625 | $550 | $475 | $375 | $335 | $300 | $280 | $635 |

MODEL 5926 STAINLESS – 9mm Para. cal., stainless variation of the Model 5924. Disc. 1992.

| | $600 | $525 | $425 | $350 | $295 | $250 | $210 | $697 |

MODEL 5943 STAINLESS – 9mm Para. cal., DAO, 4 in. barrel, aluminum alloy frame with stainless steel slide, straight backstrap, 15 shot mag. Mfg. 1990-1991 only.

| | $550 | $465 | $390 | $325 | $280 | $235 | $205 | $655 |

* ***Model 5943-SSV Stainless*** – 9mm Para. cal., similar to Model 5943 Stainless, except has 3 1/2 in. barrel, Tritium night sights. Mfg. 1990-91 only.

| | $625 | $550 | $475 | $395 | $330 | $285 | $240 | $690 |

* ***Model 5943TSW Stainless*** – 9mm Para. cal., DAO, aluminum alloy frame with stainless steel slide, includes S&W tactical features, equipment rail, and Novak Lo-Mount Carry sights, 28.9 oz. Mfg. 2000-2002.

| | $650 | $575 | $450 | $375 | $325 | $280 | $265 | $844 |

MODEL 5944 – 9mm Para. cal., similar to Model 5943 Stainless, except has blue finish slide and frame. Mfg. 1990-1991 only.

| | $625 | $550 | $475 | $400 | $350 | $300 | $280 | $610 |

MODEL 5946 STAINLESS – 9mm Para. cal., DAO, one piece Xenoy wraparound grips, all stainless steel variation of the Model 5943, 39 1/2 oz. Mfg. 1990-1999.

| | $615 | $500 | $400 | $335 | $290 | $245 | $215 | $751 |

* ***Model 5946TSW Stainless*** – 9mm Para. cal., DAO, includes S&W tactical features, equipment rail, and Novak Lo-Mount Carry sights, 38.3 oz. Mfg. 2000-2002.

| | $725 | $600 | $450 | $375 | $315 | $260 | $225 | $863 |

MODEL 6904 COMPACT – 9mm Para. cal., compact variation of the Model 5904, 3 1/2 in. barrel, DA/SA, 10 (C/B 1994) or 12* shot finger extension mag., fixed rear sight, 26 1/2 oz. Mfg. 1989-1997.

| | $550 | $475 | $400 | $350 | $325 | $300 | $280 | $625 |

MODEL 6906 COMPACT STAINLESS – 9mm Para. cal., stainless steel variation of the Model 6904, 26 1/2 oz. Mfg. 1989-1999.

| | $585 | $470 | $380 | $320 | $275 | $235 | $200 | $720 |

Add $116 for Tritium night sights (new 1992).

MODEL 6926 STAINLESS – 9mm Para. cal., 3 1/2 in. barrel, DA/SA, features frame mounted decocking lever, aluminum alloy frame with stainless slide, 12 shot mag. Mfg. 1990-1991 only.

| | $650 | $575 | $450 | $375 | $315 | $270 | $230 | $663 |

MODEL 6944 – 9mm Para. cal., DAO, 3 1/2 in. barrel, 12 shot mag., aluminum alloy frame with blue steel slide. Mfg. 1990-1991 only.

| | $600 | $525 | $450 | $375 | $325 | $300 | $280 | $578 |

MODEL 6946 STAINLESS – 9mm Para. cal., similar to Model 6944, except has stainless steel slide, semi-bobbed hammer, 26 1/2 oz. Mfg. 1990-1999.

| | $675 | $575 | $475 | $375 | $315 | $270 | $230 | $720 |

MSR	100%	98%	95%	90%	80%	70%	60%	Last MSR

SIGMA MODEL SW9F SERIES – 9mm Para. cal., DAO, SFO, 4 1/2 in. barrel, fixed sights, polymer frame and steel slide, blue finish only, 10 (C/B 1994) or 17* shot mag., 26 oz. Mfg. 1994-1996.

	100%	98%	95%	90%	80%	70%	60%	Last MSR
	$475	$400	$350	$325	$295	$280	$265	*$593*

Add $104 for Tritium night sights.

* ***Sigma Model SW9C Series Compact*** – 9mm Para. cal., similar to Sigma Model SW9F, except has 4 in. barrel, 25 oz. Mfg. 1996-1998.

	100%	98%	95%	90%	80%	70%	60%	Last MSR
	$450	$355	$325	$295	$280	$265	$240	*$541*

* ***Sigma Model SW9M Series Compact*** – 9mm Para. cal., SFO, features 3 1/4 in. barrel, 7 shot mag., fixed channel rear sight, grips integral with frame, satin black finish, 18 oz. Mfg. 1996-1998.

	100%	98%	95%	90%	80%	70%	60%	Last MSR
	$300	$270	$240	$220	$195	$175	$160	*$366*

SIGMA MODEL SW9VE/GVE (SW9E/SW9P/SW9G/SW9V) – 9mm Para. cal., DAO, SFO, features 4 in. standard or ported (SW9P, mfg. 2001-2003) barrel, 10 or 16 (new late 2004) shot mag., 3-dot sighting system, grips integral with grey (disc. 2000), Nato Green (SW9G, disc. 2003) or black polymer frame, black (SW9E, mfg. 1999-2002) or satin stainless steel (SW9VE) slide, 24.7 oz. Mfg. 1997-2012.

	100%	98%	95%	90%	80%	70%	60%	Last MSR
	$320	$275	$230	$200	$175	$150	$140	*$379*

Add $8 for Allied Forces model w/Melonite slide (mfg. 2007-2009).
Add $380 for SW9VE/SW40VE Allied Forces model w/emergency kit, including space blankets, emergency food, first aid kit, crank radio/flashlight, multi-tool, and pocket survival pack, cased (mfg. 2007-2009).
Add $48 for SW9P or SW9G with night sights (disc. 2003).
Add $210 for Tritium night sights (disc. 2000).

The Enhanced Sigma Series Model SW9VE was introduced during 1999, after the SW9V was discontinued.

SIGMA MODEL SW40F SERIES – .40 S&W cal., DAO, SFO, 4 1/2 in. barrel, fixed sights, polymer frame, blue finish only, 10 (C/B 1994) or 15* shot mag., 26 oz. Mfg. 1994-1998.

	100%	98%	95%	90%	80%	70%	60%	Last MSR
	$450	$355	$325	$295	$280	$265	$240	*$541*

Add $104 for Tritium night sights (disc. 1997).

* ***Sigma Model SW40C Series Compact*** – .40 S&W cal., similar to Sigma Model SW40F, except has 4 in. barrel, 26 oz. Mfg. 1996-1998.

	100%	98%	95%	90%	80%	70%	60%	Last MSR
	$450	$355	$325	$295	$280	$265	$240	*$541*

SIGMA MODEL SW40VE/SW40P/SW40G/SW40GVE (SW40E/SW40V) – .40 S&W cal., SFO, features 4 in. standard or ported (SW40P, mfg. 2001-2005) barrel, 10 or 14 (new mid-2004) shot mag., 3-dot sighting system, grips integral with grey (disc. 2000), Nato green (SW40G) or black polymer frame, black slide with Melonite finish (SW40E, mfg. 1999-2002) or satin stainless steel slide, 24.4 oz. Mfg. 1997-2012.

	100%	98%	95%	90%	80%	70%	60%	Last MSR
	$320	$275	$230	$200	$175	$150	$140	*$379*

Add $8 for Allied Forces model w/Melonite slide, (mfg. 2007-2009).
Add $210 for Tritium night sights (disc.).
Add $145 for Model SW40P or SW40G (includes night sights, disc. 2005).
Add $380 for SW9VE/SW40VE Allied Forces model w/emergency kit, including space blankets, emergency food, first aid kit, crank radio/flashlight, multi-tool, and pocket survival pack, cased (mfg. 2007-2009).

The Enhanced Sigma Series Model SW40VE was introduced during 1999, after the SW40V was discontinued.

MODEL SW99 – 9mm Para., .40 S&W, or .45 ACP (new 2003) cal., traditional DA, SFO, 9 (.45 ACP cal.) or 10 shot mag., similar to the Walther P99, black polymer frame with black stainless slide and barrel, 4, 4 1/8 (.40 S&W cal. only), or 4.25 (.45 ACP cal. only, new 2003) in. barrel, black finish, ambidextrous mag. release, frame equipment groove, interchangeable backstraps, decocking lever, cocking indicator, adj. 3-dot or night sights, 25.4 (9mm Para cal.) or 28 1/2 oz. Mfg. 2000-2004.

	100%	98%	95%	90%	80%	70%	60%	Last MSR
	$565	$485	$430	$380	$340	$300	$275	*$667*

Add $123 for night sights.
Add $41 for .45 ACP cal. (new 2003).

* ***Model SW99 Compact*** – similar to SW99, except is compact version, not available in .45 ACP cal., 3 1/2 in. barrel, 8 (.40 S&W cal.) or 10 (9mm Para cal.) shot mag. with finger extension, approx. 23 oz. Mfg. 2003-2004.

	100%	98%	95%	90%	80%	70%	60%	Last MSR
	$565	$485	$430	$380	$340	$300	$275	*$667*

SIGMA MODEL SW357 – .357 SIG cal., SFO, 4 in. barrel, 10 shot mag., black finish, stainless steel. Mfg. 1998 only.

	100%	98%	95%	90%	80%	70%	60%	Last MSR
	$525	$450	$375	$325	$250	$195	$165	

SIGMA MODEL SW380 – .380 ACP cal., DAO, SFO, 3 in. barrel, fixed sights, polymer frame and steel slide, striker firing system, blue finish only, 6 shot mag., shortened grip, 14 oz. Mfg. 1996-2000.

	100%	98%	95%	90%	80%	70%	60%	Last MSR
	$285	$245	$210	$190	$180	$170	$160	*$358*

MSR		100%	98%	95%	90%	80%	70%	60%	Last MSR

MODEL SW990L – 9mm Para., .40 S&W, or .45 ACP cal., DAO, SFO, 9 (.45 ACP cal. only), 10 (all cals. except .45 ACP), 12 (.40 S&W cal.) or 16 (9mm Para.) shot mag., similar to the Walther P99, black polymer frame with black stainless Melonite slide and barrel, 4 (9mm Para. cal. only), 4 1/8 (.40 S&W cal. only), or 4.25 (.45 ACP cal. only) in. barrel, black finish, approx. 25 oz. Mfg. 2005-2006.

		$610	$515	$450	$400	$350	$300	$275	$729

Add $44 for .45 ACP cal.

* **Model SW990L Compact** – similar to SW990L, except is compact version with small polymer frame, not available in .45 ACP cal., 3 1/2 in. barrel, 8 (.40 S&W cal.) or 10 (9mm Para cal.) shot mag. with finger extension, approx. 23 oz. Mfg. 2005-2006.

		$610	$515	$450	$400	$350	$300	$275	$729

MODEL SW SD9 – 9mm Para. cal., DAO, SFO, w/o hammer, 4 in. barrel, 10 or 16 shot mag., stainless steel slide/barrel, black polymer frame with Picatinny rail, front and rear slide serrations, Tritium night front sight, two-dot fixed rear sight, black Melonite finish, 22.7 oz. Mfg. 2010-2011.

		$375	$325	$295	$275	$250	$225	$200	$459

Add $40 for home defense kit that includes NanoVault lockable case and S&W Micro90 compact pistol light (disc. 2011).

MODEL SW SD40 – .40 S&W cal., DAO, striker fire action, w/o hammer, 4 in. barrel, 10 or 14 shot mag., stainless steel slide/barrel, black polymer frame with Picatinny rail, front and rear slide serrations, Tritium night front sight, two-dot fixed rear sight, black Melonite finish, 22.7 oz. Mfg. 2010-2011.

		$375	$325	$295	$275	$250	$225	$200	$459

Add $40 for home defense kit that includes NanoVault lockable case and S&W Micro90 compact pistol light (disc. 2011).

MODEL M&P SERIES – 9mm Para., .40 S&W, .357 SIG (disc. 2010), .380 (new 2014), or .45 ACP (new 2007) cal., DAO, SFO, black Melonite finished stainless steel barrel and slide with twin scalloped slide serrations, black Zytel polymer frame reinforced with stainless steel, matte black or Dark Earth brown (new 2007) finish, 6 (new 2014), 8, 10, 12, 15, or 17 shot mag., ramp front sights, Novak Lo-Mount Carry rear sight, ambidextrous manual safety became an option during 2009, 6 1/2 lbs. trigger pull, 18 degree grip angle, Picatinny rail in front of trigger guard, three interchangeable grip sizes, 24 1/4-29 1/2 oz. Approx. 25 variations in each caliber. New 2006.

Add $50 for ambidextrous manual safety with lanyard loop on non-compact models.

M&P357 – .357 SIG cal., SFO, 4 1/4 in. barrel, 10 or 15 shot mag., similar to M&P9. Disc. 2010.

		$575	$475	$375	$335	$285	$260	$230	$727

* **M&P357 Compact** – .357 SIG cal., 10 shot mag., 3 1/2 in. barrel, similar to M&P9 Compact, 22 oz. Mfg. 2007-2010.

		$575	$475	$375	$335	$285	$260	$230	$727

M&P9 – 9mm Para. cal., SFO, 10 or 17 shot mag., 4 1/4 in. standard or threaded (new 2015) barrel, full size polymer frame, white dot or steel ramp dovetail front sight, steel low profile or Novak Lo-Mount carry rear sight, stainless steel slide and barrel, black Melonite, carbon fiber (mfg. 2015 only) or FDE (new 2015) finish, with or w/o thumb safety, black grips with three interchangeable palmswell grip sizes or Crimson Trace Laser grips (new 2008), lower accessory rail, includes two magazines, 24 oz.

MSR $569		$425	$350	$315	$285	$260	$230	$200	

Add $30 for carbon fiber (mfg. 2015 only) or FDE (new 2015).
Add $120 for carry and range kit - includes Blade Tech Kydex holster, double magazine pouch, Maglula Uplula speed loader, ear plugs, and extra magazine.
Add $260 for Crimson Trace Laser grips (new 2008) or add $130 Crimson Trace green Laserguard (new 2016).
Add $100 for threaded barrel kit.

* **M&P9 JG** – 9mm Para. cal., SFO, 17 shot mag., similar to M&P9, except has fiber optic front sight, Warren tactical rear sight, five interchangeable palmswell grip sizes (three black and two pink), breast cancer awareness ribbon engraved on slide, designed in collaboration with champion Julie Goloski-Golob. Disc. 2012.

		$465	$375	$325	$300	$280	$250	$215	$619

* **M&P9L** – 9mm Para. cal., SFO, 17 shot mag., 5 in. barrel, full size polymer frame, white dot or steel ramp dovetail front sight, steel low profile carry rear sight, stainless steel slide and barrel, black Melonite finish, three interchangeable palmswell grip sizes, includes two magazines, 25 oz. Disc. 2011.

		$575	$475	$395	$350	4325	4295	$250	$758

* **M&P9 VTAC (Viking Tactics)** – 9mm Para. cal., SFO, 17 shot mag., 4 1/4 in. barrel, full size polymer frame, VTAC Warrior front and rear sights, durable PVD coated stainless steel slide, Flat Dark Earth finish, 24 oz.

MSR $799		$640	$535	$425	$375	$325	$295	$250	

* **M&P9 Compact** – 9mm Para. cal., SFO, 12 shot mag., 3 1/2 in. barrel, steel ramp dovetail mount front sight, Novak Lo-Mount carry rear sight, compact Zytel polymer frame with stainless steel slide and barrel, black Melonite, carbon fiber (new 2015) or FDE (new 2015) finish, with or w/o thumb safety, with or w/o three interchangeable

MSR	100%	98%	95%	90%	80%	70%	60%	Last MSR

palmswell or Crimson Trace Laser grips, 22 oz. New 2007.

MSR $569	$425	$350	$315	$285	$260	$230	$200	

Add $30 for carbon fiber (mfg. 2015 only) or FDE finish (new 2015).

Add $260 for Crimson Trace laser grips or $130 for Crimson Trace green Laserguard (new 2016).

Add $150 if w/o thumb safety and interchangeable grips (disc. 2011).

M&P40 – .40 S&W cal., 10 or 15 shot mag., SA or DAO, SFO, 4 1/4 in. barrel, similar to Model M&P9, with or w/o thumb safety, 24 1/4 oz.

MSR $569	$425	$350	$315	$285	$260	$230	$200	

Add $30 for carbon fiber (mfg. 2015 only).

Add $120 for carry and range kit - includes Blade Tech Kydex holster, double magazine pouch, Maglula Uplula speed loader, ear plugs, and extra magazine.

Add $260 for Crimson Trace laser grips or $130 for Crimson Trace green Laserguard (new 2016).

* **M&P40 VTAC (Viking Tactics)** – .40 S&W cal., SFO, 15 shot mag., 4 1/4 in. barrel, full size polymer frame, VTAC Warrior front and rear sights, durable PVD coated stainless steel slide, Flat Dark Earth finish, 24 oz.

MSR $799	$640	$535	$425	$375	$325	$295	$250	

* **M&P40 Compact** – 9mm Para. cal., SFO, 10 or 12 shot mag., 3 1/2 in. barrel, steel ramp dovetail mount front sight, Novak Lo-Mount carry rear sight, compact Zytel polymer frame with stainless steel slide and barrel, black Melonite, carbon fiber (new 2015), or FDE (new 2015) finish, with or w/o thumb safety, with or w/o three interchangeable palm swell or Crimson Trace Laser grips, 22 oz. New 2007.

MSR $569	$425	$350	$315	$285	$260	$230	$200	

Add $30 for carbon fiber (mfg. 2015 only) or FDE finish (new 2015).

Add $260 for Crimson Trace laser grips or $130 for Crimson Trace green Laserguard (new 2016).

M&P45 – .45 ACP cal., SFO, 10 shot mag., 4 (mid-size, disc.) or 4 1/2 in. standard or threaded (new 2015) barrel, full size black polymer frame, Melonite or Dark Earth Brown finish, otherwise similar to M&P9, 29.6 oz.

MSR $599	$450	$375	$325	$295	$260	$230	$200	

Add $120 for threaded barrel kit (new 2015).

Add $20 for ambidextrous safety with black or dark brown finish.

Add $90 for night sights (disc. 2012).

Add $230 for Crimson Trace laser grips (disc. 2012).

* **M&P45 Compact** – .45 ACP cal., SFO, 8 shot mag., 4 in. barrel, similar to M&P9 Compact, 27 oz. New 2007.

MSR $599	$450	$375	$325	$295	$260	$230	$200	

Add $20 for ambidextrous safety with either Melonite (disc.2015) or dark brown finish.

M&P C.O.R.E. (COMPETITION OPTICS READY EQUIPMENT) – 9mm Para. or .40 S&W cal., SFO, 4 1/4 or 5 in. barrel, 10 or 17 shot mag., polymer frame, stainless steel slide, striker-fire action, ambidextrous controls, black Melonite finish, lower Picatinny rail, fixed two dot rear sight, white dot dovetail front sight, accepts six different popular styles of optics, also available in Pro Series configuration, 24 oz. New 2013.

MSR $769	$650	$575	$495	$450	$360	$295	$230	

MODEL M&P 9 PRO SERIES – 9mm Para. cal., striker fire action, 4 1/4 or 5 in. barrel, black polymer frame, 17 shot, lower Picatinny rail, blue/black or satin stainless steel, plastic grips, Lo-Mount Carry, night sights, Fiber optic Green Novak reduced glare sights (disc. 2013), or optics ready, 26 oz. New 2012.

MSR $699	$575	$475	$400	$350	$300	$265	$235	

Add $140 for optic ready threaded barrel (new 2016).

Subtract $10 if satin finish stainless steel w/o night sights (5 in. barrel only).

PISTOLS: SEMI-AUTO, RIMFIRE

MODEL M&P15-22P – .22 LR cal., 6 in. threaded carbon steel barrel with A1 style compensator, 25 shot detachable mag., blowback action similar to M&P 15-22 rifle, quad rail handguard, adj. sights on top Picatinny rail, polymer lower receiver, matte black finish, black pistol grip, 51 oz. Mfg. mid-2010-2011.

	$425	$385	$360	$330	$295	$275	$250	*$519*

Product Code: 813000.

MODEL M&P 22 – .22 LR cal., SFO, 4.1 in. threaded barrel, single action hammerless, 10 or 12 shot mag., plastic grips, fixed backstrap, aluminum alloy slide, adj. rear sight, black blade front sight, ambidextrous safety, blue/black finish, ambidextrous manual safety and slide stop, reversible mag release, lower Picatinny rail, approx. 24 oz. New 2011.

MSR $419	$350	$315	$285	$260	$240	$220	$195	

MSR	100%	98%	95%	90%	80%	70%	60%	Last MSR

Rifles: Semi-Auto

The following is a listing of abbreviations with related feature codes of both centerfire and rimfire semi-auto rifles: Stock: S/6 ADJ - 6 position adj., S/BLK - black synthetic, S/CAM - camo synthetic, S/SF - solid fixed, S/W - wood stock. Pistol Grip: PG - plastic grip, RG - rubber grip, WG - wood grip, NA - no grip. Rear Sight: R/ADJ - adjustable, R/FS - folding stock, R/FSADJ - folding adjustable, NA - no rear sight. Front Sight: F/BB - Black Blade, F/BP - Black Post, F/FO - fiber optic, F/FS - folding sight, F/FSADJ - folding adjustable, F/GB - Gold Bead, F/WBF - white bead front sight, NA - no front sight. Forend: CFF - custom free float, MR - modular rail, STD - standard, NA - no forend (one piece stock). Receiver Material: AL - alloy, CA - carbon, SS - Stainless steel, POLY - polymer. Action: BA - bolt action, FA - fixed action, SAT - semi-auto.

This database does not take into consideration the state compliant variations of the M&P10 and M&P15 rifles.

M&P10 – .308 Win. cal., GIO, 18 in. barrel, enhanced flash hider, 20 shot mag., matte black finish, ambidextrous controls, 6-position CAR stock, chromed gas key, bolt carrier, and firing pin, pistol grip, 7 lbs. 11 oz. New 2013.

MSR $1,619	$1,475	$1,275	$1,050	$935	$750	$625	$525	

Product Codes: 811308.

MODEL M&P15 CENTERFIRE SEMI-AUTO SERIES – .223 Rem./5.56 NATO or 5.45x39mm cal., GIO, AR-15 style design with 16 in. or longer chrome lined barrel with muzzle brake, aluminum upper and lower receiver, 10 or 30 shot mag. (most are Mil-Spec), one-piece fixed position, skeletonized, or 6-position CAR collapsible stock, hardcoat black anodized finish, features detachable carrying handle, A2 post front sight, adj. dual aperture rear sight, thinned handguard, M&P15T features extended Picatinny rail on receiver and barrel, in addition to RAS on both sides and bottom of barrel, adj. front and rear folding battle sights, supplied with hard carry case, approx. 6 1/2 lbs. New 2006.

The lowest serial number encountered to date is SW00200.

* **Model M&P15** – 5.56 NATO cal., GIO, 16 in. carbon steel barrel, 30 shot mag., alloy receiver, black alloy finish, 6-position adj. pistol grip stock, adj. rear sight, black post front sight.

MSR $1,249	$1,250	$1,100	$950	$850	$700	$575	$450	

Product Code: 811000.

* **Model M&P15A** – 5.56 NATO cal., GIO, AR-15 style design, 16 in. barrel, 30 shot mag., similar to Model M&P15, except features a receiver Picatinny rail and adj. rear folding battle sight with ribbed handguard, 6 1/2 lbs. Mfg. 2006-2012.

	$1,275	$1,125	$950	$850	$700	$575	$450	$1,289

Product Code: 811002.

* **Model M&P15T** – 5.56 NATO cal., GIO, AR-15 style design, fixed 10 (CA compliant) or detachable 30 shot mag., 16 in. barrel, similar to Model M&P15A, except features folding (disc. 2010) or fixed black post front sight (new 2011), fixed (new 2011) or folding adj. rear sight (disc. 2010), modular rail (disc. 2010) or custom free float forend (new 2011), 6.85 lbs.

MSR $1,159	$1,150	$1,000	$875	$775	$650	$525	$425	

Product Codes: 811001 (disc. 2010), or 811041 (new 2011).

* **Model M&P15FT** – 5.56 NATO cal., GIO, AR-15 style design, 16 in. barrel, 10 shot mag. (compliant for CT, MA, MD, NJ, and NY), one-piece pistol grip fixed stock, custom free float forend (new 2012), folding adj. (new 2012) front and rear sights, modular rail (disc. 2011), alloy receiver. Mfg. 2008-2011.

MSR $1,159	$1,150	$1,000	$875	$775	$650	$525	$425	

Last MSR for product code 811004 was $1,709 in 2011.

Product Code: 811004 (disc. 2011), 811048 (new 2012).

* **Model M&P15OR** – 5.56 NATO cal., GIO, 16 in. carbon steel barrel with flat-top Picatinny rail and gas block, 30 shot mag., optics ready alloy receiver, black alloy finish, 6-position adj. stock, no rear sight. New 2008.

MSR $1,069	$950	$825	$725	$625	$525	$425	$350	

Product Code: 811003.

* **Model M&P15ORC** – 5.56 NATO cal., GIO, AR-15 style design, 16 in. barrel, 10 shot mag. (compliant CT, MA, MD, NJ and NY), black alloy finish, pistol grip stock, alloy receiver, optics ready. New mid-2008.

MSR $1,039	$925	$800	$725	$625	$525	$425	$350	

Product Code: 811013.

* **Model M&P15X** – 5.56 NATO cal., GIO, AR-15 style design, 16 in. barrel, 30 shot mag., black alloy finish, 6-position adj. pistol grip stock, folding rear and black post front sights, modular rail, alloy receiver. New 2008.

MSR $1,379	$1,375	$1,200	$1,025	$950	$775	$650	$500	

Product Code: 811008.

MSR	100%	98%	95%	90%	80%	70%	60%	Last MSR

* **Model M&P15I** – .223 Rem. cal., GIO, AR-15 style design, 17 in. barrel, 10 shot mag. (compliant CT, MA, MD, NJ, and NY), black alloy finish, pistol grip stock, adj. rear sight, black post front sight, alloy receiver, 7 lbs. Mfg. mid-2008-2011.

| | $1,000 | $875 | $775 | $675 | $575 | $500 | $450 | $1,259 |

Product Code: 811010.

* **Model M&P15R** – 5.45x39mm cal., GIO, AR-15 style design, 16 in. barrel, 30 shot mag., black alloy finish, pistol grip stock, adj. rear and black post front sight, alloy receiver, Picatinny rail, 6 1/2 lbs. Mfg. 2008-2011.

| | $1,075 | $950 | $825 | $700 | $600 | $500 | $450 | $1,089 |

Product Code: 811011.

* **Model M&P15VTAC** – 5.56 NATO cal., GIO, AR-15 style design, Viking Tactics Model, 16 in. barrel, 30 shot mag., black alloy finish, pistol grip stock, modular rail, alloy receiver. Mfg. mid-2008-2011.

| | $1,950 | $1,700 | $1,475 | $1,225 | $925 | $775 | $625 | $1,989 |

Product Code: 811012.

MODEL M&P15VTAC II – 5.56 NATO cal., GIO, 16 in. barrel, 30 shot mag., mid-length system for lower recoil, enhanced flash hider, aluminum upper and lower receivers, 13 in. TRX Extreme handguard and VLTOR IMOD 6-position collapsible stock, Melonite/hardcoat black anodized finish, 6.28 lbs. New 2012.

| MSR $1,949 | $1,700 | $1,475 | $1,225 | $925 | $775 | $625 | $550 | |

Product Code: 811025.

* **Model M&P15MOE** – 5.56 NATO cal., GIO, AR-15 style design, 16 in. barrel, 30 shot mag., black alloy finish, six position adj. stock, alloy receiver, post front sight, folding rear sight. Mfg. 2010-2011.

| | $1,250 | $1,075 | $900 | $775 | $650 | $525 | $425 | $1,249 |

Product Codes: 811020 and 811021.

MODEL M&P15 MOE MID – 5.56 NATO cal., GIO, 16 in. barrel, features Magpul hardware, 30 shot, alloy receiver, 6-position adj. stock, black post front sight and folding adj. rear sight, black or Flat Dark Earth finish. New 2012.

| MSR $1,259 | $1,075 | $900 | $775 | $650 | $525 | $425 | $375 | |

Product Codes: 811053 and 811054.

* **Model M&P15PS** – 5.56 NATO cal., GIO, AR-15 style design, 16 in. barrel, fixed 10 (CA compliant) or 30 shot mag., black alloy finish, six position adj. stock with standard forend, alloy receiver, solid handguard, Picatinny rail above gas block, no sights, flat-top upper, chrome lined bore, gas key, and bolt carrier, adj. gas plug with three settings. Mfg. 2010-2013.

| | $1,350 | $1,150 | $950 | $825 | $675 | $550 | $450 | $1,359 |

Product Code: 811022.

* **Model M&P15PSX** – 5.56 NATO cal., GIO, AR-15 style design, 16 in. barrel, 30 shot mag., black alloy finish, six position adj. stock with standard forend and tactical rail, alloy receiver. Mfg. 2010-2013.

| | $1,500 | $1,325 | $1,125 | $1,025 | $825 | $675 | $525 | $1,499 |

Product Code: 811023.

* **Model M&P15 Sport** – 5.56 NATO cal., GIO, 16 in. Melonite treated barrel, A2 flash suppressor, fixed or detachable 10 or 30 shot mag., single stage trigger, hardcoat black anodized upper and lower receiver, polymer handguard, chrome lined gas key and bolt carrier, adj. A2 post front sight, adj. dual aperture rear sight, 6-position telescoping buttstock. New 2011.

| MSR $739 | $650 | $575 | $500 | $425 | $375 | $325 | $300 | |

Product Codes: 811036 and 811037 (compliant).

* **Model M&P15 TS** – 5.56 NATO cal., GIO, AR-15 style, 16 in. barrel with flash hider, 30 shot mag., Magpul folding front and rear sights, Magpul MOE stock and mag., full Troy TRX free floating quad rail, 6 1/2 lbs. New 2011.

| MSR $1,569 | $1,550 | $1,350 | $1,175 | $1,050 | $850 | $700 | $550 | |

Product Code: 811024.

MODEL M&P15 300 WHISPER – .300 Whisper cal., GIO, 16 in. barrel with or without sound suppressor, 10 shot mag., low recoil and muzzle blast, 6-position CAR stock, black (new 2014) or Realtree APG camo on all surfaces except barrel, 6.38 lbs. New 2012.

| MSR $1,119 | $1,100 | $975 | $825 | $750 | $600 | $500 | $400 | |

Product Code: 811300 (camo) or 811302 (black).

MSR	100%	98%	95%	90%	80%	70%	60%	Last MSR

MODEL M&P15-22 RIMFIRE SEMI-AUTO – .22 LR cal., blowback action, 16 1/2 in. barrel with or w/o threading, 10 or 25 shot mag., A2 post front sight and dual aperture rear sight, fixed or six position CAR adj. stock, quad rail handguard, matte black, Pink Platinum (mfg. 2014 -2015), Black and Tan (mfg. 2014-2015), Purple Platinum (mfg. 2014-2015), Harvest Moon Orange (mfg.2014-2015), 100% Realtree APG HD (disc. 2015), Kryptek Highlander (new 2016) , or Muddy Girl (new 2016) camo finish, 5 1/2 lbs. New 2009.

| MSR $449 | $395 | $350 | $325 | $295 | $265 | $245 | $225 | |

Add 5% for threaded barrel (disc.).

Add $50 for 100% Realtree APG HD camo finish with threaded barrel (mfg. 2011-2015).

Add $50 for Pink Platinum, Black and Tan, Purple Platinum, or Harvest Moon Orange finish (mfg. 2014-2015).

Add $50 for Kryptek Highlander or Muddy Girl camo finish (new 2016).

Product Codes: 811030 (Black), 811046 (Camo), 811051 (Pink Platinum), 811059 (Black and Tan), 10041 (Purple Platinum), or 10043 (Harvest Moon Orange).

* Model M&P15-22 MOE Rimfire Semi-Auto – .22 LR cal., similar to Model M&P15-22, except has 16 in. barrel, folding front and rear sight and skeletonized MagPul MOE stock, flat black or Flat Dark Earth (new 2012) finish, approx. 5 1/2 lbs. New 2011.

| MSR $609 | $525 | $450 | $395 | $365 | $335 | $300 | $275 | |

Product Codes: 811034 and 811035.

* Model M&P15-22 PC TB

Please see listing under Performance Center rifles.

SHOTGUNS

In 1984 S&W discontinued importation of all Howa manufactured shotguns. Mossberg continued importation utilizing leftover S&W parts in addition to fabricating their own.

MODEL 3000 POLICE – 12 ga. only, 18 or 20 in. barrel, blue or parkerized finish, many combinations of finishes, stock types, and other combat accessories were available for this model.

| | | $325 | $255 | $215 | $185 | $170 | $155 | $140 | |

Add $125 for folding stock.

SOG ARMORY

Previous rifle manufacturer located in Houston, TX until late 2013.

SOG Armory also made a wide variety of components and accessories for both AR-10 and AR-15/M16 carbines and rifles.

CARBINES/RIFLES: SEMI-AUTO

All AR-15 style rifles came standard with one 10 or 30 shot magazine, manual, sling, and hard case.

SOG CRUSADER – .223 Rem. cal., GIO, 16 in. chrome lined steel barrel, 30 shot mag., Mil-Spec hardcoat anodized upper and lower, black, tan, or OD green phosphate finish, enhanced magwell and trigger guard, M16 bolt and carrier, flash hider, Ergo pistol grip, M4 6-position tactical stock, M4 stock pad, charging handle, SOG/Troy four rail handguard, SOG/Troy rear flip up sight. Disc. 2013.

| | $1,500 | $1,250 | $1,025 | $875 | $750 | $725 | $675 | *$1,700* |

SOG DEFENDER – .223 Rem. cal., GIO, 16 in. chrome lined steel barrel, 30 shot mag., Mil-Spec hardcoat anodized upper and lower, black, tan, or OD green phosphate finish, enhanced magwell and trigger guard, M16 bolt and carrier, flash hider, Ergo pistol grip, M4 6-position tactical stock, M4 stock pad, charging handle, SOG/Troy four rail handguard, detachable carry handle. Disc. 2013.

| | $1,425 | $1,175 | $1,000 | $850 | $725 | $650 | $550 | *$1,600* |

SOG ENFORCER – .223 Rem. cal., 16 in. chrome lined steel barrel, 30 shot mag., Mil-Spec hardcoat anodized upper and lower, black phosphate finish, enhanced magwell and trigger guard, M16 bolt and carrier, flash hider, Ergo pistol grip, M4 6-position tactical stock, M4 stock pad, charging handle, CAR M4 handguard with double heat shield, SOG/Troy rear slip up sight. Disc. 2013.

| | $1,350 | $1,125 | $975 | $825 | $700 | $600 | $495 | *$1,500* |

SOG GUARDIAN – .223 Rem. cal., GIO, 16 in. chrome lined steel barrel, 30 shot mag., Mil-Spec hardcoat anodized upper and lower, black phosphate finish, enhanced magwell and trigger guard, M16 bolt and carrier, flash hider, Ergo pistol grip, M4 6-position tactical stock, M4 stock pad, charging handle, CAR M4 handguard with double heat shield and detachable carry handle. Disc. 2013.

| | $1,275 | $1,075 | $925 | $800 | $700 | $600 | $495 | *$1,400* |

SOG OPERATOR – .223 Rem. cal., GIO, 16 in. chrome lined steel barrel, 30 shot mag., Mil-Spec hardcoat anodized upper and lower, black, tan, or OD green phosphate finish, enhanced magwell, M16 bolt and carrier, flash hider, Ergo

MSR	100%	98%	95%	90%	80%	70%	60%	Last MSR

pistol grip, 6-position tactical stock, M4 stock pad, charging handle, SOG/Troy four rail handguard, SOG/Troy flip up sight, Magpul Winter trigger guard, Wolf Eye's 260 Lumens tactical light, SOG mount, graphite vertical grip. Disc. 2013.

| | $2,075 | $1,825 | $1,675 | $1,450 | $1,200 | $825 | $750 | $2,300 |

SOG PREDATOR – .223 Rem. cal., GIO, 20 in. Lothar Walther fully fluted barrel with muzzle brake, SOG Extreme vent. handguard with upper and lower Picatinny rails, SOG sights, low profile gas block, Magpul trigger guard and PRS stock, 8.3 lbs. Mfg. 2011-2013.

| | $1,800 | $1,550 | $1,275 | $1,050 | $850 | $750 | $675 | $2,000 |

SOG WARRIOR – .223 Rem. cal., GIO, 16 in. chrome lined steel barrel, 30 shot mag., Mil-Spec hardcoat anodized upper and lower, black or tan phosphate finish, enhanced magwell and trigger guard, M16 bolt and carrier, flash hider, Ergo pistol grip, VLTOR EMOD stock, M4 stock pad, charging handle, SOG/Troy Extreme free float handguard with rails, SOG/Troy flip front and rear sights. Disc. 2013.

| | $1,600 | $1,375 | $1,150 | $1,000 | $875 | $725 | $600 | $1,800 |

SOMMER + OCKENFUSS GmbH

Previous manufacturer located in Baiersbronn, Germany until 2002. Previously imported by Lothar Walther Precision Tool, located in Cumming, GA. Previously imported by Intertex Carousels Corporation during 1998-2000, and located in Pineville, NC.

Sommer + Ockenfuss also produced a bolt adapter to convert the Remington 700 bolt action into a straight pull repeater, enabling the addition of a firing pin safety and firing chamber lock.

PISTOLS: SEMI-AUTO

P21 – .224 HV, 9mm Para., or .40 S&W cal., 3.11 (Combat) or 3.55 (Police) in. rotating barrel, DA/SA, release grip safety uncocks the hammer, keyed slide lock blocks firing pin and slide, 10 shot mag., approx. 24 oz. Mfg. 2001.

| | $550 | $495 | $450 | $415 | $375 | $340 | $310 | $608 |

Add approx. $320 for conversion slide assemblies.

RIFLES: SLIDE ACTION

SHORTY – most popular cals., unique slide action rifle in bullpup configuration featuring a straight line design with a grip safety pistol grip which also works the slide assembly, stainless or black coated barrel, compact 6-lug bolt with a locking surface of 0.263 sq. in., with or w/o sideplates inlet into walnut or black synthetic (new 1999) stock. Imported 1998-2002.

* ***Shorty Wilderness Rifle*** – match trigger, polymer stock, and stainless steel barrel.

| | $1,495 | $1,275 | $1,100 | $995 | $925 | $850 | $750 | $1,660 |

Add $310 for .375 H&H or .416 Rem. Mag. cal. (Shorty Safari).
Add $200 for walnut stock (Shorty American Hunter).
Add $210 for sight mounts.
Add $88 for recoil brake.

* ***Shorty Marksman Rifle*** – similar to Wilderness Rifle, except has choice of black coated or fluted heavy match barrel and recoil brake.

| | $1,875 | $1,675 | $1,450 | $1,275 | $1,100 | $995 | $850 | $2,020 |

Add $80 for .308 Win. or .300 Win. Mag. (fluted barrel), $420 for .338 Lapua Mag. with black coated barrel, or $710 for .338 Lapua Mag. with fluted stainless barrel.
Add $80 for stainless barrel.
Add $210 for sight mount, $168 for bipod, $210 for Spigot stock cap.

There were also deluxe variations, limited editions, and Marksman's packages ($4,100-$4,860 MSR) available in this model.

SOUTHERN GUN COMPANY

Current custom rifle manufacturer located in the U.K.

RIFLES

Southern Gun Company manufactures AR-15 style single shot and manual repeating action rifles in several calibers and configurations built to customer specifications. Southern Gun Company also manufactures the LA-30 semi-auto rifle with features built to customer specifications. Please contact the company directly for more information including options, pricing, and availability (see Trademark Index).

SPARTAN PRECISION RIFLES

Current rifle manufacturer established in early 2011, located in San Jose, CA. Previously located in Concord, CA.

Custom riflemaker Marc Soulie builds rifles per individual specifications, with a specialty in F-Class and sniper rifles. Please contact him directly for more information, including pricing, configurations, options, availability and delivery time (see Trademark Index).

MSR	100%	98%	95%	90%	80%	70%	60%	Last MSR

SPECIALIZED DYNAMICS

Current custom manufacturer located in Chandler, AZ since 2007.

RIFLES: SEMI-AUTO

CUSTOM RIFLE – rifle manufactured to customer's specifications including choice of caliber, barrel length, handguard, stock, trigger, and accessories, features stainless steel barrel and Specialized Dynamics lower and billet ambi side charger upper receiver.

Please contact the company directly for more information regarding a price quote for an individual customized model (see Trademark Index).

MFR (MULTI-FUNCTION RIFLE) – .17 Rem., .204 Ruger, .223 Rem., 6x45 (disc.), 20 Practical (disc.), .264 LBC, or 6.8 SPC cal., GIO, stainless barrel (choice of length), billet aluminum lower with integrated Winter trigger guard, upper receiver with aluminum free float vented and fluted handguard, single stage trigger, fixed A1 or 6-pos. stock, Ergo deluxe pistol grip.

| MSR $1,499 | $1,275 | $1,125 | $1,025 | $875 | $750 | $625 | $525 | |

LW-HUNTER – .17 Rem., .223 Rem., .204 Ruger, 20 Practical (disc.), 6x45 (disc.), .264 LBC, or 6.8 SPC cal., GIO, stainless steel barrel (choice of length), billet aluminum lower with integrated Winter trigger guard, side charge ambi upper receiver, RRA two-stage match trigger, ACE skeleton stock, Ergo deluxe pistol grip, carbon fiber free float tube, lightweight profile.

| MSR $1,599 | $1,350 | $1,200 | $1,075 | $950 | $815 | $700 | $575 | |

LONG RANGE PREDATOR – .243 Win., .260 Rem., 6.5 Creedmoor, or .308 Win. cal., GIO, stainless steel barrel (choice of length), billet large frame lower and flat-top upper receiver, RRA 2-stage match trigger, Winter trigger guard, Magpul PRS stock, Ergo deluxe pistol grip. Disc. 2014.

| | $1,820 | $1,590 | $1,325 | $1,150 | $995 | $850 | $700 | $2,149 |

SPECIALIZED TACTICAL SYSTEMS

Current manufacturer located in Ogden, UT. Previously located in Pleasant View, UT.

RIFLES: SEMI-AUTO

TITAN B – 5.56 NATO cal., GPO, 16 in. STS salt bath nitride stainless barrel, STS SX3 lower receiver, VLTOR upper receiver, Magpul MOE stock, grip, and PMAG, Magpul back up sights, two-stage match trigger, includes STS tactical case, 7 1/2 lbs.

| MSR $2,299 | $1,950 | $1,725 | $1,450 | $1,250 | $1,050 | $900 | $750 | |

TITAN B DI.L – 5.56 NATO cal., GIO, 16 in. STS salt bath Nitride stainless barrel, STS SX3 lower receiver, Mil-Spec upper, Magpul MOE stock, grip, and PMAG, Magpul back up sights, Mil-Spec trigger, hard anodized with Teflon coating, includes STS tactical case, 6 7/8 lbs.

| MSR $1,699 | $1,450 | $1,275 | $1,125 | $1,000 | $850 | $735 | $595 | |

ZOMBIE SLAYER – 5.56 NATO cal., GIO, 16 in. STS salt bath nitride stainless barrel, STS SX3 lower receiver with custom ZOMBIE logo, custom fire control, VLTOR upper receiver, STS "Zombie Muzzle Thumping Device" (ZMTD), Magpul MOE stock, grip, V-grip, and PMAG, Magpul back up sights, two-stage match trigger, Tungsten Grey cerakote finish, includes STS tactical case and "The Zombie Survival Guide" book. Only 50 mfg. 2011-2014.

| | $2,125 | $1,875 | $1,550 | $1,325 | $1,100 | $950 | $825 | $2,500 |

This Zombie themed rifle was custom built for the 2011 SHOT Show. The original model was auctioned off and proceeds went to various charities. Only a limited number of these were planned for production.

SPECIAL WEAPONS LLC

Previous tactical rifle manufacturer 1999-2002, located in Mesa, AZ. Previously located in Tempe, AZ.

Special Weapons LLC closed its doors on Dec. 31, 2002. Another company, Special Weapons, Inc., is handling the warranty repairs on Special Weapons LLC firearms (see Trademark Index).

CARBINES: SEMI-AUTO

OMEGA 760 – 9mm Para. cal., reproduction of the S&W Model 76, 16 1/4 in. partially shrouded barrel, fixed wire stock, 30 shot mag., 7 1/2 lbs. Limited mfg. 2002.

| | $495 | $450 | $425 | $395 | $375 | $350 | $325 | $575 |

SW-5 CARBINE – 9mm Para. cal., configuration styled after the HK-94 (parts interchangeable), stainless steel receiver, plastic lower housing, 16 1/4 in. stainless steel barrel, A2 style black synthetic stock with wide forearm, 10 shot mag. (accepts high capacity HK-94/MP-5 mags also), approx. 6 3/4 lbs. Mfg. 2000-2002.

| | $1,475 | $1,225 | $1,025 | $875 | $800 | $750 | $695 | $1,600 |

MSR		100%	98%	95%	90%	80%	70%	60%	Last MSR

SW-45 CARBINE – .45 ACP cal., otherwise similar to SW-5 Carbine. Mfg. 2000-2002.

		$1,550	$1,275	$1,050	$895	$825	$775	$725	$1,700

RIFLES: SEMI-AUTO

SW-3 – .308 Win. cal., styled after the HK-91 (parts interchangeable), 17.71 in. stainless steel barrel, tooled receiver, sheet steel trigger housing, A2 style stock, approx. 10 lbs. Mfg. 2000-2002.

		$1,425	$1,175	$995	$850	$800	$750	$695	$1,550

* **SW-3 SP** – similar to SW-3, except has PSG-1 style trigger assembly, 22 in. custom target barrel and Weaver rail welded to receiver top. Mfg. 2000-2002.

		$2,250	$1,975	$1,700	$1,500	$1,250	$1,050	$895	$2,500

SPHINX SYSTEMS LTD.

Current manufacturer established in 1876, and presently located in Matten b. Interlaken, Switzerland. Currently imported by Kriss Arms USA, beginning 2011 and located in Virginia Beach, VA. In late 2010, Kriss Arms acquired Sphinx Systems Ltd., including the Sphinx trademark. Previously distributed until 2009 by Sabre Defence Industries, LLC, located in Nashville, TN. Previously imported by Rocky Mountain Armoury, located in Silverthorne, CO. Previously manufactured by Sphinx Engineering S.A. located in Porrentruy, Switzerland, and by Sphinx U.S.A., located in Meriden, CT until 1996. Previously imported by Sile Distributors located in New York, NY.

PISTOLS: SEMI-AUTO

Please contact the importer directly for current U.S. availability and pricing on the following current models.

MODEL 2000S STANDARD – 9mm Para. or .40 S&W (new 1993) cal., 4.53 in. barrel, DA/SA or DAO, stainless steel fabrication, 10 (C/B 1994), 15* (9mm Para.), or 11* (.40 S&W) shot mag., checkered walnut grips, fixed sights, 35 oz. Importation disc. 2002.

		$965	$750	$625	$525	$450	$410	$375	

Add $117 for .40 S&W cal.

* **Model 2000PS Standard Police Special** – similar to Model 2000S, except has compact slide and 3.66 in. barrel.

		$850	$625	$525	$450	$410	$380	$350	

Add $40 for .40 S&W cal.
Add $87 for N/Pall finish.

* **Model 2000P Standard Compact** – similar to Model 2000 Standard, except has 3.66 in. barrel and 13 shot mag., 31 oz.

		$850	$625	$525	$450	$410	$380	$350	

Add $40 for .40 S&W cal.
Add $87 for N/Pall finish.

* **Model 2000H Standard Sub-Compact** – similar to Model 2000 Compact, except has 3.34 in. barrel and 10 shot mag., 26 oz. Disc. 1996.

		$850	$625	$525	$450	$410	$380	$350	$940

Add $40 for .40 S&W cal.
Add $87 for N/Pall finish.

MODEL 2000 MASTER – 9mm Para., 9x21mm, or .40 S&W cal., SAO, two-tone finish only, designed for Master's stock class competition.

		$1,795	$1,350	$1,100	$995	$895	$775	$650	$2,035

MODEL AT-2000 (NEW MODEL) – 9mm Para. or .40 S&W cal., 4.53 in. barrel, DA/SA, 10 shot mag., machined slide with electro deposited finish, decocking mechanism. Limited mfg. 2004-2005.

		$1,825	$1,675	$1,450	$1,225	$1,000	$800	$675	$1,995

MODEL AT-2000CS COMPETITOR – 9mm Para., 9x21mm, or .40 S&W cal., DA/SA, competition model featuring many shooting improvements including 5.3 in. compensated barrel, 10 (C/B 1994), 11* (.40 S&W), or 15* shot mag., Bo-Mar adj. sights, two-tone finish. Imported 1993-1996.

		$1,725	$1,275	$1,050	$950	$850	$750	$675	$1,902

Add $287 for Model AT-2000C (includes Sphinx scope mount).
Add $1,538 for AT-2000K conversion kit (new 1995).
Add $1,490 for Model AT-2000CKS (competition kit to convert AT-2000 to comp. pistol, disc. 1994).

MODEL 2000 COMPETITION – similar to Model 2000 Master, except is SAO and includes more advanced competitive shooting features, Bo-Mar sights, top-of-the-line competition model. Imported 1993-96.

		$2,475	$1,925	$1,725	$1,500	$1,250	$1,050	$895	$2,894

Add $78 for Model AT-2000GM (includes Sphinx scope mount).

MSR	100%	98%	95%	90%	80%	70%	60%	Last MSR

MODEL 3000 SERIES – 9mm Para., 9x21mm (disc.), .40 S&W, or .45 ACP cal., DA/SA, available in standard (4.53 in. barrel), tactical (3 3/4 in. barrel), or competition (4.53 in. barrel, adj. sights), configuration, choice of manual safety or decocker, titanium upper/lower frame with stainless slide, stainless steel slide with titanium lower frame or stainless steel frame/slide, front/rear gripstrap stippling or grooved, two-tone finish, approx. 40 oz. Imported 2001-circa 2012.

	100%	98%	95%	90%	80%	70%	60%
	$2,525	$2,275	$2,000	$1,800	$1,575	$1,375	$1,150

Add $350 for titanium frame with stainless steel slide.
Add $800 for stainless steel slide with titanium upper/lower frame (disc.).
Add $75 for tactical model.
Add $350 for competition model.

SPHINX .45 ACP – .45 ACP cal., DA/SA, steel construction, 3 3/4 in. barrel, double slide serrations, blue finish, 10 shot mag., fixed Trijicon night sights, black polymer grips, decocker mechanism, approx. 43 oz. New 2007.

MSR N/A	$2,850	$2,500	$2,150	$1,850	$1,500	$1,250	$1,000

SDP SERIES – 9mm Para. cal., 3 1/8 (Sub-Compact), 3.7 (Compact), 4 1/2 (Standard) in. barrel, DA/SA, aluminum frame and slide, full length guide rails, 13, 15, or 17 shot mag., match grade trigger, six integrated safeties including loaded chamber indicator, notched Picatinny rail avail. on compact and standard models, twin slide serrations, various sight combinations available per individual model, interchangeable aluminum/rubber grip system, 21-31 3/4 oz. New 2012.

* **SDP Standard Alpha** – 9mm Para. cal., 4 1/2 in. barrel, 17 shot mag., matte black finish only, 31 3/4 oz. New 2014.

MSR $1,295	$1,100	$965	$825	$750	$600	$495	$385

* **SDP Compact Alpha** – 9mm Para. cal., DA/SA, 3.7 in. barrel, 15 shot mag., various finishes including Alpha, Black, Krypton, Sand, Duotone, and Stainless Steel, 27 1/2 oz. New 2014.

MSR $1,295	$1,100	$965	$825	$750	$600	$495	$385

* **SDP Sub Compact Alpha** – 3 1/8 in. barrel, 13 shot mag., matte black finish only, approx. 21 oz. New 2014.

MSR $1,295	$1,100	$965	$825	$750	$600	$495	$385

SPIDER FIREARMS

Current rifle manufacturer located in St. Cloud, FL.

RIFLES: SINGLE SHOT

These models can also be custom ordered in .510 DTC, .50 Spider, .50 SFBR, .416 Barrett, .408 CheyTac, .338 Harris, .338 Lapua, and .338 Wby. Mag. cals.

SPORTSMAN FERRET 50 – .50 BMG cal., single shot bolt action, A2 style buttstock and pistol grip, Picatinny rail, choice of 18 to 36 in. barrel (LW-19 chrome moly is standard), matte black finish, perforated handguard with bipod, includes muzzle brake. New 2003.

MSR $3,511	$3,150	$2,750	$2,375	$2,150	$1,800	$1,600	$1,400

Add $291 for LW-50 stainless steel barrel (SS Sportsman)
Add $583 for LW-50 Supermatch stainless super match barrel (SM Sportsman).

SUPERCOMP FERRET – .50 BMG cal., similar to Ferret 50, features solid steel construction, fixed scope rails, 18 to 36 in. Lothar Walther stainless or chrome moly Supermatch barrels, adj. 1 lb. competition style trigger, two-axis cheekrest, and detachable rear monopod. New 2004.

MSR $3,720	$3,350	$2,930	$2,515	$2,280	$1,875	$1,650	$1,425

Add $302 for LW-50 stainless steel barrel.
Add $583 for LW-50 stainless steel Supermatch barrel.

SPIKE'S TACTICAL LLC

Current AR-15 pistol and rifle manufacturer located in Apopka, FL.

CARBINES/RIFLES: SEMI-AUTO

ST-15 M4 LE CARBINE – 5.56 NATO cal., carbine length GIO, 16 in. M4 profile barrel with A2 flash hider, ST-T2 Tungsten buffer, M4 flat-top upper, Picatinny rail, ST M4 stock, F-marked A2 front sight base, Magpul MBUS rear sight, hardcoat anodized finish, includes hard plastic carry case.

MSR $950	$800	$700	$615	$550	$485	$415	$370

* **ST-15 M4 LE Carbine w/B.A.R.** – 5.56 NATO cal., similar to M4 LE Carbine, except has 7, 9, 10, or 12 in. B.A.R.

MSR $1,125	$935	$850	$725	$625	$550	$475	$425

Add $24 for 9 in., $36 for 10 in., or $46 for 12 in. B.A.R.

MSR	100%	98%	95%	90%	80%	70%	60%	Last MSR

* ST-15 M4 LE Carbine w/S.A.R. – 5.56 NATO cal., GIO, similar to M4 LE Carbine, except available with or w/o ST Lo Profile gas block, and features 7 or 9 in. S.A.R.

MSR $1,203 — $1,025 $925 $800 $685 $595 $515 $440

Add $15 for 9 in. S.A.R. and ST Lo Profile gas block.

ST-15 MID-LENGTH LE CARBINE – 5.56 NATO cal., GIO, 16 in. Govt. profile barrel with A2 flash hider, F-marked A2 front sight base, mid-length handguards, ST-T2 Tungsten buffer, Picatinny rail, M4 feed ramps, forward assist, ST M4 stock, includes Magpul MBUS rear sight, hardcoat anodized finish, includes hard plastic case.

MSR $960 — $820 $700 $630 $570 $500 $425 $380

* ST-15 Mid-Length LE Carbine w/B.A.R. – 5.56 NATO cal., similar to Mid-Length LE Carbine, except has 9 or 10 in. B.A.R. and low profile gas block.

MSR $1,159 — $885 $785 $685 $600 $535 $465 $415

Add $12 for 10 in. B.A.R. and low profile gas block.

* ST-15 Mid-Length LE Carbine w/Heatshield – 5.56 NATO cal., similar to Mid-Length LE Carbine, except has M4 double heat shield handguards. Disc. 2014.

$800 $700 $615 $550 $485 $415 $370 *$950*

* ST-15 Mid-Length LE w/S.A.R. – 5.56 NATO cal., similar to Mid-Length LE, except has ST low profile gas block and 13.2 in. S.A.R.

MSR $1,258 — $1,050 $950 $815 $715 $625 $535 $450

PISTOLS: SEMI-AUTO

ST-15 LE PISTOL – 5.56 NATO cal., 8 in. barrel with A2 flash hider, pistol length gas system, 7 in. S.A.R.3, ST-T2 Tungsten buffer, pistol buffer tube, Magpul MBUS front and rear sights, includes hard plastic case. New late 2014.

MSR $995 — $850 $725 $650 $585 $515 $450 $395

SPIRIT GUN MANUFACTURING COMPANY LLC

Previous manufacturer located in West Palm Beach, FL until 2011.

PISTOLS: SEMI-AUTO

SGM9P – 5.56 NATO cal., GIO, 7 1/2 in. stainless steel barrel with KX3 compensator, 30 shot mag., black, green, or tan finish, SGM9 lower with integral three position sling mount and swivel, VLTOR custom CASV handguard, flip up front sight, VLTOR MUR upper receiver, National Match phosphate and chromed custom bolt carrier. Limited mfg. Disc. 2011.

$2,200 $1,950 $1,725 $1,500 $1,300 $1,100 $825 *$2,495*

RIFLES/CARBINES: SEMI-AUTO

Spirit Gun Manufacturing offered a complete line of AR-15 style rifles and carbines in law enforcement/military and civilian configurations. A variety of options and accessories were available.

SGM-15/SGM-16/SGM-17 – AR-15 style. Disc. 2011.

$2,125 $1,875 $1,550 $1,325 $1,100 $950 $825 *$2,495*

SGM-40/SGM-41 – Disc. 2011.

$2,125 $1,875 $1,550 $1,325 $1,100 $950 $825 *$2,495*

SGM-A19 – Disc. 2011.

$2,275 $1,975 $1,625 $1,375 $1,125 $975 $850 *$2,695*

SGM-A23 – Disc. 2011.

$2,375 $2,075 $1,725 $1,475 $1,200 $1,025 $895 *$2,795*

SGM-A24 – Disc. 2011.

$2,475 $2,150 $1,775 $1,525 $1,250 $1,050 $925 *$2,895*

SGM-A39 – Disc. 2011.

$2,125 $1,875 $1,550 $1,325 $1,100 $950 $825 *$2,495*

SGM-A43 – Disc. 2011.

$2,275 $1,975 $1,625 $1,375 $1,125 $975 $850 *$2,695*

SGM-A47 – Disc. 2011.

$2,375 $2,075 $1,725 $1,475 $1,200 $1,025 $895 *$2,795*

SGM-A48 – Disc. 2011.

$2,475 $2,150 $1,775 $1,525 $1,250 $1,050 $925 *$2,895*

MSR	100%	98%	95%	90%	80%	70%	60%	Last MSR

SPORT-SYSTEME DITTRICH

Current manufacturer established in 2003 and located in Kulmbach, Germany. Previously imported in North America by Wolverine Supplies, located in Manitoba, Canada until 2014, and by Marstar Canada, located in Ontario, Canada.

Sport-Systeme Dittrich manufactures high quality semi-auto reproductions of famous military guns, including the MP38 (BD 38), Sturmgewehr 44 (BD 44) and the Gerät Neumünster (BD 3008). Its latest model is a reproduction of the Fallschirmjägergewehr FG42 as the BD42 I. Please contact the importer or the company directly for more information, including pricing and U.S. availability (see Trademark Index).

SPRINGFIELD ARMORY (MFG. BY SPRINGFIELD INC.)

Current trademark manufactured by Springfield Inc., located in Geneseo, IL. Springfield Inc. has also imported a variety of models. This company was named Springfield Armory, Geneseo, IL until 1992.

Springfield Inc. manufactures commercial pistols and rifles, including reproductions of older military handguns and rifles.

COMBINATION GUNS

M6 SCOUT RIFLE – .22 LR, .22 WMR (disc.), or .22 Hornet cal. over smoothbore .410 bore w/3 in. chamber, O/U Survival Gun, 14 (legal transfer needed) or 18 1/4 in. barrels, parkerized or stainless steel (new 1995), approx. 4 lbs. Disc. 2004.

.22 LR/.22 Win. Mag. cal.	$425	$375	$325	$275	$250	$225	$195	
.22 Hornet cal.	$775	$725	$650	$550	$475	$400	$325	$215

Add approx. 10% for stainless steel.

Add 10% for lockable Marine flotation plastic carrying case.

Early mfg. does not incorporate a trigger guard while late production had a trigger guard.

M6 SCOUT PISTOL/CARBINE – .22 LR or .22 Hornet cal. over .45 LC/.410 bore, 16 in. barrels, parkerized or stainless steel. Mfg. 2002-2004.

.22 LR cal.	$425	$375	$325	$275	$250	$225	$195	
.22 Hornet cal.	$775	$725	$650	$550	$475	$400	$325	$223

Add 10% for stainless steel.

Add approx. $200 per interchangeable 10 in. pistol barrel assembly.

Add 15% for detachable stock.

This model was also available with an optional detachable stock ($49-$59 MSR, not legal with a rifled barrel less than 16 in. or smoothbore less than 18 in.).

M6 SCOUT PISTOL – .22 LR or .22 Hornet cal. over .45 LC/.410 bore, 10 in. barrels, parkerized or stainless steel. Mfg. 2002-2004.

.22 LR cal.	$425	$375	$325	$275	$250	$225	$195	
.22 Hornet cal.	$775	$725	$650	$550	$475	$400	$325	$199

Add approx. 10% for stainless steel.

Add approx. $200 per interchangeable 16 in. carbine barrel.

PISTOLS: SEMI-AUTO

OMEGA PISTOL – .38 Super, 10mm Norma, or .45 ACP cal., SA, ported slide, 5 or 6 in. interchangeable ported or unported barrel with Polygon rifling, special lockup system eliminates normal barrel link and bushing, Pachmayr grips, dual extractors, adj. rear sight. Mfg. 1987-1990.

	$775	$650	$575	$495	$425	$360	$295	$849

Add $663 for interchangeable conversion units.

Add $336 for interchangeable 5 or 6 in. barrel (including factory installation).

Each conversion unit includes an entire slide assembly, one mag., 5 or 6 in barrel, recoil spring guide mechanism assembly, and factory fitting.

Pistols: Semi-Auto - P9 Series

MODEL P9 – 9mm Para., 9x21mm (new 1991) .40 S&W (new 1991), or .45 ACP cal., patterned after the Czech CZ-75, DA/SA, blue (standard beginning 1993), parkerized (standard until 1992), or duotone finish, various barrel lengths, checkered walnut grips. Mfg. in U.S. starting 1990.

* **Model P9 Standard** – 4.72 in. barrel, 15 shot (9mm Para.), 11 shot (.40 S&W), or 10 shot (.45 ACP) mag., parkerized finish standard until 1992 - blue finish beginning 1993, 32.16 oz. Disc. 1993.

	$430	$375	$335	$295	$275	$240	$215	$518

Add $61 for .45 ACP cal.

Add $182 for duotone finish (disc. 1992).

Subtract $40 for parkerized finish.

MSR	100%	98%	95%	90%	80%	70%	60%	Last MSR

In 1992, Springfield added a redesigned stainless steel trigger, patented sear safety which disengages the trigger from the double action mechanism when the safety is on, lengthened the beavertail grip area offering less "pinch," and added a two-piece slide stop design.

* ***Model P9 Stainless*** – similar to P9 Standard, except is constructed from stainless steel, 35.3 oz. Mfg. 1991-93.

	100%	98%	95%	90%	80%	70%	60%	Last MSR
	$475	$425	$350	$285	$250	$215	$185	*$589*

Add $50 for .45 ACP cal.

* ***Model P9 Compact*** – 9mm Para. or .40 S&W cal., 3.66 in. barrel, 13 shot (9mm Para.) or 10 shot (.40 S&W) mag., shorter slide and frame, rounded trigger guard, 30 1/2 oz. Disc. 1992.

	100%	98%	95%	90%	80%	70%	60%	Last MSR
	$395	$350	$300	$275	$250	$225	$200	*$499*

Add $20 for .40 S&W cal.
Add $20-$30 for blue finish depending on cal.
Add $78 for duotone finish.

* ***Model P9 Sub-Compact*** – 9mm Para. or .40 S&W cal., smaller frame than the P9 Compact, 3.66 in. barrel, 12 shot (9mm Para.) or 9 shot (.40 S&W) finger extension mag., squared-off trigger guard, 30.1 oz. Disc. 1992.

	100%	98%	95%	90%	80%	70%	60%	Last MSR
	$395	$350	$300	$275	$250	$225	$200	*$499*

Add $20 for .40 S&W cal.
Add $20-$30 for blue finish depending on cal.

* ***Model P9 Factory Comp*** – 9mm Para., .40 S&W, or .45 ACP cal., 5 1/2 in. barrel (with compensator attached), extended sear safety and mag. release, adj. rear sight, slim competition checkered wood grips, choice of all stainless (disc. 1992) or stainless bi-tone (matte black slide), dual port compensator, 15 shot (9mm Para.), 11 shot (.40 S&W), or 10 shot (.45 ACP) mag., 33.9 oz. Mfg. 1992-93.

	100%	98%	95%	90%	80%	70%	60%	Last MSR
	$595	$525	$450	$420	$390	$360	$330	*$699*

Add $36 for .45 ACP cal.
Add $75-$100 for all stainless finish.

* ***Model P9 Ultra IPSC (LSP)*** – competition model with 5.03 in. barrel (long slide ported), adj. rear sight, choice of parkerized (standard finish until 1992 when disc.), blue (disc. 1992), bi-tone (became standard 1993), or stainless steel (disc. 1992) finish, extended thumb safety, and rubberized competition (9mm Para. and .40 S&W cals. only) or checkered walnut (.45 ACP cal. only) grips, 15 shot (9mm Para.), 11 shot (.40 S&W), or 10 shot (.45 ACP) mag., 34.6 oz. Disc. 1993.

	100%	98%	95%	90%	80%	70%	60%	Last MSR
	$555	$475	$415	$350	$300	$275	$250	*$694*

Add $30 for .45 ACP cal.

* ***Model P9 Ultra LSP Stainless*** – stainless steel variation of the P9 Ultra LSP. Mfg. 1991-92.

	100%	98%	95%	90%	80%	70%	60%	Last MSR
	$675	$525	$425	$360	$315	$260	$225	*$769*

Add $30 for .40 S&W cal.
Add $90 for .45 ACP cal.

* ***Model P9 World Cup*** – see listing under 1911-A1 Custom Models heading.

Pistols: Semi-Auto - R-Series

PANTHER MODEL – 9mm Para., .40 S&W, or .45 ACP cal., DA/SA, 3.8 in. barrel, hammer drop or firing pin safety, 15 shot (9mm Para.), 11 shot (.40 S&W), or 9 shot (.45 ACP) mag., Commander hammer, frame mounted slide stop, narrow profile, non-glare blue finish only, walnut grips, squared-off trigger guard, 29 oz. Mfg. 1992 only.

	100%	98%	95%	90%	80%	70%	60%	Last MSR
	$600	$500	$400	$350	$300	$275	$250	*$609*

FIRECAT MODEL – 9mm Para. or .40 S&W cal., SA, 3 1/2 in. barrel, 3-dot low profile sights, all steel mfg., firing pin block and frame mounted ambidextrous safety, 8 shot (9mm Para.) or 7 shot (.40 S&W) mag., checkered combat style trigger guard and front/rear gripstraps, non-glare blue finish, 35 3/4 oz. Mfg. 1992-1993.

	100%	98%	95%	90%	80%	70%	60%	Last MSR
	$550	$450	$400	$350	$300	$275	$250	*$569*

BOBCAT MODEL – while advertised in 1992, this model was never mfg.

LINX MODEL – while advertised in 1992, this model was never mfg.

Pistols: Semi-Auto - Disc. 1911-A1 Models

MODEL 1911-A1 STANDARD MODEL – .38 Super, 9mm Para., 10mm (new 1990), or .45 ACP cal., patterned after the Colt M1911-A1, 5.04 (Standard) or 4.025 (Commander or Compact Model) in. barrel, SA, 7 shot (Compact), 8 shot (.45 ACP), 9 shot (10mm), or 10 shot (9mm Para. and .38 Super) mag., walnut grips, parkerized, blue, or duotone finish. Mfg. 1985-1990.

	100%	98%	95%	90%	80%	70%	60%	Last MSR
	$400	$360	$330	$300	$280	$260	$240	*$454*

Add $35 for blue finish.
Add $80 for duotone finish.

This model was also available with a .45 ACP to 9mm Para. conversion kit for $170 in parkerized finish, or $175 in blue finish.

MSR	100%	98%	95%	90%	80%	70%	60%	Last MSR

* **Model 1911-A1 Standard Defender Model** – .45 ACP cal. only, similar to Standard 1911-A1 Model, except has fixed combat sights, beveled magwell, extended thumb safety, bobbed hammer, flared ejection port, walnut grips, factory serrated front strap and two stainless steel magazines, parkerized or blue finish. Mfg. 1988-90.

	$485	$435	$375	$340	$300	$280	$260	$567

Add $35 for blue finish.

* **Model 1911-A1 Standard Commander Model** – .45 ACP cal. only, similar to Standard 1911-A1 Model, except has 3.63 in. barrel, shortened slide, Commander hammer, low profile 3-dot sights, walnut grips, parkerized, blue, or duotone finish. Mfg. in 1990 only.

	$450	$415	$350	$325	$285	$260	$245	$514

Add $30 for blue finish.
Add $80 for duotone finish.

* **Model 1911-A1 Standard Combat Commander Model** – .45 ACP cal. only, 4 1/4 in. barrel, bobbed hammer, walnut grips. Mfg. 1988-89.

	$435	$385	$325	$295	$275	$250	$230	

Add $20 for blue finish.

* **Model 1911-A1 Standard Compact Model** – .45 ACP cal. only, compact variation featuring shortened Commander barrel and slide, reduced M1911 straight gripstrap frame, checkered walnut grips, low profile 3-dot sights, extended slide stop, combat hammer, parkerized, blue, or duotone finish. Mfg. 1990 only.

	$450	$415	$350	$325	$285	$260	$245	$514

Add $30 for blue finish.
Add $80 for duotone finish.

* **Model 1911-A1 Standard Custom Carry Gun** – .38 Super (special order only), 9mm Para., 10mm (new 1990), or .45 ACP cal., similar to Defender Model, except has tuned trigger pull, heavy recoil spring, extended thumb safety, and other features. Mfg. 1988-disc.

	$860	$725	$660	$535	$460	$420	$385	$969

Add $130 for .38 Super Ramped, 10mm was POR.

Pistols: Semi-Auto - 1911-A1, Single Action (90s Series)

The initials "PDP" refer to Springfield's Personal Defense Pistol series.

Beginning in 2000, Springfield Armory started offering a Loaded Promotion package on their 1911-A1 pistol line. Many of these features and options are found on the FBI's Hostage Rescue Teams (HRT) pistol contract with Springfield Armory. Standard features of this Loaded Promotion package are hammer forged premium air-gauged barrel, front and rear cocking serrations, Novak patented low profile sights or Bo-Mar type adj. sights, extended thumb safety, tactical beavertail, flat mainspring housing, Cocobolo grips, High Hand grip, lightweight match trigger, full length guide rod, and machine beveled mag. well. This promotion includes all pistols except the Mil-Spec Model 1911 A1.

In 2001, Springfield's Custom Loaded 1911-A1 Series pistols came equipped standard with Springfield's integral locking system, carry bevel, hammer forged premium air-gauged barrel, front and rear cocking serrations, Novak patented low profile sights (some models come equipped with Tritium sights or Bo-Mar type adj. sights), extended thumb safety, tactical beavertail, flat mainspring housing, Cocobolo grips, high hand grip, lightweight adj. match trigger, full length guide rod, machine beveled magwell, and a "loaded" coupon ($600 consumer savings). These Custom Loaded features will vary by model. All models with less than a 5 in. and all alloy pistols supplied with ramped, fully supported barrels.

Beginning 2002, every Springfield pistol is equipped with a patented integral locking system (I.L.S., keyed in the rear gripstrap) at no extra charge.

Beginning 2007, most models were shipped with an 11 gear system, including one (GI models only) or two mags., belt holster, magazine pouch, and bore brush supplied in a lockable blue plastic case.

In 2015 all Loaded pistols include the 11 Gear System which consists of a paddle holster, double magazine pouch, and a new 1911 case.

PDP DEFENDER MODEL – .40 S&W (disc. 1992) or .45 ACP cal., standard pistol with slide and barrel shortened to Champion length (4 in.), tapered cone dual port compensator system, fully adj. sights, Videcki speed trigger, rubber grips, Commander style hammer, serrated front strap, parkerized (disc. 1992), duotone/bi-tone, or blue (disc. 1993) finish. Mfg. 1991-1998.

	$850	$745	$635	$580	$465	$380	$295	$992

1911-A1 90s EDITION (CUSTOM LOADED) – .38 Super, 9mm Para., 10mm (disc. 1991), .40 S&W, or .45 ACP cal., patterned after the Colt M1911-A1, except has linkless operating system, 5.04 (Standard) or 4 (Champion or Compact Model) in. barrel, 7 shot (Compact), 8 shot (.40 S&W or .45 ACP Standard), 9 shot (9mm Para., 10mm, or .38 Super), or 10 shot (.38 Super) mag., checkered walnut grips, parkerized (.38 Super beginning 1994 or .45 ACP beginning 1993), blue or duotone (disc. 1992) finish. New 1991.

MSR	100%	98%	95%	90%	80%	70%	60%	Last MSR

* **_1911-A1 90s Edition Mil-Spec_** – .38 Super (disc. 2011) or .45 ACP cal., 5 in. stainless steel barrel, blue (disc.), parkerized, bi-tone (mfg. 2004 only), or OD Green (mfg. 2004 only) finish, 3-dot Hi-Viz fixed combat sights, standard loaded features include belt holster, double mag. pouch and extra set of grips (Mil-Spec Package), 39 oz.

| MSR $719 | $600 | $525 | $450 | $395 | $300 | $275 | $250 | |

Add $17 for blue finish (disc. 2001).

Add $21 for OD Green or bi-tone finish (mfg. 2004 only).

Subtract approx. $70 if without Mil-Spec package (became standard in 2012, includes belt holster, double mag. pouch and extra set of grips, introduced 2009).

Add $631 for .38 Super cal. in High Polish Nickel (Acusport exclusive 2004-2007).

* **_1911-A1 90s Edition Mil-Spec Operator_** – .45 ACP cal. only, similar to Mil-Spec 1911-A1, except has Picatinny light mounting system forged into lower front of frame, parkerized finish only. Disc. 2002.

| | $615 | $540 | $460 | $420 | $340 | $275 | $215 | _$756_ |

* **_1911-A1 90s Edition Loaded Operator_** – .45 ACP cal. only, similar to full size service model, except has Picatinny accessory rail forged into lower front of frame, checkered hardwood (disc. 2003), plastic grips, OD Green slide with black bi-tone Armory Kote finished frame, Novak low mount Tritium (disc.) or Trijicon night sights. New 2002.

| MSR $1,299 | $1,100 | $950 | $850 | $750 | $625 | $500 | $400 | |

* **_1911-A1 90s Edition Lightweight Operator_** – .45 ACP cal. only, 5 in. stainless steel barrel, blue finish, 7 shot mag., fixed low profile combat rear sight, dovetail front sight, Cocobolo grips, 34 oz. New 2006.

| MSR $1,209 | $1,050 | $925 | $795 | $725 | $600 | $495 | $385 | |

* **_1911-A1 90s Edition Standard or Lightweight Model_** – .45 ACP cal. (current mfg.), Standard model has parkerized, blue (disc.), or OD Green with Armory Kote (mfg. 2002-2014) finish, Custom Loaded features became standard in 2001, Lightweight Model was mfg. 1995-2012 with either matte (disc. 2002), bi-tone (mfg. 2003-2012) or blue (mfg. 1993-disc.) finish, current mfg. is w/either Novak low mount or Trijicon night sights, 28.6 or 35.6 oz.

| MSR $929 | $825 | $725 | $625 | $550 | $475 | $375 | $295 | |

Add $52 for Lightweight Model (with Trijicon night sights), disc. 2012.

Subtract approx. 10%-25% if w/o Custom Loaded features (new 2001), depending on condition.

* **_1911-A1 90s Edition Stainless Standard Model_** – 9mm Para. (mfg. 1994-2012), .38 Super (disc.), .40 S&W (mfg. 2001-2002), or .45 ACP cal., 7 (.45 ACP cal.), 8 (.40 S&W), or 9 (9mm Para.) shot mag., Custom Loaded features became standard in 2001, wraparound rubber (disc.) or checkered hardwood grips, 11 Gear system holster became standard 2009, Novak Lo-Mount (disc.), Bo-Mar type (mfg. 1996-2001), or combat 3 dot sights, beveled magwell, 39.2 oz. New 1991.

| MSR $963 | $850 | $775 | $675 | $575 | $475 | $395 | $325 | |

Add $62 for 9mm Para. cal. (disc. 2012), or $32 for .40 S&W cal. (disc.).

Add $230 for Tactical Combat Model with combat features and black stainless steel (mfg. 2005-disc.).

Add $50 for Bo-Mar type sights (disc. 2001).

Add $202 for long slide variation in .45 Super cal. with V16 porting and Bo-Mar sights (disc.).

* **_1911-A1 90s Edition Stainless Super Tuned Standard_** – .45 ACP cal. only, super tuned by the Custom Shop, 7 shot mag., 5 in. barrel, Novak fixed Lo-Mount sights, 39.2 oz. Mfg. 1997-99.

| | $875 | $765 | $655 | $595 | $480 | $395 | $305 | _$995_ |

* **_1911-A1 90s Edition Standard High Capacity_** – 9mm Para. (disc.) or .45 ACP cal., 5 in. barrel, blue (disc. 2001) or matte parkerized (new 1996) finish with plastic grips, 3-dot fixed combat sights, 10 shot (except for law enforcement) mag. Mfg. 1995-2003.

| | $635 | $555 | $475 | $430 | $350 | $285 | $220 | _$756_ |

Add $50 for blue finish (disc.).

* **_1911-A1 90s Edition Stainless High Capacity_** – similar to Standard High Capacity, except is stainless steel. Mfg. 1996-2000.

| | $675 | $590 | $505 | $460 | $370 | $305 | $235 | _$819_ |

* **_1911-A1 90s Edition XM4 High Capacity Model_** – 9mm Para. or 45 ACP cal., features widened frame for high capacity mag., blue (mfg. 1993 only) or stainless finish only. Mfg. 1993-94.

| | $595 | $520 | $445 | $405 | $325 | $270 | $210 | _$689_ |

1911-A1 TACTICAL RESPONSE PISTOL (TRP SERIES) – .45 ACP cal., forged National Match frame and slide, 5 in. stainless steel barrel, 7 shot mag., front strap checkering, low profile fixed combat 3-dot Tritium sights, extended beveled magwell, Black Armory Kote or stainless steel finish, checkered rosewood (disc.) or black/grey G10 grips, 36 oz. New 1999.

| MSR $1,646 | $1,395 | $1,225 | $1,025 | $925 | $775 | $650 | $550 | |

MSR	100%	98%	95%	90%	80%	70%	60%	Last MSR

* 1911-A1 TRP Operator – .45 ACP cal., forged National Match frame and slide, 5 in. stainless steel match grade barrel, 7 shot mag., checkered front strap, adj. Trijicon night sights, Black Armory Kote finish, checkered front strap, Black/Grey G10 grips, 4 1/2-5 1/2 lbs. New mid-2008.

MSR $1,730	$1,475	$1,275	$1,050	$950	$800	$675	$575	

MODEL 1911-A1 GI – .45 ACP cal., 5 in. barrel, parkerized, OD Green Armory Kote finish or stainless steel, 7 (standard) or 13 (high capacity) shot mag., low profile military sights, diamond checkered walnut grips with U.S. initials, includes 5.11 Gear belt holster, 36 oz. Mfg. 2004-2011.

	$565	$485	$415	$375	$300	$245	$190	*$656*

Add $52 for stainless steel.

Add $61 for high capacity magazine (parkerized finish, new 2005).

1911-A1 COMMANDER MODEL – .45 ACP cal. only, similar to Standard 1911-A1 Model, except has 3.63 in. barrel, shortened slide, Commander hammer, low profile 3-dot sights, walnut grips, parkerized, blue, or duotone finish. Mfg. 1991-92.

	$425	$370	$320	$290	$235	$190	$150	

* 1911-A1 Commander Model Combat – .45 ACP cal. only, 4 1/4 in. barrel, bobbed hammer, walnut grips. Mfg. 1991 only.

	$425	$370	$320	$290	$235	$190	$150	

1911-A1 CHAMPION MODEL – .380 ACP (Model MD-1, mfg. 1995 only) or .45 ACP cal., similar to Standard Model, except has 4 in. barrel and shortened slide, blue (disc. 2000) or parkerized (Mil-Spec Champion, new 1994) finish, Commander hammer, checkered walnut grips, 3-dot sights (Novak night sights became standard 2001), 7 shot mag., 33 1/2 oz. Mfg. 1992-2002.

	$695	$610	$520	$470	$380	$315	$245	*$856*

Add $30 for Ultra Compact slide (mfg. 1997-98).

Add $79 for ported Champion V10 with Ultra Compact slide (disc.).

Subtract approx. 10%-25% if w/o Custom Loaded features (new 2001), depending on condition.

Subtract approx. $150 for .380 ACP cal. (Model MD-1, disc.).

* 1911-A1 Champion Model (Custom Loaded) – .45 ACP cal. only, stainless steel or Lightweight bi-tone with OD Green with Black Armory Kote finish (new 2004), Trijicon night sights. Mfg. 1992-2012.

	$900	$800	$675	$615	$500	$400	$315	*$1,031*

Add $42 for stainless steel.

Add $119 for Ultra Compact slide (mfg. 1997-98).

Add $52 for ported Champion V10 with Ultra Compact slide (disc. 2000).

Subtract approx. 10%-25% if w/o Custom Loaded features (new 2001), depending on condition.

* 1911-A1 Champion Model Lightweight – .45 ACP cal., 4 in. barrel, aluminum frame, matte metal finish, night sights became standard during 2001, current mfg. has lower Picatinny rail. Mfg. 1999-disc.

	$995	$850	$725	$625	$500	$425	$350	*$1,129*

Subtract approx. 10%-25% if w/o Custom Loaded features (new 2001), depending on condition.

* 1911-A1 Champion Model Lightweight Operator – .45 ACP cal., 4 in. stainless steel match grade bull barrel, two 7 shot mags., forged aluminum alloy Operator frame with integral accessory rail, beavertail grip safety, flat mainspring housing, lightweight Delta hammer, extended ambidextrous thumb safety, extended trigger, low profile 3-dot Tritium combat sights, lowered and flared ejection port, Cross Cannon double diamond Cocobolo grips, Black Armory Kote finish, 34 oz. New 2006.

MSR $1,050	$925	$825	$725	$625	$525	$425	$350	

* 1911-A1 Champion Model GI – .45 ACP cal., parkerized or blued slide with black anodized frame (Lightweight Model, new 2005), low profile military sights, diamond checkered wood grips with U.S. initials, includes belt holster, 34 oz. Mfg. 2004-2012.

	$560	$485	$410	$375	$300	$245	$190	*$656*

* 1911-A1 Champion Model TRP – .45 ACP cal., 4 in. barrel, otherwise similar to TRP Tactical Response. Mfg. 1999-2001.

	$1,045	$915	$785	$710	$575	$470	$365	*$1,249*

* 1911-A1 Champion Model Comp PDP – .45 ACP cal. only, compensated version of the Champion Model, blue. Mfg. 1993-98.

	$780	$680	$585	$530	$430	$350	$275	*$869*

* 1911-A1 Champion Model Super Tuned – .45 ACP cal., super tuned by the Custom Shop, 7 shot mag., 4 in. barrel, blue or parkerized finish, Novak fixed Lo-Mount sights, 36.3 oz. Mfg. 1997-99.

	$850	$745	$635	$580	$465	$380	$295	*$959*

Add $30 for blue finish.

MSR	100%	98%	95%	90%	80%	70%	60%	Last MSR

* 1911-A1 Champion Model XM4 High Capacity – 9mm Para. or .45 ACP cal., high capacity variation. Mfg. 1994 only.

	$615	$540	$460	$420	$340	$275	$215	$699

1911-A1 COMPACT MODEL – .45 ACP cal. only, compact variation featuring shortened 4 in. barrel and slide, reduced M1911-A1 curved gripstrap frame, checkered walnut grips, low profile 3-dot sights, 6 or 7 shot mag., extended slide stop, standard or lightweight alloy (new 1994) frame, combat hammer, parkerized, blue, or duotone (disc. 1992) finish, standard or lightweight (new 1995) configuration, 27 or 32 oz. Mfg. 1991-96.

	$415	$365	$310	$280	$230	$185	$145	$476

Add $66 for blue finish.
Add $67 for Compact Lightweight Model (matte finish only).

* 1911-A1 Compact Model Stainless – stainless steel variation of the Compact Model. Mfg. 1991-96.

	$495	$435	$370	$335	$270	$225	$175	$582

* 1911-A1 Compact Model Lightweight – .45 ACP cal., forged alloy frame, matte metal finish, 6 shot mag., Novak night sights became standard 2001. Mfg. 1999-2003.

	$585	$510	$440	$395	$320	$265	$205	$733

Subtract approx. 10%-25% if w/o Custom Loaded features (new 2001), depending on condition.

»1911-A1 Compact Model Lightweight Stainless – similar to Compact Lightweight, except is stainless steel. Disc. 2001.

	$725	$635	$545	$495	$400	$325	$255	$900

Subtract approx. 10%-25% if w/o Custom Loaded features (new 2001), depending on condition.

* 1911-A1 Compact Model Comp Lightweight – compensated version of the Compact Model, bi-tone or matte finish, regular or lightweight alloy (new 1994) frame. Mfg. 1993-98.

	$775	$680	$580	$525	$425	$350	$270	$869

* 1911-A1 Compact Model High Capacity – blue or stainless steel, 3-dot fixed combat sights, black plastic grips, 10 shot (except for law enforcement) mag. Mfg. 1995-96 only.

	$550	$475	$400	$365	$295	$245	$190	$609

Add $39 for stainless steel.

* 1911-A1 Compact Model High Capacity PDP Comp – .45 ACP cal. only, features compensated 3 1/2 in. barrel, 10 shot (except law enforcement) mag., blue finish only. Mfg. 1995-96 only.

	$830	$725	$620	$565	$455	$375	$290	$964

1911 A-1 ULTRA COMPACT (CUSTOM LOADED) – .380 ACP (lightweight only, mfg. 1995 only), 9mm Para. (new 1998, lightweight stainless only), or .45 ACP cal., 3 1/2 in. barrel, bi-tone (.45 ACP only, disc.), matte (.380 ACP, MD-1), or parkerized (Mil-Spec Ultra Compact) finish, 6, 7 (.380 ACP cal.) or 8 (9mm Para. cal.) shot mag., Custom Loaded features and night sights became standard in 2001, 24 or 30 oz. Mfg. 1995-2003.

	$680	$595	$510	$460	$375	$305	$240	$837

Add $12 for V10 porting.
Add $12 for Novak Tritium sights (not available on 9mm Para cal.).
Add $110 for bi-tone finish (disc.).
Subtract $50 for MD-1 variation (.380 ACP only).
Subtract approx. 10%-25% if w/o Custom Loaded features (new 2001), depending on condition.

* 1911 A-1 Ultra Compact Mil-Spec – .45 ACP cal., parkerized (disc.) or blued (new 2004) finish, similar to full size Mil-Spec Model, 6 shot mag., checkered grips, 3-dot fixed Hi-Viz combat sights. Mfg. 2001-2002, reintroduced 2004 only.

	$550	$480	$410	$375	$300	$245	$190	$641

Subtract approx. 10%-25% if w/o Custom Loaded features (new 2001), depending on condition.

* 1911 A-1 Ultra Compact Stainless Custom Loaded – 9mm Para. (disc. 2004) or .45 ACP cal., stainless steel, Novak (disc.) or Fixed Combat Trijicon (current mfg.) night sights became standard 2001. Mfg. 1998-2012.

	$925	$800	$675	$615	$490	$400	$315	$1,073

Add $17 for 9mm Para cal. (lightweight, disc. 2004).
Subtract approx. 10%-25% if w/o Custom Loaded features (new 2001), depending on condition.

* 1911 A-1 Ultra Compact Lightweight – .45 ACP cal., aluminum frame, matte metal finish, night sights became standard 2001. Mfg. 1999-2001.

	$695	$610	$520	$470	$380	$315	$245	$867

Subtract approx. 10%-25% if w/o Custom Loaded features (new 2001), depending on condition.

MSR	100%	98%	95%	90%	80%	70%	60%	Last MSR

* 1911 A-1 Ultra Compact V10 Lightweight Ported – .45 ACP cal., bi-tone finish. Mfg. 1999-2001.

	$750	$655	$560	$510	$410	$335	$260	*$737*

»1911 A-1 Ultra Compact V10 Lightweight Stainless – 9mm Para. or .45 ACP (exclusive) cal., similar to Ultra Compact Lightweight, except is stainless steel, Novak Lo-Mount sights. Mfg. 1999-2002.

	$725	$635	$545	$495	$400	$325	$255	*$870*

Add $31 for night sights (.45 ACP cal. only).
Subtract approx. 10%-25% if w/o Custom Loaded features (new 2001), depending on condition.

* 1911 A-1 Ultra Compact High Capacity – 9mm Para. (disc.) or .45 ACP cal., parkerized (Mil-Spec) or blue (disc.) finish, and stainless steel (disc.) construction, 10 shot mag., 3-dot fixed combat (disc.) or Novak Lo-Mount (new 2002) sights, black plastic grips. Mfg. 1996-2002.

	$735	$645	$550	$500	$405	$330	$255	*$909*

Add $98 for stainless steel.
Add $145 for stainless steel with V10 ported barrel (disc.).
Subtract approx. 10%-25% if w/o Custom Loaded features (new 2001), depending on condition.

* 1911 A-1 Ultra Compact V10 Ported – .45 ACP cal. only, 3 1/2 in. specially compensated barrel/slide, blue (disc.), bi-tone, or parkerized (Mil-Spec Ultra Compact) finish, Novak Lo-Mount or 3-dot combat sights, 30 oz. Mfg. 1995-2002.

	$690	$605	$515	$470	$380	$310	$240	*$853*

Subtract approx. 10%-25% if w/o Custom Loaded features (new 2001), depending on condition.

* 1911 A-1 Ultra Compact V10 Super Tuned Ported – .45 ACP cal. only, super tuned by the Custom Shop, 3 1/2 in. ported barrel, bi-tone finish or stainless steel (exclusive), Novak fixed Lo-Mount sights, 32.9 oz. Mfg. 1997-99.

	$925	$810	$695	$630	$510	$415	$325	*$1,049*

Add $70 for stainless steel (exclusive).

1911-A1 MICRO COMPACT – .45 ACP cal. only, 3 in. tapered barrel w/o bushing, matte finish, checkered grips, 6 shot mag., Novak Lo-Mount night sights. Mfg. 2002 only.

	$625	$545	$470	$425	$345	$280	$220	*$749*

* 1911 A-1 Micro Compact Lightweight Custom Loaded – similar to Micro Compact 1911 A-1, except also available in .40 S&W (disc.) cal., bi-tone, OD Green (mfg. 2003 only), or black Armory Kote (mfg. 2003-2004) finish with forged steel slide (grey) and aluminum alloy frame (blue), checkered Cocobolo grips, Trijicon night sights, 24 oz. Mfg. 2002-2012.

	$1,195	$995	$875	$750	$625	$525	$425	*$1,377*

Add $71 for Operator Model with XML X-treme mini light (disc. 2011).

* 1911 A-1 Micro Compact Lightweight Stainless Custom Loaded – .45 ACP cal. only, similar to Micro Compact 1911 A-1 Custom Loaded, except is stainless or black stainless steel slide. Mfg. 2003.

	$825	$720	$620	$560	$455	$370	$290	*$993*

* 1911 A-1 Micro Compact GI – .45 ACP cal., parkerized finish, checkered diamond walnut grips with U.S. initials, includes belt holster, 32 oz. Mfg. 2004-2011.

	$615	$535	$465	$400	$325	$270	$210	*$708*

1911-A1 EMP (ENHANCED MICRO PISTOL) – 9mm Para. or .40 S&W cal., 9 shot mag., 3 in. stainless steel bull barrel, polished stainless slide with blue frame, Tritium 3-dot sights, available in Standard or Lightweight configuration, reduced dimensions result in narrower profile, Cocobolo or G10 grips, bi-tone finish, 27 (Lightweight) or 33 oz. New 2007.

MSR $1,249	$1,095	$950	$825	$725	$625	$515	$400	

Add $71 for G10 grips (new 2008).

Pistols: Semi-Auto - 1911-A1 Custom Models

In addition to the models listed, Springfield also custom builds other configurations of Race Guns that are available through Springfield dealers.

Add $100 for all cals. other than .45 ACP.

CUSTOM CARRY GUN – .45 ACP (other cals. available upon request) cal., similar to Defender Model, except has tuned trigger pull, 7 shot mag., heavy recoil spring, extended thumb safety, available in blue or phosphate (disc.) finish. New 1991.

MSR $2,095	$1,775	$1,450	$1,150	$950	$800	$700	$600	

Add $180 for Custom Carry Champion or Custom Carry Compact.

CUSTOM OPERATOR – .45 ACP cal. New 2001.

MSR $2,810	$2,495	$2,225	$1,775	$1,400	$1,100	$950	$850	

MSR	100%	98%	95%	90%	80%	70%	60%	Last MSR

PROFESSIONAL MODEL – .45 ACP cal., FBI contract model, black finish, custom fitted National Match barrel and bushing, many other custom shop features, Novak Lo-Mount rear sight, checkered Cocobolo grips, with or w/o integral light rail on lower frame. New 1999.

| MSR $3,295 | $2,825 | $2,400 | $2,100 | $1,700 | $1,325 | $1,025 | $925 | |

Add $100 for lower Picatinny rail.

1911-A1 CUSTOM COMPACT – .45 ACP cal. only, carry or lady's model with shortened slide and frame, compensated, fixed 3-dot sights, Commander style hammer, Herrett walnut grips, other custom features, blue only.

| | $1,615 | $1,325 | $1,100 | $950 | $850 | $750 | $675 | *$1,815* |

1911-A1 CUSTOM CHAMPION – similar to Custom Compact, except is based on Champion model with full size frame and shortened slide.

| | $1,615 | $1,325 | $1,100 | $950 | $850 | $750 | $675 | *$1,815* |

CUSTOM HIGH CAPACITY LTD – .40 S&W cal. Mfg. 2004-2011.

| | $2,200 | $1,775 | $1,425 | $1,125 | $975 | $875 | $775 | *$2,650* |

OPERATOR LIGHTWEIGHT – .45 ACP cal., 3 in. barrel, bi-tone finish, XML mini-light, includes Novak Trijicon night sights. Limited mfg. 2005.

| | $1,050 | $925 | $800 | $700 | $600 | $500 | $400 | *$1,247* |

OPERATOR TACTICAL RESPONSE – .45 ACP cal., 5 in. barrel, black Armory Kote finish, adj. Trijicon night sights. Limited mfg. 2005.

| | $1,395 | $1,075 | $900 | $775 | $675 | $575 | $475 | *$1,639* |

LOADED OPERATOR – .45 ACP cal., 5 in. barrel, OD Green or black Armory Kote finish and slide, Novak or Trijicon night sights. Limited mfg. 2005.

| | $1,025 | $900 | $800 | $700 | $600 | $500 | $400 | *$1,218* |

Pistols: Semi-Auto - XD Series

All XD pistols are manufactured by HS Produkt (formerly I.M. Metal) in Croatia. All XD pistols were originally shipped with two magazines. Beginning 2005, high capacity magazines are legal for civilian sales in those states that permit high cap. mags. During 2006, all XD pistols were shipped with the XD Gear System, consisting of belt holster, double magazine pouch, magazine loader, two magazines and cable lock.

In 2013, Springfield Armory USA released its XD-S Series in .45 ACP cal. with many compact features.

XD 5 IN. TACTICAL (X-TREME DUTY) – 9mm Para., .357 SIG (disc. 2014), .40 S&W, .45 ACP (new 2006), or .45 GAP (mfg. 2005-2007) cal., cold hammer forged 5 in. barrel, 9 (.45 GAP, disc.), 10, 12 (.40 S&W or .357 SIG), or 15 (9mm Para.) shot mag., lightweight polymer frame, matte black, bi-tone (.45 ACP only), Dark Earth (mfg. 2007-2012) or OD Green (disc.) finish, steel slide, single action striker fired with U.S.A. trigger system, firing pin and loaded chamber indicators, dual recoil spring system, polymer frame with lower Picatinny rail, ambidextrous mag. release, grip safety, front and rear slide serrations, external thumb safety version became separate model in 2008, approx. 29 (9mm Para. cal.) or 33 oz. Mfg. 2002-2015.

| | $475 | $400 | $350 | $300 | $265 | $235 | $200 | *$539* |

Add $31 for .45 ACP cal. (new 2006).
Add $31 for thumb safety (.45 ACP cal. only, black or bi-tone finish only).
Add $74 for bi-tone finish (.45 ACP cal. only).
Add $92 for Trijicon sights (disc.) or approx. $90 for Heinie (disc.) Tritium Slant Pro sights.
Subtract $7 for .45 GAP cal. black tactical (disc. 2007).

* *XD Tactical Pro* – limited mfg. 2003 only.

| | $875 | $775 | $675 | $575 | $475 | $400 | $350 | *$1,099* |

XD 4 IN. SERVICE (X-TREME DUTY) – 9mm Para., .357 SIG (disc. 2015), .40 S&W, .45 ACP (new 2006), or .45 GAP (mfg. 2005-2007) cal., cold hammer forged 4 in. ported or unported barrel, 9 (.45 GAP), 10 (.45 ACP), 12 (.40 S&W or .357 SIG), or 15 (9mm Para.) shot mag., lightweight polymer frame, matte black (only finish available on .357 SIG cal.), bi-tone (mfg. 2003-2015), Dark Earth (mfg. 2007-2012) or OD Green (disc.) finish, steel slide, single action striker fired with U.S.A. trigger system, firing pin and loaded chamber indicators, dual recoil spring system, polymer frame with lower Picatinny rail, ambidextrous mag. release, grip safety, front and rear slide serrations, thumb safety version became separate model during 2008, approx. 28 (9mm Para.) or 30 oz. New 2002.

| MSR $508 | $460 | $385 | $325 | $275 | $240 | $220 | $200 | |

Add $22 for .45 ACP cal.
Add $22 for thumb safety in .45 ACP cal. only.
Add $42 for bi-tone finish (mfg. 2003-2015).
Add $35 for V10 ported barrel (black or OD Green finish, not available in .45 ACP or .45 GAP cal.), disc.
Add $100 for stainless steel slide (.45 ACP cal. only), disc.

MSR	100%	98%	95%	90%	80%	70%	60%	Last MSR

Add $96 for Trijicon or Heinie Tritium Slant Pro night sights (not available on .45 GAP cal.), disc.
Subtract $7 for .45 GAP cal. (disc. 2007).

XD 3 IN. SUB-COMPACT (X-TREME DUTY) – 9mm Para. or .40 S&W (new 2004) cal., cold hammer forged 3 in. barrel, 9 (.40 S&W), 10 (9mm Para.), 13 (9mm Para.) or 16 (9mm Para.) shot mag., lightweight polymer frame, black, bi-tone (mfg. 2004-2015), satin stainless (disc.), or OD Green (disc.) finish, steel slide, single action striker fired with U.S.A. trigger system, firing pin and loaded chamber indicators, dual recoil spring system, polymer frame with lower Picatinny rail, ambidextrous mag. release, grip safety, front and rear slide serrations, 26 oz. New 2003.

| MSR $508 | $460 | $385 | $325 | $275 | $240 | $220 | $200 | |

Add $42 for bi-tone finish (mfg. 2004-2015).
Add $96 for Trijicon or Heinie Tritium Slant Pro night sights (disc.).
Add $100 for X-treme mini light (disc. 2011).

This model is not available with a thumb safety.

XD COMPACT SERIES – 9mm Para. (mfg. 2007 only), .40 S&W (mfg. 2007 only), or .45 ACP cal., 4 or 5 (disc. 2014) in. barrel, shortened grip frame, Black, OD Green (disc.2012), bi-tone (mfg. 2008-2014), or Dark Earth (disc. 2011) finish, stainless steel slide, OD Green (disc 2012) or Dark Earth (disc. 2011), 10 or extended 13 shot mag., 29 or 32 oz. New 2007.

| MSR $541 | $475 | $400 | $350 | $300 | $265 | $235 | $200 | |

Add $46 for 5 in. barrel (disc. 2014).
Add $66 for bi-tone finish (disc. 2014) or stainless steel slide (4 in. barrel only, disc. 2012).
Add $94 for Trijicon night sights (disc. 2011).
Subtract $30 for 9mm or .40 S&W cal. (4 in. barrel only), w/o night sights (disc. 2007).

XD CUSTOM SERIES – the Springfield custom shop made three variations of the XD pistol, including the XD Carry, XD Production, and XD Custom Competition. Most calibers and sizes were available.

Last MSRs in 2015 on this series were as follows - XD Carry was $795, XD Production was $1,200, and XD Custom Competition was $1,460.

XD(M) SERIES – 9mm Para., .40 S&W, or .45 ACP (new mid-2010) cal., 3.8 (available in 9mm Para. or .40 S&W only, new 2010) or 4 1/2 in. match grade barrel, 10 (.45 ACP only, new 2012), 13, 16 or 19 shot mag., polymer frame with lower Picatinny rail, minimal reset trigger, contoured frame is slightly modified from XD model, black, bi-tone, or OD Green (disc. 2014) Melonite oxide finish, deepened and diagonal slide serrations, black or stainless steel slide, includes 3 interchangeable grip straps, includes XD Gear System (disc. 2015) or two magazines, 28-31 oz. New mid-2008.

| MSR $624 | $550 | $475 | $415 | $375 | $335 | $285 | $265 | |

Add $27 for .45 ACP cal. (new 2011).
Add $62 for bi-tone finish.
Add approx. $66 for OD Green w/stainless slide (not available in .45 ACP cal.), disc. 2014.
Add $118 for night sights (Tritium or Trijicon), disc.
Subtract approx. $50 if without XD Gear System (disc. 2015).

XD(M) COMPACT SERIES – 9mm Para., .40 S&W, or .45 ACP (new 2012) cal., 3.8 in. barrel, 9 (flush, disc. 2012), 10, 11 (flush), or 13 (flush) shot mag., black or bi-tone polymer frame with lower Picatinny rail, Melonite metal finish, low profile dovetail front and rear 3 dot sights, includes the XD(M) Gear System (disc. 2015) or two mags., 26 oz. New 2011.

| MSR $631 | $550 | $475 | $425 | $375 | $335 | $300 | $265 | |

Add $28 for .45 ACP cal. (new 2012).
Add $63 for bi-tone finish.

This model is also available with an extended 16 (.40 S&W cal.) or 19 (9mm Para. cal.) shot mag. in states where legal.

XD(M) COMPETITION SERIES – 9mm Para., .40 S&W, or .45 ACP cal., 5 1/4 in. match grade select fit barrel, Melonite metal finish, fully supported chamber, 13 (.45 ACP), 16 (.40 S&W), or 19 (9mm Para.) shot mag., black polymer frame, red fiber optic front and fully adj. target rear sight, forged steel slide, black or bi-tone finish, includes the XD(M) Gear System (disc. 2015) or two magazines, 29-32 oz. New late 2011.

| MSR $769 | $650 | $575 | $525 | $450 | $375 | $325 | $295 | |

Add $27 for .45 ACP cal.
Add $62 for bi-tone finish.
Subtract approx. $80 if without XD Gear System (disc. 2015).

XD(M) CUSTOM SERIES – the Springfield custom shop makes three variations of the XD(M) pistol, including the XD(M) Carry, XD(M) Production, and XD(M) Custom Competition. Most calibers and sizes are available.

Current MSRs on this series are as follows - XD(M) Carry is $910, XD(M) Production is $1,365, and XD(M) Custom Competition is $1,525.

MSR	100%	98%	95%	90%	80%	70%	60%	Last MSR

XD(M) THREADED BARREL – .45 ACP cal., FDE polymer frame, 4 1/2 in. threaded steel barrel with thread protector, includes two 13 shot stainless steel mags., forged steel slide and barrel with Melonite finish, dovetail front and rear sights, one-piece full length guide rod, 31 oz. New 2016.

MSR $645	$565	$475	$425	$375	$335	$300	$265	

Add $28 for .45 ACP cal.

XD-S – 9mm Para. or .45 ACP cal., hammerless striker ignition system, 3.3 or 4 (new 2014) in. steel barrel, 5, 7, or 9 (single stack with extension) shot mag., polymer frame with textured grip panels, fiber optic front and low profile dovetail rear sights, black or bi-tone Melonite metal finish, loaded chamber indicator, single position Picatinny rail system, short reset trigger, rear grip safety, two interchangeable backstraps, includes XD-S Gear System, 21 1/2 oz. Mfg. 2013-2015.

	$525	$450	$400	$350	$315	$280	$250	*$595*

Add $4 for .45 ACP cal.

Add $50 for bi-tone finish.

Springfield Armory has issued a voluntary safety recall on Springfield 3.3 XDS pistols in 9mm Para. cal. with serial numbers between XS900000 and XS938700, and in .45 ACP with serial numbers between XS500000 and XS686300 due to a remote possibility of unintentional discharge. For more information, please visit www.Springfieldrecall.com, or call 800.680.6866.

* ***XD-S Essentials*** – 9mm Para., .40 S&W (new 2016), or .45 ACP cal., hammerless striker ignition system, 3.3 or 4 (new 2014) in. steel barrel, 5, 7, or 9 (single stack with extension) shot mag., polymer frame with textured grip panels, fiber optic front and low profile dovetail rear sights, black, bi-tone Melonite metal, or Flat Dark Earth (9mm or .45 ACP only, new 2016) finish, loaded chamber indicator, single position Picatinny rail system, short reset trigger, rear grip safety, two interchangeable backstraps, includes two mags., 21 1/2 oz. New 2013.

MSR $499	$450	$385	$325	$275	$240	$220	$200	

Add $50 for bi-tone finish.

Add $50 for .45 ACP cal. or $94 for .45 ACP cal. with bi-tone finish.

Add $109 for Crimson Trace Laserguard with 9mm or $153 for Crimson Trace with .45 ACP cal. (new 2016).

Springfield Armory has issued a voluntary safety recall on Springfield 3.3 XDS pistols in 9mm Para. cal. with serial numbers between XS900000 and XS938700, and in .45 ACP with serial numbers between XS500000 and XS686300 due to a remote possibility of unintentional discharge. For more information, please visit www.Springfieldrecall.com, or call 800.680.6866.

XD MOD.2 SUB-COMPACT – 9mm Para., .40 S&W, or .45 ACP cal., 3, 3.3 (.45 ACP only), 4 (new late 2015), or 5 (new 2016) in. hammer forged barrel, 9 (.40 S&W only) or 10 shot mag., ultra slim contoured polymer frame, low profile rear combat and fiber optic front sights, loaded chamber indicator, striker status indicator, posi-wedge slide serrations, ambidextrous mag. release, high-hand beavertail, accessory rail, USA trigger system, no snag trigger guard, features Gripzone grips with three zones of different textures, black Melonite, matte stainless (Bi-Tone), or Flat Dark Earth (new 2016, 3 or 3.3 in. only) finish, includes XD Gear System, 26 oz. New 2015.

MSR $565	$495	$425	$365	$315	$275	$240	$215	

Add $28 for .45 ACP cal.

Add $34 for matte stainless (Bi-Tone) finish.

Add $43 for 5 in. barrel (black, new 2016) or $86 for 5 in. Bi-Tone barrel (new 2016).

RIFLES: SEMI-AUTO, TACTICAL DESIGN

Many models listed are CA legal, since they do not have a muzzle brake. MSRs are typically the same as those guns available with a muzzle brake. Pricing on CA legal firearms is not included within the scope of this listing - please contact a Springfield dealer directly for this information.

M1 CARBINE – .30 Carbine cal., features new receiver on older military M1 GI stocks. Disc.

	$495	$435	$370	$335	$270	$225	$175	

M1 GARAND AND VARIATIONS – .30-06, .270 Win. (disc. 1987), or .308 Win. cal., semi-auto, 24 in. barrel, gas operated, 8 shot mag., adj. sights, 9 1/2 lbs.

* ***M1 Garand Rifle*** – .30-06 or .308 Win. cal., mfg. with original U.S. government issue parts, with new walnut stock, 8 shot mag., 24 in. barrel, 9 1/2 lbs. Limited mfg. 2002-2007.

	$1,175	$1,030	$880	$800	$645	$530	$410	*$1,439*

Add $30 for .308 Win. cal.

* ***M1 Garand Standard Model*** – similar to M1 Garand Rifle, except optional camo GI fiberglass stock.

	$725	$635	$545	$495	$400	$325	$255	*$761*

Subtract $65 if with GI stock.

* ***M1 Garand National Match*** – walnut stock, match barrel and sights.

	$850	$745	$635	$580	$465	$380	$295	*$897*

Add $240 for Kevlar stock.

MSR	100%	98%	95%	90%	80%	70%	60%	Last MSR

* M1 Garand Ultra Match – match barrel and sights, glass bedded stock, walnut stock standard.

	100%	98%	95%	90%	80%	70%	60%	Last MSR
	$950	$830	$710	$645	$520	$425	$330	*$1,033*

Add $240 for Kevlar stock.

* M1-D Sniper Rifle – .30-06 or .308 Win. cal., limited quantities, with original M84 scope, prong type flash suppressor, leather cheek pad and sling.

	100%	98%	95%	90%	80%	70%	60%	Last MSR
	$1,100	$960	$825	$750	$605	$495	$385	*$1,033*

* M1 Garand Tanker Rifle – similar to T-26 authorized by Gen. MacArthur at the end of WWII, 18 1/4 in. barrel, .30-06 or .308 Win. cal., GI stock standard.

	100%	98%	95%	90%	80%	70%	60%	Last MSR
	$850	$745	$635	$580	$465	$380	$295	*$797*

Add $23 for walnut full stock.

* D-Day M1 Garand Rifle – .30-06 cal., 24 in. barrel, gas operated, military square post front sight, engraved stock, 8 shot mag., two 8 shot clips, leather sling, cleaning kit, includes wooden crate and limited edition lithograph print, 9 1/2 lbs. 1,944 mfg. 2004-2005.

	100%	98%	95%	90%	80%	70%	60%	Last MSR
	$1,375	$1,205	$1,030	$935	$755	$620	$480	*$1,490*

BM 59 – .308 Win. cal., mfg. in Italy and machined and assembled in the Springfield Armory factory, 19.32 in. barrel, 20 shot detachable box mag., 9 1/2 lbs.

* BM 59 Standard Italian Rifle – with grenade launcher, winter trigger, tri-compensator, and bipod.

	100%	98%	95%	90%	80%	70%	60%	Last MSR
	$1,750	$1,530	$1,310	$1,190	$960	$785	$610	*$1,950*

* BM 59 Alpine Rifle – with Beretta pistol grip type stock.

	100%	98%	95%	90%	80%	70%	60%	Last MSR
	$2,025	$1,770	$1,520	$1,375	$1,115	$910	$710	*$2,275*

This model was also available in a Paratrooper configuration with folding stock at no extra charge.

* BM 59 Nigerian Rifle – similar to BM 59, except has Beretta pistol grip type stock.

	100%	98%	95%	90%	80%	70%	60%	Last MSR
	$2,075	$1,815	$1,555	$1,410	$1,140	$935	$725	*$2,340*

* BM 59 E Model Rifle

	100%	98%	95%	90%	80%	70%	60%	Last MSR
	$1,975	$1,730	$1,480	$1,345	$1,085	$890	$690	*$2,210*

M1A RIFLES – .243 Win. (disc.), .308 Win., or 7mm-08 Rem. (1991 mfg. only) cal., patterned after the original Springfield M14 - except semi-auto, walnut or fiberglass stock, 18 or 22 in. steel or stainless steel barrel, fiberglass handguard, "New Loaded" option (see separate listing) beginning 2001 includes NM air gauged barrel, trigger group, front and rear sights, and flash suppressor or Springfield proprietary muzzle brake, 9 lbs.

* M1A Standard/Basic Model – 7.62mm cal., 22 in. regular or National Match (disc.) barrel, two-stage military trigger, military square post front and adj. aperture rear sights, choice of Collector (original GI stock, disc. 2001), Birch (disc. 2003), Black fiberglass (M1A Basic Model, disc.), camo fiberglass (disc.), GI wood (disc. 1992), brown laminated fiberglass (disc.) or black laminated (M1A Standard Model mfg. 1996-2000) stock. Currently mfg. stock finishes for the M1A Standard model include Mossy Oak camo (new 2003), Green (new 2011), Black, Highlander Camo (new 2015), or Flat Dark Earth (new 2015) composite or walnut (new 1993) stock, approx. 9 lbs.

MSR $1,669	100%	98%	95%	90%	80%	70%	60%	
MSR $1,669	$1,425	$1,250	$1,050	$950	$825	$700	$575	

Add $10 for Green composite stock (new 2011).
Add $17 for Highlander Camo (new 2015) stock.
Add $45 for Mossy Oak camo finished stock.
Add $100 for new walnut stock.
Add $59 for birch stock (disc. 2003).
Add $44 for stainless steel barrel (disc.), $74 for bipod and stabilizer (disc.) or $159 for brown laminated stock (disc.), $59 for National Match barrel (disc.), $155 for National Match barrel and sights (disc.), $200 for folding stock (disc. 1994).
Subtract $58 for camo fiberglass stock (disc.).

Standard (entry level model) stock configuration for 1996 was black or camo fiberglass.

* M1A E-2 – standard stock is birch. Disc.

	100%	98%	95%	90%	80%	70%	60%	Last MSR
	$975	$855	$730	$665	$535	$440	$340	*$842*

Add $30 for walnut stock.
Add $120 for Shaw stock with Harris bipod.

* M1A Bush Rifle – .308 Win. cal., 18 in. shrouded barrel, 8 lbs. 12 oz., collector GI, walnut, Mossy Oak camo finished (new 2003), black fiberglass folding (disc. 1994 per C/B), and black fiberglass (disc.) or laminated black (disc.) stock. Disc. 1999, reintroduced 2003 only.

	100%	98%	95%	90%	80%	70%	60%	Last MSR
	$1,300	$1,135	$975	$885	$715	$585	$455	*$1,529*

Add $29 for walnut stock (disc.), $15 for black fiberglass stock (disc.), $86 for black laminated stock (disc.), $235 for National Match variation (disc.), and $525 for Super Match variation (disc.)

MSR	100%	98%	95%	90%	80%	70%	60%	Last MSR

* **M1A National Match** – .308 Win. cal., 22 in. steel or stainless steel (new 1999) barrel, National Match sights, mainspring guide, flash suppressor, and gas cylinder, special glass bedded oil finished match stock, two-stage tuned trigger, walnut stock became standard in 1991, 9 lbs.

| MSR $2,359 | $2,050 | $1,775 | $1,500 | $1,350 | $1,100 | $900 | $700 | |

Add $55 for stainless steel barrel.

Add $155 for heavy composition stock (disc.).

Add $250 for either fiberglass or fancy burl wood stock (disc.).

.243 Win. and 7mm-08 Rem. cals. were also available at extra charge until discontinued.

* **M1A Super Match** – .308 Win. cal., 22 in. Hart (disc.) or Douglas premium air gauged custom heavy carbon or stainless steel barrel, oversized walnut, McMillan Black fiberglass, or McMillan Marine Corps Green Camo fiberglass super match stock, modified operating rod guide, rear lugged receiver beginning 1991, approx. 11 1/2 lbs.

| MSR $2,956 | $2,575 | $2,225 | $1,900 | $1,700 | $1,375 | $1,125 | $895 | |

Add $235 for stainless steel Douglas barrel.

Add $752 for McMillan Black or Marine Corps Green camo fiberglass stock with stainless steel barrel.

Add $250 for Krieger or Hart barrel (disc.).

Add $200 for fancy burl walnut (disc.) stock.

.243 Win. and 7mm-08 Rem. cals. were also available at extra charge until discontinued.

M1A LOADED STANDARD – .308 Win. cal., 22 in. National Match steel or stainless steel barrel, features shooting upgrades such as National Match trigger assembly, front and rear sights, and National Match flash suppressor, 10 shot mag., Black or OD Green fiberglass, Collector GI walnut (disc. 2000), or new walnut stock, approx. 9 1/2 lbs. New 1999.

| MSR $1,828 | $1,625 | $1,440 | $1,225 | $1,075 | $875 | $725 | $575 | |

Add $15 for OD Green composite stock.

Add $100 for stainless steel barrel.

Add $113 for new walnut stock.

Add $213 for walnut stock with stainless steel barrel.

Add $525 for extended cluster rail with black fiberglass stock and National Match stainless steel barrel (mfg. 2006-2011).

Add $100 for Collector GI walnut (disc. 2000).

M1A PRECISION ADJUSTABLE LOADED RIFLE – .308 Win./7.62 NATO cal., 22 in. National Match carbon or stainless steel barrel, 10 shot mag., NM blade front and aperture rear sights, precision adjustable composite stock, Black or Flat Dark Earth (new 2016) finish, 11.25 lbs. New 2015.

| MSR $1,984 | $1,750 | $1,500 | $1,275 | $1,150 | $925 | $750 | $600 | |

Add $99 for stainless steel barrel.

M1A "GOLD SERIES" – .308 Win. cal., heavy walnut competition stock, gold medal grade heavy Douglas barrel. Mfg. 1987 only.

| | $1,944 | $1,700 | $1,460 | $1,320 | $1,070 | $875 | $680 | $1,944 |

Add $126 for Kevlar stock, add $390 for special Hart stainless steel barrel, add $516 for Hart stainless steel barrel with Kevlar stock.

M1A SCOUT SQUAD – .308 Win. cal., 18 in. carbon barrel, two-stage military trigger, military square post front sight and adj. aperture rear, choice of GI Collector (disc. 1998), Green (disc. 2011), Black laminated (disc. 1998), Black, Flat Dark Earth (new 2015), or Mossy Oak Composite or walnut stock, muzzle stabilizer standard, supplied with Scout mount and handguard, approx. 9 lbs. New 1997.

| MSR $1,830 | $1,595 | $1,375 | $1,150 | $1,050 | $850 | $675 | $595 | |

Add $135 for walnut stock.

Add $88 for Mossy Oak camo stock.

Add $14 for Green composite stock (disc. 2011).

M1A SOCOM 16 – .308 Win. cal., 16 1/4 in. barrel with muzzle brake, upper handguard has been cut out for sight rail, 10 shot box mag., Tritium front sight with ghost ring aperture rear sight, forward scout-style Picatinny mount, two-stage military trigger, Black, Green, Flat Dark Earth (new 2015), or Multi-Cam (mfg. 2015 only) composite stock with steel buttplate, black finish, 8.8 lbs. New 2004.

| MSR $1,965 | $1,775 | $1,525 | $1,275 | $1,150 | $925 | $750 | $650 | |

Add $15 for Green composite stock.

Subtract $148 for Multi-Cam composite stock (mfg. 2015 only).

M1A SOCOM 16 II – .308 Win. cal., 16 1/4 in. carbon steel barrel with muzzle brake, black composite stock with steel buttplate, black or urban camo (disc. 2011) finish, 10 shot box mag., Tritium front sight with ghost ring aperture rear sight, two-stage military trigger, cluster rail or extended (new 2007) cluster rail, 10 lbs. Mfg. 2005-2014.

| | $2,100 | $1,875 | $1,650 | $1,450 | $1,250 | $1,000 | $800 | $2,399 |

Add $100 for extended cluster rail (Socom II, new 2007).

MSR		100%	98%	95%	90%	80%	70%	60%	Last MSR

M1A SOCOM 16 CQB – 7.62 NATO cal., 16 1/4 in. parkerized carbon steel barrel, 10 shot mag., XS Post front sight with Tritium insert and ghost ring rear sight, 5-position CQB composite stock with adj. cheekpiece and M-Lok Rail system, 9.2 lbs. New 2016.

| | MSR $2,099 | $1,850 | $1,600 | $1,350 | $1,225 | $975 | $875 | $725 | |

    Add $297 for Vortex Venom sight and SA base.

M1A/M21 TACTICAL – .308 Win./7.62mm cal., Garand action, 22 in. barrel, tactical variation of the Super Match mfg. with match grade parts giving superior accuracy, adj. walnut cheekpiece stock, choice of Douglas carbon steel or stainless Krieger barrel, 11.6 lbs. New 1990.

| | MSR $3,619 | $3,225 | $2,875 | $2,375 | $2,100 | $1,750 | $1,450 | $1,200 | |

    Add $427 for Krieger stainless barrrel.

M25 "WHITE FEATHER" TACTICAL – .308 Win. cal., Garand action, includes black fiberglass M3A McMillan stock, 22 in. Kreiger heavy carbon steel barrel standard, Rader trigger, White Feather logo and Carlos Hathcock II signature, 10 shot box mag., includes Harris bipod, 12 3/4 lbs. Mfg. 2001-2009.

| | | $4,750 | $4,155 | $3,560 | $3,230 | $2,610 | $2,135 | $1,660 | $5,278 |

SAR-3 – .308 Win. cal., licensed copy of the pre-ban import HK-91, predecessor to the SAR-8, mfg. in Greece.

| | | $995 | $870 | $745 | $675 | $545 | $450 | $350 | |

SAR-8 – .308 Win. cal., patterned after the HK-91, roller lock delayed blowback action, fluted chamber, rotary adj. rear aperture sight, 18 in. barrel, recent mfg. incorporated a cast aluminum receiver with integrated Weaver rail, pistol grip, slim forearm, and green furniture (for law enforcement only), supplied with walnut (disc. 1994) or black fiberglass thumbhole sporter stock, 10 (C/B 1994) or 20 (disc. 1994) shot detachable mag., 8.7 lbs. Mfg. in U.S. starting 1990, disc. 1998.

| | | $1,015 | $890 | $760 | $690 | $560 | $455 | $355 | $1,204 |

    SAR-8 parts are interchangeable with both SAR-3 and HK-91 parts.

  * **SAR-8 Tactical Counter Sniper Rifle** – .308 Win. cal., tactical sniper variation of the SAR-8. Mfg. 1996-98.

| | | $1,325 | $1,160 | $995 | $900 | $730 | $595 | $465 | $1,610 |

SAR-48 MODEL – .308 Win. cal., GPO, authentic copy of the Belgian semi-auto FAL/LAR rifle, 21 in. barrel, 20 shot mag., walnut or synthetic stock, adj. sights, sling, and mag. loader. Mfg. 1985-89.

| | | $1,675 | $1,465 | $1,255 | $1,140 | $920 | $755 | $585 | |

    Add approx. 20% for Israeli configuration with heavy barrel, bipod, flash hider, and flip-up buttplate.

    The SAR-48 was disc. in 1989 and reintroduced as the Model SAR-4800 in 1990.

  * **SAR-48 Bush Rifle** – similar to SAR-48 model, except has 18 in. barrel.

| | | $1,750 | $1,530 | $1,310 | $1,190 | $960 | $785 | $610 | |

  * **SAR-48 .22 Cal.** – .22 LR cal., variation of the Sporter Model. Disc. 1989.

| | | $725 | $635 | $545 | $495 | $400 | $325 | $255 | $760 |

SAR-4800 SPORTER MODEL – .223 Rem. (new 1997) or .308 Win. cal., GPO, authentic copy of the Belgian semi-auto FAL/LAR rifle, 18 (.223 Rem. cal. only) or 21 in. barrel, 10 (C/B 1994) or 20 (disc.) shot mag., walnut (disc.) or black fiberglass thumbhole sporter stock, adj. sights, sling, and mag. loader. Mfg. 1990-1998.

| | | $1,080 | $945 | $810 | $735 | $595 | $485 | $380 | |

    All SAR - 4800 parts are interchangeable with both SAR-48 and FN/FAL parts. This model is an updated variation of the pre-WWII FN Model 49.

  * **SAR-4800 Bush Rifle Sporter Model** – similar to standard model, except has 18 in. barrel.

| | | $1,085 | $950 | $815 | $735 | $595 | $490 | $380 | $1,216 |

DR-200 SPORTER RIFLE – while advertised, this model never went into production. ($687 was planned MSR).

STAG ARMS LLC

Current rifle and accessories manufacturer located in New Britain, CT.

RIFLES: SEMI-AUTO

    All AR-15 style carbines/rifles are available in post-ban configuration for restricted states, and include one mag., instruction manual, plastic rifle case, and lifetime warranty.

    Add $50 for .300 AAC Blackout cal. upgrade for Model 1, Model 1L, Model 2, Model 2L, Model 2T, Model 2TL, Model 3, Model 3L, Model 3T, Model 3TL, or Model 3TLM (new 2016).

MSR	100%	98%	95%	90%	80%	70%	60%	Last MSR

MODEL 1 CARBINE – 5.56 NATO/.223 Rem. cal., GIO, 16 in. chrome lined barrel, A2 flash hider, 30 shot mag., A3 forged aluminum upper, A2 front post sights/removable carry handle, Picatinny rail under carry handle, standard GI carbine design, polymer handguard, 6-position collapsible stock, A2 plastic grip, available in right or left (Model 1L) hand, Type III hardcoat anodized black finish, 7 lbs.

| MSR $949 | $815 | $700 | $630 | $570 | $500 | $425 | $380 | |

Add $40 for Model 1L.

MODEL 2 CARBINE – 5.56 NATO/.223 Rem. cal., GIO, 16 in. chrome lined barrel, A2 flash hider, 30 shot mag., A3 forged aluminum upper, standard safety, F-marked A2 front sight post and Midwest Industries ERS flip up rear sight, tactical top rail, polymer handguard, 6-position collapsible stock, A2 plastic grip, available in right or left (Model 2L) hand, Type III hardcoat anodized black finish, 6 1/2 lbs.

| MSR $940 | $800 | $700 | $615 | $550 | $485 | $415 | $370 | |

Add $25 for Model 2L.

* **Model 2T Carbine** – 5.56 NATO/.223 Rem. cal., GIO, 16 in. chrome lined barrel, A2 flash hider, 30 shot mag., A3 forged aluminum upper, ambidextrous (left hand only) or standard safety, free float Picatinny quad rail, F-marked A2 front sight, A.R.M.S. flip up rear sight, 6-position collapsible stock, A2 plastic pistol grip, available in right or left-hand, Type III hardcoat anodized black finish, approx. 6.8 lbs.

| MSR $1,130 | $940 | $850 | $725 | $625 | $550 | $475 | $425 | |

Add $25 for left-hand (Model 2T-L).

MODEL 3 CARBINE – 5.56 NATO/.223 Rem. cal., GIO, 16 in. chrome lined barrel, A2 flash hider, 30 shot mag., A3 forged aluminum upper, standard safety, 6-position collapsible stock, A2 plastic grip, Picatinny railed gas block, available in right or left (Model 3L) hand, Diamondhead drop-in Versa-Base handguard, (V-RS modular rail platform became standard 2011), Type III hardcoat anodized black finish, 6.1 lbs.

| MSR $895 | $775 | $685 | $615 | $550 | $485 | $415 | $370 | |

Add $25 for Model 3L.

MODEL 3G RIFLE – 5.56 NATO/.223 Rem. cal., GIO, 18 in. stainless steel heavy fluted barrel, Stag 3G compensator, 15 in. Samson Evolution free float handguard, Geissele Super 3-Gun trigger, 30 shot mag., accessory rail, Magpul ACS buttstock and MOE pistol grip, right or left-hand action, Type III hardcoat anodized black finish, 7 1/2 lbs. New 2012.

| MSR $1,459 | $1,240 | $1,100 | $985 | $835 | $725 | $615 | $515 | |

Add $20 for left-hand (Model 3G-L).

MODEL 3T RIFLE – 5.56 NATO cal., GIO, 16 in. chrome lined barrel with A2 flash hider, 30 shot mag., Diamondhead VRS-T free float handguard, polymer Diamondhead front and rear flip-up sights, 6-position collapsible buttstock, A2 plastic grip, Type III hardcoat anodized black finish, 7.4 lbs. New 2014.

| MSR $999 | $850 | $725 | $650 | $585 | $515 | $450 | $395 | |

Add $20 for Model 3T-L (left hand).

MODEL 3T-M RIFLE – 5.56 NATO cal., GIO, 16 in. chrome lined barrel with A2 flash hider, 30 shot mag., Diamondhead VRS-T free float handguard, full length Picatinnny rail, aluminum Diamondhead front and rear flip up sights, Magpul ACS 6-pos. buttstock, Magpul MOE grip, 7 1/2 lbs. New 2014.

| MSR $1,160 | $980 | $885 | $765 | $655 | $575 | $495 | $435 | |

Add $20 for left hand (Model 3TL-M).

MODEL 4 RIFLE – 5.56 NATO/.223 Rem. cal., GIO, 20 in. chrome moly heavy barrel, A2 flash hider, 20 shot mag., A3 forged aluminum upper, Picatinny rail, rifle length polymer handguard, F-marked A2 front sight, removable carry handle, A2 buttstock with trap door for storage, A2 plastic grip, available in right or left (Model 4L) hand, Type III hardcoat anodized black finish, 8 1/2 lbs.

| MSR $1,015 | $865 | $725 | $650 | $585 | $515 | $450 | $395 | |

Add $50 for left hand (Model 4L).

MODEL 5 CARBINE – 6.8 SPC cal. with SAAMI SPEC 2 chamber, GIO, 16 in. chrome lined barrel, A2 flash hider, 25 shot mag., F-marked A2 front sight, polymer handguard, A3 forged aluminum upper, standard or ambidextrous (left-hand only) safety, 6-position collapsible stock, A2 plastic grip, available in right or left (Model 5L) hand, Type III hardcoat anodized black finish, 6.4 lbs.

| MSR $1,045 | $885 | $785 | $685 | $600 | $535 | $465 | $415 | |

Add $50 for left-hand (Model 5L).

MODEL 6 RIFLE – 5.56 NATO/.223 Rem. cal., GIO, 24 in. stainless steel heavy bull profile barrel with target crown, 10 shot mag., low profile gas block, A3 forged aluminum upper, standard or ambidextrous (left-hand only) safety, two-stage match trigger, free floating Hogue handguard, fixed A2 buttstock, tactical top rail, Hogue overmolded pistol grip, Type III hardcoat anodized black finish, 10 lbs.

| MSR $1,055 | $885 | $785 | $685 | $600 | $535 | $465 | $415 | |

Add $40 for left-hand (Model 6L).

MSR	100%	98%	95%	90%	80%	70%	60%	Last MSR

STAG 7 HUNTER – 6.8 SPC cal. with SAAMI SPEC 2 chamber, GIO, 20.8 in. stainless steel heavy profile barrel with target crown, A3 forged aluminum upper, standard or ambidextrous (left-hand only) safety, fixed A2 buttstock, railed gas block front/no rear sights, free float Hogue handguard, tactical top rail, two-stage match trigger, Hogue overmolded pistol grip, available in right or left-hand configuration, Type III hardcoat anodized black finish, 7.8 lbs.

| MSR $1,055 | $885 | $785 | $685 | $600 | $535 | $465 | $415 | |

Add $40 for left-hand (Model 7L).

MODEL 8 CARBINE – 5.56 NATO/.223 Rem. cal., GPO, 16 in. chrome lined barrel, A2 flash hider, 30 shot mag., Diamondhead flip up front and rear sights, 6-position collapsible stock, A2 plastic grip, ambidextrous (left hand only) or standard safety, A3 forged aluminum upper, polymer handguard, available in right or left (Model 8-L) hand, Type III hardcoat anodized black finish, 6.9 lbs. New 2011.

| MSR $1,145 | $975 | $885 | $765 | $655 | $575 | $495 | $435 | |

Add $30 for left-hand (Model 8L).

* ***Model 8T Carbine*** – 5.56 NATO/.223 Rem. cal., GPO, 16 in. chrome lined barrel, A2 flash hider, 30 shot mag., matched set of Diamondhead flip up sights, 6-position collapsible stock, A2 plastic grip, ambidextrous (left hand only) or standard safety, Diamondhead VRS-T free floating modular handguard, continuous top rail, Type III hardcoat anodized black finish, 7 1/4 lbs. New 2013.

| MSR $1,275 | $1,060 | $950 | $815 | $715 | $625 | $535 | $450 | |

Add $20 for Model 8TL.

MODEL 9/9L – 9mm Para cal., blowback action, 16 in. chrome lined barrel with A2 flash hider, 32 shot mag., M4 style, Picatinny railed gas block, no rear sight, 6-position collapsible stock, A2 grip, Diamondhead VRS-T 15 in. free float modular handguard, right or left (Model 9L) hand, Type III hardcoat anodized finish, 6.8 lbs. New mid-2014.

| MSR $990 | $850 | $725 | $650 | $585 | $515 | $450 | $395 | |

Add $35 for left-hand action (Model 9L).

MODEL 9T – 9mm Para. cal., GIO, blowback action, 16 in. chrome lined barrel with A2 flash hider, 32 shot mag., metal Diamondhead premium front and rear sights, right or left (Model 9T-L) hand action, Diamondhead VRS-T 13 1/2 in. free float handguard, 6-position collapsible buttstock, A2 plastic grip, Type III hardcoat anodized black finish, 7.9 lbs. New 2015.

| MSR $1,275 | $1,060 | $950 | $815 | $715 | $625 | $535 | $450 | |

Add $20 for left-hand action (Model 9T-L).

STANDARD MANUFACTURING CO. LLC

Current manufacturer located in New Britain, CT. Previously located in Newington, CT. Dealer and consumer direct sales were through FFL dealer.

RIFLES: SEMI-AUTO

THOMPSON MODEL 1922 – .22 LR cal., semi-auto rifle, 16.4 in. ribbed barrel, 10 shot (standard) or optional aluminum drum magazine, receiver milled from aircraft grade aluminum, open sights, deluxe walnut stock and forearm, pistol grip, half scale replica patterned after the Thompson Model 1927, high gloss blue finish, 5 1/2 lbs. While advertised during 2012, this gun started mfg. during 2014.

| MSR $1,299 | $1,100 | $1,000 | $900 | $800 | $700 | $600 | $500 | |

SHOTGUN: SLIDE ACTION

DP-12 – 12 ga., 3 in. chambers, twin 16 in. threaded barrels (can accept various choke tubes), 14 shot twin magazine capacity, bullpup configuration, aluminum receiver, top Picatinny rail, pistol grip, ambidextrous operation, bottom loading and ejection, inline feeding, shock absorbing recoil mechanism in butt, dual spring rubber recoil pad, black finish. New late 2014.

| MSR $1,395 | $1,325 | $1,150 | $1,000 | $900 | $825 | $750 | $675 | |

Blue Book Publications selected this model as one of its Top 10 Industry Awards from all the new firearms at the 2015 SHOT Show.

STAR, BONIFACIO ECHEVERRIA S.A.

Previous manufacturer located in Eibar, Spain. Star, Bonifacio Echeverria S.A. closed its doors on July 28th, 1997, due to the intense financial pressure the Spanish arms industry experienced during the late 1990s. Previously imported by Interarms, located in Alexandria, VA.

PISTOLS: SEMI-AUTO

MEGASTAR – 10mm or .45 ACP cal., DA/SA, larger variation of the Firestar featuring 4.6 in. barrel and 12 (.45 ACP) or 14 (10mm) shot mag., 47.6 oz. Imported 1992-1994.

| | $450 | $395 | $340 | $305 | $250 | $205 | $160 | *$653* |

Add $29 for Starvel finish.

MSR	100%	98%	95%	90%	80%	70%	60%	*Last MSR*

ULTRASTAR – 9mm Para. or .40 S&W (new 1996) cal., DA/SA, compact design, 3.57 in. barrel, 9 shot mag., blue steel metal, triple dot sights, steel internal mechanism, polymer exterior construction, 26 oz. Mfg. 1994-1997.

	$350	$300	$250	$225	$180	$145	$115	*$296*

STERLING ARMAMENT, LTD.

Previous manufacturer established c. 1900, and located in Dagenham, Essex, England. Previously imported and distributed by Cassi Inc. located in Colorado Springs, CO until 1990.

CARBINES: SEMI-AUTO

AR-180 – please refer to Armalite section for more information and pricing on this model.

STERLING MK 6 – 9mm Para. cal., blowback semi-auto with floating firing pin, shrouded 16.1 in. barrel, side mounted mag., folding stock, 7 1/2 lbs. Disc. 1989.

	N/A	$1,750	$1,500	$1,400	$1,200	$1,000	$795	*$650*

PISTOLS: SEMI-AUTO

PARAPISTOL MK 7 C4 – 9mm Para. cal., 4 in. barrel, tactical design pistol, crinkle finish, same action as MK. 6 Carbine, fires from closed bolt, 10, 15, 20, 30, 34 or 68 shot mag., 5 lbs. Disc. 1989.

	N/A	$1,500	$1,400	$1,200	$1,000	$800	$700	*$600*

Add $50 per 30 or 34 shot mag., $125 for 68 shot mag.

PARAPISTOL MK 7 C8 – 9mm Para. cal., similar to C4, except has 7.8 in. barrel, 5 1/4 lbs. Disc. 1989.

	N/A	$1,500	$1,400	$1,250	$1,050	$900	$750	*$620*

Add $50 per 30 or 34 shot mag., $125 for 68 shot mag.

STERLING ARSENAL

Current custom AR-15 manufacturer located in Sterling, VA beginning 2010.

Sterling Arsenal manufactures their own SAR-XV brand of custom AR-15 rifles. They customize the AR-10 platform, and convert and enhance Saiga-12 and AK-47 models. Sterling Arsenal also owns Critical Koting, a NIC Certified Cerakote Applicator (Sterling Arsenal brand and line of business), and operates exclusively at Sterling Arsenal's facilities.

PISTOLS: SEMI-AUTO

SAR-XV PREPR AR-15 PISTOL – 9mm Para., 5.56 NATO or .300 AAC Blackout cal., cold hammer forged chrome lined barrel, custom forged anodized receivers, Sig arm brace with KAK extended receiver extension, free float quad rail, choice of Magpul AFG or hand stop, black finish. Disc. 2015.

	$960	$875	$740	$625	$550	$475	$425	*$1,150*

Add $300 for 9mm Para. cal.

* *SAR-XV PREPR AR-15 Pistol MOD 2* – 5.56 NATO, .300 AAC Blackout, or 9mm Para. (optional upgrade) cal., upgraded variation of the SAR-XV PREPR AR-15 model, 5, 7, 8, or 10 in. QPQ Nitride barrel, custom forged anodized hardened receivers, free float KeyMod rail system, push button quick detach sling mounts, SAR custom tuned trigger, ambidextrous fire controls, Magpul MOE back up flip sights, Magpul grip, AFG or hand stop, pistol receiver extension, black finish. New 2016.

MSR $1,190	$1,000	$900	$775	$655	$575	$495	$435	

RIFLES: SEMI-AUTO

COMBAT FIELD GRADE RIFLE – .308 Win. cal., 16, 18, or 20 in. cold hammer forged barrel, compatible with Magpul mags., free float KeyMod handguard, machined and forged lower parts, Mil-Spec single stage trigger, Magpul PRS stock, QD sling mounts, black finish. New 2015.

MSR $1,600	$1,350	$1,200	$1,075	$950	$815	$700	$575	

PRECISION MATCH COMPETITION RIFLE – .308 Win. or 6.5 Creedmoor cal., 18, 20, or 22 in. JP Enterprise medium contour barrel, PWS muzzle brake or silencer mount, compatible with Magpul mags., free float KeyMod or SAR HexSphere handguard, machined and forged lower parts, SAR custom tuned JP Enterprise trigger and ambidextrous fire controls, Magpul PRS stock, QD sling mounts, Cerakote finish. New 2015.

MSR $1,250	$1,050	$950	$815	$715	$625	$535	$450	

SAR-XV COMBAT MATCH (GLADIUS V4) – 5.56 NATO, 6.8 SPC, .300 AAC Blackout (new 2016), or .458 SOCOM cal., 16 or 18 in. stainless steel barrel with phantom flash suppressor, mid-length gas ported, low profile DI gas block, front and rear alloy flip BUIS sights, custom forged and billet upper and lower receivers, SAR HexSphere modular free-float handguard, choice of Magpul CTR or STR stock, K2 pistol grip, black finish. New late 2014.

MSR $1,950	$1,650	$1,450	$1,225	$1,085	$935	$800	$660	

MSR	100%	98%	95%	90%	80%	70%	60%	Last MSR

SAR-XV PREPR (PRACTICAL READY EVERDAY PATROL RIFLE) – 5.56 NATO or .300 AAC Blackout cal., 16 in. cold hammer forged chrome lined barrel, F-marked front sight gas block and rear Magpul flip sight, custom forged anodized receivers, two-piece quad rail, machined and forged lower parts, Mil-Spec buffer tube, MFT Minimalist stock and grip, black finish. Disc. 2015.

	100%	98%	95%	90%	80%	70%	60%	Last MSR
	$725	$650	$580	$515	$450	$385	$340	$850

SAR-XV PREPR MOD 2 – 5.56 NATO, .300 AAC Blackout, 6.8 SPC, or .458 SOCOM cal., upgraded variation of Sar-XV PREPR model, mid-length ported 16 in. QPQ Nitride barrel, A2 flash hider, free float 15 in. extended KeyMod rail system, Magpul MOE back up flip sights, push button quick detach sling mounts, SAR custom tuned trigger, ambidextrous fire controls, forged anodized hardened receivers, low profile DI gas block, Mil-Spec pattern 6-position extension buffer assembly, Magpul stock and grip, black finish. New 2016.

MSR $1,250	$1,050	$950	$815	$715	$625	$535	$450

SAR-XV PREPR MOD 2 MATCH – 5.56 NATO cal., mid-length ported 16 in. stainless steel barrel, PWS muzzle brake, low profile gas block, Magpul Pro Steel back up flip sights, push button quick detach sling mounts, forged anodized hardened receivers, free float 15 in. extended KeyMod rail system, JP match tuned trigger, ambidextrous fire controls, Mil-Spec pattern 6-position extension H-Series buffer assembly, Magpul stock and grip, grey finish. New 2016.

MSR $1,650	$1,400	$1,235	$1,100	$975	$830	$720	$585

SPATHA INTERMEDIATE LONG RANGE SPR – 5.56 NATO, 6.8 SPC, or .458 SOCOM cal., GPO, 18 in. stainless steel barrel with phantom flash suppressor, billet upper receiver side charger model, single stage short travel adj. trigger, front and rear alloy flip BUIS sights, SAR HexSphere modular free-float handguard, alternative enhanced stock, K2 pistol grip, black finish. New late 2014.

MSR $1,950	$1,650	$1,450	$1,225	$1,085	$935	$800	$660

STEVENS, J., ARMS COMPANY

Current trademark of long arms produced by Savage Arms, Inc. Beginning in 1999, Savage Arms, Inc. began manufacturing/importing Stevens trademarked guns again, including rifles and shotguns. J. Stevens Arms Company was founded in 1864 at Chicopee Falls, MA as J. Stevens & Co. In 1886 the name was changed to J. Stevens Arms and Tool Co. In 1916, the plant became New England Westinghouse, and tooled up for Mosin-Nagant Rifles. In 1920, the plant was sold to the Savage Arms Corp. and manufactured guns were marked "J. Stevens Arms Co." This designation was dropped in the late 1940s, and only the name "Stevens" has been used up to 1990.

Depending on the remaining Stevens factory data, a factory letter authenticating the configuration of a particular specimen, along with dates produced may be obtained by contacting Mr. John Callahan (see Trademark Index for listings and address). The charge for this service is $25.00 per gun - please allow 8 weeks for an adequate response.

For more Stevens model information, please refer to the Serialization section in the back of this text.

SHOTGUNS

Stevens made a wide variety of inexpensive, utilitarian shotguns that, to date, have attracted mostly shooting interest, but little collector interest. A listing of these models may be found in the back of this text under "Serialization."

MODEL 350 SLIDE ACTION SECURITY – 12 ga., 3 in. chamber, 18 1/2 in. barrel, 5 shot tube mag., bottom ejection, matte black synthetic pistol grip stock, bead (disc. 2012), ghost ring, or rifle (disc. 2012) sights, 7.6 lbs. New mid-2010.

MSR $276	$225	$195	$170	$150	$135	$125	$115

STEYR ARMS (STEYR MANNLICHER)

Currently manufactured by Steyr-Mannlicher AG & Co. KG in Austria. Founded in Steyr, Austria by Joseph Werndl circa 1864. Currently imported beginning mid-2005 by Steyr Arms, Inc., located in Bessemer, AL. Previously located in Trussville, AL until 2013. Previously located in Cumming, GA. Previously imported 2004-mid-2005 by Steyr USA, located in West Point, MS. Previously imported 2002-2003 by Dynamit Nobel, located in Closter, NJ. Previously imported and distributed until 2002 by Gun South, Inc. (GSI) located in Trussville, AL.

In 2007, the firm of Steyr-Mannlicher was sold to new owners and the factory was relocated to Kleinraming, approx. 12 miles from the original site in Steyr, Austria. The new firm, Steyr Arms, was purchased by Dr. Ernst Reichmayr and his friend and partner, Gerhard Unterganschnigg.

Note: also see Mannlicher Schoenauer Sporting Rifles in the M section for pre-WWII models.

For more information and current pricing on both new and used Steyr airguns, please refer to the *Blue Book of Airguns* by Dr. Robert Beeman & John Allen (also online).

MSR	100%	98%	95%	90%	80%	70%	60%	*Last MSR*

PISTOLS: SEMI-AUTO

MODEL GB – 9mm Para. cal., DA/SA, 18 shot mag., gas delayed blowback action, non-glare checkered plastic grips, 5 1/4 in. barrel with Polygon rifling, matte finish, steel construction, 2 lbs. 6 oz. Importation disc. 1988.

	100%	98%	95%	90%	80%	70%	60%	*Last MSR*
Commercial	$675	$600	$525	$450	$400	$350	$300	
Military	$795	$725	$650	$600	$525	$450	$400	*$514*

In 1987, Steyr mfg. a military variation of the Model GB featuring a phosphate finish - only 937 were imported into the U.S.

MODEL SPP – 9mm Para. cal., SA, delayed blowback system with rotating 5.9 in. barrel, 15 or 30 shot mag., utilizes synthetic materials and advanced ergonomics, adj. sights, grooved receiver for scope mounting, matte black finish, 44 oz. Limited importation 1992-1993.

	100%	98%	95%	90%	80%	70%	60%	*Last MSR*
	$800	$675	$600	$550	$495	$450	$400	*$895*

MODEL M SERIES – 9mm Para., .357 SIG, or .40 S&W cal., DAO, SFO, features first integrated limited access key lock safety in a semi-auto pistol, 3 different safety conditions, black synthetic frame, 10 shot mag., matte black finish, loaded chamber indicator, triangle/trapezoid sights, 28 oz. Limited importation 1999-2002.

	100%	98%	95%	90%	80%	70%	60%	*Last MSR*
	$500	$450	$400	$350	$300	$275	$250	*$610*

Add $65 for night sights.

C-A1 SERIES – 9mm Para. (C9 A-1), or .40 S&W (C40 A-1, importation disc. 2011) cal., similar to M-A1 Series, 12 or 17 shot mag., compact frame.

	100%	98%	95%	90%	80%	70%	60%	*Last MSR*
MSR $560	$495	$450	$395	$350	$300	$275	$250	

L-A1 SERIES – 9mm Para., .40 S&W, or .357 SIG cal., right or left-hand action, full size polymer frame, 4 1/2 in. cold hammer forged barrel, full-length slide, adj. sights, 12 (.40 S&W or .357 SIG) or 17 (9mm Para. only) shot mag., ergonomic high grip, newly designed loaded chamber indicator, reversible magazine release, lower Picatinny rail, matte black finish. New 2014.

	100%	98%	95%	90%	80%	70%	60%	*Last MSR*
MSR $560	$475	$415	$350	$325	$260	$215	$165	

M-A1 SERIES – .357 SIG (M357 A-1, disc. 2013), 9mm Para. (M9 A-1), or .40 S&W (M40 A-1) cal., DAO, SFO, updated Model M with Picatinny rail on lower front of frame, redesigned grip frame, trigger safety and lockable safety system, black polymer frame with matte black finished slide, 3 1/2 (not available in .357 SIG cal.) or 4 in. barrel, 10, 12 (.40 S&W or .357 SIG) or 15 (9mm Para.) shot mag., white outlined triangular sights, approx. 27 oz. Imported 2004-2009, reintroduced late 2010.

	100%	98%	95%	90%	80%	70%	60%	*Last MSR*
MSR $560	$495	$450	$395	$350	$300	$275	$250	

Add $23 for triangle sights with Trilux (disc.)
Add $40 for night sights (disc. 2013).

S-A1 SERIES – 9mm Para. (S9 A-1), or .40 S&W (S40 A-1) cal., similar to M-A1 Series, 10 shot mag., smaller compact frame.

	100%	98%	95%	90%	80%	70%	60%	*Last MSR*
MSR $560	$495	$450	$395	$350	$300	$275	$250	

MODEL S – similar to Model M, except has 3 1/2 in. barrel and shorter grip frame, 10 shot mag., 22 1/2 oz. Limited importation 2000-2002.

	100%	98%	95%	90%	80%	70%	60%	*Last MSR*
	$475	$435	$385	$350	$325	$300	$280	*$610*

RIFLES: BOLT ACTION, RECENT PRODUCTION

The Steyr-Mannlicher models were in production 1968-1996.

Current production guns are now called Steyr-Mannlicher models. For models manufactured 1903-1971, please refer to the Mannlicher Schoenauer Sporting Rifles section in this text. All known calibers are listed for each model. Caliber offerings varied often throughout the 28 year run of the Steyr-Mannlicher, stock designs evolved, and sights and magazine styles changed. The only truly rare caliber is the 6mm Rem., which was always special order. Next in North American rarity is the .25-06. Certain additional European calibers are rare in the USA because they were not imported due to lack of popularity - 5.6x57mm, 6.5x57mm, 6x62mm Freres, 6.5x65mm, and 9.3x62mm.

All four action lengths, SL, L, M, S, were offered in numerous deluxe variations with engraving and stock carving on special order blued metal and highly polished engraved actions. Stock carving is heavy and elegant. The "twisted appearance" of the hammer rifles barrels on all firearms of this group lends a unique and unmistakable look to these rifles.

A major irritant for hardcore Steyr-Mannlicher collectors is the continued misidentification of Luxus models by online sellers. First, a standard USA version Luxus has the word "Luxus" engraved on the left side of the receiver. A Luxus also has a steel box magazine instead of a rotary plastic one and a rotary shotgun style safety, although some apparently early Luxus models exist with the sliding side safety.

Pricing shows the result of continued cost increases at Steyr, which finally caused the end of the production run and redesign to the SBS-96 model to save costs, regain competition, and take advantage of improved safety features.

MSR	100%	98%	95%	90%	80%	70%	60%	Last MSR

MANNLICHER/STEYR SCOUT – .223 Rem. (new 2000), .243 Win. (mfg. 2000 only, reintroduced 2005), .308 Win., 7mm-08 Rem. (new 2000), or .376 Steyr (mfg. 1999-2000, reintroduced 2005) cal., designed by Jeff Cooper, features grey, black synthetic Zytel with wood panel inserts or camo (.308 Win. cal. only beginning 2005) stock, 19 1/4 in. fluted barrel, Picatinny optic rail, integral bipod, Package includes Steyr or Leupold (disc. 2005) M8 2.5x28 IER scope with factory Steyr mounts, and luggage case. New 1998.

| MSR $2,099 | $1,850 | $1,575 | $1,375 | $1,125 | $900 | $750 | $650 | |

Add $100 for camo (disc. 2013).

Add $600 for Steyr Scout Package with Steyr or Leupold (disc. 2004) scope, mounts and luggage case (disc. 2013).

* ***Steyr Scout Jeff Cooper*** – .223 Rem., .308 Win. or .376 Steyr (disc. 2000, reintroduced 2005) cal., grey synthetic Zytel stock with Jeff Cooper logo and integral bipod, certificate of authenticity with test target, Package (disc. 2004) included Leupold M8 2.5x28 IER scope with factory Steyr mounts, and luggage case. Mfg. 1999-2009.

| | $2,375 | $2,050 | $1,750 | $1,425 | $1,175 | $1,050 | $900 | *$2,699* |

Add approx. 15% for Steyr Scout Package with Leupold scope, mounts and luggage case (disc. 2004).

»***Steyr Scout Jeff Cooper Limited Edition*** – 308 Win. cal., 20 in. fluted barrel, 10 shot polymer double stack detachable box mag., flip up iron sights, integral top rail, gray Mannox finish, Scout stock with integrated bipod and UIT rail, "JC" crest of arms, special ser. no., single stage trigger, three position safety, two removable sling swivels, includes Leupold 2.5X28mm Scout Scope, Galco Ching Sling, Boyt hard and soft case, Steyr scope mounts, extra magazine, and copy of Cooper's book *Art of the Rifle*, approx. 8 lbs., limited mfg. of 300. New mid-2010.

| MSR $2,995 | $2,625 | $2,250 | $1,875 | $1,550 | $1,275 | $1,050 | $925 | |

* ***Steyr Scout*** – .243 Win. cal., similar to Jeff Cooper Package, except does not include scope, mounts, or case. Mfg. 1999-2002.

| | $1,525 | $1,350 | $1,200 | $1,050 | $900 | $750 | $625 | *$1,969* |

Add $100 for .376 Steyr cal. (black stock only, disc. 2000).

Add $100 for Jeff Cooper grey stock.

* ***Steyr Scout Tactical*** – .223 Rem. (new 2000) or .308 Win. cal., similar to Steyr Scout, except has black synthetic stock with removable spacers, oversized bolt handle, and emergency ghost ring sights. Mfg. 1999-2002.

| | $1,600 | $1,400 | $1,250 | $1,050 | $900 | $750 | $625 | *$2,069* |

»***Steyr Scout Tactical Stainless*** – similar to Steyr Scout Tactical, except has stainless steel barrel. Mfg. 2000-2002.

| | $1,650 | $1,425 | $1,150 | $1,025 | $830 | $710 | $590 | *$2,159* |

MANNLICHER PRO VARMINT – .223 Rem. cal., 23.6 in. heavy fluted barrel, black synthetic or camo vented stock, includes tactical rail. Imported 2009-2013.

| | $1,600 | $1,450 | $1,275 | $1,075 | $900 | $775 | $650 | *$1,799* |

Add $200 for camo.

SBS TACTICAL – .308 Win. cal. only, 20 in. barrel w/o sights, features oversized bolt handle and high capacity 10 shot mag. with adapter, matte blue finish. Mfg. 1999-2002.

| | $840 | $735 | $625 | $550 | $500 | $450 | $395 | *$969* |

* ***SBS Tactical Heavy Barrel*** – .300 Win. Mag. (new 2000) or .308 Win. cal., features 20 (carbine, new 2000, .308 Win. only) or 26 in. heavy barrel w/o sights and oversized bolt handle, matte blue finish or stainless steel (carbine only, new 2000). Mfg. 1999-2002.

| | $865 | $745 | $635 | $550 | $500 | $450 | $395 | *$1,019* |

Add $30 for .300 Win. Mag. cal.

Add $40 for stainless steel.

* ***SBS Tactical McMillan*** – similar to SBS Tactical Heavy Barrel, except has custom McMillan A - 3 stock with adj. cheekpiece and oversized bolt handle, matte blue finish. Mfg. 1999-2002.

| | $1,465 | $1,245 | $1,035 | $850 | $725 | $600 | $550 | *$1,699* |

Add $30 for .300 Win. Mag. cal.

* ***SBS Tactical CISM*** – .308 Win. cal., 20 in. heavy barrel w/o sights, laminated wood stock with black lacquer finish, adj. cheekpiece and buttplate, 10 shot detachable mag., vent. forend. Mfg. 2000-2002.

| | $3,050 | $2,650 | $2,300 | $1,950 | $1,600 | $1,300 | $1,150 | *$3,499* |

Subtract approx. 35% for Swiss contract CISM Match in 7.5x55mm cal. with match diopter sights and 23 1/2 in. barrel. (Only 100 were imported.)

STEYR ELITE (SBS TACTICAL) – .223 Rem. (disc. 2008) or .308 Win. cal., 20 (carbine, disc.), 22.4 (new 2006) or 26 (disc. 2005) in. barrel with full length Picatinny spec. mounting rail, oversize bolt handle, two 5 shot detachable mags. (with spare buttstock storage), adj. black synthetic stock, matte blue finish or stainless steel. New 2000.

| MSR $2,299 | $1,950 | $1,725 | $1,500 | $1,275 | $1,050 | $875 | $775 | |

MSR	100%	98%	95%	90%	80%	70%	60%	Last MSR

* **Steyr Elite 08** – .308 Win. cal., 23.6 in. blue or stainless steel barrel, Dural aluminum folding stock, 10 shot high capacity box mag., extra long Picatinny rail. Imported 2009-2013.

	$5,325	$4,650	$4,325	$3,750	$3,250	$2,600	$1,995	$5,999

MODEL SSG – .243 Win. (disc., PII Sniper only) or .308 Win cal., for competition or law-enforcement use. Marksman has regular sights, detachable rotary mag., Teflon coated bolt with heavy duty locking lugs, synthetic stock has removable spacers, parkerized finish. Match version has heavier target barrel and "match" bolt carrier, can be used as single shot. Extremely accurate.

* **Model SSG 69 Sport (PI Rifle)** – .243 Win. or .308 Win. cal., 26 in. barrel with iron sights, 3 shot mag., black or green ABS Cycolac synthetic stock.

	$1,775	$1,500	$1,225	$1,000	$850	$725	$650	$1,989

Add 15% for walnut stock (disc. 1992, retail was $448).

* **Model SSG PII/PIIK Sniper Rifle** – .22-250 Rem. (new 2004), .243 Win. (disc.) or .308 Win. cal., 20 in. heavy (Model PIIK) or 26 in. heavy barrel, no sights, green or black synthetic Cycolac or McMillan black fiberglass stock, modified bolt handle, choice of single or set triggers.

MSR $1,899	$1,695	$1,500	$1,300	$1,050	$875	$750	$625	

Add 15% for walnut stock (disc. 1992, retail was $448).

* **Model SSG PIII Rifle** – .308 Win. cal., 26 in. heavy barrel with diopter match sight bases, H-S Precision Pro-Series stock in black only. Importation 1991-93.

	$2,300	$1,875	$1,425	$1,050	$825	$700	$600	$3,162

* **Model SSG PIV (Urban Rifle)** – .308 Win. cal., carbine variation with 16 1/2 in. heavy barrel and flash hider (disc.), ABS Cycolac synthetic stock in green or black. Imported 1991-2002, reimported beginning 2004.

MSR $1,899	$1,695	$1,500	$1,300	$1,050	$875	$750	$625	

* **Model SSG Jagd Match** – .222 Rem., .243 Win., or .308 Win. cal., checkered wood laminate stock, 23.6 in. barrel, Mannlicher sights, DT, supplied with test target. Mfg. 1991-1992.

	$1,550	$1,050	$950	$800	$675	$600	$540	$1,550

* **Model SSG Match Rifle** – .308 Win. only, 26 in. heavy barrel, brown ABS Cycolac stock, Walther Diopter sights, 8.6 lbs. Mfg. disc. 1992.

	$2,000	$1,500	$1,225	$925	$800	$700	$600	$2,306

Add $437 for walnut stock.

* **Model SPG-T** – .308 Win. cal., Target model. Mfg. 1993-98.

	$3,225	$2,850	$2,550	$2,200	$1,850	$1,500	$1,200	$3,695

* **Model SPG-CISM** – .308 Win. cal., 20 in. heavy barrel, laminated wood stock with adj. cheekpiece and black lacquer finish. Mfg. 1993-99.

	$2,995	$2,600	$2,300	$1,950	$1,700	$1,450	$1,200	$3,295

* **Model SSG Match UIT** – .308 Win. cal. only, 10 shot steel mag., special single set trigger, free floating barrel, Diopter sights, raked bolt handle, 10.8 lbs. Disc. 1998.

	$3,000	$2,500	$2,000	$1,800	$1,500	$1,200	$1,000	$3,995

UIT stands for Union Internationale de Tir.

* **Model SSG 04** – .308 Win. or .300 Win. Mag. cal., 20 (disc. 2005) or 23.6 heavy hammer forged barrel with muzzle brake, two-stage trigger, matte finished metal, black synthetic stock, adj. bipod, 8 (.300 Win. Mag.) or 10 (.308 Win.) shot mag., Picatinny rail, adj. buttstock, 10.1 lbs. Importation began 2004.

MSR $2,295	$1,950	$1,725	$1,500	$1,275	$1,050	$875	$775	

Add $1,100 for A1 model (new 2009).

* **Model SSG 08** – .308 Win., .300 Win. Mag. (new 2014), or .338 Lapua (new 2014) cal., 23.6 in. barrel, folding stock, adj. Picatinny rails.

MSR $5,895	$5,250	$4,800	$4,300	$3,750	$3,250	$2,600	$1,995	

Add $900 for .338 Lapua Mag. cal.

HS-50 – .460 Steyr (disc. 2013) or .50 BMG cal., single shot or repeater (M1) action, 33 in. barrel with muzzle brake, includes Picatinny rail and bipod, approx. 28 lbs. Importation began 2004.

MSR $5,995	$5,500	$4,950	$4,350	$3,900	$3,500	$3,150	$2,850	

Add $1,700 for M1 Repeater.

MSR		100%	98%	95%	90%	80%	70%	60%		Last MSR

RIFLES: SEMI-AUTO

AUG S.A. A3 M1 – .223 Rem. cal., gas operated, design incorporates use of advanced plastics, short stroke piston, integral Swarovski scope or Picatinny rail (24 in. heavy barrel only), 16, 20, 21, or 24 in. barrel, green composite stock (original bullpup configuration), rotating breech bolt, later mfg. was black or desert tan stock , 10, 30 or 42 shot mag., 7.9 lbs. Importation resumed mid-2006.

MSR $2,099	$1,895	$1,675	$1,425	$1,295	$1,050	$850	$675

Add approx. 10% for 24 in. heavy barrel with Picatinny rail and bipod (disc.).

Add $131 for 42 shot mag.

Add $400 for 1.5X or $500 for 3X optic.

* AUG S.A. Commercial – similar to AUG S.A., grey (3,000 mfg. circa 1997), green, or black finish.

	100%	98%	95%	90%	80%	70%	60%
SP receiver (Stanag metal)	$2,950	$2,750	$2,450	$2,150	$1,750	$1,575	$1,400
Grey finish	$3,150	$2,875	$2,600	$2,250	$1,825	$1,625	$1,450
Green finish (last finish)	$3,400	$2,975	$2,700	$2,300	$1,875	$1,675	$1,500
Black finish	$4,125	$3,750	$3,300	$2,950	$2,750	$2,500	$2,250

Last MSR was $1,362 (1989) for Green finish.

STEYR USR (UNIVERSAL SPORTING RIFLE) – .223 Rem. cal., unthreaded barrel, USR thumbhole stock, AUG barrels are not interchangeable with this model. Approx. 3,000 imported circa 1996 before the sporting arms ban began.

	$1,650	$1,450	$1,250	$1,050	$900	$775	$650

MODEL MAADI AKM – 7.62x39mm cal., copy of Soviet AKM design rifle, 30 shot mag., open sights.

	$2,250	$2,000	$1,800	$1,600	$1,450	$1,250	$1,125

STOEGER INDUSTRIES, INC.

Current importer/trademark established in 1924, and currently located in Accokeek, MD. Previously located in Wayne, NJ, until 2000. Stoeger Industries, Inc. was purchased by Beretta Holding of Italy in 2000, and is now a division of Benelli USA.

Stoeger has imported a wide variety of firearms during the past nine decades. Most of these guns were good quality and came from known makers in Europe (some were private labeled). Stoeger carried an extensive firearms inventory of both house brand and famous European trademarks - many of which were finely made with beautiful engraving, stock work, and other popular special order features. As a general rule, values for Stoeger rifles and shotguns may be ascertained by comparing them with a known trademark of equal quality and cal./ga. Certain configurations will be more desirable than others (i.e. a Stoeger .22 caliber Mannlicher with double-set triggers and detachable mag. will be worth considerably more than a single shot target rifle).

Perhaps the best reference works available on these older Stoeger firearms (not to mention the other trademarks of that time) are the older Stoeger catalogs themselves - quite collectible in their own right. You are advised to purchase these older catalogs (some reprints are also available) if more information is needed on not only older Stoeger models, but also the other firearms being sold at that time.

For more information and current pricing on both new and used Stoeger airguns, please refer to the Blue Book of Airguns by Dr. Robert Beeman & John Allen (also online).

PISTOLS: SEMI-AUTO

Stoeger Lugers can be found in the Luger section.

COUGAR – 9mm Para., .40 S&W, or .45 ACP (new 2010) cal., DA/SA, copy of Beretta, 3.6 in. barrel, 8 (.45 ACP), 11 (.40 S&W), or 15 (9mm Para.) shot mag., ambidextrous safety, 3-dot sights, Bruniton black (disc.) Nitride hardened matte black, silver, or two-tone finish, checkered plastic grips, blowback action with rotating bolt, removable front sight, approx. 32 oz. Mfg. in Turkey. Importation began 2007.

MSR $469	$385	$340	$275	$240	$215	$195	$180

Add $30 for silver or two-tone finish.

Add $40 for .45 ACP cal. in black finish with Picatinny rail.

SHOTGUNS: SxS

DOUBLE DEFENSE – 12 or 20 ga., 3 in. chambers, hammerless, matte blue finish, 20 in. ported barrels, fixed IC chokes, single trigger, non-reflective matte black hardwood or black synthetic (new 2014) stock, fiber optic front sight, top and bottom Picatinny rails, 6 1/2 lbs. New mid-2009.

MSR $499	$435	$350	$275	$225	$180	$150	$130

MSR	100%	98%	95%	90%	80%	70%	60%	Last MSR

SHOTGUNS: SLIDE ACTION

MODEL P350 – 12 ga. only, 3 or 3 1/2 in. chamber, 18 1/2 (Home Security, cyl. fixed choke, disc.), 24, 26, or 28 in. barrel, includes 5 screw-in chokes, choice of black synthetic, Timber HD (disc. 2008), Realtree APG HD, Realtree Max-4 HD, or Realtree Max-5 camo coverage, approx. 6.9 lbs. New 2005.

MSR $349	$285	$240	$200	$170	$150	$125	$110	

Add $100 for 100% camo coverage.
Add $130 for SteadyGrip stock with 24 in. barrel and Realtree APG finish.
Add $30 for pistol grip (18 1/2 in. barrel only), disc.
Add $63 for 13 oz. recoil reducer (disc. 2010).

STONER RIFLE

Please refer to the Knight's Armament Company listing in the K section.

STRAYER TRIPP INTERNATIONAL

Please refer to the STI International listing in this section.

STRAYER-VOIGT, INC.

Current manufacturer of Infinity pistols located in Grand Prairie, TX. See the Infinity listing in the I section for more information.

STREET SWEEPER

Previously manufactured by Sales of Georgia, Inc. located in Atlanta, GA.

SHOTGUNS

STREET SWEEPER – 12 ga. only, 12 shot rotary mag., tactical configuration with 18 in. barrel, double action, folding stock, 9 3/4 lbs. Restricted sales following the ATF classification as a "destructive device." Mfg. 1989-approx. 1995.

	$1,495	$1,350	$1,100	$995	$895	$795	$695	

Unless this model was registered with the ATF before May 1st, 2001, it is subject to seizure with a possible fine/imprisonment.

STURM, RUGER & CO., INC.

Current manufacturer with production facilities located in Newport, NH, Prescott, AZ, and Mayodan, NC. Previously manufactured in Southport, CT 1949-1991 (corporate and administrative offices remain at this location). A second factory was opened in Newport, NH in 1963, and still produces single action revolvers, rifles and shotguns. During September 2013, Ruger purchased a 220,000 square foot facility in Mayodan, NC. New production began in late fall of 2013.

In January of 1949, partners William B. Ruger and Alexander Sturm began manufacturing .22 pistols in a leased 4,400 square foot wooden structure on Station St. in Southport, CT. By 1956 they acquired an additional 2,300 square feet that is today affectionately known as the Red Barn. By January of 1959 they completely moved into a newly finished building on Lacey Place, not too far from Station St. The company continued to expand its product line and in 1967 began producing long guns in a factory building located in Newport, NH. By 1988 Ruger set up another facility in Prescott, AZ to make the P-series center-fire pistols. In July 1991 they completely suspended production at Southport. The corporate offices remain there to this day. Then, in 2013 Ruger opened a third large factory in Mayodan, NC. Over time production of the extensive variety of products was divided up and dispersed among these facilities.

Red Barn on Station St. 1949-1959 pistols & revolvers
Lacey Place 1959-1991 pistols, revolvers & rifles
Pinetree Casting Newport, NH 1963 - current investment castings
Newport, NH 1967 - current shotguns, rifles, and since 1992 revolvers
Prescott, AZ 1990 - current all centerfire pistols and since 1992 all rimfire pistols
Mayodan, NC 2013 - current modern rifles. In 2015 an additional line was also made up for producing SR22 pistols.

From 2004-2007 the Ruger Studio of Art & Decoration offered factory engraving on any current Ruger model. The engraving could range from presentation inscriptions to bas-relief and extensive gold in-laid masterpieces. Prices could range from a few hundred dollars to $40,000 or more.

Ruger emerged as America's largest small arms maker, and offers a complete line of firearms for sportsmen, law enforcement and military. Over a 65 year span, from five separate factories Ruger has shipped over 27 million firearms.

Alex Sturm passed away in November 1951. Bill Ruger carried on until July 6, 2002 when he too passed away at his home in Prescott, AZ. Ruger, America's greatest 20th century arms inventor is buried on his estate Corbin Park at Croydon, NH.

MSR	100%	98%	95%	90%	80%	70%	60%	Last MSR

PISTOLS: SEMI-AUTO, RIMFIRE

Many distributors and customizers have produced special/limited editions of this popular series of .22 cal. pistols; these editions are not listed in either the *Blue Book of Gun Values* or the *Blue Book of Tactical Firearms Values*. After 1999, all non-22/45 model pistols were fitted with Ruger logo medallions with a red background. Note that Ruger's 22/45 series did not have red eagle logo medallions in either grip panel until the P512MKIIRP was introduced in 2010.

* **Mark III 22/45 Threaded Barrel** – .22 LR cal., SA, 4 1/2 in. threaded bull barrel, 10 shot mag., Zytel polymer grip frame, fixed front and adj. rear sights or Picatinny rail, blue finish, 32 oz. New 2011.

MSR $499	$425	$370	$320	$290	$235	$190	$150	

Add $449 for Silent-SR suppressor (new 2016, NFA regulations apply).

22 CHARGER (CURRENT MFG.) – .22 LR cal., 10 in. cold hammer forged threaded barrel, alloy steel construction with matte black finish, brown laminate or black polymer stock, 10 shot detachable flush-mounted BX-10 rotary or 15 shot BX-15 mag. (black polymer stock only), A2-style grip, Picatinny rail, features improved ergonomics, includes adj. bipod and soft case, 3.13 lbs. New 2015.

MSR $309	$265	$230	$200	$180	$145	$120	$95	

Add $449 for Silent-SR suppressor (new 2016, NFA regulations apply).

* **22 Charger Takedown** – .22 LR cal., 10 in. cold hammer forged threaded barrel, alloy steel construction with matte black finish, Green Mountain laminate or black polymer stock, detachable flush-mounted BX-1 10 shot rotary or 15 shot BX-15 mag. (black polymer stock only), features 10/22 takedown quick disconnect feature that allows the pistol to be taken down quickly and easily, Picatinny rail, includes adj. bipod and hard plastic case, 3.22 lbs. New 2015.

MSR $419	$350	$300	$275	$250	$225	$200	$180	

Add $449 for Silent-SR suppressor (new 2016, NFA regulations apply).

PISTOLS: SEMI-AUTO, CENTERFIRE

LCP (LIGHTWEIGHT COMPACT PISTOL) – .380 ACP cal., DAO, 2 3/4 in. barrel, 6 or 7 (new 2013) shot mag., bobbed hammer, black glass filled nylon frame with molded checkering, blued steel slide, fixed sights or Crimson Trace Laserguard (new 2011), black Ruger logos inset in grip panels, includes external locking device, pocket holster, Lasermax Centerfire laser (mfg. 2012-2014), 9.65-10 oz. New 2008.

MSR $259	$220	$195	$165	$150	$120	$100	$75	

Add $170 for Crimson Trace Laserguard (new 2011).
Add $70 for Lasermax Centerfire laser (mfg. 2012-2014).

* **LCP Stainless** – .380 ACP cal., similar to LCP, except features stainless steel slide, 7 shot, fixed sights, and brushed stainless finish, 9.65 oz. New 2014.

MSR $289	$250	$220	$190	$170	$140	$115	$90	

LCP CUSTOM – .380 ACP cal., 2 3/4 in. barrel, blued alloy steel slide, 6 shot mag., photo luminescent front and drift adj. rear sights, polished stainless steel guide rod, wide red anodized skeletonized aluminum trigger, finger grip extension floorplate, black glass-filled nylon grips, 9.75 oz. New 2015.

MSR $269	$225	$195	$170	$155	$125	$100	$80	

LC9 – 9mm Para. cal., bobbed hammer, DAO, 3.12 in. barrel, alloy steel slide, blue finish, black glass filled nylon grip frame, 7 or 9 (new 2013) shot mag., 3-dot fixed front and adj. rear sights, slightly larger (less than 1 in. in both height and width) than the LCP, finger grip extension, loaded chamber indicator, includes soft case, optional Lasermax Centerfire laser (new 2012) or Crimson trace laser grips,17.1 oz. Mfg. 2011-2014.

	$375	$335	$275	$240	$215	$195	$180	*$449*

Add $80 for Lasermax Centerfire laser (new 2012).
Add $180 for Crimson trace "Laserguard" laser (new 2013).

* **LC9s** – 9mm Para. cal., SFO, 3.12 in. barrel, alloy steel slide, blue finish, black, Flat Dark Earth (new 2016), or Marsala (new 2016) glass-filled nylon checkered grip frame, 7 shot mag., adj. 3-dot sights, finger grip extension floorplate, integrated trigger safety, manual safety, and magazine disconnect, compatible with all existing LC9 accessories, including lasers, holsters and extended 9 shot mag., includes soft case, and one 7 shot mag., 17.2 oz. New mid-2014.

MSR $479	$390	$335	$275	$240	$215	$195	$180	

* **LC9s Pro** – 9mm Para. cal., SFO, 3.12 in. barrel, alloy steel slide, blue finish, black glass-filled nylon grip frame with aggressive texturing, 7 shot mag., adj. 3-dot sights, finger grip extension floorplate, visual loaded chamber view port, internal striker blocker, internal trigger safety, compatible with all existing LC9 accessories, including lasers, holsters and extended 9 shot mag., includes soft case, and one 7 shot mag., 17.2 oz. New 2015.

MSR $479	$390	$335	$275	$240	$215	$195	$180	

MSR	100%	98%	95%	90%	80%	70%	60%	Last MSR

LC380 – .380 ACP cal., DAO, 3.12 in. barrel, alloy steel slide and barrel, blued finish, 7 shot mag., black glass-filled checkered nylon grip frame, adj. 3-dot sights, Crimson Trace Laserguard Laser (new 2014) or LaserMax Centerfire (mfg. 2014 only), internal lock, manual safety, magazine disconnect, loaded chamber indicator, finger grip extension floorplate, includes one 7 shot mag. and soft case, 17.2 oz. New 2013.

	100%	98%	95%	90%	80%	70%	60%	
MSR $479	$390	$335	$275	$240	$215	$195	$180	

Add $190 for Crimson Trace Laserguard Laser (new 2014).
Add $80 for Lasermax Centerfire laser (mfg. 2014 only).

P85 – 9mm Para. cal., DA/SA, 4 1/2 in. barrel, aluminum frame with steel slide, 3-dot fixed sights, 15 shot mag., oversized trigger, polymer grips, matte black finish, 2 lbs. Mfg. 1987-1990.

	$350	$295	$265	$235	$215	$200	$185	*$410*

Subtract $30 if without case and extra mag.

Any P85 models without the "MKIIR" stamp on either the left or right side of the safety must be returned to the factory for a free safety modification.

* KP85 – stainless variation of the P85. Mfg. 1990 only.

	$375	$315	$280	$230	$200	$165	$140	*$452*

Subtract $30 if without case and extra mag.

Variants included a decocking or double action only version at no extra charge. Any KP85 models without the "MKIIR" stamp on either the left or right side of the safety must be returned to the factory for a free safety modification.

P85 MARK II – 9mm Para. cal., DA/SA, 4 1/2 in. barrel, aluminum frame with steel slide, 3-dot fixed sights, 15 shot mag., ambidextrous safety beginning in 1991, oversized trigger, polymer grips, matte black finish, 2 lbs. Mfg. 1990-1992.

	$350	$295	$265	$235	$215	$200	$185	*$410*

Subtract $30 if without case and extra mag.

Decocker and DAO models were not available in the Mark II series.

* KP85 Mark II – stainless variation of the P85. Mfg. 1990-1992.

	$375	$315	$280	$230	$200	$165	$140	*$452*

Subtract $30 if without case and extra mag.

P89 – 9mm Para. cal., DA/SA, improved variation of the P85 Mark II, 10 (C/B 1994) or 15 (new late 2005) shot mag., ambidextrous safety or decocker (Model P89D), blue finish, 32 oz. Mfg. 1992-2007.

	$380	$330	$280	$250	$215	$200	$185	*$475*

Variants were available in a decocking (P89DC) or double action only (P-89DAO, disc. 2004) version at no extra charge.

KP89 STAINLESS – stainless variation of the P89, also available in double action only (disc. 2004). Mfg. 1992-2009.

	$425	$360	$305	$250	$215	$200	$185	*$525*

Add $45 for convertible 7.65mm Luger cal. barrel (Model KP89X, approx. 5,750 mfg. during 1994 only).

P90 – .45 ACP cal., DA/SA, similar to KP90 Stainless, except has blue finish, 8 shot mag., 33 1/2 oz. Disc. 2010.

	$475	$395	$335	$265	$215	$200	$185	*$591*

Add $50 for Tritium night sights (disc. 2006).

P90 models were produced in a variety of models for law enforcement or government contracts and will be found with any combination of safety model, decocker or double action only with fingergroove tactical rubber grip and/or Tritium night sights.

KP90 STAINLESS – .45 ACP cal., DA/SA 4 1/2 in. barrel, oversized trigger, aluminum frame with stainless steel slide, 8 shot single column mag., KP90 or decocking (KP90D), polymer grips, 3-dot fixed sights, ambidextrous safety began approx ser. no. 660-12800. Mfg. 1991-2010.

	$495	$415	$360	$295	$250	$225	$200	*$636*

Add $50 for Tritium night sights (disc. 2006).

KP90 models were produced in a variety of models for law enforcement or government contracts and will be found with any combination of safety model, decocker or double action only with fingergroove tactical rubber grip and/or Tritium night sights.

KP91 STAINLESS – .40 S&W cal., similar to Model KP90 Stainless, except is not available with external safety and has 11 shot double column mag. Mfg. 1991-1994.

	$385	$335	$295	$240	$210	$180	$155	*$489*

This model was available in a decocking variation (KP91D) or double action only (KP91DAO). Approx. 39,600 of all models were mfg. before being discontinued in favor of the tapered slide KP944 model.

MSR		100%	98%	95%	90%	80%	70%	60%	Last MSR

P93 CHICAGO POLICE SPECIAL CONTRACT – produced in the late 1990s for a Chicago Police Department contract, this blued stainless P93 was ordered with a special P89M rollmark on the slide so that those who were concerned about having a "compact" pistol would not be alerted to the fact that it was indeed a P93. Extremely rare in civilian hands.

Extreme rarity precludes accurate pricing on this model, and should be examined for authenticity. NIB specimens have been noted at $550.

KP93 STAINLESS – 9mm Para. cal., compact variation with 3 9/10 in. tilting barrel - link actuated, matte blue or REM (mfg. 1996 only) finish, 3-dot sights, 10 (C/B 1994) or 15* shot mag., available with DA/SA ambidextrous decocker action or DAO, 31 oz. Mfg. 1994-2004.

		$450	$370	$315	$260	$220	$200	$185	$575

Add $50 for Tritium night sights.

KP93 models were produced in a variety of models for law enforcement or government contracts and will be found with any combination of decocker model or double action only with fingergroove tactical rubber grip and/or Tritium night sights.

P93D BLUE – similar to KP93 Stainless, except has blue finish, compact model, ambidextrous decocker, 31 oz. Mfg. 1998-2004.

		$395	$330	$285	$240	$215	$200	$185	$495

Add $50 for Tritium night sights.

P93 models were produced in a variety of models for law enforcement or government contracts and will be found with any combination of decocker model or double action only with fingergroove tactical rubber grip and/or Tritium night sights.

* P94/KP94 w/Integral Tac-Star Laser Sight – 9mm Para. cal., 10 (C/B 1994) or 15* shot mag., integral Tac-Star laser sight, Tritium night sights, ambidextrous safety, ambidextrous decocker, or double action only. Mfg. 1994 only.

		$650	$575	$495	$440	$360	$295	$225	

Add $50 for Tritium night sights.

These factory laser sighted pistol models were also produced in any combination with fingergroove tactical rubber grip and/or Tritium night sights. Some were also produced with Ruger's "REM" finish. Reportedly 1,836 made total of all models.

KP94 STAINLESS – 9mm Para. or .40 S&W cal., available with ambidextrous safety, matte stainless or REM (mfg. 1996 only) finish, DA/SA ambidextrous decocker action or DAO, 10 (C/B 1994), or 15* (9mm Para.) shot mag., 33 oz. Mfg. 1994-2004.

		$450	$370	$315	$260	$220	$200	$185	$575

Add $50 for Tritium night sights.

KP94 models have been produced in a variety of models for law enforcement or government contracts and will be found with any combination of safety model, decocker or double action only with fingergroove tactical rubber grip and/or Tritium night sights.

P94 BLUE – similar to KP94 Stainless, except has blue finish. Mfg. 1998-2004.

		$395	$330	$285	$240	$215	$200	$185	$495

Add $50 for Tritium night sights.

P94 models have been produced in a variety of models for law enforcement or government contracts and will be found with any combination of safety model, decocker or double action only with fingergroove tactical rubber grip and/or Tritium night sights.

P95PR (P95) – 9mm Para. cal., available in DA/SA ambidextrous decocker (D/DPR suffix), ambidextrous safety, or DAO configuration (DAO suffix, mfg. 1996-2004), polymer frame, 3.9 in. barrel, fixed sights, blue finish, 10 or 15 (new late 2005) shot mag., lower Picatinny rail became standard in 2006, (non-Picatinny rail models discontinued 2005), 27 oz. Mfg. 1996-2013.

		$320	$275	$235	$195	$165	$150	$135	$399

Add $50 for Tritium night sights (disc. 2006).

During 2006, this model's nomenclature changed from P95 to P95PR to reflect the Picatinny style rail.

P95 models have been produced in a variety of models for law enforcement or government contracts and will be found with any combination of safety model, decocker or double action only with fingergroove tactical rubber grip and/or Tritium night sights. The P95DAO double action only model was disc. 2004.

KP95PR STAINLESS (KP95) – stainless variation of Model P95 and P95PR. Mfg. 1997-2013.

		$355	$310	$250	$200	$175	$140	$120	$439

Add $50 for Tritium night sights.

During 2006, this model's nomenclature changed from KP95 to KP95PR to reflect the Picatinny style rail. Non-Picatinny rail models were disc. 2005. KP95 models have been produced in a variety of models for law enforcement or government contracts, and will be found in any combination of safety model, decocker, or double action only with fingergroove tactical rubber grisp and/or Tritium night sights. The KP95DAO double action only model was disc. 2004.

MSR	100%	98%	95%	90%	80%	70%	60%	Last MSR

P97D – .45 ACP cal., DA/SA, ambidextrous decocker, 8 shot mag., blue finish, 30 1/2 oz. Mfg. 2002-2004.

	$370	$315	$275	$235	$215	$200	$185	$460

Add $50 for Tritium night sights.

KP97 STAINLESS – .45 ACP cal., similar to KP95 Stainless, except has 8 shot mag., 27 oz. Mfg. 1999-2004.

	$395	$315	$265	$235	$215	$200	$185	$495

Add $50 for Tritium night sights.

P345PR (P345) – .45 ACP cal., ambidextrous safety or decocker (P345DPR, disc. 2006), DA/SA, black polymer frame with blue steel slide, 4.2 in. barrel, fixed sights, polyurethane grips, slimmer profile frame, 8 shot single column mag., with or w/o (disc. 2006) Picatinny rail, loaded chamber indicator, 29 oz. Mfg. 2005-2012.

	$485	$425	$335	$275	$225	$210	$195	$599

KP345PR (KP345) – .45 ACP cal., decocker (KP345DPR, disc. 2006), similar to P345, except has stainless steel slide, Picatinny rail became standard 2007 (KP345PR), 29 oz. Mfg. 2005-2012.

	$515	$440	$345	$280	$230	$210	$195	$639

P944 – .40 S&W cal., similar to P94, ambidextrous safety, blue finish, 34 oz. Mfg. 1999-2010.

	$445	$360	$300	$245	$215	$200	$185	$557

Add $50 for Tritium night sights (disc. 2006).

This model has been produced in many versions for law enforcement or government contracts and will be found with any combination of safety type, decocker, or double action only, fingergroove tactical rubber grip, and/or Tritium night sights.

KP944 STAINLESS – similar to P944, except is stainless steel, also available as decocker (KP944D). Mfg. 1999-2010.

	$500	$400	$345	$275	$230	$195	$170	$647

Add $50 for tritium night sights (disc. 2006).

This model has been produced in many versions for law enforcement or government contracts and will be found with any combination of safety type, decocker, or double action only, fingergroove tactical rubber grip, and/or Tritium night sights. The KP944DAO double action only model was disc. 2004.

SR9 – 9mm Para. cal., SFO, semi-double action trigger pull, 4 1/8 in. barrel, 10 or 17 shot mag., reversible backstrap, low profile 3-dot sights, glass filled nylon frame, reversible back strap, choice of black stainless (disc.), brushed stainless steel, alloy steel/Nitridox Pro Black (SR9B Model, disc.), alloy steel/Black Nitride, or OD Green (mfg. 2009-2010), Picatinny rail, ambidextrous safety, 26 1/2 oz. New late 2007.

MSR $569		$475	$415	$350	$315	$275	$240	$210

Note that all SR9 models serial numbered 330-29999 and earlier are subject to a factory recall at no charge. If your pistol has not yet had the new parts installed, please contact Sturm, Ruger & Company at 1-800-784-3701 or email SR9Recall@ruger.com and they will provide you with shipping instructions.

* **SR9C** – 9mm Para. cal., similar to the Model SR9, except has compact frame and 3 1/2 in. barrel, stainless steel/brushed stainless, alloy/Nitridox Pro Black (disc.), or alloy steel/black Nitride slide finish, 10 or 17 shot mag., adj. 3-dot sights, 23.4 oz. New mid-2010.

MSR $569		$475	$415	$350	$315	$275	$240	$210

9E – 9mm Para. cal., 4.14 in. barrel, 10 or 17 shot mag., fixed 3-dot sights, black glass-filled nylon grip frame, reversible back strap, integral accessory mounting rail, 27.2 oz. New 2015.

MSR $459		$365	$315	$280	$260	$240	$220	$195

SR40 – .40 S&W cal., hammerless SFO, 10 or 15 shot mag., 4.14 in. barrel, alloy or stainless steel slide with brushed stainless or Nitridox Pro Black finish, adj. 3-dot sights, black glass filled nylon grips, reversible backstrap, integral mounting rail, ambidextrous thumb safety, loaded chamber indicator, includes two mags., 27 1/4 oz. New 2011.

MSR $569		$475	$415	$350	$315	$275	$240	$210

* **SR40C** – .40 S&W cal., similar to SR40, except has compact frame, 3 1/2 in. barrel, brushed stainless or Nitridox Pro Black finish, 9 or 15 shot mag., adj. 3-dot sights, 23.4 oz. New mid-2011.

MSR $569		$475	$415	$350	$315	$275	$240	$210

SR45 – .45 ACP cal., 4 1/2 in. barrel, 10 shot mag., black glass -filled nylon grip frame, adj. 3-dot sights, choice of brushed stainless slide or alloy steel with black Nitride finish, includes two magazines, 30.15 oz. New 2013.

MSR $569		$475	$415	$350	$315	$275	$240	$210

SR-1911 – .45 ACP cal., SA, patterned after the Colt M1911 Series 70, 5 in. barrel, supplied with one 7 and one 8 shot stainless steel mags., matte stainless steel frame and slide, oversized beavertail grip safety, standard recoil guide system, rear slide serrations, diamond checkered Cocobolo grips with black Ruger medallion inserts, skeletonized trigger and bobbed hammer, Novak 3-dot adj. sights, approx. 40 oz. New mid-2011.

MSR $939		$785	$640	$495	$385	$325	$275	$250

MSR	100%	98%	95%	90%	80%	70%	60%	Last MSR

* **SR-1911CMD** – .45 ACP cal., Commander style, similar to SR-1911, except has 4 1/4 in. barrel, 7 shot mag., 36.4 oz. New 2013.

MSR $939	$785	$640	$495	$385	$325	$275	$250	

* **SR1911 Lightweight Commander-Style** – .45 ACP cal., 4 1/4 in. stainless steel barrel, 7 shot mag., aluminum grip frame with Black anodized finish, adj. 3-dot sights, oversized beavertail grip safety, oversized ejection port and extended mag. release, hardwood grip panels and checkered backstrap, skeletonized hammer, standard recoil guide system, rear slide serrations, includes two stainless steel mags., and soft case, 29.3 oz. New 2015.

MSR $979	$825	$720	$620	$560	$455	$370	$290	

REVOLVERS: DOUBLE ACTION

During certain years of manufacture, Ruger's changes in production on certain models (cals., barrel markings, barrel lengths, etc.) have created rare variations that are now considered premium niches. These areas of low manufacture will add premiums to the values listed on standard models.

SPEED SIX (MODELS 207, 208 and 209) – .38 Spl., .357 Mag., or 9mm Para. cal., 2 3/4, or 4 in. barrel, fixed sights, checkered walnut grips, round butt, blue finish, some guns have factory speed hammer (no hammer spur). Mfg. 1973-1988. Model 207 and 208 disc. 1988.

	$450	$375	$300	$225	$175	$150	$140	$292

Add $300 for 9mm Para. (Model 209 disc. 1984).

* **Speed Six Models 737 and 738** – stainless steel versions of Models 207 and 208, .357 Mag and .38 Spl. cals., 2 3/4, 3 (Postal Inspector contract) or 4 in. barrel. Disc. 1988.

	$475	$400	$325	$225	$175	$150	$140	$320

Add 100% for "U.S." and "N.I.S." marked with 2 3/4 in. barrel.

* **Speed Six Model 739** – stainless steel, 9mm Para. Disc. 1984.

	$700	$575	$500	$400	$275	$195	$175	

SECURITY SIX (MODEL 117) – .357 Mag. cal., 6 shot, 2 3/4, 3 (late production only), 4, 4 (heavy), or 6 in. barrel, adj. sights, checkered walnut grips, square butt. Mfg. 1970-1985.

	$450	$375	$300	$225	$175	$150	$140	$309

Add $15 for target grips.
Add 50% for .38 Special cal with 6 in. barrel and 150- prefix serial number
Add 50% for .357 Mag. Cal. With 2 3/4 in barrel, adj. sights and round butt (Model RDA-32RB - extremely rare).

Note that beginning late in the 150- serial number prefix, the grip frame was changed to have a more outward "highback" shape. Revolvers with the earlier "lowback" grip frame are generally considered more collectible. All revolvers having fixed sights and square butt grip frame with "lowback" shape to the backstrap were also marked "SECURITY-SIX". Only when the new highback gripframe came out were the fixed sight and square butt revolvers marked "SERVICE-SIX".

500 of this model were mfg. for the California Highway Patrol during 1983 (.38 Spl. cal.) in stainless steel only. They are distinguishable by a C.H.P. marking. Other Security Six Model 117 special editions have been made for various police organizations - premiums might exist in certain regions for these variations.

* **Security Six Model 717** – stainless steel version of Model 117. Disc. 1985.

	$450	$375	$300	$225	$175	$150	$140	$338

Add 30% for this model in .38 Special with 4, 4 (heavy) or 6 in. barrel.
Add 50% for .357 Mag. Cal with 2 3/4 in. barrel, adj. sights and round butt (model GA-32RB - extremely rare).

POLICE SERVICE SIX – .357 Mag, .38 Spl., or 9mm Para. cal., blue finish only, square butt, fixed sights, checkered walnut grips.

* **Police Service Six Model 107** – .357 Mag. cal., 2 3/4 or 4 in. barrel, fixed sights. Disc. 1988.

	$450	$375	$300	$225	$175	$150	$140	$287

* **Police Service Six Model 108** – .38 Spl. cal., 2 3/4 or 4 in. barrel, fixed sights. Disc. 1988.

	$400	$350	$275	$200	$175	$150	$140	$287

Add 40% for this model with low-back grip frame, 6 in. barrel, and 150- prefix serial number.
Add 125% for "U.S." marked with or without lanyard loop.
Add 100% for .380 Rim cal. With or without lanyard loop.

* **Police Service Six Model 109** – 9mm Para. cal., 2 3/4 or 4 in. barrel, fixed sights. Disc. 1984.

	$750	$550	$500	$400	$275	$195	$175	

POLICE SERVICE SIX STAINLESS STEEL – stainless construction, 2 3/4 or 4 in. barrel, fixed sights, checkered walnut grips.

* **Police Service Six Stainless Steel Model 707** – .357 Mag. cal., 2 3/4 or 4 in. barrel, square butt. Disc. 1988.

	$475	$400	$325	$225	$175	$150	$140	$310

MSR	100%	98%	95%	90%	80%	70%	60%	Last MSR

* Police Service Six Stainless Steel Model 708 – .38 Spl. cal., 2 3/4 or 4 in. barrel, square butt. Disc. 1988.

	$400	$350	$275	$200	$175	$150	$140	*$310*

GP-100 – .357 Mag. or .38 Spl. (disc.) cal., 4 (disc. 2009), 4.2, or 6 (.357 Mag. only) in. standard (disc.) or heavy full shrouded barrel, 6 shot, triple-locking cylinder, strengthened design intended for constant use with all .357 Mag. ammunition, easy takedown, rubber cushioned grip panels with polished Goncalo Alves wood inserts (disc.) or black rubber Hogue Monogrip, fixed (mfg. 1989-2006) or adj. sights with white outlined rear and interchangeable front, transfar bar safety, 35-46 oz. depending on barrel configuration. New 1986.

MSR $769	$650	$570	$490	$440	$360	$295	$230	

* GP-100 Stainless Steel – .327 Fed. Mag. (mfg. 2009-disc. 2013), .38 Spl. (disc.), or .357 Mag. cal., 3 (new 1990, .357 Mag. only), 4 (disc. 2009), 4.2, or 6 in. barrel, 6 or 7 (.327 Fed. Mag. only, disc. 2013) shot, ramp front and fixed (3 in. only) or adj. sights, satin stainless finish, 36-45 oz. New 1987.

MSR $799	$675	$590	$500	$460	$370	$300	$235	

Add $30 for adj. sights.

SP-101 STAINLESS STEEL – .22 LR (6 shot - mfg. 1990-2004), .32 H&R (6 shot - mfg. 1991-2012), .327 Federal (6 shot - mfg. 2007-2011, 2016), .38 Spl.+P (5 shot), 9mm Para. (5 shot - mfg. 1991-2000), or .357 Mag. (5 shot - new 1991) cal., 2 1/4, 3 1/16, 4 (mfg. 1990-2007), or 4.2 (new 2012) in. barrel, small frame variation of the GP-100 Stainless, fiber optic (new 2012) or black ramp front sight, fixed or adj. rear (new 1996) sights, cushioned rubber grips with black plastic or engraved hardwood insert (new 2012), satin stainless finish, 25-34 oz. New 1989.

MSR $719	$615	$540	$460	$420	$340	$275	$215	

Add $50 for fiber optic sights (new 2012, 4.2 in. barrel only).
Add $50 for .327 Fed. Mag. cal. with fiber optic front sights (new 2016).
Add $170 for Crimson Trace laser grips (mfg. 2008-2011).
Add $100 for .357 Mag. models with "125 GR. BULLET" rollmarked on barrel lug (disc. 1991).
Add $300 for 9mm Para. caliber (disc. 2000).
Add $150 for .22 LR caliber without fiber optic sights (disc. 2004).

The .327 Federal caliber configuration will also shoot .32 H&R Mag., .32 S&W, and .32 S&W Long cartridges.

The first few thousand SP-101s in .38 Special had green grip inserts. Also, approximately 3,000 total of the earliest KSP-321 and KSP-331 .357 Mag. models were rollmarked with "125 GR. BULLET" on the barrel under the caliber designation (serial range 570-59359 to 570-67976).

Ruger introduced a .357 Mag./2 1/4 in. (new 1993) or .38 Spl./2 1/4 (mfg. 1994-2005) in. configuration featuring a spurless hammer, double action only.

SP-101 barrel lengths are as follows: .22 cal. is available in 2 1/4 or 4 in. standard or heavy barrel, .32 H&R is available in 3 1/16 or 4 (mfg. 1994-2008) in. heavy barrel, .38 Spl. is available in 2 1/4 or 3 1/16 in. length only, 9mm Para. is available in 2 1/4 (mfg. 1989-2000) or 3 1/16 in. (mfg. 1989-2000) length only, and .357 Mag. is available in 2 1/4 or 3 1/16 in. length only.

* SP101 Stainless Steel .22 LR – .22 LR cal., 4.2 in. barrel, 8 shot, satin stainless steel, black rubber grips with checkered wood panel inserts, adj. rear sight, fiber optic front sight, 30 oz. New late 2011.

MSR $769	$650	$570	$490	$440	$360	$295	$230	

REDHAWK – .41 Mag. (mfg. 1984-1991), or .44 Mag. cal., 6 shot fluted cylinder, 5 1/2 and 7 1/2 (disc. 2005) in. barrel, blue finish, square butt, smooth hardwood grips, 49-54 oz. Disc. 2009.

	$615	$460	$375	$285	$225	$180	$165	*$789*

Add $40 for scope rings (disc. 2005).
.41 Mag. cals. will bring collector premium.

* Redhawk Stainless Steel – .357 Mag. (mfg. 1984-1985), .41 Mag. (mfg. 1984-1991), .44 Mag. or .45 LC (mfg. 1998-2005, 4 in. barrel only) cal., stainless steel construction, 4.2 (new 2007), 5 1/2, or 7 1/2 in. barrel, choice of hardwood, laminate (mfg. 2009-2015), or Hogue Monogrip (4.2 in. barrel only) grips, 6 shot, ramp front and adj. rear sights, satin stainless finish, 49-54 oz.

MSR $1,079	$925	$785	$655	$595	$480	$400	$315	

Add $40 for scope rings (disc.).
Models in .357 Mag., .41 Mag. or .45 LC will bring collector premiums.

The 7 1/2 in. barrel was available with or w/o integral scope mounting system (.41 Mag., .44 Mag., or .45 LC only).

SUPER REDHAWK STAINLESS – .44 Mag., .454 Casull, or .480 Ruger (mfg. 2001-2007, reintroduced 2013) cal., 6 shot, 7 1/2 or 9 1/2 in. barrel, fluted (.44 Mag. cal. only) or non-fluted cylinder, choice of regular or high gloss (mfg. 1996 only), Target Gray (.454 Casull and .480 Ruger only, disc. 2009), or satin stainless steel finish, ramp front and adj. rear sights, cushioned grip panels (GP-100 style, disc.) or Hogue Tamer Monogrips (new 2008), stainless steel scope rings, includes hard plastic case, 53-58 oz. New late 1987.

MSR $1,159	$985	$860	$740	$670	$540	$445	$345	

MSR	100%	98%	95%	90%	80%	70%	60%	*Last MSR*

Add $30 for .454 Casull or .480 Ruger cal.

Add $75 for early .44 Mag. with "SUPER REDHAWK" rollmarked on both sides of cylinder frame extension, serial range 550-00500 to at least 550-00659.

* ***Super Redhawk Stainless Alaskan*** – .44 Mag. (new 2008), .454 Casull, or .480 Ruger (disc. 2007, reintroduced 2013) cal., stainless steel, 5 shot (some .480 Ruger only) or 6 shot, 2 1/2 in. barrel, ramp front and adj. rear sights, Hogue Tamer Monogrip, unfluted cylinder, satin stainless finish, 44-45 oz. New 2005.

| MSR $1,189 | $1,000 | $875 | $750 | $680 | $550 | $450 | $350 | |

Add 50% for .480 Ruger with 5-shot cylinder (less than 30 believed to have been shipped commercially).

LCR – 9mm Para. (new 2015), .22 LR (new 2012), .22 WMR (new 2013), .38 Spl.+P, .327 Federal Mag. (new mid-2015), or .357 Mag. cal., 5 (.38 Spl. or .357 Mag.), 6 (.22 WMR or .327 Federal), or 8 (.22 LR only, new 2012) shot, DAO, hammerless, 1 7/8 in. barrel, monolithic aluminum frame, stainless steel cylinder, polymer fire control housing, matte black or blackened stainless (.357 Mag. or 9mm only) finish, Hogue Tamer Monogrip or Crimson Trace Lasergrips (disc. 2015), integral rear sight with pinned ramp front sight, 13 1/2-17 oz. New 2010.

| MSR $579 | $485 | $415 | $365 | $335 | $300 | $275 | $250 | |

Add $90 for .357 Mag., .327 Federal Mag. (new mid-2015), or 9mm Para. (new 2015) cal.

Add $280 for Crimson Trace Lasergrips (disc. 2015).

Add $50 for LCR-XS model with standard dot Tritium front sight (.38 Spl.+P cal. only) and U-notch integral rear sight (mfg. 2011-2013).

RIFLES: BOLT ACTION, CENTERFIRE

During certain years of manufacture, Ruger's changes in production on certain models (cals., barrel markings, barrel lengths, etc.) have created rare variations that are now considered premium niches. These areas of low manufacture will add premiums to the values listed on standard models.

Earlier mfg. had flat-bolt handle or hollow round bolt, and will bring $150+ premium, depending on configuration.

Early (pre-1972) mfg. with flat-bolt handle are desirable in the rarer cals. and will command a 100% premium if in 98%+ original condition.

MODEL 77-GS GUNSITE SCOUT – .308 Win. or 5.56 NATO (new 2015) cal., 16.1 in. cold hammer forged barrel with flash suppressor, 10 shot detachable box mag., alloy steel receiver, matte black finish, forward mounted Picatinny rail, protected front sight and adj. ghost ring rear sight, non-rotating Mauser type controlled round feed extractor, right or left-hand (new 2012) action, nylon trigger guard, checkered grey laminate or composite (new 2015) stock, soft rubber buttpad with 3 1/2 in. spacers, sling swivels, features the Gunsite name rollmarked on the receiver and engraved on the grip cap, approx. 7 lbs. New 2011.

| MSR $1,139 | $965 | $845 | $725 | $655 | $530 | $435 | $340 | |

* ***Model 77-GS Gunsite Scout Stainless*** – .308 Win. or 5.56 NATO (new 2015) cal., 16.1, 16 1/2 (disc. 2012) or 18 in. barrel with flash suppressor, 10 shot detachable box mag., alloy steel receiver, matte stainless finish, forward mounted Picatinny rail, checkered grey/black laminate or composite (new 2015) stock, soft rubber buttpad with 3 1/2 in. spacers, sling swivels, protected front sight and adj. ghost ring rear sight, Gunsite engraved logo grip cap, non-rotating Mauser type controlled round feed extractor, right or left-hand (new 2012) action, approx. 7 lbs. New 2011.

| MSR $1,199 | $1,020 | $895 | $775 | $675 | $575 | $475 | $350 | |

* ***Model HM77-VLEHFS Hawkeye Tactical*** – .223 Rem., .243 Win. (disc. 2010), or .308 Win. cal., 4 or 5 shot mag., matte finished blued action and 20 in. bull barrel with flash suppressor, no sights, adj. two-stage target trigger, black Hogue overmolded stock with Harris bipod, 8 3/4 lbs. Mfg. 2009-2013.

| | $1,050 | $900 | $765 | $650 | $575 | $525 | $475 | *$1,199* |

RIFLES: SEMI-AUTO, RIMFIRE

During certain years of manufacture, Ruger's changes in production on certain models (cals., barrel markings, barrel lengths, etc.) have created rare variations that are now considered premium niches. These areas of low manufacture will add premiums to the values listed on standard models. The Model 10/22 has been mfg. in a variety of limited production models including a multi-colored or green laminate wood stock variation (1986), a brown laminate stock (1988), a Kittery Trading Post Commemorative (1988), a smoke or tree bark laminate stock (1989), a Chief AJ Model, Wal-Mart (stainless with black laminated hardwood stock - 1990), etc. These limited editions will command premiums over the standard models listed, depending on the desirability of the special edition.

Note: All Ruger Rifles, except Stainless Mini-14, all Mini-30s, and Model 77-22s were made during 1976 in a "Liberty" version. Add $50-$75 when in 100% in the original box condition.

10/22 FS TACTICAL – .22 LR cal., 10 shot rotary mag., alloy steel receiver, 16 1/8 in. barrel with SR-556/Mini 14 style flash suppressor and barrel band, black synthetic stock, Picatinny rail on top of receiver, satin black finish, 4.3 lbs. New late-2010.

| MSR $359 | $285 | $240 | $200 | $185 | $150 | $125 | $110 | |

MSR	100%	98%	95%	90%	80%	70%	60%	*Last MSR*

10/22 TACTICAL w/HEAVY BARREL – .22 LR cal., 10 shot rotary mag., alloy steel receiver, 16 1/8 in. heavy hammer forged barrel w/o sights and spiraled exterior, black Hogue overmolded stock, target trigger, adj. bipod, 6.8 lbs. New late-2010.

	100%	98%	95%	90%	80%	70%	60%	Last MSR
MSR $629	$500	$395	$335	$275	$240	$215	$175	

* **K10/22-T Target Tactical** – similar to 10/22-T Target Model, except available in black matte finish, black Hogue overmolded stock, receiver with Picatinny style rail, 16.1 in. barrel with no sights, includes precision adj. bipod, 6.9 lbs. Mfg. 2010 only.

	100%	98%	95%	90%	80%	70%	60%	Last MSR
	$500	$425	$345	$295	$250	$215	$175	*$555*

SR-22 – .22 LR cal., 16.1 in. barrel with Mini-14 flash suppressor or target crown, 10 shot rotary mag., Hogue monogrip pistol grip, six position telescoping or fixed buttstock, integrated Picatinny rail on top of receiver, mid-length vented circular handguard with Picatinny rail, Ruger Rapid Deploy sights, 6 1/2 lbs. New 2013.

	100%	98%	95%	90%	80%	70%	60%	Last MSR
MSR $709	$600	$490	$425	$375	$325	$275	$250	

Add $449 for Silent-SR suppressor (new 2016, NFA regulations apply).

RIFLES: SEMI-AUTO, CENTERFIRE

Beginning 2013, all Mini-14 models and variations include a drilled and tapped receiver.

MODEL 44 STANDARD CARBINE – .44 Mag. cal., 4 shot mag., 18 1/2 in. barrel, blowback action, folding sight, curved butt. Mfg. 1959-1985.

	100%	98%	95%	90%	80%	70%	60%	Last MSR
	$750	$600	$525	$400	$300	$250	$225	*$332*

* **Model 44 Standard Carbine Deerstalker** – approx. 3,750 mfg. with "Deerstalker" marked on rifle until Ithaca lawsuit disc. manufacture (1962).

	100%	98%	95%	90%	80%	70%	60%	Last MSR
	$1,000	$850	$725	$600	$550	$475	$400	

* **Model 44 Standard Carbine 25th Year Anniversary** – mfg. 1985 only, limited production, has medallion in stock.

	100%	98%	95%	90%	80%	70%	60%	Last MSR
	$675	$575	$450	N/A	N/A	N/A	N/A	*$495*

RUGER CARBINE – 9mm Para. (PC9) or .40 S&W (PC4) cal., 16 1/4 in. barrel, 10 (PC4) or 15 (PC9) shot detachable mag., black synthetic stock, matte metal finish, with or w/o sights, with fully adj. rear sight or rear receiver sight, crossbolt safety, 6 lbs. Mfg. 1998-2006.

	100%	98%	95%	90%	80%	70%	60%	Last MSR
	$575	$475	$375	$310	$265	$240	$215	*$623*

Add $24 for adj. rear receiver sight.

Beginning 2005, this model came standard with an adjustable ghost ring aperture rear sight and protected blade front sight.

MINI-14 – .223 Rem. or .222 Rem. (disc.) cal., 5 (standard mag. starting in 1989), 10 (disc.), or 20* shot detachable mag., 18 1/2 in. barrel, gas operated, blue finish, aperture rear sight, military style stock, approx. 6 3/4 lbs. Mfg. 1975-2004.

	100%	98%	95%	90%	80%	70%	60%	Last MSR
	$535	$445	$385	$350	$325	$300	$285	*$655*

Add 20% for .222 Rem. cal.
Add $300 for folding stock (disc. 1989).
Add 25% for Southport Model with gold bead front sight.
Add 100% for Mini-14 GB (primarily used for law enforcement) with a flash hider and bayonet lug (blue or stainless) if in 95%+ original condition.

* **Mini-14 Stainless** – mini stainless steel version, choice of wood or black synthetic (new 1999) stock. Disc. 2004.

	100%	98%	95%	90%	80%	70%	60%	Last MSR
	$565	$450	$395	$365	$335	$315	$295	*$715*

Add 20% for .222 Rem. cal.
Add $300 for folding stock (disc. 1990).

MINI-14 RANCH RIFLE – .223 Rem. cal., 5 (standard mag. starting in 1989), 10 (disc.), or 20 shot detachable mag., blued finish, 18 1/2 in. barrel, choice of black synthetic or hardwood stock, receiver cut for factory rings, similar to Mini-14, supplied with scope rings, folding (disc.) or adj. ghost ring aperture rear sight, protected front sight, and flat style recoil pad (became standard 2005), 7 lbs. New 1982.

	100%	98%	95%	90%	80%	70%	60%	Last MSR
MSR $999	$850	$725	$650	$585	$515	$450	$395	

Add $51 for 20 shot mag. (new 2008).
Add $260 for Mini 14 NRA-ILA Limited Edition with 16 1/8 in. barrel and black Hogue overmolded stock (ltd. mfg. 2008-2009).

Due to 1989 Federal legislation and public sentiment at the time, the Mini-14 Ranch Rifle was shipped with a 5 shot detachable mag., 1989-2008.

MSR	100%	98%	95%	90%	80%	70%	60%	Last MSR

* Mini-14 Stainless Ranch Rifle – 5.56 NATO (current mfg.), .223 Rem. (older mfg.), or 6.8 SPC (mfg. 2007-2011) cal., stainless steel construction, 18 1/2 in. stainless steel barrel, 5 or 20 shot, blade front and adj. rear sights, choice of wood (disc.) or black synthetic (new 1999) stock, matte stainless finish, 6 3/4 lbs. New 1986.

MSR $1,069	$900	$790	$675	$610	$495	$400	$315	

Add $70 for 20 shot mag. (not available in 6.8mm SPC cal.).
Add $300 for folding stock (disc. 1990).

MINI-14 TARGET RIFLE w/THUMBHOLE STOCK – .223 Rem. cal., 22 in. stainless steel heavy barrel with adj. harmonic tuner, no sights, ergonomic black or grey (disc.) laminated thumbhole stock, stainless scope rings, 5 shot mag., 3 position rubber recoil pad with adj. LOP, 9 1/2 lbs. New 2007.

MSR $1,259	$1,070	$925	$800	$725	$585	$475	$375	

Add $16 for 20 shot mag. (mfg. 2009-disc.).

MINI-14 TARGET RIFLE w/BLACK SYNTHETIC STOCK – .223 Rem. cal., 22 in. stainless steel heavy barrel with adj. harmonic tuner, black Hogue overmolded stock, stainless scope rings, 5 shot mag., no sights, matte stainless finish, 8 1/2 lbs. New 2007.

MSR $1,259	$1,070	$925	$800	$725	$585	$475	$375	

Add $16 for 20 shot mag. (mfg. 2009-disc.).

MINI-14 TACTICAL RIFLE FIXED STOCK – 5.56 NATO or .300 AAC Blackout (new 2015) cal., blued steel or stainless steel action and barrel, compact 16 1/8 in. blue barrel with flash suppressor, 5 or 20 shot mag., fixed black synthetic stock with vents on upper forend, blade front and adj. rear sights, matte stainless finish, 6 3/4 lbs. New 2009.

MSR $1,089	$910	$795	$675	$610	$495	$400	$315	

Add $80 for stainless steel action and barrel.

MINI-14 TACTICAL RIFLE w/COLLAPSIBLE STOCK – 5.56 NATO cal., compact 16 1/8 in. blue barrel with flash suppressor, 5 (disc.) or 20 shot mag., black synthetic 6-position ATI folding/collapsible stock, includes quad Picatinny accessory rails on forend, blade front and adj. rear sights, 7 1/4 lbs. New 2009.

MSR $1,089	$910	$795	$675	$610	$495	$400	$315	

MINI-THIRTY – 7.62x39mm Russian cal., 18 1/2 in. barrel, 5 shot detachable mag., hardwood stock, includes scope rings, 7 lbs. 3 oz. Mfg. 1987-2004.

	$550	$450	$405	$375	$335	$300	$260	*$695*

* Mini-Thirty Stainless – 7.62x39mm cal., 18 1/2 in. barrel, stainless steel variation of the Mini-Thirty, black synthetic stock, adj. ghost ring aperture rear sight and protected front sight became standard 2005, 5 or 20 shot mag., integral sling swivels, 6 3/4 lbs. New 1990.

MSR $1,069	$900	$790	$675	$610	$495	$400	$315	

Add $70 for 20 shot mag.

* Mini-Thirty Tactical – 7.62x39mm cal., similar to Mini-Thirty Stainless, except has 16 1/8 in. barrel with flash suppressor, 20 shot mag., adj. ghost ring aperture rear sight and non-glare post front sight, Ruger scope bases, black synthetic stock, approx. 6 3/4 lbs. New late 2010.

MSR $1,089	$910	$795	$675	$610	$495	$400	$315	

AR-556 – 5.56 NATO cal., GIO, 16.1 in. cold hammer forged chrome moly barrel with M4 feed ramp cuts, 30 shot Magpul PMag., forged aluminum upper and lower receivers, Ruger Rapid Deploy folding rear sight, milled F-height gas block with post front sight, forward assist, dust cover, brass deflector, black synthetic 6-pos. collapsible or fixed (new 2016) stock, ergonomic pistol grip, single stage trigger, enlarged trigger guard, 6 1/2 lbs. New 2015.

MSR $799	$675	$565	$475	$425	$375	$350	$325	

SR-556/SR-556 CARBINE – 5.56 NATO or 6.8mm SPC (mfg. mid-2010-2011) cal., GPO, 10, 25 (6.8mm SPC only, disc. 2011), or 30 shot mag., 16.1 in. barrel with flash suppressor or target crown, matte black finish, four position chrome plated gas regulator, quad rail handguard, with or without Troy folding sights, fixed (556SC) or 6-position telescoping M4 style buttstock, Hogue monogrip pistol grip with finger grooves, upper receiver has integrated Picatinny rail, chrome plated bolt, bolt carrier, and extractor, includes rail covers, soft sided carry case and three magazines, 7.4 (Carbine) or 7.9 lbs. New mid-2009.

MSR $2,049	$1,830	$1,600	$1,090	$900	$775	$650	$575	

SR-762 CARBINE – 7.62 NATO cal., two-stage piston driven, AR-15 style, matte black finish, 16.1 in. heavy contour chrome lined cold hammer forged barrel, includes three 20 shot Magpul PMag magazines, folding backup iron sights, 6-position adj. M4-style stock, Hogue monogrip, lightweight adj. adapatable handguard, full length top Picatinny rail and two side rails, one piece bolt carrier, four position gas regulator, sight adjustment tool, includes soft side carry case, 8.6 lbs. New late 2013.

MSR $2,349	$2,000	$1,750	$1,500	$1,360	$1,100	$900	$725	

MSR	100%	98%	95%	90%	80%	70%	60%	Last MSR

SUN DEVIL MANUFACTURING LLC

Current rifle and billet aluminum parts and accessories manufacturer located in Mesa, AZ.

RIFLES: SEMI-AUTO

DOUBLE DEVIL TWIN AR – 5.56 NATO cal., 16 in. chrome moly barrels, Sun Devil Mfg. dual function brakes/compensators, monolithic billet heavy wall twin side by side upper receivers, B.A.D. lever compatible, free floated modular handguards with integral top Picatinny rails, billet bipod mount, black finish. New 2016.
Please contact the company directly for pricing and availability for this model.

SUPERIOR ARMS

Current manufacturer located in Wapello, IA since 2004.

PISTOLS: SEMI-AUTO

Superior Arms manufactured complete AR-style semi-auto pistols with either an A4 flattop or A2 carry handle, and 10 1/2 or 11 1/2 in. barrel.

RIFLES: SEMI-AUTO

Please contact the company directly for more information on options, delivery, and availability on the following AR-15 style carbines/rifles (see Trademark Index).

S-15 M4 CARBINE – .223 Rem. cal., GIO, 16 in. chrome moly barrel, A2 flash hider, A4 flat-top receiver with integral rail, M4 handguard, 6-position telescoping stock, A2 pistol grip, front sling swivel.

MSR $995	$850	$725	$650	$585	$515	$450	$395	

S-15 CARBINE – .223 Rem. cal., GIO, A4 flat-top receiver with integral rail, 16 in. chrome moly barrel, A2 flash hider, M4 handguard, bayonet lug, 6-position telescoping stock, A2 pistol grip, front sling swivel.

MSR $995	$850	$725	$650	$585	$515	$450	$395	

S-15 MID-LENGTH CARBINE – .223 Rem. cal., GIO, A4 flat-top receiver with integral rail, 16 in. chrome moly barrel, A2 flash hider, mid-length handguard, bayonet lug, 6-position telescoping stock, A2 pistol grip, front sling swivel.

MSR $1,010	$860	$725	$650	$585	$515	$450	$395	

S-15 H-BAR RIFLE – .223 Rem. cal., GIO, 20 in. chrome moly barrel, A2 flash hider, A4 flat-top receiver with integral rail, A2 buttstock, bayonet lug, A2 pistol grip, front sling swivel.

MSR $1,075	$895	$785	$685	$600	$535	$465	$415	

S-15 VARMINT RIFLE – .223 Rem. cal., GIO, A4 flat-top receiver with integral rail, 20 in. stainless steel bull contour barrel, Picatinny rail gas block, aluminum free floating handguard with sling swivel stud, A2 buttstock, bayonet lug, A2 pistol grip.

MSR $1,095	$925	$850	$725	$625	$550	$475	$425	

SURGEON RIFLES, INC.

Current custom rifle manufacturer located in Phoenix, AZ. Previously located in Prague, OK.

RIFLES: BOLT ACTION

REMEDY RIFLE – .300 Norma, .338 Norma, or .338 Lapua cal., Kreiger or Bartlein, stainless steel 5R, heavy Palma or MTU barrel, with or w/o fluting, AWC, PSR, Badger, or SureFire muzzle brake, AI factory mag., Jewel trigger, AI AX, McMillan A5, or Manners stock, standard, tactical, O-Ring, or round bolt knob, built-in 30 MOA Mil-Std 1913 rail and recoil lug, FDE, Pale Brown, Graphite Black, Sniper Gray, or Olive Drab finish.
Current base MSR starts at $5,720.

SCALPEL SHORT ACTION – .223 Rem., .243 Win., 6XC, 6.5x47 Lapua, 6.5 Creedmoor, .260 Rem., or .308 Win. cal., Kreiger or Bartlein, stainless steel 5R, heavy Palma or MTU barrel, with or w/o fluting, AWC, PSR, Badger FTE, or SureFire muzzle brake, AI factory mag., Jewel trigger, AI AX, McMillan A1-3, J. Allen JAE-700, Cadex Dual Strike, Manners, AI 2.0, or AI AXAICS stock, standard, tactical, O-Ring, or round bolt knob, built-in 20 MOA Mil-Std 1913 rail and recoil lug, FDE, Pale Brown, Graphite Black, Sniper Gray, or Olive Drab finish.
Current base MSR starts at $4,540.

SCALPEL LONG ACTION – 6.5x284, .284 Win. or .300 Win. Mag. cal., Kreiger or Bartlein, stainless steel 5R, heavy Palma or MTU barrel, with or w/o fluting, AWC, PSR, Badger, or SureFire muzzle brake, AI factory mag., Jewel trigger, McMillan A5, AI AX, Cadex Dual Strike, AI 2.0, or AI AXAICS stock, standard, tactical, O-Ring, or round bolt knob, built-in 20 MOA Mil-Std 1913 rail and recoil lug, FDE, Pale Brown, Graphite Black, Sniper Gray, or Olive Drab finish.
Current base MSR starts at $4,665.

MSR	100%	98%	95%	90%	80%	70%	60%	Last MSR

SURVIVAL ARMS, INC.

Previous manufacturer established in 1990 located in Orange, CT. Previously located in Cocoa, FL, until 1995.

In 1990, Survival Arms, Inc. took over the manufacture of AR-7 Explorer rifles from Charter Arms located in Stratford, CT.

RIFLES: SEMI-AUTO

AR-7 EXPLORER RIFLE – .22 LR cal., takedown or normal wood stock, takedown barreled action stores in Cycolac synthetic stock, 8 shot mag., adj. sights, 16 in. barrel, black matte finish on AR-7, silvertone on AR-7S, camouflage finish on AR-7C, 2 1/2 lbs. Disc.

	100%	98%	95%	90%	80%	70%	60%	Last MSR
	$150	$125	$100	$85	$75	$65	$55	$150

Add 20% for takedown action.

AR-20 SPORTER – similar to AR-22, except has shrouded barrel, tubular stock with pistol grip, 10 or 20 shot mag. Mfg. 1996-98.

	100%	98%	95%	90%	80%	70%	60%	Last MSR
	$195	$165	$140	$120	$105	$95	$80	$200

AR-22/AR-25 – .22 LR cal., 16 in. barrel, black rifle features pistol grip with choice of wood or metal folding* stock, includes 20 (1995 only) or 25 (disc. 1994) shot mag. Disc. 1995.

	100%	98%	95%	90%	80%	70%	60%	Last MSR
	$175	$150	$125	$100	$80	$70	$60	$200

Subtract $50 for wood stock model.

NOTES

T SECTION

TNW FIREARMS, INC.

Current firearms manufacturer located in Vernonia, OR. Consumer direct sales.

MSR	100%	98%	95%	90%	80%	70%	60%	Last MSR

PISTOLS: SEMI-AUTO

ASR – .45 ACP, 9mm Para., or .40 S&W cal., no optics, black, pink, or green finish. New 2014.

| MSR $799 | $685 | $615 | $550 | $475 | $420 | $365 | $335 | |

SDI – .223 Rem. cal., billet aluminum receivers, newly designed buffer system with rear sling attachment, black anodized finish. New 2014.

| MSR $995 | $850 | $725 | $685 | $600 | $535 | $465 | $415 | |

RIFLES: SEMI-AUTO

AERO SURVIVAL RIFLE (ASR) – 9mm Para., .40 S&W, or .45 cal., compact design, breaks down efficiently without use of tools, unique configuration allows for easy barrel removal and caliber changes, available in black, Pink Attitude, Tiger Green, tan (new 2014) or matte green (new 2014) finish.

| MSR $799 | $685 | $615 | $550 | $475 | $420 | $365 | $335 | |

Add $250 for black conversion kit or $275 for pink or green conversion kit.

MG34 – modified original German MG34s remanufactured using genuine parts, semi-auto only, shoots closed bolt, includes manual, 50 round belt, and ATF approved letter.

| MSR $3,995 | $3,750 | $3,400 | $3,000 | $2,600 | $2,200 | $1,800 | $1,400 | |

MG42 – belt fed, patterned after original WWII era rifle, lightweight design. New 2014.

| MSR $4,299 | $3,975 | $3,550 | $3,100 | $2,650 | $2,250 | $1,850 | $1,450 | |

M3HB – .50 BMG cal., modified original Browning M2/M3, heavy barrel, shoots semi-auto only, cannot be converted to full auto, fires commercial ammunition or blanks, includes IM2 training manual, head spacing gauge, 200 .50 cal. links, left and right-hand feed, ATF approval letter.

| MSR $8,600 | $8,350 | $7,600 | $6,775 | $5,825 | $5,275 | $4,275 | $3,500 | |

Add $1,199 for M3HB mount.

M37 – .30 cal., patterned after a Browning 1919, right or left feed, dual tracks for alternate operation of the belt feeding pawl. Only 125 mfg.

| MSR $4,200 | $3,900 | $3,500 | $3,050 | $2,600 | $2,200 | $1,800 | $1,400 | |

MODEL 1919 – .30 cal., modified original Browning 1919-A4 using genuine G.I. parts, shoots semi-auto only and cannot be converted to full auto, internal and external parts finished with gray military type parkerization, includes 250 links, training manual, BATF approval letter. Disc. 2013.

| | $1,850 | $1,625 | $1,400 | $1,275 | $1,025 | $850 | $650 | *$2,050* |

SGP-QCB – .223 Rem. cal., GPO, quick change barrel firearm, black anodized finish. New 2013.

| MSR $1,495 | $1,275 | $1,115 | $955 | $865 | $700 | $575 | $450 | |

SDI – 5.56 NATO cal., GIO, AR-15 style, 16.2 in. barrel, stock has quad rails, billet upper and lower receiver, black finish, 7.45 lbs. New 2014.

| MSR $995 | $850 | $745 | $640 | $580 | $470 | $400 | $350 | |

SUOMI M31 – 9mm Para. cal., 16 in. barrel, semi-auto copy of the Finnish KP31, blowback action, 36 shot stick or 71 shot drum mag., parkerized finish, metallic sights, uncheckered plain wood stock, approx. 10 lbs. Importation began 2013.

| MSR $485 | $425 | $365 | $300 | $265 | $235 | $220 | $210 | |

TACTICAL ARMS MANUFACTURER, INC.

Current manufacturer located in Huntersville, NC.

RIFLES: SEMI-AUTO

Tactical Arms Manufacturer, Inc. manufactures AR-15 M4 or M16 style rifles in various calibers and configurations. Base prices start at $1,195. Please contact the company directly for more information including options, pricing, and availability (see Trademark Index).

TACTICAL ARMZ

Current rifle and suppressor manufacturer located in Springfield, MO.

Consumer availability for these rifles may be limited in the near future as the company has secured a military contract.

MSR	100%	98%	95%	90%	80%	70%	60%	Last MSR

RIFLES: SEMI-AUTO

Consumer availability for these rifles may be limited in the near future as the company has secured a military contract.

TA-15 HAVOC – 5.56 NATO cal., 16 in. chrome moly barrel with YHM Phantom muzzle brake, YHM low profile gas block, SST, modified Battle stock, Ergo rubber pistol grip, 12 1/2 in. Tactical Armz quadrail, Magpul MBUS flip up sights, billet milled upper and lower receiver, enhanced magwell, nickel boron bolt carrier group, Cerakote Tungsten ceramic finish, includes PMAG M3 maglevel magazine w/MagGrips, hard flight case, 9 lbs.

| MSR $1,999 | $1,795 | $1,575 | $1,350 | $1,225 | $985 | $825 | $625 | |

TA-15 LANCER – 5.56 NATO cal., 16 in. chrome moly barrel with YHM Phantom flash hider, YHM low profile gas block, black nitride bolt carrier group, SST, reinforced CQB buttstock, A2 pistol grip, Magpul MBUS flip-up sights, 12 1/2 in. quad rail handguard, Cerakote Armor black ceramic finish, 7.2 lbs.

| MSR $1,199 | $1,075 | $950 | $800 | $725 | $600 | $485 | $375 | |

TA-15 RONIN – 5.56 NATO cal., 16 in. chrome moly barrel with YHM Phantom flash hider, billet milled lower and forged and milled upper receiver, nickel boron bolt carrier group, YHM low profile gas block, SST, modified Battle stock with Hogue rubber pistol grip, Magpul MBUS flip-up sights, 12 1/2 in. Tactical Armz slim rail handguard, Cerakote Armor black finish, includes PMag. M3 magazine w/MagGrips, hard case, 7 lbs.

| MSR $1,499 | $1,350 | $1,175 | $1,025 | $925 | $750 | $625 | $475 | |

TACTICAL RIFLES

Current rifle manufacturer located in Zephyrhills, FL. Previously located in Dade City, FL until 2010.

RIFLES: BOLT ACTION

Custom Hydrographic finishes are available on all rifles - price is POR.

Add $500 for Rem. 700 action. Add $895 for Chimera match grade receiver. Add $75 for extended Picatinny rail. Add $345 (short action)-$395 (long action) for TR alloy detachable floorplate or $345 for steel hinged floorplate. Add $225 for Tri-port muzzle brake.

M40 – .260 Rem., 6.5x74 Lapua, or 7.62 NATO/.308 Win. cal., Rem. 700 or TR Chimera custom match grade receiver, 17-26 in. stainless steel match grade barrel with recessed target crown, Mil-Spec parts, heavyweight steel floorplate (detachable floorplate is optional), Picatinny rail, McMillan A1, A2, A3, A4, or A5 stock, raised comb, black, green, Woodland camo, and Desert camo finish, 9 1/2 - 12 1/2 lbs.

| MSR $2,895 | $2,450 | $2,150 | $1,850 | $1,675 | $1,350 | $1,100 | $860 | |

Price does not include action.

Other precision calibers are available upon request.

* **M40-66** – .308 Win. cal., Rem. 700 action, 17-26 in. stainless steel match grade bench rest quality barrel, hand rubbed oil finished top grade American walnut stock with cheekpiece, one inch Pachmayr Decelerator pad, single stage trigger, stainless heavyweight magnum recoil lug, stainless steel hinged bottom metal assembly, glare free dull luster finish. New mid-2014.

| MSR $3,395 | $2,885 | $2,525 | $2,175 | $1,950 | $1,585 | $1,300 | $1,015 | |

* **M40-223** – .223 Rem. cal., similar to M40, except also features tactical floorplate, and tactical bolt knob. Disc. 2013.
This model was POR.

* **M40-300** – .300 WSM cal., similar to M40, long or short action, except also features dual expansion port brake.

| MSR $3,295 | $2,800 | $2,450 | $2,100 | $1,900 | $1,540 | $1,260 | $975 | |

Price does not include action.

* **M40-325** – .325 WSM cal., similar to M40, except features lighter weight barrel with muzzle brake. Disc. 2013.
This model was POR.

* **M40-338** – .338 Lapua cal., similar to M40, except has TR Chimera custom match grade receiver, 20-27 in. stainless steel match grade barrel with recessed target crown, 11-14 lbs.

| MSR $3,595 | $3,050 | $2,675 | $2,295 | $2,075 | $1,675 | $1,375 | $1,075 | |

Price does not include action.

TACTICAL CHIMERA HUNTER – .300 WSM or .308 Win. cal., Chimera stainless steel match grade action, 24 in. stainless steel select match grade barrel, recessed match grade crown, muzzle brake standard on .300 WSM, single stage adj. trigger, T7 carbon fiber/fiberglass blend stock, Picatinny rail, extreme environment corrosion resistant solid color matte finish, approx. 9 lbs. Disc. 2013.
This model was POR.

TACTICAL CLASSIC SPORTER – .243 Win., .260 Rem., .270 Win., .300 Win. Mag., .308 Win., .25-06, .30-06, 6.5 Creedmoor, 6.5 Lapua, 7mm Rem., or 7mm-08 cal., Chimera match grade stainless action, 18-26 in. stainless match grade barrel, two-piece Picatinny base, solid stainless steel heavyweight hinged floorplate assembly, XXX grade English walnut stock with hand rubbed oil finish, full length alloy bedding block, hand checkered, inlaid sling swivels, single stage adj. trigger.

| MSR $5,889 | $5,000 | $4,375 | $3,750 | $3,400 | $2,750 | $2,250 | $1,750 | |

MSR	100%	98%	95%	90%	80%	70%	60%	Last MSR

TACTICAL LONG RANGE – 7.62 NATO/.308 Win. cal., .300 Win. Mag., .325 WSM (disc. 2013), or .338 Lapua cal., Rem. 700 or TR Chimera custom action, 20-26 in. stainless steel match grade barrel with recessed target crown, Picatinny rail, adj. trigger, 3 or 5 shot mag., thumbhole stock, raised cheekpiece, includes ambidextrous sling swivel studs and soft rubber recoil pad, available in black or green finish, 12-13 1/2 lbs.

| MSR $2,995 | $2,550 | $2,225 | $1,915 | $1,735 | $1,400 | $1,150 | $895 | |

Price does not include action.

Add $355 for .300 Win. Mag. or $700 for .338 Lapua cal.

TACTICAL PARATROOPER – 7.62 NATO/.308 Win. or .300 Win. Mag. cal., Rem. 700 or TR Chimera custom match grade receiver, 16 1/2 - 26 in. stainless steel match grade barrel with recessed target crown, Picatinny rail, folding thumbhole stock with ambidextrous sling swivel studs and soft rubber recoil pad, match grade trigger, black or green finish, 10 1/2 - 12 1/4 lbs.

| MSR $3,550 | $3,000 | $2,625 | $2,250 | $2,040 | $1,650 | $1,350 | $1,050 | |

Price does not include action.

Add $245 for .300 Win. Mag. cal.

RIFLES: SEMI-AUTO

Previous models included the Dow Custom AR 10 (disc. 2004, last MSR was $2,695). Tactical Rifles also partnered with Coonan Inc. for a rifle and pistol package consisting of a special limited edition 1 of 100 rifle and Coonan pistol. Package price was $7,889.

Hydrographics or custom painted finishes are available on all rifles - price is POR.

DOW FAL 15 – .223 Rem. or 6.8 SPC cal., patterned after AR-15, GIO, medium weight match grade stainless steel barrel, matte black receiver finish, flat-top Picatinny upper, match grade trigger, hand rubbed oil finished wood stock. Disc. 2013.

This model was POR.

TACTICAL AR-15 – .223 cal., AR-15 style, GIO, Krieger heavy match grade free floating barrel with birdcage flash hider, 2-stage match trigger, Mil-Spec handguard, black, green, or sand colored stock.

| MSR $2,395 | $2,025 | $1,775 | $1,525 | $1,375 | $1,115 | $910 | $710 | |

Add $95 for titanium or chrome match bolt carrier.

Add $115 for Vortex style tempered steel flash suppressor.

Add $185 for Picatinny machined forend.

TACTICAL M4C – .223 Rem. cal., AR-15 style, GIO, 16 in. heavy match grade barrel with birdcage flash hider, free float CNC machined forend with GI foresight assembly or smooth gas block, flat-top upper, collapsible stock, extreme environment finish.

| MSR $2,285 | $1,950 | $1,700 | $1,465 | $1,325 | $1,075 | $880 | $685 | |

Add $95 for titanium or chrome match bolt carrier.

Add $115 for Vortex style tempered steel flash suppressor.

Add $50 for Harris bipod adapter stud with push button release swivel.

Add $179 for PRI folding front sight.

Add $139 for ARMS low profile folding Picatinny rail mounted rear sight.

TACTICAL M21 – .30 cal., M14 action, GIO, Krieger heavy match grade barrel, M3 bedded stock, vertical pistol grip with wrap-over thumb shelf and vertically adj. saddle type cheekpiece, butt has removable spacer system, 5 or 10 shot mag. Disc. 2013.

This model was POR.

TACTICAL SPG – .264 LBC, 6.5 CSS, 6.5mm Grendel (new 2013) or .308 (disc. 2013) cal., AR-15 style, GIO, billet upper and lower receiver, 17 shot mag., 20 in. Krieger stainless match grade contoured barrel with Surefire muzzle brake, Magpul PRS fully adj. stock, free float full length Picatinny forend, ergonomic pistol grip, two-stage trigger, zero headspace match grade black nitride coated bolt carrier group, black finish, 10 1/2 lbs.

| MSR $3,695 | $3,150 | $2,750 | $2,365 | $2,140 | $1,735 | $1,425 | $1,100 | |

Add $154 for flip-up foresight with integral gas block.

Add $129 for flip-up rear sight assembly.

TACTICAL SVR (SPECIAL VARMINT RIFLE) – .204 Ruger or .223 Rem. cal., AR-15 style, 24 in. full profile heavy match grade stainless steel barrel with target crown plain muzzle, free float forend, 20 shot mag., flat-top Picatinny rail, A2 style fixed or Magpul adj. stock, ergonomic custom grip, adj. trigger, black or green finish is standard, custom camo finishes are optional, 10 1/2 lbs.

| MSR $3,195 | $2,725 | $2,375 | $2,050 | $1,850 | $1,500 | $1,225 | $950 | |

Add $95 for titanium or chrome match bolt carrier.

Add $185 for Picatinny machined forend.

Add $249 for Magpul adj. stock.

MSR	100%	98%	95%	90%	80%	70%	60%	Last MSR

TACTICAL SOLUTIONS

Current rifle and components manufacturer located in Boise, ID. Dealer sales.

PISTOLS: SEMI-AUTO

KESTREL .22 LR AR PISTOL – .22 LR cal., 9 in. barrel with Linear compensator, 25 shot Black Dog mag., 7 in. Samson KeyMod handguard, Mil-Spec lower receiver, ALG Defense QMS trigger, pistol length buffer tube, 3.9 lbs. New 2015.

MSR $995	$850	$725	$650	$585	$515	$450	$395

RIFLES: SEMI-AUTO

Tactical Solutions makes a Pac-Lite barrel assembly for the Ruger Mark and .22/.45 Series pistol frame and conversion units for both pistols and AR-15 style rifles. Please contact the manufacturer directly for additional information, availability, and current pricing (see Trademark Index).

AR-22 LT – .22 LR cal., 16 1/2 in. barrel, 12 in. XG Pro KeyMod or M-LOK forend, TacSol lower receiver, ALG Defense QMS trigger, 2.9 lbs. New 2015.

MSR $995	$850	$725	$650	$585	$515	$450	$395

AR-22 M4 – .22 LR cal., 16.1 in. barrel, 25 shot mag., TacSol lower receiver, ALG Defense QMS trigger, two-piece polymer carbine handguard, 3.9 lbs. New 2015.

MSR $895	$775	$685	$615	$550	$485	$415	$370

AR-22 SBX – .22 LR cal., 16.6 in. barrel, 9 in. XG Pro KeyMod or M-LOK forend, TacSol lower receiver, ALG Defense QMS trigger, 2.7 lbs. New 2015.

MSR $995	$850	$725	$650	$585	$515	$450	$395

TSAR-300 – .300 AAC Blackout cal., 16.1 in. barrel with inert suppressor, 10 shot mag., Mil-Spec lower, Tacsol XG Pro forend in choice of KeyMod or M-LOK, two-piece aluminum handguard, ALG Defense QMS trigger, Hogue 6-position stock, Hogue pistol grip, 5 1/2 lbs. New 2015.

MSR $1,395	$1,200	$1,075	$950	$800	$700	$600	$495

X-RING RIFLE – .22 LR cal., 16 1/2 in. standard or threaded barrel, 10 shot mag., choice of Matte Black, Matte OD, Quicksand, Red, Blue, or Silver barrel/receiver color, Hogue overmolded stock in choice of Black, OD Green, Ghillie Green or Ghillie Tan or Vantage RS laminated stock in choice of Rose (disc.), Plum (disc.), Slate, Forest, Crimson or Royal, extended mag. release, Ruger trigger group (4.3-5.1 lbs.) or TacSol trigger group (2.5-2.75 lbs.).

MSR $900	$765	$675	$575	$525	$425	$350	$275

Add $50 for threaded barrel.
Add$100 for Vantage stock.
Add $150 for TacSol trigger group.

* **X-RING Open Sight** – .22 LR cal., 16 1/2 in. threaded barrel, Ruger or TacSol trigger group, 10 shot mag., choice of Matte Black, Matte OD, or Silver barrel/receiver color, green fiber optic and complete rear sight assembly included, Hogue overmolded stock in choice of Black, OD Green, Ghillie Green or Ghillie Tan or Vantage RS laminated stock in choice of Slate, Forest, Crimson or Royal, extended mag. release, 4.3 lbs. New 2015.

MSR $950	$810	$710	$610	$550	$450	$365	$285

Add $150 for TacSol trigger group.

X-RING TAKEDOWN RIFLE – .22 LR cal., 16 1/2 in. threaded barrel, choice of Matte Black, Matte OD, Quicksand, Red, Blue, or Silver barrel/receiver color, Ruger or TacSol trigger group, Hogue overmolded stock in choice of Black, OD Green, Ghillie Green, Ghillie Tan or Warden stock in choice of Warden Slate or Warden Forest, includes custom rifle bag, 4.3 lbs. New 2016.

MSR $1,205	$1,025	$925	$800	$685	$595	$515	$440

Add $150 for Warden stock.

TACTICAL SUPPLY

Current manufacturer located in Yakima, WA.

In addition to customized rifles, Tactical Supply offers a customized semi-auto pistol based on the Smith & Wesson M&P platform, as well as a wide variety of tactical gear, accessories, ammo, and professional gunsmithing services.

RIFLES: BOLT ACTION

Values reflect base rifle price only without options. Please contact the company directly for the wide variety of rifle options, including optics and accessories (see Trademark Index).

TS-KRG – various cals., Rem. 700, Tikka T3, or Badger Ordnance action, KRG Whiskey3 chassis, various barrel lengths, 5 or 10 shot Accuracy International mag., adj. tactical stock, comes standard with scope base rail and American Rifle Company M-10 rings.

MSR $2,000	$1,700	$1,495	$1,275	$1,150	$935	$775	$595

MSR	100%	98%	95%	90%	80%	70%	60%	Last MSR

TS-700 – various cals., Rem. 700 SPS Tactical long or short action, customer choice of barrel length, 5 or 10 shot Accuracy International mags, pistol grip synthetic stock and forearm, standard scope base rail fitted with American Rifle Company M-10 rings.

MSR $1,500	$1,275	$1,125	$950	$875	$700	$575	$450	

RIFLES: SEMI-AUTO

Values reflect base rifle price only without options. Please contact the company directly for the wide variety of rifle options, including optics and accessories (see Trademark Index).

TS-ASSAULT – 5.56 NATO, .300 AAC Blackout, or .458 SOCOM cal., customer choice of 16 in. select, premium, or match grade barrel, forged billet machined upper and lower receiver, nickel boron or chrome bolt carrier group, Timney competition trigger, Noveske 60° ambidextrous safety, Magpul furniture, 10 to 15 in. quad rail design handguard or top rail with removable pic blocks, Black, Flat Dark Earth, or OD green Cerakote finish.

MSR $1,500	$1,275	$1,125	$950	$875	$700	$575	$450	

TS-CADDY – 5.56 NATO, .300 AAC Blackout, or .458 SOCOM cal., customer choice of 16 in. select, premium, or match grade barrel, precision billet machined upper and lower receiver, nickel boron or chrome bolt carrier group, Timney competition trigger, Noveske 60° ambidextrous safety, Magpul furniture, Raptor ambi charging handle, 10 to 15 in. quad rail design handguard or top rail with removable pic blocks, customer choice of over 80 Cerakote colors.

MSR $2,500	$2,125	$1,850	$1,595	$1,450	$1,175	$950	$800	

TACTICAL WEAPONS

Current law enforcement/military division of FNH USA, located in McLean, VA.

Tactical Weapons currently manufactures machine guns only for law enforcement/military.

TACTICAL WEAPONS SOLUTIONS

Previous manufacturer located in Apopka, FL until 2015.

Tactical Weapons Solutions manufactured and sold a variety of fine quality AR-15 rifles as well as AR-15 pistols and survival supplies.

PISTOLS: SEMI-AUTO

MODEL P01 – 5.56 NATO cal., GIO, chrome moly steel barrel with A2 flash hider, forged upper and lower receivers, extended feed ramps, aluminum pistol length handguard, pistol buffer tube, forged "F" front sight base with bayonet lug, ambidextrous rear sling mount, 6.6 lbs. Disc. 2015.

	$950	$825	$725	$650	$525	$425	$350	*$1,050*

* Model P02 – 5.56 NATO cal., GIO, similar to Model P01, except features pistol length quad rail. Disc. 2015.

	$975	$850	$750	$675	$550	$450	$350	*$1,100*

MODEL P03 – 5.56 NATO cal., GIO, chrome moly steel barrel, CQB compensator, forged upper and lower receiver, extended feed ramps, carbine length quad rail, pistol buffer tube, forged "F" front sight base with bayonet lug, ambidextrous rear sling mount, 7 lbs. Disc. 2015.

	$1,195	$1,050	$900	$815	$650	$550	$425	*$1,330*

MODEL P04 – 5.56 NATO cal., GIO, 7 1/2 in. chrome moly barrel with CQB compensator, forged lower and forged M4 upper receivers, Magpul MBUS front and rear flip up sights, extended feed ramps, carbine length quad rail, pistol buffer tube, ambidextrous sling mount, extractor upgrade with Viton O-ring, black finish, 7 lbs. Disc. 2015.

	$1,250	$1,095	$950	$850	$700	$575	$450	*$1,400*

RISK TAKERS STANDARD CQB – 5.56 NATO cal., GIO, 7 1/2 in. chrome moly barrel with CQB compensator, forged lower and forged M4 upper receivers, Magpul MBUS front and rear flip up sights, extended feed ramps, carbine length quad rail, pistol buffer tube, ambidextrous sling mount, extractor upgrade with Viton O-ring, black finish, includes Risk Takers logos, 7 lbs. Disc. 2015.

	$1,075	$950	$800	$725	$595	$485	$375	*$1,202*

* Risk Takers CQB – 5.56 NATO cal., similar to Risk Takers Standard CQB, except includes Troy Medieval flash hider, Ergo Super tactical grip, Nib trigger, hammer, disconnect, FDE finish. Disc. 2015.

	$1,425	$1,250	$1,075	$975	$785	$650	$525	*$1,604*

RIFLES: SEMI-AUTO

MODEL 01 – 5.56 NATO cal., GIO, chrome moly steel barrel with A2 flash hider, forged upper and lower receiver, extended feed ramps, two piece handguard with Delta assembly, 6-position adj. stock, receiver extension tube, forged "F" front sight base with bayonet lug, ambidextrous rear sling mount, extractor upgrade with Viton O-Ring, 6 1/2 lbs. Disc. 2015.

	$795	$695	$595	$535	$435	$350	$275	*$880*

Subtract $80 for El-Model 01 without extractor upgrade with Viton O-Ring.

MSR	100%	98%	95%	90%	80%	70%	60%	Last MSR

* ***Model 02*** – 5.56 NATO cal., GIO, similar to Model 01, except features two-piece quad rail, 6.8 lbs. Disc. 2015.

	$810	$710	$610	$550	$450	$375	$285	*$900*

* ***Model 03*** – 5.56 NATO cal., GIO, similar to Model 01, except features free floating quad rail, low profile or single rail gas block, 6.7 lbs. Disc. 2015.

	$900	$795	$675	$610	$495	$400	$325	*$1,000*

MODEL 4 ALPHA – 5.56 NATO cal., GIO, 16 in. chrome moly barrel with flash hider, extended feed ramps, forged lower and forged M4 upper receivers, extractor upgrade w/Viton O-ring, free float quad rail, rec. extension tube, ambidextrous rear sling mount, nickel boron trigger, hammer, and disconnector, upgraded front and rear sights, 6-pos. adj. stock, pistol grip, black finish, 6 1/2 lbs.

	$1,275	$1,115	$950	$875	$700	$575	$450	*$1,425*

* ***Model 5 Elite*** – 5.56 NATO cal., similar to Model 4 Alpha, except includes nickel boron barrel extension, Bravo Co. "Gunfighter" charging handle, and upgraded trigger and hammer pins. Disc. 2015.

	$1,625	$1,425	$1,225	$1,100	$895	$750	$600	*$1,800*

MODEL 06 MOE – 5.56 NATO cal., chrome moly barrel with A2 flash hider, forged lower and forged M4 upper receivers, extended feed ramps, forged front sight base w/bayonet lug, ambidextrous rear sling mount, Magpul MOE handguard, buttstock, and pistol grip, Magpul MBUS rear flip-up sight, black finish, 6.4 lbs. Disc. 2015.

	$850	$750	$650	$575	$475	$385	$300	*$950*

MODEL 7 LOADED – 5.56 NATO cal., GIO, chrome moly barrel with A2 flash hider, extended feed ramps, forged lower and forged M4 upper receivers, two piece quad rail with Delta assembly, 6-position adj. stock, receiver extension tube, ambidextrous rear sling mount, forged front sight base with bayonet lug, black finish, extractor upgrade with Viton O-ring, includes 5mW green laser, 90 Lumen tactical flashlight, 6x32 scope, 5-position foldable foregrip, and tactical bipod, 6 1/2 lbs. Disc. 2015.

	$1,125	$985	$850	$775	$625	$500	$400	*$1,251*

MODEL 08/MODEL 09/MODEL 10/MODEL 11 – 5.56 NATO cal., GIO, chrome moly barrel with A2 flash hider, extended feed ramps, forged lower and forged M4 upper receivers, two piece quad rail with Delta assembly, 6-position adj. stock, receiver extension tube, ambidextrous rear sling mount, forged front sight base with bayonet lug, extractor upgrade with Viton O-ring, Cerakote FDE (Model 08), OD Green (Model 09), Pink (Model 10), or MultiCam camo (Model 11) finish, 6.8 lbs. Disc. 2015.

	$890	$775	$675	$600	$500	$400	$325	*$990*

MODEL 12/MODEL 14/MODEL 16/MODEL 18 – 5.56 NATO cal., GIO, chrome moly barrel with A2 flash hider, extended feed ramps, forged lower and forged M4 upper receivers, two piece quad rail with Delta assembly, 6-position adj. stock, receiver extension tube, ambidextrous rear sling mount, forged front sight base with bayonet lug, extractor upgrade with Viton O-ring, free floating quad rail, low profile or single rail gas block, Cerakote MultiCam (Model 12), Digital ACU (Model 14), Digital Desert (Model 16), or Reaper (Model 18) finish, 6.7 lbs. Disc. 2015.

	$1,000	$875	$750	$675	$550	$450	$350	*$1,120*

MODEL 13/MODEL 15/MODEL 17/MODEL 19/MODEL 20 – 5.56 NATO cal., GIO, chrome moly barrel with A2 flash hider, extended feed ramps, forged lower and forged M4 upper receivers, two piece quad rail with Delta assembly, 6-position adj. stock, receiver extension tube, ambidextrous rear sling mount, forged front sight base with bayonet lug, extractor upgrade with Viton O-ring, Digital ACU (Model 13), Desert Digital (Model 15), Pink (Model 10), Reaper (Model 17), Muddy Girl (Model 19), or MultiCam Pink (Model 20) finish, 6.8 lbs. Disc. 2015.

	$890	$775	$675	$600	$500	$400	$325	*$990*

.308 INTIMIDATOR – .308 Win. cal., GIO, 16 in. chrome moly steel barrel, fixed stock, pistol grip, oversized trigger guard, DPMS style upper receiver, black finish. Disc. 2015.

	$2,100	$1,850	$1,575	$1,425	$1,150	$950	$750	*$2,350*

TALON ORDNANCE

Current full-auto rifle manufacturer located in Richland, MS.

RIFLES: SEMI-AUTO

Talon Ordnance manufactures a TM4 that is select fire for military and law enforcement use. Please contact the company directly for more information on current price and availability (see Trademark Index).

TM4-A1 – 5.56 NATO cal., GIO, 16 in. barrel with removable flash hider, 30 shot stainless steel mag. with anti-tilt follower and chrome/silicon spring, hardcoat anodized Black finish, includes custom hard case, 7 1/2 lbs.

While this model was prototyped in 2015 with a projected MSR of $2,795, there are no plans to put it into production.

MSR	100%	98%	95%	90%	80%	70%	60%	Last MSR

TM4-A1SE SPECIAL EDITION – 5.56 NATO cal., GIO, 16 in. barrel with removable flash hider, 30 shot stainless steel mag. with anti-tilt follower and chrome/silicon spring, Black or OD Green Cerakote finish on upper and lower receivers, charging handle, and forearm, includes custom hard case, 7 1/2 lbs. New 2015.

While this model was prototyped in 2015 with a projected MSR of $3,195, there are no plans to put it into production.

TAR-HUNT CUSTOM RIFLES, INC.

Current custom rifled shotgun manufacturer established in 1990, and located in Bloomsburg, PA. Dealer and consumer direct sales.

In addition to rifles and shotguns, Tar-Hunt also builds custom XP-100 pistols on a customer supplied action. Contact the company directly for a price quotation (see Trademark Index).

SHOTGUNS: BOLT ACTION

Add $110 for left-hand action on all current models, $300 for high gloss metal, $495 for nickel, $250 for Jewell trigger, and $110 for dipped camouflage stock finish.

RSG-TACTICAL (SNIPER) MODEL – 12 ga. only, similar to RSG-12, except has M-86 McMillan fiberglass black tactical stock with Pachmayr Decelerator pad and heavy barrel. Mfg. 1992-98.

	100%	98%	95%	90%	80%	70%	60%	Last MSR
	$1,495	$1,250	$995	$875	$750	$700	$650	$1,595

Add $150 for Bipod.

TAURUS INTERNATIONAL MFG., INC.

Currently manufactured by Taurus Forjas S.A., located in Porto Alegre, Brazil and in Miami, FL (certain models). Currently, handguns made in Brazil are imported by Taurus International Mfg., Inc. located in Miami, FL since 1982. Beginning 2007, Taurus Tactical, a separate entity, was created for law enforcement/military sales and service. Distributor sales only.

During late 2012, Taurus Holdings purchased an exclusive global distribution agreement with Diamondback Firearms, LLC. Taurus assumed all sales and marketing efforts of the Diamondback branded products from its Miami office.

All Taurus products are known for their innovative design, quality construction, and proven value, and are backed by a lifetime repair policy.

Taurus order number nomenclature is as follows: the first digit followed by a dash refers to type (1 = pistol, 2 = revolvers, 3 = longuns, 4 = Magazines/Accessories, 5 = grips, and 10 = scope mount bases), the next 2 or 3 digits refer to model number, the next digit refers to type of hammer (0 = exposed, 1 = concealed), the next digit refers to barrel length (w/o fractions), the last digit refers to finish (1 = blue, 9 = stainless), and the suffix at the end refers to special features (T = total titanium, H = case hardened, M = matte finish, PLY = polymer, UL = Ultra-Lite, C = ported (compensation), G = gold accent, PRL = mother-of-pearl grips, R = rosewood grips, NS = night sights, MG = magnesium, and FO = fiber optic). Hence, 2-454089M refers to a Model 454 Raging Bull revolver in .454 Casull cal. with an exposed hammer and a 8 3/8 in. barrel in matte stainless finish.

PISTOLS: SEMI-AUTO

From 1990-92, certain models became available with a Laser Aim LA1 sighting system that included mounts, rings (in matching finish), a 110 volt AC recharging unit, a 9 volt DC field charger, and a high impact custom case.

Taurus incorporated their keyed Taurus security system on most models during 2000, except the PT-22 and PT-25, and this is now available with all models. When the security system is engaged (via a keyed button on the bottom of rear grip strap), the pistol cannot be fired, cocked, or disassembled, and the gun's manual safety cannot be disengaged. This security key also works for the revolvers.

Recent variations that are CA approved are not broken out separately, as pricing is usually the same as the standard model.

Add approx. $30 for the Deluxe Shooter's Pack option (includes extra mag. and custom case) on the 92, 99, 100, and 101 Series (disc. 2000).

PT-24/7 – 9mm Para., .40 S&W, or .45 ACP (new 2005) cal., DAO, SFO, large black polymer frame with blued steel or satin stainless steel slide, 4 in. barrel with 3-dot sights, grips have Ribber grip overlays, 10, 12 (.45 ACP cal.), 15 (.40 S&W cal.), or 17 (9mm Para. cal.) shot mag., built-in Picatinny rail system on bottom of frame, includes 3 safeties, 27 1/2 oz. Mfg. late 2004-2005.

	100%	98%	95%	90%	80%	70%	60%	Last MSR
	$450	$395	$345	$295	$260	$225	$195	$578

Add $16 for stainless steel.

PT-24/7 PRO FULL SIZE – 9mm Para., .40 S&W, or .45 ACP cal., SA first shot, and follows continually in SA model, SFO, large black polymer frame with blued steel, Duo Tone (new 2009), titanium (9mm Para. cal. only), or satin stainless steel slide, 4 in. barrel with Heinie front and Slant Pro rear sight, Ribber grips (.45 ACP cal.) or Ribber overmold grips (grip inlays), 10, 12 (.45 ACP cal.), 15 (.40 S&W cal.), or 17 (9mm Para. cal.) shot mag., built-in Picatinny rail system on bottom of frame, includes 3 safeties, 27.2 oz. Mfg. 2006-2010.

	100%	98%	95%	90%	80%	70%	60%	Last MSR
	$415	$350	$310	$280	$240	$210	$185	$498

Add $16 for stainless steel or $188 for titanium.

This model uses a SA trigger mechanism. However, if a cartridge does not fire, a DA feature allows the shooter a second firing pin strike via the DA trigger pull. If the cartridge still does not fire, then extraction by slide operation will insert a fresh round while reverting to the SA model automatically.

MSR		100%	98%	95%	90%	80%	70%	60%	Last MSR

* PT-24/7 Pro Long Slide – similar to Full Size 24/7-Pro, except has 5.2 in. barrel, also available in .38 Super cal. (new 2010), similar mag. capacities, Tenifer finish (2010 only), 29.1 oz. Mfg. 2006-2010.

| | | $445 | $385 | $340 | $295 | $260 | $225 | $195 | *$530* |

Add $15 for stainless steel. Add $31 for Tenifer finish (new 2010). Add $197 for Tenifer finish with night sights (.40 S&W cal. only, new 2010).

* PT-24/7 Pro Compact – similar to Full Size 24/7-Pro, except has 3 1/3 in. barrel, similar mag. capacities. Mfg. 2006-2010.

| | | $415 | $350 | $310 | $280 | $240 | $210 | $185 | *$498* |

Add $16 for stainless steel or $188 for titanium.

PT-24/7 G2 – 9mm Para., .40 S&W, or .45 ACP cal., advanced DA/SA trigger system, SFO, 4.2 in. barrel, large black polymer frame, horizontally grooved grips with metallic inserts and 3 interchangeable backstraps, ambidextrous thumb rests, matte black or stainless steel slide, Strike Two trigger with safety, ambidextrous manual decocker latch and safety, fixed front and low-profile adj. rear sight, vertical loaded chamber indicator, built-in Picatinny rail system on bottom of frame, 10, 12 (.45 ACP cal. only), 15 (.40 S&W cal. only) or 17 (9mm Para. only) shot mag., 28 oz. New 2011.

| MSR $362 | | $315 | $265 | $235 | $210 | $185 | $160 | $140 | |

Add $15 for stainless steel.

* PT-24/7 G2 Compact – 9mm Para., .40 S&W, or .45 ACP cal., similar to PT-24/7 G2, except has 3 1/2 in. barrel, 27 oz. New 2011.

| MSR $362 | | $315 | $265 | $235 | $210 | $185 | $160 | $140 | |

Add $15 for stainless steel.

PT-24/7 OSS – 9mm Para., .40 S&W, or .45 ACP cal., similar operating system as PT-24/7 Pro Full Size, including SA/DA trigger system, choice of tan or black frame, 5 1/4 in. match grade barrel, Novak sights, lower frame Picatinny rail, 10, 12, 15, or 17 shot mag., ambidextrous decocking safety, black Tenifer steel or stainless (new 2009) slide with front and rear serrations, approx. 32 oz. Mfg. 2007-2010.

| | | $475 | $415 | $370 | $325 | $285 | $240 | $210 | *$623* |

Add $63 for Novak Lo-Mount night sights.
Add $18 for matte finished stainless steel slide (new 2009).

PT-38S – .38 Super cal., 4 1/4 in. barrel, DA/SA utilizes Model PT-945 alloy frame, choice of blue, stainless steel, or stainless/gold finishes, 3-dot fixed sights, 10 shot mag., checkered rubber (standard) or smooth faux mother-of-pearl grips, 30 oz. Mfg. 2005-2010.

| | | $525 | $480 | $425 | $375 | $325 | $280 | $230 | *$695* |

Add $16 for stainless steel slide.
Add $48 for stainless steel slide, gold accents, and faux mother-of-pearl grips.

PT-58 HC PLUS – .380 ACP cal., medium frame, similar to PT-58, except has 19 shot mag., ambidextrous safety, fixed sights, 18.7 oz. Mfg. 2006-2010.

| | | $495 | $450 | $395 | $350 | $295 | $260 | $220 | *$664* |

Add $16 for stainless steel slide.

PT-92(AF) – 9mm Para. cal., DA/SA, design similar to Beretta Model 92 SB-F, exposed hammer, ambidextrous safety, 5 in. barrel, current mfg. has frame accessory rail in front of trigger guard, 10 (C/B 1994), 15*, or 17 (new late 2004) shot mag., smooth Brazilian walnut (disc.) or checkered rubber (new 1999) grips, blue or nickel (disc.) finish, fixed or night (mfg. 2000-2004) sights, loaded chamber indicator, Taurus Security System, 34 oz.

| MSR $483 | | $425 | $360 | $315 | $280 | $240 | $210 | $185 | |

Add $40 for satin nickel finish (disc. 1994).
Add $415 for Laser Aim Sight (disc. 1991).
Add $78 for night sights (disc. 2004).
Add $266 for blue or stainless conversion kit to convert 9mm Para. to .22 LR (mfg. 1999-2004).

* PT-92SS (Stainless Steel) – 9mm Para. cal., similar to PT-92(AF), except is combat matte (new 2006, high cap. mag. only) or regular stainless steel, 34 oz. New 1992.

| MSR $498 | | $435 | $365 | $320 | $280 | $240 | $210 | $185 | |

Add $78 for night sights (disc. 2004).

* PT-92AFC – compact variation of the Model PT-92AF, 4 in. barrel, 10 (C/B 1994) or 13* shot mag., fixed sights. Disc. 1996.

| | | $395 | $345 | $300 | $260 | $220 | $195 | $175 | *$449* |

Add $38 for satin nickel finish (disc. 1993).

* PT-92AFC (Stainless Steel) – similar to PT-92AFC, except stainless steel. Mfg. 1993-96.

| | | $425 | $360 | $315 | $280 | $240 | $210 | $185 | *$493* |

MSR		100%	98%	95%	90%	80%	70%	60%		*Last MSR*

PT-99 (AF) – 9mm Para. cal., similar to Model PT-92AF, except has adj. rear sight, 10 or 17 shot mag., 34 oz. Disc. 2011.

		$495	$450	$395	$350	$295	$260	$220		*$617*

Add $45 for satin nickel finish (disc. 1994).

Add $266 for blue or stainless conversion kit to convert 9mm Para. to .22 LR (mfg. 1999-2004) or .40 S&W (mfg. 2000-2004).

This action is similar to the Beretta Model 92SB-F.

* ***PT-99SS (Stainless Steel)*** – similar to PT-99, except is fabricated from stainless steel. Mfg. 1992-2011.

		$495	$450	$395	$350	$295	$260	$220		*$633*

PT-100 – .40 S&W cal., DA/SA, large frame, 5 in. barrel, 10 (C/B 1994), 11* (reintroduced late 2004) shot mag., safeties include ambidextrous manual, hammer drop, inertia firing pin, and chamber loaded indicator, choice of blue, satin nickel (disc. 1994), or stainless steel finish, accessory rail, smooth Brazilian hardwood (disc.) or rubber grips, 34 oz. Mfg. 1992-97, reintroduced 2000-2012.

		$495	$450	$395	$350	$295	$260	$220		*$641*

Add $40 for satin nickel finish (disc. 1994).

Add $78 for night sights (mfg. 2000-2004).

Add $266 for blue or stainless conversion kit to convert .40 S&W to .22 LR cal. (disc. 2004).

* ***PT-100SS (Stainless Steel)*** – .40 S&W cal., similar to PT-100, except is fabricated from stainless steel, and 16 shot mag. Mfg. 1992-96, reintroduced 2000-2013.

		$515	$460	$400	$350	$295	$260	$220		*$668*

Add $78 for night sights (disc. 2005).

PT-101 – .40 S&W cal., similar to PT-100, except has adj. rear sight., 10 or 11 shot mag., 34 oz. Mfg. 1992-96, reintroduced 2000-2011.

		$495	$450	$395	$350	$295	$260	$220		*$617*

Add $266 for blue or stainless conversion kit to convert .40 S&W to .22 LR cal. (disc. 2004).

Add $45 for satin nickel finish (disc. 1994).

* ***PT-101SS (Stainless Steel)*** – similar to PT-101, except is stainless steel. Mfg. 1992-96, reintroduced 2000-2011.

		$495	$450	$395	$350	$295	$260	$220		*$633*

PT-111 MILLENNIUM – 9mm Para. cal., DAO, SFO, 3 1/4 in. barrel with fixed 3-dot sights, black polymer frame with steel slide, striker fired, 10 shot mag. with push-button release, 18.7 oz. Mfg. 1998-2004.

		$375	$310	$265	$220	$200	$180	$165		*$422*

Add $78 for night sights (new 2000).

Add $47 for pearl or burl walnut grips (limited mfg. 2003).

* ***PT-111 Millennium Stainless*** – similar to Model PT-111, except has stainless steel slide. Mfg. 1998-2004.

		$385	$335	$295	$260	$220	$195	$175		*$438*

Add $78 for night sights (new 2000).

Add $46 for pearl or burl walnut grips (limited mfg. 2003).

* ***PT-111 Millennium Titanium*** – similar to Model PT-111, except has titanium slide and night or 3-dot (new 2004) sights. Mfg. 2000-2004.

		$435	$385	$340	$295	$260	$225	$195		*$508*

Add $78 for night sights.

PT-111 MILLENNIUM PRO – 9mm Para. cal., SA/DA trigger, SFO, 10 or 12 (new late 2004) shot mag., blue steel frame, current mfg. has Heinie Straight 8 sights, improved ergonomics, Posi-Traction slide serrations, recessed magazine release, manual safety lever, trigger block mechanism, firing pin block, and lightweight frame, 18.7 oz. Mfg. 2003-2012.

		$375	$310	$265	$220	$200	$180	$165		*$467*

Add $78 for night sights (disc. 2004).

* ***PT-111 Millennium Pro Stainless*** – similar to Model PT-111 Millennium Pro, except has stainless steel slide. Mfg. 2003-2012.

		$395	$330	$285	$260	$210	$170	$135		*$483*

Add $78 for night sights (mfg. 2004).

* ***PT-111 Ti Millennium Pro Titanium*** – similar to Model PT-111 Millennium Pro, except has titanium slide and 3 dot sights, 16 oz. Mfg. 2005-2011.

		$525	$480	$425	$375	$325	$280	$230		*$655*

PT-138 MILLENNIUM PRO – .380 ACP cal., similar to Model PT-138 Millennium, SFO, 10 or 12 shot (new 2005) mag., SA/DA trigger, current mfg. has Heinie Straight 8 sights, improved ergonomics, Posi-Traction slide serrations, recessed magazine release, manual safety lever, trigger block mechanism, firing pin block, and lightweight frame, 18.7 oz. Mfg. 2003, reintroduced 2005-2011.

		$375	$310	$265	$220	$200	$180	$165		*$467*

Add $78 for night sights (disc. 2003).

MSR	100%	98%	95%	90%	80%	70%	60%	Last MSR

* **PT-138 Millennium Pro Stainless** – similar to Model PT-138 Millennium Pro, except has stainless steel slide. Mfg. 2003, reintroduced 2005-2011.

	100%	98%	95%	90%	80%	70%	60%	Last MSR
	$395	$345	$300	$260	$220	$195	$175	*$483*

PT-140 MILLENNIUM – .40 S&W cal., DAO, SFO, 3 1/4 in. barrel, black polymer frame, manual safety, 10 shot mag., fixed 3-dot sights, blue steel slide, 18.7 oz. Mfg. 1999-2004.

	100%	98%	95%	90%	80%	70%	60%	Last MSR
	$375	$310	$265	$220	$200	$180	$165	*$461*

Add $78 for night sights (new 2000).
Add $47 for pearl or burl walnut grips (mfg. 2003).

* **PT-140 Millennium Stainless** – similar to Model PT-140, except has stainless steel slide. Mfg. 1999-2004.

	100%	98%	95%	90%	80%	70%	60%	Last MSR
	$380	$335	$295	$260	$220	$195	$175	*$476*

Add $78 for night sights (new 2000).
Add $46 for pearl or burl walnut grips (mfg. 2003).

PT-140 MILLENNIUM PRO – .40 S&W cal., similar to Model PT-140 Millennium, except has SA/DA trigger, current mfg. has Heinie Straight 8 sights, improved ergonomics, Posi-Traction slide serrations, recessed magazine release, manual safety lever, trigger block mechanism, firing pin block, and lightweight frame, 23 1/2 oz. Mfg. 2003-2012.

	100%	98%	95%	90%	80%	70%	60%	Last MSR
	$395	$345	$300	$260	$220	$195	$175	*$483*

Add $78 for night sights (disc. 2004).

* **PT-140 Millennium Pro Stainless** – similar to Model PT-140 Millennium Pro, except has stainless steel slide. Mfg. 2003-2012.

	100%	98%	95%	90%	80%	70%	60%	Last MSR
	$415	$350	$310	$280	$240	$210	$185	*$498*

Add $78 for night sights (disc. 2004).

PT-145 MILLENNIUM – .45 ACP cal., otherwise similar to Model PT-140 Millennium, 23 oz. Mfg. 2000-2003.

	100%	98%	95%	90%	80%	70%	60%	Last MSR
	$400	$350	$310	$280	$240	$210	$185	*$484*

Add $79 for night sights (new 2000).

* **PT-145 Millennium Stainless** – similar to Model PT-140, except has stainless steel slide. Mfg. 1999-2003.

	100%	98%	95%	90%	80%	70%	60%	Last MSR
	$400	$350	$310	$280	$240	$210	$185	*$500*

Add $78 for night sights (new 2000).

PT-145 MILLENNIUM PRO – .45 ACP cal., similar to Model PT-145 Millennium, except has SA/DA trigger, current mfg. has Heinie Straight 8 sights, improved ergonomics, Posi-Traction slide serrations, recessed magazine release, manual safety lever, trigger block mechanism, firing pin block, and lightweight frame, 22.2 oz. Mfg. 2003-2012.

	100%	98%	95%	90%	80%	70%	60%	Last MSR
	$395	$345	$300	$260	$220	$195	$175	*$483*

Add $78 for night sights (disc. 2004).

* **PT-145 Millennium Pro Stainless** – similar to Model PT-145 Millennium Pro, except has stainless steel slide. Mfg. 2003-2013.

	100%	98%	95%	90%	80%	70%	60%	Last MSR
	$415	$350	$310	$280	$240	$210	$185	*$498*

Add $78 for night sights (mfg. 2000-2004).

PT-400 – .400 Cor-Bon cal., similar to Model PT-940, except has 4 1/4 in. ported barrel and 8 shot mag., 29 1/2 oz. Mfg. 1999 only.

	100%	98%	95%	90%	80%	70%	60%	Last MSR
	$415	$350	$310	$280	$240	$210	$185	*$523*

* **PT-400 Stainless** – similar to Model PT-400, except has stainless steel slide. Mfg. 1999 only.

	100%	98%	95%	90%	80%	70%	60%	Last MSR
	$415	$350	$310	$280	$240	$210	$185	*$539*

PT-609/609TI-PRO – 9mm Para. cal., DA/SA, 3 1/4 in. barrel with titanium slide, fixed sights, black polymer grips, lower rail on frame, 13 shot mag., 19.7 oz. Mfg. 2007-2010.

	100%	98%	95%	90%	80%	70%	60%	Last MSR
	$535	$490	$430	$375	$325	$280	$230	*$670*

PT-638 PRO COMPACT – .380 ACP cal., SA target style trigger with trigger safety, 3.2 in. barrel, low mount sights with adj. rear, 15 shot mag., ambidextrous manual safety, loaded chamber indicator, blue or matte stainless slide, black polymer frame with Memory Pad, 28 oz. Mfg. 2011 only.

	100%	98%	95%	90%	80%	70%	60%	Last MSR
	$395	$345	$300	$260	$220	$195	$175	*$483*

Add $15 for matte stainless steel slide.

PT-709 SLIM – 9mm Para. cal., SA (disc.) or DA/SA trigger (current mfg.), 3 in. barrel, 7 shot mag., black polymer compact frame with grip texturing, 3 dot sights, loaded chamber indicator, advanced "Strike Two" trigger system, Taurus Security System, blue finish, 19 oz. Mfg. late 2008-2012, reintroduced 2014.

MSR	100%	98%	95%	90%	80%	70%	60%	Last MSR
$302	$265	$235	$210	$190	$175	$165	$155	

Add $14 for Bulldog Case (mfg. 2010-2011).

MSR	100%	98%	95%	90%	80%	70%	60%	Last MSR

* PT-709 Slim Stainless – 9mm Para. cal., similar to PT-709 Slim, except has matte finished stainless steel slide, 19 oz. New late 2008.

| MSR $317 | $275 | $240 | $215 | $195 | $175 | $165 | $155 | |

Add $15 for Bulldog Case (mfg. 2010-2011).

* PT-709 Slim Titanium – similar to Model 709 Slim, except has titanium slide, 17 oz. Disc. 2010.

| | $515 | $460 | $400 | $350 | $295 | $260 | $220 | *$623* |

Add $15 for Bulldog Case (new 2010).

PT-709 G2 SLIM – 9mm Para. cal., sub-compact frame, 7 or 9 (extended) shot mag., 3.2 in. barrel with low profile adj. rear sights, loaded chamber indicator, black polymer frame and blue or matte stainless slide, 19.4 oz. Limited mfg. 2011 only.

| | $395 | $345 | $300 | $260 | $220 | $195 | $175 | *$483* |

* PT-709 G2 Slim Stainless – similar to PT-709 G2 Slim, except has matte finished stainless steel slide. Limited mfg. 2011 only.

| | $415 | $350 | $310 | $280 | $240 | $210 | $185 | *$498* |

PT-738 TCP W/WINGS (TAURUS COMPACT PISTOL) – .380 ACP cal., 3.3 in. barrel, 6 shot mag., grooved black polymer frame, blue or stainless steel slide, hammerless, DAO trigger, low profile fixed sights, unique retractable wings that fold out from rear of slide allowing racking the slide easier, loaded chamber indicator, matte black or matte stainless finish, 10.2 oz. New 2015.

| MSR $266 | $235 | $200 | $185 | $165 | $150 | $135 | $125 | |

Add $45 for stainless steel slide.

PT-745 COMPACT MILLENNIUM PRO – .45 ACP cal., DA/SA, SFO, compact variation of Millennium Pro with 3 1/4 in. barrel, Heinie Straight 8 sights, 6 shot mag. with finger extension, matte blue steel slide, loaded chamber indicator, black polymer grip frame, Desert Tan grips were added 2006 (disc.), 20.8 oz. Mfg. 2005-2012.

| | $395 | $345 | $300 | $260 | $220 | $195 | $175 | *$483* |

* PT-745 Compact Millenium Pro Stainless – similar to PT-745 Compact Millennium Pro, except has stainless steel slide. Mfg. 2005-2012.

| | $415 | $350 | $310 | $280 | $240 | $210 | $185 | *$498* |

PT-809 – 9mm Para. cal., similar design to the PT-24/7 OSS, 4 in. barrel, DA/SA with Strike Two capability, SFO, Novak sights, 17 shot mag., external hammer, loaded chamber indicator, blue or stainless (disc. 2012), front and rear slide serrations, lower Picatinny rail, ambidextrous 3-position safety and decocker, ambidextrous mag. release, extended grip, small, medium, and large interchangeable backstraps, double stack magazines, unique takedown levers, Taurus Security System, 30.2 oz. New 2007.

| MSR $347 | $275 | $240 | $210 | $185 | $170 | $150 | $130 | |

Add $15 for stainless steel slide (disc. 2012).
Add $188 for .22 LR conversion kit (10 shot mag., mfg. 2011 only).

* PT-809 Compact – 9mm Para. cal., 3 1/2 in. barrel, 17 shot mag., 3 dot fixed sights, polymer grips with metallic inserts, loaded chamber indicator, ambidextrous mag. release, Strike Two trigger, external hammer, shortened grip frame, Taurus Security system, matte black finish, 24.7 oz. New 2011.

| MSR $347 | $275 | $240 | $210 | $185 | $170 | $150 | $130 | |

Add $15 for stainless steel slide (disc. 2012).

PT-840 – .40 S&W cal., similar design to the PT-24/7 OSS, 4 in. barrel, DA/SA with Strike Two capability, Novak sights, 15 shot mag., matte blue or matte stainless slide (disc. 2012), front and rear slide serrations, lower frame Picatinny rail, ambidextrous 3-position safety and decocker, ambidextrous mag. release, extended grip, small, medium, and large interchangeable backstraps, external hammer, double stack magazines, Taurus Security System, approx. 30 oz. New 2008.

| MSR $347 | $275 | $240 | $210 | $185 | $170 | $150 | $130 | |

Add $15 for stainless steel slide (disc. 2012).
Add $188 for .22 LR conversion kit (10 shot mag., mfg. 2011 only).

* PT-840 Compact – .40 S&W cal., 3 1/2 in. barrel, 15 shot mag., 3 dot sights, polymer grips with metallic inserts, loaded chamber indicator, ambidextrous mag. release, Strike Two capability, shortened grip frame, external hammer, matte black finish, 24.7 oz. New 2011.

| MSR $347 | $275 | $240 | $210 | $185 | $170 | $150 | $130 | |

Add $16 for stainless steel slide (disc. 2012).

MSR	100%	98%	95%	90%	80%	70%	60%	Last MSR

PT-845 – .45 ACP cal., similar design to the PT-24/7 OSS, 4 in. barrel, DA/SA with Strike Two capability, SFO, Novak sights, 12 shot mag., blue or stainless (disc.), front and rear slide serrations, lower frame Picatinny rail, ambidextrous 3-position safety and decocker, ambidextrous mag. release, extended grip, small, medium, and large interchangeable backstraps, external hammer, double stack magazines, takedown lever, approx. 30 oz. New 2008.

MSR $347	$275	$240	$210	$185	$170	$150	$130	

Add $15 for stainless steel slide (disc. 2012).

Add $188 for .22 LR conversion kit (10 shot mag., mfg. 2011 only).

PT-908 – 9mm Para. cal., compact version of the PT-92 with 3.8 in. barrel, DA/SA, 8 shot mag., fixed sights, blue or nickel finish. Mfg. 1993-1997.

	$360	$300	$260	$220	$200	$180	$165	$435

* ***PT-908D SS (Stainless Steel)*** – similar to Model PT-908, except is stainless steel. Mfg. 1993-97.

	$385	$335	$295	$260	$220	$195	$175	$473

PT-909 – 9mm Para. cal., DA/SA, 4 in. barrel, lower frame Picatinny rail, 10 or 17 shot mag., blue finish, fixed rear sight, alloy medium frame with steel slide, checkered rubber grips, 28.2 oz. Mfg. 2006-2010.

	$500	$450	$395	$350	$295	$260	$220	$648

Add $16 for stainless steel slide.

PT-911 COMPACT – 9mm Para. cal., DA/SA, 4 in. barrel, 10 or 15 (new late 2004) shot mag., checkered rubber grips, fixed sights, 28.2 oz. Mfg. 1997-2010.

	$500	$450	$395	$350	$295	$260	$220	$648

Add $79 for night sights (disc. 2004).

* ***PT-911 Compact SS (Stainless Steel)*** – stainless variation of the PT-911 Compact. Disc. 2010.

	$530	$480	$425	$375	$325	$280	$230	$664

Add $78 for night sights (disc. 2004).

* ***PT-911 Compact Deluxe*** – choice of blue/gold finish or stainless steel with gold, rosewood, or mother-of-pearl grips. Mfg. 2000-2010.

	$550	$495	$450	$395	$350	$295	$245	$702

Add $15 for stainless steel with gold or faux mother-of-pearl grips.

PT-917 COMPACT PLUS – 9mm Para. cal., DA/SA, 4 in. barrel with fixed sights, rubber grips, 19 shot mag., medium frame, blue finish or stainless steel, 31.8 oz. Mfg. 2007-2010.

	$500	$450	$395	$350	$295	$260	$220	$609

Add $18 for stainless steel.

PT-938 COMPACT – .380 ACP cal., DA/SA, 3 3/4 in. barrel, ambidextrous safety, 10 or 15 (new late 2004) shot mag., blue finish with alloy frame and steel slide, rubber grips, fixed sights, 34 oz. Mfg. 1997-2005.

	$410	$350	$310	$280	$240	$210	$185	$516

* ***PT-938 Compact SS (Stainless Steel)*** – stainless slide variation of the PT-938 Compact with matte stainless finish.

	$420	$360	$315	$280	$240	$210	$185	$531

PT-940 – .40 S&W cal., compact version of the PT-100 with 3 5/8 in. barrel, DA/SA, 10 shot mag., fixed sights, 28.2 oz. Mfg. 1996-2010.

	$500	$450	$395	$350	$295	$260	$220	$648

Add $79 for night sights (disc. 2004).

* ***PT-940 SS (Stainless Steel)*** – similar to PT-940, except is stainless steel. Mfg. 1996-2010.

	$530	$480	$425	$375	$325	$280	$230	$664

Add $80 for night sights (disc. 2009).

PT-945 – .45 ACP cal., DA/SA, 4 1/4 in. ported (mfg. 1997-2003) or unported barrel, 8 shot single stack mag., ambidextrous 3-position safety and decocker, chamber loaded indicator, 3-dot sights, 29 1/2 oz. Mfg. 1995-2010.

	$560	$495	$450	$395	$350	$295	$245	$695

Add $78 for night sights (disc. 2004).

Add $39 for ported barrel (disc. 2003).

* ***PT-945 SS (Stainless Steel)*** – stainless steel variation of the PT-945. Mfg. 1995-2010.

	$575	$510	$455	$395	$350	$295	$245	$711

Add $78 for night sights (disc. 2004).

Add $39 for ported barrel (disc. 2003).

MSR	100%	98%	95%	90%	80%	70%	60%	Last MSR

PT-957 – .357 SIG cal., DA/SA, compact model with 3 5/8 in. ported (available only with night sights or in 957 Deluxe beginning 2002) or non-ported (new 2002) barrel and slide, 10 shot mag., ambidextrous 3-position safety and decocker, blue finish, checkered rubber grips, fixed sights, 28 oz. Mfg. 1999-2003.

	$425	$360	$315	$280	$240	$210	$185	$523

Add $90 for night sights.

Add $40 for ported barrel (disc. 2002).

* **PT-957 SS (Stainless Steel)** – stainless steel variation of the PT-957. Mfg. 1999-2003.

	$430	$385	$340	$295	$260	$225	$195	$539

Add $40 for ported (disc. 2001) barrel, or $130 for ported barrel and night sights (disc. 2003).

PT-1911 – .38 Super (mfg. 2006-2011), 9mm Para. (new 2006), .40 S&W (mfg. 2006-2010) or .45 ACP cal., SA, 5 in. barrel, choice of Heinie front and rear sights or Picatinny rail, 8 (.40 S&W or .45 ACP) or 9 (.38 Super or 9mm Para.) shot mag., blue or Duo-tone (new 2008) finish, choice of steel or aluminum (new 2008) frame with steel slide, checkered diamond pattern or bull's head wood (disc. 2015) grips, bobbed hammer, front and rear serrations on slide, accurized hand tuned action, 32 oz. New mid-2005.

MSR $574	$485	$435	$375	$320	$280	$240	$210	

Add $47 for Picatinny rail (.45 ACP cal. only).

Add $70 for 9mm Para. cal. with matte black finish.

Add $85 for Duo-Tone finish (.45 ACP cal. only), not available with Picatinny rail.

Add $147 for bull's head grips (.45 ACP cal. only, disc. 2015).

Add approx. $75 for aluminum frame (disc. 2011).

* **PT-1911 Compact** – .45 ACP cal., only, similar to PT-1911, except has 4 1/4 in. barrel, 6 shot mag. Mfg. 2006 only.

	$490	$430	$365	$335	$270	$220	$170	$599

Add $20 for stainless steel slide.

* **PT-1911 Stainless** – 9mm Para. or .45 ACP cal., similar to PT-1911, except has matte stainless steel frame and slide (mirror finished beginning 2008).

MSR $682	$575	$515	$430	$375	$320	$270	$240	

Add $15 for lower frame Picatinny rail.

Subtract $23 for 9mm Para cal.

Add $68 for bull's head grips (disc. 2015).

PT-1911B SERIES – .38 Super (1911B-38, disc.), 9mm Para. (1911B-9), or .45 ACP (1911BHC-12) cal., 5 in. barrel, SA, blue, stainless, 9, 11, or 12 shot mag., with or w/o Novak night sights (disc. 2010), Heinie sights became standard 2011, 38-40 oz. Mfg. mid-2009-2011.

	$535	$490	$430	$375	$325	$280	$230	$677

Add $103 for stainless steel. Add $17 for 11 shot mag. Add $79 for .45 ACP with 12 shot mag. Add $63 for Novak night sights. Add $93 for Hi-Polish with bull's head walnut grips. Add $16 for pearl grips.

PT-2011 DT INTEGRAL – .380 ACP or 9mm Para cal., DA/SA with trigger safety, SFO, 3.2 in. barrel, 11 (.380 ACP), 13 or 15 (.380 ACP) shot mag., aluminum frame with black polymer grips, loaded chamber indicator, matte black metal finish, removable back straps, adj. rear sight, 21 or 24 oz. Mfg. 2012 only.

	$475	$415	$370	$325	$285	$240	$210	$572

* **PT-2011 DT Integral Stainless** – similar to PT-2011 DT Integral, except has stainless steel slide. Mfg. 2012 only.

	$485	$425	$375	$325	$285	$240	$210	$588

PT-2011 DT HYBRID – 9mm Para or .40 S&W cal., DA/SA with trigger safety, SFO, 3.2 in. barrel, 11 (.40 S&W) or 13 (9mm Para) shot mag., black polymer lower frame with steel upper frame and slide, loaded chamber indicator, matte black metal finish, removable back straps, adj. rear sight, 24 oz. Mfg. 2012-2013.

	$490	$425	$375	$325	$285	$240	$210	$589

* **PT-2011 DT Hybrid Stainless** – similar to PT-2011 DT Hybrid, except has stainless upper frame and slide. Mfg. 2012-2013.

	$500	$450	$395	$350	$295	$260	$220	$605

PT-2045 – .45 ACP cal., SFO, 4.2 in. barrel, blue or stainless, 12 shot mag., checkered polymer grips, with or w/o Novak night sights, approx. 32 oz. Limited mfg. 2009 only.

	$450	$395	$345	$295	$260	$225	$195	$561

Add $16 for stainless steel. Add $62 for night sights.

CURVE – .380 ACP cal., blowback action, subcompact frame, 2 1/2 in. barrel, 6 shot mag., polymer frame with metallic sub-frame, hammerless, contoured trigger, LED light and laser built into the frame, short grip frame assembly, magazine disconnect, unique curved design with belt clip that allows pistol to follow body contours, loaded chamber indicator, Taurus Security System, black oxide finish, 10.2 oz. New 2015.

MSR $392	$365	$335	$295	$275	$250	$225	$200	

Subtract $45 if without laser.

MSR	100%	98%	95%	90%	80%	70%	60%	Last MSR

REVOLVERS: RECENT PRODUCTION

From 1990-1992, certain models became available with a Laser Aim LA1 sighting system that included mounts, rings (in matching finish), a 110 volt AC recharging unit, a 9 volt DC field charger, and a high impact custom case.

The following Taurus revolvers have been listed in numerical order. All currently manufactured revolvers listed are rated for +P ammunition.

Tracker model nomenclature refers to a heavy contoured barrel with full shroud, porting, and with or w/o VR.

All currently manufactured Taurus revolvers are equipped with the patented Taurus Security System, introduced in 1998, which utilizes an integral key lock on the back of the hammer, locking the action.

Add approx. $45 for scope base mount on currently produced models that offer this option.

Add $31 for carrying case on Raging Bull & Raging Hornet Models listed (disc. 2006).

MODEL 45-410 "THE JUDGE" (44-TEN TRACKER)
– .45 LC/.410 shotshell cal., 2 1/2 or 3 (new 2008) in. chamber, DA, compact frame, 2 1/2 (disc.), 3 (new 2007), or 6 1/2 in. barrel, 5 shot, fiber optic front sight, Ribber grips, blue finish, 29 or 32 oz. New 2006.

| MSR $553 | $475 | $425 | $375 | $335 | $295 | $260 | $220 | |

Add $39 for 2 1/2 in. cylinder with ported barrel and accessory rail (mfg. 2010-2012).

Add $156 for Crimson Trace laser grips (mfg. 2010-2012).

During late 2007, this model's nomenclature changed to the Model 45-410 Judge.

* **Model 45-410 The Judge Stainless (44-Ten Tracker Stainless)** – similar to Model 45-410, except is matte stainless steel, 29, 32, or 36.8 (3 in. chamber) oz. New 2006.

| MSR $598 | $525 | $465 | $415 | $365 | $350 | $275 | $240 | |

Add $31 for 2 1/2 in. cylinder with ported barrel and accessory rail (mfg. 2010-2012).

Add $157 for Crimson Trace laser grips (mfg. 2010-2012).

* **Model 45-410 The Judge Ultra-Lite** – similar to Model 45-410 Judge, 2 1/2 in. barrel, except has alloy frame, choice of blued steel or stainless steel cylinder, not available in 3 in. cylinder, 22.4 oz. Mfg. 2008-2011.

| | $575 | $510 | $455 | $395 | $350 | $295 | $245 | *$648* |

Add $32 for stainless steel barrel and cylinder. Add $313 for Crimson Trace laser grips (new 2010).

MODEL 45-410 "THE JUDGE" PUBLIC DEFENDER
– .45/.410 shotshell, 2 in. barrel, similar to original Judge, except only available with 2 1/2 in. chamber, blue or matte stainless, steel or titanium (disc. 2011) cylinder, reduced profile hammer, Ribber grips, 28.2 oz. New mid-2009.

| MSR $553 | $475 | $425 | $375 | $335 | $295 | $260 | $220 | |

Add $45 for stainless steel cylinder or $78 for titanium cylinder (disc. 2011).

Add $47 for pink Ribber grips (mfg. 2010-2011) or $82 for pink Ribber grips and Bulldog Case (mfg. 2010-2011).

* **Model 45-410 "The Judge" Public Defender Ultra-Lite** – similar to Model 45-410 The Judge Public Defender, except has ultra-lite aluminum frame and choice of blue steel or stainless, 2 1/2 in. cylinder, 20.7 oz. Mfg. 2011 only.

| | $575 | $510 | $455 | $395 | $350 | $295 | $245 | *$648* |

Add $32 for stainless steel barrel and cylinder.

* **Model 45-410 "The Judge" Public Defender Polymer** – .45 LC/.410 shotshell, DA/SA, 2 1/2 in. barrel, 5 shot mag., black lightweight polymer frame with blue (disc. 2011) or stainless steel cylinder, spurred hammer, fiber optic front and adj. rear sights, Ribber grips, 27 oz. New 2011.

| MSR $514 | $440 | $395 | $350 | $325 | $295 | $260 | $220 | |

Subtract approx. 10% for blue cylinder (disc. 2011).

* **Model 45-410FS Polymer** – .45 LC/.410 bore, 2 1/2 in. chamber, 2 in. barrel, polymer frame with blued steel cylinder, 5 shot, fiber optic front sight, transfer bar, ribber grip, matte black finish, 27 oz. New 2013.

| MSR $483 | $425 | $360 | $315 | $280 | $250 | $225 | $195 | |

MODEL 513 RAGING JUDGE MAGNUM
– interchangeably shoots .454 Casull, .45 LC, or .410 ga., DA, large frame, 6 shot, 3 (non-ported) or 6 1/2 (VR) in. barrel with Hi-Viz fiber optic front sight, 3 in. non-fluted cylinder, rubber grips with cushion inserts and red "Raging Bull" backstrap, blue finish, 60.6 or 72.7 oz. Mfg. 2011-2013.

| | $850 | $750 | $650 | $550 | $475 | $420 | $350 | *$1,012* |

* **Model 513 Raging Judge Magnum SS** – .45 LC, .454 Casull, or .410 ga., DA/SA, large frame, 3 or 6 1/2 in. barrel, 6 shot, stainless steel, spurred hammer, fiber optic front and fixed rear sights, rubber grips with cushioned inserts, transfer bar safety, matte stainless finish, 61-73 oz.

| MSR $1,038 | $895 | $775 | $675 | $565 | $485 | $430 | $360 | |

MODEL 513 RAGING JUDGE MAGNUM ULTRA-LITE
– .45 LC cal./.410 bore with 3 in. cylinder, SA/DA, 7 shot, 3 or 6 1/2 in. barrel with high vis. fiber optic front sights, features Ultra-Lite frame, blue finish, rubber grips with cushion inserts, 41.4 or 47.2 oz. Mfg. 2011-2012.

| | $825 | $735 | $630 | $540 | $465 | $410 | $340 | *$983* |

MSR	100%	98%	95%	90%	80%	70%	60%	Last MSR

* Model 513 Raging Judge Magnum Ultra-Lite SS – similar to Model 513 Raging Judge Magnum Ultra-Lite, except is matte stainless steel. Mfg. 2011-2012.

| | $885 | $775 | $675 | $565 | $485 | $430 | $360 | *$1,030* |

MODEL 605 – .357 Mag. cal., small frame, 5 shot, 2 in. unported (new 2002), 2 1/4 (disc. 2005), or 3 (mfg. 1996-98, reintroduced 2006-disc.) in. barrel, blue steel, 4 port compensated barrel (2 1/4 in. only) with fixed sights, exposed or concealed (Model 605CH, mfg. 1997-2005, 2 1/4 in. barrel) hammer, full barrel shroud, oversized finger grooved rubber grips, 24 1/2 oz. New 1995.

| MSR $356 | $285 | $250 | $225 | $200 | $180 | $160 | $140 | |

Add $16 for ported barrel (disc. 2003).

Add $303 for Crimson Trace laser grips (disc. 2011).

* Model 605 SS (Stainless Steel) – .357 Mag. cal., stainless variation of the Model 605.

| MSR $371 | $295 | $260 | $235 | $210 | $190 | $170 | $150 | |

Add $16 for ported barrel (disc. 2003).

Add $303 for Crimson Trace laser grips (mfg. 2008-2011).

* Model 605T Titanium – similar to Model 605, except is titanium with shadow grey finish. Mfg. 2005-2006.

| | $535 | $490 | $430 | $375 | $325 | $280 | $230 | *$625* |

* Model 605 Protector (605PLYB2/Protector Ply) – .357 Mag. cal., lightweight black polymer frame, blued or stainless cylinder assembly, 1 (disc.) or 2 in. barrel with VR, 5 shot, spurred hammer, fiber optic front and fixed rear sights, Ribber grips, ambidextrous thumb safety, matte black or matte stainless finish, 19 3/4 oz. New 2011.

| MSR $356 | $285 | $250 | $225 | $200 | $180 | $160 | $140 | |

Add $15 for stainless steel cylinder (new 2012).

MODEL 608 – .357 Mag. cal., large frame, 8 shot, 3 (mfg. 1997-98), 4, 6 1/2 (VR), or 8 3/8 (VR, new 1997) in. barrel with integral compensator, rubber finger grooves, exposed or concealed (mfg. 1997-2010, 3 in. barrel) hammer, adj. sights, 44-56 oz. Mfg. 1996-2004.

| | $355 | $300 | $260 | $220 | $200 | $180 | $165 | *$469* |

Add $15 for 6.5 or 8 3/8 in. VR ported barrel.

* Model 608SS (Stainless Steel) – .357 Mag. cal., DA/SA, large frame, 3 (mfg. 1997-98), 4, 6 1/2, or 8 3/8 (disc. 2012) in. VR ported barrel, 8 shot, stainless steel, exposed or concealed hammer, adj. sights, soft rubber grips, matte stainless finish, 51 or 56 oz. New 1996.

| MSR $688 | $525 | $480 | $425 | $375 | $325 | $280 | $230 | |

MODEL 617 – .357 Mag. cal., medium frame, DA, 7 shot, 2 in. regular or ported (disc.) barrel, fixed sights, exposed or concealed (Model 617CH, disc. 2005) hammer, rubber (disc. 2006) or Ribber (new 2007) grips, 28.3 oz. Mfg. 1998-2012.

| | $415 | $350 | $310 | $280 | $240 | $210 | $185 | *$508* |

Add $15 for ported barrel (disc. 2003).

* Model 617SS (Stainless Steel) – .357 Mag. cal., similar to Model 617, except is polished (disc. 2007) or matte stainless steel, 28.3 oz. New 1998.

| MSR $560 | $450 | $395 | $345 | $295 | $260 | $225 | $195 | |

Add $15 for ported barrel (disc. 2003).

* Model 617 ULT – similar to Model 617, except is 5 shot, aluminum alloy receiver and titanium cylinder, matte stainless finish, 2 in. regular or ported barrel, soft rubber grips. Mfg. 2001-2002.

| | $455 | $395 | $345 | $295 | $260 | $225 | $195 | *$530* |

Add $15 for ported barrel.

MODEL 669 – similar to Model 66 except has fully shrouded 4 or 6 in. barrel, blue finish, 37 oz. Disc. 1998.

| | $285 | $250 | $215 | $185 | $170 | $155 | $145 | *$344* |

Add $10 for VR barrel (mfg. 1989-1992).

Add $400 for Laser Aim Sight (offered 1990-1992).

Add $19 for compensated (669CP) barrel (new 1993).

MODEL 689 – similar to Model 669, except has VR. Disc. 1998.

| | $300 | $260 | $220 | $185 | $170 | $155 | $145 | *$358* |

Add $390 for Laser Aim Sight (mfg. 1990-91 only).

MODEL 817 ULTRA-LITE – .38 Spl.+P cal., medium frame, 7 shot, 2 in. ported (disc. 2002) or unported solid rib barrel, soft rubber (disc. 2006) or Ribber (new 2007) grips, bright blue finish, 21 oz. Mfg. 1999-2012.

| | $400 | $350 | $310 | $280 | $240 | $210 | $185 | *$508* |

Add $20 for ported barrel (disc. 2002).

MSR	100%	98%	95%	90%	80%	70%	60%	Last MSR

* **Model 817 Ultra-Lite Stainless** – similar to Model 817 Ultra-Lite, except is matte stainless steel. Mfg. 1999-2012.

	100%	98%	95%	90%	80%	70%	60%	Last MSR
	$425	$360	$315	$280	$240	$210	$185	*$555*

Add $20 for ported barrel (disc. 2003).

RIFLES: SEMI-AUTO

CARBINE CT G2 SERIES – 9mm Para. (Model CT9G2L), .40 S&W (Model CT40G2M), or .45 ACP (Model GT45G2M) cal., tactical design featuring hybrid aluminum/polymer frame with steel reinforcement, 10 (.45 ACP cal), 15 (.40 S&W cal.), or 34 (9mm Para. cal) shot mag., 16 in. barrel, fixed black polymer pistol grip skeletonized stock, ribbed polymer forearm with lower Picatinny rail, flat-top aluminum upper receiver with built-in full length Picatinny rail, fixed front and adj. rear sights, 9 1/4 lbs.

While advertised in 2011, this model was never mass manufactured.

TAVOR

Current trademark imported by IWI USA, Inc., located in Harrisburg, PA.

RIFLES: SEMI-AUTO

Conversion kits are available in 9mm Para., 5.45x39mm or .300 AAC Blackout. Please contact the importer directly for pricing (see Trademark Index).

TAVOR SAR – 5.56 NATO, .300 AAC Blackout (new 2016) or 9mm Para cal., 100% ambidextrous bullpup design, non-lubricated long stroke GPO, 16 1/2, 17 (9mm Para. cal.) or 18 in. chrome lined barrel, 10 or 30 shot mag. (AR-15 compatible), reinforced polymer frame and stock, integral folding adj. backup sights with Tritium front post, flat top with full Picatinny rail or Meprolight reflex sight mounted directly to the barrel (TAR-21/IFD16) oroptional bayonet lug, short forward rail on forend, last round hold open, matte black, Flat Dark Earth or OD Green (new 2014) finish, 26 1/8-30 (with 2 3/8 in. permanently attached or 3 7/8 in. removable muzzle brake) in. OAL, approx. 8-8 1/2 lbs. Imported beginning early 2013.

MSR $1,999	$1,700	$1,495	$1,275	$1,150	$935	$765	$595	

Add $50 for .300 AAC Blackout.

Add $50 for 2 3/8 in. permanently attached or 3 7/8 in. removable muzzle brake.

Add $600 for TAR-21/IDF16 configuration with Mepro-21 reflex sight.

Available in left-hand model with all controls situated for left-hand operation including the cocking handle, safety lever, QD swivel receptacles, relocation of the forward 45° Picatinny rail to the left side and left side ejection.

TAVOR X95 – 5.56 NATO cal., ambidextrous bullpup design, non-lubricated long stroke GPO, 16 1/2 in. chrome lined barrel, 30 shot mag. (AR-15 compatible), reinforced polymer frame and stock, integral folding adj. backup sights with Tritium front post, flat-top with full Picatinny rail ambidextrous mag release in AR-15 location, forearm with Picatinny rails at the 3, 6, and 9 o'clock positions with removable rail covers, charging handle located close to center mass, modular Tavor style pistol grip, low profile bolt release button, last round hold open, matte black, Flat Dark Earth or OD Green finish, 26 1/8 in. OAL, approx. 8 lbs. Imported beginning early 2016.

MSR $1,999	$1,700	$1,495	$1,275	$1,150	$935	$765	$595	

TAYLOR'S & CO., INC.

Current importer and distributor established during 1988, and located in Winchester, VA.

Taylor's & Co. is an Uberti importer and distributor of both black powder and firearms reproductions, in addition to being the exclusive U.S. distributor for Armi Sport, located in Brescia, Italy. Taylor's is also a distributor for Bond Arms Inc. - please refer to the Bond Arms Inc. section.

For more information and up-to-date pricing regarding current Taylor's & Co., Inc. black powder models, please refer to the *Blue Book of Modern Black Powder Arms* by John Allen. This book features information, complete pricing, and reference guides.

PISTOLS: SEMI-AUTO

1911-A1 FS TACTICAL – 9mm Para. (new 2015), .45 ACP or 10mm (new 2015) cal., 5 in. barrel, 8 shot mag., combat hammer, skeletonized trigger, ambidextrous safety, extended beavertail, Picatinny underrail, green fiber optic front sight, parkerized finish, checkered walnut grips, 3 1/4 lbs. Importation began 2013.

MSR $570	$475	$415	$350	$325	$260	$215	$165	

1911 .22 – .22 LR cal., 5 in. barrel, SA, black frame with black or olive green slide, checkered wood grips, 10 shot mag., mfg. by Chiappa. Mfg. 2011-2013.

	$250	$225	$195	$175	$140	$115	$90	*$300*

Add $79 for black slide (disc. 2012).

Add $65 for target model (disc. 2012).

MSR	100%	98%	95%	90%	80%	70%	60%	Last MSR

M4 TACTICAL SERIES – .22 LR cal., GIO, 6 in. solid steel barrel, 10 or 28 shot mag., fire control group, dust cover, adj. sights, pseudo flash hider, bayonet lug, forward assist, and bolt release, quad rail capable forearm, includes two mags. Imported 2011-2012.

	$350	$315	$275	$235	$200	$180	$165	*$419*

RIFLES: SEMI-AUTO

M4 22 – .22 LR cal., blowback action, 16 in. solid steel barrel, 10 or 28 shot mag., fire control group, dust cover, adj. sights, pseudo flash hider, bayonet lug, forward assist, and bolt release, quad rail capable forearm, includes two mags, 5 1/2 lbs. Mfg. 2011-2012.

	$350	$295	$260	$230	$200	$180	$165	*$419*

SHOTGUNS: REPRODUCTIONS

SxS MODEL – 12 ga., 28 9/16 in. barrels with chokes, approx. 7 lbs. Mfg. by Pedersoli.

	$925	$800	$750	$695	$595	$400	$295	*$1,122*

TECHNO ARMS (PTY) LIMITED

Previous manufacturer located in Johannesburg, S. Africa circa 1994-1996. Previously imported by Vulcans Forge, Inc. located in Foxboro, MA.

SHOTGUNS: SLIDE ACTION

MAG-7 SLIDE ACTION SHOTGUN – 12 ga. (60mm chamber length), 5 shot detachable mag. (in pistol grip), 14, 16, 18, or 20 in. barrel, straight grip or pistol grip stock, matte finish, 8 lbs. Imported 1995-96.

	$795	$675	$625	$550	$500	$450	$400	*$875*

TEMPLAR CUSTOM, LLC (TEMPLAR CONSULTING)

Current custom AR-15 rifle and component manufacturer located in Apex, NC since 2008.

RIFLES: SEMI-AUTO

MCWS (MULTI-CALIBER WEAPONS SYSTEM) – .223 Rem./5.56 NATO (.223 Wylde chamber), 6.5 Grendel, and .50 Beowulf cal., GIO, 16 in. stainless steel button rifled barrel (.50 Beowulf), 16 in. chrome moly steel button rifled barrel (5.56 NATO), 16 in. stainless steel button rifled barrel (6.5 Grendel), all quick change barrels with stainless WCI muzzle brakes, forged lower and matched upper receiver, Magpul ACS stock, Ergo ambi grip, Geissele SSA trigger, PRI low pro witness sights, 14 in. Templar Fastrail system includes 14 in. handguard, swivel sling stud, one case hardened black oxide barrel tool and allen wrench, multi-caliber cleaning kit, choice of hard or soft case, Desert Snake Duracoat finish.

MSR $2,899	$2,600	$2,275	$1,950	$1,775	$1,425	$1,175	$925	

Add $450 for cut rifle barrel upgrade.
Add $400 for MCWS 3 caliber kit.

TEMPLAR CUSTOM SPR (SPECIAL PURPOSE RIFLE) – .223 Rem./5.56 NATO (.223 Wylde chamber) cal., GIO, 16 in. chrome moly steel medium contour barrel with A2 flash hider, forged upper and lower receiver, steel bolt carrier, 12 1/2 in. Templar FastRail, Magpul ACS or MOE stock, Ergo Ambi grip, A2 front sight assembly, other options available on this model.

MSR $2,449	$2,200	$1,925	$1,650	$1,500	$1,225	$1,000	$800	

Add $550 for single point cut rifle stainless steel barrel.

TEMPLAR CUSTOM STANDARD RIFLE – .223 Rem./5.56 NATO (.223 Wylde chamber) cal., GIO, 16 in. chrome moly steel medium contour barrel with A2 flash hider, forged lower and upper receiver, steel bolt carrier, 12 1/2 in. Templar FastRail, Magpul ACS or MOE stock, Ergo Ambi grip, A2 front sight assembly.

MSR $2,249	$2,025	$1,775	$1,525	$1,375	$1,115	$910	$710	

TEMPLAR TACTICAL ARMS LLC

Previous AR-15 manufacturer located in Bozeman, MT 2008-2014.

RIFLES: SEMI-AUTO

TTA MARK 12 RIFLE – 5.56 NATO/.223 Rem. cal., GIO, 18 in. SPR profile match barrel, billet upper and lower receivers, carbon fiber full floating forend with Picatinny rails on bottom and both sides, full length Swan Sleeve Picatinny rail, front and rear flip-up iron sights, Magpul MOE or Magpul ACS buttstock. Disc. 2014.

Base MSR was $2,150-$2,450.

MSR	100%	98%	95%	90%	80%	70%	60%	Last MSR

TTA 15 TACTICAL – 5.56 NATO/.223 Rem. or 6.8 SPC cal., GIO, 16 in. match barrel, billet upper and lower receivers, front and rear flip-up sights, choice of 10 or 12 in. Daniel Defense full floating rail, collapsible stock, custom models feature single stage trigger, Magpul grip, and Magpul ACS stock. Disc. 2014.

Base MSR was $1,700-$2,000.

TEMPLAR TACTICAL FIREARMS

Current AR-15 style rifle and suppressor manufacturer located in Spring, TX.

RIFLES: SEMI-AUTO

SENESCHAL PRECISION RIFLE – 6.5 Creedmoor or .308 Win. Mag. cal., Defiance Action, free floated match grade Bartlien barrel, stainless steel receiver, McMillan A3-5 fully adj. tactical stock, vertical pistol grip, adj. comb, tapered forend, adj. spacer system, Anschutz Rail, M16 type extractor, Badger Tactical bolt knob, matte Cerakote in Patriot Brown or Coyote Tan.

MSR $5,250	$4,725	$4,150	$3,550	$3,225	$2,600	$2,125	$1,750

Current MSR is for a base model only. Many other calibers, barrels, options, and finishes are available - custom build lead times are 6-8 months.

SERGEANT LONG RANGE HUNTING RIFLE – .308 Win. Mag. cal., Rem. 700 action, free floated medium contour threaded barrel, Tempar Tactical drop bottom magazine, oversized tactical bolt knob, Bell & Carlson Medalist A2 stock, glass bedded in Marine Tex, custom stock texturing, custom Cerakote finish.

MSR $3,400	$3,050	$2,675	$2,300	$2,075	$1,675	$1,375	$1,125

Current MSR is for a base model only. Many other calibers, barrels, options, and finishes are available - custom build lead times are 6-8 months.

TEXAS BLACK RIFLE COMPANY

Current semi-auto rifle manufacturer located in Shiner, TX.

CARBINES: SEMI-AUTO

MODEL 1836 – 5.56 NATO or .300 AAC Blackout cal., AR-15 style, 16 in. chrome lined barrel, TBRC lower and upper receiver with Delta long horn logo, Magpul MOE front and rear sights, 11.4 in. ARS KeyMod lightweight rail, M16 bolt carrier group, CMC Flat Bow trigger, Magpul ACS-L Mil-Spec side storage adjustable stock, MOE trigger guard and grip, Type III hardcoat anodized Mil-Spec finish, commemorates Texas Year of Independence in 1836, 6.6 lbs. New 2014.

MSR $1,559	$1,310	$1,150	$1,040	$875	$750	$625	$525

* **Model 1836L** – 5.56 NATO or .300 AAC Blackout cal., 16 in. barrel, TBRC lower and upper receiver with Delta long horn logo, CMC flat bow trigger, 13.2 in. KeyMod rail, Magpul MOE front and rear sights, MOE trigger guard and grip, Magpul ACS-L stock, hardcoat anodized black finish, 6.65 lbs. New 2015.

MSR $1,569	$1,320	$1,150	$1,040	$875	$750	$625	$525

* **Model 1836XL** – 5.56 NATO or .300 AAC Blackout cal., 16 in. barrel, TBRC lower and upper receiver with Delta long horn logo, CMC flat bow trigger, 15 in. KeyMod rail, Magpul MOE front and rear sights, MOE trigger guard and grip, Magpul ACS-L stock, hardcoat anodized black finish, 6.7 lbs. New 2015.

MSR $1,589	$1,335	$1,160	$1,040	$875	$750	$625	$525

MODEL 1836 MOE – 5.56 NATO cal., 16 in. barrel, Magpul MBUS rear sight, front sight gas block, Magpul MOE handguard, Magpul CTR stock, hardcoat anodized black finish, 9.75 lbs. New 2015.

MSR $995	$850	$725	$650	$585	$515	$450	$395

PISTOLS: SEMI-AUTO

MODEL 1836P – 5.56 NATO cal., AR-15 style, 7 1/2 in. barrel, TBRC upper and lower receiver with Delta long horn logo, CMC flat bow trigger, 7.2 in. ARS lightweight KeyMod rail, Magpul MOE sights, MOE trigger guard and grip, M16 bolt carrier group, black hardcoat anodized finish, commemorates Texas Year of Independence in 1836, 5 lbs. New 2015.

MSR $1,559	$1,310	$1,150	$1,040	$875	$750	$625	$525

MODEL 1836PX – 5.56 NATO cal., 10 1/2 in. barrel, TBRC upper and lower receiver with skull Delta logo, CMC flat bow trigger, ARS 9.6 in. KeyMod lightweight rail, Magpul MOE sights, MOE trigger guard and grip, black hardcoat anodized finish, 5 3/4 lbs. New 2015.

MSR $1,569	$1,320	$1,150	$1,040	$875	$750	$625	$525

MODEL 1836 .300 BLACKOUT – .300 AAC Blackout cal., 8 in. barrel, TBRC upper and lower receiver with skull Delta logo, 7.2 in. ARS lightweight KeyMod rail, CMC flat bow trigger, Magpul MOE sights, MOE trigger guard and grip, black hardcoat anodized finish, 8 1/2 lbs. New 2015.

MSR $1,559	$1,310	$1,150	$1,040	$875	$750	$625	$525

MSR	100%	98%	95%	90%	80%	70%	60%	Last MSR

TEXAS CUSTOM GUNS

Current AR-15 style custom rifle manufacturer located in Alvin, TX since 2009.

RIFLES: SEMI-AUTO

TCG-15 – 5.56 NATO cal., AR-15 style, vanadium alloy Mil-Spec steel barrel, chrome bore and chamber, parkerized finish, threaded muzzle, Mil-Spec trigger, Magpul CTR buttstock, Magpul MOE pistol grip, CNC machined aluminum alloy upper and lower receiver, nickel boron coated parts, M4 extension, free float Mil-Std 1913 rails, Type III hardcoat anodized black finish.

MSR $1,750		$1,485	$1,315	$1,150	$1,025	$875	$750	$615

THOMPSON

Current trademark of pistols and carbines manufactured by Auto Ordnance located in Worcester, MA, and corporate offices in Blauvelt, NY. Auto Ordnance became a division of Kahr Arms in 1999. Dealer and distributor sales.

Auto-Ordnance Corp. manufactures an exact reproduction of the original 1927 Thompson sub-machine gun. They are currently available from Kahr Arms in semi-auto only since production ceased on fully automatic variations (Model 1928 and M1) in 1986 (mfg. 1975-1986 including 609 M1s). All current models utilize the Thompson trademark, are manufactured in the U.S., and come with a lifetime warranty.

CARBINES: SEMI-AUTO

The Auto-Ordnance Thompson replicas listed below are currently supplied with a 15, 20, or 30 shot stick mag. Tommy Guns are not currently legal in CA, CT, or NY.

Add the following for currently manufactured Thompson 1927 A-1 models:

Add $70 for 20 or 30 shot stick mag.

Add $68 for 10 shot stick mag.

Add $193 for 10 shot drum mag. (they resemble the older 50 shot L-type drum) - new 1994.

Add $299 for 50* shot drum mag. or $577 for 100* shot drum mag. (mfg. 1990-93, reintroduced 2006).

Add $92 for Thompson rifle case with logo or $139 for padded rifle case with Thompson logo.

Add $221 for factory violin case or $204 for hard case.

1927 A3 - .22 CAL. – .22 LR cal., 16 or 18 in. finned barrel with compensator, alloy frame and receiver, fixed or detachable walnut stock, pistol grip, and forearm pistol grip, 7 lbs. Disc. 1994.

		$995	$875	$750	$650	$550	$500	$450	*$510*

1927 A5 PISTOL/CARBINE – .45 ACP cal., 13 in. finned barrel, alloy construction, overall length 26 in., 10 (C/B 1994) shot mag., 7 lbs. Disc. 1994.

		$1,050	$925	$825	$750	$650	$600	$500	*$765*

THOMPSON M1 CARBINE (.45 ACP CAL.) – .45 ACP cal., combat model, 16 1/2 in. smooth barrel w/o compensator, 30 shot original surplus mag., side-cocking lever, matte black finish, walnut stock, pistol grip, and grooved horizontal forearm, current mfg. will not accept drum mags., 11 1/2 lbs. New 1986.

MSR $1,329		$1,125	$985	$850	$775	$625	$500	$400

* ***Thompson M1-C Lightweight*** – .45 ACP cal., similar to M1 Carbine, except receiver is made of a lightweight alloy, current mfg. accepts drum mags., 9 1/2 lbs. Mfg. 2001-2002, reintroduced 2005.

MSR $1,241		$1,050	$925	$795	$715	$580	$475	$375

During 2006, this model incorporated a large machined radius on the bottom of the receiver to improve magazine insertion.

THOMPSON 1927 A-1 DELUXE CARBINE – 10mm (mfg. 1991-93) or .45 ACP cal., 16 1/2 in. finned barrel with compensator, includes one 30 shot original surplus mag., current mfg. accepts drum mags., solid steel construction, matte black finish, adj. rear sight, walnut stock, pistol grip, and finger grooved forearm grip, 13 lbs.

MSR $1,461		$1,250	$1,100	$950	$850	$700	$575	$450

Add $410 for 50 round drum, 30 shot mag., and violin case package (new 2015).

Add $715 for detachable buttstock and vertical foregrip with 50 round drum and 30 shot stick mag., or $1,048 with detachable buttstock and vertical foregrip with 100 round drum and 30 shot stick mag. (new 2016).

Add $1,502 for 50 round drum, 20 shot stick mag., and titanium gold plating (new 2016).

Add $449 for detachable buttstock and horizontal foregrip (mfg. 2007-disc).

During 2006, design changes included a more authentic spherical cocking knob, improved frame to receiver fit, and a large machined radius at the bottom of the receiver to help with magazine insertion.

MSR	100%	98%	95%	90%	80%	70%	60%	*Last MSR*

* ***Thompson 1927 A-1C Deluxe Carbine SBR*** – .45 ACP cal., 14 1/2 in. barrel with permanently affixed Cutts Compensator (approved by the BATFE), 20 shot stick mag. New 2016.

| MSR $1,461 | $1,250 | $1,100 | $950 | $850 | $700 | $575 | $450 | |

Add $449 for detachable buttstock and vertical foregrip with 20 shot stick mag.

* ***Thompson 1927 A-1C Lightweight Deluxe*** – .45 ACP cal., similar to 1927 A-1 Deluxe, except receiver made of a lightweight alloy, currently shipped with 30 shot stick mag. (where legal), current mfg. accepts drum mags., 9 1/2 lbs. New 1984.

| MSR $1,325 | $1,125 | $985 | $850 | $765 | $625 | $500 | $425 | |

Add $368 for 100 shot drum mag.

* ***Thompson 1927 A-1 Presentation Walnut Carbine*** – .45 ACP cal., similar to 1927 A-1 Deluxe, except has presentation grade walnut buttstock, pistol grip, and foregrip, supplied with plastic case. Limited mfg. 2003.

| | $850 | $675 | $525 | $425 | $350 | $325 | $295 | *$1,121* |

* ***Thompson 1927 A-1 Deluxe .22 LR Cal.*** – .22 LR cal., very limited mfg., 30 shot mag. standard.

| | $1,100 | $995 | $925 | $800 | $700 | $650 | $575 | |

THOMPSON 1927 A-1 COMMANDO – .45 ACP cal., 16 1/2 in. finned barrel with compensator, 30 shot mag., black finished stock and forearm, parkerized metal, black nylon sling, 13 lbs. New 1997.

| MSR $1,393 | $1,185 | $1,035 | $895 | $800 | $650 | $550 | $450 | |

During 2006, this model incorporated a spherical cocking knob.

THOMPSON – .45 ACP cal., 10 1/2 in. finned barrel, closed bolt, blue metal finish, pistol grip forearm, 30 shot mag., 12 lbs. New 2004.

| MSR $2,114 | $1,795 | $1,575 | $1,350 | $1,225 | $985 | $810 | $650 | |

Add $516 for detachable buttstock and horizontal foregrip (mfg. 2007-disc.) or vertical foregrip and 30 shot stick mag. (new 2016).

This carbine model may only be shipped from the factory to an NFA Class II manufacturer or NFA Class III dealer.

THOMPSON M1 – .45 ACP cal., 10 1/2 in. barrel, closed bolt, blue metal finish, regular forearm, 30 shot mag., 12 lbs. New 2004.

| MSR $2,027 | $1,725 | $1,510 | $1,295 | $1,175 | $950 | $775 | $700 | |

This carbine model may only be shipped from the factory to an NFA Class II manufacturer or NFA Class III dealer.

PISTOLS: SEMI-AUTO

1911 THOMPSON CUSTOM (1911TC) – .45 ACP cal., stainless steel or aluminum (Lightweight model, mfg. 2005-2007) construction, Series 80 design, 5 in. barrel, SA, Thompson bullet logo on left side of double serrated slide, 7 shot mag., grip safety, checkered laminate grips with medallion, skeletonized trigger, combat hammer, low profile sights, 31 1/2 (Lightweight) or 39 oz. New 2004.

| MSR $866 | $730 | $600 | $500 | $415 | $350 | $300 | $275 | |

THOMPSON 1927 A-1 DELUXE – .45 ACP cal., SA, blowback design, 10 1/2 in. finned barrel, grooved walnut forearm with sling swivel, blade front sight, adj. rear sight, 10 or 30 shot mag., also accepts 50 shot drum, 30 shot stick, 10 shot stick, and 100 shot drum magazines, approx. 6 lbs. New 2008.

| MSR $1,418 | $1,200 | $1,050 | $900 | $815 | $660 | $550 | $425 | |

Add $93 for 50 shot mag. (disc.) or $172 for 100 shot drum mag.

Subtract $95 if with 10 round drum.

This model is marked "Model of 1927A-1" and "Thompson Semi-Automatic Carbine" on the left side and Auto-Ordnance Corporation on the right side.

THOMPSON/CENTER ARMS CO., INC.

Current manufacturer established during 1967, and located in Springfield, MA. Previously located in Rochester, NH. Distributor and dealer sales.

On Dec. 18, 2006 Smith & Wesson holding corp. announced that it purchased Thompson Center Arms Co., Inc. During late 2010, Smith & Wesson moved their production to its Springfield, MA facility.

Thompson/Center also has created a custom shop to enable customers to create custom pistols, rifles, shotguns, and muzzleloaders. Please contact the factory for availability and an individualized quotation.

Please refer to the *Blue Book of Modern Black Powder Arms* by John Allen (also online) for more information and prices on Thompson/Center's lineup of modern black powder models.

RIFLES: BOLT ACTION

A recall has been issued for all Venture rifles manufactured prior to October 28, 2011. To determine if your rifle is affected, please visit Smith & Wesson's website: www.smith-wesson.com or call 1-800-713-0356.

MSR	100%	98%	95%	90%	80%	70%	60%	Last MSR

ICON PRECISION HUNTER – .204 Ruger, .223 Rem., .22-250 Rem., .243 Win., 6.5 Creedmoor (mfg. 2010-2011), or .308 Win. cal., 22 in. heavy fluted barrel with 5R button rifling, fat bolt design with tactical style handle, classic varminter style brown synthetic stock with cheekpiece and beavertail forend, detachable 3 shot mag. with single shot adapter, Picatinny rail, adj. trigger, two position safety, sling swivel studs, 8 lbs. Mfg. 2009-2012.

	$900	$775	$675	$575	$475	$425	$350	$1,019

ICON WARLORD – .308 Win. or .338 Lapua cal., 5 or 10 shot mag., hand lapped stainless steel fluted barrel, carbon fiber tactical style stock with adj. cheekpiece, available in OD Green, Flat Black, or Desert Sand, Weather Shield finish on all metal, adj. trigger, Picatinny rail, tactical bolt handle, 12 3/4 - 13 3/4 lbs. Mfg. 2010-2011.

	$3,000	$2,600	$2,200	$1,800	$1,500	$1,250	$1,125	$3,499

THOR

Current trademark manufactured by Thor Global Defense Group, located in Van Buren, AR. Distributed by Knesek Guns, located in Van Buren, AR.

PISTOLS: SEMI-AUTO

THOR 1911 SERIES – .45 ACP cal., 4 1/4 (Carry) or 5 in. (Tactical) barrel, SA, carbon steel Commander frame with bobtail, top slide, front and rear serrations, GI night sights, ambidextrous safety, black Alumagrips, matte black Melonite finish, mfg. in partnership with Guncrafter Industries.

MSR $3,230	$2,750	$2,400	$2,065	$1,875	$1,515	$1,240	$965	

Add $225 for Carry Model.

* **Thor 1911A1** – .45 ACP cal., similar to 1911 Series, except is A1 configuration not hand fitted. Mfg. 2013-2015.

	$715	$625	$535	$485	$395	$325	$250	$840

STEVEN SEAGAL LIMITED EDITION 1911A1 – .45 ACP. cal., black finish, white grips, Steven Seagal signature. Limited mfg. 2014-2015 only.

	$795	$695	$595	$540	$435	$360	$275	$935

RIFLES: BOLT ACTION

THOR M375 – .375 CheyTac cal., advanced long range interdiction system, 30 in. fluted match grade Krieger barrel with removable muzzle brake, 7 shot box mag., 10 in. top rail, carry handle, right or left-hand action, fully adj. hardened aluminum stock with sliding mechanism and adj. monopod, 26 lbs.

MSR $12,600	$10,700	$9,375	$8,025	$7,275	$5,895	$4,825	$3,750	

THOR TR375 – .375 CheyTac cal., similar to M375 Model, except has 29 inch stainless steel barrel and McMillan A5 stock. New 2014.

MSR $8,999	$7,650	$6,695	$5,750	$5,200	$4,200	$3,450	$2,675	

THOR M408 – .408 CheyTac cal., 29 in. fluted barrel, 7 shot mag., no sights, fully adj. aluminum modular stock, M1913 Picatinny rail, integral bipod, muzzle brake, polymer pistol grip, advanced long range interdiction system, 27 lbs.

MSR $12,600	$10,700	$9,375	$8,025	$7,275	$5,895	$4,825	$3,750	

THOR XM408 – .408 CheyTac cal., 30 in. fluted match grade barrel with removable muzzle brake, 5 or 7 shot detachable box mag., 10 in. Mil-Std 1913 upper rail, CNC machined receiver and bolt, adj. hardened aluminum stock with sliding mechanism, adj. mono-pod, black or camo finish, optional advanced shroud assembly, approx. 26 lbs. Disc. 2013.

	$5,850	$5,300	$4,850	$4,350	$3,900	$3,250	$2,650	$5,999

Add $6,000 for advanced shroud assembly.

THOR TR408 – .408 CheyTac cal., 29 in. fluted stainless steel barrel, fluted bolt with tactical bolt knob, Huber Concepts trigger, Harris HBRS bipod, McMillan A5 stock, 7 shot mag., beavertail forearm.

MSR $8,999	$7,650	$6,695	$5,750	$5,200	$4,200	$3,450	$2,675	

THOR TRLA 300 – .300 Win. Mag. cal., lightweight aluminum chassis with folding stock, Surefire SOCOM muzzle brake, Huber Concepts trigger, Harris HBRS bipod.

MSR $5,167	$4,395	$3,850	$3,295	$2,995	$2,400	$1,975	$1,550	

Add $479 for HS Precision chassis.
Add $815 for McMillan A3-5 stock.
Add $1,598 for Cadex chassis.

THOR TRMA338 – .338 Lapua cal., 20 in. barrel, 416R stainless steel action, Surefire muzzle brake, Huber Concepts trigger, lightweight aluminum chassis with folding stock, Harris bipod, one piece bolt, plunger ejector, mini-16 extractor, Picatinny scope rail, accept AI/AW magazines.

MSR $5,167	$4,395	$3,850	$3,295	$2,995	$2,400	$1,975	$1,550	

MSR		100%	98%	95%	90%	80%	70%	60%	Last MSR

THOR TRSA SERIES – .300 AAC Blackout or .308 Win. cal., 16 1/2 (.300 AAC Blackout cal. only), 20 or 24 in. threaded or unthreaded barrel, lightweight aluminum McMillan A3-5 (standard) chassis with folding stock, Surefire SOCOM muzzle brake, Huber Concepts trigger, Harris HBRS bipod.

MSR $5,167	$4,395	$3,850	$3,295	$2,995	$2,400	$1,975	$1,550

Add $200 for .300 AAC Blackout cal.
Add $479 for HS Precision chassis (TRSA-H)
Add $815 for McRees Precision chassis (TRSA-R).
Add $1,598 for Cadex chassis (TRSA-C).

THOR LRIM 338 LM – .338 Lapua cal., 27 in. fluted stainless steel barrel, 416R stainless steel action, Surefire muzzle brake, Huber Concepts trigger, lightweight aluminum chassis with folding stock, adj. monopod, 10 in. rail, 24 lbs. New 2014.

MSR $12,600	$10,700	$9,375	$8,025	$7,275	$5,895	$4,825	$3,750

RIFLES: SEMI-AUTO

THOR TR-15 – 5.56 NATO cal., GPO, 16.1 or 18 (DMR Model) in. barrel, 30 shot mag., detachable carry handle, M4 handguard, variety of Cerakote custom finishes available, with or w/o flash hider and muzzle brake, collapsible Mil-Spec stock, F marked front sight post, flat-top upper receiver, optional THOR rail system.

MSR $1,250	$1,125	$985	$850	$775	$625	$500	$395

Add $250 for THOR rail system.
Add $760 for 18 in. barrel.

* **Thor TR-15 CQB Carbine** – 5.56 NATO cal., GPO, 16.1 in. barrel with Noveske KX3 flash suppressor, 30 shot mag., detachable carry handle, Daniel Defense Omega X12 OFSP quad rail, Troy folding rear battle sight, Magpul MIAD grip, Vltor E-Mod stock, Knight's Armament rear sling swivel mount, black finish. New 2014.

MSR $2,350	$2,125	$1,850	$1,595	$1,450	$1,175	$950	$750

THOR TR-16 SERIES – 5.56 NATO cal., AR-15 style, 16 or 18 in. barrel with permanently attached muzzle brake, unified top rail modular forearm. New 2013.

MSR $2,750	$2,475	$2,165	$1,850	$1,685	$1,360	$1,115	$865

Add $45 for DMR model with 18 inch barrel.

* **Limited Edition Steven Seagal TR-16** – 5.56 NATO cal., 16 in. barrel, black finish, Steven Seagal signature. New 2013.

MSR $2,699	$2,425	$2,125	$1,825	$1,650	$1,335	$1,095	$850

THOR TR-17 SERIES – .308 Win. cal., similar to the TR-16 Series, 16 in. barrel only. New 2013.

MSR $11,800	$10,300	$9,015	$7,725	$7,000	$5,665	$4,635	$3,600

Add $6,650 for TR-17 System package (includes scope, rings, suppressor, bipod, cleaning kit and hard case).

* **Limited Edition Steven Seagal TR-17** – 7.62x51mm cal., 16 in. barrel, black finish, Steven Seagal signature. New 2013.

MSR $2,699	$2,425	$2,125	$1,825	$1,650	$1,335	$1,095	$850

THUNDER-FIVE

Previous trademark manufactured by MIL Inc., located in Piney Flats, TN. Previous company name was Holston Enterprises, Inc. Previously manufactured by Mil, Inc. located in Piney Flats, TN. Previously distributed by C.L. Reedy & Associates, Inc. located in Jonesborough, TN.

REVOLVERS

While previously advertised as the Spectre Five (not mfg.), this firearm was re-named the Thunder-Five.

THUNDER-FIVE – .45 LC cal./.410 bore (T-45) with 3 in. chamber or .45-70 Govt. (T-70 mfg. 1994-98) cal., single or double action, unique 5 shot revolver design permits shooting .45 LC or .410 bore shotshells interchangeably, 2 in. rifled barrel, phosphate finish, external ambidextrous hammer block safety, internal transfer bar safety, combat sights, hammer, trigger, and trigger guard, Pachmayr grips, padded plastic carrying case, 48 oz., serialization started at 1,101. Mfg. 1992-circa 2007.

	$495	$450	$400	$375	$350	$325	$300	*$545*

Sub-caliber sleeve inserts were available until 1998 for 9mm Para., .357 Mag./.38 Spl., and .38 Super cals.

THUREON DEFENSE

Current manufacturer located in New Holstein, WI.

MSR	100%	98%	95%	90%	80%	70%	60%	Last MSR

PISTOLS: SEMI-AUTO

THUREON SA PISTOL – 9mm Para. or .45 ACP cal., same operating system as the SA Carbine. New 2012.

MSR $1,019	$875	$765	$650	$595	$480	$400	$325	

THUREON GA PISTOL – 9mm Para., 357 SIG, .40 S&W, 10mm Auto, or .45 ACP cal., similar to Thureon SA pistol. New 2012.

MSR $1,069	$925	$795	$695	$625	$525	$440	$350	

RIFLES: SEMI-AUTO

Add $15 for M4 telescoping buttstock.
Add $35 for laser/tactical light mount.
Add $75 for open sights nested in sight rail.

THUREON SA CARBINE – 9mm Para. or .45 ACP cal., blowback action, 32 shot mag. (modified Uzi or Colt SMG mag.), AR-15 trigger components, integral Picatinny rail, closed bolt, aluminum upper and lower receivers, adj. buttstock, black finish, approx. 6 1/2 lbs.

MSR $1,143	$1,025	$900	$775	$700	$575	$475	$375	

THUREON GA CARBINE – 9mm Para., .357 SIG, .40 S&W, 10mm Auto, or .45 ACP cal., similar to Thureon SA Carbine, except uses Glock magazines. New 2012.

MSR $959	$875	$775	$650	$600	$475	$400	$325	

Add $40 for 10mm or .357 SIG cal.

TIKKA

Current trademark imported by Beretta U.S.A. Corp., located in Accokeek, MD. Previously imported until 2000 by Stoeger Industries, located in Wayne, NJ. Tikka rifles are currently manufactured by Sako, Ltd. located in Riihimäki, Finland. Previously manufactured by Oy Tikkakoski Ab, of Tikkakoski, Finland (pre-1989).

During 2000, Tikka was purchased by Beretta Holding of Italy. All currently produced Tikkas are imported by Beretta U.S.A. Corp., located in Accokeek, MD.

Also see listings under Ithaca combination guns and bolt action rifles for older models.

RIFLES: BOLT ACTION

About 3,000 rifles sold under the Tikka name have been recalled following catastrophic failures, but a small number of guns sold in the American market remain in the hands of consumers who have apparently not heard about the recall. A weakness in the stainless steel used to manufacture rifles during 2003-2004 has led to ruptured barrels. Consumers are urged to contact the Tikka Recall Center at 800-503-8869 with their rifle's serial number to find out if their firearm is affected.

* **T3 Scout CTR** – .223 Rem. or .308 Win. cal., 20 in. heavy barrel w/o sights, black synthetic stock with built in Monte Carlo cheekpiece, 5 or 6 shot mag., Picatinny rail on receiver. Mfg. 2010-2012.

	$825	$725	$625	$525	$425	$365	$330	*$950*

* **T3 Super Varmint** – .22-250 Rem., .223 Rem., or .308 Win. cal., 23 3/8 in. heavy stainless barrel, 3 or 4 shot mag., laminated synthetic stock with adj. comb, Picatinny rail, extra swivel stud, adj. trigger. Imported 2005-2007.

	$1,250	$1,000	$800	$695	$585	$485	$415	*$1,425*

* **T3 Tactical** – .223 Rem. or .308 Win. cal., T3 action, 20 or 24 (disc. 2007) in. free floating match grade barrel with protected threaded muzzle, 5 shot mag., fiberglass-reinforced copolymer polypropylene stock with adj. comb, wide forearm, Picatinny rail, 7 1/4 lbs. Importation began 2004.

MSR $1,775	$1,550	$1,225	$1,050	$875	$750	$650	$550	

TIPPMAN ARMS CO.

Previous manufacturer located in Fort Wayne, IN.

Tippman Arms manufactured 1/2 scale semi-auto working models of famous machine guns. All models were available with an optional hardwood case, extra ammo cans, and other accessories. Mfg. 1986-1987 only.

RIFLES: REPRODUCTIONS, SEMI-AUTO

MODEL 1919 A-4 – .22 LR cal. only, copy of Browning 1919 A-4 Model, belt fed, closed bolt operation, 11 in. barrel, tripod, 10 lbs.

	$4,750	$4,300	$3,950	$3,600	$3,250	$2,850	$2,350	*$1,325*

MODEL 1917 – .22 LR cal. only, copy of Browning M1917, watercooled, belt fed, closed bolt operation, 11 in. barrel, tripod, 10 lbs.

	$6,375	$6,000	$5,500	$5,000	$4,350	$3,750	$3,250	*$1,830*

MSR		100%	98%	95%	90%	80%	70%	60%	Last MSR

MODEL .50 HB – .22 WMR cal. only, copy of Browning .50 cal. machine gun, belt fed, closed bolt operation, 18 1/4 in. barrel, tripod, 13 lbs.

MSR		100%	98%	95%	90%	80%	70%	60%	Last MSR
		$6,625	$6,400	$5,950	$5,400	$4,950	$4,500	$4,000	$1,929

TOMAHAWK

Current trademark of shotguns manufactured by M&U, located in Konya, Turkey. No current U.S. importation.

M&U manufactures a complete line of hunting and tactical style shotguns under the Tomahawk trademark, including semi-auto, slide action, O/U, SxS, and single barrel configurations. A wide variety of configurations are available, including receiver finishes and stock options. Currently, these guns have had little or no importation into the U.S. Please contact the company directly for more information, including pricing and domestic availability (see Trademark Index).

TORNADO

Currently manufactured by AseTekno located in Helsinki, Finland.

RIFLES: BOLT ACTION

TORNADO MODEL – .338 Lapua Mag. cal., unique straight line design with free floating barrel, 5 shot mag., pistol grip assembly is part of frame, limited importation into the U.S.

The factory should be contacted directly regarding domestic availability and pricing (see Trademark Index).

TRACKINGPOINT

Current bolt action rifle manufacturer established late 2011 and located in Pflugerville, TX, previously located in Austin, TX.

RIFLES: BOLT ACTION

1000-300T (XS2) – .300 Win. Mag. cal., 24 in. Krieger barrel with AAC Blackout 90T muzzle brake, matte black finish, Surgeon Rifles XL long action, Accuracy International AX chassis system with detachable rails, Harris bipod with LaRue quick detach mount, features TrackingPoint's XactSystem with internal scope software and integrated guided trigger and tab button, includes 200 rounds of ammo. Disc. 2014.
Last MSR was $25,000.

1000-300H (XS3) – .300 Win. Mag. cal., 22 in. Krieger threaded barrel with thread protector, matte black finish, Surgeon Rifles XL long action, McMillan A5 stock, Harris bipod with LaRue quick detach mount, features TrackingPoint's XactSystem with internal scope software and integrated guided trigger, includes 200 rounds of ammo. Disc. 2014.
Last MSR was $22,500.

300 NIGHTHAWK – .300 Blackout cal.,16 in. barrel with flash hider, one second target lock time, 2.5 seconds - post - tag, 2 1/2 hours operating time, 2-14X zoom Night vision scope, multiple Picatinny rails, 12 lbs. New.
Current MSR is $6,995 (first 100 guns), standard retail price is $15,490.

BA 300H 750 SERIES – .300 Win. Mag. cal., features similar network tracking scope, guided trigger, and track button in trigger guard as 1000 Series, 26 in. fluted stainless steel barrel, 3 shot, McMillan A5 stock, Harris bipod Larue quick-detach mount, 12 lbs. New mid-2014.
Current MSR on this model is $12,995.

BA 308H 750 SERIES – .308 Win. cal., features same optics and Tracking system as 1000 Series, 26 in. fluted stainless steel barrel, 4 shot, Bell & Carlson stock with Harris bipod and Larue quick detach mount, 12 lbs. New mid-2014.
Current MSR on this model is $12,995.

BA 7MMH 750 SERIES – 7mm Rem. cal., similar optics and tracking system with integrated track button in trigger guard as 1000 Series, 26 in. fluted stainless steel barrel, 3 shot, Bell & Carlson stock, 12 lbs. Mfg. 2014 only.
Last MSR was $9,995.

BA 260 – .260 Rem. cal., 20 in. barrel, features Tag-and-Shoot scope technology, 10 lbs. New 2015.
Current MSR on this model is $7,495.

BA 338LM/XS1 1000 SERIES – .338 Lapua cal., features TrackingPoint's XactSystem with internal scope software and integrated guided trigger and tag button, 27 in. Krieger barrel with AAC Blackout 90T muzzle brake, matte black finish, Surgeon Rifles XL action, box mag., Accuracy International AX chassis system with detachable rails, Harris bipod with LaRue quick detach mount, includes hardshell case and 200 rounds of ammo.
Current MSR on this model is $27,500.

BA 338 LM/XS4 1000 SERIES – .338 Lapua cal., similar to 1000-338T, except has McMillan stock and fluted barrel. New 2014.
Current MSR on this model is $27,500.

MSR	100%	98%	95%	90%	80%	70%	60%	Last MSR

BA 338TP – .338 TP cal., 30 in. barrel, similar Tag-and-Shoot technology as the BA 338 LM, 25 lbs. New 2015.
Current MSR on this model is $49,995.

RIFLES: SEMI-AUTO

AR 300WM – .300 Win. Mag. cal., GIO, long range precision guided firearm features TrackingPoint Networked optics, 16 in. S2W profile chrome moly vanadium steel cold hammer forged barrel with Daniel Defense flash suppressor, 30 shot Magpul PMAG, Mil-Spec lower receiver with enhanced flared magwell and rear receiver QD swivel attachment point, upper receiver with indexing marks and M4 feed ramps, 12 in. Daniel Defense modular float rail, Daniel Defense low profile gas block, TrackingPoint AR Series buttstock, includes integrated Network tracking scope, TriggerLink (electronic connection between tracking optic and guided trigger), HUD (Heads Up Display - the digital display that shows the field of view and more), Tag-and-Shoot (tag button), includes cleaning kit, three batteries and chargers, 15.6 lbs. New late 2014.
Current MSR on this model is $18,995.

The networked tracking scope streams video to Android and iOS smart phones and tablets. Wind speed is the only data you'll manually input to the scope, using a toggle button.

AR 556 – 5.56 NATO cal., similar to AR 300WM, except features mid-length gas system, 12 lbs. New late 2014.
Current MSR on this model is $7,495.

AR 762 – 7.62 NATO cal., 16 in. S2W profile barrel with flash suppressor, low profile gas block, carbine gas system, lower receiver with multiple QD swivel attachment points, upper receiver with indexing marks, two 20 shot PMag. mags., Picatinny rail with rail segments, TrackingPoint AR Series buttstock, includes integrated Network tracking scope, guided trigger, and Tag-and-Shoot (tag button), cleaning kit, three batteries, and chargers, 14.6 lbs. New late 2014.
Current MSR on this model is $14,995.

The networked tracking scope streams video to Android and iOS smart phones and tablets. Wind speed is the only data you'll manually input to the scope, using a toggle button.

SA300 – .300 Win. Mag. cal., 22 in. barrel, 15.6 lbs. New 2015.
Current MSR on this model is $18,995.

TRANSFORMATIONAL DEFENSE INDUSTRIES, INC.

Previous name of a manufacturer of civilian and law enforcement firearms 2008-late 2010 and located in Virginia Beach, VA.

Transformational Defense Industries, Inc. was part of the Gamma Applied Visions Group SA. On Sept. 1, 2010, the company name was changed to Kriss USA. Please refer to the Kriss Systems SA listing for current information.

TRISTAR ARMS INC.

Current importer established in 1994, and located in N. Kansas City, MO. Distributor and dealer sales.

In 2015, the company name changed from TriStar Sporting Arms, Ltd. to TriStar Arms Inc.

PISTOLS: SEMI-AUTO

The following semi-auto pistol variations are manufactured by Canik55 in Turkey.

C-100 – 9mm Para. and .40 S&W cal., DA/SA, 3.7 in. barrel, steel slide, 10 (9mm, disc.), 11 (.40 S&W) or 15 (9mm Para.) shot mag., rear snag-free dovetail sights and fixed blade front sight, black polycoat or chrome finish, black polymer checkered grips, includes two magazines and hard plastic case, 1.53-1.63 lbs. New 2013.

MSR $460	$385	$340	$300	$275	$250	$225	$200	

Add $20 for chrome finish.

T-100 – 9mm Para. cal., DA/SA, 15 shot mag., 3.7 in. barrel, black polymer grips, rear snag-free dovetail and fixed blade front sights, Black Cerakote, Titanium Cerakote (mfg. 2014-2015), or chrome (disc. 2014) finish, includes black plastic case, 1.64 lbs. New 2013.

MSR $460	$385	$340	$300	$275	$250	$225	$200	

Add $20 for chrome (disc. 2014) or Titanium Cerakote (mfg. 2014-2015) finish.

L-120 – 9mm Para. cal., DA/SA, 4.7 in. barrel, 17 shot mag., steel slide, alloy frame, black polymer grips, rear snag-free dovetail and fixed blade front sights, Black Cerakote or chrome finish, includes black plastic case and extra mag., 1.75 lbs. Mfg. 2013-2015.

	$385	$340	$300	$275	$250	$225	$200	$459

Add $20 for chrome finish.

P-100 – 9mm Para. or .40 S&W cal., 3.7 in. barrel, 11 or 15 shot mag., black Cerakote finish, includes two mags., gun lock, cleaning kit, and hard carrying case, 2.3 lbs. New 2015.

MSR $490	$415	$350	$325	$295	$250	$225	$200	

MSR	100%	98%	95%	90%	80%	70%	60%	Last MSR

P-120 – 9mm Para. or .40 S&W (new 2015) cal., DA/SA, 4.7 in. barrel, 14 (.40 S&W) or 17 shot mag., steel slide, alloy frame, black polymer grips, rear snag-free dovetail and fixed blade front sights, Black Cerakote or chrome finish, includes two mags., gun lock, cleaning kit, and black plastic carrying case, 2.6 lbs. New 2013.

| MSR $490 | $415 | $350 | $325 | $295 | $250 | $225 | $200 | |

Add $20 for chrome finish.

S-120 – 9mm Para. cal., DA/SA, 17 shot mag., 4.7 in. barrel, steel frame, steel slide, black polymer grips, rear snag-free dovetail and fixed blade front sights, Black Cerakote or chrome finish, includes extra mag. and black plastic case, 2.26 lbs. New 2013.

| MSR $470 | $400 | $345 | $315 | $285 | $250 | $225 | $200 | |

Add $30 for chrome finish.

T-120 – 9mm Para. cal., DA/SA, full size, 17 shot mag., steel alloy frame, steel slide, 4.7 in. barrel, rail under barrel for laser or flashlight mount, scalloped ridges on slide for better grip, black polymer grips, rear snag-free dovetail and fixed blade front sights, Black Cerakote, Desert Sand Cerakote (new 2014), Titanium Cerakote (new 2014), or chrome (disc. 2014) finish, 1.88 lbs. New 2013.

| MSR $470 | $400 | $345 | $315 | $285 | $250 | $225 | $200 | |

Add $30 for Desert Sand Cerakote (new 2014), Titanium Cerakote (new 2014), or chrome (disc. 2014) finish.

TP-9C – 9mm Para. cal., DA/SA, SFO, 10 shot mag., 3 1/2 in. barrel, polymer, 1.39 lbs. Mfg. 2013 only.

| | $400 | $345 | $315 | $285 | $250 | $225 | $200 | $469 |

SHOTGUNS: SEMI-AUTO

Shim kits and fiber optic sights became standard on all hunting models beginning 2011.

PHANTOM SERIES – 12 ga. only, 3 or 3 1/2 (Phantom Field/Synthetic Mag. only) in. chamber, various VR (except Phantom HP) barrel lengths with choke tubes, available in Field (blue metal finish, gold accents, and checkered walnut stock and forearm), Synthetic (black non-glare matte metal and flat black synthetic stock and forearm), or HP (home security with open sights, matte finished metal, and synthetic stock and forearm), 6 lbs. 13 oz.-7 lbs. 6 oz. Italian mfg., limited importation 2001-2002.

| | $385 | $350 | $315 | $285 | $265 | $245 | $225 | $425 |

Subtract $44 for Phantom Synthetic.
Add $74 for 3 1/2 in. Mag. (Field).
Add $44 for Mag. Synthetic.

RAPTOR A-TAC – 12 ga., 3 in. chamber, gas operated, 20 in. barrel with extended choke, fixed pistol grip black synthetic stock, Picatinny rail, swivel studs, tactical style operating handle, bridge front sight with fiber optic bead, 7 lbs. New 2013.

| MSR $425 | $375 | $325 | $295 | $265 | $235 | $200 | $185 | |

TEC12 – 12 ga., 3 in. chamber, capable of operating in pump or semi-auto mode by the turn of a dial, inertia rotary bolt action, 20 or 28 (mfg. 2013 only) in. barrel with choke tubes, external ported cyl. choke, black synthetic stock with rubber fixed pistol grip plus one set of military sling swivels and swivel studs, matte black finish, Picatinny rail, ghost ring sight and raised front bridge sight with fiber optic bead, 7.2 lbs. New 2013.

| MSR $690 | $585 | $525 | $450 | $395 | $365 | $335 | $295 | |

* **TSA Black 3-1/2 In.** – 12 ga., 3 1/2 in. chamber, twin GPO, 26 (disc. 2015) or 28 in. chrome lined barrel, 5 shot, fiber optic front sight, black stock and forearm, flat black metal finish, 7.4 lbs. New 2012.

| MSR $640 | $565 | $500 | $450 | $415 | $375 | $350 | $325 | |

VIPER G2 SERIES – 12, 20, or 28 (wood stock or silver only) ga., 2 3/4 or 3 in. chamber, gas operated, 24, 26 or 28 in. barrel, choke tubes, 5 shot mag., G2 action became standard 2010, configurations include wood, synthetic, camo, and silver, fiber optic front sight, mag. cut off, vent. rib with matted sight plane, choice of wood, black synthetic, camo, or carbon fiber (disc. 2009) stock, approx. 5.7 - 6.9 lbs. Importation began 2007.

* **Viper G2 Camo** – 12 or 20 ga., 3 in. chamber, 26, 28, or 30 in. VR barrel with 3 Beretta Mobile choke tubes, fiber optic sights, features 100% Realtree Advantage Timber or Realtree Max-4 camo finish, 6.2-6.9 lbs. New 2012.

| MSR $610 | $515 | $450 | $365 | $315 | $275 | $235 | $185 | |

Add $60 for left-hand action (28 in. barrel, Realtree Max-4 only).

* **Viper G2 Youth Camo** – 12 (disc.) or 20 ga., 3 in. chamber, 24, 26 (disc) or 28 (disc.) in. barrel, G2 action became standard during 2010, similar to Viper Series, except has 100% Mossy Oak Duck Blind (disc.), or 100% Realtree Advantage Timber camo coverage, soft touch stock/forearm finish became standard 2011, 6 lbs. New 2008.

| MSR $610 | $515 | $450 | $365 | $315 | $275 | $235 | $185 | |

Add $16 for Viper G2 TW (Turkey/Waterfowl) Model with 12 or 20 ga., 24 or 28 in. barrel (disc.).

MSR	100%	98%	95%	90%	80%	70%	60%	Last MSR

VIPER G2 TACTICAL – 12 ga., 20 in. barrel, matte black finish, fiber optic sights, 5 shot mag., cylinder choke, swivel studs, 6 1/2 lbs. Mfg. 2010-2012.

	100%	98%	95%	90%	80%	70%	60%	Last MSR
	$395	$350	$300	$265	$235	$200	$175	*$444*

SHOTGUNS: SLIDE ACTION

COBRA SERIES – 12 ga. only, 3 in. chamber, various barrel lengths, includes 1-3 choke tubes. Importation began 2007.

* ***Cobra Field Black*** – 12 or 20 (new 2015) ga., 3 in. chamber, 26 or 28 in. barrel with 3 Beretta choke tubes, fiber optic front sight, extended forearm, swivel studs, matte black finish, 5.6-6.9 lbs.

MSR $350	$285	$250	$225	$200	$185	$175	$165	

* ***Cobra Field Camo*** – 12 or 20 ga., 3 in. chamber, 26 or 28 in. barrel, 3 Beretta Mobile choke tubes, fiber optic front sight, extended forearm, swivel studs, Next Micro Print camo finish, 5.6-6.9 lbs. New 2012.

MSR $425	$360	$315	$275	$250	$225	$200	$185	

* ***Cobra Force*** – 12 ga., 3 in. chamber, 18 1/2 (new 2014) or 20 (disc. 2013) in. barrel, one (new 2014) or 2 (disc. 2013) choke tubes, Picatinny rail under forearm and on top of receiver, fiber optic bridge front sight, rear sight, swivel studs, fixed pistol grip stock with soft rubber grip, matte black finish, 6 1/2 lbs.

MSR $400	$335	$295	$260	$240	$220	$200	$185	

* ***Cobra Tactical*** – 12 ga., 3 in. chamber, 18 1/2 (new 2014) or 20 (disc. 2013) in. barrel, spring-loaded forearm, faux extended mag tube, Beretta cyl. choke tube, blade front sight, Picatinny rail under forearm, Black synthetic stock, swivel studs, 6.3 lbs.

MSR $320	$275	$235	$215	$190	$175	$160	$150	

TROMIX CORPORATION

Previous firearms manufacturer established in 1999, and located in Inola, OK. Previously located in Broken Arrow, OK.

Tromix currently offers conversions for Saiga shotguns, as well as accessories and modifications. Please contact the company directly for its current services and conversion pricing (see Trademark Index).

RIFLES: SEMI-AUTO

Tromix manufactured AR-15 style rifles until 2008. Tromix lower receivers bear no caliber designation. Serialization was TR-0001-0405.

The models listed were also available with many custom options.

TR-15 SLEDGEHAMMER – .44 Rem. Mag. (disc. 2001), .440 Cor-Bon Mag., .458 SOCOM, .475 Tremor, or .50 AE cal., GIO, 16 3/4 in. barrel, other lengths and weights available by custom order. Mfg. 1999-2006.

	$1,175	$975	$850	$775	$700	$650	$600	*$1,350*

TR-15 TACKHAMMER – various cals., GIO, 24 in. bull barrel, other lengths and weights were available by custom order. Mfg. 1999-2006.

	$1,175	$975	$850	$775	$700	$650	$600	*$1,350*

SHOTGUNS

Tromix manufactures Class II short barrel shotguns based on the Saiga model. Please contact the company directly for more information (see Trademark Index).

TROY DEFENSE

Current firearms manufacturer located in West Springfield, MA.

Troy Defense, created in 2011, is the firearms division of Troy Industries. Troy is well-known for its high quality accessories, including sights and rails. Troy Defense offers a complete line of AR-15 style rifles for military and law enforcement, as well as some models for the civilian marketplace. A wide variety of options and accessories are available.

CARBINES/RIFLES: SEMI-AUTO

.308 RIFLE – 7.62 NATO cal., 16 in. barrel with Medieval muzzle brake, 20 shot mag., Troy rear folding BattleSight and Troy M4 folding BattleSight, BattleAx Control grip, Troy 13.8 in. Alpha 308 rail, ambidextrous charging handle, black finish only, includes one polymer magazine, 8 1/2 lbs.

MSR $1,499	$1,275	$1,125	$1,025	$875	$750	$625	$525	

5.56 CARBINE – 5.56 NATO cal., GIO, 16 in. barrel with Troy Medieval flash suppressor, 10 or 30 shot mag., forged lower and M4A4 flat-top upper receiver, M4 feed ramps, Mil-Spec trigger, 6-pos. telescoping Troy BattleAx CQB stock, BattleAx control grip, manual safety, 13 in. Alpha rail with integrated front M4 folding sight, Black or FDE finish, 6 1/2 lbs.

MSR $854	$725	$650	$580	$515	$450	$385	$340	

MSR	100%	98%	95%	90%	80%	70%	60%	Last MSR

ALPHA CARBINE – 5.56 NATO cal., AR-15 style, GIO, 16 in. barrel, Pinned Medieval flash suppressor, 30 shot mag., 13 in. Alpha BattleRail with built-in flip-up BattleSight, Troy rear folding BattleSight, Squid grips, PDW stock, black finish, includes Troy BattleMag and Proctor sling, 6 3/4 lbs. New 2015.

MSR $1,299	$1,100	$995	$875	$735	$650	$550	$465

CONQUEROR 3-GUN RIFLE – 5.56 NATO cal., AR-15 style, 18 in. barrel, Geissele Super 3 gun trigger, offset folding Battlesights, Revolution M-LOK carbon fiber BattleRail, black or tan finish. New 2015.

MSR $1,799	$1,525	$1,350	$1,175	$1,050	$900	$775	$625

Add $150 for tan finish.

CQB-SPC A3 CARBINE – 5.56 NATO cal., 16 in. barrel, no sights, forged lower receiver, M4A4 flat-top forged upper, M4 feed ramps, enhanced trigger guard, BattleAx control grip, M4 style 6-pos. stock with Troy markings, black hardcoat anodized finish. New 2015.

MSR $799	$685	$615	$550	$475	$420	$365	$335

CQB-SPC A4 CARBINE – 5.56 NATO cal., 16 in. barrel, Troy Medieval flash suppressor, TRX2 KeyMod BattleRail, Troy folding BattleSights, Troy BattleAx CQB stock and grip, black finish.

MSR $999	$850	$725	$650	$585	$515	$450	$395

DELTA CARBINE – 5.56 NATO cal., GIO, 16 in. barrel with A2 flash suppressor, 30 shot mag., enhanced trigger guard, A2 front fixed and rear fixed BattleSights, M4 6-pos. stock with Troy markings, Troy BattleAx control grip, manual safety, M4 flat-top upper receiver, M4 feed ramps, Black finish, 6 lbs.

MSR $1,099	$925	$850	$725	$625	$550	$475	$425

GAU-5/A/A – 5.56 NATO cal., 12 1/2 in. barrel with 4 1/2 in. permanently attached flash suppressor, 30 shot mag., A1 front sight, A1 drum rear, carbine handguard with single heat shield, includes small arms sling, black finish. Limited mfg. beginning 2016.

MSR $1,199	$1,025	$925	$800	$685	$595	$515	$440

This firearm replicates the weapon used by the Son Tay Raiders in the largest rescue attempt of American POWs. Portions of the proceeds for this model will go directly to the National League of POW/MIA families.

M5 9mm RIFLE – 9mm Para. cal., 16 in. barrel, Troy Medieval flash suppressor, designed for Glock magazines, Troy front and rear BattleSights, TRX3 Revolution rail, black finish, includes a built-in shell deflector. New 2016.

MSR $1,299	$1,100	$995	$875	$735	$650	$550	$465

M10A1 CSASS RIFLE – 7.62 NATO cal., AR-15 style, 16 in. heavy fluted barrel with 3-prong flash suppressor, 20 shot mag., ambidextrous mag. release, one polymer mag., nickel boron bolt carrier group, Geissele G2S trigger, Troy 45 Degree Offset folding sights, ambidextrous safety selector, Troy 15 in. 308 KeyMod rail, ambi charging handle, IC sling with two QD swivels, includes mount and Atlas bipod, tan finish only, 9 lbs.

MSR $3,045	$2,585	$2,250	$1,840	$1,575	$1,300	$1,100	$950

M10A1 GOVERNMENT CARBINE – 7.62 NATO cal., 16 in. heavy fluted match barrel, 3-prong flash hider with suppressor mount, includes one 20 shot polymer mag., rear folding and front folding M4 BattleSights, ambi charging handle, ambi safety selector, Geissele G2S trigger, Troy Alpha rail, Squid grips, BattleAx CQB stock, black finish only, 8 3/4 lbs.

MSR $2,399	$2,050	$1,800	$1,500	$1,300	$1,075	$935	$795

PROCTOR CARBINE – 5.56 NATO cal., GIO, 16 in. match grade barrrel, 30 shot mag., enhanced trigger guard, match grade CMC trigger, rear folding and front folding M4 Tritium BattleSights, Troy BattleAx CQB buttstock, BattleAx control grip, manual safety, M4A4 flat-top upper receiver, M4 feed ramps, 13 in. enhanced Troy Alpha rail, includes Proctor sling, 3 Troy BattleMags, and BattleSight adjustment tool, hardcoat anodized black or tan finish, 6 lbs.

MSR $1,749	$1,485	$1,315	$1,150	$1,025	$875	$750	$615

Add $150 for Tan finish.

SDMR – 5.56 NATO cal., AR-15 style, 16 in. match grade barrel, Troy suppressor mount pronged flash hider, 30 shot mag., Geissele trigger, nickel boron bolt carrier group, BattleAx control grip, 15 in. SDMR rail, Troy rear folding BattleSight and Troy front folding M4 Tritium BattleSight, SDMR BattleRail, BattleAx stock, black finish, includes Troy IC sling and two QD swivels, and two Troy BattleMags, 7 lbs.

MSR $1,299	$1,100	$995	$875	$735	$650	$550	$465

SGM LAMB CARBINE – 5.56 NATO cal., M-LOK BattleRail, Geissele trigger, black or tan finish.

MSR $1,749	$1,485	$1,315	$1,150	$1,025	$875	$750	$615

Add $150 for Tan finish.

MSR	100%	98%	95%	90%	80%	70%	60%	Last MSR

VTAC 308 CARBINE – .308 Win. cal., 16 in. fluted match grade barrel, 3-prong flash hider with suppressor mount, 13 in. Troy M-LOK BattleRail, Geissele Super V trigger, Troy 45 Degree Offset folding BattleSights, black or tan finish. New 2015.

	MSR $2,350	$2,000	$1,750	$1,475	$1,350	$1,100	$900	$750

Add $149 for Tan finish.

PISTOLS

P7A1 PISTOL – 5.56 NATO cal., semi-auto, 7 1/2 in. barrel, Claymore muzzle brake, utilizes proprietary patent pending spring and bolt carrier system, heavy duty latch assembly, Troy folding BattleSights, 7.2 in. Troy Alpha rail, black finish. New 2015.

	MSR $999	$850	$725	$650	$585	$515	$450	$395

PUMP ACTION PISTOL – .223 Rem. or .300 AAC Blackout cal., 10 in. Melonite barrel, Troy Claymore muzzle brake, 10 shot mag., rear folding and front folding M4 BattleSights, Alpha-style aluminum handguard with full top rail, standard trigger, BattleAx control grip, includes one Troy BattleMag, black finish, 5 lbs. New 2015.

	MSR $679	$575	$500	$435	$365	$325	$280	$265

RIFLES: SLIDE ACTION

TROY NATIONAL PAR (PUMP ACTION RIFLE) – .223 Rem. or .300 AAC Blackout cal., 16 in. barrel, double chamber muzzle brake, Troy front and rear folding BattleSights, 5-position stock, black finish. New 2015.

	MSR $1,099	$925	$850	$725	$625	$550	$475	$425

TROY OPTICS READY – .223 Rem., .300 AAC Blackout, .308 Win., 7mm-08 Rem. (new 2016), .243 Win. (new 2016), or .338 Federal (new 2016) cal., 16 or 18 (new 2016) in. barrel, with or w/o Troy BattleSights, TRX2 Alpha-Style rail (18 in. models come standard with carbon fiber rails), Troy lightweight BattleAx CQB stock, black finish. New 2015.

	MSR $799	$685	$615	$550	$475	$420	$365	$335

Add $100 for Troy BattleSights.

TROY MOSSY OAK EXCLUSIVE – .338 Federal cal., 18 in. stainless steel barrel, TRX2 carbon fiber Alpha-style rail, Mossy Oak Shadow Grass Blades finish. New 2016.

	MSR $1,199	$1,025	$925	$800	$685	$595	$515	$440

TRUVELO ARMOURY

Current manufacturer located in Midrand, South Africa. Truvelo Armoury is a division of Truvelo Manufacturers (Pty) Ltd.

Truvelo Armoury entered into the field of barrel and rifle manufacturing in 1994. The success of the manufacturing of highly accurate barrels led to the development of a combination of their own barrel range and sophisticated sniper rifle technology. The result of this combination is Truvelo's range of highly accurate, long range rifles with calibers up to 20x110 Hispano. The Truvelo range of rifles is called the Counter Measure Sniper Rifle (CMS). The CMS was developed for Urban Type Warfare at a shorter range. The rifles are compact and allow for easy maneuverability. The stock is foldable and the rifle lighter. While Truvelo's Midrand plant is home to proven technology, its designs also match space age material with classical lines. The combination of the right steel, the manufacturing process of the barrel, the bolt action and the fitment of the barrelled action into an ergonomically designed stock ensure unsurpassed accuracy. As a result, CMS rifles are lightweight, adjustable and accurate. Truvelo Armory also previously manufactured the Neostead shotgun, the BXP 9mm Tactical pistol, and various custom hunting and sporting rifles. Please contact the factory directly for more information, delivery time and availability (see Trademark Index).

NOTES

U SECTION

U.S. GENERAL TECHNOLOGIES, INC.

Previous manufacturer located in S. San Francisco, CA circa 1994-96.

MSR	100%	98%	95%	90%	80%	70%	60%	Last MSR

RIFLES: SEMI-AUTO

P-50 SEMI-AUTO – .50 BMG cal., includes 10 shot detachable mag., folding bipod, muzzle brake, matte black finish. Mfg. 1995-96.

	100%	98%	95%	90%	80%	70%	60%	Last MSR
	$5,600	$4,950	$4,475	$3,975	$3,500	$3,050	$2,600	$5,995

U.S. MACHINE GUN ARMORY LLC

Current rifle manufacturer established in the late 1990s, located in Sandy, UT. Previous company name was Practical Defense International.

RIFLES: SEMI-AUTO

U.S. Machine Gun Armory LLC also manufactures the MGA SAW line of military machine guns for military and law enforcement.

MGA MK46/48 MC – 5.56 NATO, 5.45x39mm, 6.8 SPC, or .308 Win. cal., belt fed, closed bolt rifle, utilizes standard H&K G3 style trigger pack, adj. tactical style stock, vertical pistol grip, carry handle, Picatinny top rail, MK48 Model has tripod mount and MOD 1 bipod as standard, Desert Tan finish. New 2014.

MSR $11,998	$10,800	$9,450	$8,100	$7,350	$5,950	$4,875	$3,775	

Add $3,670 for MK48 configuration.

MGA M249 – 5.56 NATO cal., belt fed, closed bolt, M16 magwell, forward tripod bushing, lower Picatinny rail adapter system, barrel heat shield, adj. tactical style stock, forward rec. quick detach sling system, M249-style top cover with rail and adj. iron sight, H&K hammer and standard H&K G3 style trigger packs.

MSR $10,298	$9,265	$8,100	$6,950	$6,300	$5,095	$4,175	$3,250	

U.S. ORDNANCE

Current manufacturer and distributor located in Reno, NV. Commercial sales through Desert Ordnance, located in Sparks, NV.

U.S. Ordnance is licensed by Saco Defense to be the exclusive manufacturer and distributor for the M60 Series machine gun and spare parts.

RIFLES: SEMI-AUTO

U.S. Ordnance manufactures semi-auto reproductions (BATFE approved) of the M-60/M-60E3 (MSR is POR), M60E4/Mk43 (MSR $12,500-$13,000, new 2004). Previous models included the .303 Vickers (last MSR was $4,500 w/o tripod), Browning M-1919 (last MSR was $1,995), and the M-1919A4 (last MSR was $2,095). These belt fed variations are machined to military specifications, and have a 5 year warranty. Please contact the distributor directly for more information, including pricing and availability (see Trademark Index).

USAS 12

Previous trademark manufactured by International Ordnance Corporation located in Nashville, TN circa 1992-95. Previously manufactured (1990-91) by Ramo Mfg., Inc. located in Nashville, TN. Previously distributed by Kiesler's Wholesale located in Jeffersonville, IN until 1994. Originally designed and previously distributed in the U.S. by Gilbert Equipment Co., Inc. located in Mobile, AL. Previously manufactured under license by Daewoo Precision Industries, Ltd. located in South Korea.

SHOTGUNS: SEMI-AUTO

USAS 12 – 12 ga. only, gas operated action available in either semi or fully auto versions, 18 1/4 in. cylinder bore barrel, closed bolt, synthetic stock, pistol grip, and forearm, carrying handle, 10 round box or 20 round drum mag., 2 3/4 in. chamber only, parkerized finish, 12 lbs. Mfg. 1987-1995.

	$1,500	$1,250	$1,050	$925	$850	$750	$650	$995

Add $300-$500 for extra 20 shot drum magazine (banned by the BATFE).

Values above are for a semi-auto model. This model is currently classified as a destructive device and necessary federal NFA Class III transfer paperwork must accompany a sale.

UMAREX SPORTWAFFEN GmbH & Co. KG.

Current firearms, airguns, air soft, and signal pistol manufacturer established in 1972 as Uma Mayer Ussfeller GmbH, with headquarters located in Arnsberg, Germany. Firearms are currently imported by Walther Arms located in Fort Smith, AR.

Initially, the company manufactured tear gas and signal pistols for eastern bloc countries, and then started producing air rifles. After acquiring Reck Sportwaffen Fabrick Karl Arndt, the company was reorganized under the Umarex name.

Umarex purchased Walther during 1993, and also manufactures ammunition, optics, and accessories. During 2006,

MSR	100%	98%	95%	90%	80%	70%	60%	*Last MSR*

Umarex purchased Hämmerli, and production equipment was moved from Lenzburg, Switzerland to Ulm, Germany. During mid-2006, Umarex purchased RUAG Ammotec USA Inc., and moved the company to Fort Smith, AR, and the company's name was changed to Umarex USA. During 2008, Colt Industries licensed Umarex to manufacture the Colt AR-15 in .22 LR cal. During 2009, H&K licensed Umarex to manufacture replicas in .22 LR cal. During 2011, Colt Industries licensed Umarex to manufacture a Govt. 1911-A1 Model in .22 LR cal. In late 2011, IWI licensed Umarex to manufacture a .22 LR copy of the UZI carbine and pistol. These guns were previously imported exclusively by Umarex USA located in Fort Smith, AR until 2013. During late 2012, Umarex and Carl Walther GmbH Sportwaffen announced the formation of Walther Arms, Inc. to import, sell, and market all Walther products in the U.S. beginning Jan. 1, 2013, except the P22 and PK380 models.

Please refer to the Colt, H&K, Hämmerli, Regent (trademark only), UZI, and Walther listings for information and values on currently imported firearms. For more information on currently manufactured (beginning circa 1984) Umarex airguns, including many major U.S. trademark mfg. under license, please refer to the *Blue Book of Airguns* by Dr. Robert Beeman & John Allen (also online).

UNERTL ORDNANCE COMPANY, INC.

Previous manufacturer located in Las Vegas, NV circa 2004-2006.

Unertl Ordnance Company manufactured a .45 ACP cal. semi-auto pistol in various configurations, including MEU (SOC) $2,795 last MSR, UCCP $2,195 last MSR, and the DLX $2,195 last MSR. The company also manufactured the UPR bolt action sniper rifle in .308 Win. cal. Last MSR was $5,900.

UNIQUE-ALPINE

Current manufacturer established in 2002, located in Bavaria, Germany, with manufacturing sites in Germany and Switzerland. No current U.S. importation.

RIFLES: BOLT ACTION

TPG-1/TPG-2/TPG-3 A1/A4 (TACTICAL PRECISION GEWEHR) – various cals. (TPG-1/TPG-2), TPG3 -A1 is chambered in .308 Win., .300 Win. Mag., or .338 Lapua Mag. cal., 20, 24, or 26 in. match grade free floating fluted barrel with muzzle brake, 8 or 10 shot mag., full length Picatinny rail, modular interchangeable rifle system allows for transfer from single shot to magazine fed rifle, tactical adj. and detachable (TPG3-A1 or TPG3-A4) stock available in right-hand or Universal configuration and a variety of colors and camo, adj. palm rest, accessory rails. 15 lbs. (TPG-3 A1).

A wide variety of options are available on these models. Please contact the company directly for more information, including options, pricing, and U.S. availability (see Trademark Index).

UNIVERSAL FIREARMS

Previous manufacturer located in Hialeah, FL 1958-1987. Previous company name was Bullseye Gunworks, located in Miami, FL. The company moved to Hialeah, FL in 1958 and began as Universal Firearms.

Universal Firearms M1 carbines were manufactured and assembled at the company's facility in Hialeah starting in the late 1950s. The carbines of the 1960s were mfg. with available surplus GI parts on a receiver subcontracted to Repp Steel Co. of Buffalo, NY. The carbines of the 1970s were mfg. with commercially manufactured parts due to a shortage of GI surplus. In 1983, the company was purchased by Iver Johnson Arms of Jacksonville, AR, but remained a separate division as Universal Firearms in Hialeah until closed and liquidated by Iver Johnson Arms in 1987.

PISTOLS: SEMI-AUTO

MODEL 3000 ENFORCER PISTOL – .30 Carbine cal., walnut stock, 11 1/4 in. barrel, 17 3/4 in. overall, 15 and 30 shot. Mfg. 1964-83. Also see listing under Iver Johnson.

	100%	98%	95%	90%	80%	70%	60%
Blue finish	$450	$375	$325	$275	$235	$200	$185
Nickel-plated	$500	$425	$350	$295	$250	$235	$220
Gold-plated	$500	$425	$350	$275	$250	$225	$200
Stainless	$600	$550	$450	$350	$275	$225	$195

Add $50 for Teflon-S finish.

RIFLES: SEMI-AUTO, CARBINES

1000 MILITARY – .30 Carbine cal., "G.I." copy, 18 in. barrel, satin blue finish, birch stock. Disc.

	100%	98%	95%	90%	80%	70%	60%
	$375	$325	$275	$235	$200	$180	$170

MODEL 1003 – 16, 18, or 20 in. barrel, .30 M1 copy, blue finish, adj. sight, birch stock, 5 1/2 lbs. Also see listing under Iver Johnson.

	100%	98%	95%	90%	80%	70%	60%	*Last MSR*
	$375	$325	$275	$235	$200	$180	$170	*$203*

* Model 1010 – nickel finish, disc.

	100%	98%	95%	90%	80%	70%	60%
	$425	$375	$325	$275	$235	$200	$180

MSR	100%	98%	95%	90%	80%	70%	60%	Last MSR

* Model 1015 – gold electroplated, disc.

Add $45 for 4X scope.

| | $425 | $375 | $325 | $275 | $235 | $200 | $180 | |

1005 DELUXE – .30 Carbine cal., custom Monte Carlo walnut stock, high polish blue, oil finish on wood.

| | $425 | $365 | $325 | $275 | $235 | $200 | $180 | |

1006 STAINLESS – .30 Carbine cal., stainless steel construction, birch stock, 18 in. barrel, 6 lbs.

| | $475 | $425 | $375 | $325 | $275 | $235 | $200 | *$234* |

1020 TEFLON – .30 Carbine cal., DuPont Teflon-S finish on metal parts, black or grey color, Monte Carlo stock.

| | $425 | $375 | $325 | $275 | $235 | $200 | $180 | |

1025 FERRET A – .256 Win. Mag. cal., M1 Action, 18 in. barrel, satin blue finish, birch stock, 5 1/2 lbs.

| | $400 | $350 | $300 | $265 | $235 | $200 | $175 | *$219* |

2200 LEATHERNECK – .22 LR cal., blowback action, 18 in. barrel, birch stock, satin blue finish, 5 1/2 lbs.

| | $350 | $300 | $250 | $215 | $185 | $170 | $160 | |

5000 PARATROOPER – .30 Carbine cal., metal folding extension or walnut stock, 16 or 18 in. barrel.

| | $550 | $475 | $400 | $350 | $295 | $250 | $225 | *$234* |

5006 PARATROOPER STAINLESS – similar to 5000, only stainless with 18 in. barrel only.

| | $650 | $575 | $500 | $425 | $350 | $285 | $250 | *$281* |

1981 COMMEMORATIVE CARBINE – .30 Carbine cal., "G.I Military" model, cased with accessories. Mfg. for 40th Anniversary 1941-1981.

| | $700 | $625 | $550 | $475 | $400 | $325 | $275 | |

USA TACTICAL FIREARMS

Current manufacturer located in Statesville, NC.

USA Tactical Firearms currently manufactures rifles, parts, and components for the AR-15 market. They also offer training classes. Please contact the company directly for more information on all their products and services (see Trademark Index).

PISTOLS: SEMI-AUTO

USA Tactical Firearms currently manufactures the USATF AR-15 Pistol . Please contact the manufacturer directly for more information including pricing and availability (see Trademark Index).

RIFLES: SEMI-AUTO

MODEL USA-15 PACKAGE A – .223 Rem./5.56 NATO cal., GIO, 16 in. M4 barrel, pinned and welded muzzle brake, multi-caliber lower receiver, flat-top upper receiver with removable carry handle, A2 front sight, single stage trigger, carbine length Picatinny handguard with covers, standard 6-position stock with buttpad, Sniper pistol grip, 10 shot mag., includes black hard case.

| MSR $1,499 | $1,350 | $1,175 | $1,025 | $925 | $750 | $625 | $500 | |

* Model USA-15 Package B – .223 Rem./5.56 NATO cal., similar to Package A, except features 16 in. H-Bar barrel.

| MSR $1,649 | $1,475 | $1,300 | $1,100 | $1,000 | $825 | $675 | $525 | |

* Model USA-15 Package C – .223 Rem./5.56 NATO cal., similar to Package A, except features single rail gas block with flip-up front sight.

| MSR $1,539 | $1,375 | $1,200 | $1,025 | $950 | $750 | $625 | $500 | |

MODEL USA-15 PACKAGE D – 7.62x39mm cal., GIO, 16 in. H-Bar barrel, pinned and welded muzzle brake, flat-top upper receiver with removable carry handle, A2 front sight, single stage trigger, carbine length Picatinny handguard with covers, standard 6-position stock with buttpad, Sniper pistol grip, 10 shot mag., includes black hard case.

| MSR $1,688 | $1,525 | $1,350 | $1,150 | $1,050 | $850 | $675 | $550 | |

UA ARMS (USELTON ARMS INC)

Current manufacturer located in Franklin, TN. Previously located in Madison, TN. Company name was changed during 2015.

PISTOLS: SEMI-AUTO, SINGLE ACTION

Beginning 2014, standard features include (except Mil-Spec model): 3-dot Novak front and rear sights, front and rear cocking serrations, high ride beavertail grip safety, IA parts ceramic coated, stainless steel parts, brushed polished bead blast, G10 black grips with medallion, classic solid or 3-hole trigger, 25 LPI front and rear checkering, one magazine, and soft case.

Damascus slides are POR on all models.

Add $119 for compact night sights or $129 for adj. compact sights.

MSR	100%	98%	95%	90%	80%	70%	60%	Last MSR

100 YEAR ANNIVERSARY 1911 LIMITED EDITION – .45 ACP cal., Officer or Government Model frame, case colored frame, mirror polished slide with fire blue accents, G10 grips, special laser engraving, limited to 100 of each type, match sets also available. Disc. 2013.

| | $3,150 | $2,750 | $2,375 | $2,150 | $1,725 | $1,425 | $1,100 | *$3,700* |

Add $300 for Government Model.

CARRY CLASSIC – .45 ACP cal., 4 1/4 in. barrel, stainless steel frame, black slide, smooth Uselton grips, skeletonized hammer and trigger, Novak low profile sights, checkered front strap, 7 shot mag., 34 oz. Disc. 2013.

| | $2,295 | $2,000 | $1,725 | $1,550 | $1,250 | $1,050 | $800 | *$2,700* |

CLASSIC NATIONAL MATCH – .45 ACP cal., Commander (4 1/4 in. barrel) or Government (5 in. barrel) style frame, 8 shot mag., Cerakote/blue finish, various grip styles available, checkered front strap, stainless steel frame, combat hammer, beavertail grip safety, 40 oz.

| MSR $2,599 | $2,200 | $1,925 | $1,650 | $1,495 | $1,200 | $995 | $775 | |

Add $200 for Commander Match.

COMPACT CLASSIC – .45 ACP cal., 3 1/2 in. barrel, 7 shot mag., available in black finish with stainless steel slide, all stainless, or blue finish with stainless slide, with or w/o Bobtail, approx. 32 oz. Disc. 2013.

| | $2,375 | $2,050 | $1,775 | $1,615 | $1,300 | $1,075 | $825 | *$2,800* |

* **Compact Classic Companion** – similar to Compact Classic, except is available in .357 SIG or .40 S&W cal., 32 oz.

| | $2,375 | $2,050 | $1,775 | $1,615 | $1,300 | $1,075 | $825 | *$2,800* |

COMPACT CLASSIC OFFICER – .45 ACP cal., 3 1/2 in. barrel, 7 shot mag., diamond checkered rosewood grips, beaver tail grip safety, 32 oz. Disc. 2011.

| | $2,850 | $2,500 | $2,150 | $1,950 | $1,575 | $1,275 | $1,000 | *$3,150* |

MATCH CLASSIC BOBTAIL – .45 ACP cal., 4 1/4 in. barrel, Bobtail stainless steel frame and polished stainless steel slide, 8 shot, extended safety, combat hammer, skeletonized trigger, checkered metal mainspring housing, 35 oz.

| | $2,425 | $2,125 | $1,815 | $1,650 | $1,325 | $1,095 | $850 | *$2,840* |

COMPACT MATCH – .45 ACP cal., 3 1/2 in. match grade barrel, available with stainless steel frame and slide or integrated aluminum (IA) frame and stainless steel slide, 8 shot, G10 grips, brushed stainless and Armor coat finish, 25-34 oz. New 2014.

| MSR $2,799 | $2,375 | $2,075 | $1,775 | $1,625 | $1,300 | $1,075 | $825 | |

Add $600 for integrated aluminum frame and stainless steel slide.

COMMANDER MATCH – .45 ACP cal., Commander style frame, 4 1/4 in. barrel, 8 shot mag., available in all stainless steel, or integrated aluminum (IA) frame (new 2014) with stainless steel slide, G10 grips, combat hammer, beavertail grip safety, brushed stainless and Armor coat finish, 28-40 oz.

| MSR $2,799 | $2,375 | $2,075 | $1,775 | $1,625 | $1,300 | $1,075 | $825 | |

Add $600 for integrated aluminum (IA) frame and stainless steel slide (new 2014).

GOVERNMENT MATCH – .45 ACP cal., Government style frame, 5 in. barrel, 8 shot mag., available in all stainless steel, integrated aluminum (IA) frame (new 2014) with stainless steel slide, or IA frame with IA slide (new 2014), G10 grips, combat hammer, beavertail grip safety, brushed stainless and Armor coat finish, 28-40 oz.

| MSR $2,599 | $2,200 | $1,925 | $1,650 | $1,500 | $1,200 | $1,000 | $800 | |

Add $900 for integrated aluminum (IA) frame and stainless steel slide (new 2014).
Add $1,100 for integrated aluminum (IA) frame and IA slide (new 2014).

DOUBLE STACK RACE GUN – .38 Super, 9mm Para., .40 S&W, or .357 SIG cal., stainless steel slide, double stack mag. Disc. 2011.

| | $2,725 | $2,395 | $2,050 | $1,850 | $1,500 | $1,225 | $950 | *$3,200* |

MIL-SPEC – .45 ACP cal., 5 in. barrel, black or blued slide, Government match frame, Armor coat finish.

| MSR $2,299 | $1,950 | $1,700 | $1,475 | $1,325 | $1,075 | $875 | $685 | |

Add $600 for integrated aluminum (IA) model with stainless steel slide, or $800 for IA slide.

IA MIL-SPEC GOVERNMENT MATCH – .45 ACP cal., 5 in. barrel, Government match integrated aluminum (IA) frame with IA or stainless steel slide, G10 grips, Armor coat finish, 28 oz. New 2014.

| MSR $2,899 | $2,475 | $2,175 | $1,850 | $1,685 | $1,350 | $1,125 | $900 | |

Add $200 for integrated aluminum (IA) frame and IA slide.

TAC RAIL – .45 ACP cal., 5 in. barrel, 8 shot mag., stainless steel or Cerakote finish, available in Black Maxx, Custom Cote 1, Custom Cote 2, or Custom Cote 3 configurations, accessory under rail, approx. 44 oz.

| | $2,375 | $2,050 | $1,775 | $1,615 | $1,300 | $1,075 | $825 | *$2,800* |

Add $100 for Cerakote finish.

MSR	100%	98%	95%	90%	80%	70%	60%	Last MSR

COMPACT TACTICAL – .45 ACP cal., 3 1/2 in. barrel, Cerakote finish, 8 shot mag., skeletonized trigger, combat hammer, stainless steel frame, G10 grips, beavertail grip safety, Novak low profile sights, Picatinny rail, brushed stainless and UA Armor coat finish, 44 oz.

MSR $2,899	$2,475	$2,175	$1,850	$1,685	$1,350	$1,125	$900	

P.U.G. COMPACT TACTICAL – .45 ACP cal., compact frame, 3 1/2 in. barrel, P.U.G. (personal utility gun) available in all stainless steel or integrated aluminum frame with stainless steel slide, G10 grips, brushed stainless and Armor coat finish. New 2014.

MSR $3,599	$3,050	$2,675	$2,300	$2,075	$1,675	$1,375	$1,075	

COMMANDER TACTICAL – .45 ACP cal., Commander style frame, 4 1/4 in. barrel, 8 shot mag., skeletonized trigger, combat hammer, stainless steel frame with stainless steel slide, or integrated aluminum (IA) frame with stainless slide (new 2014), G10 grips, beavertail grip safety, Novak low profile sights, Picatinny rail, brushed stainless and UA Armor coat finish, 44 oz.

MSR $2,899	$2,475	$2,175	$1,850	$1,685	$1,350	$1,125	$900	

Add $600 for IA frame with stainless steel slide (new 2014).

GOVERNMENT TACTICAL – .45 ACP cal., Government style frame, 5 in. barrel, 8 shot mag., skeletonized trigger, combat hammer, stainless steel frame and slide or integrated aluminum (IA) frame with stainless steel slide, G10 grips, beavertail grip safety, Novak low profile sights, Picatinny rail, brushed stainless and UA Armor or Ceramic Armor coat finish, 44 oz.

MSR $2,699	$2,295	$2,000	$1,725	$1,550	$1,250	$1,050	$800	

Add $900 for IA frame with stainless steel slide.

CQR GOVERNMENT TACTICAL – .45 ACP cal., 5 in. barrel, 8 shot mag., close quarter rail (CQR), integrated aluminum (IA) frame and IA slide, G10 grips, 3 dot Novak front and rear sights, front and rear cocking serrations, high ride beavertail grip safety, UA Armor coat finish, 28-44 oz. New 2014.

MSR $3,799	$3,225	$2,825	$2,425	$2,195	$1,775	$1,450	$1,125	

COMMANDER RECON – .45 ACP cal., 4 1/4 in. barrel with or without threading, 8 shot, available in all stainless steel or integrated aluminum (IA) frame with stainless steel slide, 30-39 oz. New mid-2014.

MSR $3,699	$3,150	$2,750	$2,375	$2,150	$1,750	$1,425	$1,100	

Add $200 for IA frame with stainless steel slide.

RIFLES: BOLT ACTION

WARRIOR MOUNTAIN LITE – 7.82/.308 Warbird cal., Warrior Mountain Lite action (new 2013), 26 in. medium contour stainless steel barrel with six flutes and removable muzzle brake, M16 extractor, Black carbon Kevlar or high grade walnut stock, drilled and tapped for scope mounts, other options are available, 6 lbs. 14 oz.

MSR $4,300	$3,875	$3,400	$2,900	$2,625	$2,125	$1,750	$1,375	

Walnut stock is POR.

Add $490 for armor coat finish on barrel and action.

* **Predator Mountain Lite** – .220 Swift cal., similar to Warrior Mountain Lite, except features 24 in. stainless steel barrel.

MSR $4,300	$3,875	$3,400	$2,900	$2,625	$2,125	$1,750	$1,375	

Add for walnut stock - POR.

* **Raptor Mountain Lite** – .270 Win. cal., similar to Warrior Mountain Lite, except features 24 in. stainless steel barrel.

MSR $4,300	$3,875	$3,400	$2,900	$2,625	$2,125	$1,750	$1,375	

Add for walnut stock - POR.

* **Stalker Mountain Lite** – 7mm Rem. Mag. cal., otherwise similar to Warrior Mountain Lite.

MSR $4,300	$3,875	$3,400	$2,900	$2,625	$2,125	$1,750	$1,375	

Add for walnut stock - POR.

* **Stealth Mountain Lite** – .300 Win. Mag. cal., otherwise similar to Warrior Mountain Lite.

MSR $4,300	$3,875	$3,400	$2,900	$2,625	$2,125	$1,750	$1,375	

Add for walnut stock - POR.

WARRIOR LITE TACTICAL LONG RANGE – 7.82/.308 Warbird Lazzeroni cal., 26 in. stainless steel button rifled and fluted barrel with removable muzzle brake, one-piece helical cut bolt, carbon Kevlar stock, 5 shot mag., Black matte finish, 10 1/2 lbs.

MSR $5,400	$4,850	$4,250	$3,650	$3,300	$2,675	$2,175	$1,700	

MSR	100%	98%	95%	90%	80%	70%	60%	Last MSR

RIFLES: SEMI-AUTO

BLACK WIDOW A3 MODEL – 5.56 NATO/.223 Rem. cal., GPO, 16 in. barrel with door jammer flash suppressor, round counter mag., adj. sight, Magpul CTR 6-position stock, quad rail with front grip, Flat Dark Earth finish.

MSR $3,200	$2,875	$2,500	$2,150	$1,950	$1,575	$1,295	$1,000	

* ***Black Widow A4 Model*** – 7.62 NATO/.308 Win. cal., 18 in. barrel with door jammer flash suppressor, otherwise similar to Black Widow A3 Model.

	$2,350	$2,050	$1,775	$1,600	$1,300	$1,050	$825	*$2,600*

UTAS

Current shotgun manufacturer located in Antalya, Turkey. The UTS-15 is currently manufactured by UTAS-USA, located in Des Plaines, IL.

SHOTGUNS: SEMI-AUTO

XTR-12 – 12 ga., 3 in. chamber, gas operated with rotating bolt, 18.7 in. barrel with muzzle, 2, 5, 7, or 10 shot mag., sights are optional, 5-position telescopic stock, integrated quad Picatinny rail, 8-position sling attachment housing, standard Cerakote black or optional Burnt Bronze, Flat Dark Earth, OD Green, or Tungsten finish, approx. 8 lbs. New 2015.

MSR $1,099	$995	$875	$800	$725	$625	$550	$475	

Add $100 for optional finishes.
Add $138 for front and rear sights.

SHOTGUNS: SLIDE ACTION

UTS-15 – 12 ga., 3 in. chamber, slide action shotgun, bullpup configuration, 18 1/2 in. barrel threaded for Beretta-style choke tubes, 7 shot, no sights, bullpup configuration with pistol grip, unique design utilizes two 7 shot alternately feeding or selectable mag.tubes with selector switch, 100% polymer receiver, top Picatinny rail, choice of black (UTS-15), Hunting Camo (UTS-15 Hunting), Desert Camo (UTS-15 Desert), or corrosion resistant Marine finish (UTS-15 Marine, disc.), choice of black (UTS-15), Hunting Camo (UTS-15 Hunting), Muddy Girl camo (UTS-15 Muddy Girl), OD Green (UTS-15 OD Green), Sand (UTS-15 Desert, disc. 2015), or Blue Camo (UTS-15 Marine, with corrosion resistant satin nickel plating on metal parts, disc. 2015), Flat Dark Earth, Tungsten, or Bronze finish, 6.9 lbs. Mfg. by UTAS in Turkey beginning late 2012.

MSR $1,099	$995	$875	$750	$625	$575	$525	$475	

Add $100 for OD Green, Sand (disc.), Bronze, FDE, or Tungsten finish.
Add $200 for Hunting Camo or Muddy Girl Camo finish.
Add $400 for Blue Camo finish with satin nickel plating on metal parts (disc.).

UZI

Current trademark manufactured by Israel Weapon Industries (IWI, previously called Israel Military Industries) and Carl Walther Sportwaffen GmbH (.22 cal. pistols/rifles only). Centerfire semi-auto pistols are currently imported beginning 2013 by IWI US, Inc., located in Harrisburg, PA. .22 cal. Uzi pistols and rifles are currently imported by Walther Arms, Inc. USA, located in Fort Smith, AR. Uzi America, a partnership between IWI and Mossberg, is currently importing a 9mm Para. and .40 S&W cal. submachine gun carbine built on the mini-Uzi receiver for the law enforcement market. During 1996-1998, Mossberg imported the Uzi Eagle pistols. These models were imported by UZI America, Inc., subsidiary of O.F. Mossberg & Sons, Inc. Previously imported by Action Arms, Ltd., located in Philadelphia, PA until 1994.

Serial number prefixes used on Uzi Firearms are as follows: "SA" on all 9mm Para. semi-auto carbines Models A and B; "45 SA" on all .45 ACP Model B carbines; "41 SA" on all .41 AE Model B carbines; "MC" on all 9mm Para. (only cal. made) semi-auto mini-carbines; "UP" on 9mm Para. semi-auto Uzi pistols, except Eagle Series pistols; and "45 UP" on all .45 semi-auto Uzi pistols (disc. 1989). There are also prototypes or experimental Uzis with either "AA" or "AAL" prefixes - these are rare and will command premiums over values listed below.

CARBINES/RIFLES: SEMI-AUTO

CARBINE MODEL A – 9mm Para. or .45 ACP (very rare) cal., semi-auto, 16.1 in. barrel, parkerized finish, 25 shot mag., mfg. by IMI 1980-1983 and ser. range is SA01,001-SA037,000.

	$1,650	$1,475	$1,325	$1,125	$975	$875	$750	

Approx. 100 Model As were mfg. with a nickel finish. These are rare and command considerable premiums over values listed above.

MSR	100%	98%	95%	90%	80%	70%	60%	Last MSR

CARBINE MODEL B – 9mm Para., .41 Action Express (new 1987), or .45 ACP (new 1987) cal., semi-auto carbine, 16.1 in. barrel, baked enamel black finish over phosphated (parkerized) base finish, 16 (.45 ACP), 20 (.41 AE) or 25 (9mm Para.) shot mag., metal folding stock, includes molded case and carrying sling, 8.4 lbs. Mfg. 1983 - until Federal legislation disc. importation 1989 and ser. range is SA037,001-SA073,544.

| | $1,500 | $1,325 | $1,200 | $1,000 | $950 | $850 | $750 | $698 |

Subtract approx. $150 for .41 AE or .45 ACP cal.
Add $150 for .22 LR cal. conversion kit (new 1987).
Add $215 for .45 ACP to 9mm Para./.41 AE conversion kit.
Add $150 for 9mm Para. to .41 AE (or vice-versa) conversion kit.
Add $215 for 9mm Para. to .45 ACP conversion kit.

MINI CARBINE – 9mm Para. cal., similar to Carbine except has 19 3/4 in. barrel, 20 shot mag., swing-away metal stock, scaled down version of the regular carbine, 7.2 lbs. New 1987. Federal legislation disc. importation 1989.

| | $2,375 | $2,175 | $1,850 | $1,600 | $1,350 | $1,150 | $995 | $698 |

UZI RIFLE – .22 LR cal., patterned after the Uzi Carbine Model B, 17.9 in. barrel with faux suppressor, blowback semi-auto action, features metal receiver, folding stock, traditional Uzi handguard, hidden Picatinny rail, adj. front and rear sights, grip safety, 10 or 20 shot mag., black finish, 7.7 lbs. Importation by Umarex began 2012.

| MSR $599 | $525 | $450 | $400 | $360 | $310 | $280 | $260 | |

PISTOLS: SEMI-AUTO

UZI PISTOL – 9mm Para. or .45 ACP (disc.) cal., 4 1/2 in. barrel, SA, parkerized finish, 10 (.45 ACP) or 20 (9mm Para.) shot mag., supplied with molded carrying case, sight adj. key and mag. loading tool, 3.8 lbs. Importation disc. 1993.

| | $1,000 | $875 | $795 | $750 | $700 | $650 | $600 | $695 |

Add $285 for .45 ACP to 9mm Para./.41 AE conversion kit.
Add $100 for 9mm Para. to .41 AE conversion kit.
Add approx. 30%-40% for two-line slide marking "45 ACP Model 45".

UZI .22 CAL. PISTOL – .22 LR cal., patterned after the Uzi centerfire pistol, blowback semi-auto action, 5 in. barrel with muzzle brake slots on top, black metal receiver, lower Picatinny rail, adj. sights, grip safety, 20 shot mag., 3.9 lbs. Importation by Umarex USA began 2012.

| MSR $499 | $440 | $385 | $340 | $300 | $275 | $250 | $225 | |

UZI EAGLE SERIES – 9mm Para., .40 S&W, or .45 ACP cal., DA/SA, various configurations, matte finish with black synthetic grips, 10 shot mag. Mfg. 1997-1998.

* *Uzi Eagle Series Full-Size* – 9mm Para. or .40 S&W cal., 4.4 in. barrel, steel construction, decocking feature, Tritium night sights, polygonal rifling. Imported 1997-98.

| | $485 | $440 | $400 | $365 | $335 | $330 | $275 | $535 |

* *Uzi Eagle Series Short Slide* – 9mm Para., .40 S&W, or .45 ACP cal., similar to Full-Size Eagle, except has 3.7 in. barrel. Imported 1997-98.

| | $485 | $440 | $400 | $365 | $335 | $330 | $275 | $535 |

Add $31 for .45 ACP cal.

* *Uzi Eagle Series Compact* – 9mm Para. or .40 S&W cal., available in double action with decocking or double action only, 3 1/2 in. barrel. Imported 1997-98.

| | $485 | $440 | $400 | $365 | $335 | $330 | $275 | $535 |

* *Uzi Eagle Series Polymer Compact* – 9mm Para. or .40 S&W cal., similar to Compact Eagle, except has compact polymer frame. Imported 1997-98.

| | $485 | $440 | $400 | $365 | $335 | $330 | $275 | $535 |

UZI PRO PISTOL – 9mm Para cal., blowback operation, closed bolt, 4 1/2 in. Mil-Spec cold hammer forged CrMoV barrel, SA, matte black finish, includes 20 and 25 shot mag., polymer pistol grip lower, firing pin block, thumb operated manual safety, approx. 3 2/3 lbs. Importation began 2013.

| MSR $1,109 | $950 | $825 | $700 | $600 | $525 | $450 | $400 | |

Add $200 for side folding stabilizing brace.

NOTES

V SECTION

VM HY-TECH LLC

Previous rifle manufacturer located in Phoenix, AZ.

MSR	100%	98%	95%	90%	80%	70%	60%	Last MSR

RIFLES

VM15 – .223 Rem. or 9mm Para. cal., AR-15 style, semi-auto, 16, 20, or 24 in. fluted and ported Wilson barrel, unique side charging on left side of receiver operated by folding lever which does not limit mounting/placement of optics, aluminum free floating handguard, forged lower receiver, A2 style buttstock with pistol grip, black finish. Mfg. 2002-2009.

	100%	98%	95%	90%	80%	70%	60%	Last MSR
	$800	$750	$675	$600	$550	$500	$400	*$865*

Add $34 for side charging loading (new 2005).
Add $310 for 9mm Para. cal.

VM-50 – .50 BMG cal., single shot, 18, 22, 30, or 36 in. Lothar Walther barrel with muzzle brake, aluminum stock, includes bipod, black finish, 22-29 lbs. Mfg. 2004-2009.

	100%	98%	95%	90%	80%	70%	60%	Last MSR
	$2,300	$2,000	$1,775	$1,600	$1,475	$1,350	$1,225	*$2,299*

Add $40-$120 for 22-36 in. barrel.

VALKYRIE ARMS LTD.

Current manufacturer located in Olympia, WA. Dealer sales.

Valkyrie Arms Ltd. manufactures custom suppressors made to order. Previously, Valkyrie Arms manufactured the DeLisle 2000, Browning M1919-SA and the DeLisle Sporter Carbine.

PISTOLS: SEMI-AUTO

M3A1 GREASE GUN – faithful reproduction of the original using USGI parts, 8 in. barrel, new and improved design.

MSR $1,450	100%	98%	95%	90%	80%	70%	60%
	$1,325	$1,200	$1,050	$950	$775	$625	$500

STEN MKII – modified AR-15 parts, one piece S-7 tool steel hardened firing pin, similar to original, semi-gloss baked on "GunKoat 2300" finish.

MSR $1,250	100%	98%	95%	90%	80%	70%	60%
	$1,050	$925	$795	$715	$580	$475	$375

RIFLES: SEMI-AUTO

M3A1 GREASE GUN – faithful reproduction using USGI parts, new and improved design, 16 1/2 in. barrel, collapsible stock.

MSR $1,550	100%	98%	95%	90%	80%	70%	60%
	$1,395	$1,250	$1,095	$975	$800	$675	$525

STEN MKII CARBINE – modified AR-15 parts, one piece S-7 tool steel hardened firing pin, similar to original, semi-gloss baked on "GunKoat 2300" finish.

MSR $1,450	100%	98%	95%	90%	80%	70%	60%
	$1,325	$1,200	$1,050	$950	$775	$625	$500

DELISLE COMMANDO CARBINE – reproduction of WWII original, uncheckered wood stock and forearm, parkerized finish, sling swivels, optional dummy suppressor.

MSR $2,495	100%	98%	95%	90%	80%	70%	60%
	$2,125	$1,850	$1,595	$1,450	$1,175	$950	$750

VALMET, INC.

Previous manufacturer located in Jyvaskyla, Finland. Previously imported by Stoeger Industries, Inc. located in South Hackensack, NJ.

The Valmet line was discontinued in 1989 and replaced by Tikka in 1990. Please refer to Tikka in the T section.

RIFLES: SEMI-AUTO

Magazines for the following models are a major consideration when purchasing a Valmet semi-auto rifle, and prices can run anywhere from $85 (.223 Rem.) up to $250 (.308 Win.). Model 76 .308 mags. will function in a Model 78, but not vice versa.

M-62S TACTICAL DESIGN RIFLE – 7.62x39 Russian cal., semi-auto version of Finnish M-62, 15 or 30 shot mag., 16 5/8 in. barrel, gas operated, rotary bolt, adj. rear sight, tube steel or wood stock. Mfg. 1962-disc.

	100%	98%	95%	90%	80%	70%	60%
	$2,500	$2,250	$1,750	$1,500	$1,250	$1,000	$900

Add approx. $200 for tube stock.

M-71S – similar to M-62S, except .223 Rem. cal., stamped metal receiver, reinforced resin or wood stock.

	100%	98%	95%	90%	80%	70%	60%
	$1,650	$1,450	$1,325	$1,175	$975	$875	$775

MSR	100%	98%	95%	90%	80%	70%	60%	Last MSR

MODEL 76 – .223 Rem., 7.62x39mm, or .308 Win. cal., gas operated semi-auto tactical design rifle, 16 3/4 in. or 20 1/2 (.308 only) in. barrel, 15 or 30 (7.62x39mm only) shot mag., parkerized finish. Federal legislation disc. importation 1989.

Plastic Stock	$1,500	$1,250	$1,100	$900	$800	$700	$600	
Wood Stock	$1,700	$1,300	$1,100	$900	$800	$700	$600	*$740*

Add approx. 10% for folding stock.
Add 100% for 7.62x39mm cal. with wood stock.
Add 20% for wood stock in .308 Win. cal.

MODEL 78 – .223 Rem., 7.62x39mm, or .308 Win. cal., similar to Model 76, except has 24 1/2 in. barrel, wood stock and forearm, and barrel bipod, 11 lbs. New 1987. Federal legislation disc. importation 1989.

	100%	98%	95%	90%	80%	70%	60%	Last MSR
	$1,750	$1,525	$1,375	$1,175	$950	$825	$700	*$1,060*

Add 10% for 7.62x39mm cal.

MODEL 82 BULLPUP – .223 Rem. cal., limited importation.

	100%	98%	95%	90%	80%	70%	60%
	$1,675	$1,425	$1,200	$995	$775	$650	$525

VALOR ARMS

Current rifle manufacturer established in 1997, located in Akron, OH.

CARBINES: SEMI-AUTO

OVR-16 – various cals. including 5.56 NATO and 6.5 Grendel, AR-15 style, GIO, 16.1 in. barrel, 30 shot mag., black Valorite coated stainless steel, single stage match trigger, six or eight (includes ambi-sling adapter) position adj. stock, rifle length forearm, free floating quad rail standard, flat-top receiver with Picatinny rail continuing into quad rail, ergonomic soft rubber grip with battery storage, with or w/o sight package, approx. 8 lbs.
  Base price on this model starts at $2,350.
  Add $200 for iron sight package.
  Add $300 for .264 LBC-AR cal.
  Add $700 for Designated Marksmen Rifle (DMR).

VALTRO

Current trademark established during 1988 manufactured by Italian Arms, located in Collebeato, Brescia, Italy. Currently imported by Valtro USA, located in Hayward, CA. Previously located in San Rafael, CA.

Valtro manufactures both excellent quality slide action and semi-auto shotguns, in addition to a very high quality semi-auto pistol, and a variety of signal pistols. Currently Valtro USA is importing only semi-auto pistols. Please contact them directly for more information and availability (see Trademark Index listing).

PISTOLS: SEMI-AUTO

1998 A1 .45 ACP – .45 ACP cal., forged National Match frame and slide, 5 in. barrel, SA, deluxe wood grips, 8 shot mag., ambidextrous safety, blue finish, flat checkered mainspring housing, front and rear slide serrations, beveled magwell, speed trigger, 40 oz., lifetime guarantee. Very limited importation.

	100%	98%	95%	90%	80%	70%	60%
	$5,500	$5,200	$4,950	$4,650	$4,250	$3,850	$3,500

SHOTGUNS: SLIDE ACTION

TACTICAL 98 SHOTGUN – 12 ga. only, 18 1/2 or 20 in. barrel featuring MMC ghost ring sights and integral muzzle brake, 5 shot mag., internal chokes, receiver sidesaddle holds 6 exposed rounds, pistol grip or standard stock, matte black finish, lightweight. Imported 1998 - disc.

	100%	98%	95%	90%	80%	70%	60%
	$790	$630	$525	$475	$425	$400	$360

PM5 – 12 ga., 20 in. barrel, 7 shot mag., black synthetic stock with matte black finish, available with or w/o ghost ring sights, optional folding stock. Limited importation.

	100%	98%	95%	90%	80%	70%	60%
	$995	$900	$800	$725	$650	$575	$500

AM5 – 16 ga., 20 in. barrel, 7 shot mag., black synthetic stock with matte black finish, ghost ring sights, optional folding stock. Limited importation.

	100%	98%	95%	90%	80%	70%	60%
	$995	$900	$800	$725	$650	$575	$500

VAN DYKE RIFLE DESIGNS

Current rifle manufacturer located in Plainville, KS.

RIFLES: BOLT ACTION

Van Dyke Rifle Designs manufactures bolt action rifles in a variety of configurations, with many options available. Prices listed represent base rifles w/o optics or available options. Please contact the company directly for more information on the variety of available options for each rifle, as well as custom made rifles (see Trademark Index).

MSR	100%	98%	95%	90%	80%	70%	60%	Last MSR

DECISION MAKER – .308 Win. cal., 25 in. Shilen stainless steel match grade barrel, Teflon coated Earth Tan desert camo finish, A-4 McMillan tactical stock with saddle cheekpiece, three baffle muzzle brake.

| MSR $3,425 | $3,085 | $2,700 | $2,315 | $2,095 | $1,695 | $1,395 | $1,075 | |

TACTICAL ELIMINATOR SUPER MAGNUM – .338 Lapua cal., Shilen match grade barrel, advanced muzzle brake, designed for extreme range, wide variety of options available.

Base price on this model is POR.

M24 SUPER MAGNUM – .338 Lapua cal., 28 1/2 or 30 in. Shilen stainless steel free floating barrel, custom chamber dimension, aluminum bedding block, many options available including rail systems, optics, muzzle brakes, trigger types and stock.

Base price on this model is POR.

REAPER CUSTOM SNIPER – various cals., Shilen stainless steel barrel, Reaper stock design includes aluminum bedding block, three-way adj. buttpad, adj. cheekpiece, long or short action, various options available.

| MSR $3,495 | $3,150 | $2,750 | $2,350 | $2,150 | $1,725 | $1,425 | $1,100 | |

AI TACTICAL ELIMINATOR I/II – .308 Win. cal., Rem. 700 short action, 22 (Eliminator I) or 24 (Eliminator II) in. Shilen stainless steel match barrel, black matte Teflon finish, multibaffled muzzle brake, Accuracy International stock with adj. cheekpiece and adj. LOP, 5 or 10 shot mag., five sling attachments.

| MSR $3,725 | $3,360 | $2,950 | $2,525 | $2,285 | $1,850 | $1,525 | $1,175 | |

Subtract $30 for Eliminator II.

* ***AI Tactical Eliminator III*** – similar to Eliminator I & II, except has Rem. long action, Magnum calibers, longer barrel length.

| MSR $3,775 | $3,400 | $2,975 | $2,550 | $2,325 | $1,875 | $1,525 | $1,195 | |

DISTANCE DOMINATOR I/II – various cals., Rem. 700 long action, 26 in. Shilen stainless steel barrel (I) or match grade barrel with heavy varmint benchrest contour (II), muzzle brake, H-S Precision heavy Kevlar tactical stock, adj. LOP, variety of options, including floorplate, detachable box mag., and optics.

| MSR $3,580 | $3,225 | $2,820 | $2,425 | $2,200 | $1,775 | $1,450 | $1,125 | |

Subtract $90 for Distance Dominator II.

RANGEMASTER SERIES – various cals., designed for long range target shooting.

* ***Rangemaster I*** – M70 short action, controlled round push feed, Shilen stainless steel match grade free floating barrel, glass pillar bedded A4 McMillan tactical stock, adj. cheekpiece, adj. spacer system, sling swivels, deep forend, various finishes.

| MSR $3,450 | $3,100 | $2,710 | $2,325 | $2,125 | $1,700 | $1,400 | $1,075 | |

* ***Rangemaster II*** – M70 short action, controlled round push feed, 24 in. Shilen stainless steel match grade heavy varmint barrel, stainless bead blast natural texture finish, muzzle brake, A2 McMillan tactical stock, vertical pistol grip, extra high comb, tapered forend, adj. cheekpiece, various finish and available optics.

| MSR $3,475 | $3,125 | $2,735 | $2,350 | $2,125 | $1,725 | $1,400 | $1,100 | |

* ***Rangemaster III*** – Rem. 700 long action, 26 in. Shilen stainless steel match grade light varmint benchrest contour barrel, triple baffle muzzle brake, bead blast natural stainless color with Teflon silver matte finish, box mag., A3 McMillan lightweight tactical stock, adj. cheekpiece, adj. spacer system, vertical pistol grip, various options available.

| MSR $3,375 | $3,050 | $2,675 | $2,285 | $2,075 | $1,675 | $1,375 | $1,075 | |

* ***Rangemaster IV*** – similar to Rangemaster III, 30 in. Shilen stainless steel barrel, A5 McMillan tactical stock, wider beavertail forend, adj. cheekpiece, Teflon OD green finish, double baffle semi-box muzzle brake, box mag., various options available.

| MSR $3,575 | $3,225 | $2,825 | $2,425 | $2,200 | $1,775 | $1,450 | $1,125 | |

DISINTEGRATOR – various varmint cals., Rem. 700 short action, based on the Anschütz Silhouette design, 26 in. stainless steel light varmint match grade barrel, Teflon black matte finish, H-S Precision black/grey web stock, double baffle muzzle brake, blind mag., two sling swivels, various options and optics available.

| MSR $2,795 | $2,525 | $2,225 | $1,900 | $1,725 | $1,395 | $1,125 | $885 | |

LONG RANGE HUNTER – various cals., Rem. 700 long action, 26 in. Shilen stainless steel sporter weight barrel, McMillan BDL style stock, Magna Port muzzle brake, bolt sleeved, glass pillar bedded, various optical options.

| MSR $3,095 | $2,785 | $2,435 | $2,100 | $1,895 | $1,525 | $1,250 | $975 | |

VECTOR ARMS, INC.

Current tactical rifle, pistol, and parts manufacturer located in N. Salt Lake, UT.

MSR	100%	98%	95%	90%	80%	70%	60%	Last MSR

PISTOLS: SEMI-AUTO

Currently, Vector Arms is offering Uzi pistols with a five year warranty.

UZI STYLE PISTOL – 9mm Para or .45 ACP cal., full size copy of Uzi pistol, parkerized or stainless steel finish, ported barrel, back plate sling swivel.

MSR $900	$800	$700	$600	$550	$475	$425	$375	

Add $59 for .45 ACP cal. Add $295 for stainless steel.

MINI UZI STYLE PISTOL – 9mm Para. cal. only, parkerized finish or stainless steel, scaled down size.

MSR $1,299	$1,175	$1,030	$875	$800	$675	$550	$450	

Add $100 for stainless steel.

V-51 PISTOL – .308 Win. cal., 9 in. barrel, gun-coating, flash hider, butt cap, sling swivel, SEF metal lower.

MSR $1,429	$1,275	$1,125	$950	$875	$700	$575	$475	

V-52 PISTOL – 7.62x39mm cal., 9 in. barrel, butt with sling swivel, flash hider and SUO lower, powder coated, 75 shot drum mag. or 30 shot clip mag. Disc. 2012.

	$1,450	$1,275	$1,095	$985	$800	$650	$510	$1,699

V-53 PISTOL – .308 Win. cal., 9 in. barrel, gun-coating, flash hider, butt cap, sling swivel, SUO polymer lower.

MSR $1,429	$1,275	$1,125	$950	$875	$700	$575	$475	

V-94/V-94S PISTOL – 9mm Para. cal., 5.9 (V94S) or 9 in. barrel, SUO lower, flash hider, butt cap, sling swivel

MSR $2,299	$1,950	$1,700	$1,465	$1,325	$1,075	$880	$685	

Add $100 for V-94S.

RIFLES: SEMI-AUTO

Until 2009, Vector Arms offered the following semi-auto tactical style rifles: V-53 (semi-auto version of the HK53 - $1,350 last MSR), V51 (semi-auto version of the HK-91, $1,024 last MSR). Vector also offered the RPD (drum or belt fed - $1,999 last MSR).

UZI STYLE RIFLE – 9mm Para. or .45 ACP cal., parkerized finish or stainless steel, fixed, folding, or side fold stock.

MSR $900	$800	$700	$600	$550	$475	$425	$375	

Add $295 for stainless steel.

MINI UZI STYLE RIFLE – 9mm Para. or .45 ACP cal., parkerized finish or stainless steel, fixed, folding, or side fold stock, scaled down frame.

MSR $1,299	$1,175	$1,030	$875	$800	$675	$550	$450	

Add $100 for stainless steel.

UZI STYLE SBR – 9mm Para. cal. only, parkerized finish, short barrel rifle configuration.

MSR $1,000	$900	$775	$675	$600	$525	$450	$395	

AK47 STYLE RIFLE – 7.62x39mm cal., AK-47 design with stamped receiver and fixed or underfolding wood or polymer stock.

MSR $895	$800	$700	$600	$550	$475	$425	$395	

V-93 RIFLE – .223 Rem. cal., semi-auto version of the HK33, fixed or collapsible stock.

MSR $1,229	$1,100	$975	$850	$750	$650	$550	$450	

Add $200 for collapsible stock.

V-94 RIFLE – 9mm Para. cal., 16 in. barrel, SUO lower, no flash hider.

MSR $2,299	$1,950	$1,700	$1,465	$1,325	$1,075	$880	$685	

VEKTOR

Current trademark established during 1953 as part of LEW (Lyttelton Engineering Work). In 1995, Vektor became a separate division of Denel of South Africa.

Vektor has manufactured a wide variety of firearms configurations, including semi-auto pistols, bolt action and slide action rifles, as well as military arms for South African law enforcement for quite some time. Currently, the company does not make any civilian small arms.

PISTOLS: SEMI-AUTO

All Vektor pistols featured polygonal rifling, excluding the Z88.

MODEL CP1 – 9mm Para. cal., 4 in. barrel, compact model with unique aesthetics and ergonomic design allowing no buttons or levers on exterior surfaces, hammerless, striker firing system, black or nickel finished slide, 10 shot mag., approx. 25 1/2 oz. Imported 1999-2000.

	$440	$400	$360	$330	$300	$280	$260	$480

Add $20 for nickel slide finish.

This model was recalled due to design problems.

MSR	100%	98%	95%	90%	80%	70%	60%	Last MSR

MODEL Z88 – 9mm Para. cal., double action, patterned after the M92 Beretta, 5 in. barrel, steel construction, black synthetic grips, 10 shot mag., 35 oz. Importation began 1999.

| | $550 | $495 | $450 | $400 | $360 | $330 | $295 | $620 |

MODEL SP1 – 9mm Para. cal., double action, 5 in. barrel with polygonal rifling, wraparound checkered synthetic grips, matte blue or normal black finish, 2.2. lbs. Imported 1999-disc.

| | $535 | $485 | $445 | $395 | $360 | $330 | $295 | $600 |

Add $30 for natural anodized or nickel finish.

Add $230 for Sport Pistol with compensated barrel.

* **Model SP1 Compact (General's Model)** – similar to Model SP1, except is compact variation with 4 in. barrel, 25.4 oz. Importation began 1999.

| | $575 | $510 | $460 | $410 | $360 | $330 | $295 | $650 |

* **Model SP1 Sport Pistol/Tuned** – similar to Model SP1, except is available with tuned action or target pistol features. Importation began 1999.

| | $1,050 | $900 | $775 | $650 | $525 | $400 | $350 | $1,200 |

Add $100 for Target Pistol with dual color finish.

MODEL SP2 – .40 S&W cal., otherwise similar to Model SP1. Importation began in 1999.

| | $575 | $510 | $460 | $410 | $360 | $330 | $295 | $650 |

Add $190 for 9mm Para. conversion kit.

* **Model SP2 Compact (General's Model)** – similar to Model SP2, except is compact variation. Importation began 1999.

| | $575 | $510 | $460 | $410 | $360 | $330 | $295 | $650 |

* **Model SP2 Competition** – competition variation of the Model SP2 featuring 5 7/8 in. barrel, additional magazine guide, enlarged safety levers, mag. catch, and straight trigger, 35 oz. Importation began 2000.

| | $850 | $775 | $675 | $575 | $510 | $460 | $395 | $1,000 |

STOCK GUN – 9mm Para. cal., normal black finish. Importation began 2000.

| | $850 | $775 | $675 | $575 | $510 | $460 | $395 | $1,000 |

ULTRA MODEL – 9mm Para. or .40 S&W (new 2000) cal., top-of-the-line double action with most performance features, optional Lynx (disc. 1999) or Tasco (new 2000) scope. Importation began 1999.

| | $1,950 | $1,700 | $1,500 | $1,300 | $1,100 | $900 | $700 | $2,150 |

Subtract $150 if w/o Tasco scope.

RIFLES: SLIDE ACTION

H5 – .223 Rem. cal., 18 or 22 in. barrel, rotating bolt, uncheckered forearm and thumbhole stock with pad, includes 4X scope with long eye relief, 9 lbs. 7 oz.-10 1/4 lbs. Imported 2000-disc.

| | $775 | $650 | $575 | $510 | $460 | $410 | $350 | $850 |

VEPR

Current trademark manufactured by Molot JSC (Vyatskie Polyany Machine Building Factory) located in Russia. Currently imported beginning 2014 by I.O., Inc., located in Palm Bay, FL, Krebs Custom, located in Wauconda, IL, Mach 1 Arsenal, located in Maryville, TN, and beginning in 2013 by Molot USA, located in Walnut Creek, CA. Previously imported by ZDF Import/Export, Inc., located in Salt Lake City, UT. Previously imported during 2004 by European American Armory, located in Sharps, FL.

RIFLES: SEMI-AUTO

VEPR HUNTER (VEPR II) CARBINE/RIFLE – .223 Rem., .270 Win. (new 2004), .30-06 (new 2004), .308 Win., or 7.62x39mm (new 2001) cal., features Vepr.'s semi-auto action, 16 (.223 Rem. or 7.62x39mm cal.), 20 1/2 (carbine, .308 Win. only, disc.), 21.6 or 23 1/4 (disc.) in. barrel with adj. rear sight, scope mount rail built into receiver top, standard or optional thumbhole checkered walnut stock with recoil pad and forend, paddle mag. release, 5 or 10 shot mag., approx 8.6 lbs.

| MSR $550 | $550 | $495 | $440 | $395 | $365 | $335 | $300 | |

SUPER VEPR – .308 Win. cal., thumbhole stock. Limited importation 2001-2007.

| | $950 | $850 | $750 | $650 | $550 | $475 | $400 | |

VEPR IV – 5.56 NATO cal., matte black finish, 23.3 in. heavy chrome lined barrel with US-made muzzle brake, 30 shot detachable mag., adj. rear sight, original RK clubfoot foldable stock, bipod, pistol grip. Importation began 2014.

| MSR $1,400 | $1,250 | $1,095 | $950 | $850 | $700 | $575 | $450 | |

MSR	100%	98%	95%	90%	80%	70%	60%	Last MSR

VEPR KREBS CUSTOM KV-13 – 7.62x39mm cal., gas operated, AK-47 design, 16 in. barrel with permanently attached four prong muzzle brake, 30 shot box mag. (accepts standard AK mags.), aperture AR style adj. sights, 6-position folding Magpul CTR stock, Tapco SAW style pistol grip, 9 1/2 in. handguard with top Picatinny rail, matte black Krebscote finish, 8 1/2 lbs. Imported and assembled by Krebs Custom.

| MSR $1,850 | $1,675 | $1,475 | $1,250 | $1,150 | $925 | $750 | $595 | |

WPA VEPR AK – 7.62x39mm, 7.62x54R, .223 Rem., or .308 Win. cal., gas operated, AK-47 design, matte black finish, 20 1/2 in. barrel, 30 shot box mag., folding stock with SGM tactical forend, Molot side mount, 9 lbs. Imported and assembled by WPA and Mach 1 Arsenal.

| MSR $999 | $900 | $795 | $675 | $625 | $495 | $400 | $350 | |

SHOTGUNS: SEMI-AUTO

VEPR 12 – 12 ga., AK-47 design, various configurations and barrel lengths, ambidextrous safety selector and bolt release lever, folding tube stock with recoil pad, pistol grip, 5 or 8 shot mag, approx. 8 1/2 lbs. New 2011.

| MSR $1,350 | $1,200 | $1,050 | $900 | $825 | $675 | $550 | $425 | |

VICTOR ARMS CORPORATION

Previous manufacturer located in Houston, TX.

Victor Arms Corporation manufactured limited quantities of a .22 LR upper unit for the AR-15. The V22 and its .22 LR cal. magazine replaced the standard .223 upper assembly/magazine. Additionally, a complete protoype gun was also manufactured.

VICTRIX ARMAMENTS

Current rifle manufacturer located in Cazzano Sant'Andrea, Brescia, Italy. No current U.S. importation.

RIFLES: SEMI-AUTO

Victrix Armaments manufactures high quality semi-autro ifles in various calibers and configurations. Current trademarks include Minerva Tactical (Stubby, Gladius, and Scorpio models), Victoria Sport (Carbon Performance, F-Class TR, F-Class Open, and Sport Series models), and Lunae Hunting (Lunae Model).

VIGILANCE RIFLES

Current rifle manufacturer located in Chino Valley, AZ beginning 2012. Previously located in Banning, and Redlands, CA.

RIFLES: BOLT ACTION

MODEL 12 WINDRUNNER – .223 Rem. or .308 Win. cal., all steel construction, 4 (disc.) or 10 shot detachable mag., collapsible stock with adjustable cheekpiece and monopod, heavy recoil pad, Picatinny rail, matte black finish, Savage AccuTrigger, includes drag bag and pivoting bipod. New late 2013.

| MSR $3,275 | $2,950 | $2,580 | $2,225 | $2,000 | $1,625 | $1,350 | $1,050 | |

RIFLES: SEMI-AUTO

M14 – .50 BMG cal., precision machined chrome moly upper receiver, carrier and bolt, chrome chamber and piston cylinder, 29 in. chrome moly barrel, M16 safety, 10 shot push button release extruded aluminum magazine with bolt catch system, M16 trigger, SRS rear stock system, front tube stock threads onto the receiver, integrated with 360° pivoting bipod, extendable cheekpiece, butt, and LOP, pistol grip, Mil-Spec actuating handle, drilled and tapped to accept standard Picatinny rails, black oxide finish, 44 lbs. New mid-2014.

| MSR $12,975 | $11,025 | $9,650 | $8,275 | $7,500 | $6,075 | $4,975 | $4,000 | |

Add $175 for match front Picatinny rail.
Add $250 for extra 10 shot magazine.
Add $400 for fifth wheel universal mounting rails.
Add $600 for aluminum hard case.
Add $2,200 for Night Force scope and rings.
Add $2,500 for Humvee mount stand for fifth wheel or boat.
Add $4,000 for any order outside the U.S.
Add $4,500 for recoiling M14 mount.
Add $9,500 for removable retractable helicopter stand and rails.

VR1 – .338 Lapua, .375 CheyTac, .408 CheyTac, or .505 Gibbs (disc. 2012) cal., GPO, stainless steel upper receiver, bull barrel, titanium muzzle brake, premium wood stock in a variety of colors or synthetic tactical stock, two-stage trigger, detachable 5 or 10 shot mag., many options available, weights vary according to configuration.

| MSR $12,975 | $11,025 | $9,650 | $8,275 | $7,500 | $6,075 | $4,975 | $4,000 | |

MSR		100%	98%	95%	90%	80%	70%	60%	Last MSR

VIGILANT ARMS

Current AR-15 manufacturer located in Florida.

Vigilant Arms manufactures high quality AR-15 pistols and rifles built to customer specifications. Please contact the company directly for more information including pricing and availability (see Trademark Index).

VIKING ARMAMENT, INC.

Current AR-15 style rifle/carbine manufacturer located in Grand Junction, CO.

Viking Armament also offers a full range of modern gunsmithing services and in-house Cerakote finishing. Please contact the company directly for more information (see Trademark Index).

RIFLES: SEMI-AUTO

CRUCIBLE AR-15/M4 RIFLE – 5.56 NATO/.223 Rem. cal., GIO, AR-15/M4 style, 16 1/2 in. SOCOM Nitride barrel, includes one Hexmag magazine, Magpul sights, Ergo grip, includes Niteride BCG, Mil-Spec fire control group, QD single point bungee sling, extended charging handle, and soft side rifle case, black anodized finish with black or FDE hardware.

| MSR $1,495 | | $1,275 | $1,125 | $1,025 | $875 | $750 | $625 | $525 | |

GUNGINR AR-15/M4 RIFLE – more research is pending for this model.

| MSR $1,095 | | $925 | $850 | $725 | $625 | $550 | $475 | $425 | |

KARA AR-15 RACE/3-GUN RIFLE – more research is pending for this model.

| MSR $2,295 | | $1,950 | $1,725 | $1,450 | $1,250 | $1,050 | $900 | $750 | |

ULFBERHT AR-15/M4 RIFLE – 5.56 NATO/.223 Rem. cal., GIO, AR-15/M4 style, 16 1/2 in. SOCOM Nitride barrel, OSS flash hider, Hexmag magazine, Magpul sights, Ergo grip, NIB BCG, ambidextrous 45 degree selector, QD single point bungee sling, extended charging handle, includes soft sided rifle case, black anodized or FDE Cerakote finish with black or FDE hardware.

| MSR $1,895 | | $1,625 | $1,425 | $1,200 | $1,075 | $925 | $795 | $650 | |

ULLR AR-15 PRECISION RIFLE – .223 Wylde cal., GIO, AR-15 style, 18 in. stainless steel heavy barrel with Viking muzzle brake, one Magpul 10 shot mag., Ergo grip, 16 in. handguard, Niteride BCG, ambidextrous 45 degree selector, multi-point bungee sling, black anodized or Kryptek Cerakote finish with black or FDE hardware, includes soft sided rifle case.

| MSR $1,895 | | $1,625 | $1,425 | $1,200 | $1,075 | $925 | $795 | $650 | |

TYR AR 10 PRECISION RIFLE – 6.5mm Creedmoor cal., GIO, OSS flash hider, one Magpul mag., Ergo grip, NIB BCG, 45 degree offset sight mounts, multi-point padded bungee sling, extended charging handle, Atlas bipod, black anodized or FDE Cerakote finish, includes soft sided rifle case.

| MSR $2,595 | | $2,200 | $1,925 | $1,600 | $1,375 | $1,125 | $975 | $850 | |

VIPER

Current trademark imported by Tristar Sporting Arms, LTD, located in North Kansas City, MO. Please refer to the Tristar Sporting Arms, LTD, listing in the T section.

VLTOR WEAPON SYSTEMS

Current manufacturer of AR-15 style rifles, receivers, parts, and related accessories located in Tucson, AZ.

CARBINES: SEMI-AUTO

PRAETORIAN – 5.56 NATO cal., Noveske stainless steel barrel, VC-A2 flash hider, VLTOR VIS extended mid-length monolithic upper with forward assist and KeyMod system, VLTOR 7-position A5 receiver extension with VLTOR A5H2 5.3oz buffer with rifle spring, Geissele SSA trigger, Diamondhead front and rear sights, five piece Picatinny rail section, Vltor/BCM Mod 4 Gunfighter charging handle, VLTOR low profile gas block with nitride surface finish, VLTOR IMOD stock, TangoDown pistol grip, VLTOR lower receiver with oversized mag. release and side saddle sling plate. New 2015.

Please contact the company directly for pricing on this model (see Trademark Index).

TS3 CARBINE – 5.56 NATO cal., AR-15 style, GIO, 16 1/4 in. barrel with muzzle brake, flat-top Vltor receiver with full length Picatinny rail, 30 shot mag., Geissele high speed National Match trigger, flip up combat sights, collapsible stock, quad rail, black finish, approx. 7 1/2 lbs. Mfg. 2011-2013.

| | | $2,125 | $1,875 | $1,550 | $1,325 | $1,100 | $950 | $825 | *$2,495* |

XVI DEFENDER – 5.56 NATO cal., GIO, 16 in. M4 barrel with A1 flash hider, extended mid-length handguard with KeyMod system, low profile gas block, flip up front and Diamondhead rear sights, BCM Mod 4 Gunfighter charging handle, lower receiver with oversized mag. release and side saddle sling plate, upper receiver with forward assist, 5-pos. receiver extension with carbine spring and buffer, standard trigger, Vltor IMOD stock, TangoDown pistol grip, black, Foliage Green, or FDE finish, includes a rifle bag, two mags., and one 2 in. Picatinny rail section. New 2014.

| MSR $1,560 | | $1,315 | $1,155 | $1,040 | $875 | $750 | $625 | $525 | |

MSR	100%	98%	95%	90%	80%	70%	60%	Last MSR

XVI WARRIOR – 5.56 NATO cal., GIO, 16 in. chrome lined Noveske barrel with VC-A2 flash hider, low profile gas block, lower receiver with oversized mag. release and side saddle sling plate, VLTOR VIS rifle length monolithic upper with forward assist and KeyMod system, 7-pos. A5 receiver extension with VLTOR A5H2 5.3 oz. buffer with rifle spring, Diamondhead sights, BCM Mod 4 Gunfighter charging handle, Geissele DMR trigger, VLTOR EMOD stock, TangoDown pistol grip, black finish, includes rifle bag, two mags., and one 2 in. Picatinny rail section, 7 1/4 lbs. New 2014.

	100%	98%	95%	90%	80%	70%	60%	
MSR $2,360	$1,950	$1,725	$1,450	$1,250	$1,050	$900	$750	

PISTOLS: SEMI-AUTO

VWS-IX DEFENDER AR PISTOL – 5.56 NATO cal., 9 in. barrel with VC-AKSU22 flash hider, VLTOR MUR-1A upper receiver with forward assist, lower receiver with oversized mag. release and side saddle sling plate, VLTOR CASV handguard in mid-length with KeyMod system, Diamondhead rear sight and VLTOR CAS-FS front sight, low profile gas block, Vltor/Bravo Company Mod 4 Gunfighter charging handle, A5 system receiver extension and spring/buffer kit, TangoDown pistol grip, black, FDE, or Foliage Green finish. New 2015.

	100%	98%	95%	90%	80%	70%	60%	
MSR $1,440	$1,225	$1,090	$950	$800	$700	$600	$495	

VWS-IX WARRIOR AR PISTOL – 5.56 NATO cal., 9 in. barrel with VC-AKSU22 flash hider, VLTOR VIS mid-length monolithic upper with forward assist and KeyMod system, Picatinny rail, Diamondhead front and rear sights, low profile gas block, BCM Mod 4 Gunfighter charging handle, VLTOR A5 system pistol receiver extension and spring/buffer kit, TangoDown pistol grip, black finish. New 2015.

	100%	98%	95%	90%	80%	70%	60%	
MSR $1,600	$1,350	$1,200	$1,075	$950	$815	$700	$575	

VWS-VII WARRIOR AR PISTOL – 5.56 NATO cal., 7 in. barrel with VC-AKSU22 flash hider, VLTOR VIS carbine length monolithic upper with forward assist and KeyMod system, Picatinny rail, Diamondhead front and rear sights, low profile gas block, BCM Mod 4 Gunfighter charging handle, VLTOR A5 system pistol receiver extension and spring/buffer kit, TangoDown pistol grip, black finish. New 2015.

	100%	98%	95%	90%	80%	70%	60%	
MSR $1,600	$1,350	$1,200	$1,075	$950	$815	$700	$575	

VWS-XII DEFENDER AR PISTOL – 5.56 NATO cal., 12 1/2 in. barrel with VC-A1 flash hider, VLTOR MUR-1A upper receiver with forward assist, VLTOR CASV handguard in extended mid-length with KeyMod system, Picatinny rail, Diamondhead rear and VLTOR CAS-FS front sights, low profile gas block, BCM Mod 4 Gunfighter charging handle, A5 system pistol receiver extension and spring/buffer kit, TangoDown pistol grip, black, Foliage Green, or FDE finish. New 2015.

	100%	98%	95%	90%	80%	70%	60%	
MSR $1,440	$1,225	$1,090	$950	$800	$700	$600	$495	

VWS-XII WARRIOR AR PISTOL – 5.56 NATO cal., 12 1/2 in. barrel with VC-A1 flash hider, VLTOR VIS extended mid-length monolithic upper receiver with forward assist and KeyMod system, Picatinny rail, Diamondhead front and rear sights, low profile gas block, BCM Mod 4 Gunfighter charging handle, A5 system pistol receiver extension and spring/buffer kit, TangoDown pistol grip, black finish. New 2015.

	100%	98%	95%	90%	80%	70%	60%	
MSR $1,600	$1,350	$1,200	$1,075	$950	$815	$700	$575	

VOLKMANN PRECISION, LLC

Current pistol manufacturer established in 2007, located in Littleton, CO. Previously located in Lakewood, CO until 2011. Consumer direct sales through FFL.

Volkmann Precision LLC was founded by Luke Volkmann, formerly a pistolsmith for Ed Brown Products. In 2011, the company name changed from Volkmann Custom Inc. to Volkmann Precision, LLC.

PISTOLS: SEMI-AUTO

All pistols are hand built, and a variety of options are available. MSRs reflect base pricing only. Please contact the company directly for more information (see Trademark Index).

Add $100 for ambidextrous safety. Add $250 for custom finish. Add $300 for engraving. Add $250 for custom serial number.

COMBAT CUSTOM – 9mm Para. or .45 ACP cal., 5 in. barrel, SA, full size frame, 7 or 8 shot mag., black Rockote or blue finish, fixed Tritium night sights, 25 LPI checkering.

	100%	98%	95%	90%	80%	70%	60%	
MSR $3,195	$2,725	$2,385	$2,050	$1,850	$1,500	$1,225	$1,000	

COMBAT CARRY – 9mm Para. or .45 ACP cal., 4 1/4 in. barrel, SA, 7 or 8 shot mag., Commander size frame and slide with Ed Brown Bobtail mainspring housing, Rockote black, OD green, titanium blue, or desert tan finish, fixed Tritium night sights, 25 LPI checkering.

	100%	98%	95%	90%	80%	70%	60%	
MSR $3,495	$2,975	$2,600	$2,225	$2,025	$1,650	$1,350	$1,050	

CLINT SMITH COMBAT SPECIAL – .45 ACP cal., SA, Clint Smith inspired and designed 1911 style, 7 or 8 shot mag., carbon or stainless steel frame, Rockote finish, Heine Ledge combat sights, gold dot front post sights, tactical accessory rail, lanyard loop mainspring, short match trigger and safety, 34-38 oz. New 2012.

	100%	98%	95%	90%	80%	70%	60%	
MSR $3,595	$3,050	$2,675	$2,300	$2,075	$1,675	$1,375	$1,100	

MSR	100%	98%	95%	90%	80%	70%	60%	Last MSR

VOLQUARTSEN CUSTOM (LTD.)

Current pistol/rifle customizer and manufacturer established in 1974, located in Carroll, IA. Dealer sales.

RIFLES: SEMI-AUTO

Current Volquartsen stock configurations include: Laminated Lightweight Thumbhole Stock, Laminated Thumbhole Silhouette Stock, Laminated Sporter Stock, Signature Series Bastogne Walnut Stock, VX-5000 Stock, McMillan Fiberglass Thumbhole Stock, McMillan Fiberglass Sporter Stock, or Hogue Overmolded Stock. Laminated stocks are available in Brown, Blue, Gray, Green, Orange, Pink, Yellow, Red, Turquoise, or Brown/Grey. Base prices listed represent standard Hogue synthetic stock.

Beginning 2014, rifles have been organized by actions and barrel combinations - Ultralite, Superlite, Lightweight, Stainless, Deluxe, IF-5, or SF-1. Previously, the nomenclature for these guns were the Standard Models listed in different calibers.

Add $120 for Hogue Overmolded Stock (Black or OD Green).
Add $250 for Laminated Sporter Stock.
Add $350 for Laminated Lightweight Thumbhole or Laminated Thumbhole Silhouette stocks.
Add $450 for VX-5000 stock.
Add $650 for McMillan Fiberglass Sporter or McMillan fiberglass Thumbhole stock.
Add $800 for Signature Series Bastogne Walnut stock.

EVOLUTION MODEL – .204 Ruger or .223 Rem. cal., gas operated, 20 or 24 (.204 Ruger only) in. standard barrel, stainless steel receiver, trigger guard, and bolt, integral machined Picatinny rail on receiver top, Brown or Gray laminate Sporter stock, Brown/Gray laminated thumbhole silhouette stock, with or w/o extended Monte Carlo cheekpiece, 10 shot AR-15 style mag., 11 1/2 lbs. New 2005.

MSR $2,483	$2,125	$1,950	$1,700	$1,475	$1,225	$1,000	$850

Add $115 for Brown/Gray laminated thumbhole silhouette stock.
Add $226 for camo (now avail. only as part of camo package w/scope), disc. 2011.
Add $1,271 for Evolution Camo package with scope (disc. 2014).

* **VM-22 Rifle** – various cals., Superlite barreled action, aluminum forward Blow compensator, black or FDE Mapgul X-22 Hunter stock, adj. LOP, integral Picatinny rail, Type III hardcoat anodized black receiver finish, 5 lbs. 4 oz. New 2016.

MSR $1,295	$1,100	$995	$875	$735	$650	$550	$465

VOLUNTEER ENTERPRISES

Previous manufacturer located in Knoxville, TN.

Volunteer Enterprises became Commando Arms after 1978.

CARBINES

COMMANDO MARK III CARBINE – .45 ACP cal., semi-auto, blowback action, 16 1/2 in. barrel, aperture sight, stock styled after the Auto-Ordnance "Tommy Gun." Mfg. 1969-1976.

	$750	$675	$625	$565	$525	$475	$425	

Add 10% for vertical grip.

COMMANDO MARK 9 – similar to Mark III in 9mm Para. cal.

	$675	$625	$565	$525	$475	$425	$375	

Add 10% for vertical grip.

VULCAN ARMAMENT, INC.

Previous rifle manufacturer located in Inver Grove Heights, MN 1991-circa 2013. Previously located in South St. Paul, MN.

Vulcan Armament specialized in tactical style firearms and offered a complete line of parts and accessories.

CARBINES/RIFLES: SEMI-AUTO

Vulcan Armament made a wide variety of AR-15 style semi-auto carbines and rifles, including configurations for military and law enforcement.

All rifles included sling, manual, cleaning kit, Vulcan knife, and hard case.

Add $20-$25 for removable carry handle.

V15 9MM CARBINE SERIES – 9mm Para. cal., GIO, 16 in. chrome moly vanadium steel barrel with threaded muzzle, A2 front sight bases with bayonet lug, all parts manganese phosphate finished, M4 contour, M4 length handguard, full heat shield, A2 upper receiver or A3 flat-top receiver, carry handle, adj. sights, Picatinny rail, black hardcoat anodized finish, forward assist, hinged ejection port cover, 6-position adj. buttstock, removable flash hider, accepts Sten magazines, 6 1/2 lbs. Disc. 2012.

	$775	$685	$585	$525	$425	$350	$275	*$860*

MSR	100%	98%	95%	90%	80%	70%	60%	Last MSR

V15 DISPATCHER SERIES – .223 Rem. cal., GIO, 16 in. chrome moly vanadium steel barrel with threaded muzzle, gas block mounted under the handguard, A2 flash hider, A2 front sight bases, bayonet lug, fixed A2 stock, A2 or A3 flat-top upper receiver, black hardcoat anodized finish, 6 1/2 lbs.

	$850	$750	$650	$575	$475	$385	$300	*$999*

V15 M4 CARBINE SERIES – .223 Rem. cal., GIO, 16 in. chrome moly vanadium steel button rifled barrel with threaded muzzle, A2 flash hider, A2 front sight bases, bayonet lug, A2 or A3 flat-top upper reciever, M4 length handguard with full heat shields, 6-position M4 buttstock, black hardcoat anodized finish, 6.4 lbs.

	$850	$750	$650	$575	$475	$385	$300	*$999*

V15 POLYMER SERIES – .223 Rem. cal., GIO, 16 or 20 in. chrome moly vanadium steel button rifled H-Bar barrel with threaded muzzle, all parts manganese phosphate finished, A2 flash hider, A2 sight bases, bayonet lug, 6-position M4 buttstock, Picatinny rail, A2 or A3 polymer receiver, forward assist, hinged ejection port cover. Disc. 2012.

	$625	$550	$475	$425	$350	$280	$225	*$700*

V15 TARGET RIFLE – .223 Rem. cal., GIO, 20 in. chrome moly vanadium steel threaded button rifled heavy barrel, A2 flash hider, all parts manganese phosphate finished, rifle length handguard, full heat shield, A2 or A3 flat-top upper receiver, Picatinny rail, black hardcoat anodized finish, fixed A2 buttstock, removable flash hider, aluminum spacer, trap door buttplate.

	$850	$750	$650	$575	$475	$385	$300	*$999*

V15 VARMINATOR SERIES – .223 Rem. cal., GIO, 16 (new 2013), 20 or 24 in. stainless steel bull barrel, full length aluminum handguard, aluminum gas block, four Picatinny rails, forged A3 upper receiver, forward assist, hinged ejection port cover, fixed A2 buttstock, aluminum spacer, trap door buttplate, hardcoat anodized finish, 9-9.2 lbs.

	$850	$750	$650	$575	$475	$385	$300	*$999*

V15 200 SERIES – 7.62x39mm cal., GIO, 16 in. chrome moly vanadium steel threaded barrel, A2 flash hider, A2 front sight bases, bayonet lug, all parts manganese phosphate finished, M4 length handguard, full heat shields, forged A2 or A3 flat-top upper receiver, forward assist, hinged ejection port, 6-position buttstock, 6.4 lbs.

	$950	$825	$715	$650	$525	$425	$325	*$1,100*

  * V15 200 Piston Series – .223 Rem. cal., similar to V15 200 Series, except has proprietary short stroke GPO.

	$1,075	$940	$800	$725	$595	$485	$375	*$1,250*

V15 202 MODULAR CARBINE – .223 Rem. cal., GIO, 16 in. chrome moly vanadium steel threaded barrel, A2 flash hider, all parts manganese phosphate finished, A3 flat-top upper receiver, four Picatinny rails, black hardcoat anodized finish, forward assist, hinged ejection port cover, modular handguard, low profile aircraft aluminum gas block, 6-position buttstock, 6 1/2 lbs.

	$835	$725	$625	$575	$450	$375	$295	*$925*

V18 SERIES – .223 Rem. cal., short stroke GPO, 16 1/2 or 20 in. chrome lined barrel, copy of the AR-180, machined gas block, front sight base, Picatinny rail, A2 flash hider, FAL style handguard, ambidextrous charging handle, carbon fiber lower, AR pistol grip, polymer FAL stock, rubber buttpad, aluminum recoil plate, last round hold open, 6.8 lbs.

	$750	$650	$565	$510	$415	$340	$265	*$889*

V73 SERIES – 7.62x39mm, .223 Rem., or .308 Win. cal., GIO, copy of Israeli Galil, 100% part interchangeability, including mags. and accessories, machined monoblock receiver, skeletonized black tactical stock, available in AR, ARM, SAR, and Micro configurations. Disc. 2012.

	$1,395	$1,220	$1,050	$950	$765	$630	$495	*$1,550*

  Add $300 for .308 Win. cal.
  Add $100 for ARM model with top carry handle.
  Add $449 for SAR or Micro configuration.

RIFLES: BOLT ACTION

  All rifles included manual, bipod, removable muzzle brake, gun lock, Vulcan knife, cleaning rod and brush, and scope rail.

V50 SERIES – .50 BMG cal., single shot, 60 degree bolt throw, capable of hits at ranges exceeding one mile, scope mounting rail, standard Mauser pattern trigger, thick recoil pad, "Shark Fin" muzzle brake, available in SS-100 (30 in. barrel, brown laminated thumbhole wood stock, disc. 2012), SS-200 (36 in. barrel, grey laminated thumbhole wood stock), SS-300 (30 in. barrel, retractable black tactical stock, disc. 2012) or the SS-400 Bullpup (30 in. barrel, bullpup stock).

	$1,725	$1,525	$1,295	$1,175	$950	$775	$600	*$1,900*

  Add $300 for SS-400 Bullpup.

W SECTION

WMD GUNS

Current manufacturer of pistols, AR-15 style rifle/carbines, and proprietary coating (NiB-X) located in Stuart, FL.

MSR	100%	98%	95%	90%	80%	70%	60%	Last MSR

PISTOLS: SEMI-AUTO

BEAST AR-15 PISTOL – 5.56 NATO cal., 10 1/2 in. barrel. New 2016.

	100%	98%	95%	90%	80%	70%	60%
MSR $1,235	$1,040	$925	$800	$685	$595	$515	$440

RIFLES/CARBINES: SEMI-AUTO

THE BEAST – 5.56 NATO, .300 AAC Blackout, .458 SOCOM, .204 Ruger, 6.5 Grendel, or 6.8 SPC cal., 16 in. match grade barrel, compensator, two 30 shot mags., low profile gas block, free float rail system with adj. optic ready Picatinny rails, forward assist, NiB-X coated barrel, receivers, fire control group, gas block, and charging handle, triangular 5-pos. ergonomic buttstock, black ceramic topcoat finish.

	100%	98%	95%	90%	80%	70%	60%
MSR $1,450	$1,235	$1,100	$985	$835	$725	$615	$515

* The Dirty Beast – similar to The Beast, except has Flat Dark Earth topcoat finish.

	100%	98%	95%	90%	80%	70%	60%
MSR $1,450	$1,235	$1,100	$985	$835	$725	$615	$515

BIG BEAST – .308 Win. cal., AR-10 rifle, GIO, 18 or 20 in. free floating barrel, Melonited bore, barrel extension, Magpul 20 shot mag., adj. (18 in. barrel) or fixed (20 in. barrel) stock, carbine length gas system, low profile gas block, billet aluminum upper and lower receivers, all exterior surfaces and key internal components are permanently coated in the NiB-X process, includes WMD/Drago tactical rifle case. New 2016.

	100%	98%	95%	90%	80%	70%	60%
MSR $2,359	$2,000	$1,750	$1,475	$1,275	$1,060	$915	$775

Add $140 for 20 in. barrel with fixed stock.

WAFFEN HIENDLMAYER

Current manufacturer located in Eggenfelden, Germany. No current U.S. importation.

Klaus Hiendlmayer specializes in custom guns and engraving, and manufactures a version of the SIG 550 sniper rifle. Prices range from €1,999-€2,750. Please contact the company directly for more information, including domestic availability (see Trademark Index).

WAFFEN SCHUMACHER GmbH

Current manufacturer of bolt action and semi-auto rifles located in Krefeld, Germany.

Waffen Schumacher GmbH also sells some original military make/models in addition to selling guns from other European manufacturers. Also see listing under Schmeisser Germany GmbH.

WALTHER

Current manufacturer established in 1886, and currently located in Ulm, Germany 1953 to date. Sport and defense models, in addition to target pistols and rifles, are currently imported by Walther Arms, Inc. located in Fort Smith, AR. Previously imported, distributed, and manufactured (Models PPK and PPK/S only) by Smith & Wesson circa 2002-2012, and located in Springfield, MA. Earl's Repair Service has imported limited quantities of Walther target pistols and rifles in the past as well. Previously imported and distributed 1998-2001 by Walther USA LLC, located in Springfield, MA, and by Interarms, located in Alexandria, VA circa 1962-1999. Previously manufactured in Zella-Mehlis, Germany 1886 to 1945. Walther was sold to Umarex Sportwaffen GmbH circa 1994, and company headquarters are located in Arnsberg, Germany. Smith & Wesson was the primary distributor for most Walther firearms and accessories in the United States from 2002-2012. During 2012, Carl Walther GmbH Sportwaffen and Umarex announced the formation of Walther Arms, Inc. located in Fort Smith, AR to import, sell, and market all Walther products in the U.S. beginning Jan. 1, 2013.

The calibers listed in the Walther Pistol sections are listed in American caliber designations. The German metric conversion is as follows: .22 LR - 5.6mm, .25 ACP - 6.35mm, .32 ACP - 7.65mm, and .380 ACP - 9mm kurz. The metric caliber designations in most cases will be indicated on the left slide legend for German mfg. pistols listed in the Walther section.

For more information and current pricing on both new and used Walther airguns, please refer to the *Blue Book of Airguns* by Dr. Robert Beeman & John Allen (also online).

PISTOLS: SEMI-AUTO, POST-WAR

Smith & Wesson has placed a recall on all Walther PPK and PPK/S pistols manufactured by Smith & Wesson from March 21, 2002-Feb. 3, 2009. Ser. no. ranges subject to this recall are as follows: 0010BAB-9999BAB, 0000BAC-9999BAC, 0000BAD-9999BAD, 0000BAE-999BAE, 0000BAF-9999BAF, 0000BAH-9999BAH, 00000BAJ-9999BAJ, 0000BAK-9999BAK, 0000BAL-5313BAL, 0000BAM-1320BAM, 0000LTD-0499LTD, 0001PPK-1500PPK, 0026REP-0219REP, and 0001WLE-0459WLE. Smith & Wesson has advised all owners to discontinue usage and return the pistol to S&W for free repair. Please contact S&W directly for more information (see Trademark Index).

MSR	100%	98%	95%	90%	80%	70%	60%	*Last MSR*

MODEL PPQ – 9mm Para. or .40 S&W cal., SFO, synthetic frame with steel slide, 4 (.40 S&W cal. only), or 4.1 (threaded barrel available on first edition only) in. barrel, 12 (.40 S&W cal. only), 15, or 17 shot mag., black finish, textured synthetic grips, night sights (first edition only) or adj. front and rear sights, Quick Defense Trigger, 24 1/2 oz. Mfg. 2011-2012.

	$525	$450	$415	$365	$325	$295	$275	$600

Add $300 for first edition model.

MODEL PPQ M2 – 9mm Para., .40 S&W, or .45 ACP (new 2016) cal., 4 (9mm Para. only), 4.1 (.40 S&W cal.), 4 1/4 (.45 ACP only), 4.6 (threaded, 9mm Para.), or 5 in. barrel, 10, 11, 12, 15, or 17 shot mag., low profile combat sights, appearance and most features similar to Model PPQ, ambidextrous mag. release button, PPQ M2 Navy SD variation with 4.6 in. threaded barrel, 24 oz. New 2013.

MSR $649	$550	$470	$425	$375	$325	$295	$275	

Add $50 for .45 ACP cal. (new 2016).
Add $100 for 5 in. barrel.
Add $50 for PPQ M2 Navy SD variation with 4.6 in. threaded barrel (9mm Para. cal. only).

MODEL PPX M1 – 9mm Para. or .40 S&W cal., hammer fired action, DAO, 4 or 4.6 (PPX SD) in. barrel, low profile 3 dot sights, lower Picatinny rail, checkered trigger guard, ergonomic textured synthetic grips, ambidextrous slide stop, bobbed hammer, polymer frame with steel or stainless steel slide, 14 or 16 shot mag., 27.2 oz. Manufactured in Ulm, Germany 2013-2014.

	$395	$350	$315	$285	$260	$240	$220	$449

Add $50 for stainless steel slide.

MODEL P88 & VARIATIONS – 9mm Para. or 9x21mm cal., DA/SA, alloy frame, 4 in. barrel, 15 shot button release mag., fully ambidextrous, decocking lever, matte finish, adj. rear sight, internal safeties, plastic grips, 31 1/2 oz. Mfg. 1987-93.

	$1,250	$925	$750	$600	$500	$450	$400	$1,129

P88 cutaways were also mfg. in small quantities for instructional use. Current pricing for a mint specimen is approx. $2,000.

* **Model P88 Compact** – 9mm Para. or 9x21mm cal., 3.93 in. barrel, 14* (disc.) or 10 (C/B 1994) shot mag., 29 oz. Imported 1993-2003.

	$975	$800	$650	$550	$500	$475	$450	$900

Add 25% for 14 shot mag.

* **Model P88 Champion** – 9mm Para. cal. only, 6 in. barrel, SA only, 14* shot mag., 30.9 oz. Very limited mfg. 1992-disc.

	$3,000	$1,850	$1,500	$1,250	$995	$775	$625	

* **Model P88 Competition** – 9mm Para. cal., 4 in. barrel, SA only, 14* shot mag., 28.2 oz. Very limited mfg. 1992-disc.

	$2,400	$1,500	$1,250	$995	$775	$625	$550	

P99 AS & VARIATIONS – 9mm Para., 9x21mm (limited importation 1996), or .40 S&W (new 1999) cal., SFO, 4 (9mm Para.) or 4.1 (.40 S&W) in. barrel, polymer frame, 10, 12 (.40 S&W cal. only), 15, or 16 (9mm Para. cal. only, disc. 2006) shot mag., standard, anti-stress (traditional double action, AS Model, new 2004), or quick action (QA, allowing consistent SA trigger performance) trigger, decocking, and internal striker safeties, cocking and loaded chamber indicators, choice of matte black, QPQ (mfg. 1999-2003) finished (silver colored) slide, or titanium coated (mfg. 2003-2006) finish, ambidextrous mag. release, ergonomic black, desert tan (disc. 2008), or green (Military model, new 1999) synthetic grip with interchangeable backstrap, adj. rear sight, 25 oz. Importation began 1995.

MSR $629	$550	$485	$435	$375	$315	$275	$250	

Add $140 for Tritium sight set with green 3-dot system (.40 S&W only), or $109 for white 3-dot metal sights (disc. 2011).
Add $260 for night sight kit (mfg. 2010-2011).
Add $31 for titanium finish (disc. 2006).
Add $125 for 9x21mm cal. (disc.).
Engraved P99s were also available in the following configurations in 9mm Para. cal. only - Grade I Arabesque ($3,700 last MSR), Grade II Goldline ($4,200 last MSR), Grade III Arabesque w/gold ($4,660 last MSR).

* **P99 Compact** – 9mm Para. or .40 S&W cal., SFO, 3 1/2 in. barrel, 8 (.40 S&W cal.) or 10 shot mag. with finger extension, available in QA, AS, or DAO (disc. 2006), Weaver rail, compact frame, blue finish only, 20 oz. New 2004.

MSR $629	$550	$485	$435	$375	$315	$275	$250	

P990 – similar to P99, SFO, except is double action only, features Walther's constant pull trigger system, black, QPQ slide finish, or Military Model (green), 25 oz. Mfg. 1998-2003.

	$550	$475	$425	$385	$350	$325	$295	$644

MSR	100%	98%	95%	90%	80%	70%	60%	Last MSR

RIFLES: DISC.

MODEL WA-2000 – .300 Win. Mag. (55 mfg., standard) or .308 Win. (92 mfg., optional) cal., ultra-deluxe semi-auto, 25.6 in. barrel, 5 or 6 shot mag., optional extras include aluminum case, spare mags., integral bipod, adj. tools and leather sling, regular or night vision scope, special order only, 16 3/4 lbs. Disc. 1988.

| | $36,000 | $32,000 | $29,000 | $27,000 | $25,000 | $22,500 | $20,000 | |

A 7.5 Swiss cal. conversion kit was also optional on this model.

RIFLES: CURRENT/RECENT MFG.

Except for the G22 and GSP rifles, the following models are available from Champion's Choice.

MODEL G22 SEMI-AUTO – .22 LR cal., bullpup design, 20 in. barrel, 10 shot mag., fire control and mag. integrated in rear of stock, black synthetic, carbon fiber, or camo (disc. 2006) thumbhole stock, adj. sliding sights, right or left-hand controls and ejection, blue or military green finish, Weaver style rails on rear sight/carry handle, lower forearm, and on front right mount, approx. 6 lbs. Mfg. 2004-2011.

| | $435 | $380 | $330 | $290 | $250 | $225 | $195 | *$509* |

Add $39 for scope or $67 for laser or $102 for red-dot sights (disc. 2009).

Add $56 for carbon fiber stock (disc. 2007) or $50 for camo stock (disc. 2006).

WAR SPORT

Current AR-15 style pistol and rifle manufacturer located in Robbins, NC. War Sport also manufacturers a line of parts and accessories including upper build kits, barrels, muzzle devices, and related small parts.

PISTOLS: SEMI-AUTO

LVOA-SP – .223 Rem./5.56 NATO cal., .223 Wylde chamber, AR-15 style, 11 3/4 in. barrel, WS Top Hat compensator, CMC 3 1/2 lb. flat trigger, MBUS Pro sights, Magpul XTM foregrip, Sig SB-15 brace, AMBI fire controls, mag. release, and charging handle, black, Foliage, FDE, or Wolf Grey finish, 6 3/4 lbs.

| MSR $3,050 | $2,585 | $2,250 | $1,840 | $1,575 | $1,300 | $1,100 | $950 | |

RIFLES: SEMI-AUTO

GPR-CC – .223 Rem./5.56 NATO cal., .223 Wylde chamber, AR-15 style, 16 in. barrel, Geissele SSA trigger, MBUS Pro sights, B5 SOPMOD stock, AMBI fire controls, mag. release, and charging handle, black, Foliage, FDE, or Wolf Grey finish, 6 1/2 lbs. New 2016.

| MSR $2,650 | $2,225 | $1,940 | $1,600 | $1,375 | $1,125 | $975 | $850 | |

WEATHERBY

Current trademark manufactured and imported by Weatherby located in Paso Robles, CA since 2006. Previously located in Atascadero, CA 1995-2006, and in South Gate, CA, 1945-1995. Weatherby began manufacturing rifles in the U.S. during early 1995. Dealer and distributor sales.

Weatherby is an importer and manufacturer of long arms. Earlier production was from Germany and Italy, and German mfg. is usually what is collectible. Rifles are currently produced in the U.S., while O/U shotguns are made in Italy and semi-autos are mfg. in Turkey.

Weatherby is well-known for their high-velocity proprietary rifle calibers.

Weatherby offers a research authentication service for Weatherby firearms. The cost is $50 per serial number ($75 for custom rifles, $100 for special editions and commemoratives), and includes a certificate signed by Roy Weatherby Jr. and company historian Dean Rumbaugh. Please contact the company directly for more information regarding this service (see Trademark Index).

Early Weatherby rifles used a Mathieu Arms action in the 1950s - primarily since it was available in left-hand action. Right-handed actions were normally mfg. from the FN Mauser type.

RIFLES: BOLT ACTION, MARK V SERIES

Pre-Mark V production started in 1945 and ended in 1961. Initially, rifles were customized from customer supplied guns, and this ended circa 1949. Between 1949-1963, Weatherby manufactured rifles in Southgate from FN Mauser actions in various cals., including the .257, .270, 7mm, .300, and .375 Wby. Mag. cals. From 1955-1959, Southgate also manufactured guns using the Mathieu left-hand action. Additionally, Schultz & Larson from Denmark was subcontracted to make rifles in .378 Wby. Mag. circa 1955-1962. Between 1956-1962, Southgate manufactured a .460 Wby. Mag. cal. using the Brevex Magnum action. Sako of Finland was also subcontracted circa 1957-1961 to produce rifles using a FN Mauser action. Initial Mark V production began in Southgate circa 1958-1959. During 1959-1973, J.P. Sauer of W. Germany was subcontracted to make the Mark V in a variety of calibers up to .460 Wby. Mag. These earlier pre-Mark V rifles will have a 20%-30% premium, depending on original condition and caliber.

In 1992, 24 in. barrels were disc. on most calibers of .300 or greater (including Models Mark V Deluxe, Fibermark, Lazermark, and Euromark). The Mark V action has also been manufactured in Japan.

All recently manufactured Weatherby Magnums in .30-378, .338-378, .378, .416, and .460 cal. are equipped with an Accubrake.

MSR	100%	98%	95%	90%	80%	70%	60%	Last MSR

In 2016, Weatherby made significant refinements to the Mark V rifle for the first time since its introduction in 1958. These changes include ergonomically enhanced stock with a slimmer forearm and more distinct lines and contours, a right-hand palm swell was added, and the overall weight was reduced. These new features also include the LXX™ trigger (precision ground/polished and wider trigger face), hand-lapped barrels, and a SUB-MOA accuracy guarantee.

MARK V TRR CUSTOM MAGNUM

– .300 Win. Mag., .300 Wby. Mag., .30-378 Wby. Mag., .338 Lapua Mag. (new 2012), or .338-378 Wby. Mag. cals., 26 (disc. 2013) or 28 in. barrel with Accubrake, fully adj. black tactical stock, adj. trigger, w/o sights, approx. 9 lbs. Mfg. 2011-2015.

| | $2,375 | $2,000 | $1,700 | $1,475 | $1,275 | $1,100 | $900 | $2,800 |

Add $200 for .30-378 Wby. Mag., .338 Lapua Mag. (new 2012) or .338-378 Wby. Mag. with 28 in. barrel and Accubrake.

MARK V TRR RC (RANGE CERTIFIED)

– .300 Win. Mag., .300 Wby. Mag., .30-378 Wby. Mag., .338 Lapua Mag. (new 2012), or .338-378 Wby. Mag. cal., 26 in. Kreiger barrel with Accubrake, adj. trigger, 2 shot mag., laminated stock with T-6 aluminum bedding system with three position buttstock, includes Leupold 4.5-14x50 LRT M1 scope (disc. 2012), Talley ring rail, bipod, and hard case, 9 1/4 lbs. Mfg. 2010-2015.

| | $3,575 | $3,050 | $2,575 | $2,250 | $1,900 | $1,650 | $1,375 | $4,200 |

Add approx. $1,700 for TRR Package including Leupold scope, ring rail, bipod, and hard case (disc. 2012).

MARK V TRR (THREAT RESPONSE RIFLE)

– .223 Rem., .308 Win., .300 Win. Mag. (disc. 2002), .300 Wby. Mag. (disc. 2002), .30-378 Wby. Mag. (disc. 2002), or .338-.378 Wby. Mag. (disc. 2002) cal., 22 in. barrel, 5 shot mag., Mark V action with black finished metal and black hybrid composite stock, various barrel lengths, optional Picatinny style ring and base system, 8 1/2-10 1/2 lbs. Mfg. 2002-2005.

| | $1,400 | $1,225 | $1,050 | $950 | $770 | $630 | $490 | $1,737 |

Add $52 for .300 Win. Mag. or .300 Wby. Mag. cals. (disc. 2002).
Add $208 for .30-378 Wby. Mag. or .338-378 Wby. Mag. cals. (disc. 2002).

RIFLES: BOLT ACTION, CUSTOM SHOP

TRCM (THREAT RESPONSE CUSTOM MAGNUM)

– .300 Win. Mag., .300 Wby. Mag., .30-378 Wby. Mag., or .338-.378 Wby. Mag. cal., Mark V action with ergonomic, fully adjustable composite stock, black finished metal, various barrel lengths, optional Picatinny style ring and base system. Mfg. 2002-2009.

| | $2,325 | $2,035 | $1,745 | $1,580 | $1,280 | $1,045 | $815 | $2,899 |

Add $270 for .30-378 Wby. Mag. or .338-378 Wby. Mag. cals.
Add $499 for desert camo stock and titanium nitride coating.

RIFLES: BOLT ACTION, VANGUARD SERIES 1

The Vanguard Series 1 rifles were discontinued in 2011. All guns were shipped with a factory three shot target, guaranteeing 1.5 in. accuracy at 100 yards.

VANGUARD SUB-MOA

– same cals. as Vanguard Synthetic, matte finished steel or stainless steel action and 24 in. barrel, choice of light tan or charcoal Monte Carlo Fiberguard stock with Pachmayr Decelerator pad, no sights, guaranteed to shoot a three shot .99 in. group at 100 yards, 3 or 5 shot mag., 7 3/4 lbs. Mfg. 2005-2011.

| | $865 | $750 | $650 | $580 | $475 | $385 | $300 | $1,019 |

Add $31 for WSM cals.
Add $150 for stainless steel action/barrel (disc. 2009).

* ***Vanguard Sub-MOA TR*** – .223 Rem. or .308 Win. cal., 22 in. contoured barrel with recessed target crown, 5 shot mag., laminated Monte Carlo composite stock with beavertail forearm and Pachmayr Decelerator pad, three swivel studs, adj. trigger, guaranteed to shoot 3-shot group of .99 in. or less with factory or premium ammo, 8 3/4 lbs. Mfg. 2010-2011.

| | $875 | $750 | $640 | $580 | $470 | $385 | $300 | $1,016 |

* ***Vanguard Sub-MOA TRR Package*** – .300 Win. Mag., .300 Wby. Mag., .30-378 Wby. Mag., or .338-378 Wby. Mag. cal., 28 in. barrel with Accubrake, adj. trigger, laminated stock with T-6 aluminum bedding system with three position buttstock, includes Leupold 4.5-14x50 LRT M1 scope, Talley ring rail, bipod, and hard case. Mfg. 2010 only.

| | $3,350 | $2,975 | $2,550 | $2,200 | $1,875 | $1,550 | $1,300 | $3,999 |

VANGUARD SUB-MOA VARMINT

– .204 Ruger (mfg. 2007-2010), .22-250 Rem., .223 Rem., or .308 Win. cal., features hand laminated composite stock with oversized vented forend and CNC machined aluminum bedding plate, Pachmayr Decelerator pad, three sling swivels, 22 in. barrel, 5 shot mag., 8 1/4 lbs. Mfg. 2006-2011.

| | $925 | $800 | $700 | $600 | $500 | $425 | $375 | $1,101 |

Add $59 for .204 Ruger cal. (disc. 2010).

RIFLES: BOLT ACTION, VANGUARD SERIES 2

Weatherby discontinued its Vanguard Series 1 in 2011, and released the Vanguard Series 2 in 2012. Differences on the Series 2 include a creep-free, match quality, two-stage trigger, 3-position safety, and Griptonite synthetic stock with special inserts and palm swell (select models). All Series 2 Vanguards come with a Sub-MOA accuracy guarantee.

MSR	100%	98%	95%	90%	80%	70%	60%	Last MSR

VANGUARD SERIES 2 TRR RC – .223 Rem. or .308 Win. cal., 22 in. barrel with recessed target crown, hand laminated Monte Carlo composite stock with aluminum bedding plate, beavertail forend, Pachmayr Decelerator recoil pad, includes factory-shot target certified and signed by Ed Weatherby and special RC engraved floor plate, 8 3/4 lbs. Mfg. 2012-2015.

	100%	98%	95%	90%	80%	70%	60%	Last MSR
	$1,025	$875	$750	$625	$525	$425	$350	*$1,199*

SHOTGUNS: SEMI-AUTO

Beginning 2008, all semi-autos are manufactured in Turkey. Previous manufacture was by ITI of Italy until 2007, and utilized the IMC choke system (integral multi-choke), which allows interchangeability with Briley choke tubes.

Add $359 for interchangeable SAS rifled 22 in. slug barrel (mfg. 2004-2007).

SA-459 TR – 12 or 20 ga., 3 in. chamber, 18 1/2 in. ported barrel, 5 or 8 (new 2015) shot mag., tactical configuration with black synthetic pistol grip stock and forearm, includes ghost ring rear sight on Picatinny receiver rail, M16 front sight, oversized bolt handle, approx. 7 lbs. New 2011.

MSR $699	$595	$525	$450	$400	$325	$275	$225	

Add $150 for 8 shot mag. (new 2015).

SHOTGUNS: SLIDE ACTION

PA-08 KNOXX HD – 12 ga., 3 in. chamber, 18 in. barrel with fixed IC choke, black synthetic Knoxx SpecOps adj. stock with pistol grip, extended mag. (5 shot capacity), 7 lbs. Mfg. in Turkey 2008 only.

	$425	$370	$320	$290	$235	$190	$150	*$499*

PA-08 TR – 12 or 20 (new 2013) ga., 3 in. chamber, 18 1/2 in. barrel with fixed cylinder choke and bladed white dot front sight, matte black finish, black synthetic stock and forearm, crossbolt trigger guard safety, 5 shot mag., dual action slide bars, 6 3/4 lbs. New 2011.

MSR $399	$350	$310	$270	$240	$210	$180	$160	

Add $20 for TR accessory rail that attaches to screw-on magazine end cap.

PA-459 HOME DEFENSE – 12 ga. only, 3 in. chamber, 19 in. barrel, black synthetic stock and forearm. Mfg. 2010 only.

	$350	$305	$265	$240	$195	$160	$125	*$469*

PA-459 TR – 12 or 20 (mfg. 2013-2015) ga. only, 3 in. chamber, 18 1/2 in. ported removeable cylinder choke tube, M16 style fiber optic front sight, black synthetic grooved pistol grip stock and forearm, alloy receiver with integral Picatinny rail and adj. ghost ring sight, 13 1/2 in. LOP, 5 (disc. 2015) or 7 (new 2015, 12 ga. only) shot mag., matte black metalwork, 6 1/2 lbs. New 2011.

MSR $599	$475	$400	$340	$295	$265	$235	$210	

Subtract approx. $100 for 20 ga. with 5 shot mag. (mfg. 2013-2015).

* **PA-459 Digital TR** – 12 ga. only, otherwise similar to PA-459 TR, except has green/tan digital camo pattern on stock (not pistol grip) and forearm, choice of 6 or 7 (new 2015) shot mag. Mfg. 2011-2015.

	$465	$400	$350	$295	$265	$235	$210	*$569*

Add $80 for 7 shot mag. (new 2015).

WEAVER ARMS CORPORATION

Previous manufacturer located in Escondido, CA circa 1984-1990.

CARBINES

NIGHTHAWK CARBINE – 9mm Para. cal., semi-auto design carbine, fires from closed bolt, 16.1 in. barrel, retractable shoulder stock, 25, 32, 40, or 50 shot mag. (interchangeable with Uzi), ambidextrous safety, parkerized finish, 6 1/2 lbs. Mfg. 1987-90.

	$675	$600	$525	$450	$375	$325	$300	*$575*

PISTOLS: SEMI-AUTO

NIGHTHAWK PISTOL – 9mm Para. cal., closed bolt semi-auto, 10 or 12 in. barrel, alloy upper receiver, ambidextrous safety, black finish, 5 lbs. Mfg. 1987-90.

	$800	$700	$625	$550	$475	$425	$350	*$475*

WEBLEY & SCOTT AG (LIMITED)

Current trademark of firearms manufactured in Turkey and airguns manufactured in England with headquarters located in Luzern, Switzerland beginning 2010. Currently imported beginning mid-2013 by Centurion International, located in Reno, NV. Previously imported mid-2011-mid-2013 by Webley & Scott USA, located in Reno, NV. Previously located in West Midlands, England, with history dating back to 1790, and Birmingham, England. SxS shotguns were

MSR		100%	98%	95%	90%	80%	70%	60%	Last MSR

previously imported and distributed late 2007-2008 by Legacy Sports International, located in Reno, NV.

Webley & Scott is one of the oldest names in the UK gun industry, being able to trace its origins back to 1790 when William Davis started making bullet moulds in his small factory in Birmingham, England. In this early period Birmingham flourished as the greatest manufacturing centre of firearms in the world. Yet the only official proof house was in London, then in 1813 the world famous Birmingham Proof House was established by an Act of Parliament.

For more information and current pricing on both new and used Webley & Scott airguns, please refer to the *Blue Book of Airguns* by Dr. Robert Beeman & John Allen (also online).

SHOTGUNS: CURRENT MFG.

Currently, Webley & Scott has a line of private label shotguns manufactured for them in Turkey by Komando Av Sa. Tic. Ltd. Sti.

MODEL 600 DELUXE TACTICAL SLIDE ACTION – 12 ga., 3 in. chamber, 20 in. chrome lined barrel with flash suppressor, matte blue receiver, 5 shot, black polymer tactical stock with pistol grip and extra ammo storage, AR style fiber optic front and ghost ring rear sights, heat shield, top Picatinny rail, spring loaded extended forend, swivel studs, rubber recoil pad, 6.6 lbs.

| | MSR $450 | | $375 | $275 | $250 | $200 | $175 | $150 | $125 | |

MODEL 612P20T TACTICAL SLIDE ACTION – 12 ga., 3 in. chamber, 20 in. chrome lined barrel with flash suppressor, matte blue receiver, 5 shot, black polymer tactical stock with pistol grip, AR style fiber optic front and ghost ring rear sights, heat shield, top Picatinny rail, spring loaded extended forend, swivel studs, rubber recoil pad, 6.6 lbs.

| | MSR $400 | | $340 | $300 | $250 | $225 | $185 | $150 | $125 | |

WESSON FIREARMS CO. INC.

Previous manufacturer located in Palmer, MA 1992-95. Previously located in Monson, MA until 1992. In late 1990, ownership of Dan Wesson Arms changed (within the family), and the new company was renamed Wesson Firearms Co., Inc.

REVOLVERS: DOUBLE ACTION

As a guideline, the following information is provided on Wesson Firearms frames. The smallest frames are Models 738P and 38P. Small frame models include 22, 722, 22M, 722M, 32, 732, 322, 7322, 8-2, 708, 9-2, 709, 14-2, 714, 15-2, and 715-2. Large frames include 41, 741, 44, 744, 45, and 745. SuperMag frame models include 40, 740, 375 (disc.), 414 (new 1995), 7414 (new 1995), 445, and 7445. Small frames are sideplate design, while large frames are solid frame construction. Dan Wesson revolvers were mfg. with solid rib barrels as standard equipment.

MODEL 8-2 SERVICE DA – similar to Model 14, except .38 Spl. cal., recessed barrel nut. Mfg. 1975-1995.

| | | | $550 | $475 | $425 | $350 | $300 | $250 | $200 | $274 |

Add approx. $6 for each additional barrel length.

MODEL 9 TARGET DA (1970s Mfg.) – similar to Model 15, except .38 Spl. cal., recessed barrel nut. Mfg. 1971-75.

| | | | $550 | $475 | $425 | $350 | $300 | $250 | $200 | |

MODEL 9-2 TARGET DA – similar to Model 15, except .38 Spl. cal. Use same add-ons as in Model 15. Mfg. 1975-1995.

| | | | $650 | $575 | $500 | $450 | $350 | $275 | $225 | $346 |

This model was also available in a Pistol Pac - same specifications and values as the Model 15 Pistol Pac.

MODEL 11 SERVICE DA – .357 Mag. cal., 6 shot, 2 1/2, 4, or 6 in. interchangeable barrels, fixed sights, blue, interchangeable grips, exposed barrel nut. Mfg. 1970-71 only.

| | | | $550 | $475 | $425 | $350 | $300 | $250 | $200 | |

Add $60 per extra barrel.

MODEL 12 SERVICE DA – similar to Model 11, with adj. sights, exposed barrel nut. Mfg. 1970-71 only.

| | | | $625 | $550 | $475 | $425 | $325 | $265 | $215 | |

MODEL 14 SERVICE DA (1970s Mfg.) – .357 Mag. cal., similar to Model 11, with recessed barrel nut. Mfg. 1971-75.

| | | | $625 | $550 | $475 | $425 | $325 | $265 | $215 | |

MODEL 14-2 SERVICE DA – .357 Mag. cal., 2 1/2, 4, 6, or 8 (disc. 1994) in. interchangeable barrels, fixed sights, blue. Mfg. 1975-1995.

| | | | $550 | $475 | $425 | $350 | $300 | $250 | $200 | $274 |

Add approx. $7 for each additional barrel length.

MODEL 15 TARGET DA (1970s Mfg.) – similar to Model 14, with adj. sights. Mfg. 1971-75.

| | | | $625 | $550 | $475 | $425 | $325 | $265 | $215 | |

MODEL 15-2 TARGET DA – similar to Model 14, except adj. sights, available with 2, 4, 6, 8, 10, 12, or 15 in. barrels. Disc. 1995.

MSR	100%	98%	95%	90%	80%	70%	60%	Last MSR

* Model 15-2 Target DA Gold Series – .357 Mag. cal., 6 or 8 in. VR heavy slotted barrel, "Gold" stamped shroud with Dan Wesson signature, smoother action (8 lb. double action pull), 18Kt. gold-plated trigger, white triangle rear sight with orange-dot Patridge front sight, exotic hardwood grips. Mfg. 1989-94.

	$800	$700	$600	$550	$450	$350	$275	$544

MODEL 38P – .38+P cal., 5 shot, 6 1/2 in. barrel, fixed sights, wood or rubber grips, 24.6 oz. Mfg. 1992-93.

	$550	$475	$425	$350	$300	$250	$200	$285

MODEL 41 – .41 Mag. cal., double action, 6 shot, 4, 6, 8, or 10 in. barrel VR. Disc. 1995.

	$800	$700	$600	$550	$450	$350	$275	$447

Add approx. $20 for heavy barrel shroud, approx. $15 for each additional barrel length.

MODEL 45 – .45 LC cal., 4, 6, 8, or 10 in. VR barrel, same frame as Model 44V, blue finish. Mfg. 1988-95.

	$650	$575	$500	$450	$350	$275	$225	$447

Add $20 for VR heavy barrel shroud, approx. $15 for each additional barrel length.

* Model 45 Pin Gun – .45 ACP cal., competition pin gun model with 5 in. vent. or heavy vent. barrel configuration, blue steel, two stage Taylor forcing cone, 54 oz. Mfg. 1993-95.

	$800	$700	$600	$550	$450	$350	$275	$654

Add $9 for VR heavy shroud barrel.

REVOLVERS: STAINLESS STEEL

Models 722, 722M, 709, 715, 732, 7322, 741V, 744V, and 745V were available in a pistol pack including 2 1/2, 4, 6, and 8 in. solid rib barrel assemblies, extra grip, 4 additional sight blades, and fitted carrying case. Last published retail prices were $712 and $785 for the standard and stainless steel models, respectively. VR or full shroud barrels were optional and were approx. priced $103 and $210, respectively.

MODEL 708 – .38 Spl. cal., similar to Model 8. Add approx. $6 for each additional barrel length. Disc. 1995.

	$550	$475	$425	$375	$300	$250	$200	$319

* Model 708 Action Cup/PPC – .38 Spl. cal., extra heavy shrouded 6 in. bull barrel with removable underweight, Hogue Gripper grips, mounted Tasco Pro Point II on Action Cup, Aristocrat sights on PPC. Mfg. 1992 only.

	$850	$750	$650	$575	$475	$375	$300	$857

Add $56 for Action Cup Model with Tasco Scope.

MODEL 709 – .38 Spl. cal., target revolver, adj. sights. Also available in special order 10, 12 (disc.), or 15 (disc.) in. barrel lengths. Disc. 1995.

	$550	$480	$415	$375	$305	$250	$195	$376

Add approx. $10 for each additional longer barrel length, approx. $19 for VR, approx. $56 for heavy VR.

MODEL 714 (INTERCHANGEABLE OR FIXED) – .357 Mag. cal., fixed sight Service Model with 2 1/2, 4, or 6 in. barrel, brushed stainless steel. Mfg. 1993-95.

	$550	$480	$415	$375	$305	$250	$195	$319

Add approx. $6 for 4 or 6 in. barrel.
Subtract $6 for fixed barrel (2 1/2 or 4 in. barrel only).

* Model 714 Action Cup/PPC – .357 Mag. cal., extra heavy shrouded 6 in. bull barrel with removable underweight, Hogue Gripper grips, mounted Tasco Pro Point II on Action Cup, Aristocrat sights on PPC. Mfg. 1992 only.

	$850	$750	$650	$575	$475	$375	$300	$857

Add $56 for Action Cup Model with Tasco Scope.

MODEL 715 INTERCHANGEABLE – .357 Mag. cal., 2 1/2, 4, 6, 8, or 10 in. barrel with adj. rear sight, brushed stainless steel. Mfg. 1993-95.

	$550	$480	$415	$375	$305	$250	$195	$376

Add approx. $10 for each additional longer barrel length, approx. $19 for VR, approx. $56 for heavy VR.

* Model 715 Fixed Target – .357 Mag. cal., 3, 4, 5, or 6 in. fixed barrel, adj. rear sight. Mfg. 1993-95.

	$550	$480	$415	$375	$305	$250	$195	$345

Add approx. $70 for compensated barrel (4, 5, or 6 in. - new 1994).

MODEL 732 – .32 H&R Mag. cal., similar to Model 32, except is stainless steel. Mfg. 1986-95.

	$650	$575	$500	$450	$350	$275	$225	$400

Add $22 for VR barrel shroud (Model 732-V), $53 for VR heavy barrel shroud (Model 732-VH), approx. $9 for each additional barrel length over 2 1/2 in.

MODEL 738P – .38 +P cal., 2, 4, or 6 1/2 in. barrel, 5 shot cylinder, stainless steel, groove in top strap rear and ramp front fixed sights, rubber or wood grips, 24.6 oz. Mfg. 1992-95.

	$550	$480	$415	$375	$305	$250	$195	$340

MSR		100%	98%	95%	90%	80%	70%	60%		Last MSR

MODEL 741V – .41 Mag. cal., similar to Model 41V. Disc. 1995.

		$800	$700	$600	$550	$450	$350	$275		$524

Add approx. $20 for heavy VR, approx. $13 for each barrel length over 4 in.

MODEL 744V – .44 Mag. cal., similar to Model 44V. Disc. 1995. - limited mfg.

		$800	$700	$600	$550	$450	$350	$275		$524

Add approx. $20 for heavy VR, $13 for each barrel length over 4 in.

* *Model 744V Target Fixed Barrel* – .44 Mag. cal., 4, 5, 6, or 8 in. barrel, brushed stainless steel. Mfg. 1994-95.

		$700	$600	$550	$500	$400	$300	$250		$493

Add approx. $4 for each barrel length over 3 in.

MODEL 745V – .45 LC cal., similar to Model 45, except in stainless steel. Disc. 1995.

		$800	$700	$600	$550	$450	$350	$275		$524

Add $20 for heavy full shroud VR barrels, $13 for each additional barrel length.

MODEL 745 PIN GUN – .45 ACP cal., similar to Model 45 Pin Gun, except is stainless steel. Mfg. 1993-95.

		$800	$700	$600	$550	$450	$350	$275		$713

Add $49 for VR heavy rib shroud.

SUPER RAM SILHOUETTE – .357 Max., .414 Super Mag., or .44 Mag. cal., silhouette variation featuring modified Iron Sight Gun Works rear sight, Allen Taylor throated barrel, factory trigger job, 4 lbs. Mfg. 1995 only.

		$1,000	$875	$750	$675	$550	$450	$350		$807

Add $43 for .414 Super Mag. cal.

HUNTER SERIES – .357 Super Mag., .41 Mag., .44 Mag., or .445 Super Mag. cal., 7 1/2 in. barrel with heavy shroud, Hogue rubber finger grooved and wood presentation grips, choice of Gunworks iron sights or w/o sights with Burris base and rings, non-fluted cylinder, with or w/o compensator, approx. 4 lbs. Mfg. 1994-95.

		$1,000	$875	$750	$675	$550	$450	$350		$849

Add $32 for compensated barrel.
Add $32 for scope mounts (w/o sights).

WILDEY, INC.

Previous manufacturer located in Warren, CT 2000-circa 2011. Previously located in New Milford, CT until 1999.

Originally, the company was named Wildey Firearms Co., Inc. located in Cheshire, CT. At that time, serialization of pistols was 45-0000. When Wildey, Inc. bought the company out of bankruptcy from the old shareholders, there had been approximately 800 pistols mfg. To distinguish the old company from the present company, the serial range was changed to 09-0000 (only 633 pistols with the 09 prefix were produced). These guns had the Cheshire, CT address. Pistols produced by Wildey, Inc., New Milford, CT are serial numbered with 4 digits (no numerical prefix).

CARBINES: SEMI-AUTO

WILDEY CARBINE – .44 Auto Mag., .45 Wildey Mag., .45 Win. Mag., or .475 Wildey Mag. cal., features 18 in. barrel with forearm and detachable skeleton walnut stock, polished or matte stainless steel. Mfg. 2003-2011.

		$2,700	$2,225	$1,750	$1,500	$1,235	$1,030	$855		$3,110

Add $237 for matte stainless steel finish.

PISTOLS: SEMI-AUTO

Add $585-$1,950 per interchangeable barrel assembly, depending on barrel length and finish.

WILDEY AUTO PISTOL – .45 Win. Mag., .45 Wildey Mag., or .475 Wildey Mag., gas operated, 5, 6, 7, 8, 10, or 14 in. VR barrel, SA, selective single shot or semi-auto, 3 lug rotary bolt, fixed barrel (interchangeable), polished stainless steel construction, 7 shot, double action, adj. sights, smooth or checkered wood grips, designed to fire proprietary new cartridges specifically for this gun including the .45 Win. Mag. cal., 64 oz. with 5 in. barrel.

Add $560-$1,148 per interchangeable barrel.

* *Wildey Survivor Model* – .357 Mag., .44 Auto Mag. (new 2003), .45 Win. Mag., 45 Wildey Mag., or .475 Wildey Mag. cal., 5, 6, 7, 8, 10, 12, 14 (new 2000), or 18 (new 2003) in. VR barrel, polished stainless steel finish. Mfg. 1990-2011.

		$1,375	$1,025	$800	$665	$560	$465	$410		$1,571

Add $26 - $125 for 5 - 12 in. barrel, depending on length, and $1,206 for 18 in. Silhouette model.
Add $26 for .45 Wildey Mag. or .475 Wildey Mag. cal.

The .475 Wildey cal. is derived from a factory cartridge.

* *Wildey Survivor Guardsman* – similar to Survivor Model, except has squared-off trigger guard, same options apply to this model as for the Survivor model. Mfg. 1990-2011.

		$1,375	$1,025	$800	$665	$560	$465	$410		$1,571

MSR	100%	98%	95%	90%	80%	70%	60%	Last MSR

* ***Wildey Hunter Guardsman*** – similar to Hunter Model, except has squared-off trigger guard, same options apply to this model as for the Hunter model. Mfg. 1990-2011.

	$1,575	$1,225	$950	$810	$670	$565	$475	*$1,829*

Add $100 for 12 in. barrel.
Add $625 for 14 in. barrel.
Add $1,175 for 18 in. silhouette barrel.

WILDEY AUTO PISTOL OLDER MFG. – .475 Wildey Mag. cal. was available in 8 or 10 in. barrel only.

* ***Older Wildey Serial Nos. 1-200.***

	$1,900	$1,700	$1,550	$1,365	$1,125	$950	$775	*$2,180*

Add $20 for 8 or 10 in. barrel.

* ***Older Wildey Serial Nos. 201-400.***

	$1,750	$1,550	$1,400	$1,235	$1,000	$870	$700	*$1,980*

Add $20 for 8 or 10 in. barrel.

* ***Older Wildey Serial Nos. 401-600.***

	$1,650	$1,375	$1,250	$1,100	$895	$785	$630	*$1,780*

Add $20 for 8 or 10 in. barrel.

* ***Older Wildey Serial Nos. 601-800.***

	$1,450	$1,200	$1,000	$885	$715	$610	$515	*$1,580*

Add $20 for 8 or 10 in. barrel.

* ***Older Wildey Serial Nos. 801-1,000.***

	$1,100	$925	$800	$695	$585	$485	$415	*$1,275*

Add $25 for 8 or 10 in. barrel.

* ***Older Wildey Serial Nos. 1,001-2,489.***

	$1,025	$850	$750	$640	$535	$450	$390	*$1,175*

Add $20 for 8 or 10 in. barrel.

WILKINSON ARMS

Previous trademark established circa 1996 and manufactured by Ray Wilkinson circa 1996-1998 (limited production), and by Northwest Arms located in Parma, ID circa 2000-2005.

CARBINES

LINDA CARBINE – 9mm Para. cal., 16 3/16 in. barrel, aluminum receiver, pre-ban configuration (limited supplies), fixed tubular stock with wood pad, vent. barrel shroud, aperture rear sight, small wooden forearm, 18 or 31 shot mag., beginning 2002, this model came standard with many accessories, 7 lbs. Mfg. circa 1996-2005.

	$1,295	$1,075	$850	$725	$600	$500	$425	*$1,800*

Only 2,200 Linda Carbines were marked "Luger Carbine" on the receiver. The last 1,500 distributed by Northwest Arms include a longer stock, and matched bolt and barrel (Rockwell 57).

TERRY CARBINE – 9mm Para. cal., blowback semi-auto action, 31 shot mag., 16 3/16 in. barrel, closed breech, adj. sights, 7 lbs. Disc.

	100%	98%	95%	90%	80%	70%	60%
With black P.V.C. stock	$475	$395	$325	$295	$260	$230	$200
With maple stock	$625	$525	$400	$350	$340	$325	$300

PISTOLS: SEMI-AUTO

DIANE MODEL – .25 ACP cal., 6 shot, 2 1/8 in. barrel, fixed sight, matte blue, plastic grips. Disc.

	$150	$125	$95	$80	$65	$55	$50

LINDA MODEL – 9mm Para. cal., blowback action firing from closed bolt, 8.3 in. barrel, 31 shot mag., PVC pistol grip, maple forearm, Williams adj. rear sight. Disc.

	$675	$625	$550	$475	$425	$350	$295

SHERRY MODEL – .22 LR cal., 2 1/2 in. barrel, aluminum frame, fully machined steel slide, trigger group, and bolt insert, available in various colors, 9 1/4 oz. Mfg. 2000-2005.

	$245	$200	$160	$140	$125	$110	$100	*$280*

Add $25 for gold anodized frame.
Add $20 for collector's edition.
Add $100 for Robar coating.

MSR	100%	98%	95%	90%	80%	70%	60%	Last MSR

WILSON COMBAT

Current firearms manufacturer, customizer, and supplier of custom firearms parts and accessories established in 1978, and located in Berryville, AR.

PISTOLS: SEMI-AUTO, SINGLE ACTION

Prices reflect .45 ACP cal. base model w/o upgrades. A wide variety of options are available - contact the company directly for pricing. Add $325 for the WCR-22 pistol suppressor (new 2016).

CONTEMPORARY CLASSIC CENTENNIAL – .45 ACP cal., 100th anniversary of the 1911, full size carbon steel frame and slide, 5 in. carbon match grade barrel and bushing, 8 shot mag., Turnbull charcoal blue finish, French walnut double diamond grips, beavertail grip safety, contoured magwell, lanyard loop mainspring housing, 30 LPI high cut checkered front grip strap, "1911-2011" engraving, battlesight with gold bead front sight, tactical thumb safety, top and rear slide serrations, special serial numbers (JMB001-JMB100) includes walnut presentation box, 45 oz. Limited edition of 100 mfg. during 2011.

	100%	98%	95%	90%	80%	70%	60%	Last MSR
	$3,550	$3,150	$2,725	$2,350	$1,950	$1,650	$1,350	*$3,995*

CLASSIC – 9mm Para., 10mm, .38 Super, 40 S&W, or .45 ACP cal., full size carbon steel frame, 5 in. stainless match grade barrel and bushing, carbon steel slide, two-tone finish, 30 LPI high cut checkered front strap, rear slide serrations, tactical thumb safety, contoured magwell, Cocobolo double diamond grips, high ride beavertail grip safety, Lo-Mount adj. rear sight with improved ramp front sight.

MSR $3,030	$2,575	$2,250	$1,925	$1,750	$1,450	$1,175	$1,000

Add $115 for 9mm Para., .38 Super, or .40 S&W cal.
Add $225 for 10mm cal.

CLASSIC SUPERGRADE – 9mm Para., 10mm, .38 Super, .40 S&W, or .45 ACP cal., full size stainless steel frame, 5 in. stainless match grade barrel and bushing, carbon steel slide, blue finish, 30 LPI high cut checkered front strap, top and rear slide serrations, Lo-Mount adj. rear sight, improved ramp front sight, ambidextrous safety, Speed-Chute magwell, Cocobolo double diamond grips, beavertail grip safety, full length guide rod, each gun hand built. Limited mfg.

MSR $5,195	$4,675	$4,225	$3,750	$3,150	$2,650	$2,200	$1,700

Add $105 for 9mm Para., 10mm, .38 Super, or .40 S&W cal.

TACTICAL SUPERGRADE – 9mm Para., 10mm (disc. 2011, 2015), .38 Super, .40 S&W (disc. 2011, 2015), or .45 ACP cal., full size stainless steel frame, 5 in. stainless match grade barrel and bushing, carbon steel slide, blue finish, 30 LPI high cut checkered front strap, top and rear slide serrations, ambidextrous safety, Speed-Chute magwell, G10 starburst grips, beavertail grip safety, battlesight with white outline Tritium front sight.

MSR $5,045	$4,550	$4,125	$3,700	$3,100	$2,600	$2,100	$1,650

Add $105 for .38 Super, 9mm Para., 10mm, or .40 S&W cal.

* **Tactical Supergrade Professional** – 9mm Para., .38 Super, or .45 ACP cal., carbon steel frame, 4 in. stainless match grade cone barrel, carbon steel slide, 8 shot mag., blue finish, 30 LPI high cut checkered front strap, top and rear slide serrations, ambidextrous thumb safety, Speed-Chute magwell, G10 starburst grips, beavertail grip safety, Battlesight with white outline Tritium front sight, full length guide rod and reverse plug, 44.8 oz. New 2010.

MSR $5,045	$4,550	$4,125	$3,700	$3,100	$2,600	$2,100	$1,650

Add $105 for .38 Super or 9mm Para. cal.

* **Tactical Supergrade Compact** – 9mm Para., .38 Super, or .45 ACP cal., compact carbon steel frame, 4 in. stainless match grade cone barrel, carbon steel slide, blue finish, 30 LPI high cut checkered front strap, top and rear slide serrations, ambidextrous thumb safety, Speed-Chute magwell, G10 starburst grips, beavertail grip safety, battlesight with white outline Tritium front sight, full length guide rod and reverse plug.

MSR $5,045	$4,550	$4,125	$3,700	$3,100	$2,600	$2,100	$1,650

Add $105 for 9mm Para. or .38 Super cal.

ULTRALIGHT CARRY – 9mm Para., .38 Super, or .45 ACP cal., full size aluminum round butt frame, 5 in. stainless match grade barrel and bushing, flush cut and crowned, carbon steel slide, blue finish, 30 LPI high cut checkered front strap, top and rear slide serrations, tactical thumb safety, contoured magwell, G10 starburst grips, beavertail grip safety and hammer, Battlesight with fiber optic front sight, countersunk slide stop.

MSR $3,650	$3,350	$2,950	$2,550	$2,150	$1,825	$1,525	$1,225

* **Ultralight Carry Compact** – 9mm Para., .38 Super, or .45 ACP cal., similar to Ultralight Carry, except has compact frame and 4 in. fluted barrel.

MSR $3,650	$3,350	$2,950	$2,550	$2,150	$1,825	$1,525	$1,225

* **Ultralight Carry Sentinel** – 9mm Para. cal., Sentinel aluminum round butt frame, 3 1/2 in. stainless match grade cone fluted barrel, 8 shot mag., carbon steel slide, blue finish, 30 LPI high cut checkered front strap, top and rear slide serrations, tactical thumb safety, contoured magwell, G10 starburst grips, beavertail grip safety and hammer, Battlesight with fiber optic front sight, shortened rounded mag. release, countersunk slide stop, approx. 31 oz.

MSR $3,875	$3,500	$3,100	$2,650	$2,225	$1,875	$1,575	$1,275

MSR	100%	98%	95%	90%	80%	70%	60%	Last MSR

CARRY COMP COMPACT – 9mm Para. (disc. 2011), .38 Super, or .45 ACP cal., full size stainless steel, lightweight aluminum, or carbon steel frame, 4 1/2 in. compensated match grade barrel, green, black, tan, or grey Amor-Tuff finish, high ride beavertail grip safety, Dymondwood grips, combat tactical sight system 30 LPI front strap checkering, skeletonized ultra light hammer.

| MSR $3,765 | $3,425 | $3,025 | $2,600 | $2,175 | $1,850 | $1,550 | $1,250 | |

Add $165 for Carry Comp Compact Lightweight (disc. 2012).

* **Carry Comp Professional** – 9mm Para. (disc. 2011), .38 Super, or .45 ACP cal., similar to Carry Comp, except has compact frame that is 1/2 in. shorter. Disc. 2012.

| | $3,425 | $3,025 | $2,600 | $2,175 | $1,850 | $1,550 | $1,250 | *$3,765* |

Add $165 for Carry Comp Professional Lightweight.

BILL WILSON CARRY PISTOL – .45 ACP cal., compact carbon steel round butt frame, 4 in. stainless match grade cone barrel, 7 shot mag., carbon steel slide, blue finish, 30 LPI high cut checkered front strap, rear slide serrations, tactical thumb safety, contoured magwell, G10 starburst grips, high ride beavertail grip safety, battlesight with fiber optic front sight, approx. 39 oz.

| MSR $3,205 | $2,775 | $2,350 | $2,025 | $1,775 | $1,475 | $1,275 | $1,075 | |

CQB – 9mm Para., .38 Super, .40 S&W (new 2012), 10mm (new 2012), or .45 ACP cal., full size aluminum round butt frame, 5 in. stainless match grade barrel and bushing, flush cut and crowned, carbon steel slide, blue finish, 30 LPI high cut checkered front strap, top and rear slide serrations, tactical thumb safety, contoured magwell, G10 starburst grips, beavertail grip safety and hammer, Battlesight with fiber optic front sight, countersunk slide stop.

| MSR $2,865 | $2,575 | $2,150 | $1,825 | $1,550 | $1,225 | $1,050 | $925 | |

Add $110 for 9mm Para., .38 Super, or .40 S&W cal.
Add $225 for 10mm cal.

* **CQB Elite** – 9mm Para., 10mm, .38 Super, .40 S&W, or .45 ACP cal., full size carbon steel frame, 5 in. stainless match grade barrel and bushing, carbon steel slide, blue finish, 30 LPI high cut checkered front strap, top and rear slide serrations, tactical thumb safety, Speed-Chute magwell with lanyard loop, G10 diagonal flat bottom grips, beavertail grip safety, Battlesight with fiber optic front sight.

| MSR $3,425 | $3,100 | $2,700 | $2,400 | $2,000 | $1,700 | $1,400 | $1,150 | |

Add $110 for 9mm Para., .38 Super, or .40 S&W cal.
Add $225 for 10mm cal.

* **CQB Tactical LE Light-Rail** – 9mm Para., 10mm, .38 Super, .40 S&W, or .45 ACP cal., full size carbon steel frame, 5 in. stainless match grade bull barrel, carbon steel slide, blue finish, integral light rail, 30 LPI high cut checkered front strap, top and rear slide serrations, tactical thumb safety, Speed-Chute magwell with lanyard loop, G10 diagonal flat bottom grips, beavertail grip safety, Battlesight with fiber optic front sight.

| MSR $3,115 | $2,700 | $2,300 | $2,000 | $1,750 | $1,450 | $1,200 | $1,050 | |

Add $115 for 9mm Para., .38 Super, or .40 S&W cal.
Add $230 for 10mm cal.

* **CQB Light-Rail** – 9mm Para., 10mm, .38 Super, .40 S&W, or .45 ACP cal., full size aluminum frame, 5 in. stainless match grade barrel and bushing, carbon steel slide, blue finish, integral light rail, 30 LPI high cut checkered front strap, top and rear slide serrations, tactical thumb safety, contoured magwell, G10 starburst grips, beavertail grip safety, battlesight with fiber optic front sight. Disc. 2012.

| | $2,625 | $2,225 | $1,950 | $1,700 | $1,400 | $1,175 | $1,025 | *$3,005* |

* **CQB Lightweight/Light-Rail Lightweight** – 9mm Para., 10mm (disc. 2014), .38 Super, .40 S&W, or .45 ACP cal., full size aluminum frame, 5 in. stainless match grade barrel and bushing, carbon steel slide, blue finish, with or w/o (disc. 2014) integral light rail, 30 LPI high cut checkered front strap, top and rear slide serrations, tactical thumb safety, contoured magwell, G10 starburst grips, beavertail grip safety, battlesight with fiber optic front sight, weighs 14% less than steel model.

| MSR $3,030 | $2,650 | $2,225 | $1,950 | $1,700 | $1,400 | $1,175 | $1,125 | |

Add $110 for 9mm Para., .38 Super, or .40 S&W cal.
Subtract approx. $115 if without light rail.

» **CQB Light-Rail Lightweight Professional** – 9mm Para., .38 Super or .45 ACP cal., similar to CQB Light-Rail Lightweight, except has professional size aluminum frame and 4 in. stainless match grade cone barrel.

| MSR $3,205 | $2,775 | $2,350 | $2,025 | $1,775 | $1,475 | $1,225 | $1,075 | |

» **CQB Light-Rail Lightweight Compact** – 9mm Para., .38 Super (disc. 2011) or .45 ACP cal., compact aluminum round butt frame, 4 in. stainless match grade cone barrel, carbon steel slide, blue finish, integral light rail, 30 LPI high cut checkered front strap, top and rear slide serrations, tactical thumb safety, contoured magwell, G10 starburst grips, high ride beavertail grip safety, Battlesight with fiber optic front sight, weighs 14% less than steel model.

| MSR $3,280 | $2,825 | $2,375 | $2,050 | $1,800 | $1,500 | $1,200 | $1,125 | |

MSR	100%	98%	95%	90%	80%	70%	60%	Last MSR

* CQB Compact – 9mm Para., .38 Super or .45 ACP cal., compact carbon steel frame, 4 in. stainless match grade cone barrel, carbon steel slide, blue finish, 30 LPI high cut checkered front strap, top and rear slide serrations, tactical thumb safety, contoured magwell, G10 starburst grips, high ride beavertail grip safety, Battlesight with fiber optic front sight.

MSR $2,890	$2,575	$2,150	$1,850	$1,575	$1,250	$1,075	$950

Add $205 for CQB Compact Lightweight.

HACKATHORN SPECIAL – 9mm Para., .38 Super, or .45 ACP cal., full size carbon steel frame, 5 in. stainless match grade barrel, 5 in. carbon steel slide, fluted chamber, 8 shot mag., checkered front strap, black G10 starburst flat bottom grips, Bullet Proof tactical thumb safety, magwell and mag. release, beavertail grip safety and hammer, Battlesight with fiber optic front sight, top and rear slide serrations, approx. 40 oz.

MSR $3,750	$3,450	$3,150	$2,700	$2,300	$1,875	$1,550	$1,250

HUNTER – 10mm or .460 Rowland cal., 5 1/2 in. single port compensated barrel with fully supported chamber, full size carbon steel frame with carbon steel slide, 30 LPI high cut checkered front strap, tactical thumb safety, contoured magwell, high ride beavertail grip safety, Crimson Trace laser grips, countersunk slide stop, full length guide rod with reverse plug, approx. 40 oz.

MSR $4,100	$3,650	$3,150	$2,750	$2,350	$1,875	$1,550	$1,350

PINNACLE – .45 ACP cal., based on the Classic Supergrade model, full size frame, 5 in. stainless match grade barrel, 8 shot, full length spiral fluted guide rod, 5 in. carbon steel slide, blued steel trigger, beavertail grip safety, deluxe burl wood smooth grips with gold plated grip medallions, lo-mount adj. rear sight with Battleblade, gold bead front sight, checkered front strap, hand fitted and finished, classic scroll pattern hand engraving, deluxe blue with polished sides of frame and slide, deluxe walnut presentation case, letter of authenticity, detailed inside & out with options selected by Bill Wilson, highest grade of craftsmanship, 45 oz.

MSR $7,995	$7,250	$6,500	$5,750	$4,995	$4,250	$3,500	$2,700

PROFESSIONAL – 9mm Para., .38 Super, 40 S&W (disc. 2011), or .45 ACP cal., professional size carbon steel frame, 4 in. stainless match grade cone barrel, carbon steel slide, blue finish, 30 LPI high cut checkered front strap, top and rear slide serrations, tactical thumb safety, contoured magwell, G10 starburst grips, high ride beavertail grip safety, battlesight with fiber optic front sight.

MSR $2,920	$2,475	$2,175	$1,850	$1,685	$1,350	$1,125	$975

* Professional Lightweight – 9mm Para., .38 Super or .45 ACP cal., similar to Professional, except has lightweight aluminum frame.

MSR $3,090	$2,625	$2,300	$1,975	$1,785	$1,450	$1,175	$1,000

ELITE PROFESSIONAL – 9mm Para., .38 Super or .45 ACP cal., professional size carbon steel frame, 4 in. stainless match grade heavy flanged cone barrel, carbon steel slide, blue finish, 30 LPI high cut checkered front strap, rear slide serrations, ambidextrous thumb safety, Speed-Chute magwell, G10 diagonal flat bottom grips, high ride beavertail grip safety, Battlesight with fiber optic front sight.

MSR $3,650	$3,350	$2,950	$2,550	$2,150	$1,825	$1,525	$1,225

Add $165 for Elite Professional Lightweight.

TACTICAL ELITE – 9mm Para., 10mm, .38 Super, 40 S&W, or .45 ACP cal., full size carbon steel frame, 5 in. stainless match grade heavy flanged cone barrel, carbon steel slide, blue finish, 30 LPI high cut checkered front strap, front and rear slide serrations, ambidextrous thumb safety, Speed-Chute magwell, G10 starburst grips, high ride beavertail grip safety, Battlesight with fiber optic front sight.

MSR $3,650	$3,350	$2,950	$2,550	$2,150	$1,825	$1,525	$1,225

Add $165 for Tactical Elite Lightweight.

TACTICAL CARRY – .45 ACP cal., full size carbon steel frame, 5 in. stainless match grade barrel, flush cut reverse crown, fluted chamber, 5 in. carbon steel slide, Baround butt one-piece magwell, slide top and rear serrations, Battlesight with fiber optic front sight, Bullet Proof beavertail grip safety and hammer, Bullet Proof magazine release G10 starburst grips. New 2015.

MSR $3,750	$3,450	$3,150	$2,700	$2,300	$1,875	$1,550	$1,250

PROTECTOR – 9mm Para., 10mm, .38 Super, 40 S&W, or .45 ACP cal., full size carbon steel frame, 5 in. stainless match grade barrel and bushing, carbon steel slide, two-tone finish, 30 LPI high cut checkered front strap, front and rear slide serrations, tactical thumb safety, contoured magwell, G10 starburst grips, high ride beavertail grip safety, Battlesight with fiber optic front sight.

MSR $2,920	$2,475	$2,175	$1,850	$1,685	$1,350	$1,125	$975

MSR	100%	98%	95%	90%	80%	70%	60%	Last MSR

STEALTH (S.D.S.) – 9mm Para., .38 Super, .40 S&W (disc. 2011) or .45 ACP cal., compact carbon steel frame, 4 in. stainless match grade heavy flanged cone barrel, carbon steel slide, blue finish, 30 LPI high cut checkered front strap, rear slide serrations, ambidextrous thumb safety, contoured magwell, G10 starburst grips, high ride beavertail grip safety, Battlesight with fiber optic front sight, full length guide rod with reverse plug.

MSR $3,535	$3,225	$2,875	$2,500	$2,100	$1,775	$1,475	$1,175	

Add $280 for Stealth Lightweight.

SENTINEL – 9mm Para. cal., carbon steel frame that is 1/2 in. shorter than compact, 3 1/2 in. stainless match grade cone barrel, 8 shot mag., carbon steel slide, blue finish, 30 LPI high cut checkered front strap, rear slide serrations, tactical thumb safety, contoured magwell, G10 slimline grips, high ride beavertail grip safety, Battlesight with fiber optic front sight, full length guide rod with reverse plug, approx. 32 oz.

MSR $3,310	$2,850	$2,375	$2,050	$1,800	$1,500	$1,225	$1,125	

Add $115 for Sentinel Lightweight.

* ***Sentinel Compact*** – 9mm Para. cal., similar to Sentinel, except has carbon steel compact frame. Mfg. 2012.

	$2,800	$2,375	$2,050	$1,800	$1,500	$1,250	$1,075	*$3,255*

Add $170 for Sentinel Compact Lightweight.

* ***Sentinel Professional*** – 9mm Para. cal., similar to Sentinel, except has professional size carbon steel frame. Mfg. 2012.

	$2,850	$2,375	$2,050	$1,800	$1,500	$1,225	$1,125	*$3,310*

Add $115 for Sentinel Professional Lightweight.

MS. SENTINEL – 9mm Para. cal., aluminum frame that is 1/2 in. shorter than compact, 3 1/2 in. stainless match grade cone fluted barrel, 8 shot mag., carbon steel slide, blue finish, 30 LPI high cut checkered front strap, rear slide serrations, tactical thumb safety, contoured magwell, Cocobolo starburst grips, concealment Bullet Proof beavertail grip safety and hammer, Bullet Proof shortened/rounded mag. release, Battlesight with fiber optic front sight, countersunk slide stop, heavy machine chamfer on bottom of slide, full length guide rod with reverse plug, approx. 31 oz.

MSR $3,875	$3,500	$3,100	$2,650	$2,225	$1,875	$1,575	$1,275	

SUPER SENTINEL – .38 Super cal., 8 shot mag., 3.6 in. match grade barrel, carbon steel slide, Sentinel aluminum frame, 30 LPI high cut checkered front strap, High Ride Bullet Proof beavertail grip safety, Bullet Proof thumb safety, contoured magwell, G10 slimline grips, fiber optic front sight, full length guide rod with reverse plug, 25.2 oz. New 2012.

MSR $3,875	$3,500	$3,100	$2,650	$2,225	$1.875	$1,575	$1,275	

SPEC-OPS 9 – 9mm Para. cal., 4 1/4 in. stainless steel match grade barrel, mid-size polymer frame with fully machined stainless steel rail insert, 16 shot mag., blue finish, 20 LPI checkered front strap, concealment Bullet Proof beavertail grip safety and Spec-Ops ultralight hammer, tactical thumb safety, Starburst grip pattern with textured grip radiuses, countersunk slide stop, contoured magwell, 30 LPI slide top serrations, Spec-Ops Lo-Profile rear sight, inline dovetail improved ramp fiber optic front sight, 37 oz.

MSR $2,285	$2,000	$1,750	$1,525	$1,300	$1,100	$900	$775	

X-TAC – .45 ACP cal., full size carbon steel frame, 8 shot mag., 5 in. stainless match grade barrel and bushing, carbon steel slide, parkerized finish, X-Tac front strap/mainspring housing, X-Tac rear cocking serrations, tactical thumb safety, contoured magwell, G10 starburst grips, beavertail grip safety, Battlesight with fiber optic front sight, 46.2 oz.

MSR $2,760	$2,495	$2,100	$1,800	$1,550	$1,225	$1,050	$925	

Add $25 for X-Tac Compact with smaller frame.

RIFLES

All rifles come standard with nylon tactical case.

A variety of accessories are available for additional cost - please contact the company directly for more information on available options (see Trademark Index).

Add $325 for WCR-22 rimfire rifle suppressor (new 2016).

.308 SUPER SNIPER – .308 Win. cal., 20 in. button rifled stainless steel fluted or non-fluted barrel, billet AR machined aluminum upper and lower receivers, 12 or 14 in. free-floating T.R.I.M. rail, customer's choice of tactical trigger unit and Armor Tuff finish colors, 9.2 lbs. New 2015.

MSR $3,095	$2,775	$2,400	$1,925	$1,650	$1,375	$1,150	$995	

Add $100 for fluted barrel.

M4 TACTICAL CARBINE – .223 Rem. cal., GIO, 16 1/4 in. fluted match grade barrel with muzzle brake, aluminum flat-top upper and lower receiver, quad rail free float aluminum handguard, black, green, tan or gray anodized finish, 20 shot mag., single stage trigger, Ergo pistol grip, 6-position collapsible stock, 6.9 lbs. Disc. 2011.

	$1,825	$1,650	$1,450	$1,250	$1,050	$875	$675	*$2,000*

MSR	100%	98%	95%	90%	80%	70%	60%	Last MSR

SPR (SPECIAL PURPOSE RIFLE) – 5.56 NATO cal., GIO, 18 in. stainless steel match grade barrel with Accu-Tac flash hider, low profile gas block, forged flat-top upper and lower receiver, quad rail free float aluminum handguard (disc.) or T.R.I.M. rail, 20 shot mag., single stage trigger, Ergo (disc.) or Bravo pistol grip, A2 fixed (disc.) or Wilson/Rogers Super-Stoc buttstock, black, green, tan or gray anodized finish, 6.9 lbs.

| MSR $2,450 | $2,250 | $1,850 | $1,675 | $1,350 | $1,100 | $875 | $750 | |

SS-15 SUPER SNIPER RIFLE – .223 Rem./5.56 NATO (.223 Wylde chamber new 2012) cal., GIO, 18 in. fluted heavy match grade stainless steel barrel with muzzle brake, aluminum flat-top upper and lower receiver, aluminum free float handguard, black, green, tan, federal brown, green base camo, or gray anodized finish, 20 shot mag., single stage trigger, Ergo pistol grip, fixed A2 stock, 8.7 lbs.

| MSR $2,225 | $1,995 | $1,725 | $1,550 | $1,250 | $1,050 | $850 | $750 | |

Add $400 for green base camo.

RECON TACTICAL – 5.56 NATO, .300 AAC Blackout, 6.8 SPC, or 7.62x40 WT cal., GIO, 16, 18, or 20 (7.62x40 WT cal. only) in. medium weight stainless steel barrel, with or without fluting, low profile gas block, quad rail, flash hider, 15 shot mag., Magpul CTR buttstock with MOE pistol grip and tactical trigger guard, Black, OD Green, FDE, or Grey finish, single stage trigger, 7 1/2 lbs.

* **Recon Tactical 5.56** – 5.56 NATO cal., 16 or 18 in. stainless barrel with or without fluting, Black, FDE, or Gray finish.

| MSR $2,460 | $2,095 | $1,835 | $1,575 | $1,425 | $1,150 | $950 | $800 | |

Add $290 for fluted barrel with FDE finish.
Add $430 for 18 in. fluted barrel with FDE finish.
Add $450 for fluted barrel with Gray finish.

* **Recon Tactical 6.8 SPC II** – 6.8 SPC cal., 16 or 18 in. fluted barrel, Black or OD Green finish.

| MSR $2,840 | $2,400 | $2,100 | $1,800 | $1,625 | $1,325 | $1,075 | $900 | |

Add $370 for 18 in. fluted barrel with billet upgrade and Black finish.

* **Recon Tactical .300 AAC Blackout** – .300 AAC Blackout cal., 16 or 18 in. fluted barrel, Black or OD Green finish.

| MSR $2,810 | $2,385 | $2,075 | $1,725 | $1,475 | $1,200 | $1,025 | $895 | |

Add $30 for 18 in. barrel.
Add $430 for 16 in. barrel with OD Green finish.

* **Recon Tactical 7.62x40WT** – 7.62x40WT cal., 16 or 20 in. barrel, Black or OD Green finish.

| MSR $2,550 | $2,165 | $1,895 | $1,625 | $1,470 | $1,190 | $975 | $825 | |

Add $210 for OD Green finish.

TACTICAL LIGHTWEIGHT – 5.56 NATO, 6.8 SPCII, or 7.62x40 WT cal., GIO, 16.2, 18 (7.62x40 WT cal. only), or 20 (7.62x40 WT cal. only) in. match grade barrel, lo-profile gas block, Picatinny rail, Ergo pistol grip, tactical trigger guard, two-stage trigger, black Armor-Tuff finish, 20 shot mag., adj. black synthetic Rogers/Wilson Super-Stoc buttstock. New 2012.

| MSR $2,250 | $2,025 | $1,750 | $1,550 | $1,250 | $1,050 | $850 | $750 | |

Add $300 for 6.8 SPCII cal.

UT-15 URBAN TACTICAL CARBINE – .223 Rem. cal., GIO, 16 1/4 in. fluted match grade barrel with muzzle brake, aluminum flat-top upper and lower receiver, quad rail free float aluminum handguard, black, green, tan or gray anodized finish, 20 shot mag., single stage trigger, Ergo pistol grip, 6-position collapsible stock, 6.9 lbs. Disc. 2011.

| | $1,825 | $1,650 | $1,450 | $1,250 | $1,050 | $875 | $675 | *$2,025* |

SHOTGUNS

Please refer to Scattergun Technologies in the S section for complete listing of shotguns and accessories.

WINCHESTER

Current trademark established in 1866 in New Haven, CT. Currently manufactured by Miroku of Japan since circa 1992, Herstal, Belgium (O/U shotguns since 2004), and in Columbia, SC (Model 70 only beginning 2008). Previously manufactured in New Haven, CT, 1866-2006, and by U.S. Repeating Arms from 1981-2006 through a licensing agreement from Olin Corp. to manufacture shotguns and rifles domestically using the Winchester Trademark. Corporate offices are located in Morgan, UT. Olin Corp. previously manufactured shotguns and rifles bearing the Winchester Hallmark at the Olin Kodensha Plant (closed 1989) located in Tochigi, Japan, Cobourg, Ontario, Canada, and also in European countries. In 1992, U.S. Repeating Arms was acquired by GIAT located in France. In late 1997, the Walloon region of Belgium acquired controlling interest of both Browning and U.S. Repeating Arms.

For more information and current pricing on both new and used Winchester airguns and current black powder models, please refer to the *Blue Book of Airguns* by Dr. Robert D. Beeman & John B. Allen, and the *Blue Book of Modern Black Powder Arms* by John Allen (also online).

MSR	100%	98%	95%	90%	80%	70%	60%	Last MSR

In addition to the models listed within this section, Winchester also offered various models/variations that were available only at the annual SHOT SHOW beginning 2004. More research is underway to identify these models, in addition to their original MSRs (if listed).

RIFLES: SEMI-AUTO

MODEL SX-AB – .308 Win. cal., 20 in. heavy barrel w/o sights, fully adj. stock with textured pistol grip and forearm, includes three interchangeable cheekpieces, 10 shot detachable mag., Picatinny bottom rail on forearm, 100% Mossy Oak Brush camo coverage, 10 lbs. Approx. 2,000 mfg. during 2009 only.

| | $1,250 | $1,075 | $950 | $825 | $700 | $600 | $550 | $1,379 |

RIFLES: BOLT ACTION - MODEL 70, 1964-2006 MFG.

Beginning 1994, Winchester began using the Classic nomenclature to indicate those models featuring a pre-1964 style action with controlled round feeding.

U.S. Repeating Arms closed its New Haven, CT manufacturing facility on March 31, 2006, and an auction was held on Sept. 27-28, 2006, selling the production equipment and related assets.

WSM cals. will bring an approx. 10% premium, and WSSM cals. will bring an approx. 15% premiums on most of the following models, if in 95%+ condition.

MODEL 70 STEALTH – .22-250 Rem., .223 Rem., .308 Win. cal., push-feed action, 26 in. heavy barrel w/o sights, non-glare matte metal finish, Accu-Block black synthetic stock with full length aluminum bedding block, 5 or 6 shot mag., 10 3/4 lbs. Mfg. 1999-2003.

| | $925 | $775 | $700 | $600 | $550 | $500 | $450 | $800 |

MODEL 70 STEALTH II – .22-250 Rem., .223 WSSM, .243 WSSM, .25 WSSM, or .308 Win. cal., push-feed action, 26 in. heavy barrel w/o sights, matte blue finish, redesigned black synthetic stock with aluminum pillar bedding, 3 or 5 shot mag., 10 lbs. Mfg. 2004-2006.

| | $825 | $675 | $550 | $425 | $375 | $325 | $300 | $886 |

Add 10% for WSSM cals.

RIFLES: BOLT ACTION - POST 1964 MODEL 70 CUSTOM GRADES

* ***Model 70 Classic Custom Grade Sharpshooter I/II*** – .22-250 Rem. (new 1993), .223 Rem. (mfg. 1993-94), .30-06, .308 Win., or .300 Win. Mag. cal., specially designed McMillan A2 (disc. 1995) or H-S Precision heavy target stock, Schneider (disc. 1995) or H-S Precision (new 1996) 24 (.308 Win. cal. only) or 26 in. stainless steel barrel, choice of blue or grey finish starting 1996. Mfg. 1992-1998.

| | $1,950 | $1,500 | $1,050 | $900 | $850 | $750 | $675 | $1,994 |

Subtract $100 if without stainless barrel (pre-1995).

This model was designated the Sharpshooter II in 1996 (features H-S Precision stock and stainless steel barrel).

This model was also available in left-hand action beginning 1998 (.30-06 and .330 Win. Mag. cals. only).

* ***Model 70 Classic Custom Grade Sporting Sharpshooter I/II*** – .270 Win. (disc. 1994), 7mm STW, or .300 Win. Mag. cal., 1/2-minute of angle sporting version of the Custom Sharpshooter, custom shop only, Sharpshooter II became standard in 1996. Mfg. 1993-98.

| | $1,875 | $1,425 | $1,000 | $875 | $825 | $750 | $675 | $1,875 |

This model was also available in left-hand action in 1998.

* ***Model 70 Classic Custom Grade Sporting Sharpshooter*** – .220 Swift cal., 26 in. Schneider barrel, controlled round feeding, available with either McMillan A2 or Sporting synthetic (disc. 1994) stock. Mfg. 1994-95 only.

| | $1,950 | $1,525 | $1,200 | $975 | $850 | $750 | $650 | $1,814 |

Shotguns: Post-1964, Semi-Auto

Winchester introduced WinChokes in 1969.

* ***Super X2 2 3/4 in. Magnum Field Practical MK I*** – 12 ga., similar to Super X2 Practical MKII, except is 2 3/4 in. chamber, has regular TruGlo iron sights, and does not have Dura-Touch, cylinder bore Invector choke standard, 8 lbs. Mfg. 2003-2007.

| | $960 | $800 | $675 | $575 | $500 | $465 | $435 | $1,116 |

* ***Super X2 3 in. Magnum Field Practical MK II*** – 12 ga., home defense configuration featuring black composite stock and forearm, black metal finish, 22 in. barrel with Invector choke system and removable LPA ghost ring sights, 8 shot extended mag., includes sling swivels, Dura-Touch armor coated composite finish became standard during 2003, 8 lbs. Mfg. 2002-2006.

| | $1,075 | $885 | $715 | $635 | $550 | $495 | $440 | $1,287 |

Subtract 10% if w/o Dura-Touch finished stock and forearm.

MSR	100%	98%	95%	90%	80%	70%	60%	Last MSR

SX3 (SUPER X3) SPORTING – 12 ga. only, 2 3/4 in. chamber, 28, 30, or 32 in. ported VR barrel with 5 extended choke tubes and TruGlo front sight, checkered adj. comb walnut stock and forearm, Active Valve gas system, gun metal grey receiver finish, Pachmayr Decelerator recoil pad, approx. 7 1/2 lbs., includes red ABS hard case with Winchester logo. Mfg. 2011-2015.

| | $1,450 | $1,175 | $1,000 | $875 | $750 | $625 | $550 | $1,700 |

This model was originally featured as a 2010 SHOT Show Special.

SHOTGUNS: SLIDE ACTION, 1964-CURRENT

Winchester introduced WinChokes in 1969.

U.S. Repeating Arms closed its New Haven, CT manufacturing facility on March 31, 2006. There may be some speculation on recently manufactured Model 1300 shotguns. All Model 1300 last MSRs listed are from the Winchester 2006 price sheet.

MODEL 1200 POLICE STAINLESS – 12 ga. only, 18 in. barrel, 7 shot mag. Disc.

| | $250 | $195 | $165 | $125 | $105 | $90 | $75 | |

MODEL 1200 DEFENDER – 12 ga. only, 18 in. cylinder bore barrel, 7 shot mag., 6 lbs. Disc.

| | $250 | $200 | $180 | $155 | $140 | $125 | $110 | |

MODEL 1300 CAMP DEFENDER – 12 ga. only, 3 in. chamber, 8 shot mag., 22 in. barrel with rifle sights and WinChoke, choice of black synthetic (disc. 2000) or hardwood (new 2001) stock and forearm, matte metal finish, 6 7/8 lbs. Mfg. 1999-2004.

| | $300 | $230 | $180 | $150 | $125 | $110 | $100 | $392 |

MODEL 1300 DEFENDER – 12 or 20 (disc. 1996, reintroduced 2001) ga., 3 in. chamber, available in Police (disc. 1989), Practical (new 2005), Marine, and Defender variations, 18 or 24 (mfg. 1994-98) in. cyl. bore barrel, 5 (disc. 1998), 7 (disc. 1998), or 8 shot mag., matte metal finish, choice of hardwood (disc. 2001), composite (matte finish), or pistol grip (matte finish, 12 ga. only) stock, TruGlo sights became standard 1999, 5 3/4-7 lbs. Disc. 2006.

| | $270 | $210 | $160 | $130 | $110 | $95 | $85 | $341 |

Add $13 for short pistol grip and full length stocks.

Add approx. $100 for Combo Package (includes extra 28 in. VR barrel - disc. 1998).

* *Model 1300 Defender NRA* – 12 or 20 ga., 18 in. barrel with removable TruGlo fiber optic front sight, composite stock, 8 shot mag., features NRA medallion on pistol grip, also available in 12 ga. combo with pistol grip stock, 6 1/4-6 1/2 lbs. Limited mfg. 2006.

| | $285 | $215 | $175 | $140 | $120 | $110 | $95 | $364 |

Add $13 for combo with pistol grip and full length stock.

* *Model 1300 Defender Practical* – 12 ga. only, 3 in. chamber, 8 shot mag., 22 in. barrel with TruGlo adj. open sights, designed for practical shooting events, black synthetic stock and forearm. Mfg. 2005.

| | $300 | $230 | $170 | $145 | $125 | $110 | $100 | $392 |

» *Model 1300 Defender Practical NRA* – 12 ga. only, 3 in. chamber, 8 shot mag., 22 in. barrel with TruGlo sights, black synthetic stock and forearm, Winchoke system, adj. open sights, NRA logo grip cap, 6 1/2 lbs. Limited mfg. 2006.

| | $315 | $240 | $180 | $150 | $130 | $110 | $100 | $414 |

* *Model 1300 Defender Stainless Coastal Marine* – 12 ga. only, 18 in. cyl. bore stainless steel barrel and mag. tube, a Sandstrom 9A phosphate coating was released late 1989 to give long lasting corrosion protection to all receiver and internal working parts, Dura-Touch armor coating stock treatment added 2004, 6 shot mag., synthetic pistol grip (disc. 2001) or full black stock configuration, approx. 6 3/8 lbs. Mfg. 2002-2005.

| | $465 | $380 | $275 | $225 | $195 | $165 | $140 | $575 |

» *Model 1300 Defender Stainless Coastal Marine NRA* – 12 ga. only, 18 in. nickel plated stainless steel barrel, anodized aluminum alloy receiver and plated parts for corrosion resistance, Dura-Touch Armor coating on composite stock, 7 shot mag., sling swivel studs, removable TruGlo fiber optic front sight, 6 1/2 lbs. Limited mfg. 2006.

| | $480 | $390 | $280 | $230 | $200 | $165 | $140 | $598 |

* *Model 1300 Lady Defender* – 20 ga. only, 3 in. chamber, choice of synthetic regular or pistol grip stock, 4 (disc. 1996) or 7 shot mag., 18 in. cyl. bore barrel (new 1996), 5 3/8 lbs. Disc. 1998.

| | $235 | $190 | $150 | $120 | $105 | $90 | $80 | $290 |

SPEED PUMP DEFENDER – 12 ga., 3 in. chamber, side ejection, 5 shot mag., 18 in. plain barrel with fixed cylinder choke, black composite stock with non-glare finish and ribbed forearm. Mfg. by Miroku during 2008.

| | $240 | $210 | $190 | $170 | $150 | $135 | $120 | $299 |

SXP (SUPER X PUMP) DEFENDER – 12 or 20 (new 2015) ga., 3 in. chamber, 18 in. fixed cylinder bore barrel, non-glare metal finish, 5 shot mag., deep groove forearm, black composite pistol grip stock, 6 1/4 lbs. New 2009.

| MSR $350 | $295 | $265 | $230 | $200 | $175 | $150 | $125 | |

Add $30 for 20 ga. (new 2015).

MSR	100%	98%	95%	90%	80%	70%	60%	Last MSR

SXP (SUPER X PUMP) MARINE DEFENDER – 12 or 20 (new 2016) ga., 3 in. chamber, 18 in. barrel with Invector Plus cylinder choke tube, black synthetic stock with textured gripping surfaces, Inflex technology recoil pad, non-glare matte black alloy drilled and tapped receiver with hard chrome barrel and mag. tube, tactical ribbed forearm, includes both brass bead and TruGlo fiber optic front sights, drop out trigger, crossbolt safety, 4-lug rotary bolt, 6 1/4 lbs. New 2013.

| MSR $400 | $350 | $315 | $285 | $250 | $220 | $195 | $175 | |

Add $30 for 20 ga. (new 2016).

WINDHAM WEAPONRY

Current manufacturer of AR-15 style pistols, rifles, receivers, parts, barrels, and related accessories established in 2011, located in Windham, ME. Windham Weaponry is located in the former Bushmaster Manufacturing plant in Windham, ME.

CARBINES/RIFLES: SEMI-AUTO

Windham Weaponry also makes several variations of the SBR (Short Barreled Rifle) for military/law enforcement. All Windham rifles and carbines carry a lifetime transferable warranty.

20 INCH GOVERNMENT RIFLE – .223 Rem./5.56 NATO cal., GIO, 20 in. Government A2 profile chrome moly barrel, A2 flash suppressor, 30 shot mag., forged aluminum flat-top upper with A4 detachable carry handle, M4 feed ramps, rifle length fiberglass handguard with aluminum heat shield, machined aluminum trigger guard, A4 dual aperture rear sight and adj. front sight base, A2 solid stock with trapdoor storage compartment, A2 black plastic pistol grip with finger groove and checkering, hardcoat anodized black finish, 7.7 lbs. New 2014.

| MSR $1,192 | $1,025 | $925 | $800 | $685 | $595 | $515 | $440 | |

.300 BLACKOUT – .300 AAC Blackout cal., GIO, 16 in. medium profile chrome lined barrel with Diamondhead "T" brake, 30 shot mag., flat-top upper receiver with Magpul enhanced trigger guard, no sights, 13 1/2 in. Diamondhead VRS-T free float forend, two Q.D. sling swivels, Hogue 6-positon telescoping buttstock, Q.D. socket endplate, Hogue overmolded beavertail pistol grip, hardcoat anodized black finish, 6.9 lbs.

| MSR $1,680 | $1,425 | $1,250 | $1,115 | $985 | $840 | $725 | $590 | |

.308 HUNTER – .308 Win. cal., GIO, 18 in. fluted chrome lined barrel with A2 flash suppressor, 5 shot mag., forged aluminum flat-top upper receiver with Picatinny rail, electroless nickel plating (new 2016) or hardcoat Coyote Brown anodized finish, integral trigger guard, no sights, laminated wood stock and forend with Nutmeg or Pepper (new 2016) finish, Hogue overmolded beavertail pistol grip, includes black web sling, QD sling swivel, and hard plastic gun case, 7.6 lbs. New 2015.

| MSR $1,587 | $1,350 | $1,180 | $1,015 | $920 | $750 | $625 | $500 | |

.308 TIMBERTEC CAMO – .308 Win. cal., GIO, 16 1/2 in. chrome lined barrel with A2 flash suppressor, 20 shot Magpul PMAG, mid-length shielded handguards, no sights, forged aluminum flat-top upper receiver with Picatinny rail, integral trigger guard, 6-pos. telescoping buttstock with Stark Grip pistol grip, TimberTec camo finish, includes black web sling and hard plastic case, 7 1/2 lbs. New 2015.

| MSR $1,533 | $1,300 | $1,140 | $975 | $885 | $715 | $585 | $475 | |

CARBON FIBER SRC – .223 Rem. cal., GIO, 16 in. M4 profile chrome moly barrel, A2 flash suppressor, 30 shot mag., M4A4 flat-top upper receiver with molded Picatinny rail, molded carbon fiber composite receiver, matte black finish, steel bolt, 6-position telescoping buttstock with A2 pistol grip, M4 double heat shield handguards, integral molded carbon fiber trigger guard, no sights, manual safety, includes black sling and hard plastic case, 5.6 lbs.

| MSR $846 | $725 | $650 | $580 | $515 | $450 | $385 | $340 | |

CDI CARBINE – .223 Rem. cal., GIO, 16 in. M4 chrome lined barrel with Vortex flash suppressor, 30 shot mag., forged aluminum lower and M4A4 flat-top upper receivers, steel bolt, Magpul MOE 6-position telescoping buttstock with pistol grip, Diamondhead free float forend, Magpul AFG angled foregrip, Magpul MOE pistol grip, machined aluminum trigger guard, Diamondhead flip up front and rear sights, manual safety, includes black sling and hard plastic case, hardcoat anodized black finish, 7 lbs.

| MSR $1,680 | $1,425 | $1,250 | $1,115 | $985 | $840 | $725 | $590 | |

DISSIPATOR M4 – .223 Rem./5.56 NATO cal., GIO, 16 in. M4 profile chrome moly standard or heavy barrel, A2 flash suppressor, 30 shot mag., aluminum trigger guard, A4 dual aperture rear sight, adj. front sight post in A2 standard base at rifle length position, 6-position telescoping buttstock with Windham Weaponry logo, rifle length heat shielded handguards, A2 black plastic pistol grip, manual safety, forged aluminum flat-top upper with A4 detachable carry handle, black web sling, hardcoat black anodized finish, 7.2 lbs. New 2015.

| MSR $1,192 | $1,025 | $925 | $800 | $685 | $595 | $515 | $440 | |

MSR	100%	98%	95%	90%	80%	70%	60%	Last MSR

HBC CARBINE – .223 Rem. cal., GIO, 16 in. heavy profile chrome lined barrel with A2 flash suppressor, 30 shot mag., M4A4 flat-top upper receiver with detachable carry handle, aluminum forged lower receiver, steel bolt, 6-position telescoping buttstock with A2 pistol grip, M4 double heat shield handguards, machined aluminum trigger guard, adj. dual aperture rear sight, adj. square post front sight, manual safety, includes black sling and hard plastic case, hardcoat anodized black finish, 7 1/2 lbs.

| MSR $1,096 | $925 | $850 | $725 | $625 | $550 | $475 | $425 | |

MODEL R16M4FTT-762 (7.62x39mm SRC) – 7.62x39mm cal., GIO, 16 in. chrome moly barrel, A2 flash suppressor, alum. trigger guard, 6-position telescoping buttstock with Windham Weaponry logo, M4 double heat shield handguards, A2 black plastic pistol grip, manual safety, forged aluminum flat-top upper, Mil-Std 1913 railed gas block, black web sling, hardcoat black anodized finish, 6.15 lbs.

| MSR $1,056 | $885 | $785 | $685 | $600 | $535 | $465 | $415 | |

MODEL R16SFST-308 – .308 Win. cal., GIO, 16 1/2 in. medium profile chrome moly barrel with A2 flash suppressor, 20 shot Magpul PMAG, forged aluminum flat-top upper with integral trigger guard, 15 in. Midwest Industries KeyMod handguard, 6-position telescoping buttstock with Windham Weaponry logo, Hogue overmolded grips, no sights, hardcoat anodized black finish, 8 lbs. Mfg. 2014-2015.

| | $1,400 | $1,235 | $1,100 | $975 | $830 | $720 | $585 | $1,645 |

MODEL R18FSFSM-308 – .308 Win. cal., GIO, 18 in. fluted chrome lined barrel with A2 flash suppressor, 20 shot Magpul PMAG, forged aluminum flat-top upper receiver with integral trigger guard, no sights, 15 in. Midwest Industries KeyMod handguard, Magpul MOE fixed buttstock, Hogue overmolded grip, hardcoat anodized black finish, 8.45 lbs. Mfg. 2014-2015.

| | $1,485 | $1,315 | $1,150 | $1,025 | $875 | $750 | $615 | $1,732 |

MODEL R18FSFST-308 – .308 Win. cal., GIO, 16 1/2 in. non-fluted or 18 in. fluted chrome moly barrel with A2 flash suppressor, 20 shot Magpul PMAG, forged aluminum flat-top upper with integral trigger guard, 15 in. Midwest Industries KeyMod handguard, 6-position telescoping buttstock with Windham Weaponry logo, Hogue overmolded beavertail pistol grip, no sights, hardcoat anodized black finish, 8 lbs. New 2014.

| MSR $1,708 | $1,450 | $1,275 | $1,125 | $1,000 | $850 | $735 | $595 | |

Subtract $63 for 16 1/2 in. non-fluted barrel.

.308 SRC – .308 Win. cal., GIO, AR-15 style, 16 1/2 in. medium profile chrome lined barrel, 20 shot Magpul PMAG, collapsible buttstock, Hogue overmolded beavertail pistol grip, matte black finish, 7.55 lbs.

| MSR $1,413 | $1,200 | $1,075 | $950 | $800 | $700 | $600 | $495 | |

MPC CARBINE – .223 Rem. cal., GIO, 16 in. M4 chrome lined barrel, A2 flash suppressor, 30 shot mag., forged aluminum lower and M4A4 flat-top upper receiver with detachable carry handle, hardcoat black anodized finish, steel bolt, 6-position telescoping buttstock with A2 pistol grip, M4 double heat shield handguards, machined aluminum trigger guard, adj. dual aperture rear sight, adj. square post front sight, manual safety, includes black sling and hard plastic case, 6.9 lbs.

| MSR $1,086 | $925 | $850 | $725 | $625 | $550 | $475 | $425 | |

* **MPC-RF Carbine** – .223 Rem. cal., similar to MPC Carbine, except does not have carry handle, includes Diamondhead rear flip up sight. New mid-2013.

| MSR $1,086 | $925 | $850 | $725 | $625 | $550 | $475 | $425 | |

Add $125 for Mission First Tactical quad rail handguard (MPC-RF MFT Model).

SRC CARBINE – .223 Rem./5.56 NATO cal., GIO, 16 in. M4 chrome lined barrel with A2 flash suppressor, 30 shot mag., forged aluminum lower and M4A4 flat-top upper receiver w/Picatinny rail, hardcoat black anodized finish, steel bolt, 6-position telescoping buttstock with Windham Weaponry logo, A2 pistol grip, M4 double heat shield handguards, machined aluminum trigger guard, no sights, manual safety, includes black sling and hard plastic case, 6.3 lbs.

| MSR $1,040 | $885 | $785 | $685 | $600 | $535 | $465 | $415 | |

* **SRC Camouflage** – .223 Rem./5.56 NATO cal., GIO, 16 in. M4 chrome lined barrel with A2 flash suppressor, 30 shot mag., machined aluminum trigger guard, no sights, 6-position telescoping buttstock, A2 pistol grip, manual safety, M4 feed ramps, forged aluminum flat-top upper receiver w/Picatinny rail, M4 double heat shield handguards, includes black sling and hard plastic case, Muddy Girl, True Timber Snowfall (disc.), King Snow (new 2015), TimberTec, or Desert Digital (mfg. 2015 only) hydrographic camo finish, 6.3 lbs. New 2014.

| MSR $1,160 | $980 | $885 | $765 | $655 | $575 | $495 | $435 | |

* **SRC .308 Carbine** – .308 Win. cal., GIO, 16 1/2 in. medium profile chrome lined barrel with A2 flash suppressor, 20 shot Magpul PMAG, M4A4 flat-top upper receiver, aluminum forged lower receiver, steel bolt, mid-length tapered heat shielded handguards, 6-position telescoping buttstock, Hogue overmolded beavertail pistol grip, integral trigger guard, hardcoat anodized black finish, includes black web sling, QD sling swivel, and hard plastic case, 7 1/2 lbs. Mfg. 2014-2015.

| | $1,250 | $1,050 | $900 | $800 | $700 | $600 | $475 | $1,413 |

MSR	100%	98%	95%	90%	80%	70%	60%	Last MSR

VEX-SS RIFLE "VARMINT EXTERMINATOR" – .223 Rem. cal., GIO, 20 in. matte finished fluted stainless steel barrel, 5 shot mag., forged aluminum flat-top upper receiver with 1913 rail and optics riser blocks, aluminum free floating forend with sling swivel, machined aluminum trigger guard, no sights, manual safety, Hogue overmolded rubber pistol grip, skeleton stock with sling swivel, hardcoat anodized black finish, includes black sling and hard plastic case, 8.2 lbs.

MSR $1,295	$1,100	$995	$875	$735	$650	$550	$465	

* **VEX-SS Camo Series** – .223 Rem. cal., GIO, 20 in. matte finished fluted stainless steel barrel, 5 shot mag., forged aluminum flat-top upper receiver, steel bolt, solid A2 stock with sling swivel, free floating tubular forend, aluminum trigger guard, no sights, Snow Camo or True Timber (new 2015) hydropgrahic printed camo pattern on forend, receiver, pistol grip and stock, 8.2 lbs.

MSR $1,470	$1,250	$1,095	$940	$850	$690	$575	$475	

* **VES-SS Wood Stocked Series** – .223 Rem. cal., GIO, 20 in. matte finished fluted stainless steel barrel, 5 shot mag., forged aluminum flat-top upper receiver with 1913 rail and optics riser blocks, receiver finish in electroless nickel (Pepper model), Olive Drab (Forest Camo model), or Coyote Brown (Nutmeg model), knurled vented aluminum free floating forend with sling swivel, machined aluminum trigger guard, no sights, manual safety, hardwood laminated stock with Pepper, Forest Camo, or Nutmeg finish, Hogue rubber pistol grip, includes black sling and hard plastic case, 8.35 lbs. New 2014.

MSR $1,480	$1,250	$1,095	$940	$850	$690	$575	$475	

WAY OF THE GUN PERFORMANCE CARBINE – .223 Rem./5.56 NATO cal., GIO, 16 in. medium profile chrome lined barrel with BCM compensator, 30 shot mag., Midwest Industries 15 in. free float KeyMod railed handguard, no sights, Magpul MOE telescoping buttstock, BCM Gunfighter Mod 2 pistol grip, charging handle, CMC trigger, includes hard plastic case, Frank Proctor's Way of the Gun DVD, and a black Way of the Gun sling. New 2015.

MSR $1,795	$1,525	$1,350	$1,175	$1,050	$900	$775	$625	

PISTOLS: SEMI-AUTO

MODEL RP11SFS-7 PISTOL – .223 Rem./5.56 NATO cal., 11 1/2 in. heavy chrome moly barrel with A2 flash suppressor, 30 shot mag., forged aluminum flat-top upper receiver with aluminum trigger guard, steel bolt, no sights, AR pistol rec. tube with foam sleeve and W.W. engraved logo, 10 in. Midwest Industries stainless steel KeyMod free float forend with 2 in. rail segment, A2 black plastic grip, hardcoat anodized black finish, 5.65 lbs. New 2014.

MSR $1,264	$1,050	$950	$815	$685	$595	$515	$440	

.300 BLACKOUT AR PISTOL – .300 AAC Blackout cal., GIO, 9 in. medium profile barrel, A2 flash suppressor, 30 shot mag., Magpul Enhanced trigger guard, Hogue overmolded pistol grip, flat-top upper with Mil-Std 1913 rail, AR pistol type rec. tube with WW laser engraved logo, QD endplate, QD sling swivel, 7 1/4 in. carbine free float vented forend, black finish, 4.85 lbs. New 2016.

MSR $1,160	$980	$885	$765	$655	$575	$495	$435	

WISEMAN, BILL AND CO.

Current custom rifle and action manufacturer established in 1980, located in College Station, TX.

Bill Wiseman also manufactures top quality actions and test barrels used throughout the firearms industry. Additionally, Wiseman/McMillan manufactures rifle barrels and custom stocks. He also performs many gunsmithing services to customer supplied rifles. Please contact the company directly for more information on these products (see Trademark Index).

RIFLES: BOLT ACTION

Add 11% excise tax to prices shown for new manufacture. Some models listed have very limited production.

TSR TACTICAL (OLDER MFG.) – .300 Win. Mag., .308 Win., or .338 Lapua Mag. cal., 5 shot detachable mag., or standard floorplate, synthetic stock with adj. cheekpiece, stainless steel fluted barrel with integral muzzle brake, guaranteed 1/2 MOA accuracy. Mfg. 1996-2003.

	$2,795	$2,200	$1,700	$1,500	$1,235	$1,030	$855	*$2,795*

Add $195 for fluted barrel.
Add $195 for muzzle brake.
Add $150 for 3 position safety.

TSR TACTICAL (NEW MFG.) – various cals., various barrel lengths with or w/o muzzle brake, receiver features integral Picatinny rail, Certa metal coating, adj. black composite Hogue stock (2 options available), detachable mag., guaranteed 1/4 MOA accuracy. New 2011.

The base MSR on this model is $3,850.

Tactical actions are available separately - the short action has an MSR of $850, and the long action has an MSR of $1,925.

MSR	100%	98%	95%	90%	80%	70%	60%	Last MSR

WYOMING ARMS LLC

Current manufacturer of AR-15 style carbines/rifles located in Cody, WY.

CARBINE/RIFLES: SEMI-AUTO

WY-12 SERIES – 7.62 NATO or 6.5mm Creedmoor cal., 18 in. stainless steel match grade fluted barrel, BCM Gunfighter Mod1 compensator, Geissele trigger, Magpul MOE pistol grip stock, ambidextrous safety selector, 12 in. Midwest Industries lightweight forend, DPMS Gen2 forged upper and lower receivers and bolt carrier group, includes custom soft gun case, black or matte sand finish. New 2016.

MSR $2,999	$2,550	$2,225	$1,825	$1,575	$1,300	$1,100	$950

WY-15 SERIES 4400 – 5.56 NATO cal., GIO, stainless steel match grade barrel with threaded muzzle, forged upper and lower receiver, Geissele two-stage trigger, Magpul MOE stock, quad rail system surrounding barrel, Picatinny rail on top of receiver.

MSR $1,999	$1,750	$1,550	$1,250	$1,100	$950	$825	$675

WY-15 SERIES 5500 – 7.62 NATO cal., GIO, 16, 18, or 20 in. barrel, 10, 20, or 30 shot mag., fixed or adj. buttstock, black, matte sand, or FDE finish. New 2016.

MSR $2,599	$2,200	$1,925	$1,600	$1,375	$1,125	$975	$850

WY-15 SERIES 6600 – 5.56 NATO/.223 Rem. cal., GIO, 16 or 18 in. stainless steel hand lapped match grade fluted barrel, threaded muzzle, titanium barrel nut and profile, billet upper with redesigned case deflector, billet lower with integral trigger guard and flared magwell, ambi safety selector, mid-length gas system, Geissele Hi Speed trigger, Geissele MK1 13 in. super modular rail, BCM Gunfighter Mod 4 charging handle and Mod 0 compensator, Magpul MOE+ grip, Wyoming Arms H4 rifle buffer, Magpul MOE stock, black finish with matte sand or gun metal gray receiver finish.

MSR $3,199	$2,725	$2,375	$1,925	$1,650	$1,375	$1,150	$995

X-Y-Z SECTIONS

XN ARMS INDUSTRY AND TRADE CO.

Current tactical semi-auto shotgun manufacturer located in Istanbul, Turkey. Currently imported by EAA Corp, located in Rockledge, FL.

SHOTGUNS: SEMI-AUTO

EKSEN MKE 1919 – 12 ga. only, 2 3/4 or 3 in. chamber, gas operated, AR-15 style, 19.7 in. barrel, 3 chokes, two 5 shot detachable mags., ribbed handguard with A2 front post sight, detachable carrying handle, integral Picatinny rail, black finish or 100% "BONZ" camo coverage, 6 1/2 lbs.

MSR $699	$625	$550	$495	$475	$450	$425	$395

XTREME MACHINING

Current rifle manufacturer located in Drifting, PA. Previously located in Grassflat, PA. Previously distributed until 2012 by American Tactical Imports, located in Rochester, NY.

MSR	100%	98%	95%	90%	80%	70%	60%	Last MSR

PISTOLS: SEMI-AUTO

XM15 – 7 1/2 in. barrel with birdcage flash hider, 30 shot mag., Xtreme Machining enhanced charging handle and 7 in. free float handguard system with low profile gas block, pistol buffer tube, black finish. New 2015.

MSR $640	$550	$480	$400	$340	$300	$265	$250

* XM15.5 – 9 1/2 in. barrel with birdcage flash hider, 20 shot mag., Xtreme Machining enhanced charging handle and 8 in. free float handguard system with low profile gas block, pistol buffer tube, black finish. New 2015.

MSR $1,375	$1,250	$1,095	$940	$850	$690	$565	$440

RIFLES: BOLT ACTION

338XT RIFLE – .338 Extreme cal., 26 in. fluted stainless steel barrel threaded for tank style muzzle brake or suppressor, 7 shot box mag., stainless steel receiver, Magnum Sako-style extractor, spring-loaded plunger ejector, fully adj. trigger, free float tube design handguard allows for four planes of accessory rail mounting, mission adaptable with a change of Picatinny rails, integral recoil lug, Mil-Spec 1913 rail, aluminum folding stock, black finish, 18 lbs. New 2015.

MSR $6,200	$5,600	$5,000	$4,400	$3,650	$3,250	$2,850	$2,200

* 338 XT Sniper Package – includes 338XT rifle, ten 7 shot mags., Xtreme Machining suppressor, tool kit, PDA loaded with ballistic software, and hard case. New 2015.

MSR $12,000	$10,800	$9,750	$8,500	$7,250	$6,000	$5,000	$4,000

.338 XTREME – .338 Xtreme cal., single shot (black or tan only) or repeater (5 or 7 shot detachable mag.) action, choice of laminated wood target, aluminum tactical, or McMillan A-5 stock, stainless steel receiver and 30 in. fluted barrel with 42-port muzzle brake, Picatinny rails, black, tan, or green finish, approx. 15 1/2 lbs. Disc.

	$4,150	$3,850	$3,500	$3,000	$2,750	$2,250	$1,750	*$4,678*

Add $414 for repeater.

.338 XTREME M100 SERIES – .338 Xtreme cal., 26 (black finish only) or 30 in. fluted barrel, M100 side folding custom stock, full length Weaver rail, 7 shot detachable box mag., available in black, tan, desert mirage, or AM tiger stripe finish. Mfg. 2011-disc.

	$5,750	$4,995	$4,300	$3,850	$3,150	$2,600	$2,000	*$6,199*

.50 BMG – .50 BMG cal., single shot or repeater, available in light gun, heavy gun, or unlimited gun configurations, 34 in. stainless steel barrel with specially designed muzzle brake, Rifle Basix trigger, aluminum steel Picatinny-style scope mounting rails, Sako-style extractor, removable plunger ejector, choice of aluminum or laminated wood stocks with forend up to 8 in. wide, options include barrel lengths, fluting, and custom stock dimensions. Disc. 2014.

Last MSR for Light Gun was $5,500, Heavy Gun was $6,000, and Unlimited Gun was P.O.R.

M38 RIFLE – .308 Win. or .300 Win. Mag. cal., 20-26 in. fluted stainless steel barrel with tank style muzzle brake or suppressor, 5 or 10 shot box mag., M38 stainless steel receiver, Sako-style extractor, spring-loaded plunger ejector, fully adj. trigger, Monolithic 1913 rail with integral recoil lug, free float tube design handguard allows for four planes of accessory rail mounting, aluminum folding stock, black finish, 11 lbs. New 2015.

MSR $2,600	$2,350	$2,050	$1,800	$1,575	$1,350	$1,075	$875

RIFLES: SEMI-AUTO

STANDARD M4 – 16 in. M4 profile barrel with birdcage flash hider and Manganese phosphate coating, 30 shot mag., standard M4 handguard with Picatinny gas block, Xtreme Machining enhanced charging handle, 6-position stock, black finish. New 2015.

MSR $610	$525	$465	$400	$340	$300	$265	$250

MSR	100%	98%	95%	90%	80%	70%	60%	Last MSR

XM15 CARBINE WITH QUAD RAIL – 16 in. M4 profile barrel with birdcage flash hider and Manganese phosphate coating, 30 shot mag., Xtreme Machining enhanced charging handle and 12 in. free float handguard system with low profile gas block, 6-position stock, black finish. New 2015.

MSR $719	$625	$540	$470	$400	$350	$310	$295	

XM47 STAINLESS – AK-47 design, stainless steel parts are made to exacting specs., most parts are interchangeable with standard AK components, laminate furniture. New 2015.

MSR $1,500	$1,275	$1,125	$1,025	$875	$750	$625	$525	

YANKEE HILL MACHINE CO., INC. (YHM)

Current manufacturer of AR-15 style rifles, receivers, parts, suppressors, and related accessories established in 1951, located in Florence, MA. Consumer direct and dealer sales.

CARBINES/RIFLES: SEMI-AUTO

YHM manufactures a complete line of AR-15 style tactical rifles and carbines, as well as upper receivers and a wide variety of accessories. Please contact the company directly for more information about available options and dealer listings (see Trademark Index).

BLACK DIAMOND CARBINE – 5.56 NATO, 7.62x39mm (mfg. 2011-2013), .300 AAC Blackout (new 2014), or 6.8 SPC (new 2010) cal., GIO, 16 in. chrome moly vanadium steel threaded barrel, Diamond fluting, Phantom flash hider, 30 shot mag., black anodized finish, aluminum lower and flat-top upper receiver, Mil-Spec bolt carrier assembly, forward assist, carbine length Diamond handguard, free floating continuous top Picatinny rail, flip up tower front and rear sights, 6-position adj. carbine stock, standard A2 grip, 6.7 lbs.

MSR $1,472	$1,295	$1,100	$1,000	$825	$675	$525	$450	

Add $80 for 6.8 SPC or 7.62x39mm (disc. 2013) cal.

BLACK DIAMOND SPECTER CARBINE – 5.56 NATO, 7.62x39mm (mfg. 2011-2013), .300 AAC Blackout (new 2014), or 6.8 SPC (new 2010) cal., GIO, similar to Black Diamond Carbine, except features Specter length Diamond handguard, 6.9 lbs.

MSR $1,498	$1,315	$1,100	$1,000	$825	$675	$525	$450	

Add $81 for 6.8 SPC or 7.62x39mm (disc. 2013) cal.

BLACK DIAMOND SPECTER XL CARBINE – 5.56 NATO, 7.62x39mm (mfg. 2011-2013), .300 AAC Blackout (new 2014), or 6.8 SPC (new 2010) cal., GIO, similar to Black Diamond Specter Carbine, except has Specter XL length Diamond handguard, approx. 7 lbs.

MSR $1,525	$1,350	$1,150	$1,050	$850	$695	$550	$475	

Add $54 for 6.8 SPC or 7.62x39mm (disc. 2013) cal.

BLACK DIAMOND RIFLE – 5.56 NATO, 7.62x39mm (mfg. 2011-2013), or 6.8 SPC cal., GIO, 20 in. chrome moly vanadium steel barrel, 30 shot mag., black anodized finish, aluminum lower and flat-top upper receiver, Mil-Spec bolt carrier assembly, forward assist, rifle length Diamond handguard, Picatinny rail risers, A2 fixed stock, A2 pistol grip, single rail gas block, two mini-risers, 8 lbs. Disc. 2015.

	$1,275	$1,085	$975	$800	$650	$500	$425	$1,445

Add $53 for 6.8 SPC or 7.62x39mm (disc. 2013) cal.

BURNT BRONZE SPECTER XL BILLET CARBINE – 5.56 NATO, 6.8 SPC, or .300 AAC Blackout cal., 16 in. steel fluted barrel with YHM Slant compensator/muzzle brake, two-stage trigger, rifle-length SLR-Slant handguard, billet aluminum lower and flat-top upper with M4 feed ramps, low profile gas block, Q.D.S. hooded front and rear sight, tactical charging handle latch, adj. Magpul CTR buttstock, Magpul MOE grip, Burnt Bronze Cerakote finish, includes 25 shot round metal mag. (6.8 SPC only), or two Magpul Gen 2 mags., a front sight adjustment tool, and hard plastic case, 7.76 lbs. Mfg. 2014-2015.

	$2,150	$1,895	$1,550	$1,325	$1,100	$950	$825	$2,395

Subtract $100 for Specter-length handguard (Burnt Bronze Specter Billet Carbine).

CUSTOMIZABLE CARBINE – 5.56 NATO, 7.62x39mm (new 2011), or 6.8 SPC (new 2010) cal., GIO, 16 in. chrome moly vanadium steel barrel, black anodized finish, aluminum lower and flat-top upper receiver, Mil-Spec bolt carrier assembly, forward assist, Phantom flash hider, carbine length customizable handguard, adj. carbine stock, flip up front tower sight and flip up rear sight, 6.3 lbs. Disc. 2013.

	$1,295	$1,100	$1,000	$825	$675	$525	$450	$1,472

Add $54 for 6.8 SPC or 7.62x39mm cal.

CUSTOMIZABLE RIFLE – 5.56 NATO, 7.62x39mm (new 2011), or 6.8 SPC (new 2011) cal., GIO, 20 in. chrome moly vanadium steel barrel, black anodized finish, aluminum lower and flat-top upper receiver, Mil-Spec bolt carrier assembly, forward assist, rifle length customizable handguard, 12 in. Co-Witness rail, fixed A2 stock, single rail gas block, two mini-risers, 8 lbs. Disc. 2013.

	$1,275	$1,085	$975	$800	$650	$500	$425	$1,445

Add $53 for 6.8 SPC or 7.62x39mm cal.

MSR	100%	98%	95%	90%	80%	70%	60%	Last MSR

DESERT ENFORCER – 5.56 NATO, 6.8 SPC (new 2016) or .300 AAC Blackout (new 2016) cal., GIO, 16 in. threaded barrel with 6 grooves and Diamond fluting, YHM Annihilator flash hider, E-Z Pull takedown pins, forged aluminum lower and flat-top A3 upper, Gen. 2 PMAG, TJ Competition Series rifle length handguard with top Picatinny rail, Quick Deploy Sights, Magpul 6-pos. adj. stock, Magpul MOE pistol grip, FDE finish with contrast of black parts, 7.1 lbs. New 2014.

MSR $2,050	$1,825	$1,625	$1,400	$1,175	$975	$825	$675	

Add $80 for 6.8 SPC cal. (new 2016).

* ***Tank Tough Desert Enforcer (OD Green SLR Specter Smooth Carbine)*** – 5.56 NATO cal., GIO, carbine length gas system, 16 in. threaded barrel with 5C2 flash hider/compensator, Gen 2 black PMAG, Tactical Q.D.S. sight system, adj. TI-7 carbine stock, Ergo grips, mid-length SLR smooth handguard, EZ Pull takedown pins, OD Green Cerakote finish with contrast of black parts. New mid-2013.

MSR $1,950	$1,650	$1,440	$1,200	$1,075	$925	$795	$650	

ENTRY LEVEL CARBINE – 5.56 NATO, 7.62x39mm (mfg. 2011-2013), .300 AAC Blackout (new 2014), or 6.8 SPC (new 2010) cal., GIO, 16 in. chrome moly vanadium steel threaded barrel, YHM Phantom flash hider, 30 shot mag., black anodized finish, aluminum lower and flat-top upper receiver, Mil-Spec bolt carrier assembly, forward assist, carbine length handguard, 6-pos. adj. carbine stock, A2 pistol grip, single rail gas block, 6.4 lbs. Disc. 2014.

	$1,095	$975	$875	$700	$575	$450	$395	*$1,284*

Add $54 for 6.8 SPC, .300 AAC Blackout (new 2014), or 7.62x39mm (disc. 2013) cal.

ENTRY LEVEL RIFLE – 5.56 NATO, 7.62x39mm (mfg. 2011-2013), or 6.8 SPC (new 2011) cal., GIO, 20 in. chrome moly vanadium steel non-fluted barrel, 30 shot mag., black anodized finish, aluminum lower and flat-top upper receiver, Mil-Spec bolt carrier assembly, forward assist, rifle length tube handguard, fixed A2 stock, A2 pistol grip, single rail gas block, two mini-risers, 8 lbs. Disc. 2015.

	$1,125	$985	$895	$725	$600	$475	$425	*$1,311*

Add $43 for 6.8 SPC or 7.62x39mm (disc. 2013) cal.

HUNT READY CARBINE – 5.56 NATO, 7.62x39mm (disc. 2013), .300 AAC Blackout (new 2014), or 6.8 SPC cal., GIO, 16 in. steel threaded and fluted barrel with YHM-28-5C2 Flash Hider, forged aluminum flat-top upper and lower receiver, low profile gas block, 5 shot mag., vented round customizable forearm, two 3 in. modular rails, bolt carrier assembly, forward assist, adj. carbine buttstock, standard pistol grip, matte black or 100% Realtree AP camo finish, includes Bushnell Banner 3-9x40mm camo scope with Circle-X reticule, Grovetec deluxe padded camo sling. New 2012.

MSR $1,531	$1,335	$1,125	$1,000	$825	$675	$525	$450	

Add $53 for 6.8 SPC or 7.62x39mm (disc. 2013) cal.

HUNT READY RIFLE – 5.56 NATO, 7.62x39mm (disc. 2013), or 6.8 SPC cal., GIO, 20 in. free floating steel barrel, diamond fluting, forged aluminum flat-top upper and lower receiver, low profile gas block, 5 shot mag., A2 Trapdoor buttstock, vented round customizable forearm, bolt carrier assembly, forward assist, matte black or 100% Realtree AP camo finish, includes Bushnell Banner 3-9x40mm camo scope with Circle-X reticule, Grovetec deluxe padded camo sling. New 2012.

MSR $1,563	$1,350	$1,175	$1,000	$825	$675	$525	$450	

Add $42 for 6.8 SPC or 7.62x39mm (disc. 2013) cal.

KR7 SERIES CARBINE – 5.56 NATO, 6.8 SPC, or .300 AAC Blackout cal., GIO, 16 in. steel threaded barrel with YHM Phantom 5C2 flash suppressor, 30 shot mag., KR7 mid-length KeyMod handguard, forged alum. lower and flat-top upper with M4 feed ramps, low profile gas block, 6-pos. adj. commercial carbine stock, matte black finish, includes hard plastic case, 6.3 lbs. New 2015.

MSR $1,284	$1,125	$975	$850	$725	$625	$495	$395	

Add $54for 6.8 SPC cal.

* ***KR7 9mm*** – 9mm Para. cal., GIO, 16 in. barrel, 32 shot mag., stainless steel hammer and trigger pins, KR7 Series mid-length handguard, dedicated 9mm lower, buffer, and bolt, matte black finish. New 2016.

MSR $1,400	$1,200	$1,075	$950	$800	$700	$600	$495	

LIGHTWEIGHT CARBINE – 5.56 NATO, 7.62x39mm (new 2011), or 6.8 SPC (new 2010) cal., GIO, 16 in. chrome moly vanadium steel barrel, black anodized finish, aluminum lower and flat-top upper receiver, Mil-Spec bolt carrier assembly, forward assist, Phantom flash hider, carbine length lightweight handguard, adj. carbine stock, forearm endcap, flip up tower front sight, flip up rear sight, 6.7 lbs. Disc. 2013.

	$1,275	$1,085	$975	$800	$650	$500	$425	*$1,445*

Add $80 for 6.8 SPC or 7.62x39mm cal.

MSR	100%	98%	95%	90%	80%	70%	60%	Last MSR

LIGHTWEIGHT RIFLE – 5.56 NATO, 7.62x39mm (new 2011), or 6.8 SPC (new 2011) cal., GIO, 20 in. chrome moly vanadium steel barrel, black anodized finish, aluminum lower and flat-top upper receiver, Mil-Spec bolt carrier assembly, forward assist, rifle length lightweight handguard, fixed A2 stock, single rail gas block, two mini-risers, 8 lbs. Disc. 2013.

| | $1,275 | $1,085 | $975 | $800 | $650 | $500 | $425 | *$1,445* |

Add $53 for 6.8 SPC or 7.62x39mm cal.

MODEL 57 CARBINE – 5.56 NATO, 6.8 SPC, or .300 AAC Blackout cal., GIO, 16 in. threaded barrel with fluting, YHM Slant Comp/Brake, mid-length top rail aluminum handguard (SLR Slant Series), Quick Deploy Sight System, two 30 shot Gen. 2 black PMAGs, EZ Pull takedown pins, Magpul CTR 6-position adj. stock, Magpul MOE pistol grip, oversized magwell, aluminum flat-top A3 upper receiver, tactical charging handle, matte black or Burnt Bronze (Limited Edition, new 2016) finish, includes three KeyMod handguard covers (new 2015). New 2014.

| MSR $2,195 | $1,950 | $1,725 | $1,475 | $1,350 | $1,075 | $895 | $695 | |

Add $70 for 6.8 SPC cal.

Add $100 for rifle-length SLR Slant handguard.

S.L.K. SPECTER CARBINE – 5.56 NATO, 6.8 SPC, or .300 AAC Blackout cal., 16 in. steel diamond fluted and threaded barrel, YHM Phantom 5C2 flash hider/compensator, SLK KeyMod mid-length handguard, forged aluminum lower and flat-top upper with M4 feed ramps, low profile gas block, Q.D.S. flip front and rear sights, EZ Pull Pin set, adj. commercial carbine stock, includes hard plastic case, 6.3 lbs. New 2014.

| MSR $1,700 | $1,525 | $1,325 | $1,150 | $1,050 | $850 | $685 | $550 | |

Add $25 for rifle-length handguard (S.L.K. Specter XL).

Add $81 for 6.8 SPC cal.

SLR SMOOTH SPECTER – 5.56 NATO, 6.8 SPC, or .300 AAC Blackout cal., GIO, 16 in. threaded barrel with Diamond fluting, Phantom flash hider, Quick Deploy Sight System, mid-length free floating handguard with continuous top Picatinny rail, EZ Pull takedown pins, 30 shot mag., forged alum. lower and flat-top A3 upper receiver, 6-pos. adj. carbine stock, A2 pistol grip, matte black finish. Disc. 2015.

| | $1,525 | $1,325 | $1,150 | $1,050 | $850 | $685 | $550 | *$1,700* |

Add $81 for 6.8 SPC or .300 AAC Blackout cal.

* **SLR Quad Specter** – 5.56 NATO, 6.8 SPC, or .300 AAC Blackout cal., GIO, similar to SLR Smooth Specter, except has mid-length quad rail handguard, 7.3 lbs. Disc. 2015.

| | $1,525 | $1,325 | $1,150 | $1,050 | $850 | $685 | $550 | *$1,700* |

Add $81 for 6.8 SPC or .300 AAC Blackout cal.

SLR SMOOTH SPECTER XL – 5.56 NATO, 6.8 SPC, or .300 AAC Blackout cal., GIO, 16 in. threaded barrel with rifling grooves and Diamond fluting, Phantom flash hider, alum. rifle length free floating customizeable handguard with continuous top Picatinny rail, 30 shot mag., Quick Deploy Sight System, EZ Pull takedown pins, forged alum. lower and flat-top A3 upper receiver, 6-pos. adj. carbine stock, A2 pistol grip, matte black finish, 7.1 lbs. Disc. 2015.

| | $1,550 | $1,350 | $1,175 | $1,050 | $850 | $700 | $550 | *$1,725* |

Add $81 for 6.8 SPC or .300 AAC Blackout cal.

* **SLR Quad Specter XL** – 5.56 NATO, 6.8 SPC, or .300 AAC Blackout cal., GIO, similar to SLR Specter XL, except features mid-length quad rail handguard, 7.4 lbs. Disc. 2015.

| | $1,550 | $1,350 | $1,175 | $1,050 | $850 | $700 | $550 | *$1,725* |

Add $81 for 6.8 SPC or .300 AAC Blackout cal.

SMOOTH CARBINE – 5.56 NATO, 7.62x39mm (mfg. 2011-2013), .300 AAC Blackout (new 2014), or 6.8 SPC (new 2010) cal., GIO, 16 in. chrome moly vanadium steel threaded barrel, Diamond fluting, Phantom flash hider, 30 shot mag., oversized magwell, black anodized finish, aluminum lower and flat-top upper receiver, Mil-Spec bolt carrier assembly, forward assist, carbine length smooth handguard, 6-position adj. carbine stock, A2 pistol grip, flip up front tower sight and flip up rear sight, 6.8 lbs.

| MSR $1,472 | $1,295 | $1,100 | $1,000 | $825 | $675 | $525 | $450 | |

Add $53 for 6.8 SPC, .300 AAC Blackout (new 2014), or 7.62x39mm (disc. 2013) cal.

SMOOTH RIFLE – 5.56 NATO, 7.62x39mm (new 2011), or 6.8 SPC (new 2011) cal., GIO, 20 in. chrome moly vanadium steel barrel, black anodized finish, aluminum lower and flat-top upper receiver, Mil-Spec bolt carrier assembly, forward assist, rifle length smooth handguard, fixed A2 stock, single rail gas block, forearm end cap, two mini-risers, 8 lbs. Disc. 2014.

| | $1,275 | $1,085 | $975 | $800 | $650 | $500 | $425 | *$1,445* |

Add $54 for 6.8 SPC or 7.62x39mm cal.

SPECTER LIGHTWEIGHT CARBINE – 5.56 NATO, 7.62x39mm (new 2011), or 6.8 SPC (new 2010) cal., GIO, 16 in. chrome moly vanadium steel barrel, black anodized finish, aluminum lower and flat-top upper receiver, Mil-Spec bolt carrier assembly, forward assist, Phantom flash hider, Specter length lightweight handguard, adj. carbine stock, forearm end cap, flip up front and rear sights, low profile gas block, 6.9 lbs. Disc. 2013.

| | $1,315 | $1,100 | $1,000 | $825 | $675 | $525 | $450 | *$1,498* |

Add $54 for 6.8 SPC or 7.62x39mm cal.

MSR	100%	98%	95%	90%	80%	70%	60%	Last MSR

SPECTER XL LIGHTWEIGHT CARBINE – 5.56 NATO, 7.62x39mm (new 2011), or 6.8 SPC (new 2010) cal., GIO, similar to Specter Lightweight Carbine, except has XL length lightweight handguard, 7.1 lbs. Disc. 2013.

	$1,350	$1,150	$1,050	$850	$695	$550	$475	$1,525

Add $54 for 6.8 SPC or 7.62x39mm cal.

SPORTSMAN SCOUT CARBINE – 5.56 NATO, 7.62x39mm, or 6.8 SPC cal., GIO, 16 in. free floating steel barrel with Phantom 5C2 flash hider, diamond fluting, aluminum lower and flat-top upper receiver with Picatinny rail, 100% Realtree AP camo coverage, forward assist, low profile gas block, M4 telescoping buttstock, includes two 3 in. modular rails, Specter length customizable handguard, forearm end cap. Mfg. 2011-2013.

	$1,195	$1,000	$900	$725	$600	$475	$425	$1,391

Add $54 for 6.8 SPC or 7.62x39mm cal.

SPORTSMAN SERIES RIFLE – 5.56 NATO, 7.62x39mm, or 6.8 SPC cal., GIO, 20 in. free floating steel barrel, diamond fluting, aluminum lower and flat-top upper receiver with Picatinny rail, 100% Realtree AP camo coverage, forward assist, low profile gas block, A2 trapdoor buttstock, includes two 3 in. modular rails, rifle length customizable handguard, forearm endcap. Mfg. 2011-2013.

	$1,275	$1,085	$975	$800	$650	$500	$425	$1,445

Add $96 for 6.8 SPC or 7.62x39mm cal.

TODD JARRETT COMPETITION SERIES CARBINE – 5.56 NATO or 6.8 SPC cal., GIO, 16 in. chrome lined threaded barrel, fluted with YHM's signature "Diamond Flute" and Phantom 5C2 flash Hider, 30 shot mag., free floating forearm, available with rifle, mid-length, or carbine length handguard, ergonomic pistol grip, padded ACE stock, Q.D.S. flip up front and rear sights, EZ Pull takedown pins, forged aluminum lower and flat-top "T" marked upper with Picatinny rail, low profile gas block, forearm end cap, matte black finish. Mfg. mid-2013-2015.

	$1,800	$1,575	$1,350	$1,225	$1,000	$825	$650	$2,007

PISTOLS: SEMI-AUTO

9mm PISTOL – 9mm Para. cal., gas blowback system, 5 1/2 in. threaded barrel with Phantom 5C2 flash hider, 30 (disc.) or 32 shot mag., forged upper and lower receivers, extended top Picatinny rail, EZ Pull takedown pins, mini KeyMod handguard, standard pistol grip, 9mm pistol buttstock assembly, caliber marked dust cover. New 2015.

MSR $1,299	$1,100	$995	$875	$735	$650	$550	$465	

5.56mm PISTOL – 5.56mm cal., GIO, 10 1/2 in. threaded and fluted barrel with Phantom 5C2 flash hider, 30 shot mag., forged upper and lower receivers, KR7 series mid-length handguard, extended top Picatinny rail, KeyMod mounting system, pistol buttstock assembly, caliber marked dust cover, EZ Pull Takedown pins, standard pistol grip, black finish. New 2015.

MSR $1,205	$1,075	$950	$800	$675	$550	$475	$400	

.300 BLK PISTOL – .300 AAC Blackout cal., GIO, 9.1 in. barrel with YHM Phantom flash hider, 30 shot mag., KR7 Series carbine length handguard, extended top Picatinny rail, KeyMod mounting system, EZ Pull takedown pins, black finish. New 2016.

MSR $1,205	$1,075	$950	$800	$675	$550	$475	$400	

7.62 NATO PISTOL – 7.62 NATO cal., GIO, 10.1 in. barrel with YHM Phantom flash hider, 20 shot mag., KR7 Series carbine length handguard, extended top Picatinny rail, KeyMod mounting system, EZ Pull takedown pins, black finish. New 2016.

MSR $1,750	$1,550	$1,350	$1,165	$1,050	$850	$700	$550	

Z-M WEAPONS

Previous rifle manufacturer and pistol components maker located in Richmond, VT. Previously located in Bernardston, MA.

PISTOLS: SEMI-AUTO

STRIKE PISTOL – .38 Super, .40 S&W, or .45 ACP cal., several configurations available, with or without compensator. Limited mfg. 1997-2000.

	$2,375	$1,825	$1,700	$1,400	$1,150	$995	$750	$2,695

RIFLES: SEMI-AUTO

LR 300 & VARIATIONS – .223 Rem. cal., modified GIO using AR-15 style action, 16 1/4 in. barrel, flat-top receiver, pivoting skeletal metal stock, aluminum or Nylatron handguard, matte finish, 7.2 lbs. Mfg. 1997-disc.

	$2,100	$1,800	$1,550	$1,300	$1,100	$900	$750	$2,208

Add $23 for Nylatron handguard.

MSR		100%	98%	95%	90%	80%	70%	60%	Last MSR

ZVI

Current manufacturer located in Prague, Czech Republic. No current U.S. importation.

ZVI manufactures the Kevin line of small frame .380 ACP cal. semi-auto pistols. ZVI also manufactures the Falcon, a .50 BMG bolt action repeater (2 shot mag.). Currently, these guns do not have any U.S. importation. Please contact the company directly for more information, including pricing and U.S. availability (see Trademark Index).

ZAKLADY MECHANICZNE TARNÓW S.A.

Current heavy industry conglomerate that also manufactures tactical bolt action rifles located in Tarnów, Poland.

RIFLES: BOLT ACTION

Zaklady currently manufactures the Alex Tactical Sport model in .308 Win. cal. It features a bullpup design, forward detachable bipod, and extended upper Picatinny rail. Please contact the company directly for current U.S. availability and pricing (see Trademark Index).

ZASTAVA ARMS

Current manufacturer established in 1853, and located in Serbia. Currently distributed exclusively by Century International Arms, located in Fairfax, VT. Some models were imported by EAA, located in Rockledge, FL; please refer to EAA in the E section. Remington previously imported certain models until 2009, as well as KBI until 2005. Previously distributed by Advanced Weapons Technologies, located in Athens, Greece, and by Nationwide Sports Distributors, located in Southampton, PA. Previously imported by T.D. Arms, followed by Brno U.S.A., circa 1990.

Zastava Arms makes a wide variety of quality pistols, rifles, and sporting shotguns. Zastava Arms was subcontracted by Remington Arms Co. to make certain bolt action rifle models.

HANDGUNS: SEMI-AUTO

MODEL CZ99 – 9mm Para. or .40 S&W cal., DA/SA, 15 shot, 4 1/4 in. barrel, short recoil, choice of various finishes, SIG locking system, hammer drop safety, ambidextrous controls, 3-dot Tritium sighting system, alloy frame, firing pin block, loaded chamber indicator, squared-off trigger guard, checkered dark grey polymer grips, 32 oz.

		$550	$400	$375	$330	$300	$285	$265	$495

While a Z9 was advertised, it was never commercially imported. All guns were CZ99 or CZ40.

Zastava CZ99 configurations (with finishes) included matte blue with synthetic grips (500 imported), commercial blue with synthetic grips (750 imported), military "painted finish" with synthetic grips (1,000 imported), matte blue finish with checkered wood grips (115 imported), high polish blue with checkered grips (115 imported), and military "painted finish" with wood grips (2 prototypes only).

MODEL CZ999 SCORPION – 9mm Para. cal., similar to CZ99, except has indicator for the last three rounds in the magazine, fire selector for pistol and revolver mode.

Please refer to the Skorpion listing in the S section for current information on this model. This pistol was imported by K.B.I. as the ZDA model.

MODEL CZ40 – .40 S&W cal., 55 prototypes were imported for testing, but most had a feeding problem due to improper magazine design, mag. design changes were planned, but were cancelled due to the Serbian/Croatian war. **Suggested retail was $495.**

MODEL CZ70 – 9mm Para. cal., SA, Tokarev style, no slide safety, blue finish, limited importation.

		$1,000	$850	$775	$675	$575	$510	$460	

MODEL M88 – 9mm Para. or .40 S&W cal., SA, 6 or 8 shot mag., 3.6 in. barrel, blue finish, compact frame, military version, not recent import, 28 oz.

		$600	$525	$465	$415	$360	$330	$295	

MODEL CZ31 – .32 Auto cal., SA, Tokarev style, no slide safety, blue finish, limited importation.

		$1,000	$850	$775	$675	$575	$510	$460	

ZELENY SPORT s.r.o.

Current manufacturer located in the Czech Republic. No current U.S. importation.

PISTOLS: SEMI-AUTO

HS SERIES – 9x19, .40 S&W, or .45 ACP cal., 12, 13, or 16 shot mag., standard or sub-compact variation. black, two-tone, or tan finish. New 2015.

These models are not currently being imported into the U.S. Please contact the company directly for more information including pricing, options, and availability (see Trademark Index).

MSR	100%	98%	95%	90%	80%	70%	60%	Last MSR

RIFLES: SEMI-AUTO

Zeleny Sport manufactures a AK-47 design Model 96 Beryl semi-auto in .223 Rem. cal., the company also makes a Works 11 Series with fixed wood, fixed synthetic, or folding stock. Please contact the company directly for possible U.S. importation, availability, and pricing (see Trademark Index).

ZENITH FIREARMS

Current pistol and rifle manufacturer located in Afton, VA.

PISTOLS: SEMI-AUTO

Z-5K – 9mm Para. cal., roller-lock, delayed blowback action, 4.6 in. cold hammer forged barrel, three 30 shot mags., front protected post sight and rear drum for elevation and windage, Picatinny style optics mount, black finish, includes factory sling and plastic carry case, 4.43 lbs. New 2015.

MSR $1,750	$1,475	$1,290	$1,125	$1,000	$850	$735	$595

Z-5P – 9mm Para. cal., roller-lock delayed blowback action, 5.8 in. cold hammer forged barrel, 30 shot mag., front protected post sight, rear drum for elevation and windage, Picatinny style optics mount, black finish, includes factory sling and plastic carry case, 4.6 lbs. New 2015.

MSR $1,800	$1,525	$1,350	$1,175	$1,050	$900	$775	$625

Z-5RS "REVERSE STRETCH" – 9mm Para. cal., roller-lock, delayed blowback action, 8.9 in. cold hammer forged barrel, three 30 shot mags., front protected post sight, rear drum for elevation and windage, Picatinny style optics mount, black finish, includes rugged plastic carry case, 5 1/2 lbs. New 2015.

MSR $1,800	$1,525	$1,350	$1,175	$1,050	$900	$775	$625

Z-43P – 5.56 NATO cal., roller-lock, delayed blowback action, 12 in. cold hammer forged barrel with threaded end and pinned muzzle brake, three 30 shot mags., front protected post sight and rear drum for elevation and windage, black, green, or camo finish, includes Picatinny style optics mount, factory sling, and plastic carry case, 7.73 lbs. New 2015.

MSR $1,600	$1,350	$1,200	$1,075	$950	$815	$700	$575

RIFLES: BOLT ACTION

BORA-12 – 7.62 NATO cal., 26 in. cold hammer forged barrel with muzzle brake, no sights, three 10 shot mags., factory Picatinny style optics mount, fully adj. buttstock, cheek, LOP, and trigger, bipod is additional, black finish, includes factory sling and plastic carry case, 14 lbs. New 2015.

MSR $6,500	$5,525	$4,850	$4,150	$3,775	$3,050	$2,500	$2,000

RIFLES: SEMI-AUTO

Z-5 – 9mm Para. cal., roller-lock delayed blowback action, 16.15 in. cold hammer forged barrel, three 10 shot mags., front protected post sight and rear drum for elevation and windage, factory Picatinny style optics mount, black finish, includes factory sling and plastic carry case, 6.88 lbs. New 2015.

MSR $1,500	$1,275	$1,125	$1,025	$875	$750	$625	$525

Z-41 – 7.62 NATO cal., roller-lock delayed blowback action, 16.15 in. barrel with threaded end and pinned muzzle brake, three 10 shot mags., front protected post sight and rear drum for elevation and windage, factory Picatinny style optics mount, black, green, or camo finish, includes factory sling and plastic carry case, 9 1/2 lbs. New 2015.

MSR $1,550	$1,310	$1,150	$1,040	$875	$750	$625	$525

Z-43 – 5.56 NATO cal., roller-lock delayed blowback action, 16.15 in. cold hammer forged barrel with threaded end and pinned muzzle brake, 10 shot mag., front protected post sight and rear drum for elevation and windage, factory Picatinny style optics mount, fixed stock, black, green, or camo finish, includes factory sling and plastic carry case, 8.9 lbs. New 2015.

MSR $1,500	$1,275	$1,125	$1,025	$875	$750	$625	$525

ZOMBIE DEFENSE

Current custom manufacturer located in Henrico, VA since 2009.

RIFLES: SEMI-AUTO

Zombie Defense builds custom rifles on the AR-15 platform to the customer's specifications using their own unique custom lower receivers. Current models with base MSRs include: Entry Level Z4 - $775, Z4 .300 Blackout - $850, Z4 6.8 SPC - $850, and Z4 18 in. SPR - $950. Please contact the company directly for more information including options, pricing, and availability (see Trademark Index).

NOTES

GLOSSARY

1989 BUSH BAN

Refers to the U.S. Federal executive branch study and resulting regulations which banned the importation of firearms which did not meet sporting criteria , i.e. certain paramilitary semi-auto only rifles and shotguns. The study was undertaken in response to the Stockton, CA tragedy in which an AK-47 type rifle was criminally used by a so-called mass murderer. The Federal regulation, U.S.C. Title 18, Section 922r, applies to imported firearms and to firearms assembled in the U.S. using imported components. It is important to note that even though the Assault Weapon Ban (which applied to U.S. manufactured firearms, not imports) has expired, Section 922r remains in effect, and has the force of U.S. Federal law, regardless of its executive branch origin as opposed to U.S. Senate and House of Representatives legislation. Also see Section 922r.

5R

Five groove rifling developed in Russia. Instead of conventional six groove rifling with opposing lands and sharp edged transitions between lands and grooves, 5R lands oppose grooves and the sides of lands are cut at a sixty-five degree angle. Claimed benefits are: decreased bullet deformation, less jacket fouling, increased velocity, and greater accuracy.

A1 STYLE

Refers to an AR style rifle in A1 configuration, or A1 specific components (triangular handguard, short fixed buttstock, receiver with integral carry handle, four slot bird cage flash hider, smooth pistol grip, rear flip sight with short and long range apertures, lighter weight 1:14 twist barrel).

A2 STYLE

Refers to an AR style rifle in A2 configuration, or A2 specific components (circular bi-lateral handguard, longer fixed buttstock, receiver with integral carry handle and spent case deflector, five slot bird cage flash hider, finger rib pistol grip, windage and elevation adjustable rear flip sight with small day and large low light apertures, heavier weight 1:7 twist barrel).

A3 STYLE

Refers to an AR style rifle in A3 configuration, or A3 specific components (circular bi-lateral handguard, collapsible buttstock, receiver with flat top Picatinny rail and detachable carry handle, A2 flash hider/pistol grip/rear sight/barrel).

A4 STYLE

Refers to an AR style rifle in A4 configuration, or A4 specific components (same as A2 except for Modular Weapons System handguard).

ACCOUTREMENT

All equipment carried by soldiers on the outside of their uniform, such as buckles, belts, or canteens, but not weapons.

ACTION

An assembly consisting of the receiver or frame and the mechanism by which a firearm is loaded, fired, and unloaded. See ACTION TYPES for the various kinds of actions.

ACTION BAR FLATS

See WATER TABLE.

ACTION TYPES

Actions are broadly classified as either manual or self-loading. Manual actions may be single shot or repeater. Single shot actions include dropping block (tilting, falling, and rolling), break, hinged, and bolt. Repeater actions include revolver, bolt, lever, pump, and dropping block. Self-loading actions may be semiautomatic or automatic. Semi-auto and automatic actions by sub-type are:

   a. blowback: simple, lever delayed, roller delayed, gas delayed, toggle delayed, hesitation locked, and chamber-ring delayed.

   b. blow-forward.

   c. recoil: short, long, and inertia.

   d. gas: short stroke piston, long stroke piston, direct impingement, and gas trap.

ADJUSTABLE CHOKE

A device built into the muzzle of a shotgun enabling changes from one choke to another.

ADJUSTABLE FRONT SIGHT

A front sight which can be moved, relative to the barrel's axis, vertically for elevation and/or horizontally for windage adjustments.

ADJUSTABLE REAR SIGHT

A rear sight which can be moved, relative to the barrel's axis, vertically for elevation and/or horizontally for windage adjustments.

ADJUSTABLE SIGHT

A firearm sight which can be adjusted so that the shooter's point of aim and the projectile's point of impact coincide at a desired target distance. On a majority of firearms only the rear sight is adjustable, but front sights may also be adjustable.

AIRGUN

A gun that utilizes compressed air or gas to launch the projectile.

AK/AKM STYLE ACTION

A gas operated rifle action with a long-stroke gas piston, a tilting breechblock locking design, and a heavy milled (early versions) or lighter sheet metal (later versions) receiver. No regulator is used; the overall design, machining, tolerances, ease of maintenance, and component durability assure reliable function in all circumstances.

ANY OTHER WEAPON

Any other firearm which is not an NFA defined machine gun, short barrel rifle, short barrel shotgun, modern shoulder stocked pistol, suppressor (BATFE uses the term "silencer"), or destructive device. An AOW is: a device capable of being concealed on a person from which a shot can be discharged through the energy of an explosive; a smooth bore barrel pistol or revolver designed or redesigned to fire a fixed shotgun shell; a weapon with combination shotgun and rifle barrels twelve inches or more but less than eighteen inches in length, from which only a single discharge can be made from either barrel without manual reloading; and any such weapon which may be readily restored to fire. AOW examples: H&R Handyguns, Ithaca Auto-Burglar guns, cane guns, and guns modified/disguised so as to be unrecognizable as firearms.

APERTURE SIGHT

An iron rear sight which has a hole or aperture in a disc or semi-circular blade instead of a rectangular or "vee" notch of an open sight. May also be a front sight, or adjustable for windage/elevation, or have adjustable/interchangeable apertures.

AR-15 STYLE ACTION

A gas operated rifle action with a direct gas impingement system (i.e. no gas piston, no regulator, no moving parts), a bolt carrier enclosing a multi-lugged rotating bolt locking design, and a two-part light-weight receiver. Propellant gas flows through a gas tube, acts directly upon the bolt carrier to cycle the action, and vents into the receiver. AR-15 style actions have fewer parts, are more adaptable/modifiable, and are significantly lighter than AK, FAL, or HK91 style actions. However, more maintenance, cleaning, and lubrication are absolutely required for reliability, in contrast to other gas operated actions.

ASSAULT RIFLE

Definition usually depends on if you're pro-gun or anti-gun. If you're pro-gun, it generally refers to a military styled, short to immediate range battle rifle capable of selective fire (semi-auto or full auto). If you're anti-gun, it can include almost anything, including sporter rifles from the turn of the 20th century.

ASSAULT SHOTGUN

Refers to a shotgun manufactured by contract for the military or law enforcement with a barrel shorter than 18 inches, usually a semi-auto or slide action configuration.

ASSAULT WEAPONS BAN

Popular title for the Violent Crime Control and Law Enforcement Act of 1994, Public Law 103-322. See VIOLENT CRIME...LAW 103-322.

AUTO LOADING/LOADER

See SEMI-AUTO ACTION.

AUTOMATIC ACTION

An action design which continuously fires and performs all steps in the operating cycle if the trigger remains fully depressed and ammunition is present in the firearm's magazine or feeding system. Also known as full auto or fully automatic. Machine guns utilize automatic actions, which may be recoil, gas, or externally powered.

AUTOMATIC EJECTOR

See SELECTIVE AUTOMATIC EJECTOR.

BACK BORE/BACK-BORED

A shotgun barrel which has been bored to a diameter greater than normal for its gauge, but not greater than SAAMI specs for that gauge. The advantages of this are: higher shot velocity, more uniform and denser patterns and fewer deformed pellets.

BACK UP IRON SIGHTS

Flip up or fixed iron sights which are not the primary sight system. They are used if the primary optical sight system fails and usually co-witness (optic sight picture and back up sight picture share the same zero).

BACKSTRAP

Those parts of the revolver or pistol frame which are exposed at the rear of the grip.

BARREL

The steel tube (may be wrapped in a sleeve of synthetic material) which a projectile travels through. May or may not be rifled.

BARREL BAND

A metal band, either fixed or adjustable, around the forend of a gun that holds the barrel to the stock.

BARREL FLATS

The lower flat surfaces under the chambers of side-by-side shotgun barrels which contact the corresponding flat areas of the shotgun's receiver. Also see WATER TABLE.

BARREL LUG

A projection which extends from a barrel and performs a locating, supporting, or energy transfer function. Lugs may be separate components, or integral to barrels.

BARREL THROAT

At the breech end of a barrel, the segment of the bore which tapers from a non-rifled projectile diameter to a fully rifled dimension. Also known as a forcing cone, leade, lede, or throat.

BATFE 922r COMPLIANT

A semi-auto paramilitary rifle (assembled with U.S. and foreign manufactured parts) which meets the statutory requirements of Section 922r of the United States code. Also refers to U.S. made parts which bring the rifle into compliance.

BATTUE

A ramped fixed rear sight assembly located on the back of the barrel, allowing quick target acquisition.

BEAVERTAIL FOREND

A wider than normal forend.

BENCH REST STOCK

A rifle stock specifically designed for a "bench rest" competition rifle which is fired from a table or bench, but supported only by sandbags or other devices. Optimized for stability, it often has a very wide flat-bottomed forend.

BESPOKE

A British term for a firearm custom-made to the purchaser's specifications. From the verb "bespeak", which means "to give order for it to be made".

BIRD'S HEAD

Refers to curved grip configuration on revolvers which resembles the outline of a bird's head, usually with 3 1/2 - 5 1/2 in. barrel lengths. Patterned after the grips on Colt's 1877 Thunderer revolver.

BLIND MAGAZINE

A box magazine which is completely concealed within the action and stock.

BLOWBACK ACTION

A semi-automatic or automatic firearm operating design which uses expanding propellant gasses to push a heavy unlocked breech bolt open, and which relies upon the inertia of its moving parts to keep the action closed until the bullet has exited the muzzle and pressure has decreased to a safe level.

BLUING

The chemical process of artificial oxidation (rusting) applied to gun parts so that the metal attains a dark blue or nearly black appearance.

BOLT

An assembly which reciprocates along the axis of a firearm's bore; it supports the cartridge case head and locks the action. Also see BOLT ACTION.

BOLT (REVOLVER)

The lug or projection which rises from a revolver's frame in order to immobilize the cylinder and align a charge hole with the bore of the barrel. Also called a cylinder stop.

BOLT ACTION

A manual action with a bolt body (usually including locking, firing pin, extractor, and ejector components) enclosed by and moving within the firearm's receiver.

BORE

Internal dimensions of a barrel (smooth or rifled) that can be measured using the Metric system (i.e. millimeters), English system (i.e. inches), or by the Gauge system (see GAUGE). On a rifled barrel, the bore is measured across the lands. Also, it is a traditional English term used when referring to the diameter of a shotgun muzzle (gauge in U.S. measure).

BOX MAGAZINE

A boxlike feed device for a firearm, which allows cartridges to be stacked one on top of the other. Most box magazines are removable for reloading.

BOXLOCK ACTION

Typified by Parker shotguns in U.S. and Westley Richards in England. Generally considered inferior in strength to the sidelock. Developed by Anson & Deeley, the boxlock is hammerless. It has two disadvantages. First, the hammer pin must be placed directly below knee of action, which is its weakest spot. Second, action walls must be thinned out to receive locks. These are inserted from below into large slots in the action body, which is then closed with a plate. If a correctly made Greener crossbolt is used, many of the boxlock's weaknesses can be negated. Also see CROSSBOLT.

BRADY ACT/BILL

See BRADY HANDGUN VIOLENCE PREVENTION ACT.

BRADY HANDGUN VIOLENCE PREVENTION ACT

1998 Federal legislation which established the National Instant Criminal Background Check System (NICS). Also commonly known as the Brady Bill, or the Brady Act. See NATIONAL INSTANT CRIMINAL BACKGROUND CHECK SYSTEM.

BREAK BARREL ACTION

A type of action where the barrels pivot on a hinge pin, allowing access to the chamber(s) in the breech. Configurations include: single shot, SxS, O/U, combination guns, drillings, and vierlings.

BREAK OPEN ACTION

See BREAK BARREL ACTION

BREECH

The rear end of a barrel where a cartridge is chambered. Also commonly used in reference to the entire chamber, breech, and receiver of long guns.

BREVETTE

French word which, in gun terminology, refers to a European copy (usually English, French, or Belgian) or patterned after a more famous design (i.e., Brevette Remington O/U derringer refers to a copy of the Remington O/U .41 cal. derringer).

BROWNING

An acid oxidation method of applying a rust-resistant finish to steel; so named because of the resultant surface color of the finished metal surface.

BUCKHORN SIGHT

Open metallic rear sight with sides that curl upward and inward.

BULL BARREL

A heavier, thicker than normal barrel with little or no taper.

BULLET BUTTON

A magazine locking device for AR-15 style rifles. It transforms a rifle with a standard manually operable magazine release and detachable magazine functionality into a fixed magazine rifle in order to comply with the State of California's firearm statutes. Depressing the "button" with a tool, e.g. bullet tip, small screwdriver, etc., is the only way to remove the magazine (which cannot hold more than ten rounds).

BUTT SPIKE

A fixed or adjustable monopod mounted near the rear on the bottom of a rifle's buttstock that, when used with forearm support of the rifle, enables the user to observe the target area for extended periods with minimal fatigue.

BUTTPAD

A rubber or synthetic composition part attached to the buttstock's end; intended to absorb recoil energy, prevent damage to the buttstock, and vary length of pull. May be fixed, solid, ventilated, or adjustable (horizontally, vertically, cant).

BUTTPLATE

A protective plate, usually steel, attached to the back of the buttstock.

BUTTSTOCK

The portion of a stock which is positioned against the user's shoulder; also known as the butt. On AR-15/M16 style or similar long guns, the separate component which is attached to the rear of the receiver. Also see STOCK.

CALIBER

The diameter of the bore (measured from land to land), usually measured in either inches or millimeters/centimeters. It does not designate bullet diameter.

CAMO (CAMOUFLAGE) FINISH

Refers to a patterned treatment using a variety of different colors/patterns that enables a gun to blend into a particular outdoors environment. In most cases, this involves a film or additional finish applied on top of a gun's wood and/or metal parts (i.e. Mossy Oak Break-Up, Mossy Oak Brush, Advantage Timber, Realtree Hardwoods, Realtree Max-4, Muddy Girl, etc.). Mossberg introduced camo finishes on its shotguns in the mid-1980s.

CARTOUCHE

Generally refers to a manufacturer's inspector marking impressed into the wood of a military gun, usually in the form of initials inside a circle or oval.

CASE COLORS

See COLOR CASE HARDENING.

CAST OFF

The distance that a buttplate is offset to the right of the line of sight for a right-handed shooter. Especially important in shotgun stocks.

CAST ON

The same as Cast Off, except that the buttplate is offset to the left of the line of sight for a left-handed shooter.

CENTERFIRE

Refers to ammunition with primers centrally positioned in the cartridge case head; or to a firearm which is chambered for centerfire ammunition.

CERAKOTE

A ceramic based firearms coating with improved performance and reliability compared to traditional firearms finishes. Offers abrasion, corrosion, and solvent protection, in many colors and designs.

CHAMBER

Rear part of the barrel which has been reamed out so that it will contain a cartridge. When the breech is closed, the cartridge is supported in the chamber, and the chamber must align the primer with the firing pin, and the bullet with the bore.

CHAMBER THROAT

See BARREL THROAT.

CHARGE HOLE

The hole bored completely through a revolver's cylinder in which cartridges are loaded.

CHARGING HANDLE

A semi-auto firearm component which is manipulated to cycle the action, but which does not fire the cartridge. Also called cocking handle, cocking knob, or operating handle.

CHECKERING

A functional decoration consisting of pointed pyramids cut into the wood or metal surfaces of a firearm. Generally applied to the pistol grip and forend/forearm areas, affording better handling and control.

CHEEKPIECE

An elevated section of the upper buttstock on which the shooter's cheek rests when holding a rifle or shotgun in firing position. It may be integral to the buttstock, or a separate component. Adjustable cheekpieces may be moved in one or more ways: up, down, fore, aft, or side-to-side.

CHOKE

The muzzle constriction on a shotgun which controls the spread of the shot.

CHOKE TUBES

Interchangeable screw-in devices allowing different choke configurations (i.e., cylinder, improved cylinder, improved modified, modified, full). While most choke tubes fit flush with the end of the barrel, some choke tubes now also protrude from the end of the barrel. Most recently made shotguns usually include three to five choke tubes with the shotgun.

CHOPPER LUMP

A method of construction of barrels for double barreled, SxS shotguns in which the "lump" extending beneath the breech of the barrel is forged as an integral part of the barrel. When the barrels are assembled, the two lumps are carefully fitted on their mating surfaces and brazed solidly together into a single unit, into which locking and other functional recesses are cut.

CLIP

A metal or synthetic material formed/shaped to hold cartridges in readiness to be loaded into a magazine or chamber. A clip is NOT a magazine (i.e., stripper clips for most variations of the Mauser Broomhandle). Also known as a stripper or cartridge clip.

COCKING INDICATOR

Any device for which the act of cocking a gun moves it into a position where it may be seen or felt, in order to notify the shooter that the gun is cocked. Typical examples are the pins found on some high-grade hammerless shotguns, which protrude slightly when they are cocked, and also the exposed cocking knobs on bolt-action rifles. Exposed hammers found on some rifles and pistols are also considered cocking indicators.

COIN FINISH

Older definition referring to a metal finish, typically on a rifle or shotgun, which resembles the finish of an old silver coin. Most coin finishes are based on nickel plating (not chrome) and are generally high polish.

COLLAPSIBLE STOCK

Mostly used in reference to a buttstock which can be shortened or lengthened along its fore to aft axis. Also applies in theory to top-folding, under-folding, and side folding buttstocks; all of which when folded reduce the weapon's length.

COLOR CASE HARDENING

A method of hardening steel and iron while imparting colorful swirls as well as surface figure. Traditional color case hardening using charcoal and bone meal is achieved by putting the desired metal parts in a crucible packed with a mixture of charcoal and finely ground animal bone to temperatures in the 800°C – 900°C range, after which they are slowly cooled. Then they are submerged into cold water, leaving a thin, colorful protective finish. Can also be achieved by treating the necessary metal parts with a cyanide liquid, which helps harden the metal surface, and can be denoted from charcoal color case hardening by a more layered color appearance.

COMB

The portion of the stock on which the shooter's cheek rests.

COMBINATION GUN

Generally, a break-open shotgun-type configuration that is fitted with at least one shotgun barrel and one rifle barrel. Such guns may be encountered with either two or three barrels, and less frequently with as many as four or five, and have been known to chamber as many as four different calibers.

COMPENSATOR

Slots, vents, or ports machined into a firearm's barrel near its muzzle, or a muzzle device, which allow propellant gasses to escape upwards and partially reduce muzzle jump.

CONTROLLED ROUND FEEDING

A bolt action rifle design in which the cartridge is mechanically secured by the extractor and bolt during all parts of the operating cycle.

CRANE

In a modern solid-frame, swing-out cylinder revolver, the U-shaped yoke on which the cylinder rotates, and which holds the cylinder in the frame. The crane/yoke is the weakest part of a revolver's mechanism.

CRIME BILL

Popular title for the Violent Crime Control and Law Enforcement Act of 1994, Public Law 103-322. See VIOLENT CRIME...LAW 103-322.

CRIMP

A turning in of the case mouth to affect a closure or to prevent the projectile(s) from slipping out of the case mouth. Various crimps include: roll, pie, star or folded, rose, stab, and taper.

CROSSBOLT

A transverse locking rod/bar used in many SxS boxlock shotguns and a few rifles, which locks the standing breech and barrels to each other. Originally designed by W.W. Greener, this term is also referred to as the Greener crossbolt. Also a transverse metal bolt which reinforces and prevents damage to the stock from recoil or abusive handling.

CROWNING

The rounding or chamfering normally done to a barrel muzzle to ensure that the mouth of the bore is square with the bore axis and that its edges are countersunk below the surface to protect it from impact damage. Traditionally, crowning was accomplished by spinning an abrasive-coated brass ball against the muzzle while moving it in a figure-eight pattern, until the abrasive had cut away any irregularities and produced a uniform and square mouth.

CRYOGENIC TEMPERING

Computer controlled cooling process that relieves barrel stress by subjecting the barrel to a temperature of -310 degrees Fahrenheit for 22 hours.

CURIO/RELIC

Firearms which are of special interest to collectors by reason of some quality other than that which is normally associated with firearms intended for sporting use or as offensive or defensive weapons. Must be older than 50 years.

CYLINDER

A rotating cartridge holder in a revolver. The cartridges are held in chambers and the cylinder turns, either to the left or the right, depending on the gun maker's design, as the hammer is cocked.

CYLINDER ARM

See CRANE.

DA/SA

A semi-auto pistol fire control design which allows an initial shot to be fired in double action mode, and subsequent shots in single action mode until the magazine is empty or the user decocks the pistol. For most modern semi-auto pistols, the cocking is either manual or automatic; and in both instances the trigger and hammer/striker are returned to their respective double action states. See also DOUBLE ACTION and SINGLE ACTION.

DAMASCENE

The decorating of metal with another metal, either by inlaying or attaching in some fashion.

DAMASCUS BARREL

A barrel made by twisting, forming, and welding thin strips of steel around a mandrel.

DE-HORNING

The removal of all sharp edges from a firearm that would cut or pinch the shooter, the shooter's clothing, and/or holster, but still maintains the nice clean lines of the firearm.

DELAYED IMPINGEMENT GAS SYSTEM

A trademarked gas operating system for AR-15 style carbines, designed by Allan Zitta. Similar to a gas piston action in concept, it has instead an operating rod and recoil spring which run through the receiver, over the barrel, and sleeve the gas tube at the gas block. The gas tube does not enter the receiver, and the recoil spring replaces the buffer and spring in the AR-15 buttstock.

DEMI-BLOC/DEMI-BLOCK

See CHOPPER LUMP.

DERRINGER

Usually refers to a small, concealable pistol with one or two short barrels.

DETACHABLE MILITARY STYLE BIPOD

A bipod designed for severe/heavy use and greater durability, with a Picatinny rail or other type of quick attach/detach mounting system.

DIRECT IMPINGEMENT GAS SYSTEM

A gas operating system in which high pressure and temperature propellant gas is routed into the firearm receiver to make contact with and move action components. There are no "moving parts" (e.g. piston, return spring, operating rod, tappet) in a direct impingement gas sytem. A typical direct impingement gas system has a gas block surrounding the barrel and covering the gas port, and a gas tube.

DOUBLE ACTION

The principle in a revolver or auto-loading pistol wherein the hammer can be cocked and dropped by a single pull of the trigger. Most of these actions also provide capability for single action fire. In auto loading pistols, double action normally applies only to the first shot of any series, the hammer being cocked by the slide for subsequent shots.

DOUBLE ACTION ONLY

A firearm action which cannot be operated in single action mode. Many newer DAO firearms are either hammerless, or their hammers and triggers cannot be positioned in a single action status.

DOUBLE UNDERLUGS

The two underlugs on the lower barrel of an over/under double barrel shotgun or rifle.

DOUBLE-BARREL(ED)

A gun which has two barrels joined either side-by-side or one over the other.

DOUBLE-SET TRIGGER

A device that consists of two triggers - one to cock the mechanism that spring-assists the other trigger, substantially lightening the other trigger's pull weight.

DOVETAIL

A flaring machined or hand-cut slot that is also slightly tapered toward one end. Cut into the upper surface of barrels and sometimes actions, the dovetail accepts a corresponding part on which a sight is mounted. Dovetail slot blanks are used to cover the dovetail when the original sight has been removed or lost; this gives the barrel a more pleasing appearance and configuration.

DRILLED & TAPPED

Refers to holes drilled into the top of a receiver/frame and threaded, which allow scope bases, blocks, rings, or other sighting devices to be rigidly attached to the gun.

DRILLING

German for triple, which is their designation for a three-barrel gun, usually two shotgun barrels and one rifle barrel.

EJECTOR

A firearm component which propels an extracted cartridge or fired case out of the receiver or chamber. Ejectors may be fixed or movable, spring loaded or manually activated. Also see SELECTIVE AUTOMATIC EJECTOR.

ELASTOMER

A synthetic elastic polymer, soft and compressible like natural rubber, used for seals, grip and stock inlays, and other molded firearm components.

ELECTROCIBLE

Unique reusable target designed like an aircraft propeller that causes it to spin and go in different directions. In competition, electrocibles come out of one of five boxes located 25 meters from the shooter, who must hit it before it crosses over the ring at 21 meters.

ELECTRO-OPTICAL SIGHT

An optical sight (see definition) with the addition of electronic battery powered components which illuminate a reticle (least complex), or which generate a reticle/optional reticles. Electro-optical sights may be: magnifying, non-magnifying, full-tube traditional optical design , or reflex types (see REFLEX SIGHT).

ELEVATION

A firearm sight's vertical distance above the barrel's bore axis; also the adjustment of a sight to compensate for the effect of gravity on a projectile's exterior ballistic path.

ENGINE TURNING

Machined circular polishing on metal, creating a unique overlapping pattern.

ENGLISH STOCK

A straight, slender-gripped stock.

ENGRAVING

The art of engraving metal in decorative patterns. Scroll engraving is the most common type of hand engraving encountered. Much of today's factory engraving is rolled on which is done mechanically. Hand engraving requires artistry and knowledge of metals and related materials.

ERGO SUREGRIP

A Falcon Industries Inc. right hand or ambidextrous replacement pistol grip for AR-15/M-16 style rifles. The grip has finger grooves, upper rear extension to support the web of the shooter's hand, is oil and solvent resistant, and a non-slip textured overmolded rubber surface.

ETCHING

A method of decorating metal gun parts, usually done by acid etching or photo engraving.

EXTRACTOR

A device which partially pulls a cartridge or fired hull/case/casing(s) from the chamber, allowing it to be removed manually.

FALLING BLOCK

A single shot action where the breechblock drops straight down when a lever is actuated.

FARQUHARSON ACTION

A single shot hammerless falling block rifle action patented in 1872 by John Farquharson.

FENCES

The hemispherical formations on a side-by-side shotgun's receiver which are adjacent to the barrel breeches. Originally fences were the curving metal flanges surrounding a percussion ignition firearm's nipple, or a flintlock ignition firearm's priming pan, which protected the shooter from sparks, smoke, and escaping gas.

FIBER OPTIC SIGHT

An iron sight with fiber optic light gathering rods or cylinders; the rod ends are perceived as glowing dots and enhance sight visibility and contrast.

FIT AND FINISH

Terms used to describe over-all firearm workmanship.

FIRE CONTROL GROUP

All components necessary to cause a cartridge to be fired; may be a self-contained assembly, easily disassembled or not user-serviceable, detachable, modular/interchangeable, and may or may not include a safety, bolt release, or other parts.

FIRING PIN

That part of a firearm which strikes the cartridge primer, causing detonation.

FLASH SUPPRESSOR/HIDER

A muzzle attachment which mechanically disrupts and reduces muzzle flash. It does not reduce muzzle blast or recoil.

FLAT-TOP UPPER

An AR-15/M16 style or other tactical semi-auto rifle with a literally flat receiver top. The majority of flat-top uppers have an extended Picatinny rail for mounting iron sights, optical sights, and other accessories, which provides much more versatility than the original "carry handle" receiver design.

FLOATING BARREL

A barrel bedded to avoid contact with any point on the stock.

FLOOR PLATE

Usually, a removable/hinged plate at the bottom of the receiver covering the magazine well.

FN FAL STYLE ACTION

A gas operated rifle action with a short-stroke spring-loaded gas piston, a tilting breechblock locking design, and a heavy receiver. A regulator valve allows the user to increase the volume of gas entering the system in order to ensure reliable operation in adverse conditions. Unlike direct gas impingement or delayed blowback operating systems, propellant gas does not vent into the receiver and fire control components.

FOLDING STOCK

Usually a buttstock hinged at or near the receiver so that it can be "folded" towards the muzzle, reducing the firearm's overall length. Not an adjustable stock as defined above, and usually does not prevent operating/firing when in its folded position.

FORCING CONE

The segment of a shotgun barrel immediately forward of the chamber where its internal diameter is reduced from chamber to bore diameter. The forcing cone aids the passage of shot into the barrel. For revolvers, the tapering portion of the barrel bore from the breech to the rifling.

FOREARM

In this text, a separate piece of wood in front of the receiver and under the barrel used for hand placement when shooting.

FOREARM/FOREND CAP

A separate piece attached to the muzzle end of a forearm; often with a colored spacer, and usually in a contrasting color/material.

FOREND/FORE-END

Usually the forward portion of a one-piece rifle or shotgun stock (in this text), but

can also refer to a separate piece of wood.

FORWARD BOLT ASSIST

A button, usually found on AR-15 type rifles, which may be pushed or struck to move the bolt carrier fully forward so that the extractor has completely engaged the cartridge rim and the bolt has locked. Mainly used to close/lock the bolt when the rifle's chamber and receiver are excessively fouled or dirty.

FRAME

The part of a firearm to which the action (lock work), barrel, and stock/grip are connected. Most of the time used when referring to a handgun or hinged frame long gun.

FREE FLOATING FOREARM

A forearm which does not contact the barrel at any point, as it attaches and places mechanical stress only on the receiver. An accuracy enhancement for AR-15/M16 style rifles, which by their modular design, are not able to have a conventionally free floated barrel in a one-piece stock.

FREE RIFLE

A rifle designed for international-type target shooting. The only restriction on design is a weight maximum 8 kilograms (17.6 lbs.).

FRONT STRAP

That part of the revolver or pistol grip frame which faces forward and often joins with the trigger guard. In target guns, notably the .45 ACP, the front strap is often stippled to give shooter's hand a slip-proof surface.

FULL AUTO

See AUTOMATIC ACTION

GAS IMPINGEMENT OPERATING SYSTEM

An action in which high pressure propellant gas is diverted from the barrel to supply the energy required to unlock the breech, extract/eject the fired case, load a cartridge, and lock the breech. This type of system generates a large amount of heat and also a considerable amount of fouling directly back into the action.

GAS PISTON OPERATING SYSTEM

A gas operation design in which a piston is used to transfer propellant gas energy to the action components. No gas enters the receiver or makes contact with other action components. Consequently, less heat is absorbed by, and less fouling accumulates in the receiver. This system also has a much different recoil pulse or "feel".

GAS PORT

A small opening in the barrel of a gas operated firearm which allows high pressure gas to flow into the gas system's components. Also an escape vent in a firearm's receiver, a safety feature.

GAUGE/GA.

A unit of measure used to determine a shotgun's bore. Determined by the amount of pure lead balls equaling the bore diameter needed to equal one pound (i.e., a 12 ga. means that 12 lead balls exactly the diameter of the bore weigh one pound). In this text, .410 is referenced as a bore (if it was a gauge, it would be a 68 ga.).

GAUGE VS. BORE DIAMETER

10-Gauge = Bore Diameter of .775 inches or 19.3mm
12-Gauge = Bore Diameter of .729 inches or 18.2mm
16-Gauge = Bore Diameter of .662 inches or 16.8mm
20-Gauge = Bore Diameter of .615 inches or 15.7mm
28-Gauge = Bore Diameter of .550 inches or 13.8mm
68-Gauge = Bore Diameter of .410 inches or 12.6mm

GCA

The Gun Control Act of 1968, 18 USC Chapter 44.

GLACIERGUARDS

AR-15/M-16 carbine length replacement handguard (two-piece) which has fifteen internal heat dispersing fins rather than the standard heat shield. The fins provide greater strength and rigidity; fiber-reinforced polymer shells resist heat and reduce weight. A DPMS product.

GRIP

The handle used to hold a handgun, or the area of a stock directly behind and attached to the frame/receiver of a long gun.

GRIPS

Can be part of the frame or components attached to the frame used to assist in accuracy, handling, control, and safety of a handgun. Many currently manufactured semi-auto handguns have grips that are molded w/checkering as part of the synthetic frame.

GRIPSTRAP(S)

Typically refers to the front and back metal attached to a handgun frame which supports the grips/stocks. Also known as the front strap and back strap.

GROOVES

The spiral depressions of the rifling in a barrel bore; created by cutting, swaging, broaching, hammering, cation action, or other methods. Also see LANDS and RIFLING.

HALF COCK

A position of the hammer in a hammer activated firing mechanism that serves as a manual safety.

HAMMER

A part of a gun's mechanism which applies force to the firing pin or other components, which in turn fires the gun.

HAMMERLESS

Some "hammerless" firearms do in fact have hidden hammers, which are located in the action housing. Truly hammerless guns, such as the Savage M99, have a firing mechanism based on a spring-powered striker.

HANDGUARD

A wooden, synthetic, or ventilated metal part attached above the barrel and ahead of the receiver to protect the shooter's hand from the heat generated during semi-auto rapid firing.

HEEL

Back end of the upper edge of the butt stock at the upper edge of the buttplate or recoil pad.

HK91/G3 STYLE ACTION

A roller locked delayed blowback rifle action. There is no gas system per se; gas pressure in the cartridge case pushes the case against the bolt and bolt carrier. Spring-loaded rollers in the bolt resist unlocking and carrier/bolt movement until chamber pressure has dropped to a safe level. Components are heavier, recoil (actual and perceived) is greater, chambers must be fluted to assure extraction, and cocking effort is much greater than direct gas or gas piston weapons.

ILAFLON

Industrielack AG trademarked ceramic reinforced enamel firearms finish coating; highly resistant to abrasion, corrosion, and chemicals/solvent.

INTEGRAL LOCKING SYSTEM

A North American Arms safety system; a key allows the user to internally lock the hammer in place, which prevents discharging the firearm.

INTRAFUSE

A trademarked system of synthetic stocks and accessories designed for tactical firearms.

IN-THE-WHITE

Refers to a gun's finish w/o bluing, nickel, case colors, gold, etc. Since all metal surfaces are normally polished, the steel appears white, hence, "in-the-white" terminology.

IRON SIGHTS

A generic term for metallic front or rear sights which do not use optical lens (magnifying or non-magnifying) components.

JUXTAPOSED

See SIDE-BY-SIDE.

KRYPTEK

A proprietary camo finish utilizing a multi-directional design to affectively conceal in a multitude of terrains that have either a lateral or vertical flow. The bi-level layering of the patterns incorporate background transitional shading and sharp random geometrical foregrounds to create a three dimensional effect that ensures the utmost in concealment at both close and long ranges. Patterns include Highlander, Typhon, and Raid.

LAMINATED STOCK

A gunstock made of many layers of wood glued together under pressure. The laminations become very strong, preventing damage from moisture or heat, and warping.

LANDS

Portions of the bore left between the grooves of the rifling in the bore of a firearm. In rifling, the grooves are usually twice the width of the land. Land diameter is measured across the bore, from land to land.

LASER SIGHT

An aiming system which projects a beam of laser light onto the target. Usually mounted so the beam is parallel to the barrel bore but not a "traditional" front or rear sight as the shooter does not look through the laser apparatus.

LENS COATINGS

Metallic coatings on optic surfaces which increase light transmission, image brightness, and color rendition. Also used to improve abrasion resistance and filter out unwanted or harmful light.

LEVER ACTION

A manual repeating action operated by an external lever.

LUMP

An English term for an underlug.

M1913 PICATINNY RAIL

Original designation for a Picatinny rail. Also see PICATINNY RAIL.

M4 STYLE

Refers to an AR style rifle in M4 carbine configuration (A2 configuration but with short handguard, short barrel, and relocated gas block).

MACHINE GUN

National Firearms Act and Gun Control Act of 1968 definition:

Any weapon which shoots, is designed to shoot, or can be readily restored to shoot, automatically more than one shot, without manual reloading, by a single function of the trigger. The term shall also include the frame or receiver of any such weapon, any part designed and intended solely and exclusively, or combination of parts designed and intended, for use in converting a weapon into a machine gun, and any combination of parts from which a machine gun can be assembled if such parts are in the possession or control of a person.

MAGAZINE (MAG.)

The container (may be detachable) which holds cartridges under spring pressure to be fed into the gun's chamber. A clip is NOT a magazine. May be a single or double or multiple column, rotary, helical, drum, or other design. The term "high capacity" denotes a magazine capable of holding more than ten rounds.

MAGNUM (MAG.)/MAGNUM AMMUNITION

A term first used by Holland & Holland in 1912 for their .375 H&H Magnum cartridge. The term has now been applied to rimfire, centerfire, or shotshell cartridges having a larger cartridge case, heavier shot charge, or higher muzzle velocity than standard cartridges or shotshells of a given caliber or gauge. Most Magnum rifle cartridges are belted designs.

MAINSPRING

The spring that delivers energy to the hammer or striker.

MANNLICHER STOCK

A full-length slender stock with slender forend extending to the muzzle (full stock) affording better barrel protection.

MELONITE

A trademarked name for a metal case hardening and surface finishing process which provides exceptional wear, abrasion, and corrosion resistance; and very high surface hardness. The generic name for this process is ferritic nitrocarburizing.

MICROMETER SIGHT

A windage and elevation adjustable sight with very precise and small increments of adjustment.

MICRO SLICK

A firearms finish coating which creates a permanently lubricated surface; it impedes galling and seizing of firearm components.

MIL

See MILRADIAN

MIL-SPEC

A series of quality control standards used by manufacturers to guarantee machine tolerances ensuring the consistency and interchangeability of parts.

MIL-DOT

A reticle with dots spaced center-to-center one milradian apart; the distance to an object of known dimension may be calculated based upon the number of milradians which are subtended by the target's known dimension.

MILRADIAN

The horizontal angle subtended by one unit of measurement at 1,000 units distance. Also called a "mil".

MINUTE OF ANGLE (MOA)

1/60 of a degree of circular angle; at 100 yards it subtends 1.047 inches. Also commonly used to describe a firearm's accuracy and precision capability, i.e. a rifle which shoots under one minute of angle. Abbreviated MOA.

MODERN SPORTING RIFLE

A National Shooting Sports Foundation term for civilian legal semiautomatic AR-15 style rifles. The NSSF promotes its usage to counter the negative anti-gun connotations, confusion, and misunderstandings which have become associated with the term "AR15". A modern sporting rifle is not an automatic or assault rifle, not a regulated NFA weapon, not a military/law enforcement M16 despite its similar cosmetic appearance, and no more powerful than other traditional configuration sporting/hunting/competition rifles of the same caliber. Sometimes called Sport Utility Rifle or SUR. Note: the letters "AR" stand for Armalite Rifle.

MODULAR WEAPONS SYSTEM

A generic term of military origin for quick attach/detach components/systems which allow flexibility and adaptability for using various sighting, illumination, and other accessories, etc. on a weapon. Also see PICATINNY RAIL.

MONOBLOC

A form of construction and assembly for double barreled shotguns wherein the breeching and locking surfaces are cut into a single separate housing or "bloc" into which the breeches of the barrels are brazed or threaded. Compare to CHOPPER LUMP.

MONTE CARLO STOCK

A stock with an elevated comb used primarily for scoped rifles.

MUZZLE

The forward end of the barrel where the projectile exits.

MUZZLE BRAKE

A muzzle device (permanent or removable) or barrel modification which reduces muzzle jump and recoil by diverting propellant gasses sideways or to the rear. Not to be confused with a flash hider or a flash suppressor. Also see COMPENSATOR.

NATIONAL INSTANT CRIMINAL BACKGROUND CHECK SYSTEM (NICS)

A U. S. federal government system established 1994 which an FFL must, with limited exceptions, contact for information on whether receipt of a firearm by a person who is not licensed under 18 U.S.C. 923 would violate Federal or state law.

NEEDLE GUN

Ignition system invented by Johan Nikolas von Dreyse in 1829. This ignition system used a paper cartridge and became obsolete with the invention of the metallic cartridge.

NFA

The National Firearms Act, 26 USC Chapter 53.

NFA FIREARM

A firearm which must be registered in the National Firearm Registration and Transfer Record, as defined in the NFA and 27 CFR, Part 479. Included are: machine guns, frames or receivers of machine guns, any combination of parts designed and intended for use in converting weapons into machine guns, any combination of parts from which a machine gun can be assembled if the parts are in the possession or under control of a person, silencers and any part designed or intended for fabricating a silencer, short-barreled rifles, short-barreled shotguns, destructive devices, and "any other weapon". NFA semi-auto carbines with less than 16 in. barrels are not listed in this book.

NICS CHECK

See NATIONAL INSTANT CRIMINAL BACKGROUND CHECK SYSTEM.

NIGHT SIGHTS

Iron sights with radioactive tritium gas capsules; the capsules are inserted into recesses in the sight body with their ends facing the shooter. The tritium glow provides sight alignment and aiming references in lowlight/no-light conditions.

NON-DETACHABLE BOX MAGAZINE

A rectangular magazine which is never removed during normal use or maintenance of the firearm. It may extend beyond/below the receiver or stock, may be high capacity, and generally is loaded from its top (single cartridges or stripper clips).

NON-DETACHABLE FOLDING BAYONET

An articulated bayonet which cannot be removed from the firearm by the end user. Normally locked into its fully folded or extended position.

NP3/NP3 PLUS

An electroless plated nickel-phosphorus alloy firearms finish which offers uniform thickness, lubricity, and hardness equivalent to hard chromium plating.

OBJECTIVE LENS

A telescopic sight's front, usually larger lens which may be adjustable to reduce parallax error.

OCULAR LENS

The rear lens of a telescopic sight, normally adjustable by rotation to focus the sight image.

OPEN SIGHT

A simple rear iron sight with a notch – the shooter aims by looking through the notch at the front sight and the target.

OPTICAL SIGHT

A generic term for a sight which has one or more optical lenses through which the weapon is aimed. Optical sights usually magnify the target image, but there are many non- magnifying optical sights.

OVER-UNDER (O/U)

A double-barrel gun in which the barrels are stacked one on top of the other. Also called Superposed.

PARALLAX

Occurs in telescopic sights when the primary image of the objective lens does not coincide with the reticle. In practice, parallax is detected in the scope when, as the viewing eye is moved laterally, the image and the reticle appear to move in relation to each other.

PARAMILITARY

Typically refers to a firearm configured or styled to resemble a military weapon with one or more of the military weapon's configurations or features, EXCEPT FOR automatic or selective fire capability. Paramilitary firearms may be slide action (primarily shotguns), bolt action, or semi-automatic (most handguns and rifles).

PARKERIZING

Matte rust-resistant oxide finish, usually dull gray or black in color, found on military guns.

PEEP SIGHT

A rear sight consisting of a disc or blade with a hole or aperture through which the front sight and target are aligned.

PEPPERBOX

An early form of revolving repeating pistol, in which a number of barrels were bored in a circle in a single piece of metal resembling the cylinder of a modern revolver. Functioning was the same as a revolver, the entire cylinder being revolved to bring successive barrels under the hammer for firing. Though occurring as far back as the 16th century, the pepperbox did not become practical until the advent of the percussion cap in the early 1800s. Pepperboxes were made in a wide variety of sizes and styles, and reached their popularity peak during the percussion period. Few were made after the advent of practical metallic cartridges. Both single and double action pepperboxes were made. Single-barreled revolvers after the 1840s were more accurate and easier to handle and soon displaced the rather clumsy and muzzle-heavy pepperbox.

PERCH BELLY

Refers to a rifle's stock configuration where the bottom portion is curved rather than straight between the buttplate and pistol grip.

PICATINNY RAIL

A serrated flat rail typically located on the top of a frame/slide/receiver, but may also be located on the sides and bottom, allowing different optics/sights/accessories to be used on the gun. Developed at the U.S. Army's Picatinny Arsenal.

PINFIRE

An obsolete ignition system; a pinfire cartridge had an internal primer and a small firing pin protruding from the rear sidewall of its metallic case.

POLYGONAL

Rifling w/o sharp edged lands and grooves. Advantages include a slight increase in muzzle velocity, less bullet deformation, and reduced lead fouling since there are no traditional lands and grooves. See RIFLING.

POPE RIB

A rib integral with the barrel. Designed by Harry M. Pope, famed barrel maker and shooter, the rib made it possible to mount a target scope low over the barrel.

PORTED BARREL

A barrel with multiple holes or slots drilled near the muzzle. See PORTING.

PORTING

Multiple holes or slots drilled into a firearm barrel near the muzzle. Porting reduces felt/perceived recoil, and if located on the upper half of the barrel reduces muzzle jump. Disadvantages are increased muzzle blast and noise.

POST-BAN

See 1989 BUSH BAN, and SECTION 922r.

PRE-BAN

See 1989 BUSH BAN, and SECTION 922r.

PRIMER

A percussion device designed to ignite the propellant charge of a centerfire cartridge or shotshell by generating flame and high temperature expanding gasses.

PRIMER RING

Refers to a visible dark ring around the firing pin hole in a breech or bolt face, created by the impact of centerfire ammunition primer cups when a cartridge is fired.

PROOF MARK

Proof marks are usually applied to all parts actually tested, but normally appear on the barrel (and possibly frame), usually indicating the country of origin and time-frame of proof (especially on European firearms). In the U.S., there is no federalized or government proof house, only the manufacturer's in-house proof mark indicating that a firearm has passed its manufacturer's quality control standards per government specifications.

PUMP ACTION

See SLIDE ACTION.

QUAD RAIL FOREARM

A rifle forearm with upper, lower, and lateral Picatinny rails which allow attachment of multiple accessories.

QUARTER RIB

A short raised portion of a ribbed barrel, which forms a base for a rear metallic or optical sight.

RATE OF TWIST

The distance in which rifling makes one complete revolution; normally expressed as one turn in a specific number of inches or millimeters. Also called rifling pitch, or merely twist.

RECEIVER

That part of a rifle or shotgun (excluding hinged frame guns) which houses the bolt, firing pin, mainspring, trigger group, and magazine or ammunition feed system. The barrel is threaded or pressed into the somewhat enlarged forward part of the receiver, called the receiver ring. At the rear of the receiver, the butt or stock is fastened. In semiautomatic pistols, the frame or housing is sometimes referred to as the receiver.

RECOIL

The rearward motion of a firearm when a shot is fired (i.e. the gun recoiled); the term for the energy or force transferred into the firearm as it discharges a projectile.

RECOIL ACTION/OPERATION

A selfloading or automatic action which uses recoil energy to unlock, extract, eject, cock the firing mechanism, and reload the chamber.

RECOIL SPRING GUIDE ROD

A metal or synthetic rod which positions the recoil spring within the firearm's receiver or slide, and prevents binding/dislocation of the spring during its compression or expansion.

RED DOT SIGHT

See REFLEX SIGHT.

REFLEX SIGHT

An optical sight which generates reticle image upon a partially curved objective lens; the reticle appears superimposed in the field of view and focused at infinity. Most reflex sights are non-magnifying and battery powered. Fiber optic light collectors or tritium may also be used to generate the reticle. Reflex sights are adjustable and virtually parallax free. Popularly known as "red dot" sights; they are NOT laser sights.

RELEASE TRIGGER

A trap shooting trigger which fires the gun when the trigger is released.

RELIC

See CURIO/RELIC.

REPEATER/REPEATING ACTION

An manual action with a magazine or cylinder loaded with more than one cartridge; all cartridges
may be fired without reloading.

RETICLE

The shapes, lines, marks, etc. which provide an aiming reference when using an optical sight. Reticles may be illuminated electronically, with tritium, or with fiber optics, and are available in a multitude of designs for many differing requirements.

REVOLVER/REVOLVING ACTION

A manual repeating action so named for its multi-chambered cylinder which rotates on an axis parallel to the barrel bore. Primarily a handgun action, but there have been long gun examples (e.g. Colt Model 1855 Revolving Rifle).

RIB

A raised sighting plane affixed to the top of a barrel.

RIFLING

The spirally cut grooves in the bore of a rifle or handgun barrel. The rifling causes the bullet to spin, stabilizing the bullet in flight. Rifling may rotate to the left or the right, the higher parts of the bore being called lands, the cuts or lower parts being called the grooves. Many types exist, such as oval, polygonal, button, Newton, Newton-Pope gain twist, parabolic, Haddan, Enfield, segmental rifling, etc. Most U.S.-made barrels have a right-hand twist, while British gun makers prefer a left-hand twist. In practice, there seems to be little difference in accuracy or barrel longevity.

RIMFIRE

Self contained metallic cartridge where the priming compound is evenly distributed within the cartridge head, but only on the outer circumference of the rim. Detonated by the firing pin(s) striking the outer edge of the case head.

RINGS

See SCOPE RINGS.

ROLLING BLOCK ACTION

A single shot action, designed in the U.S. and widely used in early Remington arms. Also known as the Remington-Rider action, the breechblock, actuated by a lever, rotates down and back from the chamber. The firing pin is contained within the block and is activated by hammer fall.

ROUND ACTION

A transitional action design, between the boxlock and sidelock, which has its lock assembly attached to the action's lower rearward projecting trigger bar. Also called a trigger plate action.

SAFETY

A mechanism(s) in/on a gun which prevents it from firing. There are many different types and variations.

SAAMI

The Sporting Arms and Ammunition Manufacturers' Institute; a branch of the National Shooting Sports Foundation.

SAW HANDLE

A distinctive squared off pistol grip design which literally is shaped like a saw handle.

SCHNABEL FOREND/FOREARM

The curved/carved flared end of the forend/forearm that resembles the beak of a bird (Schnabel in German). This type of forend is common on Austrian and German guns. In the U.S., the popularity of the Schnabel forend/forearm comes and goes with the seasons. A Schnabel forend is often seen on custom stocks and rifles.

SCOPE RINGS (BLOCKS/BASES)

Metal mounts used to attach a scope to the top of a gun's frame/receiver.

SEAR

The pivoting part in the firing or lock mechanism of a gun. The sear is linked to the trigger, and may engage the cocking piece, striker, or the firing pin.

SECTION 922r

A 1989 Federal regulation which established sporting criteria for centerfire weapons, either imported, or assembled from imported and domestic components. Firearms which do not meet the criteria are "banned", i.e. non-importable as of the regulation's effective date. Also the source of the popular terms "pre-ban" and post-ban". Due to the complexity of this regulation readers are advised to refer to the actual text of the regulation and contact the BATFE. See 1989 BUSH BAN.

SELECTIVE AUTOMATIC EJECTOR

An ejector which propels only fired cases out of a break open action firearm; and only extracts unfired cartridges. Very often found in double barrel shotguns, and also called an automatic Southgate, Holland & Holland, or Baker ejector.

SELECTIVE FIRE

Describes a firearm which has more than one firing mode; which is controlled, or "selected", by the user. Most often used in reference to firearms which can fire in semi-auto, burst, or full auto mode.

SEMI-AUTO ACTION/SEMI-AUTOMATIC/SELFLOADING/AUTOLOADING

A pistol, rifle, or shotgun that is loaded manually for the first round. Upon pulling the trigger, the gun fires, ejects the fired round, cocks the firing mechanism, and feeds a fresh round from the magazine. The trigger must be released after each shot and pulled again to fire the next round.

SHELL DEFLECTOR

A protrusion of the receiver near the ejection port which is positioned and shaped to deflect an ejected case away from the shooter's body. Especially appreciated by left-handed shooters when firing a semi-auto with right side ejection.

SHORT ACTION

A rifle action designed for short overall length cartridges.

SHORT BARREL RIFLE

Any rifle having one or more barrels less than sixteen inches in length and any weapon made from a rifle (whether by alteration, modification, or otherwise) if such weapon, as modified, has an overall length of less than twenty-six inches.

SHORT BARREL SHOTGUN

Any shotgun, which was originally equipped with a shoulder stock, with a barrel or barrels less than eighteen inches long and any weapon made from a shotgun (whether by alteration, modification, or otherwise) if such weapon as modified has an overall length of less than twenty-six inches.

SHOTSHELL

An assembly consisting of a rimmed metal head, paper or plastic base wad, 209 battery cup primer, and paper or plastic body. A shotshell cartridge is a shotshell loaded with propellant, wad column, and shot charge or a single large diameter slug.

SIDE-BY-SIDE (SxS)

A two-barrel rifle or shotgun where the barrels are horizontally arranged side-by-side. Also called juxtaposed.

SIDE FOLDING STOCK

A folding stock variation which has its buttstock rotate horizontally, usually to the right side of the firearm's receiver. See FOLDING STOCK.

SIDE LEVER

Refers to opening mechanism lever on either left or right side of receiver/frame.

SIDELOCK

A type of action, usually long gun, where the moving parts are located on the inside of the lock plates, which in turn are inlet in the sides of the stock. Usually found only on better quality shotguns and rifles.

SIDEPLATES

Ornamental metal panels normally attached to a boxlock action to simulate a sidelock.

SIGHT(S)

Any part or device which allows a firearm to be aimed, versus merely pointed, at a target. There are two main systems: "iron" and optical. Iron sights, also known as "open" sights, are now made of other substances than metal and in many variations. Optical sights have a lens, or lenses, which may or may not magnify the target image.

SINGLE ACTION

A firearms design which requires the hammer to be manually cocked for each shot. Also an auto loading pistol design which requires manual cocking of its mechanism for the first shot only.

SINGLE SHOT ACTION

An action which limits storing or loading only a single cartridge, and is manually operated.

SLIDE ACTION

A manual repeating action with a reciprocating forearm. Sliding the forearm towards the receiver opens the action and extracts/ejects the fired case; forward motion chambers a cartridge and locks the action. Also known as a pump action.

SINGLE TRIGGER

One trigger on a double-barrel gun. It fires each barrel individually by successive pulls, or may be selective, i.e., the barrel to be fired first can be selected via a control button or lever.

SLING SWIVELS

Metal loops affixed to the gun to which a carrying strap is attached.

SOUND SUPPRESSOR

See SUPPRESSOR.

SPECIAL IMPACT MUNITIONS

A class or type of firearm ammunition loaded with one or more projectiles; when fired at a human target the projectiles have a low probability of causing serious injury or death. For example: bean bag, baton, tear gas, and rubber ball rounds. A sub-class of SIMs is known as SPLLAT, or special purpose less lethal anti terrorist munitions.

SPORT UTILITY RIFLE

See MODERN SPORTING RIFLE.

SPUR TRIGGER

A firearm design which housed the trigger in an extension of the frame in some older guns. The trigger projected only slightly from the front of the extension or spur, and there was no trigger guard.

SQUARE BRIDGE ACTION

A bolt action design which has an enlarged rectangular shaped rear receiver bridge. If the front receiver bridge is also in an enlarged square, the action is termed a double square bridge.

SQUIB LOAD

A cartridge with no propellant, or so little propellant, that when fired in a semi-auto the action does not cycle; and in any type of firearm a squib load most likely results in the projectile remaining in and completely obstructing the barrel's bore.

STAMPED SHEET METAL RECEIVER

A receiver manufactured out of sheet metal which has been cut, stamped into a three-dimensional shape, and welded. An economical alternative to milling a receiver from a solid block of metal.

STANDOFF/BREACHING BARREL

Refers to a barrel that has a jagged muzzle to assist in the physical entry of a door and allows no slipping.

STATE COMPLIANT

Firearms whose features have been changed to comply with state laws/regulations such as CA, MA, MD, NJ, NY, HI, etc. are not listed in this text, as there are almost endless variations. Values of state compliant guns in the secondary marketplace will not be as high as the standard non-compliant models from which they are derived.

STOCK

Usually refers to the buttstock of a long gun, or that portion of a rifle or shotgun that comes in contact with the shooter's shoulder, and is attached to the frame/receiver.

STOCKS

Older terminology used to describe handgun grips. See GRIPS.

STRIKER

An elongated firing pin, or a separate component which imparts energy to a firing pin. Most commonly found in hammerless semi-auto pistols.

SUICIDE SPECIAL

A mass-produced inexpensive single action revolver or derringer, usually with a spur trigger. Produced under a variety of trade names, these guns earned their nickname by being almost as dangerous to shoot as to be shot at.

SUPERPOSED

Refers to an O/U barrel configuration.

SUPPRESSOR

A mechanical device, usually cylindrical and detachable, which alters and decreases muzzle blast and noise. Commonly referred to, in error, as a silencer, it acts only on the sound of the firearms discharge. It does not have any effect on the sounds generated by: the firearm's moving parts, a supersonic bullet in flight, or the bullet's impact. Legality varies per state.

TACTICAL

An imprecise term referring to certain features on handguns, rifles, and shotguns. Before 2000, a tactical gun generally referred to a rifle or carbine designed for military or law enforcement. In today's marketplace, tactical refers to certain features of both handguns and long arms.

TACTICAL REVOLVERS

Tactical revolvers have at least three of the following factory/manufacturer options or features: non-glare finish (generally but there may be exceptions), Mil Std 1913 Picatinny or equivalent rail(s), combat style grips (wood or synthetic), fixed or adjustable low profile primary sights (most often night sights), auxiliary aiming/sighting/illumination equipment, compensators or barrel porting, as well as combat triggers and hammers.

TACTICAL RIFLES

Semi-auto, bolt action, or slide action rifles which have at least two of the following factory/manufacturer options or features: magazine capacity over ten rounds, non-glare finish (generally but there may be exceptions), Mil Std 1913 Picatinny or equivalent rail(s), mostly synthetic stocks which may be fixed, folding, collapsible, adjustable, or with/without pistol grip, most have sling attachments for single, traditional two, or three point slings, tritium night sights, and some Assault Weapon Ban characteristics, such as flash suppressors, detachable magazines, bayonet lugs, etc.

TACTICAL SEMI-AUTO PISTOLS

Tactical semi-auto pistols have at least three of the following factory/manufacturer options or features: magazine capacity over ten rounds, non-glare finish (generally but there may be exceptions), Mil Std 1913 Picatinny or equivalent rail(s), combat style grips (wood or synthetic), fixed or adjustable low profile primary sights (most often night sights), auxiliary aiming/sighting/illumination devices, and compensators or barrel porting.

TACTICAL SHOTGUNS

Semi-auto or slide action shotguns which have at least two of the following factory/manufacturer options or features: higher capacity (than sporting/hunting shotguns) magazines, or magazine extensions, non-glare finish (generally but there may be exceptions), Mil Std 1913 Picatinny or equivalent rail(s), mostly synthetic stocks which may be fixed, folding, collapsible, adjustable, or with/without pistol grip, most have sling attachments for single, traditional two, or three point slings, some Assault Weapon Ban characteristics, such as bayonet lugs, or detachable high capacity magazines, rifle or night or ghost ring sights (usually adjustable), and short (18-20 inches) barrels with fixed cylinder choke.

TAKE DOWN

A gun which can be easily disassembled into two sections for carrying or shipping.

TANG(S)

Usually refers to the extension straps (upper and lower) of a rifle or shotgun receiver/frame to which the stock or grip is attached.

TARGET STOCK

A stock optimized for accuracy, consistency, ergonomics, and reliability; for firearms used primarily in formal known-distance competition shooting. Rifle versions may have many adjustment options (e.g.length of pull, cast, comb/cheek piece, buttplate, palm rest, hand stop, accessory attachment); handgun versions may have thumb or palm rests, spacers, inserts, etc.

TENIFER

A trademarked name for a metal case hardening and surface finishing process which provides exceptional wear, abrasion, and corrosion resistance; and very high surface hardness.The generic name for this process is ferritic nitrocarburizing.

THUMBHOLE STOCK (CRIME BILL)

An adaptation of the sporter thumbhole stock design which removed a weapon from semi-auto assault weapon legal status. The thumbhole was/is very large and provides the functionality of a true pistol grip stock.

THUMBHOLE STOCK (SPORTER)

A sporter/hunting stock with an ergonomic hole in the grip; the thumb of the shooter's trigger hand fits into the hole which provides for a steadier hold.

TOP BREAK

See BREAK BARREL ACTION.

TOP BREAK ACTION

See BREAK BARREL ACTION.

TOP FOLDING STOCK

A folding stock variation; the buttstock pivots upwards and over the top of the frame/receiver. See FOLDING STOCK.

TOP LEVER

Refers to the opening lever mechanism on top of the upper frame/tang.

TOP STRAP

The upper part of a revolver frame, which often is either slightly grooved - the groove serving as rear sight - or which carries at its rearward end a sight (which may or may not be adjustable).

TORQUE

The force which causes a rifled firearm to counter-rotate when a projectile travels down its bore.

TRACER

A type of military bullet that emits a colored flame from its base when fired allowing the gunner to adjust his fire onto a target.

TRAJECTORY

The curved flight path of a bullet from muzzle to target; resembling but not a true parabolic arc.

TRAJECTORY TABLE

A numerical table of computed data summarizing the down range trajectory of a projectile.

TRAP STOCK

A shotgun stock with greater length and less comb drop (Monte Carlo, in many cases) used for trap shooting, enabling a built-in height lead when shooting.

TRIGGER

Refers to a release device (mechanical or electrical) in the firing system that starts the ignition process. Usually a curved, grooved, or serrated piece of metal which is pulled rearward by the shooter's finger, and which releases the sear or hammer.

TRIGGER GUARD

Usually a circular or oval band of metal, horn, or plastic that goes around the trigger to provide both protection and safety in shooting circumstances.

TRIGGER SAFETY

A trigger assembly component which must be depressed or otherwise moved before the trigger can be pulled completely through to fire the weapon. Most often a pivoting blade in the center of a trigger which protrudes from the face of the trigger when it is engaged/"on" and automatically resets itself.

TURRETS

Cylinders on an optical sight's main tube which hold adjustment knobs or screws. A turret is dedicated to one of several functions: windage, elevation, parallax, reticle type, reticle illumination, or ranging.

TWIST BARRELS

A process in which a steel rod (called a mandrel) was wrapped with skelps - ribbons of iron. The skelps were then welded in a charcoal fire to form one piece of metal, after which the rod was driven out to be used again. The interior of the resulting tube then had to be laboriously bored out by hand to remove the roughness. Once polished, the outside was smoothed on big grinding wheels, usually turned by waterpower.

TWIST RATE

Refers to the distance required for one complete turn of rifling, usually expressed as a ratio such as 1:12 in. twist, which refers to one complete twist of rifling within 12 inches of barrel. Typically, the heavier the bullet, the faster the twist rate needs to be.

UNDER-LEVER

Action opening lever that is usually located below or in the trigger guard, can also be side pivoting from forearm.

UNDERLUG

On a break open action firearm, the lug on the chamber end of the barrel which locates the barrel in the receiver, and which locks the barrel into battery when intercepted by the bolt/underbolt. Also called a lump.

UNDER FOLDING STOCK

A folding stock variation; the buttstock rotates downwards and underneath the frame/receiver. See FOLDING STOCK.

UNLOAD

To remove all ammunition/cartridges from a firearm or magazine.

UNSERVICEABLE FIREARM

A firearm that is damaged and cannot be made functional in a minimal amount of time.

UPPER ASSEMBLY

For a semi-auto pistol this includes the barrel and slide assembly, for AR style rifles it includes the barrel, bolt and receiver housing.

VARIABLE POWER OPTICAL SIGHT

A optical sight with a multiple magnification levels, most common are 3-9 power general purpose scopes.

VENTILATED

Denotes a component with holes, slots, gaps, or other voids which reduce weight, promote cooling, have a structural purpose, or are decorative.

VENTILATED RIB

A sighting plane affixed along the length of a shotgun barrel with gaps or slots milled for cooling and lightweight handling.

VERNIER

Typically used in reference to a rear aperture (peep) sight. Usually upper tang mounted, and is adj. for elevation by means of a highly accurate finely threaded screw.

VIERLING

A German word designating a four-barrel gun.

VIOLENT CRIME CONTROL AND LAW ENFORCEMENT ACT OF 1994, PUBLIC LAW 103-322

On September 13, 1994, Congress passed the Violent Crime Control and Law Enforcement Act of 1994, Public Law 103-322. Title IX, Subtitle A, Section 110105 of this Act generally made it unlawful to manufacture, transfer, and possess semiautomatic assault weapons (SAWs) and to transfer and possess large capacity ammunition feeding devices (LCAFDs). The law also required importers and manufacturers to place certain markings on SAWs and LCAFDs, designating they were for export or law enforcement/government use. Significantly, the law provided that it would expire 10 years from the date of enactment. Accordingly, effective 12:01 am on September 13, 2004, the provisions of the law ceased to apply and the following provisions

of the regulations in Part 478 no longer apply:

- Section 478.11- Definitions of the terms "semiautomatic assault weapon" and "large capacity ammunition feeding device"
- Section 478.40- Entire section
- Section 478.40a- Entire section
- Section 478.57- Paragraphs (b) and (c)
- Section 478.92- Paragraph (a)(3) – [NOTE: Renumbered from paragraph (a)(2) to paragraph (a)(3) by TD ATF – 461 (66 FR 40596) on August 3, 2001]
- Section 478.92- Paragraph (c)
- Section 478.119- Entire section- [NOTE: An import permit is still needed pursuant to the Arms Export Control Act- see 27 CFR 447.41(a)]
- Section 478.132- Entire section
- Section 478.153- Entire section

NOTE: The references to "ammunition feeding device" in section 478.116 are not applicable on or after September 13, 2004.

NOTE: The references to "semiautomatic assault weapons" in section 478.171 are not applicable on or after September 13, 2004.

Information from BATFE Online - Bureau of Alcohol, Tobacco and Firearms, and Explosives an official site of the U.S. Department of Justice.

WAD

A shotshell component in front of the powder charge and has a cup or flat surface that the shot charge rests on. Various types of wads exist with the most common being a column of plastic.

WADCUTTER BULLET

A lead target bullet for revolvers having a flat nose and a sharp outer edge or shoulder which will cut clean holes in paper targets to aid in spotting and scoring.

WATER TABLE

The flat surfaces forward of the standing breech of a side-by-side shotgun. Also called action bar flats or action flats.

WEAVER-STYLE RAIL

A mounting rail system similar in dimensions and use as the Picatinny Rail. Weaver-style grooves are .180 wide and do not always have consistent center-to-center widths. Most Weaver-style accessories will fit the Picatinny system, however Picatinny accessories will not fit the Weaver-style system. Also see PICATINNY RAIL.

WILDCAT CARTRIDGE

An experimental or non-standard cartridge, not commercially manufactured, often using a standard cartridge case which has been significantly modified.

WINDAGE

The deflection of a projectile from its trajectory due to wind. Also, adjustment of a firearm's sight(s) to compensate for the deflection.

WING SAFETY

A bolt action rifle safety which has a horizontally rotating lever located on the rear of the bolt assembly. Also known as a Mauser safety, after its designer, Peter Paul Mauser.

WUNDHAMMER GRIP/SWELL

Originally attributed to custom gunsmith Louis Wundhammer, it consists of a bulge on the right side of the pistol grip that ergonomically fills the palm of a right-handed shooter.

YOKE

See CRANE.

YOUTH DIMENSIONS

Usually refers to shorter stock dimensions and/or lighter weight enabling youth/women to shoot and carry a firearm.

ZERO

The procedure of adjusting a firearm's sight(s) so that the point of aim coincides with the bullet's point of impact at a selected range.

*	Banned due to 1994-2004 Crime Bill (may be current again)
5R	Five (groove) Rifling
A	Standard Grade Walnut
A.R.M.S.	Atlantic Research Marketing Systems
A2	AR-15 Style/Configuration w/ fixed carry handle
A3	AR-15 Style/Configuration w/ detachable carry handle
AA	Extra Grade Walnut
AAA	Best Quality Walnut
ACB	Advanced Combat Bolt (LWRC)
ACP	Automatic Colt Pistol
ACR	Adaptive Combat Rifle
ACS	MAGPUL Adaptable Carbine/ Storage (stock)
adj.	Adjustable
AE	Automatic Ejectors or Action Express
AECA	Arms Export Control Act
AFG	MAGPUL Angled Fore Grip
AK	Avtomat Kalashnikova rifle
AMU	Army Marksman Unit
AOW	Any Other Weapon (NFA)
appts.	Appointments
AR	Armalite Rifle
ASAP	MAGPUL Ambi Sling Attachment Point
ATR	All Terrain Rifle (Mossberg)
ATS	All Terrain Shotgun (Mossberg)
AWB	Assault Weapons Ban
AWR	Alaskan/African Wilderness Rifle
B	Blue
BAC	Browning Arms Company
BAD	MAGPUL Battery Assist Device (bolt catch lever)
BAR	Browning Automatic Rifle
BASR	Bolt Action Sniper Rifle (H&K)
BB	Brass Backstrap
BBL	Barrel
BLR	Browning Lever Rifle
BMG	Browning Machine Gun
BOSS	Ballistic Optimizing Shooting System
BOSS-CR	BOSS w/o Muzzle Brake
BP	Buttplate or Black Powder
BPE	Black Power Express
BPS	Browning Pump Shotgun
BR	Bench Rest
BT	Beavertail
BT	Browning Trap shotgun
BUIS	Back-Up Iron Sight(s)
c.	Circa
C/B 1994	Introduced Because of 1994 Crime Bill
CAD	Computer Assisted Design
cal.	Caliber
CAR	Colt Automatic Rifle or Carbine
CAWS	Close Assault Weapons System
CB	Crescent Buttplate
CC	Case Colors
CCA	Colt Collectors Association
CF	Centerfire
CFR	Code of Federal Regulations
CH	Cross Hair
CLMR	Colt Lightning Magazine Rifle
CMV	Chrome Moly Vanadium Steel
CNC	Computer Numeric Controlled (machining/machinery)
COMM.	Commemorative
COMP	Compensated/Competition
COP	Continuous Optics Platform (Aero Precision USA)
CQB	Close Quarter Battle
CQC	Close Quarter Combat
C-R	Curio-Relic
CRF	Controlled Round Feed
CRPF	Controlled Round Push Feed
CSAT	Combat Shooting & Tactics

	(accessories)
CTF	Copper/Tin Frangible (bullet)
CTG/CTGE	Cartridge
CTR	MAGPUL Compact/Type Restricted (stock)
CYL/C	Cylinder
DA	Double Action
DA/SA	Double Action/Single Action
DAGR	Dual aperture Gunsite rifle scope
DAK	Double Action Kellerman Trigger (SIG)
DAO	Double Action Only
DB	Double Barrel
DBM	Detachable Box Magazine
DCM	Director of Civilian Marksmanship
DI	Direct Impingement Gas System, see Glossary
DIGS	Delayed Impingement Gas System, see Glossary
DISC or disc.	Discontinued
DLC	Diamond Like Carbon finish (STI International)
DMR	Designated Marksman Rifle (U.S Army, LWRC)
DPMS	Defense Procurement Manufacturing Services
DSL	Detachable Side Locks
DST	Double Set Triggers
DT	Double Triggers
DWM	DeutscheWaffen and Munitions Fabriken
EGLM	Enhanced Grenade Launcher Module (FNH)
EJT	Ejector or Ejectors
EMAG	MAGPUL Export MAGazine
EMP	Enhanced Micro Pistol (Springfield Inc.)
EXC	Excellent
EXT	Extractor or Extractors
F	Full Choke
F&M	Full & Modified
FA	Forearm
FAL	Fusil Automatique Leger
FBT	Full Beavertail Forearm
FDE	Flat Dark Earth (finish color)
FDL	Fleur-de-lis
FE	Forend/Fore End
FFL	Federal Firearms License
FGS	Forward Guard Shield (Radical Firearms)
FHR	First-Gen Hybrid Rail (Radical Firearms)
FIRSH	Free Floating Integrated Rail System Handguard
FK	Flat Knob
FKLT	Flat Knob Long Tang
FM	Full Mag
FMJ	Full Metal Jacket
FN CAL	FN Carabine Automatique Leger
FN GP	FN Grande Puissance (pistol)
FN LAR	Fabrique Nationale Light Automatic Rifle
FN	Fabrique Nationale
FNAR	FN Automatic Rifle
FNC	Fabrique Nationale Carabine
FNH USA	Fabrique Nationale Herstal (U.S. sales and marketing)
FNH	Fabrique Nationale Herstal
FOL	Foliage (finish)
FPS	Feet Per Second
FQR	First-Gen Quad Rail (Radical Firearms)
g.	Gram
ga.	Gauge
GCA	Gun Control Act
GIO	Gas Impingement Operation
G-LAD	Green Laser Aiming Device
GOVT	Government
GPO	Gas Piston Operation
gr.	Grain
H&H	Holland & Holland

HAMR	High accuracy multi-range rifle scope
HB	Heavy Barrel
H-BAR	H(eavy)-BARrel, AR-15/M16
HC	Hard Case
HK	Heckler und Koch
HMR	Hornady Magnum Rimfire
HP	High Power (FN/Browning pistol)
HP	Hollow Point
HPJ	High Performance Jacket
I	Improved
IAR	Infantry Automatic Rifle (LWRC)
IC	Improved Cylinder
ICORE	International Confederation of Revolver Enthusiasts
ILS	Integral Locking System (North American Arms)
IM	Improved Modified
IMI	Israel Military Industries
in.	Inch
intro.	Introduced
IOM	Individual Officer Model (FNH model suffix)
IPSC	International Practical Shooting Confederation
ISSF	International Shooting Sports Federation
ITAR	International Traffic (in) Arms Regulation
IVT	Italian Value-Added Tax
JCP	Joint Combat Pistol
KAC	Knight's Armament Co.
KMC	Knight's Manufacturing Co.
KSG	Kel Tec Shotgun
L	Long
LBA	Lightning Bolt Action (Mossberg)
LBC	Les Baer Custom (Inc.)
lbs.	Pounds
LC	Long Colt
LCW	Lauer Custom Weaponry
LDA	Light Double Action (PARA USA INC.)
LEM	Law Enforcement Model or Modification
LEO	Law Enforcement Only
LMT	Lewis Machine and Tool (Company)
LOP	Length of Pull
LPA	Lightning Pump Action (Mossberg)
LPI	Lines Per Inch
LR	Long Rifle
LT	Long Tang or Light
LTR	Light Tactical Rifle (Rem.)
LTRK	Long Tang Round Knob
LWRC	Land Warfare Resources Corporation
LWRC	Leitner-Wise Rifle Company, Inc.
M (MOD.)	Modified Choke
M&P	Military & Police
M-4	Newer AR-15/M16 Carbine Style/ Configuration
Mag.	Magnum Caliber
mag.	Magazine
MARS	Modular Accessory Rail System
MBUS	MAGPUL Back-Up Sight
MC	Monte Carlo
MCS	Modular Combat System (Rem.)
MFG or Mfg.	Manufactured/manufacture
MFT	Mission First Tactical
MIAD	MAGPUL Mission Adaptable (grip, other)
mil	see Glossary
mil-dot	See Glossary
MIL SPEC	Mfg. to Military Specifications
MK	Mark
mm	Millimeter
MOA	Minute of Angle
MOE	MAGPUL Original Equipment
MOUT	Military Operations (on) Urbanized Terrain

MR	Matted Rib
MS2	MAGPUL Multi Mission Sling System
MSR	Manufacturer's Suggested Retail
MVG	MAGPUL MOE Vertical Grip
MWS	Modular Weapons System
N	Nickel
N/A	Not Applicable or Not Available
NATO	North Atlantic Treaty Organization
NE	Nitro Express
NFA	National Firearms Act (U.S. 1934)
NIB	New in Box
NM	National Match
no.	Number
NP	New Police
NP3/NP3 Plus	Nickel-Phosphorus (firearm coating)
NSST	Non Selective Single Trigger
NVD/E	Night Vision Device/Equipment
O/U	Over and Under
OA	Overall
OAL	Overall Length
OB	Octagon Barrel
OBFM	Octagon Barrel w/full mag.
OBO	Or Best Offer
OCT	Octagon
ODG	Olive Drab Green (finish color)
ORC	Optics Ready Carbine
oz.	Ounce
P	Police (Rem. rifle/shotgun)
P99AS	Pistol 99 Anti Stress (trigger, Walther)
PAD	Personal Anti-recoil Device (Savage)
Para.	Parabellum
PBR	Patrol Bolt Rifle (FNH)
PDA	Personal Defense Assistant (PARA USA INC.)
PFFR	Percantage of factory finish remaining
PG	Pistol Grip
PGF	Precision Guided Firearm
PK	Pistol Kompact (Walther)
PMAG	MAGPUL Polymer MAGazine
POR/P.O.R.	Price on Request
POST-'89	Paramilitary mfg. after Federal legislation in Nov. 1989
POST-BAN	Refers to production after Sept. 12, 2004
PPC	Pindell Palmisano Cartridge
PPD	Post Paid
PPK	Police Pistol Kriminal (Walther 1931 design)
PPKs	Police Pistol Kriminal (Walther 1968 design)
PPQ	Police Pistol Quick (defense trigger, Walther)
PRE-'89	Paramilitary mfg. before Federal legislation in Nov. 1989
PRE-BAN	Mfg. before September 13, 1994 per C/B or before Nov. 1989.
PRS/PRS2	MAGPUL Precision Rifle/Sniper (stock)
PSD	Personal Security Detail rifle (LWRC)
PSG	PrazisionSchutzenGewehr (H&K rifle)
PSR	Precision Shooting Rifle (FNH)
PXT	Power Extractor Technology (PARA USA INC.)
QD	Quick Detachable
RACS	Remington Arms Chassis System
RAS	Rail Adapter System
RB	Round Barrel/Round Butt
RCM	Ruger Compact Magnum
RCMP	Royal Canadian Mounted Police
RDS	Rapid Deployment Stock
REC	Receiver
REM	Remington
REM. MAG.	Remington Magnum
REPR	Rapid Engagement Precision Rifle (LWRC)
RF	Rimfire
RFB	Rifle Forward (ejection) Bullpup

RFM	Rim Fire Magnum
RIS	Rail Interface system
RK	Round Knob
RKLT	Round Knob Long Tang
RKST	Round Knob Short Tang
RMEF	Rocky Mt. Elk. Foundation
RMR	Rimfire Magnum Rifle (Kel Tec)
RPD	Ruchnoy Pulemyot Degtyaryova (machine gun)
RR	Red Ramp
RSA	MAGPUL Rail Sling Attachment
RSUM	Remington Short-Action Ultra Magnum
RUM	Remington Ultra Magnum
RVG	MAGPUL Rail Vertical Grip
S	Short
S&W	Smith & Wesson
S/N	Serial Number
SA	Single Action
SAA	Single Action Army
SAAMI	Sporting Arms and Ammunition Manufacturers' Institute
SABR	Sniper/Assaulter Battle Rifle (LWRC)
SAE	Selective Automatic Ejectors
SAS	SIG Anti Snag (pistol models)
SASS	Single Action Shooting Society or (U.S. Army) Semi Automatic Sniper System
SAUM	Short Action Ultra Magnum
SAW	Semiautomatic Assault Weapon
SAW	Squad Automatic Weapon
SB	Shotgun butt or Steel backstrap
SBR	Short Barrel Rifle
SCAR	Special (Operations Forces) Combat Assault Rifle (FNH)
SCW	Sub Compact Weapon (Colt)
SDT	Super Dynamic Technology (PARA USA INC.)
ser.	serial
SFO	Striker Fire Operation
SG	Straight Grip
SIG	Schweizerische Industriegesellschaft
SIM	Special Impact Munition
SK	Skeet
SLP	Self Loading Police (FNH shotgun)
SMG	Submachine Gun
SMLE	Short Magazine Lee Enfield Rifle
SNT	Single Non-Selective Trigger
SOCOM	Special Operations Command
SOPMOD	Special Operations Peculiar Modification
SP	Special Purpose
SPC	Special Purpose Cartridge/Carbine
SPEC	Special
SPEC-OPS	Special Operations
SPG	Semi-Pistol Grip
Spl.	Special
SPLLAT	Special Purpose Low Lethality Anti Terrorist (Munition)
SPR	Special Police Rifle (FNH), Special Purpose Rifle
SPS	Special Purpose Synthetic (Remington)
SPS	Superalloy Piston System (LWRC)
sq.	Square
SR	Solid Rib
SRC	Saddle Ring Carbine
SRT	Short Reset Trigger
SS	Single Shot or Stainless Steel
SSA	Super Short Action
SSR	Sniper Support Rifle (FNH)
SST	Single Selective Trigger
ST	Single Trigger
SUR	Sport Utility Rifle - see Glossary
SWAT	Special Weapons Assault Team
SWAT	Special Weapons and Tactics
SxS	Side by Side
TAS	Tactical adjustable sight
TB	Threaded Barrel
TBA	To be Announced

TBM	Tactical Box Magazine
TD	Take Down
TDR	Target Deployment Rifle (Rem.)
TGT	Target
TH	Target Hammer
TiN	TiN coating (STI International)
TIR	Target Interdiction Rifle (Rem.)
TPS	Tactical Police Shotgun (FNH)
TRP	Tactical Response Pistol (Springfield Inc.)
TRPAFD	Take Red Pen Away From Dave!
TS	Target Stocks
TSOB	Scope Mount Rail Weaver Type
TSR XP USA	Tactical Sport Rifle - Extreme Performance Ultra Short Action (FNH)
TSR XP	Tactical Sport Rifle - Extreme Performance (FNH)
TT	Target Trigger
TTR	Tactical Target Rifle (PARA USA INC.)
TWS	Tactical Weapons System (Rem.)
UBR	MAGPUL Utility/Battle Rifle (stock)
UCIW	Ultra Compact Individual Weapon (LWRC)
UCP	Universal Combat Pistol (H&K)
UIT	Union Internationale de Tir
UMC	Union Metallic Cartridge Co.
UMP	Universal Machine Pistol (H&K)
USA	Ultra Safety Assurance (Springfield Inc.)
USAMU	U.S. Army Marksmanship Unit
USC	Universal Self-Loading Carbine (H&K)
USG	United States Government (FNH model suffix)
USP	Universal Self-Loading Pistol (H&K)
USPSA	United States Practical Shooting Association
USR	Urban Sniper Rifle (Rem.)
USSOCOM	U.S. Special Operations Command
VAT	Value Added Tax
Vent.	Ventilated
VG	Very Good
VR	Ventilated Rib
VTAC	Viking Tactics, Inc. (accessories)
VTR	Varmint Triangular Profile Barrel (Remington)
w/	With
w/o	Without
WBY	Weatherby
WC	Wad Cutter
WCF	Winchester Center Fire
WD	Wood
WFF	Watch For Fakes
WIN	Winchester
WMR	Winchester Magnum Rimfire
WO	White Outline
WRA	Winchester Repeating Arms Co.
WRF	Winchester Rim Fire
WRM	Winchester Rimfire Magnum
WSL	Winchester Self-Loading
WSM	Winchester Short Magnum
WSSM	Winchester Super Short Magnum
WW	World War
X (1X)	1X Wood Upgrade or Extra Full Choke Tube
XD	Extreme Duty (Springfield Inc.)
XDM	Extreme Duty M Factor (Springfield Inc.)
XX (2X)	2X Wood Upgrade or Extra Extra Full Choke Tube
XXX (3x)	3X Wood Upgrade
YHM	Yankee Hill Machine

TACTICAL FIREARMS TRADEMARK INDEX

We can guarantee you that no informational source has a more accurate firearms industry Trademark Index than what you are about to read. Remember, this invaluable section is also available online at no charge, so you can get the most recent contact information any time, any where, with internet access, and it is updated quarterly as things change. Why guess when you can be sure?

The following listings of domestic and international tactical firearms manufacturers, trademarks, importers, distributors, factory repair centers, and parts companies are the most complete and up-to-date ever published. Even more so than in the last edition, you will note additions and substantial changes regarding website and email listings – this may be your best way of obtaining up-to-date model and pricing information directly from some current manufacturers, importers, and/or distributors who don't post retail pricing. When online with the various company websites, it's not a bad idea to look at the date of the last web update, as this will tell you how current the online information really is.

For a complete listing of companies and contact information for airguns and modern black powder reproduction industries, please refer to the respective Trademark Indexes in the *Blue Book of Modern Black Powder Arms* and the *Blue Book of Airguns*. These Trademark Indexes are also available online at no charge (www.bluebookofgunvalues.com) – click on Information & Services.

If parts are needed for older, discontinued makes and models, it is recommended you contact either Numrich Gun Parts Corp. located in West Hurley, NY, or Jack First, Inc. located in Rapid City, SD for domestic availability and prices. For current manufacturers, it is recommended that you contact an authorized warranty repair center or stocking gun shop, unless a company/trademark has an additional service/parts listing. In Canada, please refer to the Bowmac Gunpar Inc. listing.

Hundreds of hours have been spent in this database, and we feel that this information is the most reliable source material available to contact these companies/individuals. However, if you feel that you have something to add or find an error, we would like to know about it. Simply contact us at: lisab@bluebookinc.com.

During the course of the year, the Trademark Index is constantly updated as more information becomes available. Please visit www.bluebookofgunvalues.com for the most current database (available free of charge).

If you should require additional assistance in "tracking" any of the current companies listed in this publication (or perhaps, current companies that are not listed), please contact us and we will try to help you regarding these specific requests. Again, the most up-to-date Trademark Index for the firearms, black powder reproductions, tactical, and airguns industries will be posted on our website: www.bluebookofgunvalues.com. We hope you appreciate this service – no one else in the industry has anything like it.

2 VETS ARMS CO, LLC
P.O. Box 1639
Eufaula, OK 74462
Website: www.2VetsArms.com
Email: admin@2VetsArms.com

A.M.S.D. (ADVANCED MILITARY SYSTEM DESIGN)
Factory
P.O. Box 487
Vernier/Geneva CH-1214 SWITZERLAND
Fax: 011-41-223497691
Website: www.amsd.ch
Email: sales@amsd.ch

AR-7 INDUSTRIES L.L.C.
Please refer to Armalite, Inc. listing.

AWC SYSTEMS TECHNOLOGY, LLC
23606 N. 19th Ave
Suite 10
Phoenix, AZ 85085
Phone: 623-780-1050
Toll Free: 800-401-7269
Website: www.awcsilencers.com

ACCURACY INTERNATIONAL LTD.
U.S. Office
Fredericksburg, VA
Email: aina@accuracyinternational.us
Distributor – Tac Pro Shooting Center
35100 North State Hwy. 108
Mingus, TX 76463-6405
Phone: 254-968-3112
Fax: 254-968-5857
Website: www.tacproshootingcenter.com
Distributor – Mile High Shooting Accessories
3731 Monarch Street
Erie, CO 80516
Phone: 303-255-9999
Fax: 303-254-6572
Website: www.milehighshooting.com

Distributor – SRT Supply
4450 60th Ave. N.
St. Petersburg, FL 33714
Phone: 727-526-5451
Website: www.srtsupply.com
Distributor – Euro Optic Ltd.
439 Crawford Alley
Montoursville, PA 17754
Phone: 570-368-3920
Website: www.Eurooptic.com
Email: sales@Eurooptic.com
Factory – ACCURACY INTERNATIONAL LTD.
P.O. Box 81, Portsmouth
Hampshire, UK PO3 5SJ
Fax: 011-44-23-9269-1852
Website: www.accuracyinternational.us
Email: ai@accuracyinternational.org

ACCURACY X
Phone: 540-797-4833
Website: www.accuracyx.com
Email: info@accuracyx.com

ACCURATE TOOL & MANUFACTURING
737 Werne Drive
Lexington, KY 40504
Phone: 859-983-8995
Website: www.accuratearmory.com
Email: sales@accuratearmory.com

ADAMS ARMS
612 Florida Ave
Palm Harbor, FL 34683
Toll Free: 877-461-2572
Phone: 727-853-0550
Fax: 727-853-0551
Website: www.adamsarms.net
Email: sales@adamsarms.net

ADCOR DEFENSE
P.O. Box 12239
Baltimore, MD 21224
Phone: 888-612-3267
Website: www.adcordefense.com
Email: sales@adcordefense.com

ADEQ FIREARMS COMPANY
4921 W. Cypress Street
Tampa, FL 33607
Phone: 813-636-5077
Fax: 813-281-8925
Website: www.adeqfirearms.com

ADVANCED ARMAMENT CORP.
2408 Tech Center Parkway
Suite 150
Lawrenceville, GA 30043
Phone: 770-925-9988
Website: www.advanced-armament.com
Email: salesinfo@advanced-armament.com

AERO PRECISION USA
2338 Holgate Street
Tacoma, WA 98402
Phone: 253-272-8188
Fax: 253-272-1168
Website: www.aeroprecisionusa.com
Email: sales@aeroprecisionusa.com

AKLYS DEFENSE LLC
9683 Mammoth Ave.
Baton Rouge, LA 70814
Phone: 225-448-3167
Fax: 225-448-3169
Website: www.aklysdefense.com
Email: info@aklysdefense.com

AKSA ARMS
Silah Insaat Metal San. Tic. Ltd. Sti.
Ataturk Cad. No: 87/2
Uzumlu/Beysehir, Konya, TURKEY
Phone: 011-90-546-865-3234
Website: www.aksaarms.com
Email: export@aksaarms.com

ALAN & WILLIAM ARMS, INC.
P.O. Box 415
Cheyenne Wells, CO 80810-0415
Phone: 719-343-5881
Fax: 719-767-2857
Website: www.alanandwilliamarms.com
Email: alan.william.arms@gmail.com

ALASKA MAGNUM AR'S
3875 Geist Road
Suite E PMB453
Fairbanks, AK 99709
Phone: 907-835-4868
Website: www.alaskamagnumars.com

ALBERTA TACTICAL RIFLE SUPPLY
#6, 2016 25th Ave. NE
Calgary, Alberta, CANADA T2E 6Z4
Phone: 403-277-7786
Fax: 403-277-7181
Website: www.albertatacticalrifle.com
Email: info@albertatacticalrifle.com

ALEXANDER ARMS LLC
U.S. Army - Radford Arsenal
P.O. Box 1
Radford, VA 24143
Phone: 540-639-8356
Fax: 540-639-8353
Website: www.alexanderarms.com
Email: support@alexanderarms.com

AMBUSH FIREARMS
101 War Fighter Way
Black Creek, GA 31308
Phone: 855-262-8742
Website: www.ambushfirearms.com

AMERICAN DEFENSE MANUFACTURING
2525 South 162nd Street
New Berlin, WI 53151
Phone: 262-780-9831
Fax: 262-754-0660
Website: www.adm-mfg.com
Email: sales@americandefensemfg.com

AMERICAN PRECISION ARMS
55 Lyle Field Rd.
Jefferson, GA 30549
Phone: 706-367-8881
Website: www.americanprecisionarms.com

AMERICAN SPIRIT ARMS
16001 N. Greenway Hayden Loop, Suite B
Scottsdale, AZ 85260
Phone: 480-367-9540
Fax: 480-367-9541
Website: www.americanspiritarms.com
Email: rifles@americanspiritarms.com

AMERICAN TACTICAL IMPORTS
231 Deming Way
Summerville, SC 29483
Toll Free: 800-290-0065
Fax: 843-851-2897
Website: www.americantactical.us
Email: sales@americantactical.us

AM-TAC PRECISION
4577 W. Chinden Blvd.
Garden City, ID 83714
Phone: 208-906-0585
Fax: 208-904-3887
Website: www.am-tac.com

ANDERSON MANUFACTURING
1743 Anderson Blvd.
Hebron, KY 41048
Phone: 859-689-4085
Fax: 859-689-4110
Website: www.andersonrifles.com
Email: customer.support@andersonrifles.com

ANGSTADT ARMS
Charlotte, NC - USA
Phone: 980-222-4342
Website: www.angstadtarms.com
Email: contact@angstadtarms.com

ANSCHÜTZ
Sporting Rifle Importer & Factory Service
Steyr Arms, Inc.
2530 Morgan Road
Bessemer, AL 35022
Phone: 205-417-8644
Fax: 205-417-8647
Website: www.steyrarms.com
Importers/Distributors – Match Competition Target
Rifles
Please refer to Champion's Choice listing.
Champions Shooter's Supply
11018 Camp Ohio Rd.
Utica, OH 43080
Toll Free: 800-821-4867
Fax: 740-745-1274
Website: www.championshooters.com
Importer & Repair/Warranty/Gunsmithing Services
Altius Handcrafted Firearms
125 Madison Avenue
West Yellowstone, MT 59758
Phone: 406-646-9222
Website: www.altiusguns.com
Email: altiusguns@earthlink.net
Factory - ANSCHÜTZ, J.G. GmbH & Co. KG
Postfach 1128
89001 Ulm, GERMANY
Daimlerstrasse 12
89079 Ulm, GERMANY
Fax: 011-49-731-4012700
Website: www.anschuetz-sport.com
Email: anschuetz@anschuetz-sport.com

ANZIO IRONWORKS
1905 16th Street North
St. Petersburg, FL 33704
Phone: 727-895-2019
Fax: 727-827-4728
Website: www.anzioironworks.com
Email: anzioshop@hotmail.com

ARCHER MANUFACTURING
P.O. Box 1235
Hutto, TX 78634
Phone: 512-962-2849
Website: www.archer-mfg.com
Email: sales@archer-mfg.com

ARES DEFENSE SYSTEMS, INC.
P.O. Box 120789
Melbourne, FL 32912
Phone: 321-242-8410
Fax: 321-242-8411
Website: www.aresdefense.com
Email: sales@aresdefense.com

ARIZONA ARMORY
Phoenix, AZ
Fax: 602-252-5477
Website: www.azarmory.net
Email: azarmory@msn.com

ARMALITE, INC.
P.O. Box 299
Geneseo, IL 61254
Toll Free: 800-336-0184
Fax: 309-944-6949
Website: www.ArmaLite.com
Email: info@armalite.com

ARMS ROOM LLC
19048 East Colonial Dr.
Orlando, FL 32820
Phone: 407-282-3803
Fax: 407-282-1165
Website: www.ArmsRoom.com
Email: service@armsroom.com

ARMS LLC
Oregon
Phone: 503-789-8578
Website: www.customfirearmsllc.com
Email: LarryMartin@myway.com

ARMSCOR (ARMS CORPORATION OF THE PHILIPPINES)
Importer & Distributor - Armscor Precision
International
150 N. Smart Way
Pahrump, NV 89060
Phone: 775-537-1444
Fax: 775-537-1446
Website: www.rockislandarmory.com
Email: armscor@armscor.net
Factory office - Arms Corp. of the Philippines
Armscor Avenue, Fortune
Marikina City 1800, PHILIPPINES
Phone: 632-941-6243
Fax: 632-942-0682
Website: www.armscor.com.ph
Email: info@armscor.com.ph
Executive office - Arms Corp. of the Philippines
6th Floor, Strat 100 Bldg., Emerald Ave.
Ortigas Center, Pasig City, 1600 PHILIPPINES
Fax: 632-634-3906
Email: squires@cnl.net

ARSENAL FIREARMS
Importer – please refer to EAA Corp. listing.

Factory
Gardone, ITALY
Website: www.arsenalfirearms.com

ARSENAL INC.
3395 S. Jones Blvd. #331
Las Vegas, NV 89146
Phone: 702-643-2220
Fax: 702-643-8860
Website: www.arsenalinc.com
Email: customerservice@arsenalinc.com

ASHBURY PRECISION ORDNANCE
P.O. Box 8024
Charlottesville, VA 22906-8024
Phone: 434-296-8600
Fax: 434-296-9260
Website: www.Ashburyprecisionordnance.com
Email: info@Ashburyprecisionordnance.com

ASTRA ARMS S.A.
Case Postale 103
1951 Sion SWITZERLAND
Fax: 011-41-027-322-3707
Website: www.astra-arms.ch
Email: astra@astra-arms.ch

AUTO-ORDNANCE CORP.
Please refer to the Kahr Arms listing.
Website: www.auto-ordnance.com
Website: www.tommygun.com
Website: www.tommygunshop.com

AXELSON TACTICAL
2222 Park Place, 1B
Minden, NV 89423
Phone: 855-746-7293
Website: www.axelsontactical.com
Email: donna.axelson@axelsontactical.com

AZTEK ARMS
1641 W. Alvey Drive #1
Mapleton, UT 84664
Phone: 801-491-6226
Fax: 801-704-9759
Website: www.aztekarms.com

BCM EUROPEARMS
Via Torino 15/5
10060 Roletto, Torino, ITALY
Website: www.bcmeuropearms.it
Email: info@bcmeuropearms.it

BWE FIREARMS
Longwood, FL
Phone: 407-592-3975
Website: www.bwefirearms.com
Email: Richard@bwefirearms.com

BAIKAL
Importer – please refer to RWC Group LLC listing.
Baikal Factory
Izhevsky Mekhanichesky Zavod
8, Promyshlennaya str.
Izhevsk, 426063 RUSSIA
Fax: 011-95-007-341-2665830
Website: www.baikalinc.ru
Email: worldlinks@baikalinc.ru

BARNES PRECISION MACHINE, INC.
1434 Farrington Road
Apex, NC 27523
Phone: 919-362-6805
Fax: 919-362-5752
Website: www.barnesprecision.com
Email: info@barnesprecision.com

BARRETT FIREARMS MANUFACTURING, INC.
P.O. Box 1077
Murfreesboro, TN 37133
Phone: 615-896-2938
Fax: 615-896-7313
Website: www.barrett.net
Email: mail@barrett.net

BATTLE ARMS DEVELOPMENT, INC. (B.A.D., INC.)
180 Cassia Way, Suite 510
Henderson, NV 89014
Phone: 702-802-3588
Fax: 702-948-4472
Website: www.battlearmsdevelopment.com
Email: sales@battlearmsdevelopment.com

BATTLE RIFLE COMPANY
1056 Hercules Ave.
Houston, TX 77058
Phone: 281-777-0316
Fax: 866-804-3049
Website: www.battleriflecompany.com
Email: info@battleriflecompany.com

BAZOOKA BROTHERS MFG.
472 N Union St.
Russiaville, IN 46979
Website: www.bazookabrothers.com

BENELLI
Importer - Benelli USA
17603 Indian Head Highway
Accokeek, MD 20607-2501
Toll Free: 800-264-4962
Fax: 301-283-6988
Website: www.benelliusa.com
Pistol/Airgun Importer - please refer to Larry's Guns listing.
Warranty Repair Address - Benelli USA
901 Eighth Street
Pocomoke, MD 21851
Factory - Benelli Armi S.p.A.
Via della Stazione, 50
I-61029 Urbino (PU) ITALY
Fax: 011-39-0722-307-207
Website: www.benelli.it

BERETTA, PIETRO
Importer - Beretta U.S.A. Corp
17601 Beretta Drive
Accokeek, MD 20607
Phone: 301-283-2191
Fax: 301-283-0189
Website: www.berettausa.com
Beretta Premium Grades
Website: www.berettagallery.com
Beretta Gallery
718 Madison Avenue
New York, NY 10021
Phone: 212-319-3235
Fax: 212-207-8219

Beretta Gallery
41 Highland Park Village
Dallas, TX 75205
Phone: 214-559-9800
Fax: 214-559-9805
Factory - Fabbrica d'Armi Pietro Beretta S.p.A
Via Pietro Beretta 18
25063 Gardone Val Trompia
Brescia, ITALY
Fax: 011-39-30-834-1421
Website: www.beretta.it

BERGARA
Barrels and Apex rifles – please refer to Connecticut Valley Arms listing.
Bergara Bolt Action Rifles - Bergara North America Blackpowder Products, Inc.
1685 Boggs Road, Suite 300
Duluth, GA 30096
Factory – Dikar, S.Coop.
Urate, 26
E-20570 Bergara, SPAIN
Phone: 011-34-943-769893
Website: www.bergararifles.com
Email: info@bergararifles.com

BERSA
Importer - please refer to Eagle Imports listing.
Website: www.bersa.com
Email: info@bersa.com
Factory - Bersa S.A.
Castillo 312
(1704) Ramos Mejia, ARGENTINA
Fax: 011-54-1-656-2093

BETTINSOLI, TARCISIO Srl
Importer - please refer to Franchi listing (private label models).
European Distributor - Bignami S.p.A.
via Lahn
I-39040 Ora (Bolzano), ITALY
Fax: 011-39-471-810899
Website: www.bignami.it
Factory
Via I Maggio 116
Sarezzo, Brescia, I-25068 ITALY
Fax: 011-39-030-890-0240
Website: www.bettinsoli.it
Email: info@bettinsoli.it

BLACK DAWN ARMORY (BLACK DAWN INDUSTRIES)
1511 N. Ohio
Sedalia, MO 65301
Phone: 660-851-0907
Fax: 660-851-0207
Website: www.blackdawnguns.com

BLACK RAIN ORDNANCE, INC.
P.O. Box 1111
Neosho, MO 64850
Phone: 417-456-1920
Toll Free: 888-836-2620
Fax: 417-451-2811
Website: www.blackrainordnance.com
Email: info@blackrainordnance.com

BLACKHEART INTERNATIONAL LLC
1781 Philippi Pike
Clarksburg, WV 26301
Phone: 304-622-7000
Fax: 304-622-7020
Website: www.bhiarms.com
Email: customerservice@bhigear.com

BLUEGRASS ARMORY
Good Times Outdoors
4600 West Highway 326
Ocala, FL 34482
Phone: 352-401-9070
Fax: 352-401-9667
Website: www.bluegrassarmory.com
Email: support@bluegrassarmory.com

BRAVO COMPANY MFG., INC.
P.O. Box 361
Hartland, WI 53029
Phone: 877-272-8626
Fax: 262-367-0989
Website: www.bravocompanymfg.com
Email: info@bravocompanyusa.com

BRILEY MANUFACTURING INC.
1230 Lumpkin Rd.
Houston, TX 77043
Phone: 713-932-6995 (Technical)
Toll Free: 800-331-5718 (Orders only)
Fax: 713-932-1043
Website: www.briley.com

BROWN PRECISION, INC.
P.O. Box 270 W
7786 Molinos Avenue
Los Molinos, CA 96055
Phone: 530-384-2506
Fax: 530-384-1638
Website: www.brownprecision.com
Email: info@brownprecision.com

BROWNING
Administrative Headquarters
One Browning Place
Morgan, UT 84050-9326
Phone: 801-876-2711
Product Service: 800-333-3288
Fax: 801-876-3331
Website: www.browning.com
Website: www.browningint.com
Custom Shop U.S. Representative
Mr. Ron McGhie
Email: ronm@browning.com
Browning Parts and Service
3005 Arnold Tenbrook Rd.
Arnold, MO 63010-9406
Toll Free: 800-322-4626
Fax: 636-287-9751
Historical Research (Browning Arms Co. marked guns only)
Browning Historian
One Browning Place
Morgan, UT 84050-9326
Fax: 801-876-3331
Website: www.browning.com

BUL LTD.
Importer – M1911 Parts Only
All America Sales, Inc.
8884 Hwy. 62 West
Piggot, AR 72454
Phone: 870-544-2809
Fax: 870-544-2695
Factory - Bul Transmark Ltd.
10 Rival Street
Tel-Aviv 67778, ISRAEL
Fax: 011-972-3-687-4853
Website: www.bultransmark.com
Email: info@bultransmark.com

BUSHMASTER FIREARMS INTERNATIONAL
Part of Freedom Group - Headquarters
P.O. Box 556
Madison, NC 27025
Toll Free: 800-883-6229
Fax: 207-892-8068
Website: www.bushmaster.com
Email: info@bushmaster.com

BÜYÜK HUGLU
Importer – Bud's Gun Shop
1105 Industry Rd.
Lexington, KY 40505
Phone: 859-368-0371
Fax: 800-804-5569
Website: www.budsgunshop.com
Factory – Büyük Huglu Av Tüfekleri San. Tic. Ltd. Sti.
Huglu-Beysehir, Konya TURKEY
Fax: 011-90-332-516-1182
Website: www.buyukhuglu.com
Email: info@buyukhuglu.com

CMMG, INC.
P.O. Box 369
Fayette, MO 65248
Phone: 660-248-2293
Fax: 660-248-2290
Website: www.cmmginc.com
Email: sales@cmmginc.com

CZ (CESKA ZBROJOVKA)
Firearms & Airguns Importer - CZ-USA
P.O. Box 171073
Kansas City, KS 66117-0073
Phone: 913-321-1811
Toll Free: 800-955-4486
Fax: 913-321-2251
Website: www.cz-usa.com
Email: info@cz-usa.com
Administration Offices - Ceska Zbrojovka
Svatopluka Cecha 1283
CZ-68827 Uhersky Brod CZECH REPUBLIC
Fax: 011-420-63363-3811
Website: www.czub.cz
Email: info@czub.cz

CADEX DEFENCE
U.S.A. Office
4312 Chandler Way
Valdosta, GA 31605
Phone: 229-834-4331
Canada Office
755 ave. Montrichard
St-Jean-sur-Richelieu, QC
Canada, J2X 5K8
Phone: 450-347-6774
Website: www.cadexdefence.com

CALICO LIGHT WEAPON SYSTEMS
924 N. Freemont Lane
Cornelius, OR 97113
Phone: 503-649-3010
Toll free: 888-442-2542
Fax: 503-649-3831
Website: www.calicolightweaponsystems.com

CANIK55
Importer - please refer to Tristar listing.
Importer – please refer to Century Arms listing.
Factory - Samsun Domestic Defense and Industry Corporation
Organize Sanayi Bölgesi
No: 28 Kutlukent/SAMSUN TURKEY
Fax: 011-90-362-266-6671
Website: www.canik55.com
Email: samsun@canik55.com

CARACAL
Importer – Caracal USA
Five Wilcox Way
Newington, NH 03801
Phone: 603-431-1331
Fax: 603-431-1221
Website: www.caracalusa.com
Email: info@caracalusa.com
Distributor (Italy only) – please refer to Fratelli Tanfoglio listing.
Factory
Tawazun Industrial Park
Sweihan
P.O. Box 94499
Abu Dhabi, UNITED ARAB EMIRATES
Tel: 011-971-2-5854441
Fax: 011-971-2-5854445
Website: www.caracal.ae
Email: info@caracal.ae

CENTURY ARMS
430 South Congress Ave., Ste. 1
Delray Beach, FL 33445
Toll Free: 800-527-1252
Phone: 561-265-4530
Fax: 561-265-4520
Website: www.centuryarms.com
Email: support@centuryarms.com

CHAMPIONS CHOICE, INC.
201 International Blvd.
LaVergne, TN 37086
Toll Free: (Orders Only) 800-345-7179
Phone: 615-793-4066
Fax: 615-793-4070
Email: sales@champchoice.com

CHARLES DALY (2011-PRESENT)
Importer – please refer to Samco Global Arms, Inc. (SGAI).
Website: www.charlesdaly-us.com
Email: orders@charlesdaly-us.com

CHATTAHOOCHEE GUN WORKS LLC
9th Ave., P.O. Box 2361
Phenix City, AL 36867
Phone: 334-408-2616
Fax: 334-408-2609
Website: www.c-gw.com
Email: service@cgunworks.com

CHEYTAC USA, LLC
110 Eagle Ave.
Nashville, GA 31639
Toll-Free: 844-398-9101
Fax: 408-516-9690
Website: www.cheytac.com
Email: lara@cheytac.com

CHIAPPA FIREARMS LTD.
Factory - please refer to Armi Sport listing.
U.S. Office
1414 Stanley Ave.
Dayton, OH 47404
Phone: 937-835-4894
Fax: 888-705-4570
Website: www.chiappafirearms.com
Email: info@chiappafirearms.com

CHRISTENSEN ARMS
550 North Cemetery Rd.
Gunnison, UT 84634
Phone: 435-528-7999
Fax: 435-528-5773
Website: www.christensenarms.com
Email: sales@christensenarms.com

CHRISTIAN ARMORY WORKS
Rock Spring, GA
Phone: 423-290-1799
Website: www.christianarmoryworks.com
Email: christianarmoryworks@gmail.com

CITADEL
Please refer to Legacy Sports listing.

CLARK CUSTOM GUNS, INC.
336 Shootout Lane
Princeton, LA 71067
Phone: 318-949-9884
Fax: 318-949-9829
Website: www.clarkcustomguns.com
Email: ccgweb@shreve.net

COBB MANUFACTURING, INC.
Please refer to Bushmaster listing.

COBRA
Please refer to Tristar listing.

COLT
Colt's Manufacturing Company LLC
P.O. Box 1868
Hartford, CT 06144-1868
Toll Free: 800-962-COLT
Fax: 860-244-1449
Website: www.coltsmfg.com
Colt Defense LLC (Law Enforcement & Rifles)
P.O. Box 118
Hartford, CT 06141
Phone: 860-232-4489
Fax: 860-244-1442
Website: www.colt.com
AR-15 Rifles, .22 LR cal. only - please refer to Walther Arms listing.
Historical Research - Colt Archive Properties LLC
P.O. Box 1868
Hartford, CT 01644-1868
If mailing in a request, make sure the proper research fee is enclosed (please refer to appropriate Colt section for current fees and related information).

1st and 2nd Generation SAA phone service only
Phone: 800-962-COLT
(Ask for Historical Dept. Research fees start at $150.)
Colt Cavalry & Artillery Revolver Authentication Service
Mr. John Kopec, Historian
Phone/Fax: 530-222-4440
Website: www.johnakopec.com
Email: books@johnakopec.com (book sales only)

COMMANDO ARMS
Komando Av Sil. Pat. San. Tic. A. S.
Hisarici Mah. Ahmet Toprak Cad. No. 9
Balikesir, TURKEY
Phone: 011-90-266-266-266-0
Fax: 011-90-266-243-4764
Website: www.commando-arms.com
Email: info@commando-arms.com

CONTROLLED CHAOS ARMS
8401 Hwy. S52 North
Baxter, IA 50028
Phone: 515-344-4443
Website: www.controlledchaosarms.com

CORE 15 RIFLE SYSTEMS
Good Time Outdoors, Inc.
4600 West Highway 326
Ocala, FL 34482
Phone: 352-401-9070
Fax: 352-401-9667
Website: www.core15rifles.com
Email: sales@core15rifles.com

CORONADO ARMS
450 S. Porter Road
Dixon, CA 95620
Phone: 707-678-2864
Fax: 707-678-3542
Website: www.coronadoarms.com
Email: sales@coronadoarms.com

CROSS CANYON ARMS
1010 W. Kershaw Street
Ogden, UT 84401
Phone: 801-731-0172
Website: www.crosscanyonarms.com
Email: sales@crosscanyonarms.com

CRUSADER WEAPONRY
5323 S. Baker Street
Murray, UT 84107
Phone: 801-808-6439
Website: www.crusaderweaponry.com

CZECHPOINT, INC.
P.O. Box 9207
Knoxville, TN 37940
Phone: 865-247-0184
Fax: 865-247-0185
Website: www.czechpoint-usa.com
Email: dan.brown@czechpoint-usa.com

CZECH SMALL ARMS
Jablunka 651
75623 Jablunka, CZECH REPUBLIC
Fax : 011-420-571-452-201
Website: www.csa.co.cz
Email: info@csa.co.cz

D&L SPORTS, INC.
P.O. Box 4843
Chino Valley, AZ 86323
Phone: 928-636-1726
Fax: 928-636-1757
Website: www.dlsports.com

DPMS FIREARMS
3312 12th Street SE
St. Cloud, MN 56304
Phone: 320-258-4448
Toll Free: 800-578-3767
Fax: 320-258-4449
Website: www.dpmsinc.com
Email: dpms@dpmsinc.com

DRD TACTICAL
Website: www.drdtactical.com

DSA, INC.
P.O. Box 370
Barrington, IL 60011
Phone: 847-277-7258
Fax: 847-277-7259
Website: www.dsarms.com
Email: customerservice@dsarms.com

D.Z. ARMS
3840 SW 113th
Oklahoma City, OK 73173
Phone: 405-691-1215
Fax: 405-691 5088
Website: www.dzhepburn.com
Email: dan@hepburn.com

DAKOTA ARMS, INC.
1310 Industry Road
Sturgis, SD 57785
Phone: 605-347-4686
Fax: 605-347-4459
Website: www.dakotaarms.com
Email: info@dakotarms.com

DANIEL DEFENSE
101 Warfighter Way
Black Creek, GA 31308
Phone: 866-554-4867
Phone: 912-964-4238
Fax: 912-851-3248
Website: www.danieldefense.com

DARK STORM INDUSTRIES, LLC (DSI)
4116 Sunrise Highway
Oakdale, NY 11769
Toll Free: 800-963-7700
Website: www.dark-storm.com

DAUDSONS ARMOURY
Industrial Estate, Kohat Road
Peshawar, 25210 PAKISTAN
Fax: 011-92-91-276059
Website: www.daudsons.org
Email: info@daudsons.org

DEL-TON, INCORPORATED
330 Aviation Parkway
Elizabethtown, NC 28337
Phone: 910-645-2172
Fax: 910-645-2244
Website: www.del-ton.com
Email: sales@del-ton.com

DESERT ORDNANCE
300 Sydney Drive
McCarran, NV 89434
Phone: 775-343-1330
Fax: 775-313-9852
Website: www.desertord.com
Email: questions@desertord.com

DESERT TECH (DESERT TACTICAL ARMS)
1995 W. Alexander Street
West Valley City, UT 84119
Phone: 801-975-7272
Fax: 801-908-6425
Website: www.deserttech.com

DETONICS DEFENSE TECHNOLOGIES, LLC
609 South Breese Street
Millstadt, IL 62260
Phone: 618-476-3200
Fax: 618-476-3221
Website: www.detonicsdefense.com
Email: contactus@detonics.ws

DEVIL DOG ARMS
650 Telser Road
Lake Zurich, IL 60047
Phone: 847-999-4851
Fax: 847-996-2131
Website: www.devildogarms.com
Email: sales@devildogarms.com

DEZ TACTICAL ARMS, INC.
WI
Phone: 608-547-9034
Website: www.deztacticalarms.com
Email: info@deztacticalarms.com

DIAMOND
Factory
Matsan Makina
Takim San. Ve Tic. A.S.
Halitpasa Cad. No. 2 G.O. Pasa
Istanbul TURKEY
Phone: 011-90-212-674-168687
Website: www.diamond-guns.com
Email:contact@diamond-guns.com
Importer
Adco Arms Co., Inc.
4 Draper Street
Woburn, MA 01801
Phone: 781-935-1799

DIAMONDBACK FIREARMS LLC
Marketing/Sales – please refer to Taurus International listing.
Factory
4135 Pine Tree Place
Cocoa, FL 32926
Phone: 888-380-2767
Website: www.diamondbackfirearms.com

DOUBLE D ARMORY, LTD
5650 Greenwood Plaza Blvd, Suite 205
Greenwood Village, CO 80111
Phone: 720-600-7522
Website: www.ddarmory.com
Email: sales@ddarmory.com

DOUBLESTAR CORPORATION
P.O. Box 430
Winchester, KY 40392
Phone: 888-736-7725
Fax: 859-745-4638
Website: www.jtfoc.com
Email: doug@star15.com

DRAKE ASSOCIATES
P.O. Box 1895
Shelter Island, NY 11965
Phone: 631-749-1100
Fax: 631-749-1515
Website: www.drakeassociates.us

E.D.M. ARMS
2410 West 350 North
Hurricane, UT 84737
Phone: 435-635-5233
Fax: 435-635-5258
Website: www.edmarms.com
Email: sales@edmarms.com

EAGLE ARMS
Please refer to Armalite listing.

EAGLE IMPORTS, INC.
1750 Brielle Ave., Unit B-1
Wanamassa, NJ 07712
Phone: 732-493-0333
Fax: 732-493-0301
Website: www.eagleimportsinc.com
Email: info@eagleimportsinc.com

EAST RIDGE/STATE ARMS GUN COMPANY, INC.
6319 5th Ave.
Bancroft, WI 54921
Phone: 715-366-2006
Website: www.statearms.com
Email: eastrdge@uniontel.net

ED BROWN PRODUCTS, INC.
P.O. Box 492
Perry, MO 63462
Phone: 573-565-3261
Fax: 573-565-2791
Website: www.edbrown.com
Email: edbrown@edbrown.com

EDWARD ARMS COMPANY
3020 N. 44th Street
Phoenix, AZ 85018
Phone: 602-456-9833
Website: www.edwardarms.com
Email: info@edwardarms.com

ESCORT
Importer - please refer to Legacy Sports International listing.
Factory - Hatsan Arms Company
Izmir - Ankara Karayolu 28. km. No. 289
Kemalpasa 35170, Izmir - TURKEY
Fax: 011-90-232-878-9102-878-9723
Website: www.hatsan.com.tr
Email: info@hatsan.com.tr

EMTAN KARMIEL LTD
P.O. Box 273
Karmiel, 20100 ISRAEL
Phone: 011-972-4-9987531
Fax: 011-972-4-9988981
Website: www.emtan.co.il
Email: info@emtan.co.il

EUROARMS ITALIA s.r.l.
(formerly Armi San Paolo)
via Europa 172/A
I-25062 Concesio, (BS) ITALY
Fax: 011-39-30-218-0365
Website: www.euroarms.net
Email: info@euroarms.net

EUROPEAN AMERICAN ARMORY CORP.
P.O. Box 560746
Rockledge, FL 32959
Phone: 321-639-4842
Fax: 321-639-7006
Website: www.eaacorp.com

EVANS ARMS
314 State St.
Clairton, PA 15025
Phone: 844-648-3695
Email: al@evansarms.us
Website: www.evansarms.us

EVOLUTION USA
P.O. Box 154
White Bird, ID 83554
Phone: 208-983-9208
Fax: 208-983-0944
Website: www.evo-rifles.com
Email: info@evo-rifles.com

EXCEL ARMS
1601 Fremont Ct.
Ontario, CA 91761
Phone: 909-947-4867
Fax: 909-947-0100
Website: www.excelarms.com
Email: excelind@verizon.net

F&D DEFENSE
2405 Lifehaus Industrial Dr. Suite 101
New Braunfels, TX 78130
Phone: 405-380-4346
Fax: 214-451-6380
Website: www.fd-defense.com
Email: info@fd-defense.com

FEG
Factory - FEGARMY
1095 Budapest, Soroksari ut 158
Levelcim: H-1440 Budapest Pf. 6 HUNGARY
Fax: 011-361-280-6669

FMK
P.O. Box 1358
Placentia, CA 92871
Phone: 714-630-0658
Fax: 714-630-0664
Website: www.fmkfirearms.com

FMR
3 rue Michelet
93500 Pantin FRANCE
Website: www.fmr-unique.com
Email: stephane-rolin@orange.fr

FNH USA
P.O. Box 697
McLean, VA 22101
Phone: 703-288-1292
Fax: 703-288-1730
Website: www.fnhusa.com
Email: info@fnhusa.com

Military Only
P.O. Box 896
McLean, VA 22101
Phone: 703-288-3500
Fax: 703-288-4505
Factory - F.N. Herstal S.A.
Voie de Liege, 33
Herstal, BELGIUM B4040
Fax: 011-324-240-8679
Website: www.fnherstal.com

FABARM S.p.A.
Importer – Fabarm USA
700 Lake Street
Cambridge, MD 21613
Phone: 410-901-1260
Website: www.fabarmusa.com
Factory - Fabbrica Breciana Armi
Via Averolda 31, Zona Industriale
I-25039 Travagliato, Brescia ITALY
Fax: 011-39-030-686-3684
Website: www.fabarm.com

FABRIQUE NATIONALE
Factory - Browning S.A.
Fabrique Nationale Herstal SA
Parc Industriel des Hauts Sarts
3me Ave. 25
B-4040 Herstal, BELGIUM
Fax: 011-32-42-40-5212

FAXON FIREARMS
11101 Adwood Drive
Cincinnati, OH 45240
Phone: 513-674-2580
Website: www.faxonfirearms.com

FEATHER USA
Parts/Accessories only
600 Oak Avenue
P.O. Box 247
Eaton, CO 80615
Toll Free: 800-519-0485
Fax: 970-206-1958
Website: www.featherusa.com
Email: featherawi@aol.com

FIERCE FIREARMS, LLC
321 South Main Street
P.O. Box 1045
Gunnison, UT 84634
Phone: 435-528-5080
Website: www.fiercearms.com
Email: info@fiercearms.com

FIREARMS INTERNATIONAL INC.
5200 Mitchelldale, Suite E-17
Houston, TX 77092
Phone: 713-462-4200
Fax: 713-681-5665
Website: www.highstandard.com
Email: info@highstandard.com

FIREBIRD PRECISION
P.O. Box 855
Mountainair, NM 87036
Phone: 505-847-0108
Website: www.firebirdprecision.com

FORT SOE SIA
Factory - Science Industrial Association Fort of the Ministry of Internal Affairs of Ukraine
27, 600-letiya str.
Vinnitsa 21027 UKRAINE
Fax: 011-380-432-468-016-461-002
Website: www.fort.vn.ua
Email: siafort@ukr.net

FRANKLIN ARMORY
2241 Park Place, Suite D
Minden, NV 89423
Phone: 775-783-4313
Fax: 775-783-4315
Website: www.franklinarmory.com
Email: info@franklinarmory.com

FULTON ARMORY
8725 Bollman Place Suite #1
Savage, MD 20763
Phone: 301-490-9485
Fax: 301-490-9547
Website: www.fulton-armory.com

GA PRECISION
1141 Swift Street
N. Kansas City, MO 64116
Phone: 816-221-1844
Website: www.gaprecision.net
Email: klin@gaprecision.net

G.A.C. RIFLES Srl
Loc. Bia Sot 15
25040 Corner Spa
(BS) ITALY
Phone: 011-390-364-549-140
Email: info@gacrifles.com

G.A.R. ARMS
P.O. Box 1193
Fairacres, NM 88033
Phone: 575-647-9703
Fax: 575-541-9056
Website: www.gar-arms.com

GWACS ARMORY
907 South Detroit Ave.
Suite 600
Tulsa, OK 74120
Phone: 918-970-0166
Fax: 866-941-8792
Website: www.gwacsarmory.com
Email: sales@gwacsarmory.com

GALIL
No current U.S. importation - semi-auto rifle configuration was banned April, 1998.
Israel Weapon Industries Ltd.
P.O Box 63 Ramat Hashron
47100 ISRAEL
Website: www.israel-weapon.com
Email: info@israel-weapon.com

GERMAN SPORT GUNS GmbH
Importer - please refer to American Tactical Imports listing.
Oesterweg 21
Ense-Höingen, D-59469 GERMANY
Fax: 011-49-2938-97837-130
Website: www.gsg-5.de

GIBBS RIFLE CO.
Please refer to Navy Arms listing.

GILA RIVER GUN WORKS
P.O. Box 6072
Pocatello, ID 83205
Phone: 208-241-2718
Website: www.michaelscherz.com
Email: gilagunworks@aol.com

GILBOA
Distributor – please refer to LDB Supply listing.
Factory - Silver Shadow Advanced Security Systems Ltd.
39 Jerusalem St. Ono mall
Kiryat Ono 55423 ISRAEL
Website: www.gilboa-rifle.com

GIRSAN MACHINE & LIGHT WEAPON INDUSTRY COMPANY
Factory
Teyyareduzu Mah. Sunta Sok
No: 25 Giresun, TURKEY
Fax: 011-90-454-215-3928
Phone: 0(454)215 29 31
Website: www.yavuz16.com
Email: satis@yavuz16.com
Importer -Zenith Firearms
10950 Rockfish Valley HWY
Suite C
Afton, VA 22920
Phone No: 434-202-7790
Fax: 434-202-7792
Website: www.zenithfirearms.com
Email: info@zenithfirearms.com

GRAND POWER s.r.o.
Importer - please refer to Eagle Imports listing.
Importer – please refer to Century Arms listing.
Poľovnícka 29
974 01 Banská Bystrica - Šalková
SLOVAKIA
Fax: 011-421-48-414-8754
Website: www.grandpower.eu
Email: sales@grandpower.eu

THE GUN ROOM CO., LLC
Please refer to Noreen Firearms LLC listing.

GUNCRAFTER INDUSTRIES
171 Madison 1510
Huntsville, AR 72740
Phone: 479-665-2466
Website: www.guncrafterindustries.com
Email: info@guncrafterindustries.com

H-S PRECISION, INC.
1301 Turbine Dr.
Rapid City, SD 57703
Phone: 605-341-3006
Fax: 605-342-8964
Website: www.hsprecision.com

HAGELBERG ARMS DESIGN
DENMARK
Website: www.frans-hagelber.dk
Email: info@franshagelber.dk

HAHN TACTICAL
110-H Industrial Drive
Winchester, VA 22602
Phone: 540-398-0818
Website: www.hahntactical.com
Email: sales@hahntactical.com

HATCHER GUN COMPANY
76650 Road 342
Elsie, NE 69134
Phone: 308-228-2454
Fax: 308-228-2522
Website: www.hatchergun.com
Email: th@hatchergun.com

HEAD DOWN PRODUCTS
4031 Fambrough Court, Suite 300
Dallas, GA 30770
Phone: 770-485-7015
Fax: 770-421-6345
Website: www.hdrifles.co

HECKLER & KOCH, INC.
Importer (Centerfire models) – H&K USA
5675 Transport Blvd.
Columbus, GA 31907
Phone: 706-568-1906
Fax: 706-568-9151
Website: www.hk-usa.com
Importer (Rimfire models) – Walther Arms, Inc.
7700 Chad Colley Boulevard
Fort Smith, AR 72916
Phone: 479-242-8500
Website: www.waltherams.com
Factory - Heckler & Koch GmbH
Alte Steige 7
P.O. Box 1329
D-78722 Oberndorf Neckar GERMANY
Fax: 011-49-7423-792350
Website: www.heckler-koch.com

HEINIE SPECIALTY PRODUCTS
(Repair and Sights only)
301 Oak Street
Quincy, IL 62301
Phone: 217-228-952
Fax: 217-228-9502
Website: www.heinie.com
Email: rheinie@heinie.com

HERA ARMS
Ziegelhüttenweg 5
Triefenstein D-97855 GERMANY
Fax: 011-49-0935-878158
Phone: 0049-9395 87 86 159
Website: www.hera-arms.com
Email: info@hera-arms.de

HI-POINT FIREARMS
U.S. Marketer - MKS Supply, Inc.
8611-A North Dixie Drive
Dayton, OH 45414
Phone: 877-425-4867
Fax: 937-454-0503
Website: www.hi-pointfirearms.com
Email: mkshpoint@aol.com

HIGH STANDARD MANUFACTURING CO.
5751 Mitchelldale, Ste. B-11
Houston, TX 77092
Phone: 832-516-6544
Fax: 713-681-5665
Website: www.highstandard.com
Email: stanc@highstandard.com

HOGAN MANUFACTURING LLC
Glendale, AZ 85301
Phone: 623-463-1939
Fax: 623-463-1941
Website: www.hoganguns.com

HOULDING PRECISION FIREARMS
2980 Falcon Drive
Madera, CA 93637
Phone: 559-675-9922
Website: www.houldingfirearms.com
Email: info@houldingfirearms.com

HOWA
Importer - please refer to Legacy Sports listing.

HULDRA ARMS
Mfg. – please refer to korst listing.
Distributor – Fleet Farm stores
Service
512 Laurel Street
P.O. Box 5055
Brainerd, MN 56401
Phone: 218-829-3521
Website: www.huldraarms.com
Email: service@huldraarms.com

HUNT GROUP INTERNATIONAL ARMS & SECURITY
Yoncalik (Yukari) Sk. 2-1/B
42720 Konya, TURKEY
Phone: 011-90-554-350-9098
Website: www.huntgrouparms.com
Email: info@huntgrouparms.com

I.O. INC.
2144 Franklin Drive NE
Palm Bay, FL 32905
Phone: 321-499-3819
Fax: 321-499-3822
Website: www.ioinc.us
Email: info@ioinc.us

ISSC HANDELSGESELLSCHAFT
Importer - please refer to Legacy Sports listing.
Factory
Furt 43
4754 Andrichsfurt, AUSTRIA
Fax: 011-43-7750-3842660
Website: www.issc.at
Email: office@issc.at

INTACTO ARMS
7103 Overland Rd.
Boise, ID 83709
Phone: 208-639-1270
Fax: 855-301-9349
Website: www.intactoarms.com
Email: sales@intactoarms.com

INTEGRITY ARMS & SURVIVAL
1205 Washington Street
Jefferson, GA 30549
Phone: 678-883-AR15
Website: www.customar15.net
Email: info@integrityarmssurvival.com

INTERARMS ARSENAL
Please refer to High Standard listing.

INTERSTATE ARMS CORP.
6 Dunham Road
Billerica, MA 01821
Toll Free: 800-243-3006
Phone: 978-667-7060
Fax: 978-671-0023
Website: www.interstatearms.com

INVINCIBLE ARMS, LLC
4323 Hamann Pkwy
Willoughby, OH 44094
Phone: 844-804-2767
Fax: 888-990-1339
Website: www.invinciblearms.com

IRON BRIGADE ARMORY
100 Radcliffe Circle
Jacksonville, NC 28546
Phone: 910-455-3834
Fax: 910-346-1134
Website: www.deathfromafar.com

IRON RIDGE ARMS CO.
1110 Delaware Ave.
Suite A
Longmount, CO 80501
Phone: 303-772-4365
Fax: 303-772-6204
Website: www.ironridgeguns.com
Email: tech@ironridgeguns.com

ISRAEL WEAPON INDUSTRIES LTD. (I.W.I.)
Importer – IWI US, Inc. (centerfire firearms)
P.O. Box 12607
Harrisburg, PA 17112
Phone: 717-695-2081
Website: www.iwi.us

ITHACA GUN COMPANY
420 N. Warpole St.
Upper Sandusky, OH 43351
Phone: 877-648-4222
Fax: 419-294-3230
Website: www.ithacagun.com

ITHACA GUN COMPANY LLC
Repair & Service - please refer to Ithaca Guns Company listing.

IVER JOHNSON ARMS, INC.
P.O. Box 561294
Rockledge, FL 32956
Phone: 321-636-3377
Fax: 321-632-7745
Website: www.iverjohnsonarms.com

J.B. CUSTOM INC.
16335 Lima Rd., Bldg. #5
Huntertown, IN 46748
Phone: 260-338-1894
Fax: 260-338-1585
Website: www.jbcustom.com
Email: jbcjim@gmail.com

J.L.D. ENTERPRISES, INC.
Please refer to PTR Industries listing.

JP ENTERPRISES, INC.
P.O Box 378
Hugo, MN 55038
Phone: 651-426-9196
Fax: 651-426-2472
Website: www.jprifles.com
Email: service@jprifles.com

J R CARBINES, LLC
Please refer to Just Right Carbines listing.

JAMES RIVER ARMORY
745 US Hwy 117 S.
Burgaw, NC 28425
Phone: 910-300-6462
Fax: 910-300-6463
Website: www.jamesriverarmory.com
Email: jamesriverarmory@gmail.com

JARD, INC.
3149 Nest Ave.
Sheldon, IA 51201
Phone: 712-324-7409
Website: www.jardinc.com
Email: jardusa@live.com

JARRETT RIFLES, INC.
383 Brown Road
Jackson, SC 29831
Phone: 803-471-3616
Fax: 803-471-9246
Website: www.jarrettrifles.com

JESSE JAMES FIREARMS UNLIMITED
Dripping Springs, TX
Phone: 888-269-0666
Fax: 512-857-1414
Website: www.jjfu.com
Email: jjamesfirearms@gmail.com

JUGGERNAUT TACTICAL
931 N. Parker St
Orange, CA 92867
Phone: 909-684-5822
Website: www.jtactical.com
Email: info@jtactical.com

JUST RIGHT CARBINES
231 Saltonstall Street
Canandaigua, NY 14424
Phone: 585-396-1551
Fax: 585-394-1523
Website: www.justrightcarbines.com

K-VAR CORP.
4235 W. Post Rd.
Las Vegas, NV 89118
Phone: 702-364-8880
Fax: 702-307-2303
Website: www.k-var.com

KAHR ARMS
130 Goddard Memorial Dr.
Worcester, MA 01603
Phone: 508-795-3919
Fax: 508-795-7046
Website: www.kahr.com
Website: www.kahrshop.com
Website: www.kelbly.com

KEL-TEC CNC INDUSTRIES, INC.
P.O Box 236009
Cocoa, FL 32923
Phone: 321-631-0068
Fax: 321-631-1169
Website: www.keltecweapons.com
Email: ktcustserv@kel-tec-cnc.com

KEPPELER TECHNISCHE ENTWICKLUNG GmbH
Friedrich-Reinhardt Strasse 4
D-74427 Fichtenberg, GERMANY
Fax: 011-49-07971-91-1243
Website: www.keppeler-te.de
Email: info@keppeler-te.de

KIMBER
Corporate Offices - Kimber Mfg., Inc.
555 Taxter Road, Suite 235
Elmsford, NY 10523
Phone: 888-243-4522
Fax: 406-758-2223
Website: www.kimberamerica.com
Email: info@kimberamerica.com

KING'S ARSENAL
1110 Hwy. 80 E
Abilene, TX 79601
Phone: 325-669-5064kala
Website: www.kingsarsenal.com

KNIGHT'S ARMAMENT COMPANY
701 Columbia Blvd.
Titusville, FL 32780
Phone: 321-607-9900
Website: www.knightarmco.com

KORSTOG
Mfg. – please refer to Adams Arms listing.
Exclusive U.S. Retailer – Fleet Farm stores
Service
512 Laurel Street
P.O. Box 5055
Brainerd, MN 56401
Phone: 218-829-3521
Website: www.korstog.com
Email: info@korstog.com

KRISS ARMS GROUP
Importer/US Factory – Kriss USA
565 West Lambert Road, Suite F
Brea, CA, 92821
Phone: 855-574-7787
Website: www.kriss-usa.com
Factory
Ch. De la Vuarpilliere 35 1260 Nyon
SWITZERLAND
Phone: 011-41-22-363-7820
Fax: 011-41-22-363-7821

LRB ARMS
96 Cherry Lane
Floral Park, NY 11001
Phone: 516-327-9061
Fax: 516-327-0246
Website: www.lrbarms.com

LWRC INTERNATIONAL, LLC
815 Chesapeake Dr.
Cambridge, MD 21613
Phone: 410-901-1348
Fax: 410-228-1775
Website: www.lwrci.com

LANCER SYSTEMS
2800 Milford Square Pike
Quakertown, PA 18951
Phone No: 610-973-2600
Website: www.lancer-systems.com

LARUE TACTICAL
850 Country Road 177
Leander, TX 78641
Phone: 512-259-1585
Website: www.laruetactical.com

LAUER CUSTOM WEAPONRY
3601 129th Street
Chippewa Falls, WI 54729
Toll Free: 800-830-6677
Website: www.lauerweaponry.com

LAZZERONI ARMS COMPANY
P.O. Box 26696
Tucson, AZ 85726-6696
Toll Free: 888-492-7247
Fax: 520-624-4250
Website: www.lazzeroni.com
Email: arms@lazzeroni.com

LEGACY SPORTS INTERNATIONAL LLC
4750 Longley Lane, Ste. 209
Reno, NV 89502
Toll Free: 800-553-4229
Fax: 800-786-6555
Website: www.legacysports.com

LEGEND RIFLES
Please refer to D'Arcy Echols & Co.

LEGENDARY ARMS WORKS
76 West Main Street
Reinholds, PA 17569
Phone: 717-335-8555
Website: www.legendaryarmsworks.com
Email: info@law-arms.com

LEGION FIREARMS
1901 Ramcon Drive
Temple, TX 76504
Toll Free: 855-453-4466

LEITNER-WISE DEFENSE
Parts and Accessories only
P.O. Box 25097
Alexandria, VA 22313
Phone: 703-209-0556
Fax: 703-548-1427
Website: www.leitner-wise.com
Email: info@leitner-wise.com

LES BAER CUSTOM, INC.
1804 Iowa Drive
LeClaire, IA 52753
Phone: 563-289-2126
Fax: 563-289-2132
Website: www.lesbaer.com
Email: info@lesbaer.com

LEWIS MACHINE & TOOL COMPANY (LMT)
1305 11th Street West
Milan, IL 61264
Phone: 309-787-7151
Fax: 309-787-2636
Website: www.lmtdefense.com

LITHGOW ARMS
4 Martini Parade
Lithgow, NSSW 2790 AUSTRALIA
Phone: 011-61-(0)2-6352-9900
Website: www.lithgowarms.com
Email: sales@lithgowarms.com

LOSOK CUSTOM ARMS
314 Willow Run Lane
Delaware, OH 43015
Phone: 740-363-8437

LUVO PRAGUE LTD.
Rejskova 7
Praha 2-Vinohrady, 120 00
CZECH REPUBLIC
Phone: 011-420-602-31-1552
Website: www.luvo.cz
Email: luvo@iol.cz

M+M INDUSTRIES
Northglenn, CO 80233
Phone: 303-926-5419
Toll Free: 888-236-2619
Website: www.mm-industries.com
Email: sales@mm-industries.com

MG ARMS, INC.
6030 Treaschwig Road
Spring, TX 77373
Phone: 281-821-8282
Fax: 281-821-6387
Website: www.mgarmsinc.com
Email: info@mgarmsinc.com

MGI
1168 Main Street
P.O. Box 138
Old Town, ME 04468
Phone: 207-817-3280
Fax: 207-817-3283
Website: www.mgimilitary.com
Email: mgi@mgimilitary.com

MKA ARMS
Head Office
Kayasultan Sk. No: 79/B Kozyatagi
Kadikoy, Istanbul - TURKEY
Fax: 011-90-216-527-4485
Factory
Hamidiye Mh. Kucuk San. Sit.
514 Sk. No: 3 Konya, TURKEY

MKE
Importer -Zenith Firearms
10950 Rockfish Valley HWY
Suite C
Afton, VA 22920
Phone No: 434-202-7790
Fax: 434-202-7792
Website: www.zenithfirearms.com
Email: info@zenithfirearms.com
Factory
06330 Tandogan, Ankara TURKEY
Fax: 011-90-312-222-2241
Website: www.mkek.gov.tr

MKS SUPPLY, INC.
8611-A North Dixie Drive
Dayton, OH 45414
Phone: 937-454-0363
Fax: 937-454-0503
Website: www.mkssupply.com

MMC ARMORY
10549 Mennies Lane
Mark, IL 61340
Phone: 815-339-2226
Website: www.mmcarmory.com
Email: customerservice@mmcarmory.com

MAGNUM RESEARCH, INC.
Factory (Except for Baby Eagle Series)
12602 33rd Ave SW
Pillager, MN 56473
Phone: 508-635-4273
Fax: 218-746-3097
Website: www.magnumresearch.com
Email: info@magnumresearch.com

MAKAROV
Importer - please refer to Century Arms listing.

MARLIN FIREARMS COMPANY
P.O. Box 1781
Madison, NC 27025
Phone: 203-239-5621
Gun Service No.: 800-544-8892
Repairs: 800-544-8892
Website: www.marlinfirearms.com

MASTERPIECE ARMS
P.O. Box 67
Comer, GA 30629
Phone: 866-803-0000
Fax: 770-832-3495
Website: www.masterpiecearms.com
Email: darah@masterpiecearms.com

MATCH GRADE ARMS & AMMUNITION
Please refer to MG Arms, Inc. listing.

MAUNZ MATCH RIFLES LLC
P.O. Box 104
Maumee, OH 43537
Phone: 419-832-2512
Website: www.maunzmatchrifles.com
Email: maunzmatchrifles@yahoo.com

MAVERICK ARMS, INC.
Please refer to Mossberg listing.

MAWHINNEY, CHUCK
Factory - Please refer to Riflecraft listing.
2350 Carter Street
Baker City, OR 97814
Website: www.chuckmawhinney.com
Email: cmawhinney@eoni.com

MAXIMUS ARMS, LLC
1226-C Lakeview Drive
Franklin, TN 37067
Phone: 615-595-9777
Website: www.maximusarms.com

MCCANN INDUSTRIES LLC
P.O. Box 641
Spanaway, WA 98387
Phone: 253-537-6919
Fax: 253-537-6993
Website: www.mccannindustries.com
Email: info@mccannindustries.com

MCDUFFEE ARMS
7252 Eaton Circle
Westminster, CO 80003
Phone: 303-325-3219
Fax: 866-687-6633
Website: www.mcduffeearms.com
Email: info@mcduffeearms.com

McMILLAN FIREARMS MANUFACTURING, LLC
23606 North 19th Ave. Suite 10
Phoenix, AZ 85085
Toll Free: 800-401-7269
Phone: 623-780-1050
Website: www.mcmillanfirearms.com
Email: info@mcmillanfirearms.com

METROARMS CORPORATION
Distributor – please refer to Eagle Imports, Inc. listing.
Website: www.metroarms.com

MICOR DEFENSE, INC.
P.O. Box 2175
Decatur, AL 35602
Phone: 256-560-0770
Fax: 256-341-0002
Website: www.micordefense.com
Email: orders@micordefense.com

MICROTECH SMALL ARMS RESEARCH, INC. (MSAR)
300 Chesnut Street
Bradford, PA 16701
Phone: 814-363-9260
Fax: 814-362-7068
Website: www.msarinc.com

MILLER PRECISION ARMS
3816 Hwy. 40
Columbia Falls, MT 59912
Phone: 406-892-2149
Website: www.millerprecisionarms.com

MILTAC INDUSTRIES, LLC
P.O. Box 982
Boise, ID 83701
Phone: 866-587-7130
Website: www.miltacindustries.com

MITCHELL'S MAUSERS
P.O. Box 9295
Fountain Valley, CA 92728 -9295
Toll Free: 800-274-4124
Fax: 714-848-7208
Website: www.mauser.org

MOHAWK ARMORY
995 Mowhawk Creek Rd.
Midway, TN 37809
Phone: 423-335-6528
Website: www.mohawkarmory.com

MOLOT
Please refer to Becas and Vepr. listings.

MONTANA ARMORY, INC.
Please refer to C. Sharps Arms, Inc. listing.

MOSSBERG
O.F. Mossberg & Sons, Inc.
7 Grasso Ave., P.O. Box 497
North Haven, CT 06473-9844
Phone: 203-230-5300
Fax: 203-230-5420
Factory Service Center - OFM Service Department
Eagle Pass Industrial Park
Industrial Blvd.
Eagle Pass, TX 78853
Toll Free: 800-989-4867
Website: www.mossberg.com
Email: service@mossberg.com

NAVY ARMS CO.
219 Lawn St.
Martinsburg, WV 25401
Phone: 304-262-9870
Fax: 304-262-1658
Website: www.navyarms.com
Email: info@navyarms.com

NEMESIS ARMS
102 Reed Drive
Park City, KY 42160
Phone: 270-749-2180
Website: www.nemesisarms.com

NEMO ARMS
3582 Hwy 93 S.
Kalispell, MT 59901
Phone: 406-752-NEMO
Website: www.nemoarms.com
Email: info@nemoarms.com

NESIKA
1310 Industry Road
Sturgis, SD 57785
Phone: 605-347-4686
Website: www.nesikafirearms.com
Email: info@nesikafirearms.com

NEW ENGLAND CUSTOM GUN SERVICE LTD.
741 Main Street
Claremont, NH 03743
Phone: 603-287-4836
Fax: 603-287-4834
Website: www.newenglandcustomgun.com
Email: info@necgltd.com

NEW ULTRA LIGHT ARMS LLC
P.O. Box 340
214 Price Street
Granville, WV 26534
Phone: 304-292-0600
Fax: 304-626-9947
Website: www.newultralight.com

NEWTOWN FIREARMS
103 Main Street
Placerville, CA 95667
Phone: 530-626-9945
Fax: 530-644-6684
Website: www.newtown-firearms.com

NIGHTHAWK CUSTOM
1306 W. Trimble Ave.
Berryville, AR 72616-4632
Phone: 877-268-4867
Fax: 870-423-4230
Website: www.nighthawkcustom.com
Email: info@nighthawkcustom.com

NOREEN FIREARMS LLC
131 Jetway Drive
Belgrade, MT 59714
Phone: 406-388-2200
Fax: 406-388-6500
Website: www.onlylongrange.com
Email: info@onlylongrange.com

NORINCO
European Distributor – Norconia GmbH
Zeppelinstrabe 3
D-97228 Rottendorf, GERMANY
Phone: 01149-0903-1405

Factory - China North Industries Corporation
12A Guang An Men Nan Jie
Beijing 100053 CHINA
Fax: 011-86-10-63540398
Website: www.norinco.com
Email: norinco@norinco.com.cn

NORTHERN COMPETITION
P.O. Box 44697
Racine, WI 53404-4697
Phone: 262-639-5955
Website: www.northerncompetition.com
Email: productsales@northerncompetition.com

NOSLER, INC.
107 SW Columbia St.
Bend, OR 97709
Toll Free: 800-285-3701
Fax: 800-766-7537
Website: www.nosler.com
Email: catalog@nosler.com

NOVESKE RIFLEWORKS LLC
P.O. Box 607
Grants Pass, OR 97528
Phone: 541-479-6117
Fax: 541-479-2555
Website: www.shopnoveske.com

NOWLIN MFG. INC.
Service and components only
20622 4092 Rd., Unit B
Claremore, OK 74019
Phone: 918-342-0689
Fax: 918-342-0624
Website: www.nowlinguns.com
Email: nowlinguns@msn.com

NUMRICH GUN PARTS CORP.
Parts supplier only
226 Williams Lane
P.O. Box 299
W. Hurley, NY 12491
Phone: 866-686-7424
Fax: 877-486-7278
Website: www.e-gunparts.com
Email: info@gunpartscorp.com

OBERLAND ARMS
Am Hundert 3
D-82386 Huglfing GERMANY
Fax: 011-49-8802914-751
Website: www.oberlandarms.com
Email: info@oberlandarms.com

OHIO ORDNANCE WORKS, INC.
P.O. Box 687
Chardon, OH 44024
Phone: 440-285-3481
Fax: 440-286-8571
Website: www.ohioordnanceworks.com
Email: oow@oowinc.com

OLYMPIC ARMS, INC.
624 Old Pacific Hwy. SE
Olympia, WA 98513
Toll Free: 800-228-3471
Fax: 360-491-3447
Website: www.olyarms.com
Email: info@olyarms.com

OMNI
Please refer to E.D.M. Arms listing.

ONLY LONG RANGE
Please refer to Noreen Firearms LLC listing.

ORSIS
14/8 Pod'emnaya Street
Moscow, RUSSIA 109052
Phone: 011-7-495-647-8866
Email: order@orsis.com

ORVIS
(Custom shotgun information only)
Historic Route 7A
Manchester, VT 05254
Phone: 802-362-2580
Fax: 802-362-3525
Website: www.orvis.com

OSPREY ARMAMENT
Wilmington, NC 28411
Phone: 855-741-5168
Website: www.ospreyarmament.com
Email: hello@ospreyarmament.com

PGW DEFENCE TECHNOLOGIES
Importer – Trigger Time Gun Club
3575 Stagecoach Road South
Longmont, CO 80504
Phone: 303-651-0816
Website: www.triggertimegunclub.com
Factory
#6-59 Scurfield Blvd.
Winnipeg, Manitoba, CANADA R3Y1V2
Phone: 204-487-7325
Fax: 204-231-8566
Website: www.pgwdti.com

PTR INDUSTRIES
U.S. Representative - Vincent Pestilli & Associates
193 Sam Brown Hill Rd.
Brownfield, ME 04010
Phone: 207-935-3603
Fax: 207-935-3996
Email: vapame@fairpoint.net
Factory - PTR INDUSTRIES
101 Cool Springs Dr.
Aynor, SC 29511
Phone: 843-358-2222
Fax: 843-358-2223
Website: www.PTR91.com
Email: sales@ptr91.com

PALMETTO STATE ARMORY
200 Business Park Blvd.
Columbia, SC 29203
Phone: 803-724-6950
Website: www.palmettostatearmory.com
Email: info@palmettostatearmory.com

PALMETTO STATE DEFENSE, LLC
1514 S. Hwy 14, Unit B
Greer, SC 29650
Phone: 864-469-9875
Website: www.palmettostatedefense.com
Email: sales@palmettostatedefense.com

PARA USA, LLC
Service Only – Please contact Remington's Service Dept.
Toll Free: 800-243-9700
Fax: 336-548-7801

PATRIOT ORDNANCE FACTORY (POF)
23011 N. 16th Lane
Phoenix, AZ 85027
Phone: 623-561-9572
Fax: 623-321-1680
Website: www.pof-usa.com
Email: sales@pof-usa.com

PHASE 5 TACTICAL
Roseville, CA
Website: www.phase5wsi.com

PIONEER ARMS CORP.
Importer - please refer to I.O., Inc. listing.
Factory
1905 Roku 1/9 Street
26-612 Radom, POLAND
Fax: 011-48-383-0776
Website: www.pioneer-pac.com
Email: contact@pioneer-pac.com

PISTOL DYNAMICS
2510 Kirby Ave. NE
Palm Bay, FL 32905
Phone No: 321-733-1266
Website: www.pistoldynamics.com
Email: info@pistoldynamics.com

PRECISION FIREARMS
74A Dupont Rd.
Martinsburg, WV 25404
Phone: 240-217-6875
Fax: 480-287-8094
Website: www.precisionfirearms.com
Website: www.pf15.com
Email: pf15@pf15.com

PRECISION REFLEX, INC.
710 Streine Drive
New Bremen, OH 45869
Phone: 419-629-2603
Fax: 419-629-2173
Website: www.precisionreflex.com
Email: info@precisionreflex.com

PREDATOR CUSTOM SHOP
3539 Papermill Drive
Knoxville, TN 37909
Phone: 865-321-0625
Fax: 865-521-0624
Website: www.predatorcustomshop.com
Email: sales@predatorcustomshop.com

PREDATOR TACTICAL LLC
7730 E. Redfield Rd.
Scottsdale, AZ 85260
Phone: 602-652-2864
Fax: 602-492-9987
Website: www.predatortactical.com
Email: admin@predatortactical.com

PRIMARY WEAPONS SYSTEMS
800 E. Citation Court, Ste. E
Boise, ID 83716
Phone: 208-344-5217
Fax: 208-344-5395
Website: www.primaryweapons.com

PROARMS ARMORY
Tousenska 431
25081 Nehvizdy, Praha – vychod
CZECH REPUBLIC
Phone: 011-420-602-258669
Fax: 011-420-326-997345
Website: www.proarms-armory.com
Email: hofman@proarms-armory.com

PROOF RESEARCH
10 Western Village Lane
Columbia Falls, MT 59912
Phone: 406-756-9290
Website: www.proofresearch.com
Email: info@proofresearch.com

PUMA RIFLES
*Importer - please refer to Legacy Sports
International, LLC listing.*

QUALITY PARTS CO.
Please refer to Bushmaster Firearms, Inc. listing.

R GUNS
855 Commerce Parkway
Carpentersville, IL 60110
Phone: 847-428-3569
Website: www.rguns.net
Email: rguns@rguns.net

RAAC
677 S. Cardinal Lane
Scottsburg, IN 47170
Phone: 877-752-2894
Website: www.raacfirearms.com
Email: info@raacfirearms.com

R.I.P. TACTICAL
Utah
Phone: 435-590-6036
Website: www.rip-tactical.com

RND MANUFACTURING
14399 Mead Street
Longmont, CO 80504
Phone/Fax: 970-535-4458
Website: www.rndrifles.com
Email: info@rndrifles.com

RPA INTERNATIONAL LTD.
P.O. Box 441
Tonbridge, Kent, UK TN9 9DZ
Fax: 011-44-8458803232
Website: www.rpainternational.co.uk
Email: custom@rpainternational.co.uk

RWC GROUP LLC
911 William Leigh Drive
Tullytown, PA 19007
Phone: 866-611-9576
Fax: 215-949-9191
Website: www.rwcgroupllc.com
Email: info@rwcgroupllc.com

Radical Firearms, LLC
4413 Bluebonnet
Suite 8
Stafford, TX 77477
Fax: 281-207-8910
Website: www.radicalfirearms.com
Email: info@radicalfirearms.com

RED ROCK ARMS
P.O. Box 21017
Mesa, AZ 85277
Phone: 480-832-0844
Fax: 206-350-5274
Website: www.redrockarms.com
Email: info@redrockarms.com

RED ROCK PRECISION
181 N. Commercial St.
Morgan, UT 84050
Phone: 801-391-7840
Website: www.redrockprecision.com
Email: toddredrock@comcast.net

RED X ARMS
Phone: 320-424-1362
Website: www.redxarms.com
Email: sales@redxarms.com

REMINGTON ARMS CO., INC.
Consumer Services
870 Remington Drive
P.O. Box 700
Madison, NC 27025-0700
Toll Free: 800-243-9700
Fax: 336-548-7801
Website: www.remington.com
Email: info@remington.com
Repairs
14 Hoefler Ave.
Ilion, NY 13357
Toll Free: 800-243-9700
Fax: 336-548-7801

REX FIREARMS
Importer – please refer to FIME Group LLC listing.

RHINO ARMS
St. Louis, MO 63110
Phone: 855-25-RHINO
Website: www.rhinoarms.com

RIFLES, INC.
3580 Leal Rd.
Pleasanton, TX 78064
Phone: 830-569-2055
Fax: 830-569-2297
Website: www.riflesinc.com
Email: info@riflesinc.com

RIFLECRAFT LTD.
18G Speedwell Way
Border Valley Industrial Estate
Harleston, Norfolk, IP20 9EH, UK
Website: www.riflecraft.co.uk

RITTER & STARK
Klagenfurter Strabe 19
9170 Ferlach, AUSTRIA
Phone: 011-43-4228-20512
Website: www.ritterstark.com
Email: info@ritterstark.com

RIVERMAN GUN WORKS
410 W. Neider Ave., Ste. E
Coeur d'Alene, ID 83815
Phone: 208-667-3786
Fax: 208-667-3500
Website: www.rivermangunworks.com
Email: info@rivermangunworks.com

ROBAR COMPANIES, INC.
21438 N. 7th Avenue, Ste. B
Phoenix, AZ 85027
Phone: 623-581-2648
Fax: 623-582-0059
Website: www.robarguns.com
Email: info@robarguns.com

ROBINSON ARMAMENT CO.
925 W. 100 N, Ste. A
N. Salt Lake City, UT 84116-0776
Phone: 801-355-0401
Website: www.robarm.com
Email: sales@robarm.com

ROCK ISLAND ARMORY
Please refer to Armscor listing.

ROCK RIVER ARMS, INC.
1042 Cleveland Road
Colona, IL 61241
Phone: 309-792-5780
Fax: 309-792-5781
Website: www.rockriverarms.com
Email: info@rockriverarms.com

ROCKY MOUNTAIN ARMS, INC.
1813 Sunset Place, Unit D
Longmont, CO 80501
Toll Free: 800-375-0846
Fax: 303-678-8766
Website: www.rockymountainarms.us

ROHRBAUGH FIREARMS CORP.
P.O. Box 785
Bayport, NY 11705
Toll Free: 800-803-2233
Phone: 631-242-3175
Fax: 631-242-3183
Website: www.rohrbaughfirearms.com

S.W.A.T. FIREARMS
6585 East I-30
Campbell, TX 75422
Phone: 855-862-SWAT (7928)
Website: www.swatfirearms.com

SI DEFENSE
2902 Highway 93 North
Kalispell, MT 59901
Phone: 406-752-4253
Fax: 406-755-1302
Website: www.si-defense.com
Email: info@si-defense.com

SMI ARMS
9825 W. 67th Street
Merriam, KS 66203
Phone: 913-766-0680
Website: www.SMIArms.com

SRM ARMS
Exclusive Distributor
GSA Direct LLC
802 W. Bannock St. Ste 700
Boise, ID 83702
Phone: 208-424-3141
Fax: 208-248-1111
Factory - SRM ARMS
4375A W. McMillan Rd.
Meridian, ID 83646
Phone: 888-269-1885
Website: www.srmarms.com
Email: order@srmarms.com

SSK INDUSTRIES
590 Woodvue Lane
Wintersville, OH 43953
Phone: 740-264-0176
Fax: 740-264-2257
Website: www.sskindustries.com
Email: info@sskindustries.com

STI INTERNATIONAL
114 Halmar Cove
Georgetown, TX 78628
Toll Free: 800-959-8201
Fax: 512-819-0465
Website: www.stiguns.com
Email: sales@stiguns.com

SAFETY HARBOR FIREARMS, INC.
P.O. Box 563
Safety Harbor, FL 34695-0563
Phone: 727-726-2500
Fax: 727-797-6134
Website: www.safetyharborfirearms.com
Email: sales@safetyharborfirearms.com

SAIGA
Exclusive Importer – please refer to RWC Group LLC listing.

SAKO LTD.
Importer (USA) - please refer to Beretta USA listing.
Factory - Sako, Limited
P.O. Box 149
FI-11101 Riihimaki, FINLAND
Fax: 011-358-19-720446
Website: www.sako.fi
Email: export@sako.fi

SAMCO GLOBAL ARMS, INC.
4225 NW 72nd Ave
Miami, FL 33166
Toll Free: 888-984-8678
Phone: 305-470-8090
Fax: 305-593-1014
Website: www.samcoglobal.com
Email: samco@samcoglobal.com

SAN SWISS ARMS AG
Industrieplatz 1, Postbox 1071
Neuhausen am Rheinfall
CH-8212 SWITZERLAND
Fax: 011-41-052-674-6418
Website: www.swissarms.ch
Email: info@swissarms.ch

SARCO INC.
323 Union Street
Stirling, NJ 07980
Phone: 908-647-3800
Fax: 908-647-9413
Website: www.sarcoinc.com
Email: sarcopa@sarcoinc.com
Parts Only
50 Hilton Ste.
Easton, PA 18042
Phone No. 610-250-3960

SARSILMAZ
Importer - please refer to U.S. Sporting Goods Inc. (shotguns)
Factory
Nargileci Sk. Sarsilmaz is Merkezi No.: 4
Mercan 34116, Istanbul, TURKEY
Fax: 011-90212-51119-99
Website: www.sarsilmaz.com

SAUER, J.P. & SOHN
Importer – Sauer USA, Inc.
403 East Ramsey, Ste. 301
San Antonio, TX 78216
Phone: 210-377-2527
Fax: 210-377-2533
Website: www.sauer-de.com
Factory - J.P. Sauer & Sohn GmbH
Ziegelstadel 20
88316 Isny im Allgau, GERMANY
Fax: 011-49-7562-97554-801
Website: www.sauer-waffen.de
Email: info@sauer.de

SAVAGE ARMS, INC.
100 Springdale Road
Westfield, MA 01085
Phone: 413-568-7001
Fax: 413-562-7764
Website: www.savagearms.com
Older Savage Arms Historical Research
Mr. John Callahan
P.O. Box 82
Southampton, MA 01073
$30.00/gun research fee, $25.00 per gun for
Models 1895, 1899, and 99 rifles.

SCATTERGUN TECHNOLOGIES INC.
Please refer to Wilson Combat listing.

SCHEIRING GmbH
Klagenfurter Strasse 19
A-9170 Ferlach AUSTRIA
Fax: 011-43-4227-287620
Website: www.jagdwaffen-scheiring.at
Email: waffen.scheiring@aon.at

SCHMEISSER GmbH
Importer – please refer to American Tactical Imports listing.
Adolf-Dembach-Strasse 4
D-47829 Krefeld GERMANY
Phone: 011-49-2151-457810
Fax: 011-49-2151-45781-45
Website: www.schmeisser-germany.de
Email: info@schmeisser-germany.de

SCHROEDER BAUMAN
Ft. Wayne, IN
Website: www.sbfirearms.com

SCHUETZEN PISTOL WORKS, INC.
Please refer to Olympic Arms listing.

SCHWABEN ARMS GmbH
Neckartal 95
D-78628, Rottweil, GERMANY
Fax: 011-49-0741-9429218
Website: www.schwabenarmsgmbh.de
Email: schwabenarmsgmbh@web.de

SEEKINS PRECISION
1708 6th Ave North Ste D
Lewiston, ID 83501
Phone: 208-743-3400
Website: www.seekinsprecision.com
Email: sales@seekinsprecision.com

SEMMERLING
Please refer to American Derringer Corp. listing.

SENNI ARMS CO.
Ste. 243/15 Albert Ave.
Broadbeach, Queensland, AUSTRALIA 4218
Fax: 011-07-5597-3655
Website: www.senniarms.com
Email: sales@senniarms.com

SERBU FIREARMS, INC.
6001 Johns Rd., Ste. 144
Tampa, FL 33634
Phone/Fax: 813-243-8899
Website: www.serbu.com

SERO LTD.
1106 Feher Str. 10 3/A
Budapest, HUNGARY
Fax: 011-36-1433-2182
Website: www.sero.hu
Email: info@sero.hu

**SHOOTERS ARMS MANUFACTURING
INCORPORATED**
Importer - please refer to Century Arms listing.
Factory
National Highway, Wireless
Mandaue City, Cebu, PHILIPPINES
Fax: 011-6032-346-2331
Website: www.shootersarms.com.ph
Email: rhonedeleon@yahoo.com

SIGNAL 9 DEFENSE
444 Calvert Drive
Gallatin, TN 37066
Phone: 615-989-7694
Website: www.signal9defense.com
Email: info@signal9defense.com

SIG SAUER
18 Industrial Park Drive
Exeter, NH 03833
Phone: 603-772-2302
Fax: 603-772-9082
Customer Service Phone: 603-772-2302
Customer Service Fax: 603-772-4795
Law Enforcement Phone: 603-772-2302
Law Enforcement Fax: 603-772-1481
Website: www.sigarms.com
*Factory - SIG - Schweizerische Industrie-
Gesellschaft*
Industrielplatz , CH-8212
Neuhausen am Rheinfall, SWITZERLAND
Fax: 011-41-153-216-601

SINO DEFENSE MANUFACTURING (SDM)
Distributor - Prima Armi
Viale J.F. Kennedy 8
10064 Pinerolo, ITALY
Phone: 011-39-0121-321-422
Fax: 011-39-0121-398-739
Website: www.s-defense.com
Email: export@primarmi.it

SIONICS WEAPON SYSTEMS
5118 E. Prima Street
Tucson, AZ 85712
Phone: 520-441-1260
Fax: 520-844-8329
Website: www.sionicsweaponsystems.com
Email: sales@sionicsweaponsystems.com

SISK RIFLES LLC
400 County Road 2340
Dayton, TX 77535
Phone: 936-258-4984
Website: www.siskguns.com

SKORPION
Please refer to Czechpoint, Inc. listing.

SMITH & WESSON
2100 Roosevelt Avenue
P.O. Box 2208
Springfield, MA 01104
Toll Free: 800-331-0852
Website: www.smith-wesson.com
Service email only: qa@smith-wesson.com
Smith & Wesson Research
Attn: Mr. Roy Jinks, S&W Historian
P.O. Box 2208
Springfield, MA 01102-2208
Phone: 413-747-3223 (8am-5pm)

SOUTHERN GUN COMPANY
UNITED KINGDOM
Phone: 011-44-1208-851074
Fax: 011-44-1208-850860
Website: www.southern-gun.co.uk

SPARTAN GUN WORKS
Please refer to the Remington listing.

SPARTAN PRECISION RIFLES
2128 N. First Street
Unit C
San Jose, CA 95131
Phone: 408-451-9850
Website: www.spartanrifles.com

SPECIAL WEAPONS INC.
Warranty service & repair for Special Weapons LLC
Website: www.tacticalweapons.com

SPECIALIZED DYNAMICS
925 N. California Street
Chandler, AZ 85225
Phone: 602-425-7500
Website: www.specializeddynamics.com

SPECIALIZED TACTICAL SYSTEMS
673 W. 1st Street
Ogden, UT 84404
Phone: 801-648-7004
Fax: 801-648-7357
Website: www.specializedtactical.com

SPHINX SYSTEMS LTD.
Importer – please refer to Kriss USA listing.
Factory
Gsteigstrasse 12
CH-3800 Matten Interlaken SWITZERLAND
Fax: 011-41-033-821-1006
Website: www.sphinxarms.com
Email: info@sphinxarms.com

SPIDER FIREARMS
2005-B Murcott Dr.
St. Cloud, FL 34771-5826
Phone: 407-957-3617
Fax: 407-957-0296
Website: www.ferret50.com
Email: info@ferret50.com

SPIKE'S TACTICAL LLC
2036 Apex Ct.
Apopka, FL 32703
Phone: 407-928-2666
Fax: 866-283-2215
Website: www.spikestactical.com
Email: sales@spikestactical.com

SPORT-SYSTEME DITTRICH
Burghaiger Weg 20a
D-95326 Kulmbach, GERMANY
Fax: 011-49-09221-8213758
Website: www.ssd-weapon.com

SPRINGER'S ERBEN, JOHANN
Weihburggasse 27
A-1010, Vienna AUSTRIA
Fax: 011-43-1512-0309
Website: www.springer-vienna.com

SPRINGFIELD ARMORY
Springfield Inc.
420 W. Main St.
Geneseo, IL 61254
Phone: 309-944-5631
Toll Free: 800-680-6866
Fax: 309-944-3676
Website: www.springfield-armory.com
Email: sales@springfield-armory.com
Custom Shop Email: customshop@springfield-armory.com

STAG ARMS
515 John Downey Dr.
New Britain, CT 06051
Phone: 860-229-9994
Fax: 860-229-3738
Website: www.stagarms.com
Email: sales@stagarms.com

STALLARD ARMS
Please refer to Hi-Point listing.

STANDARD MANUFACTURING COMPANY
100 Burritt Street
New Britain, CT 06053
Phone: 860-225-6581
Website: www.standardmfgllc.com
Email: info@standardmfgllc.com

STERLING ARSENAL
201 Davis Drive
Unit FF
Sterling, VA 20164
Phone: 571-926-8705
Website: www.sterlingarsenal.com
Email: support@sterlingarsenal.com

STEYR ARMS (STEYR MANNLICHER)
2530 Morgan Road
Bessemer, AL 35022
Phone: 205-417-8644
Fax: 205-417-8647
Website: www.steyrarms.com

Factory - Steyr Mannlicher A.G. & Co. KG
Ramingtal 46
Kleinraming A-4442 AUSTRIA
Fax: 01143-7252-78621
Website: www.steyr-mannlicher.com
Email: office@steyr-mannlicher.com

STOEGER INDUSTRIES
17601 Indian Head Hwy.
Accokeek, MD 20607-2501
Phone: 301-283-6981
Toll Free: 800-264-4962
Fax: 301-283-6988
Website: www.stoegerindustries.com

STONER RIFLE
Factory - please refer to Knight's Armament Co. listing.

STRATEGIC ARMORY CORPS, LLC
Please refer to Surgeon Rifles listing.

STURM, RUGER & CO., INC.
Headquarters
1 Lacey Place
Southport, CT 06490
Phone: 203-259-7843
Fax: 203-256-3367
Website: www.ruger.com
Service Center for Pistols, PC4 & PC9 Carbines
200 Ruger Road
Prescott, AZ 86301-6181
Phone: 928-778-6555
Fax: 928-778-6633
Website: www.ruger-firearms.com
Service Center for Revolvers, Long Guns & Ruger Date of Manufacture
411 Sunapee Street
Newport, NH 03773
Phone: 603-865-2442
Fax: 603-863-6165

SUN DEVIL MANUFACTURING LLC
663 West 2nd Avenue
Suite 16
Mesa, AZ 85210
Phone: 480-833-9876
Fax: 480-833-9509
Website: www.sundevilmfg.com
Email: sales@sundevilmfg.com

SUPERIOR ARMS
836 Weaver Blvd.
Wapello, IA 52653
Phone: 319-523-2016
Fax: 319-527-0188
Website: www.superiorarms.com
Email: sales@superiorarms.com

SURGEON RIFLES, INC.
23606 North 19th Ave.
Suite 10
Phoenix, AZ 85085
Phone: 623-780-1050
Toll Free: 800-401-7269
Website: www.surgeonrifles.com
Email: sales@surgeonrifles.

TNW FIREARMS INC.
P.O. Box 311
Vernonia, OR 97064
Phone: 503-429-5001
Fax: 503-429-3505
Website: www.tnwfirearms.com
Email: sales@tnwfirearms.com

TACTICAL ARMS MANUFACTURING, INC.
Huntersville, NC 28070
Phone: 704-200-2533
Fax: 978-215-8804
Website: www.tacticalarmsmfr.com

TACTICAL ARMZ
4451 E. Farm Road 132
Springfield, MO 65802
Phone: 417-883-9946
Website: www.tacticalarmz.com
Email: info@tacticalarmz.com

TACTICAL RIFLES
4918 Airport Rd.
Zephyrhills, FL 33542
Phone: 877-811-4867
Website: www.tacticalrifles.net
Email: info@tacticalrifles.net

TACTICAL SOLUTIONS
2772 S. Victory View Way
Boise, ID 83709
Phone: 866-333-9901
Fax: 208-333-9909
Website: www.tacticalsol.com

TACTICAL SUPPLY
1701 Garretson Lane
Yakima, WA 98903
Phone: 509-571-1449
Website: www.tacticalsupplier.com

TACTICAL WEAPONS
Please refer to FNH USA listing.

TALON ORDNANCE
P.O. Box 590
Madison, MS 39130
Phone: 601-856-3500 ext.228
Website: www.talonordnance.com
Email: contact@talonordnance.com

TAR-HUNT CUSTOM RIFLES, INC.
101 Dogtown Rd.
Bloomsburg, PA 17815-7544
Phone: 570-784-6368
Fax: 507-389-9150
Website: www.tarhunt.com
Email: sales@tarhunt.com

TAURUS INTERNATIONAL MANUFACTURING INC.
16175 NW 49th Ave.
Miami, FL 33014-6314
Phone: 305-624-1115
Fax: 305-623-7506
Website: www.taurususa.com

TAVOR
Importer – IWI US, Inc.
P.O. Box 126707
Harrisburg, PA 17112
Website: www.iwi.us
Email: info@iwi.us

TAYLOR'S & CO.
304 Lenoir Dr.
Winchester, VA 22603
Phone: 540-722-2017
Fax: 540-722-2018
Website: www.taylorsfirearms.com
Email: info@taylorsfirearms.com

TEMPLAR CUSTOM, LLC
P.O. Box 15
Apex, NC 27502
Phone: 919-629-8684
Website: www.templarcustom.com
Email: sales@templarcustom.com

TEMPLAR TACTICAL FIREARMS
P.O. Box 131595
Spring, TX 77393
Phone: 713-855-9874
Fax: 936-273-6652
Website: www.templartacticalfirearms.com
Email: templartactical@gmail.com

TEXAS BLACK RIFLE COMPANY
P.O. Box 1273
Shiner, TX 77984
Website: www.tbrci.com

TEXAS CUSTOM GUNS
208 E. Dumble
Alvin, TX 77511
Phone: 832-971-7140
Website: www.texascustomguns.net
Email: info@texascustomguns.net

THOMPSON
Please refer to the Kahr Arms listings.
Website: www.tommygun.com
Website: www.tommygunshop.com

THOMPSON/CENTER ARMS CO., INC.
2100 Roosevelt Avenue
Springfield, MA 01104
Customer Service Phone: 866-730-1614
Repair Only Phone: 866-730-1614
Fax: 603-30-8614
Website: www.tcarms.com
Email: tca@tcarms.com
Custom Shop - Fox Ridge Outfitters
P.O. Box 1700
Rochester, NH 03866
Toll Free: 800-243-4570

THOR GLOBAL DEFENSE GROUP
1206 Knesek Lane
Van Buren, AR 72956
Phone: 479-474-3434
Fax: 479-262-6925
Website: www.thorgdg.com

THUREON DEFENSE
2118 Wisconsin Ave.
P.O. Box 173
New Holstein, WI 53061
Phone: 920-898-5859
Fax: 920-898-5868
Website: www.thureondefense.com
Email: info@thureondefense.com

TIKKA
Importer - please refer to Beretta U.S.A. Corp. listing.
Factory - please refer to Sako listing.
Website: www.tikka.fi

TORNADO
Factory - AseTekno OY
Pälkäneentie 18/PL 94
FIN-00511 Helsinki, FINLAND
Fax: 011-358-9-753-6463
Website: www.asetekno.fi
Email: jaakko.vottonen@asetekno.fi

TRACKINGPOINT
3813 Helios Way, Suite 290
Pflugerville, TX 78660
Phone: 512-354-2114
Website: www.tracking-point.com
Email: info@tracking-point.com

TRADITIONS PERFORMANCE FIREARMS
1375 Boston Post Road
P.O. Box 776
Old Saybrook, CT 06475
Phone: 860-388-4656
Fax: 860-388-4657
Website: www.traditionsfirearms.com
Email: info@traditionsfirearms.com

TRANSFORMATIONAL DEFENSE INDUSTRIES, INC.
Please refer to Kriss USA listing.

TRISTAR ARMS INC.
1816 Linn St.
N. Kansas City, MO 64116
Phone: 816-421-1400
Fax: 816-421-4182
Website: www.tristararms.com
Email: tsaservice@tristararms.com

TROY DEFENSE
A division of Troy Industries
West Springfield, MA 01089
Phone: 866-788-6412
Fax: 413-383-0339
Website: www.troyind.com
Website: www.troydefense.com

TRUVELO MANUFACTURERS (PTY) LTD.
Factory - Truvelo Armoury
P.O. Box 14189
Lyttelton 0140 SOUTH AFRICA
Fax: 011-27-11-203-1848
Website: www.truvelo.co.za
Email: armoury@truvelo.co.za

U.S. MACHINE GUN ARMORY LLC
1914 East 9400 South
Sandy, UT 84093
Phone: 801-839-4683
Website: www.machinegunarmory.com
Email: sales@machinegunarmory.com

U.S. ORDNANCE
Commercial Distributor - see Desert Ordnance listing.

U.S. SPORTING GOODS
P.O. Box 560746
Rockledge, FL 32956
Phone: 321-639-4842
Fax: 321-639-7006
Website: www.ussginc.com
Email: ussg@eaacorp.com

UMAREX SPORTWAFFEN GmbH & CO. KG
Importer – Firearms - please refer to the Walther Arms, Inc. listing
Umarex USA (Airguns/Airsoft & Regent pistols)
7700 Chad Colley Blvd.
Ft. Smith, AR 72916
Phone: 479-646-4210
Fax: 479-646-4206
Website: www.umarexusa.com
Headquarters and Factory
Donnerfeld 2
D-59757 Arnsberg GERMANY
Fax: 011-49-2932-638224
Website: www.umarex.de

UNIQUE-ALPINE
Postfach 15 55
D-85435 Erding Bavaria GERMANY
Fax: 011-49-08122-9797-230
Website: www.unique-alpine.org
Email: info@unique-alpine.com

USA TACTICAL FIREARMS
933 Meacham Road
Statesville, NC 28677
Phone: 704-872-5150
Fax: 704-872-5122
Website: www.usatf.us

USELTON ARMS INC.
390 Southwinds Dr.
Franklin, TN 37064
Phone: 615-595-2255
Fax: 615-595-2254
Website: www.useltonarms.com

UTAS
Importer – UTAS USA
1247 Rand Road
Des Plaines, IL 60016
Phone: 847-768-1011
Fax: 847-768-1001
Website: www.utas-usa.com
Factory – UTAS Makine, Ltd.
Caglayan Mah., 2020 Sok. Uğur Apt.
No.:9/1 07230, Antalya, TURKEY
Fax: 011-90-242-323-6676
Website: www.utasturk.com

UZI
Importer (Centerfire)– IWI US, Inc.
P.O. Box 126707
Harrisburg, PA 17112
Website: www.iwi.us
Email: info@iwi.us
Importer (Rimfire)–Please refer to the Walther Arms, Inc. listing

UZKON ARMS LTD.
3651 Lindell Road Suite D488
Las Vegas, NV 89103
Phone: 1-702-326-7724
Website: www.uzkonusa.com
Email: info@uzkonusa.com

VALKYRIE ARMS LTD.
120 State Ave. NE, No. 381
Olympia, WA 98501
Phone/Fax: 360-482-4036
Website: www.valkyriearms.com
Email: info@valkyriearms.com

VALOR ARMS
2812 Riverview Road
Akron, OH 44313
Phone: 330-962-8269
Website: www.valorarms.us
Email: valorarms@gmail.com

VALTRO
Importer – Valtro USA
P.O. Box 56384
Hayward, CA 94545-6384
Phone: 510-489-8477
Website: www.valtrousa.com
Factory – Italian Arms Srl
Via de Gasperi 26/C,
25060 Collebeato (BS), ITALY
Fax: 011-39-030-2512545

VAN DYKE RIFLE DESIGNS
2324 17 RD
Plainville, KS 67663
Phone: 785-434-7577
Fax: 785-434-7517
Website: www.vandykerifles.com
Email: vandykerifles@yahoo.com

VECTOR ARMS INC.
270 West 500 North
N. Salt Lake, UT 84054
Phone: 801-295-1917
Fax: 801-295-9316
Website: www.vectorarms.com
Email: sales.vectorarms@gmail.com

VEPR. RIFLES
Importer – please refer to I.O., Inc. listing.
Importer – Krebs Custom
1000 North Rand Rd., Unit 106
Wauconda, IL 60084
Phone: 847-487-7776
Website: www.krebscustom.com
Importer – Mach 1 Arsenal
2404 East Broadway Ave., Suite B
Marysville, TN 37804
Phone: 865-982-3950
Website: www.mach1arsenal.com
Importer – Molot USA
P.O. Box 30664
Walnut Creek, CA
Phone: 775-200-1678
Website: www.molot-usa.com
Factory - MOLOT JSC
Vyatskie Polyany Machine Building Plant
135 Lenin St., Vyatski Polyany
RUS-612960 Kirov Region, RUSSIA
Fax: 011-007-83334-61832

VICTRIX ARMAMENTS
Rottigni Officina Meccanica S.r.l.
Via Giuseppe Mazzini 38/A – 24026
Brescia, ITALY
Phone: 011-39-035-7170111
Website: www.victrixarmaments.com
Email: info@victrixarmaments.com

VIGILANCE RIFLES
3795 N. Hwy 89 Ste. E
Chino Valley, AZ 86323
Phone: 877-884-4336
Website: www.vigilancerifles.com

VIKING ARMAMENT
2473 Commerce Blvd. #3
Grand Junction, CO 81505
Phone: 970-773-3494
Website: www.vikingarmament.com
Email: info@vikingarmament.com

VIPER
Please refer to Tristar listing.

VLTOR WEAPON SYSTEM
3735 N. Romero Road
Tucson, AZ 85705
Phone: 520-408-1944
Fax: 520-293-8807
Website: www.vltor.com
Email: sales@vltor.com

VOLKMANN PRECISION LLC
11160 S. Deer Creek Rd.
Littleton, CO 80127
Phone: 303-884-8654
Website: www.volkmannprecision.com
Email: volkmannprecision@yahoo.com

VOLQUARTSEN CUSTOM
P.O. Box 397
24276 240th St.
Carroll, IA 51401
Phone: 712-792-4238
Fax: 712-792-2542
Website: www.volquartsen.com
Email: info@volquartsen.com

WMD GUNS
3070 SE Dominica Terrace
Stuart, FL 34997
Phone: 772-324-9915
Website: www.wmdguns.com
Email: sales@wmdguns.com

WALTHER
Importer – Walther Arms, Inc.
7700 Chad Colley Boulevard
Fort Smith, AR 72916
Phone: 479-242-8500
Website: www.waltherams.com
*GSP/rifle conversion kits & factory repair station
– Repair - Earl's Repair Service, Inc.*
2414 Pulaski-Giles Turnpike (Rt. #100)
Pearisburg, VA 24131
Phone: 540-921-0184
Fax: 540-921-0183
Website: www.carlwalther.com
Email: info@carlwalther.com
*German Company Headquarters (Umarex)
Carl Walther Sportwaffen GmbH*
Donnerfeld 2
D-59757 Arnsberg GERMANY
Fax: 011-49-29-32-638149
Website: www.carl-walther.de
Email: sales@carl-walther.de
Factory - Carl Walther, GmbH Sportwaffenfabrik
Postfach 4325
D-89033 Ulm/Donau, GERMANY
Fax: 011-49-731-1539170

WAR SPORT
P.O. BOX 57,
Robbins, NC 27325
Website: www.warsport-us.com
Email: rick.landreth@warsport.com

WEATHERBY
1605 Commerce Way
Paso Robles, CA 93446
Technical Support: 805-227-2600
Service/Warranty: 800-227-2023
Fax: 805-237-0427
Website: www.weatherby.com

DAN WESSON FIREARMS
Distributor - please refer to CZ-USA listing.
Factory
5169 Highway 12 South
Norwich, NY 13815
Phone: 607-336-1174
Fax: 607-336-2730
Website: www.danwessonfirearms.com

WILD WEST GUNS, LLC.
7100 Homer Drive
Anchorage, AK 99518
Toll Free: 800-992-4570
Fax: 907-344-4005
Nevada Location
5225 Wynn Road
Las Vegas, NV 89118
Phone: 702-798-4570
Fax: 702-895-9850
Website: www.wildwestguns.com
Email: alaska@wildwestguns.com
Email: vegas@wildwestguns.com

WILSON COMBAT
2234 CR 719
P.O. Box 578
Berryville, AR 72616-0578
Toll Free: 800-955-4856
Fax: 870-545-3310
Website: www.wilsoncombat.com

WINCHESTER - REPEATING ARMS
Administrative Offices
275 Winchester Avenue
Morgan, UT 84050-9333
Customer Service Toll Free: 800-333-3288
Parts & Service Toll Free: 800-945-1392
Fax: 801-876-3737
Website: www.winchesterguns.com
Winchester Parts and Service
3005 Arnold Tenbrook Rd.
Arnold, MO 63010-9406
Toll Free: 800-322-4626
Fax: 636-287-9751

WINCHESTER/OLIN
Models 101 & 23 only (Disc.)
Attn: Shotgun Customer Service
427 N. Shamrock Street
East Alton, IL 62024
Fax: 618-258-3393
Website: www.winchester.com

WINDHAM WEAPONRY
999 Roosevelt Trail
Windham, ME 04062
Phone: 855-808-1888
Fax: 207-893-1632
Website: www.windhamweaponry.com

WOLF PERFORMANCE ARMS
P.O. Box 757
Placentia, CA 92871
Phone: 888-757-9653
Website: www.wolf-arms.com

WYOMING ARMS, LLC
3420 Big Horn Ave
Cody, WY 82414
Phone: 307-578-8821
Website: www.wyomingarms.com

XN ARMS INDUSTRY AND TRADE CO.
Hamidiye Mah. K. Sanayi Sitesi Sok. No. 21
42700 Beysehir/Konya TURKEY
Fax: 011-90-545-247-7394
Website: www.mka1919.com.tr.com
Email: info@xnarms.com

XTREME MACHINING
6506 Kylertown Drifting Hwy.
Drifting, PA 16834
Phone: 814-345-6290
Fax: 814-345-6292
Website: www.xtrememachining.biz
Email: xtrememachining@gmail.com

YANKEE HILL MACHINE CO., INC.
20 Ladd Ave., Ste. 1
Florence, MA 01062
Phone: 877-892-6533
Fax: 413-586-1326
Website: www.yhm.net

ZELENY SPORT s.r.o.
Slatina 116
56601 Vysoke Myto, CZECH REPUBLIC
Website: www.zelenysport.cz

ZENITH FIREARMS
10950 Rockfish Valley Highway
Suite C
Afton, VA 22920
Phone: 434-202-7790
Website: www.zenithfirearms.com
Email: info@zenithfirearms.com

ZOMBIE DEFENSE
8736 Landmark Road
Henrico, VA 23228
Phone: 804-972-3991
Fax: 804-716-1012
Website: www.zombie-defense.com
Email: info@zombie-defense.com

AMMUNITION TRADEMARK INDEX

AAA ARMS & AMMO
14717 Industrial Road
Omaha, NE 68144
www.aaa-ammo.com

ALS TECHNOLOGIES, INC.
4700 Providence Road.
Perry, FL 32347
www.lesslethal.com

ALEXANDER ARMS
US Army, Radford Arsenal
P.O. Box 1
Radford, VA 24143
www.alexanderarms.com

ALLEGIANCE AMMUNITION INC.
182 Camp Jacob Rd.
Clintwood, VA 24228
www.allegianceammo.com

ALLIANCE MACHINE LLC
1077 Mt. Gilead Road
Boonville, IN 47601

AMERICAN BULLET
P.O. Box 219
4360 East Hwy 30
Kimball, NE 69145
www.americanbullet.com

ANATOLIA CARTRIDGES COMPANY LTD.
Sanayi Cadddesi No. 110
Armutlu-Kemalpasa
Izmir, TR-35373
TURKEY
www.anatoliafisek.com.tr

AREX D.O.
Trubarjeva cesta 7
Sentjernej, 8310
SLOVENIA
www.arex.si

ARMAS Y CARTUCHOS DEL SUR S.L.
Ctra. HU-4403 Km. 1,200
Alosno (Huelva), E-21520
SPAIN
www.delsur.es

ARMS CORPORATION OF THE PHILIPPINES
6th Floor, Strata 100 Bldg.
Emerald Avenue
Ortigas Center
Pasig City, 1600
Philippines
www.armscor.com.ph

ATLANTA ARMS
7129 Wheat St. NE
Covington, GA 30014
www.atlantaarms.com

AUSTRALIAN DEFENSE INDUSTRIES
7 Murray Rose Ave.
Sydney Olympic Park
NSW 2127
AUSTRALIA
www.australian-munitions.com

AVCI CARTRIDGES
P.O. Box 5, Mustafa Ruso St. No.68
Nicosia, North Cyprus
TR00011 Mersin 10
TURKEY
www.avci-cartridges.com

AZOT
1 Rdultovskogo Square
Krasnozavodsk 141321
RUSSIA
www.azot-patron.ru

BARNES BULLETS
P.O. Box 620
Monda, UT 84645
www.barnesbullets.com

BARNAUL MACHINE TOOL PLANT
28 Kulagina St.
Barnaul 656002
RUSSIA
www.Barnaul.co.nz

BASCHIERI & PELLAGRI S.P.A.
Via frullo 26
Marano di Castenasco (BO) I-40055
ITALY
www.baschieri-pellagri.com

BECK AMMUNITION
Right to Bear Ammo.
6340 Lake Worth Blvd.
Suite 216
Ft. Worth, TX 76135
www.beckammunition.com

BITTEROOT VALLEY AMMO & COMPONENTS
3616 Eastside Highway
Stevensville, MT 59870

BLACK HILLS AMMUNITION
P.O. Box 3090
Rapid City, SD 57709-3090
www.black-hills.com

BORNAGHI S.R.L.
Via dei Giaggolo 189
57124 Livorno(LI)
ITALY
www.bornaghi.it

BRENNEKE GMBH
Ilmenauweg 2
30851 Langenhagen
GERMANY
www.brenneke.de

BUFFALO BORE AMMUNITION
366 Sandy Creek Road
Salmon, Idaho 83467
www.buffalobore.com

BUMAR SP. Z.O.O.
ZPS Pionki
Ul. Zakladowa 7
26-670 Pionki
POLAND
www.bumar.com

CAPTECH INTERNATIONAL
2441 Dakota Craft Drive
Rapid City, SD 57701
www.captechintl.com

CARTUCHOS SAGA S.A.
Caparrella, s/n
25192 Lleida
SPAIN
www.saga.es

CCC AMMO
1713 Meridian Court
Conroe, TX 77301

CCI AMMUNITION
2299 Snake River Ave.
Lewiston, ID 83501
www.cci-ammunition.com

CESARONI TECHNOLOGY INCORPORATED
P.O. Box 246
2561 Stouffville Rd.
Gormley, Ontario L0H 1G0
CANADA
www.cesaronitech.com

CHEDDITE FRANCE S.A.
Route de Lyon, 99/Box 112
Bourg-Les-Valence, F-26500
France
www.cheddite.com

CHEDDITE ITALY
Via del Giaggiolo 189
Livorno, 57124
ITALY
www.chedditeITALY.com

CHEYTAC, LLC
110 Eagle Avenue
Nashville, GA 31639
www.cheytac.com

CLEVER MIRAGE S.R.L.
Via A. De Legnago No. 9
37141 Ponte Florio Montorio (VR)
ITALY
www.clevervr.com

COMPANHIA BRASILEIRA DE CARTUCHOS
Av. Humberto de Campos, 3220 CEP
09426-900 Guapituba Ribeiro Pires/SP
BRAZIL
www.cbc.com.br

CONCHO CARTRIDGE COMPANY, INC.
P.O. Box 1430
San Angelo, TX 76902
www.conchocartridge.com

COR-BON/GLASER
1311 Industry Rd.
Sturgis, SD 57785
www.corbon.com

CROSSFIRE AMMUNITION
P.O. Box 13482
Akron, OH 44334
www.crossfireammunition.com

CUSTOM CARTRIDGE, INC.
84 East Ridge Road
Columbus, MT 59019
www.customcartridge.com

CUTTING EDGE BULLETS LLC
P.O. Box 248
Drifting, PA 16834
www.cuttingedgebullets.com

DDUPLEKS LTD.
Brivibas Gatve 197
Riga, LV-1039
Latvia
www.ddupleks.lv

DESERT TECH (DESERT TACTICAL ARMS)
P.O. Box 65816
Salt Lake City, UT 84165
www.deserttech.com

DOUBLE TAP AMMUNITION
646 S. Main St., #333
Cedar City, UT 84720
www.doubletapammo.com

DYNAMIC RESEARCH TECH.
405 N. Lyon Street
Grant City, MO 64456
www.drtammo.com

ELEY LIMITED
Selco Way
Minworth Industrial Estate
Sutton, Coldfield
West Midlands B76 1BA
ENGLAND
www.eleyammunition.com

ELEY HAWK LTD.
Selco Way, First Ave.
Minworth Industrial Estate
Sutton Coldfield
West Midlands B76 1BA
ENGLAND
www.eleyhawkltd.com

ELITE ENTERPRISES INC. DBA ELITE AMMUNITION
P.O. Box 639
Harvard, IL 60033
www.eliteammunition.net

ENGEL BALLISTIC RESEARCH, INC.
544 Alum Creek Road, Unit A
Smithville, TX 78957
www.ebrammo.com

ENVIRON-METAL INC.
1307 Clark Mill Rd.
Sweet Home, OR 97386
www.hevishot.com

ESTATE CARTRIDGE, INC.
900 Ehlen Dr.
Anoka, MN 55303
www.estatecartridge.com

EXTREME SHOCK USA
See Allegiance Ammunition Inc.

FAM - PIONKI LLC
Ul. Zakladowa 7
Pionki PL-26-670
POLAND
www.fam-pionki.pl

FEDERAL PREMIUM AMMUNITION
900 Ehlen Dr.
Anoka, MN 55303
www.federalpremium.com

FIOCCHI MUNIZIONI S.P.A.
Via Santa Barbara 4
23900 Lecco
ITALY
www.fiocchigfl.it

FIOCCHI USA
6930 N. Fremont Rd.
Ozark, MO 65721
www.fiocchiusa.com

G&L CALIBERS LTD
P.O. Box 22198
Nicosia, 1518
Cyprus
www.victorycartridges.com

GAMEBORE CARTRIDGE CO. LTD.
Great Union St.
Kingston-Upon-Hull HU9 1AR
ENGLAND
www.gamebore.com

GARRETT'S CARTRIDGE, INC.
1004 Long Road
Centralia, WA 98531
www.garrettcartridges.com

GEORGIA ARMS
P.O. Box 238
15 Industrial Court E.
Villa Rica, GA 30180
www.georgia-arms.com

GLAVPATRON CARTRIDGES LTD.
Marat 49
Tula RUS-300004
RUSSIA
www.glavpatron.ru

GOEX INC.
P.O. Box 659
Doyline, LA 71023
www.goexpowder.com

GORILLA AMMUNITION CO.
3895--39th Square
Vero Beach, FL 32960
www.gorillaammo.com

GRIZZLY CARTRIDGE CO.
See Rintoul Enterprises, LLC

GUREL HUNTING CARTRIDGES CO. LTD.
Sabanozu Saglik Mh.
Cilderesi Mevkii
Cankiri,
TURKEY
www.zuber.com.tr

GYTTORP AB
Riksvagen 15
360 44 Ingelstad
Sweden
www.gyttorp.se

HPR AMMUNITION
P.O. Box 2086
1304 W. Red Baron Rd.
Payson, AZ 85541
www.hprammo.com

HS MUNITIONS, INC.
4406 Rathbun Lane
Stevensville, MT 59870
www.thehuntingshack.com

HASLER BULLETS S.R.L.
Via Recchi 2
Como (CO) I-22100
ITALY
www.haslerbullets.com

HORNADY MANUFACTURING CO.
3625 West Old Potash Hwy
Grand Island, NE 68803
www.hornady.com

HULL CARTRIDGE CO. LTD.
Bontoft Ave., National Ave.
Hull, U.K.
www.hullcartridge.co.uk

IGMAN D.D.
Donje Polje 42
88400 Konjic
BOSNIA-HERZEGOVINA
www.igman.co.ba

IMPALA EUROPA
Dr. Karl Renner Str. 2b
Guntramsdorf A-2353
Austria
www.impalabullets.at

INDUSTRIAS TECNOS S.A. DE C.V.
Km. 6 carretera Cuernavaca a Tepoztlan
Cuernavaca, Mor. Mexico C.P. 62000
www.aguilaamo.com.mx

INTERNATIONAL CARTRIDGE CORP.
2273 Route 310
Reynoldsville, PA 15851
www.iccammo.com

ISRAEL MILITARY INDUSTRIES LTD (IMI)
Ramat Hasharon 4711001
Israel
www.imi-israel.com

JSC NOVOSIBIRSK LVE PLANT
(JSC Novosibirsk Cartridge Plant)
Stantsionnaya 30A
Novosibirsk 630108
RUSSIA
www.lveplant.ru

JAMES CALHOON
4343 U.S. Hwy. 87
Havre, MT 59501
www.jamescalhoon.com

JAMISON INTERNATIONAL V LLC
3551 Mayer Av.
Sturgis, SD 57785

KENT CARTRIDGE
P.O. Box 849
Kearneysville, WV 25430
www.kentgamebore.com

KRASNOZAVODSK CHEMICAL FACTORY
Moscow Region
Krasnovavodsk RUSS-141321
RUSSIA
www.khz-record.ru

KYNAMCO LTD.
The Old Railway Station, Station Road
Mildenhall, Suffolk IP28 7DT
U.K.
www.kynochammunition.co.uk

KYRGIAS M.G. S.A.
1 klm. Neochorouda turn
Neochorouda Thessaloniki, GR-54500
Greece

LAZZERONI ARMS COMPANY
P.O. Box 26696
Tucson, AZ 85726
www.lazzeroni.com

LEHIGH DEFENSE LLC
130 Penn Am Drive, Suite D-1
Quakertown, PA 18951
www.lehighdefense.com

LIGHTFIELD AMMUNITION CORP.
P.O. Box 162
Adelphia, NJ 07710
www.litfld.com

LUGANSK CARTRIDGE WORKS
Pochtova Str. 1M
Lugansk, 91055
UKRAINE
www.lcw.lg.ua

LYALVALE EXPRESS LTD.
Express Estate
Fisherwick Nr. Whittington
Lichfield WS13 8XA
ENGLAND
www.lyalvaleexpress.com

MFS 2000 INC.
Magyar Loszergyarto ZRt.
3332 Sirok, Pf. 9
Hungary

MAGSAFE AMMO, INC.
4700 So. U.S. Hwy. 17-92
Casselberry, FL 32707
www.magsafeonline.com

MAGTECH AMMUNITION
248 Apollo Dr. #180
Lino Lakes, MN 55014
www.magtechammunition.com

MAKINA VE KIMYA ENDUSTRISI KURUMU
Tandogan TR-06330
Ankara,
TURKEY
www.mkek.gov.tr

MAST TECHNOLOGY INC.
P.O. Box 1026
Blue Springs, MO 64013
www.masttechnology.com

MASTERCAST BULLET COMPANY
292 Anderson Road
Enon Valley, PA 16120
www.mastercast.net

MAXAM OUTDOORS S.A.
Avenida del Partenon, 16 bajo
Madrid, E-28042
SPAIN
www.maxam.net

MCMILLAN GROUP INTERNATIONAL
1638 West Knudsen Drive, Suite 101
Phoenix, AZ 85027
www.mcmillanusa.com

MELIOR S.L.
P.O. Box 46
Lerida 25080
SPAIN
www.melior-icc.com

MESKO S.A.
Zaklady Metalowe
Ul. Legionow 122
Skarzysko-Kamienna PL-26111
POLAND

METALLWERK ELISENHUTTE GMBH NASSAU (MEN)
10 Elisenhutte
Nassau/Lahn D-56377
GERMANY
Men-info@elisenhuette.de
www.men-defencetec.de

NAMMO LAPUA OY
P.O. Box 5
Lapua FIN-62101
FINLAND
www.lapua.com

NIKE FIOCCHI SPORTING AMMUNITION LTD.
Lajos Street 78
H-1036 Budapest
Hungary
www.nike-fiocchi.hu

NITRO AMMUNITION COMPANY
7560 Newkirk road
Mountain Grove, MO 65711
www.nitrocompany.com

NITRON S.A.
Zaklady Tworzyw Sztucznych
Krupski Mlyn PL-42693
POLAND

NOBEL SPORT S. A.
57 Rue Pierre Charron
Paris F-75181
France
www.nobelsport.fr

NOBEL SPORT ESPANA S.A.
Apartado 428
Villacil (Leon), E-24080
SPAIN
www.excopesa.com/nobel

NOBEL SPORT ITALIA S.R.L.
Via di Palazzetto 7/11
San Giuliano (PI) I-56017
ITALY
www.nobelsport.it

NORMA PRECISION AB
Jagargatan
SE-67040 Amotfors
Sweden
www.norma.cc

NORTHWEST S.R.L.
Via Pontevecchio, 57
Carasco (GE) I-16042
ITALY
www.northwest-ammo.com

NOSLER, INC.
107 SW Columbia St.
Bend, OR 97702
www.nosler.com

NOVOSIBIRSK MECHANICAL PLANT "ISKRA" OJSC
8 Chekalin Str.
Novosibirsk 630900
RUSSIA
www.nmz-iskra.ru

OJSC "THE TULA CARTRIDGE WORKS"
47-b Marata Str.
Tula, 300004
RUSSIA
www.en.tulammo.ru

OLD WESTERN SCOUNGER/ NAVY ARMS
219 Lawn St.
Martinsburg, WV 25401
www.ows-ammo.com

OZKURSAN LTD.
Maltepe Mah.
Cifte Havuzlar Is Merkezi Kat:3 No. 701
TR-34010 Bayrampasa- Istanbul
TURKEY
www.ozkursan.com.tr

PCP AMMUNITION CO.
3895--39th Square
Vero Beach, FL 32960
www.pcpammo.com

PNW ARMS LLC
1293 East Freeze Rd.
Potlatch, ID 83855
www.pnwarms.com

P. GAVRIELIDES LTD
P.O. Box 40217,6302
Larnaka, CYPRUS
www.olympia.com.cy

PEGORARO SPORT S.R.L.
Via F.lli Bandiera 2
Dolo (VE) I-30031
ITALY
www.pegorarosport.com

PINEY MOUNTAIN AMMUNITION CO.
122 Crest View Dr.
Cleveland, GA 30528
pineymountainammunitionco.com

POBJEDA TECHNOLOGY GORAZDE
Visegradska BB
73000 Gorazde
BOSNIA HERZEGOVINA
www.pobjeda-technology.com

POLYWAD, INC.
P.O. Box 396
Roberta, GA 31078
www.polywad.com

POONGSAN METALS CORP. (PMC)
Keuk Dong Bldg.
60-1 Chungmuro
Chung-ku
Seoul 100-705
Korea
www.poongsan.co.kr
www.pmcammo.com

PRECISION CARTRIDGE, INC.
940 Georgiana St.
Hobart, IN 46342
www.precisioncartridge.com

PRECISION DELTA CORPORATION
P.O. Box 128
Ruleville, MS 38771
www.precisiondelta.com

PRETORIA METAL PRESSINGS (PMP)
Div. of Denel Ltd.
Private Bag X334
Pretoria, 0001
Republic of South Africa
www.pmp.co.za

PROGRADE AMMO
3616 Eastside Hwy.
Stevensville, MT 59870
www.ammoland.com

PRVI PARTIZAN
Milosa Obrenovica 2
Uzice YU-31000
Serbia
www.prvipartizan.com

QUALITY CARTRIDGE
P.O. Box 445
Hollywood, MD 20636
www.qual-cart.com

RBCD PERFORMANCE PLUS
1538 SE Military Drive, Suite 206
San Antonio, TX 78214

REMINGTON ARMS CO.
P.O. Box 700
Madison, NC 27025
www.remington.com

RINTOUL ENTERPRISES, LLC
Grizzly Cartridge Co.
30201 Carmel Road
P.O. Box 1466
Rainier, OR 97048
www.grizzlycartridge.com

RUAG USA
5402 East Diana St.
Tampa, FL 33610
www.ruag-usa.com

RUAG AMMOTEC AG (RWS, NORMA, DYNAMIT NOBEL, HIRTENBERGER, GECO, ROTTWEIL, SWISS MATCH)
Kronacher Strasse 63
90765 Furth
Germany
www.ruag.com

SBR AMMUNITION
140 Indigo Dr.
Brunswick, GA 31525
www.sbrammunition.com

SAGE CONTROL ORDNANCE
3455 Kings Corner Rd.
Oscoda, MI 48750
www.sageinternationalltd.com

SAKO, LTD.
P.O. Box 149
Riihimaki, FI-11101
Finland
www.sako.fi

SAX MUNITIONS GMBH
Auer Strasse 11
Stollberg D-09366
GERMANY
www.sax-munition.de

SELLIER & BELLOT JSC
Licicka 667
Vlasim CZ-25813
Czech Republic
www.sellier-bellot.cz

SHOOTER'S PRO SHOP
107 SW Columbia St
Bend, OR 97702
www.shootersproshop.com

SIG SAUER INC.
72 Pease Blvd.
Newington, NH 03801
www.sigsauer.com

SIMUNITION OPERATIONS
P.O. Box 576
Avon, CT 06001
www.simunition.com

SINTERFIRE
200 Industrial Park rd.
Kersey, PA 15846
www.sinterfire.com

SOTIRIOS NAFPLIOTIS A.B.E.E.
P.O. Box 8- Eleon
Thiva, GR-32200
Greece

SPEER
2299 Snake River Ave.
Lewiston, ID 83501
www.speer-bullets.com.

SRC ARMS(SHARPS RIFLE CO)
1195 U.S. Hwy 20-26-87
Glenrock, WY 82637
Website: www.srcarms.com

STILLWOOD AMMUNITION SYSTEMS LLC
3308 Lee Ave.
Sanford, NC 27332
www.stillwoodammo.com

SUDDESTSCHE HULSENMANUFAKTUR
Am Zieget 5
Regensburg D093051
GERMANY
www.huelsenmanufaktur.de

SUPERIOR AMMUNITION, INC.
20788 Mossy Oak Place
Sturgis, SD 57785
www.superiorammo.com

SUPERIOR BALLISTICS, INC.
c/o Mic McPherson
10725 Road 24.4 Loop
Cortez, CO 81321

SWIFT BULLET COMPANY
One Thousand One Swift Avenue
P.O. Box 27
Quinter, KS 67752
www.swiftbullets.com

TMB DESIGNS
Highgrove Farm Industrial Estate
Unit 18
Pinvin Nr Pershore
Worcestershire WR10 2LF
UNITED KINGDOM
www.tmbdesigns.co.uk

TAKHO AMMUNITION
Baku Str. 9
Kherson City 73009
UKRAINE
www.takho.ua

TEN-X AMMUNITION
8722 Lanyard Court
Rancho Cucamonga, CA 91763
www.tenxammo.com

THIFAN INDUSTRIE S.A.R.L.
275 Rue de Malitorne, B.P. 61
18230 St. Doulchard
France
www.sauvestre.com

TOP BRASS, INC.
10325 Co. Rd. 120
Salida, CO 81201
www.topbrass-inc.com

TRAJECTORY TECHNOLOGIES, INC.
3765 Round Bottom Rd.
Newtown, OH 45244
www.trajetech.com

TRUST EIBARRES S.A.
Murrategui 9 (Azitain)
P.O. Box 32
Eibar ES-20600
SPAIN
www.cartuchostrust.com

TURAC, LTD. STI.
Tandogan Meydani Anit Cad. No. 8/15
Cankaya, Ankara
TURKEY
www.turac.com.tr

TURAN AV MALZEMELERI LTD. STI.
Uzumlu Mahallesi
Beysehir, Konya
TURKEY
www.turansilah.com

UEE CARTUCHERIA DEPORTIVA S.A.
Avda. del Partenon, 16 bajo
28042 Madrid - Espana
SPAIN

ULTRAMAX AMMUNITION
2112 Elk Vale Rd.
Rapid City, SD 57701
www.ultramaxammunition.com

ULYANOVSK MACHINERY PLANT SUE, PA
2 Metallistov St.
Ulyanovsk RUSS-32007
RUSSIA

WEATHERBY, INC.
1605 Commerce Way
Paso Robles, CA 93446
www.weatherby.com

WINCHESTER DIV.
Olin Corp.
Shamrock St.
East Alton, IL 62024
www.winchester.com

WOLF PERFORMANCE AMMUNITION
P.O. Box 757
Placentia, CA 92871
www.wolfammo.com

YAVASCALAR A.S.
Ataturk Mah. Badirma Cad N 49
Balikesir, TR-10100
Turkey
www.yavascalar.tr

YAVUZCAN FISEK SANAYI (YFS)
Golgeli Kaya Mevkii Hakimler Koyu girisi No. 4
Lalhan, Mamak 06270
Ankara,
TURKEY

ZERO AMMUNITION CO. INC
P.O. box 1188
Cullman, AL 35056
www.zerobullets.com

ACCESSORIES TRADEMARK INDEX

The following listings represent manufacturers and companies which specialize in making optics, magazines, upper and lower receivers, stocks, forends/forearms, slides, iron sights, trigger groups, weapon lights, laser sights, accessory rails, metal finishes, slings, and other accessories which enhance the functionality of tactical firearms.

5 STAR FIREARMS
Billet aluminum revolver speedloaders for 9mm, .327 Mag., .38/.357 Mag. (5,6,7, and 8 shot), .410/.45 Judge, .44 Spl./Mag., .45 Colt, .454 Casull, .460 & .500 S&W.
41666 N. Sheridan Road
Zion, IL 60099
Website: www.5starfirearms.com
Phone: 847-731-7808
Fax.: 847-731-7899

A.R.M.S. INC.
Mounting systems for day optics, night vision, thermal imagers, lasers, and lights, detachable iron sights.
230 West Center St
West Bridgewater, MA 02379
Website: www.armsmounts.com
Phone: 508-584-7816
Fax: 508-588-8045

ACCUSHOT B&T INDUSTRIES, LLC
Atlas bipods, monopods.
P.O. Box 771071
Wichita, KS 67277
Website: www.accu-shot.com
Email: sales@accu-shot.com
Phone: 316-721-3222
Fax: 316-721-1021

ACE LTD. USA
Modular folding stocks, sling mounts, vertical foregrips.
P.O. Box 430
Winchester, KY 40391
Website: www.riflestocks.com
Toll Free: 888-736-7725
Fax: 859-745-4638

ACT-MAG SRL
Pistol and rifle magazines.
Via Sardegna, 5/F I-25069
Villa Carcina, Brescia Italy
Website: www.act-mag.com
Phone: 011-390308980035
Fax: 011-390308988833

ADAMS INDUSTRIES, INC.
Night vision and thermal imaging products.
P.O. Box 641413
Los Angeles, CA 90064
Website: www.adamsindustries.com
Phone: 310-472-3017

ADCO ARMS CO., INC.
Riflescopes and red dot sights.
4 Draper Street
Woburn, MA 01801
Website: www.adcosales.com
Phone: 781-935-1799
Fax: 781-935-1011

ADDAX TACTICAL
1431 Truman Street, Unit E
San Fernando, CA 91340
Website: www.addaxtactical.com
Email: sales@addaxtactical.com
Phone: 818-361-5008

ADVANCED ARMAMENT CORPORATION
Suppressors, flash hiders, muzzle brakes, compensators, and adaptors.
1434 Hillcrest Rd
Norcross, GA 30093 USA
Website: www.advanced-armament.com
Phone: 770-925-9988
Fax: 256-327-2851

ADVANCED TECHNOLOGY INTERNATIONAL
Injection-molded synthetic gunstocks and accessories.
W60 N171 Cardinal Ave.
Cedarburg, WI 53012
Website: www.atigunstocks.com
Email: info@atigunstocks.com
Phone: 800-925-2522
Fax: 414-464-3112

ADVANTAGE TACTICAL SIGHT
"Pyramid Sight Picture" adjustable metallic sights for handguns, rifles, and shotguns.
Wrentech Industries, LLC
7 Avenida Vista Grande B-7, Suite 510
Santa Fe, NM 87508
Website: www.advantagetactical.com
Phone: 505-466-1811
Fax: 505-466-4735

AE LIGHT
HID and LED lights.
Allsman Enterprises, LLC
P.O. Box 1869
Rogue River, OR 97537
Website: www.aelight.com
Phone: 541-471-8988
Fax: 541-299-0360

AIMPOINT, INC.
Electro-optical red dot sights.
14103 Mariah Ct
Chantilly, VA 20151
Website: www.aimpoint.com
Email: sales@aimpoint.com
Phone: 703-263-9795
Fax: 703-263-9463

AIMSHOT
Laser and red dot sights, weapon lights, and mounting systems.
340 Dewpoint Lane
Alpharetta, GA 30022
Website: www.aimshot.com
Phone: 770-840-8039
Fax: 770-840-0269

AIM SPORTS, INC.
Tactical optics, lasers, muzzle brakes, bipods.
1219 E. Locust Street
Ontario, CA 91761
Website: www.aimsportsinc.com
Email: customerservice@aimsportinc.com
Phone: 909-923-2228

AIMTECH MOUNT SYSTEMS
Scope mounting systems for handguns, shotguns, and rifles.
P.O. Box 223
Thomasville, GA 31799
Website: www.aimtech-mounts.com
Phone: 229-226-4313
Fax: 229-227-0222

AJAX GRIPS, LLC
American made weapon grips.
Carrollton, TX 75247
Website: www.ajaxgrips.com

AKER INTERNATIONAL INC
Holsters
2248 Main Street, Suite 6
Chula Vista, CA 91911
Website: www.akerleather.com
Phone: 619-423-5182

ALL STAR TACTICAL
AR-15 parts, accessories, and tools.
1249 Ridgeway Ave., Suite N
Rochester, NY 14615
Phone: 585-324-0345
Website: www.allstartactical.com
Email: info@allstartactical.com

ALOT ENTERPRISE CO. LTD.
Optics
1503 Eastwood Center
5 A Kung Ngam Village Road
Shaukeiwan, Hong Kong
Website: www.alothk.com
Phone: +852 25199728

ALTAMONT COMPANY
Pistol grips and rifle stocks.
901 North Church Street
P.O. Box 309
Thomasboro, IL 61878
Website: www.altamontco.com
Email: sales@altamontco.com
Toll Free: 800-626-5774

ALUMAGRIPS
Ultra high quality handgun grips.
2851 North 34th Place
Mesa, AZ 85213
Website: www.alumagrips.com
Email: sales@alumagrips.com
Phone: 602-294-2390

AMEGA RANGES, INC.
Picatinny rail systems for Mini-14, M14, M1 Garand, M1 Carbine rifles, and Remington 870 shotguns, and tactical weapon light mounts.
6355 Stinson #202
Plano, TX 75093
Website: www.amegaranges.com
Phone: 888-347-0200

AMELON COATINGS, LLC
Micro Slick permanent lubricating firearm component coating.
227 Mount Olive Road
Amherst, VA 24521
Website: www.ameloncoatings.com
Phone: 434-946-5157
Fax: 434-946-5159

AMERICAN BODY ARMOR
13386 International Parkway
Jacksonville, FL 32218
Website: www.safariland.com
Toll Free: 800-347-1200

AMERICAN DEFENSE MFG.
Mounting solutions, firearms.
2525 S. 162nd Street
New Berlin, WI 53151
Website: www.adm-mfg.com
Phone: 262-780-9831

AMERICAN RIFLE COMPANY
Bolt actions, scope rings and mounts.
22604 58th Place S.
Kent, WA 98032
Website: www.americanrifle.com
Phone: 206-226-4387

AMERICAN SPIRIT ARMS
AR15 style uppers, lowers, barrels, parts and accessories.
16001 North Greenway-Hayden Loop, Suite B
Scottsdale, AZ 85260
Website: www.americanspiritarms.com
Phone: 480-367-9540
Fax: 480-367-9541

AMERICAN TACTICAL INC.
Tactical equipment and accessories.
231 Deming Way
Summerville, SC 29483
Website: www.americantactical.us
Phone: 800-290-0065

AMERICAN TECHNOLOGIES NETWORK, CORP.
Night vision and thermal imaging systems, tactical lights.
1341 San Mateo Ave
South San Francisco, CA 94080
Website: www.atncorp.com
Phone: 650-989-5100
Fax: 650-875-0129

AMERIGLO
Tritium self-luminous sights for pistols, rifles, and shotguns.
645 Hembree Pkwy, Suite K
Roswell, GA 30076
Website: www.ameriglo.com
Phone: 470-223-4163

AMMUNITION STORAGE COMPONENTS
150 Production Court
New Britain, CT 06051
Phone: 860-225-3548

AM-TAC PRECISION
See Trademark Index

ANZIO IRONWORKS CORP.
See Trademark Index

AR57/57CENTER
5.7x28mm caliber uppers for AR15 style rifles.
8525 152nd Avenue NE
Redmond, WA 98052
Website: www.57center.com
Phone: 888-900-5728

AREA51 PRODUCTS
Tactical weapon accessories.
5775 Montgomery Hwy., Suite 4
Dotham, AL 36303
Website: www.area51tactical.com
Phone: 334-873-4150

ARES DEFENSE SYSTEMS, INC.
See Trademark Index

ARMAMENT DYNAMICS INDUSTRIES LLC
AR15 ambidextrous charging handle.
10903 W. 84th Place
Arvada, CO 80005-5219
Phone: 303-868-6314

ARMAMENT TECHNOLOGY, INC.
ELCAN Optical Technologies sighting systems and related equipment.
3045 Robie Street, Suite 113
Halifax, Nova Scotia, B3K4P6 Canada
Website: www.armament.com
Phone: 902-454-6384
Fax: 902-454-4641

ARMASIGHT INC.
Night vision, thermal imaging, and laser devices.
815 Dubuque Av.
San Francisco, CA 94080
Website: www.armasight.com
Phone: 888-959-2259

ARMATAC INDUSTRIES INC.
150 round capacity dual drum "SAW-MAG"; 78 round capacity dual drum "SAW-LITE" AR15/M16 magazines.
836 Weaver Blvd.
Wapello, IA 32653
Website: www.armatac.com
Phone: 319-523-6046
Fax: 319-527-0188

ARMORWORKS & ATV CORP.
Body, vehicle & aircraft armor
33 South 56th Street
Chandler, AZ 85226
Website: www.armorworks.com
Phone: 480-517-1150

ARMS TECH, LTD.
Suppressors
5025 North Central Avenue, Suite 459
Phoenix, AZ 85012
Website: www.armstechltd.com
Phone: 623-936-1510
Fax: 623-936-0361

ARMYTEK OPTOELECTRONICS INC.
Flashlights & related accessories
57 Vandervoort Drive
Richmond Hill, Ontario, Canada L4E0C7
Website: www.armytek.com
Phone: 347-650-2100

ARREDONDO ACCESSORIES
AR15 and handgun action shooting/3 gun competition accessories.
2984-F First Street
La Verne, CA 91750
Website: www.arredondoaccessories.com
Phone: 909-596-9597
Fax: 909-596-3496

ASE UTRA
S Series, jet-Z, Northstar, and DUAL suppressors.
Rahkeentie 6
80100 Joensuu, Finland
Website: www.aseutra.fi
Phone: 010 4238810
Fax: 013 227347

ASHBURY INTERNATIONAL GROUP INC.
Mfr. of SABER FORSST modular rifle chassis, electro-optical weapon mounts, TACT3 field tripod.
P.O. Box 8024
Charlottesville, VA 22906
Website: www.AshburyPrecisionOrdnance.com

ASP, INC.
Weapon lights.
2511 East Capitol Dr
Appleton, WI 54911
Website: www.asp-usa.com
Phone: 800-236-6243
Fax: 800-236-8601

ATN
See AMERICAN TECHNOLOGIES NETWORK, CORP.

ATS, INC. (ADVANCED TRAINING SYSTEMS)
Live fire shooting ranges
4524 Highway 61 North
St. Paul, MN 55110
Phone: 651.429.8091
Website: www.atsusa.biz
Email: info@atsusa.biz

AWC SYSTEMS TECHNOLOGY
.22 to .50 BMG caliber suppressors for pistols, submachine guns, and rifles.
1515 West Deer Valley Road, Suite A-105
Phoenix, AZ 85027
Website: www.awcsystech.com
Phone: 623-780-1050
Fax: 623-780-2967

BADGER BARRELS, INC.
Cut-rifled and hand-lapped target-grade barrels.
8330 196 Avenue, P.O. Box 417
Bristol, WI 53104
Website: www.badgerbarrelsinc.com
Phone: 262-857-6950
Fax: 262-857-6988

BADGER ORDNANCE
Military grade rifle actions, mounting systems, rails, and scope rings.
1209 Swift Street
North Kansas City, MO 64116
Website: www.badgerordance.com
Phone: 816-421-4958
Fax: 816-421-4958

BARNES PRECISION MACHINE, INC.
AR15 style receivers, parts, and accessories.
2276 Farmington Road
Apex, NC 27523
Website: www.barnesprecision.com
Phone: 919-362-6805
Fax: 919-362-5752

BARSKA OPTICS
Riflescopes and accessories.
1721 Wright Avenue
La Verne, CA 91750
Website: www.barska.com
Phone: 909-445-8168
Fax: 909-445-8169

BATTLE ARMS DEVELOPMENT, INC.
AR10/AR15 ambidextrous safety levers.
P.O. Box 92742
Henderson, NV 89009
Website: www.battlearmsdevelopment.com
Email: sales@battlearmsdevelopment.com
Phone: 702-802-3588
Fax: 702-948-4472

BATTLECOMP ENTERPRISES, LLC
Battlecomp tactical compensators and Midnight Mounts.
101 Hickey Blvd., Suite A455
South San Francisco, CA 94080
Website: www.battlecomp.com
Phone: 650-678-0778

BCI DEFENSE
Suppressors.
545 N. Bowen Av.
Bremen, IN 46506
Website: www.bcidefense.com
Phone: 855-866-2243

BEAMSHOT-QUARTON USA, INC.
Laser sighting systems.
5805 Callaghan Road, Suite 102
San Antonio, TX 78228
Website: www.beamshot.com
Phone: 210-735-0280
Fax: 210-735-1326

BELL AND CARLSON, INC.
Hand-laminated fiberglass, carbon fiber, and aramid fiber rifle and shotgun stocks and accessories.
101 Allen Road
Dodge City, KS 67801
Website: www.bellandcarlson.com
Phone: 620-225-6688
Fax: 620-225-9095

B.E. MEYERS & CO.
"OWL" night vision scopes, "GLARE" non-lethal lasers, "IZLID" targeting/illuminating lasers.
14540 NE. 91st St.
Redmond, WA 98052
Website: www.bemeyers.com
Phone: 425-881-6648
Fax: 425-867-1759

BERGARA BARRELS
Barrels, scope mount systems, and rifle slings.
5988 Peachtree Corners East
Norcross, GA 30071
Website: www.bergarabarrels.com
Phone: 770-449-4687
Fax: 770-242-8546

BETA COMPANY, THE
"BETA C-MAG" dual drum magazines.
2137 B Flintstone Drive
Tucker, GA 30084
Website: www.betaco.com
Phone: 800-669-2382
Fax: 770-270-0559

BIRCHWOOD CASEY, LLC
Shooting and gun care products
7887 Fuller Road, Suite 100
Eden Prairie, MN 55344
Website: www.birchwoodcasey.com
Toll Free: 800-Shoot-N-C (746-6862)
Fax: 952-388-6718
Email: customerservice@birchwoodcasey.com

BIRDSONG MANUFACTURING LLC
AR-15 platforms, weapons components and suppressors
1430 Monterey Road
Florence, MS 39073
Website: www.birdsongmfg.com
Phone: 601-398-1125

BKL TECHNOLOGIES INC.
Scope mounts
P.O. Box 2478
Fort Worth, TX 76113
Website: www.bkltech.com
Phone: 817-451-8966

BLACK WEAPONS ARMORY
See Trademark Index

BLACKHAWK PRODUCTS GROUP
Rifle and shotgun stocks, slings, tactical accessories.
6160 Commander Parkway
Norfolk, VA 23502
Website: www.blackhawk.com
Phone: 800-694-5263
Fax: 757-436-3088

BLACKTHORNE PRODUCTS, LLC
AR-15, AK47 and Galil parts and accessories
P.O. Box 2441
Inver Grove Heights, MN 55076
Website: www.blackthorneproducts.com
Phone: 952-232-5832
Fax: 912-964-7701

BLUE FORCE GEAR INC.
Vickers Combat Applications Sling and weapon accessories.
P.O. Box 853
Pooler, GA 31322
Website: www.blueforcegear.com
Phone: 877-430-2583

BOYDS GUNSTOCK INDUSTRIES, INC.
Walnut and birch laminate replacement stocks.
25376 403rd Ave
Mitchell, SD 57301
Website: www.boydsgunstocks.com
Phone: 605-996-5011
Fax: 605-996-9878

BRESSER-EXPLORE SCIENTIFIC
Optics
621 Madison
Springdale, AR 72762
Website: www.bresser.com
Phone: 866-252-3811

BRILEY MANUFACTURING, INC.
1911 style pistol accessories.
1230 Lumpkin Road
Houston, TX 77043
Phone: 800-381-5718
Fax: 713-932-1043

BRITE-STRIKE TECHNOLOGIES, INC.
Tactical weapon lights.
26 Wapping Road, Jones River Industrial Park
Kingston, MA 02364
Website: www.brite-strike.com
Phone: 781-585-5509
Fax: 781-585-5332

BROWNELLS MIL/LE SUPPLY GROUP
Worldwide distributor of armorer's tools, accessories, and OEM parts.
200 South Front Street
Montezuma, IA 50171
Website: www.brownells.com
Phone: 641-623-5401
Fax: 641-623-3896

BSA OPTICS
Riflescopes and red dot sights.
3911 Southwest 47th Avenue, Suite 914
Ft. Lauderdale, FL 33314
Website: www.bsaoptics.com
Phone: 954-581-2144
Fax: 954-581-3165

B-SQUARE
Rings, bases, rail mounting systems.
13387 International Pkwy
Jacksonville, FL 32218
Phone: 904-741-5400
Fax: 904-741-5404

BUFFER TECHNOLOGIES
Recoil buffers for rifles and pistols.
P.O. Box 105047
Jefferson City, MO 65110
Website: www.buffertech.com
Phone: 877-6-BUFFER
Fax: 573-634-8522

BULLDOG BARRELS, LLC
OEM barrel blanks and finished barrels.
106 Isabella Street, 4 North Shore Center Suite 110
Pittsburgh, PA 15212
Website: www.bulldogbarrels.com
Phone: 412-322-2747
Fax: 412-322-1912

BURRIS COMPANY, INC.
Riflescopes, red dot sights, rings, and bases.
331 East 8th Street
Greeley, CO 80631
Website: www.burrisoptics.com
Phone: 970-356-1670
Fax: 970-356-8702

BUSHNELL OUTDOOR PRODUCTS
Riflescopes, red dot sights.
9200 Cody Street
Overland Park, KS 66214
Website: www.unclemikesle.com
Toll Free: 800-423-3537
Fax: 913-752-3550

BUTLER CREEK CORP.
Magazines, replacement barrels, and stocks.
9200 Cody Street
Overland Park, KS 66214
Website: www.butlercreek.com
Toll Free: 800-423-3537
Fax: 913-752-3550

BUTTON SLING, INC.
Single point shooting slings.
2913 Northwest 5th Street
Blue Springs, MO 64014
Website: www.buttonsling.com
Phone: 816-419-8100
Fax: 816-224-4040

C PRODUCTS, LLC
AR platform rifle magazines.
30 Elmwood Court
Newington, CT 06111
Website: www.cproductsllc.com
Phone: 860-953-5007
Fax: 860-953-0601

CADEX INC/CADEX DEFENSE
Rifle stocks, scope mounts, other mission essential accessories.
755 Avenue Montrichard
Saint-Jean-Sur-Richelieu
Quebec J2X 5K8 CANADA
Website: www.cadexdefense.com
Phone: 450-348-6774

CALIFORNIA COMPETITION WORKS
AR-15 accessories & parts
P.O. Box 4821
Culver City, CA 90232
Website: www.demooner.com
Phone: 310-895-0736

CAMMENGA COMPANY, LLC
Rifle magazines, AR15 rifle parts.
2011 Bailey Street
Dearborn, MI 48124
Website: www.cammenga.com
Phone: 313-914-7160
Fax: 616-392-9432

CAROLINA PRECISION ARMS LLC
Suppressors.
2725 N. Church St.
Rocky Mount, NC 27804
Phone: 252-904-0721

CASPIAN ARMS, LTD.
1911 pistol components, replacement slides for Glock pistols.
75 Cal Foster Drive
Wolcott, VT 05680
Website: www.caspianarms.com
Phone: 802-472-6454
Fax: 802-472-6709

CENTURY INTERNATIONAL ARMS, INC.
Importer of firearms parts and accessories.
430 South Congress Drive, Suite 1
Delray Beach, FL 33445
Website: www.centuryarms.com
Phone: 800-527-1252
Fax: 561-265-4520

CERAKOTE
See NIC INDUSTRIES, INC.

CHAMPION TRAPS & TARGETS
Clay and interactive targets
1 Vista Way
Anoka, MN 55303
Website: www.championtarget.com
Phone Number: 800-379-1732

CHECK-MATE INDUSTRIES, INC.
1911, Beretta 92, M-14, and other firearm magazines.
777 Mount Av.
Wyandanch, NY 11798
Website: www.checkmateindustries.com
Phone: 631-491-1777
Fax: 631-491-1745

CHIP MCCORMICK CUSTOM, LLC
Extra-capacity 1911 pistol magazines, AR-15 match and tactical trigger groups.
105 Sky King Drive
Spicewood, TX 78669
Website: www.cmcmags.com
Phone: 830-798-2863
Fax: 830-693-4975

CHOATE MACHINE & TOOL
Polymer fixed and folding stocks, and accessories for rifles and shotguns.
116 Lovers Lane
Bald Knob, AR 72010
Website: www.riflestock.com
Phone: 501-724-6193
Fax: 501-724-5873

CHRISTIE'S PRODUCTS
Collapsible stocks and accessories for Ruger 10/22 rifles, AR15 type titanium firing pins, left-handed AR15 .22 LR conversion kit.
404 Bolivia Blvd.
Bradenton, FL 34207
Website: www.1022central.com
Phone: 440-413-0031

CJ WEAPONS ACCESSORIES
Military rifle slings and buttstock cleaning kits.
317 Danielle Court
Jefferson City, MO 65109
Website: www.cjweapons.com
Toll Free: 800-510-5919
Fax: 573-634-2355

CMC TRIGGERS CORP.
Drop-in AR platform triggers.
5597 Oak St.
Fort Worth, TX 76140
Website: www.cmctriggers.com
Phone: 817-563-6611

CMMG, INC.
AR15 gas piston kits, .22 LR conversion kits, receivers, parts and accessories.
620 County Road 18
Fayette, MO 65248
Website: www.cmmginc.com
Phone: 660-248-2293
Fax: 660-248-2290

C-MORE SYSTEMS
Tubeless ultra-light and miniature red dot sights.
680-D Industrial Road
Warrenton, VA 20186
Website: www.cmore.com
Phone: 540-347-4683
Fax: 703-361-5881

COATING TECHNOLOGIES INC
NP3/NP3 Plus electroless nickel-phosphorus firearm coating.
21438 North 7th Av.
Phoenix, AZ 85027
Website:www.coatingtechnologiesinc.com
Phone: 623-581-2648
Fax: 623-581-5397

COMBAT SHOOTING AND TACTICS/CSAT
AR15/M16 rear sight aperture, CSAT glass breaking tool.
3615 Press Road
Nacogdoches, TX 75964
Website: combatshootingandtactics.com
Phone: 936-559-1605
Fax: 936-569-6840

COMMAND ARMS ACCESSORIES (CAA)
See EMA TACTICAL
Stocks, grips, rails, slings, sights, laser and weapon light mounts, shotgun forends, bipods, Glock and Uzi accessories, pistol/carbine conversions.

CONETROL SCOPE MOUNTS
Rings, bases.
Hwy 123 South
Seguin, TX 78155 USA
Website: www.conetrol.com
Email: email@conetrol.com
Phone: 830-379-3030

COUNTERSNIPER MILITARY OPTICAL GUNSIGHTS CORP.
Variable power scopes, 1-12x30, 2-16x44, 4-50x75, and other optical innovations.
2231 W. Sunset
Springfield, MO 65807
Website: www.countersniperoptics.com
Phone: 800-883-9444

CRIMSON TRACE CORPORATION
Grip-integrated laser sighting systems.
9780 Southwest Freeman Drive
Wilsonville, OR 97070 USA
Website: www.crimsontrace.com
Toll Free: 800-442-2406
Fax: 503-783-5334

CUSTOM METAL PRODUCTS, LLC
Full range product line of steel shooting targets
5781 Westwood Dr
Weldon Spring, MO 63304
Website: www.custommetalprod.com
Phone: 636-329-0142
Fax: 636-329-8937

CYLINDER & SLIDE, INC.
Custom handgun parts and accessories.
245 East 4th Street
Fremont, NE 68025
Website: www.cylinder-slide.com
Phone: 402-721-4277
Fax: 402-721-0263

D&H TACTICAL
AR10/AR15/M16 magazines and accessories.
510 S. Worthington St.
Oconomowoc, WI 53066
Website: www.dh-tactical.com
Phone: 262-569-1960

D.S.A., INC.
Accessories for AR15 and FAL rifles, B&T rail systems.
27 West 990 Industrial Avenue,
P.O. Box 370
Lake Barrington, IL 60011
Website: www.dsarms.com
Phone: 847-277-7258
Fax: 847-277-7263

DANIEL DEFENSE, INC.
Military small arms upgrade parts, integrated weapon rail systems.
6002 Commerce Boulevard, Suite 109
Savannah, GA 31408
Website: www.danieldefense.com
Phone: 912-851-3225
Fax: 912-964-3247

DANISH GUNTECH I/S
Rifle actions and Hagelberg brand suppressors.
Sverigesgade 6
DK-7430 Ikast
Denmark
Website: www.danishguntech.dk

DARK HORSE ARMS
See JOHN'S GUNS

DASAN
1911 and Glock parts, AR rifle parts.
13071 Rosecrans Av.
Santa Fe Springs, CA 90670
Website: www.dasanusa.com
Phone: 562-483-6837

DELORME
Communications satellite professional mapping solutions
2 DeLorme Drive
Yarmouth, ME 04096
Website: www.delorme.com
Phone: 207-846-7000

DEL-TON, INC.
AR15 style rifle parts and accessories.
330 Aviation Way
Elizabeth Town, NC 28337
Website: www.del-ton.com
Phone: 910-645-2172
Fax: 910-645-2244

DESERT TECH
See Trademark Index

DIAMONDHEAD USA, INC.
M4/AR15 style accessories, "Diamondhead" back-up iron sights.
44 Allston Av.
West Springfield, MA 01089
Website: www.Diamondhead-USA.com
Phone: 413-739-6970
Fax: 413-739-6973

DIPOL
Night vision scopes, IR and IR Laser illuminators.
115A, Lugo St.
Vitebsk, 210033
Republic of Belarus
Website: www.dipol.biz
Phone: +375 212 261 242
Fax: +375 212 261 414

DNZ PRODUCTS, LLC
Billet aluminum one-piece rings/base scope mounts.
2710 Wilkins Drive
Sanford, NC 27330
Website: www.dnzproducts.com
Phone: 919-777-9608
Fax: 919-777-9609

DO-ALL OUTDOORS, LLC
Targeting systems and outdoor accessories
216 19th Ave. North
Nashville, TN 37203
Phone: 615-269-4889
Fax: 615-269-4434
Website: www.doalloutdoors.com
Email: customerservice@doalloutdoors.com

DOMINION ARMS/RAUCH TACTICAL
Polymer magazines for SIG 550 rifles, M14 and VZ58 rifle upgrade components.
250 H Street, Suite 226
Blaine, WA 98230
Website: www.domarms.com
Website: www.rauchtactical.com
Phone: 877-829-1050
Fax: 866-606-2743

DOUBLESTAR CORPORATION
AR-15 parts and accessories
P.O. Box 430
Winchester, KY40392
Phone: 888-736-7725
Fax: 859-745-4638
Website: www.jtfoc.com
Email: doug@star15.com

DREADNAUGHT INDUSTRIES LLC
Parts assembler.
1648 Palo Alto Drive
Van Ormy, TX 78073
Website: www.dreadnaught-industries.com
Phone: 210-601-8149

DUOSTOCK DESIGNS, INC.
Rifle stocks for CQB weapons.
P.O. Box 32
Welling, OK 74471
Website: www.duostock.com
Phone: 866-386-7865
Fax: 918-431-3182

DUMMIES UNLIMITED, INC.
Scenario based training equipment
2435 Pine Street
Pomona, CA 91767
Website: www.dummiesunlimited.com
Phone: 909-392-7502
Fax: 909-392-7510

DURASIGHT SCOPE MOUNTING SYSTEMS
Scope mounts and rings for center-fire rifles.
5988 Peachtree Corners East
Norcross, GA 30071
Website: www.durasight.com
Phone: 770-449-4687
Fax: 770-242-8546

EAGLE GRIPS, INC.
Handgun grips.
460 Randy Road
Carol Stream, IL 60188
Website: www.eaglegrips.com
Toll Free: 800-323-6144
Fax: 630-260-0486

EAGLE INDUSTRIES
Sling, holsters, & tactical gear
1000 Biltmore Drive
Fenton, MO 64026
Website: www.eagleindustries.com
Phone: 888-343-7547

EBERLESTOCK USA LLC
Rifle stocks/chassis.
P.O. Box 862
Boise, ID 83701
Website: www.eberlestock.com
Phone: 208-424-5081

ED BROWN PRODUCTS, INC.
1911 style pistol parts.
P.O. Box 492
Perry, MO 63462
Website: www.edbrown.com
Phone: 573-565-3261
Fax: 573-565-2791

EDWARDS RECOIL REDUCER
Mechanical recoil reduction devices.
1300 Seabright Drive
Annapolis, MD 21409
Website: www.edwardsrecoilreducer.com
Phone: 443-995-2157

ELCAN OPTICAL TECHNOLOGIES
Riflescopes and other military grade optics.
1601 North Plano Road
Richardson, TX 75081
Website: www.elcan.com
Phone: 972-344-8077
Fax: 972-344-8260

ELITA ARMS AND AMMUNITION
Parts and accessories for AR-15 style rifles and carbines.
1901 Liberty Drive
Thomasville, NC 27360
Website: www.elitearmsandammunition.com
Phone: 336-847-4406

ELITE IRON, LLC
Standard and custom caliber suppressors.
1345 Thunders Trail Bldg. D
Potomac, MT 59823
Website: www.eliteiron.net
Phone: 406-244-0234
Fax: 406-244-0135

ELITE SURVIVAL SYSTEMS
Cases, bags, holsters, and tactical gear
310 West 12th Street
P.O. Box 245
Washington, MO 63090
Website: www.elitesurvival.com
Toll Free: 800-340-2778

ELITE TACTICAL ADVANTAGE
Entry and tactical shotgun rails, oversize safety and charging handle for Mossberg shotguns.
Website: www.elitetacticaladvantage.com
Phone: 888-317-8523

ELZETTA DESIGN, LLC
LED weapon lights and accessories.
P.O. Box 54364
Lexington, KY 40555
Website: www.elzetta.com
Phone: 859-707-7471
Fax: 859-918-0465

ELYSIUM ARMS/WATKINS TOOL
Rifle barrels and firearm components.
P.O. box 429
101 Bacon St.
Raton, NM 87740
Phone: 575-445-0100

EMA TACTICAL
.223 CountDown magazine, rail systems, stocks, grips, slings, and scope mounts.
1208 Branagan Drive
Tullytown, PA 19007
Website: www.ematactical.com
Phone: 215-949-9944
Fax: 215-949-9191

ENIDINE
See ITT ENIDINE INC.

ERGO GRIP
See FALCON INDUSTRIES
AR15 style pistol and forward grips, stocks, mounts, and rails; 1911 style pistol grips, shotgun tri-rail forends.

E.R. SHAW/SMALL ARMS MFG.
Firearm barrels.
5312 Thoms Run Rd.
Bridgeville, PA 15017
Website: www.ershawbarrels.com
Phone: 412-221-3636

FAB DEFENSE
Tactical equipment for military, police, and self-defense weapons.
43 Yakov Olamy Street
Moshav Mishmar Hashiva, Israel 50297
Website: www.fab-defense.com
Phone: 011 972039603399
Fax: 011 972039603312

FAILZERO
EXO Technology coatings for firearm accessories and parts.
7825 Southwest Ellipse Way
Stuart, FL 34997
Phone: 772-223-6699
Fax: 772-223-9996

FALCON INDUSTRIES
Ergonomically designed tactical weapon grips and accessories.
P.O. Box 1459
Moriarty, NM 87305
Website: www.ergogrips.net
Phone: 505-281-3783
Fax: 505-281-3991

FAXON FIREARMS
ARAK-21 gas piston upper receivers, barrels, and parts for AR-15 style rifles.
11101 Adwood Drive
Cincinnati, OH 45240
Website: www.faxonfirearms.com
Phone: 513-674-2580

FDI/FREED DESIGNS, INC.
Pateneted XGRIP adaptors which allow full-size pistol magazines to be used in compact pistols.
P.O. Box 1231
Ojai, CA 93024
Website: www.x-grips.com
Phone: 805-814-0668

F.J. FEDDERSEN, INC.
.22 through .50 BMG barrels.
7501 Corporate Park Drive
Loudon, TN 37774
Website: www.1022rifle.com
Phone: 865-408-1545

FLIR SYSTEMS, INC.
Electro-optical and infrared imaging systems.
27700 SW. Parkway Av.
Wilsonville, OR 97070
Website: www.flir.com/gs
Phone: 503-498-3547/3149
Fax: 503-684-5452

FTS TECHNOLOGIES, LTD
Fulcrum Target Systems
711 South Carson Street, Suite 4
Carson City, NV 89701
Phone Number: 775-238-3282
Website: www.fulcrumtargetsystems.com

GEISSELE AUTOMATICS, LLC
National Match and combat replacement triggers.
1920 West Marshall Street
Norristown, PA 19403
Website: www.ar15triggers.com
Phone: 610-272-2060
Fax: 610-272-2069

GEMTECH
OSHA-safe sound suppressors in most defense calibers.
P.O. Box 140618
Boise, ID 83714
Website: www.gem-tech.com
Phone: 208-939-7222

G&G
Optical mounting systems and tactical weapon accessories.
3602 East 42nd Stravenue
Tucson, AZ 85713
Website: www.gggaz.com
Phone: 520-748-7167
Fax: 520-748-7583

G. RECKNAGEL E.K.
Tactical mounts
Landwehr 4
Bergrheinfeld, GERMANY 97493
Website: www.recknagel.de
Phone: 011-49972184366

GARMIN USA
Maps & related devices
1200 East 151st Street
Olathe, KS 66062
Website: www.garmin.com
Phone: 913-397-8200

GLOCKSTORE
Custom Glock pistol parts.
4585 Murphy Canyon Road
San Diego, CA 92123
Website: www.glockstore.com
Toll Free: 800-601-8273
Fax: 858-569-0505

GRIFFIN ARMAMENT
Mil/LE/civilian suppressors.
P.O. Box 116
Wales, WI 53183
Website: www.griffinarmament.com
Email: info@griffinarmament.com
Phone: 262-501-8447

GROVETEC U.S., INC.
Slings, ammo carriers, sling swivel sets for rifles and shotguns.
P.O. Box 220060
Milwaukie, OR 97269-0060
Website: www.grovtec.com
Phone: 503-557-4689
Fax: 503-557-4936

GUNTECH USA
AR15/AK47/Saiga parts and accessories.
7850 E. Evans Rd. #105
Scottsdale, AZ 85260
Website: www.guntechusa.com
Phone: 480-478-4517

GWACS ARMORY
See Trademark Index

H-S PRECISION, INC.
Synthetic stocks, detachable rifle magazines, rifle accessories.
1301 Turbine Drive
Rapid City, SD 57703
Website: www.hsprecision.com
Phone: 605-341-3006
Fax: 605-342-8964

HARRIS ENGINEERING, INC.
Bipods and adaptors for attaching bipods.
999 Broadway
Barlow, KY 42024
Phone: 270-334-3633
Fax: 270-334-3000

HAWKE SPORT OPTICS, LLC
Rifle and shotgun scopes.
6015 Highview Drive, Suite G
Fort Wayne, IN 46818
Website: www.hawkeoptics.com
Phone: 877-429-5347
Fax: 260-918-3443

HAERING GMBH
Support live fire training in varied environments
Phone: 49 (6163) 9347-0
Fax: 49 (6163) 9347-50
Website: www.haeringtargets.com
Email: info@haering-gmbh.de

HEAD DOWN PRODUCTS
Uppers, rails, muzzle brakes, & related parts
4031 Fambrough Court, Suite 300
Powder Springs, GA 30127
Phone: 770-485-7015
Fax: 770-421-6345
Website: www.hdrifles.co

HEINIE SPECIALTY PRODUCTS
Pistol sights (low profile, tritium night, tactical), parts, and accessories.
301 Oak Street
Quincy, IL 62301
Website: www.heinie.com
Phone: 217-228-9500

HENNING SHOP
Barrels & gun parts
1629 Atwood Street
P.O. Box 6648
Longmont, CO 80501
Website: www.henningshop.com
Phone: 720-320-7890

HERA ARMS GMBH
Military, law enforcement, and sporting weapon accessories.
Ziegelhuettenweg 5
Triefenstein, GERMANY 97855
Website: www.hera-arms.com
Phone: 011 499395878724
Fax: 011 499395878723

HI LUX INC.
Leatherwood scopes.
3135 Kashiwa Street
Torrance, CA 90505
Website: www.hi-luxoptics.com
Phone: 310-257-8142

HIVIZ SHOOTING SYSTEMS
Fiber-optic firearm sights, recoil pads.
North Pass, Ltd.
1941 Health Parkway, Suite 1
Fort Collins, CO 80524
Website: www.hivizsights.com
Phone: 970-407-0426
Fax: 970-416-1208

HKS PRODUCTS INC.
Revolver speedloaders and magazine loaders.
7841 Foundation Drive
Florence, KY 41042
Website: www.hksspeedloaders.com
Phone: 800-354-9814

HOGUE, INC.
Synthetic handgun, rifle, and shotgun grips and stocks, recoil pads, sling swivels, AR15/M16 accessories.
550 Linne Road
Paso Robles, CA 93447
Website: www.hogueinc.com
Phone: 805-239-1440
Fax: 805-239-2553

HOPLITE SYSTEMS
Precision firearm components.
14000 NW 58th Court
Miami Lakes, FL 33014
Website: marktwoarms.com
Phone: 305-889-3280

HORUS VISION, LLC
Long range and CQB riflescopes.
659 Huntington Avenue
San Bruno, CA 94066
Website: www.horusvision.com
Phone: 650-588-8862; 650-583-5471
Fax: 650-588-6264

HOT SHOT TACTICAL
Lights, packs, & tactical gear
121 Interpark Boulevard #706
San Antonio, TX 78216
Website: www.hotshottactical.com
Phone: 855-357-2327

HOUSTON ARMORY
See Trademark Index

HUBER CONCEPTS
Two-stage tactical triggers.
Website: www.huberconcepts.com
Phone: 820-821-8841

HUNTER COMPANY INC
Holsters & accessories
3300 West 71st Avenue
Westminster, CO 80030
Website: www.huntercompany.com
Phone: 303-427-4626
Fax: 650-588-6264

HYPERBEAM
Riflescopes, night vision scopes.
1504 Sheepshead Bay Road, Suite 300
Brooklyn, NY 11236
Website: www.nightdetective.com
Phone: 718-272-1776
Fax: 718-272-1797

IHC, INC.
All types of aluminum color and graphic anodizing.
12400 Burt Road
Detroit, MI 48228
Website: www.ihccorp.com
Phone: 313-535-3210
Fax: 313-535-3220

INSIGHT TECHNOLOGY
Tactical lasers and illuminators.
9 Akira Way
Londonderry, NH 03053
Website: www.insighttechgear.com
Phone: 866-509-2040
Fax: 603-668-1084

INTENSITY OPTICS
Riflescopes.
Onalaska Operations
P.O. Box 39
Onalaska, WI 54650
Website: www.intensityoptics.com
Phone: 800-635-7656

IOR S.A.
Rifle scopes, red dot sights, night vision scopes, and mounts.
4 Bucovina St.
030393 Bucharest, ROMANIA
Website: www.ior.ro
Phone: +40 21 324 42 61
Fax: +40 21 324 45 12

ITAC DEFENSE, INC.
Slings, vertical foregrips, rear diopter back-up iron sights, red dot and laser sights, front/rear sights for SIG 522 rifle.
189 Lafayette Road
North Hampton, NH 03862
Website: www.itacdefense.com
Phone: 866-964-4822
Fax: 866-965-4822

ITT ENIDINE INC.
AR15/M4 style rifle hydraulic rate/recoil reduction buffers.
7 Centre Drive
Orchard Park, NY 14127
Website: www.enidine-defense.com
Phone: 716-662-1900
Fax: 716-662-1909

JAE - J. ALLEN ENTERPRISES, INC.
Precision synthetic tactical stocks for M1A/M14 and Remington 700 rifles.
21520-G Yorba Linda Blvd. #175
Yorba Linda, CA 92887
Website: www.jae100.com
Phone: 714-693-3523
Fax: 714-692-3547

JAPAN OPTICS, LTD.
Riflescopes (formerly HAKKO).
2-11-29, Ukima, Kita-ku
Tokyo, 115-0051 Japan
Website: www.japanoptics.co.jp
Phone: 011 81359146680
Fax: 011 81353922232

JOHN MASEN COMPANY, INC.
Mini 14 and AR-15 accessories, shotgun stocks.
1305 Jelmak Street
Grand Prairie, TX 75050
Website: www.johnmasen.com
Phone: 972-790-0521
Fax: 972-970-3691

JOHN'S GUNS
Suppressors for military, law enforcement and civilian applications.
Dark Horse Arms Company
1041 FM 1274
Coleman, TX 76834
Website: www.darkhorsearms.com
Phone: 325-382-4885
Fax: 325-382-4887

JONATHAN ARTHUR CIENER, INC.
.22 LR conversion units/kits for centerfire handguns and rifles.
8700 Commerce Street
Cape Canaveral, FL 32920
Website: www.22lrconversions.com
Phone: 321-868-2200
Fax: 321-868-2201

JP ENTERPRISES, INC.
JPoint red dot sight, optics mounts, rifle accessories.
P.O. Box 378
Hugo, MN 55038
Website: www.jprifles.com
Phone: 651-426-9196
Fax: 651-426-2472

KAHLES USA
Firearm scopes.
3911 SW. 47th Av., Suite 914
Fort Lauderdale, FL 33314
Website: www.kahlesusa.com
Phone: 954-581-5822
Fax: 954–581-3165

KDF INC
Scopes and muzzle brakes.
2485 State Highway 46 North
Seguin, TX 78155
Website: www.kdfguns.com
Phone: 830-379-8141

KELBLY'S INC.
Rifle stocks, tactical scopes and rings, triggers.
7222 Dalton Fox Lake Road
North Lawrence, OH 44666
Website: www.kelbly.com
Phone: 330-683-4674

KFS INDUSTRIES
Bipods and mounting adaptors, adjustable sights for 1911 style pistols.
875 Wharton Drive Southwest, P.O. Box 44405
Atlanta, GA 30336
Website: www.versapod.com
Phone: 404-691-7611
Fax: 404-505-8445

KG INDUSTRIES, LLC
High performance firearm finishes.
16790 US Highway 63 South, Building 2
Hayward, WI 54843
Website: www.kgcoatings.com
Phone: 715-934-3566
Fax: 715-934-3570

KICK-EEZ PRODUCTS
Sorbothane recoil pads.
1819 Schurman Way, Suite 106
Woodland, WA 98674
Website: www.kickeezproducts.com
Phone: 360-225-9701
Fax: 360-225-9702

KINETIC RESEARCH GROUP
Modular stocks and components for long range/ sniper rifles.
22348 Duff Lane
Middleton, ID 83644
Website: www.kineticresearchgroup.com
Phone: 720-234-1145

KLEEN-BORE INC.
Comprehensive line of gun care products
13386 International Parkway
Jacksonville, FL 32218
Phone: 800-347-1200
Fax: 800-366-1669
Website: www.kleen-bore.com

KNIGHTS MANUFACTURING COMPANY
Suppressors in popular calibers, night vision scopes.
701 Columbia Boulevard
Titusville, FL 32780
Website: www.knightarmco.com
Phone: 321-607-9900
Fax: 321-383-2143

KNS PRECISION, INC.
AR15/M16 receivers, parts and accessories; iron sights.
112 Marschall Creek Road
Fredericksburg, TX 78624
Website: www.knsprecisioninc.com
Phone: 830-997-0000
Fax: 830-997-1443

KONUS CORP USA
Optics
7530 NW 79th Street
Miami, FL 33166
Website: www.konususa.com
Phone: 305-884-7618

KREBS GUNSMITHING
SIG and AK pattern rifle accessories.
1000 N. Rand Road
Wauconcla, IL 60084
Phone: 847-487-7776

KRIEGER BARRELS, INC.
Precision single-point, cut-rifled barrels in calibers ranging from .17 cal. through 4 Bore.
2024 Mayfield Road
Richfield, WI 53076
Website: www.kriegerbarrels.com
Phone: 262-628-8558
Fax: 262-628-8748

KRUGER OPTICS INC.
251 West Barclay Drive
P.O. Box 532
Sisters, OR 97759
Website: www.krugeroptical.com
Phone: 262-628-8588

KURZZEIT USA
Bullet speed chronographs, trigger systems
3267 Valley Crest Way
Forest Grove, OR 97116
Website: www.mktactical.com
Phone: 503-577-6824

KWIK-SITE COMPANY/IRONSIGHTER COMPANY
Scope mounts, bases, rings, and extension rings.
5555 Treadwell
Wayne, MI 48184
Website: www.kwiksitecorp.com
Phone: 734-326-1500
Fax: 734-326-4120

L&G WEAPONRY
Customizes, services, and designs AR-15 & M16 style weapons.
Huntington Beach, CA
Website: www.lgweaponry.com
Email: larry@lgweaponry.com
Phone No: 714-840-3772
Fax: 714-625-4631

L-3 COMMUNICATIONS-EOTECH
Holographic red dot weapon sights.
1201 East Ellsworth Road
Ann Arbor, MI 48108
Website: www.l-3com.com/eotech
Phone: 734-741-8868
Fax: 734-741-8221

LANCER SYSTEMS
L5 translucent magazines and other firearms accessories.
7566 Morris Court, Suite 300
Allentown, PA 18106
Website: www.lancer-systems.com
Phone: 610-973-2614
Fax: 610-973-2615

LARUE TACTICAL
Quick-detach optical sight mounts, rails, AR15 style weapon handguards.
850 CR 177
Leander, TX 78641
Website: www.laruetactical.com
Phone: 512-259-1585
Fax: 512-259-1588

LASER AIMING SYSTEMS CORPORATION
Viridian brand green laser sights.
5929 Baker Road, Suite 440
Minnetonka, MN 55345
Website: www.viridiangreenlaser.com
Phone: 800-990-9390
Fax: 952-224-4097

LASER DEVICES, INC.
Laser sights and lights; rifle/shotgun/submachine gun mounts and rails, weapon lights.
70 Garden Court
2 Harris Court, Suite A-4
Monterey, CA 93940
Website: www.laserdevices.com
Phone: 831-373-0701
Fax: 831-373-0903

LASER GENETICS OF AMERICA
Laser illuminators.
3721 SW. 47th AV., Suite 305
Fort Lauderdale, FL 33314
Website: www.lasergenetics.com
Phone: 954-581-5822
Fax: 954-581-3165

LASERLYTE
Laser sights.
101 Airpark Road
Cottonwood, AZ 86326
Website: www.laserlyte.com
Phone: 928-649-3201
Fax: 928-649-3970

LASERMAX, INC.
Laser sights.
3495 Winston Place Suite B
Rochester, NY 14623
Website: www.lasermax.com
Phone: 585-272-5420
Fax: 585-272-5427

LAUER CUSTOM WEAPONRY
Firearms suppressors, Duracoat self-lubricating firearms finish.
3601 129th Street
Chippewa Falls, WI 54729
Website: www.lauerweaponry.com
Phone: 715-720-6128
Fax: 715-723-2950

LAW ENFORCEMENT TARGETS, INC.
Targets and range training products
8802 West 35W Service Dr. NE
Blaine, MN 55449-6740
Website: www.letargets.com
Toll Free: 800-779-0182
Fax: 651-645-5360

LEAPERS, INC.
Electro-optical and tactical scopes, rail mounting systems.
32700 Capitol Street
Livonia, MI 48150
Website: www.leapers.com
Phone: 734-542-1500
Fax: 734-542-7095

LEATHERWOOD/HI-LUX OPTICS
Rifle scopes, auto-ranging trajectory scopes, 30mm tactical scopes.
Hi-Lux, Inc.
3135 Kashiwa Street
Torrance, CA 90505
Website: www.hi-luxoptics.com
Phone: 310-257-8142
Fax: 310-257-8096

LEGION ARMS, LLC
Rifle and handgun rail and mounting systems.
620 Valley Forge Road, Suite B
Hillsborough, NC 27278
Phone: 919-672-8620
Fax: 919-883-5265

LEHIGH DEFENSE, LLC
AR style weapon components and accessories.
130 Penn AM Drive, Suite D-1
Quakertown, PA 18951
Website: www.lehighdefense.com
Phone: 215-536-4100

LEICA SPORT OPTICS
Optical sights.
1 Pearl Court, Suite A
Allendale, NJ 07401 USA
Website: www.leica-camera.com/usa
Phone: 201-995-0051
Fax: 201-955-1686

LEITNER-WISE DEFENSE
Weapon-mounted "Countashot" electronic shot counter.
P.O. Box 25097
Alexandria, VA 22313
Website: www.leitner-wise.com
Phone: 703-209-0556

LES BAER CUSTOM, INC.
1911 pistol frames, slides, barrels, sights, grips, scope mounts.
1804 Iowa Drive
Leclaire, IA 52753
Website: www.lesbaer.com
Phone: 563-289-2126
Fax: 563-289-2132

LEUPOLD & STEVENS, INC.
Tactical optical and electro-optical scopes, rings, and bases.
14400 Northwest Greenbriar Parkway 9700,
P.O. Box 688
Beaverton, OR 97006
Website: www.leupold.com
Toll Free: 800-538-7653
Fax: 503-526-1478

LEVELLOK SHOOTING SYSTEMS
Monopods, bipods, and tripods.
105 South 12th Street
Pittsburgh, PA 15203
Website: www.levellok.com
Phone: 412-431-5440
Fax: 412-488-7608

LEWIS MACHINE & TOOL
Tactical weapon accessories.
1305 11th Street West
Milan, IL 61264
Website: www.lewismachine.net
Phone: 309-787-7151
Fax: 309-787-7193

LIMBSAVER
LimbSaver recoil pads.
50 West Rose Nye Way
Shelton, WA 98584 USA
Website: www.limbsaver.com
Phone: 360-427-6031
Fax: 360-427-4025

LINE OF FIRE, LLC
TEGS grip system, 3.2.1. Slings.
3200 Danville Blvd., Suite 220
Alamo, CA 94507
Website: www.loftactical.com
Phone: 323-899-3016
Fax: 562-424-1562

LONE STAR TACTICAL
See Trademark Index

LONE WOLF DISTRIBUTORS, INC.
Glock pistol accessories.
57 Shepard Road, P.O. Box 3549
Oldtown, ID 83822 USA
Website: www.lonewolfdist.com
Phone: 208-437-0612
Fax: 208-437-1098

LRB ARMS
M14 and AR15 receivers.
96 Cherry Lane
Floral Park, NY 11001 USA
Website: www.lrbarms.com
Phone: 516-327-9061
Fax: 516-327-0246

LUCID
HD7 red dot sight.
235 Fairway Drive
Riverton, WY 82501
Website: www.my lucidgear.com
Phone: 307-840-2160

LUNA OPTICS, INC.
Night vision riflescopes.
54 Columbus Avenue
Staten Island, NY 10304
Website: www.lunaoptics.com
Phone No.; 718-556-5862
Fax: 718-556-5869

LWRC INTERNATIONAL, LLC
Tactical firearm accessories.
815 Chesapeake Drive
Cambridge, MD 21613
Website: www.lwrci.com
Phone: 410-901-1348
Fax: 410-228-1799

LYMAN PRODUCTS CORP.
Lyman sights; Pachmayr synthetic grips, stocks, recoil pads, and sights; Uni-Dot fiber optic sights; and TacStar weapon lights, shotgun grips/shell carriers/magazine extensions, AR style rifle grips and accessories.
475 Smith Street
Middletown, CT 06457
Website: www.lymanproducts.com
Phone: 860-632-2020
Fax: 860-632-1699

MAG-NA-PORT INTERNATIONAL INC.
Handgun, shotgun, and rifle barrel porting/muzzle brakes.
41302 Executive Drive
Harrison Twp, MI 48045
Website: www.magnaport.com
Phone: 586-469-6727
Fax: 586-469-0425

MAGPUL INDUSTRIES CORP.
Fully adjustable buttstocks, magazines, grips, rail covers, and sights for AR15 and other tactical weapons.
P.O. Box 17697
Boulder, CO 80308
Website: www.magpul.com
Phone: 877-4MAGPUL
Fax: 303-828-3469

MAJESTIC ARMS, LTD.
Ruger rimfire rifle and pistol parts, Aluma-lite 10/22 and 77/22 barrels.
101A Ellis St.
Staten Island, NY 10307
Website: www.majesticarms.com
Phone: 718-356-6765
Fax: 718-356-6835

MAKO GROUP
Tactical weapon accessories.
170-20 Central Ave.
Farmingdale, NY 11735
Website: www.themakogroup.com
Phone: 631-880-3396
Fax: 631-880-3397

MANNERS COMPOSITE STOCKS
Carbon fiber and fiber glass gunstocks.
1209 Swift
North Kansas City, MO 64116
Website: www.mannersstock.com
Phone: 816-283-3334

MANTA / MANTARAILS
Manta railguards and wire management systems, heat shield "suppressor sleeves".
326 Pearl St. NE
New Philadelphia, OH 44663
Website: www.manta.us
Phone: 330-308-6360

MARVEL PRECISION LLC
.22 LR conversions for 1911 style pistols, and associated scope mount ribs, sights, parts, and compensators.
2464 South 54th Road, Suite 2
Firth, NE 68358
Website: www.marvelprecision.com
Phone: 800-295-1987
Fax: 402-791-2246

MASTERPIECE ARMS
.22 LR/WMR, 5.7x28, 9mm, .45 ACP, 5.56 and .308 suppressors.
4904 Hwy. 98
P.O. Box 67
Comer, GA 30629
Website: www.masterpiecearms.com
Phone: 706-783-0095

MATECH, INC.
Back-up iron sights.
510 Naylor Mill Road
Salisbury, MD 21801
Website: www.matech.net
Phone: 410-548-1627
Fax: 410-548-1628

MCCANN INDUSTRIES LLC
AR-15 parts and accessories
P.O. Box 641
Spanaway, WA 98387
Phone: 253-537-6919
Fax: 253-537-6993
Website: www.mccannindustries.com
Email: info@mccannindustries.com

MCMILLAN FIBERGLASS STOCKS
Fiberglass rifle stocks.
1638 West Knudsen Drive, Suite A
Phoenix, AZ 85027
Website: www.mcmillanusa.com
Phone: 623-582-9635
Fax: 623-581-3825

MEC-GAR SRL
Handgun and rifle magazines.
Via Mandolossa, 102/a
Gussago, Brescia, 25064 Italy
Website: www.mec-gar.it
Phone: 011-390303735413
Fax: 011-390303733687

MEGA ARMS LLC
AR-15 style upper and lower receivers, rails, and accessories.
5323 Joppa St. SW
Tumwater, WA 98512
Website: mega-arms.com
Phone: 877-857-5372

MEGGITT TRAINING SYSTEMS
Supplier of integrated live fire and simulation weapons training systems
296 Brogdon Road
Suwanee, GA, 30024
Phone: 678-288-1090
Website: www.meggitttrainingsystems.com

MEOPTA USA, INC.
Riflescopes.
50 Davids Drive
Hauppauge, NY 11788
Website: www.meopta.com
Phone: 631-436-5900
Fax: 631-436-5920

MEPROLIGHT/KIMBER
Tritium night sights and red dot reflex sights.
2590 Montana Hwy 35, Suite B
Kalispell, MT 59901
Website: www.kimberamerica.com
Phone: 406-758-2222
Fax: 406-758-2223

MEPROLIGHT, LTD.
Electro-optical and optical sights and devices.
58 Hazait Street, Or-Akiva Industrial Park
Or-Akiva, 30600 Israel
Website: www.meprolight.com
Phone: 011-97246244111
Fax: 011-97246244123

MESA TACTICAL
Telescoping stock systems, shell carriers, rails, and sling loops for tactical shotguns.
1760 Monrovia Ave, Suite A14
Costa Mesa, CA 92627
Website: www.mesatactical.com
Phone: 949-642-3337
Fax: 949-642-3339

MEYERS & CO.
See B.E. MEYERS & CO.

MFI
Rails, risers, scope mounts, and accessories for tactical weapons.
563 San Miguel
Liberty, KY 42539
Website: www.mfiap.com
Phone: 606-787-0022
Fax: 606-787-0059

MGI
AR-15/M-4/M-16 lower receivers, 90 round magazines, and parts.
102 Cottage Street
Bangor, ME 04401
Website: www.MGImilitary.com
Phone: 207-945-5441
Fax: 207-945-4010

MGM TARGETS/MIKE GIBSON MANUFACTURING
Manufacturer of AR Steel Targets
17891 Karcher Rd.
Caldwell, ID 83607
Website: mgmtargets.com
Toll Free: 888-767-7371
Fax: 208-454-0666

MICOR INDUSTRIES, INC.
Flash suppressors.
1314 A State Docks Road
Decatur, AL 356601
Website: www.micorind.com
Phone: 256-560-0770
Fax: 256-341-0002

MICRO SLICK
See AMELON COATINGS, LLC

MIDWAYUSA, INC.
Shooting and gun care products
5875 West Van Horn Tavern Rd.
Columbia, MO 65203-9274
Website: www.midwayusa.com
Phone: 800-243-3220
Fax: 800-992-8312

MIDWEST INDUSTRIES, INC.
Tactical rifle accessories.
828 Philip Drive, Suite 2
Waukesha, WI 53186
Website: www.midwestindustriesinc.com
Phone: 262-896-6780
Fax: 262-896-6756

MILLETT SIGHTS
Tactical scopes, red dot sights, metallic sights, rings, and bases.
6200 Cody
Overland Park, KS 66214
Website: www.millettsights.com
Phone: 913-752-3400
Fax: 913-752-3550

MISSION FIRST TACTICAL
Tactical rifle accessories.
780 Haunted Lane
Bensalem, PA 19020
Phone: 267-803-1517
Fax: 267-803-1002

MODULAR DRIVEN TECHNOLOGIES
TAC21 and LSS chassis systems for Rem. 700, Savage, and Tikka T3 rifles.
8022 Evans Road, #103
Chilliwack, British Columbia
V2R5R8 Canada
Website: www.mdttac.com
Phone: 604-239-0800

MOUNTING SOLUTIONS PLUS
Muzzelite, LightLink, SightLink, and Glock Pistol Fiber Optic Sight.
10655 Southwest 185 Terrace
Miami, FL 33157
Website: www.mountsplus.com
Phone: 305-253-8393
Fax: 305-232-1247

MURRAYS GUNS
Replacement SKS firing pin kit, Yugoslav SKS gas valve.
12696 FM 2127
Bowie, TX 76230
Website: www.murraysguns.com
Phone: 940-928-002
Fax: 800-836-7579

N-VISION OPTICS LLC
Night vision and thermal optics.
220 Reservoir St., Suite 26
Needham, MA 02494
Website: www.nvisionoptics.com
Phone: 781-505-8360

NECG LTD. / NEW ENGLAND CUSTOM GUN SERVICE, LTD.
Rifle and shotgun iron sights, sling swivels, recoil pads, and scope mounts.
741 Main St.
Claremont, NH 03743
Website: newenglandcustomgun.com
Phone: 603-287-4836
Fax: 603-287-4832

NEW CENTURY NCSTAR, INC.
Firearms accessories, optics including precision rifle and pistol scopes, and red dot sights.
10302 Olney Street
El Monte, CA 91731
Website: www.ncstar.com
Phone: 626-575-1518
Fax: 626-575-2478

NEWCON OPTIK
Electro-optical products, night vision rifle scopes.
105 Sparks Ave
Toronto, ON M2H 2S5 Canada
Website: www.newcon-optik.com
Phone: 416-663-6963
Fax: 416-663-9065

NIC INDUSTRIES, INC.
Liquid ceramic coating developed to withstand the most extreme conditions.
7050 Sixth Street
White City, OR 97503
Website: www.nicindustries.com
Phone: 541-826-1922
Fax: 541-830-6518

NIGHTFORCE OPTICS
Nightforce precision rifle scopes.
Lightforce USA, Inc.
1040 Hazen Lane
Orofino, ID 83544
Website: www.nightforceoptics.com
Phone: 208-476-9814
Fax: 208-476-9817

NIGHT OPTICS USA, INC.
Commercial, law enforcement, and military thermal/night vision systems.
15182 Triton Lane, Suite 101
Huntington Beach, CA 92649
Website: www.nightoptics.com
Phone: 714-899-4475
Fax: 714-899-4448

NIGHT OWL OPTICS/BOUNTY HUNTER
Night vision and infrared scopes.
1465-H Henry Brennan
El Paso, TX 79936
Website: www.nightowloptics.com
Phone: 800-444-5994
Fax: 915-633-8529

NITESIGHT LTD.
NiteSite converts a conventional scope into a night vision sight.
Unit 13, West Lane
Full Sutton Airfield
York, North Yorkshire, YO41 1HS
Unite Kingdom
Website: www.nitesite.co.uk
Phone: 44-0-1759-377235

NIGHT VISION DEPOT
Night vision weapon sights and accessories.
P.O. Box 3415
Allentown, PA 18106
Website: www.nvdepot.com
Phone: 610-395-9743
Fax: 610-395-9744

NIGHT VISION SYSTEMS
Night vision, thermal imaging, combat identification, and lasers.
542 Kemmerer Lane
Allentown, PA 18104
Website: www.nightvisionsystems.com
Phone: 610-391-9101
Fax: 610-391-9220

NIKON, INC.
Riflescopes.
1300 Walt Whitman Road
Melville, NY 11747
Website: www.nikonhunting.com
Phone: 631-547-4200
Fax: 631-547-4040

NITREX OPTICS
Riflescopes.
Weaver/ATK Commercial Products
N5549 County Trunk Z
Onalaska, WI 54650
Website: www.nitrexoptics.com
Phone: 800-635-7656
Fax: 763-323-3890

NIVISYS INDUSTRIES, LLC
Night vision weapon sights, and related laser aiming and illumination systems.
400 South Clark Drive, Suite 105
Tempe, AZ 85281
Website: www.nivisys.com
Phone: 480-970-3222
Fax: 480-970-3555

NODAK SPUD LLC
AKM receivers and fire control parts, AR lowers, Picatinny rails, flash hiders, Benelli 1014/M4 extended mag tubes.
7683 Washington Ave. S.
Edina, MN 55439
Website: www.nodakspud.com
Phone: 952-942-1909
Fax: 952-942-1912

NORGON, LLC
AR15/M16 ambidextrous magazine catch.
7518 K Fullerton Road
Springfield, VA 22153
Website: www.norgon.com
Phone: 703-455-0997
Fax: 703-569-6411

NOVAK DESIGNS, INC.
Handgun sights ("LoMount", "Mega Dot"), 1911 extended safety lever, Picatinny rail, and magazines.
P.O. Box 4045
1206 30th Street
Parkersburg, WV 26104
Website: www.novaksights.com
Phone: 304-485-9295
Fax: 304-428-22676

OBERLAND ARMS OHG
Flash suppressors and compensators for tactical rifles.
Frank Satzinger & Matthias Hainich
Am Hundert 3
82386 Huglfing - GERMANY
Website: www.oberlandarms.com
Phone: 49 08802914750
Fax: 49 08802914751

OSPREY DEFENSE, LLC
AR15 style gas piston conversion kits.
6112 33rd Street E, Unit #104
Bradenton, FL 34203
Website: www.gaspiston.com
Phone: 941-322-26561
Fax: 941-322-2562

OSPREY INTERNATIONAL, INC.
Laser sights, holographic sights, and daytime riflescopes.
25 Hawks Farm Road
White, GA 30184
Website: www.osprey-optics.com
Phone: 770-387-2751
Fax: 770-387-0114

PACHMAYR
See LYMAN PRODUCTS CORP

PALMETTO STATE ARMORY
AR15 rifle accessories.
3670 Fernandina Road
Columbia, SC 29210
Website: www.palmettostatearmory.com
Phone: 803-724-6950

PARKER-HALE
Scope mounts, bipods, suppressors, and barrels.
Bedford Road
Petersfield, Hampshire, GU32 3XA
United Kingdom
Website: www.parker-hale.co.uk
Phone: 011 441730268011
Fax: 011 441730260074

PATRIOT ORDNANCE FACTORY
Gas piston weapon systems and uppers, precision sniper stocks, AR rifle magazines, AR rails/forends, and flash hiders.
23623 North 67 Ave
Glendale, AZ 85310
Website: www.pof-usa.com
Phone: 623-561-9572
Fax: 623-321-1680

PEARCE GRIP
Replacement grips for firearms.
P.O. Box 40367
Fort Worth, TX 76140
Website: www.pearcegrip.com
Phone: 817-568-9704
Fax: 817-568-9707

PENTAGONLIGHT
Tactical weapon light systems.
151 Mitchell Ave
San Francisco, CA 94080
Website: www.pentagonlight.com
Phone: 650-877-1555
Fax: 650-877-9555

PENTAX IMAGING COMPANY
Riflescopes.
600 12th Street, Suite 300
Golden, CO 80401
Website: www.pentaxsportoptics.com
Phone: 303-799-8000
Fax: 303-460-1628

PHOEBUS TACTICAL FLASHLIGHTS
LED tactical flashlights.
2800 Third Street
San Francisco, CA 94107
Website: www.phoebus.com
Phone: 415-550-0770
Fax: 415-550-2655

PHOENIX TACTICAL
"Pod Claw" bipod feet, Harris bipod rail adaptors, DLG lighted scope level indicator.
1016 W. Poplar Av., Suite 106-320
Collierville, TN 38017
Website: www.phoenixtactical.com
Phone: 901-289-1110
Fax: 901-854-0633

PHOENIX TECHNOLOGY LTD.
Kicklite stocks and accessories
P.O. Box 249
Burgaw, NC 28425
Website: www.kicklitestocks.com
Phone: 877-774-1867

POINT TECH, INC.
1911 type pistol barrels, frames, and slides, Glock barrels, Beretta barrels, Mauser barrels, AR16/M16 barrels, and .50 caliber barrels.
160 Gregg Street, Suite 1
Lodi, NJ 07644
Phone: 201-368-0711
Fax: 201-368-0133

PRECISION BARRELS
Rifle barrels
Website: www.precisionbarrels.com
Phone: 615-461-7688

PRECISION FIREARMS
AR15 upper receivers.
74 Dupont Road, Suite A
Martinsburg, WV 25404
Website: www.precisionfirearms.com

PRECISION REFLEX, INC.
Custom built AR uppers, rings, bases, carbon fiber forearms, shotgun mounts, charging handles, and auxiliary iron sights.
710 Streine Drive,
New Bremen, OH 45869
Website: www.precisionreflex.com
Phone: 419-629-2603

PREMIER RETICLES
Tactical riflescopes, scout scopes, owner of patented Gen 2 Mildot reticle.
175 Commonwealth Court
Winchester, VA 22602
Phone: 540-868-2044
Fax: 540-868-2045

PRIMARY WEAPONS SYSTEMS
AR15 receivers, parts, quad rails, Ruger 10/22 trigger groups and barrels.
800 East Citation Court, Suite C
Boise, ID 83716
Website: www.primaryweapons.com
Phone: 208-344-5217
Fax: 208-344-5395

PRO-DEFENSE
Picatinny rail mounted pepper spray.
3512 Sunny Lane
P.O. Box 3065
Columbia Falls, MT 59912
Website: www.Pro-Defense.com
Phone: 406-892-3060

PROMAG INDUSTRIES, INC.
Rifle and pistol magazines, scope rings, mounts, shotgun stocks, tactical rifle and pistol accessories.
10654 South Garfield Ave
South Gate, CA 90280
Website: www.promagindustries.com
Phone: 562-861-9554
Fax: 562-861-6377

PSI, LLC
LPA adjustable pistol sights, tactical shotgun sights, ACT-MAG/PSI and Novak pistol magazines.
2 Klarides Village Drive, Suite 336
Seymour, CT 06483
Website: www.precisionsalesintl.com
Phone: 203-262-6484
Fax: 203-262-6562

PULSAR
Thermal, Gen 2, Gen 3, and digital night vision.
2201 Heritage Parkway
Mansfield, TX 76063
Website: www.pulsarnv.com
Phone: 817-225-0310

QUAKE INDUSTRIES, INC.
Sling swivels, tactical attachments, and parts.
210 Wooden Lane
Manhattan, MT 59741
Website: www.quakeinc.com
Phone: 770-449-4687
Fax: 770-242-8546

QUICKSILVER MANUFACTURING,LLC
Ultralight titanium rifle suppressors.
1373 E. 3700 N.
Buhl, ID 83316
Website: www.qsmsilencers.com
Fax: 208-543-0913

R GUNS
See Trademark Index

RCI - XRAIL
High capacity shotgun magazines.
3825 E. Calumet St., Suite 400-173
Appleton, WI 54915
Website: www.XRAILbyRCI.com
Phone: 920-585-6534

R & D PRECISION
Oversize bolt handle knobs, replacement ambidextrous latch for Badger M5 detachable box magazine system.
942 S. Dodsworth Av.
Glendora, CA 91740
Website: www.rdprecision.net
Phone: 626-806-4389

RAINIER ARMS, LLC
Tactical rail systems, barrels, receivers, buffers, gas blocks, flash suppressors, bolt carriers, and enhanced trigger guards.
3802 N. Auburn Way, Suite 305
Auburn, WA 98002
Website: www.rainierarms.com
Phone: 877-556-4867
Fax: 253-218-2998

RAMLINE
Synthetic gunstocks.
Onalaska Operations
P.O. Box 39
Onalaska, WI 54650
Website: www.atk.com
Phone: 800-635-7656

RANCH PRODUCTS
Scope mounts and other specialty gun parts.
P.O. Box 145
Malinta, OH 43535
Website: www.ranchproducts.com
Phone: 419-966-2881
Fax: 313-565-8536

REDRING USA LLC
Optical shotgun sight.
100 Mill Plain Road
Danbury, CT 06811
Website: www.redringusa.com
Phone: 203-546-3511

RESET INC.
Picatinny riser rail with integral battery pack and contacts for central power supply of weapon accessories - RIPR/Rifle Integrated Power Rail.
49 Strathearn Place
Simi Valley, CA 93065
Website: www.reset-inc.com
Phone: 805-584-4900
Fax: 805-583-2900

RESCOMP HANDGUN TECHNOLOGIES
Compensators and mounts for all 1911 style pistols as well as AR-15, AK and Galil rifles; magazines for STI and Para Ordnance style hi-cap pistols.
P.O. Box 11786
Queenswood, 186 South Africa
Website: www.crspeed.co.za
Phone: 011 27123334768
Fax: 011 27123332112

RIVERBANK ARMORY
Coded oilers, type one bands, flip sights and other parts for M1 carbines and M1 Garands.
P.O. Box 85
Riverbank, CA 95367
Website: www.riverbankarmory.com
Phone: 209-869-5576

ROBAR COMPANIES, INC.
Polymer frame pistol grip reductions and texturizing, and NP3/NP3 Plus, Roguard, black oxide, electroless nickel, stainless steel blackening, phosphating/parkerizing, and Polymax camouflage firearm finishes.
21438 North 7th Av., Suite B
Phoenix, AZ 85027
Website: www.robarguns.com
Phone: 623-581-2648
Fax: 623-582-0059

ROCK RIVER ARMS, INC.
Parts and accessories for .223, 9mm, .458 Socom, 6.8 SPC, and .308 rifles.
1042 Cleveland Road
Colona, IL 61241
Website: www.rockriverarms.com
Phone: 309-792-5780
Fax: 309-792-5781

ROTH CONCEPT INNOVATIONS, LLC
High capacity "XRAIL" shotgun magazine tube extension system.
3825 E. Calumet St., Suite 400-173
Appleton, WI 54915
Website: www.XRAILBYRCI.com
Phone: 920-585-6534
Fax: 920-731-6660

ROYAL ARMS INTERNATIONAL INC.
Tactical accessories for shotguns and AR15 rifles, billet AR lower receivers.
1300 Graves Av.
Oxnard, CA 93030
Website: www.royalarms.com
Phone: 805-288-5250

S&K SCOPE MOUNTS
"Insta Mount" no drill/no tap scope mounting bases for ex-military rifles.
70 Swede Hollow Road
Sugar Grove, PA 16350
Website: www.scopemounts.com
Phone: 800-578-9862
Fax: 814-489-7730

S.W.A.T. FIREARMS
AR15 receivers.
6585 I-30 East
Campbell, TX 75422
Website: www.swatfirearms.com
Phone: 903-862-2408

SADLAK INDUSTRIES LLC
M-1A and M-14 parts, scope mounts, and accessories.
Nadeau Industrial Park
712 Bread & Milk Street, #7
Coventry, CT 06238
Website: www.sadlak.com
Phone: 860-742-0227

SAGE ORDNANCE SYSTEMS GROUP
EBR Aluminum Chassis Stock for M14 rifles, and accessories for law enforcement/military weapons.
3455 Kings Corner Road
Oscoda, MI 48750
Website: www.sageordnance.com
Phone: 989-739-2200
Fax: 989-739-2825

SALT RIVER TACTICAL, LLC
Support items for Combloc and Soviet-era weapons systems.
P.O. Box 20397
Mesa, AZ 85277
Website: www.saltrivertactical.com
Phone: 480-656-2683

SAMSON MFG. CORPORATION
Rail systems and other tactical accessories.
4 Forge Street
Keene, NH 03431
Website: www.samson-mfg.com
Phone: 888-665-4370
Fax: 413-665-1163

SCHERER SUPPLIES, INC.
High capacity magazines for Glock pistols.
205 Four Mile Creek Road
Tazewell, TN 37879
Phone: 423-733-2615
Fax: 423-733-2073

SCHMIDT & BENDER GMBH
High precision rifle scopes for military and law enforcement.
Am Grossacker 42
Biebertal, Hessen, 35444 GERMANY
Website: www.schmidtbender.com
Phone: 011 496409811570
Fax: 011 496409811511

SEEKINS PRECISION
See Trademark Index

SHEPHERD ENTERPRISES, INC.
Riflescopes with integral range finder, bullet drop compensator, and patented dual reticle system.
P.O. Box 189
Waterloo, NE 68069
Website: www.shepherdscopes.com
Phone: 402-779-2424
Fax: 402-779-4010

SHERLUK MARKETING
M-16/AR-15 parts and accessories.
P.O. Box 156
Delta, OH 43615
Website: www.sherluk.com
Phone: 419-923-8011
Fax: 419-923-812

SHIELD FIREARMS & SIGHTS LTD.
Combat proven red dot sights.
P.O. Box 7633
Bridport, Dorset DT6 9DW
United Kingdom
Website: www.shieldpsd.com
Phone: 44-1297-678233

SHOOTERS RIDGE
Bi-pods, Picatinny rail adaptors, rings, and bases.
N5549 County Trunk Z
Onalaska, WI 54650
Website: www.shootersridge.com
Phone: 800-635-7656
Fax: 763-323-3890

SI DEFENSE, INC.
AR15 style rifle parts.
2902 Hwy 93 North
Kalispell, MT 59901
Website: www.si-defense.com
Phone: 406-752-4253
Fax: 406-752-4082

SIERRA PRECISION RIFLES
Tactical rifle components and accessories.
24927 Bonanza Drive
Mi Wuk, CA 95346
Website: www.spaceguns.com
Phone: 209-586-6071
Fax: 209-586-6555

SIGHTMARK
Riflescopes, laser sights, red dot sights, night vision sights, and weapon lights.
201 Regency Parkway
Mansfield, TX 76063
Website: www.sightmark.com
Phone: 817-394-0310
Fax: 817-394-1628

SIGHTRON, INC.
Tactical and mil-dot scopes, and red dot sights.
100 Jeffrey Way, Suite A
Youngsville, NC 27596
Website: www.sightron.com
Phone: 919-562-3000
Fax: 919-556-0157

SILENCERCO, LLC
Suppressors.
5511 South 6055 West
West Valley City, UT 84118
Website: www.silencerco.com
Phone: 801-973-2023
Fax: 801-973-2032

SIMMONS
Rifle, shotgun, and handgun scopes.
9200 Cody Street
Overland Park, KS 66214
Phone: 913-782-3131
Fax: 913-782-4189

SLIDE FIRE SOLUTIONS
Bump fire stocks.
751 FM 2408
Moran, TX 76464
Website: www.slidefire.com
Phone: 325-945-3800

SOG ARMORY, INC.
AR upper and lower receivers, M4 carbine stocks.
11707 South Sam Houston Parkway West, Suite R
Houston, TX 77031
Website: www.sogarmory.com
Phone: 281-568-5685
Fax: 285-568-9191

SPA-DEFENSE
Night vision systems, laser systems, tactical/law enforcement equipment.
3400 NW. 9th AV., Suite 1104
Fort Lauderdale, FL 33309
Website: www.spa-defense.com
Phone: 954-568-7690
Fax: 954-630-4159

SPEEDFEED, INC.
Synthetic shotgun stocks/forends.
13386 International Parkway
Jacksonville, FL 32218
Website: www.safariland.com
Phone: 800-347-1200

SPHINX SYSTEMS, LTD.
Importer - See Kriss USA listing.
Suppressors, special mounts, parts.
Gstiegstrasse 12
Matten, Switzerland 3800
Website: www.sphinxarms.com
Phone: 011 41338211005
Fax: 011 41338211006

SPUHR AB
Scope and night vision rings/bases, tilting mounting bases, weapon light mounts, Harris bipod conversion.
Box 10
SE-24732 Dalby
Sweden
Website: www.spuhr.com
Phone: 46 0733926770
Fax: 46 046200575

SRT ARMS
Suppressors.
522 Finnie Flat Road, Suite E
PMB 138
Camp Verde, AZ 86322
Website: www.srtarms.com

STONEY POINT PRODUCTS, INC.
Monopods, bipods, quadrapods, weapon accessories.
9200 Cody
Overland Park, KS 66214
Website: www.stoneypoint.com
Phone: 913-752-3400
Fax: 913-752-3550

STRIKE INDUSTRIES
AR15, AK, Glock, and 1911 accessories.
P.O. Box 38137
Santa Ana, CA 92799
Website: www.strikeindustries.com

STURM, RUGER & CO., INC.
Integrated OEM laser device
Headquarters
1 Lacey Place
Southport, CT06490
Website: www.ruger.com
Phone: 203-259-7843
Fax: 203-256-3367
Service Center for Pistols, PC4 & PC9 Carbines
200 Ruger Road
Prescott, AZ86301-6181
Website: www.ruger-firearms.com
Phone: 928-778-6555
Fax: 928-778-6633
Service Center for Revolvers, Long Guns & Ruger
Date of Manufacture
411 Sunapee Street
Newport, NH03773
Phone: 603-865-2442
Fax: 603-863-6165

SUMMIT NIGHT VISION GROUP, INC.
Night vision, thermal, and day optics.
1845 Summit Av., Suite 403
Plano, TX 75074
Website: mwww.summitnightvision.com
Phone: 800-985-7684

SUN DEVIL MANUFACTURING, LLC
Billet aluminum AR15 components and accessories; hard anodizing, ceramic coating, and nickel Teflon finishing.
663 West Second Avenue, Suite 16
Mesa, AZ 85210
Website: www.sundevilmfg.com
Phone: 480-833-9876
Fax: 480-833-9509

SUNNY HILL ENTERPRISES INC.
Trigger guard assemblies, scope rings, and stainless steel trigger guards for Rem. 700s.
W1015 County HHH
Chilton, WI 53014
Website: www.sunny-hill.com
Phone: 920-898-4707

SUN OPTICS USA
Scopes, dot sights, scope mounts, and accessories.
P.O. Box 2225
Burleson, TX 76097
Website: www.sunopticsusa.com
Phone: 817-783-6001
Fax: 817-783-6553

SUREFIRE, LLC
Weapon lights and mounts.
18300 Mount Baldy Circle
Fountain Valley, CA 92708
Website: www.surefire.com
Phone: 714-545-9444
Fax: 714-545-9537

SWAROVSKI OPTIK NORTH AMERICA
Riflescopes and accessories.
2 Slater Road
Cranston, RI 02920
Website: www.swarovskioptik.com
Phone: 401-734-1800
Fax: 401-734-5888

SWR MANUFACTURING, LLC
.22, 9mm, .45 ACP, 5.56mm, and .30 caliber suppressors.
P.O. Box 841
Pickens, SC 29761
Website: www.swrmfg.com
Phone: 864-850-3579
Fax: 864-751-2823

TACM III, INC.
Tactical weapon lights and mounts.
2300 Commerce Park Drive, Suite 7
Palm Bay, FL 32905
Website: www.tacm3.com
Phone: 321-726-0644
Fax: 321-726-0645

TACSTAR
See LYMAN PRODUCTS CORP.

TACTICAL ARMZ
Suppressors.
4451 E Farm Road 132
Springfield, MO 65802
Website: www.tacticalarmz.com
Phone: 417-893-0486

TACTICAL INNOVATIONS, INC.
AR15 receivers, .223 suppressors.
345 Sunrise Road
Bonners Ferry, ID 83805
Website: www.tacticalinc.com
Phone: 208-267-1585
Fax: 208-267-1597

TACTICAL NIGHT VISION CO.
Night vision systems and accessories.
25612 Barton road, #328
Loma Linda, CA 92354
Website: www.tnvc.com
Phone: 909-796-7000
Fax: 909-478-9133

TACTICAL SOLUTIONS
Suppressors.
2772 S. Victory View Way
Boise, ID 83709
Website: www.tacticalsol.com
Phone: 866-333-9901

TACTICAL WEAPONS SOLUTIONS
See Trademark Index

TALLEY MANUFACTURING, INC.
Rings, bases, custom gun parts, and accessories.
9183 Old No. 6 Highway
P.O. Box 369
Santee, SC 29142
Website: www.talleyrings
Phone: 803-854-5700
Fax: 803-854-9315

TANGENT THETA INCORPORATED
Rifle scopes.
60B Otter Lake Court
Halifax, Nova Scotia B3S 1L9
CANADA
Website: www.tangenttheta.com
Phone: 902-876-2935

TANGODOWN, INC.
Mil-spec tactical weapon accessories.
4720 North La Cholla Blvd., Suite 180
Tucson, AZ 85705
Website: www.tangodown.com
Phone: 520-888-3376
Fax: 520-888-3787

TANNERITE® SPORTS LLC
Patented Binary Exploding Targets
36366 Valley Road
Pleasant Hill, Oregon 97455
Phone Number: 541-744-1406
Fax Number: 541-744-1384
Website: www.tannerite.com/

TAPCO, INC.
Synthetic stocks and forends, slings, high capacity magazines, slings, and U.S. "922r" compliance parts.
P.O. Box 2408
Kennesaw, GA 30156
Website: www.tapco.com
Phone: 770-425-1280
Fax: 770-425-1510

TASCO
Riflescopes.
9200 Cody
Overland Park, KS 66214
Website: www.tasco.com
Phone: 913-752-3400
Fax: 913-752-3550

T.A.S., LTD.
Unique single dot miniature pistol and long gun sights.
1 Eilat Street
P.O. Box 84
Tiberias, Israel 14100
Phone: 011 972507983433
Fax: 011 972467722985

TDI ARMS
Camouflage firearms finish, tactical weapon accessories.
2441 Dakota Craft
Rapid City, SD 57701
Phone: 605-415-4910

TEMPCO MANUFACTURING COMPANY, INC.
Firearm magazines, receivers, and other stamped and machined components.
2475 Hwy. 55
St. Paul, MN 55120
Website: www.tempcomfg.com

TEMPLAR CUSTOM, LLC
Barrels, Suppressors, Muzzle brakes.
P.O. Box 15
Apex, NC 27502
Phone: 877-878-2334
Website: www.templarcustom.com

TENEBRAEX, A DIVISION OF ARMAMENT TECHNOLOGY INC.
Anti-reflection devices, scope covers, and weapon sight polarizers.
3045 Robie Street, Suite 113
Halifax, B3K 4P6 Canada
Website: www.tenebraex.com
Phone: 902-454-6384

THERMOLD DESIGN & DEVELOPMENT
Zytel high capacity magazines.
115 Perimeter Center Place NE., Suite 150
Atlanta, GA 30346
Website: www.thermoldmagazines.com
Phone: 877-548-4062
Fax: 866-523-1653

THOMPSON MACHINE
Suppressors.
172 Center Street
Panacea, FL 32346
Website: www.ThompsonMachine.net
Phone: 850-766-4197

TIMNEY MANUFACTURING, INC.
Replacement triggers for rifles and Rem. 870 shotguns.
3940 West Clarendon Avenue
Phoenix, AZ 85019
Website: www.timneytriggers.com
Phone: 602-274-2999
Fax: 602-241-0361

TRIJICON, INC.
Night sights, red dot sights, riflescopes, night vision and thermal imaging systems.
49385 Shafer Avenue
P.O. Box 930059
Wixom, MI 48393
Website: www.trijicon.com
Phone: 248-960-7700
Fax: 248-960-7725

TRIPLE K MANUFACTURING COMPANY, INC.
Pistol, rifle, and shotgun magazines.
2222 Commercial Street
San Diego, CA 92113
Website: www.triplek.com
Phone: 619-232-2066
Fax: 619-232-7675

TROY INDUSTRIES, INC.
Small arms components and accessories, complete weapon upgrades.
126 Myron Street
West Springfield, MA 01089
Website: www.troyind.com
Phone: 413-788-4288
Fax: 413-383-0339

TRUGLO, INC.
Tritium fiber-optic aiming systems, red dot sights, riflescopes.
710 Presidential Drive
Richardson, TX 75081
Website: www.truglo.com
Phone: 972-774-0300
Fax: 972-774-0323

ULTIMAK
Rails, accessories, optics mounts, grips, rings, and stocks for AK, Saiga, AR, M14, Mini 14/30 and M1 rifles.
2216 S. Main, Suite B2
Moscow, ID 83843
Website: www.ultimak.com
Phone: 208-883-4734
Fax: 208-882-3896

ULTRA DOT DISTRIBUTION
Red dot, micro dot, and fiber optic sights.
6304 Riverside Drive
P.O. Box 362
Yankeetown, FL 34498
Website: www.ultradotusa.com
Phone: 352-447-2255
Fax: 352-447-2266

UNI-DOT
See LYMAN PRODUCTS CORP

URBAN-E.R.T. SLINGS, LLC
Custom weapon slings.
P.O. Box 429
Clayton, IN 46118
Website: www.urbanertslings.com
Phone: 317-223-6509
Fax: 317-539-2585

US NIGHT VISION CORPORATION
Night vision and laser sights.
1376 Lead Hill Blvd., Suite 190
Roseville, CA 95661
Website: www.usnightvision.com
Phone: 916-788-1110
Fax: 916-788-1113

U.S. OPTICS, INC.
Riflescopes, mounting systems, custom scopes, lenses, and mounts.
150 Arovista Circle
Brea, CA 92821
Website: www.usoptics.com
Phone: 714-582-1956
Fax: 714-582-1959

VALDADA OPTICS
European tactical, precision, and long range riflescopes.
P.O. Box 270095
Littleton, CO 80127
Website: www.valdada.com
Phone: 303-979-4578
Fax: 303-979-0256

VANG COMP SYSTEMS
Barrels, magazine tube extensions, oversized safeties, and sights for tactical shotguns.
400 West Butterfield Road
Chino Valley, AZ 86323
Website: www.vangcomp.com
Phone: 928-636-8455
Fax: 928-636-1538

VICKERS
See BLUE FORCE GEAR, INC.

VIKING TACTICS, INC.
AR15/M16 parts and accessories, slings, sights, and mounts.
Fayetteville, NC 28306
Website: www.vikingtactics.com
Phone: 910-987-5983
Fax: 910-565-3710

VIRIDIAN
See LASER AIMING SYSTEMS CORPORATION.

VLTOR WEAPON SYSTEMS
Modular buttstocks, and components and accessories for AR15/M16/AK rifles.
3735 North Romero Road
Tucson, AZ 85705
Website; www.vltor.com
Phone: 520-408-1944
Fax: 520-293-8807

VORTEX OPTICS
Red dot sights, riflescopes, rings and mounts.
2120 West Greenview Drive, Suite 4
Middleton, WI 53562
Website: www.vortextactical.com
Phone: 800-426-0048
Fax: 608-662-7454

WARNE MANUFACTURING COMPANY
Scope rings and mounts.
9057 SE Jannsen Road
Clackamas, OR 97015
Website: www.warnescopemounts.com
Phone: 503-657-5590
Fax: 503-657-5695

WEAVER OPTICS
Mounting systems, riflescopes, red dot sights.
N5549 County Trunk Z
Onalaska, WI 54650
Website: www.weaveroptics.com
Phone: 800-635-7656
Fax: 763-323-3890

WILCOX INDUSTRIES CORP.
Night vision mounting systems, weapon video display, thermal sights, tail cap switches, AK-SC, M4, and MP-7 rail systems, Rapid Acquisition Aiming Module (RAAM).
25 Piscataqua Drive
Newington, NH 03801
Website: www.wilcoxind.com
Phone: 603-431-1331
Fax: 603-431-1221

WILLIAMS GUN SIGHT COMPANY
Pistol, rifle, and shotgun fiber optic sights, scope mounts, open sights, receiver sights, shotgun sights, sling swivels, and tactical rifle muzzle brakes .
7389 Lapeer Road
Davison, MI 48423
Website: www.williamsgunsight.com
Phone: 810-653-2131
Fax: 810-658-2140

WILLIAMS TRIGGER SPECIALTIES
Sniper grade trigger upgrades for most semi-auto rifles.
111 SE Second Street
Atwood, IL 61913
Website: www.williamstriggers.com
Phone: 217-578-3026

WMD GUNS LLC
AR15 parts, bolt carriers, and .22 LR conversion kits.
3070 SE Dominica Terrace
Stuart, FL 34997
Website: www.wmdguns.com
Phone: 772-324-9915

WRENTECH INDUSTRIES LLC
Mfr. of the Advantage Tactical Sight.
7 Avenida Vista Grande B-7
PMB #510
Santa Fe, NM 87508
Website: www.advantagetactical.com

XGRIP
See FDI/FREED DESIGNS, INC.

X PRODUCTS
High capacity magazines and firearm accessories.
14838 NW Fawnlily Drive
Portland, OR 97229
Website: www.xproducts.com

XRAIL
See ROTH CONCEPT INNOVATIONS, LLC.

XS SIGHT SYSTEMS, INC.
XS 24/7 tritium night sights for handguns, rifles, and shotguns; tactical sights for AR15/M16/HK rifles, and mounting systems.
2401 Ludelle Street
Fort Worth, TX 76105
Website: www.xssights.com
Phone: 817-536-0136
Fax: 817-536-3517

YANKEE HILL MACHINE CO., INC.
Rail systems, forearms, flip-up sights, rifle and pistol suppressors, flash suppressors, compensators, and forward grips.
20 Ladd Av, Suite 1
Florence, MA 01062
Website: www.yhm.net
Phone: 413-584-1400
Fax: 413-586-1326

YUKON ADVANCED OPTICS
Riflescopes and night visions optics.
201 Regency Parkway
Mansfield, TX 76063
Website: www.yukonopticsusa.com
Phone: 817-225-0310
Fax: 817-394-1628

ZEL CUSTOM/TACTILITE
Bolt-action uppers for AR style rifles in .338 Lapua, .416 Barrett, and .50 BMG calibers.
11419 Challenger Av
Odessa, FL 33556
Website: www.zelcustom.com
Phone: 313-223-0411

ZEV TECHNOLOGIES, INC.
Drop-in components for Glocks.
1051 Yarnell Place
Oxnard, CA 93033
Website: www.glockworx.com
Phone: 805-486-5800

CARTRIDGE INTERCHANGEABILITY DANGEROUS COMBINATIONS

The discharge of ammunition in a firearm that is not designed to shoot that ammunition can be dangerous resulting in serious injury or even worse to the user and/or bystanders, as well as damage to the firearm. This unsafe condition is caused by an excessive buildup and/or release of high-pressure gas in a firearm's chamber, barrel, and/or action beyond which the firearm is designed to withstand. In the interest of safety, you should use only ammunition of the caliber or gauge designated by the firearm manufacturer for use in that firearm. Markings indicating the correct caliber or gauge of ammunition to be used in a firearm are usually found on the firearm's barrel, frame, or receiver. If the caliber or gauge is not clearly marked on the firearm, or if it appears the original markings have been altered or modified in any way, do not use the firearm.

Before World War I (1914-1918), each American ammunition manufacturer used dimensional, pressure, and ballistic performance standards based on individual company practices and procedures. When the U.S. entered World War I in 1917, these multiple standards caused serious difficulties. As a result, after the War, the American firearms and ammunition industry formed the Sporting Arms and Ammunition Manufacturers' Institute (SAAMI) to serve as a clearing house for standardized dimensions, practices, and procedures. Today, SAAMI continues this work under the National Shooting Sports Foundation (NSSF). In addition to developing standardized cartridge and chamber dimensions, interior ballistics, and exterior ballistics, SAAMI operates in the fields of metallurgy, chemistry, and engineering to help solve industry-wide problems. SAAMI also distributes safety brochures dealing with proper handling and storage of ammunition and components.

It is important to note that the commercial .223 Rem. cartridge is NOT the same as the 5.56x45mm NATO cartridge and they are NOT interchangeable. In a firearm chambered for .223 Rem., do not use 5.56mm NATO (military cartridges).

For more information on ammunition including an expanded SAAMI approved list of Dangerous Combinations, please refer to SAAMI at www.saami.org/index.cfm and the *Ammo Encyclopedia* available at www.bluebookofgunvalues.com.

A listing has been provided below of Field Division offices for the BATFE. You are encouraged to contact them if you have any questions regarding the legality of any weapons or their interpretation of existing laws and regulations. Remember, ignorance is no excuse when it involves Federal firearms regulations and laws. Although these various offices may not be able to help you with state, city, county, or local firearms regulations and laws, their job is to assist you on a Federal level.

U.S. Department of Justice
Bureau of Alcohol, Tobacco,
Firearms and Explosives:
Website: www.atf.gov

Atlanta Field Division
2600 Century Parkway Suite 300
Atlanta, Georgia 30345
Phone: 404-417-2600
Fax: 404-417-2601
Email: AtlantaDiv@atf.gov

Baltimore Field Division
31 Hopkins Plaza, 5th Floor
Baltimore, Maryland 21201
Phone: 443-965-2000
Fax: 443-965-2001
Email: BaltimoreDiv@atf.gov

Boston Field Division
10 Causeway Street, Suite 791
Boston, Massachusetts 02222
Phone: 617-557-1200
Fax: 617-557-1201
Email: BostonDiv@atf.gov

Charlotte Field Division
6701 Carmel Road, Suite 200
Charlotte, North Carolina 28226
Phone: 704-716-1800
Fax 704-716-1801
Email: CharlotteDiv@atf.gov

Chicago Field Division
525 West Van Buren Street,
Suite 600
Chicago, Illinois 60607
Phone: 312-846-7200
Fax: 312-846-7201
Email: ChicagoDiv@atf.gov

Columbus Field Division
230 West Street, Suite 400
Columbus, Ohio 43215
Phone: 614-827-8400
Fax: 614-827-8401
Email: ColumbusDiv@atf.gov

Dallas Field Division
1114 Commerce Street, Room 303
Dallas, TX 75242
Phone: 469-227-4300
Fax: 469-227-4330
Email: DallasDiv@atf.gov

Denver Field Division
950 17th Street, Suite 1800
Denver, Colorado 80202 USA
Phone: 303-575-7600
Fax 303-575-7601
Email: DenverDiv@atf.gov

Detroit Field Division
1155 Brewery Park Boulevard,
Suite 300
Detroit, Michigan 48207
Phone: 313-202-3400
Fax: 313-202-3445
Email: DetroitDiv@atf.gov

Houston Field Division
5825 N. Sam Houston Pkwy, Suite 300
Houston, Texas 77086 USA
Phone: 281-716-8200
Fax: 281-716-8219
Email: HoustonDiv@atf.gov

Kansas City Field Division
1251 NW Briarcliff Parkway, Suite 600
Kansas City, Missouri 64116
Phone: 816-559-0700
Fax: 816-559-0701

Los Angeles Field Division
550 North Brand Avenue
8th Floor
Glendale, California 91203
Phone: 818-265-2500
Fax: 818-265-2501
Email: LosAngelesDiv@atf.gov

Louisville Field Division
600 Dr. Martin Luther King Jr. Place, Suite 322
Louisville, KY 40202
Phone: 502-753-3400
Fax: 502-753-3401
Email: LouisDiv@atf.gov

Miami Field Division
11410 NW 20 Street, Suite 201
Miami, FL 33172
Phone: 305-597-4800
Fax: 305-597-4801
Email: MiamiDiv@atf.gov

Nashville Field Division
5300 Maryland Way, Suite 200
Brentwood, Tennessee 37027
Phone: 615-565-1400
Fax: 615-565-1401
Email: NashDiv@atf.gov

Newark Field Division
1 Garret Mountain Plaza Suite 500
Woodland Park, New Jersey 07424
Phone: 973-413-1179
Fax: 973-413-1190

New Orlearns
One Galleria Boulevard Suite 1700
Metairie, Louisiana 70001
Phone: 504-841-7000
Fax: 504-841-7039
Email: NewOrleansDiv@atf.gov

New York Field Division
Financial Square
32 Old Slip
Suite 3500
New York, New York 10005
Phone: 646-335-9000
Fax: 646-335-9001
Email: NYDiv@atf.gov

Philadelphia Field Division
The Curtis Center
601 Walnut Street, Suite 1000E
Philadelphia, Pennsylvania 19106
Phone: 215-446-7800
Fax: 215-446-7811
Email: PhilDiv@atf.gov

Phoenix Field Division
201 E. Washington Street, Suite 940
Phoenix, Arizona 85004
Phone: 602-776-5400
Fax: 602-776-5429
Email: PhoenixDiv@atf.gov

San Francisco Field Division
5601 Arnold Road, Suite 400
Dublin, California 94568
Phone: 925-557-2800
Fax: 925-557-2805
Email: SanFranciscoDiv@atf.gov

Seattle Field Division
915 2nd Avenue, Room 790
Seattle, Washington 98174
Phone: 206-204-3205
Fax: 206-204-3252
Email: SeattleDiv@atf.gov

St. Paul Field Division
30 East Seventh Street , Suite 1900
St. Paul, Minnesota 55101
Phone: 651-726-0200
Fax: 651-726-0201
Email: StPaulDiv@atf.gov

Tampa Field Division
400 North Tampa Street
Suite 2100
Tampa, Florida 33602
Phone: 813-202-7300
Fax: 813-202-7301
Email: TampaDiv@atf.gov

Washington Field Division
1401 H. Street NW, Suite 900
Washington, District of Columbia 20226
Phone: (202) 648-8010
Fax: (202) 648-8001
Email: WashDiv@atf.gov

INDEX

# #

A

B

C